WEBSTER'S
New Explorer
Crossword
Puzzle
Dictionary

Second Edition

Completely Revised and Updated

Created in Cooperation with the Editors of
MERRIAM-WEBSTER

FEDERAL
STREET
PRESS

A Division of Merriam-Webster, Incorporated
Springfield, Massachusetts

This edition published by
Federal Street Press
A Division of Merriam-Webster, Incorporated
P.O. Box 281
Springfield, MA 01102

Federal Street Press books are available for bulk purchase for sales promotion
and premium use. For details write the manager of special sales,
Federal Street Press, P.O. Box 281, Springfield, MA 01102

ISBN 10   ISBN 1-892859-94-7

ISBN 13   ISBN 978-1892859-94-5

Printed in the United States of America

05 06 07 08 09   5 4 3 2 1

Preface to the Second Edition

This new edition of our Crossword Puzzle Dictionary represents a significant revision of those that have preceded it. Every entry has been reconsidered, the content has been thoroughly updated, and the page design has been enhanced for legibility.

In updating the work, we have added many terms that have recently entered the general English vocabulary: the names of computer languages *(Java, Perl)*, new national currencies *(vatu, nakfa)*, contemporary slang *(slacker, schlep, hoser, chill out, go-to guy, brewski, nebbish)*, and much more. And numerous individuals and institutions that have emerged in recent years—soccer stars *(Hamm, Ronaldo)*, auto companies *(Kia, Daewoo)*, Nobel Prize winners *(Annan, Naipaul)*, actors and actresses *(Depp, Swank)*, and so on—have naturally also been added.

Drawing extensively on actual crossword puzzles, we have made a special effort to add examples of "crosswordese," words that show up unusually often in puzzle grids. Thus, you will find such distinctive words and names as those for Prince Valiant's wife *(Aleta)* and son *(Arn)*, a former newspaper columnist *(Eda)*, a sharp mountain ridge *(arête)*, a hare's tail *(scut)*, an eminent golfer *(Els)*, Peer Gynt's mother *(Ase, Aase)*, a puzzle-cube inventor *(Erno)*, and a Scottish uncle *(eme)*—many of which might have been omitted if frequency of use in everyday English had been our only criterion.

While crossword clues have gotten cleverer in recent years, crossword answer words have gotten simpler, and archaic and obscure terms have gradually been disappearing from puzzle grids. For this new edition, it seemed unnecessary to retain words that were unlikely to show up in even the most challenging modern puzzles, and consequently a number of words that have fallen out of use have been deleted. Their absence has been more than made up for by additional entries and answer words, which now total substantially over 300,000.

We hope our revised edition, with its new orientation, will prove to be the most useful dictionary of its kind for a new century of puzzle solving.

The principal editors of this dictionary's first two editions were James G. Lowe and Michael G. Belanger. Editorial work on the new edition was carried out by Mark A. Stevens and C. Roger Davis with freelance help from Jocelyn White Franklin, Mike Nichols, Francesca M. Forrest, and Doris Maxfield. Eileen M. Haraty and Dr. Thomas W. Adams made valuable vocabulary contributions, and Robert D. Copeland and Ted Atanowski provided essential electronic assistance.

Mark A. Stevens
Editor

Explanatory Notes

This dictionary is organized to make it easy to find answer words with a specific number of letters. Every answer word follows a numeral indicating the number of letters it contains. These words generally run from three to 13 letters. Two-letter words are omitted because such words almost never appear in crossword puzzles, and words longer than 13 letters are omitted because, when a puzzle calls for a longer answer, the answer is usually a phrase or part of a phrase rather than a single word or term. An exception to the 13-letter limit is made for multiword titles of works, which occasionally run as long as 25 letters. The exception allows for those frequent crossword clues that omit one or two words from a title, perhaps enough for a five- or ten-letter answer.

As in any crossword dictionary, a single list of answer words will often include words representing various parts of speech. The entry for **quiet**, for example, includes synonyms for the noun *(silence),* the adjective *(placid),* and the verb *(soothe),* all in a continuous list. Since clues are often intentionally ambiguous as to what part of speech or meaning is intended, listing all the possible synonyms together is probably ideal for the puzzle solver.

Words that share a root with their entry word have usually been omitted from the answer lists, because puzzle creators rarely choose a clue that is related in this way to its answer. Therefore, *singular* does not appear at **single**, *basal* does not appear at **basic**, and *papa* does not appear at **pop**. On the other hand, since clues do occasionally share a standard prefix or suffix (such as *re-* or *-ness*) with an answer word, we have retained many clue/answer-word pairs of this kind.

When one entry word simply adds a suffix to another entry word, as when **keenness** follows **keen**, the answer list for the suffixed entry word will generally omit all the words that merely add the same suffix to a word in the stem word's list. For example, because **keen** includes such answer words as *sharp* and *shrewd,* the list at **keenness** omits *sharpness* and *shrewdness*. When encountering a clue with a common suffix, therefore, the user will occasionally want to look at a neighboring entry to find all the possible synonyms.

When a personal name is entered as an answer term, the first name generally appears in parentheses and is ignored in the letter count. In cases where the first name is the one normally encountered—e.g., for historical figures such as Michelangelo and Raphael or fictional characters such as Tess Durbeyfield and Angel Clare—the last name is generally parenthesized instead. When a title begins with an article *(A, An,* or *The)*, the article is parenthesized and omitted from the letter count. In a list of geographic entities such as mountains (lakes, gulfs, etc.), the generic word *Mount (Lake, Gulf,* etc.) is parenthesized and omitted from the letter count. If you find that none of the answers as listed fits the blanks for a given puzzle clue, you should naturally check to see if any of the parenthesized elements might help provide the desired answer.

Many entries are broken into subentries by means of subheadings. Subheadings often consist of a single word, which is usually to be read as either preceding or following the main entry word. Thus, in the entry for **hair**, the subheadings include **animal** (which should be read as "animal hair") and **ornament** (which should be read as "hair ornament"). The subentry **combining form** lists the kinds of word fragments, usually Greek or Latin in origin, that are commonly called *roots*.

The dictionary is best used somewhat imaginatively. If you fail to find a word at its own entry, look up a synonym; only rarely will you fail to find one. If a clue takes a form such as **Australian tree**, **garden tool**, or **Southeast Asian lake** and the dictionary provides no such entry, check at the entry for the generic term—**tree, tool, lake**, etc.—for a list, perhaps broken down by subheadings.

WEBSTER'S
New Explorer
Crossword
Puzzle
Dictionary

A

A1 4 best, tops **5** prime **7** optimal, perfect **8** superior **9** excellent, first-rate, front-rank, matchless, top-drawer **10** blue-ribbon, first-class

Aaron *brother:* **5** Moses *father:* **5** Amram *sister:* **6** Miriam

aback 7 unaware **8** suddenly, unawares **10** by surprise **12** unexpectedly

abaft 4 back **5** after **6** astern, behind **8** rearward **9** sternward

abalone 7 mollusc, mollusk **9** gastropod

abandon 4 cede, drop, dump, ease, jilt, junk, play, quit **5** cease, chuck, ditch, leave, let go, scrap, yield **6** desert, disown, give up, laxity, maroon, reject, resign, strand, vacate **7** back out, bail out, cast off, discard, drop out, forsake, freedom, liberty, license, pull out, retreat **8** abdicate, give over, hand over, renounce, wildness, withdraw **9** looseness, repudiate, surrender, throw over **10** enthusiasm, exuberance, relinquish, wantonness **11** discontinue, leave behind, naturalness, spontaneity, unrestraint **12** carelessness, heedlessness, intemperance, recklessness, unconstraint **13** impulsiveness

abandoned 4 free, lewd, lorn, wild **5** loose **6** gave up, jilted, vacant, wanton **7** cast off, corrupt, given up, outcast, uncouth **8** cast away, depraved, derelict, deserted, desolate, forsaken, stranded **9** cast aside, debauched, destitute, discarded, dissolute, lecherous, neglected, reprobate, shameless **10** degenerate, dissipated, eliminated, friendless, lascivious, left behind, licentious, profligate, unoccupied **11** uninhibited **12** incorrigible, relinquished, uncontrolled, unrestrained

abase 5 lower, shame **6** debase, defame, demean, demote, grovel, humble, lessen, reduce **7** cheapen, degrade, devalue, put down **8** belittle **9** denigrate, discredit, disparage, downgrade, humiliate **10** depreciate, undervalue

abash 4 faze **5** mix up, shame, upset **6** dismay, puzzle, rattle **7** confuse, mortify, mystify **8** confound **9** discomfit, embarrass **10** discompose, disconcert

abashment 6 unease **7** chagrin **8** disquiet **9** confusion **12** discomfiture, discomposure **13** embarrassment

abate 3 ebb, end **4** ease, fade, fall, omit, slow, void, wane **5** allay, annul, close, let up, quash, taper **6** deduct, lessen, negate, recede, reduce, relent, weaken **7** abolish, decline, deprive, die down, dwindle, ease off, nullify, slacken, subside **8** decrease, diminish, mitigate, moderate **9** alleviate, eradicate **10** invalidate

abatement 6 ebbing, rebate, waning **8** decrease, discount **9** declining, deduction, dwindling, exemption, lessening, reduction, shrinkage **10** diminution, subsidence **11** subtraction

abattoir 8 shambles

abbey 6 friary **7** convent **8** cloister **9** monastery

abbot *female:* **6** abbess

abbreviate 3 cut **4** clip, trim **5** prune **6** cut out, reduce **7** abridge, curtail, cut back, shorten **8** compress, condense, contract, cut short, truncate

abbreviation 5 brief **6** digest, précis, sketch **7** acronym, cutting, outline **8** abstract, clipping, synopsis, trimming **10** abridgment, shortening **11** curtailment **12** condensation

abdicate 4 cede, drop, quit **5** evade, forgo, leave, waive, yield **6** abjure, give up, reject, resign **7** abandon, cast off, discard **8** abnegate, disclaim, hand over, renounce, withdraw **9** repudiate, surrender **10** relinquish

abdomen 3 gut, pot **5** belly, tummy **6** middle, paunch **7** midriff, stomach **8** potbelly **9** bay window **10** midsection **11** breadbasket *depression:* **5** navel

abduct 4 grab, take **5** seize **6** kidnap, remove, snatch **8** carry off, draw away, take away **9** carry away, steal away **10** spirit away **11** make off with

Abduction from the Seraglio composer 6 Mozart (Wolfgang Amadeus)

abecedarian 4 tyro **6** novice **7** amateur, dabbler, learner **8** beginner, initiate, neophyte **9** beginning, smatterer **10** apprentice, dilettante, elementary **11** rudimentary **12** alphabetical

Abel *brother:* **4** Cain, Seth *father:* **4** Adam *mother:* **3** Eve *slayer:* **4** Cain

Abelard *son:* 9 Astrolabe *wife:* 7 Heloise

abele 6 poplar

aberrant 3 odd 7 deviant, strange, unusual 8 abnormal, atypical, peculiar, straying 9 anomalous, deviating, different, eccentric, irregular, unnatural, untypical 11 exceptional, nonstandard

aberration 4 slip 5 quirk 6 change, oddity 7 anomaly, mistake 8 mutation, straying, 9 curiosity, deviation, exception, wandering 10 deflection, difference, distortion, divergence 11 abnormality, peculiarity 12 eccentricity, irregularity

abet 3 aid, egg 4 ally, back, help, prod, spur, urge 5 boost, egg on 6 assist, exhort, foment, incite, second, stir up 7 condone, endorse, forward, promote, support 8 advocate 9 encourage, instigate 11 countenance

abettor 4 aide, ally 6 backup, cohort, helper 7 inciter, partner 8 fomenter 9 accessory, supporter 10 accomplice, instigator 11 confederate, conspirator 12 collaborator

abeyance 4 lull, rest 5 break, lapse, pause 6 recess 7 respite, time-out, waiting 8 breather, interval 10 inactivity, quiescence, suspension 12 intermission, interruption

abeyant 7 dormant 8 deferred, inactive, recessed 9 postponed, quiescent, suspended 11 interrupted

abhor 4 hate 5 scorn 6 detest, loathe, reject, revile, vilify 7 contemn, despise, disdain, dislike 8 execrate 9 abominate, excoriate, repudiate

abhorrence 4 evil, hate 6 hatred, horror 7 disgust 8 aversion, distaste, loathing 9 repulsion, revulsion 10 repugnance 11 abomination, detestation

abhorrent 4 base, foul, vile 5 awful 6 horrid, odious 7 beastly, hateful, heinous 8 damnable, horrible, horrific 9 atrocious, execrable, invidious, loathsome, monstrous, obnoxious, repellent, repugnant, repulsive, revolting 10 abominable, deplorable, despicable, detestable, disgusting 12 contemptible 13 reprehensible

abide 4 bear, last, live, stay, wait 5 await, brook, dwell, exist, stand, tarry 6 accede, accept, comply, endure, keep on, linger, remain, reside, stay on, suffer 7 consent, hang out, inhabit, persist, sojourn, stomach, subsist, swallow, wait for 8 continue, live with, stand for, tolerate 9 put up with, withstand

abiding 4 fast, firm, sure 6 steady 7 durable, eternal, lasting, staying 8 constant, enduring, timeless 9 complying, perpetual, steadfast 10 continuing, persistent, persisting, unchanging 11 everlasting, unfaltering

abigail 4 maid

Abigail *brother:* 5 David *husband:* 5 David, Nabal *mother:* 5 Amasa *son:* 7 Chileah

ability 4 bent, gift 5 craft, flair, knack, might, savvy, skill 6 talent 7 aptness, command, faculty, know-how, mastery, prowess 8 aptitude, capacity, facility 9 adeptness, dexterity, expertise, handiness, ingenuity, potential 10 adroitness, capability, cleverness, competence, efficiency 11 proficiency, skillfulness 13 qualification

abject 3 low 4 base, mean, poor, vile 5 lowly, sorry 6 dismal, humble, shabby, sordid 7 debased, fawning, forlorn, ignoble, pitiful, servile 8 cast down, degraded, dejected, downcast, hopeless, pathetic, pitiable, rejected, resigned, wretched 9 afflicted, destitute, groveling, miserable, worthless 10 deplorable, obsequious, spiritless, submissive 11 deferential, downtrodden, subservient 12 contemptible, dishonorable, ingratiating

abjure 4 cede, deny 5 avoid, spurn 6 desert, disown, recall, recant, reject, refuse, revoke 7 abandon, disavow, decline, forsake, retract 8 disclaim, forswear, renounce, take back, withdraw 9 repudiate, surrender 10 relinquish 11 abstain from

ablaze 5 afire, aglow, fiery 6 aflame, alight, on fire 7 blazing, burning, flaming, excited, flaring, ignited, radiant

able 3 apt, fit 4 keen 5 adept, alert, sharp, smart 6 adroit, clever, expert, facile, suited 7 capable, skilled 8 skillful, talented 9 competent, effective, effectual, efficient, qualified 10 proficient 11 intelligent, resourceful 12 accomplished, enterprising

able-bodied 3 fit 4 hale 5 hardy, lusty, sound, stout 6 brawny, hearty, robust, strong, sturdy 7 capable 8 stalwart, vigorous 9 strapping

ablution 6 laving 7 bathing, washing 8 lavation 9 cleansing, immersion 12 purification

abnegate 4 cede, deny, drop 5 forgo, waive, yield 6 abjure, give up, recant, revoke, vacate 7 disavow, gainsay 8 disallow, disclaim, forswear, renounce, withdraw 9 repudiate, surrender 10 contradict, contravene, relinquish

abnegation 6 denial 9 surrender 10 abstinence, self-denial 12 renouncement, renunciation

Abner *cousin:* 4 Saul *father:* 3 Ner *slayer:* 4 Joab

abnormal 3 odd 5 freak, undue, weird 6 off-key 7 bizarre, deviant, unusual 8 aberrant, atypical, freakish, peculiar 9 anomalous, divergent, eccentric, irregular, unnatural 11 heteroclite 13 heteromorphic, preternatural

abnormality 4 flaw 6 oddity 7 anomaly 8 deviance 9 deviation, exception 10 aberration, difference 12 irregularity

abode 4 home, nest 5 house 7 address, lodging, sojourn 8 domicile, dwelling 9 residence 10 habitation

abolish 3 end 4 undo, kill, void 5 abate, annul, erase, quash 6 cancel, negate, recall, repeal, revoke, vacate 7 destroy, nullify, rescind, retract, reverse, wipe out 8 abrogate, disallow, dissolve, overturn, prohibit 9 eliminate, eradicate, terminate 10 do away with, extinguish, invalidate

abolitionist 4 Mott (Lucretia), Weld (Theodore) 5 Brown (John), Child (Lydia), Lundy (Benjamin), Smith (Gerrit), Stowe (Harriet Beecher) 6 Birney (James), Lowell (James Russell), Parker (Theodore), Tappan (Arthur), Tubman (Harriet) 7 Lincoln (Abraham) 8 Douglass (Frederick), Garrison (William Lloyd), Phillips (Wendell), Whittier (John Greenleaf)

abominable 5 awful, nasty 6 cursed, horrid, odious 7 hateful 8 horrible, shocking, terrible, wretched 9 abhorrent, loathsome, offensive, repellent, repugnant, repulsive, revolting 10 deplorable, despicable, detestable, disgusting 12 contemptible

abominable snowman 4 yeti

abominate 4 damn, hate 5 abhor, curse, scorn 6 detest, loathe, revile 7 despise 8 execrate 9 repudiate

abomination 4 evil, hate 5 scorn 6 hatred, horror, plague 7 disdain, disgust, dislike 8 anathema, aversion, contempt, distaste, loathing 9 repulsion, revulsion 10 abhorrence, repugnance, repugnancy 11 detestation

aboriginal 5 first 6 native 7 ancient, endemic, primary 8 earliest, original, primeval 9 primitive 10 indigenous, primordial 13 autochthonous

aborigine 6 native 7 ancient 8 indigene 10 autochthon

abort 4 drop, halt, stop 5 check, expel, scrap, scrub 6 arrest, cancel 7 abandon, call off 8 cut short 9 interrupt, terminate

abortive 4 vain 5 empty 6 futile, unripe 7 failing, useless 8 immature, unformed 9 fruitless, worthless 10 unavailing, unfruitful 11 ineffective, ineffectual, unavailable, undeveloped 12 unproductive, unsuccessful

abound 4 flow, teem 5 burst, crawl, crowd, flood, swarm, swell 6 be full, throng 7 bristle, jam with 8 overflow, pack with 9 crawl with 11 be plentiful

abounding 4 full, rife 5 laden 6 filled, full of, jammed, packed 7 copious, profuse, replete, stuffed, teeming 8 abundant, swarming, thronged 9 alive with, bristling, plenteous, plentiful 11 overflowing

about 4 as to, back, in re, near, nigh, over 5 again, anent, circa, round 6 almost, around, moving, nearby, nearly 7 apropos, close to, roughly, through 8 backward 9 as regards, engaged in, haphazard, in reverse, in general, regarding 10 as concerns, concerning, encircling, in regard to, more or less, on all sides, oppositely, relating to, respecting 11 any which way, dealing with, on every side, practically, referring to, relative to, surrounding 12 here and there, with regard to 13 approximately, concerned with, in reference to, with respect to

about-face 4 turn 7 reverse 8 reversal 9 turnabout, volte-face

above 3 o'er 4 over, past 5 aloft, supra 6 beyond 8 overhead 9 exceeding *prefix:* 4 over 5 hyper, super, supra

above all 7 chiefly 9 primarily 10 especially 11 principally 12 particularly

aboveboard 4 free, open 5 frank 6 candid, honest, openly 7 frankly, up front 8 candidly, honestly, straight 10 truthfully, forthright, scrupulous

abracadabra 5 charm, magic 6 babble, jargon 9 gibberish 10 double talk, mumbo jumbo 11 incantation 12 gobbledygook 13 mystification

abrade 3 bug, irk, rub 4 burn, fret, gall, rasp, wear 5 annoy, chafe, erode, grate, graze, upset, weary 6 bother, ruffle, scrape 7 corrode, eat away, perturb, provoke, roughen 8 irritate, wear away, wear down 9 aggravate, grind down

Abraham *brother:* 5 Haran, Nahor *concubine:* 5 Hagar *father:* 5 Terah *grandfather:* 5 Nahor *grandson:* 4 Esau *nephew:* 3 Lot *son:* 5 Isaac, Medan, Shuah 6 Midian, Zimran 7 Ishmael *well:* 9 Beer-Sheba *wife:* 5 Sarah 7 Keturah

abrasion 5 chafe, scuff 6 scrape 7 chafing, erosion, grating, rubbing, scratch

8 friction, grinding, scraping, scuffing 10 irritation, scratching

abrasive 5 emery, rough, sharp 6 biting, pumice 7 wearing 8 annoying 9 smoothing, polishing 10 irritating, unpleasant

abreast 6 beside, next to, versed, with-it 7 versant 8 familiar, informed, up-to-date 9 au courant 10 acquainted, conversant 13 knowledgeable

abridge 3 cut 4 pare, trim 5 limit, prune 6 lessen, narrow, reduce 7 curtail, cut back, shorten 8 boil down, compress, condense, cut short, diminish, restrict, truncate 9 summarize 10 abbreviate

abridgment 5 brief 6 digest 7 capsule, cutting, summary 8 abstract, synopsis 9 reduction, short form, 10 diminution, lessening, shortening 11 compression, contraction, curtailment, restriction 12 abbreviation, condensation

abroad 4 afar, away 5 about 6 afield, astray, widely 7 touring 8 overseas 9 elsewhere, traveling

abrogate 3 end 4 undo, void 5 abate, annul, quash 6 cancel, negate, repeal, revoke, vacate 7 abolish, blot out, nullify, rescind, reverse 8 dissolve 9 discharge 10 extinguish, invalidate, obliterate

abrupt 4 curt 5 bluff, blunt, brief, brisk, crisp, gruff, hasty, sharp, sheer, short, steep 6 cut off, snippy, sudden 7 arduous, brusque, hurried, rushing 8 headlong 9 broken off, impetuous 10 unexpected 11 precipitant, precipitate, precipitous 13 unceremonious

abruptly 5 short 6 curtly 7 quickly, steeply 8 suddenly 12 unexpectedly 13 precipitately, precipitously

abruptness 8 curtness 9 steepness 10 brusquerie 12 precipitance

Absalom *commander:* 5 Amasa *father:* 5 David *mother:* 7 Maachah *sister:* 5 Tamar *slayer:* 4 Joab

abscess 4 boil, sore 5 botch, ulcer 6 lesion, pimple, trauma 7 blister, pustule 8 furuncle 9 carbuncle

abscond 4 bolt, flee, quit 5 break, leave 6 decamp, escape, run off 7 run away, take off 8 slip away, sneak off 9 disappear, sneak away, steal away

absence 4 AWOL, lack, need, void, want 6 dearth, defect, vacuum 7 default, drought, failure, vacancy 9 privation 10 deficiency, inadequacy 11 absenteeism, inattention 13 insufficiency

absent 4 away, AWOL, gone, lost 6 no-show 7 bemused, faraway, lacking, missing, omitted, wanting, without 8 distrait, heedless 9 elsewhere, forget-

ful, wandering 10 abstracted, distracted, not present 11 inattentive, preoccupied 12 not attentive

absentminded 4 lost 7 bemused, faraway 8 distrait, dreaming, heedless, unseeing 9 forgetful, oblivious, unheeding, unmindful 10 abstracted, distracted, unnoticing 11 inattentive, inconscient, preoccupied, unconscious, unobserving 12 unperceiving

absent without leave 4 AWOL

absolute 4 full, pure, real, true 5 ideal, sheer, total, utter 6 actual, entire, simple 7 eternal, factual, genuine, perfect, supreme, unmixed 8 autarkic, complete, despotic, flawless, infinite, outright, positive, ultimate, simplest, thorough, unflawed 9 arbitrary, autarchic, boundless, downright, embodying, imperious, masterful, sovereign, unalloyed, undiluted, unlimited 10 autocratic, autonomous, consummate, impeccable, monocratic, tyrannical 11 categorical, dictatorial, domineering, fundamental, independent, unequivocal, unmitigated, unqualified 12 indefectible, indisputable, totalitarian, unrestrained, unrestricted 13 authoritarian, incontestable, unconditional

absolutely 5 fully 6 wholly 7 utterly 8 entirely 9 doubtless, perfectly 10 completely, definitely, positively, thoroughly 11 doubtlessly 13 unequivocally

absolution 6 pardon 7 amnesty, freeing, release 9 releasing, remission 10 letting off 11 exculpation, exoneration, forgiveness 12 dispensation

absolutism 9 Caesarism, despotism 12 dictatorship

absolve 4 free 5 clear, let go, remit, spare 6 acquit, excuse, exempt, let off, pardon 7 forgive, release, relieve, set free 8 dispense 9 discharge, exculpate, exonerate, vindicate

absorb 4 bear, blot 5 imbue, learn, sop up, use up 6 assume, embody, endure, engage, imbibe, infuse, ingest, soak up, sponge, suck up, take in, take up 7 acquire, consume, drink in, engross, immerse, involve, receive, sustain 8 permeate 9 preoccupy, transform 10 assimilate 11 incorporate

absorbed 4 deep, into, lost, rapt 6 intent 7 engaged, wrapped 8 caught up, immersed, involved 9 engrossed, wrapped up 10 captivated, fascinated 11 preoccupied

absorbing 9 arresting, consuming 10 engrossing, intriguing 11 captivating, fascinating, interesting **12** monopolizing, preoccupying

abstain 4 curb, deny, diet, fast, keep, pass, stop **5** avoid, forgo, spurn **6** abjure, eschew, give up, pass up, refuse, reject **7** decline, forbear, refrain **8** abnegate, forswear, hold back, keep from, renounce, swear off, teetotal, withhold **9** constrain, do without **11** deny oneself

abstemious 5 sober **6** strict **7** ascetic, austere, chaste, sparing **9** abstinent, continent, temperate **10** restrained **11** self-denying

abstinence 6 denial **7** fasting **8** chastity, sobriety **9** soberness **10** continence, self-denial, temperance **12** renunciation **13** self-restraint

abstract 5 brief, ideal **6** detach, digest, précis **7** epitome, neutral, outline, shorten, summary, utopian **8** academic, breviary, condense, detached, notional, separate, synopsis **9** disengage, summarize **10** abridgment, conceptual, conspectus, disconnect, dissociate, impersonal **11** appropriate, impractical, speculative, theoretical **12** condensation, hypothetical, transcendent **13** disinterested

abstracted 4 lost, rapt **6** absent, intent **7** bemused, faraway **8** absorbed, distrait, heedless **9** engrossed, oblivious, unheeding, unmindful, unminding, withdrawn **11** inattentive, inconscient, preoccupied, unconscious **12** absent-minded

abstruse 4 deep **5** heavy **6** knotty, occult **7** complex **8** esoteric, hermetic, involved, profound **9** difficult, intricate, recondite **11** complicated

absurd 5 balmy, comic, crazy, droll, funny, inane, loony, potty, silly, wacky **6** insane **7** asinine, fatuous, foolish, idiotic **8** farcical **9** illogical, laughable, ludicrous **10** irrational, ridiculous **11** harebrained **12** preposterous, unreasonable

absurdity 5 farce, folly **7** inanity **8** insanity, nonsense **9** craziness, dottiness, silliness **11** foolishness, incongruity, witlessness **13** irrationality, ludicrousness, senselessness

abundance 6 bounty, excess, plenty, riches, wealth **9** affluence, profusion **10** lavishness, prosperity **11** prodigality
Scottish: **5** routh

abundant 4 full, lush, rich, rife **5** ample, thick **6** filled, lavish, plenty **7** copious, crammed, crowded, liberal, profuse, replete **8** adequate, fruitful, generous, prolific **9** abounding, bounteous, boun-

tiful, extensive, luxuriant, plenteous, plentiful **10** sufficient

abuse 3 mar **4** harm, hurt, rail **5** anger, decry, shame, spoil, wrong **6** damage, debase, deride, impair, injure, misuse, revile, vilify **7** calumny, corrupt, cursing, exploit, obloquy, oppress, outrage, pervert, profane, pollute **8** belittle, berating, derision, derogate, discount, disgrace, ill-treat, maltreat, mistreat, reviling, swearing **9** blaspheme, contumely, desecrate, disparage, dispraise, harshness, invective, manhandle, mishandle, persecute, profanity, vehemence **10** defamation, depreciate, impose upon, malignment, revilement, scurrility **11** disapproval **12** billingsgate, condemnation, denunciation, vilification, vituperation

abusive 5 dirty, harsh **6** odious **7** corrupt **8** scurrile **9** injurious, insulting, invective, offending, offensive, truculent **10** calumnious, defamatory, scurrilous **11** blasphemous, castigating, opprobrious **12** calumniating, contumelious, sharp-tongued, vituperative, vituperatory

abut 4 join, link **5** flank, touch, verge **6** adjoin, border, butt on **8** border on, neighbor **9** lie beside **11** butt against, communicate

abutting 4 next **6** beside, joined, next to **7** joining, verging **8** adjacent, next door, touching **9** adjoining, bordering, impinging **10** connecting, contiguous, juxtaposed **11** bordering on, coextensive, coterminous, neighboring **12** conterminous

abysm see ABYSS

abysmal 4 deep, vast **7** endless **8** infinite, profound, unending, wretched **9** boundless, cavernous, plumbless, soundless, unplumbed **10** bottomless, fathomless, unmeasured **11** illimitable, measureless **12** immeasurable, unfathomable

abyss 3 pit **4** gulf, hell, hole, void **5** abysm, chasm, depth, gorge, hades, Sheol **6** Tophet **7** fissure, Gehenna, inferno **8** crevasse, deepness **9** perdition **10** underworld

academia 10 university **12** professoriat

academic 3 don **5** pupil, tutor **6** closet, fellow, master **7** bookish, learned, scholar, student **8** abstract, gownsman, lecturer, pedantic **9** professor, scholarly **10** scholastic **11** book-learned, conjectural, impractical, speculative, theoretical **12** conventional, hypothetical

academic period 4 term **7** quarter **8** semester **9** trimester

academy 6 lyceum 7 college, society 9 institute 10 prep school 12 conservatory

Academy Award winner

picture:

1927-28: 5 Wings *1928-29:* 14 Broadway Melody *1929-30:* 25 All Quiet on the Western Front *1930-31:* 8 Cimarron *1931-32:* 10 Grand Hotel *1932-33:* 9 Cavalcade *1934:* 18 It Happened One Night *1935:* 17 Mutiny on the Bounty *1936:* 16 The Great Ziegfeld *1937:* 15 Life of Emile Zola *1938:* 20 You Can't Take It with You *1939:* 15 Gone with the Wind *1940:* 7 Rebecca *1941:* 19 How Green Was My Valley *1942:* 10 Mrs. Miniver *1943:* 10 Casablanca *1944:* 10 Going My Way *1945:* 11 Lost Weekend (The) *1946:* 19 Best Years of Our Lives (The) *1947:* 19 Gentleman's Agreement *1948:* 6 Hamlet *1949:* 14 All the King's Men *1950:* 11 All About Eve *1951:* 15 American in Paris (An) *1952:* 19 Greatest Show on Earth (The) *1953:* 18 From Here to Eternity *1954:* 15 On the Waterfront *1955:* 5 Marty *1956:* 26 Around the World in Eighty Days *1957:* 20 Bridge on the River Kwai (The) *1958:* 4 Gigi *1959:* 6 Ben-Hur *1960:* 9 Apartment (The) *1961:* 13 West Side Story *1962:* 16 Lawrence of Arabia *1963:* 8 Tom Jones *1964:* 10 My Fair Lady *1965:* 12 Sound of Music (The) *1966:* 16 Man for All Seasons (A) *1967:* 19 In the Heat of the Night *1968:* 6 Oliver *1969:* 14 Midnight Cowboy *1970:* 6 Patton *1971:* 16 French Connection (The) *1972:* 9 Godfather (The) *1973:* 5 Sting (The) *1974:* 9 Godfather (Part Two)(The) *1975:* 25 One Flew over the Cuckoo's Nest *1976:* 5 Rocky *1977:* 9 Annie Hall *1978:* 10 Deer Hunter (The) *1979:* 14 Kramer vs. Kramer *1980:* 14 Ordinary People *1981:* 14 Chariots of Fire *1982:* 6 Gandhi *1983:* 17 Terms of Endearment *1984:* 7 Amadeus *1985:* 11 Out of Africa *1986:* 7 Platoon *1987:* 11 Last Emperor (The) *1988:* 7 Rain Man *1989:* 16 Driving Miss Daisy *1990:* 16 Dances with Wolves *1991:* 17 Silence of the Lambs (The) *1992:* 10 Unforgiven *1993:* 14 Schindler's List *1994:* 11 Forrest Gump *1995:* 10 Braveheart *1996:* 14 English Patient (The) *1997:* 7 Titanic *1998:* 17 Shakespeare in Love *1999:* 14 American Beauty *2000:* 9 Gladiator *2001:* 13 Beautiful Mind (A) *2002:* 7 Chicago *2003:* 14 Lord of the Rings

actor:

1927-28: 8 Jannings (Emil) *1928-29:* 6 Baxter (Warner) *1929-30:* 6 Arliss (George) *1930-31:* 9 Barrymore (Lionel) *1931-32:* 5 Beery (Wallace), March (Fredric) *1932-33:* 8 Laughton (Charles) *1934:* 5 Gable (Clark) *1935:* 8 McLaglen (Victor) *1936:* 4 Muni (Paul) *1937:* 5 Tracy (Spencer) *1938:* 5 Tracy (Spencer) *1939:* 5 Donat (Robert) *1940:* 7 Stewart (James) *1941:* 6 Cooper (Gary) *1942:* 6 Cagney (James) *1943:* 5 Lukas (Paul) *1944:* 6 Crosby (Bing) *1945:* 7 Milland (Ray) *1946:* 5 March (Fredric) *1947:* 6 Colman (Ronald) *1948:* 7 Olivier (Laurence) *1949:* 8 Crawford (Broderick) *1950:* 6 Ferrer (José) *1951:* 6 Bogart (Humphrey) *1952:* 6 Cooper (Gary) *1953:* 6 Holden (William) *1954:* 6 Brando (Marlon) *1955:* 8 Borgnine (Ernest) *1956:* 7 Brynner (Yul) *1957:* 8 Guinness (Alec) *1958:* 5 Niven (David) *1959:* 6 Heston (Charlton) *1960:* 9 Lancaster (Burt) *1961:* 6 Schell (Maximilian) *1962:* 4 Peck (Gregory) *1963:* 7 Poitier (Sidney) *1964:* 8 Harrison (Rex) *1965:* 6 Marvin (Lee) *1966:* 8 Scofield (Paul) *1967:* 7 Steiger (Rod) *1968:* 9 Robertson (Cliff) *1969:* 5 Wayne (John) *1970:* 5 Scott (George C.) *1971:* 7 Hackman (Gene) *1972:* 6 Brando (Marlon) *1973:* 6 Lemmon (Jack) *1974:* 6 Carney (Art) *1975:* 9 Nicholson (Jack) *1976:* 5 Finch (Peter) *1977:* 8 Dreyfuss (Richard) *1978:* 6 Voight (Jon) *1979:* 7 Hoffman (Dustin) *1980:* 6 De Niro (Robert) *1981:* 5 Fonda (Henry) *1982:* 8 Kingsley (Ben) *1983:* 6 Duvall (Robert) *1984:* 7 Abraham (F. Murray) *1985:* 4 Hurt (William) *1986:* 6 Newman (Paul) *1987:* 7 Douglas (Michael) *1988:* 7 Hoffman (Dustin) *1989:* 8 Day-Lewis (Daniel) *1990:* 5 Irons (Jeremy) *1991:* 7 Hopkins (Anthony) *1992:* 6 Pacino (Al) *1993:* 5 Hanks (Tom) *1994:* 5 Hanks (Tom) *1995:* 4 Cage (Nicholas) *1996:* 4 Rush (Geoffrey) *1997:* 9 Nicholson (Jack) *1998:* 7 Benigni (Roberto) *1999:* 6 Spacey (Kevin) *2000:* 5 Crowe (Russell) *2001:* 10 Washington (Denzel) *2002:* 5 Brody (Adrien) *2003:* 4 Penn (Sean)

actress:

1927-28: 6 Gaynor (Janet) *1928-29:* 8 Pickford (Mary) *1929-30:* 7 Shearer (Norma) *1930-31:* 8 Dressler (Marie) *1931-32:* 5 Hayes (Helen) *1932-33:* 7 Hepburn (Katharine) *1934:* 7 Colbert (Claudette) *1935:* 5 Davis (Bette) *1936:* 6 Rainer (Luise) *1937:* 6 Rainer (Luise) *1938:* 5 Davis (Bette) *1939:* 5 Leigh (Vivien) *1940:* 6 Rogers (Ginger) *1941:*

8 Fontaine (Joan) *1942:* 6 Garson (Greer) *1943:* 5 Jones (Jennifer) *1944:* 7 Bergman (Ingrid) *1945:* 8 Crawford (Joan) *1946:* 11 de Havilland (Olivia) *1947:* 5 Young (Loretta) *1948:* 5 Wyman (Jane) *1949:* 11 de Havilland (Olivia) *1950:* 8 Holliday (Judy) *1951:* 5 Leigh (Vivien) *1952:* 5 Booth (Shirley) *1953:* 7 Hepburn (Audrey) *1954:* 5 Kelly (Grace) *1955:* 7 Magnani (Anna) *1956:* 7 Bergman (Ingrid) *1957:* 8 Woodward (Joanne) *1958:* 7 Hayward (Susan) *1959:* 8 Signoret (Simone) *1960:* 6 Taylor (Elizabeth) *1961:* 5 Loren (Sophia) *1962:* 8 Bancroft (Anne) *1963:* 4 Neal (Patricia) *1964:* 7 Andrews (Julie) *1965:* 8 Christie (Julie) *1966:* 6 Taylor (Elizabeth) *1967:* 7 Hepburn (Katharine) *1968:* 7 Hepburn (Katharine) 9 Streisand (Barbra) *1969:* 5 Smith (Maggie) *1970:* 7 Jackson (Glenda) *1971:* 5 Fonda (Jane) *1972:* 8 Minnelli (Liza) *1973:* 7 Jackson (Glenda) *1974:* 7 Burstyn (Ellen) *1975:* 8 Fletcher (Louise) *1976:* 7 Dunaway (Faye) *1977:* 6 Keaton (Diane) *1978:* 5 Fonda (Jane) *1979:* 5 Field (Sally) *1980:* 6 Spacek (Sissy) *1981:* 7 Hepburn (Katharine) *1982:* 6 Streep (Meryl) *1983:* 8 MacLaine (Shirley) *1984:* 5 Field (Sally) *1985:* 4 Page (Geraldine) *1986:* 6 Matlin (Marlee) *1987:* 4 Cher *1988:* 6 Foster (Jodie) *1989:* 5 Tandy (Jessica) *1990:* 5 Bates (Kathy) *1991:* 6 Foster (Jodie) *1992:* 8 Thompson (Emma) *1993:* 6 Hunter (Holly) *1994:* 5 Lange (Jessica) *1995:* 8 Sarandon (Susan) *1996:* 9 McDormand (Frances) *1997:* 4 Hunt (Helen) *1998:* 7 Paltrow (Gwyneth) *1999:* 5 Swank (Hilary) *2000:* 7 Roberts (Julia) *2001:* 5 Berry (Halle) *2002:* 6 Kidman (Nicole) *2003:* 6 Theron (Charlize)

accede 3 let 5 admit, agree, allow, grant, yield 6 accept, assent, comply, concur, give in, permit 7 agree to, approve, concede, consent 9 acquiesce, cooperate, subscribe

accelerando 6 faster 7 speed up 10 speeding up

accelerate 3 gun, rev 4 grow, roll 5 hurry, impel, rev up, speed 6 hasten, open up, step up 7 quicken, speed up 8 expedite, go faster, increase 9 fast track, gain speed 10 move faster, peel rubber

acceleration 7 speedup 8 hurrying, spurring 9 hastening, revving up 10 increasing, quickening, speeding up, stepping up 12 moving faster

accent 4 beat, lilt, tone 5 acute, grave, meter, pulse, throb 6 rhythm, stress, weight 7 cadence 8 emphasis 9 diacritic, pulsation 10 inflection, intonation *Irish:* 6 brogue *Scottish:* 4 burr *Southern:* 5 drawl

accept 3 bow, buy, see 4 bear, gain, okay, take 5 admit, adopt, agree, catch, favor, go for, grasp, yield 6 accede, admire, affirm, assent, endure, follow, take in, take on 7 agree to, approve, believe, receive, respect, swallow, welcome 8 assent to, bear with, hold with, live with, stand for, tolerate, tough out 9 acquiesce, agree with, undertake 10 capitulate, comprehend, concur with, understand 11 acknowledge, countenance, subscribe to

acceptable 4 good, okay 6 decent, worthy 7 average, welcome 8 adequate, all right, bearable, ordinary, passable, pleasing, standard, suitable 9 endurable, tolerable 10 sufficient 11 commonplace, respectable, supportable 12 satisfactory 13 unexceptional, unimpeachable

acceptably 4 well 5 amply, right 7 capably 8 properly, suitably 9 fittingly, tolerably 10 adequately, becomingly, fairly well 11 competently 12 sufficiently 13 appropriately

acceptant 4 open 8 amenable, friendly, swayable 9 favorable, receptive, recipient, welcoming 10 open-minded, responsive 11 persuadable, persuasible, susceptible 13 influenceable

acceptation 4 gist 5 point, sense 6 import 7 meaning, message, purport 9 intention 10 intendment 12 significance, significancy 13 signification, understanding

accepted 5 usual 6 common, normal, proper 7 correct, regular, routine 8 approved, everyday, expected, habitual, ordinary, orthodox, received 9 customary 10 accustomed, recognized, sanctioned 11 established, traditional 12 conventional

access 3 fit, way 4 adit, door, gust, pang, path, road, turn 5 burst, entry, get at, onset, route, sally, spell, throe 6 attack, avenue, entrée 7 contact, flare-up, ingress, passage, seizure 8 approach, entrance, eruption, increase, outburst 9 admission, explosion 10 admittance

accessible 4 near, open 5 handy 6 public, usable 8 possible 9 available, operative, reachable 10 attainable, employable, obtainable 11 practicable 12 approachable, unrestricted

accession 4 rise 5 raise 8 addition, approach, increase, outburst, taking on 9 accretion, adherence, increment, induction 10 admittance, assumption, attainment, succession 11 acquisition 12 augmentation, inauguration

accessory 3 aid 4 aide, trim 5 extra, frill 6 helper 7 abettor, adjunct, fitting, insider, partner 8 addition, adjuvant, appendix 9 accretion, adornment, ancillary, appendage, assistant, associate, auxiliary, increment, secondary, tributary 10 accomplice, coincident, collateral, concurrent, decoration, incidental, subsidiary 11 appurtenant, concomitant, confederate, conspirator, subordinate, subservient 12 appurtenance, contributory 13 accompaniment, coconspirator, supplementary

accident 3 hap, lot 4 fate, luck, odds 5 fluke 6 chance, gamble, hazard, kismet, mishap 7 bad luck, destiny, fortune, lottery 8 calamity, casualty, fortuity, incident 9 adventure, mischance 10 misfortune 12 misadventure

accidental 3 odd 5 fluky 6 casual, chance, random 7 unmeant 8 by chance, careless 9 chromatic, dependent, extempore, impromptu, unplanned, unwitting 10 coincident, contingent, fortuitous, incidental, undesigned, unexpected, unforeseen, unintended, unpurposed 11 conditional, inadvertent 12 coincidental, nonessential, uncalculated 13 unintentional

acclaim 4 hail, clap, laud 5 cheer, éclat, exalt, extol, glory, honor, kudos, roose 6 homage, praise, salute 7 applaud, approve, commend, glorify, magnify, ovation, root for 8 applause, plaudits 10 compliment

acclimate 5 adapt 6 adjust, change, harden, season 7 toughen 9 condition, habituate

accolade 4 bays, fame 5 award, badge, honor, kudos 6 praise 7 laurels, tribute 8 approval 10 decoration 11 distinction

accommodate 3 fit 4 hold, rent, suit 5 adapt, alter, board, defer, favor, house, humor, lodge, put up, yield 6 adjust, attune, bestow, billet, change, encase, harbor, modify, oblige, please, submit, tailor, take in 7 cater to, conform, contain, enclose, furnish, indulge, quarter, receive, shelter 8 accustom, allow for, domicile 9 entertain, harmonize, integrate, reconcile 11 domiciliate, make room for

accommodating 7 amiable, helpful, willing 8 gracious, obliging 9 adaptable 10 hospitable, solicitous, thoughtful 11 considerate, cooperative

accommodations 4 digs, keep, room 5 hotel, motel 7 housing, lodging, shelter 8 lodgment, quarters 9 residence 12 room and board

accompaniment 4 back, mate 6 fellow, backup 7 adjunct, comrade, consort, partner 8 addition 9 accessory, associate, attendant, colleague, companion, corollary 10 assistance, complement, enrichment, equivalent, supplement 11 concomitant, enhancement 12 augmentation

accompany 4 join 5 bring, guide, pilot 6 attend, convoy, escort, go with 7 combine, conduct, consort 8 chaperon, come with 9 associate 10 appear with, go together 11 perform with

accompanying 8 incident 9 accessory, ancillary, attendant, attending, secondary 10 associated, coincident, collateral 11 concomitant

accomplice 4 aide, ally 5 aider 6 flunky, helper, stooge 7 abettor, partner 9 accessory, assistant, associate 11 confederate, conspirator, subordinate 13 coconspirator

accomplish 3 win 4 gain 5 reach, score 6 attain, effect, fulfil, rack up 7 achieve, execute, fulfill, perfect, pull off, realize, succeed 8 bring off, carry out, complete 9 discharge 10 bring about

accomplished 4 able 5 adept 6 expert 7 skilled 8 finished, masterly, skillful, talented 9 perfected, practiced 10 proficient 11 beyond doubt

accomplishment 3 act, art 4 deed, feat 5 craft, doing, skill 6 action, effort, finish, talent 7 ability, exploit 9 adeptness, expertise 10 attainment, capability, completion, expertness 11 achievement, acquirement, acquisition, proficiency

accord 4 deal, fuse, give, jibe, pact 5 agree, award, blend, chime, fit in, grant, match, merge, tally, union 6 affirm, assent, concur, confer, treaty 7 compact, concert, concord, conform, empathy, harmony, rapport 8 affinity, coalesce, coincide, dovetail, sympathy 9 agreement, harmonize, reconcile, vouchsafe 10 attraction, conformity, consonance, correspond, solidarity 11 concordance 13 understanding

accordant 8 agreeing 9 congruous, consonant 10 conforming, harmonious 13 correspondent

accordingly 4 duly, ergo, then, thus

5 hence **9** therefore, thereupon **12** consequently

accost 3 dog **4** call, dare, face, hail **5** annoy, cross, front, hound, worry **6** bother, call to **7** affront, apply to, bespeak, outface, outrage **8** approach, confront **9** challenge **10** buttonhole **11** memorialize

accouchement 7 lying-in **8** childbed, delivery **10** childbirth **11** confinement, giving birth, parturition

account 3 tab, use **4** bill, deem, note, rate, view **5** avail, basis, favor, score, story, track, value, worth **6** assess, client, esteem, reason, reckon, record, regard, report, repute **7** analyze, explain, expound, history, invoice, justify, recital, respect, service, utility, version **8** appraise, consider, customer, estimate **9** advantage, chronicle, narrative, probe into, rationale, reckoning, relevance, statement, valuation **10** admiration, estimation, exposition, importance, reputation, usefulness **11** consequence, distinction, explain away, explanation, performance, rationalize **13** consideration, justification *book:* **6** ledger

accountable 6 liable **8** amenable **10** answerable **11** explainable, responsible

accounting 11 bookkeeping

accoutre 3 arm, rig **4** deck, gear **5** adorn, dress, equip, fix up, ready **6** attire, fit out, outfit, supply **7** appoint, furnish, prepare, provide, turn out **9** provision

accoutrement 3 kit **4** gear **6** outfit, tackle **7** regalia **8** tackling **9** accessory, apparatus, equipment, machinery, trappings **10** provisions **11** furnishings, habiliments **12** appointments **13** paraphernalia

accredit 3 lay **4** okay **5** refer **6** assign, attest, charge, credit, enable **7** approve, ascribe, certify, commend, empower, endorse, license, warrant **8** sanction, validate, vouch for **9** attribute, authorize, recognize, recommend **10** commission, credential

accretion 4 rise **5** raise **6** growth **7** buildup **8** addition, increase **9** accession, appendage, increment **10** attachment **11** enlargement **12** accumulation, augmentation

accrue 4 grow **5** amass **6** gather, pile up **7** build up, collect, compile **8** increase **10** accumulate, amalgamate **11** agglomerate

accumulate 4 heap, grow, mass, pile **5** add to, amass, hoard, lay by, lay in, lay up, stock, store **6** accrue, garner, gather, pile up, rack up, roll up **7** acquire, backlog, collect, compile, lay down, stack up, store up **8** assemble, increase **9** stockpile

accumulation 4 bank, heap, mass, pile **5** hoard, stock, store, trove **6** growth **7** buildup, reserve **8** increase **9** accretion, amassment **10** collection **11** aggregation, enlargement **13** agglomeration

accumulative 6 heaped **7** growing **8** additive, additory **9** summative **10** collective, increasing **11** aggregative **12** augmentative

accuracy 8 veracity **9** certainty, exactness, precision **10** definition, exactitude **11** correctness, preciseness **12** definiteness

accurate 4 just, nice, true **5** exact, right **6** actual, proper **7** certain, correct, factual, precise **8** definite, reliable, rigorous **9** authentic, error-free, errorless **10** dependable

accursed 4 vile **6** odious **7** hateful **8** damnable **9** abhorrent, execrable, loathsome, offensive, repugnant, revolting **10** abominable, despicable, detestable

accusation 3 rap **6** charge **9** complaint **10** allegation, indictment **12** denunciation *false:* **7** calumny

accuse 3 tax **5** blame, brand **6** allege, charge, delate, finger, impute, indict **7** arraign, ascribe, censure, impeach **8** admonish, denounce, reproach **9** criminate, criticize, inculpate, reprobate **10** denunciate **11** incriminate

accustom 3 use **4** wont **5** adapt, inure **6** adjust, harden, season **7** conform **9** habituate **11** acclimatize, familiarize

accustomed 3 set **5** usual **6** normal **7** chronic, regular, routine **8** accepted, everyday, familiar, habitual, ordinary, standard **9** customary **10** habituated **11** commonplace, established, traditional **12** conventional

ace 3 bit, jot, pip, top **4** atom, hair, iota, mite, star **5** crumb, minim, point, score, speck **6** defeat, master, winner **7** whisker **8** molecule, particle **9** first rate, hole in one **11** hairbreadth, tennis score

ace and face card 7 natural **9** blackjack

acedia 6 apathy **7** boredom

acerbate 3 vex **5** anger, annoy, peeve **6** madden **7** incense, inflame **8** embitter, irritate **9** aggravate **10** exasperate

acerbic 4 acid, sour, tart **5** acrid, harsh, rough, sharp **7** caustic, cutting, satiric **8** stinging **9** acidulous, corrosive, sarcastic **10** astringent

acerbity 7 acidity, sarcasm **8** acrimony,

asperity, sourness, tartness **9** harshness, roughness, surliness **10** bitterness, causticity

Achates' companion 6 Aeneas

ache 3 yen **4** hurt, long, pain, pang, pine, pity, sigh **5** crave, smart, throb, yearn **6** hanker, hunger, stitch, suffer, thirst, twinge **8** yearning **11** commiserate *Scottish:* **6** stound

Acheron 5 Hades, river

achieve 3 get, win **4** gain **5** reach, score **6** attain, effect, finish, obtain, rack up, secure **7** acquire, execute, fulfill, get done, perform, realize, succeed **8** carry out, complete, conclude **9** actualize **10** accomplish

achievement 4 deed, feat **6** finish **7** exploit, success **10** attainment, completion **11** acquisition, tour de force

Achilles *adviser:* **6** Nestor *companion:* **9** Patroclus *father:* **6** Peleus *horse:* **7** Xanthus *lover:* **7** Briseis *mother:* **6** Thetis *slayer:* **5** Paris *victim:* **6** Hector *vulnerable part:* **4** heel

aching 4 hurt, sore **6** in pain **7** hurtful, hurting, painful **8** yearning **9** disturbed **10** afflictive, distressed **13** compassionate

acicular 5 acute, peaky, piked, sharp **6** peaked, pointy, spiked **7** pointed

acid 4 sour, tart **5** acerb **7** acerbic, acetose, caustic **8** stinging **9** corrosive, sarcastic, vitriolic *bleaching:* **6** oxalic *fatty:* **6** capric **7** caproic, stearic **8** caprylic *found in apples:* **5** malic *found in cranberries:* **7** benzoic *found in grapes:* **8** tartaric *found in lemons:* **6** citric *found in rhubarb:* **6** oxalic *found in sour milk:* **6** lactic *indicator:* **6** litmus *kind:* **5** amino, boric, iodic, malic, oleic **6** acetic, bromic, formic, nitric, oxalic, tannic **7** nitrous, silicic **8** carbolic, carbonic, muriatic, sulfuric **9** aqua regia **12** hydrochloric *neutralizer:* **4** base **6** alkali *tanning:* **6** tannic **8** catechin *vinegar:* **6** acetic

acidulous 3 dry **4** sour, tart **5** acerb, harsh, sharp **6** biting **7** acerbic, acetose, cutting, piquant, pungent **9** sarcastic

Acis *lover:* **7** Galatea *slayer:* **10** Polyphemus

acknowledge 3 own **4** avow, deem, tell, view **5** admit, agree, allow, grant, let on, own up **6** accede, accept, fess up, reveal **7** concede, confess, declare, divulge, profess **8** announce, consider, disclose, proclaim **9** recognize

acknowledgment 6 assent, avowal, credit, notice **9** admission **10** confession **11** affirmation, declaration, recognition

acme 3 cap, top **4** apex, peak **6** apogee,

climax, summit, tiptop, vertex, zenith **8** capstone, pinnacle, ultimate **9** high point **10** perfection **11** culmination

acorn sprouter 3 oak

acoustic 5 aural **6** audile **8** auditory **9** unplugged

acquaint 4 clue, tell, warn **6** advise, fill in, inform, notify, orient, reveal, wise up **7** apprise, divulge, present **8** accustom, disclose **9** enlighten, habituate, introduce **11** familiarize

acquaintance 4 mate **5** amigo, crony, grasp **6** friend **7** comrade, contact **9** associate, colleague, companion **10** cognizance, experience **11** familiarity

acquainted 6 versed **7** abreast, in touch **8** familiar, informed, up-to-date **9** au courant **10** conversant

acquiesce 3 bow, yes **5** agree, allow, bow to, yield **6** accede, accept, assent, comply, concur, give in, submit **7** consent, go along **9** reconcile, subscribe

acquiescence 6 assent **7** consent **8** giving in, yielding **9** deference **10** acceptance, compliance, conformity, submission **11** resignation

acquiescent 6 docile **7** passive **8** resigned, yielding **10** submissive **11** unresistant, unresisting **12** nonresistant, nonresisting

acquire 3 add, buy, get, win **4** earn, form, gain, land **5** amass, annex **6** garner, obtain, pick up, secure **7** bring in, collect, develop, procure **10** accumulate

acquirement 8 addition **9** accretion **11** acquisition

acquisition 4 gain **5** prize **7** winning **8** addition, learning, property, purchase **9** accretion

acquisitive 5 eager, itchy **6** grabby, greedy **8** covetous, desirous, grasping **10** avaricious

acquit 3 act **4** bear, free **5** carry, clear, let go **6** behave, deport, let off **7** absolve, comport, conduct, perform, release, set free **8** liberate **9** discharge, exculpate, exonerate, vindicate

acres 4 area, land **5** lands **6** estate **7** demesne, expanse, holding **8** property

acrid 4 acid, sour **5** harsh, nasty, sharp **6** biting, bitter **7** austere, burning, caustic, cutting, pungent **8** stinging **9** trenchant **10** astringent, irritating **11** acrimonious

acrimonious 3 mad **5** angry, cross, irate, sharp, testy **6** biting, bitter, cranky, ireful **7** acerbic, caustic, cutting **9** indignant, irascible, rancorous **11** belligerent, contentious, quarrelsome

acrimony 5 anger, spite **6** animus, malice, rancor **7** ill will **8** acerbity, asperity, mordancy **9** animosity, antipathy, harshness, virulence **10** bitterness **11** malevolence

Acrisius *daughter:* **5** Danaë *slayer:* **7** Perseus

acrobat 7 gymnast **9** aerialist, trapezist **11** funambulist

across 4 over **6** beyond **7** athwart **12** transversely *prefix:* **5** trans

act 3 law, run **4** bear, bill, deed, fake, feat, mime, play, pose, sham, work **5** bluff, feign, front, put-on, serve, stunt **6** affect, appear, behave, shtick **7** exploit, operate, perform, portray, pretend, routine, statute **8** function, pretense, simulate **9** officiate **10** masquerade **11** counterfeit, impersonate

acting 6 pro tem **7** interim, playing **9** ad interim, dramatics, imitating, portrayal, temporary **10** pro tempore **12** entertaining

action 4 case, deed, move, step, stir, suit, work **5** cause, doing **6** battle, bustle, combat **7** lawsuit, process, service **8** activity, behavior, conflict, fighting, function **9** execution, operation, procedure **10** engagement, proceeding **11** performance

action painting 7 tachism

activate 4 stir, wake **5** rally, rouse, set up, waken **6** arouse, awaken, call up, turn on **8** energize, mobilize, motivate, vitalize **9** stimulate

active 4 busy, live, spry **5** agile, alert, alive, brisk, going **6** at work, in play, lively, moving **7** driving, dynamic, flowing, running, working **8** animated, bustling, emitting, erupting, spirited, vigorous **9** effective, energetic, operating, operative, sprightly **11** functioning, industrious **12** enterprising

activity 6 action, bustle, motion **7** process, pursuit, venture **8** exercise, exertion **10** exercising, liveliness **11** undertaking

actor 4 mime, star **5** mimic **6** mummer, player **7** trouper **8** thespian **9** performer **11** participant **12** impersonator *name:* **3** Cox (Wally), Fox (James, Michael J.), Lee (Bruce), Lom (Herbert), Mix (Tom), Ray (Aldo) **4** Alda (Alan, Robert), Bean (Orson), Blue (Ben), Bond (Ward), Caan (James), Cage (Nicholas), Cobb (Lee J.), Coco (James), Culp (Robert), Dean (James), Depp (Johnny), Dern (Bruce), Duff (Howard), Egan (Richard), Falk (Peter), Ford (Glenn, Harrison), Foxx (Redd), Geer (Will), Gere (Richard),

Grey (Joel), Hill (Arthur), Hope (Bob), Hurt (John, William), Ives (Burl), Kaye (Danny), Kean (Edmund), Keel (Howard), Ladd (Alan), Lahr (Bert), Lord (Jack), Lowe (Rob), Lunt (Alfred), Marx (Chico, Groucho, Harpo, Zeppo), Muni (Paul), Ngor (Haing S.), Peck (Gregory), Penn (Sean), Pitt (Brad), Raft (George), Roth (Tim), Ryan (Robert), Shaw (Robert), Tati (Jacques), Tone (Franchot), Torn (Rip), Tune (Tommy), Wahl (Ken), Webb (Clifton, Jack), Wynn (Ed, Keenan), York (Michael) **5** Adler (Luther), Allen (Fred, Tim, Woody), Arkin (Adam, Alan), Asner (Ed), Autry (Gene), Ayres (Lew), Bacon (Kevin), Barry (Gene), Bates (Alan), Beery (Wallace), Benny (Jack), Berle (Milton), Boone (Richard), Booth (Edwin), Boyer (Charles), Brand (Neville), Burns (George), Caine (Michael), Candy (John), Chase (Chevy), Clift (Montgomery), Cosby (Bill), Dafoe (Willem), Davis (Clifton, Ossie, Sammy Jr.), Delon (Alain), Donat (Robert), Evans (Maurice), Ewell (Tom), Finch (Peter), Firth (Colin, Peter), Flynn (Errol), Fonda (Henry, Peter), Franz (Dennis), Gabin (Jean), Gable (Clark), Gould (Elliot), Grant (Cary, Hugh), Gwenn (Edmund), Hanks (Tom), Hardy (Oliver), Hauer (Rutger), Hawke (Ethan), Hayes (Gabby), Irons (Jeremy), Jaffe (Sam), Jones (Dean, James Earl, Tommy Lee), Kazan (Elia), Keach (Stacy), Keith (Brian, David), Kelly (Gene), Kiley (Richard), Kline (Kevin), Kotto (Yaphet), Lamas (Fernando, Lorenzo), Lanza (Mario), Lewis (Jerry, Richard), Lloyd (Harold), Lorre (Peter), Lukas (Paul), Lynde (Paul), March (Fredric), Mason (James), McCoy (Tim), Mills (John), Mineo (Sal), Moore (Dudley, Roger, Victor), Neill (Sam), Nimoy (Leonard), Niven (David), Nolte (Nick), Olmos (Edward James), O'Neal (Patrick, Ryan), Payne (John), Perry (Luke, Matthew), Pesci (Joe), Power (Tyrone), Price (Vincent), Pryce (Jonathan), Quaid (Dennis, Randy), Quayle (Anthony), Quinn (Aidan, Anthony), Rains (Claude), Reeve (Christopher), Scott (Campbell, George C., Randolph), Segal (George), Sheen (Charlie, Martin), Smits (Jimmy), Stack (Robert), Stamp (Terence), Sydow (Max von), Tracy (Spencer), Wayne (John), Wilde (Cornel), Wills (Chill), Woods (James), Young (Gig, Robert) **6** Abbott (Bud),

Albert (Eddie), Ameche (Don), Arness (James), Backus (Jim), Balsam (Martin), Barker (Lex), Baxter (Warner), Beatty (Ned, Warren), Begley (Ed), Blades (Ruben), Bogart (Humphrey), Bolger (Ray), Brando (Marlon), Brooks (Albert, Mel), Burton (Richard), Caesar (Sid), Cagney (James), Cantor (Eddie), Cariou (Len), Carney (Art), Carrey (Jim), Carvey (Dana), Chaney (Lon), Cleese (John), Coburn (Charles, James), Colman (Ronald), Conrad (Robert, William), Conway (Tim, Tom), Coogan (Jackie), Cooper (Gary), Cotten (Joseph), Coward (Noël), Crabbe (Buster), Crenna (Richard), Cronyn (Hume), Crosby (Bing), Cruise (Tom), Culkin (Macaulay), Curtis (Tony), Dailey (Dan), Dalton (Timothy), Danson (Ted), Danton (Ray), Darren (James), De Niro (Robert), de Sica (Vittorio), De Vito (Danny), Dillon (Matt), Downey (Robert), Dullea (Keir), Duryea (Dan), Duvall (Robert), Ferrer (José, Mel), Fields (W.C.), Finney (Albert), Garcia (Andy), Garner (James), Gibson (Hoot, Mel), Glover (Danny), Graves (Peter), Greene (Lorne), Grodin (Charles), Harris (Ed, Richard), Harvey (Laurence), Hayden (Sterling), Heflin (Van), Heston (Charlton), Hingle (Pat), Holden (Bill), Hopper (Dennis, William), Howard (Leslie, Ron, Trevor), Hudson (Rock), Hunter (Jeffrey, Tab), Huston (John, Walter), Hutton (Jim, Timothy), Irving (Henry), Jacobi (Derek, Lou), Jagger (Dean), Keaton (Buster, Michael), Keitel (Harvey), Kilmer (Val), Knotts (Don), Landau (Martin), Landon (Michael), Laurel (Stan), Lemmon (Jack), Liotta (Ray), Lugosi (Bela), MacRae (Gordon), Malden (Karl), Martin (Dean, Steve), Marvin (Lee), Massey (Raymond), Mature (Victor), McCrea (Joel), Meeker (Ralph), Menjou (Adolphe), Mifune (Toshiro), Modine (Matthew), Morley (Robert), Mostel (Zero), Murphy (Audie, Eddie), Murray (Bill, Don), Neeson (Liam), Nelson (Ozzie), Newley (Anthony), Newman (Paul), O'Brian (Hugh), O'Brien (Edmund, Pat), Oldman (Gary), O'Toole (Peter), Pacino (Al), Parker (Fess), Poston (Tom), Powell (Dick), Reeves (Keanu, Steve), Reiner (Carl, Rob), Reiser (Paul), Rennie (Michael), Ritter (John, Tex), Rogers (Roy, Wayne, Will), Romero (Cesar), Rooney (Mickey), Rourke (Mickey), Schell (Maximilian), Seagal (Steven), Sharif (Omar), Slezak (Walter), Snipes (Wesley), Spacey (Kevin), Spader (James), Swayze (Patrick), Taylor (Robert, Rod), Thomas (Danny, Richard), Turpin (Ben), Vallee (Rudy), Vaughn (Robert), Voight (Jon), Wagner (Robert), Walker (Robert), Warden (Jack), Wayans (Damon, Keenen Ivory), Weaver (Dennis, Fritz), Welles (Orson), Werner (Oskar), Wilder (Gene), Willis (Bruce) **7** Abraham (F. Murray), Andrews (Dana), Astaire (Fred), Aykroyd (Dan), Baldwin (Alec, Daniel, Stephen, William), Bellamy (Ralph), Bogarde (Dirk), Branagh (Kenneth), Bridges (Beau, Jeff, Lloyd), Bronson (Charles), Brosnan (Pierce), Brynner (Yul), Burbage (Richard), Bushman (Francis X.), Buttons (Red), Calhern (Louis), Calhoun (Rory), Cameron (Rod), Carroll (Leo G.), Chaplin (Charlie), Clooney (George), Connery (Sean), Connors (Chuck), Conried (Hans), Costner (Kevin), Crystal (Billy), Daniels (Jeff), da Silva (Howard), DeLuise (Dom), Dennehy (Brian), Donahue (Troy), Donlevy (Brian), Douglas (Kirk, Melvyn, Michael, Paul), Dreyfuss (Richard), Durante (Jimmy), Edwards (Vince), Feldman (Marty), Fiennes (Ralph), Freeman (Morgan), Garrick (David), Gazzara (Ben), Gielgud (John), Gleason (Jackie), Goodman (John), Gossett (Lou), Grammer (Kelsey), Granger (Farley, Stewart), Guinness (Alec), Hackman (Gene), Henreid (Paul), Hoffman (Dustin), Homolka (Oscar), Hopkins (Anthony), Hoskins (Bob), Janssen (David), Johnson (Ben, Don, Van), Jourdan (Louis), Jurgens (Curt), Karloff (Boris), Kennedy (Arthur, George), Klugman (Jack), Lawford (Peter), Leonard (Robert Sean, Sheldon), Lithgow (John), MacLane (Barton), Maharis (George), Mathers (Jerry), Matthau (Walter), McCarey (Leo), McGavin (Darren), McQueen (Steve), Milland (Ray), Mitchum (Robert), Montand (Yves), Navarro (Ramon), Newhart (Bob), O'Connor (Carroll, Donald), Olivier (Laurence), Palance (Jack), Paulsen (Pat), Peppard (George), Perkins (Anthony), Pickens (Slim), Pidgeon (Walter), Poitier (Sidney), Preston (Robert), Randall (Tony), Redford (Robert), Rickman (Alan), Robards (Jason), Robbins (Tim), Robeson (Paul), Roberts (Pernell, Tony), Sanders (George), Savalas (Telly), Scourby (Alexander), Selleck (Tom),

Sellers (Peter), Shatner (William), Shepard (Sam), Silvers (Phil), Sinatra (Frank), Skelton (Red), Skinner (Otis), Steiger (Rod), Stewart (James, Patrick), Stooges (Three), Tamblyn (Russ), Ustinov (Peter), Van Dyke (Dick, Jerry), Wallach (Eli), Widmark (Richard), Wilding (Michael), Winters (Jonathan), Woolley (Monty) **8** Banderas (Antonio), Barrault (Jean-Louis), Basehart (Richard), Belmondo (Jean-Paul), Berenger (Tom), Blackmer (Sidney), Borgnine (Ernest), Buchanan (Edgar), Buchholz (Horst), Chandler (Jeff), Costello (Lou), Crawford (Broderick, Michael), Cummings (Robert), Day-Lewis (Daniel), DiCaprio (Leonardo), Eastwood (Clint), Forsythe (John), Garfield (John), Goldblum (Jeff), Griffith (Andy), Harrison (Noel, Rex), Hemmings (David), Holbrook (Hal), Holloway (Stanley), Houseman (John), Jannings (Emil), Kingsley (Ben), Langella (Frank), Laughton (Charles), Marshall (E.G., Herbert), McDowall (Roddy), McDowell (Malcolm), McLaglen (Victor), Meredith (Burgess), Rathbone (Basil), Redgrave (Michael), Reynolds (Burt), Ritchard (Cyril), Robinson (Edward G.), Sarrazin (Michael), Scofield (Paul), Seinfeld (Jerry), Stallone (Sylvester), Stroheim (Erich von), Sullivan (Barry), Travolta (John), Turturro (John), Van Damme (Jean-Claude), Von Sydow (Max), Whitmore (James), Williams (Robin) **9** Amsterdam (Morey), Barrymore (John, Lionel), Brandauer (Klaus Maria), Broderick (Matthew), Carnovsky (Morris), Carradine (David, John, Keith, Robert), Courtenay (Tom), Depardieu (Gérard), Fairbanks (Douglas), Fishburne (Larry), Franciosa (Anthony), Hardwicke (Cedric), Harrelson (Woody), Hyde-White (Wilfrid), Lancaster (Burt), MacMurray (Fred), Malkovich (John), Montalban (Ricardo), Nicholson (Jack), Pleasance (Donald), Robertson (Cliff, Dale), Strasberg (Lee), Tarantino (Quentin), Valentino (Rudolph), Zimbalist (Efrem) **10** Fitzgerald (Barry), Hasselhoff (David), Montgomery (Robert), Richardson (Ralph), Sutherland (Donald, Kiefer), Washington (Denzel) **11** Chamberlain (Richard), Greenstreet (Sydney), Mastroianni (Marcello), Trintignant (Jean-Louis) **13** Kristofferson (Kris)

actor's quest: 4 part, role *signal:* **3** cue
actress 3 Bow (Clara), Cox (Courtney),

Day (Doris), Dee (Ruby, Sandra), Dru (Joanne), Gam (Rita), Loy (Myrna), May (Elaine), Rae (Charlotte) **4** Ball (Lucille), Bara (Theda), Barr (Roseanne), Cass (Peggy), Cher, Coca (Imogene), Cruz (Penelope), Dahl (Arlene), Daly (Tyne), Dern (Laura), Diaz (Cameron), Dors (Diana), Down (Lesley-Ann), Duke (Patty), Duse (Eleonora), Eden (Barbara), Foch (Nina), Garr (Teri), Gish (Dorothy, Lillian), Grey (Jennifer), Gwyn (Nell), Hawn (Goldie), Holm (Celeste), Hunt (Helen, Linda, Marsha), Hurt (Mary Beth), Hyer (Martha), Ivey (Judith), Kahn (Madeline), Kerr (Deborah), Lake (Veronica), Lisi (Virna), Main (Marjorie), Mayo (Virginia), Neal (Patricia), Olin (Lena), Page (Geraldine), Raye (Martha), Rigg (Diana), Ross (Diana, Katharine), Rush (Barbara), Ryan (Meg, Peggy), Shue (Elisabeth), Weld (Tuesday), West (Mae), Wood (Natalie, Peggy), Wray (Fay), York (Susannah) **5** Adams (Maude), Aimee (Anouk), Allen (Joan, Gracie, Karen, Nancy), Alley (Kirstie), Arden (Eve), Astor (Mary), Bates (Kathy), Berry (Halle), Black (Karen), Bloom (Claire), Blyth (Ann), Booth (Shirley), Brice (Fanny), Britt (May), Bruce (Virginia), Buzzi (Ruth), Caron (Leslie), Close (Glenn), Crain (Jeanne), Danes (Claire), Davis (Bette, Geena, Judy), Dench (Judi), Derek (Bo), Dunne (Irene), Eggar (Samantha), Evans (Edith), Falco (Edie), Field (Sally), Fonda (Bridget, Jane), Gabor (Eva, Zsa Zsa), Garbo (Greta), Gless (Sharon), Grant (Lee), Greer (Jane), Grier (Pam), Hagen (Uta), Hasso (Signe), Hayek (Salma), Hayes (Helen), Heche (Anne), Henie (Sonja), Howes (Sally Ann), Jones (Cherry, Jennifer, Shirley), Kazan (Lainie), Kelly (Grace, Patsy), Kurtz (Swoosie), Lahti (Christine), Lange (Hope, Jessica), Leigh (Janet, Jennifer Jason, Vivien), Lenya (Lotte), Lewis (Juliette), Loren (Sophia), Mason (Marsha, Pamela), Meara (Anne), Miles (Sarah, Vera), Moore (Demi, Julianne, Mary Tyler, Terry), North (Sheree), Novak (Kim), O'Hara (Maureen), Olson (Nancy), O'Neal (Tatum), Perez (Rosie), Picon (Molly), Pitts (Zasu), Reese (Della), Ricci (Christina), Roman (Ruth), Ruehl (Mercedes), Ryder (Winona), Saint (Eva Marie), Scott (Lizbeth, Martha), Shire (Talia), Smith (Alexis, Maggie), Stone (Sharon), Storm (Gale), Swank

(Hilary), Tandy (Jessica), Terry (Ellen), Tomei (Marisa), Tyler (Liv), Tyson (Cicely), Watts (Naomi), Welch (Raquel), Wiest (Dianne), Wyatt (Jane), Wyman (Jane), Young (Sean, Loretta) **6** Adjani (Isabelle), Angeli (Pier), Arthur (Beatrice, Jean), Ashley (Elizabeth), Bacall (Lauren), Bardot (Brigitte), Barkin (Ellen), Barrie (Wendy), Baxter (Anne), Bening (Annette), Bergen (Candice, Polly), Bisset (Jacqueline), Blaine (Vivian), Brooks (Louise), Bujold (Genevieve), Butler (Brett), Cannon (Dyan), Carter (Dixie, Lynda, Nell), Cooper (Gladys), Crouse (Lindsay), Curtin (Jane), Curtis (Jamie Lee), Danner (Blythe), Davies (Marion), Delaney (Dana), Del Rio (Dolores), Dennis (Sandy), Diller (Phyllis), Draper (Ruth), Dumont (Margaret), Duncan (Sandy), Durbin (Deanna), Duvall (Shelley), Ekberg (Anita), Ekland (Britt), Fabray (Nanette), Farmer (Frances), Farrow (Mia), Feldon (Barbara), Fisher (Carrie), Foster (Jodie), Garner (Peggy Ann), Garson (Greer), Gaynor (Mitzi), Gordon (Ruth), Grable (Betty), Grimes (Tammy), Hannah (Daryl), Harlow (Jean), Harper (Jessica, Tess, Valerie), Harris (Barbara, Julie, Rosemary), Hedren (Tippi), Hiller (Wendy), Hunter (Holly, Kim), Hussey (Ruth), Huston (Anjelica), Hutton (Betty), Irving (Amy), Keaton (Diane), Keeler (Ruby), Kidman (Nicole), Kinski (Nastassja), Knight (Shirley), Lamarr (Hedy), Lamour (Dorothy), Lasser (Louise), Laurie (Piper), Lillie (Beatrice), Louise (Tina), Lupino (Ida), MacRae (Sheila), Malone (Dorothy), Martin (Mary), Matlin (Marlee), McGraw (Ali), Merkel (Una), Merman (Ethel), Midler (Bette), Miller (Ann), Mirren (Helen), Monroe (Marilyn), Moreau (Jeanne), Moreno (Rita), Oberon (Merle), O'Brien (Margaret), Oliver (Edna May), Palmer (Lili), Paquin (Anna), Parker (Eleanor, Mary-Louise, Sarah Jessica, Suzy), Peters (Bernadette), Powers (Stephanie), Prowse (Juliet), Rainer (Luise), Rashad (Phylicia), Remick (Lee), Ritter (Thelma), Rivera (Chita), Rogers (Ginger), Scales (Prunella), Seberg (Jean), Sidney (Sylvia), Somers (Suzanne), Sommer (Elke), Spacek (Sissy), Streep (Meryl), Taylor (Elizabeth), Temple (Shirley), Theron (Charlize), Thomas (Marlo), Tiffin (Pamela), Tomlin (Lily), Turner (Kathleen, Lana), Walker (Nancy), Warren (Lesley Ann), Watson (Emily),

Weaver (Sigourney), Wilson (Marie), Winger (Debra), Wright (Teresa), Wynter (Dana) **7** Allyson (June), Andress (Ursula), Andrews (Julie), Aniston (Jennifer), Bassett (Angela), Bennett (Constance, Joan), Bergman (Ingrid), Binoche (Juliette), Blethyn (Brenda), Buckley (Betty), Bullock (Sandra), Burnett (Carol), Burstyn (Ellen), Campbell (Mrs. Patrick), Colbert (Claudette), Collins (Joan, Pauline), Cornell (Katherine), Cushman (Charlotte), Darnell (Linda), DeCarlo (Yvonne), Deneuve (Catherine), Dukakis (Olympia), Dunaway (Faye), Dunnock (Mildred), Fawcett (Farrah), Fleming (Rhonda), Fricker (Brenda), Gardner (Ava), Garland (Judy), Gingold (Hermione), Goddard (Paulette), Grahame (Gloria), Grayson (Kathryn), Hayward (Susan), Heckart (Eileen), Hepburn (Audrey, Katharine), Hershey (Barbara), Jackson (Anne, Glenda, Kate), Langtry (Lillie), Learned (Michael), Lombard (Carole), MacGraw (Ali), Madonna, Magnani (Anna), Mangano (Silvana), McGuire (Dorothy), McKenna (Siobhan), McQueen (Butterfly), Meadows (Audrey, Jayne), Mimieux (Yvette), Miranda (Carmen), Mulgrew (Kate), Natwick (Mildred), Parsons (Estelle), Perlman (Rhea), Perrine (Valerie), Plummer (Amanda), Podesta (Rosanna), Portman (Natalie), Roberts (Julia), Russell (Jane, Rosalind, Theresa), Scacchi (Greta), Sevigny (Chloë), Shearer (Norma), Shields (Brooke), Siddons (Sarah), Simmons (Jean), Sorvino (Mira), Sothern (Ann), Stevens (Connie, Stella), Stritch (Elaine), Swanson (Gloria), Swinton (Tilda), Thaxter (Phyllis), Thurman (Uma), Tierney (Gene), Ullmann (Liv), Winfrey (Oprah), Winslet (Kate), Winters (Shelley), Withers (Jane), Woodard (Alfre) **8** Anderson (Judith, Loni, Melissa Sue), Arquette (Patricia, Rosanna), Ashcroft (Peggy), Bancroft (Anne), Bankhead (Tallulah), Basinger (Kim), Blondell (Joan), Byington (Spring), Caldwell (Zoe), Channing (Carol, Stockard), Charisse (Cyd), Christie (Julie), Crawford (Joan), DeMornay (Rebecca), Dewhurst (Colleen), Dietrich (Marlene), Dressler (Marie), Fletcher (Louise), Fontaine (Joan), Fontanne (Lynn), Goldberg (Whoopi), Griffith (Melanie), Hayworth (Rita), Holliday (Judy), Lansbury (Angela), Lawrence (Gertrude), Leachman (Cloris),

Leighton (Margaret), Lindfors (Viveca), Lockhart (June), Lovelace (Linda), MacLaine (Shirley), McDaniel (Hattie), Mercouri (Melina), Minnelli (Liza), Nelligan (Kate), Neuwirth (Bebe), O'Donnell (Rosie), Pfeiffer (Michelle), Pickford (Mary), Prentiss (Paula), Redgrave (Lynn, Vanessa), Reynolds (Debbie), Roseanne, Rowlands (Gena), Sarandon (Susan), Shepherd (Cybill), Signoret (Simone), Stanwyck (Barbara), Straight (Beatrice), Sullavan (Margaret), Talmadge (Norma), Thompson (Emma, Sada), Van Doren (Mamie), Williams (Esther), Woodward (Joanne) **9** Alexander (Jane), Barrymore (Drew, Ethel), Bernhardt (Sarah), Blanchett (Cate), Cardinale (Claudia), Christian (Linda), Clayburgh (Jill), Dandridge (Dorothy), DeGeneres (Ellen), Dickinson (Angie), Fairchild (Morgan), Henderson (Florence), Kellerman (Sally), Mansfield (Jayne), McDonnell (Mary), Moorehead (Agnes), O'Sullivan (Maureen), Pleshette (Suzanne), Plowright (Joan), Schneider (Romy), Singleton (Penny), Stapleton (Jean, Maureen), Strasberg (Susan), Streisand (Barbra), Struthers (Sally), Thorndike (Sybil), Vera-Ellen, Zellweger (Renée) **10** Ann-Margret, Lanchester (Elsa), Montgomery (Elizabeth), Richardson (Miranda, Natasha), Rossellini (Isabella), Rutherford (Margaret), Tushingham (Rita) **11** de Havilland (Olivia), McCambridge (Mercedes), Riefenstahl (Leni), Silverstone (Alicia), Steenburgen (Mary) **12** Bonham-Carter (Helena), Lollabrigida (Gina), Mastrantonio (Mary Elizabeth)

actual 4 hard, live, real, true **5** exact **6** extant, living **7** certain, current, factual, genuine **8** absolute, bona fide, concrete, definite, existent, existing, material, physical, positive, tangible **9** authentic, objective **10** legitimate, phenomenal, undeniable **12** indisputable

actuality 4 fact **5** being, truth **7** reality **9** existence, substance **10** embodiment **11** incarnation, materiality

actually 4 very **5** truly **6** indeed, in fact, really **7** de facto, no doubt **9** genuinely, in reality, veritably **10** absolutely

actuate 4 move, spur, stir **5** drive, impel, rouse **6** arouse, excite, propel, set off, turn on **7** provoke, trigger **8** activate, energize, mobilize, motivate, vitalize

act up 5 cut up **7** show off **9** misbehave **11** misfunction

acumen 3 wit **6** acuity, vision, wisdom

7 insight **8** keenness **9** acuteness, sharpness **10** astuteness, perception, shrewdness **11** discernment, penetration, percipience **12** perspicacity

acute 4 dire, keen **5** sharp **6** urgent **7** crucial, exigent, intense, pointed **8** critical, incisive, piercing, shooting, stabbing **9** knifelike, observant, trenchant **10** perceptive **11** penetrating, quick-witted, sharp-witted

ad ___ 3 hoc, lib, rem **7** hominem, interim, nauseam **9** infinitum

adage 3 saw **4** rule **5** axiom, maxim, motto **6** byword, saying, truism **7** proverb **8** aphorism, apothegm

adagio 4 slow **5** tempo

Adah _husband:_ 4 Esau **6** Lamech _son:_ **5** Jabal, Jubal **7** Eliphaz

Adam _grandson:_ 4 Enos **5** Enoch _rib:_ **3** Eve _son:_ **4** Abel, Cain, Seth _wife:_ **3** Eve **6** Lilith

Adam ___ 4 Bede **5** Smith

adamant 3 set **4** firm, hard **5** rigid, stiff, stone, tough **6** flinty **8** immobile, obdurate, resolute **9** immovable, unbending, unswaying **10** determined, inflexible, unbendable, unyielding **11** unbreakable

adapt 3 fit **4** suit **5** alter, shape, yield **6** adjust, change, modify, revise, square, tailor **7** arrange, conform, remodel **9** acclimate, habituate, reconcile **11** acclimatize, accommodate

adaptable 6 mobile, pliant, supple **7** ductile, plastic, pliable **8** flexible, moldable **9** alterable, malleable, versatile **10** adjustable, modifiable **11** conformable

adaptation 6 change **8** revision **9** reworking **10** adjustment, alteration **12** modification

ad astra per ___ 6 aspera

add 3 sum, tot **4** cast, foot, join, tote **5** affix, annex, count, tally, total, unite **6** append, attach, figure, reckon, tack on, take on **7** augment, compute, count up, enlarge, improve, include **8** compound, increase, totalize **9** build onto, calculate **10** supplement

added 3 new **4** else, more **5** extra, fresh, other **7** another, farther, further **8** appended **9** accessory, increased **10** additional **13** supplementary

addendum 5 extra, rider **8** addition **10** supplement

adder 5 snake, viper **10** calculator **12** hognose snake

addict 3 fan, nut **4** bias, buff **5** hound, lover **6** abuser, devote, junkie, zealot **7** booster, devotee, fanatic, groupie, habitué **9** habituate, surrender **10** aficionado, enthusiast

addition 4 plus, rise **5** annex, extra, raise, rider **7** accrual, adjunct **8** addendum, appendix, increase **9** accession, accessory, accretion, extension, increment **10** supplement **11** enlargement **12** appurtenance, augmentation

additional see ADDED

additionally 3 too **4** also, more, then **5** again **6** as well **7** addedly, besides, further **8** likewise, moreover **9** along with **11** furthermore

additive 5 extra **8** extender **9** summative, substance

addle 5 mix up, spoil **6** muddle, puzzle **7** confuse, fluster, nonplus, perplex **8** befuddle, bewilder, confound, distract, throw off **9** dumbfound

add-on 7 adjunct **9** accessory **11** enhancement

address 3 aim, air, set, URL **4** hail, send, tact, talk **5** apply, court, grace, greet, level, place, point, poise, remit, route, skill, speak, treat **6** call to, devote, direct, pursue, relate, salute, speech **7** bearing, consign, deliver, forward, know-how, lecture, speak to, write to **8** appeal to, approach, converse, deal with, deftness, delivery, demeanor, dispatch, identify, location, petition, position, presence, talk with, transmit **9** attention, dexterity, diplomacy, expertise **10** adroitness, competence, directions, efficiency **11** communicate, comportment, designation, proficiency, savoir faire, tactfulness

adduce 3 lay **4** cite **5** claim, offer **6** allege, submit, tender **7** advance, present, proffer, propose, refer to, suggest **8** document **9** exemplify **10** illustrate

add up 3 sum **5** count, tally, total **6** amount, reckon **7** compute **9** make sense

add up to 4 mean **5** spell **6** amount, denote, import, intend **7** compute, connote, express, signify

A Death in the Family author 4 Agee (James)

adept 3 pro **4** deft, whiz **5** crack, savvy **6** adroit, expert, master, wizard **7** skilled **8** masterly, skillful, virtuoso **9** dexterous, masterful **10** proficient **11** crackerjack **12** professional

adequacy 5 might **6** enough **7** ability **8** capacity **10** capability, competence, sufficient **11** sufficiency **13** qualification

adequate 6 common, decent, enough **8** all right, passable, pleasing, standard, suitable **9** competent, sufficing **10** acceptable, sufficient **11** comfortable **12** satisfactory **13** unexceptional, unimpeachable

adequately 4 well **5** amply, right **6** enough **8** all right, passably, properly, suitably **9** fittingly, tolerably **12** sufficiently **13** appropriately

adhere 4 glue **5** cling, paste, stick **6** attach, bind to, cement, cleave, cohere, fasten **7** stick to **8** hold fast

adherence 4 bond **5** cling **7** loyalty **8** adhesion, clinging, cohesion, fidelity, sticking **9** constancy **10** attachment **12** faithfulness

adherent 6 cohort, votary **7** devotee, sectary **8** disciple, follower, henchman, partisan, stalwart **9** satellite, supporter **10** aficionado

adhering 6 clingy, gluing, sticky **7** binding **8** clinging, sticking **9** attaching, cementing

adhesive 4 glue **5** gluey, gooey, gummy, stamp, tacky **6** cement, clingy, gummed, sticky **7** holding, stickum **8** adhering, fastener, mucilage, sticking **9** attaching

adieu 5 congé **6** bye-bye, so long **7** cheerio, good-bye, parting **8** farewell **11** leave-taking

ad interim 6 acting, pro tem **9** temporary **10** pro tempore **11** temporarily

adios 4 by-by, ciao, ta-ta **5** adieu, later **6** bye-bye, so long **7** cheerio, goodbye, toodles **8** farewell, toodle-oo **10** hasta luego

adipose 3 fat **4** oily **5** fatty **6** greasy **7** fatlike

adit 3 way **4** door **5** entry **6** access, entrée, tunnel **7** ingress, passage **8** entrance **9** mine entry **10** passageway **12** mine entrance

adjacent 4 near **5** close **6** beside, nearby, next to **7** abutting, next door, touching **9** adjoining, alongside, bordering **10** contiguous, juxtaposed, near-at-hand **11** close-at-hand, neighboring **12** conterminous

adjoin 3 add **4** abut, link, line, meet **5** annex, touch, verge **6** append, attach, border, butt on, couple **7** connect, impinge **8** neighbor **11** communicate

adjourn 4 move, rise, stay **5** defer, delay **6** hold up, put off, recess, shelve **7** hold off, suspend **8** dissolve, hold over, postpone, prorogue **9** prorogate

adjudge 4 deem, rule **5** award, grant **6** decide, settle, umpire **7** mediate, referee **9** arbitrate **10** adjudicate

adjunct 5 added, affix **6** joined **8** addendum, addition, appanage, appendix, attached **9** accessory, accretion, appendage, assistant, associate, auxiliary **10** attachment **12** appurtenance

adjure 3 beg, bid **4** urge **6** exhort

7 beseech, entreat, command, implore, require **9** importune **10** supplicate

adjust 3 fit, fix, rig **4** suit, tune **5** adapt, order, right **6** accord, attune, modify, orient, settle, square, tailor, tune up **7** arrange, conform, correct, rectify, resolve **8** modulate, regulate **9** habituate, harmonize, reconcile **11** accommodate

adjuvant 4 aide **6** aiding, helper **8** enhancer, modifier **9** accessory, ancillary, assisting, auxiliary **10** collateral, subsidiary **11** appurtenant **12** contributory

ad-lib 9 extempore, improvise, impromptu **10** improvised, off-the-cuff, unprepared **11** extemporize, spontaneous, unrehearsed

Admetus *father:* **6** Pheres *wife:* **8** Alcestis

administer 3 run **4** boss, deal, give, head **5** issue **6** direct, govern, head up, manage **7** conduct, control, deal out, deliver, dole out, execute, give out, mete out, oversee, perform, provide **8** carry out, dispense, share out **9** apportion, supervise **10** distribute, portion out

administration 6 regime **7** control **9** direction **10** governance, presidency *system of:* **11** bureaucracy

administrator 4 boss, exec, head **5** chief **7** manager, officer **8** director, official, overseer **9** executive **10** supervisor

admirable 6 august, worthy **8** laudable **9** deserving, estimable, excellent, meritable **11** commendable, meritorious, outstanding **12** praiseworthy

admiral *American:* **4** Byrd (Richard), Sims (William) **5** Dewey (George), Stark (Harold) **6** Halsey (Bull), Nimitz (Chester) **7** Zumwalt (Elmo) **8** Farragut (David), Rickover (Hyman), Spruance (Raymond) *Confederate:* **6** Semmes (Raphael) *Dutch:* **5** Tromp (Maarten) *English:* **5** Drake (Francis) **6** Nelson (Horatio), Rodney (George), Vernon (Edward) **7** Hawkins (John) **8** Beaufort (Francis), Jellicoe (John), Villiers (George) **11** Mountbatten (Louis) *French:* **10** Villeneuve (Pierre-Charles) *German:* **4** Spee (Graf Maximilian von) **6** Dönitz (Karl), Raeder (Erich) **7** Doenitz (Karl), Tirpitz (Alfred von) *Japanese:* **4** Togo (Hideki) **5** Yonai (Mitsumasa) **8** Yamamoto (Isoroku) *Spanish:* **8** Menéndez (Pedro)

admiration 5 favor **6** esteem, praise, regard **7** account, delight, respect **8** applause, approval, pleasure **9** affection **10** estimation **11** approbation **12** appreciation

admire 5 adore, honor, prize, value

6 esteem, praise, regard, relish, revere **7** adulate, applaud, approve, cherish, commend, respect **8** consider, treasure **9** delight in **10** appreciate

admirer 3 fan **4** beau, buff **7** booster, devotee, fancier **8** believer, follower, partisan **9** supporter **10** enthusiast

admission 3 way **4** door **5** entry **6** access, assent, entrée **7** ingress **8** entrance **10** admittance, concession, confession **11** affirmation

admit 3 own **4** avow, take **5** agree, allow, enter, grant, let in, let on, lodge, own up **6** accept, fess up, harbor, permit, suffer, take in **7** concede, confess, receive, shelter, welcome **9** entertain, introduce, recognize **11** acknowledge

admix 5 blend, merge **6** mingle **7** combine **8** comingle, compound, immingle **9** commingle **11** intermingle

admixture 5 alloy, blend, combo **6** fusion **7** amalgam **8** compound **9** aggregate, composite **12** amalgamation

admonish 4 warn **5** alert, chide **6** lesson, monish, rebuke, talk to **7** caution, counsel, reprove, speak to **8** call down, forewarn, reproach **9** criticize, reprimand

admonition 3 tip **6** caveat, rebuke **7** caution, chiding, reproof, warning **8** reproach **9** criticism, reprimand **11** disapproval, forewarning

ado 4 fuss, stir **5** tizzy, whirl, worry **6** bother, bustle, flurry **7** concern, problem, trouble, turmoil **9** confusion **10** difficulty

adolescence 5 youth **7** puberty **8** minority **9** greenness **10** juvenility, pubescence **12** youthfulness

adolescent 4 teen **5** minor **6** teener **7** teenage **8** immature, preadult, teenager, youthful **9** pubescent

Adonai 3 God **4** YHWH **6** Elohim, Yahweh

Adonijah *brother:* **5** Amnon **7** Absalom, Chileab *father:* **5** David *mother:* **7** Haggith *slayer:* **7** Benaiah

Adonis *lover:* **5** Venus **9** Aphrodite *mother:* **5** Myrrh **6** Myrrha *slayer:* **4** boar

adopt 4 pick, take **5** raise **6** accept, affect, assume, choose, select, take on, take up **7** care for, embrace, endorse, espouse

adoption 6 choice **7** raising, support **8** espousal, taking in **9** embracing, selection **11** embracement

adorable 4 cute, dear **7** darling, lovable, winsome **8** charming, pleasing, precious **9** appealing **10** attractive, delightful

adoration 4 love **5** ardor, honor

6 esteem, praise 7 passion, worship
8 devotion, idolatry 9 adulation, affection, reverence 10 admiration 11 idolization

adore 4 love 5 honor, prize 6 admire, dote on, esteem, revere 7 cherish, idolize, respect, worship 8 dote upon, treasure, venerate 9 affection, delight in, reverence

adorn 4 deck, trim 5 fix up, grace 6 bedeck, enrich, pretty 7 dress up, enhance, enliven, furbish, garnish, smarten 8 beautify, decorate, ornament, prettify 9 embellish

adornment 5 decor, frill 6 finery 7 garnish 8 ornament, trimming 9 accessory, caparison 10 decoration 13 embellishment

ad rem 3 apt 7 apropos, fitting, germane 8 apposite, material, relevant 9 pertinent 10 applicable, relevantly, to the point 11 applicative, applicatory

adrift 4 asea, lost 5 at sea, loose 6 afloat 7 aimless, mixed up 8 confused, floating, unmoored 10 anchorless, bewildered 11 disoriented, purposeless

adroit 3 apt 4 able, deft 5 adept, canny, handy, savvy, smart 6 astute, clever, expert, nimble, shrewd 7 cunning, skilled 8 skillful, talented 9 dexterous, ingenious 11 intelligent, quick-witted, resourceful 13 perspicacious

adroitness 3 art 4 gift 5 craft, flair, knack, savvy, skill 7 address, cunning, know-how, prowess 8 deftness 9 adeptness, dexterity, expertise, ingenuity, readiness 10 cleverness, expertness 12 intelligence

adulation 7 acclaim, baloney, blarney, fawning, tribute, worship 8 applause, flattery, soft soap 9 servility, sweet talk 10 overpraise 11 false praise 12 blandishment

adulatory 7 buttery, fawning 8 unctuous 9 kowtowing, flattering, obsequious, oleaginous 11 bootlicking, sycophantic

adult 4 aged, ripe 5 grown 6 mature 7 grown-up, matured, ripened 9 fullblown 10 fully grown 11 full-fledged

adulterate 3 cut 4 thin 5 alloy, dirty, taint, water 6 debase, defile, dilute, doctor, dope up, impair, weaken 7 cheapen, corrupt, defiled, degrade, devalue, diluted, falsify, pollute, tainted, thinned 8 degraded, denature, impurify, polluted, spurious 9 water down 10 tamper with 11 contaminate

adumbrate 3 dim, fog 4 bode, call, hint, mist, veil 5 augur, cloud 6 darken, shadow, sketch 7 becloud, bespeak, betoken, obscure, outline, portend,

predict, presage, suggest 8 block out, disclose, forebode, forecast, foretell, indicate, intimate, prophesy 9 obfuscate, prefigure 10 foreshadow, overshadow 11 prefigurate 12 characterize

adumbration 4 hint, sign 5 shade, umbra 6 shadow 7 outline 8 penumbra 10 indication, intimation, suggestion

advance 3 aid 4 cite, help, lend, loan, move, rise 5 get on, march, money, raise, serve 6 assist, course, foster, mature, prefer, supply, uplift 7 deposit, develop, elevate, forward, furnish, further, headway, ongoing, present, proceed, promote, propose, upgrade 8 approach, get along, heighten, increase, progress 9 encourage, evolution, provision 10 accelerate, bring about 11 development, furtherance, improvement, progression 12 breakthrough

advanced 3 old 5 first 6 far out 7 forward, in front, leading, liberal, radical 8 far ahead, foremost 9 developed 10 precocious 11 broad-minded, progressive

advancement 4 gain, rise 5 boost 6 growth 7 headway 8 progress 9 elevation, promotion 10 betterment, preference 11 improvement, progression

advantage 4 boon, edge, gain, good, help, lead, odds 5 asset, avail, serve 6 better, profit 7 account, benefit, mastery 8 blessing, interest, leverage 9 allowance, head start, upper hand 10 ascendancy, domination, leadership, prosperity 11 superiority 12 running start

advantageous 4 good 6 timely, toward, useful 7 benefic, gainful, helpful 8 favoring, salutary 9 conducive, desirable, expedient, favorable, fortunate, promising 10 beneficial, profitable, propitious, worthwhile

advent 5 onset 6 coming 7 arrival 8 approach 9 beginning

adventitious 5 fluky 6 casual, chance 8 by chance 9 unplanned 10 accidental, contingent, fortuitous, incidental, unexpected

adventure 3 try 4 feat, risk, trip 5 quest, wager 6 chance, gamble, hazard 7 exploit 8 escapade 9 undertake 10 enterprise, experience

adventurous 4 bold, rash 5 brash, risky 6 daring 8 intrepid, reckless 9 audacious, dangerous, daredevil, foolhardy, hazardous, impetuous, imprudent 10 innovative 12 enterprising

adversary 3 con, foe 4 anti 5 enemy,

rival 7 opposer 8 opponent, opposing 10 antagonist, competitor

adverse 3 bad 4 anti 7 counter, harmful, hostile, hurtful, opposed 8 contrary, damaging, negative, opposing, opposite 9 injurious 11 deleterious, detrimental, obstructive, unfavorable 12 antagonistic, antipathetic

adversity 4 dole 5 trial 6 misery, mishap 7 bad luck, bad news, trouble 8 bad break, distress, hard time, hardship 9 mischance, suffering 10 difficulty, ill fortune, misfortune

advert 4 cite, note 5 refer 6 allude, notice, remark 7 bring up, mention, observe 8 indicate, point out

advertent 5 aware 7 heedful, mindful 9 attentive, intentive, observant, regardful

advertise 4 drum, hype, plug, puff, push 5 boost, pitch 6 blazon, herald, inform, notify, report 7 advance, apprise, build up, declare, promote, publish, sponsor 8 announce, ballyhoo, proclaim 9 broadcast, publicize 10 annunciate, promulgate

advertisement 4 bill, plug, sign 5 blurb, flyer, promo 6 notice, poster, want ad 7 affiche 8 circular 9 billboard, broadcast, promotion, publicity 10 commercial 11 declaration, publication 12 announcement, proclamation

advice 3 aid, tip 4 help, news, view, word 5 input 6 notice 7 caution, counsel, opinion, tidings, warning 8 guidance, teaching 10 admonition, suggestion 11 information, instruction 12 intelligence

advisable 4 wise 5 sound 6 seemly 7 politic, prudent 8 sensible, suitable, tactical 9 desirable, expedient, practical 10 worthwhile 11 recommended 12 advantageous

advise 3 tip 4 tell, tout, urge, warn 5 guide 6 clue in, confer, enjoin, fill in, inform, notify, tip off, wise up 7 apprise, caution, consult, counsel, suggest 8 acquaint, forewarn, instruct, point out 9 encourage, prescribe, recommend

Advise and Consent author 5 Drury (Allen)

advised 7 studied, weighed 8 designed, intended 10 calculated, considered, deliberate, thought out 11 intentional 12 premeditated

adviser 5 coach, guide 6 mentor 7 counsel, tipster 9 counselor 10 consultant, instructor

advisory 7 guiding, helping 9 educative 10 counseling 12 consultative 13 informational

advocacy 3 aid 6 urging 7 backing, defense, support 9 promotion

advocate 4 back, push, tout, urge 5 favor 6 backer, defend, preach, uphold 7 promote, propose, support 8 argue for, backstop, champion, exponent, plump for, side with 9 encourage, expounder, proponent, recommend, spokesman, supporter 11 countenance

Aeacus *father:* 4 Zeus *mother:* 6 Aegina *son:* 6 Peleus 7 Telamon

Aedon *brother:* 7 Amphion *sister-in-law:* 5 Niobe *son (victim):* 6 Itylus

Aeëtes *daughter:* 5 Medea *father:* 6 Helios

aegis 4 care, ward 5 armor, guard 6 charge, shield 7 backing, control, defense, support 8 auspices, guidance, security 9 influence, patronage, safeguard 10 protection 11 sponsorship

Aegisthus *father:* 8 Thyestes *lover:* 12 Clytemnestra *mother:* 7 Pelopia *slayer:* 7 Orestes *victim:* 6 Atreus 9 Agamemnon

Aeneas *companion:* 7 Achates *father:* 8 Anchises *mother:* 5 Venus 9 Aphrodite *son:* 5 Iulus 8 Ascanius *wife:* 6 Creusa 7 Lavinia

Aeneid *author:* 6 Vergil, Virgil *first words:* 16 arma virumque cano *hero:* 6 Aeneas

Aeolus *daughter:* 7 Alcyone 8 Halcyone *father:* 8 Poseidon

aeon 3 age 4 time 6 period 8 blue moon, duration

aerate 7 lighten, freshen, refresh 9 oxygenate, ventilate

aerial 4 high 5 lofty 6 flying, vapory 7 antenna, soaring 8 birdlike, elevated, ethereal, fanciful, towering, vaporous 9 pneumatic 10 impalpable 11 atmospheric, forward pass

aerie 4 nest 7 citadel, lookout 9 penthouse

aeronaut 4 Fogg (Phileas) 5 pilot 7 aviator 8 Zeppelin (Ferdinand, Graf von) 10 balloonist

Aerope *husband:* 6 Atreus *lover:* 8 Thyestes *son:* 8 Menelaus 9 Agamemnon

aery see AERIAL

Aesculapius *daughter:* 6 Hygeia 7 Panacea *father:* 6 Apollo *slayer:* 4 Zeus 7 Jupiter *teacher:* 6 Chiron *wife:* 6 Epione

Aeson *brother:* 6 Pelias *son:* 5 Jason

aesthete 4 buff 6 expert 7 devotee 9 authority 10 dilettante 11 appreciator, cognoscente, connoisseur

aesthetic 6 artful 8 artistic, creative, pleasing 9 beautiful, sensitive 10 attractive, harmonious

afar 5 apart 6 remote 7 distant

affable 4 kind, open, warm 6 at ease, genial, gentle, kindly, polite 7 amiable, cordial 8 friendly, gracious, obliging, pleasant, sociable 9 congenial, courteous

affair 4 case, love 5 amour, worry 6 action, matter 7 concern, liaison, palaver, romance 8 business, function, interest, intrigue, occasion 9 happening, procedure 10 proceeding 12 relationship

affect 3 act 4 fake, move, sham, stir, sway 5 adopt, alter, bluff, fancy, feign, haunt, put on, touch 6 assume, change, strike 7 act upon, disturb, impress, inspire, pretend 8 frequent, simulate 9 cultivate, influence 11 counterfeit

affectation 3 air 4 airs, pose, sham, show 6 facade 8 pretense 9 mannerism 10 pretension 13 artificiality

affected 5 false, moved, put-on 6 phoney 7 altered, assumed, changed, feigned, stilted 8 disposed, inclined, involved, mannered, precious, spurious 9 concerned, conscious, contrived, insincere, pretended, unnatural 10 artificial 11 overrefined, pretentious 13 self-conscious

affecting 3 sad 6 lively, moving 7 pitiful 8 exciting, poignant, touching 9 thrilling 10 disturbing, impressive 11 distressing, influential

affection 4 bias, love 5 trait 6 doting, liking, malady, virtue, warmth 7 ailment, concern, disease, emotion, feature, feeling, illness, leaning, passion, quality 8 devotion, disorder, fondness, interest, penchant, property, sickness, sympathy 9 attention, attribute, character, complaint, condition, sentiment 10 attachment, propensity, tenderness 12 predilection

affectionate 4 dear, fond, warm 6 caring, doting, loving, tender 7 devoted 8 friendly 11 sympathetic

affective 6 moving 7 emotive 8 stirring, touching 9 emotional

affectivity 7 emotion, feeling, passion 9 sentiment

affianced 7 engaged, pledged 8 intended, plighted, promised 9 betrothed, committed 10 contracted

affiche 4 bill, list 6 notice, poster 7 placard 8 handbill

affidavit 4 oath 9 testimony 11 affirmation, declaration

affiliate 4 ally, join 5 annex, unite 6 branch 7 combine, connect, partner 9 associate

affiliated 4 akin 5 bound 6 allied, joined, linked 7 kindred, related 9 connected, dependent 10 associated

affiliation 4 club 5 tie-in, union 6 hookup, league 7 cahoots, company, joining 8 alliance 10 connection, fellowship 11 association, combination, conjunction, partnership

affinity 6 simile 7 analogy, kinship, rapport 8 likeness, relation, sympathy 9 alikeness 10 attraction, similarity, similitude 11 resemblance 13 compatibility

affirm 3 say, yes 4 aver, avow, okay 5 state, swear, vouch 6 assent, assert, attest, depose, ratify, uphold 7 certify, confirm, declare, profess, protest, testify, witness 8 dedicate, validate 9 guarantee

affirmative 3 aye, yea, yes 4 yeah 6 assent 8 approval, positive 9 affirming, approving, asserting, assertion, endorsing, favorable, ratifying 10 confirming, supporting 11 affirmation

affix 3 add, tag 4 bind, glue, join, nail, tack 5 annex, paste, put on, rivet, stick, tag on 6 append, attach, fasten, tack on 7 impress, stick on, subjoin 8 addition 9 appendage 10 attachment

afflict 3 try, vex 4 pain, rack 5 annoy, beset, harry, press, smite, worry, wound, wring 6 bother, burden, harass, harrow, injure, martyr, pester, plague, strike, suffer 7 agonize, anguish, torment, torture, trouble 8 distress

afflicted 6 pained, rueful, woeful 7 doleful, injured, unhappy, worried 8 dolorous, stricken, troubled, wretched 9 disturbed, miserable, sorrowful, tormented 10 distressed

affliction 3 woe 4 care 5 cross, grief, trial 6 ordeal, plague, sorrow 7 anguish, illness, scourge, torment, trouble 8 distress, hardship, sickness 9 adversity, heartache, infirmity 10 misfortune 11 tribulation

afflictive 3 sad 4 dire, sore 6 aching, bitter, woeful 7 galling, hurtful, hurting, painful 8 grievous, mournful 9 sorrowful 10 calamitous, deplorable, lamentable 11 distasteful, distressing, regrettable, troublesome, unfortunate, unpalatable 13 heartbreaking

affluence 5 means, worth 6 bounty, influx, plenty, riches, wealth 8 opulence, property, richness 9 abundance, plenitude, profusion, resources 10 prosperity

affluent 4 full, rich 5 flush 6 loaded 7 copious, flowing, moneyed, opulent, wealthy, well-off 8 abundant, well-to-do

9 bountiful, plentiful, tributary, well-fixed **10** prosperous

afford 4 able, bear, give **5** allow, grant, incur, offer, spare, stand **6** bestow, confer, donate, impart, manage, supply **7** furnish, present, support, sustain

affordable 5 cheap **6** modest **7** low-cost **8** bearable **10** manageable, reasonable **11** inexpensive

affray 3 row **5** clash, fight, melee, scrap **6** fracas, rumpus **7** dispute, quarrel, ruction, scuffle **8** disorder, skirmish

affront 3 vex **4** face, meet, slap, slur **5** abuse, anger, annoy, wrong **6** injury, insult, offend, slight **7** offense, outrage, put down **8** contempt, rudeness **9** aspersion, criticize, encounter, indignity

Afghanistan *capital:* **5** Kabul *city:* **5** Herat **8** Kandahar **12** Mazar-i-Sharif *ethnic group:* **7** Pashtun *language:* **4** Dari **6** Pashto *monetary unit:* **7** Afghani *neighbor:* **4** Iran **5** China **8** Pakistan **10** Tajikistan, Uzbekistan **12** Turkmenistan

aficionado 3 fan **4** buff **5** hound, lover **6** expert **7** admirer, devotee, habitué **10** enthusiast **11** appreciator

afield 4 afar, away, awry **5** amiss, badly, wrong **6** abroad, astray **8** straying **9** elsewhere, off course

afire 3 hot **5** aglow, fiery **6** ablaze, aflame, alight, red-hot **7** blazing, burning, excited, flaming, flaring, ignited **8** inflamed, in flames **9** energized, excitable **10** passionate **11** conflagrant

afloat 4 asea **5** at sea **6** adrift, buoyed **9** supported, sustained

afraid 4 wary **5** chary, jumpy, loath, scary, sorry, timid **6** averse, scared, trepid **7** anxious, fearful, uneager, worried **8** cautious, hesitant, skittish, timorous **9** concerned, regretful, reluctant, unwilling **10** frightened **11** disinclined **12** apprehensive

afresh 3 new **4** anew, over **5** again, newly **6** de novo, encore **8** once more, repeated **9** once again

Africa *country:* **4** Chad, Mali, Togo **5** Benin, Congo, Egypt, Gabon, Ghana, Kenya, Libya, Niger, Sudan, Zaire **6** Angola, Gambia, Guinea, Malawi, Rwanda, Uganda, Zambia **7** Algeria, Burundi, Comoros, Eritrea, Lesotho, Liberia, Morocco, Namibia, Nigeria, Senegal, Somalia, Tunisia **8** Botswana, Cameroon, Djibouti, Ethiopia, Tanzania, Zimbabwe **9** Cape Verde, Mauritius, Swaziland **10** Ivory Coast, Madagascar, Mauritania, Mozambique, Seychelles **11** Burkina Faso, Côte d'Ivoire, Sierra Leone, South Africa **12** Guinea-Bissau *ethnic group:* **3** Ibo **4** Akan, Arab, Boer, Copt, Fula, Issa, Moor, Zulu **5** Bantu, Fulah, Galla, Hausa, Kongo, Mande, Pygmy, Swazi, Wolof **6** Berber, Fulani, Hamite, Herero, Kikuyu, Nubian, Somali, Tuareg, Ubangi, Yoruba **7** Ashanti, Bedouin, Bushman, Malinke, Swahili **8** Egyptian, Mandingo **9** Hottentot *language:* **3** Ibo **5** Bantu, Galla, Hausa **6** Arabic, Berber, Somali, Yoruba **7** Amharic, Bambara, Swahili **8** Malagasy **9** Afrikaans

aft 5 after **6** astern **8** rearmost, rearward **9** sternward

after 3 aft, for **4** back, hind, next, past, rear **5** below, later, since **6** astern, back of, behind, beyond, hinder **7** by and by, ensuing **8** hindmost, in view of **9** following, posterior, sternward **10** subsequent **12** subsequently

after all 3 yet **5** still **6** at last, though **7** finally, however **8** in the end **11** nonetheless **12** nevertheless

aftereffect 5 issue **6** result, upshot **7** fallout, outcome **11** consequence, eventuality

afterlife 6 beyond **8** eternity **9** hereafter

aftermath 4 wake **6** effect, result, upshot **12** consequences, repercussion

afterward 4 next, soon, then **5** later **6** behind **7** by and by, thereon **8** latterly **9** hereafter **10** thereafter **12** subsequently

afterword 8 epilogue

Agag *kingdom:* **6** Amalek *slayer:* **6** Samuel

again 4 also, anew, back, over **6** afresh, de novo, encore **8** once more

again and again 3 oft **4** much **6** often **8** ofttimes **10** frequently, oftentimes, repeatedly

against 6 contra, facing, versus **7** vis-à-vis **8** fronting, opposite, touching *prefix:* **4** anti **6** contra **7** counter

Agamemnon *avenger:* **7** Orestes *brother:* **8** Menelaus *daughter:* **7** Electra **9** Iphigenia *father:* **6** Atreus *slayer:* **9** Aegisthus *son:* **7** Orestes *wife:* **12** Clytemnestra

agape 4 love, open **6** amazed, gaping **7** yawning **8** wide open **9** astounded, love feast **10** astonished, confounded **11** dumbfounded, overwhelmed **13** thunderstruck

agate 3 taw **4** type **6** marble, quartz **7** shooter **8** type size

Agave *father:* **6** Cadmus *husband:* **6** Echion *mother:* **8** Harmonia *sister:* **3** Ino **6** Semele **7** Autonoë *son:* **8** Pentheus

age 3 eon, era **4** aeon, grow, span, time

5 epoch, ripen, stage 6 grow up, mature, mellow, period 7 develop, grow old 8 blue moon, division, interval, lifetime, long time, majority, maturate 9 become old 10 generation

aged 3 old 4 ripe, worn 5 cured, hoary, olden 6 mellow, senior 7 ancient, antique, elderly, matured, ripened 8 grown old, timeworn 9 developed, senescent, venerable 11 patriarchal 12 antediluvian

ageless 7 endless, eternal, lasting 8 dateless, enduring, immortal, timeless 9 immutable 11 everlasting

agency 4 firm 5 cause, force, means, organ, power 6 action, bureau, medium, office 7 company, channel, vehicle 8 activity, auspices, business, division, function, ministry 9 mechanism, operation 10 department, instrument 12 organization 13 establishment

agenda 6 docket, lineup 7 program 8 calendar, schedule 9 timetable *entry:* 4 item

Agenor *brother:* 5 Belus *daughter:* 6 Europa *father:* 7 Antenor, Neptune 8 Poseidon *mother:* 5 Libya *son:* 6 Cadmus

agent 3 fed, spy 4 tool 5 actor, means, organ, proxy, spook 6 deputy, factor, medium 7 channel, proctor, steward, vehicle 8 assignee, attorney, executor, minister, ministry 9 activator, go-between, middleman, operative 10 instrument, procurator

age-old 5 olden 7 ancient, antique, elderly, forever 8 timeworn 9 venerable 10 immemorial 11 time-honored, traditional

agglomerate 4 heap, mass, pile, rock 6 gather 7 cluster 9 aggregate 10 collection 11 aggregation

agglomeration 4 heap 5 hoard, trove 7 cluster 9 aggregate, amassment, gathering 10 collection, cumulation 11 aggregation

aggrandize 4 hype 5 boost 6 beef up, expand, extend, praise 7 augment, build up, enhance, enlarge, ennoble, glorify, inflate, magnify 8 heighten, increase, multiply 11 distinguish

aggravate 3 vex 4 gall 5 anger, annoy, grate, mount, peeve, pique, rouse, upset 6 burn up, deepen, nettle, worsen 7 bedevil, disturb, enhance, inflame, magnify, perturb, provoke 8 heighten, increase, irritate 9 intensify 10 exacerbate

aggravation 4 pain 5 worry 6 bother 8 increase 9 annoyance, worsening 10 irritation 11 provocation

aggregate 3 all, sum 4 body, bulk, floc 5 add up, gross, total, whole 6 amount 8 entirety, quantity, totality 9 composite 10 cumulative 11 agglomerate 12 conglomerate 13 agglomeration

aggregation 4 body, mass 5 crowd, group, hoard, total, trove 7 cluster, company 8 assembly 9 amassment, gathering 10 assemblage, collection, cumulation 11 agglomerate 12 accumulation

aggression 4 push, raid 5 fight, onset 6 attack 7 assault, offense 8 invasion 9 hostility, incursion, offensive, onslaught, pugnacity 10 assailment 12 belligerence 13 combativeness

aggressive 5 pushy 6 fierce, severe 7 hostile, scrappy, vicious, warlike 8 emphatic, forceful, militant 9 assertive, attacking, combative, energetic, intrusive, offensive 11 belligerent, contentious, domineering, hard-hitting 12 enterprising

aggrieve 4 hurt, pain 5 annoy, harry, upset, worry, wrong 6 harass, injure, plague 7 afflict, oppress, torment, trouble 8 distress 9 constrain, persecute

aghast 4 agog, awed 6 afraid, amazed, scared 7 anxious, fearful, shocked, stunned 8 appalled, dismayed, startled 9 awestruck, horrified, terrified 10 astonished, confounded, frightened 11 dumbfounded, overwhelmed 13 thunderstruck

agile 4 deft, spry 5 alert, brisk, catty, lithe, quick, zippy 6 active, adroit, limber, lively, nimble, supple 7 lissome 9 adaptable, dexterous, sprightly

agitate 4 move, rile, rock, stir, toss 5 argue, churn, peeve, shake, upset 6 arouse, bother, excite, flurry, joggle, ruffle, stir up 7 discuss, dispute, disturb, fluster, perturb, provoke, tempest, trouble, unhinge 8 disquiet, irritate 9 thrash out 10 discompose

agitation 4 flap, fuss, stir, to-do 5 clash 6 bustle, clamor, debate, flurry, lather, tumult 7 dispute, tempest, turmoil 9 commotion, confusion 10 turbulence 11 disturbance

agitator 5 rebel 6 shaker 7 inciter, stirrer 8 fomenter, inflamer 9 disrupter 10 instigator 11 provocateur

Aglaia see GRACES

Aglauros *father:* 7 Cecrops *sister:* 5 Herse 9 Pandrosos

aglow 4 warm 5 afire 6 bright, aflame, alight 7 excited, radiant, shining 8 gleaming, luminous

agnate 4 akin, like 5 alike 6 allied, joined, linked 7 cognate, connate, kindred, kinsman, related, similar **8** relation, relative **9** analogous **10** affiliated **11** consanguine **13** corresponding

agnostic 7 doubter, skeptic **8** doubting **10** questioner, undogmatic **11** uncommitted **12** noncommittal

Agnus ___ **3** Dei

ago 4 back, gone, past, yore **5** since **6** before

agog 4 avid, keen **5** eager **6** roused **7** excited, fervent **8** desirous **9** expectant, impatient **12** enthusiastic

agon 5 clash **6** battle **7** contest **8** conflict, struggle

agonize 4 fret, gall, hurt, pain, rack **5** chafe **6** harrow, squirm, suffer, writhe **7** afflict, torment, torture, trouble **8** distress, stew over, struggle **10** excruciate

agonizing 6 fierce **7** extreme, intense, painful, racking, tearing **9** harrowing, suffering, torturing, torturous **10** tormenting **12** excruciating

agony 4 pain **5** dolor, pangs **6** misery **7** anguish, passion, torment, torture **8** distress, outburst, struggle **9** suffering **10** affliction

agora 11 marketplace **12** meeting place

agrarian 5 rural **6** rustic **8** pastoral **10** campestral **12** agricultural

agree 3 buy, set, yes **4** jibe, okay, suit **5** admit, check, equal, fit in, match, tally **6** accede, accept, accord, assent, concur, settle, square **7** buy into, comport, concede, concert, concord, conform, consent **8** check out, coincide, dovetail, side with **9** acquiesce, harmonize, recognize, subscribe **10** correspond **11** acknowledge

agreeable 4 nice, open **5** ready **7** affable, welcome, willing **8** amenable, in accord, pleasant, pleasing **9** approving, congenial, congruous, consonant, favorable, receptive **10** acceptable, compatible, concurring, consenting, consistent **11** pleasurable, sympathetic

agreed 3 aye, yea, yep, yes **4** okay **6** surely **8** all right, of course **9** certainly **10** definitely, positively

agreement 4 bond, deal, pact **6** accord, assent, treaty **7** bargain, compact, concord, consent, entente, harmony **8** contract, covenant **9** concordat **10** acceptance, consonance **11** arrangement, concordance, concurrence

agree with 3 fit **4** suit **5** befit **6** assist, become **7** support **10** go together

agricultural 7 bucolic **8** agrarian, pastoral

agriculture 7 farming, tillage **8** agronomy, ranching **9** husbandry **11** cultivation, soil culture

Agrippina *brother:* **8** Caligula *husband:* **8** Claudius *son:* **4** Nero

aground 5 stuck **6** ashore, on land **7** beached, on shore **8** disabled, stranded

ague 3 flu **5** fever **7** malaria, shivers **9** influenza, shivering **10** blackwater

Ahab *daughter:* **8** Athaliah *father:* **4** Omri *wife:* **7** Jezebel

Ahasuerus *kingdom:* **6** Persia *wife:* **6** Esther, Vashti

Ahaz *kingdom:* **5** Judah *son:* **8** Hezekiah *wife:* **3** Abi

Ahaziah *father:* **4** Ahab **5** Joram **7** Jehoram *kingdom:* **5** Judah **6** Israel *mother:* **7** Jezebel **8** Athaliah *sister:* **9** Jehosheba **11** Jehosobeath

ahead 4 ante, fore **6** before, onward **7** earlier, forward, in front, leading, onwards **8** foremost, forwards, previous **9** in advance **10** beforehand **11** precedently

Ahinoam *father:* **7** Ahimaaz *husband:* **4** Saul **5** David *son:* **5** Amnon

aid 4 abet, care, hand, help, lift **6** assist, helper, relief, rescue, succor **7** backing, comfort, help out, support, sustain **9** assistant, attendant, subsidize **10** assistance, benefactor, mitigation **11** alleviation

Aida *composer:* **5** Verdi (Giuseppe) *father:* **8** Amonasro *lover:* **7** Radames *rival:* **7** Amneris

aide 6 deputy, helper, second **7** orderly **8** adjutant. **9** assistant, attendant, coadjutor **10** coadjutant, lieutenant

aikido 10 martial art

ail 4 hurt, pain **5** upset, worry **6** bother **7** afflict, disturb, trouble **8** distress

ailing 3 ill, low **4** down, sick, weak **6** in pain, poorly, sickly, unwell **8** below par, diseased **9** enfeebled **10** indisposed **11** debilitated

ailment 6 malady, unrest **7** disease, ferment, illness, turmoil **8** disorder, disquiet, sickness, syndrome **9** affection, complaint, condition, infirmity **10** inquietude, uneasiness **11** disquietude, restiveness **12** restlessness

aim 3 end, try **4** cast, goal, head, mark, mean, plan, want, wish **5** angle, essay, focus, level, point, slant, train **6** aspire, design, desire, direct, intend, object, strive, target, zero in **7** address, attempt, propose, purpose **8** ambition, endeavor **9** objective **11** contemplate

aimless 6 random **7** wayward **8** goalless **9** desultory, haphazard, hit-or-miss, irregular, pointless, unplanned **10** designless **11** purposeless

air

24

air 3 sky 4 aura, mien, mood, song, tune, vent 5 style 6 manner, melody, reveal, strain 7 bearing, divulge, express, feeling, quality 8 demeanor 9 broadcast, character, ventilate 10 atmosphere, deportment

aircraft 5 blimp, drone, plane 6 glider 7 airship, balloon, chopper 8 aerodyne, aerostat, airplane, jetliner, zeppelin 9 dirigible 10 helicopter *carrier:* 7 flattop *designer:* 6 Fokker (Anthony), Martin (Glenn) 7 Junkers (Hugo), Tupolev (Andrei) 8 Northrop (Jack), Sikorsky (Igor), Yakovlev (Alexander) 13 Messerschmitt (Willy)

airless 5 close 6 stuffy, sultry 8 stagnant, stifling 11 suffocating

airline 3 JAL, KLM, LOT, TWA 4 BOAC, El Al 5 Delta, Pan Am, USAir, Varig 6 Iberia, Qantas, United, Virgin 7 Eastern, JetBlue, Olympic 8 Aeroflot, Alitalia, American, Swissair 9 Air France, Lufthansa, Northwest, Southwest, U.S. Airways 11 Continental, Pan American

airman 5 flier, flyer, pilot 6 flyboy 7 aviator 8 aeronaut

air movement 4 gust, wind 5 draft 6 breath, breeze 7 updraft 9 downdraft

air navigation system 5 loran, navar, radar

airplane 3 jet 5 avion 6 bomber 7 fighter 8 autogiro, autogyro 9 transport *A-bomb-dropper:* 8 Enola Gay *battle:* 8 dogfight *body:* 8 fuselage *engine:* 3 jet 6 fanjet 7 propjet 8 turbofan, turbojet 9 turboprop *engine casing:* 7 nacelle *engineless:* 6 glider *instrument:* 5 radar, radio 7 compass 9 altimeter, gyroscope 10 tachometer 11 transponder *maneuver:* 4 buzz, dive, loop, roll 8 nosedive 9 chandelle 10 barrel roll *movement:* 3 yaw 4 bank, spin 5 pitch 8 tailspin *part:* 3 fin 4 flap, nose, prop, tail, wing 5 cabin, wheel 6 engine, rudder 7 aileron 8 airscrew, elevator 9 empennage, propeller 10 stabilizer *pilotless:* 5 drone *shelter:* 6 hangar *target:* 6 drogue *vapor:* 8 contrail

air plant 6 orchid 8 epiphyte 9 bromeliad, kalanchoe 11 Spanish moss 12 strangler fig

airport 5 field 7 helipad 8 heliport 9 aerodrome *building:* 8 terminal *flag:* 8 windsock
name:
> *Atlanta:* 10 Hartsfield *Boston:* 5 Logan *Chicago:* 5 O'Hare 6 Midway *Dublin:* 7 Shannon *London:* 7 Gatwick 8 Heathrow *New York:* 3 JFK 7 Kennedy 9 La Guardia *Paris:* 4 Orly 8 DeGaulle 9 Le Bourget *Rome:* 7 Da Vinci *Washington:* 6 Dulles, Reagan

8 National *part:* 5 apron, tower 6 runway 7 taxiway

airs 4 pose, show 5 front 6 vanity 7 hauteur 8 pretense 9 loftiness, mannerism, vainglory 10 pretension 11 affectation, insincerity, ostentation 13 artificiality

airship 3 jet 5 blimp, plane 8 zeppelin 9 dirigible

airtight 4 shut 6 closed, sealed 7 certain 8 hermetic, ironclad 10 impervious 11 impermeable, irrefutable 12 indisputable, invulnerable 13 incontestable

airy 4 open, rare, thin 5 blowy, fresh, gusty, light, lofty, proud, windy 6 aerial, bouncy, breezy, dainty, unreal 7 buoyant, gaseous, soaring, tenuous 8 affected, animated, delicate, ethereal, graceful, illusory, rarefied, spirited, towering, vaporous, volatile 9 expansive, frivolous, pneumatic, resilient, sprightly, vivacious 10 diaphanous, ventilated 11 atmospheric, skyscraping 12 effervescent, high-spirited

A Is for Alibi author 7 Grafton (Sue)

Ajax 4 hero 5 Greek 7 warrior *father:* 6 Oileus 7 Telamon *opponent:* 6 Hector *participant:* 9 Trojan War

akin 4 like, same 5 alike 6 allied 7 kindred, related, similar, uniform 8 parallel 9 analogous, consonant 10 affiliated, comparable, compatible 11 consanguine 13 corresponding

Alabama *capital:* 10 Montgomery *city:* 5 Selma 6 Mobile 10 Birmingham, Huntsville, Tuscaloosa 12 Muscle Shoals *college, university:* 6 Auburn 8 Tuskegee *mountain:* 6 Cheaha *nickname:* 6 Cotton (State) 12 Heart of Dixie *river:* 6 Mobile 7 Alabama 9 Tombigbee *state bird:* 12 yellowhammer *state flower:* 8 camellia *state tree:* 12 longleaf pine

alacrity 8 dispatch 9 briskness, eagerness, quickness, readiness 10 enthusiasm, expedition, liveliness, promptness 11 promptitude, willingness 12 cheerfulness

alamo 6 poplar 10 cottonwood

a la mode 4 chic, tony 6 trendy 7 dashing, stylish 8 up-to-date 9 exclusive 11 fashionable 12 with ice cream

alarm 3 SOS 4 bell, fear, horn 5 alert, dread, panic, scare, siren, spook, upset 6 dismay, excite, fright, signal, terror, tocsin 7 anxiety, disturb, startle, terrify, unnerve, warning 8 distress, frighten 9 terrorize 11 forewarning, trepidation 12 apprehension 13 consternation

alas 3 heu, woe 4 darn, drat 5 alack, oy vey 7 woe is me

Alaska *capital:* 6 Juneau *city:* 4 Nome 5 Sitka 6 Barrow 9 Anchorage, Fairbanks 10 Prudhoe Bay *island group:*

6 Kodiak 8 Aleutian, Pribilof *mountain, range:* 6 Brooks 8 McKinley, Wrangell *nickname:* 12 Last Frontier *park:* 6 Denali, Katmai *river:* 5 Yukon *state bird:* 9 ptarmigan *state flower:* 11 forget-me-not *state tree:* 11 sitka spruce

alb 4 gown 8 vestment

Albania *capital:* 6 Tirana, Tiranë *city:* 5 Korçë, Vlorë 6 Durrës 7 Shkodër *ethnic group:* 4 Gheg, Tosk *monetary unit:* 3 lek *neighbor:* 6 Greece, Serbia 9 Macedonia *part of:* 7 Balkans *peninsula:* 6 Balkan *sea:* 8 Adriatic

albatross 5 check, goony, worry 6 burden, gooney 7 anxiety, seabird 9 hindrance, millstone, restraint 11 encumbrance

Albee play 7 Sandbox (The) 8 Seascape, Zoo Story (The) 9 Tiny Alice 13 American Dream (The) 14 Three Tall Women 16 A Delicate Balance 25 Who's Afraid of Virginia Woolf?

albeit 5 still, while 6 even if, much as, though 7 despite, whereas 8 although 10 even though

Alberta *capital:* 8 Edmonton *city:* 5 Banff 7 Calgary *lake:* 6 Claire, Louise 9 Athabasca *mountain, range:* 7 Rockies 8 Columbia *provincial flower:* 8 wild rose *river:* 4 Milk 5 Peace 9 Athabasca

Albion 7 England

album 4 book 6 jacket, record 7 garland, omnibus 8 notebook, pictures, register 9 anthology, portfolio, scrapbook 10 collection, miscellany, recordings

Alcestis *father:* 6 Pelias *husband:* 7 Admetus *rescuer:* 8 Heracles, Hercules

alchemist 10 Paracelsus

alchemy 5 charm, magic 7 panacea, sorcery 8 wizardry 9 conjuring 10 necromancy

Alcina *sister:* 7 Morgana 10 Logistilla *victim:* 6 Rogero 8 Astolpho, Ruggiero

Alcinous *daughter:* 8 Nausicaa *wife:* 5 Arete

Alcmaeon *father:* 10 Amphiaraus *mother:* 8 Eriphyle *wife:* 10 Callirrhoe

Alcmene *husband:* 10 Amphitryon *son:* 8 Heracles, Hercules

alcohol 4 grog 5 booze, hooch, juice, sauce 6 hootch, liquor, red-eye, rotgut, tipple 7 spirits 8 home brew 9 aqua vitae, firewater, moonshine *name:* 4 amyl 5 butyl, cetyl, ethyl 6 glycol, methyl, sterol 7 butanol, ethanol, mannite, menthol 8 glycerin, glycerol, inositol, mannitol, methanol 9 isopropyl 11 cholesterol *used in perfumes:* 5 nerol 7 borneol 8 geraniol, linalool

alcoholic 4 hard 5 drunk 6 brewed 8 drunkard 9 distilled, fermented, inebriant, inebriate, spiritous 10 spirituous 11 dipsomaniac, inebriating 12 intoxicating

alcoholic drink see under BEVERAGE

alcove 4 nook 5 niche 6 gazebo, recess 9 belvedere 11 summerhouse *Japanese:* 8 tokonoma

Alcyone *father:* 5 Atlas 6 Aeolus *husband:* 4 Ceyx *mother:* 7 Pleione *sisters:* 8 Pleiades

ale 3 nog 4 beer, nogg

aleatory 4 iffy 5 dicey, risky, shaky 6 chancy 9 hazardous, uncertain 10 contingent, precarious, vulnerable 11 problematic, speculative 13 unpredictable

alehouse 3 bar, pub 6 bistro, saloon, tavern 7 taproom 8 beer hall 10 beer garden 11 rathskeller

alembic 5 still 6 filter 9 distiller

alert 3 SOS 4 keen, warn 5 alarm, quick, ready, sharp, smart 6 brainy, bright, clever, lively, notify, tip off, tocsin 7 heedful, mindful, on guard, red flag, wakeful 8 animated, forewarn, open-eyed, vigilant, watchful 9 attentive, mercurial, sprightly, wide-awake 10 perceptive 11 intelligent, quick-witted *Scottish:* 4 gleg 8 wakerife

Aleutian island 3 Fox 4 Adak, Atka, Attu, Near 5 Amlia, Kiska 6 Unimak 8 Unalaska 9 Andreanof *town:* 11 Dutch Harbor

alewife 4 fish 7 herring 8 menhaden

Alexander *birthplace:* 5 Pella *conquest:* 4 Tyre 5 Egypt, Issus 6 Greece, Persia 7 Parthia 8 Granicus *father:* 6 Philip *general:* 9 Antipater *horse:* 10 Bucephalus *kingdom:* 9 Macedonia *mother:* 8 Olympias *teacher:* 9 Aristotle *wife:* 6 Roxana

alfalfa 3 hay 5 plant 6 forage, legume 7 lucerne 9 perennial

alfresco 7 open-air, outdoor, outside 8 outdoors 9 out-of-door 10 out-of-doors

alga 6 desmid, diatom 7 seaweed *blue-green:* 6 nostoc *brown:* 4 kelp 5 fucus 8 rockweed *green:* 9 chlorella *red:* 4 nori

algebra term 4 root 6 factor 8 binomial, equation, monomial, variable 9 quadratic 10 polynomial

Algeria *capital:* 7 Algiers *city:* 4 Bône, Oran 6 Annaba 11 Constantine *coast:* 7 Barbary *desert:* 6 Sahara *ethnic group:* 4 Arab 6 Berber *language:* 6 Arabic, Berber *monetary unit:* 5 dinar *mountain range:* 5 Atlas 12 Saharan Atlas *neighbor:* 4 Mali 5 Libya, Niger 7 Morocco, Tunisia 10 Mauritania

Algren novel 17 Walk on the Wild Side (A) 19 Man with the Golden Arm (The)

Ali *son:* 5 Hasan 6 Husayn *wife:* 6 Fatima

alias 3 AKA 6 anonym, handle
7 moniker, pen name 8 nickname
9 false name, pseudonym, stage name
10 also called, nom de plume 11 nom
de guerre

alibi 4 plea 5 clear, cover, proof
6 answer, excuse 7 account, cover up,
defense, pretext 9 assertion, exonerate
11 explanation

alien 6 exotic 7 foreign, opposed,
strange 8 estrange, outsider, stranger,
transfer 9 estranged, extrinsic, foreigner, outlander 10 extraneous, outlandish
12 incompatible

alienate 4 part 5 repel 6 assign, convey,
divide, offend, oppose 7 break up, turn
off 8 disunify, disunite, estrange, separate, sign over, transfer 9 disaffect
10 drive apart, relinquish

alienation 5 break 6 breach 7 discord,
divorce, rupture 8 division 10 conveyance, separation 11 breaking off
12 disaffection, estrangement

alight 4 land 5 fiery 6 arrive, bright,
on fire, settle 7 blazing, burning,
deplane, descend, detrain, flaming,
flaring, get down, glowing, ignited,
shining 8 dismount 9 touch down
11 conflagrant

align 4 ally, join, line, true 5 agree,
array, order, range 6 adjust, follow, line
up 8 regulate 9 affiliate, associate
10 straighten

alike 4 akin, same 7 similar 8 parallel
9 analogous, consonant 10 comparable
13 corresponding

alikeness 6 simile 7 analogy 8 affinity,
alliance, relation 9 closeness, semblance 10 comparison, connection, similarity, similitude 11 resemblance

aliment 4 eats, fare, feed, food, grub
7 nourish, nurture, sustain 9 nutriment
10 sustenance 11 nourishment

alimentary 9 nutritive 10 nourishing,
sustaining 11 nutritional

alimentary canal 7 enteron

alimony 4 keep 5 bread 6 living, upkeep
7 support 9 allowance, provision
10 livelihood, sustenance 11 maintenance, subsistence

alive 4 rife, spry 5 alert, awake, aware,
brisk, fresh, quick, ready, vital 6 active,
extant, living, moving, viable 7 animate,
dynamic, knowing, replete, running,
teeming, working, zestful 8 animated,
existent, existing, sensible, sentient,
swarming, thronged 9 abounding,
breathing, cognizant, conscious, energetic, operative, sensitive, wide-awake
11 functioning, overflowing

alkali 4 base, salt 9 substance 11 soluble
salt *metal:* 6 cesium, sodium 7 lithium
8 francium, rubidium 9 potassium
10 monovalent *opposite:* 4 acid

alkaline 5 acrid, basic, salty 6 bitter
7 antacid, caustic, soluble 8 chemical

alkaline substance 3 lye 4 lime, soda
5 borax 6 potash 7 ammonia, antacid
8 pearl ash, saltwort 11 caustic soda

alkaloid 4 base *medicinal:* 5 ergot
7 codeine, emetine, eserine, quinine
8 atropine, caffeine, lobeline, morphine
9 ephedrine, quinidine, reserpine
11 scopolamine *narcotic:* 6 heroin
7 cocaine, codeine 8 morphine *poisonous:* 8 atropine, nicotine, solanine
11 scopolamine

all 3 sum 4 each 5 every, gross, total,
whole 6 entire, in toto, purely, wholly
7 exactly, totally, utterly 8 complete,
entirety, everyone, outright, totality
9 aggregate, everybody 10 altogether,
everything

all-around 7 general, overall, skilled
8 complete, sweeping, synoptic 9 adaptable, competent, many-sided, panoramic, universal, versatile 10 consummate, proficient 11 wide-ranging
12 encompassing 13 comprehensive

allay 4 balm, calm, ease, lull 5 abate,
quiet, still 6 lessen, reduce, settle,
soothe, subdue 7 assuage, compose,
lighten, mollify, quieten, relieve
8 decrease, diminish, mitigate, moderate 9 alleviate 11 tranquilize

all but 4 most, much, nigh 5 about
6 almost, nearly 8 as much as, in effect
9 just about, virtually 11 essentially,
practically 13 approximately

All Creatures Great and Small author
7 Herriot (James)

allegation 5 claim 6 charge, report
9 assertion, statement 10 contention,
profession 11 declaration

allege 3 say 4 avow, cite 5 claim, offer,
state 6 adduce, assert, attest, charge,
submit 7 advance, contend, declare,
present, profess 8 maintain 10 put forward

alleged 6 stated 7 accused, dubious,
reputed, suspect 8 asserted, declared,
doubtful, so-called, supposed
9 described, pretended, professed, purported, soi-disant 10 ostensible, self-
styled 12 questionable

allegiance 4 duty 5 ardor, piety 6 fealty,
homage 7 loyalty 8 devotion, fidelity
9 adherence, constancy, obedience
10 dedication, obligation 11 devotedness 12 faithfulness

allegiant 4 firm, true 5 liege, loyal

6 ardent, steady **7** devoted, dutiful, staunch **8** constant, faithful, resolute **9** steadfast **10** dependable

allegorical 5 moral **6** fabled **8** mythical, symbolic **9** legendary, spiritual **10** emblematic, exegetical, fictitious, figurative **12** iconographic, illustrative, metaphorical

allegory 4 myth, tale **5** fable, story **6** emblem, symbol **7** parable **8** apologue **9** symbolism **10** figuration **12** typification

allegro 5 brisk **6** bouncy, lively **8** animated, spirited **9** sprightly

allergy 5 dread **6** hatred **7** disgust, dislike **8** aversion, distaste **9** antipathy, disliking, rejection, repulsion

alleviate 4 cure, ease **5** allay **6** lessen, reduce, remedy **7** assuage, lighten, mollify, relieve **8** decrease, diminish, mitigate

alleviation 4 ease **6** relief **7** decline **8** decrease, easement **9** lessening, reduction **10** diminution, mitigation

alley 4 lane, walk **6** marble, street **7** passage **10** backstreet

all-fired 7 totally, utterly **9** extremely **10** absolutely, completely **11** excessively

alliance 3 tie **4** bond, pact **5** union **6** accord, league, treaty **7** compact, concord **8** affinity, relation **9** coalition **10** connection, federation **11** affiliation, association, combination, confederacy, conjunction, partnership, unification **12** relationship **13** confederation

allied 4 akin **5** bound **6** agnate, joined, linked, united **7** cognate, connate, kindred, related, unified **8** in league **9** connected **10** affiliated, associated, connatural **11** consanguine

alligator 11 crocodilian *relative:* **4** croc **6** caiman, cayman **9** crocodile

alligator pear 7 avocado

all in 4 dead, used, worn **5** spent, tired **6** bushed, done in, used up **7** drained, far-gone, worn-out **8** depleted **9** dead tired, exhausted, washed-out

all in all 5 in all **6** mainly **7** en masse, largely **9** generally **10** altogether, by and large, on the whole

allocate 4 give **5** allot, slice **6** assign, divide **7** dish out, divvy up, dole out, earmark, mete out **8** set apart **9** admeasure, apportion, designate **10** distribute

allocution 4 talk **5** spiel **6** sermon, speech **7** address, lecture, oration, oratory, pep talk **11** exhortation

allot 4 give **5** grant, share **6** accord, assign **7** deal out, divvy up, dole out, mete out **8** allocate, dispense, set aside **9** admeasure, apportion **10** distribute

allotment 3 cut, lot **4** bite, part **5** chunk, piece, quota, share, slice **6** ration **7** measure, portion **9** allowance, provision **13** apportionment

all-out 4 full **5** total **6** entire, utmost **7** maximum **8** absolute, complete, thorough **9** full-blown, full-scale, unlimited **12** totalitarian **13** thoroughgoing

all over 8 wherever **9** all around **10** everyplace, everywhere, far and near, far and wide, high and low, thoroughly, throughout

allow 3 let, lot, own **4** avow, give **5** admit, allot, brook, grant, leave, let on, stand **6** assign, endure, permit, suffer **7** concede, confess, consent, forbear, mete out **8** allocate, tolerate **9** apportion **11** acknowledge

allowance 3 aid, cut, lot, pay, sum **4** bite, edge, help, part **5** grant, leave, piece, quota, share, slice **6** amount, permit, ration **7** consent, handicap, measure, partage, portion, quantum, subsidy, vantage **8** handicap, pittance, quantity, sanction **9** advantage, allotment, head start, reduction **10** adjustment, allocation, assistance, concession, permission, sufferance, toleration **13** accommodation, apportionment, authorization

alloy 5 blend **6** fusion **7** amalgam, mixture **8** compound **9** admixture, composite **10** adulterant **11** interfusion **12** amalgamation, intermixture *brasslike:* **6** latten *copper-sulfur:* **6** niello *copper-tin:* **6** bronze *copper-zinc:* **5** brass **6** tombac *gold-like:* **6** ormolu *gold-silver:* **8** electrum *iron-carbon:* **5** steel *iron-nickel:* **5** invar *mercury:* **7** amalgam *tin-lead:* **5** terne **6** pewter, solder *used in jewelry:* **6** tombac

all-powerful 6 mighty **7** supreme **8** absolute, almighty **10** invincible, omnipotent **11** controlling

all right 3 aye, yea, yep, yes **4** good, okay, safe, well **6** agreed, decent, proper, surely **7** average **8** adequate, of course, passable, passably, pleasing, standard, very well **9** agreeable, certainly, tolerable, tolerably **10** , acceptably, adequately, definitely, positively, sufficient, well enough **12** satisfactory

all round see ALL-AROUND

All the King's Men author 6 Warren (Robert Penn)

All the Way Home author 4 Agee (James)

allude 4 hint **5** imply, point, refer **7** bring up, suggest **8** indicate, intimate

allure 4 draw, pull **5** charm, tempt **6** appeal, entice, lead on, seduce **7** attract, beguile, enchant, glamour, win over **8** charisma, inveigle, persuade

9 captivate, fascinate, magnetism, magnetize 10 attraction 11 enchantment, fascination

alluring 6 lovely 7 winning, winsome 8 charming, inviting, pleasing 9 appealing, beguiling, glamorous, seductive 10 appetizing, attractive, bewitching, enchanting 11 captivating, fascinating

ally 4 join 5 unite 6 friend, helper 7 comrade, partner 8 federate 9 accessory, affiliate, associate, auxiliary, bedfellow, colleague, supporter 10 accomplice 11 confederate 12 collaborator

almighty 4 very 6 hugely, mighty 7 awfully, godlike, supreme 8 absolute 9 extremely 10 invincible, omnipotent 11 all-powerful, exceedingly

almost 4 nigh 5 about 6 all but, nearly 8 as good as, as much as, not quite, well-nigh 9 just about, virtually 11 essentially, practically 13 approximately *Scottish:* 6 feckly

alms 4 gift 6 relief 7 present 8 donation, offering 10 assistance 11 benefaction, beneficence 12 contribution

aloe 9 emollient, succulent

Aloeus *father:* 7 Neptune 8 Poseidon *mother:* 6 Canace *son:* 4 Otus 9 Ephialtes *wife:* 9 Iphimedia

aloft 4 high, over 5 above 6 on high, upward 7 skyward 8 in flight, overhead

aloha 4 by-by, ciao, hail 5 hello, howdy 6 bye-bye, good-by, so long 7 good-bye, welcome 8 farewell, greeting 9 greetings *State:* 6 Hawaii

alone 4 only, sole, solo, stag 5 apart 6 singly, solely, unique, wholly 7 isolate, removed 8 detached, entirely, isolated, peerless, singular, solitary 9 matchless, unequaled, unmatched, unrivaled 10 nothing but, unequalled, unexampled, unexcelled 11 exclusively, unsurpassed 12 incomparable, unparalleled, unrepeatable 13 unaccompanied

aloneness 8 solitude 9 isolation, seclusion 10 uniqueness

along 3 too, yet 4 also, near, with 5 forth, there 6 as well, at hand, on hand, onward 7 besides, forward 8 likewise, moreover 11 furthermore 12 accompanying, additionally

alongside 6 beside, next to 8 touching 9 adjoining, bordering

aloof 3 shy 4 cold, cool 5 apart, proud 6 casual, chilly, frigid, offish, remote 7 distant, haughty, removed, stuck up 8 arrogant, detached, reserved, reticent, solitary 9 incurious, unbending, uncurious, withdrawn 10 disdainful, restrained, unfriendly, unsociable 11 constrained, indifferent, standoffish,

unconcerned 12 uninterested 13 disinterested

alopecia 8 baldness

alp 4 peak 5 mount 8 mountain

alpaca 4 wool 5 cloth 6 mammal *habitat:* 4 Peru 5 Andes 7 Bolivia

alpha 4 dawn 5 first, start 6 outset 7 dawning, genesis, opening 9 beginning 12 commencement

alphabet 4 ABC's 7 letters *Arabic:* 3 ayn, dad, dal, gaf, jim, kaf, kha, lam, mim, nun, qaf, sad, sin, tha, waw, zay 4 alif, dhal, shin 5 ghayn *Greek:* 3 chi, eta, phi, psi, rho, tau 4 beta, iota, zeta 5 alpha, delta, gamma, kappa, omega, sigma, theta 6 lambda 7 epsilon, omicron, upsilon *Hebrew:* 3 mem, nun, sin, taw, tet, vav, waw, yod 4 alef, ayin, beth, heth, kaph, koph, qoph, resh, shin, teth 5 aleph, gimel, lamed, sadhe, tsade, zayin 6 daleth, samekh *Old Irish:* 4 ogam 5 ogham *runic:* 7 futhark

Alpheus *beloved:* 8 Arethusa *father:* 7 Oceanus *form:* 5 river *mother:* 6 Tethys

Alpine *animal:* 4 ibex 7 chamois *dress:* 6 dirndl *house:* 6 chalet *lake:* 4 Como, Iseo 5 Garda 6 Geneva 7 Lucerne 8 Bodensee, Maggiore 9 Constance, Neuchâtel *pass:* 3 col 5 Cenis 7 Brenner, Simplon 9 St. Bernard *peak:* 5 Blanc, Eiger 7 Bernina 8 Jungfrau 10 Matterhorn *plant:* 9 edelweiss *primrose:* 8 auricula *resort:* 5 Davos 7 Bolzano, Zermatt 8 Chamonix, Grenoble 9 Innsbruck 10 Interlaken 11 Saint Moritz *river:* 5 Rhine, Rhône *snowfield:* 4 firn, névé *staff:* 10 alpenstock *state:* 5 Tirol, Tyrol 7 Bavaria *tunnel:* 5 Blanc, Cenis 7 Arlberg, Simplon 10 St. Gotthard *wind:* 4 bora, föhn 5 foehn

already 4 even, once 5 by now, prior 6 before, by then 7 earlier, just now 8 formerly 9 before now 10 by this time, heretofore, previously

also 3 and, too 4 more, plus 5 again, along 6 as well 7 besides, further 8 likewise, moreover 9 along with, including, similarly 10 in addition 11 furthermore 12 additionally

also-ran 3 dud 5 loser 7 failure, washout 8 defeated

altar 6 shrine *boy:* 6 server 7 acolyte *cloth:* 4 pall 7 frontal *constellation:* 3 Ara *hanging:* 6 dorsal, dossal *platform:* 8 predella *screen:* 7 reredos *shelf:* 7 retable *site:* 4 apse, bema *vessel:* 5 cruet, paten 7 chalice 8 ciborium 10 monstrance

alter 3 fix 4 geld, spay, turn, vary 5 adapt 6 adjust, change, doctor, modify,

mutate, neuter, revamp 7 remodel
8 castrate, moderate, modulate
9 refashion
alteration 4 turn 5 shift 6 change
8 mutation, revision 9 variation
10 adaptation, adjustment, changeover,
conversion, remodeling, transition
12 modification
altercate 4 spat, tiff 5 argue, scrap
6 bicker, hassle 7 dispute, quarrel,
wrangle 8 squabble 9 caterwaul
altercation 3 row 4 beef, flap, spat, tiff
5 brawl 6 blowup, combat, fracas, hassle 7 contest, dispute, quarrel, rhubarb,
wrangle 8 argument, squabble 9 bickering 10 falling-out 11 controversy,
embroilment
alternate 3 sub 5 proxy 6 backup, by
turn, change, fill-in, rotate, second
7 another, relieve, stand-in 8 periodic,
rotating 9 change off, fluctuate, recurrent, recurring, replacing, surrogate
10 equivalent, every other, periodical,
substitute 11 every second, pinch hitter, replacement 12 intermittent
alternately 6 in lieu, rather 7 instead
10 preferably
alternative 5 other, proxy 6 backup,
choice, option, second 7 another
8 atypical, druthers, election 9 different, selection, surrogate 10 preference,
substitute 11 contingency, nonstandard,
possibility
Althaea *father:* 8 Thestius *husband:*
6 Oeneus *son (victim):* 8 Meleager
although 4 when 5 still, while 6 albeit,
even if, much as 7 despite, howbeit,
whereas
altitude 6 height 8 eminence 9 elevation,
high level
altitudinous 4 high, tall 7 eminent 8 elevated
altogether 4 nude, well 5 fully, in all,
quite 6 in toto, wholly 7 all told, en
masse, exactly, totally, utterly 8 all in
all, entirely 9 generally, perfectly
10 absolutely, by and large, completely,
on the whole, thoroughly
altruism 7 charity 8 sympathy 10 compassion, generosity 11 benevolence
12 philanthropy, selflessness 13 unselfishness
altruistic 3 big 6 humane 8 generous
9 unselfish 10 benevolent, bighearted,
charitable, open-handed 11 considerate, magnanimous, noble-minded
12 humanitarian 13 philanthropic
alum 4 grad 6 emetic 7 styptic 8 graduate 10 astringent
always 4 ever 7 forever 8 evermore, for
keeps 9 at any rate, endlessly, eternally

10 at all times, constantly, in any event,
invariably 11 continually, forevermore,
in perpetuum, perpetually, unceasingly
12 consistently, continuously
Amahl and the Night Visitors composer
7 Menotti (Gian Carlo)
amalgamate 3 mix 4 ally, fuse, meld,
pool 5 admix, alloy, merge, unify, unite
6 mingle 7 combine 8 coalesce, compound, intermix 9 commingle, integrate 11 consolidate, intermingle
amalgamation 5 alloy, blend, union
6 fusion, merger 7 joining, melding,
merging, mixture, uniting 8 alliance,
compound 9 admixture, coalition,
composite 10 commixture 12 intermixture 13 consolidation
Amalthea *form:* 4 goat *horn:* 10 cornucopia *nursling:* 4 Zeus
amanita 8 death cap, mushroom 9 fly
agaric
amanuensis 6 scribe 7 copyist 9 scrivener, secretary 11 transcriber 12 stenographer
amass 4 bulk, heap, make, pile 5 hoard,
lay up, store, uplay 6 accrue, garner,
gather, pile up, roll up 7 acquire, collect, compile, round up, store up
8 assemble, cumulate 9 aggregate,
stockpile 10 accumulate 12 come
together
amassment 4 pile 5 clump, group,
hoard, stack, stock, store, trove 7 cluster 8 assembly, quantity 9 gathering,
stockpile 10 assemblage, collection,
cumulation 11 aggregation 12 accumulation 13 agglomeration
amateur 4 tyro 6 layman, novice, tinker,
votary 7 admirer, dabbler, devotee,
learner 8 aspirant, beginner, neophyte,
putterer 9 greenhorn, smatterer
10 apprentice, dilettante, enthusiast,
uninitiate 11 abecedarian
amateurish 3 raw 5 green 6 simple 7 artless 8 dabbling, inexpert 9 deficient,
unskilled, untutored 10 dilettante,
unfinished, unpolished, unskillful
12 dilettantist, unproficient 13 inexperienced
amative see AMOROUS
amatory 6 ardent, erotic, loving, tender
7 sensual 8 romantic 9 erogenous,
seductive 10 passionate 11 aphrodisiac
amaze 4 daze 5 floor 6 wonder
7 astound, perplex, startle 8 astonish,
bewilder, blow away, bowl over, confound, surprise 9 dumbfound 10 admiration 11 flabbergast
amazement 3 awe 6 marvel, wonder
8 surprise 9 marveling 10 admiration,

perplexity, wonderment **12** astonishment, bewilderment, confoundment

amazing 7 awesome **8** striking, stunning, wondrous **9** marvelous, startling, wonderful **10** astounding, impressive, miraculous, stupendous, surprising **11** astonishing, bewildering, spectacular **12** breathtaking

Amazon 6 parrot **7** warrior **8** giantess **12** woman warrior

ambassador 5 agent, envoy **6** legate **8** diplomat, emissary **9** messenger *papal:* **6** nuncio

amber 5 ocher, ochre, resin, rosin **6** orange, yellow **7** saffron

ambience 4 mood, tone **6** flavor, medium, milieu **7** climate **10** atmosphere **11** environment **12** surroundings

ambient 5 music **6** milieu **7** general, setting **8** everyday **9** prevalent **10** atmosphere, prevailing **11** atmospheric, environment, mise-en-scène **12** encompassing, surroundings **13** environmental

ambiguity 5 doubt **6** enigma, puzzle **7** evasion **9** equivoque, obscurity, vagueness **11** incertitude, uncertainty **12** doubtfulness, equivocality, equivocation **13** double meaning

ambiguous 5 vague **6** opaque, unsure **7** cryptic, dubious, inexact, obscure, unclear **8** doubtful, puzzling **9** enigmatic, equivocal, tenebrous, uncertain, unsettled **10** indefinite, inexplicit **11** problematic **12** inconclusive, questionable

ambit 4 area, room **5** field, limit, orbit, range, reach, scope, space, sweep **6** border, bounds, extent, limits, radius, sphere **7** breadth, circuit, compass, expanse, purview **8** boundary, confines **9** extension, perimeter, periphery **13** circumference

ambition 3 aim **4** goal, hope, itch, push, wish, zeal **5** ardor, dream, drive, vigor **6** desire, energy, hunger, spirit, target, thirst **7** avidity, craving, purpose **8** appetite, striving, yearning **9** eagerness, intention, objective **10** aspiration, enterprise, enthusiasm, get-up-and-go, initiative, pretension

ambitious 4 avid, bold, keen **5** eager, pushy **6** driven, hungry, intent **7** driving, zealous **8** aspiring, desirous, striving **9** energetic **10** aggressive **11** hardworking **12** enterprising, enthusiastic

ambivalent 5 mixed **6** unsure **7** warring **8** clashing, wavering **9** equivocal, uncertain, undecided **10** unresolved **11** fluctuating, vacillating **13** contradictory

amble 4 gait, walk **5** dally, drift, mosey **6** dawdle, linger, stroll, wander **7** meander, saunter

ambrosia 6 dainty, regale **7** dessert, perfume **8** delicacy, ointment

ambrosial 5 balmy, spicy, sweet **6** savory **7** scented **8** aromatic, fragrant, heavenly, luscious, perfumed, pleasing, redolent **9** delicious **10** delectable, delightful **11** scrumptious

ambulate 4 hoof, move, pace, step, walk **5** tread, troop **6** foot it, hoof it **7** traipse

ambulatory 6 moving, on foot, roving **7** nomadic, roaming, walking **8** vagabond **9** itinerant **11** peripatetic

ambush 4 jump, lurk, trap **5** snare **6** assail, attack, entrap, lay for, waylay **7** assault, ensnare **8** surprise **9** ambuscade **11** concealment

ameliorate 3 fix **4** help, lift, mend **5** amend, raise **6** better, perk up, remedy, reform **7** elevate, enhance, improve, lighten, relieve, upgrade **8** mitigate **9** alleviate **10** convalesce, recuperate

amenable 4 open, tame **6** docile, liable, pliant, suited **7** plastic, pliable, subdued, subject, willing **8** biddable, in accord, obedient, yielding **9** adaptable, agreeable, complying, malleable, receptive, tractable **10** answerable, consenting, responsive, submissive **11** accountable, acquiescent, cooperative, responsible

amend 3 fix **4** help **5** alter, right **6** better, change, modify, reform, remedy, repair, revise, square **7** correct, improve, rectify **8** put right **9** meliorate **10** ameliorate

amendment 5 rider **6** change, remedy, reform, repair **7** codicil **8** addendum, revision **10** alteration, attachment, correction **11** enhancement, improvement reformation **12** modification **13** rectification

amends 7 redress **8** reprisal **9** indemnity, quittance **10** recompense, reparation **11** restitution **12** compensation

amenities 5 mores **6** polish **7** decorum, manners **8** civility, courtesy **9** etiquette, propriety **12** social graces

amenity 5 charm, frill **6** luxury **7** comfort, quality **8** civility, courtesy, facility **9** advantage, etiquette, geniality, pleasance **10** affability, amiability, betterment, cordiality, enrichment, pleasantry, politeness **11** convenience, enhancement, improvement, sociability **12** agreeability, graciousness, pleasantness

ament 6 catkin

amerce 3 tax **4** dock, fine, levy **5** exact, mulct **6** punish **7** hit with, make pay **8** penalize

amercement 4 fine 5 mulct 7 damages, forfeit, penalty 10 assessment, punishment, reparation

American League *Baltimore:* 7 Orioles *Boston:* 6 Red Sox *Anaheim:* 6 Angels *Chicago:* 8 White Sox *Cleveland:* 7 Indians *Detroit:* 6 Tigers *Kansas City:* 6 Royals *Milwaukee:* 7 Brewers *Minnesota:* 5 Twins *New York:* 7 Yankees *Oakland:* 9 Athletics *Seattle:* 8 Mariners *Tampa Bay:* 9 Devil Rays *Texas:* 7 Rangers *Toronto:* 8 Blue Jays

American Samoa *capital:* 8 Pago Pago *island, island group:* 4 Rose 5 Aunuu, Manua 6 Swains 7 Tutuila *language:* 6 Samoan

America, the Beautiful *music:* 4 Ward (Samuel Augustus) *words:* 5 Bates (Katherine Lee)

Amfortas *father:* 7 Titurel *opera:* 8 Parsifal

amiability 7 amenity 9 geniality, pleasance 10 cordiality 11 sociability 12 complaisance, congeniality, friendliness, pleasantness, sociableness 13 agreeableness, enjoyableness

amiable 4 kind, warm 6 genial, gentle, kindly 7 affable, cordial, likable 8 cheerful, friendly, gracious, likeable, obliging, sociable 9 agreeable, congenial, courteous 10 responsive 11 complaisant, good-humored, good-natured, warmhearted

amicable 7 cordial, pacific 8 empathic, friendly, peaceful, sociable 9 congenial, peaceable 10 harmonious, like-minded, neighborly 11 sympathetic 13 understanding

amid 4 over 5 among, midst 6 during 7 amongst, between 10 throughout

amigo 3 pal 4 chum, mate, pard 6 friend 7 comrade, partner 8 sidekick 9 companion, confidant 12 acquaintance

amino acid 4 dopa 6 leucin, lysine, serine, toluid, valine 7 cystein, cystine, glycine, leucine, proline, toluide 8 cysteine, dopamine, histidin, thyroxin, toluidin, tyrosine

Amis, Kingsley *novel:* 8 Lucky Jim *son:* 6 Martin

amiss 3 bad 4 awry, poor 5 badly, wrong 6 afield, astray, faulty, flawed 7 wrongly 8 erringly, faultily 9 defective, imperfect 10 improperly, mistakenly, out of place 11 erroneously, imperfectly, incorrectly, unfavorably 12 inaccurately 13 inappropriate

amity 5 union 6 accord, comity, unison 7 concert, concord, harmony 8 alliance, goodwill 9 agreement 10 cordiality, friendship, kindliness 11 concurrence 12 friendliness

Ammonite 6 Semite *god:* 6 Molech, Moloch

ammunition 4 shot 5 bombs 6 rounds, shells 7 charges 8 armament, grenades, missiles, ordnance 10 cartridges 11 projectiles

Amneris's rival 4 Aïda

amnesty 6 pardon 7 freeing, release 8 immunity, reprieve 9 discharge 10 absolution 11 forgiveness 12 dispensation

Amnon *father:* 5 David *half sister:* 5 Tamar *mother:* 7 Ahinoam

amoeba 4 blob 8 rhizopod 9 protozoan

Amon *father:* 8 Manasseh *son:* 6 Josiah

Amonasro's daughter 4 Aïda

among 3 mid 4 amid 5 midst 6 amidst, within 7 between *prefix:* 5 inter

amorist 4 rake, wolf 5 lover, Romeo 7 Don Juan, gallant, playboy 8 Casanova, lothario, paramour 9 womanizer 12 heartbreaker

amorous 6 ardent, erotic, in love 7 amative, amatory, lustful 8 enamored, romantic 10 infatuated, passionate 11 aphrodisiac, impassioned

amorousness 4 love, lust 5 amour, ardor 6 desire 7 passion 9 eroticism

amorphous 7 unclear 8 formless, inchoate, nebulous, unformed, unshaped 9 shapeless, undefined 10 indistinct 11 nondescript 12 disorganized 13 characterless

amortize 5 repay 6 pay off, reduce 7 pay down 8 write off

amount 4 bulk, dose 5 add up, equal, price, total 6 dosage, matter, number, upshot 7 purport, quantum 8 quantity 9 aggregate, substance *owed:* 4 debt *small:* 3 bit, jot 4 atom, drop, iota, mite, whit 5 minim, spark, speck, trace 7 modicum, smidgen 8 molecule, particle 9 scintilla

amour 4 love 5 fling, lover 6 affair 7 liaison, passion, romance 8 intimacy, intrigue 9 dalliance 10 love affair 12 entanglement, relationship

amour propre 5 pride 6 egoism, vanity 7 conceit, egotism 8 self-love, vainness 9 vainglory 10 narcissism, self-esteem, self-regard 11 self-conceit, self-respect 12 pridefulness 13 conceitedness

amphetamines 5 speed 6 dexies, hearts, uppers 7 bennies, Dexoxyn 8 greenies, pep pills, Preludin 9 Dexedrine 10 Benzedrine, Methedrine

amphibian *burrowing:* 9 caecilian *legless:* 9 caecilian *tailed:* 3 eft 4 newt 10 salamander *tailless:* 4 frog, toad 8 bullfrog,

tree toad 10 batrachian *wormlike:* 9 caecilian *young:* 7 tadpole 8 polliwog
Amphion *brother:* 6 Zethus *conquest:*
6 Thebes *father:* 4 Zeus *mother:*
7 Antiope *sister:* 5 Aedon *wife:* 5 Niobe
amphitheater 4 bowl 5 arena 7 stadium
8 coliseum 10 auditorium, hippodrome
Amphitrite *father:* 6 Nereus *husband:*
7 Neptune 8 Poseidon *mother:* 5 Doris
son: 6 Triton
Amphitryon's wife 7 Alcmene
amphora 3 jar, jug, urn 4 ewer, vase
5 crock, flask 6 carafe, flagon, vessel
ample 4 wide 5 buxom, great, large,
roomy 6 lavish, plenty, portly 7 copious, liberal, profuse 8 abundant, generous, handsome, spacious 9 bounteous,
bountiful, capacious, expansive, extensive, plenteous, plentiful 10 commodious, sufficient 11 substantial
amplify 5 boost, raise, swell 6 dilate,
expand, extend, jack up 7 augment,
develop, distend, enhance, enlarge,
inflate, magnify 8 increase 9 elaborate,
intensify 10 supplement
amplitude 4 size 5 range, scale, scope,
space 6 amount, extent, spread 7 bigness, breadth, expanse, stretch 8 distance, fullness, wideness 9 abundance,
expansion, greatness, largeness, magnitude, roominess 12 spaciousness
13 capaciousness
amulet 4 juju, luck 5 charm 6 fetish, gri-
gri, mascot 7 periapt 8 gris-gris, talisman 10 lucky piece, phylactery
11 rabbit's-foot
amuse 4 wile 5 charm, cheer 6 appeal,
divert, engage, occupy, please, regale,
tickle 7 animate, beguile, delight,
enchant, enliven, gladden 8 distract,
interest, recreate 9 entertain, fascinate
amusement 3 fun 4 play 7 delight, pastime 8 pleasure 9 diversion, enjoyment
10 recreation 11 distraction 13 entertainment
amusing 3 fun 5 droll, funny 7 comical,
risible 8 engaging, humorous, pleasing
9 diverting, enjoyable 9 laughable
12 entertaining
Amycus *father:* 7 Neptune 8 Poseidon
friend: 8 Heracles, Hercules *mother:*
5 Melia
ana 5 varia 7 sayings 9 anecdotes 10 collection, miscellany 11 memorabilia,
miscellanea
anabasis 5 march 7 advance, headway,
retreat 8 progress 11 advancement, progression
anagogic 6 arcane, hidden, mystic,
occult, secret 7 obscure 8 esoteric,

mystical, telestic 9 spiritual 10 symbolical 11 allegorical
analects 5 album 6 digest 7 garland,
omnibus 8 treasury 9 anthology, selection 10 compendium, miscellany
11 compilation, florilegium
analgesic 6 opiate 7 anodyne 10 anesthetic, painkiller
analogous 4 akin, like 5 alike 7 kindred,
similar, related, uniform 8 parallel
9 consonant 10 comparable, equivalent,
resembling
analogue 5 match 7 cognate 8 parallel
9 correlate 10 similarity 11 correlation,
counterpart, equivalence 13 correspondent
analogy 6 simile 8 affinity, likeness,
metaphor, parallel, relation 9 agreement, alikeness, semblance 10 comparison, similarity, similitude 11 correlation, equivalence, resemblance
analysis 5 assay, audit, proof, study
6 method, review, report, survey 7 finding, inquiry 8 division 9 breakdown,
partition, statement 10 dissection,
inspection, resolution, separation
11 examination 13 clarification
analytic 6 cogent, subtle 7 logical, testing 8 studious 9 organized 10 diagnostic, scientific, systematic 11 proposition, questioning 13 investigative,
ratiocinative
analyze 4 part, test 5 assay, study
6 divide 7 dissect, examine, inspect,
resolve 8 classify, consider, separate
9 anatomize, break down, decompose,
interpret 10 decompound, scrutinize
11 deconstruct, distinguish, investigate
analyze grammatically 5 parse
Ananias 4 liar 9 falsifier 12 prevaricator
father: 9 Nedebaeus *wife (coconspirator):*
8 Sapphira
anarchism 4 riot 6 theory 7 misrule
8 disorder 9 distemper, rebellion
11 lawlessness
anarchist 5 rebel 6 rioter 8 agitator,
mutineer, provoker, revolter 9 dissident, insurgent 10 malcontent
11 provocateur 13 revolutionary
anarchy 4 riot 5 chaos 7 misrule, mob
rule, turmoil 8 disarray, disorder 9 confusion, distemper, mobocracy, rebellion 10 ochlocracy, revolution 11 lawlessness 13 nongovernment
anathema 3 ban 4 bane 5 curse, enemy,
odium, taboo 6 pariah 7 bugbear, censure, malison, outcast, reproof
8 loathing 9 damnation, bête noire
10 black beast, execration 11 abomination, commination, detestation, impre-

cation, malediction 12 condemnation, denunciation

anathematize 3 ban **4** damn, oust **5** curse, expel **6** banish **7** condemn **8** denounce, execrate **9** objurgate, proscribe **13** excommunicate

anatomical depression 5 fossa, fovea

anatomical tube 3 vas **4** duct **5** canal

anatomist 5 Wolff (Kaspar) **6** Harvey (William) **8** Vesalius (Andreas)

anatomize 5 cut up **7** analyze, dissect **8** separate **9** break down, decompose

anatomy 5 frame, mummy **6** makeup **8** analysis, division, skeleton **9** framework, histology, structure **10** dissection, morphology, physiology **11** examination

Anaxo *brother:* **10** Amphitryon *daughter:* **7** Alcmene *father:* **7** Alcaeus *husband:* **9** Electryon

ancestor 8 forebear, foregoer **9** ascendant, precursor, prototype **10** antecedent, antecessor, forefather, forerunner, progenitor **11** predecessor **12** primogenitor

ancestral 6 family, inborn, inbred, lineal **7** genetic **8** familial **9** inherited **10** bequeathed, hereditary **11** consanguine, patrimonial *sequence:* **8** pedigree **9** bloodline, genealogy

ancestry 4 line, race **5** blood, breed, stock **6** family, origin, source **7** descent, history, kindred, lineage **8** heritage, pedigree **9** parentage **10** derivation, extraction

Anchises' son 6 Aeneas

anchor 4 moor **6** secure **7** grapnel, mooring **8** mainstay *part:* **5** crown, fluke, shank

anchorage 4 port **5** haven, roads **6** harbor, refuge, riding **7** mooring, shelter **9** harborage, roadstead

anchorite 5 loner **6** hermit **7** recluse **8** solitary

anchors ___ 6 aweigh

ancient 3 old **4** aged **5** hoary, olden **6** age-old, primal **7** antique, archaic, elderly **8** Noachian, old-timer, primeval, timeworn **9** venerable **10** primordial **12** antediluvian

ancient capital 4 Susa **5** Aksum, Balkh, Calah, Isker, Kalhu, Ninus, Pella, Petra, Sibir **6** Angkor, Bactra, Nimrud, Sardis **7** Babylon, Knossos, Memphis, Nineveh, Samaria, Shushan **10** Persepolis

ancient city *Asia Minor:* **4** Nice, Teos **5** Tyana **6** Edessa, Nicaea **7** Antioch **13** Halicarnassus *Babylonia:* **4** Sura **5** Agade, Akkad, Eridu, Larsa **7** Ellasar *Bengal:* **4** Gaur **9** Lakhnauti *Canaan:*

5 Gezer *Cyprus:* **7** Salamis *Egypt:* **5** Tanis **6** Thebes **7** Memphis **10** Heliopolis *Etruria:* **4** Veii *Euphrates River:* **7** Babylon *Greece:* **5** Crisa **6** Athens, Sparta **7** Calydon **10** Lacedaemon *Ionia:* **4** Myus, Teos **5** Chios, Samos **6** Priene **7** Ephesus, Lebedos, Miletus, Phocaea **8** Colophon, Erythrae **10** Clazomenae *Italy:* **5** Locri **7** Pompeii **8** Siracusa, Syracuse **11** Herculaneum *Latium:* **5** Gabii **9** Alba Longa *Mayan:* **4** Cobá **5** Tikal, Tulum, Uxmal **8** Palenque **11** Chichén Itzá *Nile River:* **5** Meroë *North Africa:* **5** Utica **8** Carthage *Palestine:* **4** Gaza **5** Ekron, Endor, Sodom **6** Beroea, Bethel, Gilead, Hebron **7** Jericho, Samaria **8** Ashkelon **9** Capernaum, Jerusalem *Peloponnesus:* **5** Tegea **6** Sparta **7** Corinth *Sumeria:* **4** Kish, Uruk **5** Erech, Larsa **6** Lagash *Turkey:* **5** Assos, Assus **9** Byzantium

ancient country *Adriatic coast:* **7** Illyria *Africa:* **10** Mauretania *Arabian Peninsula:* **5** Sheba *Asia:* **4** Aram **5** Media, Minni, Syria **7** Armenia, Ash Sham, Bactria *Asia Minor:* **5** Lydia, Mysia **6** Aeolis, Pontus **7** Cilicia, Phrygia **8** Bithynia *Balkan:* **7** Macedon **9** Macedonia *Black Sea:* **7** Colchis *Dead Sea:* **4** Edom *Euphrates River:* **9** Babylonia *Europe:* **4** Gaul **5** Dacia **6** Gallia *gold-rich:* **5** Ophir *Italy:* **6** Latium **7** Etruria *Nile valley:* **4** Cush *Peloponnesus:* **4** Elis **7** Arcadia *Syria:* **9** Phoenicia

ancient empire 6 Median **7** Hittite, Persian **8** Assyrian, Athenian, Chaldean, Seleucid **9** Ptolemaic **10** Babylonian

ancient kingdom *Anglo-Saxon:* **6** Wessex *Asia:* **4** Ghor, Ghur *Celtic:* **7** Cumbria *China:* **3** Shu *Euphrates valley:* **4** Hira **7** Al-Hirah *Greece:* **8** Pergamon, Pergamum *North Of Assyria:* **3** Van **6** Ararat, Urartu *Palestine:* **5** Judah **6** Israel *Persian Gulf:* **4** Elam *Portugal:* **7** Algarve *Spain:* **4** Leon **6** Aragon **7** Castile, Galicia, Granada, Navarre *Syria:* **4** Moab *Welsh:* **5** Powys *West Sahara:* **4** Gana **5** Ghana

ancient monument 6 sphinx **7** obelisk, pyramid

ancient royal forest 4 Dean **8** Sherwood

ancient town *Africa:* **4** Zama *Armenia:* **4** Dwin, Tvin *Asia Minor:* **4** Soli **5** Derbe, Issus, Soloi *Attica:* **6** Icaria *Black Sea:* **5** Olbia **9** Apollonia *Greece:* **4** Abae, Opus **8** Marathon *Italy:* **4** Elea, Luna **5** Cumae, Velia *Latium:* **5** Ardea, Cures *Macedonia:* **5** Pydna, Stobi **9** Apollonia *Peloponnesus:* **5** Asine *Persia:* **6** Hormuz **8** Harmozia *Sicily:* **5** Hybla *Spain:*

5 Munda *Tatar:* 5 Isker, Sibir *Wendish:*
5 Julin

ancilla 3 aid 4 aide, ally, hand, help
6 helper 9 assistant, attendant, supporter

ancillary 5 extra 8 adjuvant, incident
9 accessory, attendant, attending, auxiliary, satellite, secondary 10 additional,
coincident, collateral, subsidiary, supporting 11 appurtenant, concomitant,
subordinate, subservient 12 accompanying, contributory 13 supplementary

andante 4 slow 5 tempo 7 relaxed, walking 8 moderate

Anderson, Maxwell *play:* 7 High Tor
8 Key Largo 9 Winterset 11 Valley
Forge 14 What Price Glory

Anderson, Sherwood *book:* 9 Poor
White 12 Dark Laughter
13 Winesburg Ohio

Andes native 4 Inca

andiron 7 firedog

Andorra *capital:* 7 Andorra *language:*
7 Catalan *liberator:* 11 Charlemagne
monetary unit: 4 euro *mountain range:*
8 Pyrenees *neighbor:* 5 Spain 6 France
river: 6 Valira

Andrea ___ 5 Doria 8 del Sarto

androgynous 7 epicene 8 bisexual 9 uni-
sexual

android 5 robot 9 automaton

Andromache *husband:* 6 Hector *son:*
8 Astyanax, Molossus

Andromeda *father:* 7 Cepheus *husband:*
7 Perseus *mother:* 10 Cassiopeia *rescuer:*
7 Perseus

___ **and warp** 4 weft, woof

anecdote 4 tale, yarn 5 story 7 account,
episode, recital 8 relation 9 narration,
narrative 12 recollection, reminiscence

anemic 3 wan 4 pale, thin, weak 5 pasty
6 feeble, pallid, sickly, watery 7 insipid
8 ischemic 9 bloodless, colorless
10 spiritless

anemone 9 buttercup 10 windflower

anent 4 as to, in re 5 about, as for
7 apropos 8 touching 9 as regards
10 concerning 13 with respect to

anesthetic 6 opiate 7 anodyne 9 analgesic 10 painkiller, palliative *medical:*
5 ether 6 spinal 8 morphine, procaine
9 halothane, novocaine 10 benzocaine,
chloroform, tetracaine 11 scopolamine
suffix: 5 caine

anesthetize 4 numb, stun 6 benumb,
deaden 8 etherize, knock out 9 narcotize 11 desensitize

anesthetized 4 dead, numb 5 inert
6 asleep, torpid 10 insensible 11 insensitive, unconscious

anew 4 over 5 again 6 afresh, de novo,
lately, of late 8 once more, recently

angel 6 backer, cherub, patron, seraph,
surety 7 sponsor 8 backer-up, guardian
9 celestial, guarantor, supporter
10 benefactor 11 underwriter *biblical:*
5 Uriel 7 Gabriel, Michael, Raphael *fall-
en:* 7 Lucifer *hierarchy:* 6 powers
7 thrones, virtues 8 cherubim,
seraphim 9 dominions *Mormon:*
6 Moroni *of death:* 6 Azrael

Angel Clare's bride 4 Tess

angelic 4 holy, pure 5 godly 6 divine
7 saintly 8 cherubic, ethereal, heavenly
9 celestial 11 beneficient

Angelica *father:* 9 Galaphron *husband:*
6 Medoro *lover:* 7 Orlando

Angelou work 13 Heart of a Woman
(The) 25 I Know Why the Caged Bird
Sings

anger 3 ire, irk, vex 4 bile, boil, burn,
fume, fury, gall, huff, rage, rant, rave,
rile 5 annoy, pique, storm, upset, wrath
6 blow up, choler, dander, enrage,
madden, nettle, offend, seethe, stir up
7 affront, bristle, dudgeon, flare up,
incense, outrage, provoke, steam up,
umbrage 8 acrimony, boil over, irritate
9 aggravate, annoyance, animosity, displease, infuriate 10 antagonism, antagonize, exasperate 11 displeasure, indignation, infuriation 12 exasperation

angle 3 aim, bow 4 axil, bend, bias, fish,
hand, skew, turn 5 facet, slant 6 aspect,
corner, crotch, dogleg 7 flexure, outlook, turning 9 direction, viewpoint
10 standpoint

angler 6 fisher 8 monkfish 9 fisherman,
goosefish

Anglo-Saxon *assembly:* 4 moot 5 gemot
6 gemote *council:* 9 heptarchy *county:*
5 shire *court:* 4 moot 5 gemot 6 gemote
crown tax: 4 geld *epic:* 7 Beowulf *free
servant:* 5 thane, thegn *god:* 3 Ing *goddess of fate:* 4 Wyrd *historian:* 4 Bede
king: 3 Ine, Ini 4 Edwy 5 Edgar, Edred
6 Alfred, Edmund, Edward, Egbert
8 Ethelred *kingdom:* 4 Kent 5 Essex
6 Mercia, Sussex, Wessex 10 East Anglia
11 Northumbria *king's council:* 5 witan
letter: 3 edh, eth, wen, wyn 4 wynn
5 thorn *nobleman:* 4 earl *poet:* 4 scop
prince: 8 atheling *sheriff:* 5 reeve *slave:*
4 esne *warrior:* 5 thane, thegn

Angola *capital:* 6 Luanda *city:* 6 Huambo
7 Lubango 8 Benguela *exclave:* 7 Cabinda *language:* 10 Portuguese *monetary
unit:* 6 kwanza *neighbor:* 5 Congo
6 Zambia 7 Namibia 11 South Africa
river: 5 Congo

angora 3 cat 4 goat, hair, wool, yarn 6 mohair, rabbit

angry 3 hot, mad 4 sore 5 irate, riled, riley, upset, vexed, wroth 6 fuming, heated, ireful, wrathy 7 enraged, furious, riled up 8 choleric, incensed, inflamed, maddened, wrathful 9 indignant, irritated 10 aggravated, infuriated 11 acrimonious, exasperated

angst 4 fear 5 worry 6 unease 7 anxiety, concern 8 distress 10 insecurity 11 disquietude, fretfulness 12 apprehension

Anguilla *island, island group:* 3 Dog 4 Seal 5 Scrub 7 Leeward *language:* 7 English *location:* 10 West Indies *territory of:* 7 Britain

anguish 3 rue, woe 4 ache, care, dole, hurt, pain, pang 5 agony, dread, grief, throe, worry 6 misery, regret, sorrow, throes 7 anxiety, torment, torture 8 distress, hardship 9 heartache, suffering 10 affliction, heartbreak 12 wretchedness

angular 4 bony, edgy, lank, lean, thin 5 gaunt, lanky, spare, stiff 6 forked, skinny, zigzag 7 pointed, scraggy, scrawny 8 cornered, rawboned, ungainly 9 roughhewn 10 unfinished, ungraceful, unpolished 13 sharp-cornered

ani 6 cuckoo

anima 4 soul 6 psyche, spirit 9 inner self

animadversion 4 slam, slur 7 censure, obloquy 9 aspersion, criticism 10 accusation, imputation, reflection 11 insinuation 12 reprehension

animadvert 6 notice 7 observe 9 criticize

animal 5 beast, brute, feral 6 brutal, carnal, ferine 7 beastly, bestial, brutish, critter, fleshly, sensual, swinish, wilding 8 creature, wildling *antlered:* 3 elk 4 axis, deer 5 moose 7 caribou 8 reindeer *aquatic:* 3 eel 4 fish, frog, seal 5 otter, whale 6 dugong, sea cow, walrus 7 dolphin, manatee, octopus 8 bryozoan, porpoise 9 alligator, crocodile *arboreal:* 4 bird 5 chimp, coati, koala, lemur, sloth 6 gibbon, monkey 7 opossum, tarsier 8 kinkajou, marmoset, squirrel 9 orangutan *burrowing:* 4 mole 5 brock, ratel 6 badger, gopher, marmot, rabbit 7 echidna 9 armadillo, groundhog, woodchuck *castrated:* 5 capon, steer 6 barrow, wether 7 gelding *draft:* 3 yak 4 mule, oxen (plural) 5 horse 6 donkey 8 elephant *exhibit:* 3 zoo *extinct:* 3 moa 4 dodo, urus 6 quagga 7 mammoth 8 dinosaur, eohippus, mastodon 9 trilobite *female:* 3 cow, dam, doe, ewe, hen, pen, roe, sow 4 mare, puss 5 bitch, goose, jenny, nanny, vixen 6 jennet 7 lioness *four-*

footed: 9 quadruped *four-limbed:* 8 tetrapod *free-swimming:* 6 nekton *hibernating:* 4 bear, frog, toad 5 skunk, snake 7 polecat 8 chipmunk 9 groundhog, woodchuck *horned:* 3 ram, yak 4 bull, goat, ibex, kudu 5 addax, bison, eland, rhino 6 cattle, koodoo 7 buffalo, gazelle, giraffe, unicorn 8 antelope *humped:* 3 elk, yak 4 zebu 5 bison, camel, moose *imaginary:* 5 snark *insect-eating:* 4 mole, newt 5 gecko, shrew 7 echidna 8 aardvark, anteater, hedgehog, pangolin, tamandua 10 salamander *male:* 3 cob, ram, tom 4 boar, buck, bull, cock, stag, stud 5 billy, steer 6 gander 7 gobbler, rooster 8 bachelor, stallion *many-celled:* 8 metazoan *many-footed:* 9 centipede, millipede *marsupial:* 5 koala 6 wombat 7 opossum, wallaby 8 kangaroo 9 bandicoot, phalanger *meat-eating:* 9 carnivore *mythical:* 5 Hydra 6 dragon, kraken, sphinx 7 centaur, griffin, mermaid, Pegasus, unicorn 8 basilisk, Cerberus, Minotaur *one-celled:* 9 protozoan *Peruvian:* 5 llama 6 alpaca, vicuña *plant-eating:* 9 herbivore *skin disease:* 5 mange *snouted:* 5 coati, tapir 8 mongoose (see also ANIMAL INSECT-EATING) *spotted:* 4 axis, paca 6 calico, jaguar, ocelot 7 cheetah, leopard, piebald 8 skewbald 9 dalmatian *striped:* 4 kudo 5 tiger, zebra 6 koodoo, quagga *trail:* 3 pug 4 foil, slot 5 spoor *tusked:* 6 walrus 7 warthog 8 elephant *two-footed:* 5 biped *web-footed:* 4 duck, frog, toad 5 goose, otter 6 beaver 8 duckbill, platypus *young:* 3 cub, kid, kit, pup 4 calf, colt, fawn, foal, joey, lamb 5 bunny, chick, kitty, poult, shoat, stirk, whelp 6 cygnet, farrow, heifer, kitten, piglet 7 bullock, gosling, lambkin 8 suckling, yeanling, yearling 9 fledgling

animal behavior *study of:* 8 ethology

animal fat 4 suet 6 tallow

animalism 4 lust 7 abandon 8 vitality 9 carnality 10 sensualism, sensuality 11 lustfulness, physicality, unrestraint

animalize 4 warp 6 debase 7 corrupt, deprave, pervert, vitiate 9 brutalize 10 bestialize, demoralize

animal life 5 fauna

animal sound 3 arf, baa, bay, caw, coo, low, mew, moo 4 bark, bray, buzz, crow, hiss, hoot, howl, meow, purr, roar, yelp 5 bleat, chirp, croak, drone, growl, grunt, miaow, neigh, quack 6 bellow, gibber, gobble, warble 7 screech, twitter

animate 4 fire, live, move, spur, stir,

urge **5** alert, alive, cheer, drive, exalt, impel, liven, nerve, spark, steel, vital **6** active, arouse, excite, inform, kindle, lively, living, moving, viable, vivify **7** actuate, chirk up, dynamic, enliven, hearten, inspire, quicken, refresh **8** activate, embolden, energize, inspirit, motivate, spirited, vitalize **9** breathing, encourage, energized, enhearten, make alive, stimulate **10** invigorate

animated 3 gay **4** keen **5** alert, alive, peppy, quick, vivid, vital **6** lively, living **7** dynamic, excited, vibrant, zestful **8** spirited, vigorous **9** activated, energetic, energized, exuberant, sprightly, vitalized, vivacious **12** high-spirited

animation 3 pep, vim **4** brio, dash, élan, life, zing **5** oomph, verve **6** energy, esprit, gaiety, spirit **8** dynamism, vitality, vivacity **10** liveliness

animato 5 brisk, tempo **6** lively **8** spirited **9** energetic, sprightly

animosity 4 hate **5** venom **6** animus, enmity, hatred, rancor **7** dislike, ill will **8** acrimony **9** antipathy, hostility **10** antagonism, resentment

animus 4 plan, soul **6** design, enmity, intent, pneuma, psyche, rancor, spirit **7** dislike, ill will, meaning, purpose **9** antipathy, élan vital, hostility, intention **10** antagonism, intendment, opposition, vital force **11** disposition, malevolence

Anjou 4 pear *capital:* **6** Angers *native:* **7** Angevin

ankle 6 tarsus

annals 6 record **7** account, history **8** archives, register **9** chronicle

annelid 4 worm **5** leech **9** earthworm

annex 3 add, arm, cop, ell, win **4** gain, hook, join, land, take, wing **5** add on, affix, seize, tag on **6** adjoin, append, attach, fasten, obtain, pick up, secure, tack on, take on **7** acquire, connect, preempt, procure, subjoin **8** accroach, addition, appendix, arrogate, superadd, take over **9** extension **10** attachment, commandeer, subsidiary, supplement **11** appropriate, expropriate, incorporate

Annie Oakley 4 pass **10** free ticket, markswoman

annihilate 4 do in, kill, raze, rout, ruin, undo **5** abate, annul, crush, erase, quash, quell, wrack, wreck **6** murder, negate, quench, rub out, squash, uproot, vanish **7** abolish, blot out, destroy, expunge, nullify, put down, root out, vitiate, wipe out **8** abrogate, demolish, massacre, suppress, vanquish **9** eradicate, extirpate, liquidate, slaugh-

ter **10** extinguish, invalidate, obliterate **11** exterminate

annihilation 7 killing **8** massacre **9** abolition **11** destruction, elimination, liquidation, termination **12** obliteration **13** extermination

anniversary *hundredth:* **9** centenary **10** centennial *tenth:* **9** decennial *thousandth:* **10** millennial

annotate 5 gloss **6** remark **7** comment, explain **8** footnote **9** elucidate, interpret **10** commentate

announce 4 call, tell **5** augur, issue, state, sound **6** attest, blazon, herald, impart, report, reveal, signal **7** bespeak, declare, divulge, forerun, give out, portend, predict, presage, present, publish, release, signify, trumpet **8** disclose, forecast, foreshow, foretell, indicate, proclaim **9** advertise, broadcast, harbinger, make known, publicize **10** give notice, make public, promulgate **11** preindicate

announcement 4 news **6** notice, report **7** message, release **8** briefing, bulletin **9** broadcast, statement **10** communiqué, disclosure **11** declaration, publication **12** proclamation, promulgation **13** advertisement, communication

announcer 5 emcee **6** deejay, herald, veejay **9** anchorman, voice-over **10** disc jockey, disk jockey, newscaster **11** anchorwoman, broadcaster, commentator **12** anchorperson, sportscaster

annoy 3 bug, irk, vex **4** bait, fret, gall, miff **5** chafe, chivy, harry, peeve, tease, upset, worry **6** badger, bother, harass, heckle, hector, needle, nettle, pester, plague, ruffle **7** agitate, bedevil, disturb, hagride, perturb, provoke, tick off **8** distress, irritate **9** beleaguer *Scottish:* **4** fash

annoyance 4 drag, to-do **5** trial, upset, worry **6** bother, nettle, plague, strain **7** problem, trouble **8** distress, headache, irritant, nuisance, vexation **10** affliction, harassment, irritation **11** aggravation, botheration, disturbance, indignation, provocation **12** exasperation

annoying 5 pesky **8** tiresome **9** troubling, vexatious **10** disturbing, irritating **11** aggravating, distressing, troublesome **12** exasperating

annual 5 plant **6** flower, yearly **7** almanac **8** each year, yearbook, yearlong **9** every year

annul 4 undo, void **5** abate, erase, quash **6** cancel, delete, efface, negate, revoke, vacate **7** abolish, blot out, expunge, nullify, redress, rescind, retract, reverse, vitiate, wipe out **8** abrogate,

dissolve 9 cancel out, discharge, frustrate **10** annihilate, counteract, extinguish, invalidate, neutralize, obliterate **11** countermand

annunciate see ANNOUNCE

anodyne 4 balm **5** bland **6** opiate, relief, remedy **7** soother **8** narcotic, nepenthe, painless, sedative **9** analgesic, calmative, innocuous, soporific **10** anesthetic, depressant, pain-killer, palliative **11** inoffensive, unoffending **12** tranquilizer

anoint 3 rub **4** daub, laud, name **5** anele, apply, bless, honor, smear **6** choose, hallow, ordain **7** confirm, massage **8** dedicate, sanctify, set apart, venerate **9** designate **10** consecrate

anomalous 3 odd **6** off-key **7** deviant, strange, unusual **8** aberrant, abnormal, atypical, peculiar **9** deviating, deviatory, divergent, irregular, unnatural, untypical **10** unexpected **11** heteroclite, incongruous, paradoxical **12** inconsistent **13** nonconforming, preternatural

anomaly 5 freak, quirk **6** oddity **9** departure, deviation, exception **10** aberration, divergence **11** abnormality, incongruity, peculiarity **12** idiosyncrasy, irregularity **13** inconsistency

anomie 4 flux **6** unrest **7** anxiety, inertia **10** alienation, insecurity **11** disquietude, instability, uncertainty **12** disaffection, estrangement, indifference, restlessness

anon 4 soon **5** later **7** by and by, shortly **8** directly **9** presently **10** before long **11** after a while

anonym 5 alias **6** handle **7** pen name **8** nickname **9** pseudonym **10** nom de plume **11** assumed name, nom de guerre

anonymous 7 unknown, unnamed **8** nameless, not named, unsigned **9** incognito **10** innominate **11** unspecified **12** undesignated, unidentified, unrecognized

anorak 5 parka

another 3 new **4** else, more **5** added, fresh **7** farther, further, one more **9** different **10** additional **11** alternative, someone else **13** something else

anschluss 5 union **6** league **8** alliance **9** coalition **10** federation **11** confederacy **13** confederation

answer 4 fill, meet, plea **5** atone, plead, rebut, reply, serve, solve **6** come in, refute, rejoin, result, retort, return **7** conform, defense, explain, fulfill, respond, satisfy **8** antiphon, rebuttal, response, solution **9** rejoinder **10** refutation **11** recriminate **13** countercharge

answerable 5 bound **6** liable **7** obliged, subject **8** amenable **9** compelled, duty-bound, obligated **11** accountable, constrained, responsible

ant 5 emmet **9** carpenter *relating to:* **6** formic

Antaean 4 huge **5** giant **6** heroic **7** mammoth, titanic **8** colossal, enormous, gigantic **9** cyclopean, Herculean **10** gargantuan

Antaeus *father:* **7** Neptune **8** Poseidon *mother:* **4** Gaea *slayer:* **8** Heracles, Hercules

antagonism 3 con **6** animus, enmity, hatred, rancor **7** discord **8** conflict, friction **9** animosity, antipathy, hostility **10** antithesis, contention, dissension, opposition, resistance **11** contrariety **12** disagreement

antagonist 3 con, foe **4** anti **5** enemy, match **6** muscle **7** opposer **8** chemical, opponent **9** adversary, contender

antagonistic 4 anti **6** averse **7** adverse, hostile, opposed **8** clashing, contrary, inimical, opposing **9** bellicose, combative, rancorous, truculent, vitriolic **10** discordant **11** belligerent, conflicting, contentious **12** antipathetic

Antarctica sea 4 Ross **7** Weddell **8** Amundsen

ante 3 bet, pay, pot **4** cost, risk **5** level, pay up, price, put up, stake, wager **6** stakes **7** produce

anteater see ANIMAL *INSECT-EATING*

antecede 7 forerun, precede, predate **8** foredate, go before

antecedence 8 priority **10** precedence, precession, preference

antecedent 4 fore, line **5** cause, prior **6** former, reason **7** earlier **8** ancestor, anterior, forebear, foregoer, occasion, previous **9** condition, foregoing, precedent, preceding, precursor, prototype **10** forerunner, progenitor **11** determinant, predecessor

antedate 7 forerun, precede **11** anachronize **12** occur earlier

antediluvian 3 old **4** aged, fogy **5** hoary, passé **6** age-old, fogram, fossil, square **7** ancient, antique, archaic **8** mossback, Noachian, obsolete, outdated, outmoded, primeval, timeworn **9** out-of-date, primitive **10** antiquated, fuddy-duddy **12** old-fashioned **13** stick-in-the-mud

antelope 3 gnu **4** kudu, oryx **5** addax, bongo, eland, nyala, serow **6** dik-dik, duiker, impala, koodoo, lechwe **7** blesbok, chamois, gazelle, gemsbok, gerenuk, sassaby **8** bushbuck, reedbuck, steinbok **9** springbok, waterbuck **10** hartebeest *female:* **3** doe *male:* 4 buck *young:* 3 kid (see also GAZELLE)

antenna 4 wire 6 aerial, device, dipole, sensor 8 monopole, receiver

antennae 4 ears 11 sensitivity 13 receptiveness

anterior 4 past 5 prior 6 former 8 previous 9 foregoing, precedent, preceding 10 antecedent

anteroom 5 entry, foyer, lobby 6 alcove 9 vestibule

Anteros *brother:* 4 Eros *father:* 4 Ares, Mars *mother:* 5 Venus 9 Aphrodite *opposite:* 4 Eros

anthem 4 hymn, song 5 chant, paean, psalm 8 canticle

anthology 3 ana 5 album 6 digest, reader 7 garland, omnibus 8 analects, treasury 9 selection 10 assortment, collection, compendium, miscellany 11 compilation, florilegium

anthropoid 3 ape 5 biped 6 monkey 7 bipedal, gorilla, manlike, primate 8 hominoid, humanoid 10 chimpanzee

anthropologist 4 Boas (Franz), Dart (Raymond), Mead (Margaret) 5 Sapir (Edward), Tylor (Edward Burnett) 6 Frazer (James George), Geertz (Clifford), Leakey (Louis), Morgan (Lewis Henry) 7 Bateson (Gregory), Kroeber (Alfred Louis) 8 Benedict (Ruth) 10 Malinowski (Bronisław) 11 Lévi-Strauss (Claude)

anti 3 con 6 averse 7 adverse, against, counter, opposed, opposer 8 contrary, opponent, opposing 9 adversary, opposed to 10 antagonist 12 antagonistic, antipathetic, in opposition

antiaircraft fire 4 flak

antibiotic 7 colicin 8 neomycin, viomycin 9 polymyxin 10 bacitracin, novobiocin, penicillin 11 bacteriocin, tyrothricin 12 streptomycin, tetracycline

antic 3 gag 4 dido, joke, lark, romp 5 caper, comic, prank, trick 6 frisky, frolic, lively 7 comical, foolish, playful 8 escapade, farcical, prankish, spirited 9 high jinks, laughable, ludicrous, sprightly 10 frolicsome, rollicking, shenanigan, tomfoolery 11 mischievous, monkeyshine 12 monkeyshines 13 practical joke

anticipate 3 see 4 wait 5 await, check 6 divine, expect 7 counter, count on, foresee, prepare, presage, prevent, wait for 8 forecast, foreknow, foretell 9 apprehend, forestall, prevision, visualize 10 prepare for

anticipation 7 inkling, outlook, promise 8 awaiting, forecast, prospect 9 aware-

ness, foresight, foretaste 10 expectancy 11 expectation, realization 12 apprehension 13 visualization

Anticlea *father:* 9 Autolycus *husband:* 7 Laertes *son:* 7 Ulysses 8 Odysseus

antidote 4 cure, drug 6 remedy 7 negator 8 medicine 9 nullifier 10 corrective, counteract, preventive 11 counterstep, neutralizer 12 counteragent 13 counteractant, counteractive

Antigone *brother:* 9 Polynices 10 Polyneices *father:* 7 Oedipus *mother:* 7 Jocasta *sister:* 6 Ismene *uncle:* 5 Creon

Antigua and Barbuda *capital:* 7 St. Johns *island:* 7 Antigua, Barbuda, Redonda *language:* 7 English *monetary unit:* 6 dollar

Antilochus *father:* 6 Nestor *friend:* 8 Achilles *slayer:* 6 Memnon

Antiope *father:* 6 Asopus *husband:* 5 Lycus 7 Theseus *queen of:* 7 Amazons *son:* 6 Zethus 7 Amphion 10 Hippolytus

antipasto 9 appetizer 11 hors d'oeuvre 12 hors d'oeuvres

antipathetic 5 loath 6 averse, loathe 7 adverse, hostile, opposed 8 aversive, clashing, contrary, inimical, opposing, opposite 9 abhorrent, disliking, loathsome, repellent, repugnant, repulsive 10 discordant, unfriendly 11 conflicting, distasteful, ill-disposed, uncongenial 12 antagonistic 13 contradictory

antipathy 4 hate 6 animus, enmity, hatred, rancor 7 allergy, dislike, ill will 8 aversion, distaste, loathing 9 animosity, hostility 10 abhorrence, antagonism, opposition, repellency

antiphon 5 psalm, reply, verse 6 answer, anthem, return 7 respond 8 response

antipodal 5 polar 7 adverse, counter, opposed, reverse 8 contrary, converse, opposite 9 diametric 11 conflicting, contrasting, diametrical 12 antithetical 13 contradictory

antipode 6 contra 7 counter, reverse 8 contrary, converse, flip side, opposite 9 other side 10 antithesis 11 counterpole

antiquate 7 make old, outdate, outmode 8 obsolete 9 obsolesce 12 superannuate

antiquated 3 old 4 aged 5 dated, fusty, hoary, moldy, passé 6 old hat 7 ancient, antique, archaic 8 obsolete, old-timey, outmoded 9 out-of-date 10 oldfangled, out-of-style 11 discredited, obsolescent 12 antediluvian, old-fashioned 13 inappropriate, superannuated

antique 3 old 4 aged 5 dated, hoary, olden, passé, relic 6 age-old, bygone, rarity 7 ancient, archaic, vintage 8 artifact, heirloom, old-timey, outdated, outmoded, timeworn 9 ancestral, objet d'art, out-of-date, venerable 10 antiquated, oldfangled 12 antediluvian, old-fashioned

antiseptic 6 iodine 7 alcohol, sterile 8 hygienic, peroxide, sanitary 9 boric acid, carvacrol, germicide, merbromin 10 gramicidin, sterilized 12 carbolic acid, disinfectant *pioneer:* 6 Lister (Joseph)

antisocial 7 ascetic, austere, hostile 8 eremitic, solitary 9 alienated, reclusive, withdrawn 10 unfriendly 11 standoffish 12 antagonistic, misanthropic

antithesis 3 con 6 contra 7 counter, reverse 8 antipode, antipole, contrary, contrast, converse, opposite 10 antagonism, opposition 11 counterpole

antithetical 5 polar 7 counter, reverse 8 contrary, converse, opposite 9 antipodal, diametric 10 antipodean 11 diametrical 13 contradictory

antitoxin 4 sera (plural) 5 serum 11 neutralizer

antiwar 6 irenic 8 pacifist 10 nonviolent, pacifistic

Antony, Mark *defeat:* 6 Actium *friend:* 6 Caesar *lover:* 9 Cleopatra *wife:* 7 Octavia

anxiety 4 care, fear 5 doubt, dread, panic, worry 6 unease 7 concern 8 distress, mistrust, suspense 9 self-doubt, suffering 10 uneasiness 11 disquietude, uncertainty 12 apprehension

anxious 4 avid, keen 5 eager 6 afraid, ardent, scared, uneasy 7 alarmed, fearful, worried 8 agitated, desirous, troubled, worrying 9 impatient, perturbed, terrified 10 breathless, disquieted, frightened 12 apprehensive

any 3 all 4 a bit, some 5 at all, every 7 a little, several 8 whatever

anyhow 6 random 7 however 8 at random, randomly 9 hit-or-miss 10 carelessly, regardless 11 any which way, haphazardly 13 helter-skelter

anymore 3 now 5 today 8 nowadays 9 presently, these days

anyone 3 all 9 everybody

anything 5 at all

anytime 4 ever 5 at all 8 whenever

anyway 4 ever, once 5 at all 7 however 12 nevertheless

anywhere 5 at all 7 all over 10 at any point

anywise 5 at all

apace 4 fast 6 versed 7 abreast, flat-out, hastily, quickly, rapidly, swiftly 8 informed, up-to-date, speedily 9 posthaste 12 lickety-split 13 expeditiously

Apache *chief:* 7 Cochise 8 Geronimo *subgroups:* 7 Cibecue 9 Jicarilla, Mescalero 10 Chiricahua

apart 5 alone, aside 6 singly 7 asunder, removed 8 detached, isolated, one by one 9 severally 10 separately 12 individually 13 independently, unaccompanied *prefix:* 3 dis

apart from 3 bar, but 4 save 6 except, saving 7 barring, besides 9 except for, excepting, excluding, other than, outside of 11 exclusive of

apartheid 8 division 9 partition 10 separation, separatism 11 segregation 12 separateness

apartment 4 flat, room 5 rooms, suite 6 rental 7 chamber, housing, lodging 8 building, dwelling 9 residence 13 accommodation

apathetic 4 dull, flat, limp 5 inert 6 stolid, torpid 7 languid, passive, unmoved 8 sluggish 9 impassive, untouched 10 anesthetic, insensible, phlegmatic, spiritless 11 emotionless, indifferent, insensitive 12 unresponsive 13 disinterested

apathy 6 torpor 8 coldness, dullness, lethargy, obduracy, stoicism 9 aloofness, disregard, inertness, lassitude, passivity, stolidity, torpidity, unconcern 10 detachment, dispassion 11 callousness, disinterest, impassivity 12 heedlessness, indifference, listlessness 13 insensibility, insensitivity

ape 4 copy, mime, mock 5 mimic 6 baboon, bonobo, gibbon, monkey, parody, pongid, simian 7 copycat, emulate, gorilla, imitate, siamang, take off 8 simulate, travesty 9 burlesque, orangutan 10 anthropoid, caricature, chimpanzee 11 impersonate

aperçu 5 brief 6 digest, précis, sketch, survey 7 insight, outline 8 syllabus 10 compendium, impression

aperitif 4 whet 5 drink 8 cocktail 9 appetizer

aperture 3 gap 4 hole, vent 6 outlet 7 opening, orifice, pinhole

apery 7 mimicry 9 imitation

apex 3 cap, tip, top 4 acme, cusp, peak, roof 5 crest, crown, limit, point 6 apogee, climax, summit, vertex, zenith 8 capstone, pinnacle, ultimate 9 crescendo, sublimity 11 culmination, ne plus ultra 12 quintessence

aphorism 3 saw 4 rule 5 adage, axiom, maxim, moral 6 dictum, saying, truism 7 precept, proverb 8 apothegm

aphrodisiac 6 erotic 7 amative, amatory, amorous, lustful 8 excitant 10 passionate

Aphrodite *Roman counterpart:* 5 Venus
consort: 4 Ares 6 Vulcan 10 Hephaestus
father: 4 Zeus 7 Jupiter *goddess of:*
4 love *mother:* 5 Dione *son:* 4 Eros
6 Aeneas 7 Priapus

apiarist 9 beekeeper

apical 3 top 7 highest, topmost 8 loftiest
9 uppermost

apiculture 10 beekeeping

apiece 3 per 4 a pop, each 6 singly, to
each 7 for each 8 one by one 9 per
capita, severally 10 separately 12 individually, respectively

apish 5 phony, silly 7 slavish 8 affected
9 emulative, imitative 10 artificial

aplenty 4 full 5 ample 6 galore, indeed
7 copious, greatly 8 abundant, very
much 9 extremely

aplomb 4 ease 5 poise 6 polish 8 coolness, easiness 9 assurance, certainty,
certitude, composure 10 confidence,
equanimity 11 nonchalance, savoir
faire 12 self-reliance 13 self-assurance

apocalypse 6 augury, oracle, vision
8 disaster, prophecy 10 Armageddon,
prediction, revelation

apocalyptic 4 dire 5 awful 7 baleful,
baneful, fateful, fearful, ominous
8 Delphian, dreadful, oracular, terrible
9 appalling, climactic, grandiose,
prophetic 10 foreboding, predicting
11 foretelling, prophetical, threatening
12 inauspicious *book:* 10 Revelation
11 Revelations

apocryphal 5 false, wrong 6 untrue
7 dubious 8 doubtful, spurious 9 incorrect, ungenuine 10 ficticious, inaccurate, unverified 11 unauthentic
12 questionable

apogee 4 acme, apex, peak 6 climax,
summit, zenith 8 capstone, meridian,
pinnacle 9 high point 11 culmination

Apollo 6 Helios 7 Phoebus *beloved:*
6 Cyrene, Daphne 8 Calliope *birthplace:*
5 Delos *father:* 4 Zeus 7 Jupiter *mother:*
4 Leto 6 Latona *oracle:* 6 Delphi *sister:*
5 Diana 7 Artemis *son:* 3 Ion 7 Orpheus
temple: 6 Delphi

apologetic 5 sorry 6 rueful 8 contrite,
penitent 9 regretful, repentant
10 remorseful 11 penitential 12 compunctious

apologia 4 plea 6 excuse, reason
7 defense 8 argument 11 elucidation,
explanation 13 clarification, justification

apologize 5 atone 6 lament, regret,
repent 7 confess 9 beg pardon 10 make
amends

apologue 4 myth, tale 5 fable, story
7 parable 8 allegory

apology 4 plea 6 amends, excuse
7 redress, regrets 8 mea culpa 9 admission, makeshift 10 concession, confession

apostasy 7 perfidy 9 defection, desertion, disavowal, falseness, rejection
11 abandonment, repudiation 12 disaffection, renunciation

apostate 7 heretic, traitor 8 defector,
deserter, recreant, renegade, turncoat
9 turnabout

apostatize 4 turn 6 defect, desert 7 abandon, forsake, sell out 8 renounce
9 repudiate

a posteriori 9 inductive

apostle 4 John, Jude, Paul 5 James,
Judas, Peter, Silas, Simon 6 Andrew,
Philip, Thomas 7 Matthew 8 Barnabas,
disciple, follower, Matthias, preacher
9 missioner 10 colporteur, evangelist,
missionary 11 Bartholomew 12 propagandist *of Germany:* 8 Boniface *of Ireland:* 7 Patrick *of the English:* 9 Augustine *of the French:* 5 Denis *of the Gauls:*
8 Irenaeus *of the Gentiles:* 4 Paul *of the
Goths:* 7 Ulfilas *to the Indians:* 9 John
Eliot

apothecary 7 chemist 8 druggist, pharmacy 9 drugstore 10 pharmacist

apothegm see APHORISM

apotheosis 6 height 7 epitome 8 exemplar, last word, ultimate 9 archetype,
elevation 10 embodiment, exaltation
11 deification, ennoblement, idolization, lionization 12 enshrinement, quintessence 13 glorification

appall 3 awe 4 faze 5 alarm, shake,
shock 6 dismay 7 horrify, outrage,
overawe, perturb 8 confound, distress
10 disconcert 11 consternate

appalled 6 aghast 11 dumbfounded

appalling 5 awful 6 horrid 7 fearful
8 daunting, dreadful, horrible, horrific,
shocking, terrible 9 atrocious, dismaying, frightful, loathsome 10 disgusting,
formidable, horrifying

appanage 5 grant, right 7 adjunct
8 property 9 endowment, privilege
10 birthright, perquisite 11 prerogative

apparatus 4 gear, tool 5 gizmo 6 device,
outfit, tackle 7 utensil 8 matériel, tackling 9 equipment, implement, machinery 10 instrument 11 contraption,
habiliments 13 accouterments, accoutrements, paraphernalia

apparel 4 clad, duds, garb, gear, robe,
suit, togs 5 adorn, array, dress, getup,
habit 6 attire, clothe, outfit 7 clothes,
costume, garment, raiment, threads
8 clothing, enclothe, glad rags, vestment 9 embellish 11 habiliments

apparent 5 clear, plain **6** patent **7** evident, obvious, seeming, visible **8** distinct, manifest, palpable **9** succedent **10** noticeable, observable **11** discernible, perceivable, unambiguous, unequivocal **12** successional

apparition 5 ghost, shade, umbra **6** shadow, spirit, vision, wraith **7** phantom, specter **8** illusion, phantasm **10** appearance, phenomenon **13** hallucination

appeal 3 ask, beg, bid **4** call, lure, plea, pray, pull, suit, urge **5** apply, brace, charm, crave, plead **6** accuse, allure, charge, excite, invoke, sue for **7** attract, beseech, entreat, glamour, implore, request **8** call upon, charisma, entreaty, interest, intrigue, petition **9** fascinate, importune, magnetism, seduction **10** allurement, attraction, supplicate **11** application, fascination, imploration **12** drawing power, solicitation, supplication

appealing 8 alluring, charming, pleading, pleasant, pleasing **9** agreeable, imploring **10** attracting, attractive, bewitching, enchanting, entreating **11** captivating, fascinating

appear 4 come, look, loom, rise, seem, show **5** arise, issue, occur, sound **6** arrive, emerge, show up **7** be clear, emanate **8** look like, resemble **9** be evident, come forth **10** be manifest **11** materialize

appearance 3 air **4** face, form, look, mien, pose, show **5** debut, dress, front, guise, image **6** advent, aspect, facade, manner **7** arrival, bearing, display, seeming **8** attitude, demeanor, illusion **9** semblance **10** impression, occurrence, simulacrum **11** countenance **13** manifestation

appease 4 calm, ease **5** allay, quiet **6** buy off, pacify, soothe **7** assuage, concede, content, gratify, mollify, placate, relieve, satisfy, sweeten **10** conciliate, propitiate

appellation 4 name **5** brand, label, nomen, style, title **7** moniker **8** cognomen **10** identifier **11** designation **12** denomination

append 3 add **5** add on, affix, annex, tag on **6** adjoin, attach, tack on **7** subjoin **10** supplement

appendage 3 arm, fin, leg, tab, tag **4** barb, flap, horn, limb, seta, tail, wing **5** extra **6** cercus, member **7** adjunct, antenna, elytron, stipule **8** pedipalp, pendicle, tentacle **9** accessory, auxiliary, extremity **10** attachment, collateral, incidental, projection, supplement

12 appurtenance, nonessential, protuberance

appendix 5 notes, rider **7** adjunct, codicil **8** addendum, addition **9** accessory, appendage **10** attachment, supplement **12** appurtenance

apperception 5 grasp **9** awareness **10** cognizance **11** realization, recognition **12** apprehension, assimilation **13** comprehension, introspection, understanding

appertain 4 bear **5** apply, refer **6** bear on, belong, relate **8** bear upon **10** be relevant **11** be connected, be pertinent

appetence 3 yen **5** taste **6** desire, hunger, relish, thirst **7** craving, longing, stomach **8** fondness

appetent 4 agog, avid, keen **5** eager **6** ardent **7** anxious, craving, lusting, thirsty **8** desirous, yearning **9** impatient **10** breathless

appetite 3 yen **4** bent, itch, lust, urge **5** taste **6** desire, hunger, liking, relish **7** craving, leaning, longing, passion, stomach **8** cupidity, fondness, gluttony, penchant, soft spot, voracity, weakness, yearning **9** hankering **10** preference, proclivity, propensity **11** inclination

appetizer 4 whet **5** snack **6** canapé, savory, tidbit **8** aperitif, cocktail, stimulus **9** antipasto **11** hors d'oeuvre

appetizing 5 tasty **6** savory **8** saporous, tempting **9** agreeable, appealing, aperitive, flavorful, palatable, relishing, toothsome **10** delectable, flavorsome **11** tantalizing **13** mouth-watering

applaud 4 clap, hail, laud, root **5** bravo, cheer, extol **6** praise, rise to **7** acclaim, approve, commend **9** recommend **10** compliment

applause 4 hand **5** round **6** bravos, cheers, praise **7** acclaim, hurrahs, ovation, rooting **8** accolade, approval, cheering, clapping, plaudits **11** acclamation **12** commendation

apple 4 crab, Fuji, Gala, pome **6** Empire, pippin, russet **7** Baldwin, costard, Duchess, Winesap **8** Braeburn, Cortland, greening, Jonagold, Jonathan, McIntosh **9** Delicious **10** Rome Beauty **11** Granny Smith, Gravenstein, Northern Spy, Transparent *dessert:* **5** crisp *juice:* **5** cider

applejack 5 cider **6** brandy, liquor **8** calvados **9** hard cider

apple knocker see RUSTIC

apple-polish 4 fawn **5** toady **6** kowtow **7** cater to, flatter, honey up, truckle **8** butter up **10** curry favor, ingratiate

apple-polisher 5 toady **6** yes-man

8 bootlick, groveler, lickspit **9** flatterer, sycophant **11** lickspittle

applesauce 5 hooey **6** bunkum **7** baloney, rubbish, twaddle **8** malarkey, nonsense **9** poppycock

appliance 6 device **7** utensil **9** implement **10** instrument **11** application *kitchen:* **4** oven **5** mixer, range, stove **6** fridge **7** blender, toaster **9** can opener, microwave **10** dishwasher **12** refrigerator

applicability 3 use **7** account, fitness, utility **9** advantage, relevance **10** usefulness

applicable 3 apt, fit **4** just, meet **5** ad rem **6** seemly, suited, useful **7** apropos, fitting, germane **8** apposite, material, relevant, suitable **9** befitting, pertinent **10** felicitous **11** appropriate

applicant 6 seeker **7** hopeful **8** aspirant, inquirer **9** candidate, job-hunter, job-seeker

application 3 use **4** form, heed, plea, suit **5** study **6** appeal, debate, effort, letter **7** request **8** entreaty, exercise, exertion, industry, petition **9** assiduity, attention, diligence, operation, treatment **10** dedication, employment **11** requisition, utilization **12** solicitation **13** concentration, consideration

appliqué 5 decal

apply 3 dab, use **4** bend, give, turn, urge **5** press, refer **6** accost, affect, appeal, assign, bear on, bestow, devote, direct, employ, engage, handle, relate, resort, take on **7** address, beseech, concern, entreat, execute, implore, involve, pertain, utilize **8** approach, bear upon, exercise, petition, set about **9** appertain, implement, importune, undertake **10** administer, buckle down

appoint 3 arm, fix, rig, set, tap **4** gear, name **5** equip **6** assign, decide, fit out, outfit, supply **7** dress up, furbish, furnish, provide, turn out **8** accouter, accoutre, accredit, delegate, nominate **9** authorize, designate, determine, embellish, provision **10** commission

appointment 3 job **4** date, meet, post, spot **5** berth, place, tryst **6** billet, choice, office **7** meeting **8** election, position **9** equipment, selection, situation **10** assignment, connection, engagement, rendezvous **11** arrangement, assignation, designation

appointments 7 fitting **8** equipage **9** equipment, trappings **12** furnishings **13** accouterments, accoutrements

apportion 3 cut, lot **4** give, mete, part **5** allot, allow, cut up, divvy, quota, serve, share, slice, split **6** assign, bestow, divide, parcel, ration **7** deal out, dish out, divvy up, dole out, measure, mete out, prorate, split up **8** allocate, dispense, separate, share out **9** admeasure, partition **10** administer, distribute

apportionment 3 cut, lot **4** part **5** piece, quota, share, slice, split **6** ration **7** measure, quantum **9** allotment, allowance **10** allocation, assignment

apposite 3 apt **4** just **5** ad rem **6** proper, suited, timely **7** apropos, fitting, germane, right on **8** material, on target, relevant, suitable **9** pertinent **10** applicable **11** appropriate

appositeness 7 aptness, fitness **9** relevance **10** pertinence, timeliness **11** suitability

appraisal 5 stock **6** rating, survey **7** pricing **8** estimate, judgment **9** valuation **10** assessment, estimation, evaluation

appraise 3 eye, fix, set **4** rate, size **5** assay, audit, gauge, judge, price, set at, value **6** assess, figure, size up, survey **7** adjudge, examine, inspect, measure, valuate **8** estimate, evaluate, look over **9** calculate, figure out

appreciable 5 clear, plain **6** marked **7** evident, obvious **8** apparent, clearcut, concrete, manifest, material, palpable, sensible, tangible **10** detectable, measurable, noticeable, observable **11** discernible, perceptible, substantial **12** considerable

appreciate 4 gain, go up, grow, know, like, love, rise **5** enjoy, grasp, judge, prize, savor, value **6** admire, esteem, fathom, regard, relish **7** apprize, cherish, cognize, enhance, improve, inflate, realize, respect **8** evaluate, increase, treasure **9** apprehend, delight in, recognize **10** comprehend, understand

appreciation 4 gain, rise **6** growth, regard, thanks **7** tribute **8** increase, judgment **9** awareness, gratitude, inflation **10** evaluation, perception **11** recognition, sensitivity, testimonial **12** gratefulness

apprehend 3 dig, get, nab, see **4** bust, fear, grab, know, nail, read, take, twig **5** catch, grasp, pinch, run in, seize, sense **6** absorb, accept, arrest, collar, detain, digest, divine, fathom, pick up, take in, wise up **7** capture, catch on, cognize, compass, foresee, make out, preknow, previse, realize **8** conceive **9** penetrate, recognize, visualize **10** anticipate, appreciate, understand

apprehensible 5 clear, lucid, plain **7** evident, obvious **8** distinct, explicit, knowable, luminous 9 graspable 10 fathomable

apprehension 3 ken 4 care, fear, idea
5 alarm, angst, dread, grasp, pinch,
worry 6 arrest, notion, pickup, unease
7 anxiety, capture, concern, seizure,
thought 8 disquiet, judgment 9 agitation, awareness, detention, knowledge,
misgiving, suspicion 10 conception,
foreboding, perception, solicitude,
uneasiness 11 disquietude, premonition
13 comprehension, understanding

apprehensive 5 alive, awake, aware,
sharp 6 afraid, astute, scared, uneasy
7 anxious, fearful, knowing, worried
8 sensible, sentient, troubled 9 cognizant, conscious, observant, sensitive
10 discerning, disquieted, insightful,
perceptive

apprentice 4 bind, tyro 5 pupil, serve
6 novice, rookie 7 learner, starter, student, trainee, work for 8 beginner,
freshman, neophyte, newcomer 9 novitiate 10 tenderfoot

apprenticed 5 bound 7 obliged, pledged
8 articled 9 obligated 10 indentured

apprise 4 clue, post, tell, warn 6 advise,
clue in, fill in, impart, inform, notify,
reveal, wise up 7 let know 8 acquaint,
announce, describe, disclose 9 make
known 11 communicate

apprize 5 value 6 admire, esteem,
regard, relish 7 cherish 8 hold dear,
treasure 10 appreciate, rate highly

approach 4 near, nigh 5 reach, rival,
touch, verge 6 access, advise, amount,
avenue, border, gain on 7 address,
advance, apply to, attempt, consult,
descent, request 8 come up to, draw
near, endeavor, overture 9 come close
11 approximate

approachable 7 affable 8 friendly, sociable 9 agreeable, congenial, reachable,
receptive 10 accessible, attainable

approaching 6 coming 7 nearing
8 expected, imminent, oncoming,
upcoming 11 forthcoming

approbate 4 back, like 5 favor 6 accept,
assent, praise 7 applaud, approve, commend, consent, endorse, support
8 sanction 9 recommend 11 countenance

approbation 3 nod 4 okay 5 favor
6 esteem, praise 7 acclaim, consent,
support 8 applause, approval, sanction
10 admiration, permission 11 endorsement, recognition 12 commendation

appropriate 3 apt, cop, due, fit 4 grab,
just, lift, meet, take, true 5 allot, annex,
claim, exact, filch, grasp, pinch, right,
seize, steal, swipe, usurp 6 assign,

assume, budget, devote, pilfer, proper,
snatch, snitch, timely, useful, worthy
7 apropos, desired, earmark, fitting,
germane, merited, preempt, purloin
8 accroach, apposite, arrogate,
deserved, eligible, entitled, relevant,
rightful, set apart, set aside, suitable
9 befitting, opportune, pertinent, requisite 10 acceptable, admissible, applicable, commandeer, compatible, confiscate, convenient, felicitous, seasonable

appropriately 4 well 5 amply, aptly, right
8 properly, suitably 9 fittingly
10 acceptably, adequately, becomingly

appropriateness 3 use 5 order
7 account, aptness, fitness, service, utility 8 meetness 9 advantage, propriety,
relevance, rightness 10 expediency, usefulness 13 applicability

appropriation 5 grant 7 funding, stipend,
subsidy 9 allotment, allowance 10 allocation, assignment, earmarking, subvention

approval 4 okay 5 favor, leave 6 assent
7 consent, go-ahead, license, support
8 applause, blessing, sanction, suffrage
10 acceptance, compliment, green light,
permission 11 approbation, benediction, concurrence, endorsement
12 commendation, ratification
13 authorization, confirmation

approve 4 okay 5 clear, favor, go for
6 accept, back up, praise, ratify, uphold
7 applaud, certify, commend, condone,
confirm, endorse, initial, mandate,
stand by, support, sustain 8 accredit,
hold with, sanction 9 approbate,
authorize, encourage 10 compliment
11 countenance

approximate 4 near 5 close, rough,
touch 6 almost 7 similar, verge on
8 approach, come near 10 resembling
11 comparative

approximately 4 most, nigh 5 about,
circa 6 all but, almost, nearly 7 close to
8 well-nigh 9 just about, very close
11 practically

approximation 8 likeness, nearness
9 closeness 10 similarity 11 resemblance

appurtenance 7 adjunct 8 addition,
appendix, ornament 9 accessory, apparatus, appendage 10 attachment 11 furnishings 13 accompaniment

appurtenant 5 extra 8 adjuvant 9 accessory, ancillary, auxiliary 10 additional,
collateral, subsidiary 11 subordinate,
subservient 12 accompanying, contributory

a priori 8 provable, reasoned 9 deducible, deductive, derivable, inferable
11 inferential, presumptive

apron 5 stage **6** shield **7** garment
8 pinafore **9** extension

apropos 3 apt **4** as to, in re, meet
5 about, ad rem, anent, aptly, as for
6 proper, timely **7** fitting, germane,
related **8** apposite, material, pointful,
relevant, suitable, suitably, touching
9 as regards, opportune, pertinent,
regarding **10** applicable, as respects,
concerning, relevantly, respecting, seasonably **11** applicative, applicatory,
bearing upon, in respect to, oppor-
tunely, pertinently **13** with respect to

apt 3 fit **4** just **5** alert, given, prone,
quick, ready, savvy, smart **6** bright,
clever, liable, likely, prompt, proper
7 apropos, fitting, germane, tending
8 apposite, disposed, inclined, relevant,
suitable **9** befitting, pertinent, qualified
10 felicitous, responsive **11** appropriate,
intelligent

aptitude 4 bent, gift **5** flair, knack, savvy
6 genius, liking, talent **7** ability, faculty,
fitness **8** capacity, tendency **10** capability, cleverness, proclivity, propensity
11 disposition, inclination, suitability
12 predilection

aptness 4 bent, gift **5** flair, knack, skill
6 genius, talent **7** ability, faculty, fitness
8 tendency **9** propriety, readiness
10 capability, cleverness, expediency,
likelihood **11** inclination, suitability
12 intelligence

aquanaut 5 diver **10** scuba diver

aqua vitae 4 grog **5** booze, drink, hooch
6 liquor, tipple **7** alcohol, spirits

aqueduct 5 canal **6** course **7** channel,
conduit, passage **8** waterway **11** watercourse

aqueous 5 fluid **6** liquid, watery **9** liquefied

Aquila 13 constellation *representation:*
5 eagle *star:* **6** Altair

Aquitaine 7 Guienne *queen:* **7** Eleanor

aquiver 5 shaky **7** quaking, shaking,
trembly **9** shivering, trembling, tremu-
lant, tremulous

Arab *chief:* **4** emir **5** sheik **6** sheikh, sul-
tan *country:* **4** Iraq, Oman **5** Egypt,
Libya, Qatar, Sudan, Syria, Yemen
6 Jordan, Kuwait **7** Algeria, Bahrain,
Lebanon, Morocco, Tunisia **11** Saudi
Arabia

arable 7 fertile **8** fruitful, tillable **10** cultivable, productive

Arachne *father:* **5** Idmon *form:* **6** spider
mother: **6** Cyrene *rival:* **6** Athena **7** Minerva

arachnid 4 mite, tick **6** acarus, spider
8 scorpion **9** arthropod, phalangid,

tarantula **10** harvestman **13** daddy longlegs

arbiter 5 judge **6** expert, umpire **7** referee **8** mediator .**9** authority, moderator
11 adjudicator

arbitrary 4 rash **6** chance, random
7 erratic, offhand, wayward, willful
8 fanciful, heedless **9** frivolous, impetuous, whimsical **10** capricious, subjective **10** irrational **12** unreasonable
13 discretionary

arbitrate 5 judge **6** settle, umpire
7 adjudge, mediate, referee **9** intervene
10 adjudicate **12** intermediate

arbitrator 5 judge **6** umpire **7** referee,
settler **8** mediator **9** moderator **11** adjudicator

arbor 4 axle, beam **5** bower, frame, shaft
7 pergola, shelter, spindle

arc 3 bow, lob **4** arch, bend, path
5 curve, round **7** rainbow **9** curvation,
curvature **11** measurement, progression

arcade 6 arches **7** gallery **10** passageway

arcadia 4 Eden, Zion **6** heaven, utopia
7 Elysium, nirvana **8** paradise **9** fairyland, Shangri-la **10** wonderland
12 promised land

arcane 6 hidden, mystic, occult, opaque,
secret **7** obscure, unknown **8** esoteric
9 recondite **10** cabalistic, mysterious,
unknowable **11** inscrutable **12** impenetrable **13** unaccountable

Arcas *father:* **4** Zeus **7** Jupiter *mother:*
8 Callisto

arch 3 bow, coy, sly **4** bend, hump, pert
5 curve, fresh, saucy, vault **6** camber,
cheeky, impish **7** playful, roguish, waggish **8** flippant, malapert **9** curvature
10 coquettish **11** mischievous *inner
curve:* **8** intrados *kind:* **4** ogee **5** ogive,
round, Tudor **6** lancet **7** rampart, trefoil
9 horseshoe, primitive, segmental
10 shouldered **11** equilateral *outer
curve:* **8** extrados *part:* **6** impost **8** keystone, springer, voussoir

archaeological site *Africa:* **8** Zimbabwe
13 Great Zimbabwe *Britain:* **7** Avebury
9 Skara Brae, Sutton Hoo **10** Stonehenge *Cambodia:* **6** Angkor **9** Angkor
Wat *Crete:* **7** Knossos *Egypt:* **4** Giza
5 Luxor **6** Abydos, Karnak, Naqada,
Thebes **7** Memphis **9** El-Bahnasa
11 Oxyrhynchus *Greece:* **6** Delphi
7 Mycenae, Olympia *Guatemala:* **5** Tikal
Honduras: **5** Copán *Indonesia* **9**
Borobudur *Iran:* **10** Persepolis *Iraq:*
4 Isin, Nuzi **6** Nimrud **7** Babylon, Nineveh, Samarra *Israel:* **7** Jericho *Italy:*
7 Pompeii **11** Herculaneum *Lebanon:*
6 Byblos **7** Baalbek *Mexico:* **5** Mitla,
Tulum, Uxmal **8** Palenque **10** Monte

Albán **11** Chichén Itzá *Peru:* **11** Machu Picchu *Syria:* **7** Palmyra *Tunisia:* **8** Carthage, Kairouan *Turkey:* **4** Troy **6** Knidos **8** Hisarlik, Pergamon **9** Hissarlik *Uzbekistan:* **9** Samarkand

archaeologist 4 Dart (Raymond) **5** Evans (Arthur) **6** Carter (Howard), Childe (V. Gordon), Kidder (Alfred), Petrie (Flinders) **7** Thomsen (Christian), Woolley (Leonard), Worsaae (Jens) **8** Breasted (James Henry), Goodyear (William) **10** Schliemann (Heinrich) **11** Champollion (Jean-François), Winckelmann (Johann)

archaic 3 old **5** dated, olden, passé **6** bygone **7** ancient, antique **8** obsolete, outdated **9** out-of-date, primitive, unevolved **10** antiquated **11** undeveloped **12** old-fashioned

archangel 5 Uriel **7** Gabriel, Michael, Raphael

arched 4 bent **5** bowed, round **6** curved **7** curving, rounded

archer 4 Tell (William) **5** Cupid **6** bowman **9** Robin Hood **11** Sagittarius

archery 9 toxophily

archetypal 5 ideal, model **7** classic, perfect, typical **9** classical, exemplary **10** consummate **12** paradigmatic, prototypical

archetype 4 idea **5** ideal, model **6** mirror **7** epitome, essence, example, pattern **8** exemplar, original, paradigm, standard **9** beau ideal, prototype **10** apotheosis, embodiment, protoplast **12** quintessence

archfiend 5 demon, devil, Satan **6** diablo **7** Lucifer

Archimedes 5 Greek **8** inventor *cry:* **6** eureka *discovery:* **5** screw **8** buoyancy **9** principle **11** water raiser

archipelago *Asian:* **5** Malay *Canada:* **6** Arctic *Japan:* **4** Goto **9** Gotoretto *Norway:* **11** Spitsbergen *Papua New Guinea:* **8** Bismarck **9** Louisiade *Philippines:* **4** Sulu *off Scotland:* **7** Orcades, Orkneys *United States:* **9** Alexander

architect 5 maker **7** creator **8** designer, inventor **9** generator **10** originator *American:* **3** Pei (I. M.) **4** Hood (Raymond), Kahn (Louis) **5** Gehry (Frank), McKim (Charles), Meier (Richard), Roche (Kevin), Stone (Edward Durell), Weese (Harry), White (Stanford) **6** Breuer (Marcel), Fuller (Buckminster), Graves (Michael), Morgan (Julia), Neutra (Richard), Rogers (Isaiah), Soleri (Paolo), Upjohn (Richard), Walter (Thomas), Warren (William), Wright (Frank Lloyd) **7** Burnham (Daniel), Gilbert (Cass), Johnson (Philip), Latrobe (Benjamin), Olmsted (Frederick Law), Renwick (James), Sturgis (John Hubbard), Venturi (Robert) **8** Bulfinch (Charles), Saarinen (Eero, Eliel), Sullivan (Louis), Thornton (William), Yamasaki (Minoru) **10** Richardson (Henry Hobson) *Austrian:* **4** Loos (Adolf) **6** Wagner (Otto) *Brazilian:* **8** Niemeyer (Oscar) *Canadian:* **6** Safdie (Moshe) *Dutch:* **8** Rietveld (Gerrit) *English:* **4** Nash (John), Shaw (Richard), Wood (John), Wren (Christopher) **5** Jones (Inigo), Scott (George Gilbert), Wyatt (James) **6** Foster (Norman), Rogers (Richard), Street (George Edmund), Voysey (Charles) **7** Lutyens (Edwin) **8** Vanbrugh (John) *Finnish:* **5** Aalto (Alvar) **8** Saarinen (Eero, Eliel) *French:* **6** Perret (Auguste) **7** Garnier (Tony), L'Enfant (Pierre-Charles) **11** Le Corbusier **12** Viollet-le-Duc (Eugène) *German:* **8** Schinkel (Karl) **10** Mendelsohn (Erich) *German-American:* **7** Gropius (Walter) *Israeli:* **6** Safdie (Moshe) *Italian:* **5** Nervi (Pier Luigi) **6** Romano (Giulio), Soleri (Paolo) **7** Alberti (Leon Battista), Bernini (Gian Lorenzo), da Vinci (Leonardo), Orcagna, Peruzzi (Baldassare), Raphael, Vignola (Giacomo da) **8** Bramante (Donato), Leonardo (da Vinci), Palladio (Andrea), Sangallo (Giuliano da), Terragni (Giuseppe) **9** Borromini (Francesco), Sansovino (Jacopo) **12** Michelangelo *Japanese:* **5** Tange (Kenzo) *Roman:* **9** Vitruvius *Scottish:* **10** Mackintosh (Charles Rennie) *Spanish:* **5** Gaudí (Antonio) *Swedish:* **7** Asplund (Erik Gunnar)

architecture 6 design, makeup **9** formation **11** composition **12** constitution, construction *ornament:* **4** boss, fret **5** gutta **6** finial, volute **7** cabling, console, crocket, diglyph **8** triglyph, vignette **9** arabesque, modillion *style:* **5** Doric, Ionic, Tudor **6** Gothic, Norman, Rococo **7** Baroque **8** Colonial, Georgian **9** Byzantine, Victorian **10** Corinthian, Romanesque

archive 4 file **6** record **7** collect, history, library, records **8** document, register **9** chronicle **10** collection, repository

archon 10 magistrate

arctic 3 icy **4** cold **5** chill, gelid **6** chilly, frigid, frosty, wintry **7** glacial, numbing **8** freezing, hibernal **11** hyperborean *animal:* **3** auk, fox **4** bear, hare, seal, vole **5** sable, whale **6** ermine, marten **7** caribou, lemming **8** reindeer **9** polar bear, ptarmigan *base:* **4** Etah **5** Thule **6** Barrow **11** Point Barrow *bird:* **3** auk

cetacean: 7 narwhal *current:* 8 Labrador
dog: 5 husky 7 Samoyed 8 malamute
explorer: 4 Byrd (Richard), Cook (Frederick) 5 Bylot (Robert), Davis (John),
Peary (Robert) 6 Baffin (William),
Bering (Vitus), Henson (Matthew),
Hudson (Henry), Nansen (Fridtjof),
Nobile (Umberto) 7 Barents (Willem),
Bennett (Floyd), Wilkins (George),
Wrangel (Ferdinand) 8 Amundsen
(Roald) 9 Ellsworth (Lincoln), Mackenzie (Alexander), MacMillan (Donald)
10 Stefansson (Vilhjalmus) *forest:*
5 taiga *jacket:* 5 parka 6 anorak *people:*
4 Lapp 5 Aleut, Inuit, Yakut 6 Eskimo,
Tungus 7 Chukchi, Samoyed *sea:*
4 Kara 6 Laptev 7 Barents, Chukchi
8 Beaufort *transport:* 7 dogsled *treeless
plains:* 6 tundra
ardent 3 hot 4 agog, avid, keen, true
5 eager, fiery, loyal 6 fervid, fierce,
heated, intent, red-hot, strong, torrid
7 blazing, burning, devoted, earnest,
fervent, flaming, glowing, intense, shining, staunch, zealous 8 constant,
desirous, faithful, powerful, resolute,
sizzling, vehement, white-hot 9 allegiant, impatient, impetuous, impulsive,
perfervid, scorching, steadfast
10 breathless, hot-blooded, passionate
11 impassioned 12 enthusiastic
ardor 4 fire, heat, zeal, zest, zing 5 gusto,
verve, vigor 6 energy, fealty, fervor,
spirit, warmth 7 avidity, loyalty, passion
8 devotion, fidelity 9 eagerness, intensity, vehemence 10 allegiance, enthusiasm, excitement 12 faithfulness
arduous 4 hard 5 harsh, rough, sheer,
steep, tight, tough 6 severe, taxing, tiring, trying, uphill 7 labored 8 grueling,
rigorous, toilsome 9 difficult, effortful,
gruelling, laborious, punishing, strenuous 10 formidable 11 precipitate, precipitous
area 4 belt, turf, zone 5 field, place,
range, realm, scene, space, tract
6 domain, locale, region, sector, sphere
7 expanse, stretch 8 district, locality,
province, vicinity 9 bailiwick, territory
12 neighborhood *unit:* 4 acre 7 hectare
arena 5 field, scene, stage 6 sphere 7 stadium, theater 8 activity, building, coliseum, province 10 hippodrome
12 amphitheater
Ares *Roman counterpart:* 4 Mars *consort:*
9 Aphrodite *father:* 4 Zeus *mother:*
4 Enyo, Hera *sister:* 4 Eris *son:*
5 Remus 7 Romulus
arête 5 crest, ridge
Arethusa 5 nymph 6 spring 9 wood
nymph *pursuer:* 7 Alpheus

argent 6 silver 7 silvern, silvery 9 whiteness
Argentina *capital:* 11 Buenos Aires *city:*
6 Paraná 7 Córdoba, La Plata, Rosario,
Santa Fe 11 Mar del Plata *desert:*
9 Patagonia *language:* 7 Spanish *leader:*
5 Perón (Juan) *monetary unit:* 4 peso
mountain, range: 5 Andes 9 Aconcagua
neighbor: 5 Chile 6 Brazil 7 Bolivia,
Uruguay 8 Paraguay *plain:* 6 Pampas
river: 5 Plata (Río de la) 6 Paraná 8 Colorado 12 Río de la Plata *volcano:*
5 Maipo 9 Tupungato
Arges 7 Cyclops *brother:* 7 Brontes
8 Steropes *father:* 6 Uranus *mother:*
4 Gaea
Argonaut 4 hero 10 adventurer 13 paper
nautilus *leader:* 5 Jason
argosy 4 ship 5 fleet 6 armada, supply
8 flotilla
argot 4 cant 5 idiom, lingo, slang 6 jargon, patois, patter 7 dialect 10 vernacular
arguable 4 moot 7 dubious 8 doubtful
9 debatable, in dispute, uncertain
10 disputable 11 contestable, problematic 12 questionable
argue 5 claim, clash, prove 6 assert,
attest, bicker, debate, differ, induce,
object, reason 7 agitate, canvass, contend, discuss, dispute, dissent, justify,
protest, quarrel, quibble, stickle, testify, witness, wrangle 8 announce, conflict, consider, disagree, indicate, maintain, persuade, polemize, squabble
9 thrash out 10 polemicize 11 expostulate, remonstrate
argument 3 row 4 case, feud, flap, fuss
5 claim, proof, set-to, theme, topic
6 debate, dustup, hassle, motive, reason, rumpus, thesis 7 defense, dispute,
polemic, sorites, subject, summary,
wrangle 8 abstract, evidence, rebuttal
9 amplitude, assertion, discourse
10 contention, discussion, dissension,
squabbling 11 controversy, disputation,
embroilment 12 disagreement
argumentation 6 debate 8 dispute, oratory 8 forensic, rhetoric 9 dialectic, reasoning 10 discussion 11 controversy,
disputation
argumentative 4 moot 9 in dispute, litigious, polemical 11 contentious, quarrelsome 12 disputatious, questionable
13 controversial
Argus *father:* 4 Zeus *mother:* 5 Niobe
slayer: 6 Hermes
Argus-eyed 5 alert 9 all-seeing
argyle 4 sock 6 design 7 diamond, pattern 8 Campbell

aria 3 air, lay 4 hymn, lied, solo, song, tune 5 ditty 6 melody 7 descant

Ariadne *father:* 5 Minos *husband:* 7 Theseus *island home:* 5 Naxos *mother:* 8 Pasiphaë

arid 3 dry 4 drab, dull, sere 5 dusty, vapid 6 barren, boring, desert, dreary, jejune 7 bone-dry, insipid, parched, sterile, tedious, thirsty 8 droughty, lifeless, weariful 9 dryasdust, infertile, unwatered, waterless, wearisome 10 lackluster, spiritless, unfruitful 12 moistureless 13 uninteresting

Ariel 6 spirit *master:* 8 Prospero

Aries 3 ram 13 constellation

aright 4 well 5 fitly 6 justly, nicely 8 decently, properly 9 correctly, fittingly, precisely 10 accurately, decorously

Ariosto *epic* 14 Orlando Furioso

arise 4 go up, lift, soar, wake 5 awake, begin, get up, issue, mount, occur, start 6 appear, ascend, aspire, come up, crop up, emerge, spring, uprear, wake up 7 emanate, proceed 8 commence 9 originate

Aristaeus *father:* 6 Apollo *mother:* 6 Cyrene *son:* 7 Actaeon *wife:* 7 Autonoe

aristocracy 5 elite, state 6 gentry, jet set 7 who's who 8 nobility, noblesse 9 beau monde, blue blood, gentility, haut monde 10 government, patricians, patriciate, upper class, upper crust

aristocrat 9 blue blood, gentleman, patrician *ancient Greek:* 8 eupatrid *Russian:* 5 boyar 6 boyard

aristocratic 5 aloof, elite, noble 6 lordly 7 courtly, elegant, genteel, haughty, refined, stately 8 highborn, well-born, well-bred 9 dignified, exclusive, patrician 10 privileged, upper-class, uppercrust 11 blue-blooded

Aristophanes *play* 5 Birds (The), Frogs (The), Wasps (The) 6 Clouds (The), Plutus

arithmetic 4 math 8 addition, counting, figuring 9 ciphering, reckoning 10 estimation 11 calculation, computation, mathematics

Arizona *capital:* 7 Phoenix *city:* 4 Mesa, Yuma 5 Tempe 6 Bisbee, Sedona, Tucson 8 Glendale, Prescott 9 Flagstaff 10 Scottsdale *mountain:* 9 Humphreys (Peak) *nickname:* 11 Grand Canyon (State) *park:* 15 Petrified Forest *river:* 4 Gila, Salt 8 Colorado *state bird:* 10 cactus wren *state flower:* 7 saguaro (cactus) *state tree:* 9 palo verde

ark 3 den 4 ship 5 chest, haven 6 adytum, asylum, refuge 7 convent, retreat, shelter 8 hideaway 9 safe house, sanctuary 10 repository, Torah chest *landfall:* 6 Ararat *wood:* 6 gopher 7 cypress

Arkansas *capital:* 10 Little Rock *city:* 4 Hope 9 Fort Smith, Pine Bluff 10 Hot Springs 11 Bentonville 12 Fayetteville *mountain, range:* 5 Ozark 8 Magazine *nickname:* 17 Land of Opportunity *river:* 3 Red 8 Arkansas *state bird:* 11 mockingbird *state flower:* 12 apple blossom *state tree:* 12 loblolly pine

arm 3 bay, ell, gun, rig 4 cove, gear, gulf, wing 5 annex, bayou, equip, firth, force, inlet, power 6 fit out, harbor, muscle, outfit, slough, weapon 7 appoint, furnish, turn out 8 accouter, strength 9 extension *bone:* 4 ulna 6 radius 7 humerus *combining form:* 6 brachi 7 brachio *muscle:* 6 biceps 7 triceps

armada 4 navy 5 boats, fleet, force, group, ships 7 vessels 8 flotilla, warships

armadillo *relative:* 5 sloth 8 anteater

armament 4 arms 5 armor 6 weapon 7 defense 8 ordnance, security, weaponry 9 munitions, safeguard 10 ammunition, protection

armamentarium 4 fund 5 stock, store 6 supply 9 inventory

armchair 6 remote 8 fauteuil 9 vicarious 11 theoretical

armed forces 4 army, navy 6 troops 8 air force, military 10 servicemen

Armenia *capital:* 7 Yerevan *city:* 6 Gyumri 8 Vanadzor *lake:* 5 Sevan *monetary unit:* 4 dram *mountain, range:* 7 Aragats 8 Caucasus *neighbor:* 4 Iran 6 Turkey 7 Georgia 10 Azerbaijan *river:* 5 Araks

armistice 5 truce 9 agreement, cease-fire 10 suspension

armor 4 mail 5 aegis, cover, guard 6 shield 7 buckler 8 security 9 safeguard 10 protection *arm:* 8 brassard *body:* 7 cuirass *armpit:* 8 pallette *buttocks:* 5 culet *coat:* 7 hauberk 10 brigandine *face:* 5 visor 6 beaver *flexible:* 4 mail *foot:* 8 solleret *hand:* 7 gantlet 8 gauntlet *head:* 6 helmet *horse:* 4 bard 5 barde 8 chamfron *leg:* 6 greave 7 jambeau *mail:* 4 coif 7 hauberk *suit:* 7 panoply *thigh:* 5 tasse 6 tuille *throat:* 6 gorget

armory 4 dump 5 depot, plant, range, store 7 arsenal, factory 8 magazine 10 collection, storehouse

armpit 6 axilla 8 underarm *Scottish:* 5 oxter

arms 7 ensigns, warfare 8 weaponry

army 4 host 5 flock, horde 6 legion 7 militia 9 multitude *combat arm:*

5 armor **8** infantry **9** artillery *commission:* **6** brevet **7** reserve *Fort:* **3** Dix, Lee, Ord **4** Drum, Hood, Knox, Myer, Polk, Sill **5** Bliss, Bragg, Irwin, Lewis, McCoy, Meade, Riley, Story **6** Carson, Eustis, Gillem, Gordon, Greely, McNair, Monroe, Rucker **7** Belvoir, Benning, Detrick, Jackson, Ritchie, Shafter, Stewart **8** Buchanan, Campbell, Hamilton, Holabird, Huachuca, Monmouth **9** McClellan, McPherson **10** Richardson, Sam Houston, Wainwright **11** Leavenworth *mascot:* **4** mule *meal:* **4** chow, mess *mine layer:* **6** sapper *NCO:* **8** corporal, sergeant *officer:* **5** major **7** captain, colonel, general, warrant **10** lieutenant *post:* **4** base, camp, fort *postal abbreviation:* **3** APO *relating to:* **7** martial **8** military *school:* **3** OCS, OTS **7** academy **9** West Point *store:* **10** commissary **12** post exchange *unit:* **5** corps, squad, troop **7** brigade, cavalry, company, platoon **8** division, regiment **9** battalion *vehicle:* **4** jeep, tank **6** Abrams, Humvee **7** Bradley **9** half-track

aroma 4 balm, odor **5** scent, smell, spice **6** flavor **7** bouquet, incense, perfume **9** fragrance, redolence

aromatic 5 balmy, spicy, sweet **6** savory **7** odorous, perfumy, pungent, scented **8** fragrant, perfumed, redolent **9** ambrosial

around 4 near, nigh **5** about, circa **6** nearby **7** through *prefix:* **4** ambi, peri **5** amphi **6** circum

around-the-clock 8 constant, unending **9** ceaseless, continual, incessant, perpetual, unceasing **10** continuous **11** unremitting **13** uninterrupted

arouse 4 fire, stir, wake, whet **5** alert, awake, pique, rally, waken **6** awaken, bestir, excite, fire up, foment, incite, kindle, work up **7** agitate, inflame **9** challenge, stimulate

arraign 3 tax, try **5** blame **6** accuse, charge, indict, summon **9** criminate, inculpate **11** incriminate

arrange 4 plan, sort **5** adapt, array, chart, order, score, unify **6** assort, codify, design, devise, lay out, line up, map out, scheme, set out, settle **7** dispose, marshal, prepare, work out **8** organize, sequence **9** blueprint, harmonize, integrate, methodize **10** bring about, categorize, instrument, symphonize, synthesize **11** choreograph, orchestrate, systematize

arrangement 5 array, order, setup **6** format, layout, lineup, series **8** grouping, ordering, sequence **9** structure **10** adaptation **11** disposition **12** distribution *floral:* **4** posy **7** bouquet, garland

arrant 4 rank **5** gross, total, utter **6** brassy, brazen **7** blatant, extreme, flat-out **8** absolute, complete, impudent, infernal, overbold **9** barefaced, downright, egregious, out-and-out, shameless, unabashed **10** immoderate, unblushing

arras 6 screen **7** drapery **8** curtains, tapestry

array 3 lot **4** clad, garb, pomp, show **5** adorn, batch, bunch, clump, dress, group, order **6** attire, bundle, clothe, draw up, finery, lineup, parade **7** apparel, arrange, cluster, display, dispose, garment, marshal, militia, panoply, raiment, variety **8** clothing, decorate, enclothe, organize, spectrum **9** formation **10** assortment **11** systematize

arrears 3 due **4** debt **5** claim, debit **7** deficit **9** liability **10** balance due, obligation **12** indebtedness

arrest 3 nab, tab, tag **4** bust, grab, halt, hold, jail, slow, snag, stay, stem, stop **5** block, catch, check, pinch, run in, seize, stall **6** collar, detain, haul in, lock up, pick up, pull in, retard, take in **7** capture, contain, seizure **8** imprison, obstruct, restrain **9** apprehend, detention, interrupt **11** incarcerate **12** apprehension

arresting 6 marked, signal **7** salient **8** striking **9** affective, appealing, prominent **10** attractive, compelling, enchanting, impressive, noticeable, remarkable **11** conspicuous, eye-catching, outstanding

arrival 6 advent, coming **7** landing, success **8** entrance, incoming **9** emergence **10** appearance

arrive 4 come, land, show **5** get in, get to, reach **6** appear, show up, thrive, turn up **7** prosper, succeed **8** flourish

arriviste 7 parvenu, upstart **8** roturier **12** nouveau riche

arrogance 3 ego **4** airs, gall **5** brass, cheek, pride **6** hubris **7** conceit, disdain, hauteur **8** self-love **9** loftiness **11** haughtiness

arrogant 5 cocky, proud **6** lordly, snooty **7** haughty, pompous **8** cavalier, fastuous, insolent, superior **9** egotistic **10** disdainful, high-handed, peremptory **11** domineering, magisterial, overbearing **12** supercilious **13** high-and-mighty, self-important

arrogate 4 grab, take **5** annex, claim, seize, usurp **6** assume, demand **7** ascribe, preempt **8** accroach, take

over 9 sequester 10 commandeer, confiscate 11 appropriate, expropriate
arrow 4 dart 5 shaft *poison:* 4 inée, upas 6 curare
arrowroot 5 plant, tuber 6 starch 7 coontie
Arrowsmith's wife 5 Leora
arroyo 3 gap 4 draw 5 brook, chasm, cleft, clove, creek, gorge, gulch, gully 6 coulee, ravine 7 channel 11 watercourse
arsenal 4 dump 5 depot, stock, store 6 armory, supply 7 factory, weapons 8 magazine, ordnance 9 stockpile 10 depository, repertoire, repository, storehouse
arson 6 firing 8 torching 9 pyromania 12 incendiarism
arsonist 5 firer, torch 7 firebug 10 incendiary
art 5 craft, skill 6 métier 7 finesse, knowhow 8 artifice, painting, vocation 9 dexterity, expertise, sculpture 10 handicraft *faddish:* 6 kitsch *style:* 3 pop 4 dada 6 cubist, rococo 7 fauvist, realist, surreal 8 abstract, futurist 9 classical 10 naturalist, surrealist 12 naturalistic, surrealistic 13 expressionist, impressionist
art deco 5 style 6 design *designer:* 4 Erté
Artemis *Roman counterpart:* 5 Diana *birthplace:* 5 Delos *brother:* 6 Apollo *father:* 4 Zeus *mother:* 4 Leto *priestess:* 9 Iphigenia
artery 3 way 4 duct, line, path, road, tube 5 aorta, track 6 avenue, course, street, vessel 7 carotid, channel, conduit, highway, passage, pathway 8 coronary 9 boulevard 12 thoroughfare
artful 3 sly 4 foxy, wily 5 adept, sharp, slick, smart, suave 6 adroit, astute, clever, crafty, shrewd, smooth, tricky 7 cunning 8 guileful, skillful 9 dexterous, ingenious 10 artificial, diplomatic
arthropod 3 bee, fly 4 crab, mite, moth, tick 6 beetle, insect, shrimp, spider 7 lobster 8 arachnid, barnacle, diplopod, myriapod, scorpion 9 butterfly, centipede, cockroach, millipede, trilobite 10 crustacean *body segment:* 6 somite, telson 8 metamere
Arthur see KING ARTHUR
article 3 the 4 bind, item, part 5 essay, paper, piece, point, theme, thing 6 matter, object 7 element, feature, passage, section 10 particular 11 composition, stipulation
articled 5 bound 10 indentured
articulate 3 say 4 join, link, oral, talk 5 clear, hinge, joint, lucid, shape,

speak, state, utter, vocal, voice 6 couple, fluent, prolix, relate, spoken, voiced 7 connect, express, jointed 8 coherent, definite, distinct, eloquent, vocalize 9 effective, enunciate, harmonize, integrate, pronounce, verbalize 10 coordinate, expressive 11 concatenate 12 intelligible, smooth-spoken
artifact 5 curio, relic 6 legacy, rarity, trophy 7 remnant, spin-off, vestige 8 creation, heirloom 9 by-product, handcraft, handiwork 10 handicraft 11 contrivance, fabrication
artifice 4 play, ploy, ruse, wile 5 craft, feint, guile, skill, trick 6 deceit, device, gambit 7 cunning, slyness 8 facility, foxiness, trickery, wiliness 9 adeptness, canniness, chicanery, duplicity, ingenuity, stratagem 10 adroitness, artfulness, cleverness, craftiness
artificial 4 fake, faux, mock, sham 5 bogus, dummy, faked, false, phony, put-on 6 ersatz, forced, hollow, unreal 7 assumed, feigned, in vitro, labored, man-made, plastic, pretend 8 affected, mannered, spurious 9 contrived, imitation, insincere, simulated, synthetic, unnatural 10 fabricated, factitious, fictitious, substitute
artillery 4 arms 5 canon, force 6 rocket 7 battery, bazooka, gunnery, weapons 8 cannonry, howitzer, ordnance, weaponry 9 munitions
artisan 6 worker 7 builder, workman 8 producer 9 carpenter, craftsman 12 craftsperson
artist 7 painter 8 sculptor, virtuoso *garb:* 5 smock *knife:* 7 spatula *medium:* 3 oil 5 paint 6 pastel 7 tempera 8 charcoal 10 watercolor *pigment board:* 7 palette *stand:* 5 easel *workshop:* 6 studio 7 atelier (see also PAINTER)
artless 4 free, open, pure, true 5 crude, naive, plain 6 direct, honest, simple 7 genuine, natural, sincere, unaware 8 trusting 9 childlike, guileless, ingenuous, unstudied 10 aboveboard, forthright, unaffected, uncultured, unschooled 12 unartificial, unsuspicious
arty 5 showy 6 pseudo 8 affected, imposing 9 overblown 11 pretentious 12 highsounding
Aruba *capital:* 10 Oranjestad *language:* 5 Dutch 10 Papiamento *monetary unit:* 6 florin *part of:* 11 Netherlands
as 3 for, who 4 coin, like, that, when 5 being, since, which, while 6 though 7 because 11 considering, for instance
___ **as a pin** 4 neat
as a rule 6 mainly, mostly 7 usually

8 commonly 9 generally 10 frequently, ordinarily

Ascanius 5 Iulus *father:* 6 Aeneas

ascend 4 go up, lift, rise, soar 5 arise, climb, crest, mount, scale 6 aspire, move up, occupy 7 lift off, take off 8 escalade, escalate, surmount

ascendancy 4 rule 5 power, reign 7 command, control, mastery 8 dominion 9 authority, dominance, influence, supremacy 10 domination, prepotency 11 preeminence, sovereignty 13 preponderance

ascendant 6 master, rising 7 regnant 8 ancestor, dominant, forebear, relative, superior 9 paramount, precursor, prevalent, sovereign 10 commanding, forefather, forerunner, prevailing, progenitor 11 controlling, overbearing, predecessor, predominant, predominate 12 preponderant, primogenitor

ascension 4 rise 6 rising 7 going up, scaling 8 climbing, mounting

ascent 4 ramp, rise 5 climb, grade, slope 6 rising 7 advance, incline 8 gradient, progress 9 acclivity, elevation, uplifting

ascertain 5 learn 7 catch on, find out, unearth 8 discover, make sure 9 determine, establish, figure out

ascetic 5 stoic 6 hermit, severe 7 austere, eremite, recluse 9 abstinent, anchoress, anchorite, mortified 10 abstemious, astringent, forbearing, restrained 11 disciplined, self-denying *ancient Hebrew:* 6 Essene *Buddhist:* 5 bonze *early Christian:* 7 stylite *Hindu:* 4 yogi 5 fakir, Yogin

Asclepius see AESCULAPIUS

ascribe 3 lay 4 cite 5 infer, refer 6 assign, charge, credit, impute 8 accredit 9 attribute, reference 10 conjecture

Asenath *husband:* 6 Joseph *son:* 7 Ephraim 8 Manasseh

aseptic 4 cool, flat 5 clean 7 sterile 8 germ-free, hygienic, sanitary 9 unfeeling 10 restrained, sterilized 11 emotionless, unemotional

asexual 6 agamic

as for 4 in re 5 about, anent 7 apropos 9 regarding 10 concerning, respecting 12 with regard to

as good as 4 nigh 6 all but, almost, nearly 8 in effect, well-nigh 9 basically, in essence, just about, virtually 11 essentially, practically

ash 4 soot, tree, wood 7 cinders, residue 8 clinkers

ashamed 6 abased, abject, guilty 7 abashed, humbled 8 contrite, penitent 9 chagrined, mortified, repentant

10 humiliated 11 discomfited, embarrassed

ashen 3 wan 4 gray, pale 5 faded, pasty, waxen 6 doughy, pallid, sallow, sickly 7 ghostly 8 blanched, bleached 9 bloodless, colorless 10 corpselike

Asher *daughter:* 5 Serah *father:* 5 Jacob *mother:* 6 Zilpah *son:* 4 Isui 6 Beriah, Ishuah, Jimnah

ashes 5 ruins 6 pallor 7 remains

ashy 3 wan 4 drab, pale 5 livid, waxen 6 doughy, leaden, pallid 7 ghastly, greyish 8 blanched 9 bloodless, colorless, washed-out 10 cadaverous

Asia *country:* 4 Laos 5 Burma, China, India, Japan, Korea, Nepal 6 Bhutan, Russia, Taiwan 7 Armenia, Georgia, Myanmar, Vietnam 8 Cambodia, Malaysia, Mongolia, Pakistan, Sri Lanka, Thailand 9 Indonesia, Kampuchea, Kazakstan, Singapore 10 Azerbaijan, Bangladesh, Kazakhstan, Kyrgyzstan, North Korea, South Korea, Tajikistan, Uzbekistan 11 Afghanistan, Philippines 12 Turkmenistan *ethnic group:* 3 Han, Lao, Tai 4 Arab, Kurd, Moor, Shan 5 Karen, Khmer, Malay, Tajik, Tamil, Uzbek 6 Burman, Lepcha, Manchu, Mongol, Sindhi 7 Baluchi, Bengali, Persian, Punjabi, Tibetan 8 Armenian, Assyrian, Javanese 9 Dravidian, Indo-Aryan, Sinhalese 10 Circassian, Montagnard, Singhalese *language:* 3 Lao 4 Urdu 5 Hindi, Malay, Tamil, Uzbek 6 Arabic, Bahasa, Korean, Nepali 7 Bengali, Burmese, Khalkha, Kurdish, Persian, Tibetan, Turkish 8 Armenian, Japanese, Javanese, Mandarin 9 Cambodian 10 Vietnamese

Asia Minor 8 Anatolia *country:* 6 Turkey

Asian inland sea 4 Aral

aside 4 away 5 apart 7 tangent 8 away from 9 in reserve, privately 10 digression, discursion 11 parenthesis

aside from 3 bar, but 4 save 6 bating, except 7 barring, besides 9 excepting, excluding, other than, outside of 11 exclusive of

Asimov, Isaac *forte:* 5 sci-fi *work:* 6 I Robot 9 Nightfall 10 Foundation (Trilogy) 14 Gods Themselves (The)

asinine 5 crazy, daffy, silly 6 absurd, simple 7 fatuous, foolish, idiotic, puerile, witless 8 mindless 9 brainless 10 irrational, ridiculous 11 nonsensical

ask 3 beg, bid 4 pray, quiz, seek 5 crave, exact, grill, plead, query 6 appeal, demand, desire, invite 7 beseech, call for, canvass, consult, enquire, entreat, examine, implore, inquire, request,

require, solicit **8** petition, question
9 catechize, importune **10** supplicate
11 interrogate *Scottish:* **5** speer, speir

askance 8 sidelong, sideways **9** cynically,
obliquely **10** critically, doubtfully,
doubtingly, scornfully **11** skeptically
12 suspiciously **13** distrustfully, mis-
trustfully

asker 6 beggar, prayer, suitor **7** speaker
9 suppliant **10** petitioner, questioner,
supplicant **11** supplicator

askew 4 awry **6** turned **8** cockeyed
9 crookedly

aslant 4 awry **5** askew **7** crooked **8** cockeyed, sideways, sidewise **9** obliquely

asleep 4 dead, idle, numb **5** inert **6** doz-
ing, numbed **7** defunct, dormant, nap-
ping **8** benumbed, deadened, inactive,
in repose, not alert, sluggish **9** senseless, unfeeling **10** insensible, slumbering, unanimated **11** indifferent, unconscious **12** anesthetized

as long as 3 for **5** since **6** seeing
7 because, whereas **10** inasmuch as
11 considering **12** provided that

as much as 6 all but, almost **8** well-nigh
11 essentially, practically

aspect 3 air **4** look, mien, side **5** angle,
facet, phase, scene, slant **6** regard, status **7** bearing, seeming **8** exposure, position **9** direction **10** appearance **11** perspective

aspen 4 tree **6** poplar

asperity 5 rigor **8** acerbity, acrimony,
grimness, hardness, hardship, mordancy, severity, tartness **9** harshness, roughness, sharpness **10** bitterness, difficulty,
unevenness **12** irregularity, irritability

asperse 4 slur **5** libel, smear, sully
6 attack, defame, insult, malign, vilify
7 baptize, slander, tarnish, traduce
8 bad mouth, dishonor, sprinkle **9** denigrate, insinuate **10** calumniate

aspersion 4 muck, slam, slur **5** abuse
7 calumny, obloquy, slander **9** invective, stricture **10** defamation, detraction **11** denigration **12** vilification, vituperation **13** animadversion

asphalt 4 pave **7** bitumen, surface
8 blacktop, pavement

asphyxiate 4 kill **5** choke, drown **6** stifle
7 smother **8** strangle, throttle **9** suffocate

aspirant 6 seeker **7** hopeful, seeking
9 applicant, candidate, contender

aspiration 3 aim **4** goal, urge, wish
5 dream **6** desire, intent, object **7** craving, longing, passion, pursuit **8** ambition, striving, yearning **9** breathing,
objective **10** pretension **13** ambi-
tiousness

aspire 3 aim, try **4** long, pant, rise, seek,
soar, want, wish **5** arise, mount, yearn
6 ascend, desire, hunger, strive, thirst

aspiring 7 longing, seeking, wanting,
wishful **8** striving, vaulting, yearning
9 ambitious

as regards 4 in re **7** apropos **8** touching
10 concerning, respecting

ass 4 dolt, fool, jerk, moke, mule
5 burro, dunce, idiot **6** donkey, nitwit
8 bonehead, imbecile **10** nincompoop
female: **5** jenny *male:* **4** jack *wild Asian:*
5 kiang **6** onager

assai 4 very

assail 4 bash, beat **5** abuse, beset, blast,
pound, storm **6** attack, berate, buffet,
charge, fall on, malign, oppugn, pummel, revile, strike, vilify **7** assault, bombard **8** fall upon, lambaste **9** break
down

assassin 3 gun **5** bravo **6** gunman, hit
man, killer **7** torpedo **8** murderer **9** cutthroat **10** hatchet man, triggerman *of
Caesar:* **6** Brutus **7** Cassius *of Garfield:*
7 Guiteau (Charles Julius) *of J. F.
Kennedy:* **6** Oswald (Lee Harvey) *of M.
L. King:* **3** Ray (James Earl) *of Lincoln:*
5 Booth (John Wilkes) *of Marat:* **6** Corday (Charlotte) *of McKinley:* **8** Czolgosz
(Leon) *of R. F. Kennedy:* **6** Sirhan
(Sirhan)

assassinate 4 do in, kill, slay **6** finish,
murder, rub out **7** bump off, execute,
gun down, put away, take out **8** dispatch, knock off **9** eliminate, liquidate

assault 3 mug, war **4** raid **5** beset, fight,
onset, set-to, storm **6** assail, attack,
charge, fall on, strike, threat **7** aggress,
besiege, mugging, offense **8** fall upon,
invasion, storming **9** incursion, offensive, onslaught, violation **10** aggression

assay 3 try **4** rate, seek, test **5** judge,
offer, prove, trial, value, weigh **6** assess,
result, rating, strive, survey **7** analyze,
attempt, examine, inspect, measure,
valuate, venture **8** analysis, appraise,
endeavor, estimate, evaluate, struggle
9 appraisal, undertake, valuation
10 assessment, evaluation, inspection,
measurement **11** examination

assemblage 5 crowd, group **6** muster
7 company, turnout **8** audience **9** gathering **10** collection **11** aggregation, composition, convergence **12** congregation

assemble 4 call, form, make, mass,
meet, mold **5** amass, build, clump,
group, shape, unite **6** gather, muster,
summon **7** cluster, collect, convene,
convoke, fashion, marshal, produce,
round up **8** congress, contrive **9** aggregate, forgather **10** accumulate, congre-

gate 11 fit together, manufacture, put together 12 call together, come together 13 bring together

assembly 4 bevy **5** bunch, covey, crowd, flock, group, party, rally, set-up **6** muster, troupe **7** cluster, meeting **8** conclave **9** congeries, gathering **10** collection **11** association, fabrication, get-together, manufacture **12** congregation, construction *American Indian:* **6** powwow *ancient Greek:* **8** ecclesia *ancient Roman:* **7** comitia *Anglo-Saxon:* **4** moot **5** gemot **6** gemote **8** folkmoot, folkmote *ecclesiastical:* **5** synod **10** consistory *legislative:* **4** diet **6** senate **8** congress **10** parliament *place:* **4** hall, room **5** agora **10** auditorium *Russian:* **4** duma *witches':* **6** sabbat **7** sabbath

assent 3 nod, yes **4** okay **5** agree **6** accede, accord, concur, say yes **7** approve, consent, embrace **8** approval, sanction, thumbs-up **9** accession, acquiesce, admission, agreement, subscribe **10** acceptance, permission **11** affirmation, concurrence **12** acquiescence

assert 3 say **4** aver, avow **5** argue, claim, posit, state, utter, voice **6** adduce, affirm, allege, attest, avouch, defend, depose, insist, submit **7** advance, contend, declare, express, justify, profess, protest, publish, warrant **8** announce, maintain, proclaim **9** broadcast, postulate, predicate **10** promulgate

assertion 6 avowal **8** averment **9** affidavit, statement **10** allegation, avouchment, contention, deposition, disclosure, insistence, profession **11** affirmation, attestation, declaration **12** asseveration **13** pronouncement

assertive 4 firm, sure **5** pushy **6** strong **7** assured, certain, decided, pushing **8** cocksure, emphatic, forceful, positive **9** confident, energetic, insistent **10** aggressive, resounding **11** affirmative, distinctive, self-assured **13** self-confident

assess 3 fix, tax **4** deem, levy, rate **5** assay, exact, judge, put on, set at, value, weigh **6** charge, figure, impose, reckon, survey **7** account, compute, subject, valuate **8** appraise, consider, estimate, evaluate **9** determine

assessment 3 fee, tax **4** duty, levy, toll **6** charge, impost, rating, tariff **8** estimate, judgment **9** appraisal, valuation **10** estimation, evaluation **12** appraisement

asset 4 boon, good **5** merit **6** credit **7** benefit **8** blessing, resource **9** advantage **11** distinction *opposite:* **9** liability

assets 5 items, means, money **6** wealth **7** capital **8** bankroll, property **9** resources, valuables **11** possessions

asseverate 4 aver, avow **5** state **6** affirm, assert, attest, avouch, depose, insist **7** certify, contend, declare, profess **8** maintain, proclaim **9** pronounce

assiduous 4 busy **5** eager **6** active **7** moiling, zealous **8** diligent, sedulous, tireless **9** attentive, laborious **10** persistent, unflagging **11** hard-working, industrious **13** indefatigable

assiduously 4 hard **6** busily **9** earnestly, intensely **10** diligently, thoroughly **11** intensively **12** exhaustively, meticulously, persistently **13** painstakingly, unremittingly

assign 3 fix, lay, set **4** cede, deed, give, name **5** allot, allow, refer **6** charge, convey, credit, define, impute, remise, settle **7** appoint, ascribe, earmark, lay down, mete out, specify, station **8** accredit, allocate, delegate, make over, relegate, sign over, transfer **9** admeasure, apportion, attribute, designate, establish, prescribe **10** pigeonhole

assignation 4 date **5** tryst **7** meeting **9** allotment **10** engagement, rendezvous **11** appointment, get-together

assignee 5 agent, proxy **6** deputy, factor **7** officer **8** attorney, delegate

assignment 3 job **4** beat, duty, post, task, work **5** chore, stint **6** office **8** homework, position, transfer **9** allotment **10** allocation, delegation, obligation **11** designation

assimilate 5 adapt, adopt, grasp, learn, liken, match **6** absorb, adjust, digest, equate, imbibe, soak up, take in, take up **7** blend in, compare, conform **8** parallel **10** comprehend, understand **11** incorporate

assimilation 8 taking in **9** awareness **10** absorption, conversion **11** mindfulness, recognition **12** apperception **13** consciousness, incorporation

assist 3 aid **4** abet, back, help, lift **5** boost, do for, serve, stead **6** relief, succor **7** backing, benefit, comfort, help out, secours, service, support, work for **8** benefact, work with **9** cooperate, open doors

assistance 3 aid **4** hand, help, lift **5** boost **6** relief, succor **7** backing, benefit, comfort, secours, service, subsidy, support **8** abetment **9** upholding **10** subvention, supporting **11** cooperation

assistant 3 aid **4** aide, ally, help **5** aider **6** backer, backup, deputy, flunky, helper, second **7** acolyte, ancilla, order-

ly 8 adjutant, henchman 9 attendant,
auxiliary, coadjutor 10 accomplice,
aide-de-camp, coadjutant, lieutenant
12 right-hand man
assistive 6 aiding, useful 7 helpful
10 beneficial 11 serviceable
assize 3 law 4 rule, writ 5 canon, edict
6 decree 7 finding, inquest, precept,
statute, verdict 8 standard 9 ordinance,
prescript 10 regulation
associate 3 pal 4 ally, chum, join, link,
mate, pair, yoke 5 blend, buddy, crony,
group, match, merge, unite 6 cohort,
comate, couple, friend, hobnob,
relate, worker 7 bracket, combine,
compeer, comrade, conjoin, connect,
consort, partner 8 confrere, coworker,
employee, familiar, federate, identify,
intimate 9 affiliate, bedfellow, colleague, companion, copartner, secondary 10 accomplice, amalgamate, compatriot, complement 11 concomitant,
confederate, correlative, counterpart,
running mate, subordinate 12 acquaintance 13 accompaniment
association 3 tie 4 band, bloc, bond,
clan, club, crew, hint 5 group, guild,
order, tie-up, union 6 hookup, league
7 circuit, concert, linkage, linking,
society 8 alliance, congress, overtone,
relation, sodality, teamwork 9 coalition, undertone 10 conference, connection, federation, fellowship, fraternity,
mental link, suggestion 11 affiliation,
brotherhood, combination, conjunction, connotation, cooperation, implication, partnership 12 conjointment,
organization, relationship, togetherness
13 collaboration
assort 5 class, group, order 6 codify,
divide 7 arrange 8 classify, stratify
9 associate, designate, harmonize,
methodize 10 categorize, distribute,
pigeonhole 11 systematize
assorted 4 like 5 mixed 6 fitted, motley,
suited, sundry, varied 7 adapted,
diverse, matched, similar, various 9 different 11 diversified, conformable
12 conglomerate, multifarious 13 heterogeneous, miscellaneous
assortment 4 olio 5 array, group
6 choice, jumble, medley 7 mélange,
mixture, variety 8 mishmash, mixed
bag, pastiche 9 diversity, potpourri,
selection 10 collection, hodgepodge,
miscellany 11 gallimaufry
assuage 4 calm, cool, ease 5 allay, quiet
6 lessen, pacify, quench, reduce, soften,
soothe, temper 7 appease, lighten, mollify, placate, relieve, sweeten

8 decrease, mitigate, moderate 9 alleviate 10 conciliate, propitiate
as such 5 per se 8 by itself 9 in essence,
virtually 11 essentially 12 by definition
13 fundamentally, intrinsically
assumably 6 likely, surely 7 no doubt
8 probably 9 doubtless 10 most likely,
presumably
assume 3 act, don 4 fake, sham, take
5 adopt, bluff, feign, put on, seize,
usurp 6 affect, draw on, expect, reckon, slip on, take in, take on, take up
7 believe, imagine, preempt, premise,
presume, pretend, receive, suppose,
suspect 8 accroach, arrogate, shoulder,
simulate, take over 9 undertake
10 commandeer, presuppose, understand 11 appropriate, counterfeit
assumed 4 fake, sham 5 bogus, false,
put on, tacit 6 made-up, phoney
7 feigned 8 affected, delusory, putative,
spurious, supposed 9 deceptive, pretended, simulated 10 artificial, fictitious
assumption 5 posit 6 belief, thesis 7 conceit, premise, seizure, surmise
8 takeover 9 arrogance, postulate
10 acceptance, arrogation, conjecture,
pretension, usurpation 11 expectation,
supposition, undertaking 13 appropriation
assurance 4 oath, word 5 nerve, troth
6 aplomb, parole, pledge, safety, surety
7 promise, support, warrant 8 audacity,
boldness, safeness, security, sureness,
temerity, warranty 9 assertion, brashness, certainty, certitude, cockiness,
composure, guarantee, hardiness, self-
trust 10 brazenness, confidence, conviction, equanimity, profession 11 affirmation, presumption
assure 4 aver 5 bet on, cinch, swear
6 affirm, attest, ensure, insure, pledge,
secure, soothe 7 certify, comfort, confirm, promise, satisfy 8 convince, persuade 9 guarantee 11 make certain
assured 3 set 4 cool 5 fixed 6 secure
7 certain, decided, settled 8 clear-cut,
composed, definite, positive, sanguine,
9 assertive, collected, confident,
undoubted, unruffled 10 guaranteed,
pronounced 11 beyond doubt, made
certain, unflappable 13 imperturbable,
self-confident, self-satisfied
assuredly 9 certainly, doubtless 10 positively 11 confidently, undoubtedly,
without fail
assuredness 6 surety 9 certainty, certitude 10 confidence, conviction
Assyria *capital:* 5 Calah 7 Nineveh *city:*
5 Ashur, Assur *god:* 3 Sin 4 Nabu

5 Ashur, Nusku 6 Tammuz 7 Ninurta
goddess: 6 Ishtar *king:* 3 Pul 6 Sargon
11 Sennacherib, Shalmaneser 12 Ashurbanipal *language:* 7 Aramaic *queen:*
9 Semiramis *river:* 6 Tigris *writing:*
9 cuneiform

asterisk 4 star 6 symbol 9 character

astern 3 aft 4 rear, tail 5 abaft 6 back of,
behind 8 backward, rearmost, rearward

asteroid 5 Ceres

Asterope *father:* 5 Atlas *mother:*
7 Pleione *sisters:* 8 Pleiades

asthma 7 allergy 8 disorder

as to 4 in re 5 about, anent 7 apropos
9 regarding 10 concerning, respecting
11 according to

astonish 4 daze, stun 5 amaze, floor,
shock 7 astound, stagger, startle, stupefy 8 blow away, bowl over, confound,
dumfound, surprise 9 dumbfound, take
aback 11 flabbergast

astonishing 7 amazing 8 stunning, wondrous 9 marvelous, startling, wonderful
10 astounding, miraculous, prodigious,
staggering, stupendous, surprising
11 spectacular 12 breathtaking

astonishment 3 awe 5 shock 6 wonder
8 surprise 9 amazement, confusion
10 perplexity, wonderment 12 bewilderment, stupefaction 13 consternation

astound 4 daze, stun 5 amaze, shock
7 confuse 8 astonish, bewilder, confound, dumfound, surprise 9 dumbfound, overwhelm, take aback 11 flabbergast

Astraea *father:* 4 Zeus 7 Jupiter *mother:*
6 Themis

astral 6 dreamy, starry 7 exalted, highest, stellar 8 elevated, sidereal 9 celestial, top-drawer, unworldly, visionary
10 top-ranking 11 high-ranking 12 otherworldly

astray 4 awry 5 amiss, badly, wrong
6 adrift, afield 7 in error 9 off course

astride 8 bridging, spanning 10 on each
side, straddling

astringent 4 acid, keen 5 acerb, acrid,
harsh, sharp, stern 6 biting, bitter,
severe, strict 7 acerbic, ascetic, austere,
caustic, cutting, puckery, pungent,
styptic 8 incisive, stinging 10 irritating
11 contracting 12 constrictive

astrolabe successor 7 sextant

astrologer 5 Dixon (Jeane), Faust
9 stargazer, Zoroaster 11 horoscopist,
Nostradamus

astrological aspect 5 trine 7 sextile
8 quartile 10 opposition 11 conjunction

astronaut 4 Ride (Sally) 5 Glenn (John),
White (Edward), Young (John) 6 Aldrin
(Edwin), Cooper (Gordon), Lovell
(James), Worden (Alfred) 7 Bluford
(Guion), Collins (Michael), Gagarin
(Yuri), Grissom (Gus), Jemison (Mae),
Schirra (Walter), Shepard (Alan),
Yegorov (Boris) 8 Stafford (Thomas)
9 Armstrong (Neil), Carpenter (Scott),
McAuliffe (Christa) 10 Tereshkova
(Valentina)

astronomer *American:* 3 See (Thomas)
Jefferson) 5 Sagan (Carl) 6 Hubble
(Edwin), Lowell (Percival) 7 Langley
(Samuel), Newcomb (Simon), Shapley
(Harlow) 8 Bowditch (Nathaniel),
Mitchell (Maria), Tombaugh (Clyde)
9 Pickering (Edward) 11 Schlesinger
(Frank) *Austrian:* 13 Schwarzschild
(Karl) *Danish:* 5 Brahe (Tycho) *Dutch:*
4 Oort (Jan Hendrik) 6 Sitter (Willem
de) 7 Huygens (Christiaan) *English:*
4 Ryle (Martin), Wren (Christopher)
6 Halley (Edmond), Lovell (Bernard)
7 Lockyer (Joseph), Parsons (William)
8 Herschel (Caroline, John, William)
French: 6 Picard (Jean) 7 Laplace
(Pierre-Simon de), Messier (Charles)
German: 4 Wolf (Maximilian) 5 Vogel
(Hermann) 6 Kepler (Johannes),
Müller (Johann), Struve (Otto) *Greek:*
12 Eratosthenes *Italian:* 7 Galileo
(Galilei) 12 Schiaparelli (Giovanni) *Persian:* 11 Omar Khayyám *Polish:*
10 Copernicus (Nicolaus) *Swedish:*
7 Celsius (Anders) *Swiss:* 6 Zwicky
(Fritz)

astute 3 sly 4 deep, foxy, keen, wily
5 cagey, canny, heady, quick, savvy,
sharp 6 artful, clever, crafty, shrewd,
tricky 7 cunning, knowing 8 guileful
9 insidious, sagacious 11 calculating
13 perspicacious

astuteness 3 wit 6 acumen 8 keenness,
wiliness 9 canniness 10 craftiness,
shrewdness 11 discernment, percipience 12 perspicacity

Astyanax *father:* 6 Hector *mother:*
10 Andromache

asunder 4 torn 5 apart, split 7 divided
9 into parts, separated

as usual 8 normally, wontedly 9 routinely 10 habitually, ordinarily 11 customarily 12 consistently

as well 3 and, too, yet 4 also, even, just,
more, plus 7 besides, further 8 likewise,
moreover 9 along with, including, similarly 10 in addition 11 furthermore
12 additionally

as well as 3 and 4 plus 7 besides 9 along
with 11 not counting 12 in addition to,
together with

as yet 5 so far, to now 7 earlier, thus far

8 hitherto, until now **10** to this time **12** to the present

asylum 4 home, port **5** cover, haven **6** covert, harbor, refuge **7** retreat, shelter **8** hospital, security **9** harborage, safe house, sanctuary **10** protection, sanatorium **11** institution

asymmetric 6 uneven **7** not even, unequal **8** lopsided **9** irregular **10** unbalanced **12** overbalanced

Atalanta *husband:* **8** Melanion *suitor:* **10** Hippomenes

at all 4 ever, once **6** anyway **7** anytime

atavism 9 reversion, throwback **10** recurrence

ataxia 5 chaos, snarl **6** huddle, muddle **7** clutter **8** disarray, disorder **9** confusion

atelier 6 studio **8** workroom, workshop

Athamas *daughter:* **5** Helle *father:* **6** Aeolus *son:* **7** Phrixos, Phrixus **8** Learchus *wife:* **3** Ino **7** Nephele

Athena *Roman counterpart:* **7** Minerva *attribute:* **3** owl **5** Aegis **7** serpent *city:* **6** Athens *father:* **4** Zeus *names:* **4** Nike **6** Pallas **9** Parthenos *shield:* **5** Aegis *statue:* **9** Palladium *temple:* **9** Parthenon

athenaeum 6 museum **7** library **8** archives **10** repository

Athens *citadel:* **9** Acropolis *founder:* **7** Cecrops *last king:* **6** Codrus *marketplace:* **5** agora *rival:* **6** Sparta *senate:* **5** boule *temple:* **9** Parthenon

athirst 4 avid, keen **5** eager **6** ardent **7** anxious **8** desiring, desirous, yearning **9** impatient

athlete 4 jock **5** sport **6** player **7** acrobat, gymnast, tumbler **9** sportsman **10** competitor **11** sportswoman

athlete's foot 8 ringworm **10** tinea pedis

athletic 6 brawny, robust, sinewy **8** sporting, vigorous **9** strapping, strenuous *contest:* **4** agon, game **5** match *field:* **4** oval, ring, rink **5** arena, court **7** diamond, stadium **8** gridiron *prize:* **3** cup **5** medal **6** trophy, wreath

athletics 5 games, races **6** events, sports **7** contest **8** exercise **9** exercises **10** gymnastics, recreation **12** calisthenics

athwart 4 over **5** cross **6** across, beyond **9** crossways, crosswise, opposed to **12** transversely

Atlanta's civic center 4 Omni

Atlas *brother:* **10** Prometheus *daughter:* **5** Hyads **6** Hyades **8** Pleiades **10** Atlantides *father:* **7** Iapetus *mother:* **7** Clymene *race:* **5** Titan *wife:* **7** Pleione

at last 7 finally

Atli *wife (slayer):* **6** Gudrun

atmosphere 3 air **4** aura, mood, tone **6** medium, milieu **7** ambient, climate, feeling, quality **8** ambiance, ambience **11** environment, mise-en-scène **12** surroundings *stratum:* **9** exosphere **10** ionosphere, mesosphere **11** chemosphere, ozonosphere, troposphere **12** stratosphere, thermosphere *sun's:* **12** chromosphere

atmospheric 4 airy **6** aerial **8** ethereal

atoll 6 island *equatorial area:* **5** Baker *Indian Ocean:* **4** Male *Kiribati:* **4** Beru *Marshall Islands:* **6** Bikini **8** Eniwetok *Tuamotu:* **4** Anaa **5** Chain *Tuvalu:* **8** Funafuti

atom 3 bit, jot **4** iota, mite, whit **5** minim, speck, touch, trace **6** tittle **7** modicum, smidgen **8** particle **9** scintilla *charged:* **3** ion **5** anion *group:* **7** radical

atomic particle 3 ion **4** beta, muon, pion **5** alpha, boson, meson **6** baryon, hadron, lepton, proton **7** fermion, hyperon, neutron, nucleon **8** electron, mesotron, neutrino, positron, thermion *hypothetical:* **5** quark **6** parton

atomize 4 nuke, ruin **5** smash, wreck **6** divide, rub out **7** break up, destroy, shatter **8** demolish, destruct, disperse, dynamite, fragment, nebulize **9** break down, devastate, pulverize **10** disconnect

at once 3 now **4** away, both **6** pronto **8** directly, first off, right now, together **9** forthwith, instantly, right away **11** immediately, straightway **12** concurrently, straightaway, without delay

atone 3 pay **6** redeem, repair, repent **7** correct, expiate, rectify, redress, satisfy **10** compensate, make amends, recompense

atoner 8 penitent

atop 4 upon

Atossa *father:* **5** Cyrus *husband:* **6** Darius **7** Smerdes **8** Cambyses *son:* **6** Xerxes

at random 5 about **6** anyhow **7** anywise **8** by chance **9** aimlessly, haphazard **10** carelessly **11** any which way, haphazardly **12** accidentally **13** helter-skelter

at rest 4 dead **5** still **8** inactive, lifeless, reposing, sleeping, tranquil, unmoving **9** quiescent **10** motionless, stationary, untroubled **11** trouble-free

Atreus *brother:* **8** Thyestes *father:* **6** Pelops *mother:* **10** Hippodamia *slayer:* **9** Aegisthus *son:* **8** Menelaus **9** Agamemnon **11** Pleisthenes *victim:* **11** Pleisthenes *wife:* **6** Aerope

atrocious 4 foul, vile **5** awful, cruel **6** brutal, horrid, odious, savage, wicked **7** heinous, noisome, obscene **8** barbaric, horrible, shocking, terrible

9 appalling, desperate, execrable, loathsome, monstrous, offensive, repulsive, revolting, sickening **10** abominable, despicable, detestable, disgusting, horrifying, outrageous, scandalous **12** contemptible

atrocity 4 evil **5** crime **6** horror, infamy **7** cruelty, outrage **8** enormity, savagery **9** barbarity, brutality **11** abomination, heinousness **13** monstrousness

atrophy 7 decline, wasting **9** decadence, waste away **10** devolution **11** declination **12** degeneration **13** deterioration

attach 3 add, fix, tie **4** bind, hook, link, take **5** affix, annex, latch, rivet, stick, unite **6** adhere, append, assign, fasten, secure **7** ascribe, connect **8** make fast **9** associate, attribute

attached 5 fixed **7** sessile

attachment 3 tie **4** bond, link, love **6** fealty **7** loyalty, seizure **8** addition, adhesion, devotion, fastener, fidelity, fondness **9** accessory, adherence, affection, connector, constancy **10** allegiance, connection **12** faithfulness

attack 4 bout, jump, raid, rush **5** beset, blitz, drive, fight, foray, onset, sally, siege, spasm, spell, storm, throe **6** access, ambush, assail, banzai, battle, charge, fall on, harass, have at, invade, irrupt, onrush, sortie, strike, tackle **7** aggress, assault, barrage, besiege, bombard, offense, seizure **8** fall upon, invasion, outbreak, paroxysm **9** beleaguer, incursion, offensive, onslaught, pugnacity **10** aggression, blitzkrieg

attain 3 get, win **4** gain **5** reach, score **6** arrive, come to, effect, make it, obtain, rack up **7** achieve, fulfill, pull off, realize, succeed **8** bring off, complete **10** accomplish

attainment 4 feat **6** finish **7** arrival **10** completion **11** achievement, acquirement, acquisition, fulfillment, realization

attempt 3 bid, try **4** seek, shot, stab **5** assay, crack, essay, offer, trial **6** attack, effort, strive, tackle **7** assault, venture **8** endeavor, striving, struggle **9** undertake **11** undertaking **12** make an effort

attend 3 aid, see **4** be at, go to, hear, heed, help, mark, mind, note **5** apply, catch, nurse, see to, serve, visit, watch **6** assist, convoy, doctor, drop in, escort, go with, listen, notice, show up, turn up, wait on **7** be there, care for, conduct, hearken, oversee, pay heed, work for **8** chaperon, stay with, wait upon **9** accompany, chaperone, companion, look after, supervise **11** concentrate

attendant 4 aide **5** valet **6** escort, helper, lackey **7** orderly, servant **9** ancillary, assistant **10** bridesmaid, coincident **11** chamberlain, concomitant **12** accompanying *ancient Roman:* **6** lictor *in court:* **7** bailiff **8** tipstaff

attendants 5 suite, train **7** cortege, retinue **9** entourage

attendee 4 goer

attention 4 care, heed, mark, note **5** study **6** notice, regard, remark **7** amenity, command, concern, respect, service, thought **8** civility, courtesy, industry, scrutiny **9** assiduity, awareness, deference, diligence, gallantry, spotlight, treatment **10** absorption, cognizance, observance, politeness **11** application, mindfulness, observation, sensibility **12** deliberation **13** concentration, consciousness, consideration

attention getter 4 ahem **5** gavel

attentive 4 kind **5** alert, awake, aware, civil **6** intent, polite **7** devoted, gallant, heedful, mindful **8** gracious, obliging, open-eyed **9** advertent, courteous, observant, regardful **10** interested, respectful, solicitous, thoughtful **11** considerate **13** concentrating

attenuate 3 sap **4** rare, slim, thin **5** abate, blunt, reedy **6** lessen, rarefy, shrink, slight, stalky, subtle, twiggy, weaken **7** cripple, deflate, disable, reduced, slender, squinny, subtile, tenuous, unbrace **8** contract, enfeeble, mitigate, rarefied, tapering, wiredraw **9** constrict, dissipate, undermine **10** become thin, become fine, become less, debilitate

attest 4 aver, show **5** argue, prove, swear, vouch **6** adjure, affirm, assert, verify **7** certify, confirm, declare, display, exhibit, point to, support, sustain, swear to, testify, warrant, witness **8** announce, indicate, manifest **9** establish **10** asseverate **11** bear witness, demonstrate **12** authenticate

attestation 5 proof **7** witness **8** evidence **9** testament, testimony **10** validation **11** declaration, testimonial **12** confirmation

attic 4 loft, room **6** garret **7** storage **8** cockloft

Attica 6 Greece *division:* **4** deme

at times 9 sometimes **10** now and then, on occasion **11** now and again **12** here and there, occasionally

attire 4 clad, duds, garb, gear, togs, wear **5** array, drape, dress, getup, habit, tog up **6** clothe, fit out, outfit **7** apparel, clothes, costume, garment, raiment, threads **8** clothing, garments, glad rags **11** habiliments

attitude 4 pose, view **5** angle, stand **6** manner, stance **7** bearing, mind-set, outlook, posture **8** carriage, demeanor, position, pretense **10** standpoint **11** inclination, perspective, point of view

attitudinize 4 mask, pose, sham **6** affect **7** pass for, pass off, posture, pretend, show off **10** masquerade

attorney 5 agent, proxy **6** deputy, factor, lawyer **7** counsel **8** advocate, assignee **9** barrister, counselor, solicitor **10** counsellor, legal eagle, mouthpiece

attract 4 draw, lure, wile **5** charm, court, tempt **6** allure, appeal, beckon, draw in, entice, invite, seduce **7** beguile, bewitch, enchant, solicit **8** appeal to, interest, intrigue, inveigle **9** captivate, fascinate, influence, magnetize

attraction 4 bait, call, draw, lure, pull **5** charm **6** allure, appeal, liking **8** affinity, cynosure, sympathy **9** affection, chemistry, magnetism, seduction **10** allurement **12** drawing power

attractive 4 cute, fair, sexy **5** bonny, dishy **6** comely, lovely, luring, pretty **7** Circean, likable, winsome **8** alluring, charming, engaging, enticing, fetching, handsome, inviting, magnetic, mesmeric, tempting **9** appealing, beauteous, beautiful, beckoning, glamorous, seductive **10** bewitching, enchanting **11** captivating, fascinating, good-looking, tantalizing **13** prepossessing

attractiveness 5 charm **6** appeal, beauty, glamor **7** glamour

attribute 3 lay **4** mark, sign **5** apply, facet, pin on, point, refer, trait **6** aspect, assign, charge, credit, emblem, impute, symbol, virtue **7** ascribe, connect, earmark, explain, feature, quality **8** accredit, classify, property **9** adjective, character, designate

attrition 3 rue **4** ruth, wear **6** sorrow **7** erosion, penance, remorse, rubbing, wearing **8** abrasion, friction, grinding **9** penitence, penitency, reduction, weakening **10** repentance **12** contriteness

attritional 5 sorry **6** rueful **8** contrite, penitent **9** regretful, repentant **10** apologetic, remorseful **11** penitential

attune 6 accord, adjust **7** balance, conform **9** harmonize, integrate, reconcile **10** coordinate, proportion **11** accommodate

atypical 3 odd **5** queer **7** deviant, strange, unusual **8** aberrant, abnormal, peculiar **9** anomalous, deviative, differ-

ent, divergent, irregular, unnatural **11** exceptional, heteroclite, nonstandard **13** preternatural

auberge 3 inn **5** hotel, lodge **6** hostel, tavern **7** hospice **8** hostelry **9** roadhouse **11** caravansary, public house

Auber opera 10 Fra Diavolo

auburn 4 rust **5** henna **6** russet **8** chestnut **11** burnt sienna **12** reddish-brown

au courant 3 mod **4** up on **5** awake, aware, hep to, hip to, savvy **6** modern, modish, versed **7** abreast, current, in touch, knowing, stylish, versant, witting **8** familiar, informed, sentient, up-to-date **9** cognizant, conscious, plugged in **10** acquainted, conversant **11** fashionable **12** contemporary **13** up-to-the-minute

auction 4 sale, sell

audacious 4 bold, rash **5** brash, brave, cocky, risky, saucy **6** brazen, cheeky, daring **7** valiant **8** arrogant, fearless, impudent, insolent, intrepid, reckless, unafraid, uncurbed **9** daredevil, dauntless, foolhardy, shameless, undaunted, venturous **10** courageous, ungoverned, unhampered **11** adventurous, impertinent, temerarious, uninhibited, untrammeled, venturesome **12** unrestrained **13** adventuresome

audacity 4 gall **5** brass, cheek, moxie, nerve, spunk **6** mettle, spirit **7** courage **8** boldness, chutzpah, rashness, temerity **9** assurance, arrogance, brashness, cockiness, disregard, hardihood, hardiness, impudence, insolence **10** brazenness, effrontery **12** recklessness

audible 5 aural, clear, heard **8** distinct **9** auricular

audibly 5 aloud **7** aurally, clearly, out loud

audience 5 crowd, group, house **6** public **7** hearing, gallery, hearers, meeting **8** admirers, assembly, audition, devotees **9** clientele, following, gathering, interview, listeners **10** assemblage, spectators

audile see AUDITORY

audio 5 sound

audit 4 scan **5** check, probe **6** go over, report, review, survey, verify **7** analyze, balance, checkup, examine, inspect **8** analysis, scrutiny **10** inspection, scrutinize **11** examination **13** investigation

audition 4 test **5** trial **6** tryout **7** hearing, reading

auditor 8 examiner, listener **9** inspector **10** accountant, controller **11** comptroller

auditory 5 aural **8** acoustic

au fait 4 able **5** right **6** decent, proper,

versed **7** abreast, capable, correct, versant **8** becoming, decorous, familiar, informed, revelant **9** befitting, competent, qualified **10** acquainted, conforming, conversant, to the point

au fond 8 at bottom **9** basically, in essence **11** essentially **13** fundamentally

Augean 9 difficult **10** formidable **11** distasteful *stable:* **3** sty **4** sink **5** filth, Sodom **7** cesspit **8** cesspool

auger 3 bit **5** borer, drill, screw **6** gimlet, trepan, wimble **9** corkscrew

Auge's son 8 Telephus

aught 3 all, nil, nix, zip **4** nada, zero **5** zilch **6** cipher **7** nothing **8** anything, goose egg **10** everything

augment 3 wax **4** grow, hike, rise **5** add to, boost, build, exalt, mount, raise **6** beef up, expand, extend **7** build up, develop, enhance, enlarge, magnify **9** intensify, reinforce **8** compound, heighten, increase, multiply **10** aggrandize, supplement **11** make greater

augmentation 4 rise **5** annex, extra, raise **7** adjunct, buildup **8** addition, increase **9** accession, accretion, increment **10** complement, enrichment **11** enhancement, enlargement

augur 4 bode, seer **6** herald, oracle **7** betoken, diviner, portend, predict, presage, promise, prophet, suggest **8** forebode, forecast, foreshow, foretell, indicate, prophesy, soothsay **9** adumbrate, foretoken, harbinger, predictor, prefigure **10** forecaster, foreshadow, foreteller, prophesier, soothsayer, vaticinate **11** Nostradamus **13** prognosticate

augury 4 omen, sign **5** token **6** herald **7** auspice, portent, presage, warning **8** bodement, forecast, prophecy **9** foretoken, harbinger **10** divination, forerunner, prediction, prognostic **11** forewarning

august 5 grand, noble, regal **6** lordly **7** eminent, stately **8** baronial, imposing, majestic, princely, splendid **9** dignified, grandiose **11** magnificent

auk 5 alcid **7** seabird *genus:* **4** Alca

___ **au lait 4** café

au naturel 3 raw **4** nude **5** naked, plain **6** unclad **8** stripped **9** unclothed, undressed **10** stark naked

aura 3 air **4** feel, glow, halo, mood, tone, vibe **5** aroma, vibes **6** nimbus **7** aureole, feeling, quality **8** ambience, mystique, radiance, stimulus **9** emanation, semblance, sensation **10** atmosphere

aural 6 audile **7** audible **8** acoustic, auditory **9** auricular

aureate 6 florid, golden **7** flowery, orotund **8** sonorous **9** bombastic, grandiose, overblown **10** euphuistic, rhetorical **11** declamatory **13** grandiloquent

aureole 4 aura, halo, ring **5** crown, light **6** circle, corona, nimbus **8** radiance

au revoir 4 by-by, ciao, ta-ta **5** adieu, adios **6** bye-bye, so long **7** good-bye **8** farewell **11** arrivederci

auricular see AURAL

Auriga star 7 Capella

aurora 4 dawn, morn **7** dawning, morning, sunrise **8** cockcrow, daybreak

Aurora *Roman counterpart:* **3** Eos *goddess of:* **4** dawn *husband:* **8** Tithonus *son:* **6** Memnon

auslander 5 alien **7** inconnu **8** outsider, stranger **9** foreigner

auspice 4 omen, sign **10** divination

auspices 5 aegis **6** charge **7** backing, support **8** guidance **9** influence, patronage **11** sponsorship, supervision

auspicious 5 lucky **6** bright, timely **7** hopeful **9** favorable, fortunate, opportune, promising, well-timed **10** prosperous **11** encouraging, propitious

Austen, Jane *novel:* **4** Emma **10** Persuasion **13** Mansfield Park **15** Northanger Abbey **17** Pride and Prejudice **19** Sense and Sensibility

Auster see NOTUS

austere 4 bare, cold, dour, firm, grim, hard **5** acrid, bleak, grave, harsh, plain, rigid, sharp, spare, stern **6** bitter, severe, simple, somber, strict **7** ascetic, serious, spartan **8** exacting **9** stringent, unadorned, unfeeling **10** astringent, restrained **11** self-denying

austerity 5 rigor **6** thrift **7** economy **8** acerbity, asperity, coldness, grimness, hardness, rigidity, severity **9** harshness, parsimony, privation, solemnity, spareness, sternness, stiffness **10** self-denial, simplicity, strictness, stringency **11** unadornment **13** self-restraint

Australia *capital:* **8** Canberra *city:* **5** Perth **6** Darwin, Sydney **8** Adelaide, Brisbane **9** Melbourne, Newcastle *desert:* **10** Great Sandy **13** Great Victoria *ethnic group:* **9** Aborigine *island:* **6** Fraser **8** Kangaroo, Melville, Tasmania *lake:* **4** Eyre *monetary unit:* **6** dollar *mountain, range:* **9** Ayers Rock **9** Kosciusko **13** Great Dividing *reef:* **12** Great Barrier *river:* **4** Swan **6** Murray **7** Darling **8** Flinders **11** Cooper Creek **12** Coopers Creek *strait:* **4** Bass **6** Torres

Austria *capital:* **6** Vienna *city:* **4** Graz, Linz **8** Salzburg **9** Innsbruck **10** Klagenfurt *lake:* **10** Neusiedler *monetary unit:* **4** euro *mountain:* **13** Grossglockner

mountain range: 4 Alps *neighbor:* 5 Italy
7 Croatia, Germany, Hungary 8 Slovakia, Slovenia 11 Switzerland 13 Czech
Republic, Liechtenstein *river:* 3 Ems
6 Danube

autarchy see AUTOCRACY

autarkic 4 free 8 separate 9 sovereign
10 autonomous, self-ruling 11 independent, self-reliant 13 self-governing

autarky 7 freedom 8 autonomy 12 independence, self-reliance

authentic 4 real, true 5 legit, pukka,
right, solid, sound, valid 6 actual,
trusty 7 certain, factual, for real, genuine 8 accurate, bona fide, credible,
faithful, reliable 9 undoubted, veritable
10 convincing, dependable, legitimate,
sure-enough 11 indubitable, trustworthy 12 questionless

authenticate 5 prove, vouch 6 adduce,
attest, verify 7 bear out, certify, confirm, justify, voucher, warrant
8 accredit, validate 11 corroborate
12 substantiate

author 5 maker 6 penman, scribe, writer
7 creator 8 inventor, novelist, prosaist
9 generator 10 originator *American:*
3 Bly (Robert), Fox (Paula), Nin
(Anaïs), Poe (Edgar Allan), Tan (Amy)
4 Agee (James), Baum (L. Frank), Buck
(Pearl S.), Cook (Robin), Dana
(Richard Henry), Fast (Howard), Ford
(Richard), Grey (Zane), Jong (Erica),
King (Stephen), Mann (Thomas), Puzo
(Mario), Rand (Ayn), Rice (Anne),
Roth (Philip), Shaw (Irwin), Uris
(Leon), West (Nathanael), Wouk (Herman) 5 Aiken (Conrad), Alger (Horatio), Banks (Russell), Barth (John),
Benét (Stephen Vincent), Blume (Judy),
Boyle (T. Coraghessan), Brown (Rita
Mae), Clark (Mary Higgins), Crane
(Hart, Stephen), Dunne (Dominick,
John Gregory), Elkin (Stanley), Ellis
(Bret Easton), Foote (Horton), Harte
(Bret), Henry (O.), Jakes (John), James
(Henry), Levin (Ira), Lewis (Sinclair),
Lurie (Alison), Mason (Bobbie Ann),
Oates (Joyce Carol), O'Hara (John),
Ozick (Cynthia), Paine (Thomas),
Paley (Grace), Potok (Chaim), Price
(Reynolds, Richard), Steel (Danielle),
Stein (Gertrude), Stone (Irving), Stout
(Rex), Stowe (Harriet Beecher), Turow
(Scott), Twain (Mark), Tyler (Anne),
Vidal (Gore), Welty (Eudora), White
(Edmund, E. B., T. H.), Wolfe (Thomas,
Tom), Wylie (Elinor) 6 Alcott (Louisa
May), Asimov (Isaac), Auster (Paul),
Bellow (Saul), Berger (Thomas), Bierce
(Ambrose), Bowles (Paul), Cabell

(James Branch), Capote (Truman),
Cather (Willa), Chopin (Kate), Clancy
(Tom), Conroy (Pat), Cooper (James
Fenimore), Dickey (James), Didion
(Joan), Ellroy (James), Ferber (Edna),
French (Marilyn), Gaddis (William),
Gaines (Ernest J.), Gilroy (Frank),
Godwin (Gail), Hailey (Arthur), Harris
(Frank, Joel Chandler), Hawkes (John),
Heller (Joseph), Hersey (John), Hinton
(S. E.), Holmes (Oliver Wendell), Hughes (Langston), Irving (John, Washington), Jewett (Sarah Orne), Kidder
(Tracy), Koontz (Dean), Krantz
(Judith), L'Amour (Louis), L'Engle
(Madeleine), Le Guin (Ursula K.), London (Jack), Mailer (Norman), McBain
(Ed), Miller (Arthur, Henry, Joaquin,
May), Morley (Christopher), Morris
(Wright), Mosley (Walter), Norris
(Frank), Parker (Dorothy), Piercy
(Marge), Porter (Katherine Anne,
William Sydney), Proulx (E. Annie),
Runyon (Damon), Sarton (May), Singer
(Isaac Bashevis), Smiley (Jane), Styron
(William), Taylor (Peter), Updike
(John), Walker (Alice), Waller (Robert
James), Warren (Robert Penn), Wilder
(Laura Ingalls, Thornton), Wilson
(August, Edmund, Harriet, Lanford),
Wister (Owen), Wright (James,
Richard) 7 Baldwin (Faith, James),
Beattie (Ann), Cheever (John), Clemens
(Samuel Langhorne), Collins (Jackie),
Connell (Evan), Cozzens (James
Gould), DeLillo (Don), Dreiser
(Theodore), Ellison (Ralph), Erdrich
(Louise), Farrell (James T.), Francis
(Dick), Franzen (Jonathan), Gardner
(Erle Stanley), Garland (Hamlin),
Glasgow (Ellen), Goldman (William),
Grafton (Sue), Grisham (John), Hammett (Dashiell), Heyward (DuBose),
Howells (William Dean), Hurston (Zora
Neale), Jackson (Shirley), Jarrell (Randall), Johnson (Diane, James), Keillor
(Garrison), Kennedy (William),
Kerouac (Jack), Kincaid (Jamaica),
Lardner (Ring), Leonard (Elmore),
Malamud (Bernard), Marquis (Don),
Masters (Edgar Lee), McCourt (Frank),
Mumford (Lewis), Nabokov (Vladimir),
O'Connor (Flannery), Pynchon
(Thomas), Rexroth (Kenneth), Richter
(Conrad), Roberts (Elizabeth Madox,
Kenneth, Nora), Saroyan (William),
Sheehan (Neil), Sheldon (Sidney), Theroux (Paul), Thoreau (Henry David),
Thurber (James), Wallace (Lew), Wharton (Edith) 8 Anderson (Maxwell, Poul,
Regina, Sherwood), Benchley (Peter),

Bradbury (Ray), Bradford (Barbara Taylor), Caldwell (Erskine), Chandler (Raymond), Cornwell (Patricia), Crichton (Michael), Doctorow (E. L.), Faulkner (William), Kingston (Maxine Hong), Marquand (John P.), McCarthy (Cormac, Mary), McMillan (Terry), McMurtry (Larry), Melville (Herman), Michener (James), Mitchell (Donald Grant, Margaret, S. Weir), Morrison (Toni), Remarque (Erich Maria), Rinehart (Mary Roberts), Salinger (J. D.), Sandburg (Carl), Sinclair (Upton), Spillane (Mickey), Stockton (Frank R.), Vonnegut (Kurt), Wambaugh (Joseph) **9** Burroughs (Edgar Rice, John, William S.), Dos Passos (John), Hawthorne (Nathaniel), Hemingway (Ernest), Hillerman (Tony), Isherwood (Christopher), McCullers (Carson), Steinbeck (John), Wodehouse (P. G.), Woollcott (Alexander) **10** Cunningham (Michael), Fitzgerald (F. Scott), Kingsolver (Barbara), Tarkington (Booth) **11** Auchincloss (Louis), Matthiessen (Peter) *Argentinian:* **6** Borges (Jorge Luis) *Australian:* **4** West (Morris L.) **5** Stead (Christina), White (Patrick) **6** Davies (Robertson) **7** Clavell (James) **8** Keneally (Thomas) **10** McCullough (Colleen), Richardson (Henry Handel) *Austrian:* **5** Kafka (Franz) **7** Jelinek (Elfriede), Suttner (Bertha) **8** Bernhard (Thomas) **10** Schnitzler (Arthur) *Canadian:* **3** Roy (Camille, Gabrielle) **5** Kirby (William), Moore (Brian), Munro (Alice) **6** Atwood (Margaret), Davies (Robertson) **7** Leacock (Stephen), Raddall (Thomas), Richler (Mordecai), Service (Robert), Shields (Carol) **8** Woodcock (George) **9** de la Roche (Mazo), MacLennan (Hugh) *Chilean:* **6** Donoso (José) **7** Allende (Isabel) *Chinese:* **5** Han Yu *Colombian:* **7** Márquez (Gabriel García) *Czech:* **5** Capek (Karel), Hasek (Jaroslav) **7** Kundera (Milan) *Danish:* **4** Rode (Helge), Wied (Gustav) **6** Jensen (Johannes Vilhelm) **7** Dinesen (Isak), Holberg (Ludwig) *Dutch:* **6** Vondel (Joost van den) *Egyptian:* **7** Mahfouz (Naguib) *English:* **4** Amis (Kingsley, Martin), Dahl (Roald), Ford (Ford Madox, John), Lyly (John), Saki, Snow (C. P.), Ward (Mrs. Humphry), West (Rebecca) **5** Byatt (A. S.), Defoe (Daniel), Doyle (Authur Conan), Eliot (George, Thomas Stearns), Evans (Mary Ann), Frayn (Michael), Hardy (Thomas), James (Henry, P. D.), Lewis (C. S., Monk, Wyndham), Lowry (Malcolm), Milne (A. A.), Munro (H. H.),

Powys (John Cowper, Llewelyn, Theodore Francis), Reade (Charles), Spark (Muriel), Waugh (Alec, Evelyn), Wells (Charles Jeremiah, H. G.), White (T. H.), Wilde (Oscar), Woolf (Leonard, Virginia), Young (Arthur, Edward, Francis Brett) **6** Ambler (Eric), Archer (Jeffrey), Austen (Jane), Belloc (Hilaire), Brontë (Anne, Charlotte, Emily), Bunyan (John), Butler (Samuel), Clarke (Arthur C.), Conrad (Joseph), Fowles (John), Graves (Robert), Greene (Graham, Robert), Hilton (James), Hudson (W. H.), Huxley (Aldous), Malory (Thomas), McEwan (Ian), O'Brian (Patrick), Orwell (George), Potter (Beatrix), Powell (Anthony), Sayers (Dorothy L.), Sterne (Laurence), Stoker (Bram), Storey (David), Walton (Izaak) **7** Ballard (J. G.), Burgess (Anthony), Burnett (Frances Hodgson), Carroll (Lewis), Collins (Wilkie), Dickens (Charles), Dodgson (Charles), Durrell (Lawrence), Fleming (Ian), Follett (Ken), Forster (E. M.), Forsyth (Frederick), Golding (Louis, William), Kipling (Rudyard), Le Carré (John), Lessing (Doris), Lofting (Hugh), Maugham (Robin, W. Somerset), Murdoch (Iris), Naipaul (V. S.), Rendell (Ruth), Rowling (J. K.), Sassoon (Siegfried), Shelley (Mary Wollstonecraft, Percy Bysshe), Sitwell (Edith, Osbert, Sacheverell), Southey (Robert), Stewart (Mary), Surtees (Robert Smith), Tolkien (J. R. R.), Walpole (Horace, Hugh), Wyndham (John) **8** Christie (Agatha), Fielding (Henry), Forester (C. S.), Koestler (Arthur), Lawrence (D. H., T. E.), Macaulay (Rose, Thomas Babington), Meredith (George), Sillitoe (Alan), Smollett (Tobias), Strachey (Lytton), Trollope (Anthony), Zangwill (Israel) **9** De Quincey (Thomas), Du Maurier (Daphne, George), Goldsmith (Oliver), Isherwood (Christopher), Mansfield (Katherine), Masefield (John), Priestley (J. B.), Radcliffe (Ann), Stevenson (Robert Louis), Thackeray (William Makepeace), Wodehouse (P. D.) **10** Chesterton (Gilbert Keith), Galsworthy (John), Richardson (Dorothy, Samuel) **12** Quiller-Couch (Arthur Thomas) *Finnish:* **7** Waltari (Mika) **9** Sillanpää (Frans Eemil) *French:* **4** Gide (André), Hugo (Victor), Kock (Charles-Paul de), Sade (Marquis de), Sand (George), Zola (Emile) **5** Beyle (Marie Henri), Camus (Albert), Dumas

(Alexandre), Genet (Jean), Sagan (Françoise), Staël (Germaine de), Verne (Jules), Vigny (Alfred-Victor) 6 Balzac (Honoré de), Daudet (Alphonse), France (Anatole), Proust (Marcel), Sartre (Jean-Paul) 7 Cocteau (Jean), Colette, Gautier (Léon, Théophile), Malraux (André), Mauriac (Claude, François), Maurois (André), Merimée (Prosper), Rolland (Romain), Romains (Jules), Simenon (Georges) 8 Beauvoir (Simone de), Flaubert (Gustave), Marivaux (Pierre), Rabelais (François), Stendhal, Voltaire 9 Giraudoux (Jean) 10 Maupassant (Guy de), Saint-Simon (Duke de) 12 Robbe-Grillet (Alain), Saint-Exupéry (Antoine de) *German:* 4 Böll (Heinrich), Mann (Thomas) 5 Grass (Gunter), Hesse (Hermann), Kafka (Franz), Storm (Theodor), Tieck (Ludwig), Zweig (Stefan) 6 Goethe (Johann Wolfgang von), Toller (Ernst) 7 Fontane (Theodor), Richter (Jean Paul), Wieland (Christoph Martin) 8 Hoffmann (E. T. A., Heinrich), Remarque (Erich Maria), Schlegel (August Wilhelm von, Friedrich von, Johann Elias) 9 Hauptmann (Gerhart), Sudermann (Hermann) 10 Wassermann (Jakob) *Greek:* 6 Lucian 11 Kazantzakis (Nikos) *Hungarian:* 5 Jókai (Mór) *Icelandic:* 7 Laxness (Halldór) *Indian:* 7 Rushdie (Salman) *Irish:* 5 Behan (Brendan), Doyle (Roddy), Joyce (James), Moore (Brian), Wilde (Oscar) 6 O'Brien (Edna), Stoker (Bram) 7 Beckett (Samuel), O'Connor (Frank), Russell (George William) 8 O'Faolain (Julia, Sean), Stephens (James) 9 O'Flaherty (Liam) *Italian:* 3 Eco (Umberto) 5 Verga (Giovanni) 6 Silone (Ignazio) 7 Calvino (Italo), Manzoni (Alessandro), Moravia (Alberto) 9 Boccaccio (Giovanni), Vittorini (Elio) 10 Pirandello (Luigi), Straparola (Gianfrancesco) *Japanese:* 7 Mishima (Yukio) 8 Kawabata (Yasunari), Murakami (Haruki), Murasaki (Shikibu) 9 Yokomitsu (Riichi), Yoshikawa (Eiji) *Lebanese:* 6 Gibran (Khalil) 7 Fuentes (Carlos) *Nigerian:* 6 Achebe (Chinua) 7 Soyinka (Wole), Tutuola (Amos) *Norwegian:* 3 Lie (Jonas) 6 Hamsun (Knut), Undset (Sigrid) 7 Rolvaag (Ole) 8 Bjornson (Bjornstjerne), Kielland (Alexander) *Peruvian:* 11 Vargas Llosa (Mario) *Polish:* 7 Reymont (Wladyslaw) 8 Zeromski (Stefan) 11 Sienkiewicz (Henryk) *Portuguese:* 6 Pessoa (Fernando) 8 Saramago (José) *Roman:* 5 Pliny, Varro (Marcus Terentius) *Russian:*

5 Gogol (Nikolai), Gorki (Maxim), Gorky (Maxim) 7 Chekhov (Anton), Pushkin (Alexander), Tolstoy (Leo) 8 Andreyev (Leonid), Turgenev (Ivan), Zamyatin (Yevgeny) 9 Ehrenburg (Ilya), Lermontov (Mikhail), Pasternak (Boris), Sholokhov (Mikhail) 10 Dostoevsky (Fyodor) 11 Dostoyevsky (Fyodor), Yevtushenko (Yevgeny) 12 Solzhenitsyn (Alexander) *Scottish:* 4 Lang (Andrew) 5 Scott (Alexander, Walter) 6 Barrie (James M.), Buchan (John) 8 Urquhart (Thomas) 9 Stevenson (Robert Louis) *South African:* 6 Fugard (Athol) 8 Gordimer (Nadine) *Spanish:* 6 Baroja (Pio) 7 Alarcón (Pedro Antonio de) 9 Cervantes (Miguel de) *Swedish:* 7 Johnson (Eyvind), Rydberg (Viktor) 8 Lagerlöf (Selma) 10 Lagerkvist (Pär), Strindberg (August) *Swiss:* 4 Wyss (Johann Rudolf) 5 Spyri (Johanna) 6 Frisch (Max) 9 Spitteler (Carl) *Trinidadian:* 7 Naipaul (V. S.) *Welsh:* 4 Owen (Alun, Daniel, Goronwy, John) 5 Evans (David, Evan), Wynne (Ellis) *Yiddish:* 4 Asch (Sholem) 6 Singer (Isaac Bashevis) 8 Aleichem (Sholem)

authoritarian 5 harsh, rigid 6 despot, severe, strict, tyrant 8 absolute, autocrat, despotic, dictator, dogmatic 9 imperious, stringent 10 absolutist, autocratic, oppressive, totalistic, tyrannical 11 dictatorial, doctrinaire, domineering, magisterial 12 totalitarian

authoritative 4 sure, true 5 legal, legit, sound 6 lawful, proven 7 factual 8 accepted, accurate, approved, attested, dogmatic, official, orthodox, reliable, verified 9 canonical, cathedral, confirmed, imperious, trustable, validated 10 autocratic, commanding, definitive, dependable, documented, dominating, ex cathedra, legitimate, sanctioned 11 dictatorial, doctrinaire, domineering, irrefutable, magisterial, overbearing, trustworthy 12 indisputable

authority 4 rule, sway 5 clout, force, power, right, say-so 6 agency, charge, credit, expert, master, weight 7 command, control, grounds, license, mastery, warrant 8 citation, decision, dominion, prestige 9 influence, testimony 10 domination, governance, government, management 12 jurisdiction

authorization 4 okay, word 5 leave 6 permit 7 consent, go-ahead, mandate 8 approval, sanction 9 agreement,

allowance, clearance **10** green light, permission, sufferance **11** approbation
authorize 3 let **4** okay, vest **5** allow **6** affirm, enable, invest, permit **7** approve, confirm, empower, endorse, entitle, license, qualify, warrant **8** accredit, sanction, vouch for **9** give leave, recognize **10** commission **11** countenance
auto see AUTOMOBILE
autobahn 7 highway **8** turnpike **10** expressway **12** superhighway
autobiography 4 life, vita **5** diary **6** memoir **7** account, journal **9** life story **11** confessions **13** reminiscences
autochthonous 6 native **7** endemic **8** original **10** aboriginal, indigenous
autocracy 7 czarism, tyranny **8** monarchy **9** despotism, monocracy **12** absolute rule, dictatorship
autocrat 4 czar, duce, emir, lord, raja, shah, tsar, tzar **5** mogul, rajah, ruler **6** caliph, despot, sultan, tyrant **7** magnate, monarch **8** dictator, oligarch, overlord **9** potentate, sovereign **10** absolutist
autocratic 7 haughty **8** absolute, arrogant, despotic **9** arbitrary, imperious, tyrannous **10** monocratic, tyrannical **11** dictatorial, domineering, overbearing
autodidactic 10 self-taught **12** self-educated
autograph 3 ink, pen **4** sign **5** write **7** endorse **8** original **9** signature, subscribe **11** endorsement, John Hancock
Autolycus *daughter:* **8** Anticlea *father:* **6** Hermes **7** Mercury
automated 7 robotic **9** by machine, motorized **10** electrical, electronic, mechanical, mechanized, programmed **12** computerized
automatic 6 reflex **8** habitual **9** impulsive, reflexive **10** mechanical, self-acting, unprompted **11** instinctive, involuntary, perfunctory, spontaneous, unmeditated *prefix:* **4** self
automaton 5 droid, golem, robot **7** android, machine **9** mechanism
automobile 3 bus, car **5** buggy, coupe, racer, sedan **6** jalopy, tourer, wheels **7** flivver, hardtop, machine **8** dragster, motorcar, roadster, runabout **9** hatchback, limousine **11** convertible *American:* **3** Reo **4** Cord, Ford, Jeep, Nash **5** Buick, Dodge, Eagle, Essex, Lexus **6** DeSoto, Hudson, Model A, Model T, Saturn, Willys **7** LaSalle, LeBaron, Lincoln, Maxwell, Mercury, Mustang, Packard, Pontiac, Rambler, Seville **8** Cadillac, Chrysler, Corvette,

Eldorado, Franklin, Plymouth **9** Chevrolet, Hupmobile **10** Duesenberg, Oldsmobile, Studebaker **11** Continental, Pierce-Arrow, Thunderbird **12** Kaiser-Frazer *British:* **4** Mini **6** Anglia, Austin, Cooper, DeSoto, Jaguar, Morris **7** Bentley, Daimler, Hillman, Sunbeam, Triumph **8** Vauxhall **10** Range Rover, Rolls-Royce **11** Aston Martin, Land Rover **12** Austin-Healey *French:* **5** Simca **7** Citroën, Peugeot, Renault *German:* **3** BMW **4** Audi, Benz, Opel **7** Daimler, Porsche **8** Mercedes **10** Volkswagen **12** Mercedes-Benz *Italian:* **4** Fiat **6** Lancia **7** Bugatti, Ferrari **8** Maserati **9** Alfa-Romeo **11** Lamborghini *Japanese:* **5** Honda, Isuzu, Mazda **6** Datsun, Nissan, Subaru, Toyota **10** Mitsubishi *Korean:* **3** Kia **6** Daewoo **7** Hyundai *Swedish:* **4** Saab **5** Volvo
automotive pioneer 4 Benz (Carl Friedrich), Ford (Henry), Olds (Ransom), Otto (Nikolaus), Pope (Albert) **5** Evans (Oliver), Rolls (Charles), Roper (Sylvester) **6** Cugnot (Nicholas Joseph), Duryea (Charles E., J. Frank), Lenoir (Etienne), Winton (Alexander) **7** Bugatti (Ettore), Citroën (André-Gustave), Daimler (Gottlieb), Peugeot (Armand), Stanley (Francis, Freelan) **8** Morrison (William) **10** Lanchester (Frederick William)
Autonoë *father:* **6** Cadmus *husband:* **9** Aristaeus *mother:* **8** Harmonia *sister:* **5** Agave *son:* **7** Actaeon
autonomous 4 free **8** autarkic, separate **9** sovereign **10** self-ruling **11** independent, self-reliant **12** self-governed, uncontrolled **13** self-contained, self-governing
autonomy 7 autarky, freedom **8** home rule, self-rule **11** sovereignty **12** independence
autopsy 6 assess **7** examine **8** evaluate, necropsy **10** assessment, dissection, evaluation, postmortem **11** examination
auto racer 4 Foyt (A. J.), Hill (Graham) **5** Clark (Jim), Mears (Rick), Petty (Richard), Unser (Al, Bobby) **6** Carter (Pancho), Fangio (Juan), Vogler (Rich) **7** Brabham (Jack), Stewart (Jackie) **8** Andretti (Mario, Michael), Johncock (Gordon) **9** Earnhardt (Dale) **10** Rutherford (Johnny)
autumn 4 fall **6** season **8** maturity
auxiliary 4 aide **5** spare **6** backup, helper **7** reserve **8** adjutant, adjuvant **9** accessory, ancillary, assistant, coadjutor, secondary **10** accomplice, additional, collateral, subsidiary **11** appurtenant,

subservient 12 contributory 13 complementary, supplementary *verb:* 3 are, can, did, had, has, may, was 4 been, does, have, must, were, will 5 could, might, ought, shall, would 6 should

avail 3 aid, use 4 gain, good, help 5 asset, serve 6 profit 7 account, benefit, fitness, satisfy, service 9 advantage, relevance 10 usefulness 13 applicability

available 5 handy, on tap, ready, valid 6 at hand, on hand, usable 7 present, willing 8 prepared 9 qualified 10 accessible, attainable, convenient, obtainable, procurable 11 purchasable

avalanche 4 mass, rush 5 drown, flood, slide 6 deluge 7 overrun, smother 8 inundate, mudslide, overflow, rockfall 9 landslide, overwhelm, rockslide, snowslide 10 inundation 12 accumulation

Avalon 8 paradise

avant-garde 7 radical 8 advanced, contempo 10 innovative, pioneering 11 cutting-edge, leading-edge, progressive 12 experimental 13 up-to-the-minute

avarice 5 greed 7 avidity 8 cupidity, rapacity, voracity 10 greediness 12 covetousness

avaricious 6 grabby, greedy, stingy 7 miserly 8 covetous, esurient, grasping, ravenous 9 mercenary, rapacious 11 acquisitive

avatar 4 type 5 image 7 epitome 8 exemplar 9 archetype 10 apotheosis, embodiment, expression 11 incarnation, reification 13 manifestation

avaunt 4 away 5 hence, leave, scram 6 beat it, depart, get out

ave 4 hail 8 farewell, greeting

avenge 5 repay, right 6 punish 7 get even, pay back, redress, requite 9 fight back, retaliate, vindicate

avenue 3 way 4 path, road 5 drive, means, route, track 6 access, artery, course, street 7 channel, parkway, pathway 8 approach 9 boulevard 10 passageway 12 thoroughfare

aver 4 avow 5 prove, state, swear 6 affirm, allege, assert, attest, avouch, depose, insist, verify 7 declare, profess, protest, testify, warrant 8 maintain 9 guarantee, predicate

average 3 par 4 fair, mean, norm 5 usual 6 common, divide, equate, figure, median, medium, middle, normal 7 balance, even out, typical 8 everyday, midpoint, moderate, ordinary 12 intermediate

averagely 4 so-so 6 enough, fairly, rather 8 passably 9 tolerably 10 moderately

averse 5 balky, loath 6 afraid 7 hostile, opposed, uneager 8 allergic, hesitant 9 reluctant, resistant, unwilling 10 indisposed 11 disinclined 12 antipathetic

aversion 4 fear, hate 5 dread 6 hatred, horror 7 allergy, disgust, dislike 8 disfavor, distaste, loathing 9 antipathy, disliking, repulsion, revulsion 10 abhorrence, antagonism, repugnance 11 abomination, detestation, displeasure 13 indisposition

aversive 8 ungenial 9 repellent, repugnant 11 uncongenial 12 antipathetic 13 unsympathetic

avert 4 foil, halt, turn, veer, ward 5 avoid, check, deter 6 thwart 7 deflect, fend off, forfend, obviate, prevent, rule out, ward off 8 go around, stave off, turn away 9 forestall, turn aside

avian 6 flying, winged 8 birdlike, ornithic

aviary 4 cage 8 birdcage, dovecote 9 birdhouse, enclosure

aviator 3 ace 4 Post (Wiley) 5 flier, pilot 6 airman, flyboy, Wright (Orville, Wilbur), Yeager (Chuck) 7 birdman, Earhart (Amelia) 8 aeronaut 9 bush pilot, Lindbergh (Charles) 10 Richthofen (Manfred von) 12 Rickenbacker (Eddie)

avid 4 agog, keen 5 eager 6 ardent, greedy, hungry 7 anxious, athirst, craving, fervent, thirsty, zealous 8 appetent, covetous, desirous, grasping 9 impatient 10 breathless, insatiable 12 enthusiastic

avidity 4 zeal 5 greed 6 fervor, thirst 7 avarice, craving 8 cupidity, keenness, rapacity 9 eagerness 10 greediness

Avis *competitor:* 5 Hertz

___ **avis** 4 rara

avocation 5 hobby 7 pastime, pursuit 8 sideline 9 amusement, diversion 10 recreation

avoid 4 bilk, duck, miss, shun, snub 5 annul, avert, dodge, elude, evade, shirk, skirt 6 bypass, divert, escape, eschew, pass up 7 abstain, prevent, refrain 8 preclude, sidestep, stay away, withdraw 9 keep clear 11 refrain from 12 keep away from

avoidance 5 dodge 6 escape 7 dodging, elusion, evasion 8 escaping, escapism, eschewal, shirking, shunning 9 runaround 10 abstinence

avouch 3 own 4 aver, avow 5 admit, claim, state, swear 6 affirm, assert, depose, insist 7 certify, confess, confirm, declare, profess, testify 9 predicate, pronounce 11 acknowledge, corroborate

avow 3 own 4 aver 5 admit, allow, grant, let on, own up, state, swear 6 affirm, assert, avouch, depose 7 concede, confess, declare, profess, protest 8 disclose, maintain, proclaim 9 predicate 11 acknowledge

avowal 6 assent 9 admission, assertion, statement 10 profession 11 affirmation, attestation, declaration

avowedly 6 openly 7 frankly 8 candidly 9 allegedly 10 apparently, ostensibly, supposedly

await 4 bide, hope, stay 5 abide 6 expect 7 count on, look for 8 watch for 10 anticipate, hang around

awake 4 stir 5 alert, alive, aware, rouse 6 active, arouse, bestir, excite, revive, roused, stir up 7 animate, aroused, excited, on guard 8 activate, sensible, sentient, vigilant, watchful 9 attentive, cognizant, conscious, observant, stimulate, stirred up

award 4 gift, give, kudo 5 allot, badge, endow, grant, honor, kudos, medal, prize 6 accord, bestow, confer, donate, trophy 7 concede, laurels, tribute 8 accolade, citation, donation 9 vouchsafe 10 blue ribbon, decoration, distribute 11 distinction *motion picture:* 5 Oscar 7 Academy 11 Golden Globe *mystery novel:* 5 Edgar *record:* 6 Grammy *science-fiction:* 4 Hugo *television:* 4 Emmy *theater:* 4 Tony

aware 4 onto 5 alert, alive, awake 7 heedful, knowing, mindful, tuned in, witting 8 informed, sensible, sentient, vigilant 9 attentive, au courant, cognizant, conscious, observant 10 conversant, perceptive 12 apprehensive 13 knowledgeable

awash 4 full 6 afloat, filled, jammed, loaded, packed 7 brimful, covered, crammed, crowded, flooded, run-over, stuffed 8 brimming, chockful 9 chockfull 11 overflowing

away 3 far, fro, now, off, out 4 afar, gone, 5 along, apart, aside, forth, hence 6 abroad, absent, afield, far off 7 distant, lacking, missing, not here 9 elsewhere 11 incessantly 12 continuously

away from 6 beyond

awe 5 alarm, amaze, scare 6 wonder 7 inspire, startle 8 astonish 9 amazement, reverence 10 veneration, wonderment 11 flabbergast 12 astonishment

aweless 4 bold 5 brave 7 valiant 8 fearless, intrepid, unafraid 9 dauntless, undaunted 10 courageous

awesome 6 august 7 amazing, sublime 8 imposing, terrific, wondrous 10 formidable, impressive 11 astonishing 12 breathtaking 13 extraordinary

awful 3 bad 4 very 5 nasty 6 odious 7 hateful 8 dreadful, horrible, horrific, shocking, terrible, terrific 9 appalling, atrocious, extremely, frightful, loathsome, offensive 10 deplorable, disgusting, formidable

awfully 4 much, very 6 hugely, vastly 7 greatly 8 terribly, whopping 9 extremely, immensely 10 dreadfully, enormously 11 exceedingly

awhile 7 briefly 8 for a time 11 temporarily

awkward 5 gawky, inept, messy, nerdy, splay 6 clumsy, gauche, klutzy, wooden 7 artless, gawkish, halting, lumpish, unhandy, unhappy 8 bumbling, bungling, tactless, ungainly 9 graceless, ham-handed, ill-chosen, inelegant, lumbering, maladroit 10 blundering, ungraceful, unskillful 11 heavy-handed, unfortunate 12 embarrassing, incommodious, inconvenient, infelicitous

awl 4 tool 7 piercer

awning 6 canopy 7 marquee 8 sunshade *ancient Roman:* 8 velarium

awry 5 amiss, askew, wrong 6 astray 7 askance, crooked 8 cockeyed 9 cock-a-hoop, crookedly *Scottish:* 5 agley

ax, axe 3 can, hew 4 adze, boot, chop, fire, sack 6 bounce 7 boot out, chopper, cleaver, dismiss, hatchet, kick out 8 tomahawk 9 discharge, terminate *blade:* 3 bit *handle:* 5 helve

axiom 3 law 4 rule 5 adage, maxim, moral, truth 6 dictum, truism 7 precept, theorem 8 aphorism, apothegm 9 postulate, principle 10 principium 11 fundamental

axiomatic 5 given 7 assumed, certain, obvious 8 accepted, absolute, manifest, provable 10 aphoristic, understood 11 fundamental, indubitable, self-evident 12 unquestioned

axis 4 line, pole, stem 5 point, pivot 8 alliance 9 continuum, plant stem 11 partnership 12 straight line, turning point

axle 3 bar, pin, rod 4 beam 5 bogie, shaft 7 spindle, support

aye 3 yea, yep, yes 4 amen, okay, ever, vote 6 agreed, always 8 all right 11 affirmative, continually

Azerbaijan *capital:* 4 Baku *city:* 5 Gäncä 8 Sumqayit *exclave:* 8 Naxçivan 11 Nakhichevan *monetary unit:* 5 manat *neighbor:* 4 Iran 6 Russia 7 Armenia, Georgia *river:* 4 Kura 5 Araks *sea:* 7 Caspian

Azores *capital:* 12 Ponta Delgada *city:*
5 Horta *island:* 4 Pico 5 Corvo, Faial,
Lajes 6 Flores 8 São Jorge, Terceura
9 São Miguel 10 Santa Maria *part of:*
8 Portugal
Aztec *capital:* 12 Tenochtitlán *conqueror:*
6 Cortés, Cortéz *emperor:* 9 Moctezu-
ma, Montezuma *god:* 4 Xipe 6 Tlaloc
9 Xipetotec 12 Quetzalcoatl *hero:*
4 Nata *language:* 7 Nahuatl *temple:*
8 teocalli
azure 3 sky 4 blue 5 color 7 sky blue

B

baa 5 bleat
Babbitt 10 conformist, middlebrow, philistine *author:* 5 Lewis (Sinclair)
babble 3 gab, jaw, yak, yap 4 blab, chat,
go on, gush, rant, rave 5 clack, prate,
run on 6 burble, drivel, gibber, gossip,
jabber, murmur, patter, piffle, rattle,
yammer 7 blabber, blather, chatter,
maunder, palaver, prattle, twaddle
8 nonsense, idle talk 9 gibberish 11 jabberwocky
babe 3 cub, tot 4 doll, girl 5 bairn,
child, chick, cutie, woman 6 infant,
hottie 7 bambino, papoose, neonate,
newborn 8 bantling, nursling
babel 3 ado, din, row 4 to-do 5 hoo-ha
6 bedlam, clamor, hubbub, jangle, outcry, racket, ruckus, tumult, uproar
7 clangor, discord, ferment, turmoil
8 brouhaha, clangour, foofaraw
9 cacophony, commotion, confusion
10 dissonance, hullabaloo, hurly-burly,
turbulence 11 pandemonium 12 vocif-
eration
baboon 3 oaf 4 clod, dolt, goon, lout
6 chacma, galoot, simian 7 palooka
8 lunkhead, mandrill, meathead
9 hamadryas
babushka 6 granny 7 bandana 8 bandanna, kerchief
baby 3 pet, tot 4 tiny 5 bairn, sissy, spoil
6 cocker, coddle, cosset, dote on,
infant, pamper 7 bambino, cater to,
indulge, neonate, newborn, papoose,
toddler 8 bantling, dote upon,
nursling, suckling, weanling 11 mollycoddle *ailment:* 5 colic, croup *bed:*
4 crib 6 cradle 8 bassinet *bedroom:*
7 nursery *breechcloth:* 6 diaper *cap:*
6 biggin, bonnet *carriage:* 4 pram
5 buggy 8 stroller 12 perambulator

doctor: 12 pediatrician *food:* 3 pap
4 milk 6 pablum 7 pabulum *garment:*
7 rompers *Italian:* 7 bambino *napkin:*
3 bib *outfit:* 7 layette *powder:* 4 talc
shoe: 6 bootee *Spanish:* 4 bebé, nene
baby grand 5 piano
babyhood 7 infancy 10 diaper days,
immaturity
babyish 5 petty 7 foolish, puerile,
spoiled 8 childish, immature, juvenile
9 infantile, infantine
Babylonian 6 lavish 9 luxurious *abode of
the dead:* 5 Aralu *capital:* 7 Babylon
chaos: 4 Apsu *city:* 5 Akkad 6 Cunaxa
crown prince: 10 Belshazzar *division:*
5 Akkad, Sumer *earth mother:* 6 Ishtar
first ruler: 6 Nimrod *god:* 3 Bel 6 Marduk, Tammuz *goddess:* 5 Belit 6 Ishtar
hero: 9 Gilgamesh *king:* 6 Sargon
9 Hammurabi 12 Ashurbanipal *river:*
6 Tigris 9 Euphrates *sun god:* 3 Bel
7 Shamash *tower:* 5 Babel 8 ziggurat
waters: 4 Apsu 6 Tiamat *winged dragon:*
6 Tiamat
baccalaureate 6 degree 9 bachelor's
10 graduation
bacchanal 6 maenad see also BACCHA-
NALIA
bacchanalia 4 bash, orgy 5 binge, revel,
spree 6 bender, excess 7 blowout,
carouse, debauch, revelry, wassail
8 carnival, festival, wingding 11 celebration, dissipation, merrymaking
bacchanalian 4 wild 7 drunken, riotous
8 frenzied 9 debauched, orgiastic
12 intoxicating *cry* 4 evoe 5 evohe
Bacchus 8 Dionysus *attendant:* 6 maenad 9 bacchante *father:* 4 Zeus
7 Jupiter *lover:* 5 Venus 9 Aphrodite
mother: 6 Semele *son:* 7 Priapus *staff:*
7 thyrsus

Bach, Johann Sebastian *birthplace:*
8 Eisenach *genre:* 5 fugue, motet, suite
6 sonata 7 cantata, chorale, partita,
prelude, toccata 8 concerto, fantasia,
oratorio, sinfonia *home:* 7 Leipzig
instrument: 5 organ 11 harpsichord
musical style: 7 baroque *religion:*
8 Lutheran

back 3 aft, aid 4 abet, fund, help, hind,
rear 5 abaft, about, dorsa (plural),
spine, stake 6 assist, astern, dorsum,
hinder, recede, uphold 7 endorse,
finance, promote, retract, retreat,
reverse, sponsor, support 8 advocate,
bankroll, champion, rearward, side
with 9 in reverse, posterior, retrocede,
subsidize 10 retrograde *ailment:* 7 lumbago 10 rheumatism *of an arthropod:*
6 tergum *of an insect:* 5 notum *of the
neck:* 4 nape 6 scruff *prefix:* 4 post
5 retro *relating to:* 6 dorsal

back answer 3 lip 6 retort 7 riposte
8 comeback, repartee 9 rejoinder,
wisecrack 10 return, shot
11 parting shot

backbite 4 slam, slur 5 abuse, decry,
knock, libel, smear, sully, taint
6 defame, defile, malign, vilify
7 asperse, put down, run down, slander, traduce 8 bad-mouth, belittle,
besmirch, derogate, diminish 9 denigrate, discredit

backbiter 6 gossip 7 defamer, traitor
9 detractor, slanderer 10 talebearer

backbiting 5 abuse, smear, spite 6 gossip
7 abusing, calumny, obloquy, scandal,
slander 8 libelous, smearing 9 aspersion, cattiness, gossiping, invective,
maligning, traducing, vilifying
10 calumnious, defamation, defamatory, scandalous, slandering, slanderous 11 denigration 12 belittlement,
depreciation, spitefulness, vituperation
13 disparagement

backbone 4 base, grit, guts, will 5 basis,
moxie, nerve, spine, spunk 6 mettle,
pillar, rachis 7 resolve, support 8 mainstay, tenacity 9 character, fortitude,
framework, toughness, vertebrae
10 foundation, moral fiber, resolution
12 spinal column 13 determination,
steadfastness

backbreaking 6 taxing, tiring 7 arduous,
onerous 8 grueling, toilsome 9 fatiguing, gruelling, laborious, punishing,
strenuous, torturous, wearisome
10 burdensome, exhausting

backchat 6 banter, gossip 10 persiflage

backcomb 5 tease

backcountry 4 bush 6 sticks 7 boonies,
outback 8 frontier, interior 9 boondocks 10 hinterland

backcourtman 5 guard

back down 4 balk 5 admit, demur,
welsh, yield 6 beg off, bow out, cry off,
give in, give up, recall, recant, renege
7 concede, disavow, retract, retreat 8
take back, withdraw 9 surrender,
weasel out 10 chicken out

backdrop 6 milieu 7 climate, context,
scenery, setting 8 stage set 10 atmosphere, background 11 environment,
mise-en-scène 12 surroundings

backer 4 ally 5 angel 6 patron, surety
7 sponsor 8 advocate, defender, exponent, follower, investor, promoter
9 auxiliary, guarantor, proponent, supporter 10 bankroller, benefactor, meal
ticket

backfire 4 fail 5 blast 6 fizzle, go awry
7 go amiss, go wrong 8 miscarry, ricochet 9 boomerang, discharge, explosion
10 disappoint, spring back 11 fall
through 13 counteraction

backgammon *board section:* 5 table
piece: 5 stone *wedge:* 5 point

background 4 base, tone 6 milieu 7 history, scenery, setting 8 heritage, training 9 education 10 experience, supporting 13 circumstances, qualification

backhanded 7 devious, oblique 8 indirect, derisive, sneering 9 insulting, sarcastic 10 roundabout 12 disingenuous
13 condescending *compliment:* 6 insult,
slight 7 put-down 9 aspersion

backing 3 aid 4 help 5 aegis, funds 7 harmony, support 8 auspices 9 patronage,
promotion 10 assistance 11 endorsement, sponsorship 13 accompaniment,
encouragement

backland see BACKCOUNTRY

backlash 5 slack 6 recoil 8 kickback,
reaction, response, ricochet 11 retaliation 12 repercussion

backlog 4 pile 5 hoard, stock, store
6 pile up, supply 7 nest egg, reserve
9 inventory, reservoir, stockpile
12 accumulation

back of 5 abaft 6 behind 9 following

back off see BACK DOWN

back out 4 quit 5 leave, welsh, yield
6 beg off, desert, give up, renege 7 forsake 8 withdraw 9 surrender

backpack 4 gear, hike 5 tramp 6 duffel,
ramble 8 knapsack, rucksack 9 haversack

backpedal see BACK DOWN

backset see SETBACK

backside 3 bum 4 butt, rear, rump, seat,
tail, tush 5 fanny, hiney, stern 6 behind,
bottom, breech, far end, heinie 8 but-

tocks, derriere, haunches 9 fundament, posterior 12 hindquarters

backslide 4 fall, sink, slip 5 lapse 6 return, revert 7 go wrong, regress, relapse 9 retrovert 10 degenerate, go downhill, recidivate 11 deteriorate

backstabbing 4 slur 5 smear 6 malice 7 calumny, scandal, slander 8 betrayal 9 treachery 10 defamation, detraction, traitorous 11 treacherous 12 belittlement, depreciation, vilification 13 disparagement

backstairs 6 covert, secret, sneaky, sordid 7 furtive 8 hush-hush 9 secretive 10 scandalous 11 clandestine, underhanded 13 surreptitious

backstop 5 fence 6 screen, uphold 7 bolster, support 8 advocate, champion, side with

back talk 3 lip 4 guff, sass 5 cheek, mouth, sauce 9 freshness, impudence, insolence 12 impertinence

backtrack 7 regress, retrace, retreat, reverse 8 turn tail

backward 4 dull, slow, rear 5 abaft, dense 6 averse, astern, behind, stupid 7 awkward, delayed, moronic 8 ignorant, inverted, rearward, retarded, reversed, stagnant 9 benighted, dimwitted, in reverse 10 half-witted, retrograde, slow-witted, uncultured 11 thickheaded, turned around, undeveloped 12 feebleminded, simpleminded, uncultivated 13 unprogressive

backwoods see BACKCOUNTRY

backwoodsman 4 hick, rube 5 swain, yokel 6 rustic 7 bumpkin, hayseed 9 hillbilly 10 clodhopper, country boy, provincial 11 mountaineer

bacon *side:* 6 flitch, gammon *slice:* 6 rasher

Bacon, Francis *work:* 12 Novum Organum

bacteria 5 cocci 7 bacilli, vibrios 8 spirilla *culture medium:* 4 agar *destroyer:* 10 antibiotic

bacterial disease 6 plague, typhus 7 anthrax, leprosy, tetanus, typhoid 8 botulism, syphilis 9 gonorrhea, infection, pneumonia 10 diphtheria, meningitis 11 shigellosis

bacteriologist *American:* 6 Enders (John Franklin) 7 Noguchi (Hideyo), Theiler (Max) *British:* 7 Fleming (Alexander) *French:* 5 Widal (Fernand) 7 Nicolle (Charles-Jean-Henri), Pasteur (Louis) *German:* 4 Cohn (Ferdinand Julius), Koch (Robert) 5 Klebs (Edwin) 7 Behring (Emil von), Löffler (Friedrich) 10 Wassermann (August von) *Japanese:* 8 Kitasato

(Shibasaburo) *Russian:* 11 Metchnikoff (Elie) *Swiss:* 6 Yersin (Alexandre-Emile-John)

bad 3 ill, low 4 evil, foul, sour 5 amiss, awful, lousy, wrong 6 crummy, putrid, rancid, rotten, sinful, wicked 7 harmful, hateful, hurtful, immoral, naughty, noisome, noxious, spoiled, tainted, vicious 8 damaging, dreadful, inferior, perverse, terrible, wretched 9 abhorrent, defective, execrable, injurious, loathsome, obnoxious, offensive, putrefied, reprobate, repulsive, sickening 10 disgusting, iniquitous 11 deleterious, detrimental, distasteful, intolerable 12 unacceptable 13 objectionable *comparative:* 5 worse *prefix:* 3 dys, mis *superlative:* 5 worst

Badebec *husband:* 9 Gargantua *son:* 10 Pantagruel

Baden 3 spa 6 resort 9 hot spring

badge 3 pin 4 arms, logo, mark, seal, sign 5 award, honor, kudos, medal, token 6 button, emblem, ensign 7 laurels 8 accolade, hallmark, insignia 10 coat of arms, decoration 11 distinction, purple heart

badger 3 bug, nag 4 bait, goad, ride 5 annoy, brock, chivy, harry, hound 6 chivvy, harass, hassle, heckle, hector, needle, pester, plague 7 torment 8 bullyrag 9 importune

Badger State 9 Wisconsin

badinage 4 play 6 banter, joking 7 jesting, joshing, kidding, ribbing, teasing 8 backchat, chitchat, repartee 9 cross talk 10 persiflage

badland 4 wild 5 waste, wilds 6 barren, desert 7 outback 8 wildness 10 wilderness 11 hill country

bad mark 3 gig 7 demerit 9 poor grade

bad-tempered 4 dour, sour 5 cross, sulky, surly, testy 6 crabby, cranky, crusty, grumpy, ornery, sullen, touchy 7 grouchy, peevish 8 choleric, petulant 9 crotchety, dyspeptic, irascible, irritable, splenetic 10 ill-humored, ill-natured, unpleasant 11 quarrelsome 12 cantankerous, curmudgeonly, disagreeable, misanthropic

Baedeker 5 guide 6 manual 8 handbook 9 guidebook, vade mecum 10 compendium 11 enchiridion, travel guide

baffle 4 balk, foil 5 addle, block, floor, mix up, stump 6 bemuse, hinder, impede, muddle, puzzle, thwart 7 barrier, confuse, flummox, mystify, nonplus, perplex 8 befuddle, bewilder, confound 9 deflector, dumbfound, frustrate 10 circumvent, disappoint, disconcert

bafflement 9 confusion 10 bemusement, perplexity 12 bewilderment

bag 3 cop, nab, kit, net, sag, win 4 flop, grip, hook, kill, land, nail, poke, sack, tote, trap 5 biddy, bulge, catch, crone, forgo, pouch, purse, seize, shoot, snare, steal, udder 6 beldam, collar, duffel, duffle, give up, secure, valise 7 abandon, acquire, capture, satchel 8 backpack, knapsack, reticule, suitcase 9 apprehend, haversack 12 protuberance

bagatelle 6 trifle, whimsy 9 plaything

baggage 4 gear 5 hussy, stuff, tramp, trull, wench 6 burden, things, wanton 7 carry-on, effects, jezebel, luggage, parcels, trollop 8 obstacle, matériel, slattern, strumpet 9 equipment, hindrance 10 impediment, prostitute 11 impedimenta 13 paraphernalia

baggy 5 loose

Baghdad *founder:* 6 Mansur *river:* 6 Tigris

bagnio 4 crib, stew 7 brothel, lupanar 8 bordello, cathouse 10 bawdy house, whorehouse

bagpipe *part:* 5 drone 7 bourdon, chanter *sound:* 5 skirl

Bahamas *capital:* 6 Nassau *island:* 3 Cat 5 Abaco 6 Andros, Inagua 7 Watling 9 Eleuthera, Mayaguana 11 Grand Bahama, San Salvador 13 New Providence *language:* 7 English *monetary unit:* 6 dollar *neighbor:* 4 Cuba

Bahrain *capital:* 6 Manama *island:* 6 Sitrah 7 Bahrain 10 Al Muharraq *language:* 6 Arabic *monetary unit:* 5 dinar

bail 3 bar, dip 4 bond, flee, lade 5 ladle, scoop 6 handle, pledge, surety 7 release 8 guaranty, security, warranty 9 guarantee 10 collateral 12 recognizance

bailiwick 4 area, turf, zone 5 field, realm 6 domain, sphere 7 demesne, purview, terrain 8 district, dominion, province 9 champaign, specialty, territory 10 discipline 12 jurisdiction

bailout 3 aid 6 relief, rescue 7 subsidy 11 benefaction, deliverance

bairn 3 kid, tot 4 babe, baby, tyke 5 child 6 infant

bait 3 nag, try, vex 4 lure, ride, trap 5 abuse, chase, chivy, decoy, harry, hound, leger, snare, taunt, tease, tempt, worry 6 allure, badger, come-on, entice, entrap, harass, heckle, hector, lead on, molest, pester, seduce 7 beguile, torment, torture 8 bullyrag, inveigle, ridicule 9 persecute, seduction, sweetener 10 attraction, allurement, enticement, temptation *and switch:* 4 lure 5 trick 8 inveigle 10 substitute

bake 4 burn, char, cook, fire, kiln 5 broil, roast, toast 6 scorch 7 scallop, scollop, swelter

baked clay 7 ceramic

baker's dozen 8 thirteen

bakers' yeast 6 leaven 9 leavening

baking 3 hot 5 fiery 6 red-hot, torrid 7 burning 8 broiling, scalding, sizzling, white-hot 9 scorching *chamber:* 4 kiln, oven

baksheesh 3 tip 4 alms 5 bribe, favor 6 grease, reward 7 payment 8 gratuity 9 emolument 12 compensation

Balaam *beast:* 3 ass 6 donkey *father:* 4 Beor

balance 4 rest 5 level, scale, weigh 6 adjust, excess, make up, offset, set off, square, stasis 7 harmony, remains, remnant, residue 8 atone for, equalize, outweigh, residual, residuum, symmetry 9 composure, congruity, equipoise, harmonize, remainder, stability 10 compensate, counteract, difference, equanimity, neutralize, proportion, steadiness 11 consistency, countervail, equilibrium, self-control 12 counterpoise

balanced 4 fair 5 equal 6 offset, stable, steady 7 equable, weighed 9 equitable, impartial 10 evenhanded, harmonized, stabilized

balcony 6 piazza 7 catwalk, gallery 8 platform 9 mezzanine *section:* 4 loge

bald 4 bare, nude 5 blunt, naked, plain, stark 6 barren, severe, shaven, smooth 8 glabrous, hairless, palpable, treeless 9 depilated, unadorned, uncovered 10 deforested, forthright 11 undisguised, unvarnished

baldachin 4 silk 6 canopy, fabric

Balder, Baldur *father:* 4 Odin *mother:* 5 Frigg 6 Frigga *slayer:* 3 Höd 4 Hoth, Loke, Loki 5 Hoder, Hothr *wife:* 5 Nanna

balderdash 3 rot 4 bosh, bull, bunk 5 bilge, crock, hooey 6 blague, bunkum, drivel 7 baloney, eyewash, garbage, hogwash, palaver, rubbish, twaddle 8 buncombe, claptrap, malarkey, nonsense, tommyrot 9 poppycock 10 tomfoolery 11 foolishness 13 horsefeathers

bald-faced 4 bold 6 arrant, brazen 7 blatant, defiant 8 impudent, insolent 9 audacious, shameless, unabashed 11 impertinent

baldness 8 alopecia 12 hairlessness

baldpate 7 widgeon 8 skinhead

Baldwin, James *essay:* 17 Nobody Knows My Name, Notes of a Native Son *novel:* 12 Fire Next Time (The)

13 Giovanni's Room 14 Another Country 21 Go Tell It on the Mountain *play:* 21 Blues for Mister Charlie

balefire 6 beacon 9 watchfire

baleful 4 dire, evil 6 deadly, malign 7 direful, fateful, harmful, hostile, malefic, ominous 8 menacing, sinister 9 ill-boding, ill-omened, malignant 10 maleficent, malevolent, pernicious 11 apocalyptic, threatening 12 unpropitious

balk 3 bar, gag, jib, shy 4 beam, dash, foil, ruin 5 block, check, demur, plank, stall 6 baffle, boggle, desist, flinch, hinder, rafter, refuse, thwart 7 prevent, scruple, stumble 8 hang back, hesitate, obstruct 9 frustrate, hindrance 10 circumvent, disappoint

balky 5 loath 6 averse, ornery, mulish, unruly 7 froward, restive, wayward, willful 8 contrary, hesitant, perverse, stubborn 9 immovable, obstinate, reluctant 10 unreliable 11 intractable, wrongheaded 12 cross-grained, recalcitrant 13 uncooperative, unpredictable

ball 3 orb, wad 4 prom 5 dance, globe, round 6 sphere 8 spheroid *batted high:* 3 fly *batted straight:* 5 liner *of thread or yarn:* 4 clew *ornamental:* 6 pom-pom, pompon *tiny:* 7 globule

ballad 3 lay 4 poem, song *singer:* 8 minstrel 10 troubadour

ballast 4 load 5 poise 6 steady 7 balance, freight 8 balancer 9 stabilize, weigh down 10 dead weight, stabilizer 12 counterpoise 13 counterweight

ballerina 6 dancer 8 coryphée, danseuse 9 toe dancer 11 dancing girl see DANCER

ballet 4 Agon 6 Apollo, Jewels, Sylvia 7 Giselle, Orpheus 8 Bayadère (La), Coppélia, Firebird (The), Raimonda, Raymonda, Swan Lake, Sylphide (La) 9 Fancy Free, Petrushka, Sylphides (Les) 10 Don Quixote, Nutcracker (The), Petrouchka 12 Rite of Spring (The) *costume:* 4 tutu 6 tights 7 leotard *dancer:* 7 danseur 8 coryphée, danseuse 9 ballerina *for two:* 9 pas de deux *handrail:* 5 barre *jump:* 4 jeté 9 entrechat *knee bend:* 4 plié *position:* 6 pointe 8 attitude 9 arabesque *step:* 3 pas 8 glissade *turn:* 6 chaîné 9 pirouette

ball game see at GAME

Ballo in Maschera composer 5 Verdi (Giuseppe)

balloon sail 9 spinnaker

ball-shaped 7 globoid, globose 8 globular, spheroid 9 globulous, spherical

ball up 4 clew, daze 5 addle 6 fuddle, jumble, muddle, puzzle, tangle 7 confuse, fluster 8 befuddle, bewilder, bollix up, confound, distract, throw off 9 disorient

ballyhoo 4 hype, tout 6 blazon, herald, hoopla, hubbub, tumult 7 promote, trumpet 8 brouhaha 9 commotion, publicity 12 extravaganza

balm 4 lull 5 aroma, cream, quiet, salve, scent, spice 6 chrism, relief, remedy, solace 7 anodyne, bouquet, comfort, incense, perfume, soother, unction, unguent 8 easement, ointment 9 emollient, fragrance, redolence 10 palliative 11 consolation, restorative

balmacaan 8 overcoat

balm of Gilead 6 poplar 7 soother 8 restorer 9 balsam fir 11 restorative 12 balsam poplar

balmy 4 calm, daft, mild, nuts, soft 5 crazy, loony, nutty, potty, silly, sweet, wacky 6 gentle, insane, smooth 7 cracked, foolish, lenient, summery 8 aromatic, deranged, fragrant, perfumed, peaceful, pleasant, pleasing, redolent, soothing, tropical 9 agreeable, ambrosial, temperate

baloney 3 rot 4 bosh, bull, bunk 5 bilge, hokum, hooey 6 bunkum, humbug 7 hogwash, rubbish 8 buncombe, claptrap, nonsense 9 poppycock 10 balderdash 11 foolishness

balsam poplar 9 tacamahac 12 balm of Gilead

Balthazar's gift 5 myrrh

Baltic *native:* 4 Lett 7 Latvian 8 Estonian 10 Lithuanian *state:* 6 Latvia 7 Estonia 9 Lithuania

Baltic native 4 Lett, Sorb, Wend 7 Latvian 8 Estonian, Prussian 10 Lithuanian

balustrade 4 rail 5 fence 7 railing 8 banister, handrail

Balzac character 4 Pons (Cousin) 5 Bette (Cousin) 6 Goriot (Père), Vidocq 7 Chabert (Colonel), Eugénie (Grandet), Grandet, Vautrin 8 Rubempré (Lucien de) 9 Birotteau, Rastignac (Eugène de) 13 Henri de Marsay

Bambi author 6 Salten (Felix)

bambino 3 kid, tot 4 babe, baby, tyke 5 bairn, child 6 cherub, Christ, infant, moppet, nipper 7 toddler

bamboozle 3 con 4 bilk, dupe, fool, gull, hoax, scam 5 stump, trick 6 baffle, befool, diddle, puzzle 7 chicane, confuse, deceive, defraud, mislead, perplex, swindle 8 befuddle, confound, flimflam, hoodwink, throw off 9 frustrate 11 hornswoggle

ban 3 bar 5 curse, taboo 6 enjoin, forbid, outlaw 7 censure, exclude 8 anathema, prohibit, suppress 9 damnation, interdict, proscribe 10 injunction 11 forbiddance, malediction, prohibition, suppression 12 denunciation, interdiction, proscription

Ban *ally:* 6 Arthur *son:* 8 Lancelot

banal 4 blah, dull, flat 5 bland, corny, ho-hum, tired, trite, usual, vapid 6 common, jejune, stupid 7 clichéd, humdrum, insipid, prosaic, sapless, trivial 8 ordinary 9 hackneyed, quotidian, wearisome 10 namby-pamby, pedestrian, uninspired, wishy-washy 11 commonplace

banality 5 ennui 6 cliché, old saw, truism 7 bromide, inanity, old song 8 chestnut, monotony, prosaism 9 platitude 10 dreariness, shibboleth, triviality 11 commonplace, old chestnut, tediousness

banausic 4 blah, drab, dull, poky 6 dreary, earthy, stodgy 7 humdrum, mundane, routine, secular, sensual, tedious, worldly 8 everyday, material, plodding, temporal, workaday 9 practical, pragmatic 10 monotonous, pedestrian 11 acquisitive, utilitarian 13 materialistic, uninteresting

band 4 belt, bevy, club, crew, gang, gird, sash, tape 5 bunch, corps, covey, group, horde, party, strap, strip, troop, unite 6 concur, fillet, girdle, league, outfit, ribbon, team up, troupe 7 cluster, combine, company, coterie 8 cincture, engirdle, ensemble, symphony 9 cooperate, orchestra 10 federation *Mexican:* 8 mariachi *neck:* 6 torque *small:* 5 combo

bandage 4 bind 5 cover, dress, gauze, truss 6 swathe 7 plaster, swaddle 8 compress, dressing

bandanna 8 babushka, kerchief 9 headscarf 11 neckerchief

bandeau 3 bra 5 strip 6 fillet, ribbon, stripe 7 tube top 8 swimwear 9 brassiere

banderilla 4 dart

banderole 4 flag, jack 6 banner, burgee, colors, ensign, pennon, scroll 7 pennant 8 bannerol, standard, streamer

bandicoot 3 rat

bandit 6 outlaw, raider, robber, sacker 7 brigand, cateran, forager, ravager 8 marauder, pillager 9 cutthroat, desperado, holdup man, plunderer 10 freebooter, highwayman 11 bushwhacker

bandleader 7 maestro 9 conductor

bandolier 4 belt, sash

bandwagon 3 fad 4 chic, mode, rage 5 craze, style, trend, vogue 7 fashion

bandy 3 bat 4 flip, swap, toss 5 argue, bowed 6 banter 7 discuss, shuffle 8 exchange 9 bowlegged, pass about 11 interchange

bane 3 woe 4 pest, ruin 5 curse, death, venom, virus 6 blight, burden, plague, poison 7 bugaboo, bugbear, scourge, torment, undoing 8 anathema, calamity, downfall, nuisance 9 bête noire, contagion, destroyer, ruination 10 affliction, pestilence 11 destruction

baneful 4 dire, evil 5 fatal 6 deadly 7 fateful, harmful, hurtful, malefic, noxious, ominous 9 ill-boding, ill-omened, injurious, malignant, pestilent, unhealthy 10 disastrous, pernicious 11 apocalyptic, deleterious, pestiferous, threatening 12 pestilential, unpropitious

bang 3 bat, box, hit, pop, rap 4 bash, beat, belt, blow, boom, bump, clap, peal, push, rape, shot, slam, sock, wham, whop 5 blast, burst, crack, crash, noise, pound, punch, smack, smash, sound, vigor, whack 6 fringe, report, strike, thrill, wallop 7 collide, exactly, resound 8 smack-dab, squarely 9 explosion 10 detonation

banger 7 athlete, sausage

Bangkok native 4 Thai

Bangladesh *capital:* 5 Dacca, Dhaka *city:* 6 Khulna 10 Chittagong *former name:* 6 Bengal *language:* 7 Bengali *monetary unit:* 4 taka *neighbor:* 5 Burma, India 7 Myanmar *river:* 5 Padma 6 Ganges, Jamuna 11 Brahmaputra

bangle 4 disk 5 charm 6 anklet, bauble 7 pendant, trinket 8 bracelet, wristlet

bang-up 3 ace 4 fine 5 dandy, primo, super 6 far-out, superb 7 capital 8 champion, fabulous, five-star, splendid, top-notch 9 excellent, first-rate 10 first-class 11 spectacular

banish 3 ban 4 oust 5 debar, eject, evict, exile, expel 6 deport, dispel, put out, run out 7 cast out, dismiss, exclude, shut out, turn out 8 drive out, relegate, send away 9 discharge, ostracize, rusticate, transport 10 expatriate 13 excommunicate

banishment 5 exile 7 banning 8 eviction 9 discharge, expulsion, ostracism 10 dispelling, relegation 11 deportation, dissolution 12 displacement

banister 3 bar 4 rail 7 railing 10 balustrade

bank 3 row 4 edge, heap, hill, mass, pile, rank, save, tier, tilt 5 amass, array, beach, coast, group, hoard, levee, mound, pitch, shore, slope, stack, stash 6 coffer, dealer, invest, margin, rivage, strand 7 deposit, incline, lay away, pyramid 8 lakeside, lay aside, salt away, seafront, set aside, sock away, squirrel, treasury 9 riverside 10 repository, storehouse 11 credit union 12 squirrel away

bank on 5 trust **7** believe

bankroll 4 back, fund **5** endow, funds, stake **6** pay for **7** capital, finance, sponsor, support **9** grubstake, subsidize **10** capitalize, underwrite

bankrupt 4 bare, bust, do in, ruin **5** break, drain, empty, strip, spent, use up, wreck **6** broken, divest, failed, fold up **7** deplete, deprive, exhaust, lacking, sterile **8** depleted, indebted **9** destitute, exhausted, pauperize, penniless **10** impoverish **12** impoverished

bankruptcy 4 lack, ruin **6** penury **7** failure **9** depletion, ruination, sterility, total loss **10** barrenness, exhaustion, insolvency **11** destitution, liquidation

banned 5 taboo **6** barred **7** illegal, illicit, tabooed **8** enjoined, verboten **9** forbidden **10** contraband, disallowed, prohibited, proscribed **11** interdicted

banner 4 flag, jack **6** burgee, ensign, pennon **7** pendant, pennant **8** banderol, gonfalon, standard, streamer **9** banderole *Roman:* **7** labarum **8** vexillum

bannerol see BANDEROLE

banquet 4 feed **5** feast **6** dinner, regale, repast, spread

banquette 4 seat, sofa **5** bench, shelf **8** platform, sidewalk

Banquo 5 ghost *murderer:* **7** Macbeth

banshee 6 keener, wailer

bantam 3 wee **4** arch, fowl, mini, pert, runt, tiny **5** dwarf, saucy, small **6** cheeky, little, petite **8** insolent, malapert **9** combative, undersize **10** diminutive, undersized

banter 3 fun, kid, rag, rib, wit **4** fool, jest, jive, joke, josh, razz **5** chaff, dally, jolly, tease **7** jesting, joshing, kidding, mockery, ragging, razzing, ribbing, teasing **8** backchat, back talk, badinage, chitchat, drollery, exchange, repartee **9** challenge, small talk **10** persiflage, pleasantry **11** give-and-take

bantling 4 babe, baby **5** bairn **6** infant **7** bambino, newborn, papoose

baptize 3 dip, dub **4** call, name, soak **5** douse, title **6** anoint, drench, purify **7** asperse, cleanse, entitle, immerse **8** christen, dedicate, initiate, sprinkle **9** designate **10** consecrate, denominate, regenerate

bar 3 ban, dam, pub, rod, tap **4** curb, dive, halt, save, stop **5** block, court, estop, ingot, limit, stick, strip **6** bistro, except, impede, lounge, saloon, tavern **7** barrier, cantina, delimit, exclude, gin mill, rule out, taproom **8** alehouse, blockade, count out, obstacle, obstruct, restrict, tribunal **9** barricade, eliminate, honky-tonk, nightclub, roadhouse

11 obstruction, rathskeller **12** circumscribe, watering hole *type:* **3** raw **4** cash, fern, open, roll, tiki **6** sports

barb 3 dig **4** dart, hook **5** quill, shaft, thorn

Barbados *capital:* **10** Bridgetown *language:* **7** English *location:* **10** West Indies *monetary unit:* **6** dollar

barbarian 3 Hun **4** Goth, lout, rude, wild **5** beast, crude, brute **6** savage, Vandal **7** lowbrow, uncouth **8** Visigoth **9** foreigner, Ostrogoth, primitive **10** uncultured **11** uncivilized **12** uncultivated

barbaric 4 wild **5** crude, rough **6** brutal, coarse, savage **7** beastly, boorish, brutish, loutish, uncouth **8** churlish **9** atrocious, monstrous, primitive, unrefined **11** uncivilized

barbarism 8 malaprop, rudeness, solecism **9** vulgarism, vulgarity **10** coarseness, corruption **11** impropriety, malapropism **12** backwardness, unseemliness

barbarity 7 cruelty **8** atrocity, savagery **9** brutality, depravity **10** inhumanity, savageness **11** viciousness **12** ruthlessness **13** monstrousness

barbarous 4 base, fell, grim, rude, vile, wild **5** cruel, harsh **6** brutal, fierce, Gothic, savage, unholy, vulgar, wicked **7** brutish, Hunnish, inhuman, lowbrow, uncivil, ungodly, vicious, wolfish **8** backward, fiendish, inhumane, ruthless, sadistic **9** benighted, ferocious, graceless, heartless, merciless, monstrous, primitive, tasteless, truculent **10** abominable, outlandish, outrageous, philistine, unmerciful **11** unchristian, uncivilized **12** uncultivated

Barbary state 5 Tunis **7** Algiers, Morocco, Tripoli

barbecue 5 grill, roast **7** cookout, roaster

barber 3 bob, cut **4** clip, crop, trim **5** shave, shear **6** shaver **7** clipper, cropper **8** coiffeur **9** coiffeuse **10** beautician, haircutter **11** hairdresser, hair stylist

Barber of Seville *author:* **12** Beaumarchais (Pierre-Augustin) *character:* **6** Figaro, Rosina, Rosine **7** Bartolo, Basilio **8** Almaviva, Bartholo *composer:* **7** Rossini (Gioacchino) **9** Paisiello (Giovanni)

bard 4 muse, poet, scop **5** skald **8** jongleur, minstrel **9** balladist **10** Parnassian, troubadour

Bard of Avon 11 Shakespeare (William)

bare 4 bald, mere, nude, void **5** empty, naked, shorn, stark, strip **6** barren, denude, devoid, expose, peeled, reveal, unclad, unveil, vacant **7** denuded, dis-

robe, emptied, exposed, uncover
8 bankrupt, disclose, stripped
9 unclothed, uncovered, undressed
barefaced 4 bald, bold, open **5** blunt,
naked **6** arrant, brassy, brazen **7** blatant, glaring, obvious **8** flagrant, impudent, overbold **9** audacious, beardless,
shameless, unabashed **10** unblushing
11 temerarious, unconcealed
barefoot 6 unshod **8** shoeless **9** discalced
bareheaded 7 hatless
barely 4 just **6** hardly, scarce **7** faintly
8 meagerly, scarcely
bargain 3 buy **4** bond, deal, pact, swap
5 agree, steal, trade, truck, value
6 barter, confer, dicker, haggle, higgle,
palter, pledge **7** chaffer, compact, savings, traffic **8** closeout, contract,
covenant, exchange, giveaway, good
deal, huckster, markdown, transact
9 agreement, good value, negotiate,
reduction **10** compromise, convention,
loss leader, pennyworth **11** arrangement, transaction **13** understanding
barge 4 scow **5** clump, stump **6** lumber
7 galumph, stumble
baritone 4 Prey (Hermann) **5** Gobbi
(Tito) **6** Bailey (Norman), London
(George), Milnes (Sherrill), Terfel
(Bryn), Warren (Leonard) **7** Hampson
(Thomas), MacNeil (Cornell), Merrill
(Robert), Tibbett (Lawrence) **8** Raimondi (Ruggero), Warfield (William)
bark 3 arf, bay, yap, yip **4** snap, woof,
yelp **5** snarl **6** bellow
barkeeper see BARTENDER
barker 6 hawker **8** pitchman
Barlow epic 9 Columbiad
barman see BARTENDER
Barmecidal 5 empty, false **6** unreal **7** fictive **8** apparent, illusive, illusory
9 imaginary **10** chimerical, ostensible
13 insubstantial
barn 6 stable *area of:* **4** loft **7** hayloft
barnacle 5 leech **7** sponger **8** hanger-on,
nuisance, parasite **9** dependent, free
rider **10** crustacean, freeloader
barnstorm 8 campaign
Barnum *elephant:* **5** Jumbo *midget:*
8 Tom Thumb *partner:* **6** Bailey
barnyard 4 foul, rude **5** crass, crude,
dirty, nasty **6** coarse, earthy, filthy, ribald, smutty, vulgar **7** obscene, raunchy,
uncouth **8** indecent **9** tasteless **10** indelicate **12** scatological
baron 4 lord, peer **5** mogul, noble
6 tycoon **7** kingpin, magnate **8** overlord
13 industrialist
baronial 5 ample, grand, noble **6** august,
lordly **7** stately **8** imposing, majestic,

princely **9** grandiose **10** commanding,
impressive **11** magnificent, resplendent
baroque 6 florid, ornate, rococo **7** complex **8** dramatic **9** excessive, grotesque,
irregular **10** flamboyant, ornamented
11 embellished, extravagant **12** ostentatious **13** overdecorated
Baroque *architect:* **4** Wren (Christopher)
7 Bernini (Gian Lorenzo), Guarini
(Guarino), Maderno (Carlo) **9** Borromini (Francesco) *composer:* **4** Bach
(Johann Sebastian) **5** Lully (Jean-Baptiste) **6** Handel (George Frideric),
Rameau (Jean-Philippe), Schütz (Heinrich) **7** Corelli (Arcangelo), Purcell
(Henry), Vivaldi (Antonio) **8** Albinoni
(Tommaso), Couperin (François), Tele-
mann (Georg Philipp) **9** Pachelbel
(Johann), Scarlatti (Alessandro,
Domenico) **10** Monteverdi (Claudio)
painter: **4** Hals (Frans) **5** Steen (Jan)
6 Claude (Lorrain), Rubens (Peter
Paul) **7** El Greco, Holbein (Hans),
Poussin (Nicolas), Van Dyck (Anthony), Vermeer (Jan) **8** Carracci (Agosti-
no, Annibale, Lodovico), Ter Borch
(Gerard) **9** Rembrandt (van Rijn),
Velázquez (Diego) **10** Caravaggio *sculptor:* **5** Puget (Pierre) **7** Bernini (Gian
Lorenzo), Coustou (Guillaume,
Nicholas), Pigalle (Jean-Baptiste)
8 Coysevox (Antoine), Girardon
(François)
barrack 4 jeer, root **5** cheer, scoff, taunt
6 billet, casern, deride, hector **7** caserne
8 quarters
barrage 3 dam **4** fire, hail, mass **5** blitz,
burst, salvo, storm, surge **6** deluge,
shower, stream, volley **7** gunfire, torrent **8** drumfire, shelling **9** broadside,
cannonade, crossfire, fusillade,
onslaught **11** bombardment
barranca 4 bank **5** bluff, gully **6** arroyo
barrel 3 keg, tun, vat **4** butt, cask, drum,
peck, race, rush, tear **5** hurry **6** firkin,
hasten **8** hogshead *maker:* **6** cooper *part:*
4 hoop **5** stave *stopper:* **4** bung *support:*
6 gantry
barrelhouse 4 dive **5** hurry, joint **7** hangout **9** honky-tonk
barren 3 dry **4** arid, bare, poor **5** bleak,
empty, stark, stony, waste **6** desert,
devoid, effete, futile, fallow **7** badland,
lacking, parched, sterile, wanting **8** desolate, heirless, impotent **9** childless,
fruitless, infertile, unbearing, unfertile,
wasteland **10** unfruitful, untillable
11 unrewarding **12** hardscrabble,
unproductive, unprofitable
barricade 5 block, fence **7** barrier
8 blockade **9** roadblock *of trees:* **6** abatis

Barrie character 4 John, Nana **5** Peter, Tommy, Wendy **7** Michael **8** Crichton **9** Tiger Lily **10** Tinker Bell **11** Captain Hook

barrier see BARRICADE

barring 3 but **4** save **6** bating, except, saving **7** besides, without **9** aside from, excluding, excepting, outside of **11** exclusive of

barrio 4 slum, turf, ward **6** ghetto **7** quarter, section **8** district, precinct **12** neighborhood

barrister 6 lawyer **7** counsel **8** advocate, attorney **9** counselor

barroom 3 pub **6** lounge, saloon, tavern **7** gin mill, rum room, taproom **8** alehouse, beer hall, dramshop, drinkery, groggery, grogshop **9** beer joint, roadhouse **12** watering hole

bartender 7 tapster **8** boniface **10** mixologist **12** saloonkeeper

barter 4 swap **5** trade, truck **7** bargain, traffic **8** exchange

Bartered Bride composer 7 Smetana (Bedrich)

Barth novel 7 Chimera **12** Giles Goat-Boy **13** Sot-Weed Factor (The)

Baruch *father:* **6** Neriah, Zabbai *occupation:* **6** scribe

basal 5 basic, vital **6** bottom, lowest **7** minimal, primary, radical **8** simplest **9** beginning, essential, undermost **10** bottommost, elementary, primordial, underlying **11** fundamental, preliminary, rudimentary **12** foundational

base 3 bad, bed, fix, key, low **4** camp, evil, foot, foul, home, mean, poor, post, prop, rest, root, seat, site, ugly, vile **5** build, cheap, dirty, found, hinge, lousy, lowly, nadir, plant, set up, sorry, stand **6** bottom, coarse, common, depend, derive, filthy, ground, humble, menial, origin, paltry, scurvy, shoddy, sleazy, sordid, source, trashy, wicked **7** bedrock, caitiff, essence, footing, ignoble, lowborn, low-down, pitiful, servile, squalid, support **8** beggarly, buttress, cowardly, garrison, inferior, pedestal, plebeian, recreant, unwashed, unworthy, wretched **9** construct, dastardly, degrading, establish, framework, loathsome, low-minded, predicate, principle **10** abominable, despicable, foundation, groundwork, substratum, unennobled **11** disgraceful, humiliating, ignominious **12** contemptible, mean-spirited, substructure, underpinning

baseball *abbreviation:* **3** ERA, LOB, MVP, RBI *reputed founder:* **9** Doubleday (Abner) *glove:* **4** mitt *official:* **3** ump **6** umpire *pitch:* **4** drop, heat **5** curve, smoke **6** change, heater, sinker, slider, slurve **7** spitter **8** change-up, fadeaway, fastball, fork ball, knuckler, palm ball, spitball **9** brushback, screwball **11** knuckleball **12** change of pace, knuckle curve *player:* **6** batter **7** baseman, catcher, fielder, pitcher **9** infielder, shortstop **10** outfielder **11** left fielder **12** right fielder **13** center fielder *term:* **3** bag, bat, box, fan, fly, out, run, tag, tap, tip **4** balk, ball, base, bean, bunt, cage, deck, foul, hook, line, mitt, pill, pole, save, walk **5** alley, apple, bench, bloop, clout, count, drive, error, flare, fungo, glove, homer, liner, mound, pop-up, slide, swing **6** assist, clutch, double, dugout, groove, ground, inning, inside, pop fly, pop-out, powder, putout, rubber, runner, single, strike, triple, windup **7** battery, blooper, bullpen, cleanup, diamond, floater, fly ball, home run, infield, manager, outside, pickoff, rhubarb, sidearm, squeeze, stretch **8** baseline, beanball, delivery, foul ball, grounder, keystone, outfield, pinch-hit, rosin bag, southpaw **9** full count, home plate, hot corner, line drive, sacrifice, strikeout, two-bagger **10** double play, frozen rope, ground ball, scratch hit, strike zone **11** knuckleball, pinch hitter, squeeze play, three-bagger

baseballer 3 Ott (Mel) **4** Bell (George), Cobb (Ty), Cone (David), Dean (Dizzy), Fisk (Carlton), Ford (Whitey), Foxx (Jimmy), Kaat (Jim), Mays (Willie), Rice (Jim), Rose (Pete), Ruth (Babe), Ryan (Nolan), Sosa (Sammy) **5** Aaron (Henry), Anson (Cap), Banks (Ernie), Belle (Albert), Bench (Johnny), Berra (Yogi), Boggs (Wade), Bonds (Barry), Brett (George), Brock (Lou), Brown (Kevin), Carew (Rod), Clark (Will), Damon (Johnny), Davis (Mark), Green (Shawn), Grove (Lefty), Gwynn (Tony), Henke (Tom), Jeter (Derek), Kiner (Ralph), Maris (Roger), Mauer (Joe), Paige (Satchel), Perez (Tony), Perry (Gaylord), Smith (Lee), Spahn (Warren), Staub (Rusty), Tiant (Luis), Viola (Frank), Weeks (Rickie), Young (Cy), Yount (Robin) **6** Dawson (Andre), Feller (Bob), Foster (George), Franco (John), Garvey (Steve), Gehrig (Lou), Gibson (Bob, Josh, Kirk), Gooden (Dwight), Herzog (Whitey), Hunter (Catfish), Koufax (Sandy), Lajoie (Nap), Maddux (Greg), Mantle (Mickey), Morgan (Joe), Murphy (Dale), Murray (Eddie), Musial (Stan), Palmer (Jim), Piazza (Mike), Raines (Tim),

Ripken (Cal), Seaver (Tom), Sisler (George), Sutter (Bruce), Sutton (Don), Thomas (Frank), Vaughn (Mo), Wagner (Honus), Walker (Larry) **7** Bagwell (Jeff), Canseco (José), Carlton (Steve), Clemens (Roger), Coleman (Vince), Collins (Eddie), Delgado (Carlos), Fingers (Rollie), Griffey (Ken), Hornsby (Roger), Hubbell (Carl), Jackson (Joe, Reggie), Johnson (Randy, Walter), Justice (David), Leonard (Buck), McGwire (Mark), Mondesi (Raul), Puckett (Kirby), Reardon (Jeff), Schmidt (Mike), Simmons (Al), Speaker (Tris) **8** Anderson (Sparky), Blyleven (Bert), Clemente (Roberto), DiMaggio (Joe), Guerrero (Vladimir), Martinez (Pedro), Mitchell (Kevin), Righetti (Dave), Robinson (Brooks, Frank, Jackie), Williams (Bernie, Ted), Winfield (Dave) **9** Alexander (Grover), Eckersley (Dennis), Gehringer (Charlie), Greenberg (Hank), Henderson (Rickey), Hernandez (Willie), Hershiser (Orel), Killebrew (Harmon), Mathewson (Christy), Mattingly (Don), Rodriguez (Alex), Sheffield (Gary) **10** Campanella (Roy), Conigliaro (Tony), Strawberry (Darryl), Valenzuela (Fernando) **11** Garciaparra (Nomar), Yastrzemski (Carl)

baseball team see AMERICAN LEAGUE; NATIONAL LEAGUE

baseboard 7 molding **8** skirting

baseless 4 idle, thin, vain **5** empty, false, wrong **6** feeble, flimsy **9** frivolous, pointless, senseless, unfounded, untenable **10** fallacious, gratuitous, groundless, inadequate, incredible, ungrounded **11** uncalled-for, unconfirmed, unnecessary, unsupported, unsustained, unwarranted **12** indefensible, contemptible, unpersuasive **13** unjustifiable

basement 6 bottom, cellar, ground **7** bedrock **10** foundation, groundwork, substratum **12** substructure

base on balls 4 walk

bash 3 bat, hit **4** belt, blow, fete, gala, slam, whop **5** blast, crack, crash, party, pound, smack, smash, thump, whack **6** attack, pummel, soiree, strike, wallop **7** blowout, shindig **8** wingding

Bashemath *father:* **7** Ishmael *husband:* **4** Esau *sister:* **8** Nebaioth

bashful 3 coy, shy **5** chary, mousy, timid **6** demure, modest **7** abashed, nervous **8** blushing, reserved, retiring, timorous **9** diffident, reluctant, shrinking, unassured **11** unassertive

basic 3 key **4** main **5** chief **6** bottom **7** capital, central, element, minimum, primary, radical **8** cardinal, inherent, rudiment **9** beginning, elemental, essential, intrinsic, primitive, principal, unadorned **10** elementary, underlying **11** fundamental **12** foundational

basically 6 au fond, mainly, mostly **7** at heart, chiefly, firstly, overall **8** in effect **9** generally, in essence, primarily

basic point 4 crux, gist, pith **5** heart **6** kernel **7** essence

basilica 6 church **7** minster **9** cathedral

basin 3 dip, pan, sag **4** bowl, sink **6** cirque, hollow **7** sinkage **8** sinkhole, washbowl **9** concavity **10** depression *liturgical:* **5** stoup **7** piscina

basis 3 bed **4** crux, root, seat, seed **5** heart, nexus **6** bottom, ground, reason **7** bedrock, essence, footing, grounds, nucleus, premise, support, warrant **9** authority, postulate, principle **10** assumption, foundation, groundwork, substratum **11** fundamental, presumption **12** substructure, underpinning **13** justification

bask 3 sun **4** loll **5** glory, revel, relax **6** lounge, wallow, welter **7** indulge **8** sunbathe **9** luxuriate

basket 6 bushel, gabion **7** pannier *angler's:* **5** creel

basketball *inventor:* **8** Naismith (James) *official:* **6** umpire **7** referee *player:* **5** cager, guard **6** center **7** forward **8** hoopster, swingman **9** point guard *team:* **4** five **7** quintet *term:* **3** gun, jam, key **4** cage, dunk, pass **5** board, lay-up, press, shoot, tip-in **6** freeze, tap-off, tip-off, travel **7** dribble, keyhole, rebound, throw-in, time-out **8** alley-oop, jump ball, slam dunk **9** backboard, backcourt, field goal, free throw **11** ball control

basketballer 3 Bol (Manute) **4** Bird (Larry), Ming (Yao), Nash (Steve), Redd (Michael), Reed (Willis), West (Jerry, Mark) **5** Allen (Ray), Barry (Rick), Brand (Elton), Cousy (Bob), Davis (Baron), Ewing (Patrick), Mikan (George), O'Neal (Shaquille), Price (Mark) **6** Baylor (Elgin), Blount (Mark), Boozer (Carlos), Bryant (Kobe), Carter (Vince), Cowens (Dave), Duncan (Tim), Erving (Julius), Gervin (George), Jordan (Michael), Malone (Jeff, Karl, Moses), McAdoo (Bob), McHale (Kevin), Miller (Brad, Reggie), Parish (Robert), Pierce (Paul, Ricky), Pippin (Scottie), Rodman (Dennis), Skiles (Scott), Thomas (Kenny), Thorpe (Otis), Walton (Bill), Worthy (James) **7** Barkley (Charles), Billups (Chauncey), Dawkins (Darryl),

Dampier (Erick), Edwards (James), Frazier (Walt), Garnett (Kevin), Hilario (Nene), Houston (Allan), Iverson (Allen), Jackson (Lauren), Jamison (Antawn), Johnson (Magic), McGrady (Tracy), Russell (Bill), Rollins (Tree), Taurasi (Diana), Wallace (Ben), Wilkins (Dominique) **8** Auerbach (Red), Cardinal (Brian), Havlicek (John), Olajuwon (Akeem), Magloire (Jamaal), Nowitzki (Dirk), Randolph (Zach), Robinson (David), Stockton (John), Thompson (Tina), Williams (Buck) **9** Donaldson (James), Ferdinand (Marie), Holdsclaw (Chamique), Robertson (Oscar) **10** Stojakovic (Predrag), Williamson (Corliss) **11** Abdul-Jabbar (Kareem), Chamberlain (Wilt)

Basmath's father 7 Solomon

Basque 6 bodice *cap:* **5** beret *game:* **6** pelota **7** jai alai *mountains:* **8** Pyrenees *province:* **5** Alava **7** Vizcaya **9** Guipúzcoa

bass 3 low **4** deep **6** singer **8** cabrilla *famous:* **5** Hines (Jerome), Pinza (Ezio), Ramey (Samuel), Siepi (Cesare), Tozzi (Giorgio) **6** Hotter (Hans), London (George), Morris (James) **7** Plishka (Paul), Robeson (Paul), Talvela (Martti) **8** Flagello (Ezio), Ghiaurov (Nicolai), Raimondi (Ruggero) **9** Chaliapin (Fyodor), Christoff (Boris)

Bassanio's beloved 6 Portia

bassinet 6 cradle, basket

bastard 5 cross **6** by-blow, hybrid **7** mongrel **9** love child **12** natural child *combining form:* **4** noth **5** notho

bastardize 4 warp **5** taint **6** debase, defile **7** corrupt, debauch, degrade, deprave, pervert, pollute, vitiate **9** brutalize **10** adulterate, bestialize, demoralize, depreciate **11** contaminate

baste 3 sew **4** beat, drub, lash, mill, pelt, rail, tack, whip **5** paste, scold **6** batter, berate, larrup, pummel, revile, stitch, thrash, wallop **7** bawl out, belabor, chew out, clobber, moisten, tell off, trounce, upbraid **8** bless out, chastise **9** dress down **10** tongue-lash

bastille 4 jail **6** prison **9** bridewell

bastinado 3 bat, rod **4** bash, beat, blow, cane, club **5** birch, crack, pound, smack, smash, stick, whack **6** cudgel, paddle, strike, switch, thwack, wallop **8** bludgeon **9** truncheon

bastion 5 tower **7** bulwark, citadel, parapet, rampart, redoubt **8** fastness, fortress **10** breastwork, stronghold **13** fortification

bat 3 bag, bop, hag **4** belt, biff, blow, bust, club, slam, sock, swat, whop,

wink **5** biddy, blink, crone, smack **6** cudgel, thwack **7** meander **8** bludgeon **9** flying fox, truncheon **10** knobkerrie, shillelagh **11** pipistrelle

batch 3 lot, set **5** array, bunch, clump, crowd, group **6** bundle, clutch, parcel **7** cluster **8** quantity, shipment **10** assemblage, assortment, collection **11** aggregation **12** accumulation

bate 3 bar **4** omit **5** check **6** deduct, except, reduce **7** cut back, exclude, suspend **8** diminish, moderate, restrain, subtract

bateau 4 boat, dory **5** craft, skiff **6** dinghy, launch **7** shallop

bath 3 spa, tub **4** soak, wash **5** hydro, wells **6** shower **7** springs **8** ablution **13** watering place

bathe 3 dip, lap, lip, sop, tub, wet **4** bask, lave, soak, soap, swim, wash **5** clean, douse, flood, rinse, flush, souse, steep **6** shower **7** cleanse, immerse, pervade, suffuse **8** irrigate

bathetic 5 mushy, soppy, stale, tired, trite **6** drippy **7** clichéd, cloying, gushing, maudlin, mawkish **9** emotional, hackneyed, schmaltzy **10** lachrymose **11** commonplace, sentimental, stereotyped, tear-jerking **13** anticlimactic, overemotional, stereotypical

bathhouse 5 sauna **6** cabana

bathing suit 6 bikini, trunks **7** bandeau, maillot

bathos 7 letdown **8** banality, comedown **9** triteness **10** anticlimax

bathroom 3 loo **4** john **5** privy **6** toilet **8** lavatory, outhouse

Bathsheba *father:* **5** Eliam *husband:* **5** David, Uriah *son:* **7** Solomon

bathtub gin 5 hooch **6** rotgut **7** bootleg **8** homebrew **9** moonshine **11** mountain dew

Batman creator 4 Kane (Bob)

baton 3 rod **4** club, mace, wand **5** billy, staff, stick **6** cudgel **7** war club **8** bludgeon **9** billy club, truncheon **10** nightstick

___ **Bator 4** Ulan

batrachian 4 frog, toad **9** amphibian

battalion 4 army, host, unit **5** force, horde **6** legion, throng, troops **8** squadron **10** contingent, detachment

batter 4 bash, beat, drub, hurt, maul, mush **5** baste, break, dough, paste, pound, wreck **6** bruise, buffet, bung up, hitter, mangle, pommel, pummel, thrash, wallop **7** assault, belabor, bombard, clobber, coating, contuse, cripple, lambast **8** demolish, lambaste

battery 3 lot, set **4** body, guns **5** abuse, array, batch, bunch, clump, group, suite 6 bundle, cannon, series 7 assault, beating, cluster 8 thumping 9 artillery, onslaught 10 energy cell 11 gunnery unit

battery terminal 5 anode 7 cathode

battle 4 fray 5 brush, clash, fight 6 action, assail, attack, combat, sortie 7 assault, contend, contest 8 conflict, skirmish, struggle 9 encounter, onslaught, scrimmage 10 engagement 11 hostilities

battle-ax 5 harpy, scold, shrew 6 virago 8 harridan 9 termagant, Xanthippe

Battle Born State 6 Nevada

battle cry 6 banzai

battlement 4 wall 7 barrier, bastion, bulwark, parapet, rampart 10 protection

batty 3 mad 4 daft, nuts, zany 5 barmy, crazy, kooky, loony, nutty, potty, wacky 6 crazed, cuckoo, insane, maniac, screwy, whacko 7 bananas, bonkers, cracked, idiotic, lunatic 8 deranged 9 bedlamite

bauble 3 toy 5 curio 6 gewgaw, trifle 7 bibelot, novelty, trinket, whatnot 8 gimcrack, ornament 9 objet d'art, plaything 10 knickknack

Baucis's husband 8 Philemon

Bavaria 6 Bayern *capital:* 6 Munich *city:* 8 Augsburg, Bayreuth, Würzburg 9 Nuremberg *king:* 6 Ludwig *patron saint:* 6 Rupert

bawd 4 drab, moll, tart 5 madam, tramp, whore 6 floozy, harlot, hooker 7 trollop 8 strumpet 10 prostitute 11 nightwalker 12 streetwalker

bawdy 4 blue, lewd 5 crude, dirty 6 coarse, erotic, ribald, risqué, smutty, vulgar 7 obscene 8 indecent, prurient 9 lecherous, offensive, salacious 10 lascivious, libidinous, licentious, suggestive

bawdy house 4 crib, stew 6 bagnio 7 brothel, lupanar 8 bordello

bawl 3 cry, sob 4 howl, roar, rout, wail, weep, yell, yowl 5 shout 6 bellow, berate, boohoo, clamor, holler, outcry, scream, shriek, squall 7 blubber, bluster

bawl out 3 wig 4 lash 5 baste, scold 6 berate, rebuke 7 censure, chew out, condemn, tell off, upbraid 8 bless out, castigate, denounce, tear into 9 dress down, reprimand 10 tongue-lash

bay 3 arm 4 cove, gulf, howl, nook, wail 5 award, bight, crown, firth, honor, inlet, niche 6 harbor, laurel, recess 7 garland, laurels 8 accolade 10 decoration *Aegean Sea:* 5 Anzac *Africa:* 6 Walvis *Alaska:* 7 Glacier *Antarctica:* 3 Ice 8 Amundsen *Argentina:* 6 Blanca

Australia: 5 Anson, Shark 6 Botany, Sharks 9 Discovery *Baltic:* 4 Hano, Kiel 6 Danzig, Kieler 9 Pomerania 10 Pomeranian, Pommersche *Beaufort Sea:* 7 Prudhoe 9 Mackenzie *Brazil:* 9 Guanabara *Bristol Channel:* 10 Carmarthen *California:* 5 Morro 8 Monterey, San Diego *Canada:* 5 Fundy *Capetown:* 5 Table *Caribbean Sea:* 5 Limon 8 Chetumal *Central America:* 7 Fonseca *Cuba:* 10 Guantánamo *East River:* 8 Flushing *Egypt:* 6 Abu Qir *Eire:* 4 Clew 7 Brandon *English Channel:* 3 Tor 4 Lyme *Europe:* 6 Biscay *Florida:* 8 Biscayne *Greenland:* 6 Baffin 8 Melville *Gulf of Alaska:* 12 Resurrection *Gulf of California:* 5 Adair *Gulf of Guinea:* 5 Benin 6 Biafra *Gulf of Mexico:* 5 Tampa 6 Mobile 7 Aransas 8 Campeche, Sarasota 9 Matagorda, Pensacola 10 San Antonio, Terrebonne 11 Atchafalaya, Ponce de Leon 12 Apalachicola 13 Corpus Christi *Gulf of St. Lawrence:* 5 Bonne, Gaspé *Hawaii:* 5 Koloa, Lawai *Hong Kong:* 4 Deep *Honshu:* 3 Ise 5 Mutsu, Osaka, Owari, Tokyo 6 Atsuta, Sagami *Indian Ocean:* 6 Bengal *Indonesia:* 8 Humboldt *Irish Sea:* 4 Luce 7 Dundalk *Jamaica:* 4 Long *Japan:* 4 Tosa *Java Sea:* 7 Batavia 8 Djakarta *Lake Erie:* 8 Sandusky *Lake Huron:* 7 Saginaw, Thunder *Lake Michigan:* 5 Green 13 Grand Traverse *Lake Ontario:* 11 Irondequoit *Lake Superior:* 5 Huron 8 Keweenaw 9 Whitefish *Long Island Sound:* 6 Oyster *Maine:* 5 Casco 7 Machias 9 Penobscot *Maryland-Virginia:* 10 Chesapeake 12 Chincoteague *Massachusetts:* 6 Boston 7 Cape Cod 8 Buzzards, Plymouth *New Brunswick:* 13 Passamaquoddy *Newfoundland:* 4 Hare 5 White 7 Fortune *New Jersey:* 5 Great 6 Newark 7 Raritan 8 Barnegat *New York:* 7 Jamaica *North Carolina:* 6 Onslow *Northwest Territories:* 5 Wager 7 Repulse 8 Franklin 9 Frobisher *Oregon:* 4 Coos *Puerto Rico:* 5 Sucia *Quebec:* 6 Ungava *Rhode Island:* 12 Narragansett *Sea of Japan:* 13 Peter the Great *South Carolina:* 4 Bull, Long *South China Sea:* 5 Subic 7 Camranh *Spain:* 5 Cadiz *Strait of Gibraltar:* 7 Tangier *Sydney:* 6 Botany *Tasmania:* 5 Storm *Texas:* 7 Trinity *Tyrrhenian Sea:* 6 Naples 7 Paestum *Wales:* 10 Caernarfon, Caernarvon *Washington:* 5 Dabob 6 Skagit *West Indies:* 5 Coral

bayou 5 creek, marsh 6 slough 9 everglade, tributary *Louisiana:* 5 Macon 9 Barataria, Lafourche 10 Terrebonne *Mississippi:* 9 Chickasaw

Bay State 13 Massachusetts

bay window 3 gut, pot **5** oriel, tummy **6** paunch **8** potbelly **9** beer belly, spare tire **11** corporation, breadbasket

bazaar 4 fair, mall, mart, souk **6** market **7** benefit **8** emporium, exchange **11** marketplace

bazooka's target 4 tank

be 4 live **5** exist

beach 4 bank **5** Cocoa, coast, shore **6** Malibu, Pebble, strand, Venice **7** seaside, shingle, Waikiki **8** cast away, lakeside, littoral, seashore **9** lakeshore **10** Clearwater, Copacabana, oceanfront, run aground

___ **Beach 3** Amy **4** Long, Palm, Vero **5** Dover, Miami, Omaha **6** Delray, Myrtle, Ormond **7** Daytona, Riviera, Waikiki **8** Imperial, Virginia

beached 6 ashore **7** aground **8** grounded, marooned, stranded **9** abandoned

beachhead 8 foothold

beachwear see BATHING SUIT

beacon 4 buoy, sign **5** flare, guide **6** pharos, signal **7** bonfire, lantern **8** balefire **9** watchfire **10** lighthouse, signal fire **11** inspiration, transmitter **12** guiding light

bead 3 dab, dot, pea **4** blob, drop **6** bubble **7** driblet, globule **8** spherule

beak 3 neb, nib **4** bill, nose **5** snoot, snout, spout **6** pecker, schnoz **7** schnozz **8** mandible **9** proboscis, schnozzle

beaker 3 cup **6** carafe, goblet, vessel **8** decanter

beaklike part 7 rostrum

be-all and end-all 3 sum **4** pith, root, soul **5** total, whole **6** bottom **7** essence **8** entirety, sum total, totality **9** aggregate, substance **10** prime cause **12** quintessence

beam 3 bar, ray **4** balk, boom, burn, glow, grin, spar **5** flare, flash, gleam, joist, plank, shaft, shine, shoot, smile, strut **6** girder, lintel, rafter, signal, streak, stream, timber **7** radiate **8** transmit **9** broadcast

beaming 6 bright, joyful, lucent **7** fulgent, lambent, radiant **8** animated, cheerful, luminous **9** brilliant, effulgent, refulgent **12** incandescent

bean 3 soy, wax **4** bush, conk, dome, head, lima, mung, navy, pate, pole, poll, snap, soya **5** baked, brain, broad, horse, jelly, pinto **6** belfry, coffee, frijol, kidney, legume, noddle, noggin, noodle, string **7** jumping **9** headpiece **10** stringless *of India:* **3** urd

beanery 4 café **5** diner, grill **9** hash

house **10** coffee shop, restaurant **11** greasy spoon **12** luncheonette

beano 5 bingo

Bean Town 6 Boston

bear 3 lug **4** tote **5** abide, allow, beget, bring, brook, bruin, carry, stand, touch **6** accept, behave, convey, deport, endure, permit, suffer **7** comport, condone, conduct, deliver, stomach, support, sustain, swallow, undergo **8** engender, generate, shoulder, tolerate **9** procreate, propagate, reproduce, transport **10** bring forth **11** countenance *Alaskan:* **5** polar **6** Kodiak *Australian:* **5** koala *genus:* **5** Ursus *kind:* **3** sun **5** black, brown, honey, koala, polar, sloth **6** Kodiak **7** grizzly **10** spectacled *relating to:* **6** ursine *young:* **3** cub

bearable 7 livable, tenable **8** adequate, passable **9** allowable, endurable, tolerable **10** acceptable, admissible, good enough, manageable, sufferable **11** supportable, sustainable

bearcat 5 panda

beard 4 dare, defy, face, fuzz **5** brave, front **6** goatee **7** outface, stubble, Vandyke **8** confront, imperial, whiskers **9** challenge *on grain:* **3** awn

bearded 5 bushy, fuzzy, hairy **6** shaggy, tufted **7** bristly, goateed, hirsute, stubbly **8** unshaven **9** whiskered **11** bewhiskered

bear down 4 rout **5** crush, quell **6** burden, defeat, reduce, subdue **7** conquer, overrun, trample **8** overcome, vanquish **9** emphasize, overpower, overwhelm, subjugate

bearer 4 mule **5** envoy **6** coolie, porter, runner **7** carrier, courier **8** conveyor, emissary **9** go-between, messenger **11** internuncio

bear hug 6 clinch

bearing 3 air, set **4** look, mien, pose **5** poise **6** aspect, manner, stance **7** address, conduct, display, posture **8** attitude, behavior, carriage, delivery, demeanor, presence, relation **9** demeanour, direction **10** connection, deportment **11** comportment

bearish 4 curt **5** gruff, rough, terse, surly **6** cranky, ornery **7** anxious, dubious, prickly, uncouth **8** cautious, vinegary **9** crotchety, irascible **10** ill-humored **11** pessimistic **12** cantankerous

bearlike 6 ursine

bear out 4 show **5** prove **6** attest, uphold, verify **7** certify, confirm, justify **8** validate, vouch for **9** vindicate **11** corroborate, demonstrate **12** authenticate, substantiate

bear up 4 cope, fare, prop 5 brace, get by 6 endure, uphold 7 bolster, support, sustain 8 buttress, get along, maintain, underpin

beast 5 brute 6 animal 7 critter, monster, varmint 8 behemoth, creature

beastly 4 foul, mean, vile 5 awful, brute, feral, nasty 6 animal, brutal, odious 7 bestial, brutish, inhuman, ogreish, swinish 8 horrible, terrible 9 barbarous, revolting 10 abominable, detestable

beat 3 box, get, gyp, hit, lam, rap, tan, top 4 balk, belt, best, cane, dash, drub, drum, dump, flap, flog, foil, lash, lick, maul, pelt, rout, ruin, stir, tick, trim, whip, whop 5 baste, cheat, cozen, excel, forge, lay on, meter, outdo, paste, pound, pulse, punch, rhyme, route, scoop, scour, smear, stick, stump, swing, throb, tread, tromp, whack, whisk 6 baffle, batter, better, buffet, cudgel, defeat, diddle, exceed, forage, hammer, larrup, muss up, patrol, pummel, rhythm, rounds, strike, thrash, thresh, thwart, wallop 7 belabor, clobber, circuit, conquer, exhaust, fashion, fatigue, lambast, lay down, prevail, pulsate, ransack, rough up, shellac, surpass, swindle, triumph, trounce 8 bewilder, bludgeon, Bohemian, lambaste, outshine, outsmart, outstrip, overcome, precinct 9 exhausted, frustrate, palpitate, pulsation, transcend, vibration 10 circumvent, pistolwhip 11 oscillation

beating 4 rout 5 lumps 6 defeat, hiding, mayhem 7 assault, setback 9 hammering, pulsation, throbbing 11 palpitation, shellacking

beatitude 3 joy 5 bliss 7 delight, ecstasy, rapture 8 euphoria, gladness, rhapsody 9 happiness, transport 10 exaltation, joyfulness 11 blessedness 12 blissfulness

Beatles 4 John (Lennon), Paul (McCartney) 5 Ringo (Starr) 6 George (Harrison)

beatnik 5 rebel 6 hippie 7 radical 8 Bohemian 9 dissident 11 flower child 13 nonconformist

beat-up 6 shabby 7 rickety, worn-out 8 decrepit, tattered 9 crumbling 10 broken-down, ramshackle, tumble-down 11 dilapidated

beau 5 dandy, flame, lover, swain, wooer 6 steady, suitor 7 admirer, beloved 8 paramour, truelove, young man 9 boyfriend 10 sweetheart

Beau Brummell 3 fop 5 dandy, swell 7 coxcomb, gallant 8 macaroni 11 petit-maître 12 lounge lizard

beau ideal 5 guide, model 6 mirror

7 epitome, example, paragon, pattern 8 exemplar, paradigm, standard 9 archetype 12 quintessence

Beaumarchais hero 6 Figaro

beau monde 5 elite 6 gentry, jet set 7 society 8 smart set 10 glitterati, upper crust

beauteous see BEAUTIFUL

beautiful 4 fair 5 bonny 6 comely, lovely, pretty 7 radiant 8 glorious, gorgeous, handsome, splendid, stunning 9 exquisite 10 attractive 11 good-looking, resplendent, well-favored

beautiful people 6 jet set 8 smart set 9 haut monde 10 glitterati 11 high society

beautify 4 deck, gild, trim 5 adorn, array, fix up, grace, prank, primp 6 bedeck, doll up 7 dress up, festoon, garland, garnish, gussy up, enhance, improve 8 decorate, ornament, prettify, spruce up 9 embellish, glamorize

beauty 5 asset, belle, dream, merit, peach 6 appeal, eyeful, looker, lovely 7 charmer, dazzler, stunner 8 knockout 9 eye-opener, good looks 10 good-looker, loveliness

beaver 6 rodent *project:* 3 dam *home:* 5 lodge *young:* 3 kit, pup

Beaver State 6 Oregon

becalm 4 hush, lull, stop 5 allay, quiet, stall, still 6 arrest, pacify, sedate, settle, soothe, steady, subdue 7 assuage, compose, quieten 11 tranquilize

because 3 for, now 4 that 5 since 7 being as, whereas 8 being how, as long as, seeing as 10 inasmuch as

because of 4 over 5 due to 7 owing to, through 8 thanks to 10 by reason of 11 on account of

Beckett work of 4 Not I, Play, Watt 6 Molloy, Murphy 7 Endgame 9 Happy Days, Unnamable (The) 10 Eleutheria, Malone Dies 14 Krapp's Last Tape 15 Waiting for Godot

beckon 3 bid, nod 4 lure, wave 6 allure, entice, invite, motion, signal, summon 7 attract

becloud 3 dim, fog 4 blur, hide, veil 5 addle, bedim, befog, cloak, muddy 6 impair, darken, muddle, puzzle, shroud 7 confuse, eclipse, obscure, perplex 8 befuddle 9 obfuscate 10 overshadow

become 3 fit, get, wax 4 grow, suit 5 befit 6 go with 7 enhance, flatter 8 turn into

becoming 3 apt 5 right 6 decent, proper, seemly 7 correct, fitting 8 decorous, suitable, tasteful 9 befitting 10 attractive, flattering, well-chosen 11 appropriate, comme il faut

bed 3 cot **4** base, bunk, crib, sack, twin **5** basis, berth, layer **6** bottom, cradle, double, ground, Murphy, pallet **7** bedrock, stratum, trundle **8** rollaway **10** foundation, substratum *of India:* **7** charpoy

bedaub 4 coat **5** cover, smear **6** smudge **7** overlay, plaster

bedazzle 4 daze **5** blind

bedcover 5 duvet, quilt **6** afghan, spread **7** blanket **8** coverlet **9** comforter **11** counterpane

bedeck 4 trim **5** adorn, array, prank **6** attire, bedaub, jazz up **7** appoint, bedizen, dress up, festoon, furbish, garland, garnish, gussy up **8** accouter, accoutre, beautify, decorate, ornament, prettify **9** embellish

bedevil 5 annoy, harry, spoil, tease, worry **6** harass, needle, nettle, pester, plague **7** hagride, provoke, torment, trouble **8** bewilder **10** exasperate

bedevilment 6 bother **7** torment, trouble **8** disorder, vexation **9** annoyance, confusion **10** irritation **11** aggravation **12** bewilderment

bedfellow 4 ally **5** crony **7** comrade **9** associate, colleague **10** compatriot **11** confederate **12** collaborator

bedim 3 fog **4** blur, mask, veil **5** befog, blear, cloud, gloom, shade, **6** darken, muddle, shadow, shroud **7** becloud, confuse, eclipse, obscure **9** obfuscate

bedizen 4 deck, garb, gild **5** adorn, array, endue **6** doll up, dude up, invest, outfit, rig out **7** costume, dandify, dress up, garnish, gussy up, turn out **8** beautify, ornament **9** caparison, embellish

bedlam 3 ado **5** chaos, furor **6** asylum, clamor, furore, hubbub, tumult, uproar, welter **7** turmoil **8** foofaraw, madhouse, upheaval **9** commotion, maelstrom **10** hurly-burly **11** pandemonium

bedlamite 3 mad, nut **4** loon, nuts **5** batty, crazy, loony **6** insane, madman, maniac **7** cracked, lunatic **8** demented, deranged

bedouin 4 Arab **5** nomad

bedraggled 5 faded, seedy **6** shabby, ragtag, untidy **7** muddied, rundown, unkempt **8** decrepit, dripping, slovenly, tattered **10** disheveled, disarrayed, disordered, down-at-heel, ramshackle, threadbare **11** dilapidated

bedridden 6 laid up, shut-in **8** confined **12** hospitalized

bedrock 4 base, core, foot, root **5** axiom, basic, basis, floor, nadir **6** bottom, depths, ground **7** footing, support **10** foundation, groundwork, substra-

tum **11** fundamental **12** substructure, underpinning

bedroom 7 boudoir, chamber

bedspread 8 coverlet **11** counterpane

bed-wetting 8 enuresis

bee *food:* **6** nectar *glue:* **8** propolis *group:* **5** swarm **6** colony *house:* **4** hive **6** apiary *kind:* **5** drone, mason, queen **6** mining, sewing, worker **8** quilting, spelling **9** carpenter *nest:* **4** hive, skep *product:* **3** wax **5** honey *relating to:* **8** apiarian *wax cells:* **9** honeycomb

beechnuts 4 mast

beef 4 crab, fuss, meat **5** bitch, brawn, gripe **6** grouse, muscle **7** grumble **9** bellyache, complaint, grievance *cut:* **3** rib **4** loin, rump, side **5** chuck, flank, plate, round, shank **7** brisket, sirloin **10** tenderloin **11** porterhouse *grade:* **5** prime **6** choice **7** utility **8** standard **10** commercial *order:* **4** rare **6** medium **8** well-done

beefeater 5 guard **6** sentry, warder, yeoman

beefy 5 bulky, burly, hefty, husky, meaty **6** brawny, fleshy, robust, stocky, sturdy **7** massive **8** muscular, thickset **9** strapping **11** substantial

Beehive State 4 Utah

beekeeper 8 apiarist **12** apiculturist

beekeeping 10 apiculture

beeline 3 fly, nip, zip **4** race, whiz **5** hurry, speed **6** bullet, hasten, hustle, rocket **7** hotfoot **8** expedite, highball **10** make tracks **12** shortest path

Beelzebub 5 devil, fiend, Satan **6** diablo **7** Evil One, Lucifer, Old Nick, serpent **8** Apollyon **9** adversary, archfiend

beer 3 ale **4** bock, brew, suds **5** draft, lager, stout, weiss **6** porter **7** brewski, cerveza, pilsner **8** pilsener *vessel:* **3** mug **4** toby **5** stein **6** flagon, seidel **7** tankard **8** schooner **9** blackjack *drinking place:* **3** bar, inn, pub **6** saloon, tavern *ingredient:* **4** hops, malt **5** yeast **6** barley *maker:* **6** brewer *mythical inventor:* **9** Gambrinus *plant:* **7** brewery *Russian:* **5** kvass *Scottish:* **10** barley-bree

beer hall 3 pub **6** saloon, tavern **7** taproom **8** alehouse **11** public house, rathskeller

Beeri *daughter:* **6** Judith *son:* **5** Hosea

beet 5 chard **6** mangel, wurzel **10** Swiss chard *family:* **9** goosefoot

Beethoven, Ludwig van *birthplace:* **4** Bonn *opera:* **7** Fidelio *overture:* **6** Egmont **7** Leonore **10** Coriolanus, Prometheus *sonata:* **7** Tempest **8** Kreutzer **9** Moonlight, Waldstein **10** Pathétique **12** Appassionata *symphony:* **6** Choral, Eroica **8** Pastoral

beetle 3 bug, jut **5** bulge **6** insect, scarab, scurry **7** project **8** overhang, protrude, stand out, stick out *click:* **6** elater **7** firefly *dung:* **6** scarab **9** tumblebug *front wing:* **6** elytra (plural) **7** elytron *fruit-eating:* **8** curculio *insect-eating:* **7** ladybug **8** ladybird *kind:* **4** bean, dung, fire, June, stag **5** click, flour, grain, tiger, water **6** carpet, chafer, ground, May bug, museum **7** blister, cadelle, carabid, firefly, goldbug, goliath, June bug, vedalia **8** ambrosia, Japanese **9** longicorn, potato bug **10** cockchafer, rhinoceros *order:* **10** Coleoptera *snouted:* **6** weevil **7** billbug **8** curculio **9** wood borer *young:* **4** grub **5** larva **6** larvae (plural) **8** wireworm

beet soup 6 borsch **7** borscht

befall 3 hap **5** ensue, occur **6** betide, chance, follow, happen **7** come off, develop, fall out **8** happen to **9** come about, eventuate, transpire

befit 4 meet, suit **6** become, go with **9** agree with, chime with **10** accord with, be right for **11** be proper for

befitting 3 apt **4** just, meet **5** happy, right **6** decent, proper, seemly **7** correct **8** becoming, decorous, suitable **10** conforming, felicitous **11** appropriate, comme il faut

befog 3 dim **4** blur, hide, veil **5** bedim, blear, cloak, cloud, muddy **6** darken, puzzle **7** becloud, confuse, eclipse, envelop, obscure, perplex **8** bewilder, confound **9** obfuscate, overcloud **10** overshadow

befool 4 dupe, gull, hoax, play **5** cozen, trick **6** delude **7** chicane, deceive, mislead **8** hoodwink **9** bamboozle, victimize **11** hornswoggle

before 3 ere **4** ante, once, till, up to **5** ahead, until **6** facing, sooner, up till **7** ahead of, already, earlier, prior to **8** formerly **9** in advance, in front of, preceding **10** previously **11** in advance of *prefix:* **3** pre, pro **4** ante, fore

befoul 3 mar, tar **4** slur, soil **5** dirty, smear, spoil, sully, taint **6** defame, defile, malign, smudge **7** blacken, pollute, profane, spatter, tarnish, traduce **8** besmirch **9** bespatter, denigrate **10** adulterate **11** contaminate

befuddle 4 daze **5** addle, mix up **6** ball up, baffle, bemuse, muddle **7** confuse, fluster, perplex, stupefy **8** bewilder, confound, distract, throw off, **9** disorient

befuddlement 3 fog **4** daze, haze, maze **5** mix-up **6** muddle, stupor **9** confusion **10** perplexity, puzzlement **11** distraction

beg 3 ask, bum, dun, nag, sue **4** pray, urge **5** apply, brace, cadge, crave, evade, hit on, mooch, plead, press, worry **6** adjure, appeal, call on, demand, invoke, pester **7** beseech, besiege, conjure, entreat, implore, request, solicit **8** petition, sidestep **9** importune, panhandle **10** supplicate

beget 4 bear, sire **5** breed, bring, cause, forge, hatch, spawn, yield **6** create, effect, father **7** produce **8** engender, generate, multiply, result in **9** procreate, propagate, reproduce **10** bring about

beggar 4 hobo, defy, ruin **5** tramp **6** bummer, cadger, fellow, pauper, prayer, sponge, suitor **7** moocher, sponger **8** bankrupt, deadbeat, vagabond **9** overwhelm, pauperize, schnorrer, suppliant **10** down-and-out, freeloader, impoverish, panhandler, petitioner, supplicant **11** bindle stiff, supplicator **12** street person

beggared 4 flat, poor **5** broke, needy **6** ruined **7** drained **8** bankrupt, dirt poor, indigent, strapped, wiped out **9** destitute, insolvent, penniless, penurious, tapped out **10** pauperized **11** impecunious, overwhelmed **12** dispossessed, impoverished

beggarly 3 low **4** base, mean, poor **5** cheap, lowly, nasty, petty, sorry **6** cheesy, meager, measly, paltry, scanty, scurvy, shabby, shoddy, trashy **7** ignoble, miserly, pitiful, squalid **8** pitiable, inferior, wretched **9** miserable, niggardly **10** despicable, despisable **11** ignominious **12** contemptible, parsimonious

Beggar's Opera *music:* **7** Pepusch (John) *painting:* **7** Hogarth (William) *text:* **3** Gay (John)

beggarweed 6 dodder **9** knotgrass **11** tick trefoil

beggary 4 need, want **6** penury **7** bumming, cadging, poverty **8** mooching, pleading **9** indigence, neediness, pauperism, privation **10** meagerness, mendicancy **11** destitution, panhandling

begin 4 dawn, open, rise **5** arise, cause, dig in, enter, found, mount, set to, start **6** appear, attack, be born, broach, create, effect, emerge, get off, induce, invent, launch, spring, sprout, tackle, take up, tee off **7** break in, embark on, emanate, jump off, kick off, lead off, prepare, usher in **8** activate, commence, embark on, engender, initiate **9** establish, instigate, institute, introduce, originate **10** embark upon, inaugurate, issue forth **11** break ground

beginner 4 colt, tiro, tyro **6** newbie, new kid, novice, rookie **7** recruit, starter, student, trainee **8** freshman, neophyte, newcomer **9** fledgling, greenhorn, novitiate **10** apprentice, catechumen, tenderfoot **11** abecedarian

beginning 4 dawn, font, rise, root **5** alpha, basal, birth, fount, onset, start **6** day one, origin, outset, primal, source, spring **7** dawning, genesis, infancy, initial, kickoff, nascent, opening **8** creation, exordium, outstart, prologue, rudiment, simplest **9** elemental, emergence, inception, incipient **10** appearance, elementary, incipiency, initiative, initiatory, opening gun, rudimental **11** origination, rudimentary **12** commencement, inauguration, introductory

begird 3 hem **4** belt, bind, ring **5** beset, fence, hem in, round **6** circle, corral, girdle, immure **7** confine, enclose, wreathe **8** encircle, engirdle, surround **9** encompass **12** circumscribe

beg off 5 demur, welsh **6** bow out, cop out, opt out, pass up, refuse, renege **7** back out, bail out, decline, drop out, pull out **8** back down, withdraw

begone 5 leave, scram, split **6** beat it, decamp, depart, get out **7** buzz off, get lost, skiddoo, take off, vamoose **8** clear out, hightail, shove off **9** skedaddle **10** make tracks

begrime 3 tar **4** foul, soil, spot **5** dirty, muddy, smear, spoil, sully, taint **6** defile, mess up, muck up, smirch, smooch, smudge, smutch **7** blacken, corrupt, pollute, tarnish **8** besmirch **11** contaminate

begrudge 4 envy **6** resent

beguile 3 con **4** draw, dupe, fool, hoax, lure, play, snow, wile **5** bluff, charm, fleet, trick **6** beckon, betray, delude, divert, entice, humbug, seduce, take in **7** attract, bewitch, deceive, enchant, engross, exploit, finesse, mislead **8** distract, hoodwink, intrigue, maneuver **9** captivate, fascinate, while away **10** manipulate **11** double-cross

beguiling 4 wily **5** false **6** artful, subtle **8** alluring, deluding, delusive, delusory **9** deceitful, deceiving, deceptive, insidious, seductive **10** bewitching, chimerical, enchanting, fallacious, misleading **11** enthralling

Behan's autobiography 10 Borstal Boy

behave 3 act, run **5** carry, react **6** acquit, be good, deport, direct, manage **7** comport, conduct, disport, perform **8** function

behavior 3 act, air, way **4** mien, tone, ways **6** action, aspect, custom, habits, manner **7** bearing, conduct **8** demeanor, presence, response **10** deportment **11** comportment

behead 4 head, kill **7** execute **9** decollate **10** decapitate, guillotine

beheaded noblewoman 8 Jane Grey (Lady) **9** Catherine (Howard) **10** Anne Boleyn

behemoth 5 giant, jumbo, whale **7** goliath, mammoth, monster **8** colossus **9** leviathan **11** monstrosity

behemothic 4 huge **5** jumbo **7** mammoth, massive, titanic **8** colossal, gigantic, towering **9** Herculean, monstrous **10** gargantuan **11** elephantine

behest 3 say **4** will, wish, word, writ **5** edict, order **6** charge, demand, urging **7** bidding, command, dictate, mandate, precept, request **9** direction, enjoinder, ordinance, prescript, prompting **10** injunction **11** commandment, exhortation, instruction **12** solicitation

behind 3 can **4** late, next, rump **5** after, fanny **6** back of, bottom, heinie **7** backing **8** backside, buttocks, derriere, trailing **9** following, posterior **10** supporting **12** subsequent to *prefix:* **4** post **5** retro

behindhand 3 lax **4** late, slow **5** slack, tardy **6** in debt, lesser, remiss **7** belated, delayed, laggard, overdue **8** backward, careless, derelict, sluggish **9** in arrears, negligent, unmindful **10** delinquent, neglectful, regardless, unpunctual **11** subordinate, undeveloped **13** unprogressive

behold 3 see **4** espy, note, view **6** descry, notice **7** discern, observe, witness *French:* **5** voilà *Latin:* **4** ecce

beholden 5 bound **7** obliged **8** grateful, indebted **9** duty-bound, obligated

beholder 4 seer **6** gawker, viewer **7** watcher, witness **8** observer, onlooker, passerby **9** bystander, spectator **10** eyewitness **12** rubbernecker

beige 3 tan **4** buff, ecru **7** vanilla

being 3 man **4** body, life, self, soul **5** human, stuff, thing **6** entity, matter, mortal, nature, object, person, spirit **7** essence **8** creature, existent, material **9** actuality, character, existence, personage, something, substance **10** individual **11** personality **12** essentiality **13** individuality

bejeweled 7 studded **8** sequined, spangled **9** encrusted **10** bespangled, gem-studded, ornamented

Bel *Sumerian counterpart:* **5** Enlil *wife:* **5** Belit **6** Beltis

Bel ___ 3 Air **5** Paese

bel ___ 5 canto **6** esprit

Bela *father:* 4 Beor 8 Benjamin *son:* 3 Ard

belabor 4 beat, drub, flog 5 baste, pound, scold 6 batter, berate, buffet, pummel, thrash, wallop 7 lambast, scourge, tell off, upbraid 8 chastise, lambaste, tear into 9 criticize, fulminate, overstate 10 flagellate 11 overexplain

Belarus *capital:* 5 Minsk *city:* 6 Homyel 7 Vitebsk 8 Mahilyow 9 Vitsyebsk *language:* 7 Russian 10 Belarusian 11 Belarussian *monetary unit:* 5 rubel, ruble *neighbor:* 6 Latvia, Poland, Russia 7 Ukraine 9 Lithuania *river:* 3 Bug 5 Neman 7 Dnieper, Pripyat

belated 4 late, slow 5 tardy 6 remiss 7 delayed, laggard, overdue 10 behindhand, behind time, unpunctual

Belau see PALAU

belch 4 burp, emit, gush, spew, vent, void 5 eject, eruct, erupt, expel, issue, spout, spurt, vomit 6 hiccup, irrupt 7 explode, extrude 8 disgorge 10 eructation 11 expectorate

beldam 3 hag 5 crone 8 old woman

beleaguer 3 bug, dog, hem, nag, vex 4 gnaw 5 annoy, beset, harry, hound, siege, storm, tease, worry 6 assail, attack, badger, bother, fall on, harass, invest, pester, plague 7 bedevil, besiege, hagride, put upon, set upon, trouble 8 blockade, fall upon

belfry 7 steeple 8 carillon 9 bell tower, campanile *dweller:* 3 bat

Belgium *capital:* 8 Brussels *city:* 4 Gent 5 Ghent, Liège 7 Antwerp 9 Charleroi *ethnic group:* 7 Fleming, Flemish, Walloon *language:* 5 Dutch 7 Flemish *monetary unit:* 4 euro *neighbor:* 6 France 7 Germany 10 Luxembourg 11 Netherlands *plain:* 8 Flanders *port:* 7 Antwerp 8 Oostende *river:* 4 Yser 5 Meuse 7 Schlede *sea:* 5 North

belie 4 deny, hide, warp 5 color, twist 6 expose, doctor, garble 7 conceal, confute, distort, falsify, gainsay, pervert, trump up 8 confront, denounce, disagree, disguise, disprove, miscolor, misstate, negative 9 disaffirm, gloss over, repudiate 10 contradict, contravene, controvert 11 dissimulate 12 misrepresent

belief 3 ism 4 idea, mind, view 5 axiom, credo, creed, dogma, faith, hunch, tenet, trust 6 assent, avowal, credit, surety, theory, thesis 7 concept, feeling, opinion, precept, surmise, theorem 8 credence, doctrine, firmness, religion, sureness 9 assurance, certainty, certitude, intuition, postulate, principle,

sentiment 10 acceptance, assumption, confidence, contention, conviction, hypothesis, impression, persuasion 11 supposition

believable 5 solid, sound, valid 6 cogent, likely, smooth, steady, trusty 7 logical, swaying, tenable, up front 8 credible, possible, probable, rational, reliable 9 authentic, colorable, plausible 10 convincing, creditable, impressive, meaningful, persuasive, presumable, reasonable, satisfying, supposable 11 conceivable, substantial, trustworthy 12 satisfactory

believe 3 buy 4 deem, hold, know 5 lap up, think, trust 6 accept, affirm, assume, credit, expect, reckon 7 fall for, imagine, profess, suppose, suspect, swallow 8 conceive, consider 10 conjecture, presuppose, understand

belittle 3 cut, pan 5 abuse, decry, knock, scorn 6 deride, insult, jeer at, revile 7 cut down, put down, run down, sneer at 8 bad-mouth, derogate, diminish, discount, minimize, write off 9 criticize, discredit, disparage, dispraise, downgrade, underrate 10 depreciate, undervalue 13 underestimate

belittlement 5 abuse, scorn 7 calumny, jeering, scandal, slander 8 derision, ridicule 9 aspersion 10 backbiting, defamation, detraction 11 denigration 12 backstabbing, depreciation 13 disparagement

Belize *capital:* 8 Belmopan *city:* 10 Belize City *ethnic group:* 4 Maya 5 Mayan *language:* 7 English, Spanish *monetary unit:* 6 dollar *mountain:* 8 Victoria *neighbor:* 6 Mexico 9 Guatemala *river:* 5 Hondo *sea:* 9 Caribbean

bell 4 peal 5 chime, knell 6 tocsin

belle 5 siren 6 beauty, eyeful 7 charmer 8 knockout, ornament 11 enchantress, femme fatale

Bellerophon *father:* 7 Glaucus 8 Poseidon *grandfather:* 8 Sisyphus *horse:* 7 Pegasus *victim:* 7 Chimera

belles lettres 10 literature

belletrist 8 novelist 4 poet 6 author, writer 9 dramatist 10 playwright

bellflower 9 campanula

___ **belli** 5 casus

bellicose 6 ornery 7 hawkish, hostile, martial, scrappy, warlike 8 factious, fighting, militant 9 assertive, combative, truculent 10 aggressive, pugnacious, rebellious 11 belligerent, contentious, hot-tempered, quarrelsome 12 disputatious, gladiatorial

belligerence 5 fight 6 attack, enmity, rancor, spleen 7 ill will 9 hostility, mili-

tancy, petulance, pugnacity **10** aggression, antagonism, truculence **11** bellicosity **12** churlishness **13** combativeness
belligerent 6 ardent, fierce **7** fighter, hostile, scrappy, soldier, warlike, warring, warrior **8** battling, churlish, fighting, invading, militant, opponent, petulant **9** aggressor, attacking, bellicose, combatant, combative, disputant, splenetic, truculent **10** aggressive, antagonist, pugnacious **11** contentious, hot-tempered, quarrelsome **12** antagonistic, disputatious
Bellini *opera:* **5** Norma **6** Pirata (II) **8** Puritani (I) **10** Sonnambula (La) *sleepwalker:* **5** Amina
bell metal 6 bronze
bellow 3 bay, cry, moo **4** bark, bawl, bray, howl, roar, rout, yowl **5** shout **6** clamor, holler **7** bluster
Bellow character 4 Rose (Billy) **5** Chick **6** Herzog (Moses E.) **7** Citrine (Charlie), Sammler (Arthur) **8** Humboldt, Fonstein (Harry) **9** Henderson **10** Ravelstein (Abe), Augie March
bell ringer 6 toller **9** Quasimodo **12** carillonneur **13** campanologist
bell ringing 11 campanology
bell-shaped 11 campanulate
bell sound 4 bong, boom, ding, dong, peal, ring, ting, toll **5** chime, clang, knell **6** tinkle
bell tower 6 belfry **7** clocher **8** carillon **9** campanile
___ **bellum 4** ante, post
bellwether 4 dean, lead **5** doyen, guide, pilot **6** leader **7** pioneer **8** lodestar **9** harbinger **10** forerunner **11** trend setter
belly 3 gut, pot **5** tummy **6** paunch, venter **7** abdomen, midriff, stomach **9** bay window **10** front porch, midsection **11** breadbasket *Scottish:* **4** wame
bellyache 4 beef, carp, crab, fret, fuss, moan, yawp **5** bitch, bleat, colic, gripe, whine **6** grouse, snivel, squawk, yammer **7** grumble **8** complain **11** let off steam **12** collywobbles
bellyacher 4 crab **5** crank **6** griper, grouch, whiner **7** grouser **8** grumbler, sourpuss **10** complainer, crosspatch, malcontent **11** faultfinder
belly button 5 navel
belong 3 fit, set **4** suit, vest **5** agree, apply, befit, chime, fit in, match, tally **6** accord, attach, become, reside **7** pertain **9** correlate, harmonize **10** correspond
belongings 3 kit **4** gear **5** goods, stuff **6** assets, estate, legacy, things **7** baggage, effects **8** chattels, movables, property **9** patrimony **11** attachments,

impedimenta, inheritance, possessions **13** appurtenances
beloved 3 pet **4** baby, beau, dear, idol, love **5** flame, honey, lover, swain, sweet **6** adored, steady **7** darling, dearest, dear one, doted on, sweetie **8** favorite, idolized, ladylove, old flame, precious, truelove **9** boyfriend, cherished, inamorata, treasured **10** girlfriend, heartthrob, sweetheart, sweetie pie
below 5 infra, under **7** beneath **10** underneath *prefix:* **3** sub **5** infra
belt 3 bat, bop **4** area, band, bash, biff, blow, gird, loop, ring, sash, slug, sock, whap, whop, zone **5** smack, smash, strap, strip **6** begird, cestus, circle, engird, girdle, region, wallop **7** baldric, clobber, stretch **8** begirdle, ceinture, cincture, encircle, engirdle **9** bandoleer, bandolier, territory, waistband **10** cummerbund *celestial:* **6** zodiac
beltway 8 ring road
Belus *brother:* **6** Agenor *daughter:* **4** Dido *father:* **7** Neptune **8** Poseidon *mother:* **5** Libya *son:* **6** Danaus **7** Cepheus, Phineus **8** Aegyptus
belvedere 6 alcove, cupola, gazebo, pagoda **7** balcony, terrace **10** widow's walk **11** garden house, summerhouse, observatory
bemedaled 9 decorated **10** beribboned
bemired 4 miry, oozy **5** boggy, dirty, grimy, gummy, gunky, muddy, stuck **6** filthy, soiled, swampy **7** swamped
bemoan 3 rue **4** wail, weep **6** bewail, grieve, lament, oppose, regret **7** deplore **8** complain, object to **10** sorrow over **12** disapprove of
bemuse 4 daze **5** addle **6** absorb, muddle, puzzle **7** confuse, mystify, nonplus, perplex **8** bewilder, distract **10** disconcert
bemused 3 wry **4** lost **6** absent, remote **7** faraway **8** distrait **9** distraite **10** abstracted, distracted **11** preoccupied **12** absentminded **13** lost in thought
bench 5 court **6** settee, settle, thwart **7** counter **8** platform **9** worktable *church:* **3** pew *outdoor:* **6** exedra *upholstered:* **9** banquette
benchmark 4 norm **5** basis, gauge, guide, model, scale **7** measure **8** exemplar, paradigm, standard **9** criterion, guideline, milestone, yardstick **10** touchstone
bend 3 arc, bow, sag **4** arch, bank, cave, curl, flex, hang, hook, lean, mold, sway, tend, tilt, turn, veer, warp **5** angle, crook, curve, round, shape, shift, stoop, twist, yield **6** compel, cor-

ner, buckle, direct, double, fasten,
kowtow, subdue, submit, zigzag
7 deflect, dispose, distort, flexure, turning 8 lean over 9 curvature, deviation,
genuflect 10 compromise, predispose

bendable 5 lithe 6 limber, pliant, supple
7 elastic, plastic, pliable 8 flexible,
moldable 9 malleable, tractable
11 manipulable

bender see BINGE

___ **bene** 4 nota

beneath 5 below, under *prefix:* 3 hyp,
sub 4 hypo 5 infra

___ **Benedict** 4 eggs

benediction 4 boon, okay 5 favor, grace
6 orison, thanks 7 benefit, benison,
godsend 8 approval, blessing 9 advantage 11 approbation 12 consecration,
thanksgiving

benefaction 4 alms, care, fund, gift, help
5 favor, grant 6 relief 7 charity, comfort, handout, largess, service, subsidy
8 donation, largesse, oblation, offering,
windfall 9 endowment, patronage
10 assistance 12 contribution, ministra-
tion

benefactor 5 angel, donor 6 backer,
patron 7 grantor, sponsor 9 supporter,
sustainer 11 contributor, underwriter

beneficence see BENEFACTION

beneficent 4 kind 6 benign, caring, giving 8 generous 10 altruistic, bighearted,
charitable, ungrudging 11 kindhearted,
magnanimous 13 compassionate, philanthropic

beneficial 4 good 5 brave, tonic
6 benign, toward, useful 7 helpful
8 favoring, salutary, valuable 9 favorable, healthful, nurturing, wholesome
10 profitable, propitious, salubrious
12 advantageous, constructive

beneficiary 4 heir 5 donee, payee
7 grantee, heiress, legatee 8 assignee
9 inheritor, recipient

beneficiate 5 treat 6 reduce 7 prepare,
process

benefit 3 aid 4 boon, gain, good, help,
perk, sake 5 avail, extra, favor, serve
6 assist, behalf, better, profit, relief,
succor 7 account, advance, charity, further, godsend, improve, promote,
relieve, welfare 8 blessing, interest
9 advantage, well-being 10 ameliorate,
fund-raiser, prosperity 11 good fortune
12 contribute to

benevolence 4 boon, gift, help 5 amity,
favor, grant 6 comity, relief 7 caritas,
charity 8 altruism, clemency, goodness,
goodwill, humanity, kindness 10 compassion, compliment, kindliness
11 magnanimity

benevolent 4 good, kind, warm 6 caring,
do-good, humane, kindly 7 helpful, liberal 8 generous, tolerant 10 altruistic,
beneficent, bighearted, charitable,
openhanded 11 considerate, magnanimous, warmhearted 12 eleemosynary,
humanitarian 13 compassionate, philanthropic, tenderhearted

Ben Hur *author:* 7 Wallace (Lew)

benighted 6 obtuse, unread 8 backward,
ignorant, untaught 9 untutored, unwitting 10 illiterate, uneducated, uninformed, unlettered, unschooled
11 know-nothing 12 uncultivated
13 unenlightened, unprogressive

benign 4 kind, mild 6 genial, gentle,
humane, kindly, mellow 7 amiable,
clement 8 gracious, harmless, merciful,
pleasant 9 favorable, fortunate, healthful, temperate, wholesome 10 auspicious, benevolent, charitable, forbearing, propitious, remediable
11 good-hearted 12 noncancerous

Benin *capital:* 9 Porto-Novo *city:* 7 Cotonou *coast:* 5 Slave *ethnic group:* 3 Fon
6 Fulani, Yoruba *former name:*
7 Dahomey *language:* 3 Fon 6 French
monetary unit: 5 franc *neighbor:* 4 Togo
5 Niger 7 Nigeria 11 Burkina Faso *river:*
5 Ouémé

benison 5 grace 8 blessing 11 benediction 12 consecration

Benjamin *brother:* 6 Joseph *father:*
5 Jacob *mother:* 6 Rachel

bent 3 set 4 bias, gift 5 arced, bowed,
flair, knack 6 arched, curved, intent,
talent 7 decided, faculty, leaning 8 aptitude, capacity, penchant, resolute,
resolved, tendency 10 determined, proclivity, propensity 11 disposition, inclination 12 predilection

benumb 4 daze, dull, stun 5 blunt, chill
6 deaden, freeze 7 petrify, stupefy
8 etherize, paralyze 10 immobilize
11 desensitize

benumbed 4 cold 6 frozen 9 unfeeling
10 insensible 11 insensitive 12 anesthetized

Beowulf *drink:* 4 mead *monster:* 7 Grendel

bequeath 4 gift, will 5 endow, grant,
leave 6 bestow, commit, confer, devise,
hand on, impart, legate, pass on 7 furnish, present 8 hand down, make over,
transmit

bequest 3 lot 4 gift 5 share, trust
6 devise, estate, legacy 7 portion 8 heritage 10 settlement 11 inheritance

berate 3 jaw 4 rail, rate 5 chide, scold
6 rebuke, revile 7 bawl out, chew out,
condemn, reprove, tell off, upbraid

8 admonish, chastise, reproach **9** castigate, criticize, reprimand **10** tonguelash, vituperate

berceuse 7 lullaby **10** cradlesong

bereave 3 rob **4** lose **5** seize, strip **6** divest, remove **7** deprive **8** take away **10** confiscate, disinherit, dispossess **11** appropriate, requisition

bereaved 8 mourning **9** sorrowful, sorrowing **10** distressed **11** heartbroken **13** grief-stricken

bereavement 3 rue, woe **4** loss **5** dolor, grief **6** misery, pining, regret, sorrow **7** anguish, despair, remorse, sadness **8** grieving, mourning **9** dejection, heartache **10** affliction, depression, desolation **11** deprivation, despondency, lamentation, tribulation

bereft 5 shorn **6** devoid, robbed **7** fleeced, forlorn, wanting **8** beggared, deprived, desolate, divested, stripped **9** destitute **10** despondent **12** disconsolate, dispossessed, impoverished

Bergen's dummy 7 Charlie (McCarthy) **8** Mortimer (Snerd)

Berger novel 12 Little Big Man

Bergman role 4 Ilsa

berm 4 path **5** ledge, mound, shelf **8** shoulder

Bermuda *capital:* **8** Hamilton *territory of:* **7** Britain

Bernice *brother:* **7** Agrippa *father:* **5** Herod *husband:* **6** Polemo *lover:* **5** Titus **9** Vespasian

berry 5 cubeb, fruit, grape **7** currant, madrona, madrone **8** allspice **9** saskatoon

berserk 3 ape **4** amok **5** amuck, crazy **6** crazed, insane **7** bonkers, lunatic **8** demented, deranged, frenzied

berth 3 bed, cot **4** dock, moor, pier, port, post, quay, slip, spot **5** cabin, jetty, levee, place, wharf **6** billet, office **8** position **9** anchorage, situation **10** connection **11** appointment, compartment **13** accommodation

beseech see BEG

beset 3 dog, hem, try, vex **4** gird, ring **5** harry, hem in, storm, worry **6** assail, attack, badger, circle, fall on, harass, infest, pester, plague, strike **7** assault, besiege, overrun, trouble, torture **8** blockade, encircle, fall upon, surround **9** beleaguer, encompass, overswarm

besetment 3 nag **4** bane, pain, pest **5** curse, trial **6** blight, bother, gadfly, pester, plague **7** torment **8** irritant, nuisance, vexation **9** annoyance **10** affliction, botherment, holy terror **11** aggravation, botheration

besetting 6 urgent **7** driving **8** dominant **9** obsessive **10** compelling, persistent **11** omnipresent **12** overwhelming

beside 4 near, nigh **6** next to

besides 3 too **4** also, else, plus, save **5** added, extra **6** and all, as well, beyond, except, to boot **7** barring, farther, further, without **8** as well as, likewise, moreover, more than **9** aside from, along with, exceeding, excluding, other than, otherwise, outside of **10** in addition **11** exclusive of, furthermore, not counting **12** additionally, together with

besiege 3 nag **4** ring, trap **5** beset, hem in, hound **6** assail, attack, circle, girdle, harass, pester, plague **7** assault, confine, environ, trouble **8** blockade, encircle, surround **9** beleaguer, encompass

besmear see SMEAR

besmirch 4 blot, foul, slur, soil **5** dirty, libel, stain, sully, taint **6** defile, damage, impugn, malign **7** asperse, slander, tarnish **8** disgrace, dishonor

besom material 5 twigs

besotted 5 dotty, drunk **7** charmed, muddled, smitten **8** enamored **9** enchanted **10** captivated, fascinated, infatuated, spellbound **11** intoxicated

bespatter see SPATTER

bespeak 3 ask **4** book, hire, show **5** imply **6** accost, attest, desire, evince, reveal **7** address, apply to, betoken, connote, lecture, portend, request, reserve, signify, solicit, suggest, testify, witness **8** announce, approach, foretell, indicate, intimate, petition **9** preengage **10** prearrange

bespoke 8 tailored **10** custom-made

best 3 gem, top **4** beat, pick, tops **5** cream, elite, excel, model, outdo, pride, prime, prize **6** choice, defeat, exceed, finest **7** conquer, leading, optimal, optimum, paragon, premium, supreme, surpass **8** exemplar, foremost, greatest, nonesuch, outshine, outstrip, overcome **9** matchless, nonpareil, number-one, paramount, transcend, unequaled **11** outstanding **12** incomparable *combining form:* **6** aristo

bestial 4 vile, wild **5** brute, cruel, feral **6** animal, brutal, carnal, fierce, malign, savage **7** beastly, brutish, inhuman, swinish, vicious **8** depraved, inhumane **9** ferocious **10** degenerate

bestialize 4 ruin, warp **5** abase **6** debase, defile **7** corrupt, debauch, degrade, deprave, pervert, pollute, subvert, vitiate, violate **9** brutalize **10** bastardize, demoralize

bestir 3 fly, rip 4 dash, flit, goad, race, rush, spur, stir, tear, urge, wake, whet 5 rally, rouse, scoot, waken, whirl 6 arouse, awaken, hasten, hustle, kindle 8 get going, scramble 9 challenge

bestow 4 give 5 apply, award, grant 6 confer, devote, donate, lavish 7 hand out, present 8 bequeath, give away *Scottish:* 7 propine

bestower 5 donor, giver 6 patron 7 donator 8 altruist 9 conferrer, patroness, presenter 10 benefactor 12 benefactress 13 good Samaritan

bestrew 3 dot, sow 6 pepper, shower 7 diffuse, disject, scatter, speckle, stipple 8 disperse, sprinkle 9 broadcast, interlard 10 distribute 11 disseminate

bestride 5 mount, tower 8 dominate, loom over, straddle 9 stand over

bet 3 pot 4 ante, game, play, risk, shot 5 put on, stake, wager 6 gamble, hazard, parlay, pledge 7 lay odds, venture *racing:* 6 exacta 8 perfecta, quinella, quiniela *taker:* 6 bookie

Betelgeuse 4 star *constellation:* 5 Orion

betel palm 5 areca

bête noire 4 hate, ruin 5 trial 6 animus, horror 7 bugbear, scourge, torment, undoing 8 anathema, aversion, downfall 9 ruination 10 black beast

bethink 4 cite, mind 6 call up, recall, remind, retain, review, revive 7 flash on 8 hark back, look back, remember, summon up 9 conjure up, recollect, reminisce 10 call to mind, retrospect

Bethuel *daughter:* 7 Rebekah *father:* 5 Nahor *mother:* 6 Milcah *son:* 5 Laban *uncle:* 7 Abraham

betide 4 fall 5 break, ensue, occur 6 befall, chance, happen 7 come off, develop, fall out 8 commence 9 come about, transpire

betimes 4 anon, soon 5 early 6 pronto, seldom, timely 7 too soon 8 directly, far ahead, fitfully, promptly 9 presently 10 before long, now and then, on occasion, seasonably 11 prematurely 12 occasionally, sporadically

betoken 4 bode, omen, show, warn 5 argue, augur 6 attest, denote, hint at 7 bespeak, point to, portend, presage, promise, signify, suggest, testify, witness 8 announce, forebode, evidence, foreshow, foretell, indicate, intimate, prophesy 9 prefigure 10 foreshadow 13 prognosticate

betray 4 dupe, jilt, name, sell, show, tell, trap 5 bluff, cheat, knife, rat on, snare, spill, split 6 delude, desert, entrap, evince, finger, inform, reveal, seduce, take in, tattle, tell on, turn in, unmask,

unveil 7 abandon, beguile, betoken, deceive, divulge, ensnare, forsake, let down, let slip, mislead, sell out, traduce, uncover 8 blurt out, denounce, disclose, discover, evidence, give away, indicate, manifest 9 deliver up 10 apostatize, break faith, lead astray 11 demonstrate, double-cross 13 inform against

betrayal 4 leak 7 perfidy, treason 8 exposure 9 duplicity, falseness, Judas kiss, treachery 10 disclosure, infidelity, revelation 13 faithlessness

betrayer 3 rat 4 fink, nark 5 Judas 6 snitch 7 stoolie, tattler, traitor 8 apostate, defector, informer, quisling, renegade, squealer, turncoat 10 talebearer, tattletale 11 backstabber, stool pigeon

betroth 3 wed 5 marry 6 pledge 7 espouse 8 affiance

betrothal 6 pledge 8 espousal 10 engagement

betrothed 6 fiancé 7 engaged, fiancée, pledged 8 intended, plighted, promised, wife-to-be 9 affianced, bride-to-be, spoken for 10 contracted 11 husband-to-be

better 3 fix, top, win 4 beat, help, mend, more, well 5 amend, cured, elder, excel, finer, outdo 6 exceed, fitter, repair 7 advance, correct, enhance, further, greater, improve, largest, mending, rectify, success, surpass, triumph, victory 8 greatest, improved, outshine, outstrip, stronger, superior, whip hand, worthier 9 advantage, desirable, excellent, healthier, improving, meliorate, preferred, transcend, upper hand 10 ameliorate, preferable, preferably, recovering, surpassing

bettor 7 gambler, wagerer

between 4 amid 5 among, twixt 6 within 7 betwixt *prefix:* 5 inter, intra

betweentimes 11 at intervals

bevel 4 bias, cant 5 angle, grade, slant, slope 7 chamfer, incline, oblique 8 diagonal

beverage 3 ade, nog, pop, tea 4 cola, maté, milk, soda 5 cider, cocoa, drink, juice, mocha, shake 6 coffee, eggnog, frappe, malted, nectar 7 potable, soda pop 8 lemonade, libation, potation 9 drinkable, milk shake *alcoholic:* 3 ale, gin, rum 4 beer, grog, mead, wine 5 cider, julep, negus, punch, stout, toddy, vodka 6 bishop, brandy, caudle, cooler, liquor, rickey, shandy, sherry, whisky 7 liqueur, martini, sangria, tequila, whiskey 8 cocktail, highball, sillabub, syllabub, vermouth *Arab:* 4 arak 6 arrack *Australasian:* 4 kava *Balkan:* 9 slivovitz *British:* 5 perry, stout *carbonated:* 4 cola, soda 6 rickey 7 soda pop 8 root beer 9 ginger ale *central Asian:* 6 kumiss 7 koumiss *Dutch:* 7 schnaps 8 schnapps *from milk:* 5 kefir 6 kumiss 7 koumiss *Greek:* 4 ouzo 7 retsina *Irish:* 6 poteen 10 usquebaugh *medicinal:* 6 elixir *Mexican:* 6 pulque 7 tequila *of the gods:* 6 nectar *Oriental:* 4 arak, sake, saki 6 arrack *Russian:* 5 kefir, kvass, vodka *Scottish:* 6 scotch *South American:* 4 maté 5 yerba 9 yerba maté *Swedish:* 5 glogg *Turkish:* 4 raki *West Indies:* 3 rum

bevy 3 mob 4 band, club, crew, gang, herd, knot, pack 5 bunch, covey, crowd, drove, flock, group, horde, party, swarm 6 clutch, gaggle, troupe 7 cluster, company, coterie 8 assembly 9 menagerie, multitude 10 assemblage, collection

bewail 3 rue 4 keen, moan, weep 5 mourn 6 bemoan, grieve, lament, regret 7 deplore

beware 4 heed, mark, mind, note, shun 5 avoid, watch 6 attend, notice 7 look out 8 take heed, watch out

bewhiskered 5 bushy 7 bearded, goateed, hirsute, stubbly 8 unshaven

bewilder 3 fog 4 daze, stun 5 addle, amaze, befog, mix up, stump 6 baffle, ball up, bemuse, fuddle, muddle, puzzle, rattle 7 confuse, fluster, mystify, nonplus, perplex, stumble 8 befuddle, confound, distract 9 disorient, dumbfound 10 disconcert

bewilderment 3 awe 4 daze 6 wonder 8 surprise 9 amazement, confusion 10 perplexity, puzzlement 11 distraction 12 astonishment, discomfiture, stupefaction 13 consternation

bewitch 3 hex 4 draw, pull, snow, take, wile 5 charm, spell, trick 6 allure, dazzle, seduce, voodoo 7 attract, bedevil, beguile, control, delight, enchant, possess 8 demonize, ensorcel, enthrall, entrance, intrigue, overlook 9 captivate, enrapture, ensorcell, fascinate, hypnotize, magnetize, mesmerize, spellbind

bewitching 4 foxy 5 siren 8 alluring, charming, engaging, enticing, magnetic, mesmeric 9 seductive 10 attractive 12 irresistible

bewitchment 3 hex 4 jinx 5 charm, magic, spell 6 trance 7 evil eye, sorcery 8 black art, wizardry 9 conjuring 10 necromancy 11 conjuration, enchantment, incantation, thaumaturgy

beyond 4 over, past 5 above, after 6 across, beside, yonder 7 besides, further, outside 8 as well as 9 afterlife, hereafter, otherwise 10 afterworld 12 over and above *prefix:* 4 meta, over, para 5 extra, hyper, super, trans, ultra 6 preter

Bhutan *capital:* 7 Thimphu *ethnic group:* 6 Bhutia 8 Assamese, Nepalese 9 Mongolian, Sharcrops *language:* 8 Dzongkha *monetary unit:* 8 ngultrum *mountain range:* 8 Himalaya 13 Great Himalaya *neighbor:* 5 China, India, Tibet *plain:* 5 Duars

bias 4 bend, bent, skew, sway, tilt, turn 5 angle, bevel, slant 7 beveled, bigotry, dispose, distort, incline, leaning, oblique, slanted 8 diagonal, penchant, slanting, tendency 9 crosswise, inclining, influence, prejudice, proneness, viewpoint 10 diagonally, favoritism, partiality, propensity, predispose, prepossess, proclivity, standpoint, transverse 11 disposition, inclination 12 onesidedness, predilection 13 preconception

biased 6 racist, swayed, unfair, warped 7 bigoted, colored, partial, slanted 8 disposed, inclined, one-sided, partisan, slanting 9 jaundiced, sectarian, unneutral 10 influenced, interested, prejudiced 11 opinionated, predisposed, tendentious

bibelot 5 curio 6 bauble, gewgaw, trifle 7 memento, novelty, trinket, whatnot 8 gimcrack, ornament 9 objet d'art 10 knickknack

Bible *abbreviation:* 3 Col, Cor, Dan, Eph, Gal, Gen, Hab, Heb, Hos, Jas, Jer, Jon, Lam, Lev, Mal, Mic, Neh, Num, Pet, Rev, Rom, Sam, Tim, Tit 4 Deut, Ezek, Josh, Judg, Obad, Phil, Prov, Zech, Zeph 5 Chron, Thess 6 Eccles, Philem *Apocrypha book:* 5 Tobit 6 Baruch, Esdras, Esther, Judith 7 Susanna 8 Manasseh, Manasses 9 Maccabees *New Testament book:* 4 Acts, John, Jude, Luke, Mark 5 James, Peter, Titus 6 Romans 7 Hebrews, Matthew, Timothy 8 Philemon 9 Ephesians, Galatians 10 Colossians, Revelation 11 Corinthians, Philippians 13 Thessalonians *Old Testament book:* 3 Job 4 Amos, Ezra, Joel, Ruth 5 Hosea, Jonah, Kings, Micah, Nahum 6 Daniel, Esther, Exodus, Haggai, Isaiah, Joshua, Judges, Psalms, Samuel 7 Ezekiel, Genesis, Malachi, Numbers, Obadiah 8 Habakkuk, Jeremiah, Nehemiah, Proverbs 9 Leviticus, Zechariah, Zephaniah 10 Chronicles 11 Deuteronomy 12 Ecclesiastes, Lamentations 13 Song of Solomon *part:* 4 book

5 verse 7 chapter 9 testament *translator:*
4 Knox (Ronald Arbuthnott) 5 Eliot
(John) 6 Jerome, Luther (Martin)
7 Erasmus (Desiderius), Tyndale
(William), Zwingli (Huldrych)
8 Andrewes (Lancelot), Wycliffe (John)
9 Coverdale (Miles) *version:* 5 Douay
6 Coptic, Gothic, Syriac 7 Vulgate
9 Jerusalem, King James, Masoretic
10 New English, Septuagint
Biblical *animal:* 8 behemoth *ascetic
order:* 6 Essene *battle:* 7 Jericho *battle
site:* 10 Armageddon *charioteer:* 4 Jehu
city, town: 4 Cana, Gaza, Tyre, Zoar
5 Endor, Gólan, Haifa, Joppa, Sidon,
Sodom 6 Asshur, Bethel, Emmaus, Gil-
gal, Hebron, Mizpah, Shiloh, Smyrna,
Tarsus 7 Antioch, Baalbec, Bethany,
Corinth, Ephesus, Ephraim, Jericho,
Magdala, Nineveh, Samaria 8 Caesarea,
Damascus, Gomorrah, Nazareth,
Philippi, Tiberias 9 Beersheba, Bethle-
hem, Capernaum, Jerusalem *coin:* (see
at HEBREW) *desert:* 5 Sinai *garden:*
4 Eden 8 Paradise *giant:* 7 Goliath *giant
slayer:* 5 David *hill:* 4 Zion 7 Calvary
hunter: 6 Nimrod *judge:* 3 Eli 4 Ehud
6 Gideon, Samson, Samuel 7 Deborah,
Jephtha 8 Jephthah *king:* 3 Asa 4 Ahab,
Amon, Elah, Jehu, Saul 5 David,
Herod, Hiram 6 Josiah 7 Azariah,
Menahem, Solomon 8 Hezekiah, Jer-
oboam, Manasseh, Rehoboam, Zedeki-
ah 9 Zechariah 11 Jehoshaphat *land:*
3 Nod 4 Aram, Elam, Moab, Seba
5 Judah, Judea 6 Canaan, Goshen,
Israel 7 Chaldea, Galilee, Samaria
9 Palestine *land of plenty:* 6 Goshen
measure: (see at HEBREW) *mountain:*
5 Horeb, Sinai 6 Ararat, Carmel,
Gilboa, Gilead, Hermon, Moriah,
Olivet, Pisgah 7 Lebanon *name:* 3 Asa,
Bel, Dan, Eli, Eve, Gad, Ham, Ira, Job,
Lot, Uri 4 Abel, Adam, Ahab, Amon,
Boaz, Cain, Elam, Enos, Esau, Jael,
Jehu, Joel, John, Lael, Leah, Levi,
Mark, Mary, Mica, Moab, Noah, Omar,
Onan, Paul, Reba, Ruth, Sara, Saul,
Seth, Shem 5 Aaron, Abner, Amram,
Asher, Caleb, David, Dinah, Elias,
Enoch, Ethan, Hagar, Heman, Herod,
Hosea, Isaac, Jacob, James, Jared,
Jesse, Jonah, Jubal, Judah, Judas,
Laban, Micah, Moses, Naomi, Peter,
Rufus, Sarah, Sheba, Simon, Tamar,
Tubal, Uriah, Uriel, Zadok 6 Ashhur,
Balaam, Baruch, Canaan, Daniel, Eli-
jah, Elisha, Esther, Gideon, Gilead,
Hannah, Hebron, Isaiah, Israel, Jeshua,
Jethro, Joanna, Joseph, Joshua, Josiah,
Judith, Martha, Miriam, Nathan, Nim-

rod, Pasach, Philip, Pilate, Rachel,
Reuben, Salome, Samson, Samuel,
Simeon, Thomas, Tobias *patriarch:* (see
at HEBREW) *people:* 6 Kenite, Levite
7 Amorite, Edomite, Elamite, Moabite
9 Israelite *plains:* 6 Sharon 7 Jericho
plotter: 5 Haman *poem:* 5 psalm *pool:*
8 Bethesda *priest:* 3 Eli 4 Levi 5 Aaron,
Annas 8 Caiaphas *Promised Land:*
6 Canaan *pronoun:* 3 thy 4 thee, thou
5 thine *prophet:* (see PROPHET)
Psalmist: 5 David *punishment:* 7 stoning
queen: 5 Sheba 6 Esther 7 Jezebel *river:*
4 Nile 6 Jordan *sacred object:* 4 urim
7 thummin *scribe:* 6 Baruch *sea:* 3 Red
4 Dead 7 Galilee *sea monster:*
9 Leviathan *spice:* 5 aloes, myrrh 6 cassia 7 calamus 8 cinnamon 12 frankincense *spy:* 5 Caleb *temptress:* 3 Eve
7 Delilah *thief:* 8 Barabbas *tree:* 5 cedar
valley: 4 Baca, Elah 6 Hinnon, Kidron,
Shaveh, Siddim *witch's home:* 5 Endor
bibliography 4 list 7 catalog, history
8 book list 13 reference list
bibliopole 7 bookman 10 book dealer,
bookseller
bibulous 6 spongy 7 thirsty 8 drinking
9 absorbent 10 absorptive
bicker 3 row 4 spar, spat, tiff 5 argue,
clack, fight, scrap 6 gurgle, hassle
7 brabble, clatter, contend, dispute, fall
out, flicker, quarrel, quibble, wrangle
8 squabble
bickering 3 row 4 spat 5 brawl, run-in
6 blowup, fracas, hassle, ruckus, rumpus, strife 7 discord, dispute, quarrel,
rhubarb, wrangle 8 squabble 11 altercation, embroilment
bicycle 4 bike *brake:* 7 caliper, coaster
for two: 6 tandem *gear shift:*
10 derailleur *rider:* 6 cycler 7 cyclist
bid 3 ask, say, try 4 call, tell, warn, wish
5 essay, greet, offer, order 6 amount,
charge, direct, effort, enjoin, invite,
render, summon, tender 7 attempt,
command, proffer, request, require,
venture 8 endeavor, instruct, proposal
10 invitation, submission 11 proposition
biddable 4 mild 6 docile, pliant 7 amiable, pliable, willing 8 amenable, obedient, obliging 9 tractable 10 governable,
manageable 11 acquiescent, cooperative, good-natured 13 accommodating
bidding 4 call, word 5 offer, order
6 behest, charge, demand, notice, tender 7 auction, command, dictate, mandate, request, summons 9 ordinance,
summoning 10 injunction, invitation
11 commandment, instruction
12 proclamation

biddy 3 bag, bat, hag, hen **4** drab, trot **5** crone, witch **6** beldam **7** chicken

bide 4 live, stay, wait **5** await, dwell, tarry **6** hang in, linger, remain, reside **7** hang out, sojourn **8** continue, sit tight, tolerate **10** hang around **11** stick around

bier 10 catafalque

biff 3 bop, box, hit, jab, zap **4** bash, belt, blow, clip, ding, nail, slam, slug, sock, swat, whop **5** blast, catch, clout, pound, slosh, smack, thump, whack **6** strike, thwack, wallop

bifurcate 3 cut **4** fork **5** halve, split **6** bisect, branch, cleave, divide **8** separate **9** branch out **11** dichotomize, dichotomous

bifurcation 4 fork **6** branch **8** division **9** dichotomy, partition, radiation **10** separation

big 3 fat **4** full, hard, huge, main, tall, vast **5** adult, ample, chief, great, grown, heavy, hefty, husky, large, lofty, major, proud, roomy **6** bumper, hugely **7** capital, copious, crammed, crowded, eminent, grown-up, hulking, leading, liberal, mammoth, massive, monster, notable, popular, replete, sizable, stuffed, swollen, weighty **8** colossal, enormous, generous, gracious, imposing, inflated, material, oversize, princely, spacious, swelling **9** capacious, chock-full, distended, extensive, heavy duty, humongous, important, momentous, overblown, paramount, ponderous, principal, prominent, unselfish **10** commodious, large-scale, preeminent, prodigious, voluminous **11** heavyweight, magnanimous, major league, overflowing, significant, substantial **12** considerable **13** comprehensive, consequential

big bang theorist 5 Gamow (George)

Big Bertha's birthplace 5 Essen

Big ___, Cal. 3 Sur

Big Dipper *constellation:* **9** Ursa Major *star:* **5** Alcor, Dubhe, Merak, Mizar

bigfoot 9 Sasquatch

biggety 4 bold, vain, wise **5** fresh, nervy, sassy **6** cheeky, snippy, snooty, uppity **7** forward, stuck-up **8** impudent, insolent, puffed up, snobbish **9** conceited **11** smart-alecky **13** self-important

bighearted 6 giving **7** liberal **8** generous **9** forgiving **10** altruistic, benevolent, charitable, munificent, openhanded **11** magnanimous **13** compassionate

big house 3 can, jug, pen **4** coop, jail **5** clink, joint **6** cooler, lockup, prison **7** slammer **8** bastille, hoosegow, stock-

ade **9** bridewell **11** reformatory **12** penitentiary

bight 3 arm, bay **4** cove, gulf **6** harbor

bigmouthed 4 loud, rude **8** boastful **10** boisterous

bigness 4 size **5** scale, scope **6** extent, volume **9** amplitude, immensity, magnitude **10** dimensions, importance

bigot 6 racist **8** jingoist **9** extremist, racialist **10** chauvinist **11** supremacist

bigoted 6 biased, narrow, unfair **9** hidebound, illiberal, sectarian **10** brassbound, intolerant, prejudiced **11** smallminded **12** narrow-minded

bigotry 4 bias **6** racism **9** apartheid, prejudice **10** xenophobia **11** intolerance

big shot 3 VIP **4** czar **5** celeb, mogul, nabob **6** bigwig, fat cat, tycoon **7** kingpin, notable, pooh-bah **8** higher-up, luminary, top brass **9** celebrity, dignitary, personage **13** high-muck-a-muck

big-time 5 major **7** eminent, greatly, leading **8** renowned **9** high-level, important, paramount, prominent **10** large-scale **11** influential, majorleague

big top 4 tent **6** circus

bigwig 3 VIP **5** heavy, mogul, nabob **6** honcho, kahuna **7** kingpin, magnate, notable **8** luminary, somebody **9** dignitary, personage **11** heavy hitter, muckety-muck **13** high-muck-a-muck

bijou 3 gem **5** jewel **8** gemstone

bijouterie 6 jewels **7** jewelry **8** trinkets **10** decoration

bike 5 cycle **7** scooter **10** motorcycle **12** motorscooter

bilge 3 rot **4** bull, bunk, guff **5** hooey, trash **6** bunkum **7** baloney, garbage, hogwash, malarky, rubbish, twaddle **8** claptrap, nonsense **9** poppycock, silliness **10** balderdash **11** foolishness

bilk 3 con, gyp **4** balk, beat, dash, duck, dupe, foil, fool, hoax, hose, kite, milk, ruin, scam, take **5** avoid, cheat, cozen, dodge, elude, evade, shake, shaft, skirt, stiff, trick **6** baffle, chisel, chouse, diddle, double, escape, eschew, fleece, rip off, sucker, thwart **7** deceive, defraud, prevent, swindle **8** flimflam, hoodwink, sidestep, stave off **9** frustrate **10** circumvent

bill 3 dun, fin, neb, nib, tab **4** beak, bone, buck, chit, list, note, skin **5** check, score, visor **6** charge, damage, dollar, notice, poster, roster **7** account, charges, invoice, placard, program, sawbuck, smacker **8** mandible **9** greenback, reckoning, smackeroo, statement

billet 3 bar, bed, gig, hut, job, rod **4** post, slab, spar, spot **5** berth, board, house,

ingot, lodge, place, put up, stick, strip
6 bestow, canton, harbor, office 7 quarter 8 domicile, position, quarters, vocation 9 entertain, situation 10 assignment, connection, employment,
encampment, livelihood, profession,
occupation 11 appointment

billet-doux 8 mash note 10 love letter

billfold 6 wallet

billiards *term* 3 cue 4 foot, head, jaws,
kiss, long, peas, pool, race, rack, spot
5 break, carom, chalk, count, masse
6 bridge, cannon, corner, crotch,
inning, miscue, nurses, pocket, stance,
string 7 bricole, cue ball, cushion, ferrule, kitchen, pyramid, scratch, shooter, snooker 8 apex ball, balkline, bank
shot, cue stick, dead ball, jump shot,
rotation, triangle 9 clean bank, eight
ball 10 chuck nurse, head string, object
ball 12 balance point

billingsgate 5 abuse 6 tirade 7 obloquy
9 contumely, invective 10 revilement,
scurrility 12 vilification, vituperation

billion *British:* 8 milliard *combining form:*
4 giga

billionth *combining form:* 4 nano

bill of fare 4 menu 7 program 11 carte
du jour

billow 4 mass, wave 5 bulge, cloud,
surge, swell 6 puff up, roller 7 balloon,
upsurge

Billy Budd's captain 4 Vere

billy club 4 cane 5 baton 6 cudgel, paddle 8 bludgeon 9 bastinado, truncheon
10 knobkerrie, nightstick

bin 4 crib 5 frame, stall 6 bunker, hamper, trough 9 container 10 receptacle

binary 4 twin, dual 5 duple 6 double,
duplex, paired 7 coupled, matched,
twofold 9 dualistic

bind 3 tie 4 frap, gird, tape, wrap
5 chain, cinch, strap, tie up, truss
6 cement, commit, fasten, fetter, ligate,
pinion 7 bandage, confine, enchain,
shackle, trammel 8 enfetter, restrain
9 constrain, constrict, indenture

binder 4 file 5 cover 6 folder, jacket
7 wrapper

binding 8 required 9 mandatory, requisite 10 obligatory

bindlestiff 4 hobo

binge 3 jag 4 orgy, riot, soak, tear, time,
toot 5 blast, booze, fling, party, revel,
souse, spree, stint 6 bender 7 blowoff,
blowout, carouse, debauch, rampage,
revelry, shindig, splurge, surfeit, wassail 8 carousal, gluttony 9 bacchanal,
brannigan 10 debauchery, indulgence
11 bacchanalia, celebration 12 intemperance

bingo 3 yes 5 beano 7 correct

biographer *American:* 5 Weems (Parson)
6 Parton (James) 7 Freeman (Douglas)
8 Bradford (Gamaliel), Sandburg (Carl)
10 McCullough (David) *English:*
6 Aubrey (John), Morley (John), Walton (Izaak) 8 Strachey (Lytton) *French:*
7 Maurois (André) *German:* 6 Ludwig
(Emil) *Greek:* 8 Plutarch *Italian:* 6 Vasari
(Giorgio) *Roman:* 9 Suetonius *Scottish*
7 Boswell (James)

biography 3 bio 4 life, obit, vita 5 diary,
story 6 memoir 7 history, profile 8 obituary 11 confessions

biological category 5 class, genus, order
6 family, phylum 7 kingdom, species,
variety 10 subspecies

bionomics 7 ecology

Bip's creator 7 Marceau (Marcel)

bird *African:* 6 barbet, bulbul, jabiru,
turaco 7 courser, marabou, ostrich,
touraco 8 hornbill, oxpecker, parakeet
9 broadbill, francolin *Antarctic:* 4 skua
7 penguin 10 sheathbill *aquatic:* 3 auk,
mew 4 coot, duck, erne, gull, loon,
skua, swan, teal, tern 5 booby, cahow,
goose, grebe, murre 6 fulmar, gannet,
petrel, puffin, scoter, wigeon 7 anhinga,
dovekie, mallard, moorhen, pelican,
penguin, skimmer, widgeon 8 baldpate,
dabchick, murrelet 9 albatross, cormorant, gallinule, guillemot, kittiwake
10 shearwater, sheathbill *arctic:* 3 auk
4 knot, skua 5 murre 6 fulmar, jaeger
7 dovekie 9 guillemot, gyrfalcon *Asian:*
4 myna, ruff, smew 5 mynah, pewit
6 chukar, drongo, dunlin, hoopoe, peewit 7 courser, lapwing, peacock 8 dotterel, hornbill, parakeet, tragopan,
wheatear 9 francolin *Australian:* 3 emu
4 lory 5 galah 6 drongo 7 bustard 8 bellbird, cockatoo, lorikeet, lyrebird, parakeet 9 cassowary *blackbird:* 3 ani, daw
4 crow, rook 5 merle, ousel, ouzel,
raven 6 chough, magpie, thrush
7 grackle, jackdaw, redwing *carrion-eating:* 6 condor 7 buzzard, vulture *Central
American:* 4 guan, ibis 5 booby, macaw
6 barbet, jabiru, toucan 7 bittern, jacamar, quetzal, tinamou 8 curassow,
troupial *chimney-nesting:* 5 swift *class:*
4 Aves *colony:* 5 roost 7 rookery *combining form:* 5 ornis 6 ornith 7 ornitho
8 ornithes (plural) *crow family:* 3 daw,
jay 4 rook 5 raven 6 chough, corbie,
magpie 7 jackdaw *diving:* 3 auk 4 smew
5 grebe, murre 6 petrel 8 murrelet
9 guillemot, merganser *European:*
3 mew 4 rook, smew, wren 5 crake,
egret, finch, merle, ousel, ouzel, pewit,
pipit 6 cuckoo, hoopoe, linnet, martin,

merlin, redleg, thrush 7 bustard, jackdaw, kestrel, lapwing, martlet, ortolan, redwing, sparrow, wagtail 8 blackcap, dabchick, nightjar, nuthatch, redstart, starling, throstle, whimbrel, woodcock 9 chaffinch, crossbill, stonechat 10 chiffchaff, goatsucker, kingfisher 11 lammergeier *extinct:* 3 moa 4 dodo 9 aepyornis, solitaire *fabulous:* 3 roc 7 phoenix *fish-eating:* 4 erne 6 osprey *flightless:* 3 emu, moa 4 dodo, kiwi, rhea 6 kakapo, ratite, takahe 7 apteryx, ostrich, penguin 8 cassowary *game:* 4 duck, rail, teal 5 brant, goose, quail, snipe 6 chukar, grouse, turkey 7 bustard, mallard, pintail, widgeon 8 baldpate, bobwhite, moorfowl, pheasant, shoveler, tragopan, wildfowl, woodcock 9 merganser, partridge, ptarmigan *ground-dwelling:* 5 quail 6 grouse, peahen, turkey 7 chicken, peacock, peafowl 8 bobwhite, moorfowl, pheasant 9 partridge, ptarmigan *Indian:* 6 bulbul 7 peacock 8 adjutant, tragopan *Jamaican:* 7 vervain *large:* 3 emu, moa 5 eagle 6 curlew 7 bustard, ostrich, pelican 8 curassow, shoebill *largest:* 7 ostrich *Madagascar:* 6 drongo 7 anhinga *marsh:* 4 coot, rail 5 crane, snipe, stilt 9 gallinule *Mexican:* 6 jacana *mythical:* 3 roc 7 phoenix *New Zealand:* 3 kea 4 kiwi 6 kakapo 7 apteryx *nocturnal:* 3 owl 5 owlet 7 oilbird 8 guacharo, nightjar 9 nighthawk 10 goatsucker *North American:* 3 ani, tit 4 coot, wren 5 booby, crane, egret, junco, murre 6 dunlin, fulmar, grouse, phoebe, towhee, turkey, verdin, willet 7 anhinga, blue jay, catbird, flicker, grackle, tanager 8 bobolink, bobwhite, cardinal, killdeer, nuthatch, thrasher, titmouse 9 chickadee, crossbill, nighthawk, partridge, snakebird 10 bufflehead 12 whippoorwill *of Arabian Nights:* 3 roc *of brilliant plumage:* 4 lory 5 macaw 6 oriole, parrot, toucan, trogon 7 jacamar 8 lorikeet, parakeet, pheasant, tragopan *of peace:* 4 dove *of prey:* 3 owl 4 hawk, kite 5 buteo, eagle, harpy 6 condor, falcon, osprey, raptor 7 buzzard, goshawk, harrier, kestrel, vulture 8 caracara 9 accipiter 11 lammergeier *passerine:* (see SONGBIRD below) *razorbilled:* 3 auk *relating to:* 5 avian 8 ornithic *shore:* 3 auk 4 gull, tern 5 snipe, stilt 6 avocet, curlew, dunlin, plover, puffin, willet 7 lapwing, skimmer 8 killdeer, whimbrel, woodcock 9 phalarope, sandpiper, turnstone *small:* 3 tit 4 wren 5 finch, pewee, pipit, vireo 6 canary,

tomtit, verdin 7 sparrow 8 titmouse 9 chickadee *songbird:* 3 jay, tit 4 chat, crow, lark, wren 5 finch, pipit, robin, veery, vireo 6 bulbul, canary, linnet, oriole, shrike, thrush 7 catbird, creeper, kinglet, redwing, skylark, sparrow, swallow, tanager, titlark, wagtail, warbler, waxwing 8 bobolink, brantail, cardinal, nuthatch, Philomel, redstart, starling, thrasher, woodlark 9 chickadee, stonechat 10 chiffchaff, flycatcher 11 nightingale *South American:* 4 guan, loro, rhea 5 egret, macaw 6 jabiru, toucan 7 jacamar, limpkin, oilbird 8 caracara, curassow, guacharo, screamer, troupial 9 trumpeter *talking:* 4 myna 5 mynah 6 parrot *tropical:* 3 ani 6 barbet, drongo, toucan, trogon 7 jacamar, quetzal, sawbill, waxbill 8 troupial *turkey-like:* 8 curassow *unfledged:* 4 eyas 5 chick 8 nestling *wading:* 4 ibis, rail 5 crane, egret, heron, stork 6 godwit, jabiru, jacana 7 bittern, limpkin, tattler 8 flamingo, shoebill 9 spoonbill *web-footed:* 3 auk 4 duck, loon, swan 5 goose, murre 6 avocet, fulmar, gannet, petrel, puffin 7 anhinga, pelican, penguin 8 shoveler 9 albatross, cormorant, guillemot, merganser, razorbill, snakebird 10 shearwater *West Indian:* 3 ani
birdbrain 4 dodo, goof 5 dummy, dunce, idiot, moron, ninny 6 nitwit 7 airhead, dullard, halfwit 8 dumbbell, imbecile, meathead, numskull 9 dumb bunny, ignoramus, numbskull, simpleton 10 nincompoop 11 featherhead
birdcage 6 aviary
birdlife 8 avifauna
bird pepper 9 chiltepin
birds' eggs *study of:* 6 oology
birth 4 dawn, stem 5 arise, issue, onset, start 6 create, outset, spring 7 emanate, genesis, lineage, opening 8 delivery, generate, geniture, nascence, nascency, nativity, pedigree 9 beginning, originate 10 extraction 11 parturition 12 commencement
birth-control leader 6 Sanger (Margaret)
birth flower *April:* 5 daisy *August:* 9 gladiolus *December:* 10 poinsettia *February:* 8 primrose *January:* 9 carnation *July:* 8 sweet pea *June:* 4 rose *March:* 6 violet *May:* 15 lily of the valley *November:* 13 chrysanthemum *October:* 6 dahlia *September:* 5 aster
birthmark 4 mole 5 nevus, point, trait 7 feature 13 discoloration
Birth of a Nation director 8 Griffith (D. W.)
birthright 3 due, lot 6 legacy 7 bequest,

portion 8 appanage, heirloom, heritage 9 patrimony 11 entitlement, inheritance

birthroot 8 trillium

birthstone *April:* 7 diamond 8 sapphire *August:* 7 peridot 8 sardonyx *December:* 6 zircon 9 turquoise *February:* 8 amethyst *January:* 6 garnet *July:* 4 ruby *June:* 5 agate, pearl 11 alexandrite *March:* 6 jasper 10 aquamarine, bloodstone *May:* 7 emerald *November:* 5 topaz *October:* 4 opal 10 tourmaline *September:* 8 sapphire 10 chrysolite

biscuit 4 rusk, snap 6 cookie 7 cracker 8 cracknel, hardtack

bishop *district:* 7 diocese *headdress:* 5 miter, mitre *seat of office:* 3 see *skullcap:* 9 zucchetto *staff:* 7 crosier, crozier *throne:* 8 cathedra

bishopric 3 see 7 diocese

bison *European:* 6 wisent 7 aurochs *family:* 7 Bovidae *North American:* 7 buffalo

bistered 4 dark 5 brown, dusky, swart, tawny 6 brunet, tanned 7 swarthy 8 brunette 11 dark-skinned

bistro 3 bar, pub 4 café 5 joint 6 nitery, tavern 7 barroom, cabaret, hot spot, niterie, taproom 8 snack bar 9 coffee bar, nightclub, night spot 10 coffee shop 11 rathskeller 13 watering place

bit 3 dab, dot, end, jot, tad 4 atom, dash, drop, iota, lump, mite, part, rein, tick, time, whet 5 borer, flake, grain, minim, pinch, scrap, shard, shred, slice, space, speck, spell, trace, while 6 minute, moment, morsel, rather, second 7 portion, segment, smidgen, stretch, trickle 8 fraction, fragment, molecule, mouthful, particle, somewhat

bit by bit 6 evenly 9 by degrees, gradually, piecemeal 12 continuously 13 slow and steady

bitch goddess 7 success

bite 3 cut, eat, lot, nip 4 chaw, chew, edge, etch, food, gnaw, kick, meal, pain, part, rust, snap, tapa, zest 5 champ, chomp, erode, munch, piece, quota, share, slice, snack, stink, taste, tooth 6 crunch, morsel, nibble 7 corrode, eat away, eat into, engrave, portion 8 dissolve, mouthful, piquancy 9 allotment, allowance, masticate, occlusion 10 laceration 11 refreshment

biting 3 raw 4 cold 5 bleak, crisp, harsh, nippy, sharp 6 bitter, severe 7 acerbic, caustic, cutting, mordant, satiric 8 freezing, incisive, piercing, scathing 9 sarcastic, trenchant 11 penetrating

bitter 4 acid, tart 5 acerb, acrid, harsh, sharp 6 severe 7 acerbic, caustic, galling, hostile, painful 8 grievous, ruthless, virulent 9 rancorous, vexa-

tious, vitriolic 11 acrimonious, unpalatable 12 antagonistic

bitterness 4 gall 6 rancor 7 ill will 8 acridity, acrimony, asperity, coldness 9 animosity, antipathy 10 resentment

bittersweet 4 vine 8 poignant 10 nightshade

bitumen 3 tar 5 pitch 7 asphalt 8 blacktop

bivalve 4 clam, spat 6 cockle, mussel, oyster 7 geoduck, mollusk, piddock, scallop 9 lampshell 10 brachiopod

bivouac 4 camp, tent 6 billet, encamp, laager, maroon 7 shelter, sojourn 10 encampment

bizarre 3 odd 5 antic, queer, weird 7 curious, oddball, strange, uncanny, unusual 8 abnormal, atypical, freakish, peculiar, quixotic, singular 9 anomalous, eccentric, fantastic, grotesque, unearthly, unnatural 10 outlandish, outrageous 11 extravagant

bizarrerie 5 freak 6 oddity 7 anomaly, caprice, oddness 9 curiosity, weirdness 10 aberration

Bizet opera 6 Carmen

blab 3 gab, gas, jaw, yak 4 chat, leak, talk, tell 5 run on, spill 6 babble, betray, burble, gabble, gossip, inform, jabber, reveal, snitch, squeal, tattle, tell on, yammer 7 blather, chatter, divulge, let slip, palaver, prattle 8 blurt out, disclose, give away, go public

blabber 3 gab, rat 4 chat, fink 5 clack, drool, prate 6 babble, canary, drivel, gabber, gabble, gossip, jabber, magpie, prater, ramble 7 blather, chatter, palaver, prattle, twaddle 8 idle talk, jabberer, prattler 9 chatterer 10 chatterbox, tattletale

blabbermouth 3 rat 4 fink 6 canary, gabber, gossip, magpie, prater, snitch 7 windbag 8 busybody, jabberer, prattler 10 chatterbox, talebearer, tattletale 11 stool pigeon

black 3 jet 4 ebon, inky, noir, onyx 5 ebony, raven, sable 6 pitchy 8 charcoal, funereal 9 pitch-dark *combining form:* 3 mel 4 atro, mela, melo 5 melam, melan 6 melano

blackball 3 bar 4 veto, shun, snub 5 block, spurn 6 ice out, refuse, reject, strike 7 boycott, exclude, keep out, rule out 9 interdict, ostracize 11 vote against

black bass 7 sunfish

black beast see BÊTE NOIRE

Black Beauty author 6 Sewell (Anna)

blackbird see BIRD

black cohosh 7 bugbane

black crappie 7 sunfish 10 calico bass

black death 6 plague 13 bubonic plague
black diamond 4 coal 8 hematite 9 carbonado
blacken 3 dim, fog, ink 4 blot, burn, char, sear, slur, soil, soot 5 cloud, libel, shade, singe, smear, sully, taint 6 bruise, darken, defame, defile, malign, scorch, vilify 7 asperse, cloud up, eclipse, slander, traduce 8 besmirch, dishonor 10 calumniate
black eye 4 blot, onus, slur 5 stain 6 bruise, defeat, shiner, stigma 7 setback
blackfish 5 whale 6 tautog 10 pilot whale
Black Forest 11 Schwarzwald *city:* 10 Baden-Baden *peak:* 8 Feldberg *river:* 5 Rhein, Rhine 6 Danube, Neckar
black gold 3 oil 9 petroleum
blackguard 4 heel, punk 5 abuse, cheat, knave, rogue 6 rascal 7 hoodlum, lowlife, ruffian, villain 8 hooligan, scalawag 9 charlatan, miscreant, reprobate, scoundrel 10 delinquent, mountebank 11 rapscallion
blackhead 3 zit 4 spot 5 sebum 6 pimple 10 larval clam
blackjack 3 oak, sap 4 bash, club, cosh 6 coerce 7 pontoon, tankard 8 bludgeon 9 twenty-one, vingt-et-un 10 sphalerite
black lead 8 graphite
black letter 6 Gothic 10 Old English
blacklist 3 bar 4 oust 5 expel, purge, smear 6 banish, impugn 7 boycott, condemn, exclude, shut out 8 denounce 9 ostracize, proscribe 10 stigmatize
blackmail 5 bleed 6 extort, payoff 7 milking, squeeze 8 chantage, coercion 9 extortion, hush money, shake down
black out 4 edit, wipe 5 annul, erase, faint, swoon 6 cancel, censor, cut off, darken, delete, efface, excise 7 conceal, eclipse, expunge 8 collapse, make dark, sanitize, suppress 9 eradicate, expurgate 10 blue-pencil, obliterate
blackpoll 7 warbler
Black Prince 6 Edward
Black Sea *city:* 5 Yalta 6 Odessa 9 Constanta *peninsula:* 6 Crimea 7 Crimean
Blackshirt 7 fascist
blacksmith 6 forger 7 farrier, striker 10 horseshoer
blacktail 8 mule deer
blackthorn 4 plum, sloe
black widow 6 spider
bladder 3 sac 4 cyst 5 pouch 7 blister, vacuole 7 vesicle
blade 4 beau, buck, dude, edge, leaf 5 knife, sword 6 runner 9 swordsman
blah 4 bosh, dull, flat, tame 5 ho-hum, hooey, tired, vapid 6 boring, bunkum, dreary, humbug, stodgy 7 humdrum

8 banausic, lifeless, mediocre, nonsense, plodding 10 balderdash, lackluster, monotonous, pedestrian 11 indifferent, uninspiring 13 uninteresting
blamable see BLAMEWORTHY
blame 3 rap 4 onus 5 fault, guilt, knock 6 accuse, charge, finger, indict 7 censure, condemn 8 denounce, reproach 9 criticize, liability, reprehend, reprobate 10 accusation, imputation 11 culpability 12 condemnation, denunciation, reprehension *Scottish:* 4 wite, wyte 6 dirdum
blameless 4 good, pure 5 clean, moral 7 perfect, upright 8 innocent, unguilty, virtuous 9 crimeless, exemplary, faultless, guiltless, honorable, lily-white, righteous, unsullied 10 immaculate, impeccable, inculpable 13 unimpeachable
blameworthy 3 lax 5 amiss 6 guilty, liable, sinful 7 at fault 8 criminal, culpable, derelict 9 negligent 10 answerable, censurable, delinquent, indictable, punishable 11 disgraceful, inexcusable, responsible 12 dishonorable 13 reprehensible, objectionable
blanch 4 fade, pale 5 quail, scald, start 6 bleach, shrink, whiten 7 decolor, lighten, parboil 8 etiolate
blanched 3 wan 4 ashy, pale 5 ashen, faded, livid, peaky, waxen, white 6 anemic, doughy, pallid, peaked 7 ghostly 9 bloodless, colorless, washed out 10 cadaverous
Blancheflor's beloved 6 Flores, Floris
bland 4 dull, flat, blah, mild, soft 5 balmy, banal, vapid 6 boring, gentle, pablum 7 insipid, restful, sapless 8 soothing 9 calmative 10 complacent, flavorless, monotonous, namby-pamby, wishy-washy 12 ingratiating 13 nonirritating
blandish 3 con, woo 4 coax, fawn, urge 5 cozen 6 cajole, stroke 7 blarney, flatter, wheedle 8 butter up, inveigle, softsoap 9 importune, sweet-talk 10 curry favor
blandishment 3 oil 5 honey 7 blarney, eyewash, incense, promise 8 flattery, soft soap 9 adulation, seduction, sweet talk 10 allurement, compliment, inducement, sycophancy, temptation
blank 3 gap 4 bare, dull, seal, skip, void 5 chasm, dazed, empty, space 6 stupid, vacant, virgin 7 deadpan, obscure, unfilled, vacuous 8 complete, omission, outright, spotless 9 impassive 10 empty space, interstice, obliterate 11 featureless 12 inexpressive, unexpressive
blanket 4 bury, hide 5 cover, quilt, throw

6 afghan, stroud 7 overlay 8 coverlet, mackinaw, sweeping 10 overspread

blankness 6 vacuum 7 nullity, vacancy, vacuity 9 emptiness 10 desolation

blare 4 roar 5 blast, shout 6 clamor, jangle 7 trumpet

blaring 4 loud 5 sharp 6 brassy, shrill 7 clarion, jarring, roaring 8 blinding, piercing, strident 9 deafening, dissonant 10 stentorian 11 ear-piercing, penetrating, stentorious 12 earsplitting

blarney 3 con, oil 4 coax, bunk 5 charm, honey, hooey 6 bunkum, cajole, humbug 7 baloney, incense, wheedle 8 blandish, buncombe, cajolery, flattery, inveigle, nonsense, soft soap 9 adulation, sweet-talk 11 compliments 12 blandishment, inveiglement

blasé 4 cool 5 bored, jaded, sated 6 breezy 7 knowing, offhand, unmoved, worldly 9 apathetic, incurious, surfeited, unexcited 10 world-weary 11 indifferent, unconcerned, worldlywise 12 disenchanted, uninterested 13 disillusioned, sophisticated

blaspheme 4 cuss 5 abuse, curse, swear 6 revile 7 pollute, profane 8 denounce, execrate 9 castigate, excoriate

blasphemous 6 coarse, sinful 7 godless, impious, obscene, profane, ungodly 10 irreverent 12 sacrilegious 13 disrespectful

blasphemy 3 sin 5 abuse, error 6 heresy 7 cursing, cussing, impiety, mockery 8 swearing 9 profanity, sacrilege, violation 10 execration, heterodoxy, iconoclasm 11 desecration, imprecation, irreverence, malediction, profanation

blast 3 din 4 bang, beat, blow, boom, clap, dash, gale, gust, kill, peal, ruin, slam, toot 5 blare, burst, crack, crash, salvo, shoot, smash, wreck 6 attack, blight, blow up, damage, squall, wallop 7 destroy, lambast, shatter, shrivel, trumpet 8 dynamite, lambaste, outburst 9 explosion, castigate, discharge, overwhelm, shock wave 10 annihilate, detonation

blat 4 bray 5 blurt 6 cry out 7 exclaim 8 blurt out

blatant 4 bald, loud 5 clear, gaudy, naked, noisy, overt, saucy 6 arrant, brassy, brazen, crying, flashy, garish, patent, tawdry, vulgar 7 glaring, jarring, obvious 8 flagrant, immodest, impudent, insolent, manifest, overbold, strident 9 barefaced, clamorous, obtrusive, shameless, unabashed 10 boisterous, outrageous, scurrilous, unblushing, vociferous 11 conspicuous, loud-

mouthed, transparent 12 ear-splitting, obstreperous

blather 3 gab, gas, jaw, rot, yak 4 bosh, gush, rave, stir 5 bleat, drool, hokum, prate 6 babble, bunkum, drivel, effuse, gabble, jabber, natter, yammer 7 blabber, chatter, enthuse, palaver, prattle, rubbish, twaddle 8 chitchat, claptrap, idle talk, nonsense 9 commotion 10 balderdash, double-talk, flapdoodle 12 gobbledygook

blaze 4 burn, fire 5 burst, flame, flare, glare, shine 7 flare up 8 eruption, outburst 10 incandesce 13 conflagration

Scottish: 3 low 4 lowe

blazer 6 marker, reefer 9 sport coat 10 sports coat 12 sports jacket

blazes 4 hell 5 abyss, Hades, Sheol 6 Tophet 7 Gehenna, inferno 9 perdition 11 netherworld

blazing 4 keen 5 afire, fiery 6 aflame, alight, ardent, fervid, on fire, red-hot 7 burning, fervent, flaming, flaring, furious, glowing, ignited, intense, lighted 8 dazzling, feverish, powerful, speeding, white-hot 9 brilliant, perfervid 11 conflagrant, impassioned 12 incandescent 13 scintillating

blazon 4 deck 5 adorn, sound 7 declare, display, publish, trumpet 8 announce, proclaim 9 advertise, broadcast 10 coat of arms, promulgate 11 ostentation

bleach 3 dim 4 fade, pale 5 white 6 blanch, blench, purify, whiten 7 decolor, launder, wash out 8 etiolate, peroxide, sanitize 9 whitewash

bleak 3 raw, sad 4 bare, cold, dour, drab, grim, wild 5 chill, drear, empty, harsh, stark 6 barren, chilly, dismal, dreary, gloomy, lonely, severe, somber, wintry 7 austere, exposed, joyless 8 blighted, desolate, funereal, hopeless 9 cheerless, windswept, woebegone 10 depressing, despondent, oppressive, melancholy

blear 3 dim, fog 4 blur, dull, mist, murk, veil 5 bedim, faint, vague 6 hidden, shroud 7 becloud, obscure, shadowy, unclear 10 indistinct

bleary 3 dim 5 all in, faint, filmy, fuzzy, milky, spent, tired, vague 6 pooped, sapped, used-up, wasted 7 blurred, drained, obscure, shadowy, unclear, worn-out 8 depleted 9 enervated, exhausted, washed-out 10 indistinct

bleat 3 baa 4 blat, carp, crab, fuss, yawp 5 gripe, whine 6 bellow, grouse, squawk, yammer 7 blather, grumble, whimper 8 complain 9 bellyache

bleed 3 sap, run 4 milk, ooze, pity, seep 5 drain, exude, leech, mulct 6 extort, fleece 7 diffuse, extract 9 blackmail 10 hemorrhage

blemish 3 mar 4 blot, flaw, harm, mark, maim, mole, scar, spot, vice, wart 5 fault, nevus, spoil, stain 6 blotch, damage, deface, defect, impair, injure, pimple, stigma 7 blacken, distort, freckle, pervert, tarnish, vitiate 8 impurity, mutilate, pockmark 9 birthmark 12 imperfection 13 disfigurement

blench 3 shy 4 balk, duck, fade 5 blink, cower, quail, quake, start, wince 6 flinch, purify, recoil, shrink, whiten 7 launder, shy away, squinch, tremble 8 draw back, etiolate 9 whitewash

blend 3 fit, mix 4 brew, fuse, meld, weld 5 admix, alloy, merge, unify, union, unite 6 commix, fusion, go with, hybrid, mingle 7 amalgam, combine, mélange, mixture 8 beverage, coalesce, compound, conflate, immingle, infusion, intermix, mishmash 9 admixture, commingle, composite, harmonize, integrate 10 amalgamate, commixture, concoction, synthesize 12 adulteration, amalgamation, intermixture

blender setting 3 mix 4 whip 5 puree 7 liquefy

blesbok 8 antelope

bless 4 laud 5 exalt, extol, endow, favor, grace 6 anoint, bestow, hallow, praise, uphold 7 approve, beatify, glorify, magnify 8 enshrine, eulogize, make holy, sanctify 10 consecrate

blessed 4 holy 5 happy, lucky 6 joyous, sacred 7 saintly 8 beatific, hallowed 9 beatified, fortunate, venerated 10 inviolable, sacrosanct, sanctified 11 consecrated

blessedness 5 bliss 8 felicity, sanctity 9 beatitude, godliness, happiness 12 blissfulness

blessing 4 boon, good, okay 5 asset, favor, grace 6 assent, bounty, thanks 7 benefit, benison, consent, fortune, godsend, support 8 approval, good luck, windfall 9 advantage 10 invocation, permission 11 approbation, benediction, endorsement, good fortune, valediction 12 commendation, consecration, thanksgiving 13 encouragement

"___ bleu!" 5 Sacré

blight 3 mar, nip 4 dash, ruin 5 blast, decay, spoil, wreck 6 canker, wither 7 disease, scourge, shrivel 9 withering 10 pestilence 13 deterioration

blimp 7 airship 8 zeppelin 9 dirigible

blind 4 daze, dull 5 decoy, front, shade, shill 6 dazzle 7 eyeless, muddled, shut-

ter 8 bedazzle, unseeing 9 sightless 10 visionless

blind alley 6 pocket 7 dead end, impasse 8 cul-de-sac, deadlock 9 stone wall 10 standstill 11 obstruction

blind god 4 Eros, Hodr, Hoth 5 Cupid, Hoder, Hodur, Hothr

blindworm 8 slowworm

blink 3 bat 4 wink 5 flash, yield 6 give in, squint 7 flicker, flutter, nictate, twinkle 9 nictitate 11 scintillate

blink at 4 omit 5 clear, let go 6 bypass, excuse, forget, ignore, slight 7 condone, connive, let pass, neglect 8 discount, overlook, pass over 9 disregard, exonerate, whitewash

blip 6 censor, screen 9 deviation, expurgate, radar spot 10 bowdlerize

bliss 3 joy 4 Zion 6 Canaan, heaven 7 ecstasy, elysium, nirvana, rapture 8 empyrean, euphoria, paradise 9 beatitude, happiness 10 exaltation 11 blessedness

blissful 5 happy 6 divine, elated, joyful, joyous 8 beatific, ecstatic, euphoric 9 ambrosial, delighted, entranced, rapturous 10 delightful, entrancing

blissfulness 3 joy 7 ecstasy 8 euphoria 9 beatitude, happiness 10 exaltation 11 contentment

blister 4 bleb, flay, lash 5 blain, bulla, slash 6 assail, canker, scathe, scorch 7 lambast, scarify, scourge, vesicle 8 lambaste 9 castigate, excoriate

blithe 3 gay 4 boon 5 happy, jolly, merry, sunny 6 bouncy, casual, cheery, chirpy, jaunty, jocund, jovial 7 gleeful 8 carefree, careless, cheerful, chirrupy, gladsome, heedless, mirthful 9 lightsome, sprightly, unworried, vivacious 10 untroubled 11 thoughtless 12 lighthearted

blithesome see BLITHE

blitz 4 raid, rush 7 air raid, bombard, bombing & shelling 9 onslaught 10 mass attack 11 bombardment

blitzkrieg 6 attack 7 assault, bombing 9 offensive, onslaught 11 bombardment

blizzard 4 gale 6 squall 8 whiteout 9 snowstorm

bloat 5 bulge, swell 6 billow, expand, fatten, puff up 7 balloon, distend, enlarge, inflate 10 distension

bloated 5 puffy 6 puffed 7 pompous, swollen 8 arrogant, enlarged, inflated 9 distended, overblown, overlarge 11 pretentious 13 self-important

bloc 4 band, ring 5 cabal, party, union 6 clique, league 7 combine, faction 8 alliance 9 coalition 10 consortium, .

contingent, federation 11 association, combination 13 confederation

block 3 bar 4 clog, fill, hunk, plug, slab, stop, wall, wing 5 brick, choke, chunk, close, ingot 6 cut off, hinder, impede 7 barrier, congest, occlude, stopper 8 obstacle, obstruct 9 barricade, hindrance, intercept

blockade 3 bar 4 stop, wall 5 beset, hem in, siege 6 shut in 7 barrier, besiege 8 close off, encircle, obstruct, stoppage 9 barricade, beleaguer, blank wall, hindrance, roadblock 10 impediment 11 obstruction

blockage 3 bar 4 clog, halt 7 barrier 8 obstacle, stoppage 10 impediment 11 obstruction

blockbuster 4 bomb 11 spectacular

blockhead 3 oaf 4 clod, dolt, dope, fool 5 dummy, dunce, idiot, moron, ninny 6 nitwit 7 halfwit, imbecile 8 clodpole, clodpoll, dumbbell, numskull 9 ignoramus, lamebrain, numbskull, simpleton 10 nincompoop 12 featherbrain

blockheaded 4 dull, dumb 5 dense, thick 6 obtuse, stupid 7 doltish 9 brainless, dim-witted 10 slow-witted

block out 4 mark 5 chart, close, draft, frame 6 hinder, screen, sketch 7 obscure, outline, prepare, repress, shut off 8 indicate, obstruct 9 adumbrate, formulate

block up 3 dam 4 clog, fill, plug, stop 5 choke 7 congest

bloke 3 guy, man 4 chap, gent 6 fellow 9 gentleman

blond 4 fair, gold, pale 5 light, sandy, straw, tawny 6 flaxen, golden 7 towhead 8 platinum 9 champagne, towheaded 10 fair-haired 11 sandy-haired 12 honey-colored

blood 4 gore 7 descent, kindred, kinship, lineage 8 ancestry 10 extraction *cancer of:* 8 leukemia *cell:* 3 red 5 white 8 hemocyte, monocyte, platelet 9 corpuscle, leukocyte 10 lymphocyte 11 erythrocyte, granulocyte *clot:* 8 thrombus *coloring matter:* 10 hemoglobin *disease:* 6 anemia 8 leukemia 10 hemophilia *fluid part:* 5 serum 6 plasma *of the gods:* 5 ichor *particle in:* 7 embolus *poisoning:* 6 pyemia 7 toxemia 10 septicemia *pressure:* 8 systolic 9 diastolic *relating to:* 5 hemic *serum:* 6 plasma *study of:* 10 hematology *sugar:* 7 glucose

bloodbath 7 carnage, slaying 8 butchery, massacre 9 slaughter 10 decimation 12 annihilation 13 extermination

bloodless 3 wan 4 ashy, dull, pale, weak 5 ashen, waxen 6 anemic, feeble, pallid,

sallow, torpid 8 listless 9 insensate, unfeeling 10 insensible, nonviolent 11 coldhearted, passionless, unemotional

bloodletting 4 gore 7 carnage, killing 8 butchery, shambles, violence 9 slaughter 10 phlebotomy 11 venesection

bloodline 6 family, strain 7 descent, lineage 8 ancestry, pedigree 10 family tree

bloodroot 7 puccoon

bloodshed 4 gore 7 carnage 9 slaughter

bloodstained 4 gory 6 grisly 7 imbrued, wounded 8 sanguine 10 sanguinary 11 ensanguined, sanguineous

bloodstone 10 chalcedony

bloodsucker 4 tick 5 lamia, leech 6 lizard, sponge 7 sponger, vampire 8 hanger-on, parasite 10 freeloader 12 lounge lizard

bloodthirsty 5 rabid 8 ravening, sanguine 9 cutthroat, homicidal, murdering, murderous, predatory, voracious 10 sanguinary 11 sanguineous

blood vessel 4 vein 5 aorta 6 artery 7 jugular 9 capillary *combining form:* 3 vas 4 angi, vasi, vaso 5 angio

bloody 4 gory, grim, very 5 cruel 6 damage, damned, deadly, grisly 7 blasted, hateful, imbrued, wounded 8 accursed, infernal, sanguine 9 cutthroat, homicidal, murdering, murderous 10 detestable, sanguinary 11 ensanguined, sanguineous 12 death-dealing, slaughtering

bloom 4 blow, glow, open, posy 5 blush 6 floret, flower, thrive, unfold 7 blossom, burgeon, coating, develop, dusting, prosper 8 flourish, rosiness 10 cloudiness, effloresce 13 discoloration

blooper 4 goof, slip, trip 5 boner, break, error, fluff, gaffe, lapse 6 boo-boo, bungle, howler, slipup 7 blunder, faux pas, fly ball, misstep, mistake, offense 8 solecism 9 indecorum, false step 11 impropriety 12 indiscretion

blossom 3 bud, wax 4 blow, glow, grow, open, posy 5 bloom, blush, flush 6 expand, flower, mature, thrive, unfold 7 burgeon, develop, prosper 8 flourish, floweret, progress 10 effloresce, peak period 13 efflorescence

blot 4 blur, mark, onus, slur, smut, soil, spot 5 brand, odium, smear, speck, stain, sully 6 absorb, smudge, stigma 7 bestain, blemish, spatter, tarnish 8 black eye, discolor, disgrace 9 bespatter, moral flaw

blotch 4 mark, spot 5 stain 6 macula,

macule, mottle, smudge **7** blemish, splotch **12** imperfection

blot out 4 raze, void **5** annul, crush, erase, quash, quell, scrub **6** cancel, delete, efface, squash **7** abolish, destroy, expunge **9** eliminate, eradicate, extirpate **10** annihilate, extinguish, obliterate **11** exterminate

blotto see DRUNK

blouse 5 middy, shell, shirt, smock, tunic **6** guimpe

bloviate 4 rail, rant, rave **5** mouth, orate, spout **7** bluster, carry on, declaim, inveigh, soapbox, talk big **8** harangue, perorate, sound off, splutter **9** hold forth **10** vociferate

blow 3 bop, fan, hit, jar **4** bang, bash, belt, biff, bump, cuff, damn, fail, gasp, gust, huff, pipe, puff, slam, slug, swat, toot, whop, wind **5** boast, botch, crack, drive, erupt, leave, pound, punch, shock, slosh, smack, smash, sound, spend, waste, whack **6** buffet, depart, impact, mishap, thwack, wallop **7** assault, breathe, chagrin, consume, debacle, explode, flutter, fritter, trumpet **8** calamity, disaster, flounder, knockout, squander **9** bombshell, collision, dissipate, throw away **10** concussion, misfortune, trifle away **11** catastrophe

blow-by-blow 4 full **5** fussy **6** minute **7** careful, precise **8** detailed, itemized, thorough **10** exhaustive, meticulous, scrupulous **13** thoroughgoing

blowhard see BOASTER

blow in 4 land **5** pop by **6** appear, arrive, drop by, show up, turn up **7** hit town **11** materialize

blowout 4 bash, fete, gala, riot, tear **5** binge, blast, break, party, split, spree **6** frolic, shindy **7** shindig, victory **8** carousal, flat tire **9** festivity

blowsy 5 dingy, ruddy **6** florid, frowsy, sloppy, untidy **7** flushed, healthy, unkempt **8** blooming, blushing **10** bedraggled

blow up 4 bomb, burn, fume, rage **5** bloat, burst, erupt, flare, go off, storm, swell **6** expand, seethe **7** bristle, distend, enlarge, explode, inflate, magnify, rupture, shatter **8** boil over, demolish, detonate, dynamite, heighten, mushroom **9** discredit, fulminate, overstate **10** aggrandize

blowy 4 airy, wild **5** fresh, gusty, windy **6** breezy, stormy **7** squally **8** blustery **9** windswept **11** tempestuous

blubber 3 cry, fat, sob **4** bawl, flab, keen, lard, pipe, wail, weep **5** flesh **6** snivel **7** carry on **8** whale fat

bludgeon 3 bat **4** club **5** baton, billy, bully **6** attack, cudgel, hector **7** bluster, war club **8** browbeat, bulldoze, bullyrag **9** bastinado, billy club, blackjack, strong-arm, truncheon **10** intimidate, nightstick *British:* **4** cosh

blue 3 low, sad, sea **4** down, glum, lewd, navy, racy **5** bawdy, ocean, royal, salty, spicy **6** cobalt, gloomy, risqué **7** naughty, profane, unhappy **8** dejected, downcast, indecent, off-color **9** depressed, woebegone **10** despondent, dispirited, melancholy, suggestive **11** downhearted *combining form:* **4** cyan **5** cyano *dark:* **5** perse **6** indigo *grayish:* **5** merle, slate *greenish:* **4** aqua, cyan, teal **5** beryl **6** cobalt **7** azurite **9** turquoise *reddish:* **5** smalt **6** marine, purple, violet **7** cyanine, gentian, lobelia *sky:* **5** azure **8** cerulean

___ **Blue 3** Ben **9** Little Boy

blue blood 4 lady, lord, peer **5** elite, noble **6** aristo **7** royalty **8** nobleman **9** gentility, gentleman, patrician **10** aristocrat, noblewoman **11** gentle birth, gentlewoman

bluebonnet 4 Scot **11** Texas lupine

Blue Boy painter 12 Gainsborough (Thomas)

bluecoat 3 cop, law **4** fuzz **5** bobby **6** copper **9** constable, patrolman, policeman

Bluegrass State 8 Kentucky

Blue Grotto site 5 Capri

bluejacket 4 mate, salt, swab **5** limey **6** sailor, seaman **7** swabbie **9** sailorman

blue jeans 5 Levis **6** denims

blue moon 3 age, eon, era **4** aeon **5** epoch **7** dog's age **8** eternity, lifetime **10** generation

bluenose 4 prig **5** prude **7** puritan **9** Mrs. Grundy, nice Nelly **10** goody-goody

bluenosed 4 prim **5** rigid **6** prissy, proper, square, stuffy **7** prudish **8** overnice, priggish **9** Victorian **10** scrupulous, tight-laced **11** puritanical, straitlaced

blue-pencil 3 cut **4** edit, trim **5** emend **6** cut out, delete, excise, remove, revise **7** clean up **8** boil down, cross out **9** strike out, tighten up

bluepoint 6 oyster

blueprint 3 map **4** cast, plan, plot **5** chart, draft, frame, model, trace **6** design, devise, rubric, scheme, set out, sketch **7** arrange, diagram, outline, picture, project **8** game plan, strategy **9** delineate **10** conception, rough draft **11** description

blue-ribbon 3 top **5** prime **6** Grade A, tiptop **7** capital, premier **8** five-star, topnotch, superior **9** excellent, first-rate, top-drawer **10** first-class, top-quality, world-class **11** outstanding **12** prize-winning

blues 4 funk **5** dumps, gloom, grief **6** lament **7** sadness, trouble **8** doldrums, glumness **9** dejection, pessimism **10** depression, desolation, low spirits, melancholy, woefulness **11** despondency, melancholia, unhappiness **12** hopelessness, mournfulness

bluff 3 act, con **4** curt, fake, fool, jive, ruse, sham, show **5** blunt, cliff, feign, frank, gruff, rough, trick **6** abrupt, betray, candid, crusty, delude, direct, hearty, humbug **7** beguile, brusque, deceive, fake out, mislead, playact, pretend **8** headland, pretense **9** deception, outspoken, precipice, steep bank **10** escarpment, forthright, no-nonsense, promontory, subterfuge **11** counterfeit, double-cross, plainspoken, short-spoken **13** unceremonious

blunder 4 bull, gaff, goof, mess, muff, slip, trip **5** boner, botch, error, fluff, gaffe, gum up, lapse, lurch **6** bobble, bollix, bumble, bungle, foul up, fumble, goof up, howler, mess up, wander **7** blooper, failure, faux pas, louse up, misstep, mistake, screw up, stumble **8** disaster, flounder **12** indiscretion, misadventure

blunderbuss 3 gun **4** dolt **5** klutz **6** galoot, lummox **7** bungler, firearm **8** bonehead, numskull **9** blockhead, numbskull **10** stumblebum **13** butterfingers

blunt 4 bald, calm, curt **5** allay, bluff, brief, frank, gruff, plain, rough, terse **6** abrupt, benumb, candid, crusty, deaden, direct, lessen, obtuse **7** brusque, rounded, uncivil **8** enfeeble, not sharp, snippety **10** forthright **11** desensitize, insensitive, plainspoken, unvarnished **12** discourteous **13** unceremonious

blur 3 dim, fog **4** blot, dull, mist **5** befog, blear, cloud, muddy, smear, stain, taint **6** smudge, stigma **7** becloud, besmear, confuse, tarnish **8** besmirch, discolor *in printing:* **6** mackle

blurb 4 hype, plug, puff **5** press **6** notice **7** write-up **8** good word **9** promotion **12** commendation

blurry 4 hazy **5** vague **6** cloudy **7** clouded, unclear **9** undefined, unfocused **10** indistinct

blurt 4 blab, blat, bolt **5** spill **6** cry out, let out **7** divulge, exclaim, let slip, spit out **8** disclose, give away **9** ejaculate

blush 4 burn, glow, rose, view **5** bloom, color, flame, flush, rouge **6** mantle,

pinken, redden **7** blossom, crimson, redness, turn red **8** mantling, rosiness

bluster 4 bawl, crow, gust, huff, rage, roar, rout **5** blast, bully, prate, storm, strut, vaunt **6** bellow, clamor, hector, lean on **7** bombast, bravado, dragoon, roister, swagger, talk big **8** boasting, browbeat, bulldoze, bullyrag, domineer **9** gasconade **10** grandstand, intimidate **11** braggadocio

blustery 4 wild **5** blowy, gusty, rough **6** drafty, raging, raving, stormy **7** furious, squally, violent **9** truculent, tumultuous, turbulent **10** boisterous **11** tempestuous

boa 5 scarf, snake

boar 3 pig **4** male **5** swine

board 4 fare, feed, food, lath, slab, slat **5** catch, get on, hop on, house, lodge, meals, panel, plank, put up, table **6** billet, embark **7** emplane, entrain, quarter **9** directors **11** directorate *artist's:* **7** palette

boarder 5 guest **6** lodger, renter, roomer, tenant

board game see at GAME

boarding house 6 hostel **7** hospice, lodging, pension **8** pensione

boardwalk 7 gangway **9** esplanade, promenade

boast 3 own **4** blow, brag, crow, have, puff **5** exalt, exult, glory, mouth, prate, preen, strut, vaunt **6** parade **7** bluster, bombast, bravado, contain, enlarge, exhibit, inflate, possess, show off, swagger, talk big **9** gasconade **10** exaggerate, grandstand **11** rodomontade **12** exaggeration

boaster 6 gascon **7** egotist, peacock, show-off **8** big mouth, blowhard, braggart **11** braggadocio, rodomontade

boastful 4 vain **5** cocky **6** braggy **8** arrogant, braggart, puffed-up, vaunting **9** bigheaded, conceited, egotistic **11** egotistical, pretentious, swellheaded **12** vainglorious **13** swelled-headed *Scottish:* **6** vaunty

boat 3 ark, hoy, tug **4** dhow, dory, junk, pram, prau, proa, punt, scow, ship, yawl **5** barge, canoe, coble, ferry, kayak, ketch, scull, shell, skiff, sloop, smack, umiak, yacht **6** bateau, bugeye, caïque, cutter, dinghy, hooker, lateen, lugger, packet, sampan, vessel, wherry **7** caravel, coracle, currach, curragh, gondola, lighter, pinnace, pirogue, pontoon, shallop, steamer, trawler, vedette, vidette **8** schooner, trimaran **9** catamaran, hydrofoil *bottom projection:* **4** keel *captain:* **5** pilot **6** master **7** skipper *dock, basin:* **6** marina *front end of:* **3** bow

4 fore, prow *motor:* 7 cruiser, inboard
8 outboard, runabout *on a ship:* 3 gig
6 launch 7 pinnace *race:* 7 regatta *rear
end of:* 3 aft 5 stern *song:* 6 chanty,
shanty 7 chantey 9 barcarole 10 barcarolle
boatman 4 mate 5 limey 6 Charon, sailor
7 mariner, oarsman, paddler 8 deckhand, water dog 9 gondolier, navigator
boat-shaped 8 scaphoid 9 navicular
Boaz's wife 4 Ruth
bob 3 jig, nod, rap, tap 4 buff, clip, crop,
dock, trim 5 bunch, float 6 bounce,
curtsy, jiggle, jounce, polish, trifle,
wobble 7 cluster, curtsey, nosegay
8 shilling 9 genuflect
bobbery 3 ado, din, row 4 fray, riot
5 babel, noise 6 bedlam, hubbub, racket, ruckus, rumpus 7 ferment, ruction
9 commotion, confusion 10 hullabaloo,
hurly-burly 11 disturbance, pandemonium
bobbin 4 pirn 5 quill, spool, wheel
7 spindle 8 cylinder
bobble 3 bob, dud 4 flub, goof, mess,
muff 5 botch, error, fluff, gum up 6 ball
up, bollix, bumble, bungle, flub up,
fumble, goof up, muff up 7 blooper,
failure, louse up, mistake
bobby 3 law 6 copper, peeler 7 officer
9 constable, patrolman, policeman
bobwhite 5 quail 9 partridge
Boccaccio *beloved:* 9 Fiammetta *tales:*
9 Decameron
bode 4 hint 5 augur 6 signal, warn of
7 betoken, portend, presage, promise,
signify, suggest 8 foreshow, indicate
9 foretoken, prefigure 10 foreshadow
bodega 3 bar, pub 6 saloon 7 barroom,
grocery 8 wineshop 12 general store
bodement 4 omen, sign 5 hunch
6 augury 7 portent, presage 8 prophecy
9 foretoken, harbinger 10 foreboding,
intimation, prediction, prognostic
11 premonition 12 presentiment
bodiless 7 ghostly 8 ethereal, spectral
9 unfleshly 10 discarnate, immaterial,
unphysical 11 disembodied, incorporeal, nonmaterial 12 apparitional
13 insubstantial
bodily 6 carnal 7 en masse, earthly,
fleshly, sensual, somatic, totally 8 corporal, entirely, physical, visceral 9 corporeal 10 altogether, completely
11 unspiritual
bodkin 4 shiv 5 blade, knife, shank
6 dagger, lancet, needle 7 poniard
8 stiletto
___ **bodkins** 4 odds
body 4 bulk, core, form, hull, mass,
soma 5 frame, stiff, stock, torso

6 corpse, corpus 7 anatomy, cadaver,
carcass, chassis, corpora (plural),
remains 8 physique 9 aggregate, substance *combining form:* 4 dema, soma,
some, somi (plural) 5 somat, somia,
somus 6 somata (plural), somato
body cavity 5 cecum, sinus 6 coelom
7 abdomen 8 hemocoel
body check 5 block
bodyguard 7 retinue 9 attendant, protector
body of water 3 bay, sea 4 cove, gulf,
lake, pond, pool 5 bight, brook, creek,
fiord, firth, fjord, inlet, ocean, river
6 harbor, lagoon, puddle, stream
7 channel, estuary 9 reservoir
body passage 4 duct, vein 5 canal
6 artery, meatus, ureter, vagina, venule,
vessel 7 trachea, urethra 8 bronchus
9 arteriole, capillary, esophagus, intestine 10 bronchiole 13 bronchial tube,
fallopian tube
body politic 5 state 6 nation 11 nation-
state
boffo 3 gag, gas, hit 4 wild 5 laugh
6 scream 7 sold-out 8 smash-hit, smashing 10 successful 11 sensational
bog 3 fen 4 mire, quag 5 delay, marsh,
swamp 6 impede, morass, muskeg,
slough, slow up 8 quagmire 9 swampland
Bogart, Humphrey *film:* 6 Sahara 7 Dead
End, Sabrina 8 Big Sleep (The), Key
Largo 10 Casablanca, High Sierra
11 Caine Mutiny (The) 12 African
Queen (The) 13 Maltese Falcon (The)
15 Petrified Forest (The) 16 To Have
and Have Not 24 Treasure of the Sierra
Madre (The) *wife:* 6 Bacall (Lauren)
bog down 4 flag, mire 5 choke, delay,
stall 6 detain, falter, hang up, hinder,
impede, retard, slow up 7 embroil, set
back, slacken 8 encumber, keep back,
obstruct, slow down 9 lose steam
10 decelerate
bogey 5 ghost, haunt, shade, spook
6 scarer, shadow, spirit, wraith 7 phantom, specter 8 phantasm, revenant
10 apparition
bogeyman 5 spook 7 bugbear, chimera,
monster, phantom, specter, spectre
10 apparition
boggle 4 balk, mess, muff, stun 5 amaze,
botch, fudge, gum up, shock, wreck
6 bollix, bungle, cobble, goof up, mess
up, strain 7 astound, louse up, nonplus,
stagger, stumble, stupefy 8 astonish,
bewilder, bowl over, confound 9 dumbfound, mishandle, mismanage, overwhelm, take aback 11 flabbergast
bogus 4 fake, mock, sham 5 false,

phony, snide 6 ersatz, forged, pseudo 7 fictive, pretend 8 invented, specious, spurious 9 brummagem, concocted, imitation, pinchbeck, simulated, trumped up 10 artificial, fabricated, fraudulent, mendacious 11 counterfeit

Bohème, La *character:* 4 Mimi 7 Rodolfo *composer:* 7 Puccini (Giacomo) *setting:* 5 Paris

bohemian 5 artsy, gypsy, hippy 6 hippie 7 beatnik, dropout, oddball, offbeat 8 maverick, vagabond, wanderer 9 eccentric 10 avant-garde, iconoclast, unorthodox 13 nonconformist

boil 3 jet 4 bolt, brew, burn, cook, dash, foam, fume, gush, moil, race, rage, rush, spew, spot, stew, vent 5 anger, churn, erupt, fling, froth, poach, shoot, storm, swirl 6 blow up, bubble, charge, canker, coddle, pimple, seethe, simmer 7 abscess, agitate, bristle, ferment, flare up, pustule, smolder 8 furuncle 9 carbuncle, discharge 10 effervesce 11 excrescence

boil down 4 pare, trim 6 amount, reduce 7 distill 8 compress, condense, simplify, truncate 9 summarize, synopsize 10 streamline 11 concentrate, encapsulate

boiler suit 8 coverall

boiling 3 hot 5 fiery 6 baking, red-hot, sultry, torrid 7 burning, febrile 8 agitated, roasting, scalding, sizzling, tropical 9 scorching 10 blistering

boil over 4 burn, fume, rage 5 erupt 6 blow up, bridle, see red, seethe 7 bristle, flare up

boisterous 4 loud, wild 5 noisy, rowdy 6 lively, stormy, unruly 7 blatant, raucous, riotous 8 strident 9 clamorous, convivial, turbulent 10 disorderly, disruptive, rollicking, tumultuous, uproarious, vociferous 11 loudmouthed, tempestuous 12 high-spirited, obstreperous, rambunctious, ungovernable, unrestrained

Boito opera 11 Mefistofele

bold 4 free, pert, rude 5 bluff, brave, fresh, gutsy, nervy, sassy, saucy, sheer, showy, steep 6 arrant, bright, brazen, cheeky, daring, heroic 7 doughty, forward, glaring, obvious, valiant 8 cocksure, fearless, impudent, insolent, intrepid, resolute, unafraid, valorous 9 audacious, dauntless, intrusive, prominent, shameless, undaunted 10 courageous, pronounced 11 adventurous, impertinent, smart-alecky, venturesome 12 enterprising, presumptuous

boldness 4 gall, grit 5 drive, nerve, valor

6 aplomb, mettle, spirit 8 audacity, backbone, chutzpah, temerity 9 arrogance, challenge, hardihood, impudence, insolence 10 brazenness, disrespect, effrontery 11 discourtesy 12 impertinence

Bolero composer 5 Ravel (Maurice)

Bolivia *ancient culture:* 4 Inca 10 Tiahuanaco *capital:* 5 La Paz, Sucre *city:* 6 El Alto 9 Santa Cruz 10 Cochabamba *conqueror:* 7 Pizarro (Hernando) *Indian people:* 6 Aymara 7 Quechua *lake:* 5 Poopó 8 Titicaca *language:* 6 Aymara 7 Quechua, Spanish *monetary unit:* 9 boliviano *mountain, range:* 5 Andes 6 Sajama *neighbor:* 4 Peru 5 Chile 6 Brazil 8 Paraguay 9 Argentina *river:* 4 Beni 5 Abuna 6 Mamoré 7 Guaporé 9 Pilcomayo

bollix 4 flub, mess, muff, ruin 5 botch, gum up, spoil, upset 6 bobble, bumble, bungle, foul up, fumble, goof up, jumble, mess up, muck up, muddle, muff up 7 confuse, louse up, screw up 8 dishevel, disorder, scramble, unsettle 9 mishandle, mismanage

bolo 5 knife 7 machete

Bolshevik 3 Red 6 commie 7 comrade 8 Leninist, tovarich, tovarish 9 communist

bolshevism 7 Marxism 8 Leninism 9 communism

bolster 3 aid 4 buoy, gird, help, prop 5 boost, brace, carry, cheer 6 assist, bear up, buoy up, pillow, upbear, uphold 7 bulwark, cushion, fortify, hearten, shore up, support, sustain 8 backstop, buttress, maintain 9 encourage, reinforce 10 strengthen 12 underpinning 13 reinforcement

bolt 3 bar, fly, rod, run 4 cram, dash, dart, flee, gulp, jump, lock, race, rush, tear, wolf 5 arrow, blurt, bound, chase, dowel, flush, rivet, scarf, scoot, shoot, skirr, slosh, start 6 charge, decamp, devour, gobble, guzzle, secure, spring 7 abscond, exclaim, hotfoot, make off, missile, rigidly, scamper, startle, take off 8 blurt out, hightail 9 skedaddle 10 make tracks, take flight 11 ingurgitate 13 thunderstroke

bomb 3 dud, hit 4 bust, dull, fail, flop, sink, zero 5 blast, blitz, lemon, loser, pound, shell 6 blow up 7 debacle, destroy, failure, home run, success, washout, wipe out 8 detonate, disaster, fall flat, long pass, long shot, spray can

bombard 4 pelt 5 blast, blitz, shell, storm 6 attack, assail, cannon, hammer, pepper, shower, strafe, strike 7 assault, barrage 8 catapult 9 cannonade

bombardment 4 hail **5** burst, salvo **6** attack, shower, volley **7** barrage, battery **8** drumfire **9** broadside, cannonade, fusillade, onslaught

bombardon 4 bass **8** bass tuba

bombast 4 rant **6** hot air **7** bluster, fustian, oration **8** rhapsody, tumidity **9** fancy talk, pomposity, turgidity **10** pretension **11** rodomontade

bombastic 5 wordy **6** prolix **7** aureate, flowery, orotund, pompous, swollen **8** inflated, puffed-up **9** overblown **10** euphuistic, rhetorical **11** declamatory, overwrought **12** magniloquent **13** grandiloquent

bombed 4 high **5** drunk, fried, stiff, tight **6** blotto, stoned, wasted **8** comatose, tanked up **9** plastered **10** inebriated **11** intoxicated

bombinate 3 hum **4** buzz, purr, whir **5** drone, strum, thrum **6** bumble, rumble **7** grumble

bombshell 4 blow, jolt **5** shock **6** marvel **8** surprise **9** curveball, sensation **10** revelation **11** thunderbolt

bona fide 4 real, sure, true **5** valid **6** actual **7** earnest, genuine, sincere **8** sterling **9** authentic, undoubted, veritable **10** legitimate, sure-enough **11** indubitable, in good faith **13** authenticated

bona fides 6 candor **7** probity **8** goodwill **9** good faith, sincerity **10** reputation **11** reliability, sincereness

bonanza 4 mine **5** catch, hoard **7** pay dirt **8** Golconda, gold mine, treasure, treasury, windfall **12** extravaganza **13** treasure trove

bonbon 5 candy, sweet **7** fondant **9** sweetmeat, sugarplum **10** confection

bond 3 tie **4** bail, fuse, knot, link, pact, yoke **5** nexus **6** cement, fetter, pledge, surety **7** bargain, compact, linkage, promise, shackle, warrant **8** adhesive, affinity, cohesion, contract, covenant, guaranty, ligament, ligature, security, vinculum, warranty **9** adherence, agreement, coherence, guarantee **10** attachment, connection, connective, obligation

bondage 4 yoke **6** chains, thrall **7** durance, fetters, helotry, peonage, serfage, serfdom, slavery **9** captivity, detention, servitude, thralldom, vassalage, villenage **10** subjection **11** enslavement, subjugation **12** imprisonment

bondsman 4 peon, serf **5** helot, slave **6** surety **7** chattel

bone *ankle:* **5** talus **6** tarsus *arm:* **4** ulna **6** radius **7** humerus *back:* **5** spine **8** vertebra **9** vertebrae (plural) *breast:* **7** sternum *calf:* **6** fibula *cavity:* **5** fossa *change into:* **6** ossify *cheek:* **5** malar **6** zygoma *chest:* **3** rib *collar:* **8** clavicle *face:* **5** malar, nasal **7** frontal *finger:* **7** phalanx **8** phalange *foot:* **6** tarsus **9** calcaneum, calcaneus **10** astragalus, metatarsus *hand:* **10** metacarpus *head:* **5** skull, vomer **7** cranium **8** parietal, sphenoid **9** occipital *heel:* **9** calcaneum, calcaneus *hip:* **5** ilium, pubis **6** pelvis **7** ischium *jaw:* **7** maxilla **8** mandible *kneecap:* **7** patella *leg:* **5** femur, tibia **6** fibula **7** patella *lower back:* **6** coccyx, sacrum *middle ear:* **5** anvil, incus **6** hammer, stapes **7** malleus, stirrup *pelvis:* **5** ilium *relating to:* **6** osteal *shin:* **5** tibia *shoulder blade:* **7** scapula *small:* **7** ossicle *substance:* **6** ossein *thigh:* **5** femur *toe:* **7** phalanx **8** phalange *U-shaped:* **5** hyoid *wrist:* **6** carpus

bonehead 4 clod **5** dunce, moron **6** cretin, dimwit, nitwit **7** halfwit **8** clodpole, clodpoll, lunkhead, numskull **9** ignoramus, lamebrain, numbskull **12** featherbrain

bonelike 7 osseous, osteoid

boner see BLOOPER

bone up 4 cram **5** study **6** review, revise **8** pore over

bong 4 bell, dong, peal, ring, toll **5** chime, knell, sound **6** hookah, strike **7** resound **9** water pipe **11** reverberate

boniface 7 barkeep **8** publican, taverner **9** barkeeper, innkeeper **12** saloonkeeper

bonkers 3 ape, mad **4** daft, loco, nuts, wild **5** batty, crazy, giddy, loony, potty **6** cuckoo, insane **7** bananas, haywire **8** demented, deranged, unhinged

bon mot 4 jest, quip **5** crack, sally **7** epigram, riposte **8** one-liner, repartee **9** witticism

bonny 4 fair, fine **6** comely, lovely, pretty **7** winsome **8** pleasing **9** beauteous, beautiful, excellent **10** attractive, delightful **11** good-looking

bon ton 4 élan **5** flair, style **6** gentry, jet set **7** fashion, society **8** elegance, smart set **9** haut monde, propriety **11** high society

bonus 4 gift, plus **6** reward **7** benefit, payment, premium **8** dividend **12** compensation **13** fringe benefit

bon vivant 7 epicure, flaneur, gourmet, trifler **8** aesthete, gourmand **10** aficionado, dilettante, gastronome **11** cognoscente, connoisseur **12** boulevardier, gastronomist, man-about-town

bony 4 lank, lean, thin **5** gaunt, lanky, spare **6** barren, skinny, twiggy **7** angular, osseous, scraggy, scrawny, starved

8 rawboned, skeletal, underfed 9 emaciated 10 cadaverous

boo 4 hiss, hoot, jeer, razz 6 bellow, deride, heckle, revile 7 catcall 9 raspberry, shout down

boob 3 oaf 4 dolt, dope, goof, goon, boor 5 chump, dunce, goose, ninny 6 bugbear, dumb ox 7 blunder, fathead, mistake, tomfool 8 lunkhead 9 simpleton 10 dunderhead, philistine

boo-boo see BLOOPER

booby hatch 6 asylum, bedlam 8 bughouse, loony bin, madhouse, nuthouse 9 funny farm 11 institution

booby trap 4 mine 5 snare 6 hazard 7 pitfall, springe 8 deadfall, land mine

boodle 3 wad 4 bilk, haul, heap, loot, mint, perk, take 5 booty, prize, spoil 6 bundle, packet, payola, spoils 7 fortune, plunder, present 8 kickback 9 incentive 10 bribe money, inducement

book 4 list, text, tome 5 album, bible, codex, enter, folio, novel, tract 6 charge, engage, enroll, folder, line up, manual, octavo, quarto, record, script, volume 7 catalog, edition, reserve 8 hardback, inscribe, register, schedule, softback, treatise 9 hardcover, monograph, paperback, preengage 10 compendium 11 publication *combining form:* 6 biblio *of hours:* 5 Horae *of psalms:* 7 psalter

bookie see BOOKMAKER

bookish 5 nerdy 6 formal 7 erudite, learned 8 academic, cerebral, literary, pedantic, studious, well-read 9 scholarly 10 longhaired 12 intellectual, professorial

bookkeeping term 4 loss 5 asset, audit, check, debit, entry, yield 6 budget, credit, equity, income, ledger, margin, profit, return 7 account, accrual, balance, expense, invoice, revenue, voucher 8 discount, dividend, interest, write off 9 inventory, liability 10 appreciate, depreciate, fiscal year 11 double entry 12 amortization, appreciation, balance sheet, depreciation, variable cost

booklet 8 brochure, opuscule, pamphlet

bookmaker 6 binder, bookie, editor 7 printer 9 bet holder, oddsmaker, publisher

book of account 6 ledger, record 7 journal 8 register

bookplate 5 label 8 ex libris

bookstall 5 kiosk 9 newsstand

boom 3 wax 4 bang, clap, grow, rise, slam, spar, wham 5 blast, boost, burst, crack, crash, sound, smash, swell 6 do well, expand, growth, rumble, thrive 7 explode, prosper, resound, thunder 8 flourish, kick hard, long beam 9 expansion 10 bull market, detonation, prosperity 11 reverberate

boomerang 6 recoil 7 rebound 8 backfire, backlash, come back, kick back, ricochet 10 bounce back

booming 4 bass, deep 6 robust 7 roaring 8 affluent, resonant, sonorous, thriving 9 deafening 10 prospering, prosperous, successful 11 flourishing

boon 3 aid, gay 4 gift, good, help 5 asset, grant, favor, jolly, merry, token 6 blithe, bounty, jocund, jovial 7 benefit, festive, gleeful, godsend, largess, present 8 blessing, largesse, mirthful, windfall 9 advantage, convivial, privilege 10 indulgence 11 benediction, benefaction

boondocks 5 wilds 6 sticks 7 outback 8 backland, frontier 9 backwater, backwoods, provinces, rural area 10 hinterland 11 backcountry, countryside 12 back of beyond

boondoggle 4 cord, hoax, scam 5 fraud, hokum 6 hustle 7 fast one, hatband, lanyard, swindle 8 flimflam 10 fool around, mess around 11 horse around

boor 3 cad, oaf 4 lout, hick, rube 5 brute, chuff, churl, clown, yahoo, yokel 6 lummox, rustic 7 buffoon, bumpkin, hayseed, peasant 9 ignoramus, vulgarian 10 clodhopper, philistine, provincial

boorish 4 rude 5 crass, crude, rough 6 coarse, common, rugged, vulgar 7 illbred, loutish, lowbred, lumpish, uncivil, uncouth 8 churlish, cloddish, clownish, impolite, insolent, lubberly, swainish 9 graceless, offensive, tasteless, unrefined 10 philistine, provincial, robustious, uncultured, ungracious, unmannerly, unpolished, unsociable 11 bad-mannered, clodhopping, illmannered, uncivilized 12 discourteous, uncultivated 13 disrespectful

boost 3 aid 4 hike, lift, jump, plug, push, rise 5 raise, steal 6 assist, beef up, expand, extend, foster, jack up 7 advance, amplify, augment, elevate, magnify, promote, support 8 heighten, increase, shoplift 9 advertise, encourage, expansion, promotion 10 assistance 11 helping hand 13 encouragement

booster 3 fan 4 hypo, shot 6 backer, patron, rocket, rooter 7 vaccine 8 champion, defender, promoter, upholder 9 amplifier, expositor, injection, proponent, supporter 10 shoplifter 11 inoculation

boot 3 can 4 bang, fire, kick, sack 5 chuck, eject, evict, expel, start 6 bounce, thrill 7 dismiss, kick out, start up 8 throw out 9 discharge, dismissal, terminate *kind:* 5 wader 6 arctic, chukka, gaiter, galosh, mukluk 7 jodhpur, shoepac 8 balmoral, cothurni (plural), overshoe, shoepack 9 cothurnus 10 Wellington

Boötes star 8 Arcturus

booth 4 nook 5 berth, bower, kiosk, stall, stand 6 carrel 9 enclosure 11 compartment

bootleg 3 hot, run 5 hooch 6 pirate 7 illicit, smuggle 9 irregular, moonshine 10 bathtub gin, contraband 11 black market, mountain dew 12 unauthorized

bootless 4 vain 5 empty 6 futile, hollow 7 useless 8 abortive, impotent, nugatory 9 fruitless, valueless, worthless 10 profitless, unavailing 11 ineffective, ineffectual 12 unproductive, unprofitable, unsuccessful

bootlick 4 fawn 5 cower, crawl, creep, toady 6 cringe, grovel, kowtow, stroke 7 cater to, flatter, truckle 8 blandish 9 brownnose, importune, seek favor 10 curry favor 11 apple-polish 12 bow and scrape

bootlicker 4 toad 5 toady 6 lackey, lapdog, minion, yes-man 7 doormat, spaniel 8 hanger-on 9 sycophant 11 lickspittle

booty 4 haul, lift, loot, pelf, swag, take 5 prize, spoil, yield 6 spoils 7 pillage, plunder, rear end, seizure, takings 8 buttocks

booze 4 brew, grog, swig 5 binge, drink, hooch, juice, quaff, sauce, souse, swill 6 guzzle, imbibe, liquor, rotgut, tank up, tipple 7 alcohol, carouse, put away, spirits, swizzle 8 cocktail, liquor up 9 aqua vitae, firewater, knock back, moonshine

boozehound 3 sot 4 lush, wino 5 drunk, hoser, souse 7 guzzler 8 drunkard 9 alcoholic, inebriate 11 dipsomaniac

boozer see BOOZEHOUND

bop 3 bat, box, hit, jab, pop, rap 4 bash, bean, belt, biff, boff, blow, clip, cuff, jive, slug, sock, swat, whop 5 clock, pound, smack, thump, whack 8 plant one

borax 4 junk

Bordeaux wine *district:* 5 Médoc 6 Graves *grape:* 6 Malbec, Merlot 8 Cabernet *name:* 5 Arsac, Ludon, Macau 6 Moulis 7 Labarde, Margaux, Pomerol 8 Cantenac, St. Julien, Pauillac 9 St. Emilion, St. Estèphe, St. Laurent *red:* 6 claret

bordello see BROTHEL

border 3 hem, lip, rim 4 abut, brim, edge, join, line, pale, trim 5 bound, brink, flank, frame, limit, march, skirt, touch, verge 6 adjoin, bounds, butt on, define, fringe, limbus, margin, trench 7 contour, outline, selvage 8 approach, boundary, frontier, neighbor, sideline, surround 9 marchland, perimeter, periphery 11 butt against, communicate *inlaid:* 8 purfling *raised:* 7 coaming

bordereau 4 note 6 record 7 account 10 memorandum

bordering 4 nigh 5 close 6 almost, next to 7 meeting, verging 8 abutting, adjacent, touching 9 adjoining, alongside, close upon, impinging 10 approximal, contiguous, juxtaposed 11 coterminous, neighboring, practically

borderland 5 march 6 fringe, margin 8 frontier 9 marchland

borderline 4 pale 6 almost, nearly 7 dubious, unclear 8 boundary, doubtful, marginal, unstable 9 ambiguous, debatable, dubitable, equivocal, perimeter, uncertain, undecided, unsettled 11 demarcation, problematic 12 intermediate 13 indeterminate

border state 8 Delaware, Kentucky, Maryland, Missouri, Virginia

bore 3 irk 4 drag, drip, mine, peer, pill, ream, sink, tire, yawn 5 auger, drill, drone, gouge, prick, punch 6 burrow, pierce, tunnel 7 bromide, caliber, fatigue 8 diameter, puncture 9 penetrate, perforate, soporific 10 dullsville

boreal 3 icy 4 cold, cool 5 chill, gelid, polar 6 arctic, bitter, chilly, frosty, frigid, tundra 7 glacial, wintery 8 freezing, northern 9 northerly

Boreas *beloved:* 8 Orithyia *brother:* 5 Notus 8 Hesperus, Zephyrus *father:* 8 Astraeus *mother:* 3 Eos *son:* 5 Zetes 6 Calais

boredom 5 blahs, ennui 6 apathy, stupor, tedium, torpor 7 fatigue 8 doldrums, dullness, flatness, monotony 9 lassitude, weariness 11 incuriosity, tediousness 12 indifference

Borgia 4 Juan 6 Alonso, Cesare 7 Alfonso, Rodrigo 8 Lucrezia

boring 3 dry 4 arid, drab, dull, flat, zero 5 ho-hum, vapid 6 dreary, stodgy, tiring 7 humdrum, tedious 8 bromidic, drudging, lifeless, tiresome 9 wearisome 10 lackluster, monotonous, pedestrian, unexciting 13 uninteresting

boring tool 5 drill, auger 6 trepan

Boris Godunov composer 10 Mussorgsky (Modest) 11 Moussorgsky (Modest)

born 3 née 6 innate, native 8 destined, inherent 9 intrinsic 10 congenital, deep-seated *combining form:* 3 gen 4 gene 6 genous 7 genetic

borne by the wind 6 aeolic, eolian 7 aeolian

Borneo *ethnic group:* 4 Dyak 5 Dayak *mountain:* 8 Kinabalu *nation:* 6 Brunei *river:* 6 Rabang

Borodin opera 10 Prince Igor

borough 4 town 5 burgh 7 village 8 township

bosh see BUNKUM

Bosnia-Herzegovina *capital:* 8 Sarajevo *language:* 7 Serbian 8 Croatian 13 Serbo-Croatian *monetary unit:* 4 mark 5 dinar *neighbor:* 6 Serbia 7 Croatia *part of:* 7 Balkans *sea:* 8 Adriatic

bosom 4 bust, core, soul, teat 5 chest, close, heart 6 breast 7 embrace 8 feelings, intimate 10 affections, conscience

bosomy 5 built, busty, buxom, curvy 6 chesty 7 shapely, stacked 9 Junoesque 11 full-figured

boss 4 head, stud 5 chief 6 direct, honcho, leader, manage, master, survey 7 command, foreman, headman, oversee 8 director, employer, overlook, overseer, superior 9 chieftain, supervise 10 supervisor, taskmaster 11 superintend *African:* 5 bwana

bossy 3 cow 4 calf 7 studded 8 despotic, imperial 9 arbitrary, assertive, imperious, masterful 10 autocratic, high-handed, imperative, oppressive, peremptory, tyrannical 11 controlling, dictatorial, domineering, magisterial, overbearing

botanist *American:* 4 Gray (Asa) 5 Sears (Paul B.) 6 Bailey (Liberty), Bessey (Charles), Carver (George Washington) 7 Bartram (John, William), Burbank (Luther) 9 Fairchild (David) *Austrian:* 6 Mendel (Gregor) *British:* 6 Sloane (Sir Hans) *Danish:* 7 Warming (Johannes) *Dutch:* 7 De Vries (Hugo) *French:* 7 Lamarck (Chevalier de) *German:* 4 Cohn (Ferdinand), Mohl (Hugo von) 5 Sachs (Julius von) *Irish:* 6 Harvey (William) *Scottish:* 5 Brown (Robert) *Swedish:* 8 Linnaeus (Carolus) *Swiss:* 6 Nägeli (Karl) 8 Candolle (Augustin)

botany branch 7 ecology 8 algology, bryology, mycology 9 phycology 10 morphology, palynology, physiology 11 hydroponics, paleobotany, pteridology, systematics 12 bacteriology

botch 4 blow, flop, flub, foul, goof, mess, muck, muff, ruin 5 fluff, gum up, mix-up, snarl, spoil 6 bobble, boggle,

bollix, bumble, bungle, fiasco, fumble, goof up, mess up, muddle 7 blunder, confuse, louse up, washout 8 bugger up, disaster, disorder, dishevel, shambles 9 mishandle, mismanage, patchwork 10 discompose, hodgepodge, misconduct, mishmash

botchy 5 messy 6 blowzy, frowsy, frowzy, sloppy, untidy 7 chaotic 8 careless, confused, slapdash, slipshod, slovenly

both *combining form:* 3 bis *prefix:* 4 ambi, amph 5 amphi

bother 3 ado, bug, irk, nag, vex 4 drag, fret, fuss, gall, pest, pain 5 annoy, eat at, harry, trial, upset 6 badger, flurry, harass, needle, pester, plague, ruffle 7 afflict, agitate, anxiety, bedevil, concern, disturb, fluster, perturb, provoke, torment, trouble 8 disquiet, headache, irritant, nuisance, vexation 9 aggravate, annoyance 10 discompose, exasperate, irritation 11 aggravation, intrude upon 12 exasperation 13 inconvenience

botheration 4 damn, pain, pest 5 trial 6 plague 7 torment 8 headache, irritant, nuisance, vexation 9 annoyance 10 difficulty, irritation 11 aggravation, provocation 12 exasperation 13 inconvenience

Botswana *capital:* 8 Gaborone *city:* 11 Francistown *desert:* 8 Kalahari *former name:* 12 Bechuanaland *language:* 6 Tswana 7 English *monetary unit:* 4 pula *neighbor:* 7 Namibia 8 Zimbabwe 11 South Africa *river:* 5 Chobe 6 Molopo 7 Limpopo 8 Okavango

bottle 4 vial 5 cruet, cruse, flask, phial 6 ampule, carafe, fiasco, flacon, magnum, vessel 7 ampoule 8 decanter, jeroboam 9 container

bottle gourd 8 calabash

bottleneck 5 choke 6 hinder, impede, narrow 7 impasse 8 obstacle, obstruct, paralyze, slowdown, throttle 9 hindrance 10 choke point, congestion, traffic jam 11 obstruction

bottom 3 bum 4 base, boat, core, foot, root, pith, rump, seat, ship, sole, soul, tail, tush 5 basal, basic, basis, fanny, found, nadir 6 behind, breech, heinie, lowest, source 7 bedrock, essence, footing, primary, rear end 8 backside, buttocks, derriere, pedestal, pediment 9 establish, fundament, lowermost, posterior, predicate, principle, underbody, undermost, underside 10 foundation, nethermost, underbelly, underlying, underneath 11 fundamental, lowest point 12 undersurface

bottomless 4 deep, vast 7 abysmal, endless **8** baseless, enduring, profound, unending **9** boundless, unlimited **10** gratuitous, groundless, unfillable, ungrounded **11** everlasting, inestimable, never-ending **12** immeasurable, incalculable, unfathomable **13** inexhaustible

bottommost 4 last **5** least **6** lowest **7** deepest

bough 3 arm **4** limb **5** shoot **6** branch **8** offshoot

boulevard 4 road **6** artery, avenue, street **7** terrace **8** main drag **9** esplanade, promenade **10** high street **12** thoroughfare

boulevardier 7 flaneur, trifler **9** bon vivant **10** aficionado, dilettante **11** cognoscente, connoisseur **12** man-about-town

bounce 3 can, hop, pep, vim, zip **4** fire, jump, leap, oust, sack, zest **5** expel, vault, verve, vigor **6** energy, hurdle, spirit, spring **7** bluster, boot out, dismiss, kick out, rebound, saltate, sparkle **8** buoyancy, ricochet, vitality **9** animation, discharge, eliminate, terminate **10** ebullience, elasticity, liveliness

bounce back 5 rally **6** perk up, pick up, recoil, return, revive **7** cheer up, improve, rebound, recover **8** backfire **9** boomerang **10** recuperate, turn around

bounce off 5 carom **7** rebound **8** ricochet

bouncer 4 goon **5** guard **8** houseman, sentinel, watchman **9** muscleman

bouncy 3 gay **4** airy **5** peppy, perky **6** blithe, cheery, jaunty, jocund, lively **7** buoyant, elastic **8** animated, volatile **9** ebullient, energetic, expansive, exuberant, resilient, sprightly **10** unsinkable **12** effervescent, high-spirited **13** irrepressible

bound 3 end, hem, hop, rim **4** bolt, edge, jump, leap, term, skip **5** caper, frisk, hem in, limit, skirt, vault, verge **6** border, bounce, define, demark, driven, finite, fringe, gambol, hurdle, margin, spring, sprint **7** confine, delimit, enclose, hotfoot, limited, mark out, obliged, pledged, rebound, saltate **8** articled, beholden, confined, confines, enslaved, resolved, restrain, surround **9** compelled, demarcate, obligated **10** determined, indentured, limitation **11** apprenticed, responsible **12** circumscribe

boundary 3 hem **4** mete, pale **5** ambit, limit **6** limits, margin **7** compass, outline **8** confines, environs, purlieus **9** perimeter, precincts **10** borderline **13** circumference

bounder 3 cad, cur, dog **4** boor, worm **5** knave, louse, rogue **6** rascal, rotter

boundless 4 vast **5** great **7** endless **8** infinite **9** excessive, limitless, unbounded, unlimited **10** indefinite, unconfined, unmeasured **11** illimitable, measureless **12** immeasurable, unrestricted **13** inexhaustible, unsurpassable

bounteous 5 ample **6** benign, lavish **7** copious, liberal, profuse **8** abundant, generous, handsome, prodigal **9** bountiful, capacious, expansive, extensive, plenteous, plentiful, unsparing **10** beneficent, big-hearted, freehanded, munificent, openhanded, voluminous **11** magnanimous, overflowing

bountiful see BOUNTEOUS

bounty 5 grant, prize, yield **6** deluge, plenty, reward, wealth **7** payment, premium **8** plethora, richness **9** abundance, affluence, plenitude, profusion **10** cornucopia, generosity, inducement, liberality, luxuriance, prosperity **11** benevolence, copiousness **12** compensation

Bounty captain 5 Bligh (William)

bouquet 4 balm, kudo, odor, posy **5** aroma, kudos, scent, spice, spray **6** eulogy, medley **7** acclaim, corsage, essence, garland, incense, nosegay, perfume **8** accolade, encomium **9** fragrance, redolence **10** compliment **11** arrangement, boutonniere **12** commendation

bourgeois 7 burgher **8** ordinary **10** conformist, philistine **11** middle-class **12** conventional

bourgeoisie 11 middle class, third estate

Bourne Identity author 6 Ludlum (Robert)

bout 3 jag, run **4** game, meet, term, tour, turn **5** match, round, shift, siege, spell, spasm, spree, stint, throe, trick **6** attack **7** contest, session **8** outbreak **10** engagement

boutique 4 shop **8** emporium

bovine 3 cow, yak **4** anoa, bull, calf, gaur, neat, zebu **5** bison, steer, stirk **6** heifer, placid, torpid, wisent **7** aurochs, banteng, buffalo, bullock, cowlike **8** longhorn *genus:* **3** Bos *sound:* **3** low, moo

bow 3 arc, bob, dip, nod **4** arch, bend, knot, lout, prow, turn **5** angle, crook, curve, debut, hunch, round, stoop, yield **6** archer, congee, curtsy, give in, kowtow, relent, salaam, salute, submit **7** concede, curtsey, flexure, incline, rainbow, succumb, turning **9** curvation, curvature, genuflect, obeisance, surrender 10 capitulate 11 buckle under 12 knuckle under

Bow, Clara 6 It girl

bowdlerize 4 blip, edit 6 censor, excise, purify, screen 7 abridge, cleanse, distort, launder 8 sanitize 9 expurgate 10 adulterate, blue-pencil

bowed 4 bent 5 arced, bandy 6 arched, curved 11 bandy-legged, curvilinear

bowel 3 gut 6 paunch 9 intestine

bower 5 arbor 6 anchor 7 enclose, pergola, retreat 9 apartment

bowery 7 skid row

bowfin 4 amia 7 mudfish

bowl 5 arena, basin, jorum, mazer, stade, tazza 6 tureen, vessel 7 stadium 8 coliseum 12 amphitheater

bowlegged 5 bandy

bowler 3 hat 5 derby 6 kegler

Bowl game 5 Super *Abilene:* 5 Pecan *Anaheim:* 7 Freedom *Atlanta:* 5 Peach *Dallas:* 6 Cotton *El Paso:* 3 Sun *Fresno:* 10 California *Honolulu:* 5 Aloha *Houston:* 10 Bluebonnet *Jacksonville:* 5 Gator *Memphis:* 7 Liberty *Miami:* 6 Orange 8 Carquest *Mobile:* 6 Senior *New Orleans:* 5 Sugar *Orlando:* 13 Florida Citrus *Pasadena:* 4 Rose *San Diego:* 7 Holiday *Shreveport:* 12 Independence *Tampa:* 10 Hall of Fame *Tempe:* 6 Fiesta *Tucson:* 6 Copper

bowling 7 kegling *British:* 8 skittles *Italian:* 5 bocce, bocci 6 boccie *term:* 3 pin 4 hook, lane, spot 5 curve, frame, spare, split 6 gutter, strike, string, turkey 7 duckpin 9 candlepin

bowl over 3 awe, wow 4 daze, fell, stun 5 floor, shock, throw 6 boggle, dismay 7 astound, flatten, impress, stupefy 8 blow away, surprise 9 bring down, dumbfound, knock down, overwhelm 10 disconcert

bow out 4 exit, fold, quit 5 leave, welsh 6 beg off, give up, retire 8 withdraw 9 surrender

box 3 bin 4 case, cell, chop, cuff, duke, loge, slap, sock, spar 5 booth, chest, clout, crate, fight, punch, smack, stall, trunk 6 buffet, carton, casket, coffer, coffin, encase, hopper, packet 7 confine, enclose, package 9 container, enclosure, rectangle 10 pigeonhole, receptacle 11 compartment

boxer 7 fighter, palooka 8 pugilist 9 flyweight 11 heavyweight, lightweight 12 bantamweight, middleweight, welterweight 13 featherweight *champ:* 3 Ali (Muhammad) 4 Bowe (Riddick) 5 Bruno (Frank), Jones (Roy), Lewis (Lennox), Louis (Joe), Moore (Archie), Tyson (Mike) 6 Hagler (Marvin),

Hearns (Thomas), Holmes (Larry), McCall (Oliver), Moorer (Michael), Seldon (Bruce), Spinks (Leon, Michael), Tunney (Gene), Walker (Mickey) 7 Charles (Ezzard), Corbett (James), Dempsey (Jack), Douglas (Buster), Foreman (George), Frazier (Joe), Johnson (Jack), LaMotta (Jake), Leonard (Sugar Ray), Sharkey (Jack), Walcott (Joe) 8 Marciano (Rocky), Robinson (Sugar Ray), Sullivan (John L.) 9 Armstrong (Henry), Holyfield (Evander), Patterson (Floyd), Schmeling (Max)

boxing 8 pugilism 10 fisticuffs 13 prizefighting *term:* 3 jab, TKO 4 blow, bout, duck, foul, hook, ring, rope, spar 5 break, count, feint, glove, match, parry, punch, round, swing 6 bucket, canvas, corner 7 low blow, referee 8 heavy bag, knockout, uppercut 9 knockdown 11 punching bag

boy 3 lad, son, tad 5 gamin, puppy, sonny 6 laddie, nipper, shaver 9 shaveling, stripling, youngster *combining form:* 3 ped 4 paed, paid, pedo 5 paedo, paido *errand:* 5 gofer 8 lobbygow *French:* 6 garçon *Latin:* 4 puer *mischievous:* 6 urchin *Spanish:* 4 niño

boyfriend 4 beau 5 swain 6 fiancé, old man, suitor 7 main man 9 inamorato

Boy Scout *founder:* 11 Baden-Powell (Robert) *gathering:* 8 jamboree *motto:* 10 be prepared *rank:* 4 Life (Scout), Star (Scout) 5 Eagle (Scout) 10 Tenderfoot *unit:* 5 troop 6 patrol

Boys Town *founder:* 8 Flanagan (Edward) *state:* 8 Nebraska

bozo 3 oaf 4 boob, clod, dodo, dolt, dope, fool, goof, jerk, mutt, simp, yo-yo 5 chump, dummy, dunce, idiot, moron, ninny, noddy, stupe 6 dimwit, donkey, dum-dum, nitwit, noodle 7 airhead, dullard, pinhead 8 bonehead, clodpoll, dumbbell, dumbhead, imbecile, lunkhead, meathead, numskull 9 birdbrain, blockhead, ignoramus, lamebrain, numbskull, simpleton, thickhead 10 dunderhead, hammerhead, nincompoop 11 chowderhead, chucklehead, knucklehead

B.P.O.E. member 3 Elk

Brabantio's daughter 9 Desdemona

brabble 3 row 4 beef, feud, flap, riot, spat, tiff 5 argue, scrap, set to 6 bicker, blowup, fracas, grouse 7 dispute, fall out, palaver, quarrel, rhubarb, scuffle, wrangle 8 argument, squabble 9 altercate, bickering, brannigan, caterwaul, wrangling 10 falling-out 11 altercation, disputation, embroilment

brace 3 arm, bar, duo, tie 4 dyad, gird,

pair, prop, stay 5 clamp, ready, shore, steel, strut, truss 6 accost, bear up, column, couple, demand, splint, steady, uphold 7 bolster, bracket, enliven, fortify, freshen, prepare, refresh, shore up, support, sustain, tighten, twosome 8 buttress 9 reinforce 10 cantilever, exhilarate, invigorate, strengthen 12 underpinning 13 underpropping

bracelet 6 bangle 7 manacle 8 wristlet

bracing 4 keen 5 brisk, crisp, fresh, nippy, sharp, tonic 6 biting, chilly 7 rousing 8 stirring 9 animating 10 energizing, quickening 11 restorative, stimulating, stimulative 12 exhilarating, invigorating

bracken 4 fern 5 brake, brush, scrub 11 undergrowth

bracket 3 arm 4 join, link, omit 5 brace 6 couple, relate, remove 7 combine, compare, conjoin, connect, embrace, enclose, include, support 8 buttress, encircle, leave out, put aside, set aside 9 associate, encompass 11 parenthesis 12 strengthener

brackish 4 sour 5 acrid, briny, salty 6 saline, salted 9 repulsive, sickening 10 nauseating

bract 4 leaf 5 glume 6 paleat, spathe 8 phyllary

brad 4 nail

Bradamant *brother:* 7 Rinaldo *husband:* 6 Rogero 8 Ruggiero

Bradbury's forte 5 sci-fi 7 fantasy

brae 4 bank, hill 5 slope 8 hillside

brag 3 gas 4 blow, crow, puff 5 boast, mouth, prate, vaunt 7 show off, swagger, talk big 9 cockiness, gasconade 10 grandstand 11 rodomontade

braggadocio 6 hot air 7 boaster, bombast, bravado, conceit, puffery, swagger, windbag 8 blowhard, boasting, braggart, bragging 9 arrogance, cockiness, pomposity 10 cockalorum, pretension, swaggering 11 fanfaronade

braggart 6 blower 7 boaster, egotist, vaunter, windbag 8 big mouth, blowhard 9 big talker, know-it-all, swaggerer, vulgarian 11 braggadocio

Brahmin 8 highbrow 9 blueblood, patrician 10 aristocrat

braid 4 plat 5 plait, queue 7 galloon, pigtail 8 soutache 9 interlace 10 intertwine, interweave

brain 3 wit 4 bean, conk, mind 7 concuss 9 intellect 10 gray matter 12 intelligence *bone:* 5 skull 7 cranium *clot:* 10 thrombosis *gland:* 6 pineal 9 pituitary *layer:* 6 cortex *lobe:* 6 limbic, vermis 7 frontal 8 parietal, temporal 9 occipital *membrane:* 3 pia 4 dura 6 meninx 8 pia

mater 9 arachnoid, dura mater *part:* 4 lobe 7 medulla 8 cerebrum, thalamus 9 sensorium, ventricle 10 cerebellum, hemisphere 12 diencephalon *relating to:* 8 cerebral 10 encephalic *ridge:* 4 gyri (plural) 5 gyrus *vertebrate:* 10 encephalon *wave record:* 3 EEG

brainchild 4 idea, opus, work 6 animus, scheme, theory 7 coinage 9 handiwork, invention 10 hypothesis, innovation 11 achievement, chef-d'oeuvre, contrivance

brainiac 4 whiz 6 genius 7 prodigy

brainless 3 dim 5 dense, silly, thick 6 simple, stupid 7 asinine, foolish, idiotic, moronic, vacuous, witless 9 dimwitted, nitwitted 10 acephalous 12 feebleminded

brainpower 3 wit 5 sense 6 smarts 8 aptitude, capacity, sagacity 9 intellect, mentality, mother wit 10 perception 11 discernment, penetration 12 intelligence 13 comprehension

brainsick 3 mad 4 daft 5 batty, crazy, manic, potty 6 crazed, insane, mental 7 cracked, haywire, lunatic 8 aberrant, demented, deranged, maniacal, unhinged 9 bedlamite, delirious, disturbed 10 disordered, incoherent, irrational, unbalanced

brainstorm 3 rap, jaw 4 idea 6 confer, huddle 7 dream up, think up 8 cogitate, discuss, mull over 9 mental fit 10 groupthink, kick around, toss around 11 inspiration, put together

brainteaser 5 poser, rebus 6 puzzle, riddle 7 stumper 9 conundrum 10 cryptogram

brainwashing 10 propaganda 11 mind control, reeducation

brainy 4 keen 5 quick, savvy, sharp, smart 6 adroit, astute, bright, clever 9 eggheaded, brilliant, sagacious 10 discerning, precocious 11 intelligent, quick-witted, ready-witted 13 knowledgeable, perspicacious

brake 4 curb, slow, stop 5 block 6 damper, hinder, impede, retard, slough 7 barrier, bracken, slacken 8 blockade, obstacle, obstruct, slow down 9 deterrent, hindrance 10 constraint, decelerate 11 bracken fern

bramble 4 burr 5 brier, furze, gorse, hedge, shrub, thorn 6 nettle 7 thistle

branch 3 arm 4 fork, limb, rami (plural), wing 5 bough, ramus 6 ramify 7 diverge, outpost 8 division 9 tributary 10 subsidiary

branched 6 ramate, ramose

brand 4 blot, blur, logo, make, mark, onus, sear, slur, sort, spot, type

5 badge, class, odium, stain, stamp, sword, taint, torch **6** accuse, charge, impute, stigma, stripe **7** species, variety **8** black eye, disgrace, insignia, logotype **9** trademark **10** stigmatize

brandish 4 wave **5** flash, shake, sport, swing, wield **6** flaunt, parade **7** display, exhibit, show off **8** flourish

brand-new 4 mint **5** fresh **6** latest, unused, virgin **8** up-to-date **9** untouched **11** cutting-edge **13** inexperienced

brandy 4 marc, ouzo, raki **5** Pisco **6** cognac, grappa, kirsch, Metaxa **7** liqueur **8** Armagnac, calvados, digestif, eau-de-vie **9** applejack, framboise, slivovitz

brannigan 3 row **4** bust, flap, spat, tiff **5** binge, fight, set-to, spree **6** bender, blowup, hassle, ruckus **7** brabble, discord, dispute, quarrel, wassail, wrangle **8** squabble **10** falling-out **11** altercation

brash 4 bold, flip, pert **5** cocky, gutsy, hasty, nervy, saucy **6** brassy, brazen, cheeky, madcap, uppish, uppity **7** brittle, forward **8** arrogant, cocksure, flippant, impudent, insolent, reckless, tactless **9** audacious, bumptious, ebullient, energetic, exuberant, hot-headed, impetuous, impolitic, maladroit, unabashed, untactful **10** ill-advised, incautious **11** overweening, thoughtless **12** high-spirited, presumptuous, undiplomatic, unrestrained **13** disrespectful, inconsiderate, irrepressible, self-assertive

brashness 4 gall, grit, guts **5** brass, cheek, crust, nerve, pluck **6** aplomb, daring, mettle, spirit **8** audacity, chutzpah, temerity **9** assurance **10** confidence, effrontery **11** presumption

brass 4 gall **5** cheek, nerve **8** audacity, chutzpah **9** brashness, impudence, insolence **10** confidence, effrontery **11** presumption **12** impertinence

brassbound 3 set **5** brash, rigid **6** brazen, narrow **7** adamant, bigoted, forward **8** obdurate **9** illiberal, presuming, obstinate, unbending **10** implacable, inflexible, intolerant, relentless, unswayable, unyielding **11** opinionated, small-minded, unrelenting **12** narrow-minded, presumptuous, single-minded **13** dyed-in-the-wool, self-asserting, self-assertive

brasserie 10 restaurant

brass hat 3 VIP **4** boss **5** elder **6** better, senior **7** big shot **8** big whell, higher-up, superior

brassica 4 kale, rape **5** colza **6** turnip **7** cabbage, mustard **8** broccoli, collards, kohlrabi, rutabaga **11** cauliflower

brass tacks 5 facts **7** details **11** nitty-gritty, particulars

brass worker 7 brazier

brassy see BRAZEN

brat 3 imp **4** punk **6** urchin **10** holy terror

bravado 5 bluff **6** hot air **7** bluster, bombast **8** audacity, boasting, boldness, bragging, defiance, vaunting **9** gasconade **10** blustering, pretension, swaggering **11** braggadocio, grandiosity **12** boastfulness

brave 4 bold, dare, defy, face, game, meet, risk **5** beard, gutsy, hardy, manly, nervy, noble, stout **6** daring, heroic, manful, plucky, spunky, take on **7** defiant, doughty, gallant, valiant, venture **8** confront, face down, fearless, intrepid, reckless, resolute, spirited, splendid, stalwart, unafraid, valorous **9** audacious, challenge, dauntless, excellent, steadfast, undaunted, withstand **10** courageous **11** boldhearted, indomitable, lionhearted, undauntable, unflinching, venturesome **12** stouthearted **13** adventuresome

Brave New World author 6 Huxley (Aldous)

bravery 4 grit, guts **5** nerve, pluck, valor **6** daring, mettle, spirit **7** courage, heroism **8** audacity, boldness, temerity **9** derring-do, fortitude, gallantry **11** intrepidity **12** fearlessness, intrepidness *false:* **7** bravado

bravo 3 olé **4** rave **5** cheer **6** gunman, hit man, killer **7** ovation, plaudit, villain **8** applause, assassin **9** desperado

bravura 4 bold **5** showy **6** daring, florid, ornate **8** dazzling, skillful, virtuoso **9** brilliant

brawl 3 row **4** feud, flap, fray, fuss, maul, riot, spar, spat, tiff **5** clash, broil, fight, melee, scrap, set-to **6** affray, battle, bicker, dustup, fracas, rumble, tussle **7** bobbery, brabble, contend, quarrel, rhubarb, ruction, scuffle, wrangle **8** dogfight, eruption, skirmish, slugfest, squabble, upheaval **9** fistfight, imbroglio, scrimmage **10** donnybrook, fisticuffs, free-for-all **11** altercation, disturbance **13** confrontation

brawn 4 beef, meat, thew **5** clout, flesh, might, power, sinew **6** muscle **8** strength **9** puissance **10** headcheese

brawny 5 beefy, burly, husky, lusty, tough **6** robust, sinewy, stocky, strong, sturdy **8** athletic, muscular, powerful, thickset, vigorous **9** strapping, well-built **10** able-bodied

bray 4 mill **5** crush, grind, pound **6** bellow, pestle, powder **7** atomize,

brazen 4 bold, loud 5 brash, gaudy, noisy, showy 6 arrant, brassy, cheeky 7 blatant, defiant, forward, glaring, jarring 8 flagrant, impudent, insolent 9 audacious, barefaced, obtrusive, shameless, unabashed 10 outrageous, procacious, unblushing 11 conspicuous, impertinent 12 contumelious, presumptuous 13 disrespectful

Brazil *capital:* 8 Brasília *city:* 5 Belém 6 Recife 8 Salvador, São Paulo 12 Rio de Janeiro 13 Belo Horizonte *discoverer:* 6 Cabral (Pedro) *island:* 6 Marajó 7 Caviana *language:* 10 Portuguese *monetary unit:* 4 real *neighbor:* 4 Peru 6 Guyana 7 Bolivia, Uruguay 8 Colombia, Paraguay, Suriname 9 Argentina, Venezuela 12 French Guiana *river:* 6 Amazon 8 Parnaíba 10 Alto Paraná 12 São Francisco

breach 3 gap 4 gash, hole, open, rent, rift, slit 5 break, chasm, cleft, crack, split 6 hiatus, lacuna, schism 7 break in, discord, disrupt, fissure, infract, interim, opening, rupture, violate 8 aperture, disunity, division, fracture, infringe, interval, trespass 9 disregard, severance, violation 10 alienation, contravene, infraction, separation, transgress 11 delinquency, dereliction 12 disaffection, disobedience, estrangement, infringement, interruption 13 contravention, discontinuity, noncompliance, nonobservance, transgression

bread 3 bun 4 food, pita, rusk 5 bagel, money, toast 6 living, muffin, sippet 7 biscuit, crouton, edibles, stollen 8 victuals, zwieback 9 provender 10 livelihood, provisions, sustenance 11 comestibles, maintenance, subsistence *communion:* 4 host 5 wafer 9 Eucharist *from heaven:* 5 manna *ingredient:* 4 meal 5 flour, yeast 6 leaven *Jewish:* 5 matzo 6 hallah, matzoh 7 challah *maker:* 4 baker *Scottish:* 7 bannock *spread:* 3 jam 4 oleo 5 jelly 6 butter 9 margarine *unleavened:* 5 matzo 6 matzoh

bread and butter 4 keep, work 6 basics, living 7 support 8 mainstay, victuals 10 employment, livelihood, occupation, sustenance 9 nutriment 11 maintenance, necessities, subsistence 12 alimentation

breadbasket 3 gut 5 belly, tummy 6 paunch 7 abdomen, stomach 8 potbelly 9 bay window, beer belly

breadth 4 area, size, span 5 range, reach, scope, space, sweep, width 6 extent, spread 7 compass, expanse, stretch 8 distance, fullness, latitude, vastness, wideness 9 amplitude, expansion, magnitude 10 liberality

break 3 gap 4 bust, dash, halt, leak, luck, rest, rift, ruin, tame 5 burst, clear, crack, inure, sever, solve, spell 6 breach, chance, decode, divide, escape, exceed, hiatus, impair, lacuna, refute, relief, reveal 7 destroy, divulge, fall out, interim, lighten, opening, respite, rupture, shatter, surpass, suspend, time-out, violate 8 accustom, bankrupt, breather, decipher, disclose, division, downtime, fracture, good luck, interval, moderate 9 interlude, interrupt 10 annihilate, controvert, impoverish 11 discontinue, disjunction, dislocation, opportunity, suspensions 12 intermission, interruption 13 discontinuity

breakable 4 weak 5 frail 6 flimsy 7 brittle, fragile, friable 8 delicate 9 frangible

breakaway 4 prop 7 escapee 8 offshoot, renegade, seceding

break down 4 fail, fold, sort, wilt 5 class, decay, index 6 cave in, digest, give in 7 analyze, clarify, crumble, crumple, elucidate, give out, give way, go crazy, succumb 8 classify, collapse, dissolve 9 anatomize, decompose, fall apart 12 disintegrate

breakdown 5 crash, decay, smash, study, wreck 6 mishap 7 crack-up, debacle, failure, smashup 8 analysis, collapse, taxonomy 9 cataclysm, partition 10 disruption, dissection, resolution 11 dysfunction, examination, prostration

breaker 4 wave 6 billow, comber, roller

Breakfast at Tiffany's *author* 6 Capote (Truman)

breakfront 7 cabinet 8 bookcase

break in 4 tame 5 train 6 breach, burgle, gentle, invade 7 intrude 8 initiate 9 condition, habituate, interfere, interpose, interrupt

breakneck 4 fast 5 fleet, hasty, quick, rapid, swift 6 racing, speedy, unsafe 8 meteoric 10 harefooted 11 precipitous

break off 3 end 4 drop, halt, kill, stop 5 abort, cease, scrub, sever 6 cancel, detach 7 curtail, scratch, suspend 8 cut short 9 terminate 11 discontinue

break out 4 bolt, flee 5 arise, erupt, flare 6 emerge, escape 7 explode 8 mushroom, separate

break through 5 burst 6 breach, emerge, pierce 7 rupture, surface 8 overcome 9 penetrate

breakthrough 4 find, gain, hike, leap, rise 5 boost 7 advance, radical, upgrade 8 advanced, increase, landmark 9 invention, milestone 10 avant-garde, innovation **11** cutting-edge, development, exceptional, progressive, quantum leap

break up 3 end **4** halt, part **6** divide, sunder **7** destroy, disband, disjoin, disrupt, rupture, scatter, shatter **8** disperse, dissever, dissolve, disunite, separate **9** decompose, dismantle, pulverize, terminate **12** disintegrate

breakup 4 rift **5** split **7** divorce, parting **8** analysis **9** dispersal **10** dissection, separation **11** dissolution

breakwater 5 jetty

breast 5 bosom, chest, heart *animal:* **7** brisket *combining form:* **3** maz **4** mast, mazo **5** masto, stern, steth **6** mastia (plural), sterno, stetho

breastbone 7 sternum

breast-feed 5 nurse **6** suckle **7** nourish

breastwork 7 barrier, bastion, bulwark, defense, parapet, rampart **9** barricade, earthwork **10** embankment **13** fortification, reinforcement

breath 4 gasp, gust, hint, puff **5** let-up, pause, trace, whiff **6** breeze **7** respite **10** exhalation, inhalation, suggestion

breathe 4 emit, sigh **5** exude, utter, voice **6** endure, exhale, expire, inhale, murmur **7** confide, express, give off, inspire, persist, radiate, respire, subsist, survive, whisper

breather 4 lull, rest, stay, vent **5** break, let-up, pause, spell **6** hiatus, recess **7** caesura, respite **8** downtime **9** remission **12** interruption

breathing *labored:* 7 dyspnea *normal:* **6** eupnea *rapid:* **8** polypnea

breathing apparatus 10 respirator *underwater:* **5** scuba

breathing orifice 4 nose **5** mouth **8** blowhole, spiracle

breathless 4 agog, avid, keen **5** eager **6** ardent **7** anxious, gasping, intense **8** gripping **9** expectant, impatient **11** short-winded **13** on tenterhooks

breathtaking 6 moving **7** awesome **8** dramatic, exciting, imposing, stunning, wondrous **9** panoramic, thrilling **10** impressive, staggering **11** astonishing, magnificent, spectacular **12** awe-inspiring, overwhelming **13** heart-stirring

Brecht play 4 Baal **13** Life of Galileo (The), Mother Courage **15** Seven Deadly Sins (The), Threepenny Opera (The) **20** Caucasian Chalk Circle (The)

breech 3 bum **4** duff, rear, rump, seat, tail **5** fanny **6** behind, bottom, heinie **7** keester, keister, rear end **8** backside, buttocks, derriere, haunches **9** fundament, posterior **12** hindquarters

breechclout 9 loincloth

breed 3 ilk **4** bear, grow, kind, make, mate, race, rear, sire, sort, type **5** beget, brand, cause, class, cross, genus, hatch, likes, raise, stock, yield **6** couple, create, father, induce, nature, strain, stripe **7** bring up, develop, educate, lineage, nurture, produce, species, variety **8** copulate, engender, generate, mate with, multiply **9** cultivate, procreate, propagate, reproduce **10** discipline, extraction, give rise to, impregnate, inseminate

breeding 4 line **5** grace, taste **6** polish **7** culture, decorum, lineage, manners **8** ancestry, civility, courtesy, pedigree **9** genealogy, gentility, propriety **10** refinement, upbringing **11** cultivation

breeding ground 6 hotbed, origin **8** hothouse **10** forcing bed, mating spot **12** forcing house

breeze 3 zip **4** flit, sail, snap, waft **5** cinch, draft, waltz **6** zephyr **8** duck soup, kid stuff **10** child's play

breezy 4 airy, cool **5** fresh, gusty, windy **6** blithe, casual, drafty **7** offhand, relaxed **8** carefree, careless, detached, informal **9** easygoing **10** insouciant, nonchalant **11** unconcerned **12** devil-may-care, lighthearted

Breton 4 Celt

___ **breve 4** alla

breviary 5 brief **6** digest, précis **7** epitome, essence, outline, rundown, summary **8** abstract, boildown, synopsis **9** reduction **10** abridgment, conspectus, prayer book **11** abridgement **12** condensation, divine office

brevity 7 economy **8** laconism **9** briefness, concision, crispness, pithiness, shortness, terseness **10** transience

brew 3 ale, tea **4** beer, loom, mull, plan, plot **5** drink **6** cook up, foment, gather, impend, infuse, scheme, stir up **7** concoct, ferment **8** contrive

briar 4 burr, pipe **5** furze, gorse, shrub, thorn **6** nettle **7** bramble, thistle

Briareus 7 Aegaeon *father:* **6** Uranus *mother:* **4** Gaea

bribe 3 buy, fix, sop **6** buy off, payoff, payola, square, suborn **7** corrupt **9** incentive **10** enticement, inducement, tamper with

bric-a-brac 6 curios **8** trinkets **9** ornaments **10** knicknacks, objets d'art **11** gingerbread **13** embellishment

brick 5 block *layer:* **5** mason *laying:* **7** masonry *material:* **4** clay, marl *oven:* **4** kiln *row:* **6** course *sun-dried:* **5** adobe *trough for carrying:* **3** hod

bridal 7 nuptial, spousal **8** conjugal **9** connubial **11** matrimonial
bridal wreath 6 spirea
bridewell 3 can, jug, pen **4** coop, jail **5** clink, joint **6** lockup, prison **7** slammer **8** bastille **12** penitentiary
bridge 4 join, link, span **5** unite **7** connect **8** overpass, traverse *great:* **8** Brooklyn **10** Golden Gate *kind:* **4** arch, draw, rope **5** swing, truss **7** bascule, covered, natural, pontoon, trestle, viaduct **10** cantilever, suspension *term:* **3** bid **4** book, east, pass, ruff, slam, suit, void, west **5** bonus, dummy, north, raise, south, trick, trump **6** double, renege, rubber **7** auction, finesse, notrump, overbid **8** contract, jump call, redouble **9** grand slam, overtrick, singleton **10** little slam, undertrick, vulnerable
bridgelike game 5 whist **6** hearts
bridle 3 bit **4** curb, fume, rein, rule **5** check, flare, quell **6** govern, halter, hold in, manage, master, rein in, ruffle, seethe, subdue **7** bristle, control, flare up, inhibit, repress **8** hold back, moderate, restrain, suppress, withhold **9** constrain, deterrent, hackamore, restraint
brief 4 curt **5** pithy, short, terse **6** abrupt, digest, inform **7** brusque, concise, epitome, laconic, outline, passing, summary **8** abstract, breviary, fleeting, succinct, synopsis **9** momentary, transient **10** abridgment, conspectus **11** abridgement, compendious **12** condensation **13** short and sweet
brig 3 can, jug, pen **4** coop, jail **5** clink **6** cooler, lockup, prison **7** slammer **8** stockade **9** guardroom **10** guardhouse
brigade 4 army, unit **5** force, group **6** troops **10** contingent, detachment
brigand 6 bandit, bummer, looter, pirate, raider **7** cateran, corsair, forager, rustler **8** marauder, pillager **9** buccaneer, plunderer **10** freebooter, highwayman
brigandage 7 pillage, sacking **10** despoiling, ransacking **11** depredation
bright 4 fair, keen **5** aglow, alert, clear, light, lucid, quick, shiny, smart, sunny, vivid **6** brainy, cheery, clever, lively, lucent **7** beaming, blazing, flaming, fulgent, glowing, lambent, lighted, radiant **8** cheerful, dazzling, gleaming, luminous, lustrous, sunshiny **9** brilliant, effulgent, favorable, refulgent, sparkling **10** auspicious, glittering, precocious, propitious, shimmering **11** illuminated, intelligent, quick-witted **12** incandescent **13** scintillating
brighten 4 buoy **5** cheer, clear, shine

6 look up, perk up, polish, revive, solace **7** burnish, cheer up, clear up, enhance, enliven, furbish, gladden, hearten, improve **8** illumine **10** illuminate
brightness 5 éclat, shine **6** luster, lustre **8** radiance, splendor **10** brilliance, effulgence, luminosity *measure of:* **3** lux **5** lumen **6** candle **7** candela **10** footcandle
brilliance see BRIGHTNESS
brilliant 6 ablaze, brainy, genius, lucent, superb **7** beaming, fulgent, lambent, radiant, shining, stellar **8** dazzling, luminous, masterly, striking **9** effulgent, ingenious, refulgent, sparkling **10** glittering **11** exceptional **12** incandescent
brilliantine 6 pomade **9** hair cream
brim 3 hem, lip, rim **4** edge, fill, well **5** brink, skirt, verge, visor **6** border, fill up, fringe, margin **7** run over **8** overflow, well over **9** perimeter, periphery **13** circumference
brimful see BRIMMING
brimming 4 full **5** awash, flush **6** filled, jammed, loaded, packed **7** crammed, crowded, replete, stuffed, teeming, welling **8** bursting, overfull, suffused, swarming, swelling **9** chock-full, jampacked **11** chockablock, running over
brimstone 6 sulfur
brine 3 sea **4** deep, main **5** ocean **8** seawater **9** salt water
bring 3 lug **4** lead, pack, tote **5** carry, fetch, gross, yield **6** convey **7** attract, produce **9** transport
bring about 3 win **5** beget, cause **6** create, draw on, effect, secure **7** procure, produce, trigger **8** engender, generate, result in **10** accomplish, effectuate, give rise to
bring around 4 hook, sway, turn **7** convert, win over **8** convince, persuade, talk into **9** argue into, prevail on, sweet-talk **11** prevail upon
bring back 5 renew **6** recall, recoup, return, revive **7** recover, reprise, restore, salvage **8** retrieve, revivify **9** reinstate **10** repatriate **11** reestablish
bring down 3 bag, hew **4** drop, fell, raze **5** floor, level, shoot **6** defeat, depose, ground, humble, lay low, reduce **7** depress, flatten **8** demolish, overturn **9** humiliate, overthrow, prostrate, undermine
bring forth 4 bear **5** beget, yield **6** create, elicit, invent **7** deliver, produce **8** generate **9** propagate, reproduce **10** give rise to
bring forward 6 adduce, submit, tender,

unveil 7 advance, present, produce, proffer 9 introduce

bring in 3 pay, net, win 4 draw, earn, gain, sell 5 fetch, gross, yield 6 garner, return, secure 7 acquire, be worth, realize 9 introduce

bring off 6 effect, finish, rescue 7 achieve, execute, realize, succeed 8 carry out 9 discharge, implement 10 accomplish, consummate, effectuate 12 carry through

bring out 4 cull 5 educe, utter, voice 6 elicit, reveal 7 declare, enhance, explain, extract 8 disclose, showcase 9 elucidate, highlight, introduce

bring together 3 mix, wed 4 herd, join, link, yoke 5 amass, batch, blend, group, marry, merge, rally, unify, unite 6 corral, muster 7 collect, compact, compile, convene, round up 8 assemble 9 aggregate, integrate, reconcile, stockpile 10 synthesize 11 consolidate

bring up 4 moot, rear 5 breed, raise, refer, teach, train, vomit 6 advert, allude, broach, foster, school 7 advance, educate, mention, nurture, propose, suggest, touch on 8 point out, instruct 9 cultivate, introduce 10 put forward 11 regurgitate

brink 3 hem 4 bank, brim, edge 5 point, skirt, verge 6 border, fringe, margin 9 extremity, perimeter, periphery, threshold

briny 5 salty 6 saline

brio 3 pep, vim, zip 4 dash, élan, fire, life, zest, zing 5 ardor, flair, gusto, oomph, style, verve, vigor 6 bounce, esprit, fervor, spirit 7 panache, passion, sparkle 8 dynamism, vivacity 9 animation

brioche 4 roll

Briseis' lover 8 Achilles

brisk 4 busy, fast, keen, spry, yare 5 agile, fresh, nippy, quick, sharp, zippy 6 lively, nimble, snappy, speedy 7 bracing 8 animated, bustling, vigorous 9 energetic, sprightly 10 refreshing 11 stimulating 12 invigorating

bristle 4 boil, burn, fume, seta 5 anger, quill, setae (plural), spine 6 arista, chaeta, seethe 7 chaetae (plural) *Scottish:* 5 birse

British *air force:* 3 RAF *cathedral city:* 3 Ely 4 York 5 Ripon, Truro, Wells 6 Durham, Exeter 7 Chester, Lincoln 8 Coventry, Hereford, St. David's 9 Lichfield, Salisbury, Wakefield, Worcester 10 Canterbury, Gloucester *Channel Island:* 4 Sark 6 Jersey 8 Alderney, Guernsey *coin, current:* 5 pence (plural), penny, pound *coin, old:* 3 bob

5 crown, groat, noble 6 bawbee, florin, George, guinea, tanner, teston 8 farthing, shilling 9 halfcrown, halfpenny, sovereign 10 threepence *colony, former:* 4 Aden, Cape 5 Adana, Kenya, Malta, Natal 6 Ceylon, Cyprus, Gambia 7 Jamaica, Sarawak 9 Gold Coast, Singapore, Transvaal 10 Basutoland, New Zealand 11 Orange River, Sierra Leone 12 Bechuanaland *county:* 4 Avon, Kent, York 5 Derby, Devon, Essex, Gwent 6 Dorset, Durham, Oxford, Surrey, Sussex 7 Bedford, Cumbria, Norfolk, Rutland, Suffolk, Warwick 8 Cheshire, Cornwall, Hereford, Hertford, Somerset, Stafford 9 Berkshire, Cleveland, Hampshire, Lancaster, Leicester, Wiltshire, Worcester 10 Cumberland, Gloucester, Humberside, Lancashire, Merseyside, Shropshire 11 Westmorland 12 Lincolnshire *court, local:* 8 hustings *court, medieval:* 4 eyre *forest:* 5 Arden, weald 8 Sherwood *king, legendary:* 3 Lud 4 Beli, Bran 6 Arthur 7 Artegal, Belinus, Elidure 8 Brannius *language, ancient:* 6 Celtic, Cymric 9 Brythonic *legislature:* 10 Parliament *news agency:* 7 Reuters *nobleman:* 4 duke, earl, peer 5 baron 6 prince 8 marquess, viscount *order:* 6 Garter *people, early:* 5 Celts, Iceni, Jutes, Picts 6 Angles, Saxons *political party:* 4 Tory, Whig 6 Labour 12 Conservative *pope:* 8 Adrian IV *prince:* 5 Harry 6 Andrew, Edward 7 Charles, William *princess:* 4 Anne 5 Diana 8 Margaret *prison:* 5 Tower (of London) 7 Newgate 8 Dartmoor *queen, ancient:* 8 Boadicea, Boudicca *resort:* 4 Bath 7 Margate 8 Brighton 9 Blackpool *royal house:* 4 York 5 Tudor 6 Stuart 7 Hanover, Windsor 9 Lancaster 11 Plantagenet *royal residence:* 7 Windsor 8 Balmoral 10 Buckingham *school:* 4 Eton 5 Rugby 6 Harrow 10 Winchester *school, military:* 9 Sandhurst *spa:* 4 Bath 5 Epsom 6 Buxton 7 Malvern, Matlock 8 Brighton 9 Harrogate 10 Cheltenham

British Columbia *capital:* 8 Victoria *city:* 6 Surrey 7 Burnaby 8 Richmond 9 Vancouver *mountain:* 11 Fairweather *provincial flower:* 7 dogwood (Pacific)

British Honduras 6 Belize

brittle 4 curt 5 crisp, frail, stiff 6 infirm 7 crumbly, fragile, friable 9 breakable, frangible, inelastic, irritable, sensitive 10 perishable, transitory

broach 3 tap 4 moot 6 open up 7 bring up, mention, propose, suggest 8 initiate 9 introduce 10 put forward

broad 4 wide 7 general, liberal 8 extended, generous, spacious, sweeping, tolerant **9** expansive, extensive *combining form:* **4** eury, lati, plat **5** platy

broadcast 3 air, sow **4** beam, show **5** radio, strew **6** blazon, report, spread **7** bestrew, declare, publish, scatter **8** announce, proclaim, televise, transmit **9** advertise, publicize **10** bruit about, promulgate **11** communicate, declaration, disseminate, publication **12** announcement, proclamation, promulgation, transmission

broaden 4 open **5** swell, widen **6** dilate, expand, extend, fatten, spread **7** amplify, augment, distend, enlarge, thicken **8** increase **10** supplement

broadloom 6 carpet

broad-minded 4 open **7** liberal **8** catholic, eclectic, flexible, tolerant, unbiased **9** accepting, indulgent, unbigoted **10** forbearing, undogmatic **11** progressive **12** unjudgmental, unprejudiced

broadsheet 7 tabloid **9** newspaper

broadside 4 hail **5** burst, salvo, sheet, storm **6** shower, volley **7** barrage, torrent **8** at random **9** cannonade, fusillade, laterally, obliquely **11** bombardment

broadtail 4 hawk **5** sheep **7** karakul **8** lambskin

Brobdingnagian 4 huge **5** giant, jumbo **7** hulking, immense, mammoth, massive, titanic **8** colossal, gigantic, towering **9** cyclopean, humongous, monstrous **10** gargantuan, prodigious **11** elephantine

brochette 4 spit **6** skewer

brochure 5 flier, flyer **7** booklet **8** pamphlet

brogue 4 lilt, shoe **6** accent, oxford **7** dialect

broil 3 row **4** bake, burn, char, cook, fray, riot, sear **5** brawl, clash, fight, grill, melee, roast, run-in, toast **6** affray, fracas, scorch, tumult **7** bobbery, rhubarb, ruction, swelter, wrangle **8** disorder, squabble **10** donnybrook, free-for-all **11** disturbance

broiling 3 hot **5** fiery **6** baking, red-hot, torrid **7** blazing, burning **8** ovenlike, scalding, sizzling, white-hot **9** scorching **10** blistering, oppressive, sweltering

broke 4 poor **5** needy, spent **6** busted, ruined **7** drained **8** bankrupt, beggared, dirt poor, indigent, strapped, wiped out **9** destitute, insolvent, out of cash, penniless, penurious, played out **10** cleaned out **11** impecunious

broke-in 4 tame **5** tamed **6** docile

broken 4 shot **5** tamed **6** beaten, busted, cut off, faulty **7** crushed, haywire,

humbled, subdued **8** bankrupt, defeated, violated, weakened **9** depressed, disrupted, fractured, heartsick, shattered, sorrowful **11** discouraged, demoralized, interrupted **12** disconnected, disheartened **13** discontinuous

broken-down 7 rickety **8** battered, decaying, decrepit **9** crumbling, neglected **10** threadbare, ramshackle **11** debilitated, dilapidated **12** deteriorated

brokenhearted 7 crushed, unhappy **8** dejected, dolorous, hopeless, wretched **9** depressed, heartsick, sorrowful **10** despairing, despondent **12** inconsolable **13** grief-stricken

broker 5 agent **6** factor **8** diplomat, mediator **9** financier, go-between, middleman **10** interagent, interceder, matchmaker, negotiator **11** intercessor **12** intermediary **13** intermediator

brolly 8 umbrella

bromide 4 bore, drip, lump, pill, yawn **5** drone, grind **6** cliché, old saw, truism **7** proverb **8** banality, chestnut, prosaism, sedative **9** platitude, soporific **10** shibboleth, triviality **11** commonplace, rubber stamp

bromidic 3 dry **4** arid, dull **5** banal, bland, dusty, stale, trite **6** boring **7** humdrum, insipid, tedious **8** shopworn, tiresome **9** dryasdust, motheaten, wearisome **10** monotonous, pedestrian, unoriginal **11** commonplace **13** unimaginative, uninteresting

bronco 5 horse **6** cayuse **7** mustang *Australian:* **6** brumby

Brontë *character:* **9** Catherine, Rochester **10** Heathcliff *novel:* **7** Shirley **8** Jane Eyre, Villette **16** Wuthering Heights *sisters:* **4** Anne **5** Emily **9** Charlotte

Bronx cheer 3 boo **4** hoot, jeer, razz **5** taunt **7** catcall **9** raspberry

brooch 3 pin **4** clip **5** clasp **8** fastener

brood 3 set, sit **4** fret, mope, muse, stew, sulk **5** cover, flock, gloom, hatch, worry **6** litter, ponder, repine **7** despond, progeny **8** children, meditate, ruminate **9** offspring

brook 4 bear, burn, gill, race, rill **5** abide, creek, stand **6** arroyo, endure, rillet, runnel, stream, suffer **7** rivulet, stomach, swallow **8** stand for, tolerate *Scottish:* **6** burnie

Brookner novel 10 Hotel du Lac

broom 5 besom, brush, shrub, sweep, whisk **7** heather

broth 5 stock **8** bouillon, consommé

brothel 4 crib, stew **6** bagnio **7** lupanar **8** bordello, cathouse **9** call house **10** bawdy house, whorehouse

brother 3 kin 4 monk 5 friar 7 comrade, sibling *French:* 5 frère *Italian:* 3 fra 5 frate 8 fratello *Latin:* 6 frater *relating to:* 9 fraternal *Spanish:* 7 hermano

brotherhood 4 club, gang 5 amity, guild, order, union 6 league 7 kinship, society 8 alliance, sodality 10 fellowship, fraternity, friendship 11 association, camaraderie, comradeship, confederacy 12 togetherness 13 consanguinity, secret society

brotherly 9 fraternal

Brothers Karamazov 4 Ivan 5 Mitya 6 Alexei, Alexey, Dmitri, Dmitry 7 Alyosha 10 Smerdyakov

brouhaha 3 din 4 coil, flap, fuss, riot, to-do 5 babel, broil, hoo-ha, whirl 6 bedlam, clamor, fracas, furore, hubbub, hurrah, jangle, pother, racket, ruckus, rumpus, shindy, tumult, uproar 7 ferment 8 foofaraw 9 agitation, commotion 10 excitement, hullabaloo, hurly-burly 11 pandemonium

brow 3 top 4 mien 5 front, crest, crown 8 forehead 9 gangplank 10 expression 11 countenance

browbeat 3 cow 5 beset, bully, harry, press 6 badger, carp at, coerce, harass, hector, lean on 7 bluster, dragoon 8 bludgeon, bulldoze, bullyrag, domineer, overbear, pressure 9 tyrannize 10 intimidate

brown 4 sear 5 dusky, toast 6 scorch, tanned 7 swarthy *dark:* 5 sepia, umber 9 chocolate *grayish:* 3 dun 6 bister, bistre *light:* 3 tan 4 ecru, fawn 5 beige, hazel, khaki, tawny *moderate:* 4 teak 6 sienna *reddish:* 3 bay 4 roan 5 henna 6 auburn, russet, sorrel, titian 8 chestnut *yellowish:* 6 bronze 12 butterscotch

Brown Bomber 5 Louis (Joe)

brown coal 7 lignite

brownie 3 elf, fay 5 fairy, pixie 6 sprite

Browning poem 8 Prospice, Sordello 11 Aurora Leigh, Pippa Passes 12 Rabbi Ben Ezra 13 Fra Lippo Lippi, My Last Duchess 14 How Do I Love Thee?

brown recluse 6 spider

brownshirt 4 Nazi 12 storm trooper

browse 4 crop, feed, scan, shop, skim 5 graze, munch 6 forage, nibble, peruse 7 dip into, pasture 8 glance at, look over 10 glance over 11 flip through, leaf through, look through, skim through 12 thumb through

bruin 4 bear

bruise 5 pound, wound 6 batter, damage, injure, injury 7 contuse 8 abrasion, discolor 9 contusion 13 discoloration

bruit about 6 blazon, gossip, report, spread 7 declare, publish 8 announce, proclaim 9 advertise, broadcast, circu-

late 10 annunciate, pass around, promulgate 11 blaze abroad

brume 3 fog 4 film, haze, mist, murk 5 vapor 6 miasma 8 haziness 11 obscuration

brummagem 4 fake, sham 5 bogus, false, gaudy, phony, showy 6 ersatz, pseudo, tinsel, tawdry 7 chintzy 8 spurious 9 imitation, pinchbeck, tasteless 10 fabricated, fictitious 11 counterfeit, make-believe

Brunei *capital:* 17 Bandar Seri Begawan *island:* 6 Borneo *language:* 5 Malay *monetary unit:* 6 dollar *neighbor:* 8 Malaysia *sea:* 10 South China

brunet 3 jet 4 dark, onyx 5 dusky, ebony, raven, sable, sooty, swart 6 swarth 7 swarthy 8 bistered, obsidian 10 dark-haired 11 brown-haired

Brunhild 5 queen 7 heroine 8 Valkyrie *husband:* 6 Gunnar 7 Gunther *lover:* 9 Siegfried

brunt 4 jolt 5 shock 6 burden, impact

brush 4 clip, kiss, skim 5 broom, clash, graze, run-in, scrap, scrub, shave, sweep, whisk 6 glance, scrape, tussle 7 contact, thicket 8 skirmish 9 encounter, shrubbery, sideswipe 11 undergrowth

brusque 4 curt, tart 5 bluff, blunt, brief, gruff, rough, short, surly, terse 6 abrupt, crusty, snippy 7 uncivil 8 impolite, snippety, succinct 10 peremptory, ungracious 11 ill-mannered 12 discourteous

brutal 4 hard 5 cruel, feral, harsh 6 rugged, savage, severe 7 beastly, bestial, callous, inhuman, swinish, vicious 8 barbaric, pitiless, ruthless, sadistic 9 barbarous, ferocious, merciless 10 relentless 11 cold-blooded, remorseless 12 bloodthirsty

brutalize 5 abuse 6 debase, harden 7 corrupt, debauch, deprave, pervert, roughen, subvert, vitiate 8 maltreat, mistreat 9 manhandle 10 bestialize

brute 4 ogre 5 beast, cruel, feral 6 animal, savage 7 beastly, bestial, inhuman, piggish, swinish, varmint 8 creature 10 troglodyte 11 instinctive

brutish 3 low 4 base, vile 5 crude, feral, gross, rough, stony 6 animal, carnal, coarse, scurvy, strong 7 beastly, bestial, boorish, inhuman, obscene, piggish, swinish, uncivil, uncouth 8 barbaric, degraded, depraved, inhumane, physical, sadistic 9 primitive, truculent, unrefined 11 animalistic, uncivilized

bryophyte 4 moss 8 hornwort 9 liverwort

Brythonic see CYMRIC

bubble 3 sac 4 blob, boil, dome, fizz, foam, moil 5 churn, froth, slosh, spume, swash 6 burble, gurgle, seethe, simmer 7 ferment, globule, vesicle 10 effervesce

bubbly 5 alive, fizzy, foamy, jolly, perky 6 cheery, frothy, lively 7 buoyant, excited 8 animated, effusive 9 champagne, ebullient, exuberant, sparkling 10 carbonated

buccaneer 5 rover 6 cowboy, pirate, sea dog 7 corsair, sea wolf 8 picaroon, sea rover 9 sea robber 10 freebooter

buck 3 fop, guy, lad, lug 4 balk, bear, bill, chap, dude, jerk, load, move, note, oner, pack, stag, tote, trip 5 cadet, carry, dandy, ferry, fight, money, pitch, repel, stark, throw 6 combat, dollar, fellow, oppose, resist, unseat 7 coxcomb, trestle 8 antelope, bank note, sawhorse, traverse 9 greenback, withstand, workhorse 10 completely 11 Beau Brummel

bucket 3 fly, run 4 pail, rush, whiz 5 hurry, speed 6 barrel, basket, hasten, hustle, vessel 9 clamshell 10 receptacle

Buckeye State 4 Ohio

buckle 4 bend, clip, fold, hasp, kink, warp 5 catch, clamp, clasp, heave, yield 6 cave in, fasten 7 contort, crumple, harness 8 collapse 9 fastening 10 coffee cake

buckle under 3 bow 4 cave, fold, give 5 defer, yield 6 cave in, submit 7 concede, succumb 8 collapse 9 surrender 10 capitulate 11 admit defeat

Buck novel 9 Good Earth (The)

buckram 4 taut 5 stiff 6 wooden 8 starched 9 cardboard, unbending 10 inflexible 11 interlining

bucks 4 kale 5 bread, dough, money, moola 6 dinero, do-re-mi, moolah 7 lettuce 10 greenbacks

buck up 4 buoy, lift 5 cheer, rally 6 solace 7 comfort, console, gladden, improve, refresh, smarten 8 brighten 9 encourage 10 strengthen

___ **buco** 4 osso

bucolic 5 rural 6 rustic 7 georgic, halcyon, idyllic 8 agrarian, arcadian, pastoral 10 campestral, provincial 11 countrified, picturesque

bud 4 germ, seed 5 gemma, spark 6 sprout 7 burgeon 9 pullulate 10 primordium *combining form:* 5 blast 6 blasto

Buddha 7 Gautama 10 Siddhartha *dialogues:* 5 sutra *disciple:* 6 Ananda *enemy:* 4 Mara *Japanese:* 5 Amida, Amita *mother:* 4 Maya *son:* 6 Rahula *teachings:* 6 dharma *wife:* 9 Yasodhara

Buddhism 3 Son, Zen 4 Chan 5 Kegon 6 Huayan, Tendai 7 Tiantai 8 Hinayana, Mahayana, Nichiren, Pure Land 9 Theravada, Vajrayana

Buddhist *chant:* 6 mantra *dialogues:* 5 sutra *enlightenment:* 6 satori *evil spirit:* 4 Mara *fate:* 5 karma *language:* 4 Pali *monk:* 4 lama 5 arhat, bonze *sacred city:* 5 Lhasa *saint:* 5 arhat *scripture:* 5 sutra 6 sutras 9 Pali canon *sect:* 3 Zen *shrine:* 4 tope 5 stupa 7 chorten *spell:* 6 mantra *spiritual leader:* 4 guru 9 Dalai Lama *state of happiness:* 7 nirvana *temple:* 6 pagoda *title:* 7 mahatma *tree of enlightenment:* 5 bodhi, pipal

buddy 3 mac, pal 4 chum, mate 5 crony 6 comate, fellow, friend 7 compeer, comrade, partner 8 coworker, playmate, sidekick 9 associate, companion 10 accomplice 11 confederate

buddy-buddy 5 close, pally, thick, tight 6 chummy 8 intimate 10 palsy-walsy 11 inseparable

budge 4 move 5 shift, yield 7 give way

budgerigar 6 parrot 8 parakeet

budget 5 funds, means 6 amount, ration, supply 8 allocate, estimate 9 allowance, apportion, resources

Buenos ___ 5 Aires

buff 3 fan, nut, rub, tan 4 fawn, sand, wipe 5 beige, brush, fiend, freak, glaze, gloss, lover, shine 6 addict, expert, polish, votary 7 admirer, burnish, devotee, fanatic, fancier, furbish, groupie, habitué 8 follower 9 yellowish 10 aficionado, altogether, enthusiast 11 connoisseur, yellow-brown

buffalo 4 bilk, faze 5 bison, bovid, stump 6 baffle, muddle, rattle 7 carabao, confuse, defraud, flummox, fluster, nonplus, perplex, swindle 8 befuddle, bewilder, confound, hoodwink 9 bamboozle, dumbfound

buffalo grass 5 grama

buffer 6 screen, shield 7 buckler, bulwark, cushion 8 absorber, mediator, polisher 9 safeguard 10 protection 12 intermediary

buffet 3 box, hit, rap 4 beat, blip, blow, bump, chop, cuff, drub, jolt, move, poke, slap, sock 5 clout, drive, force, pound, punch, smack, spank 6 batter, hammer, pummel, thrash, wallop 7 belabor, clobber, counter, lambast 8 lambaste, salad bar 9 sideboard

buffoon 3 wag 4 dolt, fool, goof, lout, zany 5 antic, clown, comic, droll, dunce, joker, yokel 6 jester 7 bumpkin, dullard 8 bonehead 9 blockhead, harlequin 10 clodhopper 11 merry-andrew

bug 3 fad, fan, irk, nag, nut, spy, tap, vex 4 buff, flaw, fret, gall, germ, rage 5 annoy, bulge, craze, fiend, freak, mania, peeve 6 badger, bother, defect, insect, malady, needle, nettle, pester, plague, zealot 7 disease, fanatic,

microbe, provoke, wiretap **8** irritate,
listen in, protrude, sickness **9** eavesdrop, infection, obsession **10** enthusiast
12 imperfection **13** microorganism

bugaboo see BUGBEAR

bugbear 4 bane, bogy, fear, ogre **5** bogey,
bogie, poser **6** goblin, teaser **7** bugaboo,
problem, specter, spectre **8** anathema,
bogeyman, phantasm **9** bête noire, boo-
german, boogeyman, hobgoblin
10 black beast **11** abomination

buggy 4 cart, tram **6** go-cart, jalopy
8 carriage

bugle *call:* **4** mess, taps **5** drill **6** sennet,
tattoo **7** fanfare, retreat, tantara
8 assembly, reveille *relative:* **6** cornet
7 trumpet **10** flugelhorn

build 3 wax **4** body, form, make, mode,
mold, rise **5** boost, erect, forge, frame,
habit, mount, put up, raise, set up,
shape, swell **6** expand, figure **7** amplify,
augment, compose, enlarge, fashion,
magnify, produce, upsurge **8** assemble,
compound, engineer, escalate, height-
en, increase, multiply, physique **9** construct, establish, fabricate, institute,
intensify, originate **10** accelerate, inaugurate, strengthen **11** fit together, manufacture **12** conformation, constitution

builder 5 mason **9** carpenter **10** bricklay-
er, contractor

builder's knot 10 clove hitch

building 3 hut **5** house **7** edifice
8 dwelling **9** structure *addition:* **3** ell
4 wing **5** annex *compartment:* **3** bay
4 room **6** office *connector:* **9** breezeway
farm: **4** barn, crib, shed, silo *for apart-
ments:* **8** tenement *for arms:* **7** arsenal
for gambling: **6** casino *for grain:* **4** silo
7 granary **8** elevator *for horses:* **6** stable
for manufacture: **4** shop **5** plant **7** factory
for music: **10** auditorium *for sports:*
3 gym **4** bowl **5** arena **7** stadium **8** coliseum **9** gymnasium **10** hippodrome
material: **4** iron, wood **5** adobe, brick,
glass, steel, stone **6** cement **8** concrete
projection: **3** bay, ell **4** wing **5** annex
6 dormer **7** cornice *round:* **7** rotunda

building kit 5 Legos **10** Erector set
11 Lincoln Logs

build up 4 hype, plug, puff **5** boost,
brace, erect **6** accrue, expand, extend,
praise **7** collect, develop, enhance, fortify, improve, promote **8** buttress,
heighten, increase **9** advertise, construct, establish, intensify, publicize
10 accumulate, aggrandize, strengthen

buildup 4 hype, puff, to-do **6** growth,
hoopla **8** increase, ballyhoo **9** accretion,
expansion, promotion, publicity
10 escalation **11** development, enhance-

ment, enlargement **12** accumulation,
augmentation **13** strengthening

built-in 6 inborn, inbred, innate **8** includ-
ed, inherent **9** essential, ingrained,
intrinsic **10** congenital, deep-seated,
indwelling **11** established, fundamental
12 constitutive, incorporated

bulb 4 leek, lily, sego **5** onion, tulip
6 allium, garlic, squill **8** daffodil,
hyacinth **9** amaryllis, narcissus *segment:* **5** clove

bulb-like bud 4 corm **5** tuber **7** rhizome

Bulgaria *capital:* **5** Sofia *city:* **4** Ruse
5 Stara, Varna **6** Burgas, Pleven, Zagora
7 Plovdiv *monetary unit:* **3** lev *mountain,
range:* **6** Balkan, Musala **7** Rhodope
neighbor: **6** Greece, Serbia, Turkey
7 Romania **9** Macedonia *part of:*
7 Balkans *river:* **6** Danube **7** Maritsa
sea: **5** Black

bulge 3 bag, jut, sac, sag **4** blob, bump,
edge, lump, poke **5** bloat, pouch, swell
6 beetle, billow, bubble, bug out, dilate,
excess, expand **7** balloon, distend,
inflate, project, puff out **8** overhang,
protrude, stand out, stick out, swelling
9 allowance, head start **10** distension,
projection, promontory, protrusion
11 excrescence, protuberate **12** protuberance

bulk 4 body, core, loom, mass **5** fiber,
swell, total **6** amount, corpus, expand,
volume **7** bigness, quantum **8** majority,
quantity, stand out **9** aggregate, magnitude, substance

bulky 3 fat **5** beefy, hefty, husky, large,
obese, stout **7** massive **8** cumbrous,
unwieldy **9** corpulent, ponderous
10 cumbersome, overweight **11** substantial

bull 4 bunk, male, slip, toro, trip
5 boner, edict, error, fluff, force, hooey,
lapse **6** bovine, bungle, decree
7 baloney, blooper, blunder, hogwash,
mistake **8** nonsense **9** detective *combining form:* **4** taur **5** tauri, tauro

bulldoze 3 cow **4** move, push, raze
5 abash, bully, clear, cream, elbow,
force, level, press, scare, shove
6 coerce, hector, hustle, jostle, lean on,
menace, propel, thrust **7** bluster, clobber, dragoon, flatten, oppress, trounce
8 bludgeon, browbeat, bullyrag, demolish, domineer, restrain, shoulder **9** terrorize, tyrannize **10** intimidate, obliterate

bullet 6 dumdum, tracer **9** cartridge
10 projectile *size:* **7** caliber, calibre

bulletin 4 news **5** flash, scoop **6** notice,
report **7** account, catalog, gazette, message, missive, release **8** briefing, calen-

dar, dispatch, magazine, register **9** catalogue, statement **10** communiqué, periodical **12** announcement

bull fiddle 10 contrabass, double bass

bullfighter 6 torero **7** matador, picador **8** toreador **11** cuadrillero **12** banderillero *famous:* **6** Arruza **7** Ordóñez **8** Belmonte, Joselito, Manolete **9** Dominguin **10** El Cordobés

bullfighting *arena:* **5** plaza *cheer:* **3** olé *hero:* **6** torero **7** matador **8** toreador *lancer:* **7** picador *red cloth:* **6** muleta *Spanish:* **7** corrida *team:* **9** cuadrilla

bullheaded 6 mulish **7** adamant, willful **8** contrary, obdurate, perverse, stubborn **9** insistent, obstinate, pigheaded **10** headstrong, refractory, self-willed, unyielding **11** intractable, stiff-necked **12** intransigent, pertinacious, strong-willed

bullish 4 rosy **6** brawny, rising, upbeat **7** booming **9** advancing, expanding, favorable **10** optimistic

bully 3 cow **4** goon, pimp, punk, thug **5** abuse, heavy, meany, tease, tough **6** harass, hector, meanie, menace, pander, pick on, rascal **7** bluster, buffalo, dragoon, harrier, oppress, ruffian, torment, torture **8** bludgeon, browbeat, bulldoze, bullyrag, harasser, threaten **9** bulldozer, persecute, victimize, tormenter, tyrannize **10** browbeater, corned beef, intimidate, persecutor **11** intimidator

bullyrag see BULLDOZE

bulrush 4 reed **5** sedge **7** cattail, papyrus

bulwark 4 wall **6** screen, shield **7** barrier, bastion, parapet, rampart, seawall **8** buttress, fortress, palisade **9** earthwork, safeguard **10** breakwater, breastwork, embankment, stronghold **13** fortification

bum 3 beg, vag **4** bust, hobo, idle, laze, lazy, loaf, loll, slug **5** binge, cadge, drunk, hit up, idler, mooch, tramp **6** bottom, dawdle, loafer, loiter, lounge, slouch, unfair **7** depress, drifter, feel low, goof off, rear end, vagrant, wheedle **8** buttocks, derelict, fainéant, slugabed, sluggard, vagabond **9** do-nothing, goldbrick, importune, lazybones, panhandle, transient

bumbershoot 8 umbrella

bumble 3 mar **4** blow, flub, muff **5** botch, fluff, gum up, lurch **6** bobble, bollix, bungle, falter, fumble, mess up, muck up, rumble, slip up, teeter, totter **7** blunder, screw up, stagger, stumble **8** flounder

bumbling 5 inept, gawky **6** clumsy, gauche, klutzy **7** awkward, halting,

unhandy **8** ungainly **9** all thumbs, graceless, ham-handed, maladroit, unskilled **11** heavy-handed, incapable, incompetent **13** butterfingers, uncoordinated

bummer 3 dud **4** drag, flop, hobo **5** tramp **6** beggar, cadger, downer, sponge, too bad **7** failure, forager, moocher, sponger **8** deadbeat, vagabond **9** tough luck **10** freebooter, panhandler, rotten luck, wet blanket

bump 3 bop, hit, jar, ram, rap, wen **4** bang, bash, bust, jolt, knot, lump, oust, slam **5** break, carom, clash, crack, crash, gnarl, knock, prang, shift, shock, shove, wound **6** demote, growth, impact, injury, jostle, jounce, nodule, remove, strike, wallop **7** collide, degrade, demerit, pothole, run into **8** demotion, dislodge, displace, swelling **9** carbuncle, collision, contusion, convexity **10** concussion, projection, protrusion **12** protuberance

bumpkin 3 oaf **4** boor, hick, lout, rube **5** clown, swain, yokel **6** rustic **7** hayseed, peasant **9** chawbacon, hillbilly, simpleton **10** clodhopper, country boy, countryman, provincial

bump off 3 ice **4** do in, kill, slay **5** erase, snuff **6** murder, rub out **7** butcher, execute, take out **8** knock off **9** eliminate, liquidate **11** assassinate

Bumppo, Natty *alias:* **7** Hawkeye **10** Deerslayer, Pathfinder *creator:* **6** Cooper (James Fenimore)

bumptious 5 cocky, pushy **8** arrogant, impudent **9** audacious, obnoxious, obtrusive, officious **13** self-assertive

bumpy 5 jerky, nubby, ridgy, rough **6** bouncy, jouncy, knobby, knotty, patchy, pimply, uneven **7** jolting, nodular **9** difficult, irregular

bun 4 load, roll **6** pastry

bunch 3 lot, set, wen **4** band, bevy, bump, clot, crew, knot, lump, mass, push **5** batch, clump, covey, crowd, flock, group, party, spray, stack, swell **6** bundle, circle, clutch, gather, huddle, parcel, throng **7** bouquet, collect, cluster **8** assembly, protrude, swelling **9** gathering **10** assemblage, assortment, collection, congregate **11** aggregation **12** accumulation

bunco steerer 3 gyp **6** con man **7** cheater, diddler, grifter, sharper **8** swindler **9** defrauder, trickster **12** double-dealer **13** confidence man

bundle 3 lot, pot, set, wad **4** bale, body, heap, mint, pack, pile, wrap **5** array, batch, bunch, clump, group, sheaf, truss **6** fardel, packet, parcel **7** cluster, fortune **10** assortment

bungalow 5 cabin, lodge **6** chalet **7** cottage

bungle 4 flub, goof, mess, muff, slip, trip **5** boner, botch, error, fluff, gum up, lapse, mix up, spoil **6** bollix, bumble, fiasco, foozle, foul up, fumble, goof up, mess up, muck up, muddle **7** blooper, blunder, failure, louse up, misstep, mistake, stumble **9** mishandle, mismanage

bungler 3 oaf **4** clod, dolt, goof **5** klutz **7** screw-up, tomfool **8** bonehead, goofball, shlemiel **9** blunderer, schlemiel **10** stumblebum **11** blunderbuss, incompetent **13** butterfingers

bunglesome 6 clumsy, klutzy **7** awkward **8** bumbling **9** all thumbs **13** uncoordinated

bung up 4 beat, hurt **5** abuse, pound **6** batter, bruise, injure **7** contuse, disable **9** disfigure, manhandle

bunion 4 lump **8** swelling **10** protrusion, tumescence **11** enlargement

bunk 3 bed, cot, kip, rot **4** bosh, bull, guff, jazz **5** bilge, board, crash, hokum, hooey, house, lodge, put up **6** humbug, pallet, piffle **7** eyewash, baloney, hogwash, rubbish, twaddle **8** claptrap, domicile, flimflam, malarkey, nonsense, tommyrot **9** poppycock **10** balderdash

bunker 3 bin **6** dugout **7** bastion, chamber **10** embankment, stronghold **11** compartment

bunkum 3 rot **4** bosh, bull, guff, jazz **5** bilge, hokum, hooey **6** humbug, piffle **7** baloney, hogwash, rubbish, twaddle **8** claptrap, flimflam, malarkey, nonsense, tommyrot **9** poppycock **10** balderdash

bunting 5 flags **9** streamers

Bunyanesque 4 huge **5** giant, jumbo **7** mammoth, massive, titanic **8** behemoth, colossal, gigantic, towering **9** Herculean **10** gargantuan, prodigious

Bunyan's ox 4 Babe

buoy 4 lift, prop **5** boost, cheer, float, raise **6** assist, beacon, bear up, buck up, signal, solace, uphold, uplift **7** bolster, comfort, gladden, hearten, support, sustain **9** encourage

buoyancy 6 bounce, levity **7** jollity **8** airiness **10** ebullience, exuberance, exuberancy, liveliness, resilience **12** floatability **13** effervescence

buoyant 3 gay **4** airy **5** sunny **6** afloat, bouncy **7** elastic **8** cheerful, floating, volatile **9** expansive, floatable, resilient

10 unsinkable, weightless **12** effervescent, lighthearted

burble 3 gas, yak **4** blab, chat, gush, talk, wash **5** clack, plash, run on, slosh, swash **6** babble, bubble, gabble, gurgle, murmur, rattle, splash, yammer **7** chatter, prattle, sparkle

burden 3 tax, try **4** care, clog, core, duty, gist, haul, lade, load, onus, pile, pith, task, text **5** brunt, cargo, press, theme, weigh **6** amount, charge, chorus, cumber, hamper, lading, lumber, saddle, strain, stress, thrust, upshot, weight **7** afflict, anxiety, freight, oppress, payload, refrain, purport **8** encumber, handicap, obligate, overload **9** millstone, substance, weigh down **10** deadweight **11** encumbrance

burdensome 5 tough **6** taxing, trying **7** arduous, exigent, irksome, onerous, weighty **8** crushing, exacting, grievous **9** demanding, difficult, fatiguing, ponderous **10** exhausting, oppressive **11** troublesome **12** backbreaking, unmanageable

bureau 4 unit **5** chest **6** agency **7** dresser, section **8** ministry **10** department, chiffonier **11** writing desk

bureaucrat 8 mandarin, minister, official **11** functionary **12** civil servant, officeholder

burg 4 city, town **7** borough **8** fortress **10** metropolis, walled town **12** municipality

burgee 4 flag **6** banner, ensign, pennon **7** pendant, pennant **8** standard, streamer

burgeon 4 blow, boom, open **5** bloom, build, mount, run up **6** emerge, expand, flower, sprout, thrive, unfold **7** augment, blossom, develop, enlarge, fill out, prosper, run riot **8** flourish, heighten, increase, multiply, mushroom, snowball **9** germinate **10** burst forth, effloresce

burghal 5 civic, urban **8** citified **9** municipal **12** metropolitan

burgher 7 citizen, denizen **8** townsman

burglar 4 yegg **5** thief *loot:* **4** swag

burglarize see BURGLE

burglary 5 heist, theft **7** larceny

burgle 3 rob **4** lift, loot **5** heist, steal, strip **6** rip off, thieve **7** despoil, plunder, ransack **9** break into, knock over **10** housebreak

burgomaster 5 mayor **10** magistrate

Burgundy wine *grape:* **5** Gamay **9** Pinot Noir **10** Chardonnay *red:* **8** Mercurey **10** Beaujolais *white:* **5** Rully **6** Chagny **7** Chablis **10** Montrachet **13** Pouilly-Fuissé

burial 4 tomb 5 grave 7 funeral 9 interment, obsequies, sepulcher, sepulchre, sepulture 10 entombment, inhumation *box:* 6 casket, coffin *ceremony:* 7 funeral, obsequy 9 obsequies *mound:* 6 barrow 7 tumulus *tomb:* 9 mausoleum, sepulcher, sepulchre

burial ground 8 boot hill, cemetery 8 boneyard, God's acre 9 graveyard 10 churchyard, necropolis 12 memorial park, potter's field *early Christian:* 8 catacomb

Burkina Faso *capital:* 11 Ouagadougou *ethnic group:* 3 Gur 5 Mossi 7 Voltaic *former name:* 10 Upper Volta *language:* 4 Moré 5 Dyula 6 French *monetary unit:* 5 franc *neighbor:* 4 Mali, Togo 5 Benin, Ghana, Niger 10 Ivory Coast *river:* 5 Volta (Black, Red) 6 Nazion 7 Mouhoun, Nakanbe 8 Red Volta 10 Black Volta

burlap 5 gunny 6 fabric 7 bagging, sacking *fiber:* 4 hemp, jute

burlesque 3 ape 4 mock, sham 5 farce, spoof 6 parody, satire, send-up 7 lampoon, mockery, mocking, takeoff 8 pastiche, skin show, travesty 10 caricature, distortion, girlie show, lampoonery

burly 4 hale 5 beefy, hefty, husky, tough 6 brawny, robust, strong, stocky 8 athletic, heavyset, muscular, powerful, stalwart, thickset, vigorous 9 strapping

Burma see MYANMAR

burn 4 bake, char, cook, fire, fume, rage, sear 5 anger, blaze, broil, creek, flame, flare, gleam, roast, scald, singe, smart, smoke, sting, toast 6 ignite, kindle, scorch, seethe 7 bristle, combust, consume, cremate, flare up, inflame, radiate, smolder, swelter 8 smoulder 9 carbonize, cauterize 10 incinerate

burnable 8 volatile 9 flammable, ignitable 10 incendiary 11 combustible, inflammable

burned-out 4 beat, shot 5 spent, weary 6 sapped 7 drained, worn-out 8 consumed, fatigued 9 destroyed, exhausted, played-out 10 broken-down 11 debilitated 12 extinguished

burner 3 hob

burning 3 hot 5 afire, aglow, fiery 6 ablaze, aflame, alight, ardent, fervid, heated, hectic, red-hot, torrid, urgent 7 blazing, fervent, fevered, glowing, ignited, kindled, searing 8 broiling, feverish, pressing, sizzling, white-hot 9 scorching 10 imperative, passionate 11 conflagrant, impassioned 12 incandescent *combining form:* 4 igni *malicious:* 5 arson

burnish 3 rub, wax 4 buff 5 glaze, gloss, scour, sheen, shine 6 luster, patina, polish, smooth 7 furbish, varnish 8 brighten

burnished 5 shiny 6 glossy, satiny, sheeny 7 lambent, radiant, shining 8 gleaming, lustrous, polished 9 brilliant 10 glistening 11 resplendent

burnsides 8 whiskers 9 sideburns 10 sideboards 11 dundrearies, muttonchops 12 side-whiskers

burp 5 belch, eruct, expel

burro 3 ass 6 donkey 7 jackass

Burroughs hero 6 Tarzan

burrow 3 den, dig 4 hole, lair, mine, nook, snug 5 delve, gouge, lodge 6 cavity, cuddle, nestle, nuzzle, tunnel 7 snuggle 10 excavation

burst 3 pop, run 4 bang, boom, clap, gush, gust, rive, rush, slam, wham 5 blast, crack, crash, erupt, flare, go off, lunge, sally, salvo, smash, spasm, split, storm, surge 6 access, blow up, emerge, launch, plunge, shiver, spring, shower, volley 7 assault, barrage, explode, flareup, fly open, rupture, shatter, torrent 8 detonate, drumfire, eruption, fragment, outbreak, splinter, splitter 9 broadside, cannonade, explosion, fusillade, onslaught 11 bombardment

Burundi *capital:* 9 Bujumbura *ethnic group:* 4 Hutu 5 Tutsi *former name:* 6 Urundi *lake:* 10 Tanganyika *language:* 5 Rundi 6 French 7 Kirundi *monetary unit:* 5 franc *neighbor:* 5 Congo 6 Rwanda 8 Tanzania

bury 4 hide, sink, stow 5 cache, cover, embed, inter, plant, stash 6 absorb, entomb, inhume, mantle, shroud 7 blanket, conceal, cover up, implant, lay away, overlay, put away, secrete 8 ensconce, submerge

bus 5 clear 7 missile, trolley, vehicle 9 hand truck 10 spacecraft

bush 4 rose 5 lilac, shrub, wahoo 6 azalea, cassis, privet 7 currant, thicket, weigela 8 backland, barberry, hazelnut 9 backwater, backwoods, forsythia, manzanita 10 gooseberry, hinterland, wilderness 11 pussy willow 12 rhododendron

bushel 3 ton 4 heap, load, pile 6 basket, hamper 7 pannier

bush-league 5 minor 6 junior, two-bit 8 inferior, mediocre, small-fry 9 smalltime 10 inadequate, second-rate 11 lightweight 13 insignificant

bushranger 6 outlaw 8 woodsman 12 frontiersman

bushwhack 4 trap 6 ambush, assail, attack, entrap, waylay 7 assault 8 surprise 9 blindside

bushwhacker 6 bandit, outlaw, raider, sniper **8** guerilla, woodsman **9** guerrilla **10** highwayman

bushy 5 bosky, fuzzy, hairy, leafy **6** fluffy, woolly **7** hirsute, unkempt **9** bristling, luxuriant, overgrown **10** disordered **11** flourishing

business 3 job **4** firm, line, work **5** trade **6** affair, custom, matter, métier, office, outfit, racket **7** calling, company, concern, pursuit, traffic **8** commerce, function, industry **9** patronage **10** employment, enterprise, livelihood, occupation **11** corporation **13** establishment *expense:* **8** overhead *syndicate:* **6** cartel

businesslike 6 formal **7** orderly, serious **8** diligent, thorough **9** competent, efficient, practical, pragmatic **10** impersonal, methodical, no-nonsense, purposeful, systematic **11** disciplined, hardworking **12** professional

businessman 6 broker, dealer, trader, tycoon **7** magnate **8** investor, merchant **9** bourgeois, financier, tradesman, executive **10** capitalist, trafficker **12** entrepreneur, merchandiser **13** industrialist

busker 8 minstrel, musician **11** entertainer

buss 4 kiss, peck **5** smack **6** smooch **8** osculate

bust 3 bag, cop, dud, hit, jag, nab, net **4** bomb, bump, fail, flop, fold, raid, ruin, slug, sock, tear, tour **5** binge, bosom, break, broke, burst, catch, chest, crash, lemon, loser, punch, smash, spell, spree, stint, torso, trash **6** arrest, bender, breast, collar, demote, pick up **7** break up, carouse, degrade, demerit, destroy, exhaust, failure, rupture, wear out **8** bankrupt, demolish, fracture **9** apprehend, break down, destitute, downgrade, penniless **10** impoverish, police raid

bustle 3 ado, fly, run **4** flit, fuss, rush, stir, tear, teem, to-do **5** hurry, whirl, whisk **6** action, be busy, bestir, clamor, flurry, furore, hassle, hasten, hubbub, hustle, motion, pother, scurry, tumult, uproar **7** ferment, turmoil **8** activity, to-and-fro **9** commotion, whirlpool, whirlwind **10** hurly-burly, excitement, liveliness

bustling 4 busy, rife **5** brisk, fussy, peppy **6** active, hectic, lively **7** dynamic, festive, hopping, humming, jumping **8** animated, swarming, vigorous **9** energetic **10** tumultuous **11** hardworking, industrious

busty 5 ample, buxom, curvy **6** bosomy, chesty, zaftig **7** shapely, stacked **10** curvaceous, voluptuous **11** full-bosomed, well-rounded

busy 5 brisk, fussy **6** active, at work, lively, on duty, tied up **7** crowded, engaged, hopping, humming, swamped, teeming, working **8** bustling, diligent, employed, hustling, meddling, occupied, overdone, sedulous **9** assiduous, congested, elaborate, energetic, intrusive, obtrusive, officious **10** meddlesome, overworked **11** impertinent, industrious, interfering, unavailable

busybody 5 prier, pryer, snoop, yenta **6** butt-in, gossip, old hen **7** meddler **8** informer, kibitzer, quidnunc **9** pragmatic **10** chatterbox, newsmonger, pragmatist, talebearer, tattletale **11** nosey parker, rumormonger **12** gossipmonger, rubbernecker, troublemaker

but 3 bar, yet **4** just, only, save **5** alone **6** except, merely, saving, unless **7** barring, besides, however **8** entirely **9** aside from, excepting, excluding, outside of **13** on the contrary

butcher 4 ruin, slay **5** botch, carve, clean, spoil, wreck **6** bollix, killer, mess up, slayer **7** cut meat, destroy, meat man **8** mutilate **9** slaughter **11** slaughterer

butcher-bird 6 shrike

butcherly 5 cruel **6** bloody, clumsy, savage **7** awkward **8** sadistic **9** ferocious, merciless **10** unskillful

butchery 7 carnage **8** abattoir, genocide, massacre **9** bloodbath, bloodshed, holocaust, slaughter **10** mass murder **12** annihilation **13** extermination

buteo 4 hawk **7** buzzard

butler 5 valet **7** steward **10** manservant

Butler, Samuel *novel:* **7** Erewhon **13** Way of All Flesh (The) *poem:* **8** Hudibras

butt 3 end, keg, tip, ram, tun, vat **4** base, cask, drum, dupe, join, push, rump, stub, tail **5** chump, fanny, patsy, stump, touch, verge **6** adjoin, barrel, border, bottom, firkin, pigeon, sucker, target, thrust, victim **7** collide, fall guy, rear end, run itno **8** derriere, hogshead, neighbor **9** cigarette, fundament, lie beside, pilgarlic, posterior, remainder **11** communicate, sitting duck **12** hindquarters **13** laughingstock

butter *artificial:* **4** oleo **9** margarine **13** oleomargarine *Indian:* **4** ghee *piece:* **3** pat *semifluid:* **4** ghee *tree:* **4** shea

butterball 5 blimp, whale **8** dumpling, elephant **10** bufflehead

butterfish 6 gunnel

butterfly 4 blue **5** diana, satyr, zebra

6 copper, morpho **7** admiral, buckeye, monarch, satyrid, skipper, sulphur, vanessa, viceroy **8** crescent, grayling, milkweed, victoria **9** aphrodite, metalmark, nymphalid, wood nymph **10** fritillary, hairstreak **11** swallowtail *bush:* **8** buddleia *fish:* **6** blenny, chiton **7** gurnard *larva:* **11** caterpillar *lily:* **8** mariposa *order:* **11** Lepidoptera *plant:* **8** oncidium *pupa:* **9** chrysalis *scientist:* **13** lepidopterist

butter up 4 coax **5** charm **6** cajole, kowtow, praise, stroke **7** adulate, beguile, blarney, flatter, massage, wheedle **8** blandish, bootlick, soft-soap **9** brownnose, sweet-talk **10** overpraise

butt in 6 kibitz, meddle **7** intrude, obtrude **8** busybody, overstep **9** interfere, interlope, interpose, interrupt

buttinsky 7 meddler **8** busybody, kibitzer, quidnunc **9** loudmouth **10** trespasser **12** troublemaker

buttocks 4 rear, rump, seat, tail **5** fanny, nates **6** behind, bottom, breech, heinie **7** hind end, hunkers, keister, rear end, tail end **8** backside, derriere, haunches **9** fundament, posterior

buttonball 8 sycamore **9** plane tree

button-down 6 square, stuffy **8** decorous, orthodox, straight **10** restrained **11** straitlaced, traditional **12** conservative, conventional

buttonwood 8 sycamore **9** plane tree

buttress 4 pier, prop, stay **5** brace, carry, shore, strut, truss **6** back up, bear up, hold up, column, uphold **7** bolster, bulwark, fortify, shore up, support, sustain **9** reinforce, stanchion **10** strengthen **12** underpinning **13** fortification, reinforcement

buxom 5 ample, busty, curvy **6** bosomy, chesty, zaftig **7** shapely, stacked **10** curvaceous, voluptuous **11** full-bosomed, full-figured, well-rounded

buy 5 bribe **6** obtain, ransom, redeem **7** acquire, bargain, believe **8** purchase

buy back 6 ransom, recoup, redeem, regain **8** retrieve **10** repurchase

buyer 6 client, patron, vendee **7** shopper **8** consumer, customer **9** purchaser

buy off 3 fix, sop **5** bribe **6** settle **7** corrupt, silence **9** influence **10** manipulate, tamper with

buzz 3 fad, hum **4** call, fizz, high, hiss, news, purr, ring, talk, whir, whiz **5** craze, drone, hurry, rumor, strum, thrum, whirr, whish **6** bumble, fizzle, gossip, murmur, natter, report, rumble, sizzle, summon, wheeze, whoosh **7** chatter, scandal, whisper **8** sibilate

9 bombinate **11** reverberate, scuttlebutt

buzzard 5 buteo **7** vulture **13** turkey vulture

by 3 per, via **4** away, near, nigh, past **5** along, aside **6** at hand, beside, next to **7** through **9** alongside **10** incidental **11** according to **12** not later than

by and by 4 anon, soon **5** after, later **7** shortly **8** directly, latterly **9** afterward, presently **10** before long **12** subsequently

by and large 7 all told, broadly, en masse, overall, usually **8** all in all, normally **9** generally, typically **10** altogether, on the whole, ordinarily **11** principally

by dint of see BY MEANS OF

bye-bye 4 ciao, ta-ta **5** adieu, adios **6** so long **7** cheerio **8** au revoir, farewell, sayonara, toodle-oo

bygone 3 old **4** dead, late, lost, once, past **5** dated, of old, olden **6** former, fossil, of yore, remote, whilom **7** antique, archaic, belated, defunct, extinct, old-time, onetime, quondam, vintage **8** departed, sometime, obsolete, outdated, outmoded, vanished **9** erstwhile, out-of-date **10** antiquated, oldfangled **12** antediluvian, old-fashioned

by means of 3 per, via **4** with **5** using **7** through **9** employing, utilizing

byname 6 handle **7** epithet, moniker **8** cognomen **9** sobriquet **10** diminutive, hypocorism **11** appellation

bypass 4 omit **5** avoid, burke, shunt, skirt **6** detour, ignore **7** highway **8** outflank, ring road, sidestep **10** circumvent, pass around **11** deviate from

by-product 5 yield **6** effect, result **7** outcome, residue, spin-off **8** offshoot **9** outgrowth **10** derivative, descendant **11** aftereffect, consequence **12** repercussion

Byron work 4 Cain, Lara **5** Beppo **6** Giaour (The), Werner **7** Corsair (The), Don Juan, Manfred **12** Childe Harold

bystander 6 gawker, viewer **7** watcher, witness **8** beholder, observer, onlooker, passerby **9** spectator **10** eyewitness **12** rubbernecker

by stealth 5 slyly **7** sub rosa **8** covertly, in secret, secretly **9** furtively, privately **10** under cover **11** insidiously **13** clandestinely

by virtue of see BY MEANS OF

by way of see BY MEANS OF

byword 3 saw **5** adage, axiom, maxim, motto, nomen **6** dictum, phrase, saying, slogan, truism **7** epigram, epithet, precept, proverb, refrain **8** aphorism, cognomen, nickname **9** platitude, prescript, sobriquet **10** hypocorism, shibboleth **11** catchphrase, commonplace, rallying cry

Byzantine 6 daedal, knotty **7** complex, devious **8** involved **9** elaborate, intricate **10** convoluted **11** complicated **12** labyrinthine **13** sophisticated, surreptitious *emperor:* **3** Leo **4** Zeno **5** Basil **6** Bardas, Justin, Phocas **7** Michael, Romanus **9** Heraclius, Justinian **10** Nicephorus, Theodosius *empress:* **3** Zoe **5** Irene **8** Theodora

C

cab 4 hack, taxi **6** jitney **7** hackney **8** carriage

cabal 3 mob **4** clan, club, plot, ring **5** coven, group, junta, mafia **6** cartel, circle, clique **7** coterie, faction, ingroup **8** intrigue **9** camarilla **10** conspiracy **11** machination

cabaletta 4 aria, song

cabalistic 6 arcane, mystic, occult **8** esoteric **9** recondite **10** mysterious **11** inscrutable **12** impenetrable

caballero 6 knight **7** paladin **8** cavalier, horseman **9** chevalier

cabana 3 hut **5** shack **7** shelter

cabaret 4 café **6** bistro, nitery **7** hot spot **9** nightclub, nightspot **10** supper club **12** watering hole

cabbage 3 nab, nip **4** cash, hook, lift, palm **5** bread, dough, filch, kraut, money, moola, pinch, steal, swipe **6** dinero, do-re-mi, moolah, pilfer **7** purloin, scratch **10** greenbacks, sauerkraut *disease of:* **6** mildew, mosaic **7** root rot, yellows **8** blackleg, club root *family:* **4** cole, kale, rape **5** colza, savoy **6** turnip **7** collard, mustard **8** broccoli, colewort, kohlrabi, rutabaga **11** cauliflower

cabbagehead see DUNCE

cabdriver 4 hack **5** cabby **6** cabbie

cabin 3 hut **4** camp, shed **5** berth, hovel, lodge, shack **6** cabana, chalet, lean-to, shanty **7** bivouac, cottage **9** stateroom

cabin cruiser 5 yacht **9** motorboat, powerboat

cabinet 4 case **6** bureau **7** armoire, chamber, commode, console, council, dresser **8** advisers, advisors, cupboard, ministry **9** presidium **10** chiffonier, collection, counselors

cabinetmaker *American:* **5** Eames (Charles), Phyfe (Duncan) **6** Belter (John Henry) **7** Goddard (John, Stephen, Thomas) **8** McIntire (Samuel), Townsend (Christopher, Edmund, James, Job, John) *English:* **4** Adam (James, Robert), Hope (Thomas), Kent (William) **8** Sheraton (Thomas) **11** Chippendale (Thomas), Hepplewhite (George) *French:* **6** Boulle (André-Charles) **8** Caffieri (Jacques, Jean-Jacques, Philippe), Cressent (Charles) *German:* **10** Weisweiler (Adam)

cable 4 rope, wire **5** braid, chain **6** stitch **8** transmit **9** telegraph

cabriolet 5 coupe **8** carriage

cache 4 bury, hide **5** cover, plant, stash, store **6** memory, wealth **7** conceal, lay away, nest egg, put away, reserve, secrete **8** ensconce, treasure **9** stockpile **10** accumulate **11** hiding place

cachet 4 rank, seal **5** motto, state **6** slogan, status **7** dignity, stature **8** approval, position, prestige, standing **11** consequence

cachinnate 4 crow, howl, roar **5** laugh, whoop **6** guffaw, shriek

cackle 3 gab, jaw **4** blab, chat, crow **5** clack, cluck **6** babble, burble, gabble, gaggle, gobble **7** blabber, blatter, chatter, prattle

cacoëthes 4 zeal **5** mania **6** desire **9** obsession

cacomistle 5 civet **7** raccoon **8** civet cat, ringtail

cacophonic 5 harsh **8** tuneless **9** dissonant, unmusical **10** discordant **11** unmelodious **12** unharmonious

cacophony 9 harshness **10** dissonance

cactus 5 nopal **6** cereus, cholla, mescal,

peyote 7 opuntia, saguaro
11 prickly pear

cad 3 cur, dog 4 boor, heel, lout, rake
5 creep, knave, louse, rogue 6 rascal,
rotter 7 bounder 9 conductor,
scoundrel

cadaver 4 body, mort 5 stiff 6 corpse
7 carcass, remains 8 deceased

cadaverous 5 ashen, gaunt, livid 6 pallid, wasted 7 deathly, ghastly, ghostly,
shadowy 8 skeletal, spectral 9 deathlike, emaciated, ghostlike 10 corpselike

caddy 3 bin, box 4 aide 5 toter 6 casket
8 canister, tea chest

cadence 4 beat, flow, lilt 5 meter, pulse
6 rhythm 9 pulsation 10 conclusion,
inflection, intonation

cadet 4 pimp 5 plebe 7 student, trainee

cadge 3 beg, bum 5 mooch 6 hustle,
sponge 8 freeload, scrounge 9 panhandle

Cadmus *daughter:* 3 Ino 5 Agave
6 Semele 7 Autonoë *father:* 6 Agenor
sister: 6 Europa *victim:* 6 dragon *wife:*
8 Harmonia

cadre 4 cell, core 5 frame, staff 6 cohort
7 in-group 9 framework

caducity 3 age 6 dotage, old age 8 senility 10 senescence 11 senectitude

Caesar *assassin:* 6 Brutus (Marcus
Junius) 7 Cassius (Gaius) *battle:* 4 Zela
9 Pharsalus *conquest:* 4 Gaul 7 Britain
eulogist: 6 Antony (Marc) 7 Anthony
(Mark) 8 Antonius (Marcus) *message:*
12 Veni vidi vici *river:* 7 Rubicon *utterance:* 9 Et tu Brute *wife:* 7 Pompeia
8 Cornelia 9 Calpurnia

Caesarism 7 tyranny 9 authority, autocracy, despotism 10 absolutism 12 dictatorship

caesura 5 break, pause 12 interruption

café 5 diner 6 bistro, nitery 7 barroom,
beanery, cabaret, hot spot 8 cookshop
9 lunchroom, nightclub, nightspot
10 coffee shop, restaurant, supper club
12 luncheonette, watering hole
13 watering place

café ___ 4 noir 6 au lait, filtre 7 society

caftan 4 gown, robe 6 muumuu 12 dressing gown

cage 3 hem, pen 4 cell, coop, jail 5 score
6 corral, immure, lock up, shut in
7 close in, enclose, impound 8 imprison
9 enclosure 11 incarcerate

cagey 3 sly 4 foxy, wary, wily 5 canny,
sharp 6 astute, clever, crafty, shrewd

cahier 6 record, report, review

cahoots 6 hookup, league 8 alliance
9 collusion 10 complicity 11 partnership

caiman 9 crocodile 11 crocodilian

Cain *brother:* 4 Abel, Seth *father:* 4 Adam

land: 3 Nod *mother:* 3 Eve *nephew:*
4 Enos *son:* 5 Enoch *victim:* 4 Abel

Caine Mutiny author 4 Wouk (Herman)

Cain novel 8 Serenade 13 Mildred Pierce
23 Postman Always Rings Twice (The)

cajole 3 con 4 coax, dupe 6 entice,
seduce 7 beguile, blarney, deceive,
wheedle 8 blandish, inveigle, maneuver,
persuade, soft-soap 9 sweet-talk

cake 3 dry, set 4 coat, loaf, rime 5 cover,
crust 6 harden, pastry 7 congeal,
encrust, incrust 8 solidify *almond:*
8 macaroon *flat:* 5 cooky 6 cookie *oatmeal:* 4 farl 5 scone 7 bannock *ring-
shaped:* 5 donut 6 jumble 8 doughnut
rum-soaked: 4 baba *Scottish:* 4 farl
5 scone *shell-shaped:* 9 madeleine *topping:* 5 icing 8 frosting, streusel *without
flour:* 5 torte *without shortening:*
6 sponge

Cakes and Ale author 7 Maugham (W.
Somerset)

cakewalk 4 romp, rout, snap 5 cinch,
dance, strut 6 breeze, prance
8 pushover, walkover

calaboose 3 can 4 brig, coop, jail, tank
5 clink, pokey 6 cooler, lockup, prison
7 slammer 8 hoosegow 9 jailhouse

calamitous 4 dire 5 fatal 6 woeful
7 ruinous 8 grievous 10 disastrous, lamentable 11 cataclysmic, devastating,
unfortunate 12 catastrophic 13 heartbreaking

calamity 4 ruin 5 wreck 7 tragedy 8 disaster, downfall 9 cataclysm 11 catastrophe, tribulation

Calamity ___ 4 Jane

calculate 4 rely 5 assay, count, gauge,
judge, solve, tally, tot up, value
6 assess, cipher, figure, intend, reckon
7 compute, measure, work out
8 appraise, estimate, evaluate, forecast
9 ascertain, determine, figure out

calculated 6 likely 7 planned 8 intended
9 worked out 10 deliberate 12 aforethought, premeditated

calculating 3 sly 4 wary, wily 5 canny,
chary, sharp 6 artful, crafty, shrewd
7 careful, cunning, devious, politic
8 cautious, discreet, guileful, scheming
9 designing 11 circumspect

calculating device 6 abacus *Peruvian:*
5 quipu

calculation 8 analysis, counting, estimate, figuring, prudence 9 ciphering,
reckoning 10 arithmetic, estimation,
prediction 11 computation

Caledonia 8 Scotland

calendar 3 log 4 card, sked 6 agenda,
docket 7 almanac, program 8 schedule
9 timetable *abbreviation:* 3 Apr, Aug,

Dec, Feb, Fri, Jan, Mar, Mon, Nov,
Oct, Sat, Sep, Sun, Tue, Wed 4 Sept
5 Thurs *ecclesiastical:* 4 ordo

calenture 4 fire, zeal 5 ardor, fever 6 fervor 7 passion 10 enthusiasm

calf *hide:* 3 kip *leather:* 3 elk *meat:* 4 veal *stray:* 5 dogie *unbranded:* 8 maverick

Caliban 5 slave *master:* 8 Prospero *witch-mother:* 7 Sycorax

caliber 4 bore 5 class, gauge, grade, merit, value, worth 6 virtue 7 ability, quality, stature 8 diameter

calibrate 3 set 6 adjust, polish 7 measure 8 fine-tune, regulate 9 ascertain 11 standardize

California *capital:* 10 Sacramento *city:* 4 Napa 6 Fresno, Sonoma 7 Anaheim, Oakland, San Jose 8 San Diego, Santa Ana 9 Long Beach, Santa Cruz 10 Los Angeles 12 San Francisco *college, university:* 3 USC 4 UCLA 5 Mills 6 Pomona 8 Berkeley, Stanford, Whittier 9 Loma Linda 10 Golden Gate, Occidental, Pepperdine, Santa Clara *desert:* 6 Mohave *fault zone:* 10 San Andreas *lake:* 5 Owens, Tahoe 9 Salton Sea *lowest spot:* 11 Death Valley *motto:* 6 Eureka *mountain, range:* 5 Coast 6 Lassen (Peak), Shasta 7 Whitney 12 Sierra Nevada *nickname:* 6 Golden (State) *park:* 7 Sequoia 8 Yosemite 11 Kings Canyon 14 Channel Islands *river:* 10 Sacramento, San Joaquin *state bird:* 5 quail *state flower:* 11 golden poppy *state tree:* 7 redwood, sequoia *wine region:* 4 Napa 6 Sonoma

caliginous 3 dim 4 dark, dusk 5 dusky, foggy, misty, murky 6 gloomy 7 obscure, sunless 8 nebulous 9 lightless, tenebrous

Caligula's mother 9 Agrippina

caliph's name 3 Ali 7 Abu Bakr

Calista's seducer 8 Lothario

calisthenics 7 workout 9 exercises

call 3 bid, cry 4 buzz, hail, lure, name, page, ring, yell 5 phone, pop in, shout, visit 6 bellow, come by, drop by, drop in, holler, salute, stop by, stop in, summon 7 convene, convoke, summons 8 estimate 9 designate, telephone

calla 4 lily

call down 5 chide, scold 6 rebuke 7 censure, reprove 8 admonish, reproach 9 reprimand

called 5 named 6 chosen, picked, yclept 7 ycleped 8 selected

caller 5 guest 6 suitor 7 visitor

call for 3 ask, beg 4 seek 5 crave, plead 6 demand, entail, pick up 7 beseech, entreat, implore, involve, require 11 necessitate

call forth 5 awake, educe, evoke, rouse 6 arouse, elicit 7 conjure, provoke 9 conjure up

calligrapher 6 penman, scribe 7 copyist 9 engrosser, scrivener

calligraphy 4 hand 6 script 7 writing 8 longhand 10 penmanship 11 handwriting

call in 5 phone 6 summon 7 convene, reclaim 8 retrieve, withdraw 9 repossess, telephone

calling 3 job 4 duty, work 5 craft, trade 6 career, métier 7 mission, pursuit, yelling 8 business, lifework, shouting, vocation 10 employment, obligation, occupation, profession

call in sick 7 book off

Calliope 4 Muse *father:* 4 Zeus 7 Jupiter *mother:* 9 Mnemosyne *son:* 7 Orpheus

Callisto *lover:* 4 Zeus 7 Jupiter *son:* 5 Arcas

Call It Sleep *author* 4 Roth (Henry)

call off 4 halt 5 abort, scrub 6 cancel, divert 8 distract

Call of the Wild *author:* 6 London (Jack) *dog:* 4 Buck

call on 5 visit 6 oblige 7 require

callosity 8 hardness 9 thickness

callous 5 stony 8 hardened, obdurate, uncaring 9 heartless, indurated, unfeeling 10 hard-bitten, hard-boiled 11 coldhearted, hardhearted, insensitive, unemotional 12 case-hardened, stonyhearted 13 unsympathetic

callow 3 raw 5 fresh, green, naive, young 7 puerile 8 immature, juvenile, youthful 9 unfledged 10 unseasoned 13 inexperienced, unexperienced

call's partner 4 beck

call up 5 draft, evoke 6 summon 8 mobilize, retrieve 9 conscript

calm 4 cool, ease, hush, lull 5 allay, peace, quiet, relax, salve, still 6 hushed, pacify, placid, poised, repose, sedate, serene, settle, smooth, soothe, stable, steady, stilly 7 appease, assuage, compose, halcyon, mollify, pacific, placate, restful, resting 8 composed, inactive, peaceful, reposing, serenity, tranquil 9 collected, composure, easygoing, impassive, possessed, quiescent, unruffled 10 phlegmatic, untroubled 11 tranquility, tranquilize, unflappable 12 even-tempered, self-composed, tranquillity 13 imperturbable, self-possessed

calmative 8 quietive, relaxing, sedative 9 soporific 12 tranquilizer

calmness 4 lull 5 quiet 6 phlegm 8 coolness, serenity 9 composure, placidity, sangfroid 10 equanimity 11 tranquility 12 tranquillity

calumet 4 pipe 9 peace pipe

calumniate 5 libel, smear 6 defame, malign, vilify 7 asperse, slander, tarnish, traduce 8 besmirch 9 denigrate 10 scandalize

calumnious 8 libelous 9 maligning, traducing, vilifying 10 backbiting, defamatory, detracting, scandalous, slanderous

calumny 7 scandal, slander 9 aspersion 10 backbiting, defamation, detraction 11 denigration 12 backstabbing, belittlement, depreciation 13 disparagement

calvados 6 brandy 9 applejack

calvary 5 agony, cross, trial 6 misery, ordeal 7 anguish 8 distress 9 suffering 10 affliction, visitation 11 tribulation

Calypso *beloved:* 7 Ulysses 8 Odysseus *island:* 6 Ogygia

calyx part 3 cup 5 sepal

camaraderie 5 cheer 7 jollity 10 affability, fellowship 12 conviviality

camarilla 3 mob 4 camp, clan, ring 5 cabal, mafia 6 circle, clique 7 coterie, ingroup

Cambodia 9 Kampuchea *capital:* 9 Phnom Penh *city:* 10 Battambang 11 Kompong Cham *ethnic group:* 8 Mon-Khmer *lake:* 8 Tonle Sap *language:* 5 Khmer *leader:* 6 Pol Pot *monetary unit:* 4 riel *neighbor:* 4 Laos 7 Vietnam 8 Thailand *river:* 6 Mekong *ruin:* 9 Angkor Wat

camel *one-humped:* 9 dromedary *two-humped:* 8 Bactrian

camel-hair fabric 3 aba

camelopard 7 giraffe

Camelot 6 palace *lord:* 6 Arthur

Camembert 6 cheese

cameo 6 brooch, relief, walk-on 8 portrait

cameraman 6 photog 7 lensman 12 photographer

Cameroon *capital:* 7 Yaoundé *ethnic group:* 4 Fang 5 Duala, Pygmy 6 Fulani 8 Bamileke *largest city:* 6 Douala *monetary unit:* 5 franc *neighbor:* 4 Chad 5 Congo, Gabon 7 Nigeria *river:* 5 Nyong 6 Sanaga

Camille's creator 5 Dumas (Alexandre)

Camino ___ 4 Real

camouflage 4 mask 5 cloak 7 conceal, deceive 8 disguise 9 dissemble 11 dissimulate

camp 3 hut 4 bloc, shed 5 cabin, lodge, shack 6 clique, shanty 7 bivouac, coterie, cottage, faction 10 settlement

campaign 4 push 5 blitz, drive, fight, lobby, stump 6 attack 7 agitate, canvass, crusade 8 movement, politick

9 barnstorm, offensive 10 engagement, expedition 11 electioneer, whistle-stop

campaigner 8 activist 9 candidate

campanile 6 belfry 8 carillon 9 bell tower

campesino 6 farmer 7 peasant

campestral 5 rural 6 rustic, sylvan 7 bucolic, country, idyllic 8 agrarian, pastoral 10 provincial 11 countrified

campus see COLLEGE

Camus work 4 Fall (The) 5 Rebel (The) 6 Plague (The) 8 Caligula, Stranger (The)

can 3 may, tin 4 boot, fire, sack 5 let go, put up 7 dismiss 9 container, discharge 10 receptacle

Canaan 4 Zion 12 Promised Land *father:* 3 Ham *grandfather:* 4 Noah

Canaanite god 3 Mot 4 Baal 6 Molech, Moloch

Canada *bay:* 5 Fundy, James 6 Baffin, Hudson, Ungava 8 Georgian 9 Frobisher *capital:* 6 Ottawa *city:* 6 London, Oshawa, Quebec, Regina, Surrey 7 Burnaby, Calgary, Halifax, Moncton, Toronto, Windsor 8 Edmonton, Hamilton, Montreal, Moose Jaw, Victoria, Winnipeg 9 Longueuil, North York, Saskatoon, Vancouver 10 Lethbridge, Thunder Bay 11 Fredericton, Scarborough 13 Charlottetown, Mississauga *district:* 6 riding *explorer:* 6 Hudson (Henry) 7 Cartier (Jacques) 9 Champlain (Samuel de) *Indian people:* 4 Cree, Inuk 5 Blood, Haida, Huron, Inuit, Métis, Niska, Slave 6 Abnaki, Beaver, Eskimo, Micmac, Mohawk, Nootka, Ojibwa, Ojibwe, Ottawa, Piegan, Seneca, Stoney 7 Kutenai, Naskapi, Ojibway, Siksika, Wyandot 8 Algonkin, Chippewa, Iroquois, Kootenai, Kootenay, Kwakiutl, Salishan, Tsattine 9 Algonkian, Algonquin, Blackfeet, Blackfoot, Chipewyan, Tsimshian 10 Algonquian, Athapascan, Gros Ventre, Montagnais 11 Assiniboine *island, island group:* 5 Banks, Devon 6 Baffin 7 Belcher 8 Melville, Victoria 9 Anticosti, Ellesmere, Vancouver 10 Cape Breton 11 Southampton 12 Newfoundland, Prince Edward *lake:* 6 Louise 7 Nipigon 8 Reindeer, Winnipeg 9 Athabasca, Champlain, Great Bear 10 Great Slave *language:* 6 French 7 English *monetary unit:* 6 dollar *mountain, range:* 5 Coast, Logan, Rocky 10 Laurentian *national park:* 5 Banff, Fundy 6 Jasper 7 Glacier, Nahanni 8 Kootenay 9 Gros Morne 10 Grasslands, Point Pelee 11 Georgian Bay, Wood Buffalo *peninsula:* 5 Bruce,

Gaspé 6 Ungava 8 Labrador *prime minister:* 4 King (W. L. Mackenzie) 5 Clark (Joe) 6 Abbott (John), Borden (Robert Laird), Bowell (Mackenzie), Martin (Paul), Tupper (Charles), Turner (John) 7 Bennett (Richard Bedford), Laurier (Wilfrid), Meighen (Arthur), Pearson (Lester), Trudeau (Pierre Elliott) 8 Campbell (Kim), Chrétien (Jean), Mulroney (Brian), Thompson (John) 9 MacDonald (John), Mackenzie (Alexander), St. Laurent (Louis) 11 Diefenbaker (John) *province:* 6 Quebec 7 Alberta, Nunavut, Ontario 8 Manitoba 10 Nova Scotia 12 New Brunswick, Newfoundland (and Labrador), Saskatchewan 15 British Columbia 18 Prince Edward Island *provincial park:* 3 Gas 7 Rondeau 9 Garibaldi *river:* 3 Red 5 Liard, Slave, Yukon 6 Albany, Fraser, Nelson, Ottawa, Severn 8 Columbia, Saguenay 9 Athabasca, Churchill, Mackenzie 10 St. Lawrence *sea:* 8 Beaufort, Labrador *symbol:* 9 maple leaf *territory:* 5 Yukon 9 Northwest

Canadian insurgent 4 Riel (Louis)

canaille 3 mob 6 masses, rabble 8 riffraff, unwashed 9 hoi polloi 11 proletarian, proletariat

canal 4 duct 6 course 7 channel, conduit 8 aqueduct 11 watercourse *Africa:* 4 Suez 8 Ismailia *Belgium:* 6 Albert *Canada:* 7 Welland *Central America:* 6 Panama *China:* 7 Da Yunhe *Florida:* 10 Saint Lucie *Germany:* 4 Kiel *Greece:* 7 Corinth *Michigan:* 3 Soo *New York:* 4 Erie 6 Oswego 9 Champlain *Ontario:* 6 Rideau *Venice:* 5 Grand

canapé 6 morsel 9 appetizer 11 hors d'oeuvre *spread:* 4 paté

canard 3 fib, lie 4 tale, yarn 5 fraud, rumor, spoof 6 deceit 7 falsity, untruth 8 chestnut 9 falsehood

canary 3 rat 4 fink, wine 5 finch 6 snitch 7 rat fink, stoolie 8 informer, squealer 11 stool pigeon

Canary Islands 5 Ferro, Lobos, Palma 6 Gomera, Hierro 7 Inferno 8 Graciosa, Tenerife 9 Alegranza, Lanzarote

cancel 3 end 4 drop, undo, x out 5 abort, annul, erase, scrub 6 delete, efface, negate, offset, repeal, revoke 7 blot out, call off, destroy, expunge, nullify, rescind, wipe out 8 black out, deletion 9 terminate 10 invalidate, neutralize, obliterate

cancer 5 tumor 9 carcinoma 10 malignancy *treatment:* 5 chemo, X-rays 9 radiation 12 chemotherapy

cancer-causing 12 carcinogenic *substance:* 10 carcinogen

candescent 7 glowing 8 dazzling 9 refulgent

Candia 5 Crete

candid 4 fair, just, open 5 blunt, frank, plain 6 honest 7 sincere 8 unbiased 9 equitable, guileless, impartial, objective 10 aboveboard, forthright, scrupulous, unreserved 11 openhearted, unconcealed, undisguised 12 unprejudiced 13 dispassionate

candidate 6 seeker 7 hopeful, nominee, stumper 8 aspirant 9 applicant, contender 10 campaigner, contestant

Candide *author:* 8 Voltaire *lover:* 9 Cunegonde *tutor:* 8 Pangloss *valet:* 7 Cacambo

candle 5 taper 6 bougie *holder:* 6 sconce 7 menorah, pricket 9 girandole 10 candelabra 11 candelabrum *material:* 3 wax 4 wick 6 tallow 7 beeswax, stearin 8 paraffin *religious:* 6 votive 7 paschal

candlefish 8 eulachon *relative:* 5 smelt

candlelit service 7 vigil

candlepins 7 bowling

candor 7 honesty 8 fairness, openness 9 frankness, sincerity, whiteness 11 artlessness 13 guilelessness

candy 7 sweeten 9 sugarcoat 10 confection *kind:* 4 rock 5 fudge, lolly, sweet, taffy 6 bonbon, comfit, dragée, jujube, nougat, toffee 7 brittle, caramel, fondant, gumdrop, penuche, praline 8 licorice, lollipop, lollypop, marzipan, sourball 9 chocolate, jelly bean, nonpareil, sweetmeat 10 confection 12 butterscotch *medicated:* 7 lozenge 9 cough drop

cane 3 rod 4 beat, drub, flog, lash, reed, stem, swat 5 flail, grass, spank, staff, stave, stick, weave, whale 6 batter, buffet, cudgel, larrup, paddle, rattan, thrash, wallop 7 lambast, sorghum 8 lambaste 12 walking stick

Canea's land 5 Crete

canine 3 dog 4 tyke 5 hound, pooch

caning material 5 istle

Canis Major star 6 Sirius

Canis Minor star 7 Procyon

canker 4 rust, sore 5 stain 6 debase, infect 7 corrupt, debauch, deprave, pervert, vitiate 8 necrosis 10 demoralize

cankered 8 infested, infected

canker sore 5 ulcer 6 lesion 10 ulceration

cannabis 3 pot 4 hemp 5 bhang, ganja, grass 7 hashish 9 marijuana

canned 5 drunk, fired 6 potted 11 prerecorded

Cannery Row author 9 Steinbeck (John)

canniness 7 caution, cunning, slyness **8** prudence, wiliness **9** cageyness, foresight **10** artfulness, cleverness, craftiness, discretion, precaution, providence, shrewdness **11** forethought

cannon 6 pom-pom **8** howitzer, ordnance **9** artillery *part:* **5** chase **6** breech **8** cascabel, trunnion

cannonade 4 bomb **5** blitz, burst, salvo, shell **6** shower, volley **7** barrage, bombard **8** drumfire, shelling **9** broadside, fusillade **11** bombardment

cannonball 4 dive **5** speed **7** missile

cannoneer 6 gunner

cannon fodder 6 troops **8** infantry, soldiers

canny 3 sly **4** wary, wise **5** acute, cagey, chary, quick, sharp, smart **6** adroit, clever, frugal, saving, shrewd **7** cunning, knowing, prudent, thrifty **9** ingenious, provident **10** economical **11** quick-witted, sharp-witted **12** nimble-witted

canoe 6 dugout **7** pirogue *ancient:* **7** coracle *Eskimo:* **5** kayak, umiak

canon 3 law **4** list, rule **5** dogma, edict, round, tenet **6** decree **7** precept, statute **8** doctrine, standard **9** clergyman, criterion, ordinance **10** regulation

canonical 5 sound **6** lawful **7** classic **8** accepted, approved, official, orthodox, received **10** authorized, recognized, sanctioned **13** authoritative

canonical hour 4 none, sext **5** lauds, prime, terce **6** matins, tierce **7** vespers **8** compline

canonicals 9 vestments

canoodle 3 hug, pet **5** spoon **6** caress, cuddle, fondle

can opener 9 church key

canopy 5 cover, shade **6** awning **7** marquee, shelter **8** covering, sunshade **9** baldachin **10** baldachino *canvas:* **4** tilt

cant 3 tip **4** heel, lean, list, tilt **5** angle, argot, bevel, idiom, lingo, piety, slang, slant, slope **6** humbug, jargon, patois, patter, speech **7** dialect, diction, incline, lexicon, palaver, recline **8** language, singsong **9** hypocrisy **10** dictionary, pharisaism, sanctimony, vernacular **11** inclination, insincerity **12** pecksniffery

cantaloupe 5 melon **9** muskmelon

cantankerous 4 dour, sour **5** cross, huffy, testy, waspy **6** crabby, cranky, crusty, grumpy, morose, ornery **7** bearish, crabbed, grouchy, peevish, prickly, waspish **8** cankered, liverish, petulant, snappish, stubborn, vinegary **9** crotchety, difficult, dyspeptic, irascible, irrita-

ble, obstinate **10** ill-natured, irritating, vinegarish **12** cross-grained

canter 3 bum **4** gait, hobo, lope **5** tramp **6** beggar **7** drifter, vagrant **8** derelict, vagabond **11** bindle stiff

Canterbury Archbishop: 3 Oda **6** Anselm, Becket (Thomas á), Parker (Matthew) **7** Cranmer (Thomas), Dunstan **9** Augustine

Canterbury Tales *author:* **7** Chaucer (Geoffrey) *character:* **8** Griselda, pardoner, summoner **10** wife of Bath *inn:* **6** Tabard

canticle 3 ode **4** hymn, song **6** Te Deum **10** Benedicite, Benedictus, Magnificat **12** Nunc Dimittis

canticles 11 Song of Songs **13** Song of Solomon

cantilever 4 beam **6** bridge **7** bracket, support

cantillate 4 sing **5** chant **6** intone, recite

cantina 3 bar, pub **6** saloon, tavern **7** barroom

canton 5 state **6** billet **7** quarter, section **8** district, division

cantor 5 hazan **6** singer **9** precentor

canvas 4 duck, sail, tarp, tent **7** tenting **8** painting **9** sailcloth, tarpaulin

canvasback 4 duck

canvass 3 con, vet **5** argue, study **6** debate, survey **7** discuss, dispute, examine, inspect, solicit **8** campaign **9** check over **10** scrutinize **11** electioneer **12** authenticate

canyon 4 Glen, Zion **5** Bryce, chasm, gorge, Grand, gulch, Hells **6** Copper, coulee, ravine, valley

cap 3 tam, top **4** best **5** beret, cover, crest, crown, limit, trump **6** beanie, exceed, top off **7** calotte **9** culminate *clergyman's:* **7** biretta **9** zucchetto *hoodlike:* **4** coif *hunter's:* **7** montero *jester's:* **7** coxcomb **9** cockscomb *Jewish:* **8** yarmulke *knitted:* **5** toque, tuque **9** balaclava *military:* **4** kepi *mushroom:* **6** pileus *part:* **4** bill, brim, flap, peak **5** visor **7** earflap *Roman:* **6** pileus *Scottish:* **3** tam **8** balmoral **9** glengarry **11** tam-o'-shanter *Turkish:* **6** calpac **7** calpack

capability 5 craft, means, skill **7** ability, potency **8** adequacy, aptitude, capacity, efficacy, facility **9** potential **10** competence, efficiency **12** potentiality **13** effectiveness, qualification

capable 3 apt **4** able **5** adept **6** adroit, au fait **9** competent, efficient, qualified **10** proficient **11** susceptible

capacious 4 wide **5** ample, roomy **7** sizable **8** abundant, spacious **9** extensive **10** commodious **11** substantial

capacitance *unit of:* **5** farad

capacity 4 bent, gift, rank, role, room
5 knack, range, reach, scope, skill,
space 6 output, status, talent 7 ability,
caliber, faculty 8 adequacy, aptitude,
facility, position, standing 10 capability,
competence 11 proficiency 13 qualification *unit of:* 4 gill, peck, pint 5 liter,
litre, minim, quart 6 bushel, gallon
10 fluid ounce, milliliter

Capaneus *slayer:* 4 Zeus *wife:* 6 Evadne

caparison 5 adorn 6 finery 7 apparel,
panoply, raiment 9 adornment, trappings

cape 4 cope, ness 5 cloak, point
6 capote, mantle, tabard, tippet 7 manteau, pelisse 8 foreland, headland, man-
telet, mantilla, pelerine 9 peninsula
10 promontory *clergyman's:* 8 mozzetta

Cape *Africa:* 4 Juby, Yubi 5 Blanc 6 Blanco 7 Agulhas *Alaska:* 3 Icy 4 Nome
11 Krusenstern *Algeria:* 3 Fer *Antarctica:*
3 Ann 4 Dart 5 Adare *Arctic:* 8 Nord-
kaap *Asia:* 5 Aniva *Australia:* 5 Byron,
Otway, Sandy, Smoky 6 Arnhem 9 Van
Diemen *Baffin Island:* 4 Dyer *Black Sea:*
5 Yasun *Borneo:* 4 Datu 6 Datoek *Brazil:*
4 Frio, Raso *California:* 9 Mendocino
Colombia: 5 Aguja *Costa Rica:* 5 Velas
Crete: 5 Plaka *Croatia:* 5 Ploca 6 Planka
Cuba: 4 Cruz 5 Maisi *Denmark:* 4 Skaw
6 Skagen *Desolación Island:* 5 Pilar 6 Pillar *Djibouti:* 3 Bir *Egypt:* 5 Banas *England:* 8 Bolerium, Lands End *Florida:*
5 Sable 7 Kennedy 9 Canaveral *Greece:*
4 Busa 5 Gallo, Malea, Papas, Vouxa
6 Araxos, Maleas 7 Akritas *Guinea:*
5 Verga *Gulf of California:* 5 Lobos *Gulf
of Guinea:* 5 Lopez *Gulf of Mexico:*
4 Rojo *Hawaii:* 5 Ka Lae 10 South Point
11 Diamond Head *Hispaniola:* 5 Beata
Honshu: 3 Iro, Oma 5 Inubo, Kyoga,
Nyudo *Indonesia:* 4 Vals 5 False *Japan:*
4 Esan, Nomo, Sata, Soya 5 Erimo,
Kamui *Libya:* 3 Tin 4 Milh *Long Island
Sound:* 10 Throgs Neck *Malay Peninsula:*
5 Bulat *Malaysia:* 4 Piai 5 Sirik *Massachusetts:* 3 Ann, Cod *Mediterranean:*
5 Ajdir *Mexico:* 4 Buey *Morocco:* 3 Sim
4 Guir, Rhir *Namibia:* 4 Fria *Newfoundland:* 5 Bauld *New Jersey:* 3 May *New
Zealand:* 5 Brett *North Carolina:* 4 Fear
7 Lookout 8 Hatteras *Northwest Territories:* 8 Bathurst *Nova Scotia:* 5 Canso
6 Breton *Oman:* 3 Nus 4 Hadd *Ontario:*
4 Hurd, Rich *Pakistan:* 5 Monze, Muari
Portugal: 4 Roca *Puerto Rico:* 4 Rojo
Quebec: 5 Gaspé *Red Sea:* 5 Kasar *Sicily:* 4 Boeo, Faro 7 Lilibeo, Passero,
Pelorus *Solomon Islands:* 5 Zelee *Somalia:* 4 Asir 5 Assir, Hafun *South Africa:*
8 Good Hope *South America:* 4 Horn
Spain: 3 Nao 4 Gata 5 Creus, Penas
Syria: 5 Basit *Taiwan:* 5 O-Iuan 7 Garam
Bi *Tierra del Fuego:* 5 Penas *Tunisia:*
5 Blanc *Turkey:* 3 Boz 4 Baba, Ince,
Kara, Krio 6 Lectum 8 Bozburun
9 Inceburun, Karaburun *Vancouver
Island:* 5 Scott *Virginia:* 5 Henry *Wash-
ington:* 5 Alava

Čapek, Karel *coinage:* 5 robot *play:*
3 R.U.R.

caper 4 dido, lark, leap, romp 5 antic,
frisk, prank, revel, shine, theft, trick
6 cavort, frolic, gambol, prance
7 roguery, rollick 8 escapade, mischief
10 shenanigan, tomfoolery 11 monkeyshine

Cape Town's famous son 5 Smuts (Jan)

Cape Verde *capital:* 5 Praia *city:* 7 Minde-
lo *island:* 3 Sal 4 Fogo, Maio 5 Brava
8 Boa Vista, São Tiago 10 São Vicente,
São Nicolau, Santa Luzia, Santo Antão
language: 7 Crioulo 10 Portuguese *monetary unit:* 6 escudo

capillary 4 tube 6 tubule 8 hairlike
11 blood vessel

capital 4 main 5 basic, chief, funds,
major, prime 6 assets, lethal, wealth
8 cardinal 9 essential, excellent, financing, first-rate, principal, resources
10 first-class, investment, preeminent,
underlying 11 fundamental, outstanding, predominant, wherewithal
Afghanistan: 5 Kabul *Albania:* 6 Tirana,
Tiranë *Alberta:* 8 Edmonton *Algeria:*
7 Algiers *Angola:* 6 Luanda *Antigua and
Barbuda:* 7 St. John's 10 Saint John's
Argentina: 11 Buenos Aires *Armenia:*
7 Yerevan *Assam:* 6 Dispur *Australia:*
8 Canberra *Austria:* 4 Wien 6 Vienna
Azerbaijan: 4 Baku *Bahamas:* 6 Nassau
Bahrain: 6 Manama *Bangladesh:*
5 Dhaka *Barbados:* 10 Bridgetown
Belarus: 5 Minsk *Belgium:* 8 Brussels
Belize: 8 Belmopan *Benin:* 9 Porto-Novo
Bhutan: 7 Thimphu *Bolivia:* 5 La Paz
Bosnia and Herzegovina: 8 Sarajevo
Botswana: 8 Gaborone *Brazil:* 8 Brasília
Bulgaria: 5 Sofia *Burkina Faso:* 11 Oua-
gadougou *Burma:* 6 Yangon 7 Rangoon
Burundi: 9 Bujumbura *Cambodia:*
9 Phnom Penh *Cameroon:* 7 Yaoundé
Canada: 6 Ottawa *Cape Verde:* 5 Praia
Central African Republic: 6 Bangui *Chad:*
8 N'Djamena *Chile:* 8 Santiago *China:*
6 Peking 7 Beijing *Colombia:* 8 Bogotá
Comoros: 6 Moroni *Congo (Zaire):*
8 Kinshasa *Costa Rica:* 7 San José *Côte
d'Ivoire:* 7 Abidjan 12 Yamoussoukro
Croatia: 6 Zagreb *Cuba:* 6 Havana
Cyprus: 7 Nicosia *Czech Republic:*
6 Prague *Denmark:* 10 Copenhagen

Dominica: 6 Roseau *Dominican Republic:* 12 Santo Domingo *East Timor:* 4 Dili *Ecuador:* 5 Quito *Egypt:* 5 Cairo *El Salvador:* 11 San Salvador *Equatorial Guinea:* 6 Malabo *Eritrea:* 6 Asmara *Estonia:* 7 Tallinn *Ethiopia:* 10 Addis Ababa *Faeroe Islands:* 8 Tórshavn *Falkland Islands:* 7 Stanley *Fiji:* 4 Suva *Finland:* 8 Helsinki *France:* 5 Paris *French Guiana:* 7 Cayenne *Gabon:* 10 Libreville *Galápagos Islands:* 12 San Cristóbal *Gambia:* 6 Banjul *Georgia, Republic of:* 6 Tiflis 7 Tbilisi *Germany:* 6 Berlin *Ghana:* 5 Accra *Greece:* 6 Athens *Greenland:* 8 Godthaab *Grenada:* 9 St. George's 12 Saint George's *Guam:* 5 Agana *Guinea:* 7 Conakry *Guyana:* 10 Georgetown *Haiti:* 12 Port-au-Prince *Honduras:* 11 Tegucigalpa *Hungary:* 8 Budapest *Iceland:* 9 Reykjavík *India:* 8 New Delhi *Indonesia:* 7 Jakarta 8 Djakarta *Iran:* 6 Tehran 7 Teheran *Iraq:* 7 Baghdad *Ireland:* 6 Dublin *Israel:* 7 Tel-Aviv 9 Jerusalem *Italy:* 4 Rome *Jamaica:* 8 Kingston *Japan:* 5 Tokyo *Jordan:* 5 Amman *Kazakhstan:* 6 Astana 7 Alma-Ata *Kenya:* 7 Nairobi *Kiribati:* 6 Tarawa 11 South Tarawa *Korea, North:* 9 Pyongyang *Korea, South:* 5 Seoul *Kuwait:* 10 Kuwait City *Kyrgyzstan:* 7 Bishkek *Laos:* 9 Vientiane *Latvia:* 4 Riga *Lebanon:* 6 Beirut *Lesotho:* 6 Maseru *Libya:* 7 Tripoli *Liechtenstein:* 5 Vaduz *Lithuania:* 7 Vilnius *Macedonia:* 6 Skopje *Madagascar:* 12 Antananarivo *Malawi:* 8 Lilongwe *Malaysia:* 11 Kuala Lumpur *Maldives:* 4 Male *Mali:* 6 Bamako *Malta:* 8 Valletta *Manitoba:* 8 Winnipeg *Marshall Islands:* 6 Majuro *Mauritania:* 10 Nouakchott *Mauritius:* 9 Port Louis *Micronesia:* 7 Palikir *Moldova:* 8 Kishinev 9 Chişinaău *Mongolia:* 9 Ulan Bator *Montserrat:* 8 Plymouth *Morocco:* 5 Rabat *Mozambique:* 6 Maputo *Myanmar:* 6 Yangon 7 Rangoon *Namibia:* 8 Windhoek *Nauru:* 5 Yaren *Nepal:* 8 Katmandu 9 Kathmandu *Netherlands:* 9 Amsterdam *Newfoundland:* 10 Saint Johns *New Zealand:* 10 Wellington *Nicaragua:* 9 Managua *Niger:* 6 Niamey *Nigeria:* 5 Abuja *Northern Ireland:* 7 Belfast *Northern Territory:* 6 Darwin *North-West Frontier Province:* 8 Peshawar *Northwest Territories:* 11 Yellowknife *Norway:* 4 Oslo *Nova Scotia:* 7 Halifax *Oman:* 6 Muscat *Pakistan:* 9 Islamabad *Palau:* 5 Koror 10 Babelthuap *Papua New Guinea:* 11 Port Moresby *Paraguay:* 8 Asunción *Peru:* 4 Lima *Philippines:* 6 Manila *Poland:* 6 Warsaw *Portugal:* 6 Lisbon

Prince Edward Island: 13 Charlottetown *Puerto Rico:* 7 San Juan *Qatar:* 4 Doha *Queensland:* 8 Brisbane *Réunion:* 7 St. Denis 10 Saint Denis *Romania:* 9 Bucharest *Russia:* 6 Moscow *Rwanda:* 6 Kigali *Saint Helena:* 9 Jamestown *Saint Kitts and Nevis:* 10 Basseterre *Saint Lucia:* 8 Castries *Samoa:* 4 Apia *Saskatchewan:* 6 Regina *Saudi Arabia:* 6 Riyadh *Scotland:* 9 Edinburgh *Senegal:* 5 Dakar *Serbia and Montenegro:* 8 Belgrade *Seychelles:* 8 Victoria *Shetland:* 7 Lerwick *Sicily:* 7 Palermo *Sierra Leone:* 8 Freetown *Sikkim:* 7 Gangtok *Sind:* 7 Karachi *Slovakia:* 10 Bratislava *Slovenia:* 9 Ljubljana *Solomon Islands:* 7 Honiara *Somalia:* 9 Mogadishu *South Africa:* 8 Cape Town, Pretoria 12 Bloemfontein *South Australia:* 8 Adelaide *South-West Africa:* 8 Windhoek *Spain:* 6 Madrid *Sri Lanka:* 7 Colombo *Sudan:* 8 Khartoum *Suriname:* 10 Paramaribo *Swaziland:* 7 Mbabane *Sweden:* 9 Stockholm *Switzerland:* 4 Bern 5 Berne *Syria:* 8 Damascus *Tahiti:* 7 Papeete *Taiwan:* 6 Taipei *Tajikistan:* 8 Dushanbe *Tanzania:* 6 Dodoma 11 Dar es Salaam *Tasmania:* 6 Hobart *Thailand:* 7 Bangkok *Tibet:* 5 Lhasa *Tirol:* 9 Innsbruck *Togo:* 4 Lomé *Tonga:* 9 Nuku'alofa *Trinidad and Tobago:* 11 Port-of-Spain *Tunisia:* 5 Tunis *Turkey:* 6 Ankara *Turkmenistan:* 8 Ashgabat 9 Ashkhabad *Tuvalu:* 8 Funafuti *Uganda:* 7 Kampala *Ukraine:* 4 Kiev *United Arab Emirates:* 8 Abu Dhabi *United Kingdom:* 6 London *Uruguay:* 10 Montevideo *Uttar Pradesh:* 7 Lucknow *Uzbekistan:* 8 Tashkent *Vanuatu:* 4 Vila *Venezuela:* 7 Caracas *Victoria:* 9 Melbourne *Vietnam:* 5 Hanoi *Wales:* 7 Cardiff *Western Australia:* 5 Perth *Yemen:* 4 Sana 5 Sanaa *Yugoslavia:* 8 Belgrade *Yukon:* 10 Whitehorse *Zambia:* 6 Lusaka *Zimbabwe:* 6 Harare

capitalist 6 backer, tycoon 7 magnate 8 investor 9 bourgeois, financier, plutocrat 12 entrepreneur

capitalistic 9 bourgeois

capitalize 4 back, fund 5 stake 6 profit 7 convert, finance, promote, sponsor, support 8 bankroll 9 grubstake, subsidize

capital sin see DEADLY SIN

capitation 3 tax 7 payment, poll tax

Capitol Hill sound 3 aye, nay

capitulate 3 bow 4 cave 5 defer, yield 6 cave in, give in, give up, relent, submit 7 concede, succumb 9 acquiesce, surrender 12 knuckle under

capitulation 9 surrender 10 submission

capo 3 bar 4 boss, head 5 chief 9 godfather

capote 4 cope 5 cloak 6 mantle, tabard 7 manteau, pelisse 8 overcoat

capper 4 lure 5 blind, decoy, shill 6 climax, finale 8 clincher

capriccio 4 whim 5 caper, fancy, prank 6 notion, vagary, whimsy 7 impulse

caprice 3 bee 4 mood, vein, whim 5 fancy, freak, humor 6 foible, maggot, megrim, notion, vagary, whimsy 7 conceit 8 crotchet

capricious 4 iffy 5 flaky, moody 6 chancy, fickle 7 erratic, flighty, wayward 8 fanciful, unstable, variable, volatile 9 arbitrary, impulsive, mercurial, uncertain, whimsical 10 changeable, inconstant 12 effervescent, incalculable 13 temperamental, unpredictable

caprid 4 goat

capriole 4 leap 5 caper

capsize 4 keel, roll, sink 5 upset 7 founder, tip over 8 collapse, overturn, turn over

capstone 4 acme, apex, peak 6 apogee, climax, coping, summit, zenith 8 pinnacle 9 high point 11 culmination

capsule 6 canned, pocket, potted 7 compact, outline 9 condensed

capsulize 6 reduce 7 enclose 8 compress, condense 9 summarize, synopsize

captain 6 master 7 skipper *fictional:* 4 Ahab, Nemo 5 Queeg *historical:* 5 Bligh (William) *pirate:* 4 Kidd (William)

Captains Courageous author 7 Kipling (Rudyard)

caption 5 title 6 legend, rubric 7 cutline, heading 8 subtitle 9 underline

captious 5 testy 7 carping, peevish 8 caviling, contrary, critical, exacting, petulant, snappish 9 demanding, irritable 10 censorious, nit-picking 12 faultfinding, overcritical 13 hypercritical

captivate 4 draw, grip, hold, take 5 charm 6 allure, dazzle, please, ravish, seduce 7 attract, beguile, bewitch, delight, enchant, gratify 8 enthrall 9 enrapture, fascinate, hypnotize, infatuate, magnetize, mesmerize, spellbind

captivating 8 charming, enticing, fetching, magnetic, riveting 9 appealing, glamorous, seductive 10 bewitching, engrossing, intriguing 11 enthralling, fascinating

captive 5 bound, caged, taken 6 jailed 7 hostage 8 confined, detainee, internee, prisoner 10 enthralled, hypnotized, imprisoned

captivity 7 bondage, custody, slavery 9 detention 10 internment 11 confinement 12 imprisonment

capture 3 bag, get, nab, net, win 4 nail, take, trap 5 catch, lasso, prize, seize, snare 6 arrest, collar, entrap, occupy, secure 7 conquer, ensnare 8 preserve

Capuan 4 lush 5 plush 6 deluxe 7 opulent 8 luscious, palatial 9 luxuriant, luxurious, sumptuous 11 upholstered

car 4 auto, heap 5 buggy, coach, crate, sedan, wreck 6 jalopy, junker, wheels 7 clunker, flivver 8 roadster 10 automobile (see also AUTOMOBILE)

carafe 4 ewer 5 cruet 6 bottle, flacon, flagon 8 decanter

caravan 6 convoy, safari

caravansary 3 inn 4 khan 5 hotel, lodge, serai 6 hostel, tavern 10 campground

carbohydrate 5 sugar 6 starch 7 amylose, glucose, lactose, maltose, sucrose 8 fructose, glycogen 9 cellulose, galactose

carbolic acid 6 phenol

carbon 4 coal, coke, soot 8 charcoal, graphite, plumbago 9 lampblack

carbonate 6 aerate

carbon copy 4 dupe, twin 5 clone, ditto, mimeo, repro, Xerox 7 replica 8 knockoff 9 duplicate, facsimile 10 dead ringer 11 replication 12 reproduction

carbonize 4 burn, char, sear 5 singe, toast 6 scorch

carbuncle 4 boil, sore 5 ulcer 6 garnet, pimple 7 abscess, pustule 8 cabochon

carcass 4 body, hulk, mort 5 frame, shell, stiff 6 corpse 7 cadaver, remains 8 skeleton

carcinoid 5 tumor 8 neoplasm

carcinoma 5 tumor 6 cancer 8 neoplasm

card 3 wag, wit 4 menu, sked 5 joker 6 agenda, docket 7 program 8 calendar, comedian, humorist, schedule 9 timetable *fortune-telling:* 5 tarot *performer's:* 3 cue *spot:* 3 pip

cardboard 5 stiff 6 unreal, wooden 7 bristol, buckram, stilted 8 lifeless 10 unlifelike 11 stereotyped, unrealistic

card-carrying 4 true 7 genuine 8 bona fide 9 authentic, certified 11 full-fledged

card game see at GAME

cardiac stimulant 7 ouabain 9 digitalis

cardinal 3 key 4 main 5 basic, chief, prime, vital 6 ruling 7 central, leading, pivotal, primary 9 essential, important, principal 10 overriding, overruling 11 fundamental 12 constitutive *point:* 4 east, west 5 north, south *suffix:* 4 teen *virtue:* 7 justice 8 prudence 9 fortitude 10 temperance

care 3 rue, woe 4 fear, heed, mind, tend,

ward **5** alarm, grief, nurse, pains, serve, trust, watch, worry **6** attend, charge, dismay, effort, mother, regard, regret, sorrow, strain, stress, unease, wait on **7** anguish, anxiety, concern, conduct, custody, keeping, trouble **8** disquiet, exertion, handling, interest, suspense **9** attention, curiosity, misgiving, oversight, vigilance **10** affliction, foreboding, management, solicitude, uneasiness **11** disquietude, heedfulness, maintenance, safekeeping, supervision **12** apprehension, guardianship, watchfulness **13** consciousness, consideration, consternation

careen 4 race, sway, tilt **5** lurch, pitch, speed, swing, weave **6** repair, wobble **7** stagger

career 3 job **4** race, rush, tear, work **5** chase, speed **6** charge, course **7** calling, passage **8** lifework, vocation **9** encounter **10** livelihood, profession

care for 4 like, love, mind, tend **5** nurse, treat **6** attend, foster **7** cherish, nurture **8** preserve **9** cultivate, look after

carefree 4 wild **6** blithe, breezy, jaunty **8** reckless **10** insouciant, untroubled **12** happy-go-lucky, lighthearted **13** irresponsible

careful 4 safe, wary **5** chary, exact, fussy **7** dutiful, guarded, precise, prudent, studied **8** accurate, cautious, critical, discreet, gingerly, thorough **9** attentive, provident **10** deliberate, meticulous, particular, scrupulous **11** calculating, circumspect, considerate, foresighted, painstaking, punctilious **13** conscientious

carefully 6 warily **8** gingerly **10** cautiously, discreetly **12** meticulously, scrupulously **13** painstakingly, punctiliously

careless 3 lax **5** hasty, messy, slack **6** casual, remiss, sloppy, untidy **7** cursory, offhand, unkempt **8** feckless, heedless, reckless, slapdash, slipshod, slovenly **9** forgetful, negligent, oblivious, unheeding, unmindful, unstudied **10** disheveled, inaccurate, incautious, neglectful, unthinking, untroubled **11** inadvertent, inattentive, indifferent, perfunctory, spontaneous, thoughtless, unconcerned **12** uninterested, unreflective **13** irresponsible

caress 3 pat, pet, toy **4** kiss, love **5** dally, touch **6** coddle, cosset, cuddle, dandle, fondle, nuzzle, pamper, stroke **7** cherish, indulge **8** canoodle **10** endearment

caressive 7 calming **8** soothing

caretaker 6 warden **7** curator, janitor **9** custodian

careworn 3 wan **5** drawn, faded, jaded **7** haggard, pinched, wearied **8** fatigued, troubled **9** exhausted **10** distressed

cargo 4 haul, load **6** burden, lading **7** freight, payload **8** shipload, shipment **11** consignment

caribe 7 piranha

caribou 4 deer **8** reindeer

caricature 4 mock, sham **5** farce, phony **6** parody **7** cartoon, lampoon, mockery, takeoff **8** travesty **9** burlesque **10** distortion, pasquinade **12** exaggeration

Carlsbad feature 4 cave **6** cavern

Carmen *author:* **7** Mérimée (Prosper) *composer:* **5** Bizet (Georges) *lover:* **7** Don José **9** Escamillo

carnage 4 gore **8** butchery, hecatomb, massacre **9** bloodbath, bloodshed, slaughter

carnal 4 lewd **6** animal, bodily, coarse, earthy, sexual, vulgar, wanton **7** earthly, fleshly, lustful, mundane, obscene, sensual, worldly **8** corporal, material, physical, sensuous, temporal **9** corporeal **10** lascivious

carnation 4 pink **5** color **6** flower

carnival 4 fair, fete **6** fiesta *attraction:* **4** ride **6** midway **9** sideshow **10** concession *character:* **5** shill **6** barker, hawker **7** grifter, spieler *New Orleans:* **9** Mardi Gras *performer:* **4** geek

carnivore 9 meat-eater **10** flesh-eater

carol 4 song **6** ballad *Christmas:* **4** noel

carom 6 bounce, glance **7** rebound **8** ricochet

Caron role 4 Gigi, Lili **5** Fanny

carotid's relative 5 aorta

carousal 3 bat, jag **4** bash, tear **5** binge, booze, drunk, fling, revel, spree **6** bender, frolic **7** blowout, debauch, shindig **8** wingding **9** brannigan *Scottish:* **6** splore

carouse 5 revel **6** cavort, frolic **7** roister *Scottish:* **4** birl

carp 3 nag **4** fuss **5** bream, cavil, scold **6** peck at, pester **7** henpeck **8** complain, cyprinid, sea bream **9** complaint, criticize, find fault

carpe ___ 4 diem

carpenter 3 ant, bee **6** joiner, wright **7** builder, workman **10** woodworker

carpentry 7 joinery **10** timberwork

carper 6 critic, nagger **7** caviler, knocker **9** nitpicker **10** complainer, criticizer **11** faultfinder

carpet 3 mat, rug **4** Agra **5** Herat, Heriz, Koula, Ladik, Sarok, tapis **6** Herati, Kerman, Keshan, Kirman, Sarouk, Tabriz, Wilton **8** moquette **9** Axminster, broadloom

carpet beetle 10 buffalo bug

carping 7 blaming, fussing, nagging, railing **8** captious, caviling, critical, scolding **9** pestering **10** censorious, upbraiding **11** criticizing, reproachful **12** faultfinding, overcritical

carrageen 7 seaweed **9** Irish moss

carrefour 5 plaza **6** square **10** crossroads

carriage 3 rig **4** pose **5** coach **6** stance **7** posture, transit **8** attitude **9** transport **10** conveyance, deportment *American:* **5** buggy **8** rockaway **9** buckboard *attendant:* **6** flunky **7** footman *baby:* **4** pram **5** buggy **8** stroller **12** perambulator *driver:* **4** hack **5** cabby **8** coachman *folding top:* **6** calash *four-wheeled:* **4** trap **5** buggy, coupe **6** calash, fiacre, landau, surrey **7** hackney, phaeton **8** barouche, brougham, carryall, rockaway, stanhope, victoria **9** buckboard *Indian:* **6** gharry *man-drawn:* **8** rickshaw **10** jinricksha, jinrikisha *Russian:* **6** troika **7** droshky *stately:* **7** caroche *three-horse:* **6** troika *two-wheeled:* **3** gig **4** shay, trap **5** buggy, sulky **6** chaise, hansom **7** calèche, dogcart, tilbury **9** cabriolet *with attendants:* **8** equipage

carriage trade 5 elite **6** gentry **7** quality **9** blue blood, gentility **10** upper class, upper crust **11** aristocracy

carrick bend 4 knot

carrier 4 mule **5** envoy **6** bearer, porter, runner, vector **7** airline, courier, shipper, vehicle **8** conveyor, emissary **9** go-between, messenger **11** internuncio, transporter

Carroll character 5 Alice, Bruno, Snark **6** Boojum, Sylvie **8** Dormouse, Red Queen **9** Mad Hatter, March Hare **10** Mock Turtle **11** White Rabbit **12** Humpty Dumpty

carrot 5 prize **6** reward **9** incentive **10** inducement

carry 3 get, lug **4** bear, haul, have, hump, keep, move, pack, send, take, tote, wear **5** bring, ferry, fetch, range, stock **6** affect, bear up, convey, uphold **7** comport, conduct, portage, possess, support, sustain **8** buttress, transfer, transmit **9** influence, transport

carrying case 7 holdall, satchel **8** carryall

carry off 4 kill **6** abduct, kidnap, remove, spirit away **7** achieve, destroy, execute, perform, realize **8** complete, conclude, dispatch, shanghai **10** accomplish

carry on 3 run **4** go on, keep, rant, rave, wage **6** direct, endure, manage, ordain **7** conduct, operate, persist, prattle, proceed **8** continue, sound off **9** persevere

carry out 6 effect, govern, render **7** achieve, execute, fulfill, oversee, perform, realize **8** bring off, complete, finalize, transact **9** discharge, prosecute **10** accomplish, administer, effectuate **12** administrate

carry over 6 deduct **7** persist **8** postpone, transfer

carry through 4 last **5** abide **6** effect, endure **7** execute, perdure, perform, persist, survive **8** bring off, complete, continue **10** accomplish, effectuate

Carson work 11 Sea Around Us (The) **12** Silent Spring

cart 3 gig **4** dray, haul **5** buggy, carry **6** barrow, convey, schlep **7** schlepp, trundle, tumbrel, tumbril **8** carriage **9** transport **11** wheelbarrow *Indian:* **5** tonga *racing:* **5** sulky

___ carte 3 à la

___ Carte 5 D'Oyly

carte blanche 3 say **5** power, right, say-so **7** freedom, license **8** free hand, free rein **9** authority **10** blank check **11** prerogative

carte du jour 4 menu

cartel 4 bloc, pool **5** trust **7** combine **9** syndicate **10** consortium **12** conglomerate

Carthaginian *goddess of the moon:* **5** Tanit **6** Tanith *queen:* **4** Dido **6** Elissa

cartilage 7 gristle

cartographer *English:* **5** Smith (William) *Flemish:* **6** Kremer (Gerhard) **8** Mercator (Gerardus), Ortelius *German:* **13** Waldseemüller (Martin) *Greek:* **7** Ptolemy

cartography 9 mapmaking

carton 3 box **4** pack

cartoonist 3 Lee (Stan) **4** Capp (Al), Kane (Bob), Nast (Thomas), Szep (Paul) **5** Adams (Scott), Booth (George), Chast (Roz), Crumb (R.), Davis (Jim), Gould (Chester), Hanna (Bill), Jones (Chuck), Kelly (Walt), Steig (William), Young (Chic) **6** Addams (Charles), Caniff (Milton), Disney (Walt), Larson (Gary), Martin (Don), Schulz (Charles), Walker (Mort) **7** Barbera (Joe), Feiffer (Jules), Ketcham (Hank), Mauldin (Bill), Thurber (James), Trudeau (Garry) **8** Goldberg (Rube), Groening (Matt), Herblock, Hokinson (Helen), MacNelly (Jeff), Oliphant (Pat) **9** Fleischer (Max) **10** Hirschfeld (Al)

cartouche 5 frame **6** shield **9** cartridge

cartridge 4 case, tube **5** shell **8** cassette, cylinder **9** cartouche, container

cartwheel 4 coin **6** dollar, tumble **10** handspring

carve 3 cut, hew **4** chip, etch, form, hack **5** shape, slice **6** chisel, cleave, incise, sculpt **7** dissect, engrave, whittle **9** sculpture

Casablanca *actor:* **5** Lorre (Peter), Rains (Claude) **6** Bogart (Humphrey) **7** Bergman (Ingrid) **11** Greenstreet (Sydney) *character:* **4** Ilsa (Lund), Rick (Blaine) **6** Laszlo (Victor) *director:* **6** Curtiz (Michael)

Casanova 4 rake, roué, wolf **5** Romeo **6** lecher, masher, tomcat **7** amorist, Don Juan, gallant, playboy, seducer **8** lothario, paramour **9** adulterer, ladies' man, libertine, womanizer **10** lady-killer, voluptuary **11** philanderer

cascade 4 fall, gush, lace, pour, spew **5** chute, falls, flood, spill **6** deluge, plunge, rapids, shower, tumble **7** Niagara, torrent **8** cataract **9** avalanche, waterfall **10** outpouring

Cascade Mountains peak 6 Lassen, Shasta **7** Rainier

case 3 box, con, vet **4** etui, hull, husk, skin, suit **5** cause, event, shell **6** action, sample, sheath **7** episode, examine, example, inspect, lawsuit **8** argument, covering, incident, instance, sampling, specimen **9** check over, condition, situation **10** occurrence, proceeding, scrutinize **11** eventuality **12** circumstance *grammatical:* **6** dative **8** ablative, genitive, vocative **9** objective **10** accusative, nominative, possessive

casebearer 5 larva **11** caterpillar

case-hardened 5 tough **7** callous **8** obdurate **9** indurated, insensate, toughened, unfeeling **11** insensitive **12** thick-skinned

casement 4 sash **6** window

Casey at the Bat poet 6 Thayer (Ernest Lawrence)

cash 4 coin, jack **5** bread, dough, money, scrip **6** dinero, redeem, wampum **7** cabbage, lettuce, scratch **8** currency **10** greenbacks, ready money **11** legal tender

cashier 3 can **4** boot, fire, oust, sack **5** clerk, eject, expel, scrap **6** banker, bounce, bursar, reject, teller **7** boot out, discard, dismiss, kick out **8** jettison, throw out **9** discharge, eliminate, terminate, throw away **10** bookkeeper **11** bean counter, comptroller

cash in 3 die **4** conk, drop **5** croak **6** expire, pop off, redeem, retire **7** kick off, succumb **8** check out, drop dead, pass away, settle up **9** liquidate

casing 4 hull, husk, pipe, rind, skin, tire **5** frame, shell, space **7** wrapper **8** membrane

casino *attendant:* **6** dealer **8** croupier *game:* **4** faro **5** craps, monte, poker **6** tierce **8** baccarat, roulette **9** blackjack

cask 3 keg, tun **4** butt, drum, pipe **6** barrel, firkin **8** hogshead

casket 3 box **5** chest **6** coffer, coffin **8** jewel box

Caspian Sea *city:* **4** Baku *feeder:* **4** Ural

Cassandra 4 seer **7** prophet, seeress **8** doomster **9** doomsayer, pessimist, worrywart **10** prophetess *brother:* **7** Helenus *father:* **5** Priam *lover:* **9** Agamemnon *mother:* **6** Hecuba *slayer:* **12** Clytemnestra

casserole 4 dish **5** crock **6** tureen

Cassiopeia 13 constellation *daughter:* **9** Andromeda *husband:* **7** Cepheus

Cassio's mistress 6 Bianca

cassock 4 robe **7** soutane **8** vestment

cast 3 add, hue, sum, tot **4** drop, face, fire, form, hurl, kind, look, mold, shed, sort, tint, tone, toss, turn, type **5** color, fling, heave, leave, pitch, range, shade, shape, strew, throw, tinge, total, touch **6** actors, design, devise, direct, figure, nature, reject, slough, troupe, visage **7** arrange, company, quality, replica, scatter **8** abdicate, disperse, jettison, sprinkle **9** character, prognosis, throw away **10** appearance, conjecture, distribute, expression, prediction, strabismus, suggestion **11** countenance *a spell on:* **3** hex **5** charm **7** beguile, bewitch **8** enthrall **9** captivate, enrapture, fascinate, hypnotize, infatuate, mesmerize, spellbind *overboard:* **7** deep-six **8** jettison

cast about 4 hunt, seek **5** grope **6** search **7** seek out **8** contrive **9** search for, search out

castaway 5 leper, tramp **6** beggar, maroon, pariah **7** Ishmael, outcast, vagrant **8** deadbeat, derelict **10** Ishmaelite

cast down see DOWNCAST

caste 5 class **6** degree, estate, status **7** station **8** division, prestige

cast head 4 bust

castigate 4 beat, flay, rail, whip **5** baste, chide, scold, slash **6** berate, pummel, punish, rebuke, scorch, thrash **7** belabor, blister, chasten, chew out, lambast, reprove, scarify, scourge, upbraid **8** chastise, lambaste, penalize **9** criticize, dress down, excoriate, reprimand **10** discipline, tongue-lash

castigation 3 rod **6** rebuke **7** reproof **8** punition, scolding **10** correction, discipline, punishment **12** chastisement

castle 5 manor, villa **7** alcazar, château, citadel, mansion **8** fortress **10** strong-

hold *adjunct:* 4 moat *gate:* 10 portcullis *ledge:* 7 rampart *structure:* 6 turret *tower:* 4 keep 6 donjon *wall:* 6 bailey 10 battlement

cast off 5 fling, flung, let go, loose, untie 6 jilted, untied 7 unhitch 8 cut loose, forsaken, rejected, unfasten, unmoored 9 discarded, unhitched 10 left behind, unfastened

Castor *brother:* 6 Pollux 10 Polydeuces *constellation:* 6 Gemini *father:* 4 Zeus 9 Tyndareus *mother:* 4 Leda *sister:* 5 Helen *slayer:* 4 Idas

castor oil 8 laxative 9 cathartic, lubricant, purgative

cast out 4 oust 5 eject, evict, exile, expel 6 banish, deport 7 discard 9 eliminate, ostracize

castrate 3 fix 4 geld, spay 5 alter, unman, unsex 6 neuter 7 unnerve 8 enervate, mutilate 9 sterilize 10 emasculate 11 desexualize

castrato singer 9 Farinelli

casual 5 light, minor 6 breezy, chance, random, remote 7 natural, offhand, relaxed, trivial, unfussy 8 detached, informal, laid-back 9 easygoing, impromptu, irregular, uncurious, unplanned, unserious 10 accidental, contingent, fortuitous, improvised, incidental, insouciant, nonchalant, occasional 11 indifferent, low-pressure, spontaneous, unconcerned, unimportant 12 uninterested 13 disinterested, insignificant

casualty 4 prey 5 death 6 mishap, victim 8 accident, calamity, disaster, fatality 9 mischance 10 misfortune 11 catastrophe 12 misadventure

casuistry 7 sophism 9 deception, sophistry 12 equivocation, speciousness 13 deceptiveness

casus ___ 5 belli

cat 4 lion, lynx, puma, puss 5 felid, kitty, liger, ounce, pussy, tiger, tigon 6 cougar, feline, jaguar, mouser, ocelot 7 caracal, cheetah, leopard, panther 12 mountain lion *Alice's:* 5 Dinah *catlike animal:* 5 civet, genet 7 linsang *combining form:* 5 ailur 6 ailuro *disease:* 9 distemper *domestic:* 3 Mau, Rex 4 Manx 5 tabby 6 Angora, Birman, calico, exotic, Ocicat, Somali 7 bobtail, Burmese, Persian, Ragdoll, Siamese 8 longhair, Wirehair 9 Himalayan, Maine coon, shorthair, Tonkinese 10 Abyssinian *extinct:* 10 saber-tooth *fastest:* 7 cheetah *female:* 5 queen 7 lioness, tigress 9 grimalkin *genus:* 5 Felis *grinning:* 8 Cheshire *male:* 3 gib, tom *relating to:* 6 feline *ring-tailed:* 6 serval *sound:*

3 mew 4 hiss, meow, purr, roar 9 caterwaul *spotted:* 4 pard 6 jaguar, margay, ocelot, serval 7 cheetah, leopard, panther *striped:* 5 tiger *tailless:* 4 Manx *young:* 6 kitten

cataclysm 5 flood 6 deluge 7 Niagara, torrent, tragedy 8 calamity, cataract, disaster, flooding 10 inundation 11 catastrophe, devastation

cataclysmic 5 fatal 7 ruinous 10 calamitous, disastrous 11 devastating 12 catastrophic

catacomb 5 crypt, vault 8 cemetery 10 necropolis, undercroft

catafalque 4 bier

catalog 4 list, roll 5 enter, index, tally 6 enroll, roster 7 itemize, program 8 classify, inscribe, register, roll call, schedule, syllabus 9 enumerate, inventory 10 prospectus *of books:* 11 bibliotheca *of saints:* 9 hagiology

catalyst 4 goad, spur 7 impetus, impulse 8 stimulus 9 incentive, stimulant 10 incitation, incitement, motivation

catamaran 4 boat, raft

catamount 4 lynx, puma 6 bobcat, cougar 7 panther, wildcat

cataract 5 falls, flood, rapid 6 deluge, rapids 7 cascade, Niagara, torrent 8 downpour 9 waterfall 10 inundation

catastrophe 3 woe 6 deluge, fiasco 7 debacle, tragedy 8 calamity, disaster, meltdown 9 cataclysm, emergency 11 devastation

catastrophic 5 fatal 6 deadly, tragic 7 ruinous 10 calamitous, disastrous 11 cataclysmic

Catawba 4 wine 5 river 6 Indian

catcall 4 hiss, hoot, jeer, razz 9 criticism, raspberry 10 Bronx cheer

catch 3 bag, get, nab, net, see, wed 4 dupe, find, fool, grab, grip, gull, haul, hoax, hook, nail, snag, sock, spot, take, trap 5 block, clasp, clout, grasp, hit on, marry, reach, round, seize, smite, snare, stick, stump, trick, watch, whack 6 accept, anchor, arrest, clutch, collar, cut off, descry, detect, engage, entrap, fasten, flurry, follow, put out, rattle, secure, snatch, strike, take in, tangle, turn up 7 capture, confuse, deceive, disturb, ensnare, grapple, hit upon, perplex, receive 8 confound, contract, entangle, flimflam, fragment, hoodwink, kick over, meet with, overhaul, overtake 9 apprehend, bamboozle, embarrass, encounter, intercept 10 comprehend, understand 12 come down with

Catch-22 author 6 Heller (Joseph)

catchall term 3 etc.

Catcher in the Rye *author:* 8 Salinger (J. D.) *character:* 9 Caulfield (Holden)

catcher's glove 4 mitt

catching 6 taking 10 contagious, infectious 12 communicable

catch on 3 see 4 hear 5 learn 7 find out 8 discover 9 ascertain, determine, figure out

catchphrase see CATCHWORD

catch up 4 hold 6 gain on 7 close in, ensnare 8 entangle, enthrall 9 fascinate, mesmerize, spellbind

catchword 5 maxim, motto 6 slogan 10 shibboleth

catchy 6 fitful, spotty, tricky 7 erratic 8 sporadic 9 appealing, desultory, irregular, memorable, spasmodic

catechist 7 teacher

catechize 3 ask 4 quiz 5 grill, query, train 7 examine, inquire 8 instruct, question 9 inculcate 11 interrogate

catechumen 6 novice 7 convert, student, trainee 8 initiate, neophyte

categorical 7 certain, decided, express 8 absolute, clear-cut, definite, emphatic, explicit, positive 9 downright 10 definitive, forthright 11 unambiguous, unequivocal, unqualified

categorize 3 peg 4 sort 5 class, group 7 put down 8 classify, identify 10 pigeonhole

category 4 rank, tier 5 class, genre, grade, group 6 league 7 section 8 division, grouping 10 pigeonhole

catenation 4 link 5 chain 6 series, string 7 linkage 10 connection, succession

catercorner 9 obliquely, slantways, slantwise 10 cornerwise, diagonally

caterpillar 5 larva 7 cutworm, webworm 8 armyworm, silkworm 10 casebearer

cater to 5 humor 6 pamper, supply 7 furnish, gratify, indulge

caterwaul 4 howl, meow, yowl 5 miaow 6 squall

catfish see FISH

catharsis 5 purge, tonic 7 purging 8 curative 9 cleansing, purgation, purgative 10 lustration 11 expurgation, restorative 12 purification

cathartic 5 purge, tonic 8 curative 9 castor oil, purgative 11 restorative, therapeutic

Cathay 5 China

cathedral 5 duomo 6 church 8 basilica *feature:* 4 apse, nave 5 altar 6 chapel 7 chancel 10 clerestory 8 buttress, transept

Cather novel 8 Lost Lady (A) 9 My Antonia, One of Ours, O Pioneers 13 Song of the Lark 15 Professor's House (The) 16 Shadows on the Rock 23 Youth and the Bright Medusa

catholic 5 broad 6 global 7 general, liberal 8 eclectic, tolerant 9 expansive, inclusive, undivided, universal, worldwide 10 ecumenical 12 cosmopolitan 13 comprehensive

catholicity 7 breadth 9 tolerance 10 liberality 11 magnanimity 12 universality

catholicon 6 elixir 7 cure-all, nostrum, panacea

catkin 5 ament

catlike 6 feline 7 furtive 8 stealthy

catnap 3 nap 4 doze 6 siesta, snooze 10 forty winks

Cato *title:* 6 aedile, censor, consul 7 praetor, tribune 8 quaestor

Cat on a ___ Tin Roof 3 Hot

cat's-paw 4 dupe, knot, pawn, tool 5 patsy 6 puppet, stooge

cattail 4 reed, rush

cattle 4 cows, kine, neat, oxen 7 bovines 9 livestock *breed:* 5 Angus, Devon, Kerry 6 Durham, Jersey, Sussex 7 Brahman, Hariana, Red Poll 8 Ayrshire, Galloway, Guernsey, Hereford, Highland, Holstein, Limousin, Longhorn 9 Charolais, Red Polled, Shorthorn, Simmental 10 Brown Swiss 11 Dutch Belted *catching rope:* 5 lasso 6 lariat *cry:* 3 low, moo *dehorn:* 4 poll *disease:* 4 loco 5 bloat 6 nagana 7 anthrax, locoism, measles, murrain 8 blackleg, lumpy jaw, mastitis, staggers 10 rinderpest, Texas fever 11 brucellosis *extinct breed:* 9 Teeswater *family:* 7 Bovidae *feed:* 6 fodder *genus:* 3 Bos *goddess:* 6 Bubona *grazing land:* 5 range 7 pasture *group:* 4 herd 5 drove *herdsman:* 6 cowboy, drover, gaucho 7 vaquero 8 wrangler 10 cowpuncher *identification:* 5 brand *pen:* 6 corral *round up:* 7 wrangle *stable:* 4 barn, byre *steal:* 6 rustle *wild flight:* 8 stampede

catty 4 mean 5 nasty 6 barbed, bitchy, feline 7 furtive, vicious 8 spiteful, stealthy 9 malicious 10 backbiting, malevolent

Caucasian *capital:* 4 Baku 6 Tiflis 7 Tbilisi, Yerevan *republic:* 7 Armenia, Georgia 10 Azerbaijan

Caucasus *peak:* 6 Elbrus *people:* 5 Osset

caucus 4 bloc, sect 5 cabal, lobby 6 parley, powwow 7 faction

caudal appendage 4 tail

caudillo 6 despot, tyrant 8 dictator 9 strongman

cauldron 3 pot 6 boiler, kettle 8 crucible

cause 4 case, make, root 5 evoke, hatch 6 compel, effect, elicit, induce, motive, origin, reason, source, spring 7 produce, provoke 8 engender, generate, movement 9 necessity, principle 10 antecedent, bring about, inducement, originator 11 determinant, precipitate 13 consideration

cause ____ 7 célèbre

causerie 4 chat 5 essay 6 column 7 article, feature 8 colloquy, dialogue 12 conversation

caustic 4 acid, keen, tart 5 acerb, acrid, sharp 6 biting, bitter, ironic 7 acerbic, cutting, mordant, pungent 8 scathing, stinging 9 corrosive, sarcastic, trenchant 10 astringent *solution:* 3 lye

cauterize 4 burn, numb, sear 6 deaden 11 anesthetize

caution 4 warn 6 caveat 7 warning 8 forewarn, monition, prudence 9 canniness, chariness, foresight, vigilance 10 admonition, discretion, providence 11 carefulness, forethought, forewarning 12 admonishment, discreetness

cautionary 7 warning 8 monitory 10 admonitory

cautious 4 wary 5 alert, cagey, canny, chary, leery 6 shrewd 7 careful, guarded, politic, prudent 8 discreet, gingerly, vigilant, watchful 9 judicious, provident 11 circumspect, considerate, foresighted

cavalcade 6 parade, series 7 cortege 8 sequence 10 procession, succession

cavalier 5 lofty, proud 6 casual, knight, lordly 7 gallant, haughty, offhand 8 arrogant, debonair, horseman, scornful, superior 9 caballero, gentleman 10 disdainful, dismissive, insouciant, nonchalant 12 aristocratic, supercilious

cavalryman 6 lancer 7 dragoon, trooper *Algerian:* 5 spahi *horse:* 5 waler *Prussian:* 5 uhlan *Russian:* 7 cossack *Turkish:* 5 spahi *weapon:* 5 lance, saber 7 carbine

cave 3 bow, den 4 bend, drop, give, grot, lair 5 antre, break, defer, yield 6 fold up, grotto, hollow, submit 7 crumple, knuckle, succumb 8 collapse 9 break down 10 capitulate, subterrane 11 buckle under 12 knuckle under, subterranean *dweller:* 3 bat 4 bear, lion 6 hermit 9 Cro-Magnon 10 troglodite 11 Neanderthal *explorer:* 9 spelunker *formation:* 10 stalactite, stalagmite *France:* 7 Lascaux 10 Rouffignac *Iceland:* 7 Singing *Indiana:* 9 Wyandotte *Iraq:* 8 Shanidar *Kentucky:* 7 Mammoth *New Zealand:* 7 Waitomo *rock:* 8 dolomite 9 limestone *Scotland:* 7 Fingal's *South Africa:* 5 Cango *Spain:* 8 Altamira *study of:* 10 speleology

caveat 6 notice 7 caution, warning 8 monition 10 admonition 11 explanation, forewarning

caveat ____ 6 emptor

caveman 5 brute 6 savage 9 barbarian, Cro-Magnon 10 troglodyte

cavern 6 grotto 12 subterranean *Capri:* 10 Blue Grotto *Montana:* 13 Lewis and Clark *New Mexico:* 8 Carlsbad *Tennessee:* 10 Cumberland *Virginia:* 5 Luray

cavernous 4 vast 6 gaping, hollow 7 yawning

caviar 3 roe 4 eggs 6 relish *source:* 6 beluga 8 sturgeon

cavil 4 carp 7 nitpick, quibble 9 criticize, find fault

caviler 6 carper, critic 7 knocker 8 quibbler 10 criticizer 11 faultfinder

caviling 5 fussy 7 carping, finicky, nagging 8 captious, contrary, critical, exacting, niggling 10 censorious, nitpicking 12 faultfinding 13 hairsplitting

cavity 3 pit 4 bore, hole, void 5 decay 6 caries, hollow 7 vacuity 10 interstice *body:* 5 antra (plural), sinus 6 antrum 8 follicle, hemocoel

cavort 4 leap, romp 5 caper, cut up, frisk, sport 6 frolic, gambol, prance 7 carry on, rollick 10 roughhouse 11 horse around

cavy 4 paca 6 rodent 9 guinea pig

caw 4 crow, yawp 6 squall, squawk

cay 3 key 4 isle, reef 5 islet 6 island

cayenne 6 pepper *genus:* 8 Capsicum

cayman see CAIMAN

Cayman Islands *capital:* 10 George Town *discoverer:* 8 Columbus (Christopher) *territory of:* 7 Britain

Cayuga chief 5 Logan (James)

cease 3 die, end 4 halt, quit, stop 5 close 6 desist, ending, finish 8 conclude, give over, knock off, leave off 9 terminate 10 conclusion 11 discontinue, termination

cease-fire 5 truce 9 armistice 10 suspension

ceaseless 7 endless, eternal, nonstop 8 constant, immortal, unending 9 continual, incessant, perennial, perpetual, sustained, unabating 10 continuing, continuous 11 everlasting, neverending, unremitting 12 interminable 13 uninterrupted

Cecrops' daughter 5 Herse 8 Aglauros, Aglaurus 9 Pandrosos, Pandrosus

cede 4 deed 5 grant, leave, yield 6 assign, convey, give up 7 abandon, concede 8 alienate, hand over, make over, part with, renounce, sign over, transfer 9 surrender, vouchsafe 10 relinquish

ceinture 4 belt, sash **6** girdle **9** waistband
Celaeno *father:* **5** Atlas *mother:* **7** Pleione
sisters: **8** Pleiades
celebrate 4 fete, hold, hymn, keep, laud
5 bless, cry up, exalt, extol, honor,
party, revel **6** praise **7** carouse, glorify,
maffick, observe, perform, rejoice
8 eulogize **9** solemnize **11** commemorate
celebrated 5 famed, great, noted
6 famous **7** eminent, notable, partied
8 caroused, rejoiced, renowned
9 prominent, well-known **11** illustrious
13 distinguished
celebration 4 bash, fete, gala **5** party
6 fiesta **7** blowout, jubilee, revelry
8 ceremony, festival, jamboree,
wingding **10** observance
____ **célèbre 5** cause
celebrity 3 VIP **4** fame, hero, lion, name,
star **5** éclat, glory **6** renown, repute
7 notable **8** eminence, luminary, prestige, somebody **9** notoriety, personage,
superstar **10** notability, prominence,
reputation
celerity 4 pace **5** speed **8** alacrity, dispatch, rapidity, velocity **9** briskness,
fleetness, quickness, swiftness **10** speediness
celestial 6 divine **7** blessed, elysian, sublime **8** beatific, empyreal, empyrean,
ethereal, heavenly, Olympian, supernal
9 unearthly **12** otherworldly
celestial body 3 sun **4** moon, star
5 comet **6** meteor, nebula, planet
8 asteroid **9** satellite
Celestial Empire 5 China
celibate 5 unwed **6** chaste, single, virgin
8 virginal, virtuous **9** abstinent, continent
cell 4 room **5** cubby, zooid **6** alcove
7 chamber, cubicle **9** corpuscle, cubbyhole **11** compartment *blood:* **8** hemocyte *disease:* **6** cancer *division:* **7** meiosis, mitosis *fertilized egg:* **6** zygote
material: **3** DNA, RNA **7** protein **9** chromatin, cytoplasm **10** protoplasm *nerve:*
6 neuron *part:* **4** gene **7** nucleus, vacuole **8** ribosome **9** centriole **10** chromosome *reproductive:* **3** egg **4** germ, ovum
5 sperm **6** gamete **8** gonidium
cellar 5 store **7** shelter **8** basement
cellist *American:* **4** Rose (Leonard)
6 Lesser (Laurence), Parnas (Leslie)
7 Nelsova (Zara), Parisot (Aldo), Stark-
er (Janos) **8** Fournier (Pierre), Schuster
(Joseph) **10** Greenhouse (Bernard) *Eng-*
lish: **5** du Pré (Jacqueline) *Russian:*
11 Piatigorsky (Gregor) **12** Rostropovich (Mstislav) *Spanish:* **6** Casals
(Pablo)

cellophane 4 wrap **7** wrapper **8** wrapping
9 packaging
celluloid 4 film **7** plastic
Celt 4 Gael, Scot **6** Breton **8** Irishman,
Welshman **10** Cornishman, Highlander
Celtic *deity:* **4** Bran **5** Epona, Lugus,
Macha **6** Brigit **8** Rhiannon **9** Cernun-
nos *festival:* **7** Beltane, Samhain
cement 4 bind, glue, join **5** grout, unify,
unite **6** mortar **8** concrete *ingredient:*
4 lime **6** silica **7** alumina **8** magnesia,
pozzolan **9** iron oxide, pozzolana
cemetery 8 boneyard, boot hill **8** God's
acre **9** graveyard **10** churchyard,
necropolis **12** burial ground, memorial
park, potter's field *underground:* **8** catacomb
cenotaph 4 tomb **6** marker **8** memorial,
monument
censer 8 thurible *carrier:* **8** thurifer
censor 3 ban, cut **4** blip, edit **5** bleep,
purge **6** cut out, delete, excise, purify,
screen **7** clean up **8** black out, restrict,
suppress, withhold **9** expurgate, red-
pencil **10** blue-pencil, bowdlerize
censorious 6 severe **7** carping **8** captious, critical **10** accusatory, condemn-
ing **11** reproachful **12** condemnatory,
denunciatory, disapproving, faultfinding, overcritical, reprehending
13 hypercritical
censurable 5 wrong **6** guilty, sinful
7 heinous **8** blamable, blameful, culpable, improper, wrongful **9** incorrect
10 deplorable, despicable, detestable
11 blameworthy, disgraceful, impeach-
able **12** unacceptable **13** discreditable,
objectionable, reprehensible
censure 5 blame, scold **6** rebuke, strafe
7 condemn, reprove, upbraid **8** chastise, denounce, disallow, reproach
9 castigate, criticize, reprehend, reprimand, reprobate **10** disapprove
centaur 6 Chiron, Nessus
Centaurus star 4 Beta **5** Alpha
Centennial State 8 Colorado
center 3 hub, mid **4** axis, core, crux,
mean, pith, root, seat **5** focus, heart,
midst, pivot **6** inside, medial, median,
middle, source **7** central, essence **8** interior, midpoint, omphalos **10** focal point
11 equidistant **12** intermediary, intermediate
centerboard 4 keel
centerfold 7 foldout **8** gatefold
central 3 hub, key, mid **4** main, mean
5 basic, chief, focal **6** medial, median,
middle **7** leading, pivotal, primary,
salient **8** cardinal, dominant, exchange,
foremost, moderate **9** essential, paramount, principal **10** overriding **11** fun-

damental, outstanding, predominant 12 intermediate

Central African Republic *capital:* 6 Bangui *former name:* 11 Ubangi-Shari *language:* 5 Sango, Zande 6 French *monetary unit:* 5 franc *neighbor:* 4 Chad 5 Congo, Sudan 8 Cameroon

Central America *country:* 6 Panama 8 Honduras 9 Costa Rica, Guatemala, Nicaragua 10 El Salvador *language:* 7 Nahuatl, Spanish

centralize 5 focus, unify 11 concentrate, consolidate

centripetal 8 afferent, focusing, unifying 10 converging 11 integrative 12 centralizing 13 concentrating, consolidating

centurion 7 officer 9 commander

century plant 5 agave

cephalopod 5 squid 7 mollusc, mollusk, octopus 10 cuttlefish

Cepheus *daughter:* 9 Andromeda *kingdom:* 8 Ethiopia *wife:* 10 Cassiopeia

cerate 4 balm 5 cream, salve 6 chrism 7 unction, unguent 8 dressing, liniment, ointment 9 demulcent, emollient

Cerberus 5 guard 8 guardian, sentinel, watchdog *father:* 6 Typhon *form:* 3 dog *mother:* 7 Echidna

cereal 4 meal, mush, samp 5 gruel 6 farina 7 oatmeal 8 cornmeal, porridge *grass:* 3 rye 4 corn, oats, ragi, rice 5 emmer, maize, spelt, wheat 6 barley, millet 7 sorghum 9 buckwheat *North African:* 8 couscous *Russian:* 5 kasha

cerebral 6 mental 7 bookish 8 highbrow 9 scholarly 10 highbrowed 12 intellectual

cerebrate 5 think 6 reason 7 reflect 8 cogitate 9 speculate 10 deliberate

cerebration 7 thought 9 brainwork 10 cogitation, reflection 11 speculation 12 deliberation

ceremonial 6 august, formal, ritual, solemn 7 courtly, stately, studied 8 mannered, stylized 10 liturgical 11 ritualistic 12 conventional

ceremonious 6 formal, proper, seemly, solemn 7 courtly, stately 8 decorous, imposing, majestic 9 dignified, grandiose 10 impressive 11 punctilious 12 conventional

ceremony 4 form, pomp, rite 6 ritual 7 decorum, liturgy, service 8 protocol 9 formality 10 observance *Jewish:* 8 habdalah, havdalah 10 bar mitzvah, bat mitzvah *university:* 8 encaenia

Ceres *Greek counterpart:* 7 Demeter *daughter:* 10 Persephone, Proserpina, Proserpine *father:* 6 Cronus, Saturn *mother:* 3 Ops 4 Rhea

certain 3 set 4 firm, some, sure, true 5 fated, fixed 6 divers, stated, sundry 7 assured, settled, several, various 8 cocksure, credible, definite, destined, positive, provable, reliable, sanguine, specific, surefire, unerring 9 authentic, certified, confident, convinced, necessary, plausible, warranted 10 conclusive, dependable, guaranteed, inarguable, inevitable, infallible, stipulated, undeniable, verifiable 11 confirmable, indubitable, ineluctable, inescapable, trustworthy, unavoidable 12 demonstrable, indisputable, well-grounded 13 incontestable, predetermined, uncontestable

certainty 5 faith 6 surety 8 firmness, sureness 9 assurance, certitude, sure thing 10 confidence, conviction 11 assuredness, staunchness 12 absoluteness, definiteness, positiveness

certificate 7 diploma, license, voucher 8 contract, document 9 affidavit 10 credential

certifier 6 notary 7 auditor 9 registrar

certify 4 aver, avow, okay 5 state, swear, vouch 6 assert, assure, attest, verify 7 approve, confirm, endorse, license, testify, warrant, witness 8 accredit, guaranty, notarize 9 authorize, guarantee, recognize 10 commission 12 authenticate

Cervantes' hero 10 Don Quixote

cessation 3 end 4 halt, rest, stop 5 break, cease, close, letup, pause 6 ending, finish, freeze, hiatus, period, recess 7 respite 10 conclusion, suspension 11 termination 12 interruption

cesspool 3 den, pit, sty 4 sink 5 sewer, Sodom 6 cloaca, gutter, pigsty 8 Gomorrah 12 Augean stable

cetacean 5 whale 7 dolphin 8 porpoise

Cetus star 4 Mira

Ceylon 8 Sri Lanka

cgs unit 3 erg 4 dyne, gram, phot 5 gauss, poise, stilb 6 second, stokes 7 lambert, maxwell, oersted 10 centimeter

Chablis 4 wine 8 Burgundy 9 white wine

Chad *capital:* 8 N'Djamena *city:* 4 Sarh 6 Abéché 7 Moundou *lake:* 4 Chad *language:* 6 Arabic, French *monetary unit:* 5 franc *neighbor:* 5 Libya, Niger, Sudan 7 Nigeria 8 Cameroon *river:* 5 Chari 6 Logone

chafe 3 irk, rub, vex 4 fret, gall, peel, rage, skin, wear 5 annoy, erode 6 abrade, bother, scrape 7 provoke 8 irritate, vexation

chaff 3 kid, rag, rib 4 jest, joke, josh, razz 5 dregs, husks, tease 6 banter,

debris, refuse 7 remains 8 detritus
9 sweepings
chaffer 6 barter, dicker, haggle, higgle,
palter 7 bargain, chatter 8 exchange,
huckster
chagrin 3 ire, irk, vex 5 abash, annoy,
peeve, pique, upset 6 dismay 7 perturb
8 disquiet, distress, unsettle, vexation
9 annoyance, discomfit, displease,
embarrass, humiliate, petulance 10 disappoint, discompose, disconcert, irritation 11 frustration, humiliation 12 discomfiture
chagrined 4 hurt 5 upset, vexed
6 shamed 7 ashamed 8 dismayed 9 disturbed, mortified, perturbed, unsettled
10 distressed, humiliated 11 discomposed, embarrassed 12 disappointed,
disconcerted
chain 3 row 4 bind, bond, gyve 5 group,
train, trust 6 cartel, catena, fetter, hobble, series, string, tether 7 combine,
manacle, shackle 8 handcuff, sequence
9 syndicate 10 succession 11 concatenate, progression 12 conglomerate
13 concatenation *adjunct:* 8 sprocket
collar: 6 torque *gang:* 6 coffle *ornamental:* 10 chatelaine *sound:* 5 clank
chain ___ 3 saw 4 gang, mail 5 store
6 letter 8 reaction
Chained Lady 9 Andromeda
chair 4 seat 5 stool 6 rocker, settee, settle 7 preside *back:* 5 splat *bishop's:*
8 cathedra *designer:* 5 Eames *portable:*
5 sedan *reclining:* 8 chaise longue,
chaise lounge *royal:* 6 throne *type:*
4 club, easy 6 morris 7 rocking 8 captain's, electric 9 director's, reclining
10 Adirondack, ladder-back
chaise 4 sofa 5 chair, coach, divan 8 carriage
chalcedony 4 onyx, sard 5 agate, chert
6 jasper, quartz 9 carnelian, cornelian
10 bloodstone 11 chrysoprase
chalet 3 hut 4 camp 5 lodge 7 cottage
chalice 3 cup 5 grail 6 goblet
chalk out 5 draft 6 sketch 7 outline
8 block out, rough out 11 skeletonize
12 characterize
chalk up 3 get, win 4 gain 6 attain, credit, impute, obtain, secure 7 achieve,
acquire, ascribe, procure, realize
9 attribute
challenge 3 try 4 dare, defy, face, stir,
wake 5 brave, claim, demur, doubt,
exact, rouse, waken 6 arouse, awaken,
demand, impugn, invite, kindle 7 calling, dispute, protest, require, solicit,
venture 8 confront, defiance, demurral,
demurrer, question, struggle 9 objec-

tion, postulate, stimulate 10 difficulty,
insistence 12 remonstrance
challenger 5 rival 8 aspirant, opponent
9 adversary, contender 10 antagonist,
competitor, contestant
chamber 4 cell, hall, room 5 haven,
house 7 cubicle 9 apartment, enclosure
11 compartment *underground:*
8 hypogeum
chambered seashell 8 nautilus
chamberlain 6 priest 7 officer, servant
9 attendant, treasurer
chameleon 6 lizard
chameleonic 6 fickle 7 protean 9 mercurial 10 changeable, inconstant
chamfer 5 bevel 6 groove
chamois 6 shammy 7 leather 8 antelope,
ruminant *habitat:* 4 Alps *Old Testament:*
6 aoudad
chamois-like animal 4 goat, ibex
champ 3 gum 4 bite, chew, mash
5 gnash, munch 7 trample 8 macerate,
ruminate 9 masticate
champagne 4 wine 6 bubbly *center:*
5 Reims 6 Rheims
Champagne *capital:* 6 Troyes
champaign 5 field, plain 7 expanse, terrain 11 battlefield
champignon 6 fungus 8 mushroom
champion 4 back, hero 5 first, prime
6 uphold, victor, winner 7 capital, contend, leading, paladin, premier, support, titlist 8 advocate, defender, exponent, fight for, foremost, medalist,
unbeaten 9 excellent, nonpareil, number one, principal, proponent, protector, supporter 11 illustrious, outstanding, titleholder, white knight
championship 5 crown, title 6 laurel,
trophy 7 contest, defense, laurels, pennant 8 advocacy 10 blue ribbon
chance 3 hap, hit, lot, odd 4 fate, luck,
meet, odds, risk, shot 5 break, fluke,
light, wager 6 befall, casual, gamble,
happen, hazard 7 fortune, offhand,
stumble, venture 8 accident, fortuity,
occasion, prospect 9 advantage, transpire 10 accidental, fortuitous, incidental, likelihood 11 contingency, opportunity, possibility, probability *even:*
6 toss-up
chancellor 5 judge 8 minister 9 secretary
German: 4 Kohl (Helmut) 6 Brandt
(Willy), Erhard (Ludwig), Hitler
(Adolf) 7 Schmidt (Helmut) 8 Adenauer
(Konrad), Bismarck (Otto von)
9 Schroeder (Gerhard)
chancy 4 iffy 5 dicey, fluky, hairy, risky
6 touchy, tricky 8 perilous, ticklish
9 dangerous, haphazard, hazardous,
uncertain 10 capricious, precarious

11 speculative, treacherous 12 incalculable 13 unpredictable

Chandler, Raymond *character:* 7 Marlowe (Philip) *novel:* 8 Big Sleep (The) 11 Long Good-Bye (The) 13 Murder My Sweet 16 Farewell My Lovely *screenplay:* 10 Blue Dahlia (The) 15 Double Indemnity

change 3 fix 4 swap, turn, vary 5 alter, coins, money, morph, shift, trade 6 adjust, evolve, modify, mutate, reform, remake, revamp, revert, revise, switch 7 commute, convert, novelty, replace, reverse 8 exchange, mutation, revision, transfer 9 alternate, deviation, diversify, fluctuate, refashion, transform, transmute, transpose, variation 10 alteration, conversion, divergence, innovation, substitute 11 interchange, permutation, transfigure, vicissitude 12 metamorphose, modification, transmogrify 13 metamorphosis, transmutation *sudden:* 8 peripety 10 peripeteia

changeable 5 fluid 6 fickle, labile, pliant, shifty 7 flighty, mutable, plastic, protean, unfixed, varying 8 restless, shifting, slippery, ticklish, unstable, unsteady, variable, volatile 9 adaptable, alterable, impulsive, mercurial, uncertain, unsettled, whimsical 10 capricious, inconstant 11 chameleonic, fluctuating, vacillating 13 kaleidoscopic, temperamental, unpredictable

change decor 4 redo 10 redecorate

changeless 5 fixed 6 steady 7 abiding, regular, uniform 8 constant, enduring, resolute 9 immutable, perpetual, steadfast, unvarying 10 invariable

change off 6 rotate 9 alternate

change of heart 8 reversal

change of life 9 menopause 11 climacteric

change of pace 5 pitch, shift 9 slow pitch

changeover 5 shift 10 alteration, conversion, transition

channel 3 way 4 band, duct, pass, path, pipe 5 agent, canal, carry 6 agency, convey, course, funnel, groove, gutter, medium, siphon, strait, trough, tunnel 7 conduct, conduit, passage, vehicle 8 aqueduct, pipeline, transmit 10 instrument 11 watercourse *Africa-Madagascar:* 10 Mozambique *Atlantic-Nantucket Sound:* 8 Muskeget *Atlantic-North Sea:* 7 English *Ellesmere-Greenland:* 7 Robeson *Ganges:* 5 Hugli 7 Hooghly *Hawaii:* 5 Kaiwi, Kauai *Japan:* 5 Bungo *Northwest Territories:* 9 M'Clintock *Pakistan:* 4 Nara *Scotland:* 5 Minch *Tierra del*

Fuego: 6 Beagle *Tigris-Euphrates:* 11 Shatt al Arab *Virginia:* 12 Hampton Roads *West Indies:* 9 Old Bahama

channel bass 4 drum 7 red drum, redfish

Channel Islands *capital:* 8 St. Helier 11 St. Peter Port *dependency of:* 7 Britain *island:* 4 Sark 6 Jersey 8 Alderney, Guernsey

chanson 4 song "Chanson ___" 6 Triste

chanson de ___ 5 geste

chant 4 sing, tune 5 drone 6 intone 8 vocalize 10 cantillate *Gregorian:* 9 plainsong 12 cantus firmus *Jewish:* 6 Hallel

chanteuse 6 singer 7 artiste 10 cantatrice

chanticleer 4 cock 7 rooster

chaos 6 bedlam, muddle 7 anarchy, clutter, entropy, turmoil 8 disarray, disorder 9 confusion 11 lawlessness

Chaos *daughter:* 3 Nox, Nyx 4 Gaea *son:* 6 Erebus

chaotic 7 jumbled, lawless 8 anarchic, confused, formless 9 amorphous, haphazard, scrambled 10 disordered, disorderly, topsy-turvy, tumultuous 11 harum-scarum, unorganized 12 disorganized 13 helter-skelter, unpredictable

chap 3 guy 4 gent 5 bloke 6 fellow

chaparral 5 scrub 7 thicket

chaparral cock 10 roadrunner

chapeau 3 hat 6 topper

chapel 5 bethel, church, shrine 7 chantry 9 sanctuary

chaperone 5 guide 6 attend, duenna, escort, matron 7 oversee 9 accompany, companion, supervise 11 superintend

chapfallen see CRESTFALLEN

chaplain 5 padre 6 pastor 8 minister, sky pilot

chaplet 5 crown 6 anadem, laurel, rosary, wreath 7 coronal, coronet, garland

chapter 4 unit 5 phase, stage 6 branch, period 7 episode, section 8 division 9 affiliate

char 4 burn 9 carbonize

character 3 ilk 4 bent, case, cast, kind, mark, mind, name, rank, role, sign, sort, type 5 state, trait 6 cipher, device, letter, makeup, nature, oddity, repute, spirit, status, stripe, symbol, temper, virtue 7 feature, oddball, persona, quality, station, variety 8 capacity, eminence, identity, position, standing 9 attribute, eccentric, rectitude, situation 10 reputation, uniqueness 11 description, disposition, personality, temperament 13 individuality *chief:*

4 hero 11 protagonist *defect:* 8 hamartia

character assassination 5 libel 7 calumny, scandal, slander 10 backbiting, defamation 12 backstabbing

characteristic 4 mark, sign 5 badge, point, token, trait 6 aspect, innate, normal, proper 7 feature, natural, quality, special, typical 8 especial, peculiar, property, specific, tendency 9 attribute, birthmark, component, mannerism, trademark 10 diagnostic, emblematic, individual, particular 11 distinction, distinctive, peculiarity, singularity 12 idiosyncrasy 13 idiosyncratic

characterize 4 mark 5 draft 6 define, sketch, typify 7 outline, portray 8 describe, identify 10 constitute, pigeonhole 11 distinguish, individuate, personalize 12 discriminate 13 differentiate, individualize

characterless 4 flat 5 mousy 7 humdrum, insipid, vacuous 8 mediocre 9 colorless 10 namby-pamby, wishy-washy 11 nondescript

charade 4 sham 5 farce, put-on 6 parody 8 disguise, pretense, travesty 9 deception 11 make-believe

chare see CHORE

charge 3 ask, bid, fee, lay, tab, tax 4 bill, care, cost, duty, fill, heap, kick, load, onus, race, rate, rush, task, tell, toll, warn 5 choke, debit, order, place, price, refer, trust 6 accuse, assign, attack, burden, credit, direct, enjoin, exhort, impugn, impute, indict, saddle, thrill 7 arraign, ascribe, bidding, command, conduct, entrust, expense, impeach, mandate, request, solicit 8 accredit, handling, instruct, price tag, reproach, stampede 9 attribute, committal, electrify, inculpate 10 accusation, allegation, commitment, injunction, management, obligation 11 incriminate, instruction, requirement, supervision

chargeable 6 liable 7 subject 11 accountable, responsible

chargeless 4 free 6 gratis 8 costless 10 gratuitous 13 complimentary

charger 5 horse, mount, steed 6 salver 7 courser, platter 8 trencher, warhorse

chariness 7 caution 8 prudence 9 integrity 10 discretion

chariot 8 carriage *four-horse:* 8 quadriga

charioteer 6 Auriga, driver

charisma 5 charm 6 allure, appeal, duende 7 glamour 9 magnetism 10 attraction 11 fascination

charitable 6 benign, giving, humane, kindly 7 clement, lenient, liberal 8 generous, merciful, obliging, tolerant

9 forgiving, indulgent 10 altruistic, beneficent, benevolent, forbearing, thoughtful 11 considerate, kindhearted, sympathetic 12 eleemosynary, humanitarian 13 philanthropic

charity 4 alms, love 5 grace, mercy 6 lenity, relief 7 caritas 8 altruism, clemency, donation, goodwill, leniency, offering 10 generosity, humaneness, kindliness 11 benefaction, beneficence, benevolence 12 contribution

charivari 5 babel, melee 6 jangle, jumble, medley, racket, ruckus, uproar 7 farrago 8 serenade, shivaree 9 cacophony, confusion 10 hodgepodge 11 celebration

charlatan 4 sham 5 bluff, faker, fraud, quack 6 con man 8 imposter, impostor, swindler 10 mountebank 11 quacksalver 13 confidence man

Charlemagne *brother:* 8 Carloman *father:* 5 Pepin *knight:* 6 Oliver, Roland 7 Olivier, paladin 8 douzeper *nephew:* 6 Roland 7 Orlando *sword:* 7 Joyeuse *traitor:* 4 Gano 7 Ganelon

Charles's Wain 9 Big Dipper, Ursa Major

charleston 5 dance

Charley's Aunt author 6 Thomas (Brandon)

Charlie and the Chocolate Factory author 4 Dahl (Roald)

Charlie Brown creator 6 Schulz (Charles)

Charlie McCarthy 5 dummy 6 stooge *friend:* 5 Snerd (Mortimer) *voice:* 6 Bergen (Edgar)

charm 3 hex 4 juju, lure, mojo, rune, take, wile 5 grace, quark, spell 6 allure, amulet, appeal, enamor, fetish, mascot, seduce, voodoo 7 attract, beguile, bewitch, enchant, glamour 8 enthrall, entrance, talisman, witchery 9 captivate, enrapture, ensorcell, fascinate, hypnotize, magnetism, mesmerize 10 allurement, attraction, phylactery, witchcraft 11 fascination, incantation 13 agreeableness

charmed 5 lucky 7 blessed 8 enamored 9 bewitched, enchanted, entranced, fortunate 10 captivated, fascinated, infatuated

charmer 4 roué 5 magus 6 wizard 7 seducer, warlock 8 conjurer, lothario, magician, sorcerer 9 enchanter 11 spellbinder

charming 7 winsome 8 adorable, alluring, inviting, magnetic 9 appealing, glamorous, seductive 10 attractive, delightful, enchanting, entrancing 11 captivating

Charon 7 boatman 8 ferryman *father:* 6 Erebus *mother:* 3 Nox *river:* 4 Styx

Charpentier opera 6 Louise
charpoy 3 bed, cot
chart 3 map 4 plan, plat, plot 5 graph, table 6 design, lay out, map out, sketch 7 arrange, diagram, outline, project 9 blueprint 10 tabulation
charter 3 let 4 deed, hire, rent 5 grant, lease 10 conveyance 12 constitution
Chartreuse 7 liqueur
chary 4 wary 5 cagey, canny 6 frugal, stingy 7 careful, guarded, miserly, prudent, sparing, thrifty 8 cautious, discreet, gingerly, hesitant 9 provident, reluctant 10 economical, restrained, suspicious, unwasteful 11 calculating, circumspect, constrained, disinclined
Charybdis 9 whirlpool *rock associated with:* 6 Scylla
chase 3 run 4 bolt, dash, game, hunt, prey, race, rush, tear 5 chivy, drive, eject, evict, hound, shoot, speed, trail 6 career, charge, course, follow, hasten, pursue, quarry 7 boot out, hunting, kick out, pursuit 8 run after, throw out
chase away 4 rout, shoo
chaser 4 wolf 6 masher 7 Don Juan 8 Casanova 9 ladies' man, womanizer 10 lady-killer 11 philanderer
chasm 3 gap 4 gulf, rift 5 abyss, cleft, clove, flume, gorge, gulch, split 6 ravine 8 crevasse
chasmal 6 gaping 7 echoing, yawning 9 cavernous
chassepot 5 rifle
chaste 4 pure 5 clean, moral 6 decent, modest, proper, seemly, vestal, virgin 7 austere, prudish 8 celibate, decorous, innocent, maidenly, platonic, spotless, virginal, virtuous 9 abstinent, continent, stainless, undefiled, unsullied 10 immaculate 11 unblemished
chasten 5 abase, scold 6 humble, punish, rebuke, refine, subdue 7 correct, upbraid 8 chastise 9 castigate, humiliate, reprimand 10 discipline
chastise 4 beat, flog, whip 5 scold 6 punish, rebuke, thrash 7 belabor, censure, chasten, correct, reprove, scourge, upbraid 9 castigate 10 discipline
chastisement 3 rod 7 reproof 8 punition 10 correction, discipline, punishment 11 castigation
chastity 6 purity, virtue 7 modesty 8 celibacy 9 innocence, integrity, virginity 10 abstention, continence, maidenhood
chasuble 8 vestment
chat 3 gab, jaw, rap, yak, yap 4 blab, gush, talk 5 prate, visit 6 babble, confab, gossip, jabber, natter, parley, pat-

ter, yak-yak 7 chatter, palaver, prattle, twaddle 8 causerie, colloquy, converse, dialogue, schmooze 9 tête-à-tête, yakety-yak 11 confabulate 12 conversation, tittle-tattle 13 confabulation
château 5 manor, villa 6 castle, estate 7 mansion 8 fortress 12 country house
chateaubriand 5 steak 10 tenderloin
Chateaubriand novel 4 René 5 Atala
chatelain 6 warden 8 governor 9 castellan
chatelaine 4 hook, wife 5 clasp 8 mistress
chattel 4 serf 5 slave 7 bondman 8 bondsman, property
chatter 3 gab, jaw, yak 4 blab, bull 5 prate 6 babble, gabble, gibber, gossip, jabber, natter, patter, yak-yak, yammer 7 blabber, blather, palaver, prattle, vibrate 9 small talk, yakety-yak 12 tittle-tattle
chatterbox 6 gabber, gossip, magpie, prater 7 blabber 8 jabberer, prattler 12 blabbermouth
chatty 5 gabby 7 voluble 9 garrulous, talkative 10 loquacious
Chaucer pilgrim 4 Cook, Monk 5 Clerk, Friar, Reeve 6 Miller, Parson, Squire 8 Franklin, Manciple, Merchant, Summoner 10 Nun's Priest, Wife of Bath
chauffeur 5 drive 6 driver 9 transport
chauvinism 6 sexism 8 jingoism 10 partiality, patriotism 11 nationalism
cheap 4 mean, poor 5 junky, tight 6 cheesy, common, cruddy, flashy, measly, paltry, shabby, shoddy, sleazy, stingy, tawdry, trashy 7 chintzy, cutrate, low-cost, reduced, thrifty 8 inferior, trifling, uncostly 9 brummagem, low-priced 10 economical 11 inexpensive 12 contemptible, meretricious
cheapen 5 decry, lower 6 debase, reduce 7 devalue 8 mark down 9 devaluate, downgrade 10 depreciate, undervalue
cheapjack 5 junky 6 hawker, cheesy, cruddy, shoddy, sleazy, tawdry, trashy 7 haggler, higgler, packman, peddler 8 huckster, inferior, rubbishy 9 worthless 13 opportunistic
cheapskate 5 miser 7 niggard, scrooge 8 tightwad 9 skinflint 11 cheeseparer
cheat 3 con, gyp 4 bilk, burn, dupe, fool, gull, hoax, milk, ream, scam 5 bunco, cozen, crook, fraud, fudge, gouge, hocus, put-on, screw, shaft, short, slick 6 chisel, chouse, con man, deceit, delude, diddle, extort, fleece, humbug, rip-off, sucker, take in 7 beguile, chicane, deceive, defraud, diddler, mislead, sharper, shyster, swindle, two-time 8 flimflam, hoodwink,

swindler, trickery **9** bamboozle, chicanery, deception, defrauder, imposture, overreach, trickster **11** doublecross **12** double-dealer **13** confidence man *on a check:* **4** kite

check 3 tab, try **4** bill, curb, halt, jibe, stay, stop, test, tick **5** block, brake, draft, prove, score, stall **6** accord, arrest, baffle, bridle, damage, desist, hold in, square, thwart, verify **7** compare, conform, control, examine, inhibit, repress, setback **8** dovetail, hold back, hold down, preclude, restrain, reversal, suppress **9** constrain, criterion, interrupt, restraint **10** correspond, inspection **11** examination **13** investigation

checkered 5 plaid **6** motley **7** mutable, spotted **9** patchwork, patterned **10** variegated **11** diversified

checklist 7 catalog **9** catalogue, inventory **11** enumeration

checkmate 4 beat **6** corner, defeat **7** outplay **8** vanquish **9** finish off

check out 3 die, eye **5** leave **6** assess **7** examine, inspect **8** appraise, evaluate, look over

check over 3 con, vet **4** scan **5** audit, study **6** review, survey **7** analyze, canvass, examine, inspect **10** scrutinize

checkup 4 exam **8** physical **10** inspection **11** examination

cheek 4 gall **5** brass, nerve **8** audacity, chutzpah, temerity **9** brashness, impudence, insolence **10** confidence, effrontery **11** presumption **12** impertinence

cheekbone 5 malar

cheeky 4 bold, flip, pert, wise **5** brash, cocky, fresh, nervy, sassy, saucy, smart **6** brazen **7** forward **8** flippant, impudent, insolent **11** impertinent, smartalecky **12** presumptuous

cheep 4 peep **5** chirp, tweet **7** chirrup, chitter, twitter

cheer 3 rah **4** buoy, hail, root **5** bravo, huzza, nerve **6** buck up, gaiety, hoorah, hooray, hurrah, hurray, huzzah, solace, spirit **7** animate, applaud, comfort, console, enliven, gladden, hearten **8** embolden, inspirit **9** animation, encourage **10** strengthen *corrida:* **3** olé

cheerful 3 gay **4** glad, rosy **5** jolly, merry, perky, sunny **6** blithe, bouncy, bright, chirpy, hearty, jaunty, jocund, lively **7** beamish, buoyant, radiant **8** animated, carefree, chirrupy **9** vivacious **12** lighthearted

cheerio 3 bye **4** ta-ta **5** adieu **6** bye-bye, good-by, so long **7** good-bye, toodles **8** farewell, toodle-oo

cheerless 4 dour, drab, grim **5** bleak **6** dismal, dreary, gloomy, somber, sombre **7** forlorn, joyless **8** desolate, dolorous, funereal, mournful **9** dejecting **10** depressing, melancholy, oppressive, tenebrific **11** dispiriting

cheers 5 salud, skoal **6** cincin, l'chaim, prosit **7** l'chayim, sláinte **8** applause, approval, chinchin **9** bottoms up **10** jubilation **11** acclamation, approbation

cheery 5 happy, jolly, merry, sunny **6** blithe, bouncy, chirpy, lively, upbeat **7** buoyant, chipper, festive, gleeful **8** animated, carefree, gladsome **9** convivial, sparkling **12** lighthearted

cheese 3 pot **4** blue, jack **5** brick, cream **6** farmer **7** cottage, process, ricotta **9** smearcase *American:* **8** Longhorn **11** Liederkranz **12** Monterey Jack *Belgian:* **9** Limburger *curdling agent:* **6** rennet, rennin *Danish:* **7** Havarti *dish:* **6** fondue **7** rarebit, soufflé *Dutch:* **4** Edam **5** Gouda **6** Leyden *English:* **7** cheddar, Stilton **8** Cheshire **10** Lancashire *French:* **4** Brie **7** fromage, Livarot **9** Camembert, Reblochon, Roquefort **10** Neufchâtel **11** Pont l'Évêque, Port du Salut *German:* **6** Tilsit **7** Munster **8** Muenster, Tilsiter *Greek:* **4** feta *green:* **7** sapsago *Italian:* **6** Asiago, Romano **7** fontina, ricotta **8** Bel Paese, Parmesan, pecorino **9** provolone **10** Gorgonzola, mozzarella *lover:* **9** turophile *main ingredient:* **6** casein *Norwegian:* **9** Jarlsberg *protein:* **6** casein *Scottish:* **6** Dunlop, Orkney **7** kebbock, kebbuck *Swiss:* **6** Saanen **7** Gruyère, sapsago **8** Vacherin **10** Emmentaler **11** Emmenthaler *uncured:* **7** cottage *Welsh:* **10** Caerphilly

cheesecloth 5 gauze

cheeselike 6 caseic **7** caseous

cheeseparer 5 miser **7** niggard, scrooge **8** tightwad **9** skinflint **10** cheapskate, pinchpenny

cheeseparing 4 mean **5** chary, cheap, mingy, tight **6** frugal, shabby, stingy **7** chintzy, miserly, thrifty **8** grudging, skimping **9** niggardly, penurious **11** closefisted, tightfisted **12** parsimonious **13** penny-pinching

cheesy 4 poor **5** cheap **6** common, shabby, shoddy, sleazy, tawdry, trashy **7** caseous **8** rubbishy

Cheever, John *novel:* **8** Falconer **14** Wapshot Scandal (The) **16** Wapshot Chronicle (The) *story:* **7** Swimmer (The)

chef 4 cook

chef d'oeuvre 7 classic **9** showpiece **10** magnum opus, masterwork **11** masterpiece, tour de force

Chekhov, Anton *play:* 6 Ivanov 7 Seagull (The) 10 Uncle Vanya 12 Three Sisters 13 Cherry Orchard (The) *story:* 9 Black Monk (The)

chelonian 6 turtle 8 tortoise

chemical *agent:* 8 catalyst *combining power:* 7 valence *compound:* 4 acid, base, diol, enol, imid, oxim, salt, tepa, urea 5 amide, amine, diene, ester, imide, imine, indol, orcin, oxime, purin, pyran, salol, tolan, triol 6 alkali, benzin, benzol, diamin, emodin, guanin, halide, hydrid, indole, inulin, ionone, isatin, isolog, isomer, ketone, lactam, maltol, metepa, natron, nitril, pterin, purine, pyrone, pyrrol, quinol, retene, silane, skatol, tannin, tetryl, thiram, thymol, tolane, triene, trimer, uracil, ureide, yttria, zeatin 7 barilla, benzene, benzole, cumarin, diamide, diamine, diazine, diazole, diester, flavone, guanine, heptose, hydride, indamin, indican, indoxyl, isatine, levulin, metamer, monomer, naphtol, nitrile, orcinol, oxazine, phytane, picolin, polyene, polymer, pyrrole, quinoid, quinone, salicin, skatole, steroid, taurine, terpene, thiazin, thiazol, thymine, tolidin, triazin, urethan, uridine, vitamer, xylidin 8 cephalin, cyanamid, disulfid, elaterin, fluorene, furfural, guaiacol, hematein, hexamine, indamine, isologue, kephalin, lichenin, limonene, melamine, naloxone, naphthol, palmitin, phenazin, phosphid, phthalin, picoline, piperine, pristane, quinolin, resorcin, salicine, santonin, siloxane, sodamide, sorbitol, spermine, squalene, stilbene, strontia, tautomer, thiazine, thiazole, thiophen, thiotepa, thiourea, tolidine, triazine, triazole, triptane, tyramine, urethane, vanillin, warfarin, xanthene, xanthine, xanthone, xylidine, ytterbia, zaratite, zirconia (see at ELEMENT) *quantity:* 4 mole *radical:* 4 acyl, amyl, cyan 5 allyl, butyl, ethyl, tolyl 6 acetyl, formyl, methyl, oxalic, phenyl, propyl, toluyl 7 benzoyl *reaction:* 5 redox *salt:* 5 niter, nitre, urate, ziram 6 haloid, humate, malate, oleate, phytin 7 ferrate, formate, gallate, maleate, pectate, persalt, picrate, tannate, toluate, zincate 8 fumarate, pyruvate, racemate, selenate, silicate, stearate, tartrate, thionate, titanate, valerate, vanadate, xanthate *suffix:* 3 ane, ase, ate, ein, ene, ide, ile, ine, ite, ium, oic, oin, one, ose, ous, yne 4 eine, idin, itol, oate, olic, onic 5 idine, onium, oside, ylene *warfare agent:* 7 tear gas 8 vesicant 10 mustard gas

chemin de fer 5 train 7 railway 8 railroad

chemise 4 slip

chemist 7 analyst 8 druggist 10 apothecary, pharmacist *American:* 4 Urey (Harold) 6 Remsen (Ira), Sumner (James) 7 Onsager (Lars), Pauling (Linus), Seaborg (Glenn) 8 Hoffmann (Roald), Langmuir (Irving), Mulliken (Robert), Richards (Theodore), Woodward (Robert) *Austrian:* 4 Kuhn (Richard) 5 Pregl (Fritz) *British:* 4 Abel (Frederick), Davy (Humphry), Todd (Alexander) 5 Boyle (Robert), Soddy (Frederick) 6 Dalton (John), Ramsay (William) 7 Faraday (Michael) 8 Smithson (James) 9 Priestley (Joseph), Wollaston (William) 10 Williamson (Alexander) *Dutch:* 8 van't Hoff (Jacobus) *French:* 5 Curie (Irene, Marie, Pierre) 7 Moissan (Henri), Pasteur (Louis) 8 Sabatier (Paul) 9 Gay-Lussac (Joseph), Lavoisier (Antoine), Berthelot (Marcellin) *German:* 5 Haber (Fritz) 6 Bunsen (Robert), Liebig (Justus von), Nernst (Walther), Wittig (Georg), Wohler (Friedrich) 7 Fischer (Emil, Ernst, Hans), Hofmann (August), Ostwald (Friedrich), Wallach (Otto), Wieland (Heinrich), Windaus (Adolf), Ziegler (Karl) 9 Zsigmondy (Richard) 10 Erlenmeyer (Richard), Staudinger (Hermann) 11 Willstatter (Richard) *Italian:* 5 Natta (Giulio) 8 Avogadro (Amedeo) *Russian:* 8 Semyonov (Nikolay), Zelinsky (Nikolay) 10 Mendeleyev (Dmitry) *Swedish:* 8 Svedberg (The, Theodor) 9 Berzelius (J. J.) *Swiss:* 6 Karrer (Paul), Werner (Alfred) (see also under NOBEL PRIZE WINNER)

chemist's vessel 4 vial 5 flask, phial 6 ampule, beaker, mortar, retort 7 ampoule 8 crucible, test tube

chemoreceptor 8 taste bud

cheongsam 5 dress

Cheops 5 Khufu

cherish 4 keep, save 5 adore, guard, honor, nurse, prize, value 6 admire, cosset, defend, dote on, esteem, foster, harbor, relish, revere, shield 7 apprize, care for, nourish, nurture, shelter, worship 8 conserve, hold dear, preserve, treasure, venerate 9 cultivate, delight in, entertain, reverence, safeguard 10 appreciate

Cherokee *chief:* 4 Ross (John) *historian:* 7 Sequoia, Sequoya 8 Sequoyah

cherry *dark:* 4 bing *family:* 4 rose 8 Rosaceae *genus:* 6 Prunus *hybrid:* 4 Duke *sour:* 7 morello *sweet:* 4 bing 7 mazzard, oxheart *wild:* 7 mazzard 10 maraschino

cherry bomb 11 firecracker
Cherry Orchard author 7 Chekhov (Anton)
cherrystone 4 clam 6 quahog
Chersonese 9 peninsula
cherub 4 babe, baby 5 angel, child, cupid, putto 6 infant 7 bambino 8 amoretto, innocent
cherubic 4 cute, rosy 6 chubby 7 angelic 8 adorable, innocent
chess champion: 3 Tal (Mikhail) 4 Euwe (Max) 6 Karpov (Anatoly), Lasker (Emanuel) 7 Fischer (Bobby), Kramnik (Vladimir), Smyslov (Vassily), Spassky (Boris) 8 Alekhine (Alexander), Kasparov (Garry), Steinitz (Wilhelm) 9 Botvinnik (Mikhail), Petrosian (Tigran) 10 Capablanca (José) draw game: 9 stalemate goal: 4 mate 9 checkmate move: 6 castle, gambit opening: 6 gambit piece: 4 king, pawn, rook 5 queen 6 bishop, knight risk: 6 gambit term: 5 check 7 capture, endgame
chest 3 box 4 kist 5 bosom, torso, trunk 6 breast, bureau, coffer, thorax 7 cabinet 8 cupboard, treasury 9 exchequer
chesterfield 4 sofa 5 divan 8 overcoat 9 davenport
chestnut 4 tree 5 color, horse 6 cliché, marron 10 chinquapin extract: 6 tannin water: 4 ling
cheval glass 6 mirror
chevalier 5 noble 6 knight 8 horseman 9 caballero, gentleman
chevet 4 apse
chevron 6 stripe
chew 3 eat, gum 4 bite, gnaw 5 champ, chomp, munch 6 crunch, devour, nibble 7 consume 8 ruminate 9 masticate
chewing gum 6 chicle
chew out 3 jaw 5 scold 6 rebuke, revile 7 bawl out, reprove, tell off, upbraid 8 lambaste, reproach 9 castigate, criticize, reprimand 10 tongue-lash, vituperate
Chiang ___ 7 Kai-shek
chic 4 mode, rage, tony 5 smart, style, swank, swish, vogue 6 modish, trendy, with-it 7 dashing, elegant, fashion, stylish 10 dernier cri 11 fashionable
chicane 4 dupe, fool, gull, hoax, ploy, ruse, wile 5 cavil, cheat, feint, fraud, trick 6 gambit 8 artifice, flimflam, hoodwink, trickery 9 bamboozle, deception, duplicity, stratagem, victimize 10 dishonesty, hanky-panky 13 double-dealing
chicanery 4 plot, ruse 5 fraud, trick 6 gambit 8 intrigue, trickery 9 deception, duplicity 10 subterfuge 11 machination, skulduggery

chichi 4 arty 5 gaudy, showy, swank 6 dressy, frilly, la-di-da 7 splashy 8 affected, précieux, precious 10 flamboyant, preciosity 11 affectation, fashionable, overrefined, pretentious 12 ostentatious 13 ornamentation
chick 3 kid, tot 4 girl 5 child 6 moppet, nipper, pullet 7 toddler 8 juvenile, young one 9 youngster
chickadee 8 titmouse family: 7 Paridae
chicken 4 fowl, funk 5 sissy, timid 6 coward, craven 7 dastard, gutless 8 cowardly, poltroon 11 lily-livered, yellowbelly 13 pusillanimous breed: 4 Java 6 Cochin 7 Cornish, Leghorn 9 Dominique, Orpington, Wyandotte 11 Jersey Giant, Rock Cornish castrated: 5 capon cooking: 5 fryer 7 broiler, roaster disease: 8 pullorum 11 coccidiosis female: 3 hen 6 pullet genus: 6 Gallus male: 4 cock 7 rooster 8 cockerel pen: 4 coop small: 6 bantam sound: 6 cackle
chicken feed 7 peanuts 8 pittance 11 chump change
chicken pox 9 varicella
chickpea 4 gram 8 garbanzo
chickweed 4 pink 7 potherb
chicle 3 gum 10 chewing gum
chicory 6 endive 7 witloof 9 radicchio
chide 3 kid 5 scold 6 berate, rebuke 7 chew out, lecture, reprove, upbraid 8 admonish, call down, reproach 9 castigate, reprimand
chiding 6 rebuke 7 reproof 8 reproach 9 reprimand 10 admonition 12 admonishment
chief 3 key 4 arch, boss, duce, head, lion, main, star 5 first, major, prime 6 führer, honcho, leader, master, primal, ruling, sachem 7 fuehrer, headman, highest, leading, premier, primary 8 cardinal, champion, dictator, dominant, eminence, foremost 9 numberone, principal, prominent 10 preeminent 11 outstanding, predominant commander: 4 CINC prefix: 4 arch Spanish: 4 jefe
Chief Justice 3 Jay (John) 4 Taft (William Howard) 5 Chase (Salmon), Stone (Harlan Fiske), Taney (Roger), Waite (Morrison), White (Edward) 6 Burger (Warren), Fuller (Melville) Hughes (Charles Evans), Vinson (Fred), Warren (Earl) 8 Marshall (John), Rutledge (John) 9 Ellsworth (Oliver), Rehnquist (William)
chiefly 6 mainly, mostly, notably 7 largely, overall 9 generally, primarily 10 especially 11 principally 12 preeminently 13 predominantly

chiffchaff 4 bird 7 warbler

chiffonier 5 chest 6 bureau 7 armoire, dresser

chigger 4 mite 6 chigoe, red bug

chignon 3 bun 4 knot

chilblain 4 sore 8 swelling 12 inflammation

child 3 kid 4 brat 5 minor, youth 6 cherub, infant, moppet, nipper, shaver, urchin 7 bambino, toddler 8 juvenile, small fry 9 youngling, youngster *combining form:* 3 ped 4 paed, pedo 5 paedo *gifted:* 7 prodigy *homeless:* 4 waif *parentless:* 6 orphan *Scottish:* 5 bairn *spoiled:* 4 brat *young:* 3 tot 4 baby, tike, tyke 6 infant, kiddie 8 bantling, weanling

childish 5 naive 7 puerile 8 arrested, immature 9 infantile

childless 6 barren 7 sterile

childlike 5 naive 6 docile, filial 7 natural, puerile 8 innocent, trustful, trusting 9 ingenuous

children 4 kids, seed 5 brood, heirs, issue 6 scions 7 progeny 9 offspring, posterity 11 descendants

child's play 4 snap 5 cinch, setup 6 breeze, picnic 8 cakewalk, duck soup, kid stuff, pushover 11 piece of cake

Chile *capital:* 8 Santiago *city:* 6 Temuco 10 Concepción, Talcahuano, Valparaíso, Viña del Mar 11 Antofagasta *conqueror:* 7 Almagro (Diego de) 8 Valdivia (Pedro de) *desert:* 7 Atacama *island:* 6 Easter 13 Juan Fernández *lake:* 10 Llanquihue *language:* 7 Spanish *leader:* 7 Allende (Salvador) 8 Pinochet (Augusto) *monetary unit:* 4 peso *mountain range:* 5 Andes *neighbor:* 4 Peru 7 Bolivia 9 Argentina *passage:* 5 Drake *river:* 6 Bío-Bío *strait:* 8 Magellan

Chileab *father:* 5 David *mother:* 7 Abigail

chili con ___ 5 carne

Chilion *father:* 9 Elimelech *mother:* 5 Naomi

chill 3 icy, raw 4 ague, cold, cool, hang 5 gelid, nippy 6 arctic, formal, freeze, frigid, frosty, wintry 7 distant, glacial, hostile 8 dispirit, freezing 10 demoralize, discourage, dishearten 11 emotionless, refrigerate

chiller 7 shocker 8 thriller

chilly 3 raw 4 cold 5 algid, brisk, crisp, nippy 6 frigid 7 bracing, coldish, hostile 10 unfriendly

chilopod 9 centipede

chime 3 din 4 bell, bong, dong, peal, ring, toll, tune 5 agree, clang, knell, sound 6 accord, strike 7 concord, harmony 8 carillon 9 agreement, harmonize 10 consonance, correspond

chime in 3 say 4 tell 5 state, utter 6 inject 7 break in, declare 9 interrupt

chimera 5 dream, fancy 7 fantasy, figment, monster, specter, spectre 8 illusion, phantasy 9 nightmare, pipe dream

Chimera *father:* 6 Typhon *mother:* 7 Echidna *slayer:* 11 Bellerophon

chimerical 6 absurd, unreal 7 fictive, utopian 8 delusive, delusory, fabulous, fanciful, illusory, mythical, spurious 9 ambitious, beguiling, deceptive, fantastic, fictional, imaginary, visionary 10 far-fetched, fictitious, improbable, outlandish 11 extravagant, unrealistic 12 preposterous, suppositious

chiming 8 harmonic 9 consonant 10 harmonious

chimney 3 lum 4 flue, tube, vent 5 stack 10 smokestack *corner:* 8 fireside 9 inglenook *output:* 4 soot 5 fumes, smoke

chimpanzee 3 ape 7 primate 10 anthropoid *kin:* 6 bonobo, gibbon 7 gorilla 9 orangutan

chin 3 gab, jaw, rap, yak 4 blab, chat, talk 8 converse

china 6 dishes 7 ceramic 8 crockery 9 porcelain, tableware 11 earthenware *maker:* 3 Bow 5 Hizen, Imari, Spode 6 Doccia, Sèvres 7 Bristol, Chelsea, Dresden, Limoges, Meissen 8 Caughley, Haviland, Wedgwood

China *bay:* 8 Hangzhou *capital:* 7 Beijing *city:* 4 Sian, Xi'an 5 Wuhan 6 Canton, Harbin, Mukden 7 Nanjing, Nanking, Tianjin 8 Shanghai, Shenyang, Tientsin 9 Chongqing, Guangzhou *desert:* 4 Gobi 10 Taklimakan *dynasty:* 3 Han, Sui 4 Ch'in, Chou, Ming, Sung, Tang, Yüan 5 Ch'ing, Shang 6 Manchu *ethnic group:* 3 Han *gulf:* 5 Bo Hai *heritage site:* 9 Great Wall *island:* 6 Hainan 8 Hong Kong *lake:* 5 Tai Hu 8 Hongze Hu, Poyang Hu 10 Dongting Hu *language:* 3 Han 8 Mandarin *leader:* 9 Mao Zedong, Sun Yat-sen 10 Kublai Khan, Mao Tse-tung 12 Deng Xiaoping 13 Chiang Kai-shek, Teng Hsiao-p'ing *monetary unit:* 4 yuan *monetary unit, former:* 4 tael *mountain, range:* 6 Kunlun 8 Himalaya 9 Altai Shan, Altay Shan, Himalayan 10 Gongga Shan *old name:* 6 Cathay *peninsula:* 7 Leizhou 8 Liaodong, Shandong *province:* 5 Anhui, Gansu, Hevei, Henan, Hubei, Hunan, Jilin 6 Fujian, Shanxi, Yunnan 7 Guizhou, Jiangsu, Jiangxi, Qinghai, Shaanxi, Sichuan 8 Liaoning, Shandong, Szechuan, Szechwan, Zhejiang 9 Guangdong 12 Heilongjiang *region:* 5 Tibet 6 Xizang 10 Nei Monggol

12 Ningxia Huizu 13 Inner Mongolia, Xinjiang Uygur *river:* 4 Amur 5 Chang, Huang, Tarim 6 Mekong, Yellow, Zangbo 7 Salween, Yangtze
china clay 6 kaolin
chinchilla 3 fur 6 rodent
chine 5 crest, ridge, spine 7 hogback 8 backbone
Chinese *aromatic root:* 7 ginseng *bamboo:* 7 whangee *boat:* 4 junk 6 sampan *bow:* 6 kowtow *cabbage:* 7 bok choy, pak choi *card game:* 6 fan-tan *cauterizing agent:* 4 moxa *prefix:* 4 Sino *conveyance:* 7 pedicab 8 rickshaw 10 jinricksha, jinrikisha *date:* 6 jujube *dialect:* 4 Amoy 8 Mandarin 9 Cantonese, Pekingese *dictator:* 9 Mao Zedong 10 Mao Tsetung 12 Deng Xiaoping 13 Teng Hsiaop'ing *dog:* 4 chow, Peke 8 chow chow 9 Pekingese *dynasty:* 3 Ch'i, Han, Qin, Sui, Wei, Yin 4 Ch'en, Ch'in, Chou, Hsia, Ming, Qing, Song, Sung, T'ang, Tsin, Yuan 5 Ch'ing, Liang, Shang 6 Manchu, Mongol, Shu Han *fabric:* 6 pongee, tussah 8 shantung *feudal principle:* 3 yin *feudal state:* 3 Wei *food:* 6 dim sum, lo mein, mantou, subgum, wonton 8 chop suey, chow mein 9 fried rice 10 egg foo yong, egg foo yung, Peking duck 11 egg foo young *fruit:* 6 lichee, litchi, lychee, loquat 7 kumquat 8 mandarin *gambling game:* 6 fan-tan *gong:* 6 tam-tam *gruel:* 6 congee *herb:* 5 ramie 7 ginseng *idol:* 4 joss *laborer:* 6 coolie *legendary emperor:* 7 Huangdi, Huang-ti *mandarin's residence:* 5 yamen *masculine principle:* 4 yang *money, silver:* 5 sycee *musical instrument:* 4 pipa *nurse:* 4 amah *official:* 8 mandarin *official seal:* 4 chop *oil:* 4 tung *ox:* 4 zebu *porcelain:* 4 Ming 7 celadon, Nankeen 8 mandarin *pottery:* 4 Kuan, Ming 5 Chien *puzzle:* 7 tangram *race:* 9 Mongoloid *religion:* 6 Taoism 8 Buddhism 12 Confucianism *sauce:* 3 soy *secret society:* 4 tong *sheep:* 5 urial *silkworm:* 6 tussah *tea:* 5 bohea, hyson 6 congou, oolong 8 souchong *temple:* 6 pagoda *tree:* 4 tung 6 ginkgo, loquat 7 kumquat *vine:* 5 kudzu
chink 4 rift, slit 5 caulk, cleft, crack, split 6 cranny 7 crevice, fissure, opening 8 aperture
chinquapin 3 nut 8 chestnut
chintzy 4 loud 5 cheap, gaudy, showy, tacky 6 flashy, garish, stingy, tawdry, vulgar 9 tasteless 12 meretricious
chip 4 flaw, nick 5 flake, notch, shard, slice, split, wafer, wedge 6 chisel, defect, paring, sliver 7 counter

chip in 6 ante up, kick in 7 pitch in 10 contribute 11 come through
chipper 4 spry 5 alert, brisk, perky, zesty 6 bright, lively, nimble 8 animated, spirited 9 sprightly, vivacious
chirk 4 buoy 5 cheer 7 animate, enliven, hearten 8 energize, inspirit 9 encourage 10 strengthen
chirography 6 script 8 longhand 10 penmanship 11 calligraphy, handwriting
chiromancy 9 palmistry
Chiron 7 centaur *father:* 6 Cronus *mother:* 7 Philyra *pupil:* 5 Jason 8 Achilles, Heracles, Hercules 9 Asclepius 11 Aesculapius
chiropody 8 podiatry
chiropractic founder 6 Palmer (Daniel)
chirp 4 chip, peep, sing 5 cheep, trill, tweet 6 warble 7 chirrup, twitter
chirpy 3 gay 5 sunny 6 blithe, cheery, sparky 7 buoyant, sparkly 8 cheerful, sunbeamy 9 lightsome
chirrup 4 chip, peep, sing 5 cheep, tweet 6 warble 7 chipper, twitter
chisel 3 gyp, hew 4 beat, bilk, scam 5 carve, cheat, cozen, cut in, gouge, trick 6 butt in, diddle, fleece, horn in, sculpt 7 defraud, engrave, intrude, swindle
chit 3 IOU, kid 4 memo, note, slip 5 child 6 moppet 7 invoice, voucher 8 notation 9 youngster 10 memorandum
chitchat 3 gab 5 chaff 6 babble, banter, gossip 7 chatter, palaver, prattle 8 badinage 9 small talk 12 tittle-tattle
chitter 4 chip, peep, sing 5 cheep, chirp, tweet 6 warble 7 chatter, chirrup, twitter
chivalric see CHIVALROUS
chivalrous 5 lofty, manly, noble 7 courtly, gallant, valiant 8 generous, gracious, knightly 9 honorable 10 benevolent, courageous 11 considerate, gentlemanly, magnanimous
chivy, chivvy 4 bait, ride 5 annoy, tease 6 badger, heckle, hector 7 torment 8 bullyrag
Chloe 11 shepherdess *beloved:* 7 Daphnis
chlordane 11 insecticide
Chloris *father:* 7 Amphion *husband:* 6 Neleus 8 Zephyrus *mother:* 5 Niobe *son:* 6 Nestor
chloroform 7 anodyne, solvent 10 anesthetic 11 anaesthetic
chockablock 4 full 6 jammed, loaded, packed 7 brimful, crammed, crowded, stuffed 9 jam-packed
chocolate 5 brown, cacao, cocoa
Chocolate Soldier composer 6 Straus (Oscar)

chocolate tree 5 cacao

choice 3 top 4 best, pick, rare, vote 5 cream, elite, prime, prize 6 chosen, dainty, option, rating, select 7 elegant, verdict 8 decision, delicate, druthers, election, judgment, selected, superior, volition 9 exquisite, selection 9 selection 10 preference 11 alternative 13 determination *even:* 6 toss-up

choir 6 chorus 7 chorale *area:* 4 loft 7 chancel, gallery *leader:* 6 cantor 8 choragus 9 precentor *member:* 9 chorister *section:* 4 alto, bass 5 tenor 7 soprano *vestment:* 4 gown, robe 5 cotta 8 surplice

choke 3 gag 4 clog, plug, stop 5 block, close 6 stifle 7 congest, occlude, silence, smother 8 obstruct, strangle, throttle 9 constrict, suffocate 10 asphyxiate

choking 8 quashing, stifling 10 repression, smothering, squelching, strangling 11 suppression

choleric 5 angry, fiery, irate 6 fierce, heated 7 enraged 8 incensed, wrathful 9 irascible, splenetic 10 infuriated 11 hot-tempered 13 quick-tempered

cholla 6 cactus 7 opuntia

Chomolungma 7 Everest (Mt.)

chomp 4 bite, chew 5 munch 6 crunch 9 masticate

choose 3 opt 4 cull, mark, pick, take, want 5 adopt, elect, favor 6 decide, desire, opt for, prefer, select 7 embrace, pick out 8 decide on, handpick 9 single out

choosy 5 fussy, picky 7 finical, finicky 9 finicking, selective 10 fastidious, particular, pernickety 11 persnickety

chop 3 cut, hew 4 dice, fell, hack, hash, seal, veer 5 cut up, grade, mince 7 quality

chop-chop 4 fast 5 quick 6 presto, pronto 7 quickly, rapidly 8 promptly, speedily 9 posthaste 12 lickety-split

chophouse 10 restaurant

Chopin, Frédéric *birthplace:* 6 Poland *instrument:* 5 piano *lover:* 4 Sand (George) *work:* 7 mazurka 8 nocturne 9 polonaise

choppy 4 wavy 5 jerky, rough 6 ripply, stormy, uneven 7 erratic 8 variable 9 turbulent, unsettled

choral section 5 altos 6 basses, tenors 8 sopranos

chord 5 triad 6 tetrad 7 harmony *sequence:* 7 cadence 11 progression

chore 3 job 4 duty, task 5 stint, trial 6 devoir, effort 7 routine 10 assignment, obligation 11 tribulation

choreograph 6 devise, direct, map out 7 arrange, compose 11 orchestrate

choreographer *American:* 4 Feld (Elliot), Holm (Hanya), Lang (Pearl) 5 Ailey (Alvin), Fosse (Bob), Limón (José), Shawn (Ted), Tharp (Twyla) 6 Duncan (Isadora), Dunham (Katherine), Fokine (Michel), Graham (Martha), Morris (Mark), Taylor (Paul), Tetley (Glen) 7 de Mille (Agnes), Jamison (Judith), Joffrey (Robert), Martins (Peter), Massine (Leonide), Robbins (Jerome), St. Denis (Ruth), Tamiris (Helen), Weidman (Charles) 8 Champion (Gower, Marge), Humphrey (Doris), Nikolais (Alwin), Villella (Edward) 10 Balanchine (George), Cunningham (Merce) *Australian:* 8 Helpmann (Robert) *Cuban:* 6 Alonso (Alicia) *Danish:* 5 Bruhn (Erik) 7 Martins (Peter) 12 Bournonville (August) *English:* 5 Dolin (Anton), Tudor (Antony) 6 Ashton (Frederick), Weaver (John) 7 Markova (Alicia), Rambert (Marie) 8 de Valois (Ninette), Helpmann (Robert) 9 MacMillan (Kenneth) *French:* 5 Lifar (Serge) 6 Béjart (Maurice), Perrot (Jules), Petipa (Marius) 7 Camargo (Marie), Massine (Léonide), Noverre (Jean-Georges) *German:* 5 Jooss (Kurt) *Hungarian:* 5 Laban (Rudolf) *Mexican:* 5 Limón (José) *Russian:* 5 Lifar (Serge) 6 Fokine (Michel), Petipa (Marius) 8 Nijinska (Bronislava), Nijinsky (Vaslav)

chorography 3 map 7 mapping 8 features 9 mapmaking

chortle 5 laugh 6 giggle, guffaw, hee-haw, titter 7 chuckle, snicker

chorus 5 choir 7 refrain

chorus girl 7 chorine

chosen 4 pick 5 elect, elite, named 6 called, marked, pegged, picked, select 7 blessed 8 selected 9 appointed, delegated, exclusive

Chou ___ 5 En-lai

chouse 3 gyp 4 bilk, clip, dupe, herd 5 cheat, cozen, drive, trick 6 diddle, fleece 7 defraud, swindle 8 flimflam

chow 4 eats, feed, food, grub, meal

chowchow 6 medley, relish 7 mélange

chowderhead 4 boob, clod, dodo, dolt, dope, fool 5 chump, dunce, idiot, noddy 6 dimwit, nitwit, noodle 7 halfwit, schnook 8 dumbbell, numskull 9 lamebrain, numbskull

chowhound 7 glutton 8 gourmand

chrism 3 oil 4 balm 5 cream, salve 6 cerate 7 unction, unguent 8 ointment

christen 3 dub 4 call, name, term 5 title

7 asperse, baptize, immerse **8** dedicate, sprinkle **9** designate

christening 7 baptism

Christian *denomination:* **6** Mormon, Quaker **7** Baptist, Friends **8** Anglican, Catholic, Lutheran, Moravian, Nazarene, Reformed **9** Calvinist, Episcopal, Mennonite, Methodist, Unitarian **10** Anabaptist **11** Pentecostal **12** Episcopalian, Presbyterian, Universalist *Eastern rite:* **5** Uniat **6** Uniate *Egyptian:* **4** Copt *love feast:* **5** agape *martyr, first:* **7** Stephen *symbol:* **3** IHS **4** fish, rood **5** cross **6** Chi-Rhos **7** ichthus

Christiania 4 Oslo

Christian Science founder 4 Eddy (Mary Baker)

Christie, Agatha *character:* **6** Marple (Jane), Poirot (Hercule) *novel:* **14** Death on the Nile **24** Murder on the Orient Express *play:* **9** Mousetrap (The) **24** Witness for the Prosecution

Christina's World *painter* **5** Wyeth (Andrew)

Christmas 4 Noel, yule **8** Nativity, yuletide *symbol:* **7** Yule log

Christmas Carol, A *author:* **7** Dickens (Charles) *character:* **7** Scrooge (Ebenezer), Tiny Tim **8** Cratchit (Bob)

Christogram 6 Chi-Rho

Christopher Robin *creator* **5** Milne (A.A.)

chromatic 8 colorful **10** accidental

chromatin thread 7 spireme

chromosome *component* **3** DNA **4** gene **8** telomere **10** centromere, chromomere

chronic 5 usual **6** wonted **7** routine **8** constant, enduring, habitual **9** ceaseless, confirmed, continual, customary, incessant, perennial, perpetual, recurrent, recurring **10** accustomed, continuing, habituated, inveterate, persisting **11** unrelenting

chronicle 4 list **6** annals, record, relate, report **7** account, history, narrate, recital, recount **8** describe **9** narration, narrative

chronicler 8 narrator, recorder, reporter **9** historian

chronograph 5 clock, watch **9** timepiece

chronology 5 annal **6** annals, record **7** history **8** calendar, register, schedule **9** timetable

chronometer 5 clock, watch **9** timepiece

chrysalis 4 pupa **8** covering

Chryseis *captor:* **9** Agamemnon *father:* **7** Chryses

Chrysippus *father:* **6** Pelops *slayer:* **6** Atreus **8** Thyestes

chthonic 6 Hadean, nether **7** hellish, satanic **8** accursed, infernal, plutonic **9** plutonian, Tartarean **10** sulphurous

chubby 5 hefty, husky, plump, podgy, pudgy, round, tubby **6** chunky, fleshy, portly, rotund, stocky, zaftig **8** plumpish, roly-poly

chuck 3 pat, tap **4** beef. cast, hurl, junk, oust, shed, toss **5** ditch, fling, heave, nudge, pitch, scrap, throw **6** give up, reject **7** abandon, boot out, discard, dismiss, kick out **8** jettison, throw out **9** throw away

chucker 7 bouncer

chuckle 5 laugh **6** giggle, guffaw, heehaw, titter **7** chortle, snicker

chucklehead see CHOWDERHEAD

chuff 3 oaf **4** boor, lout, rube **5** churl, clown, yahoo, yokel **7** bumpkin, hayseed **10** clodhopper

chum 3 pal **4** mate **5** buddy, crony **6** friend, salmon **7** comrade **8** sidekick **9** companion

chummy 4 cozy **5** close, pally, palsy, thick **8** familiar, intimate **10** buddy-buddy, palsy-walsy

chump 3 oaf, sap **4** boob, dolt, dope, dupe, fool, goof, goon, gull, mark **5** booby, dummy, dunce, patsy **6** pigeon, sucker, turkey **7** fall guy, fathead **8** dolthead, lunkhead

chunk 3 sum, wad **4** clod, hunk, lump, slab **5** clump **6** nugget

chunky 5 beefy, dumpy, hefty, husky, plump, pudgy, squat, stout **6** chubby, fleshy, portly, rotund, stocky, stubby, stumpy **8** heavyset, thickset

church 4 cult, fane, kirk, sect **5** creed, faith **6** temple **7** minster **8** basilica, religion **9** cathedral, communion **10** tabernacle **12** denomination *adjunct:* **6** belfry **7** steeple **9** bell tower *basin:* **4** font **5** stoup *bench:* **3** pew *bishop's:* **9** cathedral *calendar:* **4** ordo *caretaker:* **6** sexton *chapel:* **7** oratory *council:* **5** synod *court:* **4** rota **10** consistory *creed:* **6** Nicene **8** Apostles' *district:* **6** parish **7** diocese *father:* **5** Basil **6** Jerome, Justin, Origen **7** Ambrose, Clement **8** Ignatius **9** Augustine **10** Chrysostom, Tertullian, theologian *fund-raiser:* **6** bazaar *governing body:* **5** curia **7** classis **10** consistory, presbytery *head:* **4** pope **7** pontiff *law:* **5** canon *member:* **11** communicant *of a monastery:* **7** minster *officer:* **5** elder, vicar **6** beadle, deacon, sexton, verger, warden **9** presbyter, sacristan *part:* **4** apse, bema, loft, nave **5** aisle, altar, choir **6** vestry **7** chancel, gallery, narthex, steeple **8** sacristy, transept **9** baptistry, sanctuary **10** baptistery, clerestory *porch:* **6** parvis **7** galilee *reader:* **6** lector *recess:* **4** apse *revenue:* **5** tithe *room:* **6** vestry **8** sacristy *Scottish:*

4 kirk *seats for clergy:* 7 sedilia *service:*
4 mass 6 matins 7 vespers 8 evensong
9 communion *small:* 6 chapel *tribunal:*
4 rota *vault:* 5 crypt
Churchill, Winston *daughter:* 4 Mary
5 Diana, Sarah *father:* 8 Randolph *mother:* 6 Jennie *Order:* 6 Garter *phrase:*
11 Iron Curtain *son:* 8 Randolph *trademark:* 5 cigar *wife:* 10 Clementine
church key 9 can opener
churchman 6 bishop, cleric, divine, parson, pastor, priest 8 minister, preacher,
reverend 9 clergyman 12 ecclesiastic
churl 3 oaf 4 boor, clod, lout, rube
5 chuff, clown, yahoo, yokel 6 mucker
7 bumpkin, hayseed 10 clodhopper
churlish 4 base, curt, dour, rude 5 blunt,
crude, gruff, surly 6 coarse, crusty, oafish, vulgar 7 boorish, brusque, loutish,
lowbred, uncivil 8 cloddish, clownish
10 unmannerly 11 clodhopping, uncivilized 12 discourteous
churn 4 boil, foam, roil, stir 5 froth,
swirl 6 bubble, seethe, simmer, stir up
7 agitate, ferment, smolder
chute 4 fall, ramp 5 falls, rapid, slide,
spout 6 rapids 7 cascade, channel,
descent 8 cataract 9 spinnaker, waterfall
chutzpah 4 gall 5 brass, cheek, moxie,
nerve, spunk 8 audacity, temerity
10 effrontery
CIA *predecessor:* 3 OSS
ciao 4 by-by, ta-ta 5 adieu, adios, aloha,
hello, howdy 6 bye-bye, good-by, so
long 7 good-bye, welcome 8 farewell
9 greetings
cicatrix 4 scar 13 scarification
Cicero *forte:* 7 oratory *target:* 8 Catiline
10 Mark Antony
cicerone 4 guru 5 coach, guide, tutor
6 docent, escort, mentor 7 adviser
9 counselor, tour guide
Cid, El (Le) 4 epic, hero, play, poem
5 opera *composer:* 8 Massenet (Jules)
meaning: 4 lord *name:* 4 Díaz (Rodrigo,
Ruy) 5 Bivar *playwright:* 9 Corneille
(Pierre) *sword:* 6 Colada, Tizona *wife:*
6 Jimena, Ximena
cigar 5 stogy 6 corona, Havana, stogie
7 cheroot 8 panatela, perfecto *case:*
7 humidor *color:* 5 claro 6 maduro
8 colorado
cigarette 3 fag 4 butt 5 smoke 6 gasper
10 coffin nail
cilium 4 hair, lash 7 eyelash
Cimmerian 4 dark 5 dusky, murky
6 gloomy 7 hellish, shadowy, stygian
8 infernal, plutonic 9 plutonian
cinch 4 snap 5 girth, setup 6 assure,
breeze, ensure, fasten, insure, picnic,

secure, shoo-in 8 duck soup, kid stuff,
pushover 9 certainty 10 child's play
cinchona bark extract 7 quinine
cincture 4 band, belt, sash 6 girdle
9 waistband
cinders 3 ash 4 coal, lava, slag 5 ashes,
dross 6 embers 8 clinkers
cinema 4 film, show 5 flick, movie
6 movies 7 picture, theater, theatre
12 silver screen 13 motion picture
cinereous 4 ashy, gray, grey 5 ashen
7 ashlike
cinnabar 3 ore 7 mineral, pigment 9 vermilion *color:* 3 red
cinnamon bark 6 cassia
cinnamon stone 6 garnet 8 essonite
cipher 4 code, zero 5 aught, count, digit
6 figure, naught, nobody, number,
reckon, symbol 7 compute, integer,
numeral 8 estimate, monogram 9 calculate, nonentity 11 whole number
ciphering 8 figuring 9 computing, reckoning 10 arithmetic 11 calculation,
computation
circa 4 near, nigh 5 about 6 around
7 roughly 13 approximately
circadian 5 daily 6 cyclic 7 diurnal, regular 9 quotidian
Circe 5 siren 9 sorceress *brother:*
6 Aeëtes *father:* 3 Sol 6 Helios *home:*
5 Aeaea *lover:* 7 Ulysses 8 Odysseus
niece: 5 Medea *son:* 5 Comus
9 Telegonus
Circean 6 luring 8 alluring, enticing,
fetching, tempting 10 bewitching
circinate 6 coiled 7 rounded
circle 4 belt, gyre, hoop, loop, ring
5 crowd, cycle, group, orbit, wheel,
whorl 6 clique, corona, girdle, gyrate,
rotary, rotate 7 compass, coterie, cronies, friends, revolve, rondure 8 surround 9 encompass 10 associates, companions, revolution *bisector:* 8 diameter
colored: 6 areola *combining form:* 3 gyr
4 cycl, gyro 5 cyclo *graph:* 8 pie chart
luminous: 4 aura, halo 6 corona, nimbus 7 aureole *part:* 3 arc 6 sector
8 quadrant *small:* 4 disk 7 annulet
circlet 4 band, ring 6 bangle, diadem
8 bracelet, headband *for head or helmet:*
7 coronal
circuit 3 lap, way 4 loop, tour, trip, turn
5 ambit, cycle, orbit, round, route,
track 6 course, hookup, league 7 compass, journey, pathway, travels 8 district, rotation 9 perimeter, periphery,
round trip 10 revolution, roundabout
11 association, circulation 13 circumference
circuitous 7 devious, oblique, winding
8 circular, indirect, tortuous 10 collat-

eral, convoluted, meandering, roundabout
circuit rider 5 judge 8 minister, preacher
9 clergyman
circular 4 bill 5 flier, flyer, round 7 annular, cycloid, discoid, handout, leaflet
8 handbill 9 throwaway *file:* 11 waste-
basket *motion:* 4 eddy, gyre, spin
5 whirl 8 gyration, rotation 10 revolution *plate:* 4 disc, dish, disk
circularize 4 poll 6 survey 7 canvass
9 advertise, publicize
circulate 4 flow 6 rotate, spread 7 diffuse, radiate, revolve 8 disperse 9 propagate 10 distribute 11 disseminate
circulation 4 flow 6 spread 8 currency
9 diffusion 11 propagation 12 transmission 13 dissemination
circumciser 5 mohel
circumcision, Jewish 4 bris 9 Brit Milah
circumference 3 rim 5 ambit 6 border,
bounds, limits, margin 7 circuit, compass 8 boundary, confines 9 perimeter,
periphery
circumflex 9 diacritic
circumjacent 11 surrounding
circumlocution 8 pleonasm, verbiage
9 euphemism, loquacity, prolixity, verbosity, wordiness 10 redundancy
11 periphrasis, verboseness
circumnavigate 5 skirt 6 bypass, detour
8 sidestep
circumnavigator 4 Cook (James)
5 Drake (Francis) 8 Magellan (Ferdinand), van Noort (Olivier) 9 Cavendish
(Thomas)
circumscribe 5 cramp, limit 6 fetter,
hamper 7 confine, delimit, enclose,
mark off, outline, trammel 8 restrict,
surround 9 constrict
circumscribed 5 bound, fixed 6 finite,
narrow, strait 7 bounded, cramped,
limited, precise 8 confined, definite,
hampered 10 restrained, restricted
11 determinate
circumscription 5 cramp, limit, stint
6 border, margin 8 boundary 9 perimeter, restraint, stricture 10 constraint,
definition, limitation 11 confinement,
restriction 12 ball and chain, delimitation 13 constrainment
circumspect 4 safe, wary 5 chary 7 careful, guarded, prudent 8 cautious, discreet, gingerly 11 calculating
circumstance 4 fact, item 5 event, thing
6 detail, factor 7 adjunct, element,
episode, feature 8 accident, incident,
occasion 9 component, condition, happening 10 occurrence, particular
11 concomitant, constituent, eventuality

circumstantial 4 full 5 close, exact
6 strict 7 precise, replete 8 accurate,
complete, detailed, thorough 9 elaborate, pertinent 10 blow-by-blow, ceremonial, exhaustive, incidental, particular
circumvent 5 avoid, elude, evade, hem
in, skirt 6 bypass, detour 8 outflank,
sidestep
circumvolution 4 gyre, turn 5 wheel,
whirl 8 gyration, rotation 10 revolution
circus 4 ring 5 arena 6 big top 9 spectacle 12 amphitheater *animal:* 4 bear, flea,
lion, seal 5 horse, tiger 8 elephant
attraction: 5 freak 8 sideshow *owner:*
6 Bailey (James), Barnum (P. T.) 8 Rin-
gling (Bros.) *performer:* 5 clown, tamer
7 acrobat, athlete, juggler, tumbler
9 aerialist, fire eater *worker:*
10 roustabout
citadel 4 fort 7 redoubt 8 fastness,
fortress 10 stronghold *of Carthage:*
5 Bursa, Byrsa *Russian:* 7 Kremlin
citation 5 quote 6 eulogy 7 excerpt, mention, summons, tribute 8 accolade,
encomium 9 panegyric, quotation, reference 12 commendation
cite 4 name, tell 5 offer, quote 6 adduce,
recall, summon 7 arraign, mention,
present, refer to, specify 8 point out,
remember 9 recollect
citizen 7 burgess, burgher, subject
8 civilian, national, resident, townsman
10 inhabitant
Citizen Kane director 6 Welles (Orson)
citron 4 tree 5 melon
citrus *family:* 3 rue 8 Rutaceae *fruit:*
4 lime, ugli 5 lemon 6 citron, orange,
pomelo 7 kumquat, tangelo 8 bergamot, mandarin, shaddock 9 tangerine
10 grapefruit
city 4 burg 5 urban 7 burghal 9 municipal 10 metropolis *combining form:*
5 polis *Eternal:* 4 Rome *French:* 5 ville
heavenly: 4 Sion, Zion *Latin:* 4 urbs
Motor: 7 Detroit *of Bells:* 10 Strasbourg
of Bridges: 6 Bruges *of Brotherly Love:*
12 Philadelphia *of David:* 9 Jerusalem
official: 5 mayor 7 manager 8 alderman
10 councilman *of God:* 6 heaven 8 paradise *of Gold:* 8 Eldorado *of Kings:*
4 Lima *of Lights:* 5 Paris *of Lilies:*
8 Florence *of Masts:* 6 London *of Rams:*
6 Canton *of Refuge:* 6 Medina *of Saints:*
8 Montreal *of Seven Hills:* 4 Rome *of the
dead:* 10 necropolis *of Victory:* 5 Cairo
planner: 8 urbanist *section:* 4 slum,
ward 5 block, plaza 6 barrio, ghetto,
square, uptown 8 business, downtown,
red-light 11 residential *slicker:* 4 dude
windy: 7 Chicago

city-state, Greek 5 Argos, polis 6 Athens,
Delphi, poleis (plural), Sparta, Thebes
7 Corinth

city, town, village (see also CAPITAL)
Afghanistan: 5 Balkh, Farah, Herat,
Kushk 6 Konduz 8 Kandahar, Qanda-
har 9 Jalalabad *Alabama:* 3 Opp 4 Arab,
Boaz, Elba 5 Selma 6 Athens, Dothan,
Mobile 7 Decatur, Florala 8 Prichard
10 Birmingham, Huntsville, Scottsboro,
Tuscaloosa 12 Muscle Shoals *Alaska:*
4 Nome 5 Kenai, Sitka 6 Barrow,
Bethel, Kodiak, Valdez 9 Anchorage,
Fairbanks, Ketchikan 11 Point Barrow
Albania: 4 Fier 5 Berat, Korçë, Kukës,
Vlorë *Alberta:* 4 Olds 5 Hanna, Leduc,
Taber 7 Calgary 8 Edmonton 10 Leth-
bridge 11 Medicine Hat *Algeria:* 4 Bône,
Oran 5 Batna, Blida, Médéa, Saïda,
Sétif 6 Annaba, Bechar 11 Constantine
Angola: 6 Huambo 7 Lubango
8 Benguela *Argentina:* 4 Azul, Goya
5 Junin, Lanus, Lujan, Merlo, Salta,
Tigre 6 Parana 7 Córdoba, La Plata, La
Rioja, Mendoza, Rosario, San Juan,
Santa Fe 9 Catamarca 11 Bahía Blanca,
Mar del Plata *Arizona:* 3 Ajo 4 Eloy,
Mesa, Yuma 5 Globe, Tempe 6 Tucson
7 Sun City, Winslow 8 Glendale,
Prescott 9 Flagstaff, Tombstone 10 Casa
Grande, Scottsdale *Arkansas:* 4 Mena
5 Beebe, Cabot, Earle, Ozark, Wynne
9 Fort Smith, Pine Bluff, Texarkana
10 Hot Springs *Armenia:* 6 Gyumri
8 Vanadzor *Australia:* 3 Ayr 5 Dalby,
Dubbo, Perth, Unley 6 Darwin, Sydney
8 Adelaide, Brisbane, Randwick
9 Bankstown, Blacktown, Gold Coast,
Melbourne, Newcastle 10 Kalgoorlie,
Parramatta, Sutherland, Wollongong
12 Alice Springs *Austria:* 4 Enns, Graz,
Linz, Wels 5 Steyr, Traun 8 Salzburg
9 Innsbruck 10 Klagenfurt *Azerbaijan:*
5 Gäncä 8 Sumqayit 9 Kirovabad
Bahamas: 8 Freeport *Bangladesh:*
5 Bogra, Pabna 6 Khulna, Sylhet
7 Barisal, Comilla, Jessore, Rangpur,
Saidpur 10 Chittagong *Belarus:* 5 Brest,
Gomel, Mozyr, Pinsk 6 Grodno,
Homyel', Hrodna 7 Mogilev, Vitebsk
8 Babruysk, Mahilyow 9 Vitsyebsk *Bel-
gium:* 3 Ath, Hal, Huy, Mol 4 Amay,
Dour, Geel, Genk, Gent, Hoei, Luik,
Mons, Vise 5 Aalst, Arlon, Diest, Evere,
Ghent, Halle, Ieper, Jumet, Leuze,
Liège, Namur, Ronse, Theux, Wavre,
Ypres 6 Bruges, Brugge 7 Antwerp,
Hasselt, Louvain 8 Oostende
9 Charleroi *Benin:* 5 Kandi 6 Abomey
7 Parakou *Bolivia:* 5 Oruro, Uyuni
6 Potosí 9 Santa Cruz 10 Cochabamba

Bosnia and Herzegovina: 5 Bihac, Brcko,
Jajce, Tuzla 6 Mostar, Zenica 9 Banja
Luka *Botswana:* 4 Maun 5 Kanye
11 Francistown *Brazil:* 4 Codo, Pará
5 Bahia, Bauru, Belém, Ceara, Natal
6 Campos, Canoas, Caxias, Ilheus,
Maceio, Manaus, Olinda, Recife, Santos 7 Aracaju, Caruaru, Goiania, Jundi-
ai, Marilia, Niteroi, Pelotas, São Luis,
Uberaba, Vitória 8 Campinas, Colatina,
Curitiba, Londrina, Salvador, Santarém, São Paulo, Sorocaba, Teresina
9 Caratinga, Fortaleza, Guarulhos, Rio
Grande 10 Guarapuava, Joao Pessoa,
Juiz de Fora, Nova Iguaçu, Pernambuco, Petropolis, Piracicaba, Pôrto Velho,
Santa Maria, Santo André, São Gonça-
lo, Uberlândia 11 Campo Grande, Caxias do Sul, Ponta Grossa, Pôrto Alegre
12 Montes Claros, Rio de Janeiro, Teó-
filo Otoni, Volta Redonda 13 Belo Horizonte, Campina Grande, Duque de
Caxias, Florianopolis, Mogi das
Cruzes, Riberião Prêto *British Columbia:* 5 Comox 6 Surrey 7 Burnaby
8 Richmond 9 Vancouver *Bulgaria:*
3 Lom 4 Ruse 5 Varna, Vidin 6 Burgas
7 Plovdiv 11 Stara Zagora *California:*
4 Brea, Galt, Lodi, Ojai 5 Arvin, Azusa,
Ceres, Chico, Chino, Dixon, Hemet,
Indio, Norco, Ripon, Ukiah, Wasco,
Yreka 6 Downey, Encino, Fresno,
Oxnard, Pomona, Sonoma 7 Anaheim,
Burbank, Compton, Fremont, Hay-
ward, Modesto, Oakland, San Jose,
Seaside, Soledad, Van Nuys 8 Berkeley,
Glendale, Palo Alto, Pasadena, San
Diego, Santa Ana, Stockton, Torrance,
Yuba City 9 El Segundo, Hollywood,
Long Beach, Menlo Park, Riverside,
Sausalito 10 Chula Vista, Culver City,
Los Angeles, San Leandro, Santa Clara
11 Bakersfield, Laguna Beach, Pebble
Beach, Redwood City, San Clemente,
Santa Monica 12 Beverly Hills, Mission
Viejo, Redondo Beach, San Francisco,
Santa Barbara 13 San Bernardino, San
Luis Obispo *Cambodia:* 8 Siem Reap
10 Battambang 11 Kompong Cham
Cameroon: 4 Buea, Edea 5 Kribi, Lomie
6 Douala 7 Bamenda, Foumban
9 Bafoussam *Canada:* 4 York 5 Banff
6 London, Oshawa, Ottawa, Regina, St.
John 7 Brandon, Burnaby, Calgary,
Halifax, Iqaluit, Red Deer, St. John's,
Sudbury, Toronto, Windsor 8 Hamilton,
Montreal, Moose Jaw, North Bay, Vic-
toria, Winnipeg 9 Dartmouth, Kitchen-
er, Longueuil, North York, Saint John,
Saskatoon, Vancouver 10 Lethbridge,
Saint John's, Sherbrooke, Thunder

Bay, Whitehorse 11 Fredericton, Medicine Hat, Mississauga, Scarborough, Yellowknife 12 Peterborough, Prince Albert, Prince George 13 Charlottetown, Trois-Rivières *Central African Republic:* 5 Bouar 7 Bambari *Chad:* 4 Sarh 6 Abéché *Chile:* 4 Lebu, Lota, Tomé 5 Ancud, Angol, Arica, Maipu, Penco, Rengo, Talca 6 Temuco 7 Copiapó, Iquique 8 Rancagua 10 Concepción, Talcahuano, Valparaíso 11 Antofagasta *China:* 4 Amoy, Jian, Luan, Xi'an, Yaan 5 Hefei, Jilin, Jinan, Lhasa, Qinan, Ssuan, Wuhan, Yibin, Yumen 6 Andong, Anqing, Anshan, Anshun, Anyang, Beihai, Canton, Dalian, Datong, Foshan, Fushun, Fuzhou, Guilin, Haikou, Handan, Harbin, Hohhot, Hoihao, Jilong, Luzhou, Mukden, Ningbo, Pengbu, Suzhou, Ürümqi, Xiamen, Xining, Xuzhou, Yanggu, Yichun, Yining, Zhangi, Zhaoan 7 Baoding, Changan, Chengdu, Dandong, Guiyang, Huainan, Jiamusi, Jiaxing, Kaifeng, Kunming, Lanzhou, Luoshan, Luoyang, Nanking, Nanjing, Nanning, Shantou, Tianjin, Taiyuan, Wanxian, Weifang, Yizhang, Zhuzhou 8 Changchi, Changsha, Dangshan, Hangzhou, Hanzhong, Hengyang, Huangshi, Jiangmen, Jiujiang, Kueiyang, Liaoyang, Nanchang, Shanghai, Shangrao, Shaoyang, Shenyang, Tianshui, Yinchuan, Zhenjing 9 Changchun, Chenjiang, Chongqing, Chungking, Guangzhou, Huangshih, Zhengzhou, Zhenjiang 10 Jingdezhen, Laojunmiao 11 Qinhuangdao, Zhangjiakou *Colombia:* 4 Buga, Cali 5 Bello, Mocoa, Neiva, Ocaña, Pasto, Tuluá, Tunja 6 Cúcuta, Ibagué 7 Ciénaga, Palmira, Pereira, Popayán 8 Medellín, Montería 9 Cartagena, Manizales 10 Santa Marta 11 Bucaramanga 12 Barranquilla *Colorado:* 6 Arvada, Aurora, Golden, Salida 7 Alamosa, Boulder, Durango, Greeley, La Junta 8 Brighton, Gunnison, Lakewood, Longmont, Loveland, Montrose, Thornton 9 Englewood, Estes Park, Leadville, Littleton, Rocky Ford, Telluride 10 Broomfield, Castle Rock, Fort Lupton, Fort Morgan, Monte Vista, Northglenn, Wheat Ridge 11 Fort Collins 13 Grand Junction *Congo (Zaire):* 4 Boma 6 Bukavu 7 Kolwezi 8 Bandundu 9 Kisangani 10 Lubumbashi 12 Stanleyville *Congo-Brazzaville:* 11 Pointe-Noire *Connecticut:* 5 Byram 6 Darien, Easton, Granby, Groton,

Haddam 7 Ansonia, Bethany, Danbury, Enfield, Meriden, Milford, Newtown, Niantic, Norwalk, Norwich, Old Lyme, Pomfret, Windham 8 Branford, Cromwell, East Lyme, Guilford, New Haven, Simsbury, Stamford, Suffield, Westport 9 Greenwich, New Canaan, Newington, New London, Rocky Hill, Southbury, Waterbury, Waterford 10 Bridgeport, Brookfield, East Haddam, Farmington, Kensington, Litchfield, New Britain, New Milford, North Haven, Plainville, Ridgefield, Stonington, Torrington 11 Beacon Falls, Glastonbury, Middlefield, Old Saybrook, Southington, Wallingford, Willimantic 12 Wethersfield *Costa Rica:* 8 Alajuela 10 Puntarenas 11 Puerto Limón *Croatia:* 4 Pula 5 Sisak, Split, Zadar 6 Osijek, Rijeka, Zagreb 9 Dubrovnik *Cuba:* 5 Banes, Bauta 6 Bayamo 7 Holguín 8 Camagüey, Marianao, Matanzas, Santiago 10 Cienfuegos, Guantánamo 11 Pinar del Río *Cyprus:* 7 Kyrenia, Larnaca, Nicosia 8 Limassol 9 Famagusta *Czech Republic:* 4 Brno, Zlín 5 Plzen 7 Liberec, Olomouc, Ostrava 10 Bratislava *Delaware:* 5 Lewes 7 Seaford 10 Harrington, Wilmington, Winterthur *Denmark:* 5 Århus, Skive, Vejle 6 Alborg, Odense, Viborg 13 Frederiksberg *Dominican Republic:* 4 Azua, Bani, Moca 5 Bonao, Nagua 8 Barahona, Santiago *Ecuador:* 4 Loja 5 Canar, Daule, Manta, Pinas 7 Machala 8 Riobamba 9 Guayaquil *Egypt:* 4 Giza, Idfu, Isna, Qena 5 Aswan, Asyut, Benha, Disuq, Girga, Luxor, Minuf, Tahta, Tanta 6 Helwan 7 El Arish, Zagazig 8 Damanhur, Damietta, El Faiyum, Ismailia, Port Said 10 Alexandria *Eire:* 4 Athy, Birr, Cobh, Cork, Naas, Tuam 5 Ennis, Sligo 6 Carlow, Galway, Tralee 7 Dundalk, Kildare, Wexford, Wicklow 8 Drogheda, Kilkenny, Limerick, Monaghan 9 Castlebar, Killarney, Tipperary, Waterford 10 Balbriggan *El Salvador:* 7 La Unión 8 Santa Ana 9 Sonsonate *England:* 4 Bath, Eton, Hove, Ryde, York 5 Brent, Brigg, Colne, Corby, Cowes, Derby, Dover, Egham, Eling, Esher, Eston, Goole, Leeds, Leigh, Lewes, Luton, Poole, Ryton, Wigan 6 Bexley, Bolton, Dudley, Durham, Exeter, Merton, Oldham, Oxford, Torbay, Warley, Welwyn 7 Bristol, Bromley, Croydon, Hackney, Ipswich, Malvern, Norwich, Salford, Seaford, Walsall 8 Abingdon, Basildon, Bradford, Brighton, Coventry, Hastings, Hatfield, Havering, Hertford,

Kingston, Lewisham, Plymouth, Wallsend 9 Aylesbury, Blackpool, Cambridge, Islington, Leicester, Liverpool, Newcastle, Sheffield, Stratford 10 Birkenhead, Birmingham, Canterbury, Colchester, Manchester, Nottingham, Portsmouth, Sunderland 11 Bournemouth, Northampton, Southampton 12 Peterborough, Stoke-on-Trent, West Bromwich 13 Southend-on-Sea, Wolverhampton *Estonia:* 5 Narva, Pärnu, Tartu *Ethiopia:* 5 Aksum, Harer 6 Nazret 8 Dire Dawa *Finland:* 4 Kemi, Oulu, Pori 5 Espoo, Hango, Kotka, Lahti, Rauma, Turku, Vaasa 6 Vantaa 7 Tampere *Florida:* 5 Largo, Miami, Ocala, Ocoee, Oneco, Tampa 6 DeLand, Naples 7 Hialeah, Key West, Orlando, Sebring 8 Gulfport, Key Largo, Lakeland, Opa-Locka, Sarasota 9 Boca Raton, Bradenton, Fort Myers, Hollywood, Kissimmee, Palm Beach, Pensacola, Vero Beach 10 Clearwater, Cocoa Beach, Fort Pierce, Miami Beach, Punta Gorda, Titusville 11 Coral Gables, Gainesville, Key Biscayne, St. Augustine, Winter Haven 12 Apalachicola, Daytona Beach, Ft. Lauderdale, Jacksonville, Pompano Beach, St. Petersburg 13 Chattahoochee *France:* 3 Dax, Pau 4 Agde, Agen, Albi, Ales, Auch, Caen, Gien, Laon, Lyon, Metz, Nice, Orly, Rezé, Sens, Sète, Vire 5 Arles, Arras, Auray, Auton, Avion, Berck, Blois, Bondy, Brest, Creil, Digne, Dijon, Douai, Dreux, Flers, Gagny, Laval, Le Puy, Lille, Lunel, Lyons, Mâcon, Meaux, Melun, Muret, Nîmes, Niort, Noyon, Reims, Revin, Rodez, Rouen, Royan, Tours, Tulle, Vichy, Vitre 6 Amiens, Angers, Calais, Cannes, Dieppe, Evreux, Le Mans, Nantes, Nevers, Rennes, Rheims, Thiers, Toulon, Troyes 7 Ajaccio, Antibes, Avignon, Béthune, Bourges, Le Havre, Limoges, Lorient, Lourdes, Orléans, Roubaix 8 Beauvais, Besançon, Biarritz, Bordeaux, Chartres, Gentilly, Grenoble, Nanterre, Poitiers, Toulouse 9 Cherbourg, Dunkerque, Le Creusot, Marseille, Montreuil, Perpignan 10 Draguignan, Marseilles, Strasbourg, Versailles 11 Carcassonne, Montpellier 12 Saint-Etienne 13 Aix-en-Provence *Gabon:* 4 Oyem 5 Bitam 10 Port-Gentil 11 Franceville *Gambia:* 9 Serekunda *Georgia:* 4 Adel, Alma, Arco 5 Jesup, Macon, McRae 6 Albany, Athens 7 Augusta, Calhoun 8 Americus, Columbus, Marietta, Savannah, Val-

dosta 9 Brunswick *Georgia, Republic of:* 6 Batumi 7 Kutaisi, Rustavi, Sukhumi *Germany:* 3 Aue, Hof, Ulm 4 Bonn, Gera, Goch, Hamm, Jena, Kehl, Kiel, Köln, Marl, Suhl 5 Aalen, Ahlen, Borna, Bruhl, Calbe, Celle, Düren, Emden, Essen, Forst, Fulda, Furth, Gotha, Greiz, Hagen, Halle, Hanau, Herne, Hurth, Kleve, Lemgo, Lobau, Mainz, Neuss, Peine, Pirna, Riesa, Stade, Thale, Trier, Wesel, Zeitz 6 Aachen, Bremen, Coburg, Dachau, Dessau, Erfurt, Kassel, Lübeck, Munich, Rheydt 7 Cologne, Cottbus, Dresden, Hamburg, Hanover, Koblenz, Krefeld, Leipzig, München, Munster, Potsdam, Rostock, Zwickau 8 Augsburg, Bayreuth, Chemnitz, Cuxhaven, Dortmund, Duisburg, Freiburg, Hannover, Mannheim, Nürnberg, Würzburg 9 Bielefeld, Brunswick, Darmstadt, Frankfurt, Göttingen, Karlsruhe, Magdeburg, Nuremberg, Offenbach, Oldenburg, Osnabrück, Remscheid, Stuttgart, Wiesbaden, Wuppertal 10 Baden-Baden, Düsseldorf, Heidelberg, Oberhausen, Regensburg, Salzgitter 11 Brandenburg, Bremerhaven, Saarbrücken 12 Braunschweig 13 Gelsenkirchen *Ghana:* 4 Axim, Keta, Tema 5 Lawra, Yendi 6 Kumasi *Greece:* 3 Kos 4 Arta 5 Argos, Lamia, Nemea, Volos 6 Sparta, Thebes 7 Corinth, Khalkis, Larissa, Piraeus, Trikala 8 Salonika 12 Thessaloniki *Guatemala:* 5 Cobán 13 Quezaltenango *Guinea:* 4 Labé 6 Kankan, Kindia *Haiti:* 8 Gonaïves 10 Cap Haitien *Hawaii:* 4 Aiea, Hilo, Laie 5 Kapaa, Lihue, Maili 6 Kailua 7 Kaneohe, Waikiki, Wailuku *Honduras:* 5 Danlí 7 La Ceiba 12 San Pedro Sula *Hong Kong:* 7 Kowloon *Hungary:* 3 Ozd 4 Eger, Györ, Pécs 5 Abony, Bekes 6 Szeged 7 Miskolc 8 Debrecen *Idaho:* 4 Buhl 5 Nampa 6 Dubois, Moscow 7 Gooding, Payette, Rexburg 8 Caldwell 9 Blackfoot, Pocatello, Sandpoint, Sun Valley, Twin Falls 11 Coeur d'Alene, Grangeville 12 Mountain Home, Saint Anthony *Illinois:* 6 DeKalb, Galena, Hardin, Joliet, Macomb, Moline, Paxton, Peoria, Skokie, Urbana 7 Chicago, Decatur, Glencoe, Oak Lawn, Oak Park, Tuscola, Watseka, Wheaton 8 Carthage, Evanston, Kankakee, La Grange, Monmouth, Rockford, Vandalia, Waukegan 9 Belvidere, Effingham, Galesburg, Park Ridge, Yorkville 10 Belleville, Carbondale, Carrollton, Des Plaines,

Metropolis, Northbrook, Rock Island
11 Carlinville, Jerseyville, Lindenhurst,
Murphysboro, Taylorville 12 Highland
Park, Mount Carroll *India:* 3 Mau
4 Agra, Ahwa, Bhuj, Durg, Gaya, Kota,
Mhow, Pune, Puri, Rewa, Tonk, Ziro
5 Adoni, Aimer, Akola, Alwar, Arcot,
Arrah, Banda, Barsi, Bidar, Bihar,
Churu, Damoh, Delhi, Dewas, Eluru,
Gonda, Jalna, Jammu, Karur, Miraj,
Morvi, Nasik, Patan, Patna, Poona,
Sagar, Satna, Sikar, Simla, Surat, Thana
6 Baroda, Bhopal, Bombay, Cochin,
Guntur, Howrah, Indore, Jaipur, Jhan-
si, Kanpur, Madras, Meerut, Mysore,
Nagpur, Raipur, Rajkot, Ranchi, Ujjain
7 Aligarh, Asansol, Belgaum, Bikaner,
Burdwan, Cuttack, Gauhati, Gwalior,
Jodhpur, Kurnool, Lucknow, Madurai,
Mathura, Nellore, Patiala, Vellore
8 Amritsar, Bhatpara, Calcutta, Dehra
Dun, Kolhapur, Ludhiana, Sholapur,
Srinagar, Varanasi 9 Ahmadabad, Alla-
habad, Bangalore, Hyderabad
10 Ahmadnagar, Chandigarh, Trivandrum 11 Pondicherry *Indiana:* 4 Gary
5 Berne, Paoli, Vevay 6 Delphi, Koko-
mo, Marlon, Muncie, Tipton 7 Bedford, Corydon, Elkhart, La Porte,
Winamac 8 Bluffton, Kentland
9 Boonville, Fort Wayne, New Albany,
Rushville, South Bend, Vincennes
10 Crown Point, Evansville, Logans-
port, Scottsburg, Terre Haute, Val-
paraiso 11 Bloomington, Greencastle,
Noblesville, Shelbyville 12 Con-
nersville, Lawrenceburg, Martinsville
Indonesia: 4 Pati 5 Ambon, Bogor,
Garut, Kudus, Medan, Tegal, Turen
6 Batang, Kediri, Madiun, Malang,
Manado, Padang 7 Bandung, Kendari
8 Semarang, Surabaja, Surabaya, Tjire-
bon 9 Palembang, Pontianak, Surakar-
ta 10 Pekalongan 11 Tasikmalaja
12 Bandjarmasin *Iowa:* 5 Onawa, Pella
6 Eldora, Harlan, Keokuk, Le Mars,
Red Oak 7 Allison, Anamosa, Carroll,
Clinton, Corydon, Denison, Dubuque,
Marengo, Osceola, Waverly 8 Clarinda,
Ida Grove, Waterloo 9 Davenport, Fort
Dodge, Indianola, Mason City, Musca-
tine, Oskaloosa, Sioux City, Storm
Lake, West Union, Winterset
10 Emmetsburg, Rock Rapids, Spirit
Lake 11 Cedar Rapids, Fort Madison
13 Council Bluffs *Iran:* 3 Qom, Qum
4 Amul, Arak, Khoi, Sari, Yazd, Yezd
5 Ahvaz, Ahwaz, Babol, Rasht
6 Abadan, Meshed, Shiraz, Tabriz
7 Esfahan, Hamadan, Isfahan, Mashhad 9 Bakhtaran *Iraq:* 3 Ana, Kut

4 Kufa 5 Al Kut, Amara, Basra, Erbil,
Hilla, Mosul, Najaf, Rutba 6 Amarah,
Hillah, Kirkuk, Ramadi, Rutbah 7 Fal-
luja, Samarra 8 Fallujah, Nasiriya
9 Nasiriyah *Ireland:* (see *Eire*, above)
Israel: 5 Afula, Haifa, Holon, Jaffa
7 Rehovot 8 Ashqelon, Nazareth,
Ramat Gan 9 Beersheba *Italy:* 4 Acri,
Alba, Asti, Bari, Enna, Este, Fano,
Gela, Iesi, Lodi, Lugo, Pisa 5 Adria,
Agira, Anzio, Aosta, Arola, Cantù,
Capua, Carpi, Crema, Cuneo, Eboli,
Fermo, Fondi, Forli, Gaeta, Genoa,
Imola, Ivrea, Lecce, Lecco, Lucca,
Massa, Melfi, Menfi, Milan, Monza,
Padua, Parma, Prato, Siena, Turin
6 Ancona, Assisi, Foggia, Mantua,
Milano, Modena, Naples, Napoli, Rimi-
ni, Torino, Venice, Verona 7 Bergamo,
Bologna, Bolzano, Brescia, Catania,
Firenze, Leghorn, Messina, Palermo,
Perugia, Pescara, Potenza, Ravenna,
Salerno, San Remo, Taranto, Trieste,
Venezia 8 Brindisi, Cagliari, Florence,
La Spezia, Piacenza, Siracusa, Syracuse
Ivory Coast: 6 Bouaké *Jamaica:* 6 May
Pen 10 Montego Bay *Japan:* 3 Ina, Ise,
Ito, Ota, Tsu, Ube, Uji, Yao 4 Ageo,
Anan, Gifu, Hagi, Himi, Hofu, Iida,
Joyo, Kaga, Kobe, Kofu, Kure, Miki,
Mito, Naha, Nara, Noda, Oita, Otsu,
Saga, Saku, Soka, Tosu, Ueda, Yono
5 Akita, Atami, Beppu, Chiba, Imari,
Itami, Iwaki, Iwata, Izumi, Izumo,
Kiryu, Kochi, Kyoto, Minoo, Odate,
Ogaki, Okawa, Okaya, Omiya, Omuta,
Osaka, Otaru, Oyama, Sabae, Saiki,
Sakai, Sanjo, Suita, Tenri, Urawa
6 Akashi, Aomori, Himeji, Kadoma,
Kurume, Matsue, Mitaka, Nagano,
Nagoya, Numazu, Sasebo, Sendai,
Suzuka, Toyama, Yonago 7 Fukuoka,
Hitachi, Ibaraki, Imabari, Muroran,
Niigata, Niihama, Nobeoka, Obihiro,
Odawara, Okayama, Okazaki, Sapporo
8 Ashikaga, Fujisawa, Fukuyama,
Hirakata, Hirosaki, Ichihara, Ichikawa,
Kakogawa, Kamakura, Kanazawa,
Kawasaki, Miyazaki, Nagasaki,
Onomichi, Shizuoka, Takasaki, Toyona-
ka, Wakayama, Yamagata, Yokohama,
Yokosuka 9 Fukushima, Funabashi,
Hiroshima, Kawaguchi, Yamaguchi,
Yokkaichi *Jordan:* 5 Aqaba, Irbid
Kansas: 4 Gove, Iola 5 Colby, Hoxie,
Lakin, Leoti, Paola, Pratt 6 Atwood,
Beloit, Girard, Holton, Salina 7 Abi-
lene, Emporia, Garnett, Kinsley, Wichi-
ta 8 Cimarron, Goodland, La Crosse,
Sublette 9 Coldwater, Fort Scott, Great
Bend, Oskaloosa 10 Hutchinson

11 Leavenworth 12 Council Grove, Overland Park 13 Medicine Lodge *Kazakhstan:* 5 Semey 6 Almaty, Aqtöbe, Guryev, Uralsk 7 Alma-Ata, Zhambyl 8 Balkhash, Chimkent, Dzhambul, Kyzl Orda, Pavlodar, Shymkent 9 Karaganda 10 Aktyubinsk *Kentucky:* 4 Inez 5 Cadiz, Hyden, McKee 6 Elkton, Harlan 7 Ashland, Campton, Greenup, Hindman, Paducah, Stanton 8 Fort Knox, Mayfield 9 Bardstown, Covington, Cynthiana, Lexington, Maysville, Owensboro, Pikeville, Pineville, Southgate, Vanceburg 10 Booneville, Hawesville, Louisville, Whitesburg 11 Hardinsburg, Harrodsburg, Hodgenville, Leitchfield, Morganfield 12 Bowling Green *Kenya:* 4 Embu 5 Nyeri 6 Kisumu, Nakuru 7 Mombasa *Kyrgyzstan:* 3 Osh 5 Naryn *Laos:* 5 Pakse 11 Savannakhet *Latvia:* 7 Jelgava, Liepaja 9 Ventspils 10 Daugavpils *Lebanon:* 4 Tyre 5 Sidon, Zahlé 7 Juniyah, Tripoli *Libya:* 4 Homs 5 Derna, Zawia 6 Tobruk 8 Benghazi, Misratah *Lithuania:* 6 Kaunas 8 Klaipeda *Louisiana:* 4 Jena 5 Amite, Arabi, Houma, Mamou, Norco, Rayne 6 Colfax, Edgard, Gretna, Minden, Ruston 7 Arcadia, Bastrop, Marrero, Oberlin 8 Bogalusa, De Ridder, Metairie, New Roads, Oak Grove, Westwego 9 Abbeville, Chalmette, Hahnville, Leesville, New Iberia, Opelousas, Port Allen, Thibodaux, Winnfield, Winnsboro 10 New Orleans, Plaquemine, Shreveport 11 Lake Charles 12 Natchitoches *Macedonia:* 6 Bitola, Prilep, Tetovo *Maine:* 4 Saco 5 Orono 6 Auburn, Bangor, Gorham 7 Berwick, Kittery, Machias, Rumford 8 Lewiston, Portland, Rockland 9 Bar Harbor, Biddeford, Brunswick, Ellsworth, Kennebunk, Skowhegan, Wiscasset 11 Millinocket, Presque Isle 13 Kennebunkport *Malawi:* 5 Mzuzu, Zomba 8 Blantyre *Malaysia:* 4 Ipoh 5 Gemas, Klang 6 Kelang, Penang, Pinang 11 Johore Bahru *Mali:* 5 Kayes, Mopti, Ségou 7 Sikasso *Malta:* 10 Birkirkara *Maryland:* 5 Bowie 6 Denton, Elkton, Towson 8 Bethesda, Landover, Snow Hill 9 Baltimore, Rockville 10 Beltsville, Hagerstown 11 Chestertown, College Park, Leonardtown 12 Havre de Grace, Silver Spring *Massachusetts:* 4 Ayer 5 Acton, Lenox, Salem 6 Agawam, Boston, Dedham, Lowell, Malden, Monson, Natick, Saugus, Woburn 7 Amherst, Danvers, Duxbury, Holyoke, Hyannis, Medford, Methuen, Needham, Swansea, Taunton, Walpole, Waltham, Wareham 8 Brockton, Chicopee, Falmouth, Plymouth, Rockport, Scituate, Yarmouth 9 Attleboro, Braintree, Brookline, Cambridge, Edgartown, Fall River, Fitchburg, Haverhill, Lexington, Nantucket, Southwick, Wilbraham, Worcester 10 Barnstable, Framingham, Gloucester, Greenfield, Leominster, New Bedford, North Adams, Pittsfield, Somerville, Swampscott 11 Northampton, Springfield 12 Mattapoisett, Provincetown, Williamstown *Mauritania:* 4 Atar 5 Kaedi 6 Dakhla *Mexico:* 4 León 5 Ameca, Choix, Tepic 6 Cancún, Celaya, Colima, Jalapa, Juárez, Mérida, Oaxaca, Puebla, Toluca, Tuxtla 7 Durango, Guasave, Morelia, Obregón, Reynosa, Tampico, Tijuana, Tlalpán, Torreón, Uruapan, Zapopan 8 Chetumal, Coyoacán, Culiacán, Ensenada, Mazatlan, Mexicali, Saltillo, Tuxtepec 9 Chihuahua, Fresnillo, Ixtacalco, Monterrey, Querétaro, Salamanca, Tapachula, Zacatecas 10 Cuernavaca, Hermosillo, Ixtapalapa, Xochimilco 11 Guadalajara, Nuevo Laredo 13 San Luis Potosí *Michigan:* 4 Alma, Holt 5 Flint, Ionia, L'Anse, Niles 6 Otsego, Paw Paw, Warren 7 Allegan, Corunna, Detroit, Gladwin, Livonia, Midland, Saginaw 8 Ann Arbor, Bessemer, Dearborn, Escanaba, Grayling, Hastings, Houghton, Muskegon, Newberry, Petoskey, Sandusky 9 Cheboygan, Coldwater, Hillsdale, Kalamazoo, Menominee, Port Huron, Roscommon, Ypsilanti 10 Charlevoix, Grand Haven, West Branch, White Cloud 11 Battle Creek, Grand Rapids, Harrisville, Saint Ignace 12 Highland Park, Iron Mountain *Minnesota:* 3 Ely 4 Mora 5 Anoka, Edina, Osseo 6 Aitkin, Benson, Duluth, Waseca, Windom, Winona 7 Glencoe, Hibbing, Mankato, Red Wing, St. Cloud, Wabasha 8 Brainerd, Elk River, Moorhead, Shakopee 9 Caledonia, Crookston, Faribault, Pipestone, Rochester, Saint Paul, Silver Bay 10 Park Rapids, Saint Cloud, Saint James, Saint Peter, Stillwater, Two Harbors 11 Bloomington, Fergus Falls, Long Prairie, Minneapolis, Worthington 12 Breckenridge, Granite Falls, Redwood Falls *Mississippi:* 4 Iuka 5 Amory 6 Biloxi, Leland, McComb, Purvis, Sardis, Sumner, Tupelo, Winona 7 Belzoni, Brandon, Okolona, Quitman, Wiggins 8 Gulfport, Hernando, Meridian, Paulding, Rosedale, Walthall

9 Greenwood, Indianola, New Albany, Pittsboro, Vicksburg 10 Batesville, Booneville, Brookhaven, Clarksdale, Ellisville, Greenville, Hazlehurst, Pascagoula, Port Gibson, Starkville, Waynesboro 11 Coffeeville, Hattiesburg, Poplarville, Holly Springs *Missouri:* 3 Ava 4 Linn 5 Eldon, Hayti, Ladue, Rolla 6 Galena, Neosho, Potosi 7 Hermann, Ironton, Kennett, Linneus, Osceola, Palmyra, Sedalia, St. Louis 8 Gallatin, Hannibal 9 Boonville, Hartville, Hillsboro, Maryville, Pineville, Tuscumbia, Warrenton 10 Kansas City, Kirksville, Marble Hill, Marshfield, Perryville, Saint Louis, Springfield, Steelville, Unionville, West Plains 11 Poplar Bluff, Saint Joseph, Warrensburg 12 Independence, Saint Charles *Moldova:* 5 Balti 7 Tighina 8 Tiraspol *Mongolia:* 5 Kobdo 6 Darhan 10 Choybalsan *Montana:* 5 Butte, Havre, Libby 6 Hardin, Polson 7 Bozeman 8 Billings, Missoula, Red Lodge 10 Great Falls *Montenegro:* 8 Titograd 9 Podgorica *Morocco:* 3 Fès 4 Safi, Salé, Taza 5 Nador, Oujda 6 Agadir, Meknès 7 Kenitra, Tangier 9 Marrakech, Marrakesh 10 Casablanca *Mozambique:* 5 Beira 7 Chimoio, Nampula 9 Quelimane, Quilimane *Myanmar:* 3 Pyu 4 Paan 5 Akyab, Bhamo, Chauk, Katha, Magwe, Minbu, Mogok, Tavoy 7 Bassein 8 Mandalay, Moulmein *Namibia:* 5 Outjo 6 Tsumeb 8 Oshakati 12 Keetmanshoop *Nebraska:* 3 Ord 5 Cozad, Omaha, Ponca, Tryon, Wahoo 6 Elwood, Gering, McCook, Minden, Wilber 7 Burwell, Fremont, Kearney, Kimball, Osceola, Tekamah 8 Beatrice, Fairbury, Hastings, Ogallala, Red Cloud, Schuyler, Tecumseh, Thedford 9 Fullerton, Papillion 10 Springview, Stockville 11 Grand Island, Hayes Center, North Platte, Plattsmouth *Netherlands:* 3 Ede, Epe, Oss 4 Echt, Tiel, Uden 5 Aalst, Assen, Breda, Delft, Emmen, Hague, Soest, Vaals, Venlo, Vught, Weert, Weesp, Zeist 6 Arnhem 7 Haarlem, Tilburg, Utrecht 8 Enschede, Nijmegen, The Hague 9 Apeldoorn, Eindhoven, Groningen, Rotterdam, Zandvoort 10 Maastricht *Nevada:* 3 Ely 4 Elko, Reno 6 Fallon, Minden, Pioche 7 Tonopah 8 Las Vegas, Lovelock 9 Goldfield, Yerington 10 Winnemucca *New Brunswick:* 5 Minto 6 St. John 7 Moncton 9 Dalhousie, Saint John 10 Edmundston, Richibucto 12 Hopewell Cape, Perth Andover, Saint Andrews *Newfoundland:*

5 Burin 6 Wabana 10 Mount Pearl 11 Corner Brook *New Hampshire:* 5 Derry, Dover, Keene 6 Berlin, Exeter, Gorham, Nashua 7 Hanover, Laconia, Lebanon, Ossipee 8 Hinsdale, Seabrook 9 Littleton, Merrimack 10 Manchester, Portsmouth, Woodsville *New Jersey:* 4 Atco, Lodi 6 Camden, Newark, Nutley, Rahway, Rumson 7 Bayonne, Cape May, Clifton, Hoboken, Paramus, Passaic, Raritan, Teaneck 8 Freehold, Metuchen, Paterson, Vauxhall, Woodbury 9 Belvidere, Bridgeton, Elizabeth, Glassboro, Lakehurst, Maplewood, Menlo Park, Montclair, Princeton, Riverside, Toms River 10 Asbury Park, Bloomfield, Cherry Hill, East Orange, Flemington, Hackensack, Jersey City, Morristown, Mount Holly, Perth Amboy, Piscataway, Plainfield, Somerville, West Orange 11 Mays Landing, South Orange 12 Atlantic City, New Brunswick 13 Palisades Park *New Mexico:* 4 Taos 5 Belen, Hobbs, Raton 6 Clovis, Deming, Grants 7 Roswell, Socorro 8 Estancia, Los Lunas, Portales 9 Carrizozo, Las Cruces, Los Alamos, Lovington, Tucumcari 10 Alamogordo, Bernalillo, Fort Sumner 11 Albuquerque *New York:* 4 Elma, Ovid, Troy 5 Depew, Ilion, Islip, Le Roy, Nyack, Olean, Owego, Utica 6 Attica, Cohoes, Delmar, Elmira, Hudson, Ithaca, Oneida 7 Batavia, Buffalo, Corning, Geneseo, Katonah, Mineola, Penn Yan, Suffern, Yonkers 8 Bay Shore, Cortland, Herkimer, Hyde Park, Kingston, Lockport, Mayville, Ossining, Syracuse, Valhalla 9 Greenport, Hempstead, Patchogue, Riverhead, Rochester, Scarsdale, Schoharie 10 Binghamton, Glens Falls, Haverstraw, Huntington, Lackawanna, Lake George, Lake Placid, Mamaroneck, Massapequa, Mount Kisco, Plattsburg, Rensselaer, Watervliet 11 Canajoharie, Canandaigua, Cooperstown, Farmingdale, Hudson Falls, Plattsburgh, Port Chester, Saint George, Schenectady, Southampton, Watkins Glen, White Plains 12 Lake Pleasant, Poughkeepsie 13 Mechanicville, Port Jefferson *New Zealand:* 4 Hutt, Tawa 5 Levin, Taupo, Waihi 7 Dunedin, Manukau 8 Auckland 12 Christchurch *Nicaragua:* 4 León 5 Boaco, Rivas 6 Masaya 7 Granada *Nigeria:* 3 Aba, Ado, Ede, Ife, Ila, Iwo, Jos, Owo, Oyo 4 Kano, Ondo 5 Akure, Enugu, Gusau, Lagos, Okene, Zaria 6 Ibadan, Ilesha, Ilorin, Kaduna, Mushin, Sokoto 7 Onitsha, Oshogbo

8 Abeokuta 9 Maiduguri, Ogbomosho
12 Port Harcourt *North Carolina:*
4 Dunn 5 Ayden, Elkin, Erwin, Oteen,
Sylva 6 Dobson, Durham, Lenoir, Man-
teo, Marion, Shelby, Winton 7 Bay-
boro, Brevard, Edenton, Kinston, New
Bern, Newland, Roxboro, Sanford, Tar-
boro 8 Asheboro, Beaufort, Gastonia,
Hatteras, Snow Hill 9 Albemarle,
Asheville, Charlotte, Currituck, High
Point, Kitty Hawk, Louisburg, Lum-
berton, Morganton 10 Chapel Hill,
Greensboro, Mocksville, Smithfield,
Wilkesboro 11 Statesville, Yanceyville
12 Murfreesboro, Winston-Salem *North
Dakota:* 4 Mott 5 Cando, Fargo, Minot,
Rolla 6 Amidon, Ashley, Bowman, For-
mon, Lakota, Linton, Medora, Mohall
8 Wahpeton, Washburn 9 Dickinson,
Williston 10 Devils Lake, Grand Forks
Northern Ireland: 5 Derry, Larne, Newry,
Omagh 6 Antrim, Armagh 9 Bally-
mena, Coleraine, Craigavon, Dungan-
non 10 Ballymoney 11 Ballycastle,
Downpatrick, Enniskillen, Londonder-
ry 13 Carrickfergus *North Korea:*
5 Haeju, Nampo 6 Wonsan 7 Hamhung,
Kaesong, Sinuiju 8 Ch'ongjin, Kim-
chaek 9 P'yongyang *Northwest Territories:* 6 Dawson 10 Whitehorse 11 Yellowknife *Norway:* 4 Bodo 5 Hamar,
Skien, Vardo 6 Bergen, Tromso
8 Kirkenes 9 Stavanger, Trondheim
10 Hammerfest 12 Kristiansand *Nova
Scotia:* 5 Digby 6 Pictou 7 Arichat, Bad-
deck 8 Port Hood 9 Dartmouth,
Kentville, Lunenburg, Shelburne,
Westville 10 Antigonish 11 Guysbor-
ough *Ohio:* 4 Kent 5 Akron, Berea,
Bryan, Carey, Eaton, Heath, Logan,
Niles, Parma, Piqua, Solon, Xenia
6 Canton, Celina, Dayton, Elyria,
Euclid, Kenton, Lorain, Marion, Medi-
na, Sidney, Tiffin, Toledo 7 Ashland,
Batavia, Bucyrus, Chardon, Findlay,
Ironton, Oakwood, Pomeroy, Ravenna,
Wauseon, Wooster 8 Conneaut, Mariet-
ta, Sandusky 9 Ashtabula, Cleveland,
Coshocton, Mansfield 10 Cincinnati,
Gallipolis, Wapakoneta, Zanesville
11 Chillicothe, Circleville, Millersburg,
Mount Gilead, Painesville, Port Clinton
12 Steubenville 13 Bellefontaine, Cuya-
hoga Falls *Oklahoma:* 3 Ada 4 Alva,
Enid 5 Altus, Atoka, Sayre, Tulsa
6 Durant, El Reno, Guymon, Idabel,
Lawton, Okemah, Poteau, Wewoka
7 Antlers, Ardmore, Cordell, Eufaula,
Newkirk, Purcell, Sapulpa, Watonga
8 Anadarko, Okmulgee, Pawhuska, Sal-
lisaw, Stilwell 9 Chickasha, Claremore,

Frederick, McAlester, Wilburton
10 Stillwater, Tishomingo 11 Pauls Valley 12 Bartlesville *Oman:* 3 Sur
6 Matrah 7 Salalah *Ontario:* 4 Ajax,
Wawa, York 6 Barrie, Guelph, Kenora,
London, Oshawa, Sarnia, Simcoe
7 Cobourg, Markham, Napanee, Sudbury, Windsor 8 Brampton, Cochrane,
Goderich, Hamilton, North Bay, Pem-
broke, Prescott 9 Brantford, Etobicoke, Kitchener, L'Original, Newmarket, North York, Owen Sound,
Walkerton 10 Belleville, Brockville,
Burlington, Haileybury, Parry Sound,
Thunder Bay 11 Bracebridge, Fort
Frances, Mississauga, Scarborough
12 Peterborough, St. Catharines *Oregon:* 5 Canby, Nyssa 6 Eugene
8 Coquille, La Grande, Portland, Rose-
burg 9 Clackamas, Corvallis, Gold
Beach, Pendleton, The Dalles, Tilla-
mook 10 Grants Pass 12 Klamath Falls
Pakistan: 5 Bannu, Bhera, Kasur, Kohat
6 Gujrat, Lahore, Mardan, Multan,
Quetta, Sukkur 7 Karachi, Sialkot
8 Lyallpur, Peshawar, Sargodha
9 Hyderabad 10 Bahawalpur, Faisalabad, Gujranwala, Rawalpindi
Paraguay: 3 Itá 4 Yuty 5 Luque, Pilar
7 Caacupé, Caazapa 9 Paraguarí 10 San
Lorenzo *Papua New Guinea:* 3 Lae
10 Mount Hagen, Popondetta *Pennsylvania:* 4 Erie, York 5 Avoca, Darby,
Muncy, Paoli 6 Easton 7 Altoona, Bedford, Clarion, Hanover, Hershey,
Latrobe, Reading, Ridgway, Sunbury
8 Carlisle, Edinboro, Hazleton, Mont-
rose, Scranton, Somerset 9 Allentown,
Ebensburg, Honesdale, Jim Thorpe,
Lancaster, Lewisburg, Lock Haven,
Meadville, New Castle, Wellsboro
10 Bloomsburg, Brookville, Carbon-
dale, Clearfield, Gettysburg, Greens-
burg, Huntingdon, Kittanning, Mc-
Keesport, Middleburg, Pittsburgh,
Pottsville, Waynesburg 11 Stroudsburg,
Valley Forge, West Chester, Wilkes-
Barre 12 Philadelphia, State College,
Williamsport *Peru:* 3 Ica, Ilo 5 Ancon,
Cuzco, Jauja, Junin, Lamas, Pisco,
Piura, Tacna 6 Callao 8 Arequipa, Chi-
clayo, Chimbote, Trujillo *Philippines:*
3 Iba 4 Bago, Bais, Boac, Bogo, Cebu,
Daet, Jolo, Lipa, Mati 5 Basco, Bulan,
Cadiz, Danao, Davao, Digos, Gapan,
Gubat, Iriga, Laoag, Ormoc, Pasay,
Silay, Tagum, Vigan 6 Butuan, Iloilo,
Quezon 7 Angeles, Bacolod, Basilan
8 Batangas, Calbayog, Caloocan 9 Zam-
boanga 10 Quezon City *Poland:* 4 Lodz,
Nysa, Pila, Zary 5 Bytom, Bytow,

Chelm, Kutno, Lomza, Luban, Lubin, Plock, Radom, Torun, Tychy 6 Elblag, Gdansk, Gdynia, Kalisz, Kielce, Krakow, Lublin, Poznan, Rybnik, Zabrze 7 Chorzow, Dabrowa, Gliwice, Rzeszow, Wroclaw 8 Gornicza, Katowice, Szczecin 9 Bialystok, Bydgoszcz, Sosnowiec, Walbrzych 11 Czestochowa *Portugal:* 4 Faro 5 Braga, Evora, Porto 6 Almada, Oporto, Queluz 7 Amadora 8 Barreiro, Santarém *Prince Edward Island:* 10 Summerside *Puerto Rico:* 5 Ponce 6 Caguas 7 Arecibo, Bayamón 8 Carolina, Guaynabo, Mayagüez *Quebec:* 4 Alma 5 Amqui, Anjou, Gaspé, Laval, Lévis, Magog, Percé, Rouyn 6 Granby, Ham Sud, Matane, Ste.-Foy, Val d'Or 7 Bedford, Lachute 8 Beauport, Cap Santé, Joliette, Lac Brome, Maniwaki, Montreal, Rimouski, Roberval, Sept-Iles, Waterloo 9 Bécancour, Cookshire, Iberville, Inverness, La Malbaie, La Prairie, Longueuil, Montmagny, Sainte-Foy, Saint Jean, Tadoussac, Vaudreuil 10 Baie-Comeau, Chicoutimi 11 Beauharnois, Louiseville, Mont-Laurier 12 Charlesbourg 13 Trois-Rivières *Rhode Island:* 7 Newport, Rumford, Warwick 8 Apponaug, Coventry, Cranston, Tiverton, Westerly 9 Hopkinton, Pawtucket 10 Woonsocket 12 Narragansett, West Kingston *Romania:* 3 Dej 4 Aiud, Arad, Cluj, Deva, Husi, Iasi 5 Anina, Bacau, Buzau, Carei, Lugoj, Sibiu, Turda 6 Braila, Brasov, Galati, Oradea 7 Craiova 8 Ploiesti 9 Constanta, Timisoara 10 Cluj-Napoca *Russia:* 3 Kem, Ufa 4 Inta, Luga, Okha, Omsk, Orel, Orsk, Perm, Tula, Tura, Zima 5 Aldan, Artem, Chita, Ishim, Kansk, Kazan, Lysva, Onega, Penza, Pskov, Rzhev, Salsk, Serov, Sochi, Sokol, Tomsk, Tulun, Volsk, Yurga 6 Bratsk, Grozny, Kaluga, Kovrov, Kurgan, Rostov, Ryazan, Samara, Syzran, Tambov, Tyumen, Vyborg, Yelets 7 Irkutsk, Ivanovo, Izhevsk, Kalinin, Kolomna, Lipetsk, Magadan, Norilsk, Rybinsk, Saransk, Saratov, Shakhty, Vologda, Yakutsk, Zhdanov 8 Belgorod, Kemerovo, Kostroma, Murmansk, Nakhodka, Novgorod, Orenburg, Smolensk, Taganrog, Vladimir, Volzhski, Voronezh 9 Archangel, Astrakhan, Berezniki, Krasnodar, Serpukhov, Stavropol, Ulyanovsk, Volgograd, Yaroslavl 10 Cheboksary, Dzerzhinsk 11 Arkhangel'sk, Chelyabinsk, Cheremkhovo, Cherepovets, Kaliningrad, Krasnoyarsk, Novosibirsk,

St. Petersburg, Vladivostok 13 Yekaterinburg *Saskatchewan:* 8 Moose Jaw 9 Saskatoon 10 Assiniboia 12 Prince Albert *Saudi Arabia:* 4 Jauf, Taif 5 Jedda, Jidda, Mecca, Tabuk 6 Jeddah, Jiddah, Medina 8 Buraydah *Scotland:* 3 Ayr 4 Alva, Caol, Dyce, Oban 5 Alloa, Annan, Beith, Cowie, Cupar, Dalry, Ellon, Kelso, Kelty, Largs, Leven, Nairn, Patna, Troon 6 Dundee 7 Glasgow, Paisley 8 Aberdeen, Greenock, Hamilton 9 Inverness, Lockerbie 10 Kilmarnock 11 Dunfermline, John o'Groats *Senegal:* 5 Thiès 6 Kaolak 7 Kaolack 10 Saint-Louis *Serbia:* 3 Bor, Nis, Pec 4 Ruma 5 Becej, Cacak, Pirot, Sabac, Senta, Vrbas, Vrsac 7 Novi Sad 8 Subotica 10 Kragujevac *Slovakia:* 5 Nitra 6 Kosice, Presov, Zilina *Slovenia:* 4 Bled 5 Celje, Koper, Kranj 7 Maribor *Somalia:* 3 Eil 5 Afgoi, Alula, Brava, Burao, Marka, Obbia 7 Berbera, Kismayu 8 Hargeysa, Kismaayo *South Africa:* 5 Brits, Ceres, De Aar, Nigel, Paarl 6 Benoni, Durban, Soweto 7 Springs 8 Boksburg, Mafeking 9 Germiston, Kimberley, Ladysmith, Uitenhage 10 East London 11 Krugersdorp, Vereeniging 12 Johannesburg 13 Port Elizabeth *South Carolina:* 5 Aiken, Cayce, Saxon 6 Sumter 7 Gaffney, Laurens, Manning, Pickens 8 Beaufort, Newberry, Rock Hill, Walhalla 9 Abbeville, Allendale, Greenwood, Kingstree, McCormick, Winnsboro 10 Charleston, Darlington, Greenville, Hilton Head, Orangeburg, Walterboro 11 Bishopville, Myrtle Beach, Spartanburg 12 Moncks Corner *South Dakota:* 7 Sturgis, Yankton 8 Deadwood, Elk Point 9 Brookings, Rapid City 10 Sioux Falls *South Korea:* 3 Iri 4 Yosu 5 Cheju, Masan, Mokpo, Pusan, Suwon, Taegu, Ulson, Wonju 6 Chinju, Chonju, Inchon, Kunsan, Taejon 7 Kwangju *Spain:* 4 Adra, Baza, Elda, Jaca, Jaén, León, Loja, Lugo, Olot, Reus, Vich, Vigo 5 Albox, Alcoy, Alora, Baena, Cádiz, Ceuta, Cieza, Ecija, Eibar, Elche, Gijón, Ibiza, Jodar, Lorca, Mahon, Oliva, Osuna, Palma, Ronda, Soria, Ubeda 6 Bilbao, Burgos, Cuenca, Huelva, Lérida, Málaga, Mérida, Murcia, Oviedo, Toledo 7 Almadén, Almería, Cáceres, Córdoba, Durango, Granada, Segovia, Sevilla, Seville, Tarrasa, Vitoria 8 Albacete, Alicante, La Coruña, Pamplona, Sabadell, Valencia, Zaragoza 9 Algeciras, Barcelona, Salamanca, Santander, Saragossa, Tarragona 10 Hospitalet, Valladolid 12 San Sebastián *Sri Lanka:* 5 Galle, Kandy 6 Jaffna 8 Dehiwala, Moratuwa 10 Batticaloa *Sudan:* 4 Juba 5 Kodok, Kosti 7 El Obeid, Kassala 8 Omdurman *Sweden:* 4 Lund, Täby, Umea 5 Falun, Gävle, Lulea, Malmö, Växjö, Visby 6 Orebro 7 Uppsala 8 Göteborg, Halmstad 9 Jönköping, Linköping 12 Kristianstad *Switzerland:* 3 Zug 4 Biel, Chur, Sion, Thun 5 Aarau, Arbon, Baden, Basel, Koniz 6 Geneva, Lugano, St. Gall, Zürich 7 Lucerne, Zermatt 8 Lausanne, Montreux, St. Moritz 9 Neuchâtel, Saint Gall 11 Saint Moritz *Syria:* 4 Hama, Homs 5 Idlib 6 Aleppo, Tartus 7 Latakia *Taiwan:* 5 Chia-i 6 T'ai-nan 7 Chi-lung, Hsin-chu 8 Feng-shan, Panch'iao, San-ch'ung, T'ai-chung 9 Kaohsiung *Tanzania:* 5 Lindi, Mbeya, Tanga 6 Arusha, Dodoma, Kigoma, Mwanza 8 Morogoro, Zanzibar 11 Dar es Salaam *Tennessee:* 5 Alcoa, Erwin, Rives 6 Loudon, Ripley, Selmer 7 Memphis, Waverly 8 Gallatin, Oak Ridge, Rutledge, Tazewell, Wartburg 9 Dandridge, Dyersburg, Jacksboro, Jonesboro, Knoxville, Lewisburg, Maryville 10 Cookeville, Crossville, Somerville, Waynesboro 11 Blountville, Chattanooga, Clarksville, Greeneville, McMinnville, Rogersville, Sevierville, Shelbyville 12 Elizabethton, Lawrenceburg, Madisonville, Murfreesboro *Texas:* 4 Azle, Waco 5 Alvin, Anson, Baird, Bowie, Bryan, Clute, Cuero, Emory, Ennis, Freer, Hondo, Marfa, Mexia, Olney, Pampa, Pecos, Pharr, Plano, Sealy, Vidor, Wylie 6 Belton, Boerne, Bonham, Burnet, Conroe, Dallas, Del Rio, Denton, El Paso, Gilmer, Goliad, Jayton, Lamesa, Laredo, Linden, Lufkin, Odessa, Seguin, Sinton, Uvalde 7 Abilene, Anahuac, Bandera, Bastrop, Brenham, Denison, Dimmitt, Houston, Kaufman, Kountze, Lubbock, Midland, Wharton 8 Amarillo, Angleton, Beaumont, Beeville, Cleburne, Eastland, Giddings, Gonzales, Granbury, Groveton, Hemphill, La Grange, Lampasas, Longview, McKinney, Monahans, Montague, Pearsall, Rockwall, Stinnett 9 Arlington, Ballinger, Bellville, Big Spring, Brownwood, Corsicana, Crosbyton, Eagle Pass, Fort Worth, Galveston, Groesbeck, Henrietta, Hillsboro, Kerrville, Levelland, Palo Pinto, Plainview, San Angelo, San Marcos, Woodville 10 Brownfield, Coldspring, Gatesville, Jourdanton, Kingsville, Port Arthur,

Port Lavaca, San Antonio, Sweetwater, Waxahachie 11 Brownsville, Floresville, Littlefield, Nacogdoches, Weatherford 12 Breckenridge, Daingerfield, Fort Stockton, New Braunfels, Raymondville, Stephenville, Wichita Falls 13 Corpus Christi, Hallettsville *Thailand:* 3 Nan, Tak 5 Phrae, Roi Et, Surin 8 Songkhla 9 Chiang Mai 10 Nonthaburi *Tunisia:* 4 Béja, Sfax 5 Gabès, Gafsa, Susah 6 Ariana 7 Bizerte, Safaqis *Turkey:* 5 Adana, Bursa, Izmir, Konya, Sivas 6 Edirne, Erzurm, Samsun 7 Antakya, Antalya, Antioch, Kayseri, Malatya 8 Istanbul 9 Eskisehir, Gallipoli, Gaziantep 10 Diyarbakir *Turkmenistan:* 8 Nebit Dag 9 Chardzhou, Dashhowuz *Uganda:* 5 Jinja, Mbale 7 Entebbe *Ukraine:* 4 Lviv, Lvov, Sumy 5 Lutsk, Rovno, Yalta 6 Odessa 7 Donetsk, Kharkiv, Kharkov, Kherson, Luhansk, Poltava 8 Mariupol, Vinnitsa, Zhitomir 9 Chernigov, Chernobyl, Krivoy Rog, Krivyy Rih, Nikolayev 10 Kirovograd, Sebastopol, Sevastopol, Simferopol, Zaporozhye *United Arab Emirates:* 5 Ajman, Dubai 6 Dubayy 8 Fujairah, Fujayrah *Uruguay:* 4 Melo 5 Minas, Pando, Rocha, Salto 6 Rivera 8 Paysandú 10 Las Piedras *Utah:* 3 Loa 4 Lehi, Orem 5 Manti, Ogden, Provo, Sandy 6 Dugway, Tooele 7 Parowan 8 Duchesne 9 Coalville 11 Saint George *Uzbekistan:* 5 Nukus 6 Kokand 7 Bukhara, Fergana 8 Andizhan, Chirchik, Namangan 9 Samarkand, Samarqand *Venezuela:* 4 Coro 5 Anaco, Cagua 6 Cumaná, Mérida, Petare 7 Cabimas, Guayana, Maracay 8 Valencia 9 Maracaibo 12 Barquisimeto, San Cristóbal *Vermont:* 5 Barre 7 Rutland 8 St. Albans 10 Bennington, Burlington, Middlebury 11 Brattleboro, Saint Albans, St. Johnsbury *Vietnam:* 3 Hue 4 Vinh 5 Da Lat, Hoi An, My Tho 6 Can Tho, Da Nang, Saigon 7 Bien Hoa, Nam Dinh, Qui Nhon 8 Haiphong, Nha Trang, Thanh Hoa 9 Long Xuyen *Virginia:* 4 Tabb 5 Luray 6 Grundy 7 Accomac, Boydton, Fairfax, Hampton, New Kent, Norfolk 8 Abingdon, Culpeper, Leesburg, Manassas, Montross, Nottoway, Poquoson, Powhatan, Rustburg, Tazewell 9 Arlington, Clintwood, Courtland, Dinwiddie, Eastville, Farmville, Fincastle, Goochland, Lunenburg, Lynchburg 10 Alexandria, Appomattox, Berryville, Front Royal, Hillsville, Jonesville, King George, Lovingston, Pearisburg, Portsmouth, Rocky Mount, Wytheville 11 Heaths-

ville, King William, Newport News
12 Chesterfield, Prince George, Spotsylvania, Williamsburg *Wales:* **4** Rhyl
5 Neath, Risca, Tenby, Tywyn **7** Cardiff, Cwmbran, Denbigh, Harlech, Newport, Swansea **8** Aberdare, Bridgend **10** Caernarfon, Caernarvon, Llangollen
11 Aberystwyth *Washington:* **4** Omak
5 Brier, Camas, Kelso, Lacey, Pasco, Selah **6** Asotin, Colfax, Tacoma, Yakima **7** Ephrata, Everett, Prosser, Redmond, Seattle, Spokane **8** Chehalis, Colville, Okanogan **9** Montesano, Ritzville, Snohomish, Wenatchee
10 Bellingham, Coupeville, Ellensburg, Goldendale, Walla Walla, Waterville
11 Port Angeles, Port Orchard **12** Friday Harbor, Port Townsend *West Virginia:* **5** Nitro, Welch **6** Elkins, Hamlin, Hinton, Keyser, Ripley **7** Beckley, Weirton **8** Kingwood, Philippi, Wheeling
9 Pineville, Wellsburg **10** Buckhannon, Clarksburg, Huntington, Moorefield, Morgantown, Petersburg, Williamson
11 Harrisville, Martinsburg, Moundsville, Parkersburg **12** Harpers Ferry, Summersville **13** New Cumberland, Point Pleasant *Wisconsin:* **4** Kiel **5** Ripon, Tomah **6** Antigo, Barron, Oconto, Racine, Wausau **7** Baraboo, Chilton, Elkhorn, Hayward, Kenosha, Mauston, Merrill, Oshkosh, Shawano, Viraqua, Waupaca, Wautoma **8** Appleton, Green Bay, Kewaunee, La Crosse, Montello, Phillips, Washburn, Waukesha, West Bend **9** Eau Claire, Ellsworth, Fond du Lac, Green Lake, Ladysmith, Manitowoc, Marinette, Menomonie, Milwaukee, Sheboygan, Shell Lake, Wauwatosa, West Allis, Whitehall **10** Balsam Lake, Darlington, Dodgeville, Eagle River, Grantsburg, Janesville **11** Neillsville, Sturgeon Bay **12** Stevens Point, Whitefish Bay *Wyoming:* **6** Casper, Lander **7** Laramie, Rawlins **8** Gillette, Kemmerer, Sheridan **10** Green River
11 Rock Springs *Yemen:* **4** Aden **5** Taizz **7** Hodeida, Mukalla **8** Hudaydah *Zambia:* **5** Kabwe, Kitwe, Mansa, Mbala, Mongu, Ndola **6** Kasama **7** Chipata *Zimbabwe:* **5** Gweru **6** Hwange, Kadoma, Kwekwe, Mutare, Umtali **7** Mashava **8** Bulawayo, Masvingo
civet 3 cat *Madagascar:* **5** fossa *relative:* **5** genet
civic 5 urban **6** public, social **8** communal, national, societal **9** municipal
civil 6 polite, public, seemly, urbane **7** affable, cordial, courtly, genteel, refined **8** decorous, gracious, mannerly, national, obliging, well-bred **9** courte-

ous, political **10** diplomatic **12** well-mannered **13** accommodating
civility 6 comity **7** amenity, decency, decorum, manners **8** courtesy **9** etiquette, gentility, propriety **10** politeness **11** correctness
civilization 7 culture
civilized 6 decent, proper, urbane **7** genteel, refined **8** decorous, mannerly, tasteful **9** courteous **10** cultivated **13** sophisticated
civil rights *leader:* **4** King (Martin Luther) *organization:* **4** ACLU, CORE **5** NAACP
Civil War *admiral:* **8** Buchanan (Franklin), Farragut (David) *battle:* **6** Shiloh **7** Bull Run **8** Antietam, Manassas **9** Mobile Bay, Nashville, Vicksburg **10** Cold Harbor, Gettysburg **11** Chattanooga, Chickamauga *general:* **3** Lee (Robert E.) **4** Hood (John Bell), Pope (John) **5** Bragg (Braxton), Buell (Don Carlos), Ewell (Richard Stoddart), Grant (Ulysses S.), Meade (George), Sykes (George) **6** Hooker (Joseph) **7** Forrest (Nathan Bedford), Jackson (Thomas "Stonewall"), Sherman (Thomas West, William Tecumseh) **8** Burnside (Ambrose), Johnston (Albert Sidney, Joseph Eggleston), Sheridan (Philip) **9** McClellan (George Brinton), Rosecrans (William), Schofield (John) **10** Beauregard (Pierre) *ship:* **7** Monitor **9** Merrimack
civil wrong 4 tort
clabber 5 curds
clack 3 gab, jaw, yak **4** blab, chat **5** prate **6** babble, cackle, gabble, gossip, jabber, rattle **7** blabber, chatter, clatter, palaver, prattle **9** yakety-yak
clad 4 face, side, skin **5** dress, faced **6** clothe, decked, garbed, outfit **7** attired, clothed, covered, dressed, overlay, sheathe **8** costumed, overlaid, sheathed **9** outfitted
claim 4 call, dibs, hold, plea, take **5** argue, exact, right, share, stake, title **6** adduce, allege, assert, defend, demand, insist **7** advance, call for, contend, declare, justify, profess, purport, require, solicit, warrant **8** interest, maintain **9** assertion, challenge, postulate, privilege **10** allegation, birthright **11** affirmation, declaration, prerogative, requisition **12** protestation
clairvoyance 3 ESP **7** insight **9** intuition, telepathy **10** sixth sense **11** penetration, second sight **12** precognition
clairvoyant 4 seer **5** sibyl **7** diviner **8** telepath **10** soothsayer
clam 4 buck **5** razor **6** dollar, quahog

7 bivalve, coquina, geoduck, mollusc, mollusk, smacker, steamer 11 cherrystone *genus:* 3 Mya

clamant 4 dire 6 crying, urgent 7 blatant, burning, exigent 8 pressing 9 insistent 10 compelling, imperative

clamber 5 climb, crawl, scale, swarm 8 scrabble, scramble, struggle

clammy 4 cool, dank, damp 5 close, moist, slimy 6 sticky

clamor 3 cry, din 4 bawl, roar, to-do 5 babel, hoo-ha, noise 6 bellow, demand, hubbub, jangle, outcry, racket, ruckus, tumult, uproar 7 agitate, dispute, ferment, protest, turmoil 8 brouhaha, shouting 9 agitation, commotion 10 hullabaloo, hurly-burly 11 pandemonium

clamorous 5 noisy, vocal 6 crying, shrill, urgent 7 blatant, exigent, raucous, voluble 8 strident, vehement 9 insistent 10 boisterous, imperative, tumultuous, vociferous 11 importunate 12 obstreperous

clamp 4 grip, hold, vise 5 clasp, grasp 6 clench, clinch, clutch, fasten, secure 7 grapple

clamshell 6 bucket 7 grapple

clan 3 mob 4 camp, folk, ring, sept 5 cabal, house, stock, tribe 6 circle, clique, family 7 coterie, kindred, lineage 9 camarilla *emblem:* 5 totem

Clancy novel 12 Patriot Games 13 Sum of All Fears (The) 17 Hunt for Red October (The) 21 Clear and Present Danger

clandestine 6 covert, secret, sneaky 7 furtive, illicit 8 hush-hush, stealthy 10 undercover, under wraps 11 underhanded 12 hugger-mugger, illegitimate 13 surreptitious, under-the-table

clang 3 cry, din 4 ding, peal, slam 6 jangle 8 ding-dong

clangor 3 din 5 noise 6 clamor, jangle, racket, rattle, tumult, uproar 7 clatter, ringing 9 stridency 13 reverberation

clangorous 5 noisy 7 booming, rackety, ringing 8 clattery, sonorous 9 deafening 12 earsplitting

clap 3 pat 4 bang, blow, boom, slam, slap 5 blast, burst, crack, crash, whack 6 strike 7 applaud 8 applause

claptrap 4 bull, bunk 5 cheap, hokum, showy, trash 6 bunkum, drivel, humbug, vulgar 7 baloney, eyewash, hogwash, twaddle 8 malarkey, nonsense 9 poppycock 10 balderdash, flapdoodle

Clara Bow 6 It girl

Clare Boothe ___ 4 Luce

claret 3 red 4 wine 8 Bordeaux

clarify 5 clean, clear 6 define, filter, purify 7 analyze, cleanse, clear up, explain, resolve 8 simplify 9 elucidate 10 illuminate 13 straighten out

clarion 5 clear 7 ringing, rousing, trumpet 8 gleaming, stirring 9 brilliant

clarity 6 purity 8 accuracy, lucidity 9 clearness, limpidity, precision 10 exactitude, simplicity 12 transparency

Clarke novel 10 Earthlight 19 Fountains of Paradise (The)

clash 4 bump, jolt 5 brawl, crash, melee, set-to, smash 6 battle, fracas, impact, jangle 7 collide 8 conflict, mismatch, skirmish 9 collision, encounter 10 engagement 11 embroilment

clasp 3 hug, pin 4 clip, grip, hold 5 clamp, grasp, press 6 brooch, buckle, clench, clinch, clutch, enfold 7 embrace, grapple, squeeze 10 chatelaine

class 3 ilk 4 hold, kind, mark, part, rank, rate, sort, tier, type 5 allot, brand, caste, gauge, genre, genus, grade, grain, group, judge, order, score, stamp, style 6 assess, assign, assort, branch, course, league, nature, reckon, regard, stripe 7 bracket, caliber, quality, section, species, variety 8 appraise, category, consider, division, evaluate, grouping, separate 10 categorize, pigeonhole 11 description 12 denomination *middle:* 11 bourgeoisie *school:* 6 junior, senior 8 freshman 9 sophomore *working:* 11 proletariat

classic 5 ideal, model, prime 7 capital, typical, vintage 8 champion, enduring, standard, superior, top-notch 9 authentic, canonical, classical, excellent, exemplary, memorable, tradition 10 magnum opus, masterwork 11 chef d'oeuvre, masterpiece, tour de force, traditional 12 paradigmatic, prototypical 13 authoritative

classical 4 pure 5 Attic, Greek, ideal, Latin, Roman 7 ancient, fitting, Grecian, perfect, typical, vintage 8 Hellenic, standard, sterling 9 canonical, exemplary 10 consummate 11 traditional 13 authoritative

classical musician 4 Böhm (Karl), Hess (Myra), Lind (Jenny), Muti (Riccardo), Pons (Lily), Shaw (Robert) 5 Arrau (Claudio), Biggs (E. Power), Borge (Victor), Boult (Adrian), Davis (Colin), du Pré (Jacqueline), Gould (Glenn), Masur (Kurt), Mehta (Zubin), Melba (Nellie), Ozawa (Seiji), Patti (Adelina), Pinza (Ezio), Price (Leontyne), Ramey (Samuel), Sills (Beverly), Stern (Isaac), Szell (George) 6 Abbado (Claudio),

Battle (Kathleen), Boulez (Pierre), Callas (Maria), Caruso (Enrico), Casals (Pablo), Galway (James), Levine (James), Maazel (Lorin), Midori, Norman (Jessye), Peters (Roberta), Previn (André), Rampal (Jean-Pierre), Rattle (Simon), Reiner (Fritz), Serkin (Peter, Rudolf), Terfel (Bryn), Tucker (Richard), Upshaw (Dawn), Walter (Bruno) 7 Bartoli (Cecilia), Beecham (Thomas), Bocelli (Andrea), Brendel (Alfred), Cliburn (Van), Corelli (Franco), Domingo (Plácido), Farrell (Eileen), Fiedler (Arthur), Fleming (Renée), Glennie (Evelyn), Haitink (Bernard), Heifetz (Jascha), Karajan (Herbert von), Menuhin (Yehudi), Nilsson (Birgit), Ormandy (Eugene), Perlman (Itzhak), Pollini (Maurizio), Sargent (Malcolm), Segovia (Andrés), Tebaldi (Renata) 8 Anderson (Marian), Argerich (Martha), Bergonzi (Carlo), Carreras (José), Flagstad (Kirsten), Horowitz (Vladimir), Kreisler (Fritz), Marriner (Neville), Oistrakh (David), Schnabel (Artur), Te Kanawa (Kiri), Zukerman (Pinchas) 9 Barenboim (Daniel), Bernstein (Leonard), Chaliapin (Feodor), Klemperer (Otto), Landowska (Wanda), Pavarotti (Luciano), Stokowski (Leopold), Toscanini (Arturo) 10 Rubinstein (Arthur), Sutherland (Joan), Tetrazzini (Luisa) 11 Furtwängler (Wilhelm), Kostelanetz (André), Schwarzkopf (Elisabeth) 12 Rostropovich (Mstislav)

classification 4 sort, type 5 genre, genus, grade, order 6 family, phylum, rating 7 sorting, species 8 category, division, grouping, ordering, taxonomy, typology 11 arrangement, cataloguing

classified 6 secret, sorted 7 divided, ordered 9 top secret 11 categorized 12 confidential

classify 4 rank, rate, sort 5 grade, group 6 assort 7 arrange 9 break down 10 categorize, pigeonhole

classy 4 chic, tony 5 swank 6 modish 7 dashing, elegant, refined, stylish 8 gracious, tasteful, well-bred 9 courteous 11 fashionable

clatter 4 to-do 6 clamor, hubbub, pother, rattle, tumult, uproar 7 turmoil 9 commotion 10 hurly-burly *Scottish:* 7 brattle

clattery 5 noisy 7 rackety 10 clangorous

Claudia's husband 6 Pilate

Claudio's beloved 4 Hero

Claudius *nephew:* 6 Hamlet *predecessor:* 8 Caligula *slayer:* 6 Hamlet 9 Agrippina

successor: 4 Nero *wife:* 8 Gertrude 9 Agrippina

Clavell novel 6 Gai-Jin, Shogun, Tai-Pan 7 King Rat

claw 3 dig 4 nail, rake, tear 5 chela, talon, uncus 6 scrape 7 scratch

clay 3 cob 4 loam, lute, marl 5 argil, brick, earth, gault, loess, ocher, ochre 6 kaolin 10 terra-cotta *baked:* 4 tile 5 adobe, brick *box:* 6 saggar, sagger *building:* 5 adobe *ceramic:* 10 terra-cotta *constituent:* 6 silica 8 feldspar, silicate 9 kaolinite *in glass:* 4 tear *made of:* 7 fictile *porcelain:* 6 kaolin *red:* 8 laterite *rock:* 5 shale *tobacco pipe:* 6 dudeen *watery mixture:* 4 slip *white:* 6 kaolin

clay pigeon 6 target

clean 4 dust, fair, pure, swab, tidy, wash, wipe 5 bathe, fresh, groom, purge, scour, scrub, sweep 6 bright, chaste, decent, neaten, purify, spruce, vacuum, washed 7 clarify, launder, sinless 8 hygienic, innocent, sanitary, sanitize, spotless, unsoiled 9 blameless, faultless, sparkling, stainless, undefiled, unsullied, untainted, wholesome 10 antiseptic, immaculate 11 unblemished 12 spick-and-span

clean-cut 4 trim 7 defined, precise 8 definite, explicit, specific 9 wholesome 10 definitive 11 categorical, unambiguous, well-groomed

cleaner see CLEANSER

cleanhanded 8 innocent 9 blameless

clean-limbed 4 trim 7 shapely 8 handsome 10 statuesque

cleanse 4 wash 5 purge, rinse 6 purify, refine 7 clarify, launder 8 lustrate, sanitize 9 disinfect, expurgate, sterilize

cleanser 3 lye 4 soap 9 detergent 10 antiseptic 12 disinfectant

cleansing 7 purging 8 ablution 9 catharsis, purgation 10 lustration 11 expurgation 12 purification

clear 3 get, net, pay, rid, win 4 earn, fade, fair, fine, free, gain, leap, lose, make, pure, well 5 close, empty, exact, fully, glean, lucid, overt, pay up, plain, quite, repay, solve, stark, sunny 6 acquit, gather, hurdle, limpid, obtain, pay off, pick up, secure, settle, simple, square, vacant, vacate, vanish 7 absolve, acquire, approve, audible, clarify, clarion, cleanse, clean up, defined, evident, explain, improve, legible, obvious, precise, rule out, satisfy, utterly 8 apparent, definite, distinct, entirely, explicit, knowable, luminous, manifest, palpable, pleasant, scot-free, shake off, surmount 9 authorize, cloudless, discharge, eliminate, elucidate, evaporate, exculpate, exonerate, extricate, liquidate, meliorate, negotiate, perfectly, unblurred, unclouded, vindicate 10 ameliorate, completely, illuminate, illustrate, openhanded, seethrough 11 conspicuous, disentangle, open-and-shut, perceptible, translucent, transparent, unambiguous, unequivocal 12 recognizable, unmistakable 13 uncomplicated

clearance 3 gap 4 sale 7 go-ahead, removal 8 approval 10 green light, permission 13 authorization

clear away 6 remove 7 take out

clear-cut 5 crisp, exact, plain 7 decided, precise 8 definite, distinct, explicit, manifest 10 definitive, pronounced, undisputed 11 categorical, indubitable, unambiguous, unequivocal 12 unquestioned

clear-eyed 6 astute 9 judicious, observant 10 discerning, perceptive

clearheaded 4 calm, cool 10 perceptive

clearing 3 gap 5 field, glade 7 opening 10 settlement

clear out 5 scoot, scram, split 6 beat it, begone, bug off, decamp, depart 7 buzz off, skiddoo, take off, vamoose 8 shove off 9 drive away, skedaddle 10 hightail it

clear-sightedness 6 acuity, acumen 8 keenness, sagacity 10 astuteness, shrewdness 11 discernment, penetration, percipience 12 perspicacity

clear up 5 solve 6 cipher, unfold 7 clarify, dope out, explain, resolve, unravel 8 decipher 9 elucidate, figure out 10 illuminate

clearwing 4 moth

cleat 4 bitt 5 chock 6 batten 7 bollard, dolphin

cleavage 4 rift 5 chasm, cleft, split 6 schism 7 fissure 8 crevasse 9 splitting

cleave 3 cut, hew 4 chop, join, link, rend, rive 5 carve, cling, sever, slice, split, stick, unite 6 adhere, divide, sunder 7 combine 8 dissever, separate

cleft 3 gap 4 rift 5 chasm, chink, clove, crack, gorge, gulch, split 6 clough, ravine, schism 7 crevice, fissure 8 cleavage

clemency 5 grace, mercy 6 lenity 7 caritas, charity 8 kindness, lenience, leniency, mildness 9 tolerance 10 compassion, gentleness, indulgence, sufferance, toleration 11 forbearance

clement 4 fair, kind, mild 5 balmy 6 benign, humane, kindly 7 lenient 8 merciful, tolerant 9 indulgent 10 benevolent, charitable, forbearing 13 compassionate

clench 4 grip, grit, hold 5 clamp, clasp, grasp 6 clutch 7 grapple

Cleopatra *attendant:* 4 Iras 8 Charmian *brother:* 7 Ptolemy *husband:* 7 Ptolemy *killer:* 3 asp *lover:* 6 Antony (Marc), Caesar (Julius) 7 Anthony (Mark) *river:* 4 Nile

Cleopatra's Needle 7 obelisk

clepsydra 9 timepiece 10 water clock

clerestory 7 gallery

clergy 7 canonry 8 ministry 9 churchmen, diaconate, pastorate, rabbinate 10 priesthood 11 cardinalate 13 ecclesiastics

clergyman 5 clerk, padre, vicar 6 bishop, cleric, curate, divine, father, parson, pastor, priest, rector 7 dominie, prelate 8 chaplain, clerical, minister, preacher, reverend, shepherd, sky pilot 9 churchman, pulpiteer 10 evangelist, missionary, sermonizer 12 ecclesiastic *American:* 4 Hale (Edward Everett), King (Martin Luther, Thomas Starr) 5 Eliot (John), Moody (Dwight), Stone (Barton Warren), Weems (Parson) 6 Dwight (Timothy), Finney (Charles), Graham (Billy), Holmes (John Haynes), Hooker (Thomas), Mather (Cotton, Increase, Richard), Merton (Thomas), Parker (Samuel, Theodore), Sunday (Billy), Taylor (Edward, Graham, Nathaniel William) 7 Beecher (Henry Ward, Lyman), Edwards (Jonathan), Harvard (John), Russell (Charles Taze) 10 Muhlenberg (Frederick Augustus, Henry Melchior, John Peter Gabriel) *English:* 4 Ward (Nathaniel, Seth, William George) 5 Donne (John), Paley (William), Smith (Henry "Silver-Tongued," John "The Sebaptist," Sidney) 6 Cotton (John), Fuller (Andrew, Thomas), Taylor (Jeremy, Rowland), Wesley (Charles, John) 7 Cranmer (Thomas), Parsons (Robert) 8 Kingsley (Charles) 10 Whitefield (George) *home:* 5 manse 6 priory 7 rectory 8 vicarage 9 monastery, parsonage *traveling:* 12 circuit rider

cleric see CLERGYMAN

clerisy 8 literati 10 illuminati 13 intellectuals

clerk 7 cashier 8 salesman 9 secretary 10 accountant, bookkeeper 11 salesperson 12 stenographer

clever 3 apt, sly 4 able, deft, good, keen 5 adept, alert, canny, funny, handy, quick, savvy, sharp, smart, witty 6 adroit, astute, brainy, bright, crafty, expert, shrewd, tricky 7 amusing, capable, cunning, knowing, skilled 8 fanciful, humorous, pleasing, skillful, talented 9 competent, dexterous, ingenious 10 proficient 11 intelligent, quickwitted, resourceful 12 entertaining

cliché 3 saw 6 truism 7 bromide 8 banality, buzzword, chestnut 9 platitude 10 shibboleth, stereotype 11 commonplace

clichéd 5 banal, bland, musty, stale, tired, trite, vapid 6 old-hat 7 humdrum, insipid, worn-out 8 bromidic, shopworn, timeworn 9 hackneyed 10 pedestrian, unoriginal 11 stereotyped 13 platitudinous, unimaginative

click 3 fit 4 snap, tick, work 5 agree, match 6 go over, pan out 7 come off, succeed

client 6 patron 7 patient, protégé 8 customer 9 dependent

clientele 4 fans 5 trade, train 6 custom, market, public 7 patrons, traffic 8 audience, patients, regulars, shoppers 9 customers 10 purchasers, supporters 12 constituency

cliff 4 crag 5 bluff, scarp 8 headland, palisade 9 precipice 10 escarpment

climacteric 4 apex, crux, cusp 5 acute 6 crisis 7 crucial 8 critical 9 menopause 11 culmination 12 change of life, turning point

climactic 4 peak 7 crucial, pivotal 8 critical, decisive, dramatic 9 momentous 10 definitive 11 culminating, determining

climate 6 medium, milieu 7 ambient 8 ambience 10 atmosphere 11 environment 12 surroundings

climax 3 cap 4 acme, apex, peak 5 crown 6 apogee, summit, top off 8 capstone, meridian, pinnacle 9 culminate 11 culmination

climb 4 go up, rise, soar 5 mount, scale, slope 6 ascend 7 clamber 8 escalate, increase

climbing 8 scandent

climbing iron 7 crampon

clinch 3 hug 4 grip, hold, seal 5 clamp, clasp, grasp, sew up 6 clutch, decide, ensure, lock up 7 confirm, embrace, grapple, squeeze 8 nail down

clincher 4 tire 5 proof 6 kicker 7 quietus 9 deathblow 10 smoking gun 11 affirmation, attestation, coup de grâce 12 confirmation 13 corroboration

cling 4 bond 5 stick 6 adhere, cleave, clutch, hold on, linger 8 adhesion 9 adherence

clingstone 5 peach

clink 3 can, jug, pen 4 brig, cell, coop, jail, stir 5 pokey, pound 6 cooler, jingle, lockup, prison, tingle, tinkle 7 slammer 8 hoosegow 9 calaboose

clinker 3 dud 4 bomb, bust, flop, goof, slag 5 botch, brick, error, lemon, loser 6 bummer, bungle, fiasco, howler, turkey 7 bloomer, blunder, failure, faux pas, mistake

clinkers 3 ash 4 slag 5 ashes 7 cinders

clinquant 5 gaudy 6 flashy, garish, tawdry, tinsel 8 specious 10 glittering 11 superficial

Clio see MUSE

clip 3 bob, cut, mow, pin 4 crop, hasp, pare, snip, sock, trim 5 block, clasp, prune, punch, shave, shear, slash 6 broach, brooch, fleece, reduce 7 curtail, cut back, cut down, shorten 8 magazine, truncate 10 abbreviate, overcharge

clique 3 set 4 camp, clan, club, gang, ring 5 cabal, crowd, mafia 6 circle 7 coterie, faction, in-group 9 camarilla

cloak 4 cape, mask, robe, veil, wrap 5 cover, guise 6 facade, joseph, mantle, screen, shroud, veneer 7 blanket, conceal, curtain, dress up, manteau, obscure 8 disguise 9 dissemble, semblance 10 camouflage 11 dissimulate *ancient Greek:* 7 chlamys *ancient Roman:* 7 pallium *Arab:* 3 aba *fur:* 7 pelisse *hooded:* 6 capote 7 burnous 8 burnoose *liturgical:* 4 cope *Moroccan:* 8 djellaba *over armor:* 6 tabard 7 surcoat *Spanish:* 5 manta

clobber 4 belt, drub, flay, lick, slam, slug, whip, whup 5 blast, brain, clout, pound, smash 6 hammer, thrash, wallop 7 shellac, trounce 8 demolish, lambaste

clochard 3 bum, vag 4 hobo 5 tramp 6 beggar, canter 7 drifter, floater, moocher, vagrant 8 deadbeat, derelict, vagabond 9 transient 10 freeloader, panhandler 11 bindle stiff

cloche 3 hat 5 cover, toque, tuque

clock 4 time 9 timepiece 11 chronometer *water:* 9 clepsydra

clocklike 5 exact 6 minute, prompt, strict, timely 7 precise, regular 8 accurate, punctual, reliable, thorough 9 assiduous 10 dependable, meticulous, scrupulous 11 painstaking 13 conscientious

clockmaker 10 horologist

clockwise 6 deasil 7 dextral 11 righthanded

Clockwork Orange author 7 Burgess (Anthony)

clod 3 gob, wad 4 boob, dolt, dope, hunk, lump, soil 5 chump, chunk, clump, dummy, dunce, earth 6 dimwit 8 dumbbell 9 blockhead, lamebrain

cloddish 7 boorish, ill-bred, loutish,

uncouth **8** churlish, clownish **9** unrefined **10** uncultured, unpolished **11** uncivilized

clodhopper 4 boor, boot, hick, lout **5** chuff, churl, clown, yokel **6** rustic **7** bumpkin, hayseed, redneck **9** chawbacon

clog 3 gum, jam, tax **4** fill, glut, load, plug, stop **5** block, choke, close, stuff **6** hamper, hinder **7** congest **8** encumber, obstruct, overload **10** impediment **11** encumbrance

cloister 5 abbey, court **6** arcade, garden **7** convent, retreat, seclude, shelter **9** courtyard, monastery, sequester

Cloister and the Hearth author 5 Reade (Charles)

cloistered 7 recluse **8** confined, hermetic, secluded **9** seclusive, withdrawn **11** sequestered

cloistered one 3 nun **4** monk

clone 4 copy **5** ditto **6** double, carbon **7** replica **9** duplicate, facsimile, replicate, reproduce **10** carbon copy, simulacrum **12** reproduction

Clorinda *beloved:* **7** Tancred *father:* **6** Senapo *guardian:* **6** Arsete *slayer:* **7** Tancred

close 3 end **4** near, nigh, shut, slam **5** block, cease, choke, humid, muggy, tight **6** ending, finale, finish, narrow, nearby, sticky, stuffy, sultry, windup, wrap up **7** airless, compact, crowded, stopper **8** abutting, adjacent, complete, conclude, finalize, intimate, obstruct, stifling **9** adjoining, cessation, condensed, terminate **10** conclusion, consummate, convenient, near-at-hand **11** constricted, neighboring, termination **12** confidential

closed-minded 4 deaf **6** narrow **8** obdurate **9** hidebound, obstinate, pigheaded, unbending **10** bullheaded, hardheaded **11** intractable

closefisted 5 cheap, mingy **6** frugal, stingy **7** miserly, thrifty **9** niggardly, penurious **13** penny-pinching

close in 3 hem **4** cage **5** fence, hedge **6** corral, immure **7** advance, confine, enclose, envelop, impound **8** approach, converge, encircle, enshroud, imprison, surround

close-knit 8 intimate

closely 4 hard **7** sharply **8** intently, minutely **9** carefully **11** searchingly **12** meticulously, scrupulously, thoughtfully **13** punctiliously

close match 6 toss-up

closemouthed 3 mum **4** mute **6** silent **7** laconic **8** reserved, reticent, taciturn **12** tight-mouthed

closeness 8 intimacy

close off 4 clog, plug **5** block **6** stop up **7** isolate, occlude **8** insulate **9** segregate, sequester

closet 6 covert, inside, office **7** cabinet, chamber, furtive, private **8** wardrobe **11** speculative, theoretical

closing 3 end **4** last, stop **5** final **6** ending, finish, latest, period, windup, wrap-up **7** curtain **8** eventual, terminal, ultimate **9** cessation **10** concluding **11** termination

closure 3 cap, end, lid **6** ending, finish **8** fastener **9** cessation

clot 3 gel, set **4** curd, glob, jell, lump **5** clump **6** curdle, gelate **7** congeal **8** coagulum, thrombus **9** coagulate **10** gelatinize *combining form:* **6** thromb **7** thrombo

cloth see FABRIC

clothe 3 tog **4** deck, do up, garb, robe **5** array, cloak, couch, drape, dress, endow, equip **6** attire, bedeck, outfit, swathe **7** apparel, costume, dress up **8** accouter

clothes 3 rig **4** duds, garb, rags, togs **5** array, dress, getup, habit **6** attire, outfit, things **7** apparel, costume, raiment, rigging, threads, toggery, vesture **8** garments, glad rags **9** vestments **11** habiliments *basket:* **6** hamper *civilian:* **5** mufti

clothes-moth genus 5 Tinea

clothespress 7 armoire **8** wardrobe

cloud 3 dim, fog, tar **4** blur, haze, mist, murk **5** addle, befog, brume, gloom, muddy, plume, smear, sully, taint **6** muddle, nebula, puzzle, shadow, smudge **7** besmear, confuse, obscure, perplex, tarnish **8** befuddle, besmirch, discolor, distract, overcast **9** obfuscate *type:* **6** cirrus, nimbus **7** cumulus, stratus **11** altocumulus, altostratus **12** cirrocumulus, cirrostratus, cumulonimbus, nimbostratus **13** stratocumulus

cloudburst 6 deluge, shower **7** monsoon, torrent **8** downpour, drencher, rainfall **10** outpouring

clouded 5 dusky, murky, shady **6** dreary, gloomy, somber, sombre **7** dubious, ominous, sunless, unclear **8** doubtful, overcast **9** ambiguous, equivocal, uncertain, unsettled **11** problematic

cloudless 4 fair, fine **5** clear, sunny **7** clarion **8** pleasant, rainless, sunshiny

cloud-like mass 6 nebula

cloudy 4 dull, hazy **5** dusky, foggy, heavy, misty, murky, vague **6** gloomy, opaque, somber, sombre **7** louring, obscure, tainted, unclear **8** confused, darkened, lowering, nebulous, overcast, vaporous **10** indistinct

clout 3 box, hit, rag 4 blow, cuff, poke, pull, slam, slap, slug, sock, swat, sway 5 paste, power, punch, smack, smite, whack 6 strike 9 influence

clove 4 bulb 5 spice 7 chopped, severed

clove hitch 4 knot

clover 5 lotus 6 alsike, ladino, lucern 7 alfalfa, berseem, lucerne, melilot, trefoil 8 four-leaf, shamrock 9 lespedeza *family:* 3 pea *genus:* 9 Trifolium

clown 3 wag 4 mime, zany 5 cutup, joker, Punch 6 jester, mummer 7 buffoon 8 comedian, jokester 9 harlequin, prankster 11 merry-andrew *French:* 7 Pierrot *operatic:* 5 buffo *Spanish:* 8 gracioso

clownish 4 rude 6 clumsy, gauche, oafish 7 awkward, boorish, ill-bred, loutish, lumpish, uncouth 8 churlish, cloddish 9 unrefined

cloy 4 fill, glut, jade, pall, sate 5 gorge 6 sicken 7 satiate, surfeit 8 overfill

cloying 4 icky 5 gushy, mushy, sappy, soppy 6 sticky, sugary 7 fulsome, gushing, maudlin, mawkish 9 excessive, schmaltzy, sickening 10 disgusting, lovey-dovey, nauseating, saccharine 11 distasteful, sentimental

club 3 bat, sap 4 beat, cosh, iron, mace 5 baton, billy, guild, lodge, order, union 6 cudgel, league 7 society 8 bludgeon, sodality, sorority 9 blackjack, truncheon 10 fellowship, fraternity, knobkerrie, nightstick 11 association, brotherhood *Australian:* 5 waddy *Irish:* 10 shillelagh

clubfoot 7 talipes

cluck 4 dodo, dolt, dope, fool 5 dunce 6 dimwit, nitwit 7 pinhead

clue 3 cue 4 hint, idea, lead, sign, tell, warn 6 advise, inform, notify, notion, tip-off 7 inkling 8 evidence, telltale 10 indication, intimation, suggestion

clump 3 gob, wad 4 clod, hunk, lump, mass, mess, plod 5 batch, bunch, chunk, group, stomp, tramp 6 bumble, bundle, lumber, parcel 7 cluster, galumph, stumble

clump of grass 4 tuft 6 tuffet 7 tussock

clumsy 5 bulky, gawky, inept, splay 6 clunky, gauche, klutzy, wooden 7 awkward, hulking, lumpish, uncouth, unhandy 8 bumbling, bungling, tactless, ungainly, unsubtle, unwieldy 9 all thumbs, graceless, ham-handed, inelegant, lumbering, maladroit 11 heavy-handed, inefficient

clumsy one 3 oaf 4 clod, goon, lout, slob 5 klutz 6 baboon, galoot, lummox 7 bumpkin, bungler, palooka 13 butterfingers

clunk 4 thud 5 clout, thump, whack 6 thwack, wallop

clunker 4 bomb, heap 5 crate, wreck 6 jalopy, junker 7 stinker 10 rattletrap

cluster 3 lot, set 4 band, bevy, crew, knot, pack 5 array, batch, bunch, clump, covey, group 6 bundle, clutch, gather 7 collect, package 8 assemble, assembly 9 aggregate, associate, gathering 10 accumulate

cluster bean 4 guar

clutch 4 grab, grip, hold, keep 5 catch, clamp, clasp, grasp, pinch, seize 6 bundle, clench, clinch, snatch 7 cluster, grapple

clutter 4 hash, mash, mess, muss, ruck 5 chaos, snarl, strew 6 jumble, litter, muddle 7 mélange, rummage 8 disarray, disorder, mishmash, shambles 9 confusion 10 hodgepodge

Clydesdale 5 horse 10 draft horse

Clymene *father:* 7 Oceanus *husband:* 7 Iapetus *mother:* 6 Tethys *son:* 5 Atlas 10 Epimetheus, Prometheus

Clytemnestra *brother:* 6 Castor, Pollux 10 Polydeuces *daughter:* 7 Electra 9 Iphigenia *father:* 9 Tyndareus *husband:* 9 Agamemnon *lover:* 9 Aegisthus *mother:* 4 Leda *slayer:* 7 Orestes *son:* 7 Orestes *victim:* 9 Agamemnon, Cassandra

Clytie *beloved:* 6 Apollo *form:* 9 sunflower 10 heliotrope

coach 3 bus, car 5 drill, stage, train, tutor 6 chaise, mentor 7 prepare, trainer 8 carriage, instruct 10 instructor

coadjutor 3 aid 4 aide 6 bishop, deputy 9 assistant 10 aide-de-camp, lieutenant

coagulate 3 gel, set 4 clot, jell 6 curdle 7 congeal, jellify, thicken 8 coalesce, condense, solidify 10 gelatinize, inspissate 11 concentrate, consolidate

coal *distillate:* 3 tar *dust:* 4 smut, soot 5 slack *element:* 6 carbon *fused leavings:* 4 slag 7 clinker *glowing:* 5 ember, gleed *hard:* 10 anthracite *lump:* 3 cob *miner:* 7 collier *region:* 4 Saar *residue:* 4 coke *soft:* 6 cannel 10 bituminous

coalesce 3 mix 4 fuse, join, link 5 blend, merge, unite 6 mingle 7 combine, conjoin 10 amalgamate

coalition 4 bloc, ring 5 party, union 6 fusion, league, merger 7 combine, melding, merging 8 alliance 9 anschluss 10 federation 11 affiliation, association, combination, confederacy, integration, unification 13 confederation, consolidation

coarse 3 raw 4 rude 5 bawdy, crass, crude, dirty, gross, rough, tacky 6 common, filthy, grainy, ribald, smutty, vulgar **7** boorish, obscene, raffish, raunchy, uncouth **8** granular, indecent **9** inelegant, roughneck, unrefined **10** uncultured **11** particulate **12** uncultivated

coast 4 bank **5** beach, drift, shore, slide **6** strand **7** seaside **8** littoral, seashore *of Antarctica:* **4** Knox

coastal 7 seaside **8** littoral, riverine

coaster 4 sled, tray **6** trader

coat 5 crust, glaze, gloss, layer, parka, plate, tunic **6** blazer, duster, finish, jacket, patina, raglan, reefer, ulster, veneer **7** cutaway **8** covering, mackinaw, tegument **9** newmarket, redingote **10** integument, mackintosh **11** windbreaker *animal:* **3** fur **4** hide, pelt, wool **6** pelage *fur-lined:* **7** pelisse *kind:* **3** pea, top **5** frock **6** trench *Levantine:* **6** caftan *of arms:* **5** crest **6** blazon, emblem, shield, tabard **8** blazonry **10** escutcheon *of egg white:* **5** glair **6** glaire *of mail:* **7** hauberk *soldier's:* **5** frock, tunic **6** capote *waterproof:* **7** slicker **10** mackintosh

coating 4 film, leaf, scum, skin **5** glaze, gloss, layer **6** finish, patina, veneer **7** dusting, lacquer, overlay, surface, varnish **8** covering

coax 4 lure, urge **5** cable, press, tempt **6** cajole, entice, induce **7** blarney, wheedle **8** blandish, butter up, inveigle, persuade, soft-soap **9** importune, sweet-talk

cob 3 ear **4** swan **5** adobe, horse

cobble 4 make, mend **5** patch, stone **6** repair **11** paving stone

cobbler 3 pie **5** drink **8** cocktail **9** shoemaker

cobbler's form 4 last

cobelligerent 4 ally

cobweb 3 net **4** mesh, trap **8** gossamer **9** confusion, spiderweb **12** entanglement

coccyx 8 tailbone

cochineal 3 dye **6** insect

cock 3 tap **4** boss, head, heap, hill, lord, mass, pile, rick, tilt **5** chief, mound, stack, strut, valve **6** faucet, honcho, leader, master, spigot **7** headman, hydrant, rooster, swagger **11** chanticleer

cock-a-hoop 4 awry **5** askew **7** askance, crooked **8** boastful, exultant, exulting, jubilant **9** triumphal **10** triumphant

Cockaigne 6 utopia **7** arcadia **9** Shangrila **10** wonderland

cockalorum 7 bluster, bombast, bravado **8** blowhard, boasting, braggart, leapfrog **11** braggadocio

cockamamy 5 batty, crazy, daffy, flaky, kooky, loony, nutty, wacky **6** absurd

9 ludicrous **10** incredible, ridiculous **11** harebrained

cock-and-bull story 5 crock **6** canard **7** whopper **9** fairy tale

cockcrow 4 dawn, morn **5** sunup **7** morning, sunrise **8** daybreak, daylight

cocker 4 baby **5** humor, spoil **6** coddle, cosset, pamper **7** indulge, spaniel **11** mollycoddle

cockeyed 4 awry **5** askew **8** lopsided **11** harebrained

cockle 5 shell **6** dimple, furrow, groove, pucker, ripple **7** bivalve, mollusc, mollusk, wrinkle

cockleshell 4 boat

cockscomb see COXCOMB

cocksure 5 brash **6** cheeky **9** bumptious **13** overconfident

cocktail 5 Bronx, drink **6** gibson, gimlet, mai tai, mimosa, mojito, Rob Roy, zombie **7** gin fizz, martini, sidecar, stinger **8** aperitif, daiquiri, pink lady, salty dog, sombrero **9** Cuba libre, manhattan, margarita, mint julep, rusty nail **10** Bloody Mary, Tom Collins, wallbanger **11** grasshopper, screwdriver, whiskey sour **12** black russian, cosmopolitan, old-fashioned *fruit:* **9** macedoine *gasoline:* **7** Molotov

Cocktail Party author 5 Eliot (T. S.)

cocky 4 bold, sure **5** brash, pushy, sassy, saucy **6** brassy, cheeky, jaunty **8** arrogant, impudent, insolent **9** conceited **10** swaggering **11** self-assured **12** enterprising **13** overconfident, self-confident

coconspirator 7 abettor **9** accessory **10** accomplice **11** confederate

coconut *husk fiber:* **4** coir *meat:* **5** copra

coda 5 envoi, envoy **6** ending, finale **7** summary **8** epilogue, follow-up **9** afterword **10** conclusion

coddle 4 baby **5** humor, spoil **6** cosset, pamper **7** cater to, indulge

code 6 cipher, symbol **7** encrypt **8** encipher *kind:* **3** zip **4** area **5** Morse, legal, penal *message in:* **10** cryptogram **11** cryptograph

code word see COMMUNICATIONS CODE WORD

codger 6 duffer, fellow

codicil 5 rider **8** addendum, addition, appendix **10** postscript, supplement

codswallop see NONSENSE

coefficient 6 factor **7** measure **8** constant

coelenterate 5 coral **7** anemone, hydroid **9** cnidarian, jellyfish **10** sea anemone

coerce 3 cow **5** bully, force, impel, press **6** compel, menace, oblige **8** browbeat, bulldoze, dominate, threaten **9** blackjack, constrain, strong-arm, terrorize **10** intimidate

coercion 5 force **6** duress, menace, threat
8 pressure **10** compulsion, constraint
Coeur d'___ 5 Alene
coeval see CONTEMPORARY
coexistent see CONTEMPORARY
coffee *alkaloid:* **8** caffeine *bean:* **3** nib
cake: **6** kuchen *cup:* **9** demitasse *French:*
4 café *grinder:* **4** mill *kind:* **4** drip, java
5 decaf, latte, mocha **7** arabica, instant
8 espresso **9** Americano, macchiato
10 café au lait, cappuccino *maker:*
10 percolator *pot:* **3** urn
coffee shop 4 café **5** diner **8** snack bar
9 cafeteria, hash house, lunchroom
11 greasy spoon **12** luncheonette
coffer 5 chest **6** casket **8** treasury
9 exchequer, strongbox
coffin 3 box **4** kist **6** casket *carrier:*
6 hearse **10** pallbearer *nail:* **9** cigarette
stand: **4** bier **10** catafalque
cogency 5 force, point, power, punch
7 potency **8** strength, validity **9** relevance **10** conviction, pertinence
13 effectiveness
cogent 5 solid, sound, valid **6** potent
7 telling, weighty **8** forceful, powerful,
relevant **9** pertinent **10** compelling,
convincing, meaningful, persuasive
11 influential, well-founded **12** well-
grounded **13** consequential
cogitate 4 muse **5** think **6** ponder, reason
7 reflect **8** conceive, consider, meditate,
mull over, ruminate **9** cerebrate, speculate **10** deliberate
cogitation 7 thought **10** meditation,
reflection, rumination **11** cerebration,
speculation **12** deliberation **13** consideration
cogitative 7 pensive **10** meditative,
reflective, ruminative, thoughtful
11 speculative **13** contemplative
Cogito ___ sum 4 ergo
cognac 6 brandy
cognate 4 akin, like **5** alike **6** allied,
common **7** kindred, related, similar
8 parallel **10** affiliated, associated
cognition 9 awareness, knowledge, sen-
tience **10** perception
cognizance 4 heed, note **6** notice
9 attention, awareness, knowledge
12 jurisdiction
cognizant 5 aware **7** knowing, mindful
8 informed, sensible **9** conscious
13 knowledgeable
cognize 4 know **5** grasp **6** fathom **7** realize **8** perceive **9** apprehend **10** appreciate, comprehend, understand
cognomen 4 name **5** alias, title **7** epithet,
moniker, surname **8** nickname
11 appellation, appellative, designation
12 denomination

cognoscente 5 judge **6** critic, expert
7 epicure **8** aesthete **9** authority **10** specialist **11** connoisseur
cognoscible 8 knowable **10** fathomable
13 apprehensible
cohere 4 fuse, join **5** agree, blend, cling,
merge, stick, unite **6** accord **7** combine,
comport, conform, connect **8** coalesce,
dovetail **10** correspond **11** consolidate
coherence 4 bond **5** union, unity **8** adhesion, cohesion **9** agreement, congruity,
integrity **10** conformity, connection,
consonance, solidarity **11** consistency,
integration
coherent 5 sound **7** logical, ordered, unified **8** rational **10** consistent, integrated,
meaningful **11** coordinated
cohesion see COHERENCE
coho 6 salmon **12** silver salmon
cohort 3 pal **4** ally, band, chum, crew,
mate **5** buddy, crony, group **6** fellow,
friend **7** comrade, partner **8** adherent,
confrere, disciple, follower, henchman,
sidekick **9** assistant, associate, colleague, companion, supporter
10 accomplice **11** demographic **12** collaborator
coif 3 cap, cut **4** hood, perm **6** hairdo
7 haircut **8** skullcap
coiffeur 6 barber **10** haircutter **11** hairdresser, hairstylist
coiffure 6 hairdo *aid:* **3** net, rat **5** snood
coil 4 curl, loop, ring, turn, wind **5** helix,
twine, twist **6** rotate, spiral **7** entwine,
revolve, wreathe **8** curlicue
9 corkscrew
coiled 6 spiral, volute **7** helical, voluted,
whorled **9** circinate
coin 4 mint **6** invent, make up, strike
Afghanistan: **3** pul **7** afghani *Albania:*
3 lek **9** quindarka *Algeria:* **5** dinar **7** centime *ancient Greek:* **4** obol *ancient Muslim:* **5** dinar *ancient Roman:* **8** denarius
Argentina: **4** peso **7** centavo *Austria:*
4 euro **8** groschen **9** schilling *Bahrain:*
4 fils **5** dinar *Belgium:* **4** euro **5** franc
7 centime *Benin:* **5** franc **7** centime
Bhutan: **7** chetrum **8** ngultrum *Bolivia:*
7 centavo **9** boliviano *Botswana:* **4** pula
5 thebe *Brazil:* **4** real **7** centavo
8 cruzeiro *Bulgaria:* **3** lev **8** stotinka
Burundi: **5** franc **7** centime *Cameroon:*
5 franc **7** centime *Canada:* **6** loonie,
toonie, twonie *Cape Verde Islands:*
6 escudo **7** centavo *Chile:* **4** peso **7** centavo *China:* **3** fen **4** jiao, yuan *Columbia:*
4 peso **7** centavo *Costa Rica:* **5** colón
7 centimo *Cuba:* **4** peso **7** centavo *Czech
Republic:* **5** haler **6** koruna *defective:*
4 fido *Denmark:* **3** ore **5** krone *Dominican Republic:* **4** peso **7** centavo *Ecuador:*

5 sucre 7 centavo *edge:* 7 milling *Egypt:* 7 piastre *European gold:* 5 ducat *Finland:* 4 euro 5 penni 6 markka *former:* 3 ecu, mil, pie, sol, sou 4 anna, besa, doit, duit, kran, para, pice, reis (plural) 5 fanam, litas, mohur, paisa, rupia, shahi, soldo, toman 6 centas, denier, heller, macuta, pagoda, tangka 7 santims, sapeque 8 maravedi, skilling 9 rigsdaler 10 Indian head, reichsmark 13 reichspfennig *France:* 4 euro 5 franc 7 centime *Gambia:* 5 butut 6 dalasi *Germany:* 4 euro, mark 7 pfennig *Ghana:* 4 cedi 6 pesewa *Great Britain:* 3 bob 5 crown, penny 6 guinea 7 ha'penny 8 farthing, shilling, sixpence 9 halfpenny, sovereign 10 threepence *Greece:* 4 euro 6 lepton 7 drachma *Guatemala:* 7 centavo, quetzal *Guinea-Bissau:* 4 peso *Haiti:* 6 gourde 7 centime *Honduras:* 7 centavo, lempira *Hungary:* 5 pengo 6 filler, forint *Iceland:* 5 aurar (plural), eyrir, krona *India:* 5 paisa, rupee *Indonesia:* 3 sen 6 rupiah *Iran:* 4 rial 5 dinar *Iraq:* 4 fils 5 dinar *Ireland:* 4 euro 5 penny 8 farthing *Israel:* 5 agora 6 shekel *Italy:* 4 euro, lira 5 scudo *Japan:* 3 rin, sen, yen *Jordan:* 4 fils 5 dinar *Kenya:* 8 shilling *Korea, North and South:* 3 won 4 chon *Kuwait:* 4 fils 5 dinar *large:* 9 cartwheel *Lebanon:* 5 livre 7 piastre *Lesotho:* 4 loti 7 licente, lisente *Libya:* 5 dinar 6 dirham *Luxembourg:* 4 euro 5 franc *Madagascar:* 5 franc *Malawi:* 6 kwacha 7 tambala *Mauritania:* 5 khoum 7 ouguiya *Mauritius:* 5 rupee *Mexico:* 4 peso 7 centavo *Monaco:* 4 euro 5 franc *Morocco:* 6 dirham *Mozambique:* 7 metical *Nepal:* 5 paisa, rupee *Netherlands:* 4 euro 6 florin, gulden 7 guilder *Nicaragua:* 7 centavo, córdoba *Nigeria:* 4 kobo 5 naira *Norway:* 3 ore 5 krone *Oman:* 4 rial 5 baiza *Pakistan:* 5 paisa, rupee *Panama:* 6 balboa 9 centesimo *Papua New Guinea:* 4 kina, toea *Paraguay:* 7 centimo, guarani *Peru:* 3 sol 7 centimo *Philippines:* 4 piso 7 sentimo *Poland:* 5 grosz, zloty *Portugal:* 4 euro 6 escudo 7 centavo *Qatar:* 5 riyal 6 dirham *Roman:* 6 aureus, bezant 7 solidus *Romania:* 3 ban, leu *Russia:* 5 kopek, ruble 6 kopeck *San Marino:* 4 lira *Saudi Arabia:* 4 rial 6 halala *Seychelles:* 5 rupee *side of a:* 7 obverse *Slovakia:* 5 haler 6 koruna *South Africa:* 4 rand 10 Krugerrand *Spain:* 4 euro 6 peseta 7 centimo *Sri Lanka:* 5 rupee *stamping metal:* 8 planchet *Suriname:* 6 florin, gulden 7 guilder *Swaziland:* 9 lilangeni *Sweden:* 3 ore 5 krona 8 skilling *Switzer-land:* 5 franc 6 rappen *Syria:* 7 piastre *Tanzania:* 8 shilling *Thailand:* 4 baht 5 tical 6 satang *Tonga:* 6 pa'anga, seniti *Tunisia:* 5 dinar *Turkey:* 4 lira 5 kurus *Uganda:* 8 shilling *United Arab Emirates:* 6 dirham *United States:* 4 dime 5 penny 6 dollar, nickel 7 quarter 10 half-dollar *Uruguay:* 4 peso 9 centesimo *Vatican City:* 4 lira *Venezuela:* 7 bolivar *Samoa:* 4 sene, tala *Zambia:* 5 ngwee 6 kwacha

coinage 7 new word 8 creation, currency 9 invention, neologism 10 brainchild 11 contrivance

coincide 4 jibe 5 agree, equal, match, tally 6 accord, concur, square 7 comport, conform 8 dovetail 9 harmonize 10 correspond

coincident 7 similar 9 consonant 10 concurrent 11 concomitant, synchronous 12 accompanying, contemporary, simultaneous

coincidentally 8 by chance, together 12 accidentally, concurrently, fortuitously

coin-shaped 8 nummular

col 4 pass 5 ridge 6 saddle

___ **colada** 4 piña

colander's cousin 5 sieve 6 sifter 8 strainer

cold ___ 3 war 4 call, cash, cuts, feet, fish, sore, wave 5 cream, frame, front, patch, steel, sweat, water 6 turkey 7 comfort, storage 8 shoulder

cold 3 icy, raw 4 cool, dead, iced 5 aloof, chill, crisp, frore, gelid, nippy, polar 6 arctic, biting, chilly, frigid, frosty, frozen, wintry 7 bracing, glacial, shivery 8 chilling, comatose, freezing, lifeless 11 emotionless, passionless, unconscious, unemotional 12 unresponsive *combining form:* 4 cryo, kryo *common:* 6 coryza *symptom:* 5 cough, fever 6 sneeze 7 catarrh

cold-blooded 5 cruel 6 brutal 7 callous 8 hardened, obdurate, pitiless, ruthless 9 heartless, impassive, unfeeling 10 hard-boiled, impersonal 11 emotionless, hard-hearted 12 matter-of-fact, stonyhearted 13 dispassionate, unimpassioned

cold feet 4 fear 5 alarm, doubt, dread, panic, worry 6 dismay, fright, terror 7 anxiety, jitters 8 timidity 9 cowardice 11 trepidation 12 apprehension

coldhearted see COLD-BLOODED

cold-shoulder 3 cut 4 snub 6 ignore, slight 9 ostracize

cold storage 8 abeyance, dormancy 10 quiescence, suspension 12 intermission, interruption

cole 4 kale, rape 7 cabbage 8 brassica, broccoli, kohlrabi 11 cauliflower

Coleridge poem 9 Dejection, Kubla Khan 10 Christabel

Colette character 4 Gigi 5 Cheri 8 Claudine

colewort 4 kale 7 cabbage

colic 5 gripe 9 bellyache 11 stomachache 12 collywobbles

coliseum 4 bowl 5 arena, stade 6 circus 7 stadium

collaborate 6 team up 7 collude 8 conspire 9 cooperate

collaborator 4 ally 6 helper 7 abettor, partner, traitor 8 coworker, henchman, quisling 9 accessory, assistant, associate, auxiliary, colleague 10 accomplice 11 confederate, conspirator

collapse 4 cave, drop, fail, ruin 5 break, crash, smash, wreck 6 buckle, cave in, fold up 7 breakup, crack-up, crumple, debacle, deflate, downfall, failure, founder, give out, give way, pass out, shatter, smashup, succumb 8 condense 9 breakdown, cataclysm, fall apart, ruination 10 disruption 11 catastrophe, destruction, prostration 12 disintegrate

collar 3 bag, nab 4 grab, hook, nail, take 5 catch, seize 6 arrest, secure 7 capture 9 apprehend *armor:* 6 gorget *boy's:* 4 Eton *chain:* 4 torc 6 torque *jeweled:* 8 carcanet *lace-edged:* 6 rebato *metal:* 4 torc 6 torque *pleated:* 4 ruff

collarbone 8 clavicle

collate 5 group, order 7 arrange, collect, compare, compile 8 assemble, contrast, organize 9 integrate

collateral 4 bond 6 allied, lineal, pledge, surety 7 cognate, kindred, oblique, related, subject 8 indirect, parallel, security 9 accessory, ancillary, attendant, auxiliary, dependent, secondary, tributary 10 coincident, coordinate, reciprocal, subsidiary 11 concomitant, subordinate, subservient 12 accompanying, confirmatory, contributory 13 complementary, corresponding, corroborative

colleague 4 aide 6 cohort, fellow, helper 7 partner 8 confrere, coworker, teammate 9 assistant, associate, companion 10 compatriot 11 confederate 12 collaborator

collect 4 draw 5 group, infer, raise 6 deduce, derive, gather, muster, prayer 7 build up, compile, compose, convene, dispose, marshal, round up 8 assemble, conclude, converge 10 accumulate, congregate, rendezvous

collected 4 calm, cool 5 quiet, still 6 poised, serene 7 assured 8 complete,

composed, sanguine, tranquil 9 assembled, confident, unruffled 11 unflappable 13 imperturbable, self-possessed

collection 3 ana, kit, lot 4 band, bevy, crew, olio, ruck 5 bunch, crowd, hoard, trove 6 medley, muster 7 cluster, variety 8 assembly, caboodle 9 aggregate, anthology, congeries, gathering, stockpile 10 assemblage, assortment, cumulation, miscellany 11 aggregation 12 accumulation, congregation 13 agglomeration *miscellaneous:* 4 hash, olio 6 jumble, medley 7 mélange, mixture 8 mishmash, pastiche 9 potpourri 10 hodgepodge, salmagundi 11 olla podrida *of anecdotes:* 3 ana *of animals:* 3 zoo 9 menagerie *of artistic works:* 6 museum 7 gallery *of clothes:* 8 wardrobe *of dried plants:* 9 herbarium *of literary pieces:* 8 analects 9 anthology *of reports:* 4 file 7 dossier *of trinkets:* 10 bijouterie

collective 5 joint 7 commune, kibbutz, kolkhoz 11 cooperative

collector *of bird's eggs:* 8 oologist *of books:* 11 bibliophile *of coins:* 11 numismatist *of fares:* 9 conductor *of phonograph records:* 10 discophile *of stamps:* 11 philatelist

colleen 4 girl, lass 6 maiden *country:* 4 Eire, Erin 7 Ireland

college *building:* 3 gym, lab 4 dorm, hall *campus area:* 4 quad 10 quadrangle *class meeting:* 3 lab 7 lecture, seminar 8 tutorial, workshop *degree:* 3 BLS, DST, LLB, LLD, MBA, MEd, MFA, MLS, PhD 5 LittD *graduate:* 6 alumna, alumni (plural) 7 alumnae (plural), alumnus *official:* 4 dean 5 prexy 6 bursar, regent 7 proctor, provost 9 registrar *oldest in U.S.:* 7 Harvard *oldest women's in U.S.:* 12 Mount Holyoke *relating to:* 8 academic 10 collegiate *social group:* 4 frat 8 sorority 10 fraternity *song:* 9 alma mater *student class:* 4 soph 5 frosh 6 junior, senior 8 freshman 9 sophomore *teacher:* 3 don 4 prof 8 academic 9 professor *term:* 7 quarter, session 8 semester 9 trimester *VIP:* 4 BMOC *woman:* 4 coed

college team *Air Force:* 7 Falcons *Alabama:* 11 Crimson Tide *Arizona:* 8 Wildcats *Arizona State:* 9 Sun Devils *Arkansas:* 10 Razorbacks *Arkansas State:* 7 Indians *Army:* 6 Cadets *Auburn:* 6 Tigers *Baylor:* 5 Bears *Boston College:* 6 Eagles *Boston University:* 8 Terriers *Brigham Young:* 7 Cougars *Brown:* 5 Bears *California:* 11 Golden Bears *Central Michigan:* 9 Chippewas *Cincinnati:* 8 Bearcats *Citadel:* 8 Bulldogs *Clemson:*

6 Tigers *Colgate:* 10 Red Raiders *Colorado:* 9 Buffaloes *Colorado State:*
4 Rams *Columbia:* 5 Lions *Connecticut:*
7 Huskies *Cornell:* 6 Big Red *Dartmouth:*
8 Big Green *Davidson:* 8 Wildcats
Delaware State: 7 Hornets *Drake:* 8 Bulldogs *Duke:* 10 Blue Devils *Eastern Kentucky:* 8 Colonels *Eastern Michigan:*
6 Eagles *Florida:* 6 Gators *Florida State:*
9 Seminoles *Fresno State:* 8 Bulldogs
Furman: 8 Palidans *Georgia:* 8 Bulldogs
Georgia Tech: 13 Yellow Jackets *Harvard:*
7 Crimson *Hawaii:* 15 Rainbow Warriors
Holy Cross: 9 Crusaders *Houston:* 7 Cougars *Howard:* 6 Bisons *Idaho:* 7 Vandals
Idaho State: 7 Bengals *Illinois:* 14 Fighting Illini *Illinois State:* 8 Redbirds *Indiana:* 8 Hoosiers *Indiana State:* 9 Sycamores *Iowa:* 8 Hawkeyes *Iowa State:*
8 Cyclones *Kansas:* 8 Jayhawks *Kansas State:* 8 Wildcats *Kent State:* 13 Golden Flashes *Kentucky:* 8 Wildcats *Lehigh:*
9 Engineers *Louisiana State:* 6 Tigers
Louisiana Tech: 8 Bulldogs *Maine:*
10 Black Bears *Maryland:* 5 Terps 9 Terrapins *Massachusetts:* 9 Minutemen
Miami (Florida): 10 Hurricanes *Miami (Ohio):* 8 Redskins *Michigan:* 10 Wolverines *Michigan State:* 8 Spartans *Minnesota:* 7 Gophers *Mississippi:* 6 Rebels *Mississippi State:* 8 Bulldogs *Missouri:*
6 Tigers *Montana:* 9 Grizzlies *Montana State:* 7 Bobcats *Navy:* 10 Midshipmen
Nebraska: 11 Cornhuskers *Nevada:*
6 Rebels 8 Wolfpack *New Hampshire:*
8 Wildcats *New Mexico:* 5 Lobos *New Mexico State:* 6 Aggies *North Carolina:*
8 Tar Heels *North Carolina State:* 8 Wolfpack *Northeastern:* 7 Huskies *Northwestern:* 8 Wildcats *Notre Dame:* 13 Fighting Irish *Ohio State:* 8 Buckeyes *Ohio University:* 7 Bobcats *Oklahoma:* 7 Sooners
Oklahoma State: 7 Cowboys *Oregon:*
5 Ducks *Oregon State:* 7 Beavers *Pennsylvania:* 7 Quakers *Pennsylvania State:*
12 Nittany Lions *Pittsburgh:* 8 Panthers
Princeton: 6 Tigers *Purdue:* 12 Boilermakers *Rhode Island:* 4 Rams *Rice:*
4 Owls *Rutgers:* 14 Scarlet Knights *San Diego State:* 6 Aztecs *San Jose State:*
8 Spartans *South Carolina:* 9 Gamecocks
South Carolina State: 8 Bulldogs *Southern California:* 7 Trojans *Southern Illinois:*
7 Salukis *Southern Methodist:* 8 Mustangs *Stanford:* 9 Cardinals *Syracuse:*
9 Orangemen *Temple:* 4 Owls *Tennessee:*
10 Volunteers *Tennessee State:* 6 Tigers
Tennessee Tech: 12 Golden Eagles
Texas: 9 Longhorns *Texas A&M:*
6 Aggies *Texas Christian:* 11 Horned Frogs *Texas Southern:* 6 Tigers *Texas*

Tech: 10 Red Raiders *Toledo:* 7 Rockets
Tulane: 9 Green Wave *UCLA:* 6 Bruins
UNLV: 12 Runnin' Rebels *Utah:* 4 Utes
Utah State: 6 Aggies *Vanderbilt:* 10 Commodores *Villanova:* 8 Wildcats *Virginia:*
9 Cavaliers *VMI:* 7 Keydets *VPI:* 8 Gobblers *Wake Forest:* 12 Demon Deacons
Washington: 7 Huskies *Washington State:* 7 Cougars *West Virginia:* 12 Mountaineers *William & Mary:* 5 Tribe *Wisconsin:* 7 Badgers *Wyoming:* 7 Cowboys
Yale: 4 Elis 8 Bulldogs
collide 3 hit, ram 4 bump 5 clash, crash, smash 6 impact, strike 7 impinge 8 conflict
collision 4 bump, jolt 5 clash, crash, shock, smash, wreck 6 impact 7 crackup, smashup 10 concussion
collocate 7 arrange 8 position 9 juxtapose
collogue 6 confer, huddle, parley, powwow 7 consult
colloid 3 gel, sol 4 agar 7 mixture
8 hydrogel, hydrosol
colloquial 6 casual, vulgar 7 demotic
8 familiar, informal 9 idiomatic 10 vernacular
colloquium 5 forum 7 palaver, seminar
9 symposium 10 conference, roundtable
colloquy 4 chat, talk 5 forum 6 debate, parley 7 palaver, seminar 8 dialogue
9 symposium 10 conference, discussion, roundtable 12 conversation 13 confabulation
collude 4 plot 6 devise, scheme 7 connive 8 conspire, contrive, intrigue
9 machinate
collusion 4 plot 8 intrigue, skin game
10 conspiracy
collywobbles 5 colic, gripe 9 bellyache
11 stomachache
Colombia *capital:* 6 Bogotá *city:* 4 Cali
6 Ibagué 8 Medellín 9 Cartagena
12 Barranquilla *language:* 7 Spanish *liberator:* 7 Bolivar (Simón) *monetary unit:*
4 peso *mountain, range:* 5 Andes, Chita
6 Puracé, Tolima 9 Cristóbal *neighbor:*
4 Peru 6 Brazil, Panama 7 Ecuador
9 Venezuela *river:* 6 Chauca 7 Orinoco
9 Magdalena *sea:* 9 Caribbean
Colonel Blimp 4 fogy, Tory 6 fossil 7 old fogy 8 mossback 10 fuddy-duddy
11 reactionary
colonnade 4 stoa 9 peristyle
colony 7 outpost 9 satellite 10 settlement
color 3 dun, dye, hue, red, tan 4 aqua, blue, cast, glow, gold, gray, grey, jade, lime, navy, pink, puce, rose, teal, tint, tone 5 amber, azure, beige, belie, black, blush, brown, coral, ebony,

flush, green, hazel, henna, ivory, khaki, lilac, mauve, ocher, ochre, olive, paint, peach, rouge, shade, stain, taupe, tinge, umber 6 auburn, bronze, canary, copper, indigo, maroon, orange, purple, redden, salmon, sienna, silver, violet, yellow 7 crimson, emerald, magenta, pigment, saffron, scarlet 8 chestnut, dyestuff, lavender, tincture 9 embellish, embroider, turquoise, vermilion 10 aquamarine, exaggerate 12 pigmentation *band:* 5 facia, vitta 6 fascia *combining form:* 5 chrom 6 chromo 7 chromat 8 chromato *primary:* 3 red 4 blue 6 yellow *relating to:* 9 chromatic *secondary:* 5 green 6 orange, purple *soft:* 6 pastel

Colorado *capital:* 6 Denver *city:* 4 Vail 5 Aspen 6 Aurora, Pueblo 7 Boulder 8 Lakewood 11 Fort Collins *college, university:* 5 Regis 9 Fort Lewis *mountain, range:* 5 Longs (Peak), Pikes (Peak), Rocky 6 Elbert 7 Rockies *nickname:* 10 Centennial (State) *park:* 9 Mesa Verde *river:* 8 Arkansas, Colorado 9 Rio Grande *state bird:* 11 lark bunting *state flower:* 9 columbine *state tree:* 10 blue spruce

colorant 3 dye 5 stain 7 pigment 8 dyestuff, tincture

colored 6 biased, warped 8 one-sided, partisan 9 jaundiced 10 prejudiced 11 tendentious

colorful 3 gay 5 gaudy, showy, vivid 6 bright, flashy, florid, garish, motley 7 splashy

coloring 4 cast, tint 5 front, tinge 6 facade, nuance 7 pigment 8 overtone 10 camouflage, complexion 12 embroidering 13 embellishment

colorless 3 wan 4 ashy, drab, dull, flat, pale 5 ashen, pasty, prosy, waxen, white 6 albino, doughy, pallid 7 insipid, neutral, prosaic 8 abstract, blanched, bleached 10 achromatic, lackluster

Color Purple author 6 Walker (Alice)

colossal 4 huge, vast 7 immense, mammoth, massive, titanic 9 cyclopean, monstrous 10 gargantuan, stupendous 11 astonishing, elephantine

colossus 5 giant, titan 6 statue 7 goliath, mammoth, monster 8 behemoth 9 leviathan

Colossus of ___ 6 Rhodes

colporteur 10 evangelist, missionary 12 propagandist

colt 4 foal, tyro 6 novice, rookie 8 beginner, freshman, neophyte, newcomer 9 fledgling 10 tenderfoot

coltish 6 frisky, impish 7 playful 10 frolicsome

Columbine *beloved:* 9 Harlequin *father:* 9 Pantaloon

Columbus, Christopher *birthplace:* 5 Genoa *patron:* 8 Isabella 9 Ferdinand *ship:* 4 Niña 5 Pinta 10 Santa Maria *son:* 5 Diego *starting point:* 5 Palos

column 3 row 4 pier 5 shaft, stela 6 pillar 7 obelisk 8 pilaster *angle:* 5 arris *base:* 4 ordo 5 socle 6 plinth 9 stylobate *bulge:* 7 entasis *female figure:* 8 caryatid *male figure:* 5 atlas 7 telamon 8 atlantes (plural) *style:* 5 Doric, Ionic 10 Corinthian *top:* 7 capital 8 chapiter

coma 6 stupor, torpor 8 blackout, hebetude, lethargy 9 lassitude

comate 3 pal 4 chum 5 buddy, crony 7 comrade, partner 9 associate, colleague, companion

comatose 5 dopey 6 stupid, torpid 7 out cold 8 sluggish 9 lethargic 10 insensible 11 unconscious

comb 4 rake, sift, sort 5 crest, curry, probe, scour, sweep, tease 6 search, winnow 7 ransack 8 untangle 10 straighten 11 investigate

combat 3 war 4 buck, duel, fray 5 fight, repel 6 action, battle, oppose, resist, strife 7 contend, contest, dispute 8 skirmish, struggle 9 withstand 11 controversy

combatant 7 battler, fighter, soldier, warrior 8 militant, opponent 9 adversary, aggressor, assailant, contender, disputant, mercenary 10 antagonist, challenger, competitor, contestant 11 belligerent

combative 6 feisty 7 scrappy, warlike 8 militant 9 agonistic, bellicose, truculent 10 aggressive, pugnacious 11 belligerent, contentious, quarrelsome 12 disputatious, militaristic

combativeness 9 pugnacity 10 aggression, truculence 11 bellicosity 12 belligerence

combe 4 dale, dell, glen, vale 6 dingle, valley

combination 3 mix 4 bloc, pool, ring 5 blend, union 6 fusion, hookup, merger 7 melding, merging 8 alliance 9 aggregate, coalition, composite, synthesis 10 connection 11 affiliation, association, conjunction, partnership, unification 13 consolidation

combine 3 add, mix, wed 4 band, bloc, fuse, join, link, pool, ring 5 blend, chain, group, marry, merge, trust, unify, union, unite 6 cartel, league, mingle 7 bracket, conjoin, connect, faction 8 coadjute, coalesce 9 associate, coalition, commingle, cooperate, integrate, syndicate 10 amalgamate 11 consolidate, incorporate **12** conglomerate *Japanese:* **8** keiretsu, zaibatsu *Korean:* **7** chaebol, jaebeol

combined action 7 synergy **9** synergism

combo 4 band, trio **5** group **6** septet, sextet **7** quartet, quintet **8** ensemble

combust 4 burn **6** ignite, kindle **10** incinerate

combustible 4 edgy, fuel **8** burnable, volatile **9** excitable, flammable, ignitable **11** inflammable *material:* **3** gas, oil **4** coal, peat, wood **6** tinder

combustion 4 riot **7** burning **8** eruption, ignition, kindling **9** explosion, oxidation **13** thermogenesis

come 4 flow, hail, stem **5** arise, issue, occur **6** arrive, derive, show up, spring, turn up **7** advance, emanate, proceed **8** approach **9** originate *a cropper:* **4** fail, fall *across:* **4** find, meet **8** discover **9** encounter *apart:* **12** disintegrate *at:* **6** attack *away:* **5** leave **6** depart *before:* **7** precede *clean:* **7** confess *forth:* **5** issue **6** appear, emerge *forward:* **7** advance **9** volunteer *into:* **5** enter **7** acquire *near:* **5** verge **8** approach *round:* **5** rally **7** get well, recover *to pass:* **5** occur **6** happen *up:* **5** arise *upon:* **4** find, meet **8** discover **9** encounter

comeback 5 rally **6** answer, retort, return **7** rebound, revival, riposte **8** rebuttal, recovery, repartee, response **11** improvement **12** counterclaim, recuperation

come by 4 call **5** pop in, visit **6** drop in, look in **7** acquire, collect, inherit

comedian 3 wag, wit **4** card **5** clown, comic, droll, joker **6** jester **7** farceur **8** funnyman, humorist, jokester, quipster **11** entertainer

comedo 9 blackhead

comedown 4 dive, fall, ruin **5** crash **7** decline, descent, failure, setback **8** collapse **9** ruination

come down with 3 get **5** catch **7** develop **8** contract

comedy 5 farce, humor **6** levity **8** drollery, hilarity **9** drollness, wittiness

come in 5 enter, reply **6** answer **7** respond

comely 4 fair **5** bonny, sonsy **6** lovely, pretty, proper, sonsie **7** winsome **8** becoming, decorous, handsome, pleasing **9** beauteous, beautiful, befitting **10** attractive **11** good-looking

come off 4 fare, seem **5** click, occur **6** appear, go over, happen, pan out **7** develop, succeed **8** prove out **9** transpire

come-on 4 bait, lure, trap **5** decoy, snare **9** seduction **10** allurement, enticement,

inducement, invitation, temptation **12** blandishment, inveiglement, solicitation

come out 4 leak **5** break, debut, end up **6** emerge **9** transpire

come out with 3 say **4** tell **5** state, utter **6** report **7** declare, deliver, publish, release **8** announce, proclaim

comestible 6 edible **7** eatable **8** esculent

comestibles 4 feed, food **6** viands **7** edibles **8** victuals **9** provender **10** provisions

come through 6 chip in, endure **7** pitch in, prevail, survive **8** transmit **10** contribute

come together 4 mass, meet **5** merge, swarm **6** gather, huddle **7** cluster, collect, combine, convene **8** assemble, converge **10** congregate

come upon 4 find **7** run into, uncover, unearth **8** bump into, discover, trip over **9** encounter, run across

comeuppance 3 due **5** lumps **7** deserts

comfort 3 aid **4** help **5** cheer **6** assist, buck up, luxury, relief, solace, soothe, succor **7** amenity, cheer up, console, relieve, support **8** reassure, sympathy **10** assistance, sympathize **11** commiserate, consolation, contentment

comfortable 4 cozy, easy, homy, snug, soft **5** ample, cushy, homey, roomy **7** content, easeful, restful, well-off **8** adequate, homelike, pleasant, pleasing, spacious, well-to-do **9** agreeable, satisfied, well-fixed **10** commodious, prosperous, sufficient, well-heeled **11** substantial **12** satisfactory

comforter 4 down, pouf, puff **5** duvet, quilt **9** eiderdown

comfy 4 cozy, homy **5** cushy, homey

comic 3 wag, wit **5** antic, droll, funny, joker **6** jester **7** risible **8** comedian, farcical, funnyman, humorist, jokester, quipster **9** laughable, ludicrous **10** ridiculous

comical 4 zany **5** droll, funny, goofy, silly **6** absurd **7** amusing, foolish, risible, waggish **8** farcical **9** laughable, ludicrous **10** ridiculous

comic strip 4 Pogo, Shoe **5** Hazel, Henry, Nancy **6** Archie, Popeye **7** Blondie, Dilbert, Far Side (The), Peanuts **8** Alley Oop, Andy Capp, Garfield, Krazy Kat, Li'l Abner, Superman **9** Betty Boop, Dick Tracy, Flash Gordon, Marmaduke, Mary Worth, Spider-Man, Yellow Kid (The) **10** Doonesbury, Joe Palooka, Little Nemo **11** Bloom County, Brenda Starr, Mutt and Jeff, Rex Morgan M.D., Steve Canyon **12** Beetle

Bailey 13 Captain Marvel, Gasoline
Alley, Prince Valiant
coming 3 due 4 next 5 fated, onset
6 advent, future 7 arrival, ensuing,
nearing 8 approach, expected, foreseen, imminent 9 following, impending
11 approaching *forth:* 7 issuant
comity 5 amity 7 concord, harmony
8 goodwill 10 friendship 11 benevolence, camaraderie 12 friendliness
comma 4 lull 5 pause 8 interval
command 3 bid 4 rule, sway 5 order
6 adjure, behest, charge, compel,
direct, enjoin 7 bidding, conduct, control, dictate, mandate, mastery, precept
9 authority, direction, directive, expertise, ordinance 10 domination, injunction 11 instruction 12 jurisdiction *to go:*
4 mush 6 avaunt, begone 7 giddyap,
giddyup *to stop:* 4 whoa 5 avast
commandeer 4 take 5 annex, seize,
usurp 6 assume, hijack 7 preempt
8 accroach, arrogate 9 conscript,
sequester 10 confiscate 11 appropriate,
expropriate, requisition
commander 4 boss, head 6 honcho,
leader, master 7 captain, general, headman, officer
commandment 3 law 4 fiat, rule 5 edict,
order 6 decree 7 mitzvah, precept,
statute
commedia dell'___ 4 arte
comme il faut 6 decent, polite, proper,
seemly 7 correct 8 becoming, decorous,
suitable
commemorate 4 keep 7 observe 8 eulogize, monument 9 celebrate, solemnize
11 memorialize 13 monumentalize
commemorative 8 memorial 10 dedicatory 11 celebratory
commence 5 begin, start 6 launch, set
out 7 kick off 8 embark on, initiate
10 embark upon, inaugurate
commencement 4 dawn 5 birth, onset,
start 6 outset 7 dawning, genesis, opening 9 beginning, inception 10 graduation 12 inauguration
commend 4 hail, laud 5 extol 6 commit,
kudize, praise, salute, tender 7 acclaim,
applaud, approve, consign, entrust
8 hand over, relegate, turn over
10 compliment
commendable 6 worthy 8 laudable
9 admirable, deserving, estimable, meritable, venerable 10 creditable 11 meritorious 12 praiseworthy
commensurable see COMMENSURATE
commensurate 4 even 5 equal 10 comparable 11 coextensive 12 proportional
13 corresponding, proportionate
comment 4 note 5 opine 6 remark

7 mention, observe 8 critique, point out
9 criticism, interject 10 animadvert
11 observation 12 obiter dictum
commentary 5 gloss 6 review 8 analysis,
critique, exegesis 9 editorial, narration,
voice-over 10 annotation, exposition
11 explanation, observation 12 appreciation, obiter dictum
commerce 5 trade 7 contact, traffic
8 business, congress, dealings,
exchange, industry 9 communion
11 interchange 13 communication
commercial 6 advert 8 economic 10 mercantile 13 advertisement
commie 3 Red 5 pinko 6 bolshy 7 bolshie 9 Bolshevik
commination 5 curse 8 anathema
10 accusation, execration 11 imprecation, malediction 12 denunciation
commingle 3 mix 4 meld 5 blend, merge,
unify 8 compound, intermix 9 integrate
10 amalgamate
comminute 4 bray 5 crush, grind 9 gran-
ulate, pulverize
commiserate 4 pity 7 condole, feel for
9 empathize 10 sympathize 13 compassionate
commiseration 4 pity, ruth 7 empathy
8 sympathy 10 compassion, condolence
commission 3 bid, fee 4 name 5 board,
order 6 agency, assign, charge, enable,
engage, enjoin, enlist 7 appoint, command, council, empower, license, warrant 8 accredit, delegate, deputize
9 authorize, designate 10 delegation,
deputation, percentage 11 certificate
commit 4 bind 5 allot, grant, refer
6 assign, convey, invest, ordain, pledge,
record, reveal 7 achieve, consign,
deposit, entrust, execute, perform,
promise, pull off, trustee 8 allocate,
carry out, hand over, obligate, relegate, turn over 10 accomplish, perpetrate
commitment 3 vow 4 bond, deal, duty
6 charge, devoir, pledge 7 promise
8 contract 9 agreement, assurance,
guarantee 10 obligation 11 undertaking
committal see COMMITMENT
commixture 5 blend 6 fusion 7 amalgam,
melange 8 compound, mingling 9 composite
commodious 4 wide 5 ample, roomy
8 spacious 9 capacious, expansive, luxurious 11 comfortable
commodities 5 goods, items, wares
8 articles, products 9 vendibles 11 merchandise
common 4 park 5 banal, daily, joint,
plaza, trite, usual 6 mutual, normal,
shared 7 general, generic, prosaic, reg-

ular, routine, typical **8** adequate, communal, conjoint, conjunct, déclassé, everyday, familiar, frequent, habitual, ordinary, standard, workaday **9** customary, prevalent, tolerable, universal **10** collective, pedestrian, prevailing, unexciting, widespread **12** conventional, run-of-the-mill, satisfactory **13** unexceptional, uninteresting

commonalty 3 mob **5** plebs **6** masses, people, plebes, public, rabble **7** commune **8** populace **9** hoi polloi, multitude, plebeians **11** proletariat, rank and file, third estate

commoners see COMMONALTY

commonplace 5 stale, tired, trite, usual **6** cliché, normal, truism **7** bromide, clichéd, humdrum, mundane, obvious, prosaic, regular, routine, typical **8** banality, bromidic, chestnut, everyday, habitual, mediocre, ordinary, wellworn, workaday **9** hackneyed, platitude, prevalent **10** pedestrian, shibboleth, stereotype, uneventful **11** stereotyped **12** conventional, run-of-the-mill, unremarkable **13** stereotypical, unexceptional, uninteresting

common sense 6 wisdom **8** judgment, prudence **10** shrewdness

Common Sense author 5 Paine (Thomas)

commotion 3 ado, din, row **4** flap, fuss, moil, riot, stew, stir, to-do **5** storm, whirl **6** bustle, clamor, dither, flurry, fracas, furore, hoopla, hubbub, hurrah, lather, outcry, pother, racket, ruckus, rumpus, shindy, tumult, uproar, upturn **7** ferment, tempest, turmoil **8** brouhaha, foofaraw **9** agitation, confusion **10** convulsion, hullabaloo, hurly-burly, turbulence **11** pandemonium

commove 5 rouse **6** excite **7** agitate, inspire, provoke **9** electrify, galvanize, stimulate

communal 5 civil, joint **6** common, mutual, public, shared **10** collective **11** socialistic

commune 10 collective *Israeli:* **7** kibbutz *Russian:* **3** mir **7** kolkhoz

communicable 8 catching **10** contagious, infectious **13** transmissible, transmittable

communicate 4 tell **6** convey, impart, inform, pass on, relate, reveal, signal **7** connect, contact, divulge **8** disclose, transmit **9** make known

communication 4 talk **7** contact, message, missive, talking **8** converse, exchange **9** directive **10** discussing, discussion **11** interchange, intercourse **12** conversation *means:* **3** Web **4** drum, mail, note **5** e-mail, media, phone, radio **6** letter, medium, pigeon, speech **8** Internet **9** telegraph, telephone **10** television *system:* **8** language

communications code word 4 Alfa, Echo, Golf, Kilo, Lima, Mike, Papa, Xray, Zulu **5** Alpha, Bravo, Delta, Hotel, India, Oscar, Romeo, Tango **6** Quebec, Sierra, Victor, Yankee **7** Charlie, Foxtrot, Juliett, Uniform, Whiskey **8** November

communicative 5 vocal **6** fluent, prolix **7** verbose, voluble **8** eloquent **9** expansive, garrulous, talkative **10** articulate, expressive, loquacious

communion 7 rapport, sharing **9** Eucharist, sacrament **10** connection, fellowship *cloth:* **8** corporal *cup:* **7** chalice *plate:* **5** paten

communism 7 Marxism **8** Leninism **10** bolshevism **12** collectivism

Communist 3 red **5** lefty, pinko **6** bolshy, Maoist **7** bolshie, comrade, Marxist **8** Leninist **9** Bolshevik, Stalinist **10** Bolshevist, Trotskyist

Communist leader *Chinese:* **3** Mao **4** Deng **5** Jiang **8** Hu Jintao **9** Mao Zedong **10** Jiang Zemin, Mao Tse-tung **12** Deng Xiaoping **13** Teng Hsiao-p'ing *Russian:* **5** Lenin (Vladimir Ilyich) **6** Stalin (Joseph) **7** Kosygin (Aleksey), Trotsky (Leon) **8** Andropov (Yuri), Brezhnev (Leonid) **9** Chernenko (Konstantin), Gorbachev (Mikhail) **10** Khrushchev (Nikita)

community 4 town **7** enclave, society **12** neighborhood *ecological:* **10** biocenosis **11** biocoenosis

commute 5 alter **6** change, make up, modify, soften, travel **7** convert, curtail, shorten, shuttle **8** decrease, exchange, mitigate, transfer **9** transform, translate, transmute, transpose **10** compensate, substitute **11** interchange

Como está ___? 5 usted

Comoros *capital:* **6** Moroni *island:* **6** Mohéli **7** Anjouan **12** Grande Comore *language:* **6** Arabic, French **8** Comorian *monetary unit:* **5** franc *volcano:* **8** Karthala

compact 4 bond **5** close, dense, unify **7** bargain, bunched, crowded, pressed **8** compress, condense, contract, covenant **9** agreement, concordat **10** convention **11** concentrate, consolidate, transaction

compadre 3 pal **4** chum, mate **5** amigo, buddy, crony **6** friend **7** comrade, partner **8** confrere, sidekick, intimate **9** associate, colleague, companion

companion 3 pal **4** chum, mate **5** buddy,

crony 6 cohort, escort 7 comrade, consort, partner 8 sidekick 9 associate, attendant, colleague

companionable 6 genial, social 7 affable, amiable 8 outgoing, sociable 9 agreeable, congenial, convivial 10 gregarious 11 good-natured

companionship 7 company, society 8 intimacy 10 fellowship 11 camaraderie

company 4 band, club, crew, firm, gang, team 5 corps, group, party, troop 6 circle, clique, guests, outfit, troupe 7 concern, coterie, retinue, society, visitor 8 assembly, business, ensemble, visitors 9 gathering 10 assemblage, enterprise, fellowship 11 association, camaraderie, corporation 12 congregation 13 companionship, establishment

comparable 4 akin, like 5 alike 6 agnate 7 similar, uniform 8 parallel 9 analogous 10 equivalent, homologous 12 commensurate 13 corresponding

comparative 4 near 8 relative 11 approximate

compare 5 liken, match 6 equate, relate 7 collate 8 contrast, parallel 9 correlate 10 assimilate

comparison 6 simile 7 analogy 8 affinity, contrast, likeness 9 collation, semblance 10 similarity, similitude 11 correlation, resemblance

compartment 3 bay 4 cell, nook, part, slot 5 berth, booth, niche, stall 6 alcove, carrel, locker 7 chamber, cubicle, section 8 division 9 cubbyhole 10 pigeonhole 11 subdivision

compass 3 hem 4 ring 5 ambit, field, grasp, orbit, range, reach, scope, sweep 6 bounds, circle, domain, extent, girdle, limits, radius, sphere 7 circuit, environ, purview 8 boundary, confines, environs 9 enclosure, extension, perimeter, periphery 13 circumference *kind:* 4 gyro 5 solar 8 magnetic *stand:* 8 binnacle

compassion 4 pity, ruth 5 mercy 7 charity, empathy 8 clemency, humanity, kindness, sympathy 10 condolence, humaneness 11 benevolence 13 commiseration, fellow feeling

compassionate 4 pity, warm 6 humane, tender 7 clement 8 merciful 10 benevolent, charitable, solicitous 11 commiserate, kindhearted, softhearted, sympathetic, warmhearted

compassionless 5 stony 7 callous 8 obdurate 9 heartless, unfeeling 11 coldblooded, hard-hearted, ironhearted 12 stonyhearted

compass point 3 ENE, ESE, NNE, NNW, SSE, SSW, WNW, WSW 4 east, west 5 north, rhumb, south 7 bearing *Scottish:* 4 airt

compatible 6 proper 8 suitable 9 agreeable, congenial, congruous, consonant 10 consistent, harmonious, like-minded 11 appropriate, sympathetic

compatriot 8 confrere 9 associate, colleague, companion

compeer see COMPANION

compel 4 hale, urge 5 drive, force 6 coerce, impose, oblige 7 enforce 9 constrain

compelling 4 dire 5 acute 6 cogent, crying, urgent 7 clamant, exigent, telling, weighty 8 forceful, pressing 10 convincing, persuasive 11 importunate, significant 12 well-grounded 13 authoritative

compendious 5 brief, pithy, short 7 compact, concise, summary 8 succinct 9 condensed 11 abbreviated

compendium 4 list 5 brief, guide 6 aperçu, digest, manual, précis, sketch, survey 7 epitome, summary 8 abstract, Baedeker, handbook, overview, syllabus, synopsis 9 anthology, guidebook, vade mecum 10 abridgment, collection, conspectus 11 abridgement, compilation, enchiridion

compensate 3 pay 5 atone, repay 6 make up, offset, pay off, redeem, set off 7 balance, guerdon, requite, satisfy 8 outweigh 9 indemnify, reimburse 10 counteract, neutralize, recompense, remunerate 11 countervail

compensation 6 amends, reward, salary 7 damages, payment, redress 8 earnings, reprisal, requital, solatium 9 atonement, indemnity, quittance, repayment 10 recompense, reparation 11 restitution 12 remuneration

compete 3 vie 4 spar 5 fight 6 battle, strive 7 contend, contest 8 struggle

competence 5 skill 7 ability, know-how 8 adequacy, aptitude, capacity, facility 9 expertise 10 capability 11 proficiency, sufficiency 13 qualification

competent 3 fit 4 able 5 adept 6 au fait, decent, proper 7 capable, skilled 8 adequate 9 efficient, qualified 10 proficient, sufficient 12 satisfactory

competition 4 bout, game, meet, race 5 clash, fight, match, rival 6 strife 7 contest, matchup, rivalry 8 concours, conflict, striving, struggle, tug-of-war 10 antagonism, contention, tournament

competitor 5 enemy, rival 8 opponent 9 adversary 10 antagonist, contestant, opposition

compile 4 edit 5 amass 6 gather, select

7 build up, collate, collect **8** assemble **9** construct **10** accumulate **11** anthologize

complacency 5 pride **7** conceit **8** smugness **10** narcissism

complacent 4 smug **6** serene **7** assured **9** conceited, confident **11** self-assured, unconcerned **13** self-confident, self-contented, self-possessed, self-satisfied

complain 3 nag **4** beef, crab, fret, fuss, wail **5** gripe, grump, whine **6** grouch, grouse, lament, yammer **7** grizzle, grumble, protest **9** bellyache

complainer 4 crab **5** crank **6** griper, grouch **7** grouser **8** grumbler, sourpuss **10** malcontent **11** faultfinder

complaint 5 gripe **6** grouse, lament, malady **7** ailment, disease, protest **8** disorder, sickness, syndrome **9** condition, criticism, grievance, infirmity, objection **10** affliction, allegation **12** protestation

complaisant 4 easy, mild **7** amiable, lenient **8** generous, obliging **9** agreeable, compliant, easygoing, indulgent **11** deferential, good-humored, good-natured **12** good-tempered **13** accommodating

complement 4 crew, rest **9** correlate, remainder **10** supplement **11** counterpart

complete 3 end **4** done, full, halt **5** close, ended, total, utter, whole **6** entire, finish, intact, wind up, wrap up **7** achieve, fulfill, perfect, perform, plenary **8** absolute, conclude, finalize, finished, integral, round out, thorough **9** concluded, out-and-out, terminate **10** accomplish, consummate, exhaustive, unabridged **11** categorical, unmitigated **13** thoroughgoing

completed 4 done, over **5** ended **7** through **8** done with, executed, finished **9** concluded, fulfilled **10** terminated **11** consummated **12** accomplished

completion 3 end **6** finish, windup, wrap-up **8** fruition **10** conclusion

complex 6 daedal, knotty, system, varied **7** chelate, gordian, network **8** abstruse, compound, involved, syndrome, tortuous **9** aggregate, Byzantine, composite, elaborate, intricate **10** convoluted **11** complicated **12** conglomerate, labyrinthine **13** heterogeneous, sophisticated

complexion 3 hue **4** cast, tint, tone **5** color, humor, tinge **6** aspect, makeup, nature, temper **8** tincture **9** character **10** appearance, coloration **11** disposition, temperament **12** pigmentation **13** individuality

compliance 7 consent **8** docility **9** agreement, deference, obedience **10** acceptance, conformity, submission **11** amenability, flexibility, resignation **12** acquiescence, tractability

complicate 5 mix up, ravel, snarl **6** jumble, muddle, tangle **7** confuse, involve **8** confound, disorder, entangle **9** aggravate, convolute **10** disarrange, exacerbate

complicated 6 daedal, knotty **7** complex, gordian, tangled **8** abstruse, involved, tortuous **9** Byzantine, elaborate, intricate, recondite **10** convoluted **12** labyrinthine **13** heterogeneous, sophisticated

complicity 8 abetment **9** collusion **10** connivance **11** involvement

compliment 4 hail, kudo, laud **5** extol, honor, kudos **6** praise, salute **7** acclaim, applaud, bouquet, commend, regards, tribute **8** accolade, encomium **9** laudation, recommend **11** recognition **12** appreciation, commendation, congratulate

complimentary 4 free **6** gratis **8** costless **9** favorable, laudatory **10** chargeless, gratuitous **12** appreciative

comply 4 obey **5** yield **6** accede, submit **7** conform **9** acquiesce

component 4 part **5** piece **6** factor **7** element, segment **10** ingredient **11** constituent

comport 4 bear, jibe **5** agree, carry, fit in, match, tally **6** accord, acquit, behave, demean, square **7** conduct **8** coincide, dovetail **9** harmonize **10** correspond

comportment 3 air **4** mien **7** address, bearing, conduct **8** attitude, behavior, carriage, demeanor, presence

compose 4 calm, cool, form, lull, make **5** forge, quiet, relax, still, write **6** becalm, create, devise, draw up, indite, invent, make up, settle, solace, soothe **7** collect, console, contain, control **8** comprise **9** construct, fabricate, formulate, originate **10** constitute *type:* **3** set

composed 4 calm, cool **5** staid **6** poised, sedate, serene **9** collected, unruffled **11** unflappable **13** imperturbable, self-possessed

composer 6 scorer **8** melodist **9** balladist, songsmith, tunesmith **10** songwriter *American:* **3** Kay (Hershy, Ulysses) **4** Bock (Jerry), Cage (John), Hill (Edward Burlingame), Ives (Charles), Kern (Jerome), King

(Carole), Lane (Burton), Monk (Thelo-nious), Work (Henry Clay) **5** Adams (John), Arlen (Harold), Beach (Amy), Blake (Eubie), Bland (James A.), Bloch (Ernest), Cohan (George M.), Friml (Rudolf), Glass (Philip), Gould (Morton), Grofé (Ferde), Handy (W. C.), Loewe (Frederick), Mason (Daniel Gregory, Lowell), Moore (Douglas), Reich (Steve), Sousa (John Philip), Still (William Grant), Styne (Jule), Zappa (Frank) **6** Barber (Samuel), Berlin (Irving), Carter (Elliott), Cowell (Henry), Emmett (Daniel), Foster (Stephen), Hanson (Howard), Harris (Roy), Herman (Jerry), Joplin (Scott), Kander (John), McHugh (Jimmy), McKuen (Rod), Menken (Alan), Morton ("Jelly Roll"), Oliver ("King"), Parker (Charlie "Bird," Horatio), Piston (Walter), Porter (Cole), Previn (André), Seeger (Pete), Taylor (Deems), Varèse (Edgard), Warren (Harry) **7** Babbitt (Milton), Brubeck (Dave), Copland (Aaron), Gilbert (Henry F.), Gilmore (Patrick), Goldman (Edwin Franko), Herbert (Victor), Loesser (Frank), Mancini (Henry), Menotti (Gian Carlo), Rodgers (Richard), Romberg (Sigmund), Schuman (William), Thomson (Virgil), Tiomkin (Dimitri), Willson (Meredith), Youmans (Vincent) **8** Anderson (Leroy), Billings (William), Burleigh (Henry Thacker), Damrosch (Leopold, Walter), Gershwin (George), Hamlisch (Marvin), Herrmann (Bernard), Korngold (Erich Wolfgang), Kreisler (Fritz), Marsalis (Wynton), Schuller (Gunther), Sessions (Roger), Sondheim (Stephen), Williams (John) **9** Bacharach (Burt), Bernstein (Elmer, Leonard), Donaldson (Walter), Ellington (Duke), Hovhaness (Alan), MacDowell (Edward) **10** Blitzstein (Marc), Carmichael (Hoagy), Gottschalk (Louis Moreau) *Argentinian:* **9** Ginastera (Alberto) *Australian:* **8** Grainger (Percy) *Austrian:* **4** Berg (Alban), Wolf (Hugo) **5** Haydn (Franz Joseph) **6** Czerny (Karl), Mahler (Gustav), Mozart (Leopold, Wolfgang Amadeus), Straus (Oscar), Webern (Anton) **7** Strauss (Eduard, Johann, Josef) **8** Bruckner (Anton), Schubert (Franz) **10** Schoenberg (Arnold) *Belgian:* **5** Ysaÿe (Eugène) **6** Franck (César) *Brazilian:* **5** Jobim (Antonio Carlos) **10** Villa-Lobos (Heitor) *Czech:* **3** Suk (Josef) **6** Dvořák (Antonín) **7** Janáček (Leoš), Martinu (Bohuslav), Smetana (Bedřich) *Danish:* **7** Nielsen (Carl) *Dutch:* **9** Sweel-

inck (Jan Pieterszoon) *English:* **4** Arne (Thomas Augustine), Byrd (William) **5** Elgar (Edward), Holst (Gustav) **6** Delius (Frederick), Morley (Thomas), Tallis (Thomas), Walton (William), Wesley (Charles, Samuel) **7** Britten (Benjamin), Dowland (John), Gibbons (Orlando), Purcell (Henry), Weelkes (Thomas) **8** Sullivan (Arthur) **9** Dunstable (John) **11** Lloyd Webber (Andrew) *Finnish:* **8** Palmgren (Selim), Sibelius (Jean) *Flemish:* **5** Dufay (Guillaume), Lasso (Orlando di) **6** Lassus (Orlande de) **8** Willaert (Adriaan) *French:* **4** Indy (Vincent d'), Lalo (Edouard) **5** Auber (Esprit), Bizet (Georges), Dukas (Paul), Fauré (Gabriel), Ibert (Jacques), Jarre (Maurice), Lully (Jean-Baptiste), Ravel (Maurice), Satie (Erik), Widor (Charles-Marie) **6** Boulez (Pierre), Campra (André), Franck (César), Gounod (Charles), Rameau (Jean-Philippe), Thomas (Ambroise) **7** Berlioz (Hector), Debussy (Claude), Delibes (Léo), Machaut (Guillaume de), Milhaud (Darius), Poulenc (Francis) **8** Chabrier (Emmanuel), Couperin (François, Louis), Honegger (Arthur), Massenet (Jules), Messiaen (Olivier) **9** Meyerbeer (Giacomo), Offenbach (Jacques) **10** Saint-Saëns (Camille) *German:* **4** Bach (C. P. E., Johann Christian, Johann Sebastian, Wilhelm Friedemann), Orff (Carl) **5** Bruch (Max), Gluck (Christoph Willibald von), Reger (Max), Spohr (Louis, Ludwig), Weber (Carl Maria von), Weill (Kurt) **6** Brahms (Johannes), Handel (George Frideric), Schütz (Heinrich), Vogler (Abt), Wagner (Richard) **7** Hassler (Hans Leo), Strauss (Richard) **8** Korngold (Erich Wolfgang), Schumann (Robert), Telemann (Georg Philipp) **9** Beethoven (Ludwig van), Buxtehude (Dietrich), Hindemith (Paul), Meyerbeer (Giacomo), Pachelbel (Johann) **10** Praetorius (Michael) **11** Humperdinck (Engelbert), Mendelssohn (Felix), Stockhausen (Karlheinz) *Hungarian:* **5** Léhar (Franz), Liszt (Franz) **6** Bartók (Béla), Kodály (Zoltán), Ligeti (György) **8** Dohnányi (Erno) *Italian:* **4** Peri (Jacopo), Rota (Nino) **5** Berio (Luciano), Boito (Arrigo), Verdi (Giuseppe) **6** Busoni (Ferruccio) **7** Bellini (Vincenzo), Caccini (Giulio), Corelli (Arcangelo), Martini (Padre), Puccini (Giacomo), Rossini (Gioacchino), Salieri (Antonio), Tartini (Giuseppe), Vivaldi (Antonio) **8** Albinoni (Tomaso), Clementi (Muzio),

Gabrieli (Andrea, Giovanni), Mascagni (Pietro), Paganini (Niccolò), Respighi (Ottorino) 9 Cherubini (Luigi), Donizetti (Gaetano), Pergolesi (Giovanni Battista), Scarlatti (Alessandro, Domenico), Tommasini (Vincenzo) 10 Boccherini (Luigi), Monteverdi (Claudio), Palestrina (G. P. da), Ponchielli (Amilcare), Zingarelli (Niccolò) 11 Frescobaldi (Girolamo), Leoncavallo (Ruggero) 12 Dallapiccola (Luigi) *Mexican:* 6 Chávez (Carlos) *Norwegian:* 5 Grieg (Edvard) *Polish:* 6 Chopin (Frédéric) 7 Gorecki (Henryk) 10 Paderewski (Ignacy Jan), Penderecki (Krzysztof), Wieniawski (Henryk) 11 Lutoslawski (Witold), Szymanowski (Karol) *Romanian:* 7 Xenakis (Iannis) *Russian:* 6 Glinka (Mikhail) 7 Borodin (Aleksandr) 8 Glazunov (Aleksandr), Scriabin (Aleksandr) 9 Balakirev (Mily), Prokofiev (Sergey), Schnittke (Alfred) 10 Kabalevsky (Dmitri), Mussorgsky (Modest), Rubinstein (Anton), Stravinsky (Igor), Tcherepnin (Nikolay) 11 Tchaikovsky (Pyotr Ilich) 12 Khachaturian (Aram), Rachmaninoff (Sergey), Shostakovich (Dmitry) *Spanish:* 5 Falla (Manuel de) 7 Albéniz (Isaac), Rodrigo (Joaquin) 8 Granados (Enrique), Victoria (Tomas Luis de)

composite 3 mix 5 blend 6 fusion, hybrid 7 amalgam, complex, mixture 8 compound 11 combination 12 amalgamation

composition 4 opus 5 essay, paper, theme 6 design, layout, makeup 7 article 9 formation 11 arrangement 12 architecture, constitution, construction *choral:* 4 mass 5 motet 8 oratorio *for eight:* 5 octet *for five:* 7 quintet *for four:* 7 quartet *for nine:* 5 nonet *for one:* 4 aria, solo *for seven:* 6 septet *for six:* 6 sextet *for three:* 4 trio *for two:* 4 duet *instrumental:* 3 jig 4 reel 5 étude, fugue, gigue, march, rondo, suite 6 sonata 7 caprice, partita, prelude, scherzo 8 concerto, fantasia, overture, rhapsody, saraband, sinfonia, symphony, tone poem 9 allemande, capriccio, sarabande 10 intermezzo *vocal:* 4 aria, lied, mass, song 5 carol, chant, motet, opera, round 6 arioso, ballad, chanty 7 cantata, chanson, chantey, chorale, lullaby, requiem 8 berceuse, madrigal, oratorio 9 plainsong, spiritual

compos mentis 4 sane 5 lucid, sound 6 normal

composure 4 calm 5 poise 7 balance, dignity 8 calmness, coolness, evenness,

serenity, sobriety 9 sangfroid 10 equanimity 11 equilibrium

compound 3 mix 4 join, link 5 admix, alloy, blend, union, unite 6 expand, extend, fusion, make up, mingle 7 amalgam, augment, complex, compost, enlarge, magnify, mixture 8 coalesce, comingle, heighten, increase, intermix, multiply 9 admixture, aggravate, associate, commingle, composite, intensify, synthesis 10 commixture, exacerbate 11 intermingle 12 amalgamation *chemical:* (see at CHEMICAL) *medicinal:* 8 magnesia *protein:* 7 peptone *sulfur:* 5 thiol 7 sulfide, sulfone 8 sulfonyl, sulfuryl, sulphide

comprehend 4 know 5 catch, grasp 6 absorb, accept, embody, fathom, take in 7 cognize, compass, contain, discern, embrace, include, involve, subsume 8 comprise, perceive 9 encompass 10 appreciate, understand

comprehensible 8 knowable 9 graspable 10 fathomable 12 intelligible

comprehension 3 ken 5 grasp 9 awareness, knowledge 10 cognizance, conception, perception 11 discernment 12 apperception 13 understanding

comprehensive 4 full, wide 5 broad 6 global 7 general, overall 8 catholic, complete, sweeping 9 all-around, extensive, inclusive, universal 10 exhaustive 12 all-inclusive, encyclopedic

comprehensiveness 5 range, reach, scope 7 breadth 8 fullness 9 amplitude

compress 3 jam 4 cram, push 5 crush, press 6 reduce, shrink, squash, squish, shrink 7 bandage, compact, squeeze 8 condense, contract 11 concentrate

comprise 4 form 6 make up 7 compose, contain, embrace, include, subsume 10 comprehend, constitute

compromise 4 mean, pact, risk 6 settle 7 bargain, compact 8 contract, endanger, trade off 9 agreement, middle way 10 concession, golden mean, jeopardize, settlement 12 middle ground

compulsion 4 itch, need, urge 5 drive, force 8 coercion 9 necessity 10 constraint

compulsive 7 driving 9 besetting, obsessive 12 irresistible, overwhelming

compulsory 7 binding 8 coercive, enforced, required 9 mandatory, requisite 10 imperative, obligatory

compunction 4 pang 5 demur, qualm 6 regret, unease 7 remorse, scruple 8 distress 9 hesitancy, misgiving 10 conscience, hesitation

compunctious 5 sorry 8 contrite, penitent 9 regretful, repentant 10 apologetic, remorseful 11 penitential

computation 8 figuring 9 ciphering, reckoning 10 arithmetic, estimation 11 calculation

compute 5 tally, total 6 cipher, figure, reckon 8 estimate 9 calculate, determine

computer 6 abacus, laptop 7 desktop 9 mainframe 10 calculator *component:* 3 CPU 4 chip 5 mouse, tower 7 monitor 8 keyboard 9 hard drive *information:* 4 data *instruction:* 5 macro *inventor:* 7 Babbage (Charles) *language:* 3 Ada, APL 4 Java, Lisp, Perl 5 ALGOL, BASIC, COBOL 6 Pascal 7 FORTRAN *type:* 6 analog 7 digital

comrade 3 pal 4 ally, chum, mate 5 buddy, crony 6 cohort, comate, fellow 7 consort 8 sidekick, tovarich, tovarish 9 associate, colleague, companion

con 3 gyp, vet 4 anti, bilk, coax, dupe, fool, hoax, rook, scam 5 cheat, fraud, learn, study, trick 6 cajole, fleece, gammon, inmate, survey 7 against, blarney, canvass, chicane, convict, deceive, defraud, examine, inspect, swindle, wheedle 8 blandish, flimflam, hoodwink, inveigle, jailbird, memorize, negative, opponent, persuade, prisoner, soft-soap 9 bamboozle, check over, sweet-talk 10 antithesis, manipulate, scrutinize 11 hornswoggle 12 tuberculosis

concatenate 4 join, link 5 unite 7 connect

concavity 3 dip, sag 4 bowl, dent, sink 5 basin 6 crater, hollow, trough 7 sinkage 8 sinkhole 10 depression

conceal 4 bury, hide, mask, veil 5 cache, cloak, cover, stash 6 screen 7 obscure, secrete 8 ensconce, enshroud, palliate 10 camouflage

concealed 5 privy 6 buried, covert, hidden, secret 8 obscured, shrouded, ulterior 11 clandestine

concede 3 own 4 avow, fold 5 admit, allow, award, grant, yield 6 accept, accord 7 confess 9 surrender, vouchsafe 10 capitulate, relinquish 11 acknowledge

conceit 4 idea, whim 5 fancy, pride 6 egoism, megrim, notion, vagary, vanity 7 caprice, egotism, thought 8 crotchet, metaphor, self-love, smugness, snobbery 9 self-pride, vainglory 10 narcissism, self-esteem 11 complacence, complacency, self-opinion, swelled head

conceited 4 vain 6 snobby, snooty 7 pompous, stuck-up 8 immodest, puffed up, snobbish 12 narcissistic, vainglorious

conceitedness 6 vanity 8 self-love 9 vainglory 10 narcissism

conceivable 8 possible 9 plausible, thinkable 10 imaginable, supposable

conceive 4 form 5 beget, fancy, grasp, think 6 accept, assume, devise, expect, follow, gather, ideate, ponder 7 believe, dream up, feature, imagine, realize, suppose, suspect, think up 8 cogitate, envisage, envision, meditate, ruminate 9 apprehend, formulate, originate, speculate, visualize 10 comprehend, excogitate, understand

concentrate 4 mass 5 focus 6 gather, shrink 7 collect, compact 8 assemble, compress, condense, contract, converge 10 accumulate 11 consolidate

concentrated 5 thick 6 intent, strong 7 focused, intense 8 vehement 9 intensive, undiluted, undivided 12 undistracted

concentration 5 field, major, study 9 attention 10 absorption 11 application

concept 4 idea 5 image 6 notion, theory 7 conceit, thought 10 impression, perception

conception 4 idea 5 birth, image, start 6 notion, origin, outset, theory 7 conceit, genesis, thought 9 beginning 10 impression, perception

conceptual 5 ideal 8 abstract, notional 9 imaginary, visionary 10 ideational 11 theoretical 12 hypothetical, intellectual

concern 4 care, firm, heed 5 doubt, worry 6 affair, bear on, bother, engage, gadget, matter, occupy, outfit, regard, unease 7 anxiety, company, disturb, involve, perturb, trouble 8 business, deal with, disquiet, interest, mistrust 9 attention, curiosity, misgiving, suspicion 10 enterprise, skepticism, solicitude, uneasiness 11 carefulness, contrivance, uncertainty 12 apprehension 13 consciousness, consideration, establishment

concerned 7 anxious, worried 8 affected, involved 10 implicated, interested

concerning 4 as to, in re 5 about, anent, as for 7 apropos 9 as regards, regarding 10 relating to, relative to, respecting

concert 5 agree, union 6 accord, concur, settle, soiree 7 arrange, concord, harmony, recital 8 coincide, musicale 9 agreement, cooperate, harmonize, negotiate 11 performance

concerted 5 joint 6 mutual, united 7 unified 8 combined 11 coordinated 13 collaborative

concert hall 5 arena, odeum 7 theater, theatre 10 auditorium

concession 5 favor, grant 8 giveback 9 admission, allowance, privilege 10 compromise 12 acquiescence

conch 5 shell 7 mollusc, mollusk

concierge 6 porter, warden 7 doorman, janitor 9 custodian 10 doorkeeper

conciliate 4 calm, ease 6 disarm, pacify, soothe 7 appease, assuage, mollify, placate, sweeten, win over 9 reconcile 10 propitiate

concise 5 brief, pithy, short, terse 7 compact, laconic, summary 8 abridged, succinct 9 condensed 10 compressed, contracted 11 compendious 13 short and sweet

conclave 5 synod 6 caucus, powwow 7 meeting, session 8 assembly 9 gathering 10 conference, consistory, convention 11 convocation

conclude 3 end 4 halt, stop 5 close, infer, judge 6 decide, derive, effect, figure, finish, gather, reason, settle, wind up, wrap up 7 collect, resolve 8 complete 9 determine, terminate

concluding 4 last 5 final 6 latest, latter 7 closing 8 eventual, terminal, ultimate

conclusion 3 end 4 stop 5 cease, close 6 ending, epilog, finale, finish, period, result, windup 7 closing, closure, outcome, verdict 8 decision, epilogue, judgment, sequitur 9 cessation, deduction, inference, summation 10 completion, denouement, resolution, settlement 11 culmination, termination 13 determination

conclusive 4 last 5 final 6 cogent 8 deciding, decisive, ultimate 9 clinching 10 compelling, convincing, definitive, undeniable 11 determinant, determinate, irrefutable 12 irrefragable, unanswerable 13 determinative

concoct 3 mix 4 brew, cook 5 frame, hatch 6 cook up, create, devise, invent 7 dream up 8 conceive, contrive 9 fabricate, formulate, originate

concoction 4 brew, plan 5 blend 7 mixture, project 8 compound, creation 9 invention 11 combination, contrivance, fabrication, preparation

concomitant 7 adjunct 8 adjuvant 9 accessory, ancillary, associate, attendant, attending, companion, satellite 10 coincident, collateral 12 accompanying 13 accompaniment, supplementary

concord 4 pact 5 amity, peace, unity 6 accord, comity, treaty 7 concert, entente, harmony, rapport 8 goodwill 9 agreement 10 consonance

concordant 8 agreeing 9 congruous, consonant 10 compatible, consistent, harmonious 11 appropriate

concourse 5 foyer 6 throng 7 joining, meeting 8 junction 9 gathering 10 confluence, crossroads

concrete 5 solid 6 actual 8 specific, tangible 10 particular 11 substantial *component:* 4 sand 5 water 6 gravel

concubine 7 hetaera, hetaira 8 mistress 9 courtesan, odalisque

concupiscence 4 lust 5 ardor 6 desire 7 lechery, passion 9 prurience, pruriency 11 lustfulness 13 lickerishness

concupiscent 3 hot 7 aroused, goatish, lustful 8 prurient 9 lecherous, lickerish, salacious 10 lascivious, libidinous, lubricious, passionate

concur 4 jibe 5 agree, unite 6 accord, assent 7 approve, combine, concord, consent, go along 8 coincide 9 cooperate, harmonize

concurrent 6 coeval 8 parallel 10 coexistent, coexisting, convergent, synchronic 11 synchronous 12 contemporary, simultaneous

concurrently 6 at once 8 together 12 coincidently

concuss 3 jar 4 rock, stun 5 shake, shock 7 agitate

concussion 3 jar 4 bump, jolt 5 clout, crash, shock 6 impact 7 jarring, jolting, shaking 8 pounding 9 agitation, collision

condemn 3 rap 4 damn, doom 5 blame, decry, knock, seize 7 censure, convict, deplore 8 denounce, sentence 9 criticize, deprecate, proscribe, reprehend, reprobate 10 denunciate

condensation 3 dew 5 brief 6 digest, précis 7 epitome, outline, summary 8 abstract, synopsis 9 reduction 10 abridgment, conspectus 11 abridgement

condense 5 sum up 6 digest, reduce, shrink 7 abridge, compact, shorten 8 boil down, compress, contract 9 constrict, epitomize, summarize, synopsize 10 abbreviate 11 concentrate, consolidate, precipitate

condensed 7 concise, summary 10 boiled down 11 compendious

condescend 5 deign, stoop 6 unbend

condescending 5 lofty 6 lordly, snobby, snooty, uppish, uppity 7 haughty, pompous 8 affected, arrogant, cavalier, snobbish, superior 10 disdainful 11 patronizing, pretentious 12 supercilious

condign 3 apt, due, fit 4 fair, just 5 right 6 proper 7 fitting, merited 8 deserved,

rightful, suitable 9 equitable, justified
11 appropriate

condiment 5 curry, sauce, spice 6 catsup, relish, tamari 7 chutney, ketchup, mustard 8 dressing, soy sauce 9 seasoning 10 mayonnaise

___ **con Dios!** 4 Vaya

condition 5 shape, state, terms 6 fettle, malady, status 7 ailment, disease, fitness, proviso 8 syndrome 9 complaint, essential, exception, necessity, provision, requisite, situation 10 limitation, sine qua non 11 requirement, reservation, stipulation 12 prerequisite 13 qualification

conditional 7 reliant 8 relative 9 dependent, provisory, qualified, tentative, uncertain 10 contingent, restricted 11 provisional

condolence 3 rue 4 pity, ruth 6 solace 7 comfort 8 sympathy 10 compassion 13 commiseration

condonable 7 tenable 9 excusable, tolerable 10 acceptable, defensible, pardonable 11 justifiable

condone 5 remit 6 excuse, pardon 7 forgive 8 overlook

conduce 4 lead, tend 7 redound 10 contribute

conducive 7 helpful, leading, tending 9 favorable 10 beneficial, salubrious 11 efficacious, serviceable, stimulating 12 advantageous, contributory, instrumental 13 accommodating

conduct 3 act, run 4 bear, head, lead, show 5 guide, pilot, steer, usher 6 attend, behave, charge, convey, demean, deport, direct, escort, handle, manage 7 arrange, bearing, comport, control, manners, operate, oversee 8 behavior, demeanor, handling, shepherd, transmit 9 accompany, oversight, supervise 10 administer, deportment, management 11 comportment, supervision

conductor 5 guide 6 escort, leader 7 maestro 8 motorman 10 bandleader *American:* 4 Shaw (Robert) 5 Stock (Frederick), Szell (George) 6 Levine (James), Maazel (Lorin), Previn (André), Reiner (Fritz), Thomas (Theodore, Michael Tilson), Walter (Bruno) 7 Fennell (Frederick), Fiedler (Arthur), Monteux (Pierre), Ormandy (Eugene), Schwarz (Gerard), Slatkin (Leonard) 8 Damrosch (Leopold, Walter), Williams (John) 9 Bernstein (Leonard), Leinsdorf (Erich), Rodzinski (Artur), Steinberg (William), Stokowski (Leopold) 11 Kostelanetz (André), Mitropoulos (Dimitri) *Argen-*

tinian: 7 Kleiber (Carlos) 9 Barenboim (Daniel) *Australian:* 7 Bonynge (Richard) *Austrian:* 4 Böhm (Karl) 6 Mahler (Gustav) 7 Karajan (Herbert von) 11 Weingartner (Felix) *Belgian:* 5 Ysaÿe (Eugene) *British:* 5 Solti (Georg) *Canadian:* 6 Dutoit (Charles) 9 MacMillan (Ernest) *Czech:* 7 Kubelik (Jan, Rafael) *Dutch:* 7 Haitink (Bernard) 10 Mengelberg (Willem) *English:* 4 Wood (Henry) 5 Boult (Adrian), Davis (Colin) 6 Rattle (Simon) 7 Beecham (Thomas), Leppard (Raymond), Malcolm (George), Pinnock (Trevor), Sargent (Malcolm) 8 Goossens (Eugene), Marriner (Neville) 9 Mackerras (Charles) 10 Barbirolli (John) *Finnish:* 7 Salonen (Esa-Pekka) *French:* 5 Munch (Charles) 6 Boulez (Pierre), Prêtre (Georges) 7 Monteux (Pierre) *German:* 4 Muck (Carl, Karl) 5 Masur (Kurt) 6 Jochum (Eugen) 7 Kleiber (Erich) 9 Klemperer (Otto), Scherchen (Hermann) 10 Sawallisch (Wolfgang) 11 Furtwängler (Wilhelm), Mendelssohn (Felix) *Greek:* 11 Mitropoulos (Dimitri) *Hungarian:* 5 Seidl (Anton) 6 Doráti (Antal), Reiner (Fritz) 7 Nikisch (Arthur), Ormandy (Eugene), Richter (Hans) *Indian:* 5 Mehta (Zubin) *Italian:* 4 Muti (Riccardo) 6 Abbado (Claudio) 7 Chailly (Riccardo), Giulini (Carlo Maria) 8 Cantelli (Guido), Sinopoli (Giuseppe) 9 Toscanini (Arturo) *Japanese:* 5 Ozawa (Seiji) *Polish:* 9 Rodzinski (Artur) *Russian:* 7 Gergiev (Valery) 10 Temirkanov (Yuri) 12 Koussevitzky (Serge) *Spanish:* 6 Iturbi (José) *Swiss:* 8 Ansermet (Ernest) *stick:* 5 baton

conduit 4 duct, main, pipe 5 canal 6 course 7 channel 8 aqueduct, penstock, pipeline 11 watercourse

coney 4 pika 5 hyrax, lapin 6 rabbit 10 butterfish

confab 4 chat, talk 6 confer, huddle, parley, powwow 7 consult 8 collogue, colloquy, dialogue 10 conference, discussion 12 conversation, deliberation

confabulate see CONFAB

confabulation see CONFAB

confection see CANDY

confederacy 5 cabal, union 6 league 7 compact 8 alliance 9 coalition, syndicate 10 conspiracy, federation

confederate 3 reb 4 ally 5 rebel, unite 6 fellow 7 abettor, partner 9 accessory, associate, colleague, Johnny Reb 10 accomplice 11 conspirator 12 collaborator 13 coconspirator *admiral:* 6 Semmes *capital:* 8 Richmond *color:*

4 gray *general:* **3** Lee (Robert E.) **4** Hill (Ambrose), Hood (John Bell) **5** Bragg (Braxton), Ewell (Richard Stoddart), Price (Sterling), Smith (Edmund Kirby) **6** Morgan (John Hunt), Stuart (J. E. B.) **7** Forrest (Nathan Bedford), Hampton (Wade), Jackson (Thomas Jonathan "Stonewall"), Pickett (George) **8** Johnston (Albert Sidney, Joseph Eggleston) **9** Pemberton (John Clifford) **10** Beauregard (Pierre G. T.), Longstreet (James) *president:* **5** Davis (Jefferson) *soldier:* **9** butternut *spy:* **4** Boyd (Belle) *vicepresident:* **8** Stephens (Alexander)

confederation see CONFEDERACY

confer 4 give, meet, talk **5** allot, award, grant, speak **6** accord, advise, bestow, confab, donate, huddle, parley, powwow **7** consult, discuss, present **8** collogue, converse **10** deliberate **11** confabulate

conference 4 talk **5** forum, synod **6** caucus, league, parley, powwow **7** meeting, palaver, seminar **8** assembly, colloquy, congress **9** symposium **10** colloquium, discussion, round-robin, roundtable **11** association, convocation **12** consultation, deliberation **13** confabulation

confess 3 own **4** avow, sing **5** admit, allow, grant, let on, own up **6** reveal **7** concede, divulge, profess **8** disclose **9** come clean **11** acknowledge

confession 5 creed **6** avowal **7** peccavi **9** admission, statement **10** disclosure

confidant 8 familiar, intimate

confide 4 tell **5** trust **6** bestow, commit, reveal **7** commend, consign, entrust, whisper **8** hand over, relegate, turn over

confidence 5 faith, poise, stock, trust **6** aplomb, surety **8** credence, reliance, sureness **9** assurance, certainty, certitude **10** conviction, equanimity *game:* **4** scam **5** bunco, bunko, grift, sting **7** swindle **8** flimflam

confidence man 3 gyp **5** shark **7** diddler, grifter, scammer, sharper, sharpie **8** swindler **9** charlatan, defrauder, trickster **11** bunco artist

confident 4 bold, sure **5** brash, brave, cocky **6** secure **7** assured, certain **8** cocksure, fearless, intrepid, positive, sanguine, unafraid **9** dauntless, undaunted **10** courageous, undoubtful **11** self-assured, self-reliant **13** self-assertive, self-possessed

confidential 5 close, privy **6** hushed, inside, secret **7** private **8** familiar, hush-hush, intimate **9** auricular **10** classified

configuration 4 cast, form **5** shape **6** figure, layout, makeup **7** contour, gestalt, outline, pattern **9** structure **12** conformation

confine 3 box, mew, pen **4** cage, coop, crib, jail, term **5** bound, cramp, hem in, limit **6** immure, intern, lock up, shut in, shut up **7** delimit, enclose, impound, put away **8** encircle, imprison, localize, restrict **9** constrain **11** incarcerate **12** circumscribe

confinement 7 custody, lying-in **8** childbed **9** captivity, detention, restraint **10** constraint **12** accouchement, imprisonment **13** incarceration

confines 6 bounds, limits **7** borders, compass **8** boundary, environs, purlieus **9** precincts **10** boundaries

confirm 3 fix, set **5** check, prove, vouch **6** attest, ratify, uphold, verify **7** approve, bear out, certify, concede, endorse, justify, support **8** buttress, check out, validate **9** ascertain, reinforce **10** strengthen **11** corroborate **12** authenticate, substantiate

confirmation 5 proof **7** support, witness **8** approval, evidence **9** testimony **10** validation **11** attestation, endorsement, testimonial **12** ratification, verification **13** certification, corroboration

confirmed 3 set **5** fixed, sworn **6** proven **7** chronic, settled **8** deep-dyed, definite, habitual, hardened, ratified **10** accustomed, deep-rooted, deep-seated, entrenched, habituated, inveterate, persistent **13** bred-in-the-bone, dyed-in-the-wool

confiscate 4 grab, take **5** annex, seize, usurp **7** escheat, impound, preempt **8** arrogate **9** sequester **10** commandeer **11** appropriate, expropriate

confiture 3 jam **8** conserve, preserve **9** marmalade, preserves

conflagrant 5 afire, fiery **6** ablaze, aflame, alight **7** blazing, burning, flaming

conflagration 3 war **4** fire **5** blaze **7** inferno **8** conflict **9** holocaust

conflate 3 mix **4** fuse, join, meld, weld **5** blend, merge, mix up **6** mingle, muddle **7** combine, confuse, mistake **8** coalesce, confound **9** commingle

conflict 3 row, war **4** bout, duel, rift, vary **5** brawl, clash, fight, set-to **6** battle, combat, differ, fracas, strife **7** contend, contest, discord, dispute, rivalry, warfare **8** argument, disagree, mismatch, struggle, tug-of-war, variance **9** encounter, rencontre **10** contention, engagement **11** competition

conflicting 6 at odds **7** opposed, warring **8** clashing, contrary, opposing **9** dissonant **10** contending, discordant, discrepant **11** incongruent, incongruous, inconsonant **12** antagonistic, antipathetic, incompatible, inconsistent, inharmonious **13** contradictory

confluence 6 merger **7** joining, meeting, merging **8** junction **9** concourse, gathering **11** convergence

conform 3 fit **4** jibe, obey, suit **5** adapt, agree, fit in, match, yield **6** accord, adjust, attune, comply, follow, square, submit, tailor **8** dovetail **9** acquiesce, harmonize, reconcile **10** coordinate, correspond, proportion **11** accommodate

conformable 6 fitted, suited **7** adapted, matched **8** amenable, obedient, suitable **9** agreeable, compliant, congenial, consonant **10** submissive

conformation 4 cast, form **5** shape **6** figure **7** anatomy **9** structure **10** adaptation **11** arrangement **13** configuration

conforming 3 apt **6** decent, proper, seemly **7** correct, uniform **8** becoming, decorous, suitable **9** befitting, civilized **10** compatible, consistent **11** comme il faut

conformity 6 accord **7** decorum, harmony **9** agreement, coherence, congruity, obedience, orthodoxy **10** accordance, allegiance, compliance, consonance, observance, submission **11** consistency **12** acquiescence

confound 4 damn, faze **5** befog, mix up, stump **6** baffle, puzzle, rattle, refute **7** confuse, mistake, mystify, nonplus, perplex, stupefy **8** befuddle, bewilder, disprove **9** discomfit, dumbfound, embarrass, frustrate **10** controvert, disconcert **11** misidentify

confounded 5 utter **6** blamed, cursed, cussed, damned **7** blasted, blessed, doggone, shocked **8** absolute, accursed, dismayed, infernal, outright **9** consarned, dad-blamed, execrable, out-and-out **11** dumbfounded, overwhelmed, unmitigated **13** thunderstruck

confrere see COLLEAGUE

confront 4 defy, face, meet **5** beard, brave, cross **6** accost, breast, oppose, take on **9** challenge, encounter

Confucian way of life 3 tao

confuse 3 fog **4** blur, daze, faze **5** abash, addle, befog, cloud, dizzy, mix up, muddy, stump, upset **6** baffle, ball up, bemuse, flurry, foul up, fuddle, garble, jumble, mess up, muddle, puzzle, rattle **7** agitate, becloud, derange, disrupt, distort, flummox, fluster, mislead, mistake, mystify, nonplus, perplex, perturb, snarl up **8** bedazzle, befuddle,

bewilder, confound, disorder, disquiet, distract, throw off, unsettle **9** discomfit, disorient, embarrass **10** complicate, disarrange, discompose, disconcert **11** disorganize, misidentify **12** misrepresent

confused 4 lost **5** dazed, messy, muddy, muzzy, vague **6** addled **7** at a loss, chaotic, mixed up, muddled, puzzled **9** flustered, perplexed, unsettled **10** bewildered, nonplussed, topsy-turvy **11** disoriented **12** disconcerted

confusion 3 ado, din **4** flap, mess, stew **5** babel, chaos, havoc, mix-up, snafu, snarl **6** bedlam, dither, foul-up, hubbub, huddle, jumble, lather, muddle, tumult, unease **7** anarchy, clutter, turmoil **8** disarray, disorder, shambles **9** abashment, agitation, commotion, imbroglio **10** hullabaloo, perplexity, puzzlement, turbulence, uneasiness **11** derangement, disturbance, pandemonium **12** bewilderment **13** embarrassment

confute 4 deny **5** evert, rebut **6** defeat, negate **8** confound, disprove, puncture **10** controvert, disconfirm

congé 3 bow **5** adieu **6** good-by **7** goodbye, molding, parting, sendoff **8** farewell **9** dismissal **11** leave-taking

congeal 3 dry, gel, set **4** clot, jell **5** jelly **6** curdle, harden **7** stiffen, thicken **8** solidify **9** coagulate **10** gelatinize

congener 6 agnate **7** cognate, sibling **8** relation, relative

congenial 4 nice **6** social **7** affable, amiable, cordial, kindred, welcome **8** amicable, friendly, gracious, pleasant, pleasing, sociable, suitable **9** agreeable, congruous, consonant, favorable **10** compatible, consistent, gratifying, harmonious **11** cooperative, pleasurable, sympathetic **13** companionable

congenital 6 inborn, inbred, innate, native **7** natural **8** inherent **9** essential, ingrained, intrinsic **10** deep-seated, indigenous, indwelling

conger 3 eel

congeries 5 group **7** company **8** assembly **9** gathering **10** assemblage, collection **11** aggregation **12** congregation

congest 3 jam **4** clog, fill, plug, stop **5** block, choke, close, crowd **6** plug up **7** occlude **8** obstruct

conglobate 4 ball **6** sphere **8** ensphere **9** spherical

conglomerate 4 mass, pool **5** chain, group, mixed, trust **6** cartel, motley **7** chaebol, combine **8** keiretsu, zaibatsu **9** aggregate, syndicate **11** aggregation **12** multifarious **13** heterogeneous

conglomeration 5 hoard, trove 8 mishmash 9 aggregate 10 collection, cumulation, hodgepodge, miscellany 11 agglomerate, aggregation 12 accumulation

Congo, Democratic Republic of the *capital:* 8 Kinshasa *city:* 7 Kolwezi 9 Mbuji-Mayi 10 Lubumbashi *explorer:* 7 Stanley (Henry Morton) *former name:* 5 Zaire 12 Belgian Congo *lake:* 4 Kivu 5 Mweru 6 Albert, Edward 10 Tanganyika *language:* 6 French 7 English *monetary unit:* 5 franc *neighbor:* 5 Congo, Sudan 6 Angola, Rwanda, Uganda, Zambia 7 Burundi 8 Tanzania *river:* 5 Congo

Congo, Republic of *capital:* 11 Brazzaville *city:* 11 Pointe-Noire *former name:* 11 Middle Congo *language:* 6 French *monetary unit:* 5 franc *neighbor:* 5 Congo, Gabon 6 Angola 7 Cabinda 8 Cameroon *river:* 5 Congo

congratulate 4 laud 6 salute 10 compliment, felicitate

congregate 4 meet 5 swarm 6 gather, muster 7 collect, convene 8 assemble, converge 9 forgather 10 foregather, rendezvous

congregation 4 mass 5 crowd, flock, group 7 meeting 8 assembly, audience 9 gathering 10 assemblage, collection 11 churchgoers 12 parishioners

congress 4 diet 5 synod 6 league 7 meeting, society 8 assembly, conclave 10 convention, parliament 11 association, Capitol Hill, legislature

congressman 5 solon 7 senator 8 delegate, lawmaker 10 legislator 14 representative

congruity 9 agreement, coherence 10 conformity 11 consistency

congruous 3 apt, fit 7 fitting 9 agreeable, befitting, congenial, consonant 10 compatible, concordant, consistent, harmonious 11 appropriate, sympathetic

conifer 3 fir, yew 4 pine 5 cedar, larch 6 spruce 7 cypress, hemlock, juniper 8 softwood 9 evergreen 10 arborvitae

conjectural 7 reputed 8 putative, supposed 11 speculative, theoretical 12 hypothetical, suppositious 13 suppositional

conjecture 5 guess, infer 6 assume, theory 7 presume, suppose, surmise, suspect 8 theorize 9 inference, speculate 11 hypothesize, proposition, speculation, supposition

conjoin 3 wed 4 band, link, yoke 5 unite 6 couple 7 combine, connect 8 federate 9 affiliate, associate, cooperate 11 consolidate

conjoint 6 common, mutual, public, shared, united 7 unified 8 combined, communal 9 concerted 10 collective 11 coefficient, cooperative, intermutual

conjointly 8 mutually, together

conjugal 6 wedded 7 marital, married, nuptial, spousal 8 hymeneal 9 connubial 11 matrimonial

conjugality 7 wedlock 8 marriage 9 matrimony

conjugate 4 fuse, join, link, pair, yoke 5 yoked 6 couple, joined, linked 7 bracket, combine, conjoin, connect, coupled 9 associate, connected

conjunct 5 joint 6 common, joined, mutual, shared, united

conjunction 3 and, but, for, nor, yet 4 lest, once, than, then, when 5 after, since, union, until, where, which, while 6 before, either, though, unless 7 because, however, neither, whereas, whether 8 alliance, although, moreover, whenever 9 therefore 10 connection 11 affiliation, association, combination, concurrence

conjuration 4 oath 5 charm, spell, trick 7 sorcery 10 adjuration, hocus-pocus, invocation 11 abracadabra, incantation

conjure 3 beg 4 urge 6 appeal, invoke, summon 7 beseech, entreat, imagine, implore 8 contrive 9 importune 10 supplicate

conjurer 4 mage, seer 5 magus 6 Magian, wizard 7 warlock 8 magician, sorcerer 9 enchanter, trickster 11 illusionist, necromancer

conjuring 5 magic 7 sorcery 8 wizardry 10 hocus-pocus, necromancy 11 abracadabra, legerdemain, thaumaturgy

conk 3 die, hit, rap 4 belt, swat 5 croak, faint, knock, thump, whack 8 knock out

con man *see* CONFIDENCE MAN

connate 4 akin 6 allied, inborn, native 7 kindred, related 8 inherent 9 congenial, elemental, essential, ingrained, inherited, intrinsic 10 affiliated, congenital, indigenous, indwelling 11 consanguine

connect 3 tie, wed 4 ally, bind, join, link, yoke 5 marry, unite 6 attach, bridge, couple, fasten, relate 7 combine, conjoin 8 transfer 9 affiliate, associate, interlock

Connecticut *capital:* 8 Hartford *city:* 4 Avon 6 Darien 8 New Haven, Stamford 9 Greenwich, New London, Waterbury 10 Bridgeport *college, university:* 4 Yale 7 Trinity 8 Wesleyan 9 Fairfield 10 Quinnipiac *nickname:* 6 Nutmeg (State) 12 Constitution

(State) *river:* 6 Thames 10 Housatonic 11 Connecticut *state bird:* 5 robin (American) *state flower:* 14 mountain laurel *state tree:* 8 white oak

connection 3 tie 4 bond, link 5 joint, nexus, tie-in, union 6 hookup 7 joining, kinship, network 8 affinity, alliance, coupling, junction, juncture 9 coherence, communion, fastening 10 attachment, catenation, continuity 11 affiliation, association, combination, conjunction, partnership 12 relationship

connective 3 and, nor, not 4 then 6 either 7 neither 8 syndetic 11 conjunction, conjunctive

conniption 3 fit 4 bout 5 furor, spasm, spate, spell, throe 6 attack, frenzy 7 seizure, tantrum 8 outburst, paroxysm 10 convulsion

connivance 8 intrigue 9 collusion 10 complicity, conspiracy

connive 4 plot, wink 5 blink 6 devise, scheme, wink at 7 blink at, collude 8 conspire, contrive, intrigue 9 machinate

connoisseur 4 buff 6 expert 7 epicure, gourmet 8 aesthete, gourmand, highbrow 9 authority, bon vivant 10 dilettante, gastronome 11 cognoscente

connotation 4 hint 7 meaning 8 overtone 9 undertone 10 intimation, suggestion 11 association, implication 13 signification

connote 4 hint, mean 5 imply, spell 6 hint at, intend 7 betoken, express, signify, suggest 8 indicate, intimate 9 insinuate

connubial 6 wedded 7 marital, married, nuptial, spousal 8 conjugal, hymeneal 11 matrimonial

connubiality 7 wedlock 8 marriage 9 matrimony 11 conjugality

conquer 4 beat, best, lick, tame, whip 5 crush 6 defeat, master, subdue 8 overcome, surmount, vanquish 9 checkmate, overpower, overthrow, overwhelm, subjugate

conquest 3 win 4 rout 7 triumph, victory 9 overthrow, seduction 11 subjugation

Conrad, Joseph *character:* 3 Jim 4 Axel, Lena 5 Flora, Kurtz 6 Marlow, Verloc 7 Almayer 8 MacWhirr, Nostromo *work:* 5 Youth 6 Chance 7 Lord Jim, Typhoon, Victory 8 Nostromo 11 Secret Agent (The) 13 Almayer's Folly 15 Heart of Darkness

Conroy novel 10 Beach Music 11 Water Is Wide (The) 12 Great Santini (The) 13 Prince of Tides (The) 17 Lords of Discipline (The)

consanguineous 4 akin 6 agnate 7 cognate, connate, kindred, related

conscience 5 demur, honor, qualm 6 ethics, virtue 7 decency, remorse, scruple 8 morality, scruples 9 integrity 10 contrition 11 compunction

conscienceless 6 amoral 7 immoral 9 unethical 12 unprincipled, unscrupulous

conscientious 4 fair, just, true 5 exact 6 honest 7 careful, dutiful, upright 8 diligent, reliable, studious 9 honorable 10 high-minded, meticulous, principled, scrupulous 11 hard-working, painstaking, punctilious

conscious 5 alive, awake, aware 7 knowing, mindful, witting 8 sensible, sentient 9 attentive, cognizant 10 deliberate, perceptive

consciousness 4 heed, mind 6 regard 7 concern 9 alertness, awareness, knowledge 10 cognizance, perception 11 realization, recognition

conscribe 5 draft, limit 6 call up, enlist, enroll, muster 7 recruit

conscript 5 draft, elect 6 called, choose, chosen, enlist, enroll, induct, select 7 drafted, dragoon, impress, recruit, soldier 8 selected

consecrate 5 bless 6 anoint, devote, hallow, ordain, pledge 8 dedicate, sanctify

consecrated 4 holy 6 sacred 7 blessed 8 hallowed 10 sanctified *oil:* 6 chrism

consecution see SEQUENCE

consecutive 4 next 5 later 6 serial 7 ensuing, ordered, sequent 9 following, succedent 10 sequential, subsequent, succeeding, successive 11 progressive 12 successional

consent 3 yes 4 okay 5 agree, allow, leave, yield 6 accede, accord, assent, comply, concur, permit 7 approve, go-ahead 8 approval, sanction 9 acquiesce, agreement, allowance, subscribe 10 compliance, permission 12 acquiescence 13 authorization, understanding

consequence 4 fame, note, rank 5 issue, state 6 cachet, effect, import, moment, renown, repute, result, sequel, status, upshot, weight 7 account, conceit, dignity, fallout, outcome, stature 8 eminence, interest, position, prestige, reaction, standing 9 aftermath, inference, magnitude 10 importance, reputation 11 aftereffect, weightiness 12 repercussion, significance 13 momentousness

consequent 5 later, sound 7 ensuing, logical 8 rational 9 deduction, following, resulting

consequential 3 big 5 major 7 serious, weighty 8 egoistic, indirect, material

9 conceited, egotistic, important, momentous **10** collateral, incidental, meaningful, subsidiary **11** significant, substantial **12** considerable **13** self-important

consequently 4 ergo, thus **5** hence **9** as a result, therefore, thereupon **10** inevitably **11** accordingly

conservation 4 care **7** control **9** attention, husbandry **10** management, protection **11** safekeeping **12** guardianship, preservation

conservative 4 tory **6** proper **7** diehard, old-line **8** cautious, discreet, old-guard, orthodox, rightist, standpat **9** right-wing, temperate **10** restrained **11** circumspect, reactionary, right-winger, standpatter, traditional

conservatory 6 school **7** academy, nursery **8** hothouse **10** greenhouse **11** music school

conserve 3 can, jam **4** keep, save **5** hoard, lay up, put up, skimp, store **6** keep up **7** husband, protect, support, sustain **8** maintain, set aside, withhold **9** confiture, economize, safeguard, sweetmeat

consider 3 see **4** deem, feel, mind, muse, note, rate, view **5** fancy, judge, sense, study, think, weigh **6** credit, look at, notice, ponder, reason, reckon, regard **7** account, believe, examine, imagine, inspect, reflect, respect, suppose **8** appraise, cogitate, conceive, conclude, envisage, meditate, mull over, ruminate **9** speculate, think over **10** deliberate, excogitate, scrutinize, think about **11** contemplate

considerable 3 big **5** ample, hefty, large, major **7** notable, sizable, weighty **8** material, sensible, sizeable **9** extensive, important, momentous, plentiful **10** large-scale, meaningful **11** respectable, significant, substantial **13** consequential

considerably 3 far **4** well **5** quite **6** rather **7** notably **8** somewhat **10** noticeably **11** appreciably **13** significantly, substantially

considerate 4 kind **6** kindly, polite, tender **7** amiable, careful, patient, tactful **8** discreet, generous, obliging **9** attentive **10** chivalrous, forbearing, solicitous, thoughtful **11** circumspect, complaisant, sympathetic, warmhearted **13** compassionate

consideration 3 fee **4** heed, tact **5** cause, favor, issue, study **6** esteem, factor, motive, reason, regard **7** account, concern, payment, respect, thought **8** kindness **9** attention, awareness **10** admiration, cogitation, discussion, estimation, inducement, recompense, reflection, solicitude **11** application, forbearance, mindfulness **12** deliberation **13** attentiveness, concentration

considered 7 advised, studied, weighed **8** studious **10** deliberate, thought-out **11** intentional **12** aforethought, premeditated

consign 4 give, send, ship **5** agree, allot, award, remit, yield **6** commit, convey, devote, submit **7** address, commend, confide, deliver, entrust, forward **8** dispatch, hand over, relegate, transmit, turn over **9** surrender

consist 3 lie **4** rest **5** abide, agree, dwell, exist, fit in **6** accord, inhere, reside **7** comport, conform, consort, subsist **8** dovetail **10** correspond

consistency 7 aptness, concord, density, fitness, harmony, texture **8** evenness, firmness, likeness **9** agreement, coherence, congruity, thickness, viscosity **10** conformity, consonance, similarity **11** suitability

consistent 4 even, true **6** steady **7** regular, uniform **8** constant **9** accordant, agreeable, congenial, congruous, consonant, unfailing, unvarying **10** compatible, conforming, dependable, invariable, unchanging **11** homogeneous, sympathetic, undeviating

consistently 8 wontedly **9** regularly, routinely **10** habitually, invariably **11** customarily

console 4 calm, case **5** cheer **6** buck up, solace **7** cabinet, comfort, hearten

consolidate 3 mix, set **4** fuse, join, meld, pool **5** blend, merge, unify, unite **6** firm up, secure **7** compact, fortify **8** compress, condense, federate, solidify **9** integrate **10** amalgamate, strengthen **11** concentrate

consolidation 5 union **6** merger **7** melding, merging **9** coalition **11** combination, integration, unification **12** amalgamation

consonance 6 accord **7** concord, harmony **9** agreement, congruity, resonance **10** congruence

consonant 4 akin, like **6** agnate **7** musical, similar **8** blending, harmonic, resonant **9** congruous **10** compatible, harmonious **11** conformable **13** corresponding *kind:* **4** stop, surd **5** nasal, velar **6** atonic, voiced **7** lateral, palatal, spirant **8** alveolar, bilabial, unvoiced **9** fricative, voiceless

consort 3 set **4** mate, wife **5** agree, group, tally, unite **6** accord, attend, fellow, spouse, square, troupe **7** company,

comport, conform, husband, partner
8 assembly, chaperon, dovetail
9 accompany, associate, companion,
harmonize 10 correspond

consortium 4 bloc, club, ring 5 guild,
trust, union 6 cartel, league 7 combine,
society 8 alliance, congress 9 coalition,
syndicate 10 federation 11 association
12 conglomerate

conspectus 5 brief 6 digest, précis,
sketch, survey 7 epitome, outline, summary 8 abstract, overview, synopsis
9 reduction 10 abridgment 11 abridgement 12 condensation

conspicuous 5 clear, overt, showy
6 marked, patent, signal 7 blatant, evident, glaring, notable, obvious, pointed, salient 8 apparent, distinct, flagrant,
manifest, striking 9 arresting, egregious, notorious, obtrusive, prominent
10 celebrated, noticeable, pronounced,
remarkable 11 eye-catching, illustrious,
outstanding 12 ostentatious

conspiracy 4 plan, plot 5 cabal 6 scheme
8 intrigue 11 machination

conspirator 7 abettor, plotter, schemer
9 accessory, intriguer 10 accomplice
11 confederate

conspire 4 plot 5 cabal 6 scheme 7 collude, connive 8 intrigue 9 machinate

constable 6 deputy, lawman, warden
7 marshal, sheriff

constancy 5 faith 6 fealty 7 loyalty,
resolve 8 adhesion, devotion, fidelity,
firmness 9 adherence, diligence,
endurance, fortitude 10 allegiance,
attachment, dedication, resolution,
steadiness 11 staunchness 12 faithfulness, perseverance 13 dependability,
steadfastness

constant 4 even, fast, firm, true 5 fixed,
loyal 6 dogged, stable, steady, trusty
7 abiding, chronic, endless, equable,
lasting, nonstop, staunch, uniform
8 enduring, faithful, habitual, resolute,
unending 9 ceaseless, confirmed, continual, immovable, immutable, incessant, obstinate, perpetual, steadfast,
sustained, unceasing, unfailing, unmovable, unvarying 10 changeless, consistent, continuous, dependable, inflexible, invariable, inveterate, persistent,
persisting, unchanging, unwavering
11 everlasting, inalterable, unalterable,
unrelenting, unremitting 12 interminable, unchangeable

Constantine *birthplace:* 4 Nish *mother:*
6 Helena *son:* 7 Crispus *victim:* 6 Fausta
7 Crispus *wife:* 6 Fausta

constantly 4 ever 5 often 6 always 7 forever 9 eternally 10 frequently, invari-

ably, repeatedly 11 incessantly, perpetually 12 continuously

constellation 5 group 7 pattern
10 assemblage, collection 11 arrangement *Altar:* 3 Ara *Archer:* 11 Sagittarius
Arrow: 7 Sagitta *Balance:* 5 Libra 9 Ursa
Major *Bear, Little:* 9 Ursa Minor *Big Dipper:* 9 Ursa Major *Bird of Paradise:*
4 Apus *Bull:* 6 Taurus *Centaur:* 9 Centaurus *Chained Lady:* 9 Andromeda
Chameleon: 10 Chamaeleon *Champion:*
7 Perseus *Charioteer:* 6 Auriga *Clock:*
10 Horologium *Colt:* 8 Equuleus *Crab:*
6 Cancer *Crane:* 4 Grus *Cross:* 4 Crux
Crow: 6 Corvus *Crown:* 6 Corona *Cup:*
6 Crater *Dolphin:* 9 Delphinus *Dove:*
7 Columba *Dragon:* 5 Draco *Eagle:*
6 Aquila *Fishes:* 6 Pisces *Fly:* 5 Musca
Flying Fish: 6 Volans *Furnace:* 6 Fornax
Graving Tool: 6 Caelum *Great Bear:*
9 Ursa Major *Greater Dog:* 10 Canis
Major *Hare:* 5 Lepus *Herdsman:*
6 Boötes *Horned Goat:* 11 Capricornus
Hunter: 5 Orion *Indian:* 5 Indus *Keel:*
6 Carina *Lady in the Chair:* 10 Cassiopeia
Larger Bear: 9 Ursa Major *Larger Dog:*
10 Canis Major *Lesser Dog:* 10 Canis
Minor *Lion:* 3 Leo *Little Bear:* 9 Ursa
Minor *Little Dipper:* 9 Ursa Minor *Little
Fox:* 9 Vulpecula *Lizard:* 7 Lacerta *Lyre:*
4 Lyra *Mariner's Compass:* 5 Pyxis
Monarch: 7 Cepheus *Net:* 9 Reticulum
Painter's Easel: 6 Pictor *Pair of Com-
passes:* 8 Circinus *Peacock:* 4 Pavo
Pump: 6 Antlia *Ram:* 5 Aries *Rescuer:*
7 Perseus *River Po:* 8 Eridanus *Sails:*
4 Vela *Scorpion:* 8 Scorpius *Serpent:*
7 Serpens *Serpent Holder:* 9 Ophiuchus
Sextant: 7 Sextans *Shield:* 6 Scutum
Smaller Bear: 9 Ursa Minor *Square:*
5 Norma *Stern:* 6 Puppis *Swan:*
6 Cygnus *Table:* 5 Mensa *Toucan:*
6 Tucana *Triangle:* 10 Triangulum *Twins:*
6 Gemini *Unicorn:* 9 Monoceros *Virgin:*
5 Virgo *Water Carrier:* 8 Aquarius *Water
Monster:* 5 Hydra *Water Snake:* 6 Hydrus
Whale: 5 Cetus *Winged Horse:* 7 Pegasus
Wolf: 5 Lupus

consternate 5 alarm, daunt, shake,
shock 6 appall, dismay 7 horrify,
unnerve 8 distress

consternation 4 fear 5 alarm, dread,
panic, shock 6 dismay, fright, horror,
terror 11 trepidation 12 bewilderment

constituent 4 part 5 piece, voter 6 factor,
member 7 element, portion 8 division,
fraction 9 component, elemental, principal 10 ingredient

constitute 4 form, make 5 enact, found,
set up, start 6 create, embody, make up
7 appoint, compose 8 complete, com-

prise, organize 9 establish, institute, represent

constitution 3 law 4 code 5 build, canon 6 design, makeup, nature 7 charter 8 physique 9 formation, structure 11 composition 12 architecture, construction

constitutional 4 walk 6 inborn, inbred, innate, lawful 7 built-in, organic 8 inherent 9 essential, ingrained, intrinsic 10 congenital, deep-seated

Constitution State 11 Connecticut

Constitution, U.S.S. 12 Old Ironsides

constitutive 5 vital 8 cardinal 9 essential 11 fundamental 12 constructive

constrain 3 bar 4 curb, deny, jail 5 chain, check, crush, force, impel, limit, press 6 bridle, coerce, compel, enjoin, oblige, secure, squash, squish 7 confine, deprive, inhibit, refrain, squeeze 8 compress, hold back, hold down, imprison, restrain, restrict 11 incarcerate

constraint 4 bond 5 check, force 6 duress 8 coercion, pressure 9 captivity, detention, restraint 10 compulsion, diffidence, inhibition, limitation, repression 11 confinement, restriction, suppression 13 embarrassment

constrict 4 curb 5 cramp, limit, pinch, strap 6 hamper, narrow, shrink 7 confine, inhibit, squeeze, tighten 8 compress, condense, contract, restrain, strangle, stultify 9 constrain 12 circumscribe

constrictor 3 boa 5 snake 6 muscle 8 anaconda 9 sphincter, strangler

construct 4 form, make 5 build, erect, forge, frame, put up, raise, set up, shape 6 create, devise 7 build up, compile, fashion, produce 8 assemble, engineer 9 establish, fabricate 11 manufacture, put together

construction 6 design, makeup 7 edifice, shaping 8 assembly, building 9 formation 10 fashioning 11 arrangement, engineering, fabrication, manufacture 12 architecture, constitution

constructive 6 useful 7 helpful, implied, virtual 8 implicit, positive, valuable 9 practical 10 beneficial

construe 5 educe, gloss, parse 6 induct 7 analyze, explain, expound 9 explicate, interpret 10 paraphrase, understand

consuetude 5 habit, usage 6 custom, manner 8 practice 10 convention

consult 3 ask 6 advise, confer, huddle, parley 7 examine, refer to 8 collogue, consider 11 confabulate

consume 3 eat, use 4 down, gulp, ruin 5 drain, drink, eat up, gorge, spend, use up, waste 6 absorb, devour, expend, finish, ingest, obsess, take up 7 deplete, destroy, engross, exhaust, put away, put down, swallow 8 squander 9 dissipate, finish off, polish off 10 annihilate, extinguish, monopolize, run through

consumer 4 user 5 buyer 6 client 7 shopper, end user 8 customer 9 purchaser

consumer advocate 5 Nader (Ralph)

consuming 6 ardent 7 fervent, intense 8 gripping, riveting 9 absorbing 10 engrossing 11 enthralling 12 monopolizing

consummate 3 end 4 ripe 5 close, crown, ideal, utter 6 finish, superb, wind up, wrap up 7 achieve, perfect, supreme 8 absolute, complete, conclude, finished, flawless, peerless, ultimate 9 faultless, matchless, perfected, virtuosic 10 accomplish, impeccable, inimitable 11 superlative 12 accomplished 13 thoroughgoing

consumption 3 use 5 decay, waste 6 intake 7 wasting 8 phthisis 9 depletion, ingestion 10 absorption 11 dissipation 12 tuberculosis

contact 4 meet 5 reach, touch 8 tangency, touching 9 closeness, communion, proximity 10 connection, contiguity 11 association, contingence 13 communication

contagion 3 pox 4 bane, meme 5 taint, venom, virus 6 miasma, plague, poison 7 disease, infection, scourge 8 epidemic 9 pollution 10 corruption, pestilence 13 contamination

contagious 6 catchy 8 catching, epidemic 9 spreading 10 infectious 12 communicable, pestilential 13 transmissible, transmittable

contain 4 hold, keep 5 check, house 6 embody, take in 7 collect, control, embrace, enclose, include, receive, repress, subsume 8 comprise, restrain 9 encompass 10 comprehend 11 accommodate

container 3 bag, bin, box, can, cup, jar, keg, mug, pod, pot, tin, tub, urn, vat 4 cage, case, cask, drum, etui, ewer, pail, sack, silo, tank, vase, vial, well 5 chest, crate, cruet, flask, glass, gourd, phial, pouch 6 basket, bottle, carafe, carton, casket, coffin, cooler, goblet, hamper, hatbox, holder, inkpot, shaker 7 bandbox, capsule, chalice, inkwell, package, pitcher, thermos 8 canister, catchall, decanter, envelope, hogshead, jerrican, puncheon 10 receptacle *liturgical:* 3 pyx 7 chalice 8 ciborium

contaminate 4 foul, soil 5 dirty, spoil,

stain, sully, taint **6** befoul, debase, defile, infect, injure, poison **7** corrupt, deprave, pervert, pollute, profane, tarnish, vitiate **9** desecrate **10** adulterate

conte 4 tale **5** story **9** narrative

contemn 4 snub **5** abhor, scorn, spurn **6** deride **7** deplore, despise, disdain **8** ridicule **10** look down on

contemplate 4 mull, muse, view **5** study, think, weigh **6** behold, debate, gaze at, intend, look at, ponder, regard **7** examine, inspect, propose, reflect **8** consider, gaze upon, look upon, meditate, mull over, ruminate, think out **9** think over **10** deliberate, excogitate, scrutinize

contemplation 5 study **6** musing **7** thought **8** thinking **9** intention, pondering **10** cogitation, meditation, reflection, rumination **11** cerebration, expectation, speculation **12** deliberation **13** consideration

contemplative 6 musing **7** pensive **10** cogitative, meditative, reflecting, reflective, ruminative, thoughtful **11** speculative **13** introspective

contemporary 3 new **6** coeval, extant, modern, recent **7** current, present, topical **8** existent, existing, up-to-date **9** au courant **10** coexistent, coexisting, coincident, concurrent, present-day, synchronic **11** synchronous **12** simultaneous

contempt 5 scorn, shame **7** despite, disdain, mockery **8** aversion, defiance, disfavor, disgrace, dishonor, distaste, ignominy **9** antipathy, discredit, disesteem, disrepute **10** disrespect, opprobrium, repugnance **12** disobedience, stubbornness

contemptible 3 low **4** base, mean, poor, vile **5** cheap, sorry **6** abject, odious, paltry, scummy, scurvy, shabby, sordid **7** hateful, ignoble, pitiful, squalid **8** inferior, pitiable, shameful, unworthy, wretched **9** abhorrent, loathsome **10** despicable, detestable, disgusting **11** ignominious **12** dishonorable

contemptuous 7 haughty **8** arrogant, derisive, scornful **10** disdainful **12** supercilious **13** condescending, disrespectful

contend 3 vie, war **4** aver, avow, cope, face, urge **5** argue, brawl, claim, fight **6** affirm, allege, assert, battle, charge, combat, debate, defend, insist, oppose, report, strive **7** compete, contest **8** confront, maintain, struggle **9** encounter, withstand

contender 5 match, rival **6** player **8** opponent **9** adversary, candidate,

combatant **10** antagonist, challenger, competitor, contestant

___ **contendere 4** nolo

content 4 cozy, gist **5** happy **6** at ease, serene **7** appease, gratify, meaning, placate, satisfy **9** gratified, satisfied, substance **11** comfortable **12** significance

contention 3 war **4** beef, feud **6** combat, rumpus, strife, thesis **7** discord, dispute, dissent, quarrel, rivalry, wrangle **8** argument, conflict, disunity, squabble **10** difference, dissension, dissidence **11** altercation, competition, controversy *Scottish:* **5** sturt

contentious 5 fiery **7** carping, froward, peppery, scrappy, warlike **8** captious, caviling, contrary, militant, perverse **9** bellicose, combative, hotheaded, litigious, polemical, truculent **10** pugnacious **11** belligerent, quarrelsome **12** disputatious, faultfinding **13** argumentative, controversial

conterminous 10 coincident **11** coextensive

contest 3 vie **4** bout, duel, feud, fray, game, meet, race, tilt **5** clash, fight, match, repel, rival, trial **6** battle, combat, debate, oppose, resist, strife, strive **7** compete, dispute, rivalry, warfare **8** argument, conflict, endeavor, skirmish, struggle, tug-of-war **9** challenge, encounter, rencontre **10** engagement, tournament **11** competition

contiguity 9 adjacency, immediacy, proximity **11** propinquity

contiguous 4 next **8** abutting, adjacent, touching **9** adjoining, bordering **10** juxtaposed

continence 6 purity, virtue **8** chastity, sobriety **9** austerity **10** abnegation, abstinence, asceticism, chasteness, moderation, temperance **11** forbearance **12** renunciation **13** self-restraint

continent 4 Asia, mass **5** sober **6** Africa, chaste, Europe **8** celibate, mainland **9** abstinent, Australia, temperate **10** abstemious, Antarctica, restrained **11** abstentious **12** North America, South America *lost:* **8** Atlantis

contingence 5 touch **7** contact **8** tangency, touching

contingency 4 pass **5** event **6** chance, crisis **8** exigency, juncture, occasion **9** emergency **10** likelihood **11** opportunity, possibility, probability, uncertainty

contingent 3 odd **4** band **5** group, party, troop **6** casual, chance, likely **7** reliant **8** possible, probable, relative **9** dependent, empirical, entourage, uncertain **10** accidental, delegation, deputation, detachment, fortuitous, incidental, unforeseen **11** conditional **13** unanticipated, unforeseeable, unpredictable

continual 6 steady **7** abiding, endless, nonstop, regular, running **8** constant, enduring, timeless, unbroken, unending **9** ceaseless, incessant, perpetual, perennial, recurrent, recurring, unceasing, unfailing, unvarying **10** persistent, persisting, relentless, unchanging, unflagging **11** everlasting, unremitting **12** interminable **13** uninterrupted

continually 4 ever **6** always **7** forever **8** steadily, together **9** endlessly **10** constantly **11** incessantly, night and day **12** interminably, persistently, relentlessly, successively **13** consecutively

continuance 3 run **4** stay **5** delay **6** sequel **8** duration, survival **9** longevity **10** permanence **11** adjournment, persistence **12** postponement, prolongation

continuation 3 run **4** coda **6** sequel **8** appendix, duration, epilogue **9** endurance, extension **10** resumption **11** persistence, protraction **12** prolongation

continue 4 go on, last, stay **5** abide, renew, run on **6** endure, hang in, keep at, keep on, keep up, pick up, push on, remain, reopen, resume, retain, take up **7** carry on, persist, press on, proceed, prolong, restart, survive **8** maintain, postpone **9** carry over, persevere **10** recommence

continuing 5 fixed **6** steady **7** abiding, chronic, durable, eternal, lasting, ongoing **8** constant, enduring, lifelong, stubborn **9** long-lived, obstinate, perennial, prolonged, steadfast, tenacious, unabating **10** inveterate, persistent, persisting **11** long-lasting

continuity 4 flow **6** script **8** duration, scenario, sequence **9** endurance **11** persistence, progression

continuous see CONTINUAL

continuously see CONTINUALLY

contort 4 knot, warp **5** twist, wring **6** deform, wrench, writhe **7** distort, grimace, torture **9** convolute, corkscrew, disfigure

contortionist 7 acrobat

contour 4 form, line **5** curve, lines, shape **6** figure **7** outline, pattern, profile **9** lineament, lineation **10** silhouette **11** delineation

contra 6 facing, toward **7** against, counter, reverse, vis-à-vis **8** converse, fronting, opposite **10** conversely

contraband 3 hot **5** taboo **6** banned **7** bootleg, illegal, illicit, smuggle **8** unlawful **9** forbidden **10** prohibited,

proscribed **11** black market, bootlegging, trafficking

contract 4 bond, hire, pact, sink **5** catch, incur, lease **6** engage, induce, lessen, reduce, shrink, treaty, weaken **7** abridge, acquire, afflict, bargain, decline, dwindle, shorten, shrivel **8** compress, condense, covenant, decrease, diminish **9** agreement, constrict, succumb to **11** concentrate, transaction **12** come down with *part:* **6** clause **7** article, proviso

contraction 3 he'd, he's, I'll, it's, I've, tic **4** ain't, can't, don't, flex, he'll, isn't, let's, she'd, she's, won't, you'd **5** aren't, cramp, didn't, hadn't, hasn't, she'll, spasm, they'd, wasn't, you'll, you're, you've **6** haven't, mustn't, needn't, they'll, they've, weren't **7** couldn't, elision, mightn't, wouldn't **8** shouldn't **9** reduction, shrinkage **10** abridgment **12** abbreviation *heart's:* **7** systole *poetic:* **3** e'en, e'er, o'er, 'tis **4** ne'er, 'twas **5** 'twere, 'twill

contradict 4 deny **5** belie, cross, rebut **6** impugn, negate, refute, take on **7** confute, dispute, gainsay **8** negative, traverse **9** challenge, disaffirm

contradiction 6 denial **7** paradox **8** antinomy, negation, rebuttal, variance **9** disparity **10** gainsaying, opposition, refutation **11** discrepancy, incongruity **12** disagreement, protestation **13** inconsistency

contradictory 7 counter, reverse **8** contrary, converse, negating, opposite **9** antipodal **10** antipodean, antithesis, nullifying **12** antithetical

contraption 3 rig **5** gizmo **6** device, doodad, gadget **7** machine **9** apparatus, doohickey **11** contrivance

contrariety 10 antagonism, antithesis, opposition, perversity, unlikeness

contrariwise 9 vice versa **10** conversely, oppositely

contrary 5 balky **6** averse, ornery, unruly **7** adverse, counter, froward, reverse, wayward **8** converse, opposite, perverse, stubborn **9** antipodal, diametric, dissident, obstinate, vice versa **10** conversely, discordant, headstrong, oppositely, rebellious, refractory **11** conflicting, intractable, wrongheaded **12** antagonistic, antipathetic, antithetical, contumacious, cross-grained, recalcitrant *prefix:* **7** counter

contrast 6 differ **7** collate, compare, diverge **8** conflict, disagree **9** disparity, diversity **10** comparison, difference, divergence **11** distinction, distinguish **13** dissimilarity

contravene 4 defy, deny 5 break, cross, fight 6 abjure, breach, disown, impugn, negate, offend, oppose, reject 7 disobey, gainsay, violate 8 disclaim, infringe, renege on 9 disaffirm, go against, repudiate 10 contradict, transgress

contravention 6 breach 7 offense 8 trespass 9 violation 10 infraction 12 infringement 13 nonobservance, transgression

contretemps 3 row 4 slip, tiff 5 clash, run-in 6 dustup, mishap, slip-up 7 dispute, quarrel 8 argument 9 mischance 10 falling-out, misfortune

contribute 3 add 4 give, help, tend 5 grant 6 chip in, donate, kick in, submit, supply 7 conduce, pitch in, redound 9 subscribe 11 come through

contribution 4 alms, gift 5 input, share 7 charity, payment, present 8 donation, offering 11 benefaction, beneficence

contributory 8 adjuvant 9 accessory, ancillary, auxiliary 10 collateral, subsidiary, supporting 11 appurtenant, subservient

contrite 5 sorry 8 penitent 9 regretful, repentant 10 apologetic, remorseful 11 penitential

contriteness see CONTRITION

contrition 3 rue 4 ruth 6 regret 7 penance, remorse 9 penitence 10 repentance 11 compunction 12 self-reproach

contrivance 4 ruse 6 device, gadget 7 gimmick 8 artifice 9 apparatus, expedient, invention, stratagem 10 brainchild 11 contraption

contrive 3 rig 4 fake, make, move, plan, plot 5 frame, hatch 6 cook up, devise, invent, make up, manage, scheme, vamp up, wangle 7 arrange, concoct, connive, develop, dream up, fashion, project, work out 8 cogitate, conspire, engineer, intrigue 9 construct, elaborate, fabricate, formulate, machinate

contrived 5 hokey 6 forced 7 labored 8 strained 9 concocted, insincere 10 artificial, fabricated, factitious

control 3 run 4 curb, rein, rule, sway 5 guide, power, steer 6 bridle, direct, govern, handle, manage, master, rein in, subdue 7 command, conduct, mastery, oversee, repress, reserve 8 dominate, dominion, regulate, restrain 9 authority, direction, restraint, supervise, supremacy 10 discipline, domination, management 11 supervision 12 jurisdiction

controlled 8 discreet, reserved 9 temperate 10 restrained

controversial 5 risky 6 touchy 7 awkward, charged, eristic 8 delicate, disputed, ticklish 9 explosive, litigious, polemical 11 contentious, problematic 12 disputatious 13 argumentative

controversy 3 row 5 clash 6 debate, rumpus, strife 7 dispute, quarrel, wrangle 8 argument, squabble 10 contention, falling-out 11 altercation, disputation, embroilment

controvert 4 deny 5 rebut 6 debate, oppose, oppugn, refute 7 confute, counter, dispute, gainsay 8 disprove, question 9 challenge, repudiate

contumacious 7 froward 8 contrary, insolent, mutinous, obdurate, perverse 9 obstinate 10 rebellious, refractory 11 disobedient, intractable 12 recalcitrant 13 insubordinate

contumacy 8 contempt, defiance 9 insolence 10 perversity 12 stubbornness 13 recalcitrance

contumelious 7 abusive 8 derisive, insolent, scornful 9 insulting, truculent 10 disdainful, scurrilous 11 opprobrious 12 vituperative

contumely 5 abuse 6 insult 7 affront, mockery, obloquy 8 contempt, ridicule, sneering 9 aspersion, invective 10 scurrility 12 vituperation

contuse 6 batter, bruise, injure 7 blacken

conundrum 5 poser 6 enigma, puzzle, riddle 7 baffler, mystery, problem, puzzler, stumper 10 puzzlement 13 Chinese puzzle

convalesce 4 heal, mend 7 improve, recover 10 recuperate

convene 4 call, meet 6 call in, gather, muster, summon 7 convoke, summons 8 assemble 9 forgather 10 congregate 12 come together

convenience 4 ease 7 amenity, benefit, comfort, leisure 8 facility 9 handiness 10 assistance 13 accessibility

convenient 3 fit 4 near 5 close, handy, ready 6 at hand, nearby, proper, useful 7 close by, helpful 8 suitable 9 available, immediate, opportune 10 accessible 11 appropriate, comfortable 12 advantageous

convent 5 abbey 6 priory 7 nunnery 8 cloister 9 monastery, sanctuary

convention 3 law 4 bond, code, pact, rule 5 canon, usage 6 accord, custom, treaty 7 compact, meeting, precept 8 assembly, congress, contract, covenant, practice, protocol 9 agreement, concordat, formality, gathering, propriety, tradition 11 convocation 13 understanding

conventional 5 trite, usual **6** formal, normal, proper, seemly, solemn, square **7** correct, regular, routine, typical **8** everyday, habitual, moderate, ordinary, orthodox, standard, straight **9** bourgeois, customary **10** button-down, conforming, prevailing, restrained, unoriginal **11** commonplace, traditional **12** conservative

conventionalize 5 adapt **7** conform, stylize

converge 4 join, meet **5** focus, merge, unite **11** concentrate **12** come together

conversant 8 familiar **9** au courant **10** acquainted **11** experienced

conversation 4 chat, talk **6** confab, debate, parley **7** palaver, talking **8** causerie, colloquy, dialogue, duologue, exchange, repartee **9** discourse, tête-à-tête **10** discussion **13** confabulation

conversation piece 5 curio **6** oddity **9** curiosity

converse 3 gab **4** chat, chin, talk **5** speak, visit **6** confer, contra, parley **7** chatter, counter, reverse **8** antipode, contrary, opposite **9** antipodal, diametric **10** antithesis **12** antithetical **13** contradictory

conversely 9 vice versa **10** oppositely **12** contrariwise

conversion 5 shift **6** change, switch **7** novelty, rebirth, turning **8** mutation, reversal **9** about-face **10** alteration, changeover **11** permutation **12** modification, regeneration **13** metamorphosis, transmutation

convert 4 sway **5** alter **6** change, modify, redeem, reform, switch **7** commute, remodel, renovate **9** proselyte, transform, translate, transmute, transpose **11** transfigure **12** metamorphose, transmogrify *Christian:* **10** catechumen

convex 5 bowed, toric **6** arched, curved **7** bulging, curving, gibbous, rounded

convey 3 lug **4** bear, cart, cede, deed, pack, send, tell, tote **5** bring, carry, ferry **6** assign, impart, pass on **7** channel, conduct, consign, deliver, express, project **8** make over, sign over, transfer, transmit **9** transport **11** communicate

conveyance 3 car **4** auto, cart, deed, sled **5** coach, sedan, stage, title, wagon **7** charter, trailer, transit, vehicle **8** carriage, carrying **9** transport **10** automobile **12** transporting *public:* **3** bus, cab **4** taxi, tram **5** plane, train **6** subway **7** trolley **8** airplane, monorail, railroad, rickshaw **9** streetcar **10** jinricksha, jinrikisha

convict 5 felon, lifer **6** inmate, send up **7** condemn, put away **8** criminal, jailbird, prisoner, sentence, yardbird **10** find guilty

conviction 4 view **5** creed, faith **6** belief, surety **7** opinion **8** doctrine, sentence, sureness **9** assurance, certainty, certitude, sentiment **10** confidence, persuasion **12** condemnation

convince 6 assure, induce, prompt **7** satisfy, win over **8** persuade, talk into **9** influence, prevail on **11** bring around, prevail upon

convincing 5 solid, sound, valid **6** cogent **8** credible, faithful **9** plausible **10** believable, conclusive, persuasive, satisfying **11** trustworthy

convivial 3 gay **5** jolly, merry **6** hearty, jocund, jovial, lively, social **7** festive **8** mirthful, sociable **9** fun-loving, vivacious **10** gregarious **13** companionable

convocation 5 synod **7** council, meeting **8** assembly, conclave **9** gathering **10** assemblage **12** congregation

convoke 4 call **6** gather, invite, muster, summon **7** collect, convene **8** assemble **12** call together

convoluted 6 coiled **7** complex, tangled, winding **8** involved, tortuous **9** intricate **10** circuitous **11** anfractuous, complicated **12** labyrinthine

convoy 6 attend, escort **7** conduct **9** accompany

convulse 4 rock **5** shake **7** agitate, concuss **8** tetanize

convulsion 3 fit **5** spasm **6** attack, tumult, uproar **7** quaking, rocking, seizure, shaking **8** disaster, paroxysm, upheaval **9** commotion, trembling

cook 3 fix, fry **4** bake, boil, chef, heat, melt, stew **5** broil, grill, poach, roast, sauté, steam **6** braise, doctor, simmer **7** falsify, parboil, prepare, swelter

cooked 4 done, sham **5** bogus, faked, phony **6** made-up **7** altered **8** doctored, spurious **10** fictitious

cookery 7 cuisine *expert:* **3** Yan (Martin) **4** Chen (Joyce), Kerr (Graham), Puck (Wolfgang), Root (Waverley) **5** Beard (James), Child (Julia), David (Elizabeth), Hines (Duncan), Smith (Jeff) **6** Bocuse (Paul), Carême (Marie-Antoine), Farmer (Fannie), Fisher (M. F. K.), Franey (Pierre), Waters (Alice) **7** Crocker (Betty), Stewart (Martha) **8** Bourdain (Anthony), Rombauer (Irma) **9** Claiborne (Craig), Escoffier (Auguste), Prudhomme (Paul)

cookie 4 snap **7** biscuit, brownie **10** gingersnap

cooking *appliance:* **4** oven **5** mixer,

range, stove **7** blender, toaster
9 microwave **10** rotisserie *implement:*
3 cup, pan, pot, wok **4** olla **5** ladle,
sieve, spoon, whisk **6** grater, masher,
sifter, tureen **7** griddle, skillet, spatula,
steamer **8** colander, teaspoon **9** eggbeater, frying pan **10** rolling pin, table-
spoon **12** measuring cup *room:* **6** galley
7 kitchen

Cook Islands *capital:* **6** Avarua *dependency of:* **10** New Zealand *island:* **9** Raro-
tonga

cool 3 hep, hip, icy **4** calm, cold **5** abate,
aloof, chill, gelid, nippy **6** arctic, chilly,
frigid, frosty **7** assured, compose, control, decline, distant, dwindle, repress,
subside **8** composed, decrease,
detached, diminish, reserved, suppress
9 collected, confident, impassive,
unruffled **10** nonchalant, phlegmatic,
unsociable **11** indifferent, standoffish,
unflappable **13** dispassionate, imperturbable, self-possessed

cooler 3 fan, jug, pen **4** brig, coop, jail
5 clink, pokey **6** fridge, icebox, lockup,
prison **7** freezer, slammer **9** calaboose
11 refrigerant **12** refrigerator

cooling device 3 fan **6** fridge, icebox
7 freezer **12** refrigerator

coolness 5 chill, poise **6** aplomb,
phlegm **7** reserve **9** composure, frigidi-
ty, sangfroid **10** dispassion, equanimity
11 nonchalance, self-control

coop 3 hem, jug, mew, pen **4** brig, cage,
jail **5** cramp, fence, pokey **6** cooler, corral, lockup, prison, shut in **7** close in,
confine, enclose, slammer **9** calaboose,
enclosure

cooperate 5 agree, unite **6** concur,
league **7** combine, conjoin, pitch in
8 coincide, conspire **11** collaborate,
participate **12** work together

cooperation 8 alliance, teamwork
13 confederation

cooperative 5 joint **6** common, mutual,
shared **8** coactive, conjoint, obliging
9 collegial, concerted **10** collective, syn-
ergetic **11** coordinated **13** accommodating, collaborative, uncompetitive

Cooper hero 7 Hawkeye **10** Deerslayer,
Pathfinder **11** Natty Bumppo

coordinate 4 mate, mesh **5** align, equal,
match, order **6** adjust, relate **7** coequal,
conform **8** organize, parallel **9** companion, correlate, harmonize, integrate,
reconcile **10** proportion, reciprocal
11 accommodate, correlative, counterpart

coot 4 bird, fogy **6** dotard, duffer, fellow,
oddity, scoter, weirdo **7** oddball **9** character, eccentric

cootie 5 louse **9** body louse

cop 3 nab **4** lift, take **5** adopt, catch,
filch, pinch, steal, swipe **6** pilfer **7** capture, officer **8** bluecoat **9** patrolman,
policeman

copacetic 3 A-OK **4** fine, jake, okay
5 dandy, great, nifty **8** all right **9** excellent **12** satisfactory

cope 4 cape, hack **5** cloak, cover, get by,
match, vault **6** canopy, endure, make
do, manage, mantle **7** carry on, survive
8 vestment

copestone 5 crown

copious 4 lush, rich **5** ample **6** lavish,
plenty **7** liberal, profuse, replete
8 abundant, generous **9** abounding,
bounteous, bountiful, exuberant, luxuriant, plenteous, plentiful

Copland work 5 Rodeo **11** Billy the Kid
17 Appalachian Spring

cop-out 5 dodge **6** excuse **7** evasion, pretext, retreat

copper 4 cent, coin **5** metal, penny,
token **9** butterfly, policeman *item:*
4 cent **5** penny **6** kettle *sulfate:* **7** vitriol
9 bluestone **11** blue vitriol

copperhead 5 snake, viper **8** pit viper

coppice 4 bosk, wood **5** copse, grove,
woods **6** bosque, forest, growth **7** thicket **9** brushwood, underwood

copse see COPPICE

Copt 8 Egyptian

copula 4 bond, link **5** joint, union **7** coupler

copy 3 ape **4** echo, fake, mock, sham
5 clone, ditto, forge, mimic, model
6 carbon, parrot, repeat **7** emulate, forgery, imitate, replica, takeoff **8** knockoff, likeness, simulate **9** duplicate, facsimile, imitation, replicate, reproduce
10 impression, simulacrum, simulation,
transcribe, transcript **11** counterfeit,
counterpart, reduplicate, replication
12 reproduction

copyist 5 clerk **6** scribe **8** imitator
9 engrosser **10** plagiarist **12** transcriber

copyread 4 edit

coquet 3 toy **4** fool, vamp **5** dally, flirt,
tease **6** trifle

coquette 4 vamp **5** flirt, tease

coquettish 3 coy **6** fickle **9** frivolous, kittenish **11** flirtatious

coral 3 red **4** pink, rosy **5** polyp **9** limestone

coral reef 3 cay, key **5** atoll *off Australia:*
5 Wreck *world's largest:* **12** Great Barrier

cord 3 tie **4** band, lace, pile, rope, whip,
yarn **5** cable, nerve, stack **6** strand,
string, tendon *twisted:* **7** torsade

cordage 4 rope 5 ropes 7 rigging *fiber:*
4 bast, hemp, jute, pita 5 sisal
Corday's victim 5 Marat (Jean-Paul)
Cordelia *father:* 4 Lear *sister:* 5 Regan
7 Goneril
cordial 4 warm 6 genial, hearty, jovial,
tender 7 affable, liqueur, sincere
8 cheerful, friendly, gracious, sociable
9 congenial, convivial, heartfelt 10 hospitable 11 sympathetic, warmhearted
12 wholehearted
cordiality 6 warmth 7 amenity 9 geniality
10 amiability 12 agreeability, friendliness
cordon 4 lace, line, ring 5 braid 6 circle,
ribbon 7 barrier 8 espalier *bleu:* 4 chef,
cook 6 ribbon 10 blue ribbon, decoration, master chef
core 3 hub, nub 4 base, crux, gist, meat,
pith, root 5 basis, focus, heart, midst
6 center, depths, kernel, middle, upshot
7 essence, nucleus 8 interior, midpoint
9 substance 10 foundation
corium 5 cutis 6 dermis
cork 4 bark, plug, seal, stop 5 float
6 bobber 7 stopper, stopple
corker 4 lulu 5 beaut, dandy, dilly, doozy
6 doozie, killer 8 jim-dandy, knockout
9 humdinger 11 crackerjack 12 lollapalooza
corkscrew 4 coil, wind 5 helix, twist
6 spiral
cormorant 4 bird, shag 7 glutton
corn 5 grain, maize 6 hominy 9 granu-
late *bread:* 4 pone 7 bannock *Indian:*
5 maize 6 mealie *kind:* 3 pop 5 flint,
flour, sweet 6 Indian *pest:* 5 borer
piece: 3 cob, ear 5 spike 6 kernel, nubbin
Corncracker State 8 Kentucky
corner 3 box, fix, jam, nab 4 hole, nook,
trap, tree 5 angle, catch, coign, niche,
seize 6 collar, cranny, dogleg, pickle,
plight, recess, scrape 7 capture, dilemma, impasse, trouble 8 bottle up,
monopoly 10 bring to bay 11 predicament 12 intersection *of eye:* 7 canthus
cornerstone 4 base 5 basis 7 support
8 rudiment 10 foundation, groundwork
cornet 4 cone, horn 7 officer, trumpet
10 instrument
Cornhusker State 8 Nebraska
cornice 3 cap 4 band, eave 5 crown
7 molding
cornmeal 4 masa, samp 5 grits 6 hominy
7 hoecake *mush:* 7 polenta
cornucopia 4 cone, horn 6 bounty, plenty, wealth 9 abundance, profusion
12 horn of plenty
Cornwallis, Charles *adversary:* 6 Greene
(Nathanael) *surrender site:* 8 Yorktown

corny 5 banal, sappy, stale, trite 6 old
hat 7 clichéd, mawkish 8 shopworn
9 hackneyed, schmaltzy 11 sentimental,
stereotyped
corollary 6 effect, result, sequel, upshot
8 parallel, sequence 9 resulting 10 associated, end product, equivalent
11 aftereffect, consequence
corona 4 aura, glow, halo 5 cigar, crown,
glory 6 circle, nimbus 7 aureola, aureole
coroner 8 examiner
coronet 5 crown, tiara 6 anadem, circle,
diadem, wreath 7 chaplet, circlet, garland 8 headband
Coronis *form:* 4 crow *son:* 9 Asclepius
11 Aesculapius
corporal 3 NCO 6 bodily, carnal 7 fleshly, somatic 8 physical
corporate 7 unified 8 combined 9 aggregate
corporeal 6 bodily, carnal, mortal
7 fleshly, somatic 8 material, physical,
tangible 9 objective 10 phenomenal
11 substantial
corps 4 band, body 5 group, party, troop
6 outfit, troupe 7 company
corpse 4 body 5 bones, stiff 7 cadaver,
carcass, carrion, remains *combining
form:* 4 necr 5 necro
corpselike 4 dead 5 gaunt 7 deathly,
ghastly, macabre 8 lifeless, skeletal
10 cadaverous
corpulence 7 fatness, obesity 9 adiposity,
rotundity 10 fleshiness
corpulent 3 fat 5 bulky, gross, heavy,
obese, plump, stout 6 fleshy, portly,
rotund 7 porcine, weighty 9 overblown
10 overweight
corpus 4 body, bulk, core, mass 6 oeuvre 9 principal, substance 10 collection
11 compilation
corpuscle 4 cell 8 hemocyte, monocyte
9 blood cell, leukocyte 10 lymphocyte
11 erythrocyte, granulocyte
corral 3 mew, pen 5 fence 6 gather, shut
in 7 close in, collect, confine, enclose,
round up 8 surround 9 enclosure
correct 3 fit, fix 4 edit, just, mend, true
5 amend, emend, exact, right 6 adjust,
decent, proper, punish, reform, remedy, repair, revise, seemly 7 chasten, fitting, improve, perfect, precise, rectify,
redress 8 accurate, becoming, chastise,
decorous, flawless, set right 9 castigate,
faultless 10 conforming, discipline,
impeccable, legitimate, meticulous,
scrupulous 11 appropriate, comme il
faut, punctilious 12 conventional *combining form:* 4 orth 5 ortho
correction 3 rod 6 rebuke 7 reproof

8 revision **9** amendment **10** adjustment, discipline, emendation, punishment **11** castigation

corrective 4 cure **6** remedy **8** antidote, punitive, remedial **10** beneficial **11** counterstep, restorative **12** counteragent **13** counteractive

correctness 7 decorum **8** accuracy, fidelity **9** precision, propriety **10** exactitude

correlate 5 match **6** analog **7** pendant **8** analogue, coincide, dovetail, parallel **9** harmonize **10** complement, correspond **11** counterpart

correlative 3 and, nor **4** both, then **6** either **7** neither, related **10** complement, reciprocal **11** counterpart **13** complementary, corresponding

correspond 4 jibe **5** agree, equal, match, write **6** accord, concur **7** comport, conform **8** dovetail **9** harmonize **11** communicate

correspondence 4 mail **7** analogy, letters **8** symmetry **9** agreement, congruity **10** conformity, similarity **11** consistency, correlation *mathematical:* **7** mapping **8** function

correspondent 5 match **6** analog, pen pal, writer **7** fitting **8** analogue, parallel, reporter, suitable **9** correlate **10** conforming, journalist **11** commentator, contributor, counterpart

corresponding 4 akin, like **5** alike **6** agnate **7** related, similar **8** matching, parallel **9** analogous, consonant **10** comparable **11** correlative

correspondingly 4 also **7** equally **8** likewise **9** similarly **11** analogously

corrida 9 bullfight *shout:* **3** olé

corridor 4 hall, lane, path **5** aisle, route, strip **6** artery, avenue **7** hallway, passage **10** passageway

corroborate 5 prove **6** uphold, verify **7** approve, bear out, certify, confirm, endorse, justify, support **8** document, validate **9** vindicate **12** authenticate, substantiate

corroborative 9 ancillary, auxiliary **10** collateral, supporting, supportive **12** confirmatory

corrode 4 rust **5** eat away, eat into, oxidize **8** wear away **9** undermine

corrosive 5 acerb **6** biting **7** acerbic, caustic, cutting **9** sarcastic

corrosiveness 7 sarcasm **8** acerbity

corrugation 4 fold, ruck **5** plica, ridge **6** crease, furrow, groove **7** crinkle, wrinkle

corrupt 3 rot **5** bribe, decay, spoil, stain, taint, venal **6** befoul, debase, defile, molder, rotten, smirch **7** crooked, debauch, degrade, deprave, pervert, putrefy, tarnish, vitiate **8** bribable, degraded, depraved, infected, perverse **9** decompose, dishonest, miscreant, reprobate, unethical **10** bastardize, degenerate **12** unprincipled, unscrupulous **13** untrustworthy

corruptible 5 venal **7** buyable **8** bribable

corruption 4 vice **5** decay, fraud, graft **7** bribery, jobbery **9** barbarism, depravity, turpitude **10** immorality, wickedness **11** impropriety

corsair 5 rover **6** pirate **8** picaroon, sea rover **9** buccaneer, pickaroon, privateer **10** freebooter

corset 5 stays **6** bodice, girdle **7** support

cortege 5 train **6** parade **7** retinue **9** entourage **10** attendants, procession

cortex 4 bark, husk, peel, rind **6** casing **8** peridium

Cortland 5 apple

corundum 4 ruby **5** emery, topaz **7** emerald **8** abrasive, amethyst, sapphire

coruscate 5 flash, gleam, glint, shine **7** glisten, glitter, sparkle, twinkle **11** scintillate

corvid 3 jay **4** crow **5** raven **6** magpie **9** passerine

Corvino's wife 5 Celia

corybantic 3 mad **4** wild **5** rabid **6** crazed **7** frantic, furious **8** ecstatic, frenetic, frenzied **9** delirious

coryphée 6 dancer **8** danseuse **9** ballerina

Cosí Fan Tutte composer 6 Mozart (Wolfgang Amadeus)

cosmetic 4 kohl **5** blush, rouge **6** ceruse, makeup, powder **7** blusher, bronzer, mascara **8** lip gloss, lipstick **9** eye shadow **10** decorative, nail polish, ornamental **11** beautifying, superficial

cosmetologist 10 beautician

cosmic 4 huge, vast **7** immense **8** infinite **9** planetary, spiritual, unbounded, universal **12** astronomical, metaphysical

cosmopolitan 6 global, urbane **7** worldly **8** catholic, cultured, polished **9** civilized, universal, worldwide **10** cultivated, ecumenical **11** worldly-wise **13** sophisticated

cosmos 6 flower **8** creation, universe

Cossack *army:* **3** Don **4** Ural **5** Kuban *land:* **7** Ukraine *leader:* **5** Razin (Stenka) **6** ataman, hetman, Mazepa (Ivan) **7** Bulavin (Kondraty) **8** Pugachov (Yemelyan) *novel:* **10** Taras Bulba

cosset 3 pet **4** baby, lamb, love **5** humor, spoil **6** caress, cocker, coddle, cuddle, dandle, dote on, fondle, pamper **7** cater to, indulge **11** mollycoddle

cost 3 tab **4** rate, toll **5** price **6** charge,

damage, outlay, tariff **7** expense, payment **8** price tag **9** sacrifice **11** expenditure **12** disbursement *business:* **8** overhead

Costa Rica *bay:* **8** Coronado *capital:* **7** San José *city:* **8** Alajuela **10** Puntarenas **11** Puerto Limón *discoverer:* **8** Columbus (Christopher) *language:* **7** Spanish *leader:* **5** Arias (Oscar) *monetary unit:* **5** colón *neighbor:* **6** Panama **9** Nicaragua *peninsula:* **3** Osa **6** Nicoya *river:* **7** San Juan *volcano:* **5** Barba, Irazú **9** Turrialba

costermonger **6** hawker **7** peddler **9** barrow boy

costive **4** mean, slow **5** bound, close, tight **6** frugal, stingy **7** miserly **9** penurious **10** hardfisted, pinchpenny **11** closefisted **12** cheeseparing, parsimonious

costless **4** free **6** gratis **10** gratuitous **13** complimentary

costly **4** dear, rich **5** fancy **6** lavish, pricey **7** opulent, premium **8** precious, splendid, valuable **9** expensive, luxurious, priceless **10** exorbitant, highpriced, invaluable **11** extravagant

costume **3** rig **4** duds, garb, mode **5** dress, getup, guise, habit, style **6** attire, outfit **7** apparel, clothes, fashion, threads, turnout, uniform **8** disguise, ensemble, garments **9** trappings

cot **3** bed, hut **4** camp **5** cabin, lodge, shack **6** shanty *wheeled:* **6** gurney

coterie **4** band, camp, clan, club, ring **5** cabal **6** circle, clique **7** in-group **9** camarilla

cotillion **4** ball, prom **5** dance

cottage **3** hut **4** camp **5** cabin, lodge, shack **6** shanty **8** bungalow *Russian:* **5** dacha *Swiss:* **6** chalet

cotton *cleaner:* **3** gin **6** linter *cloth:* **4** duck, jean, mull **5** baize, chino, denim, drill, khaki, scrim, terry, wigan **6** calico, canvas, chintz, dimity, muslin, oxford, sateen, velour **7** batiste, etamine, fustian, gingham, jaconet, nankeen, organdy, percale **8** corduroy, dungaree, moleskin, nainsook, tarlatan **9** grenadine, percaline, stockinet, swansdown **10** balbriggan **11** stockinette *cloth, Indian:* **5** surah **6** madras **7** dhurrie, khaddar *comb:* **4** card *fuzz remover:* **6** linter *measure:* **4** hank, pick, yard **5** count, skein *pad:* **7** pledget *pod:* **4** boll *refuse:* **5** flock *seed separator:* **3** gin *sheet:* **4** batt *thread:* **5** lisle

Cotton State **7** Alabama

cottonwood **5** alamo **6** poplar

cottony **4** soft **6** fluffy

_____ **Coty** **4** René

couch **3** den, put **4** lair, sofa, word **5** divan, lodge **6** burrow, chaise, daybed, lounge, phrase **7** express, lie down, recline **9** davenport, formulate **12** chesterfield

couch potato **7** slacker

cougar **3** cat **4** puma **7** panther **9** catamount **12** mountain lion

cough **4** hack, hawk

cough drop **6** troche **7** lozenge

cough up **3** pay **5** spend **6** lay out, pay out **7** deliver, dole out, fork out **8** fork over, hand over, shell out

couloir **5** chasm, gorge, gulch, gully **6** ravine

council **4** diet **5** board, junta **6** powwow, senate **7** cabinet, meeting **8** assembly, conclave, congress, ministry **10** conference, federation **12** consultation *ancient Greek:* **5** boule *church:* **5** synod **10** consistory *medieval English:* **4** moot **5** gemot **6** gemote **8** hustings *Muslim:* **5** divan *Russian:* **4** duma **6** soviet *secret:* **5** cabal, junto **9** camarilla *Spanish:* **7** cabildo

counsel **4** urge, warn **6** advice, advise, charge, direct, enjoin, lawyer **7** consult, suggest **8** advocate, attorney **9** prescribe, recommend **10** advisement **12** deliberation *British:* **9** barrister, solicitor

count **3** add, sum, tot **4** bank, earl, mean, rely, tote **5** issue, score, tally, total, tot up, weigh **6** census, charge, depend, expect, figure, matter, number, reckon, result, tote up **7** compute, signify **8** estimate, militate, numerate, quantify **9** calculate, enumerate **10** allegation

countenance **3** mug **4** back, cast, face, look, mien, phiz **5** favor, go for **6** accept, visage **7** approve, commend, condone, endorse, support **8** advocate, features, hold with, sanction, tolerate **9** approbate, composure, encourage **10** expression **11** physiognomy

counter **3** pit, vie **4** anti **5** asset, check, match, polar, shelf **6** offset, oppose **7** adverse, against, hostile, obverse, opposed, reverse **8** antipode, contrary, converse, opposing, opposite **9** antipodal, diametric **10** antipodean, antithesis, contravene **12** antagonistic, antipathetic, antithetical **13** contradictory

counteract **3** fix **4** foil **5** annul **6** cancel, negate, oppose, resist, thwart **7** balance, correct, nullify, prevent, rectify, redress **8** negative **9** cancel out, frustrate **10** balance out, neutralize

counteragent **4** cure **6** remedy **8** antidote **9** antitoxin, antivenin **10** corrective

counterbalance **6** cancel, make up, offset, redeem, set off **7** ballast, correct, even out, rectify, redress **8** equalize, outweigh **10** compensate

counterblow 7 revenge **8** reprisal, requital, revanche **9** vengeance **11** retaliation, retribution

counterclockwise 4 levo **12** levorotatory

counterfeit 4 copy, fake, hoax, sham **5** bluff, bogus, dummy, false, feign, forge, fraud, mimic, phony **6** affect, assume, deceit, ersatz, forged, pseudo **7** feigned, imitate, pretend **8** delusive, delusory, knock off, simulate, spurious **9** brummagem, deception, deceptive, fabricate, imitation, imposture, insincere, pinchbeck, pretended, simulated **10** fraudulent, misleading, simulacrum *prefix:* **5** pseud **6** pseudo

counterpane 4 pouf, puff **5** duvet **6** spread **8** bedcover, coverlet **9** bedspread, comforter, eiderdown

counterpart 4 like, twin **5** equal, match **6** analog, double **7** vis-à-vis **8** analogue, parallel **9** correlate, duplicate **10** complement, coordinate, equivalent **11** correlative **13** correspondent

counterpoise 6 make up, offset, redeem, set off **7** balance, ballast **8** outweigh **9** stabilize **10** compensate

countersign 8 password **9** watchword

countervail 4 foil **6** cancel, offset, oppose, redeem, set off, thwart **7** balance, correct, nullify, rectify **8** outweigh **9** frustrate **10** compensate, neutralize

countless 6 legion, myriad, untold **7** umpteen **11** innumerable

Count of Monte Cristo 6 Dantès (Edmond) *author:* **5** Dumas (Alexandre)

count out 5 expel **6** except **7** exclude **9** disregard, eliminate

countrified 5 rural **6** rustic **7** bucolic **8** homespun, pastoral **10** campestral

country 4 home, land, soil **5** rural **6** nation, region, rustic, sticks **7** boonies, bucolic, outland **8** homeland, pastoral **9** backwoods, boondocks **10** campestral, fatherland, motherland, provincial *dance:* **3** jig **4** reel **10** strathspey *home:* **5** manor, ranch, villa **8** hacienda *music:* **9** bluegrass *road:* **4** lane, path **5** byway

coup 4 blow, feat **5** upset **6** putsch, stroke **8** takeover

couple 3 duo **4** bond, dyad, fuse, join, link, mate, pair, span, team, yoke **5** brace, hitch, marry, merge, unite **6** hook up, link up **7** bracket, combine, conjoin, connect, doublet, harness, twosome

coupler 4 link, ring **5** hitch, joint **6** hookup **7** shackle **8** ligature *railroad:* **7** drawbar

couplet 3 duo **4** dyad, pair **5** twins **7** distich, doublet, twosome

coupling 4 link, seam **5** joint, union **7** joining, pairing **8** junction, juncture **9** connector **10** connection

courage 4 dash, grit, guts **5** heart, moxie, nerve, pluck, spunk, valor **6** daring, mettle, spirit **7** bravery, heroism **8** audacity, backbone, boldness, firmness, temerity, tenacity, valiance, valiancy **9** assurance, fortitude, gallantry **10** resolution **11** doughtiness, intrepidity **12** fearlessness **13** dauntlessness

courageous 4 bold **5** brave, gutsy, nervy, stout **6** daring, heroic, manful, plucky, spunky, strong **7** doughty, gallant, valiant **8** fearless, intrepid, resolute, stalwart, unafraid, valorous **9** audacious, dauntless, tenacious, undaunted **11** venturesome **12** stouthearted

courier 5 envoy **6** legate, runner **8** emissary **9** go-between, messenger **11** internuncio

course 3 row, run, way **4** dart, dash, duct, flow, line, path, plan, race, road, rush, tack, tear **5** canal, chain, chase, class, hurry, orbit, order, range, route, scoot, scope, speed, surge, track, trend **6** career, design, hasten, hustle, manner, policy, polity, scheme, sequel, series, string, system **7** advance, channel, circuit, conduit, passage, pattern, program, regimen, routine, seminar **8** aqueduct, duration, progress, sequence, syllabus **9** procedure, racetrack **10** curriculum, succession **11** progression *dinner:* **4** soup **5** salad **6** entrée **7** dessert **9** appetizer, blue plate

courser 4 bird **5** horse **7** charger **8** huntsman, warhorse

court 3 bar, woo **4** date, quad, yard **5** charm, motel, spark, suite, tempt **6** allure, homage, invite, palace, pursue **7** address, flatter, justice, retinue, romance, solicit **8** assembly, cloister, tribunal **9** captivate, curtilage, enclosure, entourage **10** magistrate, parliament, quadrangle **11** legislature *action:* **4** suit **5** trial **6** appeal, assize **7** hearing, inquest, lawsuit **10** proceeding *calendar:* **6** docket *call to:* **7** summons **8** subpoena **11** arraignment *circuit:* **4** eyre *crier's call:* **4** oyez *decision:* **6** assize **7** finding, verdict **8** judgment *ecclesiastical:* **4** rota **5** Curia **10** consistory *Indian:* **6** durbar *kind:* **4** moot **5** civil **6** county, family **7** circuit, customs, federal, supreme **8** chancery, criminal, district, juvenile, kangaroo, superior **9** appellate, municipal **11** territorial *medieval English:* **4** eyre, moot **5** gemot **6** gemote **8** hustings *of equity:* **8** chancery *officer:* **5** clerk, crier, judge **7** bailiff, justice, marshal, sheriff **10** prosecutor *order:* **4** writ **5** edict **6** decree **7** summons **8** mandamus, subpoena *panel:* **4** jury *relating to:* **8** judicial **9** juridical *session:* **6** assize **7** sitting **8** sederunt

courteous 5 civil **6** polite **7** courtly, gallant, genteel **8** mannerly, well-bred **9** attentive **10** chivalrous, thoughtful **11** considerate **12** well-mannered

courtesy 7 amenity, decorum, manners, service **8** chivalry, civility **9** attention, etiquette, gallantry **10** cordiality, indulgence **11** courtliness **12** graciousness **13** attentiveness, consideration

court game see under GAME

courtly 5 noble **6** august, formal, urbane **7** elegant, gallant, refined, stately **8** gracious **9** dignified **10** chivalrous, flattering **11** ceremonious

courtship 4 suit **6** dating, wooing **7** romance **10** flirtation *former custom of:* **8** bundling

courtyard 4 quad **5** garth, patio **9** curtilage **10** quadrangle

cousin 3 kin **7** kinsman **8** relative

Cousteau, Jacques *ship:* **7** Calypso *vehicle:* **11** bathysphere

couturier 8 clothier, costumer, designer **10** dressmaker

cove 3 arm, bay **4** nook **5** bight, firth, inlet, niche **6** harbor, recess **9** concavity

covenant 3 vow **4** bond, pact **5** agree, swear **6** pledge, treaty **7** compact, promise **8** contract **9** agreement **10** convention

Covent Garden offering 5 opera

cover 3 cap, lid **4** bury, hide, hood, mask, wrap **5** alibi, cloak, front, guise, stash, track **6** enfold, enwrap, facade, hiding, insure, refuge, screen, secure, shield, shroud, travel **7** blanket, conceal, embrace, enclose, envelop, obscure, overlay, protect, secrete, shelter, write up **8** disguise, ensconce, enshroud, traverse **9** encompass, safeguard, sanctuary, superpose **10** overspread **11** concealment, superimpose *rooflike:* **6** awning, canopy *the eyes:* **9** blindfold *the face:* **4** mask, veil *the mouth:* **6** muzzle *with asphalt:* **4** pave *with cloth:* **5** drape *with dirt:* **7** begrime, blacken **8** besmirch *with straw:* **6** thatch

coverall 8 jumpsuit **10** boilersuit

covered wagon 9 Conestoga

covering *anatomical:* **5** theca, velum **6** tegmen **7** velamen **8** tegument **10** integument *close-fitting:* **6** sheath

9 sheathing *cloth:* **5** sheet *flap:* **9** operculum *for a book:* **4** case **6** jacket *for a cigar:* **7** wrapper *for a coffin:* **4** pall *for a corpse:* **6** shroud **8** cerement *for a package:* **7** wrapper *for concealment:* **10** camouflage *for food:* **4** cosy, cozy *for soil:* **5** mulch *metal:* **4** mail **5** armor *of a diatom:* **6** lorica *of a plant ovary:* **8** pericarp *of a seed:* **4** aril, case **5** testa *of fruits:* **4** peel, rind *of gloom:* **4** pall *of grain:* **4** hull, husk **5** chaff *shell-like:* **8** carapace *thin:* **4** film **6** patina, veneer *waterproof:* **4** tarp **9** tarpaulin

coverlet 4 pouf, puff **5** duvet **6** spread **8** bedcover **9** bedspread, comforter **11** counterpane

covert 4 lair **5** haven, privy **6** hidden, masked, refuge, secret, veiled **7** feather, furtive, retreat, shelter, sub-rosa, thicket **8** hush-hush, shrouded, stealthy **9** concealed, disguised, sanctuary, sheltered **10** undercover **11** camouflaged, clandestine, hiding place, underhanded **12** hugger-mugger **13** surreptitious, under-the-table

covertly 7 sub-rosa **9** by stealth **12** hugger-mugger

covet 4 want **5** crave **6** desire

covetous 4 avid, keen **5** itchy **6** grabby, greedy **7** envious **8** desirous, esurient, grasping, ravenous **9** rapacious, voracious **10** avaricious, gluttonous **11** acquisitive

covey 4 band, bevy, crew, nest **5** brood, bunch, flock, group, party, troop **6** gaggle, troupe **7** cluster, company

cow (see also CATTLE) **4** faze, kine (plural), neat **5** abash, bossy, bully, daunt **6** appall, bovine, dismay, hector, rattle **7** bluster, dragoon **8** bludgeon, browbeat, bulldoze, bullyrag **9** discomfit, embarrass, strong-arm **10** disconcert, intimidate *cud:* **5** rumen *French:* **5** vache *hornless:* **5** muley **7** pollard *mammary gland:* **5** udder *pen:* **6** corral *shed:* **4** barn, byre *Spanish:* **4** vaca *young:* **4** calf **5** stirk **6** heifer

coward 6 craven **7** caitiff, chicken, dastard, milksop, nebbish **8** poltroon, recreant **9** jellyfish **10** scaredy-cat **11** yellowbelly

____ **Coward 4** Noël

cowardly 5 timid, wimpy **6** afraid, craven, yellow **7** caitiff, chicken, fearful, gutless **8** poltroon, recreant, timorous **9** dastardly **11** lily-livered, milk-livered, poltroonish **12** apprehensive, fainthearted, poor-spirited, white-livered **13** pusillanimous

cowboy 5 rogue, waddy **6** drover, herder, waddie **7** puncher, rancher **8** buckaroo, herdsman, maverick,

wrangler 9 cattleman, ranch hand
10 cowpuncher 12 broncobuster *contest:* 5 rodeo *gear:* 5 cuffs, quirt, spurs
6 duster 7 bedroll, slicker, Stetson *legendary:* 9 Pecos Bill *leggings:* 5 chaps
movie: 3 Mix (Tom) 4 Hart (William S.)
5 Autry (Gene), Wayne (John) 6 Gibson
(Hoot), McCrea (Joel), Murphy
(Audie), Ritter (Tex), Rogers (Roy,
Will) 8 Cisco Kid, Eastwood (Clint)
rope: 5 lasso, reata, riata 6 lariat
Spanish-American: 6 charro, gaucho
7 vaquero

cower 5 quail, wince 6 blench, cringe,
flinch, recoil, shrink

cowfish 6 dugong, sea cow 7 grampus,
manatee 8 sirenian

cowl 4 cape, hood 5 cloak 6 mantle
7 capuche

cowpox 8 vaccinia

cowpuncher see COWBOY

coxcomb 3 fop 4 beau, buck, dude, fool
5 blood, dandy, swell 7 peacock 8 macaroni 9 exquisite 11 Beau Brummel
12 clotheshorse, fashion plate, lounge
lizard

coy 3 shy 4 arch, cute, pert 5 saucy,
timid 6 demure, modest 7 bashful, evasive, playful 8 blushing, decorous, skittish 9 diffident, kittenish 10 capricious,
coquettish 11 flirtatious, mischievous
12 noncommittal

Coyote State 11 South Dakota

coypu 6 rodent *fur:* 6 nutria

cozen 3 gyp 4 bilk, scam 5 cheat, trick
6 diddle, fleece, take in 7 beguile,
deceive, defraud, swindle, wheedle
8 flimflam 9 bamboozle 11 double-cross

cozy 4 safe, snug, soft 5 comfy, cushy,
pally, tight 6 chummy, secure 8 familiar, intimate 11 comfortable

crab 3 nag 4 beef, fuss, yawp 5 gripe,
sidle 6 grinch, griper, grouch, kvetch,
squawk, yammer 7 decapod, grouser,
growler 8 arthopod, complain, grumbler, sourpuss 9 bellyache, shellfish
10 bellyacher, complainer, crosspatch,
crustacean, curmudgeon 11 faultfinder
claw: 5 chela 6 nipper *constellation:*
6 Cancer *genus:* 3 Uca 6 Birgus 7 Limulus, Pagurus *kind:* 3 pea 4 blue, king,
pine, rock 5 ghost, purse 6 hermit, spider 7 fiddler 9 Dungeness, horseshoe
king, horseshoe: 7 limulus

crabbed 4 dour, glum, grim, sour 5 gruff,
surly 6 crusty, gloomy, morose, sullen
9 illegible, irascible, saturnine, splenetic

crablike 7 cancroid

crabwise 8 sidelong, sideward, sideways
9 laterally

crack 3 gag, gap, rap, try 4 bang, bash,
belt, blow, boom, clap, flaw, jest, joke,

open, peal, quip, rift, roll, shot, slam,
slap, snap, stab, wham, whop 5 adept,
break, burst, chink, cleft, crash, craze,
knock, smack, smash, solve, split,
whack, whirl, wreck 6 breach, cranny,
decode, expert, master, moment,
thwack 7 break up, crevice, decrypt,
destroy, fissure, instant, shatter, skilled
8 crevasse, decipher, disorder, interval,
masterly, skillful, superior 9 break into,
excellent, interrupt, masterful, witticism 10 percussion, proficient

crackbrain 3 nut 4 kook 5 crank, wacko
6 cuckoo 7 dingbat, lunatic 9 ding-a-ling, fruitcake, screwball

crackdown 5 purge 8 quashing 10 repression 11 suppression

cracked 3 mad 4 daft, nuts 5 balmy,
batty, crazy, daffy, loony, nutty 6 broken, crazed, cuckoo, insane, screwy
7 bonkers, lunatic, smashed 8 demented, deranged

cracker 5 wafer 6 hacker, rustic 7 biscuit,
saltine, snapper 8 Georgian 9 Floridian

crackerjack 3 ace 4 lulu 5 dandy, nifty,
sharp 6 corker, killer 8 jim-dandy,
knockout 9 humdinger 12 lollapalooza

crackle 4 snap 7 glitter, sparkle, twinkle
9 crepitate 10 effervesce 13 effervescence

crackpot 3 nut 4 case, kook, loon
5 crank, loony, wacko 6 cuckoo, madman 7 dingbat, lunatic, oddball 9 ding-a-ling, eccentric, fruitcake, harebrain,
screwball

crack-up, crack up 5 crash, smash, wreck
6 fiasco 7 debacle 8 accident, collapse,
disaster 9 breakdown 11 catastrophe

cradlesong 7 lullaby 8 berceuse

craft 3 art, job 5 guile, knack, skill,
trade, wiles 6 career, deceit, métier
7 ability, calling, cunning, know-how,
slyness 8 artifice, caginess, foxiness,
vocation, wiliness 9 adeptness, canniness, dexterity, duplicity, expertise,
ingenuity, technique 10 adroitness, artfulness, competence, occupation, profession, shrewdness 11 proficiency

craftiness 5 guile 7 cunning 8 artifice,
subtlety

craftsman 5 smith 6 carter, carver, potter, weaver, wright 7 artisan, builder,
cobbler, jeweler 9 carpenter 10 blacksmith

crafty 3 sly 4 foxy, keen, wily 5 acute,
cagey, canny, sharp, slick 6 adroit, artful, astute, clever, shrewd, tricky 7 cunning, devious, fawning, vulpine 8 guileful, scheming, skillful, slippery
9 deceitful, designing, ingenious, insidious 11 calculating, duplicitous *Scottish:*
7 sleekit

crag 3 tor 4 hill 5 cliff

craggy 5 harsh, rocky, rough 6 jagged, rugged, uneven

cram 3 jam, ram 4 bolt, fill, gulp, heap, load, pack, wolf 5 crowd, crush, drive, force, press, shove, study, stuff, wedge 6 gobble, review, squash, thrust 7 jam-pack, overeat, squeeze

crammed 4 full 5 awash, flush 7 brimful 8 brimming 9 chock-full

cramp 4 kink, pain, pang 5 crick, limit, spasm 6 hamper, stitch 7 confine, inhibit, shackle 8 confined, restrain, restrict 9 restraint, stricture 10 constraint, limitation 11 confinement, restriction

cramped 5 close, tight 6 narrow 9 confining, two-by-four

crane 4 bird, boom, rail 5 heron 7 derrick, stretch *arm:* 3 jib *genus:* 4 Grus *ship's:* 5 davit

Crane hero 12 Henry Fleming

cranium 5 skull 9 braincase

crank 3 nut 4 crab, kook 5 fancy 6 griper, grouch, notion, rotate, turn up, vagary 7 caprice, conceit, fanatic, grouser, oddball 8 crackpot, crotchet, grumbler, sourpuss 9 eccentric, screwball 10 bellyacher, crosspatch

cranky 5 cross, testy 6 crabby, crusty, cussed, grumpy, ornery, tetchy, touchy 7 bearish, crabbed, peevish, prickly 8 contrary, petulant, tortuous, vinegary 9 crotchety, irascible, irritable, obstinate 10 bad-humored, ill-humored 12 cantankerous, disagreeable 13 unpredictable

cranny 3 gap 4 nook, slit 5 chink, crack, niche 6 corner 7 crevice

crash 3 din, jar, ram 4 bang, boom, bump, bust, clap, fail, fold, jolt, peal, slam, wham 5 blast, break, burst, crack, shock, smash, wreck 6 impact, pileup 7 collide, crack-up, debacle, decline, failure, smashup 8 accident, collapse 9 breakdown, collision 10 concussion

crass 4 rude 5 crude, gross 6 coarse, vulgar 7 boorish, loutish, uncouth 8 churlish 9 unrefined 13 materialistic

crate 3 box 4 heap 5 wreck 6 jalopy, junker 7 clunker

crater 3 pit 4 dent, hole, pock 5 crash 6 cavity, dimple, hollow, trough 7 caldera 8 collapse 10 depression *Hawaiian:* 7 Kilauea

cravat 3 tie 4 band 5 ascot, scarf 7 necktie

crave 3 ask, beg 4 need, want, wish 5 covet 6 demand, desire 7 call for, entreat, implore, long for, require 8 yearn for

craven 4 funk 6 abject, coward 7 caitiff,

chicken, dastard, fearful, gutless, ignoble 8 cowardly, cringing, poltroon, recreant 9 dastardly 11 lily-livered, poltroonish, yellowbelly 13 pusillanimous, yellowbellied

craving 4 itch, lust, urge 6 desire, hunger, thirst 7 longing, passion 8 appetite, yearning 9 hankering

crawl 4 flow, inch, teem 5 creep, swarm 6 abound, grovel 7 slither, wriggle 9 pullulate

crawling 6 repent

craze 3 fad 4 chic, rage 5 crack, fever, furor, mania, trend, vogue 6 dement, enrage, frenzy, furore, madden 7 derange, fashion, unhinge 9 unbalance 10 dernier cri, enthusiasm

craziness 5 folly, mania 6 lunacy 8 hysteria, insanity 9 absurdity

crazy 3 fey, mad 4 daft, gaga, loco, nuts, wild 5 balmy, barmy, batty, daffy, dotty, goofy, kooky, loony, loopy, nutty, rabid, silly, wacko, wacky 6 absurd, cuckoo, fruity, insane, mental, psycho, screwy, teched, whacky 7 berserk, bonkers, cracked, foolish, frantic, lunatic, smitten, tetched, touched, unsound 8 cockeyed, crackpot, demented, deranged, frenetic, frenzied, maniacal, unhinged 9 bedlamite, delirious, eccentric, fanatical, foolhardy, ludicrous, possessed, screwball, senseless 10 crackbrain, moonstruck, ridiculous, unbalanced 11 harebrained, nonsensical 12 preposterous *British:* 5 potty 6 scatty *Scottish:* 3 wud

creak 4 rasp 5 grate, grind 6 scrape, squeak, squeal 7 grating, screech 9 squeaking

creaky 4 aged 5 rusty 7 rickety, rundown, squeaky, unsound, worn-out 8 decrepit 9 tottering 10 broken-down, ramshackle

cream 3 top 4 balm, beat, best, drub, pick, whip, whup 5 blast, elite, prime, salve 6 cerate, choice, defeat, finest, thrash 7 clobber, destroy, trounce, unguent 8 lambaste, liniment, ointment

crease 4 fold, ruck 5 graze, plica, ridge 6 furrow, groove, rumple 7 crinkle, wrinkle

create 3 dub 4 form, make, sire 5 beget, build, cause, forge, found, hatch, set up, spawn, start 6 author, design, devise, father, invent 7 compose, concoct, develop, fashion, produce 8 conceive, engender, generate, occasion 9 construct, establish, fabricate, formulate, institute, originate 10 constitute

creation 5 birth, world 6 cosmos, nature

7 genesis **8** universe **9** inception, macrocosm **10** conception **11** macrocosmos

creative 7 fertile **8** artistic, inspired, original **9** deceptive, demiurgic, ingenious, inventive **10** innovative, innovatory **11** imaginative **12** innovational

creator 3 god **6** author **8** inventor **9** architect, generator, patriarch **10** originator, progenitor

creature 3 man **5** beast, being, brute, human **6** animal, mortal, person **7** critter, varmint *fabled:* **3** elf, imp, orc, roc **4** ogre, puck, yeti **5** dwarf, fairy, ghost, giant, gnome, harpy, nymph, pixie, troll **6** dragon, goblin, gorgon, kraken, merman, sphinx, sprite **7** bigfoot, brownie, bugbear, centaur, chimera, gremlin, griffin, mermaid, monster, unicorn, vampire, wendigo **8** minotaur, werewolf **9** hobgoblin, manticore, sasquatch **10** cockatrice, hippogriff, leprechaun (see also MONSTER)

credence 5 faith, trust **6** belief, credit **8** reliance **9** sideboard **10** acceptance, confidence

credentials 6 papers **9** documents **10** references **12** certificates, testimonials **13** documentation

credenza 6 buffet **8** bookcase **9** sideboard

credible 5 solid, sound, valid **6** trusty **8** reliable **9** authentic, colorable, plausible **10** believable, convincing, persuasive, reasonable **11** trustworthy **12** satisfactory

credit 4 deem, feel **5** asset, faith, honor, refer, sense, think, trust **6** accept, assign, belief, charge, impute, notice, weight **7** ascribe, believe **8** consider, credence, prestige, reliance **9** attribute, authority, influence **10** confidence, reputation **11** recognition

creditable 6 worthy **8** laudable, reliable **9** colorable, deserving, estimable, plausible, reputable **10** believable **11** commendable, meritorious, respectable **12** praiseworthy

credo 5 canon, creed, dogma, tenet **6** belief, tenets **7** beliefs, precept **8** doctrine, ideology **9** catechism, principle

credulous 5 naive **6** unwary **8** gullible, trustful, trusting **9** believing **12** unsuspecting, unsuspicious **13** unquestioning

creed 4 sect **5** canon, dogma, faith, tenet **6** belief, church, tenets **7** beliefs, precept **8** doctrine, ideology, religion **9** catechism, communion, principle **12** denomination

creek 4 burn, rill **5** brook **6** arroyo, rillet, runlet, runnel, stream **7** freshet, rivulet **8** brooklet **9** streamlet

creep 4 drag, edge, inch, lurk, slip **5** crawl, glide, shirk, skulk, slide, slink, snake, sneak, steal **6** spread, tiptoe **7** gumshoe, slither, wriggle **9** pussyfoot

creeping 6 repent **7** gradual **9** prostrate

creepy 5 eerie, weird **6** spooky **7** anxious, macabre, ominous, strange, uncanny **8** ghoulish, menacing, sinister **9** unnerving **10** disturbing, unpleasant, unsettling **11** hair-raising

crème de la crème 4 best **5** elect, elite **6** finest **8** very best

Cremona family 5 Amati **8** Guarneri

Creon *daughter:* **6** Creusa, Glauce, Glauke *sister:* **7** Jocasta *son:* **6** Haemon *victim:* **8** Antigone

crescendo 4 acme, apex, peak, rise **5** crest, surge, swell **6** apogee, climax, growth, height, zenith **8** increase, pinnacle **9** high point **11** culmination

crescent-shaped 5 bowed **6** lunate, sickle **7** falcate *body or surface:* **8** meniscus

crest 3 cap, top **4** acme, apex, comb, noon, peak, roof, tuft **5** arête, chine, crown, plume, ridge **6** apogee, climax, summit, vertex **7** hogback **8** pinnacle, surmount **9** high point **10** coat of arms, prominence **11** culmination *of a wave:* **8** whitecap

crestfallen 3 low **4** blue, down **6** droopy **8** dejected, downcast, drooping **9** depressed **10** dispirited **11** discouraged, downhearted **12** disappointed, disconsolate, disheartened

Crete *ancient city:* **7** Cnossus, Knossos **8** Phaistos *ancient name:* **6** Candia *capital:* **5** Canea *goddess:* **8** Dictynna **11** Britomartis *guard:* **5** Talos *king:* **5** Minos **9** Idomeneus *maze:* **9** labyrinth *monster:* **8** Minotaur *mountain:* **3** Ida *princess:* **7** Ariadne

cretin 3 oaf **4** boob, clod, dolt, dope, fool, lout **5** dumbo, dummy, dunce, idiot, moron **6** dimwit, nitwit **7** half-wit **8** imbecile, lunkhead, numskull **9** lamebrain, numbskull, simpleton

Creusa *father:* **5** Priam *husband:* **6** Aeneas *mother:* **6** Hecuba *son:* **3** Ion **8** Ascanius

crevice 3 gap **4** seam, slit **5** chink, cleft, crack **6** cranny **7** fissure **8** cleavage **10** interstice

crew 4 band, bevy, gang, team **5** bunch, covey, group, party **6** rowers, rowing **7** company, sailors

crib 3 bed, bin, box, hut, key **4** pony, trot **5** cheat, crate, hovel, shack, stall, steal, theft **6** cradle, crèche, manger, pilfer **7** barrier, brothel **8** bassinet, bedstead, bordello **9** enclosure **10** plagiarism, plagiarize

Crichton novel 11 Terminal Man (The) 12 Jurassic Park 15 Andromeda Strain (The)

cricket *period of play:* 7 innings *team:* 6 eleven *term:* 3 leg, off, rot 4 bowl 5 pitch 6 bowler, wicket, yorker 7 batsman, striker 9 fieldsman *turn at bat:* 4 over

crime 3 sin 4 evil, tort, vice 5 caper 6 breach, delict, felony 7 misdeed, offense 8 atrocity, iniquity 9 diablerie, violation 10 corruption, illegality, infraction, wrongdoing 11 misdemeanor 13 transgression *instructor:* 5 Fagin

Crimea *city:* 5 Kerch, Yalta 10 Sebastopol, Sevastopol, Simferopol *river:* 4 Alma *sea:* 4 Azov *strait:* 5 Kerch

criminal 4 hood, thug 5 crook, felon, shady 6 outlaw 7 convict, corrupt, crooked, hoodlum, illegal, illicit, lawless, mobster 8 culpable, fugitive, gangster, jailbird, offender, scofflaw, unlawful, wrongful 9 desperado, felonious, miscreant, nefarious, racketeer, wrongdoer 10 delinquent, lawbreaker, malefactor, trespasser 12 illegitimate, transgressor *habitual:* 8 repeater 10 recidivist

criminate SEE INCRIMINATE

crimp 4 bend, curb, wave 5 frizz 6 crease, hamper, hold in 7 crinkle, inhibit, wrinkle 8 hold back, obstacle, restrain 9 constrain, restraint 10 impediment 11 obstruction

crimson 3 red 4 rose 5 blush, color, flush 6 redden

cringe 4 duck 5 cower, hunch, quail, wince 6 blench, flinch, recoil, shrink

crinkle 4 ruck 5 crimp, plica, ridge 6 crease, furrow, pucker, ruck up, rumple, rustle 7 crackle, crumple, scrunch, wrinkle 11 corrugation

crinkly 5 crepy 6 crepey, frizzy 7 frizzed 8 wrinkled

cripple 4 lame, maim 6 mangle 7 disable 8 mutilate, paralyze 9 hamstring, undermine 10 debilitate 12 incapacitate

crippled 4 halt, lame 6 maimed 7 gnarled, mangled 8 battered, deformed, disabled, weakened 9 enfeebled, misshapen, mutilated, paralyzed 11 debilitated, handicapped

crisis 4 crux, pass 5 pinch 6 climax, crunch, height, strait 7 impasse, straits 8 disaster, exigency, juncture, zero hour 9 emergency, extremity 10 crossroads 11 catastrophe, contingency 12 turning point

crisp 4 cold, cool, curl, deft, keen, neat, wavy 5 brisk, clean, crimp, curly, fresh, nippy, pithy, sharp, short 6 biting, chilly, lively, ripple, spruce 7 bracing, brittle, crunchy, cutting, wrinkle 8 clean-cut, clear-cut, incisive 9 trenchant 11 stimulating 12 invigorating

crisscross 3 net 4 grid, mesh 5 weave 7 network, overlap 8 reticule 9 confusion, decussate, intersect, reticular 10 reticulate

criterion 4 norm 5 canon, gauge, ideal, model, tenet 7 measure, precept 8 exemplar, paradigm, standard 9 benchmark, yardstick 10 touchstone

critic 5 judge 6 carper, pundit 7 arbiter, caviler 8 caviller, censurer, quibbler, reviewer 9 belittler, nitpicker 10 disparager, mudslinger 11 commentator, connoisseur, faultfinder

critical 4 dire 5 acute, fussy 7 carping, crucial, finicky, pivotal, weighty 8 captious, caviling, decisive 9 desperate, important, momentous 10 belittling, censorious, conclusive, precarious 11 disparaging, significant 12 faultfinding 13 consequential, determinative, hairsplitting *study:* 6 examen 8 exegesis

criticism 4 flak, slap 5 blame, cavil, swipe 6 rebuke, review 7 censure, comment, opinion, reproof 8 analysis, judgment, reproach 9 appraisal, objection 10 assessment, commentary, evaluation, nitpicking 11 examination, observation 12 faultfinding

criticize 3 pan, rap 4 bash, carp 5 blame, blast, cavil, chide, fault, judge, knock, roast, scold 6 assess, rebuke, review, scathe 7 censure, condemn, nitpick, reprove 8 appraise, badmouth, chastise, denounce, evaluate, lambaste 9 castigate, disparage, dress down, excoriate, find fault, reprehend, reprimand, reprobate

critique SEE CRITICISM

critter 5 beast 6 animal 7 varmint

Crius *father:* 6 Uranus *mother:* 4 Gaea *son:* 8 Astraeus

croak 3 die 6 cackle, expire, squawk 7 grumble

croaky 5 gruff, husky, raspy 6 hoarse 8 gravelly

Croatia *capital:* 6 Zagreb *city:* 5 Split 6 Osijek, Rijeka 9 Dubrovnik *monetary unit:* 4 kuna *neighbor:* 7 Hungary 8 Slovenia *part of:* 7 Balkans *region:* 8 Dalmatia, Slavonia

crock 3 jar, lie, pot 4 tale 6 tureen 7 cripple, disable, fiction 9 break down 11 fabrication

crocked 3 lit 4 high 5 drunk, lit up, oiled, tipsy 6 bashed, blotto, bombed, juiced, potted, soaked, soused, stewed, stoned, tanked, wasted, zonked

7 drunken, pickled, pie-eyed, sloshed, smashed **9** plastered **10** inebriated, liquored up **11** intoxicated

crocodile 7 reptile *bird:* **6** plover *Indian:* **6** gavial **7** gharial *relative:* **9** alligator *South American:* **6** caiman, cayman *Southeast Asian:* **6** mugger

Croesus' kingdom 5 Lydia

croft 4 farm **5** field

crofter 4 hind **6** farmer

Cromwell, Oliver 13 lord protector *battle:* **6** Naseby **11** Marston Moor *regiment:* **9** Ironsides *son:* **7** Richard

crone 3 hag **4** trot **5** biddy, witch **6** beldam **7** beldame

Cronus 5 Titan **6** Saturn *daughter:* **4** Hera **6** Hestia **7** Demeter *father:* **6** Uranus *mother:* **4** Gaea *sister:* **4** Rhea **6** Cybele, Tethys *son:* **4** Zeus **5** Hades **7** Jupiter, Neptune **8** Poseidon *wife:* **4** Rhea **6** Cybele

crony 3 pal **4** chum **5** buddy **6** cohort **7** comrade **8** sidekick **9** associate, companion **10** accomplice **11** confederate

crook 3 bow **4** bend, flex, hook, wind **5** angle, curve, staff, thief **6** bandit, robber **7** burglar, crosier, hoodlum, pothook **8** criminal

crooked 4 awry **5** askew, lying, shady, venal **6** curved, errant, jagged, shifty, skewed, zigzag **7** bending, corrupt, devious, illegal, illicit, slanted **8** cockeyed, criminal, ruthless, tortuous, twisting **9** deceitful, dishonest, nefarious, underhand, unethical **10** fraudulent, mendacious, untruthful **11** duplicitous, underhanded **12** unscrupulous **13** double-dealing

croon 4 sing **6** murmur, warble

crooner 4 Cole (Nat "King"), Como (Perry) **5** Laine (Frankie), Tormé (Mel) **6** Crosby (Bing), Martin (Dean), singer, Vallee (Rudy) **7** Astaire (Fred), Bennett (Tony), Sinatra (Frank) **8** Eckstine (Billy), vocalist, Williams (Andy)

crop 3 bob, cut, hew, lop, mow **4** chop, clip, pare, snip, trim **5** prune, shave, shear, stock, yield **6** gullet, handle, output **7** harvest, produce **8** fruitage, truncate **10** collection

croquet 5 roque

crosier 5 crook, staff

cross 3 mad **4** mule, rood, span **5** angry, surly, testy, trial **6** betray, bridge, crabby, cranky, grumpy, hybrid, negate, oppose, ordeal, tetchy, touchy **7** athwart, calvary, carping, gainsay, grouchy, mongrel, peevish **8** captious, choleric, confront, traverse **9** decussate, half blood, half-breed, hybridize, intersect, irascible, irritable, querulous,

splenetic **10** affliction, contradict, contravene, interbreed, transverse **11** tribulation **12** cantankerous **13** quick-tempered *a river:* **4** ford *bearer:* **8** crucifer *decoration:* **4** Iron **8** Victoria *Egyptian:* **4** ankh *kind:* **3** tau **5** Greek, Latin, papal **6** Celtic, fleury, formée, moline, pommée, potent **7** avellan, botonée, Calvary, Maltese **8** crucifix, fourchée, Lorraine, quadrate **11** patriarchal **12** Saint Andrew's **13** Saint Anthony's *section:* **5** slice *stroke of a letter:* **5** serif

crossbow 8 arbalest, arbalist

crossbreed 4 mule **6** hybrid **7** bastard, mongrel **9** half blood, half-breed, hybridize **10** interbreed

cross-eye 6 squint **10** strabismus

crossing 8 junction, overpass, traverse **9** traversal, underpass **10** transverse **11** decussation, interchange, transversal **12** intersection

cross out 5 erase **6** cancel, delete, efface, excise **7** expunge

crosspatch 4 crab **5** crank, grump **6** griper, grouch **7** grouser **8** grumbler, sorehead, sourpuss **10** complainer, curmudgeon

crossroads 4 crux, pass **5** pinch **6** crisis, strait **8** exigency, juncture, zero hour **9** carrefour, emergency **11** contingency **12** intersection, turning point *goddess:* **6** Hecate, Hekate, Trivia

cross-shaped 8 cruciate **9** cruciform

crossways 6 aslant **7** athwart, oblique **8** diagonal **9** obliquely **10** diagonally, transverse **11** kitty-corner **12** transversely

crotchet 3 bee **4** whim **5** fancy, freak, quirk, trick **6** foible, megrim, notion, vagary **7** caprice, conceit **11** quarter note **12** eccentricity

crotchety 5 testy **6** crabby, cranky, crusty, ornery, tetchy, touchy **7** bearish, peevish, prickly **8** contrary, snappish, vinegary **9** difficult, eccentric, irascible **10** vinegarish **11** ill-tempered **12** cantankerous, cross-grained

crouch 4 bend, duck **5** cower, hunch, squat, stoop **6** cringe, huddle, shrink **10** hunker down

croup 3 bum **4** butt, hack, rear, rump, seat, tail **5** cough, edema, whoop **6** behind **7** keister, rear end, tail end **8** backside, buttocks, derriere, haunches **9** posterior

crow 4 blow, brag, puff **5** boast, exult, gloat, prate, vaunt **6** cackle **7** bluster **9** gasconade, humble pie *colony:* **7** rookery *cry:* **3** caw *family:* **6** corvid **8** Corvidae *genus:* **6** Corvus *relating to:*

7 corvine *relative:* **3** daw, jay **4** rook **5** raven **6** chough, magpie **7** jackdaw

crowbar 3 pry **5** jimmy, lever

crowd 3 jam, mob **4** army, bear, cram, fill, herd, host, mass, pack, pile, push, rout, ruck **5** bunch, crush, drove, flock, flood, group, horde, hurry, press, serry, shove, surge, swarm, troop **6** circle, clique, gaggle, huddle, jostle, legion, rabble, squash, squish, stream, throng **7** cluster, collect, company, coterie, squeeze **8** assembly **9** gathering, multitude **10** assemblage, collection **11** aggregation **12** congregation

crowded 4 full **5** awash, close, dense, thick, tight **6** loaded **7** brimful, compact, teeming **8** brimming, populous, swarming **9** chock-full, congested, jam-packed

crow-like 7 corvoid

crown 3 cap, top **4** acme, apex, peak, roof **5** cover, crest, tiara **6** climax, diadem, laurel, summit, top off, vertex, wreath, zenith **7** chaplet, coronal, coronet, garland, overlay, perfect **8** pinnacle, round off, surmount **9** culminate, finish off **10** consummate **11** culmination

crucial 4 dire **5** acute, vital **6** urgent **7** central, pivotal **8** critical, deciding, decisive **9** desperate, essential, important, momentous, necessary **10** imperative **11** climacteric, significant

crucible 4 test **5** trial **6** ordeal **8** acid test **10** melting pot

crucifix 4 rood **5** cross

crucifixion site 7 Calvary **8** Golgotha

crucify 4 rack **6** impale, martyr **7** mortify, pillory, torment, torture **10** excruciate

crud 3 goo **4** glop, gook, gunk, junk, muck **5** dreck, filth, slime, trash **6** debris, sludge **7** deposit, garbage, rubbish **12** incrustation

crude 3 raw **4** poor **5** crass, dirty, gross, rough **6** coarse, earthy, impure, ribald, risqué, vulgar **7** boorish, ill-bred, loutish, lowbred, obscene, obvious, raunchy, uncivil, uncouth **8** backward, cloddish, homespun, ignorant, indecent, inferior **9** elemental, graceless, inelegant, makeshift, primitive, rough-hewn, unrefined **10** amateurish, unfinished, unpolished

cruel 4 fell, grim, mean **5** harsh **6** brutal, fierce, savage **7** bestial, brutish, callous, heinous, vicious **8** inhumane, ruthless, sadistic **9** atrocious, barbarous, ferocious, heartless, merciless, monstrous, truculent **12** bloodthirsty

cruise 4 roam, rove, sail, surf, tour **5** drift, jaunt **6** junket, voyage **9** excursion

cruiser 4 boat **5** yacht **7** warship **8** squad car **9** patrol car, powerboat

crumb 3 bit **4** iota **5** ounce, scrap, shred **6** morsel, sliver **7** smidgen **8** fragment, particle

crumble 5 decay **8** collapse **9** break down, decompose **11** deteriorate **12** disintegrate

crumbly 7 friable

crummy 4 poor **5** dingy, lousy, seedy, tacky **6** cruddy, flimsy, shoddy, sleazy **8** inferior

crumple 3 wad **4** cave **5** crimp **6** buckle, cave in, ruck up **7** crinkle, scrunch, wrinkle **8** collapse

crunch 4 chew **5** champ, chomp, grind, munch, sit-up **6** crisis **7** compute, process, squeeze **8** shortage, showdown

crusade 5 cause, drive **6** appeal **7** holy war **8** campaign, movement **9** offensive **10** expedition **11** undertaking

Crusader *English:* **7** Richard (Lionheart) *French:* **5** Louis (IX) **6** Philip, Robert **7** Baldwin, Charles, Godfrey, Raymond, Raymund **8** Boniface, Montfort, Philippe, Theobald *German:* **6** Conrad **9** Frederick, Friedrich **10** Barbarossa *Norman:* **7** Tancred **8** Bohemund *Preacher:* **5** Peter (the Hermit), Urban (II) **7** Adhémar, Bernard **8** Innocent (III), Pelagius

crusading 11 evangelical **12** evangelistic

crush 3 jam, mob **4** cram, mash, pulp, push, ruin **5** crowd, drove, grind, horde, pound, press, quash, quell, smash, wreck **6** bruise, burden, defeat, reduce, squash, squish, subdue, throng **7** conquer, destroy, mortify, oppress, passion, put down, repress, scrunch, squeeze, squelch, trample **8** bear down, beat down, demolish, overcome, suppress, vanquish **9** humiliate, multitude, overpower, overwhelm, pulverize, puppy love, subjugate **10** annihilate, extinguish, obliterate **11** infatuation

crust 4 cake, coat, rime, scab **7** coating, deposit **8** covering

crustacean 4 crab, flea **5** louse, prawn **6** isopod, shrimp, slater, sow bug **7** copepod, daphnia, decapod, lobster, pill bug **8** amphipod, barnacle, crawfish, crayfish, ostracod, sand flea **9** arthropod, beach flea, shellfish, water flea, wood louse **10** stomatopod, whale louse **11** branchiopod *aggregate of:* **5** krill *appendage:* **7** pleopod *body segment:* **6** somite, telson **8** metamere *claw:* **5** chela **6** pincer *covering substance:* **6** chitin *larva:* **8** nauplius

crusty 4 curt **5** bluff, blunt, gross, gruff, short, surly **6** cranky **7** brusque, crabbed, prickly **8** choleric **9** irascible, irritable, saturnine, splenetic

crux 3 nub **4** core, gist, meat, pith

5 focus, heart **6** kernel, thrust
7 essence, purport **9** substance
cry (see also EXCLAMATION) **3** sob
4 bawl, blub, call, howl, keen, mewl,
moan, pule, wail, weep, yawp, yell,
yowl **5** bleat, motto, mourn, shout,
whine, whoop **6** boohoo, furore, holler,
lament, scream, snivel, squall, squawk,
squeak, squeal **7** blubber, screech, ululate, whimper **10** vociferate *bacchanals':*
4 evoe *calf:* **5** bleat *cat:* **3** mew **4** meow
5 miaow *cattle:* **3** low, moo *chick:* **4** peep
5 cheep *court:* **4** oyez *crane:* **5** clang
crow: **3** caw *dog:* **3** arf **4** bark, woof *donkey:* **4** bray **6** hee-haw *duck:* **5** quack
frog: **5** croak *goat:* **5** bleat *goose:*
4 honk **5** clang *hen:* **6** cackle *horse:*
5 neigh **6** nicker, whinny **7** whicker *lion:*
4 roar *owl:* **4** hoot *pig:* **4** oink **5** grunt
raven: **5** croak *sheep:* **5** bleat *songbird:*
5 chirp, tweet *turkey:* **6** gobble
cry down 5 decry **6** defame, deride,
malign, revile, vilify **7** condemn **8** belittle, denounce, derogate, diminish
9 denigrate, deprecate, discredit, disparage **10** calumniate, depreciate
11 detract from, opprobriate
crying 4 dire **5** acute, vital **6** urgent **7** blatant, burning, clamant, exigent, heinous
8 flagrant, pressing, shocking **9** atrocious, clamorous, desperate, monstrous,
notorious **10** compelling, imperative,
outrageous, scandalous **11** importunate
crypt 5 vault **7** chamber **8** catacomb
9 mausoleum **10** undercroft
cryptic 5 vague **6** arcane, occult,
opaque, secret **7** Delphic, obscure,
unclear **8** abstruse, Delphian, esoteric,
puzzling **9** ambiguous, enigmatic, recondite, tenebrous **10** mysterious, mystifying **12** unfathomable
crystal 4 lens **5** clear, lucid **6** limpid,
lucent, quartz **8** clear-cut, luminous,
pellucid **9** glassware, unblurred **11** translucent, transparent **12** transpicuous
gazer: **4** seer **7** psychic **11** clairvoyant
Cry, the Beloved Country author 5 Paton
(Alan)
cry up 4 laud, puff **5** boost, extol **6** praise
7 acclaim
cub 3 pup **4** baby, tyro **6** novice, rookie
8 neophyte **9** offspring, youngster
10 apprentice
Cuba *capital:* **6** Havana *city:* **7** Holguín
8 Camagüey, Santiago **10** Guantánamo,
Santa Clara *discoverer:* **8** Columbus
(Christopher) *language:* **7** Spanish
leader: **6** Castro (Fidel) **7** Batista (Ful-
gencio) *monetary unit:* **4** peso **6** dollar
sea: **9** Caribbean
cubbyhole 5 niche **6** alcove, recess
7 cubicle

cube 4 dice **5** mince
Cub Scout *rank:* **4** Bear, Lion, Wolf
6 Bobcat **7** Webelos *unit:* **3** den **4** pack
Cuchulain *father:* **3** Lug **4** Lugh **5** Lugus
foe: **4** Medb **5** Maeve *kingdom:* **6** Ulster
lord: **9** Conchobar *mother:* **8** Dechtire
son: **8** Conlaoch *victim:* **8** Conlaoch
wife: **4** Emer
cuckoo 3 mad, nut **4** daft, kook, nuts
5 batty, crank, crazy, daffy, loony,
loopy, nutty, potty, silly, wacko, wacky
6 crazed, fruity, insane, screwy, whacky
7 bonkers, cracked, idiotic, lunatic,
nutcase **8** crackpot, demented **9** ding-a-
ling, harebrain, screwball **12** crackbrained *bird:* **3** ani
cucumber 4 pepo **7** gherkin
cuddle 3 hug, pet **4** neck, snug **5** spoon
6 burrow, caress, clinch, cosset, dandle,
fondle, nestle, nuzzle **7** embrace, snuggle, squeeze **8** canoodle
cuddlesome 7 lovable, snuggly **8** hugga-
ble **11** embraceable
cudgel 3 bat, sap **4** club, cosh, mace **5** baton, billy **7** war club **8** bludgeon **9** bastinado, billy club, blackjack, truncheon
10 knobkerrie, nightstick, shillelagh
cue 3 key, nod, rod, tip **4** clue, hint,
lead, prod, sign **6** insert, notion,
prompt, signal, tip-off **7** inkling, warning **8** high sign, reminder, telltale
10 indication, intimation, suggestion
cuff 3 box, hit **4** belt, blip, clip, poke,
slap, sock **5** clout, fight, punch, smack,
whack **6** bangle, buffet, wallop **7** clobber, scuffle **8** bracelet, wristlet
cul-de-sac 5 pouch **6** pocket **7** dead end,
impasse **10** blind alley **12** diverticulum
cull 4 pick, sift, thin **5** elect, glean
6 choose, garner, gather, select, winnow **7** extract, thin out
culminate 4 peak **5** crest **6** climax
culmination 3 top **4** acme, apex, peak
6 apogee, capper, climax, height, payoff, summit, zenith **8** capstone, pinnacle **11** ne plus ultra **12** consummation
culpability 4 onus **5** blame, fault, guilt
culpable 6 guilty, liable, sinful **7** at fault
8 blamable, blameful **10** censurable,
delinquent **11** blameworthy, impeach-
able, responsible **13** reprehensible
cult 3 fad **4** sect **5** creed, faith **6** church
8 religion **10** persuasion **12** denomination
cultivable 6 arable **8** tillable
cultivate 4 farm, grow, tend, till **5** breed,
nurse, raise **6** enrich, foster, refine
7 cherish, develop, further, improve,
nourish, nurture, produce, promote
9 encourage, propagate
cultivated 6 urbane **7** genteel, refined
8 cultured, polished, well-bred

cultivation 6 polish 7 culture 8 breeding 10 refinement 11 development

culture 4 grow 5 taste 6 foster 7 nurture 9 cultivate, erudition, gentility 10 refinement 11 cultivation 12 civilization 13 enlightenment

cultured 6 urbane 7 erudite, genteel, learned, refined 8 educated, highbrow, literate, polished, well-bred 9 civilized 10 cultivated 11 enlightened

culture medium 4 agar

cum ___ salis 5 grano

cumber 4 clog, lade, load 6 burden, hinder, hobble, impede, saddle 7 clutter 8 handicap 9 hindrance

cumbersome 5 bulky, heavy, hefty 6 clumsy 7 awkward 8 unwieldy 9 lumbering, ponderous 10 slow-moving

cumbrous see CUMBERSOME

cumshaw 3 fee, tip 5 bribe 6 payoff 7 present 8 gratuity, largesse 9 lagniappe, pourboire 10 perquisite

cumulate 4 heap 5 amass, hoard, lay up, store 6 garner, gather, pile up 7 collect, combine, store up 9 stockpile

cumulation 4 heap, mass, pile 5 cache, hoard, trove 9 stockpile 10 collection 11 aggregation 13 agglomeration

cumulative 8 additive, compound 9 summative 10 compounded, increasing

cunning 3 sly 4 cute, foxy, keen, wary, wily 5 acute, cagey, canny, craft, guile, savvy, sharp, skill, slick, smart 6 adroit, artful, astute, clever, crafty, deceit, shifty, tricky 7 finesse, know-how, slyness 8 artifice, deftness, facility, foxiness, guileful, slippery, subtlety, wiliness 9 adeptness, cageyness, canniness, dexterity, dexterous, duplicity, ingenious, ingenuity, insidious, sharpness, slickness 10 adroitness, artfulness, cleverness, craftiness, shiftiness, shrewdness, trickiness

cup 3 mug 4 toby 5 grail, jorum, stein 6 beaker, goblet, seidel 7 chalice, tankard 8 schooner *handle:* 3 ear, lug *liturgical:* 5 calix 7 chalice *small:* 6 noggin 8 cannikin, pannikin 9 demitasse *sports:* 5 Davis, Ryder, World 6 Curtis, Nextel 7 Stanley 8 America's, Wightman

cupbearer of the gods 4 Hebe 8 Ganymede

cupboard 5 ambry, cuddy 6 buffet, closet, larder, pantry 7 armoire, cabinet 8 credence, credenza 9 sideboard

Cupid 4 Amor, Eros 5 putto 6 cherub 8 amoretto *beloved:* 6 Psyche *brother:* 7 Anteros *father:* 6 Hermes 7 Mercury *mother:* 5 Venus 9 Aphrodite *title:* 3 Dan

cupidity 4 lust 5 greed 6 desire 7 avarice, avidity, craving, lechery, passion 8 rapacity, voracity 9 eagerness, esuri-ence 10 greediness 11 infatuation 12 covetousness 13 rapaciousness

cupola 4 dome 5 vault 6 turret 7 furnace, lookout

cur 3 dog 4 mutt 7 mongrel

curate 6 cleric, priest 9 churchman, clergyman

curative 4 pill 5 tonic 6 elixir, relief, remedy 7 healing, nostrum, panacea, therapy 8 antidote, remedial, salutary, sanative, solution 9 healthful, medicinal, remedying, treatment, wholesome 10 beneficial, corrective 11 restorative, therapeutic 12 health-giving

curator 6 keeper, warden 9 caretaker, custodian 11 conservator

curb 3 bit 4 deny 5 check, frame, leash, tie up 6 border, bridle, edging, fetter, hamper, hobble, hold in, subdue 7 abstain, contain, control, inhibit, refrain, repress 8 hold back, hold down, restrain, suppress, withhold 9 constrain, entrammel, restraint *British:* 4 kerb

curdle 4 clot, sour, turn 5 spoil 7 clabber, congeal, thicken 9 coagulate

cure 3 age, spa 4 heal, mend 5 treat 6 elixir, kipper, physic, pickle, relief, remedy 7 rectify, relieve, restore, therapy 8 antidote, medicant, medicine, preserve, recovery, solution 10 ameliorate, corrective 12 counteragent 13 counteractive

cure-all 6 elixir 7 nostrum, panacea 10 catholicon

curio 6 oddity, whimsy 7 novelty

curiosity 5 freak 6 marvel, oddity, rarity, whimsy, wonder 7 anomaly, concern, novelty 8 interest, nonesuch

curious 3 odd 4 nosy 5 nosey, novel, queer, weird 6 exotic, prying, quaint, snoopy 7 bizarre, oddball, strange, unusual 8 meddling, peculiar, puzzling, singular 9 inquiring, intrusive 11 inquisitive, questioning

curl 4 coil, kink, wind 5 frizz, twine, twist 6 spiral 7 contort, crinkle, entwine, frizzle, ringlet, wreathe 9 corkscrew

curling *match:* 8 bonspiel *period of play:* 3 end *team:* 4 four *term:* 3 tee 4 hack, rink 5 house, stone

curly 4 wavy 5 kinky 6 frizzy

currency 4 cash, coin 5 dough, lucre, money, scrip 7 coinage 8 banknote 10 acceptance, prevalence 11 legal tender *unit:* (see INDIVIDUAL COUNTRY)

current 4 eddy, flow, flux, rush, tide 5 drift, flood, spate, tenor, trend 6 extant, modern, strain, stream 7 instant, ongoing, popular, present, regnant, topical 8 accepted, existent, existing, tendency, up-to-date 9 prevalent 10 present-day, prevailing, widespread

11 fashionable 12 contemporary *air:*
4 gale, gust, wind 5 blast, draft 6 breeze,
squall, zephyr 7 cyclone, indraft,
updraft 9 downdraft 10 slipstream
ocean: 7 riptide 8 undertow 9 maelstrom, whirlpool *unit:* 3 amp 6 ampere
Currier's partner 4 Ives (James)
curry 4 beat, comb, seek, whip 5 groom
6 thrash
curse 4 bane, cuss, damn, evil, jinx, oath
5 swear 6 blight, plague, whammy
7 afflict, damning, malison, scourge,
torment 8 anathema, cussword, execrate 9 bête noire, blaspheme, blasphemy, expletive, imprecate, profanity,
swearword 10 affliction, execration,
misfortune, pestilence 11 commination,
imprecation, malediction, profanation
12 anathematize, denunciation
cursed 6 damned 7 blasted, dratted
8 damnable, infernal 9 execrable
10 confounded 13 blankety-blank
cursive 6 fluent, smooth 7 flowing, running
cursory 5 hasty, quick, rapid 6 casual
7 hurried, shallow, sketchy 8 careless
10 uncritical 11 perfunctory, superficial
curt 4 rude 5 bluff, blunt, brief, gruff,
short, terse 6 abrupt, crusty 7 brusque,
concise 8 succinct 10 peremptory
curtail 3 cut 4 clip, dock, trim 5 prune,
slash 6 lessen, reduce 7 abridge, cut
back, shorten 8 diminish, pare down,
retrench, truncate 10 abbreviate
curtain 4 drop, veil 5 drape 6 screen
7 barrier *doorway:* 8 portiere *holder:*
3 rod *Indian:* 6 purdah *rod concealer:*
7 valance *sash:* 7 tieback *stage:* 4 drop
5 scrim 8 backdrop
curtains 3 end 4 ruin 5 death 6 demise,
finish 7 decease 8 disaster
curtilage 4 quad, yard 5 court 8 cloister
9 courtyard, enclosure 10 quadrangle
curvaceous 5 buxom 7 rounded, shapely
9 Junoesque 10 statuesque, voluptuous
13 well-developed
curvature *of the spine:* 8 kyphosis, lordosis 9 scoliosis
curve 3 arc, bow 4 arch, bend, turn,
veer, wind 5 crook, round, twist 6 convex, spiral, swerve 7 concave, flexure,
rondure *of an arch:* 8 extrados, intrados
pitcher's: 4 hook *plane:* 7 cycloid,
limaçon 8 parabola, sinusoid, trochoid
9 hyperbola *S-shaped:* 3 ess 4 ogee 7 sigmoid
curved 4 bent 5 arced, bowed, round
6 arched 7 arcuate, bending, embowed,
falcate, rounded, sigmoid, sinuous,
twisted *implement:* 6 sickle *molding:*
4 ogee *sword:* 5 kukri, saber, sabre
7 cutlass 8 scimitar

curvilinear see CURVED
curvy see CURVACEOUS; CURVED
Cush *father:* 3 Ham *son:* 6 Nimrod
cushion 3 mat, pad 5 squab 6 absorb,
buffer, pillow, soften 7 bolster, hassock,
pillion 8 palliate, woolsack
cushy 4 cozy, easy, soft 11 comfortable,
undemanding
cusp 3 tip 4 apex, edge, peak 5 point,
verge 12 turning point
cuspid 6 canine 8 eyetooth
cuspidate 5 sharp 6 peaked, pointy
7 pointed
cuss 3 guy, man 4 chap, damn, dude,
oath 5 curse, swear 6 fellow 9 expletive
cussed 4 dour 5 crude, gruff 6 crusty,
cursed, grumpy, ornery 7 boorish,
brusque, grouchy 8 churlish 9 obstinate
10 unyielding 11 contentious 12 antagonistic, cantankerous
cussword 4 oath 5 curse 9 expletive,
swearword
custard 4 flan 7 pudding
custodian 5 super 6 keeper, porter, warden 7 curator, steward 8 guardian,
overseer, watchdog, watchman 9 caretaker, concierge, protector 10 supervisor 11 conservator
custody 4 care, ward 5 guard, trust
6 charge 7 keeping 9 captivity, detention 10 caretaking, management, protection 11 confinement, safekeeping,
supervision 12 guardianship
custom 3 use 4 norm 5 habit, mores
(plural), trade, usage 6 groove, manner,
praxis, ritual 7 folkway, precept, routine, traffic 8 business, habitude, practice 9 patronage 10 consuetude, convention
customary 5 usual 6 common, normal,
wonted 7 general, regular, routine
8 accepted, everyday, familiar, frequent, habitual, ordinary, orthodox,
standard 10 accustomed 11 established,
traditional 12 conventional
custom-built 7 bespoke 10 tailor-made
11 made-to-order
customer 5 buyer 6 client, patron
7 shopper 8 consumer 9 purchaser *frequent:* 7 habitué
customized see CUSTOM-BUILT
custom-made see CUSTOM-BUILT
cut 3 bob, hew, lop, mow, saw 4 bite,
chop, clip, crop, dice, dock, fell, gash,
hack, nick, pare, reap, sawn, slit, snip,
snub, trim 5 carve, filet, lathe, lower,
mince, notch, piece, prune, quota,
sawed, sever, share, shave, shear, slash,
slice, split, wound 6 cleave, delete,
dilute, divide, excise, fillet, incise,
reduce, scythe, sickle, sunder
7 abridge, curtail, dissect, operate, por-

tion, scissor, section, segment, shorten
8 amputate, decrease, dissever, division,
mark down, separate, truncate 9 allotment, allowance, reduction 10 abbreviate 12 cold-shoulder *of beef:* 3 rib
4 loin, rump 5 chine, chuck, flank,
roast, shank, steak, T-bone 6 saddle
7 brisket, sirloin 9 aitchbone 11 porterhouse

cut across 6 bisect 8 transect 9 transcend

cut-and-dried 5 stock 7 routine 9 formu-
laic 10 unoriginal 11 predictable
13 unimaginative

cutaneous 6 dermal

cutaway 4 coat, dive 5 tails

cut back 3 zag 4 clip, curb, dock, pare,
trim 5 lower, prune, shave, slash
6 lessen, reduce 7 abridge, curtail,
shorten 8 decrease, retrench, truncate
10 abbreviate

cut down 3 axe 4 chop, clip, fell, pare
5 lower, shave, slash 6 digest, reduce
7 abridge, shorten 10 abbreviate

cute 6 dainty, pretty 7 cunning 8 affected
10 attractive 11 impertinent, smart-
alecky

cut in 7 include, intrude, obtrude
9 introduce

cutlass 5 saber, sabre, sword 7 machete
8 scimitar

cut off 3 axe, bar, end, lop 4 halt, kill,
stop 5 abort, block, sever 6 disown
7 curtail, destroy, isolate, suspend
8 amputate, obstruct, renounce, separate, truncate 9 intercept, interrupt,
terminate 10 disinherit 11 discontinue

cut out 3 end 4 halt 5 leave, scram,
usurp 6 beat it, delete, depart, escape,
excise, remove, resect 7 defraud,
deprive, take off 8 displace, supplant
9 eliminate, extirpate 10 disconnect

cutpurse 5 thief 10 pickpocket

cut short 3 bob 4 clip, crop, dock, halt,
poll 5 abort, check, scrub, shear
7 abridge, curtail 8 break off 9 interrupt, terminate 10 abbreviate

cuttable 7 sectile 8 scissile

cutthroat 5 bravo 6 gunman, hit man,
killer 7 torpedo 8 assassin, murderer
10 hatchet man, triggerman

cutting 8 incisive, piercing 9 sarcastic,
trenchant 11 penetrating *edge:* 5 blade
remark: 3 dig 4 barb 5 taunt *tool:* 3 axe,
hob, saw 4 adze 5 knife, lathe, mower,
plane, razor 6 reaper, scythe, shears,
sickle 7 hatchet 8 scissors, tomahawk

cuttlefish 7 mollusc, mollusk
10 cephalopod *ink:* 5 sepia *relative:*
5 squid 7 octopus

cut up 4 dice, hash, romp 5 caper,
clown, mince, slash 6 cavort 7 carry on,
show off 9 misbehave 10 roughhouse

cutup 3 wag 4 zany 5 clown, joker
6 madcap 7 buffoon, farceur 8 jokester

cyan 4 blue

Cybele 4 Rhea *beloved:* 5 Attis *brother:*
6 Cronus *father:* 6 Uranus *husband:*
6 Cronus *mother:* 4 Gaea *son:* 4 Zeus
7 Jupiter, Neptune 8 Poseidon

cyber 5 wired 10 electronic

cybernetics founder 6 Wiener (Norbert)

cycle 3 age, lap, set 4 bike, loop, ring
5 chain, orbit, recur, round, wheel
6 circle, course, period, series 7 circuit
8 rotation, sequence 9 vibration 10 revolution, succession, two-wheeler,
velocipede 11 oscillation

cyclic 7 regular 8 periodic, repeated,
rhythmic 9 iterative, recurring, repeating 10 isochronal 12 intermittent

cyclone 7 tornado, twister

cyclopean 4 huge 7 immense, mammoth, massive, titanic 8 colossal, enormous, gigantic 9 monstrous 10 gargantuan, tremendous 11 elephantine

Cyclops 5 Arges 7 Brontes 8 Steropes
10 Polyphemus

Cycnus *father:* 4 Ares, Mars *slayer:*
8 Heracles, Hercules

cygnet 4 swan *dam (mother):* 3 pen *sire
(father):* 3 cob

Cygnus *form:* 4 swan *friend:* 7 Phaeton
star: 5 Deneb

cylinder 4 drum, pipe, tube 5 spool
6 barrel, bobbin, platen, roller

cylindrical 6 terete 7 tubular 8 tubelike

Cymbeline *daughter:* 6 Imogen *son:*
9 Arviragus, Guiderius *son-in-law:*
9 Posthumus

Cymric 5 Welsh 6 Celtic 9 Brythonic
bard: 8 Taliesin *Elysium:* 6 Annwfn *god:*
5 Lludd *of Elysium:* 5 Arawn *of the dead:*
5 Pwyll *of the seas:* 3 Ler 4 Llyr 5 Dylan
of the sky: 7 Gwydion *of the sun:* 4 Lleu,
Llew *of the underworld:* 4 Gwyn *goddess:* 3 Don 9 Arianrhod *magician:*
6 Merlin

Cymru 5 Wales

cynical 8 derisive, sardonic, scornful
12 misanthropic

Cynthia 4 Luna, moon 5 Diana
7 Artemis

cyprian 4 bawd, jade, slut, tart 5 hussy,
tramp 6 floozy, harlot, hooker, wanton
7 jezebel, trollop 8 slattern, strumpet
10 prostitute

Cyprus *capital:* 7 Nicosia 8 Lefkosia *city:*
7 Larnaca 8 Limassol *language:* 5 Greek
7 Turkish *monetary unit:* 4 lira 5 pound
mountain: 7 Olympus *port:* 9 Famagusta
sea: 13 Mediterranean

Cyrano de Bergerac 4 poet 7 duelist
8 duellist *author:* 7 Rostand (Edmond)
beloved: 6 Roxane *feature:* 4 nose *rival:*
9 Christian

Cyrus *conquest:* 5 Lydia, Media 7 Babylon *daughter:* 6 Atossa *empire:* 7 Persian
father: 8 Cambyses *son:* 8 Cambyses

cyst 3 sac, wen 4 sore 5 pouch, spore
6 growth 7 abscess, blister, capsule,
vesicle 8 swelling

Cytherea 4 isle 5 Venus 6 island
9 Aphrodite

czar 5 chief, mogul 6 despot, honcho,
tycoon, tyrant 7 emperor, kingpin,
magnate 8 autocrat *Russian:* 4 Ivan
5 Basil, Boris, Peter 6 Alexis, Dmitry,
Feodor, Fyodor, Vasily 7 Dimitri,
Michael, Romanov 8 Nicholas,
Romanoff, Theodore 9 Alexander
12 Boris Godunov

czar's wife 7 czarina

Czech Republic *capital:* 6 Prague *city:*
4 Brno 7 Ostrava *monetary unit:*
6 koruna *neighbor:* 6 Poland 7 Austria,
Germany 8 Slovakia *region:* 7 Bohemia,
Moravia *river:* 4 Labe, Oder 5 March
6 Morava

D

dab 3 bit, pat 4 blob, blow, daub, peck,
poke, spot 5 smear, touch 6 bedaub
7 besmear, plaster, splotch 8 flatfish

dabble 3 dip, dot, toy 4 fool, stud 5 fleck
6 dampen, fiddle, monkey, pepper, putter, splash, tinker 7 freckle, spatter,
stipple 8 sprinkle 9 bespeckle, muck
about 10 muck around

dabbler 4 duck, tyro 7 amateur 8 putterer, tinkerer 9 smatterer 10 dilettante

dabchick 5 grebe

dacha 5 villa 7 cottage 12 country house

dad 3 pop 4 papa 5 padre, pater 6 father,
old man, parent

Dadaist 3 Arp (Jean), Ray (Man) 4 Ball
(Hugo) 5 Ernst (Max), Grosz (George),
Tzara (Tristan) 7 Duchamp (Marcel),
Picabia (Francis) 10 Schwitters (Kurt)

daedal 6 knotty 7 complex 8 artistic,
involved, skillful 9 elaborate, intricate
11 complicated 12 labyrinthine
13 sophisticated

Daedalus 7 builder 9 architect, artificer
construction: 9 Labyrinth *father:*
6 Metion *son:* 6 Icarus *victim:* 5 Talos
6 Perdix

daffy see DAFT

daft 3 mad 4 loco, nuts 5 balmy, crazy,
dopey, flaky, loony, nutty, potty, silly,
wacko, wacky 6 absurd, crazed, cuckoo, insane, screwy 7 cracked, foolish,
idiotic, lunatic, witless 8 demented
10 unbalanced 11 harebrained

Dag *father:* 7 Delling *horse:* 9 Skinfaksi
mother: 4 Nott

Dagda *chief god of the:* 5 Gaels, Irish
daughter: 6 Brigit *instrument:* 4 harp
son: 6 Aengus *wife:* 5 Boann

dagger 4 dirk 5 skean, skene 6 bodkin,
stylet 7 dudgeon, poniard 8 stiletto *handle:* 4 hilt *Malay:* 4 kris

___ Dahl 5 Roald 6 Arlene

daikon 6 radish

daily 7 diurnal 8 everyday 9 circadian,
quotidian

dainty 5 goody, tasty, treat 6 choice,
morsel, select, tidbit 7 elegant, fragile
8 delicacy, delicate, ethereal, graceful,
kickshaw 9 exquisite, recherché
10 delightful

dairy 8 creamery

dais 5 stage 6 podium 7 rostrum 8 platform

daisy 5 oxeye 6 Shasta *British:* 10 moon-
flower *Scottish:* 5 gowan

Daisy Miller author 5 James (Henry)

Dakota dialect 5 Teton

Daksha's father 6 Brahma

dale 4 dell, glen, vale 6 dingle, valley

dally 3 lag, pet, toy 4 drag, idle, play
5 delay, flirt, tarry 6 coquet, dawdle,
diddle, linger, loiter, trifle 8 lollygag
9 hang about, waste time 10 fool
around

dam 4 weir 5 block, check 7 barrier
8 hold back, restrain *major:* 4 Oahe

6 Hoover 7 San Luis 8 Fort Peck, Garrison, Oroville 10 Bonneville, Glen Canyon 11 Grand Coulee

damage 3 mar 4 blot, harm, hurt, loss, maim, ruin 5 abuse, burst, cloud, spoil, stain, wound 6 blight, deface, impair, injure, injury, mangle, ravage, scathe 7 blemish, destroy, marring, tarnish, vitiate 8 maltreat, mischief, mistreat, mutilate, sabotage 9 devastate, vandalism 10 impairment 11 devastation

damaged 4 hurt, rent 6 broken, busted, dinged, flawed, marred 7 injured, spoiled, totaled 8 battered, impaired, ruptured 9 blemished, fractured, imperfect, shattered 10 fragmented

damaging 6 nocent 7 harmful, hurtful, nocuous 9 injurious 11 deleterious, detrimental, prejudicial

dame 4 lady 5 woman 6 gammer, matron 7 dowager 9 matriarch

Damien's island 7 Molokai

Damkina's son 6 Marduk

damn 4 cuss, darn, doom, drat 5 curse, swear 7 condemn, doggone 8 execrate, sentence 9 imprecate 10 vituperate 12 anathematize

damnable 6 blamed, cursed, cussed 7 blasted, dratted 8 accursed, infernal 9 abhorrent, execrable 10 abominable, detestable

damned 5 utter 6 blamed, cursed, cussed, darned, dashed, doomed 7 awfully, blasted, doggone, dratted, goldarn 8 accursed, infernal 9 condemned 10 confounded 13 anathematized

Damocles' ___ 5 sword

Damon's friend 7 Pythias

damp 3 wet 4 dank, dewy 5 check, choke, humid, moist, musty 6 clammy 7 bedewed 8 humidify, humidity

dampen 4 cool, curb 5 chill 6 deaden 7 depress, moisten 8 diminish

damsel 3 gal 4 girl, lass, maid, miss 5 filly, wench 6 lassie, maiden

Dan *father:* 5 Jacob *mother:* 6 Bilhah *son:* 6 Hushim

Danaë *father:* 8 Acrisius *lover:* 4 Zeus *son:* 7 Perseus

Danaus *brother:* 8 Aegyptus *daughters:* 7 Danaïds 8 Danaïdes *father:* 5 Belus *founder of:* 5 Argos *grandfather:* 7 Neptune 8 Poseidon

dance 3 hop, jig, tap 4 ball, flit, foot, heel, hoof, juba, leap, lope, reel, step, trip 5 bamba, brawl, galop, gigue, hover, lindy, mambo, mixer, polka, rumba, stomp, swing, tread 6 ballet, bolero, boogie, Boston, cancan, chassé, foot it, formal, frolic, German, hoof it,

rhumba, shimmy 7 beguine, coranto, courant, flicker, flitter, flutter, hoedown, one-step, shuffle 8 cakewalk, flamenco, galliard, glissade, rigadoon, rigaudon 9 allemande, cotillion, jitterbug, pas de deux *art of:* 12 choreography *Austrian:* 7 ländler *ballroom:* 5 rumba, tango 6 cha-cha, rhumba 7 fox-trot, mazurka, two-step 8 merengue 9 cotillion 10 Charleston *Bohemian:* 5 polka *Brazilian:* 5 samba 6 maxixe 7 lambada 8 capoeira 9 bossa nova *combining form:* 5 chore 6 choreo, chorio *country:* 4 reel 8 hornpipe *couple:* 5 polka 9 cotillion, malaguena 11 square dance *court:* 6 canary, pavane 8 saraband 9 allemande, sarabande *Cuban:* 5 conga, mambo, rumba 6 rhumba 8 habanera *designer:* 13 choreographer *English:* 6 morris *formal:* 4 ball, prom 9 cotillion *French:* 6 cancan 7 bourrée, gavotte 9 allemande 10 carmagnole *garment:* 4 tutu 7 leotard *Haitian:* 4 juba 8 merengue *Hungarian:* 7 czardas *Indian:* 6 nautch 7 bhangra *instrument:* 8 castanet *Israeli:* 4 hora *Italian:* 10 saltarello, tarantella, villanella 11 passacaglia *lively:* 3 jig 4 reel, trot 5 galop, gigue, polka, rumba 6 rhumba 7 bourrée 8 fandango, hornpipe, rigadoon, rigaudon 9 farandole, shakedown 10 Charleston, saltarello, tarantella *movement:* 4 plié, step 8 capriole, glissade 9 pirouette *Muse of:* 11 Terpsichore *1920's:* 10 Charleston *Polish:* 5 polka 7 mazurka 9 polonaise *Polynesian:* 4 hula *Scottish:* 3 bob 4 reel 5 fling 10 strathspey 11 schottische 13 Highland fling *shoes:* 5 pumps 8 slippers *slipper:* 7 toeshoe *slow:* 6 adagio, minuet, pavane 8 habanera *South American:* 7 carioca *Spanish:* 4 jota 6 bolero 7 zapateo 8 cachucha, chaconne, fandango, flamenco, saraband 9 malaguena, sarabande 10 seguidilla *springy:* 3 jig *square:* 7 hoedown, lancers 9 cotillion, quadrille *stately:* 5 pavan 6 pavane 8 saraband 9 polonaise, sarabande *step:* 3 pas *woman's:* 6 cancan

dancer 6 hoofer 7 chorine, clogger, danseur, stepper 8 coryphée, danseuse 9 ballerina, chorus boy 10 cakewalker, chorus girl *American:* 4 Feld (Elliot), Holm (Hanya), Lang (Pearl), Tune (Tommy) 5 Ailey (Alvin), Fosse (Bob), Kelly (Gene), Shawn (Ted), Tharp (Twyla) 6 Castle (Irene, Vernon), Duncan (Isadora), Dunham (Katherine), Graham (Martha), Morris (Mark), Taylor (Paul), Verdon (Gwen) 7 Astaire (Fred), Bujones (Fernando), de Mille

(Agnes), Farrell (Suzanne), Gregory (Cynthia), Jamison (Judith), Joffrey (Robert), Martins (Peter), Massine (Leonide), McBride (Patricia), Robbins (Jerome), St. Denis (Ruth), Tamiris (Helen) **8** Champion (Gower, Marge), d'Amboise (Jacques), Humphrey (Doris), Kirkland (Gelsey), Mitchell (Arthur), Nikolais (Alwin), Villella (Edward) **9** Tallchief (Maria) **10** Cunningham (Merce) *Cuban:* **6** Alonso (Alicia) *Danish:* **5** Bruhn (Erik) **7** Martins (Peter) **8** Tomasson (Helgi) *English:* **5** Dolin (Anton), Somes (Michael), Tudor (Antony) **7** Fonteyn (Margot), Markova (Alicia), Rambert (Marie) **8** de Valois (Ninette), Helpmann (Robert) *French:* **5** Lifar (Serge) **6** Béjart (Maurice), Perrot (Jules), Petipa (Marius) **7** Camargo (Marie), Massine (Leonide) *German:* **5** Jooss (Kurt) *Italian:* **5** Grisi (Carlotta) *Mexican:* **5** Limón (José) *Russian:* **5** Lifar (Serge) **6** Fokine (Michel), Petipa (Marius) **7** Massine (Leonide), Nureyev (Rudolf), Pavlova (Anna), Ulanova (Galina) **8** Danilova (Aleksandra), Makarova (Natalia), Nijinska (Bronislava), Nijinsky (Vaslav), Vaganova (Agrippina) **9** Karsavina (Tamara), Semyonova (Marina) **11** Baryshnikov (Mikhail), Plisetskaya (Maya) *Scottish:* **7** Shearer (Moira)

dancing 6 ballet **12** choreography *mania:* **9** tarantism

dandle 3 pet **4** play **6** caress, cosset, cradle, cuddle, pamper

dandruff 5 scall, scurf

dandy 3 fop **4** beau, buck, dude, fine, toff **5** nifty, swell **6** peachy **7** coxcomb, foppish **8** terrific **9** excellent, first-rate, hunky-dory **11** Beau Brummel, crackerjack **12** lounge lizard

dang 4 damn, darn **6** cursed, cussed, damned, darned **7** blasted, dratted, goldarn **8** infernal **10** confounded

danger 4 risk **5** peril **6** crisis, hazard, menace, plight, threat **7** pitfall, trouble **8** distress, jeopardy **9** emergency *signal:* **4** bell **5** alarm, siren **6** tocsin

dangerous 5 risky **6** unsafe **7** parlous **8** insecure, menacing, perilous, unstable **9** hazardous **10** precarious **11** threatening

dangle 4 hang **5** droop, swing **6** depend **7** suspend

Daniel ___ *pioneer:* **5** Boone *statesman:* **7** Webster

Danish *hero:* **5** Ogier *king:* **9** Christian, Frederick *queen:* **9** Margrethe

dank 3 wet **4** damp **5** humid, moist **6** clammy **8** dripping

Dante *beloved:* **8** Beatrice *birthplace:* **8** Florence *daughter:* **7** Antonia *deathplace:* **7** Ravenna *party:* **6** Guelph **7** Bianchi *patron:* **5** Scala *teacher:* **6** Latini *wife:* **5** Gemma *work:* **7** Inferno **8** Commedia, Paradiso **9** Vita Nuova **10** Purgatorio **12** Divine Comedy (The)

Dantean division 5 canto

Danton's colleague 5 Marat (Jean-Paul) **11** Robespierre (Maximilien)

Danzig 6 Gdańsk

Daphne *father:* **5** Ladon **6** Peneus *form:* **6** laurel **10** laurel tree *pursuer:* **6** Apollo **9** Leucippus

Daphnis' lover 5 Chloe

dapper 4 neat, trim **5** doggy, natty, sassy, smart, swank **6** classy, jaunty, rakish, snazzy, spiffy, spruce, sprucy **7** bandbox, dashing, doggish, foppish, stylish **11** well-groomed

dapple 4 spot **5** fleck, patch **6** mottle **7** speckle, stipple

dappled 4 pied **6** motley **7** flecked, mottled, patched, piebald, spotted **8** brindled **10** variegated **11** varicolored

Dardanelles 10 Hellespont

Dardanus *descendants:* **7** Trojans *father:* **4** Zeus **7** Jupiter *mother:* **7** Electra

dare 3 try **4** defy, risk **5** beard, brave **6** hazard **7** attempt, venture **8** confront, defiance **9** challenge

daredevil see DARING

darer 4 hero **6** risker

daring 4 bold, guts, rash **5** brash, brave, gutsy, moxie, nerve, nervy, pluck, valor **6** heroic, plucky **7** bravery, courage, heroism **8** audacity, boldness, fearless, reckless **9** audacious, derring-do, fortitude, venturous **10** courageous **11** adventurous, venturesome **13** adventuresome

Darius *battle:* **8** Marathon *father:* **9** Hystaspes *country:* **6** Persia **7** Parthia *son:* **6** Xerxes *wife:* **6** Atossa

Darjeeling 3 tea

dark 3 dim **4** dusk, inky, murk **5** black, blind, cloud, dingy, dusky, ebony, murky, night, sable, shady, sooty, swart, umber, unlit, vague **6** brunet, cloudy, dismal, gloomy, opaque, somber, sombre, wicked **7** obscure, ominous, rayless, satanic, shadowy, stygian, subfusc, sunless, swarthy, unclear **8** bistered, brunette, infernal, sinister **9** enigmatic, lightless, secretive, tenebrous, unlighted **10** caliginous, indistinct, mysterious, mystifying, pitch-black **11** crepuscular **13** unilluminated *poetic:* **4** ebon

darken 3 dim **5** bedim, cloud, gloom, lower, shade, sully, umber **6** shadow **7** becloud, blacken, eclipse, obscure, tarnish **8** melanize, overcast **9** obfuscate, overcloud **10** overshadow *Scottish:* **5** gloam

dark-haired *female:* **8** brunette *male:* **6** brunet

darkness 4 dusk, evil, murk **5** black, gloom, night, shade **6** shadow **8** blackout **9** nightfall, obscurity

darling 3 hon, pet **4** dear, duck, love **5** angel, deary, ducky, flame, honey, loved, sugar, sweet **7** beloved, dearest, sweetie **8** adorable, charming, favorite, precious **10** sweetheart, sweetie pie

darn 4 knit, mend **5** patch **6** blamed, cursed, cussed, damned, shucks **7** blasted, doggone, dratted **8** infernal **9** embroider **10** confounded

darn it *French:* **3** zut

Darrow client 4 Debs (Eugene), Loeb (Richard) **6** Scopes (John) **7** Haywood (William), Leopold (Nathan)

dart 3 fly, run, zip **4** barb, bolt, buzz, dash, flit, leap, rush, sail, scud, skim, tear **5** arrow, bound, hurry, lance, pitch, scamp, scoot, shaft, shoot, skirr, spear, speed, spurt **6** glance, hasten, scurry, spring, sprint **7** javelin, missile, scamper *barbed:* **10** banderilla

D'Artagnan's friends 5 Athos **6** Aramis **7** Porthos **10** musketeers

Dartmouth location 5 Devon **7** Hanover **12** New Hampshire

darts term 3 leg **4** bust **5** split **6** double, flight, hockey, treble **8** bull's-eye

Darwin, Charles *colleague:* **7** Wallace (Alfred Russel) *ship:* **6** Beagle *theory:* **9** evolution, selection

dash 3 fly, nip, run **4** bolt, brio, cast, damn, dart, élan, foil, hurl, race, ruin, rush, slam, tear, zing **5** break, chase, flair, fling, pinch, smash, style, trace **6** esprit, hyphen, pizazz, scurry, splash, sprint, thrust, thwart **7** bravura, depress, destroy, pizzazz, shatter, smidgen, spatter **8** confound **9** animation, frustrate

dashboard reading 4 fuel **5** speed **7** mileage **8** pressure **11** temperature

dashing 4 bold **5** smart **6** dapper, jaunty, lively, modish **7** gallant, stylish **8** animated, spirited **11** adventurous, fashionable

Das Kapital author 4 Marx (Karl)

dassie 4 pika **5** coney, hyrax

dastard 6 coward, craven **7** chicken, quitter **8** poltroon, recreant **9** scoundrel

dastardly 3 low **4** base, mean **6** craven, yellow **8** cowardly, shameful, skulking

11 treacherous, underhanded **13** pusillanimous

data 4 info **5** facts, input **7** figures **9** documents **11** information

date 3 age, era, woo **5** court, epoch, tryst **6** cutoff, escort **7** take out **8** deadline **9** accompany **10** engagement, rendezvous **11** anniversary, appointment, assignation

dated 3 old **5** passé **6** démodé, old hat **7** archaic, outworn **8** obsolete, outmoded **10** antiquated **12** old-fashioned **13** unfashionable

datum 4 fact

daub 4 blob, blot, spot **5** fleck, paint, smear **6** dapple, smudge, splash **7** besmear, dribble, plaster, speckle, splotch

daughter *Blythe Danner's:* **7** Paltrow (Gwyneth) *Bruce Dern's:* **5** Laura *Bush's:* **5** Jenna **7** Barbara *Carter's:* **3** Amy *Cash's:* **7** Rosanne *Cher's:* **8** Chastity *Clinton's:* **7** Chelsea *Cole's:* **7** Natalie *Coppola's:* **5** Sofia *Danny Thomas's:* **5** Marlo *Debbie Reynolds's:* **6** Carrie (Fisher) *Eddie Fisher's:* **6** Carrie *Elizabeth II's:* **4** Anne *Elvis's:* **9** Lisa Marie *Fonda's:* **4** Jane *Ford's (Gerald):* **5** Susan *Freud's:* **4** Anna *Garland's:* **12** Liza Minnelli *Goldie Hawn's:* **10** Kate Hudson *Ingrid Bergman's:* **8** Isabella (Rossellini) *Janet Leigh's:* **8** Jamie Lee (Curtis) *Joel Grey's:* **8** Jennifer *Johnson's (Lyndon):* **4** Lucy **5** Linda *Jon Voight's:* **8** Angelina (Jolie) *Kennedy's (John F.):* **8** Caroline *Klaus Kinski's:* **9** Nastassja *Maureen O'Sullivan's:* **3** Mia (Farrow) *Naomi Judd's:* **7** Wynonna *Nat King Cole's:* **7** Natalie *Nixon's:* **5** Julie **6** Tricia *Pat Boone's:* **5** Debby *Ravi Shankar's:* **10** Norah Jones *Reagan's:* **5** Patti **7** Maureen *Richard Burton's:* **4** Kate *Ryan O'Neal's:* **5** Tatum *Sinatra's:* **5** Nancy *Tony Curtis's:* **8** Jamie Lee (Curtis)

Daughter of the Moon 7 Nokomis

daunt 3 cow **5** alarm, deter **6** dismay, subdue **7** terrify **8** frighten **10** disconcert, discourage, dishearten, intimidate

daunting 7 awesome **8** imposing **9** dismaying, unnerving **10** forbidding, formidable **11** dispiriting **12** discouraging, intimidating, overwhelming

dauntless 4 bold, game **5** brave **6** daring **7** gallant, valiant **8** fearless, unafraid **9** unfearful, unfearing **10** courageous **11** lionhearted **12** stouthearted

dauntlessness 4 guts **5** heart, nerve, pluck, spunk, valor **6** daring, mettle, spirit **7** bravery, cojones, courage **8** boldness **10** resolution **12** fearlessness

davenport 4 desk, sofa 5 couch, divan 6 daybed 12 chesterfield

David *commander:* 4 Joab 5 Amasa *companion:* 8 Jonathan *daughter:* 5 Tamar *father:* 5 Jesse *rebuker:* 6 Nathan *son:* 5 Amnon 7 Absalom, Solomon 8 Adoijah *wife:* 6 Michal 7 Abigail, Ahinoam 9 Bathsheba

___ **David** 4 Camp 5 Magen, Mogen 6 Star of

David Copperfield *author:* 7 Dickens (Charles) *character:* 4 Dora, Heep 5 Uriah 6 Barkis 8 Micawber, Peggotty 9 Murdstone 10 Steerforth

Da Vinci Code author 5 Brown (Dan)

davit 5 crane

dawdle 3 lag 4 idle, laze, loaf, loll 5 dally, delay, tarry 6 diddle, linger, loiter, lounge 8 lollygag 10 dillydally

dawn 4 morn 5 sunup 6 aurora 7 morning, sunrise 8 cockcrow, daybreak, daylight 9 beginning 10 first light *goddess:* 3 Eos 6 Aurora

day *abbreviation:* 3 Fri, Mon, Sat, Sun, Thu, Tue, Wed 4 Thur, Tues 5 Thurs *before:* 3 eve *church calendar:* 5 feria *French:* 4 jour *German:* 3 Tag *holy:* 5 feast *hour:* 4 noon *Latin:* 4 dies *Spanish:* 3 día

daybreak 4 dawn, morn 5 sunup 6 aurora 7 dawning, morning, sunrise 8 cockcrow, daylight

daydream 4 muse 5 fancy 6 vision 7 fantasy, reverie 8 phantasy 9 fantasize 10 woolgather 13 woolgathering

daystar 3 Sol, sun 5 Venus 7 phoebus

daze 3 fog 4 haze, stun 5 amaze, blind 6 dazzle, stupor, trance 7 astound, confuse, stupefy 8 astonish, bedazzle, befuddle, confound 9 dumbfound

dazed 5 woozy 6 groggy, punchy 7 dazzled, stunned 8 confused 9 stupefied 10 punch-drunk

___ **d'Azur** 4 Côte

dazzle 5 amaze, blind, éclat, glitz, shine 7 impress 8 astonish, bewilder, confound, outshine 9 overpower

dazzling 6 flashy, garish 7 radiant 8 splendid, stunning 9 brilliant 11 confounding, resplendent 12 overpowering

deacon 6 clergy, cleric, layman 8 reverend 9 churchman

dead 4 cold, gone, late 5 passé, slain, stiff 6 buried, fallen 7 defunct, done for, expired, extinct 8 deceased, departed, lifeless 9 senseless 10 corpselike 11 unconscious 12 extinguished

deadbeat 3 bum 5 idler 6 debtor, loafer, slouch 7 lounger, shirker, slacker 10 delinquent, malingerer

dead duck 5 goner 8 casualty, fatality

deaden 4 dull, kill, mute, numb, stun 5 blunt, quiet 6 benumb, dampen, lessen, muffle, obtund, reduce, stifle 7 smother, stupefy 8 suppress 11 anesthetize, desensitize

dead end 4 halt, stop 6 pocket, unruly 7 impasse 8 cul-de-sac, standoff 9 stalemate, terminate 10 blind alley, bottleneck, standstill

deadened 4 numb 6 asleep, dulled, killed, numbed 7 blunted 8 benumbed, impaired 12 anesthetized

deadeye 5 block 8 marksman 12 sharpshooter

deadfall 4 trap 7 springe 9 booby trap, mousetrap

deadliness 8 fatality 9 lethality, mortality

deadlock 3 tie 4 draw 7 impasse 8 standoff, stoppage 9 checkmate, stalemate 10 standstill

deadly 5 fatal, toxic 6 lethal, mortal 7 capital, killing 8 lethally, unerring 10 implacable 11 destructive 12 pestilential

deadpan 5 blank, empty 6 vacant 9 impassive 10 poker-faced 11 inscrutable 12 inexpressive, unexpressive

Dead Souls author 5 Gogol (Nikolay)

dead to rights 9 red-handed

deadweight 4 load 6 weight

deal 4 dole, sale, sell 5 allot, serve, shake, share, trade, treat 6 barter, dicker, parcel 7 bargain, deliver, dish out, dole out, mete out, package, portion, traffic, wrestle 8 contract, disburse, dispense, share out 9 agreement, apportion, negotiate 10 administer, compromise, distribute, measure out 11 arrangement, transaction 13 understanding *great:* 4 gobs, heap, lots, tons 5 heaps, horde, loads, scads 6 oodles, plenty, stacks *out:* 8 disburse, dispense 9 apportion 10 administer, distribute *with:* 5 serve, treat 6 handle, regard 7 concern, involve

dealer 5 agent 6 broker, seller, trader, vendor 8 chandler, merchant, operator 9 tradesman 10 negotiator, trafficker 11 businessman, distributer, distributor 12 merchandiser *British:* 5 coper 6 draper, jobber, mercer 7 chapman

dealings 5 trade, truck 7 affairs, matters, traffic 8 business, commerce, concerns 11 intercourse 12 interactions, transactions, undertakings

dean 4 head 5 chief, doyen, elder 6 leader

dear 3 pet 4 fond, lamb, love 5 honey, loved, sweet 6 costly, doting, loving, prized, scarce 7 beloved, darling, devoted, lovable, machree, querida, tootsie 8 favorite, precious, valuable 9 cherished, expensive, heartfelt, treasured 10 fair-haired, honeybunch, sweetheart 12 affectionate *French:* 4 cher 5 chère 6 cherie

dearth 4 lack, want 6 famine 7 absence, default, paucity 8 scarcity, shortage, sparsity 9 privation, scantness 10 deficiency, meagerness, scantiness

death 3 end 4 exit 6 demise, ending, expiry 7 decease, passing, quietus 8 casualty, curtains, fatality, necrosis, thanatos 9 bloodshed, departure 10 expiration, extinction, grim reaper 11 dissolution, termination 12 annihilation *after:* 10 posthumous *combining form:* 6 thanat 7 thanato *music:* 5 dirge, elegy 8 threnody *notice:* 4 obit 8 obituary 9 necrology *of tissue:* 8 gangrene *personification:* 10 grim reaper *put to:* 3 gas, hit, ice, zap 4 do in, hang, kill, slay 5 drown, lynch, snuff, waste 6 murder, poison, rub out 7 bump off, butcher, execute, smother, wipe out 8 blow away, dispatch, immolate, knock off, strangle, throttle 9 slaughter, suffocate 10 asphyxiate 11 assassinate, electrocute *rate:* 9 mortality *rites:* 7 funeral 8 exequies 9 interment, obsequies

deathless 7 abiding, eternal, lasting, undying 8 enduring, immortal 11 everlasting 12 imperishable

deathlike see DEATHLY

deathly 5 fatal 6 lethal, mortal 7 macabre, stygian 12 pestilential

debacle 4 rout 6 defeat, fiasco 7 breakup, failure 8 collapse, disaster 9 breakdown, cataclysm 10 disruption

debar 3 ban 4 stop 6 forbid, outlaw 7 exclude, prevent, rule out 8 preclude, prohibit 9 interdict

debark 4 land 6 alight, get off 11 decorticate

debase 3 mar 4 harm 5 lower, stain 6 damage, defile, demean, dilute, impair, reduce, weaken 7 cheapen, corrupt, degrade, devalue, pervert, pollute, vitiate 8 dishonor 9 undermine 10 adulterate, depreciate 11 contaminate

debatable 4 iffy, moot 7 dubious 8 arguable, doubtful 9 contested, uncertain, undecided 10 disputable, unresolved 11 problematic 12 questionable

debate 4 moot 5 argue, bandy, plead 7 contend, contest, discuss, dispute, quarrel, wrangle 8 argument, consider, forensic, question 9 dialectic, thrash

out 10 controvert, toss around 11 application, controversy, disputation 12 deliberation 13 argumentation *art of:* 9 forensics *expert:* 7 eristic *place for:* 5 forum

debauch 4 orgy, warp 6 seduce 7 corrupt, deprave, pervert, vitiate 9 bacchanal, brutalize 10 lead astray, saturnalia 11 bacchanalia

debauched 6 wanton 8 degraded, depraved, vitiated 9 corrupted, dissolute, libertine, perverted 10 degenerate, licentious

debilitate 3 sap 6 impair, weaken 7 cripple, disable 8 enfeeble 9 attenuate, undermine 10 devitalize

debilitated 4 weak 6 feeble, infirm, sapped 7 run-down, worn-out 8 weakened 9 enfeebled

debility 7 disease, malaise 8 weakness 9 infirmity 10 feebleness, infirmness, sickliness 11 decrepitude

Debir *kingdom:* 5 Eglon *slayer:* 6 Joshua

debit 4 bill, levy 6 charge 7 deficit 8 drawback 9 liability 11 encumbrance, shortcoming

debonair 5 suave 6 smooth, urbane 7 dashing, elegant 10 nonchalant 12 lighthearted

Deborah's husband 9 Lappidoth

debris 4 junk, slag 5 trash, waste 6 litter, refuse, rubble, spilth 7 garbage, rubbish 8 detritus, riffraff, wreckage *rock:* 5 scree, talus 8 colluvia 9 colluvium

debt 3 due, sin 6 arrear, red ink 7 arrears, default, deficit 8 mortgage, trespass 9 arrearage, liability 10 obligation 11 delinquency *acknowledgment:* 3 IOU 4 bill 5 check

debtless 7 solvent

debunk 6 expose, reveal, show up, unmask 7 lay bare, lay open, uncloak, uncover, undress 8 unshroud 9 demystify, discredit

Debussy's La ___ 3 Mer

debut 3 bow 5 entry 6 entree 7 come out, opening, present 8 entrance, premiere 9 beginning, coming out, introduce 12 introduction, presentation

decadence 5 decay 7 decline 10 degeneracy, regression 11 degradation 12 degeneration 13 deterioration

decadent 6 effete 7 debased 8 decaying, degraded, depraved 9 debauched, declining, dissolute 10 degenerate 13 self-indulgent

Decalogue verb 5 shalt

Decameron, The *author:* 9 Boccaccio (Giovanni) *heroine:* 8 Griselda

decamp 4 blow, bolt, exit, flee 5 leave, scram, split 6 beat it, begone, cut out, escape, get out, retire 7 abscond, make off, pull out, run away, skiddoo, take off, vamoose 8 clear out, withdraw 9 skedaddle

decant 4 pour 7 draw off, pour out 8 transfer

decanter 5 cruet, flask 6 bottle, carafe, flagon, vessel

decapitate 4 head 6 behead 9 decollate 10 guillotine

decapod 7 mollusc, mollusk 10 crustacean

decathlon champ 6 Jenner (Bruce), Morris (Glenn), O'Brien (Dan), Schenk (Christian), Sebrle (Roman), Toomey (Bill), Zmelik (Robert) 7 Doherty (Ken), Johnson (Rafer), Mathias (Bob) 8 Campbell (Milton), Thompson (Daley)

decay 3 rot 4 ruin, wane 5 spoil, waste 6 molder, wither 7 atrophy, crumble, decline, putrefy, rotting 8 putresce, spoilage 9 decompose 11 deteriorate 12 dilapidation, putrefaction 13 deterioration

decayed 6 putrid, rotted, rotten, ruined 7 carious, spoiled 8 decadent, moldered, overripe 9 putrefied 10 decomposed, degenerate

decease 3 die, end 4 fail, pass 5 death, dying, sleep 6 demise, depart, expire, finish, pass on, perish 7 passing, quietus, release, succumb 8 pass away 9 departure 10 expiration

deceased 4 body, dead, late 6 corpse 7 cadaver, carcass, expired, remains 8 departed, lifeless 9 inanimate

deceit 3 gyp 4 hoax, ruse, sham 5 fraud, guile, trick 6 humbug 7 swindle 8 artifice, flimflam, trickery 9 chicanery, deception, duplicity, imposture 10 dishonesty 13 double-dealing

deceitful 3 sly 4 wily 5 false, lying 6 crafty, sneaky, tricky 7 cunning, knavish, roguish 8 guileful, two-faced 9 deceptive, dishonest, underhand 10 mendacious 11 underhanded 13 double-dealing

deceive 3 con 4 bilk, dupe, fool, gull, hoax 5 bluff, cozen, lie to, trick 6 delude, humbug, palter, take in 7 beguile, mislead, sandbag, two-time 8 flimflam, hoodwink 9 bamboozle, four-flush 11 double-cross

deceiving 5 false 6 tricky 8 deluding, delusive, delusory, guileful, two-faced 9 beguiling, deceptive 10 fallacious, misleading 11 duplicitous, underhanded

decelerate 4 slow 5 delay 6 retard, slow up 7 slacken 8 slow down

decency 7 decorum, dignity, fitness, modesty 8 civility, etiquette, propriety 10 conformity, seemliness

decennium 6 decade

decent 4 fair, good 5 right 6 honest, modest, proper, seemly 7 correct, fitting, upright 8 adequate, all right 9 competent, honorable, tolerable 10 acceptable, conforming, sufficient 11 comme il faut, presentable, respectable 12 satisfactory

deception 3 gyp 4 gaff, hoax, hype, ruse, sham, wile 5 cheat, fraud, guile, put-on, trick 6 deceit, dupery, humbug, mirage 7 chicane, cunning, fallacy, fantasm, knavery, sophism 8 flimflam, illusion, intrigue, phantasm, trickery, trumpery, wiliness 9 casuistry, chicanery, duplicity, imposture, sophistry, treachery 10 artfulness, dishonesty, hanky-panky, subterfuge 11 indirection 12 speciousness, spuriousness 13 double-dealing

deceptive 5 false, phony 6 tricky 8 deluding, delusory, illusory, specious 9 beguiling, deceitful, deceiving 10 fallacious, misleading

decide 3 opt 4 rule, will 5 judge 6 settle 7 adjudge, resolve 8 conclude 9 determine 10 adjudicate

decided 3 set 4 firm 5 fixed 6 intent 7 assured, certain, obvious, settled 8 definite, resolute, resolved 10 determined, pronounced 11 established, unequivocal

decimate 4 raze, ruin 5 wreck 7 abolish, destroy, wipe out 8 demolish, massacre 9 slaughter 10 annihilate, obliterate 11 exterminate

decipher 4 read 5 break, crack, solve 6 decode, reveal 7 decrypt, resolve, unravel 8 unriddle 9 figure out, interpret, puzzle out, translate 12 cryptanalyze

decision 4 fiat 6 choice, ruling 7 finding, resolve, verdict 8 firmness, judgment, sentence 9 selection 10 conclusion, resolution, settlement 13 determination
rabbinical: 9 responsum

decisive 3 set 7 crucial, settled 8 critical, resolute 10 conclusive, convincing, determined, imperative, peremptory 11 determining 12 unmistakable

deck 4 trim 5 adorn, array, dress, equip, floor, level, porch, prank 6 attire, blazon, clothe 7 apparel, appoint, furnish, garland, garnish, terrace 8 accouter, accoutre, beautify, decorate, emblazon, ornament, platform 9 embellish *chief:* 4 bos'n 9 boatswain *high:* 4 poop *lowest:* 5 orlop *out:* 5 array, fix up, slick, spiff, tog up **6** clothe, doll up **7** dress up, gussy up **8** spruce up *part:* **7** scupper

deckhand 3 gob **4** jack, swab **6** sailor, seaman **7** jack-tar, rouster, swabbie **10** bluejacket

declaim 4 rant **5** mouth, orate, speak **6** recite **7** deliver, lecture **8** bloviate, harangue, perorate **9** hold forth

declamatory 5 tumid, windy, wordy **6** florid, turgid **7** aureate, flowery, fustian, orotund, pompous, ranting, verbose **8** sonorous **9** bombastic, highflown, overblown **10** euphuistic, oratorical, rhetorical **12** magniloquent **13** grandiloquent

declaration 5 edict **6** avowal, notice, report **7** promise **8** document, pleading **9** affidavit, manifesto, statement, testimony **10** confession, deposition, disclosure, expression, profession **11** affirmation, attestation **12** announcement, notification, proclamation **13** advertisement, pronouncement

declare 3 say, vow **4** aver, avow, tell, vent **5** claim, sound, state, swear, utter, voice **6** affirm, allege, assert, avouch, blazon, depone, depose, herald, insist, ordain, report, reveal **7** certify, confirm, deliver, divulge, express, profess, signify, testify **8** announce, disclose, indicate, maintain, manifest, proclaim, propound **9** advertise, broadcast, enunciate, predicate, pronounce **10** annunciate, asseverate, promulgate **11** come out with, disseminate *a saint:* **8** canonize *in cards:* **3** bid **4** meld *invalid:* **5** annul

declass 4 bump, bust **5** abase, lower **6** demote, reduce **7** degrade, set back **9** downgrade

déclassé 4 mean, poor **6** common, vulgar **7** ignoble, lowered **8** inferior, lowgrade, mediocre, middling **10** secondrate **11** second-class

declension 5 class, slope **7** decline, descent **8** downfall **9** downgrade **10** inflection **12** dégringolade **13** deterioration

declination 3 ebb **5** slant, slide **6** ebbing **7** refusal, incline **8** downturn **9** downgrade **10** deflection **12** dégringolade, turning aside **13** deterioration

decline 3 dip, ebb, jib, rot, sag, set **4** balk, dive, drop, fade, fail, fall, flag, loss, sink, slip, wane **5** abate, avoid, demur, droop, lapse, lower, say no, slide, slope, slump, spurn **6** ebbing, go down, recede, refuse, reject, renege, waning, weaken, worsen **7** abstain, atrophy, descend, descent, devolve, dismiss, drop-off, dwindle, failure, falloff, forbear, refrain, relapse, sell-off, sink-

age, subside **8** comedown, decrease, downfall, downturn, languish, lowering, turn down **9** backslide, decadence, downgrade, downslide, downswing, downtrend, reprobate, repudiate, weakening **10** degeneracy, degenerate, depression, devolution, disapprove, falling off **11** backsliding, deteriorate **12** degeneration, dégringolade **13** deterioration

declivitous 5 steep **6** sloped **7** pitched, sloping **8** inclined **9** inclining **10** descending

declivity 3 dip **4** drop, fall **5** slope **7** decline, descent **8** downturn, gradient **9** downgrade **11** inclination

decode see DECIPHER

decollate 4 head, kill **6** behead **10** decapitate, guillotine

decolor 6 blanch, bleach, blench, whiten **7** wash out **11** achromatize

decompose 3 rot **5** decay, spoil, taint **6** fester, molder **7** analyze, break up, crumble, putrefy, resolve **8** dissolve, separate **9** anatomize, break down **12** disintegrate

decor 7 setting **8** backdrop, stage set **11** furnishings **13** ornamentation

decorate 4 do up, pink, trim **5** adorn, dress, frill **6** bedeck **7** bedizen, dress up, enhance, festoon, furnish, garnish **8** appliqué, beautify, emblazon, ornament **9** embellish *a border:* **6** purfle

decorated 6 ornate **7** adorned, honored, wrought **8** bemedaled, decked out, garnished **10** beribboned, ornamented **11** embellished

decoration 4 bays **5** award, badge, honor, kudos, medal **6** doodad, plaque **7** garnish, laurels **8** accolade, filigree, fretting, fretwork, frippery, furbelow, ornament, trimming, vignette **11** distinction *cutout:* **8** appliqué *furniture:* **4** buhl **6** boulle

decorous 3 fit **4** meet, prim **5** right **6** au fait, comely, decent, proper, seemly **7** correct, elegant, fitting **8** becoming, mannerly, suitable, tasteful **9** befitting, civilized, de rigueur, dignified **10** conforming **11** appropriate, respectable, well-behaved

decorously 5 fitly **7** rightly **8** decently, properly, suitably **9** correctly, fittingly **11** befittingly, respectably

decorousness 7 decency **8** civility **9** propriety, rightness **10** seemliness **11** correctness, orderliness **12** correctitude

decorticate 4 bare, bark, flay, hull, husk, pare, peel, skin **5** scale, scalp, shell, shuck, strip **6** denude **7** lay bare, pull off

decorum 5 order **7** decency, dignity, fitness, modesty, protocol **9** etiquette, propriety **10** properness, seemliness **11** correctness, orderliness **12** correctitude

decoy 4 bait, fake, lure **5** plant, shill, tempt **6** allure, capper, delude, entice, lead on, pigeon, seduce **7** deceive, mislead **8** inveigle **10** red herring

decrease 3 cut, ebb **4** bate, drop, ease, fall, loss, wane **5** allay, lower **6** lessen, reduce, shrink **7** abridge, curtail, cut back, cutback, cut down, decline, die down, drop off, dwindle, fall off, lighten, shorten, slacken, subside **8** diminish, downturn, moderate, rollback, taper off **9** abatement, alleviate, reduction **10** abbreviate, depreciate, diminution, falling off

decree 4 fiat, rule **5** canon, edict, enact, judge, order, ukase **6** behest, charge, dictum, impose, ordain, ruling **7** adjudge, appoint, bidding, command, declare, dictate, lay down, mandate, precept, statute **8** judgment, proclaim, sentence **9** directive, judgement, ordinance, prescribe, prescript, pronounce **10** adjudicate, injunction, regulation **11** declaration **12** adjudication, announcement, proclamation, promulgation **13** pronouncement *Muslim:* **5** fatwa

decrepit 4 aged, weak, worn **5** frail, seedy, tacky **6** creaky, feeble, infirm, senile, shabby, wasted, weakly **7** fragile, run-down, worn-out **8** battered, impaired, weakened **10** bedraggled, broken-down, down-at-heel, ramshackle **11** dilapidated

decrepitude 4 ruin **5** decay **7** frailty, wasting **8** collapse, debility, weakness **9** disrepair, infirmity **10** exhaustion, feebleness, infirmness **12** dilapidation, enfeeblement **13** deterioration

decretal 4 fiat, writ **5** edict, order, ukase **6** assize, dictum, letter, ruling **7** dictate **8** decision, judgment **11** declaration **13** pronouncement

decry 3 boo **4** bash, slam, slur **5** abuse **6** berate, malign, vilify **7** asperse, censure, condemn, degrade, devalue, put down **8** bad-mouth, belittle, denounce, derogate, reproach **9** criticize, deprecate, discredit, disparage, dispraise, reprehend, reprobate **10** depreciate, disapprove **11** rail against

decrypt see DECIPHER

decumbent 4 flat **5** prone **6** supine **9** lying down, prostrate, reclining **10** horizontal

decussate 5 cross **8** crosscut **9** intersect **10** crisscross, intercross

dedicate 3 vow **5** bless **6** commit, devote, hallow, pledge **7** address **8** inscribe, restrict, set apart **10** consecrate

deduce 5 infer, judge, trace **6** derive, evolve, gather, reason, reckon **7** discern, make out, surmise **8** conclude **9** figure out

deduct 4 bate **5** abate, infer, judge **6** gather, remove **7** make out, take off, take out **8** conclude, knock off, perceive, subtract, take away

deduction 3 cut **8** discount, illation, judgment, sequitur, write-off **9** abatement, inference, reasoning **10** conclusion **11** subtraction

deductive 7 a priori **8** dogmatic, illative, provable, reasoned **9** derivable, inferable **10** consequent **11** inferential **13** ratiocinative

deed 3 act **4** cede, fact, feat, pact **5** doing, title **6** action, assign, convey, escrow, remise **7** charter, exploit **8** alienate, contract, covenant, make over, sign over, transfer **9** adventure **10** conveyance, enterprise **11** achievement, performance, tour de force *brutal:* **8** atrocity *evil:* **3** sin **11** malefaction *good:* **7** mitzvah

deem 4 feel, hold **5** judge, think **7** account, adjudge, believe **8** consider

de-emphasize 8 downplay, minimize, play down **9** gloss over, soft-pedal, underplay **13** underestimate

deep 3 low **4** bass, rapt, sunk **5** abyss, grave, ocean **6** occult, orphic, secret **7** abyssal, obscure **8** abstruse, esoteric, hermetic, profound **9** engrossed, recondite **10** bottomless, fathomless, mysterious *combining form:* **5** bathy

deepen 6 darken, worsen **7** enhance, enlarge, magnify, thicken **8** heighten **9** aggravate, intensify **10** strengthen

deepness 5 abyss **9** intensity **10** profundity

deep-seated 6 inborn, inbred, innate **7** settled **8** inherent, lifelong, profound, stubborn **9** confirmed, ingrained, intrinsic **10** congenital, entrenched, indwelling, inveterate **11** established **12** long-standing **13** bred-in-the-bone, dyed-in-the-wool, thoroughgoing

deep-six 4 dump, toss **5** chuck, scrap **6** unload **7** discard **8** jettison **9** eliminate

deep water 7 trouble **8** distress **10** difficulty

deer 3 elk, roe **4** buck, musk, stag **5** moose **6** wapiti **7** caribou, venison *Asian:* **4** axis **6** sambar **7** muntjac *British:* **4** hart *female:* **3** doe **4** hind *Japanese:* **4** sika *male:* **4** buck, hart, stag **7** roebuck *meat:* **5** jerky **7** venison *path:*

3 run 5 trail *red:* 7 brocket *relating to:*
7 cervine *track:* 4 slot 5 spoor *young:*
3 kid 4 fawn

Deerslayer (The) *author:* 6 Cooper
(James Fenimore) *character:* 5 Harry
(Hurry) 6 Hutter (Thomas), Judith
(Hutter) 11 Natty Bumppo 12 Chin-
gachgook

deface 3 mar 4 harm, ruin 6 damage,
deform, impair, injure 9 disfigure, vandalize

de facto 6 actual, really 8 actually, existing

defalcation 7 default, failing, failure
10 embezzling, inadequacy, negligence
12 embezzlement

defamation 5 libel, smear 7 calumny,
obloquy, slander 10 backbiting 11 traducement 12 backstabbing 13 disparagement

defamatory 8 libelous 9 maligning, traducing, vilifying 10 backbiting, calumnious, slanderous 11 denigrating

defame 5 abase, libel, smear 6 malign,
vilify 7 asperse, blacken, blemish, slander, traduce 8 dishonor 9 denigrate,
discredit 10 calumniate

default 4 fail 5 welsh 7 absence, exclude,
failure, forfeit, neglect 9 selection

defeasance 4 deed 6 defeat 9 overthrow
11 termination

defeat 3 tan 4 beat, best, down, drub,
edge, foil, lick, loss, rout, sink, undo,
whip, whup 5 crush, outdo, skunk,
swamp, upset, waste, whomp 6 outgun,
reduce, subdue, wallop 7 beating, conquer, destroy, failure, licking, mow
down, nose out, nullify, outplay, overrun, setback, shellac, trounce, wipe out
8 knock out, outfight, outmuscle, overcome, vanquish, waterloo 9 frustrate,
overpower, overthrow, overtrump, subjugate, thrashing, trouncing 10 obliterate 11 shellacking

defeatist 8 doomster 9 doomsayer,
Gloomy Gus, pessimist, worrywart

defect 3 bug 4 flaw, lack, vice, want
5 botch, error, fault 6 damage, dearth,
desert, foible, injury 7 blemish, default,
failing 8 drawback, weakness 9 birthmark, deformity 10 apostatize, deficiency 11 shortcoming 12 imperfection,
tergiversate *timber:* 4 knot *visual:*
6 myopia, squint 9 amblyopia, hyperopia 10 presbyopia, strabismus

defection 8 apostasy 9 desertion, forsaking, recreancy 10 disloyalty 11 abandonment

defective 5 amiss 6 broken, faulty,
flawed 7 damaged, lacking, unsound,
wanting 8 impaired 9 corrupted, defi-

cient, imperfect 10 inaccurate, inadequate, incomplete 12 insufficient

defector 5 Judas 7 traitor 8 apostate,
quisling, recreant, renegade, turncoat
9 turnabout 13 double-crosser

defend 4 back, hold, save 5 argue, cover,
guard 6 screen, secure, shield, uphold
7 contend, justify, protect, support
8 advocate, champion, maintain, plead
for, preserve 9 safeguard

defendable see DEFENSIBLE

defendant 7 accused, libelee 8 libellee

defender 7 paladin, tribune 8 advocate,
champion, guardian 9 protector
11 white knight

defense 4 fort, ward 5 aegis, alibi,
armor, guard 6 excuse, sconce, shield
7 bulwark, rampart, shelter 8 apologia,
armament, fastness, fortress, muni-
ment, security 9 safeguard 10 protection, stronghold 11 exculpation, explanation 13 justification *organization:*
4 NATO 5 NORAD, SEATO
10 Warsaw Pact

defenseless 4 open 7 exposed, unarmed
8 helpless, wide open 9 unguarded
10 vulnerable 11 unprotected

defensible 5 valid 7 tenable 8 passable
9 excusable, plausible 10 condonable,
reasonable 11 justifiable

defer 3 bow 4 stay, wait 5 delay, remit,
stall, table, yield 6 accede, hold up, put
off, shelve, submit 7 hold off, lay over,
put over, suspend 8 hold over, postpone, prorogue 9 acquiesce 13 procrastinate

deference 5 honor 6 esteem, homage,
regard 7 respect 8 courtesy 9 obeisance
11 recognition

deferential 8 obliging 9 disarming,
regardful 10 respectful 11 complaisant

defiance 4 dare 5 moxie 7 bravado
8 audacity, contempt 9 challenge, contumacy, impudence, insolence 10 brazenness, effrontery 12 contrariness,
stubbornness

defiant 4 bold 5 brash, gutsy, sassy,
saucy 6 brazen, cheeky, daring 8 arrogant, impudent, insolent 9 audacious,
obstinate, resistant 10 refractory
12 recalcitrant

deficiency 4 flaw, lack, want 5 fault,
minus 6 dearth 7 absence, blemish,
demerit, failing, failure, paucity
8 scarcity, shortage, weakness 9 privation 10 inadequacy, scantiness 11 defalcation, shortcoming 12 imperfection
mental: 6 idiocy 7 amentia

deficient 3 shy 5 minus, scant, short
6 faulty, flawed, meager, meagre,
measly, scanty, scarce 7 failing, lacking,

unsound, wanting **8** exiguous, impaired **9** defective, imperfect **10** inadequate, incomplete

deficit 4 lack, loss **6** red ink **8** shortage **10** impairment, inadequacy **12** disadvantage **13** insufficiency

defile 3 tar **4** foul, pass, rape, soil **5** dirty, gorge, march, shame, smear, spoil, stain, sully, taint **6** befoul, debase, ravish **7** besmear, corrupt, pollute, profane, tarnish, violate **8** deflower, dishonor **9** desecrate **11** contaminate

defiled 5 raped **6** impure **7** stained, unclean **8** profaned, polluted, ravished, violated **9** corrupted **10** deflowered, desecrated **12** contaminated

define 3 fix, hem, rim, set **4** edge **5** limit **6** assign, border, detail **7** clarify, delimit, lay down, mark off, mark out, outline, specify **9** delineate, demarcate, determine, establish **11** distinguish **12** characterize

definite 3 set **4** sure **5** clear, final, fixed, sharp, solid **7** certain, decided, express, precise, settled **8** clear-cut, distinct, explicit, specific **10** conclusive, pronounced **11** unambiguous, unequivocal **12** unmistakable

definiteness 8 accuracy, sureness **9** certainty, certitude, exactness, precision **10** exactitude

definitive 5 final **7** express **8** clear-cut, complete, explicit, settling, specific, ultimate **10** concluding, conclusive, exhaustive **11** categorical, determining, unambiguous **13** authoritative

deflate 4 dash **6** humble, reduce, shrink **7** devalue, put down **8** contract, ridicule **9** humiliate, shoot down

deflect 5 avert, parry **6** divert **7** deviate, diverge, hold off **9** turn aside

deflection 3 yaw **4** bend, tack, turn, veer **5** carom, curve, shift **6** double, swerve **7** bending, rebound, turning, veering **8** swerving **9** departure, deviation, diversion **10** divergence

deflower 4 rape **5** spoil **6** defile, ravish **7** despoil, violate **9** desecrate

Defoe, Daniel *character:* **6** Crusoe (Robinson), Friday, Roxana **12** Moll Flanders

deform 4 warp **5** spoil **6** deface **7** contort, distort **8** misshape **9** disfigure

deformed 4 awry, bent **5** askew, bowed **6** warped **7** buckled, crooked **8** crippled **9** contorted, misshapen, unshapely

deformity 4 flaw **6** defect **7** blemish **11** abnormality **12** imperfection, irregularity, malformation **13** disfigurement

___ **de France 3** Île

defraud 3 con, gyp **4** bilk, dupe, rook,

scam **5** cheat, cozen, mulct, trick **6** fleece, rip off **7** swindle **8** flimflam **9** bamboozle

deft 3 apt **4** able **5** adept, agile, handy **6** adroit, clever **7** skilled **8** dextrous, skillful **9** dexterous

deftness 5 knack, skill **7** address, prowess **8** facility **9** adeptness, dexterity **10** capability

defunct 4 cold, dead, late **5** kaput **7** extinct **8** deceased, departed, lifeless, vanished

defy 4 dare, face, gibe, jeer, mock **5** beard, brave, flout, stump **6** resist **7** affront, outdare, outface **8** confront **9** challenge, disregard, withstand

dégagé 6 breezy, casual **7** relaxed, unfussy **8** informal **9** easygoing **10** nonchalant, unreserved **13** unconstrained

degeneracy see DEGENERATION

degenerate 4 sink **6** rotten, sunken, worsen **7** corrupt, debased, decayed, decline, descend, immoral, pervert, vicious, vitiate **8** decadent, degraded, depraved **9** backslide, dissolute **11** deteriorate

degeneration 7 atrophy, decline **8** downfall, lowering **9** decadence, depravity, downgrade **10** debasement, perversion, regression **11** degradation **12** dégringolade **13** deterioration

degradation 4 fall **7** decline, descent **8** demotion **9** abasement, decadence, depravity, downgrade, reduction **10** corruption, debasement, degeneracy, perversion **11** downgrading **12** degeneration

degrade 4 bump, bust **5** abase, break, decry, lower **6** debase, demean, demote, impair, lessen, reduce **7** corrupt, declass, pervert, put down **8** belittle, cast down, derogate, diminish **9** decompose, discredit, disparage, downgrade, humiliate

degree 3 peg **4** heat, rank, rate, rung, step, term, tier **5** grade, honor, notch, order, pitch, point, ratio, scale, shade, stage, stair **6** amount, extent, status **7** measure, station **8** standing **9** dimension, intensity, magnitude **10** proportion *academic:* **3** BFA, BSc, DDS, LLB, LLD, LLM, MBA, MFA, MSc, PhD **5** MPhil **7** master's **9** bachelor's, doctorate *highest:* **8** cum laude **13** magna cum laude, summa cum laude *of combining power:* **7** valence *of height:* **5** grade *of importance:* **7** caliber, calibre *of outward slope:* **5** splay *seeker:* **9** candidate *slight:* **4** hair *utmost:* **4** acme

dégringolade see DEGENERATION

___ **de guerre 3** nom

dehydrate 3 dry 4 sear 5 parch 9 desiccate, exsiccate

Deianira *brother:* 8 Meleager *father:* 6 Oeneus *husband:* 8 Heracles, Hercules *mother:* 7 Althaea *victim:* 8 Heracles, Hercules

deific 5 godly 6 divine 7 godlike

deification 8 idolatry 10 apotheosis, glorifying 13 glorification

deify 5 exalt 7 glorify, idolize, worship 8 sanctify, venerate 11 apotheosize

deign 5 stoop 7 descend 9 vouchsafe 10 condescend

Deiphobus *brother:* 5 Paris 6 Hector *father:* 5 Priam *mother:* 6 Hecuba *wife:* 5 Helen

Deirdre *beloved:* 5 Noisi *father:* 5 Felim

deity 3 god 4 Lord 7 goddess, godhead, godhood 8 Almighty, divinity 12 supreme being (see also at GREEK; HINDU; NORSE; ROMAN)

deject 5 chill, cloud, daunt 6 dampen, dismay 7 depress 8 dispirit 9 disparage 10 demoralize, discourage, dishearten

dejected 3 low, sad 4 blue, down, glum, sunk 6 gloomy, morose, somber, sombre 7 doleful, hangdog, humbled, unhappy 8 downcast, wretched 9 cheerless, depressed, woebegone 10 despondent, spiritless 11 crestfallen, downhearted 12 disconsolate, disheartened

dejection 5 dumps, gloom 7 despair, sadness 10 melancholy 11 despondency, unhappiness 12 mournfulness

Delaware *capital:* 5 Dover *city:* 10 Wilmington *nickname:* 5 First (State) 7 Diamond (State) *state bird:* 14 blue hen chicken *state flower:* 12 peach blossom *state tree:* 13 American holly

delay 3 lag 4 drag, hold, slow, stay, wait 5 dally, defer, stall, tarry, trail 6 dawdle, detain, hang up, hinder, holdup, impede, linger, loiter, put off, retard, slow up 7 bog down, hold off, respite, set back, slacken, suspend 8 hesitate, hold over, postpone, prorogue, reprieve, slow down 10 dillydally, moratorium, suspension 13 procrastinate

delaying 8 dawdling, dilatory 10 postponing, putting off

delectable 5 tasty, yummy 6 choice, savory 8 charming, heavenly, luscious, pleasing 9 ambrosial, delicious, enjoyable, exquisite, toothsome 10 delightful, enchanting 11 scrumptious 13 mouthwatering

delectation 3 fun, joy 4 zest 5 gusto 6 relish 7 delight 8 gladness, pleasure 9 enjoyment

delegate 4 name, send 5 agent, envoy, proxy 6 assign, depute, deputy, legate 7 appoint, consign, entrust 8 deputize, emissary, transfer 9 authorize, catchpole, designate, spokesman 10 commission, mouthpiece, procurator

delete 4 drop, omit, x out 5 erase, purge 6 cancel, censor, cut out, efface, excise, remove 7 blot out, destroy, expunge, take out, wipe out 8 black out, cross out 9 eliminate, eradicate, strike out 10 blue-pencil, obliterate

deleterious 3 bad 6 nocent 7 baneful, harmful, hurtful, nocuous, noxious, ruinous 8 damaging 9 injurious 10 pernicious 11 destructive, detrimental, mischievous, prejudicial

deletion 7 erasure, voiding 9 canceling 10 deficiency 11 elimination 12 cancellation

deliberate 4 chaw, cool, muse, pore, slow 5 chary, meant, study, think, weigh 6 chew on, ponder, reason 7 careful, heedful, planned, reflect, studied, willful, willing, witting 8 cautious, cogitate, consider, intended, measured, meditate, mull over, ruminate, talk over 9 cerebrate, conscious, unhurried 10 calculated, considered, purposeful, thought-out 11 circumspect, intentional 12 premeditated

deliberately 9 knowingly, on purpose, purposely, willfully, wittingly 11 consciously 12 purposefully 13 intentionally

deliberation 5 study 6 debate 7 thought 10 conference, discussion, reflection 13 consideration

Delibes, Léo *ballet:* 6 Sylvia 8 Coppélia, La Source *opera:* 5 Lakmé

delicacy 5 goody, treat 6 dainty, luxury, morsel, nicety, tidbit 7 frailty 8 kickshaw, fineness 9 fragility, precision 10 daintiness, difficulty, indulgence, stickiness 11 awkwardness 12 ticklishness

delicate 4 fine, lacy, weak 5 frail 6 choice, dainty, flimsy, petite, queasy, sickly, slight, subtle, tender, touchy, tricky 7 elegant, fragile, refined, tactful, tenuous 8 ethereal, feathery, finespun, gossamer, graceful, pleasing, ticklish 9 exquisite, sensitive, squeamish 10 precarious

delicatessen 11 charcuterie

delicious 5 tasty, yummy 6 choice, divine, savory 8 heavenly, luscious 9 ambrosial, exquisite, toothsome 10 delectable, delightful 11 scrumptious 13 mouthwatering

delight 3 joy 4 glee 5 amuse, bliss, charm, enjoy, exult, glory, mirth, revel

6 divert, please, regale, relish **7** ecstasy, enchant, gladden, gratify, jollity, rapture, rejoice **8** enravish, entrance, fruition, hilarity, pleasure **9** delectate, enjoyment, enrapture, entertain **11** delectation *in:* **4** love **5** adore, enjoy, savor **6** admire, relish **7** cherish **10** appreciate

delighted 4 glad **5** happy **6** joyful **8** ecstatic, euphoric

delightful 5 yummy **6** dreamy, lovely **8** charming, heavenly, luscious, pleasant, pleasing **9** congenial, enjoyable **10** delectable, enchanting, satisfying **11** captivating, fascinating, pleasurable, scrumptious **12** entertaining

Delilah's victim 6 Samson

DeLillo novel 5 Libra, Mao II **10** Underworld, White Noise

delimit 3 bar **5** bound, hem in **6** demark, define **7** confine, enclose **8** restrict **9** demarcate, determine **12** circumscribe

delineate 3 map **4** etch, limn **5** chart, image, trace **6** define, depict, detail, render **7** outline, picture, portray **8** describe, spell out **9** elucidate, interpret, represent **10** illustrate

delineation 5 draft, story **6** report **7** account, contour, drawing, outline, picture, profile **9** depiction, rendering **11** presentment

delinquency 4 debt **5** crime, fault, lapse **7** default, failure, misdeed, neglect, offense **8** omission **9** oversight **10** misconduct, nonpayment, wrongdoing **11** dereliction, misbehavior

delinquent 3 lax **5** slack **6** debtor **7** overdue **8** careless, offender **9** defaulter, in arrears, negligent **10** behindhand, neglectful

deliquesce 3 rot, run **4** flux, fuse, melt, thaw **5** decay **6** render, soften **7** liquefy, putrefy **8** dissolve, fluidize **9** decompose, disappear, waste away **12** disintegrate

delirious 3 mad **4** wild **5** crazy **6** crazed, insane, raving **7** frantic, lunatic **8** confused, demented, deranged, ecstatic, frenetic, frenzied, rambling **9** rapturous **10** bewildered, corybantic, distracted, irrational **11** lightheaded, overexcited, overwrought

delirium 5 furor, mania **6** fervor, frenzy **7** ecstasy, jimjams, rapture, seizure **8** dementia, hysteria **13** hallucination

delirium ___ 7 tremens

deliver 4 bear, deal, feed, find, give, hand, save, send, ship, sing, take **5** bring, serve, speak, state, throw, utter **6** convey, redeem, rescue, strike, sup-ply **7** consign, present, produce, provide, set free, release **8** hand over, liberate, turn over **9** pronounce, surrender **10** bring forth, emancipate **11** come out with, come through

deliverance 6 rescue **7** freeing, opinion, release, verdict **8** decision **9** acquittal, discharge, salvation **10** absolution, liberation

Deliverance author 6 Dickey (James)

delivery 4 drop **5** birth, labor **6** rescue **7** address, bearing **8** birthing, shipment **9** elocution, rendition, salvation **10** childbirth, conveyance, liberation **11** consignment, parturition, transferral **12** childbearing, transmission

dell 4 dale, glen, vale **6** dingle, hollow, valley

Delphic 4 dark **5** vatic **6** arcane, hidden, mantic, mystic, occult, veiled **7** cryptic, obscure **8** auguring, divining, esoteric, mystical, oracular **9** ambiguous, enigmatic, equivocal, prophetic, recondite, sibylline, vaticinal **10** mystifying, portentous **11** prophesying, prophetical

delta 5 plain **6** letter, symbol **7** deposit **8** triangle **9** increment

delude 3 con **4** dupe, fool, gull, hoax **5** bluff, cozen, trick **6** betray, humbug, juggle, take in **7** beguile, deceive, mislead **8** flimflam, hoodwink **11** doublecross

deluge 5 drown, flood, swamp **6** drench, engulf **7** Niagara, torrent **8** cataract, downpour, drencher, flooding, inundate, overflow **9** cataclysm, overwhelm **10** cloudburst, outpouring, inundation

delusion 4 hoax, sham **5** dream, fancy, snare **6** mirage **7** chimera, fallacy, fantasy, figment, phantom, specter **8** daydream, phantasm **9** deception **10** apparition **11** ignis fatuus **13** hallucination

delusive 5 false **8** fanciful, illusory, specious **9** beguiling, deceiving, deceptive, imaginary **10** chimerical, fallacious, misleading

delusory see DELUSIVE

deluxe 4 lush, posh **5** grand, plush, ritzy, swank **6** choice, costly, swanky **7** elegant, opulent **8** luscious, splendid **9** expensive, exquisite, luxuriant, luxurious, sumptuous **10** first class

delve 3 dig, dip **4** mine **5** probe **6** dredge, fathom, hollow, quarry, search, shovel **7** inquire **8** excavate *into:* **4** sift **5** probe **7** explore **8** prospect **11** investigate

delving 6 asking **7** inquest, inquiry, probing **8** research **9** inquiring, searching

demagnetize 7 degauss

demagogue 6 leader 7 inciter 8 agitator, fomenter 9 firebrand 10 instigator 11 provocateur 12 rabble-rouser

demand 3 ask, use 4 call, need, urge, want 5 claim, crave, exact, force, order 6 compel, direct, expect, insist 7 call for, request, require 11 requirement, requisition

demanding 4 hard 5 pushy, tough 6 taxing, trying 7 exigent, onerous, weighty 8 exacting, forceful, rigorous 9 assertive, difficult, insistent, strenuous, stringent 10 aggressive, burdensome, oppressive 11 challenging

demarcate 5 bound, limit 6 define, set off 7 delimit, mark off, outline 8 separate, set apart 9 delineate, determine 11 distinguish 12 circumscribe 13 differentiate

demarcation 9 outlining 10 border line, separation 11 distinction 12 delimitation

démarche 4 plan, ploy, ruse 5 feint 6 action, device, gambit, scheme, tactic 7 protest 8 artifice, maneuver, petition 9 stratagem 10 initiative 11 contrivance, machination

demean 4 bear 5 abase, carry, decry, lower 6 acquit, behave, debase, deport, humble 7 comport, conduct, degrade, detract 8 bad-mouth, belittle 9 disparage, humiliate

demeanor 3 air 4 look, mien 6 aspect, manner 7 address, bearing, conduct 8 behavior, carriage, presence 10 deportment 11 comportment

demented 3 mad 5 crazy, loony, nutty, wacko 6 crazed, insane, psycho 7 lunatic, unsound 8 deranged, frenzied, maniacal 9 delirious 10 hysterical, unbalanced 12 psychopathic

____ **de mer** 3 mal

demerit 4 mark 5 fault, stain 6 defect 7 blemish, penalty 9 downgrade 10 deficiency, punishment 11 shortcoming 12 imperfection

demesne 5 field, realm 6 domain, estate, region, sphere 7 terrain 8 dominion, province 9 bailiwick, champaign, territory *house:* 5 manor

Demeter see CERES

demigod 4 diva, idol 8 superman 9 superstar

demise 3 die, end 4 drop, pass 5 death, dying, sleep 6 cash in, depart, ending, expire 7 decease, passing, quietus, release, silence, succumb 8 pass away 9 cessation, departure 10 expiration, extinction

demit 4 quit 6 bow out, give up, resign

8 abdicate, renounce, step down, withdraw

demiurgic 8 creative, original 9 formative, ingenious, inventive 10 innovative 11 originative 12 innovational

demobilize 7 break up, disband, dismiss, scatter 8 disperse, separate 9 discharge, disengage, muster out

democratic 7 popular 8 populist 10 selfruling 11 egalitarian 13 self-governing

Democrats' symbol 6 donkey

démodé 5 dated, passé 7 antique, archaic 8 old-timey, outdated 9 out-of-date 12 old-fashioned

demoiselle 6 damsel, lassie, maiden 10 damselfish

demolish 4 raze, ruin 5 crush, level, smash, total, wrack, wreck 7 destroy, flatten, wipe out 8 decimate, tear down 9 finish off 10 annihilate, obliterate

demolition 6 razing 8 leveling, wrecking 10 bulldozing 11 destruction 12 annihilation

demolition bomb 11 blockbuster

demon 3 imp 5 devil, fiend, genie, ghoul, jinni, Satan 7 hellion, incubus 9 archfiend *Arabic:* 5 afrit 6 afreet *female:* 5 lamia 7 succuba, succubi (plural) 8 succubae (plural), succubus

demonic 6 wicked 7 satanic 8 devilish, diabolic, fiendish, infernal 9 possessed 10 diabolical

demonize 6 malign, revile, vilify 7 bedevil, censure, slander 8 denounce 9 diabolize

demonstrate 3 try 4 mark, show, test 5 prove, rally 7 confirm, display, exhibit, explain, make out, protest 8 evidence, manifest, proclaim, validate 9 determine, establish 10 illustrate 12 authenticate

demonstration 4 expo, show, test 5 march, proof, rally, trial 6 picket 7 display, protest 9 spectacle 10 exhibition, exposition, validation 12 presentation 13 corroboration, manifestation

demonstrative 4 open 8 effusive, outgoing, specific 9 emotional, expansive, exuberant, outspoken 10 outpouring, unreserved, validating 12 affectionate, unrestrained 13 unconstrained

demoralize 5 chill, daunt, shake, unman, upset 6 dampen, debase, deject, rattle, weaken 7 corrupt, debauch, deprave, unnerve, vitiate 8 dispirit, psych out 9 undermine 10 discourage, dishearten

Demosthenes 6 orator *oration:* 9 Philippic

demote 4 bump, bust 5 lower 6 reduce 7 declass, degrade 9 downgrade

demulcent 4 balm 5 jelly, salve

7 unguent **8** liniment, ointment, soothing **9** softening

demur 5 qualm **6** object, oppose, resist **7** dispute, protest **8** question **9** challenge, hesitancy, objection **10** hesitation, indecision, reluctance **11** compunction, remonstrate

demure 3 coy, shy **5** timid **6** modest **7** bashful **8** reserved, reticent, retiring **9** diffident **11** unassertive **12** self-effacing

demurral 7 protest **9** challenge, objection **12** remonstrance **13** remonstration

demurrer see DEMURRAL

den 4 base, cave, home, lair, nest, room **5** study **6** burrow, cavern, hollow **7** dayroom, hideout, sanctum **8** hideaway, playroom *rabbit:* **6** warren

denial 3 nay **6** heresy **7** refusal **8** disproof, negation, rebuttal **9** disavowal, rejection **10** abnegation, gainsaying, refutation **11** repudiation **12** renunciation

denigrate 5 decry, libel, smear, stain, sully **6** darken, defame, defile, impugn, malign, vilify **7** asperse, devalue, put down, slander, tarnish, traduce **8** belittle, dishonor, tear down **9** discredit, disparage **10** calumniate, scandalize

denims 5 jeans **8** overalls **9** blue jeans, dungarees

denizen 5 liver **6** native **7** dweller, habitué, haunter, resider **8** habitant, occupant, resident **9** indweller, inhabiter **10** frequenter, inhabitant

Denmark *capital:* **10** Copenhagen *city:* **5** Århus **6** Ålborg, Odense **11** Helsingborg **13** Frederiksberg *island:* **3** Fyn **7** Falster, Zealand **8** Bornholm **9** Sjaelland *monetary unit:* **5** krone *neighbor:* **6** Sweden **7** Germany *part of:* **11** Scandinavia *peninsula:* **7** Jutland *possession:* **9** Greenland **12** Faroe Islands **13** Faeroe Islands *sea:* **5** North **6** Baltic *strait:* **5** Lille, Store **9** Langeland

denominate 3 dub **4** call, name, term **5** label, style, title **7** baptize, entitle **8** christen **9** designate

denomination 4 cult, name, sect **5** creed, faith, style, title **6** church **8** category, cognomen, religion **9** communion **10** persuasion *religious:* **5** Amish **6** Mormon **7** Baptist **8** Lutheran, Moravian, Reformed **9** Adventist, Episcopal, Mennonite, Methodist, Unitarian **11** Pentecostal **12** Presbyterian, Universalist **13** Roman Catholic

denotation 4 name, sign **5** sense **6** import **7** meaning **10** indication, signifying **11** designation **13** signification, specification

denote 4 mark, mean, name, show **5** spell **6** import **7** add up to, betoken, express **8** announce, indicate **9** designate, represent

denouement 6 effect, result, upshot **7** outcome **10** conclusion **11** consequence, culmination

denounce 3 rap **4** skin **5** blame, blast, decry, knock **6** rebuke, scathe **7** censure, condemn, upbraid **8** derogate, reproach **9** castigate, criticize, dress down, excoriate, reprehend, reprobate **10** denunciate, vituperate **11** incriminate **12** anathematize

de novo 4 anew, over **5** again, newly **6** afresh **8** once more **9** over again **11** from scratch

dense 4 dull, dumb **5** close, heavy, solid, thick, tight **6** obtuse, opaque, stupid **7** compact, crammed, crowded, doltish, serried **9** fatheaded, jam-packed **10** numskulled **11** blockheaded, numbskulled, thickheaded **12** impenetrable

dent 4 bash, ding, flaw, nick **5** tooth **6** dimple, hollow **10** depression, impression

denticulate 6 ridged **7** dentate, notched, serrate, serried, toothed **8** saw-edged, sawtooth, serrated **10** saw-toothed

dentin 6 enamel

denude 4 bare **5** strip **6** divest **7** disrobe, uncover, undress **8** unclothe

denunciate see DENOUNCE

deny 5 cross, rebut **6** disown, forbid, negate, refuse, refute, reject, renege **7** disavow, gainsay **8** abnegate, disallow, disclaim, forswear, renounce, traverse, withhold **9** disaffirm **10** contradict, contravene

depart 3 die **4** exit, flee, pass, quit **5** leave, scram, split **6** begone, decamp, demise, desert, escape, expire, go away, move on, pass on, perish, skidoo **7** decease, deviate, go forth, move out, pull out, skiddoo, take off, vamoose **8** pass away, shove off, slip away, withdraw **9** skedaddle, take leave

departing 6 egress, exodus **7** good-bye **8** farewell **9** desertion **11** leave-taking, valedictory

department 5 arena **6** branch, domain, sphere **7** section **8** category, division, province **9** bailiwick, territory **11** subdivision

departure 4 exit **5** adieu, break, congé, going **6** egress, exodus, flight **7** leaving **8** farewell **9** deviation, diversion **10** aberration, decampment, deflection, divergence, embarkment, setting-out, withdrawal **11** embarkation, leave-taking *of a ship:* **6** sortie *point:* **7** outport

dependable 4 sure, true 5 loyal, solid, tried 6 secure, steady, trusty 7 certain, staunch 8 accurate, constant, faithful, reliable, surefire 9 authentic, steadfast, unfailing 11 responsible, trustworthy 12 tried and true 13 authoritative *Scottish:* 6 sicker

dependence 4 need 5 faith, habit, stock, trust 8 reliance 9 addiction 11 contingency, habituation

dependent 5 child 6 minion, vassal 7 reliant, relying 9 secondary 10 contingent, equivalent 11 conditional, subordinate

depend on 5 bet on, trust 6 bank on, hang on, look to, rely on, turn on 7 build on, count on, hinge on, stand on, swear by

depict 4 draw, limn, show 5 image, paint 6 relate, render, sketch 7 express, picture, portray 8 describe 9 delineate, represent 10 illustrate

depiction 5 image 6 sketch 7 drawing, picture 9 portrayal, rendering 11 delineation, portraiture, presentment 12 illustration, presentation

deplete 3 sap 4 milk 5 bleed, drain, eat up, empty, leech, use up 6 expend, lessen, reduce 7 consume, draw off, exhaust 8 decrease, diminish, draw down 9 undermine 10 run through

depleted 6 sapped, used up 7 drained, reduced 8 consumed, expended 9 exhausted, washed-out

deplorable 5 awful 6 rotten, woeful 8 dreadful, god-awful, grievous, terrible, wretched 9 execrable, miserable, sickening 10 calamitous, disastrous, lamentable 11 distressing, intolerable 12 contemptible, disreputable, heartrending 13 heartbreaking, reprehensible

deplore 3 rue 5 abhor, mourn 6 bemoan, bewail, grieve, lament, regret 7 condemn 8 denounce, object to 9 deprecate 10 disapprove

deploy 3 use 5 array 6 muster, unfold 7 arrange, display, dispose, marshal, utilize 8 position

___ **de plume** 3 nom

depone 5 state, swear 6 affirm, assert, attest 7 certify, confirm, declare, testify, warrant 11 corroborate 12 authenticate

deport 3 act 4 bear 5 carry, exile, expel 6 acquit, banish, behave, demean 7 conduct 8 displace, relegate 10 expatriate

deportee 5 exile 8 expellee

deportment 3 air, set 4 mien, port 6 aspect, manner 7 address, bearing, conduct, manners 8 behavior, carriage, demeanor, presence

depose 4 aver, avow, oust 5 state, swear 6 affirm, assert, avouch, remove, topple, unmake 7 declare, profess, testify, uncrown 8 dethrone, displace, throw out, unthrone 9 overthrow

deposit 3 lay 4 bank, drop, dump, fund, lees, pawn, save, stow 5 cache, chest, dregs, place, put by, stash, store 6 settle 7 consign, grounds, lay away 8 put aside, security, sediment, sock away 9 settlings 11 precipitate 13 precipitation *alluvial:* 5 delta *black:* 4 soot *calcium carbonate:* 10 stalactite, stalagmite *containing gold:* 6 placer *eggs:* 5 spawn *geologic:* 7 horizon *glacial:* 4 till 5 drift, esker 7 moraine *loam:* 5 loess *mineral:* 4 lode 10 concretion *muddy:* 6 sludge *sand:* 4 bank 5 beach *sedimentary:* 4 silt *skeletal:* 5 coral *stolen goods:* 5 fence *stream:* 8 alluvium, sediment *tooth:* 6 tartar

deposition 6 avowal 7 ousting, placing 9 affidavit, dismissal, testimony 10 testifying 11 attestation, declaration

depository 4 bank, dump, safe 5 attic, cache, depot, store, vault 7 archive, arsenal 8 magazine 9 warehouse 10 storehouse *for bones:* 7 ossuary

depot 4 dump 5 cache, store 6 armory, garage 7 arsenal, station 8 magazine, terminal, terminus 9 warehouse 10 depository, repository, storehouse 12 station house

deprave 4 warp 6 debase 7 corrupt, debauch, pervert, vitiate 9 brutalize 10 bastardize, bestialize, demoralize

depraved 3 bad, low 4 base, evil, ugly, vile 6 putrid, rotten, wanton, warped, wicked 7 bestial, corrupt, debased, immoral, twisted, vicious 8 degraded, perverse, vitiated 9 corrupted, debauched, miscreant, nefarious, perverted, reprobate 10 degenerate

depravity 4 vice 8 baseness 9 abasement, decadence 10 corruption, debasement, debauchery, degeneracy, immorality, perversion 12 degeneration

deprecate 7 frown on, put down 8 belittle, derogate, disfavor, object to, play down, pooh-pooh 9 disparage 10 disapprove 12 disapprove of

depreciate 4 drop, fall 5 abate, decry, erode, lower 6 lessen, reduce, slight 7 cheapen, devalue, put down 8 belittle, decrease, derogate, diminish, discount, mark down, write off 9 devaluate, disparage, downgrade, underrate 10 devalorize, undervalue 11 detract from

depreciation 8 discount **11** denigration **12** belittlement **13** disparagement

depreciative 9 slighting **10** derogatory, detracting, pejorative **11** disparaging, underrating **12** undervaluing

depredate 4 sack **5** waste **6** ravage **7** despoil, pillage, plunder **8** desolate, lay waste, prey upon, spoliate **9** desecrate, devastate, vandalize

depredation 4 sack **5** havoc **7** pillage, plunder, sacking **8** ravaging **9** marauding, ruination **10** spoliation **11** desecration, destruction, devastation **12** despoliation

depredator 6 looter, raider, vandal **7** forager, spoiler **8** marauder **9** plunderer **10** freebooter

depress 4 damp, dash, dent **5** chill, daunt, lower **6** dampen, deject, dismay, sadden **7** afflict, trouble **8** dispirit, enfeeble **9** disparage, weigh down **10** discourage, dishearten

depressed 3 low, sad **4** blue, down, glum, sunk **6** broody, gloomy, glumpy, lonely, somber **8** cast down, dejected, downcast **9** bummed out, flattened, woebegone **10** dispirited, lugubrious, melancholy, spiritless **11** crestfallen, downhearted, melancholic **12** disconsolate **13** disadvantaged

depressing 3 sad **5** bleak **6** dismal, dreary, gloomy, somber, sombre **7** joyless **8** funereal, mournful **9** saddening **10** melancholy, oppressive **11** melancholic **13** disheartening

depression 3 dip, low, pit, sag **4** bust, drop, funk, hole, sink, vale **5** basin, blues, dolor, dumps, ennui, gloom, scoop, slump **6** cavity, crater, hollow, pocket, valley **7** cyclone, decline, sadness, sinkage **8** downturn, sinkhole **9** concavity, dejection **10** desolation, melancholia, unhappiness *anatomical:* **5** fossa, fovea **6** foveae (plural) *geographic:* **7** Qattara *in ridge:* **3** col *in snow:* **8** sitzmark *small:* **4** dent **6** dimple

depressive 4 blue, dour, glum **6** woeful **7** doleful **8** downbeat, downcast, mournful **9** miserable, woebegone **10** despondent, melancholy **11** low-spirited

deprivation 4 lack, loss **6** denial **7** forfeit, removal **10** forfeiture **11** bereavement, divestiture **13** dispossession

deprive 3 rob **5** strip **6** divest **8** disseise, disseize **10** disinherit, dispossess *of brilliancy:* **4** dull **6** deaden *of courage:* **7** unnerve *of sensation:* **6** benumb

depth 4 base, drop, gulf **5** abyss, chasm, gorge **7** lowness **10** profundity *measure:* **6** fathom *of water:* **5** draft **7** draught

depthless 7 cursory, shallow, sketchy **10** uncritical **11** superficial

Dept. of ___ 5 Labor, State **6** Energy **7** Defense, Justice **8** Commerce, Interior, Treasury **9** Education **11** Agriculture

deputize 4 name **6** assign **7** appoint, empower, warrant **8** delegate **9** authorize, designate **10** commission

deputy 4 aide **5** agent, proxy **6** backup, factor **8** delegate **9** assistant, catchpole, surrogate

derange 4 muss **5** craze, upset **6** madden, mess up **7** confuse, perturb, unhinge **8** confound, disarray, disorder, distract, unsettle **9** interrupt, unbalance **10** discompose **11** disorganize

deranged 3 mad **4** loco **5** crazy, wacko **6** crazed, insane, maniac **7** berserk, cracked, haywire, lunatic, unsound **8** demented, maniacal **9** disturbed **10** disordered, flipped out, unbalanced

derangement 4 mess **5** chaos, mania **6** lunacy, muddle **7** madness **8** dementia, disorder, insanity **9** confusion, unbalance **10** hodgepodge **11** distraction, disturbance, psychopathy

derby 3 hat **4** race **7** contest **9** horse race

derelict 3 bum **4** hobo, lorn **5** tramp **6** remiss, shabby **7** drifter, outcast, rundown, uncouth, vagrant **8** careless, deserted, vagabond **9** abandoned, negligent **10** neglectful **11** dilapidated **12** disregardful, undependable **13** irresponsible

dereliction 5 fault **7** default, failure, neglect **9** deviation, disregard, oversight **11** abandonment, delinquency, shortcoming

deride 3 rag, rap **4** gibe, jeer, jibe, lout, mock, quiz, razz, twit **5** fleer, rally, scoff, scout, sneer, taunt **6** dump on, insult **7** catcall **8** ridicule

de rigueur 5 right **6** au fait, decent, proper **7** correct **8** becoming, decorous, required **9** essential, mandatory, requisite **10** compulsory, obligatory, prescribed **11** comme il faut

derision 5 abuse, scorn **7** disdain, mockery, ribbing **8** contempt, raillery, ridicule, scoffing **9** contumely, invective

derisive 7 abusive, jeering, mocking **8** sardonic, scoffing, scornful, taunting **9** insulting, sarcastic **10** disdainful **12** contemptuous

derivable 7 a priori **9** deducible, deductive, traceable **10** obtainable **11** extractable **12** attributable, determinable

derivation 4 root **6** origin, source

7 descent **9** etymology **10** provenance, wellspring **11** origination, provenience

derivative 5 banal **7** spin-off **8** acquired, offshoot **9** by-product, imitative, outgrowth, secondary **10** descendant, unoriginal

derive 3 get **4** draw, flow, rise, stem, take **5** adapt, arise, educe, infer, issue, trace **6** deduce, deduct, evolve, gather, obtain **7** descend, emanate, extract, proceed, work out **8** arrive at, conclude **9** formulate, originate

dernier cri 3 fad **4** chic, rage **5** craze, vogue **8** last word

derogate 5 decry **6** berate, dump on, insult **7** put down **8** bad-mouth, belittle, diminish, minimize, write off **9** disparage, dispraise **10** depreciate **11** detract from

derogatory 5 snide **8** decrying, scornful, spiteful **9** degrading, demeaning, maligning, slighting **10** belittling, detracting, disdainful, pejorative **11** disparaging **12** contumelious, depreciative

derrick 5 hoist

derriere 3 bum **4** beam, butt, rear, rump, seat, tail **5** fanny **6** behind, bottom **7** rear end **8** backside, buttocks **9** posterior

derring-do 4 guts **5** nerve, pluck, spunk, valor **6** daring, mettle **7** bravado, bravery, bravura, courage **8** boldness **9** gallantry **12** fearlessness **13** dauntlessness

dervish 4 monk, Sufi **9** mendicant *in Arabian Nights:* **4** Agib *practice:* **7** dancing **8** whirling *wandering:* **5** fakir **8** calender

descant 4 sing **6** melody, remark, treble **7** comment, discuss, melisma, melodia, oration, soprano **9** discourse, expatiate **12** counterpoint

Descartes's axiom 13 cogito ergo sum

descend 4 dive, drop, fall, pass, sink **5** slide, stoop, swoop **6** alight, derive, go down, plunge, worsen **7** decline **8** come down, dismount **9** originate **10** degenerate, retrograde *by rope:* **6** rappel

descendant 4 heir **5** scion **7** progeny, spin-off **8** offshoot, relative **9** byproduct, offspring, outgrowth **10** derivative

descendants 4 seed **5** brood, heirs, issue, spawn **6** litter **7** progeny **8** children **9** offspring, posterity **11** progeniture

descent 3 dip **4** drop, fall **5** birth, blood, slide, slope **6** origin, plunge, tumble **7** decline, drop-off, incline, lineage, sinkage **8** ancestry, comedown, gradient, pedigree **9** declivity, downgrade **10** derivation, devolution, extraction *airplane:* **8** approach *parachute:* **4** jump **7** bailout

describe 4 limn **6** denote, depict, recite,

relate, render, report **7** explain, express, mark out, narrate, outline, picture, portray, recount **9** delineate, represent **10** illustrate **12** characterize

description 3 ilk **4** kind, sort, type **6** nature, report **7** account, picture, species **9** character, depiction, narrative, portrayal **10** recounting

descry 3 see **4** espy, spot **6** behold, detect, spy out, turn up **7** discern, find out, hit upon **8** discover, meet with, perceive **9** encounter, recognize

Desdemona *father:* **9** Brabantio *husband:* **7** Othello *slanderer:* **4** Iago *slayer:* **7** Othello

desecrate 4 sack **5** stain, sully, waste **6** befoul, debase, defile, ravage **7** corrupt, degrade, despoil, pillage, pollute, profane, violate **8** spoliate **9** depredate, devastate

desecration 5 abuse **7** impiety **9** blasphemy, sacrilege **10** debasement, defilement, spoliation **11** profanation **12** despoliation

desensitize 4 dull, numb **5** blunt **6** benumb, dampen, deaden, freeze, sedate **11** anesthetize

desert 4 flee, quit **5** leave, waste **6** barren, betray, decamp, defect, escape, maroon, strand **7** abandon, abscond, badland, forsake **8** renounce **9** repudiate, wasteland **10** apostatize, wilderness **12** tergiversate *African:* **5** Namib **6** Libyan, Sahara **7** Arabian **8** Kalahari *Arizona:* **7** Painted *Asian:* **4** Gobi, Thar **6** Syrian **7** Kara-Kum **8** Kyzyl Kum, Qizilkum **10** Great Sandy *basin bottom:* **5** playa *beast:* **5** camel **9** dromedary *California:* **6** Mohave, Mojave *Chilean:* **7** Atacama *clay:* **5** adobe *dweller:* **4** Arab **5** nomad **6** Berber, Libyan, Malian, Nubian **7** bedouin **8** Algerian, Egyptian, Maghrebi, Maghribi, Sudanese **11** Mauritanian *Egyptian:* **7** Arabian *fertile area:* **5** oases (plural), oasis *garb:* **3** aba *hallucination:* **6** mirage *Israeli:* **5** Negev *region:* **3** erg *Saudi Arabia:* **7** Al-Nafud, An Nafud *Sudan:* **6** Nubian *travel group:* **7** caravan *wind:* **7** sirocco

deserted 4 bare, lorn **6** barren, vacant **8** derelict, desolate, forsaken, solitary **9** abandoned, neglected **11** uninhabited

deserter 3 rat **4** AWOL **6** bolter **7** runaway **8** apostate, defector, fugitive, renegade, runagate, turncoat

desertion 7 perfidy **8** apostasy **9** defection, forsaking **11** abandonment, dereliction

deserts 3 due **6** reward **8** requital **9** reckoning **10** recompense **11** comeuppance

deserve 3 win **4** earn, gain, rate **5** merit **6** demand **7** justify, warrant

deserved 3 apt, due **4** just **5** right **7** fitting, merited **8** rightful, suitable **9** befitting **11** appropriate **13** rhadamanthine

deserving 3 due **6** worthy **8** laudable **9** admirable, estimable **10** creditable **11** commendable, meritorious, thankworthy **12** praiseworthy

desiccate 3 dry **5** dry up, parch, wizen **6** wither **7** shrivel **9** dehydrate **10** devitalize

desiderate 4 want, wish **5** covet, crave **6** desire **7** long for, wish for **8** yearn for

design 3 aim **4** cast, draw, form, mean, mind, plan, plot, will **5** chart, draft, frame, model, motif **6** create, device, devise, figure, intend, intent, invent, lay out, makeup, map out, motive, scheme, set out, sketch, tailor **7** arrange, diagram, drawing, execute, fashion, meaning, outline, pattern, prepare, project, propose, tracing **8** contrive, creation, game plan, intrigue, strategy, thinking **9** blueprint, construct, delineate, direction, formation, intention, invention **10** decoration, figuration **11** arrangement, composition **12** architecture, construction *book:* **8** vignette *carpet:* **3** gul **9** medallion *incised:* **8** intaglio *Indonesian:* **5** batik *inlaid:* **6** mosaic *intricate:* **9** arabesque *of squares:* **5** check *openwork:* **8** filigree *perforated:* **7** stencil *raised:* **8** repoussé *skin:* **6** tattoo *textile:* **8** polka dot *velvety:* **8** flocking

designate 3 dub, tap **4** call, name, pick, term **5** allot, elect, label, style, title **6** assign, choose, denote, depute, select **7** appoint, declare, earmark, reserve, signify, specify **8** allocate, christen, delegate, identify, set aside, stand for **9** apportion, stipulate **10** decide upon **11** appropriate **12** characterize

designation 4 name, sign **5** class, nomen, style, title **6** naming **8** cognomen, monicker **11** appellation

designed 7 devised, planned **8** intended, resolved **9** contrived, patterned **10** considered, deliberate, determined, thought-out **12** premeditated

designedly 9 expressly, knowingly, on purpose, purposely, willfully, wittingly **11** consciously, purposively **12** deliberately **13** intentionally

desirable 8 enviable, fetching **9** advisable, agreeable, preferred **10** attractive, beneficial **12** advantageous

desire 3 aim, yen **4** envy, eros, itch, lust, want, wish **5** covet, crave, fancy, go for, greed **6** pining, thirst **7** avarice, craving, long for, longing, passion **8** appetite, cupidity, petition, yearn for, yearning **9** eroticism, hankering, prurience, pruriency **10** aphrodisia, attraction, preference **11** inclination, lustfulness **13** concupiscence, lickerishness

desired 6 wanted **8** hoped-for **9** preferred, requested

desirous 6 greedy **7** athirst, craving, envious, longing, wishful, wishing **8** covetous, grasping **10** solicitous

desist 4 halt, quit, stop **5** cease, yield **7** forbear, hold off, refrain **8** knock off, leave off, surcease **11** discontinue

desistance 3 end **4** halt, stop **5** cease, close **6** ending, finish, period **8** stoppage, stopping **9** cessation **10** conclusion **11** termination

desk 6 booth, stand, table **7** counter, lectern, rolltop **8** lapboard **9** secretary **10** escritoire *adjunct:* **8** inkstand, standish *item:* **3** pad **7** blotter, inkwell *library:* **6** carrel

desolate 4 bare, lorn, sack **5** alone, bleak, drear, stark, waste **6** barren, devoid, dismal, dreary, gloomy, ravage **7** despoil, forlorn, joyless, pillage, plunder **8** dejected, derelict, deserted, desolate, downcast, forsaken, lay waste, lifeless, lonesome, solitary, spoliate **9** abandoned, cheerless, deprecate, desecrate, destitute, devastate, sorrowful **10** despondent **11** dilapidated **12** inconsolable **13** disheartening

desolation 3 woe **4** ruin **5** gloom, grief, waste **6** misery, sorrow **7** anguish, despair, sadness **8** bareness **9** bleakness, dejection, wasteland **10** loneliness **11** abandonment, devastation **12** wretchedness

despair 6 give up **8** lose hope

despairing 7 anxious, doleful, forlorn **8** dejected, desolate, hopeless, wretched **9** depressed **10** despondent **11** downhearted **12** disconsolate **13** brokenhearted

desperado 6 bandit, gunman, outlaw **7** bandito, brigand, convict, ruffian **8** criminal **9** cutthroat **10** gunslinger, highwayman, lawbreaker

desperate 4 bold, dire, rash **5** acute, risky **6** daring, futile **7** crucial, forlorn, frantic, useless, violent **8** critical, headlong, hopeless, reckless, shocking **9** foolhardy, impetuous **10** despondent, frustrated, outrageous, scandalous **11** climacteric, precipitate **12** overpowering **13** irretrievable

desperation 5 agony **7** anguish, despair **8** distress **11** distraction **12** hopelessness, wretchedness

despicable 3 low 4 base, foul, grim, mean, ugly, vile 5 awful, cheap, gross, sorry 6 abject, scurvy, shabby, sordid 7 beastly, hateful, ignoble, pitiful 8 pitiable, shameful, wretched 9 degrading, loathsome 10 deplorable, detestable 11 disgraceful, ignominious 12 contemptible, disreputable 13 reprehensible

despise 4 hate, shun, snub 5 abhor, avoid, scorn, spurn 6 detest, loathe, reject 7 contemn 8 execrate 9 abominate

despised one 6 pariah 7 outcast

despisement 4 hate 5 scorn 6 hatred, malice 7 disdain, ill will 8 aversion, contempt, loathing 9 antipathy, contumely 10 abhorrence 11 detestation

despite 8 although 11 in the face of 12 regardless of

despiteful 4 evil, mean 5 catty 6 bitchy, horrid, malign, odious, wicked 7 baleful, baneful, hostile, vicious 8 vengeful 9 malicious, rancorous, repellent 10 despicable, malevolent

despoil 4 sack 5 blast, strip, waste, wreck 6 denude, devour, maraud, ravage 7 pillage, plunder 8 desolate, spoliate 9 depredate, desecrate, devastate, strip away, vandalize 10 wreak havoc

despoiler 6 looter, sacker, vandal 7 ravager, wrecker 8 marauder, pillager 9 plunderer, spoliator 10 depredator, freebooter

despond 4 fret, mope, wilt 5 brood, droop, worry 6 give up, sorrow 8 languish 9 dejection 12 hopelessness

despondency 5 blues, dumps, gloom 6 misery, sorrow 7 anguish, despair, sadness 8 glumness 9 dejection 10 depression, melancholy 11 desperation, unhappiness 12 hopelessness

despondent 3 low, sad 4 blue, down, glum 7 doleful, forlorn 8 cast down, dejected, downcast, grieving, hopeless, mourning 9 depressed, desperate, heartsick, heartsore, sorrowful, woebegone 10 dispairing, dispirited, melancholy 11 discouraged, downhearted 12 disconsolate, disheartened

despot 4 czar, duce, tsar, tzar 5 ruler 6 tyrant 7 autarch, emperor 8 autocrat, dictator 9 oppressor, strong man

despotic 8 absolute 9 arbitrary, autarchic, imperious, tyrannous 10 autocratic, monocratic, tyrannical 11 dictatorial 12 totalitarian

despotism 7 czarism, tsarism, tyranny, tzarism 8 autarchy 9 autocracy 10 absolutism, domination 12 dictatorship

desquamate 4 pare, peel 5 scale 7 peel off 8 flake off, scale off 9 exfoliate

dessert 3 ice, pie 4 cake, flan, fool, tart 5 Betty, bombe, crepe, crisp, fruit, grunt, halva, Jell-O, melba, s'more, sweet, torte 6 afters, blintz, Danish, éclair, fondue, frappe, gâteau, halvah, hermit, junket, kuchen, mousse, pastry, sorbet, sundae, trifle 7 brownie, cobbler, compote, custard, gelatin, parfait, pudding, sabayon, sherbet, soufflé, spumoni, strudel 8 ambrosia, Bismarck, crostata, flummery, ice cream, macaroon, meringue, napoleon, pandowdy, streusel, tiramisu, turnover 9 charlotte, cream puff, fruitcake, petit four, shortcake 10 blancmange, brown Betty, cheesecake, frangipane, icebox cake, zabaglione 11 baked Alaska, banana split, crème brûlée, gingerbread 12 hasty pudding, zuppa inglese *French:* 5 bombe 6 éclair, frappe, gâteau, mousse 7 parfait, sabayon 9 petit four 10 blancmange, frangipane *frozen:* 5 bombe 7 parfait, sherbet *German:* 6 kuchen 7 strudel *Italian:* 7 Fannoli, spumoni 8 tiramisu 10 zabaglione 12 zuppa inglese *Turkish:* 5 halva 6 halvah

destination 3 aim, end, use 6 object, target 7 purpose 8 terminus 9 objective 10 appointing

destine 4 fate 6 assign, direct, intend 8 dedicate, set aside 9 designate, determine, preordain 10 foreordain 12 predetermine

destiny 3 lot 4 doom, fate 5 karma 6 design, future, kismet, Moirai 7 fortune, portion 8 prospect 9 hereafter 12 circumstance

destitute 4 bare, poor, void 5 broke, empty, needy 6 bereft, devoid, ruined 7 drained, lacking 8 bankrupt, depleted, dirt poor, divested, indigent, strapped, stripped 9 deficient, exhausted, penurious 10 bankrupted, stonebroke 11 impecunious 12 impoverished

destitution 6 penury 7 poverty 9 indigence, privation

destroy 3 axe, zap 4 doom, down, kill, nuke, raze, ruin, sack, slay, undo 5 crush, erase, quash, quell, smash, total, trash, waste, wrack, wreck 6 finish, lay low, mangle, ravage, rubble, rub out 7 abolish, atomize, despoil, expunge, nullify, pillage, shatter, wipe out 8 decimate, demolish, dispatch, dynamite, lay waste, pull down, snuff out, stamp out, tear down 9 devastate, dismantle, eradicate, extirpate, liquidate, pulverize 10 annihilate, extinguish 11 exterminate

destroyer 4 bane, ruin 6 tin can, vandal 7 undoing, warship 8 downfall

destruction 4 loss, ruin 5 havoc 7 killing, sacking, undoing 8 downfall 9 ruination 10 extinction 11 devastation, liquidation 12 annihilation

destructive 7 baneful, harmful, ruinous 8 damaging 9 corrosive, injurious 10 shattering 11 deleterious, detrimental

desuetude 6 disuse 7 closure, neglect 9 cessation 11 abandonment

desultory 6 casual, chance, fitful, random, spotty 7 aimless, erratic, offhand, vagrant 8 shifting, slipshod, sporadic, wavering 9 haphazard, hit-or-miss, unplanned 10 capricious, digressive, disjointed 11 purposeless 12 unmethodical, unsystematic

detach 4 free, part, undo, wean 5 sever 6 cut off, remove, sunder 7 disjoin, divorce, release 8 separate, uncouple, withdraw 9 disengage 10 disconnect 12 disaffiliate

detached 5 alone, aloof, apart 6 remote 7 distant, neutral, removed, severed 8 abstract, isolated, separate, unbiased 9 incurious, withdrawn 10 impersonal 11 indifferent, unconcerned, unconnected 12 uninterested 13 disinterested, dispassionate, unaccompanied

detachment 5 squad 7 divorce, rupture 8 disunion, division 9 partition 10 neutrality, separation 11 dissolution

detail 4 item, list, part 5 point 6 assign, nicety, relate, report 7 appoint, article, element, itemize, listing, minutia, specify 8 allocate, spell out 9 enumerate, stipulate 10 assignment, particular 12 circumstance 13 particularize

detailed 4 full 6 minute 8 itemized, complete, thorough 10 blow-by-blow, exhaustive, meticulous, particular 13 thoroughgoing

detain 3 nab 4 bust, curb, hold, keep, mire, snag 5 check, delay, run in 6 arrest, collar, hang up, hinder, hold up, impede, pick up, retard, slow up 7 bog down, reserve, set back 8 hold back, keep back, restrain, slow down, withhold 9 apprehend 10 buttonhole *in conversation:* 10 buttonhole

detect 4 espy, find, spot 5 catch, dig up, hit on, scent 6 descry, notice, turn up 7 discern, hit upon, uncover, unearth 8 discover, meet with 9 ascertain, encounter, ferret out, track down

detectable 6 patent 7 evident, visible 8 sensible, tangible 10 noticeable, observable 11 discernible, perceptible

detection 9 discovery 10 unearthing *system:* 5 radar, sofar

detective 4 dick, G-man 6 shamus, sleuth 7 gumshoe 8 hawkshaw, informer, sherlock 9 inspector 10 private eye 12 investigator *fictional:* 4 Chan (Charlie), Gray (Cordelia), Moto (Mr.) 5 Banks (Alan), Bosch (Harry), Brown (Father), Dupin (Auguste), Lecoq, Lupin (Arsène), McGee (Travis), Morse (Inspector), Queen (Ellery), Rebus (John), Saint, Spade (Sam), Trent (Philip), Vance (Philo), Wolfe (Nero) 6 Alleyn (Roderick), Archer (Lew), Carter (Nick), Hammer (Mike), Holmes (Sherlock), Marple (Miss Jane), McCone (Sharon), Poirot (Hercule), Wimsey (Peter) 7 Campion (Albert), Charles (Nick, Nora), Maigret (Jules), Marlowe (Philip) 8 Drummond (Bulldog), Millhone (Kinsey) 9 Dalgleish (Adam) 10 Robicheaux (Dave), Warshawski (V. I.) 11 Father Brown

detective-story writer 3 Poe (Edgar Allan), Tey (Josephine) 4 Carr (John Dickson), Knox (Ronald) 5 Blake (Nicholas), Block (Lawrence), Cross (Amanda), Doyle (Arthur Conan), Green (Anna Katherine), Innes (Michael), James (P. D.), Marsh (Ngaio), Queen (Ellery), Stout (Rex) 6 Bramah (Ernest), Buchan (John), Hansen (Joseph), McBain (Ed), Mosley (Walter), Parker (Robert), Peters (Ellis), Sayers (Dorothy L.) 7 Bentley (E. C.), Biggers (Earl Derr), Collins (Wilkie), Francis (Dick), Freeman (Austin), Gardner (Erle Stanley), Grafton (Sue), Hammett (Dashiell), Hornung (E. W.), Rendell (Ruth), Simenon (Georges), Van Dine (S. S.), Wallace (Edgar) 8 Chandler (Raymond), Christie (Agatha), Gaboriau (Emile), Marquand (John), Paretsky (Sara), Rinehart (Mary Roberts), Spillane (Mickey) 9 Allingham (Margery), Hillerman (Tony), Lockridge (Frances, Richard), Macdonald (Ross) 10 Chesterton (Gilbert Keith)

detention 6 arrest 7 holding 10 internment 11 confinement 12 imprisonment

deter 5 avert, block 6 divert, hinder, impede, thwart 7 forfend, inhibit, obviate, prevent, rule out, shut out, ward off 8 dissuade, preclude, restrain, stave off 9 forestall, turn aside 10 discourage

deterge 4 wash 7 cleanse, wash off

detergent 4 soap 8 cleanser

deteriorate 3 rot 4 fade, fail, flag, sink, wear 5 decay, lapse, slide, spoil 6 weak-

en, worsen 7 decline, regress 8 languish
9 decompose, fall apart 10 debilitate,
degenerate, depreciate, go downhill,
retrograde, retrogress 12 disintegrate

deterioration 4 ruin 5 decay 6 ebbing,
waning 7 atrophy, decline, erosion, failing, rotting 8 decaying, spoiling
9 crumbling, decadence, downgrade
10 debasement, degeneracy 12 degeneration, dégringolade

determinant 4 gene 5 agent, basis, cause,
trait 6 factor, ground, reason 7 epitope,
radical 9 attribute, influence

determinate 5 fixed 6 cymose 7 limited,
precise, settled 8 constant, definite
10 definitive, restricted 11 established
13 circumscribed

determination 5 drive, spunk 6 fixing,
mettle 7 finding, opinion, purpose,
resolve, verdict 8 decision, firmness,
judgment, tenacity 9 assurance, hardihood, impulsion, intention, resolving,
willpower 10 conclusion, dedication,
definition, doggedness, resolution, settlement 11 decidedness, intrepidity
12 perseverance, resoluteness, stubbornness 13 purposiveness

determine 3 fix, set 4 rule 5 bound, limit,
prove 6 decide, figure, ordain, settle
7 control, delimit, find out, mark out,
measure, preform, unearth 8 conclude,
discover, regulate 9 ascertain, demarcate, establish, preordain, resolve on
10 delimitate, foreordain, predestine,
predispose

determined 3 set 4 bent 5 fixed 6 driven,
intent 7 decided, earnest, serious, settled 8 decisive, hellbent, resolute,
resolved, stubborn 9 tenacious 10 persistent, purposeful, unwavering
11 established, persevering, unfaltering
12 foreordained, unhesitating

detest 4 hate 5 abhor, spurn 6 loathe
7 despise, dislike 8 execrate 9 abominate, repudiate

detestable 4 foul, vile 6 damned, horrid,
odious 7 hateful, heinous 9 abhorrent,
execrable, loathsome 10 abominable,
despicable 12 contemptible

detestation 4 hate 6 hatred 8 anathema,
aversion, loathing 9 repulsion, revulsion 10 abhorrence, execration, repugnance

dethrone 4 oust 6 depose 7 uncrown
8 displace

detonate 5 blast, burst, go off, spark
6 blow up, set off 7 explode 8 touch off

detonator 3 cap 4 fuse 9 explosive
11 blasting cap

detour 5 avoid, skirt 6 bypass 9 diversion

detract 6 divert, lessen, reduce
8 decrease, diminish, minimize
10 depreciate

detraction 9 aspersion, maligning, traducing 10 backbiting, belittling, derogation, slandering 11 denigration, dep-
recation, traducement 12 backstabbing,
belittlement 13 disparagement

detractive 9 maligning, slighting, traducing, vilifying 10 defamatory, derogatory, pejorative 11 denigrating, disparaging 12 depreciative, depreciatory

detriment 4 harm, loss 6 damage, injury
7 marring 8 drawback 10 impairment
12 disadvantage

detrimental 3 bad, ill 7 adverse, harmful,
hurtful, nocuous 8 damaging, negative
9 injurious 11 deleterious, unfavorable

detritus 4 tufa, tuff 5 scree, talus
6 debris, rubble 7 remains 11 odds
and ends

Detroit *county:* 5 Wayne *founder:* 8 Cadillac (Sieur de) *lake:* 4 Erie 10 Saint Clair
sobriquet: 6 Motown 9 Motor City

de trop 5 extra, spare 7 too much, surplus 9 excessive, redundant 10 gratuitous 11 superfluous 13 supernumerary

Deucalion *father:* 10 Prometheus *kingdom:* 6 Phthia *mother:* 7 Clymene *son:*
6 Hellen *wife:* 6 Pyrrha

Deutschland über ____ 5 alles

Devaki's son 7 Krishna

____ De Valera 5 Eamon

devaluate 5 abase, decry, lower
6 reduce, weaken 7 cheapen, degrade
8 mark down, write off 9 undermine,
underrate, write down 10 depreciate

devaluation 7 decline 10 debasement,
declension 11 declination

devalue see DEPRECIATE

devastate 4 raze, ruin, sack 5 waste
6 ravage 7 despoil, pillage, plunder
8 demolish, desolate, lay waste, overcome, spoliate 9 depredate, desecrate,
overpower, overwhelm

devastation 4 loss, ruin 5 chaos, havoc,
waste 6 ravage 7 pillage, plunder 8 disorder 9 confusion, ruination 10 demolition, desolation, spoliation 11 depredation

develop 3 age 4 form, grow 5 occur,
reach, ripen 6 attain, dilate, evolve,
expand, grow up, happen, mature, mellow, open up, thrive, unfold, unfurl
7 achieve, acquire, advance, burgeon,
enlarge, expound, promote 8 flourish
9 actualize, elaborate, establish, transpire 11 come to light, materialize

development 5 phase 6 growth, result,
spread 7 advance, buildup, outcome
8 ontogeny, progress, ripening 9 evolution, expansion, flowering, phylogeny,

unfolding 10 maturation 11 elaboration, progression *of life:* 10 biogenesis

Devi 7 goddess *consort:* 5 Shiva *father:* 7 Himavat *name:* 3 Uma 4 Kali 5 Durga, Gauri 6 Chandi 7 Parvati

deviant 4 bent 5 kinky, queer 6 off-key 7 twisted, wayward 8 aberrant, abnormal, atypical, perverse 9 anomalous, different, divergent, irregular, unnatural 11 heteroclite

deviate 3 err, yaw 4 turn, vary, veer 5 sheer, stray 6 depart, swerve, wander 7 digress, diverge 8 aberrant 9 eccentric, turn aside

deviation 3 yaw 4 bend, tack, turn 5 error, shift 6 change 7 anomaly, turning, veering 8 variance 9 departure, diversion 10 aberration, alteration, deflection, divergence

device 4 ploy, tool 5 feint, gizmo, means, motif, motto, shift, thing, trick 6 dingus, doodad, emblem, figure, gadget, gambit, hickey, jigger, medium, motive, symbol, widget 7 gimmick, machine, utensil, whatnot, whatsit 8 artifice, creation, insignia 9 apparatus, appliance, doohickey, expedient, implement, invention, makeshift, mechanism, thingummy 10 instrument 11 contraption, contrivance, inclination, thingamabob, thingamajig, thingumajig *automatic:* 5 servo *binding:* 5 clamp *fastening:* 6 zipper *grasping:* 4 tong *heating:* 8 radiator *hoisting:* 5 crane, lewis 8 windlass *holding:* 4 vise 5 clamp

devil 5 beast, cloot, demon, fiend, rogue, Satan, scamp 6 Belial, diablo, dybbuk, rascal, spirit 7 Clootie, dickens, Lucifer, Old Nick, serpent, tempter, villain 8 Apollyon, Mephisto, scalawag, succubus 9 archfiend, Beelzebub, cacodemon, scoundrel, skeezicks 10 blackguard, Old Scratch 11 rapscallion

devilfish 3 ray 5 manta 7 octopus 8 manta ray 10 cephalopod

devilish 3 bad 4 evil 6 cursed, wicked 7 demonic, hellish, roguish, satanic 8 accursed, damnable, diabolic, fiendish, infernal, sinister 9 nefarious 10 diabolical, iniquitous, villainous 11 mischievous

devil-may-care 3 gay 4 rash, wild 6 rakish, sporty 7 raffish 8 carefree, rakehell, reckless 9 easygoing

devilry 7 knavery, roguery, sorcery, waggery 8 mischief 9 diablerie 10 wickedness, witchcraft 11 roguishness, waggishness 12 sportiveness

devious 3 sly 4 foxy, wily 6 artful, crafty, errant, erring, roving, shifty, sneaky,

tricky 7 bending, crooked, cunning, curving, erratic, winding 8 aberrant, guileful, indirect, scheming, sneaking, twisting 9 deceptive, underhand, wandering 10 roundabout 11 out-of-the-way, underhanded

devise 4 form, plan, plot, will 5 chart, forge, frame, shape 6 cook up, create, design, invent, legacy, legate, scheme 7 arrange, bequest, concoct, connive, dope out, dream up, hatch up, project 8 bequeath, property 9 determine, formulate 11 inheritance

devitalize 3 sap 5 drain 6 deaden, weaken 7 exhaust 8 enfeeble 9 desiccate 10 eviscerate

devoid of 7 lacking, wanting 8 free from

devoir 3 job 4 duty, task, work 5 chore, stint 6 charge 9 committal 10 assignment, commitment, obligation

devolution 5 decay 7 decline, passing 8 receding, transfer 9 conferral, decadence, recession, surrender 10 conveyance, declension, degeneracy, regression, relegation, transferal 11 degradation 12 degeneration, dégringolade, retrograding, transference 13 retrogression

devolve 4 give, pass 6 pass on 8 hand down, hand over, relegate, transfer 10 degenerate

devote 5 apply 6 commit, direct, donate, hallow 7 reserve 8 dedicate, give over, sanctify 9 confirm in, habituate 10 consecrate

devoted 4 dear, fond, true 5 loyal 6 ardent, caring, doting, fervid, loving 7 dutiful, fervent, zealous 8 constant, faithful 9 dedicated 10 thoughtful 12 affectionate *religiously:* 6 oblate

devotee 3 fan, nut 4 buff 5 hound, lover 6 addict, votary, zealot 7 admirer, amateur, fanatic, fancier, habitué 8 follower 9 supporter 10 aficionado, enthusiast

devotion 4 love, zeal 5 ardor, piety 6 fealty, fervor, prayer 7 loyalty, passion 8 fidelity, fondness 9 adherence, adoration, reverence 10 allegiance, attachment, dedication, enthusiasm 12 faithfulness

devour 3 eat 5 eat up, enjoy 6 absorb, feed on 7 consume, destroy, feast on, pillage 8 prey upon, wolf down 9 delight in, feast upon, polish off, swallow up 10 annihilate

devouring 4 avid 6 greedy 8 esurient, ravenous 9 voracious 10 gluttonous

devout 4 holy 5 godly, loyal, pious 6 ardent 7 earnest, fervent, serious, sincere, zealous 8 faithful, reverent 9 pietistic, prayerful, religious

devoutness 4 zeal 5 ardor, piety 9 reverence 10 commitment

dew 5 sweat, tears 8 moisture 11 precipitate 12 perspiration 13 precipitation

dewy 3 wet 4 damp, pure 5 fresh, moist, naive 7 artless, natural 8 innocent, wide-eyed 9 credulous, guileless, ingenuous, unworldly

dexter 5 right

dexterity 4 ease 5 craft, grace, skill 7 ability, aptness, know-how, prowess, sleight 8 deftness, facility 9 adeptness, expertise, readiness 10 adroitness, nimbleness, smoothness 12 skillfulness

dexterous 3 apt 4 able, deft 5 adept, agile, handy 6 adroit, artful, facile, nimble, smooth 7 skilled 8 masterly, skillful 10 proficient

___ **Dhabi** 3 Abu

diablerie 7 devilry, roguery, sorcery, waggery 8 deviltry, iniquity, mischief, satanism 9 devilment 10 black magic, wickedness, witchcraft, wrongdoing 11 roguishness, waggishness 12 sportiveness

diabolical 4 evil 5 awful 6 impish, wicked 7 beastly, demonic, heinous, hellish, puckish, roguish, satanic 8 demoniac, devilish, dreadful, fiendish, god-awful, hellborn, infernal, rascally, sinister 9 execrable, malicious, monstrous, nefarious 10 degenerate, demoniacal, horrendous, iniquitous, scandalous, villainous 11 mischievous

diabolism see DIABLERIE

diacritic 5 acute, breve, grave, haček, tilde 6 macron, umlaut 7 cedilla 8 dieresis 9 diaeresis 10 circumflex *Arabic:* 5 hamza 6 hamzah

diadem 5 crown 6 wreath 7 chaplet, coronal, coronet 8 headband

diagnose 4 spot 5 place 8 identify, pinpoint 9 determine, interpret, recognize 11 distinguish

diagnostic 8 analytic 10 analytical, expository, indicating, indicative 11 explanatory, exploratory 12 interpretive

diagonal 4 bias 5 bevel 6 biased 7 beveled, oblique, slanted 8 inclined, slanting 9 inclining, slantways, slantwise

diagonally 9 slantways, slantwise 10 cornerwise 11 catercorner, kitty-corner

diagram 3 map 5 chart, graph 6 design, layout, sketch 7 drawing, isotype 9 represent

dial 4 call, face, knob, tune, turn 5 phone 6 rotate 7 control 10 manipulate

dialect 4 cant, jive 5 argot, idiom, koine, lingo, slang 6 creole, jargon, patois, patter, pidgin, speech, tongue 8 language, localism 10 vernacular 11 regionalism, terminology 13 provincialism *Georgia:* 6 Gullah *London:* 7 cockney

dialectic 5 logic 6 debate 8 dialogue, forensic 9 reasoning 10 discussion 11 disputation 13 argumentation, investigation

dialogue 4 chat, talk 6 confer, parley, script 8 colloquy, converse 12 conversation 13 confabulation

diameter 4 bore 5 chord, width 7 breadth, caliber 8 bisector, wideness 9 broadness

diametric 7 counter, opposed 8 contrary, converse, opposite 12 antithetical 13 contradictory

diamond 3 gem 5 field, stone *element:* 6 carbon *famous:* 4 Hope, Pitt 5 Sancy 6 Orloff, Regent 8 Braganza, Cullinan, Kohinoor 9 Excelsior 10 Great Mogul *inferior:* 4 bort *oval:* 9 briolette *pattern:* 6 argyle *playing card:* 7 lozenge *state:* 8 Delaware *surface:* 5 facet

Diana see ARTEMIS

diapason 4 peal, stop 5 range, scale, scope 7 compass, measure 8 spectrum 10 tuning fork

diaper 5 nappy 7 pattern 8 ornament

diaphanous 5 filmy, gauzy, sheer, vague 6 flimsy 8 ethereal, gossamer 11 transparent 13 insubstantial

diaphragm 4 stop 6 septum 8 membrane 9 partition

diarist 4 Gide (André) 5 Frank (Anne), Pepys (Samuel), Scott (Walter), Swift (Jonathan), Woolf (Virginia) 6 Burney (Fanny), Evelyn (John) 7 Boswell (James) 8 Robinson (Henry Crabb) 10 chronicler, journalist

diary 3 log 6 record 7 daybook, diurnal, journal, logbook 8 notebook, register 9 chronicle

diastase 6 enzyme 8 catalyst, reactant

diatribe 6 tirade 7 polemic 8 harangue, jeremiad 9 criticism, philippic 11 castigation 12 denunciation

dibs 4 gelt 5 claim, dough, money, title 6 rights 11 reservation

dice 4 cast, cube 5 bones, cubes, ivory, mince 11 devil's-bones *game:* 5 craps *losing throw:* 7 missout *singular:* 3 die *throw:* 7 boxcars 9 snake eyes

dicer 5 loser 6 risker 7 gambler

dicey 4 iffy 5 risky 6 chancy, tricky 8 ticklish 9 uncertain, whimsical 10 precarious, speculative 11 problematic 13 unpredictable

dichotomize 5 halve 7 dissect 8 hemisect 9 bifurcate

dichotomous 5 split 6 forked 7 pronged 9 bifurcate 10 bifurcated

dichotomy 7 forking 8 division 9 bisection, branching, splitting 11 bifurcation 13 contradiction

Dickens, Charles *birthplace:* 10 Portsmouth *captain:* 6 Cuttle *character:* 3 Ada (Clare), Pip, Tim 4 Dick (Mr.), Dora, Gamp (Sairey), Heep (Uriah), Nell 5 Drood (Edwin), Emily, Fagin, Lucie (Manette), Sikes (Bill) 6 Barkis, Bumble (Mr.), Carton (Sydney), Cuttle (Capt.), Darnay (Charles), Dombey (Fanny, Florence, Paul), Dorrit (Amy), Oliver (Twist) 7 Barnaby (Rudge), Dedlock (Lady), Defarge, Gargery (Joe), Manette (Dr.), Scrooge (Ebenezer), Tiny Tim 8 Cratchit (Bob), Havisham (Miss), Jarndyce (John), Magwitch (Abel), Micawber (Mr.), Nickleby (Nicholas), Peggotty (Clara, Daniel, Ham), Pickwick (Mr.) 9 Bill Sikes, Gradgrind (Mr.), Murdstone (Mr.), Pecksniff (Mr.), Uriah Heep 10 Chuzzlewit (Anthony, Jonas, Martin), Steerforth 11 Copperfield (David) *hero:* 6 Carton (Sydney) *nationality:* 7 English *pen name:* 3 Boz *villain:* 5 Fagin *work:* 9 Hard Times 10 Bleak House 11 Oliver Twist 12 Barnaby Rudge, Dombey and Son, Little Dorrit 14 Christmas Carol (A), Pickwick Papers (The) 15 Our Mutual Friend, Tale of Two Cities (A) 16 David Copperfield, Martin Chuzzlewit, Nicholas Nickleby 17 Great Expectations

dicker 4 deal, swap 5 argue, trade 6 barter, haggle, higgle, palter 7 bargain, chaffer 8 contract, huckster 9 negotiate

dickey 10 shirtfront

Dickey novel 11 Deliverance

dictate 3 set 4 lead, rule, word 5 edict, order, tenet 6 behest, decree, direct, enjoin, govern, impose, ordain, recite 7 bidding, command, control, lay down, mandate, read off, summons 9 determine, direction, directive, prescribe, principle, pronounce, verbalize 10 injunction 12 prescription

dictative 5 bossy 8 despotic, dogmatic 9 imperious 10 peremptory 11 doctrinaire, magisterial 13 authoritarian

dictator 4 czar, duce 6 caesar, despot, tyrant 8 autocrat, martinet 9 oppressor, strongman *German:* 6 Hitler (Adolf) *Italian:* 9 Mussolini (Benito) *military:* 8 caudillo *Spanish:* 6 Franco (Francisco)

dictatorial 5 bossy 8 despotic, dogmatic 9 arbitrary, imperious, masterful 10 autocratic, iron-handed, peremptory, tyrannical 11 doctrinaire, domineering, overbearing 12 totalitarian 13 authoritarian

dictatorship 7 tyranny 9 autocracy, Caesarism, despotism, supremacy 10 absolutism

diction 6 phrase, speech 7 wordage, wording 8 delivery, language, parlance, phrasing, rhetoric, verbiage 9 elocution, verbalism 11 enunciation, phraseology

dictionary 7 lexicon 8 glossary, wordbook 10 repository 13 reference book *compiler:* 7 Johnson (Samuel), Webster (Noah) 13 lexicographer *geographical:* 9 gazetteer *of synonyms:* 8 thesauri (plural) 9 thesaurus

dictum 4 fiat 5 adage, axiom, edict, maxim, moral 6 ruling 7 mandate, opinion, precept, proverb 11 declaration 13 pronouncement

didactic 5 moral 6 teachy 7 donnish, preachy 8 advisory, edifying, pedantic, sermonic, teaching 9 hortative, pedagogic, teacherly 10 moralizing 11 informative, instructive

diddle 3 con, gyp, toy 4 beat, bilk, dupe, hoax, fool, idle, laze, loaf, loll, rook, scam 5 cheat, cozen, delay, drone, trick 6 chisel, chouse, dabble, dawdle, delude, fiddle, fleece, loiter, lounge, rope in, take in 7 deceive, defraud, goof off, mislead, swindle 8 flimflam, fool with, hoodwink, lollygag 9 bamboozle, overreach, victimize, waste time 10 dilly-dally, fool around, hang around

diddler 3 gyp 4 sham 5 cheat, faker, fraud, rogue 6 con man 7 grifter, shammer, sharper 8 swindler 9 con artist, defrauder, trickster 11 flimflammer 12 double-dealer 13 confidence man

dido 4 jest, lark 5 antic, caper, curio, frill, prank 6 bauble, frolic, gewgaw, trifle, whimsy 7 bibelot, novelty, trinket 8 furbelow, gimcrack, kickshaw, mischief 9 bagatelle, plaything 10 knickknack, tomfoolery

Dido 6 Elissa *brother:* 9 Pygmalion *city founded by:* 8 Carthage *father:* 5 Belus 6 Mutton *husband:* 7 Acerbas 8 Sichaeus *lover:* 6 Aeneas

Dido and Aeneas composer 7 Purcell (Henry)

die 4 drop, fall, mold, pass, stop, wane 5 cease, croak 6 cash in, demise, expire, go west, matrix, pass on, peg out, perish, pop off 7 decease, go south, kick off, snuff it, succumb 8 cash it in, check out, drop dead, pass away 9 disappear 10 buy the farm 12 join the choir 13 kick the bucket *from hunger:* 6 starve *loaded:* 6 fulham

___ **die** 4 sine

diehard 7 devoted, fanatic 8 true-blue 9 dogmatist 10 determined 11 bitter-ender, doctrinaire, reactionary, stand-patter 12 conservative, intransigent 13 stick-in-the-mud

___ **diem** 3 per 5 carpe

Dies ___ 4 Irae

diet 4 eats, fare, fast, feed, menu 6 ration, reduce, regime 7 regimen 8 assembly, victuals 10 parliament 11 legislature, nourishment

Diet of ___ 5 Worms 6 Speyer, Spires 8 Augsburg

Dieu ___ **(British motto)** 10 et mon droit

___**-dieu** 4 prie

differ 4 vary 5 demur 7 deviate 8 disagree

difference 7 discord, dispute, dissent 8 conflict, contrast, variance 9 departure, deviation, disparity, otherness, variation 10 dissension, divergence, unlikeness 11 controversy, discrepancy, distinction 12 disagreement 13 dissimilarity

different 5 other 6 divers, single, sundry, unlike 7 another, deviant, distant, diverse, several, special, unalike, unequal, unusual, various 8 discrete, distinct, peculiar, separate 9 disparate, divergent 10 dissimilar, individual, particular 11 contrasting, distinctive

differentiate 4 vary 5 adapt 6 change, modify 8 contrast, separate 9 diversify, transform 11 distinguish, individuate 12 characterize, discriminate

difficult 4 hard 5 tough 6 thorny, uphill 7 arduous, awkward, labored, obscure, operose 8 exacting, perverse, puzzling, stubborn 9 demanding, effortful, herculean, laborious, strenuous 10 refractory 11 problematic

difficulty 3 ado, fix, jam 4 beef 4 pass, snag 5 hitch, nodus, pinch, rigor, worry 6 bother, hang-up, hassle, pickle, plight, scrape, strait 7 dilemma, pitfall, problem, trouble 8 distress, hardness, hardship, hot water, obstacle, quandary, quagmire, question, squabble 9 adversity, bickering, challenge, deep water, objection 10 falling-out, impediment 11 aggravation, altercation, arduousness, controversy, obstruction, predicament, vicissitude 12 complication, disagreement 13 embarrassment, inconvenience

diffidence 7 modesty, reserve, shyness 8 distrust, meekness, timidity 9 quiet-ness, restraint, timidness 10 hesitation 11 bashfulness

diffident 3 shy 4 meek 5 timid 7 bashful 8 hesitant, reserved, retiring, timorous 9 reluctant, unassured 11 unassertive 12 self-effacing

diffuse 5 strew, wordy 6 prolix, spread 7 scatter, verbose 8 disperse, rambling 9 broadcast, dispersed, propagate, scattered, spreading, spread out 10 distribute, long-winded, widespread 11 disseminate, distributed

diffusion 6 spread 7 osmosis 9 broadcast, dispersal, prolixity, spreading 10 dispersion, scattering 11 circulation, propagation 12 broadcasting, promulgation

dig 3 jab 4 barb, grub, hole, like, mine, poke, prod, root, site, stab 5 delve, ditch, enjoy, gouge, nudge, probe, scoop, spade, taunt 6 burrow, plunge, quarry, relish, rootle, shovel, thrust, trench, tunnel 7 explore, root out, unearth 8 excavate, prospect 10 excavation 11 investigate *up:* 6 exhume 7 unearth

digest 5 sum up 6 absorb, codify, précis 7 consume, stomach, summate, swallow 8 abstract, boil down, classify, compress, condense, syllabus, synopsis 9 summarize, summation, synopsize 10 abridgment 12 condensation

digger 4 plow 5 miner 6 shovel 7 soldier

digit 3 toe 5 thumb 6 cipher, figure, finger, number, pinkie 7 integer, numeral 9 character 11 whole number

dignified 4 prim 6 august, formal, proper, seemly 7 courtly, elegant, stately 8 cultured, decorous, ennobled, polished 9 distingué, patrician

dignify 5 adorn, exalt, grace, honor 7 ennoble, elevate, glorify, sublime 11 distinguish

dignitary 3 VIP 4 lion 5 chief, nabob 6 leader, worthy 7 notable 8 eminence, luminary 9 personage 10 notability 11 muckety-muck 13 high-muck-a-muck

dignity 4 rank 5 honor, merit, poise, pride, worth 6 cachet, status, virtue 7 address, decorum, gravity, hauteur, majesty, stature 8 grandeur, nobility, position, prestige, standing 9 propriety 10 augustness, seemliness 11 consequence, self-respect

digress 5 stray 6 depart, ramble, swerve, wander 7 deviate, diverge 8 divagate

digression 5 aside 7 episode, tangent 8 drifting, excursus, rambling, straying 9 deviation, wandering 10 deflection, divagation, divergence 11 parenthesis

dig up 4 find 6 expose, reveal 7 nose out, root out, uncover, unearth 8 discover 9 ferret out, run across, search out, track down

dik-dik 8 antelope

dike 3 dam 4 bank 5 ditch, drain, levee 7 barrier 8 causeway 10 embankment 11 watercourse

dilapidate 4 ruin 5 decay, wreck 7 break up, crumble, decline, neglect 9 break down, decompose, disregard 10 deliquesce 12 disintegrate

dilapidated 5 dingy, seedy 6 beat-up, ragtag, ruined, shabby 7 decayed, rundown 8 battered, crumbled, decrepit 9 crumbling 10 broken-down, down-at-heel, ramshackle 12 deteriorated

dilapidation 4 ruin 5 decay 7 atrophy 8 collapse, decaying 9 crumbling, decadence, disrepair 11 decrepitude 13 decomposition, deterioration

dilate 5 swell, widen 6 expand, extend 7 distend, enlarge, expound 9 discourse, expatiate

dilatory 4 idle, slow 5 slack, tardy 7 laggard 8 dallying, delaying, sluggish 9 leisurely, lingering, unhurried 11 time-wasting

dilemma 3 box, fix, jam 4 bind, hole, spot 6 choice, corner, pickle, plight, scrape 7 catch-22, problem 8 argument, quandary 10 difficulty 11 predicament

dilettante 4 tyro 7 amateur, dabbler 8 aesthete, putterer 9 smatterer

dilettantish see AMATEURISH

diligence 4 zeal 8 industry 9 assiduity 10 commitment 11 application, persistence 12 perseverance, sedulousness 13 assiduousness

diligent 8 sedulous 9 assiduous 10 persistent, persisting, unflagging 11 hardworking, industrious, painstaking, persevering

dilly 4 lulu 5 dandy, doozy, peach 6 corker, doozie, pippin, ripper, rouser 8 jimdandy, knockout 9 humdinger 10 ripsnorter 11 crackerjack

dillydally see DELAY

dilute 3 cut 4 thin, weak 5 water 6 watery, weaken 8 diminish, weakened 9 attenuate, water down 11 watered-down

dim 4 dull, dumb, hazy, pale, slow 5 befog, blear, blind, cloud, dense, dusky, faint, muddy, murky, muted, thick, vague 6 bleary, gloomy, stupid 7 becloud, low beam, obscure, shadowy, subdued, unclear 9 tenebrous 10 ill-defined, indistinct, lackluster, lusterless 11 unpromising

dime novel 4 pulp 7 chiller, shocker

8 dreadful, thriller 12 bloodcurdler 13 penny dreadful

dimension 4 size 5 reach, scale, scope, width 6 aspect, extent, spread 7 compass, expanse, measure, quality 9 amplitude, magnitude

diminish 3 ebb 4 bate, wane 5 abate, peter, quell, taper 6 lessen, reduce, subdue, temper, weaken 7 curtail, dwindle, subside 8 belittle, decrease, minimize, moderate, restrain, taper off 9 attenuate, disparage, dispraise 10 depreciate 11 detract from

diminishing 6 waning 8 receding 9 declining, dwindling, lessening, subsiding, weakening 10 curtailing, decreasing 11 attenuating 12 depreciating

diminutive 3 wee 4 tiny 5 bitsy, dwarf, pygmy, small, teeny, weeny 6 bantam, little, midget, minute, peewee, petite, teensy 9 miniature, pint-sized, undersize 10 teeny-weeny 11 lilliputian 12 teensy-weensy

___ **dimittis** 4 Nunc

dimple 3 pit 4 dent, dint, fret, nick 5 notch 6 ripple 8 pockmark 10 depression 11 indentation

dimwit 3 oaf 4 clod, dodo, dolt, dope, fool, simp, yo-yo 5 booby, chump, cluck, dummy, dunce, idiot, moron, stupe 6 dum-dum 7 airhead, dullard, fathead, pinhead 8 bonehead, dumbbell, imbecile, lunkhead, meathead, numskull 9 birdbrain, blockhead, dumb bunny, dumb cluck, ignoramus, lamebrain, numbskull, simpleton 10 dunderhead, nincompoop 11 featherhead, knucklehead 12 featherbrain

dim-witted 4 dull, dumb, slow 6 stupid 7 doltish, foolish, idiotic, moronic 8 backward, imbecile, retarded 9 brainless, half-baked, imbecilic 11 birdbrained, lamebrained 12 feebleminded, simpleminded

din 3 row 4 roar 5 babel, clash, noise 6 bedlam, clamor, deafen, hubbub, racket, rattle, tumult, uproar 7 clangor, clatter, resound 8 brouhaha 9 commotion, stridency 10 hullabaloo, hurlyburly 11 pandemonium 13 clamorousness

Dinah *brother:* 4 Levi 6 Simeon *father:* 5 Jacob *mother:* 4 Leah

dine 3 eat, sup 4 feed 5 feast 6 eat out 7 banquet, nourish

diner 4 café 5 eater 6 eatery 7 canteen 8 snack bar 9 hash house 10 coffee shop, restaurant 11 greasy spoon 12 lunch counter, luncheonette, sandwich shop

ding 3 mar 4 dent, nick 5 clang 7 blemish

ding-a-ling 3 nut 4 kook, yo-yo 5 flake, loony, wacko 6 cuckoo, nitwit, weirdo 7 lunatic 8 crackpot 9 fruitcake, harebrain, lamebrain, screwball 10 crackbrain 12 scatterbrain

dinghy 5 skiff 7 rowboat, shallop 8 lifeboat, life raft, sailboat

dingle 4 dale, dell, glen, vale 6 ravine, valley

dingus 5 gizmo 6 doodad, gadget, jigger, widget 7 whatsit 9 doohickey, thingummy 11 thingamabob, thingamajig, thingumajig

dingy 4 foul, mean 5 dirty, seedy, tacky 6 filthy, grubby, grungy, scuzzy, shabby, soiled, sordid 7 run-down, squalid, sullied, unclean 8 begrimed

dinky 3 toy 4 tiny 5 small, teeny 9 undersize 10 locomotive

"Dinner ___" 7 at Eight

dinner 4 meal 5 feast 6 regale, repast, spread, supper 7 banquet 8 luncheon 9 collation 10 table d'hôte *course:* 4 meat, soup 5 salad 6 entrée 7 dessert 9 appetizer *jacket:* 3 tux 6 tuxedo

dinosaur 6 fossil 7 has-been 8 theropod 11 anachronism

dinosauric 4 huge 5 passé 6 bygone 7 extinct, mammoth 8 colossal, enormous, obsolete, outmoded 9 cyclopean, leviathan, out-of-date 10 antiquated, behemothic, fossilized, gargantuan, mastodonic, oldfangled 11 elephantine 12 antediluvian, old-fashioned, out-of-fashion 13 anachronistic

dint 4 nick 5 force, might, power 6 dimple, virtue 7 drive in, impress 10 impression 11 indentation

diocese 3 see 9 bishopric *Eastern Orthodox:* 7 eparchy *subdivision:* 6 parish

diode 9 rectifier 10 vacuum tube 12 electron tube *component:* 5 anode 7 cathode 9 electrode

Diomedes *city founded by:* 4 Arpi *father:* 4 Ares, Mars 6 Tydeus *foe:* 6 Aeneas, Hector *slayer:* 8 Hercules *victim:* 6 Rhesus

Dione 5 Titan *cult partner:* 4 Zeus *daughter:* 5 Venus 9 Aphrodite *father:* 7 Oceanus *lover:* 4 Zeus *mother:* 6 Tethys

Dionysus see BACCHUS

Dionyza's husband 5 Cleon

Dioscuri 5 twins 6 Castor, Gemini, Pollux *father:* 4 Zeus 9 Tyndareus *mother:* 4 Leda *sister:* 5 Helen

dip 3 sag 4 bail, draw, drop, duck, dunk, fall, lade, sink, skid, slip, slue, swim 5 basin, ladle, lower, pitch, sauce, scoop, slope, slump, spoon, stoop 6 go down, hollow, plunge 7 decline, descend, descent, falloff, immerse, sinkage 8 decrease, downturn, sinkhole, submerge, submerse 9 concavity, declivity, downswing, downtrend, immersion 10 depression

diphthong 7 digraph 8 ligature

diploma 6 degree 7 charter 8 document 9 sheepskin 10 credential

diplomacy 4 tact 7 address, finesse 8 delicacy 10 artfulness, discretion, statecraft 11 negotiation, savoir faire, tactfulness

diplomatic 4 deft 5 bland, suave 6 artful, astute, polite, smooth, urbane 7 courtly, politic, tactful 8 delicate, discreet 9 courteous 12 conciliating, conciliatory, paleographic 13 accommodating

diplomat's office 7 embassy, mission

diplopod 9 millipede

dipper 3 cup 4 bird 5 ladle, ouzel, scoop, stars 6 bucket 10 pickpocket, water ouzel

dippy 4 daft, zany 5 crazy, daffy, flaky, goofy, kooky, loony, nutty, silly, wacky 6 stupid 7 doltish, foolish, witless 9 half-baked 11 harebrained 12 preposterous

dipsomania 10 alcoholism

dire 4 grim 5 acute, awful 6 dismal, horrid, tragic, urgent, woeful 7 baleful, baneful, crucial, extreme, fateful, ominous, ruinous 8 alarming, critical, dreadful, grievous, horrible, horrific, menacing, shocking, sinister, terrible 9 appalling, desperate, frightful, illboding 10 calamitous, deplorable, depressing, foreboding, malevolent, oppressing, oppressive, pernicious 11 apocalyptic, distressing, threatening

direct 4 head, lead, show 5 apply, frank, guide, label, level, order, pilot, plain, point, route, steer, train 6 assign, charge, define, devote, divert, enjoin, escort, extend, govern, lineal, linear, manage, ordain, settle 7 address, carry on, command, conduct, control, genuine, nonstop, operate, oversee, preside, project, request 8 dispatch, instruct, regulate, shepherd, straight, unbroken, verbatim 9 determine, firsthand, immediate, prescribe 10 administer, contiguous, continuous, inevitable 11 categorical, undeviating, unequivocal, word for word *a helmsman:* 4 conn *proceedings:* 7 preside

direction 3 way 4 east, line, path, side, west 5 angle, north, point, south, trend 6 course, design 7 bearing, channel, command, purpose 8 guidance, tendency 9 clockwise, oversight, viewpoint 10 management, standpoint, trajectory

11 instruction, supervision *blowing:*
7 leeward 8 windward *horizontal:*
7 azimuth *main line of:* 4 axis (see also
COMPASS POINT)

directive 4 fiat, memo, word, writ
5 edict, order, ukase 6 charge, decree,
dictum, notice, ruling 7 bidding, command, dictate, mandate 8 deciding,
managing 9 presiding 10 assignment,
injunction, memorandum 11 instruction, supervising, supervisory 12 policy-
making 13 communication, pronouncement

directly 3 due 4 anon, soon 5 right, spang
6 at once, pronto 7 bluntly, by and by,
shortly 8 first off, in person, promptly,
squarely, straight, verbatim 9 forthwith,
instanter, instantly, presently, right
away 10 face-to-face 11 immediately,
straight off, straightway, word for word
12 contiguously, straightaway

director 4 boss, head 5 chief 6 leader,
top dog 7 manager 8 overseer 9 conductor, organizer 10 head honcho,
supervisor

directory 4 list 5 guide, index 6 folder
7 catalog 8 register 9 catalogue 11 compilation

dirge 6 lament 7 requiem 8 threnody
11 lamentation *Gaelic:* 8 coronach

dirigible 5 blimp 7 airship 8 zeppelin
9 steerable

dirk 4 stab 5 sword 6 dagger 7 poniard

dirt 3 mud 4 clay, dust, land, loam, mire,
muck, porn, smut, soil, spot 5 earth,
filth, fraud, grime, stain 6 gossip,
ground 7 chicane, squalor 9 chicanery,
excrement, indecency 10 corruption,
hanky-panky 11 pornography

dirt-poor 4 bust 5 broke 8 beggared,
indigent 9 destitute, flat broke, penniless, penurious 10 stone-broke
12 impoverished

dirty 3 low, tar 4 base, foul, lewd, smut,
soil 5 bawdy, foggy, grimy, messy,
mucky, muddy, murky, nasty, smear,
sooty, stain, sully, taint 6 basely, befoul,
coarse, debase, defile, filthy, grubby,
impure, smudge, smutty, soiled, sordid,
vulgar 7 corrupt, defiled, hateful,
immoral, obscene, raunchy, smutchy,
spotted, squalid, squally, sullied, tainted, tarnish, unclean, unkempt
8 begrimed, besmirch, blustery, indecent, off-color, polluted, unchaste,
unwashed 9 ill-gotten, uncleanly
10 abominable, blustering, scandalous,
scurrilous 11 disgraceful, distasteful,
distressing, tempestuous, unlaundered
12 contaminated, contemptible, disagreeable, dishonorable, scatological

Dis see PLUTO

disability 7 ailment 8 drawback, handicap 9 detriment, hindrance, infirmity,
unfitness 10 affliction, impairment,
impediment, incapacity 11 restriction,
shortcoming 12 disadvantage

disable 3 sap 4 maim 5 spoil 6 hobble,
weaken 7 cripple 8 enfeeble, handicap,
paralyze, sabotage 9 hamstring, undermine 10 debilitate, immobilize 12 incapacitate *a racehorse:* 6 nobble

disabled 7 hobbled 8 crippled 9 arthritic,
paralyzed, rheumatic 11 handicapped
13 incapacitated

disabuse 4 free 5 emend, purge 7 correct, deliver, rectify, redress, release,
relieve 8 liberate, unburden 9 enlight-
en, undeceive 10 illuminate 11 disencumber, disillusion

disaccharide 7 lactose, maltose, sucrose

disaccord 3 jar, war 4 vary 5 brawl,
clash 6 combat, debate, differ 7 contest,
contend, dispute, dissent, quarrel
8 conflict, disagree 12 disharmonize

disadvantage 3 bar 4 harm, loss 6 burden, damage, hamper 7 barrier, setback
8 drawback, handicap, obstacle 9 detriment, hindrance, liability, prejudice
10 impairment, impediment, imposition, limitation 11 deprivation, obstruction

disadvantaged 7 lacking 8 deprived
11 handicapped

disaffect 4 wean 5 alien, repel 8 alienate,
disquiet, disunite, estrange 10 antagonize

disaffirm 4 deny 5 annul, belie, cross
6 abjure, impugn, negate, refute, reject
7 confute, explode, gainsay, reverse
8 disclaim, disprove, negative, traverse
9 repudiate 10 contradict, contravene

disagree 4 vary 5 argue, clash 6 bicker,
differ, divide, haggle 7 contend, contest, dispute, dissent 8 conflict

disagreeable 4 ugly 7 peevish 8 annoying, petulant 9 offensive 10 unpleasant
11 disobliging, distressing, ill-tempered

disagreement 5 clash 6 debate 7 discord,
dispute, quarrel, wrangle 8 argument,
conflict, squabble, variance 9 disparity
10 contention, difference, dissension,
divergence, unlikeness 11 altercation,
controversy, discrepancy, incongruity

disallow 4 deny, veto 5 debar 6 enjoin,
forbid, refuse, reject 7 disavow, dismiss,
exclude, rule out, shut out 8 disclaim,
prohibit 9 interdict, proscribe, repudiate

disallowance 4 veto 5 taboo 6 denial
7 refusal 9 disavowal, dismissal, exclu-

sion, rejection 11 prohibition, repudiation 12 interdiction, proscription

___-disant 3 soi

disappear 3 die 5 clear, leave 6 depart, die out, vanish 8 evanesce, fade away, melt away, pass away, slip away 9 evaporate, sneak away, steal away 13 dematerialize

disappoint 4 dash, foil, ruin 6 baffle, defeat, thwart 7 let down 9 frustrate 10 discourage, dishearten

disappointment 4 blow 6 bummer, defeat, downer 7 failure, letdown 8 comedown 9 bringdown 11 frustration

disapproval 4 veto 6 rebuke 7 censure, dislike, obloquy, reproof 8 reproach 9 criticism, objection, rejection *expression of:* 3 boo 4 hiss, hoot, jeer 7 catcall 9 raspberry 10 Bronx cheer

disapprove 4 veto 6 oppose, reject 7 decline, dislike, dismiss, frown on 8 disfavor, turn down 9 dispraise

disarm 5 charm 6 allure 7 win over 8 sideline 9 captivate 10 neutralize

disarming 5 silky 6 silken 7 amiable, likable, winning, winsome 8 likeable, pleasing 9 endearing 10 convincing, persuasive, saccharine 11 deferential, insinuating 12 ingratiating

disarrange 4 mess 5 mix up, upset 6 jumble, mess up, mislay, muddle, muss up 7 confuse, disturb 8 disorder, displace, misplace, unsettle 10 discompose 11 disorganize

disarray 5 chaos 6 bedlam, jumble, mess up, muddle 7 clutter, undress 8 disorder, shambles, unsettle 9 confusion 10 discompose, dishabille

disassemble 6 detach 7 scatter 8 dismount, disperse, separate, take down, tear down 9 break down, come apart, dismantle, dismember, take apart

disassociate 5 sever, unfix 6 detach, sunder 7 back off 8 abstract, alienate, back down, disunite, liberate, separate, uncouple, withdraw 9 disengage 10 disconnect

disaster 3 woe 6 fiasco 7 debacle, failure, tragedy 8 calamity 9 cataclysm, ruination 11 catastrophe, devastation

disastrous 4 dire 5 fatal 6 tragic 7 fateful, ruinous 8 terrible 10 calamitous, horrendous 11 cataclysmic, destructive, devastating 12 catastrophic

disavow 4 deny 6 abjure, disown, impugn, negate, recant, reject 7 forsake, gainsay, retract 8 abnegate, disclaim, forswear, negative, renounce 9 repudiate

disband 3 end 4 part 5 sever 6 divide, sunder 7 break up, dissect, divorce, scatter 8 disperse, dissolve, separate

disbelieve 5 doubt, scorn, scout 6 eschew, reject 7 scoff at, suspect 8 discount, distrust, mistrust, question 9 discredit, repudiate

disbeliever 5 cynic 7 doubter, sceptic, scoffer, skeptic 9 dissenter 10 questioner 11 freethinker

disbelieving 4 wary 5 leery 6 show-me 7 cynical, dubious 8 doubting 9 quizzical, skeptical 11 incredulous, mistrustful, questioning, unconvinced

disburden 4 shed 6 unlade, unload, unship, unstow 7 off-load, relieve 8 disgorge 9 discharge

disburse 3 pay 5 allot, issue 6 lay out, pay out, supply 7 deliver, dole out, furnish, provide 8 dispense, disperse 9 apportion, partition 10 distribute, measure out

disbursement 4 cost 5 funds 6 outlay 7 expense, payment 9 allotment 11 expenditure 12 distribution

discard 4 cast, drop, dump, junk, shed, toss, waif 5 chuck, ditch, eject, let go, scrap 6 reject 7 cast off, castoff, deep-six, wash out 8 get rid of, jettison, shuck off, throw out 9 throw away, toss aside

discarnate 8 bodiless, ethereal, spectral 9 asomatous, unfleshly 10 immaterial, unembodied, unphysical, wraithlike 11 disembodied, incorporeal, nonphysical 12 otherworldly 13 insubstantial

discern 3 see 4 know, note 5 grasp, sense 6 behold, detect, divine, notice 7 observe 8 identify, perceive 9 apprehend, ascertain, recognize 10 comprehend, understand 11 distinguish 12 discriminate 13 differentiate

discernible 7 visible 8 apparent, palpable 10 detectable, noticeable, observable 11 appreciable, perceivable 12 recognizable

discerning 4 keen 5 acute, aware 6 astute 7 knowing 9 clear-eyed, insighted, observant, sagacious 10 insightful, perceptive 12 clear-sighted 13 knowledgeable, perspicacious

discernment 6 acumen 7 insight 8 keenness, sagacity 9 intuition 10 astuteness, perception, shrewdness 11 penetration, percipience, recognition 12 perspicacity 13 comprehension, sagaciousness

discharge 3 can, pay 4 drop, emit, fire, free, gush, oust, quit, sack, spew, vent, void 5 annul, clear, demob, eject, empty, expel, exude, let go, loose, pay up, quash, salvo, shoot, utter 6 bounce, excuse, exempt, let fly, let off, loosen, outlet, remove, settle, unbind, unload, vacate 7 absolve, boot out, barrage, cashier, deliver, dismiss, exclude, excrete, execute, fulfill, give off, kick out, manumit, off-load, release, relieve, removal, satisfy, unchain **8** abrogate, aquittal, dispense, displace, dissolve, ejection, emission, get rid of, liberate, separate, throw off **9** acquittal, dismissal, eliminate, explosion, expulsion, muster out, pour forth, send forth, terminate, unshackle **10** deactivate, demobilize, emancipate, inactivate, liberation, separation **11** exoneration, fulfillment *electrical:* **5** spark **6** leader **8** streamer **9** lightning

disciple 3 fan **6** minion **7** apostle, devotee, learner **8** adherent, follower, henchman, partisan, retainer **9** supporter **10** enthusiast

disciplinarian 8 enforcer, martinet **10** taskmaster **11** slave driver

disciplinary 8 punitive **9** punishing **10** corrective

discipline 4 curb, rule, will **5** check, drill, field, guide, order, teach, train **6** bridle, direct, method, punish, school, subdue **7** chasten, conduct, control, correct, educate **8** approach, chastise, instruct, penalize, restrain, training **9** castigate, obedience, subjugate, willpower **10** correction, punishment **11** castigation, self-control, self-mastery **12** chastisement **13** self-restraint

disclaim 4 deny **6** abjure, reject **7** disavow, gainsay, retract **8** disallow, forswear, renounce, traverse **9** repudiate **10** contradict

disclose 3 own **4** avow, tell **5** spill **6** expose, impart, relate, report, reveal, unmask, unveil **7** display, divulge, uncover **8** discover, give away, unclothe **9** make known

disclosure 6 exposé **8** exposure **10** revelation **11** declaration

discolor 3 tar **4** blot, dull, fade, smut, soil **5** smear, stain, sully, taint, tinge **6** defile, smudge **7** besmear, bestain, tarnish **8** besmirch

discoloration 4 spot **5** stain, taint **6** blotch, bruise, smudge **7** blemish **9** birthmark

discomfit 3 irk, vex **4** faze **5** abash, annoy, upset **6** baffle, bother, defeat, rattle, thwart **7** fluster, nonplus, perturb, unnerve **8** confound **9** embarrass **10** discompose, disconcert

discomfiture 5 upset **6** unease **8** disquiet **9** abashment, agitation, confusion **10** uneasiness **11** frustration **12** discomposure, perturbation **13** embarrassment, inconvenience

discomfort 3 irk, vex **4** ache, pain **5** annoy **6** bother, unease **7** malaise **8** vexation **9** annoyance **10** uneasiness **13** embarrassment

discomforting see UNCOMFORTABLE

discommend 5 decry **7** censure, frown on, put down **8** admonish, disfavor, object to **9** criticize, deprecate, disesteem, disparage, reprehend **10** disapprove

discommode 3 irk, vex **5** annoy, upset **6** bother, burden, flurry, put out **7** disturb, fluster, perturb, trouble **8** encumber **9** aggravate, disoblige **13** inconvenience

discompose 3 irk, vex **5** annoy, harry, upset, worry **6** bother, dismay, flurry, harass, pester, plague, ruffle, untune **7** agitate, disturb, fluster, perturb, unhinge **8** disarray, disorder, unsettle **9** embarrass **10** disarrange **11** disorganize

discomposure 5 upset, worry **6** bother, unease **8** vexation **9** abashment, agitation, annoyance, confusion **10** discomfort, irritation, perplexity, uneasiness **11** disquietude **12** discomfiture, perturbation **13** consternation, embarrassment

disconcert 4 faze **5** abash, upset, worry **6** bemuse, bother, puzzle, rattle, ruffle **7** confuse, disturb, nonplus, perplex, perturb, trouble **8** bewilder, confound, disquiet **9** discomfit, embarrass, frustrate

disconfirm 4 deny **5** rebut **6** refute, negate **7** gainsay **8** abnegate, confound, disclaim, disprove **10** contradict, controvert

disconnect 3 cut, gap **5** break, sever, unfix **6** cut off, detach **7** disjoin **8** separate, uncouple **9** disengage **10** dissociate

disconnected 7 muddled **8** detached, separate **10** disjointed, incoherent, unattached **11** fragmentary, unorganized **13** discontinuous

disconsolate 3 low, sad **4** blue, down **5** bleak, drear **6** abject, dreary, gloomy, woeful **7** doleful, forlorn, joyless, unhappy **8** dejected, downcast, wretched **9** cheerless, depressed, miserable, sorrowful, woebegone **10** dispirited, melancholy **11** comfortless, crestfallen, downhearted

discontent 4 envy **9** dysphoria **10** depression, inquietude, uneasiness **11** displeasure **12** disaffection, restlessness

discontented 5 upset **6** uneasy **7** annoyed, fretful, unhappy **8** restless **9** disturbed, irritated, perturbed **10** displeased **11** complaining, disgruntled, ungratified, unsatisfied **12** dissatisfied

discontinuation 3 end **4** stop **5** cease, close, pause **6** ending, finish **7** closing **8** abeyance **9** cessation **10** conclusion, desistance, moratorium, suspension **12** postponement

discontinue 3 end **4** halt, quit, stay, stop

5 cease, close, sever **6** desist, give up, wind up, wrap up **8** break off, close out, conclude, knock off, leave off, shut down, surcease **9** terminate

discontinuity 3 gap **4** hole, rent, rift **5** break, cleft, crack, split **6** breach, lacuna **7** fissure, opening, rupture

discontinuous 6 fitful **7** muddled **8** discrete, separate **9** spasmodic **10** incoherent, incohesive **11** unconnected **12** disconnected, intermittent **13** nonsequential

discord 5 clash **6** enmity, rancor, strife **7** rupture **8** conflict, contrast, disunity, division, friction, mismatch, variance **9** animosity, antipathy, hostility **10** antagonism, contention, difference, dissension, dissidence, dissonance, opposition **12** inconsonance, polarization **13** inconsistency *goddess:* **3** Ate **4** Eris

discordant 5 harsh **6** at odds **7** jarring **8** clashing, contrary, jangling, strident **9** dissonant **10** cacophonic, unpleasant **11** cacophonous, conflicting, disagreeing, inconsonant, quarrelsome, unmelodious **12** unharmonious

discotheque 6 bistro, nitery **7** hot spot **9** dance club, nightclub, night spot

discount 5 doubt, lower **6** deduct, ignore, reduce, slight **7** neglect, take off **8** belittle, derogate, decrease, diminish, knock off, mark down, markdown, minimize, overlook, roll back, rollback, subtract, take away **9** abatement, deduction, disregard, reduction, substract, underrate **13** underestimate

discountenance 4 faze **5** abash **6** rattle **7** frown on **8** confound, disfavor **9** deprecate, discomfit, embarrass **10** disapprove, disconcert, discourage

discourage 4 damp **5** daunt, check, chill, deter **6** dampen, deject, divert, hinder, impede **7** depress, inhibit, trouble **8** disfavor, dissuade, suppress **10** demoralize, dishearten

discouraging 5 bleak **7** unhappy **8** daunting **9** deterring, troubling **10** depressing **11** unfavorable, unpromising **12** unpropitious **13** disappointing, disheartening

discourse 4 talk **5** argue, essay, orate, speak, spiel, voice **6** sermon, speech, thesis **7** amplify, descant, enlarge, explain, expound, lecture **8** converse, harangue, perorate, rhetoric, speaking, treatise **9** expatiate, hold forth, monograph, sermonize, utterance **10** expression **11** interchange **12** conversation **13** verbalization *art of:* **8** rhetoric *religious:* **6** homily, sermon

discourteous 4 rude **6** unkind **7** boorish, brusque, ill-bred, uncivil, uncouth **8** impolite **10** ungracious, unmannerly **11** ill-mannered, impertinent **13** disrespectful

discover 4 espy, find, spot **5** learn **6** betray, detect, expose, reveal, unmask **7** divulge, find out, observe, unearth **8** come upon, perceive, proclaim, unshroud **9** ascertain, determine, encounter, make known **10** come across

discovery 4 find **5** trove **6** espial, strike **7** finding **8** locating, sighting **9** detection **10** revelation, unearthing

discredit 4 slur, ruin **5** doubt, shame **6** defame, malign, show up **7** asperse, degrade, put down, run down, slander, traduce **8** disgrace, ignominy **9** disparage, disrepute **10** disbelieve, opprobrium

discreditable 5 shady **6** shabby, shoddy **8** shameful, unworthy **9** degrading **10** inglorious **11** blameworthy, disgraceful, ignominious **12** contemptible, dishonorable, disreputable

discreet 4 wary **5** chary, muted, plain **6** modest, simple **7** careful, guarded, prudent, tactful **8** cautious, moderate **9** unadorned **10** controlled, reasonable, restrained **11** circumspect, considerate, unelaborate, unobtrusive **12** unnoticeable **13** unpretentious

discrepancy 3 gap **8** alterity, conflict, variance **9** disparity, otherness, variation **10** difference, divergence, divergency, unlikeness **12** disagreement **13** inconsistency

discrepant 6 unlike **7** diverse, varying **8** contrary **9** different, differing, disparate, divergent **11** conflicting, disagreeing **12** incompatible, inconsistent **13** contradictory

discrete 8 detached, distinct, separate **9** countable, different **12** disconnected **13** discontinuous, noncontinuous

discretion 4 care, tact **7** caution, reserve **8** delicacy, judgment, prudence, wariness **9** canniness, chariness, restraint **13** judiciousness

discriminate 5 judge **6** assess **7** compare, discern, make out **8** contrast, disfavor, evaluate, perceive, separate **9** segregate, tell apart **11** distinguish **13** differentiate

discriminating 6 choosy, select **7** finical, finicky **8** eclectic **9** judicious, selective **10** discerning **11** prejudicial

discrimination 5 taste **6** acumen **7** bigotry, insight **8** inequity, judgment **9** prejudice **10** astuteness, favoritism,

partiality, perception **11** discernment,
intolerance, penetration

discriminatory 6 biased **7** partial,
unequal **8** partisan **9** jaundiced **10** prejudiced **11** inequitable, predisposed

discursive 5 windy, wordy **6** chatty, prolix **7** diffuse, logical, verbose **8** rambling, tortuous **9** desultory **10** analytical, circuitous, digressive, long-winded,
meandering **11** wide-ranging

discuss 4 moot **5** argue, weigh **6** debate,
parley **7** canvass, expound **8** consider,
converse, hash over, talk over **9** elucidate, expatiate, interpret, talk about,
thrash out, ventilate **10** deliberate, toss
around *business:* **8** talk shop *lightly:*
5 bandy *thoroughly:* **7** exhaust

discussion 3 rap **4** chat, talk **6** confab,
debate, parley, powwow **7** canvass,
palaver **8** argument, colloquy **10** conference, rap session **11** bull session,
ventilation **12** conversation, deliberation **13** confabulation

discus thrower 6 Alekna (Virgilijus),
Marten (Maritza), Oerter (Al) **10** discobolus **11** Rashchupkin (Viktor)

disdain 5 abhor, scorn, scout, spurn
6 deride, refuse, reject, slight **7** contemn, despise, despite, hauteur, put
down **8** aversion, belittle, contempt,
disprize, misprize **9** antipathy **10** repugnance, undervalue

disdainful 5 aloof, proud **6** averse, lordly, snooty, uppity **7** haughty **8** arrogant,
cavalier, derisive, insolent, scorning,
spurning, superior, toplofty **11** overbearing **12** antipathetic, contemptuous,
supercilious **13** high and mighty

disease 3 bug, ill **5** upset, virus **6** blight,
malady **7** ailment, anthrax, illness,
malaise, mycosis, purpura **8** debility,
disorder, epidemic, myxedema, pandemic, sickness, syndrome, zoonoses
(plural), zoonosis **9** affection, black
lung, complaint, condition, contagion,
ill health, infection, infirmity, sclerosis
10 affliction, alteration, blackwater,
bronchitis, feebleness, impairment,
infirmness, sickliness **11** decrepitude,
derangement **13** unhealthiness *animal:*
5 mange, surra **6** rabies **7** bighead
8 enzootic, zoonosis **9** distemper,
tularemia **10** rinderpest *blood:*
8 leukemia, leukoses (plural), leukosis
cabbage: **8** clubroot *cattle:* **6** cowpox
7 foot rot, locoism, murrain **8** blackleg,
vaccinia **9** vibriosis **10** rinderpest
11 brucellosis *cereal grass:* **4** bunt, smut
5 ergot *children's:* **5** mumps **7** measles,
rubella **10** chicken pox **13** whooping
cough *citrus tree:* **8** tristeza *classifica-*

tion: **8** nosology *combining form:* **4** path
5 patho *communicable:* **4** mono
5 mumps, polio **6** dengue, herpes,
plague, rabies **7** cholera, leprosy,
malaria, measles, rubella, tetanus,
typhoid **8** impetigo **9** hepatitis, influenza **10** giardiasis **12** tuberculosis *deficiency:* **6** scurvy **7** rickets **8** beriberi, pellagra *disseminator:* **6** vector **7** carrier *eye:*
8 glaucoma, trachoma **9** retinitis *hair
follicle:* **7** sycoses (plural), sycosis *heart:*
11 cardiopathy *horse:* **6** nagana, spavin
7 locosim, sarcoid **8** glanders **9** strangles *identification of:* **9** diagnosis *industrial:* **10** byssinosis *infectious:* **4** mono,
yaws **6** dengue, typhus **7** leprosy, malaria, tetanus, typhoid **9** tularemia, vibriosis **10** rinderpest **13** whooping cough
liver: **9** cirrhosis, hepatitis *livestock:*
7 locoism **9** vibriosis **10** rinderpest *lung:*
8 phthisic, phthisis **9** pneumonia
10 byssinosis **12** tuberculosis *lymph
glands:* **8** scrofula *metabolic:* **4** gout
nervous system: **4** kuru **6** rabies **10** diphtheria *of beets:* **8** heartrot *of mammals:*
6 rabies **7** malaria **9** distemper
10 babesiosis, rinderpest *parasitic:* **3** rot
4 smut **5** mange **7** malaria **8** hookworm,
kala-azar **9** heartworm *plant:* **4** rust,
scab, smut, wilt **5** blast, edema, scald,
scurf, stunt **6** blight, blotch, canker,
mosaic, streak **7** blister, crinkle, foot
rot, frogeye, red leaf, root rot **8** clubroot, curly top, fusarium, gummosis,
leaf curl, leaf roll, leaf rust, leaf spot,
ring spot, root knot, stem rust
9 chlorosis, crown gall, white rust
10 blackheart, leaf scorch *poultry:*
8 leukosis *respiratory:* **6** asthma, coryza
10 byssinosis *sheep:* **3** gid **7** scrapie
9 vibriosis **10** bluetongue *skin:* **4** acne,
yaws **5** favus, hives, lupus, mange,
pinta, tinea **6** eczema, tetter **7** leprosy,
prurigo, sarcoid, scabies **8** impetigo,
miliaria, pyoderma, ringworm, vitiligo
9 pemphigus, psoriasis **10** erysipelas
11 scleroderma *syphilitic:* **5** tabes *throat:*
5 croup *thyroid:* **6** struma *tropical:*
4 yaws **5** pinta, sprue, surra **6** dengue
8 kala-azar *venereal:* **8** syphilis **9** chancroid, gonorrhea *viral:* **3** flu **4** AIDS,
noma **5** Ebola, mumps, polio **6** dengue,
grippe, herpes, rabies, zoster **7** measles,
rubella, rubeola, variola **8** morbilli,
shingles, smallpox **9** hepatitis, influenza, varicella **10** poliomyelitis

diseased 3 ill **6** ailing, infirm, sickly,
unwell **7** fevered, unsound **8** feverish,
infected

disembark 4 land **6** alight **7** deplane,
detrain **8** go ashore

disembarrass 3 rid 4 free 7 release, relieve 8 liberate, unburden, untangle 9 extricate 11 disencumber, disentangle

disembodied 7 ghostly 8 ethereal, spectral 9 asomatous, unfleshly 10 immaterial, unphysical, wraithlike 11 incorporeal, nonmaterial, nonphysical 13 insubstantial

disembogue 4 flow, gush, pour, spew 5 empty 7 pour out 9 discharge

disembowel 3 gut 10 eviscerate, exenterate

disenchanted 5 blasé, jaded 6 soured 7 cynical 9 jaundiced 10 undeceived 11 worldly-wise 12 disappointed, dissatisfied 13 disenthralled, disillusioned

disencumber 4 free 7 lighten, release, relieve, sort out 8 free from, liberate, unburden 9 alleviate, disburden, extricate

disengage 4 free, part 5 loose, unfix 6 detach, opt out, unbind 7 back out, drop out, release, unloose 8 cut loose, liberate, separate, uncouple, unfasten, unloosen, withdraw 10 disconnect

disentangle 5 untie 6 detach 7 resolve, sort out, unravel, unsnarl, untwine 8 separate 9 extricate 10 unscramble 11 disencumber 13 straighten out

disenthrall 4 free 7 manumit, release 8 liberate 10 emancipate

disfavor 7 dislike 8 aversion, distrust, mistrust 9 deprecate, disesteem, disregard, disrepute 10 disrespect 11 disapproval 12 disadvantage, unpopularity

disfigure 3 mar 4 maim, scar 6 deface, defile, deform, impair, injure, mangle 7 blemish, distort 8 mutilate

disfranchise 3 bar 7 exclude 8 take away 9 deprive of 10 disentitle

disgorge 4 barf, spew 5 belch, eject, eruct, erupt, expel, vomit 6 give up, irrupt, spit up 7 release, throw up, upchuck 9 discharge

disgrace 5 odium, shame 6 stigma 7 attaint, mortify, obloquy 8 black eye, contempt, dishonor, ignominy, reproach 9 discredit, disrepute, humiliate 10 opprobrium, stigmatize 11 degradation, humiliation

disgraceful 7 ignoble 8 shameful 9 degrading 10 deplorable, inglorious, unbecoming 11 humiliating, ignominious, reproachful 12 dishonorable, disreputable

disgruntled 5 vexed 6 cranky, put out 7 annoyed, beefing, griping 8 grousing 9 irritated 10 discontent, displeased, ill-humored, malcontent 11 ungratified 12 discontented, malcontented

disguise 4 hide, mask, sham, veil 5 belie, cloak, feign, put on 6 facade 7 conceal, falsify, obscure 8 artifice, pretense 9 deception 10 camouflage, false front, pretension 12 misrepresent

disguised 6 masked, veiled 7 cloaked, feigned 9 incognito 10 undercover 11 camouflaged

disguisement 4 mask, veil 5 cloak, front 6 facade 8 pretense 9 deception 10 false front, pretention

disgust 6 nausea, offend, revolt, sicken 8 aversion, gross out, loathing, nauseate 9 antipathy, repulsion, revulsion 10 abhorrence, repugnance 13 squeamishness

disgusted 5 fed up 8 offended, repelled, repulsed, revolted, sickened 9 nauseated, squeamish 10 grossed out

disgusting 4 foul, icky, vile 5 gross, nasty, yucky 7 noisome 9 loathsome, offensive, repellent, repugnant, repulsive, revolting, sickening 10 nauseating

dish 4 bowl, buzz, food, talk, tray 5 plate 6 course, gossip, tureen 7 chatter, hearsay, platter, scandal, slander 9 casserole, container 11 scuttlebutt *baked:* 7 soufflé *baking:* 7 cocotte, scallop 9 casserole 12 scallop shell *cheese:* 6 fondue 7 ramekin, rarebit 8 raclette, ramequin *Chinese:* 6 dim sum, lo mein, subgum, wonton 8 chop suey, chow mein 10 egg foo yong, egg foo yung 11 egg foo young *deep:* 9 casserole *Hungarian:* 7 goulash *Italian:* 5 penne, pesto, pizza 6 scampi 7 cannoli, lasagna, polenta, ravioli 8 calamari, linguine, linguini, osso buco, rigatoni 9 foccacia, manicotti 10 cannelloni, scaloppine, tortellini 11 saltimbocca *Japanese:* 7 sashimi, tempura 8 sukiyaki *Mexican:* 4 taco 5 chili 6 fajita, flauta, nachos, tamale 7 burrito, chalupa 8 frijoles 9 enchilada, guacamole 10 carne asada 11 chimichanga 12 refried beans 13 chili con carne *Middle Eastern:* 5 halva, kebab, kibbe, kibbi 6 halvah, hummus, kibbeh 7 baklava, falafel 8 couscous, moussaka 10 shish kebab 11 baba ghanouj 12 baba ghanoush *principal:* 6 entrée *rice:* 7 risotto *rice and meat:* 5 pilaf *Scottish:* 5 brose 6 haggis *shallow:* 6 saucer *Thai:* 7 pad thai

disharmonize 3 jar, war 5 clash 6 jangle 7 discord 8 conflict, mismatch 9 disaccord

disharmony 6 strife 7 discord 8 conflict, disunion, disunity, friction, variance 9 cacophony 10 contention, difference, dissension, dissonance

dishearten 3 cow 5 chill, crush, daunt, shake 6 dampen, deject, dismay, sadden 7 depress, unnerve 8 dispirit, distress 10 demoralize, discourage, intimidate

disheartening 8 daunting 9 dismaying, saddening 10 depressing 11 dispiriting 12 demoralizing, discouraging, intimidating

dishes 4 ware *clay:* 7 pottery *porcelain:* 5 china

dishevel 5 touse 6 muss up, rumple, tousle 8 disarray, disorder 10 disarrange, discompose

disheveled 5 messy 7 ruffled, rumpled, tousled, unkempt 8 ill-kempt, mussed up, uncombed 10 disarrayed, disordered 11 discomposed

dishonest 5 false, lying, rogue, snide 6 tricky, unfair 7 corrupt, crooked, knavish 8 cheating, cozening, two-faced 9 deceitful, deceiving, deceptive, swindling 10 defrauding, fraudulent, mendacious, untruthful 13 double-dealing, untrustworthy

dishonesty 5 fraud, guile 6 deceit 7 falsity, knavery, roguery 8 flimflam, pretense, trickery 9 chicanery, deception, duplicity, falsehood, hypocrisy 10 corruption 11 crookedness 13 double-dealing

dishonor see DISGRACE

dishonorable see DISGRACEFUL

dish out 5 ladle, serve 6 pile on, supply 7 deliver, present, serve up 8 allocate, disburse, dispense 10 distribute

disillusioned see DISENCHANTED

disinclination 7 dislike 8 aversion, distaste 9 antipathy, objection 10 reluctance 13 indisposition, unwillingness

disinclined 5 loath 6 averse 7 balking, opposed 8 boggling, hesitant 9 reluctant, resistant, unwilling 10 hesitating, indisposed 12 antipathetic 13 unsympathetic

disinfect 6 purify 8 sanitize 9 autoclave, sterilize 13 decontaminate

disingenuous 3 sly 4 foxy, wily 5 false 6 artful, crafty, tricky 7 cunning, devious, feigned 8 delusive, guileful, indirect, specious 9 deceitful, deceiving, deceptive, dishonest, insidious, insincere, sophistic 10 misleading 11 calculating, casuistical, sophistical

disinherit 6 cut off 7 bereave, exclude 9 deprive of, repudiate 10 dispossess

disintegrate 3 rot 4 turn 5 break, burst, decay, spoil, taint 6 molder 7 crumble, scatter, shatter 8 splinter 9 break down, decompose, fall apart 10 deliquesce

disinter 5 dig up 6 exhume, unbury 7 unearth 8 exhumate 9 resurrect

disinterest 6 apathy 7 neglect 8 coolness, lethargy 9 aloofness, disregard, unconcern 10 detachment, dispassion, neutrality 11 impassivity, inattention, insouciance, nonchalance, objectivity 12 indifference

disinterested 4 fair, just 5 aloof 6 candid 7 neutral 8 detached, unbiased 9 impartial, impassive, incurious, objective 10 even-handed, impersonal, neglectful, nonchalant 11 inattentive, indifferent, unconcerned

disjoin 4 part 5 sever, unfix 6 detach, divide, sunder, unlink 7 break up, divorce 8 disunite, separate, uncouple, unfasten 9 disengage, take apart 10 dissociate 12 disaffiliate, disassociate

disjointed 7 jumbled, muddled 8 confused, inchoate, rambling 9 displaced 10 disordered, incoherent, incohesive 11 unconnected, unorganized 13 discontinuous

disk 4 puck 5 wafer 6 record *metal:* 4 slug *ornamental:* 6 bangle, sequin

dislike 4 hate, shun 5 abhor, scorn, spurn 6 animus, detest, loathe, oppose, reject, resent 7 deplore, despise, frown on 8 aversion, disfavor, distaste, execrate 9 animosity, antipathy 10 alienation, disapprove, repugnance 11 detestation, disapproval 13 indisposition

dislimn 3 dim 5 bedim 6 darken 7 becloud, obscure 9 obfuscate

dislocate 5 break 7 disrupt, unhinge 9 disengage 10 disconnect 13 disarticulate

dislodge 4 oust 5 eject, evict, expel 6 remove, uproot 8 displace, drive out, force out

disloyal 5 false 6 untrue 8 apostate, recreant 9 alienated, faithless 10 perfidious, traitorous, unfaithful 11 disaffected, treacherous

disloyalty 7 falsity, perfidy, treason 8 apostasy 9 falseness, recreancy, treachery 10 alienation, infidelity 12 disaffection 13 faithlessness

dismal 5 bleak 6 dreary, gloomy, horrid, somber, sombre 7 joyless 8 desolate, dreadful, funereal, lowering 9 atrocious, cheerless, depressed, tenebrous 10 depressing, depressive 11 dispiriting 12 discouraging 13 disheartening

dismantle 4 raze, undo 5 strip, unrig, wreck 6 denude, divest 7 break up, destroy 8 demolish, pull down, take down 9 break down, knock down, take apart 11 disassemble

dismay 4 faze, fear 5 abash, alarm, daunt, dread, panic, scare, shake, upset 6 appall, fright, horror, rattle 7 agitate, fluster, horrify, perturb, unnerve 8 affright, bewilder, confound, dispirit, distress, frighten 9 discomfit, dumbfound, embarrass 10 discompose, disconcert, discourage, dishearten 11 trepidation 12 perturbation 13 consternation

dismayed 5 upset 6 afraid, aghast, scared, shaken 7 fearful, shocked 9 disturbed

dismember 4 maim 7 disjoin 8 mutilate 9 dismantle, take apart

dismiss 3 axe, can 4 drop, fire, oust, sack, shed 5 chuck, eject, evict, let go, scorn, spurn 6 bounce, depose, deride, lay off, reject, remove, retire, shelve, unseat 7 boot out, cashier, contemn, decline, disband, kick out, kiss off, turn off 8 displace, furlough, pooh-pooh, ridicule, throw out, turn away, turn down 9 discharge, repudiate, terminate 11 send packing

dismissal 5 congé 6 firing, layoff, ouster 7 removal 8 brush-off, bum's rush 9 discharge, expulsion 10 cashiering

dismount 6 alight, debark, get off 7 deplane, detrain 9 disembark 10 alight from 11 descend from

Disney, Walt 10 cartoonist *character:* 4 Gyro, Huey, Lady 5 Ariel, Bambi, Daisy, Dewey, Dumbo, Goofy, Louie, Mulan, Pluto, Simba, Tramp 6 Beauty, Donald, Mickey, Minnie, Mowgli 7 Aladdin, Scrooge 9 Gladstone, Pinocchio 10 Beagle Boys, Clarabelle, Pocahontas *classic:* 5 Bambi, Dumbo 8 Fantasia 9 Pinocchio 10 Jungle Book (The) 15 Lady and the Tramp

disobedient 6 unruly 7 naughty, wayward, willful 8 contrary 10 headstrong, ill-behaved, rebellious, refractory, uncompliant 11 misbehaving 12 contumacious, noncompliant, obstreperous, recalcitrant 13 insubordinate

disoblige 5 annoy 6 bother, offend, put out 7 affront, disturb, trouble 9 displease, incommode 10 discommode 13 inconvenience

disorder 3 ill 4 mess, riot 5 chaos, mix up, snarl, upset 6 ataxia, hubbub, jumble, malady, mess up, muddle, muss up, ruckus, rumple, tumble, tumult, unrest, uproar 7 ailment, anarchy, clutter, confuse, disease, embroil, illness, misdeed, shuffle, turmoil 8 disarray, sickness, syndrome, unsettle, upheaval 9 affection, agitation, commotion, complaint, confusion, infirmity 10 affliction, turbulence, untidiness *mental:* 5 mania 8 delirium, insanity, neurosis, paranoia 9 psychosis 11 psychopathy 13 schizophrenia

disordered 6 roiled 7 jumbled, muddled 8 confused, inchoate, shuffled 9 displaced 10 disjointed, dislocated, incoherent, incohesive 11 disarranged, unconnected, unorganized 13 discontinuous

disorderly 5 rowdy 6 unruly, untidy 7 jumbled, raucous, unkempt 8 confused 9 cluttered, offensive, turbulent 10 boisterous, topsy-turvy, tumultuous 12 disorganized, rambunctious, unsystematic

disorganize 5 upset 6 jumble, mess up 7 break up, confuse, derange, disband, disrupt 8 disorder, disperse, unsettle 10 disarrange

disoriented 4 lost 7 mixed up 8 confused 9 displaced, perplexed, unsettled 10 bewildered

disown 4 deny, dump 6 desert, reject 7 cast off, disavow 8 disclaim, renounce 9 repudiate

disparage 5 decry 6 defame, slight 7 condemn, degrade, devalue, dismiss, put down, run down 8 bad-mouth, belittle, derogate, discount, downplay, minimize, pooh-pooh 9 denigrate, deprecate, discredit, dispraise, downgrade, underrate 10 demoralize, depreciate, undervalue 11 detract from

disparagement 5 scorn 7 calumny, censure, despite, scandal, slander 8 contempt, despisal, reproach 9 aspersion, discredit, stricture 10 backbiting, defamation, derogation, detraction, diminution 11 degradation 12 backstabbing, depreciation 13 animadversion

disparate 6 at odds, divers, unlike, varied 7 diverse, unalike, unequal, various, varying 8 discrete, distinct, separate 9 different, divergent, unsimilar 10 dissimilar 11 distinctive, incongruous, inconsonant 12 incompatible, inconsistent

disparity 3 gap 8 contrast 9 imbalance 10 difference, divergence, divergency, inequality 11 discrepancy 13 disproportion, dissimilarity

dispassionate 4 calm, fair, just 7 neutral 8 composed, detached, unbiased 9 equitable, impartial, objective, unruffled 10 impersonal 11 unemotional 12 unprejudiced 13 disinterested

dispatch 4 kill, send, ship, slay 5 haste, hurry, scrag, speed 6 defeat, murder 7 bump off, execute, forward, killing, message, put away 8 alacrity, get rid of, shipment, transmit 9 dispose of, eliminate, swiftness 10 expedition, put to death, speediness 11 assassinate, promptitude

dispel 6 banish 7 cast out, scatter 8 disperse 9 clear away, dissipate, drive away

dispensable 5 minor 7 trivial 8 needless,

unneeded 10 disposable, expendable, unrequired 11 superfluous, unessential, unimportant, unnecessary 12 nonessential

dispensary 6 clinic

dispensation 4 plan 5 favor, share 7 license, portion, service 8 bestowal, courtesy, kindness, ordering 9 allotment, exception, exemption, privilege, remission 10 indulgence, management 12 disbursement, distribution 13 apportionment, authorization

dispense 5 allot, apply, wield 6 assign, divide, excuse, exempt, ration, supply 7 absolve, deal out, deliver, dish out, dole out, furnish, give out, mete out, portion, provide, release 8 allocate, carry out, disburse, share out, transfer 9 apportion, discharge, partition 10 administer, distribute, measure out, portion out

disperse 3 sow 5 spray, strew 6 dispel, divide, spread, vanish 7 break up, diffuse, disband, radiate, scatter 8 broadcast, dissipate, partition, propagate 10 distribute

dispersion 6 spread 7 breakup, colloid 9 diffusion, spreading 10 scattering 11 dissipation 12 distribution 13 dissemination

dispirit 3 cow 5 chill, daunt 6 deject, dismay, sadden 7 depress, oppress 8 distress 10 demoralize, discourage, dishearten

dispirited 3 low, sad 4 blue, down, glum 5 cowed 6 morose 7 daunted 8 cast down, dejected, dismayed, downcast, saddened 9 bummed out, depressed, oppressed, woebegone 10 distressed, melancholy 11 crestfallen, demoralized, discouraged, downhearted 12 disconsolate, disheartened

dispiriting 4 blue 6 dismal, dreary, gloomy 8 daunting, dolorous, funereal 9 cheerless, dismaying, saddening 10 depressing, oppressive 12 demoralizing, disconsolate, discouraging 13 disheartening

displace 4 oust, sack 5 exile, expel, usurp 6 banish, deport, depose, remove 7 succeed 8 dethrone, supplant 9 supersede, transport 10 expatriate, substitute

display 4 pomp, show 5 array, model 6 evince, expose, flaunt, lay out, parade, reveal, spread, unfold, unfurl, unveil 7 exhibit, panoply, present, showing, show off, trot out, uncover 8 brandish, evidence, manifest, showcase 9 showiness, spectacle 10 exhibiting, exhibition 11 demonstrate, ostentation 13 demonstration, manifestation

displeasing 6 vexing 7 irksome 8 annoying 10 bothersome, unpleasant 12 disagreeable 13 objectionable

displeasure 8 aversion, disfavor, vexation 9 annoyance 10 discomfort, discontent, irritation, uneasiness 11 indignation, unhappiness 13 indisposition

disport 4 show 5 amuse 6 acquit, behave, divert, expose, flaunt, frolic, parade 7 conduct, display, exhibit, show off, trot out 9 entertain

disposal 5 order 7 removal 8 bestowal, chucking, jettison, ordering, transfer 9 clearance 10 allocation, assignment, demolition, discarding, regulation, relegation 11 arrangement, consignment, destruction, disposition 12 distribution, transference

dispose 4 bend, bias, rank 5 array, order, range 6 settle 7 arrange, incline, marshal, prepare 8 organize, regulate 9 make ready 11 systematize *of:* 4 dump, junk, sell 5 chuck, scrap 6 finish, handle, unload 7 deep-six, destroy, discard 8 deal with, throw out, transfer 9 eighty-six, eliminate 10 distribute

disposed 3 apt 4 fain, game 5 prone, ready 6 biased, minded 7 partial, willing 8 arranged, inclined 9 persuaded

disposition 4 bent, cast, mood, tone, type, vein 5 being, order, stamp 6 makeup, nature, temper 7 control, leaning, mind-set 8 ordering, penchant, riddance, sequence, tendency, transfer 9 character, direction 10 management, proclivity, propensity, settlement 11 arrangement, inclination, personality, temperament 12 constitution, predilection 13 individuality *favorable:* 8 optimism *unfavorable:* 9 pessimism

dispossess 3 rob 4 oust 5 eject, strip 6 divest 7 bereave, deprive

dispossession 4 loss 6 ouster 7 seizure 9 privation 10 divestment 11 deprivation, divestiture 13 expropriation

dispraise 3 pan 5 decry 6 censor, deride, dump on 7 put down, run down 8 badmouth, belittle, derogate 9 criticize, deprecate, discredit, disparage 10 depreciate, disapprove 11 detract from 12 depreciation

disproportion 8 imparity, mismatch 9 disparity 10 inequality, unevenness 12 lopsidedness

disproportionate 6 uneven 7 unequal 8 lopsided 10 unbalanced

disprove 5 belie, rebut 6 refute, negate 7 confute, explode 8 confound, overturn, puncture, traverse 9 discredit, overthrow 10 invalidate

disputable 4 iffy, moot 7 dubious

8 arguable, doubtful 9 debatable, uncertain, unsettled 10 unresolved 11 problematic 12 questionable 13 controversial

disputation 6 debate 8 argument, forensic, polemics 9 dialectic 11 controversy 13 argumentation

dispute 4 buck, duel, moot, tiff 5 argue, fight, rebut, repel 6 bicker, combat, debate, hassle, impugn, negate, oppose, refute, resist, rumpus, strife 7 confute, contend, contest, discuss, gainsay, quarrel, quibble, wrangle 8 argument, conflict, question, squabble 9 bickering, challenge, thrash out, withstand 10 contention, controvert, falling-out 11 altercation, controversy, embroilment

disputed 7 debated 8 arguable 9 contested, uncertain 12 questionable 13 controversial

disqualified 5 unfit 8 unfitted 10 ineligible, unequipped

disqualify 3 bar 5 debar 6 except 7 exclude, rule out, suspend 9 eliminate *as judge:* 6 recuse

disquiet 5 alarm, angst, upset, worry 6 bother, flurry, unease, unrest 7 agitate, anxiety, concern, disturb, ferment, fluster, perturb, trouble, turmoil 10 discompose, uneasiness 11 disturbance, restiveness 12 restlessness 13 Sturm und Drang

disquietude 4 care 5 worry 6 unease, unrest 7 anxiety, concern, ferment, turmoil 9 agitation, misgiving 10 foreboding, uneasiness 11 nervousness, restiveness 12 apprehension, restlessness 13 Sturm und Drang

Disraeli, Benjamin *novel:* 5 Sybil 7 Lothair, Tancred 8 Endymion 9 Coningsby *opponent:* 4 Peel (Robert) 9 Gladstone (William) *queen:* 8 Victoria

disregard 6 forget, ignore, slight 7 neglect, tune out 8 overlook 9 unconcern 12 heedlessness, indifference

disregardful 3 lax 5 slack 6 remiss 8 careless, derelict, heedless 9 forgetful, unheeding, negligent, unmindful 10 neglectful, regardless, unthinking 11 indifferent, unconcerned 12 absentminded

disremember 6 forget

disreputable 4 base 5 dingy, seamy, seedy, shady 6 scurvy, shabby, shoddy, sordid 7 run-down 8 decrepit, infamous, shameful 10 inglorious 11 dilapidated, disgraceful, ignominious 12 contemptible, unprincipled 13 discreditable, unrespectable

disrepute 5 odium, shame 7 obloquy

8 disfavor, disgrace, dishonor, ignominy 9 disesteem 10 opprobrium

disrespect 6 insult 7 disdain 8 boldness, contempt, rudeness 9 disregard, flippancy, impudence, insolence 10 incivility 11 discourtesy, presumption 12 impertinence, impoliteness

disrespectful 4 flip, rude 5 sassy, saucy 7 ill-bred, uncivil 8 flippant, impolite, impudent, insolent 10 ungracious 11 ill-mannered, impertinent 12 contemptuous, discourteous

disrobe 4 bare, peel 5 strip 6 denude, divest 7 undress 8 unclothe

disrupt 5 upset 6 mess up 7 break up, rupture 8 disorder, unsettle

dissatisfaction 6 dismay 9 annoyance, complaint 10 discontent, irritation, uneasiness 11 displeasure, frustration

dissatisfied 5 irked, vexed 7 annoyed 8 bothered 10 begrudging, discontent, displeased, malcontent 11 complaining, disaffected, unfulfilled 12 disappointed, discontented, malcontented

dissect 5 probe, study 7 analyze, examine, inspect 9 anatomize, break down, take apart 10 scrutinize

dissection 7 autopsy 8 analysis, necropsy *of animals:* 7 zootomy

dissemble 4 hide, mask 5 cloak, feign 7 conceal, cover up, dress up, falsify 8 disguise, simulate 9 whitewash 10 camouflage 11 counterfeit

dissembler 4 fake 5 faker, fraud, phony 8 deceiver, imposter, impostor, pharisee 9 hypocrite, pretender

disseminate 3 sow 5 strew 6 blazon, spread 7 bestrew, diffuse, publish, scatter, send out 8 announce, disperse, proclaim 9 advertise, broadcast, circulate, propagate, publicize 10 promulgate

dissension 5 fight 6 strife 7 discord, dispute, faction, quarrel, wrangle 8 argument, clashing, conflict, disunity, friction, variance 9 bickering 10 contention, difference, quarreling 11 altercation, controversy 12 disagreement

dissent 5 demur 6 differ, heresy, object 8 conflict, variance 9 misbelief 10 contention, difference, heterodoxy, opposition, resistance 11 unorthodoxy 12 nonagreement 13 nonconformism, nonconformity

dissenter 7 heretic 8 apostate, defector, deserter, partisan, recreant 10 schismatic, separatist 11 misbeliever, schismatist 13 nonconformist

dissertation 6 thesis 8 tractate, treatise 9 discourse, monograph 10 commentary, exposition 11 disputation 12 disquisition 13 argumentation

disservice 4 harm **6** damage, injury, insult **8** disfavor, meanness, mischief **9** detriment **10** misfortune

dissever 3 cut, hew **4** hack, part **5** carve, slice, split **6** cleave, detach, divide, sunder **7** disjoin, divorce **8** disjoint, disunite, separate, uncouple **10** disconnect

dissidence 6 heresy, schism, strife **7** discord, dispute, dissent, faction **8** conflict, friction, variance **10** contention, disharmony, dissension, heterodoxy, opposition **11** discordance, unorthodoxy **12** disagreement **13** nonconformism, nonconformity

dissident 7 heretic **8** partisan, recusant **9** differing, dissenter, heretical, heterodox, protestor **10** schismatic, separatist, unorthodox **11** contentious, disagreeing, misbeliever, nonbeliever, quarrelsome, schismatist **12** disputatious, unharmonious **13** nonconformist

dissimilar 6 unlike **7** diverse, unalike, unequal, various **8** distinct **9** different, disparate, divergent **13** heterogeneous

dissimilarity 8 contrast, variance **9** disparity, diversity, variation **10** difference, divergence, divergency, unlikeness **11** incongruity **13** heterogeneity, inconsistency

dissimulate see DISSEMBLE

dissimulation 5 fraud, guile, lying **6** deceit **7** cunning **8** artifice, flimflam, pretense **9** deception, duplicity, hypocrisy, mendacity, sophistry **10** craftiness, pharisaism **11** beguilement, smoke screen

dissipate 4 blow **5** use up, waste **6** burn up, spread, vanish **7** break up, scatter **8** disperse, evanesce, melt away, misspend, squander **9** evaporate, throw away **11** fritter away

dissipated 6 rakish, wanton, wasted **8** depraved **9** debauched, reprobate **10** degenerate, licentious, profligate **11** intemperate

dissociate 4 part **5** unfix **6** cut off, detach **7** disband, disjoin **8** alienate, disunite, estrange, separate, uncouple **9** disengage **10** disconnect

dissolute 3 lax **4** fast, wild **5** loose, slack **6** rakish, wanton **7** raffish, wayward **8** decadent, depraved **9** abandoned, debauched, indulgent, reprobate **10** degenerate, dissipated, licentious, profligate **12** unprincipled, unrestrained

dissolution 5 death, decay, split **6** demise **7** breakup, divorce, rupture, split-up **8** division **9** dispersal, partition **10** detachment, disbanding, profligacy **11** evaporation **12** liquefaction

dissolvable 7 soluble **8** meltable

dissolve 3 end **4** flux, melt, thaw, undo, void **5** annul, quash **6** recess, vacate, vanish **7** adjourn, break up, destroy, diffuse, disband, liquefy, resolve, shatter, unravel **8** abrogate, demolish, disperse, evanesce, fade away, get rid of, melt away, prorogue, separate **9** decompose, dissipate, evaporate, prorogate, terminate, waste away **10** deliquesce, do away with **12** disintegrate

dissonance 6 strife **7** discord **8** clashing, conflict **9** cacophony, harshness **10** contention, difference, disharmony **11** incongruity **12** disagreement **13** inconsistency

dissonant 5 harsh **7** grating, jarring, raucous **8** strident **9** unmusical **10** cacophonic, discordant, inharmonic **11** cacophonous, conflicting, incongruous **12** incompatible, inharmonious

dissuade 5 deter **7** turn off **10** discourage, disincline

distaff 6 female **8** maternal

distance 4 area **5** ambit, lapse, orbit, range, reach, scope, space, sweep **6** course, degree, extent, length, radius, remove, spread **7** breadth, compass, expanse, horizon, mileage, reserve, spacing, stretch **8** coldness, interval **9** amplitude, disparity, expansion, extension **10** divergence, divergency, remoteness, separation **11** distinction, perspective **13** dissimilarity *angular:* **8** latitude **9** longitude *between levels:* **4** drop *between rails:* **4** gage *between supports:* **4** span *from bottom to top:* **6** height *geometric:* **8** altitude *greatest perpendicular:* **6** camber *measuring instrument:* **8** odometer **9** pedometer, telemeter **11** range finder *minute:* **4** hair *perpendicular:* **5** depth *shortest:* **7** beeline **12** straight line *the wind blows:* **5** fetch

distant 3 far, shy **4** afar, cold, cool **5** aloof, apart **6** absent, far-off, remote **7** faraway, haughty, obscure, removed, spacial, spatial **8** far-flung, isolated, outlying, reserved, secluded, solitary **9** separated, unsimilar, withdrawn **10** unsociable **11** out-of-the-way, sequestered, standoffish *combining form:* **3** tel **4** tele, telo

distaste 7 disgust, dislike **8** aversion, loathing **9** antipathy, hostility, revulsion **10** abhorrence, repugnance **13** indisposition

distasteful 8 unsavory **9** loathsome, obnoxious, offensive, repellent, repugnant, repulsive **10** abominable, unpleasant **11** displeasing, unpalatable **12** disagreeable, unappetizing **13** objectionable

distemper 6 malady **7** ailment, disease **8** disorder **9** contagion, strangles **10** affliction **11** derangement **13** panleucopenia

distend 5 bloat, bulge, swell, widen **6** dilate, expand, extend, puff up **7** amplify, augment, enlarge, inflate, stretch **8** increase, lengthen **10** stretch out

distill 6 refine **7** extract **8** boil down **11** concentrate, precipitate

distinct 4 sole **5** clear, lucid, plain **6** marked, patent, single, unique **7** audible, defined, diverse, evident, express, notable, obvious, special, unusual **8** apparent, clear-cut, definite, discrete, especial, explicit, manifest, palpable, peculiar, separate, specific **9** different, divergent **10** individual, noticeable, particular **11** categorical, unambiguous, unequivocal **12** unmistakable

distinction 4 bays, rank **5** award, badge, grade, honor, kudos **6** nicety, renown **7** laurels **8** accolade, eminence, prestige **10** difference, divergence, divergency, prominence, unlikeness **11** differentia, peculiarity, preeminence, recognition **12** significance **13** dissimilarity

distinctive 6 proper, single, unique **7** special **8** peculiar, separate, singular **10** individual **13** idiosyncratic

distingué 6 classy, urbane **7** courtly, elegant, eminent, genteel, refined **8** cultured, decorous, highbrow, mannerly, polished, well-bred **9** dignified, highclass **10** cultivated **13** sophisticated

distinguish 4 mark, note, spot, view **5** honor, place **6** descry, notice, set off **7** dignify, make out, mark off, observe, pick out **8** classify, identify, perceive, separate **9** recognize, single out **10** categorize **12** characterize, discriminate **13** differentiate, individualize

distinguished 5 famed, noted **6** famous **7** eminent, notable, stately **8** esteemed, imposing, renowned **9** dignified, prominent **10** celebrated **11** illustrious

distort 4 bend, warp, wind **5** alter, color, twist **6** deform, garble **7** contort, falsify, pervert, torture **8** misstate **11** misconstrue **12** misinterpret, misrepresent

distortion 8 twisting **9** deformity

distract 5 addle, mix up **6** ball up, bemuse, divert, puzzle **7** confuse, fluster, mislead, perplex **8** befuddle, bewilder, confound, throw off **9** sidetrack, unbalance

distracted 8 confused, deranged, maddened, troubled **9** oblivious **10** non-

plussed **11** disoriented, inattentive, preoccupied **12** absentminded

distraction 5 upset **9** agitation, amusement, confusion, diversion **10** perplexity **12** interruption **13** entertainment

distrait 5 upset **7** anxious, bemused, faraway, worried **8** confused, deranged, harassed, maddened, troubled **9** tormented, withdrawn **10** abstracted, distracted, distraught **11** inattentive, preoccupied **12** absentminded, apprehensive

distraught 5 upset **6** addled, crazed **7** anxious, frantic, muddled, rattled, shook up, unglued, worried **8** agitated, confused, demented, deranged, frenzied, harassed, troubled, worked up **9** flustered, perturbed, tormented, wigged-out **10** distressed, bewildered, freaked out, nonplussed **11** overwrought

distress 3 ail, irk, mar, try, vex, woe **4** ache, care, hurt, pain, pang, rack **5** agony, annoy, cross, dolor, grief, rigor, throe, trial, upset, worry **6** bother, grieve, harass, misery, pester, plague, sorrow, strain, strait, twinge **7** afflict, anguish, anxiety, exhaust, torment, torture, trouble **8** aggrieve, calamity, exigency, hardship **9** adversity, constrain, hard times, suffering **10** affliction, difficulty, heartbreak, misfortune, visitation **11** tribulation, vicissitude *call:* **6** Mayday *signal:* **3** SOS **5** alarm

distressing 4 dire **6** woeful **8** alarming, grievous, shocking **9** offensive **10** deplorable, lamentable **11** dispiriting, regrettable, unfortunate **13** heartbreaking

distribute 4 deal, mete **5** allot, place, strew **6** assign, assort, divide, donate, parcel, ration, spread **7** deal out, deliver, diffuse, dish out, divvy up, dole out, dribble, give out, hand out, mete out, prorate, radiate, scatter, slice up **8** allocate, classify, disburse, dispense, position, separate **9** apportion, circulate, partition, propagate, spread out **10** administer, measure out **11** disseminate *in a tournament:* **4** seed

distribution 7 density **8** delivery, dividend, grouping, ordering, sequence **9** allotment, allotting, diffusion, dispersal, marketing, placement, spreading **10** dispersion, scattering **11** arrangement, probability, propagation **12** apportioning, dispensation **13** apportionment, dissemination

distributor 5 agent **6** broker, jobber **7** carrier **10** wholesaler **12** intermediate

district 4 area, ward **5** tract **6** barrio, locale, parcel, region, sector **7** borough, quarter, section **8** division, locality, precinct, vicinage, vicinity **11** subdivision **12** neighborhood *ecclesiastical:* **5** synod **6** parish **7** diocese *Greek:* **4** deme *Indian:* **6** tahsil *judicial:* **7** circuit *London:* **4** Soho **7** Chelsea, Mayfair **9** Docklands, Greenwich, Southwark **10** Kensington, Piccadilly **11** Canary Wharf, Notting Hill **13** Knightsbridge *New York:* **4** Soho **7** Chelsea, Tribeca *theater:* **6** rialto

District of Columbia *college, university:* **6** Howard **8** American, Catholic **9** Gallaudet **10** Georgetown *motto:* **13** E Pluribus Unum *official bird:* **10** wood thrush *official flower:* **18** American Beauty rose

distrust 5 doubt **7** suspect **8** question, wariness **9** disbelief, discredit, misgiving, suspicion **10** disbelieve

distrustful 4 wary **5** chary, leery **7** cynical, dubious, jealous **8** doubtful, doubting **10** suspicious **12** questionable

distrusting 4 wary **5** chary, leery **7** cynical, dubious, jealous **8** doubtful, doubting **10** suspicious

disturb 4 faze **5** alarm, daunt, rouse, upset, worry **6** bother, harass, meddle, mess up, pester, stir up **7** agitate, break up, disrupt, fluster, perplex, trouble, unnerve **8** bewilder, distress, unsettle **9** incommode, interrupt **10** discompose, disconcert, tamper with **13** inconvenience, interfere with

disturbance 4 flap, fuss, stir, to-do **5** stink **6** clamor, hubbub, rumpus, tumult, unrest, uproar **7** bobbery, turmoil **8** disorder **9** agitation, commotion, confusion **10** alteration, disruption, turbulence **11** derangement, distraction **12** interruption *atmospheric:* **5** storm **7** cyclone, tornado **9** hurricane *mental:* **6** frenzy **8** delirium, neurosis **9** psychosis *oceanic:* **7** tsunami

disturbed 5 upset **6** insane, shaken **7** anxious, puzzled, rattled, worried **8** bothered, demented, deranged, troubled **9** concerned, psychotic, unsettled **10** distracted, distressed **12** disconcerted

disunion 7 divorce, rupture, split-up **8** division, severing, variance **9** partition **10** detachment, difference, separation **13** disconnection

disunite 4 part **6** divide, sunder **7** break up, disjoin, divorce, split up **8** dissever, separate, uncouple **9** disengage, fall apart **10** disconnect **12** disaffiliate

disunity 6 strife, schism **7** discord **8** conflict, division, variance **10** alienation, contention, disharmony, dissension **12** disaffection, disagreement, estrangement

disused 5 passé **8** obsolete, outdated, outmoded **9** abandoned, discarded **10** antiquated, superseded

ditch 4 dig, pit **4** drop, dump, foss, junk, moat **5** chuck, fosse, leave, scrap, swale **6** reject, trench, trough **7** abandon, cashier, discard, dismiss, forsake, foxhole **8** jettison, throw out **9** crash-land, dispose of, throw away **10** excavation

dither 4 fuss, stew **5** quake, shake, tizzy, waver **6** falter, flurry, quaver, shiver **7** flutter, tremble, twitter, whiffle **8** hesitate **9** agitation, commotion, confusion, vacillate **10** excitement, turbulence **12** shilly-shally

dithyramb 4 hymn, poem **5** chant

dithyrambic 6 ardent, fervid **9** perfervid, rhapsodic **10** boisterous, passionate **11** impassioned

ditto 4 copy, same **5** clone, me too, Xerox **6** carbon, repeat **7** replica, reprint, similar **9** duplicate, facsimile, photocopy **10** carbon copy, mimeograph **11** replication **12** reproduction **13** reduplication

ditty 3 air, lay **4** song, tune **5** carol, chant **6** ballad

diurnal 5 daily **7** daytime **8** daylight **9** circadian, ephemeral, quotidian

diva 7 goddess **10** prima donna **11** leading lady

divagate 4 turn, veer **5** drift, stray **6** depart, ramble, wander **7** deviate, digress, diverge

divan 4 sofa **5** couch **6** settee **7** chamber, council **9** davenport **12** chesterfield

dive 3 bar, pub **4** dash, dump, hole, jump, leap **5** joint, lunge, pitch, sound, swoop **6** header, lounge, plunge, saloon, tavern **7** barroom, decline, descend, descent, hangout, plummet, taproom **8** submerge **9** honky-tonk, roadhouse **10** cannonball *type:* **4** pike, swan, tuck **6** gainer **7** cutaway **9** belly flop, jackknife

diver 4 loon

diverge 4 part, vary **5** stray **6** depart, differ, swerve **7** deflect, deviate, digress **8** disagree, separate **9** bifurcate, branch off, draw apart

divergence 7 parting **9** departure, deviation, differing **10** aberration, deflection, difference, digression, separation **11** disagreeing, discrepancy, distinction **12** disagreement

divergent 6 unlike **8** aberrant, abnormal,

atypical **9** anomalous, different, differing, disparate, irregular **10** dissimilar

divers 6 sundry **7** several, various **8** assorted **9** different, disparate **13** miscellaneous

diverse 5 mixed **6** motley, sundry, unlike, varied **7** several, unalike, unequal, various, varying **8** assorted, discrete, distinct, manifold, separate **9** different, differing, disparate, multiform, multiplex, unsimilar **10** contrasted, dissimilar **11** contrasting, contrastive **12** multifarious **13** contradictory, miscellaneous *meanings:* **8** polysemy

diversion 5 sport **7** pastime, turning **8** pleasure, sideshow **9** amusement, deviation, enjoyment **10** aberration, deflection, recreation, red herring **11** distraction **13** entertainment

diversity 7 variety **10** assortment, difference, unlikeness **11** variegation **12** multiformity **13** dissimilarity, heterogeneity

divert 4 turn, veer **5** amuse **6** regale, swerve **7** beguile, deflect, delight, deviate, digress **8** distract, redirect **9** entertain, turn aside

divest 3 rid, rob **4** free **5** spoil, strip **6** denude **7** bereave, deprive, despoil, disrobe, undress **8** take away **9** dismantle **10** disinherit, dispossess

divide 3 cut **4** fork, part **5** allot, cut up, sever, share **6** assign, cleave, parcel, ration, sunder **7** break up, dissect, divorce, dole out, isolate, prorate, quarter, share in, split up **8** allocate, classify, dispense, disunite, separate **9** apportion, branch out, partition, watershed **10** distribute, measure out **11** dichotomize, distinguish *into four parts:* **7** quarter *into three parts:* **7** trisect *into two parts:* **5** halve **6** bisect **9** bifurcate

divided 4 rent **5** riven, split **6** cloven **7** asunder, partite **8** ruptured

dividend 5 bonus, share **6** return, reward **7** benefit, guerdon, portion, premium **9** allotment **12** dispensation

divider 6 border, screen **9** partition

divination 6 augury **7** insight **8** prophecy **11** foretelling, soothsaying *by communication with the dead:* **10** necromancy *by figures:* **8** geomancy *by lots:* **9** sortilege *by numbers:* **10** numerology *by rods:* **7** dowsing **11** rhabdomancy *by stars:* **9** astrology

divine 4 holy **5** clerk, godly, infer **6** cleric, deduce, deific, intuit, parson, priest, sacred, superb **7** foresee, godlike **8** clerical, foreknow, heavenly, luscious, minister, preacher, prophesy, reverend **9** apprehend, churchman, clergyman, marvelous, religious, visualize **10** anticipate, conjecture, sanctified, superhuman, theologian **11** scrumptious **12** ecclesiastic

diviner 4 seer **5** augur, sibyl **6** oracle **7** palmist, prophet **8** haruspex **10** forecaster, prophetess, soothsayer

divinity 3 god **5** deity, fudge **7** goddess, godhead, godhood **8** theology

division 3 cut **4** part, unit **5** class, piece, slice, split **6** branch, moiety, parcel, schism, sector **7** breakup, discord, dissent, divorce, parting, portion, rupture, section, segment, split-up **8** category, conflict, district, disunion, disunity, variance **9** partition **10** detachment, difference, disharmony, dissidence, separation **11** dissolution **12** disagreement **13** apportionment *Bible:* **5** verse *book:* **7** chapter *British territorial:* **5** shire *building:* **4** wing *cell:* **7** meiosis, mitosis *city:* **4** ward **7** borough **8** precinct *contest:* **4** heat **6** inning, period *corolla:* **5** petal *country:* **5** state **6** canton **8** province **10** department, prefecture *family:* **4** side **6** branch *geologic time:* **3** eon, era **5** epoch **6** period *hospital:* **4** ward, wing *into two:* **9** bisection **11** bifurcation, bipartition *meal:* **6** course *music:* **3** bar **4** beat **7** measure **8** movement *opera, play:* **3** act **5** scena, scene *poem:* **5** canto, verse **6** stanza *population:* **7** segment, stratum *race:* **3** lap **4** heat *social:* **5** caste, class, tribe *state:* **6** county, parish *term:* **8** quotient *time:* **3** day, eon **4** week, year **5** month **6** decade, minute, moment, second **7** century, weekend **9** fortnight **10** millennium *tribal:* **4** clan *word:* **8** syllable *zodiac:* **4** sign

divisive 8 factious **11** disunifying

divorce 4 part **5** sever, split **6** divide, sunder **7** break up, breakup, disjoin, rupture **8** disjoint, dissever, disunion, disunite, separate **9** partition, severance **10** detachment, separation **11** dissolution

divot 3 sod **4** turf **5** clump

divulge 4 blab, leak, tell **5** spill **6** betray, expose, gossip, reveal, tattle **7** let slip, uncover **8** disclose, give away

Dixie composer 6 Emmett (Daniel D.)

dizziness 7 vertigo **9** giddiness

dizzy 5 addle, dazed, giddy, mix up, silly, tipsy **6** addled **7** confuse, dazzled, flighty, foolish, fuddled, muddled, puzzled, reeling **8** confused, swimming, whirling **9** befuddled, confusing **10** bewildered, confounded, distracted, exorbitant, immoderate, inordinate

11 extravagant, light-headed, vertiginous

Djibouti *capital:* 8 Djibouti *language:*
6 Arabic, French *monetary unit:* 5 franc
neighbor: 7 Eritrea, Somalia 8 Ethiopia
sea: 3 Red

DNA *component:* 7 adenine, guanine,
thymine 8 cytosine 10 nucleotide
11 deoxyribose *segment:* 7 cistron

doable 8 feasible, possible, workable
9 realistic 10 achievable, attainable
11 performable

do away with 3 end, nix, zap 4 kill, slay
5 annul, erase, whack 6 cancel, finish,
murder, remove, repeal, revoke, rub
out 7 abolish, bump off, deep-six,
destroy, discard, expunge, rescind,
squelch, wipe out 8 abrogate, blow
away, demolish, dispatch, dissolve,
massacre, stamp out 9 dispose of, eliminate, eradicate, extirpate, finish off, liquidate, slaughter 10 extinguish, obliterate 11 discontinue, exterminate

docent 5 guide 6 leader 7 teacher 8 lecturer 10 instructor

docile 4 tame 6 pliant 7 ductile, pliable
8 amenable, biddable, obedient, yielding 9 adaptable, compliant, teachable,
tractable 10 submissive 11 acquiescent

dock 3 bob, cut 4 crop, fine, pier, quay,
rump, slip 5 berth, jetty, levee, tie up,
wharf 6 anchor, hangar, lessen, marina,
reduce 7 abridge, landing, shorten 8 cut
short, platform, truncate *worker:*
6 lumper 9 stevedore 12 longshoreman

docket 4 card 6 agenda, lineup, record
7 program 8 abstract, calendar, case-
load, register, schedule 9 timetable

doctor 3 fix, vet 4 mend 5 adapt, alter,
medic, treat 6 medico, repair 7 croaker,
dentist, falsify, scholar, surgeon 8 sawbones 9 clinician, internist, physician
10 adulterate, specialist 11 medicine
man, recondition, reconstruct *animal:*
3 vet 12 veterinarian *children's:* 12 pediatrician *famous:* 4 Koop (C. Everett)
5 Galen, Spock (Benjamin) 8 Atkins
(Robert), Chopra (Deepak), Ornish
(Dean) 9 Kevorkian (Jack)
10 Schweitzer (Albert) 11 Hippocrates,
Livingstone (David) *foot:* 10 podiatrist
11 chiropodist *heart:* 12 cardiologist
teeth: 7 dentist *women's:* 12 gynecol-
ogist

Doctor of the Church 5 Basil 6 Jerome
7 Ambrose, Gregory 9 Augustine
10 Athanasius

Doctorow novel 7 Ragtime 9 City of God
(The) 10 Waterworks, World's Fair
12 Book of Daniel (The) 13 Billy Bath-
gate 18 Welcome to Hard Times

doctrinaire 5 rigid 8 dogmatic 9 obstinate 10 unyielding 11 domineering,
magisterial 13 authoritarian

doctrine 3 ism 5 axiom, basic, canon,
credo, creed, dogma, faith, tenet 7 precept 8 teaching 9 principle 11 fundamental

document 4 deed 5 paper 6 record 8 evidence, monument 9 testimony
10 instrument 11 certificate *travel:*
8 passport

dodder 4 limp 5 shake 6 falter, hobble,
totter 7 shamble, shuffle, stagger, tremble 12 morning glory

doddering 5 shaky 6 doting, feeble,
senile 7 fragile 8 unsteady, weakened
9 faltering

dodge 4 duck, jink, ruse, slip 5 avoid,
elude, evade, fence, parry, shirk, skirt,
slide, trick 6 escape, scheme, weasel
7 evasion 8 sidestep 9 avoidance, deception, expedient

Dodger 5 Davis (Tommy) 6 Garvey
(Steve), Karros (Eric), Koufax (Sandy),
Piazza (Michael), Snider (Duke), Sutton (Don) 8 Newcombe (Don), Robinson (Jackie) 9 Hershiser (Orel) 10 Campanella (Roy) *field:* 7 Ebbetts *manager:*
6 Alston (Walter) 7 Lasorda (Tommy)

dodger 6 outlaw, screen 7 escapee 8 circular, deceiver, deserter, fugitive, handbill, runagate 9 throwaway

dodgy 4 iffy 5 fishy, vague 6 tricky
7 cryptic, obscure 8 doubtful,
unproven 9 ambiguous, enigmatic,
uncertain 10 indefinite, suspicious,
unreliable 11 problematic 12 questionable 13 controversial

dodo 3 oaf 4 bird, boob, clod, dolt,
dope, goof, yo-yo 5 chump, dummy,
dunce, idiot, moron, ninny, noddy,
stupe 6 dimwit, dum-dum, nitwit 7 airhead, dullard, pinhead 8 bonehead,
dumbbell, imbecile, lunkhead, meathead, numskull 9 birdbrain, blockhead,
ignoramus, lamebrain, numbskull, simpleton 10 dunderhead, nincompoop
11 chowderhead, chucklehead

doe 4 deer 6 female, rabbit 8 kangaroo

doff 4 shed 6 remove 7 take off

dog 3 cur, pug, pup, tag 4 bird, chow,
fice, mutt, peke, puli, tail, tyke 5 Akita,
boxer, feist, frank, hound, husky,
lemon, pooch, puppy, spitz, trail
6 Afghan, beagle, bowwow, briard,
canine, collie, detent, poodle, pursue,
rascal, saluki, setter, shadow, vizsla,
wiener, wretch 7 andiron, Maltese,
mastiff, mongrel, pointer, Samoyed,
spaniel, terrier, whippet 8 Airedale,
Brittany, inferior, keeshond, papillon,

Pekinese, pinscher, spurious, wirehair
9 Chihuahua, dachshund, dalmation,
Great Dane, greyhound, Pekingese,
retriever, schnauzer **10** bloodhound,
Pomeranian, rottweiler, Weimaraner
11 bullmastiff, frankfurter, wienerwurst
12 Newfoundland, Saint Bernard
13 cocker spaniel *Alaskan:* **8** malamute,
malemute *Australian:* **5** dingo *barkless:*
7 basenji *bird:* **6** setter **7** pointer, spaniel
9 retriever *Bush's:* **6** Millie *Buster
Brown's:* **4** Tige *Charlie Brown's:*
6 Snoopy *command:* **3** sit **4** heel, stay
Dorothy's: **4** Toto *Eskimo:* **5** husky *family:* **7** Canidae *FDR's:* **4** Fala *fictional:*
4 Buck **5** Astro, Pluto **6** Big Red
8 McBarker **9** Marmaduke, Old Yeller,
Scooby-Doo, White Fang *"Garfield":*
4 Odie *genus:* **5** Canis *Hungarian:* **6** vizsla *hunting:* **5** hound **6** beagle, borzoi,
saluki, setter, Talbot, vizsla **7** harrier,
pointer, redbone **8** elkhound, foxhound
9 wolfhound **10** bloodhound **11** basset
hound *Indian:* **5** dhole *L.B.J.'s:* **3** Her
long-bodied: **9** dachshund *movie:* **4** Asta,
Toto **5** Benji, Tramp **6** Lassie
9 Beethoven, Old Yeller, Rin Tin Tin
name: **4** Fido, Spot **5** Rover **6** Bowser
Nixon's: **8** Checkers *Odysseus's:* **5** Argos
of Hades: **8** Cerberus *Orphan Annie's:*
5 Sandy *powerful:* **11** bullmastiff *Roy
Rogers's:* **6** Bullet *Russian:* **6** borzoi
7 Samoyed *shaggy-coated:* **8** komondor,
sheepdog **9** deerhound *short-legged:*
5 corgi *small:* **3** pom, pug, pup **4** peke
8 Pekinese **9** Chihuahua, Pekingese
10 Pomeranian *space traveler:* **5** Laika
Steinbeck's: **7** Charley *television:* **4** King
5 Eddie, Tramp **6** Lassie, Murray
8 Wishbone **9** Rin Tin Tin *terrier:*
7 Scottie *three-headed:* **8** Cerberus
Tibetan: **9** Lhasa apso *tiny:* **9** Chihuahua
tooth: **4** fang *tracking:* **10** bloodhound
two-headed: **6** Orthos *Wallace's:*
6 Gromit *Welsh:* **5** corgi *Wendy's:*
4 Nana *wild:* **5** dingo *young:* **3** pup
5 puppy, whelp
dog days 6 August **9** canicular
dogfight 3 row **4** fray **5** brawl, broil,
melee, set-to **6** fracas, ruckus **7** ruction
10 donnybrook, free-for-all
dogfish 6 bowfin, burbot **8** mud puppy
dogged 7 adamant **8** obdurate, resolute,
stubborn **9** insistent, steadfast, obstinate, tenacious, unbending **10** bullheaded, hardheaded, persistent,
persisting, unshakable, unyielding
11 persevering, unremitting **12** pertinacious
doggone 4 damn, dang, darn, rank
5 utter **6** cursed, damned, darned

7 blasted, blessed, dratted **8** absolute,
accursed, infernal, outright **9** out-and-
out **10** confounded **11** unmitigated
13 blankety-blank
dogma 4 code, rule **5** canon, credo,
creed, tenet **6** belief, gospel **7** precept
8 doctrine, ideology **9** orthodoxy, postulate, teachings **10** conviction, persuasion
dogmatic 8 oracular, orthodox
9 assertive, canonical, doctrinal **11** dictatorial, doctrinaire, magisterial
13 authoritarian, authoritative
Dog of Flanders author: 5 Ouida
dog-paddle 4 swim
dog's age 3 eon **4** aeon **8** blue moon,
eternity
Dog Star 6 Sirius
dogwood 6 cornel, Cornus **8** red osier
do in 4 kill, ruin, slay **5** cheat, wreck
6 defeat, finish, murder, rub out **7** blot
out, bump off, destroy, execute,
exhaust, frazzle, take out, wear out,
wipe out **8** dispatch, knock off, knock
out **9** eliminate, liquidate, prostrate,
run ragged, shipwreck **11** assassinate
doing 3 act **6** action **8** activity *good:*
10 beneficent *evil:* **10** maleficent
doit 3 bit, jot **4** coin, damn, dram, drop,
hoot, iota, mite, whit **6** trifle **8** particle
doldrums 5 blahs, blues, dumps, ennui,
gloom, slump **6** apathy, tedium, torpor
7 boredom **9** dejection **10** depression,
inactivity, quiescence, stagnation
12 listlessness
doleful 3 sad **4** down **7** forlorn, ruthful
8 cast down, dejected, dolorous, downcast, grieving, mournful, mourning
9 afflicted, cheerless, depressed, miserable, plaintive, sorrowful, sorrowing
woebegone **10** dispirited, lamentable,
lugubrious, melancholy **11** crestfallen,
downhearted **12** disconsolate
dole out 4 deal **5** allot **6** divide, parcel,
ration **7** divvy up **8** disburse, dispense,
disperse **9** apportion, partition
10 administer, distribute
doll 3 Ken **6** Barbie, figure, Kewpie,
puppet **10** Betsy Wetsy, Raggedy Ann
11 Raggedy Andy *grotesque:* **8** golliwog
dollar 3 one **4** bill, buck, clam, oner,
peso **5** taler **6** single **7** ringgit, smacker
8 simoleon **9** cartwheel, greenback
dollop 4 blob, glob, lump **7** portion
Doll's House, A author: 5 Ibsen (Henrik)
heroine: **4** Nora
dolly 4 cart **7** stirrer **8** platform **10** locomotive
dolomite 6 marble **9** limestone
dolor 5 agony, grief **6** misery, sorrow

7 anguish, passion **8** distress **9** suffering **10** affliction

dolorous 6 rueful, woeful **7** ruthful **8** grievous, mournful, wretched **9** afflicted, anguished, miserable, plaintive, sorrowful **11** lamentable, lugubrious, melancholy **13** heartbreaking

dolphin 5 whale **7** bollard **8** porpoise

dolt 3 ass, oaf **4** boob, clod, dodo, dork, fool, goof, goon, lout, yo-yo **5** booby, chump, dunce, idiot **6** nitwit **7** dullard, fathead, halfwit, jughead, saphead, schnook **8** bonehead, dumbbell, dummkopf, imbecile, lunkhead, meathead, numskull **9** blockhead, lamebrain, numbskull, simpleton

doltish 4 dull, dumb **5** dense, thick **6** oafish, obtuse, stupid **7** idiotic, moronic **8** ignorant, mindless **9** dimwitted, fatheaded, imbecilic

domain 4 land, rule, turf **5** field, realm **6** estate, sphere **7** kingdom, terrain **8** dominion, province **9** bailiwick, territory

dome 4 head, hill, roof **5** mound **6** cupola **7** ceiling **8** mountain

domestic 4 help, home, tame **6** family, native **7** servant **8** houseboy, internal, national **9** charwoman, household **10** indigenous **11** chambermaid

domesticate 4 tame **5** adapt, adopt, train **10** housebreak

domicile 3 pad **4** home **5** abode, house, lodge, put up **6** bestow, billet, harbor **7** quarter **8** dwelling, quarters **9** residence, residency **10** habitation

domiciliate 4 bunk, tame **5** house, lodge, put up **6** billet, harbor, reside **7** quarter

dominance 4 rule, sway **5** power **7** command, control **7** mastery **9** supremacy **10** ascendancy, prepotency **11** preeminence, sovereignty

dominant 4 main **5** chief, first, major **6** ruling **7** leading, supreme **8** foremost, powerful, reigning **9** ascendant, governing, number-one, paramount, prevalent, principal **10** commanding, preeminent, prevailing, successful, surpassing **11** controlling, outweighing, overbearing **12** preponderant

dominate 4 rule **5** reign **6** direct, govern, obsess **7** control, prevail, repress **8** bestride, hold sway, look down, loom over, overlook **9** subjugate, tower over, tyrannize **10** tower above

domination 4 rule, sway **5** might, power **7** command, control, mastery **9** authority, supremacy **10** ascendancy, prepotency, suzerainty **11** preeminence, sovereignty **13** preponderancy

dominator 4 boss, head **5** chief, ruler

6 honcho, leader, master, top dog **7** headman **8** director, hierarch, kingfish **9** chieftain, commander

domineer 5 bully **6** hector **7** swagger **8** browbeat, bulldoze **9** tyrannize **10** intimidate

domineering 5 bossy **6** lordly **8** arrogant, despotic **9** imperious, masterful **10** autocratic, high-handed, oppressive, tyrannical **11** dictatorial, magisterial, overbearing

Dominica *capital:* **6** Roseau *discoverer:* **8** Columbus (Christopher) *language:* **7** English *location:* **10** West Indies *monetary unit:* **6** dollar *sea:* **9** Caribbean

Dominican Republic *capital:* **12** Santo Domingo *island:* **10** Hispaniola *language:* **7** Spanish *location:* **10** West Indies *monetary unit:* **4** peso *mountain:* **6** Duarte *neighbor:* **5** Haiti *sea:* **9** Caribbean

dominion 3 raj **4** rule, sway, turf **5** realm, power **6** domain, empery, empire, regnum, sphere **7** demesne, kingdom, terrain **8** province **9** ascendant, ownership, supremacy, territory **10** ascendancy, possession **11** preeminence, sovereignty

domino 4 mask **5** amice, cloak, visor **6** vizard **8** disguise *spot:* **3** pip

don 3 sir **4** lord **5** get on, put on, tutor **6** assume, fellow, take on **9** professor, undertake

Donalbain *brother:* **7** Malcolm *father:* **6** Duncan

donate 4 give **5** grant **6** chip in, supply **7** dish out, hand out, present, provide **8** give away, shell out, transfer **10** contribute

donation 3 aid **4** alms, gift **5** grant **7** bequest, handout **8** offering **9** endowment **11** benefaction, beneficence **12** contribution, philanthropy

Don Carlos *author:* **8** Schiller (Friedrich von) *composer:* **5** Verdi (Giuseppe) *father:* **6** Philip

done 4 over **5** all in, ended, ready, spent **6** bushed, decent, doomed, gone by, proper, used up **7** correct, drained, dressed, far-gone, settled, through, worn-out **8** becoming, complete, depleted, finished, washed-up **9** befitting, completed, concluded, exhausted **10** terminated **12** accomplished *poetic:* **3** o'er

donee 7 grantee **8** receiver **9** recipient **11** beneficiary

done for 4 gone, sunk **5** kaput **6** beaten, doomed, ruined **7** wrecked **8** finished, stricken

done in 5 spent **6** effete, used up **7** far

gone, worn out **8** depleted **9** exhausted, washed out

Don Giovanni composer 6 Mozart (Wolfgang Amadeus)

Donizetti, Gaetano *hero:* **7** Roberto (Devereux) *opera:* **5** Lucia (di Lammermoor) **10** Anna Bolena, La Favorita **11** Don Pasquale **12** Maria Stuarda

Don Juan 4 rake, roué, wolf **5** Romeo **6** chaser, masher **7** amorist, gallant, playboy, seducer **8** Casanova, lothario, paramour **9** ladies' man, libertine, womanizer **10** lady-killer, profligate **11** philanderer *drama:* **10** Stone Guest (The) *home:* **7** Seville *mother:* **4** Inez *poet:* **5** Byron (Lord) **7** Pushkin (Alexander)

donkey 3 ass **4** mule **5** burro **7** jackass *female:* **5** jenny

donkeywork 4 moil, toil **5** grind, labor **7** travail **8** drudgery

donnybrook 3 row **4** fray **5** brawl, broil, fight, melee, set-to **6** fracas, ruckus, rumpus, tumult, uproar **7** dispute, quarrel, rhubarb, ruction **10** free-for-all **11** altercation

donor 5 giver **6** patron **7** granter, grantor **8** bestower **9** conferrer, presenter **10** benefactor **11** contributor

do-nothing 3 bum **4** slug **5** idler **6** loafer, slouch **7** goof-off, slacker **8** deadbeat, fainéant, layabout, slugabed, sluggard **9** lazybones, vegetable **11** couch potato

Don Pasquale composer 9 Donizetti (Gaetano)

Don Quixote *author:* **9** Cervantes (Miguel de) *beloved:* **8** Dulcinea *companion (squire):* **11** Sancho Panza *giant:* **8** windmill *home:* **8** La Mancha *horse:* **9** Rocinante, Rosinante, Rozinante

doodad 5 gizmo, thing **6** bauble, dingus, entity, gadget, gewgaw, jigger, widget **7** trinket, whatsit **8** gimcrack **9** doohickey, thingummy **10** attachment, decoration, knickknack **11** thingamabob, thingamajig, thingumajig

doodle 6 dabble, dawdle, fiddle, potter, putter, sketch, tinker, trifle **7** cartoon, drawing **8** scribble **10** mess around

doodlebug 7 ant lion, missile **8** buzz bomb

doohickey *see* DOODAD

doom 4 damn, fate, ruin **5** death **6** decree, demise, kismet **7** condemn, destiny, tragedy **8** calamity, disaster, judgment, sentence **11** catastrophe **12** annihilation, last judgment

doomful 4 dire **7** baleful, baneful, direful, fateful, malefic, ominous, unlucky **8** dreadful, ill-fated, sinister **10** foreboding, portentous **11** apocalyptic

doomsayer 7 killjoy **9** Cassandra, defeatist, Gloomy Gus, pessimist

___ **Doone 5** Lorna

door 3 way **4** adit, exit **5** entry **6** access, egress, entrée, portal **7** gateway, ingress, opening **8** entrance, entryway **9** admission **10** admittance **11** entranceway *rear:* **7** postern

doorkeeper 6 porter

doorway 5 entry **6** portal **8** entrance, entryway **11** entranceway

doozy 3 ace, pip **5** dandy **7** paragon **8** standout **10** phenomenon **11** crackerjack

dope 3 oaf **4** clod, dodo, dolt, drug, goof, news, yo-yo **5** chump, drugs, dummy, dunce, facts, idiot, moron, ninny, noddy, stupe **6** dimwit, dumdum, heroin, nitwit, opiate, sedate, skinny **7** airhead, cocaine, details, dullard, lowdown, pinhead **8** bonehead, dumbbell, imbecile, lunkhead, meathead, narcotic, numskull **9** birdbrain, blockhead, ignoramus, lamebrain, marijuana, narcotize, numbskull, simpleton **10** dunderhead, nincompoop **11** anesthetize, chowderhead, chucklehead, information, preparation

doped 4 high **5** dazed **6** stoned, zonked **7** drugged, tuned-in **8** hopped-up, tripping, turned on, wiped out **9** spacedout, strung out, stupefied **10** narcotized

dopey 4 dumb **5** silly **6** dulled, stupid, torpid **7** fatuous, fuddled, muddled **8** comatose, sluggish **9** lethargic, senseless, stupefied

Doris *brother:* **6** Nereus *daughters:* **7** Nereids *father:* **7** Oceanus *husband:* **6** Nereus

dormancy 5 sleep **6** repose **7** latency, slumber **8** abeyance, diapause, doldrums, downtime **9** torpidity **10** inactivity, quiescence, suspension **11** cold storage **12** intermission, interruption

dormant 5 inert **6** asleep, drowsy, fallow, latent, torpid **7** abeyant **8** comatose, inactive, sluggish **9** lethargic, potential, quiescent, suspended **10** slow-moving, slumbering

dormer 3 bay **4** nook **5** niche **6** window

dorsal 6 aboral **7** abaxial

___ **d'Orsay 4** Quai

dorsum 4 back

Dorus *brother:* **6** Aeolus *father:* **6** Hellen

dory 4 bark, boat **5** craft, skiff **6** barque, bateau **7** shallop **8** lifeboat

dose 3 fix, hit **4** dram, shot, slug **7** measure, portion **8** medicate, quantity

Dos Passos trilogy 3 U.S.A.

dossier 4 file 6 folder 9 portfolio

dot 4 mark, mote, stud 5 dower, dowry, point, speck 6 bestud, pepper, period 7 freckle, speckle, stipple 8 flyspeck, sprinkle 9 bespeckle 12 decimal point

dotage 8 senility 11 decrepitude, senectitude

dote on 5 adore, enjoy, fancy, prize 7 cherish, idolize 8 treasure 9 delight in

doting 4 dear, fond 6 loving 7 adoring, devoted 12 affectionate

dotted 6 spotty 8 punctate, stippled

dotty 4 gaga 5 crazy, loony, wacky 6 absurd, insane 7 foolish, smitten 8 enamored 9 eccentric 10 captivated, enraptured, infatuated 12 preposterous

double 4 copy, dual, fold, mate, tack, twin 5 clone, duple, image, match, twice 6 bifold, binary, duplex, paired, ringer 7 dualize, enlarge, magnify, replica, twofold 8 alter ego, geminate, increase 9 companion, dualistic, duplicate, look-alike, replicate 10 dead ringer, reciprocal, simulacrum, understudy 13 spitting image

double-barreled 4 dual 5 duple 6 bifold, binary, duplex, paired 7 twofold 9 dualistic

double bass 10 bull fiddle

double-cross 3 con 4 dupe 5 cheat, trick 6 betray, delude, humbug, juggle, take in 7 beguile, deceive, sell out, two-time 8 flimflam, hoodwink 9 four-flush

double dagger 6 diesis

double-dealer 3 gyp 5 cheat, knave 6 con man 7 cozener, diddler, sharper 8 deceiver, swindler 9 defrauder 11 flimflammer 13 confidence man

double-dealing 5 fraud 6 deceit 7 chicane 8 flimflam, trickery 9 chicanery, deceitful, deception, duplicity, two-timing 10 hanky-panky 11 duplicitous

double-dome 7 egghead 8 Einstein, highbrow 10 pointy-head 12 intellectual

double-faced 9 deceitful, deceptive, equivocal, insincere 10 reversible 12 hypocritical 13 untrustworthy

doublet 3 duo 4 dyad, pair, span 5 brace 6 couple, jacket 7 twosome

double-talk 4 bosh, bunk 5 hokum, hooey 6 babble, bunkum, drivel, jabber 7 blather, hogwash, twaddle 8 flimflam, nonsense 9 gibberish, poppycock 10 balderdash 12 gobbledygook

double vision 8 diplopia

doubt 5 qualm 7 concern, dispute, dubiety, suspect 8 distrust, mistrust, question 9 challenge, disbelief, misgiving, suspicion 10 skepticism 11 dubiousness, incertitude, incredulity, uncertainty

doubtable 4 hazy, iffy, moot 7 dubious, suspect 8 arguable 9 ambiguous, debatable, equivocal, uncertain, undecided 10 disputable, borderline, indefinite 11 problematic 12 questionable

doubter 5 cynic 6 Thomas 7 skeptic 8 agnostic 10 Pyrrhonist, questioner, unbeliever 11 freethinker

doubtful 4 hazy, iffy, moot 5 fishy, shady, shaky 6 chancy, unsure 7 clouded, dubious, obscure, suspect, unclear 8 arguable, unlikely 9 ambiguous, debatable, dubitable, equivocal, uncertain, undecided, unsettled 10 borderline, disputable, improbable 11 problematic, speculative 12 questionable

doubtfulness 7 concern, dubiety 8 mistrust 9 ambiguity, misgiving, suspicion 10 indecision, skepticism, uneasiness 11 dubiousness, incertitude, uncertainty 13 indeterminacy

doubting Thomas see DOUBTER

doubtless 6 likely, surely 7 certain, clearly 8 of course, probably 10 absolutely, definitely, positively, presumably 11 indubitably 12 indisputably 13 presumptively, unequivocally

douceur 3 tip 4 gift 5 bribe 7 present 8 gratuity

dough 4 cash 5 bread, money 6 dinero, moolah 7 cabbage, lettuce, scratch 8 currency 11 legal tender *inflator:* 5 yeast

doughboy 7 dogface 11 infantryman

doughty 4 bold 5 brave, gutsy, manly, stout 6 daring, heroic, plucky, spunky, strong 7 gallant, valiant 8 fearless, intrepid, resolved, stalwart, unafraid, valorous 9 dauntless, undaunted 10 courageous 12 stouthearted

doughy 3 wan 4 pale 5 pasty, waxen 6 pallid 8 blanched 9 colorless

do up 3 can, fix 4 mend, wash, wrap 5 clean, patch 6 clothe, doctor, fasten, repair, revamp 7 exhaust, festoon, launder, package, prepare, rebuild, wear out 8 decorate, gift wrap, ornament, overhaul 9 embellish 11 recondition, reconstruct

dour 4 glum, grim 5 bleak, harsh, rigid, stern, surly 6 gloomy, morose, severe, strict, sullen 7 austere, crabbed, peevish 9 obstinate, saturnine, stringent 10 forbidding, unyielding

douse 3 sop 4 duck, dunk, soak 5 bathe, drown, plash, slosh, souse 6 drench, put out, quench, splash, strike 7 immerse, slacken 8 inundate, saturate, snuff out, submerge, submerse 10 extinguish

dove 6 culver, pigeon 8 pacifist *call:* 3 coo *genus:* 7 Columba

dovecote 6 aviary 9 birdhouse

dovetail 3 fit 4 jibe, mesh 5 agree, match, tally 6 accord, splice, square 7 comport, conform 8 check out 9 harmonize, interlock, intermesh 10 correspond

dovish 4 mild 6 gentle 7 antiwar, pacific 8 pacifist 9 peaceable 10 nonviolent, pacifistic 11 peace-loving 12 conciliatory

dowager 4 dame 5 widow 6 matron 9 matriarch 10 grande dame 11 grandmother

dowdy 4 drab 5 dated, frump, passé, seedy, tacky 6 blowsy, bygone, démodé, frowsy, frowzy, frumpy, old hat, shabby 7 rundown, unkempt 8 frumpish, outdated, outmoded, slattern, slovenly 9 out-of-date, unstylish 10 antiquated, bedraggled, slatternly 11 draggle-tail 12 old-fashioned 13 draggletailed

dowel 3 bar, peg, pin, rod 5 stick

dower 4 gift 5 endow, endue 6 legacy, talent 8 bequeath

dowitcher 5 snipe 9 sandpiper

do without 5 forgo, waive 6 abjure, eschew, give up, pass up 8 renounce

down 3 eat, fur, ill, low, off, sad 4 blue, fell, fuzz, lint, pile, sick 5 below, ended, floor, floss, fluff, level, lower, under 6 defeat, fallen, finish, lay low, nether 7 conquer, consume, destroy, flatten, swallow, unhappy 8 bowl over, complete, defeated, dejected, dispatch, feathers, finished, inferior, overcome, sluggish, surmount 9 completed, concluded, depressed, earthward, miserable 10 dispirited, groundward

down-and-out 5 broke, needy 6 hard-up, ruined 8 beggared, derelict, homeless 9 destitute, penniless, penurious 12 impoverished

down-and-outer 3 bum 6 beggar, pauper, wretch 7 have-not 9 mendicant 10 supplicant

down-at-heels 4 mean 5 dingy, ratty, seedy, tacky 6 ragged, ragtag, shabby, shoddy 7 ignoble, run-down, worn-out 8 decrepit, tattered 10 bedraggled, threadbare 11 dilapidated 12 deteriorated, disreputable

downbeat 3 low, sad 4 blue, glum 6 droopy, gloomy, morose 7 decline, doleful 8 dejected 9 depressed 10 dispirited, melancholy 11 discouraged, pessimistic 12 disconsolate, disheartened, heavyhearted

downcast 3 low, sad 4 blue, glum, sunk 5 moody, mopey 6 droopy, gloomy,

morose 7 doleful, forlorn, unhappy 8 dejected, dismayed, listless, soul-sick, troubled 9 depressed, heartsick, heartsore, miserable, oppressed, woebegone 10 chapfallen, despondent, dispirited, distressed, melancholy, spiritless 11 crestfallen, discouraged, low-spirited 12 disconsolate, disheartened

downfall 4 bane, ruin 6 demise 7 decline, undoing 8 collapse, Waterloo 9 ruination 10 devolution 11 declination, destruction 12 degeneration, dégringolade 13 deterioration

downgrade 4 bump, bust 5 abase, lower 6 demote 7 decline, demerit, descent, devalue 8 belittle, diminish, discount, minimize, relegate 9 denigrate, deprecate, devaluate, discredit, disparage, humiliate 10 depreciate, undervalue 12 degeneration, dégringolade 13 deterioration

downhearted see DOWNCAST

down-in-the-mouth see DOWNCAST

down payment 5 token 6 pledge 7 advance, deposit, earnest

downplay 8 belittle, discount, minimize, pooh-pooh 11 de-emphasize

downpour 6 deluge 7 monsoon 8 drencher 9 drenching, rainstorm 10 cloudburst, inundation 11 gully washer

downright 5 blunt, gross, total, truly, utter 7 blatant, flat-out 8 absolute, complete, explicit, positive, thorough 9 out-and-out 10 absolutely, sureenough 11 indubitable, unequivocal, unmitigated, unqualified 13 thoroughgoing

downslide 3 dip, sag 4 drop, slip 5 slump 7 decline, drop-off, falloff 8 decrease 9 declivity, reduction

downstairs 6 cellar 8 basement

down-to-earth 8 rational 9 practical, pragmatic, realistic 10 hard-boiled, hardheaded, no-nonsense, reasonable 11 common-sense, plain-spoken 12 matter-of-fact 13 unpretentious, unsentimental

downtrend see DOWNSLIDE

downtrodden 6 abject, abused 9 oppressed 10 maltreated, mistreated, persecuted, tyrannized

downturn see DOWNSLIDE

downward 8 dropping 9 declining 10 descending

downy 4 soft 5 fuzzy 6 fleecy, fluffy 7 velvety 8 feathery *filler:* 5 eider

dowry 4 gift 6 talent *French:* 3 dot

doxy 4 moll, tart 5 wench 6 floozy, harlot 7 trollop 8 mistress 10 prostitute

doyen 4 dean, head 5 chief, maven

6 expert, leader, master, wizard 7 maestro 8 virtuoso 9 authority, patriarch 10 past master

Doyle's detective 6 Holmes (Sherlock)

D'Oyly Carte offering 8 operetta

doze 3 nap 5 sleep 6 catnap, drowse, nod off, snooze 7 drop off, slumber 8 drift off 10 forty winks

dozy see DROWSY

DP 5 exile 6 émigré 7 evacuee, outcast, refugee 8 deportee, emigrant, fugitive 10 expatriate

drab 4 dull, flat 5 bleak, brown, dingy, faded, mousy, muddy, olive, vapid 6 dismal, dreary, mousey 7 subfusc 8 lifeless 9 cheerless, colorless 10 lackluster 11 dispiriting

draconian 5 cruel, harsh, rigid 6 severe, strict 7 callous 8 ironclad, rigorous, ruthless 9 merciless, stringent 10 inflexible, ironfisted, ironhanded

Dracula author 6 Stoker (Bram)

draft 3 tap 4 dose, haul, plan, plot, pull, pump, swig 5 check, claim, drink, frame, press, swill 6 breeze, call up, demand, design, devise, enlist, enroll, induct, potion, scheme, select, siphon, sketch 7 compose, concoct, current, outline, portion, prepare, project, recruit 8 block out, contrive, rough out, skeleton, traction 9 adumbrate, allowance, blueprint, conscribe, conscript, fabricate, formulate, muster out 11 delineation, skeletonize *avoider:* 6 dodger *of a law:* 4 bill

drag 3 lug, tow, tug 4 bore, haul, puff, pull, swig 5 dally, delay, draft, tarry, trail 6 burden, dawdle, harrow, loiter, schlep, search, sledge 7 schlepp 8 friction, straggle 9 lag behind 13 procrastinate

dragging 4 beat, long 5 all in, spent, weary 6 pooped 7 drained, lengthy, tedious 8 drawn-out, extended, fatigued, overlong, sluggish, wiped out 9 exhausted, lethargic, long-drawn, pooped out, prolonged, washed-out, wearisome 10 protracted, slow-moving 12 interminable, long-drawn-out

draggle 3 lag 4 rove 5 stray, trail 8 straggle, trail off 10 fall behind

draggle-tail 4 bawd, drab, slut 5 wench, whore 6 harlot 8 slattern 10 prostitute 11 nightwalker 12 streetwalker

draggletailed 6 blowsy, frowsy, frowzy, sordid, untidy 8 slattern, sluttish 10 slatternly

dragnet 4 trap 5 snare, trawl 7 network

drag off 4 cart, haul

dragon 5 beast 8 basilisk 10 cockatrice *biblical:* 5 Rahab *Canaanite:* 3 Yam

4 Yamm 5 Lotan *Chinese:* 4 lung *French:* 8 Tarasque *genus:* 5 Draco *Greek:* 5 Ladon 9 Eurythion *slayer:* 4 Baal, Enki, Zeus 5 Indra 6 Cadmus, George (St.), Marduk, Sigurd 7 Beowulf, Jupiter, Michael (St.), Ninurta, Perseus 8 Margaret (St.) *Sumerian:* 3 Kur *Wagnerian:* 6 Fafnir

dragoon 3 cow 5 bully 6 badger, coerce, harass, hector 8 bludgeon, browbeat, bulldoze, bullyrag, threaten 9 persecute, strong-arm, terrorize 10 cavalryman, intimidate

drain 3 dry, tap 4 pump, sink, sump, swig, tire, vent, wear 5 bleed, draft, drink, empty, leech, sewer, swill, use up, weary 6 burden, gutter, siphon, trench 7 conduit, culvert, deplete, dwindle, draw off, exhaust, fatigue, outflow 8 bankrupt, draw down, wear down 9 discharge 10 impoverish 11 watercourse

drain away 3 ebb 4 drop, sink, wane 5 abate 6 lessen, reduce, remove 7 draw off, dwindle, retreat, subside 8 decrease, diminish, draw back, taper off, withdraw

drained 4 beat 5 all-in, spent, weary 6 bleary, pooped, used up 7 far-gone, worn-out 8 depleted, dragging, weakened, wiped out 9 exhausted, pooped out, washed-out

drainpipe 4 duct 5 sewer, spout 7 conduit 9 downspout

dram 3 bit, dab, nip, tot 4 atom, dash, drop, iota, jolt, mite, shot, slug, spot, swig, whit 5 crumb, grain, ounce, pinch, scrap, shred, snort, speck 6 morsel, sliver 7 modicum, smidgen, snifter, snippet, soupçon 8 particle

drama 4 play 7 pageant, theater, theatre, tragedy *award:* 4 Tony *former English:* 6 masque *Japanese:* 3 Noh *main part:* 8 epitasis *musical:* 5 opera 8 operetta *suspenseful:* 11 cliff-hanger

dramatic 5 vivid 8 striking, thespian 10 histrionic, theatrical *conflict:* 4 agon

dramatis personae 4 cast 5 parts, roles 6 actors, troupe 7 company 10 characters

dramatist 10 playwright *American:* 4 Hart (Moss), Inge (William), Rabe (David), Rice (Elmer), Uhry (Alfred) 5 Albee (Edward), Barry (Philip), Foote (Horton), Guare (John), Hecht (Ben), Mamet (David), Odets (Clifford), Parks (Suzan-Lori), Payne (John Howard), Simon (Neil) 6 Ferber (Edna), Gurney (A. R.), Henley (Beth), Miller (Arthur), Norman (Marsha), O'Neill (Eugene), Thomas (Augustus), Wilder (Thorn-

ton), Wilson (August, Lanford, Robert)
7 Hellman (Lillian), Kaufman (George
S.), Kushner (Tony), Shanley (John
Patrick), Shepard (Sam) **8** Anderson
(Maxwell, Robert), Caldwell (Erskine),
Connolly (Marc), Sherwood (Robert),
Williams (Tennessee) **9** Chayefsky
(Paddy), Fierstein (Harvey), Hansberry
(Lorraine) **11** Hammerstein (Oscar),
Wasserstein (Wendy) *Austrian:*
10 Schnitzler (Arthur) *Belgian:*
11 Maeterlinck (Maurice) *Czech:*
5 Havel (Vaclav) *English:* **3** Fry
(Christopher), Gay (John) **4** Hare
(David), Rowe (Nicholas), Tate
(Nahum) **5** Frayn (Michael), Milne
(A. A.), Orton (Joe), Peele (George),
Wilde (Oscar) **6** Barrie (James), Cow-
ard (Nöel), Dryden (John), Jonson
(Ben), Pinero (Arthur Wing), Pinter
(Harold), Steele (Richard), Storey
(David) **7** Delaney (Shelagh), Marlowe
(Christopher), Marston (John),
Osborne (John), Shaffer (Anthony,
Peter), Webster (John) **8** Congreve
(William), Rattigan (Terrence), Shad-
well (Thomas), Stoppard (Tom),
Tourneur (Cyril), Vanbrugh (John),
Zangwill (Israel) **9** Ayckbourn (Alan),
Churchill (Caryl), Goldsmith (Oliver),
Middleton (Thomas), Wycherley
(William) **11** Shakespeare (William)
French: **5** Camus (Albert), Genet (Jean)
6 Musset (Alfred de), Racine (Jean),
Sardou (Victorien), Sartre (Jean-Paul),
Scribe (Eugène) **7** Anouilh (Jean),
Ionesco (Eugène), Labiche (Eugène),
Molière, Rostand (Edmond) **8** Mari-
vaux (Pierre) **9** Corneille (Pierre), Cré-
billon, Giraudoux (Jean) **12** Beaumar-
chais (P. A. Caron de) *German:* **5** Weiss
(Peter) **6** Brecht (Bertolt), Goethe
(Johann Wolfgang von), Kleist (Hein-
rich von) **8** Schiller (Friedrich von)
9 Hauptmann (Gerhart), Zuckmayer
(Carl) *Greek:* **8** Menander **9** Aeschylus,
Euripides, Sophocles **12** Aristophanes
Hindu: **8** Kalidasa *Irish:* **4** Shaw (George
Bernard) **5** Behan (Brendan), Friel
(Brian), Synge (John Millington), Yeats
(William Butler) **6** O'Casey (Sean)
7 Beckett (Samuel), Gregory (Lady
Augusta) **8** Sheridan (Richard Brinsley)
Italian: **5** Gozzi (Carlo), Verga (Giovan-
ni) **7** Alfieri (Vittorio), Ariosto (Ludovi-
co), Giacosa (Giuseppe), Goldoni
(Carlo) **8** Trissino (Gian Giorgio)
9 D'Annunzio (Gabriele) **10** Metastasio
(Pietro), Pirandello (Luigi) *Japanese:*
5 Zeami *Nigerian:* **7** Soyinka (Wole) *Nor-
wegian:* **5** Ibsen (Henrik) **8** Bjornson

(Bjornstjerne) *Roman:* **6** Seneca **7** Plautus, Terence *Romanian:* **7** Ionesco
(Eugene) *Russian:* **7** Chekhov (Anton)
8 Zamyatin (Yevgeny) *South African:*
6 Fugard (Athol) *Spanish:* **4** Vega (Lope
de) **5** Lorca (Federico García) **7** Alberti
(Rafael), Arrabal (Fernando) **8** Quin-
tero (Serafín, Joaquín) **9** Benavente
(Jacinto) **11** García Lorca (Federico),
Valle-Inclán (R. M. del) *Swedish:*
5 Sachs (Nelly) **10** Strindberg (August)
Swiss: **6** Frisch (Max)

drape 4 fold, hang, roll **5** adorn, array,
cloak, cover **6** clothe, enwrap, swathe,
wrap up **7** curtain, swaddle **8** enswathe,
envelope, swathe in

drapery 7 curtain, hanging **8** curtains,
hangings

drastic 4 dire **5** harsh **6** severe **7** extreme,
radical **9** desperate **10** exorbitant

draw 3 gut, tie, tow, tug **4** etch, haul,
limn, lure, puff, pull, pump **5** draft,
drain, infer, judge, trace **6** allure,
appeal, deduce, depict, derive, elicit,
entice, extend, gather, indite, inhale,
pencil, siphon, sketch **7** attract,
deplete, exhaust, extract, outline, portray, prolong, spin out, win over **8** conclude, contract, convince, dead heat,
deadlock, lengthen, protract, standoff
9 delineate, formulate, represent, stalemate **10** allurement, attraction, disembowel, eviscerate, exenterate *forth:*
5 educe **6** elicit **7** extract *from:* **4** milk,
pump **5** bleed *together:* **3** tie **4** join, lace

draw back 4 duck **5** cower, quail, wince
6 blench, flinch, recoil, shrink **7** back
off, retreat, take off **9** turn aside

drawback 4 flaw, snag **5** fault, hitch
6 defect, refund **7** failing, trouble
8 weakness **9** detriment, hindrance
10 deficiency, difficulty, impediment
11 shortcoming **12** disadvantage
13 inconvenience

draw down 4 milk **5** drain, spend, use up
6 expend, reduce **7** deplete, exhaust
8 decrease, diminish **9** reduction,
siphon off

drawer 9 draftsman *for money:* **4** till

drawers 5 pants **6** undies **8** trousers
10 underpants

draw in 6 enmesh, entice, induce,
prompt **7** involve, retract, win over
8 convince, persuade, pull back **9** prevail on **11** bring around, prevail upon

drawing 6 doodle, sketch **7** cartoon, outline

drawing power 4 lure, pull **6** appeal
9 magnetism **10** attraction

drawn 4 taut, worn **6** peaked **7** fraught,
haggard, pinched **8** careworn, fatigued,

pictured, strained, stressed **9** attracted **10** delineated

drawn-out 4 long **7** lengthy, tedious **8** extended, overlong **9** prolonged **10** protracted

draw off 3 tap **4** pump **5** bleed, draft, drain **6** siphon

draw out 6 extend **7** prolong, stretch **8** elongate, lengthen, protract

draw up 4 balk, halt, lift, make, stop **5** array, draft, frame, order, raise, write **6** deploy, map out **7** compose, concoct, dispose, marshal, prepare, set down **8** organize, write out **9** formulate

dray 4 cart, drag **5** wagon **6** barrow, sledge **7** travois **9** stoneboat

dread 4 fear **5** alarm, panic **6** dismay, fright, horror, phobia, terror **7** anxiety **10** foreboding **11** trepidation **12** apprehension **13** consternation

dreadful 5 awful **6** tragic **7** awesome, extreme, fearful, ghastly, hideous, ominous **8** alarming, horrible, horrific, shocking, terrible **9** appalling, frightful, revolting **11** distressing, frightening

dreadfully 7 awfully **8** horribly **9** decidedly, extremely, fearfully, hideously, seriously **10** strikingly, tragically **11** appallingly, exceedingly, frightfully

dreadnought 10 battleship

dream 4 ache, long, wish **5** crave, fancy, ideal **6** bubble, desire, hanker, vision **7** chimera, fantasy, imagine, rainbow, reverie, specter, spectre **8** ambition, delusion, illusion, phantasm, phantasy **9** fantasize, nightmare **10** aspiration *divination by:* **11** oneiromancy *god:* **8** Morpheus

dreamer 7 utopian **8** idealist **9** visionary **10** Don Quixote, lotus-eater **13** castle-builder

dreamlike 5 ideal, vague **6** unreal **7** shadowy, surreal **8** fanciful, illusory, nebulous **9** imaginary, visionary **12** otherworldly

Dream of Gerontius composer 5 Elgar (Edward)

dream up 5 frame, hatch **6** cook up, create, devise, invent **7** concoct, imagine **8** conceive, contrive, envisage, envision **9** formulate, visualize

dreamy 7 pensive **9** unworldly, visionary **10** idealistic **11** impractical **12** otherworldly **13** introspective

dreary 4 blah, drab, dull **5** bleak **6** boring, dismal, gloomy, somber, sombre **7** forlorn, humdrum, joyless, tedious **8** banausic, tiresome, wretched **9** cheerless **10** depressing, depressive, monotonous, oppressive, pedestrian **11** dispiriting **12** discouraging

dreck 3 mud **4** junk, muck, slop **5** offal, swill, trash, waste **6** litter, refuse, sewage **7** garbage, rubbish **9** sweepings

dredge 3 dig **5** barge, scoop **6** deepen, dig out, gather **8** excavate, scoop out **9** hollow out, scrape out

dregs 4 lees, scum **5** trash **6** grouts **7** deposit, grounds, remains, residue **8** sediment **9** settlings **11** precipitate

drei 5 three

dreidel 3 top

Dreiser, Theodore *character:* **5** Clyde (Griffiths) **6** Carrie (Meeber), Eugene (Witla), Sondra (Finchley) **7** Roberta (Alden) **9** Hurstwood (George) **10** Cowperwood (Frank) *novel:* **5** Stoic (The), Titan (The) **6** Genius (The) **9** Financier (The) **12** Sister Carrie **14** Jennie Gerhardt **15** American Tragedy (An)

drench 3 sop **4** dunk, soak **5** douse, souse, steep, swill **6** deluge, seethe **7** immerse **8** inundate, saturate, submerge, waterlog

dress 3 gut **4** bind, clad, deck, doll, duds, garb, gown, sack, togs **5** adorn, align, array, frock, getup, guise, habit, smock, weeds **6** attire, bedeck, caftan, clothe, dirndl, enrobe, outfit, sacque **7** apparel, bandage, bedizen, chemise, clothes, costume, garment, garnish, raiment, threads, turnout, uniform **8** beautify, clothing, covering, decorate, ensemble, ornament, wardrobe **9** embellish, make ready **11** habiliments *a wound:* **7** bandage *designer:* **4** Dior (Christian), Erté, Head (Edith) **5** Blass (Bill), Bohan (Marc), Karan (Donna), Klein (Calvin), Pucci (Emilio), Quant (Mary), Worth (Charles Frederick) **6** Armani (Giorgio), Cardin (Pierre), Jacobs (Marc), Lauren (Ralph), Miyake (Issey), Poiret (Paul) **7** Balmain (Pierre), Cassini (Oleg), Halston, Lacroix (Christian), Mizrahi (Isaac), Versace (Gianni) **8** Galliano (John), Givenchy (Hubert) **9** Courrèges (André), de la Renta (Oscar), Gernreich (Rudi), Lagerfeld (Karl), Valentino **10** Balenciaga (Cristóbal) **12** Saint-Laurent (Yves), Schiaparelli (Elsa) *finically:* **5** primp *hair:* **4** coif **6** barber *line:* **3** hem *mode of:* **5** habit *oriental:* **9** cheongsam *part:* **5** skirt **6** bodice *South Seas:* **6** sarong *with the beak:* **5** preen *with vulgarity:* **7** bedizen

dress down 5 chide, scold **6** berate, rail at, rebuke, revile **7** bawl out, reprove, tell off, upbraid **8** admonish, chastise, reproach **9** castigate, reprimand **10** tongue-lash

dresser 5 chest 6 bureau 7 commode, highboy 10 chiffonier *gaudy:* 9 butterfly

dressing 5 sauce 6 catsup 7 bandage, catchup, ketchup 8 stuffing *salad:* 5 ranch 6 French 7 Italian, Russian 10 blue cheese 11 vinaigrette 12 green goddess

dressing room 6 vestry 8 vestiary

dressmaker 7 modiste 9 couturier 10 couturiere, seamstress

dress up 6 attire, clothe, rig out, tog out 7 apparel, deck out 8 beautify, disguise, prettify, trick out 9 embellish 10 camouflage

dressy 4 chic 5 showy, smart 6 classy, formal, frilly, ornate 7 duded up, elegant, stylish 9 rigged out

Dreyfus's defender 4 Zola (Emile)

dribble 4 drip, leak, weep 5 drool 6 bounce, drivel, slaver 7 distill, drizzle, slobber, trickle 8 salivate, sprinkle

driblet 4 drop 6 gobbet 7 globule, smidgen 8 particle, pittance

dried grape 6 raisin

dried meat 5 jerky

dried plum 5 prune

drift 3 bat, gad 4 flow, flux, gist, roam, sail, skim, tide, waft, wash 5 amble, coast, creep, float, mosey, range, slide, stray, trend 6 bummel, linger, ramble, stream, stroll, wander 7 current, maunder, meander, meaning, saunter 8 movement, penchant, sideslip, tendency 9 deviation 10 propensity 11 disposition, inclination, progression 12 predilection

drifter 3 bum, vag 4 hobo 5 gypsy, nomad, tramp 7 floater, migrant, vagrant 8 derelict, vagabond 9 transient 11 beachcomber 12 rolling stone

drill 3 bit, dig 4 bore 5 auger, borer, punch, train 6 pierce, trepan, wimble 7 routine, wildcat, workout 8 exercise, practice, practise, rehearse 9 penetrate, rehearsal 10 discipline *command:* 6 at ease 8 left face 9 about face, attention, right face

drink 3 ade, lap, nip, sea, sip, tea 4 belt, brew, deep, down, grog, gulp, soak, swig, tope, toss 5 booze, draft, drain, ocean, quaff, slurp, swill, toast 6 absorb, brandy, cognac, guzzle, imbibe, jigger, liquid, liquor, pledge, potion, tank up, tipple 7 consume, potable, schnaps, spirits, swallow, swizzle, toss off 8 aperitif, beverage, libation, liquor up, schnapps 9 aqua vitae *after-dinner:* 6 frappé 7 cordial, liqueur *drugged:* 6 Mickey 10 Mickey Finn *honey:* 4 mead *hot:* 5 negus, toddy *liquor:* 5 booze, hooch 6 red-eye 9 fire-water, moonshine *mixed:* 3 nog 5 julep 6 Gibson, gimlet, mai tai, mimosa, mojito, rickey, Rob Roy, zombie 7 gin fizz, martini, sidecar, stinger 8 daiquiri, pink lady 9 alexander, Cuba libre, manhattan, margarita, mint julep, rusty nail 10 Bloody Mary, piña colada, Tom Collins 11 gin and tonic, grasshopper, screwdriver, whiskey sour 12 black Russian, old-fashioned *mixer:* 7 swirler *noisily:* 5 slurp *of liquor:* 4 dram, shot, slug 5 snort 8 highball *of the gods:* 6 nectar *soft:* 3 pop 4 cola, soda 5 tonic 7 soda pop 8 root beer 9 ginger ale 12 sarsaparilla *stimulating:* 6 bracer (see also BEVERAGE)

drinkable 6 liquor 7 potable 8 beverage, libation, potation

drinking 8 potation *fountain:* 7 bubbler *horn:* 6 rhyton *spree:* 3 jag 4 tear, toot 5 binge, spree 6 bender 7 carouse 8 carousal

drip 4 leak, plop, weep 7 dribble, droplet, trickle 8 sprinkle

dripping 3 wet 5 runny, soppy 6 soaked, soused 7 drizzly, soaking, sopping 8 drenched 9 saturated 11 wringing-wet

drippy 5 mushy, rainy, sappy, sobby, soppy, soupy, teary, weepy 6 slushy, syrupy 7 drizzly, maudlin, mawkish, soaking, sopping, tearful 9 schmaltzy 11 sentimental

drive 3 pep, ram 4 goad, herd, push, spur, taxi, trip, urge 5 chase, force, guide, impel, jaunt, lunge, motor, moxie, oomph, pilot, pound, spunk, steer, surge, vigor 6 compel, convey, exhort, hammer, outing, plunge, propel, strike, thrust 7 actuate, impetus, operate, produce 8 ambition, mobilize, momentum, navigate, shepherd, vitality 9 chauffeur, excursion, urge along 10 enterprise, get-up-and-go, initiative, motivation *away:* 4 shoo 5 exile 6 aroint *back:* 5 repel 6 defend 7 repulse *off:* 6 dispel *out:* 8 exorcise

drivel 3 rot 4 bosh, bunk 5 drool, hokum, hooey, prate 6 babble, bunkum, gabble, jabber, slaver 7 baloney, blabber, blather, dribble, hogwash, prattle, rubbish, slobber, twaddle 8 claptrap, flimflam, nonsense, salivate 9 gibberish, poppycock 10 balderdash, double-talk, flapdoodle 12 blatherskite, gobbledygook

driver 4 jehu 5 cabby 6 cabbie, cabman, hackie, mallet 7 hackman 8 coachman, motorist, muleteer, operator 9 chauffeur, dowitcher 10 taskmaster 11 tamping iron *of an elephant:* 6 mahout *Roman:* 10 charioteer *truck:* 8 teamster

driving 7 dynamic, powered 8 forceful, vigorous 9 energetic, inspiring 10 compelling

drizzle 4 mist, rain 7 dribble, spatter 8 droplets, sprinkle 10 sprinkling 13 precipitation

Dr. Jekyll and Mr. ___ 4 Hyde

droll 3 odd 5 comic, funny, nutty, witty 7 comical, risible 8 farcical, humorous 9 eccentric, laughable, ludicrous, whimsical

drollery 5 humor 6 comedy, joking, whimsy 7 jesting

dromedary 5 camel

drone 3 bee, hum 4 buzz, idle, laze, loaf, loll 5 idler 6 drudge, loiter, lounge, murmur 7 bagpipe 8 aircraft, parasite 9 bombinate 10 pedal point

drool 4 gush, rave 5 froth 6 dote on, drivel, saliva, slaver 7 blather, dribble, enthuse, slobber 8 salivate 10 rhapsodize

droop 3 sag 4 fall, flag, hang, loll, sink, swag, wilt 5 slump 6 dangle, slouch, weaken 7 decline, let down, subside 8 languish

droopy 4 blue, down, weak 5 baggy 6 gloomy 7 doleful, languid, sagging, slouchy, wilting 8 cast down, dejected, downcast 9 depressed 10 dispirited 11 downhearted

drop 3 dip, nip, sag, tot 4 down, drib, dump, fall, fell, jolt, lose, slip, slug, tear 5 cease, depth, lapse, lower, pitch, plump, scrub, slide, snort, speck, spend 6 cancel, cave in, demise, depart, expire, fumble, give up, go down, ground, plunge, reduce, smitch, topple, unload, vanish 7 abandon, decease, decline, deposit, descend, descent, distill, dribble, driblet, fall off, forfeit, give out, globule, pendant, plummet, trickle 8 bowl over, break off, collapse, comedown, downturn, keel over, nosedive 9 declivity, discharge, downslide, downswing, downtrend, prostrate, reduction, terminate 10 depository

drop by 4 call 5 pop in, visit 6 stop in 8 come over

droplet 4 drib, tear 7 globule

drop off 3 nap, sag 4 doze, fall, slip 5 slide, slump 6 catnap, drowse, lessen, snooze 7 decline, deliver, deposit, slacken 8 diminish, fall away, hand over 10 fall asleep

dropsical 5 puffy, tumid 6 turgid 7 swollen 8 inflated 9 edematous, tumescent

dropsy 5 edema 8 anasarca

dross 4 junk, scum, slag 5 dregs, offal, waste 6 debris, scoria 7 remains, residue, schlock 8 detritus, impurity, leavings

drossy 4 base 6 impure, scummy 7 trivial 8 inferior, unworthy 9 worthless

drought 4 lack, need, want 6 dearth 7 aridity, dryness 8 scarcity, shortage 10 deficiency

droughty 3 dry 4 arid, sere 7 bone-dry, dried up, parched, thirsty 10 desiccated

drove 3 mob 4 army, herd, host, mass, pack 5 crowd, flock, horde, troop 6 myriad, pushed, school, throng 7 phalanx 9 multitude

drover 6 cowboy 8 shepherd

drown 4 sink, soak 5 douse, flood, souse, swamp 6 deluge, drench, engulf 7 immerse, repress, smother 8 inundate, submerge 9 overpower, overwhelm, suffocate 10 asphyxiate, extinguish

drowse 3 nod 4 doze 5 sleep 6 catnap, snooze 7 doze off, drop off, shut-eye, slumber 10 forty winks

drowsy 4 dozy 5 dopey 6 droopy, sleepy, torpid 7 languid 8 indolent, sluggish 9 lethargic, somnolent, soporific 10 slumberous 13 lackadaisical

Dr. Seuss 6 Geisel (Theodor Seuss) _book:_ 11 Cat in the Hat (The) 15 Green Eggs and Ham, Yertle the Turtle 19 Horton Hatches the Egg 26 How the Grinch Stole Christmas

drub 3 tan, wax, zap 4 bash, beat, club, deck, drum, flay, flog, lash, lick, mash, maul, pelt, trim, whip 5 baste, cream, crush, paste, pound, score, slash, smash, smear, spank, stamp, thump, wreck 6 batter, berate, bruise, buffet, deface, hammer, master, pummel, punish, revile, scorch, thrash, thresh, wallop 7 belabor, blister, censure, clobber, cripple, lambast, scourge, shatter, shellac, trounce 8 bulldoze, lambaste, lash into, outclass, outshine 9 castigate, excoriate, overwhelm

drubbing 4 loss, rout 6 defeat 7 setback 10 defeasance 11 shellacking

drudge 4 grub, hack, moil, peon, plod, slog 5 grind, slave 6 menial, slavey 7 grubber, plodder 8 dogsbody

drudgery 4 moil, toil 5 chore, grind 7 travail 9 grunt work 10 donkeywork 11 backbreaker

drudging 6 boring, tiring 7 irksome, tedious 8 dragging, tiresome 9 fatiguing, laborious, wearisome 10 monotonous

drug 4 dope, lull 5 sulfa 6 downer, ipecac, opiate, physic, poison, potion, remedy, statin 7 fen-phen, generic, stupefy 8 biologic, medicine, narcotic, nepenthe, relaxant, sedative 9 ibuprofen, medicinal, methadone 10 antibiotic, medicament, medication 11 thalidomide *addict:* 6 junkie *agent:* 4 narc *calming:* 8 sedative *experience:* 4 trip *illicit:* 3 ice, kif, LSD, acid, coke, dope, hash, meth, scag, snow, weed 5 crack, grass, opium, smack, speed 6 heroin, peyote 7 cocaine, crystal, hashish 8 cannabis, goofball 9 mescaline 10 methadrine, psilocybin *seller:* 10 pharmacist *sleep-inducing:* 8 hypnotic 9 soporific 11 barbiturate

drugged 4 high 5 dazed, doped, dopey 6 flying, loaded, stoned, zonked 8 benumbed, hopped-up, turned on 9 spaced-out, stupefied 10 narcotized

druggist 7 chemist 10 apothecary, pharmacist

drugstore 8 pharmacy 10 apothecary

druid 4 Celt 6 priest 7 prophet *sacred object:* 3 oak 9 mistletoe

drum 3 keg, vat 4 beat, cask 5 conga, tabor 6 barrel, tom-tom, tympan 7 tambour, timpani (plural), tympani (plural) 8 cylinder *Indian:* 5 tabla 8 mridanga *Irish:* 7 bodhran *large:* 4 bass 7 timbale *small:* 5 bongo, tabor 7 timbrel *string:* 5 snare

drumbeat 4 flam, roll, tuck 6 ruffle, tattoo 7 booming, pit-a-pat, rat-a-tat 8 rataplan

drumfire 5 salvo 6 volley 7 barrage, booming 9 broadside, cannonade, fusillade 11 bombardment

drumhead 4 skin 7 summary

drummer 4 Rich (Buddy) 5 Krupa (Gene), Roach (Max), Starr (Ringo), Watts (Charlie) 6 Blakey (Art), hawker, Puente (Tito), vendor 7 peddler 8 pitchman, salesman

drum up 6 invent 7 canvass, solicit 9 originate *interest:* 8 ballyhoo

drunk 3 lit, sot 4 lush, soak, wino 5 lit up, souse, tight, tipsy 6 blotto, boozer, juiced, soused, stewed, stinko, tiddly, wasted, zonked 7 crocked, guzzler, pie-eyed, sloshed, squiffy, tippler 8 squiffed 9 inebriate, plastered 10 boozehound, inebriated 11 intoxicated

drunkard 3 sot 4 lush, soak, wino 5 rummy, souse, stiff, toper 6 bibber, boozer, soaker 7 guzzler, swiller, tippler, tosspot 9 alcoholic, inebriate, juicehead 10 boozehound 11 dipsomaniac

Drusilla *brother:* 8 Caligula *father:* 5 Herod 10 Germanicus *husband:* 5 Felix *mother:* 9 Agrippina *sister:* 8 Berenice 9 Agrippina

dry 3 set 4 arid, brut, dull, sere, sour, tart 5 baked, dusty, parch, stale, wizen 6 barren, desert, harden, stolid, thirst, wither 7 congeal, deadpan, parched, shrivel, sterile, thirsty 8 rainless, solidify, tearless, teetotal, withered 9 anhydrous, dehydrate, desiccate, evaporate, unwatered 10 dehydrated, desiccated 11 unemotional 12 matter-of-fact 13 uninteresting *combining form:* 3 xer 4 xero *goods:* 6 linens, napery 8 clothing, textiles *out:* 5 sober 8 soberize *period:* 7 drought *wine:* 3 sec 4 brut

dryasdust 4 arid, dull 5 banal, inane, vapid 6 boring, stodgy 7 insipid, prosaic, tedious 9 wearisome 10 uninspired 13 uninteresting

dry measure 4 peck, pint 5 quart 6 bushel

Dryope *form:* 5 lotus *husband:* 9 Andraemon *sister:* 4 Iole

dry up 4 wilt 5 wizen 6 wither 7 deplete, exhaust, mummify, shrivel 9 desiccate, disappear, evaporate

dual 3 two 4 twin 5 duple 6 bifold, binary, double, duplex, paired 7 coupled, matched, twofold 8 matching 9 duplicate

dualistic 5 duple 6 bifold, binary, double, duplex, paired 7 twofold 9 Manichean 10 Manichaean

dualize 4 copy, dupe 5 clone 6 double 9 duplicate, replicate, reproduce

dub 4 call, name, term, trim 5 style, title 6 duffer 7 baptize, bungler, entitle, fumbler 8 christen, nickname, rerecord 9 blunderer, designate 10 denominate

dubiety 5 doubt 7 concern 8 mistrust 9 confusion, suspicion 10 skepticism 11 incertitude, incredulity, uncertainty 12 doubtfulness

dubious 4 iffy 5 fishy 6 unsure 7 suspect, unclear 8 doubtful, hesitant, unlikely 9 equivocal, skeptical, uncertain, undecided 10 improbable, unreliable 11 mistrustful, problematic, questioning, unconvinced, unpromising 12 questionable, undependable, undetermined

dubitable 5 fishy 7 suspect 8 doubtful, marginal 9 ambiguous, uncertain, unsettled 10 borderline 11 problematic 13 indeterminate

duce 5 ruler 6 despot, leader, tyrant 8 dictator 9 Mussolini (Benito), oppressor, strongman

duck 3 bob, bow, dip, shy 4 bend, dive, dunk, shun 5 avoid, dodge, douse, elude, evade, fence, parry, shirk, stoop 6 escape, plunge 7 back out, immerse 8 sidestep, submerge, submerse 10 canvasback *Asian:* 5 Pekin 8 mandarin *dabbling:* 7 gadwall, mallard *diving:* 4 smew

7 pochard **9** merganser **10** bufflehead
Eurasian: **4** smew *European:* **8** shelduck
genus: **4** Anas *group:* **4** team **5** brace,
flock, skein **6** flight *hunter's screen:*
5 blind *male:* **5** drake *red-wattled:*
7 Muscovy *river:* **4** teal **6** wigeon **7** pintail, widgeon *scaup:* **8** bluebill *sea:*
5 eider, scaup **6** scoter

duckbill 8 platypus **9** hadrosaur,
monotreme

duck soup 4 easy, snap **5** cinch **6** breeze,
picnic, simple **8** kid stuff, painless,
pushover **10** child's play **11** piece
of cake

ducky 4 cute **5** swell **6** lovely, peachy
7 darling **9** hunky-dory **10** peachy-keen

duct 4 pipe, tube **5** canal **6** course, runway **7** channel, conduit **11** watercourse
anatomical: **3** vas **4** vasa (plural)

ductile 6 pliant, supple **7** plastic, pliable
8 flexible, moldable **9** adaptable, compliant, malleable, tractable *metal:*
4 wire

ductless gland see ENDOCRINE GLAND

dud 3 dog **4** bomb, bust, flop **5** lemon,
loser **6** bummer, misfit, turkey **7** debacle, failure, washout **8** abortion **9** valueless **11** ineffective

dude 3 fop, guy **4** beau, buck, rake
5 blood, dandy **6** fellow **7** coxcomb
8 macaroni **9** exquisite **12** Beau Brummell, lounge lizard

dudgeon 3 ire **4** fury, huff, miff, rage
5 anger, pique, wrath **7** chagrin,
offense, outrage, umbrage **8** vexation
10 resentment **11** indignation **12** exasperation

duds 3 rig **4** garb, gear, rags, togs
5 dress, getup, weeds **6** attire, things
7 apparel, clothes, raiment, threads,
toggery **8** clothing, garments **9** trappings, vestments **11** habiliments

due 4 debt, just, owed **5** lumps, owing,
right **6** direct, earned, lawful, proper,
unpaid **7** arrears, condign, deserts,
exactly, merited, payable, payment,
regular **8** adequate, deserved, directly,
expected, rightful, suitable **9** deserving,
equitable, liability, requisite, scheduled
10 ascribable, obligatory, receivable,
satisfying, sufficient **11** appropriate,
outstanding **12** compensation, satisfaction

duel 4 tilt **5** fight, joust **6** combat **7** contest, dispute **8** conflict

duenna 8 chaperon **9** chaperone, companion, governess

duet *dancer's:* **9** pas de deux

due to 4 over **7** owing to, through
9 because of **11** considering

duff 3 can **4** buns, butt, rear, rump, tail,
tush **5** fanny, slack **6** bottom **7** keister,
pudding, rear end **8** backside, buttocks,
coal dust, derriere, fine coal

duffer 4 boob, clod, dolt, dope, yo-yo
5 chump, dunce, klutz **6** dimwit, dum-
dum, lubber, nitwit **7** dullard, fumbler,
peddler, pinhead **8** bonehead, dumbbell, lunkhead, numskull **9** blockhead,
ignoramus, numbskull, simpleton
10 nincompoop, stumblebum **11** incompetent

dugout 5 canoe **6** trench **7** piragua,
pirogue, shelter

duiker 8 antelope

dukedom 5 duchy **6** domain

dulcet 5 sweet **7** melodic, tuneful
8 charming, cheerful, engaging,
euphonic, pleasant, pleasing, soothing
9 agreeable, melodious **10** euphonious
11 mellifluous

dulcimer 6 zither **8** psaltery *Hungarian:*
8 cimbalom *Persian:* **6** santir **7** santour

dull 3 dim, dun, mat **4** arid, blah, blur,
drab, flat, numb **5** blunt, dense, dusty,
faded, ho-hum, inert, matte, muddy,
muted **6** benumb, blurry, boring, dead-
en, dreary, gloomy, leaden, obtuse,
stodgy, stupid **7** blunted, humdrum,
insipid, muffled, prosaic, stupefy, subdued, tarnish, tedious **8** banausic, bromidic, deadened, discolor, lifeless, listless, monotone, plodding, sluggish
9 bloodless, colorless, dim-witted,
dryasdust, insensate, ponderous, wearisome **10** dispirited, indistinct, insensible, lackluster, lusterless, monotonous,
pedestrian **11** commonplace, desensitize, insensitive, thickheaded, thick-
witted, unsharpened **12** simpleminded
13 uninteresting

dullard 3 oaf **4** bird, boob, clod, dolt,
dope, yo-yo **5** chump, dummy, dunce,
idiot, moron, ninny, noddy, stupe
6 dimwit, dum-dum, nitwit **7** airhead,
pinhead **8** bonehead, dumbbell, imbecile, lunkhead, meathead, numskull
9 birdbrain, blockhead, ignoramus,
lamebrain, numbskull, simpleton
10 dunderhead **11** chowderhead,
chucklehead

dullness 5 ennui **6** apathy, stupor, tedium, torpor **7** boredom, languor **8** hebetude, lethargy, monotony **9** bluntness,
denseness, lassitude, stupidity, torpidity
12 indifference, listlessness, sluggishness

duly 8 properly, suitably **9** correctly, regularly **12** sufficiently **13** appropriately

duma 7 council **8** assembly, congress
11 legislature

Dumas character 5 Athos **6** Aramis,

Dantès (Edmond) 7 Camille, Porthos 9 D'Artagnan

dumb 3 mum 4 dull, mute 5 dense, quiet, thick 6 deaden, obtuse, silent, stupid 7 doltish, foolish, idiotic, moronic 8 duncical, ignorant, taciturn, wordless 9 dim-witted, fatheaded, voiceless 10 speechless, tongue-tied 11 blockheaded, thick-witted, tight-lipped 12 closemouthed, inarticulate, simple-minded, tight-mouthed, unresponsive

dumbbell see DULLARD

dumbfound 5 amaze 6 boggle, puzzle 7 astound, nonplus, perplex, stagger 8 astonish, bewilder, bowl over, confound, distract, surprise 9 take aback 11 flabbergast ·

dumbfounded 5 agape 6 amazed 7 puzzled, shocked 8 startled 9 astounded, perplexed, staggered, surprised 10 astonished, bewildered, bowled over, confounded, distracted, nonplussed, taken aback 13 thunderstruck

dummkopf 3 oaf 4 boob, clod, dodo, dolt, dope, fool, goof, jerk, mutt, simp, yo-yo 5 chump, dummy, dunce, idiot, moron, ninny, noddy, stupe 6 dimwit, donkey, dum-dum, nitwit, noodle 7 airhead, dullard, pinhead, schnook 8 bonehead, clodpoll, dumbbell, dumbhead, imbecile, lunkhead, meathead, numskull 9 birdbrain, blockhead, ignoramus, lamebrain, numbskull, simpleton, thickhead 10 dunderhead, hammerhead, nincompoop 11 chowderhead, chucklehead, knucklehead

dummy 4 boob, clod, dodo, dolt, mock, sham, yo-yo 5 chump, dunce, false, idiot, model, moron, ninny, noddy, stupe 6 dimwit, dum-dum, effigy, ersatz, layout, mock-up, nitwit, puppet, stooge 7 airhead, dullard, manikin, pinhead, stand-in 8 bonehead, dumbbell, imbecile, mannekin, meathead, numskull 9 birdbrain, blockhead, ignoramus, imitation, lamebrain, numbskull, simpleton, simulated 10 artificial, dunderhead, fictitious, nincompoop, substitute 11 chowderhead, chucklehead

dump 4 drop, junk 5 chuck, depot, ditch, scrap 6 armory, pigpen, pigsty, plunge 7 abandon, arsenal, deep-six, discard 8 jettison, magazine, throw out 9 stockpile, throw away 10 depository

dumpling 5 dough 8 quenelle 10 butterball

dumps 4 funk 5 blues, dolor, gloom, mopes, slump 7 sadness 8 doldrums 9 dejection 10 depression, gloominess,

melancholy 11 despondency, unhappiness 12 mournfulness

dumpy 5 dingy, seedy, squat, stout 6 chubby, chunky, shabby, slummy, stocky, stubby, stumpy 7 run-down 8 heavyset, thickset 9 shapeless 10 broken-down 11 dilapidated, thick-bodied

dun 3 dim, fly 4 dull, drab, gray 5 annoy, brown, dusky, horse, murky, press 6 demand, gloomy, mayfly, needle, pester, plague, somber, sombre 9 ephemerid, importune

Duncan's slayer 7 Macbeth

dunce 3 oaf 4 boob, clod, dodo, dolt, dope, goof, mutt, simp, yo-yo 5 booby, chump, dummy, idiot, moron, ninny, noddy, stupe 6 dimwit, donkey, duffer, dum-dum, nitwit, noodle, stupid 7 airhead, dullard, fathead, pinhead 8 bonehead, clodpoll, dumbbell, imbecile, lunkhead, meathead, numskull 9 birdbrain, blockhead, ignoramus, lamebrain, numbskull, simpleton 10 dunderhead, hammerhead, nincompoop 11 chowderhead, chucklehead, knucklehead

Dunciad author 4 Pope (Alexander)

dundrearies 9 burnsides, sideburns 11 muttonchops 12 side-whiskers

dune 8 sandbank *area:* 3 erg

dung 4 muck 6 manure, ordure 9 excrement *beetle:* 6 scarab 9 tumblebug

dungeon 4 jail 5 vault 6 prison 9 black hole, oubliette

dunghill 6 midden

dunk 3 dip, sop 4 soak 5 douse, drown, souse 6 drench 7 immerse 8 saturate, submerge, submerse

dunlin 9 sandpiper

duo 4 duet, dyad, pair 5 brace 6 couple 7 doublet, twosome

dupe 3 con, kid, sap 4 butt, fool, gull, hoax, mark 5 cheat, chump, cozen, patsy, spoof, trick 6 befool, delude, double, outwit, pigeon, sucker 7 chicane, deceive, defraud, mislead 8 flimflam, hoodwink 9 bamboozle, victimize 11 double-cross, hornswoggle

dupery 3 con 4 scam, sham 5 cheat, fraud 6 deceit, humbug, hustle 7 chicane 8 cheating, flimflam, trickery 9 chicanery, deception, duplicity, imposture, swindling 10 dishonesty, hanky-panky 11 hoodwinking 13 double-dealing, sharp practice

duple 4 dual, twin 6 bifold, binary, double, duplex, paired 7 coupled, doubled, twofold 9 dualistic

duplex see DUPLE

duplicate 4 copy, fake, mate, redo, same, twin 5 clone, ditto, equal, match, mimeo, repro **6** carbon, double **7** dualize, imitate, replica **8** knockoff **9** companion, facsimile, identical, imitation, look-alike, replicate, reproduce **10** carbon copy, dead ringer, equivalent, reciprocal **11** counterfeit, counterpart, replication **12** reproduction

duplicitous 5 phony **6** shifty, sneaky **7** devious **8** delusive, guileful, scheming, sneaking, two-faced **9** deceitful, deceiving, deceptive, dishonest, underhand **10** fraudulent **11** underhanded **12** disingenuous **13** double-dealing

duplicity 5 fraud, guile **6** deceit **7** cunning, perfidy **8** scheming, trickery **9** chicanery, deception, treachery **10** dishonesty, doubleness **11** skulduggery **12** dissemblance, skullduggery **13** dissimulation, double-dealing

durability 4 wear **8** firmness **9** endurance, longevity, stability **10** permanence

durable 5 stout **6** stable, strong, sturdy **7** lasting **8** enduring **9** permanent, tenacious **10** dependable **11** long-lasting

durance 7 bondage **9** captivity, detention, restraint **11** confinement **12** enthrallment, imprisonment **13** incarceration

duration 3 run **4** term, time **6** extent, period **7** interim **8** interval **11** persistence

duress 5 force **6** menace, threat **8** bullying, coercion, menacing, pressure **9** restraint **10** compulsion, constraint **11** restriction **12** intimidation

during 4 amid **10** throughout

durra 7 sorghum **12** grain sorghum

durum 5 wheat

dusk 4 dark **7** evening **8** darkness, eventide, gloaming, twilight **9** nightfall **12** semidarkness

dusky 3 dim **4** dark **5** murky, swart **6** brunet, gloomy, opaque, twilit **7** obscure, shadowy, swarthy **8** funereal, nubilous, overcast, twilight **9** tenebrous **10** caliginous **11** dark-skinned

dust 4 grit, sand, sift, soot **5** ashes, grime **6** powder **8** sprinkle **10** besprinkle, sprinkling

dustbowl victim 4 Okie

dustup 3 row **4** spat **5** fight, melee, run-in, set-to **6** battle, fracas, hassle, tussle **7** dispute, quarrel, rhubarb, scuffle **8** argument, skirmish **9** bickering, brannigan **10** falling-out **11** altercation

dusty 3 dry **4** arid, dull **5** stale **7** parched, powdery, tedious, unswept

Dutch 7 trouble **8** hot water *African:* **9** Afrikaans *ceramics:* **5** delft *cheese:* **4** Edam **5** Gouda *dog breed:* **7** griffon

8 keeshond *painter:* **3** Dou (Gerrit, Gerard) **4** Cuyp (Aelbert Jacobsz), Gogh (Vincent van), Hals (Frans) **5** Bosch (Hieronymus), Hooch (Pieter de), Steen (Jan) **7** de Hooch (Pieter), Hobbema (Meindert), van Gogh (Vincent), Vermeer (Jan) **8** Mondrian (Piet), Ruysdael (Jacob van, Salomon van), Terborch (Gerard) **9** de Kooning (Willem), Honthorst (Gerrit van), Rembrandt (van Rijn) *philosopher:* **7** Spinoza (Benedict de) *scholar:* **7** Erasmus (Desiderius)

Dutch South African 4 Boer

dutiful 7 devoted **8** faithful **9** compliant **10** respectful **13** conscientious

duty 3 job, tax, use **4** levy, onus, role, task, work **5** chare, chore, stint **6** burden, charge, devoir, impost, office, tariff **7** respect, service **8** function **10** allegiance, assessment, assignment, commitment, obligation

dwarf 4 runt **5** gnome, pygmy, stunt, troll **6** midget, peewee **7** manikin **8** Tom Thumb **9** miniature **10** diminutive, homunculus **11** hop-o'-my-thumb, lilliputian *in Snow White:* **3** Doc **5** Dopey, Happy **6** Grumpy, Sleepy, Sneezy **7** Bashful *Scottish:* **7** blastie

dwarfish 5 pygmy, small **6** midget **7** minikin, stunted **8** inferior, pint-size **9** miniature, pint-sized **10** diminutive, undersized **11** lilliputian

dweeb 4 dork, drip, geek, nerd, wimp, wuss **5** loser **7** nebbish

dwell 3 lie **4** bide, live, stay **5** abide, exist **6** locate, remain, repose, reside, settle **7** hang out

dweller 7 citizen, denizen, settler **8** habitant, occupant, resident **10** inhabitant

dwelling 3 pad **4** casa, digs, home, nest **5** abode, haunt, house **7** address, habitat, lodging **8** domicile, quarters **9** residence **10** brownstone, habitation *American Indian:* **4** tipi **5** hogan, tepee **6** pueblo, teepee, wigwam *clergyman's:* **5** manse **7** rectory **8** vicarage **9** parsonage *crude:* **3** hut **4** camp **5** cabin, hovel, shack **6** cabana, shanty **7** barrack **8** barracks *Eskimo:* **5** igloo *grand:* **5** manor, manse, villa **6** palace **7** château, mansion *Hindu:* **6** ashram *Navajo:* **5** hogan *Russian:* **5** dacha *small:* **3** cot, hut **5** hovel **7** cottage **8** bungalow

dwindle 3 ebb **4** fade, fall, wane **5** abate, taper **6** lessen, recede, reduce, shrink, weaken, wither **7** decline, die away, die down, shrivel, slacken, subside **8** decrease, diminish, taper off **9** attenuate, drain away

dyad 3 duo, two **4** pair, yoke **5** brace, twins **6** couple **7** doublet, twosome

dye 4 tint 5 color, stain, tinge 7 pigment 8 colorant, pyronine, tincture *blue:* 4 woad 6 indigo 7 cyanine *for hair:* 5 henna *plant:* 4 woad 5 sumac 6 madder *red:* 5 eosin, henna 6 kermes, ruddle 7 cudbear, fuchsin, magenta 8 alizarin, fuchsine, amaranth, safranin 9 cochineal, rhodamine, safranine 10 erythrosin *violet:* 6 archil *yellow:* 7 flavine 8 orpiment *yellowish red:* 7 annatto

dyed-in-the-wool 5 loyal, sworn 7 devoted, die-hard, old-line, settled, staunch 8 faithful, hard-core, orthodox, standpat, true-blue 9 confirmed, hard-shell, steadfast 10 deep-rooted, deep-seated, entrenched, inveterate, unwavering 11 established 13 bred-in-the-bone, thoroughgoing

dyewood 6 fustic 10 brazilwood

dying 6 demise 7 done for, quietus 8 moribund 9 departure 10 extinction, in extremis 12 annihilation

dynamic 7 driving, intense 8 forceful, forcible, powerful, vigorous 9 energetic, strenuous 10 compelling, energizing

dynamite 4 raze 5 blast 6 blow up 7 destroy, explode, shatter 8 demolish 9 explosive 10 annihilate *inventor:* 5 Nobel (Alfred)

dynamo 8 go-getter, live wire 9 generator 10 ball of fire 11 self-starter

dysentery 4 flux 6 scours 8 diarrhea

dyslogistic 7 adverse 10 derogatory, pejorative 11 deleterious, disparaging, prejudicial, unfavorable

dyspepsia 5 gloom 6 dismay 7 chagrin, pyrosis 8 glumness 9 dejection, heartburn 10 gloominess 11 frustration, indigestion

dyspeptic 5 cross, surly 6 crabby, morose, ornery 9 irritable 10 ill-humored, ill-natured 11 disgruntled, ill-tempered

dysphoria 4 funk 5 blues, dumps, gloom, mopes 6 sorrow 7 sadness 9 dejection 10 depression, gloominess, melancholy 11 unhappiness 12 mournfulness, wretchedness 13 cheerlessness

E

each 3 all, per 4 a pop 5 every 6 apiece 8 everyone 9 per capita, everybody

eager 3 hot 4 agog, avid, keen, wild 5 antsy, hyper, itchy, pushy, ready, vital 6 ardent, fervid, gung ho, heated, hungry, intent, pining, raring 7 anxious, athirst, burning, craving, earnest, fervent, longing, restive, thirsty, wishful 8 appetent, aspiring, covetous, desirous, restless, striving, vehement, yearning 9 ambitious, energetic, hankering, impatient, voracious 10 breathless, solicitous 11 impassioned 12 enthusiastic

eagerness 4 push, urge, zeal, zest, zing 5 ardor, gusto 6 desire, fervor, hunger, spirit, thirst 7 avidity, craving, itching, longing, passion 8 alacrity, ambition, appetite, fervency, vitality, yearning 9 intensity, quickness, vehemence 10 enthusiasm, impatience, resolution

eagle 4 hawk 9 accipiter *nest:* 4 aery 5 aerie, eyrie *North American:* 4 bald 6 golden *sea:* 4 erne 6 osprey

eagle-eyed 8 vigilant, watchful 9 attentive, observant 10 perceptive 12 sharp-sighted

ear 6 notice 7 auricle 9 attention *bone:* 5 anvil, incus 6 hammer, stapes 7 malleus, stirrup *canal:* 5 scala *combining form:* 3 aur, oto 4 auri, otic *doctor:* 9 otologist *inner:* 9 labyrinth *middle:* 8 tympanum *outer:* 5 pinna *part:* 4 drum, lobe 5 canal 6 tragus 7 cochlea *relating to:* 5 aural 9 auricular *science:* 7 otology

eardrum 8 tympanum

_____ **Earhart** 6 Amelia

earl 4 lord, peer 5 count, noble 8 nobleman, seigneur 9 patrician 10 aristocrat

earlier 3 ere, yet 4 once 5 as yet, so far 6 before, sooner 7 already, thus far 8 formerly, hitherto, previous 9 erstwhile, preceding 10 beforehand, heretofore, previously

earlier than 3 pre 6 before

earliest 5 first, prime 6 maiden, primal 7 initial, pioneer, primary 8 original, primeval, pristine **10** aboriginal, primordial

earlike projection 3 lug

early 3 old **5** first, prior **6** primal, timely **7** ancient, betimes **8** original, previous, primeval, pristine, untimely **9** preceding, premature, primitive **10** antecedent, antiquated, precocious, primordial **11** prematurely *prefix:* **5** paleo

earn 3 bag, get, net, win **4** gain, make, rate, reap **5** amass, clear, gross, merit, score **6** attain, come by, obtain, pick up, rack up, secure, wangle **7** acquire, bring in, collect, deserve, harvest, procure, produce, realize, receive **8** pull down **9** bring home, knock down

earnest 3 vow **4** bond, busy, firm, keen, pawn, true, warm **5** grave, sober, token **6** active, ardent, intent, pledge, solemn, somber, surety **7** deposit, genuine, intense, serious, sincere, up front, warrant, zealous **8** contract, covenant, diligent, interest, security, sedulous, studious **9** assiduous, heartfelt **10** determined, no-nonsense, passionate, sobersided, thoughtful, unaffected **11** industrious **12** enthusiastic, wholehearted

earnestly 5 madly **7** for real, like mad

earnestness 6 fervor **7** gravity, honesty, passion, resolve **8** sobriety **9** sincerity **10** absorption, doggedness **11** engrossment, persistence **12** perseverance **13** concentration, determination

earnings 3 net, pay **4** gain **5** lucre, wages **6** income, profit, return, salary **7** profits **8** proceeds, take-home **9** emolument **10** bottom line

ear shell see ABALONE

earshot 5 range, sound **7** hearing

earsplitting 4 loud **6** shrill **7** blaring, grating, raucous, roaring **8** piercing, strident **9** deafening, dissonant **10** screeching, stentorian **11** full-mouthed

earth 3 orb, sod **4** dirt, land, soil, turf **5** globe, world **6** ground, planet, sphere **7** dry land, terrain **8** creation **10** terra firma *combining form:* **3** geo **4** geog **6** tellur **7** telluro *core:* **12** centrosphere *god:* **3** Geb, Keb, Seb **5** Dagan *goddess:* **4** Erda, Gaea **5** Ceres, Nintu **6** Kishar **7** Demeter, Nerthus *relating to:* **8** telluric **9** planetary **11** terrestrial *satellite:* **4** moon *science:* **7** geology **9** geography

earthenware 4 clay **5** china, delft **7** biscuit, faience, pottery **8** clayware, crockery, majolica **9** porcelain, stoneware **10** terra-cotta

earthlike 11 terrestrial

earthly 6 likely, mortal **7** mundane, worldly **8** feasible, material, physical, possible, probable, temporal **9** corporeal, potential, practical **10** imaginable **11** conceivable, terrestrial, unspiritual

earthquake 5 shake, shock **6** tremor **7** temblor *measuring device:* **11** seismograph, seismometer *relating to:* **7** seismic *science:* **10** seismology **11** seismometry

earthwork 4 bank, wall **7** bulwark, rampart **10** embankment **13** fortification

earthworm 7 annelid **12** night crawler

earthy 3 low **4** base, real **5** crude, dirty, dusty, gross, muddy, sandy **6** clayey, coarse, common, simple **7** mundane, worldly **8** temporal **9** corporeal, inelegant, practical, pragmatic, realistic, unrefined **10** hard-boiled, hardheaded, indelicate, uncultured, unpolished **11** down-to-earth, terrestrial **12** matter-of-fact **13** materialistic, unsentimental

earwax 7 cerumen

ease 3 aid **4** bate, calm, dull, free, help, rest **5** allay, loose, peace, poise, relax, slack **6** assist, deaden, loosen, relief, repose, soften **7** assuage, comfort, fluency, improve, leisure, lighten, mollify, relieve, slacken **8** calmness, deftness, diminish, dispatch, facility, idleness, mitigate, moderate, pleasure, security, serenity **9** abundance, affluence, alleviate, expertise, reduction, untighten, well-being **10** ameliorate, artfulness, efficiency, expertness, facilitate, inactivity, mitigation, moderation, prosperity, relaxation, smoothness **11** alleviation, contentment, nonchalance, spontaneity, tranquility **12** satisfaction, skillfulness, tranquillity *off:* **3** ebb **4** bate, fade, fall, flag, wane **5** abate, let up, loose, relax, slack **6** lessen, loosen, relent, unbend, unwind **7** die away, die down, slacken, subside **8** diminish, loosen up, moderate **9** untighten

easel 4 desk **5** frame, stand **7** support **9** workbench, worktable

easement 6 relief **7** comfort **10** mitigation, palliative **11** alleviation, consolation, restorative **13** mollification

easily 6 simply **7** handily, lightly, readily **8** facilely, smoothly **11** dexterously, efficiently **12** effortlessly

East 4 Asia **6** Levant, Orient

Easter 5 Pasch *relating to:* **7** paschal *symbol:* **3** egg **4** lamb **5** bunny **6** rabbit

eastern 8 oriental **9** Levantine *countries:* **6** Orient

East Indian country 8 Malaysia **9** Indonesia, Singapore

East Timor *capital:* **4** Dili *monetary unit:* **6** dollar *neighbor:* **9** Indonesia

easy 3 lax 4 calm, cozy, glib, mild, soft, snug 5 basic, clear, comfy, cushy, light, loose, naive, plain, suave 6 breezy, facile, fluent, kindly, placid, poised, polite, secure, serene, simple, smooth, urbane 7 amiable, courtly, cursive, evident, flowing, lenient, obvious, patient, relaxed 8 apparent, composed, familiar, graceful, gullible, in clover, informal, manifest, merciful, obliging, peaceful, pleasant, sociable, tolerant, tranquil, trusting 9 collected, credulous, forgiving, indulgent, possessed 10 charitable, diplomatic, effortless, elementary, forbearing, gregarious, permissive 11 comfortable, complaisant, good-humored, good-natured, susceptible, sympathetic, unconcerned 12 good-tempered 13 compassionate, mollycoddling, self-possessed, uncomplicated

easygoing 3 lax 4 calm, cool, lazy 5 quiet 6 breezy, casual, dégagé, folksy, placid, poised, sedate, serene 7 affable, offhand, patient, relaxed, unfussy 8 amenable, carefree, composed, down home, fainéant, flexible, indolent, informal, laid-back, slothful, together, tranquil 9 apathetic, indulgent, offhanded, unhurried 10 nonchalant, permissive, unaffected 11 comfortable, complaisant, indifferent, low-pressure, pococurante, unconcerned, unflappable, uninhibited 12 devil-may-care, even-tempered, happy-go-lucky, light-hearted 13 self-possessed, unconstrained

easy mark 3 sap 4 butt, dupe, fool, gull 5 chump, patsy, sport 6 pigeon, softie, sucker, turkey, victim 7 fall guy 8 pushover 9 soft touch 11 sitting duck

eat 3 sup, vex 4 bite, chow, dine, gnaw, meal, pick, take, wolf 5 annoy, erode, feast, gorge, graze, hound, lunch, mouth, munch, scarf, scoff, scour, snack, use up 6 bother, devour, feed on, gobble, harass, hassle, ingest, inhale, nibble, pester, pick at, pig out, plague, take in 7 banquet, consume, corrode, exhaust, gorge on, swallow, torment 8 chow down, dissolve, take food, wear away 9 breakfast, decompose, masticate, partake of, polish off 10 break bread, gormandize, nibble away

eatable 6 edible 8 esculent, harmless 9 palatable 10 comestible, digestible

eatery 4 café 5 diner, grill 10 coffee shop, restaurant 11 greasy spoon 12 luncheonette

eating place 3 pub 4 café, mess 5 diner, grill, joint 6 bistro, tavern 7 automat, beanery, canteen, dinette, tearoom 8 cookshop, messroom, pizzeria, snack bar 9 brasserie, cafeteria, chophouse, hash house, lunchroom, trattoria 10 coffee shop, restaurant, steak house 11 greasy spoon 12 luncheonette

eavesdrop 3 bug, tap 4 lurk 7 monitor 8 listen in, overhear

ebb 4 drop, fade, fall, flag, tide, wane 5 abate, droop, let up 6 lessen, recede, reduce, relent, shrink, wither 7 decline, descent, die away, die down, ease off, retreat, slacken, subside 8 decrease, diminish, languish, moderate, withdraw 10 retrograde

Eblis 5 Satan *son:* 3 Tir 4 Awar 5 Dasim 8 Zalambur

ebon, ebony 3 jet 4 inky 5 black, jetty, raven, sable 6 brunet 8 brunette, jet-black 9 pitch-dark 10 pitch-black

ebullience 3 vim, zip 4 brio, élan, zing 5 gusto 6 gaiety 7 abandon, elation 8 buoyancy, vitality, vivacity 9 animation 10 enthusiasm, excitement, exuberance, liveliness 11 high spirits 12 exhilaration, spiritedness 13 effervescence

ebullient 3 mad 4 gaga 5 brash, zingy, zippy 6 bouncy, bubbly, elated, frothy, geeked, pumped, raring 7 boiling, chipper, excited, gleeful, gushing, vibrant 8 hopped-up 9 sprightly, vivacious 11 exhilarated 12 enthusiastic, high-spirited 13 irrepressible

eccentric 3 odd, nut 4 coot, kook 5 crank, crazy, droll, flaky, freak, funky, funny, goofy, kooky, nutty, queer, wacky, weird 6 far out, oddity, quaint, quirky, screwy, weirdo, whacko, whacky 7 bizarre, curious, deviant, erratic, heretic, oddball, offbeat, strange, unusual 8 aberrant, abnormal, bohemian, cockeyed, crackpot, goofball, maverick, original, peculiar, singular, uncommon 9 anomalous, character, deviating, fantastic, fruitcake, grotesque, irregular, off-center, screwball, unnatural, whimsical 10 elliptical, off-balance, unbalanced, uncentered 11 exceptional 13 idiosyncratic, nonconformist

eccentricity 4 kink 5 quirk, twist 8 crotchet, quiddity 9 deviation, weirdness 10 aberration 11 strangeness 12 idiosyncrasy

ecclesiastic see CLERGYMAN

ecclesiastical 4 holy 5 papal 6 church, sacred 8 churchly, clerical, pastoral, priestly 9 apostolic, canonical, episcopal, spiritual, synagogal 10 churchlike, pontifical, rabbinical, sacerdotal

11 ministerial, patriarchal, theological
12 episcopalian, evangelistic, tabernacular

ecdysiast see STRIPTEASER

echelon 3 row 4 file, line, rank, tier
5 grade, group, level, order, queue
6 string 7 chevron 9 formation

echidna 8 anteater 9 monotreme
13 spiny anteater

Echidna *father:* 7 Phorcys 8 Chrysaor
mother: 4 Ceto 10 Callirrhoë *offspring:*
5 Hydra 6 dragon, Orthus, Sphinx
7 Chimera 8 Cerberus, Chimaera

echinoderm 6 urchin 7 crinoid, sea star
8 starfish 9 coelomate, sea urchin
11 sea cucumber

echo 3 ape 4 mime, ring 5 evoke, mimic,
trace 6 mirror, parrot, repeat, result,
reverb, second 7 imitate, iterate,
reflect, resound, revoice, vestige 8 resonate, response 9 duplicate, imitation,
reiterate 10 reflection, repetition
11 reverberate 12 repercussion
13 reverberation

Echo 5 nymph, oread *beloved:* 9 Narcissus

echoic 7 mimetic 9 imitative 10 derivative 12 onomatopoeic 13 onomatopoetic

éclat 4 bang, dash, fame, pomp 5 glory,
honor, kudos 6 luster, lustre, praise,
renown, repute 7 acclaim, display, laurels, stardom, success 8 applause, eminence, prestige, standing 9 celebrity,
notoriety, publicity 10 brilliance, brilliancy, exaltation, prominence, reputation 11 distinction, ostentation

eclectic 5 broad, fussy, mixed, picky
6 choosy, select, varied 7 diverse,
finicky, mingled 8 assorted, catholic,
elective 9 inclusive, selective 10 discerning, fastidious, particular 11 diversified 12 dilettantish, multifarious
13 heterogeneous

eclipse 3 dim 5 bedim, cloud, cover,
excel, outdo, shade 6 darken, exceed,
shadow 7 becloud, decline, obscure,
surpass 8 downfall, outshine 9 adumbrate, obfuscate, overcloud 10 extinguish, overshadow

eclogue 3 ode 4 idyl, poem 5 idyll, lyric
8 pastoral

ecological 5 green 8 bionomic *community:* 5 biome

ecology 9 bionomics 11 environment

economic 6 fiscal 8 material, monetary
9 budgetary, financial, pecuniary
10 mercantile, profitable *doctrine:*
12 laissez-faire *system:* 9 communism,
socialism 10 capitalism 11 syndicalism
12 mercantilism

economical 4 mean 5 canny, close, spare
6 frugal, saving, stingy 7 careful, miserly, prudent, sparing, thrifty 8 skimping
9 efficient, niggardly, penny-wise, penurious, provident, scrimping 10 unwasteful 12 cheeseparing, parsimonious
13 penny-pinching

economist *American:* 5 Arrow (Kenneth), Simon (Herbert, Julian), Solow
(Robert), Tobin (James) 6 Becker
(Gary), George (Henry), Thurow
(Lester), Veblen (Thorstein), Walker
(Amasa), Weaver (Robert) 7 Krugman
(Paul), Kuznets (Simon), Stigler
(George), Volcker (Paul) 8 Friedman
(Milton), Stiglitz (Joseph) 9 Galbraith
(John Kenneth), Greenspan (Alan),
Samuelson (Paul) 10 Schumpeter
(Joseph) *Austrian:* 5 Hayek (Friedrich
von), Mises (Ludwig von) *Canadian:*
7 Leacock (Stephen) *Dutch:* 9 Tinbergen (Jan) *English:* 3 Sen (Amartya)
4 Mill (John Stuart) 5 Coase (Ronald),
Hayek (Friedrich von), Pigou (Arthur)
6 Engels (Friedrich), Keynes (John
Maynard) 7 Bagehot (Walter), Malthus
(Thomas), Ricardo (David) *French:*
3 Say (Jean-Baptiste) 6 Monnet (Jean),
Turgot (Anne-Robert-Jacques), Walras
(Léon) 7 Quesnay (François) *German:*
4 Marx (Karl) 5 Weber (Max) 6 Engels
(Friedrich) 7 Schacht (Hjalmar) *Indian:*
3 Sen (Amartya) *Scottish:* 4 Mill
(James) 5 Smith (Adam) *Swedish:*
6 Myrdal (Gunnar) *Swiss:* 8 Sismondi
(Simonde de)

economize 4 save 5 skimp, stint 6 manage, scrimp 7 husband 8 conserve
10 cut corners 12 pinch pennies

economy 6 saving, thrift 8 prudence,
skimping 9 concision, frugality, husbandry, parsimony, restraint, scrimping
10 discretion, efficiency, providence,
stinginess 11 carefulness, conciseness,
miserliness, thriftiness 13 niggardliness

Eco novel 13 Name of the Rose (The)
17 Foucault's Pendulum

ecru see BEIGE

ecstasy 3 joy 5 bliss 6 frenzy, heaven,
trance 7 delight, elation, madness, rapture 8 euphoria, paradise, rhapsody
9 beatitude, transport 10 exaltation,
joyfulness 11 blessedness, derangement,
enchantment, high spirits, inspiration
12 blissfulness, exhilaration, intoxication 13 seventh heaven

ecstatic 6 elated, joyful 7 gleeful
8 euphoric, exultant, jubilant, thrilled
9 delirious, delighted, entranced, overjoyed, rapturous 11 exhilarated, transported

Ecuador *capital:* 5 Quito *city:* 6 Ambato, Cuenca 7 Machala 9 Guayaquil *Indian people:* 7 Quechua *island group:* 9 Galápagos *language:* 7 Spanish *monetary unit:* 5 sucre 6 dollar *mountain range:* 5 Andes *neighbor:* 4 Peru 8 Colombia *volcano:* 6 Sangay 7 Cayambe 8 Cotopaxi 10 Chimborazo

ecumenical 6 cosmic, global 7 general, generic 8 catholic 9 inclusive, planetary, universal, worldwide 12 all-inclusive, cosmopolitan 13 comprehensive

ecumenical council 4 Lyon 5 Basel, Lyons, Trent 6 Nicene 7 Ephesus, Ferrara, Lateran, Vatican 8 Florence 9 Chalcedon, Constance

eczema 6 tetter

edacious see VORACIOUS

eddy 4 purl 5 swirl, twirl, whirl, whorl 6 vortex 8 backwash 9 backwater, maelstrom, whirlpool 11 counterflow

edema 5 croup, tumor 6 dropsy 8 anasarca, swelling

Eden 6 heaven, utopia 7 arcadia, elysium 8 paradise *river:* 5 Gihon 6 Pishon 8 Hiddekel 9 Euphrates

edentate 5 sloth 8 aardvark, anteater, pangolin 9 armadillo, toothless

Edessa's king 5 Abgar

edge 3 cut, end, hem, lip, rim 4 bank, bite, brim, cusp, draw, ease, hone, inch, lead, limb, line, pink, side, whet, worm 5 arris, bound, brink, bulge, force, ledge, picot, point, ridge, sidle, skirt, sting, strop, verge 6 border, fringe, margin, nosing 7 acidity, contour, chamfer, outline, serrate, sharpen, vantage 8 acerbity, acridity, boundary, emborder, handicap, keenness, surround, thinness 9 acuteness, advantage, extremity, harshness, head start, perimeter, periphery, sharpness, threshold, upper hand 10 causticity, shrillness, stringency 11 astringency 12 incisiveness 13 effectiveness

edge city 5 exurb 6 suburb

edged 4 acid, tart 5 acute, sharp 6 strong 7 cutting 8 incisive, piercing

edge in 6 inject 9 interject, interpose, insinuate 10 infiltrate 11 interpolate

edging 3 hem 4 lace 5 braid, frill, limit 6 border, fringe, lacing, margin, piping 7 flounce, selvage 8 rickrack, selvedge, trimming

edgy 3 hip 5 funky, nervy, sharp, tense, testy 6 daring, touchy, uneasy 7 excited, keyed up, offbeat, restive, uptight 8 Bohemian, out-there, renegade, restless, skittery, skittish, volatile 9 excitable, impatient, irascible, irrita-

ble 10 high-strung, outlandish 11 provocative

edible 8 esculent 9 palatable 10 comestible *root:* 3 oca, yam 4 beet, taro, yuca 6 carrot, daikon, ginger, jicama, potato, radish, turnip, wasabi 7 burdock, cassava, ginseng, malanga, parsnip, salsify 8 celeriac, galangal, kohlrabi, rutabaga 11 horseradish, sweet potato *seed:* 3 nut, pea 4 bean 6 peanut

edibles 4 chow, eats, feed, food, grub 6 viands 7 aliment, goodies, nurture 8 victuals 9 provender 10 provisions, sustenance 11 comestibles

edict 3 law 4 bull, fiat, rule 5 canon, order, ukase 6 decree, dictum, ruling 7 command, dictate, mandate, precept, statute 9 directive, manifesto, ordinance, prescript 10 injunction, regulation 12 proclamation 13 pronouncement *Islamic:* 5 fatwa *papal:* 4 bull 8 decretal

Edict of ___ 5 Milan, Worms 6 Nantes

edifice 4 pile 8 building, erection 9 structure

edify 5 teach 6 better, fill in, illume, inform, update, uplift 7 educate, elevate, enhance, improve 8 illumine, instruct 9 elucidate, enlighten 10 illuminate

edit 3 cut 4 cull, omit 5 adapt, alter, amend, emend, fix up 6 delete, doctor, excise, polish, redact, refine, review, revise, reword, select 7 abridge, compile, correct, rewrite 8 annotate, assemble, condense, copyread, fine-tune 9 proofread, rearrange 10 blue-pencil, bowdlerize

edition 4 copy, form 5 issue, print 7 reissue, reprint, version 8 printing, variorum 10 impression, reprinting 12 reproduction

editor 8 redactor 9 scrivener, wordsmith 10 copyreader 11 proofreader

Edomite's ancestor 4 Esau

educate 4 rear 5 brief, coach, drill, edify, nurse, teach, train, tutor 6 inform, school 7 explain, nurture 8 instruct 9 brainwash, enlighten 10 discipline 12 indoctrinate

education 7 culture, tuition 8 breeding, coaching, guidance, learning, literacy, pedagogy, teaching, training, tutelage, tutorage, tutoring 9 erudition, knowledge, schooling, tutorship 11 instruction, learnedness, scholarship 13 enlightenment

educational 11 informative, instructive 13 informational, instructional *institu-*

tion: 6 school 7 academy, college
10 university 12 conservatory
educator 5 tutor 7 teacher 9 professor
10 instructor *American:* 4 Mann
(Horace) 5 Dewey (John) 6 Butler
(Nicholas Murray), Conant (James
Bryant), Harris (William Torrey)
7 Barnard (Henry), Beecher
(Catharine), Peabody (Elizabeth)
8 Hutchins (Robert Maynard), McGuf-
fey (William) 10 Washington (Booker
T.) *Czech:* 8 Comenius (John Amos)
English: 6 Arnold (Thomas) 7 Spencer
(Herbert) *German:* 7 Froebel
(Friedrich), Herbart (Johann) *Italian:*
10 Montessori (Maria) *Swiss:*
10 Pestalozzi (Johann Heinrich)
educe 4 drag, draw, milk, pull 5 evoke,
wrest, wring 6 derive, elicit, evince,
evolve, extort, obtain, secure 7 distill,
draw out, extract, procure 8 bring out
10 excogitate
eel 5 moray, siren 6 conger 7 hagfish,
lamprey, sniggle *young:* 5 elver
eelpout 6 blenny, burbot 10 muttonfish
eely 5 slimy 6 slippy, wiggly 7 elusive,
wriggly 8 slippery, slithery 9 wriggling
eerie 5 scary, weird 6 creepy, spooky
7 bizarre, strange, uncanny 8 chilling, spectral 9 fantastic, grotesque,
unearthly 10 mysterious 11 frightening,
hair-raising 12 otherworldly
efface 4 dele, x out 5 annul, erase 6 cancel, delete, rub out 7 blot out, destroy,
expunge, scratch, wipe out 8 black out,
wear away 9 eliminate, eradicate, extirpate 10 obliterate
effect 3 end 4 make 5 cause, enact,
event, fruit 6 create, draw on, induce,
intent, invoke, render, result, secure,
sequel, upshot 7 achieve, bring on,
enforce, execute, fulfill, outcome, perform, produce, purport, realize, turn
out 8 bring off, carry out, complete,
conceive, generate, sequence 9 actualize, aftermath, corollary, discharge,
implement, influence, operation, outgrowth, pursuance 10 accomplish,
appearance, bring about, conclusion,
consummate, denouement, effectuate
11 consequence, development, eventuality, precipitate 12 carry through, ramification, repercussion
effective 4 able 5 sound, valid 6 causal,
cogent, direct, potent, useful 7 capable
8 adequate 9 competent, operative
10 compelling, convincing, productive
effectiveness 5 clout, force, point,
power, vigor 6 weight 7 cogency, potency 8 strength, validity 10 capability
effects 4 gear 5 goods, stuff 6 things

8 chattels, movables, property 9 equipment, moveables, trappings 10 belongings 11 impedimenta, possessions
13 accoutrements
effectual 5 sound, valid 6 potent, strong,
useful 7 capable 8 decisive, powerful,
workable 10 conclusive, fulfilling, productive 11 influential, practicable
13 authoritative, determinative
effectuate see EFFECT
effeminate 5 sappy, sissy 6 chichi, prissy
7 epicene, foppish 8 delicate, overnice,
precious 9 sissified 10 old-maidish
11 overrefined
effervescence 5 giddy 7 fizzing, foam-
ing, sparkle 8 bubbling, buoyancy,
vivacity 9 animation 10 ebullience,
ebullition, exuberance, exuberancy,
liveliness 12 exhilaration
effervescent 3 gay 4 airy 5 jolly 6 bouncy, bubbly, lively 7 boiling, buoyant,
excited 8 animated, mirthful, volatile
9 sparkling, sprightly, vivacious 10 carbonated 12 high-spirited 13 irrepressible
effete 4 soft, weak 5 frail, spent 6 barren
6 sickly 7 decayed, drained, sterile,
worn-out 8 decadent, decaying, delicate, depleted, fatigued, pampered
9 declining, dissolute, enfeebled,
exhausted, infertile, washed-out
10 degenerate, unfruitful 11 debilitated
efficacious 6 active, potent, strong
8 forceful, powerful, puissant 9 operative 10 productive 11 influential
efficacy see EFFECTIVENESS
efficiency see EFFECTIVENESS
efficient 4 able 5 adept 6 expert 7 capable, skilled 8 economic, masterly, skillful 9 competent 10 economical, productive
effigy 3 guy 4 icon, idol 5 dummy, image
6 figure 7 waxwork 8 likeness
effloresce 4 blow 5 bloom, burst
6 flower, sprout 7 blossom, burgeon
9 bear fruit
effluvium 3 air 4 odor, reek 5 smell,
vapor, waste 6 miasma 7 exhaust 8 effusion, emission 9 by-product, discharge,
emanation 10 exhalation
efflux see EFFLUVIUM
effort 3 job, try 4 feat, push, task, toil,
work 5 chore, essay, force, labor,
might, nisus, pains, sweat, while 6 energy, strain 7 attempt, travail, trouble,
venture 8 endeavor, exertion, industry,
struggle 11 application, elbow grease
effortful 4 hard 6 tiring, uphill 7 arduous, labored, operose 8 exacting, toilsome 9 ambitious, difficult, laborious,
strenuous 11 challenging

effortless 4 easy **5** adept, light, ready **6** expert, facile, fluent, simple, smooth **8** masterly, skillful **10** proficient **11** undemanding

effrontery 4 face, gall **5** brass, cheek, nerve **8** audacity, boldness, chutzpah, temerity **9** arrogance, assurance, brashness, hardihood, impudence, insolence **10** brazenness **11** presumption **12** impertinence

effulgence 4 glow **5** blaze, glory **6** luster, lustre **8** radiance, splendor **9** splendour **10** brightness, brilliance, brilliancy, luminosity

effulgent 5 vivid **6** bright, lucent **7** beaming, glowing, lambent, radiant, shining **8** dazzling, glorious, luminous, lustrous, splendid **9** brilliant **11** resplendent **12** incandescent

effuse 4 flow, gush, pour, shed **5** exude, issue **6** stream **7** emanate, enthuse, flow out, radiate

effusive 5 gushy **6** lavish, sloppy, smarmy **7** cloying, fulsome, gushing, profuse, verbose **9** expansive, exuberant **10** loquacious, outpouring, unreserved **11** extravagant **12** enthusiastic, unrestrained **13** demonstrative, unconstrained

eft 4 newt **6** triton **10** salamander

e.g. 10 for example **13** exempli gratia

egad 6 zounds **7** criminy **8** gadzooks **11** odds bodkins

egg 3 ova (plural) **4** ovum, seed **5** ovule *case:* **5** shell **7** ootheca *combining form:* **3** ovi, ovo *dish:* **6** omelet **8** omelette *fertilized:* **6** zygote **7** oospore *fish:* **3** roe **6** caviar *French:* **4** oeuf *immature:* **6** oocyte *part:* **4** yolk **5** glair, shell, white *shaped:* **5** ovate, ovoid *white:* **5** glair **7** albumen

egghead 6 pundit **8** highbrow **10** double-dome **12** intellectual

egg on 4 goad, prod, spur, urge **5** prick, rally **6** arouse, exhort, excite, incite, prompt, stir up **7** agitate **9** instigate, stimulate

eggplant 6 purple **9** aubergine **10** nightshade

egg-shaped 4 oval **5** ovate, ovoid **7** oviform

Eglah *husband:* **5** David *son:* **7** Ithream

eglantine 7 dog rose **10** sweetbriar, sweetbrier

Eglantine *father:* **5** Pepin *husband:* **9** Valentine

Eglon *king:* **5** Debir *slayer:* **4** Ehud

ego 4 self **5** pride **6** vanity **7** conceit **10** self-esteem

egocentric 7 selfish **9** conceited **10** self-loving **11** self-seeking **12** narcissistic, self-absorbed, self-affected, self-centered, self-involved, vainglorious **13** individualist, self-conceited, self-concerned, self-indulgent

egoism 5 pride **6** vanity **7** conceit **8** self-love **9** self-glory, self-pride, vainglory **10** narcissism, self-regard **11** selfishness, self-opinion

egoistic 4 smug, vain **7** selfish **9** conceited **12** self-absorbed, self-centered **13** self-concerned, self-contented, self-satisfied

egomaniacal 12 self-exalting, vainglorious

egotism 5 pride **6** vanity **7** conceit **8** boasting, bragging, self-love, vainness, vaunting **9** arrogance, pomposity, self-glory, self-pride, vainglory **10** narcissism, self-esteem **11** megalomania, self-opinion **12** boastfulness **13** conceitedness

egotistic 4 vain **5** cocky, proud **7** selfish, stuck-up **8** arrogant, boastful, inflated, puffed-up **9** conceited **11** pretentious, self-serving **12** self-absorbed, self-centered, self-involved **13** self-concerned, self-satisfied

egregious 4 rank **5** gross, stark **6** arrant, brazen **7** blatant, glaring, heinous **8** flagrant, infamous, outright, shocking **9** atrocious, notorious, shameless **10** deplorable, outrageous **11** conspicuous

egress, egression 4 door, exit **5** issue, leave **6** depart, escape, exodus, outlet **7** doorway, exiting, opening, passage **9** departure, emergence

egret 5 heron, wader

Egypt *ancient city:* **6** Thebes **7** Memphis *capital:* **5** Cairo *city:* **4** Giza **8** Port Said **10** Alexandria *dam:* **5** Aswan *desert:* **6** Libyan **7** Arabian, Western *gulf:* **4** Suez **5** Aqaba *lake:* **6** Nasser *language:* **6** Arabic *leader:* **5** Sadat (Anwar el-) **6** Nasser (Gamal Abdul) **7** Mubarak (Hosni) *monetary unit:* **5** pound *neighbor:* **5** Libya, Sudan **6** Israel *oasis:* **4** Siwa **6** Dakhla, Kharga **7** Farafra *peninsula:* **5** Sinai *river:* **4** Nile *sea:* **3** Red **13** Mediterranean

Egyptian *burial jar:* **7** canopic *Christian:* **4** Copt *cross:* **4** ankh *dam:* **5** Aswan *dynasty:* **5** Saite, Xoite **6** Hyksos, Tanite, Theban **7** Persian, Thinite **8** Memphite **9** Bubastite, Ethiopian **10** Diospolite *god:* *chief:* **6** Amen-Ra *crocodile-headed:* **5** Sebek *falcon-headed:* **4** Ment **5** Horus, Mentu **6** Sokari **7** Sokaris *ibis-headed:* **5** Thoth **6** Dhouti *jackal-headed:* **6** Anubis *of creation:* **4** Ptah **5** Phtha *of day:* **5** Horus *of earth:* **3** Geb, Keb, Seb *of evil:* **3** Set **4** Seth

5 Sebek *of life:* 4 Amen, Amon
5 Ammon *of magic:* 5 Thoth 6 Dhouti
of Memphis: 4 Ptah 5 Phtha 6 Sokari
7 Sokaris *of the heavens:* 5 Horus *of the*
morning sun: 5 Horus 7 Khepera *of the*
sun: 6 Amen-Ra *of Thebes:* 4 Amen
6 Khensu, Khonsu *of the underworld:*
6 Osiris *of war:* 4 Ment 5 Mentu *of wis-*
dom: 5 Thoth 6 Dhouti *ram-headed:*
4 Amen, Amon 5 Ammon, Khnum
6 Khnemu *snake:* 4 Apep 5 Apepi
goddess:
cat-headed: 4 Bast 5 Pakht *cow-headed:*
5 Athor 6 Hathor *lioness-headed:*
4 Bast 5 Pakht 6 Sekhet *of fertility:*
4 Isis *of love and mirth:* 5 Athor
6 Hathor *of motherhood:* 4 Apet, Isis
of Thebes: 3 Mut *of the heavens:*
3 Nut *queen of the gods:* 4 Sati *vulture-*
headed: 3 Mut 7 Nekhebt 8 Nekhebet
king: (see KING entry) *language:* 6 Arabic, Coptic *native:* 4 Arab, Copt
5 Nilot *president:* 5 Sadat 6 Nasser
7 Mubarak *queen:* 9 Cleopatra, Nefer-
titi *sacred bird:* 4 ibis *solar disk:* 4 Aten
sultan: 7 Saladin *talisman:* 6 scarab
underworld: 4 Aaru, Duat 6 Amenti
wind: 7 khamsin, sirocco
eider 4 down, duck 7 sea duck
eidetic 5 exact, vivid 7 perfect, precise
8 absolute, lifelike
eidolon 4 icon 5 ghost, ideal, image,
model, shade 6 mirage, vision, wraith
7 epitome, fantasm, figment, paragon,
phantom, specter, spectre 8 exemplar,
illusion, paradigm, phantasm 9 archetype, prototype 10 apparition
eight *group of:* 5 octet 6 octave
eight bells 4 noon
eighth note 6 quaver
eighty-six 4 boot, toss 5 chuck, eject,
evict, scrap 6 bounce 7 discard, kick
out 8 get rid of, jettison, throw out
Einstein, Albert *birthplace:* 3 Ulm *theory:*
10 relativity
Eire see IRELAND
eject 4 boot, bump, dump, fire, oust,
sack 5 chuck, evict, expel 6 banish,
bounce 7 boot out, cast out, dismiss,
kick out 8 disgorge, throw out 9 discharge
eke out 6 extend 7 augment, enhance,
fill out, squeeze, stretch 8 increase
10 supplement
elaborate 4 busy 5 fancy, showy
6 daedal, dressy, evolve, expand, knotty, minute, ornate, refine, unfold
7 amplify, build up, careful, clarify,
comment, complex, develop, discuss,
elegant, enlarge, explain, expound,
profuse, work out 8 detailed, involved,
overdone, thorough 9 Byzantine, deco-

rated, embellish, extensive, interpret,
intricate 10 overworked 11 complicated, embellished, extravagant, painstaking 12 labyrinthine
Elaine *father:* 6 Pelles *lover:* 8 Lancelot
9 Launcelot *son:* 7 Galahad
Elam *capital:* 4 Susa 7 Shushan *father:*
4 Shem *king:* 12 Chedorlaomer
élan 3 pep, vim, zip 4 brio, dash, fire,
life, zeal, zest, zing 5 ardor, flair, gusto,
oomph, verve, vigor 6 energy, esprit,
fervor, spirit 7 impetus 8 vivacity 9 animation, eagerness, intensity 10 enthusiasm
élan vital 4 soul 5 anima 6 animus, pneuma, psyche, spirit
elapse 4 go by, pass 6 expire, run out,
slip by 8 pass away
elastic 6 bouncy, limber, pliant, rubber,
supple 7 ductile, pliable, rubbery,
springy 8 animated, flexible, moldable,
stretchy, volatile 9 adaptable, expansive, malleable, resilient 10 extendable,
extensible, rubber band, rubberlike
11 stretchable
elate 4 buoy 5 cheer, exalt, flush, set up
6 excite, perk up, uplift 7 cheer up,
delight, enliven, gladden, gratify, heart-
en, inspire, overjoy 8 brighten, embold-
en, inspirit, spirit up 9 encourage
10 exhilarate, invigorate
elated 4 glad, high 5 happy 7 exalted,
excited 8 ecstatic, euphoric, exultant,
gladsome, jubilant 9 overjoyed
10 enraptured 11 exhilarated, intoxicated 12 high-spirited
elation 3 joy 4 glee 7 delight, ecstasy, rapture 8 buoyancy, euphoria 9 happiness,
transport 10 exaltation, excitement,
jubilation 12 exhilaration, intoxication
Elbe tributary 4 Eger, Iser, Ohre 5 Saale
6 Moldau, Vltava
elbow 4 push 5 joint, nudge, shove
6 hustle, jostle
eld 4 yore 6 old age 8 old times
elder 6 senior 8 old-timer 9 patriarch,
presbyter 10 golden-ager
elderliness 3 age 6 old age 8 caducity
10 senescence 11 senectitude
elderly 3 old 4 aged, gray 5 aging, hoary
7 ancient 9 declining, venerable
eldritch 5 eerie, weird 7 uncanny
Eleanor's husband 7 Henry II 8 Franklin
elect 3 opt, tap 4 name, pick 5 co-opt,
saved 6 choice, choose, chosen, decide,
opt for, ordain, picked, vote in
7 resolve, vote for 8 destined, nominate, ordained, redeemed 9 delivered,
designate, determine, exclusive, single
out 10 designated, singled out
election 6 ballot, choice, voting 7 primary 8 choosing, decision 9 balloting

10 preference, referendum 11 alternative

electioneer 5 stump 7 canvass 8 campaign, politick 9 barnstorm

elective 6 chosen 8 optional 9 voluntary 11 sympathetic 13 discretionary, noncompulsory, nonobligatory

Electra *brother:* 7 Orestes *father:* 9 Agamemnon *husband:* 7 Pylades *mother:* 12 Clytemnestra *sister:* 9 Iphigenia *victim:* 9 Aegisthus 12 Clytemnestra

electric *appliance:* 3 fan 4 iron, oven 5 clock, drier, dryer, mixer, range, stove 6 stereo, washer 7 blender, freezer, toaster 10 dishwasher, television 12 refrigerator *coil:* 5 tesla 8 solenoid *device:* 4 coil, fuse, plug 6 dynamo, magnet, switch 7 battery 8 resistor, rheostat, varistor 9 amplifier, capacitor, condenser, generator 11 transformer *generator:* 6 dynamo *particle:* 3 ion *unit:* 3 amp, ohm 4 volt, watt 5 farad, henry, joule 6 ampere 7 coulomb, faraday 8 kilowatt

electric current *kind:* 6 direct 11 alternating *power:* 7 wattage *strength:* 8 amperage

electricity 5 juice, spark 7 current 9 galvanism, lightning *kind:* 6 static 7 current

electrify 3 jar 4 jolt, stun 5 amaze, power, shock 6 charge, excite, thrill 7 astound, enthuse, inflame, provoke, stagger, startle 8 astonish, energize

electrode 6 dynode *negative:* 7 cathode *positive:* 5 anode

electron 3 ion 7 polaron *stream:* 10 cathode ray *tube:* 6 triode 7 tetrode 8 dynatron, klystron

Electryon *brother:* 6 Mestor *daughter:* 7 Alcmene *father:* 7 Perseus *mother:* 9 Andromeda *wife:* 5 Anaxo

eleemosynary 6 humane 8 generous 10 altruistic, beneficent, benevolent, charitable, munificent, openhanded 12 humanitarian 13 philanthropic

elegance 4 chic, pomp, tone 5 charm, grace, style, taste 6 luxury, polish 7 culture, dignity 8 chicness, poshness, richness, splendor, urbanity 9 gentility, precision 10 ornateness, refinement 11 cultivation 12 magnificence, tastefulness 13 sumptuousness

elegant 4 chic, fine, posh 5 fancy, grand, noble, swank 6 choice, classy, dainty, lovely, modish, ornate, swanky, urbane 7 courtly, genteel, opulent, refined, stately, stylish 8 cultured, polished, splendid, tasteful 9 exquisite, luxurious, recherché, sumptuous 10 cultivated 11 fashionable

elegiac 7 pensive 8 dactylic 9 lamenting, sorrowful 10 melancholy

elegy 4 poem, song 5 dirge 6 lament, monody 8 threnody

___ **eleison** 5 Kyrie

Elektra composer 7 Strauss (Richard)

element 4 item, part 5 basic, facet, piece, point 6 aspect, detail, factor, member, sector 7 article, feature, portion, section 8 division, particle, rudiment 9 component, essential, principle 10 ingredient, particular 11 constituent, fundamental *chemical:* 3 tin 4 gold, iron, lead, neon, zinc 5 argon, boron, radon, xenon 6 barium, carbon, cerium, cesium, cobalt, copper, curium, erbium, helium, indium, iodine, nickel, osmium, oxygen, radium, silver, sodium 7 arsenic, bismuth, bohrium, bromine, cadmium, calcium, dubnium, fermium, gallium, hafnium, hassium, holmium, iridium, krypton, lithium, mercury, niobium, rhenium, rhodium, silicon, sulphur, terbium, thorium, thulium, uranium, yttrium 8 actinium, aluminum, antimony, astatine, chlorine, chromium, europium, fluorine, hydrogen, illinium, lutecium, masurium, nitrogen, nobelium, platinum, polonium, rubidium, samarium, scandium, selenium, tantalum, thallium, titanium, tungsten, vanadium 9 americium, berkelium, beryllium, columbium, germanium, lanthanum, magnesium, manganese, neodymium, neptunium, palladium, plutonium, potassium, ruthenium, strontium, tellurium, virginium, ytterbium, zirconium 10 dysprosium, gadolinium, lawrencium, meitnerium, molybdenum, seaborgium 11 californium, einsteinium, mendelevium, phosphorous 12 darmstadtium, praseodymium 13 rutherfordium, protoactinium

elemental 3 key 4 pure 5 basal, basic, crude, prime 6 inborn, innate, primal, simple 7 central, connate, primary, radical 8 cardinal, inherent, integral, intimate, simplest 9 beginning, essential, ingrained, intrinsic, primitive 10 deepseated, primordial, underlying 11 fundamental 13 uncomplicated

elementary 4 easy 5 basal, basic 6 simple 7 initial 9 beginning, essential, primitive 10 rudimental, underlying 11 fundamental, preliminary, rudimentary 12 introductory

elemi 5 resin 9 oleoresin

elephant 6 tusker 9 pachyderm *boy:* 4 Sabu *driver:* 6 mahout *enclosure:* 5 kraal *extinct:* 7 mammoth 8 mastodon *female:* 3 cow *group:* 4 herd *keeper:* 6 mahout *male:* 4 bull *maverick:* 5 rogue *nose:* 5 trunk 9 proboscis *seat:* 6 how-

dah *sound:* 6 bellow 7 trumpet *tooth:*
4 tusk *tusk:* 5 ivory *young:* 4 calf
elephant-headed god 6 Ganesa 7 Ganesha
elephantine 4 huge 6 clumsy 7 awkward, hulking, mammoth, massive 8 colossal, enormous, gigantic 9 graceless, humongous, monstrous, ponderous 10 gargantuan, mastodonic, prodigious, ungraceful 11 heavy-footed
Elephant Man 7 Merrick (Joseph)
elevate 4 lift, rear, rise 5 boost, elate, erect, exalt, hoist, raise 6 buoy up, jack up, lift up, pick up, uplift 7 advance, dignify, ennoble, glorify, hearten, improve, inspire, promote, upgrade 8 heighten 10 exhilarate
elevated 4 high 5 grand, lofty, moral, noble 6 aerial, formal, superb 7 ethical, refined, soaring, stately, sublime 8 eloquent, majestic, virtuous 9 dignified, grandiose, high-flown, honorable, righteous 10 high-minded, upstanding 13 grandiloquent
elevation 4 hill, rise 5 boost 6 ascent, height, uplift 7 advance, raising 8 altitude, mountain 9 acclivity, promotion, upgrading 10 apotheosis, preference, preferment 11 advancement, ennoblement *indication:* 9 benchmark
elevator 4 cage, lift, silo 5 hoist *maker:* 4 Otis
elf 3 fay, imp 4 peri, puck 5 fairy, gnome, pixie, troll 6 goblin, sprite 7 brownie, gremlin 10 leprechaun
elfin 5 antic 6 frisky, impish 7 implike, playful, puckish 8 pixieish 11 mischievous
Elgin ___ 7 Marbles
Eli 4 Yale 5 Yalie
Eli ·___ 4 Yale 5 Lilly 7 Whitney
Elia 4 Lamb (Charles)
Eliab *brother:* 5 David *daughter:* 7 Abihail *father:* 5 Helon, Pallu *son:* 6 Abiram, Dathan
Eliada *father:* 5 David *son:* 5 Rezon
Eliam's daughter 9 Bathsheba
elicit 5 educe, evoke 6 derive, evince, extort 7 extract, provoke 8 bring out 9 call forth, draw forth
elide 4 fail, omit, skip 6 excise, forget, ignore, remove, slight 7 abridge, curtail, neglect 8 condense, cross out, discount, overlook, pass over, suppress 9 disregard
eligible 3 fit 6 fitted, likely, nubile, seemly, suited, worthy 7 capable 8 entitled, suitable 9 desirable, qualified 10 acceptable 11 appropriate 12 marriageable
Elihu ___ 4 Root, Yale
Elijah 5 Elias 7 prophet 8 Tishbite *father:* 5 Harim 7 Jeroham

Elimelech's wife 5 Naomi
eliminate 3 bar 4 bate, drop, oust, void 5 debar, eject, erase, evict, expel, purge 6 delete, except, remove 7 discard, dismiss, exclude, expunge, obviate, rule out, take out 8 count out 9 clear away, eradicate, liquidate 11 exterminate
Eliot, George *lover:* 5 Lewes (George Henry) *novel:* 6 Romola 8 Adam Bede 11 Middlemarch, Silas Marner 13 Daniel Deronda 14 Mill on the Floss (The) *pseudonym of:* 5 Evans (Mary Ann)
Eliot, T.S. *play:* 13 Cocktail Party (The) *poem:* 9 Gerontion, Hollow Men (The), Waste Land (The) 12 Ash Wednesday, Four Quartets
Eliphaz *father:* 4 Esau *mother:* 4 Adah *son:* 5 Teman
Elisabeth *husband:* 9 Zacharias *son:* 4 John (the Baptist)
Elisha *father:* 7 Shaphat *servant:* 6 Gehazi
Elisheba *brother:* 7 Nahshon *father:* 9 Amminadab *husband:* 5 Aaron *son:* 5 Abihu, Nadab 7 Eleazar, Ithamar
elite 3 top 4 best, pick 5 cream, elect, pride, prime, prize 6 choice, flower, gentry, select 7 quality, society 9 exclusive, gentility, patrician 10 upper class, upper crust 11 aristocracy 12 aristocratic
elixir 4 balm, cure 6 potion 7 arcanum, cure-all, nostrum, panacea, philter 10 catholicon
Elizabeth I, name for 6 Oriana 8 Gloriana
elk 4 deer 5 moose 6 sambar, wapiti 7 red deer
ell 3 arm 4 wing 5 annex, elbow, joint 8 addition 9 extension
ellipse 4 oval 5 curve, orbit
elliptical 5 brief, ovate, short 6 gnomic 7 concise, cryptic, laconic, obscure, summary 9 condensed, enigmatic 11 abbreviated
elm 5 wahoo
elocution 7 diction, oratory 8 delivery, rhetoric 11 declamation, speechcraft
elongate 4 draw 6 extend 7 draw out, lengthy, spin out, stretch 8 extended, lengthen 10 lengthened
elope 4 flee 6 escape, run off 7 abscond, run away 9 steal away
eloquence 5 force, power 6 fervor, spirit 7 fluency, oratory, passion 8 rhetoric 10 expression 12 expressivity, forcefulness
eloquent 5 lofty 6 ardent, fervid, fluent, moving 7 fervent, voluble 8 elevated, forceful, powerful, stirring 9 affecting 10 articulate, expressive, impressive, meaningful, passionate, persuasive,

rhetorical **11** impassioned, sententious **12** smooth-spoken **13** silver-tongued

El Salvador *capital:* **11** San Salvador *city:* **8** Santa Ana **9** San Miguel *ethnic group:* **5** Pipil *lake:* **8** Ilopango *language:* **7** Spanish *monetary unit:* **5** colón **6** dollar *neighbor:* **8** Honduras **9** Guatemala *river:* **5** Lempa

else 5 if not **7** besides, further **9** otherwise **10** additional **11** differently **12** additionally

elucidate 7 clarify, clear up, explain, expound **8** annotate, spell out **9** exemplify, explicate, interpret **10** illuminate, illustrate

elude 4 defy, duck, flee, foil **5** avert, avoid, dodge, evade **6** baffle, escape, outwit, thwart **8** confound **9** frustrate **10** circumvent

elusive 6 subtle, tricky **7** evasive, phantom **8** baffling, fleeting, fugitive, slippery **10** evanescent, intangible, mysterious **13** insubstantial

elute 7 extract

elver 3 eel

elvish see ELFIN

Elysium 5 bliss **6** heaven **7** nirvana **8** empyrean, paradise

elytron 4 wing

emaciated 4 bony, lean, thin **5** gaunt **6** skinny, wasted **7** scrawny, starved, wizened **8** skeletal, underfed **10** cadaverous

emaciation 5 tabes **7** atrophy **8** marasmus **10** starvation **11** attenuation

emanate 4 emit, flow, rise, stem **5** arise, exude, issue **6** derive, emerge, spring **7** come out, give off, give out, proceed, radiate **9** originate **10** derive from

emanation 4 aura, flow **6** efflux **8** effusion, emission **9** effluence

emancipate 4 free **5** let go, loose **6** loosen, redeem, unbind **7** manumit, release, set free, unchain **8** liberate, unfetter **9** discharge, unshackle **11** enfranchise

emancipation 7 release **10** liberation **11** deliverance

emancipator 5 Moses **7** Lincoln (Abraham) **9** deliverer, liberator

emasculate 3 fix **4** geld **5** alter, unman **6** neuter, soften, weaken **7** unnerve **8** castrate, enervate, unstring **10** debilitate, devitalize

embalm 7 mummify, perfume **8** preserve

embankment 4 berm, bund, dike, quay **5** levee, mound

embargo 3 ban, bar **5** edict, order **8** blockade, stoppage **10** impediment **11** prohibition

embark 5 board, enter, start **6** set out **7** set sail **8** commence

embarrass 4 faze **5** abash, upset **6** flurry, hamper, hinder, impede, rattle **7** confuse, flummox, fluster, mortify, nonplus, perturb **8** confound, distress **9** discomfit, humiliate **10** complicate, discomfort, discompose, disconcert

embarrassment 5 shame, upset **7** chagrin **8** distress **9** confusion **10** discomfort **11** humiliation **12** discomfiture, perturbation **13** mortification

embassy 5 envoy **7** mission **8** legation **10** ambassador, delegation, deputation

embay 4 trap **5** catch, seize **7** capture **8** encircle, surround

embed 3 fix, set **4** bury, root **5** infix, inlay, lodge **7** implant, ingrain **8** entrench

embellish 3 pad **4** deck, gild, trim **5** adorn, color **6** bedeck, blazon, emboss, enrich **7** amplify, dress up, enhance, festoon, garnish **8** beautify, decorate, ornament **9** elaborate, embroider **10** exaggerate **11** romanticize

embellishment 7 garnish, gilding, melisma, mordent **8** coloring, ornament **9** fioritura, floridity, hyperbole **10** decoration **11** elaboration **12** embroidering, exaggeration **13** ornamentation

ember 3 ash **6** cinder

embezzle 4 loot **5** filch, steal **6** pilfer **7** purloin **8** peculate **9** defalcate

embitter 4 sour **6** poison **7** envenom **9** acidulate

emblazon 4 laud **5** extol **7** glorify **8** inscribe **9** celebrate

emblem 4 arms, flag, logo, mace, seal, sign **5** badge, brand, crest, image, token **6** banner, device, symbol **7** pennant **8** colophon, hallmark, insignia, monogram, standard **9** attribute, trademark **10** coat of arms

emblematic 8 symbolic **10** figurative, indicative **11** allegorical **12** illustrative, metaphorical

embodiment 6 avatar **7** epitome **8** exemplar **9** archetype **11** incarnation **13** manifestation

embody 5 reify **6** evince, mirror, typify **7** compose, contain, exhibit, realize, subsume **8** manifest **9** actualize, encompass, epitomize, exemplify, incarnate, integrate, objectify, personify, represent, symbolize **10** constitute, illustrate **11** emblematize, externalize, hypostatize, incorporate, materialize **12** substantiate

embolden 5 steel **7** fortify, hearten, inspire **8** inspirit **9** encourage **10** strengthen

embolus 4 clog, clot

embosom 3 hug **7** embrace, enclose, envelop, shelter

embouchure 10 mouthpiece

embowel 3 gut **4** draw **10** eviscerate, exenterate

embrace 3 hug **4** hold, lock, love, wrap **5** admit, adopt, clasp, cling, press **6** accept, cradle, cuddle, embody, enfold, fondle, nuzzle, take in, take on, take up **7** cherish, contain, embosom, enclose, entwine, envelop, espouse, include, receive, snuggle, squeeze, subsume, welcome **8** comprise, encircle **9** encompass **10** comprehend **11** accommodate, incorporate **12** encirclement

embrangle see EMBROIL

embrocation 5 salve **7** unguent **8** liniment

embroider 3 pad, sew, tat **4** gild **5** color **6** expand, overdo, play up, stitch **7** amplify, build up, enhance, garnish, magnify, stretch **8** decorate, ornament **9** dramatize, elaborate, embellish **10** exaggerate **11** hyperbolize, romanticize

embroidery 6 crewel **7** cutwork, orphrey **8** bargello, couching, smocking, tapestry **10** crewelwork, needlework **11** needlepoint

embroil 4 mire **6** tangle **7** confuse, ensnare, involve **8** disorder, entangle **9** implicate

embroilment 4 tiff **6** fracas **7** dispute, quarrel, wrangle **8** squabble **9** bickering **10** falling-out **11** altercation, controversy

embryo 3 bud **4** germ, seed **5** fetus, spark **7** nucleus **8** blastula, gastrula

emend 4 edit **5** alter, right **6** polish, revise **7** correct, improve, rectify, retouch

emerald 3 gem **5** beryl, green, stone **8** gemstone

Emerald Isle 4 Eire, Erin **7** Ireland

emerge 4 flow, loom, rise, stem **5** arise, issue **6** appear, derive, evolve, spring **7** come out, develop, emanate, proceed, surface **9** originate, transpire **11** come to light, materialize

emergency 3 fix **4** hole, pass **5** pinch **6** climax, clutch, crisis, crunch, strait **7** squeeze **8** accident, exigency

emeritus 7 retired

Emerson, Ralph Waldo *essay:* **12** Self-Reliance *forte:* **5** essay *home:* **7** Concord *friend:* **7** Thoreau (Henry David)

emery 6 powder **8** abrasive, corundum

emetic 8 vomitive **9** cathartic, purgative

émeute 4 riot **6** mutiny, revolt, tumult **8** outbreak, upheaval, uprising **9** rebellion **12** insurrection

emigrant 7 pioneer, settler **8** colonist **10** expatriate

émigré 5 alien, exile, expat **7** evacuee, migrant, refugee **8** colonist **10** expatriate

Emilia *husband:* **4** Iago **7** Palamon *slayer:* **4** Iago

eminence 3 VIP **4** fame, peak, rise **5** honor, power **6** bigwig, esteem, height, leader, renown, repute **7** dignity, notable **8** altitude, big-timer, luminary, prestige, standing **9** authority, dignitary, elevation, greatness, loftiness **10** importance, projection, prominence, promontory, reputation **11** distinction, superiority

eminent 4 high **5** famed, grand, great, large, lofty, noble, noted **6** august, famous, exalted, notable **8** esteemed, renowned, towering **9** important, well-known **10** celebrated, noteworthy, projecting **11** conspicuous, illustrious, outstanding, prestigious **13** distinguished

eminently 4 very **6** highly **7** notably **9** extremely **10** remarkably, strikingly **11** exceedingly **12** surpassingly **13** exceptionally

emir 5 chief, ruler, sheik, title **6** sheikh **9** chieftain, commander

emissary see ENVOY

emission 4 flow **7** venting **9** discharge, effluvium, emanation, radiation

emit 4 beam, glow, ooze, pour, shed, spew, vent, void **5** eject, expel, exude, issue, loose, utter **6** exhale, let out **7** emanate, excrete, extrude, give off, give out, radiate, release, secrete, send out **8** evacuate, throw off **9** circulate, discharge

emmer 5 grain, spelt, wheat

emmet 3 ant **7** pismire

emollient 4 balm **5** salve **7** lenient **8** lenitive, liniment, sedative, soothing **9** analgesic, softening **10** mollifying

emolument 3 fee, pay **4** wage **5** wages **6** income, reward, salary **7** guerdon, stipend **8** earnings **10** recompense **11** pay envelope **12** compensation

emotion 3 ire, joy **4** fear, glee, hate, love **5** agony, ardor, grief, shame **6** affect, hatred, relief, sorrow, warmth **7** ardency, despair, disgust, ecstasy, feeling, passion, sadness **8** jealousy, surprise **9** affection, agitation, happiness, sentiment **11** affectivity, sensibility, sensitivity **12** excitability

emotional 4 warm **6** ardent, fervid, heated, moving **7** feeling, fervent, intense, soulful, zealous **8** effusive, stirring, touching, vehement **9** affecting, affective, excitable, heartfelt, impetuous, rhapsodic, sensitive **10** hysterical, passionate **11** impassioned, overwrought, rhapsodical, softhearted, susceptible, sympathetic

emotionless 3 icy **4** cold, cool **5** chill, staid, stoic, stony **6** frigid, remote, torpid **7** callous, deadpan, distant, glacial **8** detached, reserved **9** apathetic, immovable, impassive, unfeeling **10** impersonal **11** cold-blooded, indifferent **12** matter-of-fact **13** dispassionate, unimpassioned

empathy 4 pity **6** lenity, warmth **7** rapport **8** affinity, sympathy **9** communion **10** compassion **12** congeniality **13** compatibility, comprehension, fellow feeling, understanding

emperor 4 czar, shah, tsar, tzar **5** ruler **6** caesar, kaiser **7** monarch **8** autocrat, dictator **9** potentate, sovereign *French:* **8** Napoleon (Bonaparte) **9** Bonaparte (Napoleon) **11** Charlemagne *Indian:* **5** Babur *Japanese:* **6** mikado **7** Akihito **8** Hirohito *Mexican:* **8** Iturbide (Agustín de) **10** Maximilian *Roman:* **4** Nero **5** Galba, Nerva, Titus **6** Decius, Julian, Trajan **7** Gratian, Hadrian, Severus **8** Augustus, Aurelian, Caligula, Claudius, Commodus, Domitian, Honorius, Tiberius, Valerian **9** Antoninus, Caracalla, Justinian **10** Diocletian, Elagabalus **11** Constantine

emphasis 5 focus, force **6** accent, stress, weight **9** attention, intensity **10** insistence, prominence **12** accentuation

emphasize 6 accent, play up, stress **7** feature **8** pinpoint **9** highlight, italicize, spotlight, underline **10** accentuate, underscore

emphatic 4 firm **6** marked **7** decided, earnest, pointed **8** accented, decisive, forceful, positive, stressed, vigorous **9** assertive, energetic, insistent **10** resounding, underlined **11** accentuated

empire 5 realm **6** domain **7** demesne, kingdom **8** dominion *ancient:* (see ANCIENT EMPIRE)

Empire State 7 New York

empirical 7 factual **9** fact-based, pragmatic **12** experiential, experimental **13** observational

emplacement 7 battery **8** position

employ 3 job, use **4** busy, hire, work **5** apply, avail **6** devote, engage, occupy, retain, secure, take on **7** exploit, utilize **8** exercise, practice **9** make use of **10** occupation

employee 4 hand, help **5** agent **6** worker **7** servant **8** factotum **9** underling *bank:* **5** clerk, guard **6** teller *hotel:* **7** bellboy, bellhop, doorman **9** concierge, desk clerk **11** chambermaid

employer 4 boss **6** master **10** supervisor

employment 3 job, use **4** line, post, task, toil, work **5** trade, usage **6** hiring, métier, office **7** calling, mission, purpose, pursuit **8** business, exercise, function, position, vocation **9** appliance, operation, situation **10** engagement, occupation **11** application, recruitment, utilization **12** exploitation

emporium 4 mall, mart, shop **5** store **6** bazaar, market **8** exchange **11** marketplace

empower 5 endow **6** charge, enable, invest **7** entitle, entrust, license **8** accredit, delegate, deputize, sanction **9** authorize, privilege **10** commission

empress 5 queen *Byzantine:* **3** Zoe *French:* **7** Eugénie **9** Josephine *Japanese:* **5** Suiko *of India:* **8** Victoria *Mexican:* **7** Carlota *Roman:* **6** Fausta *Russian:* **4** Anna **7** czarina, tsarina, tzarina **9** Alexandra, Catherine, Elizabeth

empressement 6 fervor, warmth **10** cordiality

emprise 4 feat, gest **5** geste **7** exploit, venture **9** adventure **11** undertaking

emptiness 4 void **5** blank **6** hunger, vacuum **7** inanity, vacancy, vacuity

emptor 5 buyer **6** vendee **8** consumer, customer **9** purchaser

— **emptor 6** caveat

empty 3 rid **4** bare, dump, pour, vain, void **5** blank, clear, drain **6** barren, devoid, hollow, unload, vacant, vacate **7** deplete, drained, exhaust, vacated, vacuous **8** depleted, deserted, evacuate, forsaken **9** abandoned, destitute **10** unoccupied, untenanted *Scottish:* **4** toom

empty-headed 6 simple, vacant **7** vacuous, witless **8** ignorant, untaught **9** benighted, brainless, frivolous **10** illiterate, uneducated, unlettered, unschooled **11** know-nothing **12** uninstructed **13** rattlebrained

empyreal 4 airy, holy **6** aerial, divine **7** sublime **8** beatific, ethereal, heavenly **9** celestial, spiritual, unearthly **12** transcendent

empyrean 3 sky **4** Zion **5** bliss, ether **6** heaven, welkin **7** Elysium, heavens, nirvana **8** paradise **9** firmament

emu 4 bird, rhea **6** ratite **9** cassowary

emulate 3 ape **4** copy **5** equal, mimic, rival **6** follow, mirror **7** compete, imitate **9** challenge

emulation 7 rivalry **8** striving, tug-of-war **9** imitation **10** contention **11** competition

emulous 5 vying **8** aspiring, striving, vaulting **9** ambitious **11** competitive

emulsifier 4 soap **5** algin

enable 3 fit, let **5** allow, ready **6** permit **7** empower, entitle, license, prepare, qualify **8** accredit, sanction **9** authorize, condition 10 commission, facilitate 12 make possible

enact 4 pass, play 6 decree, depict, effect, ordain, ratify 7 execute, perform, portray 8 proclaim 9 authorize, discourse, establish, institute, legislate, represent 10 accomplish, bring about, constitute, effectuate 11 impersonate

enactment 3 law 6 action, decree 7 statute 9 depiction, ordinance, portrayal 11 legislation, performance 12 ratification

enamel 5 glaze, gloss, japan, paint 7 lacquer

enamored 4 fond 6 loving 7 devoted, smitten 8 besotted 9 bewitched, enchanted, entranced, infatuate 10 captivated, infatuated

encamp 4 tent 6 settle 7 bivouac

encampment 6 billet, laager 7 bivouac, hutment

encase 3 box 4 pack 7 confine, enclose, envelop, sheathe

enceinte 6 gravid 8 pregnant 9 expectant, expecting 10 parturient

enchain 4 bind 6 fetter 7 manacle, shackle

enchant 3 hex 4 lure, wile 5 charm, spell, witch 6 allure, enamor, seduce, thrill, voodoo 7 attract, beguile, bewitch, delight 8 ensorcel, enthrall 9 captivate, enrapture, ensorcell, fascinate, hypnotize, magnetize, mesmerize, spellbind

enchanter 4 mage 5 magus 6 wizard 7 charmer, warlock 8 conjurer, conjuror, magician, sorcerer 11 necromancer, spellbinder

enchanting 5 siren 9 glamorous, seductive 10 attractive, delectable, delightful, intriguing

enchantment 3 hex 5 charm, magic, spell 6 allure 7 glamour, sorcery 8 witchery, wizardry 9 conjuring, seduction 10 necromancy, witchcraft 11 incantation

enchantress 3 hex 5 bruja, Circe, lamia, Medea, siren, witch 9 sorceress

enchiridion 4 text 5 guide 6 manual 8 Baedeker, handbook 9 guidebook, vade mecum

encipher 4 code

encircle 3 hem 4 band, gird, halo, hoop, ring 5 girth 6 begird, engird, enlace, girdle 7 compass, embrace, enclose, environ, wreathe 8 surround 9 encompass 12 circumscribe

enclave 6 colony, ghetto, sector 7 quarter 8 district, homeland

enclose 3 box, hem, mew, pen, rim 4 cage, coop, mure, wall, wrap 5 bound, fence, hedge, limit 6 circle, closet, corral, hold in, immure, shroud, shut in, wall in 7 compass, confine, contain, embosom, include 8 fence off, imprison, surround 9 capsulize 12 circumscribe

enclosed 6 obtect

enclosure 3 box, mew, pen, sty 4 cage, camp, cell, coop, cote, fold, jail, pale, quad, tank, trap, wall, weir, yard 5 court, fence, kraal, pound, stall 6 aviary, corral, cowpen, kennel, paling, prison 7 chamber, paddock 8 cloister, stockade 9 courtyard 10 quadrangle

encomiast 7 praiser 8 eulogist 10 panegyrist

encomiastic 9 adulatory, laudative, laudatory 10 eulogistic 11 panegyrical

encomium 4 laud 5 kudos, paean 6 eulogy, homage, praise 7 acclaim, plaudit, tribute 8 accolade, citation, plaudits 9 laudation, panegyric 10 compliment, salutation 11 acclamation 12 commendation

encompass 3 hem 4 belt, gird, ring 5 bound 6 begird, circle, girdle, take in 7 contain, embrace, enclose, include, subsume 8 encircle, surround 10 accomplish, bring about, comprehend

encore 6 recall, repeat, return 10 repetition

encounter 4 face, find, fray, meet 5 brush, clash, fight, run-in, scrap, set-to 6 battle, engage, take on 7 collide, contest, meeting, quarrel, run into 8 argument, bump into, come upon, conflict, confront, meet with, skirmish, struggle 10 contention, experience

encourage 4 abet, back, buoy, push, spur, stir, urge 5 boost, cheer, egg on, rally, rouse, serve, steel 6 assist, assure, buck up, excite, foster, incite, induce, praise 7 advance, animate, approve, bolster, cheer up, endorse, fortify, further, hearten, improve, inspire, promote, provoke, quicken, support, sustain 8 advocate, embolden, energize, inspirit, reassure, sanction 9 enhearten, galvanize, instigate, patronize, reinforce, stimulate, subsidize 10 invigorate, strengthen

encouragement 4 lift, push 5 boost 7 backing, support 8 approval 11 inspiration

encouraging 4 rosy 6 bright, likely 7 hopeful 9 favorable, promising 10 auspicious, propitious

encroach 5 poach 6 invade, meddle, trench 7 impinge, intrude 8 entrench, infringe, overstep, trespass

encrypt 4 code 6 cipher, encode 7 convert 8 disguise, encipher

encumber 4 lade, load 6 burden, charge, fetter, hamper, hinder, impede, saddle, weight 7 freight, oppress 8 handicap, obstruct, overload 9 weigh down 10 overburden 13 inconvenience

encumbrance 4 lien, load, onus 5 claim 6 burden 7 baggage 8 handicap, mortgage 9 albatross, millstone 10 impediment

encyclical 6 letter 7 general 8 circular

encyclopedic 5 broad 7 general 8 complete, thorough 9 extensive, inclusive, universal 11 compendious, wide-ranging 12 all-embracing, all-inclusive 13 comprehensive

encyclopedist 7 Diderot (Denis)

end 3 aim, tip 4 coda, doom, goal, halt, quit, stop, tail, term 5 cease, close, death, finis, limit 6 demise, expire, finale, finish, object, period, result, scotch, windup, wrap up 7 abolish, closing, closure, extreme, lineman, outcome, purpose 8 boundary, complete, conclude, confines, curtains, finality, surcease, terminal, terminus 9 cessation, extremity, objective, terminate 10 borderline, completion, conclusion, denouement, expiration, extinction, limitation 11 culmination, discontinue, termination 12 consummation

endanger 4 risk 5 peril 6 expose 7 imperil 8 threaten 10 compromise, jeopardize

endeavor 3 aim, try 4 push, seek, toil, work 5 assay, essay, labor, trial 6 effort, intend, strain, strive 7 attempt, purpose, travail, venture 8 exertion, striving, struggle 9 determine, undertake 10 enterprise 11 undertaking

ended 4 done, over, past 7 through 8 complete

endemic 5 local 6 innate, native 8 homebred, inherent, primeval 9 homegrown, prevalent 10 aboriginal, indigenous, native-born

ending 4 stop 5 close 6 finale, finish, period, windup 7 closing, closure 8 terminus 9 cessation 10 completion, conclusion, denouement 11 termination

endive 7 lettuce, witloof 8 escarole

endless 7 eternal, undying 8 constant, enduring, immortal, infinite, unending 9 ceaseless, continual, incessant, limitless, perpetual, unbounded, unceasing, unlimited 10 continuous, indefinite, unmeasured 11 everlasting, illimitable, measureless 12 immeasurable, interminable

endmost 4 last 5 final 8 farthest, furthest, ultimate 10 concluding

endocrine gland 5 gonad, ovary 6 pineal, testis, thymus 7 adrenal, thyroid 8 pancreas 9 pituitary 11 parathyroid 12 hypothalamus

endomorphic 5 beefy, heavy, husky, stout 6 portly, pyknic, rotund

endorse 4 back, okay, sign 5 bless, vouch 6 attest, ratify, second, uphold 7 approve, certify, command, confirm, stand by, support, witness 8 accredit, advocate, champion, inscribe, make over, notarize, sanction 9 autograph, recommend 10 underwrite 12 authenticate

endorsement 7 backing, support 8 approval, sanction 9 signature 12 confirmation, ratification 13 authorization

endow 4 back, fund 5 found 6 bestow, confer, enrich, supply 7 empower, enhance, finance, furnish, promote, provide, sponsor, support 8 bequeath 9 subsidize

endowment 4 fund, gift 5 award, dower, dowry, grant, power, skill 6 legacy, talent 7 ability, bequest 8 appanage, aptitude, bestowal, capacity, donation 11 benefaction

end product 5 fruit, issue 6 effect, payoff, result, upshot 7 outcome 11 consequence

endue 3 don 4 vest 5 dower, equip, imbue, put on 6 clothe, invest, outfit 7 furnish, provide 8 accouter 9 crown with, transfuse

endurance 4 grit, guts, wind 5 moxie, pluck 6 mettle 7 stamina 8 patience, strength, tenacity 9 fortitude 10 permanence, resolution 11 persistence 12 perseverance

endure 4 bear, bide, go on, last 5 abide, brook, stand 6 accept, hold on, linger, pocket, remain, suffer 7 carry on, persist, ride out, stomach, survive, sustain, swallow, undergo, weather 8 continue, submit to, tolerate, tough out 9 withstand

enduring 3 old 4 fast, firm, sure 6 steady 7 abiding, durable, eternal, lasting, staunch 8 constant, lifelong 9 long-lived, perennial, permanent, steadfast 10 continuing, inveterate, persistent 11 long-lasting, unfaltering 12 never-failing

Endymion *father:* 8 Aethlius *lover:* 5 Diana 6 Selene *author:* 5 Keats (John)

enemy 3 foe 5 rival 8 attacker, opponent 9 adversary, assailant 10 antagonist, competitor

energetic 4 spry 5 brisk, fresh, hardy, lusty, peppy, zippy 6 active, lively 7 driving, dynamic, vibrant 8 spirited, tireless, vigorous **9** sprightly, strenuous, vivacious **13** indefatigable

energize 3 pep **4** fuel, stir **5** liven, pep up, rouse, spark **6** enable, excite, stir up, turn on **7** empower, enliven, fortify, inspire, juice up **8** activate, inspirit, vitalize **9** electrify, galvanize, stimulate **10** invigorate, strengthen

energy 3 pep, vim, zip **4** dash, life, tuck **5** drive, force, juice, moxie, pluck, power, sinew, steam, verve, vigor **6** effort, muscle, spirit **7** current, potency, stamina, voltage **8** activity, dynamism, efficacy, exertion, strength, vitality **9** animation, intensity, puissance **10** enterprise, get-up-and-go, initiative **11** application *unit:* **3** erg **4** dyne, volt **5** joule **7** quantum **10** horsepower

enervate 3 sap **4** jade, tire **5** weary **6** soften, weaken **7** disable, exhaust, fatigue, unnerve **8** enfeeble, unstring **10** debilitate, devitalize

enfant terrible 3 imp **5** scamp **6** urchin **9** skeezicks

enfeeble 3 sap **6** soften, weaken **7** deplete, disable, exhaust, fatigue **8** enervate **9** attenuate, undermine **10** debilitate, devitalize

enfold 3 hug **4** wrap **5** clasp, cover, press **6** shroud, swathe **7** contain, embrace, squeeze **8** surround

enforce 5 exact, impel **6** compel, effect, impose, invoke, oblige **7** execute, fulfill **8** carry out **9** constrain, discharge, implement, prosecute **10** accomplish, administer, strengthen

enfranchise 4 free **6** rescue **7** deliver, manumit, release, set free **8** liberate **10** emancipate

engage 4 bind, grip, hire, mesh **5** fight, troth **6** absorb, arrest, attack, battle, commit, employ, enlist, occupy, pledge, take on **7** assault, betroth, engross, immerse, involve, promise **8** affiance, enthrall, interact **9** captivate, encounter, fascinate, interlace, interlock, intermesh, interplay, preoccupy, undertake

engaged 4 busy, rapt **6** intent **7** working **8** absorbed, employed, immersed, intended, occupied, plighted **9** affianced, betrothed, committed, engrossed, wrapped up **10** contracted **11** preoccupied *person:* **6** fiancé **7** fiancée

engage in 4 wage **5** enter **6** pursue, tackle, take up **7** conduct **8** embark on, practice **9** prosecute, undertake

engagement 3 gig **4** date, fray, word **5** fight, troth, tryst **6** action, battle, combat, hiring, pledge, plight **7** booking, meeting, promise **8** espousal, skirmish **9** betrothal, encounter **10** commitment, employment, rendezvous **11** appointment, assignation

engaging 7 likable, winning, winsome **8** charming, pleasant, pleasing **9** appealing **10** attractive **13** prepossessing

engender 4 sire, stir **5** beget, breed, cause, hatch, rouse, spawn **6** arouse, create, excite, father, induce, lead to, work up **7** develop, produce, provoke **8** generate **9** originate, procreate, stimulate

engine 5 motor, turbo **7** turbine **10** locomotive *kind:* **3** gas, jet **5** steam **6** diesel **7** turbine **8** gasoline **9** hydraulic *jet:* **8** turbofan, turbojet *part:* **3** cam, rod **4** gear, plug, pump **5** choke **6** filter, piston, tappet **8** cylinder, manifold, throttle **9** condenser, crankcase **10** carburetor **12** transmission *siege:* **3** ram **6** onager **8** ballista, catapult **9** trebuchet **12** battering ram *sound:* **4** chug, roar **6** rattle

engineer 4 plan, plot **5** set up, swing **6** devise, driver, manage, scheme, wangle **7** arrange, finagle **8** contrive, intrigue, maneuver, motorman **9** machinate, negotiate **10** manipulate, mastermind **11** orchestrate *kind:* **5** civil **6** mining **8** chemical, sanitary **10** electrical, mechanical **12** aeronautical *military:* **6** sapper

engineers' group *abbreviation:* **4** IEEE

England 6 Albion **7** Britain **9** Britannia **12** Great Britain see also UNITED KINGDOM

English 7 British *cathedral city:* **3** Ely **4** York **5** Wells **6** Durham, Exeter **7** Lincoln, Norwich **8** Coventry, Hereford **9** Salisbury, Worcester **10** Canterbury, Winchester *coin:* **5** crown, groat, pence **6** florin, guinea **8** farthing, shilling, sixpence, twopence **9** fourpence, half crown, halfpenny, sovereign **10** threepence *combining form:* **5** Anglo *farm:* **5** croft *forest:* **5** Arden **8** Sherwood *letter:* **3** zed *measure:* **3** rod, tun **4** gill, hand, peck, span **5** chain **6** barrel, bushel, fathom, firkin **7** furlong **8** hogshead **10** barleycorn *military college:* **9** Sandhurst *patron saint:* **6** George *person:* **4** chap, mate **5** bloke **6** Briton *pirate:* **4** Kidd (Capt. William) **5** Avery (Henry), Teach (Edward) **6** Morgan (Henry) **7** Dampier (William) **10** Blackbeard *prince:* **5** Harry **6** Andrew, Edward, Philip **7** Charles, William *princess:* **4** Anne **5** Diana **8** Margaret *professor:* **3** don *royal family:* **5** Tudor **6** Stuart **7** Hanover, Windsor *saint:*

7 Dunstan 8 Cuthbert *spa:* 4 Bath *sport:* 5 rugby 7 cricket *tavern:* 3 pub *university:* 5 Leeds 6 Oxford 9 Cambridge *weight:* 5 stone 6 firkin 7 quintal 8 quartern

English Channel swimmer 6 Ederle (Gertrude)

engrave 3 cut, fix 4 etch 5 carve, chase 6 incise, scrive 7 instill 8 inscribe

engraver 6 chaser, etcher *German:* 5 Dürer (Albrecht) 10 Schongauer (Martin) *Italian:* 8 Raimondi (Marcantonio)

engraving 7 etching, linecut, woodcut 8 drypoint, intaglio 9 xylograph

engross 4 bury, busy, copy, grip 5 apply, write 6 absorb, engage, indite, occupy, scribe 7 consume, immerse, involve 8 enthrall, inscribe 9 captivate, preoccupy 10 transcribe

engrosser 6 scribe 7 copyist 9 scrivener 12 calligrapher 13 calligraphist

engulf 4 bury 5 drown, flood, swamp, whelm 6 deluge, devour 7 immerse, overrun, swallow 8 flow over, inundate, overflow, submerge 9 overwhelm, swallow up

enhance 4 lift 5 add to, adorn, exalt, raise 6 deepen 7 amplify, augment, build up, elevate, enlarge, flatter, improve, magnify 8 beautify, heighten, increase 9 aggravate, embellish, embroider, intensify, reinforce 10 exaggerate, strengthen

enigma 4 crux, knot 5 poser, rebus 6 puzzle, riddle, sphinx, teaser 7 mystery, problem, puzzler 9 conundrum 10 closed book, perplexity, puzzlement 12 question mark 13 Chinese puzzle, mystification

enigmatic 6 mystic 7 cryptic, Delphic, obscure 8 Delphian, oracular, puzzling 9 ambiguous 10 mysterious, mystifying, perplexing 11 inscrutable

enisle 6 cut off 7 isolate 8 insulate, separate 9 segregate, sequester

enjoin 3 ban, bid 4 deny, rule, tell, urge, warn 5 order, taboo 6 adjure, charge, decree, direct, forbid, impose, outlaw 7 caution, command, counsel, dictate, inhibit 8 admonish, disallow, forewarn, instruct, prohibit 9 interdict, prescribe, proscribe

enjoy 4 like, love 5 eat up, fancy, savor 6 relish 9 delight in 10 appreciate

enjoyable 3 fun 8 pleasant, pleasing 9 agreeable 10 delightful, satisfying 11 pleasurable 12 entertaining

enjoyment 4 zest 5 gusto, savor 6 relish 7 benefit, delight 8 felicity, fruition, pleasure 9 diversion 10 indulgence, recreation, relaxation 11 delectation 12 satisfaction 13 gratification

Enki *consort:* 5 Nintu *son:* 6 Ninsar

enkindle 4 fire 5 flame, light 6 ignite 7 inflame 8 touch off 9 set fire to

enlarge 3 wax 4 grow, rise 5 add to, boost, build, mount, widen 6 beef up, dilate, expand, extend 7 amplify, augment, broaden, develop, greaten, inflate, magnify, stretch 8 heighten, increase, multiply 9 elaborate, embroider 10 exaggerate

enlargement 4 node 5 tumor 6 blowup, growth, nodule 7 buildup 8 addition, increase, swelling 9 accretion, expansion, extension 12 augmentation 13 amplification

enlighten 5 edify, guide, teach 6 advise, illume, inform, uplift 7 educate, improve 8 illumine, instruct 10 illuminate

enlist 4 join 5 draft, enter 6 employ, enroll, join up, muster, sign on, sign up 7 attract, recruit 8 register 9 volunteer 11 participate

enliven 3 pep 4 buoy, fire, warm 5 amuse, cheer, pep up, renew, rouse 6 excite, jazz up, perk up, vivify, wake up 7 animate, cheer up, inspire, quicken, refresh, restore, spice up 8 energize, recreate 9 entertain, galvanize, stimulate 10 exhilarate, invigorate, rejuvenate

en masse 5 as one 6 bodily 8 together 12 collectively

enmesh 4 hook, mire, trap 5 catch, snare 6 draw in, tangle 7 embroil, ensnarl, involve, trammel 8 drag into, entangle 9 embrangle, implicate

enmity 4 hate 6 animus, hatred, rancor, spleen 7 ill will 8 aversion, bad blood, loathing 9 animosity, antipathy, hostility 10 abhorrence, antagonism 11 detestation

ennoble 5 exalt, honor, raise 6 uplift, uprear 7 dignify, elevate, glorify, magnify, sublime 10 aggrandize 11 distinguish

ennui 6 apathy, tedium 7 boredom, fatigue, languor 8 doldrums, dullness, lethargy 9 jadedness, lassitude, tiredness, weariness 11 languidness 12 listlessness

Enoch *father:* 4 Cain *son:* 10 Methuselah

Enoch Arden *author:* 8 Tennyson (Alfred)

enormity 6 infamy 7 outrage 8 atrocity, hugeness, rankness, savagery, vastness 9 barbarity, depravity, flagrancy, graveness, greatness, grossness, immensity, magnitude 11 abomination, heinousness, massiveness, monstrosity, seriousness, weightiness

enormous 4 huge, vast **5** great **7** immense, mammoth, massive, titanic **8** colossal, gigantic **9** humongous, monstrous **10** astronomic, gargantuan, prodigious, stupendous, tremendous **12** astronomical

Enos *father:* **4** Seth *grandfather:* **4** Adam *grandmother:* **3** Eve *uncle:* **4** Abel, Cain

enough 5 ample **6** fairly, plenty **8** adequate, decently, passably **9** competent, tolerably **10** acceptably, adequately, sufficient **11** comfortable, sufficiency **12** satisfactory, sufficiently *poetic:* **4** enow

enounce 3 say **5** state, utter **6** intone **8** proclaim, set forth **10** articulate

enrage 3 ire **4** rile **5** anger **6** madden **7** incense, inflame, steam up **9** infuriate

enrapture 5 charm, elate **6** ravish, trance **7** delight, enchant, rejoice **8** enthrall, entrance **9** captivate, transport

enraptured 6 elated **7** charmed **8** ecstatic, thrilled **9** bewitched, delighted, enchanted, entranced **10** captivated, enthralled, mesmerized, spellbound **11** transported

enrich 5 adorn, endow **6** fatten **7** enhance, improve **8** beautify, ornament **9** embellish, fertilize **10** supplement

enroll 4 book, file, join, list **5** draft, enter **6** enlist, induct, join up, muster, record, sign on, sign up, wrap up **7** catalog, engross, recruit **8** inscribe, register **9** conscript, subscribe **10** transcribe **11** matriculate

ensconce 4 bury, hide **5** cache, cover, place, plant, stash **6** hole up, locate, settle **7** conceal, install, secrete, shelter **9** establish

ensemble 3 duo **4** band, crew, suit, trio **5** choir, combo, decor, group, suite, troop, whole **6** chorus, outfit, septet, sextet, troupe **7** chorale, company, costume, en masse, quartet, quintet **8** together **9** aggregate, orchestra

enshrine 6 hallow, revere **7** cherish **8** dedicate, preserve, sanctify, treasure **10** consecrate **11** memorialize

enshroud 4 hide, veil, wrap **5** cloak **6** clothe, enfold, enwrap, invest **7** blanket, conceal, envelop, obscure

ensign 4 flag, jack, sign **5** badge, crest **6** banner, colors, emblem, pennon **7** officer, pennant **8** gonfalon, insignia, standard, streamer **9** oriflamme

enslave 4 yoke **5** chain **6** fetter, thrall **7** enchain, oppress, shackle, subject **8** dominate, enthrall **9** indenture, subjugate **12** disfranchise

enslavement 4 yoke **6** thrall **7** bondage,

helotry, peonage, serfdom, slavery **9** servitude, thralldom

ensnare 3 bag, net **4** hook, lure, mesh, snag, trap **5** benet, catch, decoy **6** enmesh, entrap, tangle **7** capture **8** entangle, inveigle

ensnarl 4 mire **6** enmesh, tangle **7** embroil, perplex, trammel **8** entangle **9** embrangle

ensorcell 3 hex **5** charm, spell, witch **6** allure, voodoo **7** beguile, bewitch, enchant **8** enthrall **9** captivate, enrapture, hypnotize, magnetize, mesmerize, spellbind

ensorcellment 5 magic **7** sorcery **8** witchery, wizardry **9** conjuring **10** necromancy, witchcraft **11** bewitchment, enchantment

ensphere 4 ball **8** conglobe **10** conglobate

ensue 4 stem **5** issue **6** attend, derive, follow, result **7** emanate, proceed, succeed **9** supervene

ensuing 4 next **9** later **9** resultant **10** consequent, subsequent, succeeding

ensure 5 cinch **6** clinch, secure **7** certify, confirm, warrant **9** establish, guarantee

enswathe 4 roll, wrap **5** cloak, drape **6** bundle, enwrap, shroud, wrap up **7** envelop, swaddle

entail 5 imply **6** assign, confer, demand, impose, lead to **7** call for, involve, require **8** occasion, restrict, result in, transmit **11** necessitate

entangle 4 mesh, mire, trap **5** catch, ravel, snare, snarl, tie up, twist **6** enmesh, entrap **7** capture, catch up, embroil, ensnare, ensnarl, involve, perplex, trammel **10** complicate, intertwine, interweave

entanglement 3 web **4** knot, mesh, mess, toil **5** skein, snare **6** affair, cobweb, muddle **8** intrigue **9** confusion, imbroglio **11** embroilment, involvement **12** complication

entente 4 pact **6** league, treaty **7** compact **8** alliance, covenant **9** agreement, coalition, concordat **13** understanding

enter 4 go in, join, list, open **5** admit, begin, start **6** come in, enlist, enroll, go into, insert, join up, muster, record, sign on, sign up **7** intrude **8** come into, embark on, inscribe, register **9** introduce, penetrate **10** embark upon

enterprise 4 deed, feat, firm, push, task **5** cause, drive, pluck, vigor **6** action, daring, effort, energy, hustle, outfit, scheme **7** attempt, company, concern, courage, exploit, project, pursuit, venture **8** activity, ambition, audacity, boldness, business, campaign, endeavor, gumption, industry **9** adventure, eagerness **10** enthusiasm, get-up-and-go, initiative **11** corporation, undertaking **12** organization, self-reliance **13** establishment

enterprising 4 bold **5** eager **6** daring, hungry **7** driving, go-ahead **8** aspiring, hustling **9** ambitious, audacious, energetic **10** aggressive **11** adventurous, hardworking, industrious, up-and-coming, venturesome

entertain 4 host **5** amuse **6** divert, regale **7** delight, receive **8** consider

entertainer 4 mime **5** actor, clown, comic **6** busker, dancer, jester, singer **7** actress, artiste, diseuse, trouper **8** comedian, minstrel **10** comedienne

entertaining 6 lively **7** amusing **8** engaging **9** diverting, enjoyable

entertainment 4 fete, play, show, skit **5** revue, sport **6** circus **7** banquet, concert, pastime, ridotto **8** pleasure **9** amusement, diversion, enjoyment **10** recreation **11** distraction, performance

enthrall 4 grip **5** charm **6** absorb, subdue **7** beguile, bewitch, enchant, engross, enslave **9** fascinate, hypnotize, mesmerize, spellbind, subjugate

enthralling 8 exciting, gripping, riveting **9** absorbing, arresting **10** enchanting, engrossing, entrancing **11** captivating, charismatic, provocative **12** spellbinding

enthuse 4 gush, rave **6** excite, thrill **7** animate, delight, inspire **8** energize **10** rhapsodize

enthusiasm 4 élan, fire, zeal, zest **5** ardor, craze, fever, mania, verve **6** fervor, spirit **7** ardency, passion, rapture **9** eagerness, intensity **10** ebullience, excitement, fanaticism

enthusiast 3 bug, fan, nut **4** buff **5** fiend, freak, lover, maven **6** addict, junkie, maniac, votary, zealot **7** booster, devotee, fanatic, groupie, habitué **8** believer, partisan **9** extremist **10** aficionado

enthusiastic 4 avid, gaga, keen **5** eager, rabid **6** ardent, fervid, gung ho, hearty, hipped, raring **7** devoted, excited, fervent, intense, zealous **8** hopped-up, obsessed, spirited, vascular **9** fanatical **10** passionate

entice 4 bait, coax, draw, lure, toll, wile **5** charm, decoy, tempt **6** allure, cajole, entrap, invite, lead on, seduce **7** attract, wheedle **8** inveigle, persuade

enticement 4 bait, lure, trap **5** decoy, snare **6** come-on **9** seduction **10** allurement, attraction, seducement, temptation **12** blandishment, inveiglement

enticer 4 bait, vamp **5** Circe, decoy, siren **7** Lorelei **9** attractor, temptress **10** attraction, seductress **11** enchantress, femme fatale

enticing 5 siren **8** fetching, witching **9** seductive **10** attractive, bewitching, intriguing **11** captivating, fascinating

entire 3 all **4** full **5** gross, total, whole **6** intact **7** perfect, plenary, unified **8** complete, integral, outright **10** integrated **12** consolidated

entirely 5 fully, quite **6** wholly **7** utterly **9** perfectly **10** altogether, completely, thoroughly **11** exclusively

entirety 3 sum **5** total, whole **8** sum total, totality **9** aggregate, wholeness **10** everything **12** completeness, universality

entitle 3 dub, let **4** call, name, term **5** allow **6** enable, permit **7** baptize, empower, license, qualify **8** christen **9** authorize, designate **10** denominate

entity 3 sum **4** body, item, unit **5** being, thing, whole **6** object **7** article, integer **8** quiddity, totality **9** existence, something, substance **10** individual

entomb 4 bury **5** inter **6** inhume, shrine **7** mummify **8** enshrine **9** sepulcher, sepulchre

entombment 6 burial **7** obsequy **9** obsequies, sepulture **10** inhumation

entourage 5 staff, suite, train **6** escort, milieu **7** cortege, coterie, retinue **8** henchmen **9** courtiers, followers, following, hangers-on, retainers **10** associates, attendants **12** surroundings

entr'acte 8 interval **9** interlude **12** intermission

entrails 4 guts **5** pluck, tripe **6** bowels, tripes, vitals **7** giblets, innards, insides, viscera **8** stuffing **10** intestines

entrance 4 adit, door, gate, port **5** charm, foyer, inlet, lobby, mouth **6** access, portal, ravish **7** arrival, attract, bewitch, delight, doorway, enchant, gateway, ingress, opening **8** aperture, enthrall, open door **9** admission, captivate, enrapture, fascinate, hypnotize, mesmerize, spellbind, threshold, transport, vestibule **10** admittance, ingression **11** penetration

entrant 7 starter **10** competitor, contestant **11** participant

entrap 3 bag, net **4** bait, lure, toll **5** catch, decoy, snare, tempt **6** allure, ambush, entice, entoil, lead on, seduce, tangle **7** beguile, catch up, ensnare **8** entangle, inveigle

entre ___ 4 nous

entreat 3 ask, beg, bid **4** pray, urge **5** crave, plead, press **6** adjure, appeal

7 beseech, implore, wheedle **8** blandish **9** importune **10** supplicate

entreaty 4 plea, suit **6** appeal, orison, prayer **7** request **8** petition **11** application, importunity **12** supplication

entrechat 4 leap

entrée 6 access **7** ingress **8** main dish **9** admission **10** admittance, main course

entrench 3 fix **4** root **5** embed, lodge **6** define, furrow, ground, hole up, invade, settle **7** confirm, impinge, implant, intrude **8** encroach, ensconce, infringe, trespass **9** establish **10** strengthen

entrenched 3 set **4** firm **5** rigid, sworn **8** accepted, deep-dyed **9** hard-shell **10** deep-rooted, deep-seated, inveterate **13** bred-in-the-bone, dyed-in-the-wool

entrepôt 3 hub **4** mart **5** depot **6** bazaar, market **8** emporium, exchange **9** concourse, warehouse **10** depository, storehouse **11** marketplace

entrepreneur 10 capitalist, contractor, impresario

entresol 9 mezzanine

entropy 5 chaos, decay **7** decline **8** disorder **10** randomness **11** degradation

entrust 4 give **5** allot, leave **6** assign, charge, commit, confer, impose **7** commend, confide, consign, deliver, deposit **8** allocate, delegate, hand over, relegate, turn over

entry 3 way **4** adit, door, gate, item, port **5** debit, foyer, inlet, lobby **6** access, credit, portal, record **7** doorway, ingress, opening **8** headword **9** admission, threshold, vestibule **10** admittance, enlistment, enrollment, ingression

entryway 4 door, gate **5** foyer, lobby **6** portal **7** ingress, narthex, portico **9** vestibule

entwine 4 coil, wind **5** braid, plait, twist **6** enmesh **7** wreathe **8** entangle **9** interlace **10** interweave

enumerate 3 sum, tot **4** cite, list, tell, tote **5** add up, count, tally, total, tot up **6** detail, number, recite, reckon, tote up **7** compute, itemize, recount, specify, tick off **8** identify **9** calculate, inventory **13** particularize

enunciate 3 say **5** speak, state, utter, voice **6** affirm, intone **7** declare, express, lay down **8** announce, proclaim, propound, vocalize **9** formulate, postulate, pronounce, verbalize **10** articulate

envelop 3 hem **4** hide, roll, veil, wrap **5** cloak, cover, drape **6** cocoon, enfold, engulf, enwrap, invest, sheath, shield, shroud, swathe, wrap up **7** blanket,

embrace, enclose, swaddle **8** encircle, enshroud, enswathe, surround **10** circumfuse

envenom 6 poison **8** embitter **10** exacerbate

envious 7 jealous **8** coveting, covetous, grudging **9** green-eyed, invidious, resentful **10** begrudging

environment 6 medium, milieu **7** ambient, climate, context, habitat, setting, terrain **8** ambiance, ambience, backdrop **9** situation **10** atmosphere, background **11** mise-en-scène **12** surroundings *science:* **7** ecology

environmentalist 4 Muir (John) **6** Brower (David), Carson (Rachel), Nelson (Gaylord), Wilson (Edward O.) **7** Ehrlich (Paul), Thoreau (Henry David) **8** Commoner (Barry), Cousteau (Jacques-Yves) **9** ecologist, Roosevelt (Theodore)

environs 6 bounds, limits **7** compass, fringes, suburbs **8** boundary, confines, locality, purlieus, vicinity **9** districts, outskirts, precincts **12** neighborhood, surroundings

envisage 4 view **5** dream, fancy, grasp, image, think **6** regard, vision **7** dream up, feature, foresee, imagine, picture, realize **8** conceive, look upon, summon up **9** conjure up, objectify, visualize

envoy 5 agent **6** bearer, consul, deputy, legate, nuncio **7** attaché, carrier, courier **8** diplomat, emissary, minister **9** messenger **10** ambassador **11** internuncio **12** intermediary

envy 5 covet **6** grudge **8** begrudge, grudging, jealousy **10** resentment **12** covetousness **13** invidiousness

enwrap 4 roll, veil **5** clasp, drape **6** enfold, invest, shroud, swathe **7** enclose, engross, envelop, sheathe, swaddle **8** enshroud, enswathe

enzyme 3 ase **5** ficin, lyase, renin, urase **6** kinase, ligase, lipase, mutase, papain, pepsin, rennin, urease, zymase **7** amidase, amylase, cyclase, enolase, guanase, hydrase, inulase, isozyme, lactase, maltase, oxidase, pectase, pepsine, plasmin, ptyalin, rennase, sucrase, trypsin, zymogen **8** aldolase, diastase, elastase, esterase, fumarase, lyzozyme, nuclease, protease, steapsin, thrombin, zymogene **9** cellulase, invertase

eon see AEON

Eos see AURORA

épée 5 sword

epergne 5 stand **11** centerpiece

ephemeral 5 brief, short **7** passing **8** episodic, fleeting, fugitive, volatile **9** fugacious, momentary, temporary, transient 10 evanescent, short-lived, transitory 11 impermanent

Ephialtes 5 giant *brother:* 4 Otus *father:* 6 Aloeus 8 Poseidon *mother:* 9 Iphimedia *slayer:* 6 Apollo

Ephraim *brother:* 8 Manasseh *father:* 6 Joseph *grandfather:* 5 Jacob *mother:* 7 Asenath

epic 4 poem, saga 5 grand, Iliad 6 Aeneid, heroic 7 Beowulf, Odyssey 8 imposing, sweeping 9 Gilgamesh, narrative 12 Heimskringla

epicene 10 effeminate 11 intersexual 13 hermaphrodite

epicure 7 gourmet 8 aesthete, hedonist, sybarite 9 bon vivant 10 gastronome 11 connoisseur 12 gastronomist

epicurean 7 gourmet, sensual 8 aesthete, hedonist, sensuous, sybarite 9 bon vivant, luxurious 10 gastronome, voluptuous 11 connoisseur 12 gastronomist, sensualistic

epidemic 3 flu 4 rash, wave 6 plague 7 rampant, scourge 8 catching, outbreak 9 contagion, prevalent 10 contagious, pestilence

epidermis 4 skin 7 cuticle 10 integument

epigram 3 saw 4 poem 5 adage, axiom, maxim 6 bon mot, dictum, saying, truism 7 proverb 8 aphorism, apothegm

epigrammatic 5 meaty, pithy, terse, witty 6 cogent 7 compact, concise, marrowy, piquant, pointed

epigraph 5 motto 9 quotation 11 inscription

epilogue 4 coda 5 close 6 ending, finale, windup 7 closing 8 postlude 9 afterword 10 conclusion, postscript

Epimetheus *brother:* 10 Prometheus *father:* 7 Iapetus *wife:* 7 Pandora

epiphany 6 aperçu, vision 7 insight 9 discovery, intuition 10 appearance, disclosure, revelation 11 inspiration, realization 13 manifestation

episode 5 event, phase 7 passage 8 incident, occasion 9 happening, interlude 10 occurrence 12 circumstance

episodic 5 brief 7 passing 8 fleeting, sporadic 9 ephemeral, irregular, temporary, transient 10 evanescent, occasional, short-lived 12 intermittent

epistaxis 9 nosebleed

epistle 4 note 6 letter 7 lection, missive 13 communication

epitaph 3 R.I.P. 5 elegy 6 eulogy 8 hic jacet 11 inscription

epithet 4 name 5 label, title 7 agnomen, moniker 8 cognomen, nickname 9 sobriquet 11 appellation

epitome 3 sum 4 acme, type 5 brief, short 6 digest, précis, résumé 7 essence, example, outline, summary 8 abstract, breviary, exemplar, synopsis, ultimate 9 archetype, summation, summing-up 10 abridgment, apotheosis, conspectus, embodiment 11 abridgement 12 condensation, quintessence

epitomize 5 sum up 6 digest, embody, mirror, typify 7 abridge, outline, summate 8 abstract, boil down, condense, manifest, tabulate 9 capsulize, exemplify, incarnate, inventory, objectify, personify, represent, summarize, symbolize, synopsize 10 abbreviate, illustrate 11 concentrate, emblematize, incorporate, personalize

epoch 3 age, eon, era 4 aeon, term, time 6 period 8 interval, time span

equable 4 calm, even, just 6 serene, stable, steady 7 orderly, regular, stabile, uniform 8 composed, constant 9 immutable, temperate, unvarying 10 consistent, invariable, unchanging 12 unchangeable

equal 3 tie 4 even, fair, like, mate, peer, same, twin 5 agree, alike, match 7 uniform 8 alter ego, amount to, parallel 9 duplicate, identical, impartial, objective 10 fifty-fifty 11 counterpart, symmetrical 12 commensurate, correspond to, proportional 13 commensurable, proportionate *combining form:* 3 iso 4 equi, pari *French:* 4 égal

equality 3 par 6 equity, parity 7 balance, égalité 8 evenness, fairness, sameness 10 uniformity

Equality State 7 Wyoming

equalize 4 even 5 level 6 square 7 balance 9 harmonize

equalizer 3 gun 6 pistol 8 handicap 10 tying score

equally 10 fifty-fifty 11 impartially

equanimity 4 calm, cool 5 poise 6 aplomb, phlegm 7 balance 8 calmness, coolness, evenness, serenity 9 assurance, composure, equipoise, placidity, sangfroid 10 detachment, steadiness 11 tranquility 12 tranquillity

equate 4 even 5 liken, match, treat 6 adjust, regard, relate, square 7 compare 8 consider, equalize, parallel 10 assimilate

Equatorial Guinea *capital:* 6 Malabo *island, island group:* 5 Bioko 6 Elobey, Pagulu 7 Corisco *language:* 5 Bantu 6 French 7 Spanish *mainland:* 5 Mbini 7 Río Muni *monetary unit:* 5 franc *neighbor:* 5 Gabon 8 Cameroon

equestrian 5 rider 6 horsey 8 horseman, knightly 10 horsewoman

equidistant 3 mid 6 medial, median,

middle, midway **7** central, halfway, midmost

equilibrium 5 poise **6** aplomb, stasis **7** balance **8** evenness, symmetry **9** composure, stability **10** steadiness **12** counterpoise **13** stabilization

equine 4 colt, mare **5** filly, horse, steed **6** horsey **8** stallion **9** horselike

equip 3 arm, fit, rig **5** array, dress, endow, rig up **6** attire, fit out, outfit, rig out, supply **7** appoint, furnish, prepare, provide **8** accouter, accoutre **9** provision

equipment 3 rig **4** gear **5** traps **6** attire, outfit, tackle, things **7** baggage, panoply **8** fittings, material, matériel, ordnance, supplies, tackling **9** apparatus, endowment, machinery, trappings **10** provisions **11** accessories, attachments, habiliments, impedimenta **12** accouterment, accoutrement, provisioning **13** accouterments, accoutrements, appurtenances, paraphernalia

equitable 4 even, fair, just **5** level **6** proper, square **7** condign **8** balanced, deserved, unbiased **9** identical, impartial, objective, uncolored **10** evenhanded, impersonal **12** unprejudiced **13** dispassionate

equity 3 law **7** justice **8** equality, interest, justness

equivalence 3 par **6** parity, simile **7** analogy **8** equality, identity, likeness, sameness **10** conformity **11** correlation

equivalent 4 akin, copy, like, peer, same, twin **5** alike, match **6** agnate **7** identic, similar **8** parallel **9** analogous, duplicate, identical **10** comparable, homologous, substitute, tantamount **11** convertible, correlative, counterpart **12** commensurate **13** corresponding, proportionate

equivocal 4 hazy **5** fishy, vague **6** unsure **7** clouded, dubious, obscure, suspect, unclear **8** doubtful **9** ambiguous, debatable, enigmatic, uncertain, undecided **10** ambivalent, indecisive, indistinct, irresolute, unresolved **11** problematic **12** disreputable, inconclusive, questionable **13** indeterminate

equivocate 3 fib, lie **5** cavil, dodge, evade, fudge, hedge **6** palter, waffle, weasel **7** shuffle **8** sidestep **9** pussyfoot **11** prevaricate **12** tergiversate

equivocation 3 fib **7** evasion, fibbing, hedging, sophism **8** waffling **9** ambiguity, casuistry, duplicity, sophistry **12** speciousness

equivoque 3 pun **8** wordplay

era 3 age, day **4** date, term, time **5** epoch, stage **6** period

eradicate 4 dele, raze **5** abate, erase, purge **6** delete, efface, remove, uproot **7** abolish, blot out, destroy, expunge, root out, weed out, wipe out **8** demolish, stamp out **9** eliminate, extirpate, liquidate **10** annihilate, do away with, extinguish, obliterate **11** exterminate

erase 4 dele, void, x out **6** cancel, delete, efface, excise, remove, rub out **7** abolish, blot out, expunge, nullify, scratch, take out, wipe out **8** black out, blank out, cross off, cross out **9** eliminate, extirpate, sponge out, strike out **10** obliterate

Erato see MUSE

Erbin *father:* **9** Custennin *nephew:* **6** Arthur *son:* **7** Geraint

ere 6 before

Erebus *daughter:* **3** Day **6** Hemera *father:* **5** Chaos *home:* **5** Hades *sister, wife:* **3** Nox, Nyx *son:* **6** Aether, Charon

Erec et ___ 5 Enide

Erechteus *daughter:* **8** Chthonia *father:* **6** Vulcan **10** Hephaestus *mother:* **4** Gaea *slayer:* **4** Zeus **7** Jupiter

erect 4 form **5** build, put up, raise, set up **6** create, raised **7** build up, stand-up, upright **8** assemble, elevated, standing, straight, vertical **9** construct, establish **10** upstanding **13** perpendicular

eremite 6 hermit **7** ascetic, recluse, stylite **9** anchoress, anchorite

Erewhon 6 utopia **7** nowhere *author:* **6** Butler (Samuel)

ergo 4 then, thus **5** hence **9** therefore **11** accordingly **12** consequently

Erichthonius *father:* **8** Dardanus *son:* **4** Tros

Eridanus star 8 Achernar

Erin see EIRE

Erinyes 6 Alecto, Furies **7** Megaera **9** Eumenides, Tisiphone

Eris *brother:* **4** Ares, Mars *daughter:* **3** Ate *fruit:* **5** apple *goddess of:* **6** strife **7** discord *mother:* **3** Nox, Nyx

Eritrea *archipelago:* **6** Dahlak *capital:* **6** Asmara *island:* **5** Zuqar *monetary unit:* **5** nakfa *neighbor:* **5** Sudan **8** Djibouti, Ethiopia *river:* **6** Baraka *sea:* **3** Red

ermine 3 fur **5** stoat **6** weasel

erode 3 eat, rub **4** wear **5** decay, scour **6** abrade, rub off **7** consume, corrade, crumble, eat away, rub away **8** wear away **9** scrape off **10** scrape away **11** deteriorate **12** disintegrate

Eroica composer 9 Beethoven (Ludwig van)

Eros see CUPID

erose 6 jagged, uneven **9** irregular

erotic 4 lewd, racy, sexy **5** bawdy, spicy **6** carnal, earthy, ribald, risqué **7** fleshly, obscene, profane, sensual 8 off-color, prurient, sensuous 9 salacious 10 voluptuous 11 aphrodisiac, titillating

err 3 sin 4 goof, slip, trip 5 lapse, stray 6 bungle, foul up, mess up, slip up 7 blunder, deviate, screw up, stumble 8 trespass 10 transgress

errand 3 job 4 task 5 chore 7 mission 10 assignment

errand boy 4 page 5 gofer 7 bellboy, bellhop, courier 9 go-between

errant 5 stray 6 fickle, roving 7 aimless, deviant, erratic, naughty, ranging, roaming, wayward, willful 8 drifting, fallible, rambling, shifting, straying 9 deviating, itinerant, traveling, wandering 10 meandering, unreliable 11 mischievous

erratic 5 flaky 6 fitful 7 wayward 8 freakish, shifting, unstable, variable, volatile 9 arbitrary, desultory, eccentric, fluctuant, irregular, mercurial, spasmodic, uncertain, wandering, whimsical 10 capricious, changeable, inconstant, meandering 12 inconsistent 13 idiosyncratic, unpredictable

erring see ERRANT

erroneous 3 off 4 awry 5 amiss, askew, false, wrong 6 untrue 7 unsound 8 mistaken, specious, spurious 9 defective, incorrect, misguided 10 fallacious, inaccurate, misleading

error 4 flub, goof, muff, slip, trip 5 boner, botch, fault, fluff, gaffe, lapse 6 boo-boo, bungle, fumble, howler, miscue, slipup 7 blooper, blunder, fallacy, falsity, faux pas, misstep, mistake, screwup, stumble, untruth 8 delusion, illusion, screamer 9 falsehood, indecorum, oversight 10 inaccuracy, misreading 11 impropriety, misjudgment *printing:* 4 typo 6 errata (plural) 7 erratum

ersatz 4 copy, fake, sham 5 bogus, dummy, faked, false, phony 6 pseudo 8 spurious 9 imitation, simulated, synthetic 10 artificial, factitious, simulacrum, substitute 11 counterfeit

Erse 5 Irish 6 Celtic, Gaelic

erstwhile 3 old 4 late, once, past 5 prior 6 before, bygone, former, whilom 7 already, earlier, onetime, quondam 8 formerly, previous 10 heretofore, previously

eruct 4 burp, emit, gush, spew 5 belch, eject, expel 7 explode 8 detonate, disgorge

erudite 7 bookish, learned 8 lettered, literate, studious, well-read 9 scholarly 10 scholastic

erudition 7 culture 8 learning, literacy 9 knowledge 11 bookishness, cultiva-

tion, learnedness, scholarship 12 studiousness 13 scholarliness

erupt 3 jet 4 spew 5 belch, burst, eject, expel, go off, spout, spurt 7 explode 8 break out, burst out, detonate 9 discharge 10 break forth, burst forth

eruption 4 gust, rush 5 blast, burst, flare, sally 6 access 7 flare-up 8 outbreak, outburst 9 commotion, explosion *skin:* 3 zit 4 rash 6 pimple

Esau *brother:* 5 Jacob *country:* 4 Edom *descendant:* 7 Edomite *father:* 5 Isaac *father-in-law:* 4 Elon *grandson:* 6 Amalek *mother:* 7 Rebekah *new name:* 4 Edom *son:* 5 Korha, Reuel 7 Eliphaz *wife:* 4 Adah 10 Aholibamah

escalade 5 climb, mount, scale 6 ascend 7 scaling

escalate 4 grow, rise, soar 5 boost, climb, mount, widen 6 expand, extend, spread, step up 7 amplify, augment, broaden, enlarge, inflate 8 heighten, increase, multiply 9 intensify 11 proliferate

escapade 4 lark, romp 5 antic, caper, fling, folly, prank, spree, stunt 6 frolic, vagary 7 roguery, rollick 8 mischief 9 adventure

escape 3 fly, lam 4 bolt, duck, flee, shun, skip, slip 5 avoid, break, dodge, elude, evade, shake 6 bypass, depart, eschew, flight, hegira, outlet 7 abscond, duck out, evasion, get away, make off, release, run away, skip out 8 breakout 9 avoidance, desertion, disappear, steal away 10 circumvent, liberation 11 deliverance, evasiveness *artist:* 7 Houdini (Harry) *narrow:* 9 close call 10 close shave

escargot 5 snail

escarole 6 endive

escarpment 5 bluff, cliff, slope

eschar 4 scab 5 crust 6 lesion

eschew 4 shun 5 avoid, elude, evade, forgo, spurn 6 abjure, forego, pass up, refuse, reject 7 decline 8 turn down

eschewal 7 elusion, evasion, refusal 8 shunning, spurning 9 avoidance, rejection

escort 4 beau, date, lead, show 5 guard, guide, pilot, steer, usher 6 attend, convoy, direct, gigolo, squire 7 company, conduct, consort, retinue 8 cavalier, chaperon, henchman, shepherd 9 accompany, bodyguard, chaperone, companion, entourage, safeguard 13 accompaniment

escritoire 4 desk 9 secretary 11 writing desk

escrow 4 bond, deed, fund 7 deposit

esculent 6 edible 7 eatable 10 comestible, digestible

escutcheon 6 flange, shield

Eshcol *ally:* 7 Abraham *brother:* 4 Aner 5 Mamre

esker 4 kame 5 mound, ridge

Eskimo 4 Inuk 5 Aleut, Inuit *boat:* 5 kayak, umiak *boot:* 6 mukluk *dog:* 5 husky 8 malamute *dwelling:* 5 igloo *outer garment:* 5 parka 6 anorak *sledge:* 7 komatik

esophagus 6 gullet

esoteric 5 inner 6 arcane, mystic, occult, orphic, secret 7 cryptic, private 8 abstruse, hermetic, profound 9 recondite 10 cabalistic, mysterious 12 confidential

ESP 9 telepathy 10 sixth sense 12 clairvoyance, precognition

espadrille 4 shoe 6 sandal

espalier 7 lattice, railing, trellis

esparto 5 grass

especial 4 main 5 close 7 express, notable, unusual 8 dominant, intimate, peculiar, singular, specific, uncommon 9 paramount 10 individual, particular 11 exceptional

especially 7 notably 8 markedly 9 expressly, primarily, unusually 10 peculiarly, remarkably, singularly 11 principally 12 particularly, specifically 13 distinctively, exceptionally

espial 6 notice 9 detection, discovery 11 observation

espionage 6 spying 9 sleuthing 12 surveillance

espousal 5 troth, union 6 mating 7 embrace, support, wedding 8 adoption, advocacy, approval, ceremony, marriage 9 betrothal, embracing, matrimony, promotion 10 acceptance

espouse 3 wed 4 back 5 adopt, marry 6 accept, take on, take up 7 approve, embrace, support 8 advocate

esprit 3 vim, wit 4 brio, dash, élan, zest, zing 5 oomph, verve, vigor 6 fervor, gaiety, mettle, morale, spirit 7 courage, loyalty, panache, passion, sparkle 8 devotion, vibrancy, vitality 9 animation 10 brightness, enthusiasm, fellowship 11 camaraderie

esprit de corps see MORALE

espy 3 see 4 mark, spot 5 sight 6 descry, detect, notice 7 discern, make out 9 recognize

___ es Salaam 3 Dar

essay 3 try 4 seek, test 5 labor, paper, piece, study, theme, tract, trial 6 effort, strive, thesis 7 article, attempt, venture 8 endeavor, treatise 9 undertake 10 discussion, exposition 11 composition, undertaking 12 dissertation

essayist *American:* 4 Agee (James), Will (George) 5 Baker (Russell), Cooke (Alistair), Gould (Stephen Jay), White (E. B.) 6 Brooks (Cleanth), Fisher (M. F. K.), Holmes (Oliver Wendell), Lowell (James Russell), Sontag (Susan), Thomas (Lewis) 7 Buckley (William F.), Cousins (Norman), Emerson (Ralph Waldo), Mencken (Henry Louis), Thoreau (Henry David) 8 Benchley (Robert), Lippmann (Walter), Repplier (Agnes) 10 Crèvecoeur (Jean de) *English:* 4 Elia, Lamb (Charles) 5 Bacon (Francis), Cecil (Lord David), Pater (Walter), Smith (Sydney) 6 Arnold (Matthew), Cowley (Abraham), Morris (Jan), Ruskin (John), Steele (Richard) 7 Addison (Joseph), Hazlitt (William) 8 Beerbohm (Max) 9 De Quincey (Thomas) 12 Chesterfield (Lord) *French:* 9 Montaigne (Michel de) *Scottish:* 7 Carlyle (Thomas)

essence 3 nub 4 base, core, crux, gist, odor, pith, root, soul 5 basis, being, fiber, fibre, point, stuff 6 center, entity, kernel, marrow, nature, spirit 7 extract, perfume, quality 9 substance 10 distillate 12 distillation, significance

essential 4 main, must 5 basal, basic, chief, prime, vital 6 inborn, inbred, innate, primal 7 connate, crucial, element, primary 8 cardinal, foremost, inherent, required, rudiment 9 condition, elemental, intrinsic, necessary, necessity, principal, requisite, substance 10 congenital, deep-seated, elementary, idiopathic, imperative, sine qua non, underlying 11 fundamental, requirement 12 precondition, prerequisite 13 indispensable, part and parcel

essentially 6 almost, au fond, really 7 largely 8 actually, as good as, as much as, well-nigh 9 basically, virtually 11 practically 13 fundamentally, substantially

essonite 6 garnet 13 cinnamon stone

establish 3 fix, lay, put, set 4 base, form, root, show 5 build, enact, endow, erect, found, place, prove, set up, start 6 attest, create, decree, effect, ground, impose, secure, settle, verify 7 build up, certify, clarify, confirm, find out, implant, install, instill, provide, set down 8 document, ensconce, organize 9 authorize, construct, determine, formulate, institute, legislate, originate, prescribe 10 bring about, constitute, inaugurate 11 corroborate, demonstrate 12 authenticate, substantiate

establishment 4 firm 6 outfit 7 company, concern 8 business, old guard 9 insti-

tute, workplace **10** enterprise, foundation **11** institution, ruling class
estate 4 farm, land **5** manor, ranch, villa **6** domain, legacy, quinta **7** demesne **8** dominion, hacienda, property **10** plantation *feudal:* **4** fief **7** fiefdom *first:* **6** clergy *fourth:* **5** press *manager:* **7** steward **8** executor, guardian *second:* **6** nobles **8** nobility *third:* **7** commons
esteem 4 deem **5** favor, honor, prize, think, value **6** admire, liking, regard, revere **7** account, believe, cherish, idolize, respect, worship **8** approval, consider, treasure, venerate **9** valuation **10** admiration, appreciate **12** appreciation **13** consideration
ester 6 oleate **7** acetate **8** compound **9** phosphate
Esther *cousin:* **8** Mordecai *enemy:* **5** Haman *father:* **7** Abihail *festival:* **5** Purim *Hebrew name:* **8** Hadassah *husband:* **6** Xerxes **9** Ahasuerus
estimable 5 noble **6** august, valued, worthy **7** admired **8** laudable, sterling **9** admirable, deserving, honorable, reputable, respected, venerable **10** creditable **11** commendable, meritorious, respectable **12** praiseworthy
estimate 3 put **4** call, rank, rate **5** assay, gauge, guess, infer, judge, price, set at, value **6** assess, deduce, figure, rating, reckon, survey **7** imagine, opinion, project, suppose, surmise **8** appraise, conclude, discover, evaluate, forecast, judgment, round off **9** appraisal, calculate, determine, reckoning, valuation **10** assessment, conjecture, evaluation, impression, projection **11** approximate, calculation, measurement
estimation 4 fame **5** favor, honor, stock **6** esteem, regard **7** account, opinion, respect **8** figuring, judgment **9** appraisal, reckoning, valuation **10** admiration, assessment, evaluation, impression **11** calculation **13** consideration
Estonia *capital:* **7** Tallinn *city:* **5** Tartu *gulf:* **4** Riga **7** Finland *island:* **4** Muhu **6** Vormsi **7** Hiiumaa **8** Saaremaa *lake:* **5** Pskov **6** Peipus **9** Vorts-Jarv *monetary unit:* **5** kroon *neighbor:* **6** Latvia, Russia *river:* **5** Narva, Pärnu **6** Kasari *sea:* **6** Baltic
estop 3 bar **6** enjoin, forbid **7** prevent **8** disallow, preclude, prohibit, restrain
estrange 4 part **5** split **7** break up, divorce **8** alienate, disunite, separate **9** disaffect
estrangement 4 rift **5** split **6** breach, schism **7** breakup, cooling, divorce, rupture **8** disunity, division **10** alien-

ation, falling-out, withdrawal **12** disaffection
estuary 5 firth, frith, mouth **10** tidal river
esurient 4 avid **6** greedy, hungry **8** covetous, grasping, ravening, ravenous **9** rapacious, voracious **10** avaricious, gluttonous **11** acquisitive
étagère 7 cabinet, whatnot
Etats-___ 4 Unis
etch 3 cut **5** carve, stamp **6** depict, incise **7** engrave, impress, imprint, portray **8** inscribe **9** delineate, represent
etcher *American:* **7** Pennell (Joseph) **8** Whistler (James McNeil) *Dutch:* **9** Rembrandt (van Rijn) *French:* **5** Redon (Odilon) **6** Villon (Jacques) *Italian:* **8** Piranesi (Giambattista) *Spanish:* **6** Ribera (José) *Swiss:* **4** Zorn (Anders)
Eteocles *brother:* **9** Polynices *father:* **7** Oedipus *mother:* **7** Jocasta *slayer:* **9** Polynices
eternal 7 abiding, ageless, endless, lasting, undying **8** constant, enduring, immortal, infinite, timeless, unending **9** ceaseless, continual, deathless, immutable, incessant, permanent, perpetual, unceasing **10** immemorial, unchanging **11** amaranthine, everlasting, illimitable, inalterable, neverending, unalterable, unremitting **12** imperishable, interminable
Eternal City 4 Rome
eternally 3 e'er **4** ever **6** always **7** forever **8** evermore, for keeps **11** forevermore, in perpetuum **12** in perpetuity
eternity 3 age, eon **4** aeon **7** dog's age **8** blue moon, coon's age, infinity **9** afterlife **10** infinitude, perpetuity **11** endlessness, immortality **12** infiniteness, timelessness
Etesian 4 wind **6** annual
Ethan ___ 5 Allen, Brand, Frome
Ethbaal's daughter 7 Jezebel
ether 3 air, gas, sky **6** heaven **7** heavens **8** airwaves, empyrean **10** anesthetic, atmosphere
ethereal 4 aery, airy **5** filmy, light **6** aerial **7** fragile **8** delicate, empyreal, empyrean, gossamer, heavenly, rarefied, vaporous **9** celestial, spiritual, unearthly, unworldly **10** immaterial, intangible **13** unsubstantial
ethical 4 good **5** moral, noble **6** decent **7** upright, virtual **8** elevated, virtuous **9** righteous **10** principled, upstanding **11** right-minded **13** conscientious
ethics 5 mores **6** morals, values **8** morality **9** moral code, standards **10** principles
Ethiopia *battle site:* **5** Adowa *biblical name:* **4** Cush *capital:* **10** Addis Ababa

city: 6 Gonder 8 Dire Dawa *desert:*
4 Haud 7 Danakil *emperor:* 7 Menelik,
Menilek 8 Selassie 9 Ras Tafari 13 Haile
Selassie *former name:* 9 Abyssinia *language:* 5 Oromo 7 Amharic *monetary unit:* 4 birr *mountain:* 9 Ras Dashen
neighbor: 5 Kenya, Sudan 7 Eritrea,
Somalia 8 Djibouti *region:* 5 Tigre
6 Ogaden, Tigray 7 Danakil *river:*
4 Abay 5 Awash 6 Tekeze 8 Blue Nile
ethnic 6 racial, tribal 8 minority
etiolate 4 fade, pale 6 bleach, weaken
7 lighten, wash out 8 enfeeble
etiquette 4 code, form 5 mores 7 conduct, customs, decency, decorum,
manners 8 behavior, protocol 9 amenities, propriety 10 civilities, convention,
deportment, seemliness 11 conventions,
formalities, proprieties
Etruscan *city, town:* 4 Roma, Veii
5 Caere, Vulci 6 Arezzo 7 Clusium,
Felsina, Perugia 8 Volsinii 9 Florentia,
Tarquinia, Vetulonia *deity:* 3 Tin, Tiv,
Uni 4 Turm, Usil 5 Tinia, Turan, Turms
6 Menfra, Menrva, Nethun, Trithn
7 Velchan 8 Sethlans, Voltumna *king:*
7 Porsena, Tarquin 10 Tarquinius
11 Lars Porsena *kingdom:* 7 Etruria
étude 5 study 8 exercise 11 composition
etui 4 case
etymology 11 word history
etymon 4 root 5 radix 6 source 8 morpheme
eucalyptus eater 5 koala
Eucharist *container:* 3 pyx *plate:* 5 paten
service: 4 Mass 9 Communion *vessel:*
8 ciborium *wafer:* 4 host 8 viaticum
Euclid *subject:* 8 geometry *work:* 8 Elements
____. **Eulenspiegel** 4 Till, Tyll
eulogistic 9 adulatory, laudative, laudatory 11 encomiastic, panegyrical
12 commendatory 13 complimentary
eulogize 4 hymn, laud 5 cry up, exalt,
extol 6 praise 7 acclaim, applaud, commend, glorify, magnify 9 celebrate
10 panegyrize
eulogy 5 paean 6 praise 7 oration, tribute 8 accolade, citation, encomium
9 laudation, panegyric 10 salutation
12 commendation 13 glorification
Eumenides see ERINYES
eunuch 7 gelding 8 castrate, castrato
euphony 7 harmony 8 lyricism 9 sweetness 10 consonance
euphoria 3 joy 4 glee 5 bliss 7 ecstasy,
elation, rapture 9 transport 10 exaltation, jubilation 11 high spirits 12 exhilaration, intoxication
Euphrosyne see GRACES
euphuistic 5 fancy, tumid 6 florid,

ornate, prolix, purple, turgid 7 elegant,
flowery, fustian, orotund, verbose
8 colorful, elevated, inflated, sonorous
9 bombastic, elaborate, high-flown,
overblown 10 figurative, flamboyant,
rhetorical 11 highfalutin, overwrought
12 magniloquent 13 grandiloquent
eureka 3 aha
Euridice's husband 7 Orpheus
Euripides play 3 Ion 5 Helen, Medea
6 Hecuba 7 Bacchae (The), Cyclops,
Electra, Orestes 8 Alcestis 10 Andromache, Hippolytus, Suppliants (The)
11 Trojan Women (The)
Europa *brother:* 6 Cadmus *father:*
6 Agenor 7 Phoenix *husband:* 8 Asterius
son: 5 Minos 8 Sarpedon
Europe 9 continent *country:* 4 Eire
5 Italy, Malta, Spain 6 France, Greece,
Latvia, Monaco, Norway, Poland, Russia, Sweden, Turkey 7 Albania, Andorra, Armenia, Austria, Belarus, Belgium,
Croatia, Denmark, Estonia, Finland,
Georgia, Germany, Hungary, Iceland,
Ireland, Moldova, Romania, Rumania,
Ukraine 8 Bulgaria, Portugal, Slovakia,
Slovenia 9 Lithuania, Macedonia, San
Marino 10 Azerbaijan, Luxembourg,
Yugoslavia 11 Netherlands, Switzerland, Vatican City 13 Czech Republic,
Liechtenstein, United Kingdom *ethnic group:* 4 Celt, Finn, Lapp, Lett, Pole,
Serb, Sorb, Turk, Wend 5 Croat, Czech,
Dutch, Greek, Gypsy, Irish, Latin,
Swede, Swiss, Welsh 6 Basque, Celtic,
French, German, Magyar, Polish,
Scotch, Slovak 7 Bosnian, Catalan, English, Finnish, Fleming, Italian, Lettish,
Maltese, Russian, Slovene, Spanish,
Swedish, Walloon 8 Albanian, Andorran, Armenian, Croatian, Romanian
9 Belarusan, Bulgarian, Hungarian,
Ukrainian 10 Belarusian, Macedonian,
Monegasque, Phoenician 11 Belarussian 12 Byelorussian, Scandinavian *language:* 4 Lapp 5 Czech, Dutch, Greek,
Irish, Latin, Welsh 6 Basque, Breton,
Danish, French, Gaelic, German, Magyar, Polish, Slovak 7 Catalan, English,
Finnish, Flemish, Italian, Maltese,
Romansh, Russian, Serbian, Slovene,
Spanish, Swedish, Turkish, Wendish
8 Albanian, Croatian, Lusatian,
Romanian, Rumanian 9 Bulgarian,
Hungarian, Icelandic, Norwegian
10 Macedonian, Portuguese 13 Serbo-Croatian *mountain range:* 4 Alps 8 Pyrenees 11 Carpathians
Euryale see GORGON
Eurytus *daughter:* 4 Iole *slayer:* 8 Hercules

Euterpe see MUSE

evacuate 4 exit, void **5** clear, empty, expel, leave **6** decamp, depart, remove, vacate **7** abandon, excrete, exhaust, pull out, retreat **8** clear out, pull back, withdraw **9** eliminate

evacuee 6 émigré **7** refugee **8** fugitive

evade 4 duck, flee, foil **5** avoid, dodge, elude, hedge, parry, shirk, skirt **6** baffle, bypass, escape, eschew, outwit, thwart, weasel **7** shuffle **8** sidestep, slip away **9** pussyfoot, turn aside **10** circumvent, equivocate **11** prevaricate **12** tergiversate

evaluate 4 rank, rate **5** assay, class, gauge, grade, set at, weigh **6** assess, figure, reckon, size up, survey **7** eyeball **8** appraise, classify, estimate **9** calculate, criticize

evaluation 6 rating **7** judging, opinion **8** estimate, judgment **9** appraisal **10** assessment **12** appreciation

Evander *father:* **6** Hermes **7** Mercury *mother:* **8** Carmenta **9** Carmentis *son:* **6** Pallas

evanesce 4 fade **5** clear **6** vanish **7** scatter **8** disperse, dissolve, melt away **9** disappear, dissipate, evaporate **13** dematerialize

evanescent 6 fading **7** elusive, melting, passing **8** fleeting, fugitive, volatile **9** ephemeral, fugacious, momentary, transient, vanishing **10** dissolving, short-lived, transitory **12** disappearing

evangelical 6 ardent, fervid **7** fanatic, fervent, zealous **8** militant **9** crusading **10** missionary **13** proselytizing

Evangeline *author:* **10** Longfellow (Henry Wadsworth) *beloved:* **7** Gabriel *home:* **6** Acadia

evangelist 4 John, Luke, Mark **5** Moody (Dwight) **6** Bakker (Jim, Tammy Faye), Graham (Billy, Franklin), Sunday (Billy), Wesley (John) **7** apostle, Edwards (Jonathan), Falwell (Jerry), Matthew, Roberts (Oral) **8** Schuller (Robert), Swaggart (Jimmy) **9** McPherson (Aimee Semple), missioner, Robertson (Pat) **10** colporteur, missionary, revivalist, Whitefield (George)

evangelistic 9 crusading, reforming **10** missionary, revivalist **13** proselytizing

evangelize 6 preach **7** convert **9** sermonize

evaporate 4 fade, melt **5** clear **6** vanish **8** diminish, disperse, dissolve, evanesce, melt away, vaporize **9** disappear, dissipate

evasion 5 dodge, fudge **6** escape, excuse **7** dodging, elusion, fudging **8** escaping **9** avoidance **13** circumvention

evasive 3 sly **5** cagey, dodgy, vague **6** shifty **7** elusive **8** slippery **9** ambiguous, equivocal

Eve *home:* **4** Eden *husband:* **4** Adam *son:* **4** Abel, Cain, Seth *temptation:* **5** apple, fruit

even 3 tie **4** fair, flat, just, same, tied **5** align, equal, exact, flush, grade, level, plane, still, truly **6** as well, equate, smooth, square, stable, steady **7** balance, equable, flatten, uniform **8** balanced, constant, equalize, smoothen, straight **9** equitable, expressly, identical, precisely, unvarying **10** absolutely, comparable, consistent, continuous, fifty-fifty, unchanging **13** fair and square, proportionate

evening 4 dusk **6** soiree, sunset **7** sundown **8** gloaming, twilight **9** nightfall *French:* **4** soir *Italian:* **4** sera *service:* **7** vespers *star:* **5** Venus **6** Vesper **8** Hesperus

evenness 6 equity, parity **7** balance **8** equality **9** stability **10** equanimity, uniformity **11** consistency, equilibrium

event 3 act **4** case, deed, fact, feat, meet **5** issue, match **6** action, affair, chance, effect, result, upshot **7** contest, episode, outcome, product **8** accident, function, incident, occasion **9** aftermath, happening **10** occurrence, phenomenon **11** achievement, competition, consequence, eventuality **12** circumstance, happenstance

eventful 4 busy **6** lively **9** important, momentous

eventual 4 last **5** final **6** ending **7** closing, endmost, ensuing **8** terminal, ultimate **9** resulting **10** concluding, consequent, inevitable, succeeding

eventuality 4 case **6** effect, result **7** outcome **11** consequence, contingency, possibility

eventually 6 at last, one day **7** finally, someday **8** sometime **9** hereafter **10** ultimately **13** sooner or later

eventuate 5 ensue, occur **6** befall, follow, happen, result **9** come about, take place

ever 4 once **5** at all **6** always **7** forever **9** at any time, eternally, regularly **10** constantly, invariably **11** perpetually **12** consistently, continuously

evergreen 3 fir, ivy, yew **4** ilex, pine, tree **5** cedar, holly, savin **6** laurel, myrtle, spruce **7** conifer, cypress, hemlock, juniper, lasting, redwood, sequoia, undying **8** magnolia, mangrove, timeless, unfading **9** mistletoe, perennial **10** arborvitae **12** rhododendron

Evergreen State 10 Washington
everlasting 7 abiding, endless, eternal, forever, lasting, undying **8** constant, immortal, infinite, termless, timeless, unending **9** boundless, ceaseless, continual, deathless, limitless, permanent, perpetual, unceasing **10** continuous, perdurable **11** amaranthine, never-ending, unremitting **12** imperishable
evermore 6 always **7** for good **8** for keeps **9** eternally **12** in perpetuity
every 3 all **4** each *prefix:* **3** pan
everybody 3 all **4** each
everyday 5 banal, plain, usual **6** common, normal **7** mundane, prosaic, routine **8** familiar, habitual, ordinary **9** customary, quotidian **11** commonplace **12** conventional, run-of-the-mill, unremarkable
everything 3 all *French:* **4** tout *German:* **5** alles
everywhere 7 all over, overall **8** all round, wherever **9** all around **10** far and near, far and wide, high and low, throughout
evict 3 out **4** oust **5** eject, expel **6** bounce, put out **7** boot out, dismiss, extrude, kick out **8** dislodge, force out, throw out **10** dispossess
evidence 4 clue, mark, show, sign **5** goods, proof, prove **6** attest, evince, expose, reveal **7** confirm, display, exhibit, symptom, testify, witness **8** indicate **9** testament, testimony **10** indication, smoking gun **11** attestation, demonstrate, testimonial **12** confirmation **13** documentation
evident 5 clear, overt, plain **6** marked, patent **7** obvious, visible **8** apparent, distinct, manifest, palpable, tangible **9** prominent **10** noticeable, pronounced **11** conspicuous, perceptible, unambiguous
evidently 9 outwardly, seemingly **10** officially, ostensibly
evil 3 bad, sin **4** foul, vice, vile **5** black **6** infamy, malice, sinful, wicked **7** badness, baleful, baneful, devilry, hateful, heinous, malefic, satanic, vicious **8** damnable, iniquity, satanism, villainy **9** atrocious, diablerie, diabolism, execrable, loathsome, malicious, malignant, nefarious **10** flagitious, iniquitous, maleficent, malevolent, pernicious, sinfulness, wickedness **11** maleficence *combining form:* **3** mal
evildoer 6 sinner **7** villain **8** criminal **9** miscreant **10** malefactor
evil spirit 3 imp **5** demon, devil, fiend, Satan **6** daemon
evince 4 mark, show **5** educe, evoke,

prove **6** attest, betray, elicit, expose, reveal **7** bespeak, betoken, confirm, display, exhibit, signify **8** evidence, indicate, manifest, proclaim **10** illustrate **11** demonstrate
eviscerate 3 gut **4** draw **5** bowel **7** embowel **8** protrude **10** disembowel, exenterate
evocative 6 moving **8** redolent, stirring **9** affecting, emotional, nostalgic **10** expressive, meaningful, suggestive **11** stimulating
evoke 4 cite, stir **5** educe, raise, waken **6** arouse, awaken, call up, elicit, evince, excite, induce, recall **7** conjure **8** recreate, summon up **9** call forth, conjure up, stimulate **11** summon forth
evolution 6 change, growth **8** progress, upgrowth **9** flowering, phylogeny, unfolding **10** biogenesis, maturation **11** development, progression
evolve 4 grow **5** educe, ripen **6** change, derive, emerge, mature, open up, unfold **7** advance, develop, work out **8** progress **9** elaborate
ewe 5 sheep
ewer 3 jug **4** vase **7** pitcher
ex 4 from, past **5** prior **6** former **7** earlier, without **9** erstwhile
exacerbate 6 worsen **7** envenom, inflame, provoke **8** embitter, heighten **9** aggravate, intensify
exact 4 levy, true **5** claim, force, gouge, pinch, screw, wrest, wring **6** coerce, compel, dead-on, demand, extort, spot-on, strict **7** correct, extract, literal, precise, require, solicit, squeeze **8** accurate, rigorous, selfsame **9** identical, postulate, shake down **10** meticulous, scrupulous **11** painstaking, punctilious, requisition
exacting 5 fussy, rigid, stern, tough **6** severe, strict, taxing, trying **7** exigent, finicky, onerous **8** critical, rigorous **9** demanding, stringent **10** fastidious, nitpicking, particular, scrupulous **11** persnickety **13** hypercritical
exactitude 5 rigor **8** accuracy **9** precision **10** definitude **11** correctness, preciseness **12** definiteness
exactly 4 bang, just **5** quite, right, sharp, spang **6** bang on, square, to a tee, wholly **7** totally, utterly **8** entirely, smack-dab, squarely **9** on the nose, precisely **10** absolutely, accurately, altogether, completely, positively **12** specifically
exaggerate 6 overdo **7** amplify, enlarge, inflate, magnify, overact, romance **8** overdraw, overrate **9** embellish, embroider, overstate **11** hyperbolize **13** overemphasize

exaggeration 8 travesty 9 hyperbole
10 caricature, stretching 11 enlargement, overdrawing 12 embroidering
13 embellishment, overstatement

exalt 4 fete, laud, lift 5 boost, elate,
extol, honor, raise 6 praise, uplift
7 acclaim, adulate, build up, dignify,
elevate, enhance, ennoble, glorify,
inspire, magnify, promote 8 eulogize,
heighten, inspirit 9 intensify 10 aggrandize 11 apotheosize

exaltation 3 joy 5 bliss, glory 6 homage,
praise 7 delight, ecstasy, elation, rapture, tribute 8 euphoria, rhapsody
9 panegyric, transport, uplifting
10 apotheosis, jubilation 11 deification
12 exhilaration, intoxication 13 glorification

exalted 4 high 5 grand, lofty, noble
6 august 7 eminent, highest, sublime
9 venerable 11 high-ranking, illustrious,
outstanding, prestigious

examination 4 quiz, scan, test 5 assay,
probe, trial 6 review, survey 7 canvass,
checkup, hearing, inquest, inquiry,
perusal, sifting, testing 8 analysis,
scrutiny 9 breakdown, check-over,
diagnosis 10 dissection, inspection
11 inquisition 13 catechization, investigation, perlustration *kind:* 4 oral 5 final
7 medical, midterm 8 physical *of
accounts:* 5 audit *of a corpse:* 7 autopsy
10 postmortem

examine 3 con, vet 4 pump, quiz, scan,
sift, test 5 audit, check, grill, probe,
query, study 6 go over, look at, peruse,
survey 7 canvass, check up, inquire,
inspect, observe 8 check out, look into,
look over, question 9 catechize, check
over 10 scrutinize 11 interrogate, investigate

examiner 6 censor 7 auditor, coroner
9 inspector 10 inquisitor, prosecutor
12 investigator

example 4 case 5 ideal, model 7 paragon,
pattern 8 instance, paradigm, specimen,
standard 9 archetype, precedent, prototype 11 case history 12 illustration

exanimate 4 dead 5 inert 8 lifeless, listless, sluggish, stagnant 9 lethargic
10 spiritless

exasperate 3 irk, vex 4 gall, rile, roil
5 anger, annoy, peeve, pique, upset
6 enrage, madden, nettle, rankle 7 agitate, incense, inflame, provoke 8 irritate 9 aggravate, infuriate

exasperation 8 vexation 9 annoyance
10 irritation 11 aggravation

ex cathedra 8 official 9 ex officio
13 authoritative

excavate 3 dig 4 grub 5 scoop, spade

6 dig out, dredge, expose, hollow, quarry, shovel 7 unearth 8 gouge out, scoop
out 9 hollow out, scrape out

excavation 3 dig, pit 4 hole, mine
5 ditch, stope 6 dugout, hollow, quarry,
trench, trough

exceed 3 cap, top 4 beat, best, pass
5 break, excel, outdo 6 better, outrun,
overdo 7 eclipse, outpace, overrun, surpass 8 go beyond, outreach, outshine,
outstrip, outweigh, overstep, overtake
9 overreach, transcend

exceedingly 4 very 6 hugely, vastly
7 awfully, notably, vitally 9 extremely
10 remarkably, strikingly 12 surpassingly 13 exceptionally *prefix:* 5 ultra

excel 3 cap, top 4 beat, best, pass
5 outdo, shine 6 better, exceed, outrun,
overdo 7 eclipse, outpace, overrun, surpass 8 go beyond, outclass, outreach,
outshine, outstrip, outweigh, overstep,
overtake 9 overreach, transcend

excellence 5 class, merit, value, worth
6 virtue 7 quality 8 fineness 9 greatness 10 perfection 11 distinction, superiority

excellent 3 top 4 fine 5 bully, prime
6 bang-up, banner, famous, Grade A,
superb, tip-top 7 capital, premium,
supreme 8 champion, five-star, splendid, stunning, superior, terrific, top-
notch 9 classical, first-rate, high-class,
high-grade, marvelous, number one,
wonderful 10 blue-ribbon, first-class
11 exceptional, magnificent, meritorious, sensational, superlative, unsurpassed 12 incomparable

except 3 bar, but, yet 4 omit, only, save
6 beside, exempt, object, reject, unless
7 barring, besides, exclude, however,
outside, rule out, suspend 8 pass over
9 apart from, aside from, eliminate,
excluding, outside of 11 exclusive of

exception 5 demur 7 anomaly, dissent
8 question 9 allowance, deviation,
exclusion, objection 10 aberration

exceptionable 8 unwanted 9 unwelcome
10 unsuitable 11 regrettable, undesirable 12 unacceptable 13 objectionable

exceptional 4 rare 6 scarce, unique
7 notable, special, unusual 8 abnormal,
atypical, distinct, singular, superior,
uncommon, unwonted 9 anomalous,
excellent, marvelous, wonderful
10 infrequent, noteworthy, phenomenal, remarkable 11 outstanding, uncustomary 13 extraordinary

exceptionally 4 very 6 hugely 7 notably
9 extremely 10 especially, remarkably,
strikingly 11 exceedingly 12 particularly, stupendously

excerpt 4 cite, cull, pick 5 glean, quote 6 choose, sample, select 7 extract, passage, pick out, portion, snippet 8 fragment 9 quotation

excess 3 fat 4 glut, rest 5 extra, flood, spare, waste 7 nimiety, overage, surfeit, surplus 8 leavings, leftover, overflow, overkill, overmuch 9 indulgent, overstock, redundant, remainder 10 oversupply, surplusage 11 dissipation, prodigality, superfluity, superfluous, unessential 12 extravagance, immoderation, intemperance 13 overabundance, supernumerary

excessive 4 over 5 dizzy, steep, super, undue 6 too-too 7 extreme, sky-high 8 overmuch, prodigal 10 exorbitant, immoderate, inordinate, profligate 11 extravagant, intemperate, overweening, superfluous 12 supernatural, unrestrained

excessively 3 too 6 overly, unduly 8 overmuch *prefix:* 5 hyper

exchange 4 swap, swop 5 bandy, trade, truck 6 barter, market, switch 7 bargain, commute, convert, pay back, replace, traffic 8 displace 9 transpose 10 conversion, substitute 11 reciprocate

exchequer 5 funds 8 treasury

excise 3 fee, tax 4 toll 5 elide, slash 6 cut out, delete, remove, resect 9 expurgate, extirpate, strike out, surcharge

excision 3 cut 7 removal, surgery 8 deletion 9 resection 11 extirpation

excitable 4 rash 8 volatile 9 impetuous 10 high-strung

excite 4 fire, goad, move, spur, stir 5 elate, evoke, key up, pique, prime, rouse, waken 6 appeal, arouse, elicit, fire up, induce, kindle, stir up, thrill, turn on 7 agitate, animate, commove, inflame, inspire, provoke, quicken 8 activate, charge up, energize, motivate 9 galvanize, impassion, innervate, stimulate 10 exhilarate

excited 3 hot 4 avid 5 eager 6 aflame 7 fevered 8 aflutter, worked up 10 passionate 12 enthusiastic

excitement 3 ado 4 buzz, stir, to-do 5 fever, furor 6 flurry, frenzy, furore, hubbub, thrill 7 turmoil 8 delirium, hysteria 9 agitation, commotion 10 enthusiasm, hullabaloo 11 disturbance, pandemonium 12 exhilaration

exclaim 4 blat, bolt 5 blurt 6 cry out 8 blurt out, burst out 9 ejaculate

exclamation 3 aah, aha, bah, boo, cry, eek, feh, fie, gee, hah, hey, huh, oho, ooh, pah, tsk, tut, ugh, wow 4 ahem, alas, amen, damn, dang, darn, drat, egad, gosh, heck, hell, oops, ouch, phew, pish, posh, rats, whew, yell 5 alack, bravo, faugh, golly, humph, pshaw, shout 6 clamor, hurrah, indeed, outcry, phooey, shucks 7 doggone, gee whiz, hosanna, jeepers, whoopee 9 expletive 10 hallelujah 12 interjection *of disappointment:* 4 damn, darn, rats *of disapproval:* 3 tsk 6 tsk-tsk *of disgust:* 3 bah, boo, feh, fie, ugh 4 yech, yuck 5 faugh, yecch 6 phooey *of dismay:* 4 oh no, uh-oh 5 yikes *of enthusiasm:* 4 whee 5 wahoo 7 whoopie *of fear:* 3 eek *of pain:* 4 ouch *of relief:* 4 phew *of sorrow:* 3 woe 4 alas 5 alack *of surprise:* 3 wow 4 gosh 5 golly *of triumph:* 3 aha, hah 5 yahoo 6 eureka (see also INTERJECTION)

exclude 3 ban, bar 4 oust 5 block, debar 6 banish, disbar, reject 7 keep out, lock out, obviate, prevent, rule out, shut out, suspend 8 count out, preclude, prohibit 9 blackball, blacklist, eliminate, ostracize

excluding 3 bar, but 4 less, save 6 except 7 barring, besides 9 apart from, aside from, other than, outside of

exclusion 3 bar 6 ouster 7 barring, lockout, removal 8 ejection, eviction, omission 9 blackball, expulsion, ostracism 10 banishment 12 blackballing, nonadmission

exclusive 4 lone, only, sole 5 elect, elite, prime, scoop, smart, swank, swish 6 choice, chosen, picked, select, single 7 cliquey, high-hat, stylish 8 clannish, cliquish, selected, snobbish 9 preferred, undivided 10 privileged 11 fashionable, prohibitive, restrictive 12 aristocratic, concentrated, preferential

exclusively 4 only 5 alone 6 wholly 8 entirely 10 completely 12 particularly

excogitate 6 derive, devise, invent 7 develop, think up 8 contrive, think out

excommunicate 7 cast out 8 unchurch

excoriate 4 flay, lash, skin 5 roast, slash 6 abrade, scathe, scorch 7 blister, censure, scarify, scourge 8 chastise, lambaste, lash into 9 castigate

excrement 6 ordure *of animals:* 4 dung, muck 6 manure *of sea birds:* 5 guano

excrescence 4 blot, lump, mole, wart 5 tumor 6 growth, nodule, pimple 7 blemish, process 9 by-product, outgrowth

excrete 4 emit, spew 5 eject, expel, exude 9 discharge

excruciate 4 rack 6 martyr 7 afflict, crucify, torment, torture 9 martyrize

excruciating 5 acute, sharp 6 severe 7 extreme, intense 8 piercing, shooting, stabbing 9 agonizing, harrowing, torturous 10 unbearable 11 unendurable

exculpate 4 free 5 clear, remit 6 acquit, excuse, let off, pardon 7 absolve, amnesty, condone, forgive, justify 9 exonerate, vindicate 11 rationalize

excursion 4 ride, tour, trek, trip, walk 5 aside, drive, jaunt, paseo, sally, tramp 6 cruise, junket, outing, ramble, safari 7 day trip, journey 9 round trip 10 digression, divagation, expedition 11 parenthesis 12 pleasure trip

excusable 6 venial

excuse 3 out 4 plea 5 alibi, clear, remit 6 acquit, cop-out, defend, exempt, let off, pardon, reason, wink at 7 absolve, apology, condone, defense, forgive, justify, pretext, regrets, relieve 8 mitigate, overlook, palliate, pass over, shrug off, tolerate 9 discharge, exculpate, exonerate, extenuate, gloss over, makeshift, vindicate, whitewash 10 substitute 11 explanation, rationalize 13 justification

execrable 4 base, foul, vile 7 heinous 8 accursed, damnable, horrific, infernal, wretched 9 abhorrent, atrocious, loathsome, monstrous, repulsive, revolting 10 abominable, deplorable, despicable, detestable, horrifying

execrate 4 damn, hate 5 abhor, curse 6 detest, loathe, revile, vilify 7 censure, condemn, despise 8 denounce 9 abominate, imprecate 12 anathematize

execute 3 act 4 do in, kill, play, slay 5 cause, lynch 6 effect, finish, murder, render 7 achieve, bump off, conduct, enforce, fulfill, perform, realize 8 carry out, complete, dispatch, knock off, transact 9 discharge, eliminate, implement, liquidate 10 accomplish, administer, bring about, put through, put to death 11 assassinate 12 administrate

execution 6 murder 7 killing 11 performance

executioner 7 hangman, headman 8 headsman

executive 4 dean, suit 6 leader 7 manager 8 director, governor 9 president 10 supervisor 13 administrator

exegesis 5 gloss 8 analysis 9 construal 10 commentary, exposition 11 elucidation, explanation, explication 12 construction

exemplar 4 copy 5 ideal, model 7 epitome, paragon, pattern 8 instance, paradigm, specimen, standard 9 archetype, criterion, prototype 12 illustration

exemplary 4 pure 5 ideal, model 7 classic, typical 8 laudable, monitory, virtuous 9 admirable, blameless, classical,

estimable, faultless, honorable, righteous 10 impeccable, inculpable, prototypal 11 commendable, meritorious 12 illustrative, paradigmatic, praiseworthy, prototypical

exemplify 4 copy 6 embody, mirror, typify 7 clarify 9 enlighten, epitomize, personify, represent, symbolize 10 concretize, illuminate, illustrate

exempt 4 free 5 spare 6 except, excuse, let off, spared 7 absolve, excused, relieve 8 dispense 9 discharge

exemption 7 freedom, release 8 immunity, impunity 9 discharge, exception

exenterate 3 gut 4 draw 7 embowel 10 disembowel, eviscerate

exercise 3 use, vex 4 fret, gall, hone 5 alarm, annoy, apply, drill, étude, exert, sit-up, train, upset, wield 6 chinup, crunch, employ, pull-up, push-up 7 agitate, develop, exploit, improve, prepare, problem, provoke, utilize, work out 8 activity, maneuver, practice, rehearse 9 athletics, condition, cultivate, discharge, operation 10 employment 11 application 12 calisthenics

exert 3 use 5 apply, wield 6 employ, expend, put out, strain 8 exercise, put forth

exertion 4 toil, work 5 labor, pains 6 effort, strain 7 trouble 8 activity, exercise, striving 11 application, elbow grease

exfoliate 4 peel, shed 5 scale 7 cast off, leaf out 8 flake off 10 desquamate

exhalation 6 breath 8 emission 9 breathing, effluvium, emanation

exhale 4 blow, emit 6 expire, let out 7 breathe, respire 10 breathe out

exhaust 3 fag, sap 4 do in, tire 5 drain, eat up, empty, spend, use up, waste, weary 6 expend, finish, tucker, wash up, weaken 7 burn out, consume, deplete, fatigue, frazzle, tire out, wear out 8 draw down, enervate, squander, wear down 9 discharge, dissipate, prostrate, tucker out 10 debilitate, overextend, run through

exhausted 4 beat, limp, weak 5 all in, spent, tired 6 bushed 7 run-down, worn out 8 dog-tired

exhaustion 7 burnout, fatigue 8 collapse 9 lassitude, tiredness, weariness 11 prostration

exhaustive 8 complete, sweeping, thorough 9 full-blown, full-scale, intensive 10 scrupulous 11 painstaking 13 comprehensive, thoroughgoing

exhibit 4 fair, show 6 evince, expose, flaunt, parade, reveal 7 display, feature,

show off 8 evidence, manifest, proclaim, showcase **10** exposition **11** demonstrate

exhibition 4 fair, show **7** display, pageant, showing **12** presentation **13** demonstration, manifestation

exhibitionist 3 fop **4** toff **6** hot dog **7** peacock, show-off **8** showboat **12** grandstander

exhilarate 4 buoy, lift **5** boost, cheer, elate, exalt, pep up **6** buck up, excite, thrill, uplift **7** animate, cheer up, commove, delight, enliven, gladden, inspire, refresh **8** inspirit, vitalize **9** stimulate **10** invigorate

exhilaration 3 joy **4** glee **7** ecstasy, elation **8** euphoria, gladness **10** exaltation, excitement **11** inspiration **12** vitalization, vivification **13** galvanization

exhort 4 goad, prod, spur, urge, warn **5** egg on, plead, press, prick **6** adjure, call on, incite, prompt, propel **7** beseech, entreat **8** admonish, call upon **9** stimulate

exhortation 4 plea **6** advice, urging **7** caution, warning **8** entreaty, jeremiad **10** admonition, incitement, injunction **11** inspiration **13** encouragement

exhume 5 dig up **6** redeem **7** reclaim, recover, unearth **8** disinter **9** resurrect

exigency 3 fix, jam **4** need, pass **5** pinch, rigor **6** crisis, demand, pickle, plight, strait **7** urgency **8** juncture, pressure, zero hour **9** extremity, necessity **10** compulsion, constraint, crossroads, difficulty, insistence **11** predicament, requirement

exigent 5 acute, vital **6** crying, taxing **7** burning, clamant, instant, onerous **8** exacting, grievous, pressing **9** clamorous, demanding, insistent, necessary **10** burdensome, imperative **11** importunate

exiguous 4 poor, puny, thin, tiny **5** scant, spare, token **6** meager, meagre, measly, paltry, scanty, shabby, skimpy, slight, sparse **7** minimal, scrimpy **9** miserable **10** inadequate, straitened

exile 4 oust **5** eject, expel **6** banish, deport, emigré **7** cast out, outcast, refugee **8** diaspora, displace, drive out, evacuate, expellee **9** exclusion, expulsion, extradite, migration, ostracism, ostracize **10** banishment, dispossess, expatriate, scattering **11** deportation, extradition **12** displacement, expatriation *place of:* **4** Elba **7** Siberia

exist 3 are, lie **4** live **5** occur

existence 4 life **5** being **7** reality **8** duration **9** actuality

existent 4 live, real **5** being, thing **6** actual, entity, extant, living **7** current, instant, present **10** present-day **12** contemporary

existentialist writer 5 Buber (Martin), Camus (Albert) **6** Marcel (Gabriel), Sartre (Jean-Paul) **7** Jaspers (Karl) **8** Beauvoir (Simone de) **9** Heidegger (Martin), Nietzsche (Friedrich) **11** Kierkegaard (Søren)

existing 5 alive, being, ontic **6** extant, living *from birth:* **6** innate **10** congenital *Latin:* **6** in esse

exit 3 die **4** door, gate, quit **5** death, going, leave, scram, split **6** depart, egress, escape, outlet, portal, retire **7** doorway, get away, off-ramp **8** withdraw **9** departure, egression **10** withdrawal

___ ex machina 4 deus

exodus 6 flight **9** migration **10** emigration

Exodus author 4 Uris (Leon)

exonerate 4 free **5** clear, remit **6** acquit, excuse, exempt, let off, pardon **7** absolve **8** reprieve **9** exculpate, vindicate

exorbitant 5 undue **7** extreme **9** excessive **10** immoderate, inordinate, outrageous **11** extravagant, unwarranted **12** preposterous

exordium 5 intro, proem **6** lead-in **7** opening, preface, prelude **8** foreword, overture, preamble, prologue **12** introduction, prolegomenon

exotic 4 rare **5** alien **7** bizarre, foreign, strange, unusual **8** alluring, enticing, imported, romantic **9** different, glamorous, nonnative **10** introduced, mysterious **11** fascinating

expand 3 wax **4** grow, open, rise **5** boost, mount, swell, widen **6** beef up, bulk up, dilate, pad out, spread, unfold **7** amplify, augment, bolster, develop, distend, enlarge, inflate, magnify, prolong, stretch **8** escalate, increase, lengthen, multiply, mushroom, protract **9** discourse, elaborate, expatiate, spread out

expanse 4 area, room **5** field, ocean, range, reach, scope, space, sweep, tract **6** domain, extent, sphere, spread **7** breadth, stretch **8** distance **9** territory

expansion 6 growth, spread **8** increase **9** unfolding **11** enlargement **12** augmentation

expansive 3 big **4** wide **5** ample, broad, large, roomy **6** lavish **7** buoyant, elastic, liberal, sizable **8** effusive, extended, generous, outgoing, spacious **9** capacious, garrulous, talkative **10** gregari-

ous, openhanded, unreserved 11 extroverted 13 demonstrative

expatiate 6 ramble, wander 7 dissert,
enlarge 8 dilate on, perorate 9 discourse, elaborate, sermonize 10 dilate
upon, dissertate

expatriate 5 exile, expel 6 banish,
deport, émigré 8 displace, expellee, relegate

expect 4 feel, hope, take 5 await, sense,
think, trust 6 assume, divine, gather,
look to 7 believe, count on, foresee,
imagine, look for, predict, presume,
suppose, surmise 8 forecast, foreknow
9 apprehend, count upon 10 anticipate,
presuppose

expectant 5 alert 6 gravid 7 anxious,
hopeful 8 enceinte, pregnant, vigilant,
watchful 10 breathless, parturient
12 anticipatory, apprehensive

expectation 4 hope 5 hunch 8 prospect
9 assurance, intuition 10 assumption,
likelihood 11 presumption, probability
12 anticipation, presentiment

expectorate 4 spit

expediency 5 means 6 resort, tactic
7 aptness, fitness, measure, stopgap
8 meetness, recourse, resource, strategy
9 makeshift, propriety, rightness
11 opportunism, suitability 12 appositeness, practicality, suitableness

expedient 3 fit 5 ad hoc, means, shift
6 resort, timely, useful 7 fitting, politic,
prudent, stopgap 8 feasible, recourse,
resource, suitable, tactical 9 advisable,
judicious, makeshift, opportune, practical, pragmatic, well-timed 10 convenient 11 appropriate, practicable, utilitarian 12 advantageous

expedite 4 send 5 hurry, issue, speed
6 hasten 7 quicken, speed up 8 dispatch
10 accelerate, facilitate

expedition 4 trek, trip 5 hurry, speed
6 voyage 7 journey 8 campaign, dispatch 9 excursion, swiftness 10 efficiency, speediness 11 punctuality

expeditious 4 fast 5 brisk, quick, rapid,
swift 6 prompt, speedy 9 efficient
11 efficacious

expeditiousness 5 hurry, speed 6 hustle
8 dispatch

expel 4 boot, oust, spew 5 eject, evict,
exile 6 banish, bounce, deport, disbar
7 cast out, dismiss, drum out, kick out,
turn out 8 disgorge, displace, throw out
9 discharge, eliminate 10 expatriate

expellee 5 exile 6 émigré 7 outcast
8 deportee, emigrant

expend 3 pay, sap 4 blow 5 drain, spend,
use up, waste 6 lay out, outlay, pay out
7 consume, deplete, dig into, dole out,

exhaust, fork out, utilize 8 disburse,
dispense, shell out, squander 9 dissipate
10 run through

expendable 10 disposable 11 dispensable, inessential, replaceable
12 nonessential

expenditure 4 cost 6 outlay, payoff, pay-
out 12 disbursement

expense 4 cost, loss, toll 5 debit, price
6 burden, charge, outlay 7 forfeit, payment 8 overhead 9 decrement, sacrifice
10 forfeiture 12 disbursement

expensive 4 dear, high, posh 5 fancy,
ritzy, steep, stiff 6 costly, deluxe, lavish,
pricey 7 upscale 8 precious, valuable,
wasteful 9 big-ticket, luxurious
10 exorbitant, high-priced, overpriced
11 extravagant 12 uneconomical

experience 4 know, live 5 event, savor,
skill, trial 6 ordeal, suffer, wisdom
7 episode, know-how, sustain, undergo
8 incident, practice 9 encounter, go
through 10 background 11 familiarity,
savoir faire *anew:* 6 relive

experienced 4 wise 6 mature, versed
7 old-line, veteran, worldly 8 broken in,
seasoned 9 practiced, qualified
12 accomplished

experiential see EMPIRICAL

experiment 3 try 4 test 5 assay, probe,
trial 6 try out 7 test out 8 research, trial
run 13 trial and error

experimental 9 empirical, tentative
10 innovative 11 exploratory, preliminary, preparatory, provisional 13 devel-
opmental, trial-and-error

experimentation 4 test 5 trial 7 testing
8 research, trial run 13 trial and error

expert 3 ace, pro, wiz 4 deft, whiz
5 adept, crack, doyen, maven 6 adroit,
master, wizard 7 skilled 8 masterly,
skillful, virtuoso 9 authority, dexterous,
masterful, virtuosic 10 past master,
proficient, specialist 11 crackerjack
12 passed master, professional

expertise 5 craft, skill 7 ability, command, know-how, mastery 8 facility
10 adroitness, competence 11 proficiency 12 skillfulness

expertness see EXPERTISE

expiate 6 offset, pay for, redeem
7 redress 8 atone for

expiation 9 atonement, indemnity
10 recompense, reparation 11 restitution 12 satisfaction

expiatory 7 atoning, lustral 9 purgative
11 penitential, purgatorial 12 propitiatory

expiration 3 end 5 death 10 exhalation
11 termination

expire 3 die, end **4** pass **5** lapse **6** elapse, exhale, pass on, perish, run out **7** decease **8** pass away **9** terminate **10** breathe out

explain 5 gloss, solve **7** analyze, clarify, clear up, condone, expound, justify, resolve, unravel **8** construe, decipher, spell out, unriddle, untangle **9** break down, elucidate, interpret **10** account for, illuminate, illustrate, unscramble **11** disentangle, rationalize

explain away 6 excuse **7** justify **8** minimize **9** extenuate **10** account for **11** rationalize

explanation 3 key **5** gloss **6** excuse, motive, reason **7** account, example, grounds, meaning **8** exegesis **9** construal, rationale **11** elucidation **12** significance **13** clarification

explanatory 10 discursive, exegetical **12** enlightening, illuminating, illustrative, interpretive

expletive 4 cuss, oath **5** curse, swear **8** cussword **9** swearword **12** interjection (see also EXCLAMATION)

explicate 7 amplify, develop, explain, expound **8** construe, spell out **9** elucidate, interpret

explication 5 gloss **8** exegesis **9** construal **10** commentary **11** development

explicative 10 discursive, exegetical, scholastic **12** interpretive **13** hermeneutical

explicit 4 open, sure **5** clear, exact, frank, lucid, overt, plain **7** certain, correct, express, obvious, precise **8** clearcut, definite, distinct, specific **10** definitive **11** categorical, perspicuous, unambiguous, unequivocal

explode 3 pop **4** fire **5** blast, burst, erupt, go off **6** blow up, debunk, negate, refute **7** burgeon, deflate **8** break out, burst out, detonate, disprove, dynamite, mushroom, puncture **9** discharge, discredit **10** burst forth **11** proliferate

exploit 3 act, use **4** coup, deed, feat, gest, play **5** abuse, geste, stunt **6** bestow, effort, employ, parlay, play on **7** emprise, utilize, venture **8** escapade, exercise **9** adventure, cultivate **10** enterprise, manipulate **11** achievement, performance, tour de force

explore 5 probe, scout **6** burrow, go into, search **7** dig into, examine **8** look into, prospect, traverse **9** delve into **11** inquire into, investigate

explorer *African:* **3** Cam, Cão (Diogo) **4** Park (Mungo) **5** Grant (James), Laird (Macgregor), Speke (John Hanning) **6** Akeley (Carl, Mary), Burton (Richard), Lander (John, Richard)

7 Covilhâ (Pero da), Stanley (Henry) **8** Covilhão (Pero da) **10** Clapperton (Hugh) **11** Livingstone (David) *American:* **4** Byrd (Richard), Hall (Charles Francis), Kane (Elisha Kent), Pike (Zebulon) **5** Beebe (Charles William), Clark (William), Lewis (Meriwether), Peary (Robert) **6** Henson (Matthew), Powell (John Wesley), Wilkes (Charles) **7** Frémont (John Charles) *Antarctic:* **4** Byrd (Richard), Cook (Frederick), Ross (James Clark) **5** Fuchs (Vivian), Ronne (Finn), Scott (Robert Falcon) **6** Palmer (Nathaniel), Rymill (John Riddoch), Wilkes (Charles) **7** Weddell (James), Wilkins (George) **8** Amundsen (Roald), d'Urville (Dumont) **9** Ellsworth (Lincoln) **10** Shackleton (Ernest) *Arctic:* **3** Rae (John) **4** Byrd (Richard), Cook (Frederick) **5** Davis (John), Peary (Robert) **6** Baffin (William), Bering (Vitus), Henson (Matthew), Hudson (Henry), Nansen (Fridtjof), Nobile (Umberto) **7** Barents (Willem), Bennett (Floyd), Wilkins (George), Wrangel (Ferdinand von) **8** Amundsen (Roald) **9** Mackenzie (Alexander), MacMillan (Donald) **10** Stefansson (Vilhjalmur) *Australian:* **7** Wilkins (George) *Austrian:* **9** Weyprecht (Carl) *Canadian:* **9** Mackenzie (Alexander) **10** Stefansson (Vilhjalmur) *Danish:* **9** Rasmussen (Knud) *Dutch:* **6** Tasman (Abel Janszoon) *English:* **4** Cook (James) **5** Cabot (John, Sebastian), Drake (Francis), Scott (Robert Falcon), Smith (John) **6** Baffin (William), Burton (Richard), Hudson (Henry) **7** Raleigh (Walter), Stanley (Henry) **9** Vancouver (George) **10** Shackleton (Ernest) **12** Younghusband (Francis) *French:* **7** Cartier (Jacques), La Salle (Sieur de), Nicolet (Jean) **8** Cousteau (Jacques-Yves) **9** Champlain (Samuel de), La Perouse (Comte de), Marquette (Jacques) *French Canadian:* **6** Joliet (Louis) **7** Jolliet (Louis) **9** Iberville (Sieur d') *German:* **7** Peters (Carl) **8** Humboldt (Alexander von) *Italian:* **5** Cabot (John) **6** Nobile (Umberto) **8** Vespucci (Amerigo) *New Zealand:* **7** Hillary (Edmund) *Norwegian:* **6** Nansen (Fridtjof) **8** Amundsen (Roald), Sverdrup (Otto) **9** Heyerdahl (Thor) *Portuguese:* **4** Gama (Vasco da) **5** Cunha (Tristão da) **6** Cabral (Pedro) **8** Cabrilho (João Rodrigues), Magellan (Ferdinand) *Scottish:* **3** Rae (John) **4** Park (Mungo), Ross (James Clark) **7** Thomson (Joseph) **11** Livingstone (David) *Span-*

ish: **6** Balboa (Vasco Núñez de), Cortés (Hernán, Hernando), de Soto (Hernando), Pinzón (Martín Alonso, Vicente Yáñez) **7** Mendoza (Pedro de), Pizarro (Francisco) **8** Bastidas (Rodrigo de), Coronado (Francisco de) **11** Ponce de León (Juan)

explosion 3 pop, pow **4** bang, boom, clap **5** blast, burst, crack, crash, sally, salvo, storm **6** report, volley **7** barrage, blowout, torrent **8** eruption, outburst, paroxysm **9** discharge **10** detonation

explosive 3 TNT **5** nitro, tense **6** charge, petard, powder **7** cordite, violent **8** dynamite **9** gunpowder **13** nitroglycerin *device:* **3** cap **4** bomb, mine **5** shell **6** petard **7** grenade **8** firework *expert:* **5** Maxim (Hudson), Nobel (Alfred) *sound:* **3** pop, pow **4** bang, boom **5** crack

exponent 6 backer **7** booster **8** advocate, champion, defender, partisan, promoter, upholder **9** supporter **12** practitioner

expose 3 air **4** bare, open, show **5** dig up, flash **6** debunk, flaunt, parade, reveal, show up, unmask, unveil **7** abandon, display, exhibit, lay open, publish, show off, subject, uncover, undress **8** brandish, disclose, discover, endanger, unclothe

exposé 10 disclosure, revelation, uncovering

exposed 4 bare, open **5** naked **6** liable **7** evident, subject, visible **8** manifest, stripped, unhidden **9** uncovered **11** susceptible, unconcealed, unprotected

exposition 4 fair, show **6** bazaar **7** display, exhibit

expostulate 5 argue **6** debate, reason **7** discuss, dispute

exposure 4 risk **5** peril **6** airing, baring, danger **8** betrayal, jeopardy, openness **9** liability, publicity **10** revelation **12** helplessness **13** vulnerability

expound 5 state **6** defend **7** clarify, comment, explain, present **8** construe, set forth, spell out **9** discourse, explicate, interpret

expounder 7 teacher **8** advocate, champion, defender, promoter **9** proponent, supporter

express 3 air, say **4** mean, tell, vent **5** couch, crush, frame, state, utter **6** broach, convey, denote, impart, intend, voiced **7** connote, declare, signify, special, uttered **8** announce, clearcut, definite, disclose, explicit, intended, proclaim, specific **9** enunciate, formulate, high-speed, pronounce, symbolize, ventilate **10** definitive, particular **11** categorical, communicate, intentional, unambiguous *gratitude:* **5** thank *regret:* **9** apologize

expression 4 cast, face, form, look, mien, sign, vent, word **5** idiom, issue, motto, token, voice **6** symbol, visage **7** diction, gesture **8** locution **9** eloquence, statement, utterance, verbalism, vividness **10** embodiment, indication **11** countenance, enunciation, observation **13** demonstration, manifestation *facial:* **4** grin, phiz, pout **5** frown, scowl, smile, smirk, sneer, wince **7** grimace *of assent:* **3** aye, nod, yea, yes **4** okay *of sorrow:* **4** alas, tear *trite:* **6** cliché **7** bromide **8** banality *witty:* **4** quip **5** sally **6** bon mot

expressionless 5 blank **6** stolid, vacant, wooden **7** deadpan **9** impassive **10** poker-faced **11** inscrutable

expressive 5 vivid **7** graphic **8** eloquent **9** revealing **10** meaningful, passionate

expressly 9 precisely, purposely **10** explicitly **12** particularly, specifically **13** intentionally

expressway 4 road **7** freeway, highway, parkway **8** turnpike **12** thoroughfare

expropriate 4 take **5** annex, seize **7** impound, preempt **8** arrogate **9** sequester **10** commandeer, confiscate, dispossess

expulse see EXPEL

expulsion 5 exile, purge **6** ouster **7** ousting, removal **8** ejection, eviction **9** ostracism **10** banishment, relegation **11** deportation **12** displacement

expunge 4 dele, x out **5** annul, erase **6** cancel, delete, efface **7** blot out, destroy, exclude, wipe out **8** black out **9** eliminate, eradicate, strike out **10** annihilate, obliterate

expurgate 4 blip **5** bleep, purge **6** censor, purify, screen **7** cleanse **8** sanitize **10** bowdlerize

expurgation 8 ablution **9** catharsis, cleansing **10** lustration **12** purification

exquisite 3 fop **4** fine, keen, rare **5** acute, dandy **6** choice, dainty, select, superb **7** coxcomb, elegant, extreme, intense, refined **8** delicate, finished, flawless, macaroni **9** recherché **10** fastidious, immaculate, impeccable

exsiccate 3 dry **4** sear **5** parch

extant 4 live **5** alive **6** actual, living **7** current, present **9** surviving **10** present-day **12** contemporary

extemporaneous 5 ad-lib **6** casual **7** offhand **8** ad-libbed, informal **9** impromptu, impulsive, makeshift, unplanned **10** improvised, unprepared, unscripted **11** spontaneous, unrehearsed **12** unthought-out

extempore see EXTEMPORANEOUS

extemporize 5 ad-lib 7 dash off, toss off
8 knock off 9 improvise

extend 4 draw, span, vary 5 award,
grant, offer, range, reach 6 accord,
attain, bestow, spread, tender, unbend,
unfold 7 advance, amplify, augment,
broaden, drag out, draw out, enlarge,
further, hold out, present, proceed,
proffer, project, prolong, spin out,
stretch 8 continue, elongate, increase,
lengthen, multiply, protract 10 outstretch, stretch out

extension 3 arm, ell 4 wing 5 annex,
delay, range, reach, scope, sweep
6 radius, spread 7 adjunct, compass,
purview 8 addition, increase
9 appendage, magnitude 10 broadening,
elongation 11 enlargement, lengthening, protraction 12 augmentation, continuation, postponement, prolongation

extensity 5 ambit, orbit, range, reach,
scope, sweep 6 radius 7 compass,
purview

extensive 3 big 4 long, vast, wide
5 broad, large, major 7 general,
immense, lengthy, sizable 8 far-flung,
sizeable, spacious, sweeping, thorough
9 wholesale 10 large-scale, widespread
11 far-reaching, wide-ranging 12 considerable

extent 4 size 5 ambit, limit, orbit, range,
reach, scope, sweep, width 6 amount,
degree, domain, radius 7 breadth, compass, measure, purview 8 vicinity
9 magnitude 10 dimensions, proportion

extenuate 6 dilute, excuse, lessen, soft-
en, temper, weaken 7 explain, justify,
qualify, varnish 8 diminish, enervate,
mitigate, moderate, palliate 9 gloss
over 11 rationalize

exterior 4 skin 5 outer, shell 6 facade
7 outmost, outside, outward, surface
8 apparent 9 outermost 11 superficial

exterminate 4 kill 6 rub out 7 destroy,
wipe out 8 massacre 9 eliminate, eradicate, finish off, liquidate, slaughter
10 annihilate, extinguish, obliterate

external 3 out 4 over 5 outer 7 foreign,
outside, outward, surface 9 outermost
10 peripheral 11 superficial

externalize 4 show 6 embody, evince,
excuse, expose, reveal 7 exhibit, justify
8 manifest 9 extenuate, incarnate,
objectify, personify 11 rationalize
12 substantiate

extinct 4 cold, dead, gone, late 5 passé
6 bygone 7 archaic, defunct 8 deceased,
departed, obsolete, perished, vanished
10 superseded

extinction 3 end 4 doom 5 death
6 demise 11 destruction, eradication,
liquidation 12 annihilation, obliteration
13 disappearance, extermination

extinguish 3 end 5 crush, douse, erase,
quash, quell 6 put out, quench, squash,
stifle 7 abolish, blot out, blow out,
destroy, eclipse, expunge, nullify, put
down, wipe out 8 snuff out, stamp out,
suppress 9 eliminate, eradicate, extirpate 10 annihilate, obliterate

extirpate 5 erase 6 cut out, efface,
excise, resect, uproot 7 abolish, blot
out, destroy, expunge, kill off, root out,
wipe out 8 demolish 9 eliminate, eradicate 10 annihilate, deracinate, extinguish

extol 4 hymn, laud 5 cry up, exalt
6 praise 7 acclaim, applaud, commend,
glorify, magnify 8 eulogize 9 celebrate
10 panegyrize

extort 5 wrest, wring 7 extract

extortion 8 exaction 9 blackmail

extra 3 odd 4 more, over 5 added, spare
6 de trop, rarely 7 reserve, surplus
8 leftover 9 lagniappe, redundant,
unusually 10 additional, especially
11 superfluous 12 particularly, supplemental 13 supernumerary, supplementary

extract 4 pull, yank 5 evoke, glean,
quote, wring 6 derive, eke out, elicit,
remove 7 abridge, distill, essence,
excerpt, passage, pull out, squeeze,
take out 8 citation, condense, infusion
9 quotation, selection 11 concentrate

extraction 5 birth, blood, stock 6 origin
7 descent, essence, lineage 8 ancestry,
pedigree 9 parentage 10 derivation
12 distillation

extraneous 5 alien, outer 6 exotic 7 foreign, outside 8 external 9 unrelated
10 immaterial, inapposite, incidental,
irrelevant, peripheral 11 impertinent,
inessential, superfluous, unessential
12 adventitious, inapplicable, nonessential

extraordinary 3 odd 4 rare 6 unique
7 amazing, notable, special, unusual
8 abnormal, atypical, singular, terrific,
uncommon, unwonted 9 wonderful
10 noteworthy, phenomenal, remarkable, stupendous, tremendous
11 exceptional, outstanding

extravagance 5 frill, waste 6 excess, luxury 9 hyperbole, profusion 10 indulgence, lavishness 11 ostentation, prodigality, superfluity 12 immoderation,
wastefulness

extravagant 4 wild 5 outré, undue 6 lavish 7 bizarre, extreme, profuse 8 over-

done, prodigal, reckless, wasteful
9 elaborate, excessive, fantastic,
grandiose, overblown **10** exorbitant,
hyperbolic, immoderate, inordinate,
profligate **11** exaggerated, implausible,
intemperate, nonsensical **12** ostentatious, preposterous, unrestrained
extreme 3 top **4** apex, dire, last, peak,
wild **5** crown, final, limit, ultra, undue
6 climax, excess, height, summit,
utmost, zenith **7** drastic, fanatic,
intense, maximal, maximum, outmost,
radical, violent **8** farthest, furthest, pinnacle, remotest, ultimate **9** desperate,
excessive, outermost, uttermost
10 immoderate, inordinate, outlandish,
outrageous **11** culmination, furthermost, unwarranted **12** unmeasurable,
unreasonable **13** revolutionary *degree:*
3 nth
extremely 4 very **5** ultra **6** highly, hugely,
mighty, overly, plenty **7** acutely, awfully, greatly, utterly **8** severely, terribly
9 immensely, seriously, unusually
10 remarkably, strikingly **11** exceedingly **12** terrifically
extremist 5 rabid, ultra **6** zealot **7** diehard, fanatic, radical **8** militant, ultraist
9 fanatical **10** monomaniac, ultraistic
11 reactionary **13** revolutionary
extremity 3 arm, end, leg, tip **4** acme,
apex, foot, hand, tail **5** limit, verge
6 apogee, vertex, zenith **8** terminal, terminus
extricate 4 free **5** loose **6** detach, redeem,
rescue **7** bail out, deliver, resolve, set
free, untwine **8** liberate, untangle **9** disengage **11** disencumber, disentangle,
distinguish, individuate **12** discriminate, disembarrass **13** differentiate
extrinsic 5 alien, outer **6** exotic **7** foreign, outside, outward **8** exterior, external, imported **10** incidental, extraneous
extrude 4 spew **5** eject **7** push out **8** press
out **10** squeeze out
exuberance 4 glee, life, zest **5** ardor
6 gaiety, spirit **7** abandon **8** buoyancy,
hilarity, vivacity **9** profusion **10** ebullience, enthusiasm, friskiness, liveliness
11 flamboyance, high spirits, zestfulness **12** exhilaration **13** effervescence,
sprightliness
exuberant 3 gay **4** lush, rank **5** happy
6 bouncy, elated, fecund, lavish, lively
7 buoyant, profuse, rampant, riotous,
zestful **8** fruitful, prodigal, prolific,
spirited **9** ebullient, luxuriant, sprightly, vivacious **10** flamboyant **11** exhilarated **12** effervescent, enthusiastic,
high-spirited

exude 4 emit, leak, ooze, seep, shed
5 issue **7** diffuse, display, emanate,
excrete, exhibit, give off, ooze out,
radiate, secrete **9** discharge
exult 4 crow **5** cheer, gloat, glory, revel
7 delight, rejoice **8** jubilate **9** celebrate
exultant 6 elated, joyful, joyous **7** gleeful
8 ecstatic, euphoric, jubilant **9** cock-a-hoop, overjoyed, rejoicing, triumphal
10 triumphant
exultation 3 joy **4** glee **7** delight, ecstasy,
elation, rapture, triumph **8** euphoria,
gloating **9** jubilance, rejoicing **10** jubilation
eye 3 orb **4** lamp, ogle, scan, view
5 sight, watch **6** behold, goggle, look at,
ocular, oculus, peeper, regard, size up,
vision **7** inspect **8** check out, consider,
gaze upon, scrutiny **9** headlight
10 scrutinize *defect:* **6** myopia **9** hyperopia **10** emmetropia, presbyopia
11 astigmatism *disease:* **8** cataract, glaucoma, trachoma *doctor:* **7** oculist
11 optometrist *opening:* **5** pupil *part:*
4 iris, lens, uvea **5** pupil **6** cornea, retina, sclera *relating to:* **5** optic **7** optical
socket: **5** orbit *Spanish:* **3** ojo
eyeball 4 scan **5** check, study **6** go over,
look at, peruse, survey **7** examine,
inspect, observe **8** appraise, check out,
evaluate, pore over **10** scrutinize
eye-catching 4 bold **5** gaudy, showy
6 flashy **7** salient **8** striking **9** arresting,
prominent **10** noticeable, remarkable
11 conspicuous
eyeful 6 looker **7** stunner **8** knockout
eyeglass 7 monocle
eyeglasses 5 specs **6** lenses **7** lorgnon
8 bifocals, pince-nez **9** lorgnette
10 spectacles
eyelash 6 cilium **11** hairbreadth
eyelet 4 hole **7** grommet **8** loophole,
peephole
eyepiece 4 lens **6** ocular
eye-popping 7 amazing **8** exciting, stirring **9** thrilling **10** astounding **11** astonishing, mind-blowing, spectacular
12 breathtaking
eyesore 4 blot, dump, mess **6** blight
7 blemish **8** atrocity **11** monstrosity
eyespot 6 blight, fungus **7** ocellus
eyetooth 6 canine
eyewash 3 rot **4** bunk **5** bilge, hooey,
tripe **6** bunkum **7** baloney, garbage,
hogwash, rubbish, twaddle **8** malarkey,
nonsense **9** poppycock **10** balderdash
13 horsefeathers
eyewitness 8 observer, onlooker
9 bystander, spectator
eyrie see AERIE

F

Fabergé product 3 egg 9 Easter egg
Fabian 4 Shaw (George Bernard), Webb (Beatrice, Sidney) 7 politic 8 cautious, dilatory 9 socialist 11 circumspect, calculating
fable 4 myth, tale, yarn 5 story 6 legend 7 fantasy, fiction, figment, parable 8 allegory *animal:* 8 bestiary
fabled 5 famed 6 famous, unreal 7 storied 8 fanciful, mythical, renowned 9 fictional, imaginary, legendary, pretended 10 fictitious 11 make-believe 12 mythological
fabric 3 aba, rep, web 4 lamé, repp 5 cloth, fiber, grain 7 texture 8 building, material, shirting 9 structure *coarse:* 5 crash, gunny 6 burlap, linsey, ratiné 7 cheviot, hopsack 8 homespun *corded:* 3 rep 4 repp 5 piqué 6 calico, moreen, poplin 7 pinwale 8 corduroy, paduasoy 9 bengaline *cotton:* 4 jean, leno 5 baize, chino, domet, drill, scrim, wigan 6 chintz, dimity, faille, madras, muslin 7 etamine, gingham, nankeen, percale, ticking 8 chambray, dungaree, nainsook, tarlatan *cotton and linen:* 4 huck 7 fustian 9 huckaback *crepe:* 8 marocain *dealer:* 6 draper, mercer *durable:* 4 huck, jean 5 chino, denim, drill 6 frieze, moreen 7 lasting, ticking 8 cretonne, dungaree *embroidered:* 9 baldachin 10 baldachino *finishing process:* 8 lustring 9 mercerize *flag material:* 7 bunting *glazed:* 6 chintz 7 cambric, holland *knitted:* 6 tricot 10 balbriggan *linen:* 7 cambric, lockram *looped:* 6 bouclé *lustrous:* 4 silk 5 moiré, satin, surah 7 taffeta 12 brilliantine *metallic:* 4 lamé *net:* 5 tulle 8 bobbinet, illusion *openwork:* 4 lace 8 filigree *ornamental:* 4 lace 5 braid 6 ribbon 7 bunting *pebbly-surface:* 8 barathea *pile-surface:* 5 panne, plush, terry 6 velour, velvet 7 duvetyn, velours 8 chenille, moleskin 9 velveteen *plaid:* 6 tartan *printed:* 5 batik, toile 6 calico, chintz, damask 7 allover, challis 8 cretonne, jacquard 11 toile de Jouy *puckered:* 6 plissé *raised pattern:* 4 lamé 7 brocade 10 brocatelle *satin weave:* 5 panne *sheer:* 4 lawn, mull 5 gauze, ninon, voile 6 dimity 7 batiste, chiffon, organdy, organza, tiffany 8 tar-

latan *silk:* 6 faille, pongee, samite 7 foulard, grogram 8 paduasoy, sarcenet, sarsenet, shantung 9 bombazine *striped:* 3 aba 7 ticking 8 bayadere *synthetic:* 5 ninon, nylon, Orlon, rayon 6 Dacron *twill:* 4 jean 5 chino, drill, serge 7 foulard, nankeen, ticking 8 dungaree, shalloon 9 bombazine 10 broadcloth *unfinished:* 6 greige *waterproof:* 7 oilskin *wool:* 5 baize, loden, tweed 6 alpaca, caddis, camlet, duffel, duffle, melton, merino, wadmal, wadmel, wadmol, woolen 7 woollen 8 mackinaw, prunella 9 cassimere *wool, poor quality:* 5 mungo 6 shoddy *wool mixture:* 6 saxony 7 drugget, ratteen 8 moquette, shalloon, zibeline 9 zibelline *woven:* 4 weft 7 textile
fabricate 4 form, make 5 build, erect, frame, set up, shape 6 cook up, create, devise, invent, make up 7 concoct, dream up, fashion, produce, think up 8 assemble, contrive 9 construct, structure 11 manufacture, put together
fabrication 3 fib, lie 4 bull, jive 6 canard, deceit 7 fiction, figment, hogwash, product, untruth 8 assembly, building, creation 9 deception, fairy tale, falsehood, invention 10 concoction, production 11 manufacture 12 construction
fabulist *French:* 10 La Fontaine (Jean de) *Greek:* 5 Aesop *Roman:* 8 Phaedrus *Russian:* 6 Krylov (Ivan)
fabulous 5 super 7 amazing 8 mythical, terrific, wondrous 9 fantastic, legendary, marvelous, wonderful 10 astounding, fictitious, incredible, outrageous, phenomenal, prodigious, remarkable, stupendous 11 astonishing, extravagant, spectacular 12 mythological *animal:* 6 dragon 7 centaur, unicorn *bird:* 3 roc *serpent:* 8 basilisk 10 cockatrice
facade 4 face, mask 5 color, front, guise, put-on 6 veneer 8 disguise, exterior, frontage, pretense 10 appearance, camouflage, false front
face 3 mug, pan 4 dare, defy, dial, meet, phiz, puss, show, side 5 abide, brave, front, guise, honor, image, nerve 6 endure, facade, kisser, makeup,

mazard, oppose, resist, suffer, take on, visage **7** compete, contend, dignity, surface **8** confront, cope with, deal with, disguise, features, prestige, war paint **9** assurance, encounter, lineament, semblance, withstand **10** appearance, confidence, experience, expression, maquillage, reputation **11** countenance, self-respect

face-off 5 clash, set-to **13** confrontation

facet 4 edge, item, part, side **5** angle, bezel, front, phase, plane, point, trait **6** aspect, detail **7** element, feature, surface **9** attribute, component **10** appearance, particular

facetious 4 flip **5** comic, droll, smart, witty **6** blithe, joking **7** amusing, comical, jesting, jocular, joshing, kidding, risible, waggish **8** flippant, humorous **9** ludicrous, unserious, whimsical **10** irreverent, ridiculous **12** wisecracking **13** tongue-in-cheek

face-to-face 6 direct **7** contact, present, vis-à-vis **8** directly, in person, personal **10** personally

facile 4 deft, easy, glib, snap **5** light, quick, ready **6** adroit, expert, fluent, poised, simple, smooth **7** assured, cursory, offhand, shallow, voluble **8** skillful, untaxing **9** dexterous **10** effortless, simplistic **13** uncomplicated

facilitate 3 aid **4** abet, ease, help **6** assist, enable, smooth **7** advance, forward, further, promote **8** expedite, make easy, simplify

facility 3 aid, wit **4** bent, ease **5** knack, privy, skill **6** talent, toilet **7** ability, amenity, comfort, fluency, leaning **8** aptitude, bathroom, building, capacity, lavatory, washroom **9** advantage, dexterity **10** adroitness, competence, smoothness **11** convenience, institution, proficiency **12** installation **13** accommodation, establishment

facing 5 front, panel **6** contra, lining, toward, veneer **7** surface, vis-à-vis **8** covering, opposite, paneling **11** over against *down:* **5** prone *up:* **6** supine

facsimile 4 copy, dupe, fake, twin **5** clone, ditto, match, repro **6** carbon, double **7** replica **8** knockoff, likeness **9** duplicate, imitation, photocopy **10** carbon copy, dead ringer, similitude **11** counterpart, duplication, replication **12** reproduction

fact 4 dope **5** datum, event, truth **6** detail, gospel, truism, verity **7** episode, reality **8** evidence, incident **9** actuality **10** occurrence, particular, phenomenon **11** information **12** circumstance, intelligence

faction 4 band, bloc, camp, part, ring, sect, side, wing **5** cabal, group, party **6** caucus, circle, clique, sector, strife **7** combine, coterie, discord, machine, section **8** alliance, disunity, splinter **10** contingent, disharmony

factious 7 warring **8** contrary, divisive, partisan **9** dissident, insurgent, sectarian, seditious, turbulent **10** contending, malcontent **11** contentious, disaffected, dissentious, quarrelsome **12** disputatious **13** troublemaking

factitious 4 sham **5** bogus, false, phony **6** ersatz, forced, made-up, unreal **7** assumed, created, feigned, manmade, shammed **8** affected, invented, spurious **9** concocted, contrived, fashioned, pretended, simulated, synthetic, unnatural **10** artificial, fabricated **11** constructed, counterfeit **12** manufactured **13** counterfeited

___ **facto 4** ipso **6** ex post

factor 4 gene, item **5** agent, cause, proxy **6** broker, lender, number, symbol **7** divisor, element, exclude, include, resolve **8** attorney, emissary, quantity **9** component, majordomo, substance **10** antecedent, ingredient, multiplier **11** determinant **12** intermediary

factory 4 mill, shop **5** plant, works **8** workshop **9** sweatshop **11** machine shop

factotum 4 grub **5** gofer **6** drudge **7** servant **9** assistant, operative **11** functionary

factual 4 real, true **5** exact, valid **6** actual **7** certain, genuine, literal **8** absolute, positive **9** authentic, undoubted **10** undisputed **12** indisputable

faculty 4 bent, body, gift **5** flair, knack, power **6** talent **7** ability, college **8** aptitude, capacity, facility, function, instinct **9** educators, lecturers **10** department, professors **11** instructors

fad 4 chic, kick, mode, rage, whim **5** craze, furor, style, trend **6** furore, latest, whimsy **7** caprice, fashion **9** bandwagon **10** dernier cri

faddish 3 hot **4** chic **5** today **6** modish, red-hot, trendy, with-it **7** stylish, voguish **8** contempo **9** au courant **11** cutting-edge, fashionable

fade 3 die, dim, ebb **4** fail, pale, wane, wilt **6** lessen, vanish, weaken, wither **7** decline, lighten, wash out **8** decrease, discolor, diminish **9** disappear, evaporate

faded 3 dim, wan **4** drab, dull, pale **6** pallid **8** bleached, vanished, withered **9** etiolated, washed-out

Faerie Queene, The *author:* 7 Spenser (Edmund) *character:* 3 Ate, Una 4 Alma 5 Guyon, Talus 6 Abessa, Amavia, Amoret, Arthur, Cambel, Duessa, Palmer 7 Artegal, Corceca, Fidessa, Maleger, Sansloy 8 Calidore, Florimel, Fradubio, Gloriana, Lucifera, Orgoglio, Satyrane 9 Archimago, Britomart 11 Britomartis

Fafnir 6 dragon *brother:* 5 Regin 6 Fasolt, Reginn *father:* 8 Hreidmar *slayer:* 6 Sigurd 9 Siegfried *victim:* 6 Fasolt 8 Hreidmar

fag 4 do in, moil, tire, toil 5 serve, smoke, stick, weary 6 drudge, overdo, tucker 7 exhaust, fatigue, servant, wear out 8 drudgery, knock out 9 cigarette

fag end 4 butt, edge, fray 7 remnant

faience 11 earthenware

fail 3 die, end 4 bomb, fade, lack, lose, miss, sink, slip, stop, wane 5 break, flunk 6 fizzle, forget, ignore, lessen, weaken 7 decline, default, founder, give out, go under, neglect 8 fall flat, languish, miscarry 9 break down, fall short 10 disappoint, go bankrupt 11 deteriorate

failing 4 flaw, vice 5 fault 6 defect 8 weakness 9 weak point 10 deficiency 11 shortcoming 12 imperfection

failure 3 bum, dud 4 bomb, bust, flop, miss 5 decay, loser 6 fiasco, fizzle, nogood, outage 7 default, washout 8 collapse, fracture, omission 9 breakdown, cessation, oversight, unconcern 10 bankruptcy, deficiency, insolvency, negligence 11 defalcation, dysfunction, miscarriage 12 interruption 13 deterioration

fain 3 apt 5 eager, prone, ready 6 gladly, minded 7 willing 8 amenable, inclined 9 agreeable

fainéant 3 bum 4 idle, lazy 5 idler, sloth 6 loafer, torpid 7 goof-off, slacker 8 deadbeat, inactive, indolent, layabout, slothful, sluggard, sluggish 9 do-nothing, lazybones, shiftless 11 couch potato, ineffectual 13 lackadaisical

faint 3 dim, low, wan 4 hazy, pale, soft, weak, wilt 5 dizzy, light, swoon, vague, woozy 6 feeble 7 conk out, obscure, pass out, shadowy, syncope, unclear 8 black out, collapse, keel over 9 undefined 10 ill-defined, indistinct

fair 3 due 4 even, expo, fine, join, just, mild, okay, open, so-so 5 ample, blond, bonny, clear, equal, fresh, light, sunny 6 bazaar, blonde, comely, decent, honest, kermis, lovely, market, pretty, square 7 cricket 8 adequate, all right,

balanced, carnival, festival, mediocre, middling, pleasant, pleasing, rainless, rational, sunshiny, unbiased 9 beautiful, cloudless, equitable, favorable, fortunate, impartial, objective, tolerable, unclouded 10 aboveboard, acceptable, attractive, evenhanded, exhibition, exposition, open-minded, reasonable 11 good-looking, indifferent, nonpartisan, respectable, sportsmanly 12 satisfactory, unprejudiced 13 disinterested, dispassionate, sportsmanlike

fair food 10 candy apple, candy floss, fried dough, funnel cake 11 cotton candy, elephant ear

fair-haired 3 pet 5 blond 6 blonde 7 beloved, darling, favored 8 favorite 9 fortunate

fairly 5 quite 6 nearly, rather 7 plainly 8 passably, properly, somewhat 9 tolerably 10 acceptably, deservedly, distinctly, moderately, reasonably 11 practically

fairness 6 candor 7 honesty 8 justness 9 good faith 12 impartiality

fairy 3 elf, imp, nix 4 puck 5 elfin, nixie, nymph, pixie, sylph 6 goblin, kobold, sprite 7 brownie, gremlin 10 leprechaun *king:* 6 Oberon *queen:* 3 Mab 7 Titania 8 Gloriana *shoemaker:* 10 leprechaun

fairy tale *author:* 4 Lang (Andrew) 5 Grimm (Jacob, Wilhelm), Wilde (Oscar) 7 Kipling (Rudyard) 8 Andersen (Hans Christian), Perrault (Charles) *character:* 4 Jack, Puck 6 Gretel, Hansel 8 Rapunzel, Tom Thumb 9 Snow White 10 Cinderella, Goldilocks, Thumbelina

faith 4 cult, sect 5 credo, creed, stock, troth, trust 6 belief, church, credit 8 credence, reliance, religion 9 certainty, certitude, communion, credulity 10 confidence, persuasion 12 denomination *article of:* 5 tenet

faithful 4 fast, just, true 5 liege, loyal, pious, tried 6 steady, trusty 7 devoted, dutiful, staunch 8 constant, follower, reliable, resolute, true-blue 9 religious, steadfast 10 dependable, scrupulous, unwavering 11 truehearted, trustworthy

faithfulness 5 piety, troth 6 fealty 7 loyalty 8 devotion, fidelity 9 adherence, constancy 10 allegiance, attachment

faithless 5 false, Punic 6 fickle, untrue 8 disloyal, recreant 10 perfidious, traitorous 11 treacherous 13 untrustworthy

faithlessness 7 perfidy, treason 8 betrayal 9 falseness, treachery 10 disloyalty, infidelity

fake 3 act, gyp 4 hoax, mock, sham
5 bluff, bogus, false, feign, fraud,
phony, put on, spoof 6 affect, doctor,
ersatz, forged, framed, humbug, pseudo 7 falsify, pretend 8 impostor, invented, simulate, spurious 9 brummagem,
charlatan, concocted, fabricate, imitation, imposture, pinchbeck, pretended,
simulated 10 artificial, fabricated, fictitious, fraudulent, simulation 11 counterfeit *combining form:* 5 pseud 6 pseudo
faker 4 sham 5 fraud, phony, quack
6 con man, hoaxer 8 deceiver, impostor
9 charlatan, con artist, pretender
10 mountebank 11 four-flusher 12 double-dealer 13 confidence man
fakir 7 ascetic, dervish 9 mendicant
falcon 4 hawk 5 hobby, saker 6 lanner,
merlin 7 kestrel 9 peregrine *eye cover:*
4 seel *male:* 4 jack 6 tercel 7 tiercel
8 lanneret *mature:* 7 haggard *young:*
4 eyas
falcon-headed god see at EGYPTIAN
falconry 7 hawking *equipment:* 4 bell,
hood, jess, lure *procedure:* 3 imp
4 cope, seel
Falkland Islands *capital:* 7 Stanley *colony
of:* 7 Britain
fall 3 dip, ebb, sag 4 dive, drip, drop,
dump, hang, plop, sink, slip, trip, wane
5 abate, crash, lapse, slide, slump, spill
6 autumn, drowse, give up, go down,
header, plunge, sprawl, tumble 7 cascade, decline, descend, descent,
devolve, go under, plummet, scatter,
stumble, subside 8 collapse, decrease,
diminish, keel over, nose-dive 9 hairpiece 10 depreciate 11 precipitate
fallacious 6 untrue 7 invalid 8 delusive,
delusory 9 deceitful, deceptive, erroneous, sophistic 10 fraudulent
fallacy 5 error 6 canard 7 falsity,
sophism, untruth 8 delusion 9 falsehood 11 non sequitur 13 misconception
fall apart 6 lose it 7 crumble 9 break
down, decompose 10 go to pieces
11 come unglued, deteriorate 12 disintegrate
fall back 6 recede, recoil, retire 7 retract,
retreat 8 withdraw 9 disengage, retrocede 10 retrograde
fall behind 3 lag 4 drag 5 delay, tarry,
trail 6 dawdle, linger, loiter
fall flat 4 bomb, fail, flop, miss 6 fizzle
fall guy 4 dupe, fool, goat, gull 5 chump,
front, patsy 6 stooge, sucker 8 front
man 9 scapegoat 11 whipping boy
fallible 4 iffy, weak 5 dicey, frail, human
6 errant, erring, faulty 9 imperfect
10 unreliable

falling-out 3 row 4 beef, feud, fuss, spat,
tiff 5 break, run-in, words 6 bicker, fracas, hassle 7 dispute, quarrel, rhubarb,
wrangle 8 argument, conflict, squabble
9 brannigan 11 altercation, controversy
12 disagreement, estrangement
falloff 3 sag 4 drop, slip 5 slump
7 decline 8 downturn 9 downslide,
downswing, downtrend 13 deterioration
fall out 5 argue, break, leave, occur
6 bicker 7 brabble, quarrel, wrangle
8 disagree, squabble
fallow 4 idle 5 inert 6 unsown 7 dormant,
resting 8 inactive, unseeded, untilled
9 neglected, quiescent, unplanted
12 uncultivated
false 4 fake, mock, sham 5 bogus,
dummy, hokey, lying, phony, wrong
6 ersatz, forged, hollow, pseudo, untrue
7 crooked, devious, feigned, seeming,
unloyal 8 apostate, apparent, deluding,
delusive, delusory, disloyal, recreant,
specious, spurious 9 brummagem,
deceitful, deceiving, deceptive, dishonest, distorted, erroneous, faithless,
illogical, imitation, incorrect, pinchbeck, simulated 10 artificial, fictitious,
fraudulent, inaccurate, misleading,
perfidious, traitorous, unfaithful,
untruthful 11 counterfeit, treacherous
combining form: 5 pseud 6 pseudo
falsehood 3 fib, lie 5 fable 6 canard
7 fallacy, untruth, whopper 8 roorback
9 mendacity 11 fabrication 12 misstatement 13 prevarication
falseness 7 fallacy, perfidy 8 apostasy
9 treachery 10 disloyalty, infidelity
11 insincerity
false teeth 8 dentures
falsify 3 fib, lie 4 cook, deny 5 belie,
fudge, slant 6 doctor, refute 7 deceive,
distort, mislead 8 disprove, misstate
10 contradict 11 prevaricate 12 misrepresent
falsity 3 fib, lie 4 tale, yarn 5 fable
6 canard 7 untruth, whopper 9 falsehood, mendacity 11 fabrication 13 prevarication
Falstaff *companion:* 3 Nym 4 Peto 6 Pistol 8 Bardolph *composer:* 5 Verdi
(Giuseppe) *creator:* 11 Shakespeare
(William) *play:* 7 Henry IV *prince:* 3 Hal
tavern: 9 Boar's Head
Falstaffian 3 fat 6 jovial 7 roguish
8 boastful 9 convivial, dissolute
falter 4 halt, limp, reel, sway, trip
5 quail, waver 6 flinch, teeter, totter,
wobble 7 give way, stagger, stammer,
stumble 8 hesitate 9 vacillate 12 shilly-
shally

fame 4 note 5 éclat, glory, honor, kudos 6 esteem, regard, renown, repute 7 acclaim, stardom 8 standing 9 celebrity, notoriety 10 popularity, prominence, reputation 11 acclamation, immortality, recognition

famed 5 noted 6 marked 7 eminent, notable 8 renowned 9 notorious, prominent, well-known 10 celebrated 11 illustrious 13 distinguished

familiar 4 cozy 6 common, folksy 8 domestic, everyday, frequent, informal, intimate, standard 10 accustomed 11 comfortable, commonplace 12 conventional, recognizable 13 garden-variety

familiarity 4 ease 8 intimacy 9 closeness, knowledge 11 informality 12 acquaintance

family 3 kin 4 clan, folk, home, line, race 5 brood, folks, house, issue, stirp, stock, tribe 6 ménage, strain 7 dynasty, kindred, lineage, progeny 8 pedigree 9 bloodline, household, offspring *branch:* 5 stirp *lineage:* 4 tree 6 stemma 8 pedigree 9 genealogy

famine 4 want 6 dearth, hunger 10 starvation

famished 6 hungry 7 starved 8 ravenous, starving

famous 5 famed, noble, noted 6 fabled 7 eminent, notable, popular 8 historic, renowned 9 legendary, notorious, prominent, well-known 10 celebrated 11 illustrious, prestigious, redoubtable

fan 3 bug, nut 4 blow, buff, open, wind 5 lover, rouse 6 addict, arouse, expand, extend, kindle, rooter, ruffle, spread, stir up, unfold, votary, whip up, winnow 7 admirer, devotee, habitué 8 adherent, enkindle, follower, railbird 9 stimulate 10 aficionado, enthusiast *horseracing:* 7 turfman *India:* 6 punkah *movie:* 7 cineast 8 cineaste

fanatic 3 bug, nut 4 buff 5 fiend, freak, rabid 6 addict, maniac, votary, zealot 7 devotee, die-hard, habitué 10 aficionado, enthusiast

fanatical 5 fiery, rabid 6 ardent, fervid 7 extreme, fervent, zealous 8 frenetic, frenzied, maniacal, obsessed 9 perfervid 10 passionate 11 impassioned

fanaticism 4 zeal 5 mania 6 frenzy 8 zealotry 9 extremism, monomania

fancier 6 grower 7 amateur, admirer, breeder, devotee

fanciful 6 absurd, unreal 7 bizarre, fictive 8 fabulous, illusory, imagined, mythical, notional, romantic 9 fantastic, fictional, grotesque, imaginary

10 chimerical, fictitious 11 fantastical 12 preposterous

fancy 3 bee 4 posh, whim 5 dream, ritzy, shine, smart, taste 6 liking, megrim, notion, relish, snazzy, swanky, vision, whimsy 7 caprice, chimera, conceit, concept, dream up, elegant, fantasy, feature, imagine, picture 8 conceive, daydream, envision, fondness, judgment, velleity 9 capriccio, elaborate, intricate, inventive, visualize, whimsical 10 decorative, ornamental, partiality, propensity 11 extravagant, highfalutin, imagination, inclination

fandango 5 dance 9 malaguena

fanfare 4 pomp, show 5 array 7 display, panoply 8 flourish *trumpet:* 6 tucket

fanlike 7 plicate

fanny 3 bum, can 4 buns, butt, duff, moon, rear, rump, seat, tail, tush 5 booty, nates 6 behind, bottom, breech, heinie 7 caboose, hind end, keister, rear end, tail end 8 backside, buttocks, derriere 9 fundament, posterior

fantasia 6 vision 8 daydream, illusion, rhapsody 9 fairyland 10 apparition

fantasize 4 moon 5 dream, fancy 7 imagine 8 daydream 10 woolgather

fantastic 3 odd 4 wild 6 absurd, unreal 7 bizarre, surreal 8 fanciful, singular 9 eccentric, grotesque, imaginary, marvelous, monstrous, unearthly, whimsical 10 chimerical, far-fetched, improbable, incredible, outlandish, outrageous, prodigious, stupendous, tremendous 11 implausible, nonsensical, sensational, superlative 12 preposterous, unbelievable

fantasy 4 moon, whim 5 dream, fancy, freak 6 vagary, vision, whimsy 7 caprice, chimera, fiction, reverie 8 daydream, delusion, phantasm 9 imagining, invention, pipe dream 10 bizarrerie 11 imagination 12 grotesquerie

far 4 long 6 remote 7 distant 8 outlying *combining form:* 3 tel 4 tele, telo

far and wide 7 all over 10 everyplace, everywhere, throughout

faraway 4 lost 5 moony 6 absent, dreamy, remote 7 distant, removed 8 outlying 9 oblivious, unheeding 10 abstracted, distracted 11 preoccupied, inattentive 12 absentminded

farce 6 comedy, satire 7 mockery 8 travesty 9 burlesque, slapstick 10 caricature

farceur 5 clown, cutup, joker 7 buffoon

farcical 5 comic 6 absurd 7 comical, foolish, risible 9 laughable, ludicrous 10 ridiculous 12 preposterous

fare 4 diet, dine, food, pass, rate, toll
5 get on, price, track 6 manage, travel
7 come off, journey, make out, proceed, succeed 8 get along, progress,
victuals 9 passenger, surcharge 10 provisions 11 comestibles

farewell 3 ave, bye 4 ta-ta 5 adieu, adios,
aloha, congé 6 bye-bye, pip-pip,
shalom, so long 7 aloha oe, cheerio,
good-bye 8 swan song 9 bon voyage,
departure 11 arrivederci, leave-taking,
valediction, valedictory

far-fetched 5 fishy 6 absurd 7 dubious
8 doubtful, strained, unlikely
10 improbable, incredible 11 implausible, unrealistic 12 preposterous, unbelievable

far-flung 6 remote 7 distant, removed
8 outlying 10 widespread

farinaceous 5 mealy 6 floury 7 starchy
food: 4 meal 5 flour, grits 6 cereal,
hominy 7 polenta, pudding, tapioca

farm 4 till 5 croft, ranch 6 grange, rancho 7 hennery 8 estancia, hacienda,
hatchery 9 cultivate, farmstead 10 plantation *building:* 4 barn, shed, silo *Dutch:*
6 bowery *Israeli collective:* 7 kibbutz
Russian: 7 kolkhoz, sovkhoz

farmer 6 grower, tiller, yeoman
7 granger, planter, rancher 8 ranchero,
ranchman 13 agriculturist *Russian:*
5 kulak *South African:* 4 Boer *tenant:*
6 cottar, cotter 7 crofter 12 sharecropper

farming 7 tillage 8 agronomy 9 husbandry 11 agriculture, cultivation

faro 5 monte *bet:* 7 sleeper *card:* 4 case,
hock, soda

far-off 6 remote 7 distant, removed
8 outlying

far-out 3 rad 4 cool 5 outré, weird
6 groovy 7 bizarre, offbeat, radical
9 eccentric 10 avant-garde, off-the-wall,
outlandish

farrago 4 hash, mess, olio 5 gumbo
6 jumble, medley, muddle 7 goulash,
mélange, mixture 8 mishmash, shambles 9 potpourri 10 hodgepodge, miscellany

far-reaching 5 broad 8 sweeping 9 extensive, momentous, pervasive 10 portentous, widespread 11 significant, wideranging 13 comprehensive,
consequential

farrier 5 smith 10 blacksmith, horseshoer

farsighted 4 sage, wise 9 hyperopic, prescient, sagacious 10 discerning

farthest 6 utmost 7 apogean, extreme,
outmost 8 remotest, ultimate 9 outermost, uttermost

Fasching 8 carnival

fascinate 4 draw, wile 5 charm 6 allure,
enamor, entice, please 7 attract,
beguile, bewitch, enchant 8 enthrall,
intrigue, transfix 9 captivate, enrapture, magnetize, mesmerize, spellbind

fascination 5 charm 6 allure, appeal
7 glamour 8 charisma 9 magnetism
10 attraction, witchcraft 11 enchantment 12 enthrallment

Fascist 4 Nazi 6 despot, Hitler (Adolf),
tyrant 8 autocrat 9 Falangist, Mussolini
(Benito) 10 Blackshirt

fashion 3 fad, fit, ton, way 4 chic, form,
mode, mold, suit, tone, vein, wear
5 craze, shape, style, trend, usage,
vogue 6 create, custom, design, devise,
manner, method, sculpt, tailor 7 compose, costume, pattern 8 contrive
9 bandwagon, construct, fabricate
10 dernier cri 12 haute couture

fashionable 3 hip 4 chic, cool, posh,
tony 5 fresh, ritzy, sharp, smart, swank,
swish 6 chichi, du jour, modish, trendy,
with-it 7 à la mode, current, dashing,
faddish, popular, stylish, voguish 8 upto-date 9 au courant, exclusive, happening 12 silk-stocking

fashion designer *American:* 4 Head
(Edith) 5 Beene (Geoffrey), Blass (Bill),
Dache (Lilly), Ellis (Perry), Karan
(Donna), Klein (Anne, Calvin) 6 Jacobs
(Marc), Lauren (Ralph), Mackie (Bob)
7 Galanos (James), Halston, Mizrahi
(Isaac) 8 Galliano (John), Hilfiger
(Tommy) 9 Claiborne (Liz), de la Renta
(Oscar), Gernreich (Rudi) *Anglo-French:*
5 Worth (Charles Frederick) *Dominican:*
9 de la Renta (Oscar) *English:* 5 Quant
(Mary) 8 Westwood (Vivienne) *French:*
4 Dior (Christian) 5 Bohan (Marc)
6 Cardin (Pierre), Chanel (Coco), Poiret
(Paul) 6 Ungaro (Emanuel) 7 Balmain
(Pierre), Lacroix (Christian), Montana
(Claude) 8 Givenchy (Hubert de)
9 Courrèges (André), Lagerfeld (Karl)
12 Saint-Laurent (Yves), Schiaparelli
(Elsa) *German:* 9 Lagerfeld (Karl) *Israeli:*
7 Mizrahi (Isaac) *Italian:* 5 Pucci
(Emilio), Ricci (Nina) 6 Armani (Giorgio) 7 Cassini (Oleg), Versace (Gianni)
12 Schiaparelli (Elsa) *Japanese:*
6 Miyake (Issey) *Spanish:* 10 Balenciaga
(Cristóbal)

fast 3 set 4 diet, easy, firm, Lent, soon,
sure, true, wild 5 fixed, fleet, hasty,
hitch, loose, loyal, quick, rapid, swift
6 firmly, prompt, snappy, speedy, stable
7 abstain, hastily, hurried, lasting,
quickly, rapidly, staunch, swiftly
8 chop-chop, constant, faithful, full tilt,
immobile, promptly, resolute, speedily

9 breakneck, dissolute, immovable, libertine **10** abstinence, profligate, recklessly, stationary **11** expeditious, promiscuous **12** lickety-split **13** expeditiously

fasten 3 fix, peg, pin, set, sew, tie, zip **4** bind, bolt, clip, hook, join, lace, lash, link, lock, moor, nail, seal, shut, weld **5** affix, cable, catch, chain, cinch, clamp, clasp, close, cramp, dowel, girth, hitch, latch, rivet, screw, stake, stick, strap, tie up, truss **6** anchor, attach, batten, buckle, button, couple, secure, skewer, solder, staple, tether **7** connect, mortise **8** buckle up

fastener 3 nut, peg, pin, tie **4** bolt, brad, clip, cord, frog, hasp, link, lock, nail, rope, snap, stud, tack, tape **5** catch, clamp, clasp, dowel, girth, hinge, hitch, latch, rivet, screw, spike, stake, strap **6** buckle, button, cotter, skewer, staple, tether, toggle, zipper **7** grommet, padlock, netsuke, shackle **8** coupling, cuff link, handcuff, seat belt, shoelace **9** connector, cotter pin, safety pin, thumbtack **10** clothespin

fastidious 5 fussy, picky **6** choosy, dainty, queasy **7** choosey, finical, finicky, refined **8** exacting **9** demanding, squeamish **10** meticulous, particular, pernickety **11** persnickety

fastness 4 fort, hold, keep **6** bunker, castle, refuge **7** alcazar, bastion, citadel, crannog, redoubt, sanctum **8** casemate, fortress, presidio **10** stronghold, tower house **11** strongpoint

fast-talking 4 glib **5** slick **6** facile **8** slippery **13** silver-tongued

fat 3 big, oil **4** flab, lard, suet, wide **5** beefy, broad, bulky, burly, cream, dumpy, gross, heavy, husky, large, lipid, obese, plump, pudgy, round, stout, thick, tubby **6** chunky, excess, fleshy, grease, portly, rotund, stocky, stubby, tallow **7** adipose, blubber, paunchy, porcine, surfeit, surplus, weighty **8** heavyset, oversize, thickset **9** corpulent **10** full-bodied, overweight, potbellied **11** superfluity

fatal 6 deadly, lethal, mortal **7** deathly, ruinous **8** terminal **9** incurable, pestilent **10** pernicious **12** pestilential

fatality 4 doom **5** death **8** casualty **10** deadliness

fata morgana 6 mirage **8** illusion

fat cat 5 mogul, nabob **6** big gun, bigwig, tycoon **7** big shot, magnate, pooh-bah **8** big wheel **9** moneybags, plutocrat **11** muckety-muck **13** high-muck-a-muck

fate 3 end, lot **4** doom, luck, ruin

5 death, karma **6** chance, kismet, upshot **7** destiny, fortune, outcome, portion **13** inevitability

fateful 6 deadly **7** ominous, ruinous **8** decisive **9** momentous, prophetic **10** portentous

Fates see at GREEK; NORSE; ROMAN

fathead 3 ass, oaf **4** boob, clod, dodo, dope, dolt, gawk, goof, goon, jerk, lump, mutt, yo-yo **5** cluck, clunk, dummy, dunce, idiot, moron, stock, stupe, yahoo **6** cretin, dimwit, donkey, doofus, dum-dum, nitwit, noodle, schlub, turkey **7** buffoon, dullard, jackass, schnook **8** dumbbell, imbecile, numskull **9** birdbrain, ignoramus, lamebrain, numbskull, simpleton

fatheaded 4 dull, dumb **5** dense, dopey, thick **6** obtuse, simple, stupid **7** doltish, idiotic **8** gormless **9** brainless, dimwitted, imbecilic **10** numskulled **11** numbskulled, thick-witted

father 3 dad, pop **4** dada, papa, père, sire **5** beget, breed, daddy, hatch, padre, pappy, pater, poppa, spawn **6** author, create, old man, parent, priest **7** builder, creator, founder, produce **8** ancestor, engender, generate, inventor, producer **9** architect, initiator, originate, patriarch, procreate **10** originator, prime mover *combining form:* **4** patr **5** patri, patro

Father Brown creator 10 Chesterton (Gilbert Keith)

fatherland 4 home, soil **7** country

Father Time's implement 6 scythe

fathom 4 know **5** probe, sound **7** discern, explore, measure **9** apprehend, figure out, penetrate **10** comprehend, understand **11** investigate

fathomless 7 abysmal, abyssal **8** profound **12** immeasurable

fatidic 5 vatic **6** mantic **7** Delphic, sibylic **8** Delphian, oracular, sibyllic **9** prophetic, prescient, sibylline, vaticinal **10** divinatory, predictive

fatigue 3 fag **4** poop, tire, wear **5** drain, weary **6** tucker **7** deplete, burn out, exhaust, frazzle, wear out **8** drudgery, wear down **9** tiredness, weariness **10** enervation, exhaustion *combat:* **7** frazzle **10** shell shock

Fatima *father:* **8** Mohammed, Muhammad *husband:* **9** Bluebeard *son:* **5** Hasan **6** Husayn *stepbrother:* **3** Ali

fatness 7 obesity **9** adiposity **10** corpulence, overweight

fatty 4 oily, rich **6** greasy **7** adipose **8** unctuous **10** oleaginous *combining form:* **4** lipo **5** adipo

fatuous 4 dumb, fond **5** inane, sappy,

silly 6 jejune, simple 7 asinine, foolish, puerile, witless

faucet 3 tap 4 bung, cock, gate 5 valve 6 spigot 7 hydrant, petcock 8 stopcock

Faulkner, William *character:* 3 Ike (Snopes), Joe (Christmas) 4 Eula (Varner Snopes), Flem (Snopes), Mink (Snopes) 5 Benjy (Compson), Caddy (Compson), Gavin (Stevens), Henry (Sutpen), Jason (Compson), Lucas (Beauchamp) 6 Dilsey, Temple (Drake) 7 Candace (Compson), Quentin (Compson) 8 Benjamin (Compson) *county:* 13 Yoknapatawpha *family:* 6 Benbow, Snopes, Sutpen 7 Compson 8 McCaslin, Sartoris 9 Beauchamp *novel:* 4 Town (The) 6 Hamlet (The) 7 Mansion (The), Reivers (The) 8 Sartoris 9 Sanctuary, Wild Palms (The) 11 As I Lay Dying 13 Light in August 14 Absalom, Absalom 15 Sound and the Fury (The) 17 Intruder in the Dust

fault 3 err, nag, sin 4 flaw, rift, slip, spot, vice, want 5 blame, break, knock, error, scold 6 accuse, defect, foible, miscue 7 censure, demerit, failing, fissure, frailty, mistake, upbraid 8 fracture, weakness 9 criticize, infirmity 10 San Andreas 11 culpability, dereliction, shortcoming 12 imperfection *line:* 4 rift 5 split 6 breach 7 fissure 8 crevasse

faultfinder 4 crab 5 grump 6 critic, griper, grouch, nagger, whiner 7 grouser 8 grumbler 10 bellyacher, complainer, criticizer, crosspatch

faultfinding 7 carping 8 captious, critical, nitpicky 9 criticism 10 censorious, nit-picking, pernickety 11 persnickety 12 overcritical 13 hypercritical

faultless 4 pure 7 perfect 8 innocent, unerring 9 guiltless 10 immaculate, impeccable, inculpable

faulty 4 awry 5 amiss, wrong 6 flawed, marred 7 botched, damaged, defaced, inexact, unsound 8 fallible, specious 9 blemished, defective, deficient, erroneous, imperfect, incorrect 10 fallacious, inaccurate *prefix:* 3 dys

faun 5 satyr

fauna 7 animals

Faunus *grandfather:* 6 Saturn *son:* 4 Acis 7 Latinus

Faust *author:* 6 Goethe (Johann Wolfgang von) *beloved:* 8 Gretchen *composer:* 6 Gounod (Charles)

faux 4 fake, sham 5 bogus, false, phony 6 ersatz 9 imitation, pretended, simulated, synthetic 10 substitute

faux pas 4 flub, goof, slip 5 boner, error, gaffe 6 boo-boo, howler, miscue, slipup 7 blooper, blunder, misstep, mistake, stumble 8 pratfall, solecism 9 gaucherie 11 impropriety

favor 4 baby, back, bias, boon, gift, okay 5 bless, bribe, grace, mercy, token, value 6 accept, behalf, choose, oblige, pamper, prefer, regard 7 indulge, present, support, sustain 8 courtesy, goodwill, interest, keepsake, kindness, resemble, sanction, sympathy 9 attention, patronage, privilege, take after 10 admiration, facilitate, indulgence, partiality 11 approbation, benevolence, countenance

favorable 4 fair 5 lucky 6 benign, biased, golden, timely, toward, useful 7 helpful, partial 8 pleasant, pleasing, positive 9 agreeable, benignant, fortunate, promising 10 auspicious, benevolent, propitious, prosperous 11 affirmative 12 advantageous 13 complimentary

favoring 4 rosy 6 timely, toward, useful 7 helpful 9 opportune 10 auspicious, beneficial, propitious 12 advantageous *prefix:* 3 pro

favorite 3 pet 7 dearest, popular, special 8 precious 9 preferred, well-liked 10 fair-haired, preference 11 front-runner, teacher's pet, white-haired

favoritism 4 bias 8 cronyism, nepotism 10 partiality 12 one-sidedness

fawn 3 kid 4 deer, ecru 5 beige, toady 6 bister, grovel, kowtow 7 flatter, truckle, wheedle 8 blandish, bootlick 9 sweet-talk 11 apple-polish

fawning 6 smarmy 8 unctuous 9 parasitic 10 obsequious 11 sycophantic

fay 3 elf 4 puck 5 elfin, fairy, pixie 6 elfish, goblin, sprite 7 brownie 10 leprechaun

faze 3 cow 5 abash, daunt, throw 6 dismay, rattle 7 confuse, disturb, nonplus, perturb 8 befuddle, bewilder, confound, unsettle 9 discomfit, dumbfound, embarrass 10 disconcert 11 flabbergast

FBI director 5 Freeh (Louis) 6 Hoover (J. Edgar) 7 Mueller (Robert)

fealty 5 faith, troth 7 loyalty 8 devotion, fidelity 9 adherence, constancy, vassalage 10 allegiance, attachment 11 devotedness 12 faithfulness

fear 3 awe 5 alarm, angst, dread, panic, qualm, scare, worry 6 dismay, fright, horror, phobia, terror 7 anxiety, jitters 8 cold feet, disquiet, timidity 9 agitation, cowardice, misgiving 10 foreboding 11 disquietude, trepidation 12 apprehension, cowardliness, perturbation, presentiment, timorousness *of animals:* 9 zoophobia *of being buried*

alive: 11 taphephobia **of cats:** 12 ailuro-phobia **of crowds:** 11 ochlophobia **of darkness:** 11 nyctophobia **of dirt:** 10 mysophobia **of fire:** 10 pyrophobia **of heights:** 10 acrophobia **of men:** 11 androphobia **of new things:** 9 neo-phobia **of open areas:** 11 agoraphobia **of pain:** 10 algophobia **of strangers:** 10 xenophobia **of thunder:** 12 bronto-phobia **of water:** 11 hydrophobia **of women:** 10 gynophobia

fearful 5 timid 6 afraid, aghast, scared, trepid 7 alarmed, anxious, jittery, pan-icky 8 alarmist, paranoid, timorous 9 terrified, tremulous 12 apprehensive

fearless 4 bold 5 brave 6 daring 7 gal-lant, valiant 8 intrepid, unafraid 9 dauntless 10 courageous 11 lionheart-ed 12 greathearted, stouthearted

Fear of Flying author 4 Jong (Erica)

fearsome 3 shy 5 scary, timid 6 afraid 7 extreme, intense 8 daunting, timorous 9 frightful 10 terrifying 11 frightening 12 intimidating

feasible 6 doable, likely, viable 8 possi-ble, suitable, workable 10 reasonable 11 practicable 12 tried-and-true

feast 3 eat 4 dine, meal 5 gorge 6 dinner, regale, repast, spread 7 banquet, indulge 8 potlatch **Hawaiian:** 4 luau **Scottish:** 3 foy

Feast of Lights 8 Hanukkah

Feast of Lots 5 Purim

Feast of Tabernacles 6 Sukkot 7 Sukkoth

feat 3 act 4 deed, gest 5 stunt, trick 6 action 7 exploit 11 achievement, per-formance, tour de force

feather 3 ilk 4 down, kind, sort, type 5 breed, order, pinna, plume, quill 6 fledge, fletch, pinion 7 species, vari-ety **kind:** 4 down 6 covert 7 contour, plumule, rectrix 8 scapular **part:** 3 web 4 barb, vane 5 shaft 7 barbule, calamus 8 barbicel

featherbrained 5 dizzy, giddy, silly 7 flighty, foolish 8 heedless 9 frivolous 11 light-headed, thoughtless

feathered 7 plumose

feathers 4 down 7 plumage

feature 4 item, mark, part 5 add-on, trait 6 aspect, detail, factor 7 article, ele-ment, fixture, gimmick, quality 8 hall-mark, property 9 attribute, component, lineament 10 attraction, ingredient 11 drawing card, peculiarity

febrile 3 hot 5 fiery 7 fevered, pyretic 8 feverish

feckless 4 weak 7 useless 8 carefree, impotent 11 incompetent, ineffective,

ineffectual 12 undependable 13 irre-sponsible

fecund 4 rich 7 fertile 8 fruitful, prolific 9 inventive 10 productive

fecundity 9 abundance, fertility 11 prod-igality 12 fruitfulness, productivity

Federalist writer 3 Jay (John) 7 Madison (James) 8 Hamilton (Alexander)

federation 5 union 6 league, nation 7 council 8 alliance 10 government 11 confederacy

fed up 4 sick 9 disgusted 11 exasperated

fee 3 cut, pay, tax 4 bill, cost, dues, hire, toll, wage 5 price 6 charge 7 expense, payment, rake-off, stipend, tuition 8 retainer 9 emolument 10 commission, recompense **minting:** 10 seignorage 11 seigniorage **wharf:** 7 quayage

feeble 4 puny, weak 5 frail 6 infirm, sickly, weakly 7 doddery 8 decrepit 9 doddering, unhealthy 10 inadequate

feebleminded 4 daft, dull, slow 5 dense, thick 6 stupid 7 doltish, foolish, idiotic, moronic, witless 8 imbecile, retarded 9 brainless, dim-witted, imbecilic 10 half-witted, slow-witted 11 hare-brained, thickheaded

feebleness 7 frailty 8 debility 9 fragility, infirmity 10 enervation, inadequacy 11 decrepitude

feed 3 eat 4 grub, hand, meal 5 feast, gorge, graze, stuff 6 browse, devour, fatten, fodder, ingest, regale, repast, supply, viands 7 banquet, consume, deliver, dish out, edibles, furnish, nour-ish, nurture, provide, sustain 8 dis-pense, hand over, victuals 9 partake of, provender, provision, refection 10 pro-visions

feedback 8 critique, reaction, response 9 criticism 10 evaluation

feed the kitty 4 ante

feel 5 grope, sense, touch 6 caress, fon-dle, handle, stroke 7 palpate

feeler 4 palp 5 probe 6 palpus 7 antenna 8 proposal, tentacle 12 trial balloon

feeling 3 air 4 aura, mood 5 hunch, sense, touch 6 notion, temper 7 emo-tion, inkling, opinion, outlook, passion, sensate 8 attitude, instinct, sentient 9 affection, emotional, intuition, sem-blance, sensation, sentiment, suspicion 10 atmosphere, impression, persuasion 11 affectivity, palpability, sensibility, sensitivity, tangibility

feign 3 act 4 fake, play, sham 5 bluff, put on 6 affect, assume 7 pretend 8 simu-late 9 dissemble 11 counterfeit, make believe

feigned 4 fake, sham 5 false, phony, put-on 7 assumed 8 imagined 9 imitation,

insincere, pretended, simulated 10 fabricated, fictitious 11 counterfeit
feint 4 fake, hoax, play, ploy, ruse, sham,
wile 5 trick 6 gambit 8 maneuver
9 stratagem *hockey:* 4 deke
feisty 6 frisky, plucky, spunky, touchy
7 bristly, fidgety 8 petulant, snappish,
spirited 9 fractious, irascible 10 aggressive 11 quarrelsome
feldspar 6 albite 8 andesine 9 anorthite,
moonstone 10 microcline, orthoclase
11 plagioclase *clay:* 6 kaolin
felicitate 6 salute 7 commend 10 compliment 12 congratulate
felicitous 3 apt, fit 4 meet 5 happy
6 proper, timely 7 apropos, fitting
8 apposite, pleasant, suitable 9 agreeable 10 delightful 11 appropriate
feline 3 cat, sly, tom 4 lion, lynx, pard,
puma, puss 5 catty, felid, pussy, sleek,
tiger 6 bobcat, cougar, jaguar, margay,
ocelot, serval, slinky, sneaky, tomcat
7 caracal, catlike, cheetah, furtive, leonine, leopard, lioness, panther, tigress,
wildcat 8 pussycat, stealthy *hybrid:*
5 liger, tigon 6 tiglon
fell 3 cut, hew, mow 4 down, drop, kill,
raze 5 floor 6 poleax 7 cut down, flatten 8 knock off 9 bring down,
knock down
Fellini film 8 Amarcord, Casanova, La
Strada 9 Satyricon 10 I Vitelloni 11 La
Dolce Vita 15 Nights of Cabiria 18 Juliet of the Spirits
fellow 3 bub, guy, joe, lad, man 4 buck,
chap, dude, gent, mate, peer, twin
5 bloke, match 6 codger, cohort, hombre, person 7 comrade, consort, partner 8 confrere 9 associate, companion,
copartner, gentleman 10 coordinate,
reciprocal
fellow feeling 5 agape 7 concern, empathy, rapport 8 affinity, kindness, sympathy 9 affection 10 compassion, kindliness 11 consolation 13 understanding
fellowship 4 club 5 guild 6 league
7 coterie, society, stipend 8 sodality
9 communion, community 10 fraternity
11 association, brotherhood
felon 3 con 7 convict, whitlow 8 criminal
10 malefactor
felt 6 groped, sensed
felt hat 3 fez 5 derby, terai 6 fedora, trilby 7 homburg, stetson 8 snap-brim
9 wideawake
female 4 girl 5 woman 7 girlish, woman-
ly 8 feminine *suffix:* 3 ess 4 ette, trix
Feminine Mystique author 7 Friedan
(Betty)
feminist 10 suffragist
femme fatale 5 siren 7 Lorelei 8 Mata

Hari 9 temptress 10 seductress
11 enchantress
femur 9 thighbone
fen 3 bog 4 mire, quag, wash 5 marsh,
swamp 6 morass, muskeg, slough
9 marshland
fence 3 bar, pen 4 cage, rail, pale, weir
5 hedge, parry 6 corral, paling, picket
7 barrier, enclose, railing 8 backstop,
boundary, hoarding, palisade, receiver,
sidestep, stockade 9 barricade,
stone wall
fencer 7 duelist, épéeist 8 foilsman
9 swordsman
fencing 9 swordplay *attack:* 5 lunge
6 thrust 7 reprise, riposte *cry:* 6 touché
defense: 5 parry *movement:* 4 volt *term:*
4 jury 5 forte, lunge 6 flèche, foible,
touché *touch:* 3 cut, hit *weapon:* 4 épée,
foil 5 blade, guard, saber, sabre 6 pommel
fender 4 skid 5 guard 6 buffer, bumper,
shield 7 cushion, railing 8 mudguard
fennec 3 fox
Fenrir *chain:* 8 Gleipnir *father:* 4 Loki
form: 4 wolf *mother:* 9 Angerboda
10 Angerbotha *slayer:* 5 Vidar 6 Vithar
victim: 4 Odin
Fenway Park site 6 Boston
feral 4 wild 5 brute 6 brutal, savage
7 beastly, bestial, brutish, inhuman,
untamed
Ferber novel 5 Giant, So Big 8 Cimarron, Show Boat 9 Ice Palace 13 Saratoga Trunk
Ferdinand *beloved:* 7 Miranda *father:*
6 Alonso
Ferdinand, King *conquest:* 7 Granada
daughter: 6 Joanna *wife:* 8 Germaine,
Isabella
fermata 4 hold 5 pause
ferment 4 boil, brew, stir 5 rouse, sweat
6 clamor, enzyme, excite, incite, leav-
en, seethe, simmer, unrest, work up
7 smolder, turmoil 9 agitation, commotion 12 restlessness
fermentation 7 zymosis 13 bioconversion
fern 4 tree 5 brake, holly, royal 6 Boston
7 bracken 8 polypody 10 maidenhair,
spleenwort *leaf:* 5 frond
ferocious 4 fell, grim, wild 5 brute, cruel
6 brutal, fierce, savage 7 bestial,
extreme, inhuman, intense, vicious,
violent 8 barbaric, inhumane, ruthless
9 barbarous, rapacious, truculent
ferret out 4 find 5 dig up, flush 6 elicit
7 unearth 8 discover 9 ascertain
ferrule 3 cap, tip 4 band, ring, virl 6 collet
ferry 5 carry 6 convey 7 shuttle 9 transport

ferryman 6 Charon 9 gondolier

fertile 4 lush, rich 6 fecund 8 abundant, creative, fruitful, pregnant, prolific 9 bountiful, ingenious, inventive, luxuriant, plenteous 10 productive 12 reproductive

fertilize 5 beget, breed 6 enrich 8 generate 9 fecundate, pollinate 10 impregnate, inseminate

fertilizer 4 dung 5 guano, mulch 6 manure 7 compost 9 plant food

ferule 3 rod 5 stick

fervent 3 hot 4 keen 5 eager, fiery 6 ardent, devout, gung-ho 7 blazing, burning, earnest, glowing, intense, zealous 8 vehement 9 heartfelt 10 hot-blooded, passionate 11 impassioned, warm-blooded 12 enthusiastic, wholehearted

fervor 4 fire, heat, zeal 5 ardor 6 warmth 7 passion 8 devotion, violence 9 vehemence 10 devoutness, enthusiasm

fescennine 7 obscene 10 scurrilous

fess up 3 own 5 admit 9 come clean

fester 3 rot 6 rankle 7 inflame, putrefy 8 ulcerate 9 suppurate

festina ___ 5 lente

festival 4 fair, fete, gala 5 feast 6 fiesta 7 jubilee 8 carnival, jamboree 11 celebration, merrymaking

festive 3 gay 4 gala 5 jolly, merry 6 joyful, joyous 7 gleeful 8 mirthful 11 celebratory

festivity 4 bash, fair, fete, gala 5 feast, party, revel 6 affair, frolic, gaiety 7 blowout, revelry, whoopee 8 carnival, jamboree 9 rejoicing, merriment 11 celebration, merrymaking

festoon 4 deck, hang 5 adorn 6 bedeck 7 garland 8 decorate, ornament 9 embellish

fetch 3 get 4 draw, earn 5 bring, yield 6 take in 7 attract, bring in, realize 8 retrieve

fetching 4 fair 6 comely, lovely, pretty 7 winsome 8 alluring, charming, enticing, engaging, handsome, pleasing 9 appealing 10 attractive

fete 4 ball, bash, fair, gala 5 feast, honor, party 6 affair, fiesta, soiree 7 banquet, jubilee, shindig 8 carnival, festival, jamboree, winging 9 celebrate, entertain 11 celebration, commemorate 13 entertainment

fetid 4 foul, high, rank 5 funky 6 putrid, rancid, smelly, strong 8 mephitic, stinking 10 malodorous

fetish 4 idol, juju, luck 5 charm 6 amulet 7 periapt 8 fixation, gris-gris, talisman 10 phylactery

fetor 4 odor, reek 5 stink 6 stench

fetter 3 tie 4 bind, bond, gyve 5 chain, check, irons 6 hobble, hog-tie, impede 7 enchain, manacle, shackle, trammel 8 handcuff, restrain 9 restraint

fettle 5 shape 6 health 7 fitness 9 condition 12 constitution

feud 6 enmity, strife 7 dispute, quarrel 8 argument, vendetta 9 hostility 11 controversy

feudal *estate:* 3 fee 4 feud, fief *jurisdiction:* 4 soke *laborer:* 4 serf *lord:* 5 laird, liege, thane 8 suzerain *status:* 9 vassalage *tax:* 7 tallage *tenant:* 6 vassal 7 homager, socager, vavasor 8 vavasour *tenure of land:* 6 socage *tribute:* 6 heriot

feuilleton 5 essay

fever 4 ague, fire, heat 5 flush, Lassa 6 dengue, frenzy 7 ferment, passion, pyrexia 8 delirium 9 calenture *recurrent:* 7 malaria, quartan, tertian

fevered 6 crazed, heated 7 burning, febrile, flushed 8 agitated, frenetic, restless 9 delirious 10 distracted, overheated 11 overwrought

feverish 3 hot 5 fiery 6 hectic 7 burning, febrile, flushed, pyretic 8 frenetic, frenzied 10 passionate 11 overwrought

fever tree 6 acacia 7 blue gum

few 4 rare 5 scant 6 meager, meagre, scanty, scarce, sparse 7 handful, limited 8 sporadic 9 scattered 10 infrequent, occasional, scattering, smattering, spattering, sprinkling *combining form:* 4 olig 5 oligo

fey 4 daft 5 campy, crazy, vatic 7 touched 8 oracular, precious 9 pixilated, prophetic, sibylline, visionary 11 clairvoyant 12 otherworldly

___-fi 3 sci

fiasco 3 dud 4 bomb, flop 5 farce, flask 6 bottle, defeat 7 blunder, debacle, failure, washout 8 abortion, disaster 11 miscarriage 13 embarrassment

fiat 5 edict, order 6 decree 7 command, dictate, mandate, warrant 8 sanction 11 endorsement 12 proclamation 13 authorization

fib 3 lie 4 tale 5 story 7 falsify, falsity, untruth 9 falsehood, mendacity 10 taradiddle 11 fabrication, prevaricate

fiber 3 web 4 noil, pita 5 grain, istle 6 fabric, strand, thread 7 texture *basketry:* 5 istle *brain:* 4 pons *coarse:* 4 jute 8 piassava *coconut husk:* 4 coir *rope:* 4 bast, hemp 5 sisal 8 henequen *silky:* 5 kapok *small:* 6 fibril *substructure:* 7 micelle, spongin *synthetic:* 5 nylon, Orlon, rayon, saran, vinal 6 Dacron 7 spandex *woody:* 4 bast *woollike:* 7 lanital

fibrous 4 ropy, wiry **5** tough, woody **6** sinewy **7** stringy

fibula 4 bone **5** clasp

fichu 5 scarf

fickle 7 flighty **8** unstable, variable, volatile **9** mercurial **10** capricious, changeable, inconstant, unfaithful, unreliable **12** undependable **13** temperamental, unpredictable

fiction 4 tale, yarn **5** fable, story **7** fantasy, figment **8** pretense **9** fish story, invention, narrative **10** concoction **11** fabrication

fictional 6 made-up, unreal **8** notional **9** imaginary **11** make-believe **12** suppositious

fictitious 4 fake, mock, sham **5** bogus, faked, false, phony **6** ersatz, made-up, unreal, untrue **7** assumed, created **8** cooked-up, fanciful, illusory, imagined, invented, mythical, spurious **9** concocted, fantastic, imaginary, simulated, trumped-up **10** apocryphal, artificial, chimerical, fabricated **11** make-believe **12** suppositious

fiddle 3 toy **4** play, rack **5** alter, cheat **6** dawdle, diddle, doodle, finger, meddle, monkey, potter, putter, tamper, tinker, trifle, violin **7** swindle **9** interfere **10** fool around, manipulate, mess around

fiddle-faddle 3 rot **4** bosh, bull, bunk, nuts **5** fudge, drool, hokum, hooey **6** bunkum, drivel, hoodoo, humbug, piffle **7** baloney, blarney, hogwash, rubbish, twaddle **8** nonsense, pishposh, tommyrot **9** poppycock **10** applesauce, balderdash, flapdoodle

_____ **Fideles 6** Adeste, Semper

Fidelio *composer:* **9** Beethoven (Ludwig van) *hero:* **9** Florestan *heroine:* **7** Leonora

fidelity 5 ardor, piety, troth **6** fealty **7** loyalty **8** devotion **9** adherence, constancy **10** allegiance, attachment **11** staunchness **12** faithfulness **13** dependability, steadfastness

fidget 6 fantod, fiddle, jitter, squirm, twitch **7** wriggle

fidgety 5 antsy, jumpy **6** uneasy **7** jittery, nervous, restive, squirmy, twitchy **8** restless

field 3 lea **4** area, mead, turf **5** green, milpa, orbit, range **6** domain, meadow, métier, region, sphere **7** demesne, pasture, purview, terrain **8** dominion, gridiron, precinct, vocation **9** bailiwick, champaign, specialty, territory **10** department, discipline, occupation

field crop 3 hay **4** corn, oats **5** grain, wheat **6** cotton **7** alfalfa **8** soybeans

field deity 3 Pan **4** Faun **5** Fauna **6** Faunus

field glasses 10 binoculars

field hand 4 hoer **5** sower **6** picker **7** laborer, planter

Fielding novel 6 Amelia **8** Tom Jones **13** Joseph Andrews

field marshal *Austrian:* **8** Radetzky (Joseph) *British:* **6** Napier (Robert), Raglan (Baron), Wavell (Archibald), Wilson (Henry) **7** Roberts (Frederick) **8** Wolseley (Garnet) **9** Kitchener (Horatio) **10** Montgomery (Bernard) *French:* **4** Foch (Ferdinand) **6** Joffre (Joseph-Jacques-Césaire), Pétain (Philippe) *German:* **6** Keitel (Wilhelm), Paulus (Friedrich), Rommel (Erwin), Rupert (Prince) **9** Mackensen (August von), Rundstedt (Karl von), Waldersee (Alfred von) **10** Kesselring (Albert) *Japanese:* **8** Sugiyama (Hajime) *Prussian:* **6** Moltke (Helmuth von) *Russian:* **7** Kutuzov (Mikhail), Suvorov (Aleksandr) **8** Potemkin (Grigory)

field mouse 4 vole

field officer 5 major **7** colonel

fiend 3 bug, imp, nut **5** demon, devil, freak, Satan **6** addict, Belial, diablo, maniac, zealot **7** devotee, fanatic, habitué, Lucifer, monster, Old Nick, serpent **8** Apollyon, succubus **9** Beelzebub **10** enthusiast, Old Scratch **13** Old Gooseberry

fiendish 3 bad **4** evil **5** cruel **6** malign, savage, wicked **7** baleful, demonic, hellish, inhuman, malefic, satanic, vicious **8** demoniac, devilish, diabolic, infernal, sinister **9** barbarous, difficult, ferocious, malicious, malignant **10** diabolical

fierce 4 fell, grim, wild **5** cruel **6** brutal, savage, wicked **7** brutish, hostile, inhuman, intense, vicious, violent, wolfish **8** inhumane, pitiless, ruthless, terrible, vehement **9** barbarous, bellicose, ferocious, merciless, truculent **10** aggressive, determined

fiery 3 hot, red **5** afire **6** ablaze, aflame, ardent, fervid, fierce, heated, red-hot, torrid **7** burning, febrile, fervent, flaming, flaring, igneous, intense, peppery **8** broiling, feverish, spirited, vehement, white-hot **9** flammable, hotheaded, irritable, perfervid **10** mettlesome, passionate **11** combustible, inflammable, impassioned

fiesta 4 fete **5** party **6** frolic **8** carnival, festival, jamboree **9** merriment

fife 4 pipe **5** flute

fifth *combining form:* **5** quint

fig *genus:* 5 Ficus *sacred:* 5 pipal *variety:* 5 elemi 6 Smyrna

fight 3 row, war 4 bout, buck, duel, feud, fray, spat, tiff 5 brawl, broil, clash, joust, match, melee, repel, scrap, set-to 6 affray, attack, battle, combat, fracas, oppose, oppugn, resist, rumble, tussle 7 contend, contest, dispute, quarrel, scuffle, wrangle, wrestle 8 conflict, skirmish, slugfest, squabble, struggle, traverse 10 aggression, donnybrook, free-for-all 11 altercation

fighter 3 pug 5 boxer 7 brawler, soldier, warrior 8 champion, pugilist, scrapper 9 combatant, gladiator, man-at-arms, mercenary 11 interceptor

fighter plane 3 MiG, Roc 4 Zero 5 Sabre 6 bomber, Fokker, Hawker, Mirage, Voodoo 7 Corsair, Harrier 8 Spitfire 11 interceptor

fighting fish 5 betta

figment 5 dream, fable, fancy 7 chimera, fiction 8 daydream, illusion, phantasm 9 invention, unreality 11 contrivance, fabrication

figure 3 add, sum, tot 4 cast, form, mold, rule, tote 5 count, digit, frame, image, model, motif, shape, total 6 cipher, decide, design, device, effigy, motive, number, reckon, settle, symbol 7 compute, integer, numeral, outline, pattern, resolve 8 conclude, estimate, physique 9 calculate, character, determine, enumerate *geometric:* 4 cone, cube 5 rhomb 6 circle, isogon, square 7 decagon, ellipse, hexagon, nonagon, octagon, polygon, rhombus 8 pentacle, pentagon, rhomboid, tetragon, triangle 9 rectangle 10 hexahedron, octahedron 11 icosahedron 12 dodecahedron, rhombohedron *human:* 4 nude 5 atlas 7 telamon 8 caryatid *ornamental:* 6 statue 8 gargoyle

figurehead 4 pawn, tool 5 front 6 minion, puppet 7 cat's-paw 8 creature 10 instrument, mouthpiece

figure of speech 5 trope 6 aporia, simile 7 litotes 8 metaphor, metonymy 10 synecdoche

figure out 5 crack, learn, solve 6 decide, decode, fathom 7 resolve, unravel 8 decipher, discover, unriddle 9 ascertain, determine

figure skating *jump:* 4 axel, loop, lutz 5 split 6 rocker 7 bracket, counter, salchow 11 spreadeagle *spin:* 5 camel

figurine 9 statuette

Fiji *capital:* 4 Suva *explorer:* 4 Cook (Capt. James) 6 Tasman (Abel) *island:* 3 Gau 4 Koro 6 Ovalau 8 Viti Levu 9 Vanua Levu *island group:* 3 Lau

6 Yasawa *language:* 6 Fijian 7 English *monetary unit:* 6 dollar *neighbor:* 5 Samoa 7 Vanuatu

filch 3 cop, nip 4 crib, lift, take 5 boost, pinch, steal, swipe 6 pilfer, snitch 7 purloin

file 3 row, rub 4 line, rank, rasp, tier 5 lodge, march, place, queue 6 smooth 7 archive, arrange, corrupt, dossier 10 emery board

filial 5 sonly 7 duteous, dutiful

filibuster 5 delay, stall 10 adventurer

filigree 4 lace 6 design 7 pattern 8 fretwork, openwork, ornament 10 decoration 13 embellishment, ornamentation

fill 3 jam 4 clog, cloy, cram, glut, heap, lade, load, pack, pile, plug, sate, stop 5 block, choke, close, gorge, stock, stuff 6 charge, stodge 7 congest, engorge, inflate, occlude, pervade, satiate, satisfy, stopper, surfeit 8 permeate *interstices:* 4 calk 5 caulk, chink, putty

filled 5 awash, flush, sated 6 packed 7 replete 9 saturated

filler 5 squib 7 packing, padding, tobacco, wadding 8 stuffing

fillet 4 band 5 slice, snood, strip 6 ribbon, stripe 7 bandeau, banding 8 headband *anatomical:* 9 lemniscus *architectural:* 6 listel, reglet, taenia *meat:* 10 tenderloin

fill in 3 sub 4 clew, clue, post 6 advise, detail, insert, notify 7 apprise 8 acquaint, complete 10 substitute

fill-in 3 sub 4 temp 6 backup 7 stopgap 9 alternate, expedient, makeshift, surrogate, temporary 10 substitute 11 locum tenens, pinch hitter, replacement, succedaneum

fillip 3 tap 4 goad, kick, spur 5 boost, tonic 6 buffet, strike 7 impetus, wrinkle 8 catalyst, stimulus 9 incentive, stimulant, stimulate 10 inducement, motivation 13 embellishment

film 4 coat, scum, show, skim, skin 5 flick, glaze, layer, movie, Mylar, shoot 6 cinema, lamina, patina 7 tarnish 8 membrane, pellicle 9 celluloid, photoplay 11 picture show 13 motion picture, moving picture

filmy 4 hazy 5 gauzy, misty, sheer, wispy 6 dainty 8 delicate, gossamer 10 diaphanous 11 transparent

fils 3 son

filter 4 sift 5 clean, leach, sieve 6 purify, refine, screen, strain 7 clarify, cleanse 9 percolate

filth 4 crud, dirt, dung, muck, slop, smut 5 dreck, grime, slime, trash 6 ordure, refuse, sludge 7 squalor 9 obscenity

filthy 4 base, foul, vile 5 black, dirty,

grimy, gross, gunky, mucky, muddy, nasty **6** coarse, cruddy, grubby, ribald, scuzzy, skanky, smutty, sordid **7** obscene, raunchy, squalid, unclean **8** indecent **9** loathsome, offensive, repulsive, revolting **12** scatological

filthy lucre 4 cash, loot, pelf **5** bread, bucks, dough, money, moola **6** boodle, riches, moolah, wampum **7** cabbage, scratch **8** currency

fin 3 arm **4** bill **5** fiver, pinna **7** airfoil, flipper *type:* **6** caudal, dorsal **7** ventral **8** pectoral

finagle 5 cheat, trick **6** wangle **7** snaffle, swindle, wheedle **8** fast-talk, maneuver, scrounge **9** bamboozle, machinate

final 3 end **4** last **6** ending, latest **7** closing **8** hindmost, terminal, ultimate **10** concluding, conclusive, definitive **11** examination

finale 3 end **4** coda **5** close, finis **6** capper, climax, ending, payoff, windup, wrapup **7** closing **10** conclusion, denouement **11** culmination, termination

finalize 3 end **5** close, sew up, tie up **6** decide, finish, wind up, wrap up **7** approve **8** complete, conclude, solidify **9** terminate **10** consummate

finally 6 at last, lastly **7** someday **8** at length **9** belatedly **10** at long last, eventually, ultimately **12** subsequently

finance 4 back, bank, fund **5** endow, funds, money, stake **6** credit **7** banking, promote, revenue, sponsor, support **8** bankroll **9** grubstake, patronize, subsidize **10** capitalize, investment, underwrite

financial 6 fiscal, pocket **8** business, economic, monetary **9** pecuniary **10** commercial *plan:* **6** budget *statement:* **12** balance sheet

financier *American:* **4** Hill (James Jerome), Ryan (Thomas Fortune), Sage (Russell) **5** Astor (John Jacob), Baker (George Fisher), Eaton (Cyrus), Field (Cyrus West), Gould (Jay), Grace (William Russell), Green (Hetty) **6** Biddle (Nicholas), Boesky (Ivan), Girard (Stephen), Mellon (Andrew), Morgan (John Pierpont, Junius Spencer), Morris (Robert), Rogers (Henry Huttleston), Yerkes (Charles Tyson) **7** Peabody (George) **10** Vanderbilt (Cornelius, William) *British:* **6** Baring (Alexander), Rhodes (Cecil) **7** Gresham (Thomas) *French:* **6** Necker (Jacques) **7** Colbert (Jean-Baptiste) *German:* **7** Schacht (Hjalmar) **10** Rothschild (Amschel, Jakob, Karl, Mayer, Nathan, Salomon)

finch 4 pape **5** junco, serin, zebra **6** canary, linnet, siskin, towhee

7 bunting, chewink, redpoll, sparrow **8** cardinal, grosbeak, longspur **9** crossbill, seedeater

find 3 gem **4** gain, meet, spot **5** catch, dig up, hit on, reach, sight **6** attain, detect, locate, supply, turn up **7** discern, furnish, scare up, uncover, unearth **8** bump into, come upon, discover, meet with, perceive, treasure **9** determine, discovery, encounter **10** experience **13** treasure trove

find out 4 hear **5** catch, learn **6** detect **7** catch on **8** discover, perceive **9** ascertain, determine

fine 3 end, top **4** fair, keen, levy, pure, thin **5** bonny, close, clear, dandy, mulct, sheer **6** amerce, choice, minute, ornate, punish, purify, subtle **7** clarion, damages, elegant, forfeit, penalty **8** all right, delicate, penalize, pleasant, splendid, superior **9** beautiful, enjoyable, excellent, first-rate **10** punishment, reparation

finery 5 array **6** attire **7** apparel, regalia **8** clothing, frippery, glad rags, ornament **9** caparison, full dress, trappings, trimmings **10** decoration, Sunday best

finesse 5 dodge, evade, skill, skirt **6** jockey **7** beguile, cunning, exploit **8** maneuver, subtlety **9** dexterity **10** adroitness, artfulness, manipulate

Fingal's Cave island 6 Staffa

finger 5 blame, digit, index, pinky, strum, touch **6** accuse, pinkie **7** palpate **8** identify, pinpoint *bone:* **7** phalanx *combining form:* **6** dactyl

finicky 5 fussy, picky **6** choosy, dainty, prissy **7** choosey **8** exacting **9** squeamish **10** fastidious, meticulous, particular, pernickety **11** persnickety

finis 3 end **5** close **6** finale **10** completion, conclusion

finish 3 end **4** do in, kill, slay, stop **5** cease, close, glaze, use up **6** cut off, ending, finale, murder, patina, polish, windup, wrap up **7** closing, consume, destroy, execute, exhaust, surface **8** complete, conclude, dispatch, finalize, terminus **9** cessation, liquidate, terminate **10** completion, conclusion, denouement, run through **11** termination *dull:* **3** mat **4** matt **5** matte *second:* **5** place *third:* **4** show

finished 4 done, over, ripe **5** ideal **7** done for, perfect, refined, through **8** achieved, complete, over with, polished, washed-up **9** perfected **10** consummate

finite 5 bound, fixed **7** bounded, limited, precise **9** definable **10** restricted **12** determinable

fink 3 rat **5** Judas **6** betray, snitch, squeal **7** traitor **8** betrayer, informer, quisling, snitcher **11** backstabber **13** strikebreaker

Finland 5 Suomi *Arctic region:* **7** Lapland *capital:* **8** Helsinki *city:* **5** Espoo, Turku **6** Vantaa **7** Tampere *ethnic group:* **4** Lapp, Sami *gulf:* **7** Bothnia *invader:* **9** Alexander *island:* **5** Karlö **6** Kimito **9** Vallgrund *island group:* **5** Åland *lake:* **5** Inari **6** Saimaa **7** Keitele **8** Pielinen *language:* **7** Finnish, Swedish *monetary unit:* **4** euro *monetary unit, former:* **6** markka *neighbor:* **6** Norway, Russia, Sweden

Finlandia composer 8 Sibelius (Jean)

Finnigans Wake author 5 Joyce (James)

Finnish *bath:* **5** sauna *epic:* **8** Kalevala *god:* **6** Jumala

fir 4 pine **6** balsam, Fraser **7** conifer, Douglas **9** evergreen *genus:* **5** Abies

fire 3 can, pep, vim, zip **4** bake, brio, burn, cast, dash, hurl, sack, stir, toss, zeal, zest, zing **5** ardor, blaze, drive, flame, flare, fling, glare, ingle, light, pitch, rouse, salvo, shoot, spark, throw, torch, verve, vigor **6** arouse, energy, excite, fervor, flames, ignite, kindle, spirit **7** animate, boot out, dismiss, enthuse, inferno, inflame, inspire, kick out, passion, provoke **8** enkindle **9** calenture, discharge, holocaust, terminate **10** combustion, enthusiasm, liveliness **13** conflagration *combining form:* **3** pyr **4** igni, pyro *god:* **4** Agni, Loki **6** Vulcan **10** Hephaestus

firearm see GUN

firebrand 8 agitator **10** incendiary, instigator

firebug 5 torch **8** arsonist **10** incendiary, pyromaniac

firecracker 5 squib **6** banger **9** explosive **10** cherry bomb, noisemaker

firedog 7 andiron

firedrake 6 dragon

firefly 12 lightning bug

fire opal 7 girasol

fireplace 5 grate, ingle *equipment:* **6** fender, screen **7** andiron *part:* **3** hob **6** hearth, mantel

fireplug 7 hydrant

fire up 5 anger, annoy, rouse, spark **6** excite, ignite, incite, kindle **7** enliven, inflame, inspire, provoke **8** enkindle, irritate

firework 6 petard, rocket **8** pinwheel, sparkler **11** pyrotechnic, Roman candle *cluster:* **9** girandole

firkin 3 keg, tun, vat **4** butt, cask, pipe **6** barrel, vessel **8** hogshead

firm 3 set **4** fast, hard, sure **5** fixed, rigid, solid, sound, stiff, tight, tough **6** harden, outfit, secure, settle, stable, steady, strong, sturdy **7** abiding, adamant, certain, company, concern, improve, settled, staunch, unmoved **8** business, constant, definite, enduring, faithful, resolute, specific, vigorous **9** steadfast, tenacious **10** determined, enterprise, inflexible, stipulated, strengthen, unwavering, unyielding **11** established, partnership, substantial, unfaltering, well-founded **13** establishment

firmament 3 sky **5** vault **6** sphere, welkin **7** expanse, heavens **8** empyrean

firmness 7 resolve **8** decision, security, solidity, strength, tenacity **9** constancy, stability **10** durability, resolution **13** determination

first 4 arch, head **5** alpha, chief, prime **6** maiden, primal **7** highest, initial, leading, lead-off, opening, pioneer, premier, primary, supreme **8** champion, dominant, earliest, foremost, headmost, original **9** inaugural, initially, paramount, principal, sovereign **10** aboriginal, preeminent, primordial *prefix:* **4** prot **5** proto

firstborn 4 heir **6** eldest, oldest

first-class 3 top **5** A-one, best, fine **5** prime **6** tip-top **7** capital, supreme **8** five-star, superior, top-notch **9** excellent, top-drawer

firsthand 6 direct **7** primary **9** immediate

first man in space 7 Gagarin (Yury)

first showing 5 debut **7** opening **8** premiere

First State 8 Delaware

firth 3 arm, bay **4** cove, gulf **5** inlet **6** harbor, slough **7** estuary

fiscal 8 monetary **9** budgetary, financial

fish 3 bob, net **4** cast, gill, hint **5** angle, seine, trawl, troll **7** gillnet, sniggle *angler:* **9** goosefish *aquarium:* **4** barb **5** betta, danio, guppy, platy, tetra **7** cichlid, gourami, rasbora **8** goldfish **9** angelfish *basket:* **5** creel *catfish:* **8** bullhead, hornpout *cod:* **4** cusk, hake, ling **6** burbot, tomcod **7** pollack, pollock *combining form:* **6** ichthy *croaker:* **4** drum **7** corbina **8** kingfish, sea trout, weakfish **10** squeteague *eellike:* **5** moray **6** conger **7** hagfish, lamprey *eggs:* **3** roe **5** spawn *electric:* **7** torpedo **9** stargazer *flatfish:* **3** dab **4** butt, dace, sole **5** bream, brill, fluke **6** plaice, turbot **7** halibut **8** flounder *food:* **3** cod, eel **4** bass, carp, cero, hake, ling, scup, shad, sole, tuna **5** jurel, perch, scrod, skate, smelt, trout **6** bonito, caviar, kipper, mullet, plaice, pompon, salmon, tautog, wrasse **7** alewife, catfish, cavalla, escolar, grouper, haddock, halibut, herring, pollack, pollock, pompano, sardine, sea carp, snapper **8** brisling, crevalle, flounder, mackerel *game:* **4** bass, pike, tuna **5** cobia, perch, trout **6** grilse, marlin, salmon, tarpon **8** pickerel **9** swordfish *grunt:* **7** pigfish *herring:* **4** shad, sild **5** sprat **7** alewife, sardine **8** brisling, pilchard *kind:* **3** gar, ray **4** bass, cero, chub, dory, goby, jack, opah, pike, rudd, scup, tuna **5** bream, cisco, loach, perch, porgy, shark, skate, smelt, snook, tench, tunny, wahoo **6** blenny, bonito, dorado, marlin, minnow, mullet, permit, puffer, remora, sauger, sucker, tarpon, tautog, warsaw, wrasse **7** anchovy, buffalo, capelin, cavalla, chimera, cowfish, crappie, dolphin, grunion, haddock, hogfish, jewfish, mudfish, oarfish, piranha, pupfish, sardine, sawfish, sculpin, snapper, sunfish, tilapia, whiting **8** albacore, blowfish, bluefish, bluegill, bonefish, chimaera, filefish, gambusia, grayling, halfbeak, ladyfish, lookdown, lumpfish, lungfish, mackerel, menhaden, moonfish, pickerel, pipefish, rockfish, sailfish, seahorse, skipjack, stingray, sturgeon, tilefish, warmouth, wolffish **9** amberjack, barracuda, greenling, jacksmelt, killifish, mummichog, pilotfish, spadefish, swordfish, topminnow, trunkfish, whitebait, whitefish **10** butterfish, flying fish, needlefish, parrotfish, silverside, tripletail, yellowtail **11** muskellunge, pumpkinseed, stickleback, triggerfish **12** schoolmaster *luminescent:* **11** hatchetfish, lanternfish *minnow:* **3** koi **4** carp, chub, dace **6** shiner *pan:* **5** bream, perch, trout **7** crappie, sunfish **8** bluegill, rock bass **11** pumpkinseed *porgy:* **4** scup **7** pinfish **10** sheepshead *relating to:* **7** piscine *rockfish:* **8** bocaccio, lionfish, rosefish *salmon:* **3** dog **4** chum, coho **6** sebago **7** chinook, sockeye *spear:* **3** gig **7** harpoon, trident *stew:* **8** cioppino, matelote **13** bouillabaisse *trap:* **4** weir *trout:* **4** char **5** charr **7** rainbow **9** cutthroat **11** Dolly Varden *voracious:* **6** caribe **7** piranha *young:* **3** fry **4** parr **5** larva, smolt **6** alevin, grilse

fisherman 6 angler
fish hawk 6 osprey
fishhook *adjunct:* **5** snell *part:* **4** barb **5** shank
fishing line 4 trot **7** setline **8** longline, trotline *float:* **3** bob **5** quill *leader:* **5** snell
fishing lure 3 fly **4** bait **5** spoon **7** spinner
fishing net 5 seine, trawl
fishlike mammal 4 orca **5** whale **6** dugong, sea cow **7** dolphin, grampus, manatee, narwhal **8** cetacean, porpoise
fish story 3 fib, lie **4** bunk, yarn **11** fabrication **12** exaggeration **13** overstatement
fishwife 5 harpy, scold, shrew, vixen **6** virago **9** termagant, Xanthippe
fishy 7 dubious, suspect **8** doubtful, unlikely **9** ambiguous, dubitable, equivocal, uncertain **10** suspicious **11** problematic **12** questionable
fission element 7 uranium **9** plutonium
fissure 3 gap **4** gash, hole, part, rent, rift **5** break, chasm, chink, cleft, crack, split **6** breach, cleave, divide, schism **7** crevice, discord, opening, rupture **8** crevasse, fracture **10** disharmony, separation
fist 4 duke, grip, hand **5** clamp, grasp **6** clench, clinch, clutch
fit 3 apt, set **4** hale, jibe, just, sane, suit, turn **5** adapt, agree, frame, ready, sound, spasm, spell, tally, throe **6** access, accord, adjust, attack, become, belong, decent, go with, proper, seemly, square, tailor, useful **7** capable, conform, healthy, prepare, qualify, seizure, tantrum **8** assemble, decorous, dovetail, eligible, paroxysm, suitable **9** agree with, congruous, consonant, harmonize, reconcile **10** applicable, convenient, correspond, felicitous, go together **11** accommodate, appropriate
fitful 6 random, spotty **7** erratic **8** periodic, sporadic, variable **9** haphazard, hit-or-miss, irregular, spasmodic, uncertain **10** changeable, convulsive, herky-jerky, inconstant **12** intermittent
fitness 4 trim **5** order, shape **6** fettle, health, kilter, repair **7** account, decorum, service, utility **8** capacity **9** condition, propriety, relevance **11** eligibility, suitability **13** applicability
fit out 3 arm, rig **5** equip **6** outfit **7** appoint, furnish **8** accouter, accoutre
fitting 3 apt, due **4** able, just, meet, part, true **5** happy, right **6** proper, seemly **7** apropos, germane **8** apposite, relevant, suitable **9** accessory, befitting, pertinent, qualified **10** applicable, attachment, felicitous, harmonious **11** appropriate
fit together 4 hook, join, mesh **6** hook up **7** connect **8** dovetail **9** integrate
Fitzgerald novel 10 Last Tycoon (The) **11** Great Gatsby (The) **16** Tender Is the Night **17** All the Sad Young Men, Tales of the Jazz Age **18** This Side of Paradise **21** Beautiful and the Damned (The)
five *combining form:* **4** pent **5** penta

6 quinqu 7 quinque *group of:* 6 pentad 7 quintet

five-dollar bill 3 fin

fivefold 9 quintuple

Five Nations 8 Iroquois *member:* 7 Cayugas, Mohawks, Oneidas, Senecas 9 Onondagas

five-sided figure 8 pentagon

five-star 6 deluxe, superb 8 superior, top-notch 9 excellent, first-rate 10 first-class 11 outstanding

five-year period 6 luster, lustre 7 lustrum

fix 3 jam, rig, set 4 cook, cure, geld, mend, mess, moor, root, spay, spot, work 5 affix, alter, catch, patch, ready, renew, rivet, solve, state, stick 6 adjust, anchor, assign, attach, change, decide, doctor, fasten, neuter, pickle, plight, repair, revamp, scrape, secure, settle, square, steady 7 appoint, arrange, correct, dilemma, resolve, restore, specify, work out 8 castrate, discover, overhaul, position, renovate, solution 9 condition, establish, stabilize, sterilize 11 predicament

fixation 5 craze, mania 6 fetish 9 obsession 11 fascination, infatuation

____ **fixe** 4 idée, prix

fixed 3 pat, set 4 fast, firm, sure 6 frozen, secure, stable, stated, steady 7 abiding, certain, limited, precise, settled 8 constant, definite, enduring, immobile, resolute 9 exclusive, immovable, immutable, permanent, steadfast, tenacious 10 inflexible, invariable, restricted, stationary, stipulated, unswerving, unwavering 11 determinate, unalterable 12 concentrated, unchangeable 13 circumscribed

fizz 4 buzz, foam, hiss 5 froth 6 bubble, spirit 7 bubbles, sparkle, sputter 10 effervesce, liveliness 13 effervescence

fizzle 4 bomb, fail, flop 6 fiasco 7 failure, misfire 8 miscarry, peter out 10 effervesce 11 fall through

fjord *Baffin Island:* 9 Admiralty *Denmark:* 3 Ise, Lim 5 Lamme *Iceland:* 4 Axar, Eyja 5 Horna, Skaga, Vopna *Norway:* 3 Tys 4 Bokn, Nord, Salt, Stor, Tana, Vest 5 Lakse, Ranen, Sogne 9 Stavanger, Trondheim *Spitsbergen:* 3 Ice *Svalbard:* 4 Stor

flab 3 fat 4 bulk, lard 5 flesh 7 blubber, fatness 9 cellulite 10 corpulence 11 love handles

flabbergast 3 awe 4 stun 5 amaze, shock, throw 7 astound, nonplus 8 astonish, bowl over, surprise 9 dumbfound, overwhelm

flabby see FLACCID

flaccid 4 limp, soft, weak 6 feeble, flabby, floppy 8 flexible

flag 3 ebb, lag, sag, tag 4 fade, fail, hail, iris, jack, sign, swag, tail, tire, waft, wane, wave, wilt 5 abate, color, droop, stone 6 banner, burgee, colors, ensign, guidon, pennon, signal, weaken 7 bunting, decline, pendant, pennant 8 bannerol, gonfalon, languish, Old Glory, penalize, registry, standard, streamer, tricolor 9 banderole, blue peter, oriflamme, Union Jack 10 Jolly Roger 11 deteriorate 12 Stars and Bars

flagellate 4 beat, flog, hide, lash, whip 5 whale 6 larrup, lather, stripe, switch, thrash 7 scourge 9 horsewhip

flagitious 4 evil 6 sinful, wicked 7 corrupt, vicious 8 criminal, depraved, infamous, perverse, shameful 9 miscreant, nefarious, perverted 10 degenerate, scandalous, villainous 11 disgraceful

flagon 3 jug 4 ewer 5 stoup 6 vessel 7 tankard

flagpole 4 mast 5 staff *rope:* 7 halyard

flagrant 4 bold, rank 5 gross 6 wanton 7 blatant, glaring, heinous, obvious 8 striking 9 atrocious, egregious, monstrous 10 outrageous 11 conspicuous

flagstone 5 shale, slate

flag-waver 7 patriot 8 jingoist, loyalist 10 chauvinist 11 nationalist 12 superpatriot

flail 4 club, beat, flog, whip 6 strike, thrash, thresh 7 scourge 8 flounder, thresher

flair 4 bent, chic, élan, gift 5 knack, style 6 genius, talent 7 ability, aptness, faculty 8 aptitude, tendency 10 proclivity 11 inclination

flak 4 fire 5 abuse 6 shells 7 censure, vitriol 9 brickbats, criticism, hostility 10 opposition 11 disapproval 12 condemnation, fault-finding

flake 3 bit 4 chip, kook, peel 5 scale 6 lamina 7 oddball 8 crackpot, fragment 9 eccentric

flake off 4 chip, peel 5 scale 9 exfoliate 10 desquamate

flaky 3 odd 5 goofy, nutty, wacky, weird 6 fickle, screwy 7 bizarre, erratic, offbeat 9 eccentric

flambé 6 ablaze, aflame, alight 7 blazing, flaming

flamboyant 4 loud 5 gaudy, showy 6 flashy, florid, ornate, rococo 7 baroque, splashy 8 colorful, luscious 10 over-the-top 12 ostentatious

flame 4 beau, dear, fire, glow, love 5 ardor, blaze, flare, flash, honey, light, lover 7 beloved, darling, passion, sweetie 8 ladylove, truelove 9 boyfriend, inamorata, inamorato 10 brilliance, brightness, girlfriend, heartthrob, sweetheart

flamen 6 priest

flaming 5 afire, fiery 6 ablaze, alight, ardent, red-hot 7 blazing, burning, fervent, flaring, ignited, intense 10 hot-blooded, passionate 11 conflagrant, impassioned

flammable 8 burnable 9 ignitable 10 incendiary 11 combustible *liquid:* 3 gas, oil 7 acetone, alcohol, ethanol 8 gasoline, kerosene 9 petroleum 10 turpentine

Flanders *capital:* 5 Lille *language:* 7 Flemish

flaneur 12 boulevardier, man-about-town

flank 4 abut, side 6 adjoin, border

flap 3 tab, tap 4 beat, flog, fold, slap, stew, wave, wing 5 fling, panel 6 crisis, dither, lather, pother, tumult, uproar 7 aileron, flutter, turmoil 9 agitation, commotion, confusion

flapdoodle 3 rot 4 bosh, bull, nuts 5 drool, fudge, hokum, hooey 6 bunkum, drivel 7 baloney, blarney, hogwash, rubbish 8 malarkey, nonsense, tommyrot 9 poppycock 10 applesauce, balderdash 12 blatherskite, fiddle-faddle, fiddlesticks

flapjack 7 hotcake, pancake 11 griddle cake

flare 4 burn 5 blaze, burst, flame, flash 6 signal 7 flicker 8 outburst

flare-up 5 blaze, burst, flame, flash, surge 8 eruption, outburst 9 explosion

flaring 5 afire, fiery 6 ablaze, aflame, alight 7 blazing, burning 11 conflagrant

flash 3 ray 4 beam, rush, snap, show 5 blaze, blink, crack, flame, flare, glare, gleam, glint, jiffy, shake, shine, showy, spark, speed 6 dazzle, expose, flaunt, glance, minute, moment, second 7 display, disport, exhibit, flicker, glamour, glimmer, glisten, glitter, instant, pizzazz, shimmer, show off, spangle, sparkle, twinkle 8 brandish 9 coruscate 11 coruscation, scintillate, split second 13 scintillation

flashy 4 loud 5 gaudy, jazzy, showy 6 brazen, florid, garish, glitzy, ornate, snazzy, sporty, tawdry, tinsel 7 blatant, chintzy, glaring, insipid 9 sparkling 10 flamboyant, glittering 12 meretricious, ostentatious

flask 6 bottle, fiasco, flacon 7 ampulla, canteen, costrel, thermos

flat 3 dim, mat 4 dead, drab, dull, even 5 banal, bland, exact, fixed, flush, level, muted, plane, prone, rooms, stale,

vapid 7 insipid, prosaic 8 lodgings, tenement, unsavory 9 apartment, colorless, innocuous 10 flavorless, lackluster, monotonous

flatfish see at FISH

flatland 4 mesa 5 plain 6 steppe, tundra 7 plateau 9 tableland

flat-out 8 absolute 9 downright 10 absolutely

flatten 4 deck, down, dull, even, fell, raze 5 crush, floor, level 6 smooth, squash 9 knock down, prostrate

flattened at the poles 6 oblate

flatter 4 coax, suit 5 toady 6 become, cajole, praise, stroke 7 adulate, blarney, gratify, wheedle 8 blandish, bootlick, butter up, soft-soap 9 sweet-talk

flattery 5 smarm 6 butter, praise 7 blarney 8 cajolery, soft soap, toadyism 9 adulation, sweet talk 10 sycophancy 11 compliments 12 blandishment, ingratiation, unctuousness

Flaubert, Gustave *birthplace:* 5 Rouen *heroine:* 4 Emma (Bovary) *novel:* 8 Salammbô 12 Madame Bovary

flaunt 4 show, wave 5 flash, flout, vaunt 6 expose, parade 7 display, disport, exhibit, show off 8 brandish, flourish

flavor 4 race, tang, zest, zing 5 smack, spice, taste, tinge 6 relish, season 7 variety, version

flavorless 4 flat 5 bland, stale 7 insipid 8 unsavory 11 unpalatable

flavorsome 5 sapid, tasty, yummy 6 savory 9 delicious, palatable 10 appetizing, delectable 11 good-tasting

flaw 3 gap, rip, sin 4 blot, chip, tear, vice 5 crack, fault 6 defect 7 blemish 8 weakness 9 deformity 12 imperfection

flawed 5 amiss 6 faulty, marred 7 damaged, spoiled 8 impaired 9 defective, imperfect

flawless 4 pure 5 ideal, model 6 intact 7 perfect 8 seamless, unmarred 9 exquisite 10 immaculate, impeccable 11 unblemished

flax 5 linen *fiber:* 3 tow *prepare:* 3 ret 4 card 5 dress 6 hackle, scutch

flaxen 4 fair 5 blond, straw 6 blonde, golden, yellow 7 towhead

flay 4 beat, lash, peel, skin 7 blister, censure, lambast, upbraid 8 lambaste 9 castigate, criticize, excoriate

flea 6 chigoe, jigger 7 chigger *water:* 7 daphnid

Fleance's father 6 Banquo

flèche 5 spire

fleck 3 dot 4 mark, mote, spot 5 flake, speck 6 dapple, mottle, streak, stripe 7 spatter, speckle, stipple 8 particle 9 bespeckle

Fledermaus, Die 3 bat *character:* **5** Adele, Falke, Frank **6** Alfred **9** Rosalinde **10** Eisenstein *composer:* **7** Strauss (Johann)

fledge 4 rear **7** feather

fledgling 4 colt, tyro **6** novice, rookie **8** beginner, freshman, neophyte, newcomer **10** apprentice

flee 3 fly, lam, run **4** bolt, scat, skip **5** elude, scoot, scram, skirr, steal **6** decamp, escape **7** abscond, make off, run away, scamper, vamoose **8** stampede, turn tail **9** skedaddle **10** make tracks

fleece 3 rob **4** bilk, clip, gaff, milk, rook, skin, soak, wool **5** bleed, cheat, cozen, mulct, shear, stick, sweat **6** extort, hustle, rip off **7** defraud, swindle **8** flimflam **10** overcharge

fleecy 5 downy **6** fluffy, pilose, woolly **7** hirsute **9** whiskered **10** flocculent

fleer 4 gibe, gird, jeer, jest, mock, quip **5** flout, laugh, scoff, scout, sneer, taunt

fleet 4 fast, navy, spry **5** agile, brisk, group, hasty, quick, rapid, swift **6** argosy, armada, nimble, speedy **8** flotilla **9** breakneck **10** harefooted

fleeting 5 brief **7** passing **8** fugitive, volatile **9** ephemeral, fugacious, momentary, temporary, transient **10** evanescent, short-lived, transitory

Fleming, Ian *hero:* **9** James Bond *novel:* **4** Dr. No **9** Moonraker **10** Goldfinger **11** Thunderball **12** Casino Royale **13** Live and Let Die **16** You Only Live Twice **18** From Russia with Love

flesh 4 beef, meat, skin **5** stock **7** kindred **9** offspring, relatives, substance

fleshly 5 obese **6** animal, bodily, carnal **7** lustful, profane, secular, sensual **8** corporal, physical, sensuous, temporal **9** corporeal, epicurean, luxurious, sybaritic **10** voluptuous

fleshy 3 fat **5** ample, beefy, burly, gross, heavy, hefty, husky, meaty, obese, plump, pudgy, stout, tubby **6** chubby, chunky, portly, rotund **7** porcine, weighty **9** corpulent **10** overweight, well-padded *fruit:* **4** pome **5** berry, drupe

Fletcher's partner 8 Beaumont (Francis)

fleur-de-lis 4 iris

flex 4 bend **5** tense

flexible 5 lithe, loose **6** docile, floppy, limber, pliant, supple **7** elastic, pliable, springy, willowy **8** amenable, bendable, stretchy, yielding **9** adaptable, compliant, malleable, tractable

flexion 3 bow **4** bend, fold, turn **5** angle

flexuous 5 fluid, lithe, snaky **7** sinuous, winding **8** tortuous **10** circuitous, convoluted, meandering, serpentine **11** anfractuous

flick 4 film, show **5** movie **13** motion picture, moving picture

flicker 4 bird, film, flit, hint **5** flash, gleam, glint, movie, waver **6** quiver **7** twinkle **10** woodpecker **13** motion picture, moving picture

flickering 7 lambent **8** unsteady

flier 3 ace **5** pilot **6** airman **7** aviator, birdman, handout **8** aviatrix, brochure, circular **9** throwaway

flight 3 hop, lam **4** rout, soar, slip, wing **5** flock, floor, flush, flyby, story **6** escape, flying, series **7** getaway **8** breakout

flighty 5 dizzy, giddy, silly, swift **7** foolish **8** freakish, skittish, unstable, volatile **9** frivolous, mercurial, transient **10** capricious, changeable, inconstant **11** empty-headed, harebrained **13** irresponsible

flimflam 3 con, gyp **4** bilk, dupe, fake, fool, gull, hoax, jazz, sham **5** cheat, cozen, fraud, hokum, trick **6** chouse, deceit, diddle, humbug **7** chicane, deceive, defraud, swindle **8** hoodwink, trickery **9** bamboozle, deception, moonshine **10** balderdash, double-talk **11** hornswoggle

flimflammer 3 gyp **5** cheat **6** con man **7** diddler, sharper **8** swindler **9** defrauder **11** four-flusher **12** double-dealer

flimsy 4 limp, weak **5** cheap, filmy, frail, gauzy, sheer **6** feeble, flabby, sleazy, slight, spindly **7** flaccid, fragile, rickety, tenuous, unsound **8** decrepit, delicate, gossamer **10** diaphanous, improbable **11** implausible, transparent **12** unconvincing **13** insubstantial

flinch 5 quail, start, wince **6** blench, cringe, recoil, shrink

fling 3 peg **4** cast, emit, fire, flap, hurl, plop, rush, shot, slap, stab, tear, toss **5** binge, chuck, heave, pitch, shoot, spree, throw **6** affair, charge, hurtle, launch **7** splurge **8** catapult

flip 4 glib, leaf, pert, riff, toss, wise **6** breezy, riffle, ruffle **8** turn over **10** somersault **11** impertinent, smartalecky

flip-flop 5 U-turn, waver **6** sandal, switch, waffle **7** reverse **8** reversal **9** about-face, turnabout, vacillate, volte-face **10** turnaround **11** vacillation

flippancy 5 cheek **6** levity **8** archness, pertness **9** cockiness, freshness, frivolity **10** cheekiness, impishness **11** roguishness

flippant 4 glib, pert **5** sassy, saucy

6 breezy, cheeky 11 impertinent, smart-alecky 13 disrespectful

flirt 3 toy 4 flit, fool, minx, ogle, vamp 5 dally, tease 6 coquet, trifle, wanton 8 coquette 10 experiment, mess around

flit 3 fly, zip 4 dart, pass, rush, sail, scud, whiz, wing 5 flash, hurry, scoot, speed 7 flicker, flutter, twinkle

flitter 4 dart, flap, wing 5 hover, waver 6 quiver 7 skitter 9 fluctuate

flivver 6 jalopy 9 tin lizzie

float 3 bob, fly 4 buoy, cork, hang, raft, ride, sail, scud, swim, waft 5 drift, hover 6 wander 7 pontoon, propose 8 levitate 9 negotiate

floater 3 bum, vag 4 hobo, raft 5 tramp 7 drifter, vagrant 8 derelict, vagabond 10 roustabout

floating 5 fluid, loose 6 adrift 7 buoyant, movable 8 moveable, shifting, variable 10 adjustable 11 fluctuating

flocculent 5 flaky 6 fleecy, fluffy, woolly

flock 3 mob 4 army, bevy, herd, host, mass, pack, rout 5 brood, bunch, cloud, covey, crowd, drove, group 6 flight, gaggle, gather, legion, scores, throng 8 assemble, assembly, converge 9 multitude 11 aggregation 12 congregation

floe 3 ice 4 berg 7 glacier, iceberg 8 ice field

flog 3 tan 4 beat, cane, flap, hide, lash, slog, whip 5 birch, drive, flail, whale 6 larrup, lather, stripe, switch, thrash 7 cowhide, leather, scourge 10 flagellate

flood 4 fill, flow, flux, glut, pour, rush, tide 5 burst, drown, float, spate, swamp 6 deluge, engulf, stream 7 current, freshet, immerse, Niagara, torrent 8 alluvion, cataract, inundate, overflow, submerge 9 avalanche, cataclysm, overwhelm 10 inundation, outpouring

floor 4 base, down, drop, fell 5 amaze, level, shock, story 6 ground 7 astound, flatten 8 astonish, audience, bowl down, bowl over, surprise 9 dumbfound, knock down 11 flabbergast

flop 3 dud 4 bomb, bust, fail, fall 5 lemon, loser 6 bummer, fizzle, turkey 7 clinker, failure

floppy 4 limp 6 flimsy 7 flaccid 8 diskette, flexible

flora 6 plants 10 vegetation

flora and fauna 5 biota

Florence *bridge:* 12 Ponte Vecchio *cathedral:* 5 Duomo *family:* 6 Medici *museum:* 6 Uffizi 8 Bargello *palace:* 5 Pitti *river:* 4 Arno

florid 3 red 5 flush, gaudy, ruddy, showy 6 ornate, rococo 7 baroque, flowery, flushed, glowing 8 rubicund, sanguine,

sonorous 9 bombastic, elaborate, overblown 10 euphuistic, flamboyant, rhetorical 11 declamatory 12 magniloquent 13 grandiloquent

Florida *capital:* 11 Tallahassee *city:* 5 Miami, Tampa 6 Naples, Venice 7 Hialeah, Key West, Orlando 8 Sarasota 9 Palm Beach 11 St. Augustine 12 Jacksonville, St. Petersburg *college, university:* 7 Rollins, Stetson *key:* 4 Long, Vaca, West 5 Largo 7 Big Pine 9 Matecumbe, Sugarloaf *lake:* 9 Kissimmee 10 Okeechobee *nickname:* 8 Sunshine (State) *park:* 10 Everglades *river:* 6 Indian 7 St. Johns 8 Suwannee 12 Apalachicola *state bird:* 11 mockingbird *state flower:* 13 orange blossom *state tree:* 9 sabal palm

florilegium 5 album 6 reader 7 garland, omnibus 8 analects 9 anthology 10 collection, miscellany

Florimel's husband 7 Marinel

floss 4 down, fuzz, lint 5 fluff 6 thread

flotilla 5 fleet 6 argosy, armada

Flotow opera 5 Indra 6 L'Ombre, Martha

flotsam 6 debris, jetsam 7 remains 8 wreckage 9 driftwood

flounce 5 frill, mince, strut, waltz 6 bounce, prance, ruffle, sashay

flounder 3 dab 5 slosh 6 fumble, muddle, splash, thrash, wallow 7 blunder, flounce 8 flatfish, struggle

flour 4 meal 6 pinole, powder *beetle:* 6 weevil

flourish 3 wax 4 grow, wave 5 adorn, bloom 6 flower, stroke, thrive 7 blossom, burgeon, develop, fanfare, prosper, succeed 8 brandish, curlicue, ornament 13 embellishment, ornamentation

flout 4 defy, mock 5 scorn, spurn 6 deride, insult 7 scoff at

flow 4 emit, flux, gush, ooze, pour, rill, rise, rush, stem, tide, well 5 arise, drift, flood, issue, spate, spill, surge, swarm 6 course, deluge, onrush, sluice, spring, stream 7 cascade, current, emanate, give off, outflow, proceed 8 inundate, sequence 9 discharge, originate 10 continuity, inundation, succession 11 progression 12 continuation

flower 4 best, blow, pick, posy 5 bloom, cream, elite, pride, prime, prize 6 choice, thrive 7 blossom, burgeon, develop 10 effloresce 13 inflorescence *buttonhole:* 11 boutonniere *cluster:* 4 cyme 5 spike, umbel 6 corymb, floret, raceme, spadix 7 panicle 8 spikelet 9 capitulum, dichasium, glomerule 11 monochasium 13 inflorescence *cup:* 5 calyx *garden:* 4 iris, lily, pink, rose

5 aster, canna, daisy, pansy, peony, phlox, poppy, tulip **6** azalia, cosmos, crocus, dahlia, orchid, violet **7** jonquil, petunia **8** camellia, daffodil, gardenia, geranium, gloxinia, hyacinth, larkspur, marigold, primrose **9** carnation, gladiolus, narcissus **10** delphinium, heliotrope **13** chrysanthemum *opening:* **8** anthesis *part:* **5** bract, calyx, ovary, ovule, petal, sepal, style **6** anther, pistil, spathe, stamen, stigma **7** corolla, nectary, pedicel, petiole **8** calyptra, filament, peduncle, perianth *spike:* **5** ament **6** catkin, spadix *stalk:* **7** pedicel **8** peduncle *type:* **3** ray **4** disk **6** annual, simple **9** composite, perennial *wild:* **4** flag **5** bluet, daisy, vetch **6** lupine **7** anemone, arbutus, cowslip, gentian, vervain **8** bluebell, hepatica, trillium **9** buttercup, columbine, dandelion, saxifrage **10** cinquefoil **12** lady's slipper

flower arranging 7 ikebana

flowering 6 growth **8** progress **9** evolution **11** development, florescence, progression

flowerless plant 4 fern, moss **6** lichen **9** liverwort

flowery 5 wordy **6** florid, ornate, prolix **7** aureate, diffuse, verbose **8** sonorous **9** overblown **10** euphuistic, rhetorical **11** declamatory **12** magniloquent **13** grandiloquent

Flowery Kingdom 5 China

flowing 4 easy **5** fluid **6** fluent, liquid, smooth **7** cursive, running **10** effortless *back:* **6** reflux **8** refluent *in:* **6** influx **8** influent *together:* **7** conflux **9** confluent

flow regulator 4 cock, gate **5** valve **8** throttle

flub 4 goof, mess, muff, slip **5** boner, botch, error, fluff, gaffe, lapse, snarl **6** bollix, bungle, foul up, goof up, mess up **7** blunder, faux pas, louse up

fluctuate 4 sway, yo-yo **5** swing, waver **6** seesaw **8** undulate **9** alternate, oscillate, vacillate

flue 4 pipe, vent **6** funnel, uptake **7** channel, chimney, outtake

fluent 4 easy, glib **5** fluid **6** facile, liquid, smooth, supple **7** cursive, flowing, voluble **8** eloquent, polished **10** articulate, effortless

fluff 4 down, flub, fuzz, goof, lint, mess, muff, slip, trip **5** boner, botch, error, floss, gaffe, lapse, whisk **6** bobble, bollix, bungle, goof up, mess up **7** blooper, blunder, faux pas, louse up, mistake

fluffy 5 downy **6** flossy **7** cursory, shallow **8** puffed up **10** flocculent **11** superficial **13** unsubstantial

fluid 4 free **5** lymph, water **6** liquid, mobile, molten, serous, watery **7** mutable, protean **8** flexible, shifting, unstable, unsteady, variable **9** adaptable, changeful, unsettled **10** changeable *excessive:* **5** edema

fluke 3 hap **4** lobe, worm **5** quirk **6** chance **8** flatfish, fortuity **9** trematode

fluky 3 odd **6** casual, chance, chancy, random **9** arbitrary **10** accidental, fortuitous

flume 5 chute **6** sluice, stream **7** channel **8** aqueduct **11** watercourse

flummox 5 abash, addle **6** baffle, rattle, stymie **7** confuse, fluster, perplex **8** befuddle, bewilder, confound **9** discomfit, embarrass **10** disconcert

flunk 4 fail

flunky 4 peon **5** gofer, toady **6** drudge, lackey, stooge, yes-man **7** footman, servant, steward **8** factotum, follower

flurry 3 ado, fit **4** fuss, gust, spit, stir, to-do **5** haste, whirl **6** bother, bustle, furore, pother, tumult **7** barrage, flutter, turmoil **8** snowfall **9** agitation, commotion, confusion, whirlpool, whirlwind **10** excitement, turbulence

flush 4 even, flat, glow, pink, rich, rose, wash **5** bloom, color, level, plane, raise, rinse, rouge **6** florid, filled, mantle, redden, sluice **7** cleanse, crimson, glowing, inflame, opulent, suffuse, wealthy **8** abundant, abutting, irrigate, rubicund, sanguine, squarely **9** turn color

fluster 5 addle, dizzy, shake, upset **6** ball up, bother, fuddle, muddle, rattle, ruffle **7** agitate, confuse, disturb, nonplus, perturb, unhinge **8** befuddle, bewilder, confound, disquiet, distract **10** discompose

flustered 5 upset **7** abashed, anxious, rattled **8** agitated, confused, troubled **9** chagrined, disturbed, flummoxed, perplexed, perturbed **10** bewildered, disquieted, distracted, distraught, distressed, nonplussed **11** discomposed, embarrassed **12** disconcerted

flute 4 fife, roll **5** pleat **6** goffer, groove **7** chamfer, channel, piccolo **8** recorder **9** wineglass *Japanese:* **10** shakuhachi *player:* **5** piper **7** flutist **8** flautist

flutist *American:* **5** Baker (Julius), Baron (Samuel) **7** Robison (Paula) **8** Zukerman (Eugenia) *British:* **6** Galway (James) *French:* **6** Rampal (Jean-Pierre)

flutter 4 beat, flap, flit **5** hover, quake, shake **6** flurry, quaver, quiver, wobble **7** flicker, flitter, pulsate, tremble, vibrate **9** agitation, commotion, confusion, palpitate, vibration **11** fluctuation

flu type 5 Asian, swine

flux 3 run 4 flow, fuse, melt, rush, thaw, tide 5 drift, flood, spate 6 change, stream 7 current, flowing, outflow 8 dissolve

fly 3 zip 4 bolt, dart, dash, flee, flit, lure, scud, skip, soar, whiz, wing 5 fleet, float, glide, hover, hurry, pilot, scoot, shoot, skirr, sweep, whish, whisk 6 aviate, escape, hasten, hustle 7 abscond, flutter *insect:* 4 gnat 5 midge 6 botfly, gadfly, mayfly, tsetse 7 deerfly, sandfly 8 blackfly, dipteron, horsefly, housefly, tachinid 10 bluebottle *larva:* 6 maggot

fly-by-night 5 shady 7 passing 9 transient 10 transitory, unreliable 12 disreputable, undependable 13 untrustworthy

flycatcher 5 pewee 6 phoebe, tyrant 8 bellbird, kingbird 9 passerine

flying 5 aloft 6 volant 8 airborne

Flying Dutchman, The *composer:* 6 Wagner (Richard) *heroine:* 5 Senta

flying fish 7 gurnard

flying fox 3 bat 8 fruit bat

flying horse 7 Pegasus 10 hippogriff

flying island 6 Laputa

flying lemur 6 colugo

flying mammal 3 bat

flying saucer 3 UFO

fly in the ointment 5 catch 8 drawback

foam 4 head, scud, scum, suds, surf 5 churn, froth, spume 6 bubble, lather, seethe 7 bubbles 10 effervesce

fob 4 seal 5 chain 6 pocket, ribbon 8 ornament

fob off 5 foist 6 put off 7 palm off, pass off

focus 3 fix, hub 4 zoom 5 heart, rivet 6 adjust, center, fixate, home in 8 converge, emphasis, meditate, polestar 9 concenter, epicenter 10 hypocenter 11 concentrate, nerve center

fodder 4 feed, food 6 forage, silage 9 provender *crop:* 3 hay, oat, rye 4 corn 5 maize, vetch, wheat 6 barley, clover, millet 7 alfalfa, sorghum *storage structure:* 4 silo *store:* 4 ensile

foe 5 enemy, rival 8 opponent 9 adversary 10 antagonist

fog 4 blur, daze, foam, haze, mist, murk, soup 5 brume, cloud, vapor 6 miasma, muddle 7 pea soup, pogonip

foggy 4 hazy 5 dirty, grimy, misty, murky, soupy, vague 7 brumous, muddled, obscure, tenuous 8 confused, pea soupy, vaporous

fogy 6 fossil, square 7 diehard 8 mossback 10 fuddy-duddy 12 antediluvian, conservative 11 standpatter 13 stick-in-the-mud

fogyish 7 old-line 8 outmoded, standpat 9 hidebound, out-of-date 10 antiquated, fuddy-duddy, mossbacked 11 reactionary 12 conservative, old-fashioned

foible 4 vice 5 fault 6 defect 7 failing, frailty 8 weakness 11 shortcoming 12 imperfection

foil 4 balk, beat, curb, dash, faze 5 check, sword 6 baffle, defeat, rattle, thwart 7 buffalo 8 contrast, restrain 9 discomfit, embarrass, frustrate 10 circumvent, disappoint, disconcert 11 straight man

foist 6 fob off 7 palm off, pass off

fold 3 pen, ply 4 bend, fail, tuck 5 drape, flock, pleat, plica, ridge 6 crease, double, furrow, pucker 7 flexure, plicate 9 plication 11 corrugation *skin:* 4 ruga 5 plica, rugae (plural) 6 dewlap, plicae (plural)

folder 4 file 6 binder 9 portfolio

foliage 6 growth, leaves 7 verdure 8 greenery, lushness 10 vegetation

folk 4 race 6 people 9 community

folklore 4 myth, tale 5 fable 6 belief, custom, legend, mythos, wisdom 9 mythology, tradition 12 superstition

folks 6 family 7 parents 9 relatives

folksinger 4 Baez (Joan), Ives (Burl) 5 Dylan (Bob), Niles (John Jacob), White (Josh) 6 Odetta, Seeger (Pete) 7 Collins (Judy), Guthrie (Arlo, Woody), Robeson (Paul) 9 Belafonte (Harry), Ledbetter (Huddie)

folksy 5 homey 6 casual, earthy, mellow, rustic, simple 7 natural 8 down-home, familiar, informal, laid-back, sociable 9 easygoing, ingenuous 10 unaffected, unpolished 13 unpretentious

folktale 4 myth 5 fable 6 legend 7 märchen

follow 3 dog, spy, tag 4 hunt, keep, obey, seek, tail, walk 5 catch, chase, ensue, grasp, hound, trace, track, trail 6 accept, comply, convoy, pursue, search, shadow, travel 7 conform, imitate, proceed, replace, succeed 8 postdate, practice, supplant 9 accompany, supersede 10 comprehend, understand

follower 3 fan 5 toady 6 addict, cohort, minion, sequel, votary 7 apostle, devotee, groupie, habitué, sectary, trailer 8 adherent, advocate, disciple, faithful, hanger-on, henchman, myrmidon, parasite, partisan, tagalong 9 dependent, satellite, supporter, sycophant 10 aficionado

following 4 next 5 after, below, later, since 6 behind, public 7 ensuing, retinue 8 audience, partisans 9 adherents, afterward, believers, disciples, entourage 10 afterwards, sequential, supporters, subsequent, succeeding, successive **12** subsequently, subsequent to

follow-up 6 sequel

folly 4 whim **6** lunacy, vanity **7** fatuity, foolery, inanity, madness **8** insanity, nonsense **9** absurdity, craziness, dottiness, silliness, stupidity **10** indulgence **11** foolishness **12** extravagance

foment 3 sow **4** brew, goad, spur **5** rouse, set on **6** arouse, excite, foster, incite, stir up, whip up **7** agitate, nurture, provoke **9** cultivate, encourage, instigate

fond 4 dear, warm **5** silly **6** doting, loving, tender **7** devoted, fatuous, foolish, partial **8** desirous, enamored, romantic **9** indulgent **10** infatuated **11** sentimental **12** affectionate

fondle 3 paw, pet **5** grope, touch **6** caress, cosset, dandle, stroke **7** embrace **8** canoodle

fondness 4 love **5** fancy, taste **6** liking, relish **8** appetite, devotion, penchant, soft spot, weakness **9** affection, tendresse **10** attachment, partiality, preference, propensity **11** inclination **12** predilection

font 4 root, type **6** origin, source **8** fountain **10** receptacle

food 3 pap **4** chow, diet, eats, fare, grub, meal, meat **5** bread, manna **6** fodder, viands **7** aliment, cuisine, edibles, nurture, pabulum, vittles **8** delicacy, victuals **9** nutriment, provender **10** provisions, sustenance **11** comestibles, nourishment *disorder:* **7** bulimia **8** anorexia *divine:* **8** ambrosia *element:* **5** fiber, fibre, sugar **6** starch **7** mineral, protein, vitamin **12** carbohydrate *from heaven:* **5** manna *lover:* **7** epicure, gourmet **8** gourmand *provision:* **4** mess **6** ration **7** serving *scarcity:* **6** famine *waste:* **7** garbage

foofaraw 3 ado **4** fuss, stir, to-do **5** stink **6** bother, finery, frills, furore, hurrah, pother, ruckus, rumpus **8** brouhaha **9** commotion **11** disturbance

fool 3 ass, kid, oaf, rag, rib, sap, toy **4** boob, butt, clod, dolt, dope, dupe, fish, gull, hoax, jerk, jest, joke, josh, zany **5** chump, clown, comic, dally, dummy, dunce, goose, idiot, loser, moron, ninny, patsy, schmo, trick **6** banter, cretin, dawdle, delude, diddle, dimwit, doodle, galoot, gammon, jester, lead on, meddle, monkey, motley, nitwit, pigeon, schmoe, stooge, sucker, tamper, trifle, victim **7** beguile, buffoon, chicane, deceive, fake out, fall guy, fritter, half-wit, jackass, mislead, pinhead, saphead, schmuck **8** bonehead, comedian, dumbbell, flim-

flam, hoodwink, imbecile, lunkhead, numskull, pushover **9** bamboozle, birdbrain, blockhead, interfere, simpleton **10** nincompoop **11** hornswoggle, merry-andrew, string along **13** laughingstock *around:* **4** futz, idle, laze, loaf, loll **5** flirt **6** dawdle, diddle, lounge **8** lollygag, womanize **9** philander

foolhardy 4 bold, rash **6** daring, madcap **8** headlong, reckless **9** audacious, daredevil, impetuous **11** precipitate, temerarious

foolish 3 mad **4** daft, gaga, rash, zany **5** balmy, batty, crazy, dippy, dizzy, dorky, dotty, goofy, inane, inept, kooky, loony, loopy, nutty, sappy, silly, wacky **6** absurd, insane, simple, stupid, unwise **7** asinine, doltish, fatuous, idiotic, lunatic, meshuga, moronic, witless **8** clueless, reckless, trifling **9** half-baked, brainless, fantastic, frivolous, half-baked, imbecilic, insensate, laughable, ludicrous, senseless **10** cockamamie, half-cocked, half-witted, irrational, ridiculous **11** harebrained, nonsensical **12** feebleminded

foolishness 4 bull, bunk **5** folly, fudge **6** bêtise, bunkum, lunacy **7** fatuity, inanity, rubbish **8** claptrap, drollery, insanity, nonsense, tommyrot **9** absurdity, craziness, silliness, stupidity **10** imbecility, imprudence **12** fiddle-faddle **13** horsefeathers

fool's gold 6 pyrite

foot 3 paw **4** hoof *ailment:* **4** corn **6** bunion, callus *animal:* **3** pad, paw **4** hoof *bones of:* **5** talus, tarsi (plural) **6** cuboid, tarsal, tarsus **7** phalanx **9** calcaneus, cuneiform, navicular, phalanges (plural) **10** metatarsal *combining form:* **3** ped, pod **4** podo *doctor:* **10** podiatrist **11** chiropodist *metric:* **4** iamb **5** arsis **6** dactyl, thesis **7** anapest, pyrrhic, spondee, trochee *part:* **3** toe **4** arch, ball, claw, nail **5** ankle, digit, talon **6** hallux, instep

football 5 rugby **6** rugger, soccer **7** pigskin *field:* **8** gridiron *foul:* **7** holding, offside **8** clipping **12** interference *official:* **6** umpire **7** referee **8** linesman **9** back judge, line judge **10** field judge *play:* **4** dive, trap **5** sneak, sweep **6** option, screen **7** audible, counter, handoff, rollout, runback **8** dropback **9** crossbuck, off-tackle **10** buttonhook *player position:* **3** end **4** back **5** guard **6** center, safety, tackle **7** flanker, lineman, wideout **8** fullback, halfback, slotback, split end, tailback, tight end, wingback **9** noseguard **10** cornerback, linebacker, nose tackle **11** quarterback

12 defensive end, wide receiver *scoring:*
6 safety **9** field goal, touchdown **10** conversion *starting play:* **7** kickoff *team:*
6 eleven *term:* **4** down, kick, pass, punt, rush, snap **5** blitz, block, squad **6** fumble, huddle, kicker, onside, option, safety, spiral **7** end zone, handoff, kickoff, offside, pigskin, quarter, spinner, tweener, yardage **8** clipping, crossbar, goal line, goalpost, gridiron, halftime **9** backfield, defensive, field goal, intercept, offensive, placekick, scrimmage, touchback, touchdown **11** broken field **12** interception

footballer 3 end **4** half, Kemp (Jack), Long (Howie), Lott (Ronnie), Levy (Marv), Monk (Art), Moon (Warren), Reed (Andre), Rice (Jerry), wing **5** Allen (Marcus), Baugh (Sammy), Berry (Raymond), Brady (Tom), Brown (Bob, Jim), Clark (Gary), Ditka (Mike), Elway (John), Eller (Carl), Favre (Brett), Gibbs (Joe), Groza (Lou), guard, Jones (Bert, Deacon), Kelly (Jim), Kosar (Bernie), Leahy (Pat), Lomax (Neil), Muñoz (Anthony), Shula (Don), Simms (Phil), Smith (Emmitt), Starr (Bart), Stram (Hank), Swann (Lynn), Young (Steve) **6** Aikman (Troy), Blanda (George), Butkus (Dick), Carter (Chris, Ki-Jana), center, Csonka (Larry), Dawson (Len), Ellard (Henry), Graham (Otto), Grange (Red), Greene (Joe), Harris (Franco), Jaeger (Jeff), Joiner (Charlie), kicker, Lofton (James), Lowery (Nick), Marino (Dan), Murray (Eddie), Namath (Joe), Payton (Walter), player, Rypien (Mark), safety, Sayers (Gale), Slater (Jackie), tackle, Taylor (Lawrence), Thorpe (Jim), Tittle (Y.A.), Turner (Jim), Unitas (Johnny), Walker (Herschel) **7** Bledsoe (Drew), Dorsett (Tony), Esiason (Boomer), flanker, Gifford (Frank), Hornung (Paul), Johnson (Norm), Largent (Steve), lineman, Luckman (Sid), Manning (Peyton), Montana (Joe), Newsome (Ozzie), Riggins (John), Sanders (Barry, Deion), Simpson (O. J.), Stabler (Ken), Thurman (Thomas), tweener **8** Andersen (Morten), Anderson (Gary, Ottis), Bradshaw (Terry), defender, fullback, halfback, linesman, Nagurski (Bronko), Plunkett (Jim), receiver, scatback, split end, Staubach (Roger), tailback, tight end, wingback **9** Dickerson (Eric), Jurgensen (Sonny), Hostetler (Jeff), noseguard, Tarkenton (Fran) **10** cornerback, linebacker, Stallworth (John), Singletary (Mike), Stephenson (Dwight), Youngblood (Jack) **11** ballcarrier, placekicker, quarterback, running back, snapper-back **12** strong safety, triple threat, wide receiver

Foote play 15 Trip to Bountiful (The) **19** Young Man from Atlanta (The)
footfall 4 step **5** tread
footing 4 base, rank, seat, term **5** basis, place, state **6** bottom, ground, status **7** bedrock, seating, station, warrant **8** basement, capacity, pedestal, position, standing **9** character, situation **10** foundation, groundwork, substratum **12** underpinning
footless 4 dull, dumb **5** crass, dense, inept, unfit **6** stupid **7** foolish
foot lever 5 pedal **7** treadle
footman 7 servant **10** pedestrian **11** infantryman
footpad 5 thief **6** mugger, robber **8** criminal **10** highwayman, pickpocket
footprint 3 pug **4** sign, step **5** spoor, trace, track, tract **7** pugmark, vestige
footslog 4 plod, slop, toil **5** tramp, tromp **6** trudge
footstone 6 ledger, marker **8** monument **11** grave marker
footstool 7 cricket, hassock, ottoman
fop 3 jay **4** beau **5** blade, blood, dandy, spark, swell **7** coxcomb, gallant **8** cavalier, macaroni, popinjay **9** exquisite, ladies' man, pretty boy **10** lady-killer **11** Beau Brummel, petit-maître **12** fashion plate, lounge lizard
foppish 6 chichi **8** dandyish, peacocky **10** peacockish
for 3 pro
forage 4 beat, comb, grub, prog, raid, rake, sack **5** scour **6** browse, fodder, ravage, rustle, search **7** plunder, ransack, rummage **8** finecomb, scrounge **9** pasturage (see also FODDER)
foray 4 raid **6** inroad, sortie **8** invasion **9** incursion, irruption
forbear 4 shun **5** avoid, forgo, spare **6** endure, eschew, resist, suffer **7** abstain, decline, refrain **8** hold back, restrain, tolerate
forbearance 5 grace, mercy **6** lenity **7** charity **8** clemency, lenience, leniency, mildness, patience **9** restraint, tolerance **10** abstinence, toleration **13** consideration
forbearing 4 easy, kind, mild **6** gentle **7** clement, lenient, patient **8** merciful, tolerant **9** indulgent **10** charitable, thoughtful **11** considerate, magnanimous
Forbes hero 8 Tremaine (Johnny)
forbid 3 ban, bar, nix **4** curb, deny, halt, stop, veto **5** block, check, debar **6** enjoin, hinder, impede, outlaw, refuse

7 inhibit, prevent, rule out, shut out
8 disallow, obstruct, preclude, prohibit,
restrain **9** interdict, proscribe
forbidden 5 taboo **6** banned **7** illegal,
illicit **8** verboten **10** prohibited
Forbidden City 5 Lhasa **6** Gu Gong
7 Beijing
forbidding 4 grim **5** drear, harsh **6** dreary, severe **8** daunting, menacing, sinister **9** repellent **10** formidable **11** threatening
force 3 jam **4** cram, push **5** drive, foist,
impel, might, power, press, vigor,
wreak, wreck, wrest **6** coerce, compel,
demand, duress, effort, energy, extort,
impose, legion, muscle, oblige **7** command, impetus, inflict, potency,
require, sandbag **8** coercion, man-
power, momentum, obligate, pressure,
shoehorn, strength, violence **9** constrain, intensity, puissance, strong-arm
10 compulsion, constraint *apart:*
5 wedge *unit:* **4** dyne
forced 8 strained **9** contrived, unnatural
10 artificial, compulsory **11** involuntary
forceful 5 stiff, stout **6** mighty, potent,
punchy, strong, virile **7** dynamic
8 emphatic, powerful, puissant, vigorous **9** assertive **10** compelling
forceless 4 lame, weak **5** wimpy **6** feeble
8 impotent, nugatory **9** powerless
10 inadequate **11** ineffective, ineffectual
force out see EXPEL
forcible 8 coercive **9** compelled **10** compulsory, obligatory, peremptory
ford 5 cross
Ford's folly 5 Edsel
for each 3 per **6** apiece
forearm bone 4 ulna **6** radius
forebear 8 ancestor **9** precursor
10 antecedent, progenitor **11** predecessor **12** primogenitor
forebode 5 augur **7** betoken, portend,
predict, presage **8** foretell, prophesy,
soothsay **13** prognosticate
foreboding 4 omen, sign **5** dread
6 augury **7** anxiety, portent, presage,
warning **10** prediction, prognostic
11 premonition **12** apprehension, presentiment
forecast 5 augur **6** divine **7** foresee, portend, predict, presage **8** estimate, foretell, indicate, prophecy, prophesy
9 adumbrate, calculate, prevision,
prognosis **10** prediction **13** prognosticate
forecaster 4 seer **5** augur **6** oracle
7 diviner, prophet **8** haruspex **9** predictor **10** prophesier, soothsayer, weather-
man **11** Nostradamus **13** meteorologist,
weatherperson

foreclose 3 bar **5** debar **6** cut off, hinder
7 prevent, shut out **8** preclude
forefather see FOREBEAR
forefeel 6 divine **9** apprehend, prevision
forefinger 5 index
forefront 3 van **4** lead **8** vanguard
10 avant-garde, firing line
11 cutting edge
foregoer 6 herald **8** ancestor, forebear
9 harbinger, precursor, prototype
10 antecedent, antecessor, forerunner,
progenitor **11** predecessor **12** primogenitor
foregoing 5 prior **6** former **7** earlier
8 anterior, previous **9** precedent, preceding **10** antecedent
forehanded 7 prudent, thrifty **8** well-to-
do **9** provident **10** prosperous
forehead 4 brow **5** frons, front **8** sinciput
9 sincipita (plural)
foreign 5 alien **6** exotic **7** strange **8** external, offshore, overseas **9** extrinsic, nonnative **10** accidental, extraneous, immaterial, irrelevant **11** incongruous
12 adventitious, inapplicable, incompatible, inconsistent **13** inappropriate
prefix: **4** xeno
foreigner 5 alien **8** outsider, stranger
9 outlander **10** tramontane
foreknow 6 divine **9** apprehend, prevision **10** anticipate
foreland 4 beak, cape, head, ness **5** point
10 promontory
forelock 5 bangs, quiff
foreman 4 boss **5** chief **6** gaffer, ganger,
honcho, leader **7** captain, manager,
steward **8** overseer **10** supervisor
foremost 4 arch, head, high, main
5 chief, first, front, grand **7** leading,
premier, supreme **9** number one, paramount, principal **10** preeminent **11** cutting-edge, outstanding
forenoon 4 morn **7** morning **12** ante
meridiem
forensic 8 judicial **9** debatable **10** rhetorical **13** argumentative
foreordain 4 doom, fate **9** determine
10 predestine **12** predetermine
forerunner 4 omen, sign **5** envoy
6 augury, herald **7** pioneer, portent,
presage, symptom, warning **8** ancestor,
exemplar, outrider **9** announcer, harbinger, initiator, messenger
10 antecedent, originator, prognostic
11 anticipator, predecessor
foresee 6 divine **7** predict, presage **8** perceive, prophesy **9** apprehend, prefigure,
prevision **10** anticipate **13** prognosticate
foreseer 5 augur **6** auspex, oracle
7 diviner, prophet **8** haruspex **9** predictor **10** soothsayer **11** Nostradamus

foreshadow 4 bode, hint 5 augur 6 herald 7 betoken, portend, predict, presage, promise, suggest 8 forecast, intimate 9 adumbrate, prefigure 13 prognosticate

foresight 6 vision 7 caution 8 prudence, sagacity 10 discretion, perception, precaution, prescience, providence

forest 4 bosk, wood 5 copse, grove, weald, woods 6 bosque 7 coppice, thicket, woodlot 8 wildwood, woodland 10 timberland, wilderness *deity:* 5 dryad 6 sylvan 8 Sylvanus *English:* 5 Arden 8 Sherwood *opening:* 5 glade *relating to:* 6 sylvan *subarctic:* 5 taiga *tropical:* 5 selva 6 jungle

forestall 5 avert, block, deter 6 hinder 7 obviate, preempt, prevent, rule out, ward off 8 preclude, stave off 10 anticipate

Forester, C. S. *hero:* 10 Hornblower (Horatio) *novel:* 12 African Queen (The)

foretell 4 bode, warn 5 augur 6 divine 7 portend, predict, presage, promise 8 proclaim, prophesy, soothsay 9 adumbrate, apprehend, prefigure 10 anticipate, vaticinate 13 prognosticate

forethought 8 judgment, planning, prudence 10 discretion, precaution 12 deliberation 13 premeditation

foretoken 4 bode, hint, omen, sign, warn 5 augur, augury, herald 7 portend, portent, presage, promise, symptom, warning 8 forecast 9 harbinger, precursor 10 intimation

forever 3 aye 6 always 7 endless 8 eternity, evermore 9 endlessly, eternally 10 in aeternum 11 ad infinitum, ceaselessly, continually, everlasting, incessantly, permanently, perpetually, unceasingly 12 in perpetuity 13 everlastingly

forewarning 6 caveat, tip-off 7 caution 8 monition 11 premonition

foreword 5 intro, proem 7 preface, prelude 8 exordium, overture, preamble, prologue 12 introduction, prolegomenon

for example 6 such as

for fear that 4 lest

forfeit 4 fine, lose 5 mulct 6 give up 7 penalty 9 sacrifice 10 amercement

forfend 4 ward 5 avert, deter 6 secure 7 obviate, prevent, protect, rule out, ward off 8 preclude, preserve, stave off

forge 4 copy, fake, form, make 5 pound, shape 6 smithy 7 advance, fashion, imitate, produce, turn out 8 continue 9 construct, fabricate 11 counterfeit, manufacture

forget 4 fail, omit 5 ignore, slight 7 neglect 8 discount, overlook, pass over 9 disregard

forgetful 3 lax 5 slack 6 absent, remiss 7 amnesic 8 amnesiac, careless, heedless 9 negligent, oblivious, unwitting 10 abstracted, neglectful 11 inattentive, thoughtless 12 absentminded

forgetfulness 5 lethe 7 amnesia 8 oblivion 10 negligence 11 inattention

forgivable 6 venial 10 remissible

forgive 5 remit 6 excuse, pardon 7 absolve, condone 8 overlook

forgiveness 6 pardon 7 amnesty 9 remission 10 absolution

forgo 3 bag 5 leave, waive, yield 6 eschew, give up, resign 7 abandon 8 abnegate, jettison, renounce 9 sacrifice, surrender 10 relinquish

fork 6 bisect, branch, crotch 7 diverge, utensil 9 branch off *prong:* 4 tine

fork out 3 pay 5 spend 10 contribute

forlorn 4 alone 6 bereft, futile, lonely 8 desolate, forsaken, hopeless, lonesome, solitary, wretched 9 abandoned, depressed, destitute, miserable 10 despairing, despondent 12 disconsolate

form 3 way 4 body, cast, make, mode, mold 5 build, forge, found, frame, image, model, shape, style 6 create, design, devise, figure, make up, manner 7 compose, contour, develop, fashion, outline, process, produce, profile 8 comprise, organize, practice 9 construct, establish, fabricate, framework, procedure, structure, take shape 10 constitute, convention, regulation 11 materialize 13 configuration *combining form:* 5 morph

formal 3 set 4 prim 5 exact, legal, rigid, stiff 6 dressy, lawful, proper, seemly, solemn 7 distant, orderly, regular, stately, starchy, stilted 8 abstract, black-tie, decorous, elevated, official, reserved 10 ceremonial, methodical, systematic 11 ceremonious, syntactical 12 conventional

formality 4 form, rite 6 ritual 7 liturgy, service 8 ceremony, insignia 10 ceremonial, convention, observance

formalize 6 codify 9 establish, normalize 10 regularize 11 standardize

format 4 plan, size 5 shape, style 6 makeup, method 11 arrangement 12 organization

formation 4 rank 6 design, makeup 9 structure 11 arrangement, composition, development 12 architecture, construction

former 3 old 4 late, once, past 5 prior 6 bygone, whilom 7 earlier, onetime,

quondam 8 anterior, previous, sometime **9** erstwhile, precedent, preceding **10** antecedent

formerly 4 erst, once **6** before, whilom **7** already, earlier **9** erstwhile **10** heretofore, previously

formidable 8 daunting **9** difficult **10** impressive **11** redoubtable

formless 5 vague **7** chaotic, obscure, unclear **8** inchoate, nebulous, unshaped **9** amorphous, undefined, unordered **10** immaterial, indefinite, indistinct **11** unorganized

Formosa 6 Taiwan *capital:* **6** Taipei

formula 4 rite, rule **5** canon, maxim, tenet **6** method, recipe, ritual **7** precept, theorem **8** equation **9** algorithm, blueprint, principle, yardstick **10** touchstone **12** prescription

formulate 5 couch, draft, frame, hatch **6** codify, devise, invent, make up, phrase **7** concoct, dream up, express, prepare, work out **8** contrive

forsake 4 quit **5** avoid, leave, spurn **6** defect, depart, desert, give up, reject, resign **7** abandon **8** abdicate, renounce **9** throw over **10** relinquish

forsaken 4 lorn **6** bereft **7** forlorn **8** derelict, deserted, desolate, solitary **9** abandoned

Forseti *father:* **6** Balder *palace:* **7** Glitnir

forswear 4 deny **5** unsay **6** abjure, recall, recant, reject **7** perjure, retract **8** renounce, take back, withdraw

fort 6 castle **7** bastion, bulwark, citadel, redoubt **8** fastness, fortress, garrison, martello, stockade **10** stronghold *Baltimore:* **7** McHenry *California:* **3** Ord *New Jersey:* **3** Dix *New York:* **7** Niagara, Stanwix **8** Schuyler **11** Ticonderoga *Ontario:* **9** Frontenac *San Antonio:* **5** Alamo *South Carolina:* **6** Sumter *Spanish:* **7** alcazar **8** presidio

forte 3 bag **4** loud **5** thing **6** métier **8** long suit, strength **9** specialty **10** strong suit **11** strong point

forthcoming 7 pending **8** imminent **9** impending, proximate **10** responsive **11** approaching

for the most part 9 generally, typically **10** on the whole

for the time being 3 now **6** pro tem **9** at present, currently, presently **10** pro tempore

forthright 4 open **5** blunt, frank, plain **6** candid, direct **7** up-front **8** straight **10** aboveboard, foursquare **11** openhearted, straight-out, undisguised, unvarnished

forthwith 3 now **6** at once **8** directly **9** instantly, right away, thereupon **11** immediately, straightway **12** straightaway

fortification 4 moat, wall **6** abatis, buffer, glacis **7** barrier, bastion, bulwark, citadel, parapet, rampart, redoubt **8** barbican, enceinte, fastness, garrison, palisade, presidio, stockade **9** barricade, earthwork **10** breastwork, stronghold *part:* **7** salient

fortify 3 arm **4** gird, stir **5** brace, rally, ready, renew, rouse, steel **6** enrich, secure **7** hearten, prepare, protect, refresh, restore **8** embolden, energize **9** encourage, reinforce **10** invigorate, strengthen

fortitude 4 grit, guts, pith **5** fiber, heart, nerve, pluck, spunk, valor **6** mettle, phlegm, spirit **7** bravery, courage, stamina **8** backbone, boldness, strength, tenacity **9** constancy, endurance, tolerance **10** resolution **11** intrepidity **12** fearlessness, perseverance, resoluteness, staying power **13** dauntlessness, determination

fortress see FORT

fortuitous 5 fluky, happy, lucky **6** casual, chance **10** accidental, auspicious **12** providential

fortuity 3 hap **4** luck **5** fluke **6** chance **8** accident **9** happening **10** occurrence

Fortuna 5 Tyche *symbol:* **5** wheel **6** rudder

fortunate 5 happy, lucky **9** favorable **10** auspicious, propitious **12** providential

Fortunate Islands 8 Canaries

fortune 3 lot, pot, wad **4** doom, fate, luck, mint, pile, ship **5** worth **6** boodle, bundle, chance, happen, hazard, packet, riches, wealth **7** destiny, success, weather **8** property **9** resources

Fortune founder 4 Luce (Henry)

fortune-teller 4 seer **5** augur, sibyl **7** diviner, palmist **9** wisewoman **10** soothsayer (see also FORESEER)

fortune-telling see DIVINATION

forty winks 3 nap **6** catnap, siesta, snooze **7** shut-eye

forum 5 court, panel **6** medium **8** congress, tribunal **9** symposium **10** colloquium, conference, roundtable **11** convocation, marketplace

forward 3 aid **4** abet, bold, send, ship **5** ahead, brash, eager, pushy, ready, relay, remit, sassy, saucy **6** cheeky, foster, onward, uphold **7** address, advance, consign, further, promote, support **8** advanced, champion, dispatch, impudent, transmit **9** encourage, in advance **11** smart-alecky **12** presumptuous **13** self-assertive *prefix:* **4** ante

For Whom the Bell Tolls *author:* 9 Hemingway (Ernest) *character:* 5 Maria, Pablo, Pilar 6 Jordan

Forza del Destino composer 5 Verdi (Giuseppe)

fossa 3 pit 5 fovea 6 cavity, groove 10 depression

fosse 4 dike, moat 5 canal, ditch 6 trench 7 acequia, channel

fossil 4 fogy 5 amber, relic 7 antique 8 calamite, conodont, mossback 10 antiquated, fuddy-duddy 12 antediluvian 13 stick-in-the-mud *fuel:* 3 gas, oil 4 coal, peat 9 petroleum 10 natural gas

foster 4 back, help, rear, tend 5 nurse 6 assist, harbor, parent 7 advance, bring up, nourish, nurture, promote, support, sustain 8 champion 9 cultivate, encourage

fou 5 crazy, drunk

foul 4 base, rank, soil, vile 5 botch, dirty, fetid, funky, muddy, nasty, yucky 6 coarse, defile, filthy, grubby, horrid, impure, odious, putrid, rotten, scuzzy, smutty, stormy, turbid, vulgar, wicked 7 abusive, noisome, obscene, pollute, profane, raunchy, squalid, tarnish, unclean 8 indecent, obstruct, polluted, stinking, wretched 9 collision, loathsome, obnoxious, offensive, repellent, repugnant, repulsive, revolting 10 abominable, detestable, disgusting, malodorous 11 contaminate, treacherous 12 dishonorable, scatological

foul play 3 hit 5 blood 6 murder 7 killing, outrage 8 homicide, violence 12 manslaughter

found 4 base, cast, rear 5 begin, erect, raise, set up, start 6 bottom, create, invent 7 fashion, support 8 commence, initiate, organize 9 establish, institute, originate, predicate

foundation 3 bed 4 base, rock 5 basis 6 bottom, corset, makeup 7 bedding, footing, support 8 pedestal 9 endowment 10 groundwork, substratum 11 institution 12 organization, substructure, underpinning

foundational 5 basic 6 bottom 7 primary 10 supportive, underlying 11 fundamental

founder 4 fail, sink 5 wreck 6 author, father, go down 7 creator 8 collapse, inventor, submerge, submerse 9 architect, generator, patriarch, shipwreck 10 originator

fountain 3 jet 4 head, root 5 spout 6 geyser, origin, source, spring 7 bubbler 8 wellhead 9 inception, reservoir 10 wellspring *nymph:* 6 Egeria

four 6 tetrad 7 quartet 10 quaternion *bagger:* 5 homer 7 home run *combining form:* 4 tetr 5 quadr, tetra 6 quadri, quadru, quater, tessar 7 tessara, tessera *gills:* 4 pint *hundred:* 5 elite 10 upper crust *inches:* 4 hand *pecks:* 6 bushel *quarts:* 6 gallon

four-flush 4 dupe 5 bluff 6 betray, delude, humbug, take in 7 beguile, deceive 11 doublecross

four-footed animal 8 tetrapod 9 quadruped

Four Horsemen 3 War 5 Death 6 Famine 8 Conquest 10 Pestilence

four-in-hand 3 tie 5 coach 7 necktie

fourpence 5 groat

four-poster 3 bed

fourscore 6 eighty

four-sided figure 5 rhomb 6 square 7 rhombus 9 rectangle 13 quadrilateral, parallelogram

foursquare 8 straight 10 forthright 13 quadrilateral

fourteen pounds 5 stone

fourth 7 quarter 8 quadrant, quartern *combining form:* 5 quadr, quart 6 quadri, quadru

fowl 3 hen 4 bird, cock, duck 5 chick, goose, poult 6 bantam, pullet, turkey 7 chicken, rooster (see also CHICKEN; POULTRY)

Fowles novel 5 Magus (The) 9 Collector (The) 22 French Lieutenant's Woman (The)

fox 4 fool 5 trick 6 baffle, outwit 7 confuse, reynard 8 bewilder *African:* 4 asse *female:* 5 vixen *kind:* 3 kit, red 5 swift 6 arctic, fennec, silver 8 bat-eared *Scottish:* 3 tod *young:* 3 cub

foxglove 9 digitalis

fox grape 9 muscadine 11 scuppernong

foxiness 4 wile 5 craft, guile 7 cunning, slyness 8 wiliness 10 artfulness, craftiness, cleverness

foxlike 7 vulpine

foxy 3 sly 4 wily 5 canny, slick 6 artful, astute, clever, crafty, shrewd, tricky 7 cunning, vulpine 8 guileful 9 insidious

foyer 5 lobby 8 anteroom, entrance 9 vestibule

fracas 3 row 4 feud, fray 5 brawl, broil, fight, melee, run-in, set-to 6 affray, hassle, shindy, uproar 7 dispute, quarrel, ruction 8 squabble 9 bickering 10 donnybrook, free-for-all 11 altercation

fraction 3 bit, cut 4 part 5 piece, scrap 6 divide, little 7 portion, section 8 fragment

fractious 4 wild 6 unruly 7 peevish, pettish, willful 8 contrary 9 bellicose, irritable 10 headstrong, pugnacious,

refractory **11** belligerent, contentious, intractable, quarrelsome **12** recalcitrant, ungovernable, unmanageable
fracture 4 rent, rift, tear **5** break, cleft, crack, split **6** breach, schism **7** rupture
Fra Diavolo composer 5 Auber (Esprit)
fragile 4 weak **5** frail **6** feeble, flimsy, infirm **7** brittle, friable, tenuous, unsound **8** decrepit, delicate **9** breakable, frangible
fragment 3 bit **4** chip, iota, part, rive **5** burst, crumb, flake, grain, piece, scrap, shard, shred, smash **6** morsel, shiver, sliver **7** break up, flinder, shatter **8** fraction, particle, splinter **9** fall apart **12** disintegrate
fragmentary 6 broken **7** partial **10** fractional, incomplete, unfinished
fragrance 4 musk, nose, odor **5** aroma, attar, scent, smell, spice **7** bouquet, cologne, incense, perfume **9** redolence **11** eau de parfum, toilet water **13** eau de toilette
fragrant 7 odorous, scented **8** aromatic, perfumed, redolent **11** odoriferous
frail 4 puny, slim, thin, weak **5** petty, reedy, wispy **6** feeble, flimsy, infirm, sickly, slight **7** brittle, fragile, slender, spindly, tenuous, unsound **8** decrepit, delicate **9** breakable, frangible
frailty 4 vice **5** fault **6** foible **7** failing **8** delicacy, weakness **9** infirmity **10** feebleness **11** tenuousness **12** imperfection
frame 4 body, form, mold, plan, sash **5** build, draft, erect, forge, mount, shape, shell **6** border, casing, cook up, devise, draw up, figure, invent, make up, sketch, system **7** arrange, chassis, concoct, fashion, imagine, prepare **8** assemble, casement, conceive, contrive, regulate, skeleton **9** cartouche, construct, fabricate, formulate, structure *part:* **4** sill, stud **5** joist, plate
framework 4 rack **5** shell, truss **7** trestle **8** cribbing, cribwork, scaffold, skeleton, studding, studwork, trussing **9** bare bones, structure *of crossed strips:* **7** lattice, trellis
France bay: **6** Biscay *capital:* **5** Paris *channel:* **6** Manche (La) **7** English *city:* **4** Caen, Lyon, Metz, Nice **5** Brest, Lyons **6** Amiens, Calais, Nantes, Rennes **8** Bordeaux, Grenoble, Toulouse **9** Marseille **10** Marseilles, Strasbourg, Versailles **11** Montpellier *conqueror:* **6** Caesar (Julius) *emperor:* **5** Pepin (III, the Short) **8** Napoleon (Bonaparte) **11** Charlemagne *enclave:* **6** Monaco *former name:* **4** Gaul **6** Gallia *historic province:* **4** Foix **5** Anjou, Aunis, Bearn, Berry, Maine **6** Alsace, Artois,

Marche, Poitou, Vendée **7** Gascony, Guyenne, Picardy **8** Auvergne, Bretagne, Brittany, Burgundy, Dauphine, Flanders, Gascogne, Limousin, Lorraine, Lyonnais, Normandy, Picardie, Provence, Touraine **9** Angoumois, Bourgogne, Champagne, Languedoc, Nivernois, Orléanais, Saintonge, Venaissin **10** Roussillon **11** Bourbonnais, Île-de-France **12** Franche-Comté *island:* **3** Yeu **6** Hyères, Oléron, Ushant **7** Corsica **8** Belle-Île **11** Noirmoutier *monarch:* **5** Henri, Henry, Louis **6** Philip **7** Charles **8** Philippe *monetary unit:* **4** euro *monetary unit, former:* **3** sou **5** franc *mountain, range:* **4** Alps, Jura **6** Vosges **8** Auvergne, Pyrenees **9** Mont Blanc *neighbor:* **5** Italy, Spain **7** Andorra, Belgium, Germany **10** Luxembourg **11** Switzerland *president:* **8** de Gaulle (Charles) **10** Mitterrand (François) *region:* **5** Corse **6** Alsace, Centre **7** Corsica, Picardy **8** Auvergne, Bretagne, Brittany, Burgundy, Limousin, Normandy, Picardie **9** Aquitaine, Bourgogne, Champagne, Languedoc, Normandie **10** Rhône-Alpes **11** Île-de-France **12** Franche-Comté, Midi-Pyrénées *river:* **4** Aire, Aude, Oise **5** Adour, Isère, Loire, Marne, Rhone, Saône, Seine, Somme, Yonne **7** Garonne *sea:* **13** Mediterranean *strait:* **5** Dover
Francesca's lover 5 Paolo
franchise 4 vote **6** ballot **7** freedom, license **8** suffrage **9** privilege
frangible 7 brittle, fragile, friable **8** delicate **9** breakable
frank 3 dog **4** fair, free, open **5** blunt, plain **6** candid, direct, honest, hot dog, weenie, wiener, wienie **7** upright **8** man-to-man, out-front, straight **9** barefaced, outspoken **10** forthright, scrupulous, unreserved **11** openhearted, plainspoken, transparent, unconcealed, undisguised, uninhibited, unvarnished, wienerwurst **12** heart-to-heart, unmistakable
Frankenstein author 7 Shelley (Mary)
frankfurter 3 dog **6** hot dog, weenie, wiener, wienie **11** wienerwurst
Frankie's lover 6 Johnny
Frankish hero 6 Roland
Franklin, Benjamin *birthplace:* **6** Boston *invention:* **5** stove **8** bifocals *pen name:* **11** Poor Richard
frankness 6 candor **7** honesty
frantic 3 mad **4** wild **5** upset, wired **7** fraught, shook up, unglued **8** feverish, frenetic, frenzied, maniacal, worked up **10** distraught **11** overwrought
Franzen novel 11 Corrections (The)

frappe 7 chilled, liqueur 9 milk shake
fraternal 6 clubby 8 sociable 9 brotherly, comradely, dizygotic 10 like-minded
fraternal society 3 FOE 4 BPOE, Elks 5 Lions, Moose 6 Eagles, Masons 7 Woodmen (of the World) 8 Shriners 10 Freemasons, Hibernians, Odd Fellows
fraternity 4 club 5 guild, order, union 6 league 7 company 8 sodality 10 fellowship 11 association, brotherhood 13 brotherliness
fraud 3 gyp 4 fake, gaff, hoax, sham 5 cheat, faker, phony, quack, trick 6 deceit, dupery, humbug, hustle 7 chicane, swindle 8 cozenage, flimflam, impostor, operator, trickery 9 charlatan, chicanery, deception, imposture, pretender, shell game, trickster 10 dishonesty, mountebank, subterfuge 11 counterfeit 12 double-dealer 13 double-dealing, sharp practice
fraudulence 6 deceit 8 quackery, trickery 9 chicanery, deception, phoniness 10 dishonesty
fraudulent 4 fake 5 false, phony 7 crooked 8 cheating, guileful 9 deceitful, deceptive, dishonest 10 fallacious 11 duplicitous
fraught 4 full 5 laden, tense 6 filled, uneasy 7 charged, replete, stuffed 8 pregnant 9 stressful
fräulein 4 maid, Miss 6 maiden 9 governess 12 mademoiselle
fray 3 row 4 fret 5 brawl, broil, brush, clash, fight, melee, ravel, shred 6 combat, fracas, strain, strife 7 dispute, frazzle, ruction, scuffle 8 irritate, skirmish, struggle 9 commotion, scrimmage 10 donnybrook 11 disturbance
frayed 4 worn 6 ragged, shabby 8 tattered 9 moth-eaten 10 threadbare
frazzle 4 do in, fray, poop, tire, wear 5 upset 6 tucker 7 exhaust, fatigue, wear out
frazzled 4 beat 5 upset 6 bushed, sapped 7 drained, rattled 8 agitated, confused, fatigued, tired out 9 exhausted, fagged out, unsettled 10 distressed 11 overwrought 12 disconcerted
freak 3 bug, nut 4 buff, geek, whim 5 go ape, fancy, fiend, maven 6 addict, hippie, maniac, megrim, oddity, vagary, weirdo, whimsy, zealot 7 anomaly, caprice, chimera, conceit, deviate, fanatic, monster 8 crotchet, flimflam 9 androgyne, curiosity 10 aberration, enthusiast 11 abnormality, monstrosity 12 lusus naturae, malformation
freakish 3 odd 5 kooky, outré, weird 6 far-out, quirky 7 bizarre, erratic, oddball, strange 8 aberrant, abnormal

9 arbitrary, eccentric, grotesque, whimsical 10 capricious, outlandish
freckle 3 dot 4 mole, spot 5 fleck 7 speckle, stipple
free 3 rid 4 comp, open 5 frank, loose, untie 6 acquit, exempt, gratis, loosen, unbind, untied 7 absolve, at large, liberal, manumit, movable, release, unbound, unchain, unleash, unloose 8 detached, generous, liberate, relieved, separate, unburden, unfasten, unloosen 9 at liberty, discharge, exculpate, exonerate, extricate, sovereign, unchained, unchecked, unimpeded, unshackle, unsparing 10 autonomous, democratic, emancipate, gratuitous, unconfined, unfastened, unfettered, unhampered, unshackled, voluntary 11 disentangle, emancipated, independent, spontaneous, untrammeled 12 unrestrained, unrestricted 13 complimentary, self-directing, self-governing, unconstrained
freebie 4 gift, pass 7 present 8 giveaway
freebooter 5 rover 6 bandit, pirate, raider 7 brigand, corsair 8 marauder, picaroon, pillager, rapparee, sea rover 9 buccaneer, pickaroon, plunderer, ransacker
freedom 5 right 7 liberty, license, release 8 autonomy, immunity, latitude 9 exemption, franchise, privilege 11 prerogative 12 emancipation, independence 13 outspokenness
free-for-all 4 fray 5 brawl, broil, melee 6 affray, fracas, rumble 7 ruction 10 donnybrook
freehanded 7 liberal 8 generous 9 bounteous, bountiful 10 munificent
freeloader 3 bum 5 leech 6 sponge 7 moocher 8 barnacle, hanger-on, parasite 11 bloodsucker
Free State 8 Maryland
free ticket 4 pass 11 Annie Oakley
freeze 4 halt, stop 5 chill, stall 6 benumb 7 congeal 8 glaciate, solidify, stoppage 10 immobilize
freezing 3 icy 4 cold 5 chill, gelid, nippy, polar 6 arctic, bitter, chilly, frigid, frosty, wintry 7 glacial, shivery *combining form:* 4 cryo, kryo
freight 4 haul, lade, load 5 cargo 6 burden, charge, lading 7 payload 9 transport
freighter 4 scow, ship 7 carrier, shipper
Freischütz composer 5 Weber (Carl Maria von)
French *article:* 3 les, une *attendant:* 9 concierge *back:* 3 dos *bed:* 3 lit 6 couche *boy:* 6 garçon *brother:* 5 frère *cap:* 5 beret *cardinal:* 7 Mazarin (Jules) 9 Richelieu (Duc de) *castle:* 7 château

cathedral city: 4 Albi 5 Paris, Reims, Rouen 6 Amiens, Nantes, Rheims 8 Chartres *clergyman:* 4 abbé, curé, père *coin:* 3 ecu *combining form:* 5 Gallo 6 Franco *conjunction:* 4 mais *daughter:* 5 fille *day:* 5 jeudi, lundi, mardi 6 samedi 8 dimanche, mercredi, vendredi *dear:* 4 cher *department head:* 7 prefect *direction:* 3 est, sud 4 nord 5 ouest *down with:* 4 à bas *dream:* 4 rêve *drink:* 5 boire *dynasty:* 5 Capet 6 Valois 7 Bourbon *egg:* 4 oeuf *emblem:* 10 fleur-de-lis *empress:* 7 Eugénie 9 Joséphine *evening:* 4 soir *exclamation:* 3 zut 4 eheu, hein 9 sacrebleu *farewell:* 5 adieu 8 au revoir *father:* 4 père *forest:* 7 Argonne, Belleau *friend:* 3 ami 4 amie *game:* 3 jeu 4 jeux (plural) *God:* 4 dieu *good:* 3 bon 5 bonne *hat:* 7 chapeau *here:* 3 ici *income:* 5 rente *king:* 3 roi *language:* 9 Provençal *month:* 3 mai 4 août, juin, mars, mois 5 avril 7 février, janvier, juillet *mother:* 4 mère *national anthem:* 12 Marseillaise (La) *opera:* 5 Faust, Lakmé, Manon, Thaïs 6 Carmen, Mignon 7 Werther *pancake:* 5 crêpe *pastry:* 6 éclair 8 napoleon *policeman:* 4 flic 8 gendarme *porcelain:* 6 Sèvres 7 Limoges *preposition:* 3 par, sur 4 avec, dans, pour, sans, sous *pretty:* 4 joli 5 jolie *prison:* 8 Bastille *pronoun:* 3 eux, ils, mes, moi, toi, une 4 elle, nous, vous *Protestant:* 6 Calvin (John) 8 Huguenot *pupil:* 5 élève *queen:* 5 reine *rabbit:* 5 lapin *railroad station:* 4 gare *resort:* 3 Pau 4 Nice 5 Vichy 6 Cannes, Menton 7 Antibes 8 Biarritz *resort area:* 7 Riviera *restaurant:* 6 bistro *revolutionist:* 5 Marat (Jean-Paul) 6 Danton (Georges) 11 Robespierre (Maximilien) *Revolution party:* 7 Gironde, Jacobin 8 Mountain *Revolution song:* 5 Ça Ira *saint:* 4 Joan (of Arc) 5 Denis 6 Martin (of Tours) 7 Thérèse (of Lisieux) *school:* 5 école, lycée *sea:* 3 mer *season:* 3 été 5 hiver 7 automne 9 printemps *servant:* 5 valet *shop:* 8 boutique *shrine:* 7 Lourdes *singer:* 4 Piaf (Edith) 8 chanteur 9 chanteuse *sister:* 5 soeur *small:* 5 petit 6 petite *soldier:* 5 poilu 6 soldat, Zouave 8 chasseur *son:* 4 fils *song:* 7 chanson *soup:* 6 potage *star:* 6 étoile *state:* 4 état *stock exchange:* 6 bourse *street:* 3 rue *subway:* 5 metro *there!:* 5 voilà *too much:* 4 trop *very:* 4 très *wartime capital:* 5 Vichy *water:* 3 eau *well:* 4 bien *wineshop:* 6 bistro *wood:* 4 bois *yesterday:* 4 hier

French Guiana *capital:* 7 Cayenne *department of:* 6 France *ethnic group:* 6 Creole *island:* 6 Devil's *mountain range:* 10 Tumac-Humac *neighbor:* 6 Brazil

8 Suriname *river:* 4 Mana 6 Maroni 7 Oyapock

French Polynesia *archipelago* 7 Tuamotu *capital:* 7 Papeete *island, island group:* 6 Tahiti 7 Austral, Gambier, Society 9 Marquesas *territory of:* 6 France

frenetic 3 mad 4 loco, wild 5 crazy, wired 6 crazed, hectic 7 berserk, frantic 8 agitated, feverish, frenzied, maniacal 9 delirious, orgiastic 10 corybantic

frenzied see FRENETIC

frenzy 4 amok, fury, rage 5 amuck, craze, furor, mania 6 madden 7 derange, madness, unhinge 8 delirium, distract, hysteria, insanity, paroxysm 9 unbalance 11 derangement

frequency unit 5 hertz 7 fresnel 9 gigahertz, megahertz

frequent 5 haunt, often, usual, visit 6 common, hourly 7 regular 8 everyday, familiar, habitual 9 customary

frequenter 7 denizen, habitué, haunter

frequently 5 often 8 commonly 9 routinely 10 oftentimes, repeatedly 11 customarily, recurrently

fresh 3 new, raw 4 rude 5 green, naive, novel, sassy, saucy, smart 6 callow, cheeky, recent, unused, vernal, virgin 8 brand-new, impudent, insolent, original 9 unspoiled 11 impertinent, smart-alecky 12 invigorating 13 inexperienced

freshet 5 flood, spate 6 influx

freshman 4 tyro 5 frosh, plebe 6 novice, rookie 8 beginner, neophyte, newcomer 10 apprentice, tenderfoot 13 underclassman

fret 4 fume, fuss, stew 5 brood, chafe, worry 6 dither, pother

fretful 5 angry, cross 6 crabby, cranky 7 carping, chafing, peevish, pettish, whining 8 captious, caviling, critical, perverse, petulant, restless, snappish 9 fractious, impatient, irascible, irritable, querulous

Frey *father:* 5 Njörd 6 Njörth *god of:* 3 sun 4 rain 5 peace 9 fertility *sister:* 5 Freya *wife:* 4 Gerd 5 Gerda, Gerth

Freya *brother:* 4 Frey *domain:* 9 Folkvangr *father:* 5 Njörd 6 Njörth *husband:* 4 Odin

friable 5 mealy 7 brittle, crumbly, fragile 9 frangible

friar 7 brother 8 cenobite 9 mendicant

fribble 3 toy 5 dally, flirt 6 coquet, trifle 7 trifler 8 trifling 9 dalliance, frivolity 10 dillydally, fool around

friction 4 drag 7 discord, rubbing 8 abrasion 9 animosity, attrition 10 disharmony, dissension, resistance 12 disagreement

friction match 5 vesta 7 lucifer 8 vesuvian

Friday's rescuer 6 Crusoe (Robinson)

friend 3 pal **4** ally, chum, mate **5** buddy, crony, matey, serve **6** cohort **7** comrade, partner **8** alter ego, compadre, confrere, familiar, intimate, playmate, sidekick **9** associate, colleague, companion, confidant **10** confidante **11** cater-cousin **12** acquaintance *French:* **3** ami **4** amie *Spanish:* **5** amiga, amigo

Friend 6 Quaker *founder:* **3** Fox (George)

friendly 5 happy **6** amical, chummy, folksy, genial **7** affable, amiable, cordial **8** amicable, cheerful, familiar, sociable **9** congenial, favorable **10** buddy-buddy, compatible, hospitable, neighborly **12** affectionate, well-disposed **13** accommodating

Friendly Islands 5 Tonga

friends and neighbors 4 kith

friendship 5 amity **6** accord, comity **7** concord, empathy, harmony **8** affinity, alliance, goodwill

frigate bird 3 ioa, iwa **8** alcatras **11** man-o'-war bird *genus:* **7** Fregata

Frigga, Frigg *husband:* **4** Odin *son:* **6** Balder

fright 4 fear **5** alarm, dread, panic, scare, shock **6** dismay, horror, terror **11** trepidation

frighten 3 cow **5** alarm, bully, daunt, scare, shock, spook **6** appall, dismay **7** horrify, perturb, scarify, startle, terrify, unnerve **9** terrorize **10** intimidate

frightful 4 ugly **5** awful, scary **6** horrid **7** fearful, ghastly, hideous **8** alarming, dreadful, fearsome, horrible, horrific, shocking, terrible, terrific **9** appalling, startling **10** formidable, horrendous, terrifying

frigid 3 icy **4** cold **5** chill **6** arctic, chilly, frosty **7** glacial **8** freezing **11** emotionless, indifferent, passionless, unemotional **12** unresponsive

frijoles 5 beans

frill 4 ruff **5** jabot, ruche **6** doodad, luxury, ruffle **7** flounce, ruching **8** furbelow **11** affectation, superfluity **12** extravagance

fringe 3 hem, rim **4** brim, ruff **5** bound, brink, skirt, thrum, verge **6** border, edging, margin **7** fimbria **8** penumbra, trimming **9** perimeter, periphery **10** borderland

frippery 6 finery, frills, tawdry **7** regalia **8** foofaraw, trumpery **9** trappings **11** ostentation

frisée 6 endive **7** lettuce

frisk 4 leap, play, romp, skip **5** caper, dance **6** cavort, frolic, gambol, search **7** disport, pat down, rollick

frisky 3 gay **5** antic **6** feisty, lively **7** coltish, playful **8** animated, gamesome, sportive **9** sprightly, vivacious **10** frolicsome

fritter away 4 blow **5** spend, waste **7** consume **8** squander **9** dissipate

frivolity 3 fun **4** play **6** gaiety, levity, whimsy **8** nonsense **12** childishness

frivolous 3 gay **5** dizzy, giddy, light, silly **6** frothy, yeasty **7** flighty, playful, shallow, trivial **8** carefree, careless, heedless, trifling **11** light-headed, superficial

frizzy 5 kinky **6** coiled, curled **7** twisted

frock 4 gown **5** dress, habit **6** jersey, mantle

frog 4 toad **5** ranid **6** anuran **7** croaker **9** amphibian **10** batrachian *family:* **7** Ranidae *genus:* **4** Rana *kind:* **4** hyla **6** peeper **7** leopard **8** bullfrog, tree toad *larva:* **7** tadpole

frolic 3 fun **4** lark, play, romp **5** antic, caper, dance, frisk, party, prank, revel, sport, spree **6** cavort, didoes, gaiety, gambol, prance **7** disport, skylark **8** escapade, hilarity **9** festivity, merriment **10** shenanigan, tomfoolery

frolicsome 3 gay **5** antic **6** frisky, impish **7** coltish, jocular, playful, roguish **8** sportful, sportive **9** sprightly **10** rollicking **11** mischievous

from *German:* **3** von *Scottish:* **4** frae

From Here to Eternity author 5 Jones (James)

frondeur 5 rebel **8** mutineer, renegade **9** anarchist, dissident, insurgent **10** malcontent

front 3 bow, van **4** face, fore, lend, look, mask, prow **5** beard **6** facade, facing **7** forward **8** anterior, disguise **9** challenge, encounter **10** appearance, figurehead **11** countenance

frontier 5 bound, field, march **6** border **8** backland, backwash, boundary **9** upcountry **10** borderland, hinterland **11** backcountry

frontiersman 5 Boone (Daniel), Clark (George Rogers, William) **6** Carson (Kit) **7** pioneer, settler **8** Crockett (Davy) **10** bushranger

fronton game 7 jai alai

frontward 8 anterior

frost 4 hoar, rime **6** freeze

frostfish 5 smelt **6** tomcod

frost heave 5 pingo

frosting 5 icing **7** topping **8** trimming

Frost poem 11 Mending Wall **12** Road Not Taken (The) **18** Death of the Hired Man (The) **30** Stopping By Woods on a Snowy Evening

frosty 3 icy **4** cold, rimy **5** chill, frore, hoary, nippy **6** chilly, frigid **7** glacial **8** freezing **10** unfriendly

froth 4 foam, head, suds 5 cream, spume, yeast 6 lather 8 airiness 9 frivolity, lightness

froufrou 6 frills 8 rustling

froward 5 balky 6 mulish, ornery 7 peevish, restive 8 contrary, perverse, petulant, stubborn 9 obstinate 10 headstrong, refractory 11 disobedient

frown 4 pout, sulk 5 glare, lower, scowl 6 glower

frowsy 5 dowdy, funky, fusty, messy, musty, stale 6 shabby, smelly, sordid, untidy 7 squalid, unkempt 8 slattern, slovenly 10 disheveled, disordered, slatternly 13 draggletailed

frozen 4 cold, hard 5 fixed, frore, rigid, stiff 6 frigid, numbed 7 chilled 8 benumbed, immobile 9 congealed, petrified

frugal 4 mean 5 canny, scant, spare 6 Scotch, stingy 7 careful, prudent, scrimpy, sparing, thrifty 8 discreet, stinting 9 niggardly, penurious, provident 10 economical, unwasteful 12 cheeseparing, parsimonious 13 penny-pinching

frugality 6 thrift 7 economy 8 prudence 9 husbandry 10 providence 11 thriftiness

fruit 5 issue, young 6 result 7 outcome, progeny 9 offspring *citrus:* 4 lime 5 lemon 6 citron, orange, pomelo 7 kumquat, tangelo 8 bergamot, mandarin, shaddock 9 tangerine 10 calamondin, grapefruit *dried:* 5 prune 6 raisin *drink:* 3 ade 5 juice, punch *fleshy:* 7 syconia (plural) 8 syconium *hard-shelled:* 3 nut 4 seed 5 gourd 7 coconut *residue:* 4 marc 6 pomace *seed:* 3 pip *study of:* 8 pomology 9 carpology *subtropical:* 3 fig 4 date, lime 5 lemon, olive 6 citron, orange 7 avocado, kumquat 9 tangerine 10 grapefruit *sugar:* 7 glucose 8 fructose, levulose *temperate-zone:* 4 pear, plum, sloe 5 apple, grape, melon, papaw, peach, prune 6 casaba, cherry, loquat, pawpaw, quince 7 apricot, currant 8 dewberry 9 blueberry, cranberry, muskmelon, nectarine, raspberry 10 blackberry, gooseberry, loganberry, strawberry 11 boysenberry, huckleberry, pomegranate *tropical:* 5 guava, mango 6 banana, papaya 7 acerola 8 rambutan, tamarind 9 cherimoya, persimmon, pineapple 10 calamondin, mangosteen *type:* 3 nut 4 pepo, pome 5 berry, drupe 6 achene, legume, loment, samara 7 capsule, silique, utricle 11 hesperidium *undeveloped:* 6 nubbin

fruitful 6 fecund 7 copious, fertile 8 abundant, prolific 9 bountiful, fructuous, plenteous, plentiful 10 productive 11 proliferant

fruition 7 delight 8 pleasure 9 enjoyment 10 attainment, conclusion 11 achievement, delectation, fulfillment, realization

fruitless 4 vain 6 barren, futile 7 sterile, useless 8 abortive 10 unavailing 11 ineffective, ineffectual 12 unproductive, unsuccessful

frumpy 4 drab, dull 5 dated, dowdy, tacky 6 stodgy 8 outmoded 9 out-of-date, unstylish 12 old-fashioned

frustrate 4 balk, bilk, dash, foil, halt 5 block, check, stump 6 arrest, baffle, defeat, hinder, impede, stymie, thwart 7 inhibit, prevent 8 confound, obstruct, preclude, prohibit 9 discomfit, forestall, interrupt 10 disappoint

frustration 6 defeat, dismay 7 chagrin, letdown 8 vexation 9 annoyance, hindrance 10 impediment, irritation 11 displeasure, obstruction

fry 4 burn, sear 5 frizz, grill, sauté 6 fishes, picnic 7 frizzle 11 electrocute

frying pan 6 spider 7 griddle, skillet

fuddle 5 befog, booze 6 ball up, jumble, tipple 7 confuse, fluster, stupefy 8 bewilder 10 intoxicate

fuddy-duddy 4 fogy 6 fossil, square, stodgy 8 mossback, outdated, outmoded 12 antediluvian, Colonel Blimp, old-fashioned, stuffed shirt 13 stick-in-the-mud

fudge 3 pad 4 blur, bosh, fake 5 candy, cheat, color, dodge, hedge, hooey, welsh 6 bunkum 7 distort, falsify, hogwash, penuche 8 contrive, divinity, nonsense 9 embellish, embroider, overstate, poppycock 10 equivocate, flapdoodle 11 foolishness

fuel 3 gas, oil 4 coal, coke, fire, peat, wood 5 stoke 6 biogas, diesel, petrol 7 ethanol, gasohol, inflame, propane 8 charcoal, gasoline, kerosene 9 petroleum, stimulate 10 natural gas 13 reinforcement

fugacious 7 brittle, passing 8 fleeting, fugitive, volatile 9 ephemeral, momentary, transient 10 evanescent, short-lived, transitory

fugitive 5 exile 6 outlaw 7 escapee, lamster, nomadic, passing, refugee, runaway 8 deserter, fleeting, runagate, vagabond 9 ephemeral, fugacious, momentary, transient, wandering 10 evanescent, short-lived, transitory

fugue master 4 Bach (Johann Sebastian)

Führer, der 6 Hitler (Adolf)

fulcrum 3 hub 4 axis, prop 5 hinge, nexus, pivot 7 support

fulfill 4 meet 5 honor 6 effect, finish, redeem 7 achieve, execute, perform, satisfy 8 complete 9 discharge, implement 10 accomplish

fulgent 6 bright 7 beaming, glowing, radiant, shining 8 luminous, lustrous 9 brilliant

fuliginous 4 dark 5 dingy, dusky, grimy, murky, sooty 7 obscure

full 5 sated, total, whole 6 entire, gorged, jammed, loaded, packed, utmost 7 crammed, crowded, glutted, maximum, plenary, replete, stuffed 8 brimming, complete, satiated 9 jam-packed, plentiful, surfeited 11 chockablock

full-blooded 4 rich 5 flush, ruddy 6 ardent, florid 7 flushed, genuine, glowing 8 forceful, purebred, rubicund, sanguine 9 pedigreed, pureblood 10 compelling 12 thoroughbred

full-blown 4 lush, ripe 5 adult, total 6 all-out, mature 7 grown-up

full-bodied 4 rich 5 husky, lusty, stout 6 potent, robust, strong 9 corpulent 10 meaningful 11 significant, substantial

full dress 6 finery 7 regalia 8 frippery, glad rags 10 Sunday best

full-figured 5 ample, buxom, plump 6 zaftig 10 curvaceous, Rubenesque, statuesque, voluptuous

full-fledged 4 ripe 5 adult, grown, total 6 mature 7 genuine, grown-up 8 complete 9 full-blown

full-grown 4 ripe 5 adult 6 mature

fullness 6 plenty 7 satiety 9 abundance, amplitude, repletion 10 perfection 12 completeness

full-scale 5 total 6 all-out 8 complete, life-size 9 unlimited

full tilt 7 flat-out, rapidly, swiftly 8 pell-mell, speedily 9 posthaste 12 lickety-split

fulminate 4 boil, burn, foam, fume, rage, rave 5 curse, flare 7 bluster, explode, inveigh

fulsome 4 oily 5 plump, slick, soapy, suave 6 lavish, smarmy, smooth 7 buttery, cloying, copious, profuse 8 abundant, effusive, generous, overdone, unctuous 9 excessive 10 flattering, oleaginous 11 extravagant, pharisaical 12 ingratiating, Pecksniffian

Fulton's steamboat 8 Clermont

fumarole 4 vent

fumble 3 bob, paw 4 feel, flub, mess, muff 5 botch, grope 6 bobble, bollix, bungle, muddle 7 blunder, misplay 8 flounder

fume 3 gas 4 boil, burn, odor, rage, rant, rave, reek, snit, stew 5 smoke, vapor 6 seethe, swivet 7 sputter

fun 4 play 5 sport 6 frolic, gaiety 7 amusing, jollity, pastime, whoopee 8 hilarity, pleasant, ridicule 9 amusement, diversion, diverting, enjoyment, frivolity, horseplay, jocundity, joviality, merriment 10 pleasantry 12 entertaining 13 entertainment

function 3 act, job, run, use 4 duty, goal, mark, role, task, work 5 party, power, react, serve 6 affair, behave, object, office, target 7 concern, faculty, operate, perform, purpose, service 8 activity, behavior, business, capacity, ceremony, occasion, province 9 objective, officiate, operation, reception *trigonometric:* 4 sine 6 cosine, secant 7 tangent 8 cosecant 9 cotangent

functional 5 handy, utile 6 useful 7 working 9 practical 11 practicable, serviceable, utilitarian 12 occupational

functioning 6 active 7 dynamic 9 operative

fund 4 bank, pool 5 endow, stake, stock, store 6 coffer, supply 7 capital, finance, reserve 8 bankroll, treasury 9 inventory, subsidize 10 accumulate, capitalize

fundament 4 butt, rear, rump, seat 5 basis, fanny 6 behind, bottom 8 backside, buttocks, derriere 9 posterior, principle 10 foundation, groundwork

fundamental 3 key 5 axiom, basal, basic, prime, vital 6 bottom, factor, primal, simple 7 bedrock, organic, primary, radical, theorem 8 absolute, cardinal, dominant, ultimate 9 component, essential, important, necessary, paramount, primitive, principal, principle, requisite 10 deep-rooted, elementary, grassroots, primordial, rock-bottom, underlying 11 constituent, irreducible, nitty-gritty 12 constitutive, foundational

fund-raiser 8 telethon

funeral 6 burial 7 obsequy 9 obsequies *car:* 6 hearse *director:* 9 mortician 10 undertaker *oration:* 6 eulogy 8 encomium 9 panegyric *procession:* 7 cortege *service:* 7 requiem 9 obsequies *song:* 5 dirge, elegy 8 threnody

funereal 3 sad 4 dark 5 black, bleak, grave 6 dismal, dreary, gloomy, solemn, somber, sombre 7 elegiac 8 mournful 9 deathlike, sorrowful 10 depressing, depressive, lugubrious, oppressive, sepulchral

fungus 4 conk, mold, rust, smut 5 ergot, yeast 6 agaric, dry rot, mildew 7 candida, truffle 8 mushroom, puffball 9 earthstar, stinkhorn, toadstool *combining form:* 4 myco 5 myces, mycet

6 mycete, myceto *part:* **3** cap **4** gill
5 ascus, hypha, stipe, volva **7** annulus
8 basidium, conidium, mycelium
fungus disease 3 rot **4** mold, rust, scab,
smut **5** ergot, tinea **6** blight, mildew,
thrush **7** mycosis **8** lumpy jaw, ringworm **12** athlete's foot
funk 4 odor, reek **5** blues, dolor, dumps,
ennui, gloom, smell, stink, slump
6 recoil, stench **7** sadness **9** dejection
10 depression, melancholy
funky 3 hip, odd **4** foul, rank **5** fetid,
reeky **6** earthy, frowsy, grungy, quaint,
quirky, smelly, stinky **7** natural, noisome, oddball, offbeat **8** down-home
10 malodorous
funnel 4 flue, pipe **5** stack **6** hopper
7 channel, conduct, tundish **8** transmit
10 smokestack
funny 3 odd **4** joke, zany **5** antic, comic,
droll, fishy, queer **7** amusing, bizarre,
comical, jocular, risible, strange **8** farcical, humorous, peculiar **9** facetious,
fantastic, hilarious, laughable, ludicrous **10** ridiculous
Funny Girl 5 Brice (Fanny) *composer:*
5 Styne (Jule)
funnyman 3 wag, wit **5** clown, comic,
cutup, droll, joker **6** gagman, jester
8 comedian, humorist, jokester, quipster **10** comedienne
fur 4 down, hide, pelt, pile **5** floss, fluff,
stole **6** pelage, peltry *kind:* **3** fox **4** mink,
seal **5** fitch, otter, sable **6** ermine, fisher, marten, nutria, tanuki **7** raccoon
10 chinchilla *lamb:* **7** caracul, karakul
9 broadtail *medieval:* **4** vair **7** miniver
furbelow 5 frill **7** flounce
furbish 4 buff **5** fix up, renew, shine
6 polish, revive **7** burnish, refresh,
restore **8** renovate
Furies 6 Alecto **7** Erinyes, Megaera
9 Eumenides, Tisiphone
furious 3 mad **4** wild **5** angry, livid, irate,
rabid, upset **6** crazed, fierce, insane,
raging, stormy **7** enraged, excited,
extreme, frantic, intense, violent
8 feverish, frenetic, frenzied, incensed,
maddened, vehement, wrathful
9 impetuous, turbulent **10** boisterous,
corybantic
furl 4 curl, fold, roll, wrap **6** take in
furlough 4 pass **5** leave **6** lay off **7** liberty
10 shore leave **13** authorization
furnace 4 kiln, oven **5** forge, stove
6 heater **7** smelter **8** tryworks **11** incin-
erator *part:* **4** port, vent **6** tuyere *tender:*
6 stoker
furnish 3 arm, rig **4** give, hand, lend
5 endow, endue, equip **6** fit out, outfit,
supply **7** apparel, appoint, deliver, provide, turn out **8** accouter, accoutre, dis-

pense, hand over, transfer **9** provision
10 contribute
furnishings 4 gear **5** decor **9** equipment,
trappings **10** housewares **11** appointment **13** accouterments, accoutrements, paraphernalia
furniture designer *American:* **5** Eames
(Charles, Ray), Phyfe (Duncan) **7** Goddard (John, Stephen, Thomas), Haldane
(William) **8** Stickley (Gustav) *British:*
6 Morris (William) **7** Gibbons (Grin-
ling), Shearer (Thomas) **8** Sheraton
(Thomas) **11** Chippendale (Thomas),
Hepplewhite (George) *French:* **5** Marot
(Daniel) **6** Boulle (André-Charles) *German:* **6** Breuer (Marcel) *Scottish:*
4 Adam (James, Robert)
furniture style 4 Adam **6** Empire, Shaker
7 Bauhaus, Federal, Mission **8** Colonial,
Georgian, Jacobean, Sheraton, Stickley
9 Queen Anne **11** chinoiserie, Chippendale, Duncan Phyfe, Hepplewhite
13 Arts and Crafts
furor 3 ado, cry, fad, wax **4** chic, mode,
rage, stir, to-do **5** anger, craze, mania,
style, vogue **6** flurry, frenzy, pother,
ruckus, rumpus, uproar **7** fashion, madness **8** foofaraw **9** commotion **10** dernier
cri, excitement **11** controversy
furrow 3 rut **4** ruck **5** plica, ridge, sulci
(plural) **6** course, crease, groove, sul-
cus, trench **7** channel, crinkle, wrinkle
8 entrench **9** corrugate **11** corrugation
furrowed 5 lined **6** rugose **7** grooved, sul-
cate **8** wrinkled **10** corrugated
further 4 abet, also, help **5** again, fresh
6 beyond **7** advance, besides, forward,
promote **8** engender, moreover
9 encourage, propagate **10** additional,
in addition **12** additionally
furthermore 3 and, too **4** also **6** as well,
withal **7** besides **8** likewise, moreover
9 what's more **12** additionally
furthermost 4 last **7** extreme **8** farthest,
remotest, ultimate
furtive 3 sly **4** foxy, wary, wily **6** artful,
covert, crafty, feline, masked, secret,
shifty, sneaky, stolen, tricky **7** catlike,
cunning, evasive, sub-rosa **8** guileful,
hush-hush, scheming, stealthy **9** disguised, insidious **11** circumspect, clandestine **12** hugger-mugger **13** surreptitious, under-the-table *look:* **4** peek, peep
fur trader 8 voyageur
furuncle 4 boil **7** abscess
fury 3 ire **4** burn, rage **5** anger, furor,
wrath **6** frenzy **7** madness, passion
8 violence **9** vehemence **10** fierceness
furze 4 whin **5** gorse *genus:* **4** Ulex
7 Genista
fuse 3 mix **4** flux, meld, melt, weld
5 blend, merge, smelt, unify, unite

6 anneal, solder **7** liquefy **8** coalesce, conflate, dissolve, intermix **9** commingle, integrate **10** amalgamate **11** consolidate, incorporate

fusillade 4 hail **5** burst, salvo **6** shower, volley **7** barrage **8** drumfire, outburst **9** broadside, cannonade **11** bombardment

fusion 5 alloy, blend, union **6** merger **7** amalgam, mixture **8** compound **9** coalition, immixture, synthesis

fuss 3 ado, nag, row **4** beef, crab, flap, fret, miff, stew, stir, to-do, wail **5** gripe, stink, upset, whine, worry **6** bother, bustle, hassle, hurrah, pother, ruckus, rumpus, squawk **7** protest, quarrel **8** complain, foofaraw, squabble **9** commotion, complaint, kerfuffle, objection **10** excitement **11** controversy **12** perturbation

fussbudget 3 hen **6** granny **8** stickler **10** fuddy-duddy **13** perfectionist

fusspot 8 stickler **9** nitpicker, worrywart

fussy 5 picky **6** cranky, dainty, ornate **7** careful, finicky, fretful **9** crotchety, irritable, querulous **10** fastidious, meticulous, particular, pernickety, scrupulous **11** painstaking, persnickety, punctilious **13** conscientious

fustian 4 rant **7** bombast, pompous **8** affected, inflated **9** high-flown **11** exaggerated, highfalutin, pretentious **13** grandiloquent

fusty 4 rank **5** close, dated, fetid, moldy, passé, stale **6** bygone, old-hat, smelly **7** archaic **8** outdated **10** antiquated, malodorous **11** reactionary **12** old-fashioned **13** superannuated

futile 4 idle, vain **5** empty **6** hollow, otiose **7** useless **8** abortive, bootless, hopeless, nugatory **9** fruitless, worthless **10** unavailing **11** ineffective, ineffectual **12** unproductive, unsuccessful

future 5 later **6** offing, to come **7** by-and-by **8** oncoming, tomorrow **9** hereafter

Futurism *founder:* **9** Marinetti (Filippo Tommaso) *painter:* **5** Balla (Giacomo), Carra (Carlo) **7** Russolo (Luigi) **8** Boccioni (Umberto), Severini (Gino) *sculptor:* **8** Boccioni (Umberto)

fuzz 3 cop **4** down, lint **6** police

fuzzy 3 dim **5** faint, gauzy, linty, vague, woozy **6** bleary, blurry **7** blurred, muddled, obscure, shadowy, unclear **8** confused **9** distorted, undefined **10** ill-defined, incoherent, indefinite, indistinct

fylfot 8 swastika

G

gab 3 jaw, rap, yak **4** blab, chat, talk **5** clack, drool, prate, speak **6** babble, drivel, gibber, gossip, jabber, natter, yammer **7** blabber, blather, chatter, palaver, prattle, twaddle **8** chitchat, converse, idle talk **9** gibberish, small talk

gabber 6 gossip, magpie **7** blabber **9** chatterer **10** chatterbox **12** blabbermouth, gossipmonger

gabby 4 glib **5** talky, windy **6** chatty **7** voluble **8** effusive **9** garrulous, talkative **10** long-winded, loquacious **11** loose-lipped **12** loose-tongued

gaberdine 4 coat, suit **5** cloak, cloth **6** capote, fabric **7** garment, manteau **8** material

gable 4 wall **8** pediment *ornament:* **6** finial

Gabon *capital:* **10** Libreville *city:* **10** Port-Gentil *ethnic group:* **4** Fang **5** Bantu *language:* **6** French *monetary unit:* **5** franc *neighbor:* **5** Congo **8** Cameroon *river:* **6** Ogooué

gad 3 bat **4** flit, roam, rove **5** amble, drift, mooch, range, stray, tramp **6** chisel, ramble, wander **7** maunder, meander, traipse **9** gallivant

Gad *brother:* **5** Asher *father:* **5** Jacob *mother:* **6** Zilpah *son:* **3** Eri **5** Ezbon, Haggi

Gaddis *novel* **12** Recognitions (The) **14** Frolic of His Own (A) **16** Carpenter's Gothic

gadfly 3 nag **4** pest, pill **6** bother, critic, insect, nudnik **8** nuisance

gadget 4 tool **5** gizmo, thing **6** device, dingus, doodad, hickey, jigger, widget **7** concern, gimmick, utensil **9** apparatus, appliance, doohickey, implement, mechanism **10** instrument **11** contrap-

tion, thingamabob, thingamajig, thingumajig
gadwall 4 bird, duck, fowl 9 waterfowl
gadzooks 4 drat, egad 6 crikey, zounds
Gaea *husband:* 6 Uranus *offspring:*
6 Furies, Giants, Titans, Typhon,
Uranus 7 Erinyes 8 Cyclopes
9 Eumenides *parent:* 5 Chaos
Gaelic 4 Erse 5 Irish 6 Celtic 8 Scottish
god: 3 Ler 5 Dagda *hero:* 5 Oisin 6 Ossian 11 Finn MacCool *king:* 9 Conchobar, Conchobor *language:* 4 Manx *poet:*
4 bard 6 Ossian *queen:* 4 Medb *soldier:*
4 kern 6 Fenian *spirit:* 7 banshee
gaff 3 fix, rig 4 hoax, hook, spar, spur
5 abuse, fraud, spear, trick 6 fleece,
ordeal 7 deceive, gimmick 8 raillery
12 climbing iron
gaffe 4 flub, goof, muff 5 boner, error,
fault, fluff, lapse 6 bollix, boo-boo,
bungle, foul-up, howler, slipup 7 blooper, blunder, clinker, faux pas, misstep,
mistake 8 solecism 9 gaucherie
11 impropriety, misjudgment 12 indiscretion
gag 4 balk, gasp, hoax, jape, jest, joke,
quip 5 choke, crack, heave, prank,
retch, trick 6 muffle, muzzle, shtick,
stifle, strain 7 repress, silence, squelch
8 throttle 9 restraint, wisecrack, witticism
gaga 4 agog, wild 5 crazy, giddy, nutty,
wacky 6 doting, fervid, gung ho 7 foolish, gushing, excited, smitten 8 animated, enamored, obsessed, thrilled 9 ebullient, exuberant 10 captivated,
infatuated 12 enthusiastic
gage 3 vow 4 bond 5 token 6 pledge,
surety 8 gauntlet, security (see also
GAUGE)
gaggle 4 crew, gang, pack 5 array,
bunch, flock, group 6 clutch, number
7 cluster 10 assemblage, collection
11 aggregation
Gaheris *brother:* 6 Gareth, Gawain
father: 3 Lot *mother:* 8 Margawse, Morgause *uncle:* 6 Arthur *victim:* 8 Margawse, Morgause
gaiety 3 fun, joy 4 glee 5 mirth, revel
6 finery, frolic, hoopla 7 elation, jollity,
revelry, whoopee 8 elegance, hilarity,
reveling, vivacity 9 animation, festivity,
happiness, joviality, merriment 10 ebullience, exuberance, hullabaloo, joyousness, jubilation, liveliness 11 high spirits, merrymaking 12 conviviality
gain 3 get, net, win 4 earn, land, make,
reap 5 clear, cover, lucre, reach, score
6 attain, expand, obtain, pick up, profit,
rack up, return, secure 7 achieve,
acquire, advance, attract, augment, ben-

efit, bring in, enlarge, procure 8 draw
down, earnings, increase, overtake, persuade, proceeds, traverse, windfall
10 accomplish 11 move forward
gainful 6 paying 8 fruitful, generous
9 lucrative, rewarding 10 beneficial,
productive, profitable, well-paying,
worthwhile 12 advantageous, remunerative
gainsay 4 buck, defy, deny 6 impugn,
negate, oppose, refute, resist 7 dispute
8 disclaim, disprove, negative, traverse
9 disaffirm, repudiate, withstand
10 contradict, contravene, controvert
Gainsborough *painting* 7 Blue Boy
gait 3 air, run 4 clip, dash, lope, pace,
rate, step, trot, walk 5 amble, speed,
strut, train, tread 6 canter, gallop,
stride 7 bearing 8 demeanor
gaiter 4 boot, shoe, spat 7 legging 8 overshoe
gal 4 babe, doll 5 chick
gala 4 ball, bash, fete, prom 5 merry,
party 6 lively 7 festive, jubilee, pageant,
shindig 8 festival, jamboree, wingding
9 festivity, spectacle 11 celebration
13 entertainment
galago 5 lemur 8 bush baby
Galahad *father:* 8 Lancelot 9 Launcelot
mother: 6 Elaine *quest:* 5 Grail 9 Holy
Grail
Galatea *father:* 6 Nereus *husband:* 9 Pygmalion *lover:* 4 Acis *mother:* 5 Doris
galaxy 6 nebula 8 Milky Way, universe
Galba *predecessor:* 4 Nero *successor:*
4 Otho
gale 4 blow, gust, wind 5 blast, storm
6 squall 7 cyclone, tempest, typhoon
8 outburst 9 hurricane
galena 3 ore
Galen's *forte* 7 healing 8 medicine
galilee 5 porch 6 chapel
Galilee *town* 4 Cana 7 Gergesa
8 Nazareth, Tiberias 9 Bethsaida,
Capernaum
Galileo's *birthplace* 4 Pisa 5 Italy 7 Tuscany
gall 3 irk, nag, rub, vex 4 bile, fray, fret,
rile, roil, sore, wear 5 annoy, brass,
chafe, cheek, erode, grate, graze, nerve
6 abrade, bother, burn up, harass,
pester, plague, rancor, ruffle, scrape
7 conceit, disturb, frazzle, inflame, provoke, scratch, torment 8 audacity,
boldness, chutzpah, irritate, temerity
9 aggravate, arrogance, brashness,
impudence, insolence 10 bitterness,
effrontery
gallant 3 fop 4 beau, bold, buck, dude,
hero 5 blade, blood, brave, civil, dandy,
lover, manly, Romeo, showy, suave,

swain, wooer **6** daring, heroic, suitor, urbane **7** courtly, coxcomb, dashing, Don Juan, stately, valiant **8** Casanova, gracious, lothario, paramour, spirited, valorous **9** attentive, courteous, dauntless, ladies' man **10** chivalrous, courageous

gallantry 5 honor, poise, valor **6** daring, mettle, spirit **7** amenity, bravery, courage, heroism, prowess, suavity **8** boldness, chivalry, courtesy, urbanity, valiance, valiancy **9** attention, manliness **10** resolution **11** courtliness **12** fearlessness

galleon 7 warship **12** square-rigger

gallery 5 patio, porch, salon **6** arcade, loggia, museum, piazza **7** balcony, passage, portico, veranda **8** audience, corridor, showroom **9** colonnade, onlookers, promenade *ancient Greek:* **4** stoa

galley 3 gig **4** boat, mess, ship, tray **5** cuddy, proof **6** bireme **7** canteen, kitchen, trireme, warship **8** scullery **9** cookhouse

Gallic 6 French

gallimaufry 3 mix **4** hash, mess, olio, stew **5** chaos **6** jumble, medley **7** clutter, goulash, mélange, mixture, variety **8** mishmash, pastiche **9** patchwork, potpourri **10** assortment, hodgepodge, hotchpotch, miscellany, salmagundi

gallinaceous bird 3 hen **5** quail **6** grouse, turkey **7** chicken, hoatzin, peacock **8** curassow, pheasant **9** partridge **10** guinea fowl

galling 6 bitter, vexing **8** rankling **9** upsetting, vexatious **10** afflictive, irritating, nettlesome **11** aggravating, distressing, troublesome **12** exasperating

gallivant 3 bat, bum, gad **4** flit, roam, rove **5** amble, drift, jaunt, mooch, range, stray **6** cruise, ramble, travel, wander **7** meander, traipse **8** vagabond **10** knock about

gallop 4 dash, race **6** sprint

gallows 6 gibbet *bird:* **7** villain **8** criminal

galore 4 full, lush, rich **5** ample, great **6** lavish **7** aplenty, copious, endless, profuse **8** abundant, generous **9** bountiful, expansive, plentiful **11** overflowing

galosh 4 boot, shoe **6** rubber **8** overshoe

Galsworthy work 7 Justice **11** Forsyte Saga (The)

galumph 4 plod **5** barge, clomp, clump, stomp, stump, tramp **6** lumber, trudge

galvanize 3 jar, zap **4** coat, fire, jolt, stir, spur, stun **5** pep up, pique, prime, react, rouse, shock **6** arouse, excite, perk up, thrill **7** animate, enliven, immerse, inspire, provoke, quicken **8** activate, astonish, energize, motivate,

vitalize **9** electrify, innervate, magnetize, stimulate **10** invigorate

gam 3 leg, pin, pod, rap **4** chat, flap, limb, talk **5** visit **6** confab **9** drumstick **12** conversation

Gambia *capital:* **6** Banjul *city:* **9** Serekunda *language:* **7** English *monetary unit:* **6** dalasi *neighbor:* **7** Senegal

gambit 3 con, jig **4** move, play, ploy, ruse, wile **5** dodge, topic, trick **6** design, device, remark, tactic **7** gimmick **8** artifice, maneuver, trickery **9** expedient, stratagem **10** subterfuge

gamble 3 bet, lay, set **4** dare, game, play, punt, risk **5** put on, stake, wager **6** chance, hazard, plunge, raffle **7** imperil, lottery, venture **8** cast lots, long shot **9** crapshoot, speculate **10** jeopardize

gambler 5 dicer, shark, sharp **7** sharper **9** cardsharp **10** cardplayer **11** cardsharper

gambling place 3 den **4** club, dive, Reno **5** joint, Vegas **6** casino **8** Las Vegas, pool hall **9** roadhouse **10** Monte Carlo **12** Atlantic City, betting house

gambol 3 hop **4** jump, lark, leap, romp, skip **5** bound, caper, frisk, revel, sport **6** cavort, frolic, prance, spring **7** carry on, roister, rollick

Gambrinus' invention 3 ale **4** beer **5** lager

game 3 bet, fun, lay **4** bold, jest, joke, lark, play, prey, romp **5** brave, chase, eager, hardy, sport, stake, trick, wager **6** gamble, quarry, spunky **7** contest, pastime, valiant, willing **8** fearless, intrepid, resolute, unafraid, valorous **9** amusement, dauntless, diversion, undaunted **10** courageous, recreation *ball:* **4** golf, polo, pool **5** fives, rogue, rugby **6** hockey, pelota, soccer, squash, tennis **7** cricket, croquet, jai alai **8** baseball, football, handball, hardball, lacrosse, racquets, rounders, softball **9** billiards **10** basketball, volleyball **11** racquetball *Basque:* **6** pelota **7** jai alai *bird:* **4** duck **5** quail **6** chukar, turkey **7** bustard **8** bobwhite, pheasant **9** partridge *board:* **5** chess **7** pachisi **8** checkers, Scrabble **9** crokinole, Parcheesi **10** backgammon *card:* **3** gin, loo, Uno, war **4** faro, fish, skat, solo **5** monte, ombre, pitch, poker, rummy, whist **6** Boston, bridge, casino, écarté, euchre, fan-tan, hearts, piquet **7** auction, bezique, canasta, cooncan, old maid, primero **8** baccarat, Canfield, conquian, cribbage, gin rummy, pinochle **9** blackjack, solitaire, twenty-one, vingt-et-un **11** chemin de fer *child's:* **3** tag **5** jacks **7** marbles

8 leapfrog, peekaboo **9** hopscotch *confidence:* **4** scam **5** bunco, bunko, sting *court:* **5** roque **6** pelota, squash, tennis **7** jai alai **8** handball, racquets **9** badminton **10** basketball, volleyball **11** racquetball *electric:* **7** pinball *English:* **5** rugby **7** cricket **8** draughts *Irish:* **7** hurling *of chance:* **4** faro, keno **5** beano, bingo, boule, craps, lotto, rondo **6** fan-tan, hazard, policy, raffle **7** lottery, rondeau **8** roulette *parlor:* **8** charades *racket:* **6** squash, tennis **8** lacrosse, ping-pong, racquets **9** badminton **11** racquetball, table tennis *roulette-like:* **5** boule *rule maker:* **5** Hoyle (Edmond) *string:* **10** cat's cradle *table:* **4** pool **5** craps **7** mah-jong, snooker **8** dominoes, mah-jongg, ping-pong, roulette **9** bagatelle, billiards **11** table tennis *word:* **5** rebus **6** crambo **7** anagram, hangman **8** acrostic, charades, Scrabble **9** crossword, logograph

game plan 6 scheme, tactic **8** scenario, strategy **9** blueprint **10** big picture

gamete 3 egg **4** ovum **5** sperm **8** germ cell

gamin 3 elf, imp, tad **4** brat, tyke, waif **5** scamp **6** monkey, rascal, urchin **11** guttersnipe **12** street urchin

gamine 3 elf, imp **4** brat, waif **5** scamp **6** hoyden, rascal, tomboy, urchin **11** guttersnipe **12** street urchin

gaming cubes 4 dice **5** bones

gammon 3 ham **4** dupe, fool, rook **5** bacon, feign **6** delude, fleece, humbug **7** deceive, pretend, swindle **8** flimflam, hoodwink **9** bamboozle **11** hornswoggle

gamut 5 range, scale, scope, sweep **6** extent, series, spread **7** compass **8** diapason, spectrum

gamy 3 off **4** foul, racy, rank, vile **5** brave, fetid, funky **6** plucky, putrid, rancid, rotten, smelly, sordid, stinky, strong **7** corrupt, decayed, noisome, noxious, reeking **10** decomposed, malodorous, scandalous **12** disagreeable, disreputable

gander 4 look, peek **5** goose **6** glance **7** glimpse **9** simpleton, waterfowl

___ Gandhi 5 Rajiv **6** Indira **7** Mahatma **8** Mohandas

gandy dancer 10 railroader, tracklayer

ganef 5 thief **6** rascal **9** scoundrel

Ganesa, Ganesh *father:* **4** Siva **5** Shiva *head:* **8** elephant *mother:* **7** Parvati

gang 3 lot, mob, set **4** band, clan, club, crew, pack, ring, team **5** bunch, crowd, group, horde **6** circle, clique, outfit **7** arrange, cluster, collect, combine, company, coterie **8** assemble **10** accumulate, assemblage **11** combination

gangling 4 bony, lean, slim **5** gaunt, lanky, rangy **6** meager, meagre, skinny **7** angular, scrawny, slender, spindly, stringy **8** rawboned **9** spindling

ganglion 5 tumor **7** nucleus

gangrene 3 rot **5** decay **7** mortify, putrefy **8** necrosis **9** decompose

gangster 4 goon, hood, thug **5** rough, thief, tough **6** bandit, gunman **7** hoodlum, mafioso, mobster, ruffian **8** criminal **9** cutthroat, racketeer *girlfriend:* **4** moll

gangway 4 hall, path **5** aisle **7** passage, walkway **8** corridor **10** passageway

ganja 3 kef, kif, pot, tea **4** hemp, herb, weed **5** grass, smoke **7** hashish **8** cannabis, Mary Jane **9** marijuana

gannet 4 bird **5** booby **7** seabird

ganoid fish 3 gar **6** beluga, bowfin **7** dogfish, garfish, teleost **8** billfish, sturgeon **10** paddlefish

Ganymede *abductor:* **4** Zeus **7** Jupiter *brother:* **4** Ilus *father:* **4** Tros *function:* **9** cupbearer

gaol 3 jug, pen **4** jail **5** clink, joint, pokey **6** cooler, lockup, prison **7** slammer **8** bastille **9** calaboose, jailhouse **12** penitentiary

gap 3 cut, pit **4** gash, gulf, hole, lull, pass, rent, rift, skip, slit, slot, tear, vent, void, yawn **5** abyss, blank, break, chasm, chink, cleft, clove, crack, gorge, gulch, gully, pause, space, split **6** arroyo, breach, canyon, cavity, cranny, divide, hiatus, hollow, lacuna, ravine, recess, schism, vacuum **7** caesura, crevice, fissure, interim, opening, orifice, rupture, vacancy, vacuity **8** aperture, cleavage, division, fracture, interval **9** disparity, interlude **10** deficiency, difference, interstice, separation **12** intermission, interruption **13** discontinuity

gape 3 eye, yaw **4** bore, gawk, gawp, gaze, glom, leer, look, ogle, open, part, peer, yawn **5** crack, glare, gloat, space, split, stare **6** glance, goggle **7** eyeball **10** rubberneck

gaping 4 huge, open, vast, wide **5** broad, great **7** chasmal **9** cavernous

gar 4 fish, pike **8** billfish **10** needlefish

garage 4 shop **7** cabinet, car park, carport, shelter

Garand 5 rifle

garb 4 clad, duds **5** array, cover, dress, getup, style **6** attire, clothe, outfit **7** apparel, clothes, garment, raiment, threads **9** trappings **10** appearance

garbage 4 junk, muck, slop **5** dreck, dregs, filth, offal, trash, waste **6** debris, litter, refuse, sewage **7** rubbish **8** detritus, riffraff *heap:* **6** midden

garble 4 sift, warp **5** alter, belie, color, twist **6** jumble, mangle, muddle **7** becloud, confuse, contort, distort, falsify, obscure, pervert **8** miscolor, misstate, mutilate **9** obfuscate **10** impurities **12** misrepresent

garçon 3 boy **6** waiter **7** servant

garden 4 Eden, park **7** nursery *shelter:* **5** arbor **6** arbour

gardener 6 grower **7** yardman **9** topiarist

garden house 6 alcove, gazebo **9** belvedere

Garden State 9 New Jersey

garden tool 3 hoe **4** claw, fork, rake **5** mower, spade **6** dibble, pruner, scythe, shears, shovel, sickle, trowel, weeder **8** clippers

Gardner character 10 Perry Mason

Gareth *brother:* **6** Gawain **7** Gaheris *father:* **3** Lot *mother:* **8** Margawse, Morgause *slayer:* **8** Lancelot **9** Launcelot *uncle:* **6** Arthur *wife:* **6** Liones

Gargamelle's son 9 Gargantua

Gargantua *abbey:* **7** Thélème *author:* **8** Rabelais (François) *father:* **12** Grandgousier *first word:* **5** drink *mother:* **10** Gargamelle *son:* **10** Pantagruel

gargantuan see GIGANTIC

Garibaldi follower 8 redshirt

garish 4 loud **5** gaudy, showy, vivid **6** brassy, brazen, flashy, tawdry, tinsel, vulgar **7** blatant, chintzy, glaring, raffish **12** meretricious

garland 3 ana, lei **5** album, crown **6** anadem, digest, laurel, wreath **7** chaplet, coronal, coronet, laurels, omnibus **8** analects **9** anthology, selection **10** collection, compendium, miscellany **11** florilegium

garlic 4 moly, ramp **5** clove **6** allium

garment 4 garb, gear **5** array, habit **6** attire **7** apparel, raiment **8** clothing, vestment **10** habiliment *African:* **6** kaross **7** dashiki *Arab:* **3** aba **4** haik *British:* **10** mackintosh *clergy's:* **3** alb **4** cope **7** cassock, soutane **8** vestment *close-fitting:* **6** girdle, tights **7** leotard *for sleeping:* **6** pajama **7** nightie **9** nightgown *Greek:* **5** chiton, peplos **7** chlamys **8** himation *Hindu:* **4** sari *hooded:* **8** djellaba *Japanese:* **6** kimono *lace:* **10** chemisette *Malay:* **6** sarong *men's:* **3** tie **4** vest **5** pants, shirt, socks **6** jacket, slacks **7** drawers **8** trousers *outer:* **4** cape, coat, robe, wrap **5** cloak, parka, shawl, smock, stole **6** capote, jacket, kimono, poncho, sarong, ulster, wammus **7** overall, pelisse, surtout, sweater, topcoat **8** overcoat, pinafore, pullover, scapular **9** coveralls, gaberdine, polonaise *Polynesian:* **5** pareo,

pareu *rain:* **6** poncho **7** oilskin, slicker *Roman:* **4** toga **5** tunic *Scottish:* **4** jupe, kilt **7** sporran *sleeveless:* **3** aba **4** cape **6** mantle, tabard *Turkish:* **6** dolman *women's:* **4** gown **5** dress, skirt **6** blouse, vestee **7** blouson, nightie, partlet **8** negligee, peignoir, pelerine

garner 4 cull, earn, hive, reap **5** amass, glean, hoard, lay up, store **6** gather, pick up, roll up **7** collect, extract, harvest, store up **8** cumulate, ingather **9** stockpile **10** accumulate

garnet 5 jewel, stone **6** pyrope **8** essonite **9** hessonite *black:* **8** melanite *red:* **9** almandine, almandite

garnish 4 deck, trim **5** adorn **6** bedeck **7** dress up, enhance **8** beautify, decorate, ornament **9** embellish

garret 4 loft, room **5** attic **8** cockloft

garrison 4 camp, fort, post **6** assign, billet, occupy, troops **7** station **8** fortress **10** stronghold

garrote 5 choke **8** strangle, throttle **11** strangulate

garrulous see GABBY

garter 4 band, belt **5** strap **7** support **9** supporter

garth 4 yard **5** close **9** enclosure

gas 4 fuel, fume **5** fumes, steam, vapor **6** petrol **8** gasoline **9** petroleum *atmospheric:* **4** neon **5** argon, oxide, ozone, xenon **6** helium, oxygen **7** krypton, methane **8** hydrogen, nitrogen *flammable:* **6** butane, ethane, ethyne **7** methane, propane, propene **8** ethylene *inert:* **4** neon **5** argon, radon, xenon **6** helium **7** krypton *mine:* **8** firedamp **9** black damp *oxygen:* **5** ozone *toxic:* **5** sarin, soman, tabun **6** arsine, ketene **7** mustard **8** phosgene **9** phosphine

gasconade 4 brag **7** bravado **8** boasting, bragging **11** braggadocio

gash 3 cut, rip **4** rend, slit, tear **5** carve, cleft, gouge, slash, slice, split **6** incise **8** lacerate **10** depression, laceration

gasket 4 ring, seal **5** O-ring **6** sealer

gasoline 4 fuel **6** petrol *rating:* **6** octane

gasp 4 blow, huff, pant, puff **5** heave **6** wheeze **11** exclamation

Gaspar *companion:* **8** Melchior **9** Balthazar *gift:* **12** frankincense

gassy 5 windy **7** verbose **8** inflated, vaporous **9** flatulent

gastronome 7 epicure, gourmet **8** gourmand **9** bon vivant **11** connoisseur

gastropod 4 slug **5** conch, murex, snail, whelk **6** cowrie, limpet, volute **7** abalone, mollusc, mollusk, sea slug **8** pteropod, univalve **10** periwinkle

gat 3 gun **6** pistol, roscoe **7** channel, firearm, handgun, passage **8** revolver

gate 3 tap 4 cock, door, exit, port
5 entry, hatch, toril, valve 6 faucet, portal, spigot, switch, wicket 7 hydrant,
opening, petcock 8 entrance, entryway,
stopcock 9 turnstile 10 attendance
gâteau 4 cake
gatefold 6 insert 7 foldout
Gates of Hercules 9 Gibraltar 12 prom-
ontories
gateway 4 arch, door, exit 5 pylon, toril
6 portal 7 archway, doorway, opening
8 entrance
gather 4 brew, cull, gain, grow, heap,
herd, loom, mass, meet, pick, pile,
pool, reap 5 amass, bunch, flock, glean,
group, horde, infer, judge, pluck, shirr,
swarm 6 assume, deduce, derive,
expect, garner, muster, pick up, pucker,
summon, take in 7 cluster, collect, convene, extract, harvest, marshal, round
up, suppose, surmise, suspect 8 assemble, conclude, converge, increase
9 aggregate, intensify 10 accumulate,
congregate, understand 11 concentrate
gathering 4 bevy, crew, gang, herd, mass,
ruck 5 bunch, crowd, crush, drove,
flock, group, horde, party, press, rally,
swarm 6 caucus, klatch, muster, throng
7 company, harvest, klatsch, meeting,
reunion, turnout 8 assembly, congress,
junction 9 concourse, congeries
10 assemblage, collection, conference,
confluence 11 aggregation, get-together
12 congregation
Gath's giant 7 Goliath 10 Philistine
gauche 5 crude, gawky, inept 6 clumsy
7 awkward, halting, loutish, uncouth
8 bumbling, tactless 9 graceless, ham-
handed, inelegant, maladroit 10 blundering
gaucho 6 cowboy 8 herdsman *weapon:*
4 bola 5 bolas 7 machete
gaudeamus ___ 6 igitur
gaudy 4 loud 5 showy 6 brassy, brazen,
coarse, flashy, garish, tawdry, tinsel,
vulgar 7 blatant, chintzy, glaring
9 brummagem, tasteless 10 outlandish
12 meretricious, ostentatious
Gaugamela *loser:* 6 Darius, Persia *victor:*
9 Alexander (the Great)
gauge 4 bore, rule, size 5 check, judge,
meter, scale, weigh, width 6 assess,
degree 7 compute, measure 8 diameter,
estimate, evaluate, quantify, standard
9 benchmark, criterion, dimension,
thickness, yardstick 10 instrument,
touchstone 11 measurement
Gauguin's island 7 Tahiti
Gaul 4 Celt 6 France 9 Frenchman
Gaulish 6 French *god:* 4 Esus 7 Taranis
goddess: 8 Belisama *priest:* 5 druid

gaunt 4 bare, bony, grim, lank, lean,
thin 5 harsh, lanky, spare 6 barren, gangly, skinny, wasted 7 angular, scraggy,
scrawny 8 gangling, rawboned, skeletal
9 emaciated 10 cadaverous
gauntlet 4 dare, test 5 glove, trial
6 attack, ordeal 9 challenge, onslaught
Gautama 6 Buddha 10 Siddhartha *mother:* 4 Maya 8 Mahamaya *son:* 6 Rahula
wife: 9 Yasodhara
gauze 4 film, haze, leno, mesh, mist
5 cloth, crepe, tulle 6 fabric, tissue
7 bandage, chiffon, tiffany 8 compress,
dressing 11 cheesecloth
gauzy 4 thin 5 filmy, fuzzy, sheer, vague
6 flimsy 8 delicate, pellucid 9 gossa-
mery 10 diaphanous 11 transparent
gavel 6 hammer, mallet
gavial 7 gharial, reptile 9 crocodile
gavotte 4 tune 5 dance
Gawain *brother:* 6 Gareth 7 Gaheris
father: 3 Lot *mother:* 8 Margawse, Morgause *slayer:* 8 Lancelot 9 Launcelot
uncle: 6 Arthur *victim:* 6 Uwayne
7 Lamerok 9 Pellinore
gawk 3 oaf 4 bore, gape, gaze, hick,
look, lout, lump, peer, rube 5 churl,
glare, gloat, klutz, looby, stare, yokel
6 goggle, lubber
gawky 5 inept, splay 6 clumsy, coarse,
gauche, oafish 7 awkward, loutish,
lumpish, uncouth 8 bumbling, bungling, lubberly, ungainly 9 graceless,
ham-handed, lumbering, maladroit
gay 4 glad, keen, wild 5 bonny, brash,
happy, jolly, merry, queer, showy,
sunny, vivid 6 blithe, bouncy, bright,
cheery, festal, frisky, jocund, jovial,
joyful, joyous, lively, rakish, sporty
7 animate, chipper, excited, festive, forward, gleeful, lesbian, playful, raffish
8 animated, cheerful, colorful, mirthful, rakehell, spirited, sportive 9 brilliant, exuberant, homophile, sparkling,
sprightly, vivacious 10 blithesome, frolicsome, homoerotic, homosexual,
insouciant, licentious, nonchalant
12 light-hearted
___ **Gay** 4 John 5 Enola
Gaza victor 7 Allenby (Edmund)
gaze 3 eye 4 bore, gape, gawk, leer,
look, ogle, peer, pore, scan, view
5 glare, gloat, stare, watch 6 goggle
7 eyeball, observe 8 consider 10 rubberneck 11 contemplate
gazebo 6 alcove 8 pavilion 9 belvedere
11 garden house, summerhouse
gazelle 4 kudu, oryx 5 eland, nyala
7 gemsbok 8 antelope
gazette 5 paper 6 record 7 journal, pub-

lish 9 newspaper 10 periodical 11 publication 12 announcement

gazetteer 5 atlas, guide, index

Ge see GAEA

gear 3 cam, cog, rig **5** dress, goods, shift, stuff, wheel **6** adjust, tackle, things **7** apparel, harness, rigging **8** clothing, cogwheel, garments, materiel, property, sprocket, tackling, trapping **9** apparatus, equipment, machinery **10** belongings **11** accessories, habiliments, possessions **13** accouterments, accoutrements, paraphernalia

Geats *king:* **7** Hygelac *prince:* **7** Beowulf

Geb *daughter:* **4** Isis **8** Nephthys *father:* **3** Shu *mother:* **6** Tefnut *sister:* **3** Nut *son:* **3** Set **6** Osiris *wife:* **3** Nut

gecko 6 lizard **7** reptile

Gedaliah *father:* **6** Ahikam **7** Pashhur **8** Jeduthun *slayer:* **7** Ishmael

gee 3 wow **4** gosh, turn **5** golly, right **8** goodness, gracious **9** turn right

geek 4 buff, guru, nerd, whiz **5** carny, fiend, freak **6** carney, carnie, expert, pundit, weirdo **7** devotee, egghead, fanatic, oddball **9** authority, eccentric **10** enthusiast **12** intellectual

Gehenna 3 pit **4** hell **5** abyss, hades, Sheol **6** Tophet **7** inferno **8** Tartarus **9** perdition **10** underworld **11** netherworld

Geisel *pseudonym* **7** Dr. Seuss

geisha wear 3 obi **6** kimono

gel 3 dry, set **4** clot **6** harden, mousse **7** colloid, congeal, thicken **8** solidify **9** coagulate

gelatin 3 jam **4** agar **5** jelly **7** sericin

geld 3 cut, fix, tax **5** alter, desex, unsex **6** change, neuter **7** deprive **8** castrate, mutilate **9** sterilize **10** emasculate **11** desexualize

gelid 3 icy **4** cold **5** chill, nippy, polar **6** arctic, chilly, frigid, frosty, frozen, steely **7** glacial **8** freezing

gelt 5 money

gem 3 jet **4** jade, onyx, opal, rock, ruby, sard **5** agate, amber, beryl, bijou, coral, jewel, pearl, stone, topaz **6** amulet, garnet, jasper, scarab, sphene, spinel, zircon **7** bejewel, cat's-eye, citrine, diamond, emerald, enjewel, olivine, peridot **8** amethyst, corundum, diopside, fluorite, intaglio, lazurite, obsidian, sapphire, sardonyx, sparkler, tigereye **9** carnelian, moonstone, phenakite, scapolite, spodumene, tiger's-eye, turquoise **10** aquamarine, cordierite, tourmaline **11** alexandrite, chrysoberyl, chrysoprase, lapis lazuli, masterpiece *blue:* **6** zircon **8** sapphire **9** turquoise **10** aquamarine **11** lapis lazuli *carved:*

8 intaglio *changeable:* **9** chatoyant *cut:* **7** marquis **8** baguette, cabochon, marquise **9** brilliant *face:* **5** facet *green:* **4** jade **7** emerald, peridot, smaragd **10** chrysolite **11** chrysoprase *red:* **4** ruby, sard **6** garnet, pyrope, spinel **9** carnelian *support:* **7** setting *weight:* **5** carat *yellow:* **5** amber, topaz **6** sphene **7** citrine

Gemini star 6 Castor, Pollux

gemmule 3 bud

gemsbok 4 oryx **8** antelope

Gem State 5 Idaho

gemütlich see GENIAL

gendarme 3 cop **5** bobby **7** officer, soldier **8** flatfoot **9** constable, patrolman, policeman

gender 3 sex **4** kind, male, sort, type **5** class **6** female, neuter **8** feminine **9** masculine

genealogy 5 roots, stirp, stock **6** origin, stemma **7** descent, history, lineage **8** ancestry, heredity, pedigree **9** bloodline **10** family tree

general 4 wide **5** broad, usual, vague **6** common, global, normal, public **7** blanket, generic, overall, regular, routine, typical **8** catholic, everyday, sweeping **9** all-around, inclusive, prevalent, universal **10** collective, prevailing, unspecific, widespread **11** commonplace **13** comprehensive *American:* **3** Lee (Robert E.) **4** Haig (Alexander), Pike (Zebulon), Wood (Leonard) **5** Clark (Mark, Wesley, William), Grant (Ulysses S.), Meade (George), Scott (Charles, Hugh, Winfield), Smith (Andrew Jackson, Giles, Holland, Morgan, Samuel, Walter Bedell), Stark (John), Worth (William) **6** Abrams (Creighton), Custer (George Armstrong), Franks (Tommy), Hooker (Joseph), Kearny (Philip, Stephen), Patton (George S.), Porter (Fitz-John), Powell (Colin), Slocum (Henry), Spaatz (Carl), Taylor (Maxwell, Richard, Zachary) **7** Bradley (Omar), Frémont (John Charles), Houston (Samuel), Jackson (Andrew, Thomas "Stonewall"), Lejeune (John), Ridgway (Matthew B.), Sherman (William Tecumseh), Twining (Nathaniel), Wallace (Lewis), Wheeler (Joseph) **8** Burnside (Ambrose), Goethals (George Washington), Marshall (George), Mitchell (Billy), Pershing (John J.), Sheridan (Philip), Stilwell (Joseph) **9** MacArthur (Arthur, Douglas), McClellan (George), Rosecrans (William), Schofield (John), Wilkinson (James) **10** Beauregard (P. G. T.), Eisenhower (Dwight D.), Vandegrift

(Alexander), Wainwright (Jonathan) **11** Schwarzkopf (Norman) **12** Westmoreland (William) *American Revolutionary:* **4** Knox (Henry), Ward (Artemas) **5** Gates (Horatio), Wayne ("Mad Anthony") **6** de Kalb (Baron), Greene (Nathanael), Morgan (Daniel), Putnam (Israel, Rufus) **8** Moultrie (William), Sullivan (John) **10** Washington (George) *Austrian:* **11** Wallenstein (Albrecht von) *British:* **4** Gage (Thomas), Howe (William) **5** Clive (Robert), Monck (George), Wolfe (James) **6** Rupert (Prince) **7** Amherst (Jeffery), Wingate (Orde Charles, Reginald) **8** Burgoyne (John), Cromwell (Oliver) **10** Abercromby (Ralph, Robert), Cornwallis (Charles), Wellington (Duke of) *Carthaginian:* **8** Hamilcar, Hannibal **9** Hasdrubal *Chinese:* **3** Yan (Xishan), Yen (Hsi-shan) **4** Feng (Guozhang, Kuo-chang, Yü-hsiang, Yuxiang) **5** Chang (Tso-lin), Zhang (Zuolin) *Confederate:* **3** Lee (Robert E.) **4** Hill (Ambrose), Hood (John Bell) **5** Bragg (Braxton), Ewell (Richard Stoddart), Price (Sterling), Smith (Edmund Kirby) **6** Morgan (John Hunt), Stuart (Jeb) **7** Forrest (Nathan Bedford), Hampton (Wade), Jackson (Thomas "Stonewall"), Pickett (George) **8** Johnston (Albert Sidney, Joseph Eggleston) **9** Pemberton (John) **10** Beauregard (Pierre G. T.), Longstreet (James) *French:* **3** Ney (Michel) **4** Foch (Ferdinand) **6** Moreau (Victor), Pétain (Philippe) **7** Weygand (Maxime) **8** de Gaulle (Charles), Lefebvre (Pierre), Montcalm (Marquis de), Saint-Cyr (Laurent de Gouvion-) **9** Frontenac (Comte de) **10** Rochambeau (Comte de) *German:* **4** Jodl (Alfred) **6** Kleist (Paul Ludwig von), Rommel (Erwin) **9** Rundstedt (Gerd von) **10** Kesselring (Albert), Ludendorff (Erich) *Greek:* **6** Nicias **9** Miltiades **10** Alcibiades **12** Themistocles *Japanese:* **4** Tojo (Hideki) **5** Koiso (Kuniaki) **6** Yasuda (Yoshisada) **8** Yamagata (Aritomo) **9** Yamashita (Tomoyuki) *Mexican:* **9** Santa Anna (Antonio López de) *Prussian:* **11** Scharnhorst (Gerhard von) *Roman:* **5** Sulla (Lucius Cornelius) **6** Caesar (Julius), Fabius (Quintus), Marius (Gaius), Pompey (the Great), Scipio (Gnaeus Cornelius, Publius Cornelius) **7** Regulus (Marcus Atilius), Ricimer (Flavius) **8** Agricola (Gnaeus Julius), Lucullus (Lucius Licinius), Stilicho (Flavius) **9** Marcellus (Marcus Claudius), Sertorius (Quintus) **10** Theo-

dosius (the Great) **11** Cincinnatus (Lucius Quinctius) *Russian:* **6** Zhukov (Georgy) **7** Kutuzov (Mikhail), Trotsky (Leon), Wrangel (Pyotr), Zhdanov (Andrey) **9** Yeremenko (Andrey) *Spanish:* **4** Alba (Duke of), Alva (Duke of) **6** Franco (Francisco) *Swedish:* **7** Wrangel (Karl Gustav)

general assembly 4 diet **6** plenum **8** congress **10** parliament **11** legislature

generalize 5 infer, widen **6** derive, extend, induce, spread **7** broaden **8** conclude **12** universalize

generally 6 mainly, mostly, widely **7** all told, as a rule, broadly, chiefly, en masse, largely, overall, usually **8** all in all, commonly, normally **9** on average, primarily, typically **10** altogether, by and large, frequently, on the whole, ordinarily **11** customarily, principally **12** almost always **13** predominantly

generate 4 bear, make, sire **5** beget, breed, cause, get up, hatch, spawn, yield **6** create, effect, father, induce, whip up, work up **7** achieve, develop, produce, provoke **8** engender, initiate, multiply, muster up **9** originate, procreate, propagate, reproduce **10** bring about, bring forth

generic 5 broad **6** common, global **7** blanket **9** inclusive, unbranded, universal **10** indistinct **12** nonexclusive

____ **generis 3** sui

generosity 7 charity **8** altruism, kindness, largesse **9** abundance **10** liberality **11** beneficence, benevolence, magnanimity, munificence **12** philanthropy **13** unselfishness

generous 4 free, kind **5** ample **6** lavish **7** copious, helpful, liberal, profuse, willing **8** abundant **9** bounteous, bountiful, plenteous, plentiful, unselfish, unsparing **10** altruistic, benevolent, bighearted, charitable, munificent, openhanded, ungrudging, unstinting **11** considerate, kindhearted, magnanimous, overflowing **12** greathearted

genesis 4 dawn, root **5** alpha, birth, start **6** origin, outset, source **7** dawning, opening **8** creation **9** beginning, formation, inception **10** provenance **12** commencement

genetic 10 congenital, hereditary *material:* **3** DNA, RNA **7** cistron **9** chromatid **10** chromosome *term:* **8** synapsis **9** backcross

genial 4 kind, warm **5** jolly, merry **6** benign, blithe, hearty, jocund, jovial, kindly, mellow, social **7** affable, amiable, cordial **8** amicable, friendly, gracious, pleasant, sociable **9** agreeable,

congenial, convivial, easygoing
10 neighborly 11 good-humored, good-
natured, warmhearted

genie 3 imp 4 jinn, puck 5 afrit 6 afreet,
spirit, sprite 7 servant

geniture 4 dawn 5 birth, start 6 origin
8 nativity 9 beginning, inception

genius 4 bent, gift, head, turn 5 flair,
jinni, knack 6 acumen, brains, master,
spirit, talent, wizard 7 aptness, faculty,
prodigy 8 aptitude, capacity, penchant
9 ingenuity, intellect 10 brilliance, creativity, mastermind, propensity
12 intelligence 13 inventiveness

Genoa's liberator 5 Doria (Andrea)

genre 3 ilk 4 kind, sort, type 5 class,
style 6 family, stripe 7 species, variety
8 category, division

gens 3 kin 4 clan 5 group 6 family, people 7 kinfolk 9 relations, relatives

Genseric's subjects 7 Vandals

genteel 4 nice, prim 5 civil 6 formal, la-
di-da, polite, prissy, strict, stuffy,
urbane 7 courtly, elegant, prudish,
refined, stilted, stylish 8 affected, cultured, graceful, gracious, ladylike,
mannerly, polished, precious, priggish,
well-bred 9 courteous 10 artificial, cultivated 11 fashionable, gentlemanly,
pretentious, straitlaced, well-behaved
12 aristocratic, well-mannered 13 distinguished

gentile 3 goy 5 pagan 7 heathen 9 Christian, non-Jewish

gentility 5 elite 6 gentry 7 decorum,
manners, quality, society 8 breeding,
courtesy, nobility 9 blue blood 10 aristocrat, refinement, upper class, upper
crust 11 aristocracy

gentle 4 calm, easy, kind, meek, mild,
soft, tame 5 balmy, bland, quiet, tamed
6 benign, docile, genial, kindly, mellow,
placid, serene, smooth, tender 7 amiable, lenient 8 delicate, merciful,
peaceful, pleasant, pleasing, soothing,
tranquil 9 agreeable 11 softhearted,
sympathetic, warmhearted 13 compassionate **creature:** 4 lamb

gentleman 3 sir 6 aristo, fellow, mister
8 cavalier 9 blue blood, chevalier, patrician 10 aristocrat **English:** 6 milord
French: 8 monsieur **Hindu:** 4 babu **Spanish:** 3 don 5 señor

gentleman friend 4 beau 5 lover, swain
6 fiancé, squire, suitor 7 gallant

gentlemanly 5 civil, noble, suave
6 polite, urbane 7 elegant, gallant, genteel, refined 8 mannerly, well-bred
9 courteous, honorable 10 chivalrous,
cultivated 11 considerate

gentry 5 elite, folks 7 quality, society

8 nobility 9 gentility, patrician 10 gen-
tlefolk, patriciate, upper class, upper
crust 11 aristocracy, high society, ruling class

genuflect 3 bow 4 fawn 5 kneel 6 kowtow

genuine 4 pure, real, true 5 plain,
pukka, valid 6 actual, dinkum, honest,
tested 7 factual, natural, sincere
8 absolute, bona fide, positive, true-
born 9 authentic, certified, unalloyed,
undoubted, unfeigned, veritable
10 sure-enough, unaffected

genus 3 ilk 4 kind, mode, sort, type
5 class, group, order 6 family 7 species,
variety 8 category

geode 4 rock 5 stone 6 cavity, nodule

geoduck 4 clam

geographer _American:_ 10 Huntington
(Ellsworth) _Flemish:_ 8 Mercator (Gerardus) _German:_ 6 Ratzel (Friedrich)
Greek: 6 Strabo 7 Ptolemy _Italian:_
8 Vespucci (Amerigo)

geologic period 5 azoic 6 Eocene,
Hadean 7 Archean, Miocene, Permian
8 Cambrian, Cenozoic, Devonian,
Holocene, Jurassic, Mesozoic,
Pliocene, Silurian, Triassic 9 Oligocene,
Paleocene, Paleozoic 10 Cretaceous,
Ordovician 11 Phanerozoic, Pleis-
tocene, Precambrian, Proterozoic
13 Mississippian, Pennsylvanian

geometer 6 Euclid 13 mathematician

geometric _coordinate:_ 8 abscissa, ordi-
nate _curve:_ 3 arc 6 spiral 7 ellipse, evo-
lute 8 parabola _figure:_ 5 rhomb 6 circle,
oblong, square 7 ellipse, hexagon, octagon, polygon, rhombus 8 heptagon,
pentagon, rhomboid, triangle 9 rectangle _solid:_ 4 cone, cube 5 prism 6 sphere
7 pyramid 8 cylinder, spheroid,
spherule _surface:_ 5 nappe, torus
6 toroid

geometry letters 3 QED

geophagy 4 pica

Georgia _capital:_ 7 Atlanta _city:_ 5 Macon
6 Albany, Athens 7 Augusta 8 Colum-
bus, Savannah _college, university:_
5 Clark, Emory 6 Mercer 7 Spelman
8 Valdosta 9 Morehouse _founder:_
10 Oglethorpe (James) _nickname:_
5 Peach (State) 21 Empire State of the
South _river:_ 8 Ocmulgee 13 Chattahoochee _state bird:_ 13 brown thrasher
state flower: 12 Cherokee rose _state tree:_
7 live oak _swamp:_ 10 Okefenokee

Georgia, Republic of _ancient kingdom:_
6 Iberia 7 Colchis _capital:_ 6 Tiflis 7 Tbilisi _city:_ 7 Kutaisi, Rustavi _includes:_
6 Ajaria 8 Abkhazia, Adzharia 12 South
Ossetia _monarch:_ 6 Tamara (Queen)

monetary unit: 4 lari **mountain range:**
8 Caucasus **neighbor:** 6 Russia, Turkey
7 Armenia 10 Azerbaijan **river:** 4 Kura
5 Rioni **sea:** 5 Black

Georgics author 6 Virgil

Geraint's wife 4 Enid

Gerda's husband 4 Frey

geriatric 3 old 4 aged 5 aging 6 senior
7 elderly 8 outmoded 12 old-fashioned
13 superannuated

germ 3 bud, bug 4 seed 5 spark, spore,
virus 6 embryo, origin, source
7 microbe, nucleus 8 pathogen 9 bacterium **cell:** 3 egg 4 ovum 5 sperm

German 3 Hun 4 Goth 6 Teuton **article:**
3 das, der, des, die **bomber:** 5 Gotha,
Stuka **child:** 4 Kind **coin:** 4 Mark 5 Taler
6 Thaler 7 Pfennig **empire:** 5 Reich
head: 4 Kopf **highway:** 8 Autobahn
leader: 6 Führer, Kaiser **measles:**
7 rubella **mister:** 4 Herr **no:** 4 nein
nobleman: 6 Junker **pronoun:** 3 ich, sie,
wir **rifle:** 6 Mauser **weight:** 3 Lot
5 Pfund, Stein 8 Vierling **woman:** 4 Frau
8 Fräulein

germane 3 apt 5 ad rem 7 apropos, fitting, related 8 material, relevant 9 pertinent 10 applicable 11 appropriate

Germany 11 Deutschland **capital:**
6 Berlin **city:** 3 Ulm 4 Bonn, Jena, Kiel
5 Essen, Mainz 6 Bremen, Erfurt,
Lübeck, Munich 7 Cologne, Dresden,
Hamburg, Hanover, Leipzig, München,
Potsdam 8 Augsburg, Dortmund, Duisburg, Freiburg, Hannover, Schwerin
9 Frankfurt, Nuremberg, Stuttgart,
Wiesbaden 10 Baden Baden, Düsseldorf
leader: 4 Kohl (Helmut) 6 Brandt
(Willy), Hitler (Adolf) 7 Schmidt (Helmut), Wilhelm (Kaiser) 8 Bismarck
(Otto) **monetary unit:** 4 euro **monetary
unit, former:** 4 mark 5 taler 6 thaler
12 deutsche mark **mountain, range:**
4 Harz 7 Brocken **neighbor:** 6 France,
Poland 7 Austria, Belgium, Denmark
10 Luxembourg 11 Netherlands,
Switzerland 13 Czech Republic **region:**
4 Ruhr 6 Saxony 7 Bavaria 11 Black
Forest **river:** 4 Eder, Elbe, Isar, Main,
Oder, Ruhr 5 Rhein, Rhine 6 Danube
7 Moselle **sea:** 5 North 6 Baltic **state:**
5 Hesse 6 Saxony 7 Bavaria 8 Saarland
9 Thuringia 11 Brandenburg

germinate 3 bud 6 evolve, spring, sprout
7 blossom, develop 9 originate, pullulate

Gerontion poet 5 Eliot (T. S.)

Gershom, Gershon father: 4 Levi **son:**
5 Libni 6 Shimei

Gershwin 3 Ira 6 George **opera:** 12 Porgy
and Bess **piece:** 14 Rhapsody in Blue

15 American in Paris (An) **show:** 5 Oh
Kay 9 Funny Face, Girl Crazy 10 Lady
Be Good 11 Of Thee I Sing 15 Strike
Up the Band **song:** 10 I Got Rhythm,
Summertime

Gertrude husband: 8 Claudius **son:**
6 Hamlet

Gervaise's daughter 4 Nana

Geryon dog: 6 Orthus **father:** 8 Chrysaor
mother: 10 Callirrhoë **slayer:** 8 Hercules

gestalt 4 form 5 shape 6 figure 7 pattern
9 structure 13 configuration

Gestapo chief 7 Himmler (Heinrich)

geste 4 deed, feat 7 emprise, exploit,
romance, venture 9 adventure 10 enterprise 11 undertaking

gesticulate 3 nod 4 move, wave 6 beckon, motion, signal

gesticulation 4 wave 6 motion 7 gesture
8 high sign 9 pantomime 12 body language, sign language

gesture 3 nod 4 sign, wave 5 shrug,
token 6 motion, salute, signal
8 reminder 9 signalize 10 expression,
indication **graceful:** 9 beau geste

get 3 bag 4 draw, earn, gain, land
5 catch, cause, seize 6 access, attain,
become, elicit, extort, obtain, pick up,
secure 7 achieve, acquire, bring in,
capture, chalk up, deliver, extract, procure, receive 8 contract 10 understand
12 come down with

get around 4 roam, rove, tour, trek,
walk 5 avoid, dodge, elude, evade, skirt
6 cruise, detour, escape, ramble, travel,
wander 8 ambulate, outflank, sidestep
10 circumvent

get away see GET OUT

getaway 3 lam 4 exit, slip 6 escape, flight
7 retreat 8 breakout, vacation

get back 6 go home, recoup, regain,
return, revert 7 recover, reclaim,
revenge, revisit 8 retrieve 9 repossess,
retaliate

get by 4 cope, fare 5 slide 6 eke out,
endure, manage 7 carry on, survive
8 maintain

get off 4 walk 5 leave 6 alight, depart, go
free, launch 7 pull out 8 dismount
9 disembark 10 beat the rap

get out 4 exit, kite, leak 5 break, issue,
leave, scram, split 6 alight, beat it,
begone, decamp, depart, egress, escape
7 buzz off, publish, skiddoo, take off,
vamoose 8 dispatch, hightail 9 circulate, skedaddle 10 make tracks

Gettysburg general 3 Lee (Robert E.)
5 Meade (George)

get up 4 gain 5 arise, breed, cause, dress,
hatch, mount, raise, stand 6 create,
induce, summon 7 acquire, prepare,

produce **8** engender, generate **12** rise and shine

getup 3 rig **4** duds, garb, togs **5** array, dress, guise **6** outfit **7** costume, threads

get-up-and-go 3 pep, vim, zip **4** bang, push, snap, zeal, zest **5** drive, moxie, oomph, punch, spunk, steam, verve, vigor **6** energy, spirit, starch **8** ambition **10** enterprise, initiative

gewgaw 3 toy **4** dido **5** bijou, curio **6** bangle, bauble, doodad, trifle **7** bibelot, novelty, trinket, whatnot **8** gimcrack, kickshaw **9** bagatelle, objet d'art **10** knickknack

geyser 3 jet **5** fount, spout, spurt **6** gusher, spring **8** fountain **10** wellspring **11** Old Faithful

Ghana *capital:* **5** Accra *city:* **4** Tema **6** Kumasi, Tamale *ethnic group:* **4** Akan **5** Mossi *former name:* **9** Gold Coast *gulf:* **6** Guinea *lake:* **5** Volta *language:* **7** English *monetary unit:* **4** cedi *neighbor:* **4** Togo **10** Ivory Coast **11** Burkina Faso *river:* **5** Volta

ghastly 4 grim, pale **5** awful, lurid **6** grisly, horrid, pallid **7** ghostly, hideous, macabre **8** dreadful, ghoulish, gruesome, horrible, shocking, spectral, terrible **9** appalling, deathlike, frightful, ghostlike, repulsive, sickening **10** cadaverous, corpselike, disgustful, disgusting, horrifying, nauseating, terrifying **11** frightening

ghee 3 fat **6** butter

gherkin 4 vine **6** pickle **8** cucumber

ghetto 4 slum

ghost 4 soul **5** demon, haunt, shade, spook, trace **6** kelpie, shadow, spirit, wraith, zombie **7** eidolon, phantom, specter **8** phantasm **10** apparition **11** poltergeist

ghostly 5 eerie, scary **6** spooky **7** shadowy **8** ethereal, spectral **9** deathlike, spiritual, unearthly, unworldly **10** cadaverous, corpselike, phantasmal **12** supernatural

Ghosts author 5 Ibsen (Henrik)

ghoul 4 ogre **5** fiend **7** monster **11** grave robber

GI 5 grunt **7** dogface, fighter, soldier, warrior **8** doughboy **9** man-at-arms **10** serviceman

Gianni Schicchi composer 7 Puccini (Giacomo)

giant 4 huge, hulk, ogre, Otus, vast **5** gross, Gyges, Hymir, jumbo, titan, whale **6** Cottus, Typhon **7** Aloadae (plural), Antaeus, Cyclops, Goliath, immense, mammoth, monster, titanic, whopper **8** behemoth, Briareus, colossal, colossus, enormous, gigantic,

Orgoglio **9** cyclopean, Enceladus, Ephialtes, Gargantua, Herculean, humongous, leviathan, monstrous **10** gargantuan, prodigious **11** elephantine *biblical:* **4** Anak **7** Goliath *cactus:* **7** saguaro *killer:* **4** Jack **5** David *one-eyed:* **5** Arges **7** Cyclops **10** Polyphemus *100-armed:* **9** Enceladus *100-eyed:* **5** Argus *rime-cold:* **4** Ymer, Ymir *sea god:* **5** Aegir

Giant author 6 Ferber (Edna)

giaour 7 infidel **10** unbeliever **11** nonbeliever

gib 6 tomcat

gibber 3 gab, yak **4** blab **5** prate **6** babble, drivel, gabble, jabber, yammer **7** blabber, blather, chatter, palaver, prattle, twaddle

gibberish 3 gab **5** Greek, hokum **6** babble, bunkum, burble, drivel, gabble, jabber, yammer **7** blabber, blather, chatter, palaver, prattle, twaddle **8** claptrap, flimflam, nonsense **10** balderdash, double-talk, hocus-pocus, mumbo jumbo **11** abracadabra, jabberwocky **12** gobbledygook

gibbet 4 hang **5** lynch, noose, scrag **7** execute, gallows **8** string up

gibbon 3 ape **7** primate, siamang **10** anthropoid

gibbous 6 arched, convex, humped **7** bulging, rounded, swollen **10** humpbacked **11** protuberant

gibe 4 gird, jeer, jest, mock, quip, rail **5** fleer, flout, scoff, scorn, scout, sneer, taunt, tease **6** deride, insult **8** ridicule

Gibraltar *colony of:* **7** Britain, England *conqueror:* **5** Tarik, Tariq *neighbor:* **5** Spain *opposite:* **5** Ceuta

giddy 4 gaga **5** dizzy, inane, light, silly, woozy **6** elated, yeasty **7** flighty, foolish, vacuous **8** euphoric **9** frivolous, slaphappy **10** hoity-toity **11** empty-headed, harebrained, light-headed, vertiginous **12** bubbleheaded **13** rattle-brained

___ Gide 5 André

Gideon *father:* **5** Joash *servant:* **5** Purah *son:* **9** Abimelech

gift 3 set, tip **4** alms, bent, boon, head, turn **5** award, bonus, endow, favor, flair, forte, grant, knack **6** genius, legacy, reward, talent **7** ability, aptness, cumshaw, faculty, freebie, handout, present, subsidy **8** aptitude, bestowal, capacity, donation, gratuity, largesse, oblation, offering **9** endowment, lagniappe **11** benefaction, benevolence **12** contribution, presentation

gifted 4 able **5** smart **6** expert **7** hotshot,

skilled **8** masterly, skillful, talented **9** ingenious, masterful

gig 3 jab, job, top **4** boat, fool, goad, prod, spur **5** annoy, freak, rotor, spear **6** chaise, harass **7** demerit, provoke, rowboat **8** carriage **10** engagement

gigantic 4 huge, vast **5** giant, jumbo **7** hulking, immense, mammoth, massive, titanic **8** behemoth, colossal, enormous, king-size, whopping **9** cyclopean, humongous, king-sized, monstrous, walloping **10** gargantuan, prodigious, stupendous **11** elephantine

giggle 5 laugh **6** guffaw, hee-haw, titter **7** chortle, chuckle, snicker, snigger, twitter

Gigi author 7 Colette

Gilbert and Sullivan opera 6 Mikado (The) **8** Iolanthe, Patience, Sorcerer (The) **9** Grand Duke (The), Ruddigore **10** Gondoliers (The) **11** H.M.S. Pinafore, Princess Ida, Trial by Jury

Gil Blas author 6 Lesage (Alain-René)

gild 4 coat, deck **5** adorn, cover, tinge **6** bedeck, tinsel **7** enhance, overlay **8** brighten, ornament **9** embellish, embroider

Gilda's father 9 Rigoletto

Gilead *father:* **6** Machir *grandfather:* **8** Manasseh *son:* **7** Jephtha **8** Jephthah

Gilgamesh 4 epic *companion:* **6** Eabani, Enkidu *home:* **4** Uruk **5** Erech *mother:* **6** Ninsun *victim:* **6** Huwawa **7** Humbaba

gill 4 race **5** brook, creek **6** runnel, stream, wattle **7** rivulet *relating to:* **9** branchial

gillyflower 4 pink **9** carnation, clove pink

Gilroy play 15 Subject Was Roses (The)

gilt 3 hog, pig, sow **4** bond, gold **5** swine **6** gilded, golden **10** brilliance

gimcrack 5 cheap **6** bauble, gewgaw, shoddy, trifle **7** bibelot, chintzy, trinket **8** kickshaw **10** knickknack

gimlet 4 tool **5** drill, drink **8** cocktail *ingredient:* **3** gin **5** vodka **9** lime juice

gimmick 3 con **4** ploy, ruse, wile **5** angle, catch, dodge, feint, gizmo, trick **6** device, gadget, gambit, jigger, scheme, widget **8** artifice, maneuver **9** stratagem **10** subterfuge

gimp 3 vim **4** cord, halt **5** braid, hitch **6** dodder, falter, hobble, spirit **7** cripple **8** lameness

gimpy 4 game, halt, lame **7** hobbled, limping **8** crippled

gin 3 net **4** sloe, trap **5** catch, rummy, snare **6** device, liquor **7** springe **8** beverage, generate, separate

ginger 3 fig, pep, vim, zip **4** herb, stir, zing **5** liven, spice, verve, vigor **6** ener-

gy, mettle, revive, spirit **7** sparkle *cookie:* **4** snap

gingerly 4 safe, wary **5** canny, chary **7** careful, guarded **8** cautious, delicate, discreet

gingery 4 tart **5** fiery, peppy, sharp, spicy, tangy, zesty **6** snappy, spunky **7** peppery, piquant, pungent **8** spirited **10** mettlesome **12** high-spirited

gingham 5 cloth **6** fabric **7** textile **8** material

gingiva 3 gum

gin mill 3 bar, pub **4** dive **5** joint **6** saloon, tavern **7** barroom, taproom **8** alehouse **9** roadhouse **11** public house **12** watering hole

Ginsberg poem 4 Howl **7** Kaddish

ginseng 4 herb, root

Gioconda, La 8 Mona Lisa *composer:* **10** Ponchielli (Amilcare) *painter:* **7** da Vinci (Leonardo)

giraffe 8 ruminant **9** quadruped **10** camelopard

girandole 7 earring **10** candelabra **11** candelabrum, candlestick, composition

girasol 3 gem **4** opal **5** jewel, stone **7** mineral **8** fire opal **9** artichoke

gird 3 hem **4** band, belt, bind, ring, wrap **5** brace, equip, hem in, ready, round, steel **6** circle **7** bolster, enclose, fortify, prepare, provide, shore up, wreathe **8** buttress, cincture, encircle, surround **9** encompass, reinforce **10** strengthen

girder 4 beam **5** brace **7** support **8** crossbar **9** crossbeam **10** crosspiece, transverse

girdle 4 band, belt, ring, sash **6** cestus, circle **8** ceinture, cincture, encircle, surround **9** encompass, waistband *of Aphrodite:* **6** cestus

girl 4 babe, bird, coed, doll, lass, maid, miss **5** chick, filly, missy, wench **6** damsel, lassie, maiden **8** daughter **10** sweetheart

girth 4 band, belt, bind, size **5** brace, cinch, strap **6** circle, fasten, girdle **7** measure **8** cincture, encircle, surround **9** thickness **10** dimensions **13** circumference

Giselle composer 4 Adam (Adolphe)

gist 3 nub, sum **4** core, meat, pith **5** sense **6** burden, ground, kernel, marrow, matter, thrust, upshot **7** essence **9** main point, substance

give 3 pay **4** deal, hand **5** allot, allow, award, grant, issue, offer, remit **6** accord, afford, assign, bestow, commit, confer, convey, devote, direct, donate, extend, market, pony up, render, supply, tender **7** deliver, dish out, display, dole out, fall out, fork out, furnish, hand out, mete out, present, produce, proffer, provide 8 allocate, bequeath, disburse, dispense, give away, hand over, shell out, turn over 9 apportion, sacrifice 10 administer, contribute, distribute

give-and-take 6 banter 8 exchange, repartee, trade-off 10 compromise 11 cooperation, reciprocity

give away 4 blab, leak 5 award, grant, spill 6 bestow, betray, confer, devote, donate, expose, reveal, tattle 7 deliver, divulge, hand out, let slip, present 8 bequeath, disclose

giveaway 4 deal, gift, leak 5 steal, value 6 tip-off 7 bargain, freebee, freebie, premium, present, sellout 8 betrayal, exposure 10 disclosure, revelation

give back 6 refund, retire, return 7 replace, restore, retreat 8 withdraw 9 reinstate

give in 4 fold, quit, stop 5 yield 6 assent, comply, desist, relent, submit 7 concede, deliver, indulge, succumb 8 back down, cry uncle 9 surrender 10 relinquish

given 5 prone 6 donnée 7 assumed, granted 8 inclined 9 presented, specified 10 particular 11 considering, susceptible

give off 4 beam, emit, flow, vent 5 exude, issue 6 effuse 7 emanate, radiate, release 9 discharge

give out 4 deal, dole, emit, fail, mete, vent 5 issue 6 cave in 7 declare, release, succumb 8 collapse, throw off 9 break down 10 distribute

giver 5 donor 7 donator, grantor

give up 4 cede, quit 5 allow, cease, forgo, waive, yield 6 abjure, devote, resign, vacate 7 abandon, despair 8 abdicate, hand over, renounce, withdraw 9 sacrifice, surrender 10 relinquish

give way 5 yield 6 buckle, cave in 7 retreat, succumb 8 collapse 9 surrender

gizmo see GADGET

glabrous 4 bald, bare 6 shaven, smooth 8 hairless 9 beardless 10 bald-headed 12 smooth-shaven

glacial 3 icy, raw 5 chill, gelid, nippy, polar 6 arctic, biting, chilly, frigid, frosty, frozen, wintry 8 freezing

glacier 3 ice 6 ice cap 8 ice field, ice sheet *Alaska:* 4 Muir, Taku 6 Bering 10 Mendenhall *Antarctica:* 9 Beardmore *deposit:* 4 kame 5 esker 6 placer 7 moraine *fissure:* 8 crevasse *fragment:* 4 berg 7 iceberg *Greenland:* 8 Humboldt

hill: 7 drumlin *Karakoram:* 5 Biafo 7 Baltoro *New Zealand:* 6 Tasman *pinnacle:* 5 serac

glacis 5 grade, slope 7 incline 10 buffer zone 11 buffer state

glad 3 gay 4 fain 5 happy, jolly, merry 6 blithe, bright, cheery, genial, jocund, jovial, joyful, joyous 7 beaming, gleeful, pleased, radiant, tickled, willing 8 cheerful, mirthful, pleasant, rejoiced 9 delighted, gratified, overjoyed 11 exhilarated 12 lighthearted

gladden 4 buoy 5 cheer, elate 6 buck up, perk up, please, uplift 7 cheer up, delight, gratify, hearten

glade 6 meadow 8 clearing 9 open space

gladiator 7 fighter 9 combatant, Spartacus

gladly 4 fain, lief 6 freely 7 happily, readily 8 heartily 9 willingly 10 cheerfully, with relish 12 with pleasure

gladness 3 joy 4 glee 5 bliss, cheer, mirth 6 gaiety 7 delight, jollity 9 happiness, merriment

gladstone 3 bag 8 suitcase

glamorous 7 elegant 8 alluring, charming, dazzling, enticing, magnetic 9 seductive 10 attractive, bewitching, enchanting 11 captivating, fascinating 13 sophisticated

glamour 5 charm, magic, spell 6 allure, appeal 7 romance 8 charisma, witchery 9 magnetism, sex appeal 10 attraction, witchcraft 11 fascination 12 razzle-dazzle

glance 4 peek, peep, skim, skip 5 brush, carom, flash, glaze, graze, shine 6 bounce, careen 7 glimpse 8 ricochet *lascivious:* 4 leer

gland 5 gonad, liver, organ 6 pineal, thymus 7 adrenal, mammary, parotid, thyroid 8 exocrine, pancreas, prostate, salivary 9 endocrine, pituitary 11 parathyroid *secretion:* 7 hormone *swelling:* 4 bubo

glare 4 gaze, glow, peer 5 blaze, flame, flash, frown, gleam, light, lower, scowl, shine, stare 6 dazzle, glower 7 obtrude 8 stand out 10 garishness

glaring 4 loud, rank 5 gaudy, plain, vivid 6 brazen, flashy, garish, tawdry, tinsel 7 blatant, obvious 8 blinding, flagrant 9 audacious, egregious, obtrusive 10 noticeable 11 conspicuous, outstanding 12 ostentatious

Glasgow's patron saint 5 Mungo 9 Kentigern

glass 4 lens, pane 5 image, lense, prism 6 mirror 7 reflect 9 barometer, telescope *combining form:* 5 vitro *container:* 3 jar 6 beaker, bottle *decorative:*

7 schmelz 8 schmelze *drinking:* 4 pony
5 flute 6 goblet, jigger, rummer, seidel
7 snifter, tumbler 8 schooner *gem:*
5 paste 6 strass *magnifying:* 5 loupe
milky: 7 opaline *volcanic:* 7 perlite
8 obsidian

glasses 5 specs 6 shades 7 goggles
8 bifocals, pince-nez, tumblers
9 lorgnette, trifocals 10 spectacles

glass-like 5 clear 6 glazed, limpid,
smooth 8 pellucid, vitreous 9 vitrified
11 translucent, transparent

glassmaker 6 Blenko (William)
7 Lalique (René), Tiffany (Louis Comfort) 9 Waterford

glassmaking tool 5 punty 6 pontil
8 blowpipe

Glass Menagerie author 8 Williams
(Tennessee)

glassy 5 blank, dazed, shiny 6 glazed,
smooth, vacant 7 hyaloid 8 polished,
vitreous 9 burnished

glaucous 4 waxy 7 frosted, powdery

Glaucus *beloved:* 6 Scylla *father:* 5 Minos
8 Sisyphus *mother:* 6 Merope 8 Pasiphaë
son: 11 Bellerophon

glaze 3 rub 4 buff, coat, film 5 cover,
glint, gloss, sheen, shine 6 enamel, finish, luster, patina, polish 7 burnish,
coating, furbish, lacquer, overlay

glazed 5 blank 6 glassy

gleam 3 ray 4 beam, burn, glow 5 flare,
flash, glint, sheen, shine 6 glance
7 glimmer, glisten, glitter, radiate,
shimmer, sparkle, twinkle 8 radiance
11 coruscation, scintillate 13 scintillation

gleaming 5 aglow, shiny 6 glossy, sheeny
7 beaming, burning, glowing, lambent,
radiant, shining 8 flashing, luminous,
lustrous, polished 9 brilliant, burnished, refulgent, sparkling, twinkling
10 glimmering, glistening, glittering,
shimmering 13 scintillating

glean 4 cull, reap, sift 5 amass, learn
6 garner, gather, pick up 7 extract, find
out, harvest

glebe 4 land 5 field, tract 7 acreage
8 cropland, farmland

glee 3 joy 5 mirth 6 gaiety, levity
7 delight, elation, jollity 8 gladness,
hilarity, part-song 9 enjoyment, festivity, good cheer, happiness, jocundity,
joviality, merriment 10 exuberance,
joyfulness, jubilation 12 exhilaration

gleeful 3 gay 5 jolly, merry 6 blithe, elated, jocund, jovial, joyous 8 cheerful,
exultant, jubilant, mirthful 9 exuberant
12 lighthearted

glen 4 dale, vale 5 swale 6 dingle, valley
deep: 5 gorge 6 ravine

glengarry 3 cap 6 bonnet

glib 4 easy 5 slick 6 facile, fluent,
smooth 7 offhand, shallow, voluble
8 eloquent, flippant 10 articulate, nonchalant 11 superficial

glide 3 fly 4 flow, sail, skim, slip, soar,
waft 5 coast, creep, drift, float, skate,
skirr, skulk, slide, slink, sneak, steal
7 descend, slither 8 glissade, volplane
10 portamento

glimmer 4 glow, hint 5 blink, flash,
gleam, glint, shine, spark, trace
6 glance 7 flicker, glisten, glitter,
inkling, shimmer, sparkle, twinkle
9 coruscate 10 suggestion 11 coruscation, scintillate 13 scintillation

glimpse 4 peek, peep 5 flash, glint, stime
6 glance

glint 3 ray 5 flash, glaze, gleam, sheen,
shine, trace 6 glance, luster 7 glimmer,
glisten, glitter, shimmer, sparkle, twinkle 9 coruscate 11 coruscation, scintillate 13 scintillation

glissade 4 skim, slip 5 glide, slide

glissando 3 run 5 slide 7 gliding, sliding

glisten 4 glow 5 flash, gleam, glint, shine
6 glance 7 flicker, glimmer, glitter,
shimmer, spangle, sparkle, twinkle
9 coruscate 11 coruscation, scintillate
13 scintillation

glitch 3 bug 4 flaw, snag 5 fault 6 defect
7 failing, failure, gremlin, problem
8 obstacle 10 difficulty 11 malfunction

glitter 5 flash, gleam, glint, shine 7 glimmer, glisten, shimmer, spangle, sparkle,
twinkle 9 coruscate 11 coruscation,
scintillate 13 scintillation

glittering 5 gaudy, shiny, showy 6 flashy
7 fulgent 9 brilliant, clinquant, coruscant, effulgent 11 spectacular

gloaming 3 eve 4 dusk 5 gloom
7 evening 8 eventide, twilight 9 nightfall

gloat 4 crow 5 exult, revel, vaunt 6 relish
7 triumph 9 celebrate

glob 4 clot, lump 6 dollop

global 5 grand 6 cosmic 7 blanket, general, overall 8 all-round, catholic
9 inclusive, planetary, spherical, universal, worldwide 12 encyclopedic 13 comprehensive

globe 3 orb 4 ball 5 earth, round, world
6 planet, sphere 7 rondure *half:*
10 hemisphere

globule 4 ball, bead, drip, drop 6 gobbet,
pellet 7 driblet, droplet 8 spherule

gloom 3 dim 4 dusk, funk, loom, murk
5 bedim, blues, cloud, dumps, frown,
lower, mopes, scowl 6 darken, glower,
shadow 7 becloud, despair, dimness,
obscure, sadness 8 darkness, overcast,

twilight **9** adumbrate, bleakness, dejection **10** blue devils, depression, melancholy, overshadow **11** despondency, unhappiness **12** mournfulness

gloomy 3 dim, dun, sad **4** cold, dark, dour, down, drab, dull, glum **5** black, bleak, drear, dusky, mopey, murky, muzzy, sulky, surly **6** dismal, dreary, morose, solemn, somber, sullen **7** forlorn, joyless, obscure, stygian, unhappy **8** dejected, desolate, downcast, funereal, mournful **9** cheerless, depressed, mirthless, oppressed, saturnine, tenebrous, woebegone **10** caliginous, chapfallen, depressing, depressive, dispirited, despondent, forbidding, lugubrious, melancholy, oppressive, tenebrific **11** dispiriting, pessimistic **12** disconsolate, discouraging

glorify 4 hymn, laud **5** bless, cry up, erect, exalt, extol, honor **6** admire, praise, revere **7** acclaim, dignify, elevate, ennoble, light up, lionize, magnify, sublime, worship **8** eulogize, venerate **9** celebrate **10** aggrandize

glorious 5 grand, great, noble, proud **6** august, divine, superb **7** eminent, exalted, radiant, sublime **8** esteemed, gorgeous, lustrous, majestic, renowned, splendid, stunning **9** beautiful, brilliant, effulgent, excellent, marvelous, ravishing, wonderful **11** illustrious, magnificent, resplendent, splendorous

glory 4 crow, fame, halo, pomp **5** exalt, exult, gloat, honor, revel **6** heaven, praise, relish, renown **7** acclaim, aureole, delight, majesty, rejoice, triumph **8** eminence, eternity, grandeur, jubilate, radiance, splendor **9** greatness, hereafter **10** effulgence, exaltation, exultation **11** distinction **12** magnificence, resplendence

gloss 4 buff **5** glaze, glint, sheen, shine **6** define, enamel, facade, finish, luster, patina, polish, veneer **7** burnish, comment, explain, furbish, varnish **8** annotate **9** interpret, sleekness, slickness, translate **10** annotation, appearance, brilliance, commentary, definition **11** elucidation, explanation, translation

glossary 7 lexicon **8** wordbook **9** wordhoard **10** dictionary, vocabulary

gloss over 4 mask **5** slant **6** veneer **7** conceal, cover up, distort, falsify, varnish **8** disguise, palliate **9** dissemble, extenuate, sugarcoat, whitewash **10** camouflage

glossy 5 shiny, sleek, slick **7** shining **8** gleaming, lustrous, polished **9** burnished **10** glistening *fabric:* **4** silk **5** satin *paint:* **6** enamel

glove 4 gage, mitt **5** catch, cover **6** mitten, sheath **8** covering, gauntlet

glow 4 burn, pink, rose **5** bloom, blush, flush, gleam, rouge, shine **6** mantle, redden **7** blossom, crimson, fox fire, glisten, glitter, radiate **8** brighten, radiance **10** brilliance, luminosity **13** incandescence

glower 5 frown, scowl, stare **11** look daggers

glowing 3 hot, red **4** avid **5** flush, ruddy, shiny **6** ardent, fervid, florid, heated, red-hot **7** beaming, burning, fervent, flushed, lambent, radiant, vibrant **8** blushing, dazzling, gleaming, luminous, lustrous, rubicund, sanguine, suffused **9** brilliant **10** candescent, hot-blooded, passionate **11** impassioned **12** enthusiastic, incandescent

Gluck opera 5 Orfeo **6** Armide **7** Alceste

glucose 5 sugar, syrup

glue 3 fix, gum **4** bind, join **5** epoxy, paste, stick **6** adhere, attach, cement, fasten **7** plaster, stickum **8** adhesive, mucilage

gluey 5 gummy, tacky **6** sticky, viscid **7** viscous **8** adhesive **12** mucilaginous

glum 3 sad **4** blue, dour, down **5** moody, sulky, surly **6** dismal, dreary, gloomy, morose, sullen, woeful **7** crabbed **8** brooding, dejected, downcast, taciturn **9** depressed, oppressed, saturnine, sorrowful, woebegone **10** despondent, dispirited, melancholy **11** downhearted, melancholic

glut 4 clog, cloy, cram, fill, pack, pall, sate **5** feast, flood, gorge, stuff **6** deluge, excess, stodge **7** satiate, surfeit, surplus, swallow **8** saturate **10** oversupply **13** overabundance

glutinous 4 ropy **5** gluey, gooey, gummy, pasty, tacky, thick **6** sticky, viscid **7** viscous **10** gelatinous **12** mucilaginous

glutton 3 hog, pig **8** gourmand **9** chowhound, wolverine **11** gormandizer

gluttonous 7 hoggish, piggish **8** edacious, ravening, ravenous **9** dissolute, indulgent, rapacious, voracious **10** insatiable **11** intemperate **13** overindulgent

gluttony 6 excess **7** edacity **8** gulosity, rapacity, voracity **11** piggishness

glyph 6 figure, groove, symbol **7** graphic **9** character

G-man 3 fed **4** narc, Ness (Eliot) **5** agent **6** Hoover (J. Edgar)

gnarl 4 bend, knot, warp **5** growl, snarl, twist **6** deform **7** contort, distort

gnash 4 bite **5** grind

gnat 3 bug, fly **4** pest **5** midge **6** insect **7** no-see-um

gnaw 3 eat, nag, vex 4 bite, chaw, chew 5 annoy, chomp, erode, munch, scour, tease, worry 6 bother, crunch, nibble, pester, plague, rankle 7 bedevil, corrode, eat away 8 irritate, wear away 9 masticate

gnome 3 elf, saw 4 rule 5 adage, axiom, dwarf, maxim, moral, troll, truth 6 dictum, goblin, saying, truism 7 proverb 8 aphorism, apothegm 10 shibboleth

gnostic 6 occult, secret 8 abstruse 10 mysterious

gnu 10 wildebeest

go *against:* 4 defy 5 fight 6 oppose, resist 7 counter, protest 10 contradict *ahead:* 4 lead 7 precede, proceed 8 continue, progress *along:* 5 agree, yield 6 accede, comply, concur 7 consent 9 acquiesce *around:* 5 avoid, skirt 6 bypass, detour 7 compass 8 outflank, sidestep 10 circumvent *at:* 6 assail, attack, tackle 7 assault *away:* 3 git 4 exit, scat, shoo 5 leave, scram, split 6 beat it, begone, cut out, depart, move on, retire 7 buzz off, get lost, pull out, take off 8 clear out, run along, shove off, withdraw 9 skedaddle *back:* 6 recede, return, revert 7 regress, retreat *back on:* 6 betray, renege 7 abandon 8 abrogate *back over:* 6 rehash, review, rework 7 recheck, retrace *before:* 4 lead 7 precede, predate 8 antedate *beyond:* 4 pass 5 excel, outdo 6 exceed, outrun 7 eclipse, surpass 8 outshine, outstrip, overtake 9 transcend *forward:* 6 move on, push on 7 advance, press on, proceed 8 continue, progress *in:* 5 enter 9 penetrate *out:* 4 exit 5 leave 6 expire *Scottish:* 3 gae *through:* 4 bear 5 audit, brave, check, spend 6 endure, suffer 7 consume, deplete, examine, exhaust, ride out, survive, sustain, undergo 8 squander 9 penetrate, withstand 10 experience *together:* 3 fit 4 date, jibe, suit 5 agree, match, tally 6 accord, square 7 conform 8 dovetail 9 accompany, harmonize 10 correspond *with:* 4 suit 5 befit, match 9 accompany

goad 3 egg, rod, sic 4 prod, push, spur, urge 5 drive, egg on, impel, prick, thorn 6 coerce, exhort, incite, motive, needle, prompt, propel 7 impetus, impulse 8 catalyst, motivate, stimulus 9 encourage, impulsion, incentive, stimulant, stimulate 10 inducement

go-ahead 4 okay 7 consent 8 spirited 9 ambitious, authority, clearance, energetic 10 green light, permission 11 progressive, up-and-coming 12 enterprising 13 authorization

goal 3 aim, end, use 4 duty, hope, mark 5 score 6 design, intent, object, target 7 mission, purpose 8 ambition, function 9 intention, objective

goat 3 kid, ram 4 lech 5 billy, letch, nanny 6 alpaca, angora, lecher, Saanen 8 cashmere 10 Toggenburg *female:* 3 doe 5 nanny *genus:* 5 Capra *Himalayan:* 4 tahr *male:* 4 buck 5 billy *neutered:* 6 wether *relating to:* 7 caprine *wild:* 4 ibex *wool:* 6 mohair 8 pashmina

goat antelope 5 serow 7 chamois

goatee 5 beard 7 Vandyke 8 imperial, whiskers

goatfish 6 mullet

goatish 3 hot 4 lewd 6 carnal 7 caprine, lustful, satyric 8 prurient 9 indulgent, lecherous, lickerish 10 lascivious, libidinous, passionate 12 concupiscent

goat-man deity 3 Pan

goat nut 6 jojoba, pignut

gob 3 wad 4 blob, clod, glob, hunk, lump, mass 5 chunk, mouth 6 nugget, sailor 7 extract

gobbet 4 drib, drip, drop, hunk, lump, mass 5 chunk, piece 7 driblet, droplet, globule, portion 8 fragment

gobble 3 eat 4 bolt, cram, grab, glut, gulp, slop, wolf 5 gorge 6 devour, guzzle 7 swallow 11 ingurgitate

gobbledygook see GIBBERISH

go-between 5 agent, envoy, proxy 6 broker, deputy, factor 7 liaison 8 emissary, mediator, procurer 9 middleman 10 arbitrator, interagent, interceder, matchmaker, negotiator, procurator 11 intercessor 12 intermediary, intermediate

goblet 3 cup 5 glass, grail 6 vessel 7 chalice

goblin 3 elf, fay, hob, imp 4 puck 5 bogey, bogle, fairy, ghost, gnome 6 sprite 7 brownie, bugbear 8 bogeyman

____ **go bragh** 4 Erin

gobs 4 lots, tons, wads 5 heaps, loads, lumps, piles, rafts, reams, scads 6 oodles 8 slathers 10 quantities

god 4 idol 5 deity 7 creator 8 Almighty, divinity, immortal *combining form:* 4 theo *false:* 4 baal *French:* 4 dieu *Hebrew:* 6 Elohim, Yahweh *Latin:* 4 deus *Spanish:* 4 dios (see specific entries (as GREEK; ROMAN) for names of specific gods and goddesses)

god-awful 4 foul 6 horrid, rotten 7 beastly 8 dreadful, horrible, shameful, shocking, terrible, wretched 9 appalling, atrocious, miserable 10 abominable, deplorable, despicable, detestable, disgusting, outrageous

God Bless America composer 6 Berlin (Irving)

goddess 4 idol 5 deity 8 divinity, immortal *Latin:* 3 dea (see note at GOD)

godfather 3 don 4 boss, capo 6 leader 7 sponsor

Godfather, The 8 Corleone (Don) *actor:* 6 Brando (Marlon), De Niro (Robert), Pacino (Al) *author:* 4 Puzo (Mario) *director:* 7 Coppola (Francis Ford)

God-fearing 5 pious 6 devout 8 faithful, reverent 9 pietistic, religious, righteous

godforsaken 4 bare 5 bleak 6 barren, dismal, gloomy, remote 7 pitiful 8 deserted, desolate, pitiable, wretched 9 miserable, neglected 11 unfortunate

Godiva's husband 7 Leofric

godless 5 pagan 6 unholy, wicked 7 heathen, impious, infidel, profane 8 agnostic 9 atheistic 11 irreligious, unreligious

godlike 4 holy 6 divine 7 blessed, supreme 8 almighty, immortal 10 omniscient 11 all-powerful

godliness 5 piety 6 purity 8 devotion, divinity, holiness, sanctity 9 beatitude, reverence 10 devoutness, sacredness 11 religiosity, saintliness 12 spirituality, virtuousness 13 righteousness

godly 4 holy 5 pious 6 devout, divine 7 angelic, blessed, saintly, supreme 8 almighty, hallowed, immortal, virtuous 9 pietistic, prayerful, religious 10 omniscient 11 all-powerful

go down 3 dip, set 4 drop, fall, fold, lose, sink 5 ensue, lower, occur, pitch, slide, slump 6 cave in, happen, plunge, settle, topple, tumble 7 crumple, decline, descend, founder, succumb 8 collapse, keel over, submerge, submerse 9 surrender, take place

God's acre 8 boneyard, catacomb, cemetery 9 graveyard 10 churchyard, necropolis 12 burial ground, memorial park, potter's field

godsend 4 boon, gift, good 5 manna 7 benefit 8 blessing, windfall 9 advantage 11 benevolence, serendipity

Goethe work 5 Faust 6 Egmont, Stella 7 Clavigo 10 Prometheus

gofer 4 aide, peon 5 toady 6 drudge, flunky, helper, lackey, menial 7 courier, servant 8 factotum 9 assistant, attendant

goffer 5 crimp, flute, pinch, plait, pleat

go-getter 6 dynamo 7 hustler, rustler 8 live wire 10 ball of fire, powerhouse 11 self-starter

goggle 3 eye 4 bore, gape, gawk, gaze, look, ogle, peer 5 glare, gloat, stare 10 rubberneck

goggles 5 specs 7 glasses 10 eyeglasses, spectacles

go-go 5 hyper 6 hectic 7 frantic 8 frenetic, frenzied

Gogol *novel:* 9 Dead Souls *story:* 8 Overcoat (The) 10 Taras Bulba 14 Diary of a Madman

goiter 6 struma 8 swelling

Golconda see GOLD MINE

gold 4 gilt 5 money 6 riches, wealth, yellow 7 bullion 8 treasure *bar:* 5 ingot *combining form:* 4 auri, auro 5 chrys 6 chryso *fool's:* 6 pyrite *imitation:* 6 ormolu *measure:* 5 carat, karat *Spanish:* 3 oro

goldbrick 3 bum 4 idle, laze, lazy, loaf, loll 5 cheat, dally, idler, shirk, slack 6 dawdle, loafer, loiter, lounge 7 lounger, shirker, slacker, swindle 8 lollygag, malinger, sluggard 9 lazybones 10 dillydally, malingerer

Gold Bug author 3 Poe (Edgar Allan)

gold cloth 4 lamé

gold-covered 4 gilt 6 gilded

golden 4 gilt, rich 5 auric, blond, shiny, straw 6 blonde, flaxen, gilded, mellow, superb, yellow 7 aureate, honeyed, shining 8 glorious, lustrous, resonant 9 favorable 10 auspicious, prosperous 11 flourishing

golden-ager 5 elder 6 senior 7 ancient, oldster, retiree 8 old-timer 13 senior citizen

golden-apples guardian 5 Ithun 6 Ithunn

golden bough 9 mistletoe

Golden Bough author 6 Frazer (James George)

Golden Boy playwright 5 Odets (Clifford)

golden-crowned accentor 7 warbler 8 ovenbird

goldeneye 3 bug 4 duck, fowl 6 insect 8 lacewing

Golden Fleece seeker 5 Jason 8 Argonaut

Golden Hind captain 5 Drake (Francis)

Golden Horde 6 Tatars 7 Mongols *leader:* 4 Batu

golden horse 7 Trigger 8 palomino

golden shiner 4 dace, fish

Golden State 10 California

goldfinch 4 bird 8 songbird 12 yellowhammer

gold mine 7 bonanza, pay dirt 8 El Dorado, Golconda, treasure, treasury 13 treasure trove

golem 3 oaf 4 clod, dolt, dope 5 dunce, idiot, robot 6 nitwit 7 halfwit, machine 8 imbecile 9 automaton, blockhead 10 nincompoop 11 blunderhead

golf *assistant:* 5 caddy 6 caddie *club:* 4 iron, wood 5 billy, spoon, wedge

6 driver, mashie, putter **7** niblick, pitcher **9** metal wood, sand wedge *club part:* **3** toe **4** face, grip, head, heel, neck, sole **5** hosel, shaft *course:* **5** links *cup:* **5** Ryder **6** Curtis, Walker *hazard:* **4** trap **6** bunker **8** sand trap *mound:* **3** tee *score:* **3** ace, par **5** bogey, eagle **6** birdie *stroke:* **4** baff, chip, draw, fade, hook, putt **5** drive, pitch, shank, slice **6** sclaff *target:* **3** cup, par, pin **4** flag **5** green **7** fairway *term:* **3** lie **4** club, fore, hole, loft **5** divot, rough, swing **6** hazard, marker, stance, stroke **8** foursome, handicap **9** backswing, downswing, flagstick

golfer 8 linksman *man:* **3** Els (Ernie) **4** Daly (John), Ford (Doug), Kite (Tom), Lyle (Sandy), Mize (Larry), Tway (Bob) **5** Boros (Julius), Faldo (Nick), Floyd (Ray), Grady (Wayne), Green (Hubert), Hagen (Walter), Hogan (Ben), Jones (Bobby), Irwin (Hale), North (Andy), Pavin (Corey), Peete (Calvin), Price (Nick), Shute (Denny), Singh (Vijay), Snead (Sam), Woods (Tiger) **6** Casper (Billy), Graham (David), Janzen (Lee), Langer (Bernhard), Miller (Johnny), Nelson (Byron, Larry), Norman (Greg), Ouimet (Francis), Palmer (Arnold), Player (Gary), Sluman (Jeff), Sutton (Hal), Vardon (Harry), Watson (Tom) **7** Azinger (Paul), Couples (Fred), Guldahl (Ralph), Mayfair (Billy), Sarazen (Gene), Simpson (Scott), Stewart (Payne), Strange (Curtis), Trevino (Lee), Woosnam (Ian), Zoeller (Fuzzy) **8** Crenshaw (Ben), Nicklaus (Jack), Olazabal (José), Weiskopf (Tom) **9** Rodriguez (Chi Chi), Elkington (Steve) **10** Middlecoff (Cary) **11** Ballesteros (Seve) *woman:* **4** Berg (Patty), King (Betsy) **5** Baker (Kathy), Lopez (Nancy), Rawls (Betsy), Stacy (Hollis), Suggs (Louise) **6** Alcott (Amy), Carner (Joanne), Daniel (Beth), Davies (Laura), Geddes (Jane), Mallon (Meg), Merten (Lauri), Wright (Mickey) **7** Bradley (Pat), Inkster (Juli), Mochrie (Dottie), Sheehan (Patty) **8** Zaharias (Babe) **9** Didrikson (Babe), Sorenstam (Annika), Whitworth (Kathy) **10** Stephenson (Jan)

Golgotha 7 Calvary

Goliath 5 giant **10** Philistine *deathplace:* **4** Elah *home:* **4** Gath *slayer:* **5** David

Gollum creator 7 Tolkien (J. R. R.)

gonad 5 gland, ovary **6** testis **8** testicle

gondola 3 car **4** boat **7** ski lift **11** railroad car

gone 4 away, dead, left, lost, past

5 flown **6** absent **7** defunct, extinct, lacking, missing **8** departed, vanished

gonef see GANEF

goner 8 dead duck **9** lost cause

Goneril *father:* **4** Lear (King) *husband:* **6** Albany *sister:* **5** Regan **8** Cordelia *victim:* **5** Regan

Gone with the Wind *author:* **8** Mitchell (Margaret) *character:* **5** Rhett (Butler) **6** Ashley (Wilkes) **7** Melanie (Wilkes) **8** Scarlett (O'Hara) *plantation:* **4** Tara

gonfalon 4 flag, jack **6** banner, ensign **7** pendant, pennant **8** banderol, standard **9** banderole

gong 6 cymbal, tam-tam

gonzo 6 far-out **7** bizarre, offbeat **9** wigged-out **10** outrageous

goo 4 crud, glop, guck, gunk, muck **5** slime

goober 6 peanut

good 4 pure **5** right, sound, whole **6** decent, humane, kindly, toward, worthy **7** benefit, healthy, upright, welfare **8** innocent, virtuous **9** admirable, advantage, blameless, exemplary, favorable, healthful, honorable, righteous, well-being, wholesome **10** altruistic, beneficent, beneficial, benevolent, charitable, worthwhile **11** respectable, well-behaved **12** humanitarian **13** philanthropic *French:* **3** bon **5** bonne *German:* **3** gut *Spanish:* **5** bueno

good-bye 4 ciao, ta-ta **5** adieu, congé, later **6** so long **7** cheerio, parting, send-off, toodles **8** farewell, toodle-oo **9** departing, departure **11** leave-taking, valediction, valedictory *French:* **5** adieu **8** au revoir **9** bon voyage *German:* **8** lebe wohl *Italian:* **11** arrivederci *Japanese:* **8** sayonara *Spanish:* **5** adios **12** hasta la vista

Good Earth author 4 Buck (Pearl S.)

good-for-nothing 3 bum **6** rascal, waster **7** inutile, rounder, useless, wastrel **8** feckless, rascally, unworthy **9** dissolute, scoundrel, valueless, worthless **10** ne'er-do-well, profligate, scapegrace **11** purposeless

good-looking 4 cute, fair, foxy **5** bonny, dishy, hunky **6** comely, lovely, pretty **8** alluring, drop-dead, fetching, handsome **9** beauteous, beautiful, bodacious, ravishing **10** attractive

goodly 4 fair, tidy **5** ample, hefty, large **7** sizable **8** generous **9** bountiful, plentiful **11** significant, substantial **12** considerable

good-natured 4 easy, kind, mild, warm **6** genial, jovial, mellow **7** affable, amiable, cordial, lenient **8** cheerful, friendly, laid-back, obliging, pleasant, pleasing, sanguine **9** agreeable, congenial, easygoing, gemütlich **10** altruistic, benevolent, charitable **11** complaisant

goodness 5 honor, merit, worth **6** purity, virtue **7** decency, honesty, probity, quality **8** morality **9** integrity, rectitude **11** benevolence

goods 4 gear **5** cargo, stock, stuff, wares **7** effects **8** chattels, movables, property **9** vendibles **10** belongings **11** commodities, merchandise, possessions **13** paraphernalia *smuggled:* **10** contraband *stolen:* **4** loot, swag **5** booty **6** boodle, spoils **7** plunder *thrown overboard:* **5** lagan **6** jetsam

good-tasting 5 sapid, yummy **6** delish, savory, toothy **8** luscious **9** delicious, palatable, relishing, toothsome **10** appetizing, delectable, flavorsome **11** scrumptious **13** mouthwatering

goodwill 5 amity, favor **6** comity **7** charity, rapport **8** altruism, kindness, sympathy **9** tolerance **10** compassion, friendship, generosity, kindliness **11** benevolence, helpfulness **12** friendliness

goody 5 candy, treat **6** bonbon, dainty, morsel, tidbit **8** delicacy, kickshaw

goody-goody 4 prig **5** prude **6** Grundy **7** prudish, puritan, uptight **8** bluenose, Comstock, priggish **9** Mrs. Grundy, nice-nelly **11** puritanical

gooey 5 gluey, gummy, mushy, sappy, soupy **6** cloggy, drippy, slushy, sticky, viscid **7** maudlin, viscous **8** adhesive **9** glutinous **11** sentimental **12** mucilaginous

goof 3 err, kid **4** boob, dolt, flub, fool, mess, muff **5** boner, booby, botch, chump, dunce, error, fluff, gaffe, gum up, idiot, put on **6** bobble, boggle, bollix, bumble, bungle, fumble, mess up, slip-up **7** blooper, blunder, fathead, louse up, mistake **8** dolthead, lunkhead **9** blockhead

go off 4 blow **5** blast, burst, erupt, leave, sound **6** blow up, depart **7** explode **8** detonate

goofy 5 balmy, batty, crazy, daffy, dippy, loony, nutty, potty, silly **6** simple, stupid **7** foolish, idiotic **9** ludicrous **10** ridiculous **11** harebrained

gook 4 crud, glop, gunk, muck **5** gumbo, slime **6** debris, sludge

go on 4 last, stay **5** occur **6** endure, happen, keep up **7** persist, proceed **8** continue **9** persevere

goon 3 oaf, sap **4** boob, dodo, dolt, dope, fool, hood, thug **5** dummy, idiot **6** dimwit, hit man, nitwit **7** hoodlum **8** dumbbell, enforcer **10** triggerman

gooney 7 seabird **9** albatross

goop 4 crud, gunk, muck **5** gumbo, tripe

Goops author 7 Burgess (Gelett)

goose 4 poke, spur **9** stimulate *cry:* **4** honk **5** clang *flock:* **3** vee **5** skein **6** gaggle *genus:* **5** Anser *Hawaiian:* **4** nene *male:* **6** gander *wild:* **5** brant **7** greylag **8** barnacle *young:* **7** gosling

gooseberry 7 currant

Goosebumps author 5 Stine (R. L.)

goose egg 3 nil, zip **4** nada, zero **5** aught, zilch **6** cipher, naught, nought **7** no score, nothing

gooseflesh 5 bumps **7** pimples

go over 4 scan, skim **5** study **6** peruse, review **7** examine, inspect

gopher 6 rodent **8** tortoise

Gopher State 9 Minnesota

Gordian knot cutter 9 Alexander

Gordius' son 5 Midas

gore 3 jab **4** stab **5** blood, slime, wound **6** gusset, pierce **7** carnage **12** gruesomeness

gorge 3 gap **4** cloy, fill, glut, jade, pall, sate **5** abyss, chasm, cleft, clove, flume, gulch, stuff **6** arroyo, canyon, clough, defile, pig out, ravine **7** couloir, overeat, satiate, surfeit **11** overindulge *Arizona:* **11** Grand Canyon *Colorado:* **5** Royal

gorgeous 5 grand, plush **6** comely, lavish, lovely, pretty, superb **7** opulent, sublime **8** alluring, dazzling, glorious, splendid **9** beautiful, brilliant, exquisite, luxurious, sumptuous **10** attractive, glittering **11** magnificent, resplendent, splendorous

gorgon 3 hag **5** crone, harpy, witch **6** Medusa, ogress, virago **8** battle-ax, fishwife, harridan, slattern **9** battle-axe, termagant *father:* **7** Phorcus, Phorcys *mother:* **4** Ceto

gorilla 3 ape **4** goon, hood, thug **5** tough **6** simian **7** primate **8** gangster **10** anthropoid

Gorky drama 11 Lower Depths (The)

gormless 4 dumb, slow **6** stupid

gorse 4 whin **5** furze, shrub **6** legume

gory 5 lurid **6** bloody, grisly **8** gruesome, sanguine **10** sanguinary **11** ensanguined, sanguineous, sensational **12** bloodstained **13** bloodcurdling

gosh 3 gee, wow **4** dang, darn, drat, egad, geez, heck **5** golly **6** crikey, cripes, shucks **7** doggone **8** goodness, gracious

gospel 5 truth **6** truism **7** message **8** doctrine **9** scripture **11** evangelical

gossamer 4 airy, film, fine, webs **5** filmy, gauzy, sheer **6** flimsy **7** cobwebs, tenuous 8 delicate 10 diaphanous 11 transparent

gossip 4 blab, buzz, chat, dirt, talk 5 clack, prate, rumor 6 babble, rumble, tattle 7 babbler, chatter, hearsay, prattle, tattler 8 bigmouth, busybody, informer, prattler, quidnunc, telltale 10 talebearer 11 rumormonger, scandalizer, scuttlebutt 12 blatherskite

gossipy 5 gabby, talky 6 chatty 8 babbling, blabbing 9 garrulous, talkative

Gotham 7 New York (City)

Gothic 4 dark, wild 5 crude 6 brutal, coarse, savage 7 uncouth 8 barbaric, Germanic, medieval, Teutonic 9 barbarian, barbarous, sans serif 11 black letter, uncivilized

Götterdämmerung composer 6 Wagner (Richard)

Gouda 6 cheese

gouge 3 dig 4 milk, ream, tool 5 cheat, exact, pinch, screw, wrest, wring 6 chisel, coerce, extort, groove, wrench 7 squeeze 8 scoop out 9 blackmail, extortion, shake down 10 overcharge

goulash 4 stew 6 jumble, medley 7 mélange 8 mishmash 9 potpourri 10 bridge hand, hodgepodge, salmagundi 11 gallimaufry

go under 4 fall, flop, fold, lose, sink 5 drown 6 plunge, submit 7 founder, immerse, succumb 8 collapse, submerge, submerse 9 surrender 10 capitulate

Gounod work 5 Faust 8 Ave Maria

gourd 4 pepo 5 fruit, melon 6 bottle, squash, vessel 7 chayote, gherkin, pumpkin 8 calabash, cucumber, cucurbit *instrument:* 6 maraca

gourmand see GLUTTON; GOURMET

gourmet 7 epicure 9 bon vivant 10 gastronome 11 connoisseur 12 gastronomist

gout 4 blob, clot, gush 5 spurt 6 splash 7 disease, podagra 8 eruption, swelling

govern 4 head, lead, rule 5 guide, order, reign, steer 6 direct, manage, master 7 command, conduct, control, execute, oversee 8 dominate, hold sway, regulate 9 supervise 10 administer 11 superintend

governess 5 nanny, nurse 6 duenna 8 mistress 9 nursemaid 10 babysitter 11 Mary Poppins

government 4 rule 5 power 6 polity, regime 7 regency, regimen 8 monarchy, republic, Uncle Sam 9 authority, autocracy, democracy, hierarchy, oligarchy 10 Big Brother 11 aristocracy, sovereignty *autocratic:* 7 czarism, fascism, tyranny 9 despotism 10 absolutism 12 dictatorship *by a few:* 9 oligarchy *by one:* 8 monarchy *by three:* 8 triarchy 11 triumvirate *by women:* 8 gynarchy *official:* 10 bureaucrat 11 functionary *without:* 7 anarchy

government agency 3 ATF, BIA, BLM, CDC, CIA, DEA, EPA, FAA, FBI, FCC, FDA, FEC, FHA, GAO, GPO, HUD, ICC, INS, IRS, NBS, NEA, NIH, NRC, TVA 4 FDIC, FEMA, FEPC, NASA, NOAA, NTSB, OSHA

governor 3 bey 4 head 5 chief, nabob, ruler 6 leader, regent 7 manager, viceroy 8 director 9 executive, regulator 10 commandant, magistrate *Chinese:* 6 tuchun *of a fort:* 7 alcaide, alcayde 9 castellan, chatelain *Persian:* 6 satrap

gown 4 robe, toga 5 dress, frock, habit, tunic 6 camise, kimono, kirtle, mantua 7 cassock, chemise 8 peignoir *dressing:* 8 bathrobe *hospital:* 6 johnny

goy 6 non-Jew 7 gentile

grab 3 nab 4 glom, grip, snag, take 5 catch, clasp, grasp, pluck, seize 6 clutch, collar, snatch, tackle 7 capture, grapple, seizure

grabby 6 greedy 8 covetous, desirous, grasping 9 rapacious 10 avaricious, prehensile 11 acquisitive

grace 4 ease 5 adorn, charm, favor, mercy, poise 6 allure, lenity, pardon, polish, prayer, thanks, virtue 7 charity, dignify, dignity, enhance 8 approval, blessing, clemency, easiness, elegance, goodness, kindness, leniency, petition, reprieve 9 embellish, privilege 10 indulgence, invocation, refinement 11 benediction, forbearance 12 thanksgiving

graceful 4 airy, deft, easy 5 agile, lithe 6 nimble, poised, seemly, smooth, urbane 7 elegant, flowing, genteel, refined 8 debonair, elegance, pleasing, polished

graceless 4 rude 5 crude, gawky, inept 6 clumsy, coarse, gauche, klutzy, vulgar 7 awkward, boorish, uncouth 8 barbaric, ungainly 9 barbarian, barbarous 10 outlandish, unmannered 12 infelicitous

Graces 6 Charis 8 Charites (plural) *brilliance:* 6 Aglaia *bloom:* 6 Thalia *joy:* 10 Euphrosyne *mother:* 5 Aegle

gracious 4 kind 5 suave 6 benign, genial, kindly, urbane 7 affable, amiable, cordial, courtly, gallant, stately, tactful 8 charming, generous, mannered, merciful, obliging, sociable 9 congenial, courteous 11 complaisant, good-natured 13 compassionate

grackle 5 mynah 7 jackdaw 8 starling
9 blackbird

gradation 4 rank, step 5 order, range,
scale, shade, stage 6 ablaut, change,
degree, nuance, series 8 ordering, position, spectrum 9 continuum, variation
10 difference, succession

grade 3 peg 4 cant, form, kind, lean,
mark, rank, rate, rung, sort, step, tier,
tilt 5 blend, class, group, level, notch,
order, pitch, place, slant, slope, stage
6 assess, assort, degree, league, rating
7 arrange, caliber, echelon, incline,
leaning, quality 8 appraise, category,
classify, division, evaluate, grouping,
position, standard 10 categorize
11 inclination

Grade A 3 ace, top 4 best, boss, fine,
tops 5 grand, great, prime, primo,
super 6 choice, tip-top 7 capital,
supreme 8 five-star, superior, top-notch
9 excellent, first-rate, nonpareil, number one, top-drawer 10 first-class
11 outstanding 13 par excellence

gradient 4 lean, ramp, rise, tilt 5 angle,
pitch, slant, slope 7 incline, leaning
9 acclivity, declivity 11 inclination

gradual 4 even, slow 6 Psalms, steady
7 ongoing 8 bit-by-bit, creeping 9 piecemeal, prolonged 10 continuous, developing, protracted, step-by-step 11 progressive

gradually 6 slowly 7 by steps 8 bit by bit
9 by degrees, piecemeal 10 step by step
12 deliberately 13 imperceptibly, incre-
mentally

graduate 4 alum *female:* 6 alumna
7 alumnae (plural) *male:* 6 alumni (plural) 7 alumnus

Graeae, Graiae 4 Enyo 5 Deino
8 Pephredo *father:* 7 Phorcus, Phorcys
mother: 4 Ceto *sisters:* 7 Gorgons

graft 4 join, mend, scam, skim 5 affix,
crime, fraud, scion, unite 6 attach, boodle, fasten, payola, splice 7 implant,
swindle, topwork 8 kickback 10 corruption

Grafton, Sue *character:* 8 Millhone (Kinsey) *novel:* 11 A Is for Alibi

Grahame, Kenneth *character:* 3 Rat
4 Toad, Mole 6 Badger *novel:* 16 Wind
in the Willows (The)

grail 3 cup, end 4 goal 6 goblet, object,
target 7 chalice 9 objective

grain 3 bit, jot, rye 4 corn, flax, iota,
meal, mite, oats, rice 5 crumb, fiber,
kamut, maize, speck, spelt, trace,
wheat 6 barley, cereal, millet, quinoa,
tittle 7 granule, smidgen, sorghum, texture 8 amaranth, molecule, particle
9 buckwheat, triticale *bundle:* 4 bale

5 sheaf *chute:* 6 hopper *ear:* 5 spike *elevator:* 4 silo *mixture:* 6 fodder *row:*
5 swath 7 windrow

grainy 5 rough 6 coarse 8 granular
10 unfinished, unpolished

grammarian *Roman:* 7 Donatus (Aelius)

grammatical case 6 dative 7 oblique
8 ablative, genitive, locative, vocative
9 objective 10 accusative, nominative,
possessive, subjective

grampus 5 whale 7 dolphin 8 cetacean,
porpoise, scorpion 9 blackfish 12 whip
scorpion

Granada *building:* 8 Alhambra *citadel:*
8 Alcazaba *last Moorish king:* 7 Boabdil

granary 3 bin 4 silo 9 grain area
10 repository, storehouse

grand 3 fab 4 epic, fine, huge, vast
5 gaudy, lofty, noble, regal, royal,
showy, super 6 august, flashy, garish,
lavish, lordly, mighty, ornate, superb
7 exalted, opulent, pompous, stately,
sublime 8 baronial, elevated, foremost,
gorgeous, imposing, majestic, princely,
splendid 9 first-rate, inclusive, luxurious, principal, sumptuous, wonderful
10 first-class, impressive, monumental,
prodigious, stupendous, tremendous
11 magnificent 12 ostentatious 13 comprehensive

Grand Canyon *explorer:* 6 Powell (John
Wesley) *state:* 7 Arizona

grande dame 5 queen 6 matron 7 dowager 9 matriarch

grandee 4 duke, earl, king, lord, peer
5 baron, noble, pasha 6 bashaw, prince
8 mandarin, marquess, nobleman, viscount 11 muckety-muck

grandeur 4 pomp 5 glory 7 dignity,
majesty 8 nobility, opulence, splendor,
vastness 9 greatness, immensity, largeness, loftiness, nobleness, sublimity
10 augustness 11 stateliness 12 magnificence

grandiloquent 5 lofty 7 aureate, bloated,
fustian, pompous 8 inflated 9 bombastic, flatulent, high-flown, overblown
10 histrionic, portentous 11 declamatory, highfalutin, pretentious 12 magniloquent

grand inquisitor *Spanish:* 10 Torquemada (Tomás de)

grandiose 4 epic, vast 5 lofty, noble,
regal, royal, showy 6 august, cosmic,
lavish, lordly 7 pompous, stately, sublime, utopian 8 affected, imposing,
majestic, princely, splendid 9 ambitious, high-flown 11 extravagant, highfalutin, magnificent, pretentious
12 ostentatious

grand mal 7 seizure 8 epilepsy

grandmother *Russian:* 8 babushka

grange 4 farm 9 farmhouse, farmstead

granite 3 ore 4 rock 5 stone 6 aplite 7 mineral 11 igneous rock

Granite State 12 New Hampshire

grant 3 aid 4 alms, avow, cede, dole, gift, give 5 admit, allow, award, endow, yield 6 accord, assert, assign, assume, bestow, confer, convey, donate, permit 7 charity, concede, consent, entitle, handout, present, property, subsidy, suppose 8 bequeath, donation, transfer 9 endowment, vouchsafe 10 assistance, concession, relinquish, subvention 11 acknowledge, benefaction 12 contribution 13 appropriation

granular 5 rough, sandy 6 coarse, grainy 7 powdery 8 powdered 10 unfinished, unpolished

granule 3 bit, jot 4 iota, pill, spot 5 grain 6 pellet 8 fragment, particle

grape 3 fox, uva 4 Bual 5 Gamay, Pinot, Syrah 6 Arinto, Burger, Gentil, merlot, muscat, Shiraz 7 Albillo, Aligote, Barbera, Catawba, Concord, Furmint, Niagara, sultana 8 Aleatico, Cabernet, Charbono, Delaware, Friularo, Grenache, Isabella, malvasia, muscadel, Muscadet, Nebbiolo, Riesling, Semillon, Sylvaner, Thompson, Traminer, vinifera, Viognier 9 Carmenère, Chasselas, Lambrusco, Malvoisie, muscadine, Pinot Gris, pinot noir, Sauvignon, Trebbiano, zinfandel 10 chardonnay, Grignolino, muscadelle, pinot blanc, Sangiovese, Verdicchio 11 Chenin Blanc, Petite Sirah, pinot grigio, scuppernong *disease:* 4 esca *dried:* 6 raisin *drink:* 4 wine *pulp:* 4 rape 6 pomace *residue:* 4 marc

grapefruit 6 pomelo

Grapes of Wrath, The *author:* 9 Steinbeck (John) *family:* 4 Joad *people:* 5 Okies

grapevine 4 buzz 5 rumor 6 gossip 7 hearsay 9 rumor mill 11 scuttlebutt

graph 3 map 4 plot 5 chart 6 sketch 7 diagram, outline 8 nomogram, pie chart

graphic 3 map 5 clear, lucid, photo, vivid 6 cogent, visual 7 picture, precise, telling, written 8 clear-cut, definite, detailed, explicit, incisive, striking 9 pictorial, realistic 10 compelling, photograph 11 descriptive, picturesque

graphite 4 lead 6 carbon 8 plumbago

grapnel 4 hook 6 anchor

grappa 6 brandy

grapple 3 nab 4 bind, cope, grab, grip, hold 5 catch, clamp, clasp, fight, grasp, seize 6 battle, bucket, clench, clinch,

clutch, fasten, tackle, tussle 7 contest, scuffle, wrestle 8 struggle

grasp 3 dig, ken, see 4 glom, grip, hold, know, take 5 catch, clamp, clasp, seize 6 accept, clench, clinch, clutch, fathom, follow, handle, take in, tenure 7 cognize, compass, control, embrace, grapple, realize 8 envisage, perceive 9 apprehend, awareness 10 appreciate, comprehend, take hold of, understand 12 apprehension 13 comprehension, understanding

graspable 5 clear, lucid 6 lucent 8 coherent, knowable, palpable 10 fathomable 11 perspicuous 12 intelligible 13 apprehensible

grasping 4 avid 6 grabby, greedy 8 covetous, desirous 9 rapacious 10 avaricious, prehensile 11 acquisitive

grass 3 pot, sod, tea 4 lawn, reed, turf, weed 6 redtop 7 herbage, panicum, pasture 8 cannabis, Mary Jane 9 cocksfoot, marijuana *African:* 6 imphee *annual:* 6 darnel 8 teosinte *Asian:* 7 vetiver, whangee *Australian:* 8 spinifex *beach:* 6 marram *cereal:* 3 oat, rye 4 milo, teff 5 kafir, maize, proso, sorgo, wheat 6 millet 7 sorghum 8 triticum *clump:* 4 tuft 7 tussock *dried:* 3 hay 5 straw *European:* 7 Bermuda, timothy *fiber:* 4 flax *fragrant:* 10 citronella *pasture:* 5 Bahia, grama *perennial:* 6 fescue, quitch, zoysia 7 esparto, galleta *prairie:* 8 bluestem *second growth:* 5 rowen *tropical:* 5 cogon 6 bamboo

grasshopper 6 locust 7 katydid 8 cocktail

grassland 3 lea 5 field 6 meadow 7 pasture, prairie *African:* 4 veld 5 veldt *flat:* 7 savanna 8 savannah *South American:* 5 pampa 6 pampas

Grass novel 7 Tin Drum (The)

grate 3 irk, jar, rub, vex 4 file, fray, fret, gall, rasp, rile 5 annoy, chafe, gnash, grind, peeve, pique 6 abrade, grille, nettle, rankle, scrape 7 provoke, scratch 8 irritate 9 aggravate, fireplace

grateful 7 obliged, pleased, restful, welcome 8 beholden, indebted, pleasant, pleasing, thankful 9 agreeable, congenial, favorable 10 refreshing 11 restorative 12 appreciative

Gratiano *brother:* 9 Brabantio *friend:* 7 Antonio 8 Bassanio *niece:* 9 Desdemona *wife:* 7 Nerissa

gratify 4 baby, sate 5 favor, humor, spoil 6 coddle, oblige, pamper, pander, please 7 appease, cater to, content, delight, gladden, indulge, satisfy

gratin 5 crust

grating 3 dry 4 grid, rasp 5 grill, harsh,

rough 6 grille, hoarse 7 irksome, jarring, lattice, rasping, raucous 8 gridiron, strident 9 vexatious 10 stridulous

gratis 4 comp, free 6 comped 8 costless 10 chargeless 13 complimentary, without charge

gratitude 6 thanks 12 appreciation, gratefulness, thankfulness

gratuitous 6 wanton 8 baseless 9 unfounded, voluntary 10 groundless, reasonless, ungrounded 11 uncalled-for, unnecessary, unwarranted 12 indefensible

gratuity 3 tip 4 gift, perk 5 bonus 6 reward 7 cumshaw, douceur 8 donation, largesse, offering 9 baksheesh, lagniappe, pourboire 10 perquisite 11 benefaction 12 contribution

grave 3 pit, sad 4 dire, dour, fell, grim, tomb 5 acute, awful, crypt, fatal, heavy, major, sober, staid, vault 6 burial, deadly, gloomy, sedate, severe, solemn, somber, sombre, urgent 7 austere, ghastly, ominous, ossuary, serious, subdued, weighty 8 catacomb, critical, dreadful, perilous, pressing, terrible 9 dangerous, mausoleum, momentous, ponderous, saturnine, sepulcher, sepulchre, sepulture, unsmiling *marker:* 5 stela, stele 8 memorial, monument 9 footstone, headstone, tombstone 11 sarcophagus *mound:* 6 barrow 7 tumulus *robber:* 5 ghoul

gravel 4 dirt, grit, sand *ridge:* 5 esker

gravelly 5 raspy, rough 6 gritty, hoarse 7 rasping, grating 8 abrasive, granular, gutteral, scratchy

graven image 4 icon, idol

graver 4 tool 5 burin 8 sculptor

graveyard 8 boot hill, catacomb, cemetery, God's acre 10 necropolis 12 burial ground, memorial park, potter's field

gravid 5 heavy 8 enceinte, pregnant 9 expectant, expecting, with child 10 parturient 12 childbearing

gravity 5 force 6 weight 7 dignity, urgency 8 sobriety 9 heaviness, solemnity 10 importance, somberness 11 consequence, seriousness 12 significance

gravlax 3 lox 6 salmon

gravy 4 perk 5 bonus, bribe, graft, juice, sauce 6 payola 8 dressing, windfall *French:* 3 jus

gray 3 ash, old 4 aged, ashy, blah, drab, dull 5 ashen, bleak, color, hoary, slate, slaty 6 dismal, gloomy, leaden 7 elderly, grizzly, neutral 8 grizzled, gunmetal, overcast 9 cinereous, colorless *brownish:* 5 taupe 7 fuscous

gray duck 7 gadwall, pintail

grayfish 5 shark 7 dogfish

gray matter 3 wit 4 head, mind 5 brain 6 brains, noddle, noggin, noodle 8 cerebrum 9 intellect 10 encephalon 12 intelligence, neural tissue

graze 3 eat, rub 4 feed, gall, kiss, skim, skip, wear 5 brush, chafe, erode, shave, touch 6 abrade, browse, bruise, forage, glance, scrape 7 contuse, corrade, pasture 8 abrasion, ricochet

grazier 7 rancher

grease 3 fat, oil 4 lard 5 smear 6 smooth 7 lanolin 9 lubricant, lubricate *combining form:* 4 sebi, sebo

greasy 4 oily 5 fatty, slick 8 slippery, unctuous 10 lubricious, oleaginous

greasy spoon 4 café 5 diner, grill 6 eatery 8 beanery, hashery 9 chophouse, hash house, lunchroom 10 coffee shop 12 luncheonette

great 3 big, fat 4 huge, vast 5 famed, grand, jumbo, large, noble 6 famous, heroic 7 eminent, exalted, extreme, immense, mammoth, notable, sublime, supreme, titanic 8 colossal, enormous, gigantic, glorious, oversize, renowned, terrific, towering 9 excellent, fantastic, humongous, paramount, prominent, wonderful 10 celebrated, impressive, noteworthy, prodigious, remarkable, stupendous, surpassing, tremendous, voluminous 11 illustrious, magnificent, outstanding, superlative 13 distinguished *combining form:* 4 mega 6 megalo

Great Bear 9 Big Dipper, Ursa Major 13 constellation

Great Britain see ENGLAND

Great Commoner, the 4 Pitt (William) 5 Bryan (William Jennings) 7 Lincoln (Abraham)

Great Emancipator, the 7 Lincoln (Abraham)

greater 4 more 5 metro 6 better, bigger, higher, larger 8 superior 9 exceeding 10 surpassing 12 metropolitan

greatest 4 best, most 6 utmost 7 maximum, supreme 8 foremost

Great Expectations *author:* 7 Dickens (Charles) *character:* 3 Joe (Gargery), Pip 5 Biddy 7 Estella, Jaggers 8 Havisham (Miss), Magwitch (Abel)

greathearted 4 bold, kind 5 brave, lofty, noble 6 heroic 7 gallant 8 fearless, generous, princely 10 benevolent, chivalrous, courageous, high-minded 11 considerate, magnanimous

Great Lake 4 Erie 5 Huron 7 Ontario 8 Michigan, Superior *acronym:* 5 HOMES

Great Lake State 8 Michigan

greave 7 legging

grebe 4 bird, fowl 8 dabchick 10 diving bird

Greece *ancient city-state:* 5 Argos 6 Athens, Sparta, Thebes 7 Corinth *capital:* 6 Athens *city:* 6 Patras 7 Larissa, Piraeus 8 Salonika 12 Thessaloníki *conqueror:* 6 Philip (of Macedonia) 9 Alexander (the Great) *island, island group:* 5 Crete 6 Aegean, Euboea, Ionian 8 Cyclades, Sporades *monetary unit:* 4 euro *mountain, range:* 3 Ida 4 Ossa 6 Pindus 7 Olympus 9 Parnassus *neighbor:* 6 Turkey 7 Albania 8 Bulgaria, Macedonia *part of:* 7 Balkans *peninsula:* 6 Balkan 10 Chalcidice 11 Peloponnese *region:* 6 Epirus, Thrace 8 Thessaly *sea:* 6 Aegean, Ionian 13 Mediterranean

greed 6 excess, hunger 7 avarice, avidity, craving 7 edacity, longing 8 cupidity, gluttony, rapacity, voracity 12 covetousness, ravenousness

greedy 4 avid 5 itchy 6 grabby 7 hoggish, miserly, selfish 8 covetous, desirous, edacious, esurient, grasping 10 avaricious, gluttonous 11 acquisitive

Greek 6 babble, drivel, jabber 7 Achaean 8 Hellenic, nonsense 9 gibberish *assembly:* 5 agora, boule *coin:* 4 obol 6 lepton, stater *column:* 5 Doric, Ionic 10 Corinthian *contest:* 4 agon *counselor:* 6 Nestor *dictator:* 7 Metaxas (Ioannis) *dragon:* 9 Eurythion *drink:* 4 ouzo *epic:* 5 Iliad 7 Odyssey *Fates:* 6 Clotho, Moirae 7 Atropos 8 Lachesis *god:*

  chief: 4 Zeus *messenger:* 6 Hermes *of agriculture:* 6 Cronus *of death:* 8 Thanatos *of dreams:* 8 Morpheus *of fire:* 10 Hephaestus *of healing:* 9 Asclepius 11 Aesculapius *of love:* 4 Eros *of marriage:* 5 Hymen *of the sun:* 6 Apollo *of physicians:* 6 Hermes *of the sea:* 6 Nereus, Triton 7 Oceanus 8 Poseidon *of the sun:* 6 Helios *of the underworld:* 5 Pluto *of the winds:* 5 Eurus, Notus 6 Aeolus, Boreas 8 Zephyrus *of war:* 4 Ares *of wine:* 8 Dionysus *of woods:* 3 Pan

  goddess:

  of agriculture: 7 Demeter *of beauty:* 9 Aphrodite *of dawn:* 3 Eos *of discord:* 4 Eris *of fertility:* 6 Cybele *of flowers:* 7 Chloris *of harvests:* 4 Rhea *of hunting:* 7 Artemis *of justice:* 7 Astraea *of love:* 9 Aphrodite *of marriage:* 4 Hera *of night:* 3 Nyx *of peace:* 5 Irene *of retribution:* 7 Nemesis *of ruin:* 3 Ate *of the earth:* 4 Gaea, Gaia *of the hearth:* 6 Hestia *of magic:* 6 Hecate, Hekate *of the moon:* 6 Hecate, Hekate, Selena, Selene 7 Artemis, Astarte *of the rain-*

bow: 4 Iris *of the seasons:* 5 Horae *of the underworld:* 6 Hecate, Hekate 10 Persephone *of vengeance:* 7 Nemesis *of victory:* 4 Nike *of wisdom:* 6 Athena *of witchcraft:* 6 Hecate, Hekate *of womanhood:* 4 Hera *of youth:* 4 Hebe

  hero:

  4 Aias, Ajax 5 Jason 7 Theseus 8 Achilles, Argonaut, Heracles, Hercules, Odysseus 9 Achilleus *historian:* 8 Xenophon 9 Herodotus 10 Thucydides *lawgiver:* 5 Draco, Solon *leader:* 9 Agamemnon *letter:* 3 chi, eta, phi, psi, rho, tau 4 beta, iota, zeta 5 alpha, delta, gamma, kappa, omega, sigma, theta 6 lambda 7 epsilon, omicron, upsilon *magistrate:* 6 archon *marketplace:* 5 agora *porch:* 4 stoa *sandwich:* 4 gyro *soldier:* 7 hoplite *theater:* 5 odeon, odeum *underworld:* 5 Hades *war cry:* 5 alala *warrior:* 4 Ajax 7 Ulysses 8 Achilles, Diomedes, Odysseus 9 Agamemnon, Palamedes *wine:* 7 retsina

green 3 raw 4 jade, lime, moss 5 alive, fresh, kelly, leafy, naive, virid, young 6 callow, forest, unripe 7 avocado, celadon, emerald, untried, verdant 8 immature, juvenile, unversed, youthful 9 unfledged 10 unseasoned 11 unpracticed 13 inexperienced *bluish:* 8 glaucous *combining form:* 4 verd 6 chloro *grayish:* 5 olive *yellowish:* 7 luteous 10 chartreuse

greenbacks 4 cash, jack, loot 5 bread, bucks, dough, lucre, money, moola 6 moolah, wampum 7 dollars, scratch 8 currency, smackers 11 legal tender

greenery 7 foliage, leafage 8 verdancy

green-eyed 7 envious, jealous 9 invidious *monster:* 8 jealousy

greenfly 5 aphid

greengage 4 plum

greenhead 3 fly 8 horsefly

greenheart 6 laurel 9 evergreen

greenhorn 4 babe, hick, jake, naif, rube, tyro 5 clown 6 newbie, novice, rookie 7 bumpkin, ingenue 8 beginner, newcomer 10 clodhopper, provincial

greenhouse 7 nursery 12 conservatory

Greenland *capital:* 4 Nuuk 7 Godthåb *city:* 5 Thule *ethnic group:* 5 Inuit 6 Eskimo *explorer:* 4 Eric (the Red), Erik (the Red), Leif (Eriksson) 9 Rasmussen (Knud) *language:* 6 Danish *monetary unit:* 5 krone *possession of:* 7 Denmark

green light 3 nod 4 okay 5 leave 6 assent 7 consent, go-ahead, mandate 8 approval, blessing, sanction, thumbs-up 9 authority, clearance 10 permission 11 endorsement 13 authorization

Green Mansions *author:* 6 Hudson (W. H.) *character:* 4 Rima

green monkey 6 guenon, simian, vervet

Green Mountain State 7 Vermont

greenness 5 youth 6 spring 7 puberty 8 verdancy, viridity 9 youthhood 10 immaturity, juvenility, pubescence, springtide, springtime 11 adolescence 12 inexperience

green osier 6 willow 7 dogwood

green plover 7 lapwing 9 shorebird

greenroom 6 lounge

greenstone 4 jade 7 diabase 8 nephrite 9 tremolite 10 actinolite

greet 3 bow 4 hail, meet 6 accost, call to, salaam, salute 7 address, react to, receive, welcome

greeting 3 ave, bow, nod 4 ciao, hail 5 aloha, hello, howdy 6 salaam, salute 7 address, welcome 9 handshake, reception 10 salutation

gregarious 6 clubby, genial, social 7 affable 8 outgoing, sociable 9 clubbable, congenial, convivial 11 extroverted 13 companionable

gremlin 3 bug, elf, imp 5 dwarf, gnome 6 defect, glitch 7 brownie

Grenada *capital:* 9 St. George's *discoverer:* 8 Columbus (Christopher) *former name:* 10 Concepción *language:* 7 English *location:* 10 West Indies *nickname:* 11 Isle of Spice

grenade 4 bomb 5 shell 7 missile 9 explosive, pineapple

grenadier 7 rattail, soldier

grenadine 4 pink, yarn 5 syrup 6 fabric 9 carnation

Grendel's slayer 7 Beowulf

Gretchen's lover 5 Faust

greylag 5 goose

Grey's forte 7 Western

grid 3 net 5 grate, grill 6 grille 7 grating, lattice, network, trellis

griddle 3 pan 5 grill

griddle cake 7 hotcake, pancake 8 flapjack

gridiron 3 net 5 field, grate, grill 7 grating, network

grief 3 rue, woe 4 care 5 agony, dolor, gloom, tears 6 mishap, regret, sorrow 7 anguish, chagrin, sadness, trouble 8 disaster, distress, hardship 9 adversity, heartache, suffering 10 affliction, heartbreak, misfortune 11 despondency

Grieg work 8 Peer Gynt

grievance 4 beef 5 cross, gripe, trial, wrong 6 burden, grouse, injury, squawk 8 hardship, jeremiad 9 complaint, injustice 10 affliction, allegation, unfairness 11 tribulation

grieve 3 cry 4 ache, keen, moan, wail, weep 5 mourn 6 burden, lament, sadden, sorrow, suffer 7 afflict, agonize 8 distress

grievous 3 sad 4 dire, fell, sore 5 cruel, grave, great, major 6 bitter, severe, taxing, tragic, woeful 7 galling, heinous, onerous, painful, serious, weighty 9 egregious 10 abominable, burdensome, calamitous, deplorable, lamentable, oppressive 11 distressing, regrettable, troublesome, unfortunate 12 heartrending

grift 3 con, gyp 4 bilk, rook 7 defraud, swindle 8 flimflam

grifter 3 gyp 5 cheat, crook, thief 6 con man, gouger 7 cheater, scammer, sharper, slicker 8 swindler 9 defrauder, trickster 13 confidence man

grill 3 fry, vex 4 cook, grid, pump, quiz 5 broil, grate, sauté, toast 6 eatery 7 afflict, debrief, grating, griddle, torment 8 gridiron, question 10 restaurant 11 interrogate 12 cross-examine

grilse 6 salmon

grim 3 set 4 cold, dour, fell, firm, hard 5 bleak, cruel, fixed, grave, harsh, rigid, stern 6 dismal, dogged, dreary, fierce, grisly, intent, savage, severe, somber 7 adamant, austere, inhuman, ominous 8 gruesome, inhumane, obdurate, resolute, ruthless, stubborn 9 merciless, offensive, truculent 10 determined, forbidding, implacable, inevitable, inexorable, inflexible, melancholy, relentless, unyielding, vindictive 11 unforgiving, unrelenting

grimace 3 mow, mug 4 face, moue, pout 5 frown, lower, mouth, scowl, sneer

grimalkin 3 cat 5 tabby 6 feline 9 female cat

grime 4 crud, dirt, gunk, muck, smut, soot 5 filth

grim reaper 5 death

grimy 5 dingy, dirty 6 filthy, grubby, grungy, soiled, scuzzy, smutty 10 besmirched

grin 4 beam 5 smile, smirk

grind 3 rut, vex 4 chew, grub, mill, moil, pace, plod, plug, rote, slog, toil, whet 5 crank, crush, gnash, grate, labor, slave, sweat 6 abrade, crunch, drudge, groove, harass, kibble, powder, rotate 7 oppress, routine, travail 8 drudgery, monotony, wear down 9 pulverize, treadmill 10 donkeywork

grinder 3 sub 4 gyro, hero 5 molar, tooth 6 hoagie 8 sandwich 9 submarine

grinding 5 harsh 6 severe 7 arduous, grating, wearing 9 fatiguing, strenuous *stone:* 4 mano 6 mortar, muller, pestle

griot 11 storyteller

grip 4 glom, hold, take **5** clamp, clasp, grasp, seize **6** clench, clinch, clutch, handle, tenure, valise **7** grapple **8** enthrall, suitcase **9** fascinate, mesmerize, restraint, spellbind, stagehand **10** constraint

gripe 3 bug, vex **4** beef, carp, crab, fuss, yawp **5** annoy, bitch, bleat, cavil, croak, groan, whine **6** bother, grouch, grouse, kvetch, murmur, mutter, object, squawk, yammer **7** afflict, grumble **8** complain, distress, irritate **9** bellyache, complaint, grievance, objection

griper see GRUMBLER

grippe 3 flu **9** influenza

gripper 4 clip, hand, vise **5** clamp, clasp, tongs **6** pliers

gris-gris 5 charm, spell **6** amulet, fetish **8** talisman **11** incantation

Grisham novel 4 Firm (The) **6** Broker (The), Client (The) **7** Chamber (The), Partner (The) **8** Brethren (The) **12** Pelican Brief (The)

grisly 4 gory, grim **5** awful, lurid **6** horrid **7** ghastly, hideous, macabre **8** fearsome, god-awful, gruesome, horrible, terrible, **9** frightful, repellent, repulsive, sickening **10** disgusting, horrifying, terrifying

grist 3 lot **5** grain, input, stint **6** amount, output **7** product **8** quantity

gristle 9 cartilage

grit 4 guts, sand **5** grate, grind, heart, moxie, nerve, pluck, spunk **6** gravel, mettle, powder, smooth, spirit **7** bravery, courage, granule **8** backbone, tenacity **9** fortitude **10** doggedness **13** determination

gritty 4 game **5** dirty, gutsy, rough, sandy **6** dogged, plucky, spunky **8** abrasive, gravelly, resolute, spirited **9** steadfast, tenacious **10** courageous, determined

groan 4 beef, carp, moan **5** cavil, creak, gripe **6** bemoan, grouse, lament, object, repine **7** grumble **8** complain **9** bellyache

grocery 5 store **11** supermarket *Spanish:* **6** bodega

grog 3 rum **5** booze, drink, hooch, juice, sauce **6** liquor, tipple **7** alcohol, spirits **9** firewater

groggy 4 dull, hazy, logy, weak **5** dazed, dopey, foggy, muzzy, tired, woozy **6** dulled, sleepy **7** muddled **8** befogged, confused, sluggish **9** befuddled, slaphappy, stupefied **10** punch-drunk

groin 4 fold **6** crotch

grok 6 intuit

grommet 6 eyelet **7** cringle

groom 4 comb, tend, tidy **5** brush, clean, curry, primp, ready, shave **6** neaten, ostler, polish **7** hostler, prepare, servant **8** benedict **9** attendant *Indian:* **4** syce

groove 3 rut **4** pace, rote, slot **5** canal, flute, glyph, gouge, grind, niche, score, stria **6** furrow, gutter, hollow, rabbet, rhythm **7** chamfer, channel, routine, top form **8** monotony **10** depression

groovy 3 hip **4** cool, neat **5** ducky, great, nifty, sharp, slick, super, swell **6** choice, gnarly, peachy **7** right-on **8** smashing **9** copacetic, excellent, hunky-dory, marvelous, wonderful **10** delightful, marvellous, peachy keen

grope 4 feel, grub, poke, root **6** fondle, fumble, search **7** grabble **8** scrabble

grosbeak 5 finch **8** hawfinch, songbird

gross 3 fat, raw, sum **4** earn, foul, mass, rude **5** brute, bulky, crude, obese, rough, utter, whole **6** carnal, coarse, entire, vulgar **7** blatant, boorish, capital, extreme, glaring, hulking, obscene, overall, porcine, uncouth **8** absolute, complete, flagrant, ignorant, improper, indecent, outright, sum total, tangible, totality **9** aggregate, before tax, corporeal, corpulent, downright, egregious, excessive, loathsome, offensive, out-and-out, repulsive, revolting, unrefined **10** disgusting, exorbitant, immoderate **11** twelve dozen

grotesque 6 absurd, rococo, unreal **7** baroque, bizarre, extreme **8** aberrant, abnormal, deformed, fanciful, freakish **9** distorted, fantastic, ludicrous, misshapen, monstrous **11** incongruous

grotto 4 cave, hole **5** crypt, vault **6** cavern *Capri:* **4** Blue

grouch 4 beef, carp, crab, kick, sulk, yawp **5** crank, croak, growl, grump, pique **6** carper, griper, grouse, grudge, kicker, kvetch, murmur, mutter, repine, squawk, whiner, yawper **7** crabber, grouser, growler, grumble **8** complain, grumbler, kvetcher, sorehead, sourpuss, squawker **9** bellyache, complaint **10** bellyacher, complainer, crosspatch, malcontent

ground 3 bed, sod **4** base, dirt, land, root, seat, soil, turf **5** basis, cause, earth, floor, proof **6** bottom, reason **7** bedrock, dry land, footing, support, sustain, terrain **8** argument, buttress, evidence **9** establish, testimony **10** foundation, terra firma

groundbreaking 10 innovative, innovatory, pioneering **11** cutting-edge, leading-edge

grounded 6 stable **7** beached **8** marooned, sensible, stranded **9** realistic **13** unpretentious

groundhog 6 marmot 9 woodchuck

grounding 8 practice, training, tutelage 11 instruction, preparation

groundless 4 idle 5 empty, false 6 hollow 8 baseless 9 causeless, unfounded 10 gratuitous 11 uncalled-for, unjustified, unwarranted

groundwork 3 bed 4 base, foot, root 5 basis 6 bottom 7 bedrock, footing, support 8 basement 10 foundation, substratum 11 cornerstone, preparation 12 substruction, substructure, underpinning

ground zero 5 focus, get-go 6 center, outset, target 8 bull's-eye 9 epicenter, square one

group 3 lot, set 4 band, bevy, body, club, crew, gang, pack, push, ruck, sect, team, tier 5 array, batch, bunch, class, clump, covey, crowd, grade, horde, squad, suite, troop 6 adjust, assort, bundle, cartel, circle, clique, clutch, gather, huddle, league, passel 7 battery, brigade, cluster, combine, company, coterie, council, dispose, echelon, platoon 8 assemble, assembly, category, classify, ensemble, organize 9 congeries, gathering, syndicate 10 assemblage, categorize, collection *of angels:* 4 host *of ants:* 6 colony *of bees:* 4 hive 5 swarm *of birds:* 6 flight *of cats:* 7 clowder, clutter *of cattle:* 5 drove *of chicks:* 5 brood 6 clutch *of clams:* 3 bed *of crows:* 6 murder *of ducks:* 5 brace *of eight:* 5 octet *of elephants:* 4 herd *of elks:* 4 gang *of fish:* 5 shoal 6 school *of five:* 5 quint 6 pentad 7 quintet *of four:* 6 tetrad 7 quartet *of foxes:* 5 leash, skulk *of geese:* 5 flock, skein 6 gaggle *of gnats:* 5 cloud, horde *of goats:* 5 tribe *of gorillas:* 4 band *of greyhounds:* 5 leash *of grouse:* 7 covey *of hares:* 4 down, husk *of hawks:* 4 cast *of hounds:* 3 cry 4 mute, pack *of kangaroos:* 3 mob 5 troop *of kittens:* 6 litter *of larks:* 10 exaltation *of lions:* 5 pride *of locusts:* 6 plague *of monkeys:* 5 troop *of mules:* 4 span *of nine:* 5 nonet *of oysters:* 3 bed *of partridges:* 5 covey *of peacocks:* 6 muster *of pheasants:* 4 nest *of plovers:* 4 wing 12 congregation *of quail:* 4 bevy 5 covey *of seals:* 3 pod 5 patch *of seven:* 6 pleiad, septet *of sheep:* 5 drove, flock *of six:* 6 sextet *of swans:* 4 bevy *of teals:* 6 spring *of three:* 4 trio 5 triad 7 ternary, trinity, triplet *of vipers:* 4 nest *of whales:* 3 gam, pod *of wolves:* 4 pack

grouper 8 rockfish

grouse 4 beef, carp 5 croak, gripe, quail, scold 6 mutter, yammer 7 grumble 8 complain, pheasant 9 bellyache, blackcock, ptarmigan 12 capercaillie *extinct:* 8 heath hen *red:* 8 moorfowl *strut:* 3 lek

grout 4 lees, lute 5 dregs 6 cement, filler, mortar 7 grounds, plaster 8 concrete

grove 4 holt, wood 5 copse 7 boscage, coppice, orchard, thicket

grovel 4 fawn 5 abase, cower, crawl, creep, toady 6 cajole, cringe, kowtow, snivel, wallow 7 eat dirt, truckle 8 blandish, bootlick 9 brownnose 10 curry favor, ingratiate 11 apple-polish

grow 3 age, wax 4 flow, gain, rise, tend 5 amass, breed, nurse, raise, ripen, swell 6 abound, become, expand, foster, mature, sprout, thrive 7 burgeon, care for, develop, enlarge, gestate, nurture, produce 8 escalate, flourish, increase, multiply, mushroom, spring up 9 cultivate, propagate

growl 4 beef, carp, crab, fuss, roar 5 bitch, gripe, groan, snarl 6 grouse, kvetch, mutter, repine, rumble, yammer 7 grumble 8 complain 9 bellyache

growler 3 can 4 crab, floe 5 crank, grump 6 grouch, vessel 7 ice floe, iceberg, pitcher 8 sorehead, sourpuss 9 container 10 crosspatch, malcontent 11 faultfinder

grown-up 5 adult 6 mature 8 seasoned 9 developed 11 full-fledged

grow old 3 age 4 wane 5 ripen, wizen 6 mature, mellow

growth 4 gain, rise 5 surge, swell, tumor 7 buildup 8 increase, progress, swelling 9 accretion, evolution, expansion, flowering, unfolding 11 development, enlargement, progression *malignant:* 6 cancer *skin:* 3 tag, wen 4 corn, cyst, mole, wart 5 nevus 6 bunion, callus, keloid 7 verruca

grow up 3 age 5 ripen 6 evolve, mature, mellow 7 advance, develop 8 maturate 9 come of age

grub 3 dig 4 chow, comb, eats, feed, food, hack, moil, plod, poke, rake, root, slog, toil 5 grind, larva, scour, slave, spade, stump 6 burrow, drudge, forage, menial, shovel, slavey, uproot, viands 7 edibles, ransack, rummage, unearth, vittles 8 excavate, hireling, victuals 9 provender 11 comestibles

grubby 4 foul 5 dirty, grimy, messy, seedy 6 filthy, frowsy, frowzy, grungy, scuzzy, shabby, sloppy, soiled 7 scruffy, squalid, unclean, unkempt 8 slovenly, unwashed

grubstake 3 aid 4 back, fund, help, loan 5 funds 6 assist 7 backing, capital, finance, support 8 bankroll 9 financing 10 assistance, capitalize, underwrite

grudge 4 deny, envy **5** spite **6** refuse, spleen **7** ill will **9** grievance **10** resentment **12** hard feelings, spitefulness

gruel 4 mush **5** atole, kasha **6** burgoo, congee, sowens **8** flummery, loblolly, porridge **9** stirabout

gruesome see GRISLY

gruff 4 curt, dour **5** bluff, blunt, cross, harsh, husky, stern, surly **6** abrupt, crabby, crusty, hoarse, morose, sullen **7** bearish, brusque, crabbed, grating, grouchy **8** churlish, croaking, snappish, snippety **9** saturnine **10** ill-natured **11** bad-tempered

grumble 4 beef, carp, crab, fuss, moan, yawp **5** bitch, croak, gripe, groan, growl, snarl, whine **6** bemoan, grouch, grouse, murmur, mutter, repine, squawk **8** complain **9** bellyache

grumbler 4 crab **5** crank, grump **6** grouch **8** sorehead **10** crosspatch, malcontent

grump 3 pet **4** beef, carp, crab, pout, sulk **5** crank, gripe, growl **6** griper, grouch **7** growler, grumble **8** complain, sorehead, sourpuss **9** bellyache **10** bellyacher, malcontent

grumpy 4 dour, sour **5** cross, moody, sulky, surly, testy **6** crabby, cranky, sullen **7** crabbed, peevish **8** petulant, vinegary **9** crotchety, irascible **11** bad-tempered, ill-tempered **12** cantankerous

grunion 10 silverside

grunt 5 groan, growl, snort **7** dogface, draftee, soldier

guacharo 7 oilbird

Guadeloupe *capital:* **10** Basse-Terre *department of:* **6** France *dependency:* **8** Désirade, St. Martin **12** Marie-Galante, St. Barthélemy *discoverer:* **8** Columbus (Christopher) *island:* **10** Basse-Terre **11** Grande-Terre *location:* **10** West Indies *volcano:* **9** Soufrière

Guam *capital:* **5** Agana *ethnic group:* **8** Chamorro *island group:* **7** Mariana

guanaco 5 llama **6** alpaca *kin:* **5** camel

guano 6 manure **9** excrement

guarantee 3 vow **4** bail, bond, oath, seal, word **5** token, vouch **6** assert, assure, ensure, insure, pledge, surety **7** certify, earnest, promise, warrant **8** security, warranty **9** agreement, assurance, insurance, undertake **11** stand behind, undertaking

guarantor 5 angel **6** backer, patron, surety **7** ensurer, insurer, sponsor **8** bondsman **11** underwriter

guard 4 fend, mind, tend, ward **5** aegis, alert, armor, cover, watch **6** convoy, defend, escort, jailer, keeper, minder, patrol, picket, police, screen, secure, sentry, shield, warden, warder **7** bulwark, defense, lookout, oversee, protect, turnkey **8** chaperon, overseer, preserve, security, sentinel, shepherd, watchdog, watchman **9** chaperone, custodian, look after, patrolman, protector, watch over **10** protection

guarded 4 safe, wary **5** cagey, chary, leery **7** careful, politic, prudent **8** cautious, discreet, gingerly, reserved **11** circumspect, considerate

guardhouse 4 brig, jail, keep **5** clink **6** lockup, prison **8** stockade

guardian 6 escort, keeper, patron, warden, warder **7** curator, trustee **8** Cerberus, defender, overseer, watchdog **9** custodian, protector **11** conservator

guardianship 4 care, keep, ward **5** aegis, trust **6** charge **7** custody, keeping **8** auspices **10** protection **11** safekeeping

Guare play 17 House of Blue Leaves (The) **22** Six Degrees of Separation

Guatemala *capital:* **9** Guatemala (City) *ethnic group:* **4** Maya **5** Mayan *lake:* **6** Izabal **7** Atitlán **9** Petén Itzá *language:* **7** Spanish *monetary unit:* **7** quetzal *mountain, range:* **6** Tacaná **9** Tajumulco **10** Acatenango, Santa María **11** Sierra Madre *neighbor:* **6** Belize, Mexico **8** Honduras **10** El Salvador *peninsula:* **7** Yucatán *river:* **7** Motagua **8** Polochic, Sarstoon **10** Usumacinta

guck 3 bog, goo, mud **4** clay, crud, dirt, glop, goop, mire, ooze, smut **5** filth, slime **7** stickum

gudgeon 3 pin **4** fish **5** pivot **6** socket **7** journal

Gudrun *brother:* **6** Gunnar **7** Gunther *father:* **5** Hetel *husband:* **4** Atli **5** Etzel **6** Sigurd **9** Siegfried

guerrilla 8 partisan **9** irregular *Greek:* **6** klepht

guess 4 call, shot, stab **5** fancy, hunch, infer **7** believe, predict, presume, suppose, surmise **8** estimate **9** speculate **10** conjecture, prediction **11** presumption, supposition, speculation

guest 6 caller, lodger, roomer **7** boarder, company, visitor **9** sojourner

guff 3 jaw, lip **4** bosh, sass **5** bilge, cheek, hokum, hooey, mouth, sauce, trash **6** bunkum, drivel, hot air, humbug **7** baloney, hogwash, palaver, twaddle **8** back talk, claptrap, malarkey, nonsense, tommyrot **9** poppycock **10** balderdash **13** horsefeathers

guffaw 6 cackle, hee-haw **7** chortle

guidance 6 advice **7** control, counsel **8** handling **9** direction, oversight **10** leadership, management **11** instruction, supervision

guide 4 dean, guru, help, lead, show
5 doyen, pilot, route, steer, usher **6** beacon, convoy, direct, docent, escort, handle, leader, manage, manual, mentor **7** adviser, conduct, control, marshal, oversee **8** Baedeker, chaperon, director, handbook, instruct, maneuver, navigate, shepherd, signpost **9** accompany, chaperone, conductor, vade mecum, Sacagawea **10** bellwether, compendium, instructor, pathfinder **11** enchiridion

guidebook 6 Fodor's, manual **8** Baedeker, Frommer's, handbook, Michelin **9** itinerary, vade mecum **10** compendium **11** enchiridion

guided missile 3 ABM **4** Hawk, ICBM, IRBM, Nike, Thor, Zuni **5** Atlas, drone, Snark, Titan **6** Bomarc, cruise, Exocet, Falcon, Navaho, rocket **7** Bullpup, Matador, Polaris, Regulus, Terrier **8** Redstone, Tomahawk **9** Minuteman **10** projectile, Sidewinder

Guiderius *brother:* **9** Arviragus *father:* **9** Cymbeline

guidon 4 flag **6** banner, burgee, ensign, pennon

guild 4 club **5** lodge, order, union **6** cartel, league **7** society **8** sodality **10** fellowship, fraternity **11** association, brotherhood *medieval:* **5** Hansa, Hanse

guile 4 wile **5** craft, fraud **6** deceit **7** cunning **8** artifice, trickery, wiliness **9** deception, duplicity, stratagem **10** cleverness **13** dissimulation

guileful 3 sly **4** foxy, wily **5** cagey, canny, slick **6** artful, astute, crafty, shifty, shrewd, sneaky, tricky **7** cunning, devious **8** indirect, slippery, sneaking **9** designing, insidious, underhand **11** calculating, duplicitous, underhanded

guileless 4 open **5** frank, naive **6** candid, direct, honest **7** genuine, natural, sincere, up-front **8** innocent, truthful **9** ingenuous **10** aboveboard, forthright

guillemot 3 auk **5** murre **7** seabird

guillotine 6 behead **9** decollate **10** decapitate

guilt 4 onus **5** blame, fault, shame **6** regret, stigma **7** offense, remorse **10** contrition **11** culpability **12** self-reproach

guiltless 4 pure **5** clean **6** chaste **8** innocent, virtuous **9** blameless, exemplary, faultless, righteous, stainless **10** immaculate, inculpable

guilty 6 liable, rueful, sinful **7** ashamed, at fault **8** blamable, contrite, culpable, indicted, penitent **9** impeached, regretful **10** answerable, remorseful

11 accountable, blameworthy, responsible

guimpe 6 blouse

Guinea *capital:* **7** Conakry *city:* **4** Labé **6** Kankan, Kindia *ethnic group:* **6** Fulani **7** Malinke *island, island group:* **3** Los **5** Tombo *language:* **6** French *monetary unit:* **5** franc *mountain:* **5** Nimba *neighbor:* **4** Mali **7** Liberia, Senegal **10** Ivory Coast **11** Sierra Leone **12** Guinea-Bissau *river:* **5** Niger **6** Gambia **7** Senegal

Guinea-Bissau *archipelago:* **7** Bijagós *capital:* **6** Bissau *ethnic group:* **6** Fulani **7** Malinke **8** Mandyako *language:* **10** Portuguese *monetary unit:* **5** franc *neighbor:* **6** Guinea **7** Senegal *river:* **4** Gêba

guinea fowl *genus:* **6** Numida *young:* **4** keet

guinea pig 4 cavy **6** rodent *genus:* **5** Cavia

Guinevere *court:* **7** Camelot *husband:* **6** Arthur *lover:* **8** Lancelot **9** Launcelot

guise 4 mask **5** cloak, cover, dress, getup **6** aspect, facade, outfit, veneer **7** costume, pretext **8** coloring, pretense **9** posturing, semblance **10** appearance, false front

guitar *accessory:* **4** capo *Mexican:* **5** tiple **6** cuatro **8** charango *part:* **3** nut, peg **4** fret, neck **5** brace **6** bridge, string **7** peghead *small:* **3** uke **7** ukulele *tool:* **4** pick **8** plectrum

guitarist *American:* **4** Byrd (Charlie), King (B. B., Freddie), Page (Jimmy), Pass (Joe) **5** Ellis (Herb), Isbin (Sharon) **6** Kessel (Barney), Kottke (Leo), Watson (Doc) **7** Burrell (Kenny), Hendrix (Jimi), Metheny (Pat), Vaughan (Stevie Ray) **9** Christian (Charlie), Parkening (Christopher) **10** Montgomery (Wes), Pizzarelli (Bucky, John) *Australian:* **8** Williams (John) *British:* **4** Beck (Jeff) **5** Bream (Julian) **8** Richards (Keith) *French:* **9** Reinhardt (Django) *Italian:* **7** Ghiglia (Oscar) *Spanish:* **5** Yepes (Narciso) **6** Romero (Celedonio) **7** Segovia (Andrés)

guitarlike instrument 3 uke **4** lute, vina **5** banjo, sitar **7** bandore, pandora, samisen, ukulele **8** mandolin, shamisen

gulch 3 gap **4** glen **5** gorge, gully **6** arroyo, canyon, coulee, hollow, ravine, valley **7** couloir

gules 3 red

gulf 3 bay, pit **4** cove **5** abysm, abyss, bayou, bight, chasm, firth, gorge, gulch, inlet **6** cavity, harbor, hollow, ravine, slough **8** crevasse *Adriatic Sea:* **6** Venice *Aegean Sea:* **7** Saronic **8** Salonika *Africa:* **6** Guinea *Arabian Sea:*

4 Oman 7 Persian *Australia:* 9 Van Diemen 11 Carpentaria *Baltic Sea:* . 4 Riga 6 Danzig, Gdansk 7 Bothnia, Finland *Bering Sea:* 6 Anadyr *Canada:* 13 Saint Lawrence *Central America:* 7 Fonseca *Djibouti:* 6 Tajura 8 Tadjoura *Europe:* 7 Bothnia, Gascony 8 Gascogne *Greece:* 7 Corinth, Lepanto *Indian Ocean:* 4 Aden *Ionian Sea:* 4 Arta 7 Taranto *Iran:* 7 Arabian *Italy:* 5 Genoa *Mediterranean Sea:* 5 Sidra, Tunis 8 Valencia 10 Khalij Surt 11 Syrtis Major *New Guinea:* 5 Papua 7 McCluer *New Zealand:* 7 Hauraki *North America:* 6 Mexico *Northwest Territories:* 7 Boothia 8 Amundsen 9 Queen Maud *Philippines:* 4 Asid 5 Davao, Leyte, Panay, Ragay *Red Sea:* 4 Suez 5 Aqaba 11 Aelaniticus *Russia:* 8 Sakhalin *Solomon Sea:* 4 Huon, Kula 5 Vella *South China Sea:* 4 Siam 6 Tonkin 8 Lingayen *Tyrrhenian Sea:* 7 Paestum *Yellow Sea:* 6 Chihli

Gulf State 5 Texas 7 Alabama, Florida 9 Louisiana 11 Mississippi

gull 3 con, mew, sap 4 bird, dupe, fool, hoax, scam 5 chump, cozen 6 fleece, pigeon, stooge, sucker, take in 7 chicane, fall guy 8 flimflam, hoodwink 9 bamboozle 11 hornswoggle

gullet 3 maw 4 crop, tube 6 dewlap, throat 7 channel 9 esophagus

gullible 4 easy 5 green, naive 8 innocent, trusting 9 believing, credulous 11 susceptible 12 unsuspecting

Gulliver's Travels *author:* 5 Swift (Jonathan) *horses:* 10 Houyhnhnms *land:* 6 Laputa 8 Lilliput 11 Brobdingnag *people:* 6 Yahoos

gully 3 gap 4 glen 5 gorge, gulch 6 arroyo, coulee, hollow, ravine, valley 7 couloir

gulp 4 bolt, chug, cram, glut, slop, swig, wolf 5 gorge, quaff, scarf, scoff, stuff, swill 6 devour, gobble, guzzle 7 swallow 8 mouthful 11 ingurgitate

gum 4 chew 5 botch 6 bobble, bollix, bungle, chicle, gluten, goof up, tupelo 7 exudate, gingiva, louse up 8 adhesive, mucilage 9 sapodilla 10 eucalyptus *kind:* 6 acacia, Arabic, balata, bubble 7 chewing, dextrin *resin:* 5 myrrh 7 gamboge 8 ammoniac, galbanum, scammony 9 asafetida 10 asafoetida 12 frankincense

gumbo 3 mud 4 okra, soil, soup 6 creole 7 mélange, mixture

gummy 5 gooey, pasty 6 cloggy, sticky, viscid 7 viscous 8 adhesive 9 glutinous 10 gelatinous 12 mucilaginous

gumption 5 drive, nerve, savvy 6 energy 8 industry 10 enterprise, get-up-and-go, initiative

gumshoe 3 cop 4 bull, dick, fuzz, G-man, heat, narc 6 copper, peeler, shamus, sleuth 7 officer 8 flatfoot, hawkshaw, Sherlock 9 detective, policeman 10 bloodhound, private eye 12 investigator

gun 3 gat, rod 4 Colt 5 rev up, rifle 6 cannon, Garand, heater, mortar, musket, pistol, weapon 7 bazooka, carbine, firearm 8 Browning, howitzer, revolver 9 derringer, Remington 10 Winchester *antiaircraft:* 6 ack-ack, Bofors *Austrian:* 5 Glock *British:* 4 Sten *French:* 8 arquebus 9 harquebus *German:* 5 Glock, Luger *Italian:* 7 Beretta *mount:* 6 turret *part:* 3 pin 4 bolt, bore, butt, lock 5 sight, stock 6 barrel, breech, hammer, muzzle, safety 7 chamber, trigger 8 cylinder, magazine 9 buttstock

gunfire 4 shot 5 blast, salvo 6 volley 7 barrage 9 broadside, discharge, fusillade

gung ho 4 avid, keen 6 ardent, fervid, raring 7 fervent, zealous 9 exuberant 11 impassioned 12 enthusiastic

Guni's father 8 Naphtali

gunk 3 goo 4 crud, glop, gook, goop, muck 5 slime

gunman 5 bravo 6 hit man, killer 7 shooter, torpedo 8 assassin, enforcer

Gunnar *brother-in-law:* 6 Sigurd *father:* 5 Hetel *sister:* 6 Gudrun *wife:* 8 Brunhild, Brynhild

gunner 6 sniper 7 shooter 8 marksman, rifleman 9 musketeer 11 infantryman 12 artilleryman

Gunther *sister:* 7 Gutrune 9 Kriemhild *slayer:* 5 Hagen *uncle:* 5 Hagen *wife:* 8 Brunhild 9 Brynhilde

gurgle 3 lap 4 flow, purl, wash 5 plash, slosh, swash 6 babble, bubble, burble, ripple

Gurkha knife 5 kukri

gurney 3 cot 9 stretcher

guru 4 sage 5 guide, swami, tutor 6 expert, leader, master, mentor 7 teacher 9 maharishi

gush 3 jet 4 emit, flow, pour, rave, roll, rush, spew, teem, well 5 burst, flood, flush, issue, spout, spurt, surge 6 babble, effuse, sluice, spring, stream 7 cascade, emanate 10 effervesce, outpouring

gushy 5 gooey, mushy, sappy, soppy 6 sloppy, slushy, sticky 7 cloying, maudlin, mawkish, tearful 8 bathetic, effusive 9 schmaltzy, sickening 10 nauseating, saccharine 11 sentimental

gusset 4 fold, gore, tuck 5 armor, plate, pleat 6 insert 7 bracket

gussy up 5 adorn 6 bedeck 7 furbish 8 decorate, renovate

gust 3 fit 4 blow, gale, rush, wind 5 blast, burst, draft, sally, surge, whiff 6 breeze, flurry, squall 7 bluster, delight, flare-up 8 eruption, outburst, paroxysm

gusto 3 vim 4 brio, élan, zeal, zest 5 ardor, heart, oomph, taste, verve 6 fervor, palate, relish, spirit 7 delight, passion 9 enjoyment 10 enthusiasm

gusty 5 blowy, windy 6 breezy 8 blustery

gut 4 draw, loot 5 belly, bowel, dress, empty, tummy 6 bowels, paunch 7 abdomen, ransack, stomach 8 clean out, entrails, visceral 9 intestine 10 disembowel, eviscerate, exenterate, intestines 11 instinctive

Gutenberg, Johannes *city:* 5 Mainz *invention:* 11 movable type *partner:* 4 Fust (Johann)

gutless 5 sissy, wimpy, wussy 6 coward, craven, yellow 7 chicken, unmanly 8 cowardly, timorous 9 spineless, spunkless, weak-kneed 11 lily-livered, poltroonish 12 fainthearted 13 pusillanimous

guts 4 grit, sand 5 bowel, heart, moxie, nerve, pluck, spunk, tripe 6 bowels, mettle, spirit 7 bravery, courage, innards, insides, stamina, viscera 8 backbone, entrails, stuffing 9 fortitude, intestine 10 intestines, resolution

gutsy 4 bold 5 brave 6 plucky, spunky 7 valiant 8 intrepid, resolute 10 courageous, determined, mettlesome

gutter 5 chase, ditch, flume, gully 6 furrow, groove, trench, trough 7 channel, conduit

guttersnipe 3 bum 4 hobo, scum, waif 5 gamin 6 beggar, gamine, urchin 7 outcast, vagrant, wastrel 8 derelict, riffraff, vagabond 10 ragamuffin

guttural 4 deep 5 gruff, harsh, husky, rough, velar 6 croaky, hoarse 7 grating, palatal, rasping, throaty 8 gravelly

guy 3 cat, lad, man 4 buck, chap, dude, male, rope, stud, wire 5 bloke, brace, chain, guide 6 effigy, fellow, steady 7 support

Guyana *capital:* 10 Georgetown *language:* 7 English *monetary unit:* 6 dollar *mountain range:* 9 Pacaraima *neighbor:* 6 Brazil 8 Suriname 9 Venezuela *river:* 9 Essequibo

Guys and Dolls *author:* 6 Runyon (Damon) *composer:* 7 Loesser (Frank)

guzzle 4 belt, gulp, slop, soak, swig, toss, tope 5 booze, drink, quaff, slosh, swill 6 imbibe, tank up, tipple 7 consume, swizzle

Gwendolen's husband 7 Locrine

gymnast 7 acrobat, athlete, tumbler *American:* 4 Hamm (Paul) 5 Rigby (Cathy) 6 Conner (Bart), Miller (Shannon), Retton (Mary Lou), Thomas (Kurt) *Romanian:* 8 Comaneci (Nadia) *Russian:* 3 Kim (Nelly) 6 Korbut (Olga)

gymnastics 5 sport 8 exercise, tumbling 9 athletics 10 acrobatics 12 calisthenics *apparatus:* 3 bar 4 bars, beam, buck, ring, rope 5 horse 11 balance beam *feat:* 3 kip 4 flip 5 vault 6 tumble 9 handstand, headstand 10 handspring, headspring, somersault

gyp 3 con 4 bilk, dupe, fake, hoax, rook, scam, sham 5 bunco, cheat, cozen, cross, fraud, spoof, trick 6 chisel, chouse, con man, diddle, fleece, humbug, rip off 7 cheater, deceive, defraud, diddler, finagle, sharper, swindle 8 chiseler, hoodwink, swindler 9 bamboozle, defrauder, imposture, trickster 10 mountebank 11 double-cross, flimflammer 12 double-dealer

gypsum 7 drywall, mineral 8 selenite 9 alabaster, wallboard

gypsy 3 Rom 5 caird, nomad, rover 6 roamer, Romany, tinker 7 drifter, tzigane 8 Bohemian, vagabond, wanderer *Spanish:* 6 gitano

gyrate 4 coil, purl, roll, spin, turn, wind 5 orbit, twirl, whirl 6 circle, rotate 7 revolve 9 oscillate, pirouette

gyration 4 coil, turn 5 cycle, orbit, twirl, wheel, whirl 6 circle 7 circuit, turning 8 rotation 10 revolution

gyre 4 coil, gird, ring, spin, wind 5 cycle, orbit, twirl, whirl 6 circle, girdle, rotate, spiral, vortex 7 circuit, revolve 8 rotation 10 revolution

gyro 8 sandwich

gyve 4 bond, iron 5 chain 6 fetter 7 shackle 8 restrain 9 restraint

H

Habakkuk 7 prophet
habeas corpus 4 writ **5** right **7** mandate
habiliments 4 gear **5** dress **6** attire, outfit **7** apparel, clothes **8** clothing **9** apparatus, equipment, trappings
habilitate 5 dress **6** clothe **7** qualify
habit 3 rut **4** bent, form, garb, mode, rote, wont **5** dress, quirk, style, usage **6** attire, clothe, custom, groove, manner, outfit **7** costume, fashion, pattern, routine **8** behavior, clothing, practice, tendency **9** addiction, mannerism **10** consuetude, convention, proclivity **11** disposition, inclination *riding:* **8** jodhpurs *wearer:* **3** nun **5** rider
habitable 7 livable
habitant 5 liver **7** denizen, dweller, resider **8** occupant, resident
habitat 4 home, site, turf **5** abode, haunt, range **6** locale, milieu **7** terrain **8** domicile **9** territory **11** environment **12** surroundings
habitation 3 pad **4** digs, flat, home, nest, seat **5** abode, haunt, haven, house, place, roost **7** housing, lodging, tenancy **8** domicile, dwelling, lodgment, quarters **9** homestead, residence, residency **10** settlement
habitual 3 set **5** fixed, usual **6** addict, inborn, native, normal, steady, wonted **7** chronic, regular, routine, settled **8** accepted, addicted, constant, familiar, frequent, inherent **9** automatic, confirmed, continual, customary, ingrained **10** accustomed, inveterate, persistent **11** established, instinctive, involuntary
habitually 8 commonly, normally, wontedly **9** generally, regularly, routinely **10** ordinarily **11** customarily **12** consistently
habituate 4 bear **5** inure, train **6** addict, adjust, endure, harden, school, season, take to **7** break in, prepare, support **8** accustom, tolerate **9** acclimate, condition **11** familiarize
habitué 3 fan **4** buff, user **5** hound, lover **6** addict, patron **7** denizen, devotee, haunter **8** adherent, customer **10** enthusiast, frequenter
hacienda 4 farm **5** manor, ranch, villa

6 estate, quinta **8** dwelling **9** residence **10** plantation
hack 3 cab, cut, hew, try, vex **4** blow, chip, chop, dull, gash, grub, jade, loaf, mean, ride, taxi **5** annoy, cabby, cough, grind, horse, petty, sever, slave, usual **6** cabbie, cliché, drudge, lackey, mangle, stroke, writer **7** clichéd, grating, machine, plodder, taxicab, trivial, vehicle **8** inferior, low grade, mediocre, tolerate **9** cabdriver, mercenary, potboiler **10** second-rate, uninspired **11** commonplace
hacker 4 geek, nerd **6** duffer
hackney 3 cab **4** taxi **5** horse **6** jitney **7** taxicab **8** carriage
hackneyed 3 old **4** dull, worn **5** banal, corny, stale, stock, tired, trite **6** cliché, common, old hat, old saw **7** archaic, clichéd, worn-out **8** everyday, obsolete, outdated, overused, outmoded, timeworn **9** out-of-date **10** antiquated, overworked, pedestrian **11** commonplace, meaningless
Hadad *father:* **5** Bedad **7** Ishmael *victim:* **6** Midian
Hades 4 Hell **5** Pluto, Sheol **6** blazes, Tophet **7** Gehenna, inferno **8** Tartarus **9** perdition **10** underworld **11** netherworld *Babylonian:* **5** Aralu *god:* **3** Dis **5** Orcus, Pluto *goddess:* **10** Persephone *guard:* **8** Cerberus *lake:* **7** Avernus *river:* **4** Styx **5** Lethe **7** Acheron, Cocytus **10** Phlegethon
haft 4 grip, hilt, knob **5** helve **6** handle
hag 3 hex **5** biddy, crone, harpy, shrew, vixen, witch **6** beldam, gorgon, virago **8** battle-ax, fishwife, harridan, slattern **9** hobgoblin
Hagar 9 concubine *lover:* **7** Abraham *rival:* **5** Sarah, Sarai *son:* **7** Ishmael
Hagen *father:* **8** Alberich *nephew:* **7** Gunther *slayer:* **9** Kriemhild *victim:* **9** Siegfried
haggard 3 wan **4** hawk, lank, pale, thin, weak, wild, worn **5** ashen, drawn, faded, gaunt, tired **6** fagged, pallid, skinny, wasted **7** angular, pinched, scraggy, scrawny, starved, wearied **8** careworn, fatigued, shrunken, worndown **9** emaciated, exhausted

Haggard, H. Rider *novel:* 3 She 17 King
Solomon's Mines

Haggith *husband:* 5 David *son:* 8 Adonijah

haggle 4 deal 5 argue, cavil, trade
6 barter, bicker, dicker 7 bargain, dispute, quibble, stickle, wrangle 8 squabble 10 horse-trade

hagiography *subject* 5 saint

hail 3 ave 4 ahoy, call 5 greet, salvo,
shout, storm 6 accost, call to, holler,
praise, salute, shower, volley 7 acclaim,
address, applaud, barrage, call out,
commend 8 greeting 9 broadside, cannonade, fusillade, originate, recommend 10 salutation 11 acclamation,
bombardment

Haile Selassie 9 Rastafari *follower:*
11 Rastafarian *nation:* 8 Ethiopia

hair 3 bit, jot 4 hint, mite, wool 5 cilia
(plural), pilus, trace 6 cilium, trifle
7 eyelash, whisker 8 fraction, particle
animal: 3 fur 4 mane, pelt, wool 8 vibrissa 9 vibrissae (plural) *braid:* 5 queue
7 pigtail *clip:* 8 barrette *coarse:* 7 bristle
covering of: 3 wig *cream:* 6 pomade
7 pomatum 12 brilliantine *facial:*
5 beard, patch 6 goatee 7 Vandyke
8 mustache, whiskers 9 burnsides, han-
dlebar, moustache, sideburns, soul
patch 11 muttonchops *fine:* 6 lanugo
fringe: 4 bang *head of:* 9 chevelure *knot:*
3 bun *lock of:* 4 curl 5 tress 7 cowlick
loose roll: 4 pouf *matted:* 6 dreads
10 dreadlocks *ornament:* 7 topknot
preparation: 3 gel 6 mousse, pomade
12 brilliantine *root:* 6 fibril *set:* 4 perm
stiff: 4 seta 5 setae (plural) *style:* 4 flip,
pomp, shag 5 butch, taper, wedge
6 Caesar, mullet 7 bowl cut, buzz cut,
crew cut, flattop, pageboy 9 ducktail
9 pompadour *tangled:* 7 elflock *tuft of:*
7 fetlock *unruly:* 3 mop *without:* 4 bald

haircutter 6 barber 7 stylist 8 coiffeur
9 coiffeuse

hairdo 3 bob, bun 4 afro, flip, perm,
trim 5 bangs, braid 6 Mohawk, mullet
7 beehive, bowl cut, buzz cut, chignon,
crew cut, flattop, pageboy 8 brush cut,
coiffure, cornrows, ducktail, pigtails,
ponytail, razor cut 9 permanent, pompadour 10 dreadlocks

hairdresser see HAIRCUTTER

hair-raising 5 eerie, scary 6 spooky
7 amazing, awesome 8 exciting 9 thrilling 10 terrifying 11 astonishing, frightening

hairsplitting 7 finicky 8 exacting 9 quib-
bling 10 nit-picking 12 overcritical
13 hypercritical

hairstyle see HAIRDO

hairy 5 bushy, downy, furry, fuzzy,
nappy, risky, rough 6 chancy, fleecy,
fluffy, shaggy, tufted, woolly 7 bristly,
hirsute, scraggy, unshorn, villous 8 perilous, strigose 9 dangerous, difficult,
hazardous, tomentose, whiskered
11 treacherous

Haiti *capital:* 12 Port-au-Prince *island:*
7 Tortuga 10 Hispaniola *language:*
6 Creole, French *leader:* 8 Aristide
(Jean-Bertrand), Duvalier (François,
Jean-Claude) *location:* 10 West Indies
monetary unit: 6 gourde *passage:*
8 Windward *peninsula:* 7 Tiburon *river:*
10 Artibonite

hake 4 fish, ling 7 codling, whiting *relative:* 3 cod

halcyon 4 calm 5 happy, lucky, quiet,
still 6 golden, hushed, placid, serene
8 affluent, peaceful, tranquil 9 favorable 10 auspicious, felicitous, kingfisher, prosperous, untroubled

Halcyone *father:* 6 Aeolus *husband:*
4 Ceyx

hale 3 fit 4 sane, well 5 sound, stout
6 hearty, robust 7 healthy 8 vigorous
9 strapping, wholesome

Hale character 5 Nolan (Philip)

Haley epic 5 Roots

half 6 moiety *prefix:* 4 demi, hemi, semi

half-baked 8 slapdash, slipshod 9 imbecilic, senseless, underdone 11 harebrained, impractical, nonsensical,
unrealistic 12 ill-conceived, shortsighted 13 irresponsible

half-cocked 4 rash 5 brash 8 reckless
9 foolhardy, imprudent, impulsive, misguided, premature 10 incautious,
unprepared 11 precipitate

halfhearted 4 weak 5 tepid 6 feeble
8 lukewarm 12 uninterested

half-moon 4 arch 5 curve 6 lunule 8 crescent

halfway 3 mid 6 center, medial, median,
middle 7 midmost 10 centermost
11 equidistant 12 intermediate

half-wit 4 dolt, dope, fool 5 dunce, idiot,
moron 6 cretin 8 imbecile 9 blockhead,
simpleton

half-witted 4 dull, slow 7 moronic
8 backward, imbecile 9 imbecilic 12 feebleminded, simpleminded

hall 4 dorm 5 foyer, lobby 6 lyceum
7 passage 8 corridor 9 dormitory
10 auditorium, passageway *exhibition:*
5 salon *Salvation Army:* 7 citadel

Halley's ___ 5 comet

hallmark 4 logo, seal, sign 5 badge,
stamp, trait 6 device, emblem, symbol,
virtue 7 feature, imprint, quality

8 logotype, property 9 attribute 11 distinction 13 certification

hallow 5 bless, honor 6 anoint, devote, revere 8 dedicate, make holy, sanctify, venerate 10 consecrate

hallowed 4 holy 6 sacred

hallucination 4 trip 5 ghost 6 mirage, vision, wraith 7 fantasy, phantom, specter 8 delusion, illusion, phantasm 10 apparition 11 fata morgana, ignis fatuus

hallucinogen 3 LSD 9 mescaline 10 psilocybin 11 scopolamine

halo 4 aura 5 nimbi (plural) 6 corona, nimbus 7 aureole

halogen 6 iodine 7 bromine, element 8 astatine, chlorine, fluorine

halt 3 bar, end 4 lame, limp, quit, stay, stop 5 cease, check, close, hitch, lapse, stall, waver 6 arrest, desist, dither, falter, finish, pull up 7 adjourn, bring up, stagger, suspend 8 conclude, cut short, hesitate, knock off, leave off 9 determine, interrupt, terminate, vacillate 10 standstill 11 discontinue

halter 3 bit 4 hang, rope 5 noose 6 blouse, bridle, hamper 8 restrain, trammels 9 hackamore, headstall, restraint

ham 4 hock 5 bacon, emote, thigh 7 buttock, overact 8 overplay, strutter 10 scene-eater 13 exhibitionist

Ham *brother:* 4 Shem 7 Japheth *father:* 4 Noah *son:* 4 Cush, Phut 6 Canaan 7 Mizraim

Haman's adversary 6 Esther

ham-handed 5 inept 6 clumsy, gauche 8 bumbling 9 all thumbs, graceless, inelegant, maladroit 10 blundering, unskillful

Hamilcar *conquest:* 5 Spain *home:* 8 Carthage *son:* 8 Hannibal *surname:* 5 Barca

hamlet 7 village *Irish, Scottish:* 7 clachan

Hamlet *author:* 11 Shakespeare (William) *beloved:* 7 Ophelia *castle:* 8 Elsinore *country:* 7 Denmark *friend:* 7 Horatio *mother:* 8 Gertrude *slayer:* 7 Laertes *uncle:* 8 Claudius *victim:* 7 Laertes 8 Claudius, Polonius

Hamlet, The *author:* 8 Faulkner (William) *family:* 6 Snopes

hammer 4 drub, maul, peen 5 forge, gavel, pound 6 batter, mallet, pummel, sledge 7 malleus 8 lambaste *type:* 3 air 4 claw, maul 6 sledge 8 ball-peen 9 pneumatic

hammerhead 4 dolt, dope, fool 5 dunce, idiot, shark 6 clodpoll, numskull 9 numbskull 10 thickskull

hamper 3 bin, tie 4 balk, curb, snag 5 block, check, cramp, crimp, leash, limit 6 baffle, basket, fetter, hinder, hobble, hold up, impede, retard, stymie, thwart 7 inhibit, manacle, pannier, prevent, trammel 8 encumber, handicap, obstacle, obstruct, restrain, restrict, slow down 9 frustrate

hamstring 4 lame 6 muscle, tendon 7 cripple, disable 10 immobilize 12 incapacitate

Hamutal *father:* 8 Jeremiah *husband:* 6 Josiah *son:* 8 Jehoahaz, Zedekiah

hand 3 aid, paw 4 fist, pass 5 manus 6 script, worker 7 deliver, dish out, laborer, workman 8 employee, transfer 10 assistance, penmanship 11 calligraphy, chirography *clenched:* 4 fist *combining form:* 4 chir 5 chiro *counting zero:* 8 baccarat *covering:* 5 glove 6 mitten *down:* 8 bequeath *gesture:* 5 mudra *on hip:* 6 akimbo *part:* 4 palm 5 thumb 6 finger *poker:* 5 flush 8 straight 9 full house *protector:* 5 glove 7 gantlet 8 gauntlet

handbag 4 grip 5 purse 6 clutch 8 reticule, suitcase 10 pocketbook

handbill 5 flier, flyer 6 poster 7 affiche, leaflet, placard 8 circular

handbook 5 guide 6 manual 8 Baedeker 9 vade mecum 10 compendium 11 enchiridion *religious:* 9 catechism

handcuff 6 fetter 7 manacle, shackle *British:* 7 darbies (plural)

hand down 4 will 6 bestow, pass on 7 deliver 8 bequeath, transmit

Handel, George Frideric *aria:* 5 Largo *birthplace:* 5 Halle 7 Germany *opera:* 4 Nero 5 Serse 6 Admeto, Alcina, Almira, Ottone, Xerxes 7 Arminio, Orlando, Rinaldo, Rodrigo 8 Berenice 9 Agrippina, Ariodante 12 Giulio Cesare, Julius Caesar *oratorio:* 4 Saul 6 Esther, Joshua, Samson, Semele 7 Athalia, Deborah, Jephtha, Messiah, Solomon 8 Theodora

handicap 4 edge, load, odds 6 burden, hamper, hinder, impede 8 drawback, encumber, restrict 9 advantage, allowance, detriment, head start, hindrance 10 disability, limitation 11 encumbrance 12 disadvantage

handicraft 5 skill 8 artefact, artifact

hand in 6 submit, tender 7 deliver, present

handkerchief 5 hanky 6 hankie 7 bandana 8 bandanna, mouchoir 9 accessory

handle 3 paw, use 4 feel, grip, haft, hilt, knob, name, test 5 crank, touch, trade, treat, wield 6 manage 7 control, moniker, operate 8 deal with, door-

knob, exercise, maneuver, nickname
10 manipulate *scythe:* 5 snath 6 snathe

handling 4 care 6 charge 9 packaging, treatment *partner:* 8 shipping

hand out 4 give, mete 6 bestow, donate 7 deliver, present, provide 8 disburse, dispense, give away 10 administer, distribute

hand over 4 cede, feed, give 5 leave, yield 6 commit, donate, fork up, give up, supply 7 commend, confide, consign, deliver, entrust, present 8 dispense, give back, relegate, transfer 9 deliver up, surrender 10 relinquish

handrail 8 banister

handsome 4 buff, cute, fair 5 ample, hunky, noble 6 comely, lavish 7 dashing, liberal, sizable, stately, stylish 8 abundant, generous, gracious, majestic 9 beautiful, bounteous, bountiful 10 attractive, munificent 11 fashionable, good-looking 12 considerable

handspring 6 tumble *lateral:* 9 cartwheel

handwriting 6 script 8 longhand 10 autography, manuscript, penmanship 11 calligraphy, chirography *bad:* 10 cacography *study of:* 10 graphology

handy 4 able, deft, near 5 adept, close, utile 6 adroit, clever, nearby, nimble, useful 7 close-by, skilled 8 adjacent, skillful 9 adaptable, available, dexterous 10 accessible, convenient, proficient 11 practicable, within reach

handyman 6 helper 7 go-to guy 8 factotum

hang 3 jut, sag 4 hook, idle, loll 5 cling, drape, droop, float, hoist, knack, lynch, sling, swing 6 dangle, depend 7 suspend *back:* 3 lag 4 drag, poke 5 trail 6 dawdle, schlep 7 schlepp 8 straggle *loosely:* 3 sag 6 dangle

hang around 4 stay, wait 5 abide, dally, tarry 6 dawdle, linger, loiter 7 goof off 8 frequent

hangdog 3 sad 4 blue, glum 5 cowed 6 guilty 7 ashamed, pitiful, unhappy 8 dejected, sheepish 9 chagrined, depressed 11 embarrassed

hanger-on 5 leech 6 sponge, sucker 7 sponger 8 barnacle, follower, parasite 9 sycophant 10 freeloader 11 bloodsucker

hanging 5 arras, slope 7 curtain, drapery, pendant, pendent 8 covering, tapestry 9 declivity, execution, pendulous, suspended

Hanging Gardens 7 Babylon

hang on 4 grip 5 grasp 6 clutch, endure, remain 7 persist, survive 8 continue, hold fast 9 persevere

hang out 4 idle, loaf 5 chill, dally, relax 6 loiter, lounge 7 goof off

hangout 5 haunt, joint 6 resort 7 purlieu, retreat 10 rendezvous 12 watering hole

hang up 4 mire, snag 5 delay 6 detain, impede, retard 7 bog down, set back, suspend 8 slow down

hang-up 5 block 7 dilemma, problem 9 obsession 10 difficulty, inhibition

hank 4 clip, coil, loop, ring 6 bundle

hanker 3 yen 4 ache, itch, long, lust, want, wish 5 covet, crave, yearn 6 desire, hunger, thirst

hankering 3 yen 4 ache, itch, lust, urge 5 ardor 6 desire, hunger, pining, thirst 7 craving, longing, passion 8 appetite, yearning

hanky-panky 5 fraud, trick 7 chicane 8 mischief, trickery 9 chicanery, dalliance, deception 13 double-dealing, sharp practice

Hannibal *defeat:* 4 Zama *father:* 8 Hamilcar *home:* 8 Carthage *surname:* 5 Barca *vanquisher:* 6 Scipio *victory:* 6 Cannae

Hansa 5 guild 6 league

Hans Brinker author 5 Dodge (Mary Mapes)

Hanseatic League city 6 Bremen, Lübeck, Wismar 7 Cologne, Hamburg, Rostock

Hänsel und Gretel composer 11 Humperdinck (Engelbert)

Hansen's disease 7 leprosy

hansom 5 coach 8 carriage

haole 5 white

haphazard 6 casual, chance, random 7 aimless 8 at random, careless, slipshod 9 desultory, hit-or-miss, irregular, unplanned 10 accidental, willy-nilly 11 unorganized 12 unsystematic 13 helter-skelter

hapless 4 poor 6 woeful 7 unhappy, unlucky 8 ill-fated, wretched 9 miserable 10 ill-starred 11 star-crossed, unfortunate

happen 4 pass 5 occur 6 befall, betide 7 develop, fall out, turn out 8 bechance 9 transpire *again:* 5 recur *together:* 6 concur 8 coincide

happening 3 new 5 event, scene, thing 7 episode 8 incident, occasion 9 adventure 10 experience, occurrence, phenomenon 11 fashionable 12 circumstance

happen on 4 find 8 bump into, discover

happenstance 5 event 6 chance 8 incident, occasion 9 condition, situation 11 coincidence

happiness 3 joy 4 glee 5 bliss, cheer, mirth 6 gaiety 7 aptness, content, delight, elation, jollity 8 felicity, gladness, pleasure **9** enjoyment, well-being **11** contentment **12** satisfaction

happy 4 glad **5** jolly, lucky, merry **6** joyful, joyous, upbeat **7** blessed, content, pleased **8** friendly, jubilant **9** contented, favorable, satisfied **12** enthusiastic, lighthearted

happy-go-lucky 4 easy **6** blithe, breezy, casual **8** carefree, careless, cheerful, heedless, laid-back, reckless **9** easygoing, unworried **10** insouciant, nonchalant **11** unconcerned **12** devil-may-care, light-hearted

hara-kiri 7 seppuku, suicide **8** felo-de-se

Haran *brother:* **7** Abraham *daughter:* **5** Iscah **6** Milcah *father:* **5** Terah **6** Shimei *son:* **3** Lot

harangue 4 rant, rave **5** orate, spiel **6** exhort, hassle, tirade **7** declaim, lecture, oration **8** bloviate, diatribe, jeremiad **9** discourse, philippic **11** declamation, exhortation

harass 3 irk, vex **4** bait, raid, ride **5** annoy, beset, bully, chivy, harry, hound, tease, worry **6** badger, chivvy, hassle, heckle, hector, pester, plague, stress **7** bedevil, exhaust, fatigue, torment, trouble **8** bullyrag, distress **9** beleaguer, persecute

harbinger 4 omen, sign **5** augur **6** augury, herald **7** apostle, portent **9** messenger, precursor **10** forerunner, indication

harbor 3 bay **4** cove, port **5** haven, inlet, lodge, put up **6** billet, refuge, shield, take in **7** nurture, protect, seaport, shelter **9** anchorage, safeguard, sanctuary *Hawaii:* **5** Pearl

hard 4 firm, iron **5** cruel, harsh, solid, tough **6** brutal, knotty, packed, rugged, tiring, trying **7** arduous, callous, onerous **8** absolute, concrete, exacting, granitic, grinding, indurate, pitiless, rigorous **9** demanding, difficult, fatiguing, intensely, intensive, laborious, unfeeling **10** adamantine, exhausting, spirituous, thoroughly, vigorously **11** complicated, intensively, intractable, troublesome, unrelenting, unremitting **12** backbreaking *to please:* **7** finicky

hard-boiled 4 grim **5** rough, stoic, tough **6** coarse **7** callous **8** seasoned **9** impassive, pragmatic, unfeeling **11** insensitive, unemotional **12** stonyhearted, thick-skinned **13** unsympathetic

harden 3 dry, set **5** inure, steel **6** anneal, freeze, ossify, season, temper **7** calcify, compact, congeal, densify, lithify, petrify, stiffen, toughen **8** solidify **9** acclimate, fossilize, habituate **10** strengthen

hardfisted 4 mean **5** close, tight **6** stingy, strict **13** penny-pinching

hardheaded 5 sober, tough **6** mulish, shrewd **7** willful **8** obdurate, perverse, stubborn **9** obstinate, practical, pragmatic, realistic **10** determined **11** down-to-earth, intractable

hardhearted 4 cold **8** pitiless, uncaring **9** merciless, unfeeling

hard-hitting 6 strong **8** emphatic, forceful, powerful **9** effective

hardihood 3 pep **4** gall, grit, guts **5** cheek, moxie, nerve, pluck, vigor **6** daring **7** courage **8** audacity, boldness, temerity **9** assurance, brashness, cockiness, fortitude, impudence, insolence **10** brazenness, robustness

hard-line 4 firm **5** fixed, rigid, tough **8** obdurate **9** obstinate, unbending **10** inflexible, unyielding **11** stiff-necked **12** intransigent

hardness 5 rigor **7** density **8** rigidity, severity **10** difficulty, resistance

hardscrabble 6 barren **8** marginal **9** infertile, unbearing, unfertile **12** impoverished, unproductive

hardship 4 need, toil **5** rigor, trial **6** burden **7** travail **8** asperity, distress, drudgery **9** adversity, privation, suffering **10** affliction, difficulty, discomfort, misfortune **11** tribulation

Hard Times *author:* **7** Dickens (Charles)

hard up 4 poor **5** broke, needy **6** bad off **8** beggared, bankrupt, deprived, indigent, strapped **9** desperate, destitute, penniless **10** down-and-out **11** necessitous **12** impoverished

hardy 4 bold, hale **5** brave, tough **6** daring, robust, rugged, strong **7** healthy **8** intrepid, resolute **9** audacious

Hardy, Thomas *character:* **3** Sue (Bridehead) **4** Alec (D'Urberville), Clym (Yeobright), Jude (Fawley), Tess (Durbeyfield) **5** Angel (Clare) **7** Gabriel (Oak) **8** Arabella (Donn), Eustacia (Vye), Henchard (Michael) **9** Bathsheba (Everdene) *novel:* **11** Woodlanders (The) **14** Jude the Obscure **17** Return of the Native (The) **19** Mayor of Casterbridge (The) **21** Tess of the D'Urbervilles **22** Far from the Madding Crowd *setting:* **6** Wessex

hare 5 lapin **6** rabbit *female:* **3** doe *genus:* **5** Lepus *male:* **4** buck *tail:* **4** scut *young:* **7** leveret

harebrained 5 crazy, loony, silly, wacky **6** absurd, insane, stupid **7** asinine, foolish **9** frivolous **10** ridiculous **12** preposterous

harem 5 serai **6** zenana **8** seraglio *concubine:* **9** odalisque

haricot 3 pod **4** bean **10** kidney bean

hark 4 hear, heed, mind, note 6 attend, listen, notice

harlequin 5 clown, joker 6 jester, mottle 7 buffoon 9 prankster

Harlequin *beloved:* 9 Columbine *rival:* 7 Pierrot

harm 3 mar 4 hurt, maim, ruin 5 abuse, spoil, wound, wrong 6 damage, ill-use, impair, injure, injury, misuse, molest 7 tarnish 8 ill-treat, maltreat, mischief, mistreat 9 undermine 10 disservice, misfortune

harmful 3 bad 4 evil 5 risky, toxic 6 malign, unsafe 7 noisome, noxious 8 damaging 9 dangerous, hazardous, injurious, malignant, unhealthy 10 pernicious 11 deleterious, detrimental, unhealthful

harmless 4 safe 6 benign 8 innocent, nontoxic 9 innocuous 11 inoffensive

Harmonia *daughter:* 3 Ino 5 Agave 6 Semele 7 Autonoë *father:* 4 Ares, Mars *husband:* 6 Cadmus *mother:* 5 Venus 9 Aphrodite *son:* 9 Polydorus

harmonious 5 sweet 7 chiming, chordal, musical, pacific 8 blending, friendly, in accord, peaceful, pleasing 9 agreeable, congenial, congruous, consonant, symphonic 10 compatible, concordant 11 cooperative, symmetrical, sympathetic

harmonize 3 fit 4 jibe, sing 5 agree, blend, match 6 accord, attune 7 arrange, concert, conform 8 coincide, dovetail 9 integrate 10 coordinate, correspond, synthesize 11 orchestrate

harmony 5 grace, peace, unity 6 accord 7 balance, concert, concord, oneness, rapport 8 affinity, sonority, symmetry 9 agreement, congruity, polyphony 10 accordance, concinnity, conformity, consonance, proportion 11 concordance, consistency, cooperation *lack of:* 7 discord 10 dissonance *of movement:* 8 eurythmy

harness 4 curb, gear, yoke 5 hitch, leash 6 bridle, tackle 7 utilize 11 domesticate *part:* 3 bit 4 rein 5 girth, trace 6 collar 7 blinder, crupper 9 bellyband, breeching, checkrein 12 breast collar *ring:* 6 terret

harp 4 lyre 9 harmonica *Greek:* 7 cithara, kithara

harpsichord 7 cembalo 8 clavecin

harpsichordist *American:* 6 Fuller (Albert, David), Kipnis (Igor), Newman (Anthony) 7 Marlowe (Sylvia), Pinkham (Daniel), Pinnock (Trevor), Valenti (Fernando) 11 Kirkpatrick (Ralph) *English:* 7 Malcolm (George) *German:* 7 Richter (Karl) 9 Leonhardt (Gustav) *Italian:* 7 Sgrizzi (Luciano) *Polish:* 9 Landowska (Wanda)

harpy 3 nag 5 leech, scold, shrew, vixen 6 virago 8 fishwife, harridan 9 termagant

Harpy 5 Aello 7 Celaeno, Ocypete *father:* 7 Thaumas *mother:* 7 Electra *sister:* 4 Iris

harridan 3 hag 4 fury 5 biddy, harpy, shrew, vixen, witch 6 dragon, gorgon, ogress, virago 7 hellcat 8 battle-ax, fishwife 9 battle-axe, termagant

harrier 3 dog 4 hawk 6 hector, runner 10 persecutor

harrow 3 try, vex 4 bait, rack 5 devil, tease 6 badger, heckle, hector, needle, pester, suffer 7 afflict, bedevil, torment, torture, trouble 8 distress, irritate 9 cultivate 10 excruciate

harry 3 dog, irk, vex 4 gnaw, raid, sack 5 annoy, tease, upset, worry 6 attack, badger, harass, hassle, pester, plague, ravage 7 assault, bedevil, despoil, perturb, pillage, plunder, torment 8 desolate, maltreat 9 beleaguer, depredate

harsh 5 cruel, gruff, rough, stern 6 biting, brutal, coarse, severe, uneven, unkind 7 austere, caustic, grating, jarring, painful, pungent, raucous, stubbly 8 exacting, grinding, jangling, scraping, scratchy, strident, unsmooth 9 dissonant, inclement 10 discordant, irritating, unpleasant

hart 4 deer, stag 7 red deer *mate:* 4 hind

hartebeest 8 antelope *family:* 7 Bovidae

Harte story 17 Luck of Roaring Camp (The) 19 Outcasts of Poker Flat (The)

Hartford *college:* 7 Trinity *specialty:* 9 insurance

Hart, Moss *autobiography:* 6 Act One *collaborator:* 7 Kaufman (George S.) *musical:* 13 Lady in the Dark *play:* 15 Once in a Lifetime 18 Man Who Came to Dinner (The) 20 You Can't Take It with You

haruspex 5 augur 7 diviner, prophet 8 foreseer 9 predictor 10 forecaster, foreteller, soothsayer

harvest 4 crop, pick, reap 5 amass, cache, glean, hoard, stash, yield 6 garner, gather 7 collect, reaping, store up, vintage 8 ingather, squirrel, stow away 9 garnering, gathering *bug:* 4 mite 7 chigger *fly:* 6 cicada *festival:* 6 Lammas 7 Cerelia 10 Michaelmas 12 Thanksgiving *god, goddess:* 3 Ops 5 Ceres 6 Consus 7 Demeter

harvester 7 gleaner *grain:* 6 header *of grapes:* 8 vintager

Harvey 5 pooka 6 rabbit *author:* 5 Chase (Mary) *character:* 6 Elwood (P. Dowd)

hash 4 chop, mess, stew 5 botch, mince, mix-up 6 jumble, medley, muddle, review 7 clutter, confuse, mélange, mixture 8 consider, shambles 9 patchwork 10 assortment, hodgepodge, miscellany

hash house 4 café 5 diner 6 bistro, eatery 7 pit stop 10 coffee shop 12 luncheonette

hashish 5 bhang, ganja 6 charas 8 cannabis, narcotic *plant:* 4 hemp

hash out 6 review 7 discuss 8 talk over 9 talk about

hasp 5 catch 6 fasten 8 fastener 9 fastening

hassle 3 row 4 beef, to-do 5 annoy, argue, brawl, fight, run-in 6 bicker, clamor, harass, hubbub, tumult, uproar 7 dispute, problem, quarrel, rhubarb, turmoil, wrangle 8 argument, squabble, struggle 9 commotion 11 altercation, controversy

hassock 4 pouf 7 cushion, kneeler, ottoman 9 footstool

haste 3 run 4 dash, rush 5 hurry, speed 6 barrel, bustle, flurry, hustle 7 beeline, hotfoot 8 celerity, dispatch, rapidity, velocity 9 fleetness, quickness, swiftness 10 speediness 11 hurriedness, impetuosity

hasten 3 fly, hie, run 4 rush, urge 5 hurry, press, speed 6 barrel, hustle, step up, urge on 7 hurry up, quicken, speed up 8 expedite 10 accelerate

hasty 4 fast, rash 5 brisk, eager, fleet, quick, rapid, swift 6 abrupt, rushed, speedy, sudden 7 cursory, hurried, rushing 8 careless, fleeting, headlong, heedless, reckless, slapdash 9 hotheaded, impatient, impetuous, irritable, quickened 10 ill-advised, incautious 11 expeditious, perfunctory, precipitate, precipitous, superficial, thoughtless

hat 5 derby, tuque 6 boater, cloche, fedora, panama, topper 7 bicorne, chapeau, homburg, porkpie, Stetson, tricorn 8 sombrero, tricorne 9 headpiece 11 deerstalker *ancient Greek:* 7 petasos, petasus *brimless:* 7 pillbox *close-fitting:* 4 kufi 5 toque, tuque 6 cloche, turban *felt:* 5 busby, derby 6 bowler, trilby *fur:* 5 busby 6 castor *helmetlike:* 4 topi 5 topee *maker:* 7 modiste 8 milliner *Middle Eastern:* 3 fez *military:* 4 kepi 5 busby, shako *Muslim:* 3 fez 6 turban 8 tarboosh *sheepskin:* 6 calpac 7 calpack *soft:* 5 toque *straw:* 6 boater, panama, sailor 7 bangkok, leghorn, skimmer 8 sombrero *sun:* 5 terai *tall:* 9 stovepipe *waterproof:* 9 sou'wester *woman's:* 4 coif 5 toque 6 bonnet 7 pillbox

hatch 4 door, plan, plot 5 breed, brood, cover, inlay, spawn 6 cook up, create, design, devise, emerge, invent, make up, work up 7 concoct, dream up, opening, produce, think up 8 contrive, engender, generate, incubate, occasion 9 floodgate, formulate, give birth, give forth, originate, procreate 11 compartment

hatchet 3 axe 8 tomahawk

hatchet man 6 killer 7 torpedo 8 assassin, enforcer, murderer 9 attack dog, cutthroat 10 eliminator

hate 5 abhor, scorn, spite 6 animus, detest, enmity, horror, loathe, malice, rancor 7 despise, disgust 8 aversion, execrate, loathing 9 abominate, animosity, antipathy, deprecate, repulsion, revulsion 10 abhorrence, repugnance 11 abomination, detestation

hateful 4 evil, foul, mean, vile 5 nasty 6 horrid, malign, odious, scurvy 7 vicious 8 accursed, damnable, infamous 9 abhorrent, execrable, malicious, obnoxious, repellent, repulsive 10 abominable, despicable, detestable, malevolent 11 blasphemous, opprobrious, unspeakable 13 reprehensible

Hatfields vs. ___ 6 McCoys

hatred 5 odium, spite 6 animus, enmity, rancor 7 dislike 8 aversion, loathing 9 animosity, antipathy, hostility, repulsion, revulsion 10 abhorrence, repugnance 11 abomination, detestation, malevolence *of change:* 9 misoneism *of humankind:* 11 misanthropy *of marriage:* 8 misogamy *of men:* 8 misandry *of women:* 8 misogyny

hats 9 millinery

hauberk 5 armor 9 chain mail, habergeon

haughtiness 4 airs 5 pride, scorn 7 conceit, disdain, hauteur 9 arrogance, insolence, pomposity 12 snobbishness

haughty 5 aloof, proud 6 lordly, sniffy 7 distant 8 arrogant, cavalier, scornful, snobbish, superior 9 egotistic 10 disdainful 11 overbearing 12 contemptuous, supercilious

haul 3 lug, tow, tug 4 cart, drag, draw, hump, lift, load, loot, pull, swag, take, tote 5 boost, booty, cargo, hoist, raise, truck 6 burden, lading, schlep, spoils 7 freight, payload, schlepp *with a tackle:* 5 bowse

haul up 5 hoise, hoist *with a rope:* 5 trice

haunch 3 hip 11 hindquarter

haunches 4 rump 7 hind end, rear end 8 backside, buttocks 9 posterior 12 hindquarters

haunt 4 site 5 spook 6 obsess, prey on

7 habitat, hang out, inhabit, torment, trouble **8** frequent **9** preoccupy **10** hang around, rendezvous, stay around, visit often

haunter 5 ghost **7** denizen, habitué

hautbois 4 oboe

hauteur see HAUGHTINESS

haut monde 5 elite **6** jet set **7** society, who's who **10** glitterati, upper crust **11** aristocracy, high society **13** carriage trade

have 3 own **4** hold **7** contain, include, possess

haven 4 port, roof **5** house **6** asylum, harbor, refuge **7** retreat, shelter **9** anchorage, sanctuary

haversack 3 bag **4** pack **8** backpack

havoc 4 loss, ruin, sack **5** chaos, waste **6** mayhem **8** calamity, disorder, ravaging **9** confusion, ruination **11** catastrophe, destruction, devastation, pandemonium

haw 4 left, tree **5** berry, fruit, shrub **8** turn left **10** equivocate

Hawaii *author:* **8** Michener (James A.) *capital:* **8** Honolulu *city:* **4** Hilo *coast:* **4** Kona *discoverer:* **4** Cook (Capt. James) *island:* **4** Maui, Oahu **5** Kauai, Lanai **6** Niihau **7** Molokai *mountain:* **7** Kilauea **8** Mauna Kea, Mauna Loa *nickname:* **5** Aloha (State) *park:* **9** Haleakala *state bird:* **4** nene *state flower:* **8** hibiscus *state tree:* **5** kukui **9** candlenut

Hawaiian *dance:* **4** hula *feast:* **4** luau *food:* **3** poi *god:* **4** Kane, Lono **5** Wakea **7** Kanaloa *goddess:* **4** Pele *goose:* **4** nene *instrument:* **3** uke **7** ukulele *neckwear:* **3** lei *nonnative:* **5** haole **8** malihini *resident:* **8** kamaaina *shaman:* **6** kahuna *soup:* **6** saimin *tree:* **3** koa

hawk 4 kite, sell, vend **5** buteo **6** falcon, monger, osprey, peddle **7** Cooper's, goshawk, haggard, harrier **8** caracara, huckster, roughleg **9** accipiter, redtailed, warmonger **10** militarist **11** ferruginous, rough-legged *male:* **6** tercel **7** tiercel *young:* **4** eyas

hawker 6 coster, monger, seller, vendor **7** packman, peddler **8** pitchman **12** costermonger

hawkeyed 11 keen-sighted **12** sharp-sighted

Hawkeye State 4 Iowa

hawkish 7 martial, warlike **9** combative **10** aggressive **11** belligerent **12** militaristic

___ Hawley Tariff 5 Smoot

Hawthorne, Nathaniel *birthplace:* **5** Salem *character:* **6** Hester (Prynne) **8** Clifford (Pyncheon), Hepzibah (Pyncheon),

Pyncheon (Judge) **10** Dimmesdale (Rev. Arthur) **13** Chillingworth (Roger) *novel:* **10** Marble Faun (The) **13** Scarlet Letter (The) **21** House of the Seven Gables (The)

hay 3 bed **4** feed **5** grass **6** fodder, reward **7** herbage *crops:* **6** clover **7** alfalfa, timothy

Haydn oratorio 7 Seasons (The) **8** Creation (The)

hay fever 7 allergy **10** pollenosis, pollinosis *cause:* **6** pollen **7** ragweed

haying machine 5 baler

haymaker 3 box **4** blow, sock **5** clout, punch **6** wallop

hayseed see HICK

haywire 4 amok, awry **5** amuck, crazy, upset **6** faulty **8** confused **10** out of order **12** out of control

hazard 3 bet, try **4** dare, game, luck, risk **5** peril, shoal, wager **6** chance, danger, gamble, menace **7** fortune, imperil, venture **8** accident, endanger, jeopardy, obstacle

hazardous 5 hairy, risky **6** chancy, unsafe **7** unsound **8** perilous **9** dangerous, unhealthy **10** precarious

haze 3 fog **4** film, mist, murk, smog **5** brume, cloud, drive, smoke, vapor **6** harass **7** dimness, obscure **8** dullness, initiate, overcast **9** mistiness, murkiness, vagueness **10** cloudiness

hazel 4 wood **5** birch, shrub **7** filbert

hazy 3 dim **5** faint, filmy, foggy, fuzzy, misty, murky, smoky, vague **6** cloudy, unsure **7** blurred, clouded, obscure, unclear **8** nebulous, vaporous **9** uncertain **10** indefinite, indistinct

head 3 nut **4** boss, john, main, pate, poll **5** brain, caput, chief, first, prime, privy, scalp, skull **6** climax, honcho, leader, master, noggin, noodle, set out, talent, toilet **7** cranium, faculty, latrine, leading, premier, proceed, supreme **8** director, foremost, lavatory, light out **9** chieftain, principal, strike out **10** promontory *area:* **5** crown **6** temple *back part:* **7** occiput *bone:* **5** skull **7** cranium **8** parietal *combining form:* **6** cranio **7** cephalo *covering:* **3** cap, hat **6** bonnet **8** kerchief *monastery:* **4** dean **5** abbot **8** superior *nunnery:* **6** abbess **8** superior *of hair:* **4** mane **6** fleece **9** chevelure *relating to:* **8** cephalic *shaving of:* **7** tonsure *skin:* **5** scalp *top:* **4** pate **5** crown

headache 4 pain **5** worry **6** bother, megrim **7** problem **8** migraine, nuisance, vexation **9** annoyance **10** irritation

headband 7 bandeau, circlet, coronal *ancient Greek:* **6** taenia **7** taeniae (plural)

headdress 7 topknot *American Indian:* 9 warbonnet *Arab:* 8 kaffiyeh *bishop's:* 5 miter, mitre *medieval:* 4 barb *Eastern:* 6 turban *nobleman's:* 7 coronet *royal:* 5 crown, tiara 6 diadem *Spanish women's:* 8 mantilla *women's:* 6 bonnet (see also HAT)

headland 4 cape 5 point 10 promontory

headline 6 banner 7 feature, promote 8 screamer 9 emphasize, publicize, spotlight 10 noteworthy

headlong 4 rash 5 hasty 6 abrupt, daring, rashly, sudden 7 hurried, rushing 8 heedless, reckless 9 foolhardy, impetuous, impulsive 10 heedlessly, recklessly 11 precipitate, precipitous

headmaster 6 leader 9 principal

head off 4 stop 5 avert, block 6 thwart 7 deflect, obviate, prevent, ward off 8 stave off, turn back 9 forestall, intercept

headquarters 3 hub 4 base, seat 6 center

head start 4 edge, jump, lead, odds 5 boost 7 advance, vantage 8 handicap 9 advantage, allowance

headstone 8 memorial, monument 11 grave marker

headstrong 6 dogged, mulish, unruly 7 willful 8 contrary, perverse, stubborn 9 obstinate 10 bullheaded, refractory, self-willed 11 intractable, stiff-necked

heads-up 5 alarm, alert 6 signal, tip-off 7 warning 8 high sign 11 resourceful

headway 4 gain 6 growth 7 advance 8 anabasis, progress 11 advancement, improvement

heady 4 rash, rich 5 giddy 6 elated, potent 7 willful 8 exciting 9 impetuous 11 exhilarated, intoxicated 12 intoxicating

heal 3 fix 4 cure, mend 5 sew up, treat 6 cement, remedy, repair 7 patch up, restore 8 make well

healer 6 doctor, shaman

healing 8 curative, remedial, salutary, sanative 9 vulnerary, wholesome 10 salubrious 11 restorative, therapeutic 12 convalescent *goddess of:* 3 Eir

health 7 fitness, welfare 8 haleness, vitality, wellness 9 soundness, well-being, wholeness *club:* 3 gym, spa

healthful 8 curative, hygienic, remedial, salutary 9 favorable, wholesome 10 beneficial, corrective, profitable, salubrious 11 restorative

healthy 3 fit 4 hale, spry, well 5 sound, tonic 6 benign, robust, strong, sturdy 7 chipper 8 blooming, hygienic, positive, salutary, thriving, vigorous 9 wholesome 10 able-bodied, beneficial, prosperous, salubrious 11 flourishing

heap 3 lot 4 cock, fill, gobs, hill, load, lump, mass, much, pack, pile, rick, scad 5 amass, bunch, clump, crate, loads, mound, shock, stack, wreck 6 barrel, charge, gather, jalopy, junker, lumber, oodles 7 clunker, collect, deposit, jillion 8 assemble, mountain, slathers 9 abundance, great deal, profusion, stockpile 10 quantities *combustible:* 4 pyre

hear 4 heed 5 learn 8 listen to, perceive 9 apprehend

hearing 4 test 5 trial 6 tryout 7 earshot, inquiry 8 audience, audition 9 interview 10 conference, discussion *distance:* 7 earshot

hearken 4 heed, mind, note 6 attend, listen, notice 7 observe

hearsay 4 buzz, news, talk 5 rumor 6 gossip, report 7 account, chatter 9 grapevine 11 scuttlebutt

heart 3 hub 4 core, crux, gist, guts, love, pith, root, seat, soul, zest 5 ardor, bosom, focus, gusto, moxie, pluck, spunk 6 breast, center, kernel, mettle, relish, spirit, ticker 7 courage, resolve 8 feelings, sympathy 9 character, fortitude 10 affections, compassion, conscience, enthusiasm *combining form:* 6 cardio *contraction:* 7 systole *dilation:* 8 diastole *part:* 5 valve 6 atrium, septum 9 ventricle

heartache 3 rue, woe 4 care, pain, pang 5 grief 6 regret, sorrow 7 anguish, sadness 8 distress 10 affliction

heartbeat 5 flash, jiffy, pulse, throb, trice 6 moment, second 9 pulsation *irregular:* 10 arrhythmia

heartbreak 3 rue, woe 5 agony, grief 6 misery, regret, sorrow 7 anguish, despair, torment, torture 9 suffering 10 desolation 12 wretchedness

heartbreaking 6 bitter, tragic 8 grievous 9 agonizing 10 calamitous, deplorable, lamentable 11 devastating, distressing

heartbroken 7 crushed, grieved 8 mournful, overcome, wretched 9 sorrowful 10 despairing, despondent 12 disconsolate

heartburn 7 pyrosis

hearten 4 buoy, stir 5 cheer, rally, rouse 6 arouse, buck up, buoy up, perk up 7 animate, cheer up, enliven, inspire 8 embolden, energize, inspirit 9 encourage

heartfelt 4 deep, true 6 honest 7 earnest, fervent, genuine, sincere 8 profound 9 unfeigned

hearth 4 home 5 abode 8 domicile, dwelling, fireside 9 fireplace, residence

heartily 6 wholly 9 sincerely, with gusto, zestfully 10 completely, thoroughly

heartless 4 cold, hard 5 cruel 6 unkind 7 callous 8 uncaring 9 unfeeling 10 hard-boiled 11 insensitive, unemotional 13 unsympathetic

Heart of Dixie 7 Alabama

heartsease 5 pansy, viola 6 violet 11 peace of mind, tranquility 12 johnny-jump-up, tranquillity

heart-shaped 7 cordate

heartsick 4 blue, down 8 dejected, desolate, dismayed, downcast 9 depressed 10 despondent, dispirited 11 demoralized 12 disconsolate

heartthrob 4 idol, love 5 flame, honey, sweet 7 beloved, darling, passion 10 sweetheart

heart-to-heart 4 open, talk 5 frank 6 candid, honest 7 sincere 8 truthful 12 conversation

hearty 4 hale, warm 5 ample 6 jovial, robust, sailor, strong 7 cordial, healthy, profuse, sincere 8 abundant, vehement, vigorous 9 approving, energetic, exuberant, flavorful, unfeigned 12 enthusiastic, unrestrained

heat 4 cook, rage, warm, zeal 5 ardor, fever 6 fervor, simmer, warmth 7 caloric, inflame, passion, swelter 8 pyrolyze *combining form:* 4 pyro 6 calori, thermo 7 thermia *measuring device:* 11 calorimeter, thermometer *quantity:* 3 BTU

heated 3 hot, mad 5 angry, fiery, irate 6 ardent, fervid, fierce, ireful, raging, steamy 7 boiling, burning, fevered, furious 8 broiling, feverish, scalding, sizzling, vehement, wrathful 9 indignant, scorching 10 passionate 11 acrimonious

heater 3 gun, rod 5 stove 6 boiler, pistol 7 furnace 8 fastball, radiator

heath 4 moor 5 shrub 9 wasteland

heathen 5 pagan 7 infidel 8 barbaric 11 irreligious, uncivilized

heat-producing 9 calorific

heave 3 lob 4 cast, draw, fire, gasp, haul, heft, huff, hurl, lift, pant, puff, pull, push, toss 5 fling, hoist, labor, pitch, raise, retch, sling, surge, throw, vomit 6 launch

heave-ho 4 boot 6 ouster 8 bum's rush 9 dismissal

heaven 3 God 4 Zion 5 bliss, glory 6 utopia 7 arcadia, delight, ecstasy, elysium, nirvana, rapture 8 empyrean, eternity, paradise 9 firmament, Shangri-la 10 wonderland 11 immortality, kingdom come 12 promised land

heavenly 4 lush 6 divine, sacred 7 blessed 8 beatific, empyreal, empyrean, ethereal 9 ambrosial, celestial, delicious 10 delectable, delightful, enchanting

heavy 3 big, fat 4 rich 5 beefy, bulky, gross, hefty, obese, stout 6 bad guy, chunky, drowsy, fleshy, gravid, leaden, portly 7 arduous, intense, labored, massive, porcine, villain, weighty 8 burdened, cumbrous, enceinte, pregnant, sluggish, unwieldy 9 corpulent, expectant, expecting, laborious, lumbering, ponderous, strenuous 10 burdensome, cumbersome, formidable, oppressive, overweight

heavy-handed 5 crude, harsh, inept 6 clumsy, gauche, klutzy 7 awkward 8 bumbling, despotic 9 maladroit 10 oppressive 11 domineering, overbearing

heavyhearted 3 sad 4 glum 5 sorry 7 unhappy 8 dejected, downcast, mournful, saddened 9 depressed, miserable, sorrowful 10 despondent, dispirited, melancholy

heavyset 5 beefy, husky, stout, thick 6 chunky, portly, stocky 11 thick-bodied

heavyweight 3 VIP 4 lion 5 boxer, chief 6 big gun, bigwig, leader 7 big shot, notable 8 big-timer

Hebe *father:* 4 Zeus 7 Jupiter *husband:* 8 Hercules *mother:* 4 Hera, Juno *successor:* 8 Ganymede

hebetude 6 stupor, torpor 7 languor 8 dullness, lethargy 9 lassitude, torpidity 10 drowsiness

hebetudinous 4 dull, logy 5 dopey 6 drowsy, stupid, torpid 8 listless, sluggish 9 lethargic

Hebrew 3 Jew 6 Jewish *coin:* 6 lepton, shekel *festival:* 5 Purim 6 Pesach, Sukkot 7 Hanukah, Sukkoth 8 Chanukah, Lag b'Omer, Passover, Shabuoth 9 Tishah-b'Ab, Yom Kippur 12 Rosh Hashanah, Simchas Torah *God:* 6 Adonai, Elohim, Yahweh 7 Jehovah *judge:* 6 Gideon *lawgiver:* 5 Moses *letter:* (see at ALPHABET) *measure:* 5 cubit, ephah *month:* 4 Adar, Elul, Iyar 5 Nisan, Sivan, Tebet 6 Kislev, Shebat, Tammuz, Tishri 6 Veadar (in leap year) 7 Heshvan *patriarch:* 3 Dan, Gad 4 Cain, Levi, Seth 5 Asher, David, Isaac, Jacob, Judah 6 Joseph, Reuben, Simeon 7 Abraham, Zebulun 8 Benjamin, Issachar, Naphtali *sacred city:* 5 Safad, Safed 6 Hebron 8 Tiberias 9 Jerusalem (see also JEWISH)

Hebrides island 4 Eigg, Rhum, Skye, Uist 5 Lewis 6 Harris

Hecate *father:* 6 Perses *goddess of:*

5 night 10 underworld, witchcraft **mother:** 7 Asteria

hecatomb 7 killing, slaying 8 butchery 9 bloodbath, sacrifice, slaughter

heck 4 darn, drat, geez, gosh, hell, jeez 5 golly 6 shucks

heckle 3 nag 4 bait, faze, gibe, ride 5 annoy, chivy, hound, tease, worry 6 badger, bother, harass, hassle, hector, molest, needle, pester, plague, rattle 7 disrupt, disturb, torment 9 interrupt 10 disconcert

hectic 3 red 6 fervid 7 burning, excited, fevered, flushed 8 confused, exciting, feverish, frenetic, restless 9 turbulent 10 persistent

hector 3 cow, nag 4 bait, ride 5 bully, chivy, hound 6 badger, harass, lean on 7 bedevil, swagger 8 browbeat, bullyrag, domineer 10 intimidate

Hector *brother:* 5 Paris 7 Helenus, Troilus 9 Deiphobus, Polydorus *father:* 5 Priam *mother:* 6 Hecuba *sister:* 6 Creusa 8 Polyxena 9 Cassandra *slayer:* 8 Achilles *victim:* 9 Patroclus *wife:* 10 Andromache

Hecuba *daughter:* 6 Creusa 8 Polyxena 9 Cassandra *father:* 5 Dymas *husband:* 5 Priam *son:* 5 Paris 6 Hector 7 Helenus, Troilus 9 Deiphobus, Polydorus *victim:* 11 Polymnestor

hedge 4 trim 5 avoid, evade, fence, guard, hem in, limit 6 hinder 7 barrier, defense, enclose, evasion, protect 8 boundary, encircle, restrict 9 shrubbery 10 protection

hedgehog 9 porcupine 10 stronghold

hedonist 4 rake 7 epicure, gourmet 8 gourmand, sybarite 9 bon vivant, epicurean, libertine 10 sensualist, voluptuary

heebie-jeebies 5 jumps 6 creeps, nerves, shakes 7 jitters, shivers, willies 11 nervousness

heed 4 care, hark, mark, mind, note, obey 5 watch 6 attend, harken, listen, notice, regard, remark 7 be aware, concern, hearing, hearken, observe, respect 8 consider, interest 9 attention 10 observance

heedful 5 alert, aware 7 on guard 8 vigilant 9 attentive, observant, observing 10 interested, meticulous, scrupulous 13 conscientious

heedless 9 negligent, oblivious, unmindful 10 unthinking 11 inadvertent, inattentive, unobservant 12 unreflective 13 inconsiderate

heedlessness 7 neglect 9 disregard, unconcern 11 disinterest, inattention, insouciance 12 indifference

hee-haw 4 bray 5 laugh 6 guffaw 10 horse laugh

heel 3 bum, cad, tip 4 cant, hock, lean, list, tilt 5 creep, knave, louse, rogue, skunk, slope 6 rascal, rotter 7 incline, lowlife, villain 9 scoundrel *bone:* 8 calcanea (plural), calcanei (plural) 9 calcaneum, calcaneus

heft 4 lift, load 5 hoist, raise, weigh 6 weight 7 heave up 9 heaviness, influence 10 importance

hefty 3 big 5 beefy, burly, bulky, heavy, husky, large, major 6 brawny, mighty, rugged, strong 7 massive, sizable 8 imposing, powerful 9 extensive, good-sized, plentiful, ponderous, strapping 11 substantial

hegira 6 escape, exodus, flight 7 journey 10 emigration, evacuation 11 deliverance

Heidi *author:* 5 Spyri (Johanna) *goatherd:* 5 Peter *setting:* 4 Alps

heifer 4 calf

___ **Heifetz** 6 Jascha

height 3 top 4 acme, apex, cusp, peak, rise 6 apogee, climax, heyday, summit, vertex, zenith 7 stature 8 altitude, pinnacle 9 elevation, loftiness 10 prominence *combining form:* 4 acro

heighten 3 wax 5 boost, mount, raise 6 beef up, expand, extend 7 amplify, augment, build up, elevate, enhance, enlarge, improve, magnify 8 increase 9 highlight, intensify 10 aggrandize

heinie 3 bum 4 butt, rear, rump 5 fanny 6 bottom 7 rear end 8 backside

heinous 4 evil 6 odious 7 hateful 8 infamous, shocking 9 abhorrent, atrocious, execrable, monstrous 10 abominable, detestable, outrageous

heinousness 4 evil 6 horror, infamy 8 atrocity, enormity 13 monstrousness

heir 4 scion 7 grantee, heritor, legatee 9 inheritor, successor 11 beneficiary *joint:* 8 parcener 10 coparcener

heist 3 cop, rob 4 lift, loot 5 boost, caper, filch, pinch, steal, swipe, theft 6 holdup, rip off 7 larceny, purloin, robbery 8 burglary 9 strong-arm

Helen of Troy *abductor:* 5 Paris *husband:* 8 Menelaus

Helenus *brother:* 5 Paris 6 Hector 7 Troilus 9 Deiphobus, Polydorus *father:* 5 Priam *mother:* 6 Hecuba *sister:* 6 Creusa 8 Polyxena 9 Cassandra *wife:* 10 Andromache

Hel, Hela *father:* 4 Loki *hall:* 7 Niflhel 8 Niflheim *mother:* 9 Angerboda

helical 6 spiral

helicopter 7 chopper 9 eggbeater

10 whirlybird *armed:* **7** gunship *blade:*
5 rotor

Helios 6 Apollo *daughter:* **5** Circe
8 Pasiphaë *father:* **8** Hyperion *mother:*
5 Theia *sister:* **3** Eos **6** Aurora, Selene
son: **8** Phaethon

heliotrope 4 herb **5** shrub **6** borage
10 bloodstone

hell 5 hades, Sheol **6** blazes, Tophet
7 Gehenna, inferno **9** perdition

hell-bent 6 driven, intent **8** obsessed,
resolved **10** determined

Hellen *father:* **9** Deucalion *mother:*
6 Pyrrha *son:* **5** Dorus **6** Aeolus, Xuthus

hellhole 3 pit **8** dystopia, snake pit
9 mare's nest

hellion 3 elf, imp **4** puck, punk **5** demon,
rogue, scamp **6** rascal **7** gremlin

hellish 6 horrid **7** ghastly, hideous, satanic, stygian **8** damnable, diabolic, dreadful, gruesome, horrible, infernal, terrible **9** appalling, frightful, monstrous,
plutonian **10** diabolical

Hellman *play* **11** Little Foxes (The)
13 Children's Hour (The) **15** Watch on
the Rhine

hello 3 hey **4** ciao, hail **5** aloha, howdy
7 hi there, welcome **8** greeting **9** greetings

helm 5 wheel **7** cockpit **8** controls

helmet 6 casque, sallet, tin hat **7** mor-
rion **8** burgonet, headgear *medieval:*
6 sallet **7** basinet *part:* **7** ventail **8** aven-
tail *sun:* **4** topi **5** topee

helmsman 5 pilot

Heloïse *husband:* **7** Abelard (Peter) *son:*
9 Astrolabe

helot 4 peon, serf **5** slave **6** vassal
7 laborer, peasant, servant

helotry 4 yoke **6** thrall **7** bondage, peonage, serfdom, slavery **9** servitude,
thralldom **11** enslavement

help 3 aid **4** abet, back, mend **5** avail,
boost, guide, serve **6** assist, relief, remedy, succor **7** advance, benefit, bolster,
further, promote, relieve, secours, service, support **8** mitigate, palliate **9** alleviate, meliorate **10** ameliorate, assistance, facilitate **11** cooperation *forward:*
7 further *hired:* **5** labor

helper 4 aide **6** deputy, server **7** ancilla,
servant **8** employee **9** assistant, associate, attendant, auxiliary **10** apprentice
11 subordinate

helpful 5 of use **6** usable, useful **8** salutary, valuable **9** effective, favorable,
practical **10** beneficial, profitable, propitious **11** encouraging **12** advantageous, constructive

helping 4 dose **5** share **7** portion, serving
9 auxiliary

helpless 4 weak **6** feeble, futile, unable
7 forlorn **8** desolate **9** abandoned,
dependent **11** unprotected

helter-skelter 6 anyhow **7** anywise,
flighty, hastily, turmoil **8** at random,
disorder, pell-mell, randomly **9** confusion, haphazard, hit-or-miss **11** any
which way, haphazardly, in confusion,
precipitate

helve 4 haft **6** handle

Helvetian 5 Swiss

hem 3 pen, rim **4** brim, edge, gird, ring,
seam, shut **5** bound, brink, fence,
hedge, skirt, verge **6** border, circle, corral, edging, fringe, immure, margin,
stitch **7** close in, enclose, selvage, short-
en **8** encircle, surround **9** encompass,
perimeter, periphery *turned-back:* **4** cuff

Heman *father:* **4** Joel *grandfather:*
6 Samuel

hematite 3 ore **7** mineral **12** black diamond

Hemingway, Ernest *novel:* **9** In Our Time
12 Sun Also Rises (The) **13** Moveable
Feast (A) **14** Farewell to Arms (A)
15 Old Man and the Sea (The) **16** To
Have and Have Not **18** Islands in the
Stream, Snows of Kilimanjaro (The)
19 For Whom the Bell Tolls *sobriquet:*
4 Papa

hemlock 4 drug, herb, tree, wood **6** poison

hemophiliac 7 bleeder

hemp 3 kef, kif **7** hashish **8** cannabis
9 marijuana *fiber:* **5** oakum *kind:* **4** aloe

hen 5 biddy *broody:* **6** sitter *spayed:*
8 poularde *young:* **6** pullet

hence 4 away, ergo, thus **5** since **9** as a
result, from now on, therefore, thereupon **11** accordingly **12** consequently

henceforth 9 from now on, hereafter

henchman 6 cohort, lackey, minion,
stooge **7** abettor **8** adherent, disciple,
follower, partisan, retainer **9** attendant,
supporter **10** accomplice

Henley poem 8 Invictus

henpeck 3 nag **4** carp, fuss **5** annoy
6 badger, carp at, harass, hector **8** domineer **9** find fault

Henry II *adversary:* **6** Becket (Thomas à)
son: **7** Richard (Lionheart) *surname:*
5 Anjou **11** Plantagenet *wife:* **7** Eleanor

Henry IV *surname:* **9** Lancaster *victim:*
10 Richard III

Henry VIII *archbishop:* **7** Cranmer
(Thomas) **10** Thomas More *daughter:*
9 Elizabeth *son:* **6** Edward *surname:*
5 Tudor *victim:* **4** Anne (Boleyn)
9 Catherine (Howard) **10** Thomas More
wife: **4** Anne (Boleyn, of Cleves), Jane

(Seymour) **9** Catherine (Howard, of Aragon, Parr)

hepatic 9 liverwort

Hephaestus 6 Vulcan *father:* **4** Zeus **7** Jupiter *mother:* **4** Hera, Juno *wife:* **5** Venus **6** Charis **9** Aphrodite

Hephzibah *husband:* **8** Hezekiah *son:* **8** Manasseh

hepped up 5 eager **7** excited, fervent **12** enthusiastic

Hera 4 Juno *father:* **6** Cronus, Saturn *husband:* **4** Zeus **7** Jupiter *messenger:* **4** Iris *mother:* **4** Rhea

Heracles *beloved:* **4** Iole *brother:* **8** Iphicles *charioteer:* **6** Iolaus *father:* **4** Zeus **7** Jupiter *mother:* **7** Alcmene *son:* **6** Hyllus *victim:* **5** Hydra, Ladon **6** Geryon, Megara, Orthus **10** Nemean lion *wife:* **4** Hebe **6** Megara **8** Deianira

herald 4 hail, tout **5** crier, greet **6** signal **7** courier, declare, portend, precede, presage, trumpet **8** announce, ballyhoo, exponent, outrider, proclaim **9** advertise, harbinger, messenger, precursor, publicize, spokesman **10** forerunner, foreshadow

heraldic *border:* **7** bordure *cross:* **6** fleury, formée, moline, pommée **8** fourchée *term:* **4** bend, fess, orle, pale, seme, vert **5** crest, flank, gules **6** argent, blazon, canton, charge, device, dexter, emblem, impale, manche, sejant, voided, volant **7** chevron, nombril, passant, purpure, rampant, saltire, statant **8** guardant, sinister, tincture **9** regardant **10** escutcheon

heraldry 6 armory **9** pageantry

herb 3 oca **4** dill, flax, forb, hemp, leek, mint, nard, sage, wort **5** basil, chive, tansy, thyme **6** allium, arnica, borage, catnip, endive, eryngo, fennel, garlic, hyssop, lovage, orpine, squill, yarrow **7** boneset, caraway, catmint, chervil, chicory, comfrey, episcia, ginseng, milfoil, mullein, oregano, parsley, pinesap, pussley, salsify, sanicle **8** angelica, camomile, capsicum, cardamom, centaury, cilantro, costmary, feverfew, freewort, hepatica, lungwort, mandrake, marjoram, origanum, pokeweed, purslane, rapeseed, selfheal, tarragon, turmeric, euphrasy, valerian, woodruff, wormwood **9** birthwort, bush basil, chamomile, patchouli, spikenard **10** basil thyme **12** balm of Gilead *mythical:* **4** moly *poisonous:* **7** aconite, dogbane, hemlock, henbane **8** veratrum **9** hellebore

herbicide 6 dioxin, diquat, diuron **7** monuron **8** picloram, simazine **11** Agent Orange

Herculean 4 huge, vast **5** giant **7** arduous, immense, mammoth, titanic **8** colossal, enormous, gigantic, powerful **10** formidable, superhuman

Hercules see HERACLES

herd 3 mob **4** bevy, lead **5** covey, crowd, drive, drove, flock, swarm **6** gather, throng **9** associate, multitude

herdsman 6 Boötes, cowboy **7** breeder **8** shepherd

here and there 6 passim **7** at times **9** sometimes **11** irregularly

hereditary 6 inborn, inbred, innate, lineal **7** genetic **9** ancestral, inherited **10** congenital **11** traditional, transmitted

heredity 7 lineage **8** ancestry **9** tradition **11** inheritance *unit:* **4** gene

heresy 6 schism **7** dissent, fallacy, impiety **9** defection, deviation, misbelief **10** dissidence, heterodoxy, infidelity, radicalism **11** revisionism, unorthodoxy **13** nonconformism, nonconformity

heretic 7 infidel **8** apostate, defector, recusant, renegade **9** dissenter, dissident **10** iconoclast, schismatic, separatist, unbeliever **11** misbeliever, nonbeliever, revisionist **13** nonconformist

heretical 7 infidel **8** apostate **9** dissident, heterodox, miscreant, sectarian **10** dissenting, schismatic, unorthodox **11** revisionist **12** misbelieving **13** nonconformist

heritage 6 legacy **7** bequest **9** patrimony, tradition **10** birthright

Hermes 7 Mercury *attribute:* **7** petasos, petasus **8** caduceus *father:* **4** Zeus **7** Jupiter *mother:* **4** Maia

hermetic 6 closed, occult, secret **7** recluse **8** abstruse, airtight, profound, secluded, solitary **9** recondite **10** cloistered, impervious **11** sequestered

Hermia *beloved:* **8** Lysander *father:* **5** Egeus

Hermione *father:* **8** Menelaus *husband:* **7** Orestes, Pyrrhus **11** Neoptolemus *mother:* **5** Helen

hermit 5 loner **6** cookie **7** eremite, recluse **8** solitary **9** anchorite

hermitage 7 retreat **8** cloister, hideaway **9** monastery

hernia 6 breach **7** rupture **10** protrusion *support:* **5** truss *type:* **6** cystic, hiatal **7** femoral **9** umbilical **10** incisional

hero 4 idol **6** knight **7** demigod, paladin **8** champion **11** protagonist *American:* **6** Bunyan (Paul) **8** Superman *Armenian:* **10** Skanderbeg *Babylonian:* **9** Gilgamesh *Celtic-French:* **7** Tristan **8** Tristram *Crusades:* **7** Tancred **8** Tancredi *English:* **6** Arthur **7** Beowulf **9** Robin Hood

French: 6 Roland 11 Charlemagne *German:* 5 Etzel 8 Arminius 9 Siegfried *Greek:* 4 Ajax 5 Jason 7 Perseus, Ulysses 8 Achilles, Heracles, Hercules, Leonidas, Odysseus 11 Bellerophon *Hebrew:* 5 David 6 Daniel, Samson *Hungarian:* 5 Arpad 7 Hunyadi (János) *Irish:* 9 Cuchulain, Cuchulinn, Cuchullin *Italian:* 7 Orlando *Roman:* 7 Romulus 8 Horatius *Scandinavian:* 6 Sigurd 9 Siegfried *Scottish:* 5 Bruce (Robert) 6 Rob Roy *Spanish:* 5 El Cid *Spartan:* 8 Leonidas *Trojan:* 6 Aeneas, Hector

Herod *daughter:* 6 Salome *father:* 7 Antipas 9 Antipater *kingdom:* 5 Judea 6 Judaea *mother:* 6 Cyprus *son:* 5 Herod (Antipas) 6 Joseph 7 Pheroas 9 Phasaelus

Herodias *daughter:* 6 Salome *father:* 11 Aristobulus *husband:* 5 Herod (Antipas)

heroic 4 bold, huge 5 brave, noble 6 daring, mighty 7 drastic, extreme, radical, valiant 8 colossal, enormous, fearless, gigantic, intrepid, unafraid, valorous 9 dauntless, Herculean, undaunted 10 courageous

heroin 4 gear, skag 5 horse, smack 8 narcotic 11 diamorphine

heroism 5 valor 6 daring, spirit 7 bravery, courage, prowess 8 boldness, chivalry, nobility, valiance 9 gallantry 11 intrepidity

heron relative 5 egret 7 bittern

Hero's lover 7 Leander

herring 7 sardine 8 brisling, pilchard *smoked:* 7 bloater

Herse *father:* 7 Cecrops *sister:* 8 Aglauros *son:* 8 Cephalus

Hersey *novel:* 4 Wall (The) 12 Bell for Adano (A) *town:* 5 Adano

Hesione *brother:* 5 Priam *father:* 8 Laomedon *husband:* 7 Telamon *rescuer:* 8 Heracles, Hercules *son:* 6 Teucer

hesitant 4 slow 5 chary, loath, timid 6 afraid, averse, unsure 7 halting, uneager 9 faltering, reluctant, tentative, uncertain, unwilling 10 irresolute 11 disinclined, vacillating

hesitate 4 balk 5 delay, demur, hedge, pause, stall, stick, waver 6 dawdle, dither, falter, waffle 7 stammer, stutter 8 hang back, hold back 9 temporize, vacillate 12 shilly-shally

Hesperides 6 nymphs

Hesperus 5 Venus 11 evening star *father:* 8 Astraeus *mother:* 3 Eos

Hesse *novel:* 6 Demian 10 Siddhartha 11 Steppenwolf 12 Magister Ludi

Hestia 5 Vesta *father:* 6 Cronus, Saturn *mother:* 4 Rhea

heterodox 9 dissident, heretical, sectarian 10 schismatic, unorthodox 13 nonconformist

heterodoxy 6 heresy, schism 7 dissent 9 misbelief 10 dissidence 13 nonconformism, nonconformity

heterogeneous 5 mixed 6 motley, sundry, varied 7 diverse, various 8 assorted 9 disparate 12 conglomerate

het up 5 irate, upset 7 excited 8 agitated

hew 3 axe, cut 4 chop, fell, form 5 shape, stick 6 adhere 7 conform, cut down

hex 4 jinx 5 charm, curse, spell, witch 6 voodoo, whammy 7 bad luck, bewitch, enchant 9 sorceress 11 enchantment, enchantress

heyday 4 acme, peak 5 prime 6 height, zenith 9 high point

Hezekiah *father:* 4 Ahaz 7 Neariah *mother:* 3 Abi *son:* 8 Manasseh *wife:* 9 Hephzibah

hiatus 3 gap 5 break, space 6 breach, lacuna 7 interim 8 aperture, downtime, interval 10 suspension 12 interruption 13 discontinuity

Hiawatha *author:* 10 Longfellow (Henry Wadsworth) *grandmother:* 7 Nokomis *mother:* 7 Wenonah *tribe:* 6 Ojibwa, Ojibwe 7 Ojibway *wife:* 9 Minnehaha

hibernal 6 wintry 8 winterly

Hibernia 4 Eire, Erin 7 Ireland

hick 4 rube 5 yokel 6 rustic 7 bumpkin, hayseed 8 cornball 10 clodhopper, provincial

hidden 5 privy 6 buried, covert, occult, secret, veiled 7 obscure 8 obscured, shrouded, ulterior 9 concealed 11 undisclosed *combining form:* 6 crypto, krypto

hide 3 fur 4 bury, lurk, mask, pelt, skin, veil 5 cache, cloak, cover, inter, shade, stash 6 harbor, lie low, screen, shroud 7 conceal, cover up, leather, obscure, seclude, secrete, shelter 8 ensconce

hideaway see HIDEOUT

hidebound 8 obdurate 9 parochial 10 inflexible, provincial 11 reactionary, straitlaced 12 conservative, narrow-minded 13 straightlaced

hideous 4 ugly 5 awful, gross, lurid, nasty 6 grisly, horrid 7 ghastly, hateful 8 gruesome, horrible, shocking, terrible 9 appalling, dismaying, frightful, loathsome, monstrous, offensive, repellent, repugnant, repulsive, revolting, sickening 10 disgusting, horrifying

hideout 3 den 4 lair 5 cache, haven 6 covert, refuge 7 retreat, shelter 9 hermitage, safe house, sanctuary

hie 3 run 4 dash, push, trot 5 hurry, scoot 6 hasten, hustle

hierarch 4 boss, head 5 chief 6 honcho, leader, master 7 headman 9 chieftain 10 high priest

hierarchy 5 group, order, ranks 6 ladder, system 7 pyramid 9 food chain, structure 11 bureaucracy 12 pecking order

hieratic 6 formal 8 priestly, stylized 10 priestlike, sacerdotal

high 4 tall 5 drunk, giddy, grand, lofty, noble, tipsy 6 elated, raised, stoned, treble, zonked 7 drugged, keyed up, soaring, supreme 8 abstruse, elevated, eloquent, euphoric, hopped-up, piercing, towering 9 climactic, delirious, prominent, spaced-out 11 extravagant, intoxicated *combining form:* 4 alti

high ___ 3 hat, tea 4 five, noon, road, sign, tech, tide, time 5 chair, heels, jinks 6 priest, roller, school

high-and-mighty 5 bossy, proud 6 lordly 7 haughty 8 arrogant, cavalier, insolent, superior 9 imperious 10 disdainful 11 domineering, overbearing 12 supercilious

highball 3 fly, run 4 dash, rush, whiz 5 hurry, speed 6 barrel, hustle, signal 7 hotfoot 8 cocktail

highboy 5 chest 6 bureau 7 dresser 9 furniture

highbrow 4 snob 7 egghead 8 cerebral, cultured, educated 9 intellect 12 intellectual

high-class 7 elegant 8 five-star, superior 9 exclusive, exquisite, first-rate, patrician 11 fashionable 12 aristocratic 13 sophisticated

highest 3 top 5 chief 6 apical, upmost 7 exalted, supreme, topmost 9 top-drawer, uppermost 10 top-ranking *point:* 4 acme, apex 5 crest 6 summit, zenith 8 pinnacle

highfalutin 5 fancy, windy 6 florid 7 aureate, flowery, fustian, orotund, pompous 8 affected 9 bombastic, grandiose, overblown, rhapsodic 10 oratorical, rhetorical 11 declamatory, pretentious

high-flown 5 showy, tumid, windy 6 turgid 7 aureate, flowery, fustian, orotund, pompous, swollen 8 elevated, inflated, sonorous 9 bombastic, grandiose, overblown 10 flamboyant 11 declamatory, pretentious 12 magniloquent, ostentatious 13 grandiloquent

high-handed 5 bossy 8 dogmatic, imperial 9 arbitrary, imperious 10 autocratic, disdainful, imperative, peremptory 11 dictatorial, domineering, magisterial, overbearing

high-hat 4 snub 6 slight, snobby, snooty 7 disdain, haughty 8 arrogant, snobbish 9 conceited, disregard 11 pretentious 12 supercilious

high jinks 3 fun 6 antics 7 fooling, revelry 9 horseplay, rowdiness, whoop-de-do

Highlander 4 Gael, Scot

highlight 4 mark 5 focus 6 accent, stress 7 feature 8 point out 9 emphasize, underline 10 accentuate, focal point

high-minded 5 lofty, moral, noble 7 ethical, upright 8 elevated 10 principled

high-muck-a-muck 3 VIP 5 nabob 6 bigwig 7 big shot, notable

high-pitched 6 shrill 7 excited 8 agitated, feverish, frenetic, piercing

high point 3 top 4 acme, peak 6 apogee, summit, zenith 8 best part, pinnacle

high-powered 6 driven, strong 7 dynamic 8 animated, forceful, vigorous 9 energetic, strenuous 10 aggressive, compelling 12 enterprising

high-pressure 8 forceful 9 insistent, stressful 10 aggressive

high roller 7 gambler, spender, wastrel 8 prodigal 10 big spender, profligate, squanderer 11 spendthrift

high sign 3 nod, tip 4 wink 5 alarm 6 signal, tipoff 7 gesture, warning

Highsmith novel 11 Ripley's Game 16 Talented Mr. Ripley (The)

high-sounding 7 pompous 8 affected, imposing, inflated, puffed-up 9 grandiose, overblown 11 pretentious

high-spirited 4 bold 5 brash, fiery, jolly, merry 6 bubbly, daring, joyful, lively, plucky, spunky 7 excited, gleeful 9 ebullient, energetic, exuberant, vivacious 12 effervescent, lighthearted

high-strung 4 edgy, taut 5 hyper, jumpy, nervy, tense, tight, wired 6 touchy 7 fidgety, jittery, keyed up, nervous, uptight 8 restless 9 excitable, sensitive

hightail it 3 run 4 bolt, dash, flee 5 scoot, scram 6 get out, run off 7 take off 8 clear out 9 skedaddle

highway 4 pike, road 5 track 6 artery 8 corridor, turnpike 10 interstate 12 thoroughfare *German:* 8 autobahn *Italian:* 10 autostrada

highwayman 5 thief 6 bandit, robber 7 brigand

hijack 5 seize, steal 6 abduct, kidnap 8 take over 10 commandeer 11 appropriate

hike 4 jump, rove, snap, trek, walk 5 boost, raise, tramp, tromp 6 jack up, rise up, travel 7 journey, traipse, upgrade 8 backpack, increase

hilarious 5 funny, merry 7 comical

8 humorous, mirthful 9 laughable, priceless 10 rollicking

hilarity 4 glee 5 cheer, mirth 6 gaiety 7 delight 8 jocosity, laughter 9 merriment 12 cheerfulness

hill 4 bank, bump, cock, dune, heap, knob, pile, rick, rise 5 bluff, butte, knoll, mound, ridge, shock, slope, stack 6 cuesta, height 7 hummock, incline 8 mountain 9 elevation, monadnock *African veld:* 5 kopje 6 koppie *Boston:* 6 Bunker *craggy:* 3 tor *Cuba:* 7 San Juan *D.C.:* 7 Capitol *elongate:* 7 drumlin *level-topped:* 4 mesa 5 butte *of stratified drift:* 4 kame *rounded:* 5 swell *sand:* 4 dune *small:* 5 knoll, kopje, mound 6 koppie *surrounded by ice:* 7 nunatak

hillbilly 4 rube 5 yokel 6 rustic 7 bumpkin, hayseed 10 clodhopper 12 backwoodsman

hillock 4 rise 5 knoll, mound

hillside 5 slope *Scottish:* 4 brae

hilt 4 grip, haft 6 handle 8 handgrip

Himalayan country 5 Nepal 6 Bhutan

hind 3 doe 4 back, deer, rear 5 after 7 grouper 9 posterior *mate:* 4 hart

hinder 4 balk, curb, mire 5 block, check, delay, deter 6 baffle, burden, fetter, hamper, hold up, impede, retard, thwart 7 inhibit, prevent, shackle, trammel 8 handicap, hold back, obstruct, restrain 9 frustrate, hamstring, interfere, interrupt

hindmost 3 end 4 back, last, rear 5 after, final 6 latter 7 closing 8 farthest, terminal, ultimate 9 posterior 10 concluding

hindquarters 8 haunches

hindrance 3 bar 4 snag 8 obstacle 9 impedance 10 impediment 11 obstruction

Hindu *age:* 4 yuga *ascetic:* 4 yogi 5 fakir, swami *caste (varna):* 5 Sudra 6 Vaisya 7 Brahman 9 Kshatriya *class:* 5 caste, varna *community:* 6 ashram *demon:* 4 Rahu 6 Ravana *essence:* 5 atman *force:* 5 karma *garment:* 4 sari *gentleman:* 4 babu *god:* 4 deva, Siva 5 Shiva 6 Brahma, Vishnu *goddess:* 4 devi *goddess of beauty:* 7 Lakshmi *goddess of destruction:* 4 Kali *god of destruction:* 4 Siva 5 Shiva *god of fire:* 4 Agni *god of love:* 4 Kama *god of the heavens:* 7 Krishna *god of war:* 6 Skanda 10 Karttikeya *god of wisdom:* 6 Ganesa, Ganesh *hell:* 6 Naraka *holy man:* 5 sadhu *instrument:* 5 sitar, tabla *leader:* 6 Gandhi (Mahatma) *lowest caste:* 5 Sudra *nobleman:* 4 raja 5 rajah *philosophy:* 7 Vedanta *precept:* 5 sutra *prince:* 4 raja 5 rajah 8 maharaja 9 maharajah *queen:* 4 rani

5 ranee 8 maharani 9 maharanee *salvation:* 7 nirvana *scripture:* 4 Veda 6 Purana 12 Bhagavad Gita *social group:* 5 caste, varna *teacher:* 4 guru 5 swami 9 maharishi *term of respect:* 5 sahib *title:* 3 sri *treatise:* 3 Upanishad *twice-born:* 6 Vaisya 7 Brahman 9 Kshatriya

hinge 4 pawl 5 joint, mount 12 turning point *kind:* 4 butt 5 piano 10 hook-and-eye

hint 3 cue, tip 4 clue, dash, sign, wisp 5 imply, taste, tinge, touch, trace 6 allude, notion, shadow, tipoff 7 inkling, soupçon, suggest 8 allusion, indicate, innuendo, intimate 9 insinuate, scintilla, suspicion 10 indication, intimation, suggestion 11 implication, insinuation

hinterland 4 bush 6 sticks 8 frontier, interior 9 backwater, backwoods, boondocks, up-country 10 wilderness 11 backcountry

hip 3 hot 4 chic, coxa 5 aware, savvy 6 haunch, trendy, with-it 7 tuned in 11 fashionable *bone:* 5 ilium, pubis 6 pelvis 7 ischium *cattle:* 5 thurl *disorder:* 8 sciatica

hippie 8 bohemian, longhair 11 flower child 13 nonconformist

Hippocratic ___ 4 oath

Hippodamia *father:* 8 Oenomaus *husband:* 6 Pelops 9 Pirithous 10 Peirithous *son:* 6 Atreus 8 Thyestes

Hippolytus *father:* 7 Theseus *mother:* 7 Antiope 9 Hippolyte *stepmother:* 7 Phaedra

hire 3 fee, pay 4 rent, wage 5 lease, wages 6 employ, engage, retain, sign on, take on 7 charter, payment, recruit 8 contract 10 employment 11 contract for

hireling 4 hack 6 worker 7 servant 8 employee 9 mercenary

Hirschfeld's daughter 4 Nina

hirsute 5 hairy 6 shaggy, woolly 9 whiskered

Hispania 6 Iberia 9 peninsula *part:* 5 Spain 8 Portugal

Hispaniola country 5 Haiti

hiss 4 boo 4 hoot, jeer 5 decry 6 deride, revile, sizzle, wheeze 7 catcall, whisper, whistle 8 sibilate

historian 8 annalist 10 chronicler *American:* 4 Webb (Charles Richard) 5 Adams (Brooks, Charles Kendall, Hannah, Henry, Herbert Baxter), Beard (Charles, Mary), Foote (Shelby) 6 Brooks (Van Wyck), Catton (Bruce), DeVoto (Bernard), Durant (Ariel, Will), Malone (Dumas), Miller (Perry), Muzzey (David), Nevins (Allen), Sarton (George Alfred), Shirer (William), Sparks (Jared), Turner (Frederick Jackson) **7** Ambrose (Stephen), Morison (Samuel Eliot), Parkman (Francis), Ridpath (John Clark), Tuchman (Barbara), Woodson (Carter G.) **8** Bancroft (George), Boorstin (Daniel), Channing (Edward), Commager (Henry Steele), Prescott (William H.), Robinson (James Harvey), Woodward (C. Vann) **10** McCullough (David) **11** Schlesinger (Arthur) *Arab:* **10** Ibn Khaldun *Danish:* **4** Saxo (Grammaticus) *Dutch:* **8** Huizinga (Johan) *English:* **4** Bede (Venerable), Stow (John), Ward (Adolphus) **5** Acton (Lord), Grote (George), Wells (Herbert George) **6** Camden (William), Gibbon (Edward), Keegan (John), Namier (Lewis Bernstein), Stubbs (William), Taylor (A. J. P.) **7** Hakluyt (Richard), Raleigh (Walter), Toynbee (Arnold), Whewell (William) **8** Geoffrey (of Monmouth), Macaulay (Thomas Babington) **9** Holinshed (Raphael), Trevelyan (George) *French:* **5** Bloch (Marc), Renan (Ernest), Taine (Hippolyte) **6** Guizot (François), Thiers (Louis-Adolphe), Volney (Comte de) **7** Braudel (Ferdinand) **8** Hanotaux (Gabriel), Michelet (Jules) *German:* **5** Ranke (Leopold von) **7** Mommsen (Theodor), Niebuhr (Barthold Georg) **8** Spengler (Oswald) *Greek:* **8** Plutarch, Polybius, Xenophon **9** Dionysius, Herodotus **10** Thucydides *Italian:* **4** Vico (Giovanni) **5** Croce (Benedetto) **9** Salvemini (Gaetano) *Jewish:* **8** Josephus (Flavius) *Roman:* **4** Livy **7** Sallust, Tacitus (Cornelius) **9** Suetonius *Scottish:* **7** Carlyle (Thomas) **9** Robertson (William) *Swiss:* **6** Müller (Johannes von) *Welsh:* **7** Nennius

historical period 3 age, era **5** epoch

history 4 past, saga **5** diary **6** annals, memoir, record **7** account, done for, journal **9** chronicle, narrative, treatment **10** chronology

histrionic 5 showy, stagy **6** staged **8** affected, dramatic **10** artificial, theatrical

hit 3 bop, jab, rap **4** bang, bash, bean, biff, blow, bump, bunt, butt, conk, cuff, ding, lick, slap, slug, sock, swat **5** clout, knock, paste, pound, punch, smack, smash, smite, swipe, whack **6** batter, buffet, chance, larrup, strike, stroke, thwack, wallop **7** clobber, sellout, success **8** bludgeon, lambaste **9** collision, sensation *baseball:* **5** homer, liner **6** double, single, triple **7** home run **9** line drive *golf ball:* **5** shank

hitch 4 jerk, join, halt, hook, knot, lift, limp, snag, yoke **5** delay, thumb, unite **6** attach, couple, fasten, hobble, tether **7** connect, harness **8** make fast, stoppage **10** connection, difficulty, impediment **11** obstruction **12** entanglement

Hitchcock, Alfred *film:* **4** Rope **5** Birds (The), Topaz **6** Frenzy, Marnie, Psycho **7** Rebecca, Vertigo **8** Lifeboat, Sabotage **9** Notorious, Suspicion **10** Rear Window, Spellbound **12** Lady Vanishes (The) **13** To Catch a Thief **14** Shadow of a Doubt **16** North by Northwest *forte:* **8** suspense

hitchhike 5 thumb

hither 4 here **6** nearer **11** to this place

hitherto 5 as yet, so far **7** earlier, thus far, till now **8** formerly, until now **10** previously

Hitler, Adolf *follower:* **4** Nazi *title:* **6** Führer **7** Fuehrer *wife:* **5** Braun (Eva)

hit man 5 bravo **6** killer **7** torpedo **8** assassin, enforcer, murderer **9** cutthroat

hit-or-miss 6 casual, chance, random **7** aimless, erratic **8** careless **9** desultory, haphazard, irregular, unplanned

hive 6 apiary, colony **7** cluster **9** stockpile

HMS Pinafore *composer:* **8** Sullivan (Arthur) *librettist:* **7** Gilbert (W. S.)

hoagie 3 sub **4** hero **5** po'boy **7** grinder, torpedo **8** sandwich **9** submarine

hoar 4 rime **5** frost

hoard 4 save **5** amass, cache, lay by, lay up, stash, stock, store, trove **6** supply **7** collect, lay away, nest egg, reserve **8** squirrel, treasure **9** stockpile **10** accumulate, collection, cumulation **11** aggregation **12** accumulation

hoarder 5 miser **7** scrooge

hoarse 5 gruff, husky, rough, thick **6** croaky **7** grating, rasping, raucous, throaty **8** croaking, gravelly, guttural

hoary 3 old **4** aged **5** stale **6** age-old **7** ancient, antique **8** timeworn **9** venerable

hoax 3 con **4** dupe, fake, fool, gull, sham **5** fraud, phony, trick **6** befool, delude, humbug, take in **7** deceive, mislead **8** flimflam, hoodwink, trickery **9** bamboozle, deception, imposture

Hobbit creator 7 Tolkien (J. R. R.)

hobble 4 lame, limp **6** fetter, hamper, hinder, hog-tie, impede **7** cripple, trammel **8** handicap

hobby 6 falcon **7** pastime, pursuit **8** activity, sideline **9** avocation, diversion

hobgoblin 5 bogey **7** bugaboo

hobnob 3 mix **6** mingle **7** consort **9** associate, rub elbows, socialize 10 fraternize 11 get together

hobo 3 bum 5 gypsy, tramp 7 drifter, floater, swagman, vagrant 8 derelict, vagabond

hock 4 debt, pawn 5 ankle 6 prison

hockey 6 shinny *arena:* 4 rink *cup:* 7 Stanley *implement:* 4 puck 5 stick *official:* 7 referee 8 linesman *player:* 3 Orr (Bobby), Roy (Patrick) 4 Bure (Pavel), Fuhr (Grant), Howe (Gordie), Hull (Bobby, Brett), Jagr (Jaromir), wing 5 Bossy (Mike), Bucyk (John), Hasek (Dominik), Kurri (Jari), Maruk (Dennis), Sakic (Joe), Shore (Eddie), Shutt (Steve) 6 center, Clarke (Bobby), Coffey (Paul), Dionne (Marcel), Dryden (Ken), goalie, Harvey (Doug), Juneau (Joe), Kariya (Paul), Leetch (Brian), Mikita (Stan), Morenz (Howie), Parent (Bernie), Potvin (Denis), Recchi (Mark), Savard (Denis), Sundin (Mats) 7 Belfour (Ed), Bourque (Ray), Brodeur (Martin), Chelios (Chris), Fedorov (Sergei), forward, Francis (Ron), Gretzky (Wayne), Lafleur (Guy), Lemieux (Claude, Mario), Lindros (Eric), Messier (Mark), Mogilny (Alexander), Richard (Maurice), Richter (Mike), Selanne (Teemu), Stastny (Peter), Yzerman (Steve) 8 Beliveau (Jean), Esposito (Phil, Tony), Forsberg (Peter), Nicholls (Bernie), pointman, Shanahan (Brendan), Trottier (Bryan), Ysebaert (Paul) 9 Hawerchuk (Dale) 10 Carbonneau (Guy), defenseman, goalkeeper *team:* 4 Jets 5 Blues, Kings, Stars 6 Bruins, Devils, Flames, Flyers, Oilers, Sabres, Sharks 7 Canucks, Rangers, Whalers 8 Capitals, Panthers, Penguins, Red Wings, Senators 9 Canadiens, Islanders, Lightning, Nordiques 10 Black Hawks, Maple Leafs, North Stars 11 Mighty Ducks *term:* 3 box 4 cage, goal, puck, rink 5 bandy, bench, check, icing, stick 6 charge, crease, shinny 7 face-off, offside 8 blue line 9 back-check, body-check 10 center line, penalty box *variation of:* 9 broomball

hocus-pocus 4 sham 8 artifice, nonsense, trickery 9 conjuring, deception, imposture 10 mumbo jumbo 11 abracadabra, incantation, legerdemain 13 sleight of hand

hod 4 tray 6 trough 7 scuttle 11 coal scuttle

Hoder, Hoth *brother:* 6 Balder *slayer:* 4 Vali *victim:* 6 Balder

hodgepodge 4 hash 6 jumble, medley 7 mélange, mixture 8 mishmash, mixed

bag 9 patchwork, potpourri 10 assortment, miscellany 11 gallimaufry

hoe 4 till, weed 6 tiller, weeder 9 cultivate

hoedown 9 barn dance 11 contra dance, square dance

hog 3 pig, sow 4 boar 5 swine *family:* 6 Suidae *female:* 3 sow 4 gilt *genus:* 3 Sus *red:* 5 duroc *young:* 5 shoat

hogback 5 crest, ridge

hogshead 3 keg, tun 4 butt, cask 6 barrel 9 container

hog-tie 4 bind 6 fetter 7 shackle, trammel

hogwash 3 rot 4 bunk, slop 5 bilge, hokum, hooey, swill 6 piffle 7 baloney, garbage, rubbish 8 nonsense 9 moonshine, poppycock 10 applesauce, balderdash, flapdoodle, taradiddle 12 gobbledygook

hog wild 5 crazy 6 crazed, madcap 7 berserk

ho-hum 4 dull 5 bored 6 boring 7 tedious 8 tiresome 10 unexciting 11 indifferent

hoi polloi 3 mob 5 horde 6 masses 8 populace 9 multitude 10 lower class 11 proletariat

hoist 4 lift 5 drink, raise, winch 6 lift up, pick up, take up 7 derrick, elevate 8 windlass

hoity-toity 4 smug 5 dizzy, giddy, silly 7 flighty, pompous 9 conceited, frivolous 11 highfalutin

hokey 4 fake, mock, sham 5 banal, bogus, corny, hammy, phony, stale, stagy, trite 6 ersatz, pseudo 7 clichéd 8 cornball, outdated 9 contrived, hackneyed 12 melodramatic

hokum 4 bosh 5 hooey 7 baloney, hogwash 8 malarkey, nonsense 9 moonshine, poppycock 10 applesauce, balderdash, flapdoodle, taradiddle 11 foolishness 12 gobbledygook

hold 3 own 4 bear, deem, grab, grip, keep 5 carry, clamp, clasp, cling, grasp, gripe, judge, sense, think, value 6 arrest, clench, clinch, clutch, detain, harbor, regard, retain 7 contain, convene, convoke, fermata, grapple, keep out, possess, reserve, support, sustain 8 keep back, maintain, preserve, restrict *close:* 6 cuddle *dear:* 7 cherish *in check:* 7 repress *in common:* 5 share *out:* 4 last 6 endure *together:* 4 bond 5 clamp 6 fasten *wrestling:* 6 nelson 8 headlock, scissors 10 full nelson, half nelson

hold back 4 curb, keep, stop 5 check, delay 6 bridle, detain, impede, retain 7 inhibit, keep out, prevent, refrain, reserve 8 restrain, suppress, withhold 9 constrain

hold forth 4 rant **5** orate, speak, spout **7** declaim, expound, lecture **8** harangue, proclaim **9** expatiate **10** dilate upon

hold off 4 stay, wait **5** defer, delay, pause, repel **6** rebuff, resist **7** abstain, adjourn, repulse, suspend **8** hesitate, postpone, prorogue **9** withstand **11** discontinue

hold up 3 rob **4** halt, lift, stay **5** check, defer, delay, raise **6** hinder, impede, put off, retard **7** support, suspend **8** postpone, prorogue, slow down

hole 3 den, gap, jam, pit **4** cave, flaw, lair, rent, spot, void **5** fault, niche **6** breach, burrow, cavity, cranny, defect, eyelet, lacuna, outlet **7** dilemma, opening, orifice **8** aperture, weakness **9** perforate **10** excavation, interstice **11** perforation, predicament

hole in one 3 ace

holiday 5 leave **6** May Day **7** Flag Day **8** Labor Day, New Year's, vacation **9** Christmas, Halloween **10** Father's Day, Mother's Day **11** Memorial Day, Veterans Day **12** All Saints' Day, Groundhog Day, Thanksgiving **13** Presidents' Day, St. Patrick's Day, Valentine's Day *British:* **9** Boxing Day *Canadian:* **11** Dominion Day, Victoria Day *Jewish:* **8** Passover

holiness 5 piety **6** purity **8** devotion, divinity, sanctity **9** beatitude **11** religiosity **12** consecration, spirituality

Holland see NETHERLANDS

holler 3 cry **4** call, yell **5** shout **6** bellow, clamor, cry out, outcry **7** call out **8** complain **9** complaint

hollow 3 dip, sag **4** void **5** basin, empty, false **6** cavity, ravine, sunken, vacant **7** concave, echoing, sinkage **8** sinkhole, thorough **9** cavernous, concavity **10** depression, sepulchral *out:* **3** dig, gut **4** mine **5** gouge **8** excavate

holly 4 tree **5** shrub *genus:* **4** Ilex

holocaust 4 fire **7** inferno **8** genocide **9** sacrifice **10** mass murder **11** destruction **13** conflagration

Holofernes' slayer 6 Judith

holy 6 adored, divine, sacred **7** angelic, blessed, revered, sainted, saintly, sublime **8** hallowed **9** glorified, religious, spiritual, venerated, worshiped **10** reverenced, sacrosanct, sanctified **11** consecrated *combining form:* **5** hagio, hiero *communion:* **9** Eucharist *oil:* **6** chrism *person:* **5** saint **6** zaddik **7** tzaddik *Spirit:* **9** Paraclete *vessel:* **5** grail **7** chalice **8** ciborium

holy place 6 church, shrine, temple **7** sanctum **9** sanctuary

Holy Roman Emperor 4 Karl, Otto **5** Adolf, Franz, Henry, Louis **6** Albert, Arnulf, Conrad, Joseph, Lothar, Ludwig, Philip, Rudolf, Rupert, Wenzel **7** Charles, Francis, Leopold, Lothair **8** Heinrich **9** Ferdinand, Frederick, Friedrich, Sigismund **10** Maximilian **11** Charlemagne

Holy Thursday 6 Maundy (Thursday) **9** Ascension (Day)

holy writ 5 Bible **9** Scripture

homage 5 honor **6** praise **7** respect, tribute **9** deference, obeisance, reverence

hombre 3 cat, guy, lad, man **4** buck, chap, dude, gent, stud **6** fellow, honcho **7** comrade

home 4 digs, land, site **5** abode, haunt, house, range **6** family, hearth **7** country, habitat, housing **8** domicile, dwelling, locality **9** household, residence **10** fatherland, habitation, motherland **12** headquarters *country:* **5** cabin **7** cottage **8** bungalow

homeless 5 stray **6** exiled **7** outcast, vagrant **8** derelict **9** abandoned, displaced, wandering **12** dispossessed

homely 4 cozy **5** plain **6** direct, modest, simple **7** natural **8** familiar, ordinary **11** comfortable, commonplace **12** unattractive **13** unpretentious

Homer *epic:* **5** Iliad **7** Odyssey

homesickness 7 longing **9** nostalgia

homespun 5 plain **6** fabric, folksy, simple **8** ordinary **9** practical **13** unpretentious

Home, Sweet Home *music:* **6** Bishop (Henry) *words:* **5** Payne (John Howard)

homicidal 6 bloody **8** sanguine **9** murdering, murderous **10** sanguinary **11** sanguineous **12** bloodthirsty

homicide 5 blood **6** killer, murder, slayer **7** killing **8** foul play, murderer **9** manslayer **12** manslaughter

homily 6 sermon **7** lecture **9** discourse

homogeneous 7 uniform **10** consistent

Homo sapiens 3 man **7** mankind **8** humanity **9** humankind, human race

homunculus 5 dwarf, pygmy **6** midget, peewee **7** manikin **8** Tom Thumb

honcho 4 boss, head **5** chief **6** leader, master **7** big shot, foreman, headman **8** hierarch, overseer **9** chieftain

Honduras *capital:* **11** Tegucigalpa *city:* **7** La Ceiba **9** Choluteca **10** El Progreso **12** San Pedro Sula *coast:* **8** Mosquito *discoverer:* **8** Columbus (Christopher) *Indian people:* **4** Maya **5** Mayan *language:* **7** Spanish *monetary unit:* **7** lempira *neighbor:* **9** Guatemala, Nicaragua **10** El Salvador *river:* **4** Coco, Ulúa **5** Aguán **6** Patuca *sea:* **9** Caribbean

hone 4 edge, whet **6** finish, polish,

refine, smooth 7 perfect, sharpen
9 whetstone

honest 4 fair, just, open, real, true
5 frank, plain 6 candid, simple 7 genuine, sincere, upright 8 innocent, reliable, truthful 9 objective, reputable, unfeigned, veracious 10 creditable, forthright, legitimate, scrupulous
11 respectable 12 praiseworthy 13 conscientious, dispassionate, unimpeachable

honesty 4 herb 5 honor 6 candor, virtue
7 probity 8 fairness, goodness, justness, veracity 9 integrity, rectitude, sincerity
11 uprightness 12 truthfulness

honey *combining form:* 4 meli, mell
5 melli *drink:* 4 mead

honeybee genus 4 Apis

honeycomb 3 pit 4 fill, fret 5 cells
6 impair, infest, riddle, weaken 7 subvert 9 perforate

honeydew 5 melon

honeyed 5 sweet 6 golden, liquid, mellow 9 sweetened 10 flattering 11 mellifluous

honeysuckle 6 azalea 9 columbine
13 pinxter flower

honk 4 blow, toot 5 blare, blast 7 trumpet

honky-tonk 4 dive 5 joint 7 hangout
9 juke joint, roadhouse 11 barrelhouse

honor 4 fete, laud 5 adorn, asset, award, badge, exalt, glory, kudos, medal
6 credit, esteem, homage, praise, purity, regard, trophy 7 commend, dignify, ennoble, fulfill, glorify, laurels, respect 8 accolade, approval, carry out, chastity, decorate, devotion, good name
9 adulation, deference, integrity, privilege, recognize, reverence 10 admiration, decoration, reputation, veneration
11 distinction, distinguish, recognition
12 commendation

honorable 4 just, true 5 moral, right
6 honest, worthy 7 ethical, upright
8 laudable 9 dignified 10 creditable, scrupulous 11 illustrious 13 conscientious

honorarium 7 payment 8 gratuity 10 recompense 12 compensation 13 consideration

hooch 6 liquor, rotgut 7 bootleg
8 dwelling, home brew 9 firewater, moonshine 10 bathtub gin

hood 4 cowl, thug 5 tough 6 bonnet, helmet 7 capuche 8 covering, gangster, hooligan 10 delinquent

hoodlum 4 punk, thug 5 bully 7 mobster, ruffian 8 criminal, gangster, hooligan
10 delinquent

hoodoo 3 hex 4 jinx, juju, rock 5 curse,

haunt, hokum, magic, spell, spook
6 harass, voodoo, whammy 7 bewitch, evil eye, sorcery, terrify, torment
8 nonsense 9 conjuring 10 black magic, hocus-pocus, mumbo jumbo, witchcraft

hoodwink 3 con 4 dupe, fool, gull, hoax
5 trick 6 befool 7 deceive, mislead
8 flimflam 9 bamboozle

hooey 3 rot 4 bunk 5 bilge 6 bunkum
7 baloney, hogwash 8 claptrap, malarkey, nonsense

hoof 4 foot, walk 5 troop 7 traipse
8 ambulate *cloven:* 5 cloot

hoofer 6 dancer 7 danseur 8 coryphée, danseuse 9 ballerina, tap dancer

hooflike 6 ungual

hook 3 nab, nip 4 gore, hasp 5 catch, curve, hitch, pinch, steal 6 anchor, fasten, pilfer 7 hamulus 8 crotchet *a fish:*
4 gaff, snag *for keys:* 10 chatelaine

hooklike 7 falcate 8 unciform, uncinate
part: 5 uncus 7 hamulus

hookup 7 circuit, linkage 8 alliance
10 assemblage, connection 11 affiliation, association, combination, conjunction, partnership

hooky 6 truant 7 truancy 8 truantry

hooligan see HOODLUM

hoop 4 band, ring 6 circle 7 circlet

hoopla 4 bash, fuss, stir, to-do 6 bustle, frolic 7 revelry, shindig, whoopee 8 ballyhoo, wingding 9 commotion, festivity, merriment, promotion 13 entertainment

hoops 5 b-ball 10 basketball

hooray 3 rah, yay 5 cheer, huzza 6 huzzah, yippee 7 acclaim 10 hallelujah

hoosegow 3 jug, pen 4 brig, cage, coop, jail, keep, stir 5 clink, pokey 6 cooler, lockup, prison 7 slammer 8 bastille, big house 9 calaboose, jailhouse 12 penitentiary

Hoosier State 7 Indiana

hoot 3 bit, boo, jot 4 hiss, iota, jeer, whit
5 laugh, scrap, shout, whoop 6 assail, deride, heckle 7 catcall, modicum
8 particle

hooter 3 owl 5 owlet

Hoover Dam lake 4 Mead

hop 4 jump, leap, trip, vine 5 bound, dance 6 bounce, spring, wait on
7 rebound 8 jump over

hope 4 goal, wish 5 await, dream, faith, trust 6 aspire, desire, expect 7 count on, longing, promise 8 ambition, optimism, prospect 9 count upon 10 anticipate, aspiration, confidence *loss of:*
7 despair

hopeful 4 rosy 5 eager, sunny 6 bright, cheery, golden, seeker, upbeat

7 assured **8** aspirant, aspiring **9** candidate, confident, expectant, promising **10** auspicious, contestant, optimistic, propitious **11** encouraging **12** advantageous

hopeless 4 glum, lost, vain **6** futile, gloomy, morose **7** forlorn **8** downcast **9** desperate, incurable, insoluble **10** despairing, despondent, impossible **11** ineffectual, irreparable, pessimistic **12** incorrigible, irredeemable, irremediable

hoper 7 truster **8** optimist **9** expectant, Pollyanna

hopped-up 4 high **5** giddy **6** stoned, zonked **7** drugged, excited **9** delirious **12** enthusiastic

hopper 3 box, mix **4** frog, hare, tank, toad **5** bunny, chute **6** rabbit **7** cricket **10** freight car, receptacle

___ **Hopper 5** Grace (Murray), Hedda **6** Edward

hopping 4 busy **5** irate, livid **6** lively **7** furious **9** extremely, violently **10** infuriated

Horae 4 Dike **6** Eirene **7** Eunomia, seasons

Horam *kingdom:* **5** Gezer *slayer:* **6** Joshua

horde 3 mob **4** army **5** crowd, crush, drove, press, swarm **6** throng **9** multitude

horizon 4 goal **5** limit, range, reach, scope, vista **6** extent **7** purview, skyline **8** prospect **11** perspective

horizontal 4 flat **5** level **8** parallel

hormone 4 ACTH **5** kinin **6** estrin **7** estriol, estrone, gastrin, insulin, relaxin **8** autacoid, estrogen, glucagon, kallidin, secretin *female:* **8** estrogen *insect:* **8** ecdysone *pituitary:* **8** oxytocin

horn 4 toot **5** cornu **6** antler, klaxon, shofar **7** trumpet **10** cornucopia, projection *ancient Greek:* **5** rhyta (plural) **6** rhyton *animal:* **6** antler

___ **Hornblower 7** Horatio

horn in 6 meddle **7** intrude, obtrude **9** insinuate, interfere, interlope, interrupt

hornlike 8 corneous **10** keratinous

hornswoggle 3 con **4** dupe, fool, gull, hoax **5** trick **7** deceive **8** flimflam, hoodwink **9** bamboozle

horrendous 5 awful **7** fearful, ghastly, heinous, hideous **8** alarming, dreadful, gruesome, horrible, horrific, shocking, terrible **9** abhorrent, appalling, execrable, frightful, repugnant, revolting **11** distressing, unspeakable

horrible 4 grim **5** awful, lurid **6** grisly **7** fearful, ghastly, hateful, hellish, hideous **8** dreadful, gruesome, shocking **9** abhorrent, appalling, frightful, loathsome, repellent, repugnant, repulsive, revolting **10** abominable, disgusting, terrifying

horrid 5 nasty **7** noisome **8** shocking **9** loathsome, offensive, repulsive, sickening **10** detestable, disgusting

horrific 5 awful **7** fearful **8** dreadful, shocking, terrible **9** appalling, dismaying, frightful, harrowing

horrify 5 daunt, shock **6** appall, dismay **7** disgust

horrifying 4 grim **5** awful, lurid **6** grisly **7** ghastly, hideous **8** gruesome, terrible **9** appalling, atrocious

horror 4 fear, hate, pain **5** alarm, dread, panic, shock **6** dismay, fright, hatred, terror **7** disgust **8** aversion, loathing **9** repulsion, revulsion **10** abhorrence, repugnance **11** abomination, detestation, trepidation

hors d'oeuvre 4 whet **6** canape **7** crudité **9** antipasto, appetizer

horse 4 buck, roan **5** bronc, pacer, steed **6** bronco, brumby, equine **7** cavalry, palfrey, sawbuck, trestle, trotter **8** footrope, jackstay, palomino, skewbald, stallion, traveler *Australian-bred:* **5** waler *battle:* **7** charger *breed:* **5** pinto **6** Morgan **7** Arabian, Belgian, Iceland **8** Palomino, Shetland **9** Appaloosa, Percheron **10** Lippizaner **12** standardbred, Thoroughbred *champion:* **7** Man o' War **8** Affirmed, Citation **10** Seabiscuit **11** Seattle Slew, Secretariat, Smarty Jones *collar part:* **4** hame *color:* **3** bay **6** sorrel **8** chestnut *combining form:* **4** hipp **5** hippo *covering:* **8** trapping *draft:* **10** Clydesdale *extinct:* **8** eohippus *farm:* **6** dobbin *female:* **4** mare **5** filly *foot part:* **7** pastern *gait:* **4** trot **6** canter, gallop *gear:* **3** bit **4** rein **6** saddle **7** harness **9** checkrein *leg joint:* **7** fetlock *leg part:* **6** gaskin **7** gambrel *male:* **4** colt **8** stallion *mark:* **5** blaze *of the movies:* **4** Fury **6** Flicka, Silver **7** Trigger **8** Champion **11** Black Beauty *race:* **5** Ascot, derby **7** Belmont **9** Preakness *rump:* **7** crupper *small:* **4** pony **6** garron, jennet *spotted:* **5** pinto **7** piebald *tan:* **8** palomino *thoroughbred:* **8** hotblood *war:* **8** destrier *wild:* **7** mustang

horsefeathers 3 rot **4** bull, bunk **5** bilge, hokum, hooey, trash **6** bunkum, drivel, piffle **7** baloney, garbage, hogwash, rubbish, twaddle **8** claptrap, flimflam, nonsense, tommyrot **9** poppycock **10** applesauce, balderdash

horseman 5 rider **6** cowboy **7** vaquero **8** cavalier **9** caballero, chevalier **10** equestrian

horsemanship 6 manège **10** equitation

horse opera 5 oater **7** western

horseplay 7 fooling **8** clowning, rowdyism **9** high jinks, rowdiness **10** buffoonery, roughhouse **11** shenanigans **12** roughhousing

horseshoer 6 smithy **10** blacksmith

hortative 8 advisory **9** exhorting, homiletic

horticulturist 7 Burbank (Luther)

Horus *brother:* **6** Anubis *father:* **6** Osiris *mother:* **4** Isis *victim:* **3** Set **4** Seth

hose 4 sock, tube, wash **5** cheat, spray, trick, water **6** tights **8** stocking

hoser 6 barfly, boozer **7** redneck

hospice see HOSTEL

hospitable 4 kind, open **6** social **7** cordial **8** friendly, generous, gracious **9** convivial, receptive, welcoming **10** gregarious

hospital 6 clinic **7** lazaret **9** infirmary, lazaretto *attendant:* **7** orderly *ship's:* **7** sickbay

Hospitallers' island 5 Malta **6** Rhodes

host 4 army **5** array, cloud, crowd, emcee, flock, horde **6** angels, legion, myriad, scores, server **7** present, receive **8** assemble **9** innkeeper, introduce, moderator, multitude, presenter

hostage 4 pawn **5** token **6** pledge, surety **7** captive, earnest **8** guaranty, prisoner, security **9** guarantee

hostel 3 inn **4** stay **5** lodge **6** tavern, travel **7** auberge, lodging **11** caravansary, public house

hostile 4 anti, mean **5** enemy **6** bitter, fierce **7** adverse, opposed, warlike **8** contrary, inimical, opposite **9** bellicose, combative, resistant, resisting **10** malevolent, pugnacious, unfriendly **11** belligerent, contentious **12** antagonistic **13** argumentative

hostility 3 war **6** animus, enmity, hatred, rancor **7** ill will **8** conflict **9** antipathy **10** aggression, antagonism, opposition, resistance **12** belligerence

hot 3 new **4** fast, heat, sexy **5** angry, close, eager, fiery, lucky, spicy **6** ardent, baking, banned, heated, hectic, on fire, raging, stolen, sultry, torrid, urgent **7** boiling, burning, excited, fevered, illicit, lustful, peppery, popular, pungent, zealous **8** broiling, feverish, in demand, scalding, sizzling, tropical, vehement **9** energized, lecherous, scorching **10** blistering, contraband, passionate, sweltering **11** radioactive

hot air 4 bosh **6** bunkum **7** blather, prattle, twaddle **8** malarkey, nonsense **9** empty talk, poppycock **10** double-talk

hotbed 3 hub **4** core, seat **5** heart **6** center **7** nucleus **10** focal point **11** nerve center

hot-blooded 5 fiery **6** ardent **7** burning, fervent, flaming **9** excitable, impetuous, impulsive **10** passionate **11** impassioned **12** high-spirited

hotchpotch see HODGEPODGE

hot dog 5 frank **6** weenie, wiener, wienie **7** sausage, show-off **11** frankfurter, wienerwurst

hotel 3 inn **5** lodge **6** tavern **7** auberge, hospice, pension **8** motor inn **11** public house **12** lodging house, rooming house **13** boardinghouse *chain:* **5** Hyatt **6** Hilton, Ramada, Westin **7** Days Inn **8** Marriott, Radisson, Sheraton, Stouffer **10** Holiday Inn **11** Best Western, Four Seasons *inferior:* **7** fleabag **9** flophouse

hothead 5 rebel **7** fanatic, inciter, radical **8** agitator **9** demagogue, firebrand **10** incendiary **12** rabble-rouser, troublemaker **13** revolutionary

hotheaded 4 rash **5** brash, fiery, hasty **6** madcap **8** reckless **9** excitable, impetuous, imprudent, impulsive, irritable

hotshot 3 ace **4** star, whiz **5** comer **6** expert, master, wizard **8** virtuoso **10** powerhouse **11** heavyweight

hot-tempered see QUICK-TEMPERED

hot water 3 box, fix, jam **4** bind, hole **6** corner, pickle **7** dilemma, problem, trouble **9** tight spot **10** difficulty **11** predicament

___ **Houdini 5** Harry

hound 3 dog, fan **4** bait, buff, ride **5** chivy **6** badger, basset, beagle, bowwow, canine, harass, hassle, heckle, hector, pester, pursue, Talbot **7** devotee **8** bullyrag **9** dachshund, persecute **10** aficionado *Russian:* **6** borzoi

hourglass 5 timer

house 3 cot, hut, ken **4** home, shed **5** abode, board, cabin, dwell, hovel, lodge, put up, shack **6** billet, chalet, harbor, shanty **7** contain, cottage, enclose, mansion, quarter, saltbox, shelter, theater **8** audience, bungalow, domicile, dwelling, quarters **9** residence *clergyman's:* **5** manse **7** rectory **9** parsonage *country:* **5** manor **7** cottage **8** bungalow *dog:* **6** kennel *earth:* **5** adobe *Eskimo:* **5** igloo *mean:* **5** hovel, shack *of prostitution:* **4** crib **6** bagnio **7** brothel **8** bordello *religious:* **5** abbey **6** priory **7** convent, nunnery **9** monastery *rooming:* **5** lodge *Russian:* **5** dacha *small:* **4** camp **5** cabin, shack **6** shanty **7** cottage **8** bungalow *Spanish:* **4** casa

housebreaker 4 yegg 5 thief 7 burglar, prowler 8 picklock

household 4 home 5 folks 6 family, ménage 8 domestic, familiar **gods (Roman):** 5 lares 7 penates

house of worship 6 bethel, chapel, church, mosque, pagoda, shrine, temple 7 chantry, minster, oratory 8 basilica 9 cathedral, sanctuary, synagogue 10 tabernacle 11 conventicle

housing 4 case, room 7 shelter 8 barracks, quarters 9 enclosure

hovel 3 hut, sty 4 dump, shed 5 hutch, shack 6 burrow, pigpen, pigsty, shanty 7 shelter

hover 4 flit, hang 5 dance, drift, float, poise, waver 7 flitter, flutter, suspend 9 fluctuate, hang about

howbeit 3 yet 4 when 5 still, while 6 even if, much as, though 7 whereas 8 after all, although 11 nonetheless 12 nevertheless

however 3 but, yet 4 only 5 still 6 except, though 8 after all 11 nonetheless

howl 3 bay, cry 4 bark, keen, wail, yell, yelp 6 cry out 9 caterwaul

howler 4 flub, gaff, goof 5 boner, fluff, gaffe 6 boo-boo 7 blooper, blunder

huarache 6 sandal

hub 4 axis, core 5 focus, heart, pivot 6 center 8 polestar 10 focal point 11 nerve center **opposite:** 3 rim

hubbub 3 din 4 fuss, stir, to-do 5 babel, furor, hoo-ha, noise 6 clamor, furore, hassle, jangle, pother, racket, rumpus, tumult, uproar 7 turmoil 8 brouhaha, foofaraw 9 commotion, confusion 10 hullabaloo, hurly-burly 11 disturbance, pandemonium

hubris 3 ego 4 gall 5 brass, cheek, nerve, pride 7 conceit, hauteur, swagger 8 audacity, chutzpah 9 arrogance, cockiness, vainglory 11 braggadocio

hubristic 4 vain 5 cocky, proud 7 haughty 8 arrogant, insolent, superior 11 overbearing, overweening 13 overconfident

Huckleberry Finn **author:** 5 Twain (Mark) 7 Clemens (Samuel) **character:** 3 Jim, Tom (Sawyer) 4 Duke, King **river:** 11 Mississippi

huckster 4 hawk, plug, vend 5 pitch 6 dicker, haggle, hawker, peddle, vendor 7 bargain, chaffer, haggler, packman, peddler, promote 8 pitchman

huddle 4 lump, mass 5 bunch, crowd, group, hunch 6 confab, confer, crouch, curl up, gather, parley, powwow 7 cluster, consult, meeting 8 assemble 10 conference, discussion

Hudson's ship 8 Half Moon

hue 4 cast, tint, tone 5 color, shade, shape, tinge, value 6 aspect, manner 8 coloring, tincture 10 coloration, complexion

huff 3 pet 4 blow, gasp, pant, rile, roil, snap, snit, tiff 5 annoy, grate, heave, peeve, pique, storm 6 nettle, put out 7 bluster, inflate 8 irritate

huffy 5 angry, proud, testy 6 piqued, touchy 7 annoyed, fretful, haughty, peevish, prickly, waspish 8 arrogant, petulant, snappish 9 irritable, irritated, querulous

hug 4 hold 5 clasp, press, prize, value 6 clinch, clutch, cuddle, enfold 7 cherish, embrace, envelop, squeeze 8 hold fast, hold onto 12 congratulate

huge 4 vast, wide 5 bulky, giant, grand, great, jumbo 6 heroic, mighty, untold 7 immense, mammoth, massive, titanic 8 colossal, enormous, gigantic, whopping 9 extensive, monstrous 10 monumental, prodigious, stupendous, tremendous 11 magnificent, mountainous

hugeness 8 enormity 9 immensity, magnitude

hugger-mugger 4 hash 6 jumble, muddle, secret, tangle 7 clutter, furtive, jumbled, secrecy 8 confused, covertly, disorder, secretly 9 by stealth, confusion, furtively 10 disordered, disorderly, stealthily, undercover 11 clandestine 13 clandestinely

Hugo, Victor **character:** 6 Javert (Inspector) 7 Cosette, Fantine, Valjean (Jean) 9 Esmeralda, Quasimodo **novel:** 13 Les Misérables 20 Hunchback of Notre Dame (The)

Huguenot 10 Protestant **leader:** 5 Condé (Prince de), Rohan (Henri) 6 Mornay (Philippe) 7 Coligny (Gaspard II de)

Huguenots composer 9 Meyerbeer (Giacomo)

hulk 4 body, loom, ship 5 shell, wreck 8 skeleton 9 shipwreck

hulking 4 huge 5 beefy, bulky, burly, husky 7 immense, mammoth, massive 8 colossal, enormous, gigantic, oversize 9 humongous, lumbering, monstrous, ponderous, strapping 11 heavyweight

hull 3 pod 4 bark, body, case, husk, peel, rind, skin 5 chaff, frame, shell, shuck 6 casing 8 covering 11 decorticate

hullabaloo 3 din 4 to-do 5 hoo-ha, noise 6 clamor, hubbub, jangle, pother, racket, tumult, uproar 8 ballyhoo, foofaraw 9 commotion, hue and cry 11 pandemonium

hum 4 buzz, purr, sing, zing 5 drone 6 murmur 7 vibrate

human 5 being, party 6 mortal, person 7 hominid 8 hominoid 10 individual *race:* 7 mankind

Human Comedy author 6 Balzac (Honoré de) 7 Saroyan (William)

humane 4 kind 6 gentle, kindly, tender 8 merciful 10 altruistic, benevolent, charitable 11 considerate, kindhearted, soft-hearted, sympathetic, warmhearted 13 compassionate, philanthropic

humanitarian 5 giver 8 generous 10 altruistic, benefactor, beneficent, benevolent, charitable 13 compassionate, philanthropic

humanity 6 people 7 mankind 8 kindness, sympathy 10 compassion, generosity 11 benevolence, Homo sapiens

humble 3 low 4 meek 5 abash, crush, lowly, quiet 6 demean, modest, simple 7 chagrin, deflate, degrade, subdued 8 cast down, disgrace, ordinary 9 compliant, diffident, discomfit, embarrass, humiliate 10 submissive, unassuming 11 acquiescent, deferential 13 insignificant, unpretentious

humbug 3 con, rot 4 fake, fool, hoax, sham 5 faker, fraud, hokum, phony, spoof, trick 6 bunkum, delude, drivel, take in 7 beguile, deceive, mislead 8 flimflam, impostor, malarkey, nonsense, pretense, quackery 9 deception, hypocrite, imposture, pretender, trickster 10 balderdash

humdinger 3 gem 5 beaut, dandy, dilly, doozy, jewel, prize 6 doozie 8 jim-dandy 11 crackerjack

humdrum 4 blah, dull, flat 6 boring, dreary, stodgy 7 prosaic, tedious 8 monotone, monotony, plodding, unvaried, workaday 10 monotonous, uneventful 13 uninteresting

humid 3 wet 4 damp, dank 5 close, moist, muggy, soggy 6 clammy, sodden, steamy, sticky, stuffy 10 oppressive

humidify 6 dampen 7 moisten

humiliate 5 abase, crush, lower, shame 6 bemean, debase, demean, humble 7 chagrin, degrade, mortify 8 belittle, cast down, disgrace 9 embarrass

humiliation 5 shame 7 chagrin, put-down 8 disgrace, ignominy, reproach 9 abasement, disrepute, indignity 11 degradation 13 embarrassment, mortification

humility 7 modesty, shyness 8 meekness 9 abasement, lowliness 10 diffidence, submission 12 subservience 13 self-abasement

humming 4 busy 5 brisk 6 active, lively 8 bustling, hustling 9 energetic

hummock 4 hump 5 couch, knoll, mound 7 hillock

humongous 4 huge, vast 5 giant, jumbo 7 immense, mammoth, massive, titanic 8 colossal, enormous, gigantic 9 monstrous 10 gargantuan, prodigious, tremendous

humor 3 wit 4 baby, bent, mind, mood, tone, vein, whim 5 fancy, fluid, spoil, yield 6 banter, coddle, comedy, cosset, esprit, joking, levity, nature, pamper, temper 7 caprice, cater to, conceit, gratify, indulge, jesting, kidding 8 crotchet, drollery, jocosity, repartee 9 character, drollness, flippancy, funniness, witticism, wittiness 10 complexion, jocularity, pleasantry 11 disposition, temperament

humorist 3 Ade (George), wag, wit 4 card, Nash (Ogden), Shaw (Henry Wheeler), Ward (Artemus, Edward) 5 Adams (Franklin Pierce), Allen (Fred), Barry (Dave), clown, comic, cutup, droll, Dunne (Finley Peter), joker, Twain (Mark), White (E. B.) 6 Blount (Roy), Browne (Charles Farrar), Diller (Phyllis), gagman, jester, kidder, Parker (Dorothy), Rogers (Will), Rourke (P. J.), Runyon (Damon), Thorpe (Thomas Bangs) 7 buffoon, Bombeck (Erma), Burgess (Gelett), Clemens (Samuel Langhorne), gagster, Hubbard (Kin), Keillor (Garrison), Marquis (Don), punster, Sedaris (David), Thurber (James), Trillin (Calvin) 8 Aleichem (Shalom), Benchley (Robert), comedian, funnyman, jokester, Perelman (S. J.), quipster 9 jokesmith, prankster, Wodehouse (P. G.) *Canadian:* 7 Leacock (Stephen)

humorous 5 comic, droll, funny, jokey, merry, witty 6 jocose 7 amusing, comical, jocular, risible, waggish 8 mirthful 9 facetious, laughable, whimsical

hump 3 lug 4 bump, race, tote 5 bulge, carry, hunch, mound, range 6 hustle, schlep 7 hummock, schlepp 8 mountain, obstacle, swelling 9 transport 10 protrusion

humpback 5 whale 8 kyphosis 10 pink salmon

humpbacked 6 convex, curved 7 gibbous

Humperdinck opera 15 Hansel and Gretel

humus 3 mor 4 mull, soil 7 compost 8 material

hunch 4 arch, clod, idea, lump, hump, push 5 chunk, clump, crook, squat, stoop 6 crouch, curl up, huddle, jostle, notion, nugget 7 feeling, inkling 9 intuition

Hunchback of Notre Dame author: 4 Hugo (Victor) *character:* 9 Esmeralda, Quasimodo

hundred *combining form:* 5 centi, hecto
Hungary *capital:* 8 Budapest *city:* 4 Pécs
6 Szeged 7 Miskolc 8 Debrecen *ethnic group:* 6 Magyar *lake:* 7 Balaton *monetary unit:* 6 forint *mountain range:*
10 Carpathian *national hero:* 5 Árpád *neighbor:* 6 Serbia 7 Austria, Croatia, Romania, Ukraine 8 Slovakia, Slovenia *plain:* 11 Great Alföld *river:* 5 Tisza
6 Danube
hunger 3 yen 4 ache, itch, long, lust, need, pine, want 5 crave, greed, yearn 6 desire, hanker, thirst 7 craving, longing
hungry 4 avid, keen, poor 5 eager 6 barren 7 craving, starved, thirsty
8 desirous, famished, ravenous, starving, underfed, yearning 9 hankering, motivated
hunk 3 gob, wad 4 clod, lump 5 chunk, clump, piece, wedge 6 nugget 7 portion
hunker down 5 dig in, squat 6 crouch 8 settle in
hunky 4 buff 5 burly 6 buffed 8 athletic, muscular 9 strapping, well-built
hunky-dory 4 fine, okay 5 dandy, ducky, nifty, swell 6 peachy 10 peachy keen 12 satisfactory
Hunnish 4 rude, wild 6 savage 7 fearful, uncivil 9 barbarian, barbarous, ferocious 11 uncivilized
hunt 3 dog, run 4 hawk, seek 5 chase, hound, prowl, quest, shoot, snare, stalk, track, trail 6 battue, course, dig out, prey on, pursue, safari, search 7 explore, pursuit, rummage 9 ferret out, search for, search out *birds:* 4 fowl *illegally:* 5 poach
hunter 6 jaeger, nimrod 8 predator *biblical:* 6 Nimrod *cap:* 7 montero *constellation:* 5 Orion *mythological:* 5 Orion 7 Actaeon
hunting 5 chase 6 venery 7 gunning, hawking 8 coursing, falconry 9 predatory 10 predacious *bird:* 6 falcon *call:* 7 recheat *cry:* 6 yoicks 7 tallyho 10 view halloo *dog:* 5 hound 6 basset, beagle, borzoi, saluki, setter, vizsla 7 harrier, pointer, spaniel 9 ridgeback, wolfhound 10 bloodhound *expedition:* 6 safari *horn:* 5 bugle
huntress 5 Diana 7 Artemis 8 Atalanta
hurdle 3 bar 4 leap, snag 5 bound, clear, vault 6 hamper, spring 7 barrier 8 leap over, obstacle, overcome, overleap, surmount, traverse 9 negotiate 10 difficulty, impediment 11 obstruction
hurl 4 cast, fire 5 chuck, fling, heave, pitch, sling, throw, vomit 6 launch, thrust 8 catapult
hurly-burly 3 din 4 riot, to-do 5 melee

6 clamor, furore, hassle, hubbub, racket, rumpus, tumult, uproar 7 turmoil
8 confused 9 commotion, confusion
hurrah 4 fuss, to-do, zeal 5 cheer 6 fervor, rumpus 7 fanfare, ovation
8 approval 9 commotion 10 enthusiasm
11 acclamation
hurricane 7 typhoon
hurried 4 fast, sped 5 hasty, quick, swift
6 abrupt, rushed, sudden 7 cursory, rushing 8 headlong 9 impetuous 11 precipitant, precipitate
hurry 3 fly, hie, jog, run, zip 4 post, prod, push, rush 5 fleet, haste, scoot, speed, whirl, whish, whisk 6 barrel, breeze, bullet, bustle, hasten, hustle, rocket, rustle, step up, tumult 7 beeline, hotfoot, quicken, shake up, skelter, speed up, swiften 8 celerity, dispatch, expedite, highball, make time
9 commotion, make haste, swiftness
10 accelerate, speediness
hurt 3 mar 4 ache, blow, harm, pain
5 wound, wrong 6 damage, grieve, hamper, harmed, impair, injure, injury, in pain, misuse, offend, pained, suffer
7 afflict, anguish, blemish, damaged, wounded 8 aggrieve, distress, mischief, mistreat 9 constrain, detriment, prejudice, resentful, suffering 10 resentment
hurtful 4 mean, sore 6 aching, unkind
7 harmful, painful 8 damaging, wounding 9 injurious 11 deleterious, destructive, detrimental, distressing, prejudicial
hurtle 3 fly 4 race, rush, tear 5 fling, shoot, speed, throw 6 charge, plunge, rocket
husband 3 man 4 mate, save 6 manage, mister, spouse 7 consort, partner 8 conserve, helpmate, helpmeet 9 economize, other half 10 bridegroom
husbandry 6 thrift 7 control, economy, farming 8 prudence 9 frugality 10 management 11 agriculture, thriftiness
12 conservation, preservation
hush 4 calm 5 quell, quiet 6 shut up, stifle 7 cover up, mollify, secrecy, silence
8 choke off, suppress 9 cessation, quietness, stillness
hush-hush 6 covert, secret 7 private, sub-rosa 9 top secret 11 clandestine
12 confidential 13 surreptitious, under-the-table
husk 3 pod 4 case, peel, rind, skin
5 shell, shuck, strip 6 casing
husky 3 big, dog 5 beefy, burly, great, hefty, large, rough, stout 6 brawny, croaky, hoarse, mighty, robust, strong, sturdy 7 throaty 8 muscular, oversize, stalwart, thickset 9 strapping

hustings 5 stump

hustle 3 fly, rob, run 4 earn, move, push, rush, sell, urge, work 5 cheat, elbow, fraud, haste, hurry, press, shove, speed 6 hasten 7 hotfoot, promote, solicit, swindle 8 bulldoze, deception, dispatch 9 swiftness

hustler 4 doer 6 dynamo, vendor 8 go-getter, live wire 10 powerhouse

hustling 4 busy 5 eager 6 active, lively, speedy 7 hopping, humming 9 energetic 10 aggressive

hut 3 cot 4 camp, crib, shed 5 cabin, dacha, hooch, hovel, hutch, jacal, lodge, roost, shack 6 cabana, chalet, lean-to, shanty 7 cottage 8 bungalow *American Indian:* 6 wigwam 7 wickiup *Scottish:* 5 bothy, shiel 8 shieling

hutch 3 bin, pen 4 cage, coop 5 chest, shack 6 locker, shanty 8 cupboard 9 enclosure

Huxley novel 8 Antic Hay 11 Crome Yellow 13 Brave New World, Eyeless in Gaza

Hyacinthus *father:* 7 Amyclas *slayer:* 6 Apollo

hybrid 5 blend, cross, mixed 7 amalgam, mixture 8 combined, compound 9 composite, crossbred 10 crossbreed 11 combination

hybridize 4 join 5 blend, cross 7 combine 10 crossbreed, interbreed, intercross

Hydra 5 polyp 6 plague 7 monster, serpent 13 constellation *father:* 6 Typhon *mother:* 7 Echidna *slayer:* 8 Heracles, Hercules

hydrant 3 tap 4 pipe 5 valve 6 faucet, spigot 7 petcock 8 fireplug

hydraulic device 3 ram 4 jack, lift, pump 5 brake, press 8 elevator

hydrocarbon 5 xylol 6 dioxin, ethane, xylene 7 benzene, methane, styrene, toluene 8 biphenyl, butylene, ethylene *liquid:* 6 octane 7 retinol, styrene 8 menthene

hydroid 5 polyp 6 medusa, obelia 9 jellyfish

hydrometer scale 4 Brix 5 Baumé

hydrophobia 5 lyssa 6 rabies

hyena 5 dingo 6 jackal 9 scavenger

Hygeia 5 Salus *father:* 9 Asclepius 11 Aesculapius *goddess of:* 6 health

hygiene 6 health 10 sanitation 11 cleanliness

hygienic 5 clean 7 aseptic, healthy, sterile 8 sanitary 9 healthful 10 antiseptic, unpolluted

Hyllus' father 8 Heracles, Hercules

hymeneal 6 bridal, wedded 7 marital, married, nuptial, spousal 8 conjugal 9 connubial 11 matrimonial

hymn 4 laud, song 5 bless, carol, chant, extol, paean, psalm 6 anthem, choral, praise 7 chorale, glorify 8 canticle, doxology, eulogize

hype 4 plug, tout 5 boost, thump 7 acclaim, enliven, glorify, promote, puffery, trumpet 8 ballyhoo, increase 9 advertise, excellent, publicity, publicize, stimulate 11 advertising

hyper 4 edgy 5 antsy, jumpy, wired 6 on edge 7 anxious, frantic 8 agitated, frenetic, hopped-up 9 excitable 10 highstrung, overactive 11 overwrought

hyperbole 6 excess 12 embroidering, exaggeration 13 embellishment, overstatement

hypercritical 6 severe 7 carping 8 captious, exacting 10 censorious, nitpicking 12 faultfinding

Hyperion *daughter:* 3 Eos 6 Aurora, Selene *father:* 6 Uranus *mother:* 4 Gaea *son:* 6 Helios *wife:* 5 Theia

hypnotic 6 opiate, sleepy 8 mesmeric, narcotic, sedative 9 somnolent, soporific 11 mesmerizing, somniferous 12 somnifacient, spellbinding

hypnotize 4 drug 5 charm 6 dazzle, trance 8 enthrall, entrance, overcome 9 captivate, mesmerize, overpower, spellbind

hypocorism 7 pet name 8 nickname 9 sobriquet

hypocrisy 4 cant, sham 6 deceit, humbug 7 falsity, pietism 8 quackery 9 deception, duplicity, phoniness 10 sanctimony 11 insincerity, religiosity

hypocrite 4 fake, sham 5 actor, faker, fraud, phony, poser 6 humbug, poseur 7 bluffer, pietist 8 deceiver, impostor, pharisee 9 charlatan, pretender 10 dissembler 11 masquerader 12 dissimulator

hypocritical 5 false 7 canting 8 affected, specious, two-faced 9 deceitful, insincere, pietistic 10 Janus-faced 11 dissembling, double-faced, duplicitous 12 mealymouthed, xpecksniffian 13 sanctimonious

hypothesis 6 belief, theory 7 premise 8 position, supposal 9 condition, inference 10 antecedent, assumption, conjecture 11 explanation, speculation, supposition

hypothetical 7 assumed 8 abstract, academic, supposed 10 assumptive 11 conditional, conjectural, suppositous, theoretical 12 suppositious 13 suppositional

hyrax 4 cony 5 coney 6 dassie, mammal 8 ungulate

hysteria 4 fear **5** craze, furor, mania, panic **6** excess, frenzy **7** madness **8** delirium

hysterical 5 rabid **6** crazed, madcap, raving **7** berserk, frantic **8** agitated, frenzied, neurotic **9** delirious, disturbed, hilarious, impetuous **10** convulsive, distraught, uproarious **11** impassioned, overexcited, overwrought **13** side-splitting

I

Iago *general:* **7** Othello *victim:* **6** Cassio, Emilia **7** Othello **9** Desdemona *wife:* **6** Emilia

Iapetus *father:* **6** Uranus *mother:* **4** Gaea *son:* **5** Atlas **9** Menoetius **10** Epimetheus, Prometheus *wife:* **7** Clymene

Iasion *brother:* **8** Dardanus *father:* **4** Zeus **7** Jupiter *lover:* **5** Ceres **7** Demeter *mother:* **7** Electra *son:* **6** Plutus

ibex 4 tahr **8** wild goat *family:* **7** Bovidae *genus:* **5** Capra

Ibhar's father 5 David

ibis-headed god 5 Thoth

ibis relative 5 heron, stork

Ibsen, Henrik *character:* **3** Ase **4** Nora (Helmer) **5** Brack (Judge), Brand, Hedda (Gabler), Helen (Alving), Werle (Gergers) **6** Ejlert (Lovberg), Hedvig (Ekdal), Jorgen (Tesman), Oswald (Alving) **7** Solness (Halvard), Solveig, Torvald (Helmer) **8** Peer Gynt **9** Stockmann (Thomas) *country:* **6** Norway *play:* **6** Ghosts **8** Peer Gynt, Wild Duck (The) **10** Doll's House (A) **11** Hedda Gabler, Little Eyolf, Rosmersholm **13** Master Builder (The) **16** Enemy of the People (An)

Icarus' father 8 Daedalus

ice *area:* **4** rink *dessert:* **6** sorbet **7** sherbet *floating:* **4** berg, floe *hanging:* **6** icicle *pinnacle:* **5** serac

icebox 6 cooler, fridge **12** refrigerator

ice cream 7 spumoni, tortoni *dish:* **6** sundae **11** baked Alaska *drink:* **4** soda **6** frappe

iced 5 glacé **6** glazed **7** chilled

ice field 4 floe **7** glacier

ice game 6 hockey **7** curling

ice house 5 igloo

Iceland *capital:* **9** Reykjavik *monetary unit:* **5** krona *sea:* **9** Norwegian *snow-*

field: **11** Vatnajökull *strait:* **7** Denmark *volcano:* **5** Hekla

Icelandic *epic:* **4** Edda, saga *hero:* **5** Njáll **6** Gunnar **7** Grettir

Ichabod Crane's beloved 7 Katrina

icing 7 topping **8** frosting

icky 4 vile **5** awful, gross, nasty **9** loathsome, offensive, repellent, repulsive, revolting, sickening **10** disgusting **11** distasteful

icon 4 idol, sign **5** image **6** emblem, symbol

iconoclastic 9 dissident, heretical **10** rebellious, unorthodox **13** nonconformist

icy 4 cold **5** gelid, polar **6** arctic, chilly, frigid, frosty, steely **7** glacial **8** freezing **11** emotionless, unemotional

Idaho *capital:* **5** Boise *city:* **6** Moscow **9** Pocatello, Twin Falls **10** Idaho Falls **11** Coeur d'Alene *mountain:* **5** Borah (Peak) **9** Gem (State) *river:* **5** Snake **6** Salmon *state bird:* **8** bluebird *state flower:* **7** syringa *state tree:* **9** white pine

Idas *brother:* **7** Lynceus *father:* **8** Aphareus *slayer:* **4** Zeus *victim:* **6** Castor *wife:* **8** Marpessa

idea 4 whim **5** fancy, guess, motif **6** belief, notion, theory, thesis, vagary **7** caprice, conceit, concept, inkling, meaning, opinion, subject, surmise, thought **8** estimate **9** sentiment, suspicion **10** assumption, brainstorm, conception, conclusion, conjecture, conviction, estimation, hypothesis, impression, perception, reflection **11** abstraction, formulation, supposition

ideal 4 best, goal **5** model **7** chimera, classic, epitome, paragon, perfect, utopian **8** absolute, ensample, exemplar, flawless, nonesuch, paradigm, standard, ultimate **9** archetype, classical, exemplary, nonpareil **10** archetypal, conceptual, consummate **11** theoretical

idealist 7 dreamer, quixote, utopian **9** ideologue, visionary

idealistic 6 dreamy **7** utopian **8** poetical, quixotic, romantic **9** visionary **10** starry-eyed **11** impractical, unrealistic

idealize 5 deify, exalt, extol **7** elevate, ennoble, glorify, worship **8** venerate

ideate 5 think **7** imagine **8** conceive, envisage, envision

idée fixe 5 mania **6** fetish, phobia **7** complex **8** fixation **9** obsession **13** preoccupation

identical 3 one **4** like, same, very **5** alike, equal, exact **8** selfsame **9** duplicate **10** equivalent, synonymous

identification mark 4 logo **5** badge, brand, label **6** emblem

identify 3 tag **4** mark, name, spot **5** brand, place **6** finger, select **7** make out, pick out **9** pinpoint **9** determine, recognize **11** distinguish

identity 4 name, self **7** oneness **8** sameness, selfhood **9** character **10** congruence, uniformity, uniqueness **11** personality, singularity **13** individuality, particularity

ideological 8 notional **10** conceptual, ideational **11** speculative **13** philosophical

ideologue 8 believer, idealist, partisan, theorist

ideology 3 ism **5** credo, creed **7** beliefs **8** doctrine **10** philosophy, principles

idiocy 7 fatuity **9** cretinism, stupidity **10** imbecility **11** foolishness

idiomatic 7 demotic **8** peculiar **9** dialectal **10** colloquial, vernacular

idiosyncrasy 5 quirk **6** oddity **7** anomaly **11** peculiarity, singularity **12** eccentricity

idiosyncratic 3 odd **5** kooky, queer, weird **6** quirky **7** erratic, oddball, offbeat, unusual **8** peculiar, singular **9** eccentric **11** distinctive

idiot 3 ass **4** dolt, fool, jerk, simp **5** dummy, dunce, moron, ninny **6** cretin, nitwit, stupid **7** airhead, dullard, half-wit, jackass, natural, tomfool **8** dumbbell, imbecile, numskull **9** ignoramus, numbskull, simpleton **10** nincompoop

idiotic 5 dopey **6** stupid **7** foolish, moronic **8** ignorant **9** brainless, imbecilic, senseless

idle 3 bum **4** laze, lazy, loaf, loll, rest, vain **5** dally, drone, empty, inert, slack,

tarry **6** asleep, dawdle, diddle, fallow, futile, linger, loiter, lounge, otiose, unused, vacant **7** aimless, dormant, passive **8** inactive, indolent, slothful **9** shiftless **10** unoccupied

idleness 4 ease **5** sloth **6** vanity **7** leisure, loafing **8** lethargy **9** indolence **10** inactivity

idler 3 bum **4** slug **5** drone **6** loafer, slouch **7** dawdler **8** deadbeat, fainéant, loiterer, slugabed, sluggard **9** do-nothing, lazybones **11** couch potato

Idmon *daughter:* **7** Arachne *father:* **6** Apollo *mother:* **6** Cyrene

idol 3 god **4** hero, icon, star **5** deity, image, totem **6** fetish, minion, symbol **8** likeness *Chinese:* **4** joss

idolatry 7 worship **8** devotion **9** adoration **10** exaltation, veneration **11** deification **13** glorification

idolize 5 adore, deify, exalt **6** revere **7** glorify, worship **8** venerate

Idomeneo composer 6 Mozart (Wolfgang Amadeus)

idyllic 5 ideal **6** rustic **7** bucolic, halcyon, perfect, utopian **8** arcadian, heavenly, pastoral, peaceful, romantic **9** idealized, unspoiled **11** picturesque, sentimental

Idylls of the King *author:* **8** Tennyson (Alfred) *character:* **4** Enid **6** Arthur, Elaine, Gareth, Merlin, Vivien **7** Geraint, Lynette **8** Lancelot

iffy 5 dicey, risky **6** chancy, unsure **7** dubious, erratic **8** doubtful **9** uncertain **10** unreliable **12** inconsistent **13** unpredictable

igneous rock 4 lava **5** magma **6** basalt, gabbro **7** diabase, granite **8** porphyry

ignis fatuus 6 mirage **7** chimera **8** delusion, illusion, phantasm **9** pipe dream **12** will-o'-the-wisp **13** hallucination

ignitable 8 burnable **9** excitable, flammable **10** incendiary **11** combustible, inflammable

ignite 4 fire **5** light, spark **6** excite, kindle **7** inflame **8** enkindle, touch off

ignited 3 lit **5** afire, fiery **6** ablaze, aflame, alight **7** blazing, burning, flaming, flaring **11** conflagrant

ignoble 3 low **4** base, mean, poor, vile **5** lowly **6** abject, coarse, common, scurvy, sordid, vulgar **7** lowborn, servile **8** baseborn, indecent, inferior, plebeian, shameful, unwashed, wretched **10** despicable, inglorious **11** disgraceful **12** contemptible, dishonorable

ignominious 6 odious **8** infamous, shameful **9** degrading **10** despicable, inglorious **11** disgraceful, humiliating, opprobrious **12** contemptible, dishonorable, disreputable **13** discreditable, unrespectable

ignominy 5 odium, shame **6** infamy **7** obloquy, scandal **8** disgrace, dishonor **9** discredit, disesteem, disrepute **10** opprobrium **11** humiliation **13** mortification

ignoramus 4 dolt **5** dummy, dunce, idiot, moron **6** dimwit, nitwit, stupid **7** airhead, dullard, half-wit **8** dumbbell, imbecile, numskull **9** numbskull, simpleton

ignorance 7 naiveté **9** innocence, nescience, stupidity **10** illiteracy, simpleness, simplicity **11** unawareness **12** incognizance

ignorant 5 naive **6** simple **7** unaware **8** nescient, untaught **9** benighted, ingenuous, oblivious, unknowing, unlearned, untutored, unwitting **10** illiterate, uncultured, uneducated, uninformed, unlettered, unschooled **11** incognizant, know-nothing **12** uninstructed **13** unenlightened

ignore 4 omit, snub **5** avoid **6** forget, reject, slight **7** neglect **8** overlook **9** disregard

Igraine *husband:* **5** Uther **7** Gorlois *son:* **6** Arthur

iguana 5 anole **6** lizard **8** basilisk **10** chuckwalla

ilex 4 maté **5** holly **6** yaupon **7** holm oak **8** inkberry

Iliad 4 epic *author:* **5** Homer *character:* **4** Ajax **5** Helen, Paris, Priam **6** Aeneas, Hector **8** Achilles, Diomedes, Odysseus **9** Agamemnon, Patroclus *city:* **4** Troy

Ilium 4 Troy

ilk 4 kind, sort, type **5** breed, class, genre **6** family, kidney, nature, stripe **7** variety

ill 4 sick **6** ailing, infirm, laid up, malady, peaked, queasy, unwell **7** ailment, disease, trouble, unlucky **8** diseased, disorder, distress, feverish, nauseous, scarcely, sickness, syndrome **9** afflicted, infirmity, nauseated, unhealthy **10** misfortune

ill-adapted 8 unfitted, unsuited **10** unsuitable

ill-advised 4 rash **5** brash, hasty **6** madcap, unwise **7** foolish **8** careless, heedless, reckless **9** foolhardy, impolitic, imprudent **10** incautious, indiscreet, unthinking **11** inexpedient, injudicious, thoughtless

ill at ease 3 shy **4** edgy **6** on edge **7** anxious, awkward, fidgety, nervous **8** insecure, restless **9** unsettled **11** discomfited **12** apprehensive **13** self-conscious, uncomfortable

ill-boding 4 dire **7** baleful, doomful, fateful, ominous, unlucky **8** sinister **10** portentous **11** apocalyptic **12** inauspicious, unpropitious

ill-bred 4 rude **5** crude **7** boorish, loutish, uncivil, uncouth **8** impolite **9** unrefined **10** uncultured, ungracious, unmannered, unmannerly, unpolished **11** uncivilized **12** discourteous

ill-defined 5 faint, fuzzy, vague **7** shadowy **10** indistinct

illegal 3 hot **6** banned **7** bootleg, illicit, lawless **8** criminal, outlawed, unlawful, wrongful **9** felonious, forbidden **10** actionable, prohibited, proscribed, unlicensed **12** illegitimate *act:* **5** crime **6** felony *scheme:* **4** scam

illegible 8 scrawled **10** unreadable **11** inscrutable

illegitimacy 8 bastardy **11** bar sinister **12** unlawfulness

illegitimate 7 bastard, bootleg, erratic, invalid, lawless, natural **8** criminal, improper, spurious, unlawful **11** misbegotten **12** unauthorized

ill-fated 6 cursed, doomed **7** unhappy, unlucky **8** accursed, luckless, untoward **10** disastrous **11** star-crossed, unfortunate

ill-favored 4 ugly **5** plain **6** homely **12** unattractive

ill-humored 4 dour, sour **5** cross, surly, testy **6** crabby, cranky, crusty, grumpy, morose, ornery, sullen, tetchy, touchy **7** crabbed, grouchy, peevish, prickly **8** choleric, churlish, snappish **9** dyspeptic, irascible, irritable, saturnine, splenetic **12** cantankerous, disagreeable, misanthropic

illiberal 6 biased, narrow **7** bigoted, insular **9** hidebound, parochial, penurious **10** intolerant, prejudiced, provincial **11** reactionary, small-minded **12** conservative, narrow-minded, uncharitable

illicit 7 bootleg, crooked, lawless **8** criminal, unlawful **9** forbidden **10** contraband, prohibited **11** black-market, clandestine **12** unauthorized

illimitable 7 endless **8** infinite, unending **9** boundless **11** measureless

Illinois *capital:* **11** Springfield *city:* **6** Aurora, Cicero, Joliet, Peoria **7** Chicago **8** Rockford *college, university:* **4** Knox **6** DePaul **7** Wheaton **12** Northwestern *nickname:* **7** Prairie (State) *river:* **6** Wabash *state bird:* **8** cardinal *state flower:* **6** violet *state tree:* **8** white oak

illiterate 6 unread **8** untaught **9** untutored **10** uneducated, unlettered, unschooled

ill-mannered 4 rude 6 coarse 7 boorish, loutish, uncivil, uncouth 8 churlish, impolite 10 ungracious 12 discourteous

ill-natured 4 sour 5 cross, huffy, surly, testy 6 bitchy, crabby, grumpy, ornery, tetchy 7 grouchy, peevish, waspish 8 choleric, churlish, snappish, spiteful 9 dyspeptic, fractious, irascible, irritable 10 malevolent 11 belligerent, contentious, quarrelsome 12 cantankerous, disagreeable

illness 6 malady 7 ailment, disease, malaise 8 cachexia, disorder, sickness 9 infirmity 10 affliction 13 indisposition

illogical 6 absurd 7 invalid, unsound 8 specious 9 plausible, senseless, sophistic 10 fallacious, irrational, unreasoned 11 nonrational 12 preposterous, unreasonable

ill-starred 6 cursed, doomed, malign 7 fateful, ominous, unhappy, unlucky 8 luckless, untoward 10 disastrous, foreboding, portentous 11 unfavorable, unfortunate, unpromising 12 inauspicious, unpropitious

ill-tempered 4 sour 5 cross, huffy, surly 6 crabby, bitchy, grumpy, ornery, snippy 7 grouchy, peevish, waspish 8 choleric, churlish, petulant, shrewish, snappish, spiteful 9 dyspeptic, fractious, irascible, irritable 11 belligerent, contentious, quarrelsome 12 cantankerous, disagreeable

ill-timed 11 inopportune 12 unseasonable

ill-treat 4 harm, hurt 5 abuse 6 injure, misuse, molest 7 torment 8 aggrieve 10 traumatize

illuminate 5 clear, edify, exalt, gloss, light 6 uplift 7 clarify, clear up, explain, lighten 8 brighten, decorate 9 elucidate, embellish, enlighten, highlight, irradiate, spotlight

illuminati 5 elite 7 clerisy, scholar 8 academic 11 academician 13 intellectuals

illumination 8 lighting *unit of:* 3 lux 4 phot 5 lumen 6 candle 7 candela 10 footcandle

illusion 4 myth 5 dream, fancy, ghost 6 facade, mirage 7 chimera, fantasy 8 phantasm, phantasy 9 invention, pipe dream, semblance 11 ignis fatuus 12 will-o'-the-wisp 13 hallucination

illusionist 8 conjurer, magician 9 trickster

illusive see ILLUSORY

illusory 4 sham 6 unreal 7 seeming 8 apparent, fanciful 9 deceptive, fictional, imaginary, visionary 10 chimerical, fallacious, fictitious, misleading, ostensible

illustrate 4 mark, show 6 depict, evince, expose, reveal 7 clarify, display, exhibit, explain, picture, portray 8 decorate, describe, evidence, instance, manifest 9 elucidate, epitomize, exemplify 11 demonstrate

illustration 4 case 6 sample 7 diagram, drawing, example, picture, problem 8 instance

illustrative 7 graphic 9 pictorial 10 clarifying 11 descriptive 12 iconographic

illustrator *American:* 4 Kent (Rockwell), Pyle (Howard) 5 Abbey (Edwin Austin), Flagg (James Montgomery), Smith (Jessie Willcox), Wyeth (Newell Convers) 6 Gibson (Charles Dana) 7 Burgess (Gelett), Parrish (Maxwell) 8 Rockwell (Norman) 9 Remington (Frederic) *English:* 5 Crane (Walter) 6 Morris (William), Potter (Beatrix) 7 Nielsen (Kay), Rackham (Arthur), Tenniel (John) 9 Beardsley (Aubrey), Caldecott (Randolph), du Maurier (George), Greenaway (Kate) *French:* 4 Doré (Gustave) 5 Dulac (Edmund) *German:* 5 Dürer (Albrecht)

illustrious 5 famed, great, lofty, noted 6 famous 7 eminent, exalted, notable, sublime 8 glorious, renowned, splendid 9 acclaimed, prominent 10 celebrated, preeminent 11 outstanding, prestigious 13 distinguished

illustriousness 4 fame 5 glory 6 renown 8 eminence, prestige 9 celebrity 10 prominence 11 distinction, preeminence

ill will 5 spite, venom 6 animus, enmity, malice, rancor, spleen 7 despite, dislike 8 acrimony, aversion, bad blood 9 animosity, antipathy, malignity 10 resentment 11 malevolence 12 spitefulness 13 maliciousness

Ilus *father:* 4 Tros *grandson:* 5 Priam *mother:* 10 Callirrhoë *son:* 8 Laomedon

image 4 copy, form, icon, idea, idol 5 equal, match 6 double, effigy, figure, mirror, notion, ringer, vision 7 concept, fantasm, feature, picture 8 likeness, phantasm, portrait 9 facsimile, semblance 10 conception, equivalent, impression, reflection, simulacrum 12 illustration *Polynesian:* 4 tiki *Semitic:* 6 teraph 8 teraphim (plural)

imaginary 5 ideal 6 made-up, unreal 7 fancied, fictive 8 abstract, fabulous, fanciful, illusive, illusory, notional, quixotic 9 dreamlike, fantastic, fictional, legendary, visionary 10 apocryphal, chimerical, fictitious, phantasmal 11 make-believe 12 hypothetical, suppositious

imagination 5 fancy 7 fantasy 8 phantasy

9 invention 10 creativity 11 inspiration 13 inventiveness

imaginative 5 false 7 blue-sky, fictive 8 artistic, creative, fanciful, original, poetical 9 ingenious, inventive, visionary, whimsical 11 resourceful 12 enterprising

imagine 5 dream, fancy 6 assume, invent, make up 7 dream up, feature, picture, suspect 8 conceive, envisage, envision 9 fabricate, visualize 10 conjecture

imbecile 4 dodo, dolt, dull, fool, jerk 5 dunce, idiot, moron, ninny 6 cretin, dimwit, nitwit 7 half-wit, jackass, moronic, pinhead, tomfool 8 numskull 9 birdbrain, blockhead, numbskull 10 dunderhead, nincompoop

imbibe 3 sip, sup 4 chug, soak, swig, toss 5 booze, drink, quaff, swill 6 absorb, guzzle, tipple 7 consume, swallow, swizzle 10 assimilate

imbricate 3 lap 7 overlap, shingle 11 overlapping

imbroglio 3 row 4 maze, mess, spat, to-do 5 brawl, mix-up 6 fracas, muddle, tangle 7 dispute, quarrel, rhubarb, scandal, wrangle 8 argument, disorder, squabble 9 confusion, intricacy 10 falling-out 11 altercation, predicament 12 complication, entanglement

imbrue 4 soil 5 stain 8 discolor

imbue 3 dye 4 soak 5 bathe, endow, steep, tinge 6 infuse, invest, leaven 7 ingrain, instill, pervade, suffuse 8 permeate, saturate 9 influence, inoculate

imitate 3 ape 4 copy, echo, mime, mock 5 forge, mimic, spoof 6 parody 7 emulate, take off 8 resemble, simulate, travesty 9 burlesque, duplicate, replicate, reproduce 11 counterfeit, impersonate

imitation 4 copy, fake, mock, sham 5 clone, ditto, dummy, false, match, phony 6 ersatz, parody, ringer 7 forgery, replica 8 likeness, parallel, spurious, travesty 9 duplicate, semblance, simulated 10 artificial, simulacrum, simulation, substitute 11 counterfeit, counterpart 12 reproduction, substitution

imitative 4 mock 5 apish 6 echoic 7 copycat, mimetic, parodic, slavish 11 counterfeit 12 onomatopoeic 13 onomatopoetic

immaculate 4 pure 5 clean 6 chaste, virgin 7 cleanly, perfect, sinless 8 flawless, spotless, unsoiled, virtuous 9 stainless, undefiled, unsullied 11 spic-and-span, unblemished 12 spick-and-span

immaterial 7 trivial 8 bodiless, ethereal 10 extraneous, inapposite, intangible,

irrelevant 11 disembodied, incorporeal, nonphysical, unimportant 12 inapplicable 13 insignificant, insubstantial, unsubstantial

immature 3 raw 5 crude, green, young 6 callow, infant, unripe 7 puerile 8 childish, juvenile, youthful 9 infantile, primitive, unfledged 10 unfinished 11 undeveloped

immaturity 6 nonage 7 infancy 8 minority 9 childhood, salad days 11 adolescence 12 juvenescence

immeasurable 4 vast 6 untold 7 endless 8 infinite 9 boundless, extensive, limitless, unbounded, unlimited 11 illimitable, inestimable, uncountable 12 incalculable, unfathomable

immediate 4 next, nigh 5 close 6 at hand, direct, nearby, urgent 7 current, instant, ongoing, primary 9 firsthand, proximate 10 unmediated 12 straightaway 13 instantaneous

immediately 3 now, PDQ 4 anon, stat 6 at once, presto, pronto 8 directly, promptly 9 forthwith, instanter, instantly, right away 11 straightway 12 straightaway

immense 4 huge, vast 5 great, large 6 mighty 7 mammoth, massive, titanic 8 colossal, enormous, gigantic 9 humongous, monstrous 10 gargantuan, monumental, prodigious, tremendous 11 elephantine

immensely 4 a lot 8 terribly 9 extremely 11 exceedingly 12 inordinately

immensity 8 enormity, hugeness, vastness 9 greatness 12 enormousness

immerse 3 dip 4 duck, dunk, sink, soak 5 bathe, douse 6 drench, engage, plunge 7 baptize, engross, involve 8 saturate, submerge

immigrant 5 alien 7 settler 8 newcomer 10 transplant *Japanese:* 5 issei

imminent 6 at hand 6 coming 7 brewing, nearing, ominous, pending 8 upcoming 9 gathering, proximate 11 approaching, overhanging

immobile 3 set 5 fixed, inert, still 6 frozen, stable, static 9 unmovable 10 motionless, stationary

immobilize 5 still 7 cripple, disable 8 paralyze 9 hamstring 12 incapacitate

immoderate 5 undue 7 extreme 9 excessive 10 exorbitant, inordinate, untempered 11 extravagant, intemperate 12 unreasonable, unrestrained 13 extraordinary, overindulgent

immoderation 6 excess 11 exorbitance, prodigality 12 extravagance, intemperance

immodest 4 lewd, vain 7 stuck-up

8 arrogant, boastful, indecent, puffed-up, unchaste **9** conceited, egotistic **11** pretentious

immolate 4 burn, kill **7** destroy **9** sacrifice

immoral 4 evil, vile **5** dirty, wrong **6** sinful, wanton, wicked **7** corrupt, unclean, vicious **8** depraved, indecent, unchaste **9** dissolute, reprobate, uncleanly **10** degenerate, iniquitous, licentious

immorality 3 sin **4** vice **8** iniquity **9** depravity **10** corruption, unchastity, wickedness

immortal 7 endless, eternal, godlike, undying **8** timeless, unending **9** ceaseless, deathless, perpetual **11** amaranthine, everlasting, sempiternal

immotile 5 fixed, inert **6** rooted, static **9** paralyzed **10** stationary

immovable 3 pat, set **4** fast, firm **5** fixed, rigid **6** rooted, stable **7** adamant **8** constant, obdurate, stubborn **9** steadfast **10** inflexible, invariable, stationary, unyielding

immune 4 free, safe **6** exempt, secure **9** protected **10** impervious **12** invulnerable, unassailable

immunity 7 defense, freedom **9** exemption, privilege **10** protection

immure 3 pen **4** cage, coop, jail, wall **6** entomb, intern, shut in **7** confine, enclose **8** imprison **11** incarcerate

immutable 4 firm **5** fixed **8** constant **9** permanent, steadfast **10** changeless, inflexible, invariable, unchanging **11** inalterable, unalterable **12** unchangeable

Imogen *father:* **9** Cymbeline *husband:* **9** Posthumus

imp 3 elf **4** brat, puck **5** demon, devil, fiend, gamin, gnome, pixie, scamp **6** goblin, kobold, sprite, urchin **7** gremlin **9** hobgoblin

impact 3 hit, jar, rap **4** blow, bump, jolt, rock, slam, slap **5** brunt, embed, pound, punch, shock, smash, smite **6** affect, buffet, strike, wallop **9** collision, influence **10** concussion, percussion

impair 3 mar, sap **4** harm, hurt **5** spoil **6** damage, injure, lessen, weaken, worsen **7** cripple, tarnish, vitiate **8** enfeeble **9** prejudice, undermine **10** debilitate

impala 8 antelope

impale 4 gore, spit, stab **5** lance, prick, spear, spike, stick **6** pierce, skewer **8** puncture, transfix **11** transpierce

impalpable 4 fine **7** powdery **8** ethereal **10** intangible **11** disembodied, incorporeal **12** imponderable **13** imperceptible, indiscernible

impart 4 cede, give, lend, tell **5** grant, share, yield **6** afford, bestow, confer, convey, pass on, relate, render **8** disclose, transmit **11** communicate *knowledge:* **5** teach **6** inform **7** educate **8** instruct

impartial 4 even, fair, just **5** equal **7** neutral **8** detached, unbiased **9** equitable, objective, uncolored **10** evenhanded **12** unprejudiced **13** disinterested, dispassionate

impassable 6 closed **7** blocked **10** obstructed **12** impenetrable

impasse 3 box, fix, jam **6** aporia, corner, logjam, pickle, pocket **7** catch-22, dead end, dilemma **8** cul-de-sac, deadlock, standoff **9** stalemate **10** blind alley, bottleneck

impassioned 3 hot **5** fiery **6** ardent, fervid, fierce, heated, red-hot, torrid **7** blazing, burning, fervent, flaming, intense, violent, zealous **8** feverish, romantic, vehement, white-hot **9** emotional, perfervid **10** hot-blooded, overheated **11** dithyrambic **12** melodramatic **13** overemotional

impassive 4 calm, cold, cool **5** stoic **6** stolid, vacant **7** deadpan **8** composed, hardened, reserved, reticent, taciturn **9** heartless **10** insensible, insentient, phlegmatic, poker-faced **11** cold-blooded, emotionless, insensitive, passionless, unconcerned, unemotional, unexcitable, unflappable **12** inexpressive, unexpressive, unresponsive **13** dispassionate, self-possessed, unsusceptible

impassivity 6 apathy, phlegm **8** stoicism **9** stolidity **12** indifference **13** insensibility

impatient 4 edgy **5** antsy, eager, hasty **7** anxious, fretful, restive **8** restless **9** irascible, irritable **10** intolerant

impeach 5 blame, doubt **6** accuse, charge, indict **7** censure **9** inculpate, reprehend **11** incriminate

impeccable 4 pure **5** exact **7** perfect, precise **8** absolute, accurate, flawless, unerring **9** blameless, errorless, faultless, guiltless **10** infallible **11** unblemished

impecunious 4 poor **5** broke, needy **7** pinched **8** bankrupt, beggarly, indigent **9** destitute, insolvent, penniless, penurious **10** down-and-out **11** necessitous

impecuniousness 4 need, want **6** penury **7** poverty **9** indigence, neediness, pauperism, privation **11** destitution

impedance 3 bar **4** clog **5** block **8** blockage, obstacle **9** hindrance **10** opposition **11** obstruction

impede 3 bar, dam 4 clog, slow 5 block, check, debar, delay, deter, stall 6 hinder, hang up, hold up, stymie, thwart 7 bog down 8 encumber, obstruct 9 embarrass, interfere, stonewall

impediment 3 bar 4 clog, snag 5 block, hitch 6 hurdle 7 barrier 8 obstacle 9 barricade, hindrance, roadblock 10 difficulty 11 encumbrance, obstruction

impel 4 goad, prod, push, spur, urge 5 drive, force, rouse 6 excite, incite, prompt 7 actuate, inspire 8 mobilize, motivate 9 instigate, stimulate

impend 4 loom, near 6 menace 8 approach, overhang, threaten

impenetrable 5 dense 6 arcane 7 obscure 9 enigmatic, recondite 10 impervious, invincible, mysterious, unknowable 11 impermeable, bulletproof, inscrutable, ungraspable 12 unfathomable

imperative 4 duty, need, rule, writ 5 acute, vital 6 crying, urgent 7 burning, clamant, command, crucial, exigent 8 critical, pressing, required 9 clamorous, essential, insistent, mandatory, necessary, necessity, requisite 10 compulsory, obligation, obligatory 11 fundamental, necessitous 12 prerequisite

imperceptible 3 dim 5 faint, vague 6 slight, subtle 7 gradual 9 invisible 10 impalpable, indistinct, insensible, intangible, unapparent 12 undetectable, unnoticeable, unobservable 13 inappreciable, inconspicuous, indiscernible

imperceptive 4 dull 7 shallow, unaware 11 inattentive, insensitive

imperfect 6 faulty, flawed 9 defective, deficient, irregular 10 defeasible, inadequate

imperfection 3 sin 4 flaw, wart 5 fault 6 defect, foible 7 blemish, demerit, failing, frailty 8 weakness 10 deficiency 11 shortcoming

imperial 5 regal, royal 6 kingly, lordly 7 haughty 8 absolute, majestic 9 masterful, sovereign 10 high-handed, peremptory 11 domineering, magisterial, monarchical

imperil 4 risk 6 hazard, menace 7 venture 8 endanger, threaten 10 jeopardize

imperious 5 bossy 6 urgent 7 haughty 8 absolute, arrogant, despotic, dominant 9 arbitrary, masterful 10 autocratic, commanding, high-handed, oppressive, peremptory, tyrannical 11 dictatorial, domineering, heavy-handed, magisterial, overbearing

impermanent 7 passing 8 fleeting, fugitive 9 ephemeral, fugacious, momentary, temporary, transient 10 evanescent, short-lived, transitory

impersonal 4 cold 5 aloof 8 abstract, detached 11 cold-blooded, emotionless 13 dispassionate, unimpassioned

impersonate 3 ape 4 play 5 mimic 6 act out 7 imitate, playact, portray 9 represent 11 counterfeit

impersonator 4 mime 5 actor, mimic 6 mummer, player, ringer 7 actress, copycat 8 thespian

impertinence 3 lip 4 gall, guff, sass 5 brass, cheek 8 audacity, boldness, chutzpah, rudeness, temerity 9 brashness, impudence, insolence 10 brazenness, effrontery, incivility 11 discourtesy, irrelevance

impertinent 4 bold, busy, rude 5 brash, fresh, sassy, saucy 6 brazen, cheeky 7 uncivil 8 insolent, meddling 9 audacious, intrusive, obtrusive, officious 10 inapposite, irrelative, irrelevant, meddlesome 11 ill-mannered 12 discourteous, inapplicable, presumptuous

imperturbability 5 poise 6 aplomb, phlegm 8 calmness, coolness, serenity, stoicism 9 composure, placidity, sangfroid 10 dispassion, equanimity 11 equilibrium, nonchalance 12 tranquillity

imperturbable 4 calm, cool 5 stoic 6 placid, poised, serene, smooth, steady, stolid 7 unmoved 8 composed, tranquil 9 collected, unruffled 10 nonchalant, phlegmatic, unaffected 11 unflappable

impervious 4 safe 6 immune 8 hardened 10 inviolable 12 inaccessible, invulnerable

impetuous 3 hot 4 rash, wild 5 fiery, hasty 6 ardent, fervid, madcap, sudden 8 headlong, vehement, volatile 9 hotheaded, mercurial 10 irrational, passionate 11 precipitant, precipitate, precipitous, spontaneous 13 temperamental

impetus 4 goad, push, spur 5 force 6 motive 8 catalyst, momentum, stimulus 9 incentive, stimulant 10 incitement, motivation 13 encouragement

impinge 5 press 6 border 7 intrude, obtrude 8 encroach

impious 6 sinful, unholy, wicked 7 godless, infidel, profane, secular, ungodly 8 agnostic, apostate 9 atheistic 10 irreverent, unfaithful, unhallowed 11 blasphemous, irreligious, unrighteous 12 iconoclastic, sacrilegious 13 unconsecrated

impish 4 arch 5 elfin 6 elvish 7 playful,

puckish, roguish, waggish 11 mischievous

impishness 7 devilry, roguery, waggery 8 deviltry, mischief 9 devilment 11 roguishness, waggishness

implacable 4 grim 8 ruthless 9 merciless 10 inexorable, unyielding 11 intractable 12 unappeasable

implant 3 fix 4 root 5 embed, graft, infix 6 enroot, infuse, insert 7 ingrain, inspire, instill 9 establish, inculcate, inoculate, introduce 10 inseminate 12 augmentation

implausible 5 fishy 6 flimsy 7 dubious, suspect 8 doubtful, fanciful, unlikely 10 far-fetched, incredible 12 questionable, unbelievable, unconvincing

implement 4 tool 6 device, effect, enable, gadget 7 enforce, execute, fulfill, perform, realize, utensil 8 carry out, complete, make good 9 actualize, apparatus, appliance 10 accomplish, instrument, supplement 11 contraption, contrivance *carpentry:* 3 die, saw 4 file 5 brace, clamp, drill, punch, tongs 6 chisel, hammer, pliers, reamer, sander, wrench 7 hacksaw, scraper 9 blowtorch 11 screwdriver *cleaning:* 3 mop 5 broom, brush, whisk 6 duster, vacuum 7 sweeper 10 whiskbroom *cutting:* 5 knife, mower, razor 6 scythe, shears, sickle 8 scissors *digging:* 5 spade 6 dibber, dibble, shovel *drawing:* 3 pen 6 eraser, pencil 7 compass 8 template *eating:* 4 fork 5 knife, spoon *engraving:* 5 burin 6 graver *farm:* 4 plow 6 binder, harrow, plough, scythe, seeder, sickle 8 gangplow, reaphook, spreader, thresher 9 pitchfork 10 cultivator *fireplace:* 5 poker, tongs 7 andiron *fishing:* 3 rod 4 hook, lure, reel 6 sinker 7 harpoon, trident *garden:* 3 hoe 4 rake 5 spade 6 dibber, dibble, digger, tiller, trowel 7 mattock 11 wheelbarrow *grooming:* 4 comb, file 5 brush, razor 7 clipper 8 clippers, nail file, tweezers 10 toothbrush *kitchen:* 3 pan, pot 4 mold 5 mixer, whisk 6 grater, kettle, mortar, pestle 7 blender, skillet, spatula 8 colander, saucepan, stockpot *logging:* 5 peavy 6 peavey 8 cant hook *measuring:* 3 cup 4 gage, rule 5 gauge, ruler, scale 7 caliper, divider, trammel, T-square 10 micrometer, protractor *stone:* 5 burin 7 neolith 9 paleolith

implicate 4 link, mire 5 blame 6 tangle 7 concern, embroil, entwine, include, involve 8 entangle, intimate 11 incriminate

implication 4 hint 8 allusion, overtone 9 inference, undertone 10 connection,

intimation, suggestion 11 association, connotation 12 significance

implicit 5 tacit 6 unsaid 8 inherent, unspoken 9 doubtless, potential, unuttered 10 undeclared, understood 11 unexpressed 13 unquestioning

implied 5 tacit 6 unsaid 8 unspoken 9 suggested 10 undeclared, understood 11 unexpressed

implore 3 ask, beg 4 coax, pray 5 crave, plead 6 adjure, appeal 7 beseech, entreat, solicit 10 supplicate

imply 4 hint, mean 7 connote, include, involve, signify, suggest 8 indicate, intimate 9 insinuate

impolite 4 rude 5 crude 7 ill-bred, uncivil, uncouth 10 ungracious, unladylike, unmannered, unmannerly 11 ill-mannered 12 discourteous 13 ungentlemanly

impolitic 5 brash 6 unwise 8 tactless 9 imprudent, maladroit, untactful 10 ill-advised, indiscreet 11 inadvisable, inexpedient, injudicious 12 shortsighted, undiplomatic

import 4 bear, gist, mean, pith 5 sense, value, worth 6 convey, denote, intend, intent, matter, moment, stress, thrust, weight 7 concern, connote, express, meaning, message, purpose, signify 8 emphasis, indicate, transfer 9 magnitude, substance 10 intendment 11 acceptation, consequence 12 significance 13 signification

importance 4 mark, note, pith 5 value, worth 6 moment, weight 7 account, gravity 8 eminence, priority, salience, standing 9 greatness, magnitude, substance 10 prominence, worthiness 11 consequence, distinction, seriousness, weightiness 12 significance

important 3 big 5 chief, grave, great, heavy, major, noted, vital 6 famous, marked, potent, urgent, worthy 7 bigtime, capital, crucial, eminent, fateful, notable, salient, serious, telling, weighty 8 critical, eventful, foremost, material, powerful, pressing, valuable 9 essential, estimable, imperious, memorable, momentous, prominent 10 meaningful, noteworthy, preeminent, worthwhile 11 outstanding, significant, substantial 12 considerable 13 consequential, distinguished, indispensable

importune 3 beg 4 pray, urge 5 annoy, plead, worry 6 appeal, invoke, plague 7 beseech, besiege, entreat, solicit, trouble 8 petition

impose 3 fob 4 lade, levy 5 abuse, enact, exact, foist, force, order, place, put on, visit, wreak **6** assess, burden, charge, compel, decree, demand, enjoin, fob off, ordain, saddle **7** command, dictate, exploit, inflict, intrude, lay down, obtrude, palm off, pass off, require **8** encroach, encumber, infringe, trespass **9** authorize, constrain, establish

imposing 4 huge **5** grand, noble, regal, royal **6** august **7** awesome, massive, pompous, stately **8** baronial, majestic, towering **9** dignified **10** commanding, monumental **11** magnificent, outstanding **12** high-sounding **13** distinguished

imposition 3 tax **4** duty, fine, levy **6** burden, demand **7** penalty **9** deception **13** inconvenience

impossible 6 absurd **8** hopeless **10** infeasible, unfeasible, unworkable **11** unthinkable **12** preposterous, unacceptable, unattainable, unbelievable, unimaginable, unrealizable, unreasonable **13** inconceivable

impost 3 fee, tax **4** duty, levy, toll **6** charge, tariff **7** tribute **9** surcharge **10** assessment

impostor 4 fake, sham **5** actor, cheat, faker, fraud, mimic, phony, poser, quack **6** humbug, poseur **8** deceiver **9** charlatan, con artist, hypocrite, pretender **10** dissembler, mountebank **11** masquerader **12** impersonator

imposture 4 fake, hoax, sell, sham, wile **5** cheat, fraud **6** deceit, humbug **8** flimflam **9** deception, mare's nest, stratagem **11** counterfeit

impotence 8 weakness **9** sterility **10** inadequacy **12** helplessness **13** powerlessness

impotent 4 lame, weak **6** effete, feeble **7** sterile **8** helpless **9** forceless, incapable, powerless **11** ineffective, ineffectual **12** invertebrate

impound 5 seize **6** immure, lock up **7** confine, enclose, put away **8** imprison **10** confiscate

impoverish 4 bust, ruin **5** break **6** beggar **8** bankrupt **9** pauperize

impoverished 4 poor **5** broke, needy **8** bankrupt, indigent **9** destitute, penniless, penurious

impoverishment 4 need, want **6** penury **9** indigence, neediness, privation **11** destitution

impracticable 8 unusable **10** infeasible, unfeasible, unworkable **11** insuperable, unrealistic **12** inaccessible, unattainable

impractical 7 utopian **8** quixotic, romantic, unusable **9** visionary **10** idealistic, infeasible, ivory-tower, starry-eyed, unfeasible, unworkable **11** theoretical, unrealistic

imprecation 3 hex **4** cuss **5** curse **7** malison **8** anathema **11** malediction

imprecise 5 rough, vague **7** inexact **9** estimated **10** indefinite **11** approximate, unspecified

impregnable 4 safe **6** immune, secure **9** protected **10** invincible, inviolable, unbeatable **11** indomitable, insuperable **12** unassailable **13** unconquerable

impregnate 3 sop **4** fill, soak **5** imbue, souse, steep **6** drench, infuse **7** pervade **8** conceive, permeate, saturate **9** fecundate, fertilize, penetrate, transfuse **10** inseminate

impresario 4 Bing (Rudolf) **5** Carte (Richard D'Oyly), Hurok (Sol) **6** Pastor (Tony) **7** manager **8** director, Kirstein (Lincoln), producer, promoter **9** Diaghilev (Sergei) **10** D'Oyly Carte (Richard)

impress 3 fix, set **4** dent, etch, mark, move, seal, sway **5** brand, carry, drive, exert, force, grave, infix, print, stamp, touch **6** affect, effect, excite, strike **7** engrave, ingrain, inspire **8** inscribe, transfer, transmit **9** establish, influence, stimulate

impressible 8 gullible, immature, moldable **9** malleable, receptive, sensitive **10** affectable, susceptive, vulnerable **11** persuadable, suggestible, susceptible

impression 4 dent, idea, mark, sign **5** image, print, stamp, trace, track **6** effect, hollow, notion **7** concept, edition, feeling, reissue, thought, vestige **8** printing, reaction **9** influence

impressionable 8 sensible, sentient **9** malleable, receptive, sensitive **10** responsive **11** suggestible, susceptible

impressionist *composer:* **5** Ravel (Maurice) **7** Debussy (Claude) *mimic:* **6** Carvey (Dana), Little (Rich) *painter:* **5** Degas (Edgar), Manet (Edouard), Monet (Claude) **6** Renoir (Auguste), Sisley (Alfred) **7** Cassatt (Mary), Morisot (Berthe) **8** Pissarro (Camille) (see also POSTIMPRESSIONIST)

impressive 5 grand, noble **6** moving, superb **7** amazing, awesome, notable, stately, sublime **8** dazzling, dramatic, gorgeous, majestic, powerful, splendid, stirring, striking, touching **9** admirable, affecting, arresting, inspiring **11** magnificent

imprimatur 6 permit **7** license **8** approval, sanction **10** permission **13** authorization

imprint 3 fix **4** dent, etch, mark **5** grave, press, stamp **6** dimple, effect **7** engrave **8** inscribe **9** engraving, influence

10 depression 11 indentation, inscription

imprison 3 jug 4 cage, jail 6 coop up, detain, immure, intern, send up 7 confine, enclose 8 restrain, restrict, stockade 9 constrain 11 incarcerate

improbable 5 fishy 7 dubious 8 doubtful, fanciful, unlikely 10 far-fetched 11 implausible

impromptu 5 ad-lib 7 offhand 9 extempore, makeshift, unplanned, unstudied 10 off-the-cuff, unprepared, unscripted 11 extemporary, spontaneous, unrehearsed

improper 5 inapt, inept, outré, undue, wrong 6 gauche, risqué 7 illicit, naughty 8 ill-timed, indecent, tactless, unseemly, untimely, untoward 9 incorrect, unethical, unfitting 10 inaccurate, inapposite, indecorous, indelicate, malapropos, unbecoming, undecorous, unsuitable 11 impertinent, unbefitting 12 illegitimate, inadmissible, inapplicable, infelicitous, unseasonable 13 inappropriate

impropriety 5 gaffe 7 blooper, blunder, faux pas 8 solecism 9 barbarism, gaucherie, indecorum, vulgarism 12 unseemliness 13 incorrectness

improve 4 edit, help, mend 5 amend, boost, edify, emend, raise 6 better, enrich, look up, perk up, refine, reform, remedy, revise, revive, uplift 7 advance, amplify, augment, build up, correct, develop, enhance, enlarge, further, perfect, recover, rectify, upgrade 8 increase, progress 9 cultivate, intensify, meliorate 10 aggrandize, ameliorate, recuperate, strengthen

improvident 4 rash 6 lavish 8 careless, feckless, heedless, prodigal, reckless, wasteful 9 impetuous, negligent, unthrifty 10 profligate 11 extravagant, spendthrift 12 shortsighted, uneconomical

improvise 5 ad-lib 6 cook up, invent, make up 7 concoct 8 contrive 9 fabricate 11 extemporize

improvised 7 offhand 9 extempore, unstudied 10 off-the-cuff, unprepared, unscripted 11 extemporary, unrehearsed

imprudent 4 rash 6 unwise 7 foolish 8 reckless 9 foolhardy 10 ill-advised, incautious, indiscreet 11 inadvisable, inexpedient, injudicious 12 shortsighted

impudence 4 gall 5 brass, cheek, nerve 8 audacity, boldness, chutzpah, temerity 9 brashness, cockiness, hardihood, insolence, nerviness 10 disrespect, effrontery 11 presumption

impudent 4 bold, flip, pert, wise 5 brash, cocky, fresh, nervy, sassy, saucy, smart 6 brassy, brazen, cheeky 7 blatant, forward 8 flippant, insolent, overbold 9 audacious, barefaced, bold-faced 11 brazen-faced, smart-alecky 12 contumelious 13 disrespectful

impugn 5 cross 6 assail, attack, defame, malign, oppose, vilify 7 asperse, gainsay, impeach 8 chastise, reproach, traverse 9 castigate, denigrate, deprecate, disparage, reprehend 9 criticize, denigrate

impugnable 5 fishy, shady 6 guilty 7 suspect 8 doubtful 9 equivocal, uncertain 10 assailable, suspicious 11 problematic 12 disreputable

impulse 4 goad, push, spur, urge, whim 5 drive, force 6 motive, thrust, whimsy 7 caprice, passion 8 catalyst, excitant, stimulus 9 actuation, incentive, stimulant 10 incitation, incitement, motivation 11 inspiration, instigation

impulsive 4 rash 5 hasty 6 abrupt, fickle, sudden 7 erratic, flighty, offhand 8 headlong, volatile 9 automatic, extempore, mercurial, unplanned, whimsical 10 capricious 11 instinctive, involuntary, precipitate, spontaneous

impunity 7 freedom, liberty, license 8 immunity 9 exception, exemption, indemnity, privilege 10 absolution, protection 12 dispensation

impure 3 raw 5 mixed 6 soiled, sordid, unholy 7 alloyed, defiled, profane, sullied, unclean 8 indecent, polluted, unchaste 9 uncleanly, unrefined 10 desecrated, unhallowed 11 adulterated

impute 3 lay 4 cite 5 blame, refer 6 accuse, adduce, assign, charge, credit, indict 7 ascribe 8 accredit 9 attribute, implicate

inaccessible 5 aloof 6 arcane, closed, far-off, remote 7 cryptic, distant, faraway, obscure 8 abstruse, esoteric, hermetic 9 recondite 11 unavailable, unreachable 12 unattainable, unobtainable

inaccurate 5 false, wrong 6 all wet, faulty, untrue 7 unsound 8 specious 9 distorted, erroneous 10 fictitious

inaction 6 repose 7 latency 8 dormancy, idleness, lethargy 9 indolence, passivity, slackness, torpidity 10 quiescence 12 slothfulness

inactive 4 idle, lazy 5 inert, quiet, slack, still 6 asleep, latent, sleepy, static, torpid 7 abeyant, dormant, passive, resting 8 slothful, sluggish 9 do-nothing, lethargic, quiescent, sedentary

in addition 4 also 6 as well, to boot,

withal 7 besides, further 8 moreover 11 furthermore

inadequacy 4 lack, want 6 dearth 7 deficit, failure, paucity 8 shortage, weakness 9 impotence 10 deficiency, scantiness 11 shortcoming

inadequate 3 shy 5 scant, short 6 meager, scanty, scarce, skimpy 7 lacking, scrimpy, wanting 8 impotent 9 defective, deficient 10 emasculate

inadmissible 5 unapt, unfit 8 unusable, unworthy 9 unwelcome 10 unsuitable 11 unqualified 12 unacceptable

inadvertent 8 careless, heedless 9 negligent, unmindful, unplanned, unwitting 10 accidental, unintended, unthinking 13 unintentional

inadvisable 4 rash 6 unwise 7 foolish 8 careless, reckless 9 foolhardy, impolitic, imprudent, pointless 10 illadvised 11 harebrained

inalterable 5 fixed 6 stable 8 constant 9 immovable, immutable, steadfast, unmovable, unvarying 12 unchangeable

inamorata, inamorato 4 beau, dear 5 flame, honey, lover 6 steady 7 beloved, darling, squeeze, sweetie 8 ladylove, mistress, paramour, truelove 9 boyfriend 10 girlfriend, heartthrob, sweetheart

inane 4 flat, idle, vain 5 blank, dotty, empty, silly, vapid 6 absurd, hollow, jejune, vacant 7 asinine, fatuous, foolish, idiotic, insipid, lunatic, trivial, vacuous, witless 8 mindless 9 frivolous, pointless, senseless

inanimate 4 dead, dull 5 inert 5 still 6 asleep, torpid 7 dormant 8 immotile, lifeless 9 quiescent 10 motionless 11 unconscious

inanity 5 folly 6 idiocy, lunacy 7 fatuity, vacuity 8 vapidity 9 absurdity, dottiness, emptiness, silliness 10 hollowness 11 foolishness, vacuousness, witlessness 13 senselessness

inappreciable 6 meager, scanty, skimpy, slight 10 impalpable, unapparent 13 imperceptible

inappropriate 5 amiss, undue, unfit 6 unmeet 8 improper, unseemly, untimely, untoward 9 ill-suited 10 malapropos, unsuitable 11 impertinent

inapt 5 unfit 6 clumsy, gauche, jejune, unmeet 7 awkward, unhandy 8 improper, unfitted, unsuited, untimely 9 maladroit, unfitting, unskilled 10 amateurish, irrelevant, malapropos, unskillful, unsuitable

inarticulate 4 dumb, mute 5 tacit 6 silent 7 halting, unvocal 8 mumbling, unspoken, wordless 9 voiceless 10 maundering, speechless, tongue-tied, undeclared 11 unexpressed

inasmuch as 5 since 7 because, whereas 11 considering

inattentive 6 absent, remiss 8 distrait, heedless 9 forgetful, negligent, unheeding, unmindful 10 abstracted, distracted, unthinking 12 absentminded

inaugural 5 first 6 maiden, speech 7 address, initial, leading, opening, premier 8 foremost 9 beginning

inaugurate 5 begin, set up, start 6 launch 7 kick off 8 commence, dedicate, initiate 9 establish, institute, originate 10 consecrate

inauspicious 4 dire 7 adverse, baleful, direful, fateful, ominous, unlucky 8 sinister 9 ill-boding 11 threatening, unfavorable, unpromising 12 unpropitious

inborn 6 innate, native 7 connate, natural 8 inherent 9 intrinsic 10 congenital, connatural, hereditary, unacquired

inbred 7 connate, genetic, natural 8 inherent 9 intrinsic 10 congenital, connatural, deep-seated, hereditary

Inca *capital:* 5 Cuzco *conqueror:* 7 Pizarro (Francisco) *god:* 4 Inti 9 Viracocha 10 Pachacamac *language:* 7 Quechua *record:* 5 quipu *ruler:* 9 Atahualpa, Pachacuti 10 Atahuallpa

incalculable 4 huge, iffy, vast 6 untold 8 enormous 9 boundless, countless, limitless, uncertain 10 tremendous, unnumbered 11 illimitable, measureless, uncountable 12 immeasurable, unmeasurable 13 unpredictable

in camera 7 privily, sub rosa 8 covertly, secretly 9 furtively, privately 10 stealthily 13 clandestinely

incandescent 3 hot 5 lucid 6 ardent, bright, lucent 7 beaming, fulgent, glowing, intense, lambent, radiant 8 dazzling, luminous 9 brilliant, effulgent, refulgent 11 resplendent

incantation 3 hex 4 rune 5 chant, charm, magic, spell 10 hocus-pocus, mumbojumbo, necromancy 11 abracadabra, conjuration, enchantment *Buddhist, Hindu:* 6 mantra

incapable 5 unfit 6 unable 8 impotent, unexpert, unfitted 9 powerless, unskilled 10 unequipped, unskillful 11 unqualified 12 disqualified

incapacitate 6 disarm 7 cripple, disable 8 paralyze 10 debilitate, devitalize, disqualify, immobilize

incapacity 9 impotence, unfitness 10 impairment 11 disablement 12 fecklessness

incarcerate 3 jug 4 jail 6 coop up, immure, intern, send up 7 confine, enclose, impound 8 imprison

incarnadine 3 red 4 rosy 5 ruddy 6 redden 7 pinkish 8 bloodred

incarnate 5 human, reify 6 embody 7 realize 8 embodied, manifest 9 actualize, corporeal, personify 11 materialize, personalize 12 substantiate

incarnation 6 avatar 10 embodiment 11 reification *of Christ:* 7 kenosis

incautious 4 rash 5 brash, hasty 6 daring, madcap, unwary 8 careless, heedless, reckless 9 daredevil, foolhardy, impetuous, imprudent, negligent, unmindful 10 ill-advised, neglectful, regardless 11 precipitate, thoughtless

incendiary 5 fiery, torch 7 firebug 8 agitator, arsonist, arsonous 9 explosive, firebrand, ignitable 10 pyromaniac 12 pyromaniacal

incense 3 ire, mad, oil 4 balm, burn, rile 5 anger, aroma, scent, spice 6 arouse, enrage, homage, incite, madden 7 inflame, provoke 8 irritate 9 infuriate *vessel:* 6 censer 8 thurible

incentive 4 goad, spur 5 spark 6 motive 7 impetus, impulse 8 catalyst, stimulus 9 stimulant 10 inducement, motivation 11 provocation 13 encouragement

inception 4 root 5 birth, start 6 origin, outset, source 7 genesis, kickoff, opening 9 beginning 10 derivation, provenance 11 provenience 12 commencement

inceptive 7 initial, leadoff, nascent 9 beginning 10 initiatory

incertitude 5 doubt 7 dubiety 8 mistrust 9 suspicion 10 skepticism 11 dubiousness, uncertainty, vacillation 12 irresolution

incessant 6 steady 7 endless, eternal, nonstop 8 constant 9 ceaseless, continual, perpetual, unceasing 10 continuous 11 everlasting, unremitting 12 interminable 13 uninterrupted

inch 3 bit 5 crawl, creep 7 modicum

inchoate 8 formless, immature, unformed, unshaped 9 amorphous, embryonic, incipient, potential, shapeless 10 disjointed, incoherent 11 rudimentary, unorganized 12 disconnected

incident 5 event 6 moment 7 episode 8 occasion 9 ancillary, attendant, happening, satellite 10 affiliated, collateral, consequent, occurrence 11 concomitant, subordinate 12 circumstance

incidental 5 fluky, minor 6 casual, chance 9 accessory 10 contingent, fortuitous 11 subordinate 12 nonessential

incidentally 7 by the by 8 by the bye, by the way, casually 12 fortuitously

incinerate 4 burn 7 cremate

incipient 7 nascent 9 beginning, embryonic 10 commencing

incipit 5 start 7 opening 9 beginning

incise 3 cut 4 etch, gash, kerf, slit 5 carve, slash, slice 6 chisel, pierce 7 engrave

incision 3 cut 4 gash, slit 5 blaze, notch 10 laceration

incisive 4 keen 5 acute, crisp, sharp, terse 6 direct 7 cutting, mordant 8 clear-cut, piercing, slashing, succinct 9 trenchant 11 penetrating 13 perspicacious

incite 3 egg 4 abet, goad, prod, spur, urge 5 egg on, raise, rouse, set on 6 arouse, exhort, foment, kindle, set off, spur on, stir up, whip up 7 actuate, agitate, provoke, trigger 8 motivate 9 instigate, stimulate

incitement see INCENTIVE

inclement 3 raw 5 harsh, rough 6 bitter, brutal, severe, stormy 8 rigorous

inclination 3 bow, nod 4 bent, bias, lean, tilt, will 5 fancy, grade, pitch, slant, slope, taste, trend 6 ascent, liking 7 descent, incline, leaning 8 affinity, appetite, fondness, gradient, penchant, soft spot, tendency, velleity, weakness 9 affection 10 attachment, partiality, proclivity, propensity 11 disposition 12 predilection

incline 3 tip 4 bend, bias, cant, cast, heel, lean, list, sway, tend, tilt, turn 5 grade, impel, slant, slide, slope 6 affect, induce 7 dispose, leaning 8 gradient, persuade 9 influence, prejudice

inclined 3 apt 5 given, prone, raked 6 liable, likely, minded 7 dipping, leaning, oblique, sloping, tilting, willing 8 diagonal, pitching 11 predisposed *way:* 4 ramp

include 5 admit, bound, cover 6 enfold, number, take in 7 confine, contain, embrace, enclose, receive, subsume 8 comprise, encircle 9 encompass 10 comprehend 11 accommodate

inclusive 5 broad 6 global 7 general, overall 8 complete, sweeping 9 allaround, embracive 11 compendious 12 encompassing, encyclopedic 13 comprehensive

incognito 6 veiled 7 cloaked 9 anonymous, disguised 11 camouflaged

incognizant 7 unaware 8 ignorant 9 oblivious, unknowing, unmindful, unwitting 10 unfamiliar, uninformed 11 unconscious 12 unacquainted

incoherent 5 loose 6 broken, raving

7 muddled, unclear 8 confused 9 illogical 10 disjointed, disordered, irrational, maundering, tongue-tied 11 unconnected, unorganized 12 disconnected, disorganized 13 discontinuous

incombustible 9 fireproof 10 unburnable 12 nonflammable

income 4 gain, take 5 wages 6 profit 7 revenue 8 entrance, proceeds, receipts 9 emolument

incommode 3 irk, vex 5 annoy, upset 6 bother, burden, hinder, plague, put out 7 disturb, perturb, trouble 8 disquiet, distress, irritate 9 disoblige 10 disconcert

incommodious 7 awkward, cramped, crowded 8 confined 9 congested

incommunicable 8 reserved, taciturn 9 ineffable, withdrawn 11 unspeakable, unutterable 13 undescribable, unexpressible

incomparable 6 unique 7 supreme 8 peerless, singular, ultimate 9 matchless, nonpareil, paramount, unequaled, unmatched, unrivaled 10 preeminent, surpassing, unequalled, unrivalled 11 outstanding, superlative, unequalable, unmatchable 12 transcendent, unparalleled 13 unsurpassable

incompatible 7 adverse, counter 8 contrary, opposite 9 dissonant, unmixable 10 discordant, discrepant 11 conflicting, disagreeing, uncongenial, unfavorable 12 antagonistic, antithetical 13 contradictory, unsympathetic

incompetence 9 unfitness 10 disability, ineptitude 12 fecklessness

incompetent 5 inept, unfit 6 clumsy 8 helpless, inexpert, unfitted 9 incapable, maladroit, unskilled 10 unequipped 11 inefficient, unqualified

incomplete 4 part 5 short 6 broken, undone 7 partial, sketchy 8 abridged, immature 9 truncated 10 unfinished 11 fragmentary

incompliant 5 rigid, stiff 6 mulish 7 defiant 8 perverse, stubborn 9 obstinate, pigheaded, resistant, unbending 10 bullheaded, headstrong, inflexible, self-willed, unyielding 11 intractable 12 pertinacious, recalcitrant

incomprehensible 7 cryptic, obscure, unclear 8 abstruse, baffling, esoteric 9 fathomless, mysterious, mystifying, unknowable 11 ungraspable 12 impenetrable, unfathomable, unimaginable

inconceivable 10 improbable, unknowable 11 implausible, unthinkable 12 unbelievable, unconvincing, unimaginable

in conclusion 6 lastly 7 finally

inconclusive 4 open 9 equivocal, uncertain, undecided, unsettled 10 unfinished

incongruous 5 alien 6 absurd 7 foreign, variant 9 anomalous, dissonant 10 discordant, discrepant, unsuitable 11 conflicting, disagreeing 12 disconsonant

inconsequential 5 petty, small 6 measly, paltry 7 trivial 8 picayune, trifling 9 illogical, small-time 10 immaterial, irrelevant, negligible 11 impertinent, superficial, unimportant

inconsiderable 4 puny 5 minor, petty 6 meager, meagre, paltry, scanty, skimpy, slight 7 scrimpy, trivial 8 picayune, trifling 9 frivolous, smallbeer 10 negligible 11 unimportant

inconsiderate 4 rash 5 brash, hasty 6 unkind 8 careless, heedless, impolite, reckless 9 hotheaded, impulsive 10 illadvised, ungracious 11 precipitate, thoughtless 12 discourteous, uncharitable

inconsistent 6 fickle 8 contrary 9 dissonant, illogical, mercurial 10 capricious, changeable, discordant, discrepant 11 conflicting 13 contradictory

inconsolable 7 forlorn 8 desolate 9 heartsick 11 comfortless, heartbroken

inconspicuous 6 hidden, subtle 7 obscure 9 concealed 11 unobtrusive 12 unnoticeable

inconstant 6 fickle, untrue 7 erratic, mutable, protean, vagrant 8 unstable, unsteady, variable, volatile, wavering 9 changeful, faithless, fluctuant, irregular, mercurial, uncertain, unsettled 10 capricious, changeable, irresolute, perfidious, unfaithful 11 chameleonic, vacillating 13 temperamental

incontestable 4 sure 7 certain 8 absolute, clear-cut, ironclad, positive 9 apodictic, undoubted 10 conclusive, inarguable, undeniable 11 irrefutable, unequivocal 12 unassailable, undisputable 13 unimpeachable

incontinent 5 loose 6 wanton 9 dissolute 10 licentious, profligate 12 unrestrained

incontrovertible 4 sure 7 certain 8 absolute, clear-cut, definite, positive 10 conclusive, undeniable 11 irrefutable, unequivocal 12 undisputable

inconvenience 3 irk, vex 5 annoy 6 bother, meddle, put out 7 disrupt, disturb, trouble 8 handicap, vexation 9 aggravate, annoyance, disoblige 10 discomfort, discommode, disruption, exasperate 11 aggravation, awkwardness 12 disadvantage, discomfiture, exasperation 13 embarrassment

inconvenient 7 awkward, unhandy
8 annoying 10 bothersome, unsuitable
11 pestiferous, troublesome

incorporate 3 mix 4 form, fuse, join
5 blend, merge, unite 6 absorb,
embody, imbibe, mingle 7 combine
8 organize 9 establish 10 amalgamate,
assimilate

incorporeal 8 bodiless, formless 9 spiritual 10 discarnate, immaterial, unphysical 11 disembodied, nonmaterial, nonphysical 12 metaphysical
13 unsubstantial

incorrect 5 false, wrong 6 faulty, untrue
7 unsound 8 improper, specious 9 erroneous, imprecise 10 fallacious, inaccurate, unbecoming

incorrigible 6 unruly 8 depraved 9 incurable 10 delinquent, inveterate 11 unalterable 12 irredeemable

increase 3 add, eke, wax 4 gain, grow,
hike, jump, plus, push, rise, teem
5 boost, build, mount, put up, raise,
run up, surge, swarm, swell 6 accrue,
amount, beef up, dilate, expand,
extend, gather, growth, jack up,
markup 7 accrual, advance, amplify,
augment, burgeon, distend, enhance,
enlarge, inflate, magnify, prolong,
upsurge 8 addition, compound, escalate, flourish, heighten, lengthen, manifold, multiply, protract, snowball
9 accession, accretion, aggravate,
expansion, extension, increment, inflation, intensify, pullulate, reinforce
10 accelerate, accumulate, aggrandize,
appreciate, strengthen 11 enlargement
12 augmentation, breakthrough
13 amplification

incredible 7 amazing, awesome 8 unlikely 9 cockamamy, fantastic 10 astounding, cockamamie, far-fetched,
impossible, improbable, outlandish,
phenomenal, remarkable 11 astonishing, implausible 12 preposterous, unbelievable, unconvincing, unimaginable
13 extraordinary

incredulity 7 unfaith 8 distrust, mistrust,
unbelief 9 disbelief, nonbelief, suspicion 10 skepticism

incredulous 6 show-me 7 dubious
8 doubting 9 quizzical, skeptical 10 suspicious 11 distrustful, mistrustful,
questioning, unbelieving, unconvinced
12 disbelieving

increment 4 gain, hike, rise, step 5 raise
6 degree, growth 7 quantum 8 addition
9 accession, accretion 11 enlargement
12 augmentation

incriminate 6 accuse, charge 7 arraign,
impeach 9 implicate

incrustation 4 film, rime, scab 5 scale
6 tartar 7 coating

incubus 5 demon, fiend 9 nightmare

inculcate 5 teach, train 6 impart 7 educate, implant, impress, instill

inculpable 4 pure 5 clean 8 innocent,
spotless, virtuous 9 blameless, guiltless,
righteous 10 impeccable

incumbent 7 leaning, resting 8 occupant,
required 9 overlying 10 obligatory
12 officeholder

incur 7 acquire, bring on 8 contract

incurable 5 fatal 6 deadly, lethal 8 hopeless, terminal 9 immutable 11 immedicable, irreparable 12 irremediable,
unchangeable 13 uncorrectable

incursion 4 raid 5 blitz, foray, sally
6 attack, sortie 7 assault 9 irruption

incus 4 bone 5 anvil

indebted 5 bound 7 obliged 8 beholden
9 obligated

indebtedness 3 due, IOU 7 arrears
9 arrearage, gratitude, liability 10 obligation 11 delinquency 12 thankfulness

indecent 4 blue, foul, lewd, racy
5 bawdy, dirty, gross, nasty 6 coarse,
filthy, impure, risqué, smutty, vulgar
7 obscene, profane, raunchy 8 immodest, improper, off-color, unseemly,
untoward 9 offensive 10 malodorous,
scurrilous 12 scatological 13 objectionable

indecision 5 doubt 8 wavering 9 hesitancy 11 ambivalence, uncertainty, vacillation 12 equivocation, irresolution,
shilly-shally

indecisive 5 vague 6 unsure 7 dubious,
unclear 8 wavering 9 equivocal, tentative, uncertain, undecided, unsettled
10 irresolute 11 problematic, vacillating

indecorous 4 rude 5 gross, rough
6 coarse, vulgar 7 uncivil 8 impolite,
improper, unseemly, untoward 9 graceless, irregular, offensive, tasteless, unrefined 10 unbecoming 11 ill-mannered,
undignified 12 discourteous

indecorum 5 gaffe 6 breach 7 blooper,
blunder, faux pas, offense 8 solecism
11 impropriety

indeed 4 amen 5 truly 6 really, surely,
verily 8 forsooth, honestly 9 assuredly,
certainly 10 positively, undeniably
11 doubtlessly, undoubtedly
13 unequivocally

indefatigable 6 dogged 8 tireless, untiring, vigorous 9 energetic, tenacious
10 persistent, relentless, unflagging,
unwearying 11 unrelenting

indefensible 9 unguarded, untenable
10 assailable, vulnerable 11 unpro-

tected **12** unforgivable, unpardonable
13 unjustifiable
indefinable 5 vague **7** elusive **9** uncertain
11 unspeakable, unutterable **13** undescribable
indefinite 4 wide **5** broad, loose, vague
7 endless, general, inexact, obscure,
unclear, unfixed **8** infinite **9** ambiguous, boundless, imprecise, limitless,
unbounded, uncertain, undefined,
unlimited **10** indistinct, inexplicit,
unmeasured, unspecific **12** inconclusive
13 indeterminate *pronoun:* **3** all, any,
few **4** each, many, most, none, some
6 anyone, nobody **7** anybody, several,
someone **8** everyone, somebody
9 everybody
indehiscent fruit 3 key, nut **4** pepo
5 berry, grain, grape, melon **6** achene,
loment, samara, squash **7** pumpkin
8 cucumber **9** caryopsis **10** schizocarp
indelible 4 fast **5** fixed **7** lasting **8** enduring **9** memorable, permanent **13** unforgettable
indelicate 3 raw **4** lewd, rude **5** crude,
gross, rough **6** coarse, vulgar **7** uncouth
8 impolite, improper, tactless, unseemly,
untoward **9** unrefined **10** unbecoming
indemnify 5 repay **6** secure **7** redress,
requite **9** reimburse **10** compensate,
recompense, remunerate
indemnity 6 amends **7** redress **8** requital,
security **9** exemption, quittance, reprisals **10** protection, recompense, reparation **11** restitution **12** compensation,
remuneration **13** fee-for-service
indentation 4 dent, nick **5** notch **6** dimple, recess **10** depression
indenture 4 nick **5** notch **8** contract
9 agreement **11** certificate
indentured 5 bound **10** controlled
11 apprenticed
independent 4 free **8** absolute, autarkic,
separate **9** autarchic, sovereign
10 autonomous **11** self-reliant **13** self-
contained
indescribable 11 unspeakable, unutterable **13** unexplainable
indestructible 7 lasting **8** enduring,
immortal **9** permanent **12** imperishable,
irrefragable, unperishable
indeterminate 5 vague **9** imprecise,
uncertain, unlimited
index 4 list, mark, sign **5** ratio, table
7 catalog, symptom **8** classify, evidence,
regulate **9** catalogue **11** systematize
India *bay:* **6** Bengal *capital:* **8** New Delhi
city: **5** Delhi **6** Bombay, Kanpur,
Madras, Mumbai, Nagpur **7** Chennai,
Kolkata, Lucknow **8** Calcutta **9** Ahmadabad, Bangalore, Hyderabad *coast:*

7 Malabar **10** Coromandel *European discoverer:* **4** Gama (Vasco da) *language:*
5 Hindi *leader:* **5** Nehru (Jawaharlal)
6 Gandhi (Indira, Mohandas, Rajiv)
monetary unit: **5** rupee *mountain range:*
7 Vindhya **9** Himalayas *neighbor:*
5 Burma, China, Nepal **6** Bhutan
7 Myanmar **8** Pakistan **10** Bangladesh
pass: **5** Bolan, Gumal **6** Khyber *plateau:*
6 Deccan *river:* **5** Indus **6** Ganges, Yamuna **7** Krishna **11** Brahmaputra *sea:*
7 Arabian
Indian *bread:* **3** nan **4** naan **7** chapati *butter:* **3** ghi **4** ghee *caste:* **5** Sudra **6** Vaisya
7 Brahman **9** Kshatriya *female dancer:*
8 bayadere *groom:* **4** syce *harem:*
6 zenana *instrument:* **4** vina **5** sarod,
sitar, tabla **7** tambura *lady:* **4** bibi
5 begum **8** memsahib *nurse:* **4** amah,
ayah *outcast:* **6** pariah *prince:* **4** raja,
rana **5** rajah **8** maharaja **9** maharajah
princess: **4** rani **5** begum, ranee *scholar:*
6 pandit, pundit *screen:* **6** purdah *seal,
stamp:* **4** chop *soldier:* **4** peon **5** sepoy
teacher: **4** guru *viceroy:* **5** nabob, nawab
weight unit: **3** ser **4** cash, dhan, pank,
pice, powe, rati, tank, tola **5** adpao,
fanam, hubba, masha, maund, pally,
pouah, ratti **6** dhurra, pagoda, pollam
7 chinnam, chittak
Indiana *capital:* **12** Indianapolis *city:*
4 Gary **6** Muncie **9** Fort Wayne, South
Bend **10** Evansville, Terre Haute
11 Bloomington *college, university:*
6 DePauw, Purdue **9** Ball State, Notre
Dame *nickname:* **7** Hoosier (State) *river:*
5 White **6** Wabash *state bird:* **8** cardinal
state flower: **5** peony *state tree:* **5** tulip
Indian, American *baby:* **7** papoose *ball
game:* **8** lacrosse *carrier:* **7** travois *Central and South American:* **3** Ona **4** Cuna,
Inca, Maya **5** Arara, Aztec, Carib,
Huave, Olmec, Yagua **6** Arawak,
Aymara, Jivaro, Omagua, Toltec, Yahgan **7** Chibcha, Quechua, Zapotec
8 Tarascan, Yanomamo **10** Araucanian
11 Tupi-Guaraní *food:* **4** samp **5** maize
8 pemmican *home:* **5** hogan, lodge,
tepee **6** pueblo, teepee, wigwam **7** wickiup *leader:* **4** Popé **6** Wovoka **7** Cochise,
Osceola, Pontiac, Sequoia, Sequoya
8 Geronimo, Hiawatha, Powhatan,
Sequoyah, Tecumseh **9** Black Hawk,
Massasoit **10** Crazy Horse **11** Cornplanter, Sitting Bull *money:* **6** wampum
North American: **3** Fox, Oto, Sac, Ute
4 Cree, Crow, Erie, Hopi, Hupa, Iowa,
Otoe, Pima, Pomo, Sauk, Taos, Yuma,
Zuni **5** Aleut, Caddo, Creek, Haida,
Huron, Kansa, Kiowa, Maidu, Miami,
Modoc, Omaha, Osage, Sioux, Uinta

6 Apache, Cayuga, Dakota, Lenape, Mandan, Micmac, Mohawk, Munsee, Navaho, Navajo, Nootka, Oglala, Ojibwa, Oneida, Paiute, Pawnee, Pueblo, Quapaw, Salish, Santee, Seneca, Siwash **7** Anasazi, Arapaho, Arikara, Bannock, Chilkat, Chinook, Choctaw, Dakotah, Esselen, Klamath, Kutenai, Mohican, Naskapi, Natchez, Ojibway, Pontiac, Shawnee, Tlingit **8** Cherokee, Cheyenne, Chippewa, Comanche, Delaware, Illinois, Iroquois, Kickapoo, Kwakiutl, Nez Percé, Onondaga, Powhatan, Seminole, Shoshoni **9** Blackfoot, Chickasaw, Menominee, Tsimshian, Tuscarora, Wampanoag, Winnebago **10** Assiniboin, Chiricahua, Gros Ventre, Potawatomi **11** Massachuset, Narraganset *pipe:* **7** calumet *spirit:* **5** totem **6** manitu **7** kachina, manitou

Indian paintbrush 8 hawkweed **10** painted cup

indicate 4 bode, hint, mark, mean, show **5** augur, imply, point, prove **6** attest, convey, denote, evince, import, reveal **7** bespeak, betoken, connote, display, exhibit, express, presage, signify, suggest **8** disclose, evidence, foretell, manifest, register **9** designate **10** foreshadow, illustrate **11** demonstrate

indication 3 cue **4** clue, hint, mark, sign **5** proof, token, trace **6** augury, signal **7** gesture, inkling, portent, symptom **8** evidence, reminder, telltale **9** testimony **10** expression, suggestion **13** foreshadowing, manifestation

indicative 10 expressive, suggestive **11** evidentiary, symptomatic **12** illustrative **13** demonstrative

indicia 5 marks, signs **8** imprints, markings

indict 5 blame **6** accuse, charge **7** arraign, censure, impeach **9** criticize

indifference 6 apathy **9** aloofness, unconcern **10** detachment, dispassion **11** disinterest **12** carelessness, impartiality

indifferent 4 cold, cool, numb, so-so **5** aloof, blasé, stoic **6** casual, remote **7** average, neutral **8** careless, detached, mediocre, middling, moderate, ordinary, passable, unbiased, uncaring **9** apathetic, impartial, impassive, objective **10** nonchalant, unaffected **11** unconcerned, unemotional **12** uninterested, unprejudiced **13** disinterested, dispassionate

indigence 4 need, want **6** penury **7** poverty **9** neediness, pauperism, privation **11** deprivation, destitution

indigene 6 native **9** aborigine **10** aboriginal

indigenous 6 native **7** endemic, natural **10** aboriginal, congenital, connatural, unacquired **13** autochthonous

indigent 4 poor **5** broke, needy **9** destitute, penniless **11** impecunious, necessitous **12** impoverished

indigestion 9 dyspepsia, heartburn

indignant 3 mad **5** irate, riled, upset, vexed **6** galled, heated **7** annoyed **8** offended, outraged, provoked **9** affronted, irritated, resentful

indignation 5 pique **7** dudgeon **10** irritation, resentment

indignity 3 cut **4** slap **6** injury, insult, slight **7** affront, outrage **9** contumely, grievance **10** disrespect **11** humiliation **13** disparagement, embarrassment

indigo 4 blue **8** deep blue

indigo bird 5 finch **7** bunting

Indira's father 5 Nehru (Jawaharlal)

indirect 7 devious, oblique, vagrant, winding **8** circular, sidelong, tortuous **9** deceitful, underhand, wandering **10** backhanded, circuitous, collateral, meandering, roundabout **11** duplicitous, underhanded

indiscreet 5 gabby **6** unwise **7** foolish, gossipy **8** tactless **9** impolitic, imprudent, untactful **10** ill-advised **11** loose-lipped

indiscretion 4 slip **5** folly, gaffe, lapse **7** blunder, faux pas, mistake, misstep **8** solecism **10** imprudence **11** impropriety

indiscriminate 5 mixed **6** hybrid, motley, random, varied **7** aimless, jumbled, vagrant **8** assorted, careless **9** arbitrary, desultory, haphazard, hit-or-miss, unplanned, wholesale **10** uncritical **11** promiscuous **12** conglomerate, multifarious, unrestrained **13** heterogeneous, miscellaneous

indispensable 5 basic, vital **6** needed **7** crucial, needful, pivotal **8** cardinal, critical **9** essential, necessary, requisite **10** imperative, obligatory **11** fundamental

indisposed 3 ill **4** down, sick **5** loath **6** ailing, averse, poorly, sickly, unwell **7** uneager **8** hesitant **9** reluctant, resistant, unwilling **11** disinclined

indisposition 6 malady **7** ailment, dislike, illness, malaise **8** aversion, disfavor, distaste, sickness, unhealth **10** affliction, reluctance

indisputable 4 sure, true **7** certain, evident, obvious **8** absolute, ironclad, positive **9** apodictic **10** undeniable **11** irrefutable, unequivocal **12** irrefragable, unassailable

indistinct 3 dim **4** hazy **5** faint, foggy,

misty, murky, vague **6** bleary, blurry, cloudy **7** blurred, obscure, shadowy, unclear **8** confused **9** uncertain, undefined **12** undetermined

indistinguishable 4 same **5** alike, equal, vague **7** unclear **9** duplicate, identical **10** equivalent

indite 3 pen **5** write **6** record, scribe **7** compose, engross **10** transcribe

individual 3 one **4** body, lone, self, sole, soul, unit **5** being, human, party, thing **6** entity, mortal, person, proper, single **7** special **8** creature, discrete, distinct, peculiar, personal, separate, singular, solitary, specific **10** particular, respective **11** distinctive **13** idiosyncratic *combining form:* **4** idio

individualist 5 loner **6** hermit **8** lone wolf, maverick **13** nonconformist

individuality 4 self **7** essence, oneness **8** identity, selfhood **9** character **10** uniqueness **11** personality, singularity **12** idiosyncrasy, separateness

individualize 4 mark **7** specify **9** customize **10** specialize **11** distinguish, personalize, singularize **12** characterize **13** differentiate, particularize

Indochinese country 4 Laos **5** Burma **7** Myanmar, Vietnam **8** Cambodia, Thailand **9** Kampuchea

indoctrinate 5 teach, tutor **7** educate, program **8** convince, persuade **9** brainwash, inculcate

indolence 4 laze **5** sloth **7** inertia, languor **8** idleness, laziness, lethargy **9** torpidity **12** slothfulness, sluggishness **13** shiftlessness

indolent 4 idle, lazy **6** torpid **8** fainéant, slothful, sluggish **9** lethargic, shiftless

indomitable 7 staunch **9** steadfast **10** invincible, unbeatable **11** impregnable **13** unconquerable

Indonesia *archipelago:* **5** Malay *capital:* **7** Jakarta **8** Djakarta *city:* **5** Medan **7** Bandung, Cilacap **8** Semarang, Surabaja, Surabaya **9** Palembang *island group:* **5** Sunda **8** Moluccas *language:* **6** Bahasa *leader:* **7** Suharto, Sukarno *monetary unit:* **6** rupiah *regions:* **4** Bali, Java **5** Ceram, Timor **6** Bangka, Borneo, Flores, Lombok, Madura **7** Celebes, Sumatra **8** Sulawesi **9** Irian Jaya *volcano:* **8** Krakatau, Krakatoa

indubitable 4 sure **6** patent **7** certain, evident, obvious **8** definite, ironclad, positive **9** apodictic, veritable **10** undeniable **11** irrefutable, self-evident, unequivocal **12** irrefragable

induce 5 cause **6** effect, elicit, prompt **7** actuate, procure **8** convince, engender, generate, motivate, occasion, persuade **9** encourage

inducement 4 bait, lure **6** come-on, motive **10** attraction, motivation **13** consideration

induct 4 lead **5** admit **6** enlist, enroll **7** appoint, install

inductance unit 5 henry

induction 8 entrance **9** accession, reasoning **10** enlistment **11** appointment **13** ratiocination

inductive 7 logical **9** prefatory, prelusive **11** a posteriori

indulge 3 pet **4** baby, bask **5** allow, favor, humor, spoil **6** cocker, coddle, cosset, oblige, pamper, permit, please, wallow **7** cater to, delight, gratify, satisfy **9** luxuriate **11** mollycoddle

indulgence 5 favor, mercy, treat **6** luxury **7** charity **8** clemency, courtesy, kindness, lenience, leniency **9** allowance, remission, tolerance **10** compassion, kindliness, permission, toleration **11** forbearance, forgiveness **12** dispensation, mercifulness **13** gratification

indulgence seller 5 Tezel (Johann) **6** Tetzel (Johann)

indulgent 4 easy, kind **7** clement, lenient **8** generous, merciful, tolerant **9** forgiving **10** charitable, permissive

indurate 6 harden **7** callous, confirm, congeal **8** hardened, solidify, stubborn **9** unfeeling **11** hard-hearted

industrialist 6 tycoon **7** magnate **12** manufacturer

industrious 4 busy **8** diligent, sedulous **9** assiduous, laborious

industry 4 work **5** labor **8** business, commerce **9** assiduity, diligence **10** enterprise

inebriant see INTOXICANT

inebriate 3 sot **4** lush, soak **5** drunk, souse, tipple, tipsy, toper **6** bibber, boozer **7** stupefy, tippler, tosspot **9** drunkard **10** intoxicate

inebriated 3 lit **5** drunk, lit up, oiled, stiff, tight, tipsy **6** blotto, juiced, loaded, plowed, potted, soused, stewed, tanked, wasted **7** crocked, pickled, pie-eyed, sloshed, smashed **8** polluted **9** plastered

inedible 9 poisonous **12** unappetizing

ineffable 5 taboo **9** forbidden **11** unspeakable, unutterable **13** undescribable

ineffaceable 7 lasting **8** enduring **9** indelible, permanent

ineffective 4 vain, weak **6** futile **7** useless **8** abortive, bootless, feckless, impotent **9** fruitless, powerless **10** emasculate, unavailing 12 unproductive, unsuccessful

ineffectiveness 8 futility 9 impotence

ineffectual see INEFFECTIVE

inefficient 5 slack 6 clumsy 8 careless, slipshod, wasteful 9 negligent

inelastic 5 rigid, stiff 7 brittle 9 unbending 10 unyielding

inelegant 5 crass, crude, gross, rough 6 coarse, gauche, vulgar 7 awkward, uncouth 9 graceless, unrefined 10 uncultured, ungraceful 12 uncultivated

ineligible 5 unfit 8 unfitted, unworthy 10 unequipped, unsuitable 11 unqualified 12 disqualified

ineluctable 4 sure 5 bound, fated 6 doomed 7 certain 8 destined 9 necessary 10 inevitable, unevadable 11 unavoidable, unescapable 13 unpreventable

inept 5 unfit 6 clumsy, gauche, klutzy 7 artless, awkward, foolish, halting, unhandy 8 bumbling, bungling 9 all thumbs, ham-handed, maladroit, unskilled 10 malapropos, unskillful, unsuitable 11 heavy-handed, undexterous, unfortunate

inequality 8 imparity 9 disparity 10 unevenness 12 irregularity, variableness 13 disproportion, heterogeneity

inequitable 6 biased, unfair, unjust 7 partial 10 prejudiced 11 unjustified, unrighteous

inequity 4 bias 5 wrong 9 prejudice 10 unfairness, unjustness

ineradicable 6 innate 7 chronic 8 constant, inherent, stubborn 9 ingrained 10 deep-rooted, deep-seated, entrenched, inveterate 11 established, ever-present, never-ending

inert 4 calm, dead, idle 5 quiet, still 6 asleep, sleepy 7 dormant, passive 8 immobile, lifeless, sluggish 9 apathetic, lethargic 10 motionless

inert gas 4 neon 5 argon, radon, xenon 6 helium 7 krypton

inertia 5 sloth 6 apathy, stupor, torpor 7 languor 8 idleness, laziness, lethargy 9 indolence, inertness, lassitude, passivity, torpidity 10 immobility, inactivity 11 disinterest 12 listlessness, sluggishness

inescapable see INEVITABLE

inessential see UNESSENTIAL

inestimable 9 priceless 11 measureless 12 immeasurable, unmeasurable, unfathomable

inevitable 4 sure 5 bound, fated 6 doomed 7 certain 8 destined 9 necessary 11 unavoidable, unescapable 12 foreordained 13 unpreventable

inevitably 8 perforce 10 willy-nilly 11 like it or not, unavoidably

inexcusable 6 guilty 8 blamable, culpable 9 untenable 10 censurable 11 blameworthy, condemnable 12 criticizable, unforgivable, unpardonable 13 reprehensible, unjustifiable

inexhaustible 8 tireless, untiring 9 unfailing, weariless 10 bottomless, unflagging 13 indefatigable

inexorable 5 rigid 6 strict 7 adamant 8 immobile, obdurate, stubborn 9 immovable, unbending 10 relentless, unyielding 11 unrelenting

inexpensive 3 low 5 cheap 7 cut-rate 8 moderate 10 reasonable

inexperience 7 naïveté, rawness 8 verdancy 9 freshness, greenness 10 callowness

inexperienced 3 raw 5 fresh, green, naive, young 6 callow 7 untried 8 unversed 9 unskilled, untrained, unworldly 10 amateurish, unseasoned

inexpert 9 maladroit, unskilled, untrained 10 amateurish

inexplicable 6 arcane, obtuse, opaque 7 cryptic 9 enigmatic 10 mysterious, mystifying, unsolvable 11 undefinable 12 impenetrable, unfathomable 13 unaccountable, unexplainable

inexpressible 8 nameless 11 unspeakable, unutterable 13 undescribable, unexplainable

inexpressive 5 blank, stoic 6 stolid, vacant, wooden 7 deadpan 9 impassive 10 poker-faced 13 straight-faced

inextricable 9 insoluble 10 unsolvable

infallible 4 sure 5 exact 6 trusty 7 certain, correct, perfect 8 absolute, accurate, flawless, surefire, unerring 9 errorless, unfailing 10 dependable, impeccable 11 trustworthy 12 tried-and-true 13 unimpeachable

infamous 4 evil, vile 6 odious 7 hateful, heinous 8 flagrant, shameful 9 abhorrent, miscreant, nefarious, notorious 10 abominable, despicable, detestable, flagitious, scandalous, villainous 11 disgraceful, ignominious, opprobrious 12 contemptible, disreputable

infamy 5 odium, shame 7 obloquy 8 disgrace, dishonor, ignominy 9 disrepute, notoriety 10 opprobrium

infancy 8 babyhood 9 childhood

infant 4 babe, baby 5 bairn, child, green 7 bambino, neonate, newborn, papoose, toddler 8 bantling, immature, nursling 9 unfledged *bed:* 4 crib 6 cradle 8 bassinet *food:* 3 pap 4 milk 7 pabulum *room:* 7 nursery

infanta 8 princess

infantile 7 babyish, puerile 8 childish, immature

infantryman 7 dogface 8 doughboy 11 foot soldier *Algerian:* 6 Zouave

infatuated 5 dotty, silly 7 foolish 8 besotted, enamored, obsessed 9 bewitched, rapturous 10 captivated, passionate

infatuation 4 rage 5 ardor, craze, crush, folly 7 passion, rapture 8 devotion 9 obsession, puppy love 11 fascination

infect 5 taint 6 defile, poison 7 corrupt, pollute 11 contaminate

infection 3 bug 6 sepses (plural), sepsis *fungous:* 8 mycetoma

infectious 8 catching, epidemic, virulent 9 pestilent 10 contagious, corrupting 12 communicable 13 contaminating, transmittable

infelicitous 5 unapt, unfit 6 unmeet 7 awkward, unhappy 8 improper 9 imperfect 10 malapropos, unsuitable 11 regrettable, unfortunate

infer 5 judge 6 deduce, deduct, derive, gather, reason 7 collect, make out, suppose, surmise 8 conclude, construe 10 conjecture 11 hypothesize

inference 7 surmise 8 illation, sequitur 9 deduction 10 assumption, conclusion, conjecture, derivation 11 presumption, supposition

inferior 3 low 4 base, fair, hack, mean, poor, puny 5 cheap, lousy, lower, minor, petty, scrub, sorry, under, worse 6 common, deputy, feeble, impure, junior, lesser, nether, no-good, paltry, satrap, shoddy, sleazy, tawdry, tinpot, vassal 7 average, subject, unequal 8 declassé, low-grade, mediocre, middling, ordinary, unworthy, wretched 9 attendant, auxiliary, no-account, satellite, secondary, subaltern, subjacent, underling, worthless 10 inadequate, second-rate 11 substandard *prefix:* 3 sub 4 demi 5 infra

infernal 6 Hadean 7 hellish, satanic 8 chthonic, damnable, demoniac, devilish, diabolic, plutonic 9 chthonian, plutonian, Tartarean 10 diabolical, sulphurous

inferno 3 pit 4 fire, hell 5 Hades, Sheol 6 blazes, Tophet 7 Gehenna 9 holocaust, perdition 10 underworld 11 netherworld 13 conflagration

Inferno *division:* 5 canto *poet:* 5 Dante (Alighieri) *verse form:* 9 terza rima

infertile 6 barren, effete 7 sterile 8 impotent 10 unfruitful 12 hardscrabble, unproductive

infest 4 teem 5 beset, swarm 6 plague 7 overrun 10 parasitize

infidel 5 pagan 7 atheist, heathen, heretic, skeptic 8 agnostic 10 unbeliever

infidelity 7 perfidy, treason 8 adultery, betrayal, cheating 9 disbelief, treachery 10 disloyalty 13 faithlessness

infinite 4 vast 7 endless, eternal, immense 8 unending 9 boundless, countless, limitless, perpetual, unlimited 11 everlasting, illimitable, measureless, sempiternal 12 immeasurable

infinity 8 eternity 10 perpetuity 11 endlessness 12 sempiternity 13 boundlessness, limitlessness

infirm 4 lame, sick, weak 5 frail 6 ailing, feeble, sickly 7 failing, fragile, unsound 8 decrepit, unstable 9 doddering 11 debilitated

infirmity 3 ill 4 flaw 5 decay 6 malady 7 ailment, disease, frailty, illness, malaise 8 debility, disorder, sickness, syndrome, weakness 9 complaint, condition 10 affliction, feebleness, sickliness 11 decrepitude 12 debilitation, enfeeblement

infix 4 root 5 embed, lodge 6 fasten, pierce 7 engrave, implant, impress

inflame 4 fire, gall, goad, rile, roil 5 anger, light, rouse 6 arouse, enrage, excite, foment, ignite, kindle, madden, redden, stir up 7 provoke 8 enkindle, irritate 9 aggravate 10 exacerbate, exasperate

inflammable 5 fiery 6 ardent 8 burnable, volatile 9 excitable, ignitable, irascible 11 combustible

inflammation 4 gout, sore 6 otitis, quinsy 7 catarrh, colitis 8 adenitis, bursitis, cystitis, neuritis, pleurisy, rachitis, swelling 9 arthritis, chilblain, gastritis, nephritis, phlebitis 10 bronchitis, cellulitis, combustion, dermatitis, gingivitis, laryngitis, tendinitis 12 encephalitis 13 poliomyelitis *eye:* 6 iritis 7 pinkeye 9 keratitis *horse:* 7 fistula, quittor *intestines:* 7 ileitis 9 enteritis *suffix:* 4 itis

inflammatory 8 exciting 9 explosive, seditious 11 provocative 13 rabble-rousing, revolutionary

inflate 4 fill 5 bloat, elate, swell 6 expand 7 amplify, distend 10 aggrandize

inflated 5 tumid, windy 6 turgid 7 bloated, swollen, verbose 9 bombastic, distended, dropsical, flatulent, overblown 10 heightened 11 exaggerated, pretentious

inflection 4 bend, tone 5 curve, pitch 6 accent, change, stress, timbre 8 emphasis, tonality 9 accidence 10 modulation

inflexible 3 set 4 grim, hard, iron 5 fixed, rigid, stiff 6 strict 7 adamant, die-hard

8 granitic, hard-line, immobile, iron-clad, obdurate, stubborn **9** immovable, immutable, obstinate, steadfast, unbending **10** adamantine, brassbound, implacable, rock-ribbed, unbendable, unyielding **11** unalterable, unrelenting **12** unchangeable **13** dyed-in-the-wool

inflict 5 visit, wreak **7** mete out, subject **8** dispense **10** administer

inflow 4 rush **7** arrival

influence 4 move, pull, sway **5** alter, bribe, clout, force, impel, lobby, touch **6** affect, compel, impact, modify, moment, strike, weight **7** command, control, impress, mastery **8** dominate, militate, persuade, prestige **9** authority, dominance

influenceable 8 gullible **9** malleable, receptive, tractable **11** persuadable, persuasible, suggestible

influential 6 potent **8** forceful, powerful **9** effective **10** persuasive **13** authoritative

influx 7 arrival **8** entrance, invasion **9** accession

inform 3 rat **4** blab, clue, leak, post, tell, warn **5** brief, edify, endow, endue, imbue, teach **6** advise, betray, fill in, impart, leaven, notify, reveal, snitch, squeal, tattle, turn in, update **7** animate, apprise, caution, educate **8** acquaint, disclose, forewarn **9** advertise, enlighten **10** illuminate **11** familiarize

informal 6 casual, dégagé, folksy **7** natural, offhand, relaxed **8** down-home, familiar, laid-back **9** easygoing **10** colloquial, unofficial **13** unceremonious

information 4 data, fact, lore, news, poop, word **5** scoop **6** advice, notice, skinny, wisdom **7** lowdown, tidings **9** knowledge **12** intelligence *second-hand:* **7** hearsay

information bureau *abbreviation:* **4** USIA, USIS

informative 8 edifying, exegetic **10** exegetical **11** educational, elucidative, explanatory **12** enlightening, illuminating

informed 4 wise **5** aware **6** au fait, versed **7** abreast, knowing **8** apprised, educated **9** au courant, cognizant **10** acquainted, conversant **11** enlightened **13** knowledgeable

informer 3 rat, spy **4** fink, mole **5** stool **6** canary, gossip, snitch **7** rat fink, stoolie, tattler, tipster **8** squealer, telltale **10** deep throat, talebearer, tattletale **11** stool pigeon **13** whistle-blower

infra 5 after, below, later, under **7** beneath

infract 3 sin **6** breach, offend **7** violate **8** trespass **10** contravene, transgress

infraction 3 sin **4** foul **5** crime, error **6** breach **7** faux pas, misdeed, offense **8** trespass **9** violation **12** encroachment **13** contravention, transgression

infrastructure 4 base **5** basis **9** framework **10** foundation, groundwork, substratum **12** underpinning

infrequent 3 odd **4** rare **6** scarce, seldom **7** unusual **8** isolated, sporadic, uncommon, unwonted **10** occasional **11** exceptional

infringe 6 breach, impose, meddle, offend **7** disturb, obtrude, violate **8** encroach, entrench, trespass **10** transgress

infuriate 3 ire, mad **4** rile **5** anger, pique **6** enrage, madden, rankle **7** incense, inflame, outrage, provoke, steam up

infuse 4 fill, soak **5** imbue, steep **6** leaven **7** animate, implant, pervade, suffuse **8** permeate, saturate **10** impregnate

ingenious 5 acute, canny, sharp, smart **6** adroit, clever, crafty **7** cunning, fertile **8** creative, original **11** imaginative, resourceful

ingenuity 5 knack, savvy, skill **6** acumen, smarts, talent **7** know-how, mastery **8** deftness, keenness **9** adeptness, handiness **10** adroitness, capability, cleverness, perception, shrewdness **11** proficiency **12** intelligence, skillfulness **13** inventiveness

ingenuous 4 open **5** naive **6** simple **7** artless, natural **8** innocent **9** childlike, guileless, unstudied **10** unaffected

ingest 3 eat **4** feed **6** devour **7** consume, partake, swallow

Inge work 6 Picnic **7** Bus Stop **18** Splendor in the Grass **19** Come Back Little Sheba

inglorious 8 shameful **11** disgraceful, ignominious, opprobrious **12** dishonorable, disreputable **13** discreditable, unrespectable

ingot 3 bar, rod **4** mold **6** billet

ingrained 6 innate **8** inherent **9** essential **10** congenital, deep-rooted, deep-seated

ingratiating 5 silky **6** silken, smarmy **7** fawning **8** pleasing, unctuous **9** adulatory **10** flattering **11** sycophantic

ingredient 4 part **5** piece **6** factor **7** element **9** component **11** constituent

ingress 4 door **5** entry **6** access, entrée, portal **7** doorway, passage **8** entrance, entryway **9** admission, vestibule **10** admittance **11** entranceway

ingurgitate 4 bolt, cram, gulp, slop, wolf **5** gorge, scarf, stuff, swill **6** devour, gobble, guzzle **7** swallow

inhabit 4 live **5** dwell, haunt **6** occupy, people, settle, tenant **8** populate
inhabitant 5 liver **6** inmate, native **7** citizen, denizen, dweller, resider **8** indigene, resident **9** aborigine **10** autochthon *foreign:* **5** alien *indigenous:* **6** native **9** aborigine
inhale 7 breathe, consume, respire, swallow
inharmonious 6 atonal **7** jarring **9** dissonant, unmusical **10** discordant **11** cacophonous, conflicting, conflictive, disagreeing, quarrelsome, uncongenial **12** antagonistic
inhere 3 lie **5** dwell **6** belong, reside
inherent 4 born **5** basic **6** native **7** built-in, connate, natural **8** immanent **9** elemental, essential **10** congenital, deep-seated **11** fundamental
inherit 4 acquire, receive, succeed
inheritance 3 DNA **4** gene, gift **6** devise, estate, legacy **7** bequest **8** heirloom, heritage **9** patrimony, tradition **10** birthright **13** primogeniture
inherited 6 native **7** connate, genetic, natural **10** bequeathed, congenital, connatural, handed-down, hand-me-down
inheritor 4 heir **7** heiress, legatee **11** beneficiary
inhibit 4 curb, slow **5** check **6** arrest, bridle, enjoin, fetter, hamper, hinder, hobble, impede **7** prevent, repress, trammel **8** hold back, obstruct, restrain, suppress, withhold **9** constrain **10** discourage
inhibition 4 curb **5** taboo **6** hang-up **7** barrier **9** hindrance, restraint, stricture **10** impediment, repression **11** suppression
inhuman 5 cruel, feral **6** brutal, savage **7** beastly, bestial, brutish **8** fiendish **9** barbarous, monstrous **10** diabolical
inhumane 4 fell, grim **5** cruel **6** brutal, fierce, malign, savage **8** ruthless, sadistic **9** barbarous, ferocious, heartless, merciless, truculent
inhumation 6 burial **9** interment, sepulture **10** entombment
inhume 4 bury **5** plant **6** entomb **7** put away **9** lay to rest
inimical 7 adverse, harmful, hostile **10** malevolent, unfriendly **11** belligerent, contentious **12** antagonistic, antipathetic
iniquitous 3 bad **4** base, evil, vile **5** wrong **6** sinful, unjust, wicked **7** immoral, vicious **9** nefarious
iniquity 3 sin **4** evil **5** crime, wrong **7** offense **9** turpitude **8** trespass **10** immorality, wickedness, wrongdoing **13** transgression

initial 5 first, prime **6** anlage, letter, maiden **7** approve, engrave, leading, opening, primary **8** earliest, foremost, monogram, original **9** beginning
initiate 4 open **5** begin, enter, set up, start **6** enroll, get off, induct, invest, launch, take up **7** install, kick off, usher in **8** commence **9** originate **10** inaugurate
initiation 5 debut **7** baptism **9** admission, beginning, induction **10** admittance **11** investiture, origination **12** commencement, introduction
initiative 4 push **5** drive, spunk **6** energy **8** ambition, aptitude, gumption **9** beginning **10** enterprise, get-up-and-go
inject 3 add **6** insert **7** implant, instill **9** inoculate, introduce, vaccinate
injection 3 fix **4** hypo, shot **5** serum **7** booster, vaccine **10** hypodermic **11** inoculation, vaccination
injudicious 4 rash **5** hasty **6** unwise **8** heedless, reckless **9** ill-judged, impolitic, imprudent **10** ill-advised, indiscreet **11** inexpedient **12** short-sighted
injunction 3 ban, bar **4** writ **5** order **6** behest, charge **7** bidding, command, dictate, mandate **9** direction **11** prohibition
injure 3 mar **4** foul, harm, hurt, maim, pain **5** spoil, wound, wrong **6** blight, bruise, damage, deface, deform, foul up, impair, mangle **7** afflict, contort, cripple, disable, torture **8** distress, maltreat, mutilate **9** disfigure **12** incapacitate
injurious 6 nocent **7** abusive, adverse, harmful, hurtful **8** damaging **9** offensive **10** defamatory **11** detrimental
injury 3 ill **4** harm, hurt **5** wound, wrong **6** damage, trauma **8** distress **9** detriment
injustice 4 tort **5** crime, wrong **6** breach, damage **7** outrage **8** inequity, trespass **9** grievance, violation **10** favoritism, wrongdoing
ink 3 dye, pen **4** sign **8** inscribe **9** autograph, signature, subscribe
inkling 3 cue, tip **4** clue, hint, idea, lead, wind **5** hunch **6** notion, tip-off **8** telltale **9** suspicion **10** indication, intimation, suggestion
inky 3 jet **4** ebon **5** black, ebony, jetty, raven, sable **9** Cimmerian, pitch-dark **10** pitch-black
inlaid 5 piqué **6** boolle **7** hatched **8** enchased, nielloed **9** damascene, incrusted
Inland Empire 8 Illinois
inlet 3 arm, bay **4** cove, gulf **5** bayou,

bight, creek, fiord, firth, fjord, sound
6 harbor, slough, strait 7 estuary *Admiralties:* 4 Kali *Adriatic Sea:* 5 Vlorë
Aegean Sea: 7 Saronic *Africa:* 6 Walvis
Alaska: 4 Cook 5 Cross, Taiya 7 Glacier
8 Chilkoot *Aleutians:* 5 Holtz, Nazan
Angola: 5 Bengo, Tiger 6 Tigres *Antarctica:* 3 Ice 7 McMurdo 8 Amundsen
10 Shackleton *Arabian Sea:* 4 Qamr
5 Kamar *Australia:* 4 King 6 Botany
9 Discovery 10 Broad Sound *Baffin Bay:*
8 Melville *Baffin Island:* 9 Admiralty
Baltic Sea: 4 Hano 6 Danzig, Gdansk
9 Pomerania 10 Pomeranian *Barents
Sea:* 4 Kola 7 Pechora *Beaufort Sea:*
7 Prudhoe 9 Mackenzie *Bismarck Sea:*
5 Kimbe *Brazil:* 9 Guanabara *Bristol
Channal:* 10 Carmarthen *California:*
5 Morro 8 Monterey *Canada:* 5 Fundy
9 Howe Sound *Cape Breton Island:*
4 Mira *Caribbean Sea:* 5 Limón *Central
America:* 7 Fonseca *Chile:* 5 Otway
Crete: 4 Suda 5 Canea *Denmark:* 3 Ise
Djibouti: 6 Tajura 8 Tadjoura *East River:*
8 Flushing *Ecuador:* 5 Manta *Eire:*
4 Clew 7 Brandon *English Channel:*
3 Tor *Florida:* 8 Biscayne 10 Saint Lucie
Georgia: 8 Altamaha *Greenland:* 6 Baffin
Gulf of Alaska: 3 Icy 5 Woman 12 Resurrection *Gulf of Mexico:* 7 Aransas
8 Suwannee 9 Matagorda, Pensacola
10 Terrebonne 11 Atchafalaya
12 Apalachicola *Gulf of St. Lawrence:*
5 Bonne *Hawaii:* 11 Pearl Harbor *Honshu:* 3 Ise 5 Owari 6 Atsuta *Hudson Bay:*
7 Repulse *Iceland:* 4 Axar, Eyja, Huna
5 Horna, Skaga, Vopna 8 Hunafloi
Indonesia: 4 Bima 5 Saleh *Ionian Sea:*
7 Taranto *Irish Sea:* 4 Luce 7 Dundalk
Japan: 4 Tosa *Java:* 4 Lada 5 Peper *Java
Sea:* 7 Batavia *Kara Sea:* 6 Enisei 7 Yenisei *Labrador:* 8 Hamilton *Lake Erie:*
8 Put-in-Bay, Sandusky *Lake Huron:*
7 Saginaw, Thunder *Lake Ontario:*
11 Irondequoit *Lake Superior:* 5 Huron
8 Keweenaw 9 Whitefish *Long Island:*
8 Rockaway *Long Island Sound:* 6 Oyster *Madagascar:* 8 Antongil *Maine:*
5 Casco 7 Machias *Maryland-Virginia:*
10 Chesapeake *Massachusetts:* 8 Buzzards, Plymouth 9 Annisquam *Massachusetts Bay:* 10 Lynn Harbor *Mediterranean Sea:* 8 Valencia 9 Famagusta
10 Khalij Surt 11 Syrtis Major *Mozambique:* 5 Memba, Pemba *Nantucket
Sound:* 5 Lewis *Newfoundland:* 4 Hare
5 White 7 Fortune *New Guinea:* 3 Oro
5 Berau, Hansa 11 McCluer Gulf *New
Jersey:* 7 Raritan 8 Barnegat 9 Little
Egg *New Zealand:* 5 Hawke 6 Tasman
North Carolina: 9 Albemarle *Northern Ire-

land: 12 Belfast Lough *North Sea:* 4 Lyse
9 Hardanger *Northwest Territories:*
5 Wager 8 Bathurst, Franklin 9 Frobisher 12 Prince Albert *Norway:* 3 Tys
4 Bokn, Tana 5 Lakse, Sogne *Norwegian
Sea:* 4 Nord, Salt, Stor, Vest 5 Ranen
8 Scoresby 9 Trondheim *Ontario:*
4 Owen *Oregon:* 4 Coos *Philippines:*
5 Baler, Pilar, Sogod 6 Butuan 9 Davao
Gulf, Leyte Gulf, Panay Gulf *Puget
Sound:* 4 Carr, Case *Quebec:* 6 Ungava
Red Sea: 4 Foul *Rhode Island:* 12 Narragansett *Russia:* 5 Chaun 8 Sakhalin
Santo Cruz Islands: 8 Basilisk *Solomon
Islands:* 4 Deep 8 Huon Gulf *South
Africa:* 5 Table *South Carolina:* 4 Bull
South China Sea: 4 Bias, Datu, Siam,
Taya 5 Dasol, Subic, Subig 6 Brunei,
Paluan 7 Camranh 8 Lingayen *Spain:*
5 Cádiz *Spitsbergen:* 3 Ice 4 Bell 5 Kings
Sumatra: 5 Bajur 10 Koninginne
Tyrrhenian Sea: 6 Naples 7 Paestum
Wales: 5 Burry *Washington:* 5 Dabob
6 Skagit 11 Grays Harbor

inmate 7 convict 8 occupant, prisoner,
resident 10 inhabitant

inmost part 4 core, pith 5 heart 6 center,
depths, kernel, marrow 7 nucleus

inn 5 hotel, lodge, motel, serai 6 hostel,
tavern 7 auberge, hospice, pension
8 hostelry 9 roadhouse 11 caravansary,
public house 12 caravansarai 13 boardinghouse *German:* 7 Gasthof 8 Gasthaus
Spanish: 5 fonda 6 posada 7 parador
Turkish: 6 imaret

innards 4 guts 5 belly 6 bowels, tripes
7 viscera 8 entrails, stuffing 10 intestines

innate see INHERENT

inner 3 gut 5 focal 6 hidden, middle,
secret 7 central, nuclear, private
8 familiar, interior, internal, personal,
visceral 9 concealed, essential

innervate 4 jolt, move 5 pique, rouse
6 excite 7 animate, provoke, quicken
8 motivate, vitalize 9 electrify, galvanize, stimulate

Innisfail 4 Eire, Erin 7 Ireland

innkeeper 4 host 8 boniface, hosteler,
hotelier, landlord, publican

innocence 6 purity 7 naiveté 8 chastity
10 simplicity 11 artlessness, sinlessness

innocent 4 good, lamb, naïf, pure, void
5 clean, legal, licit, naive 6 chaste,
devoid, lawful 7 artless, natural,
unaware 8 harmless, ignorant, virtuous
9 blameless, childlike, exemplary, faultless, guileless, guiltless, ingenuous,
innocuous, righteous, stainless,
unstained, unsullied, untainted

10 inculpable, legitimate **12** unsuspecting

innocuous 5 banal, bland **6** pallid **7** insipid **8** harmless **11** inoffensive, unoffending **13** insignificant

innovation 6 change **7** novelty

innovative 3 new **5** novel **8** creative, original **9** inventive **10** newfangled **11** cutting-edge, leading-edge **12** trailblazing

innovator 9 architect, developer **10** originator **11** trailblazer **13** revolutionary

innuendo 4 clue, hint, slur **7** calumny **8** allusion **9** aspersion **10** backbiting, intimation **11** implication, insinuation

innumerable 4 many **6** legion, myriad, untold **7** umpteen **9** countless, uncounted **10** numberless **13** multitudinous

Ino *brother:* **9** Polydorus *father:* **6** Cadmus *grandfather:* **6** Agenor *husband:* **7** Athamas *mother:* **8** Harmonia *sister:* **5** Agave **6** Semele **7** Autonoë *son:* **8** Learchus, Palaemon **10** Melicertes

inobtrusive 5 muted, quiet **6** modest **7** subdued **8** discreet, tasteful **10** restrained

inoculate 5 imbue, shoot, steep **6** infuse **7** implant, suffuse **9** vaccinate

inoffensive 5 bland **7** neutral **8** harmless **9** innocuous, peaceable

inopportune 8 ill-timed, mistimed, untimely **12** unseasonable

inordinate 5 undue **6** wanton **7** extreme **8** overmuch **9** excessive **10** exorbitant, gratuitous, immoderate, irrational **11** extravagant, intemperate, superfluous, uncalled-for **12** unreasonable **13** extraordinary

inorganic 7 mineral **10** artificial

in passing 5 aside **6** obiter **7** by the by **8** by the bye, by the way **12** incidentally

in perpetuum 4 ever **6** always **7** forever, for good **8** evermore, for keeps **9** eternally **10** enduringly **11** forevermore

input 4 data **6** advice, energy **7** comment, counsel, opinion **8** feedback, guidance, material, stimulus **11** information

inquest 5 probe **7** hearing, inquiry **11** examination **13** investigation

inquietude 5 angst **6** unease, unrest **7** anxiety, ferment, turmoil **8** distress **10** uneasiness **11** restiveness **12** restlessness **13** Sturm und Drang

inquire 3 ask, pry **4** seek **5** probe, query **7** examine **8** question **9** catechize **11** interrogate, investigate

inquiry 5 audit, probe, query **7** hearing **8** grilling, question, research, scrutiny **11** examination, questioning **13** investigation

inquisition 4 hunt **5** probe, quest, trial **6** search **7** inquiry **8** grilling, research **11** examination **13** interrogation, investigation

inquisitive 4 nosy **6** prying, snoopy **7** curious **8** meddling, snooping **9** intrusive **10** meddlesome **11** questioning

inquisitor 10 Torquemada (Tomás de)

in re 4 as to **5** about, as for **7** apropos **9** as regards, regarding **10** as respects, concerning, respecting **12** with regard to **13** with respect to

in respect to see IN RE

inroad 4 raid **5** foray **7** advance **8** invasion **9** incursion **12** encroachment

ins and outs 5 ropes **6** quirks **7** details **8** minutiae, oddities **11** incidentals, particulars **12** lay of the land **13** peculiarities, ramifications

insane 3 mad, off **4** daft, nuts **5** batty, crazy, daffy, dotty, loony, manic, nutsy, nutty, rabid, silly, wacky **6** absurd, crazed, cuckoo, maniac, raving, schizo, screwy, teched **7** berserk, bonkers, cracked, haywire, lunatic, tetched, touched, unsound **8** demented, deranged, unhinged **9** eccentric, psychotic **10** disordered, irrational, moonstruck, unbalanced **11** harebrained **12** crackbrained, preposterous, unreasonable

insane asylum 6 bedlam **8** loony bin, madhouse, nuthouse, snake pit **10** sanatorium, sanitarium

insanity 5 folly, mania **6** frenzy, lunacy **7** madness **8** delirium, delusion, dementia, hysteria, illusion **9** craziness, dottiness, psychosis **11** derangement, psychopathy

insatiable 6 crying, greedy, urgent **7** exigent **8** pressing, ravenous **9** clamorous, demanding, voracious **10** quenchless **11** importunate **12** unappeasable, unquenchable

inscribe 4 etch, list **5** carve, enter, print, write **6** enroll, record **7** engrave, engross, impress, imprint **8** dedicate, enscroll, register

inscription 5 title **6** legend **7** epigram, epitaph, heading **8** epigraph **10** dedication

inscrutable 6 arcane **7** deadpan **10** mysterious, poker-faced, sphinxlike, unknowable, unreadable **12** impenetrable, unfathomable

insect 3 bee, bug, fly **6** beetle *adult:* **5** imago *antenna:* **4** palp **6** feeler, palpus *combining form:* **5** entom **6** entomo *covering:* **6** chitin *immature:* **4** grub, pupa **5** larva, nymph **6** larvae (plural), maggot **8** wriggler **9** chrysalis **11** caterpillar

kind: 3 ant, bee 4 flea, moth, wasp
5 aphid, scale 6 bedbug, beefly, beetle,
cicada, earwig, hornet, mantid, mantis,
mayfly 7 ant lion, cricket, firefly, June
bug, katydid, ladybug, termite 8 honeybee, horsefly, housefly, lacewing, mosquito, stinkbug 9 bumblebee, butterfly,
damselfly, dragonfly 10 silverfish,
springtail 11 grasshopper 12 walking-
stick *luminous:* 7 firefly 8 glowworm
molt: 7 ecdysis *moth:* 4 luna 5 gypsy
6 miller, sphinx 7 noctuid, pyralid, tor-
trix, tussock 8 cecropia, cinnabar,
forester, sphingid 9 clearwing, geo-
metrid, saturniid, tortricid 10 Polyphemus *multi-legged:* 8 diplopod 9 centipede, millipede *part:* 4 palp 5 cerci
(plural) 6 cercus, labium, labrum, ocel-
li (plural), palpus, thorax 7 antenna,
maxilla, ocellus 8 antennae (plural),
mandible, maxillae (plural) 9 proboscis, spiracles 10 ovipositor
11 exoskeleton *pest:* 4 flea, lice (plural),
mite 5 louse, midge, scale 7 blowfly,
termite 8 horsefly, housefly, mealybug
9 cockroach, gypsy moth 10 boll weevil, Hessian fly, silverfish *science:*
10 entomology *winged:* 5 alate *wingless:*
4 flea, lice (plural) 5 louse 8 firebrat
10 silverfish, springtail 11 bristletail
insecticide 3 DDT 5 mirex, naled
6 aldrin, endrin 7 lindane, phorate
8 carbaryl, dieldrin, rotenone 9 chlordane, malathion, parathion 10 per-
methrin
insecure 5 shaky 6 unsafe, unsure, wobbly 7 anxious 8 unstable 9 uncertain
10 precarious 11 unconfident 12 apprehensive
inseminate 7 implant, instill 9 fertilize,
pollinate 10 impregnate
insensate 4 dull, hard, numb 5 stony
6 brutal, numbed 7 callous 8 comatose
9 bloodless, heartless, impassive,
unfeeling
insensibility 4 coma 6 apathy, torpor
8 lethargy, stoicism 12 indifference
insensible 4 cold, dead, dull, hard,
numb, rapt 5 stoic 6 asleep, intent,
numbed, obtuse, stolid 7 callous
8 absorbed, comatose, deadened, hardened, obdurate 9 apathetic, bloodless,
engrossed, impassive, unfeeling
11 unconscious 12 anesthetized
insensitive 4 dull, hard, numb, rude
5 crass 6 numbed, obtuse, unkind 7 callous 8 benumbed, deadened, hardened,
tactless, uncaring 9 bloodless, heartless,
unfeeling 10 anesthetic, impossible
11 indifferent, unconcerned 12 anesthetized, unresponsive

insert 5 enter 7 implant, obtrude 9 interpose 10 interleave 11 intercalate, interpolate
insertion 8 addendum, addition 13 interpolation
in short 7 briefly, tersely 9 concisely
10 succinctly
inside 6 closet, secret, within 7 private
8 hush-hush, interior 12 confidential
combining form: 4 endo
insidious 3 sly 4 foxy, wily 6 artful,
crafty, subtle, tricky 7 cunning, gradual
8 creeping, guileful 9 deceitful 13 surreptitious
insight 6 acumen, aperçu, wisdom
8 sagacity, sapience 9 intuition 11 discernment, penetration 13 understanding
insightful 4 keen, sage, wise 7 gnostic,
knowing 9 intuitive, sagacious 10 discerning, perceptive 11 penetrating
insignia 4 mark, sign 5 badge 6 emblem
8 brassard 10 decoration
insignificant 4 puny 5 dinky, minor,
petty, small 6 casual, little, minute, paltry 7 minimal, trivial 8 nugatory, trifling 9 secondary, small-time 10 negligible 11 minor-league, unimportant
insincere 5 false, lying, phony 6 double,
forced, hollow, shifty, tricky 7 feigned
8 mala fide, slippery, spurious 9 deceitful, deceptive, dishonest, pretended,
simulated 10 left-handed, mendacious,
untruthful 11 dissembling, double-
faced 12 hypocritical
insinuate 4 hint 5 imply 6 inject, insert,
work in, worm in 7 implant, instill,
suggest 9 introduce
insipid 3 dry 4 arid, dull, flat, mild, pale,
thin, weak 5 banal, bland, vapid
6 jejune, watery 7 mundane, prosaic,
subdued, tedious 8 bromidic, lifeless,
ordinary 9 innocuous, tasteless 10 flavorless, monotonous, namby-pamby,
wishy-washy 11 commonplace
insist 4 hold 5 argue, claim, swear
6 affirm, assert, demand, stress 7 certify, contend, declare, require, testify
8 maintain
insistent 6 crying, dogged, urgent
7 adamant, burning, clamant, exigent
8 emphatic, forceful, pressing, resolute
9 assertive, clamorous, obtrusive
10 determined, imperative, relentless
11 persevering
insolence 4 gall, guff, sass 5 brass,
cheek, nerve 8 audacity, boldness,
chutzpah, contempt, rudeness 9 arrogance, impudence 10 brazenness, disrespect, effrontery 11 haughtiness, presumption 12 impertinence

insolent 4 bold, flip, pert, rude **5** cocky, lofty, sassy, saucy **6** brazen, cheeky **7** haughty, uncivil **8** arrogant, cavalier, flippant, impolite, impudent, superior **9** audacious, barefaced, bold-faced **10** disdainful, peremptory **11** impertinent, overbearing **12** contumelious, discourteous, supercilious **13** high-and-mighty

insouciance 6 aplomb **9** disregard, unconcern **10** breeziness **11** disinterest, nonchalance **12** carelessness, heedlessness, indifference

insouciant 4 airy, flip **6** blithe, breezy, casual, jaunty **8** carefree, flippant, heedless **9** easygoing **10** nonchalant, untroubled **11** indifferent, thoughtless, unconcerned **12** devil-may-care, happy-go-lucky, lighthearted

inspect 3 con, vet **4** scan, view **5** audit, check, probe, study **6** review, size up, survey **7** canvass, examine, observe **8** appraise, check out, look over, question **9** check over **10** scrutinize **11** investigate

inspiration 4 muse **6** animus, genius, vision **7** insight **8** afflatus **9** brainwave, influence **10** brainchild, brainstorm, creativity **13** enlightenment

inspire 4 fire, stir **5** elate, exalt, imbue, rouse **6** arouse, excite, foment, incite, prompt, strike **7** animate, enliven, impress, instill, quicken **8** motivate **9** encourage, galvanize, influence, stimulate **10** exhilarate

inspiring 6 moving **7** awesome, rousing **8** exalting, stirring **9** animating, uplifting **10** vitalizing

inspirit 4 fire, lift, spur, stir **5** cheer, exalt, liven, rally, rouse, spark, steel **6** arouse, excite, incite, kindle, revive, uplift, vivify **7** animate, comfort, console, delight, enliven, gladden, hearten, nourish, quicken, refresh, restore **8** activate, embolden, energize, revivify, vitalize **9** encourage, stimulate **10** invigorate, strengthen

instability 8 fluidity **9** shakiness **10** insecurity, volatility **11** inconstancy **12** unsteadiness

install 4 seat, vest **5** put in, set up **6** induct, invest **8** ensconce, enthrone, entrench **9** establish

instance 4 case, cite, item **6** detail, ground, reason, sample **7** example **8** specimen **10** particular **12** illustration

instant 3 sec **4** wink **5** flash, jiffy, point, shake, trice **6** moment, second, urgent **7** current, exigent, present **8** existent, occasion, pressing **9** heartbeat, immediate, insistent, twinkling **10** imperative, present-day

instantaneous 4 fast **5** quick, rapid **9** immediate, ligntning, momentary **11** hair-trigger, split-second

instanter 3 now **6** at once **8** directly **9** forthwith, right away **11** immediately

instantly 3 now **6** at once **8** directly **9** forthwith, right away **11** immediately

instead 4 else **6** in lieu, rather **11** alternately **13** alternatively

instigate 4 abet, fire, goad, plan, plot, prod, spur, urge **5** egg on, impel, raise **6** excite, foment, incite, stir up, whip up **7** provoke, suggest **8** motivate **9** stimulate **10** bring about

instill 5 imbue **6** impart, infuse, inject **7** implant, suffuse **8** engender **9** inculcate, introduce

instinct 4 nose **5** hunch, sense **7** feeling, impulse **8** aptitude, behavior **9** intuition **10** proclivity, sixth sense **11** gut reaction

instinctive 3 gut **6** inborn, innate, normal **7** natural **8** habitual, inherent, visceral **9** automatic, ingrained, intrinsic, intuitive, reflexive, unlearned **10** congenital, unprompted **11** involuntary, spontaneous, unmeditated

instinctual 6 reflex **7** natural, routine **8** habitual, knee-jerk, untaught **9** automatic, impulsive, intuitive, reflexive **10** mechanical, unthinking **11** involuntary, spontaneous, unconscious

institute 5 begin, found, set up, start **6** decree, launch, ordain **7** academy, pioneer, usher in **8** initiate, organize **9** establish, introduce, originate **10** inaugurate **12** organization

institution 4 firm, rite **5** habit **6** custom **9** enactment **10** foundation **13** establishment *kind:* **6** asylum, school **7** academy, college **8** hospital **10** sanatorium, sanitarium, sanitorium, university

instruct 4 show **5** coach, drill, guide, order, steer, teach, train, tutor **6** direct, enjoin, inform, school **7** apprise, command, counsel, educate, lecture **9** enlighten, prescribe

instruction 5 drill **6** advice, lesson **7** precept **8** coaching, guidance, teaching, training, tutelage **9** catechism, education, schooling **10** directions *place of:* **6** school **7** academe, academy, college **10** university

instructive 8 didactic, edifying, pedantic **9** pedagogic **11** educational, explanatory, explicative, informative **12** enlightening

instructor 3 don **4** guru **5** coach, guide, swami, tutor **6** mentor **7** teacher, trainer **8** educator, lecturer **9** pedagogue, preceptor

instrument 4 deed, gear, mean, tool **5** agent, means, organ **6** agency, device, gadget, medium **7** utensil, vehicle **9** apparatus, appliance, machinery, mechanism **11** contraption, contrivance **13** paraphernalia *aircraft:* **5** radar, radio **7** compass **9** altimeter, gyroscope **10** altazimuth, tachometer **11** transponder *calculating:* **6** abacus **8** computer **9** slide rule *graphic:* **6** camera **8** otoscope **9** telescope **10** binoculars, microscope **11** fluoroscope, stethoscope, stroboscope **12** bronchoscope, oscilloscope, spectrograph, spectroscope *measuring:* **4** gage **5** clock, gauge, radar, scale, sonar **7** alidade, ammeter, balance, caliper, sextant, transit **8** quadrant **9** altimeter, astrolabe, barometer, bolometer, manometer, pedometer, sonometer, voltmeter **10** anemometer, Fathometer, hydrometer, hygrometer, micrometer, radiometer, radiosonde, spirometer, tachometer, theodolite **11** chronometer, lie detector, range finder, seismograph, speedometer, thermometer **12** electroscope, galvanometer, oscillograph, oscilloscope **13** Geiger counter, potentiometer *medical:* **6** lancet, trocar **7** curette, forceps, specula (plural) **8** tenacula (plural) **9** tenaculum *radiation-producing:* **5** laser, maser (see also IMPLEMENT; MUSICAL INSTRUMENT; TOOL)

instrumental 5 vital **6** useful **7** crucial, helpful **9** conducive, essential, necessary, requisite **10** imperative **13** indispensable

instrumentality 5 agent, force, means, organ **6** agency, energy, medium **7** channel, vehicle **8** ministry **9** mechanism

insubordinate 6 unruly **8** factious, mutinous **9** fractious, seditious **10** headstrong, rebellious, refractory **11** disobedient, intractable, uncompliant **12** contumacious, recalcitrant, ungovernable

insubstantial 4 airy, weak **5** frail **6** feeble, flimsy **7** fragile, tenuous **8** bodiless, ethereal **9** imaginary, unfleshly **10** intangible **11** disembodied **12** apparitional

insufferable 10 unbearable **11** intolerable, unendurable **13** insupportable

insufficiency 4 lack **6** dearth **7** paucity, poverty **8** scarcity, shortage **10** deficiency, inadequacy, scantiness, scarceness **11** defalcation

insufficient 5 scant **6** scanty, scarce,

skimpy **7** lacking, wanting **10** inadequate, incomplete

insular 5 local **6** narrow **7** bigoted, limited **8** confined, isolated, secluded **9** illiberal, parochial, sectarian, small-town **10** prejudiced, provincial, restricted

insulate 6 cut off, enisle **7** isolate **8** close off **9** segregate, sequester

insult 4 gibe, jeer, mock, slap, slur **5** abuse, fleer, scoff, scorn, shame, sneer, taunt **6** debase, deride, offend, revile **7** affront, disdain, obloquy, offense, outrage **8** derision, disgrace, ignominy, ridicule **9** contumely, humiliate **10** opprobrium **12** vituperation

insurance 8 guaranty, warranty **10** protection *agency:* **7** actuary **8** adjuster **11** underwriter *term:* **6** policy **7** annuity **8** coverage **9** bordereau **11** beneficiary

insure 5 cinch, guard **6** shield **7** confirm, protect **9** guarantee, safeguard **10** underwrite

insurgent 5 rebel **6** anarch **8** factious, frondeur, mutineer, mutinous, revolter **9** anarchist, seditious **10** incendiary, rebellious **12** contumacious **13** insubordinate, revolutionary

insurrection 4 coup **6** mutiny, putsch, revolt, rising **8** uprising **9** rebellion

insurrectionist 5 rebel **6** anarch **8** frondeur, mutineer, revolter **10** malcontent

insusceptible 6 exempt, immune **9** resistant **10** impervious **11** unreceptive

intact 5 sound, whole **6** entire, unhurt, virgin **7** perfect **8** complete, unbroken, unmarred, virginal **9** undamaged, uninjured, untouched **10** unimpaired

intangible 4 airy **5** vague **7** elusive, ghostly **8** ethereal **10** evanescent, immaterial, impalpable **11** incorporeal

integer 4 unit **5** digit **6** entity, figure, number **7** numeral **11** whole number

integral 4 full **5** whole **6** entire **7** perfect **8** complete, inherent **9** composite, elemental, essential, necessary, requisite **11** constituent **13** indispensable

integrate 3 mix **4** fuse, join, link **5** blend, merge, unify, unite **6** embody, mingle **7** combine, conjoin **8** coalesce **9** harmonize, reconcile **10** amalgamate, assimilate, coordinate, synthesize **11** consolidate, desegregate

integrity 5 honor **6** virtue **7** honesty, probity **8** cohesion **9** coherence, constancy, rectitude, soundness, wholeness **12** completeness

integument 4 coat **5** testa **7** coating, cuticle **8** covering, envelope

intellect 3 wit **4** mind **5** brain **6** acumen, brains, genius, reason, smarts **9** intuition, mentality 12 intelligence 13 comprehension, understanding

intellectual 5 brain 6 brainy, mental, pundit 7 bookish, egghead, erudite, psychic, thinker 8 academic, cerebral, highbrow, longhair 9 scholarly

intelligence 3 wit 4 dope, info, mind, news, word 5 brain, savvy, sense 6 acuity, acumen, brains, notice, reason, smarts, wisdom 7 hearsay, tidings 8 aptitude, judgment, learning, sagacity 9 knowledge, mentality, mother wit 10 brainpower, shrewdness

intelligent 4 keen, wise 5 acute, alert, aware, quick, sharp, smart, sound 6 adroit, astute, brainy, bright, clever, shrewd 7 cunning, knowing, logical 8 rational, sensible 9 brilliant, ingenious, sagacious 10 reasonable 11 quickwitted, ready-witted 13 perspicacious

intelligentsia 7 clerisy 8 literati, vanguard 10 avant-garde, illuminati

intelligible 5 clear, lucid, plain

intemperance 6 excess 7 license 9 depravity 10 debauchery, profligacy 11 dissipation, drunkenness 12 immoderation, incontinence

intemperate 5 harsh 6 bitter, brutal, severe 7 drunken, extreme, violent 8 bibulous 9 crapulous, dissolute, excessive 10 dissipated, exorbitant, gluttonous, immoderate, inordinate, profligate 12 unrestrained 13 overindulgent

intend 3 aim, try 4 mean, plan 5 essay, spell 6 assign, denote, design, scheme, strive 7 attempt, connote, propose, purpose, signify 8 endeavor 9 designate

intended 6 fiancé 7 engaged, fiancée 8 destined, plighted, promised, proposed 9 affianced, betrothed 10 calculated, deliberate

intense 4 keen 5 acute, vivid 6 ardent, fervid, fierce, severe, strong 7 extreme, fervent, furious, violent, zealous 8 powerful, vehement 9 assiduous, excessive, exquisite 10 heightened 12 concentrated

intensify 4 rise 5 mount, rouse 6 accent, heat up, stress 7 enhance, sharpen 8 escalate, heighten, increase, redouble 9 aggravate, emphasize 10 accentuate, aggrandize, exacerbate 11 concentrate

intensity 6 energy, fervor 7 passion 8 emphasis, ferocity, fervency, loudness 9 vehemence

intensive 6 all-out 7 zealous 8 sweeping, thorough 10 exhaustive 12 concentrated *pronoun:* 6 itself, myself 7 herself, himself 8 yourself 9 ourselves 10 themselves, yourselves

intent 3 aim, set 4 goal, plan, rapt, will 5 eager, fixed 6 design, import, object 7 decided, earnest, engaged, meaning, purport, purpose, riveted, wrapped 8 absorbed, conation, decisive, diligent, immersed, resolute, resolved, sedulous, volition 9 engrossed, objective, wrapped up 10 determined

intention 3 aim, end 4 goal, hope, plan, wish 6 design, desire, object 7 meaning, purpose 8 ambition 9 objective 10 aspiration

intentional 5 meant 7 advised, studied, willful, willing, witting 8 designed, proposed 9 voluntary 10 considered, deliberate 12 premeditated

intentionally 9 on purpose, purposely

inter 4 bury 5 plant 6 entomb, inhume 9 lay to rest

interact 9 cooperate 11 collaborate

interbreed 5 cross 9 hybridize 10 mongrelize

intercede 6 step in 7 mediate 9 arbitrate

intercept 4 grab 5 catch, seize, steal 6 cut off, hijack

intercessor 5 agent 6 broker 8 advocate, mediator 9 go-between, middleman

interconnect 4 join, link 5 unite 6 couple, hook up, link up

intercourse 3 sex 5 trade, truck 7 contact, dealing, traffic 8 business, commerce, dealings 9 communion 10 connection, networking 11 give-and-take 12 conversation 13 communication

intercross 9 hybridize 10 mongrelize

interdict 3 ban, bar 4 veto 5 block, taboo 6 cut off, enjoin, forbid, outlaw 7 censure, condemn, embargo 8 disallow, prohibit, sanction 9 proscribe 11 prohibition

interest 4 gain, grab, hook, lure, pull 5 pique, stake, tempt 6 appeal, arouse, behalf, engage, profit, regard 7 attract, concern, engross, involve, welfare 8 appeal to, intrigue 9 attention, curiosity, fascinate, tantalize, well-being 10 prosperity

interested 4 rapt 5 drawn 7 curious, partial 8 invested, partisan 9 attentive

interface 3 GUI 6 border 8 boundary 9 cooperate 11 communicate

interfere 6 butt in, horn in, meddle, step in 7 barge in, intrude

interim 3 gap 5 break, pause 6 acting, breach, hiatus, lacuna, pro tem 7 stopgap, time-out 8 downtime, meantime 9 makeshift, temporary 10 pro tempore 11 provisional

interior 3 gut 4 pith 5 belly, bosom, heart, inner 6 center, inland, inside, inward, marrow 8 visceral 9 heartland 10 hinterland

interject 3 add 6 fill in, insert 7 throw in

interjection *agreement:* 4 amen 5 roger
6 righto 7 right on *attention-getter:* 3 hey
4 ahem, ahoy, psst 6 yoo-hoo *calling
pigs:* 5 sooey *cheer:* 3 rah 5 wahoo
6 hooray, hurrah, hurray *contempt:*
4 pooh 5 pshaw *disappointment:* 4 rats
5 shoot 6 shucks *disapproval:* 3 boo, fie
disbelief: 3 huh *disgust:* 3 bah, boo,
pah, ugh 4 rats, yuck 5 faugh, yecch
6 phooey *dismay:* 4 oh no, uh-oh *dismissal:* 3 git 4 shoo *farewell:* 3 bye 4 ciao
5 adios 6 bye-bye, so long 7 cheerio
greeting: 4 ciao 5 aloha, hello, howdy *in
golf:* 4 fore *in hunting:* 6 yoicks *in march-
ing:* 3 hup, hut *joy:* 4 whee 6 hooray,
hurrah, hurray, yippee 7 hosanna,
whoopee 8 alleluia 10 hallelujah *mild
apology:* 4 oops 6 whoops *mild oath:*
3 gad 4 darn, drat, egad, geez, gosh,
heck, jeez 5 egads, golly, zooks
6 jiminy, zounds 7 begorra, gee whiz,
jeepers 8 gadzooks 13 gee whillikers
O.K.: 5 roger, wilco *pain:* 4 ouch *peace:*
6 shalom *regret:* 3 woe 4 alas 5 alack
8 lackaday *relief:* 4 phew *request:*
7 prithee *silence:* 3 shh *sneeze:* 5 achoo
6 atchoo 7 kerchoo *sorrow:* 4 alas
5 alack 8 lackaday *stop:* 4 whoa *surprise:* 3 aha, huh, oho, wow 4 gosh,
oops 5 blimy, yikes, yipes, zowie
6 blimey *to a horse:* 4 whoa 7 giddyap
toast: 5 salud, skoal 6 cheers, prosit,
l'chaim 7 l'chayim *triumph:* 3 aha, hah
6 eureka (see also EXCLAMATION)

interlace 3 mix 5 braid, plait, twine,
weave 7 entwine 9 alternate

interlard 3 mix 6 mingle

interlocuter 4 host 5 emcee

interlope 6 butt in, horn in, meddle 7 intrude 8 encroach, infringe 9 interfere

interlude 4 halt, lull, rest 5 break, idyll,
letup, pause, spell 6 recess 7 episode,
respite 8 breather, entr'acte, meantime,
stoppage 9 meanwhile 10 suspension

intermediary 3 mid 4 mean 5 agent,
envoy, organ 6 agency, broker, center,
medium, middle, midway 7 central,
channel, vehicle 8 delegate, emissary,
mediator, ministry 9 go-between, middleman

intermediate 3 mid 4 fair, mean, so-so
6 broker, center, medium, middle, midway, step in 7 average, between, central
8 middling 9 arbitrate, go-between,
middleman

intermediator 6 broker 7 liaison, referee
9 go-between, middleman

interment 6 burial 9 sepulture 10 inhumation

intermesh 4 lock 6 engage 8 dovetail

interminable 7 endless, eternal, lasting
8 constant, infinite, unending 9 boundless, ceaseless, continual, limitless, permanent, perpetual, unceasing 10 protracted 11 everlasting, never-ending

intermission 4 lull, rest, stop 5 break,
pause, spell 6 recess 7 latency, respite,
time-out 8 abeyance, dormancy, interval 10 quiescence, suspension 11 parenthesis

intermit 4 halt, stay 5 break, defer, delay
6 arrest, hold up, put off 7 suspend
8 postpone, prorogue 9 interrupt 11 discontinue

intermittent 6 broken, cyclic, fitful, serial
8 cyclical, metrical, periodic, seasonal,
sporadic 9 irregular, recurrent, recurring, spasmodic, stop-and-go 10 occasional

intermix 4 meld 5 blend 6 mingle
8 comingle, compound 9 commingle,
integrate 10 amalgamate 11 intermingle

intermixture 4 brew 5 blend 7 amalgam
8 compound 9 composite, synthesis
12 amalgamation 13 miscegenation

intern 4 jail 6 immure 7 confine,
impound, put away, trainee 8 imprison
11 incarcerate

internal 6 native 7 private 8 visceral
10 subjective *prefix:* 5 intra

internal organs 4 guts 6 bowels, vitals
7 innards, viscera 8 entrails 10 intestines, penetralia

international organization 3 FAO, IAM,
ICJ, IFC, ILO, ITO, ITU, OAS, WHO,
WMO, WTO 4 IAAF, IABA, IAEA,
IARU, IATA, ICAO, IFIP, IMCO,
NATO 5 ICFTU, SEATO 6 UNESCO,
UNICEF

internuncio 5 envoy 6 bearer, legate
7 carrier, courier 8 delegate, emissary
9 go-between, messenger, middleman

interpolate 3 add 5 admit, annex, enter
6 append, fill in, inject, insert 7 throw
in 9 introduce

interpose 6 butt in, fill in, insert, meddle, step in 7 intrude, mediate, obtrude,
throw in 8 moderate 9 arbitrate, insinuate, introduce, negotiate 11 come
between

interpret 5 gloss 6 decode 7 explain,
expound 8 annotate, construe 9 elucidate, explicate 10 paraphrase

interpretation 5 gloss 7 meaning, reading, version 8 exegesis 9 construal, rendering 11 explanation, translation

interpretive 8 exegetic 10 diagnostic,
exegetical, expository 11 explanatory,
explicatory

interregnum 5 break, lapse, pause 6 hiatus 7 time-out

interrogate 3 ask 4 pump, quiz 5 grill, query 7 examine 8 question 9 catechize 12 cross-examine

interrupt 4 halt, stay, stop 5 abort, break, cut in 7 break in, chime in, suspend 8 cut short

interruption 3 gap 4 halt 5 break, pause, split 6 breach, cutoff, hiatus, lacuna, recess 7 caesura 8 stoppage

intersect 4 meet 5 cross 9 decussate 10 crisscross

intersection 8 crossing, junction 10 crossroads

intersperse 7 diffuse, scatter 8 sprinkle

interstice 3 gap 4 slit, slot, vent 5 chink, cleft, crack, space 6 breach, cavity, cranny 7 crevice, fissure, opening, orifice 8 aperture

intertwine 4 mesh 5 braid, plait, twist, weave 7 network 9 convolute 10 crisscross

interval 3 gap 4 lull, wait 5 break, comma, delay, letup, pause, space 6 breach, hiatus, lacuna 7 caesura, interim, respite, time-out 8 downtime 9 pausation 11 parenthesis *music:* 4 rest

intervene 6 butt in, meddle, step in 7 intrude, mediate, obtrude

interweave 3 mix 4 fuse, join, knit, link, mesh 5 blend, plait, twine 6 enmesh 7 entwine, wreathe

intestinal fortitude 4 grit, guts 5 nerve, pluck, spunk 6 mettle, spirit 7 courage 8 backbone 10 resolution

intestine 3 gut 4 tube 5 bowel, canal 7 viscera (plural) *combining form:* 4 coli, colo 6 entero *part:* 5 cecum, colon, ileum 7 jejunum 8 duodenum

in the same place 6 ibidem

intimacy 9 closeness 11 familiarity 12 acquaintance

intimate 3 gut 4 cozy, dear, fond, hint 5 amigo, close, crony, imply, inner, privy 6 attest, friend, impart, loving, secret 7 comrade, connote, devoted, nearest, suggest 8 familiar, inherent 9 close-knit, companion, confidant, ingrained, insinuate, intrinsic 12 confidential

intimation 3 cue 4 clue, hint 5 shade, tinge, trace 6 breath 7 inkling 8 telltale 10 suggestion

intimidate 3 awe, cow 4 bait 5 bully, chivy, daunt, scare 6 badger, coerce, hector 7 buffalo, overawe 8 browbeat, bulldoze, bullyrag 9 strong-arm, terrorize

intolerable 10 unbearable 11 unendurable 12 insufferable 13 insupportable

intolerant 6 narrow 7 bigoted 8 dogmatic 9 hidebound, illiberal 10 inflexible, prejudiced 11 small-minded 12 narrowminded

intonation 5 chant, pitch 6 accent, timbre 7 cadence 8 chanting 10 inflection, modulation, recitation

intone 5 chant, croon, drone 10 cantillate

in toto 3 all 6 wholly 7 all told, en masse 10 altogether

intoxicant 5 booze, drink, hooch, sauce 6 hootch, liquor, rotgut 7 alcohol, spirits 9 aqua vitae, firewater, moonshine

intoxicated 3 lit, wet 4 high 5 blind, drunk, fried, giddy, lit up, oiled, stiff, tight, tipsy 6 blotto, bombed, canned, elated, juiced, loaded, looped, potted, sodden, soused, stewed, stoned, tanked, tiddly, zonked 7 blitzed, crocked, drunken, excited, maudlin, muddled, pickled, pie-eyed, sloshed, smashed, sozzled 8 cockeyed, polluted, squiffed 9 crapulous, plastered 11 exhilarated

intoxication 3 joy 5 bliss 6 frenzy 7 ecstasy, elation, rapture 8 delirium, euphoria 9 transport 10 exaltation 11 drunkenness, inebriation

intractable 4 wild 5 balky 6 mulish, ornery, unruly 7 froward, willful 8 mutinous, obdurate, perverse, stubborn 9 fractious, obstinate, pigheaded, unbending 10 bullheaded, headstrong, inflexible, rebellious, refractory, unyielding 12 pertinacious, recalcitrant, ungovernable 13 undisciplined

intransigent 5 rigid, tough 7 willful 8 obdurate, resolute, stubborn 9 obstinate, unbending, unpliable 10 refractory, self-willed, unyielding 12 contumacious, pertinacious

intrepid 4 bold, game 5 brave, gutsy, hardy 6 daring, heroic 7 doughty, gallant, valiant 8 fearless, resolute, stalwart, unafraid, valorous 9 audacious, dauntless, undaunted 10 courageous 11 adventurous, temerarious

intricate 4 mazy 6 daedal, knotty 7 complex, gordian, tangled 8 abstruse, involved, tortuous 9 Byzantine, elaborate 10 circuitous, convoluted 11 complicated 12 labyrinthine 13 sophisticated

intrigue 4 plot, wile 5 amour, cabal, cheat, pique, trick 6 affair, appeal, excite, scheme 7 attract, beguile, collude, connive, liaison, romance 8 cogitate, conspire, contrive, interest 9 machinate 10 conspiracy 11 machination

intriguing 8 enticing 9 absorbing, beguiling 10 engrossing, entrancing 11 captivating, fascinating, stimulating

intrinsic see INHERENT

intrinsically 5 per se **6** as such **7** at heart **10** inherently

introduce 5 begin, enter, found, set up **6** broach, fill in, insert, launch, unveil, work in **7** bring up, implant, install, instill, pioneer, precede, preface, present, throw in, usher in **8** initiate, innovate, organize **9** establish, insinuate, institute, interject, interpose, originate

introduction 5 debut, proem **6** lead-in **7** introit, opening, preface, prelude **8** entrance, exordium, foreword, overture, preamble, prologue, protases (plural), protasis **12** prolegomenon

introductory 5 basic **7** initial, nascent, opening **8** proemial **9** beginning, prefatory **10** elementary **11** preliminary, preparatory

intrude 5 cut in **6** butt in, horn in, impose, invade, meddle **7** barge in, burst in, presume **8** encroach, infringe, trespass **9** interfere, interlope, interrupt

intrusive 4 busy, nosy **5** nosey **6** prying, snoopy **7** curious **8** meddling, snooping **9** officious **10** meddlesome **11** impertinent

in truth 6 indeed, really, verily **8** actually, candidly **9** veritably

intuit 5 infer, sense **6** deduce, divine **7** surmise

intuition 5 hunch **7** feeling, inkling, insight **8** instinct **10** sixth sense **11** second sight **12** presentiment

intuitive 6 innate **7** natural **8** unwilled, visceral **10** unthinking **11** instinctive, instinctual, involuntary, spontaneous, unconscious

Inuit 6 Eskimo

inundate 4 glut **5** drown, flood, swamp, whelm **6** deluge, engulf **7** overrun **8** overflow, submerge **9** overwhelm

inundation 5 flood, spate **6** deluge **7** Niagara, torrent **8** cataract, flooding, overflow **9** avalanche, cataclysm, landslide **10** cloudburst

inure 5 steel, train **6** harden, season **7** prepare, toughen **8** accustom **9** acclimate, habituate **10** discipline **11** familiarize

inutile 6 no-good **7** useless **8** unusable **9** valueless, worthless

invade 4 loot, raid **6** breach, occupy, ravage **7** overrun, pillage, plunder **8** encroach, infringe, trespass **9** penetrate

invader 8 intruder **10** encroacher, interloper, trespasser **11** infiltrator

invalid 3 bad **4** null, sick, void **5** false **6** ailing, infirm, shut-in, sickly **7** unsound **8** baseless, disabled **9** bedridden, illogical, sophistic **10** fallacious, irrational **11** null and void **12** convalescent

invalidate 4 undo, void **5** annul, quash **6** cancel, offset, vacate **7** abolish, nullify **9** discredit, repudiate **10** counteract, disqualify, neutralize

invaluable 7 crucial **8** precious **9** essential, priceless **11** beyond price, inestimable **13** irreplaceable

invariable 4 same **5** fixed **6** static, steady **7** uniform **8** constant **9** continual, immovable, immutable, unfailing, unvarying **10** changeless, consistent, unchanging **11** inalterable, unalterable **12** unchangeable

invariably 4 ever **6** always **7** forever

invasion 4 raid **5** foray **6** attack, inroad **7** assault, offense **8** trespass **9** incursion, intrusion, offensive, onslaught **12** encroachment

invective 5 abuse **6** tirade **7** abusive, obloquy **8** diatribe, jeremiad **9** contumely, philippic, truculent **10** opprobrium, scurrility, scurrilous **11** opprobrious **12** billingsgate, contumelious, vituperation, vituperative

inveigh 4 kick, rail, rant **6** object **7** protest **8** complain **9** fulminate **11** expostulate, remonstrate

inveigle 4 coax, lure **5** decoy, snare, tempt **6** allure, cajole, entice, entrap, lead on, rope in, seduce, wangle **7** blarney, win over **8** blandish, butter up, maneuver, persuade

invent 4 coin, mint **6** cook up, create, design, devise, make up, patent, vamp up **7** concoct, dream up, fashion, hatch up, pioneer, think up **8** conceive, contrive, discover, engineer, envision **9** fabricate, formulate, originate

invention 7 coinage, fiction **8** creation **10** brainchild, innovation **11** contrivance

inventive 7 fertile, teeming **8** creative, fruitful, original **9** demiurgic, ingenious **10** innovative, innovatory **11** imaginative

inventor 5 maker **6** author, father, mother **7** creator, founder **8** engineer **9** architect, generator, innovator **10** discoverer, introducer, originator *air brake:* **12** Westinghouse (George) *air conditioning:* **7** Carrier (Willis) *automobile:* **7** Daimler (Gottlieb) *ballpoint pen:* **4** Loud (John) *barbed wire:* **7** Glidden (Joseph Farwell) *barometer:* **10** Torricelli (Evangelista) *bifocal lens:* **8** Franklin (Benjamin) *camera:* **7** Eastman (George) *cash register:* **5** Ritty (James) *cotton gin:* **7** Whitney (Eli) *cylinder lock:* **4** Yale

(Linus) *dirigible:* 8 Zeppelin (Ferdinand von) *dynamite:* 5 Nobel (Alfred) *electric battery:* 5 Volta (Alessandro) *electric fan:* 7 Wheeler (George) *electric organ:* 7 Hammond (Laurens) *electric razor:* 6 Schick (Jacob) *electric stove:* 7 Hadaway (W. S.) *elevator:* 4 Otis (Elisha) *fountain pen:* 8 Waterman (Lewis) *friction match:* 6 Walker (John) *gyrocompass:* 6 Sperry (Elmer) *helicopter:* 8 Sikorsky (Igor) *hot-air balloon:* 11 Montgolfier (Jacques, Joseph) *incandescent lamp:* 6 Edison (Thomas Alva) *induction motor:* 5 Tesla (Nikola) *lawn mower:* 5 Hills (Amariah) *Linotype:* 12 Mergenthaler (Ottmar) *logarithm:* 6 Napier (John) *machine gun:* 7 Gatling (Richard) *microphone:* 8 Berliner (Emile) *microwave oven:* 7 Spencer (Percy) *movable type:* 9 Gutenberg (Johannes) *parachute:* 9 Blanchard (Jean-Pierre) *pendulum clock:* 7 Huygens (Christiaan) *phonograph:* 6 Edison (Thomas Alva) *photography:* 6 Niepce (Nicéphore), Talbot (W. H. Fox) 8 Daguerre (Louis) *piano:* 10 Cristofori (Bartolomeo) *radio:* 7 Marconi (Guglielmo) *reaper:* 9 McCormick (Cyrus) *revolver:* 4 Colt (Samuel) *rocket engine:* 7 Goddard (Robert) *safety pin:* 4 Hunt (Walter) *safety razor:* 8 Gillette (King) *sewing machine:* 4 Howe (Elias) *sleeping car:* 7 Pullman (George) *spinning jenny:* 10 Hargreaves (James) *steamboat:* 5 Fitch (John) 6 Fulton (Robert), Miller (Patrick), Rumsey (James) 8 Jouffroy (Claude de) *steam engine:* 4 Watt (James) *steam locomotive:* 10 Stephenson (George) *stethoscope:* 7 Laënnec (René) *submarine:* 7 Holland (John Philip) *synthesizer:* 4 Moog (Robert) *tank:* 7 Swinton (Ernest) *telegraph:* 5 Morse (Samuel F. B.) *telephone:* 4 Bell (Alexander Graham) *telescope:* 10 Lippershey (Hans) *television:* 5 Baird (John) 6 Nipkow (Paul) 8 Zworykin (Vladimir) 10 Farnsworth (Philo) *thermometer:* 7 Galileo (Galilei) *torpedo:* 9 Whitehead (Robert) *tractor:* 5 Deere (John) *transistor:* 7 Bardeen (John) 8 Brattain (Walter), Shockley (William) *vulcanized rubber:* 8 Goodyear (Charles) *writing for the blind:* 7 Braille (Louis) *zipper:* 6 Judson (Whitcomb)

inventory 3 sum 4 fund, list 5 hoard, stock, store, tally 6 assets, digest, record, supply, survey 7 account, backlog, catalog, itemize, reserve, specify, summary 8 register, tabulate 9 catalogue, checklist, enumerate, reservoir, stockpile, summarize, synopsize

inverse 8 contrary, opposite

inversion 7 reverse 8 flipping, reversal, upending 9 about-face, turnabout, volte-face

invert 4 flip 5 upend 7 reverse 8 overturn, turn over 9 transpose

invertebrate 4 weak 5 timid 7 chicken, doormat, milksop 8 boneless, impotent, weakling 9 jellyfish, spineless 10 namby-pamby 11 ineffectual, milquetoast *kind:* 4 worm 6 insect, sponge 7 mollusc, mollusk 8 arachnid 9 arthropod 12 coelenterate

invest 4 gird, veil, wrap 5 adorn, array, dress, endow, imbue 6 clothe, confer, enfold, induct, infuse, ordain 7 empower, enclose, envelop, ingrain, install, suffuse

investigate 3 pry 4 sift 5 audit, probe, study 6 go into, search 7 dig into, examine, explore, inquire, inspect 8 check out, look into, muckrake, prospect, research 9 delve into 10 scrutinize 11 inquire into

investigation 5 audit, probe 6 survey 7 inquest, inquiry 8 research, scrutiny 11 fact-finding, inquisition

investigator 3 spy 4 dick 5 hound 6 shamus, sleuth 7 gumshoe 8 hawkshaw, sherlock 9 detective

investiture 9 inaugural, induction 10 initiation, ordination 12 inauguration, installation, ratification

inveterate 3 old, set 5 fixed, sworn 6 rooted 7 abiding, chronic, settled 8 deep-dyed, enduring, habitual, hardcore, hardened, lifelong 9 confirmed, ingrained, perennial 10 continuing, deep-rooted, deep-seated, entrenched, habituated, persistent, persisting 11 established 12 incorrigible 13 dyed-in-the-wool

Invictus author 6 Henley (William Ernest)

invidious 7 envious, envying, jealous 9 green-eyed, obnoxious, resentful

invigorate 4 stir 5 brace, pep up, rally, renew, rouse 6 perk up, vivify 7 animate, brace up, enliven, fortify, juice up, refresh, restore 8 energize, vitalize 9 reinforce, stimulate 10 rejuvenate, revitalize, strengthen

invincible 10 inviolable, unbeatable 11 impregnable, indomitable, insuperable 12 invulnerable, unassailable, undefeatable 13 unconquerable

in vino ___ 7 veritas

inviolable 4 safe 6 secure 10 impervious, sacrosanct 11 consecrated, impregnable 12 unassailable 13 incorruptible

invisible 6 hidden **9** concealed **10** intangible **12** unnoticeable **13** imperceptible

Invisible Man *author:* **5** Wells (H. G.) **7** Ellison (Ralph) *character:* **7** Griffin

Invisible Man, The *author:* **5** Wells (Herbert George) *character:* **7** Griffin (Herbert)

invitation 4 call, lure **6** come-on **7** bidding, proffer **8** entreaty, proposal **10** enticement **11** proposition **12** solicitation

invite 3 ask, bid **4** call, lure **5** tempt **6** allure, call in, entice, summon **7** propose, request, solicit

inviting 8 engaging, enticing, tempting **9** appealing, beguiling, seductive **10** attractive, intriguing

invocation 6 appeal, prayer **8** entreaty, petition **11** conjuration, incantation **12** supplication

invoice 3 tab **4** bill, list **5** score **7** account **8** manifest **9** reckoning, statement **11** consignment

invoke 3 beg **4** pray **5** crave, plead **6** appeal, call on, effect **7** beseech, conjure, enforce, entreat, implore, solicit **8** call upon, petition **9** call forth, conjure up, implement, importune **10** supplicate

involuntary 6 forced, reflex **8** knee-jerk **9** automatic, impulsive, reflexive, unwitting **10** compulsory, unintended, unprompted **11** instinctive, spontaneous, unconscious, unmeditated **13** unintentional

involve 4 mire **6** affect, embody, engage, entail, take in **7** call for, concern, contain, embrace, embroil, include, require, subsume **8** comprise, entangle **9** encompass, implicate **10** complicate, comprehend **11** necessitate

involved 6 daedal, knotty **7** complex, gordian **8** confused **9** Byzantine, elaborate, intricate **10** convoluted **11** complicated **12** labyrinthine

invulnerable 6 immune, secure **10** impervious, invincible, unbeatable **11** impregnable, indomitable **12** unassailable

Io *father:* **7** Inachus *guard:* **5** Argus *son:* **7** Epaphus

iodine source 4 kelp

Iolanthe *composer:* **8** Sullivan (Arthur) *librettist:* **7** Gilbert (W. S.)

Iolcus king 5 Aeson **6** Pelias

Iole *captor:* **8** Heracles, Hercules *father:* **7** Eurytus *husband:* **6** Hyllus

ion 6 ligand *kind:* **5** anion **6** cation **8** thermion

Ion *father:* **6** Apollo *mother:* **6** Creusa *stepfather:* **6** Xuthus

Ionesco, Eugène *play:* **6** Chairs (The), Lesson (The) **10** Rhinoceros **11** Bald Soprano (The)

iota 3 bit, jot, ray **4** atom, hint, mite, whit **5** crumb, grain, ounce, scrap, shred, speck, trace **6** tittle **7** smidgen **8** molecule, particle **9** scintilla

IOU 4 chit, debt *part:* **3** owe, you

Iowa *capital:* **9** Des Moines *city:* **4** Ames **7** Dubuque **8** Waterloo **9** Davenport, Sioux City **11** Cedar Rapids **13** Council Bluffs *college, university:* **5** Drake **8** Grinnell *nickname:* **7** Hawkeye (State) *river:* **9** Des Moines *state bird:* **9** goldfinch *state flower:* **15** wild prairie rose *state tree:* **3** oak

Iphicles *brother:* **8** Heracles, Hercules *mother:* **7** Alcmene *son:* **6** Iolaus

Iphigenia *avenger:* **12** Clytemnestra *brother:* **7** Orestes *father:* **9** Agamemnon *mother:* **12** Clytemnestra *sister:* **7** Electra

Iran *ancient civilization:* **4** Elam **5** Medes, Media **6** Persia *capital:* **6** Tehran **7** Teheran *city:* **3** Qom, Qum **6** Shiraz, Tabriz **7** Esfahan, Isfahan, Mashhad *conqueror:* **9** Alexander (the Great) *gulf:* **4** Oman **7** Persian *island:* **5** Qeshm *language:* **5** Farsi **7** Persian *leader:* **7** Pahlavi (Mohammad Reza, Reza Shah) **8** Khomeini (Ayatollah Ruholla) *monetary unit:* **4** rial *mountain, range:* **6** Elburz, Zagros **8** Damavand **9** Hindu Kush *neighbor:* **4** Iraq **6** Turkey **7** Armenia **8** Pakistan **10** Azerbaijan **11** Afghanistan **12** Turkmenistan *river:* **5** Atrek, Karun, Safid **7** Karkheh *sea:* **7** Caspian *strait:* **6** Hormuz

Iranian 7 Persian *parliament:* **6** Majlis *religious movement:* **5** Baha'i *sect:* **4** Shia *sect member:* **6** Shiite

Iraq *ancient civilization:* **5** Akkad, Sumer **8** Akkadian, Sumerian **9** Babylonia **10** Babylonian *ancient name:* **11** Mesopotamia *capital:* **7** Baghdad *city:* **5** Basra, Mosul, Najaf **6** Kirkuk **7** Falluja, Karbala **8** Fallujah *conqueror:* **9** Alexander (the Great) *desert:* **6** Syrian *gulf:* **7** Persian *leader:* **6** Faisal **7** Hussein (Saddam) *monetary unit:* **5** dinar *neighbor:* **4** Iran **5** Syria **6** Jordan, Kuwait, Turkey **11** Saudi Arabia *river:* **6** Tigris **9** Euphrates

irascible 4 tart **5** huffy, surly, testy **6** crabby, cranky, feisty, tetchy, touchy **7** bristly, grouchy, peevish, peppery, prickly **8** choleric, petulant, snappish **9** crotchety, fractious, irritable, querulous, splenetic **11** hot-tempered **12** cantankerous **13** quick-tempered

irate 3 mad **5** angry, livid, riled, vexed,

wroth 6 fuming 7 enraged, furious, steamed 8 choleric, incensed, provoked, wrathful 9 indignant 10 infuriated

ire 4 fury, rage, rile 5 anger, wrath 6 choler, enrage, madden, temper 7 incense, steam up, umbrage 9 infuriate 10 exasperate 11 indignation 12 exasperation

Ireland 4 Eire, Erin 8 Hibernia *capital:* 6 Dublin *city:* 4 Cork 5 Kerry, Louth, Meath, Sligo 6 Galway 7 Donegal, Kildare, Wexford, Wicklow 8 Kilkenny, Limerick 9 Waterford 12 Dun Laoghaire *county:* 4 Mayo 5 Clare 6 Galway 8 Limerick *island group:* 4 Aran 8 Hibernia *lake:* 3 Ree (Lough) 4 Derg (Lough) 5 Neagh (Lough) 6 Corrib (Lough) *language:* 5 Irish 6 Gaelic 7 English *monetary unit:* 4 euro *monetary unit, former:* 5 pound *nickname:* 11 Emerald Isle *river:* 6 Barrow, Liffey 7 Shannon

Irene 3 Pax *father:* 4 Zeus 7 Jupiter *mother:* 6 Themis

irenic 4 calm 7 pacific 8 pacifist 9 peaceable, placative, placatory 10 nonviolent 12 conciliatory, propitiatory

Iris *father:* 7 Thaumas *mother:* 7 Electra

Irish 4 Erse 6 Celtic, Gaelic *accent:* 6 brogue *cattle:* 5 Kerry *clan:* 4 sept *combining form:* 7 Hiberno *coronation stone:* 7 Lia Fail *cudgel:* 10 shillelagh *death spirit:* 7 banshee *dog:* 6 setter 7 terrier *elf:* 10 leprechaun *flag color:* 5 green, white 6 orange *flower:* 8 shamrock *girl:* 4 lass 6 lassie 7 colleen *god:* 3 Ler 5 Dagda 6 Aengus *goddess:* 4 Badb, Bodb 6 Brigit 8 Morrigan *hero:* 9 Cuchulain 10 Cú Chulainn *heroine:* 7 Deirdre *king:* 9 Brian Boru *lake:* 5 lough *language:* 6 Gaelic *legislature:* 4 Dail *militant force:* 3 IRA *nationalist:* 4 Tone (Wolfe) 6 Pearse (Padraig) 7 Collins (Michael), Parnell (Charles) 8 De Valera (Eamon), O'Connell (Daniel) 9 Sarsfield (Patrick) *nationalist society:* 8 Sinn Fein *patron saint:* 7 Patrick *theater:* 5 Abbey *writing system:* 4 ogam 5 ogham (see also GAELIC; CELTIC)

Irish moss 7 seaweed 9 carrageen

irk 3 try, vex 4 fret, gall, pain, rile 5 annoy, peeve, pique, upset 6 abrade, bother, harass, nettle, ruffle, strain, stress 7 provoke, trouble 8 exercise, irritate 10 exasperate

irksome 6 vexing 7 tedious 8 annoying, rankling 9 provoking, upsetting, vexatious 10 bothersome, irritating, nettle-some, unpleasant 11 aggravating, troublesome, unpalatable

iron 4 firm, gyve, hard 5 press, rigid 6 fetter, strong 7 adamant, manacle, shackle 8 handcuff, obdurate 9 unbending 10 inexorable, inflexible, *combining form:* 5 ferro 6 sidero *German:* 5 Eisen *relating to:* 6 ferric 7 ferrous

ironbound 5 harsh, rocky, rough, stern 6 craggy, jagged, rugged, severe, strict, uneven 7 scraggy 8 asperous, exacting, rigorous, scabrous 9 stringent 10 inflexible

Iron City 10 Pittsburgh

ironclad 5 fixed 7 binding 8 constant 9 immovable, immutable 10 inflexible, invariable 11 inalterable, irrefutable, unalterable 12 indisputable, irrefragable, unchangeable 13 unimpeachable

ironfisted 4 grim, hard, mean 5 harsh 6 brutal, severe, stingy 7 callous, miserly 8 pitiless, ruthless 9 penurious 10 implacable, unmerciful 11 hardhearted, intractable, remorseless 12 unappeasable

ironhanded 5 harsh, rigid 6 severe, strict 8 despotic, rigorous 9 draconian, stringent 10 tyrannical 12 unpermissive

ironhearted 5 stony 7 callous 8 hardened, obdurate, ruthless 9 merciless, unfeeling 10 hard-boiled 11 cold-blooded 13 unsympathetic

iron horse 10 locomotive

ironic 3 wry 6 biting 7 caustic, cutting, cynical, mordant, satiric 8 sardonic 9 sarcastic, trenchant

iron ore 8 goethite, hematite, limonite, siderite, taconite 9 magnetite

Iron Pants 6 Patton (George)

irons 5 bonds, gyves 6 chains 7 bilboes, darbies, fetters 8 manacles, shackles

Iroquois tribe 6 Cayuga, Mohawk, Oneida, Seneca 8 Onondaga 9 Tuscarora

irradiate 4 beam, glow 5 edify, light, shine 6 uplift 7 light up 8 illumine 9 enlighten 10 illuminate

irrational 3 mad 5 crazy 6 absurd, insane 7 invalid 8 demented 9 illogical, senseless, sophistic 10 cockamamie, fallacious, ridiculous 12 preposterous, unreasonable

irrefutable 4 sure 6 proven 7 certain 8 airtight, ironclad, positive 9 apodictic, veracious 10 conclusive, inarguable 11 indubitable 12 indisputable 13 incontestable

irregular 3 odd 5 queer 6 fitful, patchy, random, spotty, uneven 7 aimless, erratic, unequal 8 aberrant, abnormal, atypical, informal, lopsided, peculiar, singular, sporadic, unstable, unsteady, variable **9** anomalous, desultory, divergent, eccentric, guerrilla, haphazard, hit-or-miss, spasmodic, unregular, unsettled **10** asymmetric, capricious, changeable, inconstant, off-balance, unbalanced, unofficial **11** exceptional, fluctuating **12** intermittent, unsystematic

irregularity 5 freak, quirk **6** oddity **7** anomaly **8** deviance **9** deviation, roughness **10** aberration, inequality, unevenness **11** abnormality

irrelevant 5 inapt **9** unrelated **10** extraneous, immaterial, inapposite, peripheral **11** inessential, unessential, unimportant **12** inapplicable **13** insignificant

irreligious 6 unholy **7** godless, impious, profane, ungodly **11** blasphemous

irreparable 8 cureless, hopeless **9** incurable **11** immedicable **12** irredeemable, irremediable **13** irretrievable, unrecoverable

irreproachable 4 pure **8** flawless, innocent, spotless, virtuous **9** blameless, errorless, exemplary, faultless, guiltless, righteous **10** immaculate, impeccable, inculpable, unblamable

irresolute 5 shaky **6** fickle, unsure, wobbly **7** halting **8** doubtful, hesitant, unstable, waffling, wavering **9** equivocal, faltering, tentative, uncertain, undecided **10** ambivalent, changeable, inconstant, wishy-washy **11** fluctuating, half-hearted, vacillating

irresponsible 4 rash, wild **8** carefree, careless, feckless, reckless **10** incautious, unreliable **12** undependable **13** unaccountable, untrustworthy

irreverent 4 flip **7** impious, profane, ungodly **8** flippant **9** satirical **11** blasphemous **12** sacrilegious

irrevocable 4 firm **5** final **9** immutable **11** unalterable **12** irreversible, unchangeable **13** nonreversible

irrigation ditch 5 flume **6** sluice **7** acequia

irritability 5 pique **6** choler **8** edginess **9** petulance **10** crabbiness, impatience **11** fretfulness, peevishness *abnormal:* **8** erethism

irritable 4 edgy, sour **5** cross, huffy, testy, waspy, whiny **6** crabby, cranky, crusty, grumpy, ornery, snappy, tetchy, touchy **7** fretful, grouchy, peevish, pettish, prickly, waspish **8** captious, choleric, petulant, snappish **9** crotchety, fractious, impatient, irascible, querulous, splenetic **12** cantankerous, disagreeable

irritant 4 itch, pest **5** nudge **6** bother, gadfly, noodge, nudnik, pester, plague

8 headache, nuisance, vexation **9** annoyance **11** botheration

irritate 3 bug, irk, rub, vex **4** fret, gall, goad, rile, roil **5** anger, annoy, chafe, grate, peeve, pique, spite **6** abrade, badger, bother, burn up, harass, hector, madden, needle, nettle, offend, ruffle **7** inflame, provoke **9** aggravate, stimulate **10** exacerbate, exasperate

irritated 5 irate, testy **7** fretful, peevish **8** choleric **9** impatient, irascible

irritation 4 itch, pest, rash, sore **6** bother, plague **7** chagrin **8** nuisance, vexation **9** annoyance

irrupt 5 belch, eruct, surge **6** invade **7** intrude

irruption 4 raid **5** foray **6** inroad **7** upsurge **8** invasion **9** incursion, intrusion

I.R.S. employee 7 auditor **10** accountant

Irving novel 15 Cider House Rules (The) **17** Hotel New Hampshire (The) **20** World According to Garp (The)

Isaac *father:* **7** Abraham *mother:* **5** Sarah *son:* **4** Esau **5** Jacob *wife:* **7** Rebekah

Isabella I *country:* **5** Spain *home:* **7** Castile *husband:* **9** Ferdinand

Isaiah 7 prophet *father:* **4** Amoz

Iscah *brother:* **3** Lot *father:* **5** Haran *sister:* **6** Milcah

Iseult, Isolde *beloved:* **7** Tristan **8** Tristram *husband:* **4** Mark

Ishbak *father:* **7** Abraham *mother:* **7** Keturah

Ishbosheth's father 4 Saul

Ishmael 6 pariah **7** outcast **8** castaway, outsider **11** untouchable *father:* **7** Abraham *mother:* **5** Hagar

Ishtar *brother:* **7** Shamash *father:* **3** Anu, Sin *lover:* **6** Tammuz

Ishui's father 4 Saul **5** Asher

Isis *brother:* **6** Osiris *father:* **3** Geb *husband:* **6** Osiris *mother:* **3** Nut *son:* **4** Sept **5** Horus

Islam *adherent:* **6** Moslem, Muslim *founder:* **8** Mohammed, Muhammad *god:* **5** Allah *holy city:* **5** Mecca *holy month:* **7** Ramadan *law:* **6** Sharia *place of worship:* **6** mosque *priest:* **4** imam *scriptures:* **5** Koran, Quran *sect:* **4** Shia, Sufi **5** Sunni **6** Shiite, Sufism **7** Ismaili, Wahhabi (see also MUSLIM)

island 3 ait, cay, key **4** holm **5** atoll, oasis **6** skerry **7** crannog *Admiralty group:* **5** Manus *Adriatic Sea:* **3** Vis **4** Brac, Cres, Hvar **5** Brach, Ciovo, Mljet, Solta **6** Lesina, Pharus *Aegean Sea:* **4** Scio **5** Chios, Khios, Samos, Thira **6** Ikaria, Lemnos, Lesbos, Limnos **7** Nikaria **8** Mitilini, Mytilene, Santorin **10** Sakis-Adasi, Susam-Adasi *Alaska:* **4** Adak,

Atka, Attu, Kuiu **8** Wrangell *Aleutian group:* **3** Rat **4** Adak, Akun, Attu **5** Amlia, Kiska, Umnak **6** Kanaga, Tanaga, Unimak **8** Amchitka, Unalaska *American Samoa:* **3** Ofu, Tau **4** Rose **6** Swains *Andaman Sea:* **4** Mali **5** Tavoy *Antarctica:* **5** Scott, Young *Apostle group:* **3** Oak **4** Long, Sand **5** Outer **8** Madeline, Michigan, Stockton *Arafura Sea:* **5** Dolak *Arctic Archipelago:* **6** Baffin **8** Victoria *Arctic Ocean:* **5** Senja *Australian:* **5** Cocos **8** Tasmania *Azores:* **4** Pico **5** Corvo, Faial *Bahamas:* **3** Cat, Rum **4** Long **5** Abaco, Exuma **6** Andros, Inagua **7** Acklins, Crooked **8** Watlings **9** Eleuthera, Mayaguana **11** San Salvador *Bahrain:* **5** Sitra **8** Muharraq *Balearic group:* **5** Ibiza **7** Majorca, Menorca, Minorca **8** Mallorca *Baltic Sea:* **4** Moon, Muhu **5** Faron, Mukhu, Rugen, Worms **6** Vormsi **7** Gotland **8** Bornholm, Gothland, Gottland *Barents Sea:* **4** Bear *Bay of Naples:* **5** Capri *Bay of Panama:* **4** Naos *Bering Sea:* **5** Medny **7** Nunivak **10** Big Diomede **13** Little Diomede *Bismarck Archipelago:* **5** Lihir **10** New Britain *Bristol Channel:* **5** Lundy *Buzzards Bay:* **9** Cuttyhunk *Canadian:* **5** Banks, Devon **6** Baffin **8** Bathurst, Melville, Somerset, Victoria **9** Anticosti, Ellesmere **10** Cape Breton **11** Axel Heiberg, Southampton **12** Newfoundland, Prince Edward *Canaries:* **6** Gomera **7** La Palma **8** Tenerife **9** Lanzarote *Cape Verde:* **4** Fogo, Maio, Mayo **5** Brava, Rombo *Caribbean Sea:* **4** Cuba **5** Aruba, Utila, Vache **6** Tobago **7** Antigua, Curaçao, Jamaica **8** Barbados, Dominica, Trinidad **10** Guadeloupe, Martinique, Puerto Rico (see also VIRGIN GROUP) *Carolines:* **5** Sorol **6** Ponape **9** Ascension *Chagos Archipelago:* **11** Diego Garcia *Channel group:* **4** Herm, Sark **5** Lihou, Sercq **6** Jersey **8** Guernsey *Chesapeake Bay:* **4** Deal, Kent **5** Smith, Watts *Chukchi Sea:* **6** Herald *Comoro group:* **7** Mayotte *Congo River:* **4** Bamu *Cook group:* **4** Atiu **5** Mauke *Croatia:* **3** Krk, Pag, Rab **5** Susak, Unije *Cyclades:* **3** Ios, Kea, Nio **4** Ceos, Keos, Milo **5** Delos, Melos, Milos, Naxos, Paros, Siros, Syros **6** Andros, Dhilos **7** Amorgos, Cythnos, Kithnos, Kythnos, Mykonos *Denmark:* **3** Als, Fyn, Mon **4** Aero, Fano, Moen, Mors **5** Alsen, Funen, Moers, Samso **8** Bornholm **13** Fanum Fortunae *D'Entrecasteaux group:* **8** Kaluwawa **9** Fergusson *Dodecanese group:* **3** Coo, Cos, Kos **4** Caso, Lero, Simi, Syme **5** Kasos,

Leros, Lipso, Lisso, Patmo, Telos **6** Calino, Lipsos, Nisiro, Patmos **7** Calimno, Nisiros, Nisyros **8** Kalymnos *East River:* **5** Ward's **7** Welfare **9** Roosevelt *England's:* **7** Britain **9** Britannia **12** Great Britain *English Channel:* **5** Wight *Faeroes:* **4** Vago **5** Bordo, Sando *Fiji:* **4** Koro **5** Mango, Vatoa *Florida Keys:* **4** Long, Vaca, West **5** Largo **7** Big Pine **9** Matecumbe, Sugarloaf *Fox group:* **5** Umnak **6** Akutan, Unimak **8** Unalaska *French:* **7** Corsica **12** New Caledonia *French Polynesia:* **4** Rapa, Reao, Ua Pu **5** Ua Pau *Frisian group:* **3** Rom **4** Föhr, Sylt **5** Amrum, Juist, Mando, Texel **6** Borkum **7** Ameland **8** Langeoog, Pellworm, Vlieland **9** Helgoland, Norderney *Futunas:* **5** Alofi *Galápagos:* **5** Pinta **7** Chatham, Isabela **8** Abingdon **10** Albermarle *Georgia:* **5** Tybee *Germany:* **4** Fohr **7** Fehmarn **9** Helgoland **10** Heligoland *Greater Antilles:* **4** Cuba **7** Jamaica **10** Hispaniola, Puerto Rico *Greece:* **4** Milo, Rodi **5** Creta, Crete, Hydra, Idhra, Kriti, Rodos, Tenos, Tinos **6** Euboea, Evvoia, Hydrea, Lesbos, Rhodes, Rhodus **9** Negropont **10** Negroponte *Grenadines:* **5** Union *Gulf of Alaska:* **6** Kodiak *Gulf of Bothnia:* **5** Karlö *Gulf of Carpentaria:* **5** Maria **6** Groote **7** Eylandt *Gulf of Guinea:* **7** Sao Tomé **8** Príncipe, Sao Thomé **11** Saint Thomas *Gulf of Mexico:* **3** Cat **5** Lobos *Gulf of Panama:* **3** Rey *Gulf of St. Lawrence:* **5** Brion *Gulf of Thailand:* **3** Kut **5** Samui *Haiti:* **6** Gonâve *Hawaii:* **4** Maui, Oahu **5** Kauai, Lanai **6** Niihau **7** Molokai **9** Kahoolawe *Hudson Bay:* **5** Coats *Indian Ocean:* **4** Mahé, Nias **5** Heard, Pemba **7** La Dique, Praslin, Réunion **8** Sri Lanka, Zanzibar **9** Mauritius **10** Madagascar *Indonesia:* **4** Bali, Biak, Java, Maja, Muna, Nias, Rhio, Riau, Roma, Roti, Savu, Sawu **5** Batam, Boano, Buton, Djawa, Japen, Lakor, Moena, Riouw, Rotti, Rupat, Sawoe, Solor, Sumba, Wetar, Wokam **6** Butung, Flores, Jappen, Lombok, Madura, Padang, Roepat, Romang, Soemba **7** Celebes, Madoera, Sumatra, Sumbawa **8** Boetoeng, Soembawa, Sulawesi **10** Bandanaira, Banda Neira, Sandalwood *Inner Hebrides:* **4** Coll, Eigg, Iona, Jura, Muck, Mull, Skye **5** Canna, Gigha, Islay, Tiree, Tyree *Ionian group:* **5** Corfu, Paxos, Zante **6** Cerigo, Ithaca, Leukas, Levkas **10** Santa Maura *Iran:* **5** Shahi *Ireland:* **4** Aran *Irish Sea:* **3** Man *Italy:* **4** Elba **6** Sicily **8** Sardinia *Japan:* **3** Iki, Uku **4** Naru, Yezo

5 Awaji, Fukae, Fukue, Hondo, Shodo 6 Honshu, Kyushu 7 Shikoku 8 Hokkaido 10 Shodoshima *Java Sea:* 4 Laut *Kiribati:* 6 Tarawa *Kuril group:* 4 Urup 5 Ketoi, Matua 6 Iturup 7 Etorofu, Matsuwa 8 Kunashir 9 Kunashiri *Lake Champlain:* 5 Grand *Lake Erie:* 9 North Bass, South Bass 10 Middle Bass *Lake Huron:* 8 Drummond 10 Manitoulin *Lake Michigan:* 3 Hog 4 High 6 Beaver *Lake Ontario:* 5 Wolfe *Lake Superior:* 4 Sand 6 Royale 7 Manitou *Lake Winnipeg:* 5 Hecla *largest:* 9 Greenland *Leeward group:* 5 Nevis 7 Antigua, Barbuda, Redonda 8 Anguilla, Sombrero 10 Montserrat, Saint Kitts 13 St. Christopher *legendary:* 7 Cipango *Lesser Sundas:* 4 Alor 5 Ombai *Leti group:* 3 Moa 5 Lakor *Line group:* 5 Flint 6 Malden, Vostok 7 Fanning, Palmyra 8 Starbuck 9 Christmas *Long Island Sound:* 4 City, Hart 5 Goose, Harts *Loyalty group:* 3 Uea 4 Lifu, Maré, Uvea 5 Lifou *Malay Archipelago:* 5 Kisar, Larat, Timor 6 Borneo 9 New Guinea *Malaysia:* 6 Penang, Pinang 13 Prince of Wales *Malta:* 4 Gozo *Marianas:* 4 Maug, Rota 5 Pagan 6 Saipan *Marquesas group:* 4 Eiào, Ua Pu 6 Hatutu, Hiva Oa, Ua Huka 7 Tahuata 8 Fatu Hiva, Nuku Hiva *Marshall group:* 5 Wotho, Wotje 8 Eniwetok 9 Kwajalein *Massachusetts:* 9 Nantucket *Mediterranean Sea:* 4 Elba 5 Corfu, Crete, Malta 6 Cyprus, Euboea, Rhodes, Sicily 7 Corsica 8 Sardinia *Midway group:* 4 Sand 7 Eastern *Moluccas:* 4 Buru 5 Ambon, Ceram, Seram 6 Boeroe *Mozambique channel:* 10 Juan de Nova *Myanmar:* 5 Daung, Kadan, Lanbi *Narragansett Bay:* 5 Rhode 8 Prudence 9 Aquidneck, Conanicut *Netherlands:* 5 Texel 7 Ameland 8 Vlieland *Netherlands Antilles:* 7 Curaçao *New York:* 4 Fire, Long 9 Gardiners, Roosevelt *New York Bay:* 5 Ellis 6 Staten 7 Liberty 9 Governors, Manhattan *New Zealand:* 5 South, White 7 Chatham, Stewart 8 D'Urville *Niagara River:* 4 Goat *Nile River:* 4 Argo, Roda, Ruda 5 Rhoda 6 Rawdah 11 Elephantine *North Channel:* 3 Mew *Northern Cook group:* 7 Penrhyn 8 Manihiki 9 Tongareva *North Pacific:* 4 Wake *Northwest Territories:* 5 Banks, Bylot, Devon 8 Bathurst, Melville 9 Ellesmere 10 Cornwallis, Resolution 13 Prince of Wales *Norwegian:* 8 Jan Mayen *Norwegian Sea:* 5 Donna, Smola, Vikna *Nova Scotia:* 5 Sable 10 Cape Breton *off Alaska:* 4 Dall 5 Kayak *off Albania:* 5 Sazan 6 Saseno *off Australia:* 4 Dunk *off Belize:*

9 Ambergris *off Brazil:* 4 Apeu 5 Rocas *off British Columbia:* 4 King, Pitt 9 Vancouver *off Cape Cod:* 8 Muskeget 9 Nantucket *off Chile:* 5 Guafo, Mocha *off China:* 4 Amoy 5 Ma-tsu 6 Hainan, Quemoy, Taiwan *off Crete:* 3 Dia *off Ecuador:* 4 Puna *off England:* 3 Man 5 Wight 6 Walney *off Florida:* 3 Dog 4 Pine 6 Amelia 7 Pelican, Sanibel 9 Anastasia *off French Guiana:* 6 Devil's *off Georgia:* 10 Cumberland 11 Saint Simons *off Germany:* 4 Sylt *off Greenland:* 5 Disko *off Guinea:* 5 Tombo *off Hispaniola:* 5 Beata *off Honduras:* 5 Tigre *off Iceland:* 7 Surtsey *off India:* 5 Sagar *off Ireland:* 4 Tory 5 Clare, Clear *off Kenya:* 4 Lamu *off Long Island:* 7 Fishers *off Louisiana:* 5 Marsh *off Maine:* 4 Deer, Orrs 5 Swans 8 Monhegan 11 Mount Desert *off Malay Peninsula:* 6 Phuket 9 Singapore *off Maryland:* 10 Assateague *off Massachusetts:* 4 Plum 7 Naushon *off Mexico:* 7 Cozumel *off Mississippi:* 4 Horn, Ship *off Mozambique:* 3 Ibo *off New Brunswick:* 10 Campobello *off Newfoundland:* 4 Bell *off Nigeria:* 5 Lagos *off North Carolina:* 5 Bodie *off Norway:* 5 Bomlo, Froya, Hitra, Sotra, Stord, Vardo 8 Hitteren *off Panama:* 5 Coiba 6 Parida *off Poland:* 5 Wolin 6 Wollin *off Puerto Rico:* 4 Crab 7 Culebra, Vieques *off Rhode Island:* 5 Block *off Scotland:* 4 Bute 5 Arran *off South Carolina:* 5 North 6 Parris 10 Hilton Head *off Sri Lanka:* 5 Delft *off Staten Island:* 7 Hoffman *off Sumatra:* 3 Weh *off Sweden:* 5 Graso, Oland, Vaddo *off Syria:* 5 Arvad, Arwad, Rouad 6 Aradus *off Tanzania:* 5 Mafia, Pemba *off Tasmania:* 5 Bruni, Bruny *off Tunisia:* 5 Jerba 6 Djerba, Meninx *off Venezuela:* 5 Aruba 7 Bonaire 8 Buen Aire *off Virginia:* 5 Wreck *off Wales:* 5 Caldy 6 Caldey *Okinawa group:* 4 Kume *Orkneys:* 3 Hoy *Outer Hebrides:* 5 Barra, Scarp *Palmer Archipelago:* 6 Anvers 7 Antwerp, Brabant *Pearl Harbor:* 4 Ford *Persian Gulf:* 4 Qeys 5 Kharg, Khark *Philippines:* 4 Buad, Cebu, Fuga, Ilin, Poro, Sulu 5 Balut, Batan, Bohol, Coron, Daram, Leyte, Luzon, Panay, Samal, Samar, Sugbu, Talim, Ticao, Verde 6 Negros 7 Masbate, Mindoro, Palawan, Paragua 8 Limasawa, Mindanao 10 Corregidor *Phoenix group:* 4 Hull, Mary 6 Birnie, Canton 9 Enderbury *Puerto Rico:* 4 Mona *Quebec:* 4 Alma *Queen Charlotte group:* 7 Moresby *Red Sea:* 5 Tiran, Zugur, Zuqar *Russia:* 7 Wrangel *Ryukyu group:* 7 Okinawa *St. Lawrence River:* 4 Hare 5 Jesus

8 Montreal *San Francisco Bay:* 5 Angel
Santa Cruz: 5 Anuda, Ndeni 6 Cherry
Sea of Japan: 4 Sado 5 Rebun *Sea of
Marmara:* 4 Avsa *second largest:* 9 New
Guinea *Senegal:* 5 Gorée *Seychelles:*
4 Mahé 7 La Digue, Praslin *Shetland
archipelago:* 4 Unst, Yell 5 Foula *Shumagin group:* 4 Unga *Sierra Leone:* 5 Tasso
Society group: 5 Eimeo, Tahaa, Tahao,
Taiti 6 Moorea, Tahiti 8 Otaheite
Solomon group: 4 Buka, Gizo, Savo
7 Malaita 11 Guadalcanal
12 Bougainville *South Atlantic:* 5 Gough
6 Gough's 11 Saint Helena *South Korea:*
5 Cheju *South of Tokyo:* 3 Iwo 7 Iwo
Jima, Naka Iwo *South Orkneys:*
10 Coronation *South Pacific:* 3 Hiu
4 Niue 5 Raoul 6 Savage, Sunday
7 Norfolk 8 Pitcairn *Spitsbergen archipelago:* 4 Edge *Strait of Hormuz:*
5 Qeshm, Qishm *Sulu Archipelago:*
4 Jolo 5 Lapac *Svalbard:* 4 Hope *Sverdrup:* 11 Axel Heiberg 12 Amund
Ringnes *Swedish:* 3 Ven 4 Hven
5 Hveen, Orust *Tanzania:* 8 Zanzibar
Texas: 5 Padre *Thames River:* 7 Sheppey
third largest: 7 Borneo *Tierra del Fuego:*
5 Hoste *Tonga:* 3 Eua, Foa 4 Uiha
5 Haano *Treasury group:* 4 Mono *Truk
group:* 3 Tol 4 Haru, Moen, Udot,
Uman 5 Fefan *Tuamotu Archipelago:*
4 Anaa 5 Chain *Turkish:* 5 Imroz
6 Imbros *Tuvalu:* 7 Nanumea 9 Nukufe-
tau *Tyrrhenian Sea:* 6 Ischia 11 Monte-
cristo *Vanuatu:* 3 Api, Epi, Oba 4 Aoba,
Gaua, Tana, Vate 5 Efate, Maewo,
Tanna *Venezuelan:* 5 Patos 9 La Tortuga
Virgin group, American: 9 Saint John
10 Saint Croix 11 Saint Thomas *Virgin
group, British:* 5 Peter 6 Norman 7 Anegada, Tortola 11 Jost Van Dyke *volcanic:* 5 Tofua 7 Iwo Jima *Wales:*
8 Anglesea, Anglesey, Holyhead *Weddell
Sea:* 4 Ross 6 Hearst *Western Samoa:*
5 Upolu 6 Savaii *West Indies:* 4 Mona,
Saba, Salt 5 Nevis, Peter, Saona 6 Tobago, Tortue 7 Grenada, Tortuga
8 Trinidad 9 Santa Cruz 10 Concepción,
Hispaniola, Montserrat, Saint Croix
(see also BAHAMAS; GREATER
ANTILLES; LEEWARD GROUP; VIRGIN
GROUP; WINDWARD GROUP) *West of
England:* 7 Ireland *West Pacific:* 5 Dyaul,
Fauro, Ocean 6 Banaba, Marcus 7 Iwo
Jima, Kita Iwo 9 Minami Iwo *Windward
group:* 10 Martinique *with former peni-
tentiary:* 8 Alcatraz
island group *Alaska:* 3 Rat 8 Aleutian,
Pribilof 9 Andreanof, Catherine *Aleu-
tians:* 4 Near *American Samoa:* 5 Manua
Arabian Sea: 9 Laccadive *Arctic Archipel-*

ago: 8 Sverdrup *Arctic Ocean:* 8 Svalbard 12 Novaya Zemlya *Bahamas:*
5 Berry, Exuma 6 Bimini *Banda Sea:*
5 Damar *Bangladesh:* 5 Hatia, Hatya
Bay of Bengal: 7 Andaman, Nicobar
between England and France: 7 Channel
Bismarck Archipelago: 4 Feni 5 Tabar,
Tanga *Bismarck Sea:* 4 Vitu *British:*
7 Bermuda *Caribbean Sea:* 4 Swan
5 Pearl 6 Cayman, Perlas, Pigeon
8 Pichones 10 Grenadines, West Indies
Carolines: 3 Uap, Yap 4 Truk 5 Nomoi
7 Hogoleu *Central Pacific Ocean:* 4 Line
5 Samoa, Union 6 Danger, Midway
7 Phoenix, Tokelau 8 Manihiki 9 Polynesia 12 Northern Cook *Coral Sea:*
4 Huon *Cuba:* 8 Camagüey *east of
Philippines:* 10 Micronesia *East Siberian
Sea:* 4 Bear 8 Medvezhi *Ecuador:*
·5 Colón 9 Galápagos *England:* 5 Farne
Fiji: 3 Lau 7 Eastern *Formosa Strait:*
4 Hoko 5 Peng hu 10 Pescadores
French: 5 Salut 6 Safety 9 Kerguelen
French Polynesia: 3 Low 6 Tubuai 7 Austral, Paumotu, Société, Society, Tuamotu 9 Marquesas, Touamotou *Germany:*
8 Halligen *Greece:* 6 Aegean, Ionian
8 Cyclades 10 Dodecanese 11 Dode-
canesus *Hudson Bay:* 7 Belcher *Indian
Ocean:* 7 Aldabra *Indonesia:* 4 Asia,
Batu, Pagi, Sula 5 Babar, Batoe, Pagai,
Pageh, Penju, Spice, Wakde 6 Maluku
Ireland: 4 Aran *Japan:* 5 Osumi *largest:*
5 Malay 8 Malaysia *Lesser Antilles:*
8 Windward *Malay Archipelago:* 5 Sunda
6 Soenda *Mediterranean Sea:* 8 Baleares,
Balearic *Moluccas:* 3 Kai, Kei, Obi
4 Leti 5 Banda, Leti 8 Tanimbar 9 Ti-
morlaut *New Caledonia:* 7 Loyalty
9 Loyalties *north of Australia:* 9 Melane-
sia *north of British Isles:* 5 Faroe
7 Faeroes *north off Fiji:* 5 Hoorn 6 Futuna *north off Madagascar:* 7 Aldabra
8 Farquhar *north of New Caledonia:*
5 Belep *north of New Guinea:* 8 Bismarck
9 Admiralty 11 Admiralties *Northwest
Territories:* 5 Parry *off Alaska:* 3 Fox *off
Alaska Peninsula:* 8 Shumagin *off Cape
Cod:* 9 Elizabeth *off eastern Asia:*
5 Kuril 6 Kurile *off England:* 6 Scilly *off
Florida:* 11 Dry Tortugas *off Guinea:*
3 Los 4 Loos *off Honduras:* 5 Bahia *off
Morocco:* 7 Madeira *off New Guinea:*
3 Aru 4 Aroe *off Nicaragua:* 4 Corn *off
northern Africa:* 6 Canary 8 Canaries *off
northern Australia:* 6 Wessel 7 Dampier
off Sicily: 5 Egadi 8 Aegadian *Outer
Hebrides:* 4 Uist *Papua New Guinea:*
5 Green *Persian Gulf:* 4 Tunb *Philippines:*
4 Cuyo 5 Tapul 6 Lubang 7 Basilan,
Bisayas, Visayan *Portuguese:* 6 Azores

Quebec: 8 Magdalen 9 Madeleine
Ryukyus: 5 Amami *St. Lawrence River:*
8 Thousand *Sea of Japan:* 3 Oki *Sea of Marmara:* 5 Kizil 7 Princes 11 Kizil
Adalar *South Atlantic Ocean:* 8 Falkland,
Malvinas *South China Sea:* 6 Hirata
7 Paracel, Spratly *south of New Zealand:*
8 Auckland *South Pacific:* 11 Austronesia *Sulu Sea:* 7 Cagayan 9 Cagayanes
Tonga: 5 Vavau *Tyrrhenian Sea:* 5 Ponza
Venezuelan: 4 Aves, Bird 9 Los Roques
West Europe: 12 British Isles *West Indies:*
6 Virgin 10 Guadeloupe *west of French Polynesia:* 4 Cook *west of Scotland:*
7 Western 8 Hebrides *west Pacific Ocean:* 4 Duff 5 Bonin, Mapia, Palau,
Pelew 7 Ladrone, Mariana, Solomon,
Vanuatu 8 Marshall, Treasury 9 Ogasawara 10 Saint David

island nation *Atlantic Ocean:* 9 Cape
Verde *Indian Ocean:* 8 Malagasy, Malgache, Sri Lanka 9 Mauritius 10 Madagascar, Seychelles *Mediterranean Sea:*
6 Cyprus *Mozambique Channel:*
6 Comoro 7 Comores *off southern China:* 6 Taiwan *south of Greenland:*
7 Iceland *West Indies:* 4 Cuba 7 Jamaica
8 Barbados 10 Saint Lucia *West Pacific Ocean:* 5 Nauru *Windward group:*
8 Dominica
island province 12 Prince Edward
island state 6 Hawaii
isle see ISLAND
Ismene *brother:* 9 Polynices *father:*
7 Oedipus *mother:* 7 Jocasta *sister:*
8 Antigone *uncle:* 5 Creon
isochronous 7 regular 8 cyclical, periodic, rhythmic 9 recurrent, recurring
10 periodical 12 intermittent
isolate 6 cut off, detach, enisle 7 seclude
8 close off, insulate, pinpoint, separate,
set apart 9 segregate, sequester 10 quarantine
isolated 5 alone 6 random, remote,
unique 7 unusual 8 solitary, sporadic
9 separated, withdrawn 11 exceptional,
quarantined
Isolde see ISEULT
Israel *ancient name:* 4 Zion 5 Judea
6 Canaan, Judaea 9 Palestine *capital:*
9 Jerusalem *city:* 4 Acre 5 Haifa, Jaffa
7 Tel Aviv 9 Beersheba *desert:* 5 Negeb,
Negev *gulf:* 5 Aqaba *lake:* 8 Tiberias
12 Sea of Galilee *language:* 6 Arabic,
Hebrew *monetary unit:* 6 shekel *neighbor:* 5 Egypt, Syria 6 Jordan 7 Lebanon
plain: 9 Esdraelon *river:* 6 Jordan *sea:*
4 Dead 13 Mediterranean
Israeli 5 Sabra
Israelite see HEBREW; JEWISH
Issachar *father:* 5 Jacob *mother:* 4 Leah

issue 4 emit, flow, gush, pour, rise, seed,
stem, vent 5 arise, birth, brood, child,
fruit, scion, topic 6 affair, appear,
effect, emerge, get out, matter, put out,
result, scions, sequel, source, spring,
upshot 7 concern, descent, edition,
emanate, give off, give out, outcome,
problem, proceed, progeny, publish,
release, subject 8 bulletin, children,
question, throw off 9 come forth, offspring, originate, posterity 10 derive
from, distribute, end product, promulgate 11 consequence, descendants,
progeniture, publication
Istanbul *ancient name:* 9 Byzantium *business section:* 6 Galata *country:* 6 Turkey
foreign quarter: 4 Pera 7 Beyoglu *park:*
8 Seraglio *residential section:* 7 Uskudar
isthmus *Africa-Asia:* 4 Suez *Greece:*
7 Corinth *America:* 6 Panama *Malay Peninsula:* 3 Kra
Italian *automobile:* 4 Fiat 6 Lancia 7 Ferrari 8 Maserati 9 Alfa Romeo 11 Lamborghini *cathedral:* 5 duomo *dialect:*
6 Tuscan 8 Sicilian *dictator:* 9 Mussolini
(Benito) *family:* 4 Este 5 Cenci, Savoy
6 Borgia, Medici, Orsini, Pepoli,
Savoia, Sforza 7 Colonna, Gonzaga,
Spinola 8 Visconti *fascist:* 10 Blackshirt
game: 5 bocce, bocci 6 boccie *gentleman:* 6 signor 7 signore *highway:*
10 autostrada *lady:* 5 donna 7 signora
9 signorina *magistrate:* 7 podestà *meat:*
6 salami 8 pancetta 9 pepperoni, salsiccia 10 mortadella, prosciutto *opera house:* 7 La Scala *patriot:* 6 Cavour
(Conte di), Rienzo (Cola di) 7 Mazzini
(Giuseppe) 9 Garibaldi (Giuseppe) *religious reformer:* 9 Savonarola (Girolamo) *resort:* 4 Lido 5 Abano, Capri
8 Sorrento, Taormina *road:* 6 strada
soup: 10 minestrone *square:* 6 piazza
street: 3 via 5 corso *weight:* 5 libra,
oncia
Italy *bay:* 6 Naples *capital:* 4 Rome *city:*
4 Asti, Bari, Pisa 5 Aosta, Genoa,
Milan, Padua, Parma, Siena, Turin
6 Genova, Mantua, Milano, Modena,
Naples, Napoli, Padova, Torino, Venice,
Verona 7 Bergamo, Bologna, Bolzano,
Catania, Cremona, Firenze, Leghorn,
Livorno, Mantova, Palermo, Perugia,
Ravenna, Salerno, Taranto, Trieste,
Venezia 8 Florence, Siracusa, Syracuse
enclave: 9 San Marino 11 Vatican City
gulf: 5 Gaeta 7 Salerno, Taranto 11 Sant'
Eufemia *island, island group:* 4 Elba
5 Capri 6 Ischia, Lipari, Sicily 7 Aeolian, Capraia 8 Sardinia *lake:* 4 Como
5 Garda 7 Bolsena 8 Maggiore 9 Bracciano *leader:* 9 Mussolini (Benito)

monetary unit: 4 euro **monetary unit, former:** 4 lira **mountain, range:** 4 Alps, Etna 9 Apennines, Mont Blanc, Monte Rosa 10 Monte Corno **neighbor:** 6 France 7 Austria 8 Slovenia 11 Switzerland **peninsula:** 9 Salentina **river:** 4 Arno, Liri 5 Adige, Piave, Tiber 6 Isonzo, Tevere 8 Volturno **sea:** 6 Ionian 8 Adriatic, Ligurian 10 Tyrrhenian 13 Mediterranean **strait:** 7 Messina, Otranto **volcano:** 4 Etna 8 Vesuvius **wine region:** 4 Asti

itch 3 yen 4 ache, long, lust, pine 5 crave, yearn 6 desire, hanker, hunger, thirst 7 craving, longing 8 appetite, pruritus, yearning 9 hankering

itchy 4 avid, edgy, keen 5 antsy, eager, jumpy 6 fidgety, restive 8 prurient, pruritic, restless 9 impatient

item 3 bit 5 entry, point, scrap, story, thing, topic 6 detail, matter 7 account, article, element, feature, product 8 clipping 9 commodity 10 particular

itemize 4 list 5 count, tally 6 number 7 catalog, run down, specify, tick off 8 document, spell out 9 catalogue, enumerate, inventory

iterate 5 drill, recap, renew 6 rehash, repeat, replay, retell 7 reprise, restate 12 recapitulate

Ithaca king 8 Odysseus

Ithamar's father 5 Aaron

itinerant 5 gypsy, nomad 6 roving 7 migrant, nomadic, roaming, vagrant 8 drifting, rambling, traveler, vagabond, wanderer 9 migratory, transient, unsettled, wandering, wayfaring 11 peripatetic

itty-bitty 3 wee 4 tiny 5 teeny, weeny 6 teensy 10 teeny-weeny 12 teensyweensy

Ivanhoe author: 5 Scott (Walter) **character:** 5 Isaac 6 Cedric, Rowena, Ulrica 7 Rebecca, Wilfred 9 Robin Hood

Ivory Coast 11 Côte d'Ivoire **capital:** 7 Abidjan 12 Yamoussoukro **city:** 6 Bouaké **language:** 6 French **monetary unit:** 5 franc **mountain:** 5 Nimba **neighbor:** 4 Mali 5 Ghana 6 Guinea 7 Liberia 11 Burkina Faso **river:** 7 Bandama 9 Sassandra

ivory-tower 8 academic 11 conjectural, impractical, theoretical, unrealistic

J

jab 3 hit 4 blow, poke, prod, sock, stab 5 nudge, prick, punch 6 pierce, strike, thrust 8 puncture

jabber 3 gab, jaw, yak 6 babble, drivel, gabble 7 blather, chatter, prattle 8 nonsense 9 gibberish

jabberer 6 gabber, magpie 7 babbler, blabber, gabbler 8 prattler 9 chatterer 10 chatterbox

Jabberwocky author 7 Carroll (Lewis)

jabot 4 fall 5 frill 6 ruffle

___ **jacet** 3 hic

jack 3 tar 4 bird, card, fish, flag, hike, lift, move, salt 5 boost, brace, bread, dough, knave, knife, money, put up, raise 6 brandy, cheese, device, donkey, rabbit, sailor, seaman 7 laborer, mariner, servant 8 increase, standard 9 criticize, mechanism 10 take to task

jackal 4 dupe, pawn 5 agent, canid, patsy

6 canine, flunky, lackey, minion, stooge 7 cat's-paw 9 accessory, auxiliary 10 accomplice 11 stool pigeon **god:** 4 Anpu 6 Anubis

jackanapes 3 ape 4 brat, fool 6 monkey

jackass 4 dolt, dope, fool, jerk 5 burro, dunce, idiot, schmo 6 donkey, nitwit 7 nebbish 8 bonehead, imbecile, numskull 9 blockhead, numbskull 10 nincompoop **deer:** 3 kob 8 antelope

jackdaw 7 grackle 9 blackbird

jacket 4 Eton 5 parka, tunic 6 anorak, blazer, bolero, jerkin, reefer, sacque, tuxedo 7 doublet, Norfolk, peacoat, spencer 8 camisole 10 roundabout **armored:** 7 hauberk 9 habergeon **sleeveless:** 4 vest 6 bolero, jerkin 9 waistcoat

jackhammer 5 drill 9 rock drill

jackknife 4 dive 6 barlow **game:** 11 mumblety-peg

jackleg 6 make-do, novice 7 amateur,

shyster, stopgap **9** dishonest, green-horn, makeshift, temporary, unskilled **10** substitute **11** pettifogger **12** unscrupulous

jack-of-all-trades 6 tinker **7** go-to guy **8** factotum, handyman

jack-o'-lantern 6 fungus **7** pumpkin

jackpot 3 sum **4** pool **5** award, kitty, prize **6** reward, stakes **7** bonanza, success **8** windfall

jackrabbit 4 hare

jackstay 3 bar, rod **4** rope **7** rigging, support

Jacob *brother:* **4** Esau *daughter:* **5** Dinah *father:* **5** Isaac *father-in-law:* **5** Laban *mother:* **7** Rebekah *new name:* **6** Israel *son:* **3** Dan, Gad **4** Levi **5** Asher, Judah **6** Joseph, Reuben, Simeon **7** Zebulun **8** Benjamin, Issachar, Naphtali *variant:* **5** James *wife:* **4** Leah **6** Rachel

Jacobin 7 radical **9** Dominican, extremist

Jacob's ladder 4 herb **5** phlox **9** perennial

jade 3 gem, nag **4** bore, cloy, dull, minx, pall, tire, wear **5** color, drain, flirt, green, hussy, jewel, stone, tramp, weary, wench **6** wanton **7** fatigue, jezebel, mineral, trollop, wear out **8** gemstone, nephrite, strumpet, wear down

jaded 4 worn **5** blasé, bored, sated, tired, weary **6** dulled **7** cynical, wearied, worn-out **8** fatigued, satiated, worn down **9** apathetic, exhausted, surfeited **10** overworked

jaeger 4 skua **6** hunter **8** huntsman

Jael *husband:* **5** Heber *victim:* **6** Sisera

jag 3 cut **4** barb, jerk, load, pink, tear **5** binge, notch, prick, spell, spree **6** bender, indent, thrill, thrust **7** serrate

jagged 5 harsh, rough, sharp **6** broken, craggy, rugged, spiked, uneven **7** scraggy **8** serrated, unsmooth **9** irregular

___ Jagger 4 Mick

jai alai 6 pelota *basket:* **5** cesta *court:* **6** cancha **7** fronton

jail 3 can, jug, pen **4** coop, gaol, poky **5** clink, pokey **6** cooler, lockup, prison **7** confine, freezer, slammer **8** hoosegow, imprison, stockade **9** constrain **11** confinement, incarcerate

jailbird 3 con **5** felon, loser **7** convict **8** criminal, prisoner, repeater **10** recidivist

jailer 5 guard, screw **6** keeper, warden **7** turnkey **8** overseer

jakes 5 privy **8** outhouse **9** backhouse

jalopy 3 car **4** auto, heap **5** crate, wreck **6** beater, junker **7** clunker, vehicle **10** automobile, rattletrap

jalousie 5 blind **6** window **7** shutter

jam 3 box, fix **4** bind, clog, cram, dunk, pack, push **5** block, crowd, crush, force, jelly, press, stuff, wedge **6** bruise, impede, plight, scrape, squash, squish **7** dilemma, squeeze **8** compress, conserve, obstacle, preserve **9** confiture, preserves **10** difficulty **11** predicament

Jamaica *capital:* **8** Kingston *cay:* **5** Pedro **6** Morant *city:* **10** Montego Bay **11** Spanish Town *discoverer:* **8** Columbus (Christopher) *language:* **7** English *location:* **10** West Indies *mountain range:* **4** Blue **10** Dry Harbour *sea:* **9** Caribbean

Jamaican *export:* **3** rum **5** sugar *hair style:* **10** dreadlocks *music:* **3** dub, ska **6** reggae *musician:* **5** Cliff (Jimmy) **6** Marley (Bob, Ziggy) **7** Wailers *nationalist:* **6** Garvey (Marcus)

jambalaya 4 olio **5** gumbo **7** mélange, mixture **8** mishmash

jamboree 4 gala **5** revel **6** fiesta, frolic **7** carouse, shindig **8** carnival, festival, wingding **9** merriment **11** celebration **13** entertainment

James *brother:* **4** John **5** Jesus, Joses *cousin:* **5** Jesus *father:* **7** Zebedee **8** Alphaeus *mother:* **4** Mary **6** Salome

James novel 8 American (The) **9** Europeans (The) **10** Bostonians (The), Confidence, Golden Bowl (The), Tragic Muse (The) **11** Ambassadors (The), Daisy Miller **14** Turn of the Screw (The), Wings of the Dove (The) **15** Portrait of a Lady (The) **16** Washington Square

Jammu and ___ 7 Kashmir

Jane Eyre *author:* **6** Brontë (Charlotte) *lover:* **9** Rochester

jangle 3 jar **4** ring **5** babel, clash **6** clamor, excite, hubbub **7** discord, quarrel **8** conflict **11** discordance, discordancy **12** disharmonize

jangling 5 harsh, noisy, tense **7** grating **9** dissonant **10** discordant, quarreling

janitor 5 super **6** porter **7** cleaner **9** caretaker, concierge, custodian **10** doorkeeper

japan 4 coat **7** coating, varnish **11** lacquerware

Japan 5 Nihon **6** Nippon *capital:* **3** Edo **5** Tokyo *city:* **4** Kobe **5** Kyoto, Osaka, Otaru **6** Nagoya **7** Fukuoka, Okinawa, Sapporo **8** Kawasaki, Nagasaki, Yokohama **9** Hiroshima *island:* **6** Honshu, Kyushu **7** Shikoku **8** Hokkaido *lake:* **4** Biwa **8** Chuzenji *monetary unit:* **3** yen *mountain:* **4** Fuji **8** Fujiyama

Japanese *aborigine:* **4** Ainu *art:* **6** bonsai **6** ukiyo-e *baron:* **6** daimyo *battle cry:*

6 banzai *Buddha:* 5 Amida, Amita *cartoons:* 5 anime *comics:* 5 manga *dancing girl:* 6 geisha *dish:* 4 miso, soba 5 gyoza, katsu, kombu, sushi 7 sashimi, tempura 8 sukiyaki, teriyaki *drama:* 3 Noh 6 Bugaku, Kabuki 7 Bunraku *drink:* 4 sake, saki *emperor:* 6 Mikado 7 Akihito 8 Hirohito *fencing:* 5 kendo *festival:* 3 Bon *fish:* 4 fugu *flower arrangement:* 7 ikebana *garment:* 6 kimono *gateway:* 5 torii *god:* 5 Ebisu, Hotei 7 Daikoku, Jurojin 8 Bishamon *goddess:* 6 Benten 9 Amaterasu *governor:* 6 shogun *grill:* 7 hibachi *immigrant:* 5 issei *instrument:* 4 biwa, koto 7 samisen 8 shamisen 10 shakuhachi *martial art:* 4 judo 5 kendo 6 aikido, karate 7 jujitsu *martial artist:* 5 ninja *money:* 3 sen, yen *plum:* 6 loquat *poem:* 5 haiku, tanka *porcelain:* 5 imari *pottery:* 4 raku 7 satsuma *radish:* 6 daikon *religion:* 6 Shinto 8 Buddhism 9 Shintoism *rice wine:* 4 sake, saki *robe:* 6 kimono *samurai clan:* 5 Taira 8 Minamoto *sash:* 3 obi *song:* 3 uta *suicide:* 7 seppuku 8 harakiri, kamikaze *theater:* 3 Noh 6 Bugaku, Kabuki 7 Bunraku *tidal wave:* 7 tsunami *vehicle:* 8 rickshaw *warrior:* 7 samurai *warrior code:* 7 bushido *wrestling:* 4 sumo *writing:* 4 kana 8 hiragana, katakana *zither:* 4 koto
Japanese-American 5 Issei, Nisei *second-generation:* 6 Sansei
jape 3 gag, kid, rib 4 gibe, jest, jibe, joke, mock, quip 5 crack, laugh, prank, tease 7 waggery 8 drollery 9 wisecrack, witticism
Japheth *brother:* 3 Ham 4 Shem *father:* 4 Noah *son:* 5 Gomer, Javan, Madai, Magog, Tiras, Tubal 7 Meshech
jar 4 bump, jolt, olla 5 cruse, quake, shake, shock, upset 6 jangle, jounce 7 tremble, vibrate 8 mismatch 9 container *ancient:* 6 krater 7 amphora *Egyptian:* 7 canopic
jardiniere 5 stand 6 holder 7 garnish
jargon 4 cant 5 argot, idiom, lingo, slang 6 patois, pidgin 7 dialect, lexicon, palaver 8 language 9 gibberish 10 mumbo-jumbo, vernacular, vocabulary 11 terminology *lawyer's:* 8 legalese
jarl 4 earl 5 noble 8 nobleman 12 Scandinavian
jarring 5 harsh, rough 6 hoarse, jangly 7 grating, rasping, raucous 8 strident 9 dissonant 10 discordant, unsettling
jasmine 3 tea 4 vine 5 shrub 6 flower, yellow 7 perfume
Jason *father:* 5 Aeson *helper:* 5 Medea *lover:* 6 Creusa, Glauce, Glauke *quest:* 6 Fleece 12 Golden Fleece *ship:* 4 Argo

shipmate: 8 Argonaut *teacher:* 6 Chiron 7 Cheiron *uncle:* 6 Pelias *wife:* 5 Medea
jasper 6 morlop, quartz 9 stoneware 10 chalcedony
jaundice 4 bias 7 disease, icterus 9 prejudice
jaundiced 6 biased, warped, yellow 7 colored, cynical, envious, hostile, jealous 9 distorted 10 suspicious
jaunt 4 ride, trip 5 drive, sally 6 junket, outing, ramble 7 journey 9 excursion
jaunty 4 airy, pert 5 fresh, light, peppy, perky 6 breezy, lively 7 buoyant 8 debonair 9 sprightly 10 nonchalant
java 6 coffee
Java *almond:* 7 talisay *cotton:* 5 kapok *jute:* 5 kenaf *plum:* 5 jaman 6 jambul 7 jambool
Javanese *civet:* 5 rasse *orchestra:* 7 gamelan *tree:* 4 upas
Javan squirrel 8 jelerang
javelin 5 lance, shaft, spear 6 weapon 7 assagai, assegai, harpoon
Javert's prey 7 Valjean (Jean)
jaw 3 gab, yak 4 chat, rail, talk 5 clack, prate 6 babble, gabble 7 chatter, prattle 9 yakety-yak
jawbone 7 maxilla 8 arm-twist, mandible, persuade, talk into
jawbreaker 9 hard candy
jay 4 bird, blue, hick, rube 5 dandy 6 rustic 7 bumpkin, hayseed 9 chatterer, greenhorn
Jayhawker 9 guerrilla *State:* 6 Kansas 8 Missouri
jazz 3 bop 4 guff, jive 5 bebop, stuff, swing 6 boogie 7 ragtime 8 malarkey, nonsense *up:* 5 rouse 6 vivify 7 animate, enliven 9 stimulate
jazz musician 4 Cole (Nat "King"), Getz (Stan), Hirt (Al), Monk (Thelonious), O'Day (Anita), Rich (Buddy), Shaw (Artie) 5 Baker (Chet), Basie (Count), Brown (Clifford), Corea (Chick), Davis (Miles), Evans (Bill, Gil), Hines (Earl "Fatha"), Jones (Hank), Krall (Diana), Krupa (Gene), McRae (Carmen), Roach (Max), Smith (Jimmy), Sun Ra, Tatum (Art), Tormé (Mel), Young (Lester) 6 Bechet (Sidney), Blakey (Art), Burton (Gary), Carter (Benny), Dorsey (Jimmy, Tommy), Farmer (Art), Garner (Erroll), Gordon (Dexter), Herman (Woody), Jordan (Louis), Kenton (Stan), Mingus (Charles), Morton (Jelly Roll), Oliver (King), Parker (Charlie), Pepper (Art), Powell (Bud), Puente (Tito), Silver (Horace), Waller (Fats) 7 Brubeck (Dave), Coleman (Ornette), Connick (Harry), Goodman (Benny), Hampton (Lionel), Hancock (Herbie),

Hawkins (Coleman), Holiday (Billie), Jarrett (Keith), Metheny (Pat), Rollins (Sonny), Rushing (Jimmy), Shorter (Wayne), Vaughan (Sarah), Webster (Ben) **8** Adderley (Cannonball), Calloway (Cab), Coltrane (John), Eldridge (Roy), Marsalis (Wynton), Mulligan (Gerry), Peterson (Oscar), Williams (Mary Lou) **9** Armstrong (Louis), Ellington (Duke), Gillespie (Dizzy), Reinhardt (Django) **10** Fitzgerald (Ella), Montgomery (Wes), Washington (Dinah) **11** Beiderbecke (Bix)

jazzy 5 gaudy **6** brassy, flashy, glitzy, lively, rakish **7** raffish, splashy **8** animated, colorful, exciting, spirited **9** vivacious **10** flamboyant

jealous 5 green **7** envious, hostile **8** doubting, vigilant **9** demanding, green-eyed, invidious, resentful **10** intolerant, possessive, suspicious **11** distrustful, mistrustful

jeer 4 gibe, jibe, mock **5** fleer, flout, scoff, scorn, sneer, taunt **6** deride, heckle, hector, insult **7** contemn, laugh at, mockery **8** derision, ridicule

Jeeves *creator:* **9** Wodehouse (P. G.) *employer:* **7** Wooster (Bertie) *position:* **5** valet **6** butler

jeez 4 gosh, heck **5** golly, shoot **6** shucks **7** jeepers

jefe 4 boss, head, lord **5** chief, ruler **6** honcho, leader **9** chieftain, commander

Jefferson, Thomas *home:* **10** Monticello *lover:* **5** Sally (Hemings) *state:* **8** Virginia

Jehoram *brother:* **7** Ahaziah *father:* **4** Ahab **11** Jehoshaphat *kingdom:* **5** Judah *slayer:* **4** Jehu *wife:* **8** Athaliah

Jehoshaphat *father:* **3** Asa **6** Ahilud, Nimshi, Paruah *father-in-law:* **4** Ahab *son:* **4** Jehu **7** Jehoram *wife:* **8** Athaliah

Jehovah 3 God **6** Adonai, Elohim, Yahweh

Jehu 6 driver *father:* **6** Hanani **11** Jehoshaphat *grandfather:* **6** Nimshi *son:* **8** Jehoahaz *victim:* **5** Joram **7** Jehoram

jejune 4 dull, flat **5** banal, bland, empty, inane, silly, trite, vapid **7** insipid, puerile **8** childish, juvenile, lifeless **9** colorless, innocuous **10** spiritless **13** uninteresting

Jekyll's alter ego 4 Hyde (Mr.)

jell 3 set **4** form **6** cohere, gelate **7** congeal, thicken **8** coalesce **9** coagulate, take shape

jelly 3 set **4** mass **5** aspic **6** spread **7** congeal, thicken **9** coagulate

jellyfish 6 coward, medusa **7** doormat, medusan **8** medusoid, pushover, weak-

ling **10** ctenophore **12** coelenterate, invertebrate, siphonophore

je ne ___ quoi 4 sais

jennet 3 ass **5** hinny, horse **6** donkey

jenny 4 bird **6** donkey (female) **7** machine

jeopardize 4 risk **5** peril **6** chance, expose, hazard **7** imperil **8** endanger

jeopardy 4 risk **5** peril **6** danger, hazard, menace **8** exposure **9** liability **12** endangerment

jeremiad 6 lament, tirade **7** lecture **8** diatribe, harangue **9** complaint, philippic **11** declamation, lamentation

Jeremiah *scribe:* **6** Baruch

Jericho's conqueror 6 Joshua

jerk 3 ass, lug, tic, tug **4** dolt, dope, fool, jolt, pull, push, snap, twit, yank **5** brute, idiot, lurch, ninny, spasm, twist, wrest **6** bounce, nitwit, thrust, twitch, wrench **7** jackass **8** preserve **10** nincompoop

jerkin 6 jacket

jerky 4 meat **5** inane **6** abrupt, stupid, sudden **7** foolish, idiotic, jolting **8** saccadic **9** senseless

Jerome's Bible 7 Vulgate

jersey 3 cow **6** fabric **7** garment, sweater **8** pullover

Jerusalem 4 Sion, Zion **5** Salem **8** Holy City *hill:* **4** Sion, Zion **6** Moriah *mosque:* **4** Omar **6** Al-Aqsa **13** Dome of the Rock *pool:* **6** Siloam **8** Bethesda

Jerusalem artichoke 5 tuber **8** girasole **9** sunflower

Jerusalem thorn 5 shrub **9** horsebean

jess 5 strap

Jesse *daughter:* **7** Abigail, Zeruiah *father:* **4** Obed *grandfather:* **4** Boaz *son:* **4** Ozem **5** David, Eliab, Elihu **6** Raddai **7** Shammah **8** Abinadab, Nethanel *youngest son:* **5** David

Jessica *father:* **7** Shylock *husband:* **7** Lorenzo

jest 3 fun, gag, kid, rag, rib **4** butt, game, gibe, jape, jeer, joke, josh, mock, quip, razz **5** crack, fleer, flout, humor, prank, scoff, sneer, spoof, sport, tease **6** banter, gaiety **7** mockery, waggery **8** derision, drollery, ridicule **9** merriment, wisecrack, witticism

jester 3 wag, wit **4** fool **5** actor, clown, comic, joker **7** buffoon **8** comedian, funnyman, humorist, jokester, quipster **9** prankster **11** entertainer

Jesuit *founder:* **6** Loyola (Ignatius) *leader:* **6** Xavier (St. Francis)

jet 4 coal, ebon, emit, gush, inky, rush, spew **5** black, ebony, plane, spout, spurt **6** engine, nozzle, squirt, stream,

travel 7 current, jewelry 8 airplane
9 pitch-dark 10 pitch-black

Jethro *daughter:* 8 Zipporah *son-in-law:*
5 Moses

jetsam 7 flotsam 8 wreckage 9 driftwood

jet set 5 A-list, elite 9 beau monde, haut
monde 10 glitterati

jettison 4 drop, dump, junk, omit
5 eject, forgo, scrap 6 reject, remove
7 deep-six, discard 8 disposal, get rid
of, throw out 9 sacrifice, throw away

jetty 4 dock, ebon, inky, pier, quay
5 black, ebony, groin, wharf 7 project
9 pitch-dark 10 pitch-black

Jew 6 Essene, Hebrew, Semite 7 Israeli,
Judaist 9 Israelite

jewel 3 gem 4 rock 5 adorn, bijou, ideal,
prize, stone 7 bearing 8 gemstone,
ornament, treasure 9 embellish

jeweler 8 lapidary *famous:* 7 Tiffany
(Charles Lewis)

jewelry 10 bijouterie *artificial:* 5 glass,
paste 6 strass 7 costume *piece:* 3 pin
4 ring 6 brooch 7 earring 8 bracelet,
cufflink, necklace, tieclasp 9 lavaliere
set: 6 parure

Jewish *bread:* 5 matzo 6 matzoh *ceremony:* 4 bris 8 havdalah 10 bar mitzvah,
bas mitzvah *combining form:* 5 Judeo
6 Judaeo *credo:* 5 shema *doctrine:*
6 Mishna 7 Mishnah *New Year:* 12 Rosh
Hashanah *organization:* 8 Hadassah
9 B'nai B'rith *prayer:* 7 kaddish, kiddush *prayer book:* 6 siddur *sabbath:*
8 Saturday *scripture:* 5 Torah 6 Talmud
synagogue: 4 shul *teacher:* 5 rabbi,
rebbe 6 Hillel *village:* 6 shtetl (see also
HEBREW)

Jezebel 4 slut 5 hussy, tramp, trull,
wench 6 wanton 7 trollop 8 slattern,
strumpet *father:* 7 Ethbaal *home:*
5 Sidon *husband:* 4 Ahab *slayer:* 4 Jehu
victim: 6 Naboth

jib 3 arm, shy 4 balk, boom, sail, stop
5 demur 6 refuse 9 stop short

jibe 5 agree, fit in, match, shift, tally
6 accord, concur, square 7 conform
8 dovetail 9 harmonize 10 correspond,
go together 12 change course

jiffy 3 sec 4 tick, wink 5 flash, hurry,
shake, trice 6 minute, moment, second
7 instant 11 split second

jig 4 fish, game, hoax, hook, jerk, play,
ploy, ruse, sham, wile 5 catch, dance,
feint, trick 6 device, gambit 7 gimmick
9 deception

jigger 4 jerk, mold, sail 5 alter, gizmo
6 device, dingus, doodad, gadget, widget 7 gimmick, machine, measure
9 doohickey, rearrange, shot glass,
thingummy 10 manipulate

jiggle 4 jerk 5 shake 7 agitate 9 oscillate

jigsaw 3 cut 4 tool 6 puzzle 7 arrange,
machine

jihad 3 war 6 strife 7 crusade, holy war
8 campaign, struggle

jilt 4 drop 5 ditch, leave 6 desert, reject
7 abandon, cast off, discard

jim-dandy 5 great, ideal, nifty, super
7 perfect 8 knockout 9 excellent, first-
rate, humdinger 11 outstanding

jimmy 3 bar, pry 4 open 5 crack, force,
lever 7 crowbar 9 break open,
force open

jimsonweed 6 datura 10 thorn apple

jingle 4 call, ring, song 5 clink, rhyme,
sound, verse 6 tinkle

jingoistic 7 hawkish 11 belligerent
12 chauvinistic, militaristic 13 national-
istic

jinn 5 afrit, genie 6 afreet, spirit

jinx 3 hex 5 charm, curse, spell 6 plague,
whammy 7 bad luck, evil eye 8 fore-
doom 10 affliction, misfortune

jitters 5 jumps, panic 6 nerves, shakes
7 anxiety, shivers, willies 9 whim-
whams 11 nervousness, stage fright
13 heebie-jeebies

jittery 5 jumpy, nervy 6 goosey, spooky
7 anxious, fearful, fidgety, nervous,
panicky 10 high-strung

jive 3 kid 4 fool, jazz, talk 5 dance,
music, swing, tease 6 cajole, hot air,
jargon

Joab *brother:* 6 Asahel 7 Abishai *father:*
7 Seraiah, Zeruiah *slayer:* 7 Benaiah
uncle: 5 David *victim:* 5 Abner, Amasa

Joan of Arc *birthplace:* 7 Domremy *epithet:* 7 Pucelle (La) 13 Maid of Orléans
king: 10 Charles VII *victory:* 7 Orléans

Joan's husband 5 Darby

Joash *father:* 4 Ahab 7 Ahaziah 8 Jehoahaz *son:* 6 Gideon 7 Amaziah 8 Jeroboam *victim:* 9 Zechariah

job 4 duty, hire, item, post, role, spot,
task, work 5 chore, stint, trade 6 effort,
office 7 calling, deprive, posting, pursuit, robbery 8 business, function,
penalize, position, vocation 9 situation,
speculate, victimize 10 assignment, difficulty, employment, engagement,
livelihood, occupation, profession
11 undertaking

Job *daughter:* 6 Keziah 7 Jemimah
father: 8 Issachar *friend:* 6 Bildad,
Zophar 7 Eliphaz

jobber 6 broker, dealer, seller, trader
8 merchant 10 contractor, wholesaler

job-safety agency 4 OSHA

job-training program 4 JTPA

Jocasta *daughter:* 6 Ismene 8 Antigone

husband: 5 Laius 7 Oedipus **son:** 7 Oedipus 8 Eteocles 9 Polynices

jock 5 pilot 7 athlete

jockey 4 play 5 rider, trick 7 beguile, exploit, finesse 8 maneuver 10 manipulate **famous:** 5 Baeza (Braulio) 6 Arcaro (Eddie), Bailey (Jerry), Murphy (Isaac), Pincay (Laffit) 7 Cauthen (Steve), Cordero (Angel), Hartack (Bill), Longden (Johnny), Stevens (Gary) 8 McCarron (Chris), McHargue (Darrel), Turcotte (Ron) 9 Shoemaker (Willie)

jocular 5 comic, funny, jolly, merry, witty 6 jocose, jocund, jovial, lively 7 amusing, comical, jesting, playful 8 cheerful, humorous 9 facetious

jocularity 3 fun, wit 4 glee 5 humor, mirth 6 gaiety 7 jollity 8 hilarity 9 jocundity, joviality, merriment 11 high spirits, playfulness

jocund 3 gay 5 happy, jolly, merry 6 elated, jovial, lively 7 festive, gleeful, playful 8 mirthful 12 lighthearted

joe 3 guy 4 java 6 coffee, fellow

jog 3 dig, jab, run 4 lope, move, pace, poke, prod, push, ride, stir, trot 5 nudge, punch, rouse, shake 6 bounce, change, jounce, prompt, remind

joggle 4 join, trot 5 dowel, joint, notch, shake, tooth 6 jostle

john 4 head 5 privy 6 toilet 7 latrine 8 bathroom, lavatory 11 water closet

John Hancock 9 autograph, signature

Johnson, Samuel biographer: 7 Boswell (James) **work:** 8 Rasselas 10 dictionary

John the Baptist father: 9 Zacharias **mother:** 9 Elisabeth

John the Evangelist brother: 5 James **father:** 7 Zebedee **mother:** 6 Salome

join 3 tie, wed 4 abut, ally, bind, bond, fuse, line, link, mate, yoke 5 affix, align, blend, marry, merge, piece, touch, unify, union, unite 6 attach, border, couple, engage, enlist, enroll, sign on, sign up, splice 7 combine, connect 8 compound, side with 9 affiliate, associate, integrate 12 come together

joint 3 bar, ell, hip, tie 4 butt, crux, dive, knee, link, node, seam 5 ankle, elbow, hinge, nexus, union, wrist 6 common, mutual, public, shared, suture, united 7 hangout, knuckle, shiplap 8 abutment, combined, communal, conjunct, coupling, junction, juncture, shoulder 9 concerted, honky-tonk 10 collective, connection 11 cooperative 12 articulation **combining form:** 5 arthr 6 arthro, condyl 7 condylo **disease:** 9 arthritis 10 rheumatism

joist 4 beam 6 rafter, timber 7 support

joke 3 gag, kid, pun, rag, rib, yak 4 fool,

jape, jest, josh, quip, razz 5 crack, humor, prank, sally 6 banter, corker, parody 7 mockery, sarcasm, waggery 8 drollery, one-liner 9 burlesque, wisecrack, witticism 11 monkeyshine **stale:** 8 chestnut

joker 3 guy, wag, wit 4 card, fool 5 catch, clown, comic, cutup 6 fellow, jester, kicker 7 proviso 8 comedian, humorist 9 condition 10 limitation 11 stipulation

jollity 3 fun, joy 4 glee 5 cheer, mirth 6 gaiety, revels 7 revelry, whoopee 8 hilarity 9 festivity, jocundity, joviality, merriment 10 ebullience, jocularity, liveliness 11 high spirits, merrymaking 12 cheerfulness, conviviality

jolly 3 fun, gay, kid 4 glad, jest, josh, very 5 humor, merry 6 banter, blithe, jocund, jovial, joyful, joyous 7 festive, gleeful, jocular, playful, roguish, waggish 8 cheerful, mirthful, splendid 9 convivial 10 frolicsome 12 lighthearted

Jolly Roger 4 flag 6 ensign **user:** 6 pirate

jolt 3 hit, jar 4 blow, bump, jerk, shot, slug, stun 5 check, clash, crash, knock, lurch, shake, shock, snort, upset 6 impact, jounce, rattle 7 disturb, reverse, shake up, startle 8 astonish, surprise 9 collision

Jonah 7 prophet **swallower:** 4 fish 5 whale

Jonathan brother: 7 Johanan **father:** 4 Saul **friend:** 5 David

Jones, John Paul ship: 15 Bonhomme Richard **victim:** 7 Serapis

Jones novel 11 Thin Red Line (The) 15 Some Came Running 18 From Here to Eternity

jongleur 4 bard 6 singer 7 juggler 8 minstrel 10 troubadour 11 entertainer

jonquil 8 daffodil 9 narcissus, perennial

Jonson play 7 Volpone 9 Alchemist (The) 15 Bartholomew Fair

Joplin creation 3 rag 7 ragtime

Joram brother: 7 Ahaziah **father:** 3 Toi 4 Ahab 11 Jehoshaphat **slayer:** 4 Jehu **son:** 7 Ahaziah

Jordan capital: 5 Amman **city:** 5 Irbid, Zarqa **gulf:** 5 Aqaba **language:** 6 Arabic **monarch:** 7 Hussein **monetary unit:** 5 dinar **mountain:** 4 Ramm **neighbor:** 4 Iraq 5 Syria 6 Israel 11 Saudi Arabia **river:** 6 Jordan **sea:** 4 Dead

jorum 3 cup, jug 6 vessel

Joseph brother: (see JACOB son) **buyer:** 8 Potiphar **father:** 5 Asaph, Jacob 9 Zacharias 10 Mattathias **mother:** 6 Rachel **son:** 5 Jesus 7 Ephraim 8 Manasseh **wife:** 4 Mary 7 Asenath

josh 3 kid, rag, rib 4 jest, joke, razz
5 chaff, jolly, tease 6 banter
Joshua's victory 7 Jericho
Joshua tree 5 yucca
joss 4 idol 5 image
Jo's sister 3 Amy, Meg 4 Beth
jostle 3 jar, jog 4 bump, push 5 crowd,
elbow, nudge, press, shove 7 agitate,
collide, compete, contend, vie with
8 shoulder
jot 3 bit 4 atom, iota, note, whit 5 grain,
minim, speck, write 6 tittle 7 smidgen
8 particle
joule component 3 erg
jounce 3 bob, jar, jog 4 bump, jolt
5 shake, shock, thump 6 impact
journal 3 log 5 diary, organ, paper
6 ledger, record, review 7 account,
gazette, minutes 8 magazine, register
9 chronicle, newspaper 10 periodical
journalist 3 Bly (Nellie) 4 Dowd (Maureen), Drew (Elizabeth), King (Larry),
Pyle (Ernie), Reed (John), Rose (Charlie), Will (George F.), Zahn (Paula)
5 Baker (Russell), Brown (George),
Cooke (Alistair), Dunne (Finley Peter),
Evans (Rowland), Hersh (Seymour),
Novak (Robert), Rowan (Carl), Royko
(Mike), Safer (Morley), Smith
(Hedrick), Stahl (Lesley), Stone (I. F.),
Szulc (Tad), White (William Allen),
Wolfe (Tom) 6 Arnett (Peter), Bierce
(Ambrose), Broder (David), Brokaw
(Tom), Ephron (Nora), Koppel (Ted),
Kuralt (Charles), Lehrer (Jim), Moyers
(Bill), Murrow (Edward R.), Osgood
(Charles), Rather (Dan), Reston
(James), Reuter (Paul Julius), Rivera
(Geraldo), Runyon (Damon), Safire
(William), Shirer (William L.), Thomas
(Helen, Lowell), Zenger (John Peter)
7 Blitzer (Wolf), Bradlee (Benjamin),
Breslin (Jimmy), Cousins (Norman),
Greeley (Horace), Gunther (John),
Huntley (Chet), Kempton (Murray),
McGrory (Mary), Mencken (H. L.),
Pearson (Drew), Royster (Vermont),
Russert (Tim), Tarbell (Ida), Trillin
(Calvin), Wallace (Chris, Mike), Wal-
ters (Barbara) 8 Amanpour (Christi-
ane), Anderson (Jack, Terry), Atkin-
son (Brooks), Brinkley (David),
Cronkite (Walter), Garrison (William
Lloyd), Jennings (Peter), Lippmann
(Walter), Pulitzer (Joseph), Salinger
(Pierre), Sevareid (Eric), Steffens (Lin-
coln), Thompson (Dorothy, Hunter),
Winchell (Walter), Woodward (Bob)
9 Bernstein (Carl), Donaldson (Sam),
Frederick (Pauline), Salisbury (Harri-
son), Schieffer (Bob)

journey 3 hie 4 hike, roam, tour, trek,
trip 5 jaunt, quest 6 cruise, junket,
push on, safari, travel, voyage 7 caravan, odyssey, proceed, travels
8 progress 9 excursion 10 expedition,
pilgrimage *route:* 9 itinerary *stage:* 3 leg
joust 4 duel, feud, spar, tilt 5 clash, fight
6 combat 7 contest 8 conflict 10 tournament *arena:* 5 lists 8 tiltyard
Jove see JUPITER
jovial 5 happy, jolly, merry 6 cheery
7 amiable 8 cheerful 9 convivial
11 good-humored, good-natured
jowl 3 jaw 5 cheek 6 dewlap, wattle
8 mandible
joy 4 glee 5 bliss, mirth 6 gaiety
7 delight, elation 8 felicity, fruition,
gladness, pleasure 9 enjoyment, happiness, merriment 11 delectation
Joyce, James *birthplace:* 6 Dublin *character:* 5 Bloom (Leopold), Bloom
(Molly) 7 Dedalus (Stephen) *work:*
6 Exiles 7 Ulysses 9 Dubliners
13 Finnegans Wake
joyful 3 gay 4 glad 5 happy, jolly, merry
6 elated, jocund 7 buoyant, festive,
gleeful, pleased 8 ecstatic, jubilant,
mirthful 9 delighted, rapturous
12 lighthearted
jubilant 5 happy 6 elated, joyful, joyous
8 euphoric, exultant, exulting 9 cock-a-
hoop, delighted, overjoyed, triumphal
10 triumphant
jubilate 5 exult, glory 7 delight, rejoice
9 celebrate
jubilation 3 joy 4 glee 7 ecstasy, rapture
8 euphoria, rhapsody 9 rejoicing, transport 10 exaltation, exultation, joyfulness, joyousness 11 celebration
12 exhilaration
jubilee 6 flambé 8 festival 9 festivity
10 indulgence 11 anniversary, celebration 13 commemoration
Judah *brother:* (see JACOB son) *father:*
5 Jacob *king:* 3 Asa 4 Ahaz, Amon
5 Joash 6 Abijam, Josiah, Jotham
Uzziah 7 Ahaziah, Amaziah, Jehoram
8 Hezekiah, Jehoahaz, Manasseh,
Rehoboam, Zedekiah 9 Jehoiakim
10 Jehoiachin 11 Jehoshaphat *mother:*
4 Leah *son:* 4 Onan 6 Shelah
Judas 7 traitor 8 informer, turncoat
father: 5 Simon 7 Chalphi 10 Mattathias
replacement: 8 Matthias *suicide place:*
8 Aceldama, Akeldama
judge 3 ref, try, ump 4 call, deem, rule,
test 5 infer 6 critic, decide, deduce,
jurist, reckon, settle, umpire 7 arbiter,
justice, mediate, referee 8 assessor, critique, estimate, mediator 9 arbitrate,
criticize, determine, moderator

10 adjudicate, arbitrator, chancellor, magistrate, negotiator 11 conciliator 12 intermediary *bench:* 4 banc *chamber:* 6 camera *in Hades:* 5 Minos 6 Aeacus 12 Rhadamanthus *mallet:* 5 gavel *Muslim:* 5 mufti

judgment 5 award, sense 6 acumen, decree, ruling, result, wisdom 7 finding, insight, opinion, verdict 8 decision, sagacity, sentence 9 appraisal, deduction, good sense, inference 10 assessment, conclusion, discretion, estimation, evaluation, horse sense, punishment 11 common sense, discernment 13 determination

judgmental 7 carping 8 captious, critical 10 belittling, censorious, derogatory 11 disparaging, reproachful 12 disapproving, faultfinding 13 hypercritical

Judgment Day 8 doomsday

____ **judicata** 3 res

judicial *assembly:* 5 court *document:* 4 writ

judicious 3 apt 4 fair, just, sage, sane, wise 5 right, sound 6 astute 7 careful, prudent, sapient 8 accurate, discreet, rational, sensible 9 equitable, objective, sagacious 10 discerning, reasonable

Judith *father:* 5 Beeri *home:* 8 Bethulia *husband:* 4 Esau *victim:* 10 Holofernes

judo 10 martial art *teacher:* 6 sensei

Judy's husband 5 Punch

jug 3 jar, pen 4 coop, ewer, gaol, jail, stew, stir, toby 5 pokey 6 cooler, flagon, immure, intern, lockup, prison, vessel 7 confine, pitcher, slammer 8 demijohn, imprison 9 constrain, container 11 incarcerate

jug-band instrument 5 kazoo 6 bottle 7 washtub 9 stovepipe, washboard

juggernaut 11 steamroller

juggle 3 fix 4 fool, toss 5 bluff, trick 6 change, delude, doctor, handle, humbug, take in 7 balance, beguile, deceive, mislead, shuffle 9 rearrange 10 manipulate

juice 3 sap 4 fuel, must 5 fluid 7 current, essence 8 vitality 10 succulence 11 electricity *fermented:* 4 wine 5 cider, perry

juicy 3 fat 4 racy, rich 5 lusty, vital 7 piquant 8 colorful, dripping, exciting 9 delicious, rewarding, succulent 10 profitable 11 fascinating, sensational

juju 4 luck 5 charm, magic 6 amulet, fetish, mascot 8 talisman 10 lucky charm

jujube 4 tree 5 fruit 7 gumdrop, lozenge

julep 5 drink

Juliet *betrothed:* 5 Paris *father:* 7 Capulet *lover:* 5 Romeo

July 14 11 Bastille Day

jumble 3 mix 4 cake, hash, mess, olio 5 chaos, mix up, shake 6 cookie, medley, mess up, muddle, muss up 7 clutter, confuse, disturb, mélange, rummage, shuffle 8 disarray, disorder, mishmash, pastiche, scramble 9 confusion, patchwork, potpourri 10 assortment, hodgepodge, hotchpotch, miscellany

jumbo 4 huge, vast 5 giant 6 mighty 7 immense, mammoth, massive 8 colossal, enormous, gigantic, oversize 9 oversized 10 prodigious 11 elephantine

jump 3 hop 4 bolt, hike, leap, move, trip 5 avoid, begin, boost, bound, clear, flush, hurry, leave, put up, raise, shift, start, vault 6 attack, bounce, bustle, change, hurdle, hustle, jack up, pounce, spring 7 bail out, elevate, startle 8 increase, leap over 9 advantage

jumper 4 sled 5 dress, horse, smock 6 blouse, jacket

jumping-frog county 9 Calaveras

jumpy 6 on edge 7 anxious, jittery, nervous 9 excitable 10 high-strung

junction 4 seam 5 joint, union 7 joining, meeting 8 coupling 9 interface 10 confluence, connection, crossroads 12 intersection

juncture 4 seam 5 joint, point, union 6 crisis, moment 7 instant, joining 8 coupling 10 connection, crossroads 11 concurrence, convergence 12 turning point

jungle 3 web, zoo 4 hash, mash, maze 5 snarl 6 jumble, morass, muddle, tangle 7 clutter, thicket 8 mishmash 9 labyrinth

Jungle Books, The *author:* 7 Kipling (Rudyard) *bear:* 5 Baloo *boy:* 6 Mowgli *panther:* 8 Bagheera *python:* 3 Kaa *tiger:* 9 Shere Khan *wolf:* 5 Akela

Jungle, The *author:* 8 Sinclair (Upton) *locale:* 7 Chicago 10 stockyards

junior 3 son 5 lower, minor, sonny, youth 6 lesser 7 student, younger 8 inferior, young man, youthful 9 secondary, youngster 11 subordinate

juniper 4 cone 5 cedar, fruit, savin, shrub 7 conifer 9 evergreen

junk 4 boat, dope, drug, ship 5 scrap, trash, waste 6 debris, heroin, litter, refuse, reject 7 cashier, clutter, discard, rubbish, rummage 8 get rid of, jettison, throw out 9 narcotics, throw away

junker 4 heap 5 crate, wreck 6 jalopy

junket 4 trip 5 feast, jaunt, spree 6 outing, picnic 7 banquet, dessert, journey 9 excursion

junk mail 4 spam

Juno *bird:* 7 peacock *epithet:* 6 Moneta
Greek equivalent: 4 Hera *husband:*
7 Jupiter (see also HERA)

Junoesque 7 stately 10 curvaceous, statuesque

junta 5 cabal, group 7 council, faction
9 committee

Jupiter 4 Jove, Zeus *angel:* 7 Zadkiel
cupbearer: 8 Ganymede *daughter:*
5 Venus 7 Minerva *epithet:* 6 Fidius,
Fulgur, Stator, Tonans 7 Pluvius *father:*
6 Saturn *lover:* 6 Europa 8 Callisto
mother: 3 Ops *satellite:* 6 Europa 8 Callisto, Ganymede *son:* 5 Arcas 6 Castor,
Pollux *temple:* 7 Capitol *wife:* 4 Juno

Jurgen *author:* 6 Cabell (James Branch)
trade: 10 pawnbroker

juridical 5 legal 6 lawful 8 juristic
10 legalistic

jurisdiction 3 law, see 4 sway, zone
5 might, orbit, power, range, reach,
scope, venue 6 county, domain, parish,
sphere 7 circuit, command, compass,
control, diocese, mastery, purview
8 dominion, hegemony, province
9 authority, bailiwick, territory 10 domination 11 supervision

jurisprudence 3 law

jurist 5 judge

jury 5 panel *decision:* 7 verdict

jury-rigged 6 make-do 7 stopgap
9 makeshift, temporary 10 improvised

just 3 apt, due, fit 4 even, fair, good,
meet, only, true, very 5 equal, legal,
quite, right 6 barely, hardly, honest,
lawful, nearly, proper, simply, square
7 correct, ethical, exactly, fitting, merited, perhaps, precise, totally, upright
8 accurate, deserved, directly, possibly,
recently, rightful, scarcely, squarely,
suitable, unbiased 9 equitable, expressly, honorable, impartial, justified,

objective, precisely, requisite, righteous
10 accurately, completely, legitimate,
reasonable, scrupulous 11 appropriate,
immediately, well-founded 12 unprejudiced 13 conscientious

justice 3 law 5 court, judge, right 6 equity 7 honesty 8 evenness, fairness, fair
play 10 lawfulness, magistrate 11 correctness 12 impartiality

justification 6 excuse, reason 7 account,
apology, defense, grounds 8 apologia
9 rationale 10 validation 11 explanation, vindication

justify 5 argue, claim, prove 6 assert,
defend, uphold, verify 7 account, bear
out, confirm, contend, explain, support, warrant 8 maintain, make even,
validate 9 vindicate 10 legitimate, legitimize 11 corroborate, rationalize
12 authenticate, legitimatize, substantiate

jut 4 hang, poke 5 bulge, pouch 6 beetle,
thrust 7 project 8 extend up, overhang,
protrude, stand out, stick out 9 extend
out, extension 10 projection, protrusion 12 protuberance

jute 5 gunny 6 burlap 7 sacking

Juvenal 4 poet 5 Roman *forte:* 6 satire

juvenile 3 kid 5 actor, child, green,
young, youth 6 callow, jejune, junior,
moppet 7 preteen, puerile 8 childish,
immature, youthful 9 childlike, fledgling, youngling, youngster 11 undeveloped

juvenility 5 youth 9 childhood, greenness
10 immaturity, springtide, springtime
12 youthfulness

juxtaposed 4 next 8 abutting, adjacent,
neighbor, proximal, touching 9 adjoining, bordering 10 appositive, contiguous, side-by-side 11 coterminous,
neighboring 12 conterminous

kabob see KEBAB

kachina 4 doll 6 spirit 12 impersonator

kaddish 6 prayer

Kafka, Franz *character:* 4 Olga 6 Gregor
(Samsa), Joseph (K.) *novel:* 5 Trial

(The) 6 Castle (The) 7 Amerika *story:*
8 Judgment (The) 12 Hunger Artist (A)
13 Metamorphosis (The)

kaiser 5 ruler 7 emperor, monarch
8 autocrat 9 sovereign

kaka 6 parrot

kale 4 cash, cole 5 bucks, money, moola 6 moolah 7 cabbage 8 colewort

kaleidoscopic 8 changing, colorful 10 variegated

Kali *aspect:* 5 Durga 7 Parvati *husband:* 4 Siva 5 Shiva

Kama *god of:* 4 love *mount:* 6 parrot 7 sparrow *wife:* 4 Rati

kamikaze 7 suicide 8 suicidal

kampong 6 hamlet 7 village

Kampuchea see CAMBODIA

kangaroo 6 leaper 7 wallaby 8 wallaroo 9 marsupial *herd:* 3 mob *young:* 4 joey

Kansas *capital:* 6 Topeka *city:* 6 Olathe, Salina, Topeka 7 Abilene, Emporia, Shawnee, Wichita 8 Lawrence *nickname:* 9 Jayhawker (State), Sunflower (State) *prison:* 11 Leavenworth *river:* 8 Arkansas *state bird:* 10 meadowlark *state flower:* 9 sunflower *state tree:* 10 cottonwood

kaolin 4 clay

kaput 5 spent 6 ruined 7 done for, useless 8 defeated, finished, outmoded 9 destroyed

karakul 5 sheep 9 broadtail

karma 4 fate 9 emanation

kaross 3 rug 7 garment

kasha 5 grain 8 porridge 9 buckwheat

Katharina *father:* 8 Baptista *suitor:* 9 Petruchio

Katrina's suitor 9 Brom Bones 12 Ichabod Crane

katydid 3 bug 6 insect 11 grasshopper

katzenjammer 3 din 5 noise 6 clamor, hubbub, racket 8 distress, hangover, headache 9 commotion

kava 5 shrub 6 pepper 8 beverage

kayo 6 defeat, finish 8 knockout 9 finish off 11 coup de grace

Kazakhstan *capital:* 6 Akmola, Astana *city:* 5 Semey 8 Pavlodar, Shymkent *lake:* 6 Tengiz 8 Balkhash *language:* 6 Kazakh 7 Russian *monetary unit:* 5 tenge *mountain:* 10 Khan-Tengri *neighbor:* 5 China 6 Russia 10 Kyrgyzstan, Uzbekistan 12 Turkmenistan *river:* 4 Ural 6 Irtysh 8 Syr Dar'ya *sea:* 4 Aral 7 Caspian

Kazantzakis hero 5 Zorba (Alexis)

kea 6 parrot

Keats poem 5 Lamia 8 Endymion, Hyperion, Isabella, To Autumn 11 Ode to Psyche 12 Eve of St. Agnes (The) 16 Ode on a Grecian Urn 17 Ode to a Nightingale

kebab 8 shashlik

kedge 6 anchor

keel 4 boat, lean, ship 5 barge, pitch,

ridge, slump 6 carina 7 capsize 8 overturn 11 centerboard

keen 4 avid, fine, wail, yowl 5 acute, alert, eager, honed, mourn, sharp, smart 6 ardent, astute, bewail, bright, clever, gung ho, intent, lament, shrewd 7 anxious, fervent, intense, whetted, zealous 8 animated, spirited 9 fine-edged, impatient, sensitive, wonderful 10 perceptive, razor-sharp 11 lamentation, penetrating, quick-witted, sharp-witted 12 enthusiastic, sharp-sighted

keenness 3 wit 4 edge, zeal 6 acuity, acumen 10 enthusiasm 11 discernment, penetration 12 incisiveness, perspicacity

keep 3 own 4 hold, jail, mind, obey, save, stay, tend 5 lodge, stock 6 castle, comply, detain, living, lockup, manage, prison, retain 7 abstain, conduct, confine, forbear, fulfill, possess, refrain, reserve 8 conserve, fortress, maintain, preserve, withhold 9 constrain 10 livelihood, sustenance 11 maintenance, subsistence

keep back 3 bar, dam 4 curb, hold, save, stay 6 detain, retain, retard, stifle 7 contain, inhibit, repress, reserve 8 restrain, restrict, suppress, withhold

keeper 5 guard 6 warden 7 big fish, curator 8 Cerberus, guardian, watchdog 9 custodian, protector

keeping 4 care, ward 5 aegis, trust 6 charge 7 custody, support 8 wardship 9 provision 10 caretaking, conformity, observance 11 maintenance 12 conservation, guardianship

keep on 4 last 5 abide 6 endure 7 persist 8 continue 9 hang tough, persevere

keep out 3 ban, bar 4 hold, stop 5 block, check, debar 6 forbid 7 embargo, exclude 8 prohibit, turn back 9 blackball

keepsake 5 token 6 trophy 7 memento 8 memorial, reminder, souvenir 11 remembrance

keep up 7 persist, prolong, sustain 8 continue, maintain, preserve 9 persevere

kef 4 hash, hemp 7 hashish 10 dreaminess 12 tranquillity

keg 3 tun 4 butt, cask, pipe 6 barrel, firkin, vessel 8 hogshead 9 container

kegler 6 bowler

keister 3 bum, end 4 buns, duff, rear, rump, seat, tail, tush 5 fanny 6 behind, bottom 8 backside, buttocks, derriere 9 posterior

keloid 4 scar

kelp 4 alga 7 seaweed

kelpie 3 dog 5 naiad, nixie 6 sprite

ken 4 view 5 grasp, range, reach, scope,

sight 7 horizon, purview 9 knowledge
10 perception 13 comprehension,
understanding
kenaf 5 fiber, plant 8 hibiscus
Kenilworth author 5 Scott (Walter)
Kennedy novel 8 Ironweed
kennel 4 pack 5 board 6 gutter 7 shelter
9 enclosure
keno 4 game *similar to:* 5 beano, bingo,
lotto
Kentucky *capital:* 9 Frankfort *city:* 9 Lexington 10 Louisville 12 Bowling Green
nickname: 9 Bluegrass (State) *park:*
11 Mammoth Cave *racecourse:*
14 Churchill Downs *river:* 4 Ohio *state
bird:* 8 cardinal *state flower:* 9 goldenrod
state tree: 11 tulip poplar
Kentucky bluegrass 3 Poa
Kenya *capital:* 7 Nairobi *city:* 6 Kisumu,
Nakuru 7 Mombasa *lake:* 7 Turkana
8 Victoria *language:* 7 English, Swahili
monetary unit: 8 shilling *mountain:*
5 Elgon, Kenya *neighbor:* 5 Sudan
6 Uganda 7 Somalia 8 Ethiopia, Tanzania *river:* 4 Tana
kepi 3 cap
kerchief 6 hankie 7 bandana 8 babushka,
bandanna, kaffiyeh *Scottish:* 5 curch
kerf 3 cut 4 nick, slit 5 cleft, notch
6 groove
kerfuffle 3 ado, row 4 flap, fuss, stir, to-
do 5 hoo-ha 6 dust-up, ruckus, rumpus
7 turmoil 8 foofaraw 11 disturbance
kermis 4 fair 8 carnival, festival
kernel 3 nub, nut 4 core, crux, gist,
meat, pith, seed 5 grain 6 nubbin,
upshot 7 essence, nucleus 9 substance
Kerouac novel 6 Big Sur 9 On the Road
10 Dharma Bums (The) 13 Subter-
raneans (The)
Kesey novel 21 Sometimes a Great
Notion 25 One Flew over the
Cuckoo's Nest
kestrel 4 bird, hawk 6 falcon 9 wind-
hover
ketch 4 boat 6 vessel 8 sailboat 10 watercraft
ketone 7 acetone, camphor
kettle 3 pot 6 hollow, vessel 7 caldron,
marmite, pothole 8 cauldron
kettledrum 5 naker 7 timpani (plural),
timpano
key 4 clue, isle, reef 5 basic, islet, vital
6 cotter, island, legend, master, opener,
samara, spline, ticket, tip-off 7 central,
crucial, digital, pivotal 8 critical, passport, password, skeleton, solution,
tonality 9 essential, important 10 open
sesame 11 fundamental *combining form:*
5 clavi, clavo *notch:* 4 ward
keyboard 6 manual 7 clavier

key fruit 6 samara
key man 5 chief 7 kingpin 9 locksmith
keynote 4 core, crux, gist, pith, tone
5 theme, tonic
keynoter 6 orator 7 speaker
Keystone State 12 Pennsylvania
khaki 3 tan 5 brown, cloth, color 7 garment, uniform
khamsin 4 wind
khan 5 chief, ruler 9 chieftain, sovereign
11 caravansary
khedive 5 ruler 7 viceroy
Khomeini 4 imam 9 ayatollah
Ki *mother:* 5 Nammu *son:* 5 Enlil
kiang 3 ass
kibble 4 meal 5 grain, grind 9 pulverize
kibbutz 4 co-op, farm 7 commune
10 collective, settlement 11 cooperative
kibe 4 heel, sore 8 swelling 9 chilblain
kibitz 4 chat 6 banter, butt in, meddle
7 comment, intrude, obtrude 9 interfere
kibitzer 7 meddler 8 busybody, observer
9 buttinsky, spectator 10 rubberneck
kibosh 3 hex 4 jinx, stop 5 check, curse
kick 4 bang, boot, carp, fuss, punt, wail
5 gripe, rebel, whine 6 object, recoil,
repine, resist, thrill, wallop 7 grumble,
protest 8 complain
kicker 5 catch 6 clause, punter 9 condition, fine print
kick in 3 die, pay 4 give 5 begin, put up,
start 6 donate, pony up 7 cough up,
fork out 8 fork over, hand over 10 contribute
kick off 3 die 4 open 5 begin, croak, start
6 launch 8 commence, drop dead,
embark on, initiate 10 inaugurate
kick out 3 axe, can 4 fire, oust, sack
5 eject, evict 6 bounce 7 boot out,
cashier, dismiss 8 throw out 9 discharge
kickshaw 5 goody, treat 6 bauble, dainty,
gewgaw, morsel, tidbit, trifle 7 bibelot,
trinket 8 delicacy 9 bagatelle
kid 3 guy, rag, rib 4 dupe, fool, gull,
hoax, jest, joke, josh, razz 5 child, jolly,
trick, youth 6 banter, befool, moppet,
nipper 7 deceive, younger 8 flimflam,
hoodwink, juvenile 9 bamboozle,
youngling, youngster
kidnap 6 abduct, snatch 8 shanghai
kidney 5 gland, organ *combining form:*
4 reni, reno 5 nephr 6 nephro
kidney-shaped 8 reniform
kielbasa 7 sausage
kilderkin 3 keg 4 cask 6 barrel 9 container
kilim 3 mat, rug 6 carpet
kill 3 end, off, zap 4 do in, prey, slay,
stop, veto 5 creek, croak, scrag, snuff,
waste 6 defeat, delete, finish, murder,
quarry, stifle 7 bump off, butcher,

channel, destroy, execute **8** blow away, carry off, dispatch, knock off, massacre **9** sacrifice, slaughter **10** annihilate **11** assassinate, exterminate

killer 6 gunman, hit man **7** butcher, torpedo **8** assassin, homicide *combining form:* **4** cide

Killer Angels author 6 Shaara (Michael)

killer whale 4 orca **8** cetacean

killing 5 blood, fatal **6** deadly, lethal, mortal, murder **7** carnage **8** butchery, foul play, homicide **9** bloodbath, bloodshed, slaughter **12** manslaughter *of a race:* **8** genocide *of bacteria:* **11** bactericide *of a brother:* **10** fratricide *of a father:* **9** patricide *of a king:* **8** regicide *of a mother:* **9** matricide *of a relative:* **9** parricide *of a sister:* **10** sororicide *of oneself:* **7** suicide *of plants:* **9** herbicide

killjoy 6 downer, grinch, grouch **7** spoiler **8** doomster, sourpuss **9** Cassandra, defeatist, doomsayer, gloomy Gus, pessimist, worrywart **10** spoilsport, wet blanket

Kilmer poem 5 Trees

kiln 4 oast, oven **7** furnace

kilt 5 skirt *accessory:* **7** sporran *fabric:* **5** plaid **6** tartan

kilter 4 trim **5** order, shape **6** fettle, repair **7** fitness **9** condition

kimono 4 gown, robe *sash:* **3** obi

kin 3 sib **4** clan, folk, kind **5** blood, flesh, house, stock, tribe **6** family **7** lineage, related **8** relation, relative

kind 3 ilk **4** good, like, sort, type, warm **5** breed, class, genre **6** benign, genial, gentle, humane, loving, nature, stripe, tender **7** affable, amiable, clement, essence, feather, helpful, lenient, quality, species, variety **8** category, merciful, tolerant **9** character **10** altruistic, benevolent, charitable, forbearing, responsive **11** considerate, description, good-hearted, good-humored, good-natured, openhearted, softhearted, sympathetic, warmhearted **12** affectionate, good-tempered, humanitarian **13** compassionate, philanthropic

kindle 4 bear, fire, stir, wake, whet **5** light, rally, rouse, spark, start, waken **6** arouse, awaken, bestir, excite, foment, ignite, incite **7** inflame, provoke **8** activate **9** instigate, stimulate **10** illuminate

kindliness 8 goodwill, sympathy **9** affection **10** solicitude **11** benevolence

kindly 6 benign, gentle **7** benefic **8** friendly, generous, gracious, pleasant **9** agreeable, attentive, benignant **10** beneficent, beneficial, neighborly

11 considerate, good-hearted, sympathetic

kindness 5 favor, mercy **7** service **8** clemency, courtesy, goodwill, sympathy **10** compassion, generosity, indulgence **11** benevolence **13** consideration

kind of 5 quite **6** fairly, pretty, rather **8** passably, somewhat **9** tolerably **10** more or less, reasonably, relatively

kindred 3 sib **4** clan, folk, like, sept **5** alike, blood, flesh, house, stock, tribe **6** agnate, allied, family **7** cognate, connate, lineage, related, similar **9** relatives **10** affiliated, connatural **11** consanguine

king 3 rex **4** czar, tsar **5** mogul, ruler **6** tycoon **7** magnate, monarch **9** sovereign *Albanian:* **3** Zog **7** William *Assyrian:* **6** Sargon **11** Sennacherib, Shalmaneser *Babylonian:* **6** Sargon **9** Hammurabi **10** Belshazzar *Belgian:* **6** Albert **7** Leopold **8** Baudouin *Bohemian:* **9** Wenceslas **10** Wenceslaus *Bulgarian:* **5** Boris **6** Simeon *Damascus:* **8** Benhadad *Danish:* **4** Abel, Eric, Gorm, Hans, John, Olaf **5** Sweyn **6** Canute, Harold, Magnus **8** Nicholas, Waldemar **9** Christian, Frederick **11** Christopher *Dutch:* **7** William *Egyptian:* **3** Tut **4** Pepi, Seti **5** Khufu, Menes, Necho **6** Cheops, Ramses **7** Harmhab, Osorkon, Psamtik, Ptolemy **8** Ikhnaton, Thothmes, Thutmose **9** Amenhotep, Sesostris **11** Tutankhamen *English:* **4** John **5** Henry, James **6** Alfred, Canute, Edmund, Edward, Egbert, George, Harold **7** Charles, Richard, Stephen, William **8** Ethelred **9** Athelstan, Ethelbald, Ethelbert *French:* **3** Odo, roi **4** Jean, John **5** Henri, Henry, Louis, Pepin, Raoul **6** Philip, Robert, Rudolf **7** Charles, Francis, Lothair **8** François **9** Hugh Capet **11** Charlemagne *German:* **4** Carl, Karl **5** König, Louis **6** Lothar, Ludwig **7** Charles, Lothair *Greek (modern):* **4** Paul **6** George **9** Alexander **11** Constantine *Hawaiian:* **10** Kamehameha *Hungarian:* **6** Attila *Indian:* **4** raja **5** rajah *Irish:* **9** Brian Boru *Italian:* **7** Humbert, Umberto *Jordanian:* **5** Talal **7** Hussein **8** Abdullah *Judah:* (see at JUDAH) *Judean:* **5** Herod *Lydian:* **5** Gyges **7** Croesus **8** Alyattes *Norwegian:* **4** Eric, Erik, Inge, Olaf **5** Sweyn **6** Haakon, Harald, Harold, Magnus, Sigurd, Sverre *Ostrogothic:* **9** Theodoric *Persian:* **5** Cyrus **6** Darius, Xerxes *Portuguese:* **4** John **5** Henry, Louis, Peter **6** Carlos, Edward, Manuel, Sancho **7** Alfonso **9** Ferdinand, Sebastian *Prussian:* **7** Wilhelm, William **9** Frederick, Friedrich *relating to:* **5** regal, royal

Saudi Arabian: 4 Saud 6 Faisal 9 Abdul-Aziz *Scottish:* 4 John 5 David, Edgar, James 6 Duncan 7 Macbeth, Malcolm, William 9 Alexander, Donalbane 10 David Bruce 11 Robert Bruce *Spanish:* 3 rey 5 Louis 6 Philip 7 Alfonso, Amadeus, Charles 9 Ferdinand 10 Juan Carlos *Spartan:* 8 Leonidas *Swedish:* 4 Eric, John 5 Oscar 6 Birger, Gustav, Haakon, Magnus 7 Charles 8 Gustavus, Waldemar 9 Frederick, Sigismund, Sten Sture *Visigothic:* 6 Alaric

King Arthur *birthplace:* 8 Tintagel *chronicler:* 8 Geoffrey (of Monmouth) *court site:* 7 Camelot 8 Caerleon *deathplace:* 6 Camlan *father:* 5 Uther *father-in-law:* 9 Laodogant, Leodegran 11 Leodegrance *foster father:* 5 Ector *jester:* 7 Dagonet *knight:* 3 Kay 4 Bors 5 Balan, Balin 6 Gareth, Gawain, Modred 7 Galahad, Geraint, Lamerok, Mordred, Tristan 8 Bedivere, Lancelot, Parsifal, Percival, Tristram 9 Launcelot *lance:* 3 Ron *last abode:* 6 Avalon *last name:* 9 Pendragon *magician:* 6 Merlin *mother:* 6 Ygerne 7 Igraine *nephew:* 6 Gareth, Modred 7 Mordred *queen:* 9 Guinevere *shield:* 7 Pridwin *sister:* 7 Morgain 11 Morgan le Fay *slayer:* 6 Modred 7 Mordred *son:* 6 Modred 7 Mordred *steward:* 3 Kay *sword:* 9 Excalibur *victim:* 6 Modred 7 Mordred *wife:* 9 Guinevere

king crab 7 limulus

kingdom 5 realm 6 domain, empire 7 demesne 8 monarchy

kingdom come 4 Zion 6 heaven 8 paradise 9 hereafter 10 afterworld

kingfish 4 boss 6 bigwig, honcho, master 7 big shot, croaker 8 mackerel

kingfisher 7 halcyon 10 kookaburra

kingly 5 regal, royal 6 august, lordly, regnal 7 exalted 8 imperial, majestic 9 imperious, masterful, monarchal, sovereign 10 monarchial 11 monarchical

King novel 6 Carrie 7 Shining (The) 8 Dead Zone (The) 9 Dark Tower (The), Green Mile (The), Salem's Lot 11 Firestarter, Pet Sematary

King Philip 9 Metacomet

kingpin 4 boss, guru, head 5 chief, mogul 6 bigwig, top dog 7 magnate 9 top banana 10 mastermind

Kings Peak range 5 Uinta

Kingu *consort:* 6 Tiamat *slayer:* 6 Marduk

kink 4 bend, curl, knot, whim 5 cramp, crick, quirk, snarl, spasm, twist 6 tangle 11 peculiarity 12 eccentricity, imperfection

kinky 3 odd 4 bent 5 curly, outré, ultra, weird 6 curled, far-out, frizzy, quirky 7 bizarre, deviant, knotted, strange, twisted 9 eccentric 10 outlandish

kiosk 5 booth 8 pavilion 9 newsstand 11 summerhouse

kip 3 bed, nap 4 hide, pelt, skin 5 sleep

Kipling, Rudyard *work:* 3 Kim 6 L'Envoi 8 Gunga Din, Mandalay 10 Fuzzy Wuzzy 11 Jungle Books (The), Recessional 13 Just So Stories, Soldiers Three 15 Light That Failed (The), Puck of Pook's Hill 18 Captains Courageous

Kiribati *capital:* 6 Tarawa *island, island group:* 4 Line 6 Banaba 7 Gilbert, Phoenix *language:* 7 English *location:* 7 Oceania *monetary unit:* 6 dollar

kirk 6 church

kirsch 6 brandy, liquor

kirtle 4 coat, gown 5 dress, tunic 7 garment

Kish *father:* 3 Ner 4 Abdi 5 Abiel, Jeiel 6 Jehiel *son:* 4 Saul

kismet 3 lot 4 doom, fate, luck 5 weird 6 Moirai 7 destiny, fortune

kiss 4 buss, neck, peck 5 graze, smack 6 cookie, glance, smooch 7 lip-lock 8 osculate, pucker up 10 osculation

kisser 3 mug 4 face, lips 5 mouth

Kiss sculptor 5 Rodin (Auguste)

kit 3 set 4 gear, pelt 5 group 6 outfit, tackle, violin 7 package 8 caboodle 9 container 10 collection

kitchen 4 mess 6 galley 7 cuisine 8 scullery *appliance:* (see at APPLIANCE) *boss:* 4 chef (see also COOKING)

kite 4 hawk, sail, soar 5 check, glede, hurry, mosey 7 saunter, take off 8 clear out, hightail, predator 9 spinnaker

kith 3 kin, sib 4 clan, folk 6 family 7 friends, kindred, kinfolk 9 neighbors, relatives

kitsch 4 camp, junk 9 vulgarity

kittenish 3 coy 6 elvish, frisky, impish 7 coltish, playful 10 frolicsome 11 mischievous

kitty 3 cat, pot 4 fund, pool, puss 5 pussy 6 feline, stakes 7 jackpot

kiwi 4 bird 5 fruit 7 Apteryx 12 New Zealander

klatch 5 bunch, group 7 meeting 9 gathering 11 get-together

kleptomaniac 5 thief 7 booster 10 shoplifter

klutz 3 oaf 4 boob, clod, gawk, lout, lump 5 looby 6 lubber, lummox 7 bungler, palooka 8 shlemiel 9 schlemiel 10 stumblebum

klutzy 5 inept 6 clumsy 7 awkward 9 all thumbs, maladroit 10 blundering

knack 4 bent, gift, head 5 flair, forte, skill, trick 6 genius, talent 7 ability, apt-

ness, command, faculty, know-how,
mastery **8** aptitude, capacity, facility
9 dexterity, expertise, stratagem
10 expertness

knapsack 4 pack **8** backpack

knave 4 heel, jack **5** fraud, rogue, scamp
6 rascal, varlet **7** lowlife, villain
8 scalawag, swindler **9** scoundrel
10 blackguard **11** rapscallion

knavery 5 fraud **6** deceit **8** mischief,
trickery, villainy **9** chicanery, deception, rascality **10** dishonesty

knavish 5 lying **6** shifty, tricky **7** devious,
roguish **8** rascally **9** deceitful, deceptive, dishonest **10** mendacious
12 unscrupulous

knead 4 form, mold, work **5** press, shape
7 massage **10** manipulate

knee 5 joint *bend:* **9** genuflect **12** genuflection *bone:* **7** patella

kneeler 5 stool **7** cushion **8** prie-dieu
9 footstool

knell 4 bong, peal, ring, toll **5** chime
6 summon **7** warning **8** announce, proclaim

knickknack 3 toy **4** dido **5** curio
6 bauble, gadget, gewgaw, trifle
7 bibelot, novelty, trinket, whatnot,
whatsit **8** gimcrack, ornament, souvenir **9** bagatelle, bric-a-brac, objet
d'art

knife 4 bolo, shiv, snee **5** blade, bowie,
panga, shank, sword **6** barong, cutter,
dagger, parang, sickle **7** cleaver,
machete, scalpel **8** stiletto, yataghan
11 switchblade *case:* **6** sheath *handle:*
4 haft, hilt *maker:* **6** cutler **7** grinder

knifelike 4 keen **5** acute, sharp **7** cutting
8 piercing, stabbing **11** penetrating

knight 3 dub, sir **5** eques **8** cavalier,
chessman, horseman **9** caballero,
chevalier *code:* **8** chivalry *competition:*
7 listing, tilting **8** jousting **10** tournament *German:* **6** Ritter *servant:* **4** page
5 valet **6** squire *title:* **3** sir *wife:* **4** lady

knighthood 8 chivalry

knightly 4 bold **5** brave, noble **6** heroic
7 gallant, valiant **10** chivalrous

Knight of the Round Table see KING
ARTHUR

Knight of the Rueful Countenance
10 Don Quixote

knit 4 bind, heal, join, link, mend, purl
5 plait, unite, weave **6** fabric, stitch
7 conjoin, crochet **8** contract **9** interlace **10** intertwine

knitting *material:* **4** yarn *stitch:* **3** rib
4 purl **6** garter *tool:* **6** needle

knob 3 bun, bur, nub **4** bump, burl,
burr, dial, hill, hump, lump, node,
umbo **5** bulge, gnarl, knoll, mound

6 button, finial, handle, nubble, pommel **7** hillock **12** protuberance

knobkerrie 3 bat **4** club, mace **5** billy
6 cudgel, weapon **7** war club **8** bludgeon **9** billy club, truncheon

knock 3 bob, hit, rap, tap **4** bash, blow,
bump, cuff, lick, swat **5** blame, clout,
fault, pound, swipe, thump **6** strike
7 censure, condemn, setback
8 denounce, reversal **9** criticize
10 denunciate

knock down 4 drop, earn, fell, gain, raze
5 floor, level, lower **6** lay low, reduce
7 acquire, bring in, flatten **9** dismantle
11 disassemble

knocker 6 carper, critic **7** caviler **8** quibbler **10** complainer, criticizer **11** faultfinder

knock off 3 rob **4** copy, do in, halt, kill,
quit, slay, stop **5** cease **6** deduct, defeat,
desist, finish, murder **7** execute, imitate, take out **8** discount, overcome,
subtract **9** liquidate **11** assassinate, call
it quits, counterfeit

knockout 4 kayo **5** dandy, final **6** beauty,
eyeful, looker, lovely **7** stunner **8** decisive, jim-dandy, striking, stunning
9 deathblow, finishing, humdinger
10 attractive **11** coup de grace, crackerjack

knock over 3 rob **4** down, drop, fell
5 amaze, floor, steal, upset **6** boggle,
hijack, hold up, lay low, topple **7** flatten, stick up **9** bring down, eliminate,
overpower, overthrow, overwhelm,
prostrate

knoll 4 hill, knob **5** mound **7** hillock

knot 3 bow, tie **4** bond, burr, link, loop,
lump, node **5** bunch, gnarl, hitch,
nexus **6** jungle, tangle **8** ligament, ligature, vinculum *in fiber:* **3** nep *kind:*
4 bend, loop, slip **5** hitch **6** granny,
splice, square **7** bowline **9** sheet bend
10 clove hitch, sheepshank

knotty 4 hard **6** sticky **7** complex,
gnarled, Gordian **8** involved **9** byzantine, difficult, elaborate, intricate
10 formidable **11** complicated, problematic

knout 4 flog, lash, whip **7** scourge

know 3 wot **5** grasp **6** fathom, intuit
7 discern, realize **9** apprehend, recognize **10** appreciate, comprehend, experience, understand *Scottish:* **3** ken

knowable 9 graspable **10** cognizable,
fathomable **12** intelligible **13** apprehensible

know-how 5 craft, knack, skill **6** talent
7 ability, cunning, faculty, mastery
8 aptitude **9** dexterity, expertise
10 adroitness, expertness **11** proficiency

knowing 3 hep, hip 4 sage, wise 5 aware, blasé, canny, smart 6 bright, clever 7 witting, worldly 8 sentient 9 cognizant, conscious, sagacious 10 conversant, discerning, insightful, perceptive 11 worldly-wise 13 sophisticated

know-it-all 6 smarty 7 wise guy 8 wiseacre 10 smart aleck 11 smartypants, wisenheimer

knowledge 3 ken 4 lore, news 5 facts 6 wisdom 7 science 8 learning 9 cognition, education, erudition 10 cognizance 11 information, scholarship 12 intelligence 13 enlightenment *lack of:* 9 ignorance *mystical:* 6 gnosis

knowledgeable 5 savvy 8 educated, informed

know-nothing 4 dolt, dope, fool 5 dummy, dunce, idiot, yahoo 6 dimwit 7 pinhead 8 agnostic, ignorant, numskull 9 benighted, blockhead, brainless, ignoramus, lamebrain, numbskull 10 illiterate, uneducated 11 empty-headed

knuckle 5 joint *combining form:* 6 condyl 7 condylo

knucklehead 4 dolt, dope, fool 5 dummy, dunce, idiot, yahoo 6 dimwit 8 clodpole, numskull 9 ignoramus, lamebrain, numbskull

knuckle under 3 bow 4 cave 5 yield 6 cave in, give in, submit 7 succumb 8 say uncle 9 surrender 10 capitulate

knurl 3 nub 4 bead, knob 5 ridge 12 protuberance

KO 4 kayo 8 knockout

koan 7 paradox

kobold 5 dwarf, gnome 6 goblin, spirit, sprite

Kohinoor 3 gem 7 diamond

kohlrabi 7 cabbage

kola 3 nut 4 tree

komatik 4 sled 6 sledge

kook 3 nut 5 crank, loony, wacko 6 cuckoo, weirdo 7 dingbat, lunatic, oddball 8 crackpot 9 ding-a-ling, fruitcake, screwball 10 crackbrain

kooky 4 daft, nuts 5 batty, crazy, daffy, dotty, flaky, loony, nutty, silly, wacky, weird 6 freaky, fruity, insane, screwy 7 bizarre, idiotic, lunatic, offbeat, touched 8 demented 9 eccentric, fantastic 10 flipped out, freaked-out, off-the-wall, outlandish

kopeck 4 coin *one hundred:* 5 ruble

Koran *chapter:* 4 sura *revealer of:* 7 Gabriel *scholar:* 5 ulama, ulema

Korea see *Korea, North; Korea, South*

Korean *dynasty:* 5 Silla 7 Koguryo *national dish:* 6 kimchi

Korea, North *capital:* 9 P'yongyang *city:*

7 Hamhung 8 Ch'ongjin *leader:* 9 Kim Il-sung, Kim Jong Il 10 Kim Chong-Il *monetary unit:* 3 won *mountain:* 6 Paektu *neighbor:* 5 China 6 Russia 10 South Korea *sea:* 6 Yellow

Korea, South *capital:* 5 Seoul *city:* 5 Pusan, Taegu 6 Inch'on, Taejon 7 Kwangju *island:* 5 Cheju *monetary unit:* 3 won *neighbor:* 10 North Korea *river:* 3 Han 7 Naktong *sea:* 5 Japan 6 Yellow

kosher 3 fit 4 pure 5 clean 6 proper 10 acceptable, legitimate, sanctioned 12 satisfactory

Kosinski novel 5 Steps 10 Being There 11 Painted Bird (The)

Koussevitzky 5 Serge 6 Sergei 9 conductor

kowtow 3 bow 4 fawn 5 cower, defer, kneel, toady 6 cringe, grovel 7 honey up, truckle 8 bootlick 11 apple-polish

kraal 3 pen 6 corral 7 village 9 enclosure

kraken 5 squid 9 leviathan 10 giant squid, sea monster

krater 3 jar 4 vase 6 vessel

Kriemhild *brother:* 7 Gunther *husband:* 5 Etzel 6 Attila 9 Siegfried *slayer:* 10 Hildebrand *victim:* 5 Hagen

kris 6 dagger

Krishna *avatar of:* 6 Vishnu *brother:* 8 Balarama *father:* 8 Vasudeva *mother:* 6 Devaki *uncle:* 5 Kansa *victim:* 5 Kansa

Krupp works site 5 Essen

kudos 4 bays, fame 5 award, glory, honor 6 honors, praise, renown 7 acclaim, bouquet, laurels 8 accolade, bouquets 10 compliment 11 distinction, recognition

kudu 8 antelope

kukri 5 sword

kumquat 5 fruit *kin:* 6 orange

Kushner play 15 Angels in America

Kuwait *capital:* 6 Kuwait *gulf:* 7 Persian *island:* 7 Bubiyan 8 Faylakah *language:* 6 Arabic 7 Persian *monetary unit:* 5 dinar *neighbor:* 4 Iraq 11 Saudi Arabia *oasis:* 8 Al-Jahrah

kvass 4 beer

kvetch 4 beef, crab, fret, fuss 5 gripe, whine 6 grouch, grouse 7 grumble 8 complain 9 bellyache

___ kwon do 3 tae

kyphosis 8 humpback 9 curvature, hunchback

Kyrgyzstan *capital:* 7 Bishkek *city:* 3 Osh *conqueror:* 9 Jöchi Khan *lake:* 8 Issyk-Kul *language:* 6 Kyrgyz 7 Russian *monetary unit:* 3 som *mountain, range:* 4 Alai 6 Pobedy 7 Victory 8 Tian Shan 10 Khan-Tengri 11 Kok Shaal-Tau *neighbor:* 5 China 10 Kazakhstan, Tajikistan, Uzbekistan *river:* 5 Naryn

L

Laadah *father:* 6 Shelah *grandfather:*
5 Judah

laager 4 camp 6 encamp 7 bivouac

lab 13 proving ground

Laban *daughter:* 4 Leah 6 Rachel *father:*
7 Bethuel *grandfather:* 5 Nahor *sister:*
7 Rebekah

label 3 tag 4 band, mark 6 marker, ticket
7 epithet, hallmark, sticker 8 classify,
identify, insignia

labium 3 lip

labor 4 moil, task, toil, work 5 chore,
grind, sweat 6 drudge, effort, strain,
strive 7 slavery, travail 8 drudgery,
endeavor, exertion, struggle 10 birth
pangs, childbirth, donkeywork
12 childbearing *group:* 3 AFL, CIO
5 ILGWU, union 6 AFL-CIO *leader:*
5 Hoffa (James, Jimmy), Lewis (John
L.), Meany (George) 6 Chavez (Cesar)
7 Gompers (Samuel), Reuther (Walter),
Sweeney (John J.) 8 Kirkland (Lane),
Randolph (A. Philip)

laboratory *device:* 5 flask 6 beaker, mortar, pestle, retort 7 burette, pipette
8 crucible, test tube 12 Bunsen burner

labored 4 hard 6 forced, taxing, tiring
7 arduous 8 strained 9 difficult, effortful, fatiguing, strenuous

laborer 4 hack, hand, peon 5 grind,
navvy 6 coolie, menial 7 workman
10 roustabout, workingman *Mexican:*
7 bracero

laborious 4 hard 6 tiring, uphill 7 arduous, onerous, operose 8 diligent, grueling, sedulous, toilsome 9 assiduous, difficult, effortful, strenuous
10 burdensome, unflagging 11 hardworking, industrious, persevering
12 backbreaking

La Brea 4 pits 7 tar pits *fossil:* 7 mammoth 8 mastodon 10 saber-tooth

labyrinth 3 web 4 coil, knot, maze, mesh
5 skein, snarl 6 jungle, morass, tangle
builder: 8 Daedalus *hero:* 7 Theseus
monster: 8 Minotaur

labyrinthine 4 mazy 6 daedal, knotty
7 complex, gordian 8 involved, maze-
like, tortuous 9 Byzantine, elaborate,
intricate 10 convoluted, perplexing
11 bewildering, complicated

lace 3 net, tat, tie 4 cord, trim 5 adorn,
braid, frill, plait, twine 6 fasten, string
7 entwine, netting, tatting 8 filigree,
openwork 9 embroider 10 embroidery,
intertwine 11 needlepoint *edge:* 5 picot
ground: 6 reseau *into:* 5 abuse 6 attack
7 condemn *kind:* 6 bobbin 7 Alençon,
guipure, macramé, Maltese, Mechlin,
torchon 8 Brussels, Venetian 9 Chantil-
ly 11 needlepoint 12 Valenciennes
make: 3 tat *pattern:* 5 toilé

Lacedaemon 6 Sparta

lacerate 3 cut, rip 4 gash, rend, tear
5 slash, wound 6 mangle, pierce
7 afflict, mangled, torment 8 distress

lachrymose 3 sad 5 teary, weepy 7 doleful, tearful, weeping 8 dolorous,
mournful 11 tear-jerking

lack 4 need, want 6 dearth, defect
7 absence, default, deficit, failure,
paucity, poverty, require 8 scarcity,
shortage 9 privation 10 deficiency, inadequacy, scantiness 13 insufficiency

lackadaisical 4 idle, lazy, limp, slow
5 moony 6 dreamy 7 languid, passive
8 fainéant, indolent, listless, slothful
9 apathetic, enervated 10 languorous,
spiritless 11 daydreaming, halfhearted,
languishing

lackey 5 toady 6 fawner, flunky, minion,
vassal 7 footman, servant 8 truckler
9 attendant, sycophant

lacking 3 shy 4 sans 5 minus, short
6 absent, flawed, needed 7 missing,
needing, omitted, wanting, without
8 devoid of, impaired 9 defective, deficient 10 deprived of, inadequate,
incomplete 11 halfhearted 12 insufficient

lackluster 3 dim 4 arid, blah, drab, dull,
flat 5 blind, ho-hum, matte, muted,
prosy, rusty, vapid 6 boring, leaden
7 prosaic 8 lifeless, mediocre 9 colorless, tarnished, wearisome 10 uninspired 13 unimaginative

Laconian 7 Spartan *king:* 5 Lelex, Myles
8 Menelaus

laconic 4 curt 5 bluff, blunt, brief, pithy,
short, terse 7 brusque, concise 8 succinct

lacquer 5 glaze, gloss 6 enamel, finish
7 shellac, varnish

lacrosse *related game:* 7 jai alai *term:*

5 clamp **6** crease, crosse, pocket **7** face-off *team:* **3** ten

lactate 4 salt **5** ester, nurse **6** suckle
7 secrete **8** wet-nurse **10** breast-feed

lacteal 5 milky **6** cloudy, pearly

lacuna 3 gap, pit **4** void **5** blank, break,
space **6** breach, cavity, hiatus **7** caesura
10 deficiency **12** interruption **13** discontinuity

lacy 5 meshy **6** dainty **7** netlike **8** delicate, gossamer **9** filigreed

lad 3 boy, son, tad **5** youth **6** shaver
9 shaveling, stripling *Irish:* **4** boyo
5 bucko *Scottish:* **5** chiel **7** callant

ladder 3 run **5** ranks, scale **6** series
7 ranking **9** hierarchy *adjunct:* **4** rung
6 rundle

ladderlike 6 scalar, scaled **7** stepped
11 scalariform

lade 3 dip, tax **4** bail, load, pack, ship,
stow **5** ladle, scoop **6** burden, saddle,
weight **8** encumber

la-di-dah 6 too-too **7** elegant, genteel,
stuck-up **8** affected, snobbish **9** conceited, grandiose, high-flown **10** hoity-toity
11 pretentious

lading 4 haul, load **5** cargo, goods **6** burden **7** bailing, dipping, freight, loading,
payload **8** shipment **11** consignment

ladle 3 dip **4** bail **5** scoop, spoon **6** dipper

Ladon 6 dragon *father:* **7** Phorcus, Phorcys *mother:* **4** Ceto *slayer:* **8** Heracles,
Hercules

lady 4 dame **5** madam, woman **6** female,
matron *French:* **4** dame *German:* **4** Frau
Italian: **5** donna **7** signora *Muslim:*
5 begum *Spanish:* **4** doña **6** señora

lady ___ 4 luck **5** apple **6** beetle, chapel

ladybug 6 beetle *Australian:* **7** vedalia

Lady Chatterley's Lover *author:*
8 Lawrence (David Herbert) *character:*
6 Connie **7** Mellors (Oliver) **9** Constance

lady-killer 4 dude, hunk, roué, stud
7 playboy, seducer **8** Casanova, lothario
12 heartbreaker

Lady of the Lake, The 5 Ellen (Douglas),
Nimue **6** Vivien *author:* **5** Scott (Walter)

Lady Windermere's Fan *author:* **5** Wilde
(Oscar)

Laertes *father:* **8** Acrisius, Polonius *sister:* **7** Ophelia *son:* **7** Ulysses **8** Odysseus
victim: **6** Hamlet *wife:* **8** Anticlea

La Fontaine's forte 5 fable

lag 4 drag, flag, last, poke, slow, tire
5 dally, delay, tarry, trail **6** dawdle,
linger, loiter **7** slacken **8** hang back,
hindmost, interval **10** dillydally **13** procrastinate

lager 4 beer, brew, malt, suds **7** brewski

laggard 3 lax **4** slow **5** tardy **6** loafer

7 dawdler **8** dallying, dawdling, delaying, dilatory, flagging, lingerer, loiterer,
slowpoke, sluggish, tarrying **9** apathetic, lazybones, lethargic, loitering, straggler **10** behindhand

La Gioconda 8 Mona Lisa *composer:*
10 Ponchielli (Amilcare) *painter:* **7** da
Vinci (Leonardo) **8** Leonardo (da Vinci)

lagniappe 3 tip **4** gift, perk **5** bonus
7 cumshaw, largess **8** dividend, gratuity
9 baksheesh, pourboire **10** perquisite

lagomorph 4 hare, pika **6** rabbit

lagoon 4 pond, pool **5** bayou, sound
6 strait **7** channel, narrows

___ La Guardia 8 Fiorello

Lahmi *brother:* **7** Goliath *slayer:*
7 Elhanan

laid-back 4 cool **6** breezy, casual
7 relaxed **8** carefree, informal **9** easygoing, hang-loose **10** nonchalant

lair 3 den **4** cave **5** haunt, lodge **6** burrow, refuge **7** hideout, retreat **8** hideaway **9** sanctuary

Laius *father:* **8** Labdacus *slayer, son:*
7 Oedipus *wife:* **7** Jocasta

lake 4 loch, mere, pond, pool, tarn
5 lough **6** lagoon *Adriatic:* **6** Varano
Alberta: **6** Louise *Algeria:* **5** Hodna *Alps:*
6 Annecy *Arizona-Nevada:* **4** Mead *Armenia:* **5** Sevan **6** Gokcha, Sevang **9** Lychnitis *Aswan's:* **6** Nasser *Australia:* **4** Eyre
5 Carey, Cowan, Frome, Wells **6** Barlee
7 Amadeus, Everard, Torrens **8** Gairdner *Austria:* **5** Atter, Traun **6** Kammer
8 Attersee **9** Kammersee *Bolivia:*
5 Poopó *Botswana:* **5** Ngami *British
Columbia:* **4** Pitt **5** Atlin *California:*
4 Mono, Tule **5** Clear, Eagle, Honey
Cambodia: **8** Tonle Sap *Canada:* **4** Dyke
8 Manitoba *central Africa:* **4** Kivu
5 Mweru **6** Albert *Central America:*
5 Guija *central Europe:* **5** Leman
6 Geneva, Lugano **7** Ceresio
8 Bodensee **9** Constance *central North
America:* **5** Rainy *Chile:* **4** Laja **5** Ranco
China: **6** Poyang **8** Dongting *Colorado:*
5 Grand *Denmark:* **5** Esrum *east Africa:*
6 Rudolf **7** Turkana *east Asia:* **6** Khanka
7 Xingkai **8** Hsingkai *east central Africa:*
8 Victoria **10** Tanganyika *east China:*
3 Tai **5** Dalai, Hulun *Ethiopia:* **4** Tana,
Zwai **5** Abaya, Shala, Shamo, Tsana
8 Stefanie **9** Chew Bahir *Finland:* **5** Inari
Florida: **5** Worth **10** Okeechobee *Germany:* **5** Ammer, Chiem **8** Ammersee,
Chiemsee *Ghana:* **5** Volta *Great:* **4** Erie
5 Huron **7** Ontario **8** Michigan, Superior *Greece:* **5** Bolbe, Volvi *Guatemala:*
7 Atitlán *Honduras:* **5** Yojoa *Honshu:*
3 Omi **4** Biwa, Suwa, Yodo *Hungary:*
7 Balaton **10** Plattensee *Idaho:* **4** Waha

5 Grays 6 Priest 11 Coeur d'Alene, Pend Oreille *India:* 3 Dal 5 Wular 6 Chilka *Indonesia:* 4 Poso, Toba 5 Ranau *Iowa:* 5 Storm *Iran:* 5 Niriz, Shahi, Urmia 8 Matianus, Urumiyeh 9 Bakhtigan *Ireland:* 3 Gur, Ree 4 Conn, Derg, Mask 5 Allen, Arrow, Leane *Israel:* 12 Bahr Tabariya, Sea of Galilee *Israel-Jordan:* 7 Dead Sea *Italy:* 4 Como, Iseo, Nemi 5 Garda 6 Albano 7 Bolsena, Perugia 8 Maggiore 9 Trasimene *Japan:* 4 Imba 8 Imbanuma *Kazakhstan:* 7 Balqash 8 Balkhash *Louisiana:* 4 Soda 9 Catahoula 13 Pontchartrain *Maine:* 6 Sebago 9 Moosehead *Mali:* 4 Debo *Manitoba:* 4 Gods 5 Cedar, Moose 8 Winnipeg *Mexico:* 7 Chapala *Michigan:* 4 Burt *Minnesota:* 3 Red 4 Cass, Gull, Swan 5 Leech 6 Itasca 9 Mille Lacs 10 Minnetonka, of the Woods 11 Lac qui Parle *Minnesota-Wisconsin:* 5 Pepin *Mongolian:* 3 Har 5 Har Us, Khara 8 Khara Usu *Montana:* 8 Medicine *mountain:* 4 tarn *Myanmar:* 4 Inle *Nevada:* 4 Ruby 7 Pyramid *New Hampshire:* 5 Squam 13 Winnipesaukee *New Jersey:* 5 Union *New York:* 4 Long 5 Chazy, Keuka 6 Cayuga, George, Oneida, Otsego, Owasco, Placid, Seneca 7 Crooked, Saranac 8 Onondaga, Saratoga 10 Chautauqua 11 Canandaigua, Skaneateles *New Zealand:* 4 Ohau 5 Hawea, Taupo 6 Pukaki, Wanaka 8 Wakatipu *Nicaragua:* 7 Managua *North Africa:* 4 Chad *Northern Ireland:* 5 Neagh *Northwest Territories:* 4 Gras 5 Baker, Garry, Pelly 9 Great Bear 10 Great Slave *Norway:* 5 Mjosa *Nova Scotia:* 7 Bras d'Or *Ontario:* 4 Rice, Seul 5 Trout *Oregon:* 5 Abert 6 Crater 7 Malheur, Wallowa *Paraguay:* 4 Ypoá *Peru:* 5 Junín 13 Chinchaycocha *Philippines:* 4 Bato, Taal 5 Lanao 6 Bombon *Poland:* 5 Mamry, Mauer *Quebec:* 5 Minto, Payne *Russia:* 3 Seg 5 Chany, Ilmen, Lacha, Onega 6 Baikal, Ladoga 7 Rybinsk 10 Eltonskoye 11 Ladozhskoye *Saskatchewan:* 4 Cree 5 Ronge *Scotland:* 3 Ard, Awe 4 Doon, Earn, Ness, Oich, Shin, Sloy 5 Leven, Lochy, Maree, Morar, Shiel 6 Lomond *Siberia:* 6 Baikal, Baykal *South Africa:* 4 Kosi *South America:* 5 Merin, Mirim 8 Titicaca *South Carolina:* 7 Wateree *South Dakota:* 5 Andes *southeast Africa:* 5 Nyasa 6 Nyassa *southwest Europe:* 5 Ohrid 7 Okhrida *Sweden:* 5 Asnen, Roxen 6 Siljan, Vänern, Vetter 7 Malaren, Vattern *Switzerland:* 3 Zug 4 Biel, Joux 5 Zuger 6 Bieler, Bienne, Brienz, Sarnen, Sarner, Zurich

7 Lucerne, Lungern 8 Brienzer, Züricher 9 Neuchâtel, Zürichsee *Tajikistan:* 7 Karakul *Tanzania:* 5 Rukwa *Texas-Louisiana:* 5 Caddo *Tibet:* 4 Na-mu 6 Nam Tso, Tengri *Turkey:* 3 Tuz, Van 4 Bafa, Nice 5 Iznik, Sugla 6 Nicaea *Uganda:* 5 Kyoga *Utah:* 6 Powell, Sevier 9 Great Salt *Wales:* 4 Bala *Washington:* 4 Omak 5 Moses 6 Chelan 9 Wenatchee *western China:* 4 Ai-pi 6 Ebinur *western United States:* 4 Bear 5 Tahoe *Wisconsin:* 5 Green 9 Winnebago *Yellowstone National Park:* 5 Heart, Lewis 8 Shoshone *Zaire:* 5 Tumba *Zambia:* 9 Bangweolo, Bangweulu

lake group *central North America:* 5 Great *Connecticut:* 4 Twin *Egypt:* 5 Balah *Maine:* 8 Rangeley *New Hampshire:* 11 Connecticut *New York:* 6 Finger *Saskatchewan:* 5 Quill *Twin:* 8 Washinee 9 Washining *Wisconsin:* 4 Four

lake herring 5 cisco

Lake poet 7 Southey (Robert) 9 Coleridge (Samuel Taylor) 10 Wordsworth (William)

Lake Wobegon Days author 7 Keillor (Garrison)

Lakmé *aria:* 8 Bell Song *composer:* 7 Delibes (Léo)

Lakshmi *husband:* 6 Vishnu *son:* 4 Kama

lam 3 hit 4 beat, blow, bolt, drub, flay, flee, flog, pelt, skip, whip 5 baste, paste, pound, scram, smack, split, whale 6 batter, beat it, buffet, cut out, decamp, escape, flight, hammer, pummel, strike, thrash, wallop 7 getaway, take off, vamoose 8 breakout, escaping 9 skedaddle

La Mancha's knight 10 Don Quixote

lamb 4 cade 5 sheep 6 cosset 8 yeanling *leg of:* 5 gigot

lambaste 3 pan 4 beat, drub, flay, flog, lash, lick, pelt, slam, slap, trim, whip 5 paste, pound, roast, scold, score, slash, smear 6 assail, attack, berate, cudgel, hammer, pummel, scathe, scorch, thrash, wallop 7 assault, blister, censure, clobber, reprove, scourge, shellac, upbraid 8 bludgeon, denounce, harangue, lash into 9 castigate, criticize, excoriate 10 tongue-lash

lambent 5 aglow 6 ardent, bright, lucent 7 beaming, glowing, radiant, shining 8 gleaming, luminous, lustrous 9 brilliant, effulgent, refulgent, twinkling 10 flickering, glittering, shimmering 12 incandescent

lamblike 4 meek 6 docile

lamb of God 5 Jesus 6 Christ 8 Agnus Dei

Lamb's pseudonym 4 Elia

lame 4 gimp, halt, limp 5 gimpy, stiff

6 feeble, flimsy **7** cripple, disable, halting, limping **8** crippled, disabled, hobbling, inferior **10** inadequate **11** ineffectual **12** contemptible, unconvincing **13** incapacitated

lamebrain 3 oaf **4** dolt, dope, goof, mutt, simp, yo-yo **5** chump, dummy, dunce, idiot, moron, ninny, noddy, stupe **6** dimwit, donkey, dum-dum, nitwit, noodle **7** airhead, dullard, pinhead, schnook **8** bonehead, clodpoll, dumbbell, dumbhead, imbecile, lunkhead, meathead, numskull **9** blockhead, ignoramus, numbskull, simpleton, thickhead **10** dunderhead, hammerhead, nincompoop **11** chowderhead, chucklehead, knucklehead

Lamech *daughter:* **6** Naamah *father:* **10** Methuselah *son:* **4** Noah **5** Jabal, Jubal **9** Tubalcain *wife:* **4** Adah **6** Zillah

lament 3 cry, rue **4** keen, moan, pine, wail, weep **5** dirge, elegy, mourn **6** bemoan, bewail, grieve, plaint, regret, repent, sorrow **7** deplore, elegize, wailing **8** jeremiad, threnody **9** complaint, ululation

lamentable 6 rueful, woeful **7** doleful, pitiful **8** dolorous, grievous, mournful **9** plaintive, sorrowful **10** afflictive, deplorable, lugubrious, melancholy **11** distressing, regrettable, unfortunate **13** heartbreaking

lamentation 5 elegy, grief **7** anguish, remorse, wailing **8** grieving, mourning, threnody **9** sorrowing, ululation **13** mortification

Lamerok *father:* **9** Pellinore *lover:* **8** Margawse *slayer:* **6** Gawain

lamia 3 hag, hex **5** witch **7** hellcat, vampire **9** sorceress **11** enchantress, necromancer

Lamia *country:* **5** Libya *form:* **7** serpent *lover:* **4** Zeus

lamina 5 blade, flake, layer, plate, scale

lamp 3 arc **4** bulb **5** klieg, light, torch **7** lantern **10** candelabra **11** candelabrum *floor:* **8** torchère **9** torchiere *hanging:* **10** chandelier

lampblack 4 soot **6** carbon

Lampetia *father:* **6** Apollo, Helios *husband:* **9** Asclepius *mother:* **6** Neaera *sister:* **9** Phaethusa

lampoon 4 mock **5** roast, spoof, squib **6** parody, satire, send-up **7** take off **8** ridicule, satirize **9** burlesque **10** caricature, pasquinade

lamprey 3 eel

lanai 5 patio, porch **6** piazza **7** terrace, veranda

lance 4 gash, hurl **5** slash, spear **6** impale, pierce, skewer **7** javelin **8** transfix

Lancelot, Launcelot *father:* **3** Ban *lover:* **6** Elaine **9** Guinevere *son:* **7** Galahad *victim:* **6** Gawain

lancer 10 cavalryman *Prussian:* **5** uhlan

lancet 4 arch **5** blade, knife **6** cutter, window **7** scalpel

land 4 dirt, dock, gain, soil **5** acres, berth, earth, light, manor, shore, terra, tract **6** alight, estate, ground, obtain, pick up, secure **7** acquire, acreage, country, expanse, grounds, procure, set down, terrain, terrene **9** touch down **10** terra firma *alluvial:* **5** delta *barren:* **5** waste **6** desert *cultivated:* **4** farm **5** tilth **7** tillage *for grazing:* **3** lea, ley **5** range **6** meadow **7** pasture *high:* **4** hill, mesa **7** plateau **8** mountain *level:* **4** mesa **5** plain **7** plateau *low:* **4** vale **6** valley **9** intervale *measure:* **3** rod **4** acre *open:* **3** lea **5** field, green, plain **6** meadow **7** pasture *piece:* **3** lot **4** plot **5** tract **6** estate, parcel *reclaimed:* **6** polder *sloping:* **6** cuesta *strip:* **7** isthmus *wet:* **3** bog, fen **5** marsh, swamp **6** marish

land east of Eden 3 Nod

landed 4 alit

landlord 6 lessor, squire **9** innkeeper **10** freeholder

landmark 5 cairn, guide **9** benchmark, milestone, watershed **11** achievement **12** breakthrough, turning point

Land of Enchantment 9 New Mexico

Land of Lakes 8 Michigan

Land of Opportunity 3 USA **8** Arkansas **12** United States

Land of the Midnight Sun 6 Norway

landowner 6 squire, yeoman *Anglo-Saxon:* **5** thane, thegn *Dutch:* **7** patroon *Scottish:* **5** laird

landscape 5 scene, vista **7** scenery, setting, terrain **8** backdrop, prospect

lane 3 way **4** path, road **5** aisle, alley, byway, track **6** street **7** pathway, roadway **8** footpath **10** passageway

lang syne 4 past, yore **10** yesteryear

language 4 cant **5** argot, idiom, lingo, prose, slang **6** jargon, patois, speech, tongue **7** dialect, lexicon, palaver **10** vernacular, vocabulary **11** terminology *ambiguous:* **8** newspeak **10** doubletalk *ancient:* **5** Greek, Latin **6** Hebrew **8** Etruscan, Sanskrit *artificial:* **3** Ido **7** Volapük **9** Esperanto *classical:* **5** Greek, Latin *combining form:* **5** gloss, glott **6** glosso, glotto *expert:* **8** linguist *informal:* **4** jive **5** lingo, slang *meaningless:* **6** babble, jabber **7** blather **9** gibberish **10** mumbo-jumbo *mixed:* **6** creole, pidgin *pretentious:* **7** bombast, fustian **8** claptrap *regional:* **7** dialect

relating to: 10 linguistic *Romance:*
6 French 7 Catalan, Italian, Spanish
8 Romanian, Rumanian 10 Portuguese
secret: 4 cant, code 5 argot *structure:*
6 syntax 7 grammar *suffix:* 3 ese *written:*
5 prose

languid 4 lazy, limp 5 inert 6 draggy,
supine, torpid 8 drooping, flagging,
inactive, listless, slothful, sluggish
9 apathetic, enervated, impassive,
lethargic 10 languorous, phlegmatic,
spiritless 13 lackadaisical

languish 4 fade, fail, pine, tire, wilt
5 brood, droop 6 weaken 7 decline
9 waste away

languishing 4 limp, weak 6 feeble, pining 7 languid 8 fainéant, indolent, listless, weakened 9 depressed, enervated,
enfeebled 10 dispirited, languorous,
spiritless 11 debilitated, devitalized
13 lackadaisical

languor 3 kef, kif 5 ennui 6 stupor, tedium, torpor 7 fatigue 8 doldrums, dullness, hebetude, lethargy 9 heaviness,
inertness, lassitude, torpidity, weariness
10 exhaustion

languorous 4 lazy, limp 5 inert 6 draggy,
supine, torpid 7 laggard, languid, passive, relaxed 8 dilatory, drooping,
fainéant, flagging, inactive, indolent,
indulged, listless, pampered, slothful,
sluggard 9 apathetic, enervated, impassive, lethargic 10 phlegmatic, spiritless
11 languishing 13 lackadaisical

lank 4 bony, lean, thin 5 rangy, spare
6 gangly 7 angular, scraggy, slender
8 gangling 10 attenuated

lanky 4 lean, thin 5 gaunt, spare 6 gangly
7 scrawny 8 gangling, rawboned

lanyard 4 cord, line, rope 7 cordage

Laocoön *city:* 4 Troy *killer:* 8 serpents

Laodamia *father:* 7 Acastus *husband:*
11 Protesilaus

Laomedon *daughter:* 7 Hesione *father:*
4 Ilus *kingdom:* 4 Troy *mother:* 8 Eury-
dice *slayer:* 8 Heracles, Hercules *son:*
5 Priam 8 Tithonus

Laos *capital:* 9 Vientiane *city:* 11 Savannakhet *ethnic group:* 5 Hmong *monetary
unit:* 3 kip *neighbor:* 5 Burma, China
7 Myanmar, Vietnam 8 Cambodia,
Thailand 9 Kampuchea *river:* 6 Mekong

lap 3 sip 4 fold, join, wind 6 cuddle,
splash, swathe 7 circuit, control, custody, shingle 9 imbricate

lapidary 6 cutter 7 elegant, jeweler
8 engraver, polisher

lapillus 4 lava 6 cinder

lapin 6 rabbit

Lapiths *foes:* 8 centaurs *king:* 5 Ixion

lappet 4 flap, fold 5 lapel

Lapsang 3 tea 6 Fujian

lapse 3 err, gap, sin 4 fall, flub, goof,
sink, slip, vice 5 boner, cease, error,
fluff, gaffe, slide 6 breach, bungle,
expire, foible, miscue 7 blooper, blunder, decline, descend, failing, failure,
faux pas, forfeit, frailty, mistake,
screwup, subside 8 apostasy, interval,
trespass 9 backslide, deviation, oversight, violation 10 apostatize 11 backsliding, impropriety 12 indiscretion,
interruption 13 retrogression, transgression

lapsed 4 sunk 5 ended 6 ceased
7 expired 8 obsolete 9 forfeited

Laputan 6 absurd 9 visionary

Lar 3 god 6 spirit

larboard 4 left, port 8 leftward

larcenist 5 thief 6 bandit, robber 7 burglar, filcher, stealer 8 pilferer 9 embez-
zler, plunderer, purloiner 10 pickpocket, shoplifter

larcenous 7 robbing 8 thieving 9 pilfer-
ing 10 plunderous 13 light-fingered

larceny 5 theft 7 looting, robbery 8 burglary, stealing, thievery, thieving *kind:*
5 grand, petty

lard 3 fat 6 fatten, grease 10 shortening

larder 6 pantry

large 3 big, fat 4 bull, huge, vast 5 ample,
bulky, giant, grand, great, gross, hefty,
husky, jumbo, major 6 goodly 7 copious, extreme, immense, mammoth,
massive, outsize, sizable 8 colossal,
enormous, gigantic, king-size, oversize,
spacious, whopping 9 capacious, excessive, extensive, humongous, monstrous
10 exorbitant, immoderate, inordinate,
large-scale, monumental, prodigious,
stupendous, tremendous, voluminous
11 extravagant, substantial *combining
form:* 4 macr, mega 5 macro 6 megalo

largesse 4 alms, gift 6 bounty 7 bequest,
charity, cumshaw, gifting, present
8 donation, gratuity 9 endowment,
pourboire 10 almsgiving, generosity,
liberality 11 benefaction, benevolence,
benificence, magnanimity, munificence
12 philanthropy

largo 4 slow 5 broad, tempo

lariat 4 rope 5 lasso, noose, reata, riata
user: 6 cowboy, drover 10 cowpuncher

lark 4 bird, dido, romp 5 antic, caper,
prank, shine, stunt, trick 6 frolic 7 rollick 8 escapade, songbird 9 diversion
10 tomfoolery 11 distraction, shenanigans 12 monkeyshines

larrup 3 tan 4 beat, cane, drub, dust,
flay, flog, hide, lash, lick, whip, whup
5 pound, spank, whale 6 cudgel, lather,
paddle, thrash, wallop 7 clobber,

scourge, shellac, trounce 8 lambaste
10 flagellate

larva 3 bot 4 grub, worm 6 dobson, maggot 8 cercaria, hornworm, mealworm
10 casebearer 11 caterpillar 12 hellgrammite *amphibian:* 7 tadpole *crustacean:* 4 zoea *flatworm:* 5 redia *freeswimming:* 7 planula *mollusk:* 7 veliger
moth: 8 leafworm *tapeworm:* 6 measle

larynx 7 trachea 8 voice box

lasagna 5 pasta 7 noodles

lascivious 4 lewd 5 bawdy, loose, randy
6 carnal, coarse, rakish, wanton 7 fleshly, goatish, immoral, lustful, satyric
8 depraved, prurient 9 lecherous, libertine, lickerish, salacious 10 libidinous,
licentious, lubricious, profligate
12 concupiscent

lash 4 beat, bind, dash, flay, flog, hide,
whip 5 baste, birch, fling, pound, scold,
slash, whale 6 assail, berate, buffet,
pummel, scathe, strike, stripe, switch,
thrash 7 blister, scarify, scourge,
upbraid 8 lambaste 9 castigate, excoriate, horsewhip 10 flagellate

lass 3 gal 4 girl, maid 5 wench 6 damsel,
maiden 7 colleen

lassitude 5 ennui, sloth 6 apathy, stupor,
tedium, torpor 7 fatigue, languor
8 debility, doldrums, dullness, hebetude, laziness, lethargy 9 indolence,
tiredness, torpidity, weariness
10 exhaustion 11 disinterest, insouciance 12 heedlessness, indifference,
listlessness, sluggishness

lasso see LARIAT

last 3 end, lag 5 abide, final 6 endure,
latest, latter, utmost 7 closing, extreme,
perdure, persist 8 continue, crowning,
eventual, farthest, furthest, hindmost,
rearmost, remotest, terminal, ultimate
9 umpteenth, uttermost 10 concluding,
conclusive 11 terminating *French:*
7 dernier *next to:* 6 penult 11 penultimate

last-ditch 5 final 7 defiant 8 ultimate
9 desperate 10 concluding

lasting 6 stable 7 abiding, durable, undying 8 enduring, lifelong, long-term,
longtime 9 continual, indelible, perennial, permanent, unceasing 10 continuing, continuous, perdurable, persisting
12 indissoluble, long-standing

Last of the Mohicans, The 5 Uncas
author: 6 Cooper (James Fenimore)
character: 4 Cora 5 Alice, Magua, Uncas
11 Natty Bumppo 12 Chingachgook

Last Supper, The *painter:* 7 da Vinci
(Leonardo)

latch 4 bolt, hasp, hook 5 catch 6 fasten,
secure 8 fastener *British:* 5 sneck

latchet 4 band, cord, lace 5 strap, thong
8 shoelace

late 4 dead, past, slow 5 tardy 6 former,
recent, whilom 7 defunct, delayed, onetime, overdue, quondam 8 deceased,
departed, sometime 9 preceding

Late George Apley, The *author:* 8 Marquand (John P.)

latent 4 idle 5 inert 6 covert, fallow, hidden, innate, unripe 7 abeyant, dormant, lurking 8 immature, inactive,
inherent 9 concealed, intrinsic, potential, quiescent

later 4 anon, soon 5 after, infra 6 behind
7 by and by, ensuing 9 afterward, following, posterior 10 subsequent, succeeding 12 subsequently

lateral 4 pass, side 6 branch 8 crabwise,
flanking, sidelong, sideward, sideways,
sidewise

laterally 8 crabwise, sideward, sideways,
sidewise

latest 6 newest, red-hot 7 current 8 contempo 9 au courant 10 dernier cri
13 up-to-the-minute

latex 6 balata 8 emulsion *product:* 5 paint
6 chicle, rubber

lath 4 slat 5 board, frame, stave, stick,
strip

lather 4 flap, flog, foam, hide, lash, soap,
stew, suds, whip 5 froth, spume, tizzy,
yeast 6 dither, hoopla, pother, thrash,
welter 7 scourge, turmoil 8 soapsuds

Latin 5 Roman 7 Italian 8 Hispanic *after:*
4 post *always:* 6 semper *before:* 4 ante,
prae *book:* 5 liber *boy:* 4 puer *brother:*
6 frater *but:* 3 sed *day:* 4 dies *dog:*
5 canis *foot:* 3 pes *friend:* 6 amicus *god:*
4 deus *goddess:* 3 dea *grammarian:*
7 Donatus (Aelius) *hand:* 5 manus *is:*
3 est *law:* 3 ius, jus, lex *light:* 3 lux *love:*
3 amo 4 amas, amat, amor *peace:* 3 pax
pronoun: 3 ego, nos, vos *road:* 3 via *see:*
4 vide *that is:* 5 id est *thing:* 3 res *this:*
3 hic, hoc 4 haec *thus:* 3 sic *war:* 6 bellum *wife:* 4 uxor *woman:* 6 femina *year:*
5 annus

Latin American *country:* 4 Cuba, Peru
5 Chile 6 Belize, Brazil, Guyana, Mexico, Panama 7 Bolivia, Ecuador,
Uruguay 8 Colombia, Honduras,
Paraguay, Suriname 9 Argentina, Costa
Rica, Guatemala, Nicaragua,
Venezuela 10 El Salvador *revolutionary:*
6 Castro (Fidel) 7 Bolívar (Simón),
Guevara (Ché), Hidalgo (Father
Miguel) 8 O'Higgins (Bernardo) 9 San
Martín (José de)

Latinus *daughter:* 7 Lavinia *father:*
6 Faunus 8 Odysseus *son-in-law:*
6 Aeneas *wife:* 5 Amata

latitude 4 play, room 5 range, scope, space, width 6 leeway, margin 7 breadth, compass, freedom, liberty, license 9 elbowroom 10 discretion 12 independence

latke 7 pancake 13 potato pancake

Latona 4 Leto *daughter:* 5 Diana 7 Artemis *father:* 5 Coeus *mother:* 6 Phoebe *son:* 6 Apollo

Latter-day Saint 6 Mormon

lattice 4 grid, mesh 5 grate, grill 7 grating, network, trellis 12 reticulation

Latvia *capital:* 4 Riga *city:* 7 Liepaja 10 Daugavpils *gulf:* 4 Riga *monetary unit:* 3 lat *neighbor:* 6 Russia 7 Belarus, Estonia 9 Lithuania *river:* 7 Daugava 12 Western Dvina *sea:* 6 Baltic

Latvian 4 Lett 7 Lettish

laud 5 adore, bless, cry up, extol, glory, honor 6 admire, praise, revere 7 acclaim, flatter, glorify, magnify, worship 8 eulogize, venerate 9 celebrate, reverence

laudable 6 worthy 9 admirable, deserving, estimable 11 commendable, meritorious, thankworthy 12 praiseworthy

laudatory 7 glowing 9 adulatory, approving 10 eulogistic, flattering 11 approbative, encomiastic, panegyrical 12 complimentary 13 complimentary

laugh 3 yuk 4 ha-ha, roar, yuck 5 tehee, whoop 6 cackle, giggle, guffaw, heehaw, titter 7 chortle, chuckle, snicker 10 cachinnate

laughable 4 rich 5 comic, droll, funny, goofy, witty 6 absurd, jocose 7 amusing, comical, jocular, mocking, risible 8 derisive, derisory, farcical, humorous 9 ludicrous 10 ridiculous

laughing 5 merry, riant 6 blithe 8 mirthful 9 sparkling

laughingstock 4 butt, dupe, fool, jest, joke, mark, mock 5 sport 6 target 7 mockery 8 derision

launch 4 boat, cast, fire, hurl 5 begin, debut, fling, heave, pitch, sling, start, throw 6 get off 7 jump off, kick off, lift off, release, take off, usher in 8 blast off, catapult, commence, embark on, initiate 9 inception, institute, introduce, motorboat, set afloat 10 inaugurate, initiation 12 inauguration

launder 4 wash 5 clean 6 trough 7 cleanse 8 sanitize, transfer

Laura's lover 8 Petrarch

laurels 4 bays, fame 5 award, honor, kudos, prize 6 awards, badges, honors, prizes, renown 7 acclaim 8 accolade, citation 9 accolades, citations 10 decoration, reputation 11 decorations, distinction 12 achievements, distinctions

laurel-tree nymph 6 Daphne

lava 4 slag 5 magma 6 scoria 8 andesite, trachyte *fragment:* 8 lapillus *stream:* 4 flow 6 coulee

lavalava 5 cloth, skirt

lavaliere 7 pendant 8 necklace

lavatory 4 head, john 5 basin, potty, privy 6 johnny, toilet 7 latrine 8 bathroom, restroom, washroom 11 water closet

lave 4 pour, wash 5 bathe

Lavinia *father:* 7 Latinus *husband:* 6 Aeneas *mother:* 5 Amata

Lavinium's founder 6 Aeneas

lavish 4 lush, pour 5 plush, spend, waste 6 swanky 7 liberal, opulent, profuse 8 effusive, prodigal, splendid, squander 9 bountiful, excessive, exuberant, luxuriant, luxurious, sumptuous 10 immoderate, inordinate, munificent 11 extravagant

law 3 act, lex 4 bill, code, rule 5 axiom, canon, edict, Torah 6 assize, decree, equity 7 dictate, justice, mandate, precept, statute, theorem 8 exigency 9 enactment, ordinance, principle 10 principium, regulation 11 commandment, fundamental 12 prescription *body of:* 4 code 7 pandect 12 constitution *degree:* 3 LLB, LLD *expert:* 5 judge 6 jurist 7 justice *practitioner:* 6 lawyer 7 counsel 8 attorney 9 barrister, solicitor *relating to:* 5 jural, legal 7 canonic 8 forensic, juristic 9 judiciary *violation of:* 4 tort 5 crime 6 felony 11 misdemeanor

law-abiding 6 decent 7 duteous, dutiful, orderly, upright 8 obedient, obliging, straight 9 compliant, peaceable 10 forthright, respectful 11 respectable, well-behaved

lawbreaker 3 con 4 hood, thug 5 crook, felon 6 outlaw, sinner 7 convict, hoodlum, mobster 8 criminal, gangster, hooligan, jailbird, offender, scofflaw, violator 9 desperado, wrongdoer 10 malefactor, trespasser 12 transgressor

lawful 3 due 4 just 5 legal, legit, licit, valid 6 kosher 7 condign 8 bona fide, innocent, mandated, ordained 9 allowable, canonical, juridical, legalized 10 authorized, legitimate 11 permissible

lawgiver 5 Draco, Moses, solon 7 senator 8 alderman 10 councilman, legislator 11 congressman

lawlessness 5 chaos 6 strife 7 anarchy, discord, misrule, turmoil 8 conflict, disorder 9 mobocracy 10 illegality, misconduct, ochlocracy, unruliness, wrongdoing **11** criminality, pandemonium

lawman 7 marshal, officer, sheriff **9** policeman

Lawrence novel 7 Rainbow (The) **8** Kangaroo, Lost Girl (The) **9** Aaron's Rod **11** Women in Love **13** Sons and Lovers

lawsuit 4 case **5** cause, claim **6** action **8** replevin **9** assumpsit **10** litigation, proceeding **11** presentment, prosecution

lawyer 6 jurist, legist **7** counsel, pleader **8** advocate, attorney **9** barrister, counselor, solicitor *dishonest:* **7** shyster **11** pettifogger *fictional:* **7** Matlock (Ben) **10** Perry Mason *French:* **6** avocat

lax 5 loose, slack **6** casual, remiss, sloppy **7** lenient **8** careless, derelict, lacrosse **9** deficient, forgetful, negligent **10** neglectful **11** inattentive

lay 3 bet, put, set **5** apply, hatch, place, wager **6** assert, assign, ballad, charge, credit, devise, impute, settle, spread **7** amateur, arrange, ascribe, concoct, deposit, prepare, present **11** nonclerical

lay by 4 keep, save **5** amass, hoard, store **7** deposit, discard, store up **8** preserve, salt away, set aside **10** accumulate

lay down 3 set **4** rule **5** order, store, yield **6** assert, decree, define, give up, impose, ordain, record, resign **7** abandon, command, dictate, specify **8** hand over, preserve, proclaim **9** establish, prescribe, surrender **10** relinquish

layer 3 hen, ply **4** coat, film, seam, tier **5** paver, sheet **6** folium, lamina, veneer **7** coating, stratum **8** covering, laminate, membrane, sandwich, stratify *inner:* **6** lining *of skin:* **6** dermis **9** epidermis *outer:* **4** skin **6** veneer

lay for 6 ambush **8** surprise

lay in see LAY BY

layman 6 novice **7** amateur, secular **11** parishioner

lay off 4 halt, quit, stop **5** avoid, cease, let go, lie by **6** desist **7** dismiss, measure, release **9** discharge, terminate **10** inactivity **11** discontinue

lay out 3 pay **4** give, plan **5** chart, dummy, place, spend **6** design, expend **7** arrange, display, exhibit, prepare **8** disburse

lay waste 4 ruin **6** ravage **7** destroy **8** desolate **9** devastate

lazar 5 leper

Lazarus' sister 4 Mary **6** Martha

laze 3 bum, lag **4** bask, hang, idle, loaf, loll **5** chill **6** dawdle, loiter, lounge, slouch **7** goof off, hang out **8** chill out **9** goldbrick **10** hang around

laziness 5 sloth **6** torpor **7** inertia, languor, laxness, loafing **8** idleness, lethargy, otiosity **9** indolence, lassitude, loitering, slackness **10** inactivity **11** languidness **12** listlessness

lazy 3 lax **4** idle **5** inert, slack **6** droopy, remiss, supine, torpid **7** languid, loafing, passive **8** fainéant, inactive, indolent, listless, slothful, sluggish **9** lethargic, negligent, shiftless, slowgoing **10** languorous

lazy Susan 4 tray **9** turntable

leach 4 drip, leak, ooze, perk, seep, suck, weep **5** bleed, drain, exude, issue **7** draw out, dribble, trickle **8** filtrate, perspire **9** discharge, lixiviate, percolate

lead 3 tip **4** head, hint, show, star **5** guide, metal, plumb, route, steer, trace, usher **6** bullet, ceruse, direct, escort, leader **7** captain, conduct, precede, preface **8** graphite, persuade, shepherd **10** bellwether *combining form:* **5** plumb **6** plumbo *ore:* **6** galena **9** anglesite *oxide:* **6** sinter *sounding:* **5** plumb **7** plummet

lead astray 6 seduce **7** corrupt

leaden 4 drab, dull, flat, gray **5** heavy, inert **6** gloomy, somber **7** languid, weighty **8** dragging, lifeless, sluggish **9** ponderous

leader 4 boss, dean, duce, guru, head, jefe, lord **5** chief, guide, pilot **6** despot, honcho, rector **7** captain, foreman, general, headman, manager, warlord **8** chairman, director, hierarch, superior **9** chieftain, commander, conductor, demagogue, harbinger, precursor, president, principal, straw boss **10** bellwether, forerunner, pacesetter *authoritarian:* **10** Big Brother *Cossack:* **6** ataman, hetman *German:* **6** führer **7** fuehrer *Japanese:* **6** shogun *military:* **7** admiral, general, warlord **9** commander **12** field marshal *Muslim:* **3** aga **4** agha, emir **6** caliph, mullah *national:* **7** premier **9** president **12** chief of state

leading 4 arch, head, main **5** chief, first, major **6** famous, master **7** premier, primary **8** champion, foremost, headmost, peerless **9** paramount, principal, prominent, well-known **10** preeminent

lead on 3 con **4** bait, dupe, fool, gull, hoax, lure, scam, tole, toll, wile **5** cozen, flirt, tempt **6** allure, betray, cajole, coquet, delude, entice, entrap, humbug, seduce, suck in, take in, trifle **7** beguile, deceive, toy with **8** coquette, hoodwink, inveigle **9** bamboozle **11** string along

leaf 4 flip, foil, page, riff, scan, skim **5** blade, bract, folio, frond, petal, scale, sepal, thumb **6** browse, glance, riffle, spathe *aperture:* **5** stoma *axis:* **6** rachis *combining form:* **5** phyll **6** phyllo **7** phyllum *edge:* **9** crenation *lily:* **3** pad *part:* **4** lobe, vein **5** blade, costa, stoma **7** petiole, stipule, tendril *pine:* **6** needle *vein:* **5** costa

leafage 7 foliage, umbrage, verdure

leaflet 5 flier, flyer, pinna, sheet, tract **6** folder **7** handout **8** circular, handbill, pamphlet

leafy 4 lush **5** green, shady **6** shaded, wooded **7** foliate, verdant **8** foliated, laminate **9** verdurous

league 4 band, bond, club, crew **5** class, grade, group, guild, order, union, unite **6** circle **7** circuit, combine, society **8** alliance, category, division, grouping, sodality **9** coalition **10** conference, consortium, federation, fellowship, fraternity **11** association, brotherhood, confederacy **13** confederation

Leah *daughter:* **5** Dinah *father:* **5** Laban *husband:* **5** Jacob *sister:* **6** Rachel *son:* **4** Levi **5** Judah **6** Reuben, Simeon **7** Zebulun **8** Issachar

leak 4 drip, ooze, seep **5** break, crack, spill **6** escape, get out, reveal, source **7** come out, divulge, seepage **8** disclose **9** discharge **10** make public

leaky 6 broken, faulty, porous **7** cracked, damaged

lea, ley 4 veld **5** field, veldt **6** fallow, meadow **7** pasture **9** grassland, pasturage

lean 3 sag, tip **4** bend, bony, cant, heel, lank, list, slim, thin, tilt **5** gaunt, lanky, shift, slant, slope, spare **6** meager, meagre, skinny, slight, wasted **7** angular, deviate, haggard, incline, pinched, scraggy, scrawny, slender, stringy, wizened **8** gradient, rawboned **9** deficient **11** inclination

Leander's beloved 4 Hero

Leaning Tower site 4 Pisa

lean-to 3 hut **4** shed **5** shack **6** shanty **7** bivouac, shelter

leap 3 hop **4** buck, jump, loup, rise, soar **5** bound, caper, clear, mount, vault **6** ascend, gambol, hurdle, spring **7** saltate **8** capriole, surmount *ballet:* **4** jeté **9** entrechat *by a horse:* **7** gambado

Lear, King *daughter:* **5** Regan **7** Goneril **8** Cordelia *servant:* **4** Kent

learn 3 con **4** hear **5** grasp, study **6** attain, detect, master, pick up **7** acquire, catch on, discern, find out, realize, uncover, unearth **8** discover, memorize **9** ascertain, determine **10** comprehend, understand **11** stumble onto

learned 4 sage, wise **6** expert, versed **7** bookish, erudite, sapient, studied **8** abstruse, academic, cultured, educated, esoteric, highbrow, lettered, pedantic, well-read **9** recondite, scholarly **10** cultivated, scholastic **12** intellectual

learner 4 tyro **5** pupil **6** novice, rookie **7** student, trainee **8** beginner, disciple, initiate, neophyte **9** greenhorn, postulant **10** apprentice, catechumen **11** abecedarian

learning 4 lore **6** wisdom **7** science, tuition **8** booklore, pedantry **9** education, erudition, knowledge **11** scholarship *person of:* **7** egghead, scholar **9** professor **12** intellectual

lease 3 let **4** hire, rent **6** sublet **7** charter, compact **8** contract, covenant, document **11** continuance

leash 3 tie **4** bind, cord, curb, rein, rope **5** strap **6** bridle, fetter, hamper, tether **7** shackle, trammel **8** restrain **9** entrammel

least 6 fewest **7** minimal, minimum **8** smallest

leather 3 tan **4** hide, skin, whip **6** thrash *kind:* **3** kid, kip, oak **4** bock, buff, calf, roan **5** crown, grain, mocha, strap, suede, whang **6** castor, latigo, oxhide, patent, roller, saddle, skiver **7** buffalo, chamois, morocco, ostrich, peccary **8** capeskin, cordovan, cordwain, shagreen *maker:* **5** tawer **6** tanner **7** tannery *piece:* **4** welt **5** strap, thong *prepare:* **3** tan, taw **5** curry *soft:* **5** mocha, suede **8** cabretta

leatherneck 6 marine

Leatherstocking Tales, The *author:* **6** Cooper (James Fenimore) *hero:* **5** Natty (Bumppo) *title:* **7** Prairie (The) **8** Pioneers (The) **10** Deerslayer (The), Pathfinder (The) **17** Last of the Mohicans (The)

leave 3 fly, let **4** blow, cede, exit, flee, move, part, quit, will **5** allow, scram, split **6** assent, assign, beat it, commit, cut out, decamp, depart, desert, devise, escape, get off, legate, permit, resign, retire, set out, vacate **7** abandon, abscond, absence, consent, consign, entrust, forsake, get away, liberty, pull out, take off, vamoose **8** bequeath, clear out, farewell, furlough, hand down, transmit, vacation, withdraw **9** departure, disappear, surrender, terminate **10** permission, relinquish, sabbatical **13** authorization

leaved 5 green **7** foliate, verdant **8** foliated

leaven 5 imbue, steep, yeast **6** infuse, invest, modify, temper, vivify **7** enliven,

ingrain, lighten, suffuse **8** moderate **9** alleviate, inoculate, sourdough **12** baking powder
leave of absence 8 furlough
leave off 3 end **4** halt, quit, stop **5** cease **6** desist, give up **7** abstain **8** give over, surcease **9** terminate **11** discontinue
leave out 4 omit, skip **5** elide **7** exclude
Leaves of Grass author 7 Whitman (Walt)
leavings 4 lees, orts, rest **5** dregs, scrap **6** debris, grouts **7** balance, remains, remnant, residue, rubbish **8** discards, oddments, remnants, residual, residuum **9** fragments, leftovers, remainder
Lebanon *capital:* **6** Beirut *city:* **4** Tyre **5** Sidon **6** Zahlah **7** Tripoli *language:* **6** Arabic, French *monetary unit:* **5** pound *mountain:* **6** Hermon *neighbor:* **5** Syria **6** Israel *river:* **6** Litani **7** Orontes *sea:* **13** Mediterranean *valley:* **5** Bekáa
Le Carré, John *character:* **6** Smiley (George) *novel:* **11** Russia House (The) **17** Little Drummer Girl (The) **22** Tinker, Tailor, Soldier, Spy **23** Spy Who Came in from the Cold (The)
lecher 4 rake, roué, wolf **7** Don Juan, seducer **8** Casanova, lothario **9** debauchee, reprobate, libertine, womanizer **10** degenerate, profligate, voluptuary **11** philanderer
lecherous 4 lewd **5** bawdy, loose, randy **6** carnal, coarse, rakish, wanton **7** fleshly, goatish, immoral, lustful, satyric **8** depraved, prurient, scabrous **9** debauched, libertine, lickerish, salacious **10** lascivious, libidinous, licentious, lubricious, profligate **11** promiscuous **12** concupiscent
lectern 4 desk **5** stand **6** podium
lecture 4 talk **5** chide, scold, speak **6** berate, preach, rebuke, sermon, speech **7** address, declaim, expound, oration, reproof, reprove, upbraid **8** admonish, briefing, harangue, scolding **9** chalk talk, criticism, criticize, discourse, hold forth, reprimand, talking-to **10** allocution **12** disquisition, dressing-down
lecturer 3 don **6** docent, fellow, master, orator, reader **7** scholar, speaker, teacher, trainer **9** pedagogue, preceptor, professor **10** instructor **11** academician
Leda *daughter:* **5** Helen **12** Clytemnestra *father:* **8** Thestius *husband:* **9** Tyndareus *lover:* **4** swan, Zeus *son:* **6** Castor, Pollux
ledge 3 bar, rim **4** berm, lode, reef, sill, vein **5** bench, ridge, shelf **6** mantle **7** bedrock, molding **10** projection

ledger 4 book **5** tally **6** record **7** account, balance **8** register **9** reckoning
lee 5 haven **7** shelter **9** protected, sheltered
leech 4 milk, worm **5** bleed, drain **6** sponge, sucker **7** exhaust, sponger **8** barnacle, hanger-on, parasite **10** freeloader **11** bloodsucker **12** lounge lizard
leer 3 eye **4** ogle **5** fleer, gloat, smirk, sneer, stare **6** glance, goggle, squint **7** grimace
leery 4 wary **5** chary **6** unsure **7** dubious, guarded **8** cautious, doubtful, doubting **10** suspicious **11** circumspect, distrustful, mistrustful
lees 5 dregs **6** grouts, refuse **7** deposit, grounds, residue **8** leavings, residual, residuum, sediment **9** settlings **11** precipitate
leeward 8 downwind *opposite:* **8** windward
leeway 4 play, room **5** scope, space **6** margin **7** breadth, compass, freedom, liberty **8** latitude **9** elbowroom, tolerance
left 4 port **7** liberal, radical **8** departed, deserted, larboard, residual, sinister **9** abandoned, discarded, remaining, sinistral
left-handed 5 inept **6** clumsy, gauche **7** awkward, dubious **8** fumbling, southpaw **9** ambiguous, equivocal, insincere, maladroit **10** morganatic
left-hand page 5 verso
leftover 5 extra, spare **6** excess, unused **7** remnant, reserve, residue, surplus, uneaten, vestige **8** residual, unneeded **9** redundant, remainder, remaining **10** unconsumed **11** superfluous
leftovers see LEAVINGS
leftward 4 levo **5** aport *go:* **3** haw
leg 3 gam **4** limb **5** shank **7** support, upright **8** cabriole **9** appendage, drumstick *bone:* **4** shin **5** femur, tibia **6** fibula **7** patella *part:* **4** calf, crus, foot, knee, shin **5** ankle, thigh
legacy 4 gift **5** trust **6** devise, estate **7** bequest **8** heirloom, heritage **9** endowment, patrimony, tradition **10** birthright **11** benefaction, inheritance
legal 5 legit, licit **6** lawful **7** allowed **8** innocent **9** juridical, statutory **10** legitimate, sanctioned *matter:* **3** res **4** case, suit *order:* **4** writ **7** summons **8** subpoena *party:* **6** suitor **8** litigant **9** defendant, plaintiff *restraint:* **8** estoppel
legal tender 3 wad **4** cash **5** bread, dough, money, moola, notes **6** moolah, specie **7** coinage **8** banknote, currency **9** long green

legate 4 will 5 endow, envoy, grant, leave 6 bestow, commit, devise, deputy, devise, pass on 7 entrust, leave to 8 bequeath, delegate, emissary, hand down, transmit 10 ambassador

legatee 4 heir 7 devisee 9 inheritor

legato 5 fluid 6 smooth 7 flowing

legend 3 key 4 lore, myth, saga, tale, yarn 5 fable, motto, story 6 mythos 7 caption, fiction 8 epigraph, folklore, folktale 9 mythology, tradition 11 inscription

legendary 5 famed 6 fabled, famous, mythic 7 fabular, fancied, fictive, storied 8 fabulous, mythical, renowned, supposed 9 well-known 10 apocryphal, celebrated 11 illustrious, traditional 12 mythological

legerdemain 5 magic 8 trickery 9 chicanery, conjuring, deception 13 sleight of hand

leggings 5 chaps 7 puttees 9 gambadoes

leghorn 3 hat 4 fowl 5 straw 7 chicken

legible 5 clear 8 distinct, readable 12 decipherable, intelligible

legion 4 army, host, many, mass, rout 5 cloud, crowd, drove, flock, horde 6 myriad, scores, sundry, throng 7 phalanx, various 8 numerous, populous 9 countless, multitude 10 numberless

legislate 5 enact, order 6 codify, decree, ordain, permit, ratify 7 empower, mandate 8 legalize, regulate, sanction 9 establish

legislation 3 act, law 4 acts, bill, code, laws 5 bills, codes, rules 6 edicts 7 statute 8 charters, dictates, statutes 9 enactment, lawmaking 10 enactments, ordinances, regulation 11 regulations 12 codification

legislator 5 solon 7 senator 8 alderman, lawgiver, lawmaker 10 councilman 11 assemblyman, congressman

legislature 4 diet 5 house, junta 6 senate 7 council 8 assembly, congress 10 parliament *Communist:* 6 soviet 7 politburo, presidium *czarist Russian:* 4 duma *Danish:* 9 Folketing *Finnish:* 9 Eduskunta *German:* 9 Bundesrat, Bundestag *Iceland:* 7 Althing *Israel:* 7 Knesset *Norway:* 8 Storting *one-house:* 10 unicameral *Poland:* 4 Sejm *Spain:* 6 Cortes *Sweden:* 7 Riksdag *two-house:* 9 bicameral

legitimate 4 fair, just, true 5 legal, licit, sound, usual, valid 6 kosher, lawful, normal, proper 7 genuine, regular, typical 8 accepted, innocent, orthodox, rightful 9 allowable, authentic, canonical, customary 10 admissable, autho-

rized, reasonable, recognized 11 justifiable, well-founded

Le Guin novel 7 Telling (The) 18 Left Hand of Darkness (The)

legume 3 pea, pod 4 bean, guar, seed 5 pulse 6 clover, lentil 7 soybean

leg up 3 aid 4 edge, lift 5 boost 6 assist 9 advantage, head start

lei 6 wreath 7 garland 8 necklace

Leibniz's invention 8 calculus

Leif Eriksson *discovery:* 7 Vinland *father:* 4 Eric, Erik (the Red)

leisure 4 ease, rest, time 6 casual, chance, repose 7 freedom, liberty 10 relaxation 11 opportunity

leisurely 4 easy, slow 6 lazily, slowly 7 relaxed, restful 8 laid-back 9 unhurried

leitmotiv 4 idea 5 theme, topic 6 burden, motive, thesis 7 subject

lemma 5 bract, theme 7 heading, premise, theorem 8 argument 11 proposition

lemon 3 dud 4 bomb, bust, flop 5 fruit, loser, scent 6 flavor, yellow 7 failure

lemur 5 indri, loris, potto 6 aye-aye, colugo, galago 7 tarsier 8 bush baby

lend 4 give, loan 5 allow, grant 6 afford, oblige, supply 7 advance, furnish, provide 11 accommodate

length 4 span 5 ambit, range, reach, realm, scope 6 extent, radius 7 compass, expanse, measure, purview, section, stretch, yardage 8 distance, duration

lengthen 6 expand, extend, let out 7 draw out, prolong, spin out, stretch 8 elongate, increase, protract 9 string out *Scottish:* 3 eke

lengthy 4 long 8 dragging, drawn-out, extended, overlong 9 elongated, prolonged 10 long-winded, protracted, voluminous 12 interminable

leniency 5 mercy 7 quarter 8 clemency 9 tolerance 10 indulgence, toleration 11 forbearance

lenient 4 easy, kind, mild, soft 6 benign, gentle, kindly 7 amiable, clement 8 merciful, obliging, tolerant 9 benignant, forgiving, indulgent 10 forbearing, permissive

lenity 5 mercy 7 quarter 8 clemency 9 tolerance 10 humaneness, indulgence 11 forbearance

lens 5 glass 6 lentil 8 meniscus *kind:* 5 toric 6 convex 7 bifocal, concave 8 trifocal

lento 4 slow 5 tempo

Leofric's wife 6 Godiva

Leoncavallo opera 9 Pagliacci (I) 10 Chatterton

leonine 8 lionlike

Leonora 7 heroine *alias:* 7 Fidelio *husband:* 9 Florestan

leopard 3 cat 4 pard 5 ounce 7 panther

leper 6 pariah 7 Ishmael, outcast 8 castaway, derelict 9 incurable 10 Ishmaelite 11 untouchable

Leper Priest 6 Damien (Father)

lepers' hospital 9 lazaretto

lepers' island 7 Molokai

lepidoptera 5 moths 8 skippers 11 butterflies 12 caterpillars

Leporello's master 11 Don Giovanni

leprechaun 3 elf 5 dwarf, fairy 6 sprite 7 brownie *trade:* 8 cobbling

Lesage hero 7 Gil Blas

Lesbos poet 6 Sappho 7 Alcaeus

___ **LeShan** 3 Eda

lesion 3 cut 4 boil, flaw, harm, sore 5 ulcer, wound 6 injury 7 blister

Lesotho *capital:* 6 Maseru *ethnic group:* 5 Sotho *former name:* 10 Basutoland *language:* 5 Sotho *monetary unit:* 4 loti *mountain:* 9 Ntlenyana *neighbor:* 11 South Africa *river:* 6 Orange 7 Caledon

lessen 3 cut 4 clip, crop, ease, thin, wane 5 abate, erode, lower, taper 6 dilute, impair, minify, recede, reduce, shrink, weaken 7 abridge, assuage, curtail, degrade, dwindle, lighten, relieve, subside 8 decrease, diminish, minimize, mitigate, taper off 9 attenuate

lessening 4 drop, fall 5 letup 8 decrease, slowdown 9 abatement, reduction 10 curtailing, diminution 11 degradation

lesser 5 lower, minor 7 smaller 8 inferior 9 secondary, small-time, subjacent 11 minor-league, subordinate 13 insignificant

lesson 4 text 5 chide, moral, study 6 rebuke 7 example, lecture, reading, reprove, warning 8 admonish, exercise, homework, reproach 9 reprimand 10 admonition, assignment 11 instruction

lessor 8 landlady, landlord 9 landowner 10 freeholder

let 4 make, rent 5 allow, grant, lease, leave 6 assign, permit, suffer 9 authorize 11 obstruction

letdown 5 slump 7 decline, descent, failure, reverse, setback 10 anticlimax, depression, misfortune 11 frustration

let go 3 can 4 boot, fire, free, sack 5 remit 6 unhand 7 dismiss, neglect, release, set free 8 liberate 9 discharge, terminate

lethal 4 fell 5 fatal 6 deadly, mortal, poison 7 baleful, deathly 8 poisoned, virulent 9 murderous, poisonous 11 destructive, devastating

lethargic 4 dull, idle, slow 5 dopey, heavy, inert 6 draggy, supine, torpid 7 dormant, laggard, languid, passive 8 comatose, dilatory, inactive, listless, slothful, sluggish 9 apathetic, impassive 10 languorous, phlegmatic, spiritless 11 indifferent 12 hebetudinous 13 lackadaisical

lethargy 5 sloth 6 apathy, phlegm, stupor, torpor 7 inertia, languor, slumber 8 dullness, hebetude, idleness, laziness 9 disregard, inanition, indolence, inertness, lassitude, torpidity 10 inactivity, supineness 11 impassivity, passiveness 12 listlessness

lethe 7 amnesia 8 oblivion 13 forgetfulness

Leto see LATONA

let off 5 spare 6 excuse, exempt 7 absolve, relieve 8 dispense 9 discharge

let on 3 own 5 admit, allow, grant, own up, spill 6 betray, fess up, reveal 7 concede, confess, confirm, divulge, pretend 8 disclose, give away

let out 5 blurt, loose 6 exhale 7 release, set free, unloose 8 lengthen, liberate, set loose 9 discharge, turn loose

letter 3 bee, cee, cue, dee, ess, gee, jay, kay, pee, tee, vee, wye, zed, zee 4 line, mail, memo, note, rune 5 aitch, print, vowel 6 report, screed, symbol 7 epistle, message, missive 8 dispatch, inscribe 9 consonant *airmail:* 8 aerogram *Anglo-Saxon:* (see ANGLO-SAXON) *Arabic:* (see ALPHABET) *Greek:* (see ALPHABET) *Hebrew:* (see ALPHABET) *kind:* 5 chain, roman 6 italic, uncial 8 Dear John *large:* 7 capital 8 majuscule, uppercase *small:* 9 lowercase, minuscule

lettuce 3 cos 4 Bibb, head 6 Boston 7 iceberg, romaine, Simpson 10 butterweed

let up 3 ebb 4 fall, stop, wane 5 abate, cease 6 lessen, relent 7 die away, die down, ease off, slacken, subside 8 decrease, diminish, moderate, taper off

letup 4 lull 5 break, pause 7 respite 9 abatement, cessation, lessening, reduction 10 slackening

levee 4 dike, dock, pier, quay 5 jetty, ridge, wharf 7 seawall 8 assembly, function 9 reception 10 breakwater, embankment, riverfront

level 3 aim, lay, par 4 calm, even, flat, raze, same, tier 5 equal, floor, flush, grade, plane 6 direct, ground, smooth, status, steady 7 aligned, flatten, mow down 8 balanced, bulldoze, demolish,

equalize, parallel, smoothen, standing
9 bring down, intensity, knock down,
magnitude **10** equivalent, horizontal,
reasonable **11** equilibrium

lever 3 bar, pry **4** jack, tool **5** jimmy,
peavy, prize **6** peavey, tappet **7** crowbar

leverage 5 clout, power **7** exploit
9 advantage, dominance, influence
11 superiority **13** effectiveness

leveret 4 hare

Levi *father:* **5** Jacob *mother:* **4** Leah *son:*
6 Kohath, Merari **7** Gershon

leviathan 4 huge **5** giant, jumbo, large,
titan, whale **7** Goliath, immense, mammoth, massive, monster, titanic **8** behemoth, colossal, colossus, enormous,
gigantic **9** cyclopean, monstrous **10** formidable, gargantuan **11** elephantine,
monstrosity

Leviathan author 6 Hobbes (Thomas)

levitate 4 lift, rise **5** float, raise **7** elevate,
suspend

levity 5 folly, humor **8** buoyancy
9 absurdity, flippancy, frivolity, giddiness, lightness, silliness **10** jocularity,
volatility

levy 3 tax **4** duty, toll, wage **5** exact, lay
on **6** assess, charge, custom, enlist,
impose, impost, tariff **7** carry on, collect **9** conscript **10** assessment, enlistment **12** conscription

lewd 5 bawdy, gross **6** coarse, ribald,
smutty, vulgar **7** fleshly, goatish, lustful, obscene, satyric **8** depraved,
improper, indecent, prurient, unchaste
9 debauched, lecherous, libertine, lickerish, salacious **10** indelicate, lascivious, libidinous, licentious, lubricious

Lewis and Clark interpreter 9 Sacagawea

Lewis novel 7 Babbitt **9** Dodsworth
10 Arrowsmith, Main Street **11** Elmer
Gantry

Lewis work 18 Chronicles of Narnia
(The)

lexicographer 8 compiler *American:*
6 Porter (Noah) **7** Webster (Noah)
9 Worcester (Joseph) *English:* **4** Wyld
(Henry) **6** Fowler (Francis, Henry),
Murray (James), Onions (Charles)
7 Craigie (William), Johnson (Samuel)
9 Partridge (Eric) *French:* **6** Littré
(Paul-Emile) **8** Larousse (Pierre) *German:* **5** Grimm (Jakob, Wilhelm)

lexicon 4 cant **6** jargon **8** glossary, language, wordbook **9** inventory, word-
hoard **10** dictionary, repertoire, vocabulary **11** terminology

liable 3 apt **4** open **5** given, prone **6** likely
7 exposed, subject **8** inclined **9** sensitive
10 answerable, assailable, vulnerable
11 accountable, responsible, susceptible

liaison 4 bond, link **5** amour, fixer
6 affair, broker, hookup **7** contact,
romance **8** intrigue **9** go-between
10 connection **12** entanglement, intermediary, relationship **13** communication

liana 4 vine

liar 6 fibber **7** Ananias **8** fabulist, perjur-
er **9** falsifier **12** prevaricator *female:*
8 Sapphira

libation 5 drink **6** liquid, liquor **7** potable
8 beverage, oblation, offering, potation

libel 4 slur **5** smear **6** defame, malign,
vilify **7** asperse, calumny, obloquy,
slander, traduce **8** bad-mouth, tear
down **9** aspersion, denigrate **10** calumniate, defamation, scandalize **11** denigration

libelous 6 untrue **9** injurious, invidious,
maligning, traducing, vilifying **10** backbiting, calumnious, defamatory, dero-
gative, derogatory, detracting, detractive, malevolent, pejorative,
scandalous, slanderous

liberal 4 full, open **5** ample, broad, loose
6 lavish **7** copious, profuse, radical
8 abundant, generous, prodigal, tolerant **9** bounteous, bountiful, indulgent,
plentiful, unsparing **10** benevolent, bighearted, charitable, freehanded, munificent, openhanded, permissive,
unorthodox **11** broad-minded

liberate 4 free **5** loose **7** manumit,
release, unchain **9** discharge, unshackle
10 commandeer, emancipate **11** appropriate, expropriate

liberator 6 savior **7** messiah **9** deliverer *of
Argentina:* **9** San Martín (José de) *of
Chile:* **8** O'Higgins (Bernardo) *of
Ecuador:* **5** Sucre (Antonio José de) *of
Scotland:* **5** Bruce (Robert the) *of South
America:* **7** Bolívar (Simón)

Liberia *capital:* **8** Monrovia *coast:* **3** Kru
5 Grain *language:* **7** English *neighbor:*
6 Guinea **10** Ivory Coast **11** Sierra
Leone

Liberian *language:* **3** Kwa *native:* **3** Kru,
Vai **4** Gola, Toma **5** Bassa, Grebo
6 Kruman

libertine 4 lewd, rake, roué **5** bawdy,
loose, randy **6** carnal, rakish, wanton
7 lustful, raffish, satyric **9** debauched,
debauchee, dissolute, lecherous, salacious **10** degenerate, dissipated, lascivious, libidinous, licentious, profligate
11 promiscuous

liberty 4 risk **5** leave **6** chance **7** freedom,
license **8** autonomy **9** franchise, privilege **10** permission **11** familiarity
12 emancipation, independence

libidinous 4 lewd **5** bawdy, loose, randy

6 carnal, rakish, wanton **7** fleshly, goatish, lustful, satyric **8** depraved, prurient **9** debauched, lecherous, libertine, lickerish, salacious **10** lascivious, licentious, lubricious, profligate **11** promiscuous **12** concupiscent

librarian 5 Dewey (Melvil)

library 7 archive **8** atheneum **9** athenaeum **11** bibliotheca *desk:* **6** carrel

Libya *capital:* **7** Tripoli *city:* **8** Benghazi *desert:* **6** Sahara *gulf:* **5** Sidra *language:* **6** Arabic **7** Hamitic *leader:* **7** Gadhafi, Qaddafi (Mu'ammar) *monetary unit:* **5** dinar *neighbor:* **4** Chad **5** Egypt, Niger, Sudan **7** Algeria, Tunisia *sea:* **13** Mediterranean

lice 7 cooties

license 3 let, tag **5** allow, grant, leave **6** enable, laxity, permit, suffer, ticket **7** certify, empower, freedom, go-ahead, liberty **8** accredit, document, sanction, variance **9** authority, authorize, slackness **10** permission, profligacy **11** certificate, impropriety **12** carte blanche **13** authorization

licentious 4 lewd **5** bawdy, loose, randy **6** amoral, carnal, rakish, wanton **7** fleshly, goatish, immoral, lustful, satyric **8** depraved, prurient, scabrous **9** abandoned, debauched, dissolute, lecherous, libertine, salacious **10** lascivious, libidinous, lubricious, profligate **11** promiscuous **12** concupiscent

lichen 4 moss **6** archil, litmus **7** oakmoss *genus:* **5** Usnea

licit 4 okay **5** legal **6** lawful **7** allowed **8** approved, innocent, licensed **9** allowable, permitted **10** admissible, authorized, legitimate, sanctioned **11** permissible

lick 3 bit, dab, dig, hit, lap, rap, tan **4** beat, dash, deck, down, drub, hint, swat, whip, wipe **5** cream, pinch, pound, smack, smear, spank, taste, touch, trace, whiff **6** defeat, master, punish, thrash, tongue, wallop **7** clobber, conquer, shellac, trounce **8** lambaste, outstrip, overcome, surmount **9** overwhelm

lickerish see LIBIDINOUS

lickety-split 4 fast **5** apace **6** presto, pronto **7** flat out, hastily, quickly, rapidly, swiftly **8** chop-chop, full tilt, headlong, pell-mell, speedily **9** posthaste **13** expeditiously, precipitately

licorice 4 root **5** candy *pill:* **6** cachou

lid 3 cap, top **5** cover **8** covering *moss:* **9** operculum

lie 3 fib **4** rest, tale **5** exist, fable, libel **6** belong, canard, covert, delude,

extend, inhere, remain, repose, reside **7** consist, falsify, falsity, perjure, recline, untruth **8** misspeak, misstate **9** dissemble, falsehood, fish story, mendacity **10** inaccuracy, taradiddle **11** prevaricate **12** misstatement

Liechtenstein *capital:* **5** Vaduz *language:* **6** German *monetary unit:* **4** euro *mountain range:* **4** Alps *neighbor:* **7** Austria **11** Switzerland *river:* **5** Rhein, Rhine

lied 4 song **7** art song

lief 4 fain, soon **6** freely, gladly **7** happily, readily **9** willingly **11** contentedly

liege 4 lord, true **5** loyal **6** ardent, master, vassal **7** abiding, staunch **8** constant, enduring, faithful, reliable, resolute, stalwart **9** dedicated, steadfast **10** dependable

lien 5 claim **6** charge, demand **8** interest, mortgage **10** imposition

lieu 5 place, stead

lieutenant 4 aide **6** backup, deputy **7** officer **9** assistant, coadjutor **10** aide-de-camp, coadjutant **11** subordinate

life 3 vim **4** brio, dash, élan, soul **5** verve **6** energy, esprit, spirit **8** vitality **9** animation, existence *animal:* **5** fauna *animal and plant:* **5** biota *combining form:* **3** bio *plant:* **5** flora *relating to:* **5** vital **8** biologic **10** biological *science:* **7** biology

life jacket 7 Mae West

lifeless 4 dead, drab, dull **5** inert **6** asleep, barren, torpid, wasted **7** defunct, extinct **8** comatose, deceased, departed **9** inanimate, inorganic, insensate **10** lackluster

lifelike 5 exact **7** natural, precise **8** accurate, faithful, veristic **9** realistic

life of ___ 5 Riley **8** the party

Life with Father author 3 Day (Clarence)

lift 4 heft, hike, jack, load, rear, rise **5** boost, exalt, filch, heave, hoist, pinch, raise, steal, swipe, theft **6** assist, pick up, pilfer, repeal, revoke, snitch, take up **7** elevate, purloin, rescind, reverse, support **8** levitate, stealing, thievery **10** plagiarize

lift-off 6 ascent, launch **7** takeoff **9** launching

ligament 3 tie **4** band, bond, link, yoke **5** nexus **8** ligature, vinculum **10** connection

ligature see LIGAMENT

Ligeia author 3 Poe (Edgar Allan)

light 4 airy, dawn, deft, easy, fair, fire, lamp, land, luck, neon **5** blond, flash, minor, perch, roost, sunny, torch **6** beacon, blithe, bright, candle, casual, facile, flimsy, fluffy, ignite, kindle, settle, simple, slight, strobe **7** lantern, sunrise, trivial **8** cheerful, daybreak, enkindle, illumine, luminous, trifling **9** frivolous, touch down **10** chandelier, effortless, illuminate *combining form:* **4** luci, phos, phot **5** lumin, photo **6** lumini, lumino *measure:* **3** lux **4** phot **5** lumen **6** candle **7** candela *refractor:* **5** prism *relating to:* **6** photic *ring:* **4** halo **6** corona **7** aureola, aureole *science:* **6** optics *source:* **3** sun **4** lamp

light-emitting 6 lucent **7** fulgent, lambent, shining **8** luminous **9** effulgent, refulgent

lighten 4 dawn, ease, fade **5** allay, cheer **6** bleach, lessen, reduce **7** assuage, gladden, hearten, mollify, relieve **8** decrease, mitigate, unburden **9** alleviate, attenuate, extenuate **11** disencumber

light-headed 5 dizzy, faint, giddy, silly **6** swimmy **7** flighty **9** frivolous, slaphappy **10** unbalanced **11** disoriented, vertiginous

lighthearted 3 gay **4** glad **5** happy, jolly, merry, sunny **6** blithe, jocund, jovial, joyful, joyous, lively, upbeat **7** buoyant, festive, gleeful, playful, winsome **8** carefree, cheerful, mirthful, spirited, volatile **9** easygoing, expansive, resilient, sprightly, vivacious **10** blithesome, insouciant **12** effervescent, happy-go-lucky, high-spirited

lighthouse 6 beacon **7** warning

lightless 4 dark **5** unlit **7** aphotic, stygian **9** tenebrous, pitch-dark **10** caliginous, pitch-black **11** unillumined

lightness 6 bounce, gaiety, levity **8** buoyancy, vivacity **9** animation, frivolity **10** cheeriness, liveliness, resiliency, volatility **12** cheerfulness **13** effervescence

lightning bug 7 firefly

lignite 4 coal **9** brown coal

likable 4 nice **6** genial **7** affable, amiable, popular, winning, winsome **8** charming, engaging, friendly, pleasant, pleasing **9** agreeable, appealing, congenial **10** attractive, personable **11** good-natured

like 3 à la, dig **4** akin, same, such **5** close, enjoy, equal, match **6** admire, agnate, allied, prefer, relish **7** approve, cognate, kindred, related, similar, uniform **8** parallel, selfsame **9** analogous, consonant, identical **10** appreciate, comparable, comprehend, equivalent, resembling

likelihood 6 chance **8** prospect **11** eventuality, possibility, presumption, probability

likely 3 apt **5** given, prone **6** liable, odds-on **7** assumed **8** credible, inclined, possible, presumed, probable, probably, reliable, suitable **9** doubtless, plausible, promising **10** achievable, attractive, believable, presumably

liken 5 match **6** equate **7** compare **8** parallel **10** assimilate

likeness 4 copy, twin **5** clone, image **6** double, effigy **7** analogy, picture, replica **8** affinity, portrait, sameness **9** depiction, facsimile, look-alike, semblance **10** appearance, similitude, uniformity **11** resemblance

likewise 3 and, too **4** also **6** as well, withal **7** besides **8** moreover **9** similarly **10** in addition **11** furthermore

liking 4 bent **5** fancy, taste **6** desire **8** affinity, appetite, fondness, penchant, pleasure, soft spot, weakness **9** affection **10** attraction, partiality **11** inclination **12** appreciation, predilection

Lilith *husband:* **4** Adam *successor:* **3** Eve

lilliputian 3 wee **4** runt, tiny **5** dwarf, petty, pygmy, small **6** bantam, little, midget, peanut, peewee, shrimp **7** manikin **8** pint-size, Tom Thumb **9** miniature, pint-sized, undersize **10** diminutive, homunculus

lilt 3 air **4** flow, purl, sing, song, tune **5** carol, pulse, swing, tempo **6** melody, rhythm **7** cadence **8** buoyancy

lily 3 pad **4** aloe, sego **5** calla, tiger, yucca **6** flower **7** leopard **8** mariposa

lily-livered 5 sissy, wimpy **6** craven, yellow **7** caitiff, chicken, fearful, gutless **8** cowardly, cowering, poltroon, recreant, timorous **9** spineless, spunkless, weak-kneed **12** fainthearted, poor-spirited **13** pusillanimous

lily-white 4 pure **7** upright **8** innocent, virtuous **9** blameless, estimable, exclusive, exemplary, guiltless, righteous, untainted **10** inculpable **11** uncorrupted

limb 3 arm, fin, gam, leg **4** lobe, twig, wing **5** bough, shoot, spray, sprig **6** branch, member, pinion **7** flipper **8** offshoot **9** appendage, dismember, extremity

limber 4 spry **5** agile, lithe, loose **6** nimble, pliant, supple **7** elastic, lissome, pliable, springy **8** flexible **9** lithesome, resilient

limbo 5 dance **7** neglect **8** oblivion **9** detention, purgatory **11** confinement, uncertainty

lime 4 tree **5** color, fruit, green **6** citrus, linden **7** calcium

limen 8 doorsill, doorstep **9** threshold

limerick 4 poem **5** verse *writer:* **4** Lear (Edward)

limestone 4 tufa, tuff **5** chalk **6** marble, oolite **7** coquina **10** travertine

lime tree 6 linden

limit 3 bar, cap, end, fix, set **4** curb **5** check, quota **6** border, bounds, curfew, define, extent, hinder, lessen **7** confine, curtail, enclose, extreme, mark out, measure **8** boundary, deadline, restrain, restrict **9** constrict, demarcate, determine, extremity, prescribe **12** circumscribe

limitless 4 vast **7** endless **8** infinite, wide-open **9** boundless, unbounded **10** indefinite **11** illimitable, innumerable, measureless **12** immeasurable, incalculable **13** inexhaustible

limn 4 draw **5** image, paint **6** depict, render, sketch **7** outline, picture, portray **8** describe **9** delineate, interpret, represent

Limoges product 9 porcelain

limp 3 lax **4** bent, halt, lame, wilt **5** hitch, loose, slack, spent, weary **6** dodder, droopy, falter, hobble **7** flaccid, languid, shamble, shuffle, slumped **8** drooping **9** enervated, exhausted **10** spiritless

limpid 4 pure **5** clear, lucid **6** glassy, serene **8** pellucid **10** see-through, untroubled **11** crystalline, translucent, transparent, unambiguous **12** crystal clear

limping 4 halt, lame **5** gimpy **7** halting **8** hobbling, lameness **9** faltering **12** claudication

linchpin 8 backbone, mainstay

Lincoln *assassin:* **5** Booth (John Wilkes) *biographer:* **8** Sandburg (Carl) *debater:* **7** Douglas (Stephen) *law partner:* **7** Herndon (William) *mother:* **5** Nancy (Hanks) *nickname:* **5** Honest Abe **12** Railsplitter *photographer:* **5** Brady (Mathew) *secretary of state:* **6** Seward (William) *secretary of war:* **7** Stanton (Edwin) *wife:* **8** Mary Todd

line 3 row **4** file, rank, rope **5** array, goods, queue, route **6** border, column, series, strain, string **7** contour, descent **8** business, pedigree, sequence **10** employment, occupation, succession *curved:* **3** arc *mathematical:* **6** vector *metrical:* **5** verse **6** verset **8** versicle *weather map:* **6** isobar

lineage 3 kin **4** clan, folk, race **5** birth, blood, breed, house, stirp, stock, tribe **6** family, origin, strain **7** descent, kindred **8** ancestry, breeding, pedigree **9** forebears, genealogy **10** derivation, extraction, succession **11** forefathers, progenitors

lineal 6 direct **8** familial **9** ancestral, inherited **10** bequeathed, hereditary

lineament 4 form **6** figure, relief **7** contour, feature, outline, profile **10** figuration, silhouette

lined 5 drawn, ruled **7** aligned, striate, striped **8** streaked, wrinkled

linen 4 lawn **5** cloth, toile **6** byssus, damask, fabric, napery, sheets **7** batiste, bedding, cambric, taffeta **8** cretonne, lingerie *fiber:* **3** tow *source:* **4** flax

linger 3 lag **4** bide, drag, loll, mope, poke, stay, wait **5** abide, dally, delay, mosey, tarry **6** dawdle, loiter, put off, remain **7** saunter **10** dillydally **11** stick around **13** procrastinate

lingerie 8 negligee

lingo 4 cant **5** argot, idiom, slang **6** jargon, patois, patter, speech, tongue **7** dialect **10** vernacular, vocabulary

linguist 8 polyglot **11** philologist

linguistics 9 philology

liniment 3 oil **4** aloe, balm **5** salve **6** lotion **7** anodyne, unction, unguent **8** aloe vera, lenitive, ointment **9** demulcent **11** embrocation

lining 6 facing, insert **8** wainscot

link 3 tie **4** bind, bond, join, knot, ring, yoke **5** hitch, nexus, unite **6** attach, copula, couple, hookup, relate, splice **7** bracket, combine, conjoin, connect, contact, joining **8** catenate, division, vinculum **9** associate, conjugate **10** attachment, connection **11** association **12** relationship

linksman 6 golfer

linnet 5 finch

lint 3 fur, nap **4** down, fuzz, pile **5** floss, fluff **9** ravelings

lion 3 cat **4** puma **6** cougar **7** notable **8** eminence, luminary **9** carnivore, personage *group:* **5** pride *young:* **3** cub

lionhearted 4 bold **5** brave **6** heroic **7** valiant **8** fearless, intrepid, stalwart, unafraid, valorous **9** dauntless **10** courageous

lionize 4 fete **5** exalt, extol, honor **6** glorify **8** venerate **9** celebrate

lion monkey 7 tamarin **8** marmoset

Lion of Judah 8 Selassie (Haile)

lip 3 rim **4** brim, edge, guff, sass **6** labium, labrum, margin **8** back talk *relating to:* **6** labial

lipid 3 fat, wax

lipped 7 labiate **9** bilabiate

liquefy 3 run **4** flux, melt, thaw **5** smelt **6** render **8** dissolve **10** deliquesce

liqueur 4 arak, ouzo, raki **5** crème **6** brandy, Kahlua, kirsch, kummel, pastis, Pernod **7** cordial, curaçao, ratafia, sambuca, sloe gin **8** absinthe, amaretto, anisette, Drambuie, Galliano **10** Chartreuse, pousse-café

liquid 5 drink, fluid, sauce, water **6** watery **7** flowing **8** beverage, emulsion **11** mellifluous *container:* **3** cup, jug, keg, mug **4** vial **5** glass **6** bottle, goblet **7** pitcher, tumbler *flammable:* **3** gas, oil **5** ether, furan **6** butane, toluol **7** alcohol, toluene **8** gasoline, pyridine *measure:* **3** cup, gal **4** pint **5** liter, ounce, quart **6** gallon *thick:* **5** syrup **8** molasses

liquidate 3 pay **4** do in, kill **5** pay up, purge **6** murder, remove, rub out, settle, square **7** bump off, convert, gun down, satisfy **8** amortize, dispatch, dissolve, knock off **9** eliminate, terminate **10** annihilate **11** assassinate

liquor 5 booze, drink, hooch **7** alcohol, potable, spirits **8** potation **9** firewater, inebriant **10** intoxicant *add:* **4** lace **5** spike *Asian:* **4** arak **6** arrack *home-made:* **9** moonshine **10** bathtub gin *inferior:* **5** hooch **6** red-eye, rotgut *Japanese:* **4** sake, saki *kind:* **3** gin, rum, rye **5** vodka **6** brandy, geneva, scotch **7** aquavit, bourbon, schnaps, whiskey **8** schnapps, vermouth **9** aqua vitae **10** barley-bree *malt:* **3** ale **4** beer **5** nappy, stout **6** porter *measure:* **4** dram, shot **6** jigger **7** shooter *Mexican:* **5** sotol **6** mescal **7** tequila

lissome 5 agile, lithe **6** limber, nimble, supple, svelte **7** slender **8** flexible, graceful

list 3 tip **4** book, cant, file, heel, lean, menu, note, post, roll, tilt **5** arena, count, index, slant, slate, slope, tally **6** agenda, census, docket, lineup, record, roster **7** catalog, incline, itemize, specify **8** calendar, glossary, manifest, register, roll call, schedule, tabulate **9** chronicle, enumerate, inventory **13** particularize

listen 4 hark, hear, heed, note **5** audit **6** attend, harken **7** hearken, monitor **8** overhear **9** eavesdrop

listeners 8 audience

listless 4 dull, limp, weak **5** inert, slack **6** torpid, vacant **7** languid **8** indolent, sluggish **9** apathetic, enervated, lethargic, lymphatic **10** languorous, phlegmatic, spiritless **11** indifferent, languishing **13** lackadaisical

listlessness 6 apathy, stupor, torpor **7** fatigue, inertia, languor **8** doldrums, lethargy **9** indolence, lassitude, torpidity **10** enervation

litany 4 list **5** chant **6** prayer **7** account, listing, recital, refrain **8** petition, roga-

tion **9** catalogue **10** invocation, recitation **11** enumeration **12** supplication

literal 4 bald, bare **5** blunt, exact, stark **6** actual, simple, strict **7** precise **8** accurate, bona fide, faithful, verbatim **9** authentic **11** unvarnished, word-for-word **13** unembellished

literally 5 truly **6** direct, indeed, openly, simply **7** plainly, totally, utterly **8** candidly, directly, verbatim **9** genuinely, virtually **11** word for word

literary 7 bookish, erudite, learned **8** lettered, well-read **9** authorial, scholarly **12** belletristic

literary work 4 book, opus, play, poem **5** drama, essay, novel **10** short story

literature 5 prose **6** poetry **7** fiction **13** belles-lettres

lithe 4 lean, slim **5** agile, spare **6** limber, supple, svelte **7** lissome, pliable, slender **8** flexible, graceful

lithographer 4 Ives (James Merritt) **7** Currier (Nathaniel)

Lithuania *capital:* **7** Vilnius *city:* **6** Kaunas **8** Klaipeda *monetary unit:* **5** litas *neighbor:* **6** Latvia, Poland, Russia **7** Belarus *river:* **5** Neman, Venta **7** Lielupe *sea:* **6** Baltic

litigant 4 suer **6** suitor **9** defendant, disputant, plaintiff

litigate 3 sue **6** indict **7** arraign, contest, dispute **9** prosecute

litigation 4 case, suit **7** lawsuit **11** prosecution, proceedings

litter 3 bed **4** cubs, junk **5** brood, couch, issue, strew, trash, waste, young **6** clutch, debris, refuse **7** bedding, clutter, garbage, kittens, piglets, progeny, puppies, rubbish, scatter **8** detritus **9** offspring, stretcher **10** scattering

little 3 bit, dab, toy, wee **4** dash, hint, mean, puny, tiny **5** brief, dinky, minor, petty, pinch, short, small, taste, trace, young **6** bantam, meager, meagre, minute, narrow, paltry, petite, skimpy **7** trivial **8** dwarfish, slightly, smallish, trifling **9** miniature, small-beer **10** diminutive, short-lived, undersized **11** microscopic, unimportant

Little Bighorn *state:* **7** Montana *victim:* **6** Custer (George Armstrong) *victor:* **11** Sitting Bull

little by little 6 slowly **8** inchmeal, steadily **9** gradually, piecemeal

Little Dipper *constellation:* **9** Ursa Minor *star:* **5** North **7** Polaris

Little Women *author:* **6** Alcott (Louisa May) *character:* **3** Amy, Meg **4** Beth **6** Laurie, Marmee *surname:* **5** March

littoral 5 beach, coast, shore **6** strand

7 coastal, seaside **8** seaboard, sea front, seashore **9** shoreline **10** oceanfront

liturgy 4 rite **6** ritual **7** service **8** ceremony **9** sacrament **10** ceremonial, observance, repertoire

livable 6 viable **8** adequate, bearable, passable **9** endurable, habitable, tolerable **11** inhabitable, supportable

live 4 fare, stay **5** abide, dwell, exist, vital, vivid **6** actual, reside, thrive **7** breathe, current, subsist, survive

livelihood 3 job **4** keep, work **5** craft, trade **7** support **8** business, vocation **10** employment, handicraft, occupation, profession, sustenance **11** subsistence

liveliness 3 pep, zip **4** brio, élan, zing **5** verve, vigor **6** energy, hustle, spirit **8** dispatch, vibrance, vibrancy, vitality, vivacity **9** animation

lively 3 gay **4** busy, keen, pert, spry, yare **5** agile, alert, brisk, fresh, jazzy, jolly, merry, peppy, zippy **6** active, bouncy, bright, chirpy, frisky, jocund, nimble **7** animate, buoyant, chipper, intense, rousing **8** animated, bustling, hustling, spirited, vigorous, volatile **9** energetic, resilient, sparkling, sprightly, vivacious **11** stimulating

liven 5 pep up **6** jazz up, vivify **7** animate, freshen, quicken **8** energize, inspirit, vitalize **10** invigorate

liver 7 denizen **8** habitant, occupant, resident **10** inhabitant *combining form:* **5** hepat **6** hepato *disease:* **9** cirrhosis, hepatitis *French:* **4** foie *lobster's:* **8** tomalley

liverwort 8 hepatica **9** bryophyte

livestock 4 cows, hogs, pigs **5** bulls, goats, sheep **6** beasts, calves, cattle **7** animals *feed:* **6** silage **8** ensilage

live wire 6 dynamo **7** hustler, rustler **8** go-getter, promoter **9** energizer, generator **11** self-starter

livid 3 hot, mad, wan **4** ashy, pale **5** ashen, lurid, waxen **6** fuming, leaden, pallid, sultry **7** boiling, bruised, enraged, furious, reddish **8** blanched, contused, incensed **9** colorless **10** discolored, infuriated **12** black-and-blue **13** beside oneself

living 5 means, vital **6** extant, income **8** animated, existent **10** livelihood, sustenance

living room 6 parlor **10** lebensraum

lizard 3 eft **4** gila, newt **5** anole, gecko, skink, teiid **6** dragon, goanna, iguana **7** monitor, reptile, saurian **8** basilisk, mosasaur, slowworm, squamate, whiptail **9** alligator, blindworm, chameleon, crocodile **10** chuckwalla, salamander *combining form:* **4** saur **5** saura, sauro

llama 6 alpaca, vicuña **7** camelid, guanaco *country:* **4** Peru *habitat:* **5** Andes

Lloyd's business 9 insurance

lo 4 hark, heed, look, mark, mind **6** attend **7** observe

load 3 tax **4** bias, copy, fill, haul, heap, lade, onus, pack, pile, task **5** cargo, laden, swamp, weigh **6** burden, debase, doctor, dope up, eyeful, lading, saddle, weight **7** freight **8** encumber, shipment, transfer **9** liability, millstone, transport **11** consignment, encumbrance

loaded 4 full, high, rich **5** awash, doped **6** aboard, biased, filled, packed, stoned **7** boarded, brimful, crowded, wealthy **8** affluent, brimming, chockful, tripping, turned on **9** chock-full

loaf 3 bum, bun **4** idle, laze, lazy, loll **5** bread, dough **6** dawdle, lounge **7** goof off **8** lollygag **9** bum around, goldbrick **10** fool around

loafer 3 bum **4** shoe, slug **5** idler **6** slouch **7** goof-off, lounger **8** deadbeat, dolittle, fainéant, slugabed, sluggard **9** do-nothing, goldbrick, lazybones **11** beachcomber, lollygagger

loam 4 clay, dirt, sand, silt, soil **7** topsoil *deposit:* **5** loess

loan 3 pay **4** lend **6** credit **7** advance, imprest **9** grubstake

loan shark 6 lender, usurer **7** Shylock **10** pawnbroker **11** moneylender

loath 6 afraid, averse **8** hesitant **9** reluctant, unwilling **10** indisposed **11** disinclined **12** antipathetic

loathe 4 hate **5** abhor, scorn, spurn **6** detest, refuse, reject **7** despise **8** execrate **9** abominate

loathsome 4 foul, ugly, vile **5** gross, nasty **6** odious **7** beastly, hateful, hideous **8** horrible **9** abhorrent, execrable, obnoxious, offensive, repellent, repugnant, repulsive, revolting **10** abominable, deplorable, detestable, disgusting, nauseating

lob 4 loft, toss **5** chuck, fling, heave, pitch, sling, throw **6** propel

lobby 4 hall **5** foyer **7** promote **8** anteroom, corridor **9** influence, vestibule **10** passageway **11** waiting room

lobe 4 flap **7** pendant

lobo 4 wolf **8** gray wolf **10** timber wolf

lobster 8 crawfish **10** crustacean *claw:* **5** chela **6** pincer *female:* **3** hen *male:* **4** cock *trap:* **3** pot **5** creel

local 6 native **7** endemic, insular, topical **9** parochial **10** provincial

locale 4 area, belt, site, turf, ward **5** place, scene, venue **6** milieu, parish, region, sector 7 commune, quarter, setting 8 district, precinct, vicinage, vicinity 9 community, territory 11 mise-enscène 12 neighborhood

locality 4 area, belt, city, site, turf, zone 5 block, field, haunt, place, tract 6 county, domain, hamlet, region, sector, sphere, square 7 habitat, section 8 district, environs, precinct, province, purlieus, township, vicinage, vicinity 9 bailiwick, situation, territory 12 neighborhood

localize 4 mass 5 amass, focus 7 cluster, collect 8 coalesce, pinpoint 10 accumulate 11 concentrate, consolidate 12 conglomerate

locate 3 fix, spy 4 espy, find, site, spot 5 dwell, place, trace 6 detect, reside, settle 7 nose out, situate, station, uncover 8 come upon, discover, pinpoint, position 9 establish, ferret out, search out 10 come across

location 4 area, site, post, spot 5 locus, place, point, scene, venue, where 7 bearing, habitat, setting 8 position 9 situation 11 mise-en-scène, whereabouts

loch 3 bay 4 lake

lock 4 bolt, curl, hank, hold, tuft 5 latch, tress 6 fasten, secure 7 ringlet 8 fastener 9 enclosure, fastening

lockjaw 7 tetanus, trismus

lockup 3 jug, pen 4 brig, cell, coop, jail, stir, tank 5 clink, pokey, pound 6 cooler, prison 7 slammer 8 bastille

loco 3 ape, mad 4 nuts 5 balmy, batty, crazy, kooky, loony, nutty 6 crazed, insane, screwy 7 bananas, berserk, bonkers, cracked, flipped, lunatic 8 demented, deranged, frenzied, unhinged 10 flipped out

locomotive 5 cheer, dolly, train 6 engine *small:* 5 dinky 6 dinkey *type:* 5 steam 6 diesel 8 electric

locum tenens 3 sub 5 proxy 6 backup, fill-in, supply 7 stand-in 9 alternate, auxiliary, surrogate 10 substitute 11 pinch hitter, replacement, succedaneum

locus 3 hub 4 seat, site 5 focus, heart, stage 6 center 7 setting 8 cynosure, location, polestar 10 focal point 11 nerve center 12 headquarters

locust 4 tree, wood 5 carob 6 cicada, insect 11 grasshopper

locution 4 word 5 argot, idiom, lingo 6 jargon, patois, phrase 7 dialect 8 parlance, phrasing 9 utterance 10 expression 11 phraseology

lode 4 seam, vein 5 store 6 source, supply 7 deposit

lodestar 4 guru 5 gauge, guide, ideal, model 6 beacon, leader, mentor 7 epitome 8 exemplar, paradigm 9 archetype, guidepost 11 inspiration

lodestone 6 magnet 9 magnetite

lodge 3 den, fix, inn 4 bunk, camp, club, file, lair, nest, root, stay 5 abide, abode, board, cabin, couch, dwell, embed, guild, hotel, house, motel, order, put up 6 billet, burrow, hostel, league, remain, shanty, tavern, wigwam 7 auberge, contain, cottage, deposit, hospice, quarter, receive, shelter 8 domicile, hostelry, sodality 9 gatehouse 10 fellowship 11 accommodate, brotherhood, caravansary, public house

lodger 5 guest 6 renter, roomer, tenant 7 boarder, resider

lodging 3 inn, pad 4 dorm, room 5 abode, hotel, motel, place 7 shelter 8 chambers, diggings, domicile, dwelling, quarters 9 apartment, residence 10 pied-à-terre 13 accommodation

loess 4 clay, loam, marl 7 deposit

loft 4 rise 5 attic, raise 6 dormer, garret, propel 7 gallery

loftiness 5 pride 6 height 7 disdain, hauteur, stature 8 altitude, eminence 9 aloofness, arrogance, elevation, pomposity, sublimity 11 haughtiness, superiority 13 condescension

lofty 4 airy, epic, high, tall 5 grand, noble, proud 6 aerial, august, raised, remote, superb 7 exalted, haughty, soaring, stately, sublime, utopian 8 arrogant, cavalier, elevated, eloquent, imposing, insolent, majestic, superior, towering 9 ambitious, grandiose, visionary 10 disdainful 11 overbearing, pretentious, skyscraping 12 supercilious

log 5 diary, tally 6 record, timber 7 journal 8 register *mover:* 5 peavy 6 peavey 7 cant dog

loge 3 box 5 booth, stall 7 balcony 9 mezzanine

logger 9 lumberman 10 lumberjack, woodcutter *legendary:* 10 Paul Bunyan

loggerhead 6 shrike, turtle

loggia 6 arcade 7 balcony, gallery, veranda

logic 6 reason 9 reasoning 10 syntactics *specious:* 7 sophism 9 sophistry

logical 5 sound, valid 6 cogent 8 analytic, sensible 9 deducible, deductive, plausible 10 analytical, compelling, convincing, diagnostic, reasonable, scientific, systematic

logjam 5 crowd 7 impasse 8 blockage, deadlock, stoppage 11 obstruction

logo 5 badge, brand, motto **6** cipher, device, emblem, symbol **8** colophon, hallmark, monogram **9** trademark

logogriph 6 puzzle **7** anagram

logroll 4 birl

logy 4 dull, slow **5** dopey, heavy **6** drowsy, groggy, torpid **8** listless, sluggish

Lohengrin *composer:* **6** Wagner (Richard) *father:* **8** Parsifal, Parzival *wife:* **4** Elsa

loincloth 5 dhoti **11** breechcloth, breechclout

Loire city 5 Blois, Tours **6** Nantes **7** Orléans

loiter 3 bum, lag **4** drag, idle, laze, lazy, loaf, loll, poke **5** dally, delay, tarry, trail **6** dawdle, diddle, linger, lounge, put off, putter **8** lollygag **10** dillydally, fool around, hang around **13** procrastinate

Loki *father:* **8** Farbauti *mother:* **3** Nal **6** Laufey *offspring:* **3** Hel **4** Hela **6** Fenris **7** Midgard *slayer:* **8** Heimdall *victim:* **6** Balder *wife:* **5** Sigyn **9** Angurboda

Lolita author 7 Nabokov (Vladimir)

loll 3 bum, lag **4** drag, idle, laze, lazy, loaf, poke **5** chill, dally, delay, droop, slump, tarry, trail **6** dawdle, diddle, linger, lounge, putter, slouch **8** chill out **10** dillydally, fool around, hang around **13** procrastinate

Lollards' leader 8 Wycliffe (John)

lollygag 4 idle, loaf, loll, poke, drag **6** dawdle, diddle, loiter, piddle, putter **10** dilly-dally, fool around **11** horse around **12** monkey around

Lombard 6 banker **11** moneylender *king:* **5** Cleph **6** Alboin, Audoin **7** Aistulf, Aripert, Authari **9** Liudprand

London *borough:* **5** Brent **6** Barnet, Bexley, Ealing, Harrow, Sutton **7** Barking, Bromley, Chelsea, Croydon, Enfield, Hackney, Lambeth **8** Haringey, Havering, Hounslow, Lewisham **9** Greenwich, Islington, Redbridge **10** Kensington **11** Westminster *cathedral:* **7** St. Paul's *clock:* **6** Big Ben *district:* **4** Soho **5** Acton **7** Chelsea, Mayfair **9** Belgravia, Southwark *gallery:* **4** Tate *policeman:* **5** bobby *prison:* **7** Newgate *river:* **6** Thames *square:* **9** Leicester, Trafalgar *street:* **4** Bond **5** Fleet **6** Strand **7** Downing **9** Whitehall **10** Piccadilly *subway:* **4** tube

London novel 7 Sea Wolf (The) **8** Iron Heel (The) **9** White Fang **10** Martin Eden **13** Call of the Wild (The)

lone 4 only, sole, solo **5** alone **6** single, unique **8** deserted, forsaken, isolated, secluded, separate, singular, solitary **13** unaccompanied

lonely 4 left, lorn **5** alone **7** forlorn **8** deserted, forsaken, homesick, lonesome, rejected, solitary **9** abandoned

loneness 8 solitude **9** isolation **10** detachment **12** separateness, solitariness

loner 6 hermit **7** isolate, outcast, recluse **8** outsider, solitary **13** individualist

Lone Ranger, The *creator:* **7** Striker (Fran) *companion:* **5** Tonto *horse:* **6** Silver *trademark:* **4** mask **12** silver bullet

Lone Star State 5 Texas

long 3 far, yen **4** ache, itch, lust, pine, sigh, tall **5** large, wordy, yearn **6** hanker, hunger, prolix, strong, thirst **7** endless, lengthy, tedious **8** dragging, drawn-out, extended, unending **9** extensive **10** full-length, protracted

long-drawn-out 7 endless, lengthy **8** dragging, unending **10** protracted **12** interminable

Longfellow poem 8 Christus, Hiawatha, Hyperion, Kavanagh **10** Evangeline **11** My Lost Youth, Psalm of Life (A)

long for 4 want **5** covet, crave, mourn **6** desire **8** aspire to

longing 3 yen **4** itch, lust, urge, wish **5** greed **6** desire, hunger, thirst **7** avidity, craving, passion **8** appetite

longshoreman 9 stevedore **10** roustabout

long-suffering 7 patient, stoical **8** enduring, resigned **9** compliant **10** forbearing, submissive **13** accommodating, uncomplaining

long suit 3 bag **4** gift **5** forte, thing **6** métier, talent **8** strength **9** specialty

long-winded 5 wordy **6** prolix **7** diffuse, lengthy, verbose **8** rambling **9** garrulous, redundant **10** loquacious

look 3 air, eye **4** gape, gawk, leer, mien, ogle, peek, peep, peer, seem, view **5** glare, stare, watch **6** admire, appear, aspect, behold, expect, eyeful, glance, glower, goggle, regard, squint, survey, visage **7** bearing, examine, eyeball, glimpse, observe **8** demeanor, onceover **10** appearance, expression, rubberneck **11** countenance, physiognomy

look after 4 mind, tend **5** nurse, serve, watch **6** attend, wait on **7** care for, husband **8** wait upon **9** watch over **10** provide for

look-alike 4 twin **5** clone **6** double **7** similar **8** matching **9** duplicate

look at 3 eye, see **4** face, ogle, scan, view **5** check **6** behold, ponder **7** examine, inspect **8** confront, consider **11** investigate

look back 6 recall, review **7** reflect **8** remember **9** reminisce

look down on 5 abhor, scorn, scout,

spurn 7 contemn, despise, disdain
8 dominate **9** tower over **10** tower
above

looker 6 beauty, eyeful, lovely, vision
7 stunner, witness **8** knockout, ornament **9** bystander, sightseer, spectator
10 eyewitness

looker-on 5 gaper **6** viewer **7** watcher,
witness **8** beholder, observer
9 bystander, spectator **10** eyewitness
12 rubbernecker

look for 4 seek **5** await **6** expect, plan on
9 search out **10** anticipate

looking glass 6 mirror **9** reflector

look into 5 check, probe, study **6** pursue,
survey **7** examine, explore, inspect
8 check out, question, research **10** scrutinize **11** investigate

look out 4 mind **6** beware

lookout 4 view **5** guard, scout, tower,
vista, watch **6** affair, cupola, picket,
sentry **7** spotter **8** panorama, prospect,
sentinel, watchman **9** belvedere, crow's
nest, firetower **10** watchtower, widow's
walk **11** observatory, perspective

look over 3 vet **4** read **5** check **6** review,
size up **7** examine, inspect **8** appraise,
evaluate

loom 4 brew, bulk, near, rear **5** hover,
mount, tower **6** appear, come on,
emerge, gather, impend **7** portend
8 approach, overhang, stand out,
threaten **9** take shape *part:* **6** heddle
7 harness, shuttle, treadle, trundle

loon 3 nut, oaf **4** bird, clod, dodo, dolt,
goof, lout, yo-yo **5** chump, dummy,
dunce, ninny, noddy, stupe, yokel
6 dimwit, dum-dum, nitwit **7** airhead,
buffoon, dullard, pinhead **8** bonehead,
dumbbell, crackpot, imbecile,
lunkhead, meathead, numskull **9** birdbrain, blockhead, ignoramus, lamebrain, numbskull, simpleton **10** dunderhead, nincompoop **11** chowderhead,
chucklehead

loony 3 nut **5** balmy, batty, crazy, daffy,
dippy, goofy, inane, nutty, silly, wacky
6 absurd, insane, madman, maniac,
screwy **7** fatuous, foolish, idiotic,
lunatic **8** demented, reckless **9** bedlamite, half-baked, ludicrous, senseless
10 ridiculous **11** harebrained **12** preposterous

loony bin 6 asylum, bedlam **8** bughouse,
madhouse, nuthouse **9** funny farm
10 booby hatch, crazy house

loop 3 arc, eye **4** ring **5** curve, noose,
picot **6** circle, eyelet, league, staple
7 circlet, circuit **13** circumference

looped 4 high **5** bowed, drunk, stiff
6 blotto, bombed, curved, juiced,

loaded, potted, stewed, tanked, zonked
7 crocked, pickled, pie-eyed, sloshed,
smashed **9** plastered **10** inebriated
11 curvilinear, intoxicated

loophole 3 out **6** escape, outlet **7** opening

loopy 4 daft, nuts, wavy **5** arced, batty,
bowed, crazy, daffy, dotty, flaky, nutty,
silly, snaky, wacky **6** arched, curved,
freaky, fruity, screwy, swirly **7** bizarre,
idiotic, lunatic, offbeat, sinuous,
touched **8** demented **9** eccentric
10 flipped out, off-the-wall, outlandish

loose 3 lax **4** easy, fast, free, lewd, limp
5 baggy, slack, vague **6** flabby, wanton
7 flaccid, relaxed **8** flexible
9 debauched, desultory, dissolute,
imprecise **10** disjointed, dissipated, ill-
defined, licentious, unattached, unconfined **12** disconnected, unrestrained

loose end 6 detail **8** fragment

loose-lipped see LOQUACIOUS

loosen 4 ease, free, undo **5** relax, slack,
untie **6** unbind **7** ease off, manumit,
release, slacken, unchain **8** liberate,
unbuckle, unfasten **10** emancipate

loosen up 5 relax **6** unbend, unwind
7 ease off, stretch

loot 3 rob **4** haul, lift, pelf, raid, sack,
swag **5** boost, booty, dough, lucre,
money, moola, reave, rifle, spoil **6** boodle, moolah, ravish, spoils **7** despoil,
pillage, plunder, ransack, stick up
9 knock over

looter 5 thief **7** brigand **8** marauder

lop 3 cut **4** chop, clip, crop, trim
5 prune, sever **6** excise **8** amputate,
truncate **9** dismember **10** guillotine

lope 3 jog, run **4** gait, romp, trot **5** amble
6 canter

lopsided 4 awry **5** askew **6** uneven
7 crooked, leaning, tilting **8** top-heavy
10 asymmetric, off-balance, unbalanced
12 asymmetrical **13** unsymmetrical

loquacious 5 gabby, talky, wordy **6** chatty, mouthy, prolix **7** verbose, voluble,
yakking **8** babbling **9** garrulous, jabber-
ing, talkative **10** blathering, chattering,
long-winded **11** loose-lipped **12** motor-
mouthed

lord 3 sir **4** boss, duke, earl, peer
5 noble, ruler **6** master **7** marquis **8** governor, marquess, nobleman, viscount
9 sovereign, tyrannize *feudal:* **5** liege
8 seigneur, suzerain *Muslim:* **6** sayyid

Lord High Executioner 4 Koko

Lord Jim author 6 Conrad (Joseph)

lordly 5 grand, lofty, noble, proud
6 august, uppity **7** exalted, haughty,
pompous, stately, swollen **8** affected,
arrogant, cavalier, gracious, imposing,

insolent, majestic, princely, snobbish, superior **9** dignified, egotistic, grandiose **10** disdainful, high-handed **11** dictatorial, magisterial, magnificent, overbearing, patronizing **12** aristocratic, supercilious **13** authoritarian, high-and-mighty

Lord of the Flies *author:* **7** Golding (William) *character:* **4** Jack **5** Piggy, Ralph

Lord's Prayer 9 Our Father **11** Paternoster

lore 6 mythos, wisdom **7** history **8** folkways, learning **9** knowledge, mythology, tradition **11** information **12** superstition

Lorelei 5 siren **9** temptress **10** seductress **11** femme fatale *poet:* **5** Heine (Heinrich) *river:* **5** Rhein, Rhine *victim:* **6** sailor **7** mariner

lorgnette 10 eyeglasses, spectacles **12** opera glasses

Lorna Doone *author:* **9** Blackmore (Richard) *hero:* **4** Ridd (John)

___ **Lorraine 6** Alsace

lorry 3 rig, van **4** semi **5** truck

lose 4 miss **5** evade, shake, waste, yield **6** escape, give up, mislay **7** destroy, forfeit, succumb **8** misplace, shake off, throw off **9** sacrifice, surrender

lose it 7 crack up, flip out, go crazy **8** freak out

loser 3 dud **4** bomb, bust, flop **5** lemon **6** bummer, fiasco, misfit, turkey **7** also-ran, debacle, failure, washout **8** deadbeat **11** incompetent

loss 4 harm, ruin **5** waste **6** damage, defeat, injury **7** deficit, failure, forfeit **8** casualty, decrease, fatality **9** depletion, privation, sacrifice, shrinkage **10** divestment, forfeiture, misfortune, misplacing **11** bereavement, deprivation, destruction **13** disappearance

lost 4 dead, gone, rapt **6** absent, astray, bygone, damned, doomed, futile, hidden, wasted **7** defunct, faraway, lacking, mislaid, missing **8** absorbed, departed, distrait, helpless, hopeless, vanished **9** condemned, desperate, destroyed **10** abstracted, insensible, overlooked **11** irrevocable, preoccupied **12** irredeemable, unregenerate

Lost Horizon *author:* **6** Hilton (James) *character:* **6** Conway (Hugh) *land:* **9** Shangri-La

lot 3 cut, ilk, set **4** doom, fate, give, heap, kind, mass, part, plat, sort, type, yard **5** allow, batch, block, bunch, field, group, moira, patch, quota, share, slice, tract, weird **6** assign, barrel, bundle, clutch, kismet, parcel, stripe **7** acreage, cluster, destiny, fortune, mete out, portion, species **8** allocate, clearing, frontage **9** aggregate, allowance, apportion

Lot *father:* **5** Haran *sister:* **5** Iscah **6** Milcah *son:* **4** Moab **5** Ammon *uncle:* **7** Abraham

lothario 4 stud, wolf **5** letch, Romeo **6** lecher, tomcat **7** amorist, Don Juan, gallant, seducer **8** Casanova, paramour **9** debaucher, womanizer **10** lady-killer **11** philanderer

lotion 3 oil **4** balm **5** cream, salve **6** cerate **7** unguent **8** ablution, cosmetic, lenitive, liniment, ointment **9** demulcent **11** embrocation

lottery 6 raffle **7** drawing **11** sweepstakes

lotus-eater 7 dreamer **8** escapist, romantic **10** daydreamer **13** castle-builder

loud 5 forte, gaudy, noisy, showy **6** brassy, brazen, flashy, garish, glitzy, tawdry, vulgar **7** blaring, blatant, booming, chintzy, glaring, pealing, raucous, roaring **8** piercing, resonant, sonorous, strident **9** clamorous, deafening, obnoxious, obtrusive, offensive, tasteless **10** bigmouthed, boisterous, flamboyant, resounding, stentorian, thunderous, vociferous **12** earsplitting

loudmouth 6 ranter **7** stentor **8** blowhard, braggart **9** blusterer

loudspeaker 6 woofer **7** tweeter **9** amplifier

Louisiana *capital:* **10** Baton Rouge *city:* **10** New Orleans, Shreveport *college, university:* **6** Tulane *county:* **6** parish *lake:* **13** Pontchartrain *nickname:* **7** Pelican (State) *river:* **11** Mississippi *state bird:* **12** brown pelican *state flower:* **8** magnolia *state tree:* **11** bald cypress

lounge 3 bar, bum, lie, pub, tap **4** idle, laze, loaf, loll, sofa **5** couch, dally, drift, lobby, relax **6** dawdle, loiter, parlor, repose, saloon **7** barroom, goof off, lie down, recline, taproom **8** restroom, kill time **10** living room

lounge lizard 3 fop **4** rake, toff **5** blade, dandy, leech **6** gigolo, sponge **9** ladies' man

Lourdes saint 10 Bernadette

louse 3 cur, dog, rat **4** toad **5** aphid, creep, skunk, snake **6** cootie, psylla, rotter, slater, wretch **7** stinker *egg:* **3** nit

louse up 4 blow, flub, muff, ruin **5** botch, spoil, wreck **6** bobble, bollix, bumble, bungle, fumble

lousy 3 ill **4** poor, rife **5** awful **6** shoddy, rotten **7** replete, teeming **8** crawling, horrible, inferior, infested, terrible **9** miserable, repulsive **10** despicable **12** contemptible

lout 3 oaf 4 boob, boor, dolt, gawk, hick, rube 5 brute, chuff, churl, klutz, looby, scorn, yokel 6 galoot, lubber, lummox, rustic 7 bumpkin, hayseed, palooka 9 simpleton 10 clodhopper

Louvre masterpiece 8 Mona Lisa 11 Venus de Milo

lovable 4 dear 5 sweet 6 cuddly 7 winning, winsome 8 adorable 9 appealing, endearing 11 embraceable

love 4 zeal 5 adore, ardor, crush, Cupid, exalt, prize, value 6 desire, dote on, fervor, revere 7 adulate, cherish, idolize, passion, romance, worship 8 devotion, fondness, idolatry, treasure, venerate, yearning 9 adoration, adulation, affection, delight in, sentiment 10 allegiance, appreciate, attachment, enthusiasm 11 amorousness, infatuation *combining form:* 5 phily 6 philia *French:* 5 amour *Italian:* 5 amore

love apple 6 tomato

lovebird 6 budgie, parrot 10 budgerigar

love feast 5 agape

love god 4 Amor, Eros, Kama 5 Bhaga, Cupid

love goddess 5 Athor, Freya, Venus 6 Hathor, Inanna, Ishtar 7 Astarte 9 Aphrodite, Ashtoreth

love letter 8 mash note 9 valentine 10 billet-doux

lovely 4 fair 5 sweet, swell 6 comely, dainty, pretty 7 elegant 8 adorable, alluring, charming, delicate, engaging, graceful, knockout 9 beauteous, beautiful, exquisite 10 attractive, delightful, enchanting, entrancing 11 captivating, good-looking

love potion 7 philter, philtre 11 aphrodisiac

lover 3 fan 4 beau, buff 5 flame, leman, Romeo, swain 6 addict, steady, suitor, votary 7 amorist, darling, devotee, Don Juan, gallant, habitué, squeeze 8 fancy man, lotharjo, mistress, paramour 9 boyfriend, inamorata, inamorato 10 aficionado, girlfriend, sweetheart

lovey-dovey 5 mushy 6 doting 7 amorous 12 affectionate

loving 4 dear, fond 6 ardent, erotic, tender 7 amatory, amorous, cordial, devoted, fervent 8 attached, enamored, faithful 10 benevolent, infatuated, passionate, solicitous 11 impassioned 12 affectionate

low 3 moo 4 base, blue, dead, deep, down, flat, mean, neap, poor, weak 5 cheap, short 6 abject, ailing, humble, hushed, lesser, nether, poorly, sickly, sordid, sparse, unwell 7 cut-rate, reduced, scrubby 8 cast down, dejected, depleted, downcast, inferior, mediocre, wretched 9 declining, depressed, miserable, subnormal, woebegone 10 economical, inadequate, indisposed, marked down, spiritless 11 crestfallen, downhearted, substandard, unfavorable

lowbred 4 base, rude 6 coarse, oafish, vulgar 7 boorish, brutish, loutish, uncouth 8 churlish, cloddish, lubberly 11 uncivilized

low-cost 5 cheap 6 budget, cheapo 7 bargain, cut-rate 10 affordable, reasonable 11 inexpensive

low-down 4 base, mean, ugly, vile 6 odious, scurvy 7 ignoble 8 shameful, wretched 9 abhorrent, worthless 10 despicable, disgusting 11 ignominious 12 contemptible

lowdown 4 dope, info 5 facts, scoop, specs 6 skinny 8 briefing 11 information

lower 3 cut 4 clip, drop, fall, sink 5 frown, gloom, scowl, shave, slash, under 6 debase, demean, demote, humble, lesser, menace, nether, reduce 7 cut down, deflate, degrade, demerit, depress, descend, devalue, let down 8 inferior, mark down, overcast, submerge, threaten 9 devaluate, downgrade *prefix:* 5 infra

Lower Depths author 5 Gorki, Gorky (Maksim, Maxim)

lowest point 5 nadir *in the U.S.:* 11 Death Valley *on earth:* 7 Dead Sea

low-grade 4 hack 5 junky, lousy 6 cheesy, cruddy, shabby, shoddy, sleazy, tawdry 8 below par, déclassé, inferior, mediocre 9 deficient 10 second-rate 11 second-class, substandard 12 second-drawer

low-key 4 soft 5 muted, quiet 7 relaxed, subdued 8 laid-back, softened, tasteful 9 easygoing, minimized, temperate, toned down 10 played down, restrained 11 understated

lowland 4 flat, sump, vale 5 basin 6 bottom, slough, valley 7 bottoms *Scottish:* 6 lallan 7 lalland

lowlife 4 fink, heel 5 knave, rogue 6 no-good, outlaw, rascal, wretch 7 hoodlum, ruffian, villain 9 miscreant, reprobate, scoundrel 10 blackguard, black sheep, sleazeball 11 rapscallion, slimebucket 12 bottom-feeder

lowly 4 base, mean, meek 6 abject, humble, menial, modest 7 ignoble, mundane, obscure, prosaic, servile 8 baseborn, plebeian, unwashed

low-pressure 4 calm 6 casual, dégagé, folksy, mellow 7 relaxed 8 flexible, informal, laid-back **9** easygoing **10** nonchalant

low-spirited 3 sad **4** blue, down, glum **6** abject, droopy, gloomy, morose **7** doleful **8** cast down, dejected, downcast, saddened **9** bummed out, cheerless, depressed, woebegone **10** dispirited, melancholy **11** discouraged, downhearted **12** disheartened, heavyhearted

low tide 3 ebb **4** neap

loyal 4 firm, true **5** liege **6** ardent, trusty **7** devoted, dutiful, staunch **8** constant, faithful, resolute, true-blue **9** allegiant, steadfast, unfailing **10** dependable **11** trustworthy

loyalist 4 Tory **7** patriot **8** partisan **10** countryman **11** nationalist

loyalty 6 fealty **8** adhesion, devotion, fidelity **9** adherence, constancy **10** allegiance, attachment, dedication **11** staunchness **12** faithfulness **13** dependability, steadfastness

lozenge 4 pill **6** troche **7** diamond, rhombus **8** pastille

LSD 4 acid *user:* **8** acidhead

lubricate 3 oil **6** grease, smooth **7** moisten

lubricious 4 lewd, oily **5** slick **6** carnal, greasy, slippy, wanton **8** prurient, slippery, slithery, ticklish **9** lecherous, salacious **10** lascivious, libidinous **12** concupiscent

lucent 5 clear **6** bright, limpid **7** beaming, crystal, glowing, lambent, radiant, shining **8** clear-cut, luminous, pellucid **9** brilliant, effulgent, refulgent **11** unambiguous

Lucia di Lammermoor *character:* **7** Edgardo *composer:* **9** Donizetti (Gaetano) *novelist:* **5** Scott (Walter)

lucid 4 sane **5** clear **6** bright, limpid **7** crystal, lambent, radiant **8** clear-cut, knowable, luminous **9** brilliant, effulgent, graspable, refulgent, unblurred **10** articulate, fathomable **11** translucent, transparent, unambiguous **12** compos mentis, incandescent, intelligible, transpicuous **13** apprehensible

lucidity 6 acumen, sanity **7** clarity **8** sagacity, saneness **9** clearness, plainness, soundness **10** cognizance, perception **12** clairvoyance

Lucifer 5 devil, fiend, Satan, Venus **7** Old Nick **8** Apollyon **9** archfiend, Beelzebub **10** Old Scratch **13** Old Gooseberry

Lucinde *beloved:* **7** Leandre **9** Clitandre *father:* **7** Geronte **10** Sganarelle

luck 3 hap, hit **4** juju, meet **5** fluke, light **6** chance, happen, hazard, kismet **7** fortune, godsend, stumble **8** fortuity,

occasion, windfall **9** advantage **11** opportunity *token:* **5** charm **6** amulet, clover, fetish, mascot **8** talisman **9** horseshoe **11** rabbit's foot

luckless 7 adverse, hapless, unhappy **8** ill-fated, untoward, wretched **9** miserable **10** ill-starred **11** star-crossed, unfavorable, unfortunate **12** misfortunate, unpropitious

lucky 6 golden, timely **7** favored **9** favorable, fortunate **10** auspicious, beneficial, felicitous, fortuitous, propitious **12** advantageous, providential **13** serendipitous *Scottish:* **5** canny

Lucky Jim author 4 Amis (Kingsley)

lucrative 6 paying **7** gainful **8** fruitful **10** high-income, productive, profitable, well-paying, worthwhile **11** moneymaking **12** advantageous, remunerative

lucre 3 pay **4** cash, gain, jack, loot **5** dough, green, money, moola **6** dinero, do-re-mi, moolah, profit, wampum **7** cabbage, revenue **9** long green **10** greenbacks

Lucrezia ___ 6 Borgia

ludicrous 4 zany **5** antic, comic, droll, funny, goofy, nutty, silly **6** absurd **7** amusing, bizarre, comical, foolish, risible **8** farcical **9** fantastic, grotesque, laughable **10** off-the-wall, outlandish, ridiculous **11** incongruous **12** preposterous

Ludlum novel 14 Bourne Identity (The) **15** Bourne Supremacy (The) **16** Holcroft Covenant (The) **19** Prometheus Deception (The)

lug 3 nut, oaf, tow, tug **4** bear, buck, drag, draw, haul, hump, jerk, pull, tote **5** carry, ferry, shlep **6** convey, schlep **9** transport

luggage 4 bags, gear **7** baggage

lugubrious 3 sad **4** blue, dour, down, glum **5** bleak **6** dismal, dreary, gloomy, morose, rueful, somber, sullen, woeful **7** doleful, joyless **8** cast down, dejected, dolesome, downcast, mournful **9** cheerless, depressed, plaintive, saturnine, sorrowful, woebegone **10** depressing, despondent, lamentable, melancholy, oppressive **11** discouraged, dispiriting, downhearted **12** disconsolate

lukewarm 5 blasé, tepid **7** dubious, offhand **8** hesitant **9** uncertain, undecided **10** wishy-washy **11** halfhearted, indifferent

lull 3 ebb **4** balm, calm, hush, wane **5** letup, pause, quiet, still **6** becalm, pacify, soothe, temper **7** compose, decline, ease off, slacken **8** abeyance, interval **9** stillness **10** quiescence **11** tranquilize

lullaby 8 berceuse **10** cradlesong

lulu 3 ace 5 dandy, doozy, dream 6 doozie, wonder 7 delight 8 knockout 9 sensation

lumber 3 tax 4 clog, lade, load, logs, plod, slog, wood 5 barge, clump, stump, weigh 6 burden, charge, rumble, saddle, timber, trudge 8 encumber

lumberjack see LOGGER

luminance 10 brightness

luminary 3 sun, VIP 4 lion, name, star 5 celeb, light, nabob 6 leader, worthy 7 big name, notable 8 big-timer, eminence, somebody 9 celebrity, dignitary, superstar 10 notability 12 leading light

luminous 5 clear, lucid 6 bright, lucent 7 beaming, crystal, fulgent, lambent, radiant, shining 8 clear-cut, lustrous, pellucid 9 brilliant, effulgent, refulgent 11 illustrious, translucent, transparent 12 enlightening, incandescent

lummox 3 oaf 4 boor, clod, gawk, lout 5 klutz, looby 6 lubber 7 palooka

lump 3 gob, lot, oaf, wad 4 blob, bulk, chip, clod, gawk, glob, heap, hunk, lout, mass, pile, welt 5 abide, batch, block, brook, bulge, bunch, chunk, hunch, klutz, knurl, looby, piece, scrap, stand, tumor 6 digest, endure, entire, lubber, morsel, nugget 7 handful, palooka, portion, stomach, swallow 8 swelling, totality 9 aggregate 10 protrusion, tumescence 12 protuberance

lumpy 5 crude, gawky, rough 6 choppy, clumsy, coarse, oafish 8 clumpish, unformed 9 roughhewn

lunacy 5 folly, mania 6 idiocy 7 fatuity, foolery, inanity, madness 8 delirium, dementia, insanity 9 absurdity, craziness, silliness, stupidity 10 imbecility 11 derangement, foolishness 13 senselessness

lunar *dark area:* 4 mare 5 maria (plural) *valley:* 4 rill 5 rille

lunatic 3 mad, nut 4 daft, kook, loco, yo-yo, zany 5 balmy, batty, crank, crazy, nutty, raver, wacko, wacky 6 absurd, crazed, cuckoo, insane, madman, maniac, nitwit, psycho, screwy 7 bonkers, cracked, foolish 8 crackpot, demented, demoniac, deranged, frenzied, maniacal, paranoid, schizoid, unhinged 9 bedlamite, ding-a-ling, fruitcake, harebrain, screwball 10 crackbrain 11 nonsensical

lunch 3 eat 4 meal, nosh 5 snack

luncheonette 4 café 5 diner 6 bistro, eatery 7 beanery, canteen, tearoom 8 snack bar 9 cafeteria 10 coffee shop, restaurant 11 greasy spoon

lune 3 bow 5 curve 6 sickle 8 crescent, meniscus

lung *combining form:* 5 pneum, pulmo 6 pneumo, pulmon *disease:* 9 emphysema, pneumonia 10 byssinosis 12 tuberculosis

lunge 3 jab 4 dash, dive, stab 5 bound, drive, pitch, surge 6 charge, plunge, pounce, thrust

lunkhead 3 oaf 4 boob, clod, dodo, dolt, goof, yo-yo 5 booby, chump, dummy, dunce, idiot, moron, ninny, noddy, stupe 6 dimwit, dum-dum, nitwit 7 dullard 8 dumbbell, imbecile, numskull 9 birdbrain, ignoramus, lamebrain, numbskull, simpleton 10 nincompoop

lupine 5 feral 6 brutal, fierce 7 wolfish 8 ravening 9 predatory, rapacious 10 bluebonnet, sanguinary

lurch 3 bob, yaw 4 jerk, lean, list, reel, rock, roll, sway, tilt, toss 5 heave, pitch, slide, swing 6 bumble, careen, falter, plunge, seesaw, swerve, teeter, totter 7 blunder, stagger, stumble 8 flounder

lure 3 bag 4 bait, call, draw, fake, hook, pull, rope, toll, trap, wile 5 blind, catch, charm, decoy, snare, tempt, trick 6 appeal, cajole, come-on, draw in, draw on, entice, entrap, invite, lead on, seduce 7 attract, beguile, bewitch, capture, con game, enchant, ensnare, gimmick, wheedle 8 blandish, delusion, illusion, inveigle 9 captivate, fascinate, incentive, seduction, siren song 10 attraction, camouflage, enticement, inducement, seducement, temptation *fishing:* 3 fly 4 worm 5 spoon 6 minnow 8 bucktail

lurid 3 wan 4 ashy, gory, gray, grim, pale 5 ashen, fiery, gross, livid, waxen 6 doughy, grisly, malign, sultry, yellow 7 baleful, ghastly, graphic, hideous, macabre, malefic, tabloid 8 blanched, gruesome, horrible, shocking, sinister, terrible 9 colorless 10 horrifying, maleficent, terrifying 11 sensational 12 melodramatic

Lurie novel 14 Foreign Affairs 18 War Between the Tates (The)

lurk 4 hide, slip 5 creep, prowl, skulk, slide, slink, sneak, snoop, steal 9 pussyfoot

luscious 4 rich, sexy 5 sapid, sweet, tasty, yummy 6 delish, divine, ornate, savory 7 opulent, piquant, sensual 8 sensuous 9 ambrosial, epicurean, exquisite, flavorful, luxurious, seductive, sumptuous, toothsome 10 delectable, delightful, flamboyant, flavorsome, voluptuous 11 scrumptious 13 mouth-watering

lush 3 sot 4 rank, rich, wino 5 dense, drink, drunk, yummy 6 bibber, boozer, deluxe, lavish, savory 7 fertile, opulent, profuse, sensual, teeming, tippler 8 abundant, drunkard, palatial, prodigal, sensuous, thriving 9 ambrosial, delicious, epicurean, exuberant, inebriate, luxuriant, luxurious, plentiful, sumptuous, toothsome 10 boozehound, delectable, delightful, profitable, prosperous, voluptuous 11 extravagant, flourishing

Lusitania 8 Portugal

lust 3 rut, yen 4 ache, itch, pine, urge, wish, zeal, zest 5 ardor, crave, drive, greed, letch, yearn 6 desire, fervor, hanker, hunger, libido 7 avidity, craving, lechery, longing, passion 8 appetite, coveting, cupidity, lewdness, priapism, salacity, satyrism, yearning 9 carnality, eagerness, eroticism, lubricity, prurience, pruriency 10 enthusiasm, excitement, satyriasis, wantonness 11 nymphomania 13 concupiscence, lecherousness, salaciousness

luster 4 glow 5 glaze, gleam, glint, gloss, sheen, shine 6 polish 7 burnish, shimmer 8 lambency, radiance 9 afterglow 10 brightness, brilliance, brilliancy, effulgence, luminosity, refulgence 11 candescence, iridescence

lusterless 3 dim, wan 4 blah, drab, dull, flat, gray, matt 5 brown, dingy, dusky, faded, matte, muddy, muted, vapid 6 boring 10 uninspired

lustful 3 hot 4 lewd 5 bawdy, horny 6 carnal, erotic, wanton 7 burning, goatish, itching, ruttish, satyric 8 prurient 9 debauched, lecherous, libertine, lickerish, salacious 10 hot-blooded, lascivious, libidinous, licentious, lubricious, passionate 12 concupiscent

lustrate 5 purge 6 purify 7 cleanse

lustration 6 ritual 8 ablution 9 catharsis, cleansing, purgation 10 sprinkling 12 purification

lustrous 5 nitid, shiny 6 bright, gleamy, glossy, sheeny 7 fulgent, glowing, lambent, radiant, shining 8 gleaming, luminous, polished, splendid 9 brilliant, burnished, effulgent, refulgent 10 glimmering, glistening 11 resplendent 12 incandescent

lusty 4 hale 5 hardy, vital 6 brawny, hearty, mighty, potent, robust, strong, virile 7 dynamic, healthy, rousing 8 vigorous 9 energetic, strapping, strenuous 10 prodigious, red-blooded 12 enthusiastic

lute 4 clay, seal 5 grout 6 cement 7 bandora 8 mandolin 10 chitarrone, instrument *Arabic:* 3 oud *two-necked:* 7 theorbo

lutenist 5 Bream (Julian) 7 Dowland (John) 8 Gaultier (Denis)

Lutetia 5 Paris

Luxembourg *capital:* 10 Luxembourg *monetary unit:* 4 euro *mountain range:* 8 Ardennes *neighbor:* 6 France 7 Belgium, Germany *river:* 4 Sûre 7 Alzette

luxuriant 4 lush, rank, rich 5 dense 6 fecund, lavish 7 copious, fertile, opulent, profuse, rampant, riotous, teeming 8 abundant, fruitful, luscious, prodigal, prolific 9 excessive, exuberant, sumptuous

luxuriate 4 bask 5 bloom, enjoy, feast, revel 6 abound, relish, thrive, wallow 7 delight, indulge 8 flourish

luxurious 4 lush, posh, rich 5 fancy, grand, plush, ritzy, showy 6 costly, deluxe, lavish, plushy 7 opulent, sensual, stately 8 imposing, majestic, palatial, splendid 9 elaborate, epicurean, expensive, grandiose, sumptuous 10 impressive 11 extravagant, magnificent *situation:* 7 fat city 10 bed of roses, easy street

luxury 5 frill, treat 6 dainty 7 amenity, comfort 8 delicacy, opulence 9 abundance, affluence 10 indulgence 11 superfluity 12 extravagance

lycée 6 school 10 high school

lyceum 4 hall 6 school 7 academy, chamber 9 institute

Lycidas *author:* 6 Milton (John)

Lycomedes *daughter:* 8 Deidamia *victim:* 7 Theseus

Lycus *brother:* 7 Nycteus *father:* 7 Pandion *slayer:* 6 Zethus 7 Amphion *wife:* 5 Dirce

Lydian *king:* 5 Gyges 7 Croesus 8 Alyattes *queen:* 7 Omphale

lye 7 caustic 9 hydroxide

lynch 4 hang 5 scrag 6 gibbet, murder 7 execute 8 string up

Lynette see LINE

lynx 4 puma 6 bobcat, cougar 7 caracal, wildcat 9 catamount

Lyra *star:* 4 Vega

lyre 4 harp

lyric 3 ode 4 odic, poem 5 melic, verse 6 poetic 7 melodic, musical 8 operatic 9 exuberant, rhapsodic

lyrical 7 lilting, melodic, musical, songful, tuneful 8 operatic

lyricist 4 poet 10 librettist

Lysander's beloved 6 Hermia

M

Maacah *father:* 5 Nahor 6 Talmai 7 Absalom *husband:* 5 David 6 Jehiel, Machir 8 Rehoboam *son:* 5 Hanan 6 Abijam, Achish 7 Absalom 10 Shephatiah

macabre 4 grim 5 lurid 6 grisly, horrid, morbid 7 deathly, ghastly, hideous 8 ghoulish, gruesome, horrible 9 deathlike 10 horrifying

macadam 3 tar 7 asphalt, roadway 8 pavement

macaque 6 monkey, rhesus

macaroni 3 fop 4 beau, buck, dude, toff 5 dandy, pasta, swell 7 coxcomb, gallant

macaw 6 parrot

Macbeth *character:* 4 Ross 5 Angus 6 Hecate, Lennox 7 Fleance *slayer:* 7 Macduff *successor:* 7 Malcolm *title:* 5 thane *victim:* 6 Banquo, Duncan

mace 4 club 5 baton, staff 6 cudgel, nutmeg 8 bludgeon

Macedonia *capital:* 6 Skopje *city:* 6 Tetovo *monetary unit:* 5 denar *neighbor:* 6 Greece, Serbia 7 Albania 8 Bulgaria *part of:* 7 Balkans *peninsula:* 6 Balkan

macerate 4 soak 5 steep 6 drench, soften 7 immerse, suffuse 8 saturate

machete 4 bolo 5 knife 6 scythe

Machiavellian 4 wily 6 shrewd 7 cunning, devious 8 guileful, scheming 9 conniving, deceitful, insidious 10 conspiring 11 duplicitous, treacherous 12 unscrupulous

Machiavelli work 6 Prince (The) 8 Mandrake (The) 10 Mandragola (La)

machinate 4 plot 6 scheme 7 connive, finagle 8 conspire, intrigue, maneuver

machination 4 plot, ploy, ruse 5 cabal, dodge 6 gambit, scheme 8 artifice, intrigue, maneuver, scheming, trickery 9 chicanery, collusion, deception, dirty work, expedient, stratagem 10 hankypanky, subterfuge 11 contrivance, skulduggery 12 gamesmanship, skullduggery

machine 6 device, engine, gadget 9 apparatus, appliance, automaton 11 contraption

machine-gun 4 rake 6 strafe 8 enfilade 9 rapid-fire

machine-gun inventor 7 Gatling (Richard)

machinery 5 works 9 apparatus, equipment, mechanism

machismo 7 swagger 8 virility 9 manliness 11 masculinity

macho 5 manly 6 virile 9 masculine

Machu Picchu resident 4 Inca

mackinaw 4 coat 5 cover, trout 7 blanket

mackintosh 7 slicker 8 raincoat

macrocosm 5 world 6 cosmos 8 creation, universe

mad 4 daft, nuts, rash, sore, wild 5 angry, crazy, irate, irked, kooky, livid, loony, nutty, rabid, wacky 6 absurd, crazed, cuckoo, heated, insane, ireful, screwy 7 berserk, bonkers, cracked, enraged, foolish, frantic, furious, lunatic 8 choleric, demented, deranged, frenetic, frenzied, incensed, offended, outraged, unhinged, worked up, wrathful 9 delirious, fanatical, fantastic, hilarious, illogical, senseless 10 distracted, infuriated, irrational, unbalanced

Madagascar *capital:* 12 Antananarivo *channel:* 10 Mozambique *city:* 9 Mahajanga, Toamasina *language:* 6 French 8 Malagasy *monetary unit:* 5 franc *mountain range:* 9 Ankaratra

madame 3 Mrs. 4 wife 6 milady, missus

Madame Bovary *author:* 8 Flaubert (Gustave) *character:* 4 Emma (Bovary) 7 Charles (Bovary) 8 Rodolphe

Madame Butterfly *character:* 9 Cho-Cho-San, Cio-Cio-San, Pinkerton, Sharpless *composer:* 7 Puccini (Giacomo)

madcap 4 rash, wild 5 antic 7 foolish 8 reckless 9 frivolous, hotheaded 10 capricious, incautious

Mad Cavalier 6 Rupert (Prince)

madden 3 ire, vex 4 goad 5 anger, craze 6 enrage 7 derange, incense, inflame, outrage, possess, steam up, unhinge 9 infuriate, unbalance

Madeira Islands *capital:* 7 Funchal *export:* 4 wine *part of:* 8 Portugal

mademoiselle 4 girl, Miss 6 maiden 9 governess 10 yellowtail 11 silver perch

made-to-order 6 custom 7 bespoke 10 customized, custom-built

made-up 5 bogus, false 7 painted 8 invented, mythical, specious 9 fictional, imaginary, pretended, trumpedup 10 fabricated, fictitious 11 makebelieve 12 cosmeticized

madhouse 6 asylum, bedlam 8 loony bin 9 funny farm 10 booby hatch

madman 3 nut 4 kook, loon 5 loony, raver 6 cuckoo, maniac, psycho 7 lunatic, nutcase 9 bedlamite, psychotic, fruitcake

madness 4 rage 5 folly 6 lunacy 8 insanity 9 psychosis 11 derangement

Madonna initials 3 BVM

Madras 9 Tamil Nadu *founder:* 3 Day (Francis)

Madrid museum 5 Prado

madrigal 4 glee, poem, song 8 part-song

madrigalist *English:* 4 Byrd (William) 6 Morley (Thomas), Wilbye (John) 7 Tomkins (Thomas), Weelkes (Thomas) *Flemish:* 8 Willaert (Adriaan) *Italian:* 8 Marenzio (Luca) 10 Monteverdi (Claudio)

maelstrom 4 eddy 5 whirl 6 vortex 7 turmoil 9 whirlpool

maenad 9 bacchante, priestess

maestro see CONDUCTOR

Mafia 3 mob 4 ring 6 clique 7 rackets 8 gangland 9 Black Hand, syndicate 10 Cosa Nostra, underworld

mafioso 4 goon 6 hit man 7 mobster 8 gangster 9 racketeer

magazine 4 dump 5 cache, depot, organ, store 6 armory, digest, review, weekly 7 arsenal, gazette, journal, monthly 8 biweekly 9 bimonthly, quarterly, warehouse 10 depository, periodical, repository, storehouse 11 publication

mage 6 priest 8 magician, sorcerer

maggot 4 grub, whim 5 fancy, larva 6 vagary 7 caprice, conceit

Magi 6 Caspar, Gaspar 8 Melchior 9 Balthasar, Balthazar *gift:* 4 gold 5 myrrh 7 incense 12 frankincense

Magian see MAGUS

magic 4 juju 5 wicca 6 hoodoo, voodoo 7 alchemy, devilry, sorcery 8 satanism, witchery, witching, wizardry 9 conjuring, diablerie, diabolism, occultism, sortilege 10 hocus-pocus, mumbo jumbo, necromancy, witchcraft 11 abracadabra, bewitchment, enchantment, legerdemain, thaumaturgy

magical 6 occult 8 wizardly 10 bewitching, entrancing 11 necromantic 12 thaumaturgic

Magic Flute composer 6 Mozart (Wolfgang Amadeus)

magician 5 brujo, witch 6 shaman, wizard 7 Houdini, warlock 8 conjurer, satanist, sorcerer 9 diabolist, enchanter, trickster, voodooist 11 medicine man, necromancer, thaumaturge *Arthurian:* 6 Merlin *Shakespearean:* 8 Prospero

stage: 5 Randi (James) 11 Copperfield (David), illusionist *Tolkien's:* 7 Gandalf

Magic Mountain, The *author:* 4 Mann (Thomas) *character:* 7 Castorp (Hans)

magisterial 6 lordly 7 pompous 8 dogmatic 9 imperious, masterful 10 highhanded 11 doctrinaire, domineering, overbearing 13 authoritative, self-important

Magister Ludi author 5 Hesse (Hermann)

magistrate 5 court, judge 7 bencher, justice 8 official *ancient Greek:* 5 ephor 6 archon *ancient Roman:* 6 aedile 7 duumvir, praetor, questor 8 quaestor *Italian:* 7 podesta *Scottish:* 6 bailie

Magna Carta *king:* 4 John *place signed:* 9 Runnymede

magnanimous 5 noble 7 liberal 8 generous, princely 9 forgiving, unselfish 10 benevolent, bighearted, charitable, chivalrous, high-minded, munificent

magnate 5 baron, mogul, nabob 6 fat cat, prince, tycoon 9 personage, plutocrat

magnet 9 lodestone 10 attraction

magnetic 8 alluring 9 appealing, seductive 10 attractive 11 captivating, charismatic, fascinating 12 irresistible *substance:* 4 iron 7 ferrite

magnetism 4 draw, lure, pull 5 charm 6 allure, appeal 7 glamour 8 charisma 10 attraction 11 fascination

magnetize 4 draw, lure, wile 5 charm 7 attract, bewitch, enchant 9 captivate, fascinate

magnification unit 8 diameter

magnificence 4 pomp 7 majesty 8 grandeur, splendor 9 pageantry 13 sumptuousness

magnificent 5 grand, noble, regal, royal 6 august, lavish, lordly, superb 7 exalted, opulent, stately, sublime 8 glorious, imposing, majestic, palatial, princely, splendid 9 brilliant, grandiose, luxurious, sumptuous 11 extravagant, resplendent, splendorous 13 splendiferous

magnifier 4 lens 9 telescope *jeweler's:* 5 loupe

magnify 4 hymn, laud 5 add to, boost, cry up, exalt, extol, honor, swell 6 expand, extend, praise 7 amplify, augment, enhance, enlarge, ennoble, glorify, inflate 8 eulogize, heighten, increase, maximize, multiply, overplay 9 aggravate, celebrate, embellish, embroider, intensify, overstate 10 aggrandize, exaggerate, panegyrize 13 overemphasize

magniloquent 5 tumid, windy 6 florid, turgid 7 aureate, flowery, fustian, orotund, pompous, swollen **8** sonorous **9** bombastic, high-flown, overblown, rhapsodic **10** euphuistic, rhetorical **11** declamatory

magnitude 4 size **5** order, range **6** extent, import, number, volume **7** bigness, caliber, measure, quality **8** enormity, hugeness, quantity, vastness **9** greatness, immensity, largeness **10** dimensions, importance, proportion **11** consequence

Magnolia State 11 Mississippi

magnum opus 7 classic **10** masterwork **11** chef d'oeuvre, masterpiece, tour de force

Magog's king 3 Gog

magpie 3 jay **4** bird **6** gabber, prater **7** blabber, hoarder **8** jabberer, prattler **9** chatterer, collector **10** chatterbox **12** blabbermouth

maguey 5 agave, fiber **7** cantala *relative:* **4** aloe

magus 6 wizard **7** diviner, warlock **8** conjurer, sorcerer **9** enchanter **10** astrologer **11** necromancer

Magyar 9 Hungarian

Mahalath *father:* **7** Ishmael **8** Jerimoth *husband:* **4** Esau **8** Rehoboam

mah-jongg piece 4 tile

Mahlon *father:* **9** Elimelech *mother:* **5** Naomi *wife:* **4** Ruth

Maia *father:* **5** Atlas *mother:* **7** Pleione *sisters:* **8** Pleiades *son:* **6** Hermes **7** Mercury

maid 4 amah, girl, lass, miss **5** biddy, bonne, wench **6** au pair, damsel, lassie, live-in, virgin **7** servant **8** domestic **9** charwoman, hired girl **10** au pair girl *Indian:* **4** ayah *lady's:* **7** abigail *stage:* **9** soubrette

maiden 3 gal **4** girl, lass, miss **5** first, fresh, missy, prime, wench **6** damsel, lassie, unused, virgin **7** initial, pioneer, primary **8** earliest, original, spinster, virginal **10** spinsterly *Norse mythological:* **8** valkyrie

maidenhair tree 6 ginkgo

maidenhead 5 hymen **6** purity **9** virginity

maidenhood 9 virginity

Maid of Astolat 6 Elaine

Maid of Orleans, The 4 Joan (of Arc) **7** Pucelle (La) *author:* **8** Schiller (Friedrich von)

mail 4 post **5** armor **7** hauberk, letters **8** messages

___ **mail 3** air **4** junk **5** chain

maim 4 maul **6** mangle **7** cripple, disable **8** mutilate, paralyze **9** disfigure

main 3 sea **5** chief, great, major, ocean, prime, trunk, vital **7** central, high sea, leading, premier, primary **8** cardinal, foremost, high seas **9** essential, paramount, principal **10** preeminent, pre-

vailing **11** fundamental, outstanding, predominant

Maine *capital:* **7** Augusta *city:* **6** Bangor **8** Lewiston, Portland *college, university:* **5** Bates, Colby **7** Bowdoin *lake:* **6** Sebago *motto:* **6** Dirigo *mountain:* **8** Cadillac, Katahdin *nickname:* **8** Pine Tree (State) *park:* **6** Acadia *river:* **8** Kennebec **9** Penobscot *state bird:* **9** chickadee *state flower:* **22** white pine cone and tassel *state tree:* **9** white pine

mainly 6 mostly **7** chiefly, largely **8** above all **9** primarily **10** especially **11** principally **13** predominantly

mainstay 4 prop **5** brace **6** pillar **7** bulwark, standby, support **8** backbone, buttress **9** supporter, sustainer

Main Street author 5 Lewis (Sinclair)

maintain 4 aver, avow **5** argue, claim **6** affirm, allege, assert, back up, defend, insist, keep up, manage, stress, uphold **7** care for, carry on, contend, declare, justify, persist, profess, support, sustain, warrant **8** continue, preserve **9** cultivate, emphasize, look after **10** provide for

maintenance 4 care, keep **6** living, upkeep **7** alimony, support **10** livelihood **11** subsistence **12** alimentation *worker:* **7** janitor **9** custodian

maize 4 corn, milo **10** Indian corn

majestic 5 grand, noble, regal, royal **6** august, kingly, lordly, superb **7** exalted, stately **8** elevated, imperial, imposing, princely, splendid **9** dignified, grandiose, sumptuous **11** ceremonious, magnificent

majesty 4 pomp **5** glory **8** eminence, grandeur, splendor **9** greatness, loftiness **11** stateliness **12** magnificence

major 3 big **4** main, star **5** chief, grave, large **6** higher, larger **7** capital, greater, notable, primary, serious, sizable **8** sizeable, superior **9** principal, prominent **10** large-scale, preeminent **11** outstanding, predominant, significant **12** considerable

Major Barbara author 4 Shaw (George Bernard)

majority 4 bulk, edge **6** margin **13** preponderance

make 3 act, net, set **4** earn, form, gain, mold **5** build, cause, erect, forge, frame, hatch, shape, spawn **6** compel, create, derive, draw up, effect, output, parent **7** achieve, bring in, compose, fashion, prepare, produce **8** comprise, conclude, draw down, generate **9** construct, establish, fabricate, originate **10** constitute **11** manufacture, put together *amends:* **5** atone *believe:* **7** pretend *certain:* **6** assure **8** convince *fast:* **3** fix **4** gird

6 secure *good:* **7** succeed **9** indemnify
known: **3** air **6** expose, reveal, spread
7 declare, divulge, uncover **8** announce,
disclose, proclaim *use of:* **6** employ

make-believe 4 mock, sham **7** charade,
feigned, fiction **8** disguise, pretense
9 fictional, imaginary, insincere, pretended, simulated **10** fictitious

make do 4 cope **5** get by, get on, shift
6 endure, fake it, manage, wing it
7 survive **8** get along **9** improvise
11 extemporize **13** muddle through

make off 3 fly, run **4** flee, skip **5** leave,
scoot, scram **6** decamp, depart, escape
7 abscond, run away **9** skedaddle

make out 3 see **4** fare, neck **5** grasp, infer
6 accept, deduce, derive, follow, gather,
manage, take in, thrive **7** discern, prosper, succeed **8** conclude, flourish, get
along, perceive **9** apprehend, determine, establish, interpret **10** comprehend, understand

make over 4 cede, deed **6** assign, convey,
reform **7** remodel, reshape **8** renovate,
transfer

maker 7 builder, creator **8** borrower,
designer, inventor, producer **10** originator **11** constructor **12** manufacturer

makeshift 6 resort **7** stopgap **8** recourse,
resource **9** expedient, temporary
10 expediency, substitute **11** provisional
13 quick-and-dirty, rough-and-ready

make up 4 form **5** atone **6** devise, invent
7 arrange, compile, compose, concoct,
fashion, prepare **8** comprise, contrive
9 apologize, construct, fabricate, formulate, improvise, reconcile **10** compensate

makeup 4 cast, form, kohl, mold
5 blush, fiber, gloss, grain, paint, rouge,
shape, stamp, style **6** design, nature,
powder, stripe, temper **7** blusher, mascara **8** lip gloss, war paint **9** character,
formation **10** complexion, maquillage
11 arrangement, composition, disposition, greasepaint, personality, temperament **12** architecture, constitution,
construction, organization

maladroit 5 inept **6** clumsy, gauche,
klutzy **7** awkward, unhandy **8** bumbling, bungling, tactless **9** ham-handed,
impolitic **10** blundering, ungraceful
11 heavy-handed **12** undiplomatic

malady 3 ill **7** ailment, disease, illness
8 disorder, sickness, syndrome **9** complaint, condition, infirmity **10** affliction

malaise 4 funk **5** dumps, ennui **8** debility, doldrums **10** enervation

Malamud, Bernard *novel:* **5** Fixer (The)
7 Natural (The) **9** Assistant (The) *story:*
11 Magic Barrel (The)

malapert 4 rude **5** brash, fresh, nervy,
sassy, saucy, smart **6** brassy, brazen,
cheeky **7** forward **8** impudent, insolent
12 presumptuous

Malaprop creator 8 Sheridan (Richard
Brinsley)

malapropos 5 inapt, undue **8** improper,
unseemly, untimely **10** unsuitable
11 inopportune **13** inappropriate, inopportunely

malaria 4 ague **6** miasma *medicine:* **7** quinine **8** cinchona *mosquito:* **9** anopheles

malarkey 4 guff **5** bilge, hokum, hooey,
tripe **6** bunkum, drivel **7** hogwash, rubbish, twaddle **8** nonsense **9** poppycock
10 balderdash **12** blatherskite

Malawi *capital:* **8** Lilongwe *city:* **8** Blantyre *explorer:* **11** Livingstone (David)
former name: **9** Nyasaland *lake:* **5** Nyasa
6 Malawi *language:* **7** English
8 Chichewa *monetary unit:* **6** kwacha
neighbor: **6** Zambia **8** Tanzania
10 Mozambique *river:* **5** Shire

Malaysia *capital:* **11** Kuala Lumpur *city:*
4 Ipoh **6** Penang **11** Johor Baharu
island: **6** Borneo *monetary unit:* **7** ringgit
neighbor: **8** Thailand **9** Indonesia *peninsula:* **5** Malay *sea:* **10** South China *strait:*
7 Malacca

malcontent 5 rebel **6** griper, grouch,
unruly **8** agitator, factious, frondeur,
grumbler, mutinous, restless **9** alienated **10** bellyacher, complainer, rebellious **11** disaffected, disgruntled, disobedient, ungratified **12** contumacious,
dissatisfied

mal de mer 6 nausea **8** vomiting **10** queasiness **11** seasickness

Maldives *capital:* **4** Male *language:*
6 Divehi *monetary unit:* **7** rufiyaa

male 3 guy, tom **4** gent **5** macho, manly
6 manful, virile **7** manlike **9** masculine,
staminate

malediction 4 jinx, oath **5** curse **7** malison **8** anathema **10** execration **11** imprecation

malefactor 5 felon, knave, rogue **6** sinner **8** criminal, evildoer, offender **9** miscreant, reprobate, scoundrel, wrongdoer **10** blackguard, lawbreaker

maleficent 4 evil, vile **5** toxic **6** malign,
sinful, wicked **7** baleful, baneful, beastly, harmful, noxious, vicious
8 damnable, sinister, virulent **9** execrable, injurious, nefarious, repugnant
10 pernicious, villainous **11** destructive

malevolence 4 evil **5** spite **6** grudge, malice, spleen **7** ill will **9** hostility, malignity **12** spitefulness **13** maliciousness

malevolent 4 evil **6** malign, wicked
7 baleful, hateful, hurtful, vicious **8** sinister, spiteful, venomous **9** injurious,
malicious, malignant, poisonous

malfunction 6 glitch 7 misfire

Mali *capital:* 6 Bamako *city:* 5 Mopti, Ségou 7 Sikasso 8 Timbuktu 10 Tombouctou *desert:* 6 Sahara *former name:* 11 French Sudan *language:* 6 French *monetary unit:* 5 franc *neighbor:* 5 Niger 6 Guinea 7 Algeria, Senegal 10 Ivory Coast, Mauritania 11 Burkina Faso *river:* 5 Niger

malice 4 bile, hate 5 spite, venom 6 animus, enmity, grudge, hatred, poison, spleen 7 ill will 8 meanness 9 animosity, antipathy 10 bitterness, resentment 11 hatefulness, malevolence 12 spitefulness 13 invidiousness

malicious 4 evil, mean 5 nasty, petty 6 wicked 7 baneful, hateful, heinous, jealous 8 spiteful, vengeful, venomous, virulent 9 poisonous, poison-pen, rancorous 10 malevolent

maliciousness see MALEVOLENCE

malign 4 evil, soil 5 abuse, decry, libel, smear, stain, sully, taint 6 befoul, defame, defile, revile, smirch, vilify, wicked 7 asperse, baleful, baneful, blacken, detract, hateful, hostile, noxious, slander, tarnish, traduce, vicious 8 besmirch, derogate, inimical, sinister, spiteful, tear down, virulent 9 denigrate, disparage, injurious, rancorous 10 calumniate, depreciate, maleficent, malevolent, pernicious, scandalize, vituperate 11 deleterious, opprobriate 12 antagonistic, antipathetic

malignant 4 evil 5 fatal 6 deadly, lethal, wicked 7 baleful, hateful, vicious 8 devilish, fiendish, spiteful 9 injurious, rancorous 10 diabolical, malevolent

malison 5 curse 8 anathema 11 commination, imprecation, malediction

mall 4 lane 5 alley, plaza, strip 7 passage 9 concourse, esplanade, promenade 10 passageway 11 median strip

malleable 6 pliant, supple 7 ductile, plastic, pliable 8 flexible 9 adaptable

mallet 6 hammer

malodorous 4 foul, gamy, rank 5 fetid, fuggy, funky, fusty, musty, stale 6 frowsy, putrid, rancid, rotten, smelly, stinky 7 noisome, noxious, reeking, spoiled 8 mephitic, stinking 9 offensive 10 nauseating 11 ill-smelling 12 pestilential

Malta *capital:* 8 Valletta *city:* 5 Qormi 10 Birkirkara *island:* 4 Gozo 6 Comino *language:* 6 French 7 Maltese *monetary unit:* 4 lira *sea:* 13 Mediterranean

Maltese Falcon, The *actor:* 5 Astor (Mary), Lorre (Peter) 6 Bogart (Humphrey) 11 Greenstreet (Sydney) *author:* 7 Hammett (Dashiell) *detective:* 5 Spade (Sam) *director:* 6 Huston (John)

maltreat 5 abuse 6 ill-use, misuse, molest

mama 4 dame, doll, wife 5 broad, femme, hussy, madam, woman 6 matron, mother

Mamet play 7 Oleanna 14 Boston Marriage 15 American Buffalo 17 Glengarry Glen Ross

mammal 3 ass 5 camel, hippo, hyrax 6 alpaca, colugo, dassie, rabbit 7 primate 8 elephant 12 hippopotamus *African:* 5 okapi, zebra 8 aardvark, aardwolf *aquatic:* 6 dugong, sea cow 7 cowfish, manatee, narwhal, platypi (plural) 8 cetacean, platypus, porpoise, sirenian *arboreal:* 5 lemur 6 sifaka 7 opossum 8 kinkajou *Australian:* 5 koala 8 kangaroo *burrowing:* 8 starnose *carnivorous:* 3 cat, dog, fox 4 bear, lion, mink, seal, wolf 5 genet, hyena, otter, panda, ratel, sable, tiger 6 badger, grison, marten, racoon, walrus 7 linsang, polecat, raccoon 8 mongoose *catlike:* 5 civet *doglike:* 6 jackal *extinct:* 6 quagga 8 mastodon, stegodon *feline:* 4 lion 5 tiger, tigon 6 ocelot, tiglon 7 leopard, lioness, tigress *flying:* 3 bat *gnawing:* 3 rat 6 beaver, rodent 8 squirrel *goatlike:* 4 tahr 5 takin *harelike:* 5 hyrax 7 hyraces (plural) *hoofed:* 3 cow, pig 4 deer, goat, oxen (plural) 5 camel, sheep, tapir 6 alpaca 7 peccary 8 ruminant, ungulate 12 hippopotamus *horned:* 4 goat *insect-eating:* 4 mole 5 shrew 6 tenrec 8 hedgehog *long-necked:* 7 giraffe *marine:* 4 orca, seal 6 walrus 7 dolphin, grampus *marsupial:* 9 bandicoot *nocturnal:* 6 wombat *raccoon-like:* 10 cacomistle *ruminant:* 4 deer 5 llama, moose, sheep 6 vicuña *small:* 4 pika 8 hedgehog, hedgepig *South American:* 7 guanaco *toothless:* 5 sloth 8 edentate, pangolin 9 armadillo *tropical:* 5 coati *unweaned:* 8 suckling *with flippers:* 8 pinniped *wolflike:* 5 hyena

mammon 4 pelf 5 lucre 6 riches, wealth 8 treasure 9 abundance, affluence 10 prosperity 11 possessions

mammoth 4 huge, vast 5 giant, jumbo 6 mighty 7 immense, massive, monster, titanic 8 colossal, enormous, gigantic 9 leviathan, monstrous 10 gargantuan, mastodonic, monumental 11 elephantine

man 3 guy 4 buck, chap, cuss, dude, gent 5 being, bloke 6 fellow, mister, mortal, person 7 husband 8 creature, paramour 9 boyfriend, mortality, personage 10 individual 11 Homo sapiens *castrated:* 6 eunuch *combining form:*

4 andr 5 andro, homin 6 homini *French:*
5 homme *Italian:* 4 uomo *Latin:* 3 vir
4 homo *old:* 6 codger, geezer *Spanish:*
6 hombre *Yiddish:* 6 mensch *young:*
3 boy, lad 6 shaver 9 stripling

manage 3 run 4 cope, fare, head, keep
5 get by, get on, guide, shift 6 afford,
direct, effect, govern, handle 7 achieve,
carry on, conduct, control, execute,
finagle, operate, oversee, succeed
8 carry out, contrive, cope with, deal
with, dominate, engineer, get along,
maintain 9 cultivate, supervise
10 accomplish, administer, bring about
11 superintend

manageable 6 docile 8 amenable, bearable, biddable, passable 9 agreeable,
compliant, endurable, tractable
10 responsive 11 cooperative, supportable, sustainable 13 accommodating

management 4 care 5 brass 6 charge
7 conduct, control, running 8 guidance,
handling 9 direction, oversight 10 con-
ducting 11 front office, supervising,
supervision

manager 4 boss, exec 6 gerent 7 handler,
officer 8 director, official, overseer,
producer 9 conductor, executive
10 impresario, supervisor 13 administrator *museum:* 7 curator

mañana 7 someday 8 sometime, tomorrow

Man and Superman author: 4 Shaw
(George Bernard)

Manassas battle 7 Bull Run

Manasseh, Manasses *brother:* 7 Ephraim
father: 6 Hashum, Joseph 8 Hezekiah
10 Pahathmoab *grandfather:* 5 Jacob
grandson: 6 Gilead *mother:* 7 Asenath
son: 6 Machir

man-at-arms 7 fighter, soldier, warrior
10 serviceman

Mandalay author 7 Kipling (Rudyard)

mandarin 5 elder 6 orange 8 official
9 tangerine 10 bureaucrat, panjandrum

mandate 4 fiat, word 5 edict, order,
ukase 6 behest, charge, decree 7 bidding, command, dictate 9 authority,
directive 10 imperative, injunction
13 authorization

mandatory 6 forced 7 binding 8 required
9 de rigueur, necessary, requisite
10 compulsory, imperative, obligatory
11 involuntary

mandible 3 jaw 8 lower jaw

man-eater 4 lion, ogre 5 shark, tiger
8 cannibal 13 mackerel shark

Manette's daughter 5 Lucie

maneuver 3 ply 4 move, plan, plot, ploy,
step 5 feint, trick, wield 6 design,
device, gambit, handle, jockey, scheme,

tactic, wangle 7 exploit, finagle, finesse
8 artifice, démarche, engineer, exercise,
intrigue, movement, navigate 9 machinate, procedure, stratagem 10 manipulate, proceeding, subterfuge 11 contrivance, machination 12 manipulation

maneuvering room 8 latitude

Man for All Seasons, A *author:* 4 Bolt
(Robert) *subject:* 4 More (Thomas)

manganese *ore:* 10 pyrolusite

manger 4 rack 6 cratch, feeder, trough

mangle 3 mar 4 iron, maim, maul
5 press 6 damage, deface, deform,
impair, injure 7 butcher, contort, distort 8 lacerate, mutilate 9 disfigure

mangy 5 seedy 6 ragtag, shabby
7 scruffy, squalid 8 decrepit, tattered
9 moth-eaten 10 down-at-heel, threadbare

manhandle 5 abuse 6 batter 7 rough up
8 maltreat, mistreat 10 push around,
slap around

Manhattan *building:* 11 Empire State *district:* 4 Soho 6 Harlem 7 Chelsea,
Tribeca *entertainment district:* 11 Times
Square *financial district:* 10 Wall Street
museum: 7 Whitney 10 Guggenheim
12 Metropolitan *opera house:* 12 Metropolitan *purchaser:* 6 Minuit (Peter)
river: 4 East 6 Hudson *school:* 3 NYU
8 Columbia 9 Juilliard

mania 4 rage, zeal 5 craze, fancy 6 frenzy, lunacy 7 madness, passion 8 fixation, idée fixe, insanity 9 cacoëthes,
obsession 10 compulsion, enthusiasm
11 infatuation

maniac 3 bug, nut 4 loon 5 fiend, freak
6 madman, psycho, zealot 7 fanatic,
lunatic, nutcase 8 crackpot 9 bedlamite
10 enthusiast

manifest 4 show 5 clear, overt, plain,
shown, utter, voice 6 appear, embody,
evince, expose, patent, reveal 7 display,
evident, evinced, exhibit, express,
invoice, obvious, visible 8 apparent,
distinct, evidence, palpable, proclaim,
revealed 9 evidenced, incarnate, objectify, prominent 10 illustrate, noticeable,
observable 11 demonstrate, exteriorize,
externalize, perceptible, unambiguous

manifestation 4 show, sign 5 proof 7 display, symptom 8 epiphany 10 appearance, revelation

manifesto 4 fiat, rule, writ 5 credo,
creed, edict, ukase 6 decree, dictum,
gospel, notice, policy, ruling 7 mandate, statute 8 doctrine, document,
platform 9 affidavit, directive, statement, testament, testimony, ultimatum
10 deposition, indictment, injunction,
regulation, resolution 11 declaration

12 announcement, denunciation, notification, proclamation 13 pronouncement

manifold 7 diverse, various 8 compound, multiple, multiply, numerous 9 multiform, multiplex 10 multiphase 12 multifarious

manikin 4 runt 5 dummy, dwarf, gnome, model, pygmy 6 midget, peewee 8 Tom Thumb 10 homunculus

Manila *founder:* 7 Legazpi (Miguel López de) *site:* 11 Phillipines *victor:* 5 Dewey (George)

manipulate 3 ply, rig 4 play 5 steer, swing, wield 6 direct, doctor, handle, jockey, juggle, manage 7 beguile, conduct, control, exploit, finagle, finesse, massage 8 engineer, maneuver 9 machinate 10 tamper with

Man, Isle of *capital:* 7 Douglas *cat:* 4 Manx *possession of:* 7 Britain *sea:* 5 Irish

Manitoba *capital:* 8 Winnipeg *lake:* 8 Winnipeg 12 Winnipegosis *mountain:* 5 Baldy *provincial flower:* 13 prairie crocus *river:* 6 Nelson 9 Churchill

mankind 6 humans, people 8 humanity 11 Homo sapiens

manlike 4 male 6 virile 8 hominoid, humanoid 9 masculine 10 anthropoid

manly 4 male 5 macho 6 virile 9 masculine

man-made 9 synthetic 10 artificial, factitious *object:* 8 artefact, artifact

Mann *character* 6 Joseph 10 Aschenbach (Gustav von), Felix Krull 11 Hans Castorp, Tonio Kröger

manner 3 air, use, way 4 form, kind, look, mien, mode, sort, vein, wont 5 habit, modus, style, usage 6 aspect, custom, method 7 bearing, conduct, fashion, p's and q's 8 behavior, demeanor, habitude, practice, presence 9 demeanour, etiquette, technique 10 consuetude, deportment 11 affectation, comportment, peculiarity 12 idiosyncrasy

mannered 7 stilted 8 affected 10 artificial 13 self-conscious

mannerism 3 tic 4 pose 5 quirk 10 preciosity 11 affectation, peculiarity, singularity 12 eccentricity, idiosyncrasy 13 artificiality

mannerless 4 rude 6 coarse 7 boorish, ill-bred, uncivil, uncouth 8 impolite 12 discourteous

mannerly 5 civil 6 polite 7 genteel, refined 8 decorous, gracious, well-bred 9 civilized, courteous 10 respectful

Manon *composer* 8 Massenet (Jules)

Manon Lescaut *author:* 7 Prévost (Abbé)

composer: 7 Puccini (Giacomo) 8 Massenet (Jules) *lover:* 9 des Grieux

manor 5 villa 6 estate, quinta 7 château, demesne 12 landed estate

manservant 5 valet 6 butler

mansion 4 hall 5 villa 6 palace 7 château

manslayer 6 killer 8 homicide, murderer

manta 3 ray 5 cloak, cloth, shawl 7 blanket

manteau 4 coat, robe, wrap 5 cloak 6 capote, mantle, tabard

mantic 5 vatic 7 Delphic, fatidic 8 Delphian, oracular 9 prophetic, sibylline, vaticinal 10 divinatory

mantilla 4 cape, wrap 5 cloak, fichu, scarf, shawl

mantle 4 cope, glow, pink, robe, rose 5 blush, cloak, color, cover, flush, rouge 6 capote, casing, pinken, redden 7 crimson

man-to-man 4 open 5 frank, plain 6 candid, direct, honest 10 forthright, unreserved 11 openhearted

mantra 5 chant, motto 6 prayer, slogan 9 watchword 10 invocation 11 incantation

manual 4 text 5 guide 6 primer 8 Baedeker, handbook, hornbook, textbook 9 guidebook, vade mecum 10 compendium 11 abecedarium, enchiridion *religious:* 9 catechism *worker:* 6 menial 7 laborer

manufacture 4 form, make 6 create, invent 7 fashion, produce 8 assemble 9 fabricate 11 put together

manumit 4 free 6 unbind 7 release, set free, unchain 8 liberate 9 unshackle 10 emancipate

manure 4 dung 6 ordure 7 excreta 9 excrement 10 fertilizer

manuscript 4 hand 6 scrawl 8 longhand 9 autograph 10 penmanship 11 calligraphy, handwriting *ancient:* 5 codex 6 scroll 7 codices (plural) *red part:* 6 rubric

Man Without a Country, The *author:* 4 Hale (Edward Everett) *character:* 5 Nolan

many 5 scads 6 divers, legion, myriad, sundry 7 copious, diverse, umpteen, various 8 abundant, manifold, multiple, numerous 9 abounding, bounteous, bountiful, countless, multitude, plentiful 12 multifarious 13 multitudinous *combining form:* 4 poly 5 multi, pluri

many-sided 7 diverse 8 all-round, talented 9 all-around, versatile 10 variegated 11 diversified 12 multifaceted, multifarious 13 comprehensive

Mao's successor 3 Hua (Guofeng, Kuofeng) 4 Deng (Xiaoping), Teng (Hsiao-p'ing)

map 4 plan, plat 5 chart, draft, globe, graph 6 design, lay out, set out, sketch, survey 7 arrange, diagram, drawing, outline, tracing 9 delineate *collection:* 5 atlas *line:* 6 isobar 7 contour, isogram, isohyet 8 isogloss, isogonic, isopleth, isotherm *maker:* 12 cartographer *making:* 11 cartography

maple *genus:* 4 Acer *product:* 5 syrup *type:* 3 red 5 sugar 8 box elder

map projection 5 conic 8 Mercator 9 polyconic 10 sinusoidal 12 orthographic 13 stereographic

maquillage 6 makeup

mar 4 ding, harm, hurt, scar, warp 5 spoil, stain 6 bruise, damage, deface, deform, impair, injure 7 blemish, scratch, tarnish, vitiate 9 disfigure

marabou 5 stork

Marat/Sade author 5 Weiss (Peter)

Marat, Jean-Paul *colleague:* 6 Danton (Georges) 11 Robespierre (Maximilien) *slayer:* 6 Corday (Charlotte)

maraud 4 loot, raid, sack 5 foray, harry 6 harass, ravage, ravish 7 despoil, pillage, plunder, ransack

marauder 6 bandit, pirate 7 brigand, spoiler, wrecker 9 buccaneer, desperado 10 freebooter

marble 3 mib, mig, taw 4 immy, migg 5 agate, aggie, alley, rance 6 blotch, miggle, mottle, streak 7 cipolin, glassie, steelie 9 limestone

marbled 6 veined 7 dappled, flecked, mottled 8 speckled, streaked

Marble Faun, The *author:* 9 Hawthorne (Nathaniel) *character:* 5 Hilda 6 Kenyon, Miriam 9 Donatello *setting:* 4 Rome

marcel 4 wave

march 3 hem, rim 4 abut, file, line 5 skirt 6 adjoin, border, parade 7 advance, headway, proceed 8 anabasis, boundary, frontier, outlands, progress, traverse 9 periphery 10 borderland

March *date:* 4 ides *mother:* 6 Marmee *sisters:* 3 Amy, Meg 4 Beth

March Hare creator 7 Carroll (Lewis)

March King 5 Sousa (John Philip)

Mardi Gras 8 carnival 10 Fat Tuesday *city:* 10 New Orleans

Marduk *city:* 7 Babylon *consort:* 8 Zarbanit, Zarpanit *victim:* 5 Kingu 6 Tiamat

mare 3 sea 5 horse 6 equine

mare's nest 3 con, din 4 hoax, scam 5 babel, cheat, fraud, put-on, spoof 6 bedlam, clamor, hubbub, humbug, racket, ruckus, tumult, uproar 7 swin-

dle, turmoil 8 brouhaha, flimflam, illusion 9 confusion, imposture 10 hullabaloo 11 pandemonium

margarine 4 oleo

margin 3 hem, rim 4 brim, edge, join, line, play, room, side 5 bound, brink, frame, scope, shore, skirt, verge 6 border, fringe, leeway 7 minimum, outline, selvage 8 boundary, latitude, selvedge, surround, trimming 9 elbowroom, perimeter, periphery 13 circumference *tiny:* 4 hair

marginal 5 minor 7 limited, minimal 9 bordering 10 borderline, negligible, peripheral, subsidiary 13 insignificant

Marguerite's lover 5 Faust

Maria ___ 5 Elena 7 Stuarda

Marianas *discoverer:* 8 Magellan (Ferdinand) *island:* 4 Guam, Rota 5 Pagan 6 Guguan, Saipan, Tinian 7 Agrihan, Aguijan

marijuana 3 pot 4 hash, hemp, weed 5 bhang, grass 6 reefer 7 hashish 8 cannabis

marina 4 dock, pier, quay 5 basin, berth, wharf 8 boatyard

marinate 4 soak 5 steep 6 drench, pickle 7 immerse 8 macerate

marine 5 naval 7 abyssal, aquatic, deep-sea, oceanic, pelagic 8 nautical, seagoing 9 seafaring, thalassic 10 oceangoing 12 hydrographic 13 oceanographic *crustacean:* 6 shrimp 7 lobster 8 barnacle *deposit:* 5 coral *plant:* 4 kelp, nori 5 dulse 6 wakame 7 seaweed

mariner 3 gob, tar 4 jack, salt, swab 5 limey 6 hearty, rating, sailor, sea dog, seaman 7 jack-tar, old salt, swabbie 8 seafarer 9 sailorman, shellback, tarpaulin 10 bluejacket

marital 6 wedded 7 married, nuptial, spousal 8 conjugal, hymeneal 9 connubial

maritime 7 oceanic, pelagic 8 nautical 9 thalassic 12 navigational

mark 3 aim, jot, sap 4 butt, dupe, fool, goal, gull, heed, look, nick, note, pick, show, sign, view 5 blaze, bound, brand, chart, chump, elect, grade, label, notch, stamp, token, trait 6 behold, choose, denote, evince, lay off, notice, object, opt for, rating, record, select, sucker, target, victim, virtue 7 betoken, delimit, discern, exhibit, fall guy, feature, gudgeon, indicia, initial, measure, observe, qualify, scratch, signify, symptom 8 function, indicate, perceive, register 9 attribute, character, designate, objective, single out 10 indication 11 differentia, distinction, distinguish 12 characterize *distinctive:* 7 indicia 8 indicium *identifying:* 4 logo, seal 6 emblem, signet, symbol 8 colophon, logotype *of insertion:* 5 caret *of omission:* 8 ellipsis 10 apostrophe *over a vowel:* 5 breve 6 accent, macron *over n:* 5 tilde *punctuation:* 4 dash 5 brace, colon, comma, slant, slash 6 hyphen, period 7 bracket, solidus 9 backslash, guillemet, semicolon 10 apostrophe *under a letter:* 7 cedilla

Mark 6 Gospel *cousin:* 8 Barnabas *mother:* 4 Mary

mark down 3 cut 4 pare 5 shave, slash 6 reduce 7 devalue 8 discount 9 devaluate 10 depreciate, undervalue

marked 5 noted 6 patent, signal 7 evident, notable, obvious, pointed, salient 8 distinct, manifest, striking 9 arresting, prominent 10 noticeable, remarkable 11 conspicuous, outstanding 12 considerable 13 distinguished *man:* 4 Cain

market 4 fair, mall, sell, shop, vend 5 store 6 bazaar, outlet, retail 8 emporium, exchange, showroom 9 advertise, traffic in, wholesale 11 merchandise *kind:* 4 flea 5 money, stock

marketable 5 sound 7 salable 8 vendible 10 commercial

marketplace 4 mall, souk 5 agora 6 bazaar, rialto 8 emporium

marksman 4 shot 7 deadeye, shooter 12 sharpshooter

marl 4 clay, silt

marlin 8 billfish 9 spearfish

Marlowe play 8 Edward II 9 Dr. Faustus 10 Jew of Malta (The) 11 Tamburlaine 13 Doctor Faustus

marmot 6 rodent 9 woodchuck 10 prairie dog

maroon 3 red 6 claret, desert, strand 7 abandon, crimson, forsake, isolate, outcast 8 burgundy, castaway

Marquand character 4 Gray (Charles), Moto (Mr.) 5 Apley (George), Wayde (Willis) 6 Pulham (H.M.) 7 Goodwin (Melville)

Marquis, Don *cat:* 9 Mehitabel *cockroach:* 5 Archy

marriage 5 match, union 6 bridal 7 nuptial, spousal, wedding, wedlock 8 coupling, espousal, monogamy, nuptials, polygamy 9 matrimony 11 conjugality 12 connubiality *combining form:* 4 gamy 6 gamous *notice:* 5 banns *outside a group:* 7 exogamy *within a group:* 8 endogamy

marriageable 6 nubile 8 eligible

marriage broker 9 go-between 10 matchmaker

Marriage of Figaro composer 6 Mozart (Wolfgang Amadeus)

marrow 4 core, meat, pith, soul 5 heart, stuff 6 kernel 7 essence 12 quintessence

marry 3 tie, wed 4 join, link, mate, wive, yoke 5 hitch, merge, unite 6 couple, splice, spouse 7 combine, conjoin, espouse 9 conjugate

Mars 4 Ares 6 planet *lover:* 5 Venus *mission:* 6 Viking 7 Mariner 10 Pathfinder *moon:* 6 Deimos, Phobos *relating to:* 7 martian (see also ARES)

Marseillaise composer 13 Rouget de Lisle (Claude-Joseph)

marsh 3 bog, fen 4 mire, ooze, quag 5 bayou, glade, swale, swamp 6 morass, muskeg, slough 7 wetland 8 quagmire 9 swampland

marshal 5 align, array, guide, order, rally, usher 6 deploy, direct, escort, muster 7 arrange, officer, round up 8 assemble, mobilize, organize, shepherd 9 methodize, systemize

Marshall Islands *atoll:* 6 Bikini 8 Enewetak 9 Kwajalein *capital:* 6 Majuro *ethnic group:* 11 Micronesian *island chain:* 5 Ralik, Ratak 6 Sunset 7 Sunrise *language:* 7 English 11 Marshallese *monetary unit:* 6 dollar

marsupial 5 koala 6 possum, wombat 7 opossum 8 kangaroo 9 bandicoot

marten 6 fisher, weasel

Martha *brother:* 7 Lazarus *sister:* 4 Mary

martial 7 warlike 8 militant, military, spirited 9 bellicose, combative, soldierly 11 belligerent 12 militaristic

martial art 4 judo 5 kendo 6 aikido, karate, kung fu, tai chi 7 shaolin 8 capoeira, jiujitsu 9 tae kwon do 11 tai chi chuan *school:* 4 dojo

Martial's forte 7 epigram

Martin Chuzzlewit author 7 Dickens (Charles)

Martinique *capital:* 12 Fort-de-France *department of:* 6 France *discoverer:* 8 Columbus (Christopher) *island group:* 8 Windward *location:* 10 West Indies *neighbor:* 8 Dominica 10 Saint Lucia *volcano:* 5 Pelée

martyr 4 Paul, rack 5 Agnes, Alban, James, Peter, saint, wring 6 George, harrow, Justin 7 afflict, agonize, Clement, crucify, Cyprian, Stephen, torment, torture 8 Ignatius, Lawrence, Polycarp, sufferer 9 Joan of Arc, Sebastian 10 excruciate, Thomas More *Protestant:* 6 Ridley (Nicholas) 7 Cranmer (Thomas), Latimer (Hugh)

marvel 4 gape 6 wonder 7 miracle, portent, prodigy, stunner 9 curiosity, sensation 10 phenomenon 12 astonishment

marvelous 5 super, swell 6 divine 7 amazing, awesome, ripping 8 glorious, striking, stunning, superior, terrific, wondrous 9 excellent, wonderful 10 astounding, incredible, miraculous, phenomenal, prodigious, remarkable, staggering, stupendous, surprising 11 astonishing, exceptional, sensational, spectacular 12 awe-inspiring, supernatural 13 extraordinary

Marx brother 5 Chico, Harpo, Zeppo 7 Groucho

Marxist 9 socialist 9 communist

Marx, Karl *book:* 7 Kapital (Das) *collaborator:* 6 Engels (Friedrich)

Mary *husband:* 6 Clopas, Joseph 8 Alphaeus *kinswoman:* 9 Elisabeth *son:* 4 Mark 5 James, Jesus

Maryland *bay:* 10 Chesapeake *capital:* 9 Annapolis *city:* 9 Baltimore, Frederick *college, university:* 6 Towson 7 Goucher 9 Annapolis 12 Johns Hopkins 12 Naval Academy (U.S.) *fort:* 7 McHenry *nickname:* 7 Old Line (State) *river:* 7 Potomac 8 Patuxent *state bird:* 15 Baltimore oriole *state flower:* 14 black-eyed Susan *state tree:* 8 white oak

mascot 4 juju 5 charm 6 amulet, fetish, symbol 8 talisman

masculine 4 male 5 macho, manly 6 manful, virile 7 manlike

masculinity 8 machismo, virility 9 manliness

mash 4 pulp 5 crush, smash 6 squish 8 macerate 9 pulverize

masher 4 wolf 5 flirt 6 chaser 7 Don Juan, seducer 8 Casanova 9 ladies' man, womanizer 10 lady-killer 11 philanderer

mash note 10 billet-doux, love letter

mask 4 hide, pose, sham, veil 5 cover, front, guard, guise, visor 6 facade, screen, vizard 7 dress up, frisket, pretext 8 coloring, disguise, pretense 9 dissemble, semblance 10 appearance, camouflage, false front, simulation 11 dissimulate 13 dissimulation

masonry 9 brickwork, stonework *in a frame:* 7 nogging

masquerade 4 pose 6 facade 7 costume, posture 8 carnival, disguise 10 camouflage, masked ball 11 costume ball

mass 3 lot, sum, wad 4 bank, body, bulk, clot, core, glob, heap, hill, lump, pack, peck, pile 5 clump, group, mound 6 corpus, volume 7 expanse, globule, wadding 8 assemble 9 aggregate, great deal, stockpile, substance 11 aggregation 12 conglomerate *for the dead:* 7 requiem *of individuals:* 3 mob 4 host 5 crowd, crush, flock, horde, swarm 6 throng 12 congregation 13 agglomeration *part:* 6 proper 8 ordinary

Massachusetts *cape:* 3 Ann, Cod *capital:*

6 Boston *city:* 6 Lowell, Quincy 9 Cambridge, Worcester 10 New Bedford 11 Springfield *college, university:* 3 MIT 5 Clark, Smith, Tufts 6 Boston 7 Amherst, Berklee, Harvard 8 Brandeis, Williams 9 Hampshire, Radcliffe, Wellesley 12 Mount Holyoke, Northeastern *island:* 9 Nantucket 15 Martha's Vineyard *mountain, range:* 8 Greylock 9 Berkshire *nickname:* 3 Bay (State) 9 Old Colony (State) *river:* 11 Connecticut *state bird:* 9 chickadee *state flower:* 9 mayflower *state tree:* 3 elm (American)

massacre 4 kill 6 mangle, murder, pogrom 7 butcher, carnage 8 butchery, decimate, genocide, mangling, mutilate 9 bloodbath, bloodshed, slaughter 10 annihilate, blood purge, decimation, mutilation 11 exterminate 12 annihilation

massage 3 rub 5 knead 7 flatter, rubdown 8 blandish 10 manipulate

Massenet opera 5 Le Cid, Manon, Sapho, Thaïs 7 Werther

massive 4 huge, vast 5 bulky, giant, jumbo, solid 6 mighty 7 hulking, immense, mammoth, weighty 8 colossal, cumbrous, enormous, gigantic, towering 9 humongous, monstrous 10 gargantuan, monumental, prodigious, stupendous, tremendous 11 elephantine, mountainous

master 4 best, boss, guru, head, lick, rule, tame 5 adept, bwana, chief, crack, learn, ruler, sahib, tutor 6 artist, expert, genius, honcho, leader, subdue, victor 7 captain, conquer, headman, maestro, padrone, prevail, skilled, triumph 8 dominant, dominate, employer, governor, overcome, overlord, overseer, regulate, skeleton, skillful, superior, surmount, virtuoso 9 authority, chieftain, conqueror, dominator, paramount, principal, sovereign 10 proficient 11 predominant

masterful 4 deft 5 adept, bossy 6 adroit, expert 7 skilled 8 despotic, skillful 9 imperious 10 autocratic, high-handed, proficient, tyrannical 11 dictatorial, domineering, magisterial, overbearing 13 authoritarian, authoritative, high-and-mighty

masterly 5 adept, crack 6 adroit, expert 7 skilled 8 skillful 9 dexterous 10 proficient 11 crackerjack 12 accomplished

Master of Ballantrae, The 6 Durrie *author:* 9 Stevenson (Robert Louis)

masterpiece 7 classic 10 magnum opus 11 chef d'oeuvre, tour de force

mastery 5 knack, skill 7 ability, com-

mand, control, know-how, prowess
8 dominion 9 authority, expertise
10 ascendancy, domination, expertness,
virtuosity 11 proficiency, superiority

masticate 4 chaw, chew, pulp 5 champ,
chomp, crush, munch 6 crunch
7 scrunch 8 macerate, ruminate
9 break down

mat 3 rug 4 felt 6 border, carpet

matador 6 torero 8 toreador 11 bullfighter *adjunct:* 6 muleta *move:* 4 pase
5 faena 8 veronica

Mata Hari 3 spy

match 3 pit 4 bout, game, like, meet,
peer, suit, twin 5 array, equal, liken,
rival, touch, union 6 double, equate,
oppose 7 compare, compeer, contest,
counter, opposer, paragon, play off
8 alliance, analogue, marriage, opponent, parallel 9 adversary, correlate,
duplicate, encounter, measure up, partake of 10 antagonist, complement,
coordinate, engagement, equivalent,
reciprocal, supplement, tournament
11 counterpart 12 correspond to 13 correspondent, harmonize with *a bet:* 3 see
friction: 7 lucifer

matchless 6 unique 7 supreme 8 peerless, singular 9 nonpareil, unequaled,
unrivaled 10 inimitable 12 incomparable, unparalleled

matchmaker see MARRIAGE BROKER

mate 3 pal, tie, wed 4 chum, pair, twin
5 amigo, breed, buddy, crony, equal,
hitch, marry 6 cohort, couple, double,
fellow, friend, helper, splice, spouse
7 compeer, comrade, consort, partner
8 confrere, sidekick 9 associate, companion, copartner, duplicate, procreate
10 complement, equivalent, reciprocal
11 concomitant

maté 3 tea 5 holly 8 beverage

mater 3 mom, mum 6 mother 9 matriarch

___ **mater** 4 alma

material 4 real, true 5 cloth, stuff 6 actual, fabric, matter, object 7 earthly, element, germane, worldly 8 apposite, palpable, physical, relevant, sensible,
tangible 9 component, corporeal,
equipment, essential, important, objective, pertinent, substance 10 applicable,
individual, ingredient, meaningful,
phenomenal 11 appreciable, constituent, fundamental, perceptible, significant, substantial 12 considerable
13 consequential *building:* 5 adobe,
brick 6 stucco 7 lagging, plaster, ply-
wood, shingle 8 concrete

materialistic 7 secular, worldly
11 acquisitive

materialize 4 loom, rise 5 arise, issue,
reify 6 appear, embody, emerge, evolve,
show up, typify 7 develop, surface
8 manifest 9 come about, incarnate,
objectify, take shape 11 exteriorize
12 substantiate

matériel 4 gear 5 stock 8 supplies 9 apparatus, equipment, machinery 10 provisions 13 accouterments, accoutrements,
paraphernalia

maternal 8 motherly

matey 5 pally, tight 6 clubby 7 affable
8 amicable, familiar, friendly, intimate,
sociable 9 congenial

mathematician *American:* 5 Wiles
(Andrew) 6 Peirce (Charles S.), Veblen
(Oswald), Wiener (Norbert) *Austrian:*
5 Gödel (Kurt) *British:* 6 Stokes
(George) *Dutch:* 7 Huygens (Christiaan)
English: 6 Newton (Isaac), Taylor
(Brook), Turing (Alan), Wallis (John)
7 Pearson (Karl), Russell (Bertrand)
8 Hamilton (James Rowan) 9 Sylvester
(James Joseph), Whitehead (Alfred
North, Henry) *French:* 5 Borel (Emile),
Comte (Auguste), Viète (François)
6 Galois (Evariste), Pascal (Blaise),
Picard (Charles-Emile) 7 Fourier (Jean-
Baptiste), Laplace (Marquis de),
Vernier (Pierre) 8 Painlevé (Paul), Poin-
caré (Jules-Henri) 9 Descartes (René)
German: 5 Gauss (Carl), Wolff (Freiherr
von) 6 Staudt (Karl von) 7 Leibniz
(Gottfried Wilhelm), Riemann (Georg)
11 Weierstrass (Karl) *Greek:* 6 Euclid
10 Archimedes, Pythagoras *Hungarian:*
5 Erdos (Paul) *Italian:* 8 Volterra (Vito)
10 Torricelli (Evangelista) *Norwegian:*
7 Stormer (Fredrik) *Russian:*
11 Lobachevsky (Nikolay) *Scottish:*
4 Tait (Peter) 6 Napier (John) 8 Stirling
(James) *Swiss:* 5 Euler (Leonhard),
Sturm (Jacques) 7 Steiner (Jakob)

mathematics *branch:* 4 trig 7 algebra
8 calculus, geometry, topology 10 arithmetic, statistics 12 trigonometry *proven
statement in:* 7 theorem

___ **Mather** 6 Cotton 7 Richard
8 Increase

matriarch 4 dame 6 mother 7 dowager
10 grande dame

matriculate 4 join 5 enter 6 enroll, sign
on 8 register

matrimonial 6 bridal, wedded 7 marital,
married, nuptial, spousal 8 conjugal,
hymeneal 9 connubial 11 epithalamic

matrimony 7 wedlock 8 marriage 11 conjugality 12 connubiality

matrix 3 die, net, web 4 grid, mesh
5 array 6 cradle, gangue 7 complex,
network 10 groundmass, truth table

matron 4 dame 7 dowager 8 chaperon 9 chaperone 10 grande dame

Mattathias *father:* 5 Simon 6 Ananos 7 Absalom, Boethus 10 Theophilus *son:* 8 Josephus

matter 4 being, body, core, gist, meat, pith, text 5 being, cause, order, point, sense, stuff, theme, thing, topic, value, weigh 6 affair, amount, burden, entity, import, object 7 concern, signify, subject 8 argument, material 9 grievance, magnitude, substance 11 constituent 12 circumstance

matter-of-fact 3 dry 5 plain, prose, prosy, sober, stoic 6 stolid 7 prosaic 9 impassive, objective, practical, pragmatic, realistic 10 hard-boiled, hardheaded, impersonal, phlegmatic, unaffected 11 cold-blooded, down-to-earth, emotionless 13 unimpassioned, unsentimental

mattress 3 pad 4 sack *case:* 4 tick *fabric:* 7 ticking *straw:* 6 pallet

mature 3 age, due 4 grow, ripe 5 adult, grown, owing, ready, ripen 6 flower, grow up, mellow, season, unpaid 7 advance, blossom, decline, develop, grown-up, overdue, payable, ripened 8 progress 9 developed, full-blown, full-grown 11 full-fledged

maudlin 5 gushy, mushy, silly, sappy, soppy 6 slushy, sticky 7 cloying, gushing, mawkish 8 bathetic 11 sentimental, tear-jerking

Maugham character 4 Kear, Liza 5 Carey, Rosie, Sadie 7 Mildred 8 Ashenden, Craddock 10 Strickland

maul 4 bang, bash, beat, club, drub, flog, whip 5 abuse, flail, pound 6 batter, bruise, buffet, cudgel, hammer, injure, mangle, molest, pummel, sledge, thrash 7 clobber, rough up 8 bludgeon, lambaste, maltreat 9 manhandle

Mauna ___ 3 Kea, Loa

maunder 3 bat, gad 4 rove 5 drift, mooch, range 6 mumble, mutter, ramble, wander 7 blather, digress, traipse 8 divagate

Mauritania *capital:* 10 Nouakchott *desert:* 6 Sahara *language:* 5 Wolof 6 Arabic, Fulani 7 Soninke *monetary unit:* 7 ouguiya *neighbor:* 4 Mali 6 Guinea 7 Senegal 7 Algeria 13 Western Sahara *river:* 7 Senegal

Mauritius *capital:* 9 Port Louis *island group:* 9 Mascarene *language:* 6 Creole 7 English *monetary unit:* 5 rupee

Maurois biographee 4 Hugo (Victor), Sand (George) 5 Byron (Lord), Dumas (Alexandre) 6 Balzac (Honoré de),

Proust (Marcel) 7 Shelley (Percy Bysshe) 8 Disraeli (Benjamin)

mauve 5 lilac 6 purple, violet

maven 3 ace 4 buff, whiz 5 adept, freak, shark 6 addict, expert, master, savant 7 devotee, fanatic, hotshot 8 virtuoso 9 authority 10 enthusiast 11 connoisseur

maverick 5 stray 7 heretic 8 unmarked 9 dissident, unbranded 10 iconoclast 11 independent 13 nonconformist

maw 4 crop 5 chasm, mouth 6 cavity, gullet 7 stomach

mawkish 5 gushy, mushy, sappy, soppy 6 sloppy, slushy, sticky, syrupy 7 cloying, gushing, insipid, maudlin 8 bathetic, romantic 9 schmaltzy, sickening 10 lovey-dovey, nauseating 11 sentimental, tear-jerking

maxilla 3 jaw 4 bone

maxim 3 law, saw 4 rule 5 adage, axiom, gnome, moral, motto, tenet, truth 6 byword, dictum, saying, truism 7 precept, proverb, theorem 8 aphorism, apothegm 9 platitude, prescript, principle 11 commonplace

maximal 3 top 6 utmost 7 highest, largest, supreme, topmost 8 complete, greatest, ultimate 9 paramount

maximum 3 top 6 utmost 7 highest, largest, supreme, topmost 8 extremum, greatest, ultimate 9 paramount

may 5 might, shrub 6 spirea 8 hawthorn

maybe 7 perhaps 8 possibly 9 perchance 11 conceivably, uncertainty

Mayflower *document:* 7 Compact *passengers:* 8 Pilgrims

mayhem 4 maim, riot 5 chaos, havoc 7 cripple, dislimb 8 mutilate 9 dismember 10 mutilation

mayor 11 burgomaster *Chicago (former):* 5 Daley (Richard) *New York (former):* 4 Koch (Edward) 6 Walker (Jimmy) 7 Lindsay (John) 8 Giuliani (Rudolph) 9 La Guardia (Fiorello) *Spanish:* 7 alcalde

Mayor of Casterbridge, The *author:* 5 Hardy (Thomas) *character:* 8 Henchard (Michael)

maze 3 web 4 knot, mesh 5 skein, snarl 6 jungle, morass, tangle 7 confuse, network, perplex 8 bewilder, mishmash 9 labyrinth

Mazel ___ ! 3 tov

McCarthy novel 8 Crossing (The) 16 Cities of the Plain 18 All the Pretty Horses

McCullers, Carson *novel:* 18 Ballad of the Sad Cafe (The) 18 Member of the Wedding (The) 20 Heart Is a Lonely Hunter (The) 23 Reflections in a Golden Eye

McCullough novel 10 Thorn Birds (The)

McMurtry novel 12 Buffalo Girls, Lonesome Dove 14 Horseman Pass By 15 Last Picture Show (The) 17 Terms of Endearment

McTeague author 6 Norris (Frànk)

MD 3 doc 6 doctor, medico 8 sawbones 9 physician

mea culpa 5 error, fault 7 apology 9 admission 10 concession, confession

meadow 3 lea, ley 5 green 7 pasture 9 grassland *historic:* 9 Runnymede *lowlying:* 5 haugh

meadow mushroom 6 agaric

meager 4 bare, bony, lean, mere, thin 5 gaunt, lanky, scant, short, spare 6 paltry, scanty, shabby, skimpy, skinny, slight, sparse 7 angular, minimum, scraggy, scrawny, scrimpy 8 exiguous, rawboned 9 deficient, miserable 10 inadequate 12 insufficient

meal 4 chow, fare, feed, grub 5 board, feast, lunch, snack 6 brunch, dinner, farina, picnic, repast, spread, supper 7 high tea, nooning 8 victuals 9 breakfast, collation, refection *army:* 4 mess

mealy 6 spotty, uneven 11 farinaceous

mean 3 low, mid, par 4 base, fair, hint, norm, poor, want, wish 5 cheap, cruel, imply, lousy, lowly, mingy, petty, rough, small, snide, spell, tight, weigh 6 attest, center, common, denote, design, humble, intend, matter, medial, medium, middle, paltry, scummy, scurvy, shabby, shoddy, sleazy, stingy, unwell 7 average, betoken, connote, express, lowborn, miserly, pitiful, portend, propose, purport, signify, suggest, vicious 8 déclassé, indicate, inferior, mediocre, middling, midpoint, moderate, ordinary, pitiable, plebeian, stand for 9 designate, penurious, represent, symbolize 10 despicable, second-rate 11 closefisted, tightfisted 12 contemptible, intermediary, intermediate

meander 4 roam, rove, turn, wind 5 amble, drift, range, snake, stray, twist 6 ramble, wander 7 traipse, winding 8 vagabond 9 gallivant, labyrinth

meandering 5 snaky 7 sinuous 8 flexuous, tortuous 10 convoluted, serpentine 11 anfractuous

meaning 3 aim 4 gist, pith 5 drift, force, point, sense 6 effect, import, intent 7 essence, message, purport 9 intention, substance 10 definition, denotation, intimation 11 connotation, implication 12 significance 13 signification

meaningful 5 valid 7 pointed, serious, weighty 8 eloquent, material 9 important, momentous 10 expressive 11 sententious, significant, substantial 13 consequential

meaningless 5 empty, inane 6 absurd, futile, hollow 7 trivial 8 nugatory 11 nonsensical 13 insignificant

meanings *diverse:* 8 polysemy *study of:* 9 semantics

means 5 funds, money 6 agency, assets, avenue, income 7 backing, capital 8 finances, holdings, property, reserves 9 apparatus, equipment, resources, substance 10 instrument 11 wherewithal

meantime 7 interim 8 interval

measly 4 poor, puny 5 petty, scant 6 meager, meagre, paltry, scanty 7 pitiful, trivial 8 niggling, pathetic, picayune, piddling, trifling 9 miserable 10 picayunish 13 insignificant

measure 3 bar 4 bill, size, step, test 5 bound, gauge, index, quota, scale, share, shift, weigh 6 amount, bounds, degree, effort, extent, figure, ration, reckon, resort, size up, survey 7 caliper, compute, delimit, mark out, portion, stopgap 8 calliper, estimate, regulate, resource, standard 9 allotment, benchmark, calculate, calibrate, criterion, demarcate, determine, expedient, magnitude, yardstick 10 dimensions, indication, proceeding, proportion, touchstone 11 proposition 13 apportionment *area:* 4 acre 7 hectare *capacity:* 4 gill, peck, pint 5 liter, minim, quart 6 bushel, gallon 8 fluidram 9 fluid dram 10 fluid ounce, milliliter *cloth:* 3 ell *combining form:* 6 metric 8 metrical *depth:* 5 plumb, sound *dry:* 4 peck 6 bushel *electrical:* 3 amp 4 watt 6 ampere 7 coulomb *horse height:* 4 hand *interstellar space:* 6 parsec *length:* 3 rod 4 foot, inch, link, mile, yard 5 chain, cubit, meter 6 league 7 furlong 9 kilometer 10 centimeter *liquid:* 4 gill, pint 5 minim, quart 6 gallon *mixed drinks:* 6 jigger *of comparison:* 8 standard *paper:* 4 ream *printer's:* 4 pica 5 point *radioactive decay:* 8 halflife *rotation:* 5 angle *strength of solution:* 7 titrate *surface:* 3 are *thermodynamic:* 7 entropy 8 enthalpy

measured 7 regular, stately 8 metrical 9 regulated, temperate, unhurried 10 calculated, controlled, deliberate, restrained 13 proportionate

Measure for Measure *character:* 6 Angelo, Juliet 7 Claudio, Mariana 8 Isabella 9 Vincentio *setting:* 6 Vienna

measurement 4 area 6 degree 8 capacity, quantity 9 dimension, magnitude 11 calibration, mensuration

measure up to 3 tie 4 meet 5 equal, match, rival, touch 7 emulate 10 qualify for

measuring device 4 gage 5 buret, gauge, scale 7 burette, caliper, sextant, venturi 8 calipers 8 dipstick 9 altimeter, barometer, dosimeter, pedometer 11 tensiometer, velocimeter

meat 4 core, food, gist, pith, pork, veal 5 flesh, jerky, steak 6 thrust, upshot 7 edibles 8 victuals 9 foodstuff, provender, substance 10 provisions 11 comestibles *broth:* 8 bouillon *cake:* 6 burger 9 hamburger *cured:* 7 biltong *cut:* 3 rib 4 loin, rump 5 chuck, flank, plate, round, shank 7 brisket, sirloin 8 rib roast 9 club steak, rump roast, short loin, short ribs 10 blade roast, flank steak, round steak, T-bone steak 12 boneless neck, pinbone steak, sirloin steak 13 blade rib roast, crosscut shank *dealer:* 7 butcher *deer:* 7 venison *dried:* 5 jerky *fastening pin:* 6 skewer *holding rod:* 4 spit 10 rotisserie *juices:* 5 gravy *packer:* 5 Swift 6 Armour *raw:* 6 gobbet *roasted:* 8 barbecue *roasting shop:* 10 rotisserie *seasoned:* 7 sausage 8 pastrami, scrapple *sheep:* 6 mutton *side:* 8 sowbelly *skewered:* 5 kebab, kebob *slice:* 6 cutlet, rasher *small portion:* 6 collop *tough part:* 7 gristle

meat-eating 11 carnivorous

meathead 3 lug, oaf 4 clod, dodo, dolt, gawk, goon, lout 5 chump, klutz, looby 6 dimwit, lubber 7 bungler, palooka 8 dumbbell, numskull 9 birdbrain, ignoramus, lamebrain, numbskull 10 nincompoop

Mebd *husband:* 6 Ailill *victim:* 10 Cuchulainn

Mecca 4 goal *country:* 11 Saudi Arabia *pilgrimage:* 4 hadj, hajj *port:* 5 Jedda, Jidda 6 Jeddah, Jiddah *shrine:* 5 Kaaba

mechanic 7 artisan 9 machinist

mechanical 4 cold 7 cursory, robotic 8 lifeless 9 automated, automatic, unfeeling 10 impersonal 11 emotionless, instinctive, involuntary, perfunctory, unemotional

mechanism 4 gear 5 gizmo, means, works 6 agency, doodad, jigger, medium, widget 7 whatsit 8 dohickey 9 apparatus, appliance, procedure, technique, thingummy 10 instrument 11 contraption, contrivance, thingamabob, thingamajig, thingumajig

medal 5 badge, honor, prize 6 reward 7 laurels 8 accolade 10 decoration 13 commemoration

meddle 3 pry 4 fool, nose 5 snoop 6 butt in, dabble, horn in, kibitz, monkey,

putter, tamper, tinker 7 intrude, obtrude 8 trespass 9 interfere, interlope, intervene 10 mess around

meddler 5 snoop, yenta 7 snooper 8 busybody, intruder, kibitzer 9 buttinsky 12 troublemaker

meddlesome 4 busy, nosy 6 prying 9 intrusive, obtrusive, officious 11 impertinent, interfering

Medea 5 witch 9 sorceress 11 enchantress *aunt:* 5 Circe *brother:* 8 Absyrtus *father:* 6 Aeëtes *husband:* 5 Jason 6 Aegeus *sister:* 5 Circe *son:* 6 Medeus *victim:* 6 Creusa, Glauce, Glauke

medial 3 mid 4 mean 6 center, middle 7 average, central, halfway, midmost 8 middling, moderate 10 centermost, middlemost 11 equidistant 12 intermediary, intermediate

median see MEDIAL

mediate 5 judge 6 broker, convey, liaise, settle, step in, umpire 7 adjudge, referee, resolve 8 moderate, transmit 9 arbitrate, intercede, interfere, interpose, intervene, negotiate 10 conciliate

mediator 5 judge 6 broker, umpire 7 arbiter, liaison, referee 9 go-between, middleman 10 interceder, negotiator, peacemaker 11 intercessor

medical instrument 6 needle 7 forceps, scalpel, scanner, syringe 8 otoscope 9 endoscope, speculum 11 cardiograph, stethoscope

medical practitioner 3 doc 5 nurse 6 doctor, intern 7 surgeon 9 physician

medicament 4 cure, pill 6 elixir, physic, remedy 7 nostrum 8 antidote, curative 10 palliative *inert:* 7 placebo

medicate 4 cure, dose, drug, heal 5 treat

medicinal 8 curative, remedial, salutary, sanative 9 healthful 12 health-giving, pharmaceutic

medicine 4 cure, pill 5 bromo 6 physic, remedy 7 anodyne, nostrum 8 busulfan, poultice 11 antipyretic *bottle:* 4 vial *branch:* 7 surgery 8 oncology 9 neurology, pathology 10 bariatrics, cardiology, geriatrics, gynecology, nephrology, obstetrics, pediatrics, psychiatry *cathartic:* 8 evacuant 9 purgative *combining form:* 5 iatro 8 pharmaco *quantity of:* 4 dose 6 dosage *shell:* 7 capsule *soothing:* 7 anodyne 8 lenitive, narcotic, sedative 9 calmative, soporific

medicine man 6 doctor, kahuna, shaman 9 curandero

medieval study 5 logic 7 grammar, trivium 8 rhetoric 10 quadrivium

mediocre 4 dull, fair, hack, so-so 6 common 7 average, fairish 8 inferior, mid-

dling, moderate, ordinary, passable
9 tolerable 10 pedestrian, uninspired
11 commonplace, indifferent 12 run-of-
the-mill 13 unexceptional

meditate 4 mull, muse 5 weigh 6 intend,
ponder 7 purpose, reflect, revolve
8 cogitate, consider, mull over, ruminate, turn over 9 reflect on 10 deliberate 11 contemplate

meditative 6 broody 7 pensive 8 brooding
10 reflective, ruminative, thoughtful

meditator 4 yogi

Mediterranean 11 Mare Nostrum
12 Mare Internum *coastal region:* 7 Riviera *eastern shores:* 6 Levant *island:*
(see at ISLAND) *wind:* 7 mistral, sirocco

medium 3 par 4 fair, mean, so-so
5 agent, organ 6 agency, métier, milieu,
normal 7 ambient, average, channel,
climate, culture, neutral, vehicle
8 ambience, middling, moderate, passable, standard 9 tolerable 10 atmosphere 11 clairvoyant, environment
12 run-of-the-mill *of exchange:* 5 money
8 currency 11 legal tender

medley 4 brew, olio 5 combo, gumbo
6 jumble, ragout 7 farrago, mélange,
mixture 8 mishmash, pastiche 9 pasticcio, patchwork, potpourri 10 assortment, hodgepodge, miscellany, salmagundi 11 gallimaufry

Medusa 6 Gorgon *father:* 7 Phorcus,
Phorcys *hair:* 6 snakes *mother:* 4 Ceto
offspring: 7 Pegasus 8 Chrysaor *sister:*
6 Stheno 7 Euryale *slayer:* 7 Perseus

medusa 9 jellyfish

meed 3 due 4 part 5 quota, share
6 amount, desert, ration, return,
reward 7 guerdon, measure, portion
8 dividend 9 allotment, allowance
10 recompense 13 apportionment

meek 3 shy 4 mild, tame 5 lowly, timid
6 docile, gentle, humble, modest
7 patient 8 tolerant 10 submissive,
unassuming 11 deferential 13 long-
suffering

meerschaum 4 pipe 9 sepiolite

meet 3 apt, fit 4 face, fair, fill, find, join,
just, open, spot 5 cross, event, hit on,
match, right, touch, unite 6 answer,
chance, engage, oppose, proper, settle,
take on, useful 7 contest, convene, fitting, fulfill, hit upon, satisfy, stumble,
undergo 8 approach, assemble, come
upon, concours, conflict, confront,
converge, suitable 9 encounter,
impinge on, measure up 10 congregate,
provide for 11 appropriate, competition *a bet:* 3 see *a need:* 7 suffice *athletic:* 8 gymkhana 10 tournament *by
appointment:* 10 rendezvous

meeting 4 moot, talk 5 tryst 6 huddle,
parley, powwow 7 session 8 assembly,
conclave, concours, congress, junction
9 concourse, encounter, gathering, rencontre 10 conference, confluence, convention, rendezvous 11 competition,
convocation, get-together 12 intersection *Anglo-Saxon:* 5 gemot 6 gemote
place: 5 forum *spiritual:* 6 séance

Mefistofele composer 5 Boito (Arrigo)

Megaera see ERINYES

megaphone 8 bullhorn 10 mouthpiece

Megara *father:* 5 Creon *husband:* 8 Heracles, Hercules *king:* 5 Nisus

megillah 5 story 7 account

megrim 4 urge, whim 5 fancy, freak,
humor 6 notion, vagary, whimsy
7 caprice, conceit, impulse, vertigo
8 crotchet, migraine 9 dizziness

Mehitabel 3 cat *creator:* 7 Marquis (Don)
friend: 5 Archy

Mein Kampf author 6 Hitler (Adolf)

meiosis 7 litotes 12 cell division

Meissen 5 china 6 ceramics 9 porcelain

Meistersinger 5 Sachs (Hans) 9 Frauen-
lob

Meistersinger, Die *beloved:* 3 Eva *composer:* 6 Wagner (Richard) *hero:* 6 Walter *mentor:* 5 Sachs (Hans)

melancholia 5 gloom 6 sorrow 7 despair,
sadness 9 dejection, morbidity
10 depression, desolation, gloominess
11 despondency, dolefulness

melancholic 3 low, sad 4 blue, glum
6 gloomy, morose, triste 7 joyless
8 dejected, downcast, mournful
9 depressed, saddening 10 depressing,
despondent, dispirited

melancholy 3 low, sad 4 blue, funk,
glum 5 blues, dumps, ennui, gloom
6 dismal, dreary, gloomy, misery,
morose, rueful, somber, tedium, triste,
woeful 7 boredom, despair, doleful,
joyless, pensive, sadness, unhappy
8 dejected, dolorous, downcast, funereal, mournful, saddened 9 black bile,
dejection, depressed, plaintive, saddening, sorrowful 10 depressing, depression, despondent, dispirited, lachrymose, lamentable, lugubrious,
reflective, thoughtful 11 despondency,
unhappiness 12 heavyhearted, wretchedness

mélange see MEDLEY

Melanippus *father:* 7 Theseus *slayer:*
10 Amphiaraus *victim:* 6 Tydeus

Melchior *companion:* 6 Caspar, Gaspar
9 Balthasar, Balthazar *gift:* 4 gold

Melchizedek's kingdom 5 Salem

meld 3 mix 4 fuse 5 blend, merge 6 mingle 7 combine, mixture 8 compound

9 commingle, interfuse **10** amalgamate **11** intermingle

Meleager *beloved:* **8** Atalanta *father:* **6** Oeneus *mother:* **7** Althaea *victim:* **4** boar

melee 3 row **4** fray, riot **5** brawl, broil, clash, fight **6** affray, fracas, ruckus, rumpus **7** scuffle **8** skirmish **9** scrimmage **10** donnybrook, free-for-all

meliorate 4 help **5** amend **6** better, soften **7** improve **8** mitigate, palliate

Mélisande's lover 7 Pelléas

melisma 7 cadenza, descant

mellifluous 5 sweet **6** dulcet, fluent, golden, liquid, smooth **7** flowing, honeyed, silvery **8** euphonic, soothing **10** euphonious **13** silver-tongued

mellow 3 age **4** aged, ripe **5** ripen **6** genial, golden, grow up, mature, season, smooth **7** honeyed, matured, ripened **8** laid-back, pleasant, seasoned **9** agreeable

melodic 5 sweet **6** dulcet **7** musical, songful, tuneful **8** canorous, euphonic **10** euphonious

melodious 5 lyric, sweet **6** dulcet **7** musical, songful, tuneful **8** euphonic **9** cantabile **10** euphonious

melody 3 air, lay **4** aria, song, tune **5** canto, music, theme **6** chorus, strain, warble **7** descant, refrain **11** tunefulness

melon 4 pepo **5** gourd **6** casaba, profit **8** crenshaw, honeydew, windfall **10** cantaloupe

Melpomene see MUSE

melt 3 run **4** flux, fuse, thaw **6** relent, soften **7** liquefy **8** dissolve, liquesce, unfreeze **9** disappear **10** deliquesce *down:* **6** render *together:* **4** fuse

Melville, Herman *character:* **3** Pip **4** Ahab, Toby **5** Bembo, Chase **6** Cereno (Benito), Jermin, Pierre **7** Fayaway, Ishmael **8** Bartleby, Queequeg, Starbuck *work:* **4** Omoo **5** Mardi, Typee **6** Pierre **7** Redburn **8** Moby Dick **11** White-Jacket **12** Benito Cereno **13** Confidence-Man (The)

member 3 cut **4** part **5** piece **6** clause, parcel **7** portion, section, segment **8** division **9** appendage, component **10** ingredient *political party:* **4** Tory, Whig **7** Liberal **8** Democrat, Laborite **9** Labourite **10** Republican **12** Conservative *service club:* **4** Lion **8** Kiwanian, Rotarian

membrane 4 film **6** pleura **7** pleurae (plural) *bodily:* **6** serosa *brain:* **3** pia *diffusion through:* **7** osmosis *dividing:* **5** septa (plural) **6** septum *ear:* **8** tympanum *enclosing:* **8** indusium *thin:* **6** lami-

na **7** lamella, laminae (plural) **8** lamellae (plural) *wing:* **8** patagium

memento 5 relic, token, trace **6** trophy **7** vestige **8** keepsake, reminder, souvenir **11** remembrance

Memnon *father:* **8** Tithonus *mother:* **3** Eos **6** Aurora *slayer:* **8** Achilles

memoir 3 bio **4** life **5** diary **6** record, report, thesis **7** account, journal **8** anecdote **9** biography **11** confessions **12** recollection, reminiscence **13** autobiography

memoirist 7 Boswell, diarist **10** biographer

memorable 7 lasting, notable **8** historic **9** deathless, indelible, momentous, red-letter **10** noteworthy **11** significant **13** distinguished

memorandum 4 chit, note **6** minute, notice, record **7** tickler **8** notation, reminder **12** announcement

memorial 4 note **5** relic, token, trace **6** record, trophy **7** relique **8** keepsake, monument, reminder, souvenir **10** dedicatory **11** celebrative, remembrance **12** consecrative, remembrancer **13** commemoration, commemorative *mound:* **5** cairn

memorial park see CEMETERY

memorize 3 con, get **6** retain **8** remember

memory 6 recall **8** mind's eye, souvenir **9** anamnesis, awareness, flashback, retention **10** reflection **11** remembrance **12** recollection, reminiscence **13** retentiveness, retrospection *assisting:* **8** mnemonic *loss:* **7** amnesia

menace 4 risk **5** alarm, peril, scare **6** danger, hazard, threat **7** imperil, jeopard, torment **8** endanger, frighten, jeopardy, threaten **9** terrorize **10** intimidate, jeopardize

ménage 4 clan **5** house **6** family **8** quarters **9** household **12** housekeeping

menagerie 3 zoo **7** mixture

mend 3 fix, sew **4** cure, darn, heal **5** patch, renew **6** cobble, doctor, look up, perk up, reform, remedy, repair, revamp **7** correct, improve, patch up, rebuild, rectify, redress, restore **8** overhaul, renovate **9** condition, refurbish **10** ameliorate, convalesce, recuperate **11** recondition, reconstruct

mendacious 5 false, lying **6** shifty **7** fibbing **9** deceitful, deceptive, dishonest, paltering **10** untruthful **11** dissembling **13** prevaricating

mendacity 3 lie **6** deceit **9** deception, duplicity, falsehood **10** dishonesty **12** equivocation **13** truthlessness

mendicancy 7 beggary, begging, bumming, cadging **8** mooching, sponging **11** panhandling

mendicant 5 friar **6** beggar **7** begging

Mending Wall author 5 Frost (Robert)

Menelaus *brother:* **9** Agamemnon *father:* **6** Atreus *kingdom:* **6** Sparta *mother:* **6** Aerope *wife:* **5** Helen

menial 4 dull **5** lowly **6** humble **7** servant, servile, slavish **8** obeisant, retainer **9** unskilled **10** obsequious **11** subservient, undignified

meniscus 4 lens **9** cartilage

Menlo Park inventor 6 Edison (Thomas Alva)

menopause 11 climacteric **12** change of life

menorah 10 candelabra

Menotti, Gian Carlo *character:* **5** Amahl *opera:* **6** Consul (The), Medium (The) **9** Telephone (The)

men's store 12 haberdashery

mental 5 inner **7** psychic **8** cerebral, rational, thinking **9** reasoning, spiritual **10** immaterial, telepathic **11** intelligent **12** intellective, intellectual **13** psychological *faculty:* **6** memory

mentality 3 wit **5** sense **6** brains **7** mindset, outlook **9** intellect, mother wit **10** brainpower **12** intelligence

mention 4 cite, name, note **7** refer to, specify **8** advert to, allude to, citation, instance **9** reference

mentor 4 guru **5** coach, guide, tutor **7** teacher **9** counselor **10** counsellor

Mentor's pupil 10 Telemachus

menu 4 card, diet **5** carte **10** bill of fare **11** carte du jour *item:* **4** soup **5** salad **6** entrée **7** dessert **9** appetizer

Mephibosheth *father:* **4** Saul **8** Jonathan *mother:* **6** Rizpah

Mephistophelian 7 satanic **8** devilish, diabolic **10** diabolical

mephitic 4 rank **5** fetid, funky, musty **6** putrid, smelly **7** noisome, noxious, reeking **8** stinking **9** poisonous **10** malodorous

Merab *father:* **4** Saul *husband:* **6** Adriel

mercenary 4 hack **5** venal **6** greedy **7** corrupt, soldier **8** hireling

merchandise 4 line, sell **5** cargo, goods, stock, trade, wares **6** deal in, job lot, market, retail **7** effects, promote, staples, traffic **8** products **9** publicize, vendibles **11** commodities

merchandiser 6 dealer, trader, vendor **8** retailer **9** tradesman **10** wholesaler **11** businessman **13** businesswoman

merchant 5 buyer **6** dealer, jobber, seller, trader, vendor **7** peddler **8** purveyor, retailer **9** tradesman **10** trafficker, wholesaler **11** businessman, storekeep-

er *guild:* **5** Hansa, Hanse *League:* **9** Hanseatic *ship:* **5** oiler **6** argosy, coaler, galiot, packet, tanker, trader **7** collier, galliot, steamer **8** Indiaman **9** freighter *wine:* **7** vintner

Merchant of Venice, The 7 Antonio *character:* **6** Portia **7** Jessica, Lorenzo, Nerissa, Shylock **8** Bassanio

merciful 4 kind **6** benign, humane, kindly **7** clement, lenient **8** tolerant **9** forgiving, indulgent **10** charitable, forbearing **11** softhearted **13** compassionate

merciless 4 grim **5** cruel, harsh **6** brutal, savage, wanton **9** cutthroat, ferocious, unfeeling **10** gratuitous, implacable, ironfisted, unyielding **11** hardhearted, unrelenting **12** unappeasable

mercurial 5 flaky **6** fickle, mobile **7** erratic **8** unstable, variable, volatile **9** impulsive **10** capricious, changeable, inconstant **13** temperamental, unpredictable

mercury 5 azoth **11** quicksilver *ore:* **8** cinnabar

Mercury 6 planet (see also HERMES)

Mercutio *friend:* **5** Romeo *slayer:* **6** Tybalt

mercy 4 pity, ruth **5** grace **6** lenity **7** caritas, charity **8** clemency, goodwill, kindness, leniency **9** benignity, tolerance **10** compassion, generosity, kindliness **11** benevolence, forbearance **13** commiseration *petition for:* **5** kyrie **8** miserere

mere 4 bare, lake, pool, pure **8** boundary, landmark **9** undiluted

merely 4 just, only **6** simply, solely, wholly

meretricious 4 loud, sham **5** gaudy, phony, showy **6** flashy, garish, glitzy, sleazy, tawdry, tinsel, trashy **7** chintzy **8** delusive, delusory, illusory **9** contrived, deceptive **10** misleading **11** counterfeit, pretentious

merganser 4 duck, smew

merge 3 mix **4** fuse, join **5** blend, unify, unite **6** mingle **7** combine **8** coalesce, compound **9** commingle, interfuse **10** amalgamate, assimilate **11** consolidate, intermingle

merger 5 union **6** fusion **7** melding **8** alliance, takeover **9** coalition **10** absorption **11** combination, unification **12** amalgamation **13** consolidation

meridian 4 acme, apex, peak **6** apogee, climax, summit, zenith **8** pinnacle

merit 3 due **4** earn, rate **5** arete, value, worth **6** virtue **7** caliber, deserts, deserve, entitle, justify, quality, stature, warrant **10** excellence, perfection, recompense **11** achievement

merited 3 due **4** fair, just **5** right

7 condign, fitting **8** deserved, rightful, suitable **9** justified, requisite **11** appropriate

meritorious 6 worthy **8** laudable **9** admirable, deserving, estimable, honorable **10** creditable **11** commendable, thankworthy **12** praiseworthy

Merlin 4 seer **5** augur, magus **6** shaman, wizard **7** prophet **8** magician **10** soothsayer **11** necromancer, thaumaturge

merlin 6 falcon **10** pigeon hawk

mermaid 3 nix **5** Ariel, nixie **7** manatee **8** sirenian **10** water nymph **11** water sprite

Merope *father:* **5** Atlas **8** Oenopion *husband:* **7** Polybus **8** Sisyphus **11** Cresphontes *lover:* **5** Orion *mother:* **7** Pleione *sisters:* **8** Pleiades *son:* **7** Aepytus, Glaucus

merriment 4 glee **5** mirth, revel **6** gaiety **7** jollity, revelry, whoopee **8** hilarity, reveling **9** festivity, jocundity, joviality **10** jocularity, jubilation **13** entertainment

merry 3 gay **4** glad **5** happy, jolly **6** blithe, jocund, jovial, joyful, joyous, lively **7** festive, gleeful **8** animated, cheerful, mirthful **9** hilarious, sprightly, vivacious **12** high-spirited, lighthearted

merry-andrew 4 fool, zany **5** clown, joker **6** jester, madcap **7** buffoon **9** harlequin **10** mountebank

merrymaker 7 partyer, reveler **8** carouser

merrymaking 5 party, revel **6** frolic, gaiety **7** jollity, revelry, whoopee **8** hilarity **9** festivity **12** conviviality

Merry Widow composer 5 Lehár (Franz)

Merry Wives of Windsor, The *character:* **3** Nym **4** Ford, Page **5** Caius **6** Fenton, Pistol **7** Slender **8** Falstaff

mesa 5 bench, butte **7** plateau **9** tableland

mescal 5 agave **6** cactus, liquor, maguey, peyote

mesh 3 net, web **4** jibe, maze **5** skein, snare, snarl **6** engage, morass, tangle **7** netting, network **8** dovetail, entangle **9** harmonize, interlock, labyrinth **10** coordinate **12** reticulation

meshuga 3 mad **4** nuts **5** crazy, goofy, kooky, loony, nutty, wacky **6** insane, screwy **7** foolish

mesmeric 8 alluring, hypnotic **9** glamorous **10** bewitching, enchanting **11** captivating

mesmerize 4 vamp **6** dazzle, seduce **7** bewitch **8** ensorcel, enthrall, entrance **9** captivate, ensorcell, fascinate, hypnotize, spellbind

Mesopotamia 4 Iraq *civilization:* **4** Elam **5** Akkad, Sumer **7** Assyria, Elamite **8** Akkadian, Assyrian, Sumerian **9** Babylonia **10** Babylonian *river:* **6** Tigris **9** Euphrates

mess 4 hash **5** botch, snafu **6** fright, jumble, muddle **7** eyesore **8** botchery, disarray, disorder, shambles, wreckage **9** confusion **10** hodgepodge, miscellany *around:* **4** idle **5** chill, dally **6** dawdle, doodle, fiddle, potter, putter **7** goof off, hang out **8** chill out, lollygag **10** dillydally *up:* **4** blow, flub, muff, ruin **5** botch, fluff, fudge, spoil, touse **6** bungle, fumble, tousle **7** butcher

message 4 note **5** sense, theme **6** letter, report **7** epistle, mission, missive, purport **8** bulletin, dispatch, telegram **9** directive, telegraph **10** communiqué **12** significance **13** communication, signification

Messalina's husband 8 Claudius

mess around 4 fool, idle **5** flirt **6** dabble, dawdle, fiddle, meddle, monkey, potter, putter, tamper, tinker **8** womanize **9** associate, interfere, interlope, philander

messenger 4 post **5** envoy **6** herald, runner **7** apostle, courier **8** emissary **9** gobetween, harbinger **10** ambassador **11** internuncio **12** intermediary *God's:* **5** angel *of the gods:* **6** Hermes **7** Mercury *Turkish:* **6** chiaus

messiah 6 savior **7** saviour **8** defender **9** deliverer, liberator

Messiah composer 6 Handel (George Frideric)

messy 6 frowsy, frowzy, sloppy, unneat, untidy **7** chaotic, rumpled, unkempt **8** careless, confused, ill-kempt, slapdash, slipshod, slovenly **10** disheveled, disorderly **11** dishevelled *abode:* **3** sty **6** pigpen, pigsty

mestizo 5 métis **6** ladino **10** mixed-blood

Mestor *father:* **7** Perseus *mother:* **9** Andromeda

metal 4 gold, iron **5** steel **6** bronze *alloy:* (see ALLOY) *casting mold:* **5** ingot *corrosion:* **4** rust *fuse:* **6** solder *in mass:* **7** bullion *layer:* **6** nugget *magnetic:* **4** iron *refuse:* **4** slag **5** dross **6** scoria *sheath:* **5** armor *thin:* **4** foil, leaf **5** plate *worker:* **5** smith **10** blacksmith

metallic element 3 tin **4** gold, iron, lead, zinc **6** barium, cobalt, copper, nickel, radium, silver, sodium **7** arsenic, bismuth, cadmium, calcium, lithium, mercury, uranium **8** aluminum, chromium, platinum, titanium, tungsten, vanadium **9** magnesium, manganese, potassium, strontium **10** molybdenum

metamere 6 somite 7 segment

metamorphic rock 5 slate 6 gneiss, marble, schist 9 quartzite, soapstone

metamorphose 6 change, mutate 7 convert, develop 9 transform, translate, transmute 11 transfigure 12 transmogrify

metamorphosis 6 change 8 changing, mutation 9 evolution, sea change 10 changeover 13 transmutation

Metamorphosis author 5 Kafka (Franz) ___ me tangere 4 noli

metaphor 5 trope 6 simile, symbol 7 analogy 8 allegory 10 comparison, similitude

metaphorical compound 7 kenning

metaphysical 8 bodiless, numinous 9 unearthly, unfleshly 10 immaterial, suprahuman 12 supermundane, supramundane, supranatural, transcendent 13 preternatural *poet:* 5 Donne (John) 6 Cowley (Abraham) 7 Crashaw (Richard), Herbert (George), Marvell (Andrew), Vaughan (Henry) 9 Cleveland (John)

mete 4 deal, dole, give 5 allot, bound 6 border, parcel, ration 7 portion 8 allocate, boundary, disburse, dispense 9 apportion 10 distribute

meteor 8 fireball 12 shooting star *exploding:* 6 bolide *shower:* 5 Lyrid 6 Leonid, Taurid 7 Aquarid, Geminid, Orionid, Perseid 10 Quadrantid

meteorite 8 aerolite 10 siderolite

meter 4 beat, scan 6 rhythm 7 cadence, measure, pattern

metheglin 4 mead 8 beverage *ingredient:* 5 honey

method 3 way 4 mode, modi (plural), plan 5 means, modus, order, style 6 course, design, manner, schema, scheme, system 7 fashion, formula, pattern, process, routine, wrinkle 8 practice 9 procedure, technique 11 orderliness 13 modus operandi *careful:* 8 strategy *of employing troops:* 6 tactic 7 tactics *of procedure:* 4 game

methodical 5 exact 7 careful, logical, orderly, precise, regular 9 efficient, organized 10 deliberate, scrupulous, systematic, systemized 12 systematized

Methuselah *father:* 5 Enoch *grandson:* 4 Noah *son:* 6 Lamech

meticulous 5 exact, fussy, picky 6 strict 7 careful, finicky, precise 8 detailed, thorough 10 fastidious, nitpicking, pernickety, scrupulous 11 microscopic, painstaking, persnickety, punctilious 13 conscientious

métier 4 work 5 craft, field, forte, trade 7 calling, pursuit 8 business, strength, vocation 9 specialty 10 employment, occupation, profession

metrical foot 4 iamb 5 ionic, paeon 6 cretic, dactyl, iambic, iambus 7 anapest, pyrrhic, pyrrhus, spondee, triseme, trochee 8 bacchius, choriamb, dactylic, spondaic, tribrach, trochaic 9 anapestic 10 tribrachic

metric unit *area:* 3 are 7 hectare *capacity:* 5 liter, litre 9 decaliter, deciliter, kiloliter 10 centiliter, hectoliter, milliliter *length:* 5 meter 9 decameter, decimeter, dekameter, kilometer 10 centimeter, hectometer, millimeter *mass and weight:* 4 gram 7 quintal 8 decagram, decigram, dekagram, kilogram 9 centigram, hectogram, metric ton, milligram

metro 4 tube 6 subway 11 underground

metropolis 4 city 7 capital

metropolitan 5 urban 6 urbane 7 primate 9 municipal 10 archbishop

mettle 4 fire, grit, guts 5 heart, moxie, nerve, pluck, spunk, steel, valor, vigor 6 daring, spirit, starch, temper 7 cojones, courage, resolve, stamina 8 backbone, boldness, tenacity, vitality 9 fortitude 10 resolution

mettlesome 4 bold, game 5 brave, fiery, gutsy 6 plucky, spunky 7 staunch, valiant 8 intrepid, resolute, spirited, vigorous 9 tenacious 10 courageous, determined

mew 3 hem, pen 4 cage, coop, gull 5 alley, fence 6 corral, immure, shut in, stable 7 enclose 8 hideaway

mewl 4 moan, pule 5 whine 6 snivel 7 whimper

Mexican *crop:* 5 sisal *estate:* 8 hacienda *food:* 4 masa, taco 5 chili, salsa 6 tamale 7 burrito, panocha, penuche, tostada 8 frijoles, tortilla 9 enchilada, guacamole 10 quesadilla 11 chimichanga *house:* 5 jacal *liquor:* 7 tequila

Mexico *ancient city:* 12 Tenochtitlán *ancient culture:* 4 Maya 5 Aztec, Mayan, Olmec 6 Toltec *bay:* 8 Campeche *capital:* 10 Mexico City *city:* 4 León 6 Juárez, Mérida, Oaxaca, Puebla 7 Nogales, Tijuana 8 Acapulco, Mexicali, Saltillo 9 Chihuahua, Matamoros, Monterrey 10 Cuernavaca 11 Guadalajara 12 Ciudad Juárez *conqueror:* 6 Cortés (Hernán, Hernando) *discoverer:* 7 Córdoba (Fernández de) *emperor:* 10 Maximilian *gulf:* 10 California *island:* 7 Cozumel *island group:* 13 Revillagigedo *lake:* 7 Chapala, Cuitzeo, Texcoco 9 Pátzcuaro *language:* 7 Spanish *leader:* 4 Díaz (Porfirio) 6 Juárez (Benito) 8 Carranza (Venustiano) *monetary unit:* 4 peso *mountain, range:* 8 Malinche 11 Sierra Madre *neighbor:* 6 Belize 9 Guatemala *peninsula:* 4 Baja 7 Yucatán *port:* 7 Tampico 8 Ensenada, Mazatlán, Veracruz *resort:* 6 Cancún 8 Acapulco *revolutionist:* 5 Villa (Pancho) 6 Zapata (Emiliano) 7 Hidalgo (Padre Miguel) *river:* 4 Mayo 5 Bravo, Yaquí 6 Balsas, Grande, Pánuco 7 Conchos 8 Grijalva, Río Bravo, Santiago 9 Rio Grande 10 Usumacinta *ruined city:* 5 Uxmal 7 Mayapán 8 Palenque 11 Chichén Itzá *sea:* 9 Caribbean *volcano:* 6 Colima 9 Paricutín 11 Ixtacihuatl 12 Citlaltépetl, Ixtaccíhuatl, Popocatépetl

mezzanine 5 story 7 balcony 8 entresol

mezzo 4 half 6 singer 7 soprano

mezzo-soprano *American:* 5 Elias (Rosalind), Horne (Marilyn), Jones (Sissieretta) 6 Bumbry (Grace), Graves (Denyce) 7 Stevens (Risë), Verrett (Shirley) 8 Troyanos (Tatiana), von Stade (Frederica) *Austrian:* 6 Ludwig (Christa) *English:* 5 Baker (Janet) *Italian:* 7 Bartoli (Cecilia) 8 Cossotto (Fiorenza)

Miami *bowl:* 6 Orange *chief:* 12 Little Turtle *county:* 4 Dade *stadium:* 9 Joe Robbie *team:* 4 Heat 7 Marlins 8 Dolphins, Panthers

miasma 3 fog 4 haze, mist, murk, smog 5 brume, vapor 9 effluvium

mica 7 biotite 8 silicate 9 isinglass, muscovite

Michelangelo Buonarotti *painting:* 10 Holy Family (The) 12 Last Judgment (The) *statue:* 5 David, Moses, Pietà 7 Bacchus

Michener novel 5 Space, Texas 6 Hawaii, Poland, Source (The) 8 Caravans, Covenant (The), Drifters (The), Sayonara 10 Centennial, Chesapeake 13 Fires of Spring (The) 15 Bridges at Toko-Ri (The)

Michigan *capital:* 7 Lansing *city:* 5 Flint 7 Detroit, Lansing, Pontiac 8 Ann Arbor, Dearborn 9 Kalamazoo 11 Grand Rapids 13 Sault Ste. Marie 16 Sault Sainte Marie *college, university:* 6 Calvin 9 Kalamazoo 10 Wayne State *lake:* 4 Erie 5 Huron 8 Michigan, Superior *nickname:* 9 Wolverine (State) 10 Great Lakes (State) *state bird:* 5 robin *state flower:* 12 apple blossom *state tree:* 9 white pine

mickey 5 flask, split

microbe 3 bug 4 germ 5 virus 8 bacillus, pathogen 9 bacterium 13 microorganism

microfilm sheet 5 fiche

Micronesia *capital:* 7 Palikir *island, island group:* 3 Yap 5 Chuuk 6 Kosrae 7 Pohnpei 8 Caroline *language:* 7 English

microorganism 4 germ 5 virus 6 aerobe 7 bacilli (plural), microbe, protist 8 bacillus, bacteria (plural), pathogen, protozoa (plural) 9 bacterium, protozoan, protozoon

microphone 3 bug 4 mike *shield:* 4 gobo

microscope 9 magnifier *inventor:* 11 Leeuwenhoek (Antoni van) *part:* 5 stage 6 mirror 8 eyepiece 9 objective

microscopic 4 tiny 5 small 6 minute

Mid-Atlantic state 7 New York 8 Delaware, Maryland, Virginia 9 New Jersey 12 Pennsylvania, West Virginia

midday 4 noon, sext 8 high noon, noontide, noontime

middle 4 core, mean 5 mesne, waist 6 center, medial, median 7 average, central, halfway 8 interior 10 centermost 11 equidistant, intervening 12 intermediary, intermediate

Middle American country 4 Cuba 5 Haiti 6 Belize, Mexico, Panama 7 Bahamas, Grenada, Jamaica 8 Barbados, Dominica, Honduras 9 Costa Rica, Guatemala, Nicaragua 10 El Salvador

middlebrow 7 Babbitt

middle class 11 bourgeoisie

middle-class 9 bourgeois

middle ear *bone:* 5 incus 6 stapes 7 malleus *membrane:* 7 eardrum 8 tympanum

Middle Eastern country 4 Iran, Iraq, Oman 5 Egypt, Qatar, Sudan, Syria, Yemen 6 Cyprus, Israel, Jordan, Kuwait, Turkey 7 Bahrain, Lebanon 11 Saudi Arabia

Middle Kingdom 5 China

middleman 5 agent 6 broker 8 mediator 9 go-between 11 intercessor 12 intermediary, intermediate

Middlemarch author 5 Eliot (George), Evans (Mary Ann)

middle-of-the-road 7 neutral 8 moderate 9 impartial 11 nonpartisan

middling 4 fair, okay, so-so 6 fairly, medium, rather 7 average, fairish, typical 8 adequate, mediocre, moderate, ordinary, passable 9 tolerable 10 moderately, second-rate 11 indifferent 12 intermediate, run-of-the-mill

midge 3 fly 6 punkie 7 no-see-um 8 dipteran 10 chironomid *larva:* 9 bloodworm

midget 4 runt 5 dwarf, pygmy 6 bantam, peewee 7 manikin 8 Tom Thumb 10 homunculus 11 hop-o'-my-thumb, Lilliputian

Midian *father:* 7 Abraham *mother:* 7 Keturah

midpoint 3 par 4 mean, norm 6 center, median, middle 7 average, centrum, halfway 8 bull's-eye, standard

midwife 6 granny, Lucina 10 accoucheur

mien 3 air, set 4 look 6 aspect, manner 7 address, bearing 8 carriage, demeanor, presence 9 mannerism 10 appearance, deportment, expression 11 comportment

miff 3 fit, irk, vex 4 beef, flap, spat 5 annoy, pique, run-in, upset 6 bother, fracas, nettle, offend, put out 7 dispute, provoke, quarrel, rhubarb 8 irritate, squabble 10 conniption, falling-out 11 altercation

might 3 may 4 sway 5 brawn, clout, force, means, power 6 energy, muscle 7 ability, command, control, mastery, potency 8 capacity, strength 9 authority, resources 12 forcefulness

mighty 4 huge, very 5 grand, great 6 heroic, potent, strong 7 eminent, immense, massive, titanic 8 enormous, forceful, gigantic, imposing, powerful, puissant 10 impressive, monumental, prodigious, stupendous, tremendous 11 illustrious 13 extraordinary

Mignon *composer* 6 Thomas (Ambroise)

mignonette 4 herb 5 sauce 6 annual 6 reseda

migrant 5 exile, mover, nomad 7 drifter, nomadic, refugee 8 traveler, wanderer 9 itinerant, transient 10 expatriate

migrate 4 move, trek 5 drift, range, shift 6 wander 8 transfer

migration 6 exodus 8 diaspora *of professionals:* 10 brain drain

migratory 5 nomad 6 errant, mobile, moving, roving 7 nomadic, ranging 9 wandering

Mikado, The *composer:* 8 Sullivan (Arthur) *librettist:* 7 Gilbert (W. S.)

milady 6 madame 10 noblewoman 11 gentlewoman

Milan *family:* 6 Sforza 8 Visconti *opera house:* 7 La Scala

Milcah *brother:* 3 Lot *father:* 5 Haran 10 Zelophehad *husband:* 5 Nahor *son:* 7 Bethuel

mild 4 calm, easy, meek, soft, tame 5 balmy, bland, faint, tepid 6 benign, docile, gentle, placid, serene, smooth, tender 7 amiable, clement, equable, insipid, lenient, patient, subdued 8 moderate, obliging 9 benignant, temperate 10 forbearing, submissive

mildew 4 mold, rust 6 fungus, growth

___ **mile** 7 statute 8 nautical

mileage recorder 8 odometer

milestone 5 event 6 marker 8 landmark, occasion

milieu 5 scene 6 medium, sphere 7 ambient, climate, setting 8 ambience 10 atmosphere, background 11 environment, mise-en-scène 12 surroundings

militant 7 fighter, martial, warlike, warrior 8 activist, fighting 9 assertive, bellicose, combatant, combative, truculent 10 aggressive, pugnacious 11 belligerent, contentious, quarrelsome 12 gladiatorial

military 5 troop 6 forces, troops 7 martial, warlike 8 soldiery 9 soldierly 10 servicemen 11 armed forces, soldierlike *alliance:* 4 NATO *base:* 4 camp, fort, post 5 depot, field 6 billet 8 barracks, garrison, quarters 10 encampment *officer:* 5 major 7 captain, colonel, general 9 brigadier 10 lieutenant *prisoner:* 3 POW *school:* 3 OCS, OTS 4 ROTC, USMA 9 Annapolis, West Point *sector:* 10 combat zone, front lines 11 battlefront *store:* 10 commissary *storehouse:* 5 depot 6 armory 7 arsenal *supplies:* 8 matériel, ordnance *unit:* 5 corps, squad, troop 7 company, platoon 8 division, regiment 9 battalion 11 battle group *vehicle:* 4 jeep, tank 6 Abrams, Humvee 7 Bradley 9 Blackhawk, half-track

militate 4 tell 5 count, weigh 6 matter 11 carry weight

militia 7 reserve

milk 4 pump, rook, suck 5 drain, educe, empty, evoke, exact, mulct, nurse, wring 6 elicit, extort, fleece 7 exhaust, exploit, extract *coagulated:* 4 curd *combining form:* 4 lact 5 lacti, lacto *curdled:* 7 clabber *fermented:* 5 kefir 6 kumiss, yogurt 7 koumiss, yoghurt *liquid part:* 4 whey *store:* 5 dairy *sugar:* 7 lactose

milk shake 6 frappe 7 frosted

milky 4 fair, meek, mild, pale, tame 5 white 6 chalky, cloudy, gentle 7 lacteal, whitish 8 timorous

mill 5 grind, plant, shape, works 7 factory, machine 9 circulate, pulverize 11 manufactory

millenary 8 thousand

Miller, Arthur *film:* 7 Misfits (The) *play:* 5 Price (The) 9 All My Sons 8 Crucible (The) 12 After the Fall 16 Death of a Salesman 17 View from the Bridge (A) *salesman:* 5 Loman (Willy)

milliner 6 hatter

million *combining form:* 3 meg 4 mega

millionth *combining form:* 4 micr 5 micro

Mill on the Floss *author* 5 Eliot (George), Evans (Mary Ann)

millstone 4 duty, load, onus 6 burden,

charge, weight 9 albatross 10 affliction, deadweight

Milne bear 4 Pooh

milord 8 nobleman 9 gentleman, patrician 10 aristocrat 12 silk stocking

Milquetoast, Caspar *creator:* 7 Webster (Harold Tucker) (see also MILKSOP)

Miltiades' victory 8 Marathon

Milton work 5 Comus 7 Lycidas 8 L'Allegro 12 Areopagitica, Paradise Lost

mime 3 act 5 actor 6 act out 7 Marceau (Marcel) 9 performer, represent 11 impersonate 12 impersonator

mimic 3 act, ape 4 copy, mock, play 5 actor, enact 6 mummer, parody, parrot, player 7 copycat, imitate 8 resemble, simulate, travesty 9 burlesque, pantomime 11 impersonate 12 impersonator

mimicry 4 echo 6 parody 8 travesty 9 imitation, parroting 10 caricature 13 impersonation

minatory 4 dire, grim 7 baleful, baneful, direful, hostile, malefic, ominous 8 menacing, sinister 9 ill-boding 10 forbidding, foreboding, maleficent 11 frightening, threatening 12 intimidating

mince 4 chop, dice, hash 5 cut up, strut 6 prance, sashay, soften 8 moderate, restrain, tone down 9 euphemize

mincing 5 fussy 6 dainty, la-di-da, tootoo 7 finical, finicky, stilted 8 affected, delicate 10 fastidious, pernickety 11 persnickety

mind 3 wit 4 mood, obey, soul, tend, will, wits 5 brain, fancy, watch, weigh 6 attend, belief, beware, brains, follow, memory, notice, psyche, reason, senses, spirit 7 care for, discern, dislike, feeling, observe, oversee, purpose 8 consider 9 intellect, intention, mentality, supervise 10 brainpower, gray matter 11 disposition, temperament 12 intelligence 13 consciousness *combining form:* 5 psych 6 psycho

mindful 5 alert, awake, aware 7 knowing 8 sensible, vigilant 9 attentive, cognizant, conscious, observant 10 conversant 13 conscientious

mindless 4 rash 5 silly 6 simple, stupid 7 asinine, foolish, unaware, vacuous 9 nitwitted, oblivious 10 irrational, unthinking 13 unintelligent

mine 3 dig, pit, sap 4 fund, lode, vein, well 5 delve, drill, hoard, stock, store 6 burrow, quarry, spring 7 bonanza, deposit, extract 8 eldorado, excavate, Golconda 10 excavation, wellspring 13 treasure trove *coal:* 8 colliery *entrance:* 4 adit

miner 6 pitman 7 collier

mineral 5 beryl, topaz, trona 6 augite, barite, garnet, iolite, pinite, rutile, sphene, spinel, sulfur, zircon 7 apatite, azurite, bornite, calcite, citrine, coesite, cyanite, jadeite, kernite, kunzite, olivine, zeolite 8 boracite, cinnabar, dolomite, epsomite, fayalite, feldspar, fluorite, hematite, lazulite, lazurite, siderite, sodalite, stibnite, triplite, wellsite 9 aragonite, celestite, cerussite, danburite, fosterite, kaolinite, lawsonite, magnetite, malachite, muscovite, phenakite, scapolite, tridymite, turquoise, wulfenite 10 chalcedony, orthoclase, pyrrhotite, tourmaline 11 alexandrite, chrysoberyl, melanterite 12 brazilianite, chalcopyrite, tincalconite 13 rhodochrosite

flaky: 4 mica *greasy:* 4 talc 10 serpentine *hard:* 6 spinel 7 diamond 8 corundum *iridescent:* 4 opal *nonmetallic:* 5 boron 6 gypsum, halite 8 asbestos, graphite *shiny:* 4 gold 6 galena, pyrite, silver *soft:* 4 talc 6 gypsum 8 graphite *transparent:* 6 quartz

mineral water 7 seltzer 8 club soda

Minerva see ATHENA

mingle 3 mix 4 meld 5 blend, merge 6 commix 7 combine 8 intermix 9 associate, socialize

mingy 4 mean 5 cheap, tight 6 stingy 7 chintzy, miserly, scrimpy 8 grudging, ungiving 9 niggardly, penurious 10 pinchpenny 11 closefisted, tightfisted

miniature 3 wee 4 tiny 5 small, teeny, weeny 6 little, minute, petite, teensy 9 itsy-bitsy, itty-bitty 10 diminutive, small-scale, teeny-weeny 11 Lilliputian 12 illumination

minify 4 trim 6 lessen, shrink 7 abridge, curtail 8 decrease, diminish 10 abbreviate

minim 3 bit, jot 4 atom, iota 5 grain, speck 7 modicum, smidgen 8 particle *music:* 8 half note

minimal 5 basic, least, token 6 lowest 7 nominal 8 littlest, smallest 9 slightest

minimize 5 decry 6 reduce 7 run down 8 belittle, derogate, discount, downplay, play down 9 disparage, soft-pedal, underrate 10 depreciate 13 underestimate

minimum 3 dab, jot 4 iota, whit 5 least, speck 6 lowest, margin 7 smidgen 8 particle, pittance, smallest

minion 4 idol 5 toady 6 flunky, lackey, vassal, yes-man 7 darling, devotee, spaniel 8 creature, favorite, follower, parasite, truckler 9 sycophant, toadeater, underling **10** bootlicker **11** lickspittle, subordinate

minister 4 tend **5** agent, clerk, serve **6** cleric, curate, divine, parson **8** clerical, preacher, reverend **9** churchman, clergyman **10** ambassador **12** ecclesiastic *of state:* **10** chancellor *plenipotentiary:* **5** envoy **6** consul **8** diplomat, emissary

ministry 5 agent, organ **6** agency, clergy, medium **7** cabinet **10** department, instrument **11** bureaucracy

Minnehaha's husband 8 Hiawatha

Minnesota *capital:* **6** St. Paul *city:* **5** Edina **6** Duluth **9** Rochester **11** Minneapolis *college, university:* **8** Carleton **9** Saint Olaf **10** Macalester *nickname:* **6** Gopher (State) **9** North Star (State) *park:* **9** Voyageurs *river:* **7** St. Croix **9** Minnesota **11** Mississippi *state bird:* **4** loon (common) *state flower:* **12** lady's slipper *state tree:* **7** red pine

minor 5 lower, petty, small, youth **6** casual, lesser, little, paltry, slight **7** trivial **8** inferior, mediocre, piddling, small-fry, trifling, underage **9** dependent, secondary, small-beer, small-time **10** bush-league, second-rate, shoestring **11** indifferent, unimportant **13** insignificant

minority 5 youth **6** nonage **7** infancy **9** childhood **10** immaturity

minor-league 5 small **6** lesser **9** secondary, small-time **11** unimportant

Minos *daughter:* **7** Ariadne, Phaedra *father:* **4** Zeus **7** Jupiter *kingdom:* **5** Crete *monster:* **8** Minotaur *mother:* **6** Europa *son:* **9** Androgeos *wife:* **8** Pasiphaë

Minotaur *father:* **4** bull *home:* **9** labyrinth *mother:* **8** Pasiphaë *slayer:* **7** Theseus

minstrel 4 bard, wait **6** harper, singer **7** gleeman **8** jongleur **9** balladist **10** troubadour *end man:* **5** Bones (Mr.), Tambo (Mr.) *instrument:* **4** lute, lyre **5** rebec, shawm, tabor **8** crumhorn, psaltery **9** krummhorn **10** tambourine

mint 3 pot **4** cast, coin, heap, pile, sage **5** basil, bugle, forge, issue, stamp, trove **6** boodle, bundle, create, intact, packet, savory, strike, unused **7** fortune, likenew, menthol, perfect, produce **8** brand-new, lavender, marjoram, original **9** blue curls, bugleweed, undamaged

Minuit's purchase 9 Manhattan

minus 4 flaw, lack, less, sans **6** absent, defect **7** lacking, missing, wanting, without **8** drawback, negative, subtract **10** deficiency

minuscule 4 tiny **5** small **6** letter, little, minute **7** trivial **9** lowercase, miniature

10 negligible, small-scale **11** meaningless, microscopic **13** imperceptible, inappreciable, insignificant

minute 3 wee **4** jiff, memo, note, tiny **5** draft, flash, jiffy, small, teeny, weeny **6** little, moment, record, teensy **7** careful, instant, precise, trivial **8** detailed, itemized, thorough, trifling **9** itsy-bitsy, itty-bitty, miniature, minuscule **10** diminutive, memorandum, meticulous, scrupulous, teeny-weeny **11** Lilliputian, punctilious **13** infinitesimal

minutes 3 log **6** annals, record **7** summary **10** transcript **11** proceedings

minutiae 6 trivia **7** details **10** fine points, triviality **11** particulars

minx 4 bawd, moll, slut, tart **5** bimbo, tramp, wench, whore **6** floozy, harlot, hooker **7** hustler, trollop **8** strumpet **10** prostitute

miracle 4 boon, feat **6** marvel, wonder **7** godsend, portent, prodigy, stunner **8** windfall **9** sensation **10** phenomenon

miraculous 7 amazing **8** wondrous **9** marvelous, unearthly, wonderful **10** astounding, prodigious, superhuman **11** astonishing, spectacular **12** inexplicable, supernatural **13** preternatural

mirage 6 vision, wraith **8** delusion, illusion, phantasm **11** fata morgana, ignis fatuus **13** hallucination

Miranda *father:* **8** Prospero *lover:* **9** Ferdinand

mire 3 bog, fen, mud **4** muck, ooze, sink, trap **5** delay, marsh, slush, swamp **6** detain, enmesh, entrap, hang up, morass, slough, tangle **7** bog down, embroil, ensnare, involve, set back **8** entangle **9** imbroglio, implicate, quicksand

Miriam's brother 5 Aaron, Moses

mirror 5 glass **6** embody, typify **7** reflect **8** speculum **9** exemplify, personify, reflector, represent **10** illustrate **11** cheval glass **12** looking glass *signaling:* **10** heliograph

mirth 3 fun, joy **4** glee **5** cheer **6** gaiety, levity **7** jollity, revelry **8** gladness, hilarity **9** festivity, frivolity, happiness, jocundity, joviality, merriment **10** jocularity **11** merrymaking **12** cheerfulness

mirthful 3 gay **5** jolly, merry, riant **6** jocund, jovial **7** festive **9** exuberant, hilarious **12** lighthearted

miry 4 oozy **5** boggy, mucky, muddy **6** marshy, slushy, swampy

misadventure 4 slip **5** boner, error, lapse **6** howler, mishap **7** blunder, faux pas **8** accident, calamity, casualty, disaster **9** cataclysm **10** misfortune **11** catastrophe

misanthrope 5 cynic, grump, loner 6 grinch 7 killjoy, recluse, scoffer 10 curmudgeon

misanthropic 7 cynical 10 antisocial

misappropriate 5 filch, steal 6 pilfer 7 purloin 8 embezzle, peculate 9 defalcate

misbegotten 7 bastard, illicit, natural 8 baseborn, deformed, spurious 10 fatherless, unfathered 12 contemptible, disreputable, ill-conceived, illegitimate

misbehave 5 act up, cut up, lapse, rebel, stray 6 act out, offend 7 carry on, disobey 8 trespass 10 roughhouse, transgress

misbehavior 7 misdeed 8 rudeness 9 high jinks 10 misconduct, wrongdoing 11 delinquency, dereliction, naughtiness 13 transgression

miscalculate 3 err 8 miscount, misgauge

miscarry 4 fail, flop 5 abort 6 fizzle 7 go wrong

miscellaneous 3 odd 5 mixed 6 motley, sundry, varied 7 diverse 8 assorted 9 different, disparate, scrambled 13 heterogeneous

miscellany 3 ana 4 hash, olio, stew 5 salad 6 jumble, medley, motley, muddle 7 farrago, mélange, mixture, omnibus 8 mixed bag, pastiche 9 anthology, congeries, pasticcio, patchwork, potpourri 10 assortment, hodgepodge, hotchpotch, salmagundi 11 aggregation, gallimaufry, odds and ends, olla podrida, smorgasbord

mischance 6 mishap 7 bad luck, tragedy 8 accident, casualty 9 adversity 10 misfortune 11 contretemps

mischief 3 ill 4 evil, harm 5 prank 6 damage, strife 7 devilry, roguery, trouble, waggery 8 deviltry, sabotage 9 devilment, diablerie, vandalism 10 wrongdoing 11 naughtiness, shenanigans 12 monkeyshines

mischief-maker 3 imp 4 puck 5 devil, knave, rogue, scamp 6 rascal 7 villain 8 agitator, scalawag 9 prankster, trickster 11 rapscallion 12 rabble-rouser

mischievous 3 sly 4 arch, foxy 5 antic, saucy 6 artful, bratty, impish, tricky, vexing 7 harmful, irksome, larkish, naughty, playful, puckish, roguish, tricksy, waggish 8 annoying, damaging, perverse, prankish, rascally, sportive 9 injurious, malicious 10 bothersome, frolicsome, ill-behaved

misconception 5 error 7 fallacy, mistake 8 delusion, illusion

misconduct 8 adultery 10 wrongdoing 11 dereliction, impropriety, malfeasance, malpractice, misbehavior 12 malversation 13 transgression

miscreant 4 heel 5 felon, knave, rogue 6 outlaw, rascal, sinner, wretch 7 corrupt, culprit, heretic, hoodlum, infidel, lowlife, vicious, villain 8 apostate, criminal, depraved, infamous, perverse 9 heretical, nefarious, scoundrel, unhealthy, wrongdoer 10 blackguard, degenerate, delinquent, unbeliever, villainous

miscue 4 goof, miss, slip, trip 5 error, fluff, lapse 6 slipup 7 blooper, blunder, mistake

misdeed 3 sin 5 crime, wrong 6 breach 7 offense 9 violation 10 infraction 13 transgression

misdoubt 4 fear 5 dread 7 suspect

mise-en-scène 3 set 4 site 6 locale, medium, milieu 7 ambient, climate, context, scenery, setting 8 ambience, stage set 10 atmosphere, background 11 environment 12 stage setting, surroundings

miser 5 piker 7 hoarder, niggard, scrooge 8 tightwad 9 skinflint 10 cheapskate, pinchpenny

miserable 6 gloomy, meager, meagre, paltry, rueful, sordid, woeful 7 doleful, forlorn, piteous, pitiful, squalid 8 desolate, dolorous, downcast, hopeless, shameful, tortured, wretched 9 afflicted, destitute, sorrowful, worthless 10 despairing, despondent, melancholy 12 contemptible

Miserables, Les *author:* 4 Hugo (Victor) *character:* 6 Javert (Inspector) 7 Cosette, Fantine, Valjean (Jean)

miserly 4 mean 5 close, tight 6 greedy, stingy 7 scrimpy 8 covetous, grasping 9 niggardly, penurious, scrimping 10 avaricious 11 closefisted, tightfisted 12 cheeseparing, parsimonious 13 penny-pinching

misery 3 woe 5 agony, dolor, grief 6 sorrow 7 anguish, squalor 8 calamity, distress 9 adversity, dejection, suffering 10 affliction, depression, desolation 11 despondency 12 wretchedness

misfit 6 oddity, weirdo, zombie 7 oddball 8 maverick 9 eccentric, screwball

misfortune 3 woe 4 blow, harm, loss 5 cross, trial 7 reverse, setback, tragedy, trouble 8 accident, calamity, casualty, disaster, hardship 9 adversity, cataclysm 10 affliction, visitation 11 catastrophe, contretemps, tribulation

misgiving 4 fear 5 doubt, dread, qualm 6 unease 7 anxiety 8 distrust 9 suspicion 10 foreboding 11 premonition, trepidation 12 apprehension, presentiment

misguided 5 wrong **9** erroneous **10** ill-advised **11** injudicious **12** short-sighted

mishandle 4 flub **5** abuse, botch **6** bungle, fumble, mess up **7** rough up **8** maltreat **10** knock about, slap around

mishap 7 bad luck, tragedy **8** accident, casualty **9** adversity **11** contretemps

mishmash 6 jumble, litter, medley, muddle **7** clutter, mélange, mixture, rummage **8** pastiche, scramble **9** pasticcio, patchwork, potpourri **10** hodgepodge, hotchpotch

misidentify 5 mix up **7** confuse **8** confound

misinterpret 7 confuse, misread

mislay 4 lose

mislead 4 dupe, fool, gull, lure **5** bluff, cheat **6** betray, delude, entice, seduce, take in **7** beguile, deceive **8** hoodwink, inveigle **11** double-cross

misleading 5 false, wrong **8** delusive, delusory, specious **9** deceitful, deceptive **10** fallacious, inaccurate **11** casuistical, sophistical

mismatch 3 jar **5** clash **6** jangle **7** discord **8** conflict

misplace 4 lose

misprint 4 typo

misprision 5 scorn **7** despite, disdain, neglect **8** contempt, sedition **9** contumely, disregard **10** misconduct, negligence **11** concealment, dereliction, impropriety, malpractice

misrepresent 4 warp **5** twist **6** garble **7** distort, falsify, varnish **8** disguise **9** embellish, embroider **10** camouflage **11** counterfeit

misrepresentation 3 fib, lie **4** tale **5** story **6** canard **7** falsity, untruth **9** falsehood **10** distortion

miss 3 err, gal **4** fail, girl, lass, maid, omit, skip **5** avoid **6** damsel, escape, forget, ignore, lassie, maiden **7** failure, misfire, neglect **8** discount, leave out, overlook **9** disregard

Missa Solemnis composer 9 Beethoven (Ludwig van)

misshape 4 warp **6** deform **7** contort, distort, torture **9** disfigure

missile 4 bolt, dart **5** arrow, shell, spear **6** bullet, rocket **10** cannonball, projectile *underwater:* **7** torpedo (see also GUIDED MISSILE)

missing 4 AWOL **6** absent

mission 3 aim, job **4** duty, goal, task **5** quest **6** charge, errand, object **7** calling, embassy, purpose **8** legation, lifework, ministry, vocation **9** objective **10** assignment

missionary 7 apostle **8** emissary **10** evan-gelist, revivalist **12** propagandist, prose-lytizer

Mississippi *capital:* **7** Jackson *city:* **6** Biloxi **8** Gulfport **10** Greenville *college, university:* **12** Jackson State **8** Mill-saps *nickname:* **8** Magnolia (State) *river:* **5** Pearl **11** Mississippi *state bird:* **11** mockingbird *state flower:* **8** magnolia *state tree:* **8** magnolia

missive 4 memo, note **6** letter, report **7** epistle, message **8** dispatch

Miss Julie author 10 Strindberg (August)

Miss Lonelyhearts author 4 West (Nathanael)

Missouri *capital:* **13** Jefferson City *city:* **7** St. Louis **10** Kansas City **11** Springfield **12** Independence *college, university:* **10** Washington *lake:* **15** Lake of the Ozarks *nickname:* **6** Show Me (State) *river:* **8** Missouri **11** Mississippi *state bird:* **8** bluebird *state flower:* **8** hawthorn *state tree:* **7** dogwood

misstate 4 warp **5** color, twist **6** garble **7** distort, falsify

misstatement 3 fib, lie **4** tale **7** falsity, untruth **9** falsehood **13** prevarication

misstep 4 flub, goof, slip **5** boner, error, fluff, gaffe, lapse **6** slipup **7** blooper, blunder, faux pas

mist 3 dim, fog **4** blur, film, haze, murk **5** befog, brume, cloud **7** becloud, obscure

mistake 4 flub, slip **5** boner, error, fluff, folly, gaffe **6** boo-boo, bungle, howler, slipup **7** blooper, blunder, confuse, faux pas, take for **8** confound **10** inaccuracy

mistaken 5 false, wrong **6** all wet, faulty, flawed, untrue **7** invalid **8** specious **9** defective, incorrect, misguided, unfounded **10** fallacious, fraudulent, inaccurate **11** misinformed

mister 3 sir **7** husband *French:* **8** monsieur *German:* **4** Herr *Italian:* **6** signor *Spanish:* **5** señor

Mister Roberts author 6 Heggen (Thomas)

mistreat 5 abuse **6** ill-use, molest **7** rough up **9** brutalize, manhandle

mistress 4 doxy, moll **5** lover, woman **7** hetaira **8** dulcinea, ladylove, paramour **9** concubine, courtesan, inamorata, kept woman **10** chatelaine, girl friend *of Charles II:* **4** Gwyn (Nell) **8** Villiers (Barbara) *of Edward III:* **7** Perrers (Alice) *of Henry II (England):* **8** Clifford (Rosamund) *of Henry II (France):* **9** de Poitiers (Diane) *of Louis XV:* **9** Pompadour (Madame de)

mistrust 5 doubt **7** concern, dispute, dubiety, surmise, suspect **8** wariness

9 apprehend, misgiving, suspicion **10** foreboding, skepticism **11** incertitude, uncertainty **12** apprehension

mistrustful 4 wary **5** leery **6** uneasy **7** dubious, jealous **8** doubting **9** skeptical **10** disquieted, suspicious **12** apprehensive

misty 3 dim **4** hazy **5** foggy, vague **6** cloudy, vapory **7** blurred, obscure, tearful, unclear **8** confused, nebulous, vaporous **10** indistinct

misunderstanding 4 rift, spat, tiff **5** mixup **6** breach **7** dispute, quarrel, rupture **8** squabble **10** falling-out **12** disagreement

misuse 5 waste *of a word:* **8** malaprop **11** malapropism

mite 3 bit, jot **4** atom, iota **5** grain, minim, ounce, speck **6** acarid, tittle **7** chigger, modicum, smidgen **8** molecule, particle *family:* **8** oribatid

miter 5 crown, joint **9** headdress

mitigate 4 ease **5** abate, allay, relax, slake **6** lessen, soften, subdue, temper **7** assuage, lighten, mollify, relieve **8** palliate, moderate, tone down **9** alleviate, extenuate, meliorate

mitigation 4 ease **6** relief **8** easement

mitosis 12 cell division, karyokinesis *stage:* **8** anaphase, prophase **9** metaphase, telophase

mix 4 fuse, link, lump, meld, stir **5** blend, merge, unite **6** fusion, jumble, mingle, tangle, work in **7** amalgam, combine, concoct, confuse, conjoin **8** coalesce, compound, confound **9** associate, commingle, interfuse **10** amalgamate, crossbreed **11** intermingle **12** amalgamation

mixed 6 hybrid, impure, motley, sundry, varied **7** diluted, diverse, mongrel **8** assorted, compound **9** composite, interbred, irregular **12** multifarious **13** heterogeneous, miscellaneous

mixed bag 4 olio **5** salad **6** jumble, medley **7** mélange **8** mishmash, pastiche **9** potpourri **10** assortment, hodgepodge, miscellany **11** gallimaufry

mixed-up 5 fazed **7** jumbled **8** confused **9** flustered, perplexed **10** bewildered, disjointed, distracted, incoherent, nonplussed **12** disconcerted

mixologist 6 barman **7** tapster **9** barkeeper, bartender

mixture 4 brew, hash, olio, stew **5** alloy, blend **6** fusion, hybrid, jumble, medley **7** amalgam, farrago, mélange **8** compound, mishmash, solution **9** composite, potpourri **10** concoction, confection, miscellany, salmagundi **11** combination **12** amalgamation

mix up 5 addle **6** fuddle, jumble, muddle **7** confuse, fluster, mistake **8** befuddle, bewilder, confound **10** disarrange, discompose **11** disorganize, misidentify

mix-up 4 hash, mess, muss **5** botch, chaos, error, melee **6** muddle, tangle **7** mistake **8** shambles **9** commotion, confusion

mks unit 3 lux, ohm **4** mole, volt, watt **5** farad, henry, hertz, joule, lumen, meter, metre, tesla, weber **6** ampere, kelvin, newton, pascal, second **7** candela, coulomb, siemens **8** kilogram

Mnemosyne 6 Memory *daughters:* **5** Muses *father:* **6** Uranus *lover:* **4** Zeus *mother:* **4** Gaea

Moabite *city:* **3** Kir *god:* **7** Chemosh *king:* **5** Eglon, Mesha

Moab's father 3 Lot

moan 4 wail, weep **5** gripe, groan, whine **6** bewail, grieve, grouse, lament **7** deplore **8** complain

mob 3 jam **4** clan, gang, herd, pack, push, ring, riot **5** crowd, crush, horde, mafia, press, swarm **6** jostle, masses, rabble, throng **8** canaille, riffraff **9** hoi polloi, multitude **11** proletariat

mobile 5 fluid **6** moving **7** migrant, movable, protean **8** cellular, moveable, unstable, unsteady, variable **9** adaptable, changeful, itinerant, mercurial, migratory, unsettled, versatile **10** ambulatory, capricious, changeable, inconstant **11** peripatetic

mobile home 6 camper **7** trailer **9** Airstream

mobile-phone area 4 cell

mobilize 5 drive, impel, rally, ready, rouse **6** arouse, call up, muster, prompt, propel **7** actuate, animate, marshal **8** activate, assemble, organize **9** circulate

mobster 4 goon, thug **6** hit man **7** mafioso **8** criminal, gangster **9** godfather, racketeer

Moby Dick 5 whale **10** white whale *author:* **8** Melville (Herman) *character:* **3** Pip **6** Daggoo, Parsee **7** Ishmael **8** Queequeg, Starbuck, Tashtego *pursuer:* **4** Ahab *ship:* **6** Pequod

moccasin 6 loafer **7** slipper **8** larrigan

mock 3 ape **4** defy, fake, gibe, jape, jeer, razz, twit **5** bogus, chaff, dummy, false, feign, mimic, phony, quasi, sneer, taunt, tease **6** deride, ersatz, parody, pseudo, send up **7** deceive, feigned, imitate, lampoon, mislead **8** ridicule, satirize, so-called, spurious **9** imitation, simulated **10** artificial **11** counterfeit

mockery 4 sham **5** farce, scorn, sport **6** japery, parody, satire **7** take-off **8** contempt, derision, raillery, ridicule, travesty **9** burlesque, imitation **10** caricature **13** laughingstock

mocking 8 derisive, sardonic, scornful **9** sarcastic

mode 3 fad, way **4** chic, rage **5** state, style, vogue **6** custom, manner, method, status, system **7** fashion **9** condition, procedure, situation, technique **10** convention, dernier cri

model 4 copy, type **5** dummy, ideal, shape **6** design, effigy, mirror, mockup, symbol **7** classic, epitome, example, imitate, manikin, paragon, pattern, perfect, replica, typical **8** ensample, exemplar, flawless, mannikin, maquette, nonesuch, paradigm, standard **9** archetype, beau ideal, blueprint, classical, criterion, exemplary, miniature, nonpareil **10** apotheosis, embodiment, prototypal, touchstone **12** paradigmatic, prototypical, reproduction

moderate 3 ebb **4** calm, cool, curb, even, fair, mild, slow, so-so, wane **5** abate, bland, let up, sober **6** gentle, lessen, medium, paltry, reduce, relent, slight, soften, steady, subdue, temper **7** average, chasten, control, cushion, die away, die down, ease off, equable, lighten, limited, neutral, relieve, slacken, subside, trivial **8** centrist, constant, decrease, diminish, discreet, mediocre, middling, mitigate, restrain **9** alleviate, constrain, temperate **10** abstemious, controlled, reasonable, restrained **11** indifferent **12** conservative

moderation 7 control, measure **9** restraint **10** abstinence, constraint, limitation, temperance **13** temperateness

moderator 5 judge **7** arbiter **8** chairman, examiner, governor, mediator **10** peacemaker **11** chairperson

modern 3 new **5** fresh, novel **6** recent **7** current **8** neoteric, up-to-date **10** newfangled, present-day **12** contemporary

modernize 5 renew **6** update **8** renovate **9** refurbish **10** rejuvenate

modest 3 coy, shy **4** meek, prim **5** lowly, plain, timid **6** decent, demure, humble, prissy, proper, seemly, simple **7** bashful, prudish **8** decorous, discreet, moderate, priggish, reserved, reticent, retiring **9** diffident **10** unassuming **11** puritanical, straitlaced, unassertive, unelaborate **12** self-effacing, unornamented **13** unembellished, unembroidered, unpretentious

Modest Proposal author 5 Swift (Jonathan)

modesty 7 decency, reserve **8** chastity,

humility, timidity **9** propriety, reticence **10** diffidence

modicum 3 bit, jot **4** atom, iota, mite, whit **5** grain, minim, ounce, pinch, scrap, speck, trace **7** smidgen, soupçon **8** particle

modify 4 vary **5** adapt, alter, amend, limit, tweak **6** adjust, change, mutate, revise, rework, temper **7** qualify **8** mitigate, moderate, restrain **9** refashion

modish 4 chic **5** smart, swank **6** chichi, trendy, with-it **7** dashing, stylish **11** fashionable

Modred *father:* **6** Arthur *mother:* **8** Margawse *slayer, victim:* **6** Arthur

modulate 4 vary **5** tweak **6** adjust, attune, temper **8** fine-tune, regulate, restrain

modus ____ **7** vivendi **8** operandi

modus operandi 5 style **6** custom, manner, method, system **7** process, program, routine **8** approach, practice, strategy **9** procedure, technique

mogul 4 czar, king, lord **5** baron, nabob, ruler **6** bigwig, prince, sachem, tycoon **7** kingpin, magnate **9** plutocrat, potentate

Mohammed see MUHAMMAD

Mohawk chief 5 Brant (Joseph) **8** Hiawatha

Mohican chief 5 Uncas

moiety 3 cut **4** half, part **5** piece **7** element, portion, section, segment **8** division **9** component

moil 3 tug, wet **4** grub, to-do, work **5** churn, dirty, drive, grind, labor, swirl **6** bustle, clamor, drudge, hubbub, lather, seethe, strain, strive, uproar **7** ferment, travail, trouble, wrangle **8** drudgery **9** agitation, commotion, confusion **10** hurly-burly, turbulence

moist 3 wet **4** damp, dank, dewy **5** humid **6** clammy, steamy, sticky **7** dampish, maudlin, tearful, wettish

moisten 3 wet **6** dampen **8** humidify, saturate

moisture 4 damp **5** vapor **7** wetness **8** humidity **13** precipitation

mojo 3 hex **4** jinx **5** charm, magic, power, spell **6** hoodoo, whammy

molar 5 tooth **7** grinder *neighbor:* **6** canine

molasses 7 treacle **10** blackstrap

mold 3 die **4** cast, form, sort, type **5** forge, knead, shape, stamp **6** design, fungus **7** fashion, pattern **8** template **9** construct **11** description

moldable 6 pliant, supple **7** ductile, plastic, pliable **9** adaptable, malleable

molder 3 rot **5** decay, waste **7** crumble

9 break down, decompose 11 deteriorate 12 disintegrate

molding 4 bead, ogee 5 congé, ogive, talon, torus 6 reglet 7 annulet, beading, cavetto, cornice, reeding 8 cincture 9 baseboard *compound:* 4 beak, cyma, ogie 10 serpentine *edge:* 4 arris *flat:* 5 bevel, splay 6 fascia, fillet, listel, regula 7 chamfer *simple curve:* 4 roll 5 flute, ovolo, torus 6 scotia 8 astragal

Moldova *capital:* 8 Chisinau, Kishinev *former name:* 8 Moldavia *language:* 8 Romanian *monetary unit:* 8 Romanian *monetary unit:* 7 Romania, Ukraine *river:* 8 Dniester

moldy 5 dated, fusty, musty, passé 6 bygone, old hat 7 ancient, antique, archaic, outworn 8 mildewed, outdated 9 crumbling, moth-eaten 10 antiquated 12 old-fashioned

mole 3 spy 4 pier, quay 5 jetty, nevus 6 burrow, tunnel 9 birthmark 10 breakwater

molecule 3 bit, jot 4 iota 5 minim, speck 7 modicum 8 particle

molest 3 vex 4 bait 5 abuse, annoy, harry, tease 6 badger, bother, harass, heckle, hector, pester, plague 7 disturb, torment, trouble 9 persecute

Moll Flanders author 5 Defoe (Daniel)

mollify 4 calm, ease 5 allay 6 pacify, soften, soothe, temper 7 appease, assuage, lighten, placate, relieve, sweeten 8 mitigate 9 alleviate 10 ameliorate, conciliate, propitiate

mollusk 6 chiton *bivalve:* 4 clam 6 cockle, mussel, oyster, teredo 7 geoduck, scallop 8 shipworm *cephalopod:* 5 squid 7 octopus 8 argonaut, nautilus 10 cuttlefish *part:* 6 mantle, radula, siphon *tooth shell:* 9 dentalium *univalve:* 4 slug 5 conch, cowry, murex, snail, whelk 6 cowrie, limpet, triton 7 abalone 10 nudibranch, periwinkle

Molly ___ 7 Maguire, Pitcher

mollycoddle 3 pet 4 baby 5 humor, spoil 6 cocker, cosset, dandle, pamper 7 cater to, indulge

Moloch's pit 6 Tophet

molt 4 cast, shed, slip 6 change, slough 7 cast off, discard, ecdysis 9 slough off

molted skins 7 exuviae

molten 6 melted 7 glowing 9 liquefied

molten rock 4 lava 5 magma

moment 5 flash, jiffy, point, shake, trice 6 import, minute, second 7 instant 8 juncture, occasion 9 magnitude 10 importance 11 consequence, split second 12 significance

momentary 5 brief, quick 8 fleeting, fugitive 9 ephemeral, fugacious, transient 10 evanescent, short-lived, transitory

momentous 5 grave 7 epochal, fateful, serious, weighty 9 important 10 meaningful 11 significant, substantial 12 considerable 13 consequential

momentousness 6 import, weight 9 magnitude 10 importance 11 consequence, weightiness 12 significance

momentum 5 drive 6 energy, thrust 7 impetus, impulse 10 propulsion

Momo author 4 Ende (Michael)

momus 6 carper, critic, mocker 7 caviler 8 caviller 9 detractor 11 faultfinder

Monaco *commune:* 10 Monte Carlo *language:* 6 French *monetary unit:* 4 euro *neighbor:* 6 France *prince:* 6 Albert 7 Rainier *princess:* 5 Grace

monad 3 one 4 atom, unit 8 zoospore 9 protozoan

Mona Lisa 10 La Gioconda *painter:* 7 da Vinci (Leonardo) 8 Leonardo (da Vinci)

monarch 4 czar, king, raja, tsar, tzar 5 queen, rajah, ruler 6 kaiser, prince 7 emperor, empress, majesty 9 butterfly, potentate, sovereign

monarchical 5 regal, royal 6 kingly 8 imperial, kinglike, majestic 9 sovereign

monarch's daughter 8 princess *Portuguese, Spanish:* 7 infanta

monarch's son 6 prince *French:* 7 dauphin *Portuguese, Spanish:* 7 infante

monarchy 4 rule 5 realm, reign 7 kingdom 8 kingship 9 autocracy, monocracy 11 sovereignty

monastery 5 abbey 6 friary, priory 7 convent, nunnery 8 cloister *Buddhist:* 8 lamasery *Eastern Orthodox:* 5 laura *head:* 5 abbot, prior

monastic 4 abbé, monk 7 ascetic, brother 8 isolated, secluded 9 reclusive 10 cloistered 11 sequestered

___ Mondrian 4 Piet

monetary 6 fiscal 9 financial, pecuniary 10 numismatic

monetary rate 7 millage

monetary unit see at individual countries

money 4 cash, coin, gelt, jack, kale, loot, pelf, swag 5 bread, chips, dough, funds, lucre, moola, rhino 6 boodle, change, dinero, do-re-mi, mammon, moolah, riches, specie, wampum, wealth 7 cabbage, capital, coinage, lettuce, needful, scratch, stipend 8 bankroll, currency, finances, treasure 9 resources 10 greenbacks 11 filthy lucre, legal tender

moneyed 4 rich 5 flush 6 loaded 7 opulent, wealthy, well-off 8 affluent, well-to-do 10 prosperous, well-heeled

money-grubber 5 miser 7 hoarder, niggard, scrooge 8 tightwad 9 skinflint 10 cheapskate 12 penny-pincher

moneymaking 6 paying 7 gainful 9 lucrative 10 profitable, well-paying, worthwhile 12 advantageous, remunerative

monger 4 hawk, sell, vend 6 broker, dealer, hawker, peddle, trader, vendor 7 higgler, packman, peddler 8 huckster

Mongol conqueror 9 Tamerlane 10 Kublai Khan 11 Genghis Khan, Tamburlaine

Mongolia *capital:* 9 Ulan Bator 11 Ulaanbaatar *conqueror:* 6 Ögödei 11 Genghis Khan *desert:* 4 Gobi *lake:* 6 Baikal *monetary unit:* 6 tugrik *mountain range:* 5 Altai, Altay 6 Kentai 7 Hentiyn 9 Altai Shan, Altay Shan *neighbor:* 5 China 6 Russia *river:* 5 Orhun 7 Selenga

mongrel 3 cur 4 mule, mutt 5 cross 6 hybrid 7 bastard, mixture 8 half-bred 9 crossbred, half blood, half-breed 10 crossbreed

moniker 3 tag 4 name 6 handle 8 cognomen, nickname 9 sobriquet 11 appellation, designation

monish 4 warn

monition 6 caveat 7 caution, portent, warning 11 forewarning

monitor 4 test 5 check, watch 6 screen 7 adviser, observe, oversee 8 watchdog 11 keep track of

Monitor *designer:* 8 Ericsson (John) *opponent:* 8 Virginia 9 Merrimack

monitory 7 warning 8 advisory 10 cautionary

monk 4 abbé 5 friar 7 brother 8 cenobite, monastic 9 anchorite *Buddhist:* 4 lama 5 bonze *Hindu:* 8 sannyasi *Roman Catholic:* 8 Capuchin, Salesian, Trappist 9 Carmelite, Dominican 10 Carthusian, Cistercian, Franciscan 11 Augustinian *room:* 4 cell *shaven crown:* 7 tonsure *title:* 3 Dom, Fra 5 Padre

monkey 3 imp 4 mess 5 gamin 6 meddle, simian, tamper, urchin 8 busybody 9 interfere, interlope *New World:* 4 titi 6 howler, spider, uakari, woolly 7 sapajou, tamarin 8 capuchin, marmoset, squirrel 11 douroucouli *Old World:* 5 Diana, drill 6 guenon, langur, rhesus, vervet 7 colobus, hanuman, macaque 8 mandrill, mangabey 9 proboscis 10 Barbary ape

monkeyshine 3 gag 4 dido, jape, lark 5 antic, caper, prank, stunt, trick 6 frolic 10 shenanigan, tomfoolery

monocratic 5 absolute, despotic 9 arbitrary, autarchic, tyrannous 10 autocratic, tyrannical

monogram 8 initials

monograph 5 study 6 thesis 8 tractate, treatise 9 discourse 12 disquisition, dissertation

monopolize 3 hog 5 sew up 6 absorb, corner 7 control, engross 8 dominate, take over

monopoly 5 trust 6 cartel, corner 7 control 9 ownership, syndicate 10 consortium, domination 11 exclusivity

monotone 5 drone

monotonous 4 blah, dull 6 boring, dreary 7 droning, humdrum, one-note, uniform 8 singsong, unvaried 9 unvarying 10 pedestrian, repetitive 11 repetitious

monotony 6 tedium 7 humdrum 8 flatness, sameness 10 uniformity

monsoon 6 deluge 8 downpour 9 rainstorm 10 cloudburst

monster 4 ogre 5 beast, freak, giant, whale 6 mutant, ogress 8 behemoth, bogeyman, colossus, giantess 9 hellhound, leviathan, manticore *biblical:* 5 Rehab 8 Behemoth 9 Leviathan *female:* 6 Gorgon, Medusa, Scylla *fire-breathing:* 6 dragon, Typhon 7 Chimera 8 Chimaera *fowl-dragon:* 10 cockatrice *French:* 8 Tarasque *horse-fish:* 11 hippocampus *hundred-armed:* 9 Enceladus *hundred-eyed:* 5 Argus *hundred-handed:* 8 Briareus *lion-eagle:* 7 griffin *serpent-headed:* 6 gorgon *study of:* 10 teratology *three-bodied:* 6 Geryon *three-headed dog:* 8 Cerberus *two-headed dog:* 6 Orthos *water:* 6 kraken *woman-bird:* 5 Harpy *woman-lion:* 6 Sphinx *woman-serpent:* 7 Echidna (see also DRAGON)

___ **monster** 4 Gila

monstrosity 4 mess 5 freak 6 fright, horror 7 eyesore, outrage, prodigy 8 atrocity, enormity 11 abomination 12 malformation

monstrous 4 huge, vast 5 awful, giant, large 7 glaring, heinous, hellish, hideous, immense, mammoth, massive, titanic 8 aberrant, abnormal, colossal, deformed, dreadful, enormous, fiendish, freakish, gigantic, god-awful, gruesome, horrible, infamous, shocking, towering 9 atrocious, egregious, fantastic, frightful, grotesque, loathsome, malformed, unnatural 10 diabolical, flagitious, gargantuan, horrendous, impressive, monumental, outrageous, prodigious, scandalous, stupendous, tremendous 11 elephantine

montage 6 jumble, medley 7 mélange, mixture 9 composite, patchwork, potpourri 10 assortment, miscellany 12 conglomerate

Montagues' enemies 8 Capulets

Montaigne's forte 5 essay

Montana *capital:* 6 Helena *city:* 5 Butte 7 Bozeman 8 Billings, Missoula 10 Great Falls *lake:* 8 Flathead *motto:* 9 Oro y plata *mountain:* 7 Granite (Peak) *nickname:* 8 Treasure (State) *park:* 7 Glacier *river:* 8 Missouri 11 Yellowstone *state bird:* 10 meadowlark *state flower:* 10 bitterroot *state tree:* 13 ponderosa pine

Monteverdi opera 5 Orfeo 7 Arianna

Montezuma *capital:* 12 Tenochtitlán *conqueror:* 6 Cortés, Cortéz (Hernán, Hernando) *people:* 6 Aztecs *revenge:* 8 diarrhea

month *Hindu:* 3 Pus 4 Asin, Jeth, Magh 5 Aghan, Chait, Sawan 6 Asargh, Bhadon, Kartik, Phagun 7 Baisakh *Jewish:* 4 Adar, Elul, Iyar 5 Nisan, Sivan, Tebet 6 Kislev, Shebat, Tammuz, Tishri 7 Heshvan *Muslim:* 4 Rabi 5 Rajab, Safar 6 Jumada, Sha'ban 7 Ramadan, Shawwal 8 Muharram 9 Dhu'l-Hijja, Dhu'l-Qa'dah

Montmartre church 10 Sacré Coeur

Montserrat *capital:* 8 Plymouth *discoverer:* 8 Columbus (Christopher) *location:* 10 West Indies *territory of:* 7 Britain *volcano:* 9 Soufrière

monument 5 cairn, stela, stupa 7 memento, tribute 8 archives, cenotaph, document, memorial 9 footstone, headstone, tombstone 10 gravestone 11 grave marker, testimonial *prehistoric:* 6 dolmen, menhir 7 cromlech, megalith

monumental 4 huge, vast 6 mighty, mortal 7 awesome, immense, mammoth, massive 8 enormous, gigantic, historic, majestic, towering 9 monstrous 10 prodigious, stupendous, tremendous 11 mountainous, outstanding 12 overwhelming

mooch 3 bat, beg, bum 4 grub, roam, rove 5 amble, cadge, drift, range, slink, sneak, steal, stray 6 ramble, sponge, wander 7 maunder, meander, saunter 8 freeload, scrounge 9 panhandle

mooching 7 beggary 9 mendicity 10 mendicancy

mood 3 air 4 aura, feel, tone, whim 5 fancy, humor 6 spirit, temper, vagary 7 caprice, emotion, feeling, mind-set 8 ambiance, ambience 9 character, semblance 10 atmosphere 11 disposition, personality, temperament

moody 4 glum 5 mopey 6 fickle, gloomy 7 pensive 8 unstable 9 mercurial, whimsical 10 capricious, changeable, depressive, inconstant, melancholy 13 temperamental

moola 4 cash, coin, pelf, swag 5 bread, dough, money 6 dinero, specie, wampum 7 cabbage, scratch 9 long green

moon 4 gape, mope 5 dream 6 dawdle 8 languish 9 satellite *dark area:* 4 mare 5 maria (plural) *farside god:* 3 Sin 5 Nanna 6 Meztli *goddess:* 4 Luna 5 Diana, Tanit 6 Hecate, Hekate, Selena, Selene, Tanith 7 Artemis, Astarte *valley:* 4 rill *vehicle:* 3 LEM (see also SATELLITE)

Moon and Sixpence author 7 Maugham (W. Somerset)

mooncalf 4 dolt, fool 5 dunce, ninny 7 jackass, tomfool 9 simpleton

Moon River composer 7 Mancini (Henry)

moonshine 4 bosh, jake 5 hokum 6 bunkum, humbug 7 bootleg, eyewash, hogwash 8 homebrew, malarkey, nonsense, tommyrot 9 poppycock 10 balderdash, bathtub gin, contraband, flapdoodle 11 mountain dew 12 blatherskite

Moonstone, The *author:* 7 Collins (Wilkie) *detective:* 4 Cuff

moonstruck 4 daft, nuts 5 batty, corny, flaky, kooky, mushy, nutty, sappy, wacko, wacky 6 crazed, cuckoo, fruity, insane, screwy 7 berserk, bonkers, lunatic, maudlin, touched 8 romantic 9 nostalgic, schmaltzy 10 lovey-dovey, saccharine, unbalanced 11 sentimental

moor 3 bog, fen 4 dock, fell 5 berth, catch, tie up 6 anchor, Berber, fasten, Muslim, secure, tether 7 peat bog 8 make fast, Moroccan *fictional:* 7 Othello

moose 6 cervid *female:* 3 cow *male:* 4 bull *relative:* 3 elk 4 deer

moot 5 argue, plead 6 broach, debate 7 agitate, bring up, canvass, discuss, dispute, dubious, suggest, suspect 8 abstract, academic, arguable, disputed, doubtful 9 debatable, introduce, thrash out, uncertain, unsettled, ventilate 10 disputable, unresolved 11 problematic 12 questionable 13 controversial

mop 4 swab, wipe

mope 4 fret, idle, moon, pine, pout, sigh, stew, sulk 5 brood, drift, mosey 6 dawdle, linger 7 maunder, meander, saunter 8 languish

mopes 4 funk 5 blues, dumps, ennui, slump 7 dismals, malaise, sadness 8 dolefuls 10 depression, melancholy 11 unhappiness

mopey 3 low 4 blue, down, glum 6 broody, droopy, morose 7 doleful

8 cast down, dejected, downcast
9 depressed **10** dispirited, melancholy,
spiritless
moppet 3 kid, tot **4** tyke **5** chick, child
7 toddler **8** juvenile **9** youngster
mop up 4 beat, drub, dust, lick, whip
6 absorb, garner, gather **7** shellac,
trounce **8** complete, lambaste **9** overwhelm
moral 3 saw **4** good, just, pure, rule
5 adage, axiom, gnome, maxim, noble,
right **6** chaste, decent, dictum, honest,
lesson, proper, saying, truism **7** epigram, ethical, preachy, precept,
proverb, upright, virtual **8** aphorism,
apothegm, didactic, elevated, sermonic,
virtuous **9** honorable, righteous
10 high-minded, principled, scrupulous, upstanding **11** right-minded
13 conscientious
morale 4 mood **5** heart **6** esprit, mettle,
spirit, temper **7** resolve **10** confidence
13 esprit de corps
moralistic 5 noble, pious **7** canting, ethical **8** didactic, virtuous **9** righteous
10 principled **11** pharisaical, right-
minded **13** sanctimonious
morality 5 ethic, honor, mores **6** purity,
virtue **7** decency, probity **8** goodness
9 integrity, rectitude, rightness **11** saintliness, uprightness **13** righteousness
moralize 6 preach **7** lecture **9** preachify,
sermonize **11** pontificate
morals 5 mores **6** ethics, ideals **8** scruples **9** integrity, standards **10** principles
morass 3 bog, fen, web **4** knot, maze,
mesh, mire, quag, trap **5** marsh, skein,
snarl, swamp **6** jungle, muddle, tangle
8 quagmire **9** imbroglio
moratorium 3 ban **5** delay **8** interval
10 suspension
moray 3 eel
morbid 4 dark, sick **5** moody **6** gloomy,
grisly, morose, sickly, sullen **7** unsound
8 diseased, gruesome **9** saturnine,
unhealthy **11** melancholic, unwholesome **12** pathological
mordancy 7 acidity **8** acerbity, acridity,
acrimony, asperity, pungency **9** harshness, sharpness **10** causticity, tren-
chancy **11** astringency, sardonicism
12 incisiveness
mordant 4 keen **5** acrid, salty, sharp
6 biting **7** burning, caustic, cutting,
pungent **8** incisive, sardonic, scathing
9 sarcastic, trenchant
Mordecai *cousin:* **6** Esther *father:* **4** Jair
mother: **6** Esther
more 3 new, too **4** also, else, plus
5 added, again, along, extra, fresh,
older, other, spare **6** as well, better,

nearer, withal **7** another, besides, farther, further, greater **8** likewise, moreover **9** increased **10** additional
More book 6 Utopia
more or less 5 about **7** roughly
13 approximately
moreover 3 and, too **4** also **6** as well,
withal **7** besides, further **8** likewise
10 in addition **11** furthermore **12** additionally
mores 6 ethics, habits, values **7** beliefs,
customs, manners **8** folkways **9** amenities, etiquette **10** civilities **11** proprieties
Morgana's brother 6 Arthur
Morgan le Fay 9 sorceress *brother:*
6 Arthur (King)
moribund 5 dying **6** ebbing, fading **7** dormant, outworn **8** decaying, expiring,
inactive **9** declining **11** obsolescent
13 deteriorating
Mormon Church *administrative unit:*
4 ward **5** stake *founder:* **5** Smith
(Joseph) *leader:* **5** Young (Brigham)
priest: **5** elder
Mormon State 4 Utah
morning 4 dawn **5** sunup **6** aurora
7 dawning, sunrise **8** cockcrow, daybreak, daylight, forenoon *moisture:*
3 dew **8** dewdrops *song:* **6** aubade
Morocco *capital:* **5** Rabat *city:* **3** Fès
6 Meknès **9** Marrakech, Marrakesh
10 Casablanca *coast:* **7** Barbary *language:* **6** Arabic, Berber *monetary unit:*
6 dirham *mountain:* **7** Toubkal *mountain
range:* **3** Rif **5** Atlas *neighbor:* **5** Spain
7 Algeria **13** Western Sahara *sea:*
13 Mediterranean
moron 4 dodo, dolt, dope, fool
5 dummy, dunce, idiot **6** cretin, dimwit,
stupid **7** dullard, half-wit **8** dumbbell,
imbecile, numskull **9** ignoramus, lamebrain, numbskull, simpleton
moronic 4 dull, dumb **6** simple, stupid
8 backward, retarded **9** brainless, dim-
witted, imbecile **10** half-witted, slow-
witted **12** feebleminded, simpleminded
morose 4 dour, glum, sour **5** moody,
sulky **6** cranky, crusty, gloomy, morbid,
sullen **7** crabbed, unhappy **9** depressed,
saturnine **10** depressive, ill-humored,
melancholy
morph 6 change, mutate **7** convert
9 transform, transmute **12** metamorphose, transmogrify
Morpheus *father:* **6** Hypnos *god of:*
5 sleep
Morrison novel 4 Jazz, Love, Sula
7 Beloved **9** Bluest Eye (The) **13** Song
of Solomon
Morse code *dash:* **3** dah *dot:* **3** dit
morsel 3 bit **4** bite **5** crumb, goody,

piece, scrap, snack, taste, treat **6** dainty, nibble, tidbit **7** soupçon **8** delicacy, fragment, kickshaw, mouthful

mortal 3 man **5** awful, being, fatal, frail, human, party **6** deadly, lethal, person **7** deathly, earthly, extreme, fleshly, tedious, worldly **8** creature, ruthless, temporal **9** merciless, personage **10** implacable, individual, perishable **11** conceivable

mortality 5 flesh **7** mankind **8** fatality, humanity **9** death rate, humankind, lethality **10** deadliness

mortar 5 grout **6** binder, cannon, cement, vessel **7** plaster, sealant **8** howitzer, ordnance

Morte d'Arthur author 6 Malory (Thomas)

mortgage 4 hock, lien, pawn **6** pledge **10** obligation

mortician 8 embalmer **10** undertaker

mortified 6 shamed **7** ascetic, ashamed, austere **8** red-faced **9** chagrined **10** humiliated, shamefaced **11** embarrassed

mortify 5 abash, shame **6** dismay **7** chagrin, perturb **8** disgrace **9** discomfit, embarrass, humiliate

mortuary 8 funereal **10** sepulchral **11** funeral home

mosaic 5 inlay **7** chimera **8** terrazzo **9** composite, patchwork **12** tessellation *piece:* **6** smalto **7** tessera **8** tesserae (plural)

Moscow *cathedral:* **11** Saint Basil's *citadel:* **7** Kremlin *resident:* **9** Muscovite

Moses *brother:* **5** Aaron *brother-in-law:* **5** Hobab *deathplace:* **4** Nebo *father-in-law:* **6** Jethro *sister:* **6** Miriam *son:* **7** Eliezer, Gershom *spy:* **5** Caleb *successor:* **6** Joshua *wife:* **8** Zipporah

mosey 4 mope **5** amble, drift **6** dawdle, linger, ramble, stroll, wander **7** maunder, meander, saunter

mosh 4 slam **9** slam-dance

Moslem see MUSLIM

mosque 6 masjid *niche:* **6** mihrab *prayer caller:* **7** muezzin *turret:* **7** minaret

mosquito 5 culex *genus:* **5** Aëdes, Culex **9** Anopheles

moss 9 bryophyte *kind:* **4** peat **8** sphagnum *part:* **4** seta **7** capsule, rhizoid *study of:* **8** bryology

mossback 4 fogy **6** fossil **10** fuddy-duddy **11** reactionary **12** antediluvian, conservative **13** stick-in-the-mud

mostly 6 mainly **7** chiefly, largely, overall, usually **9** generally, primarily **11** principally **13** predominantly

mote 3 bit, dot, jot **4** iota, whit **5** grain, point, speck, trace **8** flyspeck, particle

moth *immature:* **5** larva **6** larvae (plural) **11** caterpillar *kind:* **4** luna **7** codling, tussock **8** Cecropia, silkworm **9** browntail *order:* **11** Lepidoptera

moth-eaten 4 worn **5** dated, dingy, faded, mangy, moldy, musty, passé, ratty, seedy **6** bygone, old hat, patchy, shabby **7** antique, archaic, raggedy, run-down, unkempt **8** decrepit, outdated, outmoded, tattered, timeworn **10** antiquated, down-at-heel, threadbare **11** dilapidated

mother 3 dam, mom **4** mama, root **5** fount, mammy, mater, momma, mommy, mummy, nurse **6** origin, source **7** care for, nurture **9** prototype, rootstock **10** provenance, wellspring *combining form:* **4** matr **5** matri, matro

mother country 8 homeland **10** fatherland

Mother Courage author 6 Brecht (Bertolt)

motherly 8 maternal **9** nurturing **10** protective

mother-of-pearl 5 nacre

Mother of Presidents 8 Virginia

Mother of the Gods 3 Ops **4** Rhea **6** Cybele

motif 4 idea, text **5** point, theme, topic **6** design, device, figure, matter **7** pattern, subject **13** subject matter

motion 4 stir, sway **6** signal **7** gesture **8** movement, proposal, stirring **9** agitation

motionless 5 fixed, inert, still **6** frozen, static **7** stalled **8** becalmed, immobile, stagnant, unmoving **9** immovable, steadfast **10** stationary, stock-still

motion picture see MOVIE

motivate 4 fire, goad, move, spur **5** impel, pique, rouse **6** arouse, excite, incite, induce, prompt **7** actuate, inspire, provoke, quicken, trigger **8** inspirit, persuade **9** galvanize, influence, stimulate

motivation 4 spur **5** drive **7** impetus, impulse **8** ambition, catalyst, stimulus **9** impulsion, incentive, stimulant **10** incitation, incitement **11** inspiration, instigation, provocation

motive 3 aim, end **4** spur **5** cause, point, theme, topic **6** design, device, figure, intent, matter, object, reason, spring **7** impulse, pattern, purpose, subject **8** stimulus **9** incentive, intention, rationale **10** incitement, inducement **11** inspiration

motley 5 mixed, salad **6** jumble, medley, varied **7** dappled, diverse, piebald **8** assorted, pastiche **9** disparate, multihued **10** assortment, hodgepodge, miscellany, multicolor, variegated **11** galli-maufry, varicolored **12** conglomerate, multicolored, multifarious, parti-colored **13** heterogeneous, miscellaneous, polychromatic

motor 3 car **4** auto, ride **5** buggy, drive **6** cruise, engine **7** machine **10** automobile

motorboat 6 launch **7** cruiser, inboard **8** outboard, runabout **12** cabin cruiser

motorcycle 7 chopper **8** minibike **9** trail bike *adjunct:* **7** sidecar

Motown 7 Detroit

mottle 4 spot **5** fleck **6** blotch, dapple, marble **7** spatter, speckle, stipple, splotch

mottled 5 tabby **7** blotchy, dappled, flecked, spotted **8** blotched, brindled, speckled **9** checkered **10** variegated

motto 3 cry **5** adage, axiom, maxim **6** byword, saying, slogan, war cry **7** precept, proverb **8** aphorism **9** battle cry, catchword, watchword **10** shibboleth **11** catchphrase

moue 3 mow, mug **4** face, pout **7** grimace

mound 4 bank, cock, heap, hill, hump, mass, pile **5** cairn, drift, knoll, shock, stack **6** barrow, tumuli (plural) **7** bulwark, hillock, rampart, tumulus **9** elevation **10** embankment *Buddhist:* **5** stupa *burial, Eastern Europe:* **6** kurgan *of detritus:* **4** kame *of sand:* **4** dune *of stones:* **5** cairn

mount 3 alp, wax **4** lift, peak, rise, show, soar **5** arise, build, climb, frame, horse, put on, raise, rouse, scale, set up, stage, steed, swell **6** ascend, aspire, deepen, expand, launch, uprear **7** advance, augment, display, enhance, enlarge, install, magnify, produce, support, upsurge **8** bestride, escalade, escalate, heighten, increase, multiply, redouble **9** aggravate, intensify **10** promontory

mountain 3 alp, lot **4** bank, crag, dome, heap, hill, hulk, lump, mass, mesa, much, peak, pile, slew **5** bluff, butte, drift, mound, shock, stack **6** height *Alaska:* **4** Bona **6** Denali **7** Foraker, Sanford **8** McKinley, Wrangell *Alberta:* **6** Castle **10** Eisenhower *Alps:* **4** Rosa (Monte) **5** Blanc, Eiger **8** Jungfrau **10** Matterhorn *Angola:* **4** Moco *Antarctica:* **4** Mohl **6** Vinson (Massif) **7** Gardner **9** Elizabeth *Appalachians:* **8** Mitchell **10** Kittatinny **10** Washington **13** Clingmans Dome *Argentina:* **9** Aconcagua *Australia:* **4** Ziel **5** Bruce **6** Cradle **9** Kosciusko *biblical:* **5** Horeb, Tabor **6** Hermon **8** Har Tavor *Black Hills:* **6** Harney (Peak) *Bolivia:* **6** Sorata **8** Illi-

mani *Borneo:* **8** Kinabalu, Kinabulu *California:* **5** Guyot **6** Shasta, Sonora (Peak) **7** Palomar, Whitney **8** Tuolumne **10** Buena Vista, Stanislaus *Canada:* **5** Logan *China:* **4** Emei, Song *Colorado:* **5** Pikes (Peak) **9** Purgatory (Peak) *Costa Rica:* **6** Blanco **14** Chirripó Grande *Cyprus:* **7** Olympus, Troodos *depression:* **3** col *Dominican Republic:* **6** Duarte **8** Trujillo *Egypt:* **4** Musa **5** Sinai *Fiji:* **8** Victoria **9** Tomaniivi *foot:* **8** piedmont *France:* **5** Blanc (Mont) *Gabon:* **8** Iboundji *Georgia:* **8** Springer **10** Oglethorpe *Germany:* **7** Zollern **9** Zugspitze **11** Fichtelberg *Greece:* **3** Ida **5** Athos, Levka **7** Helicon, Olympus **9** Parnassus, Psiloriti **10** Pendelikon, Pentelicus *Greenland:* **9** Gunnbjorn *Himalayas:* **6** Lhotse **7** Everest **9** Annapurna *India:* **5** Japvo *Indonesia:* **4** Lawu **5** Kwoka, Lawoe, Raung **6** Raoeng, Semeru **7** Kerinci *Israel:* **5** Meron **6** Carmel *Ivory Coast:* **5** Nimba *Japan:* **4** Fuji **5** Iwate **7** Fujisan **8** Fujiyama *Java:* **5** Liman *Jordan:* **3** Hor **5** Hārūn *Maine:* **8** Katahdin *Malaysia:* **5** Ophir, Tahan **6** Ledang *Mediterranean entrance:* **5** Calpe **7** Gibraltar *Mexico:* **7** Orizaba (Pico de) *New York:* **4** Bear **5** Marcy *North America's highest:* **6** Denali **8** McKinley *North Carolina:* **8** Mitchell *Oman:* **4** Sham *Oregon:* **4** Hood *Pakistan:* **9** Tirich Mir *Papua New Guinea:* **7** Wilhelm *Pennine Alps:* **4** Rosa (Monte) *Philippines:* **3** Apo, Iba **4** Labo **5** Silay *ridge:* **4** spur **5** arête, crest **7** sawbuck *Romania:* **11** Moldoveanul *South America:* **7** Roraima **9** Aconcagua *South Dakota:* **6** Custer (Peak) *Switzerland:* **3** Dom **4** Rosa (Monte) **5** Eiger **8** Jungfrau **10** Matterhorn *Syria:* **4** Druz **5** Duruz *Tanzania:* **11** Kilimanjaro *Tasmania:* **4** Ossa *Tennessee:* **13** Clingmans Dome *Togo:* **4** Agou *Utah:* **5** Kings *Vermont:* **9** Mansfield *Vietnam:* **8** Ngoo Linh *Virginia:* **6** Rogers *Western Hemisphere's highest:* **9** Aconcagua *world's highest:* **7** Everest *Wyoming:* **5** Cloud **7** Gannett (Peak) (see also PEAK)

mountain climbing *equipment:* **3** axe, nut **5** piton **7** crampon **9** carabiner *maneuver:* **6** rappel **10** rappelling

mountain dew see MOONSHINE

mountain formation 7 orogeny **10** orogenesis

mountainous 4 huge, vast **6** alpine, mighty **7** immense, mammoth, massive **8** enormous, gigantic, towering **10** monumental, prodigious

mountain pass 3 col *Afghanistan-Pakistan:* **6** Khyber *Alps:* **5** Gries *Califor-*

nia: 4 Muir 6 Sonora *China-Myanmar:*
5 Namni *Colorado:* 3 Ute 5 Mosca,
Muddy, Music, Raton *Europe:* 8 Moravian *Greece:* 5 Rupel *Hindu Kush Mts.:*
5 Dorah, Durah *Pakistan:* 5 Bolan,
Gomal, Gumal *Sierra Nevada:* 4 Mono
Switzerland: 5 Furka, Gemmi 7 Grimsel
8 Lötschen *Tunisia:* 4 Faïd *Ukrainian:*
5 Uzhok *Wyoming:* 5 Union
mountain range *Asia:* 5 Altai, Altay
8 Himalaya, Tien Shan 9 Altai Shan,
Altay Shan, Himalayan, Himalayas,
Hindu Kush *Australia:* 8 Flinders
Europe: 4 Alps 10 Carpathian *Germany:*
4 Harz 5 Hartz *Greece:* 4 Oeta *India:*
5 Ghats *Iran:* 6 Zagros *Italy:* 9 Apennines
Mexico: 11 Sierra Madre *North Africa:*
5 Atlas *North America:* 5 Rocky 7 Rockies 11 Appalachian *Russia:* 4 Ural *Scotland:* 9 Grampians *Sinai:* 9 Gebel Musa
Slovakia: 5 Tatra, Tatry 9 High Tatra
South America: 5 Andes *Turkey:* 6 Taurus
United States: 5 Rocky, White 6 Brooks
7 Cascade, Olympic, Rockies, Sawatch,
Wasatch 8 Absaroka, Aleutian, Catskill,
Wrangell 9 Blue Ridge, Wind River
10 Adirondack, Bitterroot, Black Hills,
Clearwater, Grand Teton *Zimbabwe:*
6 Matopo (Hills) 7 Matoppo (Hills)
Mountain State 7 Montana 12 West Virginia
mountebank 5 quack 6 con man 8 swindler 9 charlatan 11 flimflammer, quacksalver 13 confidence man
Mount St. Helens 7 volcano
mourn 3 rue 6 bemoan, bewail, grieve,
lament, sorrow 7 deplore, protest
mournful 3 sad 6 dismal, gloomy, rueful,
somber, triste, woeful 7 doleful, forlorn, joyless, unhappy 8 dejected,
desolate, dolorous, funereal, grievous,
wretched 9 dirgelike, plaintive 10 depressing, despondent, dispirited,
lugubrious, melancholy 11 distressing,
melancholic, regrettable, unfortunate
12 heavyhearted
mournfulness 5 blues, dumps, gloom
7 dismals, sadness 9 dejection
10 depression, melancholy
mourning 5 grief 7 keening, remorse,
wailing, weeping 8 grieving 9 lamenting, morbidity, sorrowing, ululation
10 heartbreak 11 bereavement, lamentation
Mourning Becomes Electra *author:*
6 O'Neill (Eugene)
mourning period, Jewish 5 shiva 6 shivah
mourning symbol 7 armband
mouse 6 rodent, shiner 8 black eye
mousy 3 shy 4 drab, dull 5 plain, quiet,

timid 7 bashful 8 retiring, timorous
9 colorless, diffident, shrinking
11 unassertive 12 self-effacing
mouth 3 gob 4 trap 5 chops 6 kisser
8 entrance 10 embouchure
mouthlike opening 5 stoma 7 stomata
(plural)
mouthpiece 5 organ 6 puppet 7 speaker
8 front man 9 spokesman 10 figurehead
11 spokeswoman 12 spokesperson
mouthwatering 5 sapid, tasty, yummy
6 savory, toothy 8 tasteful 9 delicious,
palatable, succulent, toothsome
10 appetizing, delectable 11 good-tasting
mouthy 4 glib 5 gabby, talky, windy
7 verbose, voluble 8 effusive 9 bombastic, garrulous, talkative
movable 5 loose 6 mobile, motile, roving
8 portable 10 changeable
movables 5 goods 7 effects 8 chattels
10 belongings 11 furnishings
move 3 act 4 lead, spur, stir, sway
5 bring, budge, carry, drive, impel,
leave, march, rouse, shift, start, touch
6 affect, convey, depart, excite, incite,
induce, kindle, prompt, propel 7 actuate, advance, animate, conduct,
impress, inspire, migrate, proceed, propose, provoke, request, suggest 8 activate, dislodge, displace, evacuate, get
along, maneuver, motivate, persuade,
progress, relocate, resettle, transfer,
withdraw 9 dislocate, galvanize, influence, instigate, stimulate, transport
movement 4 flow, stir 5 tempo, trend
6 action, motion 7 crusade 8 activity,
campaign, dynamism, maneuver,
progress, stirring, tendency, velocity
9 migration *music:* 4 moto *reflex:* 5 taxis
stimulated: 7 kinesis
movie 4 cine, film, show 5 flick 6 cinema, talkie 7 picture 9 photoplay 11 picture show 13 motion picture *cowboy:*
5 oater 7 western *short:* 4 clip 8 newsreel
movie director *American:* 3 Lee (Spike),
Ray (Nicholas) 4 Coen (Joel), Ford
(John), Hill (George Roy), Mann
(Anthony), Penn (Arthur), Ritt (Martin), Ross (Herbert), Sirk (Douglas),
Wise (Robert) 5 Allen (Woody), Ashby
(Hal), Brown (Clarence), Capra
(Frank), Cukor (George), Demme
(Jonathan), Donen (Stanley), Fosse
(Bob), Hawks (Howard), Ivory (James),
Jonze (Spike), Kazan (Elia), LeRoy
(Mervyn), Logan (Joshua), Lucas
(George), Lumet (Sidney), Lynch
(David), Moore (Michael), Roach
(Hal), Stone (Oliver), Vidor (King),

Walsh (Raoul), Whale (James), Wyler (William), Zwick (Ed) **6** Altman (Robert), Beatty (Warren), Benton (Robert), Brooks (Richard), Burton (Tim), Cimino (Michael), Curtiz (Michael), Fuller (Samuel), Gibson (Mel), Hanson (Curtis), Howard (Ron), Huston (John), Kramer (Stanley), Malick (Terrence), Pakula (Alan), Parker (Alan), Welles (Orson), Wilder (Billy) **7** Borzage (Frank), Cameron (James), Chaplin (Charlie), Coppola (Francis Ford, Sofia), Costner (Kevin), De Mille (Cecil B.), De Palma (Brian), Fleming (Victor), Gilliam (Terry), Jewison (Norman), Kubrick (Stanley), McCarey (Leo), Nichols (Mike), Pollack (Sydney), Redford (Robert), Siodmak (Robert), Stevens (George), Sturges (Preston), Van Sant (Gus), Wellman (William) **8** Avildsen (John), Eastwood (Clint), Flaherty (Robert), Friedkin (William), Griffith (David Wark), Jarmusch (Jim), Levinson (Barry), Lubitsch (Ernst), Marshall (Penny), Minnelli (Vincente), Mulligan (Robert), Scorsese (Martin), Zemeckis (Robert) **9** Carpenter (John), Hitchcock (Alfred), Milestone (Lewis), Peckinpah (Sam), Preminger (Otto), Spielberg (Steven), Sternberg (Josef von), Streisand (Barbra), Tarantino (Quentin), Zinnemann (Fred) **10** Cassavetes (John), Heckerling (Amy), Mankiewicz (Joseph), Soderbergh (Steven) **11** Bogdanovich (Peter) **13** Frankenheimer (John) *Australian:* **4** Weir (Peter) **6** Noonan (Chris) **9** Armstrong (Gillian), Beresford (Bruce) *Austrian:* **4** Lang (Fritz) **8** Stroheim (Erich von), Sternberg (Josef von) *British:* **4** Lean (David), Reed (Carol) **5** Leigh (Mike), Losey (Joseph), Reisz (Karel), Scott (Ridley) **6** Figgis (Mike), Frears (Stephen), Jordan (Neil), Newell (Mike), Parker (Alan), Powell (Michael) **7** Boorman (John), Branagh (Kenneth), Forsyth (Bill) **8** Anderson (Lindsay) **9** Hitchcock (Alfred) **10** Richardson (Tony) **11** Schlesinger (John) *Chinese:* **3** Lee (Ang) **4** Chen (Kaige) **5** Zhang (Yimou) *French:* **4** Demy (Jacques), Tati (Jacques), Vigo (Jean) **5** Malle (Louis) **6** Godard (Jean-Luc), Ophüls (Marcel), Renoir (Jean), Rohmer (Eric) **7** Bresson (Robert), Chabrol (Claude), Cocteau (Jean), Resnais (Alain), Rivette (Jacques) **8** Truffaut (François) *German:* **6** Herzog (Werner), Ophüls (Max) **7** Winders (Wim) **8** Petersen (Wolfgang) **10** Fass-

binder (Rainer Werner) **11** Riefenstahl (Leni), Schlöndorff (Volker) *Italian:* **5** Leone (Sergio) **6** De Sica (Vittorio) **7** Fellini (Federico) **8** Pasolini (Pier Paolo), Visconti (Luchino) **9** Antonioni (Michelangelo) **10** Bertolucci (Bernardo), Rossellini (Roberto), Wertmüller (Lina), Zeffirelli (Franco) *Japanese:* **3** Ozu (Yasujiru) **5** Itami (Juzo) **8** Kurosawa (Akira), Miyazaki (Hayao) **9** Mizoguchi (Kenji) *New Zealand:* **7** Campion (Jane) *Polish* **5** Wajda (Ardrzej) **7** Holland (Agnieszka) **8** Polanski (Roman) *Russian:* **9** Tarkovsky (Andrei) **10** Eisenstein (Sergei) *Spanish:* **6** Buñuel (Luis) **9** Almodóvar (Pedro) *Swedish:* **7** Bergman (Ingmar) **10** Zetterling (Mai)

movie producer *American:* **3** Fox (William) **4** Cohn (Jack) **5** Lasky (Jesse), Mayer (Louis B.), Zukor (Adolph) **6** Warner (Jack L.), Zanuck (Darryl, Richard) **7** Goldwyn (Samuel), Laemmle (Carl) **8** Selznick (David O.) *Austrian:* **9** Reinhardt (Max)

moving 5 astir **6** mobile **7** emotive, rousing **8** arousing, exciting, gripping, pathetic, poignant, stirring, touching **9** affecting, emotional, inspiring, transient **11** stimulating

moving stairs 9 escalator

mow 3 cut **4** clip, crop, fell, heap, pile, raze, rick **5** level, shave, shear, stack **7** grimace **9** knock down

moxie 3 pep, vim, zip **4** grit, guts **5** brass, heart, nerve, oomph, pluck, savvy, spunk, vigor **6** energy, mettle, spirit, starch **7** cojones, courage, know-how **8** backbone **9** fortitude **10** get-up-and-go, resolution **13** determination

Mozambique *capital:* **6** Maputo *language:* **5** Bantu **7** Swahili **10** Portuguese *monetary unit:* **7** metical *neighbor:* **6** Malawi, Zambia **8** Tanzania, Zimbabwe **9** Swaziland **11** South Africa *river:* **6** Ruvuma **7** Limpopo, Zambezi

Mozart, Wolfgang Amadeus *birthplace:* **8** Salzburg *cataloger:* **6** Köchel (Ludwig) *deathplace:* **6** Vienna *opera:* **8** Idomeneo **10** Magic Flute (The) **11** Don Giovanni, Il Rè Pastore **12** Così Fan Tutte **16** Marriage of Figaro (The)

MP's prey 4 AWOL **8** deserter

Mr. Moto star 5 Lorre (Peter)

Mrs. Grundy 4 prig **5** prude **7** puritan **8** bluenose

much 3 oft **4** long, many, most **5** often **6** highly, hugely, plenty **7** greatly, notably **8** abundant **9** eminently, extremely, great deal **10** frequently, oftentimes, repeatedly *combining form:* 4 poly 5 multi

Much Ado About Nothing *character:* 4 Hero 7 Claudio, Don John 8 Beatrice, Benedick, Dogberry

muck 3 goo, mud 4 crap, crud, dirt, dung, gook, goop, grub, gunk, junk, mess, mire, murk, plod, slog, slop, soil, toil 5 dirty, dreck, filth, grime, gumbo, slave, slime, swill, trash, waste 6 drudge, litter, manure, meddle, putter, sleaze, sludge, smirch, tinker 7 garbage, rubbish 8 nonsense 9 interfere

muckety-muck 3 VIP 5 nabob 6 bigwig, fat cat 7 big shot, kingpin, notable 8 kingfish, somebody 9 dignitary

mucky 4 foul 5 dirty, grimy, muddy, muggy, murky, nasty, soggy 6 cruddy, filthy, grubby, grungy 7 squalid, unclean

mucous 5 slimy 6 viscid

mud 4 dirt, mire, muck, ooze 5 dregs, slime 6 depths, sludge

muddle 3 mix 4 hash, mess, muck, rile, roil 5 addle, botch, mix up, snarl 6 ataxia, bungle, drivel, foul up, fumble, jumble, jungle, litter, mess up, tangle, tumble 7 clutter, confuse, fluster, perplex, rummage, shuffle, snarl up, stumble, stupefy 8 befuddle, bewilder, confound, disarray, disorder, distract, entangle, mishmash, scramble, shambles, throw off, unsettle 9 confusion, throw away 10 complicate, disarrange, discompose 11 disorganize

muddled 5 drunk, tight, tipsy, vague 7 mixed-up 8 inchoate 10 disjointed, disordered, incoherent, inebriated 11 intoxicated, unorganized

muddle through 4 cope, fare 5 get by, get on 6 manage 7 carry on, make out 8 get along

muddy 3 dim, fog 4 base, blur, drab, dull, fade, foul, hazy, oozy, roil, soil 5 befog, cloud, dingy, dirty, grime, grimy, murky 6 cloudy, gloomy, grubby, sordid, turbid 7 becloud, begrime, confuse, obscure, squalid, tarnish, unclean, unclear 8 confused

muff 4 blow, flub 5 botch, fluff 6 bobble, bollix, bungle, fumble, goof up, mess up 7 louse up, misplay, screw up 9 mishandle

muffle 4 dull, mute, veil 5 shush 6 dampen, deaden, lessen, shroud, soften, stifle, subdue, wrap up 7 envelop, repress, silence, smother, squelch 8 bundle up, suppress, tone down

muffled 5 muted 6 dulled 7 stifled, subdued 8 deadened, obscured, silenced

9 distorted, enveloped 10 indistinct, suppressed

muffler 4 mask, veil 5 cloak, scarf

mug 3 cup, ham, mop, mow, rob 4 boob, dolt, dope, face, fool, moue, phiz, punk, puss, thug 5 dunce, idiot, mouth, rowdy, stein, tough 6 ambush, dimwit 7 assault, grimace, tankard 8 bullyboy, dumbbell, features, numskull 9 blockhead, bushwhack, ignoramus, roughneck

mugger 4 thug 6 robber 9 assailant, crocodile

muggy 4 damp 5 humid, moist 6 sticky, sultry 7 dampish

Muhammad *adopted son:* 3 Ali *birthplace:* 5 Mecca *camel:* 5 Kaswa *daughter:* 6 Fatima *deathplace:* 6 Medina *deity:* 5 Allah *father:* 8 Abdallah, Abdullah *father-in-law:* 7 Abu Bakr *flight:* 6 hegira, hejira *follower:* 6 Moslem, Muslim *horse:* 5 Buraq 7 Alborak *religion:* 5 Islam *son:* 7 Ibrahim *son-in-law:* 3 Ali *successor:* 6 caliph 7 Abu Bakr *tribe:* 7 Koreish, Quraysh *uncle:* 8 Abu Talib *wife:* 5 Aisha 6 Ayesha 7 Khadija

mulatto 5 métis, mixed 7 mestizo 9 halfbreed, half-caste 10 crossbreed

mulberry 3 fig 10 breadfruit *type:* 6 banyan 11 India rubber, osage orange

mulct 4 fine, milk, rook 5 bleed, cheat, gouge 6 extort, fleece 7 deceive, defraud, forfeit, penalty, swindle 8 penalize 9 blackmail

mule 5 cross, scuff 6 bagman, hybrid 7 bastard, courier, mongrel 8 smuggler 9 crossbred, half blood, half-breed 10 crossbreed

mulish 3 contrary, perverse, stubborn 9 obstinate, pigheaded 10 bullheaded, headstrong, inflexible, refractory, unyielding 11 stiff-necked

mull 4 hash, muse 5 brood, think, weigh 6 ponder 7 reflect 8 cogitate, consider, meditate, ruminate, turn over 9 pulverize 10 deliberate 11 contemplate

multicolored 4 pied 6 motley 7 dappled 9 prismatic 10 variegated 13 polychromatic

multifarious 5 mixed 6 motley, sundry, varied 7 diverse, various 8 assorted, manifold 13 heterogeneous, miscellaneous

multiform 6 sundry, varied 7 diverse, various 8 assorted, manifold 9 disparate 12 multifarious

multilateral 9 many-sided

multiple 4 many 6 shared, sundry 7 diverse, several, various 8 assorted, manifold, numerous 9 composite

multiplicity 3 lot 4 heap, load, mass,

peck 5 flood, hoard, horde 6 barrel
7 variety 8 mountain, plethora 9 diversity, great deal, profusion

multiply 3 wax 4 rise 5 boost, breed, build, mount 6 expand, extend, spread 7 amplify, augment, enlarge, magnify 8 generate, heighten, increase 9 procreate, propagate, reproduce 10 aggrandize 11 proliferate

multitude 3 mob 4 army, herd, host, mass, slew 5 crowd, crush, drove, flock, horde, swarm 6 legion, myriad, public, throng 8 populace

multitudinous 4 many 6 legion, myriad, sundry 7 copious, various 8 abundant, manifold, numerous, populous 9 countless 10 numberless, voluminous 11 innumerable

mum 4 dumb, mute 5 quiet 6 silent 8 wordless 10 speechless, tongue-tied

mumble 6 murmur, mutter 7 maunder

mumbo jumbo 4 juju 6 fetish 9 gibberish 10 hocus-pocus 11 abracadabra 12 gobbledygook, superstition

mummer 4 mime 5 actor, mimic 12 impersonator

mummify 5 dry up, wizen 6 embalm, wither 7 shrivel 9 desiccate

munch 3 eat 4 chaw, chew 5 champ, chomp, snack 6 crunch 9 masticate

mundane 5 lowly 6 earthy, normal 7 earthly, humdrum, prosaic, routine, terrene, worldly 8 banausic, day-to-day, everyday, familiar, ordinary, telluric, workaday 9 practical, sublunary, tellurian 11 commonplace, terrestrial, uncelestial 13 materialistic

municipal 5 civic, local, urban 12 metropolitan

munificent 6 lavish 7 liberal 8 generous, handsome 9 bounteous, bountiful 10 benevolent, freehanded, openhanded 11 magnanimous 13 philanthropic

munitions maker 5 Krupp

muralist 4 Sert (José María) 6 Benton (Thomas Hart), Giotto, Orozco (José Clemente), Rivera (Diego) 7 La Farge (John) 9 Siqueiros (David Alfaro) 12 Michelangelo (Buonarotti)

murder 3 hit, off 4 do in, kill, slay 5 blood, lynch, scrag, snuff, waste 6 rub out 7 bump off, execute, garrote, killing, smother, take out 8 foul play, homicide, knock off, strangle 9 eradicate, liquidate, slaughter 10 annihilate, asphyxiate, decapitate, extinguish 11 assassinate, electrocute, exterminate 12 manslaughter *brother:* 10 fratricide *father:* 9 patricide *king:* 8 regicide *mother:* 9 matricide *parent:* 9 parricide *sister:* 10 sororicide

murderer 6 hit man, killer, slayer 7 butcher 8 assassin, homicide 9 cutthroat, manslayer 11 slaughterer

Murder in the Cathedral *author:* 5 Eliot (Thomas Stearns) *character:* 5 Henry (II) 6 Becket (Thomas à)

murderous 6 deadly, lethal 10 sanguinary 12 bloodthirsty

murk 3 fog 4 haze, mist 5 brume, gloom 6 miasma 8 darkness 9 obscurity

murky 3 dim 4 dark, dull, foul, gray 5 dirty, dusky, foggy, misty, muddy, roily, vague 6 cloudy, gloomy, opaque, somber, turbid 7 obscure 8 nebulous 9 ambiguous, equivocal, tenebrous 10 caliginous

murmur 3 hum 4 buzz, purr 5 drone, rumor 6 grouch, grouse, mumble, mutter, rumble 7 grumble, whisper 8 complain 9 grumbling, undertone 11 scuttlebutt, susurration

Muscat sultanate 4 Oman

muscle 4 beef, thew 5 brawn, force, might, power, sinew 6 energy 7 potency 8 strength 9 strong arm *abdomen:* 7 abdomen *arm:* 6 biceps 7 triceps *back:* 9 trapezius *calf:* 6 soleus *chest:* 10 pectoralis *jaw:* 8 masseter *kind:* 6 flexor, tensor 7 dilator, evertor, levator, rotator 8 abductor, adductor, extensor *loin:* 5 psoas *neck:* 8 platysma *shoulder:* 7 deltoid 10 deltoideus *study of:* 7 myology *thigh:* 8 gracilis 9 sartorius

muscle-bound 5 rigid, stiff 6 wooden

muscular 4 ropy 5 beefy, burly, husky 6 brawny, mighty, robust, sinewy, strong, sturdy 8 athletic, forceful, powerful, resolute, stalwart, vigorous 9 Herculean, strapping, well-built

muse 5 angel, brood, guide, think 6 genius, ponder, trance 7 reflect, reverie 8 cogitate, meditate, mull over, ruminate, turn over 10 deliberate 11 contemplate

Muse *father:* 4 Zeus 7 Jupiter *mother:* 9 Mnemosyne *of astronomy:* 6 Urania *of choral song:* 11 Terpsichore *of comedy:* 6 Thalia *of dancing:* 11 Terpsichore *of epic poetry:* 8 Calliope *of history:* 4 Clio *of love poetry:* 5 Erato *of lyric poetry:* 5 Erato *of music:* 7 Euterpe *of pastoral poetry:* 6 Thalia *of sacred poetry:* 8 Polymnia 10 Polyhymnia *of tragedy:* 9 Melpomene

museum 5 salon 7 archive, exhibit, gallery 8 atheneum 10 collection, repository

mush 4 slop 5 grits, gruel, hokum 6 bathos, drivel, hominy 8 porridge, schmaltz

mushroom 4 grow 6 expand, spread

7 burgeon, explode, inflate **8** snowball
11 proliferate *combining form:* **3** myc
4 myco **5** mycet **6** myceto *edible:*
5 enoki, morel **6** bolete **7** cremini, crim-
ini, porcini **8** shiitake **9** mousseron
10 champignon, portabella, portabello,
portobello **11** chanterelle *kind:* **6** agaric,
bolete **7** inky cap, russula *part:* **3** cap
4 gill, ring **5** stipe, volva **6** pileus
7 annulus **8** mycelium *poisonous:*
7 amanita **8** death cap **9** fly agaric,
toadstool

mushy 4 soft **5** pulpy, soppy, vague
6 quaggy, spongy **7** amorous, maudlin,
mawkish, squashy, squishy **8** bathetic,
effusive, romantic, squooshy
9 schmaltzy **10** lovey-dovey, saccharine
11 sentimental

music *abbreviation:* **3** fff, ppp, sfz **5** cresc
bass staff lines: **5** GBDFA *bass staff
spaces:* **4** ACEG *characteristic phrase:*
9 leitmotif, leitmotiv *chord:* **5** major,
minor, tonic **7** harmony **8** dominant
9 augmented **10** diminished *embellishment:* **3** run **4** turn **5** trill **7** cadenza,
mordent, roulade **8** arpeggio, flourish
9 grace note *for eight:* **5** octet *for five:*
7 quintet *for four:* **7** quartet *for nine:*
5 nonet *for one:* **4** solo *for seven:*
6 septet *for six:* **6** sextet *for three:* **4** trio
for two: **3** duo **4** duet *god:* **6** Apollo *hall:*
7 cabaret, theater *instrumental form:*
3 jig **4** jazz, reel **5** étude, fugue, gigue,
march, polka, rondo, suite, swing,
waltz **6** minuet, pavane, sonata **7** bourrée, gavotte, mazurka, prelude, ragtime, toccata **8** chaconne, concerto,
courante, fantasia, galliard, nocturne,
overture, rhapsody, ricercar, saraband,
serenade, symphony, tone poem **9** allemande, polonaise **11** rock and roll *medley:* **4** olio *morning:* **6** aubade *Muse:*
7 Euterpe *night:* **8** nocturne, serenade
note: **4** half **5** breve, minim, neume,
whole **6** eighth, quaver **7** quarter
8 crotchet **9** sixteenth **10** semiquaver
patron saint: **7** Cecilia *period:* **6** Modern,
Rococo **7** Baroque **8** Medieval, Romantic **9** Classical *symbol:* **3** bar, key **4** clef,
flat, note, rest, slur, turn **5** sharp, staff
7 fermata, mordent **9** alla breve **10** accidental *treble staff lines:* **5** EGBDF *treble
staff spaces:* **4** FACE *vocal form:* **3** air
4 aria, hymn, lied, mass, song **5** chant,
motet, opera, round **6** anthem, ballad
7 cantata, chanson, chorale **8** cavatina,
madrigal, operetta, oratorio, serenade
9 cabaletta

musical 4 show **5** revue **6** choral **7** lyrical, melodic, songful, tuneful **8** har-

monic, operetta, zarzuela **9** melodious,
symphonic **10** euphonious, harmonious
musical composition 4 aria, hymn, lied,
opus, song, trio **5** chant, canon, carol,
étude, fugue, march, motet, opera,
rondo, suite **6** anthem, ballad, sextet,
sonata **7** cantata, chanson, chorale,
prelude, quartet, quintet, requiem,
scherzo, toccata **8** concerto, fantasia,
madrigal, nocturne, operetta, oratorio,
overture, postlude, serenade, sonatina,
symphony **9** bagatelle, cabaletta, interlude **10** intermezzo, recitative
musical direction *accented:* **7** marcato
8 sforzato **9** sforzando *all:* **5** tutti *brisk:*
4 vivo **6** vivace **7** allegro, animato *connected:* **6** legato *detached:* **8** spiccato,
staccato *dignified:* **8** maestoso *disconnected:* **8** staccato *emotional:* **12** appas-
sionato *emphatic:* **7** marcato *excited:*
7 agitato *fast:* **4** vite, vivo **6** presto,
veloce, vivace **7** allegro *faster:* **7** stretto
11 accelerando *fluctuating tempo:*
6 rubato *forcefully:* **7** furioso *freely:* **9** ad
libitum *gay:* **7** giocoso *gentle:* **5** dolce
7 amabile, amoroso **10** affettuoso *graceful:* **8** grazioso *half:* **5** mezzo *heavy:*
7 pesante *held firmly:* **6** tenuto *less:*
4 meno *little:* **4** poco *little by little:*
9 poco a poco *lively:* **4** vite **6** vivace
7 allegro, animato, giocoso *loud:* **5** forte
louder: **9** crescendo *majestic:* **8** maestoso
moderate: **7** andante **8** moderato *moderately loud:* **10** mezzo forte *moderately
soft:* **10** mezzo piano *playful:*
10 scherzando *plucked:* **9** pizzicato
quick: **4** vite, vivo **6** presto, veloce,
vivace **7** allegro *quickening:* **11** affrettan-
do *repeat:* **3** bis **6** da capo *run:* **8** arpeggio **9** glissando *sad:* **7** dolente
8 doloroso *separate:* **9** divisi *silent:*
5 tacet *singing:* **9** cantabile *sliding:*
9 glissando *slow:* **5** grave, largo **6** adagio
7 andante **9** larghetto *slowing:* **3** rit
6 ritard **10** ritardando **11** rallentando
smooth: **6** legato *soft:* **5** dolce, piano
softening: **10** diminuendo **11** decrescendo *solemn:* **5** grave *spirited:* **4** vivo
6 vivace **7** animato **9** spiritoso *stately:*
7 pomposo **8** maestoso *sustained:*
6 tenuto **9** sostenuto *sweet:* **5** dolce *tender:* **7** amabile, amoroso **10** affettuoso
together: **4** a due **5** tutti *very:* **5** assai
very fast: **11** prestissimo *very loud:*
10 fortissimo *very soft:* **10** pianissimo
musical drama 5 opera **8** operetta,
zarzuela **9** singspiel
musical group 4 band, trio **5** choir, combo **6** chorus, sextet **7** quartet, quintet
8 ensemble, glee club **9** orchestra
musical instrument *African:* **5** mbira

7 kalimba *ancient:* **4** lyre, rote **5** crwth
6 syrinx **7** cithara, kithara, panpipe,
sistrum *Arabic:* **3** oud *bagpipe:*
7 musette, pibroch *biblical:* **6** cymbal
7 timbrel **8** psaltery *brass:* **4** horn, tuba
5 bugle **6** cornet **7** althorn, clarion, helicon, saxhorn, trumpet **8** trombone
10 French horn *Indian:* **4** vina **5** sarod,
sitar, tabla *Japanese:* **4** biwa, koto
7 samisen **8** shamisen **10** shakuhachi
keyboard: **5** organ, piano **6** spinet
7 celesta, cembalo, clavier **8** calliope,
melodeon, virginal **9** accordion
10 clavichord, concertina, pianoforte
11 harpsichord *medieval:* **4** lute **5** naker,
rebab, rebec, shawm, tabor **7** gittern,
mandola, panpipe **8** cornetto, dulcimer,
gemshorn, hornpipe, Jew's harp,
oliphant, recorder **9** monochord
10 clavichord, hurdy-gurdy *percussion:*
4 bell, drum **5** anvil, güiro, piano
6 cymbal, maraca **7** marimba, timbrel,
timpani, tympani **8** bass drum, castanet, triangle **9** snare drum, xylophone
10 kettledrum, tambourine, vibraphone
Persian: **6** santir *pipe:* **6** syrinx **7** bagpipe, musette, panpipe *reed:* **4** oboe
7 bassoon **8** clarinet **9** harmonica, saxophone **11** English horn *Renaissance:*
4 viol **5** regal, shawm **6** curtal, spinet
7 bagpipe, bandora, cittern, rackett,
sackbut, serpent, theorbo, vihuela, vio-
lone **8** crumhorn, recorder, virginal
10 chitarrone, colascione **11** harpsichord *Russian:* **9** balalaika *stringed:*
3 oud **4** harp, lute, lyre, vina, viol
5 banjo, cello, piano, rebec, sitar, viola
6 fiddle, guitar, violin, zither **7** bandora,
cittern, gittern, kantele, pandura,
ukulele **8** autoharp, dulcimer, mandolin **10** contrabass, double bass
11 harpsichord, violoncello *toy:* **5** kazoo
7 ocarina *two-necked:* **7** theorbo *woodwind:* **4** oboe **5** flute **7** bassoon, piccolo
9 flageolet, saxophone **11** English horn
musical interval 5 fifth, major, minor,
sixth, third **6** fourth, octave, second
7 perfect, seventh, tritone
musical syllable 3 sol
musician 4 bard **5** piper **6** player
7 jazzman, maestro **8** minstrel, virtuoso
9 performer **10** troubadour
muskeg 3 bog, fen **4** mire, quag **5** marsh,
swamp **6** morass, slough **8** quagmire
musket 5 fusil **9** flintlock, matchlock
12 muzzleloader
Musketeer 5 Athos **6** Aramis **7** Porthos
author: **5** Dumas (Alexandre) *friend:*
9 d'Artagnan
muskmelon 10 cantaloupe
Muslim *ascetic:* **4** Sufi **5** fakir **7** dervish

8 marabout *body of scholars:* **5** ulama,
ulema *branch:* **4** Shia **5** Sunni **6** Shiite
caller to prayer: **7** muezzin *decree:*
5 fatwa, irade *devil:* **5** Iblis *garment:*
6 chador *god:* **5** Allah *holy city:* **5** Mecca
6 Medina *holy war:* **5** jihad *judge:*
5 mufti *leader:* **3** aga **4** agha, amir, emir
5 ameer *mendicant:* **5** fakir *messiah:*
5 Mahdi *month:* (see at MONTH) *month
of fasting:* **7** Ramadan *mosque:* **6** masjid
mystic: **4** Sufi *pilgrim:* **5** hajji *pilgrimage:*
4 hajj *prayer:* **5** salat *priest:* **4** imam
prophet: **8** Mohammed, Muhammad
religion: **5** Islam *scripture:* **5** Koran,
Quran *shrine:* **5** Kaaba *temple:*
6 mosque *title:* **3** aga **4** emir **6** caliph *tradition:* **5** sunna (see also MOSQUE;
MUHAMMAD)
muss 3 row **4** mess **5** botch, chaos, mix-
up, upset **6** jumble, mess-up, muddle,
rumple, tousle **7** disrupt, rummage
8 disarray, dishevel, disorder, shambles
9 confusion **10** disarrange **11** disorganize
mussel 5 naiad *genus:* **4** Unio **7** Mytilus
8 Anodonta *larva:* **9** blackhead
Mussolini, Benito 4 Duce (Il) *son-in-law:*
5 Ciano (Galeazzo)
mussy 6 sloppy, untidy **7** tousled,
unkempt **8** slovenly **9** cluttered
10 disheveled
must 4 duty, mold, need, want **5** juice,
ought **6** devoir, should **9** condition,
essential, necessity, requisite **10** obligation, sine qua non **11** requirement
12 precondition, prerequisite
muster 4 call, roll **5** crowd, group, raise,
rally, rouse **6** enlist, enroll, gather,
induce, invoke, join up, roster, sample,
sign on, sign up, summon, work up
7 collect, convene, develop, include,
marshal, produce **8** assemble, assembly,
comprise, congress, generate, mobilize,
organize, roll call, specimen **9** gathering, inventory, nose count **10** accumulate, assemblage, collection, congregate, rendezvous **12** accumulation,
congregation
muster out 5 demob, let go **9** discharge
10 demobilize
musty 4 dank, dull, sour **5** funky, moldy,
stale, tired, trite **6** frowsy, frowzy, old
hat, smelly **7** airless, antique, mildewy,
squalid **8** shopworn, timeworn **10** antiquated, malodorous, threadbare
Mut *husband:* **4** Amen, Amon *son:*
5 Chons **6** Chonsu, Khonsu
mutable 5 fluid **6** fickle, mobile, shifty
7 erratic, protean **8** slippery, unstable,
unsteady, variable, volatile, wavering
9 changeful, mercurial, unsettled

10 capricious, changeable, inconstant **11** fluctuating, vacillating **12** inconsistent

mutate 4 vary **5** alter, morph **6** change, modify **9** refashion, transform, transmute **11** transfigure **12** metamorphose, transmogrify

mutation 5 sport **6** change **7** novelty **9** deviation, variation **10** alteration **11** vicissitude **12** modification **13** metamorphosis

mute 3 mum **4** dumb **5** quiet **6** dampen, deaden, muffle, muzzle, reduce, silent, soften, stifle, subdue **7** silence **8** silencer, wordless **9** voiceless **10** speechless, tongue-tied

muted 3 dim, mat **4** dull **6** low-key, silent **10** speechless

mutilate 3 mar **4** maim **6** damage, deface, injure, mangle **7** cripple **9** disfigure, dismember

mutineer 5 rebel

mutinous 6 unruly **8** factious **9** insurgent, seditious, turbulent **10** rebellious **12** contumacious **13** insubordinate

mutiny 5 rebel **6** revolt, rise up **8** uprising **9** rebellion **12** insurrection

mutt 3 cur, dog **4** mule **5** cross **6** hybrid **7** mixture, mongrel **9** half blood, half-breed **10** crossbreed

Mutt and ___ 4 Jeff

mutter 5 growl **6** grouch, grouse, mumble, murmur **7** grumble **9** undertone

muttonchops 9 burnsides, sideburns **10** sideboards **11** dundrearies **12** sidewhiskers

mutual 5 joint **6** common, public, shared, united **7** related **8** communal, conjoint, conjunct **9** bilateral, connected **10** associated, reciprocal, respective *prefix:* **5** inter

muumuu 6 caftan

muzzle 3 gag **4** hush, mute, nose, phiz **5** snout **7** silence, squelch

muzzy 3 dim **4** dull, hazy **5** faint, vague **6** blurry, gloomy **7** blurred, muddled, unclear **8** confused, nebulous **9** imprecise

myalgia 4 ache, pain **5** cramp **6** strain **8** soreness

Myanmar 5 Burma *bay:* **6** Bengal *capital:* **6** Yangon **7** Rangoon *monetary unit:* **4** kyat *neighbor:* **4** Laos **5** China, India **8** Thailand **10** Bangladesh *peninsula:* **9** Indochina *river:* **7** Salween **9** Irrawaddy *sea:* **7** Andaman

My Antonia author 6 Cather (Willa)

My Last Duchess author 8 Browning (Robert)

My Lost Youth author 10 Longfellow (Henry Wadsworth)

Myra Breckenridge author 5 Vidal (Gore)

myriad 3 lot **4** heap, host, raft, slew **5** flood, horde, swarm **6** throng **9** countless, multitude **10** infinitude, numberless **11** innumerable **12** incalculable **13** multitudinous

myrmecology subject 3 ant **4** ants

myrmidon 6 minion **8** follower, retainer **9** attendant, underling **11** subordinate

Myron's statue 10 Discobolos, Discobolus **13** Discus Thrower (The)

Myrrha's son 6 Adonis

mysterious 6 arcane, mystic, occult, secret **7** cryptic, obscure, strange **8** abstruse, esoteric, numinous **9** ambiguous, enigmatic, equivocal, recondite **10** cabalistic, unknowable **11** inscrutable **12** impenetrable, inexplicable, unfathomable **13** unaccountable

mystery 5 poser **6** enigma, puzzle, riddle, secret **7** arcanum, problem, stumper **8** whodunit **9** conundrum **10** closed book, perplexity, puzzlement **13** Chinese puzzle

mystic 4 seer **6** arcane, medium, occult, oracle, secret **7** obscure **8** anagogic, esoteric, hermetic, numinous **9** enigmatic, visionary **10** cabalistic, unknowable **11** inscrutable, necromantic **12** impenetrable, thaumaturgic **13** unaccountable

mystical 4 holy **6** arcane, covert, divine, occult, orphic, sacred, secret **7** cryptic, sub-rosa **8** anagogic, esoteric, hermetic, oracular, profound **9** recondite, spiritual **10** miraculous, symbolical **11** clandestine **12** supernatural, supranatural

mysticism 7 Orphism **8** cabalism, quietism **11** hermeticism

mystify 6 baffle, puzzle **7** confuse, obscure, perplex **8** befuddle, bewilder, confound **9** obfuscate

mystifying 7 cryptic, delphic **8** Delphian **9** enigmatic

mystique 5 charm, magic **7** glamour **8** charisma **9** magnetism

myth 4 lore, saga, tale **5** fable, story **6** legend **7** fiction, figment, parable **8** allegory, folklore **9** tradition **11** fabrication

mythical 6 fabled, made-up, unreal **7** created, fictive **8** fabulous, fanciful, invented **9** fantastic, fictional, imaginary, legendary **10** apocryphal, fictitious

mythologist 4 Jung (Carl Gustav), Ovid **5** Tylor (Edward Burnett) **6** Eliade (Mircea), Frazer (James George), Müller (Friedrich Max) **8** Campbell (Joseph) **9** Euhemerus **10** Malinowski (Bronislaw)

mythology see MYTH

N

Naamah *brother:* 9 Tubalcain *father:*
6 Lamech *husband:* 7 Solomon *mother:*
6 Zillah *son:* 8 Rehoboam

nab 4 grab 5 catch, pinch, run in, seize
6 arrest, clutch, collar, pick up, pull in,
snatch 7 capture 9 apprehend

nabob 3 VIP 5 mogul, noble 6 bigwig, fat
cat, tycoon 7 big shot, magnate,
notable 8 big chief, eminence, governor
9 big cheese, dignitary, personage
10 notability

Nabokov novel 3 Ada 4 Gift (The), Pnin
6 Lolita 7 Defense (The), Despair 8 Pale
Fire 14 King Queen Knave

nacre 13 mother-of-pearl

nada 3 nil, zip 5 zilch 6 naught 7 nothing, nullity 11 nothingness

nadir 4 base, foot 5 depth 6 bottom
8 low point *opposite:* 6 zenith

nag 3 irk, vex 4 bait, carp, goad, ride
5 annoy, chivy, harry, horse, hound,
worry 6 badger, bother, carp at, harass,
heckle, hector, needle, peck at, pester,
plague 7 henpeck, torment 8 complain,
harangue, irritate

naiad 5 nymph

naïf 7 ingenue

nail 3 bag, get, nab 4 brad, grab, stud,
tack, trap 5 catch, clone, spike, sprig
6 arrest, collar, secure 7 capture
9 apprehend

naive 6 simple 7 artless, natural
8 gullible, innocent, wide-eyed 9 childlike, credulous, guileless, ingenuous,
unstudied 10 self-taught, unaffected,
unschooled 11 susceptible

naked 3 raw 4 bald, bare, mere, nude,
pure 5 clear, sheer 6 peeled, scanty,
simple, unclad 7 denuded, evident,
exposed, obvious 8 revealed, stripped
9 au naturel, disclosed, unclothed,
uncovered, undressed *combining form:*
4 gymn 5 gymno

Naked and the Dead author 6 Mailer
(Norman)

namby-pamby 4 weak 5 banal, bland,
inane, sissy, vapid 6 effete, jejune
7 insipid 8 nebbishy, weakling 9 spineless 10 effeminate, indecisive, panty-
waist, wishy-washy 12 milk-and-water
13 characterless

name 3 dub, nom, tab, tag, tap 4 call,
cite, race, term 5 alias, label, nomen,
quote, state, style, title 6 byword, finger, handle, report, repute, rubric
7 appoint, baptize, declare, entitle, epithet, mention, moniker, publish, specify 8 announce, christen, identify,
instance, nominate 9 advertise, character, designate, incognito, recognize,
sobriquet, stipulate 10 denominate,
reputation 11 appellation, appellative,
designation *ancient Rome:* 7 agnomen
8 prenomen *assumed:* 5 alias 9 sobriquet *family:* 8 cognomen *fictitious:*
9 pseudonym *giver:* 6 eponym

nameless 6 unsung 7 obscure, unknown
9 anonymous 11 indefinable, unutterable 12 uncelebrated, unidentified

namely 3 viz. 5 to wit 6 that is 8 scilicet
9 expressly, specially, videlicet 10 especially 12 particularly, specifically

Namibia *capital:* 8 Windhoek *city:*
8 Oshakati, Rehoboth *desert:* 5 Namib
8 Kalahari *language:* 5 Bantu 6 German
9 Afrikaans *neighbor:* 6 Angola 8 Botswana 11 South Africa *river:* 6 Cunene,
Orange 8 Okavango

nana 7 grandma 11 grandmother

Nana *author:* 4 Zola (Emile) *mother:*
8 Gervaise

Nanna *brother:* 6 Nergal, Ninazu *father:*
5 Enlil *husband:* 6 Balder *mother:*
6 Ninlil *son:* 3 Utu *wife:* 6 Ningal

nanny 7 nurse 9 caregiver, governess,
nursemaid

Naomi 4 Mara *daughter-in-law:* 4 Ruth
5 Orpah *husband:* 9 Elimelech *son:*
6 Mahlon 7 Chilion

nap 4 doze, pile, rest, shag, wale, warp,
weft, woof 5 sleep, weave 6 drowse,
nod off, siesta, snooze 7 drop off, surface 10 forty winks

nape 6 scruff

Naphtali *brother:* 3 Dan *father:* 5 Jacob
mother: 6 Bilhah *son:* 4 Guni 5 Jezer
7 Jahzeel, Jahziel, Shallum

naphtha 7 solvent 9 petroleum

napkin 5 cloth, doily, towel 9 serviette

napoleon 4 boot 6 pastry 8 card game
9 solitaire *bid:* 7 blucher 10 wellington

Napoleon *adversary:* 6 Nelson (Horatio)
7 Kutuzov (Mikhail) 10 Wellington
(Duke of) *birthplace:* 7 Ajaccio, Corsica

brother: 5 Louis 6 Jérome, Joseph, Lucien *brother-in-law:* 5 Murat (Joachim) *deathplace:* 8 St. Helena *defeat:* 7 Leipzig 8 Waterloo 9 Trafalgar *father:* 5 Carlo *island of exile:* 4 Elba 8 St. Helena *marshal:* 3 Ney (Michel) 5 Murat (Joachim), Soult (Nicolas-Jean) 6 Suchet (Louis-Gabriel) *sister:* 5 Maria 8 Carlotta, Carolina *victory:* 3 Ulm 4 Jena, Lodi 5 Ligny 6 Abukir, Abu Qir, Arcole, Wagram 7 Bautzen, Dresden, Marengo 8 Borodino 10 Austerlitz *wife:* 9 Josephine 11 Marie Louise

narcissism 6 egoism, vanity 7 conceit, egotism 8 self-love, vainness 9 vainglory 11 egocentrism, self-conceit 13 conceitedness

narcissistic 4 vain 7 stuck-up 9 conceited, egotistic 10 self-loving 11 egotistical 12 self-absorbed, self-admiring, self-centered, vainglorious

Narcissus *admirer:* 4 Echo *father:* 9 Cephissus *mother:* 7 Liriope

narcotic 3 hop 4 dope, drug, junk 5 opium 6 heroin, opiate 7 anodyne, cocaine, hashish 8 hypnotic, morphine, nepenthe 9 somnolent, soporific 10 somnorific 11 somniferous *peddler:* 6 dealer, pusher

narrate 4 tell 5 state 6 depict, detail, recite, relate, report 7 express, outline, portray, recount 8 describe, rehearse 9 chronicle, delineate

narrative 4 epic, myth, saga, tale, yarn 5 fable, story 6 legend, report 7 account, history, recital, version 8 anecdote 9 chronicle *medieval French:* 5 roman 7 romance *prose:* 5 novel 7 novella

narrator 6 teller 7 reciter 8 reporter 9 describer, performer 10 chronicler

narrow 5 close, small, taper 6 lessen, strait 7 bigoted, limited, precise, slender 8 contract, decrease, straiten 9 confining, constrict, hidebound, illiberal 10 brassbound, inflexible, intolerant, prejudiced, restricted

narrowly 6 barely 7 closely 8 scarcely, strictly

narrow-minded 5 petty 7 bigoted, insular 9 hidebound, illiberal 10 brassbound, intolerant, prejudiced, provincial

nasal 6 rhinal, twangy 9 nosepiece *combining form:* 4 rhin 5 rhino

nascency 5 birth 6 origin 7 genesis 8 birthing, creation, nativity 9 inception 11 parturition

nascent 7 budding, growing, newborn 8 emergent 9 beginning, embryonic, fledgling, incipient, sprouting 10 blossoming, burgeoning, initiative, initiatory

Naseby victor 7 Fairfax (Thomas) 8 Cromwell (Oliver)

___ **Nastase** 4 Ilie

nasty 4 evil, foul, icky, mean, vile 5 awful, dirty, gross, snide 6 coarse, filthy, grubby, horrid, malign, odious, wicked 7 beastly, harmful, hateful, ill-bred, painful, raunchy, squalid, vicious 8 god-awful, improper, indecent, spiteful 9 hazardous, loathsome, malicious, malignant, obnoxious, offensive, repugnant, repulsive, vexatious 10 disgusting, malevolent 11 distasteful 12 disagreeable

natant 8 floating, swimming

Nathan *father:* 4 Bani 5 Attai, David *son:* 5 Zabad

nation 4 race 5 realm, state, tribe 6 domain, people, polity 7 country, kingdom, society 8 dominion, populace, republic 11 sovereignty 12 commonwealth, principality

national 6 native 7 citizen, federal, subject 8 resident 10 countryman 11 countrywide

National Basketball Association *Atlanta:* 5 Hawks *Boston:* 7 Celtics *Charlotte:* 7 Hornets *Chicago:* 5 Bulls *Cleveland:* 9 Cavaliers *Dallas:* 9 Mavericks *Denver:* 7 Nuggets *Detroit:* 7 Pistons *Golden State:* 8 Warriors *Houston:* 7 Rockets *Indiana:* 6 Pacers *Los Angeles:* 6 Lakers 8 Clippers *Miami:* 4 Heat *Milwaukee:* 5 Bucks *Minnesota:* 12 Timberwolves *New Jersey:* 4 Nets *New York:* 6 Knicks *Orlando:* 5 Magic *Phoenix:* 4 Suns *Portland:* 12 Trail Blazers *Sacramento:* 5 Kings *San Antonio:* 5 Spurs *Seattle:* 11 SuperSonics *Toronto:* 7 Raptors *Utah:* 4 Jazz *Vancouver:* 9 Grizzlies *Washington:* 7 Bullets

National Football League *Arizona:* 9 Cardinals *Atlanta:* 7 Falcons *Baltimore:* 6 Ravens *Buffalo:* 5 Bills *Carolina:* 8 Panthers *Chicago:* 5 Bears *Cincinnati:* 7 Bengals *Cleveland:* 6 Browns *Dallas:* 7 Cowboys *Denver:* 7 Broncos *Detroit:* 5 Lions *Green Bay:* 7 Packers *Houston:* 5 Oilers *Indianapolis:* 5 Colts *Jacksonville:* 7 Jaguars *Kansas City:* 6 Chiefs *Miami:* 8 Dolphins *Minnesota:* 7 Vikings *New England:* 8 Patriots *New Orleans:* 6 Saints *New York:* 4 Jets 6 Giants *Oakland:* 7 Raiders *Philadelphia:* 6 Eagles *Pittsburgh:* 8 Steelers *St. Louis:* 4 Rams *San Diego:* 8 Chargers *Seattle:* 8 Seahawks *Tampa Bay:* 4 Bucs 10 Buccaneers *Tennessee:* 6 Oilers *Washington:* 8 Redskins

national historical park *Alaska:* 5 Sitka

Idaho: 8 Nez Percé *Kentucky-Tennessee:* 13 Cumberland Gap *Maryland-West Virginia:* 12 Harpers Ferry *Massachusetts:* 9 Minute Man *New York:* 8 Saratoga

National Hockey League *Anaheim:* 11 Mighty Ducks *Atlanta:* 9 Thrashers *Boston:* 6 Bruins *Buffalo:* 6 Sabres *Calgary:* 6 Flames *Carolina:* 10 Hurricanes *Chicago:* 10 Blackhawks *Colorado:* 9 Avalanche *Columbus:* 11 Blue Jackets *Dallas:* 5 Stars *Detroit:* 8 Red Wings *Edmonton:* 6 Oilers *Florida:* 8 Panthers *Los Angeles:* 5 Kings *Minnesota:* 4 Wild *Montreal:* 9 Canadiens *Nashville:* 9 Predators *New Jersey:* 6 Devils *New York:* 7 Rangers 9 Islanders *Ottawa:* 8 Senators *Philadelphia:* 6 Flyers *Phoenix:* 7 Coyotes *St. Louis:* 5 Blues *San Jose:* 6 Sharks *Tampa Bay:* 9 Lightning *Toronto:* 10 Maple Leafs *Vancouver:* 7 Canucks *Washington:* 8 Capitals

nationalism 8 jingoism 10 chauvinism, patriotism

National League *Arizona:* 12 Diamondbacks *Atlanta:* 6 Braves *Chicago:* 4 Cubs *Cincinnati:* 4 Reds *Colorado:* 7 Rockies *Florida:* 7 Marlins *Houston:* 6 Astros *Los Angeles:* 7 Dodgers *Milwaukee:* 7 Brewers *New York:* 4 Mets *Philadelphia:* 8 Phillies *Pittsburgh:* 7 Pirates *St. Louis:* 9 Cardinals *San Diego:* 6 Padres *San Francisco:* 6 Giants *Washington:* 9 Nationals

national military park *Alabama:* 13 Horseshoe Bend *Arkansas:* 8 Pea Ridge *Mississippi:* 9 Vicksburg *Pennsylvania:* 10 Gettysburg *South Carolina:* 13 Kings Mountain *Tennessee:* 6 Shiloh

national monument *Alabama:* 11 Russell Cave *Alaska:* 9 Aniakchak *Arizona:* 5 Tonto 6 Navajo 7 Saguaro, Wupatki 8 Tuzigoot 10 Chiricahua, Pipe Spring, Tumacacori 11 Hohokam Pima 12 Sunset Crater, Walnut Canyon *California:* 8 Cabrillo, Lava Beds 9 Muir Woods, Pinnacles 10 Joshua Tree 11 Death Valley *Colorado:* 10 Yucca House *Colorado-Utah:* 8 Dinosaur 9 Hovenweep *Florida:* 12 Fort Matanzas 13 Fort Jefferson *Georgia:* 8 Ocmulgee 11 Fort Pulaski 13 Fort Frederica *Iowa:* 12 Effigy Mounds *Louisiana:* 12 Poverty Point *Maryland:* 11 Fort McHenry *Minnesota:* 9 Pipestone 12 Grand Portage *Nebraska:* 9 Homestead 11 Scotts Bluff *New Mexico:* 5 Pecos 7 El Morro 9 Bandelier, El Malpais, Fort Union 10 Aztec Ruins, White Sands *New York:* 11 Fort Stanwix 13 Castle Clinton *South Carolina:* 10 Fort Sumter 13 Congaree Swamp *South Dakota:* 9 Jewel Cave *Utah:*

11 Cedar Breaks 13 Rainbow Bridge *Wyoming:* 11 Devils Tower, Fossil Butte

national park *Alaska:* 6 Denali, Katmai 9 Lake Clark 10 Glacier Bay 11 Kenai Fjords, Kobuk Valley *Angola:* 4 Iona, Mupa *Arizona:* 11 Grand Canyon *Arkansas:* 10 Hot Springs *Botswana:* 5 Chobe *California:* 7 Redwood, Sequoia 8 Yosemite 11 King's Canyon *Chad:* 5 Manda *Colombia:* 5 Uraba *Colorado:* 9 Mesa Verde 13 Rocky Mountain *eastern Africa:* 10 Mount Kenya *Florida:* 8 Biscayne 10 Everglades *Hawaii:* 9 Haleakala *India:* 5 Kanha *Japan:* 5 Nikko *Kentucky:* 11 Mammoth Cave *Kenya:* 4 Meru 5 Tsavo 10 Royal Tsavo *Lake Superior:* 10 Isle Royale *Maine:* 6 Acadia *Malaysia:* 8 Kinabalu *Minnesota:* 9 Voyageurs *Montana:* 7 Glacier *Nevada:* 10 Great Basin *Oregon:* 10 Crater Lake *Poland:* 5 Ojcow, Tatra *South Africa:* 6 Kruger *South Dakota:* 8 Badlands, Wind Cave *Sri Lanka:* 4 Yala *Sweden:* 5 Sarek *Tanzania:* 5 Ruaha 9 Serengeti *Texas:* 7 Big Bend *Utah:* 4 Zion 6 Arches 11 Bryce Canyon, Canyonlands, Capitol Reef *Virginia:* 10 Shenandoah *Washington:* 7 Olympic 12 Mount Rainier 13 North Cascades *Wyoming:* 10 Grand Teton *Wyoming-Idaho-Montana:* 11 Yellowstone *Zambia:* 5 Kafue *Zimbabwe:* 13 Rhodes Inyanga, Victoria Falls

native 3 raw 4 wild 5 local 6 inborn, innate 7 connate, endemic, natural 8 domestic, indigene, inherent, internal, national 9 inherited 10 aboriginal, congenital, connatural, indigenous, unacquired *Acadian Louisiana:* 5 Cajun *China:* 3 Han 9 Celestial *India:* 5 sepoy *Japan:* 9 Nipponese *London:* 7 Cockney *New England:* 4 Yank 6 Yankee *New York:* 13 Knickerbocker

Native Son author 6 Wright (Richard)

Nativity 4 Noel, Xmas, yule 8 yuletide 9 Christmas

nativity 5 birth, start 6 origin, outset 7 genesis 8 delivery 9 beginning, horoscope, inception 11 parturition

natter 3 gab, jaw, yak, yap 4 blab, buzz, chat, go on 5 prate, run on 6 babble, gabble, gossip, tattle 7 chatter, prattle, twaddle 8 chitchat, converse

natty 4 neat, tidy, trim 5 doggy, sassy, smart, swank 6 classy, dapper, jaunty, snazzy, spiffy, spruce, sprucy, swanky 7 bandbox, doggish, stylish 9 turned out 11 well-groomed

natural 4 pure, wild 5 naive, usual 6 candid, inborn, innate, native, normal, simple 7 artless, connate, organic

8 homespun, inherent, innocent
9 childlike, ingenuous, ingrained, primitive 10 congenital, indigenous, legitimate, unaffected 11 commonplace, instinctive, spontaneous
naturalist *American:* 4 Muir (John)
5 Hyatt (Alpheus) 7 Audubon (John James), Verrill (Addison, Alpheus) *English:* 3 Ray (John) 5 White (Gilbert)
6 Darwin (Charles) 7 Wallace (Alfred)
10 Williamson (William) *French:*
5 Fabre (Jean-Henri) 7 Lamarck (Chevalier de), Réaumur (René-Antoine) *Scottish:* 6 Wilson (Alexander)
10 Richardson (John)
nature 3 ilk, way 4 kind, sort, type
6 makeup, manner, stripe, temper
7 essence, scenery 8 creation, tendency, universe 9 character, landscape
10 complexion 11 description, disposition, personality, temperament 12 constitution
naught 3 nil, zip 4 love, nada, zero
5 zilch 6 cipher 7 nothing, nullity
8 goose egg 11 nothingness
naughty 3 bad 4 lewd 5 bawdy 6 unruly, ribald, risqué, smutty, vulgar
7 froward, obscene, raunchy, wayward, willful 8 contrary, improper, perverse, rascally 10 ill-behaved 11 disobedient, mischievous 12 obstreperous, recalcitrant
Nauru *capital:* 5 Yaren *former name:*
8 Pleasant (Island) *monetary unit:* 6 dollar
nauseate 5 repel 6 offend, sicken 7 disgust, repulse
nauseated 6 queasy 7 carsick 8 qualmish
9 disgusted, squeamish 10 grossed out
nauseating 6 putrid 7 noisome 9 loathsome, offensive, repellant, repugnant, repulsive, revolting, sickening 10 disgusting
Nausicaa *father:* 8 Alcinous *mother:*
5 Arete
nautical 5 naval 6 marine 7 oceanic
8 maritime 12 navigational *instrument:*
3 aba 7 compass, pelorus, sextant
Navajo dwelling 5 hogan
naval hero 5 Jones (John Paul), Perry (Matthew, Oliver Hazard) 8 Farragut (David, George), Lawrence (James)
navel 6 middle 7 nombril 9 umbilicus
11 belly button *combining form:*
6 omphal 7 omphalo
navigate 4 helm, plot, sail 5 guide, pilot, steer 6 cruise 8 maneuver, traverse
navigation 8 piloting 10 seamanship
12 helmsmanship
navigational system 5 loran
navigator 5 flyer, pilot 6 airman 7 co-

pilot *Danish:* 6 Bering (Vitus) *Dutch:*
6 Tasman (Abel) 7 Barents (Willem)
English: 4 Cook (Captain James)
5 Cabot (John, Sebastian), Drake (Francis) 6 Hudson (Henry) 7 Gilbert (Humphrey), Raleigh (Walter) 9 Vancouver (George) *French:* 7 Cartier (Jacques) 9 La Perouse (Comte de) *Italian:* 6 Caboto (Giovanni) 8 Columbus (Christopher), Vespucci (Amerigo)
9 Verrazano (Giovanni) 10 Verrazzano (Giovanni) *Norwegian:* 4 Eric (the Red)
8 Ericsson (Leif) 12 Leif Ericsson, Leif Eriksson *Portuguese:* 4 Dias (Bartolomeu, Dinis) 6 Cabral (Pedro Alvares), da Gama (Vasco) 8 Magellan (Ferdinand) *Spanish:* 9 Fernández (Juan)
navy 4 blue 5 fleet 6 argosy, armada
8 flotilla
Nazi 9 Hitlerite 10 brownshirt *admiral:*
6 Dönitz (Karl), Raeder (Erich)
7 Doenitz (Karl) *air force:* 9 Luftwaffe
armed forces: 9 Wehrmacht *collaborator:*
5 Laval (Pierre) 8 Quisling (Vidkun)
concentration camp: 6 Belsen, Dachau
9 Auschwitz, Treblinka 10 Buchenwald, Nordhausen *field marshal:* 5 Model (Walter) 6 Keitel (Wilhelm), Paulus (Friedrich), Rommel (Erwin) 9 Rundstedt (Karl von) 10 Kesselring (Albert)
greeting: 4 heil *leader:* 3 Ley (Robert)
4 Hess (Rudolf), Röhm (Ernst)
5 Roehm (Ernst) 6 Führer, Göring (Hermann), Hitler (Adolf) 7 Fuehrer, Goering (Hermann), Himmler (Heinrich) 8 Goebbels (Joseph), Heydrich (Reinhard) 9 Rosenberg (Alfred) *police:*
7 Gestapo *propagandist:* 8 Goebbels (Joseph) *submarine:* 5 U-boat *surrender signer:* 4 Jodl (Alfred) 6 Keitel (Wilhelm) *symbol:* 6 fylfot 8 swastika *tactic:*
10 blitzkrieg *tank:* 6 Panzer
NCO 3 cpl, sgt 8 corporal, sergeant
neap 3 low 4 low tide
near 4 nigh 5 about, circa, close, round
6 almost, around 7 close by, close on
8 adjacent, approach 9 immediate, proximate 11 approximate
nearby 4 nigh 5 about, aside, close, handy 6 around, beside 8 adjacent
9 adjoining, proximate 10 contiguous, convenient 11 neighboring
nearest 4 next 7 closest 8 adjacent, proximal 9 proximate 10 contiguous
nearsighted 6 myopic
neat 4 deft, nice, prim, snug, tidy, trig, trim 5 clean, clear, kempt 6 clever, smooth, spruce 7 orderly, precise, unmixed 8 straight, well-kept 9 shipshape, undiluted 10 methodical, sys-

tematic 11 spic-and-span, uncluttered, well-groomed 12 spic-and-span 13 unadulterated

neb 3 tip 4 beak, bill, nose, prow 5 snoot, snout 9 proboscis

Nebraska *capital:* 7 Lincoln *city:* 5 Omaha *college, university:* 9 Creighton *nickname:* 10 Cornhusker (State) *river:* 6 Platte 8 Missouri *state bird:* 10 meadowlark *state flower:* 9 goldenrod *state tree:* 10 cottonwood

nebula 6 galaxy

nebulous 4 hazy 5 vague 6 cloudy, turbid 7 clouded, obscure, unclear 9 ambiguous, amorphous, uncertain 10 indefinite, indistinct 13 indeterminate

necessary 5 basic, vital 6 needed 7 crucial, needful 8 cardinal, integral, required 9 de rigueur, essential, mandatory, requisite 10 compulsory, imperative, inevitable, obligatory, undeniable 11 fundamental, ineluctable, inescapable, unavoidable 12 all-important, prerequisite 13 indispensable

necessitate 5 cause, exact, force 6 compel, demand, entail 7 call for, involve, require 8 occasion

necessity 4 must, need 6 crisis, duress 7 poverty 8 exigency 9 essential, privation, requisite 10 compulsion, imperative, obligation, sine qua non 11 dire straits, needfulness, requirement 12 precondition, prerequisite

neck 3 pet 4 kiss 6 fondle, smooch *back of:* 4 nape 5 nucha 6 scruff *ornament:* 6 gorget, torque

necklace 5 chain 6 choker 7 rivière 8 carcanet

necktie 5 ascot 6 cravat 10 four-in-hand

necrology 4 obit 8 obituary

necromancy 4 juju 5 magic, vodun 6 hoodoo, voodoo 7 devilry, sorcery 8 witchery, wizardry 9 conjuring, diabolism, magicking 10 black magic, witchcraft 11 bewitchment, conjuration, enchantment, incantation, thaumaturgy

necropolis 8 boneyard, boot hill, cemetery, God's acre 9 graveyard 10 churchyard 12 memorial park, potter's field

necropsy 7 anatomy, autopsy 10 dissection, postmortem

née 4 born 10 originally

need 3 use 4 call, duty, lack, must, want 5 crave 6 demand, devoir, hunger, penury, thirst 7 poverty, require 8 distress, exigency, occasion, shortage 9 indigence, necessity, privation, requisite 10 compulsion, deficiency, obligation 11 deprivation, destitution, requirement

neediness 4 want 6 penury 7 poverty 9 indigence, privation 11 deprivation, destitution 13 insufficiency

needle 3 rib 5 annoy, tease 6 harass, pester, plague 7 bedevil, hagride, obelisk, pricker, syringe 10 hypodermic *case:* 4 etui *hole:* 3 eye

needlefish 3 gar 8 pipefish

needlelike 7 styloid 8 belonoid *part:* 7 acicula

needlepoint 4 lace 7 alençon, crochet, tatting 8 bargello 10 embroidery 11 cross-stitch

needlework 4 lace 6 sewing 7 alençon, crochet, sampler, tatting 8 bargello, knitting 9 stitching 10 crocheting, embroidery 11 cross-stitch

needy 4 poor 5 broke 6 hard up 8 beggared, dirt-poor, indigent, strapped 9 destitute, penniless, penurious 10 down-and-out 11 impecunious, necessitous 12 impoverished

ne'er-do-well 3 bum, dud 5 loser 6 loafer, no-good 7 failure, wastrel 8 derelict 9 shiftless 10 profligate, scapegrace

nefarious 4 evil, vile 6 savage, wicked 7 heinous, impious, noxious 8 depraved, dreadful, flagrant, infamous, perverse 9 execrable, miscreant, monstrous, offensive 10 abominable, degenerate, detestable, iniquitous, outrageous, villainous 11 opprobrious 13 reprehensible

negate 4 deny, undo, void 5 annul, quash, rebut 6 cancel, impugn, refute, vacate 7 abolish, gainsay, nullify, redress, vitiate 8 abrogate, disallow, disprove, overturn, traverse 9 cancel out, disaffirm, repudiate 10 contradict, contravene, counteract, invalidate, neutralize 12 countercheck

negative 3 nix 4 deny, kill, veto 5 annul, cross, minus 6 impugn 7 adverse, gainsay, nullify, redress, refusal 8 abrogate, disprove, traverse 9 cancel out, frustrate 10 contradict, contravene, counteract, invalidate, neutralize 11 detrimental, unfavorable *battery terminal:* 5 anode *ion:* 5 anion *Scottish:* 3 nae *sign:* 5 minus

neglect 4 fail, omit 5 let go, shirk 6 forget, ignore, laxity, slight 7 failure, laxness 8 omission, overlook, overpass, pass over 9 avoidance, disregard, oversight, pretermit 10 negligence 11 dereliction, inattention 12 carelessness 13 pretermission

neglectful see NEGLIGENT

negligee 4 gown 5 teddy 7 chemise, nightie 8 camisole, peignoir 9 nightgown

negligent 3 lax **5** slack **6** remiss **8** careless, derelict, heedless **9** forgetful, imprudent **10** delinquent, neglectful, nonchalant, regardless, unthinking **11** inattentive, pococurante, unconcerned **12** disregardful **13** irresponsible, lackadaisical

negligible 4 puny, slim **5** minor, petty, small **6** meager, meagre, minute, remote, paltry, skimpy, slight **7** minimal, slender, trivial **8** nugatory, picayune, trifling **9** minuscule **11** meaningless, unimportant **13** imperceptible, insignificant

negotiable 8 passable **11** convertible **12** transferable

negotiate 4 cash **6** confer, dicker, hurdle, manage, parley, settle **7** arrange, bargain, develop, mediate, work out, wrangle **8** contract, covenant, moderate, surmount, transact, transfer **9** arbitrate **10** horse-trade

neigh 6 nicker, whinny

neighbor 4 abut **5** flank, frame, skirt **6** adjoin, border **7** abutter **8** border on

neighborhood 4 area, turf, ward **5** block, range **6** parish **8** district, locality, precinct, purlieus, vicinage, vicinity **9** community, proximity

neighborly 6 genial **7** amiable, cordial, helpful **8** amicable, friendly, obliging, sociable **9** congenial **10** gregarious, hospitable **11** considerate, cooperative, good-natured **13** accommodating

nematode 4 worm **7** eelworm **9** roundworm

Nemean predator 4 lion

nemesis 4 bane, doom **5** curse, enemy, rival **8** opponent **9** bête noire **11** retribution

neologism 7 coinage, new word

neophyte see NEWCOMER

Neoptolemus 7 Pyrrhus *father:* **8** Achilles *slayer:* **7** Orestes *victim:* **5** Priam *wife:* **8** Hermione

neoteric 6 modern, recent

Nepal *capital:* **8** Katmandu **9** Kathmandu *city:* **7** Pokhara **8** Lalitpur *monetary unit:* **5** rupee *mountain, range:* **7** Everest **8** Himalaya **9** Himalayan, Himalayas **10** Dhaulagiri **11** Gauri Sankar **12** Kanchenjunga *neighbor:* **5** China, India *river:* **6** Ganges

nepenthe 6 opiate, potion **7** anodyne **8** lenitive, narcotic **9** analgesic **10** anesthetic, painkiller

Nephthys *brother, husband:* **3** Set **4** Seth

nepotism 10 favoritism, partiality

Neptune 6 planet *satellite:* **6** Nereid, Triton (see also POSEIDON)

nerd 4 drip, geek **6** misfit **7** egghead, nebbish, oddball **10** pointy-head

Nereid 6 Thetis **7** Galatea **10** Amphitrite *father:* **6** Nereus *mother:* **5** Doris

Nereus *daughters:* **8** Nereides *emblem:* **7** trident *father:* **6** Pontus *mother:* **4** Gaea *wife:* **5** Doris

Nergal *brother:* **5** Nanna **6** Ninazu *father:* **5** Enlil *mother:* **6** Ninlil

Nero *birthplace:* **4** Rome *mother:* **9** Agrippina *successor:* **5** Galba *tutor:* **6** Seneca *victim:* **5** Lucan **6** Seneca **7** Octavia, Poppaea **9** Agrippina *wife:* **7** Octavia, Poppaea

Nero Wolfe *creator* **5** Stout (Rex)

nerve 4 face, gall, grit, guts **5** brass, cheek, crust, heart, moxie, spunk **6** daring **7** sciatic **8** audacity, backbone, boldness, chutzpah, temerity **9** assurance, brashness, fortitude, hardihood, hardiness **10** confidence, effrontery **11** presumption *cell:* **6** neuron *cell group:* **7** ganglia (plural) **8** ganglion *combining form:* **4** neur **5** neura, neuro *cranial:* **4** vagi (plural) **5** optic, vagus **8** abducens *ending:* **8** receptor *lesion:* **8** neuritis

nerve center 3 hub **4** core, seat **5** focus, heart, locus **7** capital **8** cynosure, polestar **10** crossroads, focal point **12** headquarters

nerve gas 5 sarin, soman, tabun

nervous 4 edgy **5** jerky, jumpy, tense, timid **6** fitful, goosey, on edge, spooky, uneasy **7** erratic, fidgety, fretful, jittery, restive, twitchy, uptight **8** aflutter, agitated, forcible, skittery, skittish, spirited, twittery, unsteady, vigorous, volatile **9** excitable, irregular, irritable **10** high-strung **12** apprehensive

nervy 4 bold, edgy, pert **5** brash, cocky, fresh, jerky, jumpy, sassy, tense **6** brassy, cheeky, goosey, plucky, spooky, uneasy **7** fidgety, forward, jittery, restive, twitchy, uptight **8** impudent, intrepid, twittery **9** excitable **10** high-strung **11** smart-alecky

ness 4 cape **8** foreland, headland **9** peninsula **10** promontory

Nessus' *victim* **8** Heracles, Hercules

nest 3 den **4** aery, home, lair, nidi (plural) **5** aerie, eyrie, nidus **7** hangout, shelter **11** aggregation *eagle's:* **4** aery **5** aerie, eyrie *wasp's:* **8** vespiary

nest egg 5 cache, funds, hoard, kitty, stash **6** assets **7** reserve

nestle 4 snug **6** bundle, burrow, cuddle, huddle, nuzzle **7** snuggle

Nestor *father:* **6** Neleus *kingdom:* **5** Pylos

net 4 gain, gist, mesh **5** basic, catch, clear, seine, tulle, yield **6** maline **7** clean

up, essence, malines *conical:* 5 trawl
fishing: 5 seine *hair:* 5 snood
Nethanel *brother:* 5 David *father:* 5 Jesse
7 Pashhur 8 Obededom *son:* 8 Shema-
iah
nether 3 low 4 down 5 below, lower,
under 6 lesser 8 chthonic, inferior
9 subjacent 10 underworld 11 underground 12 subterranean
Netherlands 7 Holland *capital:* 9 Amsterdam *city:* 5 Hague (The) 7 Utrecht
8 The Hague 9 Rotterdam *former inlet:*
9 Zuider Zee *island group:* 11 West
Frisian *lake:* 10 IJsselmeer *language:*
5 Dutch *monetary unit:* 4 euro *monetary
unit, former:* 7 guilder *neighbor:* 7 Belgium, Germany *river:* 4 Maas 5 Meuse,
Rhein, Rhine 7 Scheldt *sea:* 5 North
Netherlands Antilles *capital:* 10 Willem-
stad *discoverer:* 8 Columbus (Christopher) *former name:* 7 Curaçao *island:*
4 Saba 7 Bonaire 7 Curaçao *location:*
10 West Indies *part of:* 11 Netherlands
netherworld 3 pit 4 hell 5 abyss, hades,
Sheol 6 blazes, Tophet 7 Gehenna,
inferno 8 hellfire 9 perdition 10 no-
man's-land, underworld 11 underground
netlike 9 reticular 10 reticulate
nettle 3 nag, vex 4 gall, huff, rile, roil
5 annoy, chafe, peeve, pique, upset
6 abrade, badger, harass, incite, put
out, pester, ruffle, stir up 7 agitate, disturb, perturb, provoke 8 irritate
10 exasperate
nettle rash 5 hives 9 urticaria
nettlesome 5 pesky 6 vexing 7 galling,
irksome, prickly 8 annoying, rankling
9 irritable, upsetting, vexatious 10 irritating
network 3 web 4 mesh 8 gridiron 9 reticulum *anatomical:* 4 rete 5 retia (plural)
neurotic 6 phobic, touchy 7 anxious
8 abnormal, unstable 9 disturbed,
obsessive 10 compulsive, disordered
neuter 3 fix 4 geld, spay 5 alter, unsex
7 sexless 8 castrate, mutilate 9 sterilize
11 desexualize 12 intransitive
neutral 7 hueless 8 detached, middling,
unbiased 9 colorless, impartial,
unaligned 10 achromatic, disengaged,
even-handed, impersonal, nonaligned,
pokerfaced 11 indifferent, nonpartisan
13 disinterested, dispassionate
neutralize 4 undo 5 annul 6 negate, offset 7 balance, nullify, redress, reverse
9 cancel out 10 counteract, invalidate
11 countervail 12 countercheck, counterpoise
Nevada *capital:* 10 Carson City *city:*
4 Elko, Reno 8 Las Vegas *dam:*

6 Hoover 7 Boulder *lake:* 4 Mead
5 Tahoe *mountain:* 8 Boundary (Peak)
nickname: 6 Silver (State) *river:* 8 Humboldt *state bird:* 8 bluebird (mountain)
state flower: 9 sagebrush *state tree:*
5 piñon 6 pinyon 15 bristlecone pine
névé 4 firn, snow
never-ending 7 eternal 8 immortal
9 ceaseless 11 everlasting
Never-Ending Story author 4 Ende
(Michael)
nevertheless 3 but, yet 5 still 6 anyhow,
anyway, though, withal 7 howbeit,
however 8 after all 10 regardless
11 nonetheless, still and all
nevus 4 mole 9 birthmark
new 5 fresh, novel 6 modern, recent
7 another, revived 8 neoteric, pristine
10 additional, unfamiliar 11 modernis-
tic 12 contemporary *combining form:*
3 neo, nov 4 novo *word:* 7 coinage
9 neologism
New Brunswick *capital:* 11 Fredericton
city: 6 St. John 7 Moncton *mountain:*
8 Carleton *provincial flower:* 12 purple
violet *river:* 9 Miramichi, Saint John
10 Nepisiguit 11 Restigouche
New Caledonia *capital:* 6 Nouméa *department of:* 6 France *discoverer:* 4 Cook
(Capt. James) *island:* 7 Loyalty, Walpole
11 Isle of Pines
newcomer 4 colt, tyro 6 novice, rookie
8 beginner, freshman, initiate, neophyte 9 greenhorn, immigrant, novitiate 10 apprentice, tenderfoot
New Deal agency 3 CCC, NRA, SEC,
TVA, WPA 4 FDIC, NLRB
Newfoundland and Labrador *capital:*
7 St. John's *mountain:* 8 Caubvick
provincial flower: 12 pitcher plant *river:*
6 Gander 8 Exploits 9 Churchill
New Hampshire *capital:* 7 Concord *city:*
6 Nashua 10 Manchester, Portsmouth
college, university: 9 Dartmouth *motto:*
13 Live Free or Die *mountain, range:*
5 White 10 Washington *nickname:*
7 Granite (State) *river:* 9 Merrimack
11 Connecticut *state bird:* 11 purple
finch *state flower:* 11 purple lilac *state
tree:* 10 white birch
New Jersey *capital:* 7 Trenton *city:*
6 Camden, Newark 7 Cape May
8 Paterson 9 Elizabeth 10 Jersey City
college, university: 4 Drew 7 Rutgers
9 Princeton, Seton Hall 18 Fairleigh
Dickinson *nickname:* 6 Garden (State)
river: 6 Hudson 7 Raritan 8 Delaware
state bird: 9 goldfinch *state flower:* 6 violet *state tree:* 6 red oak
New Mexico *capital:* 7 Santa Fe *caverns:*
8 Carlsbad *city:* 4 Taos 7 Roswell 9 Las

Cruces, Los Alamos 10 Farmington 11 Albuquerque *mountain, range:* 7 Wheeler (Peak) 14 Sangre de Cristo *nickname:* 17 Land of Enchantment *river:* 5 Pecos 9 Rio Grande *state bird:* 10 roadrunner *state flower:* 5 yucca *state tree:* 5 piñon 6 pinyon

news 4 dope, poop, word 5 rumor 6 advice, gossip, report, tattle 7 low-down, tidings 9 knowledge, speerings 11 information, scuttlebutt 12 announcement, intelligence 4 TASS 7 Reuters 8 ITAR-TASS

newspaper 5 daily, organ 6 review 7 journal, tabloid 8 magazine 10 period-ical *publisher:* 6 Hearst (William Randolph) 7 Murdoch (Rupert) 11 Beaver-brook (Lord)

newt 3 eft 6 triton *green:* 5 ebbet

New Testament see at BIBLE

New York *capital:* 6 Albany *city:* 4 Rome, Troy 5 Utica 6 Elmira, Ithaca 7 Buffalo, Yonkers 8 Saratoga, Syracuse 9 Rochester 11 New York City *college, university:* 3 RPI 4 Pace, CUNY, SUNY 5 Pratt, Siena 6 CW Post, Hunter, Vassar 7 Adelphi, Barnard, Colgate, Cornell, Fordham, Hofstra, St. Johns, Yeshiva 8 Columbia, Skidmore, Syracuse 9 Juilliard, West Point 13 Sarah Lawrence *island:* 4 Long, Fire *lake, lake group:* 4 Erie 6 Cayuga, Finger, Oneida 7 Saranac 9 Champlain *motto:* 9 Excelsior *mountain, range:* 7 Marcy 8 Catskill 10 Adirondack *nickname:* 6 Empire (State) *river:* 6 Hudson 7 Niagara 10 St. Lawrence *state bird:* 8 bluebird *state flower:* 4 rose *state tree:* 10 sugar maple

New York City 6 Gotham 8 Big Apple *borough:* 5 Bronx 6 Queens 8 Brooklyn, Richmond 9 Manhattan 12 Staten Island

New Zealand *capital:* 10 Wellington *city:* 8 Auckland 12 Christchurch *ethnic group:* 5 Maori *explorer:* 4 Cook (Capt. James) 6 Tasman (Abel) *island:* 5 North, South 7 Chatham, Stewart *island group:* 4 Cook 8 Manihiki 12 Northern Cook *lake:* 5 Taupo *language:* 5 Maori 7 English *monetary unit:* 6 dollar *mountain, range:* 4 Cook 6 Egmont 12 Southern Alps *native:* 4 Kiwi *strait:* 4 Cook *volcano:* 7 Ruapehu 9 Ngauruhoe

next 4 then 5 after, later 6 behind, beside, second 7 closest, ensuing, nearest 8 abutting, adjacent, touching 9 adjoining, afterward, alongside, following, proximate 10 contiguous, subsequent, succeeding 11 neighboring

next to 4 near 6 almost, beside 7 abreast, close by 8 abutting, adjacent, opposite, touching 9 adjoining, alongside, bordering 11 neighboring

nexus 3 tie 4 bond, knot, link, yoke 5 focus 6 center 8 ligament, ligature, vinculum 10 connection

Nez Percé chief 6 Joseph

Niagara 5 flood, spate 6 deluge 7 torrent 8 alluvion, cataract, flooding, overflow 9 cataclysm, waterfall 10 inundation

nib 3 neb, tip 4 beak, bill, nose, prow 5 prong, snoot, snout, tooth 8 pen point 9 proboscis

nibble 3 eat, nip 4 bite, chew, crop, gnaw, nosh, peck, pick 5 graze, munch, snack, taste 6 morsel, tidbit

Nicaragua *capital:* 7 Managua *city:* 4 León 6 Masaya *coast:* 8 Mosquito *ethnic group:* 4 Maya 5 Mayan *discoverer:* 8 Columbus (Christopher) *language:* 7 Spanish *monetary unit:* 7 córdoba *neighbor:* 8 Honduras 9 Costa Rica *sea:* 9 Caribbean

nice 4 fine, good, kind, mild, neat 5 right 6 benign, comely, dainty, decent, polite, proper, seemly 7 affable, clement, cordial, correct, fitting, refined 8 becoming, charming, decorous, obliging, pleasant, pleasing, suitable, virtuous, well-bred 9 admirable, agreeable, courteous, congenial, enjoyable, favorable, judicious 10 attractive, personable 11 appropriate, respectable

niche 4 nook 6 alcove, corner, cranny, recess 7 calling 8 vocation 9 cubbyhole 11 compartment

Nicholas Nickleby author 7 Dickens (Charles)

nick 3 cut 4 chip, gash 5 cheat, notch, score 6 groove, record 10 overcharge 11 indentation

nickname 3 tag 5 label 6 byword, handle 7 agnomen, epithet, moniker 8 cognomen 9 sobriquet 10 diminutive, hypocorism

Nicomede *conquest:* 10 Cappodocia *dramatist:* 9 Corneille (Pierre) *half-brother:* 6 Attale *stepmother:* 7 Arsinoë

nictitate 3 bat 4 wink 5 blink 7 flutter, twinkle

nifty 4 cool, keen, neat 5 dandy, ducky, super, swell 6 clever, groovy, peachy 7 stylish 8 jim-dandy, splendid, terrific 9 ingenious

Niger *capital:* 6 Niamey *city:* 6 Maradi, Zinder *desert:* 5 Sahel 6 Sahara *ethnic group:* 5 Hausa *language:* 5 Hausa 6 Arabic, French *monetary unit:* 5 franc *neighbor:* 4 Chad, Mali 5 Benin, Libya 7 Algeria, Nigeria 11 Burkina Faso *river:* 5 Niger

Nigeria *capital:* 5 Abuja, Lagos *city:*

4 Kano 6 Ibadan, Ilorin 7 Oshogbo
9 Ogbomosho *ethnic group:* 4 Igbo
5 Hausa 6 Fulani, Yoruba *gulf:* 6 Guinea
lake: 4 Chad *language:* 5 Hausa 7 English *monetary unit:* 5 naira *neighbor:*
4 Chad 5 Benin, Niger 8 Cameroon
river: 5 Benue, Niger 6 Kaduna

niggard 5 churl, miser, piker, screw
7 hoarder, scrooge 8 tightwad 9 skinflint 10 cheapskate, curmudgeon
12 money-grubber, penny-pincher

niggardly 5 tight 6 scanty, stingy
7 chintzy, miserly 9 penurious
10 begrudging 11 closefisted, tightfisted
12 cheeseparing, parsimonious
13 penny-pinching

niggling 5 minor, petty 6 measly, paltry,
two-bit 7 trivial 8 picayune, piddling,
tiresome, trifling 9 small-time 10 bothersome, picayunish 11 small-minded

nigh 4 near 5 about, close, round 6 all
but, almost, around, beside, nearby,
nearly 7 close to 8 approach 9 immediate, just about, proximate, virtually
10 near at hand, pretty much 11 practically

night blindness 10 nyctalopia

nightclub 5 disco 6 bistro, casino
7 cabaret 9 honky-tonk, speakeasy
11 discotheque

nightfall 3 eve 4 dusk, even 6 sunset
7 evening, sundown 8 eventide, gloaming, twilight

nighthawk 6 petrel 7 bullbat 10 goatsucker

nightjar 9 nighthawk 10 goatsucker
12 whip-poor-will

nightly 9 nocturnal

nightmare 5 dream, fancy, worry
6 fright, horror, ordeal, vision 7 bugbear, fantasy, incubus, torment 8 phantasm, phantasy, succubus 12 apprehension 13 hallucination

nightshade 6 tomato 7 henbane 10 belladonna 11 bittersweet

nightstick 3 bat 4 club, mace 5 baton,
billy, staff 6 cudgel 8 bludgeon 9 billy
club, blackjack, truncheon 10 shillelagh

Nike *father:* 6 Pallas *goddess of:* 7 victory
mother: 4 Styx

nil 3 nix, zip 4 love, wind, zero 5 zilch
6 naught 7 nothing

Nile 6 Al-Bahr *dam:* 5 Aswan 6 Makwar
10 Gebel Aulia *explorer:* 5 Baker (Sir
Samuel), Bruce (James), Grant (James
Augustus), Speke (John Hanning)
queen: 4 Cleo 9 Cleopatra *section:*
4 Abay 5 Abbai

nilgai 8 antelope

nimble 4 deft, spry, yare 5 agile, alert,
fleet, handy, light, quick, zippy

6 adroit, limber, lively 7 lissome 9 dexterous, sprightly 10 responsive
11 quick-witted

Nimrod 6 hunter *father:* 4 Cush

Ninazu *brother:* 5 Nanna 6 Nergal *father:*
5 Enlil *mother:* 6 Ninlil

nincompoop 3 oaf 4 boob, clod, dodo,
fool, goof, mutt, simp, yo-yo 5 chump,
dummy, dunce, idiot, moron, ninny,
noddy, stupe 6 dimwit, donkey, dumdum, nitwit 7 airhead, dullard, pinhead, schnook, tomfool 8 bonehead,
clodpoll, dumbbell, dumbhead, imbecile, lunkhead, meathead, numskull
9 birdbrain, blockhead, ignoramus,
lamebrain, numbskull, simpleton,
thickhead 10 dunderhead, hammerhead 11 chowderhead, chucklehead,
knucklehead

nine 12 baseball team *combining form:*
3 non 4 nona *goddesses:* 5 Muses
group: 6 ennead *inches:* 4 span *instruments:* 5 nonet

Nine Worlds 3 Hel 6 Asgard 7 Alfheim,
Midgard 8 Niflheim, Vanaheim
10 Jotunnheim 12 Muspellsheim
13 Svartalfaheim

ninny see NINCOMPOOP

Ninsum's son 9 Gilgamesh

Nintu *consort:* 4 Enki *son:* 6 Ninsar

Ninurta *father:* 5 Enlil *victim:* 3 Kur

Ninus *father:* 5 Belus *wife:* 9 Semiramis

Niobe *brother:* 6 Pelops *father:* 8 Tantalus
husband: 7 Amphion *sister-in-law:*
5 Aedon

nip 3 bit, nab, sip 4 bite, dart, dash,
dram, drop, jolt, peck, shot, slug, swig
5 chill, clamp, hurry, pinch, sever,
snort, steal 6 imbibe, snatch, thwart,
tipple 7 cabbage, snifter, swallow
9 frustrate

nipper 3 kid 4 tyke 5 child 6 moppet,
shaver 7 pincers 8 young one
9 youngling, youngster

nipple 3 pap 4 teat

Nippon 5 Japan

nippy 3 icy, raw 4 cold, cool 5 algid,
chill, crisp, sharp 6 arctic, biting, bitter,
chilly, frosty, wintry 7 caustic, glacial,
numbing, shivery 8 chilling, freezing

nirvana 5 bliss, dream 6 heaven 7 Elysium 8 empyrean, oblivion, paradise
9 Shangri-la

Nisus *betrayer, daughter:* 6 Scylla *father:*
7 Pandion

nitid 6 bright, glossy, lucent 7 fulgent,
glowing, shining 8 gleaming, glinting,
luminous, lustrous, polished 9 burnished

nitpick 4 carp 5 cavil 7 quibble 10 split
hairs

nitrogen 5 azote *combining form:* 3 azo
nitwit 3 oaf 4 boob, clod, dodo, dolt, dope, goof, mutt, simp 5 chump, cluck, dummy, dunce, idiot, moron, ninny, noddy, stupe 6 donkey, dum-dum 7 airhead, dullard, pinhead, schnook 8 bonehead, clodpoll, dumbbell, imbecile, lunkhead, meathead, numskull 9 birdbrain, blockhead, ignoramus, lamebrain, numbskull, simpleton, thickhead 10 dunderhead, hammerhead, nincompoop 11 chowderhead, chucklehead, knucklehead
nix 3 nay, zap 4 kill, nope, veto 5 quash 6 cancel, naught, reject, scotch, sprite 7 call off, nothing, nullify
Njord, Njorth *daughter:* 5 Freya *son:* 4 Frey *wife:* 6 Skadhi, Skathi
no 3 nay, nix 6 denial 7 refusal 8 negative 10 thumbs-down *German:* 4 nein
no-account see NO-GOOD
Noachian 3 old 4 aged 5 fusty, hoary 6 age-old 7 ancient, antique, archaic 8 timeworn 9 venerable 10 antiquated, oldfangled 12 antediluvian, old-fashioned 13 superannuated
Noah *father:* 6 Lamech 10 Zelophehad *grandson:* 4 Aram 6 Canaan *great-grandson:* 3 Hul *landing place:* 6 Ararat *son:* 3 Ham 4 Shem 6 Canaan 7 Japheth
Nobel Prize winner
chemistry:
1901: 8 van't Hoff (Jacobus) *1902:* 7 Fischer (Emil) *1903:* 9 Arrhenius (Svante) *1904:* 6 Ramsay (William) *1905:* 9 von Baeyer (Adolf) *1906:* 7 Moissan (Henri) *1907:* 7 Buchner (Eduard) *1908:* 10 Rutherford (Ernest) *1909:* 7 Ostwald (Wilhelm) *1910:* 7 Wallach (Otto) *1911:* 5 Curie (Marie) *1912:* 8 Grignard (François), Sabatier (Paul) *1913:* 6 Werner (Alfred) *1914:* 8 Richards (Theodore) *1915:* 11 Willstatter (Richard) *1918:* 5 Haber (Fritz) *1920:* 6 Nernst (Walther) *1921:* 5 Soddy (Frederick) *1922:* 5 Aston (Francis) *1923:* 5 Pregl (Fritz) *1925:* 9 Zsigmondy (Richard) *1926:* 8 Svedberg (Theodor) *1927:* 7 Wieland (Heinrich) *1928:* 7 Windaus (Adolf) *1929:* 6 Harden (Arthur) 12 Euler-Chelpin (Hans von) *1930:* 7 Fischer (Hans) *1931:* 5 Bosch (Karl) 7 Bergius (Friedrich) *1932:* 8 Langmuir (Irving) *1934:* 4 Urey (Harold) *1935:* 11 Joliot-Curie (Frédéric, Irene) *1936:* 5 Debye (Peter) *1937:* 6 Karrer (Paul) 7 Haworth (Walter) *1938:* 4 Kuhn (Richard) *1939:* 7 Ruzicka (Leopold) 9 Butenandt (Adolf) *1943:* 6 Hevesy (Georg de) *1944:* 4 Hahn (Otto) *1945:* 8 Virtanen

(Artturi) *1946:* 6 Sumner (James) 7 Stanley (Wendell) 8 Northrop (John Howard) *1947:* 8 Robinson (Robert) *1948:* 8 Tiselius (Arne) *1949:* 7 Giauque (William) *1950:* 5 Alder (Kurt), Diels (Otto) *1951:* 7 Seaborg (Glenn) 8 McMillan (Edwin) *1952:* 5 Synge (Richard) 6 Martin (Archer) *1953:* 10 Staudinger (Hermann) *1954:* 7 Pauling (Linus) *1955:* 10 du Vigneaud (Vincent) *1956:* 7 Semenov (Nikolay) 11 Hinshelwood (Cyril) *1957:* 4 Todd (Alexander) *1958:* 6 Sanger (Frederick) *1959:* 9 Heyrovsky (Jaroslav) *1960:* 5 Libby (Willard) *1961:* 6 Calvin (Melvin) *1962:* 6 Perutz (Max) 7 Kendrew (John) *1963:* 5 Natta (Giulio) 7 Ziegler (Karl) *1964:* 7 Hodgkin (Dorothy) 8 Woodward (Robert) *1966:* 8 Mulliken (Robert) *1967:* 5 Eigen (Manfred) 6 Porter (George) 7 Norrish (Ronald) *1968:* 7 Onsager (Lars) *1969:* 6 Barton (Derek), Hassel (Odd) *1970:* 6 Leloir (Luis) *1971:* 8 Herzberg (Gerhard) *1972:* 5 Moore (Stanford), Stein (William) 8 Anfinsen (Christian) *1973:* 7 Fischer (Ernst) 8 Wilkinson (Geoffrey) *1974:* 5 Flory (Paul) *1975:* 6 Prelog (Vladimir) 9 Cornforth (John) *1976:* 8 Lipscomb (William) *1977:* 9 Prigogine (Ilya) *1978:* 8 Mitchell (Peter) *1979:* 5 Brown (Herbert) 6 Wittig (Georg) *1980:* 4 Berg (Paul) 6 Sanger (Frederick) 7 Gilbert (Walter) *1981:* 5 Fukui (Kenichi) 8 Hoffmann (Roald) *1982:* 4 Klug (Aaron) *1983:* 5 Taube (Henry) *1984:* 10 Merrifield (R. Bruce) *1985:* 5 Karle (Jerome) 8 Hauptman (Herbert) *1986:* 3 Lee (Yuan) 7 Polanyi (John) 10 Herschbach (Dudley) *1987:* 4 Cram (Donald), Lehn (Jean-Marie) 8 Pedersen (Charles) *1988:* 5 Huber (Robert) 6 Michel (Hartmut) 11 Deisenhofer (Johann) *1989:* 4 Cech (Thomas) 6 Altman (Sidney) *1990:* 5 Corey (Elias) *1991:* 5 Ernst (Richard) *1992:* 6 Marcus (Rudolph) *1993:* 5 Smith (Michael) 6 Mullis (Kary) *1994:* 4 Olah (George) *1995:* 6 Molina (Mario) 7 Crutzen (Paul), Rowland (F. Sherwood) *1996:* 4 Curl (Robert) 5 Kroto (Harold) 7 Smalley (Richard) *1997* 4 Skou (Jens) 5 Boyer (Paul) 6 Walker (John) *1998:* 4 Kohn (Walter) 5 Pople (John) *1999:* 6 Zewail (Ahmed) *2000:* 6 Heeger (Alan) 9 Shirakawa (Hideki) 10 MacDiarmid (Alan) *2001:* 6 Noyori (Ryoji) 7 Knowles (William) 9 Sharpless (K. Barry) *2002:* 4 Fenn (John) 6 Tanaka

(Koichi) 8 Wüthrich (Kurt) *2003:*
4 Agre (Peter) 9 MacKinnon (Roderick) *2004:* 4 Rose (Irwin) 7 Hershko (Avram) 11 Ciechanover (Aaron)

economics:
1969: 6 Frisch (Ragnar) 9 Tinbergen (Jan) *1970:* 9 Samuelson (Paul) *1971:* 7 Kuznets (Simon) *1972:* 5 Arrow (Kenneth), Hicks (John) *1973:* 8 Leontief (Wassily) *1974:* 5 Hayek (Friedrich von) 6 Myrdal (Gunnar) *1975:* 8 Koopmans (Tjalling) 11 Kantorovich (Leonid) *1976:* 8 Friedman (Milton) *1977:* 5 Meade (James), Ohlin (Bertil) *1978:* 5 Simon (Herbert) *1979:* 5 Lewis (Arthur) 7 Schultz (Theodore) *1980:* 5 Klein (Lawrence) *1981:* 5 Tobin (James) *1982:* 7 Stigler (George) *1983:* 6 Debreu (Gerard) *1984:* 5 Stone (Richard) *1985:* 10 Modigliani (Franco) *1986:* 8 Buchanan (James) *1987:* 5 Solow (Robert) *1988:* 6 Allais (Maurice) *1989:* 8 Haavelmo (Trygve) *1990:* 6 Miller (Merton), Sharpe (William) 9 Markowitz (Harry) *1991:* 5 Coase (Ronald) *1992:* 6 Becker (Gary) *1993:* 5 Fogel (Robert), North (Douglass) *1994:* 4 Nash (John) 6 Selten (Reinhard) 8 Harsanyi (John) *1995:* 5 Lucas (Robert) *1996:* 7 Vickrey (William) 8 Mirrlees (James) *1998:* 3 Sen (Amartya) *1999:* 7 Mundell (Robert) *2000:* 7 Heckman (James) 8 McFadden (Daniel) *2001:* 6 Spence (Michael) 7 Akerlof (George) 8 Stiglitz (Joseph) *2002:* 5 Smith (Vernon) 8 Kahneman (Daniel) *2003:* 5 Engle (Robert) 7 Granger (Clive) *2004:* 7 Kydland (Finn) 8 Prescott (Edward)

literature:
1901: 9 Prudhomme (Sully) *1902:* 7 Mommsen (Theodor) *1903:* 8 Bjornson (Bjornstjerne) *1904:* 7 Mistral (Frédéric) 9 Echegaray (José) *1905:* 11 Sienkiewicz (Henryk) *1906:* 8 Carducci (Giosue) *1907:* 7 Kipling (Rudyard) *1908:* 6 Eucken (Rudolf) *1909:* 8 Lagerlof (Selma) *1910:* 5 Heyse (Paul) *1911:* 11 Maeterlinck (Maurice) *1912:* 9 Hauptmann (Gerhart) *1913:* 6 Tagore (Rabindranath) *1915:* 7 Rolland (Romain) *1916:* 10 Heidenstam (Verner von) *1917:* 9 Gjellerup (Karl) 11 Pontoppidan (Henrik) *1919:* 9 Spitteler (Carl) *1920:* 6 Hamsun (Knut) *1921:* 6 France (Anatole) *1922:* 9 Benavente (Jacinto) *1923:* 5 Yeats (William Butler) *1924:* 7 Reymont (Wladyslaw) *1925:* 4 Shaw (George Bernard) *1926:* 7 Deledda (Grazia) *1927:* 7 Bergson (Henri) *1928:* 6 Undset

(Sigrid) *1929:* 4 Mann (Thomas) *1930:* 5 Lewis (Sinclair) *1931:* 9 Karlfeldt (Erik Axel) *1932:* 10 Galsworthy (John) *1933:* 5 Bunin (Ivan) *1934:* 10 Pirandello (Luigi) *1936:* 6 O'Neill (Eugene) *1937:* 12 Martin du Gard (Roger) *1938:* 4 Buck (Pearl) *1939:* 9 Sillanpää (Frans Eemil) *1944:* 6 Jensen (Johannes) *1945:* 7 Mistral (Gabriela) *1946:* 5 Hesse (Hermann) *1947:* 4 Gide (André) *1948:* 5 Eliot (Thomas Stearns) *1949:* 8 Faulkner (William) *1950:* 7 Russell (Bertrand) *1951:* 10 Lagerkvist (Pär) *1952:* 7 Mauriac (François) *1953:* 9 Churchill (Winston) *1954:* 9 Hemingway (Ernest) *1955:* 7 Laxness (Halldór) *1956:* 7 Jiménez (Juan Ramón) *1957:* 5 Camus (Albert) *1958:* 9 Pasternak (Boris) *1959:* 9 Quasimodo (Salvatore) *1960:* 5 Perse (Saint-John) *1961:* 6 Andric (Ivo) *1962:* 9 Steinbeck (John) *1963:* 7 Seferis (George) *1964:* 6 Sartre (Jean-Paul) *1965:* 9 Sholokhov (Mikhail) *1966:* 5 Agnon (Shmuel Yosef), Sachs (Nelly) *1967:* 8 Asturias (Miguel Angel) *1968:* 8 Kawabata (Yasunari) *1969:* 7 Beckett (Samuel) *1970:* 12 Solzhenitsyn (Alexander) *1971:* 6 Neruda (Pablo) *1972:* 4 Böll (Heinrich) *1973:* 5 White (Patrick) *1974:* 7 Johnson (Eyvind) 9 Martinson (Edmund) *1975:* 7 Montale (Eugenio) *1976:* 6 Bellow (Saul) *1977:* 10 Aleixandre (Vicente) *1978:* 6 Singer (Isaac Bashevis) *1979:* 6 Elytis (Odysseus) *1980:* 6 Milosz (Czeslaw) *1981:* 7 Canetti (Elias) *1982:* 13 García Márquez (Gabriel) *1983:* 7 Golding (William) *1984:* 7 Seifert (Jaroslav) *1985:* 5 Simon (Claude) *1986:* 7 Soyinka (Wole) *1987:* 7 Brodsky (Joseph) *1988:* 7 Mahfouz (Naguib) *1989:* 4 Cela (Camilo José) *1990:* 3 Paz (Octavio) *1991:* 8 Gordimer (Nadine) *1992:* 7 Walcott (Derek) *1993:* 8 Morrison (Toni) *1994:* 2 Oe (Kenzaburo) *1995:* 6 Heaney (Seamus) *1996:* 10 Szymborska (Wislawa) *1997:* 2 Fo (Dario) *1998:* 8 Saramago (José) *1999:* 5 Grass (Günter) *2000:* 3 Gao (Xingjian) 11 Gao Xingjian *2001:* 7 Naipaul (V. S.) *2002:* 7 Kertész (Imre) *2003:* 7 Coetzee (J. M.) *2004:* 7 Jelinek (Elfriede)

peace:
1901: 5 Passy (Frédéric) 6 Dunant (Jean-Henri) *1902:* 5 Gobat (Charles Albert) 8 Ducommun (Elie) *1903:* 6 Cremer (William) *1905:* 7 Suttner (Bertha von) *1906:* 9 Roosevelt (Theodore) *1907:* 6 Moneta (Ernesto)

7 Renault (Louis) *1908:* 5 Bajer (Fredrik) 9 Arnoldson (Klas Pontus) *1909:* 9 Beernaert (Auguste) 13 d'Estournelles (Paul) *1911:* 5 Asser (Tobias), Fried (Alfred) *1912:* 4 Root (Elihu) *1913:* 10 La Fontaine (Henri) *1919:* 6 Wilson (Woodrow) *1920:* 9 Bourgeois (Léon) *1921:* 5 Lange (Christian Louis) 8 Branting (Karl Hjalmar) *1922:* 6 Nansen (Fridtjof) *1925:* 5 Dawes (Charles) 11 Chamberlain (Austen) *1926:* 6 Briand (Aristide) 10 Stresemann (Gustav) *1927:* 6 Quidde (Ludwig) 7 Buisson (Ferdinand) *1929:* 7 Kellogg (Frank) *1930:* 9 Soderblom (Nathan) *1931:* 6 Addams (Jane), Butler (Nicholas Murray) *1933:* 6 Angell (Norman) *1934:* 9 Henderson (Arthur) *1935:* 9 Ossietzky (Carl von) *1936:* 13 Saavedra Lamas (Carlos de) *1937:* 5 Cecil (Robert) *1945:* 4 Hull (Cordell) *1946:* 4 Mott (John) 5 Balch (Emily Greene) *1949:* 3 Orr (John Boyd) *1950:* 6 Bunche (Ralph) *1951:* 7 Jouhaux (Léon) *1952:* 10 Schweitzer (Albert) *1953:* 8 Marshall (George) *1957:* 7 Pearson (Lester) *1958:* 4 Pire (Dominique Georges) *1959:* 9 Noel-Baker (Philip) *1960:* 7 Luthuli (Albert John) *1961:* 12 Hammarskjold (Dag) *1962:* 7 Pauling (Linus) *1964:* 4 King (Martin Luther) *1968:* 6 Cassin (René) *1970:* 7 Borlaug (Norman) *1971:* 6 Brandt (Willy) *1973:* 8 Le Duc Tho 9 Kissinger (Henry) *1974:* 4 Sato (Eisaku) 8 MacBride (Sean) *1975:* 8 Sakharov (Andrey) *1976:* 8 Corrigan (Mairead), Williams (Betty) *1978:* 5 Begin (Menachem), Sadat (Anwar el-) *1979:* 12 Mother Teresa *1980:* 8 Esquivel (Adolfo Pérez) *1982:* 6 Myrdal (Alva) 12 García Robles (Alfonso) *1983:* 6 Walesa (Lech) *1984:* 4 Tutu (Desmond) *1986:* 6 Wiesel (Elie) *1987:* 7 Arias Sánchez (Oscar) *1989:* 9 Dalai Lama *1990:* 9 Gorbachev (Mikhail) *1991:* 13 Aung San Suu Kyi *1992:* 6 Menchú (Rigoberta) *1993:* 7 de Klerk (F. W.), Mandela (Nelson) *1994:* 5 Peres (Shimon), Rabin (Yitzhak) 6 Arafat (Yasir) *1995:* 7 Rotblat (Joseph) *1996:* 10 Ramos-Horta (José) 11 Ximenes Belo (Carlos Felipe) *1997:* 8 Williams (Jody) *1998:* 4 Hume (John) 7 Trimble (David) *2000:* 3 Kim (Daejung) 10 Kim Dae-jung *2001:* 5 Annan (Kofi) *2002:* 6 Carter (Jimmy) *2003:* 5 Ebadi (Shirin) *2004:* 7 Maathai (Wangari)

physics:
1901: 8 Roentgen (Wilhelm) *1902:*

6 Zeeman (Pieter) 7 Lorentz (Hendrik Antoon) *1903:* 5 Curie (Marie, Pierre) 9 Becquerel (Antoine-Henri) *1904:* 6 Strutt (John) 8 Rayleigh (Lord) *1905:* 6 Lenard (Philipp von) *1906:* 7 Thomson (Joseph) *1907:* 9 Michelson (Albert) *1908:* 8 Lippmann (Gabriel) *1909:* 5 Braun (Karl) 7 Marconi (Guglielmo) *1910:* 11 van der Waals (Johannes) *1911:* 4 Wien (Wilhelm) *1912:* 5 Dalen (Nils) *1914:* 4 Laue (Max von) *1915:* 5 Bragg (William) *1917:* 6 Barkla (Charles) *1918:* 6 Planck (Max) *1919:* 5 Stark (Johannes) *1920:* 9 Guillaume (Charles) *1921:* 8 Einstein (Albert) *1922:* 4 Bohr (Niels) *1923:* 8 Millikan (Robert) *1924:* 8 Siegbahn (Karl) *1925:* 5 Hertz (Gustav) 6 Franck (James) *1926:* 6 Perrin (Jean-Baptiste) *1927:* 6 Wilson (Charles) 7 Compton (Arthur) *1928:* 10 Richardson (Owen) *1929:* 7 Broglie (Louis-Victor de) *1930:* 5 Raman (Chandrasekhara) *1932:* 10 Heisenberg (Werner) *1933:* 5 Dirac (Paul) 11 Schrödinger (Erwin) *1935:* 8 Chadwick (James) *1936:* 4 Hess (Victor) 8 Anderson (Carl) *1937:* 7 Thomson (George) 8 Davisson (Clinton) *1938:* 5 Fermi (Enrico) *1939:* 8 Lawrence (Ernest) *1943:* 5 Stern (Otto) *1944:* 4 Rabi (Isidor Isaac) *1945:* 5 Pauli (Wolfgang) *1946:* 8 Bridgman (Percy) *1947:* 8 Appleton (Edward) *1948:* 8 Blackett (Patrick) *1949:* 6 Yukawa (Hideki) *1950:* 6 Powell (Cecil) *1951:* 6 Walton (Ernest) 9 Cockcroft (John) *1952:* 5 Bloch (Felix) 7 Purcell (Edward) *1953:* 7 Zernike (Frits) *1954:* 4 Born (Max) 5 Bothe (Walther) *1955:* 4 Lamb (Willis) 5 Kusch (Polykarp) *1956:* 7 Bardeen (John) 8 Brattain (Walter), Shockley (William) *1957:* 3 Lee (Tsung Dao) 4 Yang (Chen Ning) *1958:* 4 Tamm (Igor) 5 Frank (Ilya) 9 Cherenkov (Pavel) *1959:* 5 Segrè (Emilio) 11 Chamberlain (Owen) *1960:* 6 Glaser (Donald) *1961:* 9 Mossbauer (Rudolf) 10 Hofstadter (Robert) *1962:* 6 Landau (Lev) *1963:* 5 Mayer (Maria) 6 Jensen (J. Hans), Wigner (Eugene) *1964:* 5 Basov (Nikolay) 6 Townes (Charles) 9 Prochorov (Alexander) *1965:* 7 Feynman (Richard) 8 Tomonaga (Shinichiro) 9 Schwinger (Julian) *1966:* 7 Kastler (Alfred) *1967:* 5 Bethe (Hans) *1968:* 7 Alvarez (Luis) *1969:* 8 Gell-Mann (Murray) *1970:* 4 Néel (Louis) 6 Alfven (Hannes) *1971:* 5 Gabor (Dennis) *1972:* 6 Cooper (Leon) 7 Bardeen (John) 10 Schrieffer

(John) *1973:* 5 Esaki (Leo) 7 Giaever
(Ivar) 9 Josephson (Brian) *1974:* 4 Ryle
(Martin) 6 Hewish (Antony) *1975:*
4 Bohr (Aage) 9 Mottelson (Ben),
Rainwater (L. James) *1976:* 4 Ting
(Samuel) 7 Richter (Burton) *1977:*
4 Mott (Nevill) 8 Anderson (Philip),
Van Vleck (John) *1978:* 6 Wilson
(Robert) 7 Kapitsa (Pyotr), Penzias
(Arno) *1979:* 5 Salam (Abdus)
7 Glashow (Sheldon) 8 Weinberg
(Steven) *1980:* 5 Fitch (Val) 6 Cronin
(James) *1981:* 8 Schawlow (Arthur),
Siegbahn (Kai) 11 Bloembergen
(Nicholaas) *1982:* 6 Wilson (Kenneth)
1983: 6 Fowler (William) 13 Chan-
drasekhar (Subrahmanyan) *1984:*
6 Rubbia (Carlo) 11 van der Meere
(Simon) *1985:* 8 Klitzing (Klaus von)
1986: 5 Ruska (Ernst) 6 Binnig (Gerd),
Rohrer (Heinrich) *1987:* 6 Müller
(K. Alex) 7 Bednorz (J. Georg) *1988:*
8 Lederman (Leon), Schwartz
(Melvin) 11 Steinberger (Jack) *1989:*
4 Paul (Wolfgang) 6 Ramsey (Norman)
7 Dehmelt (Hans) *1990:* 6 Taylor
(Richard) 7 Kendall (Henry) 8 Friedman (Jerome) *1991:* 8 De Gennes
(Pierre-Gilles) *1992:* 7 Charpak
(Georges) *1993:* 5 Hulse (Russell)
6 Taylor (Joseph) *1994:* 5 Shull (Clif-
ford) 10 Brockhouse (Bertram) *1995:*
4 Perl (Martin) 6 Reines (Frederick)
1996: 3 Lee (David) 8 Osheroff (Douglas) 10 Richardson (Robert) 3 Chu
(Steven) 8 Phillips (William) 14 Cohen-
Tannoudji (Claude) *1998:* 4 Tsui
(Daniel) 7 Störmer (Horst) 8 Laughlin
(Robert) *1999:* 6 't Hooft (Gerardus)
7 Veltman (Martinus) *2000:* 5 Kilby
(Jack) 7 Alferev (Zhores), Kroemer
(Herbert) *2001:* 6 Wieman (Carl)
7 Cornell (Eric) 8 Ketterle (Wolfgang)
2002: 5 Davis (Raymond) 7 Koshiba
(Masatoshi) 8 Giacconi (Riccardo)
2003: 7 Leggett (Anthony) 8 Ginzburg
(Vitaly) 9 Abrikosov (Alexei) *2004:*
5 Gross (David) 7 Wilczek (Frank)
8 Politzer (David)

physiology or medicine:
1901: 7 Behring (Emil von) *1902:*
4 Ross (Ronald) *1903:* 6 Finsen (Niels
Ryberg) *1904:* 6 Pavlov (Ivan) *1905:*
4 Koch (Robert) *1906:* 5 Golgi (Camillo) 11 Ramón y Cajal (Santiago) *1907:*
7 Laveran (Alphonse) *1908:* 7 Ehrlich
(Paul) 11 Metchnikoff (Elie) *1909:*
6 Kocher (Emil) *1910:* 6 Kossel
(Albrecht) *1911:* 10 Gullstrand (All-
var) *1912:* 6 Carrel (Alexis) *1913:*
6 Richet (Charles) *1914:* 6 Barany

(Robert) *1919:* 6 Bordet (Jules) *1920:*
5 Krogh (August) *1922:* 4 Hill
(Archibald) 8 Meyerhof (Otto) *1923:*
7 Banting (Frederick), Macleod (John)
1924: 9 Einthoven (Willem) *1926:*
7 Fibiger (Johannes) *1927:* 13 Wagner-
Jauregg (Julius) *1928:* 7 Nicolle
(Charles) *1929:* 7 Eijkman (Christiaan), Hopkins (Frederick) *1930:*
11 Landsteiner (Karl) *1931:* 7 Warburg
(Otto) *1932:* 6 Adrian (Edgar) 11 Sher-
rington (Charles) *1933:* 6 Morgan
(Thomas) *1934:* 5 Minot (George)
6 Murphy (William) 7 Whipple
(George) *1935:* 7 Spemann (Hans)
1936: 4 Dale (Henry) 5 Loewi (Otto)
1937: 12 Szent-Györgyi (Albert) *1938:*
7 Heymans (Corneille) *1939:*
6 Domagk (Gerhard) *1943:* 3 Dam
(Henrik) 5 Doisy (Edward) *1944:*
6 Gasser (Herbert) 8 Erlanger (Joseph)
1945: 5 Chain (Ernst) 6 Florey
(Howard) 7 Fleming (Alexander) *1946:*
6 Muller (Hermann) *1947:* 4 Cori
(Carl, Gerty) 7 Houssay (Bernardo)
1948: 7 Mueller (Paul) *1949:* 4 Hess
(Walter) 5 Moniz (Antonio) *1950:*
5 Hench (Philip) 7 Kendall (Edward)
10 Reichstein (Tadeus) *1951:* 7 Theiler
(Max) *1952:* 7 Waksman (Selman)
1953: 5 Krebs (Hans) 7 Lipmann
(Fritz) *1954:* 6 Enders (John), Weller
(Thomas) 7 Robbins (Frederick) *1955:*
8 Theorell (Hugo) *1956:* 8 Cournand
(André), Richards (Dickinson)
9 Forssmann (Werner) *1957:* 5 Bovet
(Daniel) *1958:* 5 Tatum (Edward)
6 Beadle (George) 9 Lederberg
(Joshua) *1959:* 5 Ochoa (Severo)
8 Kornberg (Arthur) *1960:* 6 Burnet
(Macfarlane) 7 Medawar (Peter) *1961:*
6 Bekesy (Georg von) *1962:* 5 Crick
(Francis) 6 Watson (James) 7 Wilkins
(Maurice) *1963:* 6 Eccles (John), Huxley (Andrew) 7 Hodgkin (Alan) *1964:*
5 Bloch (Konrad), Lynen (Feodor)
1965: 5 Jacob (Francois), Monod
(Jacques) 5 Lwoff (André) *1966:*
4 Rous (Francis) 7 Huggins (Charles)
1967: 4 Wald (George) 6 Granit (Ragnar) 8 Hartline (H. Keffer) *1968:*
6 Holley (Robert) 7 Khorana (H. Gobind) 9 Nirenberg (Marshall) *1969:*
5 Luria (Salvador) 7 Hershey (Alfred)
8 Delbruck (Max) *1970:* 4 Katz
(Bernard) 5 Euler (Ulf von) 7 Axelrod
(Julius) *1971:* 10 Sutherland (Earl)
1972: 6 Porter (Rodney) 7 Edelman
(Gerald) *1973:* 6 Frisch (Karl von),
Lorenz (Konrad) 9 Tinbergen (Niko-
laas) *1974:* 4 Duve (Christian)

6 Claude (Albert), Palade (George) *1975:* 5 Temin (Howard) 8 Dulbecco (Renato) 9 Baltimore (David) *1976:* 8 Blumberg (Baruch), Gajdusek (D. Carleton) *1977:* 5 Yalow (Rosalyn) 7 Schally (Andrew) 9 Guillemin (Roger) *1978:* 5 Arber (Werner), Smith (Hamilton) 7 Nathans (Daniel) *1979:* 7 Cormack (Allan) 10 Hounsfield (Godfrey) *1980:* 5 Snell (George) 7 Dausset (Jean) 10 Benacerraf (Baruj) *1981:* 5 Hubel (David) 6 Sperry (Roger), Wiesel (Torsten) *1982:* 4 Vane (John) 9 Bergstrom (Sune) 10 Samuelsson (Bengt) *1983:* 10 McClintock (Barbara) *1984:* 5 Jerne (Niels) 7 Koehler (Georges) 8 Milstein (Cesar) *1985:* 5 Brown (Michael) 9 Goldstein (Joseph) *1986:* 5 Cohen (Stanley) 14 Levi-Montalcini (Rita) *1987:* 8 Tonegawa (Susumu) *1988:* 5 Black (James), Elion (Gertrude) 9 Hitchings (George) *1989:* 6 Bishop (J. Michael), Varmus (Harold) *1990:* 6 Murray (Joseph), Thomas (E. Donnall) *1991:* 5 Neher (Erwin) 7 Sakmann (Bert) *1992:* 5 Krebs (Edwin) 7 Fischer (Edmond) *1993:* 5 Sharp (Phillip) 7 Roberts (Richard) *1994:* 6 Gilman (Alfred) 7 Rodbell (Martin) *1995:* 5 Lewis (Edward) 9 Wieschaus (Eric) 15 Nüsslein-Volhard (Christiane) *1996:* 7 Doherty (Peter) 11 Zinkernagel (Rolf) *1997:* 8 Prusiner (Stanley) *1998:* 5 Murad (Ferid) 7 Ignarro (Louis) 9 Furchgott (Robert) *1999:* 6 Blobel (Günter) *2000:* 6 Kandel (Eric) 8 Carlsson (Arvid) 9 Greengard (Paul) *2001:* 4 Hunt (Tim) 5 Nurse (Paul) 8 Hartwell (Leland) *2002:* 7 Brenner (Sydney), Horvitz (Robert), Sulston (John) *2003:* 9 Lauterbur (Paul), Mansfield (Peter) 4 Axel (Richard), Buck (Linda)

Nobel's invention 8 dynamite

nobility 6 virtue 7 dignity, peerage, royalty 8 eminence, noblesse 9 loftiness 10 exaltation, excellence, worthiness 11 aristocracy, superiority, uprightness

noble 4 peer 5 grand, lofty, moral 6 august, lordly, titled, worthy 7 courtly, eminent, exalted, notable, stately, sublime, upright 8 baronial, elevated, generous, gracious, heroical, highborn, highbred, imposing, magnific, majestic, princely, sterling, virtuous, wellborn 9 dignified, estimable, excellent, grandiose, honorable, righteous 10 high-minded, impressive, principled 11 illustrious, magnanimous, magnifi-

cent, outstanding, right-minded 12 aristocratic

nobleman 4 duke, earl, peer 5 baron, count 6 prince 7 baronet, marquis 8 marquess, viscount *French:* 5 comte 7 vicomte *German:* 4 Graf 8 margrave 9 landgrave *Indian:* 6 sardar, sirdar 8 maharaja 9 maharajah *Italian:* 8 marchese *Japanese (former):* 6 daimyo *Scandinavian:* 4 jarl *Spanish:* 7 hidalgo

noblewoman 4 lady 7 baronne, duchess, peeress 8 baroness, countess, princess 11 marchioness, viscountess *French:* 8 marquise *Italian:* 8 marchesa

nobody 4 zero 6 cipher 7 nothing, nullity, upstart 9 nonentity 11 lightweight, small potato

nocturnal 7 nightly 9 nighttime

nocuous 3 bad 6 nocent 7 harmful, hurtful 8 damaging 9 injurious 11 deleterious, destructive, detrimental, mischievous

nod 3 bob, err 4 doze, okay 5 agree, droop, slump 6 assent, invite, signal 7 approve 8 approval 10 acceptance

nodding 6 casual, slight 7 passing 8 drooping 9 pendulous 11 superficial

noddle 3 nob, nut 4 bean, head, pate, poll 6 noggin

noddy 3 oaf 4 boob, clod, dodo, dolt, dope, fool, goof, mutt, simp, yo-yo 5 chump, dummy, dunce, moron, ninny, stupe 6 dimwit, donkey, dumdum 7 airhead, dullard, pinhead, schnook 8 bonehead, clodpoll, dumbbell, dumbhead, imbecile, lunkhead, meathead, numskull 9 birdbrain, blockhead, ignoramus, lamebrain, numbskull, simpleton, thickhead 10 dunderhead, hammerhead, nincompoop 11 chowderhead, chucklehead, knucklehead

node 4 bump, burl, knob, knot, lump, mass 5 bulge, point 6 growth, vertex 8 swelling 11 enlargement, predicament 12 entanglement, protuberance

Noel 4 Xmas 5 carol 9 Christmas

nog 3 ale 4 beer, brew, malt, suds 5 lager, stout

noggin 3 cup, mug, nip, nob, nut 4 bean, gill, head, pate, poll 6 noddle, noodle

no-good 3 bum, dud 4 base, vile, worm 5 loser 6 scurvy, wretch 7 dirtbag, inutile, lowlife, rounder, wastrel 8 deadbeat, shameful, unworthy, wretched 9 no-account, valueless, worthless 10 ne'er-do-well, profligate, scapegrace 11 ignominious 12 contemptible, disreputable 13 reprehensible

noise 3 din 4 blab, talk 5 babel, rumor,

sound 6 clamor, gossip, hubbub, racket, ruckus, rumpus, tattle, uproar 7 ruction, sonance, stridor 8 resonant 11 pandemonium

noiseless 4 hush, mute 5 muted, quiet, still, whist 6 hushed, silent, stilly 9 soundless

noisemaker 4 horn 6 rattle 7 clapper

noisome 4 foul, rank, vile 5 fetid, funky, fusty, musty, nasty 6 filthy, horrid, putrid, rancid, smelly 7 harmful, noxious, squalid 8 stinking 9 obnoxious, offensive, repulsive, revolting, sickening 10 disgusting, malodorous, nauseating

noisy 4 loud 5 rowdy 7 blatant, booming, clamant, rackety, raucous, squeaky 8 clattery, strident 9 clamorous, deafening, turbulent 10 boisterous, chattering, clangorous, tumultuous, uproarious, vociferous 11 conspicuous 12 earsplitting, obstreperous

nomad 5 gypsy, rover 7 migrant, rambler 8 vagabond, wanderer *Arabic:* 7 bedouin

nomadic 5 gypsy 6 roving 7 roaming, vagrant 8 drifting, vagabond 9 itinerant, migratory, wandering, wayfaring 11 peripatetic 13 perambulatory

nom de plume see PEN NAME

nomen 4 name 7 moniker 11 appellation, designation

nomenclature 4 list, name 7 catalog 8 glossary, taxonomy 11 appellation, designation, phraseology, terminology 12 codification

nominal 3 low 5 given, named, rated, small 6 formal, puppet 7 alleged, minimal, seeming, titular 8 apparent, socalled, trifling 9 pretended, professed 10 ostensible 11 approximate, inexpensive 12 satisfactory, substantival 13 insignificant

nominate 3 tap 4 call, name 5 offer, put up 7 appoint, propose, suggest 9 designate, recommend

nominee 6 choice 8 aspirant 9 candidate, contender 10 contestant

nonage 5 youth 7 infancy 8 minority 9 childhood 10 immaturity, juvenility

nonchalant 4 cool, easy 5 blase 6 casual, mellow, serene 7 offhand 8 carefree, careless, cheerful, composed, laid-back 9 collected, easygoing, incurious, unruffled 10 effortless, insouciant, untroubled 11 indifferent, unconcerned, unflappable, unperturbed 12 lighthearted 13 dispassionate, imperturbable, lackadaisical

noncommittal 7 neutral 8 reserved 9 impassive 10 disengaged

nonconformist 5 rebel 7 beatnik, heretic, oddball, offbeat, radical 8 bohemian, maverick 9 dissenter, dissident, eccentric, heretical, heterodox, protester, sectarian 10 schismatic, separatist, unorthodox 11 misbeliever, schismatist

nonconformity 6 heresy, schism 7 dissent 9 misbelief, recusancy 10 dissidence, heterodoxy, opposition 11 unorthodoxy 12 disaffection 13 individualism, noncompliance

nonentity 4 zero 5 aught, zilch 6 cipher, nobody 7 nothing, nullity, whiffet 8 unperson 10 figurehead, mouthpiece

nonesuch 5 ideal 7 epitome, paragon, pattern 8 exemplar, paradigm, standard 9 archetype, matchless, nonpareil, unequaled, unrivaled

nonetheless 3 yet 5 still 6 anyway, though, withal 7 howbeit, however 8 although, after all 10 regardless 11 still and all

nonexistence 4 nada, void 7 nullity, vacuity 11 nothingness

nonflammable 9 fireproof 10 unburnable 13 incombustible

non-Hawaiian 5 haole

non-Jewish 3 goy 6 goyish 7 gentile

non-Muslim 6 giaour

no-nonsense 5 grave, sober 6 solemn 7 earnest, serious 8 resolute 9 pragmatic, realistic 10 determined, hardheaded, sobersided 11 plainspoken 12 businesslike 13 unsentimental

nonpareil see NONESUCH

nonpartisan 7 neutral 8 unbiased 9 equitable, impartial, objective, uncolored 10 nonaligned 11 independent 12 unprejudiced

nonplus 4 faze 5 stump 6 baffle, boggle, muddle, puzzle, rattle, stymie 7 buffalo, confuse, dilemma, flummox, fluster, mystify, perplex, stagger 8 bewilder, confound, distract, overcome, paralyze, quandary 9 discomfit, dumbfound, frustrate 10 disconcert

nonresistant 6 docile, pliant 7 passive, pliable 8 resigned, yielding 9 complying, tractable 10 conforming, submissive 11 acquiescent, conformable 13 accommodating

nonsense 3 rot 4 blah, bosh, bull, bunk, crap, gook, guff, jazz, punk, tosh 5 bilge, crock, drool, folly, fudge, Greek, hokum, hooey, trash 6 babble, blague, bunkum, drivel, hot air, humbug, jabber, piffle 7 baloney, blather, eyewash, flubdub, foolery, fooling, hogwash, inanity, rubbish, trifles, twaddle 8 buncombe, claptrap, falderal, folderol, flimflam, malarkey, pishposh, slipslop, tommyrot, trumpery **9** gibberish, moonshine, poppycock **10** applesauce, balderdash, double-talk, flapdoodle, tomfoolery **11** jabberwocky **12** blatherskite, fiddle-faddle, fiddlesticks **13** horsefeathers *British:* **10** codswallop

nonsensical 5 crazy, daffy, flaky, goofy, inane, kooky, loony, nutty, silly, wacky **6** absurd, screwy **7** foolish, idiotic, risible **9** illogical, laughable, ludicrous, senseless **10** irrational **12** preposterous, unreasonable

nonviolent 6 irenic **7** pacific **8** pacifist **9** peaceable **10** pacifistic

noodle 3 oaf **4** bean, boob, clod, dodo, dope, goof, head, mutt, poll, simp, yo-yo **5** chump, dummy, dunce, idiot, moron, ninny, noddy, stupe **6** dimwit, donkey, dum-dum, nitwit, noggin **7** airhead, dullard, pinhead, schnook **8** bonehead, clodpoll, dumbbell, dumbhead, imbecile, lunkhead, meathead, numskull **9** birdbrain, blockhead, ignoramus, lamebrain, numbskull, simpleton **10** dunderhead, hammerhead, nincompoop **11** chowderhead, chucklehead, knucklehead

nook 3 bay **4** cove **5** hutch, niche **6** alcove, cavity, corner, cranny, recess **9** cubbyhole **11** compartment

noose 3 tie **4** bait, bind, hang, loop, lure, trap **5** lasso, snare **6** entrap, secure

norm 3 par **4** mean, rule, type **5** gauge, maxim, model **6** median **7** average, measure, pattern **8** paradigm, standard **9** benchmark, criterion **10** touchstone

Norma *composer:* **7** Bellini (Vincenzo) *librettist:* **6** Romani (Felice)

normal 4 sane **5** usual **6** common **7** average, general, natural, regular, typical **8** ordinary, standard **9** customary, prevalent **11** commonplace, traditional **12** conventional **13** perpendicular

Normandy's capital 5 Rouen

Norns 5 fates, Skuld, Urdur **9** Verthandi

Norris novel 3 Pit (The) **4** Blix **7** Octopus (The) **8** McTeague

Norse *abode of the dead:* **8** Niflheim *alphabet:* **5** Runic *archer:* **4** Egil *bard:* **5** scald, skald *chieftain:* **4** jarl, Rolf **5** Rollo *demon:* **4** Mara, Surt **5** Surtr *dragon:* **6** Fafnir **8** Nithhogg *epic:* **4** Edda *explorer:* **4** Erik, Leif **8** Ericsson (Leif), Eriksson (Leif) *first man:* **3** Ask **4** Askr *first woman:* **5** Embla *giant:* **4** Egil, Wade, Wate, Ymer, Ymir **5** Aegir, Egill, Hymir, Jotun, Mimir **6** Fafnir, Jotunn *giantess:* **4** Egia, Norn, Nott *god:* **3** Asa, Ass **4** Surt, Vali, Vili

5 Aesir (plural), Surtr, Vanir (plural) **6** Hoenir, Vithar **7** Vitharr *blind:* **4** Hoth **5** Hoder, Hodur, Hothr *chief:* **4** Odin **5** Othin, Wodan, Woden, Wotan *guardian:* **7** Heimdal **8** Heimdall **9** Heimdallr *messenger:* **6** Hermod **7** Hermodr *of beauty:* **5** Baldr **6** Balder, Baldur *of evil:* **4** Loke, Loki *of fertility:* **4** Frey **5** Freyr *of justice:* **7** Forsete, Forseti *of light:* **3** Dag *of peace:* **5** Baldr **6** Balder, Baldur *of poetry:* **5** Brage, Bragi *of the hunt:* **3** Ull **4** Ullr *of the seas:* **5** Njord **6** Njoerd, Njorth **4** Hler **5** Aegir, Gymir *of the sky:* **4** Odin **5** Othin *of thunder:* **4** Thor **5** Donar *of war:* **3** Tiu, Tiw, Tyr, Zio, Ziu *wolf:* **6** Fenrir *goddess:* **3** dis **4** Saga **5** disir (plural) **7** Asynjur *of fate:* **3** Urd **4** Norn, Urth, Wyrd **5** Skuld **9** Verthandi *of healing:* **3** Eir *of love:* **5** Freya *of marriage:* **5** Frigg **6** Frigga *of night:* **4** Natt, Nott *of storms:* **3** Ran *of the earth:* **5** Joerd, Jorth *of the moon:* **5** Nanna *of the sea:* **3** Ran *of the sky:* **5** Frigg **6** Frigga *of the underworld:* **3** Hel **4** Hela *of youth:* **4** Idun **5** Ithun **6** Ithunn *gods' abode:* **6** Asgard *hall of heroes:* **8** Valhalla *king:* **4** Atli, Olaf *nobleman:* **4** jarl *patron saint:* **4** Olaf *poem:* **4** rune *poet:* **5** scald, skald *rainbow bridge:* **7** Bifrost *sea serpent:* **4** Wade, Wate **6** kraken **7** Midgard *smith:* **6** Völund *tale:* **4** saga *toast:* **5** skoal *watchdog:* **4** Garm **5** Garmr *world's destruction:* **8** Ragnarok *world tree:* **8** Ygdrasil **10** Yggdrasill

north *combining form:* **4** arct **5** arcto

North African *country:* **5** Egypt, Libya **7** Algeria, Morocco, Tunisia *fruit:* **3** fig **4** date *garment:* **4** haik *grass:* **4** alfa **7** esparto *jackal:* **4** dieb *language:* **6** Arabic, Berber *Muslim sect:* **6** Sanusi **7** Senussi *people:* **6** Berber, Hamite **7** bedouin *seaport:* **4** Oran, Sfax **6** Annaba **7** Tangier **10** Casablanca

North America *country:* **6** Canada, Mexico, Panama **8** Honduras **9** Costa Rica, Guatemala, Nicaragua **10** El Salvador **12** United States

North Carolina *capital:* **7** Raleigh *city:* **6** Durham **9** Asheville, Charlotte **10** Greensboro **12** Winston-Salem *college, university:* **4** Duke, Elon **10** Wake Forest *mountain, range:* **8** Mitchell **9** Blue Ridge **10** Great Smoky *nickname:* **7** Tar Heel (State) *state bird:* **8** cardinal *state flower:* **7** dogwood *state tree:* **4** pine

North Dakota *capital:* **8** Bismarck *city:* **5** Fargo, Minot **10** Grand Forks *nickname:* **5** Sioux (State) **11** Flickertail (State) *river:* **3** Red **8** Missouri *state bird:*

10 meadowlark *state flower:* **11** prairie rose *state tree:* **3** elm (American)

northern 4 pike **6** boreal **11** hyperborean

Northern Mariana Islands *commonwealth of:* **12** United States *discoverer:* **8** Magellan (Ferdinand) *island:* **4** Rota **6** Saipan, Tinian

North Star State 9 Minnesota

Northwest Passage author 7 Roberts (Kenneth)

Northwest Territories *capital:* **11** Yellowknife *gulf:* **8** Amundsen *island:* **5** Banks **8** Victoria *lake:* **9** Great Bear **10** Great Slave *river:* **9** Mackenzie *sea:* **8** Beaufort

north wind see at WIND

Norway *Arctic region:* **7** Lapland *cape:* **7** Nordkyn *capital:* **4** Oslo *city:* **6** Bergen **9** Stavanger, Trondheim *inlet:* **9** Skagerrak *island:* **5** Senja **6** Sørøya **8** Magerøya, Steinsøy **10** Nord-Kvaløy, Ringvassøy *island group:* **7** Lofoten **10** Vesterålen *lake:* **5** Mjøsa *monetary unit:* **5** krone *mountain range:* **6** Kjølen **11** Jotunheimen *neighbor:* **6** Russia, Sweden **7** Finland *part of:* **11** Scandinavia *port:* **5** Vardø **6** Tromsø **8** Kirkenes **10** Hammerfest *river:* **4** Tana **5** Glåma, Lågen **9** Dramselva *sea:* **5** North

Norwegian *goblin:* **5** nisse *language:* **5** Norse **6** Bokmal **7** Bokmaal, Nynorsk, Riksmal **8** Landsmal, Riksmaal **9** Landsmaal

nose 3 pry **4** beak, bent, bump, gift, head, poke **5** aroma, flair, knack, scent, smell, sniff, snift, snoop, snoot, snout, snuff **6** genius, muzzle, nuzzle, talent **7** aptness, faculty, smeller, sneezer **8** smell out **9** olfaction, proboscis, schnozzle *French:* **3** nez *kind:* **3** pug **5** Roman **8** aquiline *lengthener:* **3** lie *opening:* **7** nostril

nosebleed 9 epistaxis

nosedive 4 drop, fall **6** header, plunge **7** plummet

nosegay 4 posy **6** flower **7** bouquet, corsage **11** boutonniere

nosh 4 bite **5** graze, munch, snack **6** nibble

Nostradamus 7 prophet

Nostromo author 6 Conrad (Joseph)

nostrum 4 cure **6** elixir, remedy **7** cure-all, panacea **8** antidote, medicine **10** catholicon, corrective **11** restorative

nosy 6 prying, snoopy **7** curious, peeping **8** snooping **9** intrusive **11** inquisitive, inquisitory

notability 3 VIP **4** lion, star **5** celeb, chief **6** leader, worthy **7** big name, big shot **8** big-timer, eminence, luminary, presence, somebody **9** celebrity, chieftain, dignitary, personage, superstar **11** personality

notable 3 VIP **4** star **5** celeb, chief, famed, mogul, nabob, power **6** big boy, biggie, big gun, bigwig, famous, fat cat, leader, prince **7** big name, big shot, eminent, magnate, pooh-bah **8** big chief, big-timer, big wheel, eminence, luminary, renowned, somebody, striking **9** big cheese, celebrity, character, dignitary, distingué, personage, prominent, superstar **10** celebrated, celebrious, noteworthy, remarkable **11** conspicuous, heavyweight, illustrious, muckety-muck, personality **13** distinguished, high-muck-a-muck

notarize 7 certify, endorse **8** validate **12** authenticate

notch 3 cut, gap, jag **4** gash, mark, nick, nock, rung, slit, step **5** cleft, grade, score, stage **6** degree, groove, indent, rabbet, record **7** achieve, scratch **8** incision, undercut **11** indentation

note 3 jot **4** bond, chit, heed, mark, memo, show, sign, tone **5** catch, sound, token **6** letter, notice, record, regard **7** comment, discern, jotting, missive, observe, promise, set down **8** eminence, indicate, perceive, reminder **9** attention, knowledge **10** cognizance, commentary, memorandum, observance, reputation **11** distinction, distinguish, observation

notebook 3 log **5** diary **7** journal

noted 6 famous **7** eminent, leading, popular **8** esteemed, renowned, striking **9** acclaimed, prominent, well-known **10** celebrated, recognized, remarkable **11** illustrious **13** distinguished

noteworthy 7 salient **8** singular, striking **9** arresting, bodacious, memorable, prominent, red-letter **10** impressive, meaningful, remarkable **11** conspicuous, exceptional, high-profile, major-league, outstanding, significant **12** considerable **13** extraordinary

nothing 3 nil, nix **4** zero **5** aught, nihil, zilch **6** cipher, naught, nobody, nought, trifle **7** nullity, whiffet **8** goose egg, whipster **9** no-account, nonentity *French:* **4** rien *German:* **6** nichts *Latin:* **5** nihil *Spanish:* **4** nada

nothingness 4 nada, void **5** death **6** vacuum **7** nullity, vacuity **9** emptiness **12** nonexistence

notice 3 see **4** espy, heed, mark, memo **5** catch, sight **6** descry, regard, review **7** discern, observe, respect **8** handbill, perceive **9** attention, directive, recognize **10** cognizance, evaluation **11** dec-

laration, information, observation
12 announcement, proclamation
13 communication

noticeable 6 marked, patent, signal
7 evident, obvious, pointed, salient
8 apparent, manifest, striking **9** arresting, prominent **10** noteworthy, observable, remarkable **11** appreciable, conspicuous, eye-catching, outstanding, perceptible, significant **12** unmistakable

notify 3 cue **4** tell, warn **5** alert, brief
6 advise, clue in, fill in, inform
7 apprise **8** acquaint **9** enlighten

notion 4 clue, hint, idea, whim **5** fancy
6 belief, maggot, theory, vagary
7 caprice, conceit, concept, inkling, thought **8** crotchet **10** conception, impression, intimation, perception
11 inclination

notional 5 ideal **6** unreal **7** fancied, fictive **8** fanciful, illusory, imagined
9 imaginary, visionary, whimsical
10 capricious, conceptual **11** speculative, theoretical **12** hypothetical

notoriety 4 fame **6** infamy, renown
7 obloquy **9** disrepute **10** opprobrium, prominence **11** recognition

notorious 5 noted **6** famous **8** ill-famed, infamous **9** prominent, well-known
10 outrageous, scandalous **12** disreputable

Notus 6 Auster *brother:* **5** Eurus **6** Boreas
8 Zephyrus *father:* **6** Aeolus **8** Astraeus
mother: **3** Eos

noun 4 name **7** nominal **11** substantive
inflectional form: **4** case *verbal:* **6** gerund

nourish 4 feed, rear **5** nurse, raise **6** foster **7** bring up, build up, nurture, promote, support **8** maintain **9** cultivate, encourage **10** provide for, strengthen

nourishment 3 pap **4** diet, eats, feed, food, grub **6** viands **7** aliment, pabulum, vittles **8** victuals **9** nutriment, provender **10** sustenance

___ **nous 5** entre

nouveau riche 7 parvenu, upstart
9 arriviste

Nova Scotia *capital:* **7** Halifax *city:*
9 Dartmouth *island:* **10** Cape Breton
lake: **7** Bras D'Or *provincial flower:*
9 mayflower

novel 3 new, odd **5** fresh **6** unique **7** offbeat, unusual **8** atypical, original, peculiar, singular, uncommon **9** different, narrative **10** avant-garde, innovative, newfangled

novelist see AUTHOR

novelty 5 curio **6** bauble, gewgaw, oddity, trifle **7** bibelot, gimmick, newness, trinket, whatnot **8** gimcrack, souvenir

9 bagatelle, curiosity, objet d'art
10 innovation, knickknack

novice 3 cub **4** colt, punk, tyro **6** rookie
7 amateur, learner, recruit, student, trainee **8** aspirant, beginner, freshman, neophyte, newcomer, prentice **9** fledgling, greenhorn, novitiate, postulant
10 apprentice, tenderfoot **11** probationer

Novum Organum *author:* **5** Bacon (Francis)

now 3 PDQ **4** soon **5** today **6** at once, pronto **7** anymore, present **8** directly, first off, promptly **9** forthwith, instanter, instantly, presently, right away, sometimes **11** immediately, straightway
12 straightaway

now and then 7 at times, betimes
9 sometimes **12** infrequently, occasionally, periodically, sporadically

Nox *brother:* **6** Erebus *daughter:* **3** Day
4 Eris **5** Light *father:* **5** Chaos *husband:*
6 Erebus *son:* **6** Charon, Hypnos
8 Thanatos

noxious 4 foul **5** fetid, toxic **6** deadly, putrid **7** baneful, harmful, noisome
8 stinking **9** dangerous, pestilent, poisonous, unhealthy **10** corrupting, pernicious **11** deleterious, destructive, detrimental, pestiferous **12** disagreeable, pestilential

nozzle 4 nose, vent **5** spout **7** channel

nuance 4 hint **5** shade, tinge, touch, trace **6** nicety **7** shading, soupçon
8 overtone, subtlety **9** gradation, suspicion **10** refinement, suggestion **11** distinction

nub 4 core, crux, gist, knob, knot, lump, meat, node, pith **5** bulge, point, short
6 kernel, upshot **8** swelling **9** substance
10 projection **12** protuberance

Nubian 5 Mahas **6** Birked, Kenuzi, Midobi **7** Dongola **8** Cushitic
9 Chari-Nile

nubile 4 ripe **10** attractive **12** marriageable

nuchal 4 nape

nuclear agency 3 AEC, NRC

nuclear particle 5 meson **6** proton **7** neutron

nucleus 3 bud **4** core, germ, head, kern, ring, seed **5** focus, spark **6** embryo
material: **8** karyotin

nude 3 raw **4** bald, bare **5** naked, stark
6 barren, peeled, unclad **8** disrobed, stripped **9** au naturel, buck naked, unattired, unclothed, uncovered, undressed **10** stark naked

nudge 3 dig, jab, jog **4** near, poke, prod, push **5** elbow, punch, shove **8** approach

nudnik 4 bore, drip, pill, twit **8** nuisance

nugatory 4 idle, vain 5 empty, inane, vapid 6 futile, hollow, otiose 7 invalid, vacuous 8 trifling 9 fruitless, worthless 11 inoperative, meaningless

nugget 3 gob, wad 4 hunk, lump, plum 5 chunk 6 tidbit

nuisance 4 pain, pest, pill 6 bother, nudnik 8 headache, irritant, pesterer, vexation 11 botheration

nuke 4 bomb 5 crush, smash 6 attack 7 destroy 8 demolish 9 eradicate, microwave 10 annihilate 11 exterminate

null 4 void, zero 5 annul, empty 6 futile 7 invalid, useless 8 nugatory 9 worthless 10 invalidate, obliterate, unavailing 11 ineffective, ineffectual, inoperative

nullify 3 zap 4 undo, veto, void 5 abate, annul, limit, quash, scrub, trash 6 cancel, efface, negate, offset, repeal, revoke, squash 7 abolish, rescind, scratch, take out, wipe out 8 abrogate 10 annihilate, compensate, counteract, invalidate, neutralize 11 countervail

nullity 4 nada, zero 5 zilch 6 cipher, nobody 7 nothing, vacuity, whiffet 9 annulment, nonentity 11 nothingness 12 nonexistence

numb 5 chill, dazed 6 deaden, freeze 7 callous 8 deadened, detached 9 insensate, paralyzed, stupefied, unfeeling 10 insensible, insentient 11 desensitize, indifferent 12 anesthetized, desensitized

number 5 add up, count, digit, run to, sum to, tally, total 6 amount, cipher, come to, figure 7 chiffer, include, integer, numeral, ordinal, run into, several, sum into 8 cardinal, numerate, paginate 9 aggregate, enumerate *added to another:* 6 augend *resulting from division:* 8 quotient *resulting from multiplication:* 7 product *resulting from subtraction:* 10 difference *science:* 11 mathematics

number one 4 best, main 5 chief, major 6 finest, Grade A, top dog 7 capital, highest, leading, primary, stellar 8 dominant, five-star, foremost, superior 9 excellent, first-rate, front-rank, numero uno, principal, top-drawer 10 blue-ribbon, first-class, preeminent 11 first-string, outstanding, predominant

numbness 5 shock 6 stupor 10 anesthesia 12 stupefaction *combining form:* 4 narc 5 narco

numeral 5 digit 6 cipher, figure, number 7 integer 11 whole number

numerate 4 list 5 count, tally 6 number 7 compute, itemize, tick off 8 tabulate 9 calculate

numerous 4 many 6 legion 7 profuse, umpteen 8 abundant, populous 9 plentiful 10 voluminous 13 multitudinous

Numitor *brother:* 7 Amulius *daughter:* 9 Rea Silvia 10 Rhea Silvia *grandson:* 5 Remus 7 Romulus

numskull 3 oaf 4 boob, clod, dodo, dolt, dope, goof, mutt, simp 5 chump, dummy, dunce, idiot, moron, ninny, noddy, stupe 6 dimwit, donkey, dumdum, nitwit 7 airhead, dullard, pinhead, schnook 8 bonehead, clodpate, clodpoll, dumbbell, dumbhead, imbecile, lunkhead, meathead 9 birdbrain, blockhead, ignoramus, lamebrain, simpleton, thickhead 10 dunderhead, hammerhead, nincompoop 11 chowderhead, chucklehead, knucklehead

nun 6 sister *headcloth:* 6 wimple

Nunavut *capital:* 7 Iqaluit *island:* 5 Devon 6 Baffin 9 Ellesmere 11 Southampton *mountain:* 7 Barbeau (Peak) *peninsula:* 7 Boothia 8 Melville *provincial flower:* 11 Arctic poppy

nunnery 7 convent 10 sisterhood *head:* 8 superior

nuptial 6 bridal, wedded 7 marital, married, spousal, wedding 8 conjugal, espousal, hymeneal, marriage 9 connubial 11 matrimonial

nurse 4 feed, nana, rear, suck 5 nanny, serve 6 attend, foster, pamper, suckle 7 care for, cherish, nourish, nurture 9 cultivate 10 minister to *children's:* 5 nanny *English:* 11 Nightingale (Florence) *Indian:* 4 ayah *Chinese:* 4 amah

nursemaid 4 nana 5 nanny 6 minder, sitter 9 governess 10 babysitter *Indian:* 4 ayah *Chinese:* 4 amah

nursery 6 crèche 7 brooder 8 hothouse 9 fosterage 10 greenhouse 12 conservatory

nurture 4 care, feed, rear, tend 5 nurse, raise, train 6 cradle, foster 7 bring up, care for, develop, educate, nourish, rearing 8 breeding, instruct, training, tutelage 9 cultivate 10 upbringing

nut 3 bug 4 kook, loon 5 acorn, crank, fiend, freak, loony, pecan 6 almond, cashew, cuckoo, madman, maniac, zealot 7 fanatic, filbert, hickory, lunatic 8 crackpot 9 bedlamite, ding-a-ling, macadamia, pistachio, screwball 10 enthusiast, Tom o' Bedlam *of a violin bow:* 4 frog, heel

Nut *consort:* 3 Geb, Keb *daughter:* 4 Isis 8 Nephthys *son:* 6 Osiris

nuthouse 6 asylum, bedlam 8 loony bin 9 funny farm 10 booby hatch 11 institution 12 insane asylum

Nutmeg State 11 Connecticut

nutria 5 coypu

nutriment 4 diet, fare, food, grub, keep
6 viands **7** aliment, pabulum **8** victuals
9 provender **10** provisions, sustenance
11 comestibles, nourishment, subsistence

nutrition 4 diet **7** vittles **8** victuals **10** sustenance **11** nourishment

nutritious 9 healthful, wholesome **10** alimentary, nourishing

nuts 3 mad **4** daft, keen, wild **5** batty,
crazy, kooky, loony, rabid, wacky
6 absurd, cuckoo, insane, screwy
7 bonkers, cracked, excited, foolish,
idiotic **8** animated, demented, deranged
9 exuberant, fanatical, screwball

10 passionate, unbalanced **12** enthusiastic

nutty see NUTS

nuzzle 3 rub **4** root, snug **5** nudge **6** burrow, cuddle, nestle **7** snuggle

Nycteus *brother:* **5** Lycus *daughter:*
7 Antiope

nymph 3 nix **5** dryad, larva, naiad, nixie,
sylph **6** kelpie, maiden, sprite **7** mermaid *changed into a bear:* **8** Callisto
changed into a laurel: **6** Daphne *changed
into a rock:* **4** Echo *mountain:* **5** oread
sea: **6** Nereid **7** Calypso *water:* **5** naiad
6 undine *wood:* **5** dryad

Nyx see NOX

O

oaf 4 boob, boor, bull, clod, dodo, dolt,
goof, goon, hulk, lout, lump, slob
5 booby, chump, clown, dummy,
dunce, klutz **6** dum-dum, galoot, lubber, lummox **7** fathead, palooka **8** bonehead, lunkhead, meathead **9** blockhead,
blunderer, lamebrain, simpleton

oafish 5 dense **6** clumsy, klutzy, rustic
7 boorish, doltish, loutish **8** bungling,
churlish, clownish, lubberly

oak *African:* **7** turtosa *fruit:* **5** acorn
genus: **7** Quercus *kind:* **3** bur, pin, red
4 bear, cork, holm, ilex, live **5** black,
holly, roble, white **6** barren, cerris,
encina **7** durmast, English, moss-cup,
valonia **9** blackjack *Mexican:* **8** chaparro
young: **8** flittern

oar 3 row **4** pole, pull **5** rower, scull
6 paddle **7** paddler *part:* **4** loom, palm
5 blade, shaft **6** button, collar *pin:*
5 thole

oarsman 3 bow **5** rower **6** stroke
7 sculler *director:* **3** cox **8** coxswain

oasis 3 spa **4** wadi **6** refuge, relief
ancient: **4** Merv *Egypt:* **4** Siwa **5** Gafsa
6 Dakhla **7** Farafra **8** Ammonium *Libya:*
5 Mizda, Sebha **6** Sabhah **7** Gadames
8 Ghudamis *Niger:* **5** Bilma *Saudi Arabia:* **5** Hofuf, Taima **7** Al-Hufuf

oast 4 kiln, oven

oat 5 grain, grass **6** cereal *genus:* **5** Avena
Scottish: **3** ait

oater 7 western **10** horse opera

oath 3 vow **4** cuss **5** curse, swear
6 pledge **7** promise **8** cussword **9** expletive, profanity, swearword *mild:* **3** gee
4 darn, drat, egad, geez, gosh, jeez
5 golly **6** jiminy **7** gee whiz

oatmeal 5 gruel **6** burgoo **8** porridge
Scottish: **8** drammock

obdurate 3 set **4** firm, hard **5** harsh,
rigid, stony **6** dogged, mulish
7 adamant, callous **8** stubborn **9** heartless, immovable, unbending, unfeeling
10 hard-boiled, inflexible, unshakable,
unyielding **11** coldhearted, hardhearted, insensitive, unemotional **12** intransigent, stonyhearted **13** unsympathetic

obeah 5 charm, magic

Obed *father:* **4** Boaz **6** Ephlal **8** Shemaiah
mother: **4** Ruth *son:* **5** Jesse **7** Azariah

obedient 5 loyal **6** docile **7** devoted,
duteous, dutiful, willing **8** amenable,
biddable, obliging, yielding **9** compliant, tractable **10** law-abiding, manageable, respectful, submissive **11** acquiescent, cooperative, deferential,
subservient

obeisance 3 bow **5** honor **6** curtsy,
esteem, fealty, homage, kowtow,
salaam **7** gesture, loyalty, respect **9** deference, reverence **10** allegiance, submission

obelisk 6 dagger, pillar, symbol

Oberon *messenger:* 4 Puck *wife:* 7 Titania

Oberto composer 5 Verdi (Giuseppe)

obese 3 fat 5 bulky, gross, heavy, tubby 6 fleshy 7 adipose, outsize, porcine 9 corpulent 10 overweight

obey 3 bow 4 heed, keep, mind 5 agree, defer, serve, yield 6 accede, accept, assent, comply, follow, regard, submit 7 abide by, conform, execute, fulfill, observe, satisfy 8 adhere to, carry out 9 acquiesce

obfuscate 4 blur 5 cloud, muddy 6 darken 7 becloud, conceal, confuse, cover up, obscure 9 adumbrate

obi 4 sash

obiter dictum 4 note 6 remark 7 comment, opinion 10 commentary, incidental 11 observation

obituary 9 necrology 11 death notice

object 3 aim, end, use 4 goal, idea, item, kick, view, wish 5 being, cause, demur, focus, frown, point, thing 6 design, entity, except, intent, matter, motive, oppose, target 7 article, dissent, protest, purpose 8 complain, disagree, function, material 9 criticize, intention, something 10 disapprove

objection 5 demur 7 protest 8 argument, demurral, demurrer, question 9 challenge, complaint, exception 10 difficulty, opposition 11 disapproval 12 disagreement, remonstrance 13 remonstration

objectionable 5 unfit 8 unwanted 9 abhorrent, invidious, loathsome, obnoxious, offensive, repellent, repugnant, repulsive, revolting, unwelcome 10 ill-favored, unpleasant 11 displeasing, distasteful, undesirable 12 disagreeable

objective 3 aim, end 4 fair, goal, just, lens, mark 6 actual, design, intent, target 7 mission, purpose 8 ambition, function, material, physical, sensible, unbiased 9 corporeal, equitable, impartial, intention 10 impersonal 11 independent, substantial 12 unprejudiced 13 dispassionate

objet d'art 5 curio, virtu (plural) 7 bibelot, novelty 10 knickknack

objurgate 5 chide, decry, scold 6 rebuke 7 censure, reprove, upbraid 8 admonish, reproach 9 castigate, reprimand

oblate 7 lay monk 9 flattened, religious

oblation 4 gift 6 corban 8 holy gift, offering 9 sacrifice 12 presentation

obligate 4 bind 7 require 8 encumber, restrict 9 constrain

obligated 5 bound, owing 6 liable 8 beholden, indebted 11 accountable, responsible

obligation 3 IOU, vow 4 bond, call, debt, dues, duty, need, oath 5 cause 6 burden, charge, pledge 7 promise 8 business, contract 9 committal, liability, necessity, restraint 10 commitment, compulsion, constraint 11 requirement 12 indebtedness

obligatory 7 binding 8 required 9 essential, mandatory, necessary, requisite 10 compulsory, imperative 11 unavoidable

oblige 3 aid 4 bind, help, make 5 avail, favor, force 6 assist, coerce, compel, please, profit 7 benefit, command, gratify, require 9 constrain 10 contribute 11 accommodate, necessitate

obliged 4 made 5 bound 6 forced 8 beholden, grateful, indebted, thankful 11 constrained 12 appreciative

obliging 4 kind 5 civil 7 amiable, helpful, willing 8 friendly, pleasant 11 complaisant, considerate, cooperative, good-humored, good-natured 12 good-tempered

oblique 6 sloped, tilted 7 devious, leaning, obscure, sloping, tilting 8 inclined, indirect 9 inclining 10 roundabout

obliterate 4 raze, x out 5 erase 6 cancel, delete, efface, remove, rub out 7 blot out, destroy, expunge, wipe out 8 black out, cross out 10 annihilate

oblivion 5 lethe, limbo 7 amnesia, nirvana, nowhere 9 emptiness 11 nothingness 13 forgetfulness, insensibility

oblivious 4 lost 5 blind 7 unaware 8 absorbed, heedless, ignorant 9 forgetful, unknowing, unmindful, unwitting 10 unfamiliar, uninformed 11 inattentive, incognizant, unconscious

oblong 4 oval 5 ovate 7 ellipse 8 elongate 9 elongated, rectangle 11 rectangular

obloquy 4 slam, slur 5 abuse, odium, shame 6 infamy, rebuke 7 calumny, censure 8 disgrace, dishonor, ignominy 9 aspersion, contumely, discredit, disrepute, invective, stricture 10 defamation, opprobrium, scurrility 11 disapproval 12 billingsgate, condemnation, vituperation

obnoxious 4 vile 5 awful 6 odious, rotten 7 hateful 9 abhorrent, invidious, loathsome, offensive, repellent, repugnant, revulsive, sickening 10 abominable, detestable, disgusting

oboe 4 reed 7 hautboy 8 hautbois, woodwind 10 double reed *early:* 5 shawm *relative:* 7 bassoon 11 English horn

O'Brian character 6 Aubrey (Jack) 7 Maturin (Stephen)

obscene 4 foul, lewd, rank, vile

5 bawdy, crass, crude, dirty, gross, lurid, taboo 6 coarse, filthy, impure, ribald, risqué, smutty, vulgar 7 immoral, noisome, profane, raunchy 8 indecent, scabrous 9 abhorrent, appalling, excessive, offensive, repellent, repugnant, repulsive, salacious 10 disgusting, lascivious, scurrilous 11 foulmouthed, unprintable 12 pornographic, scatological

obscure 3 dim 4 blur, hide, mask, veil 5 blind, cloak, cloud, cover, dusky, faint, minor, murky, shade, shady, vague 6 cloudy, darken, hidden, opaque, remote, screen, secret, shadow, shroud, veiled 7 clouded, conceal, cryptic, eclipse, removed, shadowy, unclear, unknown, unnoted 8 disguise, nameless, overcast, puzzling, secluded, shrouded 9 ambiguous, enigmatic, tenebrous, uncertain, undefined 10 camouflage, ill-defined, indefinite, indistinct, mysterious, overshadow 11 out-of-the-way, unimportant 12 inaccessible, unnoticeable 13 inconspicuous

obscurity 3 fog 4 haze, mist, murk 5 gloom 6 enigma, miasma, puzzle 7 dimness, mystery, shadows 8 darkness 9 ambiguity

obsequies 4 rite 5 rites 7 funeral 10 burial rite

obsequious 4 oily 6 abject 7 fawning, servile, slavish 8 obedient, obeisant, toadying, unctuous 9 parasitic 10 flattering, submissive 11 deferential, subservient, sycophantic

observance 4 rite, rule 6 custom, notice, regard, ritual 7 liturgy, service 8 ceremony, practice 9 adherence, attention, formality 10 ceremonial

observant 4 keen 5 alert, awake, aware, sharp 7 heedful, mindful 8 watchful 9 advertent, attentive 10 perceptive

observation 4 note, notice, record, regard, remark 7 comment, finding, opinion 8 judgment, notation 9 attention, inference 10 commentary 12 obiter dictum

observatory 5 tower 7 lookout, outlook 8 overlook *famous:* 4 Lick 6 Wilson, Yerkes 7 Palomar *instrument:* 9 telescope

observe 3 see 4 espy, keep, look, mark, mind, note, obey, twig, view 5 honor, opine, sight, state, study, watch 6 behold, comply, follow, look at, notice, remark 7 abide by, comment, conform, discern, respect 8 perceive 9 celebrate, solemnize 10 comply with 11 commemorate

obsess 5 beset, haunt, hound, rivet

6 absorb, plague 7 consume, possess 9 captivate, preoccupy

obsessed 6 dogged, driven, hipped, hooked 7 gripped, haunted, plagued 8 overcome, troubled 9 dominated, possessed 11 preoccupied 12 prepossessed

obsession 5 craze, mania 6 fetish, hangup 8 fixation, idée fixe 11 infatuation 13 preoccupation

obsessive 5 rabid 8 frenetic, maniacal, neurotic 9 fanatical, possessed 10 passionate 11 preoccupied

obsolete 3 old 5 dated, passé, stale 6 old hat 7 disused, worn-out 8 outmoded, time-worn 9 out-of-date 10 antiquated, superseded 12 antediluvian, old-fashioned

obstacle 3 bar 4 bump, clog, snag 5 block, catch, check, crimp, hitch 6 hurdle 7 barrier 8 handicap, hardship 9 hindrance, impedance, roadblock 10 difficulty, impediment 11 encumbrance, vicissitude 12 interference

obstinate 4 deaf, firm 5 balky, fixed 6 dogged, mulish 7 staunch, willful 8 obdurate, perverse, resolute, stubborn 9 pigheaded, resistant, unbudging, immovable 10 hardheaded, headstrong, inflexible, persistent, refractory, unyielding 11 intractable, opinionated, stiff-necked, wrongheaded 12 intransigent, pertinacious, recalcitrant

obstreperous 4 loud 5 noisy, rowdy 6 unruly 7 blatant, raucous 8 strident 9 clamorous, insistent 10 boisterous, disorderly, vociferant, vociferous 11 disobedient, loudmouthed 12 rambunctious

obstruct 3 bar, dam 4 clog, hide, plug, stop 5 block, check, choke, close 6 cut off, hamper, hinder, impede, stymie, thwart 7 congest, occlude, prevent, shut off, shut out, trammel 9 interfere

obstruction 3 bar 4 snag 5 hitch 6 hamper, hurdle 7 barrier 8 blockage, obstacle, stoppage 9 hindrance, impedance 10 impediment

obtain 3 buy, get, win 4 earn, gain, have, reap 5 annex, reach 6 pick up, secure 7 achieve, acquire, chalk up, procure 8 purchase

obtrude 5 cut in 6 butt in, horn in, impose, meddle 7 presume, push out 8 chisel in, infringe 9 interfere, thrust out

obtrusive 4 nosy 5 pushy 6 prying 7 forward 8 meddling 9 bumptious, officious 10 meddlesome, protruding 11 impertinent, interfering

obtuse 4 dull, dumb, slow 5 blunt,

dense, thick 6 stupid 7 rounded, unclear 11 insensitive

obverse 4 face, side 5 front 8 opposite 9 other side 10 complement 11 counterpart

obviate 4 ward 5 avert, deter, block 7 forfend, prevent, rule out 8 preclude, stave off 9 forestall, interfere, interpose, intervene 10 anticipate

obvious 5 clear, overt, plain 6 patent, simple 7 blatant, evident, glaring 8 apparent, clear-cut, distinct, manifest, palpable 10 undeniable 11 conspicuous, self-evident, transparent, unambiguous, unequivocal

oca 5 tuber 6 sorrel

O'Casey, Sean 9 dramatist 10 playwright *plays:* 17 Juno and the Paycock, Plough and the Stars (The)

occasion 4 call, need, shot, show, time 5 basis, break, cause, event 6 chance, demand, effect, excuse, ground, lead to, moment, reason 7 episode, instant, opening, produce 8 ceremony, incident, instance 9 condition, happening, necessity 10 bring about, foundation, obligation, occurrence 11 celebration, determinant, opportunity 12 circumstance 13 justification

occasional 3 few, odd 4 rare 6 casual, random, scarce, seldom 7 special, unusual 8 specific, sporadic, uncommon 9 irregular 10 incidental, infrequent

Occidental 7 Western 8 European 9 Westerner

occlude 4 clog, fill, hide, plug, stop 5 block, choke, close, cover 6 screen, stop up 7 close up, conceal, congest, 8 block off, obstruct

occult 5 eerie, magic 6 arcane, orphic, secret 8 abstruse, esoteric, hermetic, mystical 9 recondite, unearthly 10 cabalistic, mysterious 12 supernatural

occupant 5 liver 6 inmate, tenant 7 denizen, dweller, resider 8 habitant, resident 10 inhabitant

occupation 3 job, use 4 line, work 5 trade 6 career, métier, office 7 calling, control, pursuit, seizure 8 activity, business, position, vocation 9 occupancy, residence 10 employment, habitation, possession, settlement

occupy 3 use 4 busy, fill, hold, take 5 seize, tie up 6 absorb, employ, engage, live in, people, take up, tenant 7 control, engross, immerse, inhabit, involve, possess 8 populate, reside in, take over

occur 3 hap 4 pass 5 arise, ensue, pop up 6 appear, befall, betide, chance, dawn on, happen, result, strike 7 come off, develop 9 take place, transpire

occurrence 3 hap 4 pass 5 event, state 7 episode 8 exigency, incident, juncture, occasion 9 adventure, condition, emergency, happening, situation

ocean 3 sea 4 blue, deep, main 5 brine, drink 6 Arctic, Indian 7 Pacific 8 Atlantic 9 Antarctic *movement:* 4 tide, wave

Oceania *country:* 4 Fiji 5 Belau, Nauru, Palau, Samoa, Tonga 6 Tuvalu 7 Vanuatu 8 Kiribati 9 Australia 10 New Zealand *territory:* 7 Tokelau 12 New Caledonia 13 American Samoa *ethnic group:* 6 Fijian, Papuan, Samoan 10 Melanesian, Polynesian 11 Micronesian *language:* 5 Maori 6 Fijian, Papuan, Pidgin, Samoan 10 Melanesian

oceanic 4 huge, vast 5 great 6 marine 7 immense, pelagic 8 enormous, maritime 9 saltwater, thalassic

Ocean State 11 Rhode Island

Oceanus *daughter:* 5 Doris 7 Oceanid 8 Eurynome *father:* 6 Uranus *mother:* 4 Gaea *sister:* 6 Tethys *son:* 6 Peneus 7 Alpheus *wife:* 6 Tethys

ocellus 3 eye 7 eyespot

ocelot 3 cat 7 wildcat

octave 5 eight, scale 6 eighth, stanza 8 interval

Octavia *brother:* 8 Augustus *grandson:* 8 Caligula *husband:* 4 Nero 6 Antony

octopus 7 mollusc, mollusk 9 devilfish 10 cephalopod *arm:* 8 tentacle *genus:* 7 Polypus *kin:* 5 squid 10 cuttlefish

ocular 4 seen 5 optic 6 visual 7 eyelike, optical, visible 8 eyepiece, viewable 9 perceived

Odalisque painter 6 Ingres (Jean-Auguste-Dominique) 7 Matisse (Henri)

odd 4 lone, rare 5 extra, fluky, queer, rummy, weird 6 casual, chance, single, uneven 7 curious, erratic, strange, unusual 8 peculiar, singular 9 eccentric, unmatched 13 idiosyncratic

oddball 4 kook 5 kooky, weird 6 weirdo 7 bizarre, curious, offbeat, strange, unusual 8 original, peculiar 9 character, eccentric 10 outlandish 13 idiosyncratic

oddity 5 freak, quirk 6 weirdo 7 anomaly 9 character, curiosity, departure, deviation, eccentric, weirdness 10 aberration, difference 11 abnormality, peculiarity, strangeness 12 eccentricity, idiosyncrasy, irregularity

odds 4 edge 5 favor, ratio 7 benefit, chances 8 handicap, variance 9 advantage, allowance, disparity 10 difference, likelihood, partiality 11 probability 12 disagreement

odds and ends 4 bits, olio 6 jumble, medley, motley, scraps 7 mélange, mixture 8 remnants, sundries 9 etceteras, leftovers, potpourri 10 assortment, hodgepodge, miscellany 13 paraphernalia

ode 4 hymn, poem 5 lyric, psalm, verse *part:* 5 epode 7 strophe 11 antistrophe

Odets play 9 Golden Boy 11 Country Girl (The) 12 Awake and Sing 15 Waiting for Lefty

odeum 4 hall 7 theater 11 concert hall

Odin *brother:* 4 Vili *daughter-in-law:* 5 Nanna *father:* 3 Bor *hall:* 8 Valhalla *horse:* 8 Sleipnir *maiden:* 8 Valkyrie *mansion:* 8 Gladsheim *mother:* 6 Bestla *raven:* 5 Hugin, Munin *ring:* 8 Draupnir *son:* 3 Tyr 4 Thor, Vali 6 Balder *spear:* 7 Gungnir *sword:* 4 Gram *wife:* 4 Fria, Rind 5 Frigg 6 Frigga *wolf:* 4 Geri 5 Freki

odious 4 foul, vile 6 horrid 7 hateful 8 horrible 9 abhorrent, execrable, invidious, loathsome, malicious, repellent, repugnant 10 abominable, despicable, detestable

odium 4 hate, onus 5 shame 6 hatred, infamy, stigma 7 censure, obloquy 8 contempt, disgrace, dishonor, ignominy, loathing 9 disrepute 10 abhorrence, opprobrium 11 detestation 12 condemnation

odor 4 funk 5 aroma, scent, smell, stink, whiff 6 stench 7 bouquet, perfume 9 fragrance, redolence

odorous 5 heady, sweet 6 smelly, strong 7 pungent, scented 8 aromatic, fragrant, perfumed, redolent, unsavory 9 offensive

Odysseus 7 Ulysses *dog:* 5 Argos *enchantress:* 5 Circe *father:* 7 Laertes *friend:* 6 Mentor *harasser:* 8 Poseidon *herb:* 4 moly *kingdom:* 6 Ithaca *mother:* 8 Anticlea *son:* 9 Telegonus 10 Telemachus *swineherd:* 7 Eumaeus *voyage:* 7 odyssey *wife:* 8 Penelope

odyssey 4 trek 5 quest 6 voyage 7 journey 9 wandering 13 peregrination

Odyssey author 5 Homer

Oedipus *brother-in-law:* 5 Creon *daughter:* 6 Ismene 8 Antigone *father:* 5 Laius *foster father:* 7 Polybus *foster mother:* 8 Periboea *kingdom:* 6 Thebes *mother:* 7 Jocasta *son:* 8 Eteocles 9 Polynices 10 Polyneices *victim:* 5 Laius *wife:* 7 Jocasta

Oeneus *kingdom:* 7 Calydon *son:* 8 Meleager *wife:* 7 Althaea

Oenomaus *charioteer:* 8 Myrtilus *daughter:* 10 Hippodamia *kingdom:* 4 Pisa *slayer:* 6 Pelops

Oenone *husband:* 5 Paris *rival:* 5 Helen

oeuvre 4 work 6 corpus, output 8 lifework 10 collection 11 compilation

of *German:* 3 aus, von *Italian:* 5 degli, della, delle

off 4 away, kill 5 aside 6 depart, murder, remote, slight 7 seaward, spoiled 9 eccentric, incorrect

offal 4 guts 4 junk 5 gurry, trash, waste 6 debris, litter, refuse, spilth 7 carrion, garbage, innards, rubbish, viscera 8 entrails 9 sweepings 10 intestines

offbeat 3 odd 5 fresh, outré, weird 6 way out 7 bizarre, oddball, strange, unusual 8 bohemian, peculiar, singular, uncommon 9 different, eccentric, whimsical 10 outlandish, unorthodox 11 distinctive 13 idiosyncratic

off-color 3 ill, low 4 blue, racy 5 bawdy, broad, salty, shady 6 ailing, peaked, poorly, risqué, sickly, unwell 7 dubious, naughty 8 improper, indecent 10 indisposed, suggestive

offend 3 sin, vex 4 gall, hurt, miff, pain 5 anger, annoy, pique, repel, shock, upset 6 appall, breach, insult, nettle 7 affront, disturb, provoke, violate 8 aggrieve, distress, irritate 9 displease 10 antagonize, transgress

offender 5 felon 6 sinner 7 culprit 8 criminal, violator 9 wrongdoer 10 lawbreaker, malefactor 12 transgressor

offense 3 sin 4 huff, hurt, miff, tort, vice 5 crime, fault, pique, wrong 6 attack, breach, felony, injury, insult 7 affront, assault, dudgeon, misdeed, mistake, outrage, umbrage 9 indignity, onslaught, violation 10 aggression, infraction, resentment 11 displeasure, indignation, misdemeanor

offensive 3 bad 4 foul, rank, vile 5 drive, onset 6 attack, odious 7 assault, noisome, obscene, painful 8 nauseous, unsavory 9 loathsome, obnoxious, onslaught, repellent, repugnant, repulsive, sickening 10 aggression, aggressive, disgusting, nauseating, unpleasant 11 uncongenial, unpalatable, unwholesome 12 disagreeable, unappetizing 13 objectionable

offer 3 bid, try 4 seek, show 5 assay, essay, pitch, put up 6 afford, extend, submit, tender 7 advance, attempt, display, exhibit, hold out, present, propose, provide, suggest 8 endeavor, proposal, threaten 9 sacrifice 10 submission 11 proposition

offering 4 alms, gift 5 grant 6 course, corban 7 charity, present 8 donation,

oblation 9 sacrifice 11 benefaction, beneficence 12 contribution

offhand 5 ad-lib 6 blithe, breezy, casual 8 informal 9 extempore, impromptu, unstudied 10 improvised, nonchalant, unprepared 11 extemporary, spontaneous, unrehearsed

office 3 job 4 duty 5 berth, suite 6 agency, billet, bureau 7 station 8 business, cube farm, function, province 9 situation, workplace 10 department *head:* 4 boss 7 manager *machine:* 3 fax 6 copier 7 printer 8 computer 10 calculator, fax machine 11 photocopier *seeker:* 9 candidate 10 politician *worker:* 5 clerk 6 typist 9 file clerk, secretary 10 bookkeeper

officer 3 cop 4 exec 6 noncom, police 7 John Law, manager 8 official 9 executive *abbreviation:* 3 Adm., Col., Ens., Gen., Maj. 4 Capt., Cmdr. 5 Comdr., Lieut. *army:* 5 major 7 captain, colonel, general 10 lieutenant *British:* 9 brigadier *court:* 7 bailiff *king's:* 11 chamberlain *law-enforcement:* 3 cop 6 deputy, police 7 marshal, sheriff 9 constable, patrolman, policeman *naval:* 4 mate 6 ensign 7 admiral, captain 9 commander, commodore 10 lieutenant *noncommissioned:* 5 sarge 8 corporal, sergeant *petty:* 5 bosun 6 yeoman 9 boatswain *prison:* 5 guard 6 warden

official 4 exec 7 cleared, manager 8 approved, bona fide, endorsed 9 authentic, canonical, cathedral, certified, executive 10 accredited, authorized, ex cathedra, magistrate, sanctioned 13 administrator, authoritative *city or town:* 5 mayor 8 alderman 9 councilor, selectman 10 councillor *diplomatic:* 5 envoy 6 consul 7 attaché 10 ambassador *governmental:* 6 syndic *parish:* 6 beadle *sports:* 3 ref, ump 6 umpire 7 referee 8 linesman *university:* 4 dean 6 bursar 7 provost 9 registrar 10 chancellor

officiate 5 chair, serve 6 direct, umpire 7 conduct, oversee, preside, referee 9 supervise 11 superintend

officious 4 busy, nosy 5 pushy 7 forward 8 meddling 9 assertive, intrusive, obtrusive 10 meddlesome 11 impertinent 13 self-important

offing 6 future 7 by-and-by 9 aftertime, hereafter 10 near future

off-key 3 odd 4 sour 7 jarring 9 anomalous, dissonant, unnatural 10 discordant 12 inharmonious

off-putting 8 daunting 9 dismaying, offensive, repellent 10 forbidding, foreboding 11 distasteful 12 disagreeable, discouraging 13 disconcerting, disheartening, objectionable

offscouring 5 trash 6 pariah, refuse, reject 7 outcast 8 castaway, derelict 11 untouchable

offset 6 square 7 balance 8 equalize 10 balance out, compensate, neutralize 11 counterpose, countervail 12 counterpoise, displacement

offshoot 4 twig 5 scion 6 branch 7 product, spin-off 9 affiliate, by-product, outgrowth 10 derivative, descendant

offspring 3 kid 4 kids, seed 5 brood, child, hatch, issue, scion, spawn, swarm, young 7 produce, product, progeny 8 children 9 posterity 10 descendant 11 progenitute

off-the-wall 3 odd 5 kooky, weird 6 farout, way-out 7 bizarre, oddball, unusual 8 freakish 9 eccentric, fantastic, grotesque 10 outlandish

off-white 4 bone 5 cream, ivory 6 oyster, vellum 9 parchment

Of Human Bondage *author* 7 Maugham (W. Somerset)

Of Mice and Men *author:* 9 Steinbeck (John) *character:* 6 George (Milton), Lennie (Small)

often 9 generally 10 frequently, habitually, repeatedly 11 recurrently

ogee 3 ess 4 arch 5 curve 7 molding

Ogier the ___ 4 Dane

ogive 3 rib 4 arch 5 graph

ogle 3 eye 4 gape, gaze, leer, look 5 stare 6 goggle 10 rubberneck

ogre 5 bogey, giant 7 bugbear, monster 8 bogeyman 9 boogeyman *Algonquian:* 7 windigo

ogress 5 harpy, scold, shrew, vixen 6 amazon, virago 8 fishwife 9 termagant, Xanthippe

O'Hara novel 7 Pal Joey 12 Butterfield 8 17 Ten North Frederick

Ohio *capital:* 8 Columbus *city:* 5 Akron, Xenia 6 Canton, Dayton, Toledo 9 Cleveland 10 Cincinnati *college, university:* 5 Miami 6 Kenyon 7 Antioch, Denison, Oberlin 9 Kent State 12 Bowling Green *nickname:* 7 Buckeye (State) *river:* 4 Ohio 6 Maumee 8 Sandusky *state bird:* 8 cardinal *state flower:* 16 scarlet carnation *state tree:* 7 buckeye

Oholibamah *father:* 4 Anah *husband:* 4 Esau

oil 3 fat, gas 4 balm, fuel, lube, oleo 5 oleum, slick 6 anoint, grease, pomade 7 blarney, incense, lanolin 8 flattery, soft soap 9 adulation, lubricant, lubricate, petroleum *combining form:* 3 ole 4 olei, oleo *consecrated:* 6 chrism *fra-*

grant: **5** attar **6** neroli *fuel:* **3** gas **6** petrol **8** gasoline, kerosene *relating to:* **5** oleic *ship:* **6** tanker *source:* **5** olive, shale *well:* **6** gusher

Oil! author 8 Sinclair (Upton)

oilbird 8 guacharo

oily 5 fatty, slick, soapy, suave **6** greasy, smarmy, smooth **7** fulsome **8** slippery, unctuous **10** lubricious, obsequious, oleaginous

ointment 4 balm **5** cream, salve **6** lotion **7** unction, unguent **8** calamine, liniment **9** emollient **11** embrocation

Okinawa capital 4 Naha

Oklahoma *capital:* **12** Oklahoma City *city:* **3** Ada **4** Enid **5** Tulsa **6** Norman *college, university:* **11** Oral Roberts *mountain:* **9** Black Mesa *nickname:* **6** Sooner (State) *river:* **3** Red **8** Arkansas, Canadian *state bird:* **10** flycatcher *state flower:* **9** mistletoe *state tree:* **6** redbud

OK, okay 3 aye, yea, yes **4** fine, good, safe, well **5** agree, allow, favor **6** agreed, assent, decent, permit **7** approve, certify, endorse, support **8** accredit, adequate, all right, approval, blessing, high sign, passable, sanction, thumbs-up **9** authorize, hunky-dory **10** acceptable, permission **11** endorsement **12** satisfactory

okra 4 herb, soup **5** gumbo **6** mallow

old 4 aged, gray, late, past **5** dated, hoary, passé, stale **6** bygone, démodé, former, mature, senior, whilom **7** ancient, antique, archaic, elderly, lasting, onetime, overage, quondam, veteran **8** enduring, lifelong, Noachian, outmoded, timeworn **9** erstwhile, geriatric, long-lived, perennial, perpetual, primitive, venerable **10** antiquated, inveterate **13** superannuated *Scottish:* **4** auld

old age 6 dotage **8** caducity **10** senescence **11** decrepitude, elderliness, senectitude

Old Bailey 5 court

Old Colony State 13 Massachusetts

Old Curiosity Shop author 7 Dickens (Charles)

Old Dominion State 8 Virginia

Old Faithful 6 geyser

old-fashioned 4 aged **5** dated, dowdy, fusty, moldy, passé, stale, tired **6** bygone, démodé, quaint, stodgy **7** ancient, antique, archaic, outworn, vintage **8** cocktail, obsolete, outdated, outmoded **9** out-of-date, unstylish **10** antiquated

old hand 3 pro, vet **6** expert, master **7** veteran **9** authority **10** past master, specialist

old hat 5 dated, passé, stale, tired, trite **6** démodé **7** antique, clichéd, vintage **8** outmoded, timeworn, well-worn **9** hackneyed, out-of-date **10** antiquated

Old Ironsides 12 Constitution (U.S.S.) *poet:* **6** Holmes (Oliver Wendell)

Old Line State 8 Maryland

old maid 6 fusser **7** fusspot **8** card game, spinster **10** fussbudget

Old North State 13 North Carolina

Old Rough and Ready 6 Taylor (Zachary)

Olds' car 3 Reo

old-time 5 dated **6** bygone **7** antique, vintage **10** antiquated **12** long-standing

old-timer 3 vet **5** elder **6** senior **7** ancient, antique, veteran

Old World 6 Europe

oleaginous see OILY

oleaster 5 shrub **12** Russian olive

olecranon 9 funny bone

oleo 9 margarine

oleoresin 10 turpentine

oleum 3 oil

olfaction 5 sense, smell **8** smelling

olid 4 rank **5** fetid **6** putrid, rancid, rotten **7** stenchy **8** stinking **9** offensive **10** malodorous

olio 3 mix **4** stew **5** umble **6** medley **7** mélange, mixture **8** mishmash, mixed bag **9** potpourri **10** assortment, collection, hodgepodge, miscellany

Oliver Twist *author:* **7** Dickens (Charles) *character:* **5** Fagin, Nancy, Sikes (Bill) **6** Bumble (Mr.) **12** Artful Dodger

Ollie's partner 4 Stan

Olympian 3 god **5** lofty, noble **6** lordly **7** athlete, exalted, godlike **8** majestic, superior **10** competitor

Olympics 5 games **6** sports **9** athletics *place of origin:* **6** Greece *symbol:* **5** flame, torch

Oman *capital:* **6** Masqat, Muscat *language:* **6** Arabic **7** Baluchi *monetary unit:* **4** rial *mountain range:* **7** Al-Hajar *neighbor:* **5** Yemen **11** Saudi Arabia *peninsula:* **7** Arabian *sea:* **7** Arabian

Omar 4 poet **7** Khayyám *country:* **6** Persia *father:* **7** Eliphaz *poem:* **8** Rubaiyat

omega 3 end **6** ending, finale, letter *kin:* **3** zed, zee

omen 4 sign **5** augur, token **6** augury, boding **7** auspice, portent, presage, warning **8** bodement, prophecy **9** foretoken **10** foreboding, prediction, prognostic

ominous 4 dark, dire, grim **6** dismal **7** baleful, direful, doomful, fateful **8** alarming, lowering, menacing, sinister **9** ill-boding, prophetic **10** forbidding, foreboding, portentous **11** frightening, threatening **12** inauspicious, unpropitious

omission 3 cut, gap **4** lack, skip, slip **5** blank, break, chasm, error, lapse **6** hiatus, lacuna **7** elision, failure **8** eclipsis, ellipsis, overlook **9** exclusion *mark:* **5** caret **8** ellipsis **10** apostrophe

omit 4 drop, fail, skip **5** elide **6** except, forget, ignore, slight **7** exclude, neglect **8** leave out, overlook, pass over **11** leave undone

omnibus 3 ana **4** posy **5** album **7** garland **8** analects, treasury **9** anthology **10** miscellany **11** florilegium

omnipotent 6 divine **7** godlike, supreme **8** almighty **9** unlimited **11** all-powerful

omnipresent 7 allover, endless **8** infinite, unending **9** boundless, limitless, universal **10** ubiquitous

omniscient 4 wise **7** learned **9** know-it-all **10** all-knowing

omnium-gatherum see OLIO

Omphale *domain:* **5** Lydia *slave:* **8** Heracles, Hercules

omphalos 3 hub **5** navel **9** umbilicus **10** focal point

on 4 atop, over **5** above, along **7** working **9** operating **11** functioning

onager 3 ass **5** kiang **8** catapult

Onan's father 5 Judah

once 4 ever, late, past **5** at all **6** before, bygone, former, whilom **7** already, earlier, long ago, onetime, quondam **8** formerly, sometime

once-over 4 look **5** check **6** gander, glance, survey **10** inspection **11** examination

one 4 lone, only, sole, unit **5** monad **6** single, unique **7** numeral **8** separate, singular, solitary **9** undivided **10** individual, particular *combining form:* **4** mono *French:* **3** une *German:* **3** ein **4** eine *prefix:* **3** uni *Scottish:* **3** ane *Spanish:* **3** una, uno

one and a half *combining form:* **6** sesqui

one-eyed giant 7 Cyclops **10** Polyphemus

one-handed god 3 Tiu, Tyr

one-horse town 4 burg **6** hamlet, Podunk **11** whistle-stop

one hundred 6 centum *years:* **7** century

O'Neill, Eugene *heroine:* **4** Anna, Nina *play:* **3** Ile **4** Gold **8** Hairy Ape (The) **12** Ah Wilderness, Anna Christie, Emperor Jones, Iceman Cometh (The) **13** Great God Brown (The), Marco Millions **16** Strange Interlude **18** Desire Under the Elms **22** Mourning Becomes Electra **24** Long Day's Journey into Night

oneiric 6 dreamy **8** anagogic **9** dreamlike

oneness 3 all **5** union, unity, whole

7 harmony **8** entirety, identity, sameness, totality **9** integrity, unanimity **10** singleness, uniformity **11** singularity, unification **13** individuality

onerous 4 hard **5** heavy, tough **6** taxing, trying **7** arduous, exigent, wearing, weighty **8** exacting, grievous, imposing, pressing, toilsome **9** demanding, difficult, laborious **10** burdensome, cumbersome, oppressive **11** troublesome

one-sided 6 biased, uneven **7** colored, partial, unequal **8** inclined, partisan, weighted **10** prejudiced, unbalanced, unilateral

onetime 3 old **4** once, past **6** bygone, former, whilom **7** quondam **8** previous **9** erstwhile

ongoing 7 current, growing **8** evolving **9** advancing, in process **10** continuing, continuous, developing, in progress, unfinished **11** progressing

on hand 4 here **5** ready **6** nearby **7** pending, present **9** available

onion 4 bulb **7** shallot *bulb:* **3** set *genus:* **6** Allium *kin:* **4** leek **6** garlic *kind:* **7** Bermuda, Danvers, Spanish *roll:* **5** bialy *young:* **8** scallion

online 5 wired **9** connected *business:* **5** e-tail *guffaw:* **3** LOL *system:* **3** Web **8** Internet

onlooker 6 viewer **7** watcher, witness **8** beholder, kibitzer, observer **9** bystander, spectator **10** eyewitness **12** rubbernecker

only 3 but, few, one, yet **4** just, lone, mere, save, sole, solo **5** alone **6** and yet, at most, except, merely, simply, single, solely, unique **7** however, utterly **8** entirely, singular, solitary **11** exclusively

onomasticon 7 lexicon **8** wordbook

onomatopoeic 5 mimic **6** echoic **7** mimetic **9** emulative, imitative **10** simulative

onset 4 dawn, rush **5** birth, start **6** attack, coming, origin **7** arrival, assault, dawning, offense, opening **8** invasion **9** beginning, inception, offensive **10** aggression **12** commencement

onslaught 5 blitz **6** attack, charge, deluge **7** assault, barrage, offense, torrent **8** invasion **9** offensive **10** aggression

on-target 5 exact, right **7** correct, perfect, precise **8** accurate **11** appropriate

Ontario *bay:* **8** Georgian *capital:* **7** Toronto *city:* **4** York **6** London, Ottawa **7** Markham, Windsor **8** Hamilton **9** Etobicoke, Kitchener, North York **10** Thunder Bay **11** Mississauga, Scarborough **13** Sault Ste. Marie *lake:* **4** Erie

5 Huron **7** Nipigon, Ontario **8** Superior *provincial flower:* **13** white trillium *river:* **5** Moose **6** Albany, Severn, Winisk

on the house 4 free **6** gratis **13** complimentary

on the nose 5 bingo **6** dead-on, spot-on **7** exactly **8** accurate **9** precisely **10** accurately

on the other hand 3 but **7** however

on the rocks 4 iced **7** with ice, wrecked

on the whole 6 mainly, mostly **7** usually **8** all in all **9** generally, in general, typically **10** altogether, by and large

onus 3 tax **4** duty, load, task **5** blame, brand, fault, guilt, odium, stain **6** burden, charge, stigma, weight **8** black eye **9** liability **10** obligation, oppression

onward 5 ahead, along, forth **7** forward **9** advancing

onyx 5 agate **10** chalcedony

oodles 4 gobs, lots, tons **5** heaps, loads, rafts, scads **6** plenty

oolong 3 tea

oomph 3 pep, vim, zip **4** brio, dash, élan, life, push, zest, zing **5** charm, drive, punch, verve, vigor **6** esprit, pizazz, spirit **7** glamour, pizzazz **8** strength, vitality **9** magnetism, sex appeal

ooze 3 goo, mud **4** emit, goop, leak, seep, weep **5** bleed, exude, issue, marsh, slime, sweat **7** secrete, seepage **8** transude

opacity 8 dullness **9** murkiness, obscurity **10** obtuseness

opal 3 gem **5** jewel, stone **6** silica **7** girasol, hyalite, mineral **8** gemstone

opaque 3 dim **4** dull, hazy **5** dense, filmy, murky, vague **6** cloudy **7** clouded, obscure, unclear **8** abstruse

OPEC nation 3 UAE **4** Iran, Iraq **5** Libya, Qatar **6** Kuwait **7** Algeria, Nigeria **9** Indonesia, Venezuela **11** Saudi Arabia

open 4 ajar, bare, free, wide **5** frank, naked, overt **6** broach, candid, expand, expose, public, reveal, spread, unfold, unlock, unseal, unveil **7** convene, outdoor, uncover, unlatch **8** disclose, outdoors, stripped, unclothe, unlocked, unsealed **9** available, uncovered **10** out-of-doors, unfastened **11** susceptible, unconcealed, undisguised **12** unrestricted

open-air 7 outdoor, outside **8** alfresco, outdoors **9** out-of-door **10** out-of-doors

open-and-shut 4 easy **5** clear, plain **6** patent, simple **7** evident, obvious

openhanded 6 giving, lavish **7** liberal **8** generous **9** bounteous, bountiful, unselfish, unsparing **10** beneficent, big-hearted, charitable, munificent **11** magnanimous

openhearted 4 kind, warm **5** frank, plain **6** candid, honest **8** generous **10** responsive **11** sympathetic

opening 3 gap **4** dawn, door, gate, hole, pass, pore, slit, slot, vent **5** break, chasm, chink, cleft, crack, debut, mouth, onset, start, stoma **6** breach, chance, lacuna, outlet, outset **7** crevice, dawning, fissure, orifice, pinhole **8** aperture, overture **9** beginning **11** opportunity *ship's:* **5** hatch **8** hatchway, porthole

open-minded 7 liberal **8** tolerant, unbiased **9** receptive **12** freethinking, unprejudiced

openmouthed 4 agog, awed, rapt **5** agape **6** amazed, gaping **7** stunned **9** astounded, surprised **10** astonished, speechless

open sesame 3 key **5** charm **6** ticket **8** passport, password

open up 4 fire, talk **5** shoot **6** reveal **7** cut into, divulge **8** disclose **9** make plain, spread out **11** communicate

opera *comic:* **5** buffa **6** bouffe *glasses:* **9** lorgnette *kind:* **4** soap **5** comic, grand, horse, space *part:* **3** act **4** aria **5** scena *solo:* **4** aria *star:* **4** diva **10** prima donna *text:* **8** libretto (see also individual titles and composers)

operant 8 behavior **9** effective **10** measurable, observable, productive **12** conditioning

operate 3 act, cut, run, use **4** work **5** drive, exert, steer **6** behave, direct, effect, handle, manage **7** carry on, conduct, control, perform, produce **8** function, maneuver **9** influence **10** bring about, manipulate

operation 3 use **4** step **6** action **7** concern, mission, process, surgery **8** activity, business, exercise, exertion, function, maneuver **9** procedure **10** employment, engagement, enterprise **11** performance, transaction

operative 3 key **4** hand, live, open **5** agent, alive **6** active, artisan, moving, usable, worker **7** dynamic, in force, laborer, running, working, workman **8** mechanic, relevant **9** effective, essential, important **10** functional **11** efficacious, influential, secret agent, significant

operator 5 agent, fixer, pilot **6** doctor, driver **7** schemer, surgeon **9** conductor

operculum 3 lid **4** flap **6** covering

operetta composer 5 Friml (Rudolf), Lehár (Franz), Suppé (Franz von) **6** Straus (Oscar) **7** Gilbert (William S.), Herbert (Victor), Romberg (Sigmund),

Strauss (Johann) 8 Sullivan (Arthur)
9 Offenbach (Jacques)

operose 4 dull 6 boring, tiring 7 tedious
8 tiresome, toilsome, weariful 9 difficult, laborious, wearisome

Ophelia *beloved:* 6 Hamlet *brother:*
7 Laertes *father:* 8 Polonius

ophidian 5 snake 9 snakelike

opiate 4 dope, drug 7 anodyne 8 hypnotic, narcotic, nepenthe, sedative 9 analgesic, soporific 10 anesthetic, painkiller
11 somniferous 12 somnifacient, tranquilizer *type:* 7 codeine 8 morphine

opine 4 deem, hold, view 5 judge, state,
think 6 advise, assert 7 believe, express,
suppose 8 point out 9 recommend

opinion 4 idea, view 5 tenet 6 belief,
notion, theory 7 feeling, thought 8 attitude, estimate, judgment, reaction
9 sentiment 10 assumption, conclusion,
conjecture, conviction, estimation,
hypothesis, persuasion 11 speculation,
supposition *express an:* 4 vote 5 judge
9 criticize

opium 4 dope, drug 8 narcotic *derivative:*
6 heroin 7 codeine 8 laudanum, morphine 9 paregoric *source:* 5 poppy

opossum 9 marsupial *kin:* 8 kangaroo

opponent 3 con, foe 4 anti 5 enemy, rival
6 muscle 7 nemesis 9 adversary, assailant, combatant 10 antagonist, challenger, competitor 12 counteragent

opportune 3 apt, fit 6 timely 8 suitable
9 favorable, well-timed 10 auspicious,
convenient, felicitous, propitious
11 appropriate

opportunity 4 turn 5 break, space, spell
6 chance 7 opening 8 juncture, occasion, prospect 12 circumstance

oppose 4 buck, defy, deny, duel 5 cross,
fight, repel 6 attack, combat, debate,
differ, object, refute, resist 7 assault,
contest, counter, dispute, prevent,
protest 8 confront, contrast, disagree,
obstruct 9 withstand 10 contradict,
contravene, controvert, disapprove

opposite 4 foil 5 polar 6 contra, facing
7 antonym, counter, inverse, obverse,
opposed, reverse 8 antipode, antipole,
contrary, contrast, converse 9 antipodal, diametric 10 antipodean, antithesis
11 contrasting, counterpole 12 antithetical, counterpoint 13 contradictory *prefix:* 3 dis 5 retro 6 contra 7 counter

opposition 3 con, foe 5 enemy 7 rivalry
8 conflict, defiance 9 adversary, animosity, hostility, other side 10 antagonism, antithesis, resistance 11 contrariety, disapproval

oppress 5 abuse, crush, wrong 6 burden, injure, sadden, subdue 7 afflict,

torment, torture, trouble 8 aggrieve,
distress, overload 9 persecute, subjugate, weigh down

oppressive 5 harsh, heavy 6 brutal, dismal, gloomy, severe, somber, sombre,
taxing 7 exigent, onerous, weighty
8 crushing, exacting, grievous, stifling
9 demanding 10 burdensome, depressing, tyrannical 11 dispiriting, overbearing, suffocating 12 discouraging, overwhelming

oppressive force 4 onus, yoke 6 burden,
weight

oppressor 5 bully 6 despot, tyrant
8 autocrat, dictator 9 strongman

opprobrious 4 evil, vile 6 odious, vulgar
7 abusive, hateful 8 infamous 9 notorious, truculent 10 despicable, scurrilous
11 disgraceful, ignominious 12 contemptible, contumelious, vituperative

opprobrium 5 abuse, blame, odium,
scorn, shame 6 infamy 7 obloquy 8 contempt, disgrace, dishonor, ignominy,
reproach 9 discredit, disesteem, disrepute 10 scurrility 12 vituperation

oppugn 5 argue, fight 6 battle, combat
7 contend, contest, dispute 8 question

Ops 4 Rhea *consort:* 6 Cronus, Saturn
daughter: 5 Ceres 7 Demeter

opt 3 tap 4 pick 5 elect, favor 6 choose,
decide, prefer, select

optical 6 ocular, visual 8 visional *instrument:* 4 lens 5 scope 7 transit 9 magnifier, periscope, telescope 10 microscope

optimal 4 best 5 ideal 6 choice, finest
7 perfect 8 choicest, superior

optimist 5 hoper 7 dreamer 8 idealist,
Micawber 9 Pollyanna 10 positivist

optimistic 4 rosy 5 happy, merry, sunny
6 bright, hoping, upbeat 7 assured,
buoyant, hopeful 8 cheerful, positive,
sanguine, trusting 9 confident, promising 11 rose-colored 12 Pollyannaish

option 4 pick 5 claim, extra, grant, right
6 choice 7 license 8 contract, election
9 accessory, privilege, selection 10 preference 11 alternative, prerogative

optional 4 free 5 extra 8 elective 9 voluntary 11 alternative 13 discretionary
item: 5 add-on, extra

opulence 6 bounty, luxury, plenty, riches, wealth 7 fortune 9 abundance, affluence, plenitude, profusion

opulent 4 lush, rich 5 plush, showy,
swank 6 deluxe, lavish 7 moneyed, profuse, wealthy 8 affluent, palatial 9 luxuriant, luxurious, plentiful, sumptuous
11 extravagant 12 ostentatious

opuntia 6 cactus

opus 4 work 5 piece 6 oeuvre 7 product
8 creation 11 composition

or 4 else, gold 6 golden, yellow 9 otherwise

oracle 4 sage, seer 5 augur, sibyl 6 augury, medium, Pythia, vision 7 prophet 8 haruspex, prophecy 10 apocalypse, revelation, soothsayer *site:* 6 Claros, Delphi, Didyma, Dodona 7 Olympia 9 Epidaurus

oracular 5 vatic 6 mantic, orphic 7 cryptic, Delphic, fatidic, obscure 8 Delphian, dogmatic 9 ambiguous, arbitrary, prophetic, sibylline, vaticinal

oral 4 exam 5 vocal 6 spoken, verbal, voiced 8 narrated, viva voce 9 unwritten 11 examination

orange 6 citrus *brownish:* 6 Titian *deep:* 11 bittersweet *genus:* 6 Citrus *kin:* 4 lime 5 lemon 7 kumquat, satsuma 8 mandarin 9 tangerine 10 grapefruit *kind:* 4 sour 5 blood, chino, navel, Osage, sweet 7 Seville 8 bergamot, mandarin, Valencia *oil:* 6 neroli *seed:* 3 pip *skin:* 4 rind

orangutan 3 ape 6 pongid 7 primate 10 anthropoid

orate 4 rant 5 mouth, speak, spiel 6 preach 7 address, declaim, lecture 8 bloviate, harangue, perorate 9 discourse, sermonize, speechify 11 pontificate

oration 6 homily, sermon, speech 7 address, lecture 9 discourse *funeral:* 6 eulogy

orator 7 speaker *American:* 4 Clay (Henry) 5 Bryan (William Jennings), Henry (Patrick) 7 Calhoun (John C.), Douglas (Stephen), Webster (Daniel) *British:* 5 Burke (Edmund) 8 Disraeli (Benjamin) 9 Churchill (Winston), Gladstone (William) *French:* 8 Mirabeau (Comte de) *Greek:* 5 Corax 8 Pericles 11 Demosthenes *Roman:* 6 Cicero

oratory 6 chapel, speech 7 bombast 8 rhetoric 9 discourse, elocution, eloquence 10 expression 11 exhortation, speechcraft

orb 3 eye 4 ball 5 globe, round 6 circle, sphere

orbit 4 path 5 ambit, range, reach, scope, sweep, track 6 extent, radius 7 ellipse *farthest point:* 5 apsis 6 apogee 8 aphelion *nearest point:* 5 apsis 7 perigee 10 perihelion

orchard 5 trees 10 plantation

orchestra 4 band 7 gamelan 8 ensemble, symphony 12 philharmonic *leader:* 9 conductor *section:* 5 brass 6 string 7 brasses, strings 8 woodwind 9 woodwinds 10 percussion

orchestrate 5 blend, score, unify 6 manage 7 arrange, compose 8 organize 9 harmonize, integrate 10 coordinate

orchid *kind:* 7 calypso, pogonia 8 cattleya, oncidium 9 cymbidium 11 cypripedium *petal:* 3 lip 8 labellum *product:* 5 salep *tuber:* 5 salep

ordain 4 will 5 enact, order 6 decree, direct, impose, invest 7 appoint, command, conduct, destine, dictate, install, lay down 9 establish, prescribe, pronounce 10 predestine

ordeal 4 test 5 agony, cross, trial 7 calvary, torment, trouble 8 crucible 9 suffering 10 affliction, difficulty, visitation 11 tribulation

order 4 book, rank 5 array, caste, class, genre, range 6 decree, lineup, method, scheme, series, system 7 command, harmony, mandate, marshal, pattern, reserve 8 classify, neatness, position, shipment, tidiness 9 directive, hierarchy, procedure, structure 10 injunction, regularity 11 progression *lack of:* 5 chaos 6 ataxia 7 anarchy, clutter 9 confusion 11 pandemonium *of business:* 6 agenda, docket *of preference:* 8 priority

orderly 4 aide, calm, neat, tidy, trim 6 batman 7 correct, precise, regular, soldier, uniform 8 methodic, peaceful 9 attendant, organized, peaceable, regulated, shipshape 10 methodical, systematic 11 uncluttered, well-behaved 12 businesslike

ordinance 3 law 4 code, rule 5 edict 6 decree 7 precept, statute 9 direction, prescript 10 regulation

ordinary 4 so-so 5 banal, cheap, judge, plain, trite, usual 6 common, normal 7 average, humdrum, mundane, natural, popular, prelate, prosaic, regular, routine, typical 8 everyday, familiar, inferior, mediocre, workaday 9 clergyman, customary, quotidian 10 uneventful, unoriginal 11 commonplace 12 unnoteworthy

ordnance 4 arms, guns 6 cannon 7 weapons 8 armament, supplies, weaponry 9 artillery, munitions 10 ammunition

ore 4 gold, rock 5 metal 6 copper, silver 7 mineral 8 platinum *analysis:* 5 assay *deposit:* 4 lode, vein *excavation:* 5 stope *iron:* 5 ocher, ochre 8 goethite, hematite, limonite *lead:* 6 galena *process:* 8 leaching, smelting *refuse:* 4 slag 5 dross, matte 6 scoria *smelted:* 7 regulus

oread 5 nymph

Oregon *capital:* 5 Salem *city:* 4 Bend 6 Eugene 7 Coos Bay, Medford 8 Portland *college, university:* 4 Reed *lake:*

6 Crater *mountain, range:* 4 Hood 7 Cascade *nickname:* 6 Beaver (State) *river:* 5 Snake 8 Columbia *state bird:* 10 meadowlark *state flower:* 11 Oregon grape *state tree:* 10 Douglas fir

Orestes *father:* 9 Agamemnon *friend:* 7 Pylades *mother:* 12 Clytemnestra *sister:* 7 Electra 9 Iphigenia *victim:* 9 Aegisthus 12 Clytemnestra *wife:* 8 Hermione

organ 5 agent, means 6 agency, medium, review 7 channel, journal, vehicle 8 magazine, ministry 9 newspaper 10 instrument, periodical *ancient:* 9 hydraulus *barrel:* 10 hurdy-gurdy *bodily:* 3 ear, eye 4 lung, nose, skin 5 gland, heart, liver 6 kidney, larynx, spleen, tongue, tonsil, viscus 9 intestine *mouth:* 9 harmonica *part:* 4 pipe, reed, stop 5 pedal, valve 6 blower 7 console, tremolo 8 keyboard 9 wind chest *reed:* 8 melodeon 9 harmonium *stop:* 4 oboe, sext 5 gamba, quint, viola 6 dulcet 7 bassoon, celesta, melodia, subbass, tertian 8 carillon, diapason, dulciana, gemshorn *tactile:* 6 feeler 8 tentacle

organ cactus 7 saguaro

organic 5 basic 6 innate 7 natural, primary 8 inherent, integral 9 essential 10 structural 11 fundamental

organism 5 being, plant 6 animal *disease-producing:* 4 germ 5 virus 8 pathogen 9 bacterium *single-celled:* 5 monad 6 amoeba 9 protozoan

organist *American:* 3 Fox (Virgil) 5 Biggs (E. Power) 6 Newman (Anthony) *Dutch:* 9 Sweelínck (Jan) *English:* 6 Wesley (Samuel) 7 Gibbons (Christopher, Edward, Ellis, Orlando) *French:* 5 Alain (Marie-Claire), Widor (Charles) 6 Franck (César) 8 Messiaen (Olivier) 10 Schweitzer (Albert) *German:* 4 Bach (Johann Sebastian) 6 Handel (George Frideric), Walcha (Helmut) 7 Richter (Anton, Ernst, Ferdinand, Johann, Karl) *Swiss:* 4 Rogg (Lionel)

organization 4 body, club, unit 5 group, guild, setup 6 agency, system 7 pattern 9 framework, structure 11 arrangement, association, corporation, institution 13 establishment *college:* 4 frat 8 sorority 9 fraternity *criminal:* 4 gang 5 Mafia *fraternal:* (see FRATERNAL SOCIETY) *government:* (see GOVERNMENT AGENCY) *lack of:* 5 chaos *political:* 4 bloc 5 party 7 apparat, machine

organize 4 form 5 array, group, order, rally, set up, start 6 create, line up 7 arrange 8 classify, unionize 9 construct, establish, institute, integrate 10 constitute, coordinate 11 put together

orgulous 5 proud

orgy 4 rite 5 binge, revel, spree 7 blowout, carouse, debauch, rampage, revelry, splurge 8 carousal 9 bacchanal 10 indulgence, saturnalia 11 bacchanalia

oriel 3 bay 6 window

orient 3 set 4 face 5 adapt, align, pearl, sheen 6 adjust, direct, inform, locate, luster 7 arrange 8 acquaint, lustrous 9 sparkling 11 accommodate, familiarize

Orient 4 Asia, East 7 Far East

Oriental 3 rug 5 Asian 6 carpet 7 Eastern 10 Far Eastern

orientation 7 bearing 8 location, position 9 alignment, direction 10 adjustment 11 arrangement

orifice see OPENING

oriflamme 4 flag 5 ideal 6 banner, pennon, symbol 7 pendant, pennant 8 standard, streamer

origami 12 paper folding *bird:* 5 crane

origin 4 root, seed, well 5 birth, blood, start 6 source 7 descent, genesis, lineage 8 ancestry, fountain, pedigree 9 beginning, inception, maternity, parentage, paternity 10 derivation, extraction, provenance, wellspring

original 3 new 5 first, model, novel, prime 6 native, unique 7 initial, pattern, pioneer, primary 8 creative, earliest 9 archetype, ingenious, innovator, inventive, precursor, primitive, prototype 10 archetypal, forerunner, innovative

originally 5 first 7 at first 8 formerly 9 initially, primarily

originate 4 coin, flow, hail, make, rise, stem 5 arise, begin, found, hatch, issue, set up, start 6 create, derive, invent, launch, spring 7 emanate, proceed, produce, think up 8 commence, generate, initiate, innovate 9 institute, introduce

originator 5 maker 6 author 7 creator, founder, planner 8 inventor, producer 9 initiator, innovator 10 institutor, introducer

oriole 4 bird 8 troupial *European:* 6 loriot *genus:* 7 Icterus *golden:* 6 loriot *kind:* 6 golden 7 orchard 8 Bullock's 9 Baltimore

Orion 6 hunter 13 constellation *beloved:* 3 Eos *belt:* 7 Ellwand *father:* 7 Hyrieus 8 Poseidon *slayer:* 5 Diana 7 Artemis *star:* 5 Rigel 9 Bellatrix 10 Betelgeuse

orison 6 prayer 8 entreaty, petition 12 supplication

Orithyia *lover:* 6 Boreas *son:* 5 Zetes 6 Calais

Orlando author 5 Woolf (Virginia)
Orlando Furioso author 7 Ariosto (Ludovico)
Orléans heroine 9 Joan of Arc
orlop 4 deck
ormolu 5 brass **6** bronze
ornament 3 gem **4** bead, deck, trim **5** adorn, jewel **6** bedeck, finial, tassel **7** dress up, garnish, jewelry, pendant, whatnot **8** beautify, decorate, filigree **9** embellish, embroider, lavaliere *Christmas tree:* **4** bulb **5** angel **6** tinsel *lip:* **6** labret *shoulder:* **7** epaulet
ornamental case 4 etui
ornate 4 lush, rich **5** fancy, gaudy, showy **6** florid, frilly, gilded, glitzy, rococo **7** baroque, flowery, opulent **8** overdone **9** elaborate, luxuriant, sumptuous **10** flamboyant
ornery 5 balky, cross, testy **6** crabby, cranky, crusty, grumpy **7** bearish, froward, grouchy **8** contrary, perverse, stubborn, vinegary **9** crotchety, difficult, irascible, irritable **10** inflexible, vinegarish **12** cantankerous
ornithic 5 avian **8** birdlike
ornithologist *American:* **4** Bond (James) **7** Audubon (John James), Bartram (William) **8** Peterson (Roger Tory) *English:* **5** Gould (John) *Scottish:* **6** Wilson (Alexander)
orotund 4 full, loud **5** round **7** flowery, pompous, ringing **8** resonant, sonorous **9** bombastic, high-flown, overblown **10** euphuistic, oratorical, resounding, rhetorical, stentorian **11** declamatory **12** magniloquent **13** grandiloquent
Orpah *husband:* **7** Chilion *sister-in-law:* **4** Ruth
orphan 4 waif **5** Annie, gamin, stray **6** bereft, gamine, urchin **7** cast-off, ignored **8** forsaken, homeless **9** abandoned, foundling, neglected **10** motherless, parentless
Orpheus *father:* **6** Apollo **7** Oeagrus *home:* **6** Thrace *instrument:* **4** lyre *mother:* **8** Calliope *wife:* **8** Euridice
orphic 6 arcane, mystic, occult **7** cryptic, Delphic, obscure **8** abstruse, Delphian, esoteric, hermetic, mystical, oracular, profound **9** enigmatic, recondite
ort 3 bit **4** bite **5** crumb, piece, scrap **6** morsel **7** remnant **8** leftover
orthodox 6 proper **8** accepted, approved, official, received, standard **9** canonical, customary **10** conformist, recognized, sanctioned **11** established, traditional **12** acknowledged, conservative, conventional **13** authoritative
orthography 7 writing **8** spelling
ortolan 7 bunting

Orwell novel 10 Animal Farm **18** Nineteen Eighty-four
oryx 7 gemsbok **8** antelope
os 3 ora (plural) **4** bone, ossa (plural) **5** mouth **7** orifice
Osborne play 15 Look Back in Anger
oscillate 4 sway, vary **5** swing, waver **6** change, seesaw **7** vibrate **9** alternate, fluctuate
oscillation 4 sway **5** swing **9** variation, vibration **10** undulation **11** fluctuation, periodicity
osculate 3 lip **4** buss, kiss, peck **5** smack **6** smooch
osier 3 rod **6** willow **7** dogwood
Osiris *brother:* **3** Set **4** Seth *father:* **3** Geb, Keb, Seb *mother:* **3** Nut *scribe:* **5** Thoth *sister:* **4** Isis *slayer:* **3** Set **4** Seth *son:* **5** Horus **6** Anubis *wife:* **4** Isis
osmosis 4 flow **8** transfer **9** diffusion **10** absorption **12** assimilation **13** incorporation
osprey 4 hawk **8** fish hawk
osseous 4 bony **8** bonelike
ossicle 4 bone **5** incus **6** stapes **7** malleus
ossify 3 set **6** harden **7** stiffen **8** solidify **9** fossilize
osso ___ 4 buco
ossuary 4 tomb **5** vault **8** boneyard, cemetery **9** sepulcher, sepulchre
ostensible 6 stated **7** alleged, seeming **8** apparent, asserted, illusive, illusory, so-called, supposed **9** pretended, professed, purported, semblable **11** superficial
ostentation 4 show **5** flash, swank **7** display **9** pomposity, showiness, vainglory **10** flashiness, pretension **11** flamboyance
ostentatious 4 loud **5** gaudy, showy, swank **6** flashy, garish, swanky **7** pompous, splashy **8** overdone, peacocky **10** flamboyant, peacockish **11** pretentious **12** vainglorious
ostiole 4 pore **7** orifice **8** aperture
ostracism 5 exile **7** removal **9** exclusion **10** banishment, relegation **11** deportation
ostracize 3 bar, cut **4** shun, snub **5** exile **6** banish, deport **7** exclude, keep out, shut out **8** throw out **9** blackball **10** expatriate **12** cold-shoulder
ostrich 6 ratite
Ostrogoth king 9 Theodoric
otalgia 7 earache
Otello composer 5 Verdi (Giuseppe) **7** Rossini (Gioacchino)
O tempora! O ___! 5 mores
Othello *author:* **11** Shakespeare (William) *ensign:* **4** Iago *lieutenant:* **6** Cassio *maid:* **6** Emilia *victim, wife:* **9** Desdemona

others 4 rest 9 remainder *and:* 4 et al 6 et alia, et alii 7 et aliae

other than 3 but 4 save 6 except 7 besides 9 apart from, aside from, except for, excepting, excluding

otherwise 3 not 5 if not 6 or else 7 changed 9 different 11 differently 12 anything else 13 alternatively

otic 5 aural 8 auditory 9 auricular

otiose 4 idle, vain 5 empty 6 futile, hollow 7 surplus, useless 8 nugatory 9 fruitless, pointless, worthless 11 ineffective, purposeless, superfluous 12 functionless 13 supernumerary

Ottawa chief 7 Pontiac

ottoman 4 seat 5 couch 6 fabric 9 footstool

Ottoman 4 Turk 7 Turkish *ruler:* 5 Osman, Selim 8 Suleiman, Süleyman

Otus 5 giant *brother:* 9 Ephialtes *father:* 6 Aloeus 8 Poseidon *mother:* 9 Iphimedia *slayer:* 6 Apollo

ouch 3 cry 5 bezel, jewel 6 brooch, buckle 7 setting 8 ornament 11 exclamation

ounce 3 bit, cat 4 dram 5 pinch, scrap, shred 6 amount, splash, weight 7 measure, modicum, smidgen 8 fraction, particle 11 snow leopard

our *French:* 5 notre *Italian:* 6 nostra

Our Town author 6 Wilder (Thornton)

oust 4 fire, sack 5 eject, evict, expel 6 banish, deport, remove, topple, unseat 7 boot out, cast out, deprive, dismiss, kick out 8 displace, drive out, force out, relegate, supplant, take away, throw out 10 dispossess

ouster 7 removal 8 ejection, eviction 9 discharge, dismissal, expulsion 10 banishment

out 4 away, exit 5 forth, loose 6 absent, excuse *of control:* 4 wild 7 chaotic *of gas:* 5 tired 7 drained 9 exhausted *of line:* 4 awry, rude 5 askew, fresh *of place:* 13 inappropriate *of sorts:* 5 cross 7 grouchy, peevish 9 irritable *of the ordinary:* 3 odd 7 bizarre, strange, unusual

outage 4 loss 5 break 7 failure 8 blackout 12 interruption

out-and-out 5 gross, sheer, total, utter 7 perfect 8 absolute, complete; positive 9 downright 10 consummate 11 unmitigated, unqualified 13 thoroughgoing

outback 4 bush 6 sticks 7 boonies 9 boondocks 10 hinterland, wilderness

outboard 4 boat 5 motor 6 engine

outbreak 4 rash, rise, rush 5 burst, flare, spike, surge 6 attack, blowup, plague, revolt 7 flare-up 8 epidemic, eruption, increase, uprising 9 rebellion 12 insurrection

outburst 3 fit 4 gush, gust 5 flare, sally, scene, spasm, storm, surge 6 frenzy, tirade 7 flare-up, tantrum, torrent 8 eruption, paroxysm, upheaval 9 explosion

outcast 4 hobo 5 exile, leper, tramp 6 pariah 7 Ishmael, vagrant 8 castaway, derelict, vagabond 9 reprobate 10 expatriate, Ishmaelite 11 offscouring, untouchable

outclass 3 top 4 best 5 excel 6 exceed 7 surpass

outcome 3 end 5 event, fruit, issue 6 effect, result, sequel, upshot 9 aftermath 10 conclusion 11 aftereffect, consequence, development

outcrop 4 rock 5 ledge 6 appear 7 project 8 protrude 10 projection, protrusion 12 protuberance

outcry 4 yell 5 noise, shout 6 clamor, tumult, uproar 7 auction, ferment, protest 8 upheaval 9 commotion, objection 11 exclamation

outdated 3 old 5 passé 6 démodé, old hat 7 antique 12 old-fashioned

outdistance 3 top 4 beat, best, pass 5 trump 6 better 7 eclipse, surpass

outdo 3 top 4 beat, best 5 excel, trump 6 better, defeat, exceed 7 eclipse, surpass, triumph 8 overcome 9 transcend

outdoor 4 open-air 8 alfresco

outer 6 remote 7 surface 8 exoteric, exterior, external 9 extrinsic 10 extraneous 11 superficial

outermost 4 last 5 final 6 far-off 7 distant, extreme 8 farthest, furthest, remotest

outfit 3 kit, rig, set 4 band, firm, gear, suit, team, togs, unit 5 corps, dress, equip, getup, group, squad, troop 6 clothe, supply, tackle, troupe 7 appoint, company, concern, costume, furnish 8 accouter, accoutre, business, clothing, ensemble, matériel, tackling 9 equipment, provision 10 enterprise 12 organization 13 accouterments, accoutrements, establishment

outflank 5 evade 6 bypass 9 get around 10 circumvent

outflow 6 efflux 8 drainage, effluent 9 effluence

out-front 4 open 5 frank 6 candid, honest 10 forthright

outgoing 4 open 7 affable 8 friendly, sociable 9 departing, expansive 10 gregarious, responsive 11 extroverted

outgrowth 6 effect, result 7 product, spin-off 8 offshoot 9 by-product, offspring 10 derivative 11 aftereffect, consequence

outhouse 5 jakes, privy 7 latrine

outing 4 spin, trip **5** drive, jaunt, sally **6** junket, picnic **9** excursion **10** appearance, disclosure

outlandish 3 odd **4** wild **5** alien, outré, ultra, weird **6** exotic, quaint, remote, vulgar **7** bizarre, curious, extreme, foreign, offbeat, strange, uncouth, unusual **8** peculiar, singular **9** eccentric, fantastic, tasteless **10** ridiculous, unorthodox **11** extravagant

outlast 6 endure **7** survive, weather **9** withstand

outlaw 3 ban, con **4** wild **5** crook **6** bandit, banned, enjoin, forbid **7** exclude, illegal **8** criminal, disallow, fugitive, prohibit, renegade, restrict **9** desperado, illegalize, interdict, proscribe **10** rebellious

outlay 3 pay, tab **4** cost, give **5** spend **6** amount, expend **7** expense, payment **8** disburse **11** expenditure **12** disbursement

outlet 4 exit, hole, mart, shop, vent **5** issue, store **6** avenue, egress, escape, market **7** channel, opening, passage, release **8** aperture **10** discounter, receptacle

outline 4 edge, form, limn, plan **5** brief, draft, shape, trace **6** bounds, border, précis, schema, sketch **7** contour, profile, summary **8** abstract, boundary, skeleton, syllabus, synopsis **9** delineate, summarize **10** figuration, silhouette **11** skeletonize

outlive 7 survive, weather

outlook 4 side, view **5** angle, scope, sight, slant, vista **6** aspect, future **7** promise **8** attitude, forecast, position, prospect **9** direction, viewpoint **10** standpoint **11** expectation, observatory, perspective, point of view

outlying 3 far **6** far-off, remote **7** distant, faraway, removed **8** far-flung

outmoded 4 dead **5** dated, passé, tired **8** obsolete **9** moth-eaten, unstylish **10** oldfangled **11** obsolescent **12** old-fashioned

Out of Africa author 7 Dinesen (Isak)

out-of-date 3 old **4** past **5** passé, stale **6** démodé, old hat, square **7** antique, archaic, old-time, vintage **8** obsolete **9** unstylish **10** antiquated **12** old-fashioned

out of it 4 lost **5** dazed **7** muddled **8** confused **10** bewildered

out-of-the-way 4 rare **6** remote **7** distant, obscure, removed, unusual **8** secluded, uncommon

outpost 4 base **6** branch, colony **8** foothold **10** detachment, settlement

outpouring 4 flow, gush, rush **5** burst, flood, spate, spurt **6** deluge, stream **7** torrent **8** effusion

output 4 crop, gain, take **5** power, yield **6** amount, profit **7** harvest, produce, product **10** production **11** achievement, information

outrage 4 fury, rape **5** abuse, shock, wrong **6** injury, insult, offend **7** affront, incense, violate **8** aggrieve, atrocity, ill-treat, mischief, violence **9** brutality, infuriate **10** resentment, scandalize

outrageous 5 awful, gross **6** horrid, insane, odious, unholy, wicked **7** beastly, ghastly, heinous, ignoble, obscene **8** dreadful, flagrant, horrible, shocking, terrible **9** atrocious, egregious, excessive, fantastic **10** abominable, inordinate, scandalous **11** intolerable

outré 3 odd **5** ultra **6** far-out **7** bizarre, extreme, off-beat, strange **8** peculiar **9** eccentric

outrigger 4 beam, boat, prau, proa, spar

outright 4 pure **5** total, utter, whole **6** entire **7** perfect **8** absolute, complete, entirely, positive **9** on the spot **10** completely, consummate **11** unequivocal, unmitigated, unqualified **13** thoroughgoing

outrun 3 top **4** beat, pass **6** exceed **7** surpass

outset 4 dawn **5** birth, start **7** opening **9** beginning, inception **12** commencement

outshine 3 top **4** beat, best **5** excel **6** exceed **7** surpass

outside 5 alien **7** foreign, open-air **8** alfresco, exterior, external

outsider 5 alien **7** inconnu **8** newcomer, stranger **9** foreigner

outsmart see OUTWIT

outspoken 4 free, open **5** blunt, frank, plain, vocal **6** candid, direct, honest **7** up front **8** explicit **10** forthright, point-blank, unreserved **11** unequivocal

outstanding 3 due **4** star **5** noted, owing **6** signal, superb, unpaid **7** capital, eminent, notable, salient, stellar **8** dominant, striking, superior **9** arresting, excellent, prominent, unsettled **10** noticeable, preeminent, remarkable, unresolved **11** conspicuous, distinctive, exceptional, magnificent, superlative, uncollected **13** extraordinary

outstrip 3 top **4** beat, best, pass **5** excel **6** better, exceed **7** surpass **8** distance, go beyond, overtake **9** transcend **11** leave behind

outward 5 overt **7** evident, visible **8** apparent, exterior, external **10** noticeable, ostensible **11** superficial

outweigh 6 exceed 8 overbear 10 overshadow 11 overbalance 12 preponderate

outworn see OUTMODED

ouzel 6 dipper, thrush 9 blackbird

oval 5 track 6 oblong 7 ellipse 8 elliptic 9 egg-shaped, racetrack 10 elliptical 11 ellipsoidal

ovation 5 kudos 6 homage, praise 7 acclaim, tribute 8 applause, approval, cheering, clapping, plaudits 11 acclamation

oven 4 kiln, oast 5 range, stove

over 4 anew, atop, done, past, upon 5 above, again, aloft, ended 6 across, beyond 8 finished, once more *French:* 3 sur *German:* 4 über *prefix:* 3 epi, sur 5 extra, hyper, super, supra *Spanish:* 5 sobre

overabundance 4 glut 6 excess 7 surfeit, surplus 8 plethora 10 surplusage 11 superfluity

overact 3 ham, mug 4 rant 5 emote 10 exaggerate

overage 6 excess 7 surplus

overall 5 smock, total 6 global, mainly, mostly 7 chiefly, general, largely 8 as a whole, sweeping 9 generally, inclusive, in general, primarily 10 far and wide 11 principally 13 comprehensive, predominantly

overalls 5 pants 8 trousers

over and above 4 also 6 as well, beyond 7 besides 8 as well as 10 in addition

over and over 3 oft 5 often 8 ofttimes 10 frequently, oftentimes, repeatedly 11 continually, recurrently

overbearing 5 bossy 6 lordly 7 haughty, pompous 8 absolute, arrogant, despotic, dogmatic, dominant, imperial, insolent, scornful, superior 9 imperious, tyrannous 10 autocratic, disdainful, dominating, high-handed, oppressive, peremptory, tyrannical 11 dictatorial, domineering, magisterial 12 supercilious 13 high-and-mighty

overblown 6 turgid 7 flowery, hyped up, orotund, pompous 8 inflated 9 bombastic, excessive, high-flown 10 euphuistic, oratorical, rhetorical 11 declamatory, exaggerated, pretentious 12 magniloquent 13 grandiloquent

overcast 3 sew 4 dull, gray, hazy 5 cloud, cover 6 cloudy, darken, shadow 7 becloud, blanket, clouded, obscure 8 covering, lowering 9 adumbrate

overcharge 3 pad 4 bilk, clip, skin, soak 5 cheat, stick 6 fleece 7 inflate

overcoat 5 paint 6 capote, raglan, ulster 7 surtout 9 balmacaan, outerwear 12 chesterfield

overcome 4 beat, best, lick 5 drown, throw 6 defeat, hurdle, master 7 conquer, prevail, triumph 8 surmount 9 prostrate

overconfident 4 rash 5 brash, cocky, pushy 8 arrogant, cocksure, reckless 9 hubristic, presuming 12 presumptuous

overdo 7 exhaust, fatigue, wear out 9 embellish 10 exaggerate

overdue 4 late 5 owing, tardy 6 behind, unpaid 7 belated, delayed, payable 8 dilatory 9 unsettled 10 behindhand, delinquent, unpunctual 11 outstanding

overemphasize 7 magnify 8 heighten 9 dramatize, embellish 10 exaggerate

overflow 4 pour 5 cover, drown, flood, slosh, spate, spill, swamp 6 deluge, engulf, excess, outlet 7 surfeit, surplus, torrent 8 flooding, inundate, spillage, submerge 10 inundation, surplusage 11 superfluity

overgrown 4 lush 5 dense, thick 6 brushy 7 hulking 8 ungainly 9 excessive, ponderous 10 junglelike

overhang 3 jut 4 loom 5 bulge 6 beetle, extend, impend 7 project 8 protrude, stick out, threaten 10 projection

overhaul 3 fix 4 mend, redo 5 patch, renew 6 doctor, remake, repair, revamp, revise 7 rebuild, restore 8 renovate 11 recondition, reconstruct

overhead 4 atop 5 above, aloft, smash 7 ceiling, expense 8 expenses

overheated 5 fiery 7 fervent 8 inflated 9 perfervid 11 impassioned

overindulgence 6 excess 7 surfeit 8 gluttony 11 dissipation 12 immoderation, intemperance

overjoyed 6 elated 7 gleeful 8 ecstatic, euphoric, exultant, jubilant, thrilled 9 rapturous 11 transported

overkill 4 glut 6 excess 7 surfeit, surplus, too much 8 plethora 10 obliterate, redundancy, surplusage 11 superfluity

overlap 5 shingle 9 imbricate

overlay 3 cap 4 coat 5 cover, glaze 6 finish, veneer 7 blanket, coating, lacquer, varnish 8 covering 11 superimpose 12 transparency

overload 4 glut 5 stuff 6 burden, excess, pile on, strain 7 surfeit

overlook 4 fail, miss, omit, skip 5 check, let go 6 excuse, forget, ignore, pass by, slight, slip up, survey, wink at 7 blink at, condone, forgive, inspect, let pass, neglect 8 discount, dominate, surmount 9 disregard, supervise 11 superintend

overlord 4 czar, tsar, tzar 5 chief, mogul, ruler 6 tycoon 7 magnate 8 suzerain 9 potentate, sovereign

overly 3 too 6 unduly 11 exceedingly, excessively 12 immoderately, inordinately

overpass 5 cross 6 bridge 8 crossing, traverse 9 traversal 11 interchange

overplay 4 hype 6 expand 7 enlarge, inflate, magnify, point up, stretch 8 maximize 9 dramatize 10 exaggerate 11 hyperbolize

overpower 4 rout 5 crush, swamp, whelm 6 defeat, master, subdue 7 conquer 8 vanquish 9 prostrate, subjugate

overreach 3 con 4 beat, bilk 5 cheat, outdo 6 defeat, outfox, outwit 7 defraud 8 flimflam, outsmart 10 exaggerate 11 outmaneuver

override 4 veto 5 annul 6 cancel 7 nullify 10 counteract, neutralize

overriding 3 key 4 main 5 chief, major, prime, vital 7 central, crucial, pivotal, primary, supreme 8 cardinal, dominant, foremost 9 paramount, principal

overrule 4 undo, veto 5 upset 6 negate, revoke 7 reverse 8 set aside 11 countermand

overrun 4 beat, raid, teem, whip 5 swamp, swarm 6 defeat, excess, infest, invade, occupy, ravage, spread, thrash 7 clobber, conquer

overseas 6 abroad 11 transmarine, ultramarine 12 transoceanic

oversee 3 run 4 boss 5 watch 6 direct, manage, survey 7 command, examine, inspect 9 supervise 11 superintend

overseer 4 boss, exec, head 5 chief 7 foreman, manager 8 director 9 executive 10 supervisor 13 administrator

overshadow 4 veil 5 cloud, dwarf, shade 6 darken, exceed 7 becloud, eclipse, obscure, surpass 8 dominate, outshine, outweigh 9 adumbrate

overshoe 4 boot 6 arctic, galosh, patten, rubber

oversight 4 care, slip 5 aegis, check, error, lapse 6 charge, slip-up 7 control, failure, mistake, neglect 8 omission 10 intendance, management 11 supervision

overspread 3 cap 5 beset, cover, flood, swarm 6 infest, invade 7 blanket, obscure, pervade 8 permeate

overstate 3 pad 7 amplify, enlarge, magnify 9 embellish, embroider 10 exaggerate

overstep 6 exceed, offend 7 surpass, violate 8 infringe, trespass 10 transgress

overstock 4 glut 5 extra 6 excess 7 surplus 9 remainder 10 surplusage

overstress 7 magnify 8 maximize 10 exaggerate

overt 4 open 5 clear 6 patent 7 evident, obvious, outward, visible 8 apparent, manifest 10 observable

overtake 4 pass 5 catch 6 pass by 7 outpace, surpass 8 come upon, outstrip 11 outdistance

Over the Rainbow *composer:* 5 Arlen (Harold) 7 Harburg (E. Y.) *singer:* 7 Garland (Judy)

over there 3 yon 6 yonder

over-the-top 7 extreme 8 reckless 9 egregious, excessive 10 exorbitant, flamboyant, outrageous 11 extravagant

overthrow 4 fell, oust, rout 5 purge, upset 6 defeat, depose, remove, topple, unseat 7 conquer 8 dethrone, downfall 9 bring down

overtone 4 hint 5 sense 8 coloring, harmonic 9 inference 10 suggestion 11 association, connotation, implication 12 undercurrent

overture 3 bid 5 proem 7 advance, preface, prelude, present 8 approach, foreword, preamble, prologue, proposal 9 prelusion 10 initiative 11 proposition 12 introduction, presentation

overturn 3 tip 4 flip, void 5 upend, upset 6 topple, tumble 7 capsize, nullify, reverse 8 set aside 10 invalidate

overused 5 stale, tired, trite 7 clichéd, worn-out 9 hackneyed

overview 6 aperçu, précis, survey 7 epitome, summary 10 conspectus

overweening 5 brash, pushy 6 lordly, uppish, uppity 7 forward 8 arrogant 9 conceited, presuming 10 immoderate 11 exaggerated 12 presumptuous

overweight 3 fat 5 beefy, burly, dumpy, gross, heavy, husky, obese, plump, pudgy, stout 6 chubby, chunky, flabby, fleshy, portly, rotund 7 outsize 8 heavyset, thickset 9 corpulent

overwhelm 4 beat, bury, rout, ruin, sink, whip 5 crush, drown, flood, swamp, upset, wreck 6 defeat, deluge, engulf, thrash 7 conquer, destroy, oppress, shatter, shellac, smother 8 inundate, submerge 9 devastate, prostrate 10 demoralize 11 subordinate

overwhelmed 6 aghast, 7 shocked, stunned, touched 8 defeated, helpless 10 distressed 13 thunderstruck

overwhelming 4 huge 5 great 7 extreme 8 numerous

overwrought 5 hyper, upset 7 anxious, frantic, wound up 8 agitated, frenetic, stressed, troubled 9 disturbed, emotional 10 distracted, freaked out, highstrung, hysterical 11 discomposed

Ovid work 5 Fasti 6 Amores 7 Tristia 8 Heroides 13 Metamorphoses

ovine 5 sheep 9 sheeplike

ovoid 4 oval 5 ovate 9 egg-shaped

ovule 3 egg *fertilized:* 4 seed

ovum 3 egg 6 gamete 7 egg cell 11 macrogamete

owing 3 due 6 in debt, mature, unpaid 7 overdue, payable 9 unsettled 11 outstanding

owing to 4 over 7 through 9 because of 10 by reason of 11 on account of

owl *cry:* 4 hoot *genus:* 4 Otus *kind:* 3 elf 4 barn, gray, lulu 5 eagle, gnome, madge, pygmy, snowy 6 barred, horned 7 saw-whet, screech 9 long-eared 10 short-eared 11 great horned

Owl and the Pussycat author 4 Lear (Edward)

own 4 avow, have, hold 5 admit, allow, enjoy, grant, let on 6 accept, fess up, retain 7 concede, confess, possess 8 disclose 9 recognize 11 acknowledge

owner 6 holder 8 landlady, landlord 9 possessor, purchaser 10 proprietor

ownership 4 hand 5 title 8 dominion, property 10 possession 11 proprietary *perpetual:* 8 mortmain

ox 3 yak 4 anoa, gaur, musk, zebu 5 bison, steer 6 bovine 7 banteng, buf-falo *Asian:* 4 zebu *attachment:* 4 yoke *extinct:* 4 urus 7 aurochs *family:* 7 Bovidae *relating to:* 6 bovine *wild:* 4 anoa, gaur 7 banteng

oxeye 5 daisy 6 flower

oxford 4 shoe 5 cloth, sheep 6 cotton, fabric

oxide *calcium:* 4 lime 9 quicklime *ferric:* 4 rust *sodium:* 4 soda

oxidize 4 rust

oxygen 3 air, gas 5 ozone 7 element *discoverer:* 9 Lavoisier (Antoine) *form:* 5 ozone *liquid:* 3 lox

oyster 7 bivalve, mollusc, mollusk *bed:* 4 park 6 claire, cultch *eggs:* 5 spawn *genus:* 6 Ostrea *Long Island:* 9 bluepoint *product:* 5 pearl *shell:* 4 test 5 shuck *young:* 4 spat

oyster plant 7 salsify

Oz *creator:* 4 Baum (L. Frank) *inhabitant:* 8 Munchkin *princess:* 4 Ozma

Ozark State 8 Missouri

Ozem *brother:* 5 David *father:* 5 Jesse 9 Jerahmeel

Ozymandias author 7 Shelley (Percy Bysshe)

P

pabulum 3 pap 4 food 7 aliment 8 nutrient 9 blandness, nutriment 10 insipidity, sustenance 11 nourishment

paca 4 cavy

pace 3 set 4 beat, clip, gait, lead, rate, step, time, walk 5 speed, tempo, tread, troop 6 motion, stride, timing 7 example, fluency, measure, precede, proceed, routine, step off 8 ambulate, antecede, movement, progress, regulate

pachyderm 8 elephant

pacific 4 calm, mild 6 gentle, irenic, placid, serene 8 dovelike, peaceful, soothing, tranquil 9 peaceable, temperate 12 conciliatory

Pacificator, Great 4 Clay (Henry)

Pacific nation 5 Belau, Japan, Nauru, Palau, Tonga 6 Tuvalu 7 Vanuatu 8 Kiribati

Pacific Ocean discoverer 6 Balboa (Vasco Núñez de)

pacifist 4 dove 6 irenic 8 appeaser, peaceful, peacenik 9 peaceable 10 nonviolent 11 peacemonger

pacify 4 calm, cool, ease, lull 5 allay, quell, quiet, still 6 disarm, settle, soften, soothe, subdue, temper 7 appease, assuage, mollify, placate 9 subjugate 10 conciliate, propitiate

pack 3 jam, kit, lot, lug, ram, set, wad 4 band, bear, cram, deck, fill, gang, heap, load, lump, mass, pile, stow, tamp, tote, unit 5 bunch, carry, cover, crowd, ferry, group, store, stuff, troop 6 bundle, charge, clique, convey, depart, gather 7 possess 8 assemble, compress, knapsack 9 container, equipment, influence, transport 10 collection, congregate

package 3 box 4 deal, unit, wrap 5 array, combo, whole 6 bundle, parcel 7 enclose, present, wrapper 8 shipment 9 container 10 collection 11 combination

pack animal 3 ass 4 mule 5 burro, camel, horse, llama 6 donkey 7 jackass 13 beast of burden

packed 4 full 5 awash, dense, flush 6 filled, jammed 7 brimful, crowded, stuffed 8 brimming 9 chock-full 10 compressed

packet 3 wad 4 boat, mass, pile 5 group 6 bundle, parcel 7 cluster

pact 4 bond, deal 6 accord, treaty 7 bargain, concord 8 alliance, contract, covenant 9 agreement

pad 3 bed, mat, wad 4 foot, mute 5 fudge, guard, paper, stuff 6 buffer, expand, muffle, shield, tablet 7 augment, bolster, cushion, stretch 8 dressing, increase 9 embellish, embroider, overstate 10 exaggerate, overcharge

paddle 3 oar, row 4 beat, stir 5 spank 6 propel, thrash

paddock 5 field 7 pasture 9 enclosure

paddy wagon 10 Black Maria

padre 3 Fra 6 father, priest 8 chaplain, minister 9 clergyman, confessor

paean 4 hymn, song 6 anthem, eulogy, praise 7 tribute 8 accolade, encomium 9 panegyric

page 4 book, call, leaf 5 folio, sheet 6 locate, summon 7 bellhop, equerry *left-hand:* 5 verso *right-hand:* 5 recto

pageant 4 sham, show 7 charade, display, tableau 8 pretense 9 spectacle 10 exhibition

pageantry 4 pomp, show 7 display, panoply 8 flourish, splendor 9 spectacle 10 exhibition 11 flamboyance, ostentation 12 magnificence

Pagliacci, I *character:* 5 Canio, Nedda, Tonio 6 Silvio *composer:* 11 Leoncavallo (Ruggero)

pagoda 6 temple

pail 6 bucket, piggin, vessel

pain 3 irk 4 ache, care, hurt, pang 5 agony, cramp, grief, throe, upset 6 grieve, harass, stitch, twinge 7 afflict, anguish, torture, travail, trouble 8 aggrieve, distress 9 suffering 10 affliction, discomfort *back:* 7 lumbago *muscular:* 7 myalgia

painful 3 raw 4 hard, sore 5 acute, sharp 6 aching, trying 7 arduous, irksome 8 annoying, piercing, stinging 9 agonizing, difficult, laborious, torturous, upsetting, vexatious 10 afflictive, tormenting

painkiller 4 drug 6 opiate 7 anodyne, codeine 8 morphine, narcotic 9 analgesic 10 anesthetic

painstaking 5 exact 7 careful, heedful 8 diligent, exacting, thorough 9 assiduous, diligence, laborious 10 meticulous, scrupulous 11 punctilious

paint 4 coat, daub, limn, swab, tint 5 adorn, brush, color, cover, horse, pinto, rouge, stain 6 depict, makeup 7 coating, pigment, portray, produce, touch up 8 cosmetic, decorate 9 delineate, represent 10 maquillage

painter 6 artist *American:* 4 Cole (Thomas), Haas (Richard), West (Benjamin), Wood (Grant) 5 Abbey (Edwin Austin), Davis (Stuart), Gorky (Arshile), Grosz (George), Henri (Robert), Hicks (Edward), Homer (Winslow), Johns (Jasper), Kline (Franz), Kroll (Leon), Marin (John), Marsh (Reginald), Moses (Grandma), Peale (Anna, Charles Willson, James, Raphaelle, Rembrandt, Sarah, Titian), Ryder (Albert Pinkham), Shahn (Ben), Sloan (Eric, John), Weber (Max), Wyeth (Andrew, Jamie, Newell Convers) 6 Albers (Josef), Benton (Thomas Hart), Catlin (George), Church (Frederick Edwin), Coburn (Alvin Langdon), Copley (John Singleton), Durand (Asher), Eakins (Thomas), Hassam (Childe), Hopper (Edward), Inness (George), Leutze (Emanuel), Martin (Agnes, Homer), Newman (Barnett), Rivers (Larry), Rothko (Mark), Stella (Frank), Stuart (Gilbert), Tanguy (Yves), Thorpe (Thomas), Warhol (Andy) 7 Allston (Washington), Bearden (Romare), Bellows (George), Bingham (George Caleb), Cassatt (Mary), Duchamp (Marcel), Harnett (William), Hartley (Marsden), Kinkade (Thomas), La Farge (John), O'Keeffe (Georgia), Parrish (Maxfield), Pollock (Jackson), Sargent (John Singer), Sheeler (Charles), Tiffany (Louis Comfort), Tworkov (Jack), Wiggins (Carleton) 8 Melchers (Gari), Rockwell (Norman), Sullivan (Patrick), Trumbull (John), Whistler (James McNeill) 9 Bierstadt (Albert), de Kooning (Willem), Feininger (Lyonel), Reinhardt (Ad), Remington (Frederic), Twachtman (John Henry), Vanderlyn (John) 10 Motherwell (Robert), Whittredge (Thomas) 12 Lichtenstein (Roy), Rauschenberg (Robert) *Austrian:* 5 Klimt (Gustav) 9 Kokoschka (Oskar) *Belgian:* 5 Ensor (James) 6 Campin (Robert) 8 Magritte (René) *Canadian:* 4 Kane (Paul) 6 Harris (Lawren), Watson (Homer) **7** Jackson (Alexander Young), Thomson (Tom) **9** MacDonald (James Edward Hervey) *Chinese:* **4** Wu Li **6** Ma Yüan **7** Wang Wei **8** Yen Li-pen *Dutch:* **3** Dou (Gerrit) **4** Hals (Frans), Lely (Peter), Maas (Nicolas) **5** Bosch (Hieronymus), Hooch (Pieter de), Steen (Jan) **6** Potter (Paul) **7** de Hooch (Pieter), de Witte (Emanuel), Hobbema (Meindert), van Gogh (Vincent), Vermeer (Jan) **8** Mondrian (Piet), Ruisdael (Jacob van, Salomon), Ruysdael (Salomon), Terborch (Gerard) **9** de Kooning (Willem), Rembrandt (van Rijn), Wouwerman (Philips) **11** Terbrugghen (Hendrik) *English:* **4** John (Augustus), Lear (Edward) **5** Bacon (Francis), Blake (William), Brown (Ford Madox), Lewis (Wyndham), Watts (George Frederick) **6** Romney (George), Turner (Joseph Mallord William), Wilson (Richard) **7** Hogarth (William), Kneller (Godfrey), Millais (John) **8** Lawrence (Thomas), Reynolds (Joshua), Rossetti (Dante Gabriel) **9** Constable (John), Nicholson (Ben, William) **12** Gainsborough (Thomas) *Finnish:* **9** Järnefelt (Edvard) *Flemish:* **4** Eyck (Hubert van, Jan van), Goes (Hugo van der) **6** Rubens (Peter Paul), Weyden (Rogier van der) **7** Memling (Hams), Teniers (David), Van Dyck (Anthony), van Eyck (Hubert, Jan) **8** Breughel, Brueghel (Abraham, Ambrose, Jan, Pieter) *French:* **4** Doré (Gustave), Dufy (Raoul), Erté **5** Corot (Camille), David (Jacques-Louis), Degas (Edgar), Léger (Fernand), Manet (Edouard), Monet (Claude), Redon (Odilon), Vouet (Simon) **6** Braque (Georges), Breton (André), Claude (of Lorrain), Clouet (François, Jean), Gérôme (Jean-Léon), Greuze (Jean-Baptiste), Ingres (Jean-Auguste-Dominique), Le Brun (Charles), Le Nain (Antoine, Louis, Mathieu), Millet (Jean-François), Renoir (Pierre-Auguste), Seurat (Georges), Sisley (Alfred), Tanguy (Yves), Vernet (Carle, Horace, Joseph) **7** Balthus, Bonheur (Rosa), Bonnard (Pierre), Boucher (François), Cézanne (Paul), Chardin (Jean-Baptiste), Courbet (Gustave), Daumier (Honoré), Duchamp (Gaston, Marcel), Gauguin (Paul), Matisse (Henri), Morisot (Berthe), Poussin (Nicolas), Rouault (Georges), Utrillo (Maurice), Watteau (Antoine) **8** Dubuffet (Jean), Magritte (René), Pissarro (Camille), Rousseau (Henri, Théodore), Vlaminck (Maurice de), Vuillard (Edouard) **9** Delacroix (Eugène), Fragonard (Jean-Honoré), Géricault (Théodore), Laurencin (Marie) **10** Bouguereau (William), Meissonier (Jean-Louis) **11** Caillebotte (Gustave) **13** Claude Lorrain *German:* **5** Dürer (Albrecht), Ernst (Max), Grosz (George), Nolde (Emil) **6** Albers (Josef), Müller (Friedrich "Maler") **7** Cranach (Lucas), Holbein (Hans), Lochner (Stefan), Schwind (Moritz von), Zoffany (Johann) **8** Kirchner (Ernst), Kollwitz (Käthe) **9** Grünewald (Matthias), Kandinsky (Wassily) **10** Schongauer (Martin), Wohlgemuth (Michael) *Greek:* **6** Zeuxis **7** Apelles **10** Polygnotus *Irish:* **5** Yeats (Jack, John Butler) *Italian:* **4** Reni (Guido), Rosa (Salvator), Tura (Cosme) **5** Campi (Antonio, Bernardino, Giulio, Vincenzo), Lippi (Fra Filippo, Filippino, Lorenzo), Piero (della Francesca, di Cosimo), Sarto (Andrea del) **6** Andrea (del Sarto), Cosimo (Agnolo di, Piero di), Giotto, Romano (Giulio), Sodoma (Il), Titian, Vasari (Giorgio) **7** Bellini (Gentile, Giovanni, Jacopo), Chirico (Giorgio De), Cimabue, da Vinci (Leonardo), Fiesole (Giovanni da), Martini (Simone), Orcagna, Peruzzi (Baldassare), Raphael, Tiepolo (Giovanni), Uccello (Paolo), Zuccari (Taddeo) **8** del Sarto (Andrea), Fabriano (Gentile da), Giordano (Luca), Leonardo (da Vinci), Mantegna (Andrea), Masaccio, Montagna (Bartolommeo), Perugino, Pontorno (Jacopo da), Severini (Gino), Veronese (Paolo), Vivarini (Alvise, Antonio, Bartolomeo) **9** Carpaccio (Vittore), Correggio, Francesca (Piero della) **10** Caravaggio, Modigliani (Amedeo), Signorelli (Luca), Tintoretto, Verrocchio (Andrea del), Zuccarelli (Francesco) **11** Ghirlandaio (Domenico), Ghirlandajo (Domenico) **12** Michelangelo (Buonarotti), Parmigianino *Japanese:* **5** Korin **6** Sesshu *Lithuanian:* **7** Soutine (Chaim) *Mexican:* **6** Orozco (José), Rivera (Diego), Tamayo (Rufino) **9** Siqueiros (David) *Norwegian:* **5** Munch (Edvard) *Russian:* **7** Chagall (Marc), Roerich (Nikolay) **9** Kandinsky (Wassily) *Scottish:* **6** Ramsay (Allan) **7** Nasmyth (Alexander), Raeburn (Henry) *Spanish:* **4** Dalí (Salvador), Goya (Francisco), Gris (Juan), Miró (Joan), Sert (José Maria) **6** Ribera (José), Rincón (Antonio del), Tapiés (Antonio) **7** El Greco, Herrera (Francisco de), Murillo (Bartolomé Esteban), Picasso (Pablo), Zuloaga (Ignacio) **8** Zurbarán (Francisco de) **9** Velázquez (Diego) *Swedish:* **4** Zorn (Anders) **6** Roslin (Alexander) *Swiss:* **4** Klee (Paul), Witz (Konrad)

painting 3 oil **7** acrylic, picture **10** watercolor *circular:* **5** tondo *one-color:* **8** monotint **10** monochrome *plaster:* **5** secco **6** fresco *style:* **4** Dada **5** fauve **6** cubism, cubist, Gothic, pop art, rococo **7** baroque, Bauhaus, dadaism, fauvism, fauvist, realism, realist **8** Barbizon, futurism, futurist, romantic **9** Byzantine, geometric, mannerism, mannerist **10** classicism, classicist, surrealism, surrealist **11** romanticism **13** expressionism, expressionist, impressionism, impressionist *technique:* **3** oil **6** fresco, pastel **7** gouache, polymer, tempera **9** encaustic **10** watercolor *tool:* **5** brush, easel, knife, paint **6** canvas **7** palette *wall:* **5** mural

pair 3 duo, two **4** dyad, join, mate, span, team, twin, yoke **5** brace, match, twins, unite **6** couple **7** doublet, twosome **8** geminate

Pakistan *capital:* **9** Islamabad *city:* **6** Lahore, Multan **7** Karachi **9** Hyderabad **10** Faisalabad, Rawalpindi *language:* **4** Urdu *leader:* **6** Bhutto (Benazir) *monetary unit:* **5** rupee *mountain, range:* **8** Himalaya **9** Himalayan, Himalayas **11** Nanga Parbat *neighbor:* **4** Iran **5** China, India **11** Afghanistan *sea:* **7** Arabian

pal 4 chum, mate **5** amigo, buddy, crony **6** comate, friend **7** comrade, partner **9** companion

palace 5 court, manor, manse **6** castle **7** alcazar, château, mansion

paladin 6 leader **8** advocate, champion, defender, official

Palamedes *brother:* **6** Sforza **8** Achilles *father:* **8** Nauplius *slayer:* **7** Corinda, Ulysses **8** Odysseus

palatable 5 sapid, tasty **6** savory **8** pleasing, savorous, tasteful **9** agreeable, appealing, delicious, toothsome **10** acceptable, appetizing **12** satisfactory

palate 5 taste **6** liking **6** relish

palatial 4 rich **5** grand, large, noble, plush, regal **6** deluxe, ornate **7** opulent, stately **8** imposing, majestic, splendid **9** grandiose, luxuriant, luxurious, sumptuous **10** impressive **11** magnificent

Palau *capital:* **5** Koror *former name:* **5** Pelew *island:* **5** Koror **6** Angaur **7** Eli Malk **10** Babelthuap, Urukthapel *language:* **7** English, Palauan

palaver 3 gas, yak **4** blab, cant, chat, guff, talk **6** babble, cajole, hot air, jargon, parley, powwow, speech **7** chatter, prattle **8** colloquy, converse, dialogue **10** conference, discussion, rap session **12** conversation

pale 3 dim, wan **4** area, ashy, dull, fade, sick, weak **5** ashen, faded, faint, fence, field, light, livid, pasty, stake, waxen **6** anemic, blanch, chalky, doughy, feeble, pallid, picket, sallow, sickly, weaken, whiten **7** enclose, ghastly, insipid **8** blanched, district, encircle **9** bloodless, colorless, enclosure

palinode 10 retraction **11** recantation

pall 4 bore, cloy, damp, jade, sate, tire **5** cloak, cloth, cloud, drape, ennui, gloom, weary **6** coffin, damper, mantle, shadow **7** dwindle, satiate, surfeit **8** covering

palladium 9 safeguard

Pallas 6 Athena *brother:* **6** Aegeus *father:* **7** Pandion *slayer:* **7** Theseus *wife:* **4** Styx (see also ATHENA)

palliate 4 ease, help **5** cover, salve **6** excuse, lessen, reduce, soften, soothe, temper **7** assuage, cover up, lighten **8** mitigate, moderate **9** alleviate, sugarcoat, whitewash **10** ameliorate

pallid 3 wan **4** ashy, dull, pale, weak **5** ashen, pasty, waxen **6** anemic, doughy, sickly **8** blanched, lifeless **9** bloodless, colorless

pallor 8 lividity, paleness **9** pastiness, whiteness **10** etiolation **12** glaucousness

pally 4 cozy **5** close, matey **6** chummy **7** devoted **8** familiar, friendly, intimate

palm 5 prize, steal, swipe **6** trophy **7** conceal, triumph, victory *beverage:* **4** nipa *fiber:* **4** bass, bast **8** piassava *fruit:* **4** date **7** coconut **11** coquilla nut *kind:* **3** fan, wax **4** coco, date, doom, hemp, nipa, sago **5** areca, betel, ivory, royal **6** raffia, rattan **7** cabbage, feather, palmyra **8** carnauba, palmetto, piassava **12** Washingtonia *leaf:* **4** olla **5** frond *starch:* **4** sago *vine:* **6** rattan

palmer 7 pilgrim

Palmetto State 13 South Carolina

palmistry 6 augury **8** prophecy **10** divination **11** soothsaying

palm off 5 foist **7** deceive, pretend **8** disguise

palmy 6 golden **7** booming, halcyon, opulent **8** affluent, thriving **10** prospering, prosperous **11** flourishing

Palmyra's queen 7 Zenobia

palooka 3 oaf **4** boob, dolt, goon, lout, lump **5** boxer, klutz **6** baboon, galoot, lummox **7** bruiser

palpable 4 real, sure **5** clear, plain **6** patent **7** certain, concrete, evident, obvious, tactile **8** apparent, definite, distinct, manifest, material, positive, tangible **10** noticeable **11** discernible, perceptible, unequivocal

palpate 4 feel **5** touch **6** finger **7** examine

palpitate 4 beat **5** pulse, throb **6** quiver **7** flutter, pulsate **12** pitter-patter

palsy-walsy 4 cozy **5** close, thick, tight **6** chummy **8** intimate **10** buddy-buddy

palter 3 fib, lie **5** evade **6** dicker, haggle **7** bargain, chaffer, deceive, falsify, wrangle **10** equivocate **11** prevaricate **12** misrepresent

paltry 3 low **4** base, mean, poor, puny, vile **5** cheap, petty, tatty **6** meager, measly, narrow, shabby, shoddy, sleazy, trashy **7** low-down, pitiful, trivial **8** beggarly, inferior, picayune, piddling, rubbishy, trifling **9** worthless **10** despicable, picayunish **11** unimportant **12** contemptible **13** insignificant

paludal place 3 fen **5** marsh

Pamela author 10 Richardson (Samuel)

pampa 5 plain **7** prairie **9** grassland

pamper 3 pet **4** baby **5** humor, spoil **6** caress, cocker, coddle, cosset, cuddle, dandle, fondle **7** cater to, cherish, gratify, indulge **9** spoon-feed **11** mollycoddle

pamphlet 5 flier, flyer, tract **6** folder **7** leaflet **8** brochure, circular **9** throwaway **10** broadsheet

pan 3 pot, rap **4** slam, wash **5** basin, knock, roast, trash **6** attack, vessel **7** censure, condemn, skillet **8** denounce, ridicule **9** betel leaf, container, criticism, criticize **10** receptacle

Pan 5 Inuus **6** Faunus *father:* **6** Hermes *invention:* **6** syrinx *lower part:* **4** goat *mother:* **8** Penelope *pipe:* **6** syrinx *seat of worship:* **7** Arcadia *son:* **7** Silenus

panacea 4 cure **6** remedy **7** cure-all, nostrum **10** catholicon

Panacea's father 9 Asclepius **11** Aesculapius

panache 4 brio, dash, élan, tuft, zest **5** ardor, crest, flair, style, verve, vigor **6** esprit, polish, spirit **8** aigrette, flourish, vivacity **11** flamboyance

panama 3 hat

Panama *capital:* **10** Panama City *discoverer:* **6** Balboa (Vasco Núñez de) **8** Columbus (Christopher) *gulf:* **7** San Blas **8** Mosquito *language:* **7** Spanish *leader:* **7** Noriega (Manuel) *monetary unit:* **6** balboa *neighbor:* **8** Colombia **9** Costa Rica *peninsula:* **6** Azuero *sea:* **9** Caribbean *volcano:* **8** Chiriquí

pancake 8 flapjack, slapjack *French:* **5** crepe *Jewish:* **5** latke **6** blintz **7** blintze *Russian:* **5** blini

Pandarus 6 archer **8** procuror *father:* **6** Lycaon *slayer:* **8** Diomedes

pandect 4 code, laws **8** treatise **10** compendium **11** compilation

pandemic 4 rife **7** general, rampant **9** contagion, extensive, prevalent **10** contagious, widespread **11** wide-ranging

pandemonium 3 din **5** babel, chaos, furor **6** bedlam, clamor, hubbub, tumult, uproar **7** anarchy, discord, inferno, misrule, turmoil **8** disorder **9** confusion **10** hullabaloo

pander 4 pimp **5** cater **9** exploiter, go-between

Pandion *daughter:* **6** Procne **9** Philomela *son:* **6** Pallas

Pandora *creator:* **10** Hephaestus *husband:* **10** Epimetheus

pane 4 side **5** sheet **7** section

panegyric 6 eulogy, praise **7** tribute **8** citation, encomium **9** laudation **10** compliment **12** commendation

panegyrical 8 praising **9** laudative, laudatory **10** eulogistic **11** encomiastic **12** commendatory **13** complimentary

panel 4 jury **5** board, frame **6** hurdle **7** section **9** dashboard

panfry 5 sauté

pang 4 ache, pain, stab **5** agony, prick, spasm, throe **6** stitch, twinge **7** anguish, torment **8** distress

Pangloss's pupil 7 Candide

panhandle 3 beg, bum, tap **5** cadge, hit up, touch **6** hustle **7** solicit

panhandler 6 beggar

panic 4 fear, riot, rush **5** alarm, scare **6** dismay, frenzy, fright, horror, terror **7** anxiety, terrify **8** frighten, hysteria, stampede

pannier 4 hoop, pack **6** basket, hamper **9** overskirt

panoply 4 pomp, show **5** armor, array **6** attire **7** display, fanfare **9** trappings

panorama 4 view **5** range, reach, scene, scope, sweep, vista **7** display, expanse, picture, purview **12** presentation

panoramic 8 sweeping, synoptic **12** all-inclusive, unobstructed **13** comprehensive

pan out 4 work **5** click, prove, score **7** come off, succeed

pant 4 blow, gasp, gulp, huff, puff **5** chuff, heave **6** wheeze

Pantagruel 5 giant *companion:* **7** Panurge *father:* **9** Gargantua *mother:* **7** Badebec

pantaloon 7 buffoon, trouser

Pantaloon's daughter 9 Columbine

pantheon 4 gods **5** Aesir **6** temple **9** hierarchy **10** hall of fame

panther 4 pard, puma 6 cougar, jaguar 7 leopard 12 mountain lion

pantomime 5 drama, mimic 6 act out, ballet, dancer 7 charade 12 harlequinade *clown:* 7 Pierrot

pantry 6 closet, larder 7 buttery 9 storeroom

pants 5 jeans 6 slacks 7 drawers, garment 8 breeches, britches, knickers, trousers

Panurge's companion 10 Pantagruel

Paolo's lover 9 Francesca

pap 4 food, mash, mush 7 aliment, pabulum 8 soft food 9 blandness, nutriment 10 sustenance 11 nourishment

papal 8 pontific 9 apostolic 10 pontifical *court:* 5 Curia *decree:* 8 decretal *envoy:* 6 nuncio *letter:* 4 bull 10 encyclical

paper 5 essay, sheet, theme 6 letter, report 7 article 8 document 9 monograph, newsprint 10 memorandum 11 composition, publication 12 dissertation *measure:* 4 ream 5 quire *roll:* 6 scroll *scrap:* 4 chad *size:* 3 cap 5 atlas, crown, folio, legal, royal, sexto, sixmo 6 octavo, quarto 7 emperor 8 elephant, foolscap, imperial *stiff:* 7 bristol 9 cardboard 12 bristol board *strong:* 5 kraft 6 manila *thin:* 6 tissue 9 onionskin *transparent:* 8 glassine *writing:* 3 rag 6 vellum 9 parchment

paper folding 7 origami

paperwork 7 red tape

papillon 7 spaniel 9 butterfly

Papua New Guinea *archipelago:* 8 Bismarck *capital:* 11 Port Moresby *city:* 3 Lae *island:* 12 Bougainville *language:* 4 Motu 8 Tok Pisin *monetary unit:* 4 kina *neighbor:* 9 Indonesia, Irian Jaya

par 4 mean, norm 5 equal, score, usual 6 median, normal 7 average, typical 8 equality, standard

parable 4 myth, tale 5 fable, moral, story 7 example 8 allegory

parachute 7 bailout, skydive *part:* 5 riser 6 canopy 7 harness, ripcord

Paraclete 9 Holy Ghost 10 Holy Spirit

parade 4 brag, pomp, show 5 array, boast, flash, march, shine, strut 6 expose, flaunt, ground, reveal, review 7 display, disport, exhibit, fanfare, marshal, panoply, show off, trot out 8 brandish, ceremony, movement, proclaim 9 advertise, cavalcade, pageantry, promenade 10 exhibition, masquerade, procession 11 demonstrate

paradigm 5 ideal, model 6 mirror 7 example, pattern 8 exemplar, standard 9 archetype, beau ideal, framework, prototype

paradise 4 Eden, Zion 5 bliss 6 heaven, utopia 7 arcadia, elysium, nirvana 8 empyrean 9 Shangri-la 10 wonderland 12 New Jerusalem, promised land

Paradise Lost author 6 Milton (John)

paragon 3 gem 4 tops 5 champ, cream, ideal, jewel, match, model, peach, saint 6 beauty 7 compare, epitome 8 champion, exemplar, last word, nonesuch, parallel, ultimate 9 archetype, beau ideal, nonpareil 10 apotheosis

Paraguay *capital:* 8 Asunción *lake:* 4 Ypoá *language:* 7 Guarani, Spanish *monetary unit:* 7 guarani *neighbor:* 6 Brazil 7 Bolivia 9 Argentina *river:* 9 Pilcomayo

parallel 4 akin, copy, even, like 5 agree, align, alike, along, equal, liken, match 6 double, equate, line up 7 aligned, compare, similar 8 analogue 9 alongside, analogous, companion, consonant, corollary, correlate, duplicate 10 comparable, comparison, correspond, equivalent, similarity 11 coextensive, counterpart, duplication, resemblance 13 correspondent, corresponding

parallelogram 5 rhomb 6 oblong, square 7 rhombus 8 rhomboid 9 rectangle 13 quadrilateral

paralysis 5 palsy 7 inertia 9 impotence

paralyze 3 awe 4 daze, numb, stun 6 benumb, deaden, dismay 7 cripple, disable, nonplus, petrify, stupefy 8 shut down 10 immobilize 12 incapacitate

paramount 5 chief, ruler 6 master 7 capital, leading, primary, regnant, supreme 8 cardinal, crowning, dominant, foremost, headmost, superior 9 principal, sovereign, uppermost 10 commanding, preeminent 11 predominant

paramour 5 lover, Romeo 7 Don Juan, gallant 8 Casanova, lothario, mistress 9 courtesan, inamorata, inamorato

parapet 4 wall 7 bastion, bulwark, rampart 10 battlement, breastwork *part:* 6 merlon 12 crenellation

paraphernalia 4 gear 5 items 6 outfit, tackle 7 effects 8 property 9 equipment, trappings 10 belongings 11 accessories, furnishings 13 accouterments, accoutrements, appurtenances

paraphrase 6 reword 7 restate, version 9 interpret, rendering, translate 11 restatement, translation

parasite 5 leech, toady 6 sponge, sucker 7 sponger 8 barnacle, deadbeat, hanger-on 9 dependent, exploiter, sycophant 10 freeloader, self-seeker 11 bloodsucker

parasitic 8 sponging, toadying 9 leech-

like 11 freeloading, sycophantic
12 bloodsucking
parasol 8 umbrella
____ **paratus** 6 semper
Parcae 5 Fates, Norns 6 Moirai *name:*
4 Nona 5 Morta 6 Decuma
parcel 3 box, cut, lot 4 body, deal, land,
mete, pack, part, plot, wrap 5 allot,
array, batch, bunch, group, piece,
share, tract 6 assign, bundle, divide,
packet, ration 7 package, partial, portion, prorate, section, segment 8 allocate, disburse, disperse, division, part-
time 9 apportion, partition 10 distribute
parch 3 dry 4 burn, sear 5 dry up, roast,
toast 6 dry out, scorch 7 shrivel 9 dehydrate, desiccate
parched 3 dry 4 arid, sere 5 dusty
7 bone-dry, thirsty 8 scorched, withered
9 shriveled, waterless 10 dehydrated
parchment 4 skin 5 paper 6 vellum
7 diploma 8 document
pardon 4 free 5 remit, spare 6 excuse, let
off 7 absolve, amnesty, condone, forgive, release 8 liberate, reprieve, tolerate 9 acquittal, exculpate, indemnity,
remission 10 absolution, indulgence
11 exculpation, exoneration, forgiveness
pardonable 6 venial 9 allowable, excusable 11 permissible
pare 3 cut 4 clip, crop, peel, trim
5 lower, prune, shave 6 reduce, remove
7 curtail, cut back, cut down, trim off,
whittle 8 diminish
parent 4 make, rear 5 beget, cause,
hatch, raise, spawn 6 author, create,
father, mother, origin 7 bring up, care
for, produce 8 begetter, generate 9 originate, procreate 10 progenitor
parenthetically 7 by the by 8 by the bye,
by the way 9 in passing 12 incidentally
parentless 6 orphan 8 orphaned
par excellence 3 top 5 prime 7 premier,
supreme 8 foremost, peerless, superior
9 number one, unmatched 10 first-
class, preeminent 11 outstanding
pariah 5 leper 7 Ishmael, outcast 8 castaway 10 Ishmaelite 11 offscouring,
untouchable *Japanese:* 3 eta
Paris *ancient name:* 7 Lutetia *avenue:*
13 Champs-Elysées *basilica:* 10 Sacré
Coeur *cathedral:* 9 Notre Dame *city hall:*
12 Hôtel de Ville *college:* 8 Sorbonne
garden: 9 Tuileries 10 Luxembourg
island: 11 Île de la Cité *museum:*
5 Cluny 6 Louvre *palace:* 6 Louvre
7 Bourbon *patron saint:* 9 Geneviève
racecourse: 7 Auteuil *river:* 5 Seine *section:* 8 Left Bank 9 Right Bank
10 Montmartre 12 Latin Quarter *stock

exchange: 6 Bourse *subway:* 5 Métro
tower: 6 Eiffel
Paris *beloved:* 5 Helen *betrothed:* 6 Juliet
father: 5 Priam *mother:* 6 Hecuba *slayer:*
11 Philoctetes *wife:* 6 Oenone
parish 6 county 8 district 9 community
12 congregation, neighborhood
Parisina *author:* 5 Byron (Lord) *husband:*
3 Azo *lover:* 4 Hugo *slayer:* 3 Azo
parity 8 equality, sameness, symmetry
10 similarity, similitude 11 equivalence,
equivalency, parallelism
park 4 stop 5 green, plaza 7 deposit, fun-
fair, reserve 8 carnival, preserve
9 esplanade 11 reservation
parka 6 anorak, jacket 7 garment
8 pullover 9 outerwear
park designer 4 Vaux (Calvert) 6 Paxton
(Joseph) 7 Alphand (Jean), Le Nôtre
(André), Olmsted (Frederick Law)
parlance 4 talk 5 idiom, style, usage
6 phrase, speech 7 wording 8 language,
locution, phrasing 9 verbalism
11 phraseology
parlay 3 bet 4 risk 5 bid up, boost, stake,
wager 6 expand, extend, hazard 7 build
up, enhance, enlarge, exploit, venture
8 increase, leverage 9 transform
parley 4 talk 5 speak 6 confab, confer,
huddle, powwow 7 discuss, meeting
8 colloquy, converse, dialogue 9 discourse, negotiate 10 conference, discussion 11 confabulate 12 conversation
13 confabulation
parliament see LEGISLATURE
parlor 4 room 5 salon 11 drawing room
13 reception room
parlous 5 hairy, risky 6 chancy, unsafe
8 critical 9 dangerous, hazardous
10 precarious
Parnassian 4 poet 6 poetic
parochial 5 local 6 narrow 7 insular, limited 9 sectarian, small-town 10 provincial, restricted
parody 3 rib 4 mock 5 mimic, spoof
6 satire 7 imitate, lampoon, mockery,
takeoff 8 ridicule, travesty 9 burlesque,
imitation 10 caricature
parole 4 free, word 6 let out, pledge
7 promise, release 9 discharge, proba-
tion, watchword 11 performance
paronomasia 3 pun 11 play on words
paroxysm 3 fit 4 bout 5 spasm, throe
6 attack, frenzy 7 flare-up, seizure
8 eruption, outbreak, outburst 9 explosion 10 conniption, convulsion
parrot 3 ape 4 aper, copy, echo 5 mimic
6 repeat 7 chatter, copycat, imitate
kind: 3 ara, kea 4 kaka, lory 5 macaw
6 Amazon, budgie, kakapo 8 cockatoo,

lorikeet, lovebird, parakeet **9** cockatiel **10** budgerigar

parrot fever 11 psittacosis

parry 4 duck, fend **5** avert, avoid, block, dodge, elude, evade **7** counter, deflect, evasion, fend off, prevent, respond, ward off **8** sidestep, stave off **9** turn aside **10** circumvent

parse 4 scan **7** analyze, dissect, examine, resolve **8** construe **9** anatomize, explicate, interpret

Parsi 11 Zoroastrian

Parsifal *composer:* **6** Wagner (Richard) *magician:* **8** Klingsor *quest:* **5** Grail *son:* **9** Lohengrin *temptress:* **6** Kundry

parsimonious 4 mean **5** cheap, close, tight **6** frugal, stingy **7** chintzy, miserly, sparing, thrifty **9** penurious **10** restrained **11** closefisted, tightfisted **13** penny-pinching

parsley 4 herb **7** garnish *family:* **6** carrot *piece:* **5** sprig

parson 6 cleric, pastor, rector **8** clerical, minister, preacher, reverend **9** clergyman **12** ecclesiastic

parsonage 5 manse **7** rectory

part 3 bit, cut **4** chip, unit **5** chunk, piece, quota, scrap, sever, share, slice **6** detail, divide, member, moiety, ration, sector **7** element, measure, portion, quantum, quarter, section, segment **8** division, fraction, fragment, function, separate **9** component

partake 3 eat **5** savor, share **6** accept, sample **7** acquire, consume, receive **9** enter into **11** participate

Parthenon *sculptor:* **7** Phidias **8** Pheidias *sculpture:* **6** frieze *site:* **9** Acropolis

partial 6 biased, unfair, warped **7** colored, half-way **8** inclined, one-sided **9** jaundiced **10** fractional, incomplete, prejudiced **11** fragmentary, predisposed

partiality 4 bent, bias **5** favor, taste **6** liking **7** leaning **8** affinity, fondness, tendency **10** favoritism, preference **11** inclination **12** one-sidedness, predilection

participant 5 party **6** fellow, member, player, sharer **7** partner, sharing **11** contributor, shareholder

participate 4 join, play **5** share **6** engage, join in **7** partake **8** take part

particle 3 ace, bit, dot, jot, tad **4** atom, doit, dram, drop, hint, hoot, iota, mite, mote, spot, whit **5** atomy, crumb, fleck, grain, minim, ounce, scrap, shred, speck **6** morsel, tittle **7** granule, modicum, smidgen, soupçon **8** fragment **9** scintilla *atomic:* **3** ion **5** anion **6** cation *elementary:* **3** psi, tau **4** kaon, muon, pion **5** boson, meson **6** baryon, hadron,

lambda, lepton, photon, proton **7** fermion, hyperon, neutron, nucleon, upsilon **8** electron, mesotron, neutrino, positron *hypothetical:* **5** gluon, quark **6** parton **8** graviton *virus:* **6** virion *with negative charge:* **8** electron *with positive charge:* **6** proton **8** positron

particular 3 one **4** fact, full, item, lone **5** exact, fussy, picky, point, thing **6** detail, marked, minute, single, unique **7** careful, correct, element, feature, finicky, notable, precise, several, special, unusual **8** accurate, concrete, detailed, distinct, especial, exacting, itemized, separate, solitary, specific, uncommon **10** blow-by-blow, fastidious, individual, meticulous, pernickety, scrupulous **11** distinctive, exceptional, persnickety, punctilious **12** circumstance

particularize 4 list **6** detail **7** catalog, itemize, specify **8** spell out **9** enumerate, inventory **13** individualize

parting 4 last **5** adieu, break, congé, final **6** good-by **7** good-bye **8** division, farewell **10** divergence, separation **11** leave-taking, valedictory

partisan 6 backer, biased, warped **7** devotee, die-hard, fanatic, patriot, sectary **8** adherent, advocate, disciple, follower, one-sided, stalwart, upholder **9** factional, guerrilla, irregular, satellite, sectarian, supporter

partition 4 wall **6** divide, screen **7** divider, section, wall off **8** disunion, division, fence off, separate **10** separation

partner 4 ally, chum, mate **5** buddy, crony **6** cohort, fellow **7** comrade **8** confrere, sidekick **9** assistant, associate, colleague, companion **10** accomplice **11** confederate

partnership 4 firm **5** union **7** cahoots, company, sharing **8** alliance, business, marriage, relation **11** affiliation, association, combination **12** consociation, togetherness **13** participation

parturient 6 gravid, parous **8** enceinte, pregnant **9** expecting

parturition 5 birth **8** delivery **10** childbirth **12** childbearing

party 4 ball, band, bash, bevy, bloc, crew, fete, gala, orgy, side **5** actor, corps, covey, feast, group, revel, troop **6** fiesta, frolic, kegger, mortal, person, social, soiree, troupe **7** blowout, carouse, faction, roister, shindig **8** carousal, litigant, wingding **9** bacchanal, gathering, make merry, raise hell **10** detachment, individual, saturnalia **11** bacchanalia, celebration, participant

parvenu 7 upstart 9 arriviste 12 nouveau riche

Pascal essay 6 Pensée

Pasiphaë *daughter:* 7 Ariadne, Phaedra *husband:* 5 Minos *son:* 8 Minotaur

pass 3 die, end 4 fare, hand 5 cease, lapse, occur, relay, spend, while 6 crisis, depart, elapse, exceed, expire, hand on, happen, permit, push on, slight, slip by, strait 7 come off, develop, journey, proceed, succumb 8 bequeath, fork over, hand down, juncture, outshine, outstrip, transmit 9 while away *Afghanistan:* 5 Murgh *Afghanistan-Pakistan:* 6 Khyber *Alaska:* 5 White *Alps:* 3 col 5 Cenis, Loibl 7 Brenner, Ljubelj, Simplon 9 St. Bernard *California:* 5 Cajon *China-India:* 9 Karakoram *Colorado:* 3 Ute *Pakistan:* 5 Kilik *Russian:* 12 Caspian Gates *Tennessee:* 10 Cumberland *Turkey:* 13 Cilician Gates

passable 4 okay, open, so-so 6 decent 8 adequate, all right 9 tolerable, unblocked 10 accessible, good enough 12 satisfactory

passably 6 enough 8 all right, somewhat 10 moderately

passage 3 way 4 exit, fare, hall, path, text 5 route, shift 6 access, arcade, avenue, course, egress, strait, travel, tunnel, voyage 7 channel, excerpt, hallway, journey, transit 8 corridor, transfer, traverse 9 enactment, quotation 10 transition 11 transmittal 12 transference, transmission *air:* 7 windway *arched:* 6 arcade *Atlantic-Pacific:* 9 Northwest *roofed:* 6 arcade 9 breezeway

Passage to India author 7 Forster (E. M.)

pass away 3 die, end 6 demise, depart, elapse, expire, perish 7 decease, succumb 9 disappear

pass by 4 miss, omit 6 forget, ignore 7 neglect 8 overlook 9 disregard

passé 4 dead 5 dated, stale 6 démodé, old hat 7 demoded, disused, extinct, outworn 8 obsolete, outdated, outmoded 9 out-of-date 10 antiquated, superseded 12 old-fashioned

passel 3 lot 4 heap, pack 5 bunch 6 bundle 9 multitude

passing 5 brief, death, quick 6 demise, highly 7 cursory, decease 8 fleeting 9 ephemeral, fugacious, extremely, momentary, transient 10 evanescent, short-lived, transitory 11 exceedingly, superficial 12 satisfactory

passion 4 fire, fury, heat, itch, love, lust, rage, urge, zeal 5 agony, amour, anger, ardor, craze, crush, drive 6 desire, fervor, hunger 7 avidity, craving, ecstasy, emotion, feeling, rapture 8 appetite, devotion, outburst, yearning 9 affection, eagerness, suffering, transport 10 enthusiasm, excitement, heartthrob 11 amorousness, infatuation

passionate 3 hot 5 angry, fiery 6 ardent, fervid, heated 7 amorous, aroused, blazing, burning, excited, fervent, furious, intense 8 incensed, vehement 9 impetuous, steamed up 10 hot-blooded, stimulated 11 hot-tempered 12 enthusiastic 13 quick-tempered

passive 4 idle 5 inert 6 docile, latent 8 enduring, immobile, inactive, listless, resigned, yielding 9 apathetic, compliant, lethargic, quiescent 10 motionless, nonviolent, phlegmatic, submissive 11 acquiescent, complaisant, indifferent, unresistant

pass out 3 die 5 faint, swoon 7 divvy up 8 disburse, keel over 10 distribute

pass over 4 miss, omit, skip 6 forget, ignore 7 dismiss, neglect 8 discount, leave out 9 disregard

Passover 5 Pasch 6 Pesach *bread:* 5 matzo 6 matzoh *meal:* 5 seder

pass up 5 forgo 6 refuse, reject 7 decline

past 3 ago, old 4 gone, late, once, yore 5 above, after, prior 6 beyond, bygone, former, whilom 7 onetime, quondam 8 anterior, foretime, lang syne, previous, sometime 9 antiquity, erstwhile, foregoing, precedent, preceding, yesterday 10 antecedent, yesteryear

pasta 5 dough *kind:* 4 ziti 7 gnocchi, lasagna, ravioli 8 linguine, linguini, macaroni, rigatoni 9 cannelloni, fettucine, fettucini, manicotti, spaghetti 10 cannelloni, fettuccine, fettuccini, tortellini, vermicelli 11 cappelletti

paste 3 fix, hit 4 beat, clay, drub, food, glue, sock 5 affix, dough, pound, stick, stuff 6 adhere, attach, cement, defeat, fasten, thrash, wallop 7 trounce 8 adhesive, material

Pasternak hero 7 Zhivago (Dr.)

pastiche 4 olio 6 jumble, medley 7 farrago, mélange, mixture 8 mishmash 9 potpourri 10 assortment, hodgepodge, hotchpotch, miscellany, salmagundi 11 gallimaufry

pastime 4 game 5 hobby, sport 9 amusement, diversion 10 recreation 13 entertainment

past master 4 whiz 5 adept, maven 6 expert, wizard 9 authority

pastor 5 padre 6 cleric, parson 8 minister, preacher, reverend, sky pilot 9 clergyman

pastoral 5 idyll, rural 6 rustic 7 bucolic,

country, crosier, idyllic **8** agrarian, clerical, innocent, peaceful **10** campestral

pastor's assistant 6 curate

pastry 3 bun, pie **4** baba, cake, flan, tart **5** torte **6** cornet, Danish, éclair, gâteau, pirogi **7** baklava, beignet, bouchée, dariole, fritter, gâteaux (plural), palmier, savarin, strudel, tartlet **8** napoleon, papillon, piroshki, pirozhki, turnover **9** barquette, cream puff, madeleine, petit four, vol-au-vent **10** cheesecake **11** profiterole **12** millefeuille *kind:* **4** filo, puff **5** flaky **6** phyllo *shell:* **7** timbale **8** meringue

pasture 3 lea, ley **4** feed, land **5** field, grass, graze **6** browse, meadow **9** grassland

pasty 3 wan **4** pale **6** doughy, pallid, sickly **7** meat pie **8** turnover **9** unhealthy

pat 3 apt, dab, set **4** firm **5** fixed, slice, stiff, trite **6** dead-on **7** apropos, fitting **8** apposite, standard, suitable **9** contrived, pertinent, rehearsed

patch 3 bit, fix **4** area, fill, mend, plot **5** cover, piece, scrap, spell **6** doctor, emblem, fill up, repair, shield **7** connect, plaster **8** material **10** connection

patchwork 4 olio **5** quilt **6** jumble **7** mixture **8** covering, mishmash, mixed bag **10** assortment, hodgepodge, hotchpotch, miscellany, salmagundi

patchy 6 fitful, random, spotty, uneven **7** erratic **8** sporadic **9** haphazard, hit-or-miss, irregular **12** intermittent

pate 4 bean, dome, head, poll **5** brain, crown **6** noddle, noggin, noodle

pâté de ___ 8 foie gras

patella 7 kneecap, kneepan

patent 4 open **5** clear, plain, right **6** secure **7** evident, license, obvious, visible **8** apparent, distinct, manifest, unclosed **9** exclusive, privilege, prominent, protected **11** proprietary **12** intelligible, unobstructed

paternal 8 fatherly *relative:* **6** agnate

paternity 7 lineage **8** ancestry **10** fatherhood, provenance **11** progenitors

Pater Noster 9 Our Father

path 3 way **4** lane, line, road, tack, walk **5** byway, orbit, route, track, trail **6** avenue, bridle, course **7** passage, walkway **9** direction **10** trajectory

pathetic 3 sad **4** poor **5** sorry **6** absurd, moving, paltry, rueful **7** piteous, pitiful, risible, useless **8** inferior, pitiable, poignant, touching **9** affecting, laughable, miserable **10** inadequate, lamentable, ridiculous

Pathfinder *author:* **6** Cooper (James Fenimore) *hero:* **6** Bumppo (Natty)

pathogen 4 germ **5** virus **9** bacterium

pathological 7 deviant **8** aberrant, abnormal, diseased, maniacal, schizoid **9** psychotic

pathos 4 pity **7** emotion **8** sympathy **9** poignance, poignancy

pathway 4 line, walk **5** route, track, trail **6** course **7** channel, conduit, network, passage

patience 4 cool **8** calmness, stoicism **9** composure, endurance **10** equanimity, sufferance **11** forbearance, resignation, self-control

Patience *composer:* **8** Sullivan (Arthur) *librettist:* **7** Gilbert (W. S.)

patient 4 case, meek **7** enduring **9** easygoing **10** persistent **11** susceptible **13** long-suffering *man:* **3** Job

patina 4 aura, coat, film **6** finish, polish **7** coating **8** covering **10** appearance, coloration

patio 5 court **6** atrium **7** terrace **9** courtyard

patois 4 cant **5** argot, lingo, slang **6** jargon **7** dialect **10** colloquial, vernacular

patriarch 4 sire **6** father **7** creator, founder **9** architect, graybeard *biblical:* **5** David, Isaac, Jacob **7** Abraham

patrician 5 noble **6** aristo **9** blue blood, gentleman **10** aristocrat, upper-class

patriciate 5 elite **6** gentry **9** blue blood, gentility **10** upper crust **11** aristocracy

patrimony 6 estate, legacy **8** heritage **9** endowment **10** birthright **11** inheritance

patriot 5 jingo **8** jingoist, loyalist **9** flagwaver **10** chauvinist **11** nationalist

patriotism 8 jingoism **10** chauvinism **11** nationalism

Patroclus *friend:* **8** Achilles *slayer:* **6** Hector

patrol 5 guard, round, scout, troop, watch **7** protect **8** sentinel **9** keep watch

patrolman 3 cop **5** guard **6** police **7** officer

patrol wagon see PADDY WAGON

patron 5 angel **6** backer, client **7** sponsor **8** customer, guardian **9** protector, supporter **10** benefactor

patronage 4 help **5** aegis, trade **6** custom **7** backing, subsidy, support, traffic **8** activity, advocacy, auspices, business, cronyism **9** clientage, clientele, influence **10** pork barrel, protection **11** benefaction, sponsorship **12** guardianship

patronize 3 aid, use **4** back **5** deign, favor **6** assist, shop at **7** protect, support **8** frequent **10** condescend

patron saint *of beggars, cripples:* **5** Giles *of children:* **8** Nicholas *of England:*

6 George *of fishermen:* 5 Peter *of France:*
5 Denis *of Ireland:* 7 Patrick *of lawyers:*
4 Ives *of musicians:* 7 Cecilia *of Norway:*
4 Olaf *of physicians:* 4 Luke *of sailors:*
4 Elmo 8 Nicholas *of Scotland:*
6 Andrew *of shoemakers:* 7 Crispin *of
Spain:* 5 James 8 Santiago *of Wales:*
5 David *of winegrowers:* 7 Vincent *of
workers:* 6 Joseph

patsy 3 sap 4 dupe, fool, mark 5 chump
6 pigeon, sucker, victim 8 easy mark,
pushover

patter 4 cant 5 argot, lingo, slang, spiel
6 babble, jargon, patois 7 chatter, prattle

pattern 4 copy, form, plan 5 guide, ideal,
model, motif, order, shape 6 design,
figure, follow, method, mirror, system
7 diagram, emulate, example, imitate
8 exemplar, grouping, paradigm, standard, template 9 archetype, incidence,
prototype 10 flight path 11 arrangement, orderliness 12 distribution
13 configuration

paucity 4 lack, want 6 dearth 7 poverty
8 scarcity, shortage 9 scantness, small-
ness 10 deficiency, meagerness, mea-
greness 13 insufficiency

___ **Paulo** 3 São

Paul the Apostle *birthplace:* 6 Tarsus
companion: 5 Silas, Titus 7 Artemas,
Timothy 8 Barnabas *original name:*
4 Saul *place of conversion:* 8 Damascus
prosecutor: 9 Tertullus *teacher:*
8 Gamaliel *tribe:* 8 Benjamin

paunch 3 gut, pot 5 belly, tummy
7 abdomen, stomach 8 potbelly 9 bay
window, beer belly 11 breadbasket

paunchy 3 fat 5 beefy, plump, tubby
6 chunky, portly, rotund 8 thickset
10 overweight, potbellied

pauper 6 beggar 7 have-not 8 bankrupt,
indigent 9 mendicant

pauperism 4 need, ruin, want 6 penury
7 beggary, poverty 9 indigence, neediness, privation 11 destitution

pause 3 gap 4 halt, hush, lull, rest, stop,
wait 5 break, comma, delay, lapse,
letup 6 hiatus, linger, recess 7 caesura,
respite, time out 8 breather, hesitate,
inaction, interval, take five 9 cessation,
interlude 10 hesitation, suspension
12 intermission, interruption

pave 3 lay, tar 5 cover 7 asphalt, surface
8 blacktop, concrete

pavement 6 tarmac 7 asphalt, macadam,
surface 8 concrete, sidewalk

pavilion 4 tent 5 kiosk 6 canopy, gazebo
9 belvedere 11 summerhouse

paw 4 feel, foot, grab, hand 5 grope,
touch 6 fondle, handle, molest, scrape

pawn 4 hock, tool 6 pledge, puppet,
stooge, victim 7 deposit, hostage, warrant 8 guaranty, security 9 guarantee
10 chess piece, instrument

pax 5 peace 6 tablet

Pax ___ 3 Dei 6 Romana 10 Britannica

pay 3 fee 4 wage 5 clear, offer, remit,
serve, spend 6 answer, defray, employ,
expend, kick in, lay out, pony up, profit, render, return, salary, settle, square,
tender, reward 7 benefit, bring in,
cough up, forfeit, fork out, requite,
satisfy, stipend 8 defrayal, disburse,
earnings, shell out 9 discharge, emolument, indemnify, liquidate, reimburse
10 compensate, recompense, remunerate 12 compensation, remuneration

payable 3 due 4 owed 5 owing 6 mature,
unpaid 7 overdue 9 unsettled 10 obligatory 11 outstanding, uncollected

paycheck 5 wages 6 salary

payload 4 haul 5 cargo, goods 6 burden,
lading, weight 7 freight, tonnage 8 shipment

payment 3 fee 4 dues 5 award, money
6 amends, outlay, return, reward
7 penance 8 defrayal, requital 11 restitution 12 compensation, remuneration,
satisfaction

payoff 3 fix 5 bribe 6 climax, profit,
result, reward, upshot 7 outcome
8 clincher, decisive 10 conclusion, conclusive, denouement 11 retribution

payola 5 bribe

PDQ 4 ASAP 6 at once, pronto 8 directly,
right now, right off 9 forthwith, instanter, instantly, right away 11 immediately, straightway 12 straightaway

peace 3 pax 4 calm, ease, pact 5 amity,
order, quiet 6 accord, repose 7 concord, harmony, silence 8 serenity
11 tranquility 12 tranquillity

peaceable 6 dovish, irenic 7 amiable,
pacific 8 amicable, friendly, pacifist,
tranquil 10 nonviolent 11 complaisant
12 conciliatory

peaceful 4 calm 5 still, quiet 6 irenic,
placid, serene 7 equable, pacific 8 composed, tranquil 9 unruffled 10 harmonious, nonviolent, untroubled

peacemaker 7 arbiter 8 mediator, pacifier, placater 10 arbitrator, negotiator
11 conciliator, pacificator

peace officer 3 cop 6 police 9 policeman
11 policewoman

peach 3 rat 4 blab, tree 5 fruit 6 betray,
inform, reveal, snitch, squeal 9 free-
stone, humdinger, nectarine 10 clingstone 11 crackerjack *family:* 4 rose

Peach State 7 Georgia

peachy 4 fine, good, nice 5 dandy, nifty,

super, swell **8** pleasant, pleasing
9 excellent, hunky-dory, marvelous, wonderful

peacockish 5 showy, swank **6** chichi, flashy, swanky **7** splashy **8** show-offy **10** flamboyant **11** pretentious **12** ostentatious

peak 3 alp, top, tor **4** acme, apex, bill, crag, roof **5** crest, crown, mount, visor **6** apogee, summit, vertex, zenith **8** capsheaf, capstone, meridian, mountain, pinnacle *Adirondack:* **9** Whiteface *Africa's highest:* **4** Kibo *Alaska-Canada:* **12** Mt. Saint Elias *Andes:* **4** Ruiz **5** Torrá *Apennines:* **5** Amaro *Argentina:* **4** Azul **5** Negra, Payún *Bavaria:* **5** Arber *Berkshires:* **8** Greylock *Black Hills:* **8** Rushmore *Bolivia:* **5** Cuzco, Tahua, Ubina **6** Sajama *Borneo:* **4** Raja *California:* **6** Shasta, Sonora **7** Palomar, Whitney **8** Half Dome **9** Excelsior *Canada:* **5** Keele *Canaries:* **5** Teide **8** Tenerife *Carpathian:* **4** Rysy *Cascades:* **7** Rainier *Catskill:* **6** Pisgah *Caucasus:* **5** Ushba **6** Elbrus *Chile:* **4** Mayo, Pili **5** Paine, Pular *Colombia:* **4** Tama **5** Neiva *Colorado:* **3** Ute **5** Pikes **9** Purgatory *Cuba:* **8** Turquino *Ecuador:* **10** Chimborazo *England:* **11** Scafell Pike *Ethiopia:* **4** Guna **5** Holla *France:* **5** Pilat *French Guiana:* **5** Amana *Georgia:* **8** Springer *Glacier National Park:* **8** Kootenai *Greece:* **4** Ossa **6** Pelion *Himalayas:* **3** Api **5** Kamet **6** Lhotse **10** Gasherbrum *Honshū:* **4** Yari **10** Yarigatake *Idaho:* **11** Pend Oreille *Iran:* **8** Damavand *Italy:* **4** Etna **8** Vesuvius *Japan:* **4** Sobo **5** Oyama **7** Sobozan *Java:* **6** Slamet *Jordan:* **6** Gilead *Karakoram Range:* **7** Dapsang **10** Masherbrum **12** Godwin Austen *Maine:* **8** Katahdin **10** Saddleback *Montana:* **8** Gallatin *Nevada:* **3** Ely *Newfoundland:* **9** Gros Morne *New Hampshire:* **9** Monadnock *New Zealand:* **3** Una **4** Cook **7** Aorangi **8** Aspiring *Oahu:* **5** Kaala *Oregon:* **4** Hood *Papua New Guinea:* **8** Victoria *Pennine Alps:* **10** Matterhorn, Mont Cervin *Philippines:* **4** High *Pyrenees:* **11** de Vignemale *Russia's highest:* **6** Elbrus *Scotland:* **8** Ben Nevis *Sicily:* **4** Etna *Spain:* **5** Yelmo **8** Mulhacén *Switzerland:* **3** Dom **4** Dôle, Tödi **5** Eiger, Mönch **6** La Dôle, Rusein **7** Pilatus **8** Jungfrau *Tanzania:* **11** Kilimanjaro *Utah:* **5** Kings *Venezuela:* **5** Icutú *Vermont:* **8** Haystack, Stratton **8** Ascutney **9** Mansfield *Washington:* **7** Olympus, Rainier **11** Saint Helens *White Mts.:* **10** Washington *Wyoming:* **3** Elk **10** Grand Teton *Yukon:* **4** King **5** Logan

peaked 3 ill, wan **4** ashy, pale, sick **5** acute, ashen, drawn, sharp **6** ailing, pallid, sickly **7** pointed **9** emaciated

peal 4 bell, bong, ring, toll **5** chime, knell, sound **7** ringing **8** ding-dong

peanut 6 goober, legume **10** foam pellet

pear 4 Bosc **5** Anjou, Hardy **6** Comice, Garber, Seckel **7** Kieffer, LeConte **8** Bartlett *cider:* **5** perry

pearl 3 gem **4** dear **5** jewel **7** paragon **8** treasure

Pearl Mosque site 4 Agra

pearly 8 lustrous, nacreous, precious **10** iridescent, opalescent

pear-shaped 8 pyriform

peasant 4 carl, kern, peon, serf **5** churl **6** rustic **7** bumpkin, hayseed, villein *Arab:* **6** fellah *Latin-American:* **9** campesino *Russian:* **6** muzhik

peccary 8 javelina *genus:* **7** Tayassu

peck 3 lot, nag **4** buss, carp, fuss, heap, kiss, load, mess, pile, poke **6** carp at, nibble, pick at, pick up, pierce, strike **8** quantity

pecking order 6 ladder **7** pyramid **9** food chain, hierarchy

peculate 5 steal **8** embezzle **9** defalcate **11** appropriate

peculiar 3 odd **4** rare **5** queer, weird **6** unique **7** bizarre, curious, oddball, offbeat, special, strange, unusual **8** abnormal, singular, specific, uncommon **9** eccentric **10** individual, particular **11** distinctive

peculiarity 4 mark **5** quirk, trait **6** oddity **7** feature, quality **8** property **9** attribute, character, mannerism **12** eccentricity, idiosyncrasy

pecuniary 6 fiscal **8** economic, monetary **9** financial

pedagogue 5 tutor **6** pedant **7** teacher **8** educator **12** schoolmaster

pedagogy 8 teaching **9** education

pedal 5 lever **7** bicycle, treadle *digit:* **3** toe

pedant 7 teacher **9** formalist **10** schoolmarm **12** precisionist

pedantic 3 dry **4** arid, dull **6** stodgy **7** bookish, donnish, erudite, learned, tedious **8** academic, didactic, priggish **9** ponderous **10** pedestrian, scholastic **11** pedagogical **13** unimaginative

peddle 4 hawk, push, sell, vend **5** pitch **6** monger **8** huckster

peddler 6 coster, dealer, hawker, monger, vendor **8** huckster, merchant, promoter **9** tradesman **12** costermonger

pedestal 4 base, foot **5** stand **7** footing, support **10** foundation **12** underpinning *part:* **4** dado **6** plinth **7** subbase

pedestrian 4 blah, dull **5** banal **6** dreary,

stodgy, walker **7** humdrum, mundane, prosaic **8** everyday, ordinary **11** commonplace **13** unimaginative

pedigree 6 origin, purity **7** descent, history, lineage **8** ancestry, purebred **9** bloodline, genealogy **10** background, extraction, family tree

peduncle 4 stem **5** stalk **7** pedicel

peek 3 spy **4** look **6** glance **7** glimpse

peel 4 bark, pare, rind, skin **5** flake, scale, strip **7** take off **8** flake off **9** break away, exfoliate

peeled 4 bare, open **5** naked **7** denuded, exposed **8** stripped **9** uncovered

peep 3 see, spy **4** look **5** chirp, tweet, watch **6** glance, squeak **7** glimpse, twitter **9** sandpiper

Peeping Tom 5 snoop **6** voyeur **7** prowler, snooper

peer 3 pry **4** gaze, lord **5** equal, glare, noble, stare **6** goggle, squint **9** associate *British:* **4** duke, earl **5** baron **7** marquis **8** marquess, viscount

Peer Gynt *author:* **5** Ibsen (Henrik) *beloved:* **7** Solveig *composer:* **5** Grieg (Edvard) *mother:* **3** Ase **4** Aase

peerless 4 best **6** unique **7** perfect, supreme **8** superior **9** matchless, nonpareil, paramount, unequaled, unmatched, unrivaled **12** incomparable, unparalleled

peeve 3 bug, irk, vex **4** miff, rile **5** anger, annoy, pique **6** bother, nettle, put out **7** disturb, provoke **8** irritate, nuisance, vexation **9** aggravate, annoyance, grievance **10** exasperate **11** aggravation

peevish 4 sour **5** cross, testy **6** cranky, grumpy, ornery **7** fretful, whining **8** petulant **9** fractious, irritable, obstinate, querulous **11** ill-tempered

peewee 4 runt, tyke **5** dwarf, pygmy, small **6** midget, shaver, shrimp, squirt **9** miniature **10** diminutive, flycatcher **11** lilliputian

Peewee ___ 5 Reese

peg 3 fix, pin **4** hold, mark, plod, plug, step, work **5** dowel, place, prong, stake, throw **6** attach, degree, fasten, hustle, marker, reason **7** pin down, pretext, support **8** identify, restrict

Pegasus 5 horse, steed *rider:* **11** Bellerophon

pejorative 7 adverse **8** critical, debasing **9** slighting **10** belittling, derogatory, detractive **11** denigrating, deprecatory, disparaging, opprobrious, unfavorable **12** depreciatory

pelagic 6 marine **7** oceanic **8** maritime

Peleus *brother:* **7** Telamon *father:* **6** Aeacus *half brother:* **6** Phocus *son:* **8** Achilles *victim:* **8** Eurytion *wife:* **6** Thetis

pelf 4 loot, swag **5** booty, money, moola **6** boodle, moolah, riches, spoils **7** plunder

Pelias *country:* **6** Iolcus *father:* **8** Poseidon *half brother:* **5** Aeson *son:* **7** Acastus

Pelican State 9 Louisiana

Pelléas *beloved:* **9** Mélisande *brother, slayer:* **6** Golaud

Pelles *daughter:* **6** Elaine *grandson:* **7** Galahad

pellet 3 wad **4** ball, shot **6** sphere **10** projectile

Pellinore *slayer:* **6** Gawain *son:* **5** Torre **6** Dornar **7** Lamerok **8** Percival **9** Agglovale

pell-mell 5 chaos, snarl **6** muddle, rashly **7** chaotic, clutter, hastily **8** confused, disarray, disorder, headlong, reckless **9** confusion, haphazard, hurriedly **10** carelessly, heedlessly **11** hurry-scurry **13** helter-skelter

pellucid 5 clear, plain, sheer **6** limpid **7** crystal, evident, obvious **8** clear-cut, luminous **9** unblurred **10** see-through **11** crystalline, transparent

Pelops *father:* **8** Tantalus *son:* **6** Atreus **8** Pittheus, Thyestes *wife:* **10** Hippodamia

pelota 4 ball **7** jai alai

pelt 3 fur, run **4** beat, blow, dash, drub, hide, hurl, rush, skin, whop **5** hurry, pound, scoot, speed, strip, throw, whack **6** assail, batter, pepper, pummel, strike, wallop **7** bombard, hotfoot

pen 3 sty **4** cage, coop, jail, swan **5** pound, quill, write **6** cooler, corral, indite, prison, shut in, stylus, writer **7** close in, confine, enclose, fence in **9** ballpoint, enclosure

penal 8 punitive **12** correctional, disciplinary

penalize 4 dock, fine **5** mulct **6** punish **7** deprive **8** handicap **10** discipline **12** disadvantage

penalty 4 fine, loss **5** mulct **7** damages, forfeit **8** hardship **10** amercement, forfeiture, punishment **12** disadvantage

penance 4 rite **7** penalty **8** hardship **9** atonement **10** punishment

penchant 4 bent **5** taste **6** liking **7** leaning **8** affinity, fondness, tendency **9** inclining **10** partiality, proclivity, propensity **11** inclination **12** predilection

pendant 4 flag, jack, rope **7** fixture **8** ornament **10** supplement

pendent 7 hanging **9** suspended, undecided, unsettled **11** overhanging **12** undetermined

pending 6 during **8** awaiting, imminent **9** undecided, unsettled **12** undetermined

___ **Pendragon** 5 Uther

pendulous 7 hanging 8 dangling, drooping, wavering 9 faltering, suspended, tentative, uncertain 10 hesitating, indecisive 11 vacillating

Penelope *father:* 7 Icarius *father-in-law:* 7 Laertes *husband:* 7 Ulysses 8 Odysseus *mother:* 8 Periboea *son:* 10 Telemachus *suitor:* 7 Agelaus

penetrable 6 porous 8 pervious 9 permeable

penetrate 3 jab 4 bore, go in, stab 5 break, drive, enter, probe, touch 6 affect, charge, invade, pierce 7 pervade 8 discover, encroach, perceive, permeate, puncture, saturate 9 percolate, perforate 10 understand

penetrating 4 keen 5 acute, sharp 6 astute, shrewd 8 incisive, piercing 9 trenchant 10 discerning, insightful, perceptive 11 quick-witted, sharp-witted 12 sharp-sighted

Peneus *daughter:* 6 Daphne *father:* 7 Oceanus *mother:* 6 Tethys

penguin type 6 Adélie

___ **Penh** 5 Phnom

peninsula 4 neck 10 chersonese *Alaska:* 5 Kenai 6 Seward *Australia:* 6 Tasman *Barents Sea:* 5 Kanin *British colony:* 9 Gibraltar *Canada:* 8 Labrador *Chile:* 5 Swett *Costa Rica:* 3 Osa *Croatia:* 6 Istria *Denmark:* 7 Jutland *eastern United States:* 8 Delmarva *Estonia:* 5 Sorve *Florida:* 8 Pinellas 9 Canaveral *France:* 5 Giens *Greece:* 4 Acte 10 Chalcidice 11 Peloponnese 12 Peloponnesus *Guam:* 5 Orote *Hong Kong:* 7 Kowloon *Honshu:* 3 Izu 5 Miura *Massachusetts:* 7 Cape Ann, Cape Cod *Mexico:* 7 Yucatan 14 Baja California *Michigan:* 8 Keweenaw *Middle East:* 5 Sinai *New Guinea:* 4 Huon *New Jersey:* 9 Sandy Hook *New Zealand:* 5 Banks, Mahia *Nunavut:* 7 Boothia 8 Melville *Ontario:* 5 Bruce *Persian Gulf:* 9 Ras Tanura *Quebec:* 5 Gaspé *Russia:* 4 Kola 5 Taman, Yamal 6 Kolski, Taimyr 9 Kamchatka *Scotland:* 7 Kintyre *South Australia:* 4 Eyre 5 Yorke *Southeast Asia:* 5 Malay 9 Indochina *southeastern Europe:* 6 Balkan *southwestern Asia:* 6 Arabia 7 Arabian *southwestern Europe:* 7 Iberian *Texas:* 9 Matagorda *Tierra del Fuego:* 5 Mitre *Turkey:* 8 Anatolia 9 Asia Minor *Ukraine:* 5 Kerch *Wales:* 5 Gower, Lleyn *Washington:* 7 Olympic *Wisconsin:* 4 Door

Peninsular State 7 Florida

penitence 3 rue 4 ruth 6 regret, sorrow 7 anguish, remorse 8 distress, humbling 10 contrition, repentance 11 compunction, self-reproof 12 self-reproach

penitent 5 sorry 6 rueful 8 contrite 9 regretful, repentant 10 apologetic, remorseful

penitentiary see PRISON

penman 5 clerk 6 author, scribe, writer 7 copyist 9 scrivener 12 calligrapher

penmanship 4 hand 5 style 6 script 7 writing 11 calligraphy, chirography, handwriting

pen name 6 anonym 9 pseudonym 10 nom de plume *Addison, Joseph:* 4 Clio *Arouet, François-Marie:* 8 Voltaire *Beyle, Marie-Henri:* 8 Stendhal *Blair, Eric:* 12 George Orwell *Brontë, Anne:* 9 Acton Bell *Brontë, Charlotte:* 10 Currer Bell *Brontë, Emily:* 9 Ellis Bell *Clemens, Samuel:* 9 Mark Twain *Dickens, Charles:* 3 Boz *Dodgson, Charles Lutwidge:* 12 Lewis Carroll *Dupin, Amandine-Aurore:* 10 George Sand *Evans, Mary Ann:* 11 George Eliot *Faust, Frederick:* 8 Max Brand *Franklin, Benjamin:* 11 Poor Richard *Geisel, Theodore:* 7 Dr. Seuss *Glidden, Frederick:* 9 Luke Short *Lamb, Charles:* 4 Elia *Munro, Hector Hugh:* 4 Saki *Poquelin, Jean-Baptiste:* 7 Molière *Porter, William Sidney:* 6 O. Henry *Ramé, Maria Louise:* 5 Ouida *Thibault, Jacques-Anatole-François:* 13 Anatole France *Viaud, Louis-Marie-Julien:* 10 Pierre Loti

pennant 4 flag, jack 5 color 6 banner, ensign 8 standard, streamer 9 banderole 12 championship

penniless 4 poor 5 broke, needy 8 bankrupt, indigent 9 destitute, insolvent 11 impecunious

pennon 4 flag, jack, wing 5 color 6 banner, ensign 8 bannerol, gonfalon, streamer 9 banderole, oriflamme

Pennsylvania *capital:* 10 Harrisburg *city:* 4 Erie 7 Reading 8 Scranton 9 Allentown 10 Pittsburgh 12 Philadelphia *college, university:* 6 Drexel, Lehigh, Temple 7 LaSalle 8 Bryn Mawr, Bucknell 9 Dickinson, Lafayette, Penn State, Villanova 10 Swarthmore 14 Carnegie Mellon *mountain range:* 6 Pocono *nickname:* 8 Keystone (State) *river:* 9 Allegheny 10 Schuylkill 11 Monongahela, Susquehanna *state bird:* 12 ruffed grouse *state flower:* 14 mountain laurel *state tree:* 7 hemlock

penny-pincher 5 miser 7 niggard, scrooge 8 tightwad 9 skinflint 10 cheapskate

penny-pinching 4 mean 6 frugal, stingy, thrift 7 miserly, thrifty 9 frugality, niggardly, parsimony, penurious 11 tightfisted 12 cheeseparing, parsimonious

penny-wise 5 canny, tight **6** frugal, stingy **7** prudent, sparing, thrifty **9** provident **10** economical **12** parsimonious

pen point 3 neb, nib

pension 3 inn **5** hotel, lodge **6** hostel, reward **7** annuity, auberge, payment, stipend **8** gratuity **9** allowance **12** room and board, roominghouse **13** boardinghouse

pensioner 7 retiree

pensive 3 sad **6** dreamy, musing **7** wistful **10** meditative, melancholy, reflective, ruminative, thoughtful **11** preoccupied **13** contemplative

Pentateuch 5 Torah *books:* **6** Exodus **7** Genesis, Numbers **9** Leviticus **11** Deuteronomy

Penthesilea *queen of:* **7** Amazons *slayer:* **8** Achilles

Pentheus *grandfather:* **6** Cadmus *king of:* **6** Thebes *mother:* **5** Agave

penumbra 4 veil **5** cover, shade **6** fringe, screen, shadow, shroud **7** curtain

penurious 4 mean, poor **5** needy, tight **6** frugal, stingy **7** miserly **8** indigent, stinting **9** destitute, niggardly **11** impecunious, tightfisted **12** impoverished, parsimonious **13** penny-pinching

penury 4 need, want **7** beggary, poverty **8** distress **9** indigence, privation, pauperism **11** destitution, needfulness

peon 4 serf **5** slave **6** drudge, toiler **7** laborer, peasant **11** galley slave *Anglo-Saxon:* **4** esne

peonage 4 yoke **6** thrall **7** bondage, helotry, serfdom, slavery **9** servitude, thralldom, villenage **11** enslavement

people 3 kin **4** folk **5** plebs **6** public **7** society **8** populace **9** commoners, community, plebeians **10** commonalty **11** inhabitants, rank and file, third estate

pep 3 vim **4** brio, dash **5** moxie, punch, verve, vigor **6** energy **7** sparkle **8** vitality, vivacity **10** get-up-and-go, liveliness **11** high spirits

pepo 5 gourd, melon **6** squash **7** pumpkin **8** cucumber

pepper 4 pelt **5** chili **6** season, shower **7** cayenne, paprika, pimento, tabasco **8** capsicum, cascabel, chipotle, habanero, jalapeño, pimiento, sprinkle **9** condiment, seasoning **12** Scotch bonnet

peppery 3 hot **5** cross, fiery, sharp, spicy, testy, zesty **6** biting, lively, snappy, touchy **7** piquant, pungent **8** choleric, poignant, seasoned, stinging **9** irascible, irritable **11** hot-tempered **13** quick-tempered

peppy 5 alert, perky **6** active, bright, lively **7** vibrant **8** animated, spirited, vigorous **9** energetic, sprightly, vivacious

___ **Pepys 6** Samuel

Pequod *cabin boy:* **3** Pip *captain:* **4** Ahab *harpooner:* **6** Daggoo **8** Queequeg, Tashtego *mate:* **8** Starbuck

per 3 via **4** a pop, each, with **6** apiece **7** by way of, for each, through **9** by means of **12** individually

perambulate 4 walk **6** ramble, stroll **8** traverse **9** promenade

per capita 4 each **6** apiece, by each **7** equally, for each

perceive 3 see **4** espy, feel, know, mark, note **5** grasp, seize, sense **6** detect, notice, remark **7** discern, observe, realize **8** identify **9** apprehend, recognize **10** comprehend, understand

percentage 3 cut **4** part **5** piece, share, slice **6** profit **7** portion **9** advantage **10** commission, proportion **11** probability

perceptible 5 clear **6** marked **7** visible **8** apparent, definite, distinct, palpable, sensible, tangible **10** detectable, noticeable, observable **11** appreciable, discernible **12** recognizable

perception 4 idea **5** grasp, image **6** acumen, notion **7** concept, feeling, insight, thought **9** awareness, cognition **10** impression **11** discernment, observation **12** appreciation **13** understanding

perceptive 4 keen, sage, wise **5** acute, alert, aware, sharp **7** knowing **9** intuitive, observant, sagacious, sensitive **10** discerning, insightful, responsive **13** understanding

perch 3 bar, peg, set **4** fish, land, rest, seat **5** light, roost, sit on **6** alight, settle **7** set down, sit atop, sit down

perchance 5 maybe **7** perhaps **8** possibly **11** conceivably

percipience 6 acumen **8** keenness **9** cognition, intuition **10** astuteness **11** discernment **12** appreciation, perspicacity **13** comprehension

percolate 4 drip, ooze, seep **5** exude **6** charge, filter, simmer, spread **7** pervade, trickle **9** penetrate

percussion 3 jar **4** bump, jolt **5** clash, crash, shock **6** impact **9** collision **10** concussion *instrument:* (see at MUSICAL INSTRUMENT)

Perdita *father:* **7** Leontes *mother:* **8** Hermione

perdition 4 hell **5** hades **7** inferno **9** damnation **10** underworld **11** netherworld

Père Goriot *author* **6** Balzac (Honoré de)

peregrination 4 trek, trip, walk 7 journey, travels 9 traversal 10 expedition

peremptory 5 bossy, final 7 haughty 8 absolute, arrogant, decisive, dogmatic, imperial 9 imperious, masterful 10 autocratic, commanding, disdainful, high-handed, imperative 11 dictatorial, domineering, magisterial, overbearing

perennial 7 durable 8 constant, enduring, lifelong 9 continual, long-lived, permanent, perpetual, recurrent, unceasing 10 continuing, persistent, persisting, unchanging 11 long-lasting

Perez *brother:* 5 Zerah *father:* 5 Judah *mother:* 5 Tamar

perfect 4 full, pure 5 exact, ideal, model, right, sound, total, utter, whole 6 entire, expert, intact, polish, proper, refine 7 correct, improve, precise 8 absolute, accurate, complete, finished, flawless, outright, peerless, spotless, unbroken, unflawed 9 downright, excellent, faultless, matchless, stainless, unalloyed, undamaged, undiluted 10 consummate, impeccable, proficient 11 unequivocal, unmitigated, unqualified

perfection 4 acme 5 ideal 6 purity, virtue 7 paragon 9 integrity, wholeness 10 excellence, excellency 11 saintliness 12 completeness, flawlessness, transcendence 13 faultlessness

perfectly 5 fully, quite 6 wholly 7 to a turn, utterly 8 entirely 10 altogether, completely, thoroughly

perfidious 5 false 6 untrue 8 disloyal 9 deceitful, dishonest, faithless 10 treasonous, traitorous, unfaithful, unreliable 11 treacherous

perfidy 6 deceit 7 falsity, sellout, treason 8 betrayal 9 falseness, treachery 10 disloyalty, infidelity 13 faithlessness

perforate 3 pit 4 bore 5 drill, prick, punch 6 pierce 8 puncture 9 penetrate

perform 3 act 4 play, work 5 enact 6 behave, comply, effect 7 achieve, execute, fulfill, operate, playact, present, satisfy 8 bring off, carry out, complete, function 9 discharge, entertain, implement 10 accomplish

performance 3 act 4 deed, feat, show, work 6 acting, action 7 conduct, display 8 behavior, efficacy, exercise 9 discharge, execution, operation 10 efficiency, exhibition 11 achievement, fulfillment 12 presentation

performer 4 doer, mime 5 actor, mimic 6 mummer, player 7 actress, artiste, trouper 8 thespian 9 playactor 12 impersonator

perfume 4 balm 5 aroma, cense, scent, smell, spice 6 sachet 7 bouquet, incense, odorize 9 aromatize, fragrance, redolence *source:* 4 musk 5 attar, myrrh, orris 8 bergamot

perfumer 6 Chanel (Coco)

perfunctory 7 cursory, routine 8 careless 9 automatic 10 impersonal, mechanical 11 superficial

pergola 5 arbor, bower 7 trellis

perhaps 5 maybe 8 feasibly, possibly 9 perchance 11 conceivably

periapt see AMULET

Pericles *father:* 10 Xanthippus *mistress:* 7 Aspasia *mother:* 8 Agariste

peril 4 risk 6 danger, hazard, menace 8 exposure, jeopardy 9 liability 12 endangerment

perilous 5 hairy, risky 6 chancy, unsafe 7 unsound 9 dangerous, desperate, hazardous, uncertain 11 treacherous

___ **Perilous** 5 Siege

perimeter 4 edge 5 limit, verge 6 border, bounds, margin 8 boundary

period 3 age, end, era 4 span, stop, term, time 5 cycle, phase, point, spell, stage 6 extent 8 division, duration, interval, sentence

periodic 6 cyclic, fitful 7 regular 8 cyclical, repeated, sporadic 9 recurrent, recurring 10 occasional 11 fluctuating 12 intermittent

periodical 5 organ 6 cyclic, review 7 journal 8 cyclical, magazine 9 alternate, newspaper, recurrent, recurring 10 isochronal 11 isochronous, publication 12 intermittent

peripatetic 6 moving, roving 7 nomadic, walking 8 ambulant, vagabond 9 itinerant, traveling, wayfaring 10 ambulatory, pedestrian, travelling 13 perambulatory

peripheral 6 remote 7 lateral, surface 8 far-flung, marginal, outlying 9 auxiliary, secondary 10 borderline, tangential 11 out-of-the-way 13 supplementary

perish 3 die, end 4 pass 5 cease 6 be lost, demise, depart, expire, vanish 7 decease, decline, go under, succumb 8 collapse, pass away 9 disappear

perjure 3 lie 6 delude 7 deceive, distort, falsify, mislead 8 forswear 9 misinform 10 equivocate 11 prevaricate

perk 4 gain, mend, plus 5 cheer, extra 7 benefit, freshen, improve, refresh, smarten 8 brighten

perky 5 alert, cocky, happy 6 bouncy, bubbly, cheery, chirpy, frisky, jaunty, lively, upbeat 7 buoyant, chipper 8 animated, cheerful, spirited, sportive 9 energetic, sparkling, sprightly, vivacious 12 effervescent, high-spirited

permanent 5 fixed 6 stable 7 abiding, durable, lasting 8 constant, enduring, hair wave 9 continual, perennial 10 changeless, invariable, unchanging 11 established, everlasting 12 imperishable

permeable 6 porous, spongy 8 pervious 9 diffusive 10 penetrable

permeate 5 imbue 6 drench, infuse, spread 7 diffuse, pervade, suffuse 8 saturate 9 penetrate, percolate 10 impregnate, infiltrate 11 pass through

permissible 4 okay 5 legal 7 allowed 8 approved 9 allowable, tolerable, tolerated 10 acceptable, authorized, sanctioned

permission 5 leave 6 assent, permit 7 consent, license 8 approval, sanction 9 agreement, allowance 11 approbation, endorsement 12 acquiescence 13 authorization

permissive 3 lax 4 open 7 lenient, liberal 8 tolerant 9 easygoing, forgiving, indulgent 10 forbearing 11 acquiescent, complaisant

permit 3 let 4 okay, pass 5 agree, allow, grant, leave 6 accede, enable, say yes, suffer 7 consent, license, warrant 8 sanction, tolerate 9 allowance, authorize, give leave 10 permission 13 authorization

permutation 6 change 7 variety, version 9 variation 10 alteration, innovation 11 arrangement, vicissitude 12 modification

pernicious 4 evil 5 fatal, toxic 6 deadly, lethal, malign, wicked 7 baleful, baneful, harmful, hurtful, killing, malefic, noxious, ruinous 8 damaging, sinister, virulent 9 injurious, malignant, offensive, poisonous 10 maleficent 11 deleterious, destructive, detrimental, devastating

Pernod flavor 5 anise 8 licorice

perorate 5 speak 7 declaim, lecture 8 bloviate, harangue, proclaim 9 hold forth

perpend 5 study, weigh 6 ponder 7 examine, reflect 8 consider, think out 9 reflect on, think over 10 excogitate, think about 11 contemplate

perpendicular 5 plumb, sheer, steep 7 upright 8 straight, vertical 11 precipitate, precipitous

perpetrate 6 commit, effect 7 inflict, execute, perform 8 carry out 10 bring about

perpetual 7 endless, eternal, undying 8 constant, unending 9 ceaseless, continual, incessant, perennial, recurrent, unceasing 10 continuous 11 everlasting, unremitting

perpetuate 7 sustain 8 conserve, continue, eternize, maintain, preserve 9 keep alive 10 eternalize 11 immortalize

perplex 5 befog, mix up, stump 6 baffle, bemuse, muddle, puzzle 7 buffalo, confuse, mystify, nonplus, perturb 8 befuddle, bewilder, confound, distract, entangle 9 dumbfound 10 discompose

perquisite 3 tip 4 gain 5 right 6 profit 7 benefit, payment 8 gratuity 9 privilege

per se 6 as such, solely 8 in itself 11 essentially 13 intrinsically

persecute 4 bait, ride 5 annoy, harry, hound, worry, wrong 6 badger, harass, hector, injure, molest, pester, pick on, plague, punish, pursue 7 afflict, oppress, torment, torture 8 aggrieve

Persephone 4 Kore 10 Proserpina *father:* 4 Zeus 7 Jupiter *husband:* 5 Hades, Pluto *mother:* 5 Ceres 7 Demeter

Perseus *father:* 4 Zeus 7 Jupiter *grandfather:* 8 Acrisius *mother:* 5 Danaë *victim:* 6 Medusa 8 Acrisius *wife:* 9 Andromeda

perseverance 8 tenacity 9 diligence, endurance 10 dedication 11 persistence 13 steadfastness

persevere see PERSIST

Persia 4 Iran

Persian *ancient:* 4 Mede *fairy:* 4 peri *governor:* 6 satrap *language:* 5 Farsi, Parsi *mystic:* 5 sufi *poet:* 5 Hafez, Hafiz 7 Firdusi 8 Ferdowsi, Firdausi, Firdawsi, Firdousi 11 Omar Khayyám *prophet:* 9 Zoroaster *robe:* 6 caftan *sacred books:* 6 Avesta *sun-god:* 7 Mithras *title:* 4 shah *writing:* 9 cuneiform

persiflage 6 banter, joking 7 jesting, kidding, ribbing 8 badinage, raillery, repartee

persist 4 go on, last 5 abide 6 endure, hang on, keep on, linger 7 carry on, prevail 8 continue 9 persevere

persistence 8 duration 9 endurance 10 continuity 11 continuance 12 continuation

persistent 6 dogged 7 lasting 8 enduring, obdurate, stubborn 9 continual, steadfast, tenacious 10 continuing, determined, relentless, unshakable 11 persevering, unremitting

persnickety 5 fussy, picky 6 choosy 7 finicky 8 exacting 10 fastidious, particular

person 3 guy 4 self, soul 5 being, human 6 entity, mensch, mortal 8 creature, specimen 10 individual

personable 4 nice 6 genial 7 affable, amiable 8 charming, friendly, pleasant,

pleasing 9 appealing, congenial
10 attractive

personage 3 VIP 5 human 6 bigwig, figure 7 big shot, notable 8 creature, luminary, somebody 9 celebrity, character, dignitary 10 individual

personal 3 own 5 privy 7 private, special 8 peculiar 10 individual, particular

personal effects 5 stuff 10 belongings 11 possessions

personality 3 ego, VIP 4 self 6 makeup, nature, temper, traits 7 notable 8 identity, selfhood, selfness 9 celebrity, character, dignitary, qualities 10 complexion 11 disposition, singularity, temperament 13 individualism, individuality

personate 3 act 4 play 5 enact 6 embody, typify 7 perform 9 epitomize, exemplify, represent 10 illustrate

personify 6 embody, typify 8 stand for 9 actualize, epitomize, exemplify, incarnate, represent, symbolize 11 emblematize

perspective 4 view 5 angle, scene, slant, vista 7 outlook 8 position, prospect 9 viewpoint 10 standpoint 11 point of view

perspicacious 4 keen 5 acute, quick, savvy, sharp 6 astute, clever, shrewd 9 observant, sagacious 10 discerning, insightful, perceptive 11 penetrating

perspicacity 6 acumen 7 insight 8 keenness 10 astuteness, shrewdness 11 discernment, penetration, percipience

perspicuous 5 clear, lucid, plain 6 lucent, simple 7 crystal, precise 8 clear-cut, pellucid 11 unambiguous

perspiration 5 sweat

perspire see SWEAT

persuadable 4 open 7 willing 9 receptive 11 suggestible, susceptible

persuade 3 win 4 coax, lead, sell, sway, urge 5 argue 6 entice, induce, prompt 7 convert, impress, win over 8 convince 9 influence, prevail on 11 bring around

persuasion 4 kind, mind, sort, type, view 5 group 6 belief, school 7 faction, opinion 8 argument 9 character, prejudice, sentiment 10 connection, conviction 11 affiliation, description

Persuasion author 6 Austen (Jane)

persuasive 6 cogent 7 telling, winning 8 credible 10 compelling, convincing 11 influential

pert 4 bold, chic, flip, trim 5 alert, cocky, fresh, sassy, saucy, smart 6 brazen, bright, cheeky, jaunty, lively 7 forward 8 animated, flippant, spirited 9 audacious, sprightly, vivacious

pertain 5 apply, refer 6 affect, bear on,

belong, regard, relate 7 concern 8 bear upon 9 touch upon

pertinacious 4 firm 5 fixed 6 dogged, mulish 7 willful 8 resolute, stubborn 9 obstinate, tenacious 10 inflexible, persistent, unshakable, unyielding

pertinent 3 apt, fit 5 ad rem 7 apropos, fitting, germane 8 apposite, material, relevant 10 applicable 11 appropriate

perturb 5 upset, worry 6 bother 7 agitate, disturb, fluster, trouble 8 disorder, disquiet, unsettle 10 discompose, disconcert

Peru *ancient civilization:* 4 Inca *capital:* 4 Lima *city:* 5 Cusco, Cuzco 6 Callao 8 Arequipa, Trujillo *conqueror:* 7 Pizarro (Francisco) *ethnic group:* 7 Quechua *lake:* 8 Titicaca *language:* 6 Aymara 7 Quechua, Spanish *leader:* 8 Fujimori (Alberto) *monetary unit:* 3 sol *mountain, range:* 5 Andes 9 Huascarán *neighbor:* 5 Chile 6 Brazil 7 Bolivia, Ecuador 8 Colombia *river:* 6 Amazon 7 Marañón *volcano:* 5 Misti 7 El Misti 8 Yucamani

peruse 4 read, scan 5 study 6 survey 7 examine 8 consider, look over, pore over

pervade 5 imbue 6 spread 7 diffuse 8 permeate, saturate 9 penetrate, percolate, transfuse 10 impregnate

perverse 5 balky 6 cranky, mulish, ornery 7 corrupt, deviant, froward, peevish, wayward, willful 8 contrary, depraved, improper, stubborn 9 incorrect, irritable, obstinate 10 degenerate, headstrong, refractory 11 stiff-necked, wrongheaded 12 cross-grained, unreasonable

pervert 4 ruin, skew, warp 5 abuse, twist 6 debase, divert, garble, misuse 7 corrupt, debauch, deprave, distort, deviant, falsify, vitiate 8 misstate, mistreat 9 misdirect 11 misconstrue 12 misinterpret, misrepresent

pervious 4 open 6 porous 9 permeable 10 accessible, penetrable

pesky 6 vexing 7 irksome 8 annoying 9 vexatious 10 bothersome 11 troublesome

pessimist 5 cynic 9 Cassandra, defeatist, doomsayer, worrywart 11 misanthrope

pessimistic 6 gloomy, morose 7 cynical 10 despairing 11 distrustful 12 misanthropic

pest 4 bane 5 trial, worry 6 bother, plague, vermin 7 nudnick, trouble 8 irritant, nuisance, vexation 9 annoyance, tormentor

pester 3 bug, irk, nag 4 ride 5 annoy, harry, tease, worry 6 badger, bother, harass, hassle, plague **7** bedevil, disturb, torment **8** irritate

pestiferous 7 baneful, noxious **8** annoying, infected **9** infective, pestilent **10** pernicious **11** troublesome **12** pestilential

pestilence 5 curse **6** plague **7** scourge

pestilential 5 fatal **6** deadly, lethal, vexing **7** baneful, deathly, noxious, ruinous **8** annoying **10** pernicious

pestle 4 mano **6** muller *vessel:* **6** mortar

pet 3 cat, dog, hug **4** dear, kiss, love, neck, pout, sulk **5** loved **6** caress, cosset, dandle, fondle, pamper, stroke **7** beloved, cherish, darling, indulge **8** favorite, treasure **9** cherished, endearing, sulkiness

petcock 3 tap **5** valve **6** faucet, spigot

Peter Grimes composer 7 Britten (Benjamin)

peter out 4 fade, wane **5** abate, cease **6** lessen, recede, run dry **7** dwindle **8** decrease, diminish, taper off **9** drain away

Peter Pan *author:* **6** Barrie (James) *character:* **5** Wendy **7** Michael **9** Tiger Lily **10** Tinker Bell *dog:* **4** Nana *pirate:* **4** Hook, Smee

Peter the Apostle *brother:* **6** Andrew *father:* **5** Jonah *original name:* **5** Simon

Peter the Great *father:* **6** Alexis *wife:* **7** Eudoxia **9** Catherine

petite 5 small **6** little **8** smallish **10** diminutive

petition 3 ask **4** plea **5** plead **6** appeal **7** beseech, entreat, implore, request, solicit **8** entreaty **10** supplicate **11** application **12** supplication

Petrarch's beloved 5 Laura

Petrified Forest author 8 Sherwood (Robert)

petrify 4 daze, numb, stun **5** chill, scare **6** benumb, deaden, harden **7** startle **8** confound, frighten, paralyze

Petruchio's wife 9 Katharina, Katharine

pettifogger 7 shyster **8** quibbler **9** nitpicker

petty 4 mean **5** minor, small **6** measly, narrow, paltry **7** trivial **8** niggling, picayune, piddling, trifling **9** frivolous, secondary **10** irrelevant, negligible **11** small-minded, subordinate, unimportant **13** insignificant

petty officer 6 noncom

petulant 5 huffy, moody, sulky, testy, whiny **6** touchy **7** grouchy, peevish **8** snappish **9** irascible, irritable, querulous **10** ill-humored

pew 3 row **4** seat **5** bench

peyote 6 cactus, mescal *drug:* **9** mescaline

Phaedra *father:* **5** Minos *husband:* **7** Theseus *mother:* **8** Pasiphaë *sister:* **7** Ariadne *stepson:* **10** Hippolytus

Phaëthon's father 6 Helios **7** Phoebus

phalanx 4 army, host, mass **5** horde **6** myriad, throng **6** troops

phantasm 5 dream, fancy, ghost **6** spirit, vision **7** fantasy, fiction, figment, specter, spectre **8** daydream, delusion, illusion **9** invention **10** apparition **11** fabrication **13** hallucination

phantom 5 dummy, ghost, shade, spook **6** goblin, shadow, spirit, vision **7** bugbear, chimera, eidolon, specter, spectre **8** illusory **9** imaginary **10** apparition, fictitious **12** will-o'-the-wisp

pharaoh 3 Tut **4** Seti **5** Menes, ruler **6** Ahmose, Ramses, tyrant **7** Harmhab **8** Ikhnaton, Thutmose **9** Amenhotep, Merneptah **11** Tutankhamen

pharisee 9 hypocrite

pharmacist 8 druggist **10** apothecary *British:* **7** chemist

pharos 6 beacon **10** lighthouse

Pharsalus, battle of *vanquished:* **6** Pompey *victor:* **6** Caesar (Julius)

phase 4 part, side, view **5** point, stage, state **6** adjust, aspect **7** conduct **8** carry out, position **9** condition, situation, viewpoint **10** appearance

PhD exam 5 orals

Phèdre author 6 Racine (Jean)

phenomenal 6 actual **7** unusual **8** material, physical, sensible, singular, tangible, uncommon **9** corporeal, fantastic, objective **10** remarkable **11** exceptional, outstanding, perceivable, perceptible, substantial **13** extraordinary

phenomenon 4 fact **5** event **6** marvel, object, rarity, wonder **7** miracle, reality **9** actuality, sensation **10** experience, uniqueness **11** peculiarity, singularity

Phi ___ Kappa 4 Beta

philander 8 womanize

philanthropic 6 giving, humane **8** generous **10** altruistic, benevolent, bighearted, charitable **11** magnanimous **12** eleemosynary, humanitarian

philanthropist *American:* **5** Gates (Bill) **6** Cooper (Peter), Girard (Stephen), Mellon (Andrew) **7** Cornell (Ezra), Eastman (George), Packard (David), Whitney (Gertrude Vanderbilt) **8** Carnegie (Andrew), Stanford (Leland) **9** Rosenwald (Julius) **10** Vanderbilt (Cornelius) **11** Rockefeller (J. D.) *English:* **11** Wilberforce (William) *Swedish:* **5** Nobel (Alfred)

Philemon's wife 6 Baucis

philharmonic 8 symphony **9** orchestra, symphonic

Philip of Macedonia *father:* 7 Amyntas *son:* 9 Alexander

philippic 6 tirade 8 diatribe, harangue, jeremiad 12 condemnation

Philippics author 6 Cicero

Philippines *capital:* 6 Manila *city:* 4 Cebu 5 Davao 10 Quezon City *discoverer:* 8 Magellan (Ferdinand) *island:* 4 Cebu 5 Leyte, Luzon, Panay, Samar 6 Negros 7 Masbate, Mindoro, Palawan 8 Mindanao *language:* 7 Ilocano, Tagalog 8 Filipino, Pilipino *leader:* 6 Aquino (Corazon), Marcos (Ferdinand) *liberator:* 9 MacArthur (Douglas) *patriot:* 5 Rizal (José) *monetary unit:* 4 peso *sea:* 4 Sulu 5 Samar 7 Celebes, Sibuyan, Visayan 8 Mindanao 10 Philippine, South China *volcano:* 4 Taal 5 Mayon

Philippi victor 6 Antony (Marc, Mark) 8 Octavian

Philip the Tetrarch *father:* 5 Herod *mother:* 9 Cleopatra

philistine 4 boob 7 Babbitt 9 bourgeois, vulgarian 10 capitalist 11 materialist

Philistine *champion:* 7 Goliath *city:* 4 Gath, Gaza 5 Ekron 6 Ashdod 8 Ashkelon *foe:* 5 David 6 Samson *god:* 5 Dagon

Philoctetes *father:* 5 Poeas *victim:* 5 Paris

Philomela 11 nightingale *father:* 7 Pandion *ravisher:* 6 Tereus *sister:* 6 Procne

philosopher *American:* 5 Adler (Mortimer), Dewey (John), James (William), Quine (Willard), Rorty (Richard), Royce (Josiah) 6 Langer (Susanne), Peirce (C. S.) 7 Marcuse (Herbert), Mumford (Lewis), Strauss (Leo) 9 Santayana (George) *Arab:* 8 Averroës, Avicenna *Austrian:* 6 Popper (Karl) 12 Wittgenstein (Ludwig) *Chinese:* 5 Laoxi 6 Lao-tsu 7 Dai Zhen, Mencius, Tai Chen 9 Confucius *Danish:* 11 Kierkegaard (Soren) *Dutch:* 7 Erasmus (Desiderius), Spinoza (Baruch de) *English:* 4 Ayer (A. J.), Mill (John Stuart), More (Henry, Thomas), Watt (James) 5 Bacon (Francis), Burke (Edmund), Locke (John), Moore (G. E.), Occam (William of), Paine (Thomas) 6 Berlin (Isaiah), Hobbes (Thomas), Huxley (Thomas), Ockham (William), Popper (Karl) 7 Bentham (Jeremy), Russell (Bertrand), Spencer (Herbert), Whewell (William) 9 Whitehead (Alfred North) 12 Wittgenstein (Ludwig) *Finnish:* 11 Westermarck (Edward) *French:* 4 Weil (Simone) 5 Comte (Auguste), Taine (Hippolyte) 6 Pascal (Blaise), Sartre (Jean-Paul), Valéry (Paul) 7 Abelard (Peter), Bergson (Henri), Derrida (Jacques), Diderot (Denis), Fourier (Charles) 8 Foucault (Michel), Maritain (Jacques), Rousseau (Jean-Jacques), Voltaire 9 Descartes (René), Montaigne (Michel de) 10 Saint-Simon (Comte de) 11 Montesquieu (Baron de) 12 Merleau-Ponty (Maurice) *German:* 4 Kant (Immanuel), Marx (Karl) 5 Frege (Gottlob), Hegel (Georg Wilhelm Friedrich), Wolff (Christian von) 6 Carnap (Rudolf), Fichte (Immanuel, Johann), Herder (Johann von) 7 Husserl (Edmund), Jaspers (Karl), Leibniz (Gottfried) 8 Spengler (Oswald) 9 Heidegger (Martin), Nietzsche (Friedrich), Schelling (Friedrich von) 12 Schopenhauer (Arthur) 14 Albertus Magnus *Greek:* 4 Zeno 5 Plato, Timon 6 Thales 7 Gorgias, Proclus 8 Diogenes, Epicurus, Longinus, Socrates 9 Aristotle, Epictetus 10 Anaxagoras, Democritus, Empedocles, Heraclitus, Parmenides, Protagoras, Pythagoras, Xenocrates, Xenophanes 11 Anaximander 12 Theophrastus *Irish:* 8 Berkeley (George) *Italian:* 5 Croce (Benedetto) 6 Ficino (Marsilio) 11 Machiavelli (Niccolo) *Jewish:* 5 Buber (Martin), Philo 10 Maimonides (Moses) 12 Philo Judaeus *Roman:* 6 Seneca (Lucias Annaeus) 8 Boethius (Anicius), Plotinus 9 Lucretius *Scottish:* 4 Hume (David), Mill (James), Reid (Thomas) 7 Stewart (Dugald) *Spanish:* 6 Suárez (Francisco) 7 Unamuno (Miguel de) 13 Ortega y Gasset (José) *Swedish:* 10 Swedenborg (Emanuel)

philosopher's stone 3 key 6 elixir

philosophical 4 calm 7 stoical 8 composed, rational, resigned 9 unruffled 10 thoughtful

philosophy 6 system, theory, values 7 beliefs, inquiry 8 attitude, calmness 10 discipline *component:* 5 logic 6 ethics 10 aesthetics 11 metaphysics 12 epistemology

philter 4 drug 5 charm, tonic 6 potion 9 stimulant 10 love potion 11 aphrodisiac, restorative

Phineas *beloved:* 9 Andromeda *tormentors:* 7 Harpies *wife:* 9 Cleopatra

phlegm 5 humor, mucus 6 apathy 8 calmness, coolness, dullness 9 composure, sangfroid 10 equanimity 11 impassivity, nonchalance 12 indifference

phlegmatic 4 calm, cool, dull 5 aloof, stoic 6 stolid 8 detached 9 apathetic, impassive, lethargic 11 indifferent, unconcerned

Phlegyas *daughter:* 7 Coronis *father:* 4 Ares, Mars *son:* 5 Ixion

phobia see FEAR

Phobos 4 moon 9 satellite *brother:* 6 Deimos *father:* 4 Ares, Mars

Phocus *father:* 6 Aeacus 8 Ornytion *half brother:* 6 Peleus 7 Telamon *mother:* 8 Psamathe *slayer:* 6 Peleus 7 Telamon *wife:* 7 Antiope

Phoebe 5 Diana 7 Artemis *daughter:* 4 Leto *father:* 9 Leucippus *mother:* 4 Gaea

Phoebus see APOLLO

Phoenician *city:* 4 Acre, Tyre 5 Sidon *colony:* 8 Carthage *god:* 4 Baal 6 Eshmun *goddess:* 6 Baltis 7 Astarte

Phoenix *pupil:* 8 Achilles *sister:* 6 Europa *team:* 4 Suns 7 Coyotes 9 Cardinals 12 Diamondbacks

phony 4 fake, sham 5 bogus, cheat, faker, false, fraud 6 humbug, pseudo 8 impostor, specious, spurious 9 charlatan, dishonest, pretender 10 ficticious, suspicious 11 counterfeit 12 hypocritical

photograph 3 pic 4 film, snap 5 shoot 6 glossy 7 picture, tintype 8 snapshot *three-dimensional:* 8 hologram

photographer 8 photoist 9 cameraman 10 shutterbug *famous:* 3 Ray (Man) 4 Capa (Cornell, Robert), Haas (Ernst), Hine (Lewis), Penn (Irving), Riis (Jacob) 5 Adams (Ansel), Arbus (Diane), Atget (Eugène), Brady (Mathew), Evans (Frederick, Walker), Horst (Horst Peter), Karsh (Yousuf), Lange (Dorothea), Model (Lisette), Nadar, Parks (Gordon), Ritts (Herb), Smith (W. Eugene), Weber (Bruce), White (Clarence, Minor) 6 Abbott (Berenice), Avedon (Richard), Beaton (Cecil), Brandt (Bill), Coburn (Alvin), Curtis (Edward S.), Newton (Helmut), Porter (Eliot), Rowell (Galen), Siegel (Eliot), Strand (Paul), Talbot (William Henry Fox), Weegee, Wegman (William), Weston (Brett, Edward) 7 Brassaï, Cameron (Julia Margaret), Emerson (Peter), Halsman (Philippe), Jackson (William Henry), Kertész (André), Salomon (Erich), Siskind (Aaron), Snowdon (Earl of), Thomson (John), Watkins (Carleton) 8 Callahan (Harry), Cosindas (Marie), Daguerre (Louis-Jacques-Mandé), Kasebier (Gertrude), Scavullo (Francesco), Steichen (Edward), Steinert (Otto) 9 Caponigro (Paul), Feininger (Andreas), Leibovitz (Annie), Meyrowitz (Joel), Muybridge (Eadweard), O'Sullivan (Timothy), Rejlander (Oscar), Rothstein (Arthur), Stieglitz (Alfred), Winogrand (Garry) 10 Cunningham (Imogen), Heartfield (John), Moholy-Nagy (Laszlo) 11 Bourke-White (Margaret), Eisenstaedt (Alfred) 12 Mapplethorpe (Robert)

photographic 5 exact, vivid 7 graphic 8 accurate, detailed 9 pictorial 11 picturesque *solution:* 4 hypo 5 fixer, toner 7 reducer 9 developer

phrase 5 couch, frame, idiom 6 slogan 7 diction, express, styling, wording 8 locution, verbiage 9 catchword, formulate, verbalism, watchword 10 expression

Phrygian *god:* 4 Atys 5 Attis *goddess:* 6 Cybele *king:* 5 Midas 7 Gordius

phylactery 5 charm 6 amulet 7 periapt 8 talisman

physic 4 cure, heal 5 purge 6 remedy 8 medicine 9 cathartic, purgative 10 medication

physical 4 real 5 lusty, rough 6 actual, bodily, carnal, sexual 7 fleshly, natural, somatic 8 concrete, corporal, material, sensible, tangible 9 corporeal, objective 10 phenomenal 11 perceivable, perceptible, substantial

physician 3 doc 5 medic 6 doctor, medico 7 surgeon 8 sawbones *American:* 4 Rush (Benjamin), Salk (Jonas) 5 Minot (George), Spock (Benjamin), Still (Andrew) 6 Jarvik (Robert), Murphy (John), Weller (Thomas) 7 Huggins (Charles), Robbins (Frederick), Theiler (Max) 8 Richards (Dickinson) 9 Sternberg (George Miller) *Arab:* 8 Avicenna *Canadian:* 5 Osler (William) *English:* 4 Ross (Ronald) 6 Harvey (William), Jenner (Edward, William), Willis (Thomas) 8 Sydenham (Thomas) *French:* 5 Widal (Fernand) 7 Laveran (Charles) 10 Schweitzer (Albert) *German:* 7 Sylvius (Franciscus) *Greek:* 5 Galen 11 Hippocrates *Italian:* 7 Galvani (Luigi) *South African:* 7 Barnard (Christiaan) *Swiss:* 10 Paracelsus (see also NOBEL PRIZE WINNER *physiology or medicine;* SURGEON)

physicist *American:* 4 Rabi (I. I.), Ting (Samuel) 5 Fermi (Enrico), Gibbs (J. Willard), Kusch (Polykarp), Mayer (Maria-Goeppert), Pauli (Wolfgang), Pupin (Michael), Segré (Emilio), Smyth (Henry DeWolf), Stern (Otto) 6 Teller (Edward), Townes (Charles), Wigner (Eugene) 7 Alvarez (Luis), Feynman (Richard), Goddard (Robert), Purcell (Edward) 8 Einstein (Albert), Gell-Mann (Murray), McMillan (Edwin), Millikan (Clark, Robert), Mulliken (Robert), Shockley (William), Van Allen (James) 9 Michelson (Albert),

Schwinger (Julian) 11 Oppenheimer (J. Robert) *Austrian:* 4 Mach (Ernst) 7 Doppler (Christian) 11 Schrödinger (Erwin) *British:* 4 Snow (C. P.) 5 Dirac (P. A. M.), Jeans (James), Joule (James) 6 Dalton (John), Kelvin (Baron), Newton (Isaac), Powell (Cecil), Stokes (George) 7 Faraday (Michael), Hodgkin (Dorothy), Thomson (George, Joseph, William), Tyndall (John) 8 Rayleigh (Lord), Robinson (Robert), Thompson (Benjamin, Silvanus) 9 Wollaston (William) 10 Richardson (Owen), Rutherford (Ernest), Wheatstone (Charles) *Chinese:* 4 Yang (Chen Ning) *Danish:* 4 Bohr (Aage, Niels) *Dutch:* 6 Zeeman (Pieter) 7 Huygens (Christian), Lorentz (Hendrik), Zernike (Frits) 11 Van der Waals (Johannes) *French:* 4 Néel (Louis) 5 Arago (François) 6 Ampère (André-Marie), Perrin (Jean-Baptiste) 7 Coulomb (Charles-Augustin de), Kastler (Alfred), Réaumur (René-Antoine de) 8 Lippmann (Gabriel) *German:* 3 Ohm (Georg) 4 Laue (Max von), Wien (Wilhelm) 5 Hertz (Gustav, Heinrich), Stark (Johannes) 6 Jensen (Hans), Lenard (Philipp), Nernst (Walther), Planck (Max) 7 Meitner (Lise) 8 Roentgen (Wilhelm) 9 Helmholtz (Hermann von), Kirchhoff (Gustav), Mossbauer (Rudolf) 10 Fahrenheit (Daniel), Hofstadter (Robert) *Indian:* 5 Raman (Chandrasekhara) *Irish:* 6 Walton (Ernest) *Italian:* 5 Rossi (Bruno), Volta (Alessandro) 7 Galileo (Galilei), Galvani (Luigi) 10 Torricelli (Evangelista) *Japanese:* 6 Yukawa (Hideki) 8 Tomonaga (Shinichiro) *Mexican:* 8 Vallarta (Manuel) *Russian:* 4 Tamm (Igor) 6 Landau (Lev) 9 Prokhorov (Aleksandr) *Scottish:* 4 Tait (Peter) 6 Wilson (Charles) 7 Maxwell (James Clerk) *Swedish:* 7 Rydberg (Johannes) 8 Angstrom (Anders), Siegbahn (Kai, Karl) *Swiss:* 6 Zwicky (Fritz) 7 Piccard (Auguste) (see also NOBEL PRIZE WINNER *physics*)

physiognomy 3 mug 4 face 5 front 6 aspect, visage 7 profile 8 features 9 character 10 lineaments 11 countenance, temperament

physiologist *English:* 8 Starling (Ernest) *German:* 5 Weber (Ernst), Wundt (Wilhelm) 7 Schwann (Theodor) 9 Helmholtz (Hermann von) *Italian:* 11 Spallanzani (Lazzaro) (see also NOBEL PRIZE WINNER *physiology or medicine*)

physique 4 body, form 5 build, shape

6 figure, makeup 7 anatomy 9 structure 12 constitution

pianist *American:* 4 Nero (Peter), Wild (Earl) 5 Arrau (Claudio), Janis (Byron), Watts (André) 6 Duchin (Peter), Joplin (Scott), Serkin (Peter, Rudolf) 7 Cliburn (Van), Istomin (Eugene), Ohlsson (Garrick), Perahia (Murray), Winston (George) 8 Graffman (Gary), Horowitz (Vladimir), Pennario (Leonard) 9 Fleischer (Leon) 10 Johannesen (Grant), Rubinstein (Arthur) *Argentinian:* 8 Argerich (Martha) *Austrian:* 6 Czerny (Karl) 7 Brendel (Alfred) 8 Schnabel (Artur) *Bulgarian:* 11 Weissenberg (Alexis) *Canadian:* 5 Gould (Glenn) *Cuban:* 5 Bolet (Jorge) *English:* 4 Hess (Myra) 5 Ogdon (John) 6 Curzon (Clifford) *French:* 6 Cortot (Alfred) 7 Cziffra (Gyorgy) 9 Casadesus (Robert), Entremont (Philippe) 10 Saint-Saëns (Camille) *German:* 6 Kempff (Wilhelm) 8 Schumann (Clara) 9 Gieseking (Walter) *Hungarian:* 5 Liszt (Franz) 7 Cziffra (Gyorgy) *Italian:* 6 Busoni (Ferruccio) 7 Pollini (Maurizio) 8 Clementi (Muzio) *Japanese:* 6 Uchida (Mitsuko) *Polish:* 6 Chopin (Frédéric) 7 Hofmann (Josef) 10 Paderewski (Ignacy), Rubinstein (Arthur) *Romanian:* 4 Lupu (Radu) 7 Lipatti (Dinu) *Russian:* 6 Berman (Lazar), Gilels (Emil), Kissin (Evgeny) 7 Richter (Sviatoslav) 8 Horowitz (Vladimir), Pachmann (Vladimir von) 9 Ashkenazy (Vladimir) 10 Rubinstein (Anton) 12 Rachmaninoff (Sergey) *Spanish:* 6 Iturbi (José) 8 Granados (Enrique) 10 de Larrocha (Alicia) *Swiss:* 4 Anda (Geza)

piano 5 grand 6 softly, spinet 7 quietly, upright 9 baby grand *builder:* 5 Knabe (William), Stein (Johann), Zumpe (Johann) 7 Baldwin (Dwight) 8 Steinway (Henry) 9 Bechstein (Friedrich) 10 Chickering (Jonas), Silbermann (Johann) *inventor:* 10 Cristofori (Bartolomeo) *pedal:* 6 damper 9 sostenuto

piazza 5 patio, plaza, porch 6 square 7 balcony, gallery, portico, terrace, veranda 9 courtyard

picaroon 5 rogue, rover, thief 6 pirate 7 brigand, corsair 8 sea rover 9 buccaneer 10 freebooter

picayune 5 petty 6 measly, paltry, trifle 7 trivial 8 piddling 11 small-minded 13 insignificant

pick 3 rob, tap 4 best, carp, cull, open, pull, take, tool 5 elect, pluck, probe, prize 6 choice, choose, chosen, option, pierce, pilfer, remove, select, unlock

7 harvest, provoke 8 selected 9 exclusive, single out

picket 4 pale, post 5 fence, guard, stake, watch 6 sentry, tether 7 enclose, lookout, protest 8 palisade, sentinel, watchman 11 demonstrate

pickle 3 fix, jam 4 dill, spot 5 brine, treat 6 plight, scrape 7 dilemma, gherkin, trouble 8 marinate, preserve 10 difficulty 11 predicament

pick on 5 bully, harry, taunt, tease 6 hector, pester 9 criticize, single out

pick out 4 espy, name, spot 6 choose, descry, detect, select, take in 7 discern 8 identify, perceive 9 apprehend, ascertain, recognize 11 distinguish

pickpocket 3 dip 5 thief 6 dipper 8 cutpurse

pick up 3 buy, get 4 cull, gain, earn, land, lift, tidy 5 catch, glean, hoist, learn, raise, run in 6 arrest, detain, gather, notice, obtain, pull in, resume, revive 7 acquire, clean up, collect, restart 8 perceive 9 apprehend 10 appreciate, understand

pickup 5 truck 9 detention 10 hitchhiker 11 improvement 12 acceleration

picky 5 fussy 6 choosy 7 finicky 10 fastidious, particular, pernickety 11 persnickety

picnic 4 snap 5 cinch 6 breeze, outing 7 cookout 8 cakewalk 11 piece of cake

picture 4 limn, show 5 image, photo, pinup 7 drawing, tableau 8 describe, painting, portrait 9 depiction, portrayal 10 simulacrum 11 delineation, description 13 spitting image *stand:* 5 easel

picturesque 5 vivid 6 quaint, scenic 8 artistic, charming

piddling 4 puny 5 petty 6 meager, meagre, measly, paltry 7 trivial 8 picayune, trifling 11 Mickey Mouse, unimportant 13 insignificant

pie 4 flan, tart 5 pasty 6 pastry 7 cobbler, dessert 8 turnover

piebald 5 mixed 6 motley 7 mottled 10 multicolor

piece 4 part 5 patch, slice 6 member, parcel 7 firearm, portion, section, segment 8 division, fraction, fragment 9 allotment 10 allocation

pièce de résistance 8 main dish 9 showpiece 11 centerpiece, chef d'oeuvre, masterpiece

piecemeal 5 apart 6 slowly 7 gradual 8 bit by bit 9 by degrees, gradually 11 fragmentary

pied 6 motley 7 blotchy, brindle, dappled, mottled 8 brindled, speckled 9 multihued 10 variegated 11 varicolored 12 parti-colored

pier 4 anta, dock, quay, slip 5 berth, jetty, levee, wharf 6 column, pillar 8 pilaster *architectural:* 4 anta

pierce 3 cut 4 stab 5 probe, spear 6 impale, incise, skewer 8 puncture 9 penetrate, perforate 10 run through

piercing 4 high, keen 5 acute, sharp 6 piping, shrill 8 shooting, stabbing, strident 9 knifelike 12 earsplitting *tool:* 3 awl

piety 6 fealty 7 loyalty 8 devotion, fidelity, sanctity 9 reverence 10 allegiance, dedication, devoutness 12 faithfulness

piffle 4 bosh, bunk 5 hooey 6 drivel 7 baloney, rubbish, twaddle 8 malarkey, nonsense 10 balderdash

pig 3 hog 4 slob 5 shoat, swine 6 farrow, piglet, porker 7 casting, glutton *breed:* 5 Duroc 8 Tamworth 9 Berkshire, Hampshire, Yorkshire *female:* 3 sow 4 gilt *feral:* 9 razorback *litter:* 6 farrow *male:* 4 boar 6 barrow *meat:* 3 ham 4 pork 5 bacon 7 sausage 8 chitlins 12 chitterlings *wild:* 7 peccary, warthog 8 babirusa

pigeon 3 sap 4 dupe, fool, gull, mark 5 chump, decoy, patsy 6 culver, stooge, sucker 7 fall guy 8 rock dove *genus:* 7 Columba *house:* 4 cote, loft *kind:* 4 barb, rock 5 homer 6 homing, pouter, roller 7 carrier, crowned, fantail, tumbler *relative:* 4 dove *young:* 5 squab

pigeon hawk 6 merlin

pigeonhole 4 slot, sort 5 class, cubby, grade, group, niche 6 recess, shelve 7 catalog 8 category, classify, grouping 10 categorize 11 compartment

piggish 6 greedy 7 selfish, swinish 10 gluttonous

pigheaded 5 rigid 6 dogged, mulish 7 willful 8 contrary, perverse, stubborn 9 obstinate 10 inflexible, unyielding

piglet 5 shoat

pigment 3 dye 4 tint 5 color, paint, stain 8 colorant, dyestuff, tincture *black:* 9 lampblack *blue:* 4 cyan 5 azure, smalt 6 indigo 7 cyanine 8 cerulean 9 verdigris 11 ultramarine *brown:* 5 sepia *umber:* 6 bister, sienna *combining form:* 5 chrom 6 chromo *dark:* 7 melanin *green:* 7 celadon 8 viridian 10 biliverdin *orange:* 7 realgar 8 carotene *red:* 4 lake *toxic:* 8 gossypol *yellow:* 5 ocher, ochre 6 flavin, lutein 7 flavine, xanthin

pigpen 3 sty 4 dump, mess 5 hovel

pigskin 6 saddle 8 football

pike 4 dive, fish 5 spear 7 highway 8 pickerel

piker 5 miser 7 scrooge 8 tightwad 9 skinflint 10 cheapskate 12 pennypincher

pilaster 4 pier 6 column, pillar

pilchard 7 herring, sardine

pile 3 fur, lot, nap 4 coat, fill, heap, hill, load, mass, much, pack, peck, pyre 5 amass, crowd, drive, stack 6 bundle, column, jumble 7 collect, fortune, reactor 8 quantity 9 great deal 10 assemblage, collection 11 aggregation 12 accumulation

pileup 4 mass 5 crash, smash 8 accident 9 collision 12 accumulation

pilfer 3 rob 4 lift, take 5 filch, pinch, steal, swipe 6 finger, snitch, thieve 7 purloin 11 appropriate

pilgarlic 4 butt 8 baldhead 13 laughingstock

Pilgrim 5 Alden (John) 6 Carver (John) 7 Puritan, Winslow (Edward) 8 Bradford (William), Brewster (William), Standish (Myles)

pilgrim 5 hadji, hajji 6 palmer 8 traveler, wanderer, wayfarer

pilgrimage 4 hajj, trip 7 journey

Pilgrims' interpreter 7 Squanto

Pilgrim's Progress 8 allegory *author:* 6 Bunyan (John) *hero:* 9 Christian

pill 4 ball, bore, pain, pest 5 bolus 6 pellet 7 capsule, lozenge 8 medicine, nuisance 9 annoyance

pillage 4 lift, loot, sack 5 booty, prize, spoil, steal 6 maraud, ravage, thieve 7 despoil, plunder, purloin 8 spoliate 9 depredate, desecrate

pillar 4 pier, post, prop 5 pylon, shaft, stela, stele 6 column, stelae (plural) 7 obelisk, support, upright 8 backbone, mainstay, pedestal, pilaster

pillory 6 stocks

pillow 3 pad 4 rest 7 bolster, cushion, support

pilot 4 lead, show, tool 5 drive, flier, guide, steer 6 airman, direct, leader 7 aviator, conduct, guiding, tracing 8 aviatrix, helmsman, shepherd

pimple 3 dot, zit 4 acne, boil, spot, stud 6 papule 7 blemish, blister, pustule, speckle 8 sprinkle, swelling

pin 3 leg, peg 4 clip, hold, join 5 affix, blame, stake 6 attach, broach, brooch, cotter, emblem, fasten, secure, trifle 8 fastener, hold down, ornament, restrain

pinafore 5 apron, dress, frock

pinch 3 bit, nab, nip 4 dash, lift, pain, take 5 filch, press, prune, run in, skimp, steal, swipe, taper, theft, tweak 6 arrest, crisis, narrow, pilfer, snatch, stress 7 confine, deficit, larceny, squeeze, straits 8 compress, exigency, hardship, juncture, pressure, stealing, straiten 9 apprehend, constrict, emer-

gency, privation, tight spot 10 substitute

pinchbeck 4 fake, sham 5 alloy, bogus, false, phony 6 pseudo 8 spurious 9 brummagem 11 counterfeit

pinch hitter 3 sub 6 backup, fill-in, relief 7 stand-in 9 alternate, surrogate 10 substitute 11 alternative, replacement

pinchpenny 4 mean 5 cheap, close, mingy, tight 6 stingy 7 chintzy, costive, miserly, scrimpy 9 niggardly, penurious 11 closefisted, tightfisted 12 parsimonious

Pindar *home:* 6 Thebes *poem:* 3 ode

pine 4 ache, long, mope, sigh, tree, wish, wood 5 brood, crave, dream, yearn 6 desire, grieve, hanker, hunger, lament, thirst 7 conifer 8 languish 9 evergreen

Pine Tree State 5 Maine

pinhead 4 dolt, dope, fool 5 dunce 6 dimwit, nitwit 7 dullard 8 dumbbell 9 birdbrain

pinion 3 cog 4 bind, gear, wing 5 quill, tie up, truss 6 fetter, tether 7 disable, feather, shackle 8 cogwheel, restrain 9 hamstring

pink 3 cut 4 best, peak, stab 5 blush 6 flower, height, pierce 7 excited, paragon 9 perforate

pinna 3 ear, fin 4 wing 7 feather, leaflet

pinnacle 3 top, tor 4 acme, apex, peak 5 crest, crown, serac, spire 6 apogee, climax, height, summit, zenith 7 steeple 8 capsheaf, meridian 11 culmination

pinniped 4 seal 6 walrus

Pinocchio author 7 Collodi (Carlo) 9 Lorenzini (Carlo)

pinochle *card:* 3 ace, ten 4 jack, king, nine 5 queen *term:* 4 meld 5 widow 7 auction *two-handed:* 7 goulash

pinpoint 3 aim, fix 4 spot, tiny 5 exact, place 6 locate 7 precise 8 identify, stand out 9 determine, highlight, recognize 11 distinguish

Pinter play 8 Betrayal 9 Caretaker (The) 10 Homecoming (The)

pinto 4 pied, pony 5 horse, paint 7 mottled, piebald 8 skewbald

pint-size 3 wee 5 dwarf, small 6 midget, pocket 7 miniature 10 diminutive

pioneer 5 first, prime 6 maiden 7 explore, founder, initial, primary, settler 8 colonist, earliest, explorer, original 9 innovator 10 avant-garde, pathfinder 11 trailblazer 12 frontiersman *famous:* 5 Boone (Daniel), Bowie (Jim), Clark (William), Lewis (Meriwether) 6 Carson (Kit), Colter (John) 7 Bridger (Jim), Chapman (John),

Frémont (John C.), Whitman (Marcus) 8 Crockett (Davy)

pious 4 holy 5 godly 6 devout, worthy 7 devoted, dutiful 8 reverent, virtuous 9 hypocrite, pietistic, prayerful, religious 10 devotional 12 hypocritical

pip 3 dot 4 blip, peep, seed, spot 5 speck 9 break open

pipe 3 keg, tun 4 butt, cask, duct, hose, tube 6 barrel, convey, funnel, siphon 7 channel, conduct, conduit 8 aqueduct, hogshead *ceremonial:* 7 calumet *part:* 4 bowl, stem

pipe down 4 hush 5 dry up, quiet 6 shut up 7 be quiet

pipe dream 4 wish 7 chimera, fantasy 8 illusion

pipeline 5 works 6 system 7 channel, conduit, process 8 activity, supplier 10 connection

pipsqueak 6 shaver, squirt 7 tadpole 8 half-pint, small fry

piquant 4 tart 5 sharp, spicy, tangy, zesty 6 biting, lively, savory, snappy 7 peppery, pungent 8 poignant, spirited 9 flavorful, sparkling 10 appetizing 11 provocative, stimulating

pique 3 irk, vex 4 huff, miff, move 5 anger, annoy, peeve, pride, rouse 6 arouse, excite, nettle, offend, put out 7 dudgeon, offense, provoke, quicken 8 irritate, motivate, vexation 9 aggravate, annoyance, challenge, stimulate 10 exasperate, irritation, resentment

piracy 5 theft 7 lifting, looting, pillage, plunder, robbery 8 stealing, thievery 10 plagiarism

piranha 6 caribe

pirate 5 rover 6 looter, raider, robber, sea dog 7 brigand, corsair, sea wolf 8 marauder, picaroon, pillager, sea rover 9 buccaneer, plunderer, privateer, sea robber 10 freebooter *English:* 4 Read (Mary) 5 Bonny (Anne), Teach (Edward) 6 Morgan (Henry) 7 Dampier (William) 10 Blackbeard *flag:* 10 Jolly Roger *French:* 7 Laffite (Jean), Lafitte (Jean) *Scottish:* 4 Kidd (William)

Pirates of Penzance, The *composer:* 8 Sullivan (Arthur) *librettist:* 7 Gilbert (W. S.)

pirogue 5 canoe 6 dugout

pirouette 4 spin, turn 5 twirl, whirl

piscator 6 angler 9 fisherman

pismire 3 ant

pistol 3 gat, rod 4 Colt 5 Glock, Luger 6 Magnum, Mauser, roscoe 7 bulldog, handgun 8 revolver, small arm 9 derringer, pepperbox *case:* 7 holster

pit 3 vie 4 dent, hell, hole, scar 5 arena, hades, match, shaft, stone 6 cavity, hollow, oppose 7 counter, play off 8 pockmark 11 indentation

Pit and the Pendulum author 3 Poe (Edgar Allan)

pitch 3 dip, set 4 buck, dive, drop, fall, hurl, line, play, plug, tilt, tone, toss 5 erect, fling, heave, lurch, put up, resin, slant, sling, slope, spiel, throw 6 encamp, go down, plunge 7 discard, incline, present, promote 8 distance 9 advertise, declivity 13 advertisement

pitch-dark 3 jet 4 ebon, inky 5 black, ebony, jetty

pitcher 4 ewer, olla, toby 5 cruse 6 beaker, flagon 7 creamer *area:* 5 mound *handle:* 3 ear 4 ansa (see also BASEBALLER)

pitch in 3 aid 4 help 5 begin, set to, start 6 fall to 8 commence, get going, start off 9 subscribe, volunteer 10 contribute

piteous 3 sad 4 poor 8 pathetic 9 affecting 10 lamentable 11 distressing

pitfall 4 risk, snag, trap 5 catch, peril, snare 6 danger, hazard 9 booby trap 10 difficulty 12 entanglement

pith 3 nub 4 core, kill, meat, pulp 5 focus, heart 6 center, import, kernel 7 essence, nucleus 9 substance 10 importance 12 significance

pith helmet 5 topee

pithy 5 brief, crisp, meaty, short, terse 6 cogent 7 compact, concise, pointed 8 succinct 12 epigrammatic 13 short and sweet

pitiable 4 poor 5 cheap, sorry 8 shameful 10 deplorable, lamentable 12 contemptible

pitiful 3 sad 4 mean, poor 5 cheap, sorry 6 meager, meagre, paltry, shabby 7 forlorn 8 beggarly, pathetic, wretched 9 miserable 10 despicable, inadequate 12 contemptible 13 heartbreaking

pitiless 4 cold, hard 5 cruel, harsh, stony 6 brutal 8 inhumane, uncaring 9 barbarous, unfeeling 10 unmerciful 11 coldhearted, hardhearted

pittance 4 wage 5 scrap, trace 6 trifle 7 modicum, peanuts 9 allowance

pity 3 rue 4 ache, ruth 5 mercy 6 regret, sorrow 7 empathy, feel for, sadness 8 distress, sympathy 10 compassion, condolence, sympathize 11 commiserate 13 commiseration

pivot 3 pin 4 turn 5 hinge, shaft, swing, wheel 6 center, swivel

pivotal 3 key 5 chief, vital 7 central, crucial 8 critical, decisive 9 essential, important

pixie 3 elf, fay, imp 5 antic, fairy, scamp 6 elvish, impish, rascal, sprite 7 brown-

ie, coltish, playful, puckish **8** prankish
11 mischievous

pixilated 3 fey **7** bemused, erratic,
flighty, muddled, touched **9** eccentric,
whimsical **10** capricious

Pizarro, Francisco *brother:* **7** Gonzalo
city founded: **4** Lima *conquest:* **4** Peru
victims: **5** Incas **9** Atahualpa
10 Atahuallpa

pizzazz 3 pep, vim, zip **4** bang, brio,
dash, snap, zest, zing **5** éclat, flair,
flash, gusto, moxie, oomph, punch,
verve **6** dazzle, energy, hoopla, sizzle,
spirit **7** glamour, panache **8** vitality
10 excitement

placard 4 bill, post **6** notice, plaque,
poster **7** affiche **8** handbill

placate 4 calm, ease **6** pacify, soothe
7 appease, assuage, comfort, mollify,
satisfy, sweeten, win over **10** conciliate,
propitiate

place 3 lay, put, set **4** area, lieu, loci
(plural), post, rank, site, spot, zone
5 locus, point, stead, tract **6** region, status **7** situate, station **8** district, identify,
locality, location, pinpoint, position,
standing **9** establish, recognize *combining form:* **3** top **4** loco, topo, topy

placid 4 calm, easy, mild **5** quiet, still
6 gentle, serene **7** halcyon **8** composed,
peaceful, tranquil, waveless, windless
9 unruffled **10** complacent, unagitated,
untroubled **11** undisturbed **13** imperturbable

plagiarize 4 copy, crib **5** steal **6** pirate
11 appropriate

plague 3 vex **4** bane, evil, pest **5** annoy,
beset, curse, harry, hound, smite, trial,
worry **6** blight, bother, infest, harass,
hassle, hector, pester **7** afflict, bedevil,
disease, disturb, scourge, torment,
trouble **8** calamity, distress, epidemic,
invasion, irritant, irritate, nuisance,
outbreak, pandemic **9** annoyance,
beleaguer **10** affliction, black death,
pestilence **11** infestation

plaid 6 tartan

plain 3 lea **4** bald, bare, open, pure
5 blunt, clear, field, frank, usual **6** candid, common, homely, modest, patent,
severe, simple, tundra **7** expanse, evident, obvious, prairie, savanna **8** apparent, distinct, everyday, homespun,
manifest, ordinary, straight **9** outspoken, unadorned **10** absolutely, forthright, unaffected **11** undecorated,
unvarnished **13** uncomplicated

plainclothesman 4 dick **6** shamus, sleuth
7 gumshoe **8** hawkshaw **9** detective
12 investigator

____ **Plaines 3** Des

plainness 6 candor, purity **7** clarity,
honesty **8** lucidity **10** simplicity

plainsong 5 chant **12** cantus firmus

plainspoken 4 open **5** frank **6** candid,
direct, honest **8** straight, truthful
10 forthright **11** undisguised, unvarnished

plaintive 3 sad **4** glum **6** woeful **7** doleful,
piteous, pitiful **8** dolorous, downcast,
mournful **9** sorrowful **10** dispirited,
lamentable, lugubrious, melancholy

plait 4 fold **5** braid, pleat, weave **7** pigtail
10 intertwine, interweave

plan 3 aim, map, way **4** cast, goal, idea,
mean, plot **5** chart, frame **6** design,
devise, intend, intent, lay out, map out,
method, scheme, set out **7** arrange, diagram, drawing, outline, pattern, program, project, propose, purpose, work
out **8** contrive, engineer, organize,
strategy, think out **9** blueprint, formulate, intention, procedure **11** arrangement, formulation

plane 3 fly, jet **4** even, flat, tool, tree
5 flush, level **6** smooth **8** aircraft, air-
liner

planet 4 Mars **5** Earth, Pluto, Venus
6 Saturn, Uranus **7** Jupiter, Mercury,
Neptune *path:* **5** orbit *satellite:* **4** moon
shadow: **5** umbra *small:* **8** asteroid

planetary 4 vast **6** global **7** erratic,
immense **8** colossal, enormous **9** universal, wandering, worldwide **11** terrestrial

plangent 7 orotund, ringing, vibrant
8 resonant, sonorous **9** consonant,
plaintive **10** expressive, resounding
11 reverberant

plank 4 item, wood **5** board, floor **6** lumber, timber **7** article, support

plant 3 fix, pot, set, sow **4** bury, grow,
hide, mill, park, root, seed, tomb
5 cache, cover, imbed, inter, place,
plunk, put in, stash, works **6** entomb,
inhume, occult, screen **7** conceal, factory, install, lay away, put away, secrete
8 colonize, populate **9** cultivate
angiosperm: **5** dicot **7** monocot *aquatic:*
4 reed **5** lotus, sedge **7** awlwort, cattail,
fanwort, papyrus **8** duckweed, eelgrass,
hornwort, pondweed **9** water lily
10 watercress **11** bladderwort **12** pick-
erelweed *Australian:* **6** mallee **7** banksia
8 blackboy **10** eucalyptus *body:* **4** stem
7 thallus *bulbous:* **4** lily **5** camas, onion,
tulip **7** jonquil **8** hyacinth **9** narcissus
carnivorous: **6** sundew **10** butterwort
12 pitcher plant, Venus flytrap *cell
layer:* **7** phellem *climbing:* **3** ivy **4** vine
5 betel, liana, vetch **6** bryony, derris,
smilax **7** creeper, jasmine **8** bignonia,

fumitory, moonseed, scammony, wisteria 12 morning glory *coloring agent:*
8 carotene 11 chlorophyll, xanthophyll
combining form: 4 phyt 5 phyto *cone-bearing:* 3 fir, yew 4 pine 5 cedar, cycad
6 ginkgo, spruce 7 conifer, cypress, redwood 10 arborvitae, gymnosperm
desert: 4 aloe 5 agave 6 cactus, cholla
8 mesquite, ocotillo 9 paloverde 11 brittlebush *disease:* 3 rot 4 gall, mold, rust,
scab, smut, wilt 5 ergot 6 blight,
mildew, mosaic 7 blister 8 clubroot
9 black spot 10 black heart *extinct:*
8 calamite *flowerless:* 4 alga, fern, kelp,
moss 5 algae (plural), fungi (plural)
6 fungus, lichen 7 seaweed 8 clubmoss
9 bryophyte, equisetum, horsetail, liverwort *fluid:* 3 gum, sap 4 milk 5 latex,
resin *gland:* 7 nectary *hallucinogenic:*
4 hemp 5 poppy 6 mescal 8 cannabis
9 marijuana *largest:* 7 sequoia *life:*
5 flora *marine:* 4 kelp, nori 5 dulse,
fucus 6 wakame 7 seaweed 8 gulfweed
10 sea lettuce *marsh:* 4 reed 5 carex,
sedge 7 bogbean, bulrush, calamus,
cattail 8 red maple, sphagnum
11 loosestrife *medicinal:* 4 aloe, sage
5 poppy, senna, tansy 6 catnip, fennel,
garlic, hyssop, ipecac, nettle 7 aconite,
boneset, burdock, camphor, comfrey,
ginseng, hemlock, henbane, juniper,
lobelia, mullein, mustard, parsley
8 camomile, capsicum, cinchona, feverfew, licorice, pilewort, plantain, wormwood 9 asafetida, chamomile, dandelion, echinacea, fenugreek, monkshood
10 asafoetida, goldenseal, peppermint
microscopic: 4 mold 6 diatom 7 euglena
8 bacteria (plural) 9 bacterium *oldest:*
11 bristlecone *onion-like:* 4 leek 5 chive
7 shallot 8 scallion *opening:* 5 stoma
7 stomata (plural) *parasitic:* 6 dodder,
fungus 7 pinesap 8 gerardia 9 broomrape, mistletoe, rafflesia, witchweed
10 beechdrops *part:* 3 bud, nut, sap
4 bark, bulb, cell, cone, corm, leaf,
pome, root, seed, stem, wood 5 drupe,
fruit, grain, spore, thorn, tuber, xylem
6 catkin, flower, nectar, phloem,
raceme 7 rhizome 8 lenticel 9 cellulose,
cotyledon 11 chlorophyll, chloroplast
13 inflorescence *pest:* 5 aphid, scale
6 chafer, thrips, weevil 7 cutworm
8 fruit fly, wireworm 9 gypsy moth
10 cankerworm, leafhopper, phylloxera
11 codling moth *poisonous:* 4 poke,
upas 5 sumac 6 castor, croton, datura
7 amanita, cassava, cowbane, henbane,
lobelia, tobacco 8 foxglove, larkspur,
locoweed, mayapple, oleander, pokeweed 9 baneberry, monkshood 10 bel-

ladonna, jimsonweed, manchineel,
nightshade *saprophytic:* 5 fungi (plural)
6 fungus 7 pinesap 9 pinedrops, snow
plant 10 beechdrops, Indian pipe *succulent:* 4 aloe 5 agave 6 cactus 10 bitterroot *thorny:* 4 rose 5 briar 6 cactus, nettle, teasel 7 caltrop, thistle 9 cocklebur
tissue: 5 xylem 6 phloem 7 cambium,
medulla 8 meristem *young:* 5 scion,
shoot 6 sprout 7 cutting 8 seedling
plantain 5 fruit 6 banana
plantation 5 manor 6 colony, estate,
quinta 7 acreage, demesne 8 hacienda
10 encampment, habitation, settlement
plant louse 5 aphid
plaque 4 film 5 badge, patch 6 brooch,
lesion, tablet 7 tribute 8 bacteria,
memorial 13 commemoration
plaster 3 dab 4 coat 5 affix, cover, gesso
6 stucco 7 coating, conceal, overlay
8 dressing *of paris:* 5 gesso 6 gypsum
plastered 3 lit 4 high 5 drunk, lit up,
oiled 6 bashed, blotto, bombed, juiced,
potted, soaked, soused, stewed, stoned,
tanked, wasted, zonked 7 crocked,
drunken, pickled, pie-eyed, sloshed,
smashed, sottish 10 inebriated, liquored
up 11 intoxicated
plastic 4 soft 5 vinyl 6 pliant, supple
7 ductile, pliable 8 creative, flexible,
moldable, workable 9 adaptable, formative, malleable, synthetic 10 artificial,
credit card, sculptural
plat 3 lot, map 4 plan 5 chart, tract
6 parcel 7 quadrat
plate 4 base, coat, disc, dish, disk, gild,
tile 5 layer, paten, scute, slice 6 enamel,
fascia, lamina, plaque 7 anodize, lamella, overlay
plateau 4 mesa 5 table 6 upland 9 altiplano, tableland *arid:* 4 puna *barren:*
5 field 6 paramo *dry:* 5 karoo 6 karroo
platform 3 map 4 bank, base, dais, deck,
plan 5 bimah, forum, ledge, riser, shelf,
stage, stump 6 design, perron, podium,
pulpit, scheme 7 balcony, pattern, rostrum 8 hustings, scaffold 9 banquette,
manifesto 11 declaration *temporary:*
7 staging 8 scaffold *wooden:* 9 boardwalk
Plath, Sylvia *novel:* 7 Bell Jar (The)
poem: 5 Ariel, Daddy
platitude 6 cliché, truism 7 bromide
8 banality, prosaism 10 shibboleth
Plato *father:* 7 Ariston *literary form:* 6 dialog 8 dialogue *original name:* 10 Aristocles *school:* 7 Academy *work:* 3 Ion
4 Meno 5 Crito, Lysis 6 Laches, Phaedo
7 Apology, Gorgias 8 Phaedrus, Republic (The) 9 Charmides, Symposium
platter 5 plate 6 record 8 trencher

platypus 8 duckbill

plaudits 5 kudos **6** cheers, praise **7** acclaim, ovation **8** applause, approval, encomium **9** accolades **11** acclamation

plausible 8 credible, specious **10** believable, convincing, creditable, persuasive, reasonable

play 3 act, fun **4** game, jest, joke, romp **5** drama, feint, serve, sport, treat, trick, wager **6** cavort, comedy, fiddle, frolic, gambit, gambol, leeway, margin **7** delight, disport, perform, twiddle **8** latitude, maneuver, pleasure **9** amusement, diversion, enjoyment, stratagem **10** manipulate, recreation *kind:* **5** farce **6** comedy **7** musical, tragedy **8** one-acter **9** melodrama, pantomime *part:* **3** act **5** scene **8** epilogue, prologue

playact 5 put on **7** perform, posture, pretend **9** personate **11** impersonate, make believe

playboy 4 rake, roué **8** hedonist **9** bon vivant

play down 8 minimize **9** deprecate, soft-pedal, underrate **11** de-emphasize

player 5 actor **6** mummer **7** actress, athlete, trouper **8** musician, thespian **9** contender, performer **10** competitor, contestant **11** participant

playful 5 antic, jolly, merry, pixie **6** elvish, frisky, impish, jocund, joking, jovial, lively **7** coltish, jocular, puckish, waggish **8** humorous, sportive **9** kittenish, sprightly **10** frolicsome

play off 3 pit, vie **5** match **6** oppose **7** counter **8** contrast

plaything 3 toy

play up 6 stress **7** feature **9** dramatize, emphasize, highlight, overstate, underline **10** accentuate, exaggerate, underscore

playwright 9 dramatist **10** dramaturge (see also DRAMATIST)

plaza 6 circus, common, square, zocalo **9** carrefour **11** marketplace

plea 4 suit **5** alibi **6** appeal, excuse, orison, prayer **7** apology, defense, pretext, request **8** entreaty, overture, petition **11** application, imploration **12** supplication *defendant's:* **4** nolo **6** guilty **8** innocent **9** not guilty

plead 3 beg **4** pray **5** argue **6** allege, answer, appeal **7** beseech, entreat, implore **8** advocate, maintain **9** importune **10** supplicate

pleasant 4 fair, fine, good, nice **5** clear, sunny, sweet **6** cheery, genial, pretty **7** amiable, clarion, likable, welcome **8** amicable, charming, cheerful, engaging, gracious, grateful, likeable, pleas-

ing, sunshine, sunshiny **9** agreeable, appealing, cloudless, congenial, convivial, enjoyable, favorable, unclouded **10** delightful, gratifying

pleasantry 3 fun **4** jest, joke **6** banter, levity **8** badinage, repartee **9** wittiness **10** jocularity

please 4 like, suit, wish **5** agree, amuse, enjoy, serve **6** choose **7** content, delight, gladden, gratify, indulge, satisfy *French:* **12** s'il vous plait *German:* **5** bitte *Spanish:* **8** por favor

pleasing 4 good, nice **6** pretty **7** welcome **8** suitable **9** agreeable, congenial, favorable, palatable **10** attractive, delightful, gratifying **12** satisfactory

pleasure 3 fun, joy **4** will **5** bliss, fancy **6** desire, liking, relish **7** delight, gladden, gratify **8** felicity, gladness, hedonism **9** amusement, diversion, enjoyment, happiness, merriment **11** inclination

pleat 4 fold **5** crimp **6** crease

plebe 5 frosh **8** freshman

plebeian 3 low **4** base **5** crude, lowly **6** coarse, common, humble, menial **8** commoner, everyday, ordinary **10** lower-class

plectrum 4 pick

pledge 3 vow **4** bail, bind, bond, gage, hock, oath, pawn, seal, sign, word **5** drink, swear, toast, token **6** parole, plight, surety **7** chattel, earnest, promise, warrant **8** bailment, contract, covenant, guaranty, security, warranty **9** agreement, assurance, certainty, guarantee, undertake

pledget 3 pad **8** compress

Pleiades 4 Maia **6** Merope **7** Alcyone, Celaeno, Electra, Sterope, Taygeta **8** Asterope *brightest star:* **7** Alcyone

plenary 4 full **5** whole **6** entire **7** general **8** absolute, complete **9** inclusive **11** unqualified **12** unrestricted

plenitude 4 glut **6** excess **7** satiety, surfeit **8** fullness **9** abundance, profusion, repletion **11** copiousness, sufficiency, superfluity **12** completeness

plenteous 7 fertile **8** abundant, fruitful, prolific **9** abounding **10** productive

plentiful 4 full, rich **5** ample, flush **7** copious, profuse **8** abundant, affluent, generous **9** abounding, bounteous, unstinted **10** sufficient

plenty 3 lot **4** heap, pack, peck, pile **6** stacks, wealth **8** adequacy, fullness, mountain **9** abundance, affluence, great deal **10** cornucopia

pleonasm 8 verbiage **9** prolixity, tautology, verbosity, wordiness **10** redundancy **11** periphrasis, superfluity

plethora 4 glut 5 flood 6 excess 7 over-run, surfeit, surplus 8 fullness, over-flow 9 abundance, profusion, repletion 11 superfluity 13 overabundance

plexus 4 rete 7 network

pliable 6 supple 7 plastic 9 adaptable 10 adjustable 11 complaisant, manipulable

pliant 5 lithe 6 limber, supple 7 ductile, plastic, springy 8 flexible, moldable, workable, yielding 9 adaptable, malleable, tractable 10 manageable

plica 4 fold 6 crease, groove

plight 3 fix, jam, vow 4 hole, spot, word 5 swear 6 engage, pickle, pledge, scrape 7 betroth, dilemma, promise 8 quandary 9 betrothal 10 difficulty, engagement 11 predicament

plod 4 slog, toil 5 grind, slave, tramp, tread, tromp 6 drudge, lumber, trudge 8 plug away

plot 3 map 4 area, land, mark, note, plan 5 cabal, chart, story, tract 6 design, devise, invent, lay out, locate, parcel, scheme 7 collude, compact, connive, diagram, outline 8 conspire, contrive, intrigue, scenario 9 collusion, conniving, machinate 10 complicity, connivance, conspiracy 11 machination

plover 5 pewit, stilt 6 peewit 7 lapwing 8 dotterel, killdeer *relative:* 9 sandpiper, turnstone

plow 3 dig 4 till, turn 5 break 6 furrow, harrow, trench 8 turn over 9 cultivate *part:* 4 beam, frog 5 share 7 coulter 8 landside 9 moldboard

ploy 4 ruse, scam, wile 5 feint, trick 6 device, frolic, gambit, tactic 7 gimmick 8 artifice, escapade, maneuver 9 stratagem 11 contrivance

pluck 3 rob, tug 4 grit, guts, pick, pull, yank 5 cheek, grasp, heart, moxie, nerve, spunk 6 daring, fleece, mettle, remove, snatch, spirit, tweeze 7 bravery, courage, pull out 8 gameness 10 resolution

plucky 4 bold, game 5 brave 6 feisty, spunky 7 doughty 8 fearless, spirited, unafraid 9 dauntless 10 courageous

plug 3 tap 4 bung, clog, core, cork, fill, hype, pack, push, stop, tout 5 block, blurb, boost, choke, close, cry up, shoot 6 device, remedy 7 congest, fitting, hydrant, promote, stopper 8 obstruct 9 advertise, publicity, publicize 10 connection

plug-ugly 4 thug 5 bully, rowdy, tough 7 hoodlum, ruffian 9 roughneck

plum 5 prize 6 purple, reward 7 guerdon, premium 8 dividend *dried:* 5 prune

kind: 6 damson 7 bullace 9 greengage *spiny:* 10 blackthorn

plumage 8 feathers *early:* 4 down

plumb 5 delve, probe, sound 6 fathom, weight 7 exactly, examine, explore, install, measure 8 absolute, complete, thorough, vertical 10 absolutely, vertically 11 immediately 13 perpendicular

plume 4 tail 5 array, preen, pride, prize 6 column 7 feather 8 aigrette

plummet 4 dive, drop, fall 5 crash 6 plunge, tumble 8 collapse, nose-dive 11 precipitate

plump 3 fat 4 drop, fall, full 5 ample, buxom, favor, pudgy, round, stout, tubby 6 chubby, portly, rotund 7 rounded, support 8 abundant, directly, roly-poly 10 Rubenesque

plumply 7 frankly, plainly 8 candidly 12 forthrightly

plunder 3 rob 4 loot, sack, swag, take 5 booty, prize, seize, spoil, steal, strip 6 boodle, rapine, spoils 7 despoil, pillage, ransack, relieve, stick up 9 pillaging

plunge 3 bet, ram, run 4 dive, drop, fall, jump, rush, sink, stab, swim 5 drive, lunge, pitch, stick 6 charge, gamble, hasten, hurtle, thrust, topple, tumble 7 descend, immerse, plummet 8 nose-dive, submerge 9 penetrate

plus 3 and 4 more, perk 5 added, asset, bonus, boost, extra 6 excess 7 benefit 8 addition, increase, positive

plush 4 full, rich 6 deluxe, fabric, lavish, velvet 7 opulent 8 luscious, palatial 9 expensive, luxuriant, luxurious, sumptuous

Pluto 3 Dis 5 Hades *brother:* 4 Zeus 7 Jupiter, Neptune 8 Poseidon *father:* 6 Cronus, Saturn *mother:* 3 Ops 4 Rhea *wife:* 10 Persephone, Proserpina

plutocrat 5 mogul 6 fat cat, tycoon 7 magnate 9 financier, moneybags 10 capitalist

plutonian 8 infernal 10 underworld

Plutus *father:* 6 Iasion *god of:* 6 riches, wealth *mother:* 5 Ceres 7 Demeter

ply 3 use 4 bias, sail 5 apply, exert, layer, wield 6 employ, handle, strand, supply, travel, voyage 7 furnish, perform 8 maneuver, practice 11 inclination

pneuma 4 soul 5 anima 6 psyche, spirit

pneumatic 4 airy 5 ample, buxom, plump 6 aerial, zaftig 9 spiritual 10 curvaceous 11 atmospheric

poach 4 cook 5 steal 6 coddle, simmer 7 intrude 8 encroach, trespass 9 interlope 11 appropriate

Pocahontas *father:* 8 Powhatan *husband:* 5 Rolfe (John)

pock 3 pit 4 hole, spot 7 pustule

pocket 3 bag 4 lift, sack 5 filch, pinch, pouch, purse, steal, swipe 6 cavity 7 capsule, dead end, impasse 8 cul-de-sac 9 condensed 10 blind alley *billiards:* 4 pool

pocketbook 3 bag 4 poke 5 purse 6 clutch, income, wallet 7 handbag 8 billfold 9 clutch bag

pocket bread 4 pita

pocket money 6 change 9 petty cash 11 small change

pocket-size 4 tiny 5 small 9 miniature 10 diminutive

pod 3 bag, gam, sac 4 boll, case, hull, husk, skin 5 shell, shuck 6 cocoon 7 capsule, silique 8 seedcase *plant:* 3 pea 4 bean, okra 5 chili, gumbo 6 cassia, cowpea, legume, lentil, peanut, pepper 8 capsicum, mesquite, milkweed 9 lespedeza

pod-bearing tree 5 carob 6 locust 7 catalpa

podiatry 9 chiropody

podium 4 dais 6 pulpit 7 lectern, rostrum 8 platform

___ **podrida** 4 olla

Poe, Edgar Allan *detective:* 5 Dupin (C. Auguste) *poem:* 5 Bells (The), Raven (The) 6 Lenore 7 Israfel, To Helen, Ulalume 8 Eldorado, For Annie 10 Annabel Lee *tale:* 6 Ligeia, Shadow 7 Gold-Bug (The), Morella, Silence 8 Black Cat (The) 13 Tell-tale Heart (The) 15 Purloined Letter (The) 17 Cask of Amontillado (The), Pit and the Pendulum (The) 19 Masque of the Red Death (The) 21 Fall of the House of Usher (The)

poem 3 ode 4 epic, epos, idyl, rime, rune, song 5 ditty, elegy, epode, idyll, lyric, rhyme, verse 6 ballad, epopee, jingle, rondel, sonnet 7 eclogue, rondeau 8 limerick, madrigal *closing:* 5 envoi, envoy *division:* 4 foot, line 5 canto, epode, stich, verse 6 stanza 7 refrain 8 epilogue, prologue *Japanese:* 5 haiku, tánka *of eight lines:* 6 octave 7 triolet *of four lines:* 8 quatrain *of fourteen lines:* 6 sonnet *of three lines:* 7 triplet *pastoral:* 7 eclogue, georgic *short:* 5 ditty 7 epigram

poet 4 bard, muse, scop 5 skald 6 lyrist 7 elegist 8 idyllist, lyricist 9 balladist, sonneteer 10 Parnassian *American:* 3 Poe (Edgar Allan) 4 Dove (Rita), Hass (Robert), Nash (Ogden), Read (Thomas), Rich (Adrienne), Tabb (John Banister), Tate (Allen) 5 Auden (Wystan Hugh), Benét (Stephen Vincent), Crane (Hart), Field (Eugene), Frost (Robert), Guest (Edgar), Moore (Marianne), Plath (Sylvia), Pound (Ezra), Riley (James Whitcomb), Wylie (Elinor) 6 Barlow (Joel), Bishop (Elizabeth), Brooks (Gwendolyn), Bryant (William Cullen), Ciardi (John), Dickey (James), Dunbar (Paul Laurence), Hughes (Langston), Kilmer (Joyce), Lanier (Sidney), Lowell (Amy, James Russell, Robert), McKuen (Rod), Millay (Edna St. Vincent), Pinsky (Robert), Ransom (John Crowe), Seeger (Alan), Strand (Mark), Taylor (Edward), Warren (Robert Penn), Wilbur (Richard) 7 Angelou (Maya), Ashbery (John), Emerson (Ralph Waldo), Freneau (Philip), Halleck (Fitz-Greene), Jeffers (Robinson), Lindsay (Vachel), Markham (Edwin), Merrill (James), Nemerov (Howard), Roethke (Theodore), Shapiro (Karl), Stevens (Wallace), Whitman (Walt) 8 Berryman (John), Cummings (E. E.), Ginsberg (Allen), MacLeish (Archibald), Robinson (Edwin Arlington), Sandburg (Carl), Teasdale (Sara), Wheatley (Phillis), Whittier (John Greenleaf), Williams (C. K., William Carlos) 9 Dickinson (Emily), Santayana (George) 10 Bradstreet (Anne), Longfellow (Henry Wadsworth) 12 Wigglesworth (Michael) *Anglo-Saxon:* 7 Caedmon, Cynwulf 8 Cynewulf, Kynewulf *Arab:* 5 Jarir 6 Hariri 8 al-Hariri *Australian:* 8 Paterson (Andrew Barton) *Belgian:* 11 Maeterlinck (Maurice) *Canadian:* 5 Pratt (Edwin John) 6 Hébert (Anne) 7 Roberts (Charles G. D.), Service (Robert) 8 Drummond (William Henry) 9 Fréchette (Louis-Honoré) *Chilean:* 6 Neruda (Pablo) 7 Mistral (Gabriela) *Chinese:* 4 Li Po, Tu Fu 7 Wang Wei *Danish:* 4 Rode (Helge) 5 Ewald (Johannes) *English:* 3 Gay (John) 4 Gray (Thomas), Owen (Wilfred), Pope (Alexander), Rowe (Nicholas), Tate (Nahum), Wyat (Thomas) 5 Blake (William), Byron (Lord), Carew (Thomas), Clare (John), Donne (John), Eliot (Thomas Stearns), Gower (John), Hardy (Thomas), Keats (John), Noyes (Alfred), Wilde (Oscar), Wyatt (Thomas), Young (Edward) 6 Arnold (Matthew), Austin (Alfred), Belloc (Hilaire), Brooke (Rupert), Butler (Samuel), Clough (Arthur Hugh), Cowper (William), Dryden (John), Graves (Robert), Larkin (Philip), Milton (John), Savage (Richard), Sidney (Philip), Surrey (Earl of), Symons (Arthur), Waller (Edmund), Warton

(Thomas), Watson (William), Wotton (Henry) **7** Bridges (Robert), Campion (Thomas), Chaucer (Geoffrey), Gilbert (W. S.), Herbert (George), Herrick (Robert), Hopkins (Gerard Manley), Housman (A. E.), Kipling (Rudyard), Layamon, Marvell (Andrew), Patmore (Coventry), Quarles (Francis), Shelley (Percy Bysshe), Skelton (John), Southey (Robert), Spender (Stephen), Spenser (Edmund) **8** Betjeman (John), Browning (Elizabeth Barrett, Robert), de la Mare (Walter), Langland (William), Lovelace (Richard), Meredith (George), Rossetti (Christina, Dante Gabriel), Suckling (John), Tennyson (Alfred Lord), Thompson (Francis) **9** Coleridge (Samuel Taylor), Masefield (John), Swinburne (Algernon Charles) **10** Chatterton (Thomas), FitzGerald (Edward), Wordsworth (William) **11** Shakespeare (William) *Finnish:* **8** Runeberg (Johan Ludvig) *French:* **5** Marot (Clément) **6** Musset (Alfred de), Valéry (Paul), Villon (François) **7** Bourget (Paul), Chénier (André de, Marie-Joseph), Gautier (Théophile), Rimbaud (Arthur), Ronsard (Pierre de) **8** Malherbe (François de), Mallarmé (Stéphane), Verlaine (Paul) **9** Lamartine (Alphonse de) **10** Baudelaire (Charles) **11** Apollinaire (Guillaume) *German:* **5** Heine (Heinrich), Rilke (Rainer Maria), Sachs (Hans), Storm (Theodor) **6** Brecht (Bertolt), Goethe (Johann Wolfgang von), Uhland (Ludwig) **7** Walther (von der Vogelweide), Wolfram (von Eschenbach) **8** Schiller (Friedrich von) **9** Klopstock (Friedrich Gottlieb) *Greek:* **5** Arion, Homer **6** Elytis (Odysseus), Erinna, Hesiod, Pindar, Ritsos (Yannis), Sappho **7** Agathon, Alcaeus, Orpheus, Seferis (George), Thespis **8** Anacreon **9** Simonides **10** Apollonius, Theocritus *Hindu:* **5** Naidu (Sarojini) **6** Tagore (Rabindranath) **8** Kalidasa, Tulsidas *Hungarian:* **6** Petofi (Sandor), Zrinyi (Miklos) *Irish:* **5** Moore (Thomas), Wolfe (Charles), Yeats (William Butler) **6** Heaney (Seamus) **7** Dunsany (Lord) **8** Drummond (William Henry), MacNeice (Louis) *Italian:* **4** Rosa (Salvator), Vida (Marco) **5** Dante (Alighieri), Tasso (Torquato) **7** Ariosto (Ludovico), Manzoni (Alessandro), Montale (Eugenio) **8** Carducci (Giosuè), Leopardi (Giacomo), Petrarch **9** Boccaccio (Giovanni), D'Annunzio (Gabriele), Marinetti (Filippo Tommaso), Quasimodo (Salvatore), Ungaretti (Giuseppe) *Japanese:*

5 Basho **6** Matsuo *medieval:* **8** minstrel, trouvère **10** troubadour *Mexican:* **3** Paz (Octavio) *nonsense:* **4** Lear (Edward) *Norwegian:* **8** Bjornson (Bjornstjerne), Welhaven (Johan) **9** Wergeland (Henrik) *Persian:* **4** Sadi **5** Attar, Hafez, Hafiz **11** Omar Khayyám *Roman:* **4** Ovid **6** Horace, Vergil, Virgil **7** Juvenal, Martial, Statius **8** Catullus, Tibullus **9** Lucretius *Russian:* **4** Blok (Aleksandr) **7** Brodsky (Joseph), Pushkin (Aleksandr), Yesenin (Sergey) **9** Akhmatova (Anna), Kheraskov (Mikhail), Pasternak (Boris), Tsvetaeva (Marina) **10** Mandelstam (Osip), Mayakovsky (Vladimir) **11** Yevtushenko (Yevgeny) *Saint Lucian:* **7** Walcott (Derek) *Scottish:* **4** Hogg (James), Muir (Edwin) **5** Burns (Robert), Scott (Alexander, Walter) **6** Dunbar (William), Ramsay (Allan) **7** Thomson (James) **10** MacDiarmid (Hugh) *Spanish:* **5** Lorca (Federico García) **7** Jiménez (Juan Ramón) **8** Figueroa (Francisco) **10** Aleixandre (Vicente) **11** García Lorca (Federico) *Swedish:* **5** Sachs (Nelly) **6** Tegner (Esaias) **8** Snoilsky (Carl Johan) **9** Karlfeldt (Erik Axel) *Swiss:* **5** Amiel (Henri Frédéric) **9** Spitteler (Carl) *Welsh:* **6** Thomas (Dylan) **7** Aneurin, Watkins (Vernon)

poetic 5 lyric **6** dreamy **8** romantic **9** aesthetic, beautiful

poet laureate *British:* **3** Pye (Henry) **4** Rowe (Nicholas), Tate (Nahum) **6** Austin (Alfred), Cibber (Colley), Dryden (John), Hughes (Ted), Jonson (Ben), Motion (Andrew) **7** Bridges (Robert), Southey (Robert) **8** Betjeman (John), Davenant (William), Day-Lewis (Cecil), Shadwell (Thomas), Tennyson (Alfred) **9** Masefield (John), Whitehead (William) **10** Wordsworth (William) *American:* **4** Dove (Rita), Hass (Robert) **5** Glück (Louise) **6** Kooser (Ted), Kunitz (Stanley), Merwin (W. S.), Pinsky (Robert), Strand (Mark), Warren (Robert Penn), Wilbur (Richard) **7** Brodsky (Joseph), Collins (Billy), Nemerov (Howard), Van Duyn (Mona)

Pogo creator 5 Kelly (Walt)

poi 4 taro

poignancy 6 pathos **7** emotion, sadness **9** sentiment

poignant 3 sad **4** keen **5** acute, sharp **6** biting, moving **7** painful, piquant, pointed, pungent **8** incisive, piercing, stirring, touching **9** affecting, emotional **11** penetrating, stimulating

point 3 aim, bit, dot, end, jag, nib, tip **4** apex, barb, crux, goal, item, mark,

show, site, spot, step, tine, turn, unit
5 brink, motif, place, stage, theme,
topic, trace, verge **6** credit, detail,
direct, intent, moment, motive, object,
period, reason **7** cogency, decimal, element, essence, feature, instant, meaning, purpose, sharpen, subject **8** headland, juncture, locality, location,
particle, position **9** direction, emphasize, punctuate **10** promontory **12** significance

Point Counter Point author 6 Huxley
(Aldous)

pointed 5 acute, sharp **6** barbed,
marked, signal **7** salient **8** incisive,
striking **9** arresting, pertinent, prominent **11** conspicuous, penetrating

pointer 3 dog, tip **4** clue, hint **5** arrow,
guide **6** gundog **9** indicator **10** suggestion

pointillist 6 Seurat (Georges), Signac
(Paul) **8** Pissarro (Camille)

pointless 4 idle, vain **5** inane, silly
6 futile **7** useless **8** bootless **9** fruitless,
senseless, worthless **10** immaterial,
irrelevant, unavailing, unfruitful
11 meaningless **12** unprofitable

point of view 5 angle, slant **7** outlook
8 position, prospect **11** perspective

poise 4 ease, hang, tact **5** brace, grace,
hover, skill **6** aplomb, steady **7** address,
balance, bearing, dignity, support, suspend **8** calmness, carriage, elegance,
serenity **9** assurance, composure, diplomacy **10** confidence, equanimity **11** del-
icatesse, equilibrium, savoir faire, tactfulness

poised 4 calm **6** at ease, serene, steady
7 assured, equable **8** composed, tranquil **9** collected, confident **13** self-possessed

poison 4 bane, upas **5** toxin, venom
6 toxoid **7** arsenic, botulin, cyanide,
envenom **8** toxicant **9** botulinum, contagion **10** strychnine **13** contamination
arrow: **4** inée, upas **6** curare **7** ouabain
combining form: **3** tox **4** toxi, toxo **6** tox-
ico

poisoning *food:* **8** botulism *lead:*
8 plumbism

poisonous 5 toxic **7** baneful, miasmal,
nocuous, noxious **8** mephitic, venomous, virulent **9** pestilent **10** pernicious

poke 3 dig, hit, jab, jut, lag, pry **4** cuff,
nose, prod, push, sock, stab, stir, urge
5 bulge, dally, delay, elbow, nudge,
punch, snoop, tarry **6** dawdle, meddle,
pierce, putter, thrust **7** intrude, project,
rummage **8** stick out **9** interfere, interject, interpose

poker *bet total:* **3** pot *form:* **4** stud *hand:*
4 pair **5** flush **8** straight **9** full house
10 royal flush **13** straight flush *stake:*
4 ante *term:* **3** see **4** call, draw, open
5 raise *token:* **4** chip

poker-faced 5 blank, staid **7** deadpan,
neutral **9** impassive **11** inscrutable, noncommittal **12** inexpressive

pokey 3 can, jug, pen **4** brig, coop, jail,
stir **5** clink **6** cooler, prison **7** slammer
9 calaboose

poky 4 slow **5** dingy, seedy **6** dreary,
shabby **7** cramped, laggard, run-down
8 dilatory, plodding, sluggish

Poland *capital:* **6** Warsaw *city:* **4** Lódz
6 Gdansk, Kraków, Poznan **7** Wroclaw
8 Katowice, Szczecin *leader:* **6** Walesa
(Lech) *monetary unit:* **5** zloty *mountain
range:* **10** Carpathian *national hero:*
10 Kosciuszko (Thaddeus) *neighbor:*
6 Russia **7** Belarus, Germany, Ukraine
8 Slovakia **9** Lithuania **13** Czech
Republic *river:* **4** Oder **7** Vistula *sea:*
6 Baltic

polar 6 arctic **7** pivotal **8** opposite **9** diametric

pole 4 punt, spar **5** shaft, staff, stick, stilt
Indian: **5** totem *Scottish:* **5** caber

polecat 5 fitch, skunk **6** ferret **7** fitchet

polemic 6 attack, debate, screed, tirade
7 defense, dispute **8** argument, diatribe,
harangue, jeremiad **9** assertion, philippic **10** contention, refutation **11** controversy, disputation **12** denunciation,
remonstrance

polemical 7 scrappy **10** pugnacious
11 contentious, opinionated **12** disputatious **13** argumentative, controversial

polestar 3 hub **5** focus, guide **10** focal
point

police 3 cop, law, man **4** fuzz, heat
6 copper, govern, lawman, patrol
7 control, monitor, trooper **8** bluecoat,
flatfoot, gendarme, regulate **9** patrolman **12** peace officer

police officer 3 cop **4** fuzz, heat **5** bobby
6 copper, peeler **7** John Law, sheriff,
trooper **8** bluecoat, Dogberry, flatfoot,
gendarme **9** constable, patrolman *Ital-
ian:* **11** carabiniere *Parisian:* **4** flic **8** gendarme

policy 4 plan **6** course, method, number
7 lottery, program **8** contract, practice
9 procedure **10** management

polio vaccine developer 4 Salk (Jonas)
5 Sabin (Albert)

polish 3 rub, wax **4** buff **5** glaze, glint,
gloss, sheen, shine **6** luster, refine,
smooth, soften **7** burnish, culture,
enhance, improve, perfect, touch up
8 brighten **10** refinement

Polish *dumpling:* 7 pierogi *leader:* 6 Walesa (Lech) *patriot:* 9 Kosciusko (Thaddeus) *pope:* 8 John Paul *sausage:* 8 kielbasa *soldier:* 7 Pulaski (Casimir)

polish off 5 eat up 6 devour 7 consume, put away 8 dispatch 9 dispose of

polite 5 civil 7 courtly, genteel, refined 8 cultured, mannerly, polished, well-bred 9 attentive, courteous 10 thoughtful 11 considerate 12 well-mannered

politeness 7 manners 8 civility, courtesy 10 refinement

politic 4 wise 5 suave 6 adroit, shrewd, smooth 7 prudent, tactful 8 tactical 9 advisable, expedient, judicious, sagacious 10 diplomatic

political *meeting:* 6 caucus *party:* 3 GOP 10 Democratic, Republican *system:* 7 fascism 9 communism, democracy, socialism

poll 4 cast, clip, crop, head, nape 5 count, shear, tally, votes 6 record, sample, survey 7 canvass, pollard 8 question 9 interview 10 canvassing

pollack 4 fish 6 saithe 8 bluefish *family:* 3 cod

pollard 3 top 4 crop, tree 7 cut back

pollen-producing organ 6 stamen

pollex 5 thumb

___ **polloi** 3 hoi

pollster 5 Zogby (John) 6 Gallup (George), Harris (Lou)

pollute 4 foul, soil 5 dirty, spoil, stain, sully, taint 6 befoul, damage, debase, defile 7 corrupt, profane 10 adulterate 11 contaminate

pollution 4 smog 5 abuse 8 impurity 10 defilement

Pollux 10 Polydeuces *brother:* 6 Castor *father:* 4 Zeus *mother:* 4 Leda *sister:* 5 Helen 12 Clytemnestra

Pollyanna 8 optimist *author:* 6 Porter (Eleanor)

Pollyannaish 6 blithe, cheery, upbeat 8 cheerful, positive 10 optimistic 11 rose-colored

pollywog 7 tadpole

Polonius *daughter:* 7 Ophelia *slayer:* 6 Hamlet *son:* 7 Laertes

poltergeist 5 ghost 6 spirit

poltroon 6 coward, craven, yellow 7 chicken, dastard, gutless 8 cowardly 9 dastardly 11 lily-livered

Polydorus *father:* 5 Priam 6 Cadmus *mother:* 6 Hecuba 8 Harmonia *slayer:* 8 Achilles 10 Polymestor 11 Polymnestor

polygon *eight-sided:* 7 octagon *five-sided:* 8 pentagon *four-sided:* 8 tetragon *nine-sided:* 7 nonagon *seven-sided:* 8 heptagon *six-sided:* 7 hexagon *ten-sided:* 7 decagon *three-sided:* 8 triangle *twelve-sided:* 9 dodecagon

Polyhymnia 4 Muse *invention:* 4 lyre

Polynesian 5 Maori 6 Samoan, Tongan 8 Hawaiian, Tahitian 9 Marquesan

Polynices *brother:* 8 Eteocles *father:* 7 Oedipus *mother:* 7 Jocasta *wife:* 5 Argia 6 Argeia

polyp 5 tumor, zooid 6 growth 7 hydroid *freshwater:* 5 hydra

Polyphemus 7 Cyclops *beloved:* 7 Galatea *father:* 8 Poseidon *victim:* 4 Acis

pome 4 pear 5 apple, fruit

pommel 4 knob 6 handle

pomp 4 show 5 array 6 parade, ritual 7 display, fanfare, panoply 8 ceremony, grandeur, splendor 9 pageantry, vainglory 11 ostentation

pompano 4 fish 8 carangid 10 butterfish

Pompeii's volcano 8 Vesuvius

pompous 4 vain 5 proud, showy 6 lordly, ornate, stuffy 7 stuck-up 8 arrogant, boastful, inflated 9 bombastic, conceited, important, overblown 10 egocentric, flamboyant, pontifical 11 magisterial, pretentious 12 ostentatious, vainglorious

pond 4 mere, pool, tarn 5 stank 6 lagoon

ponder 4 mull, muse 5 study, think, weigh 6 reason 7 examine, perpend, reflect 8 appraise, cogitate, consider, evaluate, meditate, mull over, ruminate 9 reflect on, speculate 10 deliberate, think about 11 contemplate

ponderous 4 dull 5 heavy 6 clumsy, dreary, stodgy, wooden 7 labored, massive, weighty 8 cumbrous, lifeless, plodding, unwieldy 9 lumbering 10 burdensome, cumbersome, oppressive

poniard 6 dagger

Ponte Vecchio *city:* 8 Florence *river:* 4 Arno

Pontiac 5 chief *tribe:* 6 Ottawa

pontiff 4 pope

pontifical 7 pompous 8 dogmatic 9 episcopal 11 magisterial

pony 4 crib, trot 5 horse 6 bronco, cayuse 7 mustang *breed:* 6 Exmoor 8 Shetland

pony up 3 pay 6 lay out, pay out 7 dish out, dole out, fork out 8 hand over, shell out, turn over 10 compensate, remunerate

pooch 3 dog, pup 4 tyke 5 hound, puppy 6 bowwow, canine

Pooh *creator:* 5 Milne (A. A.) *illustrator:* 7 Shepard (Ernest)

pooh-bah 3 VIP 4 czar, king, star, tsar, tzar 5 baron, heavy, mogul 6 big gun, bigwig, honcho, kahuna, prince, worthy **7** big name, big shot, kingpin, magnate, notable **8** big wheel, eminence, luminary **9** big cheese, personage, superstar **11** heavyweight

pooh-pooh 5 scorn **6** deride **7** disdain, dismiss, sneer at **8** minimize, play down

pool 3 pot **4** mere, pond, tarn **5** chain, group, kitty, merge, trust **6** cartel, lagoon, laguna, puddle **7** combine, jackpot **9** syndicate *player:* **7** Mosconi (Willie) **13** Minnesota Fats

poop 4 dirt, info, tire **7** fatigue

poor 4 base, mean **5** broke, needy, scant, skimp, spare **6** humble, meager, meagre, paltry, scanty, skimpy, sparse **8** bankrupt, beggarly, indigent, strapped **9** destitute, insolvent, penniless, penurious **10** down-and-out, pauperized, stone-broke **11** impecunious, necessitous

poorly 3 ill, low **4** sick **5** badly **6** ailing, sickly, unwell **10** indisposed **11** imperfectly

pop 3 dad, dot, gun, hit, try **4** dada, dart, ding, shot, slap, slog, sock, soda **5** catch, crack, daddy, drink, fling, shoot, whack, whirl **6** attack, bug out, effort, father, strike **7** assault, attempt, explode **8** backfire

pop artist 5 Blake (Peter), Johns (Jasper) **6** Warhol (Andy) **7** Hockney (David), Indiana (Robert) **9** Oldenburg (Claes), Wesselman (Tom) **10** Rosenquist (James) **12** Lichtenstein (Roy)

pope 3 Leo **4** John, Mark, Paul, Pius **5** Caius, Conon, Donus, Felix, Gaius, Lando, Linus, Peter, Soter, Urban **6** Adrian, Agatho, Fabian, Julius, Lucius, Martin, Sixtus, Victor **7** Anterus, Clement, Damasus, Gregory, Hadrian, Hyginus, Marinus, Paschal, Pontian, Romanus, Sergius, Stephen, Zosimus **8** Agapetus, Anicetus, Benedict, Boniface, Calixtus, Eugenius, Eusebius, Formosis, Gelasius, Hilarius, Honorius, Innocent, John Paul, Liberius, Nicholas, Pelagius, Siricius, Theodore, Vigilius, Vitalian **9** Adeodatus, Alexander, Anacletus, Callistus, Celestine, Cornelius, Densdedit, Dionysius, Eutychian, Evaristus, Hormisdas, Marcellus, Miltiades, Severinus, Silverius, Silvester, Sisinnius, Sylvester, Symmachus, Valentine, Zacharias **10** Anastasius, Melchiades, Sabinianus, Simplicius, Zephyrinus **11** Christopher, Constantine, Eleutherius, Eutychianus, Marcellinus, Telesphorus

Pope poem 7 Dunciad (The) **10** Essay on Man (An) **13** Rape of the Lock (The)

Popeye *accessory:* **4** pipe *baby:* **7** Swee'-Pea **8** Sweet Pea *energizer:* **7** spinach *friend:* **5** Wimpy **8** Olive Oyl *occupation:* **6** sailor *rival:* **5** Bluto

pop in 4 call **5** visit **6** drop by, look up, stop by **8** come over

popinjay 3 fop **4** toff **5** dandy, swell **7** peacock **8** macaroni

poplar 5 abele, alamo, aspen **6** balsam **9** tulip tree **10** cottonwood **12** balm of Gilead

Poppaea's husband 4 Nero

poppycock 3 rot **4** bosh, bunk, guff **5** bilge, hokum **6** bunkum **7** baloney **8** malarkey, nonsense **10** balderdash

populace 5 plebs **6** masses, people, public **9** citizenry, commonage, commoners, plebeians **10** commonalty **11** commonality, rank and file, third estate

popular 5 cheap, noted **6** common, famous **7** admired, current, favored, general, leading **8** accepted, approved, favorite, ordinary **9** preferred, prevalent, prominent, well-known, well-liked **10** democratic, prevailing, widespread **11** inexpensive

populate 6 occupy, people, settle **7** inhabit

populous 6 packed **7** crowded, teeming **8** numerous **9** congested **13** multitudinous

porcelain *Chinese:* **9** Lowestoft *English:* **3** Bow **5** Derby, Spode **6** Minton **7** Aynsley, Belleek, Bristol, Chelsea **8** Caughley, Wedgwood *French:* **6** Sèvres **7** Limoges *German:* **7** Dresden, Meissen *ingredient:* **6** kaolin *Italian:* **6** Doccia *Japanese:* **5** Imari

porch 4 deck **5** lanai **6** piazza **7** gallery, veranda **8** verandah

porcupine 8 hedgehog

pore 6 outlet **7** opening, orifice, reflect **8** meditate **10** interstice

pore over 4 read, scan **5** study **6** peruse **10** scrutinize

porgy 4 fish, scup **6** sparid **8** menhaden

Porgy and Bess *composer:* **8** Gershwin (George) *librettist:* **7** Heyward (DuBose) **8** Gershwin (Ira)

Po River city 5 Milan, Padua, Turin **6** Milano, Padova, Torino, Verona **7** Brescia

pork 3 ham, pig **5** bacon, swine **8** sowbelly *cut:* **3** ham **4** jowl, loin, side **7** fatback **8** forefoot, hind foot, spare rib **9** picnic ham **10** Boston butt

pork-barreling 9 patronage

pornographic 7 obscene

porous 5 leaky **6** spongy **8** pervious **9** permeable **10** penetrable

porpoise 5 whale **7** dolphin

porridge 4 mush **5** gruel, kasha **6** bur-

goo, cereal, congee, pablum, sowens
7 oatmeal, pabulum 8 flummery, loblolly 9 stirabout

port 4 hole, jack, left, wine 5 cover,
haven 6 harbor, refuge 7 bearing, opening, retreat, shelter 8 larboard, left side
9 anchorage, harborage, roadstead,
sanctuary 11 comportment *opposite:*
9 starboard

portable 5 handy 6 mobile, wieldy

portal 4 door, gate 5 entry 7 doorway,
gateway 8 approach, entrance, entryway

portcullis 4 gate 7 grating, lattice

portend 4 bode 5 augur 6 signal 7 betoken, predict, presage, promise, signify
8 forebode, forecast, foretell, indicate,
prophesy 9 adumbrate, foretoken
10 foreshadow, vaticinate

portent 4 omen, sign 6 augury, boding
7 presage, prodigy 9 foretoken, sensation 10 foreboding, indication 11 premonition

portentous 5 grave 6 solemn 7 ominous,
pompous, serious, weighty 8 inflated
9 marvelous, momentous, ponderous
10 prodigious

porter 5 hamal, stout 6 bearer, redcap,
skycap 7 bellboy, bellhop, carrier
9 transport 10 doorkeeper

Portia 6 lawyer *husband:* 6 Brutus 8 Bassanio *maid:* 7 Nerissa

portico 4 stoa 9 colonnade

portion 3 cut, lot 4 bite, part 5 dower,
moira, piece, quota, share, slice 6 moiety, parcel 7 measure, quantum, segment 8 division *largest:* 10 lion's share
unused: 8 leftover

portly 3 fat 5 bulky, heavy, large, stout
6 fleshy 7 rotound, stately, weighty
8 imposing 9 corpulent 10 overweight

portmanteau 8 carryall, suitcase

portrait 4 bust 5 image 6 figure, statue
7 picture 8 painting 9 depiction

portray 4 draw, limn, play 5 enact, paint
6 depict, render 7 picture 8 describe
9 delineate, interpret, represent

portrayal 5 image 7 account, picture
8 likeness, painting 9 depiction
11 delineation, description, performance 12 illustration

Portugal *capital:* 6 Lisbon *city:* 5 Porto
6 Oporto 7 Amadora *former name:*
9 Lusitania *island group:* 6 Azores
7 Madeira *leader:* 7 Salazar (Antonio
de) *monetary unit:* 4 euro *monetary unit,
former:* 6 escudo *neighbor:* 5 Spain
peninsula: 7 Iberian *river:* 5 Tagus

pose 3 act, air, ask, set, sit 4 airs, fake,
role, sham 5 feign, front, offer, place,
stand, state, strut 6 affect, assume, pass

as, stance 7 pass for, pass off, present,
pretend, show off, suggest 8 attitude,
pretense, set forth 9 mannerism 10 pretension 11 affectation

Poseidon 7 Neptune *brother:* 4 Zeus
5 Hades, Pluto 7 Jupiter *consort:* 4 Tyro
6 Medusa 7 Demeter *father:* 6 Cronus
mother: 4 Rhea *offspring:* 7 Pegasus *son:*
5 Orion 6 Neleus, Pelias, Triton
7 Antaeus 10 Polyphemus *weapon:* 7 trident *wife:* 10 Amphitrite

poser 6 puzzle, riddle 7 problem
9 conundrum 11 brainteaser

poseur 4 fake 5 bluff, decoy, fraud,
phony, quack 7 bluffer 8 deceiver,
imposter 9 charlatan, hypocrite, pretender 10 mountebank 11 masquerader
12 impersonator

posh 4 chic, rich, tony 5 fancy, grand,
smart, swank 7 elegant, stylish 9 exclusive, expensive, luxurious 11 fashionable, highfalutin, pretentious

posit 3 fix 5 offer 6 affirm, assert,
assume 7 premise, present, presume,
propose, suggest 9 postulate

position 3 job 4 rank, site, spot 5 locus,
place, point, situs, stand, state 6 belief,
locate, stance 7 emplace, footing,
stature 8 attitude, capacity, location,
prestige, standing 10 standpoint

positive 4 firm, real, sure 5 clear, sound
6 actual, useful 7 assured, certain,
decided, factual, genuine, helpful, reality 8 absolute, complete, constant, definite, forceful, outright 9 confident,
doubtless, downright, effective, favorable, realistic 10 beneficial, inarguable,
optimistic, prescribed, undeniable
11 categorical, irrefutable, unequivocal,
unmitigated, unqualified 12 indisputable, unmistakable 13 incontestable

possess 3 own 4 have, hold, keep
5 carry 6 retain 7 acquire, control

possessed 3 mad 6 crazed, hooked
8 frenzied 9 bewitched

possession 7 control 8 property 9 occupancy, ownership 10 occupation

possessive 7 jealous 8 watchful 10 protective 11 proprietary

possibility 4 odds 6 chance 8 instance
9 potential 10 likelihood 11 contingency, feasibility

possible 6 doable, likely, viable 7 earthly 8 feasible 9 expedient, potential
10 imaginable, realizable 11 practicable

possibly 5 maybe 7 perhaps 8 by chance
9 perchance 11 conceivably

post 3 set 4 camp, mail, pole, ride, spot,
task 5 affix, hurry, newel, place, put up,
score, stage, stake 6 advise, column, fill
in, inform, notify, office, pillar

7 apprise, express, placard, publish, station **8** announce, denounce, position **9** advertise **10** assignment

poster 4 bill, sign **6** notice **7** affiche, placard **9** broadside, signboard
12 announcement **13** advertisement

posterior 4 back, hind, rear, rump, seat, tail **5** after, fanny, later **6** behind, caudal, dorsal, hinder **7** ensuing, rear end, tail end **8** backside, buttocks, derriere, hindmost, rearward **9** following **10** subsequent

posterity 6 future **7** progeny **8** children **9** offspring **11** descendants

posthaste 4 fast **6** at once, pronto **7** fleetly, quickly, rapidly, swiftly **8** promptly, speedily **11** immediately

Postimpressionist painter 6 Seurat (Georges) **7** Cezanne (Paul), Gauguin (Paul), Van Gogh (Vincent) **8** Pissarro (Camille), Rousseau (Henri)

postmortem 7 autopsy **8** necropsy

postpone 5 defer, delay, table **6** hold up, put off, shelve **7** hold off, lay over, suspend **8** hold over, prorogue

postulate 5 axiom, claim **6** assert, assume, demand, thesis **7** premise, suppose **10** assumption, hypothesis, presuppose **11** hypothesize, presumption, supposition

posture 4 mode, pose **5** state **6** affect, assume, manner, stance, status **7** bearing, outlook **8** attitude, carriage, position **9** condition, situation **12** attitudinize

posy 5 bloom **6** flower **7** blossom, bouquet, corsage, nosegay **9** sentiment

pot 3 bet, pan, wad **4** ante, hemp, olla **5** grass, kitty, stake, wager **6** boodle, bundle, pipkin **8** cannabis **9** marijuana

potable 5 clean, drink, fresh **6** liquid, liquor **8** beverage **9** drinkable

potassium ore 7 sylvite

potato 3 yam **4** spud **5** tater *bud:* **3** eye

pot-au-___ 3 feu

potbelly 3 gut **4** stove **6** paunch **9** bay window, spare tire

potency 3 pep **5** force, might, power, vigor **6** energy, muscle **8** strength **9** influence, puissance **10** capability **13** effectiveness

potent 4 rich **6** mighty, robust, strong, virile **7** dynamic **8** forceful, forcible, powerful **9** effective **10** persuasive **11** influential

potential 6 latent **7** ability, promise **8** capacity, possible **9** plausible, promising **10** imaginable **11** conceivable, possibility

pother 3 ado **4** flap, fret, fuss, stir, to-do **5** furor, whirl, worry **6** bustle, flurry,

furore, hassle, hubbub, tumult, uproar **7** fluster, turmoil **9** agitation, annoyance, commotion, confusion

potion 6 liquid **7** mixture, philter, philtre **8** medicine **10** concoction

Potiphar's slave 6 Joseph

Potiphera *daughter:* **7** Asenath *son-in-law:* **6** Joseph

Potok novel 6 Chosen (The) **16** My Name Is Asher Lev

potpourri 4 olio **5** blend **6** medley **7** grab bag, mélange, variety **8** mishmash, pastiche **10** assortment, collection, hodgepodge, miscellany, salmagundi

potshot 3 cut, dig **4** gibe, jibe **5** crack, shoot, swipe **6** attack, insult **9** criticism

potter see PUTTER

Potter character 5 Mopsy, Mr. Tod **6** Flopsy, Jemima (Puddleduck) **10** Cotton-tail, Hunca Munca **11** Peter Rabbit **12** Jeremy Fisher

potter's field 8 cemetery, God's acre **9** graveyard

pottery 4 raku **5** delft **7** redware **8** ceramics, clayware, slipware **10** lusterware, terra-cotta, yellowware **11** earthenware

pouch 3 bag, sac **4** sack **5** bulge, bursa, burse **6** pocket **7** saccule **8** sacculus

pouf 5 quilt **7** ottoman **9** comforter

poultry 4 fowl *type:* **4** duck, swan **5** goose, quail **6** grouse, pigeon, turkey **7** chicken, ostrich, peacock **8** pheasant **9** partridge

pounce 5 seize, swoop, talon **6** attack, powder **7** assault, stencil

pound 4 bang, bash, beat, slam, slug, sock **5** drive, money, stamp, throb, thump, tramp **6** batter, buffet, hammer, pummel, strike, thrash, wallop **7** belabor, impress, pulsate **9** enclosure

Pound work 6 Cantos (The)

poupée 4 doll

pour 4 flow, gush, rain, rill, rush, teem **5** flood, issue, skink, spate, surge, swarm **6** decant, deluge, drench, sluice, spring, stream **7** cascade, torrent **8** inundate, overflow

pourboire 3 tip **7** cumshaw **8** gratuity

pout 3 pet **4** fish, moue, sulk **5** grump **8** protrude **10** expression, protrusion

poverty 4 need, want **6** dearth, penury **7** beggary, paucity **8** hardship, poorness, scarcity, shortage **9** indigence, neediness, pauperism, privation **10** mendicancy, scarceness **11** destitution **13** pennilessness

POW camp 6 stalag

powder 4 bray, dust, talc **5** crush **6** talcum **8** sprinkle **9** comminute, pulverize, triturate **10** besprinkle

power 3 vis **4** sway **5** force, might, sinew,

steam, vigor, vires (plural) **6** energy, muscle **7** command, ability, control, potency, voltage **8** dominion, dynamism, imperium, strength **9** authority, influence, privilege, puissance, strong arm **10** ascendancy, domination **11** prerogative, sovereignty, superiority **12** jurisdiction, potentiality *combining form:* **5** dynam **6** dynamo *unit:* **4** watt

powerful 5 great **6** mighty, potent, strong **7** dynamic **8** dominant, puissant, vigorous **9** energetic, strenuous **10** convincing, impressive, invincible, persuasive **11** efficacious, influential, prestigious **13** authoritative

powerless 4 weak **5** inert **6** feeble, unable **7** passive **8** impotent **9** incapable **11** incompetent, ineffective

powwow 4 chat, talk **6** confab, confer, huddle, parley **7** discuss, meeting **8** ceremony **9** gathering **10** discussion **11** confabulate, get-together

practicable 5 utile **6** doable, likely, usable, useful **8** feasible, possible **9** operative **10** functional

practical 5 handy, utile **6** active, useful, versed **7** applied, skilled, trained, virtual **8** sensible **9** pragmatic, realistic **10** functional **11** down-to-earth, experienced **12** businesslike

practically 5 about **6** all but, almost, near to, nearly **7** close to **8** in effect **9** in essence, just about

practice 3 use, way **4** form, mode, wont **5** drill, habit, usage **6** custom, manner, method, repeat, system, tryout, warm up **7** perform, process **8** drilling, engage in, exercise, habitude, rehearse **9** procedure, rehearsal **10** convention

pragmatic 7 factual, logical **8** rational **9** practical, realistic **11** down-to-earth

prairie 4 veld **5** plain, veldt **7** plateau **9** grassland

prairie chicken 6 grouse

prairie wolf 6 coyote

praise 4 hail, hymn, laud, puff **5** bravo, cry up, exalt, extol, honor, kudos **6** belaud, kudize **7** acclaim, adulate, applaud, commend, enhance, flatter, glorify, hosanna, magnify, ovation, plaudit, puffery, sublime **8** accolade, applause, approval, citation, encomium, eulogize, flattery **9** celebrate, laudation, panegyric, recommend **10** aggrandize, compliment, panegyrize **11** acclamation **12** commendation

praiseworthy 8 laudable **9** admirable, deserving, estimable **11** commendable, meritorious

prance 4 step **5** mince, strut **6** sashay, spring **8** cakewalk

prank 3 gag **4** deck, dido, lark, whim **5** adorn, antic, caper, fancy, spiff, sport, trick **6** doll up, frolic, gambol, levity, shavie, vagary, whimsy **7** caprice, deck out, doll out, dress up, garnish, rollick, spiff up **8** beautify, decorate, escapade, ornament, spruce up **9** embellish, frivolity, horseplay, smarten up **10** shenanigan, tomfoolery **11** monkeyshine

prankster 3 wag **5** cutup, joker

prate 3 gab, jaw, yak **4** blab, chat, go on **5** run on **6** babble, gabble, jabber **7** blabber, blather, chatter **9** yakety-yak

prater 6 gossip, magpie **10** chatterbox **12** blabbermouth

pratfall 6 mishap, tumble **7** blunder, stumble **11** humiliation

prawn 6 shrimp **11** langoustine *French:* **8** crevette

praxis 5 habit **6** action, custom, manner **7** conduct **8** exercise, habitude, practice

Praxiteles statue 5 Satyr **6** Hermes **9** Aphrodite

pray 3 ask, beg **5** plead **6** appeal **7** beseech, entreat, implore, request **8** petition **10** supplicate

prayer 4 plea, suit **6** appeal, litany, orison **7** angelus, begging, worship **8** blessing, devotion, entreaty, petition, pleading, rogation **9** adoration **11** application, imploration, imprecation **12** supplication *beads:* **6** rosary *ending:* **4** amen *for the dead:* **7** requiem *Jewish:* **7** kaddish, kiddush *period:* **6** novena **7** triduum *shawl:* **7** tallith

prayer book 6 missal, siddur **8** breviary

prayerful 4 holy **5** godly, pious **6** devout **7** earnest, sincere

preach 4 urge **6** exhort **7** address, deliver, lecture **8** admonish, advocate, moralize **9** sermonize **10** evangelize

preacher 5 padre **6** cleric, divine, parson, pastor **8** chaplain, clerical, minister, reverend **9** churchman, clergyman **10** evangelist, sermonizer **12** ecclesiastic

preaching friar 9 Dominican

preachy 4 smug **7** donnish **8** didactic, sermonic, unctuous **9** homiletic, hortative, pedagogic, pietistic **10** moralizing **11** exhortative, sermonizing **13** sanctimonious, self-righteous

preamble 5 intro, proem **8** exordium, foreword, overture, prologue **12** introduction

precarious 4 iffy **5** dicey, risky, shaky **6** chancy, touchy, tricky, unsafe **7** dubious **8** delicate, doubtful, insecure, ticklish, unstable **9** dangerous, hazardous, sensitive, uncertain **10** unreliable

precaution 4 care 8 prudence 9 foresight, insurance, provision, safeguard 11 forethought

precede 4 lead, rank 5 usher 6 herald 7 forerun, outrank, surpass 8 announce, antedate, go before 9 introduce

precedence 5 order 8 priority 9 seniority

precedent 4 past, rule 5 model, prior 6 former 7 earlier, example 8 anterior 9 foregoing 10 convention

preceding 4 past 5 prior 6 before, former 7 ahead of, prior to 8 anterior, hitherto 9 erstwhile 10 heretofore 11 in advance of *prefix:* 4 ante

precept 3 law 4 rule 5 axiom, edict, order, tenet 6 behest, decree 7 bidding, command 8 doctrine 9 principle 10 injunction, regulation 11 fundamental

preceptive 8 didactic

preceptor 4 head 5 tutor 7 teacher 9 principal 10 headmaster

precinct 4 area 6 domain, region, sector, sphere 7 quarter, section 8 district, division, township 9 bailiwick, enclosure

precious 3 pet 4 dear, nice, rare, rich, very 5 fussy, great, loved, showy 6 adored, choice, costly, la-di-da, prized 7 beloved, darling 8 affected, esteemed, favorite, valuable 9 cherished, exquisite, extremely, priceless 10 invaluable

precipice 5 brink, cliff 8 overhang

precipitancy 4 rush 5 haste, hurry 9 hastiness 10 abruptness, suddenness 11 hurriedness

precipitate 4 fall, hurl 5 hasty, sheer, steep, throw 6 abrupt, madcap, result, sudden, upshot 7 bring on, deposit, falling, flowing, grounds, hurried, outcome, product 8 condense, headlong, sediment, separate 9 breakneck, impatient, impetuous, impulsive 10 unexpected, unforeseen 11 consequence

precipitation 4 hail, mist, rain, snow 5 sleet 7 deposit 8 sediment

precipitous 4 rash 5 hasty, sheer, steep 6 abrupt, sudden 7 hurried, rushing 8 headlong, heedless, plunging 9 breakneck 13 perpendicular

précis 6 digest, survey 7 summary 8 abstract, overview, syllabus 10 abridgment, compendium 11 abridgement 12 condensation

precise 4 nice 5 exact, fixed, right 6 narrow, strict 7 correct, limited 8 accurate, clear-cut, definite, rigorous, specific 9 clocklike, stringent 10 particular

precisely 4 just 5 right 7 exactly 8 strictly

precision 4 care 5 rigor 8 accuracy

9 exactness 10 exactitude, refinement 11 correctness

preclude 5 avert, deter 7 forfend, obviate, prevent, rule out 8 prohibit, stave off 9 forestall

precocious 5 smart 6 brainy, bright, mature 7 forward 8 advanced

precondition 4 must, need 7 proviso 9 essential, necessity, provision, requisite 10 sine qua non 11 requirement, stipulation

precursor 6 herald 8 ancestor, forebear 9 harbinger, indicator, prototype 10 antecedent, forerunner

predator 6 hunter, preyer, raptor 7 stalker 8 devourer 9 destroyer 10 bird of prey

predatory 6 greedy 9 pillaging, rapacious 10 plundering 12 exploitative

predecessor 8 ancestor, forebear 9 precursor, prototype 10 antecedent, forerunner

predicament 3 fix, jam 4 bind, hole, spot 5 pinch, state 6 corner, muddle, pickle, plight, puzzle, scrape, strait 7 dilemma, impasse, trouble 8 hardship, nuisance, quagmire 9 condition, situation 10 difficulty

predicate 4 aver, avow, base, rest 5 found, imply 6 affirm, assert, avouch 7 declare, profess 9 establish

predict 5 augur, guess, infer 6 expect 7 forbode, foresee, portend, surmise 8 announce, conclude, forebode, forecast, foretell, indicate, prophesy, soothsay 10 conjecture, vaticinate 13 prognosticate

prediction 6 augury 8 forecast, prophecy 9 prognosis 10 expectancy 11 expectation

predilection 4 bent, bias 5 fancy, taste 6 liking 7 leaning 8 fondness, penchant, tendency 9 inclining 10 partiality, proclivity, propensity 11 inclination

predispose 4 bend, bias, tend, sway 5 prime 6 affect 7 incline 9 influence

predisposed 5 prone, ready 6 biased 7 partial, willing 8 inclined 11 susceptible

predisposition 4 bent, bias 7 leaning 8 penchant, tendency 9 inclining 10 partiality, proclivity, propensity 11 inclination

predominant 4 main 5 chief, major 6 master, ruling 7 capital, general, leading, primary 8 reigning, superior 9 number one, paramount, principal, sovereign 10 prevailing 11 outstanding

predominate 4 rule 5 reign 6 govern, master 7 command, control, prevail 8 outweigh

preeminence 6 renown 7 primacy 8 dominion, prestige 9 supremacy 10 ascendancy, domination, excellence, importance 11 distinction, superiority

preeminent 4 main 5 chief 7 capital, stellar, supreme 8 dominant, foremost, peerless, towering, ultimate 9 matchless, number-one, paramount, principal, unrivaled 10 surpassing, unrivalled 11 outstanding, unmatchable 12 incomparable, transcendent *prefix:* 4 arch

preempt 4 bump, take 5 annex, seize, usurp 6 assume 7 acquire, replace 8 arrogate 9 forestall 10 confiscate, substitute 11 appropriate, expropriate

preen 5 gloat, groom, pride, primp, swell 6 smooth

preface 4 lead, open 5 begin, proem, usher 6 herald 8 exordium, foreword, overture, preamble, prologue 9 introduce 11 preliminary 12 introduction

prefatory 7 opening 8 proemial 12 introductory

prefect 7 head boy, monitor 8 head girl 10 magistrate

prefer 5 elect, favor 6 choose, opt for, select 7 advance, elevate, promote, upgrade

preferable 5 finer 6 better 8 superior, worthier

preference 4 pick 6 choice, option 8 election, priority 9 advantage, elevation, promotion, selection, upgrading 10 favoritism, partiality

prefigure 4 hint 7 foresee 8 indicate 9 adumbrate 10 foreshadow

pregnancy 9 gestation, gravidity

pregnant 4 full, rich 5 heavy 6 gravid, parous 7 teeming, weighty 8 eloquent, enceinte, profound 9 expectant, expecting, gestating, inventive, momentous, with child 10 expressive, meaningful, parturient 11 significant

prehensile 8 grasping

prejudice 3 mar 4 bias, harm, hurt, sway 5 color, favor 6 damage, injure, injury, racism, sexism 7 bigotry, leaning 8 aversion 9 antipathy, hostility, influence 10 partiality 11 intolerance 12 onesidedness

prejudicial 6 biased 7 bigoted 8 damaging 9 injurious 11 deleterious, detrimental

prelate 5 abbot 6 bishop 7 primate 8 cardinal, diocesan 9 patriarch 10 archbishop 12 ecclesiastic

preliminary 4 heat 5 basic, match, trial 7 initial, opening 8 proemial 9 beginning 10 qualifying 11 fundamental 12 introductory

prelude 5 intro, proem 8 exordium, foreword, overture, prologue 12 introduction, prolegomenon

premature 5 early 8 untimely 10 beforehand

premeditated 5 set up 7 planned, studied, willful 8 designed, intended 9 conscious 10 calculated, considered, deliberate, thought-out 11 intentional

premier 4 head, main 5 chief, first 7 leading, primary 8 earliest, foremost, original 9 principal 13 prime minister

premiere 5 debut 7 opening 8 earliest, original 9 beginning 10 first night

premise 4 base 5 posit 6 assume, thesis 8 building, property, set forth 9 postulate 10 assumption 11 postulation, proposition, supposition

premium 5 bonus, extra, prize 6 reward 8 dividend, superior 9 excellent 10 recompense 11 exceptional

premonition 4 omen 9 misgiving, suspicion 10 foreboding 11 forewarning 12 apprehension, presentiment

preoccupied 4 deep, lost, rapt 6 absent, intent 7 engaged, faraway, worried 8 absorbed, immersed 9 concerned, engrossed, wrapped up 10 abstracted, distracted 11 inattentive 12 absentminded

prep 5 basic, coach, drill, equip, groom, prime, ready, train, trial 8 get ready 11 preliminary 12 introductory

preparation 4 base, plan 5 study 7 fitness, measure 8 compound, medicine, training 9 alertness, foresight, readiness 10 background, concoction

preparatory 5 basic 11 preliminary, rudimentary 12 introductory

prepare 3 fit, fix 4 gird 5 draft, prime, ready, train 6 draw up, make up, outfit 7 fortify, furnish 9 formulate

prepared 3 set 4 up on 5 fixed, ready 6 primed 7 treated 9 processed

preponderance 4 bulk 8 dominion, majority, main part 9 ascendant, dominance, supremacy 10 ascendancy, domination 11 superiority

preponderant 7 supreme 8 dominant, superior 9 paramount 10 prevailing

preponderate 4 rule 5 reign 6 exceed 7 command, dictate, outrank, prevail 8 dominate, outweigh

prepossess 4 bias, sway 5 favor 6 absorb, engage, occupy 7 engross, immerse, involve 9 influence

prepossessing 7 likable 9 appealing 10 attractive

preposterous 4 wild 5 crazy, wacky 6 absurd, insane 7 asinine, foolish, idiotic 9 fantastic, laughable, senseless

10 irrational, ridiculous 11 harebrained
12 unreasonable
prerequisite 4 must, need 5 vital
8 required 9 condition, essential,
mandatory, necessary, necessity
10 imperative, sine qua non 11 requirement 13 indispensable
prerogative 5 power, right 8 appanage,
immunity 9 authority, exemption, privilege 10 birthright, perquisite
presage 4 bode, omen, warn 5 augur,
sense 6 augury, boding, herald, intuit
7 portend, portent, predict, promise,
warning 8 announce, forebode, forecast, foretell, forewarn, indicate,
prophesy, soothsay 9 foretoken, harbinger, intuition, misgiving 10 foreboding, foreshadow, prediction, prognostic,
vaticinate
presbyter 5 elder 6 priest
prescience 9 foresight 12 anticipation,
clairvoyance 13 foreknowledge
prescribe 3 fix, set 4 rule 5 guide, order
6 assign, choose, decide, decree, define,
direct, impose, ordain, select 7 dictate,
lay down, pick out, require, specify
9 designate, determine, stipulate
prescript 3 law 4 rule 5 edict, order
6 decree 10 regulation
prescription 4 drug, rule 5 claim, right,
title 6 custom, remedy 8 medicine
9 direction 10 medication
presence 3 air 4 look, mien 5 poise
6 aspect, spirit 7 address, bearing 8 carriage, demeanor 9 composure
present 3 act, aim, now 4 boon, gift,
give, here, pose, show 5 award, bring,
favor, offer, point, stage, tense, today
6 at hand, bestow, confer, convey,
direct, donate, extend, in view, modern, submit, tender 7 hand out, largess,
perform, proffer 8 existing, nominate
9 introduce 12 contemporary
presentable 3 fit 6 decent, proper
8 becoming 9 befitting 10 acceptable
11 appropriate 12 satisfactory
present-day 6 living, recent 7 current,
ongoing, popular, topical 8 contempo,
existent, existing, pressing, up-to-date
9 prevalent, surviving 10 prevailing
12 contemporary
presently 3 now 4 anon, soon 5 today
6 in time, one day 7 by and by 9 forthwith, these days 10 before long
preservation 4 care 6 saving, shield
7 defense, keeping 8 pickling 10 hus-
banding, protection 11 conservancy,
maintenance, safekeeping
preserve 3 can, jam 4 save 5 jelly, put up
6 keep up, pickle 7 protect, shelter, sustain 8 keep safe, maintain 9 confiture

preside 3 run 4 head, lead 5 chair
6 direct, handle, manage 7 conduct,
control, operate, oversee 8 moderate
9 officiate
president *United States:* 4 Bush (George,
George W.), Ford (Gerald R.), Polk
(James K.), Taft (William H.) 5 Adams
(John, John Quincy), Grant (Ulysses
S.), Hayes (Rutherford B.), Nixon
(Richard M.), Tyler (John) 6 Arthur
(Chester A.), Carter (Jimmy), Hoover
(Herbert), Monroe (James), Pierce
(Franklin), Reagan (Ronald), Taylor
(Zachary), Truman (Harry S.), Wilson
(Woodrow) 7 Clinton (Bill), Harding
(Warren), Jackson (Andrew), Johnson
(Andrew, Lyndon), Kennedy (John F.),
Lincoln (Abraham), Madison (James)
8 Buchanan (James), Coolidge (Calvin),
Fillmore (Millard), Garfield (James),
Harrison (Benjamin, William Henry),
McKinley (William), Van Buren (Mar-
tin) 9 Cleveland (Grover), Jefferson
(Thomas), Roosevelt (Franklin D.,
Theodore) 10 Eisenhower (Dwight D.),
Washington (George)
presidio 4 fort 7 bastion, citadel 8 fastness, fortress, garrison 10 stronghold
13 fortification
press 3 hug, jam, ram 4 cram, iron,
mass, pack, pile, push, rush, urge
5 clasp, crowd, crush, drive, force,
horde, hurry, media, shove 6 demand,
hustle, insist, jostle, propel, squash,
stress, throng, thrust 7 beseech,
entreat, imprint, printer, squeeze
9 constrain, influence, multitude
pressing 5 acute, vital 6 urgent 7 crucial, earnest, exigent, serious 8 critical
9 immediate, important, insistent
10 compelling, imperative
pressure 4 push, rush 5 drive, impel
6 burden, strain, stress 7 tension
10 constraint *combining form:* 5 piezo
instrument: 9 barometer *unit:* 3 bar
6 pascal
prestige 4 fame, rank, sway 5 power
6 cachet, credit, esteem, regard,
renown, repute, status, weight 7 dignity, stature 8 eminence, position, standing 9 authority, influence 10 importance, prominence 11 consequence,
distinction
prestigious 5 famed, great 6 famous
7 eminent, honored, notable
8 esteemed, renowned 9 prominent,
respected 10 celebrated 11 influential
13 distinguished
presto 4 fast 7 hastily, quickly, rapidly
8 suddenly 9 posthaste 11 immediately

presumably 6 likely, surely 8 probably 9 doubtless

presume 4 dare 5 guess, imply, infer, think, trust 6 expect, gather, impose, reason 7 believe, intrude, suppose, surmise, venture 8 infringe 9 postulate 10 conjecture

presumption 4 gall 5 brass, cheek, nerve 6 belief, daring, ground, reason, thesis 7 conceit 8 audacity, chutzpah, evidence 9 brashness, inference, postulate 10 confidence, effrontery

presumptuous 4 bold, smug 5 brash, fresh, pushy 6 cheeky, uppity 7 forward 8 arrogant 9 audacious, confident 11 overweening, self-assured

presuppose 5 posit 6 assume, expect 7 imagine, require, surmise 9 postulate

pretend 3 act 4 fake, pose, sham 5 bluff, claim, false, feign, guess, put on 6 affect, assume, delude, invent 7 deceive, imitate, mislead, playact, profess, purport, suppose, surmise 8 simulate 9 imaginary 11 counterfeit, make-believe

pretender 4 fake, sham 5 actor, faker, fraud, phony 6 humbug 8 claimant, impostor 9 hypocrite

pretense 3 act, air 4 face, fake, mask, pose, sham 5 claim, cloak, cover, front, guise 6 deceit, facade, humbug 7 charade, fiction 8 disguise 9 deception, false show, imposture 10 masquerade, simulation 11 affectation, make-believe, ostentation

pretension 5 claim, right 6 vanity 8 ambition 10 allegation, aspiration 11 affectation

pretentious 5 lofty, put-on, showy 6 chichi, la-di-da, too-too 7 pompous, stilted 8 affected, inflated, puffed up, snobbish, specious 9 bombastic, conceited, grandiose, overblown 10 euphuistic, rhetorical 11 highfalutin 12 high-sounding, magniloquent, vainglorious

preternatural 7 psychic, unusual 8 abnormal, atypical 9 anomalous, unearthly, untypical 10 mysterious 12 inexplicable, supernatural 13 extraordinary

pretext 4 mask, ploy 5 alibi, cloak, cover, front, guise 6 device, excuse 7 apology 10 subterfuge

pretty 3 apt, pat 4 cute, fair, nice, some 5 bonny, quite 6 adroit, artful, clever, comely, fairly, kind of, lovely, mainly, rather, seemly, sort of 7 cunning, darling 8 graceful, handsome, pleasant, pleasing, skillful, somewhat 9 appealing, beautiful 10 attractive, moderately,

more or less 11 good-looking 12 considerable

prevail 4 beat, rule 5 reign 6 master 7 conquer, impress, persist, triumph 8 convince, dominate, domineer, overcome, override, persuade 9 influence

prevalent 4 rife 6 ruling 7 favored, popular, regnant 8 accepted, dominant, superior 9 ascendant, customary, paramount, sovereign 10 accustomed, widespread

prevaricate 3 fib, lie 5 avoid, evade 6 palter 7 confuse, deceive, distort, falsify, quibble 12 misrepresent

prevarication 3 fib, lie 4 tale 5 lying, story 6 canard, deceit 7 falsity 9 deception, falsehood

prevent 3 bar, dam 4 balk, foil, ward 5 avert, avoid, block, check, debar, deter 6 arrest, baffle, forbid, hinder, impede, thwart 7 forfend, head off, inhibit, obviate 8 obstruct, prohibit, stave off 9 forestall, frustrate, interdict 10 anticipate

previous 4 fore, past 5 early, prior 6 before, former 7 earlier, onetime 8 anterior 9 erstwhile, foregoing, in advance 10 antecedent, beforehand

previously 4 once 5 afore, ahead 6 before 7 already, earlier 8 formerly 9 erstwhile 10 heretofore

prewar 10 antebellum

prey 4 feed, game, mark 5 chase 6 quarry, target, victim 8 casualty, distress

Priam *daughter:* 6 Creusa 8 Polyxena 9 Cassandra *father:* 8 Laomedon *grandfather:* 4 Ilus *kingdom:* 4 Troy *slayer:* 7 Pyrrhus 11 Neoptolemus *son:* 5 Paris 6 Hector, Lycaon 7 Helenus, Troilus 9 Deiphobus, Polydorus *wife:* 6 Arisbe, Hecuba

Priapus *father:* 7 Bacchus 8 Dionysus *mother:* 5 Venus 9 Aphrodite

price 3 fee, fix, tab 4 cost, fare, rate, toll 6 amount, assess, charge, figure, outlay, reward, tariff 7 expense, payment 8 appraise

priceless 4 rare, rich 5 droll, funny, witty 6 absurd, costly, prized, valued 7 amusing 8 precious, valuable 9 cherished, treasured 10 invaluable

pricey 4 dear 5 steep 6 costly 9 expensive

prick 3 jab 4 goad, mark, prod, spur, urge 5 egg on, point, sting, thorn 6 affect, excite, exhort, pierce, prompt 7 pinhole 8 puncture 9 perforate

prickly 5 burry, sharp, spiny 6 briary, thorny, tingly, touchy, trying 7 brambly, waspish 8 annoying, nettling, snappish, stinging 9 difficult, fractious, irritable, vexatious **10** bothersome, irritating, nettlesome **11** troublesome

pride 3 ego, top **4** best, brag, pack, pick **5** boast, cream, elite, exult, group, preen, prime, prize, vaunt **6** choice, egoism, vanity **7** conceit, delight, elation, dignity, disdain, egotism **8** smugness, treasure **9** arrogance, cockiness, vainglory **10** self-esteem, self-regard **11** self-respect **12** congratulate

Pride and Prejudice author 6 Austen (Jane)

prideful 6 elated **7** haughty **8** exultant **10** disdainful

prier 5 snoop **7** meddler **8** busybody, quidnunc **9** buttinsky

priest 6 cleric, divine, rector **8** chaplain **9** clergyman, presbyter *ancient Roman:* **6** flamen **8** pontifex *Buddhist:* **4** lama *Celtic:* **5** druid *French:* **4** abbé, curé *Muslim:* **4** imam *tribal:* **6** shaman

priestly 8 clerical, hieratic **10** sacerdotal

prig 5 prude, thief **6** pedant **8** bluenose **9** Mrs. Grundy **10** goody-goody

priggish 5 fussy **6** stuffy **7** genteel, pompous, prudish **8** affected, pedantic **11** puritanical, straitlaced

prim 4 neat, nice, snug, tidy, trig **5** stiff **6** formal, proper, strict, stuffy, wooden **7** correct, genteel, orderly, precise, prudish **8** decorous, priggish **11** straitlaced

prima donna 4 diva, snob, star **7** artiste **9** chanteuse **10** narcissist **11** leading lady

prima facie 4 true **5** valid **8** apparent **11** self-evident

primal 5 basic **6** age-old **7** ancient, premier **8** cardinal, original **9** atavistic, paramount, primitive **10** preeminent **11** prehistoric

primary 4 main **5** basal, basic, chief, first **6** direct **7** initial, pioneer, radical **8** cardinal, earliest, original **9** elemental, essential, firsthand, immediate, number-one, paramount, principal **10** aboriginal, underlying **11** fundamental, rudimentary **12** foundational, introductory *combining form:* **4** prot **5** proto *prefix:* **4** arch **5** archi

primate 3 ape, man **5** human, lemur, loris **6** aye-aye, bonobo, monkey **7** gorilla **10** anthropoid, chimpanzee, human being **11** Homo sapiens *nocturnal:* **5** loris **7** tarsier *small:* **6** galago

prime 3 top **4** best, dawn, fill, load, morn, peak, pick, rate **5** coach, cream, elite, first, paint, sunup, tonic, youth **6** choice, excite, height, spring, symbol **7** capital, highest, initial, morning, prepare, provoke, quicken **8** earliest, moti-

vate, original, superior **9** excellent, first-rate, principal, stimulate **10** first-class

primer 4 book **5** guide **6** manual, reader **8** hornbook

primeval 7 ancient **8** earliest, original **10** aboriginal

primitive 3 raw **4** rude **5** basic, crude, early **6** savage **7** archaic, Spartan **8** barbaric, original, primeval **9** atavistic, barbarian, barbarous, elemental, essential, unevolved **10** elementary, primordial, underlying **11** fundamental, preliterate, uncivilized, undeveloped **12** uncultivated *combining form:* **5** palae, paleo **6** archae, archeo, palaeo **7** archaeo *prefix:* **4** arch **5** arche, archi

primogenitor 8 ancestor, forebear **9** precursor **10** forefather

primordial 5 basic, early, first **7** ancient **8** earliest, original

primp 4 fuss **5** adorn, dress, fix up, preen **7** dress up

prince *Anglo-Saxon:* **8** atheling *Arab:* **4** amir, emir *Austrian:* **8** archduke *Ethiopian:* **3** ras *Indian:* **4** raja **5** rajah *of demons:* **9** Beelzebub *of Monaco:* **7** Rainier *of the church:* **8** cardinal *of Wales:* **7** Charles

Prince and the Pauper author 5 Twain (Mark) **7** Clemens (Samuel)

Prince ___ Coast, Antarctica 4 Olav

Prince Edward Island *capital:* **13** Charlottetown *provincial flower:* **12** lady's slipper

Prince Igor composer 7 Borodin (Aleksandr)

princely 5 grand, noble, royal **8** generous, imposing, majestic **9** dignified **11** magnificent

princess 7 infanta *mythical:* **3** Ino *of Monaco:* **5** Grace

Prince Valiant *artist:* **6** Foster (Hal) *son:* **3** Arn *wife:* **5** Aleta

principal 4 arch, dean, head, main, star **5** chief, first, major, prime **6** assets **7** capital, leading, premier, primary, stellar **8** cardinal, champion, dominant, foremost **9** paramount **10** headmaster, preeminent **11** outstanding, predominant *combining form:* **4** prot **5** proto *prefix:* **4** arch **5** archi

principium 3 law **5** axiom, basis **7** element, theorem **10** foundation **11** fundamental

principle 3 law **4** code, form, rule **5** axiom, basis, canon, ethic, tenet **6** ground, origin, source **7** conduct, faculty, precept **8** doctrine, polestar, rudiment **10** assumption, convention, foundation **11** fundamental

principled 5 moral, noble 6 honest 7 ethical, upright 8 virtuous 9 righteous 10 moralistic

print 4 type 5 issue, litho, stamp, write 7 engrave, impress, publish, typeset 10 impression *style:* 4 bold 5 roman 6 italic 7 cursive 8 boldface

printer *English:* 6 Caxton (William) *German:* 9 Gutenberg (Johann, Johannes) *Italian:* 6 Bodoni (Giambattista) 8 Manutius (Aldus)

printing 7 edition, reissue 10 impression *measure:* 4 pica 5 agate *process:* 4 roto 7 gravure

priority 4 lead 5 order 8 ordering 9 supremacy 10 importance, precedence, preference

prison 3 can, pen 4 brig, coop, jail, keep 5 clink 6 cooler, lockup 7 dungeon, slammer 8 bastille, big house, stockade 9 calaboose 11 reformatory 12 penitentiary *California:* 8 Alcatraz 10 San Quentin *New York:* 6 Attica 8 Sing Sing 12 Rikers Island *Northern Ireland:* 4 Maze *resident:* 6 inmate 7 convict 8 jailbird

prisoner 7 captive, convict, hostage 8 criminal, detainee, jailbird

prissy 5 picky 7 finicky, precise, prudish 8 exacting 10 fastidious, particular 11 straitlaced

pristine 4 pure 5 clean, fresh 8 earliest, original 9 unspoiled

privacy 6 secret 7 retreat, secrecy 9 seclusion 11 concealment

private 5 inner 6 secret 7 soldier 8 eyes-only, hush-hush, intimate, personal 9 concealed 10 closed-door, restricted, unofficial 11 independent, sequestered 12 confidential

privateer 4 ship 7 gunship 9 mercenary

private eye 3 spy 4 G-man, tail 6 sleuth, shamus 7 gumshoe 9 detective 12 investigator

privately 7 sub rosa 8 covertly, in camera, in secret, secretly

privation 4 lack, loss, need, want 6 dearth, penury 7 absence, poverty 8 distress 9 indigence, neediness, suffering

privilege 4 boon 5 favor, grant, right 7 license 8 appanage 9 allowance, exemption 10 birthright, concession, perquisite 11 entitlement, opportunity, prerogative *pope-granted:* 6 indult

privy 3 can, loo 4 head, john 5 jakes 6 secret, toilet 7 latrine 8 bathroom, informed, lavatory, outhouse, personal 9 concealed, withdrawn 11 water closet

prize 3 pry, top 4 best, loot, pick, plum, rate, swag 5 award, booty, cream, elite, force, lever, spoil, value 6 choice, esteem, reward, spoils, trophy 7 capture, cherish, jackpot, plunder, premium 8 treasure 10 appreciate 11 outstanding

prizefighting 6 boxing 8 pugilism

pro 3 for 6 expert, master 8 skillful 9 authority, in favor of 11 affirmative

probable 6 likely 7 seeming 8 apparent, credible, expected, feasible, rational, reliable 10 reasonable

probe 4 poke, quiz, test 5 query, study 6 search 7 dig into, examine, explore, feel out, inquest, inquire, inquiry 8 check out, look into, research, sound out 9 delve into, penetrate 11 exploration, investigate, reconnoiter 13 investigation

probity 5 honor 6 virtue 7 honesty 8 fairness, goodness 9 integrity, rectitude 11 uprightness

problem 4 mess 5 hitch, issue, poser 6 enigma, puzzle, riddle 7 dilemma, example, mystery, puzzler, trouble 8 hardship, headache, question 10 difficulty

problematic 4 iffy, moot, open 7 dubious 8 arguable, doubtful 9 debatable, uncertain, unsettled 10 precarious 12 questionable

proboscis 4 beak, nose 5 snoot, snout, trunk

procedure 4 plan, step 6 course, custom, method, policy, system 7 formula, measure, routine 8 protocol 9 operation 11 instruction

proceed 4 flow, move, rise, stem, wend 5 arise, get on, issue, segue 6 emerge, push on, spring, travel 7 advance, carry on, emanate, journey 8 continue, get along 9 originate 10 derive from

proceedings 8 goings-on *recorded:* 4 acta 6 annals 7 minutes

proceeds 4 gain, take 5 yield 6 profit, result, return 8 earnings

process 3 way 4 mode, wise 5 modus, treat 6 handle, manner, method, refine, system 7 fashion, prepare, recycle, routine 8 workings 9 evolution, operation, outgrowth, procedure, technique 11 development

procession 5 march, order, train 6 parade, series, string 7 caravan, cortege 8 sequence 9 cavalcade, marchpast, motorcade 11 consecution

proclaim 5 extol 6 assert, insist 7 declare, exhibit, glorify, publish 8 announce, evidence, manifest 9 advertise, broadcast, make known 10 annunciate, bruit about

proclivity 4 bent 6 liking 7 leaning 8 penchant 9 proneness 11 inclination

Procne *father:* 7 Pandion *husband:* 6 Tereus *sister:* 9 Philomela *son:* 4 Itys

procrastinate 5 dally, delay 6 dawdle

procreate 5 beget, breed 7 produce 8 conceive, generate, multiply 9 reproduce

Procris' husband 8 Cephalus

Procrustean ___ 3 bed

proctor 7 monitor, oversee 9 supervise 10 supervisor

procure 3 buy, get 4 gain 6 obtain, pick up 7 achieve, acquire 8 purchase 10 bring about

prod 3 dig, jab, jog 4 goad, poke, push, spur, stir, urge 5 elbow, nudge, point, prick, rouse 6 excite, exhort, incite, thrust 8 motivate 9 stimulate 10 incitement

prodigal 4 lush 6 lavish 7 opulent, profuse, riotous, spender, wastrel 8 reckless, wasteful 9 exuberant, luxuriant 10 profligate, squanderer 11 extravagant, spendthrift

prodigious 4 huge, vast 6 mighty, unreal 7 amazing, immense, mammoth, massive, strange, unusual 8 colossal, enormous, gigantic 9 fantastic, marvelous, wonderful 10 astounding, impressive, monumental, phenomenal, remarkable, staggering, stupendous, surprising 11 astonishing 13 extraordinary

produce 4 bear, form, grow, make, show, sire 5 beget, breed, build, cause, erect, frame, hatch, mount, put on, raise, spawn, stage, yield 6 create, effect, father, output, parent, secure, work up 7 deliver, fashion, turn out 8 engender, generate, multiply 9 construct, fabricate, originate, procreate, propagate 10 bring about 11 manufacture, put together

product 5 fruit, issue, yield 6 effect, legacy, output, result, upshot 7 harvest, outcome, turnout 8 artifact, creation, multiple, offshoot 9 handiwork, outgrowth 11 consequence, manufacture

production 5 fruit, yield 6 output 7 staging, turnout 8 artifact, assembly, creation 9 execution, handiwork, rendering 11 achievement, manufacture, realization

productive 4 rich 6 fecund, useful 7 fertile 8 abundant, fruitful, prolific 9 rewarding 10 beneficial

proem 7 preface, prelude 8 exordium, foreword, overture, prologue 11 preliminary

profane 3 lay 4 damn, foul 5 abuse, dirty, pagan 6 coarse, debase, defile, filthy, impure, unholy, vulgar 7 impious, obscene, secular 8 indecent, temporal, unsacred 9 desecrate 10 irreverent, unhallowed 11 blasphemous, irreligious 12 sacrilegious, unsanctified

profanity 4 oath 5 abuse, curse 7 cursing, cussing 8 swearing 9 blasphemy, sacrilege 10 execration 11 imprecation, irreverence

profess 4 aver, avow 5 claim, teach 6 affirm, allege, assert, avouch 7 declare, pretend, protest, purport 8 maintain, practice

profession 3 art, job, vow 5 craft, trade 6 avowal, career, métier 7 calling 8 business, vocation 9 assertion, specialty, statement, testimony 10 handicraft, occupation 11 affirmation

professional 4 paid 6 expert, master 7 learned, skilled 9 authority 10 proficient, specialist 11 experienced 12 businesslike

professor 3 don 6 expert 7 teacher 8 academic, educator

proffer 4 give, pose 6 extend, submit, tender 7 hold out, present, suggest 10 invitation, suggestion

proficiency 5 savvy, skill 7 ability, advance 8 progress 9 adeptness, expertise, knowledge 10 competence

proficient 4 able 5 adept 6 expert 7 capable, skilled 8 advanced, masterly, skillful 9 authority, competent, effective, masterful, qualified 11 crackerjack, experienced 12 accomplished

profile 5 chart 6 sketch, survey 7 contour, diagram, outline 8 exposure, portrait, side view 9 biography 10 silhouette 11 description

profit 3 net 4 gain, take 5 serve, yield 6 excess, income, payoff, return 7 benefit, receipt 8 earnings, proceeds 10 percentage 12 compensation

profitable 6 paying, useful 7 gainful 8 fruitful 9 lucrative, rewarding 10 beneficial, well-paying, worthwhile 11 moneymaking 12 advantageous, remunerative

profligate 4 wild 6 waster 7 immoral, spender, wastrel 8 prodigal, reckless, wasteful 9 abandoned, dissolute, indulgent, reprobate 10 dissipated, immoderate, licentious, squanderer 11 extravagant, promiscuous, spendthrift 13 self-indulgent

profound 4 deep, wise 5 heavy, total, utter 7 abysmal, intense 8 absolute, abstruse, complete, esoteric, thorough 9 intensive 10 deep-seated, insightful

profundity 5 depth 6 wisdom 7 insight 8 deepness 12 abstruseness

profuse 4 lush 6 lavish 7 copious, fulsome, liberal, opulent 8 abundant, generous, prodigal 9 abounding, bounteous, bountiful, excessive, exuberant, luxuriant, plentiful 10 munificent 11 extravagant

profusion 4 glut, riot 5 flood, spate, surge 6 bounty, deluge, excess, wealth 7 nimiety, satiety, surfeit, surplus, torrent 8 overflow, overload, plethora 9 abundance, plenitude 10 lavishness, luxuriance, oversupply, plentitude, redundancy 11 copiousness, prodigality, sufficiency, superfluity 12 extravagance 13 overabundance

progenitor 4 sire 6 author, father, mother 8 ancestor, forebear 9 initiator, precursor 10 antecessor, forefather, forerunner, originator 11 predecessor

progeny 4 line 5 issue 6 litter, result, scions 7 outcome, product 8 children 9 offspring, posterity 11 descendants

prognosis 8 estimate, forecast, prophecy 9 prevision 10 estimation, prediction 11 expectation 12 anticipation

prognostic 4 omen, sign 6 augury 7 portent, presage 10 foreboding, indication

prognosticate 6 divine 7 foresee, predict, presage 8 forecast, foretell, prophesy

program 4 bill, book, plan, show 5 plans, slate 6 agenda, course, docket, lineup, policy 7 listing 8 calendar, playbill, schedule, syllabus 9 broadcast, procedure, timetable 10 bill of fare, curriculum

progress 4 fare, gain, grow 5 get on, march 6 course, growth 7 advance, headway, passage, proceed 8 anabasis, get along, momentum 9 evolution, flowering, unfolding 11 advancement, development, improvement *planned:* 7 telesis

progressing 5 afoot 7 en route 8 under way

progression 5 chain 6 course, growth, series 7 advance 8 sequence 9 evolution, unfolding 11 development

progressive 6 modern 7 growing, liberal, radical 8 advanced, tolerant 9 advancing 10 developing, increasing

prohibit 3 ban, bar 4 stop 5 block, debar 6 enjoin, forbid, outlaw 7 prevent 8 preclude 9 interdict

prohibited 5 taboo 6 banned, barred 7 illegal, illicit 8 verboten 9 forbidden

prohibition 3 ban, bar 5 taboo 7 embargo 8 sanction 9 interdict 10 constraint, forbidding, injunction 12 disallowance, interdiction, proscription

prohibitive 5 steep 6 costly 7 sky-high 9 excessive 10 exorbitant, forbidding 11 restrictive

project 3 jut 4 cast, feat, plan 5 bulge 6 affair, design, devise, extend, intend, scheme, vision 7 arrange, concern, emprise, exploit, feature, imagine, propose, purpose, venture 8 business, conceive, envisage, envision, game plan, overhang, protrude, stand out, stick out, strategy 9 blueprint, visualize 10 enterprise 11 proposition, undertaking

projection 3 jut 4 bump, knob, view 5 bulge 7 display 8 estimate, forecast, overhang, scheming, swelling 9 extension 10 jutting out, perception 11 expectation

proletariat 6 masses 7 workers 8 laborers 9 commoners, hoi polloi 12 working class

prolific 4 rich 6 fecund, gifted, lavish 7 fertile 8 abundant, creative, fruitful 9 abounding, bountiful, inventive 10 generating, generative 11 reproducing 12 reproductive

prolix 4 long 5 windy, wordy 7 diffuse, lengthy, tedious, verbose 8 drawn out, rambling, tiresome 9 redundant, wearisome 10 long-winded

prologue 7 opening, preface, prelude 8 exordium, foreword, overture, preamble 9 beginning 12 introduction

prolong 6 extend 7 drag out, draw out, spin out, stretch 8 continue, elongate, lengthen

prolonged 7 lasting, lengthy 8 drawn-out 9 lingering 10 continuing, persistent, persisting

prom 4 ball, fete, gala 5 dance 6 formal

promenade 4 deck, walk 6 parade, stroll 9 boardwalk

Prometheus *brother:* 5 Atlas 9 Menoetius 10 Epimetheus *creation:* 3 man 7 mankind *father:* 7 Iapetus *gift:* 4 fire *mother:* 7 Clymene *rescuer:* 8 Heracles, Hercules *tormentor:* 5 eagle

prominence 4 crag, fame, rise, spur 5 bulge 6 height, renown, status 8 eminence, headland, prestige, salience, standing 9 celebrity, elevation 10 importance, projection 11 distinction

prominent 5 famed, great, noted 6 famous, marked, signal 7 eminent, jutting, leading, notable, popular, salient 8 renowned, striking 9 arresting, notorious, well-known 10 celebrated, noticeable, pronounced, remarkable 11 conspicuous, eye-catching, illustrious, outstanding 13 distinguished *person:* 3 VIP 4 BMOC, lion 5 mogul, nabob 6 bigwig, honcho 7 big shot,

grandee 8 luminary, mandarin, somebody 9 dignitary 13 high-muck-a-muck
promiscuous 5 mixed 6 casual, random,
varied 7 immoral 8 careless 9 haphazard, hit-or-miss, irregular 10 licentious
11 unselective 12 unrestrained
promise 3 vow 4 bode, bond, oath
5 agree, augur, swear, vouch 6 assure,
engage, ensure, expect, insure, parole,
pledge, plight 7 betroth, compact, consent, declare, outlook, portend,
presage, suggest 8 contract, covenant,
indicate 9 assurance, betrothal, potential, undertake 11 declaration, expectation
promised land 4 Zion 6 Canaan, heaven
8 paradise 11 kingdom come
promising 6 likely 7 hopeful 9 favorable
10 auspicious 11 encouraging
promissory note 3 IOU
promontory 4 beak, bill, cape, head,
ness 5 bulge, point 8 foreland, headland
promote 3 aid 4 help, plug, puff, push,
sell, tout 5 boost, favor, raise 6 foster,
launch, prefer 7 advance, build up, elevate, endorse, forward, further, nurture, present, support 8 advocate,
champion 9 advertise, encourage, publicize, recommend
promotion 6 step up 7 advance, buildup,
puffery 9 elevation, publicity, upgrading 10 preference, preferment
11 advancement, advertising, improvement 13 advertisement
prompt 3 apt, cue, jog 4 fast, goad, help,
hint, move, spur, urge 5 alert, quick,
rapid, ready 6 assist, incite, induce, on
time, remind, speedy, stir up, timely
7 suggest 8 convince, persuade, punctual, reminder 10 responsive
promulgate 5 issue 6 decree 7 declare,
publish 8 announce, proclaim 9 advertise, broadcast 10 annunciate 11 disseminate
prone 3 apt 4 flat, open 5 given, level
6 liable, likely, supine 7 subject, tending, willing 8 disposed, facedown,
inclined 9 lying down, reclining,
recumbent 10 horizontal 11 predisposed, susceptible
prong 4 barb, fang, fork, spur, stab, tine
5 point, thorn 6 pierce
pronghorn 8 antelope
___ **pro nobis** 3 ora
pronoun *archaic:* 3 thy 4 thou 5 thine
demonstrative: 4 that, this 5 these, those
indefinite: 3 all, any, few, one 4 both,
each, none, some 5 no one, other
6 anyone, either, nobody 7 another,
anybody, neither, nothing, someone
8 anything, somebody 9 everybody,

something 10 everything *personal:*
3 her, him, she, you 4 them, they *pos-*
sessive: 3 her, his, its, our 4 hers, mine,
ours, your 5 their, yours 6 theirs *reflex-*
ive: 6 itself, myself 7 herself, himself,
oneself, ourself 8 yourself 9 ourselves
10 themselves, yourselves *relative:*
3 who 4 that, what, whom 5 which,
whose, whoso 6 whomso 7 whoever
8 whatever, whomever 9 whichever,
whosoever 10 whatsoever, whomsoever
11 whichsoever
pronounce 3 say 5 judge, sound, speak,
utter 6 affirm, assert, decree, recite
7 declare 9 enunciate 10 articulate
pronounced 5 clear 6 marked, strong
7 assured, decided, evident, obvious
8 clear-cut, definite, distinct 12 unmistakable
pronouncement 5 edict 6 decree 9 manifesto, statement 11 declaration, publication 12 notification
pronto 3 now, PDQ 4 ASAP, fast, stat 6 at
once 7 quickly 8 directly 9 forthwith,
posthaste, right away 11 immediately
pronunciation *distinctive:* 4 burr, lilt
5 drawl, twang 6 accent, brogue *study:*
8 orthoepy 9 phonetics
proof 4 test 5 facts, goods 6 galley
8 argument, evidence 9 testament, testimony 10 impression 11 attestation
12 confirmation
proofreaders' mark 4 dele, stet 5 caret
prop 4 stay 5 brace, shore 6 buoy up,
hold up 7 bolster, shore up, support,
sustain 8 buttress 10 strengthen
12 underpinning
propaganda 4 hype 8 agitprop, lobbying
propagandize 4 tout 5 boost, extol
7 advance, promote, trumpet 9 brainwash, catechize, inculcate 10 promulgate 11 proselytize 12 indoctrinate
propagate 5 beget, breed, raise, strew
6 extend, spread 7 diffuse, publish,
radiate 8 disperse, generate, increase,
multiply, transmit 9 circulate, cultivate,
publicize, reproduce 10 distribute
11 disseminate
propel 4 goad, move, push, spur, urge
5 drive, egg on, power, shoot, shove
6 exhort, launch, thrust 7 actuate
8 activate
propellant 3 gas 4 fuel, spur 7 impetus,
impulse 8 catalyst, stimulus 9 explosive,
incentive, stimulant 10 motivation
propensity 7 leaning 8 penchant 10 preference 11 inclination
proper 3 apt, due, fit 4 good, just, meet,
nice, prim, true 5 exact, happy, right
6 au fait, decent, prissy, seemly, useful
7 correct, desired, fitting, genteel, pre-

cise **8** accurate, becoming, decorous, peculiar, priggish, rightful, rigorous, suitable **9** befitting **10** applicable, convenient, felicitous, individual **11** appropriate, comme il faut, distinctive *combining form:* **4** orth **5** ortho

property 4 land, mark **5** acres, trait, worth **6** assets, estate, realty, riches, virtue, wealth **7** acreage, chattel, effects, feature, fortune, quality **8** chattels, dominion, hallmark, holdings, premises **9** attribute, ownership, resources, substance **10** belongings, possession, real estate *conveyor:* **7** alienor *recipient:* **7** alienee *seller:* **7** Realtor *transfer:* **8** alienate

prophecy 6 vision **8** forecast **10** divination, prediction **11** foretelling

prophesy 5 augur **6** divine, preach **7** foresee, portend, predict, presage **8** forecast, foretell, instruct, soothsay **9** adumbrate, prefigure **10** vaticinate **13** prognosticate

prophet 4 seer **5** augur, sibyl **6** auspex, oracle **7** diviner, seeress **8** foreseer, haruspex **9** predictor **10** forecaster, foreteller, prophesier **11** soothsayer **11** Nostradamus **13** fortune-teller *Arthurian:* **6** Merlin *Major:* **6** Daniel, Isaiah **7** Ezekiel **8** Jeremiah *Minor:* **4** Amos, Joel **5** Hosea, Jonah, Micah, Nahum **6** Haggai **7** Malachi, Obadiah **8** Habakkuk **9** Zechariah, Zephaniah

Prophet author 6 Gibran (Khalil)

prophetess 5 sibyl **7** Deborah **9** Cassandra

prophetic 5 vatic **6** orphic **7** Delphic **8** Delphian, oracular **9** presaging, prescient, sibylline, vaticinal **10** predictive, revelatory **11** apocalyptic, foretelling

propinquity 7 kinship **8** nearness **9** closeness, proximity **10** contiguity

propitiate 5 adapt, atone **6** adjust, pacify, soothe **7** appease, assuage, gratify, mollify, placate, satisfy **9** intercede, reconcile **10** conciliate

propitious 4 good, rosy **5** lucky **6** benign, bright **7** benefic, helpful **8** favoring **9** favorable, fortunate, opportune, promising **10** auspicious, beneficent, beneficial, benevolent **12** advantageous

proponent 6 backer **8** advocate, champion, defender **9** expounder, supporter **10** enthusiast

proportion 4 rate, size **5** allot, ratio, quota, share **6** adjust, divide **7** balance, conform, harmony **8** symmetry **9** dimension **10** percentage **12** relationship

proportional 5 scale **7** in scale **8** relative **9** equalized **10** contingent, equivalent,

reciprocal **11** correlative, symmetrical **12** commensurate **13** commensurable, corresponding

proposal 3 bid **4** idea, plan **6** motion, scheme **7** outline, proffer, project **8** scenario **10** invitation, suggestion **11** proposition *final:* **9** ultimatum

propose 3 aim, ask, put **4** name, plan, pose **5** offer **6** design, intend, submit, tender **7** advance, move for, present, request, solicit, suggest **8** nominate, put forth, set forth, theorize **9** recommend **10** put forward

proposition 4 plan **5** offer **6** scheme, thesis **7** premise, suggest, theorem **10** invitation, suggestion

propound 3 put **4** pose **5** offer **7** present, suggest **8** put forth

proprietor 5 owner **8** landlord **9** possessor

propriety 7 aptness, decency, decorum, manners **8** behavior, civility, good form **9** etiquette, rightness **10** seemliness **11** correctness, fittingness, suitability **12** decorousness

propulsion 4 fuel, push **5** drive, force, power **6** energy, thrust

prorate 5 allot, divvy, quota, share, split **6** assess, divide, parcel, ration **7** divvy up, portion **9** apportion, partition **10** distribute

prorogue 3 end **4** rise, stay **5** defer, delay **6** hold up, put off, recess, shelve **7** adjourn, hold off, suspend **8** dissolve, hold over, postpone **9** terminate

prosaic 4 dull, flat **5** banal, prose, prosy, trite, vapid **6** boring, common **7** factual, literal, mundane, tedious **8** everyday, lifeless, ordinary, workaday **9** colorless **10** lackluster, uneventful **11** commonplace **13** unimaginative

proscenium 5 frame, stage **9** forestage **10** foreground

proscribe 3 ban **4** damn **6** enjoin, forbid, outlaw **7** condemn **8** prohibit, sentence **9** interdict

proscription 3 ban **5** taboo **11** prohibition **12** condemnation, interdiction

prosecute 3 sue **4** wage **5** press **6** charge, indict, pursue **7** carry on, perform **8** continue **9** bring suit, persevere

proselyte 7 convert, recruit **8** neophyte

proselytize 5 draft **6** enlist, enroll, sign up **7** convert, recruit, win over **8** convince **9** brainwash, catechize **11** prevail upon **12** indoctrinate

___ **prosequi 5** nolle

prospect 4 mine, view **5** scene, vista **6** chance, survey, vision **7** dig into, explore, lookout, outlook **8** customer, exposure **9** candidate **10** expectancy

11 expectation, possibility 12 anticipation

prospective 6 coming, future, likely 7 awaited, ensuing, nearing, pending, planned, would-be 8 destined, eventual, expected, hoped-for, intended, proposed, soon-to-be 9 impending, looked-for, potential, scheduled 10 consequent, succeeding 11 anticipated, approaching, predestined, forthcoming

prospectus 4 list, plan 6 design, layout, précis 7 epitome, outline, program, summary 8 bulletin, synopsis 9 catalogue, timetable 10 projection 11 description 12 announcement

prosper 5 score, yield 6 arrive, do well, thrive 7 make out, produce, succeed, turn out 8 flourish, grow rich

prosperity 4 ease 6 riches, wealth 7 success 8 thriving 9 abundance, advantage, affluence, well-being

Prospero *daughter:* 7 Miranda *servant:* 5 Ariel *slave:* 7 Caliban

prosperous 4 rich, well 5 happy, lucky 6 robust, strong 7 booming, halcyon, opulent, wealthy, well-off 8 affluent, thriving, well-to-do 9 desirable, favorable, fortunate, promising, well-fixed 10 auspicious, successful, well-heeled 11 comfortable, flourishing

prostitute 4 bawd, doxy, drab, moll 5 abuse, B-girl, madam, quean, whore 6 callet, debase, floozy, harlot, hooker, misuse, wanton 7 chippie, cocotte, corrupt, cyprian, floozie, hustler, Paphian 8 call girl, meretrix, strumpet 9 courtesan, party girl 11 fille de joie, nightwalker 12 camp follower, streetwalker *reformed:* 8 magdalen 9 magdalene

prostitution 8 harlotry, whoredom 13 streetwalking *house of:* 4 crib, stew 6 bagnio 7 brothel, lupanar 8 bordello, cathouse 10 bawdy house 13 sporting house

prostrate 4 fell, flat 5 abase, level, prone 6 humble, lay low, submit, supine 7 exhaust, wear out 8 helpless, overcome 9 decumbent, exhausted, overpower, overwhelm, powerless, recumbent 10 procumbent, submissive

protagonist 4 hero, lead, star 5 actor 6 leader 7 heroine, sponsor 8 advocate, champion 9 principal

protean 6 mobile, varied 7 diverse, mutable 8 variable 9 adaptable, versatile 10 changeable

protect 4 save 5 cover, guard 6 defend, screen, secure, shield 7 shelter 8 preserve, restrict 9 safeguard

protection 4 care 5 aegis, armor, bribe, graft, guard 6 safety, shield 7 bulwark, defense, shelter, support 8 armament, coverage, immunity, security 9 extortion, insurance, safeguard 11 supervision

protector 5 armor, guard 6 patron, regent, shield 8 guardian 9 caretaker

protégé 4 ward 5 pupil 7 student, trainee 8 disciple

protein 4 zein 5 actin, opsin 6 avidin, enzyme, fibrin, globin 7 albumin, elastin, fibroin, histone, keratin, legumin, sericin 8 creatine, globulin, glutelin, prolamin, protamin, proteose, vitellin *complex:* 6 mucoid *derivative:* 7 peptone *poisonous:* 5 abrin, ricin

pro tem 6 acting 7 interim 9 ad interim, temporary

protest 4 aver, avow, beef 6 affirm, assert, avouch, except, object, oppose, picket, resist 7 declare, profess 8 maintain 9 challenge, complaint, objection 10 disapprove 11 demonstrate, disapproval 13 demonstration

Protestant 5 Amish 6 Mormon, Quaker, Shaker 7 Baptist, Lollard, Pilgrim, Puritan 8 Anglican, Lutheran, Moravian 9 Adventist, Mennonite, Methodist, Unitarian 11 Pentecostal 12 Episcopalian, Presbyterian *Bohemian:* 7 Hussite *French:* 8 Huguenot

protocol 4 code, form, rule 5 custom, ritual 7 compact, conduct, decorum, manners 8 courtesy 9 concordat, etiquette, politesse, propriety 11 conventions, formalities

prototype 4 norm 5 model 6 design 7 example, pattern 8 original, paradigm, standard

prototypical 5 ideal, model 7 classic 9 classical, exemplary 10 archetypal

protozoan 4 cell 5 ameba 6 amoeba 7 ciliate, stentor 10 flagellate, paramecium

protract 6 drag on, extend 7 drag out, draw out, prolong, stretch 8 continue

protrude 3 jut 4 poke, pout 5 bulge 6 jut out 7 project 8 overhang, stand out, stick out

protrusion 3 jut, nub 4 bump 5 bulge 8 swelling 10 projection

protuberant 5 bulgy 7 bulging 9 prominent 11 conspicuous

proud 4 vain 5 huffy, lofty, noble 6 lordly, stuffy, superb 7 haughty, pleased, pompous, stuck-up, stately 8 arrogant, exultant, glorious, scornful, snobbish, spirited, splendid, superior, vigorous 9 conceited, delighted, imperious 10 disdainful, high-handed 11 magnificent, pretentious, resplendent 12 ostentatious, supercilious

Proulx novel 9 Postcards 12 Shipping News (The)

prove 3 try 4 show, test 5 argue, check 6 attest, pan out, verify 7 bear out, certify, confirm, examine, explain, turn out 8 document, indicate, validate 9 determine, establish 11 corroborate, demonstrate 12 substantiate

provenance 4 root, well 6 origin, source 7 history 9 inception 10 derivation

provender 4 feed, food 8 victuals 10 provisions

proverb 3 saw 5 adage, axiom, maxim 6 byword, saying 7 epigram 8 aphorism

provide 4 give, hand 5 endow, equip, serve, state 6 afford, outfit, supply 7 deliver, furnish, prepare, specify, support 8 dispense, hand over, maintain 9 stipulate

provided 5 given 6 if only 8 equipped, supplied

providence 4 care 6 thrift 7 caution, economy 8 prudence 9 foresight, frugality 11 forethought, thriftiness

provident 5 canny, chary 6 frugal, saving 7 careful, prudent, sparing, thrifty 8 prepared 10 economical, unwasteful 11 foresighted

providential 5 happy, lucky 9 benignant, fortunate 10 auspicious, fortuitous

province 4 area, duty, role, work 5 field, shire 6 canton, county, domain, office, region, sphere 7 demesne, pursuit, terrain 8 district, dominion, function 9 bailiwick, champaign, territory 10 department 12 jurisdiction

provincial 5 local, rural 6 narrow, rustic, simple 7 country, insular, limited 8 pastoral 9 parochial, sectarian, small-town 11 countrified

provision 5 stock, store 6 supply 9 condition 11 preparation, requirement, reservation, stipulation

provisional 5 stamp 6 acting, pro tem 9 temporary 10 contingent 11 conditional

provisions 4 feed, food, grub 5 stock 6 viands 7 aliment, edibles, nurture, vittles 8 supplies, victuals 9 provender 10 sustenance 11 comestibles *dealer:* 8 chandler

proviso 6 clause 7 article 9 condition 11 stipulation

provocation 5 cause, wrong 7 offense 8 stimulus, vexation 9 annoyance, incentive 10 incitement 11 instigation

provocative 5 heady 8 alluring, annoying, arousing, exciting 9 offensive 10 intriguing 11 challenging, stimulating

provoke 3 bug, irk, vex 4 abet, rile, stir,

wake 5 anger, annoy, cause, evoke, pique, rouse, upset, waken 6 arouse, awaken, bother, excite, foment, harass, incite, induce, kindle, nettle, stir up, whip up 7 incense, inflame, inspire, outrage, quicken 8 generate, irritate, motivate, occasion 9 challenge, galvanize, instigate, stimulate

provost 4 head 6 keeper 7 marshal 8 director 10 magistrate 13 administrator

prow 3 bow 4 stem 5 front 10 projection

prowess 5 skill, valor 7 bravery, command, courage, heroism, mastery 9 expertise, gallantry 10 excellence

prowl 4 hunt, roam 5 skulk, slink, sneak, steal 6 search, wander

proximate 4 near, next 5 close 6 nearby 8 adjacent, imminent 9 following, immediate, preceding 10 near-at-hand 11 forthcoming

proximity 8 nearness, vicinity 9 adjacency, closeness, immediacy 10 contiguity 11 propinquity

proxy 5 agent 6 deputy 7 stand-in 8 attorney 9 surrogate 10 substitute

pro ___ 3 tem 4 bono, rata 5 forma 7 tempore

prude 4 prig 7 old maid, Puritan 8 bluenose 9 Mrs. Grundy

prudence 4 care 5 skill 6 acumen, reason, thrift, wisdom 7 caution, economy 8 sagacity 9 foresight, frugality 10 astuteness, discretion, expediency, precaution, providence, shrewdness 11 calculation, forethought, thriftiness

prudent 4 sage, sane, wary, wise 5 canny, chary 6 frugal 7 careful, politic 8 cautious, discreet, sensible 9 expedient, judicious 11 circumspect

prudish 4 prim 5 stern 6 narrow, prissy, proper, severe, strict, stuffy 7 austere, genteel 8 affected, decorous, priggish 11 puritanical, straitlaced

prune 3 cut, lop 4 clip, crop, pare, plum, thin, trim 5 shear 6 cut off, reduce, remove 7 cut away, cut back, shorten 8 pare down, truncate

prurience 4 lust 6 desire, libido 7 lechery, passion 8 cupidity 9 carnality, eroticism 11 lustfulness 13 concupiscence

prurient 4 lewd 5 bawdy 6 erotic 7 goatish, lustful, satyric, sensual 9 lickerish 10 lascivious, libidinous, passionate 12 concupiscent

pruritic 5 itchy

Prussian *aristocrat:* 6 Junker 12 Hohenzollern *prime minister:* 8 Bismarck (Otto von) *ruler:* 7 Wilhelm 9 Frederick (the Great)

pry 4 nose, open, poke 5 jimmy, lever, snoop 6 meddle 7 inquire 9 interfere

prying 4 nosy 6 snoopy 7 curious 8 meddling, snooping 9 intrusive, obtrusive, officious 10 meddlesome 11 impertinent, inquisitive

psalm 3 ode 4 hymn, poem, song 5 paean *book:* 7 psalter *selection:* 6 Hallel *word:* 5 selah

psalmist 4 poet 5 Asaph, David 6 cantor

pseudo 4 fake, mock, sham 5 bogus, false, phony 7 pretend 8 spurious 9 imitation 10 artificial 11 counterfeit

pseudonym 5 alias 7 pen name 9 false name, stage name 10 nom de plume 11 nom de guerre

psyche 4 mind, soul 5 anima 6 animus, pneuma, spirit *part:* 3 ego 8 superego

Psyche's beloved 4 Eros 5 Cupid

psychiatrist 6 shrink 8 alienist 11 neurologist *American:* 3 May (Rollo) 5 Reich (Wilhelm) 6 Kramer (Peter), Rogers (Carl) 7 Erikson (Erik) 8 Sullivan (Harry Stack) 9 Menninger (Karl) 10 Bettelheim (Bruno) *Austrian:* 5 Adler (Alfred), Freud (Anna, Sigmund), Reich (Wilhelm) *British:* 5 Laing (R. D.) *French:* 5 Lacan (Jacques) *German:* 5 Fromm (Erich) 6 Horney (Karen) *Swiss:* 4 Jung (Carl) 9 Rorschach (Hermann)

psychic 4 seer 6 medium, mental, occult 8 cerebral 9 mentalist, prophetic, spiritual 10 mind reader, telepathic 11 clairvoyant, telekinetic 12 intellectual, supersensory *American:* 5 Cayce (Edgar), Dixon (Jeane) 10 Montgomery (Ruth) *power:* 3 ESP

psycho 3 nut 5 crazy, sicko, wacko 6 madman, maniac, mental, schizo, weirdo 7 berserk, haywire, lunatic, nutcase 8 crackpot, demented, deranged, head case 9 fruitcake, screwball, sociopath

psychoanalyst 4 Jung (Carl Gustav), Rank (Otto) 5 Adler (Alfred), Freud (Sigmund), Fromm (Erich), Klein (Melanie), Kohut (Heinz), Lacan (Jacques) 6 Horney (Karen) 7 Erikson (Erik) 8 Ferenczi (Sandor)

psychologist 6 shrink 9 therapist *American:* 5 James (William) 6 Terman (Lewis), Watson (John), Yerkes (Robert) 7 Skinner (B. F.) 9 Thorndike (Edward L.) *English:* 4 Ward (James) 8 Spearman (Charles), Tichener (Edward) *German:* 5 Wundt (Wilhelm) 6 Müller (Georg), Stumpf (Carl) 10 Wertheimer (Max)

psychotic 3 mad 5 crazy 6 insane

8 demented, deranged, schizoid 13 schizophrenic

ptarmigan 6 grouse

ptomaine 6 poison

pub 3 bar, inn 4 dive 5 joint 6 tavern 7 barroom, gin mill, taproom 8 grogshop 9 roadhouse 11 rathskeller

puberty 11 adolescence

public 4 open 5 civic, civil, state 6 common, mutual, people, shared, social 7 general, popular, society 8 communal, national, populace 9 community, municipal, universal 10 accessible, government

publican 7 barkeep 8 landlord, licensee, taverner 9 bartender, collector, innkeeper 12 tax collector

publication 4 book 7 article, journal 8 magazine, pamphlet 9 broadside, newspaper 10 periodical *list:* 12 bibliography

public house 3 bar, inn 6 hostel, saloon, tavern 7 auberge, hospice 8 hostelry

publicity 3 ink 4 hype, plug 5 blurb, press, promo 6 hoopla, notice 7 billing, write-up 8 ballyhoo 9 attention, promotion 11 advertising 12 announcement 13 advertisement

publicize 4 bill, hype, plug, puff, push, tout 5 boost 7 promote, trumpet 8 announce 9 advertise, broadcast 10 press-agent, promulgate

publish 3 air 5 issue, print 6 get out, inform, put out, report 7 release 8 announce, bring out, proclaim 9 advertise, broadcast, make known 10 distribute, promulgate 11 disseminate

Puccini, Giacomo *opera:* 5 Tosca 7 Le Villi 8 La Bohème, Turandot 12 Manon Lescaut 15 Madame Butterfly

puck 3 elf, imp 4 disk 5 fairy 6 spirit, sprite 9 hobgoblin, prankster

pucker 4 fold 5 purse 6 cockle, crease 7 wrinkle 8 compress, contract 9 constrict

puckish 5 antic, elfin, larky, pixie 6 elvish, impish 7 playful 8 prankish 9 whimsical 11 mischievous

Puck's master 6 Oberon

pudding 4 duff 6 burgoo 7 custard, tapioca *baked:* 5 kugel 10 brown Betty

pudgy 3 fat 5 plump, round, stout, tubby 6 chubby, chunky, flabby, rotund 8 plumpish, roly-poly

pueblo 4 town 7 village 8 dwelling *ceremonial room:* 4 kiva

puerile 5 inane, silly 6 jejune 7 foolish 8 childish, immature, juvenile

Puerto Rico *capital:* 7 San Juan *city:* 5 Ponce 7 Bayamon 8 Mayagüez *discov-*

erer: **8** Columbus (Christopher) *language:* **7** Spanish *location:* **10** West
Indies

puff 3 pad **4** blow, brag, crow, drag, emit,
huff, pant, plug, pouf, push, tout, waft
5 blurb, boast, boost, elate, expel, quilt,
swell, vaunt, whiff **6** exhale, pastry,
praise **7** flatter, inflate **8** swelling
9 advertise, comforter, publicize
10 exaggerate

puffer 8 blowfish **9** globefish, swellfish

puffery 4 hype, plug **9** promotion, publicity **11** advertising **12** exaggeration,
press-agentry

puffin 4 bird **7** seabird **9** sea parrot
10 shearwater *cousin:* **3** auk

puffy 7 swollen **8** inflated

pug 3 bun, dog **4** nose **5** boxer, track
9 footprint

pugilism 6 boxing **13** prizefighting

pugilist 5 boxer **7** fighter **12** prizefighter

pugnacious 7 defiant, scrappy **8** brawling, fighting, militant **9** bellicose, combative, truculent **10** aggressive, rebellious **11** belligerent, contentious,
quarrelsome **13** argumentative

pugnacity 9 hostility **10** aggression, truculence, truculency **12** belligerence
13 combativeness

puisne 6 junior **8** inferior

puissance 5 force, might, power **6** energy **7** potency **8** strength

puissant 6 mighty, potent, strong
8 forceful, powerful

pukka 4 real, tops **7** genuine **8** bona fide
9 authentic **10** first-class

pule 3 cry **4** mewl **5** whine **7** whimper

Pulitzer Prize fiction winner *1918:*
5 Poole (Ernest) *1919:* **10** Tarkington
(Booth) *1921:* **7** Wharton (Edith) *1922:*
10 Tarkington (Booth) *1923:* **6** Cather
(Willa) *1924:* **6** Wilson (Margaret) *1925:*
6 Ferber (Edna) *1926:* **5** Lewis (Sinclair)
1927: **9** Bromfield (Louis) *1928:*
6 Wilder (Thornton) *1929:* **8** Peterkin
(Julia) *1930:* **7** La Farge (Oliver) *1931:*
6 Barnes (Margaret) *1932:* **4** Buck
(Pearl) *1933:* **9** Stribling (T. S.) *1934:*
6 Miller (Caroline) *1935:* **7** Johnson
(Josephine) *1936:* **5** Davis (Harold)
1937: **8** Mitchell (Margaret) *1938:*
8 Marquand (John) *1939:* **8** Rawlings
(Marjorie Kinnan) *1940:* **9** Steinbeck
(John) *1942:* **7** Glasgow (Ellen) *1943:*
8 Sinclair (Upton) *1944:* **6** Flavin (Martin) *1945:* **6** Hersey (John) *1947:* **6** Warren (Robert Penn) *1948:* **8** Michener
(James) *1949:* **7** Cozzens (James Gould)
1950: **7** Guthrie (A. B.) *1951:* **7** Richter
(Conrad) *1952:* **4** Wouk (Herman) *1953:*
9 Hemingway (Ernest) *1955:* **8** Faulkner
(William) *1956:* **6** Kantor (MacKinlay)
1958: **4** Agee (James) *1959:* **6** Taylor
(Robert Lewis) *1960:* **5** Drury (Allen)
1961: **3** Lee (Harper) *1962:* **7** O'Connor
(Edwin) *1963:* **8** Faulkner (William)
1965: **4** Grau (Shirley Ann) *1966:*
6 Porter (Katherine Anne) *1967:*
7 Malamud (Bernard) *1968:* **6** Styron
(William) *1969:* **7** Momaday (N. Scott)
1970: **8** Stafford (Jean) *1972:* **7** Stegner
(Wallace) *1973:* **5** Welty (Eudora) *1975:*
6 Shaara (Michael) *1976:* **6** Bellow
(Saul) *1978:* **9** McPherson (James Alan)
1979: **7** Cheever (John) *1980:* **6** Mailer
(Norman) *1981:* **5** Toole (John
Kennedy) *1982:* **6** Updike (John) *1983:*
6 Walker (Alice) *1984:* **7** Kennedy
(William) *1985:* **5** Lurie (Alison) *1986:*
8 McMurtry (Larry) *1987:* **6** Taylor
(Peter) *1988:* **8** Morrison (Toni) *1989:*
5 Tyler (Anne) *1990:* **8** Hijuelos (Oscar)
1991: **6** Updike (John) *1992:* **6** Smiley
(Jane) *1993:* **6** Butler (Robert Olen)
1994: **6** Proulx (E. Annie) *1995:*
7 Shields (Carol) *1996:* **4** Ford
(Richard) *1997:* **10** Millhauser (Steven)
1998: **4** Roth (Philip) *1999:* **10** Cunningham (Michael) *2000:* **6** Lahiri (Jhumpa)
2001: **6** Chabon (Michael) *2002:* **5** Russo
(Richard) *2003:* **9** Eugenides (Jeffrey)
2004: **5** Jones (Edward P.)

pull 3 oar, row, tow, tug **4** drag, draw,
haul, lure, root, yank **5** clout, draft,
drive, force, pluck, put on **6** appeal,
assume, entice **7** attract, draw out,
extract, stretch **9** advantage, influence
10 attraction

pull back 6 rein in **7** retreat **8** withdraw

pull down 4 draw, earn, raze, ruin
5 lower, wreck **6** reduce **7** depress,
destroy **8** demolish, overcome **9** dismantle

pullet 3 hen **5** chick **7** chicken

pulley 5 wheel **6** sheave *watch's:* **5** fusee

pull in 3 nab **4** stop **5** check, pinch
6 arrest, arrive, collar, detain, pick up
7 inhibit **8** hold back, restrain **9** apprehend

pulling 6 towage **7** draught, haulage
8 traction *cable:* **7** towline

Pullman 3 car **7** sleeper **8** suitcase **11** railroad car

pull off 6 attain, manage **7** achieve, succeed **8** carry out **10** accomplish

pull out 4 exit, quit **5** leave **6** depart
7 abandon, retreat, take off **8** shove off,
withdraw

pull through 5 rally **7** get over, recover,
ride out, survive, weather **9** get better

pullulate 4 teem **5** breed, crawl, swarm

6 abound, sprout **7** produce **9** germinate

pull up 4 halt, stop **5** check **6** rebuke **8** draw even **9** reprimand

pulp 4 mash, pith **5** crush **6** bruise, squash **7** tabloid **8** soft part

pulpit 4 ambo, dais **6** podium **7** lectern, rostrum **8** ministry, platform

pulpy 4 soft **5** cheap, juicy, lurid, mushy **6** spongy **11** sensational

pulsate 4 beat, pump **5** pound, throb **7** vibrate **9** oscillate, palpitate

pulse 4 beat **5** throb **6** rhythm

pulverize 4 beat, ruin **5** crush, grind, smash, wreck **6** crunch, powder **7** atomize, destroy **8** demolish **9** micronize **10** annihilate

puma 3 cat **6** cougar **7** panther **12** mountain lion

pumice 5 glass, stone **8** polisher

pummel 3 hit **4** beat, drub **5** pound, punch **6** batter, buffet, hammer, thrash, wallop **7** belabor

pump 4 draw, shoe, quiz **5** exert, grill, heart, raise **6** device, elicit **7** operate **8** energize, question

pumpernickel 3 rye **5** bread

pumpkin 4 pepo **6** orange, squash **12** jack-o'-lantern *family:* **5** gourd

pump up 4 fill **6** excite, expand **7** enthuse, inflate **8** energize, increase, motivate **9** stimulate

pun 4 joke **11** paronomasia, play on words **13** double meaning

punch 3 box, cut, die, dig, hit, jab, jog, pep **4** bang, blow, cuff, poke, prod, push, snap, sock **5** clout, drive, notch, smack, vigor **6** buffet, emboss, energy, impact, pummel, strike, thrust **8** uppercut, vitality **9** emphasize, perforate

punch bowl 8 monteith

punch-drunk 5 dazed, dizzy, woozy **6** addled, groggy **8** unsteady **9** befuddled, slaphappy **10** staggering **11** disoriented

puncheon 3 log **4** cask, slab, tool **6** timber

puncher 5 boxer **6** cowboy

Punch's wife 4 Judy

punchy 5 dazed, dizzy, vivid **6** addled, lively **7** dynamic, vibrant **8** forceful, spirited, vigorous **9** befuddled, energetic, slaphappy **11** light-headed

punctilious 5 exact, fussy **7** careful, precise **9** attentive, observant **10** meticulous, particular, scrupulous **11** painstaking

punctual 5 ready **6** on time, prompt, timely

punctuate 4 mark **5** point **6** accent, divide, stress **8** separate **9** emphasize, interrupt **10** accentuate

punctuation mark 4 dash **5** brace, colon, comma, slant, slash **6** hyphen, parens, period **7** bracket, solidus, virgule **8** diagonal, ellipsis **9** backslash, guillemet, semicolon **10** apostrophe **11** parenthesis

puncture 3 jab **4** bore, flat, hole, stab **5** burst, drill, prick, punch **6** blow up, debunk, riddle **7** deflate, explode **8** disprove **9** discredit, perforate **11** perforation

pundit 4 guru, sage **5** maven, swami **6** critic, expert **7** teacher, wise man **9** authority

pungency 4 bite **5** sting **8** piquancy **9** intensity, sharpness

pungent 5 acrid, acute, harsh, sharp, spicy, tangy, zesty **6** barbed, biting **7** caustic, cutting, intense, mordant, painful, peppery, piquant, pointed **8** exciting, incisive, poignant, stinging **9** trenchant **10** irritating **11** provocative, stimulating

punish 4 fine, hurt **5** mulct, spank **6** amerce, avenge **7** chasten, correct, put down, reprove, revenge, scourge, torture **8** chastise, penalize **9** castigate, criticize **10** discipline

punishment 3 rod **4** fine **5** lumps, mulct **7** penalty, reproof **10** amercement, chastening, correction, discipline **11** castigation, comeuppance, just deserts **12** chastisement

punitive 5 penal **11** castigating, vindicative **12** correctional, disciplinary

punk 4 hood, thug **5** rowdy, tough **6** novice, rookie, tinder **7** hoodlum, ruffian, toughie **8** beginner, gangster, inferior **9** roughneck **10** delinquent

punkah 3 fan

punt 4 boat, boot, kick, play **6** gamble, propel

Punta del ___ 4 Este

puny 4 weak **5** dinky, petty, small **6** feeble, little, measly, paltry, slight **7** trivial **8** inferior, niggling, picayune, piddling, trifling

pupa 9 chrysalid, chrysalis

pupil 5 cadet, tutee **7** learner, scholar, student **8** disciple **9** schoolboy **10** apprentice, schoolgirl *French:* **5** élève

puppet 4 doll, dupe, pawn, tool **6** figure, stooge **10** figurehead, marionette

puppy 3 dog **5** whelp

Purcell opera 13 Dido and Aeneas

purchase 3 buy **4** hold **6** obtain, pay for **7** acquire, procure **9** advantage **11** acquisition

pure 5 clean, fresh, plain, sheer, total,

utter 6 chaste, decent 7 a priori, genuine, perfect, unmixed 8 absolute, abstract, innocent, spotless, virtuous 9 authentic, continent, exemplary, inviolate, stainless, unalloyed, undiluted, untainted 10 immaculate 11 theoretical, unblemished, unmitigated, unqualified 13 unadulterated

purebred 8 pedigree 9 full-blood, pedigreed 10 registered 11 full-blooded

puree 4 soup 5 paste

purely 4 just 5 quite 6 merely, simply, wholly 7 exactly, totally, utterly 8 entirely 10 altogether, completely 11 exclusively

purfle 4 trim 6 border 8 decorate, ornament

purgation 9 catharsis, cleansing 10 lustration

purgative 5 jalap 7 lustral 9 cathartic

purge 3 rid 4 oust 5 clear, expel 6 purify, remove 7 cleanse, wipe out 8 get rid of, lustrate 9 eliminate, liquidate

purification 8 ablution 9 catharsis, cleansing, expiation, purgation 10 absolution, lustration 11 expurgation 12 regeneration *sacrament:* 7 baptism

purify 5 clean, purge 6 filter, refine 7 clarify, cleanse

Purim 11 Feast of Lots *queen:* 6 Esther

puritan 4 prig 5 prude 8 bluenose 9 Mrs. Grundy

puritanical 4 prim 5 rigid 6 severe, strict 7 ascetic, austere, prudish 8 priggish 9 bluenosed 11 straitlaced

purity 8 chastity 9 innocence

purl 4 eddy, edge, knit 5 swirl, whirl 6 border, murmur, stitch 9 embroider

purlieu 5 haunt 7 hangout

purlieus 6 bounds, limits 7 suburbs 8 boundary, confines, environs 9 outskirts, precincts 12 neighborhood

purloin 3 nip 4 lift, take 5 filch, pinch, steal, swipe 6 pilfer, remove, rip off, snitch 11 appropriate

purloiner 5 crook, thief 8 larcener 9 larcenist

purple 4 plum, robe 5 cloth, grape, lilac, mauve, regal 6 florid, maroon, orchid, ornate, turgid, violet 7 flowery, pigment, pompous 8 imperial, lavender 9 bombastic, high-flown, overblown 10 rhetorical

Purple Heart 5 award, medal 10 decoration

purport 4 gist, mean 5 claim, drift, sense, tenor 6 allege, intend, thrust 7 meaning, message, profess, purpose 8 maintain 9 substance 11 connotation, implication 12 significance, significancy

purported 7 alleged, reputed, seeming

8 apparent, so-called, supposed 9 professed 10 ostensible

purpose 3 aim, end, use 4 goal, plan 5 point 6 action, design, intent, object 7 meaning, mission, resolve, subject 8 ambition, function, proposal 9 direction, intention, objective 10 aspiration, resolution 13 determination

purposeful 6 driven, intent 7 earnest, planned, studied, willful 8 resolute 9 conscious, dedicated 10 calculated, considered, deliberate, determined 11 intentional 12 premeditated

purposeless 6 random 9 desultory, haphazard, hit-or-miss, irregular, unplanned

purposely 9 expressly 10 explicitly 12 deliberately 13 intentionally

purr 3 hum 6 murmur

purse 3 bag, sum 4 knit 5 money, pouch, prize 6 pucker, wallet 7 handbag 8 reticule 9 clutch bag 10 pocketbook, prize money *Scottish:* 7 sporran

pursue 3 woo 4 hunt, seek 5 chase, haunt, hound, stalk, track, trail 6 badger, follow 7 afflict, go after, proceed 8 continue, engage in 9 persecute, persevere

pursuit 3 job 4 hunt, work 5 chase, quest, trade 6 search 8 activity, business, vocation 9 avocation, following 10 employment, occupation, profession

purvey 6 obtain, peddle, supply 7 furnish, provide 9 provision

purview 5 ken 5 ambit, limit, orbit, range, reach, scope, sweep 6 extent 8 boundary

push 3 pep 4 goad, plug, prod, sell, spur, urge 5 boost, drive, elbow, exert, force, impel, press, punch, shove, vigor 6 attack, effort, energy, expand, peddle, propel, throng, thrust 7 advance, assault, impetus, promote 8 ambition, pressure, vitality 9 incentive, influence, offensive 10 enterprise, get-up-and-go, initiative

Pushkin, Alexander *novel:* 12 Eugene Onegin *play:* 10 Stone Guest (The) 12 Boris Godunov *story:* 13 Queen of Spades (The)

push off 4 exit 5 leave, start 6 depart, set out

push on 6 travel 7 advance, journey, proceed 8 continue, progress

pushover 4 snap 5 chump, cinch, softy 6 breeze, picnic, stooge, sucker 9 soft touch

pushy 4 bold 5 brash, nervy 7 forward 8 forceful 9 assertive, obnoxious 10 aggressive 12 presumptuous

pusillanimous 5 timid 6 coward, craven

7 chicken, gutless 8 cowardly, poltroon, timorous 9 spineless 11 lily-livered

puss 3 cat, mug 4 face 6 kisser, kitten

pussycat 5 sissy, softy 6 softie 8 pushover, weakling 9 soft touch 10 namby-pamby 13 bleeding heart

pussyfoot 5 creep, dodge, evade, glide, skulk, slink, sneak, steal 6 tiptoe 10 equivocate

pustule 4 boil 6 pimple 7 abscess, blister 8 furuncle 9 carbuncle

put 3 lay, set 4 park 5 place 8 position

putative 7 assumed, reputed 8 accepted, believed, presumed, supposed 11 conjectural 12 hypothetical

put away 3 eat 4 stow 5 eat up, swill 6 commit, devour, lock up 7 confine, consume 9 polish off 11 incarcerate

put by 4 save 5 lay in, store 7 lay away 8 lay aside, salt away

put down 5 crush, quash, quell 6 demean, demote, depose, squash, subdue 7 squelch 8 belittle, suppress 9 criticize, disparage, downgrade, humiliate

put forth 5 issue 6 assert 7 present, propose

put off 5 defer, delay 7 suspend 8 hold over, postpone

put on 3 act, don, kid 4 fake 5 apply, bluff, feign, mount, stage 6 affect, assume 7 mislead, perform, pretend, produce

put-on 3 act 4 fake, sham, show 5 faked, phony, spoof 6 parody 7 assumed, feigned 8 affected, disguise 9 pretended 10 artificial, false front

put out 3 vex 4 gall 5 annoy, douse, issue, upset 6 bother, quench 7 disturb, produce, publish, trouble 8 irritate 9 aggravate, displease, embarrass 10 disconcert, exasperate, extinguish 13 inconvenience

putrefy 3 rot 5 decay, spoil, taint 6 molder 7 corrupt 9 break down, decompose

putrid 4 foul 5 fetid 6 rancid, rotten 7 corrupt, decayed, noisome, spoiled

putsch 4 coup 6 revolt 8 takeover, uprising 9 coup d'état, overthrow, rebellion 10 usurpation

putter 4 club, idle 6 fiddle, golfer, tinker 8 golf club

putting area 5 green

putto 6 cherub 8 amoretto

put together 4 form, join, make 5 build, unite 7 combine, connect, fashion, produce 8 assemble 9 construct, fabricate

putty 3 mud 4 clay 6 cement

put up 4 bunk 5 board, build, erect, house, lodge, raise 6 billet, harbor 7 quarter 8 domicile 9 construct

put up with 4 bear 5 stand 6 endure 8 tolerate

Puzo novel 6 Omerta 7 Last Don (The) 8 Fools Die, Sicilian (The) 9 Godfather (The)

puzzle 3 why 4 foil 5 poser, rebus 6 baffle, enigma, fuddle, muddle, riddle 7 anagram, confuse, mystery, mystify, nonplus, perplex, problem, tangram 8 acrostic, befuddle, bewilder, confound 9 conundrum, crossword, dumbfound, frustrate 10 disconcert 11 brainteaser

puzzle out 5 solve 6 answer, decode 7 clarify, clear up, explain, unravel 8 decipher, unriddle

puzzling 6 knotty 7 cryptic 8 baffling 9 confusing, difficult, enigmatic 10 mystifying, perplexing 11 bewildering, paradoxical 12 inexplicable

Pygmalion *beloved:* 7 Galatea *father:* 5 Belus *playwright:* 4 Shaw (George Bernard) *sister:* 4 Dido *victim:* 8 Sichaeus

pygmy 4 tiny 5 dwarf 6 bantam, little, midget 8 dwarfish 10 diminutive, homunculus 11 lilliputian

Pylades *companion:* 7 Orestes *father:* 9 Strophius *wife:* 7 Electra

pylon 4 post 5 tower 6 marker 7 gateway

Pym's creator 3 Poe (Edgar Allan)

Pynchon novel 15 Gravity's Rainbow

pyramid builder 5 Khufu 6 Cheops

Pyramus' beloved 6 Thisbe

pyre 4 heap, pile

pyretic 3 hot 7 burning, febrile, fevered 8 feverish

pyromaniac 5 torch 8 arsonist 10 incendiary

pyrosis 9 heartburn

pyrotechnics 7 display 9 fireworks, spectacle

Pyrrha's husband 9 Deucalion

Pyrrhonist 7 doubter, skeptic 10 unbeliever

Pyrrhus *kingdom:* 6 Epirus *victory:* 7 Asculum

Pythias' friend 5 Damon

python 3 boa 5 snake *slayer:* 6 Apollo

pyx 3 box 4 case 6 vessel 9 container 10 receptacle

Q

Qatar *capital:* 4 Doha *gulf:* 7 Persian *language:* 6 Arabic *monetary unit:* 5 riyal *neighbor:* 11 Saudi Arabia *peninsula:* 7 Arabian

QED *word* 4 erat, quod 13 demonstrandum

q.t., on the 8 covertly, secretly 13 under the table

quack 3 cry 4 honk, sham 6 con man, humbug 7 shammer 9 charlatan 10 mountebank 12 saltimbanque

quackery 4 hoax, scam 5 fraud, hokum 6 deceit 8 flimflam, pretense 9 deception, duplicity, imposture 11 dissembling

quad see QUADRANGLE

quadrangle 4 yard 5 close, court, patio 6 square 7 polygon 9 courtyard, curtilage, enclosure

quadrant 3 arc 6 fourth 9 one-fourth 10 instrument

quadratic 4 boxy 6 square 7 boxlike 10 foursquare

quadriga 7 chariot

quadrille 5 dance, ombre 8 card game

quadrivium *subject* 5 music 8 geometry 9 astronomy 10 arithmetic

quaestor 6 bursar 8 official 9 paymaster, treasurer

quaff 3 sip 4 swig, toss 5 drink, sup up 6 guzzle, imbibe, sup off 7 carouse, swallow

quagga 3 ass

quaggy 4 soft 5 boggy, mushy, pulpy 6 flabby, marshy, spongy 7 flaccid, squashy, squishy 8 squooshy, yielding

quagmire 3 bog, fen, fix, jam 4 mire 5 marsh, pinch, swamp 6 morass, pickle, plight, scrape, slough 7 dilemma 8 quandary 9 imbroglio, marshland, swampland 11 predicament

quahog 4 clam 7 mollusc, mollusk 9 shellfish 11 cherrystone

quail 5 cower, wince 6 blanch, blench, cringe, flinch, recoil, shrink 7 shudder, squinch, tremble 8 bobwhite *flock of:* 4 bevy

quaint 3 odd 5 funny, queer 7 antique, archaic, curious, oddball, strange, unusual 8 peculiar, singular 9 different, eccentric, whimsical 10 antiquated, unfamiliar 12 old-fashioned

quake 5 shake, waver 6 dither, quaver, quiver, shiver, tremor 7 shudder, temblor, tremble, twitter, vibrate 8 trembler

Quaker 6 Friend *city:* 12 Philadelphia *colonizer:* 4 Penn (William) *founder:* 3 Fox (George) *poet:* 6 Barton (Bernard) 8 Whittier (John Greenleaf) *State:* 12 Pennsylvania

qualification 6 caveat 7 ability, fitness 8 adequacy, aptitude, capacity, criterion, standard 9 condition 10 capability, competence 11 requirement, restriction, stipulation

qualified 3 fit 4 able 6 au fait, proper, proved, proven, tested 7 capable, limited, partial, skilled, trained 8 eligible, modified, reserved 9 competent 10 restricted 11 conditional 12 accomplished

qualify 3 fit 5 limit 6 lessen, modify, reduce, soften, temper 7 certify, entitle, license, mollify, prepare 8 describe, mitigate, moderate 9 authorize 12 characterize

quality 4 rank 5 class, elite, grade, merit, prime, savor, state, trait, value, worth 6 factor, flower, gentry, status, virtue 7 caliber, element, feature, stature 8 position, property, standing 9 attribute, blue blood, character, gentility, parameter 10 excellence, patriciate, perfection

qualm 4 fear 5 demur, doubt 6 nausea, unease 7 illness, scruple 8 mistrust 9 faintness, misgiving, objection 10 conscience, foreboding, reluctance, uneasiness 11 compunction, nervousness, uncertainty 12 apprehension, remonstrance 13 unwillingness

qualmish 3 ill 4 sick 6 queasy, uneasy, unwell 8 hesitant, nauseous 9 nauseated, reluctant, squeamish, uncertain 10 scrupulous 12 apprehensive

quandary 3 fix, jam 4 bind, hole, spot 5 pinch 6 pickle, plight, scrape 7 dilemma 8 quagmire 10 difficulty 11 predicament

quantity 4 body, bulk, dose 5 total 6 amount, degree, volume 9 abundance, aggregate, magnitude *fixed:*

8 constant *small:* **3** bit **7** modicum, smidgen

Quantrill's ___ **7** Raiders

quantum 5 quota, share, total **6** amount, budget, ration **7** measure, portion **9** aggregate, allotment, allowance, increment **13** apportionment *of gravity:* **8** graviton *of radiant energy:* **6** photon *of vibrational energy:* **6** phonon *theory originator:* **6** Planck (Max)

quarantine 6 detain **7** confine, isolate **8** restrain **9** isolation, restraint **10** detainment **11** confinement

quarrel 3 row **4** beef, bolt, dust, feud, fray, fuss, miff, spar, spat, tiff **5** argue, arrow, brawl, broil, clash, fight, melee, run-in, scrap, set-to **6** affray, battle, bicker, differ, dustup, fracas, ruckus, squall, strife **7** brabble, discord, dispute, dissent, fall out, rhubarb, ruction, scuffle, wrangle **8** argument, catfight, conflict, disagree, skirmish, squabble **9** altercate, bickering, brannigan, disaccord, lock horns, imbroglio, scrimmage **10** contention, difference, dissension, donnybrook, falling-out, free-for-all **11** altercation, battle royal, embroilment **12** disagreement

quarrelsome 6 brawly **7** adverse, counter, hostile, scrappy, warlike **8** brawling, choleric, inimical, militant **9** bellicose, combative, irascible, irritable, rancorous, truculent **10** pugnacious **11** bad-tempered, belligerent, contentious **12** cantankerous, disputatious **13** argumentative

quarry 3 dig, pit **4** game, mine, pane, prey **5** chase, delve **6** source, victim **8** excavate **10** excavation

quarter 4 area, bunk, part **5** board, house, lodge, mercy, put up **6** barrio, billet, canton, fourth, ghetto, harbor, sector **7** barrack, section, shelter **8** clemency, district, division, locality, precinct, quadrant *circle:* **8** quadrant *note:* **8** crotchet *pint:* **4** gill *ship's:* **6** fo'c'sle **10** forecastle

quarterback 4 boss, head, lead **6** direct, leader, player **7** athlete, oversee **8** director, overseer **9** supervise **10** footballer, supervisor

quartet 4 four **5** group **6** tetrad **8** ensemble, foursome **10** quadruplet, quaternion **11** composition

quart, metric 5 liter, litre

quartz 4 onyx, sard **5** agate **6** jasper **7** citrine, mineral **8** amethyst, sardonyx **9** cairngorm, carnelian **10** chalcedony

quash 4 undo, void **5** annul, crush, quell **6** defeat, negate, quench, stifle, subdue **7** abolish, nullify, put down, repress, smother, squelch **8** abrogate, dissolve, suppress **10** extinguish, invalidate

quasi 6 almost **7** nominal, seeming, virtual **8** apparent

Quasimodo 9 hunchback *creator:* **4** Hugo (Victor) *occupation:* **10** bell ringer *residence:* **9** Notre Dame

quaver 4 note **5** quake, shake, trill, waver **6** dither, shiver, tremor **7** shudder, tremble, twitter **10** eighth note

quay 4 dock, pier, slip **5** berth, jetty, levee, wharf **6** marina **7** moorage

quean 4 bawd, slut, tart **5** tramp, wench, whore **6** harlot, hooker **7** chippie, hustler **8** strumpet **9** courtesan **10** prostitute **12** streetwalker

queasy 3 ill **4** sick **6** qualmy, uneasy, unwell **7** dubious **8** delicate, doubtful, hesitant, nauseous, qualmish, troubled **9** hazardous, nauseated, reluctant, squeamish

Quebec province *capital:* **6** Quebec *city:* **5** Laval **8** Montreal **9** Longueuil *island:* **9** Anticosti *mountain:* **9** Tremblant **10** D'Iberville *peninsula:* **5** Gaspé *provincial flower:* **10** fleur-de-lys **11** madonna lily *river:* **10** St. Lawrence

Queeg's ship 5 Caine

queen *Austria-Hungary:* **12** Maria Theresa *Belgian:* **6** Astrid *Danish:* **8** Margaret, Margrete *Egyptian:* **9** Cleopatra **10** Hatshepsut *English:* **4** Anne, Mary **8** Victoria **9** Elizabeth *French and English:* **7** Eleanor *Netherlands:* **7** Beatrix, Juliana **10** Wilhelmina *of heaven:* **4** Mary, moon **7** Astarte *of Isles:* **6** Albion *of Ithaca:* **8** Penelope *of Navarre:* **8** Margaret *of Scots:* **4** Mary *of Sheba:* **6** Balkis *of the Adriatic:* **6** Venice *of the Antilles:* **4** Cuba *of the East:* **7** Zenobia *of the fairies:* **3** Mab **7** Titania *of the gods:* **4** Hera, Juno, Sati *of the Nile:* **9** Cleopatra *of the North:* **9** Edinburgh *of the underworld:* **3** Hel **4** Hela **10** Persephone, Proserpina *Spanish:* **8** Isabella *Swedish:* **9** Christina

Queen Anne's lace 6 carrot **10** wild carrot

Queen of Spades *author:* **7** Pushkin (Alexander) *composer:* **11** Tchaikovsky (Peter Ilyich)

Queensland *capital:* **8** Brisbane *explorer:* **4** Cook (Captain James)

queer 3 odd **4** ruin **5** bogus, droll, funny, spoil, weird **6** qualmy, queasy, unwell **7** bizarre, curious, dubious, oddball, strange, touched, unusual **8** doubtful, obsessed, peculiar, qualmish, singular **9** eccentric, squeamish, worthless **10** outlandish, suspicious **11** counterfeit **12** questionable

quell 4 calm, stop 5 check, crush, quash, quiet 6 pacify, quench, squash, subdue 7 conquer, put down, squelch 8 overcome, suppress, vanquish 9 overwhelm, subjugate 10 extinguish

Quemoy's neighbor 4 Amoy 5 Matsu

quench 4 sate 5 allay, douse, quash, quell, slake 6 lessen, put out, reduce 7 appease, assuage, gratify, lighten, put down, relieve, satiate, satisfy 8 mitigate, suppress 9 alleviate, eliminate 10 extinguish

quenelle 8 dumpling, meatball 9 forcemeat

quern 4 mill

querulous 5 whiny 7 fretful, peevish, pettish, whining 8 petulant 9 lamenting 10 whimpering 11 complaining

query 3 ask 4 quiz 5 doubt, grill 7 dubiety, inquire, inquiry 8 question 9 catechize 11 interrogate 13 interrogation

quest 4 hunt 5 probe 6 pursue, search 7 delving, inquire, inquiry, probing, pursuit, seeking 8 research 9 pursuance 11 inquisition 13 investigation

question 3 ask, pry 4 poll, pump, quiz 5 doubt, grill, issue, probe, query 6 chance, matter 7 debrief, dispute, examine, inquire, inquiry, problem, suspect 8 distrust, mistrust 9 catechize, challenge, objection 10 difficulty, puzzle over 11 interrogate, possibility 13 interrogation, interrogatory

questionable 4 iffy, moot 5 shady, vague 6 unsure 7 dubious, obscure, suspect 8 arguable, doubtful, unproven 9 debatable, equivocal, refutable, uncertain 10 disputable, fly-by-night, improbable, unreliable 11 problematic 12 undependable

questioning 5 probe, query 6 show-me 7 delving, dubious, inquiry, probing 8 doubtful, grilling 9 inquiring, quizzical, skeptical, uncertain 11 incredulous, inquisitive, unbelieving 12 disbelieving 13 interrogation, interrogatory, investigative

quetzal 4 bird, coin 6 trogon

queue 3 row 4 file, line, rank, wait 5 braid 6 column 8 sequence

quibble 4 carp 5 argue, cavil 6 argufy, bicker, niggle, object 7 dispute, evasion, nitpick, wrangle 8 squabble 9 criticism, criticize, objection 10 split hairs

quick 4 core, deft, fast, keen, pith, root 5 acute, agile, brisk, fleet, hasty, rapid, sharp, smart, swift 6 abrupt, clever, nimble, prompt, speedy, sudden 7 hurried 9 breakneck, impetuous 10 harefooted 11 expeditious 12 lickety-split
combining form: 5 tachy

quick bread 6 muffin 7 biscuit

quicken 4 goad, grow, move, spur, stir, wake 5 hurry, liven, pique, rouse, speed 6 arouse, awaken, excite, hasten, incite, induce, kindle, revive, step up, vivify 7 actuate, animate, enliven, provoke, shake up, sharpen, speed up 8 activate, energize, motivate, vitalize 9 galvanize, stimulate 10 accelerate, exhilarate, invigorate

quickly 5 apace 6 at once, pronto 9 forthwith, posthaste 12 straightaway

quickness 5 haste, speed 8 alacrity, celerity, dispatch, legerity, rapidity, velocity 9 fleetness, rapidness, swiftness 10 promptness

quicksand 3 bog 4 mire 6 morass

quicksilver 7 mercury 9 mercurial 10 inconstant

quick-tempered 5 cross, fiery, ratty, testy 6 cranky, touchy 7 peppery 8 choleric, petulant 9 irascible, irritable, splenetic 10 passionate

quick-witted 3 apt 4 keen 5 acute, agile, alert, canny, ready, sharp, smart 6 astute, brainy, bright, clever, prompt 9 brilliant 10 perceptive 11 intelligent, penetrating

quid 3 cut, wad 4 chew, coin 5 money, pound 9 sovereign

quiddity 3 nub 4 gist, meat, pith 6 trifle 7 essence, quibble 8 crotchet 12 eccentricity, quintessence

quidnunc see RUMORMONGER

quiescent 4 calm 5 quiet, still 6 benign, hushed, latent, placid, serene, stilly 7 abeyant, dormant, halcyon, lurking 8 inactive, tranquil 10 untroubled

quiet 4 calm, hush, idle, lull, mute, stop 5 abate, allay, inert, muted, shush, still, whist 6 asleep, becalm, gentle, hushed, lessen, placid, serene, settle, silent, sleepy, soothe, subdue 7 compose, halcyon, pacific, passive, restful, silence, subdued 8 decrease, inactive, peaceful, reserved, secluded, taciturn, tranquil 9 cessation, easygoing, noiseless, soundless, stillness, unruffled 10 restrained, untroubled 11 tranquility, tranquilize, unobtrusive 12 tranquillity

quietus 3 end 5 death, sleep 6 damper, demise, finish 7 decease, passing, silence 8 curtains 10 inactivity, settlement 11 termination

quill 3 pen 5 float, shaft, spine, spool 6 bobbin 7 feather, spindle

quilt 4 pouf, puff 5 duvet 8 coverlet 9 comforter, eiderdown 11 counterpane
design: 8 trapunto

quintessence 4 gist, meat, pith, soul

5 ideal, model, stuff **6** marrow **7** epitome **8** exemplar, last word, quiddity, ultimate **9** substance **10** apotheosis **12** essentiality

quintessential 5 ideal, model **7** classic, typical **8** ultimate **9** classical, exemplary **10** archetypal, consummate, prototypal **12** prototypical

quintuple 8 fivefold

quip 3 dig, gag, kid **4** gibe, gird, jape, jeer, jest, jibe, joke **5** crack, fleer, sally, scoff, sneer, tease **6** banter, oddity, retort **7** quibble **8** drollery, repartee **9** wisecrack, witticism **12** equivocation

quipster 3 wag, wit **4** card **5** clown, comic, droll, joker **6** jester **8** comedian, funnyman, humorist, jokester **11** wisecracker

quirk 3 tic **4** bend, kink, quip, whim **5** crook, curve, twist **6** groove, oddity, vagary **7** caprice **8** accident, crotchet **9** mannerism **11** peculiarity **12** idiosyncrasy

quirky 3 odd **7** erratic, offbeat **8** peculiar **9** eccentric, irregular, whimsical **10** capricious **13** idiosyncratic

quirt 4 lash, whip

quisling 5 Judas, rebel **7** traitor **8** apostate, betrayer, defector, turncoat **10** copperhead **11** backstabber **12** collaborator

quit 3 end, pay **4** drop, free, halt, stop **5** cease, chuck, leave **6** depart, desert, desist, give up, resign, retire, settle **7** abandon, drop out, forsake, release, relieve, satisfy **8** knock off, leave off, released, renounce, withdraw **9** discharge, liquidate, surrender, terminate **10** relinquish **11** discontinue

quite 3 all **4** just, very, well **5** fully, in all **6** in toto, purely, rather, wholly **7** exactly, totally, utterly **8** entirely **9** perfectly **10** absolutely, altogether, completely, positively, thoroughly **12** considerably

quittance 6 amends **7** redress **8** reprisal, requital **9** atonement, discharge, expiation, repayment **10** recompense, reparation **11** restitution **12** compensation

quitter 4 funk **6** coward, craven **7** chicken, dastard **8** poltroon, recreant **9** defeatist **11** yellowbelly

quiver 4 beat, case **5** pulse, quake,

shake, throb, waver **6** arrows, dither, jitter, quaver, shiver, tremor **7** pulsate, shudder, tremble, twitter, vibrate **9** palpitate, vibration

Quixote see DON QUIXOTE

quixotic 7 foolish **8** fanciful, illusory, romantic **9** fantastic, imaginary, visionary **10** capricious, chimerical, idealistic **11** impractical **13** unpredictable

quiz 3 ask **4** exam, test **5** grill, query **7** examine, inquire **8** question **9** catechize **11** interrogate **12** cross-examine

quizzical 5 odd **5** queer **6** quaint, showme **7** curious, dubious, mocking, probing, puzzled, teasing **8** doubtful, doubting, sardonic **9** inquiring, skeptical **11** incredulous, inquisitive, questioning, unbelieving **12** disbelieving

quodlibet 5 issue, point **6** debate, medley **7** mélange **8** fantasia, question **11** disputation

quoin 5 angle, block, wedge **6** corner **8** keystone, voussoir

quoit 4 game, ring **6** circle

quoits peg 3 hob

quondam 4 late, once, past **6** bygone, former, whilom **7** defunct, onetime **8** sometime **9** erstwhile **10** occasional

quorum 4 body **5** group **7** council **8** majority

quota 3 cut, lot **4** bite, meed, part **5** share, slice, whack **6** amount, parcel, ration **7** measure, portion, quantum **9** allotment, allowance **10** allocation, percentage, proportion

quotation 3 bid **5** offer, price **7** excerpt, extract, passage **8** citation

quotation mark, French 9 guillemet

quote 3 bid **4** cite, list **5** offer, price, refer **6** adduce, borrow, repeat **7** excerpt, extract, passage **8** citation

quotidian 5 daily, plain, usual **6** common **7** average, diurnal, prosaic, regular, routine, vanilla **8** day-to-day, everyday, ordinary, workaday **9** circadian **11** commonplace **12** unremarkable

quotient 5 ratio, share **7** caliber, portion **9** allotment, magnitude **10** percentage, proportion

Quo Vadis *author:* **11** Sienkiewicz (Henryk) *character:* **4** Nero **5** Lygia, Peter **8** Vinicius **9** Petronius

R

Ra *son:* 6 Khonsu *wife:* 3 Mut

Raamah *father:* 4 Cush *son:* 5 Dedan, Sheba

Rabbi Ben Ezra *author* 8 Browning (Robert)

rabbit 4 cony, hare 5 bunny, coney *female:* 3 doe *fictional:* 5 Fiver, Hazel, Mopsy, Peter 6 Flopsy, Harvey 7 Thumper 8 Crusader, Ricochet 9 Bugs Bunny 10 Cotton-tail 11 Easter Bunny *food:* 5 salad 6 carrot 7 lettuce *neutered:* 5 lapin *tail:* 4 scut

rabble 3 mob 4 mass, rout 5 crush, horde 6 masses 8 canaille, populace, riffraff, unwashed 9 hoi polloi 10 lower class 11 proletariat, rank and file

rabble-rouser 7 inciter 8 agitator, fomenter 9 demagogue 10 incendiary 12 troublemaker

Rabelais character 7 Panurge 9 Gargantua 10 Pantagruel

rabid 3 mad 4 wild 5 crazy, ultra 6 crazed, insane 7 extreme, fanatic, frantic, furious, radical, zealous 8 demented, deranged, frenetic, frenzied, obsessed, ultraist 9 delirious, extremist 10 corybantic 11 hydrophobic

rabies 11 hydrophobia

raccoon 8 ringtail *dog:* 6 tanuki *relative:* 5 civet, coati, panda 8 civet cat, kinkajou 10 cacomistle, coatimundi

race 4 bolt, dart, dash, gill, lash, meet, rush, tear, type 5 brook, chase, creek, fling, hurry, match, rally, relay, shoot, speed, spurt 6 charge, course, gallop, runnel, scurry, sprint, stream 7 channel, contest, rivalry, rivulet, scamper 8 marathon 9 grand prix 11 competition, watercourse

racecourse 4 oval, turf 5 track

racehorse 5 Alsab, Kelso 6 Forego 7 Assault, Man O' War 8 Affirmed, Citation 9 Riva Ridge, War Emblem 10 War Admiral 11 Forward Pass, Seattle Slew, Secretariat, Smarty Jones 12 Native Dancer

Rachel *father:* 5 Laban *husband:* 5 Jacob *servant:* 6 Bilhah *sister:* 4 Leah *son:* 6 Joseph 8 Benjamin

rachis 4 back 5 chine, spine 8 backbone 12 spinal column

rachitic 5 shaky 6 wobbly 7 rackety, rickety, tenuous 9 tremulous 10 ramshackle, rattletrap

___ Rachmaninoff 6 Sergei, Sergey

racing enthusiast 8 railbird

racism 7 bigotry, jim crow 9 apartheid, prejudice 11 segregation

racist 4 nazi 5 bigot 7 bigoted 10 intolerant, prejudiced 11 supremacist

rack 3 bed 4 buck, bunk, pace, pain, sack, scud 5 frame, wring 6 harass, harrow, martyr, strain, wrench 7 afflict, agonize, antlers, crucify, ratchet, sawbuck, stretch, torment, torture 8 distress, sawhorse 9 framework, persecute 10 excruciate

racket 3 con, din 4 game 5 babel, fraud, hoo-ha, noise 6 clamor, hubbub, rattle, scheme, tumult, uproar 7 pursuit, swindle 8 ballyhoo, brouhaha, foofaraw 10 hullabaloo 11 pandemonium

racketeer 7 mafioso, mobster 8 extorter, gangster 9 godfather

rack up 3 win 4 gain 5 reach, score 6 attain 7 achieve, realize 10 accomplish

raconteur 11 storyteller

racy 4 blue, gamy 5 bawdy, broad, juicy, salty, spicy, vampy, zesty 6 purple, risqué, smutty, snappy, vulgar, wicked 7 piquant, pungent 8 indecent, offcolor, vigorous 10 suggestive

Radames' beloved 4 Aïda

radar image 3 pip 4 blip, spot 5 trace

Raddai *brother:* 5 David *father:* 5 Jesse

radiance 3 ray 4 glow 5 glory, shine 6 luster 7 aureola, aureole 8 splendor 10 brightness, brilliance

radiant 4 glad 5 beamy, shiny 6 bright, cheery, lucent 7 beaming, fulgent, glowing, lambent 8 cheerful, luminous, lustrous 9 brilliant, effulgent 10 effulgence 12 incandescent

radiate 4 beam, glow 5 gleam, shine, strew 6 spread 7 diverge 8 illumine 10 illuminate

radiation unit 3 rad, rem, rep 7 langley, sievert 8 roentgen

radiator 6 cooler, heater 9 convector 11 transmitter 13 heat exchanger

radical 4 acyl, root 5 basal, basic, rebel, ultra 7 extreme, fanatic, primary 8 agitator, cardinal, inherent, militant, ultraist **9** anarchist, essential, extremist, intrinsic **10** subversive, underlying **11** fundamental **12** foundational, iconoclastic **13** revolutionary *mathematical:* **4** surd

radicle 4 root **5** radix **9** hypocotyl

radio 8 wireless *frequency range:* **8** wave band

radioactive 3 hot **7** nuclear

radius 5 ambit, orbit, range, reach, sweep **6** extent **7** compass, purview **9** extension

radix 5 base, root **6** source

raffish 6 coarse, jaunty, rakish, sporty, vulgar **9** dissolute **12** devil-may-care

raffle 7 drawing, lottery

raft 3 lot, ton **4** heap, mess, pile, scad, slew **5** balsa, float **6** bundle

rafter 4 balk, beam, viga

rag 3 jaw, kid, rib **4** bait, jive, josh, rail, razz, rock **5** baste, cloth, scold, tease **6** berate, harass, hector, needle, pester **7** tabloid, torment **9** newspaper

ragamuffin 3 bum **4** hobo, waif **5** gamin, tramp **6** beggar, gamine, orphan, urchin **7** wastrel **8** vagabond **9** scarecrow **11** guttersnipe

rage 3 cry, fad, ire, mad, wax **4** chic, fume, fury, mode, rant **5** anger, craze, fancy, furor, mania, storm, style, vogue, wrath **6** blow up, frenzy, furore, seethe **7** fashion, madness, passion **8** boil over, hysteria, violence **10** dernier cri **11** indignation

ragged 4 rent, torn **5** seedy **6** frayed, jagged, shabby, uneven **7** unkempt, worn-out **8** frazzled, straggly, tattered **10** threadbare

raging 4 wild **6** stormy **7** furious, extreme, intense, violent **8** blustery **9** ferocious, turbulent **10** blustering **11** tempestuous

ragout 4 stew **5** salmi **6** burgoo, jumble, medley **7** farrago, goulash, mélange, mixture **8** mishmash **9** potpourri **10** hodgepodge, salmagundi **11** gallimaufry

rags 4 duds, garb **5** dress **6** attire, shreds **7** apparel, clothes, raiment, threads **8** clothing **10** attirement **11** habiliments

ragtag see RABBLE

ragwort 7 senecio **9** cineraria, groundsel **10** butterweed

raid 4 bust, loot, sack **5** foray, harry **6** attack, forage, harass, inroad, invade, maraud, ravage, sortie **7** assault, despoil, overrun, plunder **8** invasion, spoliate **9** incursion, onslaught

raider 6 pirate **10** freebooter

rail 3 bar, jaw **5** fence, scold, track **6** berate, revile **7** barrier, inveigh,

upbraid **8** banister **10** tongue-lash, vituperate

rail bird 4 sora **5** crake **7** clapper **8** marsh hen, water hen

railing 8 banister **10** balustrade *part:* **8** baluster

raillery 5 scorn **6** banter **7** mockery, teasing **8** badinage, derision, ridicule, taunting **10** lampoonery, persiflage

railroad *branch:* **6** siding *car:* **5** coach, diner, stock **6** hopper **7** caboose, gondola, Pullman *engine:* **10** locomotive *locomotive:* **9** iron horse *station:* **5** depot *underground:* **4** tube **5** metro **6** subway *worker:* **6** porter **7** fireman **8** brakeman, engineer **9** conductor **11** gandy dancer

raiment 4 duds, garb, gear, togs **5** array, dress **6** attire **7** apparel, clothes, threads, vesture **8** clothing, garments, glad rags, vestiary **9** caparison **10** attirement **11** habiliments

rain 6 deluge, mizzle, shower **7** drizzle **8** downpour, sprinkle **10** cloudburst **13** precipitation

rainbow 3 arc **4** iris **5** array, gamut **7** fantasy **8** illusion, spectrum **9** pipe dream *bridge:* **7** Bifrost *chaser:* **9** visionary *goddess:* **4** Iris

rainbow fish 5 guppy, trout **6** wrasse

raincoat 3 mac **4** mack **6** poncho, trench **7** oilskin, slicker **10** mackintosh

rain leader 9 downspout

rain tree 9 monkeypod

raise 4 ante, grow, hike, jack, jump, lift, pump, rear **5** boost, breed, erect, exalt, hoist, put up **6** foment, incite, jack up, muster **7** augment, bring up, collect, elevate, enhance, inflate, produce **8** heighten, increase **9** construct, cultivate, increment, propagate

raisin 5 grape **7** currant, sultana **10** dried grape

Raisin in the Sun author 9 Hansberry (Lorraine)

raison d'___ 4 état, être

raja 4 king **5** chief, ruler **6** prince **9** dignitary

rake 3 rip **4** comb, roué **5** angle, blood, pitch, rifle, scamp, scour, slope **6** forage, glance, lecher, rascal, scrape, search, strafe **7** incline, playboy, ransack, rummage, scratch **8** enfilade, lothario **9** debauchee, libertine **10** profligate

rakehell 4 fast, wild **5** blood **6** rascal, sporty **7** playboy, raffish **8** lothario, rascally **9** debauchee, dissolute, lecherous, libertine **10** licentious, profligate

rake-off 3 cut **4** bite, take **5** chunk, share **7** portion **9** baksheesh, lagniappe **10** commission, percentage

rake's look 4 leer, ogle
Rake's Progress artist 7 Hogarth (William)
rakish see RAKEHELL
rally 4 race, stir, wake **5** harry, renew, rouse, waken **6** arouse, awaken, bestir, kindle, muster, perk up, pick up, repair, volley **7** convene, enliven, marshal, rebound, recover **8** assemble, clambake, comeback, mobilize, recovery **9** challenge, re-collect **10** invigorate, reorganize
rallying cry 5 motto **6** byword, slogan **9** watchword **10** shibboleth **11** catchphrase
ram 5 Aries, crash, crowd, drive, pound, sheep, stuff **6** batter, plunge, strike, thrust **7** warship
Rama's wife 4 Sita
ramble 3 gad **4** roam, rove **5** drift, range, stray, troll **6** stroll, wander **7** blather, digress, diverge, maunder, meander, saunter, traipse **8** divagate, straggle **9** gallivant
rambler 4 rose **5** gypsy, hiker, nomad, rover **6** roamer, walker **7** drifter, vagrant **8** stroller, vagabond, wanderer **9** itinerant **10** ranch house
rambunctious 5 rowdy **6** unruly **7** raucous, willful **10** boisterous, headstrong **11** intractable **12** recalcitrant, ungovernable
ramification 5 shoot **6** branch, offset **8** offshoot **9** outgrowth, offspring **11** consequence
ramify 6 branch, divide, extend **7** develop, radiate **9** branch out, propagate **11** proliferate
Ramona author 7 Jackson (Helen Hunt)
ramose 8 branched
ramp 5 apron **7** incline
rampage 4 rage, riot, tear **5** binge, fling, spree, storm
rampageous 4 wild **6** unruly **7** riotous
rampant 4 rank, rife, wild **7** rearing, regnant **9** prevalent, unbridled **10** widespread **12** uncontrolled, unrestrained
rampart 4 wall **5** ridge **7** bulwark, parapet **9** barricade **10** breastwork
ramshackle 6 flimsy **7** rickety, run-down **8** decrepit **10** tumbledown **11** dilapidated
ram's mate 3 ewe
ranch 5 finca **8** estancia, hacienda **worker: 6** cowboy, gaucho **7** cowgirl, cowhand, cowpoke **10** cowpuncher
rancher 6 cowboy **7** breeder **9** cattleman
rancid 4 high, rank, sour **5** fetid **6** putrid, skunky, smelly **7** noisome, spoiled **8** stinking **9** offensive **10** malodorous
rancor 4 gall **6** animus, enmity, hatred **7** ill will **9** animosity, antipathy, hostility **10** antagonism, bitterness
rancorous 6 bitter **7** hateful, hostile **8** spiteful, venomous **9** malicious, malignant, vitriolic **10** malevolent **11** acrimonious **12** antagonistic
Rand, Ayn *novel:* **6** Anthem **12** Fountainhead (The) **13** Atlas Shrugged
random 6 casual **7** aimless **8** slapdash **9** arbitrary, desultory, haphazard, hit-or-miss, unplanned **10** accidental, contingent, hit-and-miss, incidental **11** purposeless
randy 4 lewd **5** bawdy, lusty **7** lustful, satyric **9** lecherous, libertine, lickerish, salacious **10** lascivious, libidinous, licentious
range 3 row, run **4** area, band, roam, rove, shot, site, sort, span, vary **5** align, ambit, carry, drift, field, gamut, orbit, order, reach, realm, ridge, scale, scope, space, stove, stray, sweep, width **6** assort, domain, extent, length, limits, ramble, sierra, sphere, spread, wander **7** compass, earshot, expanse, eyeshot, habitat, meander, purview, stretch **8** confines, distance, latitude, locality, panorama, province, stovetop, traverse, vicinity **9** amplitude, extension, gallivant, magnitude, territory **12** distribution
range finder 9 telemeter
ranger 3 spy **5** scout **6** lawman, patrol, warden **8** overseer **9** caretaker, protector
rangy 4 lean **5** lanky **6** gangly **7** spindly **8** gangling
rani's mate 4 raja **5** rajah
rank 3 row **4** file, foul, lush, rate, sort, tier **5** class, fetid, funky, grade, gross, humid, order, place, queue **6** assort, cachet, coarse, filthy, lavish, putrid, rancid, rating, smelly, status **7** arrange, dignity, echelon, footing, noisome, perfect, profuse, rampant, reeking, station, stature **8** absolute, classify, evaluate, flagrant, outright, position, standing, stinking **9** downright, egregious, loathsome, luxuriant, overgrown, repulsive **10** consummate, malodorous **11** conspicuous, outstanding, unmitigated
rank and file 5 plebs **6** people, plebes **8** populace **9** commonage, commoners, plebeians **10** commonalty **11** enlisted men
rankle 3 irk, vex **4** rile **5** annoy **6** bother, fester, nettle, seethe **8** embitter, irritate **9** aggravate **10** exasperate
ransack 3 rob **4** comb, grub, loot, rake **5** rifle, scour **6** forage, ravage **7** plunder, rummage

Ran's husband 5 Aegir

ransom 3 buy **4** free **6** redeem, regain, rescue **7** deliver, recover **8** liberate **13** consideration

rant 3 jaw, rag **4** huff, rage, rail, rate, rave **5** mouth, scold **7** bluster, bombast, declaim, fustian **8** bloviate, harangue, perorate **10** vituperate **11** rodomontade

ranula 4 cyst

rap 3 hit, tap **4** blow, chat, swat, talk, wipe **5** blame, chide, knock, swipe **6** charge, patter, rebuke **7** censure, condemn, reproof **8** causerie, denounce, reproach, sentence **9** criticize, criticism, reprehend, reprimand, reprobate **10** discussion **12** conversation

rapacious 6 greedy **8** covetous, grasping, ravening, ravenous **9** predatory, raptorial, voracious **10** gluttonous, predaceous

rapacity 5 greed **7** avarice, avidity **8** cupidity, voracity **10** greediness **12** covetousness, ravenousness

rape 4 ruin **5** colza, force, spoil **6** canola, defile, ravage, ravish **7** assault, debauch, despoil, outrage, plunder, violate **9** violation **10** ravishment, spoliation

Rape of the Lock, The *author:* **4** Pope (Alexander) *heroine:* **7** Belinda

Raphael *birthplace:* **6** Urbino *subject:* **7** Madonna *teacher:* **8** Perugino

rapid 4 fast **5** brisk, chute, fleet, hasty, quick, swift **6** speedy **7** hurried **9** breakneck **11** expeditious

rapidity 5 haste, hurry, speed **8** celerity, velocity

rapids 5 chute **8** cataract **10** white water

rapine 4 loot, swag **5** booty, prize, spoil **6** boodle, spoils **7** pillage, plunder **10** spoliation

Rappaccini's Daughter 8 Beatrice *author:* **9** Hawthorne (Nathaniel)

rapport 5 unity **6** accord **7** concord, harmony **8** affinity **9** communion **13** communication

rapscallion see RASCAL

rap session 6 confab, parley **7** palaver **8** colloquy **10** discussion

rapt 6 intent **7** engaged **8** absorbed, immersed **9** engrossed **11** carried away, preoccupied, transported

raptor 3 owl **4** hawk **5** eagle **6** condor, falcon, merlin, osprey **7** kestrel, vulture **9** gyrfalcon **10** bird of prey **11** deinonychus

rapture 5 swoon **6** heaven **7** delight, ecstasy, nirvana **9** transport **10** exaltation **13** seventh heaven

rara ___ 4 avis

rare 3 few, red **4** pink, thin **6** choice, dainty, exotic, scarce, seldom, select **7** elegant, unusual **8** delicate, singular, sporadic, superior, uncommon, unwonted **9** exquisite, recherché, underdone **10** infrequent, occasional **11** distinctive, exceptional **13** extraordinary

rarefied 4 fine, thin **7** tenuous **8** esoteric **10** attenuated

rarefy 4 thin **6** refine **9** attenuate

rarely 6 little, seldom **9** extremely, unusually **12** infrequently

raring 4 avid, keen **5** eager **6** gung-ho **12** enthusiastic

rarity 5 curio **6** oddity **7** curiosa **8** scarcity **9** curiosity **10** aberration **11** collectible

rascal 3 imp **4** rake **5** devil, knave, rogue, scamp **7** lowlife, villain, wastrel **8** scalawag **9** miscreant, reprobate, scoundrel, skeezicks **10** blackguard **11** rapscallion *Irish:* **8** spalpeen

rash 5 hasty, heady **6** abrupt, daring, madcap, plague, sudden, unwary, unwise **7** foolish **8** careless, epidemic, eruption, headlong, heedless, outbreak, reckless **9** audacious, daredevil, foolhardy, hotheaded, impetuous, imprudent, impulsive **10** ill-advised, incautious, indiscreet, unthinking **11** injudicious, precipitate, temerarious, thoughtless

rasp 4 file, fret **5** annoy, chafe, grate **6** abrade, scrape **7** scratch **8** irritate

raspberry 7 catcall **8** blackcap **10** Bronx cheer

raspy 3 dry **5** harsh, rough **6** hoarse **7** grating, jarring, raucous **8** scrabbly, scratchy

rat 4 fink, heel, scab **5** louse **6** defect, desert, inform, rodent, snitch, squeak, squeal, tattle **7** stoolie **8** apostate, defector, informer, recreant, renegade, squealer, turncoat **9** bandicoot, repudiate, turnabout **11** stool pigeon **12** tergiversate *female:* **3** doe

rate 3 fee, set, tab **4** cost, earn, rank **5** assay, class, grade, merit, price, scale, set at, value **6** amount, assess, charge, degree, esteem, regard, survey, tariff **7** apprize, deserve, valuate **8** appraise, classify, consider, estimate, evaluate, price tag **9** valuation **10** proportion

rather 4 a bit **5** quite **6** fairly, in lieu, kind of, pretty, sort of **7** instead **8** somewhat **9** tolerably **10** moderately, more or less, preferably **11** alternately **12** considerably **13** alternatively

rathskeller 3 bar, inn, pub **4** dive **6** saloon, tavern **7** barroom, taproom **8** alehouse, basement

ratify 4 seal 5 enact 7 approve, certify, confirm, endorse, license 8 accredit, sanction, validate

rating 4 mark, rank 5 class, grade 6 number 8 estimate, standing

ratio 5 scale 7 percent 8 fraction, quotient 10 percentage, proportion

ratiocination 8 judgment, sequitur 9 inference, reasoning 10 conclusion

ration 4 dole, food, meal, mete 5 allot, divvy, quota, share 6 divide, parcel 7 measure, mete out, prorate 8 allocate 9 allotment, allowance 10 provisions 13 apportionment

rational 4 calm, cool, sane 5 lucid, sober, sound 6 stable 7 logical, prudent 8 sensible, thinking 9 judicious 10 consequent, reasonable 11 circumspect, intelligent, level-headed 12 intellectual

rationale 5 basis, logic 6 reason 7 grounds 9 reasoning 11 explanation 13 justification

rationalize 7 explain, justify 10 account for 11 externalize

ratite 3 emu, moa 4 kiwi, rhea 7 ostrich

rattail 3 cod 9 grenadier

rattan 4 cane, palm 6 switch 7 malacca

Rattigan play 10 Winslow Boy (The) 14 Separate Tables

rattle 3 gab, jaw, yak 4 chat, faze 5 abash, addle, clack, noise, rouse, run on, upset 6 babble, gabble, jangle, racket 7 chatter, clatter, confuse, disturb, flummox, perplex 8 bewilder, confound, distract 9 discomfit, embarrass 10 noisemaker

rattlebrained 5 dizzy, giddy, silly 7 flighty 8 skittish 9 frivolous

rattling 4 very 5 brisk, quick 6 damned, lively, mighty 8 whacking, whopping 9 energetic, extremely 11 exceedingly

ratty 4 mean 5 dowdy, dumpy, tacky 6 cheesy, scurvy, shabby 7 unkempt 8 slovenly 10 despicable 11 treacherous 12 contemptible

raucous 4 loud 5 harsh, noisy, rough, rowdy 6 hoarse, unruly 7 grating, jarring, squawky 8 rowdyish, strident 9 termagant, turbulent 10 boisterous, disorderly, stridulent, stridulous, tumultuous 11 cacophonous 12 rambunctious

raunchy 4 foul 5 dirty, nasty 6 coarse, filthy, sloppy, smutty, vulgar 7 obscene 8 indecent 9 salacious

ravage 4 loot, raze, ruin, sack 5 foray, harry, spoil, strip, waste, wreck 6 forage, invade, ravish 7 despoil, overrun, pillage, plunder, ransack, scourge 8 desolate, spoliate 9 depredate, desecrate, devastate

rave 4 gush, rant 5 storm 6 babble, jabber 7 enthuse 10 rhapsodize

ravel 3 run 4 fray 5 snarl 6 muddle, tangle 7 perplex, untwine 8 entangle 9 extricate 10 complicate 11 disentangle

ravelings 4 lint 7 threads

Ravel work 6 Boléro 7 La Valse 14 Daphnis et Chloé 17 Rapsodie espagnole

raven 3 jet 4 ebon, inky, prey 5 black, ebony, jetty, sable 7 despoil, plunder 9 pitch-dark 10 pitch-black *relative:* 3 jay 4 crow 6 magpie 7 blue jay

Raven, The *author:* 3 Poe (Edgar Allan) *lost love:* 9 Lenore *refrain:* 9 Nevermore

ravenous 6 greedy, hungry 7 starved 8 edacious, famished, starving 9 rapacious, voracious 10 gluttonous

ravine 3 cut, gap 4 gulf, pass 5 abyss, chasm, cleft, clove, flume, gorge, gulch, gully, notch 6 arroyo, canyon, clough, coulee, defile, gutter, nullah 7 crevice, fissure 8 barranca, crevasse *Mt. Washington's:* 9 Tuckerman

raving 3 mad 5 manic, rabid, upset 6 crazed 7 frantic, lunatic, unglued 8 demented, deranged, frenetic, frenzied, maniacal, obsessed, unhinged, worked up 9 ravishing 10 distraught, flipped out, hysterical, irrational 11 overwrought

ravish 4 rape 5 force, spoil 6 defile 7 assault, despoil, outrage, pillage, plunder, violate 8 deflower, entrance, overcome 9 enrapture, transport

raw 4 cold, nude, rude 5 bleak, chill, crass, crude, fresh, green, naked, rough, young 6 callow, coarse, impure, native, unclad, unripe, vulgar 7 uncouth 8 immature, uncooked, unformed 9 au naturel, inelegant, irritated, run-of-mine, unbridled, unclothed, undressed, unrefined 10 unfinished, unpolished 13 inexperienced

rawboned 4 bony, lank, lean 5 gaunt, gawky, lanky, spare 6 skinny 7 angular, scraggy, scrawny

ray 4 beam 5 gleam, manta, shaft, skate, trace 6 radius, streak, stream 7 radiate, sawfish, sunbeam, torpedo 8 moonbeam 9 devilfish, thornback 10 guitarfish

raze 4 ruin 5 level 7 destroy 8 demolish, pull down, tear down

razor 6 shaver

razz 3 rag, rib 4 bait, josh, mock, twit 5 scout, taunt 6 badger, banter, deride, heckle, hector 8 ridicule (see also RASPBERRY)

RBI 11 run batted in 12 runs batted in

re 4 as to 5 as for 7 apropos 9 apropos

of, as regards, regarding 10 as respects, concerning, relating to, respecting 12 with regard to 13 with respect to

reach 4 beat, gain, pass, span, tack 5 carry, get at, get to, grasp, level, range, scope, sweep, touch 6 arrive, attain, extend, extent, rack up, thrust 7 achieve, horizon, project, stretch 9 encompass, influence 10 accomplish, get through

___ **reaction** 4 dark 5 alarm, chain, light 7 nuclear 8 chemical

reactivate 5 renew 6 revive 8 rekindle, revivify 9 resurrect 10 revitalize 11 resuscitate

read 4 scan, skim 6 peruse 8 pore over *inability to:* 8 dyslexia

readable 7 legible

reader 6 lector, primer 7 proofer, scanner 8 bookworm 9 anthology

readily 4 well 6 easily, freely 7 lightly 9 willingly 12 effortlessly

readiness 4 ease 5 skill 7 aptness 8 alacrity, dispatch, facility 9 dexterity, quickness 10 promptness 11 inclination, promptitude 12 preparedness

reading 6 lesson 7 lection, version, vulgate 9 rendition 10 recitation

ready 3 set 4 prep, ripe 5 equip 6 active, gear up, make up, primed, prompt 7 prepare 8 prepared 9 available, inclined

real 4 true, very 5 pukka, sound, valid 6 actual, honest 7 certain, genuine, sincere 8 bona fide, concrete, existent, tangible 9 authentic, undoubted, veridical 10 sure-enough, undeniable 11 substantive 12 indisputable

realism 6 verism 7 verismo 10 naturalism, pragmatism 11 objectivism, objectivity

realistic 4 sane 5 sober, sound 7 genuine, natural 8 lifelike, rational, sensible, veristic 9 practical, pragmatic 10 bottom-line, hard-boiled, hardheaded, reasonable, unromantic 11 down-to-earth 12 matter-of-fact 13 unsentimental

reality 4 fact, true 5 being, sooth, truth 9 actuality, existence, substance 13 flesh and blood

realize 4 gain 5 grasp, reach, score 6 attain, rack up 7 achieve, feature, imagine, reflect 8 conceive, envisage, envision 9 actualize, recognize 10 accomplish, comprehend

really 4 very 5 truly 6 indeed, verily 7 awfully, clearly 8 actually, honestly 9 assuredly, certainly, decidedly, genuinely 10 definitely, positively 11 exceedingly, indubitably, undoubtedly 12 unmistakably

realm 5 orbit, range, scope, sweep 6 domain, empire, estate, extent, radius, sphere 7 compass, demesne, kingdom, purview 8 dominion

ream 4 load, scad 5 widen 7 enlarge 11 countersink

reanimation 7 rebirth, revival 10 renascence, resurgence 11 reawakening, renaissance 12 risorgimento

reap 3 cut 4 earn, gain 5 glean, shear 6 garner, gather, obtain, sickle, thresh 7 harvest

rear 3 aft 4 back, butt, hind, lift, ramp, rump, seat, tail 5 after, breed, build, erect, fanny, hoist, nurse, put up, raise, set up 6 behind, bottom, fledge, foster, uphold 7 bring up, caboose, elevate, nurture 8 backside, buttocks, hindmost 9 construct, posterior

rear end 3 bum, bun, can 4 duff, moon, rump, seat, tail, tush 5 booty, fanny 6 behind, bottom, heinie 7 caboose, keister, tail end 8 backside, buttocks, derriere 9 posterior

rearmost 3 end 4 last 5 final 8 terminal, ultimate

rearrange see READJUST

rearward 3 aft 4 back 6 behind 8 backward 9 posterior 10 retrograde

Rea Silvia *father:* 7 Numitor *son:* 5 Remus 7 Romulus

reason 3 why, wit 4 mind, nous 5 basis, cause, infer, proof, think 6 excuse, ground, motive, sanity, senses 7 account, reflect 8 argument, cogitate, conceive, persuade 9 inference, intellect, rationale, soundness, speculate, wherefore 10 antecedent, deliberate 11 determinant, explanation 12 intelligence 13 consideration, justification, ratiocination, understanding

reasonable 4 fair, just 5 cheap, level, sound 6 modest 7 logical, low-cost, tenable 8 credible, feasible, moderate, rational, sensible 9 equitable, plausible 10 acceptable, affordable, restrained 11 inexpensive, intelligent

reasoning 4 case 5 logic 8 argument 9 deduction

reasonless 7 invalid 8 baseless 9 illogical, senseless, unfounded 10 fallacious, groundless, irrational 11 meaningless, purposeless

reawaken 5 renew 6 revive 7 refresh 8 revivify 9 reanimate 10 regenerate 12 reinvigorate

rebate 6 lessen, refund, return 8 decrease, diminish, give back 9 deduction, reduction

Rebecca *beloved:* 7 Ivanhoe *father:* 5 Isaac

Rebekah *brother:* 5 Laban *father:* 7 Bethuel *husband:* 5 Isaac *nurse:* 7 Deborah *son:* 4 Esau 5 Jacob

rebel 6 anarch, mutiny, resist, revolt 7 disobey 8 frondeur, mutineer 9 insurgent 10 malcontent 13 revolutionary, revolutionist

rebellion 6 émeute, mutiny, revolt, rising 8 defiance, intifada, sedition, uprising 10 insurgence, insurgency, resistance, revolution 12 insurrection

rebellious 6 unruly 8 mutinous, stubborn 9 insurgent 10 refractory 11 disaffected, disobedient 12 contumacious, unmanageable 13 insubordinate

rebirth 7 revival 9 awakening 10 conversion, renascence, resurgence 11 reanimation, reawakening, renaissance 12 resurrection, risorgimento

rebound 5 rally 6 bounce, reecho, recoil, repeat 7 recover 8 comeback, recovery, ricochet, snap back 10 convalesce

rebozo 5 scarf, shawl

rebuff 4 slap, snub 5 repel 6 reject 7 fend off, repulse, ward off 8 turn away

rebuild 6 repair, revamp 7 remodel, restore 8 overhaul, renovate, retrofit 9 modernize, refurbish 11 recondition, reconstruct 12 rehabilitate

rebuke 3 rap 4 snub 5 chide, scold, scorn 6 bawl out, berate, earful, lesson, rebuff 7 lecture, reproof, reprove 8 admonish, call down, reproach, scolding 9 reprimand, talking-to 10 tongue-lash 11 comeuppance, objurgation 12 admonishment, dressing-down 13 tongue-lashing

rebut 5 repel 6 refute, reject 7 confute, fend off, repulse, ward off 8 confound, disprove, stave off 10 controvert, disconfirm

rebuttal 5 reply 6 answer, retort 7 defense, riposte 8 argument, comeback, response 9 rejoinder 10 refutation 11 repudiation

recalcitrant 6 unruly 7 froward, willful 8 contrary, perverse, stubborn, untoward 9 fractious, obstinate, resistant 10 headstrong 11 intractable 12 ungovernable, unmanageable

recall 4 stir 5 evoke, renew, rouse, waken 6 arouse, awaken, cancel, memory, remind, repeal, revive, revoke 7 bethink, rescind, restore, retract, reverse 8 callback, remember, resemble, take back, withdraw 9 anamnesis, recollect, reinstate, reminisce, represent, reproduce 10 revocation 11 bring to mind, countermand, remembrance 12 recollection, reminiscence

recant 5 unsay 6 abjure, revoke 7 retract 8 forswear, renounce, take back, withdraw 9 backtrack, repudiate

recap 5 sum up 6 précis, résumé 7 reprise, retread, summary 8 overview 9 summarize 10 retrograde

recapitulate 5 sum up 6 resume 9 summarize 10 retrograde

recapitulation 5 sum-up 6 précis, résumé 7 epitome, reprise, summary 9 summing-up

recede 3 ebb 4 back 5 abate, taper 6 lessen, reduce, retire 7 dwindle, regress, retract, retreat 8 decrease, diminish, fall back, withdraw 10 retrograde, retrogress

receipts 4 gate, take 5 sales 6 income 7 revenue, takings 8 earnings, proceeds

receive 4 host 5 admit, catch, greet 6 accept, endure, suffer, take in 7 acquire, sustain, welcome 10 experience

received 5 plain, sound 6 common 7 popular 8 accepted, familiar, ordinary, orthodox 12 acknowledged, conventional

receiver 4 dish 5 donee, fence, pager 6 aerial 7 antenna, catcher, scanner 9 recipient, treasurer

recent 3 new 4 late 5 fresh, novel 6 latest, modern 8 neoteric

receptacle 6 hamper, holder, hopper, trough, vessel 9 container 10 repository

receptive 4 open 7 passive 8 amenable 9 sensitive 10 accessible, hospitable, open-minded, responsive 11 persuadable, persuasible, suggestible, susceptible

recess 4 cove, nook 5 break, cleft, niche 6 alcove, grotto, hiatus 7 adjourn 8 prorogue 9 prorogate, terminate 11 indentation

Recessional *author:* 7 Kipling (Rudyard)

recessive 3 shy 8 retiring 9 reclusive, withdrawn 10 unsociable

recherché 4 rare 5 novel 6 choice, dainty, exotic, select 7 elegant, unusual 8 affected, delicate, original, superior, uncommon 9 exquisite 11 pretentious

recipe 7 formula 9 procedure 12 prescription

reciprocal 4 mate, twin 5 match 6 double, fellow, mutual 8 requited 9 companion, duplicate 10 coordinate 11 interactive *prefix:* 5 inter

reciprocate 5 repay 6 retort, return 7 requite 8 exchange 9 retaliate 10 compensate, recompense 11 interchange

recital 5 story 6 soiree 7 concert, reading 9 discourse, narration 10 recounting 11 enumeration, performance

recite 4 tell 5 chant, count, state 6 detail, number, relate, repeat, report, set out 7 declaim, narrate, recount, reel off 8 describe, rehearse 9 pronounce

reckless 4 rash, wild 5 brash, hasty 6 daring, madcap 8 carefree, heedless 9 audacious, daredevil, foolhardy, hotheaded 10 ill-advised, incautious 11 harebrained, temerarious, thoughtless 12 devil-may-care 13 irresponsible

reckon 3 sum 5 count, gauge, guess, judge, tally, total 6 cipher, figure, number, regard 7 account, compute, suppose, surmise 8 consider, estimate 9 calculate, enumerate 10 conjecture 11 approximate

reckoning 3 tab 4 bill 5 tally, score 7 account, invoice 9 statement 10 arithmetic, estimation 11 calculation, computation

reclaim 4 save, tame 6 redeem, reform, rescue 7 deliver, recover, restore 9 restitute 11 recondition, reconstruct 12 rehabilitate

recline 3 lie 4 rest, tilt 5 couch, slant, slope 6 lounge, repose 7 lie down 10 stretch out

reclining 4 flat 5 prone 6 supine 9 decumbent, prostrate, recumbent

recluse 5 loner 6 hermit, shut-in 7 eremite 8 cenobite, solitary 9 anchorite *female:* 7 ancress 9 anchoress

reclusive 8 eremitic, hermetic, reserved, solitary 9 withdrawn 10 antisocial, eremitical, unsociable 12 misanthropic

recognition 6 credit, esteem, notice 9 attention, awareness, gratitude 10 cognizance, perception 11 realization 12 appreciation

recognize 4 note, spot 5 admit 6 notice 7 observe, realize 8 diagnose, identify 9 apprehend 10 appreciate 11 acknowledge, determinate, distinguish

recoil 4 balk, kick 5 cower, dodge, quail, start, wince 6 blench, cringe, flinch, shrink 7 rebound, retract, squinch 8 reaction

recollect 5 evoke 6 recall, remind, revive 7 bethink 8 remember 9 reminisce

recollection 6 memory, recall 9 anamnesis, flashback 11 remembrance 12 reminiscence

recommence 5 renew 6 pick up, reopen, resume, take up 7 restart 8 continue

recommend 4 tout 6 advise, praise, prefer 7 acclaim, commend, counsel, endorse, entrust, propose, suggest 8 advocate

recommendation 4 plug 5 pitch 6 advice 7 counsel 11 endorsement, testimonial

recompense 3 pay 4 wage 5 repay 6 amends, reward 7 guerdon, premium, redress, requite 8 gratuity, requital 9 indemnify, indemnity, quittance, reimburse, repayment 10 compensate, remunerate, reparation 11 reciprocate, restitution, retribution 12 compensation, remuneration 13 consideration, gratification

reconcile 4 suit, tune 5 adapt 6 accept, accord, adjust, attune, make up, resign, settle, square, submit, tailor 7 conform, get over, resolve 9 harmonize, integrate 10 conciliate, coordinate 11 accommodate

recondite 4 deep 6 hidden, mystic, occult, orphic, secret 7 cryptic, erudite, learned, obscure 8 abstruse, academic, esoteric, hermetic, profound 9 concealed, difficult, enigmatic, scholarly

recondition 3 fix 4 mend 6 doctor, repair, revamp 7 rebuild, restore 8 make over, overhaul, retrofit 9 restitute 10 rejuvenate 12 rehabilitate

reconnoiter 5 scout 6 survey

reconsider 6 review, revise 7 rethink, reweigh 8 reassess 9 reexamine 10 reevaluate 13 think better of

reconstruct 6 recast, re-form, remake, revamp 7 rebuild, reclaim, remodel, restore 8 make over, overhaul, readjust, renovate 9 refashion, restitute 10 reassemble, reorganize

record 4 disc, disk 5 album 6 annals, enroll 7 archive, journal, platter 8 archives, document, register 9 chronicle 10 transcript *of a meeting:* 7 minutes *of proceedings:* 4 acta *ship's:* 3 log 7 logbook

recorder 5 flute 9 registrar *flight:* 8 black box

record player 5 phono 8 Victrola 9 turntable 10 gramophone, phonograph

recount 4 tell 5 state 6 recite, relate, report, retail 7 narrate 8 describe, rehearse 9 enumerate

recoup 6 regain 7 get back, reclaim, recover 8 retrieve 9 repossess

recourse 6 backup, refuge, resort 7 standby, stopgap, support 8 resource 9 expedient, makeshift

recover 4 heal, mend 5 evict, rally, renew 6 recoup, redeem, regain, revive 7 get back, get over, improve, rebound, recycle, reclaim, restore 8 retrieve, snap back 9 come round, reacquire, recapture, re-collect, repossess, restitute 10 bounce back, convalesce, recuperate

recreant 3 rat 5 false 6 coward, craven,

untrue 7 chicken, dastard, unloyal
8 apostate, cowardly, defector, deserter, disloyal, poltroon, renegade, turncoat
9 dastardly, faithless, turnabout 10 perfidious, traitorous, unfaithful 13 pusillanimous

recreate 4 play 5 evoke, renew 7 freshen, refresh, restore 11 reconstruct

recreation 4 play 5 hobby, sport
7 leisure, pastime 8 activity 9 avocation, diversion 10 relaxation 13 entertainment

recrudesce 5 recur 6 return, revert, revive 7 reoccur 8 break out

recruit 4 boot, hire 5 raise 6 engage, enlist, enroll, muster, novice, rookie
7 draftee 8 beginner, enlistee, freshman, headhunt, neophyte, newcomer 9 conscript, fledgling, reinforce, replenish
10 apprentice, tenderfoot

rectifier 4 tube 5 diode 8 detector, ignitron

rectify 3 fix 4 mend 5 amend, emend
6 adjust, remedy, repair 7 correct

rectitude 6 virtue 7 honesty, probity
8 morality 9 rightness 11 uprightness
13 righteousness

rector 6 parson, pastor, priest 9 clergyman 10 headmaster

rectory 5 manse 8 benefice 9 parsonage

recumbent 4 flat 5 prone 6 supine 7 leaning, resting 8 reposing 9 lying down, prostrate, reclining

recuperate 4 heal, mend 5 rally 6 regain, revive 7 rebound, recover 8 snap back
10 convalesce

recur 5 cycle, haunt 6 repeat, resort, return 7 iterate, revolve 8 turn back

recurring 7 chronic 8 periodic 10 continuous, isochronal, periodical, persistent
11 isochronous 12 intermittent

red 4 puce, ruby 5 coral, gules, rouge, ruddy 6 cerise, claret, florid, maroon
7 carmine, crimson, flushed, glowing, magenta, oxblood, scarlet, vermeil
8 burgundy, sanguine 9 vermilion *combining form:* 4 rhod 5 rhodo

Red 6 Bolshy, commie 7 Bolshie, comrade 9 Bolshevik, Communist

redact 4 edit 6 censor, revise

Red and the Black author: 8 Stendhal

red ape 9 orangutan

red arsenic 7 realgar

red-backed sandpiper 6 dunlin

Red Badge of Courage *author:* 5 Crane (Stephen) *hero:* 7 Fleming (Henry)

red-bellied snipe 9 dowitcher

redbird 7 tanager 8 cardinal 13 summer tanager

red blood cell 11 erythrocyte

red-blooded 5 juicy, lusty, manly
6 hearty, robust, virile 8 vigorous
9 energetic

redbreast 4 knot 5 robin 7 sunfish

red-breasted snipe 9 dowitcher

Redburn author 8 Melville (Herman)

red carp 8 goldfish

red cobalt 9 erythrite

red copper ore 7 cuprite

Red Cross *founder:* 6 Barton (Clara)
Knight: 6 George

redden 5 blush, color, flush, rouge
6 mantle, ruddle 11 incarnadine

red dog 5 blitz

redecorate 4 redo 5 fix up 9 refurbish

redeem 4 free, save 5 atone, loose, renew 6 offset, pay off, ransom, reform, rescue 7 expiate, reclaim, recover, restore 9 exonerate

redeemer 5 Jesus 6 Christ, savior 7 messiah, saviour

redemption 6 ransom 7 release 9 atonement, expiation, salvation 11 deliverance

red-eye 5 hooch 6 flight, rotgut
7 whiskey 8 rock bass 9 moonshine

red-faced 5 ruddy 6 florid, shamed
7 abashed, flushed, glowing 8 blushing, rubicund, sanguine, sheepish 9 mortified 11 embarrassed

redfish 4 bass, drum 5 perch 6 salmon
10 ocean perch 11 channel bass

red hickory 6 pignut

red-hot 5 fiery 6 ardent, fervid 7 blazing, boiling, burning, fervent, flaming, glowing 8 brand-new, scalding, sizzling
9 scorching 10 blistering, passionate, sweltering 11 impassioned

red Indian paint 9 bloodroot 11 sanguinaria

red ink 7 arrears, deficit 8 shortage

red inkberry 8 pokeweed

red ironbark 8 eucalypt 10 eucalyptus

red iron ore 5 ocher, ochre 8 hematite

red lauan 8 mahogany

red-legged crow 6 chough

red-legged sandpiper 9 turnstone

red-letter 7 notable 8 historic 9 important, memorable 10 noteworthy, observable, remarkable 11 significant

red-light district 5 stews 10 tenderloin

red mite 7 chigger

redneck 4 clod, hick, rube 5 Bubba, yahoo, yokel 6 rustic 7 bumpkin, hayseed 9 hillbilly 10 clodhopper, good old boy, good ole boy

redo 5 renew 6 repeat, revamp 7 remodel, restyle 8 make over, overhaul, refinish, renovate 9 refurbish 10 redecorate

red ocher 8 hematite

redolence 4 balm, odor **5** aroma, attar, scent, spice **7** bouquet, incense, perfume **9** fragrance

redolent 5 balmy, spicy, sweet **7** odorous, scented **8** aromatic, fragrant, perfumed **9** ambrosial, evocative **10** suggestive **11** reminiscent

redouble 4 dupe **7** dualize, enhance, magnify **8** heighten **9** duplicate, intensify, reinforce **10** strengthen

redoubt 4 fort **7** bastion, citadel **8** fastness, fortress **10** stronghold

redoubtable 5 famed, great **6** famous, mighty **7** awesome, eminent **8** imposing, puissant, renowned **9** prominent **10** celebrated, formidable, impressive **11** illustrious **12** intimidating, overwhelming **13** distinguished

redound 6 accrue, recoil **7** conduce, reflect **10** contribute

red pigment 5 ocher, ochre **6** ruddle

Red Planet 4 Mars

redpoll 5 finch **6** linnet

redraft 6 revamp, revise, rework **7** restyle, rewrite **8** make over, overhaul, rescript, revision, work over **9** recension

redress 4 heal **6** amends, avenge, negate, offset, relief, remedy **7** correct **8** reprisal, requital **9** cancel out, indemnity, quittance, vindicate **10** compensate, counteract, correction, neutralize, recompense, reparation **11** restitution, retribution **12** compensation

red roe 5 coral **6** caviar

redroot 7 alkanet, pigweed **9** bloodroot **12** New Jersey tea

red sable 8 kolinsky

red silver ore 9 proustite

red squirrel 9 chickaree

reduce 3 cut **4** cull, diet, melt, pare **5** abate, force, lower, shade, shave, slash, smelt **6** humble, lessen, recede, weaken **7** abridge, curtail, cut back, cut down, dwindle, liquefy, squeeze **8** boil down, compress, contract, decrease, diminish, discount, mark down, minimize, simplify, taper off **10** depreciate, slenderize **11** consolidate

reductio ad ___ 8 absurdum

reduction 6 digest, précis, rebate **7** cutback, cutdown, epitome, summary **8** abstract, discount, markdown, synopsis **9** abatement **10** shortening **11** curtailment **12** condensation

redundancy 6 excess **7** nimiety, surfeit **8** pleonasm **9** abundance, profusion, prolixity, tautology **10** repetition **11** periphrasis, reiteration, superfluity **13** supernumerary

redundant 5 extra, spare, windy, wordy

6 prolix **7** surplus, verbose **9** duplicate, excessive, iterative **11** duplicative, reiterative, repetitious, superfluous, tautologous **13** supernumerary

redux 7 revived **8** restored

redwing 6 thrush **9** blackbird

redwood 7 amboyna, sequoia **8** mahogany

reed 4 pipe **5** arrow, grass

reedy 4 thin **6** skinny, stalky, twiggy **7** spindly

reef 3 bar, cay, key **4** lode, vein **5** atoll, ledge **6** reduce, skerry **7** sandbar

reek 4 funk **5** fetor, smell, stink **6** stench **9** effluvium

reeking 4 rank **5** fetid, funky, fusty **6** putrid, rancid, smelly, stinky **7** noisome, stenchy **10** malodorous

reel 4 spin, sway, turn **5** lurch, spool, weave, whirl **6** bobbin, careen, teeter, totter, waggle, wobble **7** stagger, stumble **8** fall back

reestablish 5 renew **6** revive **7** restore **9** reinstate **10** reinscribe **11** reintroduce

reevaluate 6 review **7** rethink, reweigh **8** reassess **9** reexamine **10** reconsider

reeve 4 ruff **6** thread **9** sandpiper **10** magistrate

reexamine see REEVALUATE

refashion 5 alter **6** change, modify, recast, remake, revamp **7** remodel **8** make over, overhaul **9** transmute

refection 4 feed, meal **6** repast **11** nourishment, refreshment

refectory 10 dining hall

refer 6 advert, allude, assign, relate, submit **7** ascribe **9** attribute

referee 3 ump **5** judge **6** umpire **7** adjudge, arbiter, mediate **8** mediator **9** arbitrate, officiate **10** adjudicate, arbitrator

reference 5 atlas **6** credit, source **7** almanac, meaning, mention **8** allusion, citation, innuendo, relation, resource **9** directory **10** dictionary **11** testimonial **12** encyclopedia

reference book 5 atlas, bible, guide **6** manual **7** almanac **8** handbook **9** guidebook **10** dictionary **11** enchiridion **12** encyclopedia

reference guide 5 index **12** bibliography

referendum 4 poll, vote **10** plebiscite

refine 5 smelt, prune **6** polish, purify, smooth **7** elevate, improve, perfect, process **8** civilize **9** cultivate

refined 4 pure **6** subtle, urbane **7** elegant, genteel, raffiné **8** cultured, elevated, ladylike, raffinée, well-bred **9** civilized **10** cultivated, fastidious **13** sophisticated

refinement 5 couth, grace, taste **6** finish,

polish 7 culture, finesse, suavity
8 breeding, civility, courtesy, elegance,
subtlety, urbanity 9 politesse 10 politeness 11 cultivation 12 civilization, distillation, purification 13 clarification

reflect 4 echo, pore, show 5 weigh
6 bounce, mirror, ponder, reason,
return 7 redound 8 chew over, cogitate,
consider, ruminate 9 cerebrate 10 deliberate, retrospect 11 contemplate,
demonstrate

reflection 4 slur 5 image 6 musing
7 replica, thought 8 reproach 9 aspersion 10 cogitation, meditation, rumination, simulacrum 11 cerebration
12 deliberation, reproduction 13 animadversion, consideration, contemplation

reflective 7 pensive 9 reflexive 10 cogitative, indicative, meditative, ruminative,
thoughtful 12 deliberative 13 contemplative

reflux 3 ebb 4 GERD 8 backflow

reform 5 amend, emend 6 redeem, revise
7 correct, improve, reclaim, shape up
8 make over 10 correction, houseclean,
regenerate

Reformation leader 4 Knox (John)
6 Calvin (John), Luther (Martin)
7 Zwingli (Huldrych)

reformatory 3 pen 6 prison 7 borstal
8 big house, remedial 10 corrective
12 penitentiary

refractory 6 mulish, unruly 7 froward,
restive 8 contrary, perverse, stubborn
9 obstinate 10 bullheaded, headstrong,
rebellious, unyielding 11 intractable,
stiff-necked 12 unmanageable

refrain 4 keep, stop 6 burden, chorus,
shrink 7 abstain, forbear 8 hold back

refresh 5 renew 6 revive 7 animate,
enliven, quicken, restore 8 irrigate,
recreate, renovate 9 replenish, stimulate 10 rejuvenate

refresher 5 drink, tonic 6 bracer
8 reminder 9 stimulant 11 restorative

refreshing 5 brisk, tonic 7 bracing
8 reviving 9 analeptic, animating
10 delightful, energizing 11 restorative,
stimulating 12 invigorating, rejuve-
nating

refrigerant 3 ice 5 freon 7 coolant, cryo-
gen 12 fluorocarbon 13 sulfur dioxide

refrigerator 6 cooler, fridge, icebox,
walk-in 9 condenser 10 Frigidaire

refuge 4 lair, port 5 cover, haven 6 asylum, covert, harbor, resort 7 hideout,
protect, retreat, shelter 8 hideaway,
recourse, resource 9 expedient, harborage, sanctuary, safe house

refugee 5 exile 6 émigré 7 evacuee

8 emigrant, fugitive 10 boat person,
expatriate

refulgent 6 bright 7 glowing, radiant
8 luminous 9 brilliant

refund 5 repay 6 rebate 8 give back
9 reimburse, repayment, restitute
11 restitution

refurbish 4 redo 5 fix up, renew
6 revamp 7 restore 8 make over, overhaul, renovate 10 redecorate, rejuvenate 11 recondition

refusal 4 veto 6 denial 7 regrets 8 negative, negation 9 disavowal 10 abnegation 11 declination, repudiation

refuse 3 jib, nix 4 deny, junk, scum
5 dreck, dross, offal, spurn, swill, trash,
waste 6 debris, litter, reject, scraps,
spilth 7 decline, garbage, residue, rubbish 8 disallow, leavings, remnants,
turn down, withhold 9 reprobate, repudiate, sweepings 10 disapprove

refutation 8 disproof, elenchus, rebuttal

refute 4 deny 5 rebut 7 confute 8 confound, disprove 10 controvert, disconfirm

regain 6 recoup 7 get back, recover
8 reoccupy, retrieve 9 recapture, repossess *possession:* 7 replevy 8 replevin

regal 5 grand 6 august, kingly, purple
7 queenly, stately, sublime 8 glorious,
imperial, imposing, kinglike, majestic,
princely, splendid 9 monarchal, sovereign 10 monarchial 11 magnificent,
monarchical, resplendent

regale 4 feed 5 amuse, feast 6 dinner,
divert, spread 7 banquet 9 entertain

regalia 5 array 6 finery 8 frippery,
insignia 9 caparison, full dress, trappings 10 decoration 11 habiliments

Regan *father:* 4 Lear *husband:* 8 Cornwall *sister:* 7 Goneril 8 Cordelia

regard 4 deem, heed, mark, note, rate,
view 5 assay, favor, honor, judge, value
6 admire, assess, esteem, homage, liking, notice, reckon, repute 7 account,
concern, respect 8 approval, consider,
devotion, estimate, fondness 9 attention 10 admiration, cognizance, estimation, observance, solicitude 11 approbation, contemplate, observation
12 appreciation, satisfaction 13 consideration

regardful 7 heedful 8 watchful 9 advertent, attentive, observant 10 perceptive,
respectful

regarding 4 as to, in re 5 about, anent,
as for 7 apropos 8 touching 9 apropos
of 10 as respects, concerning, relative
to, respecting 11 in respect to 13 with
respect to

regatta 4 race

regenerate 5 renew 6 reform, revive 7 rebirth, restore 8 recreate 9 reproduce

regent 5 ruler 6 warden 8 governor 9 protector

regicide's victim 4 king

regime 4 rule, term 5 reign 6 empire, tenure 7 dynasty 10 government, leadership

regimen 4 diet, plan, rule 6 course 10 government

region 4 area, belt, part, zone 5 field, tract 6 domain, locale, sector, sphere 7 demesne, terrain 8 locality, province, vicinity 9 bailiwick, territory 12 neighborhood

regional 5 local 9 localized, sectional 10 provincial 11 territorial

register 4 file, list, note, roll, till 5 enter, range, tally 6 annals, docket, enroll, ledger, record, roster 7 catalog, check in, express 8 indicate 9 catalogue

regnant 4 rife 6 ruling 7 current, popular 8 dominant, reigning 9 paramount, prevalent, sovereign 10 prevailing, widespread

regress 6 revert 9 backslide 10 retrograde

regret 3 rue, woe 4 care 5 grief, mourn 6 bemoan, bewail, excuse, grieve, lament, repent, sorrow 7 anguish, apology, deplore, remorse 9 heartache, penitence 10 contrition, heartbreak 11 compunction

regretful 5 sorry 6 rueful 8 contrite, mournful, penitent 9 repentant, sorrowful 10 apologetic, remorseful 11 penitential

regrettable 3 sad 6 too bad, woeful 8 grievous 10 lamentable 11 distressing, unfortunate 13 heartbreaking

regular 3 due, set 4 even 5 fixed, usual 6 common, normal, steady 7 average, equable, general, natural, orderly, typical, uniform 8 complete, constant, everyday, methodic, ordinary, standard 9 clocklike, customary, prevalent 10 methodical, systematic 11 commonplace 12 run-of-the-mill

regulate 5 order, scale 6 adjust, direct, govern, police, square, temper 7 arrange, control 8 organize 9 methodize, systemize 11 systematize

regulation 3 law 4 rule 5 canon, edict, order 6 decree 7 precept, statute 9 ordinance, prescript 11 restriction 12 codification

regulator 8 governor

rehabilitate 4 cure, heal 7 reclaim, recover, restore 8 renovate 9 reeducate, restitute 11 recondition

rehash 5 reuse 6 repeat, review, rework 7 restate, version 8 chew over, rehearse, talk over 9 rendering, rendition, rewording 11 restatement 12 recapitulate

rehearse 5 drill, train 6 repeat 7 run over 8 exercise, practice 10 run through

Rehoboam *father:* 7 Solomon *kingdom:* 5 Judah 6 Israel *mother:* 6 Naamah

reign 4 rule, sway 6 govern 7 prevail 8 dominate, dominion 11 predominate, sovereignty

reimburse 3 pay 5 repay 6 recoup, refund 7 requite 9 indemnify 10 compensate, remunerate

rein 4 curb, stem 5 check 6 bridle 7 compose, control, repress 8 hold back, restrain, suppress

reinforce 4 prop 5 brace 7 augment, bolster, enlarge, fortify, recruit, sustain 8 buttress, increase, redouble 10 invigorate, strengthen

reinstate 6 recall 7 restore 11 reestablish, reintroduce 12 rehabilitate

reintroduce 6 recall, revive 7 restore 9 reinstate 11 reestablish

reinvestment 4 DRIP 8 plowback

reiterate 5 renew, resay 6 repeat, resume, retell 7 reprise

reject 3 nix 4 jilt, junk, shed 5 debar, scorn, scrap, spurn 6 abjure, pariah, pass up, rebuff, refuse 7 cashier, cast-off, decline, discard, dismiss, exclude, outcast, repulse, shut out 8 castaway, jettison, throw out, turn away, turn down 9 eliminate, repudiate, shoot down, throw away 10 disapprove

rejoice 5 cheer, exult, glory 7 delight, gladden 8 jubilate

rejoinder 5 reply 6 answer, retort 8 comeback, rebuttal, repartee, response

rejuvenate 5 green, renew 7 refresh 8 renovate 9 modernize 10 revitalize

rekindle 5 renew 6 revive 7 restart 8 reawaken, reignite, revivify 10 reactivate, revitalize

relate 4 link, tell 5 apply, refer 6 assign, detail, recite, report 7 connect, express, pertain, recount 8 describe, disclose, interact, rehearse 9 appertain, chronicle

related 4 akin 5 alike, enate 6 agnate, allied 7 cognate, connate, germane, kindred 8 incident 9 analogous, connected, identical, pertinent 10 associated, connatural, homologous 11 consanguine

relation 3 kin 6 agnate 7 hinship, kinsman 8 affinity 9 kinswoman, reference 11 propinquity

relationship 3 tie 4 bond, link 5 ratio, tie-in, union 6 affair 7 analogy, contact, liaison 8 affinity, alliance 10 connection 11 affiliation, association 13 confederation, consanguinity

relative 3 mom, sib, sis, son 4 aunt, mama, papa 5 blood, madre, mamma, momma, niece, pappy, pater, poppa, uncle 6 agnate, cousin, father, mother, nephew, parent, sister 7 apropos, brother, cognate, germane, kinsman, sibling 8 ancestor, daughter, grandson, relation, relevant 9 ascendant, dependent, kinswoman, pertinent 10 applicable, collateral, descendant, grandchild 11 comparative, conditional, grandfather, grandmother, grandparent 13 granddaughter

relatives 3 kin 4 kith 5 folks 7 kindred, kinfolk 8 kinfolks 9 relations

relax 4 bask, ease, loll, rest 5 chill, let go, loose, remit 6 loosen, lounge, modify, unkink, unwind 7 slacken 8 chill out, kick back, loosen up, unbuckle, wind down 9 untighten 10 decompress

relaxation 3 fun 4 ease, rest 5 hobby 6 repose 7 leisure, pastime 9 amusement, diversion, enjoyment 10 recreation

relaxed 5 loose, slack 6 casual, dégagé, mellow 8 informal 9 easygoing 11 low-pressure

release 4 emit, free, vent 5 issue, loose, untie, yield 6 acquit, loosen, pardon, ransom, unbind, uncage 7 give off, give out, manumit, set free, unchain, unleash 8 liberate, unfetter 9 acquittal, discharge, exculpate, exonerate, surrender 10 emancipate 11 manumission 12 emancipation *conditional:* 6 parole

relegate 5 exile, expel 6 assign, banish, charge, commit, demote, resign 7 commend, confide, consign, entrust 8 delegate, hand over, transfer, turn over

relent 3 ebb 4 cave, ease, wane 5 abate, let up, yield 6 give in, submit 7 die away, die down, ease off, slacken, subside 8 moderate 9 acquiesce 10 capitulate

relentless 5 cruel, rigid, stern 6 dogged 7 adamant, nonstop 8 constant, obdurate, rigorous, unabated 9 ferocious, incessant, stringent 10 implacable, inexorable, inflexible, unyielding 11 remorseless, unfaltering

relevant 3 apt, fit 5 ad rem 6 cogent 7 apropos, germane 8 apposite, material, relative 9 pertinent 10 admissible, applicable 11 applicative, appropriate 12 proportional

reliable 4 safe, sure 5 solid, sound, tried,

valid 6 proven, secure, trusty 7 bedrock, certain 8 constant, verified 9 foolproof, validated 10 dependable 11 trustworthy 12 tried-and-true

reliance 4 hope 5 faith, stock, trust 10 dependence

relic 5 token 6 corpse 7 antique, memento, remains, remnant, vestige 8 artifact, fragment, keepsake, memorial, reminder, souvenir 11 remembrance

relict 5 widow 8 survivor

relief 3 aid 4 ease, fret, hand, help, lift 5 break, cameo 6 assist, raised, remedy, succor 7 comfort, redress, respite, support, welfare 8 breather, fretwork, repoussé 9 abatement, diversion 10 assistance, mitigation 11 alleviation, deliverance *pitcher:* 6 closer 7 fireman, stopper

relieve 3 rid 4 calm, ease, free, help, quit, vent 5 allay, relax, spell 6 assist, exempt, lessen, loosen, reduce, remedy, soften, solace, soothe, succor, supply 7 absolve, assuage, comfort, deprive, lighten, mollify

religion 4 cult, sect 5 cause, creed, dogma, faith 6 belief, church 8 devotion, doctrine

religious 3 nun 4 holy, monk 5 friar, godly, pious 6 devout, priest, sacred, votary 7 staunch, upright 8 cenobite, faithful, monastic, priestly, reverent 9 pietistic, prayerful, spiritual, steadfast 10 scriptural, scrupulous, worshipful

relinquish 4 cede, quit, shed 5 forgo, leave, waive, yield 6 desert, give up, resign 7 abandon, discard, lay down, release 8 abdicate, hand over, renounce 9 quitclaim, sacrifice, surrender

relish 4 like, tang, zest 5 enjoy, fancy, flair, gusto, savor, taste 6 flavor, liking, palate 7 delight 8 fondness, penchant, pleasure, sapidity 9 appetizer, condiment, enjoyment 10 appreciate 11 delectation, hors d'oeuvre

relucent 6 bright 7 glaring, radiant, shining 10 reflecting

reluctant 3 shy 4 wary 5 chary, loath 6 afraid, averse 8 cautious, grudging, hesitant 9 unwilling 10 indisposed 11 disinclined *prophet:* 5 Jonah

rely 3 bet 4 bank, plan 5 count 6 depend, gamble, reckon

rely on 5 trust 6 expect 10 anticipate

remain 4 bide, last, live, stay, wait 5 abide, tarry 6 endure, linger, loiter 7 persist, survive 8 continue 10 hang around 11 stick around

remainder 4 rest 5 dregs, trace 6 excess 7 balance, residue, remnant, surplus, vestige 8 leavings, leftover, residual, residuum

remains 4 body 5 ashes, bones, ruins 6 corpse, debris, relics 7 balance, cadaver, carcass, flotsam 8 leavings, remnants 9 reliquiae

remand 8 send back

remark 4 gibe, note 5 aside, crack 7 comment, mention 9 utterance, wise-crack, witticism 10 annotation 11 observation 12 obiter dictum

remarkable 4 rare 5 great 6 signal, unique 7 salient, strange, unusual 8 sin-gular, striking, uncommon 9 arresting, bodacious, momentous, prominent 10 impressive, noteworthy, noticeable 11 conspicuous, exceptional, outstand-ing, significant 13 extraordinary

___ **Remarque** 5 Erich (Maria)

remedial 8 curative, salutary, sanative 9 medicinal 10 corrective 11 restorative, therapeutic 12 recuperative

remedy 3 fix 4 cure, drug, heal 5 salve, solve 6 elixir, relief, repair 7 correct, cure-all, nostrum, panacea, rectify, redress, relieve 8 antidote, medicine, specific 9 alleviate, treatment 10 cor-rective, medicament, medication

remember 5 educe, evoke 6 recall, record, relive, retain, reward 7 bethink 9 flash back, recollect, reminisce 10 bear in mind 11 commemorate, memorialize

remembrance 4 gift 5 favor, relic, token 6 memory, recall, trophy 7 memento, present, thought 8 keepsake, memorial, reminder, souvenir 9 anamnesis, flash-back 12 recollection, reminiscence

remind 6 advise, prompt 7 bethink 8 admonish

reminder 4 hint, memo 5 relic, token 6 prompt, trophy 7 memento 8 keep-sake, memorial, monument, souvenir 9 refresher 10 admonition, memoran-dum 11 remembrance

reminisce see REMEMBER

reminiscence 6 memory, recall 8 anec-dote 9 anamnesis, flashback 11 remem-brance 12 recollection

remise 4 cede, deed 5 alien, grant 6 assign, convey 8 make over, transfer 9 quitclaim

remiss 3 lax 4 lazy 5 slack 8 careless, derelict, heedless, indolent, slothful 9 negligent 10 delinquent, neglectful, slatternly 11 inattentive

remit 4 send, ship, stay, stop 5 abate, defer, delay, relax 6 desist, hold up, pardon, put off, remand, shelve 7 con-done, consign, forgive, forward, hold off 8 dispatch, moderate, postpone

remnant 3 end 4 heel, husk, part, rest, rump 5 relic, trace, wrack 6 fag end, relict 7 balance, oddment, residue 8 leavings, leftover, residuum 9 remain-der

remodel 4 redo 6 recast, revamp 8 make over, overhaul, redesign 9 refashion 11 reconstruct

remonstrance 5 demur 7 protest 8 demurral, demurrer 9 challenge, objection

remonstrate 5 argue, demur, plead 6 combat, object, oppose, reason 7 protest 9 challenge

remora 4 clog, drag 6 sucker 9 hin-drance 10 impediment 11 encum-brance, shark sucker

remorse 3 rue 4 ruth 5 guilt, smart 6 regret, sorrow 9 penitence 10 contri-tion, repentance 11 compunction 12 self-reproach

remorseful see REGRETFUL

remote 3 far, off 4 slim 5 aloof 6 far-off, slight 7 distant, faraway, obscure, out-side, slender 8 detached, far-flung, frontier, isolated, lonesome, off-lying, outlying, secluded 9 backwoods, with-drawn 10 negligible 11 godforsaken, out-of-the-way *combining form:* 3 tel 4 tele

remotest 6 utmost 7 extreme, outmost 8 farthest 9 outermost, uttermost 11 furthermost

remove 4 doff, skim 5 purge 6 unseat 7 extract, take off, take out 8 dislodge, evacuate, take away, withdraw 9 clear away, eliminate *from office:* 6 depose *hair:* 8 depilate *surgically:* 6 resect

removed 5 aloof, apart 6 far-off, remote 7 devious, distant, faraway, obscure 8 detached, far-flung, isolated, outly-ing, separate 10 distracted 11 uncon-nected

remunerate 3 pay 5 repay 7 requite 9 indemnify, reimburse 10 compensate, recompense

remunerative 6 paying 7 gainful, payable 9 lucrative 10 productive, profitable 11 moneymaking

Remus *brother:* 7 Romulus *father:* 4 Mars *mother:* 9 Rea Silvia 10 Rhea Silvia *slay-er:* 7 Romulus

renaissance see REBIRTH

renal 7 nephric 9 nephritic

rend 3 rip 4 rive, tear 5 split 6 cleave, divide

render 3 pay 4 cede, limn 5 yield 6 depict, give up, impart, return, sub-mit 7 deliver, execute, pay back, pic-ture, portray, provide, restore 8 carry out, describe, hand over, turn over

9 delineate, interpret, represent, translate, transpose 10 administer, relinquish 12 administrate

rendering 4 copy 7 version 9 depiction 10 paraphrase 11 description, performance, restatement, translation 12 reproduction

rendezvous 4 date 5 haunt, tryst 6 gather, muster 7 collect, hangout, meeting 8 assemble 10 congregate, engagement 11 appointment, assignation, get-together

rendition 7 reading, version 10 adaptation 11 performance, translation

renegade 3 rat 5 rebel 6 outlaw 7 heretic 8 apostate, defector, deserter, maverick, recreant, turncoat 9 turnabout 10 schismatic

renege 4 deny 5 welsh 6 cry off, recall, recant, revoke 7 back off, back out, retract 8 renounce, withdraw 9 backpedal

renew 6 redeem, reform, revamp, revive 7 freshen, refresh, remodel 8 make over, overhaul, recharge, recreate, rekindle, renovate, revivify 9 refurbish, resurrect 10 reactivate, recommence, regenerate, rejuvenate, revitalize

rennet 8 abomasum

renounce 4 deny, quit 5 demit 6 abjure, defect, desert, give up, recant, renege, resign 7 abandon, decline, forsake, put away, retract 8 abdicate, abnegate, disclaim, forswear, swear off 9 repudiate, sacrifice 10 apostatize

renovate 4 redo 5 renew 6 remake, repair, revamp, revive 7 furbish, refresh, restore 8 overhaul, revivify 9 modernize, refurbish, resurrect 10 rejuvenate, revitalize 12 rehabilitate

renown 4 fame 5 éclat, glory, kudos 6 repute 7 acclaim 8 eminence, prestige 9 celebrity, notoriety 10 prominence, reputation 11 distinction

renowned 5 famed, great, noted 6 fabled, famous 7 eminent, notable 8 extolled 9 acclaimed, legendary, notorious, prominent, well-known 10 celebrated 11 illustrious, outstanding 13 distinguished

rent 3 let, rip 4 hire, rift, tear, torn 5 lease, split 6 breach, sublet 7 charter, fissure, rupture 8 fracture

rental 4 hire 7 tenancy

renter 6 lessee, tenant 11 leaseholder

renunciation 6 denial 7 refusal 8 apostasy, eschewal, forgoing 9 disavowal, sacrifice, surrender 10 abdication, abnegation, disclaimer, self-denial 11 abandonment, forswearing, repudiation, resignation

reorder 5 shift 7 permute 9 rearrange, reshuffle

reorganization 7 shake-up 8 turnover

repair 3 fix 4 mend 5 patch 6 cobble, doctor 7 fitness, service 8 overhaul 9 condition 11 recondition

reparations 6 amends 7 redress 9 indemnity, quittance 10 recompense, settlement 11 restitution 12 satisfaction

repartee 4 quip 6 banter, retort 7 riposte 8 backchat, badinage, comeback 9 cross talk, rejoinder 10 persiflage

repast 3 eat 4 feed, meal 5 feast 9 refection

repay 6 offset, return, reward 7 requite 9 indemnify, reimburse 10 compensate, recompense, remunerate 11 get even with

repeal 4 lift, void 5 annul 6 recall, revoke 7 abandon, abolish, nullify, rescind, reverse 8 abrogate, renounce

repeat 4 copy, echo 5 recap, recur, rerun, resay 6 go over, parrot, reecho, recite, rehash, relate, retell 7 imitate, iterate, reprise, restate 9 duplicate, reiterate, replicate 11 reduplicate 12 recapitulate

repeater 7 firearm 10 recidivist

repeating 7 iterant 9 perennial, recurrent 11 reiterative, repetitious

repel 5 rebut 6 rebuff, reject, revolt, sicken 7 disgust, fend off, hold off, repulse, ward off 8 nauseate, stave off

repellent 4 foul, vile 5 nasty 7 noisome 8 aversive 9 abhorrent, loathsome, obnoxious, offensive, repulsive, revolting 10 forbidding, disgusting, off-putting 11 rebarbative

repent 3 rue 6 regret

repentance 3 rue 4 ruth 6 sorrow 7 remorse 10 contrition 11 compunction

repentant see REGRETFUL

repetition 4 copy, echo 5 rerun 7 recital, reprise 11 duplication

rephrase 6 recast, reword 7 restate

repine 4 beef, fuss, kick, long, moan, wail 5 gripe, yearn 6 grouse, hanker, murmur 7 grumble 8 complain

replace 7 put back, restore 8 exchange, supplant 9 supersede 10 substitute

replacement 3 sub 6 fill-in, makeup 7 stand-in 9 alternate, surrogate, temporary 10 substitute 11 locum tenens, pinch hitter, succedaneum

replenish 4 fill 5 renew, stock 6 refill 7 refresh, restore

replete 4 full, rife 5 awash, lousy 7 brimful, crammed, stuffed 8 brimming 9 chock-full 11 overflowing

replica 4 copy, dupe, fake 5 clone, ditto 6 carbon 9 duplicate, facsimile, imitation 10 carbon copy, simulacrum 12 reproduction

replicate 4 copy 5 clone 6 repeat 9 reproduce

reply 4 echo 6 answer, rejoin, retort 7 respond 8 comeback, repartee, response 9 rejoinder

report 4 bang, boom, news, tell 5 crack, relay, rumor, study 6 record, relate, return, review, show up 7 account, article, check in, hearsay, narrate, recount, rundown 8 advisory, bulletin, describe, dispatch 9 broadcast, chronicle, narrative, statement 11 compte rendu

reporter 7 newsman 8 pressman 9 newshound, newswoman 10 journalist *inexperienced:* 3 cub

repose 3 lie 4 calm, rest 5 peace, poise, quiet, sleep 7 lie down, recline 8 quietude 9 composure, stillness 10 inactivity, quiescence, relaxation 11 restfulness, tranquility 12 tranquillity

repository 3 ark 5 depot, store 7 archive, arsenal 8 magazine, treasury 10 storehouse

repossess see REGAIN

reprehend 3 rap 4 rate, skin 5 blame, chide, fault, knock, scold 6 berate, rebuke 7 censure, condemn, upbraid 8 admonish, denounce 9 criticize 10 denunciate

reprehensible 4 base, evil 6 guilty, sinful, unholy, wicked 8 blamable, criminal, culpable 10 censurable 11 blameworthy, disgraceful

represent 3 act 6 denote, depict, embody, mirror, recall, relate, render, sketch, typify 7 display, exhibit, express, hold out, imitate, make out, narrate, outline, picture, portray, present, protest, realize, signify, suggest 8 describe, stand for 9 delineate, epitomize, exemplify, interpret, personify, symbolize 10 constitute, illustrate, substitute 11 emblematize, impersonate

representation 5 draft, image 6 effigy, symbol 7 picture 8 likeness 9 portrayal, statement 10 caricature, delegation

representative 5 agent, envoy, model, proxy 6 deputy, sample 7 burgess, example, typical 8 delegate, emissary, sampling, specimen 9 exemplary, spokesman 10 ambassador, legislator, prototypal, substitute 11 congressman 12 illustrative, prototypical 13 congresswoman

repress 4 curb 5 check, sit on 6 bridle, muffle, stifle, subdue 7 smother, squelch, swallow 8 keep down, restrain, suppress

repression 4 curb 7 amnesia, control 8 stifling 9 clampdown, crackdown, restraint 10 constraint

reprieve 4 stay 5 grace 7 respite, suspend

reprimand 3 rap 4 rate, ream, task 5 chide, scold 6 rebuke 7 bawl out, censure, chew out, reproof, reprove 8 admonish, call down, reproach, scolding 9 reprimand, talking-to 10 admonition 12 admonishment, dressing-down 13 tongue-lashing

reprisal 7 redress, revenge 8 revanche 9 vengeance 11 counterblow, retaliation, retribution

reprise 5 recap 6 repeat 9 reiterate 10 recurrence, repetition

reproach 3 rap 4 rail 5 blame, chide, scold 6 berate, rebuke 7 bawl out, censure, chew out, remorse, reprove, upbraid 8 admonish, call down 9 reprimand 10 admonition, opprobrium 12 admonishment

reprobate 3 rap 4 skin 5 blame, scamp, spurn 6 refuse, reject, sinner 7 censure, condemn, lowlife, villain 8 denounce, scalawag 9 miscreant, scoundrel 10 blackguard, degenerate

reproduce 4 bear, copy 5 beget, breed, spore 7 imitate 8 multiply 9 duplicate, procreate, propagate, replicate 10 regenerate 11 reduplicate

reproduction see REPLICA

reproductive cell 3 egg 4 ovum 5 sperm, spore 6 gamete 12 spermatozoid, spermatozoon

reproof 3 rap 6 rebuke 7 censure, lecture 8 scolding 9 criticism, reprimand 10 admonition 11 castigation 12 admonishment, reprehension 13 remonstration

reprove 5 chide, scold 6 rebuke 7 censure, chasten 8 admonish, call down, lambaste, reproach 9 criticize, dress down, reprimand

reptile 5 snake 6 caiman, cayman, gavial, iguana, lizard, turtle 7 tuatara 8 tortoise 9 alligator, crocodile, sphenodon *combining form:* 6 herpet 7 herpeto *extinct:* 8 dinosaur

republic 5 state 6 nation 9 democracy

Republican Party 3 GOP *mascot:* 8 elephant

Republic author 5 Plato

repudiate 4 deny 5 spurn 6 abjure, disown, recant, refuse, reject 7 decline, disavow, dismiss 8 disclaim, renounce 9 disaffirm 10 apostatize, disapprove

repugnance 6 horror 7 disgust 8 aversion, loathing 9 repulsion, revulsion 10 abhorrence, antagonism, odiousness 11 abomination, detestation

repugnant 4 foul, vile 5 nasty, yucky 6 creepy, horrid, skanky 7 noisome 8 aversive, gruesome 9 abhorrent, loathsome, obnoxious, offensive, repulsive, revolting 10 disgusting

repulse 5 rebut, repel, spurn 6 rebuff, reject, revolt, sicken 7 disgust, fend off, hold off, ward off 8 nauseate, stave off

repulsion see REPUGNANCE

repulsive see REPUGNANT

reputable 7 eminent, upright 8 esteemed 9 estimable, honorable 10 creditable, legitimate, recognized, sanctioned 11 respectable, trustworthy 13 well-thought-of

reputation 4 fame, name, note 5 éclat, honor 6 esteem, renown, report 8 position, prestige, standing 9 celebrity, character, notoriety

reputed 6 honest 7 alleged 8 putative, supposed 9 estimable, purported 10 creditable, ostensible 11 respectable 12 hypothetical

request 3 ask, dun, sue 4 pray, seek 5 plead, press 6 appeal, demand, invite 7 entreat, solicit 8 entreaty, petition 10 invitation

Requiem for a Nun author 8 Faulkner (William)

require 3 ask, beg 4 lack, need, want 5 claim, crave 6 demand, desire 7 call for, dictate, mandate, solicit 11 necessitate

required 3 due 5 vital 7 crucial 9 essential, mandatory, necessary, requisite 10 compulsory, obligatory 11 fundamental

requirement 4 must, need, want 5 claim 6 charge, demand 9 condition, essential, necessity, requisite 10 imperative, sine qua non 11 stipulation

requisite 3 due 4 must 5 vital 7 crucial, needful 9 cardinal 9 condition, essential, necessity 10 imperative, sine qua non 11 fundamental 12 precondition 13 indispensable

requisition 4 call 5 claim, exact 6 demand 7 solicit 11 application

requite 3 pay 5 repay 6 return 7 revenge, satisfy 9 indemnify, reimburse 10 compensate, recompense, remunerate 11 reciprocate

reredos 6 screen 9 partition

rescind 4 lift 5 annul 6 cancel, recall, repeal, revoke 7 retract, reverse 8 roll back, take back

rescue 4 free, save 6 ransom, redeem 7 bailout, deliver, reclaim, recover, release, salvage 8 liberate, preserve 9 extricate 11 deliverance

rescuer 6 savior 7 saviour

research 5 probe, study 7 inquest, inquiry 8 look into 9 delve into 10 experiment 11 examination, inquisition, investigate 13 investigation

resect 6 cut out, excise 8 amputate 9 extirpate

resemblance 7 analogy 8 likeness 9 alikeness 10 comparison, similarity, similitude 11 parallelism

resemble 5 favor 6 recall 8 look like, simulate 9 take after 11 approximate

resembling 4 like 6 akin to

resentful 4 sore 6 bitter, piqued, sullen 7 envious

resentment 5 pique 6 animus, grudge, malice, rancor 7 dudgeon, offense, umbrage 9 animosity 11 indignation

reservation 5 doubt 7 booking, proviso 8 homeland, preserve 9 condition, misgiving, sanctuary 10 limitation

reserve 4 book, fund, hold, keep 5 hoard, put by, stash, stock, store, tract 6 retain, supply 7 nest egg, savings, standby 8 contract, distance, fallback, hold back, postpone, set aside, squirrel, withhold 9 inventory, restraint, reticence, stockpile 10 constraint, discretion, diffidence 13 qualification

reserved 4 cool 5 aloof, stiff 6 demure, formal, remote 7 distant 8 reticent, retiring, taciturn 9 diffident, reclusive, secretive, withdrawn 10 unsociable 11 tight-lipped 12 closemouthed 13 self-contained

reservoir 5 hoard, stock, store 6 supply 7 nest egg 9 inventory, stockpile

reside 3 lie 4 live, stay 5 dwell, exist 6 inhere 7 consist

residence 4 home, stay 5 abode, house 7 address 8 domicile, dwelling 9 occupancy 10 habitation

resident 5 liver 6 inmate, lodger, native, tenant 7 citizen, denizen, dweller, present 8 inherent, occupant 10 inhabitant 11 householder

residential area 9 community 12 neighborhood

residual 7 balance, payment, remnant 8 leavings, leftover 9 remainder

residue 3 ash 4 heel, lees, rest, silt, slag 5 ashes, dregs, grout 6 debris, excess, scraps 7 balance, grounds, remains, remnant, surplus 8 leavings, remnants, residuum 9 leftovers, remainder, scourings

resign 4 cede, quit 5 demit, leave, yield 6 give up, retire, submit 7 abandon, consign 8 abdicate, hand over, relegate, renounce, step down **9** reconcile, surrender **10** relinquish

resignation 8 meekness **9** demission, surrender **10** abdication, compliance, submission **12** acquiescence, renunciation

resigned 9 compliant **10** submissive **11** acquiescent, complaisant

resile 6 recede, recoil, spring **7** rebound, retract, retreat **8** draw back, snap back

resilient 6 bouncy, supple, whippy **7** buoyant, elastic, springy **8** flexible, stretchy **9** adaptable

resin 4 balm **5** copal, damar, roset **6** dammar **7** acrylic, copaiba *aromatic:* **6** balsam, mastic **8** sandarac *fragrant:* **5** elemi **6** storax, styrax **7** ladanum **8** labdanum *gum:* **5** myrrh **7** benzoin *medicinal:* **6** guaiac **8** guaiacum *of an insect:* **3** lac *synthetic:* **8** phenolic *used by bees:* **8** propolis

resist 4 buck, defy, kick **5** rebel **6** baffle, combat, oppose, revolt **7** contest, counter, gainsay **8** traverse **10** contradict, contravene

resistance 7 dissent **8** defiance, variance **10** dissension, dissidence, opposition **11** contrariety, obstruction

resistance unit 3 ohm

resistor 8 rheostat, varistor **10** thermistor

resolute 3 set **4** bent, bold, fast, firm, true **6** intent, steady, sturdy **7** decided, staunch **8** constant, decisive, faithful, intrepid, stubborn **9** obstinate, steadfast, tenacious, undaunted **10** determined, persistent **12** pertinacious, single-minded

resolution 4 guts **5** heart, nerve, pluck, spunk **6** mettle, spirit **7** courage, outcome **8** decision, firmness, tenacity **10** conclusion **12** perseverance **13** determination, steadfastness

resolve 5 clear, crack **6** decide, settle **7** clear up, iron out, unravel, work out **8** boldness, conclude, decipher, firmness **9** breakdown, determine, intention, reconcile **10** unscramble **13** determination, steadfastness

resonant 4 deep, full, rich **6** silver **7** booming, echoing, orotund, vibrant **8** powerful, sonorous **11** reverberant

resonate 4 echo, peal, ring **7** resound, vibrate **11** reverberate

resort 3 spa **5** haven, hotel, lodge, shift **6** harbor, refuge **7** retreat, riviera, stopgap **8** recourse **9** expedient, makeshift **10** substitute

resound 4 boom, echo, peal, ring **11** reverberate

resounding 7 booming, echoing, oro-

tund, vibrant **8** emphatic, sonorous **10** clangorous, resonating, thunderous **11** unequivocal

resource 3 aid **5** asset, means, shift **6** supply **7** standby

resourceful 5 adept **6** adroit, artful, clever, shrewd **7** capable, cunning **8** creative, skillful **9** ingenious, inventive **10** innovative **11** imaginative **12** enterprising

resources 5 funds, means, purse **6** assets, riches, wealth **7** capital, fortune, reserve **8** bankroll, finances, property, reserves **9** substance **11** wherewithal

respect 3 awe **5** favor, honor, props **6** admire, detail, devoir, esteem, homage, regard, revere **7** account, concern **8** venerate **9** deference **10** admiration, estimation, particular, veneration

respectable 4 fair **5** ample **6** decent, proper, worthy **8** adequate **9** admirable, estimable, honorable **10** sufficient **11** appropriate, presentable **12** satisfactory **13** well-thought-of

respectful 5 civil **6** polite **8** obeisant, reverent **9** courteous **11** deferential, reverential

respecting 3 per **4** as to, in re **5** about **7** apropos **9** as regards, regarding **10** as concerns, concerning, relating to **11** considering

respire 7 breathe

respite 4 lull, rest **5** break, delay, pause, spell, truce **6** hiatus, recess, relief **8** breather, reprieve, surcease **12** intermission

resplendent 5 regal **7** glowing, shining **8** glorious, gorgeous **9** brilliant, refulgent **11** magnificent

respond 5 react, reply **6** answer, rejoin, retort **8** come back

response 5 reply **6** answer, retort, return **7** riposte **8** antiphon, comeback, reaction **9** rejoinder

responsibility 4 buck, duty, onus **5** blame, brief, fault **6** burden, charge, devoir **10** obligation **11** reliability

responsible 6 liable **8** amenable, reliable **10** answerable, chargeable, dependable **11** accountable, trustworthy

responsive 4 open **8** sentient **9** sensitive **11** susceptible, sympathetic

rest 3 sit **4** calm, ease, loaf, loll, lull, stay **5** let up, pause, peace, quiet, relax, spell **6** depend, excess, lounge, repose **7** balance, leisure, lie down, recline, remains, remnant, surplus **8** breather, interlude, leavings, vacation **9** predicate, remainder

restate 4 echo 6 reword 8 rephrase
9 translate 10 paraphrase 12 recapitulate

restatement 10 paraphrase 11 translation

restaurant 4 café 5 diner 6 eatery 7 beanery 9 brasserie, cafeteria 10 coffee shop
11 coffeehouse, greasy spoon *price:* 8 à
la carte, prix fixe 10 table d'hôte *worker:* 4 chef, cook 6 busboy, server, waiter
7 maître d', waitron 8 waitress 10 dishwasher, headwaiter, waitperson
12 maître d'hôtel

___ **Restaurant** 6 Alice's

restful 4 calm 5 quiet 6 placid 8 peaceful, tranquil

restitute 6 refund, return 7 reclaim,
recover, restore 8 give back 11 recondition, reconstruct 12 rehabilitate

restitution 6 amends, refund, return
7 redress 8 reprisal 9 indemnity, quittance 10 recompense, reparation
11 restoration 12 remuneration, satisfaction

restive 4 edgy 5 balky, nervy, tense
6 ornery, uneasy 7 fidgety, froward,
uptight, wayward 8 contrary, perverse,
skittish

restiveness 7 anxiety, ferment, turmoil
8 disquiet 9 balkiness 10 inquietude,
perversity 11 contrariety, disquietude,
waywardness 12 contrariness

restless 5 antsy, itchy, jumpy 6 fitful,
uneasy 7 anxious, fidgety, fretful, jittery, nervous, unquiet 8 agitated, troubled 9 disturbed, perturbed, unsettled
12 discontented, dissatisfied

restorative 4 balm 5 tonic 7 healing
8 curative, remedial, sanative 12 recuperative

restore 4 cure, heal, mend 5 amend,
remit, renew, right 6 recall, recoup,
reform, remedy, render, repair, return,
revive 7 get back, improve, reclaim,
recover, rectify, refresh, replace 8 give
back, recreate, renovate, revivify
9 refurbish, reinstate, replenish, restitute 10 regenerate, rejuvenate 11 recondition, reestablish 12 rehabilitate

restrain 3 bit, gag 4 curb, rein 5 check,
leash 6 arrest, bridle, halter, hamper,
hinder, hold in, impede, muzzle, temper 7 collect, control, harness, inhibit,
repress 8 hold back, hold down, moderate, suppress *trade:* 7 embargo

restrained 4 cool 6 low-key 5 canny,
quiet 6 modest 7 subdued 8 discreet,
reserved, reticent, retiring, tasteful
9 contained, inhibited, temperate
10 controlled, reasonable

restraint 6 bridle 7 durance, embargo,
reserve 8 estoppel, pullback 9 hindrance 10 deterrence, inhibition, limitation, moderation 11 confinement, forbearance 12 straitjacket

restrict 3 bar, tie 4 bind, curb 5 hem in,
limit 6 hamper, hobble, impede, narrow, shrink 7 confine, curtail, delimit,
inhibit, trammel 8 hold back, prelimit
10 delimitate 12 circumscribe *a will:*
6 entail

restriction 4 curb 5 check, limit, stint
7 control 9 restraint 10 constraint, limitation, regulation 11 confinement, prohibition 12 proscription 13 qualification

restyle 4 redo 6 revamp, revise, rework
8 make over

result 3 end 4 flow, stem 5 close, ensue,
fruit, issue 6 effect, emerge, finish, follow, payoff, sequel, upshot 7 outcome,
product 8 sequence, solution 9 aftermath, come about, eventuate 10 conclusion, denouement, production
11 aftereffect, consequence, eventuality
incidental: 7 spinoff

resume 4 go on 5 renew 6 pick up,
reopen 7 carry on, proceed, restart
8 continue 10 recommence

résumé 4 vita 5 sum-up 7 summary
9 summation, summing-up

resurgence 5 rally 7 rebirth, revival
8 comeback, recovery 10 renascence
11 renaissance 12 risorgimento

resurrect 5 raise, renew 6 come to,
revive 8 retrieve, revivify 10 reactivate

resurrection 7 rebirth, revival 10 renascence 11 renaissance 12 risorgimento

resuscitate see RESURRECT

retail 4 sell, tell, vend 6 market 7 narrate
11 merchandise

retailer 6 dealer, seller, trader, vendor
8 merchant 9 tradesman 10 shopkeeper
11 storekeeper 12 merchandiser

retain 3 own 4 hire, hold, keep 6 detain
7 reserve 8 hold over, preserve, remember, withhold

retainer 3 fee 6 lackey, menial, minion,
yeoman 7 deposit, servant 8 employee,
follower 9 bite plate, dependent, pensioner

retaliate 7 get back, get even

retaliation see REPRISAL

retaliatory 8 punitive, vengeful 10 vindictive

retard 4 clog, mire, slow 5 delay, stunt
6 detain, fetter, hamper, hang up, hinder, impede, slow up 7 set back, slack-
en 8 decrease, hold back, restrain
10 decelerate

retarded 3 dim 4 dull, dumb, slow
6 opaque, simple, stupid 8 backward
9 dim-witted 10 half-witted, slow-witted
11 exceptional

retch 3 gag 4 barf, hurl, puke, spew 5 heave, vomit 6 spit up 7 bring up, throw up, upchuck 8 disgorge

retention 6 memory 7 storage

reticent see RESERVED

reticulate 4 vein 6 veiny 6 meshed, netted 7 netlike 10 crisscross

retinue 4 band, tail 5 suite, train 6 livery 7 company, cortege 9 entourage, following

retire 4 exit, quit 5 leave, yield 6 bow out, depart, recede, resign, turn in 7 dismiss, pension 8 step down, withdraw 9 discharge, strike out, terminate 10 relinquish

retired person 7 emerita 8 emeritus 9 pensioner

retiree 9 pensioner 10 golden-ager 13 senior citizen

retirement allowance 3 SEP 7 pension

retiring 3 shy 5 mousy, timid 6 demure, modest 7 bashful 8 reserved 9 diffident, withdrawn 11 unassertive

retool 7 reequip 10 reengineer

retort 5 reply, sally 6 answer, rejoin 7 counter, respond, riposte 8 comeback, repartee, response 9 rejoinder, retaliate, wisecrack

retouch 5 alter, emend, renew 6 repair 7 correct, enhance, improve, restore

retract 4 deny 5 unsay 6 abjure, recall, recant, recede, renege, resile, revoke 7 disavow, rescind, retreat, swallow 8 forswear, renounce, take back, withdraw

retreat 3 den, ebb 4 flee, quit 5 cover, haven, leave 6 ashram, asylum, bow out, covert, decamp, depart, escape, recede, recoil, refuge, shrink, vacate 7 abandon, back off, back out, pull out, shelter 8 back down, draw back, evacuate, fall back, hideaway, withdraw 9 backtrack, climb down, sanctuary 10 give ground, withdrawal

retrench 3 cut 4 pare 5 slash 6 excise, lessen, reduce 7 abridge, curtail 9 economize

retribution 6 return, reward 7 deserts, revenge 8 avenging, reprisal, requital, revanche 9 vengeance 10 punishment, recompense 11 counterblow, retaliation *goddess of:* 3 Ate 4 Fury 7 Nemesis

retrieve 5 fetch 6 recall, recoup, redeem, rescue 7 get back, recover, restore, salvage 9 resurrect

retro 7 antique, revival, vintage 9 nostalgic 12 old-fashioned

retrograde 4 back 7 inverse, reverse 8 backward, inverted, rearward

retrogress see REVERT

retrospect 9 hindsight 12 recollection 13 reexamination

retrospective 6 review 8 backward 10 exhibition, reflective, ruminative

return 5 recur, repay, reply, yield 6 answer, rebate, regain, rejoin, render, repeat, retort, revert 7 bring in, get back, rebound, recover, reprise, requite, respond, reverse, riposte 8 comeback, dividend, earnings, give back, proceeds, reappear, response 9 rejoinder, repayment, reversion 10 recompense, recurrence 11 reciprocate, restitution

Return of the Native *author:* 5 Hardy (Thomas) *character:* 4 Clym 8 Eustacia

Reuben *brother:* 6 Joseph *father:* 5 Jacob *mother:* 4 Leah *son:* 5 Carmi 6 Hanoch, Hezron, Phallu

Réunion *capital:* 7 St.-Denis *city:* 6 St.-Paul 7 St.-Louis 8 St.-Pierre *department of:* 6 France *ethnic group:* 6 Creole *former name:* 7 Bourbon 9 Bonaparte *island group:* 9 Mascarene

revamp 4 redo 5 renew 6 remake, repair, revise, rework 7 remodel, restyle, rewrite 8 make over, overhaul, redesign, renovate 9 refurbish 11 recondition

reveal 4 bare, blab, jamb, leak, open, show, tell 5 admit, let on, peach, spill 6 betray, evince, expose, impart, unmask, unveil 7 confess, declare, display, divulge, exhibit, publish, uncover, undress 8 announce, decipher, disclose, discover, give away, unclothe 9 broadcast 11 acknowledge, communicate 12 bring to light

revel 4 bask, orgy, riot 5 binge, feast, party, spree 6 boogie, frolic, gaiety, hoopla, wallow 7 carouse, delight, indulge, jollity, roister, rollick, wassail, whoopla 8 carnival, carousal, festival 9 bacchanal, celebrate, festivity, luxuriate, merriment, whoop-de-do 11 bacchanalia, celebration, merrymaking

revelation 6 kicker 8 epiphany, giveaway, prophecy, surprise 9 discovery 10 apocalypse, disclosure 13 manifestation

reveler 7 orgiast 8 bacchant, carouser 9 bacchante, wassailer 10 merrymaker

revelry 4 orgy, riot 6 gaiety 7 carouse, jollity, wassail, whoopee, whoopla 8 carousal, partying 9 festivity, high jinks, merriment, whoop-de-do 10 whoop-de-doo 11 merrymaking

revenant 5 ghost, haunt, shade, spook 6 shadow, spirit, wraith, zombie 7 phantom, specter, spectre 8 phantasm, prodigal, visitant 10 apparition

revenge 5 right 6 defend 7 get back, get even, redress, requite 8 reprisal,

requital, revanche **9** retaliate, vindicate
11 retaliation, retribution

revenue 4 rent **5** gains, issue, yield
6 income, profit, return **7** comings
8 earnings, interest, proceeds, receipts,
taxation

reverberant 6 hollow **7** booming, echoing **8** resonant **10** resounding

reverberate 4 echo, ring **6** reecho
7 resound

revere 4 laud **5** adore, exalt, extol,
honor, prize, value **6** admire, esteem,
regard **7** cherish, magnify, respect, worship **8** treasure, venerate **10** appreciate

revered 9 venerable

reverence 3 awe **5** adore, dread, honor,
piety **6** esteem, fealty, homage **7** loyalty,
respect, worship **8** devotion, venerate
9 deference, obeisance, solemnity
10 veneration *gesture of:* **3** bow **6** kowtow **8** kneeling **12** genuflection

reverend 4 abbé, holy **5** clerk, vicar
6 clergy, cleric, deacon, divine, parson,
rector **8** chaplain, clerical, minister,
preacher **9** churchman, clergyman
11 clergywoman **12** ecclesiastic

reverent 5 godly **6** devout **7** dutiful
9 prayerful **10** God-fearing, respectful,
worshipful

reverie 4 muse **5** dream **6** trance, vision
7 fantasy **8** daydream **10** absorption,
brown study, meditation **11** abstraction
13 woolgathering

reversal 4 turn **5** U-turn **6** double,
switch **7** setback, undoing **8** backfire,
flip-flop **9** about-face, inversion, turnabout, volte-face **10** switcheroo
12 solarization **13** change of heart

reverse 4 lift **6** change, contra, defeat,
invert, recall, repeal, revoke **7** capsize,
counter, rescind, setback **8** antipode,
backward, contrary, disaster, exchange,
opposite, overrule, overturn **9** about-
face, backwards, diametric, overthrow,
transpose, turnabout, volte-face
10 antithesis, misfortune

reversion 4 turn **5** lapse **6** return
7 atavism, escheat **9** about-face, throwback, turnabout, volte-face **10** regression, succession

revert 4 turn **6** return **7** decline, devolve,
escheat, inverse, regress **8** turn back
9 backslide **10** degenerate, retrograde,
retrogress

revetment 6 bunker, riprap **9** barricade,
earthwork **10** embankment

review 4 scan **5** audit, recap, study
6 assess, go over, parade, report, revise,
survey **7** analyze, journal, rethink
8 analysis, critique, magazine, revision,
scrutiny, talk over **9** criticism, reexam-

ine, refresher **10** evaluation, inspection,
periodical, reconsider, reevaluate
11 examination **13** reexamination, retrospective

revile 4 rail, rate **5** abuse, scold **6** attack,
berate, defame, malign, vilify **7** asperse,
bawl out, chew out, upbraid **8** belittle,
disgrace, execrate **9** blaspheme
10 tongue-lash, vituperate

revise 4 edit **5** alter, amend, emend,
proof, renew **6** change, polish, redraw,
reform, retool, revamp, rework **7** correct, improve, redraft, restore, restyle,
rewrite **8** overhaul, redesign, work over
9 red-pencil **10** blue-pencil

revision 6 change, revamp, update
7 redraft **8** facelift, overhaul, updating
10 alteration, correction, emendation
11 overhauling **12** modification

revitalize see REVIVE

revival 7 rebirth, renewal **8** comeback
10 renascence, resurgence **11** reanimation, renaissance, restoration **12** regeneration, rejuvenation, resurrection,
risorgimento **13** recrudescence, resusci-
tation

revive 4 wake **5** rally, renew, rouse
6 arouse, awaken, come to, recall
7 bring to, enliven, freshen, quicken,
refresh, restore **8** reawaken, rekindle,
renovate, retrieve **9** reanimate, resurrect **10** reactivate, recuperate, regenerate, rejuvenate **11** bring around, reintroduce, resuscitate **12** reinvigorate

revoke 4 lift, void **5** annul, erase
6 abjure, cancel, recall, recant, renege,
repeal **7** abolish, nullify, rescind,
retract, reverse **8** abrogate, call back
10 invalidate **11** countermand

revolt 4 riot **5** rebel, repel, shock
6 mutiny, resist, sicken **7** disgust,
repulse **8** nauseate, outbreak, uprising
9 jacquerie, rebellion **10** insurgence,
insurgency **12** insurrection

revolter 5 rebel **6** anarch **8** frondeur,
mutineer **9** anarchist, insurgent **10** malcontent

revolting 4 foul, ugly, vile **5** nasty **6** horrid **7** hideous, noisome, obscene
8 shocking **9** atrocious, loathsome,
repellent, repugnant, repulsive **10** disgusting, nauseating

revolution 4 gyre, reel, riot, roll, spin,
turn **5** cycle, orbit, twirl, wheel, whirl
6 mutiny **7** circuit **8** gyration, rotation,
uprising **9** pirouette, rebellion **10** barrel
roll, changeover, somersault **12** insurrection

revolutionary 5 rebel, ultra **7** extreme,
radical **8** mutineer, rotating, ultraist
9 extremist, insurgent *American:* **4** Reed

(John) **5** Shays (Daniel) *French:* **5** Marat (Jean-Paul) **6** Danton (Georges) **8** Mirabeau (Comte de) **9** Saint-Just (Louis) **11** Robespierre (Maximilien) *Irish:* **4** Tone (Wolfe) **6** Pearse (Padraig, Patrick) **7** Collins (Michael), Parnell (Charles Stewart) **8** Casement (Roger), de Valera (Eamon), Griffith (Arthur), O'Connell (Daniel) *Mexican:* **5** Villa (Pancho) **6** Zapata (Emiliano) **7** Hidalgo (Padre Miguel) *Russian:* **5** Kirov (Sergey), Lenin (Vladimir Ilyich) **7** Trotsky (Leon) **8** Kerensky (Aleksandr) **9** Kropotkin (Pyotr)

revolutionize 9 transform **11** transfigure

revolve 4 spin, turn **5** twirl, wheel, whirl **6** circle, gyrate, rotate

revolver 3 gun, rod **4** Colt **5** Glock, Luger, Ruger **6** Magnum, pistol, six-gun **7** firearm, handgun, shooter, sidearm **10** six-shooter

revue 4 show **9** burlesque **10** production, vaudeville **13** entertainment

revulsion 4 hate **6** hatred, horror **7** disgust **8** aversion, loathing **10** abhorrence, repugnance **11** abomination, detestation

reward 5 bonus, booty, crown, medal, price, prize **6** bounty, carrot, payoff, trophy **7** guerdon, jackpot, premium **8** dividend **10** compensate, honorarium, recompense, remunerate **12** compensation, remuneration

rewarding 7 gainful **8** edifying, fruitful, valuable **9** lucrative **10** beneficial, fulfilling, gratifying, productive, profitable, satisfying, worthwhile **12** advantageous, remunerative

reword SEE RESTATE

rework 6 revamp, revise **7** restyle, rewrite

Reynard 3 fox

rhadamanthine 3 due **4** just **5** right **6** strict **7** condign, fitting, merited **8** deserved, rigorous, rightful, suitable **9** requisite, stringent **11** appropriate

Rhadamanthus 5 judge *brother:* **5** Minos *father:* **4** Zeus **7** Jupiter *mother:* **6** Europa

rhapsodic 5 lyric **8** ecstatic, effusive **9** emotional, exuberant

rhapsodize 4 gush, rave **5** drool **6** effuse **7** enthuse

Rhea 3 Ops *daughter:* **4** Hera, Juno **5** Ceres, Vesta **6** Hestia **7** Demeter *father:* **6** Uranus *husband:* **6** Cronus, Saturn *mother:* **4** Gaea *son:* **4** Zeus **5** Hades, Pluto **7** Jupiter, Neptune **8** Poseidon

Rheingold, Das *character:* **4** Loki **5** Freya, Wotan **6** Fafner, Fafnir, Fasolt

8 Alberich *composer:* **6** Wagner (Richard)

rheostat 8 resistor

rhesus 6 monkey **7** macaque

rhetoric 4 rant **6** speech **7** bombast, fustian, oratory **8** rhapsody **9** elocution, eloquence, verbosity **11** rodomontade, speechcraft *term:* **6** aporia, simile **7** litotes **8** metaphor **10** apostrophe, digression **12** alliteration, onomatopoeia

rhetorical 4 glib **5** gassy, grand, tumid, windy **6** florid, fluent, ornate, purple, turgid **7** aureate, flowery, orotund, pompous, stilted **8** eloquent, forensic, inflated, overdone, sonorous **9** bombastic, grandiose, high-flown, overblown, tumescent **10** euphuistic, flamboyant, oratorical **11** declamatory, highfalutin, overwrought, pretentious **12** high-sounding, magniloquent **13** grandiloquent

rhetorician 6 orator, writer **7** speaker *Roman:* **10** Quintilian

Rhine River *city:* **4** Bonn, Köln **5** Basel, Mainz **7** Coblenz, Cologne, Koblenz **8** Duisburg, Mannheim **9** Rotterdam, Weisbaden **10** Düsseldorf *nymph:* **7** Lorelei *tributary:* **3** Aar, Ill, Lek **4** Aare, Lahn, Main, Ruhr, Waal

rhizome 4 root **5** tuber

Rhode Island *bay:* **12** Narragansett *capital:* **10** Providence *city:* **7** Newport, Warwick **9** Pawtucket *college, university:* **4** RISD **5** Brown *island:* **5** Block *nickname:* **5** Ocean (State) **11** Little Rhody *river:* **8** Pawtuxet *state bird:* **14** Rhode Island red *state flower:* **6** violet *state tree:* **8** red maple

Rhodesia 8 Zimbabwe

rhombus 7 diamond, lozenge **13** parallelogram

rhonchus 5 snore

Rhône River *city:* **4** Lyon **5** Arles, Lyons **6** Geneva **7** Avignon *lake:* **6** Geneva *mountain range:* **4** Jura *tributary:* **5** Isère, Saône

rhubarb 3 row **4** flap **5** run-in **6** ruckus, tangle **7** dispute, quarrel, wrangle **8** argument, pieplant **11** altercation, controversy

rhyme 4 poem, song **5** agree, ditty, verse **6** accord, jingle, poetry **7** conform **8** dovetail **9** harmonize **10** coordinate, correspond

rhymer 4 bard, poet **5** odist **7** metrist **9** poetaster, rhymester, sonneteer, versifier

rhythm 4 beat, flow, lilt, time **5** meter, pulse, swing **6** accent, groove **7** cadence, measure, pattern **8** sequence

rhythmic 7 pulsing, regular 8 measured, metrical

rialto 6 market 8 district, exchange 11 marketplace

riant 3 gay 5 jolly, merry 6 blithe, bright, jocund, jovial 7 buoyant, gleeful 8 cheerful, mirthful 10 blithesome

riata 4 rope 5 lasso 6 lariat

rib 3 fun, kid, rag 4 band, bone, dike, fool, jape, jest, joke, josh, purl, razz, stay, wale 5 chaff, costa, ridge, tease 6 banter, costae (plural), lierne, needle

ribald 3 raw 4 blue, racy, rude 5 bawdy, crude, dirty 6 coarse, earthy, filthy, purple, risqué, smutty, vulgar 7 obscene, profane, raunchy 8 indecent, off-color 9 offensive, reprobate 10 suggestive

ribbon 3 bow 4 band, tape 5 braid, shred, strip 6 cordon, fillet, stripe, tatter 7 bandeau

rice 7 arborio, risotto *dish:* 5 pilaf 6 congee 7 risotto 9 jambalaya *drink:* 4 sake, saki 5 mirin 6 arrack *field:* 5 paddy *husk:* 5 lemma

rich 4 dear, lush, oily, posh 5 ample, fatty, flush, grand, heavy, plush, swank, vivid 6 costly, creamy, deluxe, fecund, gilded, lavish, loaded, monied, ornate, potent, rococo 7 baroque, copious, elegant, fertile, filling, moneyed, opulent, orotund, profuse, wealthy, well-off 8 abundant, affluent, eloquent, fruitful, palatial, well-to-do 9 abounding, bountiful, elaborate, luxuriant, luxurious, plentiful, sumptuous, well-fixed 10 productive, prosperous, well-heeled 11 extravagant *person:* 5 Midas, mogul, nabob 6 fat cat 7 Croesus, magnate 9 moneybags, plutocrat

Richardson work 6 Pamela 8 Clarissa

Richelieu's successor 7 Mazarin

riches 4 gold, pelf 5 booty, lucre, worth 6 mammon, wealth 7 fortune 8 opulence, property, treasure 9 resources *demon of:* 6 Mammon

rick 4 cock, heap, pile 5 shock, stack

rickety 4 weak 5 shaky 6 wobbly 7 unsound 8 decrepit, insecure, rachitic, unstable, unsteady 10 ramshackle, rattletrap

ricochet 4 ping, skim, skip 5 carom 6 bounce, glance 7 rebound 9 boomerang

rid 6 divest 7 relieve 8 unburden 11 disencumber

riddle 5 rebus 6 enigma, puzzle 7 mystery, perplex, problem 9 conundrum, perforate 10 closed book, puzzlement 11 brainteaser

ride 4 spin, tour, trip 5 drive, jaunt, mount 7 journey 8 carousel 9 excursion

ride out 6 endure 7 outlast, survive, weather 9 withstand

rider 6 clause, cowboy, jockey 7 codicil 8 addendum, addition, appendix, horseman, reinsman 9 amendment 10 equestrian, horsewoman, supplement

ridge 3 rib, top 4 bank, brow, fold, keel, reef, roll, ruck, seam, wave 5 arête, arris, chine, crest, knurl, plica, spine 6 crease, divide, furrow, rimple, saddle, summit 7 annulet, breaker, crinkle, hogback, wrinkle 8 shoulder 9 razorback 11 corrugation *gravelly:* 5 esker *on the skin:* 4 welt *sharp:* 7 hogback

ridicule 3 pan 4 gibe, haze, jape, jeer, mock, razz, ride, twit 5 chaff, flout, mimic, roast, scoff, scout, sneer, squib, taunt 6 deride, satire 7 lampoon, mockery, pillory, sarcasm 8 derision, raillery, satirize, travesty 9 burlesque 10 caricature *god of:* 5 Momus *object of:* 4 butt 13 laughingstock

ridiculous 5 comic, daffy, dotty, goofy, silly, wacky 6 absurd, insane 7 bizarre, comical, foolish, risible 8 derisory, farcical 9 cockamamy, fantastic, grotesque, laughable, ludicrous, monstrous 10 cockamamie, outrageous 11 for the birds, harebrained 12 preposterous, unbelievable

riding *academy:* 6 manège *costume:* 5 habit *pants:* 8 jodhpurs *whip:* 4 crop 5 quirt

Rienzi composer 6 Wagner (Richard)

rife 4 full 5 flush 6 common 7 replete, teeming 8 abundant, swarming 9 abounding, plentiful, prevalent 10 widespread 11 overflowing

riff 4 flip, leaf, scan, skim 5 thumb 6 browse 8 ostinato

riffle 4 flip, leaf, fret, scan, skim, wave 5 shoal, sluice, thumb 6 browse 7 shallow, shuffle 10 interstice

riffraff 3 mob 5 trash, waste 6 debris, kelter, litter, masses, rabble, refuse 7 garbage, rubbish 8 canaille, unwashed 11 proletariat

rifle 3 arm, gun, rob 4 loot, sack 5 steal 6 burgle, groove, weapon 7 carbine, despoil, firearm, pillage, plunder, ransack, rummage 9 chassepot *accessory:* 6 ramrod *kind:* 6 Garand, Mauser 7 Enfield 8 Browning 9 Remington 10 Winchester 11 Springfield

rift 3 gap 4 rent 5 break, chasm, chink, cleft, crack, fault, space, split 6 breach, cleave, divide, hiatus, schism 7 fissure, opening, rupture 8 crevasse, division, fracture, interval **9** fault line **10** separation **12** estrangement

rig 3 arm, fit, fix **4** fake, gear **5** dress, equip, getup, trick **6** adjust, clothe, doctor, outfit, tackle **7** apparel, arrange, costume, derrick, furnish, turn out **8** accouter, accoutre, clothing, equipage **9** apparatus, construct, equipment **10** manipulate

rigging 3 net **4** duds, gear, togs **5** dress, lines, ropes **6** attire, chains, tackle, things **7** apparel, clothes, raiment **8** clothing **9** apparatus, equipment

right 3 apt, due, fit **4** fair, just, sane, true, well **5** amend, amply, claim, droit, emend, exact, sound, title **6** at once, common, decent, dexter, direct, equity, honest, lawful, proper, square, strict **7** condign, correct, exactly, fitting, freedom, genuine, healthy, liberty, license, merited, old-line, rectify, redress **8** accurate, becoming, bona fide, decorous, easement, faithful, interest, orthodox, smack-dab, straight, suffrage, suitable **9** authentic, befitting, equitable, forthwith, honorable, privilege, requisite, veracious, veritable **10** altogether, applicable, felicitous, perquisite, scrupulous **11** appropriate, correctness, prerogative *combining form:* **4** orth, rect **5** dextr, ortho, recti **6** dextro *feudal:* **4** soke *legal:* **5** droit **8** usufruct *royal:* **7** regalia (plural)

right away 3 now **6** at once, pronto **8** directly, promptly **9** forthwith, instanter, instantly **11** immediately, straight off, straightway **12** then and there

righteous 4 good, holy, just, pure **5** godly, moral, noble, pious **6** devout, worthy **7** ethical, genuine, sinless, upright **8** innocent, virtuous **9** blameless, guiltless **10** inculpable, principled

righteousness 6 equity, virtue **7** justice, probity **8** holiness, morality **9** rectitude

rightful 3 apt, due, fit **4** fair, just, true **5** legal **6** honest, lawful, proper **7** condign, fitting **8** deserved, suitable **9** befitting, equitable, impartial **10** applicable, legitimate **11** appropriate

right-handed 6 dexter **7** dextral **9** clockwise

right-hand page 5 recto

rightist 4 tory **11** reactionary **12** conservative

right-minded 5 moral, noble **6** decent, honest **7** ethical **8** virtuous **10** upstanding

Rights of Man author 5 Paine (Thomas)

rigid 3 set **4** firm, hard, taut **5** fixed, stiff, tense **6** severe, strict **7** austere, precise, hard-set **8** cast-iron, ironclad, obdu-rate, rigorous **9** draconian, immovable, inelastic, rockbound, stringent, unbending **10** adamantine, brassbound, inflexible, relentless, unyielding **11** unbudgeable **13** rhadamanthine

rigidity 6 turgor **7** buckram **8** hardness **9** stiffness *muscular:* **8** myotonia

rigmarole 6 bunkum, drivel, ramble **8** nonsense **9** gibberish, procedure **10** balderdash, mumbo jumbo

Rigoletto *composer:* **5** Verdi (Giuseppe) *daughter:* **5** Gilda

rigor 7 cruelty **8** asperity, hardness, hardship, severity **9** austerity, exactness, harshness, roughness, sharpness, sternness **10** affliction, difficulty, exactitude, strictness **11** tribulation **13** inflexibility

rigorous 5 exact, harsh, rigid, rough, stern, stiff **6** bitter, brutal, proper, rugged, severe, strict **7** ascetic, drastic, onerous, precise **8** accurate, exacting **9** draconian, ironbound, stringent **10** burdensome, inflexible, ironhanded, oppressive **13** rhadamanthine

rile 3 bug, rub, vex **4** roil **5** anger, annoy, grate, muddy, peeve, pique, upset **6** muddle, nettle, put out, rankle **7** agitate, disturb, fluster, inflame, perturb, provoke **8** disorder, disquiet, irritate **9** aggravate **10** discompose, exasperate

rill 3 run **4** burn, purl **5** bourn, brook, creek **6** runnel, stream, valley **7** freshet, rivulet **8** brooklet **9** streamlet **11** watercourse

rim 3 hem, lip **4** bank, boss, brim, edge, ring **5** bezel, bezil, bound, brink, skirt, verge **6** border, flange, fringe, margin, shield **7** annulus, horizon, outline **8** boundary, surround **9** perimeter, periphery *of a basket:* **4** hoop *of a cask:* **5** chime *of an insect's wing:* **6** termen *of a spoked wheel:* **5** felly **6** felloe

rime 3 ice **4** hoar **5** crust, frost **7** coating, encrust **9** hoarfrost, Jack Frost **12** incrustation

Rinaldo *beloved:* **8** Angelica *cousin:* **7** Orlando *father:* **5** Aymon *horse:* **6** Bayard *mother:* **3** Aya *sister:* **10** Bradamante *uncle:* **11** Charlemagne

rind 4 bark, husk, peel, skin **5** crust **9** crackling

ring 3 eye, hem, rim **4** band, bloc, bong, echo, gird, gyre, hoop, loop, peal, toll **5** arena, bezel, cabal, chime, clang, cycle, group, knell, knoll, round, sound **6** circle, clique, collar, girdle, staple **7** annulus, clangor, combine, compass, resound, vibrate **8** bracelet, cincture, encircle, surround **9** coalition, encompass **11** combination, reverberate *around sun or moon:* **6** corona *curtain:* 3 eye *for a compass:* 6 gimbal *harness:* 3 dee 6 button, terret *heraldic:* 7 annulet *in a hinge:* 7 gudgeon *of chain:* 4 link *of color:* 8 stocking *of leaves or flowers:* 6 wreath 7 garland *of light:* 4 halo 5 glory 6 corona, nimbus 7 aureole 8 halation *of rope or metal:* 4 hank 6 becket 7 garland, grommet, thimble *of two hoops:* 6 gimmal *relating to:* 7 annular *used as a valve or diaphragm:* 5 wafer *wedding:* 4 band

Ring and the Book author 8 Browning (Robert)

ringed 8 annulate, bordered 9 encircled 10 surrounded

ringer 4 fake, spit 5 clone, image 6 double 7 clapper, picture 8 impostor, portrait 10 simulacrum 13 spitting image

ringing 7 orotund, vibrant 8 decisive, emphatic, plangent, resonant, sonorous 10 clangorous, resounding 11 reverberant, unequivocal

ringleader 4 boss 5 chief 6 honcho 7 kingpin 9 godfather 10 head honcho, instigator, mastermind

ringlet 4 curl, lock 5 crimp, tress 7 circlet, earlock, tendril

Ring of the Nibelung composer 6 Wagner (Richard)

rinse 4 dunk, lave, wash 5 bathe, douse, swill 6 shower, sluice 7 cleanse *the mouth:* 6 gargle

riot 5 brawl, melee, revel, spree 6 bedlam, émeute, jumble, revolt, tumult, uproar 7 carouse, debauch, rampage, revelry, roister, wassail 8 carousal, disorder, uprising 9 commotion 10 debauchery, donnybrook, revolution 11 disturbance

riotous 4 lush, wild 6 stormy, unruly, wanton 7 bacchic, profuse 8 abundant 9 abounding, clamorous, exuberant, luxuriant, plentiful, turbulent 10 boisterous 11 saturnalian, tempestuous 12 unrestrained

rip 4 gash, hole, rend, rent, rive, spit, tear 5 shred, slash, split 6 attack, cleave 7 current, sputter 8 lacerate, undertow 9 criticize, disparage 12 undercurrent *into:* 5 go for 6 assail, attack 8 lambaste *off:* 3 con, rob 4 copy 5 cheat, steal, theft 7 defraud, imitate, swindle 9 imitation

ripe 4 aged, full, late 5 adult, grown, ready, ruddy, plump 6 mature, mellow, smelly, timely 7 grown-up 8 prepared, suitable 9 developed, full-blown, fullgrown, offensive, opportune 10 seasonable 11 appropriate, full-fledged

ripen 3 age 4 cure, grow 6 better, grow up, mature, mellow, season 7 develop, enhance, improve, perfect 8 heighten, maturate

riposte 5 parry, reply 6 retort, return, thrust 8 back talk, comeback, repartee 13 counterattack

ripping 4 fine 5 grand, nifty, super, swell 6 divine, peachy 7 capital 8 glorious, splendid, terrific 9 admirable, delicious, excellent, fantastic, marvelous, wonderful 10 delightful, delectable, remarkable 11 scrumptious, sensational

ripple 3 lap 4 curl, fret, riff, wave 6 cockle, dimple, lipper, popple, ruffle, spread, wimple 7 crinkle, wavelet, wrinkle 8 undulate

rip-roaring 5 noisy 6 lively 8 exciting 9 hilarious 10 boisterous, rollicking, uproarious

ripsnorter 5 dandy 6 hummer 8 jimdandy 9 humdinger 11 crackerjack

riptide 7 current 8 undertow 12 undercurrent

Rip Van Winkle *author:* 6 Irving (Washington) *dog:* 4 Wolf

rise 3 wax 4 flow, grow, lift, rear, soar, stem, well 5 awake, begin, climb, get up, issue, mount, rouse, stand, surge, swell, tower 6 ascend, ascent, awaken, emerge, expand, growth, spring, thrive, uprear 7 advance, augment, develop, emanate, enhance, enlarge, stand up, succeed, surface, upsurge 8 eminence, heighten, increase 9 ascension; increment, intensify, originate, terminate *above:* 8 surmount *again:* 7 resurge 9 resurrect *against:* 5 rebel 6 mutiny, revolt *and fall:* 4 tide 5 heave 6 welter *and shine:* 5 get up *gradually:* 4 loom

Rise and Fall of the Third Reich author 6 Shirer (William)

Rise of Silas Lapham author 7 Howells (William Dean)

riser 4 step 8 platform

risible 4 rich 5 comic, droll, funny, jokey 6 absurd 7 comical 8 farcical 9 laughable, ludicrous 10 ridiculous

risk 4 ante, dare, defy 5 peril, stake, throw, wager 6 chance, danger, gamble, hazard, menace, stakes 7 imperil, jeopard, venture 8 endanger, exposure, jeopardy 9 adventure, encounter, liability 10 jeopardize

risky 4 bold 5 dicey, hairy 6 chancy, daring, touchy, tricky 7 parlous, unsound 8 delicate, perilous, ticklish 9 dangerous, hazardous, unhealthy 10 jeopardous, precarious 11 adventurous, speculative, treacherous

risqué 4 blue, lewd, racy, sexy 5 broad, crude, dirty, salty, spicy, vampy 6 coarse, daring, earthy, purple, ribald,

vulgar **7** naughty, obscene, raunchy
8 indecent, off-color, scabrous **9** salacious **10** indecorous, indelicate, suggestive

rite 6 office **7** liturgy, mystery, service
8 ceremony **9** formality, ordinance, sacrament, solemnity **10** ceremonial, initiation, observance **11** celebration, sacramental *funeral:* **6** exequy **7** obsequy **8** exequies **9** obsequies *Jewish:* **4** bris *of initiation or purification:* **7** baptism *of knighthood:* **8** accolade (see also SACRAMENT)

ritual see RITE

ritzy 4 posh **5** fancy, swank **6** chichi, classy, modish, snazzy, swanky **7** elegant, high-hat, stylish **9** au courant, exclusive, expensive, luxurious **11** fashionable **12** ostentatious

rival 3 tie, try, vie **4** even, peer, side
5 equal, match **6** strive **7** attempt, compete, contend, contest, emulate
8 approach, opponent **9** adversary, competing, contender, measure up
10 antagonist, competitor, contending, contestant **11** comparative, competition

rivalry 6 strife **7** contest, warfare **8** conflict, jealousy, tug-of-war **9** emulation
10 contention, opposition **11** competition

rive 3 rip **4** rend, tear **5** break, burst, crack, sever, smash, split **6** cleave, divide, shiver, sunder **7** fissure, shatter
8 fracture, fragment, lacerate, separate, splinter

river *Africa:* **4** Bomu, Juba **5** Chari, Congo, Shari, Tsavo, Zaire **6** Atbara, Mbomou, Songwe, Ubangi **7** Aruwimi, Limpopo, Zambesi, Zambezi **9** Astaboras, Crocodile *Alabama:* **5** Coosa
6 Mobile **7** Conecuh, Perdido **9** Tombigbee **10** Tallapoosa *Alaska:* **5** Kobuk
6 Copper, Noatak, Tanana **7** Koyukuk, Susitna **9** Kuskokwim *Albania:* **4** Drin
5 Drini *Argentina:* **5** Negro **6** Paraná
7 Matanza *arm:* **6** branch **9** tributary
Asia: **3** Ili **4** Amur, Oxus **5** Indus **6** Jayhun, Sutlej **7** Oedanes **8** Amu Darya
9 Dyardanes **11** Brahmaputra *Australia:*
4 Daly **5** Roper, Yarra **6** Barwon, Culgoa, Dawson, DeGrey, Murray **7** Darling, Fitzroy, Lachlan **8** Victoria
10 Yarra Yarra *Austria:* **4** Enns *bank:*
5 levee *Belgium:* **5** Rupel, Senne, Weser
6 Dender, Dindar, Ourthe **8** Visurgis
Bolivia: **4** Beni **5** Abuná **6** Mamoré *Borneo:* **5** Kajan *bottom:* **3** bed *Brazil:* **3** Ica
4 Pará, Paru **5** Negro, Xingu **6** Paraná
7 Madeira, Tapajos, Tapajoz *British Columbia:* **6** Skeena **10** Bella Coola *California:* **3** Eel, Pit **4** Kern, Yuba **6** Merced

7 Feather, Salinas, Trinity **8** Tuolumne
Cambodia: **8** Tonle Sap *Canada:* **3** Bow
4 Back **5** Moose, Peace, Slave **6** Beaver, Fraser, Nelson **8** Gatineau, Saguenay
9 Athabasca, Great Fish, Mackenzie, Richelieu **11** Assiniboine *Carolinas:*
7 Catawba *central United States:* **3** Fox
5 Grand **6** Neosho, Platte, Wabash
8 Keya Paha, Missouri, Niobrara **9** Tennessee, Verdigris **10** Republican, Saint Croix **11** Mississippi *channel:* **6** alveus
Chile: **3** Loa **5** Itata, Maule **6** Bío-Bío
8 Valdivia *China:* **3** Bei, Hun, Wei
4 Dong **5** Baihe, Chang, Huang, Tarim
6 Yellow **7** Kashgar, Yangtze *China-North Korea:* **4** Yalu *Colombia:* **4** Tomo
6 Atrato **9** Magdalena *Colorado:*
5 Yampa **8** Gunnison *Connecticut:*
6 Thames **7** Niantic, Shepaug **9** Naugatuck **10** Farmington, Housatonic, Quinnipiac **11** Willimantic *crossing:*
4 ford *current:* **4** eddy **6** rapids *Czech Republic:* **4** Iser **6** Jizera, Moldau, Vltava
dam: **4** weir *Denmark:* **4** Stor *dried bed:*
4 wadi *East Asia:* **4** Yalu **5** Amnok
7 Oryokko *Ecuador:* **4** Napo **10** Esmeraldas *England:* **3** Esk, Exe, Nen, Ure
4 Aire, Avon, Eden, Nene, Ouse, Tees, Tyne, Wear, Yare **5** Swale, Trent
6 Mersey, Ribble, Thames *Ethiopia:*
3 Omo **4** Baro, Dawa *Europe:* **4** Eger, Elbe, Labe, Oder, Ohre **5** Albis, Saale
6 Danube, Ticino *Florida:* **6** Indian
9 Kissimmee **10** Saint Johns
12 Apalachicola *France:* **3** Ain, Lot, Var
4 Aire, Aude, Cher, Eure, Gers, Loir, Oise, Orne, Saar, Tarn, Yser **5** Adour, Aisne, Drôme, Indre, Isère, Loire, Marne, Rhône, Saare, Sâone, Seine, Somme, Yonne **6** Allier, Ariège, Scarpe, Vienne **7** Durance, Garonne, La Riège
8 Charente, Dordogne *Georgia:*
6 Etowah, Oconee **8** Altamaha, Ocmulgee **13** Chattahoochee *Germany:* **3** Ems, Rur **4** Eder, Eger, Elbe, Isar, Main, Rems, Ruhr **5** Hunte, Lippe, Rhine, Spree, Werra, Weser **6** Neckar *Germany-Poland:* **4** Oder *Ghana:* **5** Volta *god:*
7 Alpheus, Inachus **8** Achelous *Greece:*
3 Iri **4** Arta **5** Lerna, Lerne **7** Alpheus, Eurotas **8** Achelous **9** Arakhthos *Honduras:* **4** Ulúa **5** Aguán **6** Patuca *Iberian:*
5 Douro, Duero *Idaho:* **5** Lemhi *Illinois:*
8 Mackinaw *India:* **4** Sind **5** Sindh, Tapti
6 Chenab, Ganges, Jhelum, Kaveri, Kistna **7** Cauvery, Krishna **8** Acesines, Godavari *inlet:* **5** bayou **6** slough *Iran:*
3 Kor **4** Mand, Mund **5** Karun **8** Safid Rud, Sefid Rud *Ireland:* **3** Lee **4** Deel, Erne, Suir **5** Boyne, Clare, Foyle **6** Barrow, Liffey **7** Shannon *Italy:* **4** Adda,

Arno, Liri, Nera 5 Adige, Arnus, Etsch, Liris, Oglio, Padus, Piave, Tiber 6 Ollius, Rapido, Tevere, Trebia 7 Athesis, Rubicon, Secchia, Tiberis, Trebbia 8 Rubicone, Volturno *Kansas:* 6 Pawnee *Kazakhstan-Russia:* 4 Ural 5 Tobol 6 Irtysh *Kenya:* 4 Athi, Tana *Kubla Khan's:* 4 Alph *land:* 4 holm 5 flats 7 bottoms *Latvia:* 5 Gauja *Latvia-Lithuania:* 7 Lielupe *Lebanon:* 6 Litani *Little Rock's:* 8 Arkansas *living on the bank of:* 8 riparian *longest:* 8 Nile *Louisiana:* 11 Atchafalaya *Maine:* 8 Kennebec 9 Aroostook, Penobscot *Malaysia:* 9 Trengganu *Maryland:* 8 Monocacy, Patapsco, Patuxent 9 Nanticoke *Massachusetts:* 7 Charles, Taunton 5 Westfield 10 Housatonic *Mexico:* 6 Pánuco, Sonora 7 Tabasco 8 Grijalva *Michigan:* 4 Cass 5 Huron 7 Saginaw 8 Manistee, Muskegon 9 Cheboygan, Kalamazoo 10 Michigamme, Shiawassee *Mississippi:* 5 Pearl, Yazoo 10 Pascagoula *Moldova-Ukraine:* 8 Dneister *Missouri:* 5 Osage *mouth:* 5 delta *Myanmar (Burma):* 4 Pegu 8 Chindwin, Irrawady *Nebraska:* 4 Loup 6 Nemaha, Platte 7 Elkhorn *Netherlands:* 4 Waal 5 Issel, Yssel 6 IJssel 7 Vahalis *New England:* 4 Saco 6 Nashua 9 Merrimack 10 Blackstone 11 Connecticut 12 Androscoggin *New Jersey:* 6 Rahway 7 Passaic, Raritan 8 Tuckahoe *New York:* 5 Tioga 6 Hudson, Mohawk, Oneida, Oswego, Seneca 7 Chemung, Niagara 8 Chenango *New Zealand:* 7 Waikato *Nicaragua:* 4 Coco 7 Segovia *Nigeria:* 5 Benin *North Carolina:* 3 Haw, Tar 5 Neuse 6 Chowan 8 Alamance *northeast United States:* 4 Ohio 6 Hoosic 7 Genesee, Hocking 8 Delaware, Mahoning 9 Allegheny 11 Monongahela, Susquehanna *Northern Ireland:* 4 Bann 6 Mourne *North Korea:* 5 Daido 7 Taedong *northwest United States:* 5 Snake 7 Klamath 8 Columbia 11 Pend Oreille *Norway:* 4 Tana, Teno *nymph:* 5 naiad *of fire:* 10 Phlegethon *of forgetfulness:* 5 Lethe *of ice:* 7 glacier *of woe:* 7 Acheron *Ohio:* 5 Miami 8 Cuyahoga, Sandusky 9 Muskingum 10 Tuscarawas *Oklahoma:* 8 Cimarron *Oregon:* 5 Rogue 6 Owyhee 7 Malheur 8 McKenzie 9 Clackamas, Deschutes 10 Willamette *Panama:* 5 Tuira 7 Chagres *Papua New Guinea:* 3 Fly 5 Sepik *Paraguay:* 3 Apa 9 Pilcomayo *Pennsylvania:* 6 Lehigh 10 Schuylkill *Peru:* 5 Rímac, Santa 7 Marañón 8 Apurímac, Huallaga, Urubamba *Philippines:* 4 Abra, Agno 5 Pasig 7 Cagayan 8 Cotabato, Min-

danao, Pampanga *Poland:* 3 San 7 Vistula *Portugal:* 4 Sado 7 Mondego *relating to:* 7 fluvial *Rhode Island:* 7 Seekonk 8 Sakonnet 10 Providence *Romania:* 5 Arges *Russia:* 3 Don, Oka, Ufa, Usa 4 Kama, Kara, Lena, Msta, Neva, Sura, Svir 5 Onega, Terek, Volga 6 Anadyr, Angara, Belaya, Kolima, Kolyma, Ussuri, Vyatka 7 Dnieper, Pechora, Yenisey 8 Barguzin, Kostroma, Voronezh, Vychegda *Russia-Ukraine:* 6 Donets *sacred:* 6 Ganges *Scotland:* 3 Dee, Don, Esk, Tay 4 Doon, Nith, Spey, Tyne 5 Afton, Annan, Clyde, Forth, Tweed 6 Teviot 7 Deveron 8 Findhorn *Shanghai's:* 7 Huangpu, Hwang Pu *Sicily:* 5 Salso 6 Simeto *siren:* 7 Lorelei *Slovakia:* 3 Vag, Vah 4 Gran, Hron, Waag 5 Garam, Nitra 6 Neutra, Nyitra *South Africa:* 4 Vaal 6 Orange *South America:* 3 Apa 6 Amazon 8 Amazonas, Orellana 9 Pilcomayo *South Carolina:* 6 Saluda, Santee 7 Wateree 8 Congaree *South Dakota:* 3 Bad *Southeast Asia:* 6 Dza-chu, Mekong 7 Salween 8 Lan-ts'ang *southeast United States:* 6 Pee Dee 7 Noxubee, Washita 8 Escambia, Ouachita, Suwannee 10 Okanoxubee *southern United States:* 6 Sabine *South Korea:* 3 Kum *southwest United States:* 4 Gila, Zuni 5 Pecos 8 Colorado *Spain:* 4 Ebro 6 Aragon 12 Guadalquivir *Sweden:* 4 Göta 5 Kalix *Switzerland:* 3 Aar 4 Aare 5 Reuss *Syria:* 6 Khabur 7 Orontes *Tasmania:* 4 Huon *Tbilisi's:* 4 Kura *Texas:* 5 Llano 6 Brazos, Nueces 7 San Saba, Trinity 9 Guadalupe *Texas-Mexico:* 8 Rio Bravo 9 Rio Grande *tidal:* 7 estuary *Tokyo's:* 6 Sumida *Turkey:* 4 Aras 5 Araks 6 Seihun, Seyhan *Ukrainian:* 3 Bug 4 Alma *underworld:* 4 Styx 5 Lethe 7 Acheron, Cocytus 10 Phlegethon *Uruguay:* 5 Negro *Utah:* 5 Provo, Uinta, Weber 6 Jordan, Sevier *valley:* 6 strath *Venezuela:* 5 Apure, Caura 6 Caroní 7 Orinoco *Vermont:* 3 Mad 5 Onion, White 8 Winooski *Virginia:* 3 Dan 5 James 7 Rapidan 9 Nansemond 10 Appomattox, Shenandoah 12 Chickahominy, Rappahannock *wailing:* 7 Cocytus *Wales:* 4 Dyfi 5 Clwyd, Dovey, Teifi *Washington:* 6 Skagit, Yakima 9 Klickitat, Snohomish, Wenatchee *West Africa:* 5 Niger 6 Gambia 7 Senegal *western United States:* 7 Laramie 8 Columbia, Flathead 11 Yellowstone *West Virginia:* 7 Kanawha *Wisconsin:* 8 Kickapoo 9 Menominee *Wyoming:* 8 Shoshone 10 Gros Ventre 11 Medicine Bow

___ **Rivera 5** Diego
river duck 4 teal **6** wigeon **7** dabbler, mallard, widgeon **8** shoveler **9** greenwing
river horse 5 hippo **12** hippopotamus
riverine 8 riparian
river island 3 ait
rivet 3 fix, pin **4** bolt, brad, stud **5** affix **6** absorb, attach, clinch, fasten **7** engross **8** fastener
Riviera city 4 Nice **6** Cannes, Monaco **7** Antibes, San Remo **8** St. Tropez **10** Monte Carlo
rivulet 3 run **4** beck, burn, gill, race, rill **5** bourn, brook, creek **6** runlet, runnel, stream **9** streamlet
Rizpah *father:* **4** Aiah *lover:* **4** Saul *son:* **6** Armoni **12** Mephibosheth
roach 3 hog **6** shiner **7** sunfish
road 3 way **4** fare, lane, line, path **5** drive, going, route, track **6** artery, avenue, career, causey, course, street **7** highway, journey, passage **8** causeway, chaussée, crossway, highroad, pavement, speedway, turnpike **9** boulevard **12** thoroughfare *along a cliff:* **8** corniche *around a city:* **6** bypass **7** beltway *bend:* **7** hairpin *edge:* **4** berm **8** shoulder *French:* **6** chemin *Irish:* **6** boreen *machine:* **5** paver **6** grader **9** bulldozer *Roman:* **3** via **4** iter *side:* **6** branch **8** shunpike *Spanish:* **6** camino *surface:* **3** tar **6** gravel **7** macadam **8** pavement
roadblock 7 barrier **8** blockade **9** barricade **11** obstruction
road book 3 map **5** atlas **9** gazetteer, itinerary
roadhouse 3 bar, inn **4** dive **5** hotel, lodge **6** tavern **9** nightclub
roadrunner 6 cuckoo **13** chaparral cock
road rut 6 kettle **7** pothole **9** chuckhole
roam 3 bat, bum, gad, run **4** rove, walk **5** drift, prowl, range, stray **6** ramble, stroll, travel, wander **7** meander, traipse **8** straggle, vagabond **9** gallivant
roamer 3 bum **5** gipsy, gypsy, nomad, rover **6** ranger, walker **7** drifter, prowler, rambler, vagrant **8** marauder, stroller, traveler, vagabond, wanderer **11** nightwalker
roar 3 din **4** bawl, bell, boom, bray, howl, yell **5** shout **6** bellow, clamor, outcry **7** bluster **10** vociferate *bullring:* **3** olé
roast 4 bake, mock, rack, sear **5** broil, grill, joint, parch **6** scathe, scorch **7** banquet, blister, mockery, swelter **8** barbecue, ridicule **9** criticize
rob 3 cop, mug **4** lift, loot, nick, raid, roll, sack **5** boost, filch, heist, pinch, pluck, reave, steal **6** burgle, fleece,

hijack, hold up, pilfer, rip off, snitch, thieve **7** defraud, deprive, despoil, pillage, plunder, purloin, ransack, stick up, swindle **8** knock off **9** knock over **10** burglarize
robber 4 yegg **5** crook, thief **6** bandit, looter, mugger, reiver **7** brigand, burglar, footpad, rustler **8** hijacker, swindler **9** holdup man **10** cat burglar, highwayman, sandbagger, stickup man **12** housebreaker *grave:* **5** ghoul
robbery 5 heist, theft **6** holdup, piracy **7** larceny, mugging, stickup **8** banditry
robe 3 aba **4** cape, gown, wrap **5** cloak, habit **6** caftan, mantle **7** garment, manteau **8** covering, dalmatic, vestment *baptismal:* **7** chrisom *bishop's:* **7** chimere *of Roman emperors:* **6** purple *Turkish:* **6** dolman
Robinson Crusoe *author:* **5** Defoe (Daniel) *character:* **6** Friday
robot 5 golem **7** android **8** automata (plural) **9** automaton
Rob Roy author 5 Scott (Walter)
robust 4 hale, rude **5** hardy, husky, lusty, rough, sound, stout **6** hearty, potent, rugged, sinewy, strong, sturdy **7** healthy **8** athletic, muscular, vigorous **9** strapping **10** boisterous, red-blooded, full-bodied, prosperous
robustious 4 rude **5** lusty, rough, rowdy, wooly **6** rugged **7** boorish, ill-bred, loutish **8** churlish, clownish **9** unrefined **10** boisterous, unpolished
rock 4 crag, reel, roll, sway, toss **5** geode, pitch, quake, shake, swing **6** totter **7** boulder, breccia **8** astonish, convulse, undulate **9** oscillate *basaltic:* **5** wacke *cavity:* **3** vug *combining form:* **4** lite, lith, lyte, petr **5** clast, petri, petro *decomposed:* **6** gossan *fissile:* **5** shale *formation:* **5** nappe **6** pluton **7** rimrock, terrane **8** isocline, syncline *fragment:* **8** xenolith *igneous:* **4** lava **6** basalt, gabbro, pumice **7** diabase, diorite, granite **8** eruptive, felstone, obsidian, porphyry, traprock **10** travertine *layer:* **10** mantlerock *mass:* **5** scree **9** batholith *metamorphic:* **5** slate **6** gneiss, marble, schist **9** quartzite, soapstone *molten:* **4** lava *sedimentary:* **4** clay, coal **5** chalk, chert, coral, flint, shale **8** mudstone **9** limestone, sandstone, siltstone *volcanic:* **4** tuff **6** basalt
rock bass 7 sunfish
rock-bottom 4 root **6** lowest **8** cheapest **9** lowermost **11** fundamental
rocket 3 fly, zip **4** soar, whiz, zoom **5** mount **6** ascend, bullet **7** missile, shoot up **8** firework, starship **10** projectile *landing:* **7** reentry **10** splashdown

launcher: 7 bazooka *launching:* 7 liftoff 8 blastoff *scientist:* 5 Braun (Wernher von) 7 Goddard (Robert)

rockfish 4 cony, hind 5 coney 7 grouper, jewfish, sea bass 8 bocaccio 10 scorpaenid 11 striped bass

Rockies resort 4 Vail 5 Aspen 8 Snowmass 9 Telluride

___ Rockne 5 Knute

rock rabbit 4 cony, pika 5 coney, hyrax 6 dassie

rock-ribbed 5 rigid 8 dogmatic, obdurate 9 unbending 10 inflexible, unyielding

rockweed 5 algae, fucus 7 seaweed 12 bladder wrack

rocky hill 3 tor 5 kopje

rococo 4 busy 5 showy 6 florid, frilly, ornate 7 baroque, elegant, opulent 9 elaborate, intricate 10 decorative, flamboyant 11 overwrought

rod 3 bar 4 cane, pole, wand 5 baton, dowel, spoke, staff, stave, stick 6 pistol 7 scepter 8 revolver 10 correction, discipline, punishment 11 castigation 12 chastisement *bundle of:* 6 fasces

rodent 3 rat 4 cavy, cony, mole, paca, pika, vole 5 cavie, coney, coypu, mouse, shrew 6 agouti, beaver, gerbil, gopher, jerboa, marmot, murine, nutria, rabbit 7 hamster, lemming, leveret, muskrat 8 capybara, chipmunk, dormouse, squirrel, tuco tuco, viscacha, vizcacha, water rat 9 guinea pig, porcupine 10 chinchilla, field mouse, prairie dog 11 kangaroo rat, meadow mouse, pocket mouse 12 pocket gopher *aquatic:* 5 coypu 6 beaver, nutria 7 muskrat 8 musquash *burrowing:* 6 gerbil, gopher 7 hamster 8 viscacha, vizcacha *family:* 5 murid 6 murine 7 sciurid *genus:* 3 Mus 5 Lepus

rodeo 7 contest, roundup 9 enclosure 10 exhibition 11 competition *animal:* 5 horse, steer 10 Brahma bull *event:* 10 calf roping 11 bulldogging 12 bronco riding *performer:* 5 clown 6 cowboy

___ Rodin 7 Auguste

rodomontade 4 blow, brag, rant 5 boast, swash, vaunt 7 bluster, swagger 9 gasconade 11 braggadocio

Rodomonte *beloved:* 8 Doralice *slayer:* 8 Ruggiero

Rodrigo Díaz de Bivar 5 El Cid

rod-shaped 7 virgate 8 bacillar 9 bacillary

roe 4 deer, eggs 6 beluga, caviar, osetra 7 sevruga

Roentgen's discovery 4 X-ray

rogation 6 litany, prayer 8 entreaty, petition 10 beseeching 12 supplication

___ Rogers 3 Roy 4 Carl, Fred, Will 6 Ginger, Robert

rogue 5 cheat, gypsy, knave, scamp 6 rascal 7 lowlife, sharper, villain 8 picaroon, scalawag, swindler 9 defrauder, miscreant, reprobate, scoundrel, skeezicks, trickster 10 blackguard, mountebank 11 rapscallion *relating to:* 10 picaresque

roguery 5 fraud 7 devilry, knavery, waggery 8 deviltry, mischief, trickery 9 devilment, diablerie 11 waggishness 12 sportiveness

roguish 3 sly 4 arch 6 impish, wicked 7 knavish 8 devilish, espiègle, scampish 10 picaresque 11 mischievous

roil 3 mud, vex 4 foul, rile, romp 5 annoy, dirty, grate, muddy, peeve, upset 6 befoul, muddle, nettle, stir up 7 agitate, disturb 8 disorder, irritate 9 aggravate 10 exasperate

roily 5 muddy, riley 6 turbid 9 turbulent

roister 4 riot 5 revel 6 frolic 7 carouse, reveler, wassail 9 wassailer

Roland 7 Orlando *beloved:* 4 Aude *betrayer:* 4 Gano 7 Ganelon *friend:* 6 Oliver 7 Olivier *horn:* 7 Olivant *sword:* 8 Durandal, Durendal *uncle:* 11 Charlemagne

role 3 bit 4 duty, lead, part, pose 5 cameo, cloak, guise, niche 6 aspect, office 7 quality 8 capacity, function, position 9 character 13 impersonation

roll 3 bun, rob 4 bolt, coil, flow, furl, gyre, list, pour, rock, toss, turn, wind, wrap 5 heave, pitch, surge 6 bundle, roster, rotate, stream, swathe, wallow, wrap up 7 biscuit, brioche, envelop, revolve, swaddle, trundle 8 involute, register, schedule, turn over

roll about 6 wallow, welter

roll back 6 lower 6 reduce, repeal 7 curtail, rescind

roller 3 rod 4 bowl, drum, wave 6 canary, caster, platen 7 breaker, carrier, tumbler 8 cylinder

Roller-Derby round 3 jam

rollick 4 lark, play, romp 5 caper, frisk, party, revel, sport 6 cavort, frolic, gambol 7 disport, skylark 8 escapade 9 merriment

rollicking 4 wild 5 antic, merry 6 frisky, lively 8 sportive 10 boisterous, frolicsome 12 high-spirited

rolling stock 4 cars 7 coaches, engines 8 cabooses, Pullmans, sleepers, trailers 11 locomotives

rolling stone 5 rover 6 roamer 7 drifter, rambler, vagrant 8 wanderer, vagabond

roly-poly see ROTUND

Roman 5 Latin 7 Italian *amphitheater:* 9 Colosseum *assembly:* 5 forum 6 senate 7 comitia *building:* 5 Forum 6 Circus 8 basilica, Pantheon *clan:* 4 gens

comedy writer: 7 Plautus (Titus), Terence conspirator: 6 Brutus (Marcus
Junius) 7 Cassius (Gaius) 8 Catiline
date: 4 Ides 7 calends, kalends emperor:
4 Nero, Otho 5 Galba (Servius Sulpi-
cius), Nerva (Marcus Cocceius), Titus,
Verus (Lucius Aurelius) 6 Julian, Trajan
7 Hadrian, Maximus (Magnus Clemens,
Marcus Clodius, Petronius), Severus
(Lucius Septimius) 8 Augustus, Caligula, Claudius, Commodus (Lucius
Aelius), Domitian, Tiberius, Valerian
9 Caracalla, Vespasian 10 Diocletian,
Theodosius 11 Constantine, Valentinian
entrance hall: 5 atria (plural) 6 atrium
epic: 6 Aeneid epigrammatist: 7 Martial
family: 7 Gracchi Fates: 4 Nona 5 Morta
6 Decuma, Parcae founder: 5 Remus
7 Romulus fountain: 5 Trevi 6 Triton
garment: 4 toga 5 tunic general: 5 Sulla
(Lucius Cornelius), Titus 6 Antony
(Marc), Marius (Gaius), Scipio (Publius
Cornelius) 8 Agricola (Gnaeus Julius)
god: 4 deus blind: 6 Plutus chief: 4 Jove
7 Jupiter messenger: 7 Mercury of agriculture: 6 Saturn of animals: 6 Faunus of
death: 4 Mors of dreams: 8 Morpheus of
fire: 6 Vulcan of gates and doors: 5 Janus
of healing: 9 Asclepius 11 Aesculapius of
heaven: 6 Uranus of households: 5 Lares
7 Penates of love: 4 Amor 5 Cupid of
medicine: 9 Asclepius 11 Aesculapius of
mirth: 5 Comus of regeneration: 7 Priapus of sleep: 6 Somnus of the sea:
6 Pontus 7 Neptune, Proteus of the sun:
3 Sol 6 Apollo of the underworld: 3 Dis
5 Orcus, Pluto 8 Dispater of the wind:
5 Eurus, Notus 6 Aeolus, Aquilo,
Auster, Boreas 8 Favonius, Zephyrus of
war: 4 Mars 8 Quirinus of wealth: 6 Plutus of wine: 7 Bacchus of woods:
6 Faunus two-faced: 5 Janus goddess:
3 dea of agriculture: 5 Ceres of beauty:
5 Venus of dawn: 6 Aurora of flowers:
5 Flora of handicrafts: 7 Minerva of harvests: 3 Ops of health: 7 Minerva of
hope: 4 Spes of hunting: 5 Diana of justice: 7 Astraea of love: 5 Venus of marriage: 4 Juno of night: 3 Nox of peace:
3 Pax of springs: 7 Juturna of strife:
9 Discordia of the earth: 6 Tellus of the
hearth: 5 Vesta of the moon: 4 Luna of
the sea: 10 Amphitrite of the underworld:
10 Proserpina of victory: 6 Vacuna of
war: 7 Bellona of wisdom: 7 Minerva of
womanhood: 4 Juno greeting: 3 ave hero:
6 Caesar (Julius) 11 Cincinnatus
(Lucius Quinctius) hill: 7 Caelian, Vimi-
nal 8 Aventine, Palatine, Quirinal
9 Esquiline 10 Capitoline historian:
4 Livy 5 Nepos 7 Sallust, Tacitus 9 Suetonius king: 7 Romulus, Servius, Tullius

12 Ancus Martius 13 Numa Pompilius
marketplace: 5 agora military formation:
3 ala 6 alares (plural) 7 phalanx military
unit: 6 cohort, legion 7 maniple officer:
9 centurion official: 5 augur, edile
6 aedile, censor, consul, lictor 7 praetor, prefect, tribune 8 quaestor people:
5 Laeti, plebs 7 populi (plural) 7 popu-
lus, Sabines 9 plebeians philosopher:
4 Cato 6 Seneca 8 Apuleius 9 Epictetus,
Lucretius physician: 9 Asclepius 11 Aesculapius port: 5 Ostia procurator:
6 Pilate (Pontius) racecourse: 6 circus
road: 4 iter slave: 9 Spartacus statesman:
4 Cato 5 Pliny 6 Caesar, Cicero, Pompey, Seneca 7 Agrippa 8 Augustus,
Gracchus, Maecenas 9 Flaminius symbol of authority: 6 fasces
roman à ___ 4 clef
romance 3 woo 4 gest, love 5 amour,
court, fling, geste, novel 6 affair 7 fantasy, fiction 8 stardust 10 love affair
12 bodice ripper
Romance language 6 French 7 Catalan,
Italian, Spanish 8 Romanian, Rumanian 9 Sardinian 10 Portuguese
Romania capital: 9 Bucharest city: 4 Iasi
6 Brasov, Galati 7 Craiova 9 Constanta,
Timisoara monetary unit: 3 leu mountain
range: 10 Carpathian neighbor: 6 Serbia
7 Hungary, Moldova, Ukraine 8 Bulgaria part of: 7 Balkans peninsula: 6 Balkan
river: 5 Tisza 6 Danube sea: 5 Black
romantic 5 gauzy, ideal, idyll, mushy
6 ardent, dreamy, exotic, gothic, poetic,
unreal 7 amorous, maudlin, mawkish
8 fanciful, quixotic 9 fantastic, imaginary, visionary 10 idealistic, lovey-
dovey 11 sentimental
Romany 5 Gipsy, Gypsy
Romeo 7 amorist, Don Juan, gallant
8 Casanova, lothario, paramour
beloved: 6 Juliet enemy: 6 Tybalt father:
8 Montague friend: 8 Mercutio
Rommel, Erwin 9 Desert Fox
romp 4 lark, play 5 caper, frisk, sport
6 cavort, frolic, gambol, hoyden 7 rollick, runaway, skylark 8 escapade
Romulus brother: 5 Remus father: 4 Mars
mother: 9 Rea Silvia 10 Rhea Silvia victim: 5 Remus
rondure 3 arc, orb 4 arch, ball, ring
5 curve, globe, round 6 circle, sphere
9 curvature
rood 5 cross 8 crucifix
roof 3 hip, top 4 apex, peak 5 cover,
crest, crown 6 summit 7 ceiling 8 covering, housetop material: 3 tar, tin 4 tile
5 slate, straw, terne 6 copper, thatch
7 shingle of a cavern: 4 dome of the
mouth: 6 palate part: 3 hip 4 eave structure: 9 penthouse type: 5 gable 7 gam-

brel, mansard **9** butterfly *vaulted:*
4 dome
roofer 5 tiler
rook 4 bilk, colt, crow, scam, tyro
5 cheat, mulct, raven, stick **6** castle,
fleece, novice **7** amateur, defraud,
recruit, swindle, trainee **8** beginner,
flimflam, freshman, neophyte, newcomer **10** apprentice, tenderfoot
rookery 5 roost **6** colony
rookie 4 colt, tyro **6** novice **7** amateur,
recruit, trainee **8** beginner, freshman,
neophyte, newcomer **10** apprentice,
tenderfoot
room 3 den **4** cell, hall, play, rein
5 divan, house, lodge, put up, salon,
scope, space **6** alcove, billet, leeway,
margin, reside, studio **7** chamber, cubicle, expanse, gallery, lodging **9** clearance *ancient Roman:* **5** atria (plural)
6 atrium *eating:* **4** nook **6** alcove **7** commons, kitchen **8** mess hall **9** refectory
food storage: **6** larder, pantry *for paint-
ings:* **7** gallery *in a monastery:* **4** cell
9 refectory **11** calefactory *in a prison:*
4 cell *on a ship:* **5** cabin **6** galley *round:*
7 rotunda
roomer 5 guest **6** lodger, renter, tenant
7 boarder
roomy 4 wide **5** ample, broad, large
8 spacious **9** capacious **10** commodious
Roosevelt, Franklin D. *birthplace:* **8** Hyde
Park *dog:* **4** Fala *message:* **12** fireside
chat *mother:* **4** Sara *predecessor:*
6 Hoover (Herbert) *program:* **7** New
Deal *successor:* **6** Truman (Harry) *wife:*
7 Eleanor
roost 3 sit **4** land, nest, rest **5** perch
6 alight, settle **7** rookery **8** dovecote
rooster 4 cock **5** capon **8** cockerel, game-
cock **10** cockalorum **11** chanticleer
root 3 dig, fix **4** base, bulb, core, grub,
pith, stem, well **5** basis, cheer, embed,
grout, lodge, plant, radix, tuber **6** bottom, etymon, ground, marrow, origin,
settle, source **7** applaud, bedrock,
essence, footing, radical **8** radicate
9 beginning, establish, inception
10 foundation *aromatic:* **7** ginseng *edible:* **3** oca, yam **4** beet **6** carrot, daikon,
ginger, jicama, potato, radish, turnip
7 burdock, parsnip, salsify **8** celeriac,
kohlrabi, rutabaga, tuckahoe **11** horseradish *fragrant:* **5** orris **7** vetiver *main:*
7 taproot *medicinal:* **5** jalap **7** ginseng
relating to: **7** radical *starch:* **4** arum *tropical:* **4** taro *word:* **6** etymon
rootlet 7 radicle, rhizoid
root out 4 grub **9** eradicate, extirpate
10 deracinate
Roots author 5 Haley (Alex)
rope 3 guy, tie **4** bind, cord, line, stay

5 belay, bight, brace, cable, chord,
lasso, riata, sheet **6** binder, fasten, halter, hawser, lariat, marlin, shroud,
strand, string, tether **7** halyard, lashing,
marline, painter, towline **8** buntline,
lifeline *loop:* **7** cringle *mooring:*
6 hawser *ship's:* **6** marlin, parral, parrel
7 lanyard, marline, ratline
ropedancer 11 funambulist
rope off 6 cordon
ropes 10 ins and outs, procedures, tech-
niques
ropy 4 wiry **6** sinewy **7** stringy, viscous
8 muscular
roque 7 croquet
rorqual 5 whale **7** finback **8** fin whale
11 baleen whale
Rosalind's beloved 7 Orlando
rosary 5 beads **7** chaplet **8** beadroll,
devotion **11** prayer beads
rose 4 glow, pink **5** blush, color, flush,
rouge **6** mantle, pinken, redden **7** crimson **10** erysipelas *Chinese:* **8** Cherokee
cotton: **7** cudweed *feature:* **5** thorn *kind:*
4 moss **5** Peace, Vogue **6** Circus,
damask **7** Fashion, Granada, Iceberg,
New Dawn, Pascali, Tiffany **8** Rubaiyat
9 Floradora, Montezuma, polyantha,
Tropicana **10** Floribunda **11** grandiflo-
ra, Mount Shasta **12** Crimson Glory
roseate 3 red **4** pink **5** sunny **6** bright,
upbeat **7** beamish **8** cheerful, sanguine
10 optimistic
rose-colored see ROSEATE
Rosenkavalier composer 7 Strauss
(Richard)
rose of ___ 6 Sharon
rose oil 5 attar
Rose Tattoo author 8 Williams (Tennessee)
rosette 7 cockade **8** ornament
Rosinante's master 7 Quixote (Don)
Rosmersholm author 5 Ibsen (Henrik)
___ Rossetti 5 Dante (Gabriel) **9** Christina *work:* **8** Sing-Song **11** Annus Domini,
House of Life (The), Seek and Find,
Sister Helen **12** Beata Beatrix, Goblin
Market
Rossini opera 6 Otello **8** Tancredi
11 Cenerentola (La), William Tell
14 Siege of Corinth (The) **15** Barber of
Seville (The)
Rostand hero 6 Cyrano (de Bergerac)
roster 4 list, roll, rota **5** slate **6** muster,
scroll **8** register, roll call, schedule
9 honor roll **10** muster roll **11** waiting list
rostrum 4 dais **5** bimah **6** pulpit
7 lectern, tribune **8** platform
rosy see ROSEATE
rot 4 bosh, bull, mold **5** decay, hooey,
spoil, taint, trash **6** fester, molder **7** cor-

rupt, crapola, crumble, garbage, hogwash, putrefy, rubbish **8** gangrene,
nonsense **9** break down, decompose,
poppycock **10** balderdash, degenerate
11 deteriorate, putrescence **12** disintegrate, putrefaction **13** decomposition

rotary 6 circle **8** gyratory, spinning,
whirling **10** roundabout **11** vertiginous
13 traffic circle

rotate 4 gyre, roll, spin, turn **5** pivot,
twirl, wheel, whirl **6** gyrate, swivel
7 revolve, trundle **9** alternate, pirouette
a log: **4** birl

rotation 4 gyre, loop, turn **5** cycle, orbit,
pivot, round, wheel, whirl **7** circuit,
turning **8** gyration **10** revolution, succession

rote 5 crowd, grind **6** custom, groove,
memory **7** routine **8** practice **9** automatic, treadmill **10** mechanical, repetition **12** memorization

Roth novel 11 Call It Sleep **15** Goodbye
Columbus **16** American Pastoral
17 Portnoy's Complaint

rotten 4 foul **5** fetid, lousy **6** crummy,
putrid **7** corrupt, decayed, spoiled,
tainted **9** nefarious, offensive, putrified
10 decomposed, degenerate, putrescent

rotter 3 cad, cur **4** lout **5** creep, louse
7 bounder **9** scoundrel **10** blackguard

rotund 3 fat **5** obese, plump, podgy,
pudgy, round, stout, thick, tubby
6 chubby, chunky, portly, stocky
7 rounded **8** heavyset, roly-poly, thickset **9** corpulent **10** potbellied

roué 4 lech, rake, wolf **6** lecher **7** Don
Juan, seducer, swinger **8** Casanova,
lothario, sybarite **9** bon vivant, debauchee, libertine, womanizer **10** sensualist, voluptuary **11** philanderer

rouge 3 red **4** glow, pink, rose **5** blush,
color, flush **6** mantle, pinken, redden
7 crimson

rough 3 raw **4** rude, wild **5** brute,
bumpy, crass, crude, hairy, harsh,
raspy, rowdy, yahoo **6** choppy, coarse,
craggy, crusty, hoarse, jagged, rugged,
stormy, uneven **7** cragged, grating, jarring, rasping, raucous, ruffian, scraggy,
uncivil, uncouth **8** bullyboy, churlish,
impolite, scabrous, unformed **9** difficult, imperfect, strenuous, turbulent,
unrefined **10** boisterous, tumultuous,
unfinished, unpolished **11** approximate,
tempestuous

rough-and-ready 5 crude **6** make-do
7 stopgap **8** slapdash **9** expedient,
impromptu, makeshift **10** improvised
11 provisional **13** quick-and-dirty

rough-hewn 4 rude **5** crude, plain
10 unfinished, unpolished **12** uncultivated

roughly 5 about **9** virtually **10** more or
less **13** approximately

roughneck see RUFFIAN

rough out 5 block, chalk, draft **6** sketch
7 outline **9** adumbrate **11** skeletonize

rough up 4 beat, maul **6** batter, pummel
8 maltreat **9** brutalize, manhandle
10 slap around

round 4 gyre, tour, turn **5** bowed, cycle,
globe, wheel **6** circle, curved, rotund
7 annular, circuit **8** circular, globular,
roly-poly, rotation **9** orbicular, spherical **10** conglobate

roundabout 6 circle, detour, rotary **7** circuit, compass, curving, devious,
oblique, winding **8** circular, indirect
10 circuitous, meandering **13** traffic circle

rounded 5 bowed, plump **6** arched, convex, curved, zaftig **7** concave **9** developed **10** curvaceous, Rubenesque
13 well-developed

rounder 4 rake, roué, waif **6** no-good,
waster **7** wastrel **8** vagabond **9** libertine
10 profligate

roundly 4 well **5** fully, quite **6** widely,
wholly **7** bluntly, sharply, smartly,
utterly **8** candidly, entirely **9** brusquely
10 altogether, completely, rigorously,
scathingly, thoroughly, vigorously

round off 3 cap, top **5** crown **6** climax,
finish **8** conclude **9** culminate

round-robin 6 appeal, letter, series
7 protest **8** petition, sequence **9** statement **10** tournament

round trip 4 tour **7** circuit **9** excursion

round up 4 herd **5** drive, group **6** gather
7 cluster, collect **8** assemble

rouse 3 jog **4** call, goad, rock, stir, wake,
whet **5** alarm, awake, pique, rally,
roust, waken **6** awaken, bestir, excite,
foment, incite, kindle, muster, rattle,
recall, revive, vivify, work up **7** agitate,
animate, commove, disturb, enliven,
provoke, quicken **8** motivate **9** aggravate, challenge, galvanize, instigate,
stimulate

rousing 5 brisk, peppy **6** lively **8** animated, exciting, spirited, stirring **9** inspiring **11** stimulating **12** exhilarating,
intoxicating

Rousseau work 5 Émile

roustabout 4 hand **6** worker **7** laborer,
workman **8** deckhand **10** workingman
12 longshoreman, troublemaker

route 3 way **4** path, road, send, ship
5 guide, pilot, steer, track, trail
6 avenue, bypass, course, detour,
direct, divert, escort, flyway, seaway,
skyway **7** channel, circuit, conduct,
consign, forward, highway, journey,

passage, portage, sea-lane **8** corridor, dispatch, transmit, traverse **9** direction, itinerary

routine 3 act, bit, rut **4** dull, pace, rote **5** chore, drill, grind, habit, ho-hum, plain, round, trial, usual **6** course, groove, improv, shtick, wonted **7** chronic, formula, program, regular, utility **8** accepted, everyday, habitual, ordinary, standard, workaday **9** customary, procedure, quotidian, treadmill **10** accustomed, donkeywork, mechanical, monologue **11** commonplace, cut-and-dried, housekeeping, perfunctory **12** unremarkable

rove 3 gad **4** roam **5** drift, range, stray **6** ramble, wander **7** meander, traipse **8** straggle, vagabond **9** gallivant

rover 5 stray **6** pirate, roamer, viking **7** corsair, drifter, floater, rambler, vagrant **8** picaroon, runabout, traveler, wanderer **9** buccaneer, meanderer **10** freebooter **12** rolling stone

roving 6 errant, mobile **7** movable, nomadic, vagrant **8** straying, vagabond **9** itinerant, migratory, wayfaring **11** peripatetic

row 3 oar, way **4** bank, crew, file, fray, fuss, line, muss, rank, spat, tier, tiff **5** align, brawl, broil, chain, fight, melee, order, queue, range, run-in, scrap, scull, strip, swath **6** bicker, clamor, column, dustup, fracas, kickup, paddle, propel, ruckus, series, string, stroke **7** brabble, dispute, quarrel, rhubarb, wrangle **8** argument, diagonal, sequence, squabble **9** commotion **10** falling-out, single file, succession **11** altercation, disturbance, progression

rowdy 4 punk, rude **5** bully, crude, rough, yahoo **6** unruly **7** hoodlum, rackety, raffish, raucous, ruffian **8** bullyboy, hooligan **9** roughneck **10** boisterous, disorderly, robustious **11** rumbustious **12** rambunctious

Rowena *father:* **7** Hengist *guardian:* **6** Cedric *husband:* **7** Ivanhoe **9** Vortigern

Rowling character 11 Harry Potter

Roxana *husband:* **9** Alexander *rival:* **7** Statira

royal 5 grand, noble, regal **6** kingly, lordly **7** stately **9** glorious, imperial, imposing, majestic, princely, splendid **9** grandiose, monarchal, sovereign **10** monarchial **11** magnificent, monarchical

rub 4 buff **5** chafe, grate, shine **6** abrade, polish, smooth, stroke **7** burnish, massage

Rubaiyat author 4 Omar (Khayyám)

rubber 4 buna **5** crepe **6** eraser

10 caoutchouc *basis:* **5** latex *hard:* **7** ebonite *synthetic:* **8** neoprene *tree:* **4** Para

Rubber City 5 Akron

rubberneck 3 eye **4** gape, gawk, gaze **5** snoop, stare **6** goggle **8** sightsee

rubber-stamp 7 approve, certify, endorse **9** authorize

rubbish 3 rot **4** bosh, crap, crud, junk, muck, slop **5** bilge, dreck, hooey, offal, trash, truck, waste **6** debris, litter, refuse, raffle, rubble, spilth **7** crapola, garbage, hogwash **8** nonsense, riffraff, tommyrot **9** poppycock, sweepings **11** foolishness

rubbishy 5 cheap, tatty **6** paltry, shoddy, sleazy, trashy **9** worthless

rubble 5 ruins, scree **6** debris, litter **8** detritus, wreckage

rube 4 boor, hick, naïf **5** churl, cluck, swain, yahoo, yokel **6** rustic **7** bumpkin, hayseed, redneck **9** greenhorn, hillbilly **10** clodhopper **12** apple-knocker, backwoodsman

rubicund 3 red **5** flush, ruddy **6** florid **7** glowing, reddish **8** sanguine **11** full-blooded, incarnadine

____ **Rubik 4** Erno

rub out 3 ice, off, zap **4** do in, kill, slay **5** erase, smoke, waste, whack **6** finish, murder **7** bump off, destroy, put away **8** dispatch, knock off **9** liquidate, terminate **10** extinguish, obliterate **11** assassinate

rubric 4 name, rule **5** canon, class, gloss, style, title **6** custom **7** concept, heading **8** category, headline **9** tradition **11** appellation, designation **13** interpolation

ruck 3 mob **4** fold, heap, mass, pile **5** crimp, crowd, group, purse, ridge **6** cockle, crease, furrow, gather, jumble, pucker, rumple **7** crinkle, crumple, scrunch, wrinkle **10** generality **11** corrugation

rucksack 4 pack **6** kit bag **7** musette **8** backpack

ruckus 3 row **4** fuss, to-do **5** brawl, melee, scrap **6** fracas, furore, hassle, pother, rumpus, shindy, uproar **7** dispute, quarrel, rhubarb, shindig, wrangle **8** squabble **9** commotion **10** falling-out **11** altercation, controversy, disturbance

ruddle *see* REDDEN

ruddy 3 red **4** ripe, rosy **5** flush **6** blowsy, florid **7** flushed, glowing **8** rubicund, sanguine **11** full-blooded, incarnadine

rude 3 raw **4** curt **5** crass, gross, gruff, harsh, rough, rowdy, surly **6** abrupt, callow, clumsy, coarse, crusty, robust, rugged, rustic, sturdy, unhewn, vulgar **7** boorish, brusque, ill-bred, loutish, lowbred, uncivil, uncouth **8** arrogant, churlish, clownish, impolite, tactless **9** barbarian, barbarous, elemental, inelegant, primitive, rough-hewn, unrefined **10** ungracious, unmannered, unmannerly, unpolished **11** ill-mannered, impertinent, uncivilized **12** discourteous, uncultivated **13** disrespectful

rudimentary 5 basal, basic **6** simple **7** initial, primary **8** simplest **9** beginning, elemental, vestigial **10** elementary **11** fundamental, undeveloped **12** introductory

rudiments 6 basics **10** essentials **12** fundamentals

rue 3 woe **4** pity, ruth **5** dolor, grief, mourn, prick **6** grieve, lament, regret, repent, sorrow **7** anguish, deplore, remorse **8** sympathy **9** heartache, penitence **10** affliction, compassion, contrition, heartbreak, repentance **11** compunction

rueful 5 sorry **6** woeful **8** contrite, penitent **9** regretful, sorrowful **10** remorseful

ruff 5 frill, perch, trump **6** collar, fringe **9** sandpiper **11** pumpkinseed *female:* **5** reeve

ruffian 4 goon, hood, punk, thug **5** beast, brute, bully, rowdy, tough, yahoo **6** Apache, hector **7** gorilla, hoodlum **8** bullyboy, hooligan **9** muscleman, roughneck, swaggerer

ruffle 3 bug, irk, rub, vex **4** fret, gall, wear **5** annoy, brawl, chafe, frill, graze, jabot, pleat, ruche **6** abrade, bother, nettle, ripple **7** agitate, bristle, disturb, flounce, provoke, trouble, wrinkle **8** drumbeat, furbelow, irritate, skirmish **9** commotion

rug 3 mat **6** carpet, runner **7** laprobe *kind:* **3** rag, rya **6** hooked **7** braided, dhurrie, flokati, Persian **8** Aubusson, bearskin, Oriental **10** Savonnerie

rugby *formation:* **5** scrum **9** scrummage *goal:* **7** dropped, penalty *period:* **4** half *player:* **6** center, hooker, winger **8** standoff **9** scrum half *scoring:* **3** try **4** goal **10** conversion *team:* **7** fifteen *term:* **4** heel **5** match **7** convert, dribble, hand off, knock on **9** fair catch *time-out:* **8** stoppage *version:* **5** union **6** league

rugged 5 burly, hardy, harsh, heavy, husky, rough, tough **6** brawny, coarse, craggy, jagged, robust, severe, stable, stormy, strong, sturdy, uneven **7** arduous, austere, scraggy **8** leathery, muscular, rigorous, scabrous, stalwart, vigor-

ous **9** difficult, inclement, strenuous, unrefined, weathered **10** formidable, unpolished **11** tempestuous

Ruggiero *guardian:* **7** Atlante *sister:* **7** Marfisa *slayer:* **11** Tisaphernes *wife:* **10** Bradamante

rug rat 3 tot **4** tyke **6** moppet **7** toddler

Ruhr industrial city 5 Essen

ruin 4 bane, bust, dash, do in, doom, fall, loss, rape, raze, sack, undo **5** decay, havoc, smash, spoil, trash, use up, waste, wrack, wreck **6** beggar, finish, pauper, perish, ravage **7** corrupt, deplete, despoil, destroy, exhaust, failure, nemesis, pillage, shatter, undoing, wipe out **8** bankrupt, collapse, decimate, demolish, downfall, spoliate **9** depredate, devastate, disrepair, overthrow, pauperize, shipwreck **10** desolation, impoverish **11** destruction, devastation, dissolution **12** degeneration **13** deterioration

ruination 4 bane, loss, rack **5** havoc **7** undoing **8** calamity, disaster, downfall **10** decimation **11** destruction, devastation

ruinous 5 fatal **7** baneful **10** calamitous, disastrous, pernicious **11** destructive **12** catastrophic

rule 3 law **4** lead, sway **5** axiom, bylaw, canon, edict, habit, judge, maxim, moral, order, reign **6** assize, custom, decree, deduce, dictum, direct, govern, regime, truism **7** brocard, command, control, precept, prevail, regency, regimen, resolve, statute **8** decretum, doctrine, dominate, domineer, dominion **9** authority, determine, etiquette, ordinance, principle, procedure **10** regulation *absolute:* **7** autarky **8** autarchy *by a god:* **8** theonomy

Rule Britannia composer 4 Arne (Thomas)

rule out 3 bar **5** block, debar **6** forbid, refuse, reject **7** exclude, forfend, head off, obviate, prevent **8** preclude, prohibit, stave off **9** eliminate

ruler 4 king, lord **5** queen **6** archon, dynast, ferule, gerent, prince, regent, satrap, sultan **7** emperor, monarch, viceroy **8** governor, hierarch, oligarch, pentarch, princess, theocrat **9** dominator, imperator, matriarch, patriarch, potentate, sovereign **12** straightedge *absolute:* **6** despot, tyrant **8** autocrat, dictator, overlord *Arab:* **4** amir, emir **5** sheik **6** sharif, sheikh, sultan *Asian:* **4** khan *Byzantine Empire:* **6** exarch *Egyptian:* **7** pharaoh *family:* **7** dynasty *Iranian:* **4** shah *one of four:* **8** tetrarch *one of seven:* **8** heptarch *one of three:*

7 triarch 8 triumvir *Persian:* 6 satrap
Russian: 4 czar, tsar, tzar *Turkish:*
3 bey, dey

ruling 3 law 4 call 5 chief, edict, order,
ukase 6 decree 7 current, finding, popular, regnant, verdict 8 decision, judgment 9 directive, judgement, prevalent,
statement 10 prevailing, widespread
11 predominant 12 adjudication

Rumania see ROMANIA

rumble 4 buzz, roar, roll 5 brawl, drone,
fight, growl, rumor 6 murmur, report
7 hearsay, quarrel, resound, thunder
8 feedback 9 complaint 11 altercation,
disturbance, reverberate, scuttlebutt

ruminant 3 cow, yak 4 deer, goat, tahr
5 bison, camel, okapi, serow, sheep,
takin 6 alpaca, cattle, musk ox, vicuña
7 buffalo, chamois, chewing, giraffe,
guanaco 8 antelope *stomach:* 5 rumen
6 omasum 8 abomasum 9 reticulum

ruminate 4 chew, mull, muse 5 champ,
chomp, weigh 6 ponder 7 reflect 8 cogitate, consider, meditate 9 masticate
10 deliberate 11 contemplate

ruminative 7 pensive 8 thinking 9 pondering 10 cogitative, meditative, reflective, thoughtful 11 speculative 13 contemplative, introspective

rummage 4 comb, fish, grub, hash,
hunt, poke, rake, rout, seek 5 delve,
scour 6 ferret, forage, jumble, litter,
search 7 clutter, ransack 8 mishmash
9 potpourri 10 hodgepodge, hotchpotch, miscellany

rummy 3 gin, odd, sot 4 lush, soak, wino
5 drunk, souse, toper 6 boozer
7 bizarre, canasta, curious, guzzler,
strange, swiller, tippler, tosspot
8 drunkard, peculiar 9 eccentric, inebriate 10 boozehound

rumor 4 blab, buzz, talk 5 bruit, story
6 canard, gossip, murmur, mutter,
report, rumble, tattle 7 hearsay, tidings,
whisper 9 grapevine 11 scuttlebutt,
susurration

rumormonger 6 gossip 8 gossiper,
informer, quidnunc, telltale 9 whisper-
er 10 talebearer, tattletale

rump 3 can 4 beam, butt, duff, hind,
rear, tush 5 fanny 6 behind, bottom,
breech, heinie 7 keister, rear end
8 backside, buttocks, derriere, haunches 9 posterior

rumple 4 fold, muss, ruck 5 crimp,
screw, touse 6 pucker, tousle 7 crimple,
crinkle, scrunch, wrinkle 8 dishevel,
disorder

rumpus see RUCKUS

run 3 fly, hie, jog 4 bolt, dart, dash, flee,
flow, race, rush, scud, tear 5 chase,

haste, hurry, scoot, skirr, speed
6 career, gallop, hasten, scurry, sprint,
streak, stream 7 scamper, scuttle,
smuggle 9 skedaddle

run across 4 meet 8 bump into, discover
9 encounter, stumble on

runagate 4 hobo 5 tramp 6 outlaw
7 drifter, floater, lamster, vagrant,
wastrel 8 bohemian, fugitive, rapparee,
vagabond, wanderer 11 guttersnipe

run along 5 leave, scram 6 beat it,
begone, cut out, depart 7 get lost, skiddoo, take off, vamoose 8 shove off
9 skedaddle 10 make tracks

runaround 4 duck, slip 5 dodge 7 elusion, evasion

run away 4 bolt, flee, skip 5 elope, leave,
scram, skirr, split, steal 6 depart,
desert, escape 7 abscond, make off
8 clear out, light out, stampede
9 skedaddle 10 make tracks

runaway 4 wild 5 loose 6 outlaw
7 escapee, lamster 8 deserter, fugitive
10 delinquent 12 uncontrolled

run down 3 hit, ram, tag 5 catch, knock,
trace 6 pursue 7 decline 8 belittle, derogate, diminish 9 apprehend, disparage
10 depreciate 11 catch up with

run-down 5 dingy, seedy, tacky, tired
6 beat-up, bushed, shabby 7 rickety,
ruinous, worn-out 8 decrepit, tattered,
untended 9 burned-out, exhausted,
neglected 10 bedraggled, down-at-heel,
ramshackle, uncared-for 11 dilapidated

rundown 4 dope, poop 5 recap, scoop
6 report, review, skinny, update 7 outline, summary 8 briefing, synopsis

runes 4 ogam 5 ogham 7 futhark

rung 3 bar 4 step 5 grade, notch, round,
spoke, staff, stage, stair, tread 6 degree,
rundle 10 crosspiece

run-in 3 row 4 tiff 5 brush, fight, set-to
6 hassle, scrape, tangle 7 dispute, quarrel, rhubarb, wrangle 8 skirmish,
squabble 9 encounter 10 falling-out
11 altercation

run into 3 hit, ram 4 meet 9 encounter,
stumble on 11 collide with

runner 3 rug 5 miler, racer 6 carpet,
stolon 7 carrier, courier 8 smuggler,
sprinter 9 go-between, messenger
10 marathoner 11 ballcarrier

running 6 active, fluent 7 cursive,
dynamic, flowing, working 9 operative
10 continuous 11 functioning

run-of-the-mill 4 dull, so-so 5 usual
6 common, normal 7 average, humdrum, regular, typical 8 everyday,
familiar, mediocre, middling, moderate, ordinary 9 prevalent 10 monoto-

nous 11 commonplace, indifferent 12 intermediate 13 unexceptional

run on 3 gab, yak 4 blab 5 clack 6 babble, cackle, gabble, jabber, rattle 7 chatter, prattle 8 continue

run out of 5 use up 6 finish 7 exhaust

run over 5 spill 6 exceed, repeat 7 examine 8 overfill, overflow, rehearse

runt 5 dwarf, pygmy 6 midget, peanut, peewee, shrimp, squirt 7 manikin 8 Tom Thumb 10 homunculus 11 hop-o'-my-thumb, lilliputian

run through 3 jab 4 blow, gore, read, scan, stab 5 spend, use up, waste 6 expend, finish, impale, pierce 7 consume, examine, exhaust 8 rehearse, squander, transfix

runty 3 wee 4 puny 6 peewee 7 stunted 8 dwarfish 10 diminutive, undersized

run up 5 build, erect, mount 6 expand 7 augment, enlarge 8 increase, multiply 9 construct 10 accumulate

runway 4 duct, path 5 strip, track, trail 6 sluice, tarmac 7 channel, conduit 8 airstrip, platform

rupture 4 rend, rent, rift, rive 5 break, burst, cleft, sever, split 6 breach, cleave, hernia, schism, sunder 7 blowout, break up, disrupt, divorce, fissure, parting, split-up 8 division, fracture, separate 9 partition 10 separation 11 dissolution 12 estrangement

R.U.R. *author:* 5 Capek (Karel) *character:* 5 robot

rural 6 rustic 7 bucolic, country, idyllic 8 agrarian, arcadian, down-home, pastoral 10 campestral 11 countrified

ruse 3 con, jig 4 hoax, ploy, wile 5 dodge, feint, fraud, stall, trick 6 deceit, gambit 7 gimmick, swindle 8 artifice, maneuver, trickery 9 deception, stratagem 10 subterfuge 13 double-dealing

rush 3 fly, rip, run 4 boil, bolt, dart, dash, flit, flow, hurl, lash, race, roar, scud, tear, tide, whiz 5 blitz, break, carry, chase, court, daily, flash, haste, hurry, lunge, onset, sally, scoot, shoot, spate, speed, storm, surge 6 attack, barrel, beat it, bustle, career, charge, course, hasten, hurtle, hustle, irrupt, plunge, streak, stream, thrill, whoosh 7 assault, cattail, current, rampage, torrent 8 stampede 9 whirlwind, wire grass 13 precipitation

Rushdie novel 5 Shame 13 Satanic Verses (The) 17 Midnight's Children

rushing 5 hasty 6 abrupt, sudden 7 hurried 8 headlong 9 impetuous 11 precipitate, precipitous

rusk 7 biscuit 8 biscotto

Russia *capital:* 6 Moscow *city:* 3 Ufa 4 Omsk, Perm' 5 Kazan', Kursk 6 Grozny, Samara 7 Groznyy, Izhevsk, Ivanovo 8 Murmansk 9 Leningrad, Volgograd 10 Stalingrad 11 Chelyabinsk, Novosibirsk, Vladivostok 12 St. Petersburg 13 Yekaterinburg *emperor:* 5 Boris (Godunov), Peter (the Great) 7 Godunov (Boris), Michael (Romanov), Romanov (Michael) 8 Nicholas *empress:* 4 Anna (Ivanovna) 9 Catherine (the Great), Elizabeth (Petrovna) *ethnic group:* 7 Cossack *island:* 8 Sakhalin *island group:* 5 Kuril 6 Kurile *lake:* 5 Il'men', Onega 6 Baikal, Ladoga *leader:* 5 Lenin (Vladimir), Putin (Vladimir) 6 Stalin (Joseph) 7 Trotsky (Leon) 8 Brezhnev (Leonid) 10 Khrushchev (Nikita) *monetary unit:* 5 ruble *mountain, range:* 4 Ural 5 Altai, Altay, Sayan 6 Elbrus, Kolyma, Koryak 8 Caucasus, Stanovoy *neighbor:* 5 China 6 Latvia, Norway 7 Belarus, Estonia, Finland, Georgia, Ukraine 8 Mongolia 9 Kazakstan 10 Azerbaijan, Kazakhstan, North Korea *peninsula:* 4 Kola 5 Gydan, Kanin, Yamal 6 Taymyr 7 Chukchi 9 Kamchatka *region:* 7 Siberia 9 Circassia 11 Golden Horde *revolution:* 9 Bolshevik *river:* 3 Don 4 Amur, Lena, Ural 5 Desna, Dvina, Vitim, Volga 6 Belaya, Kolyma, Vilyui, Vilyuy 7 Pechora, Yenisey 9 Indigirka *sea:* 4 Azov, Kara 5 Black, White 6 Laptev, Okhotsk 7 Barents, Caspian, Chukchi *strait:* 6 Bering

Russian *aristocrat:* 5 boyar *family:* 7 Romanov 9 Stroganov *grandmother:* 8 babushka *monk:* 8 Rasputin *peasant:* 5 kulak, mujik 6 muzhik, muzhik *ruler:* (see CZAR) *saint:* 15 Alexander Nevsky *urn:* 7 samovar *vehicle:* 6 troika *villa:* 5 dacha

rustic 4 hick, rube, rude 5 churl, clown, plain, rough, rural, swain, yokel 6 farmer 7 bucolic, bumpkin, country, granger, hayseed, peasant, plowboy, plowman, red-neck, uncouth 8 agrarian, pastoral 9 chawbacon, hillbilly 10 campestral, clodhopper, countryman, husbandman 11 countrified 12 apple-knocker, backwoodsman

rustle 5 haste, hurry, speed, steal, swish 6 forage, swoosh 7 crackle, crinkle 8 susurrus

rustler 5 thief 6 duffer, robber 7 forager 8 marauder

Rustum's son 6 Sohrab

rusty 4 slow 6 bygone, creaky 7 outworn 8 outdated, outmoded 10 antiquated, discolored 12 old-fashioned

rut 5 gouge, grind, track 6 furrow, groove 7 channel, routine 9 treadmill

rutabaga 5 swede 6 turnip

ruth 3 rue, woe 4 pity 5 grief, mercy 6 regret, sorrow 7 anguish, remorse, sadness 8 distress, sympathy 9 attrition, penitence 10 compassion, contrition, repentance 11 compunction 13 commiseration

Ruth *husband:* 4 Boaz 6 Mahlon *mother-in-law:* 5 Naomi *son:* 4 Obed

ruthful 6 woeful 7 doleful 8 dolorous, wretched 9 miserable, sorrowful

ruthless 4 hard 5 cruel, harsh 6 brutal, savage 7 inhuman 8 pitiless 9 barbarous, cutthroat, dog-eat-dog, ferocious, heartless, merciless, unsparing 10 implacable, ironfisted

ruttish 4 lewd 5 lusty, randy 6 wanton 7 goatish, lustful, satyric 9 lecherous, lickerish, salacious 10 lascivious, libidinous 12 concupiscent

Rwanda *city:* 6 Kigali *ethnic group:* 4 Hutu 5 Tutsi *language:* 6 French, Rwanda *monetary unit:* 5 franc *neighbor:* 5 Congo 6 Uganda 7 Burundi 8 Tanzania

S

___ **Saarinen** 4 Eero 5 Eliel

Sabatini novel 11 Scaramouche 12 Captain Blood

sabbatical 4 rest 5 leave 7 time off 8 vacation

saber 5 sword 7 cutlass 8 scimitar

sabertooth 3 cat 5 tiger

sable 3 fur 4 dark, inky 5 black, ebony, raven 6 gloomy, somber, sombre, weasel 8 mourning

sabot 4 clog, shoe 10 wooden shoe

sabotage 5 wreck 6 damage, hamper, hinder 7 cripple, disable, subvert, torpedo 8 obstruct, wreckage, wrecking 9 frustrate, undermine, vandalize 10 subversion 11 undermining

Sabra *father:* 7 Ptolemy *rescuer:* 8 St. George *son:* 3 Guy 5 David 9 Alexander

sac 4 caul, cyst 5 pouch 7 vesicle

saccharine 5 mushy, sweet 6 sugary, syrupy 7 candied, cloying, honeyed, maudlin, mawkish, sugared 9 oversweet, schmaltzy 11 sentimental, sugarcoated 12 ingratiating

sacerdotal 8 hieratic, pastoral, priestly 10 priestlike 11 ministerial

sachem 4 boss 5 chief 6 leader

sachet 3 bag 6 powder 7 perfume 9 potpourri

sack 3 bag, bed, can 4 bunk, drop, fire, loot, raid, wine 5 expel, pouch, strip, waste 6 pocket, ravage 7 boot out, cashier, despoil, dismiss, hammock, kick out, pillage, plunder 8 desolate, spoliate 9 container, depredate, desecrate, devastate, white wine

sackbut 8 trombone

sacque 6 jacket

sacrament 4 rite 6 ritual 7 baptism, penance 8 ceremony, marriage 9 Communion, Eucharist, matrimony 10 holy orders 12 confirmation

sacrarium 6 chapel, shrine 7 oratory, piscina 8 sacristy 9 sanctuary

sacred 4 holy 5 godly 6 divine, immune 7 angelic, blessed, saintly 8 hallowed, numinous 9 inviolate, spiritual 10 inviolable, sacrosanct, sanctified 11 consecrated, sacramental *combining form:* 4 hagi, hier, sacr 5 hagio, hiero, sacro *monkey:* 6 baboon, rhesus 7 hanuman *place:* 7 sanctum *weed:* 7 vervain

sacrifice 4 bunt, cede, lose, loss 5 forgo, yield 6 devote, donate, eschew, give up, martyr, victim 7 forfeit, offer up 8 dedicate, hecatomb, immolate, oblation, offering 12 renunciation

sacrilege 6 heresy 7 impiety, offense 9 blasphemy, violation 11 desecration, irreverence, profanation

sacrilegious 7 impious, profane, ungodly 10 irreverent 11 blasphemous

sacristan 6 sexton

sacristy 6 vestry

sacrosanct 9 inviolate 10 inviolable

sad 4 blue, down 5 sorry 6 dismal, dreary, gloomy, morose, triste, woeful **7** doleful, joyless, piteous, pitiful, unhappy **8** dejected, desolate, dolorous, downbeat, downcast, grieving, mournful, pathetic, pitiable **9** depressed, sorrowful, woebegone **10** depressing, dispirited, lamentable, melancholy **11** melancholic **12** heavyhearted

sadden 7 depress, oppress, trouble **8** aggrieve, dispirit **9** weigh down **10** discourage

saddle 3 tax **4** lade, load, task **5** weigh **6** burden, charge, hamper, impede, impose, weight **7** aparejo, inflict **8** encumber, restrict *adjunct:* **7** stirrup *part:* **6** cantle, pommel *strap:* **5** cinch, girth **6** latigo **7** harness

sadness 3 woe **4** funk **5** blues, dolor, dumps, gloom, grief, mopes **6** misery, sorrow **7** dismals, megrims **8** doldrums, glumness, mourning **9** dejection, dysphoria, heartache **10** blue devils, depression, desolation, melancholy **11** despondency, melancholia, unhappiness

safari 4 hunt, trek, trip **7** caravan, journey **10** expedition

safe 4 snug, wary **5** chary **6** secure, unhurt **7** careful, guarded **8** cautious, defended, shielded, unharmed **9** innocuous, protected, sheltered, uninjured, unscathed **10** inviolable, sheltering **11** impregnable **12** invulnerable, unassailable

safecracker 4 yegg **8** picklock **9** cracksman

safeguard 4 ward **6** convoy, defend, escort, shield, surety **7** bulwark, defense, protect **8** armament, preserve **10** precaution, protection

safety 4 asylum, refuge **7** defense, shelter **8** immunity, security **9** assurance, sanctuary **10** protection **13** inviolability

sag 3 dip **4** bend, drop, flag, flap, flop, hang, sink, slip, wilt **5** droop, slide, slump **6** dangle, hollow, slouch **7** decline, drop off, falloff, sinkage, sinking **8** downturn, settling, sinkhole **9** concavity, downswing **10** depression

saga 4 edda, epic, myth, tale **5** story **6** legend **9** chronicle, narrative **12** Heimskringla

sagacious 4 keen, wise **5** acute, smart **6** astute, clever, shrewd **7** knowing, prudent, sapient **8** critical **9** far-seeing, judicious **10** discerning, insightful, perceptive **11** intelligent **13** perspicacious

sagacity 5 grasp **6** acuity, acumen, wisdom **7** insight **8** judgment, keenness, prudence, sapience **10** perception, shrewdness **11** discernment, penetra-

tion, percipience, perspicuity **12** perspicacity **13** comprehension, judiciousness, understanding

sagamore 5 chief **6** sachem

Sagan work 6 Cosmos **16** Bonjour tristesse

sage 4 guru, mint, wise **6** expert, master, nestor, pundit, savant, shrewd **7** gnostic, knowing, learned, prudent, sapient, scholar, wise man **8** polymath, profound, sensible **9** judicious **10** discerning, insightful, perceptive **11** penetrating, philosophic *Hindu:* **6** pandit **7** mahatma

Sage *of Chelsea:* **7** Carlyle (Thomas) *of Concord:* **7** Emerson (Ralph Waldo) *of Emporia:* **5** White (William Allen) *of Ferney:* **8** Voltaire *of Monticello:* **9** Jefferson (Thomas) *of Pylos:* **6** Nestor

Sagebrush State 6 Nevada

Sagittarius 6 archer **7** centaur **13** constellation

sago 4 palm **6** starch

saguaro 6 cactus

sahib 3 sir **6** master **9** gentleman

sail 3 fly **4** dart, flit, scud, skim, wing **5** fleet, float, shoot, skirr, sweep **6** cruise, mizzen **7** spencer **9** spinnaker *triangular:* **3** jib **5** genoa

sailboat 4 bark, yawl **5** ketch, skiff, sloop, yacht **6** dinghy **8** schooner, skipjack

sailing vessel 4 bark, brig **5** xebec **6** barque **7** frigate, galleon **8** schooner **10** barkentine, brigantine **11** barquentine

sailor 3 gob, tar **4** jack, mate, salt, swab **6** hearty, sea dog, seaman **7** jack-tar, mariner, matelot, old salt, swabbie **8** flatfoot, seafarer, shipmate, water dog **9** shellback, tarpaulin, yachtsman **10** bluejacket *British:* **5** limey *fictional:* **6** Sinbad *patron saint:* **4** Elmo *song:* **6** chanty **7** chantey **9** barcarole

saint 7 paragon *biography:* **11** hagiography *list:* **9** hagiology (see also PATRON SAINT)

Saint, The 12 Simon Templar *creator:* **9** Charteris (Leslie)

Saint Anthony's cross 3 tau

Saint Elmo's Fire 9 corposant

Saint Helena *capital:* **9** Jamestown *colony of:* **7** Britain *island:* **9** Ascension

Saint Joan author 4 Shaw (George Bernard)

Saint John's bread 5 carob

Saint Kitts and Nevis *capital:* **10** Basseterre *island group:* **7** Leeward *language:* **7** English *location:* **10** West Indies *monetary unit:* **6** dollar

Saint Lucia *capital:* **8** Castries *island*

group: 8 Windward **language:** 6 French
7 English **location:** 10 West Indies **monetary unit:** 6 dollar **volcano:** 8 Quilabou

saintly 4 holy, pure 5 godly, pious
6 devout, worthy 7 angelic, blessed,
upright 8 beatific, seraphic, virtuous
9 righteous

Saint Paul's architect 4 Wren (Christopher)

Saint Peter's Basilica **architect:** 7 Bernini
(Gian Lorenzo) 12 Michelangelo
(Buonarotti) **sculpture:** 5 Pietà

Saint-Pierre and Miquelon **capital:** 8 St.-
Pierre **department of:** 6 France

Saint Vincent and the Grenadines **capital:** 9 Kingstown **island group:** 8 Windward **language:** 6 French 7 English **location:** 10 West Indies **monetary unit:**
6 dollar **volcano:** 9 Soufrière

Saint Vitus' dance 6 chorea

sake 3 end 4 good 5 drink 7 benefit, purpose, welfare

Saki 5 Munro (H. H.)

salaam 3 bow 6 kowtow 8 greeting
9 obeisance

salacious 4 fast, lewd 5 bawdy 6 erotic,
ribald, risqué 7 lustful, satyric 8 indecent, prurient 9 lecherous, libertine
10 lascivious, libidinous, licentious

salad **item:** 3 egg 4 bean, cuke, herb
5 cress, olive, onion 6 carrot, celery,
cheese, endive, pepper, potato, radish,
tomato 7 anchovy, cabbage, crouton,
lettuce, parsley, spinach 8 chickpea,
coleslaw, cucumber, garbanzo, mushroom, scallion 10 watercress **type:**
5 chef's 6 Caesar

salamander 3 eft 4 newt 7 urodele 8 mud
puppy, water dog 10 hellbender **Mexican:** 7 axolotl

salary 3 pay 4 take, wage 6 income
7 stipend 8 earnings 9 emolument
10 recompense 12 compensation, remuneration

sale 6 bazaar, demand 7 auction 8 closeout, disposal, transfer 9 clearance
11 transaction

salient 6 marked, signal 7 obvious,
weighty 8 striking 9 arresting, important, obtrusive, pertinent, prominent
10 impressive, noticeable, projecting,
pronounced, remarkable 11 conspicuous, outstanding, significant

saline 5 briny, salty 8 brackish

Salinger, J. D. **character:** 4 Esmé 6 Holden (Caulfield) **novel:** 14 Franny and
Zooey 15 Catcher in the Rye

saliva 4 spit 6 slaver, sputum 7 spittle

salivate 5 drool 6 drivel, slaver 7 slobber

___ **Salk** 5 Jonas

sallow 3 wan 4 pale, waxy 5 pasty 6 pallid, sickly, willow, yellow 7 bilious
9 jaundiced

sally 3 gag 4 gust, jape, jest, joke, quip
5 blast, burst, crack, jaunt 6 depart,
junket, outing, set out, sortie, volley
7 barrage, flare-up 8 drollery, eruption,
outbreak, outburst, paroxysm 9 discharge, excursion, explosion, wisecrack, witticism

salmagundi see HODGEPODGE

salmon 4 parr, pink 5 smolt 6 grilse
7 sockeye 9 brandling **cured:** 7 gravlax
8 gravlaks **male:** 6 kipper **smoked:** 3 lox

Salome **composer:** 7 Strauss (Richard)
father: 5 Herod **husband:** 6 Philip
7 Zebedee 11 Aristobulus **mother:**
8 Herodias **son:** 4 John 5 James **victim:**
4 John (the Baptist)

salon 4 hall, shop 5 suite 6 parlor
7 gallery 9 apartment, reception
10 exhibition

saloon 3 bar, pub 6 tavern 7 barroom,
cantina, gin mill, taproom 9 beer joint
12 watering hole

salt 3 tar 4 jack, keep, NaCl 5 brine
6 sailor, saline, seaman 7 jack-tar,
mariner 8 salinize 9 sailorman

salt away 4 bank, save 5 hoard, lay by,
lay up, put by, stash, store 7 deposit
8 lay aside, squirrel

saltpeter 5 niter, nitre

salty 4 blue, racy 5 briny, crude, spicy,
tangy 6 earthy, purple, risqué, saline
7 caustic, mordant, pungent 8 brackish,
off-color, scathing 9 trenchant

salubrious 5 tonic 7 bracing, healthy
8 hygienic, salutary 9 healthful, wholesome 10 beneficial 11 restorative
12 invigorating

Salus see HYGEIA

salutary 5 tonic 6 benign 7 bracing, healing 8 curative, remedial, sanative
9 analeptic, healthful, vulnerary,
wholesome 10 beneficial, salubrious
11 restorative, therapeutic 12 advantageous, health-giving

salutation 4 hail 5 hello, howdy 7 welcome 8 greeting **Arab:** 6 salaam **French:**
5 salut **Hawaiian:** 5 aloha **Italian:** 4 ciao
Latin: 3 ave **Spanish:** 4 hola

salute 4 hail 5 greet, honor 6 praise
7 address, commend 8 greeting 12 congratulate

salvage 4 save 6 ransom, recoup,
redeem, regain, rescue 7 deliver,
reclaim, recover 8 retrieve

salvation 6 saving 7 keeping 10 redemption 11 deliverance 12 conservation,
preservation

Salvation Army founder 5 Booth (General William)

salve 4 balm 5 cream, quiet 6 cerate, chrism, lotion, remedy 7 assuage, unction, unguent 8 ointment 9 emollient
salver 4 tray
salvo 4 hail 5 burst, spray, storm 6 attack, shower, volley 7 barrage, proviso 9 broadside, cannonade, discharge, fusillade 11 bombardment
Samaritan 6 helper 10 benefactor
same 4 idem, like, very 5 equal, exact 7 coequal, similar 8 constant 9 duplicate, identical, unvarying 10 consistent, equivalent, invariable, unchanging
Samoa *capital:* 4 Apia *island:* 5 Upolu 6 Savai'i *language:* 6 Samoan 7 English *monetary unit:* 4 tala
samovar 3 urn
samp 6 cereal, hominy
sampan 4 boat 5 skiff
sample 3 try 4 case, part, test, unit 5 piece, taste 7 element, example, excerpt, portion, segment 8 fragment, instance, specimen 10 indication 11 case history, constituent 12 illustration
Samson *betrayer:* 7 Delilah *birthplace:* 5 Zorah *deathplace:* 4 Gaza *father:* 6 Manoah *tribe:* 3 Dan
Samson Agonistes author 6 Milton (John)
Samuel *father:* 7 Elkanah *grandson:* 5 Heman *mother:* 6 Hannah
samurai code 7 Bushido
San Antonio *team:* 5 Spurs *landmark:* 5 Alamo
sanatorium 3 spa 8 hospital, rest home
sanctify 5 bless 6 hallow, ordain, purify 8 dedicate 10 consecrate
sanctimonious 5 pious 7 canting, preachy 8 unctuous 9 pharisaic 11 pharisaical 12 hypocritical, Pecksniffian 13 self-righteous
sanction 4 fiat, okay 5 bless, leave 6 assent, decree, permit, ratify 7 approve, backing, boycott, certify, consent, embargo, endorse, license, penalty, support 8 accredit, approval 9 allowance, authorize 10 commission, permission, sufferance 11 approbation, endorsement 12 confirmation, ratification 13 authorization, encouragement
sanctity 8 holiness 9 godliness 11 saintliness, uprightness 13 inviolability, righteousness
sanctuary 5 haven, oasis 6 asylum, covert, harbor, refuge, shrine, temple 7 reserve, retreat, shelter 8 preserve 9 holy place
sanctum 4 lair 6 shrine 7 retreat, shelter 9 holy place, sanctuary
sand 3 tan 4 buff, ecru, fawn, grit

5 beach, beige, camel, grind, khaki, scour, shore 6 gravel, polish, smooth 7 burnish 8 granules
sandal 4 clog, zori 5 sabot, thong 6 patten 8 flip-flop, huarache 10 espadrille
sandbag 6 ambush, waylay
sandbar 4 reef, spit 7 tombolo
Sand County Almanac author 7 Leopold (Aldo)
sandpiper 4 knot, ruff 5 reeve 6 dunlin 9 shorebird
sandstone deposit 6 flysch
sandwich 3 BLT, sub 4 club, gyro, roti 5 butty, Cuban 6 Denver, hoagie, Reuben 7 grinder, Western 9 submarine 10 muffuletta *shop:* 4 deli
sandy 4 fair 5 blond 6 blonde, grainy, gritty
sane 3 fit 4 good, hale, sage, well, wise 5 lucid, right, sober, sound 6 cogent, normal 7 healthy, logical, prudent, sapient 8 all there, balanced, oriented, rational, sensible 9 judicious, wholesome 10 reasonable 11 levelheaded 12 compos mentis
San Francisco *hill:* 3 Nob 7 Russian *tower:* 4 Coit
sangfroid 4 calm 5 poise 6 aplomb, phlegm 9 composure 10 equanimity 11 self-control
sanguinary 4 gory 6 bloody 9 homicidal, murdering, murderous 12 bloodstained, bloodthirsty
sanguine 4 gory 5 flush, ruddy 6 bloody, florid, secure, upbeat 7 assured, buoyant, flushed, glowing, hopeful 8 bloodred, cheerful, rubicund 9 confident, homicidal, murdering, murderous 10 optimistic 11 self-assured 12 bloodstained, bloodthirsty, Pollyannaish 13 self-confident
sanitary 5 clean 7 sterile 8 hygienic 9 healthful 10 antiseptic, salubrious
sanitize 5 clean, purge 6 bleach, censor, purify 7 cleanse, launder 8 black out 9 disinfect, expurgate, sterilize 10 bowdlerize
sanity 6 health, reason 7 balance 8 lucidity, prudence 9 normality, soundness, stability
San Marino *capital:* 9 San Marino *monetary unit:* 4 euro *monetary unit, former:* 4 lira *neighbor:* 5 Italy
sans 7 lacking, missing, wanting, without
Sanskrit *dialect:* 4 Pali *epic:* 8 Ramayana *Scripture:* 4 Veda
Santa Lucia composer 5 Denza (Luigi)
São Tomé and Príncipe *capital:* 7 São Tomé *language:* 10 Portuguese *location:*

12 Gulf of Guinea *monetary unit:* **5** dobra

sap 4 dupe, fool, gull, mark **5** chump, drain **6** pigeon, sucker, weaken **7** cripple, deplete, disable, exhaust, fall guy **8** enervate, enfeeble **9** attenuate, schlemiel, undermine **10** debilitate

sapid 5 tasty **6** savory **9** delicious, flavorful, palatable, toothsome **10** appetizing **11** scrumptious

sapience *see* SAGACITY

sapient *see* SAGACIOUS

sapling 4 tree **5** child, youth **9** youngster

Sapphira's husband 7 Ananias

Sappho *forte:* **6** poetry *island:* **6** Lesbos

sappy 5 ditzy, flaky, mushy, silly, soupy **6** drippy, slushy, sticky, syrupy **7** cloying, foolish, maudlin, mawkish **8** bathetic **11** sentimental

Saracen hero 9 Rodomonte

Sarah *husband:* **7** Abraham *maid:* **5** Hagar *son:* **5** Isaac

sarcasm 3 wit **4** gibe **5** irony, scorn **6** satire **7** mockery **8** acerbity, mordancy, ridicule, sneering **10** causticity

sarcastic 4 acid, tart **5** acerb, sharp **6** biting, ironic **7** acerbic, caustic, cutting, cynical, jeering, mocking, mordant, satiric **8** sardonic, scathing, scornful, stinging **9** corrosive

sarcophagus 4 tomb **6** coffin

sardine 4 sild **7** anchovy, herring **8** pilchard

Sardinia's capital 8 Cagliari

sardonic 3 wry **6** ironic **7** caustic, cynical, jeering, mocking, satiric **8** derisive, scornful, sneering **9** corrosive, sarcastic **10** disdainful **12** contemptuous

sarong 5 skirt **7** garment

Sarpedon *brother:* **5** Minos **12** Rhadamanthus *father:* **4** Zeus **7** Jupiter *mother:* **6** Europa **8** Laodamia

Sartor ___ 8 Resartus

Sartre work 4 Wall (The) **5** Flies (The) **6** Nausea, No Exit **8** Huis Clos **10** Saint Genet

sash 4 belt **6** girdle **8** ceinture, cincture **9** waistband **10** cummerbund

sashay 5 mince, strut **6** prance **7** flounce, saunter, swagger

Saskatchewan *capital:* **6** Regina *city:* **8** Moose Jaw **9** Saskatoon **12** Prince Albert *mountain range:* **12** Cypress Hills *provincial flower:* **7** red lily **11** prairie lily *river:* **9** Churchill **11** Assiniboine

sass 3 lip **4** guff **5** brass, cheek, mouth, sauce **8** back talk **9** impudence, insolence **12** impertinence

sassy 4 bold, flip, pert, wise **5** fresh, lippy, nervy, smart **6** brazen, cheeky **7** forward **8** flippant, impudent, insolent, malapert **9** audacious, unabashed **11** smart-alecky

Satan 5 demon, devil, fiend **6** diablo **7** Lucifer, Old Nick, serpent, villain **9** archfiend, Beelzebub **10** Old Scratch

satanic 4 evil **6** wicked **7** demonic, hellish **8** demoniac, devilish, diabolic, fiendish, infernal

satanism 9 diabolism

satchel 3 bag **4** case, tote **5** pouch **6** valise **7** handbag **9** briefcase

sate 4 cloy, fill, glut, jade, pall **5** gorge, stuff **6** stodge **7** appease, overeat, placate, surfeit **8** overfill **9** overstuff **10** conciliate

sated 4 full **6** filled, gorged **7** glutted, overfed, replete, stuffed **8** appeased, chockful **9** chock-full, surfeited

satellite 4 moon **5** toady **6** cohort, minion **7** Sputnik **8** adherent, disciple, follower, henchman, partisan **9** attendant, supporter, sycophant, tributary *of Jupiter:* **6** Europa **8** Callisto, Ganymede *of Mars:* **6** Deimos, Phobos *of Neptune:* **6** Nereid, Triton *of Saturn:* **4** Rhea **5** Dione, Janus, Mimas, Titan **6** Phoebe, Tethys **7** Iapetus **8** Hyperion **9** Enceladus *of Uranus:* **5** Ariel **6** Oberon **7** Miranda, Titania, Umbriel

satiate *see* SATE

satire 3 wit **5** irony, spoof, squib **6** parody **7** lampoon, mockery, takeoff **8** raillery, ridicule, spoofery, travesty **9** burlesque **10** caricature, lampoonery, pasquinade, persiflage

satiric 6 ironic **7** mocking **8** farcical, ironical

satirist *English:* **5** Swift (Jonathan) **7** Marston (John) *French:* **8** Rabelais (François), Voltaire *Greek:* **8** Menippus *Italian:* **7** Aretino (Pietro) *Roman:* **6** Horace **7** Juvenal, Martial, Persius **9** Petronius

satirize 4 mock **5** spoof **6** parody, send up **7** lampoon **8** ridicule **10** caricature

satisfaction 6 amends **7** redress **8** pleasure, serenity **9** atonement **10** reparation **11** contentment, fulfillment, restitution, vindication **12** propitiation **13** gratification

satisfactory 4 fair, good, okay **5** sound **6** decent **8** adequate, all right, passable **9** competent, tolerable **10** acceptable, sufficient **13** unexceptional

satisfy 3 pay **4** fill, meet, sate, suit **5** clear, humor, pay up, serve **6** answer, assure, dispel, pacify, please, settle, square **7** appease, content, fulfill, gladden, gratify, indulge, placate, satiate, suffice, win over **8** convince, persuade

9 conform to, discharge, indemnify **10** comply with

satori 12 illumination **13** enlightenment

satrap 5 ruler **6** cohort **7** viceroy **8** governor, henchman, sidekick **11** subordinate

saturate 3 sop, wet **4** fill, soak **5** bathe, douse, imbue, souse, steep **6** charge, drench, infuse **7** pervade, suffuse **8** permeate, waterlog **9** transfuse

Saturn *moon:* **4** Rhea **5** Dione, Janus, Mimas, Titan **6** Phoebe, Tethys **7** Iapetus **8** Hyperion **9** Enceladus *see also* CRONUS

saturnalia 4 orgy **5** party, revel **6** excess **7** debauch **9** bacchanal **11** bacchanalia, dissipation

saturnine 4 dour, glum, grim **5** sulky, surly **6** gloomy, moping, morose, somber, sombre, sullen **7** crabbed **8** funereal, sardonic

satyr 4 goat, rake, wolf **6** lecher **9** butterfly

satyric 4 lewd **5** randy **6** wanton **7** goatish, lustful **8** prurient **9** lecherous, libertine, lickerish, salacious **10** lascivious, libidinous, licentious, lubricious **11** promiscuous **12** concupiscent

sauce 4 guff, sass **5** mouth **6** relish **7** topping **8** back talk **9** condiment, impudence *kind:* **3** soy **4** hard, mole **5** chili, curry, gravy, melba, pesto, salsa **6** Mornay, panada, tamari, tartar **7** chutney, marengo, Newburg, piquant, soubise, tartare, velouté **8** béchamel, duxelles, marinara, matelote, noisette, normande **9** béarnaise, lyonnaise, rémoulade **10** bordelaise, Provençale **11** hollandaise, vinaigrette

saucy *see* SASSY

Saudi Arabia *capital:* **6** Riyadh *city:* **5** Jedda, Jidda, Mecca **6** Jeddah, Jiddah, Medina *desert:* **7** Arabian **10** Rub Al-Khali **12** Empty Quarter *gulf:* **7** Persian *monetary unit:* **5** riyal *neighbor:* **3** UAE **4** Iraq, Oman **5** Qatar, Yemen **6** Jordan *peninsula:* **7** Arabian *sea:* **3** Red

Saul *concubine:* **6** Rizpah *cousin:* **5** Abner *daughter:* **5** Merab **6** Michal *father:* **4** Kish *son:* **8** Jonathan *successor:* **5** David *uncle:* **3** Ner *wife:* **7** Ahinoam

saunter 4 mope, roam, rove **5** amble, drift, mosey **6** loiter, ramble, sashay, stroll, wander **7** meander, traipse

sausage 5 wurst **6** banger, kishke, salami, Vienna, wiener **7** baloney, bologna, boloney, chorizo, saveloy **8** cervelat, kielbasa **9** andouille, bratwurst, frankfurt, pepperoni, Thuringer **10** knack-wurst, knockwurst, liverwurst, mortadella **11** frankfurter

sauté 3 fry **4** sear **5** brown, grill **6** sizzle **7** frizzle

savage 4 grim, wild **5** brute, cruel, feral **6** bloody, brutal, fierce, Gothic, rugged **7** bestial, brutish, inhuman, untamed, vicious, wolfish **8** barbaric, inhumane, primeval, ravenous, unbroken **9** barbarian, barbarous, ferocious, heartless, murderous, primitive, rapacious, truculent, voracious **10** implacable, relentless **11** uncivilized **12** bloodthirsty, uncontrolled, uncultivated, unsocialized

savagery 7 cruelty **8** atrocity **9** barbarity, brutality, depravity **10** bestiality, inhumanity **11** abomination, monstrosity, viciousness **12** ruthlessness

savanna 5 plain **9** grassland

savant 4 sage **7** scholar, thinker, wise man

save 3 bar, but, yet **4** bank, keep, only, stow **5** amass, avoid, cache, guard, hoard, lay by, lay in, lay up, put by, set by, skimp, spare, store **6** defend, except, gather, keep up, manage, ransom, redeem, rescue, scrimp, shield, unless **7** barring, besides, collect, deliver, deposit, however, husband, lay away, protect, reclaim, reserve, salvage, set free, store up **8** conserve, lay aside, liberate, maintain, preserve, salt away, set aside, squirrel **9** aside from, economize, excluding, safeguard, stash away, stockpile **10** accumulate

savior 7 messiah, paladin, rescuer **8** defender **9** deliverer, liberator, preserver, protector, salvation **11** white knight

savoir faire 4 tact **5** grace, poise **6** aplomb **7** address, dignity, finesse, manners **8** urbanity **10** confidence, refinement **13** self-assurance

savor 4 odor, tang **5** enjoy, scent, smack, smell, spice, taste, tinge **6** flavor, relish, season **8** sapidity

savory 5 sapid, spicy, tangy, tasty **7** piquant **9** flavorful, palatable, toothsome **10** appetizing

savvy 4 deft **5** adept, craft, handy, knack, skill **6** clever, talent **7** ability, know-how, skilled **8** deftness **9** adeptness, expertise, handiness, ingenuity **10** capability, cleverness, competence

saw 3 cut, hew **5** adage, axiom, maxim **6** byword, cliché, saying **7** precept, proverb **8** aphorism, apothegm

___ saw 3 bow, jig, pit, rip **4** band, buck, buzz, fret, hack, whip **5** chain, crown, saber **6** coping, scroll **7** compass, keyhole **8** circular, crosscut

sawbones 3 doc 6 doctor 7 surgeon 9 physician

sawbuck 6 tenner 7 trestle

sawhorse see SAWBUCK

saw-toothed 7 serrate, serried 8 serrated 11 denticulate

Saxon *assembly:* 4 moot 5 gemot 6 gemote *nobleman:* 8 atheling *serf:* 4 esne *warrior:* 5 thane

say 4 talk, tell 5 mouth, speak, state, utter, voice 6 affirm, assert, assume, recite, remark 7 comment, declare, express 8 announce, proclaim 9 enunciate, pronounce 10 articulate

Sayers character 6 Wimsey (Lord Peter)

saying 3 mot, saw 5 adage, axiom, maxim 6 byword, dictum, truism 7 precept, proverb 8 apothegm

scab 5 crust 6 eschar 13 strikebreaker

scabbard 6 sheath

scabrous 4 lewd 5 harsh, rough, salty, scaly 6 craggy, grubby, jagged, knobby, knotty, rugged, scabby, scurfy, sordid, uneven 7 bristly, prickly, scraggy, squalid 8 indecent 10 scandalous

scads 4 gobs, lots, wads 5 loads, piles, reams 6 oodles 8 slathers 10 quantities

scaffold 5 stage, truss 7 staging 8 platform 9 framework

Scala, La *city:* 5 Milan *production:* 5 opera

scalawag see SCAMP

scald 4 boil, burn 6 scorch

scale 4 peel, rate, skin 5 climb, flake, gamut, gauge, mount, ratio, scute, strip 6 ascend, degree, extent, ladder, lamina, scutum, squama 7 measure, ranking 8 escalade, flake off, spall off 9 exfoliate, hierarchy 10 desquamate, proportion 11 decorticate *auxiliary:* 7 vernier *earthquake:* 7 Richter *temperature:* 6 Kelvin 7 Celsius 10 centigrade, Fahrenheit *wind:* 8 Beaufort

scallion 4 leek 5 onion 7 shallot 10 green onion

scalp 4 flay, skin 5 cheat 6 resell, trophy

scam 3 con, gyp 4 bilk, dupe, fool, hoax 5 cheat, fraud, stick, trick 6 delude, diddle, take in 7 beguile, deceive, defraud, swindle 8 flimflam, hoodwink 11 double-cross

scamp 3 imp 4 brat, rake, tyke 5 devil, joker, knave, rogue 6 rascal, urchin 7 hellion 8 scalawag, slyboots 9 prankster, skeezicks 11 rapscallion

scamper 3 run 4 dash, skip 5 scoot 6 scurry 7 scuttle

scan 3 eye 4 skim, view 5 audit, check 6 browse, review, survey 7 examine, eyeball, inspect 8 glance at 10 run through, scrutinize

scandal 5 rumor 6 gossip, infamy 7 calumny, obloquy, offense, slander 8 disgrace, dishonor, reproach 9 aspersion, discredit, disrepute 10 backbiting, defamation, detraction, opprobrium

scandalize 5 libel, shock, smear 6 defame, malign 7 asperse, slander 9 denigrate 10 calumniate

scandalmonger 6 gossip 8 busybody, gossiper, quidnunc, telltale 9 backbiter, muckraker 10 talebearer

scandalous 7 heinous 8 infamous, libelous, shameful, shocking 9 notorious, offensive 10 defamatory, outrageous, scurrilous 11 disgraceful

Scandinavian see NORSE

Scandinavian country 6 Norway, Sweden 7 Denmark, Finland, Iceland

scant 5 short, skimp, spare, stint, tight 6 meager, meagre, paltry, scarce, scrimp, skimpy, slight, sparse 7 scrimpy, wanting 8 exiguous 10 inadequate 12 insufficient

scantiness 4 lack 6 dearth 7 deficit, paucity 8 scarcity, shortage, sparsity 10 deficiency, inadequacy, scarceness, sparseness 13 insufficiency

scanty see SCANT

scapegoat 6 target, victim 7 fall guy 9 sacrifice 11 whipping boy

scapegrace 5 knave, rogue, scamp 6 bad egg, rascal 7 ruffian, varmint, villain 8 hooligan, recreant, scalawag 9 miscreant, reprobate, scoundrel 10 blackguard, black sheep, delinquent 11 rapscallion

Scapin 5 rogue, valet 6 rascal *author:* 7 Molière *employer:* 7 Léandre

scar 3 mar 4 flaw 5 score 6 deface, defect, keloid 7 blemish, scratch 8 cicatrix, pockmark 9 cicatrize, disfigure *on a seed:* 5 hilum

scarab 6 beetle

scaramouch see SCAMP

scarce 3 few 4 rare 5 scant 6 barely, hardly, scanty, sparse 7 limited, wanting 8 sporadic, uncommon 9 deficient 10 inadequate, infrequent, occasional 12 insufficient

scarcity see SCANTINESS

scare 5 alarm, panic, spook 6 fright 7 horrify, petrify, shake up, startle, terrify 8 frighten, paralyze 9 terrorize

scaredy-cat 4 wimp, wuss 5 mouse, sissy 6 coward 7 chicken, dastard 8 alarmist, poltroon 11 milquetoast, yellowbelly

scare up 4 find, snag 5 rally 6 corral, gather, locate, obtain, secure 7 acquire, collect, procure, unearth 8 smoke out 9 ferret out, track down

scarf 4 gulp, wolf 5 ascot, fichu, plaid,

shawl, stole **6** cravat, devour, gobble, inhale **8** babushka, liripipe, mantilla, puggaree **10** lambrequin *Mexican:* **6** rebozo

Scarlet Letter, The *author:* **9** Hawthorne (Nathaniel) *character:* **5** Pearl **6** Hester (Prynne) **10** Dimmesdale (Arthur) **13** Chillingworth (Roger)

Scarlet Pimpernel author 5 Orczy (Baroness Emmuska)

Scarlett's home 4 Tara

scary 6 creepy, spooky **8** chilling **9** frightful

scathe 4 burn, flay, flog, harm, lash, sear **5** roast, slash **6** assail, berate, scorch, thrash **7** blister, scarify, scourge, upbraid **8** lambaste **9** castigate, excoriate

scathing 6 biting, brutal **7** caustic, mordant **8** stinging **9** trenchant

scatter 3 sow **4** cast, part, shed **5** strew **6** divide, spread **7** bestrew, break up, diffuse, disband, diverge **8** disperse, sprinkle **9** broadcast, dissipate **10** besprinkle, distribute **11** disseminate

scatterbrained 5 dizzy, giddy, silly **7** flighty, foolish **8** heedless **9** frivolous

scattering 8 diaspora **10** dispersion

scavenger 5 hyena **6** jackal **7** vulture

scenario 4 plot **6** script **7** outline **8** libretto, synopsis **10** screenplay

scene 3 row, set **4** fuss, site, spot, view **5** arena, field, place, sight, vista **6** locale, milieu, sphere **7** episode, outlook, setting, tableau, tantrum **8** backdrop, locality, location, stage set **9** commotion, landscape, situation **10** background **11** environment **12** stage setting

scenery 3 set **5** decor, props **7** setting **8** stage set **10** properties **11** furnishings **12** stage setting

scent 4 nose, odor **5** aroma, smell, sniff, snuff, whiff **7** bouquet, essence, incense, odorize, perfume **9** aromatize, fragrance, redolence

scepter 4 mace **5** baton, staff **11** sovereignty

schedule 4 list, roll **5** chart, slate, table **6** agenda, docket, record, roster **7** catalog, program, reserve **8** calendar, register, roll call **9** catalogue, timetable

scheme 4 plan, plot, ploy, ruse **5** cabal, order **6** design, device, devise **7** collude, connive, diagram, program, project **8** cogitate, conspire, contrive, game plan, intrigue, proposal, strategy **9** blueprint, expedient, machinate **10** conspiracy **11** arrangement, contrivance, machination

schism 4 rent, rift **5** break, chasm, cleft, split **6** breach, heresy **7** discord, dissent, fissure, rupture **8** cleavage, division, fracture **10** disharmony, dissidence, divergence, falling-out, heterodoxy, separation **11** unorthodoxy **12** estrangement

schlemiel 4 fool **5** chump, klutz **7** bungler

schlep 3 lug, tow **4** drag, haul, hump, plod, pull, slog, tote **5** carry, truck **6** trudge **7** shamble, shuffle **8** straggle

schlock 4 junk, mean **5** cheap, dreck, gaudy, junky, tacky, tatty **6** cheesy, common, kitsch, shoddy, sleazy, tawdry, trashy **8** inferior, low-grade **11** second-class, substandard

schmaltzy 5 mushy, soppy **6** drippy **7** maudlin, mawkish **11** sentimental

schmo 4 dolt, dope, dork, fool, goof, jerk, mutt, simp, twit, yo-yo **5** brute, chump, idiot, moron, ninny, noddy, scamp **6** dimwit, donkey, dumdum, nitwit, noodle, nudnik, rascal **7** dullard, halfwit, jackass, schmuck, schnook **8** bonehead, clodpoll, imbecile, lunkhead, meathead, numskull **9** birdbrain, blockhead, ignoramus, lamebrain, numbskull, thickhead **10** dunderhead, hammerhead, nincompoop **11** chowderhead, chucklehead, knucklehead

schmooze 3 gab, yak **4** chat **6** chat up **8** converse

schnoz 4 beak, nose **6** honker

scholar 4 sage, wonk **5** pupil **6** savant **7** bookman, egghead, student, wise man **8** bookworm, polymath **12** intellectual *Hindu:* **6** pandit, pundit *Muslim:* **5** ulama, ulema

scholarly 7 bookish, erudite, learned **8** academic, educated, studious **10** scholastic **12** intellectual

scholarship 5 award, grant **7** stipend **8** learning **9** education, erudition, knowledge **11** learnedness

scholastic 7 bookish, erudite, learned **8** academic, lettered, literary, pedantic **9** scholarly *life:* **8** academia

school 3 gam, pad **5** shoal, teach, train, tutor **7** academy, borstal, college, educate **8** instruct **9** alma mater, institute **10** discipline, university *French:* **5** école, lycée *grounds:* **6** campus *Jewish:* **5** heder **7** yeshiva *judo:* **4** dojo *organization:* **3** PTA, PTO *religious:* **8** seminary *term:* **7** quarter **8** semester **9** trimester

schoolbook 4 text **6** primer, reader **7** speller

School for Scandal author 8 Sheridan (Richard Brinsley)

schooner 4 ship 5 stoup 6 goblet, seidel 7 tumbler 8 sailboat

Schubert forte 4 lied, song

science *of agriculture:* 8 agronomy *of animals:* 7 zoology *of armorial bearings:* 8 heraldry *of criminal punishment:* 8 penology *of environment:* 7 ecology *of fermentation:* 8 zymology *of health:* 7 hygiene 9 hygienics *of heredity:* 8 genetics *of human behavior:* 10 psychology *of measuring time:* 8 horology 11 chronometry *of motion:* 8 kinetics *of mountains:* 7 orology *of plants:* 6 botany *of projectiles:* 10 ballistics *of the earth:* 7 geology

scientific classification 8 taxonomy

sci-fi writer 3 Lem (Stanislaw) 4 Card (Orson Scott), Dick (Philip K.), Pohl (Frederik) 5 Disch (Thomas M.), Lewis (C. S.), Niven (Larry), Verne (Jules), Wells (H. G.) 6 Aldiss (Brian), Asimov (Isaac), Bester (Alfred), Bishop (Michael), Butler (Octavia), Clarke (Arthur C.), Delany (Samuel), Farmer (Philip José), Gibson (William), Le Guin (Ursula), Leiber (Fritz), Miller (Walter) 7 Ballard (J. G.), Clement (Hal), Ellison (Harlan), Herbert (Frank), Hubbard (L. Ron), Van Vogt (A. E.), Zelazny (Roger) 8 Anderson (Poul), Bradbury (Ray), Heinlein (Robert A.), Sterling (Bruce), Sturgeon (Theodore), Vonnegut (Kurt) 9 Gernsback (Hugo), Kornbluth (C. M.) 10 Silverberg (Robert)

scimitar 5 saber, sabre, sword 7 cutlass

scintilla 3 bit, jot 4 iota, whit 5 grain, spark, speck, trace 8 particle

scintillate 5 flash, gleam, glint, spark 6 glance 7 glimmer, glisten, glitter, shimmer, sparkle, twinkle 9 coruscate

scion 4 heir 5 child, graft, issue 7 progeny 8 offshoot 9 inheritor, offspring, successor 10 descendant

scoff at 4 mock, twit 5 fleer, scorn 6 deride 7 contemn, disdain 8 belittle, pooh-pooh, ridicule

scold 3 rag 4 chew, lash, rail, rant 5 baste, blame, chide, grill, harpy, hound, shrew, vixen 6 berate, grouch, grouse, harass, murmur, mutter, rebuke, revile, virago 7 bawl out, blister, censure, chasten, chew out, grumble, lecture, reprove, tell off, upbraid 8 admonish, execrate, fishwife, lambaste, reproach, Xantippe 9 criticize, dress down, excoriate, objurgate, reprehend, reprimand, termagant, Xanthippe 10 tongue-lash, vituperate

scoop 3 dig, dip 4 bail, beat, lift 5 gouge, ladle, spade 6 dig out, pick up, shovel 8 excavate 9 exclusive

scoot 3 fly, run, zip 4 dash, flee, race, rush, skip 5 hurry, scram, skirr, slide 6 hustle, scurry, sprint 7 scamper 9 skedaddle

scope 4 area, room 5 ambit, gamut, orbit, range, reach, sweep 6 extent, leeway, margin, radius 7 breadth, compass, purview 8 capacity, fullness, latitude 9 amplitude, extension

Scopes trial lawyer 5 Bryan (William Jennings) 6 Darrow (Clarence)

scorch 4 bake, burn, char, flay, sear 5 broil, roast, singe 6 scathe 7 blacken, blister, scarify, scourge, swelter 8 lambaste 9 castigate, excoriate

score 3 cut, tab, win 4 bill, gain, goal, line, mark, nick, slit 5 cleft, count, notch, reach, tally, total 6 attain, furrow, groove, grudge, rack up, record, thrive, twenty 7 account, achieve, invoice, prosper, scratch, succeed 8 flourish 9 reckoning 10 accomplish

scorn 4 gibe, jeer, mock 5 abhor, flout, scoff, spurn, taunt 6 deride 7 contemn, despise, despite, disdain, jeering, mockery 8 contempt, derision, ridicule, scoffing, taunting 9 contumely

Scorpius star 7 Antares

Scotch cocktail 6 Rob Roy 9 Rusty Nail

scoter 7 sea coot, sea duck

Scotland *capital:* 9 Edinburgh *city:* 6 Dundee 7 Glasgow 8 Aberdeen 9 Inverness 11 Dunfermline *firth:* 5 Clyde, Forth, Moray 6 Solway *former capital:* 5 Perth *island, island group:* 4 Iona, Jura, Mull, Skye, Uist 5 Arran, Islay 7 Orkneys 9 Shetlands 8 Hebrides *lake:* 8 Loch Ness 10 Loch Lomond *mountain, range:* 8 Ben Nevis 9 Grampians *patron saint:* 6 Andrew *river:* 3 Dee, Esk

Scott, Sir Walter *novel:* 5 Abbot (The) 6 Rob Roy 7 Ivanhoe 8 Talisman (The), Waverley 9 Woodstock 10 Kenilworth 11 Redgauntlet 12 Old Mortality 14 Quentin Durward *poem:* 7 Marmion 13 Lady of the Lake (The)

____ Scott case 4 Dred

Scottish *cap:* 3 tam 9 glengarry 11 tam-o'-shanter *child:* 5 bairn *dance:* 4 reel 5 fling 10 strathspey *guide:* 6 gillie *hero:* 5 Bruce (Robert) 7 Wallace (William) *hill:* 4 brae *lake:* 4 loch *landowner:* 5 laird *outlaw:* 6 Rob Roy *patron saint:* 6 Andrew *plaid:* 6 tartan *pudding:* 6 haggis *skirt:* 4 kilt *spirit:* 6 kelpie 7 banshee *sword:* 8 claymore *trousers:* 5 trews

scoundrel see SCAMP

scour 4 comb, rake 5 erode, purge,

range, scrub **6** forage, search **7** corrode, eat away, ransack, rummage **8** wear away **9** ferret out

scourge 4 bane, flay, flog, hide, lash, whip, whop **5** curse, flail, slash, whale **6** plague, ravage, scathe, stripe, thrash **7** afflict, blister, despoil, pillage, scarify **8** chastise, lambaste **9** castigate, depredate, desecrate, devastate, excoriate **10** affliction, flagellate, pestilence

Scourge of God 6 Attila

scout 3 spy **6** ranger, survey **7** explore, lookout **8** searcher, watchman **11** investigate, reconnoiter

scouting group 3 BSA, GSA

scow 3 hoy **5** barge **6** garvey **7** lighter

scowl 5 frown, glare, lower **6** glower

scrabble 5 grope **6** scrawl **7** clamber **8** flounder

scraggly 6 ragged, shaggy, uneven **7** unkempt **9** irregular

scraggy 4 bony, lank, lean **5** gaunt, harsh, lanky, rocky, rough **6** jagged, rugged, skinny, uneven **7** angular, scrawny, spindly, unlevel **8** gangling, rawboned, scabrous

scram 5 scoot, split **6** beat it, get out **7** buzz off, get lost, skiddoo, take off, vamoose **8** clear out **9** skedaddle

scramble 4 hash **6** jumble, jungle, muddle, scurry, tumble **7** clamber, clutter, rummage, scuttle, shuffle **8** mishmash, scrabble, straggle **9** confusion

scrambled 7 chaotic, jumbled, mixed-up **8** confused **9** corrupted **10** disordered, disorderly

scrap 3 bit, jot, row **4** chip, dump, fray, junk, spat, tiff, whit **5** brawl, chuck, crumb, fight, melee, piece, set-to, shred, speck **6** bicker, fracas, reject, sliver, tittle **7** brabble, cutting, discard, fall out, quarrel, scuffle, smidgen, wrangle **8** fragment, jettison, leftover, particle, squabble, throw out **9** throw away

scrape 3 fix, jam, rub **4** mess, rasp, spot **5** chafe, fight, grate, graze, pinch, scour, scuff, shave, skimp, spare, stint **6** abrade, pickle, plight, scrimp **7** dilemma, scratch, trouble **8** abrasion, struggle **11** predicament

scrappy 6 feisty **8** brawling **9** combative, truculent **10** pugnacious **11** belligerent, contentious, quarrelsome

scratch 4 claw, rake, rasp **5** grate, score, scrup **6** scotch, scrape, scrawl **7** call off **8** scrabble, scribble

scratchy 5 rough **6** gritty **7** itching, prickly, rasping **8** abrasive, granular, tingling **10** irritating

scrawl 6 doodle **7** scratch **8** scrabble, scribble

scrawny 4 bony, lank, lean **5** gaunt, lanky **6** skinny **7** scraggy **8** rawboned

scream 3 cry **4** yell, yowl **5** shout **6** screak, shriek, shrill, squeal **7** screech

screech 6 screak, scream, shriek, shrill, squeal

screed 5 level, spiel **6** letter, tirade **8** diatribe, harangue, jeremiad **9** discourse, philippic **11** disputation **12** disquisition

screen 4 cull, sift, veil **5** blind, sieve **6** facade, filter, movies, shroud, winnow **7** conceal, obscure, pick out **9** partition **10** camouflage *Japanese:* **5** shoji

screw 9 propeller

screwball 3 nut, wag **4** kook, zany **5** clown, crazy, cutup, flake, flaky, freak, gonzo, joker, kooky, loony, nutty, silly, wacko, wacky **6** madcap, weirdo **7** buffoon, dingbat, farceur **8** crackpot, jokester **9** ding-a-ling, eccentric, fruitcake, whimsical

Screwtape Letters author 5 Lewis (C. S.)

screwy 3 mad **4** daft, nuts **5** batty, crazy, goofy, loony, nutty, wacky **6** absurd, insane **7** bizarre, cracked, lunatic **9** eccentric **10** unbalanced

scribble 5 write **6** scrawl **7** scratch **8** squiggle

scribe 5 clerk, write **6** author, writer **7** copyist **9** scrivener, secretary

scrimmage 4 fray **5** brawl, broil, clash, fight, melee, scrap, set-to **6** battle, fracas, ruckus, rumpus **7** scuffle **8** skirmish **10** donnybrook, free-for-all

scrimp 4 save **5** stint **6** save up, scrape **8** conserve **9** economize

script 4 hand, text **5** write **8** longhand, scenario **10** penmanship, screenplay **11** calligraphy, chirography, handwriting, orchestrate

scrivener 6 notary, scribe, writer **7** copyist

scrooge 5 miser **7** niggard **8** tightwad **9** skinflint **10** cheapskate **12** moneygrubber

scrounge 3 beg, bum, tap **4** grub, hunt, loot **5** cadge, filch, mooch, pinch, steal, swipe, touch **6** forage, hustle, pilfer, snitch, sponge, thieve **7** finagle, solicit, wheedle **8** freeload **9** panhandle

scroungy 5 dirty, seedy **6** grubby, grungy, scurvy, scuzzy, shabby, sleazy, sordid **7** scruffy, squalid, unkempt **8** slovenly **10** slatternly

scrub 3 rub **4** buff, drop, wash **5** abort, brush, scour **6** cancel, mallee, maquis, polish **7** abandon, call off, cleanse, scratch **9** chaparral, eliminate

scrubby 4 drab, mean **5** dingy, dowdy,

runty 6 paltry, ragged, shabby, shoddy
7 rundown, runtish, stunted 8 inferior
9 neglected 10 bedraggled,
broken-down

scruff 4 nape, neck

scruffy 5 mangy, seedy, tacky 6 frowsy,
frowzy, shabby, shaggy 7 run-down,
scrubby, unkempt 8 slovenly, tattered
10 down-at-heel, threadbare

scrumptious 5 tasty, yummy 8 heavenly,
luscious 9 ambrosial, delicious, succulent, toothsome 10 delectable, delightful 13 mouthwatering

scruple 3 bit, jot 4 balk, iota 5 demur,
doubt, grain, qualm, scrap, shred,
worry 7 concern, modicum 8 particle,
question 9 hesitancy 11 compunction

scrupulous 5 exact, fussy 6 honest,
minute, strict 7 careful, heedful,
upright 8 critical, punctual, rigorous
9 honorable 10 fair-minded, fastidious,
meticulous, principled, upstanding
11 painstaking, punctilious 12 con-
scionable 13 conscientious

scrutinize 4 comb, scan 5 audit, probe,
study 6 peruse 7 analyze, canvass, dig
into, dissect, examine, eyeball, inspect
8 look over, pore over 9 check over
11 contemplate, investigate

scrutiny 4 scan 5 audit 6 review, survey
7 perusal 8 analysis 10 inspection
11 examination 12 surveillance

scuba diver 7 frogman 8 aquanaut

scud 3 fly 4 race, rain, rush, sail, skim
5 brume, froth, scoot, speed, spray,
spume 6 clouds, scurry, shower

scuff 6 scrape 7 scratch, shamble, shuffle

scuffle 3 row 4 fray 5 brawl, broil, fight,
scrap, set-to 6 affray, fracas, hubbub,
tussle 7 bobbery, grapple, shamble,
shuffle, wrestle 10 roughhouse

scull 3 oar, row 4 boat 5 shell 6 propel

sculpt 3 hew 5 carve, shape 6 chisel

sculptor *American:* 3 Lin (Maya) 4 Gabo
(Naum), Taft (Lorado) 5 Andre (Carl),
Koons (Jeff), Pratt (Bela), Segal
(George), Serra (Richard), Smith
(David), Story (William) 6 Aitkin
(Robert), Calder (Alexander), French
(Daniel Chester), Powers (Hiram),
Zorach (William) 7 Borglum (Gutzon),
Cornell (Joseph), Noguchi (Isamu)
8 Lachaise (Gaston), Lipchitz
(Jacques), Nadelman (Elie), Nevelson
(Louise) 9 Bourgeois (Louise), Mestro-
vic (Ivan), Oldenburg (Claes), Reming-
ton (Frederic) 12 Saint-Gaudens
(Augustus) *Czech:* 6 Stursa (Jan) *Dan-
ish:* 11 Thorvaldsen (Bertel), Thorwald-
sen (Bertel) *Dutch:* 6 Sluter (Claus) *Eng-
lish:* 5 Moore (Henry), Watts (George)

7 Epstein (Jacob), Flaxman (John)
8 Hepworth (Barbara) *French:* 3 Arp
(Hans, Jean) 4 Bloc (André) 5 Rodin
(Auguste) 6 Dubois (Paul), Houdon
(Jean-Antoine) 7 Maillol (Aristide),
Pevsner (Antoine) 9 Bartholdi
(Frédéric-Auguste), Roubillac (Louis-
François) *Greek:* 5 Myron 7 Phidias
8 Pheidias 10 Polyclitus, Praxiteles
11 Polycleitus *Italian:* 5 Leoni (Leone),
Salvi (Niccolò, Nicola) 6 Canova
(Antonio), Pisano (Andrea, Nino),
Robbia (Andrea, Giovanni, Girolamo,
Luca della) 7 Bernini (Gian Lorenzo),
Cellini (Benvenuto), da Vinci (Leonar-
do), Orcagna, Quercia (Jacopo della)
8 Ghiberti (Lorenzo), Leonardo (da
Vinci), Vittoria (Alessandro) 9 Donatello, Sansovino (Jacopo) 10 Verrocchio
(Andrea del) 12 Michelangelo (Buonar-
roti) *Rhodian:* 9 Polydorus *Romanian:*
8 Brancusi (Constantin) *Russian:* 7 Zad-
kine (Ossip) *Swedish:* 6 Milles (Carl)
9 Oldenburg (Claes) *Swiss:* 10 Gia-
cometti (Alberto)

scum 5 algae, dregs, dross 6 refuse, vermin 8 riffraff

scummy 3 low 4 base, mean, vile 5 dirty,
mucky, slimy 6 grubby, odious, sleazy,
sordid 7 squalid 10 despicable 12 contemptible

scurrilous 4 foul 5 dirty, gross, nasty
6 coarse, filthy, vulgar 7 abusive,
obscene, profane 8 indecent 9 insulting,
offensive 10 outrageous 11 opprobrious
12 contumelious, vituperative

scurry 3 run 4 dart, dash 5 scoot, shoot
6 bustle 7 scamper, scuffle, scuttle

scurvy see SCUMMY

scut 4 tail

scuttlebutt 4 buzz, talk 5 rumor 6 gossip,
report 7 chatter, hearsay 9 grapevine

Scylla 4 rock *counterpart:* 9 Charybdis
father: 5 Nisus *lover:* 5 Minos

scythe handle 5 snath 6 snathe

sea 4 blue, deep, main 5 brine, drink,
ocean *Antarctica:* 4 Ross 5 Davis 7 Weddell 8 Amundsen *Arctic:* 4 Kara
7 Chukchi 8 Beaufort, Karskoye
9 Chuckchee, Norwegian 11 Chukot-
skoye 12 East Siberian *Asia-Europe:*
5 Black *Asia Minor:* 7 Icarian *Atlantic:*
5 North 7 Weddell 9 Caribbean *Aus-
tralia-Indonesia:* 7 Arafura *Balkan Penin-
sula-Italy:* 8 Adriatic *Bay of Bengal:*
7 Andaman *China-Korea:* 5 Huang,
Hwang 6 Yellow *combining form:* 3 mer
4 mari 5 pelag 6 pelago 7 thalass 8 tha-
lasso *Corsica-Italy:* 10 Tyrrhenian *Den-
mark-Norway:* 9 Skagerrak *Denmark-
Sweden:* 8 Kattegat *England-Ireland:*

5 Irish *Fiji:* 4 Koro *France-Italy:* 8 Ligurian *Greece:* 5 Crete *Greece-Italy:* 6 Ionian *Greece-Turkey:* 6 Aegean 8 Thracian *Honshu:* 6 Sagami *Indian Ocean:* 5 Timor 7 Arabian *Indonesia:* 4 Bali 6 Flores *inland:* 3 Red 4 Aral 7 Caspian *Japan:* 3 Suo 6 Inland *Malay Archipelago:* 5 Banda *Mexico:* 6 Cortés *Netherlands:* 6 Wadden *North Atlantic:* 8 Sargasso *Northern Europe:* 6 Baltic, Ostsee 8 Suevicum *North Pacific:* 6 Bering *off Scotland:* 8 Hebrides *off Sweden:* 5 Aland *Pacific:* 4 Java 5 China, Coral 6 Maluku 7 Celebes, Eastern, Molucca, Solomon 9 East China 10 South China *Philippine:* 4 Sulu *Russia:* 5 White 7 Okhotsk *Russia-Ukraine:* 4 Azov *South Pacific:* 4 Ross 6 Tasman 8 Amundsen *Turkey:* 7 Marmara 9 Propontis *West Pacific:* 5 Ceram, Japan 8 Bismarck 10 Philippine

sea anemone 5 polyp

seabird see BIRD *aquatic*

seacoast 5 beach, coast, shore 6 strand 8 littoral 9 shoreline

sea cucumber 7 trepang 11 holothurian

sea dog see SAILOR

sea duck 5 eider, scaup 6 scoter 9 merganser

sea eagle 4 erne 6 osprey 8 fish hawk

seafarer 3 tar 4 salt 6 sailor 7 jack-tar, mariner

seafood dish 4 clam, crab 5 clams, squid 6 mussel, oyster, shrimp 7 lobster, mussels, oysters, scallop 8 calamari, scallops

seagoing 8 maritime, nautical

seal 5 sigil, stamp 6 cachet, signet 7 sticker *female:* 3 cow *herd:* 3 pod 5 patch *young:* 3 pup

sealant 4 lute 5 caulk, grout 6 luting, mastic 8 caulking

sea lily 7 crinoid

seam 4 bond 5 joint, union 8 coupling, juncture 10 connection

seaman see SAILOR

sea monster 3 Orc 6 kraken 9 leviathan

seamount 5 guyot

seamy 5 dirty, rough, seedy 6 sordid 7 squalid 12 disreputable

séance 7 meeting, session, sitting *holder:* 6 medium

seaport *Alaska:* 6 Juneau 9 Anchorage *Albania:* 5 Vlorë 6 Durres, Valona *Algeria:* 4 Bône, Oran 6 Annaba *Angola:* 6 Lobito, Luanda 7 Cabinda 8 Benguela *Argentina:* 11 Buenos Aires, Mar del Plata *Australia:* 4 Eden 5 Bowen, Perth 6 Darwin, Hobart, Sydney 8 Brisbane 9 Melbourne 10 Wollongong *Azores:* 5 Horta *Balearic:* 5 Ibiza *Belgium:* 6 Ostend 7 Antwerp *Benin:* 7 Cotonou

9 Porto-Novo *Black Sea:* 5 Varna 6 Burgas, Odessa 9 Constanta *Brazil:* 3 Rio 4 Pará 5 Bahia, Belém, Natal 6 Recife, Santos 7 Vitoria 8 Salvador 9 Fortaleza 10 Pernambuco 11 Pôrto Alegre, São Salvador 12 Rio de Janeiro *Bulgaria:* 5 Varna 6 Burgas *Cameroon:* 6 Douala *Canaries:* 8 Arrecife 9 Las Palmas *Chile:* 5 Arica 8 Coquimbo 10 Valparaíso *China:* 4 Amoy 6 Dalian, Fuzhou, Lüshun, Xiamen 7 Foochow, Hsia-men, Qingdao, Tianjin 8 Shanghai, Tientsin, Tsingtao 9 Guangzhou, Zhenjiang 10 Chen-chiang, Port Arthur *Colombia:* 6 Lorica 9 Cartagena 12 Barranquilla *Corsica:* 5 Calvi 7 Ajaccio *Costa Rica:* 5 Limón 10 Puntarenas *Crimean:* 5 Kerch, Yalta 10 Sebastopol, Sevastopol *Croatia:* 5 Rieka, Split 6 Rijeka 9 Dubrovnik *Cuba:* 6 Havana 8 Matanzas, Santiago *Cyprus:* 9 Famagusta *Denmark:* 5 Arhus 6 Aarhus, Alborg 7 Aalborg 8 Elsinore 10 Copenhagen *Ecuador:* 9 Guayaquil *Egypt:* 4 Said 10 Alexandria *England:* 4 Hull 5 Dover 9 Liverpool 10 Portsmouth 11 Southampton *Equatorial Guinea:* 4 Bata *Eritrea:* 4 Aseb *Estonia:* 5 Pärnu 7 Tallinn *Finland:* 3 Abo 4 Kemi, Oulu, Pori, Vasa 5 Hango, Kotka, Rauma, Turku, Vaasa 6 Vyborg *Florida:* 5 Miami, Tampa 9 Pensacola 12 Apalachicola, Jacksonville *France:* 4 Nice 5 Brest, Havre 6 Calais, Cannes, Toulon 7 Dunkirk, Le Havre 8 Bordeaux, Boulogne 9 Cherbourg, Dunkerque, Marseille 10 Marseilles *French Polynesia:* 7 Papeete *Georgia:* 8 Savannah 9 Brunswick *Georgia, Republic of:* 4 Pot'i *Germany:* 4 Kiel 5 Emden 6 Bremen, Lübeck, Wismar 7 Hamburg, Rostock 8 Cuxhaven 11 Bremerhaven *Ghana:* 4 Tema 5 Accra *Greece:* 5 Pylos, Syros, Volos 7 Piraeus *Guatemala:* 7 San José 10 Livingston *Haiti:* 5 Cayes 10 Cap Haitien *Honduras:* 7 La Ceiba 8 Trujillo *India:* 3 Goa 4 Puri 5 Marud 6 Bombay, Madras, Mumbai, Old Goa 7 Calicut, Chennai 8 Calcutta 9 Jagannath 10 Trivandrum *Iran:* 4 Jask 7 Bushehr *Iraq:* 5 Basra *Ireland:* 4 Cork 5 Sligo 6 Dingle, Dublin, Galway, Tralee 8 Drogheda, Limerick 9 Waterford 10 Balbriggan *Israel:* 4 Acre, Akko, Elat, Yafo 5 Accho, Eilat, Haifa, Jaffa, Joppa 6 Ashdod 8 Ashqelon *Italy:* 4 Bari 5 Anzio, Gaeta, Genoa 6 Naples, Pesaro, Rimini, Venice 7 Leghorn, Livorno, Marsala, Messina, Rapallo, Salerno, Taranto, Trieste 8 Brindisi, Sorrento, Syracuse *Ivory Coast:* 5 Tabou

7 Abidjan *Jamaica:* 8 Kingston 10 Montego Bay *Japan:* 4 Kobe 5 Kochi, Osaka, Rumoi, Ujina, Uraga 6 Sasebo 7 Fukuoka 8 Nagasaki, Yokohama 9 Hiroshima *Java:* 5 Tegal, Tuban 7 Cilacap, Jakarta 8 Semarang, Surabaya *Jordan:* 5 Aqaba, Elath 6 Aelana *Latvia:* 4 Riga *Lebanon:* 4 Tyre 5 Saida, Sidon 6 Beirut 7 Tripoli *Libya:* 6 Tobruk 7 Tripoli 8 Benghazi *Lithuania:* 5 Memel 8 Klaipeda *Madagascar:* 8 Tamatave *Maine:* 7 Belfast 8 Portland *Malaysia:* 4 Miri, Weld 5 Pekan 6 Melaka, Pinang 7 Malacca 10 George Town *Massachusetts:* 6 Boston 9 Fall River 10 New Bedford *Mauritius:* 9 Port Louis *Mediterranean:* 4 Gaza, Oran 5 Genoa, Haifa, Jaffa 6 Beirut, Naples, Venice 7 Algiers, Bizerte, Catania, Palermo, Piraeus, Tripoli 8 Benghazi, Port Said 9 Barcelona, Marseille 10 Alexandria, Marseilles *Mexico:* 7 Tampico 8 Acapulco, Mazatlán, Veracruz *Minorca:* 5 Mahón *Moluccas:* 5 Ambon *Montenegro:* 5 Kotor *Morocco:* 4 Safi, Salé 5 Ceuta 6 Agadir 7 Tangier, Tétouan 10 Casablanca *Mozambique:* 5 Beira, Pemba 6 Amelia, Maputo, Xai Xai 11 Porto Amelia *New Hampshire:* 10 Portsmouth *New Zealand:* 8 Auckland 10 Wellington *Nicaragua:* 5 Brito *Nigeria:* 5 Lagos 8 Harcourt *Niger mouth:* 5 Bonny *North Korea:* 4 Yuki 5 Nampo, Unggi 6 Wonsan *Norway:* 4 Bodo, Moss 5 Vadso 6 Bergen, Tromso 9 Stavanger, Trondheim 11 Fredrikstad *Oman:* 6 Masqat, Muscat *Pakistan:* 5 Pasni 6 Gwadar 7 Karachi *Papua New Guinea:* 3 Lea *Peru:* 3 Ilo 4 Eten 5 Paita, Pisco 6 Callao *Philippines:* 4 Cebu 5 Davao, Laoag 6 Aparri, Cavite, Iloilo, Manila 7 Legaspi 8 Tacloban 9 Zamboanga *Poland:* 6 Danzig, Gdansk, Gdynia 7 Stettin 8 Szczecin *Portugal:* 4 Faro 5 Porto 6 Oporto 7 Funchal *Puerto Rico:* 5 Ponce 7 Arecibo, San Juan 8 Mayagüez *Russia:* 6 Vyborg 8 Murmansk 11 Kaliningrad, Vladivostok *Ryukyu:* 4 Naha, Nawa *Sakhalin Island:* 8 Korsakov *Saudi Arabia:* 5 Jedda, Jidda, Yanbu, Yenbo 6 Jeddah, Jiddah *Scotland:* 3 Ayr 5 Leith, Leven 6 Dundee 7 Glasgow 8 Aberdeen *Sicily:* 7 Catania, Marsala, Messina, Palermo 8 Syracuse *Slovenia:* 5 Kopar, Koper, Piran *Somalia:* 7 Berbera 9 Mogadishu *South Africa:* 5 Natal 6 Durban 8 Cape Town *South Carolina:* 8 Savannah 10 Charleston *South Korea:* 5 Masan, Mokpo, Pusan 6 Inchon 7 Incheon, Masampo *Spain:* 5 Cádiz, Gijón 6 Abdera, Málaga 8 Alicante 9 Algeciras, Barcelona, Cartagena, Las Palmas *Sri Lanka:* 7 Colombo 10 Batticaloa *Sumatra:* 5 Medan 6 Padang 9 Banda Aceh *Sweden:* 4 Umea 5 Gavle, Lulea, Malmö, Pitea, Ystad 8 Göteborg 9 Stockholm 10 Gothenburg 11 Helsingborg *Tanzania:* 5 Lindi, Tanga 8 Zanzibar 11 Dar es Salaam *Thailand:* 4 Trat 8 Bang Phra *Tunisia:* 4 Sfax 5 Gabès 6 Sousse 7 Bizerta, Bizerte *Turkey:* 4 Rize 5 Izmir, Sinop 6 Samsun, Smyrna 7 Antalya 8 Istanbul *Ukraine:* 5 Kerch, Yalta 6 Odessa 7 Kherson *Vanuatu:* 4 Vila 8 Port-Vila *Vietnam:* 3 Hue 6 Da Nang 7 Tourane 8 Haiphong, Nha Trang *Virginia:* 7 Norfolk 10 Portsmouth *Yemen:* 4 Aden 5 Mocha

seaport capital 4 Aden, Apia, Dili, Lomé, Suva 5 Accra, Adana, Dakar, Lagos 6 Banjul, Belize, Bissau, Dublin, Havana, Kuwait, Lisbon, Maputo, Masqat, Muscat, Roseau 7 Algiers, Batavia, Colombo, Jakarta, Moresby, San Juan 8 Castries, Djakarta, Freetown, Hamilton, Helsinki, Honolulu, Kingston, Monrovia, Valletta 9 Mogadishu, Nuku'alofa, Porto-Novo, Reykjavík, Singapore 10 Bridgetown, Daressalem, Libreville, Mogadiscio, Paramaribo 11 Dar es Salaam, Port of Spain 12 Port-au-Prince

sear 3 dry 5 parch, singe 6 burn up, scorch, sizzle 7 shrivel 9 cauterize, dehydrate, desiccate

search 4 beat, comb, grub, hunt, scan, seek 5 chase, check, delve, frisk, grope, quest, rifle, scour 6 ferret, forage 7 fossick, hunting, manhunt, pursuit, ransack, rummage, run down 8 finecomb, scavenge, scout out 9 cast about, ferret out 10 scrutinize

searing 3 hot 5 harsh 6 severe 7 blazing, burning, intense 8 scathing 9 agonizing, scorching 10 blistering 12 excruciating

sea robber 5 rover 6 pirate 7 corsair 8 picaroon 9 buccaneer 10 freebooter

seasickness 6 nausea 8 mal de mer

season 3 fit 4 fall, term, time 5 spice, train, treat 6 autumn, harden, pepper, period, school, spring, summer, winter 7 prepare, toughen 8 marinade, marinate 9 acclimate 10 case-harden, discipline 11 acclimatize

seasonable 3 apt 6 timely 7 welcome 9 favorable, opportune, pertinent, well-timed 10 auspicious, convenient, propitious 11 appropriate

seasoned 6 inured, mature, tested, versed 7 adapted, matured, veteran 8 flavored, hardened 9 flavorful, prac-

ticed **10** acclimated, habituated
11 experienced **12** acclimatized, accomplished

seasoning 3 bay **4** dill, herb, mace, sage, salt **5** anise, basil, chili, clove, cumin, spice, thyme **6** cloves, fennel, garlic, ginger, nutmeg, pepper, savory **7** cayenne, chervil, mustard, oregano, paprika, parsley, saffron **8** allspice, cardamom, cinnamon, rosemary, tarragon, turmeric **9** condiment, coriander

seat 3 hub **4** base, beam, duff, rear, rest, rump **5** basis, chair, place, usher **6** behind, bottom, center, settee **7** fulcrum **8** backside, buttocks, derriere **9** fundament, posterior **10** foundation *church:* **3** pew *on a camel or elephant:* **6** howdah *upholstered:* **9** banquette

sea urchin 7 echinus **8** echinoid

seaweed 4 kelp, nori, ulva **5** dulse, fucus, kombu **6** fucoid, wakame **8** sargasso **9** carrageen, Irish moss **12** bladder wrack

Sea Wolf, The *author:* **6** London (Jack) *captain:* **10** Wolf Larsen *ship:* **5** Ghost

Sebastian *brother:* **6** Alonso *sister:* **5** Viola

secco 3 dry **8** painting, staccato

secede 4 quit **5** leave **8** separate, withdraw

seclude 4 hide **6** closet, immure, retire, screen **7** confine, enclose, isolate, shut off **8** cloister, separate, withdraw **9** sequester

secluded 6 hidden, remote **7** private, recluse, shut off **8** hermetic, isolated, screened, solitary **9** concealed, reclusive, withdrawn **10** cloistered, tucked away **11** out-of-the-way, quarantined, sequestered

seclusion 7 privacy **8** solitude **9** isolation **10** separation, withdrawal

second 4 wink **5** flash, jiffy, trice **6** moment **7** endorse, instant, support **9** twinkling

secondary 3 sub **6** lesser **7** derived **8** borrowed, inferior **9** resultant, tributary **10** collateral, derivative, subsequent **11** subordinate, subservient

second-class 6 common **8** déclassé, inferior, low-grade, mediocre

secondhand 4 used, worn **7** derived **8** borrowed **10** derivative

second-string 3 sub **6** backup **9** alternate **10** substitute

secrecy 7 silence, stealth **10** covertness, subterfuge **11** concealment, furtiveness

secret 5 sneak **6** arcane, closet, covert, hidden, occult **7** cryptic, furtive, obscure, sub-rosa **8** abstruse, backdoor, discreet, hermetic, hush-hush, stealthy

9 concealed, recondite **10** classified, restricted, undercover **11** clandestine, out-of-the-way, underhanded **12** confidential, hugger-mugger **13** surreptitious, under-the-table *combining form:* **5** crypt, krypt **6** crypto, krypto

secret agent 3 spy **8** emissary

secretary 4 aide, desk **5** clerk **6** scribe **9** assistant **10** amanuensis, escritoire *king's:* **10** chancellor

secrete 4 bury, emit, hide **5** cache, exude, plant, stash **6** screen **7** conceal, deposit, emanate

secretive 7 furtive **8** reticent, taciturn **10** backstairs, buttoned-up **11** tight-lipped **12** close-mouthed **13** unforthcoming

secretly 7 sub rosa **9** furtively **10** stealthily

secret society 3 KKK **4** tong **5** cabal, Mafia, Triad **6** Mau Mau, Yakuza **7** camorra **9** camarilla, Carbonari **10** Cosa Nostra, Freemasons, Ku Klux Klan

sect 4 cult **5** creed, party **7** faction **8** division, religion **12** denomination

sectarian 5 local **8** splinter **9** dissident, heretical, heterodox, parochial **10** provincial, schismatic, unorthodox **13** nonconformist

sectary 5 rebel **7** heretic **8** adherent, disciple, follower, partisan **9** dissenter, dissident **10** schismatic, separatist **13** nonconformist, revolutionary

section 3 cut **4** area, belt, part, zone **5** chunk, piece, slice, tract **6** member, moiety, parcel, region, sector, sphere **7** portion, quarter, segment **8** district, division, locality, precinct **11** subdivision

sector 4 area, zone **7** quarter, section **8** district, precinct **11** subdivision

secular 3 lay **7** earthly, profane, worldly **8** temporal, unsacred **11** nonclerical, terrestrial **12** nonreligious

secure 3 fix **4** bind, fast, firm, gain, land, lock, moor, nail, safe **5** catch, cinch, clamp, cover, fixed, guard, solid, sound, tried **6** anchor, assure, cement, clinch, defend, effect, ensure, fasten, insure, obtain, shield, stable **7** acquire, assured, capture, procure, protect, tie down **8** reliable, sanguine **9** confident, safeguard **10** batten down, bring about **11** established, impregnable

security 4 bail, bond, pawn **5** guard, token **6** pledge, safety, shield, surety **7** defense, earnest, warrant **8** guaranty, immunity, warranty **9** assurance, guarantee, safeguard, soundness, stability

10 collateral, protection, steadiness
13 certification

sedate 4 calm **5** grave, sober, staid
6 placid, proper, seemly, serene, steady
7 earnest, serious **8** composed, decorous, tranquil **9** collected, dignified, unruffled **10** sobersided **13** dispassionate, imperturbable

sedative 4 balm **6** downer, Valium
7 calmant, Librium, Miltown, Seconal
8 barbital, hyoscine, Nembutal **9** calmative **10** depressant **11** barbiturate
12 sleeping pill, tranquilizer

sedentary 4 lazy **6** seated **7** settled, sitting **8** inactive **10** stationary

sediment 4 lees, silt **5** dregs, dross **7** bottoms, deposit, grounds, heeltap, residue
8 residuum **9** settlings **11** precipitate
layer: **5** varve

sedition 4 coup **6** mutiny, putsch, revolt,
strike **7** protest, treason **8** intrigue,
uprising **9** coup d'état, rebellion **10** revolution **12** insurrection

seditious 8 disloyal, factious, mutinous
9 dissident, insurgent **10** rebellious,
traitorous **11** treacherous

seduce 4 bait, coax, lure **5** decoy, tempt
6 allure, betray, delude, entice, entrap,
lead on, ravish **7** corrupt, debauch,
deceive **8** entrance, inveigle

seducer 4 roué, vamp **7** Don Juan, playboy **8** lothario **9** libertine

seduction 4 lure **8** conquest **9** siren song
10 allurement, attraction, ravishment,
temptation

seductive 5 siren **8** alluring, magnetic,
tempting **9** beguiling **10** attractive,
bewitching, enchanting **11** captivating

seductress 5 siren **7** Lorelei **9** temptress
11 femme fatale

sedulous 8 diligent, tireless **9** assiduous,
laborious **10** persistent **11** industrious,
persevering, unremitting

see 4 call, date, espy, gape, gaze, look,
mark, peer, scan, view **5** grasp, sight,
visit, watch **6** behold, come by, descry,
divine, drop by, drop in, go with, look
in, notice, stop by, stop in, take in
7 discern, examine, find out, glimpse,
imagine, make out, observe, realize
8 conceive, consider, envisage, envision, perceive **9** apprehend, ascertain,
determine, recognize, visualize **10** comprehend, scrutinize, understand

seed 3 sow **4** core, germ **5** brood, grain,
issue, ovule, plant, spark, spawn
6 embryo, kernel, notion **7** concept,
nucleus, progeny **8** children **9** offspring
11 descendants *aromatic:* **6** fennel *coating:* **5** testa **6** testae (plural) *covering:*
4 aril *of a bean:* **7** haricot *of a vine:*

6 peanut *poisonous:* **10** castor bean *vessel:* **3** pod **5** fruit, pyxis **7** silicle, silique

seedcase 3 pod

seedy 5 dingy, faded, mangy, ratty, tired
6 droopy, frowsy, frowzy, shabby, used
up, wilted **7** run-down, scruffy, squalid,
unkempt, wilting **8** decaying, decrepit,
drooping, flagging, inferior, slovenly,
tattered **9** neglected, overgrown
10 bedraggled, down-at-heel, threadbare **12** disreputable

seek 3 try **4** fish, hunt, root **5** assay,
delve, essay, offer, quest, sniff **6** pursue,
strive **7** attempt, inquire, look for,
request **8** endeavor, smell out **9** search
for, search out, undertake

seem 3 act **4** look **5** imply **6** appear,
behave **7** suggest **8** resemble

seemly 3 fit **6** decent, proper, suited
7 apropos, correct, fitting **8** becoming,
decorous, suitable **9** befitting, congenial, congruous **10** compatible, conforming **11** appropriate, comme il faut

seep 4 drip, leak, ooze, weep **5** bleed,
exude, leech, sweat **6** filter, strain **7** diffuse, dribble, trickle **8** transude **9** percolate

seer 5 augur, sibyl **6** oracle **7** diviner,
prophet **8** foreseer, haruspex **9** predictor **10** forecaster, foreteller, soothsayer
11 clairvoyant, Nostradamus

seesaw 3 yaw **4** rock, veer **5** lurch,
pitch, swing **6** teeter **7** bascule **8** flipflop **9** alternate, fluctuate, oscillate
11 teeterboard

seethe 3 sop **4** boil, burn, foam, fret,
fume, rage, soak, stew **5** churn, erupt,
froth, souse, steam, steep **6** bubble,
drench, simmer, sizzle **7** bristle, ferment, parboil, smolder **8** saturate,
smoulder, waterlog

see-through 5 clear **6** limpid **8** pellucid
11 translucent, transparent

segment 3 cut **4** part **5** piece **6** divide,
member, moiety **7** portion, section
8 division, separate **10** categorize

sego 4 lily

segregate 6 enisle, select **7** isolate **8** separate **9** sequester **10** disconnect

segregation 9 apartheid, isolation **10** jim
crowism, separatism **13** ghettoization

segue 7 proceed **8** continue **10** transition
11 progression

seidel 5 stoup **8** schooner

seine 3 net **5** trawl

Seine tributary 4 Oise **5** Marne, Yonne

seismologist 7 Richter (Charles)

seize 3 bag, nab **4** grab, take **5** annex,
catch, clasp, grasp, usurp **6** abduct,
arrest, clinch, clutch, kidnap, occupy,
secure, snatch **7** capture, grapple,

impound 8 arrogate, carry off 9 apprehend, sequester 10 commandeer, confiscate 11 appropriate, expropriate

seizure 3 fit 4 turn 5 spasm, spell, throe 6 access, attack, taking 7 capture 8 paroxysm, takeover 9 breakdown 10 annexation, convulsion, usurpation 12 confiscation

seldom 6 hardly, rarely 8 scarcely 10 hardly ever 12 infrequently, occasionally, sporadically

select 4 best, cull, fine, pick, rare 5 cream, elite, prime 6 choice, choose, chosen, culled, opt for, picked 7 favored, pick out 8 screened, superior 9 exclusive, exquisite, preferred, recherché, single out

selection 6 choice 7 culling, excerpt, picking 8 choosing 10 assortment, preference

selective 5 fussy, picky 6 choosy 7 choosey, finicky 8 specific 10 discerning, particular, scrupulous 11 persnickety

Selene 4 Luna 6 Hecate 7 Artemis *beloved:* 8 Endymion *brother:* 6 Helios *father:* 8 Hyperion *mother:* 4 Thea

self 3 ego *combining form:* 3 aut 4 auto

self-absorbed 4 smug 8 egoistic 9 conceited, egotistic 10 complacent, egocentric 11 egotistical, introverted 12 narcissistic 13 inner-directed

self-acting 9 automatic

self-assertive 4 bold 5 brash, pushy 6 cheeky 7 forward 8 cocksure, militant 9 audacious, obtrusive, officious 10 aggressive 11 impertinent, overweening 12 presumptuous

self-assurance 5 poise 6 aplomb 8 coolness 9 composure, sangfroid 10 confidence, equanimity 13 collectedness

self-assured 4 smug 6 poised 8 sanguine 9 confident

self-centered 9 conceited, egotistic 10 egocentric 11 egotistical 12 narcissistic

self-composed 4 calm 6 poised, serene 7 assured 9 collected, confident, possessed 10 controlled

self-confidence 5 poise 6 aplomb 9 assurance

self-confident 5 cocky 6 jaunty, poised 7 assured 8 sanguine

self-conscious 4 prim 5 stiff 6 formal, uneasy 7 awkward, stilted, studied 8 affected, mannered 9 contrived, ill at ease 10 artificial

self-contained 6 closed, formal 7 built-in 8 composed, enclosed, reserved, reticent 9 exclusive 10 restrained 11 independent

self-control 7 balance, dignity, reserve 9 restraint, stability, willpower 10 abstinence, constraint, discipline, temperance 11 forbearance

self-defense art 4 judo 6 aikido, karate, kung fu 7 jujitsu 9 tai kwan do

self-destruction 7 suicide 8 felo-de-se, hara-kiri

self-discipline 4 will 8 stoicism 9 willpower 10 abstinence

self-educated 12 autodidactic

self-effacing 3 shy 5 timid 6 modest 7 bashful 8 retiring, sheepish 9 diffident, unassured 11 unassertive

self-esteem 5 pride 6 vanity 7 conceit, dignity, egotism 10 narcissism 11 amour propre

self-evident 5 clear, plain 6 patent 7 obvious 8 manifest, palpable 10 prima facie, undeniable 12 demonstrable, unmistakable

self-explanatory 5 clear, plain 7 evident, obvious 8 manifest 11 perspicuous, transparent

self-governing 7 popular 9 sovereign 10 autonomous, democratic

self-importance 3 ego 5 pride 6 egoism, hubris 7 conceit, egotism 9 arrogance, pomposity, vainglory

self-important 4 smug, vain 6 lordly 7 bloated, haughty, pompous 8 arrogant 9 conceited, egotistic 10 pontifical 11 magisterial, pretentious

self-indulgent 9 libertine, sybaritic 10 hedonistic

self-interest 6 egoism

selfish 6 stingy 8 egoistic 9 egotistic 10 egocentric, ungenerous 11 egomaniacal 12 self-centered 13 self-indulgent

selfless 8 generous 10 altruistic, benevolent, charitable

self-love 6 egoism, vanity 7 conceit, egotism 8 vainness 9 vainglory 10 narcissism 11 amour propre 13 conceitedness

self-possessed 4 calm 6 poised, serene 7 equable 8 composed, sanguine 9 collected, unruffled 11 unflappable 13 imperturbable

self-proclaimed 8 so-called 9 soi-disant 10 self-styled

Self-Reliance author 7 Emerson (Ralph Waldo)

self-respect 5 pride 7 dignity 11 amour propre

self-restraint 8 chastity, sobriety 9 willpower 10 abnegation, abstention, abstinence, continence, discipline 11 forbearance

self-righteous 5 pious 7 canting, preachy 8 unctuous 9 pharisaic 10 complacent, goody-goody 11 pharisaical 12 hypocritical, pecksniffian 13 sanctimonious

self-sacrificing 8 generous, selfless 9 unselfish

self-satisfied 4 smug 8 priggish 10 complacent

self-seeking 6 greedy 7 selfish 8 egoistic 9 egotistic 10 egocentric 11 egotistical

self-serving see SELF-SEEKING

self-starter 7 hustler 8 go-getter

self-styled 7 nominal, would-be 8 socalled 9 soi-disant

self-taught 12 autodidactic

sell 4 hawk, vend 5 trade 6 barter, deal in, hustle, market, peddle, retail, unload 7 auction 8 exchange

sell out 4 dump, move 6 betray, turn in, unload 7 deceive 8 inform on 11 double-cross

selvage, selvedge 3 hem 4 edge 6 border

semblance 3 air 4 face, look, mask, pose, show, veil 5 front, guise, image 6 aspect, facade, simile, veneer 7 analogy, feeling, modicum 8 affinity, disguise, likeness, pretense 10 apparition, appearance, comparison, false front, masquerade, similarity, similitude, simulacrum 11 countenance

Semele *father:* 6 Cadmus *mother:* 8 Harmonia *sister:* 3 Ino 5 Agave 7 Autonoë *son:* 7 Bacchus 8 Dionysus

semi 3 rig 4 demi, half, hemi 5 truck 6 partly

seminar 5 forum 8 colloquy 10 colloquium, conference, roundtable

Seminole *chief* 7 Osceola

Semiramis *husband:* 5 Ninus *kingdom:* 7 Babylon

Semite 3 Jew 4 Arab 6 Hebrew 7 Moabite 8 Akkadian, Assyrian 9 Canaanite 10 Babylonian, Phoenician

Senapo *daughter:* 8 Clorinda *kingdom:* 8 Ethiopia

senate 7 chamber, council 8 assembly 11 legislature

senator 5 solon 8 lawmaker 10 legislator

send 4 mail, post, ship 5 relay, remit, route 6 commit, export, launch 7 address, advance, airmail, consign, forward, traject 8 dispatch, transmit *back:* 6 remand

Sendak *book* 17 In the Night Kitchen 21 Where the Wild Things Are

send in 6 submit

send-up 5 roast, spoof 6 parody, satire 7 lampoon, takeoff 9 burlesque 10 caricature, pasquinade

Senegal *capital:* 5 Dakar *enclave:* 6 Gambia *ethnic group:* 5 Wolof 6 Fulani 7 Malinke *language:* 6 French *monetary unit:* 5 franc *neighbor:* 4 Mali 6 Guinea

10 Mauritania 12 Guinea-Bissau *river:* 6 Gambia 7 Senegal

senescence 6 old age 8 caducity 11 elderliness, senectitude

senior 5 doyen, elder, older, prior 7 ancient, doyenne, oldster 8 higher-up, old-timer, superior 10 golden-ager

Sennacherib *domain:* 7 Assyria *father:* 6 Sargon *kingdom:* 7 Assyria *slayer, son:* 8 Sharezer 11 Adrammelech

sensation 4 bomb 6 marvel, tingle, wonder 7 feeling, miracle, prodigy, stunner 8 response 9 bombshell 10 impression, perception, phenomenon 13 consciousness

sensational 3 hot 5 boffo, juicy, lurid 6 purple, vulgar 7 tabloid 8 dramatic, exciting, fabulous, glorious, slambang, smashing, stunning 9 hunky-dory, marvelous, thrilling 10 astounding, impressive, incredible, remarkable, scandalous 11 astonishing, extravagant, outstanding, spectacular 12 electrifying

sense 3 wit 4 feel 5 sight, smell, taste, touch 6 divine, intuit, pick up 7 believe, discern, feeling, hearing, meaning, message, realize 8 consider, judgment, perceive, prudence 9 awareness, foresight, intuition 10 anticipate, cognizance, discretion, perception 12 intelligence, significance 13 comprehension, consciousness, understanding *sixth:* 3 ESP

Sense and Sensibility *author* 6 Austen (Jane)

senseless 4 cold, numb 5 silly 6 absurd, numbed, simple, stupid 7 fatuous, foolish, idiotic, moronic, trivial, witless 8 benumbed, comatose, deadened, mindless 9 brainless, pointless 10 irrational 11 meaningless, purposeless, unconscious

senselessness 5 folly 7 inanity 8 insanity 9 absurdity, stupidity 12 illogicality

sense organ 3 ear, eye 4 nose, skin 6 tongue 8 receptor

sensibility 5 taste 7 emotion, feeling, insight 8 judgment, keenness 9 affection, awareness, sensation 11 discernment, penetration 12 appreciation

sensible 4 sage, sane, wise 5 solid, sound 6 astute, shrewd 7 logical, prudent, sapient 8 rational 9 judicious, objective, sagacious 10 reasonable

sensitive 4 keen, sore 5 aware, prone 6 liable, tender, touchy, tricky 7 feeling, nervous 8 delicate, sensible, sentient, ticklish 9 emotional 10 high-strung, perceptive, precarious, responsive 11 susceptible 13 understanding

sensitive plant 6 mimosa *family:* 3 pea

sensual 4 lush 6 animal, carnal, earthy 7 fleshly, mundane, worldly 8 temporal 9 epicurean, luxurious, sybaritic 10 hedonistic, voluptuous 11 irreligious, unspiritual

sensuality 4 lust 6 desire, luxury 7 lechery, license 8 hedonism, lewdness, pleasure 9 carnality, depravity, eroticism, prurience 10 debauchery, degeneracy, immorality, indulgence, perversion, profligacy, sybaritism 11 dissipation 12 incontinence 13 dissoluteness, gratification, salaciousness

sensuous 4 lush 6 carnal 7 fleshly 8 luscious 9 epicurean, luxurious, sybaritic 10 hedonistic, voluptuous 13 self-indulgent

sentence 3 rap 4 damn, doom 5 blame, judge 6 dictum, ordain, punish 7 adjudge, condemn, convict, verdict 8 decision, denounce, judgment, penalize 10 adjudicate, punishment

sententious 5 crisp, pithy, terse 7 concise, piquant, pointed 8 eloquent, pregnant, succinct 10 aphoristic, expressive, meaningful, moralistic, moralizing

sentient 5 alert, aware, savvy 7 knowing 8 sensible 9 attentive, cognizant, conscious, receptive, sensitive 10 conversant, discerning, perceptive, percipient, responsive 12 appreciative

sentiment 4 view 6 belief 7 emotion, feeling, leaning, opinion, passion, posture 8 penchant, position, tendency 9 affection, inclining, sensation 10 conception, conviction, partiality, persuasion, propensity 11 disposition, inclination, sensibility

sentimental 4 soft 5 corny, gooey, gushy, mushy, sappy, soupy, sweet 6 dreamy, drippy, slushy, sticky, sugary, syrupy, tender 7 cloying, gushing, insipid, maudlin, mawkish 8 bathetic, effusive, romantic 9 misty-eyed, nostalgic, schmaltzy 10 idealistic, lovey-dovey, moonstruck, namby-pamby, saccharine, soft-boiled 11 tear-jerking 12 affectionate

sentimentality 4 mush 8 schmaltz

sentinel see SENTRY

sentry 5 guard, watch 6 picket 7 lookout 8 sentinel, watchman

separate 4 comb, only, part, sift, sole, sort 5 apart, sever, split 6 cut off, detach, divide, single, sunder, unique, winnow 7 asunder, disjoin, diverse, divided, divorce, isolate, several, split up, unravel, various 8 alienate, detached, discrete, disjoint, disperse, distinct, insulate, isolated, solitary, splinter, uncouple 9 different, divergent, extricate, segregate, sequester 11 compartment, distinctive, distinguish, independent, unconnected 12 disconnected, discriminate 13 differentiate

separation 3 gap 4 rift 5 break, split 6 schism 7 breakup, divorce, parting, rupture, split-up 8 disunion, disunity, division 9 apartheid, dichotomy, partition 11 disjunction, dissolution, segregation 12 dissociation, estrangement 13 disconnection, sequestration

separatism 9 apartheid 11 segregation

separatist 10 schismatic 12 secessionist

sepia 3 ink 5 brown, umber 6 sienna

sepulchral 4 grim 5 bleak, grave 6 dismal, gloomy, solemn, somber 7 doleful, macabre 8 funereal, ghoulish, mortuary 9 tenebrous

sepulchre 4 tomb 5 grave, vault 9 mausoleum

sequel 3 end 5 close 6 effect, ending, finish, result, upshot 7 closing, outcome 8 epilogue 9 aftermath 10 succession 11 aftereffect, consequence, development, eventuality, progression, termination 12 continuation

sequence 3 row, run, set 4 flow 5 chain, order, train 6 course, series, string 8 disposal, ordering 9 placement 10 procession, succession 11 arrangement, disposition, progression 12 distribution

sequential 6 serial 9 succedent 10 continuous, succeeding, successive 11 consecutive 12 successional 13 chronological

sequester 4 hide, take 5 annex, seize 6 attach, cut off, enisle 7 impound, isolate, preempt, seclude, secrete 8 accroach, arrogate, cloister, close off, insulate, separate, set apart, withdraw 9 segregate 10 commandeer, confiscate, dispossess 11 appropriate, expropriate

sequoia 7 big tree, redwood 12 coast redwood

seraglio 5 harem

serape 5 shawl

seraph 5 angel 8 guardian 9 messenger

seraphic 4 pure 7 angelic, sublime 8 beatific, cherubic, ethereal

Serbia and Montenegro *capital:* 8 Belgrade *city:* 3 Bar 5 Kotar, Tivat 7 Novi Sad, Pancevo 9 Podgorica 11 Pristinauzi *monetary unit:* 4 euro 5 dinar *neighbor:* 6 Bosnia, Kosovo 7 Albania, Croatia, Hungary, Romania 8 Bulgaria 9 Macedonia *part of:* 7 Balkans *peninsula:* 6 Balkan *province:* 9 Vojvodina *province, former:* 6 Kosovo *river:* 4 Sava 6 Danube *sea:* 8 Adriatic

sere 3 dry 5 dried 7 parched, thirsty
8 withered 9 shriveled, unwatered
serenade 7 lullaby 8 shivaree 9 charivari
serene 4 calm 5 quiet, still 6 limpid,
placid, poised, sedate 7 halcyon 8 composed, tranquil 9 unruffled 10 untroubled
serenity 4 calm 5 peace 8 calmness, quietude 9 composure, placidity, stillness
10 equanimity 11 contentment, tranquility 12 peacefulness, tranquillity
serf 4 esne, peon 5 churl, helot, slave
6 thrall 7 bondman, villein *freeborn:*
7 colonus
serial 10 sequential, successive 11 consecutive, installment
series 3 row, run, set 4 list, tier 5 chain,
range, scale, train 6 catena, column,
parade, sequel, string 8 sequence 9 cavalcade, gradation 10 procession, succession 11 progression 12 continuation
serious 4 grim, hard 5 grave, heavy,
major, sober, staid, stern, tough
6 intent, sedate, severe, solemn,
somber, sombre, steady 7 austere,
earnest, intense, pensive, sincere,
unfunny, weighty 8 funereal, menacing,
resolute, sobering 9 difficult, humor-
less, important, laborious, strenuous,
unamusing 10 determined, formidable,
meditative, no-nonsense, poker-faced,
purposeful, reflective, sobersided,
thoughtful, unhumorous 11 significant,
threatening 12 businesslike 13 contemplative
sermon 6 homily, speech, tirade
7 address, lecture, oration 8 harangue
9 preaching 10 preachment 11 exhortation
sermonize 5 orate 6 dilate, exhort,
preach 7 dissert, lecture 8 moralize
9 discourse, expatiate, preachify 10 dissertate, evangelize 11 pontificate
serpent 5 fiend, Satan, snake *fabled:*
8 basilisk *mythical:* 10 cockatrice *sound:*
4 hiss
serpentine 4 rock, wily 5 snaky 7 cunning, devious, mineral, sinuous, winding 8 flexuous, tempting, tortuous
9 snakelike 10 circuitous, convoluted,
meandering
serrated 7 notched, toothed 8 saw-
edged, sawtooth 10 saw-toothed 11 denticulate
servant 4 maid, peon 5 slave, valet
6 butler, flunky, helper, lackey, menial
7 famulus, footman 8 domestic, hand-
maid, hireling, houseboy 9 attendant
11 chamberlain, chambermaid *India:*
4 syce *kitchen:* 8 scullion *Wodehouse:*
6 Jeeves

serve 3 act, fit, use 4 help, make, play,
suit, work 5 nurse, spend, treat 6 foster,
handle, wait on 7 advance, benefit,
care for, present, promote, provide,
satisfy, suffice, work for 8 deal with,
function 9 encourage, officiate 10 minister to
service 3 use 4 duty, help, rite 5 favor
6 employ, repair, ritual 7 account, benefit, fitness, liturgy 8 ceremony, courtesy, disposal, maintain 10 active duty,
assistance, ceremonial, observance,
usefulness 11 maintenance 12 dispensation
serviceable 5 handy, utile 6 decent,
usable, useful 7 durable, helpful 8 adequate, suitable 9 efficient, practical
10 acceptable, beneficial, convenient,
dependable, functional 11 utilitarian
12 satisfactory
servile 6 abject, craven, humble, menial
7 fawning, slavish 8 obedient, obeisant
9 groveling 10 obsequious, submissive
11 subservient
servility 7 bondage, helotry, peonage,
serfdom, slavery 9 thralldom
11 enslavement
serving 6 dollop 7 helping, portion
servitude 5 labor 6 corvée, thrall
7 bondage, helotry, peonage, serfdom,
slavery 9 captivity, indenture, thralldom, villenage 10 subjection
11 enslavement 12 enthrallment
sesame 3 til *grass:* 4 gama
sessile 5 fixed 6 rooted 7 settled
8 attached 11 established
session 6 assize, séance 7 meeting, sitting
set 3 aim, dry, fix, gel, lay, lot, put
4 firm, jell 5 array, batch, bunch, fixed,
group, place, put on, ready, rigid, scene
6 belong, harden, impose, placed, rooted, secure, stated 7 arrange, certain,
cluster, congeal, decided, deposit, dictate, jellify, lay down, located, prepare,
scenery, situate, specify, station 8 prepared, resolute, resolved, situated,
solidify, specific 9 confirmed, designate, establish, prescribe, specified,
stipulate, tenacious 10 assortment,
determined, gelatinize, inflexible, posi-
tioned, prescribed, stipulated 11 established, mise-en-scène *a gem:* 6 collet
right: 7 redress
set aside 4 void 5 annul 7 discard, dismiss, reserve 8 overrule
set back 4 mire 5 delay 6 detain, hang
up, hinder, retard, slow up
setback 5 check, hitch 6 defeat, rebuff
7 reverse 8 obstacle, reversal 9 hindrance 10 impediment, regression

set down 4 land 5 light, perch, roost 6 alight, record 9 establish, touch down

set fire to 4 burn 6 ignite 7 emblaze, inflame 8 enkindle, touch off

set forth 4 cite 5 state 6 adduce, affirm, allege, avouch, depart, embark, launch, submit 7 advance, declare, express, present, proffer, propose, take off 8 proclaim, spell out 9 introduce 10 account for

set free 5 loose 6 redeem, rescue, unbind 7 deliver, manumit, unchain, unloose 8 liberate, unloosen 9 unshackle 10 emancipate

Seth *brother:* 4 Abel, Cain *father:* 4 Adam *mother:* 3 Eve *son:* 4 Enos

set out 5 start 6 embark, intend 7 take off 9 undertake

Set's victim 6 Osiris

settee 4 seat, sofa 5 bench, divan 6 lounge

setting 5 scene 7 context, scenery 8 ambience 10 background 11 mise-en-scène *for a stone:* 4 ouch

settle 3 fix, lay, pay, put 4 calm 5 allay, judge, light, pay up, perch, place, quiet, roost, still 6 alight, clinch, decide, soothe, square, verify, wind up 7 arrange, compose, confirm, dispose, install, mediate, resolve, satisfy, work out 8 colonize, conclude, ensconce, nail down 9 determine, discharge, establish, negotiate, reconcile, touch down

settlement 4 deal 6 colony, hamlet 7 outpost, quietus, village 8 decision 9 agreement 10 conclusion, encampment, habitation, resolution 11 arrangement 13 determination *Israeli:* 6 moshav

settler 7 pioneer 8 colonist, squatter 9 colonizer

set-to 3 row 4 fray, spat 5 brawl, broil, brush, fight, run-in, scrap 6 affray, blowup, fracas, tussle 7 dispute, quarrel, rhubarb, scuffle 8 argument, skirmish 9 encounter 10 falling-out 11 altercation

set up 4 open 5 erect, found, raise, start 6 create, launch 7 arrange, install 8 assemble, generate, initiate, organize 9 construct, establish, institute, originate

setup 4 plan 5 array, trick 6 layout, scheme, shoo-in 7 pattern, project, setting 8 assembly, carriage, position, slam dunk 9 alignment, apparatus, structure, sure thing 11 arrangement, preparation 12 constitution

seven *combining form:* 4 hept, sept 5 hepta, septi *group of:* 6 heptad 8 hebdomad

seventeenth century 8 seicento

sever 3 cut, lop 4 part, rend 5 slice, split 6 cleave, cut off, detach, divide, sunder 7 break up, divorce 8 amputate, disjoint, separate

several 4 a few, many, some 6 divers, plural, sundry, varied 7 certain, diverse, various 8 assorted, discrete, distinct, manifold, numerous, separate, specific 9 different 10 respective

severe 4 dour, grim, hard 5 acute, grave, harsh, heavy, rigid, sober, stern, tough 6 bitter, brutal, rugged, strict 7 arduous, ascetic, austere, extreme, intense, onerous, serious, weighty 8 exacting, pitiless, rigorous 9 demanding, difficult, laborious, strenuous, stringent, unbending 10 forbidding, implacable, inflexible, iron-willed, oppressive, unyielding 11 disciplined, heavy-handed

severity 5 rigor 7 gravity, urgency 8 exigency, grimness, obduracy, rigidity 9 austerity, harshness, intensity, plainness, privation, restraint, spareness, starkness, sternness 10 strictness, stringency 11 seriousness

sew 4 darn, mend, seam 5 baste 6 needle, stitch, suture

sewer 4 duct 5 ditch, drain 6 tailor 7 cesspit, conduit 8 cesspool, stitcher

sewing *aid:* 7 thimble *case:* 4 etui *kit:* 9 housewife

sewing-machine inventor 4 Howe (Elias)

sexless 6 neuter 7 epicene 8 neutered

sex manual 9 Kama-sutra

sexton 6 deacon 9 custodian, sacristan

sexual 4 blue, lewd, racy 6 carnal, erotic, ribald, risqué, smutty 7 obscene 8 venereal 9 salacious 12 pornographic

sexual desire 4 eros, lust 6 libido

sexy 4 blue, racy 5 bawdy, spicy 6 erotic, purple, ribald, risqué, steamy, sultry 7 naughty 8 alluring, off-color, sensuous 9 appealing, salacious, seductive 10 attractive, suggestive

Seychelles *capital:* 8 Victoria *island:* 4 Mahé 7 La Digue, Praslin *language:* 6 Creole, French *monetary unit:* 5 rupee

Sganarelle *brother:* 6 Ariste *daughter:* 7 Lucinde *ward:* 7 Leonore 8 Isabelle *wife:* 7 Martine

shabby 5 dingy, dowdy, faded, mangy, ratty, seedy, sorry, tacky, tired 6 frayed, scurvy, shoddy, sleazy, sordid 7 outworn, rickety, run-down, scrubby, scruffy, squalid, worn-out 8 beggarly, decaying, decrepit, dog-eared, tattered 9 miserable, moth-eaten, neglected, worm-eaten 10 bedraggled, down-at-heel, ramshackle, threadbare 11 dilapidated 12 deteriorated, disreputable 13 deteriorating, unrespectable

shack 3 cot, hut 4 camp, shed 5 cabin, hovel, lodge 6 shanty 7 cottage

shackle 4 gyve 5 bilbo, chain, leash, strap 6 fetter, hobble, hog-tie, impede, pinion, secure 7 enchain, leg-iron, manacle, trammel 8 handcuff 9 entrammel

shad 7 clupeid, herring

shade 3 hue 4 cast, tint, tone, veil 5 ghost, tinge, trace, umbra 6 awning, darken, nuance, screen 7 dimness, eclipse, phantom, shelter, specter, spectre, umbrage 8 darkness, penumbra, phantasm, tincture 9 gradation, intensity, obscurity 10 apparition 11 distinction

shadow 3 dim, dog, tag 4 haze, hint, tail 5 cloud, shade, tinge, touch, trace, trail, umbra 6 screen, spirit, wraith 7 eidolon, obscure, phantom, specter, umbrage, vestige 8 overcast, penumbra, phantasm, revenant, tincture 9 inumbrate, overcloud, suspicion 10 apparition, intimation, suggestion 11 adumbration

shadowy 3 dim 4 dark 5 dusky, faint, murky, vague 6 gloomy, shaded 7 ghostly, obscure 9 tenebrous 10 indistinct

shady 4 dark 5 bosky, dusky, fishy 6 purple, shabby, shoddy 7 clouded, dubious, suspect 8 doubtful, screened 9 equivocal, sheltered, uncertain 10 suggestive, suspicious, umbrageous, unreliable 12 disreputable

Shaffer play 5 Equus 7 Amadeus

shaft 3 jab, ray, rod 4 axle, barb, beam, dart, pole, stem 5 arrow, lance, shoot, spear, stalk, thill 6 thrust 7 chimney, spindle 8 short end

shag 3 nap, rug 4 pile 5 chase, fetch 7 thicket, tobacco 9 cormorant

shaggy 5 bushy 7 unkempt 8 uncombed

shake 3 jar, jog, rid 4 deal, jerk, jolt, lose, rock, roil, sway 5 avoid, churn, daunt, elude, jiffy, quail, quake, shock, upset, waver, worry 6 escape, frappe, jiggle, joggle, outwit, quaver, quiver, rattle, ruffle, shimmy, shiver, stir up, tremor 7 agitate, chatter, disturb, perturb, shingle, shudder, temblor, tremble, unnerve, vibrate 8 brandish, convulse, throw off, unsettle 9 oscillate, palpitate 10 earthquake

shake down 5 frisk, gouge, screw, wrest, wring 6 coerce, extort, fleece, search 7 squeeze 9 blackmail

shakedown 3 bed 4 test 5 dance, trial 6 pallet, search, tryout 7 pursuit, testing 8 exaction 9 blackmail, extortion 10 inspection

Shakers leader 3 Lee (Ann) 9 Mother Ann

Shakespearean actor 4 Kean (Edmund) 5 Booth (Edwin), Dench (Judi), Evans (Maurice), Terry (Ellen) 6 Irving (Henry) 7 Branagh (Kenneth), Burbage (Richard), Garrick (David), Gielgud (John), Olivier (Laurence), Siddons (Sarah) 8 Ashcroft (Peggy), Macready (William), Redgrave (Michael), Scofield (Paul) 9 Barrymore (Ethel, John, Lionel, Maurice) 10 Richardson (Ralph)

Shakespeare, William *mother:* 9 Mary Arden *play:* 6 Hamlet, Henry V 7 Henry IV, Henry VI, Macbeth, Othello, Tempest (The) 8 King John, King Lear, Pericles 9 Cymbeline, Henry VIII, Richard II 10 Coriolanus, Richard III 11 As You Like It, Winter's Tale (The) 12 Julius Caesar, Twelfth Night 13 Timon of Athens 14 Comedy of Errors (The), Romeo and Juliet 16 Love's Labour's Lost, Merchant of Venice (The), Taming of the Shrew (The) 17 Measure for Measure 18 Antony and Cleopatra 19 Much Ado About Nothing 20 All's Well That Ends Well, Midsummer Night's Dream (A) *theater:* 5 Globe *wife:* 12 Anne Hathaway

shaky 4 weak 6 infirm, unsure, wobbly 7 aquiver, dubious, jittery, quaking, rackety, rickety, suspect, trembly, unsound 8 doubtful, insecure, rachitic, unstable, unsteady, wavering 9 quivering, tottering, trembling, tremulous, uncertain, unsettled 10 indecisive, precarious, rattletrap, unreliable 11 problematic, vacillating

shale 4 rock 5 slate

shallot 4 herb 5 onion 10 green onion

shallow 4 idle, vain 5 petty, shoal 7 cursory, sketchy, trivial 8 trifling 9 depthless, frivolous 11 perfunctory, superficial

shallows 6 lagoon, shoals

Shallum *father:* 5 Shaul, Zadok 6 Jabesh, Josiah, Sismai, Tikvah 8 Colhozeh, Naphtali 9 Hallohesh *mother:* 6 Bilhah *nephew:* 8 Jeremiah *slayer:* 7 Menahem *son:* 6 Mibsam 7 Hilkiah 8 Maaseiah *victim:* 9 Zechariah

shalom 5 peace

sham 3 act, ape 4 fake, hoax, mock 5 bluff, bogus, bunco, cheat, dummy, false, farce, feign, fraud, phony, put on, spoof 6 deceit, ersatz, facade, fakery, forged, invent, pseudo 7 assumed, feigned, forgery, imitate, mislead, mockery, pretend **8** affected, flimflam, simulate, spurious, travesty **9** brummagem, burlesque, deception, hypocrisy, imitation, imposture, pinchbeck, simulated **10** artificial, caricature, false front, fictitious, fraudulent, sanctimony, substitute **11** counterfeit, make-believe **12** pecksniffery *combining form:* **5** pseud **6** pseudo

shaman 6 healer, priest, wizard **7** diviner **8** conjurer, conjuror, magician, sorcerer **9** enchanter, priestess **10** high priest, soothsayer **11** faith healer, necromancer, thaumaturge, witch doctor

Shamash 6 sun-god *father:* **3** Sin *sister:* **6** Ishtar *wife:* **3** Aya

shamble see SHUFFLE

shambles 4 mess **5** chaos **6** jumble, muddle **8** disarray, disorder, wreckage **9** confusion

shame 4 pity **5** abash, guilt, odium **6** infamy, stigma **7** chagrin, mortify, obloquy, remorse, scandal **8** disgrace, dishonor, ignominy **9** disrepute, embarrass, humiliate, ill repute **10** opprobrium **11** humiliation **12** self-reproach **13** embarrassment, mortification

shamefaced 7 abashed **8** blushing, sheepish **9** mortified **10** humiliated **11** crestfallen, embarrassed

shameless 6 arrant, brazen, wanton **7** blatant, immoral **8** depraved, flagrant, immodest, impudent **9** abandoned, bald-faced, barefaced, dissolute, unabashed **10** outrageous, profligate, unblushing **11** brazen-faced, disgraceful **12** presumptuous

Shammah *brother:* **5** David *father:* **4** Agee **5** Jesse, Reuel *grandfather:* **4** Esau **7** Ishmael *son:* **7** Jonadab **8** Jonathan

Shammua *father:* **5** David, Galal **6** Bilgah, Zaccur *mother:* **9** Bathsheba *son:* **4** Abda

shamus 3 cop **4** dick, tail **6** copper, shadow, sleuth **7** gumshoe **8** flatfoot, sherlock **9** constable, detective, operative, policeman **10** private eye **12** investigator **13** police officer

shanghai 6 abduct, hijack, kidnap

Shangri-la 5 Tibet **6** utopia **7** arcadia **8** paradise **9** Cockaigne, fairyland **10** wonderland

shank 3 leg **4** shin, stem **5** stalk, tibia

shanty 3 cot, hut **4** camp, shed **5** cabin, hovel, lodge, shack **7** cottage

shape 3 fit **4** case, cast, form, mold, plan, trim **5** forge, frame, state, whack **6** aspect, devise, fettle, figure, kilter, repair, sculpt, tailor, work up **7** contour, fitness, outline, pattern, profile **8** assemble **9** condition, construct, fab-ricate, semblance **10** appearance, silhouette **12** conformation **13** configuration *combining form:* **5** morph **6** morpho

shapeable 6 pliant, supple **7** ductile, plastic, pliable **8** flexible **9** tractable

shapeless 8 inchoate, unformed **9** amorphous

shapely 4 trim **5** buxom **9** Junoesque **10** curvaceous, statuesque, well-turned **11** clean-limbed

shard 4 chip **5** chunk, scale, scrap, shell **6** sliver **7** elytron **8** carapace, fragment

share 3 cut, lot **4** part **5** chunk, claim, quota, slice, stake **6** divide, parcel, ration **7** dole out, give out, helping, partake, portion, prorate, quantum **8** dispense, fraction, interest, quotient **9** allotment, allowance, apportion **10** experience, percentage, proportion **11** participate

shared 5 joint **6** common, mutual, public **8** communal, conjoint, conjunct **9** concerted **10** collective **11** cooperative

Sharezer *father, victim:* **11** Sennacherib

shark 5 cheat **8** swindler *kind:* **4** mako, sand, tope **5** nurse, tiger **7** basking, dogfish, leopard **8** mackerel, man-eater, thresher **9** porbeagle **10** great white, hammerhead *skin:* **8** shagreen

sharp 3 sly **4** acid, keen, tony, trig **5** acrid, acute, alert, canny, crisp, honed, quick, slick, smart, swank **6** biting, bitter, brainy, bright, clever, jagged, nimble, peaked, shrewd, shrill, snappy **7** caustic, dashing, intense, pointed, prickly, stylish, whetted **8** clean-cut, clear-cut, incisive, piercing, shooting, stabbing, stinging **9** agonizing, brilliant, ingenious, knifelike, vitriolic **10** astringent, perceptive **11** intelligent, penetrating, quick-witted, resourceful **12** excruciating, nimble-witted

sharpen 4 edge, file, hone, whet **5** grind, strop

sharper 6 con man **7** diddler **8** chiseler, swindler **9** defrauder, trickster **10** mountebank **12** double-dealer

sharp-eyed 4 keen **5** alert **8** vigilant, watchful **9** attentive, observant **10** discerning, perceptive

sharpie see SHARPER

sharpness 4 edge **6** acumen **9** precision

sharpshooter 8 marksman

sharp-sighted 8 hawk-eyed, lynx-eyed **9** eagle-eyed

sharp-witted 4 keen **5** acute, canny, quick, smart **6** astute, clever, shrewd **11** intelligent

shatter 4 dash **5** break, burst, crush, smash **6** shiver **8** demolish, fragment, splinter 9 pulverize 10 annihilate 11 fragmentize 12 disintegrate

shatterable 7 brittle, fragile 9 breakable, frangible

shave 3 cut 4 clip, crop, pare, peel, skim, trim 5 lower, prune, shear, skive 6 barber, cut off, deduct, reduce, scrape, sliver 7 cut back, whittle 8 mark down

shaveling 3 boy, kid, lad, tad 6 laddie, squirt 9 stripling, youngster

shaver 3 boy, kid, lad, tad 5 child, razor 6 barber, laddie, squirt 9 stripling, youngster

shawl 4 wrap 5 fichu, manta 6 chador, serape 7 tallith 8 mantilla

shawm's descendant 4 oboe

Shawnee chief 8 Tecumseh, Tecumtha 9 Cornstalk

Shaw play 6 Geneva 7 Candida 9 Pygmalion, Saint Joan 11 Misalliance 12 Major Barbara 13 Arms and the Man

shay 6 chaise 8 carriage

shear 3 cut, mow 4 clip, crop, pare, snip, trim 5 prune, shave, skive 6 barber

shears 8 scissors

shearwater 4 bird 6 petrel 7 skimmer

sheath 4 case, skin 5 cover 7 holster 8 scabbard

sheathe 4 case, clad, face, side, skin, wrap 5 cover, panel 6 encase, jacket

Sheba *father:* 6 Bichri *queen:* 6 Balkis

shebang 4 mess 6 affair 7 schmear 8 business, caboodle 9 ball of wax, enchilada

shed 3 hut 4 cast, doff, drop, emit, molt 5 exude, hovel, hutch, scrap, shack, stall 6 divest, lean-to, reject, slough 7 cast off, diffuse, discard, radiate, take off 8 jettison, throw out 9 throw away

sheen 5 glaze, gleam, glint, gloss, shine 6 finish, luster, lustre, polish 7 burnish, glitter, shimmer 8 radiance 9 shininess 10 brightness

sheeny see SHINY

sheep 5 ovine *breed:* 5 Tunis 6 Dorper, Dorset, Merino, Navajo, No-Tail, Oxford, Panama, Romney 7 Cheviot, Colbred, Karakul, Lincoln, Ryeland, Suffolk 8 Columbia, Cotswold, Polwarth 9 Hampshire, Leicester, Montadale, Southdown 10 Corriedale, Debouillet 11 Rambouillet *coat:* 4 wool 6 fleece *disease:* 3 gid *female:* 3 ewe *male:* 3 ram 6 wether *meat:* 6 mutton *relating to:* 5 ovine *Scottish:* 9 blackface *sound:* 5 bleat *tender:* 8 shepherd *wild:* 5 urial 6 aoudad, argali, bharal 7 bighorn, mouflon *young:* 4 lamb

sheepish 4 meek 5 timid 7 abashed, ashamed, bashful 8 timorous 9 diffident 10 shamefaced 11 embarrassed

sheepskin 4 roan 6 mouton 7 diploma 9 parchment *prepare:* 3 taw

sheer 4 pure, skew, thin, turn, veer 5 filmy, gauzy, steep, utter 6 abrupt, arrant, flimsy, simple, swerve 7 chiffon, deflect, deviate, perfect, unmixed 8 absolute, complete, gossamer, outright 9 out-and-out, unalloyed, undiluted 10 diaphanous, see-through 11 precipitate, precipitous, transparent, unmitigated

sheet 3 ply 4 film, leaf, page, sail, slab 5 cover, linen, paper 6 lamina, veneer 8 membrane 9 newspaper

sheet ___ 3 ice 4 film 5 glass, metal, music 6 anchor

shelf 3 hob 4 bank, edge, reef, sill 5 ledge, shoal 6 mantel 7 counter 8 sandbank

shell 3 pod 4 boat, bomb, case, hull, husk, rake, skin 5 blitz, conch, shuck 6 pepper 7 bombard, capsule, grenade, mollusc, mollusk 8 carapace 9 cannonade, cartridge *defective:* 3 dud *explosive:* 4 bomb *layer:* 5 nacre *ornamental:* 6 cowrie *study:* 10 conchology

shellac 4 beat, drub, flay, lick, rout, trim, whap, whip, whop, whup 5 resin, smear, whomp 6 defeat, thrash 7 clobber, smother, trounce 8 lambaste, vanquish

Shelley, Percy Bysshe *poem:* 5 Cloud (The) 7 Adonais, Alastor 8 Queen Mab 10 Ozymandias, To a Skylark 16 Ode to the West Wind

shellfish 4 clam, crab 5 conch, cowry, prawn, snail, whelk 6 cockle, limpet, mussel, oyster, quahog, triton 7 abalone, crawdad, geoduck, lobster, mollusc, mollusk, scallop 8 barnacle, crayfish, escargot 10 crustacean, periwinkle

shell out 3 pay 4 give 5 spend 8 fork over, hand over

shell-shaped 6 spiral 9 cochleate

shelter 3 den, hut, lee 4 cote, fold, hide, port, roof, shed, tent 5 arbor, bower, cloak, cover, haven, house, shack, tower 6 asylum, burrow, covert, defend, harbor, refuge, shield 7 chamber, defense, foxhole, hideout, hospice, housing, lodging, pergola, pillbox, protect, retreat 8 hideaway, hidy-hole, security 9 dwellings, hermitage, hidey-hole, sanctuary 10 retirement *for aircraft:* 6 hangar *for cows:* 4 barn, byre *toward:* 4 alee

shelve 4 dish, drop, stay, tilt 5 defer,

delay, slope, stock, waive **6** freeze, give up, hold up, put off **7** hold off, suspend **8** hold over, mothball, postpone, prorogue, set aside

Shem *brother:* **3** Ham **7** Japheth *father:* **4** Noah

Shema's father 4 Joel **6** Hebron

Shemida's father 6 Gilead

shenanigan 4 dido, lark **5** antic, caper, prank, stunt, trick **6** frolic **8** escapade, mischief **10** tomfoolery **11** monkeyshine

Sheol see HADES

shepherd 4 lead, show, tend **5** guide, pilot, route, steer, watch **6** direct, escort, leader **7** conduct **8** guardian *dog:* **6** collie **12** border collie *stick:* **5** crook, staff

Sheridan play 6 Critic (The), Rivals (The) **7** Pizarro **16** School for Scandal (The)

sheriff 5 reeve **6** lawman **7** marshal, officer *aide:* **6** deputy

sherlock 4 dick, tail **5** snoop **6** shadow, shamus, sleuth **7** gumshoe **8** hawkshaw **9** detective **10** private eye **12** investigator

Sherlock Holmes *creator:* **5** Doyle (Arthur Conan) *sidekick:* **6** Watson (Dr.)

sherry 4 fino, wine **7** oloroso **10** manzanilla **11** amontillado

Sherwood play 10 Road to Rome (The) **13** Idiot's Delight **14** Waterloo Bridge **15** Petrified Forest (The)

shibboleth 3 saw, tag **5** axiom, maxim **6** byword, cliché, phrase, saying, slogan, truism **7** bromide **8** banality, chestnut, password, prosaism **9** catchword, platitude, watchword **11** catchphrase, commonplace

shield 4 fend, roof, ward **5** aegis, armor, cover, guard, haven, house **6** buffer, defend, harbor, screen, secure **7** buckler, bulwark, defense, protect, shelter **8** defilade **9** safeguard **10** escutcheon *band:* **4** fess *bullfighter's:* **9** burladero *light:* **5** targe *part:* **4** boss, umbo **7** bordure *Roman:* **7** testudo

shield-like 7 peltate

shift 3 yaw **4** bend, bout, move, stir, tack, time, tour, turn, vary, veer **5** alter, budge, get by, spell, stint, trick **6** change, make do, manage, remove, resort, swerve **7** deviate, replace, shuffle, stopgap **8** get along, relocate, resource, transfer **9** deviation, expedient, fluctuate **10** alteration, changeover, conversion, transition **11** fluctuation

shiftless 4 idle, lazy **5** inept **8** feckless, indolent, slothful **11** inefficient

shifty 3 sly **4** foxy, wily **5** cagey, lying, shady, slick **6** crafty, sneaky, tricky **7** cunning, devious, elusive, evasive, furtive **8** guileful, slippery, sneaking **9** conniving, deceitful, deceptive, dishonest, insidious, underhand **10** inconstant, untruthful **11** duplicitous, underhanded **12** equivocating

shill 5 blind, decoy, pitch **6** capper **8** promoter **10** accomplice, sales pitch

shillelagh 3 bat **4** club, cosh, mace **5** baton, billy, stick **6** cudgel **8** bludgeon **9** bastinado, billy club, blackjack, truncheon **10** nightstick

shilling 3 bob

shilly-shally 5 fudge, hedge, stall, waver **6** dawdle, dither, waffle **7** whiffle **8** hesitate **9** temporize, vacillate **11** prevaricate **12** tergiversate

Shimea *brother:* **5** David *father:* **5** David, Jesse *son:* **7** Jonadab **8** Jonathan

shimmer 5 flash, gleam, glint, sheen **6** luster, lustre **7** glimmer, glisten, glitter, spangle, sparkle, twinkle **9** coruscate **11** coruscation, scintillate **13** scintillation

shimmy 5 dance, shake **6** quiver, shiver, tremor **7** chemise, shudder, tremble, vibrate **9** vibration

shin 3 run **4** dash **5** scoot, tibia **6** scurry, sprint **7** scamper

shindig 4 ball, bash, fête, gala **5** binge, dance, party, revel **6** affair, frolic **7** blowout **8** wingding

shine 3 ray, rub **4** beam, buff, burn, glow **5** blaze, flare, flash, glare, glaze, gleam, glint, gloss, sheen **6** luster, lustre, polish **7** burnish, glimmer, glisten, glitter, radiate, shimmer, sparkle, twinkle **9** luminesce **10** incandesce

shiner 4 fish **8** black eye, cyprinid

shingle 5 beach, coast, shore **7** haircut, overlap, overlay **8** detritus **9** signboard

shiny 6 bright, glossy **7** fulgent, radiant **8** dazzling, gleaming, lustrous, polished **9** burnished, effulgent **10** glistening

ship 4 boat, send **5** remit, route **6** export **7** consign, forward, freight **8** dispatch, transfer, transmit *ancient:* **6** galley **7** galleon, trireme *attendant:* **7** steward *beam:* **7** keelson *berth:* **4** dock, slip *boat:* **6** dinghy *body:* **4** hull *cabin:* **9** stateroom *commercial:* **5** liner, oiler **6** argosy, tanker, trader **9** freighter *crew member:* **4** hand, mate **6** sailor *deck:* **4** boat, main, poop **5** orlop **6** bridge **10** forecastle *fishing:* **6** lugger **7** trawler *fleet:* **6** armada *floor:* **4** deck *front:* **3** bow **4** prow, stem **8** cutwater *hoister:* **4** boom **5** davit **7** capstan *kitchen:* **6** galley *left side:* **4** port **8** larboard *military:* **6** cutter,

PT boat 7 carrier, cruiser 9 destroyer, submarine *officer:* 4 mate 5 bosun 6 purser 7 captain, steward 9 boatswain *part:* 3 bow 4 beam, deck, helm, hold, hull, keel, mast, stem 5 bilge, hatch, stern 6 bridge, rudder 7 scupper *partition:* 7 bulwark 8 bulkhead *personnel:* 4 crew *platform:* 9 crow's nest, gangboard, gangplank *post:* 4 mast 7 bollard *prison:* 4 brig *projection:* 7 sponson *rear:* 5 stern *record:* 3 log *right side:* 9 starboard *room:* 4 brig 5 cabin 6 galley *rope:* 4 line 5 sheet 7 halyard *sailing:* 3 hoy 4 brig, dhow, prau, proa, yawl 5 ketch, sloop, xebec, yacht 6 lugger 7 caravel, galleon 8 schooner *steerer:* 4 helm 6 tiller *storage area:* 4 hold *to the rear of:* 3 aft 5 abaft 6 astern *valve:* 7 seacock *window:* 4 port 8 porthole

shipment 5 cargo 6 lading 7 freight, payload 8 delivery 11 consignment

Ship of Fools *author* 6 Porter (Katherine Anne)

Shipping News *author* 6 Proulx (Annie)

ships, group of 4 navy 5 fleet, flota 6 armada 8 flotilla

shipshape 4 neat, snug, tidy, trig, trim 7 orderly 11 spic-and-span, uncluttered 12 spick-and-span

shipworm 6 teredo

shire 5 horse 6 county 8 district 10 draft horse

shirk 4 duck, lurk, shun 5 avoid, creep, dodge, elude, evade, skulk, slink, sneak, steal 8 sidestep

shirker *see* SLACKER

shirt 4 polo, sark 5 dress, kurta, sport 6 blouse, jersey 9 guayabera

shirty 3 mad 5 angry, cross, irate 6 heated, ireful 7 annoyed 8 choleric, incensed, offended 9 indignant, irritated

shiv 5 blade, knife, shank 6 dagger 8 stiletto

Shiva *consort:* 3 Uma 4 Devi, Kali 5 Durga, Gauri 6 Ambika, Chandi 7 Parvati 9 Haimavati *son:* 6 Ganesa, Skanda 7 Ganesha 10 Karttikeya

shiver 5 burst, quake, shake, smash 6 quaver, quiver, tremor 7 shatter, shudder, tremble, twitter 8 fragment, splinter, splitter

shoal 3 bar 4 bank, hook, reef, spit 6 school 7 barrier, sandbar, shallow, tombolo 8 sandbank, sand reef

shoat 3 hog, pig 5 swine 6 piglet, porker

Shobab *father:* 5 Caleb, David *mother:* 6 Azubah 9 Bathsheba

shock 3 jar 4 blow, bump, daze, jolt, pile, rick, stun 5 amaze, clash, crash, mound, quake, shake, sheaf 6 appall,

dismay, impact, insult, offend, trauma, tremor 7 astound, disgust, horrify, outrage, stagger, startle, stupefy, temblor 8 astonish, surprise 9 collision, electrify 10 concussion, earthquake, percussion, scandalize, traumatize 11 flabbergast 12 stupefaction

shock absorber 6 spring 7 dashpot, snubber

shocker 4 blow 7 stunner 8 surprise, thriller 9 bombshell, eye-opener, sensation 11 showstopper

shocking 5 awful, lurid 6 horrid 7 glaring, heinous 8 dreadful, horrible, horrific, shameful, terrible 9 appalling, atrocious, frightful, monstrous, revolting 10 outrageous, scandalous 11 disgraceful, distressing, unspeakable

shoddy 4 base, mean, poor 5 cheap, dingy, gaudy, junky, seedy, tacky, tatty 6 cheesy, common, paltry, shabby, sleazy, tawdry, trashy 7 run-down, scruffy 8 inferior, rubbishy, shameful 9 makeshift 10 broken-down, down-at-heel 11 dilapidated, disgraceful, ignominious, pretentious 12 dishonorable, disreputable 13 discreditable

shoe 4 boot, clog, geta, mule, pump 5 sabot, wedge 6 brogan, brogue, buskin, gaiter, galosh, gillie, loafer, oxford, patten, sandal 7 chopine, ghillie, slipper, sneaker 8 balmoral, moccasin, platform, plimsoll 10 clodhopper, espadrille *armored:* 8 solleret *athlete's:* 7 sneaker *form:* 4 last, tree *kind:* 8 elevator, open-toed 10 high-heeled *part:* 3 tip, toe 4 arch, heel, lace, lift, sole, vamp 5 shank, upper 6 box toe, collar, foxing, insole, lining, throat, tongue 7 counter, outsole 8 backstay *protective:* 6 galosh, rubber *shiner:* 6 polish 9 bootblack *wooden:* 5 sabot 7 chopine

shoelace tip 5 aglet

shoeless 6 unshod 8 barefoot 9 discalced

shoemaker 7 cobbler *patron saint:* 7 Crispin *Scottish:* 6 souter

Shogun *author* 7 Clavell (James)

Sholem Aleichem *character* 5 Tevye

shoo 4 scat 5 drive, leave, scare, scram, split 6 beat it, begone, bug off, skidoo 7 buzz off, get lost, skiddoo, vamoose 8 clear out 9 skedaddle, take a hike 10 hit the road

shoo-in 6 winner 7 sure bet 8 slam dunk 9 sure thing

shoot 3 bud, fly, gun, ray 4 beam, bolt, dart, dash, fire, lash, race, rush, sail, scud, skim, spew, tear 5 blast, chase, fling, photo, shaft, skirr, snipe, spurt

6 branch **7** project **9** discharge **10** photograph

shoot down 3 pan, rap **4** bash, kill, slam **5** blast, decry, knock, scorn, trash **6** assail, deride, dump on, reject, squash **7** deflate, squelch, torpedo **8** bad-mouth, belittle, derogate, discount, disprove, puncture, ridicule **9** discredit

shooting 4 keen **5** acute, sharp **7** gunplay **8** piercing, stabbing

shooting star 6 meteor **8** fireball

shoot up 4 soar **6** inject, rocket **7** burgeon **8** mushroom **9** skyrocket

shop 4 hunt **5** store **6** browse, market, outlet, search **8** boutique, emporium, showroom

shoplift 3 bag, cop **4** lift, palm **5** filch, pinch, steal, swipe **6** pilfer, rip off, snitch

shop owner 8 merchant, retailer **9** tradesman **10** proprietor

shopworn 5 banal, faded, stale, tired, trite **6** cliché, soiled **7** clichéd **8** overused **9** hackneyed **10** threadbare

shore 4 bank, prop, stay **5** beach, brace, brink, coast **6** bear up, strand, uphold **7** bolster, shingle, support, sustain **8** buttress, littoral, seacoast **9** coastland, coastline, riverbank, riverside, waterside **10** embankment, waterfront

shorebird see at BIRD

short 3 shy **4** curt **5** blunt, brief, crisp, scant, skimp, spare, squat, stint, terse **6** abrupt, meager, meagre, scanty, scarce, skimpy, stubby **7** brusque, compact, concise, lacking, laconic, stunted, wanting **8** abridged, succinct **9** deficient **10** inadequate **11** abbreviated **12** insufficient

shortage 4 lack **5** pinch **6** dearth, ullage **7** deficit, paucity **8** scarcity **10** deficiency, inadequacy, scantiness

shortcoming 3 bug, sin **4** flaw, lack **5** fault, lapse **6** defect **7** demerit, failing **8** weakness **9** weak point **10** deficiency **12** imperfection

shortcut 6 bypass, cutoff

shorten 3 bob, cut **4** clip, dock **5** elide, slash **6** lessen, reduce, shrink **7** abridge, curtail, cut back, cut down, excerpt **8** boil down, compress, condense, contract, decrease, diminish, minimize, truncate **10** abbreviate

shorthand 11 stenography *method:* **5** Gregg **6** Pitman

shorthanded 7 wanting **11** undermanned **12** understaffed

short-lived 5 brief **7** passing **8** fleeting **9** ephemeral, fugacious, momentary, temporary **10** evanescent, transitory

shortly 4 anon, soon **6** pronto **7** briefly, by and by, in brief, quickly, tersely **8** directly **9** concisely, presently **10** succinctly **11** laconically

shortness 7 brevity **9** concision

shortsighted 6 myopic **8** heedless, reckless **10** astigmatic

short-spoken 4 curt **5** bluff, blunt, brief, gruff, terse **6** abrupt, crusty, snippy **7** brusque **8** snippety

short-tempered 5 testy **6** touchy **7** prickly **8** snappish **9** irascible, irritable

Shoshone chief 8 Washakie **9** Pocatello

shot 3 nip, pop, try **4** dose, dram, drop, jolt, stab **5** blast, break, carom, crack, fling, guess, ounce, photo, range, reach, snort, swipe, whack, whirl **6** chance, effort, stroke **7** attempt, snifter **8** marksman, occasion **9** discharge **11** opportunity

shoulder 4 bear, edge, push, side **5** elbow, press, shove **6** assume, hustle, jostle, take on **8** bulldoze *bone:* **7** scapula **8** clavicle *covering:* **6** tippet **8** scapular *muscle:* **7** deltoid *relating to:* **7** humeral **8** scapular

shoulder blade 7 scapula

shout 3 cry **4** bark, bawl, bray, call, roar, yell **5** blare, whoop **6** bellow, clamor, holler, scream **7** exclaim **10** vociferate

shove 3 dig, jab, jam **4** cram, prod, push **5** crowd, drive, elbow, press **6** jostle, propel, thrust **8** bulldoze, shoulder

shovel 3 dig **4** grub **5** delve, scoop, spade **6** dig out, dredge, trowel **8** excavate

shoveler 4 duck **9** broadbill

shove off 3 git **4** blow, exit **5** leave, scoot, scram, split **6** beat it, cut out, decamp, depart, move on **7** move out, pull out, vamoose **8** clear out, run along

show 4 fair, film, lead, pomp, sham **5** array, flick, front, guide, mount, movie, offer, prove, revue, sport, stage **6** appear, arrive, direct, effect, evince, expose, flaunt, lay out, parade, reveal, set out, submit, unveil **7** conduct, display, divulge, exhibit, explain, fanfare, panoply, picture, present, produce, project, trot out **8** brandish, disclose, evidence, illusion, indicate, instruct, manifest, proclaim **9** determine, establish, pageantry, represent, semblance, spectacle **10** appearance, exhibition, exposition, illustrate, production **11** demonstrate, materialize, performance **13** demonstration, manifestation

Show Boat *author:* **6** Ferber (Edna) *composer:* **4** Kern (Jerome) *lyricist:* **11** Hammerstein (Oscar)

showcase 6 flaunt, parade **7** cabinet, exhibit, feature, vitrine

shower 4 hail, rain, wash 5 bathe, burst, party, salvo, spray, storm 6 deluge, lavish, volley 7 barrage, cascade, shatter, spatter 8 cataract, downpour, fountain, rainfall 9 broadside, cannonade, fusillade 10 cloudburst 11 bombardment

showman 8 producer, promoter 10 impresario *famous:* 4 Cody (William F.) 6 Barnum (Phineas T.)

Show Me State 8 Missouri

show off 4 brag 5 boast, flash, model, vaunt 6 expose, flaunt, hotdog, parade 7 display, exhibit, swagger, trot out 8 brandish 10 grandstand

show-off 3 ham 6 hotdog 7 boaster, hotshot, peacock 8 blowhard, braggart 9 swaggerer 13 exhibitionist

showpiece 3 gem 5 jewel, prize 10 magnum opus, masterwork 11 chef d'oeuvre, masterpiece

show up 4 come 6 appear, arrive, debunk, expose, reveal, unmask 8 discover 9 discredit, embarrass 10 invalidate 11 materialize

showy 4 loud 5 gaudy, jazzy 6 flashy, garish, ornate, sporty, tawdry 7 opulent, splashy 8 gorgeous, overdone, striking 9 luxurious, sumptuous 10 flamboyant 11 overwrought, pretentious, resplendent, sensational 12 meretricious, orchidaceous, ostentatious

shred 3 bit, dag, jot, rag 4 iota, whit 5 crumb, grain, grate, ounce, scrap, shave, speck, trace 6 sliver, tatter 7 modicum, smidgen, snippet 8 demolish, fragment, particle 9 scintilla

shrew 3 nag 4 mole 5 harpy, scold, vixen, witch 6 dragon, gorgon, ogress, rodent, virago 7 hellcat 8 battle-ax, fishwife, harridan, she-devil, spitfire, Xantippe 9 battle-axe, termagant, Xanthippe

shrewd 3 sly 4 foxy, keen, wily, wise 5 acute, cagey, canny, savvy, sharp, slick, smart 6 artful, astute, clever, crafty, smooth 7 knowing, prudent 8 sensible 9 ingenious, judicious, sagacious 10 discerning 11 intelligent, penetrating, quick-witted 13 perspicacious

shrewish 5 cross, testy 6 cranky, snappy 7 peevish, peppery 8 choleric, petulant 9 crotchety, fractious, irascible, splenetic 10 ill-natured 11 contentious, intractable, quarrelsome 12 disputatious 13 quick-tempered, short-tempered

shriek 3 cry 4 yell 6 screak, scream, shrill, squawk, squeal 7 screech

shrill 4 keen 5 acute, sharp 6 piping 8 piercing, strident 9 deafening 12 earsplitting

shrimp 4 runt 5 prawn 6 peanut, scampi 10 crustacean

shrine 5 altar 6 temple 7 sanctum 9 reliquary, sacrarium, sanctuary *Buddhist:* 5 stupa 7 chorten

shrink 3 shy 4 wane 5 cower, quail, slink, start, wince 6 blench, boggle, cringe, flinch, huddle, recede, recoil, wither 7 analyst, dwindle, refrain 8 compress, condense, contract, draw back, withdraw 9 constrict, shrivel up, therapist, waste away 12 psychiatrist, psychologist

shrinking 3 shy 5 mousy, timid 7 bashful 8 retiring, skittish 9 withdrawn

shrive 5 purge 6 pardon, purify 7 absolve, confess, expiate 8 lustrate

shrivel 4 wilt 5 dry up, parch, wizen 6 shrink, wither 7 dwindle, wrinkle 9 dehydrate, desiccate

Shropshire Lad author 7 Housman (A. E.)

shroud 4 hide, rope, veil, wrap 5 cloak, cover, shade 6 enfold, enwrap, screen 7 conceal, enclose, envelop, obscure 8 cerement, obstruct 9 cerecloth 12 winding-sheet

shrouded 5 privy 6 covert, hidden, secret 7 obscure 10 mysterious

shrub 4 bush 5 elder, erica, hazel 6 muskit, privet 7 arboret, dyeweed, guayule 8 barberry, bluewood, boxthorn, inkberry, ironweed, rosebush 9 bearberry 10 bladdernut *Asian:* 4 bago 6 kerria 8 caragana, japonica *desert:* 7 ephedra *dwarf:* 6 bonsai *East Indian:* 3 aal 4 sunn *European:* 4 cade 8 woodbine *evergreen:* 3 box, kat, yew 4 ilex, khat, titi 5 furze, heath, holly, pyxie, savin, taxus 6 kalmia, laurel, myrtle, nandin, protea, sabine, savine 7 boxwood, heather, jasmine, juniper, rosebay 8 lambkill, oleander, rosemary, tamarisk *flowering:* 5 ribes, tiara, wahoo 6 daphne, laurel, myrtle, spirea 7 chamise, chamiso, mahonia, maybush, rhodora, spiraea, weigela 8 magnolia, mezereon, nineback, oleander, oleaster, shadblow, shadbush, snowball, snowbush, tornillo, viburnum, wisteria *genus:* 4 Inga, Itea 7 Solanum 8 Euonymus *hardwood:* 6 cornel *Mexican:* 8 ocotillo *ornamental:* 6 privet 7 syringa 9 bluebeard *pasture:* 8 cowberry *prickly:* 5 briar, chico, furze, gorse 7 bramble 8 hawthorn, mesquite 9 buckthorn *thicket:* 6 maquis 7 macchia 9 chaparral *tropical:* 4 kava 5 henna 7 lantana 8 buddleia 10 frangipani *West Indian:* 4 anil 7 acerola

shrug off 8 belittle, downplay, minimize

shtick 3 act, bag, bit **5** spiel **6** number **7** routine **9** specialty **11** performance

Shuah *father:* **7** Abraham *mother:* **7** Keturah

shuck 3 pod **4** case, cast, hull, husk, junk, peel, shed, skin **5** ditch, scrap, shell, strip **6** reject, remove, slough **7** discard, peel off, take off **8** jettison **11** decorticate

shudder 5 quake, shake **6** quaver, quiver, shimmy, shiver, tremor **7** frisson, tremble, twitter, vibrate

shuffle 3 mix **4** hash **5** dodge, evade, hedge, scuff, shift **6** jumble, mess up, muddle, weasel **7** clutter, reorder, rummage, shamble **8** disarray, disorder, intermix, mishmash **9** rearrange **10** disarrange, equivocate **11** disorganize

shun 3 cut **4** duck, snub **5** avoid, dodge, elude, evade, scorn **6** escape, eschew, refuse, reject **7** decline, disdain

shunt 4 turn **5** avert, shift **6** change, divert, switch **7** deflect, shuttle **8** transfer **9** sidetrack

shush 4 hush **5** quiet, still **6** muffle, muzzle, shut up, stifle **7** repress, silence, squelch **8** suppress

shut 3 bar **4** lock, seal, slam **5** close **6** fasten **9** close down **10** batten down

Shute novel 10 On the Beach

shut in 3 hem, mew, pen **4** cage, coop, wall **5** fence **6** coop up, immure **7** confine, enclose **8** imprison

shut-in 7 invalid **8** confined **9** withdrawn **12** convalescent

shut out 3 bar **6** screen **7** exclude **9** ostracize

shutter 5 blind **6** screen

shuttle 5 ferry, shunt **6** bobbin **7** commute, spindle **9** alternate

shuttlecock 4 bird **6** bandy

shut up 3 gag, mew, pen **4** cage, hush, jail, mute **5** burke, choke, quiet, shush, still **6** muzzle, stifle **7** confine, enclose, impound, silence, squelch **8** choke off, imprison, pipe down, suppress **9** quiet down **11** incarcerate

shy 3 coy **4** balk, duck, meek, shun, wary **5** avoid, chary, elude, evade, mousy, quail, scant, short, timid **6** averse, blench, demure, modest, recoil, scanty, scarce, shrink **7** bashful, fearful, lacking, wanting **8** hesitant, reserved, reticent, retiring, sheepish, timorous **9** diffident **11** introverted, unassertive **12** apprehensive, insufficient, self-effacing **13** self-conscious

Shylock 6 usurer **9** loan shark *daughter:* **7** Jessica

shyster 11 pettifogger

Siam see THAILAND

sib 3 bro, kin, sis **4** akin **6** sister **7** brother, kindred, kinsman, related **8** relation, relative **9** relatives

Sibelius composition 9 Finlandia **11** Valse Triste

Siberian *dog:* **5** husky **7** Samoyed *native:* **5** Tatar, Yakut **6** Tartar, Tungus **7** Chukchi **9** Mongolian *plain:* **6** steppe *tent:* **4** yurt

sibilate 4 buzz, fizz, hiss, whiz **6** fizzle, sizzle **7** whisper

sibling 3 bro, sis **6** sister **7** brother

sibyl 4 seer **6** oracle **7** prophet **10** prophetess, soothsayer **13** fortuneteller

sic 3 set **4** thus **5** chase **6** attack

Sicilian *secret organization:* **5** Mafia *volcano:* **4** Etna

Sicily *capital:* **7** Palermo *city:* **7** Catania, Messina **8** Siracusa, Syracuse, Taormina *volcano:* **4** Etna

sick 3 ill **5** fed up, tired, weary **6** ailing, laid up, morbid, peaked, rotten, unwell, wobbly **7** fevered, invalid **8** confined, diseased **9** bedridden, defective, disgusted, unhealthy **10** indisposed **11** debilitated

sicken 5 upset **7** afflict, disgust, fall ill **8** nauseate

sickle 5 blade, mower **6** scythe **8** crescent

sickle-shaped 7 falcate

sickly 3 ill, low, wan **4** puny, weak **5** frail **6** ailing, anemic, feeble, infirm, morbid, peaked, poorly, unwell **8** delicate, diseased **9** unhealthy **10** indisposed **11** unhealthful, unwholesome **12** insalubrious

sickness 3 bug **6** malady **7** ailment, disease, illness **8** disorder, syndrome **9** complaint, condition, infirmity **10** affliction **13** indisposition

sic transit gloria ___ 5 mundi

side 4 clad, team **5** angle, facet, flank **6** aspect **9** direction **10** standpoint *combining form:* **5** later **6** lateri, latero *exposed:* **8** windward *sheltered:* **3** lee

sideboard 5 table **6** buffet **8** credence, credenza *for wine:* **8** cellaret **10** cellarette

sideburns 9 burnsides **10** sideboards **11** dundrearies, muttonchops

sidekick 3 pal **4** chun **5** buddy, crony **7** partner **9** assistant, companion **10** accomplice

sideline 5 eject, hobby **6** injure **7** disable, pastime, take out **9** avocation, diversion **10** recreation **11** distraction **12** incapacitate

sidereal 6 astral, starry **7** stellar

side road 5 byway **8** bystreet, shunpike

sideshow 9 diversion 11 distraction

sidestep 4 duck 5 avoid, burke, dodge, evade, hedge, skirt 6 bypass, swerve, weasel 10 circumvent, equivocate 12 tergiversate

sideswipe 5 brush, carom, graze, shave 6 glance, scrape

sidetrack 5 shunt 6 divert, switch 7 deflect

sidewhiskers see SIDEBURNS

side with 4 back 5 favor 6 second, uphold 7 endorse, support 8 backstop, champion

sidle 4 edge, slip

siege 4 bout 5 spell 6 attack 7 assault, seizure 8 blockade 9 onslaught

Siegfried *composer:* 6 Wagner (Richard) *lover:* 8 Brunhild *mother:* 9 Sieglinde *slayer:* 5 Hagen *sword:* 7 Balmung *vulnerable spot:* 4 back 8 shoulder *wife:* 9 Kriemhild

Sienkiewicz novel 8 Quo Vadis

sierra 3 saw 4 fish 5 range 8 mackerel 13 mountain range

Sierra Leone *capital:* 8 Freetown *ethnic group:* 5 Mende, Temne *language:* 4 Krio 7 English *monetary unit:* 5 leone *neighbor:* 6 Guinea 7 Liberia

Sierra Nevada lake 5 Tahoe

Sierra ___ 5 Ancha, Leone, Madre 6 Blanca, Nevada

siesta 3 nap 4 doze 5 sleep 6 catnap, snooze 10 forty winks

sieve 4 sift 6 filter, screen, winnow 8 colander, filtrate, strainer

Sif's husband 4 Thor

sift 3 pan 4 comb, cull, sort 5 glean, sieve 6 filter, screen, strain, winnow 8 filtrate, separate

sigh 3 sob 4 gasp, long, moan, pine 5 groan, sough, whine, yearn 6 exhale, grieve, hanker, murmur 7 breathe, respire, suspire

sight 3 aim, eye, spy 4 espy, view 5 scene, vista 6 notice, vision 7 make out, outlook *relating to:* 5 optic 6 ocular, visual 7 optical

sightseer 7 tourist 10 rubberneck 12 rubbernecker

sign 3 cue, ink 4 flag, hint, mark, omen 5 index, proof, token, trace 6 motion, signal, symbol 7 endorse, gesture, indicia, initial, symptom, vestige, warning 8 evidence, exponent, reminder 9 autograph, indicator 10 expression, indication, suggestion *directional:* 5 arrow *of the zodiac:* (see ZODIAC SIGN)

signal 3 cue, nod 4 flag 5 alarm, alert 6 beckon, wigwag 7 gesture 8 high sign 9 indicator *distress:* 3 SOS 6 Mayday

signature 4 name 9 autograph 11 John Hancock *flourish:* 6 paraph

signet 4 ring, seal 5 stamp 6 device 8 hallmark, intaglio

significance 4 pith 5 merit, point, sense 6 credit, import, moment, weight 7 gravity, meaning 9 authority, magnitude 10 importance 11 consequence, weightiness

significant 5 sound, valid 7 notable, telling, weighty 8 material, powerful 9 important, momentous 10 compelling, convincing, meaningful, noteworthy 11 substantial 12 considerable 13 consequential

signification 4 gist 5 point, sense 6 import 7 essence, meaning, message, purport 9 substance 10 intendment 11 implication 12 notification 13 understanding

signify 4 mean, show 5 count, imply, spell, weigh 6 convey, denote, intend, matter 7 add up to, bespeak, connote, express, purport, suggest 8 indicate

sign on 4 book, hire, join 5 draft 6 engage, enlist, enroll, induct, join up, retain, secure 7 recruit 9 conscript

sign over 4 cede, deed 5 alien, grant 6 assign, convey, remise 7 consign 8 alienate, transfer

sign up 4 join 5 enter 6 enlist, enroll, muster

Sigurd *horse:* 5 Grani *slayer:* 5 Hogni *victim:* 6 Fafner, Fafnir *wife:* 6 Gudrun

Sigyn's husband 4 Loki

Sikhism *deity:* 4 Akal *founder:* 5 Nanak 9 Guru Nanak *leader:* 5 Arjan 9 Guru Arjan 11 Gobind Singh *scripture:* 9 Adi Granth *shrine:* 12 Golden Temple

silage 6 fodder

silence 3 gag 4 calm, hush, lull, mute 5 quash, quell, quiet, shush, still 6 dampen, deaden, muffle, muzzle, shut up, squash, stifle 7 secrecy, squelch 8 choke off, muteness, quietude, suppress 9 quietness, reticence, stillness

silent 3 mum 4 dumb, mute 5 muted, quiet, still, tacit, whist 6 hushed, stilly 8 reticent, taciturn, unspoken, wordless 9 noiseless, soundless, voiceless 10 speechless 11 close-lipped, tight-lipped 12 closemouthed, tight-mouthed

silhouette 6 shadow 7 contour, outline, profile 9 lineament, lineation 10 figuration 11 delineation

Silicon Valley city 8 Palo Alto

silk 5 fiber 7 foulard 8 sarcenet, sarsenet *fabric:* 4 gros 5 caffa, ninon, Pekin, satin, surah, tulle 6 mantua, pongee, samite, sendal, tussah 7 taffeta *factory:*

8 filature *hat:* **6** topper *maker:* **4** worm *raw:* **6** greige *source:* **6** cocoon *waste:* **4** noil **5** floss *wild:* **6** tussah

sill 5 bench, ledge, shelf **9** threshold

silliness 5 folly **6** idiocy **7** inanity **9** absurdity, stupidity

silly 4 daft **5** balmy, crazy, daffy, dippy, dizzy, funny, giddy, inane, loony, sappy, wacky **6** absurd, simple **7** asinine, fatuous, flighty, foolish, idiotic, vacuous, witless **9** brainless, frivolous, ludicrous, nitwitted, senseless **10** irrational, ridiculous, weak-minded **11** empty-headed, harebrained, light-headed **12** preposterous, simpleminded **13** rattlebrained

silt 5 dregs **7** deposit, residue **8** alluvium, sediment

silver 4 coin **5** money, shiny **6** argent, dulcet **7** bullion, element **8** flatware, lustrous, sterling **9** argentine, tableware *relating to:* **9** argentine

silverfish 6 insect, tarpon

silversmith 6 Revere (Paul) **11** metal-worker

silver-tongued 4 glib **6** fluent **7** voluble **8** eloquent

silvery 6 argent **7** shining **9** argentine, brilliant **10** glittering, shimmering

Silvia's beloved 9 Valentine

___ **Simbel 3** Abu

Simenon character 7 Maigret (Inspector)

Simeon *father:* **5** Jacob *mother:* **4** Leah *son:* **4** Ohad **6** Nemuel

simian 3 ape **5** chimp, lemur, loris **6** baboon, bonobo, galago, monkey **7** apelike, gorilla, primate, tarsier **9** orangutan **10** anthropoid, chimpanzee, monkeylike

similar 4 akin, like **5** alike **6** agnate **7** uniform **8** parallel, suchlike **9** analogous, consonant **10** comparable, reciprocal **11** correlative **13** complementary, corresponding

similarity 6 parity **7** analogy, harmony, kinship **8** affinity, likeness, parallel, sameness **9** alikeness, closeness, congruity, semblance **10** conformity, congruence **11** coincidence, correlation, homogeneity, parallelism, resemblance

similarly 8 likewise

simile 7 analogy **8** affinity, likeness, metaphor **9** alikeness, semblance **10** comparison **11** correlation, resemblance *word:* **4** like

similitude 4 copy **5** image **6** double **7** analogy, kinship, replica **8** affinity, likeness, metaphor, relation, sameness **9** alikeness, congruity, semblance **10** comparison, similarity **11** correla-

tion, counterpart, equivalence, resemblance

simmer 4 boil, fret, fume, stew, stir **5** churn **6** bubble, seethe **7** ferment, smolder

simmer down 5 relax

Simon *brother:* **5** Jesus **6** Andrew *father:* **5** Jonah *new name:* **5** Peter *son:* **5** Judas, Rufus **9** Alexander

Simon ___ **5** Magus **6** Legree **8** of Cyrene **9** the Zealot

Simon Maccabaeus *father:* **10** Mattathias *nickname:* **6** Thassi *slayer:* **7** Ptolemy

Simon play 9 Odd Couple (The) **10** Chapter Two, Plaza Suite **11** Biloxi Blues **12** Sunshine Boys (The) **13** Lost in Yonkers **16** Come Blow Your Horn **17** Barefoot in the Park **20** Brighton Beach Memoirs **21** Last of the Red Hot Lovers **22** Prisoner of Second Avenue (The)

simp 4 dope **5** dunce, idiot, moron **6** dimwit, nitwit **7** pinhead **8** bonehead, imbecile, lunkhead, numskull **9** blockhead, lamebrain, numbskull **10** nincompoop

simple 4 easy, mere, pure **5** basic, lucid, naive, plain, sheer **6** modest **7** artless, natural, unmixed **8** absolute, trusting **9** childlike, credulous, ingenuous, unadorned **10** effortless, elementary, unaffected **11** fundamental, undecorated, unelaborate **13** unpretentious *combining form:* **4** hapl **5** haplo

simpleminded 4 dull, slow **5** naive **6** stupid **7** foolish, idiotic, moronic **8** gullible, retarded **9** dim-witted, imbecilic **10** half-witted, slow-witted

simpleton 4 dolt, dope, fool **5** dummy, dunce, idiot, moron **6** cretin, dimwit, nitwit **7** dullard, half-wit, pinhead **8** bonehead, dumbbell, imbecile, lunkhead **9** blockhead, ignoramus, lamebrain **10** nincompoop

simplify 4 ease **7** clarify, clear up **8** boil down **10** facilitate, streamline, unscramble **11** disentangle **13** straighten out

simply 4 just, only **6** merely

simulacrum 4 copy **5** clone, ditto, guise, image, trace **6** double, ersatz, mirror, ringer **7** picture, replica **8** likeness, portrait **9** facsimile, imitation, semblance **10** appearance **12** reproduction **13** impersonation, spitting image

simulate 3 ape **4** fake, sham **5** feign, mimic **6** embody, mirror, parody, parrot **7** imitate **8** resemble **9** incarnate **11** counterfeit

simulated 4 fake, mock, sham **5** bogus, dummy, false, phony **6** ersatz **8** spurious 9 imitation, insincere, pretended 10 artificial, fictitious, substitute 11 counterfeit

simultaneous 6 coeval 10 coexistent, coexisting, coincident, coinciding, concurrent, synchronic 11 synchronous 12 contemporary

simultaneously 6 at once 7 jointly 8 together 9 meanwhile

sin 3 err 4 debt, evil, tort, vice 5 crime, fault, guilt, lapse, stray, wrong 6 offend 7 demerit, misdeed, offense 8 hamartia, iniquity, trespass 10 deficiency, peccadillo, transgress, wickedness, wrongdoing 11 shortcoming 12 imperfection *deadly:* 4 envy, lust 5 anger, greed, pride, sloth 8 gluttony 12 covetousness

Sin 7 moon-god *daughter:* 6 Ishtar *son:* 7 Shamash *wife:* 6 Ningal

since 3 ago 5 after 6 behind 7 because, whereas 8 as long as 9 following 10 inasmuch as 11 considering *Scottish:* 4 syne

sincere 4 real, true 5 frank, plain 6 actual, candid, devout, honest 7 artless, earnest, genuine, serious 8 bona fide, truthful 9 authentic, heartfelt, ingenuous, unfeigned 10 aboveboard, forthright 12 wholehearted 13 unpretentious

sincerity 6 candor 7 honesty 8 goodwill, openness 9 frankness, good faith 11 artlessness, earnestness

sine qua non 4 must 9 condition, essential, necessity, requisite 11 requirement 12 precondition, prerequisite

sinew 6 tendon

sinewy 4 ropy, wiry 5 tough 6 brawny 7 fibrous, stringy 8 muscular

sinful 3 bad 4 base, evil, vile 5 wrong 6 guilty, unholy, wicked 7 immoral, peccant, vicious 8 blamable, culpable, damnable, depraved, shameful 9 reprobate 10 iniquitous 11 blameworthy, disgraceful 13 reprehensible

sing 3 rat 4 fink, hymn 5 carol, chant, chirp, croon, troll, yodel 6 inform, intone, snitch, squeal, warble 7 confess, descant, lullaby 8 serenade, vocalize 10 cantillate

Singapore *capital:* 9 Singapore *language:* 5 Malay, Tamil 8 Mandarin *monetary unit:* 6 dollar

singe 4 burn, char, sear 6 scorch

singer 4 alto, bass 5 mezzo, tenor 6 canary 7 crooner, soloist, soprano 8 baritone, choirboy, songbird, songster, vocalist 9 balladeer, chorister, contralto 10 troubadour *cabaret:* 11 chansonnier *female:* 9 chanteuse *opera:* 4 diva 10 cantatrice *religious:* 6 cantor

singing *exercise:* 7 solfège *group:* 3 duo 4 trio 5 choir 6 chorus 7 chorale, quartet, quintet *voice:* 4 alto, bass 5 mezzo,

tenor 7 soprano 8 baritone 9 contralto 12 mezzo-soprano

single 3 hit, odd, one 4 free, lone, only, sole 5 unwed 6 maiden, unique 7 base hit, unitary 8 distinct, isolated, separate, solitary, specific 9 exclusive, unmarried 10 individual, particular, unattached *combining form:* 3 mon 4 hapl, mono 5 haplo *prefix:* 3 uni

single-minded 5 rigid 6 dogged, driven, intent 7 adamant, devoted, diehard 8 hell-bent, obdurate, resolute, resolved, stubborn 9 dedicated, steadfast, unbending 10 brassbound, determined, inexorable, inflexible, purposeful, relentless, unyielding

single out 4 cull, mark, pick 5 elect, favor 6 choose, opt for, select 9 designate 11 distinguish

singular 3 odd 4 lone, only, rare, sole, solo 5 weird 6 unique 7 bizarre, oddball, strange, unusual 8 peculiar, solitary, uncommon 9 exclusive 10 individual, outlandish, particular, unexampled 11 exceptional 13 extraordinary

singularity 5 quirk, unity 6 oddity 7 anomaly, oneness 8 identity 9 exception 11 peculiarity, personality 12 idiosyncrasy 13 individuality, particularity

singularize 4 mark 11 distinguish, individuate 12 characterize 13 differentiate, individualize

sinister 4 dark, dire, evil, left 6 creepy, malign 7 baleful, fateful, malefic, ominous 8 lowering, menacing 9 illomened, malicious 10 foreboding, maleficent, portentous 11 apocalyptic, threatening 12 inauspicious, unpropitious

sink 3 dip, pit, sag 4 bore, bury, dive, drop, fall, sump, wane 5 basin, drill, droop, lower, sewer, slope, slump, stoop, swamp 6 hollow, invest, plunge, settle, thrust, worsen 7 capsize, cesspit, decline, depress, descend, founder, go under, immerse, let down, scuttle, subside, torpedo 8 cesspool, hellhole, submerge, submerse 9 concavity, disappear 10 depression

sinker 3 bob 5 plumb 6 weight 8 doughnut, fastball, plumb bob

sinkhole 3 dip, sag 4 bowl 5 basin 6 hollow 8 cesspool 9 concavity 10 depression

sinless 4 pure 6 chaste 8 innocent 9 righteous 10 impeccable

sinner 5 rogue, scamp 6 bad egg, outlaw, rascal, wretch 7 lowlife, villain 8 criminal, evildoer, offender 9 libertine, miscreant, reprobate, scoundrel, wrongdoer 10 black sheep, delinquent, profligate, malefactor 11 rapscallion

Sinn ___ 4 Fein

sinuous 4 wavy 5 lithe, snaky 7 winding 8 flexuous, tortuous 10 convoluted, meandering, serpentine 11 anfractuous, snake-shaped

sinus 6 cavity, hollow, recess

Sioux 6 Dakota *chief:* 8 Red Cloud 10 Crazy Horse 11 Sitting Bull *people:* 3 Ofo 4 Crow 6 Biloxi, Tutelo 7 Catawba, Hidatsa 9 Winnebago

sip 5 drink, savor, taste 6 imbibe

siphon 3 tap 4 draw, pipe, pump 5 draft, drain 6 convoy, divert, funnel 7 channel, conduct, draw off 8 transmit

sir 4 lord 5 title 6 knight, mister 9 gentleman

sire 4 lord 5 beget, breed, hatch, spawn 6 father, parent 7 founder 8 engender 9 patriarch, procreate, propagate 10 forefather

siren 4 vamp 5 alarm 7 Lorelei 9 temptress 10 seductress 11 femme fatale *film:* 4 Bara (Theda)

Siren 5 Ligea 8 Leucosia 10 Parthenope *German:* 7 Lorelei

sirenian 6 dugong, sea cow 7 manatee

siren song 4 lure 5 decoy, snare 6 come-on 10 allurement, enticement, temptation

Sirius 7 Dog Star

sister 3 nun 7 sibling *French:* 5 soeur *Latin:* 5 soror *Spanish:* 7 hermana

Sister Carrie author 7 Dreiser (Theodore)

sisterly 7 sororal

Sisyphus *brother:* 7 Athamas 9 Salmoneus *father:* 6 Aeolus *mother:* 7 Enarete *son:* 7 Glaucus

sit 4 pose 5 perch, roost

Sita *abductor:* 6 Ravana *husband, rescuer:* 4 Rama

sitarist 7 Shankar (Ravi)

site 3 dig 4 home, spot 5 haunt, locus, place, point, scene, venue 6 locale 7 station 8 locality, location, position

sit-in 7 protest

sitting 6 séance 7 session *prolonged:* 8 sederunt

Sitting Bull's tribe 5 Sioux

sitting duck 4 butt, mark 6 target

situate 3 put, set 5 place 6 locate 7 install 8 position

situation 3 job 4 post, rank 5 point, state 6 plight, status 7 footing, setting, station 8 location, position, standing 9 condition 13 circumstances

situs 5 place, venue 6 locale

Siva see SHIVA

six *combining form:* 3 hex, sex 4 hexa, sexi 5 sexti *group of:* 6 sestet, sextet 9 sextuplet *relating to:* 6 senary

sixfold 8 sextuple

six-shooter 3 gun 6 pistol 8 revolver

sixth sense 3 ESP 7 insight 9 intuition, telepathy 12 clairvoyance

sizable 3 big 5 ample, hefty, large, major, roomy 8 spacious 9 capacious, extensive 10 commodious, large-scale 11 substantial 12 considerable

size 4 area, bulk, mass 5 range, scope, width 6 extent, height, length, spread, volume 7 bigness, breadth, caliber, expanse, measure, stature 9 amplitude, dimension, extension, greatness, largeness, magnitude 10 dimensions, proportion 11 measurement, proportions

size up 3 peg 4 rate, read 5 assay, gauge, judge, value 6 assess, review, survey 7 adjudge, dope out 8 appraise, estimate, evaluate 9 figure out

sizzle 3 fry 4 buzz, fizz, hiss, whiz 5 grill 6 hoopla, seethe 7 pizzazz 8 sibilate 10 excitement

sizzling 3 hot 6 red-hot, torrid 7 burning 8 scalding, white-hot 9 scorching

skald 4 bard, poet

Skanda 6 war-god *brother:* 6 Ganesa 7 Ganesha *father:* 4 Siva 5 Shiva

skate 3 nag, ray 4 skid, skim 5 glide, skirr, slide 8 glissade 11 Rollerblade *blade:* 6 runner *kind:* 6 figure, hockey

skating site 3 ice 4 rink

skedaddle 3 run 4 bolt, flee, skip 5 scoot, scram, split 6 beat it, begone, bug off, cut out, decamp, get out 7 make off, run away, scamper, skiddoo, take off, vamoose 8 clear out 10 make tracks

skein 4 coil 5 flock, snarl, twist 6 tangle 12 entanglement

skeletal 4 bony 5 gaunt 6 wasted 7 angular, scraggy, starved 8 rawboned 9 emaciated 10 cadaverous

skeleton 5 bones, draft, frame 6 sketch 7 diagram, outline 9 bare bones, framework *marine:* 5 coral, shell

skeptic 5 cynic 7 doubter, scoffer 8 agnostic 10 Pyrrhonist, questioner, unbeliever 11 disbeliever

skeptical 4 wary 5 leery 6 show-me 7 cynical, dubious 8 doubtful, doubting 9 quizzical 10 dissenting, suspicious 11 mistrustful, questioning, unbelieving 12 disbelieving, freethinking

skepticism 5 doubt 7 dubiety 8 distrust, mistrust, wariness 9 dubiosity, misgiving, suspicion 11 incertitude, uncertainty

skerry 4 isle, reef 6 island

sketch 4 draw, plot 5 draft, rough, trace 6 depict, design, doodle, lay out, map out, précis 7 develop, diagram, outline, portray 8 block out, chalk out, rough out 9 blueprint, delineate 12 character-ize

sketchy 4 iffy 5 crude, rough, vague 6 skimpy, slight 7 cursory, shallow 8 skeletal 10 incomplete 11 preliminary, superficial 12 questionable

skew 4 bias, veer 5 angle, fudge, slant, slide 6 swerve 7 distort

skewer 3 rod 4 spit 5 lance, spear, spike 6 impale, pierce 8 puncture, ridicule, transfix 9 brochette, criticize

ski 5 glide, slide *lift:* 4 J-bar, T-bar 5 chair 7 gondola

skid 5 glide, skate, slide 6 pallet, runner 7 spinout 8 sideslip

skiddoo 4 scat 5 leave, scram, split 6 beat it, begone, bug off, decamp, depart, vacate 7 buzz off, take off, vamoose 8 clear out, shove off 9 skedaddle, take a hike 10 hit the road, make tracks

skid row 6 bowery

skier *American:* 3 Moe (Tommy) 4 Kidd (Billy) 5 Mahre (Phil, Steve) 6 Miller (Bode) 7 Johnson (Bill) *Austrian:* 5 Maier (Hermann) 6 Proell (Annemarie), Sailer (Toni) 7 Klammer (Franz), Schranz (Karl) 10 Girardelli (Marc) 11 Moser-Proell (Annemarie) *French:* 5 Killy (Jean-Claude) *Italian:* 5 Tomba (Alberto) 6 Thoeni (Gustavo) *Luxembourg:* 10 Girardelli (Marc) *Swedish:* 8 Stenmark (Ingemar) *Swiss:* 10 Zurbriggen (Pirmin)

skiff 4 boat 7 rowboat

skiing *area:* 3 run 5 slope *cross-country:* 7 touring *event:* 6 schuss, slalom 8 downhill 11 giant slalom *horse-drawn:* 9 skijoring *kind:* 6 Alpine, Nordic *position:* 7 vorlage *technique:* 6 wedeln 8 snowplow, traverse *turn:* 7 christy 8 christie

skill 3 art 5 craft, knack 7 ability, address, command, cunning, finesse, know-how, mastery, prowess, sleight 8 deftness, facility 9 dexterity, expertise, ingenuity, readiness, technique 10 adroitness, competence 11 proficiency

skilled 3 apt 4 able 5 adept 6 expert 7 capable, trained 8 masterly, talented 9 competent, masterful, practiced 10 proficient 12 accomplished

skillet 3 pan 6 spider 9 frying pan

skillful 4 deft 5 adept, crack, handy 6 adroit, clever, daedal, expert 7 skilled 8 masterly 9 competent, dexterous, masterful, practiced, workmanly 10 proficient 11 crackerjack, workman-like 12 accomplished

skim 4 sail, scan, scud, skip 5 brush, carom, glide, graze, skirr 6 browse 8 embezzle, ricochet

skimp 4 save 5 pinch, scant, spare, stint 6 meager, scanty, scrape, sparse 7 slender 8 begrudge, conserve, retrench, withhold 9 economize

skimpy 5 scant, spare 6 meager, meagre, paltry, scanty, scarce, sparse 7 limited, wanting 8 exiguous 9 deficient 10 inadequate 12 insufficient

skim through 4 scan 6 browse

skin 3 fur, gyp, pod, rap 4 clad, clip, husk, hide, pare, peel, pelt, rind, soak 5 blame, cheat, cover, scale, shell, stiff, strip 6 fleece, sheath, slough 7 censure, condemn, sheathe 8 denounce 9 epidermis, sheathing 10 integument, overcharge 11 decorticate *animal:* 4 coat, hide, pelt 6 hackle, peltry *combining form:* 3 cut 4 cuti, derm 5 derma, dermo, dermy 6 dermat, dermia, dermis 7 cutaneo, dermata (plural), dermato, epiderm 8 epidermo *depression:* 6 dimple *disease:* 4 acne 5 hives, mange 6 eczema 10 dermatitis *dry:* 5 scurf *fold:* 5 plica *layer:* 5 derma 6 corium, dermis 7 cuticle 9 epidermis *opening:* 4 pore *protuberance:* 3 tag, wen 4 mole, wart 6 pimple *rabbit:* 5 coney *relating to:* 6 dermal 9 cuticular, epidermal *spot:* 7 freckle

skin-deep 7 shallow, trivial 11 superficial

skinflint 5 miser 7 niggard, scrooge 8 tightwad 10 cheapskate, pinchpenny

skin game 3 con 4 scam 5 bunco, bunko, cheat, fraud, sting, trick 6 hustle, racket 7 swindle 8 flimflam

skink 6 lizard

skinny 4 bony, dope, info, lank, lean, thin 5 gaunt, lanky, scoop, spare, weedy 6 twiggy 7 angular, lowdown, scraggy, scrawny 8 rawboned, skeletal 9 emaciated

Skin of Our Teeth author 6 Wilder (Thornton)

skip 3 hop, run 4 flee, jump, leap, omit, trip 5 bound, caper, carom, frisk, leave, scoot, skirr 6 cavort, gambol, pass up, spring 7 misfire, scamper, skitter 8 leave out, overlook, pass over, ricochet 9 skedaddle

skipjack 4 boat, fish, tuna 8 bluefish, ladyfish, sailboat

skipper 5 pilot 6 leader 7 captain 9 butterfly, commander

skirmish 3 row 4 fray 5 broil, brush, clash, melee, run-in, scrap, set-to 6 affray, battle, fracas 7 assault, dispute 8 conflict, struggle 9 encounter, scrimmage

skirr 3 run 4 bolt, flee, sail, scud, skim,

skip 5 float, scoot, shoot 7 make off, scamper 9 skedaddle

skirt 3 hem, rim 4 brim, duck, edge 5 avoid, bound, brink, burke, dodge, elude, evade, hedge, verge 6 border, bypass, define, detour, escape, fringe, ignore, margin 8 sidestep, surround 9 perimeter, periphery 10 circumvent *ballet:* 4 tutu *feature:* 3 hem 4 slit *long:* 4 maxi *Scottish:* 4 kilt *short:* 4 mini *style:* 5 A-line 6 sheath

skit 6 shtick, sketch 9 burlesque

skitter 3 hop 4 flit, skip, trip 6 scurry, spring 7 scamper

skittery see SKITTISH

skittish 3 coy, shy 4 edgy, wary 5 chary, dizzy, jumpy, leery 6 fickle 7 bashful, fidgety, flighty, nervous, rabbity, restive 8 unstable, volatile 9 excitable, frivolous, impulsive, mercurial, whimsical 10 capricious, unreliable

skive 4 pare 5 carve, shave, slice

skivvies 9 underwear

skoal 5 toast 6 health

skua 4 bird 6 jaeger 7 seabird

skulduggery 5 fraud 8 foul play, trickery 9 chicanery, duplicity 10 hanky-panky

skulk 4 lurk, slip 5 creep, prowl, shirk, slink, sneak, steal

skull 4 head, mind 5 brain 7 cranium 8 brainpan 9 braincase *back of:* 7 occiput *bone:* 5 vomer 6 zygoma 7 ethmoid, frontal 8 parietal, sphenoid, temporal *jawless:* 9 calvarium *joint:* 6 suture *part:* 3 jaw 5 inion

skullcap 6 beanie, pileus 7 calotte 8 yarmulke 9 calvarium, zucchetto

skunk 4 beat, drub, lick, scum, whip, whup 6 thrash, wallop 7 clobber, polecat, shellac, stinker, trounce 8 civet cat, lambaste 9 overwhelm, slaughter *genus:* 8 Mephitis

sky 5 azure 6 heaven, welkin 7 heavens 8 empyrean 9 firmament

sky-blue 5 azure 8 cerulean

skylarking 5 revel 7 revelry, whoopee 9 high jinks, horseplay, rowdiness, whoop-de-do 10 roughhouse 12 roughhousing

skylight 6 window

skyline 7 horizon, outline

sky pilot 5 padre 6 cleric, parson, pastor 8 chaplain, minister, preacher 9 churchman, clergyman

skyrocket 4 rise, soar 7 shoot up 8 catapult

sky sighting 3 UFO

slab 5 block, chunk, slice, strip 8 pavement

slack 3 lax 4 lazy, slow, soft 5 inert, loose, relax 6 remiss 7 ease off, laggard, passive, relaxed 8 careless, derelict, dilatory, inactive, indolent, slothful, sluggish, stagnant 9 leisurely, lethargic, negligent 10 neglectful

slacken 3 ebb, lax 4 ease, slow, wane 5 abate, let up, loose, relax 6 detain, ease up, lessen, loosen, relent, retard, slow up 7 die down, dwindle, ease off, subside 8 diminish, moderate, slow down 9 untighten 10 decelerate

slacker 3 bum 4 slug 5 idler, sloth 6 loafer 7 goof-off, shirker, wastrel 8 deadbeat, layabout, slugabed, sluggard 9 goldbrick, lazybones 10 delinquent 11 couch potato

slag 4 lava 5 dross 6 cinder, debris, scoria

slake 5 allay 6 deaden, quench 7 crumble, hydrate, relieve, satisfy 9 alleviate

slam 3 bat, hit, jab, pan, rap 4 bang, bash, beat, belt, blow, boom, dash, drub, flay, slug, slur, swat, wham 5 blast, crack, crash, fling, knock, pound, slash, smack, smash, swipe, whack 6 batter, cudgel, hammer, scathe, strike, thwack, wallop 7 clobber, potshot 8 lambaste 9 castigate

slam-dance 4 mosh

slam dunk 5 cinch, setup 6 shoo-in 7 safe bet 9 certainty, sure thing

slammer 3 can, jug, pen 4 brig, coop, jail, stir 5 clink, pokey 6 cooler, lockup, prison 9 calaboose 12 penitentiary

slander 4 slur, tale 5 libel, slime, smear, sully 6 defame, malign, smirch, vilify 7 calumny, scandal, tarnish, traduce 8 besmirch 9 denigrate 10 backbiting, calumniate, defamation, detraction, scandalize 11 mud-slinging 12 backstabbing

slang 4 cant, jive 5 argot, lingo 6 jargon, patois, patter 7 dialect 10 vernacular

slant 3 tip 4 bank, bias, cant, heel, lean, list, skew, tilt, veer, warp 5 angle, aside, bevel, grade, slope, splay 7 distort, incline, leaning, outlook 8 gradient 9 prejudice, viewpoint 10 standpoint 11 inclination 12 predilection *combining form:* 4 clin 5 clino

slap 3 hit, pop 4 bash, blow, cuff, shot, slam, swat 5 clout, smack, spank, whack 6 buffet, insult, rebuff, strike 7 affront, putdown 8 brickbat, lambaste, penalize 9 castigate

slapdash 5 hasty, messy 6 random, sloppy 7 cursory 8 careless, slipshod 9 halfbaked, haphazard, hit-or-miss, makeshift

slap down 5 quell 6 kibosh 7 squelch 8 prohibit, suppress

slaphappy 5 dazed, dizzy, woozy 6 punchy 10 punch-drunk

slash 3 cut 4 clip, gash, hack, pare, slit 5 lower, shave, slice 6 reduce, scathe, scorch 7 abridge, blister, curtail, cut back, cut down, scarify, scourge, shorten 8 lacerate, lambaste, mark down 9 castigate, excoriate 10 abbreviate

slat 4 lath 5 board, stave, strip 6 louver, louvre 7 airfoil

slate 4 gray, list, rock, tile 6 lineup, record, tablet, ticket 7 shingle 8 schedule 9 designate

slather 5 smear 6 spread 8 squander

slattern 4 bawd, moll, slut, tart 5 hussy, tramp, wench 6 floozy, harlot 7 chippie, jezebel, trollop 8 strumpet 10 prostitute 11 painted lady 12 scarlet woman, streetwalker

slaughter 4 kill, slay 6 murder 7 butcher, carnage, killing, wipe out 8 butchery, decimate, demolish, hecatomb, massacre 9 bloodbath, bloodshed, liquidate 10 annihilate, butchering 11 destruction, exterminate, liquidation 12 annihilation

slaughterhouse 8 abattoir

Slav 4 Pole, Serb, Sorb, Wend 5 Croat, Czech 6 Bulgar, Slovak 7 Russian, Serbian, Slovene 8 Bohemian, Croatian, Moravian 9 Bulgarian, Ruthenian, Ukrainian

slave 4 grub, help, peon, plod, serf, slog, toil 5 grind, helot, swink 6 drudge, menial, thrall, toiler, vassal 7 bondman, chattel, servant *feudal:* 4 serf *harem:* 9 odalisque *liberated:* 8 freedman *Muslim:* 6 Mamluk 8 Mameluke *Spartan:* 5 helot

slave driver 6 tyrant 7 foreman 8 martinet, overseer 10 taskmaster 11 Simon Legree

slaver 4 spit 5 drool, froth 6 drivel, saliva 7 dribble, slobber, spittle 8 salivate

slavery 6 thrall 7 bondage, helotry, peonage, serfdom 9 indenture, servitude, thralldom 11 subjugation

Slavic apostle 5 Cyril 9 Methodius

slavish 6 abject, menial 7 servile 8 obeisant, wretched 9 groveling, imitative, laborious 10 obsequious, unoriginal 11 subservient

slay 4 do in, kill 6 murder 7 bump off, butcher, execute, put away 8 dispatch, knock off 9 liquidate, slaughter 11 assassinate

slayer 7 butcher 11 executioner

sleazy 3 low 5 cheap, dingy, seedy, tacky, tatty 6 cheesy, flimsy, shabby, shoddy, trashy 7 run-down, squalid 8 gimcrack 10 down-at-heel 11 dilapidated 12 disreputable

sled 4 luge, pung 6 sleigh 7 coaster, travois 8 toboggan *Russian:* 6 troika

sled dog 5 husky 8 malamute

sledge 4 maul 6 hammer, sleigh *Eskimo:* 7 komatik

sleek 4 oily 6 glassy, glossy, smooth 7 elegant, stylish 8 lustrous, polished 10 glistening

sleep 3 nap 4 doze, rest 6 catnap, repose, siesta, snooze 7 shut-eye, slumber 11 slumberland *bringer:* 7 sandman *combining form:* 4 hypn, narc 5 hypno, narco, somni *god:* 6 Hypnos, Somnus

sleeper 4 beam, mole 7 Pullman 8 long shot 11 double agent, stringpiece

sleeping 7 dormant 8 comatose *disease:* 10 narcolepsy

sleepless 7 wakeful 8 vigilant 9 insomniac

sleeplessness 8 insomnia

sleepwalker 12 somnambulist

sleepy 4 dozy 6 drowsy 7 nodding 9 somnolent 10 slumberous

sleigh 4 pung 6 sledge

sleight 4 ploy, ruse, wile 5 skill, trick 7 gimmick, prowess 8 artifice, deftness, maneuver 9 dexterity, stratagem 10 adroitness

sleight of hand 11 legerdemain

slender 4 lean, slim, thin, trim 5 lithe, reedy, spare 6 skinny, slight, svelte, twiggy 7 spindly, willowy

sleuth 4 dick, Drew (Nancy) 5 Brown (Encyclopedia, Father), Kojak, Morse, Queen (Ellery), Saint (The), snoop, Spade (Sam), Tracy (Dick), Wolfe (Nero) 6 Hammer (Mike), Holmes (Sherlock), Marple (Miss), Poirot (Hercule), shamus, Wimsey (Peter) 7 Cadfael (Brother), Columbo, Fansler (Kate), gumshoe, Maigret, Marlowe (Philip) 8 hawkshaw, Millhone (Kinsey), Rockford (Jim), sherlock 9 Dalgliesh (Adam), detective, Scarpetta (Kay) 10 private eye 12 investigator

slew 3 lot, mob, ton 4 army, heap, host, load, mess, pile, raft, skid, turn, veer 5 batch, bunch, crowd, flock, pivot, twist 6 myriad, passel, swerve, throng 9 abundance, multitude

slice 3 cut 4 gash, slit 5 allot, carve, divvy, quota, sever, share, slash, split, wedge 6 cleave, divide, incise, sample 7 dissect, portion, segment 8 allocate 9 allotment, allowance

slick 4 film, glib, oily, slip, wily 5 sharp, sleek, soapy 6 crafty, glossy, greasy, shrewd, smarmy, smooth, tricky 7 cunning 8 slippery, slithery, unctuous 10 lubricious, oleaginous

slicker 4 dude 5 dandy, shark 6 con man

7 cheater, diddler, grifter, oilskin, sharper **8** raincoat, swindler **9** trickster **11** flimflammer

slide 3 dip, sag **4** flow, ramp, skid, slip **5** chute, coast, chute, drift, glide, skate, slump, spill **6** scooch, stream **7** decline, slither **8** downturn **9** downswing, downtrend **12** transparency

slight 4 omit, skip, slim, snub, thin **5** frail, reedy, scorn, small **6** flimsy, ignore, meager, meagre, modest, offend, paltry, remote, skinny **7** contemn, neglect, outside, put-down, slender, tenuous, trivial **8** brush-off, delicate, discount, overlook, smallish, trifling **9** disregard, pint-sized **10** disrespect, negligible

slim 4 thin **5** lithe, reedy, small, spare **6** meager, meagre, minute, narrow, paltry, remote, skinny, slight, svelte, twiggy **7** lissome, outside, slender, tenuous **9** lithesome **10** negligible

slim down 4 diet, fast **6** reduce **10** slenderize

slime 3 goo, mud **4** glop, gunk, muck, ooze, scum **5** filth **6** sleaze, sludge **7** slander

slimy 4 oozy **6** mucous **7** viscous

sling 3 lob **4** cast, fire, hang, hurl, sock, toss **5** chuck, heave, march, pitch, throw **6** dangle, launch **7** suspend **8** catapult

slink 4 lurk **5** creep, prowl, skulk, slide, sneak, steal **7** gumshoe

slinky 4 sexy **5** lithe, sleek **6** svelte **7** furtive, lissome, sinuous, slender, willowy **8** graceful, sensuous, stealthy

slip 3 sag **4** dock, drop, fall, flow, flub, goof, lurk, shed, sink, skid **5** berth, boner, creep, error, fluff, gaffe, glide, lapse, slide, slink, slump, sneak, steal **6** escape **7** blooper, blunder, decline, drop off, fall off, faux pas, mistake, slither **8** downturn, throw off **9** downswing, downtrend

slipper 4 mule, shoe **5** scuff **6** bootee, bootie, sandal **8** flip-flop, pantofle

slippery 3 icy **4** eely, oily **5** slick **6** greasy, shifty, smooth **7** devious, evasive **8** illusive, slithery **10** lubricious

slipshod 6 blowsy, blowzy, frowsy, frowzy, shabby, shoddy, sloppy, untidy **7** rumpled, scrubby, scruffy, unkempt **8** careless, ill-kempt, slapdash, slovenly, tattered **9** haphazard, negligent **10** bedraggled, disheveled, downat-heel

slipup 4 goof **5** boner, error, fluff, lapse **6** bungle, glitch, miscue, mishap **7** blooper, blunder, faux pas, misstep, mistake, setback, stumble **8** accident

9 mischance, oversight **10** misfortune **11** misjudgment

slit 3 cut, gap **4** gash, rent **5** chink, crack, slash, slice **6** cranny, incise **7** crevice, fissure, opening

slither 4 slip **5** creep, glide, sidle, slide, slink, snake, sneak, steal **7** wriggle **8** undulate

slithery see SLIPPERY

sliver 5 scrap, shard, shave, shred, slice **6** paring **7** shaving, snippet **8** splinter

slob 3 oaf **4** boor, clod, goon, lout **6** galoot, sloven

slobber 4 gush **5** drool, froth **6** drivel, effuse, slaver **7** dribble, enthuse **8** salivate

sloe 4 plum **10** blackthorn

slog 4 grub, moil, plod, plug, toil **5** chore, grind, labor, slave, sweat **6** drudge, schlep, trudge **7** schlepp

slogan 5 motto **6** byword **9** catchword, watchword **10** shibboleth **11** catchphrase

sloop 4 boat **8** sailboat

slop 3 mud, pap **4** gush, muck **5** douse, dreck, dregs, offal, slosh, slush, spill, swill **6** guzzle, pablum, refuse, splash, sludge **7** garbage, pablum, rubbish **8** splatter

slope 3 tip **4** bend, cant, heel, lean, list, rise, skew, swag, sway, tilt **5** grade, pitch, scarp, slant **6** ascent, glacis **7** descent, incline, leaning, recline **8** gradient **9** acclivity, declivity, obliquity **11** inclination *combining form:* **5** cline **6** clinal

sloppy 5 dowdy, gushy, messy **6** slushy, untidy **7** gushing, unkempt **8** careless, effusive, ill-kempt, slapdash, slipshod, slovenly **10** bedraggled, disheveled **11** dishevelled

slosh 4 gush, slop, wash **5** churn, swash **6** gurgle, splash **8** flounder, splatter

slot 4 vent **5** niche, notch **6** groove, keyway **7** keyhole, opening, passage **8** aperture **10** pigeonhole

sloth 4 laze **5** idler **6** acedia, apathy, idling, lazing, loafer, slouch, torpor **7** goof-off, languor, loafing, slacker **8** idleness, laziness, lethargy **9** heaviness, indolence, lassitude, lazybones, torpidity **11** couch potato **12** listlessness, sluggishness **13** shiftlessness

slothful 4 idle, lazy **8** fainéant, indolent **9** shiftless

slouch 3 bum, oaf, sag **4** laze, loaf, loll, lout, mope, slug **5** droop, idler, sloth, slump, stoop **6** loafer, loiter, lounge **7** saunter, shamble, shuffle **8** fainéant, slugabed, sluggard **9** do-nothing, lazybones

slough 3 bog, fen **4** cast, mire, molt, quag, shed, sump **5** inlet, marsh, scrap, swamp **6** morass, reject **7** discard **8** jettison, quagmire, throw out **9** backwater, marshland, swampland, throw away

Slovakia *capital:* **10** Bratislava *city:* **6** Kosice *monetary unit:* **6** koruna *mountain range:* **10** Carpathian *neighbor:* **6** Poland **7** Austria, Hungary, Ukraine **13** Czech Republic *river:* **3** Váh **4** Hron **6** Danube, Morava

Slovenia *capital:* **9** Ljubljana *city:* **7** Maribor *monetary unit:* **5** tolar *neighbor:* **5** Italy **7** Austria, Croatia, Hungary *part of:* **7** Balkans *peninsula:* **6** Balkan

slovenly 5 dingy, messy, mussy, seedy, slack **6** frowsy, frowzy, grubby, grungy, scuzzy, shabby, skanky, sleazy, sloppy, untidy **7** squalid, unkempt **8** careless, slapdash, slipshod **10** bedraggled, slatternly

slow 4 late, poky **5** brake, check, lento, tardy **6** adagio, hinder, impede, leaden, retard, torpid **7** halting, lagging, slacken **8** dilatory, dragging, plodding, sluggish, stagnant **9** leisurely, snaillike, unhurried **10** decelerate, snail-paced, straggling

slowpoke 5 snail **6** lagger **7** dawdler, laggard **8** lingerer, loiterer **9** straggler

sludge 3 mud **4** crud, gunk, mire, muck, ooze, slop **5** slime **6** sewage **8** sediment

slug 3 bum, hit, nip, tot **4** bash, belt, dram, drop, jolt, shot, slam, swat **5** blast, clout, idler, larva, pound, punch, smack, smash, snail, snort, thump **6** buffet, loafer, slouch, thwack, wallop **7** clobber, goof-off, slacker **8** fainéant, toothful **9** do-nothing, lazybones **11** couch potato *genus:* **5** Limax

slugfest 4 bout **5** brawl, set-to **6** rumble **8** dogfight **10** donnybrook, prizefight

sluggard 3 bum **5** idler **6** loafer, slouch **7** dawdler, goof-off, laggard, shirker, slacker **8** deadbeat, fainéant, slowpoke, slugabed **9** do-nothing, goldbrick, lazybones

slugger 5 boxer **6** batter, hitter **7** palooka

sluggish 4 lazy, logy, slow **5** inert, slack **6** draggy, leaden, stupid, torpid **7** lumpish **8** dragging, indolent, listless, slothful **9** apathetic, lethargic

sluice 4 duct, flow, gush, pour, race, wash **5** flush, surge **6** trough **7** channel **8** spillway **9** floodgate

slum 6 ghetto **7** skid row

slumber 3 nap **4** doze **5** sleep **6** catnap, drowse, snooze, stupor, torpor **8** dor-

mancy, hebetude, lethargy **9** lassitude, torpidity

slumberous see SLEEPY

slumgullion 4 stew **6** burgoo, ragout **7** goulash

slump 3 dip, sag **4** drop, fall, flag, funk, loll, sink, slip **5** droop, hunch, slide **6** slouch, trough **7** decline, drop off, falloff **8** collapse, downturn **9** downslide, downswing, downtrend, recession **10** depression, stagnation

slur 4 blot, blur, lisp, onus, slam, spot **5** brand, knock, libel, odium, smear, stain **6** befoul, defame, insult, malign, stigma, vilify **7** blacken, calumny, obloquy, obscure, slander, spatter, traduce **8** black eye, brickbat, innuendo, tear down **9** aspersion, bespatter, denigrate, discredit, disparage **10** accusation, calumniate

slurp 3 lap **4** gulp, suck **5** lap up, swill **6** guzzle

slush 3 mud **4** mire, muck, slop **6** drivel **8** schmaltz

sly 4 foxy, wily **5** cagey, saucy, shady, slick **6** artful, clever, crafty, shifty, shrewd, smooth, sneaky, subtle, tricky **7** cunning, devious, furtive, roguish, vulpine **8** guileful, scheming, slippery, stealthy **9** designing, insidious, underhand **11** mischievous, underhanded

slyboots see SCAMP

slyness 4 wile **5** guile **7** cunning **8** caginess, foxiness, wiliness **9** canniness **10** craftiness

smack 3 bat, bop, box **4** bang, bash, belt, biff, blow, buss, chop, clip, cuff, dash, hint, kiss, peck, reek, slam, slap, sock, tang, whop **5** clout, crack, plumb, punch, savor, smell, spank, stink, taste, tinge, trace, whack **6** buffet, heroin, relish, smooch, square, strike, thwack **7** clobber, soupçon

smack-dab 4 bang, just **5** plumb, right **7** exactly **8** squarely **9** perfectly, precisely

small 3 wee **4** mean, mini, puny, tiny **5** bitty, dinky, dwarf, micro, minor, petty, runty, short, teeny **6** bantam, little, meager, meagre, minute, monkey, narrow, paltry, petite, slight, teensy **7** cramped, stunted, trivial **8** picayune, piddling, pint-size, trifling **9** miniature, minuscule, pint-sized **10** diminutive, negligible, undersized **11** ineffectual, unimportant *combining form:* **4** micr, mini **5** micro

small fry 4 kids, tots **8** children **10** youngsters

small-minded 4 mean **5** petty **6** narrow **7** bigoted **9** hidebound, illiberal, parochial **10** brassbound, intolerant, provincial

smallpox 7 variola

small talk 4 chat **6** banter **7** chatter, palaver, prattle **8** badinage, chitchat, raillery, repartee **10** persiflage

small-time 5 minor, petty **6** paltry, two-bit **7** trivial **8** picayune, piddling, trifling **10** bush-league, negligible, shoestring **11** minor-league, unimportant **13** insignificant

smalt 4 blue

smarmy 4 glib, oily **5** slick **6** sleazy **7** buttery, fawning, fulsome **8** unctuous **10** obsequious, oleaginous **12** ingratiating

smart 3 apt **4** ache, chic, keen **5** acute, alert, canny, fresh, natty, quick, sassy, saucy, sharp, slick, sting, swank, throb **6** brainy, bright, cheeky, clever, dapper, shrewd, spruce, suffer **7** dashing, stylish **8** impudent **11** fashionable, intelligent, quick-witted, ready-witted, sharp-witted

smart aleck 7 show-off, wise guy **8** wiseacre **9** know-it-all **11** wisecracker, wisenheimer

smart-alecky 4 wise **5** fresh, sassy, saucy **6** cheeky **8** impudent, insolent **9** bold-faced **11** impertinent

smart set 5 elect, elite **6** bon ton, gentry **7** in crowd, quality, society, who's who **9** beau monde, haut monde **10** blue bloods, upper crust **11** aristocracy, Four Hundred, high society

smarty-pants 7 wise guy **9** know-it-all, swellhead **11** wisenheimer

smash 3 hit, jar **4** bang, bash, belt, blow, boom, clap, jolt, raze, ruin, slam, slug, sock, wham, whop **5** blast, burst, clash, crack, crash, crush, pound, shock, whack, wreck **6** batter, impact, pileup, shiver, wallop **7** clobber, crack-up, debacle, destroy, shatter, smashup, success **8** collapse, decimate, demolish, fragment, knockout, overhand, splinter, tear down **9** breakdown, collision, pulverize, sensation, succès fou **10** annihilate **12** disintegrate

smashup 5 crash, wreck **6** fiasco, pileup **7** crack-up, debacle **8** accident, collapse, disaster **9** breakdown, collision

smattering 3 few **7** handful **10** sprinkling

smear 3 dab, tar **4** beat, coat, daub, drub, lick, slur, soil, whip **5** cover, libel, stain, sully, taint **6** befoul, defame, defile, malign, smirch, smudge, spread, thrash, vilify **7** asperse, blacken, calumny, plaster, shellac, slander, tarnish, traduce **8** besmirch **9** bespatter, denigrate **10** calumniate

smell 4 funk, nose, odor, reek **5** aroma, scent, sense, smack, sniff, snuff, stink, trace, whiff **6** detect, stench **7** bouquet, perfume **9** fragrance, redolence

smell, sense of 9 olfaction

smelly 4 rank **5** fetid, funky, reeky **6** foetid, putrid, rancid, stinky **7** noisome, reeking, stenchy **8** mephitic, stinking **10** malodorous

smelt 4 flux, fuse, slag **6** reduce, refine, tomcod **8** sparling **9** sand lance, whitebait

smidgen see PARTICLE

smile 4 beam, grin **5** smirk **6** simper

smirch see SMUDGE

smirk 4 grin, leer **5** fleer, sneer **6** simper **7** grimace

smite 3 hit **4** belt, kill, sock **5** clout, whack **6** assail, attack, strike **7** afflict, assault, clobber, torment

smithereens 4 bits **6** pieces **9** fragments, particles

smitten 5 taken **6** hooked **8** besotted, enamored **9** enamoured, enchanted, entranced **10** captivated, enraptured, infatuated **11** intoxicated

smock 5 apron, dress, frock **8** pinafore

smoke 4 cure, fume **5** fumes, vapor **8** fastball, fumigate **9** cigarette

smoky 4 fumy, gray, hazy **5** murky, sooty **6** turbid **7** reeking **10** caliginous, smoldering

smolder 4 glow **5** churn **6** bubble, seethe, simmer **7** ferment **9** fulminate

smooch 4 buss, kiss, neck, peck **5** smack **8** osculate

smooth 4 easy, even, flat **5** fluid, flush, level, plane, sleek, slick, suave **6** facile, fluent, glassy, glossy, polish, urbane **7** cursive, flatten, flowing, running **8** glabrous, hairless, soothing, unbroken **10** effortless, unwrinkled

smooth-spoken 4 glib **6** fluent **8** eloquent **10** articulate **13** silver-tongued

smorgasbord 4 hash, olio **6** buffet, jumble, medley **7** farrago, mélange **8** mishmash, mixed bag, pastiche **9** potpourri **10** hodgepodge, miscellany, salmagundi **11** gallimaufry

smother 5 choke, douse, quell **6** hush up, muffle, quench, stifle **7** blanket, repress, squelch **8** inundate, restrain, suppress **9** overwhelm, suffocate **10** asphyxiate

smudge 3 dab **4** blot, blur, daub, foul, soil **5** dirty, smear, stain, sully, taint **6** bedaub, blotch, defile, smirch **7** begrime, besmear, blacken, blemish, splotch, tarnish **8** besmirch

smug 8 priggish **9** conceited **10** complacent **13** self-satisfied

smuggle 3 run 7 bootleg

smut 4 porn 5 filth 9 obscenity
11 pornography

smutty 4 blue, foul, lewd, racy 5 bawdy,
dirty, nasty, sooty 6 coarse, filthy,
risqué, vulgar 7 obscene, raunchy
8 indecent, off-color, prurient 9 salacious 12 pornographic, scatological

Smyrna 5 Izmir

snack 3 tea 4 bite, nosh, tapa 6 morsel,
nibble 11 refreshment

snaffle 3 bit, cop 4 lift 5 filch, pinch,
swipe 6 pilfer, pocket 7 purloin

snafu 5 botch, error, mix-up, snarl
6 bungle, foul up, mess up, muddle
7 chaotic, screwup 9 confusion

snag 3 nab 4 curb, grab, hook, nail, tear
5 catch, hitch 6 glitch, holdup, hurdle,
obtain, secure 7 capture 8 drawback,
obstacle 9 apprehend 10 impediment
11 obstruction

snail 5 whelk 6 limpet 7 mollusc, mollusk 8 escargot, ramshorn, slowpoke
9 gastropod 10 periwinkle

snake 3 boa 4 fink 5 crawl, creep, racer,
slide 6 python, writhe 7 hognose, serpent, slither 8 anaconda, ophidian,
undulate *poisonous:* 3 asp 5 adder,
cobra, coral, krait, mamba, viper
6 elapid, taipan 7 rattler 8 pit viper
10 bushmaster, copperhead, fer-de-
lance 11 cottonmouth 13 water moccasin

snakebird 6 darter 7 anhinga

snake-eater 8 mongoose
13 secretary bird

snakelike 7 sinuous 8 ophidian 10 serpentine

snakeroot 7 bugbane 10 wild ginger
11 blazing star

snakeweed 7 bistort 13 poison hemlock

snaky 7 sinuous, winding 8 flexuous,
tortuous 10 convoluted, meandering,
serpentine 11 anfractuous

snap 4 bang, bark 5 break, cinch, crack
6 breeze, picnic 7 crackle 8 duck soup,
kid stuff, pushover 10 child's play

snap back 6 revive 7 rebound, recover
10 convalesce, recuperate

snappy 4 edgy, fast, tart 5 brisk, hasty,
huffy, natty, quick, rapid, sharp, smart,
swank, swift, testy 6 lively, prompt,
speedy, touchy 7 dashing, stylish,
waspish 8 animated, petulant, vigorous
9 breakneck, fractious, irritable, vivacious

snare 3 bag 4 bait, hook, lure, trap
5 catch, decoy, tempt 6 come-on,
enmesh, entice, entrap, seduce, tangle
7 capture, catch up, chicane, embroil,
ensnare, ensnarl, involve, pitfail, tram-

mel 8 entangle, inveigle 9 chicanery,
deception 10 enticement, temptation

snarl 3 jam, web 4 bark, knot, maze,
mesh 5 chaos, growl, ravel, skein 6 jungle, morass, muddle, tangle 7 perplex
8 disarray, disorder, entangle, mishmash 9 confusion, labyrinth 10 com-
plexity, complicate 12 complication,
entanglement

snatch 3 bit, nab 4 grab, jerk, take, yank
5 catch, pluck, seize, swipe 6 abduct,
clutch, kidnap, wrench 8 fragment

snazzy 4 chic 5 fancy, gaudy, jazzy,
nobby, ritzy, sassy, sharp, smart, showy,
swank 6 chichi, classy, flashy, garish,
glitzy, jaunty, spiffy, swanky 7 elegant

sneak 3 cur, pad 4 lurk, slip, worm
5 crawl, creep, glide, mooch, prowl,
shirk, skulk, skunk, slide, slink, steal
6 covert, secret, tiptoe, weasel
7 furtive, gumshoe, slither, smuggle
8 hush-hush, slyboots, stealthy 9 pussyfoot, scoundrel 10 undercover 11 clandestine

sneaky 4 foxy 6 shifty, tricky 7 devious,
furtive 8 guileful, indirect, slippery,
stealthy 9 underhand 11 duplicitous,
underhanded

sneer 4 gibe, jeer 5 fleer, scoff, smirk
7 grimace, snigger

snicker 5 laugh 6 giggle, titter 7 chortle,
chuckle

snide 4 mean 5 nasty 8 spiteful 9 malicious 11 insinuating

sniff 4 jeer, nose 5 scent, scoff, smell,
snoop 6 inhale

sniffy 4 smug 5 aloof, lofty 6 lordly,
snooty, uppity 7 haughty, pompous,
stuck-up 8 scornful, superior 10 disdainful, hoity-toity 12 contemptuous,
supercilious

snifter 3 nip, sip, tot 4 dram, drop, jolt,
shot, slug 5 glass, snort 6 finger, goblet

snip 3 bit, cut 4 clip, crop, trim 5 notch,
scrap 8 fragment

snipe 4 carp 9 sandpiper

sniper 6 gunman, killer 7 shooter
8 marksman, rifleman 12 sharpshooter

snippety see SNIPPY

snippy 4 curt 5 bluff, blunt, brief, gruff,
short, terse 6 abrupt, crusty 7 brusque
8 snappish

snit 3 fit 4 flap, fume, huff, stew 5 panic,
pique, sweat, tizzy 6 dither, frenzy,
lather, pother, swivet 10 conniption

snitch 3 cop, nip, rat 4 beak, fink, hook,
lift, palm, sing, tell 5 filch, peach,
pinch, spill, steal, swipe 6 inform, pilfer, pocket, squeal, tattle 7 purloin, rat
fink, tattler, tipster 8 betrayer,
informer, squealer 11 stool pigeon

snivel 3 sob **4** weep **5** cower, whine **6** cringe, whinge **7** blubber, snuffle, whimper

snob 5 snoot **6** poseur **7** parvenu

snobbish 6 snooty, uppity **7** haughty, high-hat, stuck-up **10** hoity-toity **11** patronizing, pretentious **12** supercilious **13** condescending

snook 5 cobia **6** robalo **12** sergeant fish

snooker 3 con **4** dupe, fool, hoax, pool **5** trick **6** delude **7** beguile, deceive, defraud **8** flimflam, hoodwink **9** bamboozle **11** hornswoggle

snoop 3 pry, spy **4** nose, peek, peep, peer, poke **5** prier, pryer **6** ferret, meddle, sleuth **7** gumshoe, intrude, meddler **8** busybody, quidnunc **9** detective, inspector, interfere **10** rubberneck

snooper 3 spy **9** detective, inspector **12** investigator

snoopy 4 nosy **6** prying **7** curious **8** meddling **9** intrusive **10** meddlesome **11** inquisitive

snoot see SNOUT

snooty see SNOBBISH

snooze 3 kip, nap **4** doze **5** sleep **6** catnap, drowse, nod off, siesta **7** drop off, slumber **10** forty winks

snore 8 rhonchus

snort 3 nip, tot **4** dram, drop, jolt, shot, slug **5** scoff, snarl **6** exhale, inhale **7** snifter

snout 4 beak, nose **6** muzzle **9** proboscis

snow *glacial:* **4** firn, névé *melted:* **5** slush *pellet:* **7** graupel *ridge:* **8** sastruga

snow apple 8 mushroom

snowball 5 mount, run up **6** expand **7** augment, burgeon, explode, inflate **8** increase, multiply, mushroom, viburnum **10** accumulate **11** proliferate

snowbird 5 finch, junco **6** thrush **7** bunting **9** fieldfare, ivory gull

Snow-Bound author 8 Whittier (John Greenleaf)

snow finch 9 brambling

snow grouse 9 ptarmigan

snow leopard 5 ounce

Snow Leopard author 11 Matthiessen (Peter)

snowstorm 8 blizzard

snub 3 cut **4** shun **5** blunt, scorn, spite, spurn **6** rebuff, rebuke, slight, stubby **7** put down **9** ostracize, repudiate **12** cold-shoulder

snuff 3 ice, off **4** kill, nose **5** pinch, scent, smell **6** murder, rappee **7** execute **10** extinguish **11** exterminate

snug 4 cozy, neat, taut, tidy, trim **5** comfy, cushy, tight **6** burrow, cuddle, nestle, nuzzle, secure **7** orderly **9** sheltered, shipshape **11** comfortable

snuggle 5 spoon **6** burrow, cuddle, curl up, huddle, nestle, nuzzle

so 3 sae **4** ergo, then, thus **5** hence **6** indeed **9** similarly, therefore **11** accordingly **12** consequently

soak 3 sot, wet **4** bilk, clip, lush, skin, swig, wino **5** douse, drink, gouge, imbue, souse, steep **6** boozer, drench, fleece, infuse, seethe **7** drinker, guzzler, immerse **8** drunkard, permeate, saturate, submerge **9** alcoholic, penetrate **10** boozehound, impregnate, overcharge *flax:* **3** ret

soap 4 suds **6** stroke **7** flatter, wheedle **8** blandish, butter up, inveigle **9** sweet-talk *hard:* **7** castile *ingredient:* **3** lye

soapbox 4 dais **6** podium **7** rostrum **8** hustings, platform, scaffold

soap plant 5 amole

soapstone 8 steatite

soapwort 7 cowherd **11** bouncing bet

soar 3 fly **4** lift, rise **5** arise, climb, glide, hover, mount, shoot **6** ascend, rocket **7** shoot up **8** increase **9** skyrocket

sob 3 cry **4** bawl, blub, wail, weep **7** blubber, whimper

sober 4 calm, cool **5** grave, staid **6** lowkey, proper, sedate, serene, solemn **7** austere, earnest, serious, subdued **8** composed, decorous, low-keyed, moderate, rational, reserved **9** abstinent, collected, practical, pragmatic, realistic, temperate **10** abstaining, abstemious, controlled, forbearing, hardheaded, no-nonsense, reasonable, restrained **11** disciplined, down-to-earth **12** matter-of-fact **13** imperturbable, self-possessed, unimpassioned

sobriety 7 gravity **10** abstinence, continence, sedateness, temperance **11** seriousness

sobriquet 3 tag **5** alias **6** byname **7** epithet, moniker **8** cognomen, nickname **10** hypocorism

so-called 6 formal **7** alleged, nominal, titular **8** supposed **9** pretended, professed, purported **10** ostensible, self-styled

soccer *cup:* **5** World *official:* **7** referee **8** linesman *player:* **6** booter, goalie, kicker, winger **7** forward, link man, striker, sweeper **8** defender, fullback, halfback **10** goalkeeper *star:* **4** Hamm (Mia), Pelé **5** Akers (Michelle) **7** Beckham (David), Ronaldo **8** Maradona (Diego) **11** Beckenbauer (Franz) *term:* **3** net **4** boot, chip, kick, trap **6** corner, header, tackle, volley **7** dribble, kickoff, throw-in **8** back-heel, free kick, goal kick, goal line **9** touchline **10** center spot, corner flag, corner kick

11 dropped ball, halfway line, penalty kick, penalty spot

sociable 5 close **6** genial **7** affable, amiable, cordial **8** familiar, gracious **9** clubbable, congenial, convivial **10** gregarious, hospitable **11** good-natured

social 5 civic, civil **8** communal **9** clubbable, convivial **10** collective, gregarious, hospitable **11** extroverted **13** companionable *class:* **5** caste

Social Contract author 8 Rousseau (Jean-Jacques)

socialist *American:* **4** Debs (Eugene) **6** Ripley (George), Thomas (Norman) *British:* **4** Owen (Robert, Robert Dale), Webb (Beatrice, Sidney) **6** Morris (William) *French:* **7** Fourier (Charles), Viviani (René) **10** Saint-Simon (Henri de) *German:* **4** Marx (Karl) **6** Engels (Friedrich) **9** Luxemburg (Rosa) **10** Liebknecht (Wilhelm)

socialize 3 mix **5** party **6** hobnob, mingle **7** consort **9** associate **10** fraternize

social worker 4 Riis (Jacob), Wald (Lillian D.) **6** Addams (Jane) **7** Alinsky (Saul), Lathrop (Julia C.)

society 4 club **5** elite, guild **6** gentry, league, people, public **7** company, quality, who's who **8** populace, sodality **9** beau monde, community, haut monde **10** fellowship, fraternity, upper class, upper crust **11** aristocracy, association, brotherhood **13** companionship

sociologist *American:* **4** Bell (Daniel), Ward (Lester Frank) **5** Balch (Emily Green), Whyte (William H.) **6** Du Bois (W. E. B.), Glazer (Nathan), Sumner (William Graham) **7** Johnson (Charles Spurgeon), Riesman (David) *English:* **7** Spencer (Herbert) *French:* **8** Durkheim (Emile) *German:* **5** Weber (Max) *Italian:* **6** Pareto (Vilfredo) *Swedish:* **6** Myrdal (Alva, Gunnar)

sock 3 bop, box, hit **4** bash, belt, blow, chop, cuff, ding, slap, slog **5** clout, punch, smack, smash, whack **6** argyle, buffet, strike, thwack **8** stocking

sock away 4 bank, save, stow **5** cache, hoard, lay by, put by, stash **8** lay aside

socks 4 hose **7** hosiery

Socrates *birthplace:* **6** Athens *poison:* **7** hemlock *pupil:* **5** Plato *wife:* **8** Xantippe **9** Xanthippe

Socratic 8 maieutic

sod 4 land, peat, turf **5** earth, grass **6** ground

soda 3 pop **4** cola **5** tonic **7** seltzer

sodality 4 club **5** guild, lodge, order, union **6** league **7** society **9** community **10** fellowship, fraternity **11** association, brotherhood

sodden 3 wet **5** soggy, soppy **6** soaked, soused **7** soaking, sopping **8** drenched, dripping **9** saturated **11** waterlogged, wringing-wet

Sodom and ___ 8 Gomorrah

sofa 5 couch, divan **7** ottoman **9** banquette, davenport

so far 3 yet **5** as yet, still **6** to date **7** till now **8** hitherto, until now **10** heretofore

Sofia native 6 Bulgar **9** Bulgarian

soft 4 cozy, easy, mild, snug **5** balmy, comfy, cushy, downy, faint, mushy, silky **6** doughy, flabby, gentle, low-key, pliant, satiny, silken, simple, smooth, spongy, tender **7** cottony, lenient, pillowy, pliable, squashy, squishy, subdued, velvety **8** cushiony, workable, yielding **9** malleable **11** comfortable

softcover 9 paperback

soften 4 ease, tame **5** abate, allay, blunt, relax **6** dampen, lessen, mellow, soothe, subdue, temper, weaken **7** assuage, lighten, mollify **8** diminish, enfeeble, mitigate, moderate, palliate, tone down, turn down **9** alleviate

soft hail 7 graupel

softhearted 4 kind, warm **6** humane, kindly, tender **7** lenient **10** responsive **11** sympathetic **13** compassionate

soft palate 5 velum

soft-pedal 4 mute **6** dampen, hush up, muffle, subdue **8** minimize, play down, suppress, tone down **9** underplay **11** deemphasize

soft-soap 3 con **4** coax **6** cajole, soothe, wangle **7** blarney, flatter, wheedle **8** blandish, butter up, inveigle **9** sweet-talk

soggy 3 wet **6** doughy, soaked, sodden **7** soaking, sopping **8** drenched, dripping **9** saturated **10** bedraggled **11** waterlogged

Sohrab and Rustum author 6 Arnold (Matthew)

soi-disant 7 alleged **8** putative, so-called, supposed **9** pretended, professed, purported **10** ostensible, self-styled

soil 3 mud, tar **4** daub, dirt, foul, land, loam, mess, muck, murk **5** dirty, earth, grime, muddy, smear, stain, sully, taint **6** defile, ground, smirch, smudge **7** blacken, country, pollute, tarnish **8** besmirch, discolor, homeland **10** fatherland, motherland, terra firma **11** contaminate *aggregate:* **3** ped *clay:* **5** gault *dark:* **9** chernozem *deposit:* **5** loess **7** eluvium *infertile:* **6** podzol *layer:* **4** gley, sola (plural) **5** solum *rich:* **6** hotbed *tropical:* **7** latosol

soiree 4 fete, gala **5** party **6** affair, social

7 shindig **8** function **9** festivity, reception **11** celebration **13** entertainment
sojourn 4 bide, stay, stop **5** abide, lodge, tarry, visit **6** linger **7** layover **8** stopover
Sol 3 sun **7** daystar, phoebus *horse:* **4** Eous **5** Ethon **9** Erythreos (see also HELIOS)
solace 5 allay, amuse, cheer **6** buck up **7** comfort, console, hearten **8** inspirit **10** condolence
solar disk 4 Aten, Aton
solarium 7 sunroom
solder 4 fuse, weld **5** braze
soldier 5 grunt, sepoy **7** dogface, draftee, fighter, private, recruit, trooper, veteran, warrior **8** bluecoat, doughboy, fusilier, rifleman **9** free lance, guerrilla, man-at-arms, mercenary **10** carabineer, carabinier, serviceman **11** condottiere, infantryman *ancient Greece:* **7** hoplite *British:* **5** Tommy **7** redcoat *cavalry:* **6** hussar **8** chasseur *Confederate:* **3** reb *French:* **5** poilu **6** Zouave *German:* **5** jerry *irregular:* **8** guerilla **9** guerrilla *Prussian:* **5** uhlan *Turkish:* **9** janissary
sole 3 one **4** lone, only **5** alone **6** bottom, single, unique **8** flatfish, singular **9** exclusive
solecism 4 goof, slip **5** boner, error, gaffe, lapse **6** misuse **7** blooper, blunder, faux pas, mistake **9** barbarism, indecorum, vulgarism **11** impropriety
solemn 5 grand, grave, sober, staid, stern **6** august, formal, ritual, sedate, somber, sombre **7** earnest, plenary, serious, stately, weighty **8** funereal, imposing, majestic **9** dignified **10** ceremonial, impressive, no-nonsense, sobersided **11** ceremonious, magnificent
solemnize 4 keep **5** bless, honor **6** hallow **7** dignify, observe **8** venerate **9** celebrate, ritualize **10** consecrate **11** commemorate
solicit 3 ask, beg **4** lure, tout, urge **5** apply **6** demand, drum up, entice **7** beseech, bespeak, canvass, entreat, implore, request **8** petition **9** importune **11** proposition, requisition
solicitor 6 jurist, lawyer, suitor **7** pleader **8** advocate, attorney **9** counselor
solicitous 4 avid, keen **5** eager, fussy **6** ardent, tender **7** anxious, careful, devoted, fearful, finicky, worried **8** rigorous **9** assiduous, attentive, concerned, impatient **10** fastidious, meticulous, scrupulous **11** considerate, punctilious, sympathetic **12** apprehensive **13** conscientious
solicitude 4 care, heed **5** qualm, worry **6** unease **7** anxiety, concern, scruple **9** attention, vigilance **10** uneasiness

11 compunction **12** watchfulness **13** consideration
solid 4 firm, hard **5** dense, sound, valid **6** cogent, secure, stable, sturdy, united **7** compact **8** reliable, unbroken **9** steadfast, unanimous, undivided **10** convincing **11** substantial
solidarity 5 union, unity **6** esprit **7** concord, oneness **8** cohesion **9** integrity **10** singleness **12** cohesiveness, togetherness **13** esprit de corps
solidify 3 dry, fix, gel, set **4** cake, jell **6** freeze, harden, secure **7** compact, congeal **8** compress, contract, indurate **11** consolidate
solitary 4 lone, lorn, only, solo **5** alone **6** hermit, lonely, single, unique **7** recluse **8** derelict, deserted, desolate, eremitic, forsaken, isolated, lonesome, separate, singular **9** abandoned, reclusive, withdrawn **10** antisocial, particular, unsociable **11** standoffish **12** misanthropic **13** unaccompanied
solitude 7 privacy **8** loneness **9** aloneness, isolation, seclusion **10** detachment, loneliness, quarantine, retirement, withdrawal **11** confinement **12** separateness
solo 4 lone **5** alone **6** single **7** unaided **8** solitary **13** independently, unaccompanied
Solomon *brother:* **8** Adonijah *daughter:* **7** Taphath **8** Basemath *father:* **5** David *kingdom:* **6** Israel *mother:* **9** Bathsheba *son, successor:* **8** Rehoboam *victim:* **4** Joab **8** Adonijah
Solomon Islands *capital:* **7** Honiara *ethnic group:* **10** Melanesian *island:* **7** Florida, Malaita, Rennell **8** Choiseul **11** Guadalcanal, Santa Isabel **12** San Cristóbal *language:* **5** Pijin **7** English *monetary unit:* **6** dollar
solon 8 lawgiver **10** legislator
so long 4 by-by, ciao, ta-ta **5** adieu, adios **6** bye-bye **7** cheerio, goodbye, toodles **8** farewell, Godspeed, toodle-oo
solution 6 answer, result *salt:* **6** saline
solve 3 fix **5** break, crack **6** decode, reveal, settle **7** clarify, clear up, dope out, explain, unravel, work out **8** construe, decipher, unriddle, untangle **9** elucidate, figure out, interpret, puzzle out **11** disentangle
Somalia *capital:* **9** Mogadishu *gulf:* **4** Aden *language:* **6** Arabic, Somali *location:* **12** Horn of Africa *monetary unit:* **8** shilling *neighbor:* **5** Kenya **8** Djibouti, Ethiopia
somatic 6 bodily, carnal **7** fleshly **8** corporal, parietal, physical **9** corporeal
somber 3 dim **4** dark, drab, dull, grim

5 bleak, dusky, grave, heavy, murky, staid **6** dismal, dreary, gloomy, sedate, solemn **7** doleful, joyless, obscure, serious, weighty **8** funereal, mournful **9** tenebrous **10** caliginous, depressing, depressive, lugubrious, melancholy, sepulchral, sobersided, tenebrific **11** dispiriting

somewhat 5 quite **6** fairly, kind of, rather, sort of **7** a little **8** slightly **9** partially, tolerably **10** moderately

sommelier's offering 4 wine

somniferous see SLEEPY

somnolent see SLEEPY

Somnus *brother:* **4** Mors *god of:* **5** sleep *mother:* **3** Nox

son *French:* **4** fils *Italian:* **6** figlio *Spanish:* **4** hijo

song 3 air, lay **4** aria, glee, hymn, lied, tune **5** carol, chant, ditty, lyric, paean **6** ballad, melody, number **7** chanson **8** madrigal *biblical:* **8** canticle *boat:* **9** barcarole **10** barcarolle *French:* **7** chanson *German:* **4** lied **6** lieder (plural) *lamentation:* **5** dirge **8** threnode, threnody *medieval:* **8** sirvente **9** sirventes *morning:* **6** aubade *of joy:* **5** paean *operatic:* **4** aria **8** cavatina **9** cabaletta *Portuguese:* **4** fado *sacred:* **5** psalm *sailor's:* **6** chanty, shanty **7** chantey *short:* **8** canzonet *wedding:* **8** hymeneal

song and dance 5 pitch, spiel

songbird see at BIRD

Song of Myself author 7 Whitman (Walt)

Song of Solomon 9 Canticles

songwriter 8 composer, lyricist

Sonja ___ 5 Henie

Sonnambula composer 7 Bellini (Vincenzo)

sonnet *developer:* **8** Petrarch *part:* **5** octet **6** octave, sestet

sonorous 7 ringing, vibrant **8** resonant **10** oratorical, resounding, rhetorical **11** declamatory **12** magniloquent **13** grandiloquent

Sontag novel 9 In America **12** Volcano Lover (The)

soon 4 anon **6** any day, pronto **7** betimes, quickly, rapidly, shortly **8** directly, promptly, speedily **9** forthwith, presently, right away **10** before long

Sooner State 8 Oklahoma

soothe 4 balm, calm, ease, hush, lull **5** allay, quiet, salve, still **6** becalm, pacify, settle, solace, subdue **7** appease, assuage, comfort, compose, console, massage, mollify, placate, relieve **8** calm down, reassure **9** alleviate **10** conciliate, propitiate **11** tranquilize

soothsay 5 augur **8** prophesy **9** adumbrate **10** vaticinate **13** prognosticate

soothsayer 4 seer **5** sibyl **6** oracle **7** diviner, prophet **8** foreseer **9** predictor **10** forecaster, foreteller *ancient Roman:* **5** augur **6** auspex **8** haruspex *blind:* **8** Tiresias (see also PROPHET)

sop 3 wet **4** gift, soak **5** bribe, douse, goody, souse, steep **6** deluge, drench, reward, seethe **7** douceur **8** gratuity, saturate, waterlog **9** incentive, lagniappe, sweetener **10** enticement

sophism see SOPHISTRY

sophistic 5 false, phony **7** invalid, seeming, unsound **8** delusive, illusory, spurious **9** beguiling, casuistic, deceptive, plausible **10** fallacious, fraudulent, misleading, ostensible

sophisticated 5 blasé, jaded, suave **6** smooth, svelte, urbane **7** complex, knowing, refined, worldly **8** cultured, involved, schooled, seasoned **9** Byzantine, elaborate, intricate, practiced **10** world-weary **11** complicated, experienced, worldly-wise **12** cosmopolitan

sophistry 12 casuistry **12** equivocation **13** dissimulation, prevarication

Sophocles play 4 Ajax **7** Electra **8** Antigone **10** Oedipus Rex

Sophonisba *brother:* **8** Hannibal *father:* **9** Hasdrubal *husband:* **6** Syphax

soporific 4 dozy **6** drowsy, opiate, sleepy **7** anodyne, calming, numbing **8** hypnotic, narcotic, sedative **9** calmative, deadening, somnolent **10** anesthetic, slumberous **11** somniferous **12** somnifacient **13** tranquilizing

soprano *American:* **4** Pons (Lily) **5** Costa (Mary), Gluck (Alma), Moffo (Anna), Moore (Grace), Price (Leontyne), Sills (Beverly) **6** Arroyo (Martina), Battle (Kathleen), Callas (Maria), Curtin (Phyllis), Donath (Helen), Farrar (Geraldine), Garden (Mary), Munsel (Patrice), Norman (Jessye), Peters (Roberta), Piazza (Marguerite), Resnik (Regina) **7** Farrell (Eileen), Fleming (Renée), Kirsten (Dorothy), Stevens (Risë), Traubel (Helen) **8** Ponselle (Rosa) *Australian:* **5** Melba (Nellie) **10** Sutherland (Joan) *Austrian:* **4** Popp (Lucia) **7** Rysanek (Leonie) **8** Sembrich (Marcella) *Canadian:* **7** Stratas (Teresa) *French:* **7** Crespin (Régine) *German:* **6** Leider (Frida) **7** Lehmann (Lilli, Lotte) **11** Schwarzkopf (Elisabeth) *Italian:* **5** Freni (Mirella), Grisi (Giuditta, Giulia), Patti (Adelina) **6** Scotto (Renata) **7** Bartoli (Cecilia), Tebaldi (Renata) **10** Tetrazzini (Luisa) **11** Ricciarelli (Katia) *Korean:* **6** Sumi Jo *Mexican:*

8 Cruz-Romo (Gilda) *New Zealand:* 8 Te Kanawa (Kiri) *Norwegian:* 8 Flagstad (Kirsten) *Romanian:* 8 Cotrubas (Ileana) *Spanish:* 7 Caballé (Montserrat) 8 Berganza (Teresa) 12 de los Angeles (Victoria) *Swedish:* 4 Lind (Jenny) 7 Nilsson (Birgit) (see also MEZZO-SOPRANO)

sorcerer 4 mage 5 magus 6 wizard 7 warlock 8 conjurer, conjuror, magician 9 enchanter 11 necromancer, thaumaturge 13 thaumaturgist

sorceress 3 hag, hex 5 Circe, witch

sorcery 5 magic 8 diablery, wizardry 9 conjuring 10 necromancy, witchcraft 11 bewitchment, enchantment, thaumaturgy *West Indian:* 5 obeah

sordid 3 low 4 base, foul, mean, vile 5 dirty, nasty, seamy, shady, venal 6 blowsy, blowzy, filthy, frowsy, frowzy, grubby, scurvy, shabby, sleazy 7 ignoble, low-down, squalid, unclean 8 degraded, shameful, wretched 9 loathsome, mercenary 10 despicable, scandalous, slatternly 11 disgraceful 12 contemptible, disreputable 13 reprehensible

sore 3 raw 4 boil 5 angry, irked, ulcer, upset, vexed 6 aching, bitter, canker, peeved, tender 7 abscess, chancre, hurting, painful 8 inflamed, smarting 9 chilblain, irritated, rancorous, resentful, sensitive 10 affliction

sorehead 4 crab 5 grump 6 griper, grouch 7 grouser 8 grumbler, sourpuss 10 bellyacher, complainer, crosspatch, malcontent

sorrel 4 dock 8 chestnut, sourwood

sorrow 3 rue, sob, woe 4 moan, ruth 5 dolor, grief, mourn 6 grieve, lament, misery, regret 7 anguish, remorse, sadness 8 distress, grieving, mourning 9 dejection, heartache, suffering 10 affliction, heartbreak, melancholy 11 lamentation, unhappiness 12 mournfulness

sorrowful 3 sad 6 rueful, triste, woeful 7 doleful, forlorn, piteous, ruthful, unhappy 8 dolorous, downcast, grieving, mournful, tristful, wretched 9 afflicted, miserable, plaintive, woebegone 10 lamentable, lugubrious, melancholy 11 heartbroken 12 disconsolate

sorry 3 bad, sad 4 mean, poor 5 cheap 6 cheesy, paltry, scummy, scurvy, shabby, shoddy 7 scruffy, unhappy 8 beggarly, contrite, mournful, penitent, pitiable, saddened, trifling, wretched 9 miserable, regretful, repentant 10 apologetic, despicable, inadequate, melancholy, remorseful 11 disgraceful,

penitential 12 contemptible, heavy-hearted

sort 3 ilk, lot, set 4 comb, cull, kind, pick, sift, type 5 class, order 6 choose, screen, select, stripe, winnow 7 arrange, catalog, species, variety 8 classify, separate 9 catalogue, character 10 categorize, pigeonhole

sortie 4 dash, raid 5 foray, sally 7 assault, mission 9 excursion 10 expedition

sortilege 6 augury 7 sorcery 8 divining, witchery 10 divination, necromancy, witchcraft 11 thaumaturgy

so-so 4 fair, okay 6 decent, enough, fairly, medium, rather 7 average, fairish 8 adequate, mediocre, middling, moderate, passable, passably 9 tolerably 10 moderately 11 indifferent 12 run-of-the-mill

sot 4 lush, wino 5 drunk, souse 6 bibber, boozer 7 guzzler, tippler, tosspot 8 drunkard 9 alcoholic, inebriate 10 boozehound

sotto voce 3 low 5 aside 6 softly 7 faintly, mutedly, quietly 9 privately

souchong 3 tea

sough 4 sigh 7 suspire, whisper

soul 4 pith 5 anima, being, heart, stuff 6 animus, breast, marrow, pneuma, psyche, spirit 7 essence 9 élan vital, substance 10 conscience, vital force 12 quintessence *combining form:* 5 psych 6 psycho

soulful 6 moving, tender 7 emotive, fervent 8 poignant, stirring, touching 9 affecting, emotional 11 impassioned, sentimental

soul singer 4 Gaye (Marvin) 5 Bland (Bobby), Brown (James), Cooke (Sam), Flack (Roberta), Green (Al), Hayes (Isaac) 6 Butler (Jerry), Knight (Gladys), Sledge (Percy) 7 Charles (Ray), Pickett (Wilson), Redding (Otis) 8 Franklin (Aretha), Mayfield (Curtis)

sound 4 fit 4 firm, hale, safe, sane 5 audio, legit, noise, plumb, probe, right, sober, solid, valid, whole 6 cogent, fathom, intact, secure, stable, sturdy, unhurt 7 correct, earshot, healthy, logical, prudent 8 rational, reliable, sensible, unharmed 9 judicious, resonance, undamaged, vibration, wholesome 10 convincing, reasonable 11 well-founded 12 satisfactory, well-grounded 13 reverberation *combining form:* 3 son 4 phon, soni, sono 5 audio, audit, phone, phony 6 audito, phonia *high-pitched:* 4 ping, ting *pleasant:* 7 euphony *quality:* 6 timbre *repeating:* 7 rat-a-tat 8 rataplan 10 rat-a-tat-tat *science:* 6 sonics 7 phonics 9 acoustics

Sound *Alaska:* 5 Cross *Antarctica:*
7 McMurdo *Australia:* 4 King 5 Broad
Bahamas: 5 Exuma *Canada:* 4 Howe
6 Nansen *Connecticut-New York:* 10 Long
Island *English Channel:* 8 Plymouth
Georgia: 8 Altamaha *Greenland:* 5 Smith
Gulf of Mexico: 8 Suwannee 11 Mississippi *Massachusetts:* 8 Vineyard 8 Nantucket *New England:* 11 Block Island
North Carolina: 4 Core 5 Bogue 7 Pamlico, Roanoke 9 Albemarle, Currituck
Northwest Territories: 4 Peel 8 Melville
9 Lancaster 8 Prince Albert *Norwegian
Sea:* 8 Scoresby *Ontario:* 4 Owen *Scotland:* 3 Hoy 4 Jura, Mull 5 Inner *Spitsbergen:* 4 Bell *Washington:* 5 Puget

Sound and the Fury, The *author:*
8 Faulkner (William) *character:* 5 Benjy
(Compson), Caddy (Compson), Jason
(Compson) 6 Dilsey 7 Quentin (Compson)

soundness 6 health, sanity 7 balance
8 lucidity, prudence, security, solidity,
strength 9 integrity, stability 11 reliability 12 practicality

sound off 7 speak up 8 speak out

soup *beet:* 6 borsch 7 borscht *bowl:*
6 tureen *clear:* 5 broth 8 bouillon, consommé, julienne *cold:* 8 gazpacho
11 vichyssoise *curry:* 12 mulligatawny
okra: 5 gumbo *seafood:* 7 chowder *thick:*
5 gumbo, puree 6 bisque, burgoo *vegetable:* 10 minestrone

soupçon see PARTICLE

soupy 5 foggy, gooey, gushy, murky,
mushy 6 drippy, slushy, smoggy 7 cloying, maudlin, mawkish 8 cornball
9 schmaltzy 10 saccharine 11 sentimental, tear-jerking

sour 4 acid, dour, tart 5 acerb, acrid,
tangy, testy 6 acidic, bitter, crabby,
cranky, curdle, grumpy, morose, rancid, rotten, sullen, turned 7 acerbic,
grouchy, peevish, prickly, spoiled,
unhappy 8 embitter, vinegary 9 acidulous, fermented 12 disagreeable

source 4 font, root, well 5 basis, cause,
fount, model, onset, start 6 mother, origin, spring 7 dawning, genesis 8 begetter, fountain, wellhead 9 beginning,
inception, informant, precursor, prototype, reference, rootstock 10 antecedent, authorship, birthplace, derivation, originator, progenitor,
provenance, wellspring 11 origination,
provenience 12 fountainhead

sourness 7 acidity 8 acerbity, asperity

sourpuss 4 crab 5 crank, grump
6 griper, grouch 7 grouser, killjoy
8 grumbler, sorehead 10 bellyacher,
complainer, crosspatch, curmudgeon
11 misanthrope

souse 3 dip, sop, sot 4 lush, soak, wino
5 binge, drown, steep 6 boozer, drench,
pickle, plunge, seethe 7 immerse
8 drunkard, inundate, marinate, preserve, saturate, submerge, submerse
9 alcoholic, immersion, inebriate
10 boozehound, intoxicate 11 dipsomaniac

soused 3 lit 4 high 5 drunk, lit up, oiled
6 bashed, blotto, bombed, juiced, potted, soaked, soused, stewed, stoned,
tanked, wasted, zonked 7 crocked,
drunken, pickled, pie-eyed, sloshed,
smashed, sottish 8 polluted 9 plastered
10 inebriated, liquored up 11 intoxicated

south *combining form:* 5 austr 6 austro
French: 3 sud *Spanish:* 3 sur

South Africa *capital:* 8 Cape Town, Pretoria 12 Bloemfontein *city:* 6 Durban
12 Johannesburg *desert:* 8 Kalahari
enclave: 7 Lesotho *grassland:* 4 veld
5 veldt *language:* 5 Bantu 7 English
9 Afrikaans *monetary unit:* 4 rand *mountain range:* 11 Drakensberg *neighbor:*
7 Namibia 8 Botswana 9 Swaziland,
Zimbabwe 10 Mozambique *plateau:*
5 Karoo 6 Karroo *river:* 6 Molopo,
Orange *settlers:* 5 Boers

South America *country:* 4 Peru 5 Chile
6 Brazil, Guyana 7 Bolivia, Ecuador,
Uruguay 8 Colombia, Paraguay, Suriname 9 Argentina, Venezuela *ethnic
group:* 6 Aymara, Creole, Indian 7 mestizo, mulatto, Quechua, Spanish
10 Amerindian, Portuguese *language:*
6 Aymara 7 Guaraní, Quechua, Spanish
10 Portuguese

South Carolina *capital:* 8 Columbia *city:*
10 Charleston, Greenville *college, university:* 7 Citadel, Clemson *fort:*
6 Sumter *island, island group:* 3 Sea
6 Edisto, Parris 10 Hilton Head *nickname:* 8 Palmetto (State) *river:* 6 Edisto,
Pee Dee, Santee 7 Tugaloo 8 Savannah
state bird: 12 Carolina wren *state flower:*
13 yellow jasmine *state tree:* 8 palmetto

South Dakota *capital:* 6 Pierre *city:*
9 Rapid City 10 Sioux Falls *mountain:*
6 Harney (Peak) 8 Rushmore 10 Black
Hills *nickname:* 6 Coyote (State) 10 Mt.
Rushmore (State) *park:* 8 Badlands,
Wind Cave *river:* 8 Missouri 11 Belle
Forche *state bird:* 18 ring-necked pheasant *state flower:* 12 pasqueflower *state
tree:* 6 spruce

southerly 7 austral

South-West Africa 7 Namibia

south wind see at WIND

souvenir 5 relic, token **6** trophy
7 memento **8** keepsake, memorial, reminder **11** remembrance

sovereign 4 coin, czar, free, king, tsar
5 queen, regal, royal, ruler **6** kingly, ruling **7** emperor, empress, highest, monarch, regnant, supreme **8** absolute, autarkic, autocrat, dominant, imperial, kinglike, majestic **9** ascendant, autarchic, monarchal, number one, paramount, potentate **10** autonomous, monarchial **11** independent, monarchical, predominant **12** self-governed

soviet 7 council **9** committee

sow 4 seed, toss **5** drill, fling, plant, strew **7** bestrew, scatter **9** broadcast
11 disseminate

spa 5 baths, hydro, wells **6** hot tub, resort, spring, waters **7** springs
13 watering place *Czech:* **6** Bilina
8 Karlsbad *English:* **4** Bath **6** Buxton
9 Harrogate *French:* **3** Dax **5** Evian *German:* **3** Ems **5** Baden **6** Bad Ems
9 Kissingen

space 3 gap **4** area, room **5** blank, scope
6 cavity, extent, spread, volume
7 breadth, expanse, stretch **8** capacity, distance, interval, universe **9** amplitude, expansion

spaced-out 4 high **5** doped **6** stoned, zonked **7** drugged **8** hopped-up, turned on

spacious 3 big **4** vast, wide **5** ample, large, roomy **7** immense **8** enormous, extended **9** boundless, capacious, cavernous, expansive, extensive **10** commodious, voluminous

spade 3 dig **4** grub **5** dig up, scoop **6** dig out, shovel **8** excavate

Spade, Sam 4 dick **6** shamus, sleuth
7 gumshoe **9** detective **10** private eye *creator:* **7** Hammett (Dashiell) *novel:*
13 Maltese Falcon (The)

Spain *ancient name:* **8** Hispania *capital:*
6 Madrid *city:* **6** Málaga **7** Seville
8 Valencia, Zaragoza **9** Barcelona, Saragossa *island group:* **6** Canary
8 Balearic *king:* **10** Juan Carlos *leader:*
6 Franco (Francisco) *monetary unit:*
4 euro *monetary unit, former:* **4** real
6 peseta *mountain:* **8** Mulhacén **11** Pico de Aneto *mountain range:* **8** Pyrenees *neighbor:* **6** France **8** Portugal *peninsula:*
7 Iberian *region:* **8** Valencia **9** Catalonia *river:* **4** Ebro **12** Guadalquivir *sea:*
13 Mediterranean *strait:* **9** Gibraltar

spall 4 chip **5** flake **7** shaving **8** fragment
9 exfoliate

spam 8 junk mail

span 4 arch, term, time **5** cross, reach
6 extent, length, period, spread **7** compass, measure, stretch **8** duration, interval, lifetime, straddle, traverse

spangle 4 trim **5** flash, gleam **6** sequin
7 glitter, shimmer, sparkle, twinkle
9 coruscate **11** scintillate

Spaniard 9 Castilian

Spanish *boss:* **7** cacique *chaperone:*
6 duenna *combining form:* **7** hispano *dictator:* **8** caudillo *folksong:* **6** tonada *fortress:* **7** alcazar *garrison:* **8** presidio *hors d'oeuvre:* **4** tapa *inn:* **6** posada *mayor:* **7** alcalde *national hero:* **3** Cid
(El) **5** El Cid *nobleman:* **7** grandee *operetta:* **8** zarzuela *penal settlement:*
8 presidio *plain:* **5** llano, pampa *plantation:* **8** hacienda *princess:* **7** infanta *ranch:* **5** finca **8** estancia *saint:*
7 Dominic **8** Ignatius *scarf:* **8** mantilla *shawl:* **6** serape *title:* **3** don **4** doña
5 señor **6** señora **8** señorita *wine:* **4** sack
6 sherry

Spanish fly 9 cantharis

spank 4 cane, flog, lash, slap **5** smack
6 larrup, paddle, punish, thrash
7 scourge **8** chastise

spar 3 box, vie **4** pole **5** joust, stall **7** dispute, wrangle **8** longeron *ship's:*
4 boom, gaff, mast, yard **7** yardarm
8 bowsprit

spare 4 lank, lean, pity, save, slim
5 avoid, extra, gaunt, lanky **6** backup, excess, excuse, exempt, let off, meager, meagre, pardon, scanty, scrape, scrimp, skimpy, skinny, slight, unused
7 absolve, relieve, reserve, scrawny, scrimpy, surplus **8** leftover **10** additional **11** superfluous

sparing 4 bare, wary **5** canny, chary, tight **6** frugal, meager, meagre, saving, stingy **7** prudent, thrifty **9** provident
10 economical, restrained, unwasteful
11 tightfisted **12** parsimonious

spark 3 woo **5** court, ember, glint
6 foment, incite, kindle, set off **7** provoke, trigger **8** activate, touch off
9 instigate, scintilla

sparkle 4 zing **5** flash, gleam, glint, verve
7 glimmer, glisten, glitter, shimmer, twinkle **8** vivacity **9** animation, coruscate **10** effervesce, liveliness **11** coruscation, scintillate **13** scintillation

sparkling 6 bubbly, lively **8** animated, bubbling **9** brilliant **12** effervescent

Spark novel 11 Memento Mori **21** Prime of Miss Jean Brodie (The)

sparse 4 rare, thin **5** scant **6** meager, meagre, scanty, scarce, skimpy **7** limited, scrimpy **8** exiguous, sporadic, uncommon **9** dispersed, scattered
10 inadequate, infrequent, occasional
12 insufficient

Sparta 10 Lacedaemon *country:* **7** Laconia *king:* **8** Leonidas *opponent:* **6** Athens

Spartacus *author:* **4** Fast (Howard) *slayer:* **7** Crassus

spasm 3 fit, tic **4** pang **5** burst, crick, throe **6** twitch **8** paroxysm **10** convulsion *muscular:* **6** clonus

spasmodic 5 jerky **6** fitful, spotty **7** erratic **8** sporadic **9** desultory, excitable **10** convulsive **12** intermittent

spat 3 row **4** flap, miff, tiff **5** fight, scene, scrap **6** bicker, gaiter, hassle, oyster **7** brabble, dispute, fall out, quarrel, rhubarb, wrangle **8** argument, outburst, squabble **10** falling-out **11** altercation

spate 4 flow, flux, gush, pour, rain, rush, tide **5** flood, river, spurt, surge **6** deluge, series, shower, stream **7** current, freshet, torrent **8** cataract, outburst, overflow **10** inundation, outpouring

spatter 4 slop, slur, spit **5** douse, fleck, plash, slosh, smear, spray, spurt, swash **6** befoul, defame, malign, splash, splosh, vilify **7** asperse, blacken, handful, slander, speckle, splurge, stipple, traduce **8** besmirch, sprinkle **9** denigrate, disparage

spawn 4 eggs, sire **5** beget, breed, brood, hatch, issue **6** create, father, parent **7** produce, product, progeny, provoke **8** engender, generate **9** offspring, originate, procreate, propagate, reproduce, stimulate

speak 3 gab, jaw, say, yak **4** blab, chat, chin, talk **5** blurt, drawl, mouth, orate, spiel, spout, utter, voice **6** assert, convey, intone, mumble, murmur, mutter, parley **7** address, declaim, declare, lecture, phonate, whisper **8** converse, dilate on, perorate, vocalize **9** discourse, enunciate, expatiate, hold forth, verbalize *confusedly:* **7** stammer, stutter **8** splutter *for:* **7** testify

speaker 4 voice **9** spokesman **10** mouthpiece **12** spokesperson

spear 3 gig **4** pike, spit **5** gouge, lance, spike **6** impale, pierce, skewer **7** harpoon, leister, trident **8** puncture, transfix **9** penetrate

special 4 rare **6** unique **7** express, notable, unusual **8** peculiar, uncommon **10** designated, individual, noteworthy, particular **11** distinctive, exceptional, outstanding

species 4 kind, sort, type **5** breed, class, order

specific 3 set **5** exact **6** strict, unique **7** express, limited, precise, special **8** clean-cut, clear-cut, definite, distinct, especial, explicit **10** individual, particular **11** categorical, unambiguous

specify 3 fix, set **4** cite, list, name **6** detail **7** itemize, mention, pin down, tick off **8** instance, spell out **9** determine, enumerate, establish, inventory, stipulate **13** particularize

specimen 4 case, sort, type **6** sample **7** example, neotype, variety **8** exemplar, holotype, instance, sampling **12** illustration

specious 5 empty, false **6** hollow **8** spurious **9** casuistic, plausible, sophistic **10** misleading, ostensible **11** sophistical

speciousness 7 sophism **9** casuistry, sophistry

speck 3 bit, dot, jot **4** atom, iota, mite, mote, spot, tick, whit **5** crumb, fleck, grain, point, shred, trace **7** freckle, smidgen **8** molecule, particle, pinpoint

speckle 3 dot **4** spot **5** flake, fleck **6** dapple, pepper **7** stipple **8** sprinkle

spectacle 4 pomp, show **5** drama, sight **6** parade **7** display, pageant, panoply, tableau **10** exhibition, exposition **12** extravaganza

spectacular 5 stagy **7** amazing, pageant **8** dazzling, dramatic, striking, wondrous **9** marvelous, thrilling, wonderful **10** astounding, eye-popping, histrionic, miraculous, phenomenal, prodigious, staggering, stupefying, stupendous, theatrical **11** astonishing, sensational **12** extravaganza

spectator 5 gazer **6** viewer **7** watcher, witness **8** beholder, observer, onlooker **9** bystander **10** eyewitness

Spectator author 6 Steele (Richard) **7** Addison (Joseph)

specter 5 ghost, shade **6** shadow, spirit, wraith **7** eidolon, phantom **8** phantasm, revenant, visitant **10** apparition

spectral 6 spooky **7** ghastly, ghostly, phantom **9** ghostlike, unearthly **10** shadowlike **11** disembodied, phantomlike

spectrum 5 ambit, gamut, range, scale, sweep **7** compass **8** diapason **9** continuum

speculate 4 muse **5** study, think, weigh **6** ponder, reason, review, wonder **7** reflect **8** cogitate, consider, meditate, ruminate, theorize **9** cerebrate **10** conjecture, deliberate **11** contemplate

speculation 5 guess, hunch **6** gamble, review, theory **7** surmise **9** brainwork **10** conjecture

speculative 7 curious, pensive **8** academic **10** thoughtful **11** conjectural, theoretical **12** hypothetical

speech 4 talk **5** idiom, spiel, voice

6 debate, homily, parley, sermon, tirade, tongue **7** address, dialect, diction, lecture, oration, palaver **8** dialogue, diatribe, harangue, language, parlance, rhetoric **9** discourse, monologue, utterance **10** allocution, expression, vernacular **11** declamation **12** articulation, disquisition, vocalization **13** verbalization *defect:* **4** lisp **7** stutter

speechcraft 7 oratory **8** rhetoric **9** elocution

speechless 3 mum **4** dumb, mute **6** silent **7** aphonic **10** dumbstruck, tongue-tied

speed 3 fly, run, zip **4** clip, gait, pace, race, rush, tear, whiz **5** chase, haste, hurry, tempo **6** barrel, burn up, career, hasten, hustle, whoosh **7** quicken **8** alacrity, celerity, dispatch, expedite, highball, legerity, momentum, rapidity, velocity **9** fleetness, quickness, swiftness **10** accelerate, cannonball, facilitate, promptness

speedway 5 track **8** turnpike **9** racetrack **10** racecourse

speedy 4 fast **5** brisk, fleet, hasty, quick, rapid, swift **6** nimble, prompt **8** headlong **9** breakneck **11** expeditious

spell 3 hex **4** bout, jinx, mojo, time, tour, turn **5** charm, hitch, shift, stint, throe, while **6** attack, period, streak, voodoo **7** relieve, stretch **11** conjuration, incantation

spellbind 3 hex **4** grip, vamp **5** charm **7** bewitch, catch up, enchant **8** enthrall, entrance **9** enrapture, fascinate, hypnotize, mesmerize

spelling 11 orthography *bad:* **10** cacography

spell out 7 clarify, explain, expound **8** construe, set forth **9** elucidate, explicate, interpret

spend 3 pay **4** blow, drop, pass **5** use up, waste **6** lavish, lay out, outlay **7** consume, exhaust, fork out, hand out, splurge **8** disburse, shell out, squander **9** dissipate, go through, throw away, while away **10** contribute, run through

spender 7 wastrel **8** prodigal **10** high roller, profligate, squanderer **11** scattergood

spendthrift see SPENDER

spent 4 shot **5** all in **6** effete, pooped, used-up, wasted **7** drained, worn-out **8** burnt out, consumed, depleted, washed-up **9** exhausted, washed-out

spew 4 gush, ooze **5** belch, eject, eruct, erupt, expel, exude, flood, heave, shoot, spray, vomit **6** irrupt, spit up, squirt **7** throw up, upchuck **8** disgorge

sphagnum 4 moss

sphere 3 orb **4** area, ball, star, turf, zone **5** arena, field, globe, range, realm, round, scope **6** circle, domain, planet **7** demesne, rondure, terrain **8** dominion, province **9** bailiwick, territory **12** jurisdiction

spherical 5 round **6** global **7** globose **8** globular **9** orbicular

Sphinx *builder:* **6** Khafre *father:* **6** Typhon *mother:* **7** Echidna *query:* **6** riddle *site:* **4** Giza **6** Thebes

spice 3 pep, zip **4** kick, mace, tang, zest **5** anise, aroma, clove, cumin, poppy, savor, scent, smack, smell, taste **6** cloves, fennel, ginger, nutmeg, pepper, relish, sesame **7** bouquet, caraway, perfume **8** cardamom, cinnamon, piquancy **9** fragrance, redolence, seasoning

Spice Islands 8 Moluccas

spick-and-span 3 new **4** mint, neat, snug, tidy, trig, trim **5** clean, fresh **6** spruce **7** orderly **8** brand-new, spotless **9** shipshape **10** immaculate **11** well-groomed

spicy 3 hot **4** racy **5** bawdy, fiery, salty, tangy, zesty **6** lively, purple, ribald, risqué, savory, snappy, wicked **7** gingery, peppery, piquant, pungent, scented, zestful **8** aromatic, fragrant, off-color, perfumed, redolent, seasoned, spirited **9** flavorful, salacious **10** scandalous, suggestive **11** titillating

spider 6 frypan **7** skillet **8** arachnid **9** frying pan **10** black widow

spiel 4 jive, line **5** pitch **6** patter **12** song and dance

spieler 4 tout **6** barker, hawker, talker **8** huckster

spigot 3 tap **4** cock, gate **5** valve **6** faucet **7** hydrant, petcock, shutoff **8** stopcock

spike 3 pin **4** heel, nail **5** lance, piton, spear **6** antler, impale, needle, skewer **7** spindle **8** increase, mackerel, puncture, transfix

spile 4 bung **5** spout

spill 4 blab, drip, drop, fall, flow, slop, tell **5** spray **6** betray, inform, reveal, splash, squeal, tattle **7** divulge, dribble, run over, spatter **8** disclose, overflow

Spillane detective 10 Mike Hammer

spilth 5 dregs, dross, swill, trash, waste **6** debris, refuse, scraps **7** garbage, rubbish **8** leavings

spin 4 gyre, reel, ride, swim, turn **5** dizzy, swirl, twirl, wheel, whirl **6** gyrate, rotate **7** revolve **8** rotation **9** pirouette, whirligig **10** revolution *a log:* **4** birl *out:* **4** draw **6** extend **7** prolong, stretch 8 elongate, lengthen, protract 10 prolongate

spinal column 5 chine 6 rachis *curvature:* 8 lordosis *part:* 8 vertebra (see also SPINE)

spindle 3 pin, rod 5 newel, shaft, spike 6 impale, rachis

spindly 5 frail, lanky, rangy, shaky, weedy 6 flimsy, gangly, skinny, twiggy, wobbly 7 fragile, rickety, tottery 8 gangling, skeletal, unsteady 9 emaciated 10 jerry-built

spine 4 back 6 rachis 7 spicule 8 backbone 9 vertebrae

spineless 5 timid 8 cowardly, timorous 9 weak-kneed 10 weak-willed 12 invertebrate

spin-off 8 offshoot 9 by-product, outgrowth 10 derivative, descendant

___ **Spinoza** 6 Baruch

spinster 7 old maid 10 maiden lady

spiny 6 barbed, thorny 7 prickly 8 echinate 10 nettlesome

spiral 4 coil, curl, wind 5 helix, twine, twist 6 volute 7 helical, helices (plural) 8 gyroidal, volution 9 cochleate, corkscrew *combining form:* 3 gyr 4 gyro 5 helic 6 helico

spire 4 coil 5 twist, whorl 7 steeple 8 pinnacle

spirit 3 pep, vim, zip 4 brio, dash, élan, gimp, grit, guts, life, mood, snap, soul, zeal, zest, zing 5 anima, ardor, drive, force, heart, moxie, oomph, pluck, shade, spunk, tenor, verve, vigor 6 animus, daimon, energy, esprit, fervor, ginger, mettle, morale, pneuma, psyche, starch, temper, wraith 7 passion, phantom, specter, spectre 8 phantasm, revenant, vitality 9 animation, élan vital, substance 10 apparition, enthusiasm, get-up-and-go, liveliness *away:* 6 abduct, kidnap, snatch *evil:* 5 afrit, demon 6 afreet 7 erlking, shaitan *female:* 5 nymph 7 banshee *Hopi:* 7 kachina *Persian:* 4 peri

spirited 4 bold, game, keen 5 eager, fiery, peppy 6 ardent, gritty, lively, plucky, spunky 7 chipper, fervent, gingery, peppery, valiant, zealous 8 animated, cheerful, intrepid, resolute 9 audacious, dauntless, energetic, sprightly, vivacious 10 courageous, mettlesome, passionate 12 enthusiastic

spirits 5 booze, drink 6 liquor, tipple 9 aqua vitae, firewater *low:* 5 blues, dumps, ennui 8 doldrums 10 blue devils, depression, melancholy

spiritual 6 sacred 7 saintly 8 churchly, mystical, numinous, platonic 9 religious 10 high-minded, immaterial, unphysical 11 disembodied, incorporeal, nonmaterial, nonphysical 12 metaphysical, supernatural, transcendent

spiritualist 6 medium, mystic 7 psychic

spit 5 spear 6 impale, saliva, skewer, slaver, sputum 7 spatter, sputter 8 splutter 9 brochette 11 expectorate

spite 5 venom 6 grudge, malice, rancor, spleen 7 ill will, revenge 9 pettiness, vengeance 11 malevolence 13 maliciousness

spiteful 4 mean 5 catty, nasty, snide 6 malign, wicked 7 vicious, waspish 8 venomous 9 malicious, malignant, rancorous 10 malevolent, vindictive

spitfire 4 fury 5 harpy, shrew, vixen 6 dragon, virago 7 hellcat, tigress 8 fishwife, harridan 9 termagant

spitting image 4 twin 5 clone 6 double, ringer 9 duplicate 10 carbon copy, dead ringer, simulacrum

spittoon 8 cuspidor

splash 3 sop, wet 4 slop, soak 5 douse, slosh, spray, swash 6 drench 7 spatter 8 sprinkle

splashy 5 gaudy, jazzy, showy 6 flashy, garish, glitzy, tawdry 7 blatant, dashing 8 colorful, dazzling, striking 10 flamboyant, theatrical 11 sensational 12 meretricious, ostentatious

splatter 4 slop 5 douse, plash, slosh, spray, swash 6 splash 8 sprinkle

splay 4 cant, tilt 5 angle, bevel, gawky, slant, slope 6 clumsy, extend, spread 7 awkward, incline 8 ungainly 9 expansion 11 inclination

spleen see SPITE

splendid 4 fine 5 grand, showy 6 superb 7 shining 8 glorious, gorgeous 9 brilliant, excellent, marvelous, wonderful 10 first-class, impressive 11 illustrious, magnificent, outstanding 12 transcendent

splendor 4 pomp 5 glory 6 dazzle 7 panoply 8 grandeur, richness 9 pageantry, spectacle 10 brilliance, brilliancy 12 magnificence

splenetic 5 cross, surly 6 fuming 8 incensed, spiteful 9 malicious 10 ill-natured, malevolent 11 ill-tempered

splice 3 tie 4 join, mate, mesh 5 braid, graft, plait, unite

splint 5 brace, strip 7 support 10 immobilize

splinter 4 rive 5 burst, smash 6 shiver, sliver 7 faction, shatter 8 fragment 12 disintegrate

split 3 rip 4 part, rend, rent, rift, rima, rime, rive, tear 5 break, carve, chasm, chink, cleft, crack, sever, slice 6 breach, cleave, cloven, divide, schism, sunder **7** break up, disjoin, dissect, diverge, divorce, divvy up, fission, fissure, rupture **8** cleavage, dissever, fracture, separate **11** dichotomize *combining form:* **5** schiz **6** schizo **7** schisto

splotch 4 blob, blot, spot **5** fleck, stain **6** smudge

splurge 4 orgy **5** binge, fling, spree **7** blowout, rampage **10** indulgence **12** extravagance

splutter 4 spit **6** babble, jabber **7** stammer

spoil 3 mar, rob, rot **4** baby, harm, prey, ruin, sack **5** decay, humor, taint, waste, wreck **6** coddle, cosset, curdle, damage, defile, impair, molder, pamper, ravish **7** blemish, cater to, destroy, indulge, pillage, putrefy, tarnish, vitiate **8** demolish **9** break down, decompose **11** mollycoddle

spoiled 4 rank, sour **6** putrid, rancid, rotten, ruined **7** coddled, decayed **8** impaired, indulged, pampered **9** indulgent

spoils 4 haul, loot, swag **5** booty **7** pillage, plunder

spoilsport 7 killjoy

spoken 4 oral, said, told **6** verbal, voiced **7** uttered **8** phonetic, viva voce **9** delivered, unwritten **11** articulated

sponge 4 grub **5** cadge, leech, mooch **7** moocher **8** freeload, parasite, scrounge **10** freeloader *material:* **8** mesoglea *opening:* **6** oscula (plural) **7** osculum, ostiole

sponger 5 leech **7** moocher **8** parasite **10** freeloader

spongy 4 soft **5** mushy, pulpy **6** porous, quaggy **7** squashy, squishy **9** absorbent

sponsor 4 back, fund **5** angel, stake **6** backer, patron, surety **7** endorse, finance **8** advocate, bankroll, champion, Maecenas, mainstay, promoter, vouch for **9** grubstake, guarantee, guarantor, patronize, subsidize, supporter **10** benefactor, underwrite **11** underwriter

sponsorship 5 aegis **7** backing, support **8** advocacy, auspices **9** patronage

spontaneous 5 ad-lib **7** natural, offhand **8** ad-libbed, unforced **9** automatic, extempore, impromptu, impulsive, unstudied **10** improvised, off-the-cuff, unprompted **11** instinctive, unmeditated **13** unconstrained

spontoon 4 pike **5** lance, spear

spoof 4 sham **5** farce, put-on **6** parody, satire, send-up **7** lampoon, takeoff **8** travesty

spook 3 spy **5** agent, alarm, ghost, haunt, scare **7** specter, spectre, startle, terrify **8** frighten

spooky 5 eerie, weird **6** creepy **7** ghostly, ominous, uncanny **9** unearthly

spool 4 wind **6** bobbin

spoon 3 pet, woo **4** neck **5** court, ladle, scoop **6** cuddle

spoonbill 4 ibis **8** shoveler **9** ruddy duck **10** paddlefish

Spoon River poet 7 Masters (Edgar Lee)

spoony 5 mushy, silly **6** simple, slushy, syrupy **7** fatuous, foolish, mawkish, smitten, witless **9** schmaltzy **10** saccharine **11** sentimental

spoor 5 scent, trace, track, tract, trail **7** vestige **8** footstep **9** droppings, footprint

sporadic 4 rare **6** catchy, fitful, random, scarce, sparse, spotty **7** erratic **8** episodic, isolated, uncommon **9** desultory, irregular, scattered, spasmodic **10** infrequent, occasional

sport 3 fun **4** game, jest, joke, mock, play **6** frolic, racing, trifle **7** mockery, show off **9** diversion, high jinks, horseplay **10** recreation *indoor:* **6** boxing, hockey, squash **7** bowling **8** handball **9** wrestling **10** acrobatics, basketball, gymnastics **11** racquetball, table tennis *Olympic:* **4** judo **6** boxing, diving, hockey, rowing **7** archery, cycling, fencing, shot put **8** canoeing, football, high jump, long jump, marathon, shooting, swimming, yachting **9** decathlon, pole vault, water polo, wrestling **10** basketball, gymnastics, pentathlon, triple jump, volleyball **11** discus throw, hammer throw **12** javelin throw, steeplechase **13** weightlifting *water:* **6** diving, rowing **7** sailing, surfing **8** canoeing, swimming, yachting *winter:* **4** luge **6** hockey, skiing **7** curling, lugeing, skating **8** biathlon, sledding **10** ski jumping **11** bobsledding, tobogganing

sporting house 6 bagnio **7** brothel **8** bordello

sportive 5 antic **6** frisky, impish **7** playful, roguish, waggish **10** frolicsome **11** mischievous

sportiveness 7 devilry, roguery, waggery **8** deviltry, mischief **9** devilment, rascality

sporty 4 fast **5** peppy **6** breezy, casual, jaunty, lively **7** dashing, relaxed **8** debonair, informal **10** insouciant **11** streamlined

spot 3 fix, jam, nip, see **4** espy, post, site **5** fleck, hit on, locus, place, point, speck **6** blotch, detect, pickle, plight, scrape **7** dilemma, smidgen, spatter, speckle **8** diagnose, flyspeck, identify, location, pinpoint, position **9** recognize, situation **11** predicament

spotless 4 pure 5 clean 6 chaste 8 hygienic, sanitary, unsoiled 9 undefiled, unstained, unsullied 10 immaculate 11 unblemished

spotlight 5 focus 6 notice 7 feature, point up 8 interest, point out 9 attention, emphasize, public eye, publicity 10 illuminate 12 illumination

spotted 4 seen 6 motley 7 brindle, dappled, piebald 8 brindled, speckled, stippled

spouse 4 mate, wife 5 bride, groom, hubby 7 consort, husband

spout 3 jet 4 gush 5 chute, eject, spray, spurt 6 nozzle, squirt

sprain 4 pull, tear, turn 5 twist 6 wrench 7 stretch

sprawl 4 flop, loll 5 drape, slump 6 extend, lounge, slouch, spread 7 stretch 11 spread-eagle

spray 3 fog 4 hose, mist 6 shower, spritz 7 aerosol, atomize, diffuse, spatter 8 atomizer, droplets, fumigate, nebulize 9 spindrift

spread 3 jam, lay, set, sow 4 deal, oleo, open, pâté, push 5 apply, feast, jelly, space, splay, strew, sweep 6 butter, expand, extend, fan out, pass on, retail 7 banquet, breadth, diffuse, expanse, overrun, pervade, radiate, scatter, slather, stretch, suffuse 8 bedcover, coverlet, dispense, disperse, mushroom, permeate 9 amplitude, broadcast, circulate, diffusion, dissipate, expansion, extension, profusion, propagate, radiation 10 dispersion, distribute, outstretch 11 counterpane, disseminate 12 transmission 13 proliferation

spree 3 jag 4 bash, bust, lark, orgy, riot, tear 5 binge, drunk, fling, revel 6 bender, frolic 7 blowout, carouse, rampage, splurge 8 carousal, wingding 10 indulgence 11 bacchanalia

sprig 4 brad, heir, twig 5 scion, shoot 7 pintail 9 ruddy duck

sprightly 3 gay 4 keen, spry, yare 5 agile, alert, antic, brisk, peppy, perky, zesty, zingy, zippy 6 active, breezy, chirpy, frisky, jaunty, lively, nimble 7 animate, chipper, coltish, piquant, playful, pungent 8 animated, cheerful, spirited, sportive 9 energetic, vivacious 10 frolicsome, rollicking 13 scintillating

spring 3 hop 4 flow, jump, leap, lope, rise, root, skip, stem, trip, well 5 arise, begin, bound, cause, fount, issue, start 6 appear, bounce, emerge, hurdle, reason, source, uncoil, vernal 7 come out, emanate, proceed, rebound, startle 8 commence, fountain, stimulus, well-

head 9 originate 10 incitement, resilience 12 fountainhead *back:* 6 resile

springe 4 trap 5 noose, snare 7 pitfall 9 booby trap

springlike 6 vernal

springy 6 supple 7 elastic 8 flexible, stretchy 9 recoiling, resilient

sprinkle 3 dot 4 rain, spot 5 shake, speck, spray, strew 6 pepper, powder, spritz 7 asperse, drizzle, freckle, scatter, speckle, stipple 9 bespeckle

sprint 3 run 4 dart, dash, race, shin, tear 5 scoot 6 gallop, hurtle, scurry 7 scamper

sprite 3 elf, fay, nix 4 puck 5 dryad, fairy, naiad, nixie, nymph, pixie, sylph 6 kelpie 7 brownie 9 hamadryad

spritz 3 jet 5 spray, spurt 6 shower, squirt

sprout 3 bud 4 grow 5 scion, shoot 6 ratoon, sucker 7 burgeon 8 offshoot 9 germinate

spruce 4 trim 5 natty, sassy, spiff 6 dapper, spiffy 11 well-groomed

spry 4 yare 5 agile, brisk, sound, zesty, zippy 6 active, lively, nimble, robust 7 healthy 8 animated, spirited, vigorous 9 energetic, vivacious

spud 6 potato

___ **Spumante** 4 Asti

spume 4 fizz, foam, head, scum, suds 5 froth, spray, yeast 6 lather

spunk 4 grit, guts 5 heart, moxie, nerve, pluck 6 mettle, spirit, tinder 7 cojones, courage 8 backbone, gumption 9 fortitude, toughness 10 liveliness, resolution

spunky 4 bold 5 brave, fiery 6 daring 7 doughty, gingery, peppery 8 fearless, spirited 9 dauntless 10 courageous, mettlesome 12 high-spirited

spur 4 goad, prod, stir, urge 5 egg on, impel, prick, rally, rouse, spine 6 arouse, branch, exhort, motive, prompt, propel 7 impetus, impulse 8 buttress, catalyst, excitant, stimulus 9 actuation, incentive, instigate, stimulant, stimulate 10 incitement, inducement, motivation, projection *part:* 5 rowel

spurious 4 fake, mock, sham 5 bogus, dummy, false, phony, put-on 6 ersatz, pseudo 7 assumed, feigned, pretend 8 affected 9 brummagem, imitation, pinchbeck, pretended, simulated 10 apocryphal, artificial, substitute 11 counterfeit, make-believe 12 illegitimate *combining form:* 5 pseud 6 pseudo

spurn 4 snub 5 flout, scoff, scorn, scout, sneer 6 rebuff, refuse, reject 7 contemn, decline, despise, disdain, dismiss, repulse 8 turn down 9 disregard, reprobate, repudiate **10** disapprove **12** cold-shoulder

spurt 3 jet **4** gush, jump **5** burst, expel, spout, surge **6** shower, spritz, squirt **7** upsurge **8** eruption, increase **9** discharge

sputter 4 fizz, fume, rage, rant, rave, spew, spit **6** gibber, jabber **7** bluster, stammer

spy 5 agent, scout, snoop, spook **6** beagle, sleuth **7** gumshoe **8** informer, saboteur **9** detective **12** investigator **13** undercover man *name:* **4** Ames (Aldrich), Boyd (Belle), Hari (Mata) **5** André (John), Blunt (Anthony), Fuchs (Klaus) **6** Philby (Kim), Smiley (George) **7** Burgess (Guy), Hanssen (Robert), Maclean (Donald), Pollard (Jonathan)

spyglass 9 telescope

spying 9 espionage

Spyri's heroine 5 Heidi

squab 5 couch **6** pigeon **7** cushion

squabble see SPAT

squalid 3 low **4** base, foul, mean, vile **5** dingy, dirty, nasty, seedy **6** filthy, frowsy, frowzy, grubby, scurvy, shabby, shoddy, sleazy, sordid **7** ignoble, lowdown, run-down, scrubby, unclean, unkempt **8** slovenly, wretched **10** despicable, disheveled **11** dilapidated **12** disreputable

squall 3 caw, row, yap, yip **4** bark, bawl, beef, feud, fuss, gust, howl, roar, tiff, wail, yawp, yell, yelp, yowl **5** brawl, fight, hoo-ha, shout **6** bellow, clamor, flurry, fracas, hubbub, ruckus, rumpus, scream, shriek, squeal, yammer **7** dispute, flare-up, quarrel, rhubarb, screech **8** brouhaha, squabble **9** bickering, caterwaul, commotion **10** falling-out, hullabaloo **11** altercation

squalor 5 filth **6** misery **7** neglect, poverty **8** baseness, iniquity **9** depravity, dirtiness **10** sordidness **11** degradation **12** wretchedness

squander 4 blow **5** spend, waste **7** consume, exhaust, fritter, scatter **9** dissipate, throw away **10** trifle away **11** fritter away

squanderer see SPENDER

square 3 fit, fix **4** bang, boxy, even, fair, jibe, just, tied **5** adapt, agree, align, clear, equal, exact, fit in, match, pay up, plaza, right, sharp, spang, tally **6** accord, adjust, settle **7** balance, conform, exactly, satisfy, settled **8** check out, coincide, dovetail, orthodox, quadrate, smack-dab, straight, unbiased **9** discharge, equitable, harmonize, impartial, liquidate, objective, precise-

ly, quadratic, reconcile, rectangle **10** accurately, correspond

squash 3 jam **4** cram, mash, pepo, pulp **5** crush, gourd, press, quell **7** flatten, put down, squeeze, squelch **8** suppress *variety:* **5** acorn **6** cushaw, Sibley, turban **7** Hubbard, scallop **8** pattypan, zucchini **9** butternut, crookneck **10** Marblehead

squat 3 low **5** dumpy, hunch, stoop, stout, thick **6** chunky, crouch, hunker, stocky, stubby **8** heavyset, thickset **10** hunker down **11** thick-bodied

squawfish 4 chub **8** cyprinid **10** pikeminnow

squawk 3 caw, yap, yip **4** beef, crab, fuss, yawp **5** bleat, gripe **6** yammer **7** protest, screech **8** complain **9** bellyache, complaint

squeak 3 rat **4** blab, fink, peep, pipe, sing **5** cheep, creak **6** escape, inform, snitch, tattle **10** tattletale

squeal 3 rat, yip **4** blab, howl, sing, yell, yelp, yowl **5** bleat, creak, grate, gripe, peach **6** inform, screak, scream, shriek, shrill, snitch, squawk, tattle **7** protest, screech **8** complain **10** tattletale

squealer 3 rat **4** fink **6** canary, snitch, weasel **7** ratfink, stoolie, tattler, tipster **8** betrayer, informer **10** talebearer, tattletale **11** stool pigeon

squeamish 5 fussy, upset **6** queasy **7** finical, finicky **8** nauseous **9** nauseated **10** fastidious, particular, pernickety **11** persnickety

squeeze 3 hug, jam **4** bind, cram, grip, milk, pack, push **5** clasp, crowd, crush, exact, gouge, juice, pinch, press, screw, wring **6** clutch, coerce, compel, crunch, eke out, enfold, extort, jostle, squash, squish **7** dilemma, embrace, extract **8** compress, contract, pressure, quandary **9** shake down **11** compression, predicament

squelch 5 quell, shush, sit on **6** muffle, muzzle, squash, squish, stifle, subdue **7** repress, silence, smother **8** strangle, suppress **10** extinguish

squib 4 fire **6** filler **7** lampoon **8** shoot off **9** detonator **11** firecracker

squid 7 mollusc, mollusk **8** calamari, calamary **10** cephalopod *kin:* **7** octopus **10** cuttlefish

squiggle 4 worm **6** doodle, scrawl, squirm, writhe **7** scratch **8** curlicue, scrabble, scribble

squinch 5 quail, start, wince **6** blench, crouch, recoil, shrink

squint 4 peek, peep, peer **10** hagioscope, strabismus

squire 6 attend, escort, lawyer **7** consort,

squirm 4 worm 6 fidget, wiggle, writhe 7 wriggle

squirrel 4 stow 5 cache, hoard, stash 7 secrete *red:* 9 chickaree

squirt 3 jet, kid, pup, tot 4 brat, tyke 5 sprat, spray, spurt, twerp 6 shaver, shrimp, splurt, spritz 7 spatter

squish 3 jam 4 cram, mash, mush, pack, push 5 crush, press, quash, smash 7 flatten, scrunch, squeeze, squelch, trample

squishy 4 soft 6 flabby, quaggy, slushy, spongy

Sri Lanka *bay:* 6 Bengal *capital:* 7 Colombo *city:* 8 Moratuwa *ethnic group:* 9 Sinhalese *former name:* 6 Ceylon *language:* 5 Tamil 9 Sinhalese *monetary unit:* 5 rupee *shoals:* 11 Adam's Bridge *strait:* 4 Palk

SRO 7 sellout

SS chief 7 Himmler (Heinrich)

S-shaped 7 sigmoid

stab 3 dig, pop, try 4 pang, poke, shot 5 crack, drive, fling, prick, spear, stick, whack, whirl 6 effort, pierce, thrust, twinge 7 attempt 8 puncture 9 penetrate

Stabat ___ 5 Mater

stabile 6 steady 9 sculpture 10 stationary

stabilize 3 fix, set 4 prop 5 brace, poise 6 cement, firm up, fixate, prop up, secure, settle, steady 7 balance, ballast, support, sustain 8 solidify 9 reinforce

stable 3 set 4 barn, fast, firm, mews, safe, sure 5 fixed, solid, sound 6 secure, steady, sturdy 7 abiding, durable, lasting, staunch 8 balanced, constant, enduring, resolute 9 immutable, permanent, steadfast, unvarying 10 perdurable, stationary, unchanging, unshakable

stack 4 cock, heap, hill, load, mass, pile, pipe 5 mound, sheaf 7 chimney, pyramid

stack up 3 add 5 equal, total 6 equate, gather 7 compare, measure

stadium 4 bowl, rink, ring 5 arena 6 garden 8 coliseum 10 hippodrome 12 amphitheater

staff 3 rod 4 club, prop, rung, team, wand 5 baton, billy 6 cudgel 7 faculty, support 9 personnel *bishop's:* 7 crosier, crozier *medical:* 8 caduceus

stage 3 lot 4 play, rung, show, step 5 grade, level, mount, notch, phase, put on 6 degree, period, status 7 execute, perform, present, produce *direction:* 4 exit 5 enter 6 exeunt *scenery:* 3 set 8 backdrop *show:* 4 play 5 drama, revue 7 musical 9 burlesque 10 vaudeville *signal:* 3 cue *whisper:* 5 aside

stage set 5 decor, scene 7 scenery 8 backdrop 11 mise-en-scène

stagger 4 daze, reel, stun, sway 5 amaze, floor, lurch, pitch, stump, waver, weave 6 boggle, careen, dither, falter, teeter, topple, totter, wobble, zigzag 7 astound, nonplus, perplex, shatter, stumble, stupefy 8 astonish, bowl over 9 dumbfound, overwhelm, vacillate 11 flabbergast

stagnant 5 musty, stale 6 static 8 immobile, unmoving 10 motionless, stationary

stagnate 4 idle 5 stall 6 fester 8 languish, stultify, vegetate

stagy 10 artificial, histrionic, theatrical 11 pretentious 12 melodramatic

staid 5 grave, sober 6 formal, sedate, solemn, somber, sombre, stuffy 7 earnest, serious, starchy 8 composed, decorous, priggish 9 dignified

stain 3 dye, tar 4 blot, daub, onus, slur, soil, spot 5 brand, color, odium, shame, smear, sully, taint, tinge 6 blotch, defile, embrue, imbrue, smirch, smudge, stigma 7 blemish, pigment, tarnish 8 besmirch, colorant, discolor, dishonor, dyestuff, tincture

staircase *handrail:* 8 banister *outdoor:* 6 perron *post:* 5 newel 8 baluster

stake 3 bet, lay, pot, set 4 ante, back, game, pale, play, post, risk 5 claim, put on, share, wager 6 gamble, paling, picket, pledge, tether 7 finance 8 bankroll, interest 10 capitalize, investment

stalag 7 POW camp 10 prison camp

stale 5 banal, dusty, faded, fusty, moldy, musty, passé, tired, trite 7 clichéd, tedious, worn-out 8 overused, shopworn, timeworn 9 hackneyed, tasteless 11 commonplace, stereotyped

stalemate 3 tie 4 draw 7 impasse 8 deadlock, gridlock, standoff

stalk 4 hunt, prey 5 chase, track 6 ambush, follow, pursue, stride 8 flush out *flower:* 8 peduncle *leaf:* 7 petiole *short:* 5 stipe

stall 3 bay, pew 4 halt 5 booth, brake, check, delay, hedge, kiosk, stand 6 arrest, put off 7 conk out, counter, hold off 8 obstruct 9 stonewall 10 filibuster 11 compartment, prevaricate

stalwart 4 bold 5 brave, gutsy, husky, stout, tough 6 brawny, robust, sinewy, strong, sturdy 7 valiant 8 fearless, intrepid, unafraid, valorous, vigorous 9 dauntless, tenacious, undaunted 10 courageous

stamen *part* 6 anther 8 filament

stamina 8 tenacity 9 endurance, fortitude, tolerance 11 persistence 12 staying power

stammer 6 gibber, jabber 7 sputter, stutter 8 hesitate, splutter

stamp 3 ilk, lot 4 etch, kind, mark, mint, mold, seal, sort, type 5 clomp, clump, pound, print, tromp 6 hammer, stripe 7 impress, imprint, trample 8 hallmark, inscribe 9 character 10 impression 12 characterize

stampede 4 bolt, dash, rout, rush, tear 5 crush, panic, rodeo 6 charge

stamps 7 postage

stance 4 pose 7 bearing, posture 8 attitude, carriage, position 10 deportment

stanch 4 stem, stop 5 check 6 stop up 8 hold back

stanchion 4 post, prop 5 brace 7 support

stand 4 bear 5 abide, booth, brook, kiosk, stall, treat 6 endure, handle, suffer 7 counter, stomach, swallow, weather 8 attitude, platform, position, tolerate *artist's:* 5 easel *three-legged:* 6 tripod, trivet *ornamental:* 7 étagère

standard 3 law, par 4 flag, jack, mean, norm, rule 5 color, gauge, ideal, model, stock, usual 6 banner, belief, common, ensign, median, normal, pennon 7 average, classic, example, general, measure, pattern, pennant, regular, typical, uniform 8 accepted, everyday, exemplar, familiar, ordinary, orthodox, paradigm 9 archetype, benchmark, criterion, customary, principle, yardstick 10 definitive, prevailing, recognized, regulation, touchstone 11 established, fundamental

standardize 6 adjust 7 conform 8 regulate 9 reconcile

stand for 4 bear, mean 5 allow 6 denote, permit 7 signify 8 indicate, tolerate 9 put up with, represent, symbolize

stand-in 3 sub 5 proxy 6 backup, second 9 alternate, surrogate 10 substitute, understudy 11 pinch hitter, replacement 12 impersonator

standing 4 rank, term 5 erect, fixed, place 6 cachet, credit, repute, status 7 dignity, footing, station, stature, upright 8 capacity, duration, eminence, position, prestige, stagnant 9 character, permanent, situation 10 estimation, reputation 11 consequence, established

standoff see STALEMATE

standoffish 5 aloof 6 chilly 7 distant, haughty 8 detached, reserved 9 reclusive, withdrawn 10 unfriendly, unsociable 12 misanthropic

stand out 3 jut 4 bulk, loom 5 bulge 7 project 8 protrude

standpatter 4 fogy, tory 7 diehard

8 mossback 11 bitter-ender 12 conservative

standpoint 4 side 5 angle, slant 7 outlook 9 direction 11 perspective

standstill 4 halt, stop 5 check, pause 7 impasse 8 deadlock, dead stop 9 cessation, stalemate

Stanford site 8 Palo Alto

Stanley Kowalski's wife 6 Stella

Stanleys' car 7 steamer

Stan's partner 5 Ollie

stanza 7 strophe *combining form:* 5 stich *of eight lines:* 6 octave *of four lines:* 6 ballad 8 quatrain *of six lines:* 6 sestet *of three lines:* 6 tercet 7 triplet *Persian:* 8 rubaiyat

star 4 icon, idol, lead, main, nova 5 actor, chief, major 6 étoile 7 actress, capital 8 asterisk, dominant, luminary 9 celebrity, headliner, principal 10 preeminent 11 outstanding *bright:* 4 Vega 5 Deneb, Rigel, Spica 6 Altair, Pollux, Sirius 7 Antares, Canopus, Capella, Procyon 8 Arcturus 9 Aldebaran, Archernar, Fomalhaut 10 Beta Crucis, Betelgeuse 11 Alpha Crucis 12 Beta Centauri 13 Alpha Centauri *combining form:* 4 astr 5 aster, astro 6 astero, sidero *five-pointed:* 8 pentacle 9 pentagram *giant:* 10 Betelgeuse *six-pointed:* 8 hexagram

starch 3 pep 4 push, snap 5 drive, moxie, punch, spunk, vigor 7 stiffen 8 gumption, vitality 9 formality *combining form:* 4 amyl 5 amylo

starchy 4 prim 5 aloof, stiff 6 doughy, formal, wooden 7 stilted

star-crossed 6 doomed 7 hapless, unlucky 8 ill-fated, luckless 10 illstarred 11 unfortunate 12 misfortune

Stardust composer 10 Carmichael (Hoagy)

stare 3 eye 4 gape, gawk, gaze, ogle, peer 6 goggle 10 rubberneck

stark 3 raw 4 bare, nude, pure 5 bleak, blunt, clear, harsh, naked, quite, rigid, sheer, utter 6 barren, strict, unclad, vacant, wholly 8 absolute, complete, desolate, stripped 9 au naturel, outand-out 10 absolutely

starry 6 astral 7 stellar 8 sidereal

starry-eyed 6 dreamy, unreal 7 utopian 8 ecstatic 9 rapturous, visionary 11 impractical, unrealistic 13 impracticable

Star-Spangled Banner writer 3 Key (Francis Scott)

start 4 bolt, dawn, draw 5 arise, begin, crank, found, issue, onset, quail, react, set up, wince 6 blench, create, embark, flinch, launch, outset, recoil, shrink, spring, take up **7** actuate, genesis, infancy, kickoff, opening, trigger **8** activate, commence, embark on, initiate, organize, reaction **9** beginning, establish, institute, originate **10** inaugurate **12** commencement

startle 4 jolt, jump **5** alarm, scare, shock, spook **8** astonish, frighten, surprise

starved 6 hungry **8** famished, ravenous, underfed

stash 4 bury, hide **5** cache, hoard, plant, store **7** conceal, lay away, nest egg, secrete **8** lay aside, sock away, squirrel **9** stockpile

stasis 7 balance, inertia **9** equipoise **10** immobility, stagnation **11** equilibrium

state 3 air, put, say **4** aver, mode, rank, tell, vent **5** utter **6** affirm, assert, recite, relate, report **7** declare, dignity, explain, expound, express, posture, recount **8** attitude, capacity, describe, position, set forth, standing **9** condition, enunciate, situation, ventilate *subdivison:* **6** county

state *easternmost:* **5** Maine *largest:* **6** Alaska *smallest:* **11** Rhode Island *southernmost:* **6** Hawaii

state abbreviation *Alabama:* **3** Ala. *Alaska:* **4** Alas. *Arizona:* **4** Ariz. *Arkansas:* **3** Ark. *California:* **3** Cal. **5** Calif. *Colorado:* **3** Col. **4** Colo. *Connecticut:* **4** Conn. *Delaware:* **3** Del. *Florida:* **3** Fla. *Idaho:* **3** Ida. *Illinois:* **3** Ill. *Indiana:* **3** Ind. *Kansas:* **3** Kan. **4** Kans. *Kentucky:* **3** Ken. *Massachusetts:* **4** Mass. *Michigan:* **4** Mich. *Minnesota:* **4** Minn. *Mississippi:* **4** Miss. *Montana:* **4** Mont. *Nebraska:* **3** Neb. **4** Nebr. *Nevada:* **3** Nev. *New Mexico:* **4** N. Mex. *North Carolina:* **4** N. Car. *North Dakota:* **4** N. Dak. *Oklahoma:* **4** Okla. *Oregon:* **3** Ore. **4** Oreg. *Pennsylvania:* **4** Penn. **5** Penna. *South Carolina:* **4** S. Car. *South Dakota:* **4** S. Dak. *Tennessee:* **4** Tenn. *Texas:* **3** Tex. *Vermont:* **4** Verm. *Virginia:* **4** Virg. *Washington:* **4** Wash. *West Virginia:* **3** W. Va. *Wisconsin:* **3** Wis. **4** Wisc. *Wyoming:* **3** Wyo.

stately 5 grand, lofty, noble, regal, royal **6** august, formal, kingly, lordly, solemn **7** courtly, elegant, gallant, haughty **8** gracious, imperial, imposing, majestic, palatial, princely **9** dignified **10** ceremonial, impressive, monumental **11** ceremonious, magnificent

statement 3 tab **4** bill **5** score **6** avowal, charge, dictum, remark, report **7** account, comment, invoice, recital **8** averment **9** affidavit, assertion, manifesto, narrative, reckoning, testimony,

utterance **10** deposition, expression **11** description *introductory:* **7** preface **8** foreword, prologue

stateroom 5 cabin

statesman 10 politician *American:* **3** Hay (John Milton) **4** Clay (Henry), Hull (Cordell), Otis (James), Root (Elihu) **5** Adams (Samuel), Henry (Patrick), Lodge (Henry Cabot), Vance (Cyrus) **6** Bunche (Ralph), Bunker (Ellsworth), Dulles (John Foster), Kennan (George F), Morris (Gouverneur), Powell (Colin), Sumner (Charles) **7** Acheson (Dean), Hancock (John), Kellogg (Frank B.), Lansing (Robert), Sherman (John, Roger), Stimson (Henry L.), Webster (Daniel) **8** Franklin (Benjamin), Hamilton (Alexander), Harriman (Averell), Pinckney (Charles, Thomas), Randolph (Edmund Jennings, John, Payton), Rutledge (John), Trumbull (Jonathan, Joseph) **9** Kissinger (Henry), Stevenson (Adlai) **10** Stettinius (Edward Reilly) *Australian:* **9** Wentworth (William Charles) *Austrian:* **6** Renner (Karl) **7** Kaunitz (Wenzel von) **8** Dollfuss (Engelbert), Stevenson (Adlai) **10** Metternich (Klemens von) **13** Schwarzenberg (Felix zu) *Canadian:* **4** King (W. L. Mackenzie) **7** Laurier (Wilfrid) **8** Thompson (John Sparrow) **9** Macdonald (John Alexander, John Sandfield), Mackenzie (Alexander, William Lyon) *Chinese:* **3** Yen (Hsishan) **4** Deng (Xiaoping), Kung (Hsiang-hsi), Teng (Hsiao-p'ing), Wang (Anshih, Chingwei), Yuan (Shih-kai) **9** Sun Yat-Sen *Dutch:* **6** de Witt (Johan de) **7** Grotius (Hugo), Stikker (Dirk) *East German:* **8** Ulbricht (Walter) *English:* **3** Fox (Charles, Henry) **4** Eden (Anthony, George, William), More (Thomas), Peel (Arthur, Robert, William), Pitt (William), Vane (Henry) **5** Cecil (Robert, William), North (Francis, Frederick, Roger) **6** Morley (John), Sidney (Algernon, Henry, Philip, Robert), Temple (Henry, William), Wolsey (Thomas) **7** Halifax (Earl of), Reading (Marquis of), Russell (John, William), Stanley (Edward George, Edward Henry), Stewart (Robert), Warwick (Earl of) **8** Cromwell (Oliver, Thomas), Disraeli (Benjamin), Robinson (George Frederick Samuel), Villiers (George) **9** Cavendish (Spencer, William), Churchill (Randolph, Winston), Gladstone (William), Salisbury (Earl, Marquis of), Strafford (Earl of), Wellesley (Arthur, Richard Colley) **10** Palmerston (Lord), Rockingham

(Marquis of), Sunderland (Earl of), Walsingham (Francis), Wellington (Duke of) 11 Chamberlain (Austen, Joseph, Neville), Shaftesbury (Earl of) 12 Chesterfield (Earl of) *Finnish:* 9 Stahlberg (Kaarlo Juho) *French:* 5 Sully (Duc de) 6 Guizot (François-Pierre-Guillaume), Thiers (Louis-Adolphe), Turgot (Anne-Robert-Jacques) 7 Herriot (Edouard), Mazarin (Jules), Schuman (Robert), Viviani (René) 8 Hanotaux (Gabriel) 9 Lafayette (Marquis de), Millerand (Alexandre), Richelieu (Duc de) 10 Clemenceau (Georges) 11 Tocqueville (Alexis de) *German:* 5 Wirth (Joseph) 10 Stresemann (Gustav) *German-Danish:* 9 Struensee (Johann Friedrich) *Greek:* 6 Zaimis (Alexandros) 8 Pericles 9 Aristides 11 Cleisthenes, Demosthenes 12 Themistocles *Israeli:* 4 Eban (Abba) 5 Begin (Menachem), Dayan (Moshe) *Italian:* 6 Cavour (Conte di), Crispi (Francesco) 7 Orlando (Vittorio Emanuele) 11 Machiavelli (Niccolo) *Japanese:* 5 genro, Kanoe 6 Kanoye *Norwegian:* 6 Nansen (Fridtjof) *Polish:* 7 Zaleski (August) 9 Pilsudski (Jozef) 10 Paderewski (Ignacy) *Prussian:* 5 Stein (Karl) *Roman:* 4 Cato (Marcus Porcius) 6 Cicero (Marcus Tullius), Pompey, Seneca (Lucius Annaeus) 7 Agrippa (Marcus Vipsanius) 8 Gracchus (Gaius, Tiberius), Maecenas (Gaius) 9 Symmachus (Quintus Aurelius) *Russian:* 5 Witte (Sergey) 7 Molotov (Vyacheslav) 8 Potemkin (Grigory) 9 Vyshinsky (Andrey) *Scottish:* 4 Knox (John) *South American:* 7 Bolívar (Simón) 9 San Martín (José de) *Swiss:* 4 Ador (Gustave) 5 Welti (Emil)
static 5 fixed, inert 6 stable, steady 7 stabile, stalled, stopped 8 constant, immobile, inactive, stagnant, unmoving 9 immovable, unvarying 10 changeless, unchanging
station 4 post, rank, site, spot 5 depot, locus, place, point 6 assign 7 footing 8 capacity, standing 9 character 10 white noise
stationary 5 fixed 6 static 8 immobile, stagnant, unmoving 9 immovable 10 motionless, stock-still
statue *base:* 6 plinth 8 pedestal *gigantic:* 8 Colossus *Greek:* 5 atlas 7 telamon 8 caryatid *religious:* 5 Pietà *small:* 8 figurine
stature see STATUS
status 4 rank 5 merit, place, worth 6 cachet, rating, renown 7 caliber, dig-

nity, footing, posture, quality 8 capacity, eminence, position, prestige, standing 9 character, condition, situation 10 prominence 11 consequence, distinction
statute 3 act, law 4 bill 5 canon, edict 9 enactment, ordinance
staunch 4 fast, firm, sure, true 5 liege, loyal, solid, sound 6 secure, stable, strong, trusty 8 constant, faithful, reliable, resolute, stalwart 9 steadfast 10 dependable 11 substantial, trustworthy
stave off 4 foil 5 avert, block, deter, dodge, elude, parry, rebut, repel 6 rebuff, thwart 7 forfend, obviate, prevent, repulse 8 preclude 9 forestall 10 circumvent
stay 3 guy, lag 4 bide, halt, prop, rest, stop, wait 5 abide, brace, check, defer, delay, dwell, lodge, tarry, visit 6 linger, put off, remain 7 sojourn, support, suspend 8 hold over, postpone, stop over 9 interrupt 10 suspension 11 stick around
steadfast 4 firm, sure, true 5 fixed, liege, loyal 7 abiding, adamant, patient, staunch 8 constant, enduring, faithful, immobile, reliable, resolute, stubborn 9 immovable, unbending, unmovable 10 dependable, unwavering, unyielding 11 unfaltering, unflinching 12 neverfailing, single-minded, wholehearted 13 unquestioning
steady 3 set 4 even, fast, firm, sure 5 fixed, liege, loyal, sober 6 stable, static 7 abiding, ballast, certain, durable, equable, nonstop, regular, stabile, staunch, uniform 8 constant, enduring, faithful, habitual, reliable, resolute, unbroken, unshaken 9 ceaseless, incessant, stabilize, unvarying 10 changeless, consistent, continuous, dependable, persistent, sweetheart, unchanging, unswerving, unwavering 11 unfaltering 12 unchangeable, wholehearted
steak 4 club, cube, loin 5 chuck, flank, round, T-bone 6 rib eye 7 brisket, sirloin 9 Delmonico, hamburger, Salisbury 10 tenderloin 11 filet mignon, London broil, porterhouse 13 chateaubriand
steal 3 bag, cop, nab, nip, rob 4 grab, hook, kite, lift, loot, lurk, slip, take 5 creep, filch, glide, heist, pinch, poach, prowl, seize, shirk, sidle, skulk, slide, slink, sneak, swipe 6 burgle, fleece, hijack, pilfer, pocket, snatch, snitch, thieve, tiptoe 7 bargain, pillage, plunder, purloin 8 embezzle, shanghai, shoplift 9 pussyfoot 10 burglarize, pla-

giarize 11 appropriate *a vehicle:*
6 hijack 8 highjack

stealing 5 theft 6 piracy 7 larceny, robbery 8 burglary

stealthy 3 sly 4 wily 6 covert, crafty, feline, secret, shifty, silent, slinky, sneaky 7 catlike, cunning, furtive, subrosa 8 hush-hush, skulking, slinking, sneaking 9 noiseless 10 undercover 11 clandestine 13 surreptitious

steam bath 5 sauna

steamboat structure 5 texas

steamer 4 boat, clam, ship

steam organ 8 calliope

steed 5 horse, mount 7 charger

steel 4 gird 5 brace, nerve, rally 6 buck up, harden 7 fortify, hearten, stiffen 8 embolden, inspirit 9 reinforce 10 strengthen

steep 3 sop 4 high, soak 5 bathe, dizzy, imbue, sheer 6 abrupt, drench, infuse 7 arduous, extreme, immerse, suffuse 8 elevated, marinate, saturate 9 excessive 10 exorbitant, immoderate, impregnate, inordinate 11 precipitate, precipitous

steeple 5 spire, tower 6 flèche

steer 4 helm, lead 5 guide, pilot, point, route 6 direct, escort, tip-off 7 channel, conduct, skipper 8 shepherd *a ship:* 4 conn, helm, luff

Stegner novel 13 Angle of Repose, Spectator Bird (The) 20 Big Rock Candy Mountain (The)

stein 3 mug 5 stoup 6 goblet 7 tankard

Steinbeck novel 5 Pearl (The) 10 Cannery Row, East of Eden 12 Of Mice and Men, Tortilla Flat 13 Grapes of Wrath (The)

Stein's companion 6 Toklas (Alice B.)

Steinway product 5 piano

stellar 6 astral, starry 7 leading, shining 8 sidereal, standout, starlike 10 preeminent 11 outstanding, predominant, superlative

stem 4 flow, head, rise, stop 5 arise, check, issue 6 arrest, derive, spring, stanch 7 control, develop, emanate, proceed 8 peduncle 9 originate *plant:* 5 haulm *underground:* 5 tuber 7 rhizome

stench 4 funk, reek 5 smell, stink

stentorian 4 loud 7 blaring, booming, orotund, raucous, roaring 8 sonorous, strident 9 clamorous, deafening 10 thundering 12 earsplitting

step 4 hoof, pace, rung, walk 5 grade, level, notch, stage, stair, track, tread 6 degree 7 measure, traipse 8 footfall 9 gradation *dance:* 3 pas

step-by-step 7 gradual 9 piecemeal

steppe 5 plain 6 tundra

Steppenwolf author 5 Hesse (Hermann)

stereotype 4 mold 7 pattern 10 categorize, pigeonhole 11 standardize

stereotypical 4 hack 5 banal, stale, trite 7 clichéd 8 shopworn, timeworn 9 hackneyed 11 commonplace

sterile 4 arid, bare, vain 6 barren, fallow 7 aseptic, worn-out 8 desolate, hygienic, impotent, lifeless, sanitary 9 fruitless, infertile 10 antiseptic, unfruitful, uninspired 11 disinfected 12 unproductive

sterilize 3 fix 4 geld, spay 5 alter 6 neuter, purify 7 cleanse 8 sanitize 9 disinfect 10 emasculate

sterilized 7 aseptic

sterling 4 pure, true 5 noble 6 worthy 8 virtuous 9 estimable, exemplary, honorable

stern 4 grim 5 harsh, rigid, sober, stony 6 gloomy, severe, strict 7 ascetic, austere 8 obdurate 10 forbidding, implacable, inexorable, inflexible 11 unrelenting

sternward 3 aft

Sterope *father:* 5 Atlas *mother:* 7 Pleione *sisters:* 8 Pleiades

Stevenson novel 9 Kidnapped

stew 4 boil, brew, flap, fret, fume, fuss, hash, olio, olla, snit 5 daube, salmi, sweat, tizzy, worry 6 burgoo, dither, jumble, lather, medley, pother, ragout, seethe, simmer, swivet, tumult 7 brothel, goulash, mélange, mixture, parboil, swelter, turmoil 8 bordello, mishmash, mulligan, pot-au-feu 9 Brunswick, cassoulet, commotion, confusion, pasticcio, potpourri 10 hodgepodge, hotchpotch, miscellany, turbulence 11 olla podrida, ratatouille, slumgullion 13 bouillabaisse

steward 6 manage 7 manager 8 overseer 10 supervisor

stewed 3 lit 4 high 5 drunk, lit up, oiled 6 bashed, blotto, bombed, cooked, juiced, potted, soaked, soused, stewed, stoned, tanked, wasted, zonked 7 crocked, drunken, pickled, pie-eyed, sloshed, smashed, sottish 8 simmered 9 plastered 10 inebriated, liquored up 11 intoxicated

Stheno see GORGON

stick 3 put, rod 4 glue, pole, stab 5 affix, baton, cling 6 adhere, attach, cleave, cohere, fasten 7 scruple 10 overcharge

stick around 4 bide, stay, wait 5 abide, dally, tarry 6 linger, remain

sticker 3 pin 4 barb, seal, shiv, spur 5 point, prong, shank, spike, spine, stamp 6 dagger 8 stiletto

stick-in-the-mud 4 fogy 6 fossil 8 mossback 10 fuddy-duddy

stick out 3 jut 5 bulge 6 beetle 7 project 8 overhang, protrude

stick up 3 mug, rob 6 waylay 7 project 8 protrude

sticky 5 gluey, gooey, gummy, humid, muggy, mushy, soggy, tacky 6 clammy, knotty, slushy, sultry, thorny, viscid 7 awkward, cloying, maudlin, mawkish, viscous 8 adhesive, bathetic, clinging, romantic 9 difficult 11 problematic, sentimental, tear-jerking

stiff 3 guy, lit, set 4 body, firm, hard, lush 5 cheat, drunk, harsh, oiled, proud, rigid, stark, steep, stick, tense, tight, tipsy 6 buzzed, corpse, frozen, jelled, juiced, person, plowed, potent, potted, severe, soused, stewed, wooden 7 cadaver, carcass, sloshed, starchy, stilted 8 hardened, reserved, stubborn 9 cardboard, excessive, inelastic, obstinate, petrified, plastered, unbending 10 exorbitant, inebriated, inflexible, mechanical, unyielding 11 intoxicated, intractable

stiffen 5 tense 6 harden 7 thicken 8 rigidify, solidify 9 stabilize 10 immobilize

stifle 3 gag 4 hush, mute 5 burke, choke, deter 6 dampen, deaden, hush up, muffle, muzzle 7 repress, silence, smother, squelch 8 stultify, suppress 9 suffocate 10 asphyxiate, discourage

stigma 4 blot, onus, spot 5 brand, odium, shame, stain, taint 6 smudge, smutch 8 black eye, disgrace, dishonor, petechia, tainting

stigmatize 5 brand, label, stamp

still 3 yet 4 calm, even, hush, lull 5 allay, inert, quiet, shush, whist 6 becalm, hushed, placid, serene, settle, silent, though, withal 7 halcyon, however, silence 8 after all, likewise, peaceful, stagnant, tranquil 9 noiseless, quietness, soundless 10 motionless, stationary 11 furthermore, nonetheless, tranquility 12 nevertheless

stilt 4 bird, pile, pole 8 longlegs 9 shorebird

stilted 4 prim 5 stiff 6 formal, wooden 7 pompous, starchy 8 affected 9 cardboard

stilt-like bird 6 avocet

stimulant 4 goad, spur 5 tonic 7 impetus, impulse 8 caffeine, catalyst, excitant 9 analeptic, energizer, incentive 10 incitement, motivation

stimulate 4 fire, goad, move, prod, spur, urge, whet 5 impel, pique, rouse, set up, spark 6 arouse, excite, fire up, foment, incite, prompt, vivify, work up 7 agitate, enliven, inspire, provoke, quicken, trigger 8 activate, energize, motivate, vitalize 9 galvanize 10 exhilarate

stimulus 4 goad, kick, push, spur 5 boost, cause 6 charge, motive 7 impetus, impulse 8 catalyst 9 incentive 10 incitement, inducement, motivation 11 instigation, provocation 13 encouragement

sting 3 con 4 trap 5 cheat, prick, smart, snare 6 hustle, tingle 7 con game 8 skin game

stinging 8 aculeate

stingy 4 mean 5 close, tight 6 frugal, narrow, paltry, skimpy 7 chintzy, costive, miserly, niggard, scrimpy, sparing, thrifty 8 grudging 9 niggardly, pennywise, penurious 10 economical, ironfisted, pinchpenny, ungenerous 11 tightfisted 12 cheeseparing, parsimonious 13 penny-pinching

stink 4 flap, funk, fuss, reek 5 smell 6 stench

stinker 3 dog, dud 4 bomb, bust, flop 5 lemon, skunk 6 petrel

stinking see SMELLY

stinky see SMELLY

stint 3 job 4 bout, task, time, tour, turn 5 chore, cramp, pinch, scant, share, shift, skimp, spare, spell 6 amount, scrape, scrimp 8 quantity, restrict 9 allotment, stricture 10 assignment, limitation 11 restriction

stipend 3 fee, pay 4 hire, wage 5 award 6 salary 7 payment 9 allowance, emolument 13 consideration

stipple 3 dot 5 fleck, speck 6 pepper 7 freckle, speckle 8 sprinkle

stipulate 5 state 6 detail 7 specify 8 contract, spell out 13 particularize

stipulation 5 limit, terms 7 proviso, strings 9 condition, provision 11 requirement

stir 3 ado, din, mix 4 beat, fuss, rout, to-do, wake, whet 5 awake, blend, budge, churn, evoke, impel, raise, rally, rouse, roust, set on, spark, waken, whirl 6 arouse, awaken, bustle, excite, flurry, foment, hubbub, incite, kindle, pother, seethe, simmer, tumult, whip up 7 actuate, agitate, disturb, ferment, inspire, provoke, quicken 8 activate, activity, energize 9 agitation, commotion, galvanize, stimulate 11 disturbance

stirrup 6 stapes 8 footrest

stithy 5 anvil

stoat 6 ermine, weasel

stock 4 butt, fund, hope, race 5 brace, carry, faith, goods, hoard, store, trunk,

trust **6** family, supply **7** furnish, lineage
8 pedigree, reliance **9** inventory, selection **10** confidence, dependence **11** merchandise

stockade 4 jail **5** fence **6** paling, prison
8 palisade **9** enclosure, guardroom

stock exchange 6 bourse

stockings 4 hose **5** socks **7** hosiery

stockpile 4 bank, heap, mass **5** amass,
cache, hoard, lay up, store **6** garner,
supply **7** backlog, collect, nest egg,
reserve, store up **9** inventory, reservoir
10 accumulate, repository

stocky 3 fat **5** beefy, burly, dumpy,
husky, plump, pudgy, squat, stout,
thick **6** chunky, stubby, stumpy
8 heavyset, thickset **9** corpulent

stodge 4 fill, sate **5** gorge, stuff
7 overeat, surfeit

stodgy 5 fusty **6** stuffy **9** hidebound, out-
of-date **12** old-fashioned

stogie 4 shoe **5** cigar **6** brogan

stoic 6 stolid **7** Spartan **9** apathetic,
impassive **10** phlegmatic **11** indifferent,
unconcerned

stoicism 9 stolidity **11** impassivity
founder: **4** Zeno

stoke 3 fan **4** feed, fuel, poke, stir, tend
6 supply

Stoker novel 7 Dracula

stolid 3 dry **4** dull, flat **5** stoic **6** wooden
8 rocklike **9** apathetic, impassive,
unruffled **10** phlegmatic **11** unemotional

stomach 3 gut **4** bear, craw **5** abide,
belly, brook, stand, taste, tummy
6 digest, endure, paunch, venter
7 abdomen, swallow **8** appetite, tolerate
combining form: **5** gastr **6** gastro, ventri,
ventro *enzyme:* **6** pepsin, rennin *muscle:*
7 pylorus *ruminant:* **6** omasum **8** abomasum **9** reticulum *Scottish:* **4** kyte

stomachache 5 colic, gripe **12** collywobbles

stomp 5 clomp, clump, pound, tramp,
tromp **7** trample

stone 3 gem **4** rock **5** lapis **6** pebble
7 boulder *base:* **6** plinth *block of:*
8 monolith *chip:* **5** spall *combining form:*
4 lite, lith, lyte *cosmic:* **6** meteor
9 chondrite, meteorite *for grinding
grains:* **6** metate *fruit:* **5** drupe *memorial:*
7 obelisk *monument:* **8** megalith *of a
fruit:* **3** pit

___ **Stone 7** Blarney, Rosetta

Stone novel 11 Lust for Life **18** Agony
and the Ecstasy (The)

stonecrop 5 sedum

stoned 3 lit **4** high **5** boozy, doped,
drunk, fried, oiled, tight, tipsy
6 buzzed, canned, juiced, loaded,

plowed, potted, soused, stewed, tanked,
wasted, zonked **7** crocked, drugged,
muddled, pickled, pie-eyed, sloshed,
smashed **8** hopped-up, turned on,
wiped out **9** pixilated, plastered,
spaced-out, strung out **10** inebriated,
tripped out **11** intoxicated

stooge 3 act, sap **4** dupe, foil, gull,
mark, pawn, tool **5** chump, dummy,
patsy, proxy **6** puppet, sucker, victim
7 fall guy **8** sidekick **9** represent
11 stool pigeon, straight man **12** second
banana

Stooge 3 Moe (Howard) **5** Curly
(Howard), Larry (Fine)

stool pigeon 3 rat **4** fink, nark **5** decoy
6 canary, snitch **7** ratfink, tipster
8 informer

stoop 3 dip **4** bend, duck, sink **5** deign,
hunch, porch, slump **6** resort, slouch
7 descend, portico, veranda **8** stairway
10 condescend

stop 3 bar, can, dam, end **4** clog, fill,
halt, plug, quit, stay, stem **5** block,
brake, cease, check, close, stall, tarry
6 arrest, cut off, desist, draw up, ending, kibosh, stanch **7** disrupt, occlude,
prevent, shut off, sojourn, suspend,
turn off **8** knock off, leave off, obstruct
9 cessation, interrupt, terminate
10 conclusion, standstill **11** discontinue,
refrain from, termination *up:* **4** cork,
plug **7** occlude

stopgap 5 shift **6** resort **8** recourse,
resource **9** expedient, makeshift
10 expediency, substitute

stopover 4 stay **5** visit **7** sojourn

stoppage 4 halt **6** cutoff, strike **7** walk-
out **8** shutdown **10** standstill **11** obstruction

stopper 4 bung, cork, fill, plug **5** close

store 3 bin **4** fund, mart, pack, shop,
tank **5** amass, cache, depot, hoard, lay
up, stash **6** ensile, garner, market, outlet, shoppe, supply **7** arsenal, backlog,
bootery, deposit, reserve **8** boutique,
cumulate, emporium, mothball, showroom, squirrel **9** abundance, chandlery,
inventory, reservoir, stockpile, warehouse **10** accumulate, depository, five-
and-ten, repository **11** five-and-dime
12 accumulation

storehouse 5 depot **7** arsenal, granary
8 magazine **9** stockpile **10** depository,
repository

storekeeper 8 merchant, retailer
9 tradesman

storeroom 6 larder, pantry **7** buttery

storm 3 row **4** fury, gale, hail, rage, rant,
rave, roar, rush, to-do **5** beset, blast,
blitz, burst, furor, onset, salvo **6** assail,

attack, charge, clamor, fall on, flurry, furore, hubbub, outcry, pother, racket, rumpus, shower, squall, strike, tumult, volley 7 assault, barrage, bluster, cyclone, monsoon, ruction, tempest, thunder, tornado, turmoil, twister, typhoon 8 blizzard, downpour, drumfire, fall upon, outbreak, outburst, paroxysm, upheaval 9 broadside, cannonade, commotion, discharge, fusillade, hurricane, nor'easter, onslaught 10 blitzkrieg, cloudburst, hurly-burly 11 bombardment, northeaster, northwester

storm trooper 10 brownshirt

stormy 4 foul 5 rainy, rough 6 raging 7 furious 8 blustery 9 turbulent 10 tumultuous 11 tempestuous, threatening

story 3 fib, lie 4 epic, saga, tale, yarn 5 conte, fable 6 canard, legend, report 7 account, fiction, märchen, parable, version 8 allegory, anecdote, folktale, megillah, tall tale 9 chronicle, fairy tale, narration, narrative 11 description, fabrication

storyteller 4 liar 6 fibber 8 fabulist 9 raconteur

stoup 4 font 5 basin 6 flagon, goblet 7 chalice, tankard

stout 3 ale, fat 4 brew 5 beefy, bulky, burly, heavy, husky, obese, plump, thick 6 fleshy, portly, strong, sturdy 9 corpulent 10 overweight

Stout detective 5 Wolfe (Nero)

stouthearted 4 bold, game 5 brave, gutsy 7 doughty, valiant 8 fearless, intrepid, resolute, stalwart, stubborn, unafraid 9 audacious, dauntless, undaunted 10 courageous

stove 4 kiln, oven 5 range 8 Franklin, potbelly

stow 4 load, pack 5 stash, store 7 deposit

stower 9 stevedore

Stowe work 4 Dred

strabismus 6 squint

straddle 4 span 6 sprawl 8 bestride 11 spread-eagle

strafe 4 rake 6 attack 8 enfilade 10 machine-gun

straggle 3 lag 4 poke, roam, rove 5 drift, range, stray 6 dawdle, loiter, ramble, wander 7 maunder, meander 8 trail off 9 string out

straight 4 even, fair, neat, pure, true 5 erect, plain, plumb, right 6 at once, candid, direct, honest, linear, square 7 unmixed, upright 8 orthodox 9 bourgeois, forthwith, undiluted 10 aboveboard, button-down, forthright 12 conventional 13 unadulterated *combining form:* 4 orth, rect 5 ortho, recti

straightaway 3 now 6 at once 7 stretch 8 directly, first off, promptly 9 forthwith, instanter 11 immediately

straighten 4 even, tidy 5 align 6 neaten, unbend, uncurl 7 rectify

straightforward 5 frank, lucid 6 candid, direct, honest 7 genuine, precise, sincere 8 clear-cut 9 outspoken 10 forthright 11 undeviating

strain 3 air, tax, try 4 hint, kind, pull, sort, toil, tune, vein 5 exert, stock, sweat, tinge, touch, trace, twist 6 filter, melody, screen, streak, stress, strive, wrench 7 lineage, overtax, tension, trouble 8 ancestry, exertion, overwork, pedigree, pressure, struggle 9 overexert

strait 4 bind, pass 5 pinch 6 crisis, plight 7 channel, dilemma, narrows, squeeze 8 exigency, hardship, juncture 9 crossroad, emergency 10 difficulty 11 contingency *Adriatic Sea-Ionian Sea:* 7 Otranto *Alaska:* 3 Icy *Alaska-Russia:* 6 Bering *Albania-Greece:* 5 Corfu *Asia-Europe:* 11 Dardanelles *Atlantic-Baffin Island:* 5 Davis *Atlantic-Mediterranean:* 9 Gibraltar *Atlantic-Nantucket Sound:* 8 Muskeget *Atlantic-North Sea:* 7 English *Atlantic-Pacific:* 5 Drake 8 Magellan *Atlantic-Saint Lawrence:* 5 Cabot *Baffin Island-Quebec:* 6 Hudson *Bering Sea-Sea of Okhotsk:* 5 Kuril 6 Kurile *Bismarck Sea-Solomon Sea:* 6 Vitiaz *Canada:* 3 Rae 5 Dease *East China Sea:* 5 Korea 8 Tsushima *East China-South China:* 6 Taiwan 7 Formosa *England-France:* 5 Dover *Flores Sea-Indian Ocean:* 4 Sape *Flores Sea-Savu Sea:* 4 Alor *Indian Ocean-Java Sea:* 5 Sunda *India-Sri Lanka:* 4 Palk *Indonesia:* 4 Alas, Alor, Bali 5 Tioro 6 Lombok 7 Dampier 8 Macassar, Makassar, Surabaya *Inner Hebrides:* 5 Tiree *Iran-Oman:* 6 Hormuz *Italy:* 7 Messina *Japan:* 4 Yura 5 Bungo, Kitan 7 Hayasui *Japan-Sakhalin Island:* 4 Soya *Lake Huron:* 10 Mississagi *Lake Huron-Lake Michigan:* 8 Mackinac *Malay Archipelago:* 5 Wetar *Malaysia-Singapore:* 6 Johore *Malay-Sumatra:* 7 Malacca *New Jersey-Staten Island:* 7 van Kull *New South Wales-Tasmania:* 4 Bass *New Zealand:* 4 Cook *Northwest Territories:* 6 Barrow 8 Franklin, Victoria 13 Prince of Wales *Nova Scotia:* 5 Canso *Pacific-San Francisco Bay:* 10 Golden Gate *Pacific-South China Sea:* 5 Luzon *Philippines:* 5 Bohol, Tanon 6 Iloilo 7 Basilan *Russia:* 4 Kara *Suvu Sea-Timor Sea:* 4 Roti *Sea of Azov-Black Sea:* 5 Kerch 7 Enikale *Sea of Japan:* 5 Tatar *Solomon*

Islands: 12 Bougainville *South China Sea:* 7 Mindoro 9 Singapore *Turkey:* 8 Bosporus 9 Bosphorus, Karadeniz *Vancouver-Washington:* 10 Juan de Fuca *Wales:* 5 Menai *Washington Sound:* 4 Haro

straitened 7 lacking, pinched, wanting 8 deprived, strapped 9 deficient, destitute 10 distressed, inadequate 12 impoverished

straitlaced 4 prim 5 staid, stiff 6 formal, narrow, prissy, strict, stuffy 7 genteel, prudish, starchy, stilted 8 priggish 9 hidebound, Victorian 11 puritanical

strand 4 bank 5 beach, coast, fiber, leave, shore, wreck 6 desert, maroon, thread 7 abandon, shingle 8 cast away, littoral, seacoast, seashore 9 shipwreck 10 run aground, waterfront

strange 3 odd 5 alien, crazy, fishy, funny, kinky, kooky, nutty, outré, queer, weird 6 exotic, far-out, freaky 7 bizarre, curious, oddball, offbeat, uncanny, unknown, unusual 8 aberrant, abnormal, atypical, peculiar, singular, wondrous 9 eccentric, fantastic, grotesque 10 mysterious, off-the-wall, outlandish, surprising, unfamiliar 11 exceptional 12 unaccustomed

Strange Interlude author 6 O'Neill (Eugene)

stranger 5 alien, guest 7 visitor 8 newcomer, outsider, wanderer 9 auslander, foreigner, immigrant, transient

strangle 5 burke, choke, shush 6 muffle, quelch, stifle 7 garotte, garrote 8 suppress, throttle 10 asphyxiate

strap 4 band, beat, belt, bind 5 leash 6 attach, punish, secure, suffer 7 binding, leather 8 distress 9 constrict

strapping 5 beefy, burly, hardy, husky 6 brawny, robust, rugged, sturdy 8 muscular, vigorous 10 able-bodied

stratagem 4 play, plot, ploy, ruse, wile 5 feint, trick 6 device, gambit, scheme, tactic 8 artifice, intrigue, maneuver 10 conspiracy, subterfuge 11 machination

strategy 4 plan 6 design, method, scheme 7 project, tactics 8 game plan 9 blueprint

stratum 3 bed 4 rank 5 class, grade, layer, level

Strauss, Richard *opera:* 6 Salome 7 Elektra 13 Rosenkavalier (Der) 15 Ariadne auf Naxos 16 Frau ohne Schatten (Der) *tone poem:* 7 Don Juan 10 Don Quixote 11 Heldenleben (Ein) 20 Thus Spake Zarathustra 23 Death and Transfiguration

straw 3 hay 5 blond 6 flaxen, golden,

thatch *braided:* 6 sennit *mat:* 6 tatami *plaited:* 7 leghorn

stray 3 err, gad 4 lost, roam, rove, waif 5 drift, range 6 depart, errant, ramble, random, wander 7 deviate, digress, diverge, erratic, meander, runaway, traipse, vagrant 8 divagate, homeless, sporadic 9 vagabond

streak 4 hint, vein 5 fleck, tinge, trace 6 dapple, marble, mottle, strain, stripe 7 striate 8 tincture 9 suspicion, variegate 10 intimation, suggestion

streaked 5 upset 7 brindle, marbled, striped 8 brindled, grizzled 9 disturbed

stream 3 run 4 beck, burn, flow, flux, gill, gush, pour, race, rill, rush, sike, tide 5 bourn, brook, creek, spate, surge 6 bourne, branch, rindle, runnel, sluice 7 current, freshet, rivulet, torrent 8 affluent

streamer 4 flag, jack 6 banner, burgee, ensign, pennon 7 pennant 8 banderol, bannerol, standard 9 banderole

streamline 7 contour 8 organize, simplify 9 modernize

street 3 way 4 drag, road, wynd 5 alley, drive 6 artery, avenue 7 roadway 9 boulevard 12 thoroughfare *border:* 4 curb 7 curbing *material:* 6 cobble 7 asphalt, macadam 11 cobblestone

streetcar 4 tram 7 trolley

Streetcar Named Desire, A *author:* 8 Williams (Tennessee) *character:* 6 Stella (Kowalski) 7 Blanche (DuBois), Stanley (Kowalski)

Street Scene author 4 Rice (Elmer)

strength 5 brawn, force, might, power, sinew, vigor 6 energy, muscle 7 potency 8 firmness, security 9 fortitude, intensity, soundness, stability, toughness 10 steadiness, sturdiness

strengthen 4 gird 5 brace, steel 6 anneal, harden, prop up 7 bolster, enhance, fortify, support, toughen 8 buttress, embolden, energize 9 intensify, reinforce, undergird 10 invigorate, rejuvenate

strenuous 4 hard 5 tough 6 taxing, uphill 7 arduous, operose 9 demanding, difficult, effortful, Herculean, laborious 12 backbreaking

Strephon 8 shepherd *beloved:* 5 Chloe 6 Urania

stress 6 accent, burden, import, play up, strain, weight 7 anxiety, feature, tension, trouble, urgency 8 emphasis, pressure 9 emphasize, italicize, underline 10 accentuate, underscore 12 accentuation *in poetry:* 5 ictus

stretch 4 area, draw, time 5 range, reach, scope, space, spell, sweep, tract, while

6 extend, extent, length, limber, region, spread **7** breadth, compass, draw out, expanse, magnify, prolong, purview, spin out, tighten **8** distance, elongate, lengthen, protract **9** embellish, embroider, expansion, overstate **10** exaggerate *on a frame:* **6** tenter *out:* **6** sprawl **7** lie down, recline

stretchable 7 ductile, elastic, tensile

stretched 4 taut

stretcher 4 yarn **6** gurney, litter **8** tall tale

strew 3 sow **4** dust **5** cover **6** pepper, spread **7** scatter **8** disperse, sprinkle **9** broadcast, circulate, propagate **10** distribute **11** disseminate

stricken 3 hit, ill **4** hurt, sick **7** injured, wounded **9** afflicted **11** overwhelmed

strict 4 firm **5** exact, harsh, rigid, stern, tough **6** narrow, severe **7** precise **8** exacting, faithful, rigorous **9** draconian, stringent, unsparing **10** inflexible, ironhanded, meticulous, scrupulous **11** punctilious

stricture 5 cramp, stint **7** censure, reproof **8** reproach **9** aspersion, criticism, reprimand **10** constraint, limitation **11** restriction **13** animadversion

stride 4 gait, pace, step **5** march, stalk **7** advance **8** straddle

strident 4 loud **5** harsh **6** shrill **7** grating, jarring, rasping, raucous, squawky **8** piercing **9** clamorous, insistent, obtrusive **10** boisterous, discordant, stentorian, vociferous **11** loudmouthed **12** earsplitting, obstreperous

strife 4 fray **5** broil, fight **6** battle, combat **7** discord, dispute, dissent, quarrel, rivalry, warfare, wrangle **8** argument, conflict, disunity, friction, struggle, tug-of-war **10** contention, difference, dissension, dissidence **11** altercation, competition, controversy

strike 3 hit, pop, rap **4** bash, beat, find, poke, slam, slap, slug, sock, swat, whap, whop **5** clout, knock, punch, smack, smite, swipe, thump, whack **6** affect, assail, attack, cudgel, delete, hammer, pummel, thrash **7** assault, impress, inflict, inspire **8** discover, stoppage

striking 5 showy, vivid **6** cogent, marked, signal **7** salient, telling **8** forceful **9** arresting, prominent **10** compelling, noticeable, remarkable **11** conspicuous, outstanding

Strindberg play 6 Easter, Father (The) **8** Comrades **9** Creditors (The), Dream Play (A), Miss Julie **10** Master Olaf **11** Ghost Sonata (The) **12** Dance of Death (The), Gustavus Vasa

string 3 row **4** file, line, rank, tier **5** chain, order, queue, train, twine

6 sequel, series **7** echelon **8** recourse, resource, sequence **10** succession *up:* **4** hang **5** noose, scrag **6** gibbet

stringent see STRICT

stringy 4 lean, ropy, wiry **6** sinewy **7** fibrous **8** muscular

strip 4 band, bare, doff, flay, husk, peel, sack, skin **5** scale **6** billet, denude, divest, expose, fillet, ravage, ribbon **7** bandeau, deprive, disrobe, pillage, uncover, undress **8** unclothe *leather:* **5** thong *of wood:* **4** lath, slat *skin:* **6** flense

stripe 3 ilk **4** band, kind, lash, sort, type **5** order **6** strake, streak **7** banding, chevron, lineate, striate, variety

stripling 3 boy, lad **5** youth **9** youngster **10** adolescent

stripper 6 peeler, teaser **9** ecdysiast

stripteaser see STRIPPER

strive 3 try, vie **4** seek **5** labor **6** strain **7** attempt, contend **8** endeavor, struggle **9** undertake

stroke 3 fit, hit, pet, rub **4** blow, hone, whet **5** swing **6** attack, caress, fondle, soothe **7** flatter **8** apoplexy, ischemia **9** heartbeat

stroll 4 rove, turn, walk **5** amble, drift, mosey, paseo **7** cruise, linger, ramble, wander **7** saunter, traipse **9** promenade

stroller 4 pram **6** go-cart **8** carriage **12** baby carriage, perambulator

strong 4 fast, firm, hard **5** burly, hardy, lusty, solid, sound, stout, tough **6** brawny, hearty, heroic, mighty, potent, robust, rugged, secure, sinewy, stable, sturdy **7** durable, intense, staunch **8** forceful, muscular, powerful, stalwart, vigorous **9** resilient, strapping, tenacious **10** able-bodied, full-bodied, spirituous **12** concentrated

strong-arm 5 bully **6** bounce, hector, lean on **7** assault, dragoon **8** browbeat, bulldoze, bullyrag **9** terrorize **10** intimidate

strongbox 4 safe **5** chest **6** coffer **13** treasure chest

stronghold 4 fort **7** bastion, bulwark, citadel, redoubt **8** fastness, fortress

strong point 5 forte **6** métier

strong suit see STRONG POINT

strophe 5 verse **6** stanza

structure 4 form **5** frame **6** format, makeup, system **7** anatomy, complex, edifice, network **8** building, erection, skeleton **9** framework **10** morphology **11** arrangement, composition

struggle 3 try, vie **4** agon **5** trial **6** battle, effort, hassle, strain, strife, strive, tussle **7** attempt, compete, contest, grapple, scuffle **8** endeavor, exertion, flounder,

skirmish, striving **9** undertake
11 undertaking
strumpet 4 bawd, jade, slut, tart **5** hussy,
tramp, trull, wench **6** floozy, harlot,
hooker, wanton **7** jezebel, trollop **8** slattern
strut 6 flaunt, parade, prance, sashay
7 flounce, peacock, show off, swagger
stub 3 end **4** butt, tail **5** stump **6** put out,
strike **7** remnant **10** extinguish
stubborn 5 balky, rigid **6** cussed, dogged,
mulish, ornery **7** adamant, lasting, willful **8** obdurate, perverse **9** obstinate,
pigheaded, steadfast, unbending
10 bullheaded, determined, headstrong,
inexorable, inflexible, persistent, rebellious, refractory, relentless, unyielding
11 intractable **12** cantankerous, contumacious, pertinacious, single-minded
stubby 5 dumpy, short, squat, stout
6 stocky, stumpy **8** heavyset, thickset
stuck 5 clung, glued **6** jammed, wedged
7 adhered, baffled, blocked, saddled,
stabbed, stopped, stumped **8** attached,
held fast **11** overcharged
stuck-up 4 vain **6** sniffy, snippy, snooty
7 haughty **8** snobbish **9** conceited
12 narcissistic, supercilious
stud 3 guy **4** dude, hunk, male, nail,
post **5** cleat **6** button, pillar **7** earring,
speckle, upright **8** sprinkle, stallion
student 5 pupil **6** novice **7** protégé,
scholar **8** disciple **10** apprentice *college:*
9 undergrad **13** undergraduate *female:*
4 coed *first-year:* **5** frosh **8** freshman
fourth-year: **6** senior *French:* **5** élève
8 étudiant *military:* **5** cadet, middy
10 midshipman *second-year:* **9** sophomore *third-year:* **6** junior *wandering:*
7 goliard
studio 4 shop **7** atelier **8** workroom,
workshop
studious 7 bookish, learned **9** scholarly
Studs Lonigan creator 7 Farrell
(James T.)
study 3 con, den, vet **4** cram, muse
6 ponder, survey **7** analyze, examine,
inspect, reverie **8** consider **9** attention,
think over **10** excogitate, scrutinize
11 application
stuff 3 jam, ram **4** cram, fill, glut, junk,
pack, sate, tamp **5** crowd, gorge, shove
6 matter, things **7** essence, jam-pack,
squeeze, surfeit **8** material, overfill
9 substance **11** possessions
stuffy 4 dull, prim **5** close, fuggy, heavy,
humid, stale, thick **6** narrow, stodgy
7 airless, bloated, genteel, humdrum,
pompous, prudish, stilted **8** priggish,
stagnant, stifling **9** hidebound, Victorian **10** oppressive, pontifical **11** puritanical, suffocating **12** narrow-minded
13 self-important, self-righteous
stultify 4 dull **6** deaden, impair, stifle,
weaken **7** inhibit, nullify, repress,
smother, trammel **8** restrain, stagnate,
suppress **9** suffocate **10** discourage,
invalidate
stumble 3 err **4** reel, slip, trip **5** error,
fluff, gaffe, lapse, lurch **6** falter, muddle, slipup, totter **7** blunder, faux pas,
mistake, stagger, stammer **8** flounder
stump 3 end **4** beat, butt, dare, defy,
plod, stub **5** barge, clomp, clump, stick
6 baffle, outwit, puzzle, stymie, trudge
7 buffalo, flummox, galumph, mystify,
nonplus, perplex **8** bewilder, campaign,
confound, hustings, politick **9** barnstorm, challenge **11** electioneer
stun 4 daze **5** amaze, floor, shock **6** dazzle **7** astound, nonplus, stagger, stupefy
8 astonish, bewilder, bowl over, knock
out, paralyze **9** dumbfound **11** flabbergast
stunning 6 superb **7** amazing, awesome
8 gorgeous, striking **9** excellent, wonderful **10** astounding, impressive,
remarkable, staggering, surprising
11 astonishing
stunt 4 curb, feat **5** antic, caper, check,
dwarf, prank, trick **6** hinder, impair,
retard **8** escapade, hold back, suppress
stupefy 4 daze, dull, faze, stun **5** addle,
amaze **6** muddle, rattle **7** astound, nonplus, petrify, stagger **8** astonish, bewilder, paralyze **9** disorient, dumbfound
11 flabbergast
stupendous 7 amazing, awesome, massive, titanic **8** colossal, enormous,
gigantic, stunning, towering, wondrous
9 fantastic, marvelous, monstrous,
wonderful **10** astounding, miraculous,
monumental, phenomenal, prodigious,
staggering, tremendous **11** astonishing,
spectacular **12** breathtaking, mind-
boggling, overwhelming
stupid 3 dim **4** dull, dumb, slow **5** dense,
dopey, inane, silly, thick **6** oafish,
obtuse, simple, torpid **7** asinine, doltish, fatuous, foolish, idiotic, moronic,
witless **8** backward, ignorant, mindless,
retarded **9** brainless, fatheaded, imbecilic, laughable, ludicrous, pinheaded,
senseless **10** half-witted, slow-witted
11 blockheaded, thickheaded, thick-
witted **13** chuckleheaded
stupor 6 torpor **7** languor **8** dullness,
hebetude, lethargy, narcosis **9** lassitude,
torpidity **10** anesthesia, somnolence
13 insensibility *combining form:* **4** narc
5 narco
sturdy 5 hardy, solid, sound, stout,

tough 6 robust, rugged, secure, strong 7 durable, healthy, staunch 8 stalwart, vigorous 9 strapping

sturgeon 6 beluga *roe:* 6 caviar

Sturm und Drang 5 angst 6 unease, unrest 7 anxiety, ferment, turmoil 8 disquiet 9 agitation 10 inquietude, turbulence 11 disquietude, restiveness 12 restlessness

St. Vitus' ___ 5 dance

sty 3 pen 4 coop, cyst 6 pigpen 7 piggery

stygian 4 dark 6 gloomy 7 hellish, sunless 8 infernal, plutonic 9 Cimmerian, plutonian

style 3 fad, way 4 élan, mode, rage, vein 5 craze, decor, flair, trend, vogue 6 manner 7 fashion, panache 10 dernier cri 11 savoir-faire *hair:* 4 coif 8 coiffure

stylish 3 mod 4 chic, posh, tony, trig 5 doggy, natty, ritzy, sassy, sharp, showy, sleek, slick, smart, swank, swell 6 chichi, dapper, dressy, modern, modish, snappy, snazzy, spiffy, trendy, with-it 7 à la mode, dashing, doggish 8 spiffing, up-to-date 10 newfangled 11 fashionable

stymie 4 stop 5 block 6 hamper, hinder, impede, thwart 7 flummox, prevent 8 confound, obstruct 9 frustrate, hamstring

Stymphalides' slayer 8 Heracles, Hercules

Styron novel 13 Sophie's Choice 22 Confessions of Nat Turner (The)

Styx *father:* 7 Oceanus *ferryman:* 6 Charon *location:* 5 Hades *mother:* 6 Tethys

Styx's counterpart 5 Lethe 7 Acheron, Cocytus 10 Phlegethon

suave 4 oily 5 slick 6 smooth, urbane 7 cordial, courtly, gallant, politic, refined, tactful, worldly 8 debonair, gracious, polished, unctuous, well-bred 9 courteous 10 cultivated, diplomatic 12 ingratiating 13 sophisticated

sub 5 below, proxy, under 6 backup, fill-in 7 stand-by, stand-in 8 pinch-hit 9 alternate, secondary, surrogate 10 understudy 11 locum tenens, pinch hitter, replacement

subaltern 8 inferior 9 secondary, underling

subdue 4 curb, tame 5 crush, quash, quell 6 defeat, master, quench 7 conquer, control, put down, repress, squelch 8 beat down, overcome, suppress, tone down, vanquish 9 overpower, overthrow, subjugate

subdued 4 soft, tame 5 muted, quiet, sober 6 low-key, mellow, subtle 7 neutral, serious 8 low-keyed, softened,

tasteful, tempered 9 moderated, toned down 10 controlled, restrained, submissive 11 unobtrusive

subjacent 3 low 5 lower, under 6 lesser, nether 8 inferior

subject 3 apt 4 core, open 5 motif, point, prone, theme, topic 6 expose, liable, likely, matter, motive, vassal 7 citizen, exposed, lay open, problem 8 argument, inferior, material, question 9 dependent, leitmotif, secondary, sensitive, subjugate, substance, tributary 11 subordinate, subservient, susceptible

subjective 6 biased 10 prejudiced

subjugate see SUBDUE

sublime 4 holy 5 ideal, lofty, noble, proud 6 august, divine, sacred, superb 7 blessed, exalted 8 elevated, glorious, heavenly, majestic, splendid 9 celestial, spiritual 11 magnificent, resplendent 12 transcendent

submarine 4 hero 5 po'boy, U-boat 6 hoagie 7 grinder *detector:* 5 sonar

submerge 3 dip 4 duck, dunk, sink 5 drown, flood, swamp 6 deluge, engulf, plunge 7 founder, go under, immerse 8 inundate, overflow

submerse see SUBMERGE

submissive 4 meek, tame 6 abject, docile, pliant 7 servile, slavish, subdued 8 amenable, obedient, obeisant, yielding 9 compliant, tractable 10 obsequious 11 acquiescent, deferential, subservient, unresisting 12 nonresisting

submit 3 bow 4 cave, fold, obey 5 defer, offer, yield 6 accede, comply, give in, hand in, relent, send in, tender 7 concede, deliver, go under, present, proffer, provide, subject, succumb, suggest 9 acquiesce, surrender 10 capitulate 11 buckle under 12 knuckle under

subordinate 5 minor, scrub, under 6 junior 7 adjunct, subject 8 inferior 9 accessory, ancillary, auxiliary, dependent, secondary, subaltern, tributary, underling 10 collateral, submissive, subsidiary 11 subservient

sub rosa 6 covert, secret 7 furtive, private 8 covertly, in camera, secretly, stealthy 9 by stealth, furtively, privately, secretive, underhand 10 stealthily 11 clandestine, underhanded 13 clandestinely, surreptitious

subscribe 3 ink 4 sign 5 agree 6 accede, adhere, assent, attest, pledge 7 approve, consent, endorse, support 8 sanction 9 acquiesce

subsequent 4 next 5 after, later 6 serial 7 ensuing 9 following, resultant, resulting 10 sequential, succeeding, successive 11 consecutive *prefix:* 4 post

subsequently 4 next, then 5 after, later 9 afterward 10 afterwards, thereafter

subservient 6 abject, docile 7 fawning, ignoble, servile, slavish 8 adjuvant, obeisant 9 accessory, ancillary, auxiliary, compliant, truckling 10 collateral, obsequious, submissive 11 acquiescent, deferential, subordinate, sycophantic

subside 3 ebb 4 ease, fall, lull, sink, wane 5 abate, let up, taper 6 ease up, recede, settle 7 decline, descend, die away, die down, dwindle, ease off, slacken 8 decrease, diminish, moderate

subsidiary 5 minor 6 backup, branch 7 subject 8 adjuvant 9 accessory, ancillary, auxiliary, secondary, tributary 10 collateral 11 subordinate 12 supplemental 13 supplementary

subsidize 4 back, fund 5 endow, stake 7 finance, promote, sponsor, support 8 bankroll 9 grubstake 10 underwrite

subsidy 4 gift 5 grant 6 reward 10 subvention 13 appropriation

subsistence 4 keep, salt 5 bread, means 6 income, living 7 support 9 resources 10 livelihood, sustenance 11 maintenance, wherewithal 12 alimentation

substance 3 nub 4 bulk, core, crux, gist, mass, meat, pith, soul 5 being, drift, focus, heart, point, sense, stuff, tenor 6 amount, burden, entity, import, kernel, marrow, matter, nubbin, object, thrust, upshot, wealth 7 essence, meaning, nucleus, purport 8 material, property, sum total 9 resources 12 essentiality, quintessence

substantial 3 big 4 full 5 ample, hefty, large, solid 6 strong, sturdy 7 massive, sizable, weighty 8 abundant, concrete, material, physical, sensible, tangible 9 corporeal, important, objective 10 meaningful, phenomenal 11 significant 12 considerable

substantiate 5 prove 6 embody, evince, verify 7 bear out, confirm, justify 8 evidence, manifest, validate 9 establish, incarnate, objectify, vindicate 11 corroborate, demonstrate 12 authenticate

substantive 4 firm, noun, real 5 solid 8 definite 9 essential

substitute 4 mock, sham, swap 5 dummy, locum, proxy, trade 6 acting, backup, deputy, double, ersatz, fill-in, refuge, resort, second, switch 7 replace, reserve, standby, stand-in, stopgap 8 exchange, recourse, resource, spurious 9 alternate, expedient, imitation, makeshift, simulated, surrogate, temporary 10 artificial, expediency, understudy 11 alternative, locum tenens,

pinch hitter, replacement, succedaneum

substratum 4 base 5 basis 6 bottom, ground 7 bedrock, footing 10 foundation, groundwork 12 underpinning

substructure 4 base, seat 5 basis 6 bottom 7 footing 10 foundation, groundwork 12 underpinning

subsume 6 embody, take in 7 contain, embrace, include, involve 8 comprise 9 encompass 10 comprehend

subterfuge 4 ploy, ruse, sham 5 cheat, feint, fraud 6 deceit, dupery 7 chicane 8 trickery 9 chicanery, deception 10 dishonesty

subterranean 11 underground

subtle 4 fine 5 faint 6 artful, astute 7 cunning, refined 8 delicate, finespun, guileful, skillful 9 insidious 10 indistinct 13 inconspicuous

subtract 6 deduct, remove 7 take off 8 discount, knock off, take away, withdraw, withhold

subtraction 6 rebate 8 discount 9 abatement, deduction 10 diminution, withdrawal *term:* 7 minuend 9 remainder 10 subtrahend

suburb 8 edge city

suburbs 7 fringes 8 environs, purlieus 9 outskirts

subversion 8 sabotage 11 undermining 12 undercutting

subvert 5 upset 6 debase 7 corrupt, deprave, vitiate 8 overturn, sabotage 9 overthrow, undermine

subway *British:* 4 tube 11 underground *French:* 5 métro

succeed 3 win 4 boom 5 click, ensue, score 6 arrive, follow, go over, make it, pan out, thrive, win out 7 catch on, come off, make out, prevail, prosper, replace, triumph 8 displace, flourish, get ahead, make good, supplant 9 supervene

succes ___ 3 fou 7 d'estime

success 3 hit 5 smash 7 arrival, fortune, killing, triumph, victory 8 fruition 10 attainment, prosperity 11 achievement, fulfillment

successful 5 smash 7 booming 8 fruitful, thriving 9 effective, lucrative 10 prosperous, triumphant, victorious 11 flourishing

succession 3 row 5 chain, cycle, march, order, round, suite, train 6 course, sequel, series, string 8 sequence 11 progression

successive 4 next 7 ensuing 9 following 10 subsequent

successor 4 heir 8 claimant, follower 9 inheritor 11 beneficiary

succinct 4 curt 5 blunt, brief, pithy, short, terse 7 brusque, compact, concise, laconic, summary 11 compendious

succor 3 aid 4 help, lift 6 assist, relief 7 comfort, relieve, support 10 assistance, sustenance

succulent 5 juicy 8 luscious

succumb 3 bow, die 4 cave, fold, wilt 5 defer, yield 6 accede, buckle, cave in, expire, give in, perish, relent, resign, submit 7 give out, go under, knuckle 8 collapse 9 break down, surrender 10 capitulate 11 buckle under 12 knuckle under

sucker 3 con, gyp, sap 4 bilk, dupe, fool, gull, mark, rook 5 cheat, chump, patsy, shoot 6 diddle, pigeon 7 defraud, fall guy, swindle 8 hoodwink, pushover 9 bamboozle

suckle 5 nurse 7 nourish, nurture 10 breast-feed

Sudan *capital:* 8 Khartoum *desert:* 6 Libyan *language:* 6 Arabic *monetary unit:* 5 dinar *neighbor:* 4 Chad 5 Congo, Egypt, Kenya, Libya 6 Uganda 7 Eritrea 8 Ethiopia *river:* 4 Nile *sea:* 3 Red

sudden 4 rash 5 hasty, swift 6 abrupt, prompt 7 hurried 8 headlong 9 impetuous, impromptu, impulsive 10 unexpected, unforeseen 11 precipitant, precipitate, precipitous

suddenly 5 aback 7 hastily, shortly, unaware 8 abruptly, promptly, unawares 10 by surprise 12 unexpectedly

suds 4 beer, fizz, foam, head, soap 5 froth, spume 6 lather

sue 8 litigate

suer 8 litigant

suet 3 fat 4 lard 6 tallow

Suez Canal *builder:* 7 Lesseps (Ferdinand de) *city:* 8 Ismailia, Port Said

suffer 4 ache, bear, lump 5 abide, admit, allow, brook, leave, stand, yield 6 accept, endure, permit, submit 7 agonize, anguish, stomach, sustain, swallow, undergo 8 tolerate 10 experience 11 countenance

sufferer 6 victim

suffering 4 ache 5 agony, dolor 6 misery, ordeal 7 anguish, passion, torment, torture 8 distress 10 affliction, misfortune

suffice 5 avail, serve

sufficient 3 due 5 ample 6 common, decent, enough, plenty 8 adequate, all right 9 competent 10 acceptable, tolerable 11 comfortable 12 commensurate, satisfactory 13 commensurable, proportionate *poetic:* 4 enow

suffocate 5 burke, choke 6 stifle 7 smother 8 snuff out, strangle 10 asphyxiate

suffrage 4 vote 5 voice 6 ballot 9 franchise

suffragist 4 Catt (Carrie Chapman), Howe (Julia Ward), Mott (Lucretia), Paul (Alice) 5 Stone (Lucy) 7 Anthony (Susan B.), Bloomer (Amelia), Stanton (Elizabeth Cady) 8 Woodhull (Victoria Claflin) 9 Pankhurst (Emmeline)

suffuse 4 fill 5 flush, imbue, steep 7 pervade 8 permeate, saturate 10 impregnate

sugar 6 aldose, fucose, xylose 7 glucose, lactose, maltose, mannose, pentose, sorbose, sucrose, sweeten 8 fructose, furanose, levulose 10 saccharose *combining form:* 4 gluc, glyc, sucr 5 gluco, glyco, sucro 7 sacchar 8 sacchari, saccharo *from palm sap:* 7 jaggery *Mexican:* 7 panocha, penuche *source:* 4 beet, cane, corn 5 maple

sugarcane refuse 7 bagasse

sugarcoat 5 candy 6 veneer 7 sweeten, varnish 8 palliate 9 extenuate, gloss over, gloze over, whitewash

sugary 6 syrupy 7 cloying, honeyed, mawkish 10 saccharine 11 sentimental

suggest 4 hint 5 evoke, imply 6 submit 7 connote, propose, signify 8 indicate, intimate 9 adumbrate, insinuate

suggestion 3 cue 4 clue, hint 5 shade, smack, tinge, trace 6 advice 7 inkling 8 allusion, innuendo, overtone, proposal, reminder 9 suspicion, undertone 10 indication, intimation 11 implication, insinuation

suggestive 4 racy 5 salty, spicy 6 ribald, risqué 8 off-color 9 evocative 10 indicative 11 reminiscent

suicidal pilot 8 kamikaze

suicide 8 felo-de-se, hara-kiri 10 self-murder 13 self-slaughter *Japanese:* 7 seppuku

suit 3 fit 4 case, jibe, plea 5 adapt, agree, befit, cause, check, serve, tally 6 accord, action, adjust, appeal, become, go with, please, prayer, square, tailor 7 conform, enhance, flatter, lawsuit, request, satisfy 8 entreaty, petition 9 agree with, reconcile 10 go together 11 accommodate, application, imploration, imprecation 12 solicitation, supplication *type:* 4 zoot 6 monkey, vested 9 paternity 10 pin-striped 11 class-action

suitable 3 apt, due, fit 4 just, meet 5 right 6 proper, seemly, useful 7 condign, fitting 8 apposite, becoming, deserved, eligible 9 pertinent, qualified,

requisite **10** acceptable, felicitous
11 appropriate

suitcase 3 bag **4** grip **6** valise **7** carry-on,
holdall **8** carryall

suite 3 lot, row, set **4** flat **5** array, group,
rooms, staff, train **6** sequel, series,
string **7** lodging, retinue **8** chambers,
sequence **9** apartment, entourage, following

suitor 4 beau **5** lover, spark, swain,
wooer **7** admirer, gallant, sparker **8** cavalier, paramour **9** boyfriend **10** petitioner

sulfur 9 brimstone

sulk 4 mope, pout **5** brood, gloom

sulky 4 cart, dour, glum **5** moody
6 gloomy, morose, sullen **7** crabbed
9 saturnine

sullen 4 dour, glum, mean, sour
5 moody, pouty, surly **6** crabby, dismal,
gloomy, grumpy, morose, somber, sombre **7** crabbed, pouting **8** lowering,
scowling **9** glowering, saturnine **10** ill-
humored **11** pessimistic

Sullivan's partner 7 Gilbert (William
Schwenk)

sully 3 tar **4** soil **5** dirty, shame, smear,
stain, taint **6** defame, defile, malign, vilify **7** asperse, blacken, pollute, slander,
tarnish, traduce **8** besmirch, disgrace,
dishonor **9** denigrate

Sultan of Swat 8 Babe Ruth

sultry 3 hot **4** sexy **5** close, humid,
muggy **6** steamy, sticky, stuffy, torrid
7 airless **8** stifling **9** seductive **10** passionate, sweltering, voluptuous

sum 3 add, all, tot **4** mass, tote **5** gross,
total, whole **6** amount, digest, entity,
figure, resumé **7** epitome **8** entirety,
integral, nutshell, totality **9** aggregate,
epitomize

Sumatra *country:* **9** Indonesia *highest
peak:* **7** Kerinci **8** Kerintji *largest city:*
5 Medan *shrew:* **4** tana

Sumerian *city:* **4** Umma *dragon:* **3** Kur
god: **3** Abu, Kur, Utu **4** Enki **5** Enlil,
Lahar, Nanna, Nintu **6** Dumuzi, Nergal, Ninazu **7** Enkimdu *goddess:* **6** Ningal, Ninlil

summarize 5 recap **6** digest **7** abridge,
outline **8** boil down, condense **9** epitomize, synopsize **11** encapsulate **12** recapitulate

summary 5 recap **6** aperçu, digest, précis, résumé, review, wrap-up **7** com-
pend, epitome, outline, roundup, run-
down **8** abstract, overview, scenario,
synopsis **9** inventory **10** abridgment,
compendium, conspectus **12** condensation

summer *French:* **3** été

summerhouse 6 alcove, gazebo, pagoda
9 belvedere

summery 7 estival

summit 3 top **4** acme, apex, peak, roof
5 crest, crown **6** apogee, climax, height,
vertex, zenith **8** capstone, meridian,
pinnacle **11** culmination

summon 3 bid **4** call, cite **5** evoke, order
6 beckon, call in, invite, muster
7 arraign, command, conjure, convene,
convoke, send for **8** assemble, subpoena

sump 4 sink **8** cesspool

sumptuous 4 lush, rich **5** grand **6** costly,
deluxe, lavish, superb **7** opulent **8** gorgeous, luscious, palatial, splendid
9 grandiose, luxurious **11** extravagant,
resplendent **12** awe-inspiring

sun 3 orb, Sol **4** bask, star **7** daystar,
phoebus **8** daylight, luminary, radiance
9 radiation *combining form:* **4** heli
5 helio *disk:* **4** Aten *god:* **3** Lug, Sol,
Tem, Utu **4** Amen, Atmu, Atum, Inti,
Lleu, Llew, Lugh, Utug **5** Horus,
Sunna, Surya **6** Apollo, Babbar, Helios,
Marduk **7** Khepera, Ninurta, Phoebus,
Shamash **8** Hyperion, Merodach

Sun Also Rises, The *author:* **9** Hemingway (Ernest) *character:* **6** Ashley
(Brett), Barnes (Jake)

sunder 3 cut **4** rend, rive **5** break, sever,
slice, split **6** cleave, divide **8** dissever,
disunite, separate

sundial part 6 gnomon

sundown 4 dusk **7** evening **8** eventide,
gloaming, twilight

sundries 7 notions **8** oddments **9** etceteras **11** odds and ends

sundry 4 many, some **6** varied **7** diverse,
several, various **8** assorted, manifold,
numerous **9** different, disparate **12** multifarious **13** miscellaneous, multitudinous

sunfish 4 opah **7** pompano **8** bluegill
11 pumpkinseed

Sunflower State 6 Kansas

sun-god see at SUN

Sun King 8 Louis XIV

sunny 4 fair, fine, warm **5** clear, happy
6 blithe, bright, cheery, chirpy, golden
7 beaming, clarion, radiant **8** cheerful,
pleasant, rainless **9** brilliant, cloudless,
unclouded **10** optimistic

sunrise 4 dawn, morn **6** aurora **7** dawning, morning **8** cockcrow, daybreak,
daylight *goddess:* **3** Eos **6** Aurora

sunroom 8 solarium

sunset 3 eve **4** dusk **7** evening **8** gloaming, twilight

Sunset State 6 Oregon

Sunshine State 7 Florida

sunup see SUNRISE

sup 3 eat **4** dine **5** feast

super 4 very **5** great **8** powerful, splendid, terrific **9** excellent, extremely, fantastic, first-rate, wonderful **11** outstanding

superannuated 4 aged **5** hoary, passé **6** bygone **7** ancient, archaic, elderly, outworn **8** obsolete, outdated, outmoded **9** out-of-date **10** antiquated **11** obsolescent **12** old-fashioned

superb 4 rich **5** grand, lofty, noble, prime, super **7** elegant, exalted, optimal, optimum, opulent, stately, sublime, supreme **8** glorious, gorgeous, imposing, majestic, peerless, splendid, standout **9** excellent, marvelous, matchless, wonderful **11** magnificent, outstanding, resplendent, sensational, splendorous, superlative **13** splendiferous

supercilious 5 lofty **6** lordly, sniffy, snippy **7** haughty, stuck-up **8** cavalier, snobbish, superior **10** disdainful **11** patronizing **13** condescending, high-and-mighty

superficial 5 hasty **6** casual, slight **7** cursory, shallow, sketchy, trivial **8** external, skin-deep **9** depthless **11** perfunctory

superfluity 4 glut **5** frill **6** excess **7** nimiety, overrun, surfeit, surplus **8** overflow, overkill, overload, overmuch, overplus, plethora **10** oversupply, redundancy, surplusage **11** prodigality **12** extravagance **13** overabundance

superfluous 5 extra, spare **6** de trop, excess **7** surplus **8** needless **9** excessive, redundant **10** gratuitous **11** uncalled-for, unnecessary

superintend 4 boss **6** direct, manage **7** control, oversee **10** administer

superintendence 4 care **6** charge **7** conduct, running **8** handling **9** authority, direction, oversight **10** management

superior 4 rare **5** above, lofty, major, prime, proud, upper **6** better, choice, higher, lordly, select, senior, sniffy, snippy, snooty **7** capital, greater, haughty, premium, stuck-up **8** arrogant, brass hat, cavalier, dominant, higher-up, insolent **9** excellent, first-rate, marvelous **10** disdainful, first-class, noteworthy, preeminent, preferable, remarkable **11** exceptional, overbearing, patronizing, predominant **13** condescending, high-and-mighty

superiority 9 advantage, dominance, seniority, supremacy, upper hand **10** ascendancy

superjacent 4 over **6** higher **7** greater **9** overlying

superlative 4 best **8** peerless, standout **10** consummate **11** magnificent, outstanding

Superman 9 Clark Kent *cartoonist:* **7** Shuster (Joe) *girlfriend:* **8** Lois Lane

supernatural 5 magic **6** divine, mystic **7** magical, psychic, uncanny **8** heavenly **9** celestial, unearthly **10** miraculous, paranormal, phenomenal **12** metaphysical, transcendent **13** extraordinary

supernatural being 3 elf, fay, god, hob, imp, nix **4** jinn, ogre, peri, puck **5** afrit, angel, bogle, deity, demon, fairy, gnome, jinni, lamia, naiad, nixie, nymph, pixie, satyr, sylph, Titan, troll **6** afreet, goblin, kelpie, seraph, spirit, sprite **7** banshee, brownie, bugbear, goddess, incubus, silenus, vampire **8** bogeyman, demiurge, succubus **9** hobgoblin **10** leprechaun

supernumerary 5 extra, spare **6** de trop, excess, walk-on **7** reserve, surplus **8** leftover **9** redundant

supersede 5 usurp **7** replace, succeed **8** displace, supplant

supervene 5 ensue, occur **6** befall, follow, result **7** succeed **9** eventuate, transpire

supervise 3 run **4** boss **5** steer **6** direct, govern, manage **7** conduct, control, monitor, oversee, proctor, referee **8** chaperon, overlook **10** administer

supervision 4 care **6** charge **7** control, running **8** auspices, handling **9** direction, oversight **10** intendance, management **11** stewardship

supervisor 7 foreman, manager **8** director, overseer **13** administrator

supine 5 inert, prone, slack **7** passive **8** inactive, indolent **9** prostrate, recumbent **10** horizontal **12** outstretched

supper club 6 nitery **7** cabaret **9** night spot

supplant 4 oust **5** usurp **6** cut out, unseat **7** replace, succeed **8** crowd out, displace, force out **9** overthrow, supersede

supple 5 agile, lithe, withy **6** limber, nimble, pliant, whippy **7** ductile, elastic, lissome, plastic, pliable, springy, willowy **8** flexible, graceful, moldable **9** adaptable, malleable, resilient

supplement 3 add, pad **5** rider **6** append, beef up, enrich, extend, sequel **7** adjunct, augment, codicil, enhance, fill out, fortify **8** addendum, addition, appendix, buttress, increase **9** accessory, reinforce **10** postscript, strengthen

suppliant 5 asker **6** beggar, suitor **9** solicitor **10** petitioner

supplicant see SUPPLIANT

supplicate 3 ask, beg, sue **4** pray **5** crave,

plead 6 appeal, invoke **7** beseech, entreat, implore, solicit **8** petition **9** importune

supplication 4 plea, suit **6** appeal, orison, prayer **8** entreaty, petition **11** application

supplies 6 stores **8** matériel **9** equipment, materials **10** provisions

supply 3 man **4** fund, hand, help **5** cache, equip, hoard, stock, store **6** afford, outfit, purvey **7** deliver, fulfill, furnish, provide, reserve, satisfy, surplus **8** dispense, hand over, transfer, turn over **9** inventory, provision, reservoir, stockpile **10** contribute **12** accumulation

support 3 aid **4** back, base, bear, hand, help, lift, prop, root, side, stay **5** abide, adopt, boost, brace, bread, brook, carry, favor, shore, strut, truss **6** anchor, assist, bear up, buoy up, column, crutch, defend, endure, girder, pillar, second, suffer, uphold, verify **7** alimony, applaud, approve, backing, bolster, comfort, confirm, embrace, endorse, espouse, fortify, fulcrum, nourish, nurture, pull for, shore up, stiffen, sustain **8** abutment, advocate, backstop, buttress, champion, mainstay, maintain, sanction, side with, underpin **9** encourage, reinforce, underprop **10** assistance, foundation, livelihood, provide for, strengthen, sustenance **11** corroborate, maintenance, subsistence **12** underpinning

supporter 4 ally **6** patron **7** booster, sectary **8** adherent, advocate, champion, disciple, exponent, follower, henchman, partisan **9** proponent

suppose 4 deem **5** allow, guess, infer, opine, posit, think **6** assume, expect, gather, reckon **7** believe, imagine, presume, pretend, surmise, suspect **8** consider **9** postulate, speculate **10** conjecture **11** hypothesize

supposed 7 alleged, seeming **8** apparent, putative **10** ostensible

supposition 5 guess, hunch, posit **6** notion, theory, thesis **7** premise, surmise **9** postulate **10** assumption, conjecture, hypothesis **11** postulation, presumption, speculation

supposititious 6 unreal **7** dubious, fictive, reputed **8** doubtful, fanciful, illusory, putative, spurious **9** fantastic, fictional, imaginary, pretended, simulated **10** chimerical, fictitious, fraudulent **11** conjectural **12** hypothetical, illegitimate, questionable

suppress 4 curb, stop **5** burke, check, choke, crush, drown, quash, quell, shush, spike, stunt **6** arrest, censor, cut off, hush up, muffle, muzzle, quench, retard, squash, stifle, subdue **7** abolish, collect, conceal, control, prevent, put down, silence, smother, squelch, swallow **8** prohibit, restrain, snuff out, withhold **9** overthrow **10** extinguish

suppurate 6 fester

supra 5 above

supremacy 7 control, mastery **8** dominion **9** authority, dominance **10** ascendancy, domination, mastership, prepotency **11** preeminence, sovereignty **12** predominance **13** preponderance

supreme 4 best **5** chief, final, prime **6** superb, utmost **7** highest, leading, maximum, perfect **8** absolute, cardinal, crowning, foremost, greatest, peerless, towering, ultimate **9** matchless, paramount, principal, sovereign, unequaled, unmatched, unrivaled **10** preeminent, surpassing **11** culminating, predominant, superlative, unmatchable, unsurpassed **12** incomparable, transcendent, unparalleled **13** unsurpassable

Supreme Being 3 God **5** Allah **7** creator, Jehovah **8** Almighty

surcease 3 end **4** halt, quit, rest, stay, stop **6** desist **7** refrain, respite, suspend **8** knock off, leave off, postpone, stoppage **9** cessation, remission **10** suspension **11** discontinue **12** postponement

sure 3 set **4** fast, firm, safe **5** fixed **6** indeed, secure, stable, steady, strong **7** certain, staunch **8** absolute, definite, enduring, positive, reliable, unerring **9** confident, convinced, steadfast **10** convincing, dependable, inevitable, infallible, undeniable, unshakable, unwavering **11** indubitable, trustworthy, unequivocal, unfaltering **12** indisputable **13** incontestable, unquestioning

surefire 7 assured, certain **8** reliable **10** dependable, guaranteed

sure thing 6 shoo-in, winner **9** certainty

surety 4 bail, bond **5** angel **6** backer, patron, pledge **7** sponsor **8** guaranty, security, warranty **9** certainty, certitude, guarantee, guarantor **10** confidence, conviction

surface 3 top **4** face, pave, rise, skin **5** cover **6** appear, come up, facade, facing, finish, patina, show up, veneer **7** outside **8** covering, exterior **11** superficial

surfeit 4 cloy, fill, glut, jade, pall, sate **5** gorge, stuff **6** excess **7** replete, satiate, surplus **8** overfill, overflow, overkill, overmuch, overplus, plethora **10** surplusage **11** overindulge, superfluity **13** overabundance

surge 4 flow, gush, pour, rise, roll, rush, tide, wave 5 flood, swell 6 billow, deluge, sluice, stream 7 torrent

surgeon 8 sawbones *American:* 4 Mayo (Charles, William), Reed (Walter) 6 Thorek (Max) 7 Cushing (Harvey), DeBakey (Michael) 8 McDowell (Ephraim) *British:* 6 Hunter (John) *English:* 5 Paget (James) 6 Lister (Joseph) *French:* 4 Paré (Ambroise) 5 Broca (Paul) *South African:* 7 Barnard (Christiaan) *Swiss:* 6 Kocher (Emil Theodor)

surgery 9 operation *instrument:* 5 clamp, curet, lance, laser, probe 6 gorget, lancet, splint, stylet, trocar 7 forceps, scalpel

surgical removal 8 ablation *combining form:* 6 ectomy

Suriname *capital:* 10 Paramaribo *former name:* 11 Dutch Guiana *language:* 5 Dutch, Hindi 6 Sranan *monetary unit:* 7 guilder *mountain range:* 10 Tumac-Humac *neighbor:* 6 Brazil, Guyana 12 French Guiana *river:* 6 Maroni 8 Suriname 10 Courantyne

surly 4 dour, glum 5 cross, gruff, sulky 6 crusty, grumpy, morose, sullen 7 bearish, crabbed, grouchy 8 churlish, menacing, snappish, saturnine 9 irritable, saturnine 10 ungracious 11 ill-mannered, threatening 12 discourteous

surmise see SUPPOSE

surmount 3 cap, top 4 best, down, leap, lick 5 clear, climb, crest, crown, excel, outdo, vault 6 better, hurdle, master 7 conquer, surpass 8 outstrip, overcome, vanquish 9 negotiate, transcend

surpass 3 cap, top 4 beat, best 5 excel, outdo, trump 6 better, exceed, outrun 7 eclipse, outpace 8 go beyond, outclass, outshine, outstrip, outweigh, overstep 9 transcend 10 overshadow 11 outdistance

surplice 5 cotta, ephod 8 vestment

surplus 5 extra, spare 6 excess 7 overage, overrun, reserve, surfeit 8 leftover, overflow, overkill, overmuch, plethora 9 overstock, remainder 10 oversupply 11 superfluity, superfluous 13 overabundance, supernumerary

surprise 4 faze, stun 5 amaze, floor 6 ambush, dismay, rattle, waylay, wonder 7 astound, capture, nonplus, stagger, startle, stupefy 8 astonish, bewilder, bowl over 9 amazement, dumbfound, overpower, take aback 11 flabbergast 12 astonishment, stupefaction

surreal 5 weird 7 bizarre 9 dreamlike, fantastic 10 outlandish 12 unbelievable

surrender 4 cave, cede, fold 5 waive, yield 6 cave in, give in, give up, resign,

submit 7 abandon, concede, succumb 8 cry uncle, hand over 10 abdication, capitulate, relinquish, submission 12 capitulation, renunciation *sign:* 7 hands up 9 white flag

surreptitious see STEALTHY

surrogate 3 sub 5 proxy 6 acting, deputy, fill-in 7 stand-in, stopgap 9 alternate, makeshift 10 substitute 11 alternative, locum tenens, pinch hitter, replacement, succedaneum

surround 4 hem, rim 4 edge, gird, loop, ring 5 beset, bound, hem in, limit, round, skirt, verge 6 border, circle, fringe, girdle, margin 7 besiege, compass, confine, enclose, envelop, outline 8 encircle 9 encompass 12 circumscribe

surrounding 5 about 7 ambient 12 circumjacent *prefix:* 4 peri 6 circum

surroundings 6 milieu 7 ambient 8 ambience 11 environment, mise-en-scène

surveillance 3 eye, tab 4 tail 5 vigil, watch 7 lookout 8 scrutiny, stakeout 9 vigilance 11 supervision

survey 3 con, vet 4 case, scan, view 5 assay, audit 6 assess, précis, review, size up 7 canvass, examine, inspect, pandect, perusal, preview 8 analysis, appraise, estimate, evaluate, look over, overlook, overview, scrutiny, syllabus 9 check over 10 inspection, scrutinize 11 reconnoiter, superintend

survive 4 keep, last 6 endure 7 carry on, hold out, outlast, outlive, outwear, persist, recover, ride out, weather 8 continue, live down 9 withstand 11 come through, live through, pull through

Surya 6 sun-god *son:* 4 Manu, Yama 5 Karna 6 Asvins 7 Sugriva *temple site:* 7 Konarak

susceptible 4 open 5 naive, prone 6 liable 7 exposed, pliable, subject 8 disposed, inclined, sensible 9 malleable, receptive, sensitive 10 responsive, vulnerable 11 impressible, persuadable, predisposed 12 nonresistant

suspect 5 doubt, fishy, guess 6 assume, unsure 7 believe, dubious, imagine, suppose, surmise 8 distrust, doubtful, mistrust 9 doubtable, uncertain 10 disbelieve 11 problematic 12 questionable

suspend 3 bar 4 bate, halt, hang, stay, stop 5 debar, defer, delay, hover, sling 6 dangle, depend, hold up, put off, shelve 7 adjourn, hold off 8 intermit, postpone, prorogue 9 eliminate 11 discontinue

suspended 6 frozen 7 hanging, pendant, pendent, stopped 8 dangling, swinging 9 pendulous

suspenders 6 braces 8 galluses
suspense 7 anxiety, mystery, tension 10 expectancy 11 expectation, uncertainty 12 apprehension
suspension 4 halt, stay, stop 5 delay, letup, pause 6 cutoff, freeze 7 latency, respite, time-out 8 abeyance, dormancy, stoppage 9 remission 10 moratorium, quiescence 11 cold storage, withholding 12 intermission, interruption, postponement
suspicion 4 hint 5 doubt, dread, guess, hunch, qualm, shade, smell, tinge, touch, trace, whiff 7 concern, dubiety, surmise 8 distrust, mistrust, wariness 9 chariness, misgiving 10 foreboding, intimation, skepticism, suggestion 11 incertitude, premonition, supposition, uncertainty
suspicious 4 wary 5 chary, fishy, leery 7 dubious, jealous, suspect 8 doubtful, watchful 9 doubtable, skeptical 11 distrustful, mistrustful, problematic 12 apprehensive, questionable
suspire 4 sigh 5 sough
sustain 4 bear, feed, prop, save 5 brace, carry, stand 6 bear up, buoy up, endure, foster, hold up, keep up, succor, suffer, uphold 7 bolster, confirm, nourish, nurture, prolong, relieve, shore up, support, undergo 8 buttress, preserve, tolerate 9 withstand 10 experience, strengthen
sustenance 3 pap 4 food, keep, meat 5 bread, means 6 living, viands 7 aliment, alimony, pabulum, support 8 victuals 9 nutriment, provender 10 livelihood, provisions 11 maintenance, nourishment, subsistence, wherewithal 12 alimentation
susurration 4 purr 6 mumble, murmur, mutter, rustle 7 whisper 9 undertone
suture 3 sew 4 seam 6 stitch
suzerain 5 ruler 8 overlord 9 sovereign
svelte 4 slim 5 lithe, sleek, suave 6 smooth, urbane 7 elegant, slender 8 graceful
swab 3 mop 5 clean 6 sponge
swaddle 4 roll, wrap 5 drape 6 enfold, enwrap, swathe, wrap up 7 blanket, envelop 8 enshroud, enswathe
swag 3 yaw 4 loot, tilt 5 booty, droop, lurch, money, pitch, prize 6 boodle, seesaw, spoils 7 cluster, festoon, garland, pillage, plunder, profits 10 contraband
swagger 4 brag 5 boast, bully, strut, swank, swash, swell 7 bluster, bravado, peacock, saunter 9 arrogance, cockiness, gasconade 11 braggadocio, swashbuckle

swagman 4 hobo 5 rover, tramp 7 drifter, vagrant 8 vagabond, wanderer
swain 4 beau 5 lover, spark, wooer 6 rustic, suitor 7 admirer, peasant, sparker 8 shepherd 9 boyfriend
swallow 3 buy, sip 4 bear, belt, bolt, down, gulp, swig, take, toss, wolf 5 abide, brook, drink, quaff, slurp, stand, swill 6 absorb, accept, digest, endure, guzzle, imbibe, ingest, inhale 7 believe, consume, fall for, repress, retract, stomach 8 chugalug, take back, tolerate 11 ingurgitate
swamp 3 bog, fen 4 holm, mire, moss, muck, quag 5 drown, flood, glade, marsh, whelm 6 deluge, engulf, morass, muskeg, slough 7 bottoms 8 inundate, overcome, overflow, quagmire, submerge 9 everglade, marshland, overwhelm *Everglades:* 10 Big Cypress *Georgia:* 10 Okefenokee *North Carolina-Virginia:* 6 Dismal
Swamp Fox 6 Marion (Francis)
swan *female:* 3 pen *male:* 3 cob 4 cobb *young:* 6 cygnet
Swanhild *father:* 6 Sigurd *mother:* 6 Gudrun
swank 4 posh, tony, trig 5 boast, fancy, ritzy, sharp, showy, smart, swell, swish 6 chichi, classy, dapper, deluxe, lavish, plushy, snappy, trendy 7 elegant, peacock, show off, splashy, stylish, swagger 8 peacocky 9 glamorous, luxurious 10 flamboyant, peacockish 12 orchidaceous, ostentatious
swap 5 trade, truck 6 barter, change, switch 7 bargain, traffic 8 exchange 10 substitute
swarm 3 jam, mob 4 army, bevy, herd, host, mass, pack, push, shin, teem 5 crawl, crowd, crush, drove, flock, group, horde, mount, press 6 abound, gather, myriad, throng 7 climb up, cluster, overrun 9 multitude, pullulate 10 congregate
swarthy 4 dark 5 dusky, sooty 6 brunet 8 bistered 11 dark-skinned
swash 3 lap 4 brag, dash, gush, rush, slop 5 boast, churn, douse, froth, plash, slosh 6 bubble, burble, gurgle, seethe, splash 7 bluster, channel, saunter, spatter, splurge, swagger 8 splatter
swat 3 bat, box, hit, rap 4 bash, belt, blow, cuff, lick, slap, slog, slug, sock 5 blast, clout, homer, knock, smack, smash, smite, swipe, whack 6 buffet, larrup, strike, wallop 7 clobber, home run
swath 4 belt, path 5 strip, sweep 6 stroke
swathe see SWADDLE

sway 4 bend, bias, rock, rule **5** lurch, might, power, range, reach, reign, scope, sweep, swing, waver, weave **6** affect, direct, govern, induce, totter, wobble **7** command, control, dispose, impress, incline, mastery, stagger, win over **8** dominate, dominion, overrule, persuade, undulate **9** authority, dominance, fluctuate, influence, oscillate, prevail on, vacillate **10** domination, predispose **11** fluctuation

Swaziland *capital:* **7** Lobamba, Mbabane *city:* **7** Manzini *language:* **5** Swazi **7** English *monetary unit:* **9** lilangeni *neighbor:* **10** Mozambique **11** South Africa *river:* **5** Usutu **6** Komati **8** Umbeluzi

swear 3 vow **4** avow, bind, cuss, damn, oath, rail, rant **5** abuse, curse, vouch **6** adjure, affirm, assert, attest, depone, depose, pledge, plight **7** declare, promise, testify, warrant **8** covenant, maintain **9** blaspheme, imprecate **10** asseverate, vituperate

swearword 4 cuss, oath **5** curse **9** expletive, obscenity **10** scurrility

sweat 4 emit, glow, moil, ooze, seep, toil, weep **5** exude, grind, labor **6** strain, swivet **7** excrete **8** perspire, transude **12** perspiration

sweater 8 cardigan, pullover, slipover **10** turtleneck

sweaty 6 clammy, sticky **7** glowing **10** perspiring

Sweden *Arctic region:* **7** Lapland *capital:* **9** Stockholm *city:* **5** Malmö **8** Göteborg *gulf:* **7** Bothnia **8** Kattegat *island:* **5** Öland **7** Gotland *lake:* **6** Vänern **7** Mälaren, Vättern **9** Hjälmaren *monetary unit:* **5** krona *mountain range:* **5** Kölen *neighbor:* **6** Norway **7** Finland *part of:* **11** Scandinavia *river:* **3** Dal *sea:* **6** Baltic

Swedish Nightingale 4 Lind (Jenny)

sweep 3 arc, fly, mop, win **4** flit, sail, scud, skim, wing **5** ambit, broom, brush, clean, clear, curve, drive, orbit, range, reach, scope, surge, whisk **6** extent, radius, search **7** compass, purview, victory **9** extension

sweeping 5 broad **6** all-out **7** blanket, general, overall, radical **8** thorough, whole-hog **9** extensive, inclusive, out-and-out, universal, wholesale **12** all-embracing **13** comprehensive, thoroughgoing

sweepings 4 dust **5** trash, waste **6** debris, litter, refuse **7** garbage, residue, rubbish **8** detritus

sweet 5 candy, honey **6** bonbon, dulcet, lovely, sugary, syrupy **7** angelic, cloying, dessert, melodic, scented, sugared, winning, winsome **8** aromatic, fragrant, heavenly, luscious, perfumed **9** ambrosial, delicious **10** delectable, saccharine *combining form:* **4** glyc **5** glyco

Sweet ___ 7 Adeline, Charity **8** Caroline

sweeten 5 candy, honey, sugar **6** soften **7** appease, assuage, enhance, mollify, placate **9** sugarcoat, sugar over **10** conciliate, propitiate

sweet potato 3 yam

sweet-talk 4 coax **5** charm **6** banter, cajole, wangle **7** blarney, flatter, wheedle **8** blandish, butter up, inveigle, soft-soap

swell 4 fine, grow, keen, neat, pout, puff **5** bloat, bulge, dandy, nifty, pouch, super, surge, swank **6** abound, billow, blow up, dilate, expand, groovy **7** amplify, augment, balloon, distend, inflate, peacock, swagger, upsurge **8** increase, terrific **9** crescendo, marvelous, wonderful *British:* **3** nob **4** toff

swelled head 5 pride **6** egoism, vanity **7** conceit, egotism **8** smugness **9** arrogance, vainglory **10** narcissism **11** amour propre, self-conceit **13** conceitedness

swelling 3 sty **4** boil, bubo, bump, corn, gall, node **5** bulge, edema, tumid, tumor **6** bunion, growth, nodule **7** gibbous **8** tubercle **9** carbuncle, chilblain, expansion, tumescent **10** tumescence **11** excrescence **12** inflammation, protuberance

sweltering 3 hot **5** fiery **6** baking, sultry, torrid **7** burning, searing **8** broiling, roasting, sizzling, tropical **9** scorching

swerve 4 skew, turn, veer **5** sheer, shift, stray, waver **6** depart, wander **7** deflect, deviate, digress, diverge

swift 4 fast **5** fleet, hasty, quick, rapid, ready **6** prompt, snappy, speedy, sudden **8** full-tilt, headlong **9** breakneck

___ Swift 3 Tom **8** Jonathan *character:* **8** Gulliver

swiftness 4 gait, pace **5** haste, hurry, speed **6** hustle **8** celerity, dispatch, legerity, rapidity, velocity **9** quickness, rapidness **10** expedition, speediness

swig 4 belt, down, drag, gulp, pull, slug **5** booze, draft, drain, drink, quaff, swill **6** guzzle, imbibe, tipple **7** swallow, swizzle

swill 4 bolt, gulp, slop, swig, tope, wolf **5** booze, draft, drink, gorge, scarf, scoff, slops, trash, waste **6** debris, gobble, guzzle, ingest, inhale, refuse, spilth, tank up, tipple **7** consume, garbage, hogwash, put away, rubbish, swizzle **8** chow down **9** polish off

swim 3 dip **4** reel, spin, turn **5** bathe, crawl, float, swoon, whirl **9** dizziness, dog-paddle

swimmingly 6 easily **8** smoothly **10** splendidly

swimming stroke 5 crawl **7** dolphin, trudgen **9** butterfly, dog paddle

swindle 3 con, gyp **4** bilk, clip, dupe, fake, hoax, rook, scam, sell, sham, skin, soak **5** bunco, bunko, cheat, cozen, fraud, gouge, phony, rogue, shaft, skunk, sting **6** chouse, diddle, fleece, humbug, hustle, take in **7** defraud **8** flimflam, hoodwink **9** bamboozle, imposture, victimize **11** hornswoggle

swindler 5 cheat, crook, ganef, gonif, shark **6** con man, goniff **7** sharper, shyster **8** deceiver **9** charlatan, defrauder **10** mountebank

swine see HOG

swing 4 sway, veer **5** flail, lurch, pivot, twirl, waver, weave, whirl, wield **6** dangle, divert, rhythm, rotate, seesaw, stroke, swerve, switch **7** revolve, suspend **8** brandish **9** alternate, fluctuate, oscillate, vacillate

swinish 5 feral **6** animal, coarse **7** beastly, bestial, porcine

swipe 3 cop, hit, nab, rap **4** blow, clip, conk, grab, hook, lick, lift, nick, sock, swat, wipe **5** clout, filch, heist, knock, pinch, smack, steal **6** pilfer, snatch, snitch, strike, wallop

swirl 4 eddy, purl, roil **5** curve, twist, whirl, whorl **6** swoosh, vortex **9** whirlpool **11** convolution

swish 4 buzz, chic, fizz, hiss, posh, tony, whiz **5** ritzy, smart, swank, whisk **6** classy, dressy, sizzle, trendy, whoosh **7** elegant, stylish **8** sibilate **9** exclusive

Swiss Family Robinson author **4** Wyss (Johann David)

switch 3 rod, wag **4** beat, flay, flog, lash, swap, veer, wand, whip **5** shift, shunt, trade, whisk **6** change, strike, waggle **7** scourge **8** exchange, flip-flop, reversal **9** about-face, sidetrack **10** substitute **12** substitution

Switzerland capital: **4** Bern city: **5** Basel **6** Geneva, Zürich **8** Lausanne lake: **6** Geneva, Wallen **7** Lucerne **9** Constance, Neuchâtel, Thunersee, Zürichsee language: **6** French, German **7** Italian monetary unit: **5** franc mountain, range: **4** Alps, Jura **9** Monte Rosa neighbor: **5** Italy **6** France **7** Austria, Germany **13** Liechtenstein resort: **5** Davos, Vevey **7** Zermatt **8** Montreux, St. Moritz **10** Interlaken river: **4** Aare **5** Rhine, Rhône state: **6** canton

swivel 4 spin, turn **5** pivot, swing, twirl, whirl **6** rotate **7** revolve **9** pirouette

swivet see SNIT

swizzle see SWIG

swollen 5 puffy, tumid **6** turgid **7** bloated, bulbous, bulging, pompous **8** enlarged, inflated, varicose **9** bombastic, distended, tumescent **10** rhetorical **12** magniloquent **13** grandiloquent

swoon 4 coma, daze, fade **5** droop, faint **6** torpor **7** pass out, rapture, syncope **8** black out

swoosh 4 eddy, gush, purl, rush **5** swirl, whirl, whorl

sword 4 épée, foil **5** saber, sabre **6** barong, bilboa, rapier, Toledo **7** cutlass **8** claymore, falchion, scimitar, yataghan

sword of ___ 8 Damocles

sword-shaped 8 ensiform

sworn 6 avowed **7** devoted **8** affirmed **9** committed, confirmed **10** deep-rooted, deep-seated, entrenched, inveterate

sybarite 7 epicure **8** hedonist **9** libertine **10** sensualist, voluptuary

sybaritic 6 carnal **7** sensual **8** sensuous **9** epicurean, libertine, luxurious **10** hedonistic, voluptuous **13** self-indulgent

sycophancy 7 fawning **8** flattery, toadying **9** truckling **11** bootlicking

sycophant 5 leech, toady **6** flunky, lackey, minion, yes-man **8** groveler, hanger-on, parasite, truckler **9** easy rider, flatterer, toadeater **10** bootlicker, self-seeker **11** lickspittle **13** apple-polisher

sycophantic 7 fawning, servile, slavish **8** toadying, unctuous **9** groveling, kowtowing, parasitic, truckling **10** obsequious **11** bootlicking

Sycorax's son 7 Caliban

syllable deletion: **7** apocope last: **6** ultima lengthening of: **7** ectasis next to last: **6** penult shortening of: **7** elision, systole stressed: **5** arsis

syllabus 6 aperçu, digest, précis, sketch, survey **7** epitome, outline, pandect, summary **8** abstract, headnote, synopsis **10** compendium

sylph 5 fairy, nymph **6** sprite

sylvan 5 bosky, woody **6** rustic, wooded deity: **3** Pan **4** Faun **5** dryad, satyr **6** Faunus **7** Silenus **8** Arethusa, Silvanus, Sylvanus

symbol 4 logo, mark, sign **5** badge, motif, stamp, token **6** design, device, emblem, mascot **9** attribute **10** indication chemical: see individual element musical: **4** clef, flat, hold, note, rest, turn **5** shake, sharp, trill **7** fermata, mordent, natural 8 arpeggio 9 crescendo 10 diminuendo 11 decrescendo

symbolic 5 token 10 emblematic 11 allegorical

symbolist poet 7 Rimbaud (Arthur) 8 Mallarmé (Stéphane), Verlaine (Paul)

symbolize 4 mean 6 embody, mirror, typify 7 signify 8 stand for 9 epitomize, exemplify, personify, represent 10 illustrate 11 emblematize

symmetrical 5 equal 7 regular 8 balanced 12 commensurate, proportional 13 commensurable

symmetry 5 order 6 parity 7 balance, harmony 8 equality, evenness 9 agreement, congruity 10 conformity, proportion, regularity 11 arrangement

sympathetic 4 kind, warm 6 benign, caring, humane, kindly, tender 8 amenable, friendly 9 agreeable, approving, benignant, congenial, congruous, consonant, favorable, receptive 10 compatible, consistent, responsive 11 considerate, kindhearted, softhearted, warmhearted 12 well-disposed 13 compassionate, understanding

sympathize 4 pity 7 condole 11 commiserate 13 compassionate

sympathy 4 pity, ruth 5 heart 6 accord, solace, warmth 7 comfort, harmony, rapport 8 affinity, kindness 9 agreement 10 benignancy, compassion, condolence, kindliness, tenderness 11 consolation, sensitivity 13 commiseration

symphonic 10 orchestral

symphony 9 orchestra 12 philharmonic

symposium 5 forum 7 meeting, seminar 9 gathering 10 conference, discussion

symptom 4 mark, sign 5 index, token 8 evidence 10 indication

symptoms 7 indicia 8 syndrome

synagogue 6 temple

sync 4 jibe 5 agree, match 7 harmony 8 coincide 9 harmonize 10 concurrent 12 simultaneous

synchronize 5 agree 6 concur 8 coincide

synchronous 6 coeval 10 coetaneous, coexistent, coexisting, coincident, concurrent 11 concomitant 12 contemporary, simultaneous 13 geostationary

syncope 4 coma 5 faint, swoon 8 blackout

syndicate 3 mob 4 pool 5 chain, group, mafia, trust, union 6 cartel, league 7 combine 11 association, partnership 12 conglomerate, organization 13 confederation

syndrome 3 ill 6 malady 7 ailment, disease 8 disorder, sickness 9 complaint, condition, infirmity

synergic 5 joint 6 shared 8 coacting, coactive, conjoint 9 collusive, concerted 11 cooperating, cooperative, coordinated

synod 4 body, diet 7 council, meeting 8 assembly, conclave, congress 10 conference, convention 11 convocation

synopsis 5 brief, recap 6 aperçu, digest, précis, review 7 capsule, epitome, outline, rundown, summary 8 abstract, breviary, syllabus 10 abridgment, compendium, conspectus 12 condensation

synopsize 5 recap, sum up 6 digest 7 outline, summate 8 abstract, boil down, compress, condense 9 epitomize, inventory, summarize 11 encapsulate

synthesis 5 blend, union 6 fusion, merger 7 amalgam 8 blending, compound 9 composite 11 combination 12 amalgamation 13 incorporation

synthesize 4 fuse, meld 5 blend, merge, unify 7 combine 8 compound 9 harmonize, integrate 10 amalgamate 11 incorporate

synthetic 6 ersatz 7 man-made 9 unnatural 10 artificial, fabricated 11 counterfeit

Syria *capital:* 8 Damascus *city:* 4 Homs 6 Aleppo *desert:* 6 Syrian *language:* 6 Arabic, French *monetary unit:* 5 pound *mountain range:* 7 Lebanon *neighbor:* 4 Iraq 6 Israel, Jordan, Turkey 7 Lebanon *plain:* 11 Mesopotamia *river:* 9 Euphrates *sea:* 13 Mediterranean

syringe 6 needle

Syrinx 5 nymph *pursuer:* 3 Pan

syrinx 7 panpipe 8 panpipes

syrup 6 orgeat 9 grenadine

syrupy 5 gooey, mushy, sappy, sweet 6 drippy, dulcet, slushy, sticky, sugary 7 cloying, maudlin, mawkish 9 schmaltzy 10 saccharine 11 sentimental

system 3 way 4 mode, plan 5 modus, order, setup 6 entity, manner, method, scheme 7 complex, network, pattern, process, regimen, routine 8 strategy 9 procedure, structure, technique 10 regularity 11 arrangement, disposition, orderliness

systematic 7 logical, ordered, orderly, regular 8 arranged 9 organized 10 analytical, methodical 12 businesslike

systematize 5 array, order 6 codify 7 arrange, catalog, dispose, marshal 8 classify, organize, regiment 9 catalogue, methodize

system of weights 4 troy 11 avoirdupois 12 apothecaries

T

tab 4 bill, cost, flap, list, loop, rate
5 check, count, price, score 6 charge,
record 7 account, invoice 8 eagle eye,
price tag, scrutiny 9 appendage, designate, extension, reckoning, statement
12 surveillance

tabard 4 cape, coat 5 tunic 10 coat
of arms

tabby 3 cat 6 feline, cement 8 brindled

tabernacle 4 tent 5 hovel 6 church, temple

tabes 7 atrophy, wasting 12 degeneration

Tabitha's Greek name 6 Dorcas

table 4 fare, list 5 bench, board, chart,
defer, stand 6 buffet, put off, record,
shelve, teapoy 7 counter 8 mahogany,
postpone 9 sideboard *ornament:*
7 epergne 11 centerpiece *writing:* 4 desk
9 secretary 10 escritoire

table d' ___ 4 hôte

tableland 4 mesa 5 butte 6 upland
7 plateau *Alabama-West Virginia:*
10 Cumberland *Arizona:* 5 Kanab 6 Kai-
bob *England:* 8 Dartmoor *India:*
5 Malwa (see also PLATEAU)

tablet 3 bar, pad 4 cake, disk, pill, slab
5 panel, slate 6 pellet, plaque, troche
7 lozenge, notepad 8 steno pad

Table Talk author 6 Selden (John)

tableware 4 cups 5 bowls, china, forks
6 dishes, knives, plates, silver, spoons
7 glasses, saucers 8 settings, utensils
9 stainless

tabloid 3 rag 5 lurid, pulpy 6 digest
7 summary 9 condensed, newspaper
11 sensational 12 scandal sheet

taboo 3 ban 4 no-no 6 banned, enjoin,
forbid 7 inhibit, obscene 9 forbidden,
ineffable, interdict, off-limits, restraint
10 inhibition 11 restriction, unspeakable 12 interdiction

tabor 4 drum

tabulate 4 list 5 count, order 6 codify,
figure, record 7 arrange 9 enumerate
11 systematize

tabulation 4 list 5 chart, tally 6 record
7 account

tabula ___ 4 rasa

tacit 6 silent, unsaid 7 assumed, implied
8 implicit, inferred, unspoken 9 intimated, suggested 10 subtextual, unde-

clared, underlying, understood
11 acquiescent, unexpressed 12 inarticu-
ulate

taciturn 4 dumb 6 silent 7 laconic
8 reserved, reticent, wordless 9 secretive 11 tight-lipped 12 closemouthed

Tacitus work 7 Annales 8 Dialogus, Ger-
mania 9 Historiae

tack 3 pin, yaw 4 beat, brad, gear, join,
nail, stay, turn 5 baste, reach, shift
6 attach, double, stitch, swerve, turn
up, zigzag 7 tangent 8 put about 9 come
about, deviation 10 alteration, deflection, digression, sea biscuit 11 ship biscuit 12 pilot biscuit

tackle 3 cat, rig 4 gear, sack 6 outfit,
take on, take up 7 halyard, lineman,
rigging 8 set about 9 apparatus, equipment, machinery, undertake 10 footballer, linebacker, plunge into 13 paraphernalia

tacky 5 cheap, crude, dingy, dowdy,
gaudy, messy, seedy, ratty, tatty
6 blowsy, frowsy, frumpy, kitsch, shabby, sleazy, sloppy, sticky, frumpy,
tawdry, untidy, vulgar 7 run-down,
unkempt 8 adhesive, frumpish, slovenly 9 inelegant, tasteless, unstylish
10 broken-down, down-at-heel, threadbare

tact 5 poise, touch 6 acumen 7 address,
finesse, suavity 8 civility, courtesy, delicacy, urbanity 9 diplomacy, politesse
10 adroitness, politeness, smoothness
11 savoir faire, sensitivity

tactful 5 civil, suave 6 adroit, urbane
7 politic 8 delicate, discreet, polished
9 courteous, sensitive 10 diplomatic,
perceptive, thoughtful 11 considerate

tactical 7 politic, prudent 9 advisable,
expedient, strategic

tactics 4 plan 6 method, scheme
8 maneuver, playbook, strategy 9 stratagem

tactile 8 palpable, tangible 9 touchable

taction 4 feel 5 touch 7 contact 9 palpation

tactless 4 rude 5 blunt, crude, inept
6 candid, clumsy, gauche 7 awkward
8 impolite 9 impolitic, maladroit
10 indiscreet 11 insensitive

tad 3 bit, boy, lad, son 4 lick, mite, snap,

spot, whit **5** child, crumb, sonny, speck **6** laddie, nipper, shaver **7** smidgen **8** fraction

tadpole 8 polliwog, pollywog

taffy 5 candy **8** flattery

tag 3 bit, dog, end **4** cost, flag, game, logo, mark, name, tail **5** aglet, brand, label, price, trail **6** append, charge, follow, select, shadow, slogan, tassel, tatter, ticket **7** license, run down **8** graffito, identify, insignia

Tahiti *city:* **7** Papeete *painter:* **7** Gauguin (Paul)

tail 3 dog, end, tag **4** butt, rear **5** hound, stalk **6** follow, pursue, shadow **7** hind end, rear end **8** backside, buttocks **9** posterior *bone:* **6** coccyx *relating to:* **6** caudal *short:* **4** scut

tailed 7 caudate

tailor 3 fit, sew **4** suit **5** alter **8** clothier, seamster **11** haberdasher

tailor-made 6 fitted, suited **7** bespoke, fitting **8** suitable **10** well-suited **11** appropriate

taint 3 rot **4** blot, blur, foul, harm, hurt, smut, soil, spot, turn, vice **5** brand, cloud, color, decay, dirty, fault, smear, spoil, stain, sully, touch **6** befoul, darken, defile, poison, smudge, smutch **7** blacken, blemish, corrupt, pollute, putrefy, tarnish **8** besmirch, discolor **9** discredit **10** adulterate, stigmatize **11** contaminate

taipan 5 snake **8** merchant **11** businessman

Taiwan 7 Formosa *capital:* **6** Taipei *channel:* **5** Bashi *city:* **6** T'ai-nan **8** Panch'iao, T'ai-chung **9** Kao-hsiung *language:* **8** Mandarin *leader:* **13** Chiang Kai-shek *monetary unit:* **6** dollar *mountain:* **6** Yü Shan

Tajikistan *capital:* **8** Dushanbe *monetary unit:* **5** ruble *mountain, range:* **6** Pamirs **9** Communism (Peak), Trans Alai **10** Revolution (Peak) *neighbor:* **5** China **10** Kyrgyzstan, Uzbekistan **11** Afghanistan *river:* **8** Amu Dar'ya, Syr Dar'ya

Taj Mahal 9 mausoleum *builder:* **9** Shah Jahan *site:* **4** Agra

take 3 get, nab **4** grab **5** annex, catch, seize **6** gather, obtain, secure **7** capture, receive **8** proceeds, receipts *account of:* **6** notice *advantage of:* **5** abuse **7** exploit *after:* **6** follow **8** resemble *apart:* **7** analyze, dissect **9** dismantle *care:* **6** beware *care of:* **3** fix **4** tend **5** nurse **6** attend *exception:* **6** object *five:* **4** rest *from:* **7** deprive, detract **8** subtract *it easy:* **5** relax *on the:* **7** corrupt *part:* **4** join **5** share **11** participate *place:* **5** occur

6 happen *to task:* **5** scold **7** reprove *turns:* **9** alternate *unawares:* **8** surprise

take away 4 grab **5** wrest **6** arrest, commit, deduct, detach, detain, remove **7** deprive, detract **8** diminish, discount, minimize, subtract, withdraw

take back 5 unsay **6** abjure, recall, recant, return **7** replace, restore, retract, swallow **8** forswear, withdraw **9** repossess

take down 4 note **5** lower, write **6** humble, record, reduce **7** deflate **8** dismount **9** dismantle **11** disassemble

take in 3 con **4** dupe, fool, furl, jail **5** admit, bluff, board, house, trick **6** absorb, accept, arrest, attend, betray, delude, embody **7** beguile, compass, contain, deceive, embrace, include, involve, mislead, observe, receive, shelter, snooker, subsume **8** flimflam, hoodwink, perceive **9** apprehend, bamboozle, encompass, four-flush **10** assimilate, comprehend, understand **11** double-cross

take off 4 doff, exit, quit **5** leave, scram **6** begone, deduct, depart, remove, set out **7** pull out, skiddoo, vamoose **8** clear out, discount, hightail, light out, subtract, withdraw **9** skedaddle

takeoff 5 spoof **6** launch, parody, satire, send-up **7** lampoon **8** travesty **9** burlesque **10** caricature *area:* **3** pad **6** runway

take on 3 don **4** face, hire, meet **5** adopt, annex, fight **6** accept, append, assume, attack, battle, employ, engage, strike, tackle **7** contest, embrace, espouse, venture **8** endeavor, set about **9** encounter, undertake

take out 4 date, kill, omit **5** loose **6** deduct, remove **7** destroy, release, unleash **8** discount, knock off, separate, subtract, withdraw, withhold **9** eliminate **10** annihilate

take over 5 seize, spell, usurp **6** assume **7** capture, relieve

take up 3 use **4** fill, open **5** adopt, begin, enter, raise, renew, set to, start **6** absorb, accept, assume, gather, occupy, resume, shrink, tackle **7** embrace, espouse, kick off, restart, shorten, tighten **8** commence, continue, initiate **10** recommence

talc 6 powder **8** steatite **9** soapstone

tale 3 fib, lie **4** myth, saga, yarn **5** fable, rumor, story **6** canard, legend **7** fiction **8** anecdote **9** narration, narrative

talebearer 3 rat **4** fink **6** canary, gossip, snitch **7** rat fink, tattler **8** busybody, gossiper, informer, quidnunc, squealer, telltale **9** informant **10** newsmonger, tat-

tletale 11 rumormonger, stool pigeon
12 blabbermouth 13 scandalmonger
talent 4 bent, gift, head, nose 5 craft,
dowry, flair, forte, knack, skill 6 genius
7 ability, aptness, faculty 9 endowment,
expertise
talented 4 able 6 clever, expert, gifted
8 skillful
Tale of Two Cities, A *author:* 7 Dickens
(Charles) *character:* 5 Lucie (Manette)
6 Carton (Sidney), Darnay (Charles)
7 Defarge (Madame), Manette (Alexander)
Tales of a Traveller author 6 Irving
(Washington)
Tales of a Wayside Inn author
10 Longfellow (Henry Wadsworth)
Tales of Hoffman composer 9 Offenbach
(Jacques)
talisman 4 juju, luck 5 charm 6 amulet,
fetish, mascot, scarab 7 periapt 10 phylactery
Talisman author 5 Scott (Walter)
talk 3 gab, rap, yak 4 blab, buzz, chat,
chin, yarn 5 prate, rumor, run on,
speak, utter, voice 6 babble, gabble,
gossip, parley, patter, report, speech
7 address, chatter, declaim, hearsay,
lecture, prattle 8 colloquy, converse,
dialogue, harangue 9 discourse, utterance 10 discussion 12 conversation
about: 7 discuss *back:* 4 sass *foolish:*
4 bunk 6 babble 7 chatter, palaver
indistinctly: 6 mumble, mutter *over:*
7 discuss *slowly:* 5 drawl *small:*
8 chitchat *wildly:* 4 rant, rave
talkative 4 glib 5 gabby, vocal 6 chatty,
fluent 7 gossipy, voluble 9 garrulous
10 loquacious 13 communicative
talk over 6 debate 7 discuss, hash out
8 consider 9 thrash out 10 deliberate
talky 5 gabby, windy, wordy 6 chatty,
prolix 7 verbose, voluble
tall 4 high, long 5 lanky, large, lofty,
rangy 6 absurd 7 pompous 8 towering
9 high-flown 10 far-fetched 11 skyscraping 12 altitudinous
tallow 3 fat 4 lard, suet 6 grease
tally 3 tab 4 jibe, list, tale 5 agree, count,
match, score, total 6 accord, census,
number, reckon, square 7 account, balance, catalog, compute, conform, itemize 8 check off, register, tabulate
9 agreement, catalogue, enumerate,
harmonize, inventory, reckoning
10 complement, correspond
talon 4 claw, hand 5 stock 6 finger
talus 5 ankle, scree, slope 9 anklebone
10 astragalus
tam 3 cap
Tamar *brother:* 7 Absalom *father:* 5 David

7 Absalom *father-in-law:* 5 Judah *half
brother:* 5 Amnon *seducer:* 5 Amnon
son: 5 Perez, Zerah
tamarisk 9 salt cedar
tambour 3 cup 4 drum 9 embroider
10 embroidery
Tamburlaine the Great author 7 Marlowe
(Christopher)
tame 4 bust, dull, meek, mild 5 break,
train, vapid 6 bridle, docile, gentle,
humble, soften, subdue 7 harness,
insipid, reclaim, subdued 8 domestic,
familiar, obedient 9 tractable 10 housebreak, submissive 11 domesticate,
housebroken 12 domesticated
Taming of the Shrew, The *character:*
6 Bianca 8 Baptista 9 Katharina, Petruchio
Tammany boss 5 Tweed (William)
Tammuz's lover 6 Ishtar
tam-o'-shanter 3 cap
tamp 3 ram 4 pack 5 pound, press, stuff
tampion 4 plug 5 cover
tan 3 sun, taw 4 beat, ecru, flog, whip
5 beige, brown, tawny, toast 6 bronze,
darken, thrash 7 biscuit
Tan novel 11 Joy Luck Club (The)
15 Kitchen God's Wife (The) 19 Bonesetter's Daughter (The)
tanager 7 redbird
Tancred, Tancredi *beloved:* 8 Clorinda
father: 3 Odo *mother:* 4 Emma *victim:*
8 Clorinda
tandem 4 pair 7 bicycle, concert 8 carriage
tang 3 nip 4 bite, fang, odor, ring, zest
5 aroma, clang, prong, sapor, savor,
shank, smack, taste, trace 6 flavor, relish 8 piquancy, pungency, sapidity
9 spiciness
tangible 4 real 7 tactile 8 concrete, material, palpable, physical, sensible 9 corporeal, touchable 10 detectable,
observable, phenomenal 11 appreciable, discernible, perceptible, substantial
tangle 3 mat, web 4 foul, knot, maze,
mesh, shag 5 clash, ravel, skein, snare,
snarl 6 entrap, foul up, hamper, jumble, jungle, morass, muddle, pileup,
raffle 7 dispute, embroil, ensnare,
ensnarl, involve, perplex, seaweed,
thicket 8 obstruct 9 embarrass, implicate 10 complicate 11 altercation,
predicament 12 bewilderment, complication
Tanglewood Tales author 9 Hawthorne
(Nathaniel)
tango 5 dance 8 circuity 11 indirection
13 deceitfulness
tangy 5 sharp 6 lively 7 piquant, pungent, zestful 9 flavorful

tank 3 vat 5 basin 7 cistern 8 aquarium 9 reservoir *American:* 6 Abrams 7 Bradley, Sherman *German:* 6 panzer *part:* 6 turret

tankard 3 mug 5 stoup 6 flagon 9 blackjack

tanked 3 lit 4 high, lost 5 drunk, lit up, oiled 6 bashed, blotto, bombed, failed, gave up, juiced, potted, soaked, soused, stewed, stoned, tanked, wasted, zonked 7 crocked, drunken, pickled, pie-eyed, sloshed, smashed, sottish 9 collapsed, plastered 10 inebriated, liquored up 11 intoxicated

tanker 4 ship 5 oiler

Tannhäuser composer 6 Wagner (Richard)

tantalize 3 rag 4 bait, lure 5 tease, tempt 6 entice, needle 7 torment 9 frustrate

Tantalus *daughter:* 5 Niobe *father:* 4 Zeus *son:* 6 Pelops

tantamount 4 same 5 alike, equal 8 parallel, selfsame 9 duplicate, identical 10 equivalent 12 commensurate

tantara 5 blare 7 fanfare

tantivy 3 run 6 gallop

tantrum 3 fit 6 blowup 8 outburst, paroxysm 9 hysterics 10 conniption

Tanzania *capital:* 6 Dodoma 11 Dar es Salaam *city:* 6 Arusha *former name:* 10 Tanganyika *island:* 5 Mafia, Pemba 8 Zanzibar *lake:* 5 Rukwa 6 Malawi 8 Victoria 10 Tanganyika *language:* 7 English, Swahili *monetary unit:* 8 shilling *mountain:* 11 Kilimanjaro *neighbor:* 5 Congo, Kenya 6 Malawi, Rwanda, Uganda, Zambia 7 Burundi 10 Mozambique *plain:* 9 Serengeti *river:* 6 Kagera, Rufiji, Ruvuma 7 Pangani *volcano:* 6 Lengai

Taoism founder 5 Laozi 6 Lao Tzu

tap 3 hit, pat 4 cock, draw, flap, name, plug, tick 5 chuck, draft, drain, nudge, touch, valve 6 faucet, select, siphon, spigot, strike 7 appoint, draw off, hydrant, percuss, petcock 8 drumbeat, half sole, nominate, stopcock 9 designate

tape 4 band, belt, bind 5 strip 6 fillet, ribbon 7 bandage *kind:* 5 inkle 6 ferret 7 masking 8 adhesive *machine:* 4 deck 8 recorder

taper 4 wane, wick 5 abate, close, draft, pinch, spire 6 candle, lessen, narrow, reduce 7 dwindle, glimmer 8 decrease, diminish

tapering 5 conic, spiry 6 spired, terete 7 conical 8 ensiform, fusiform, napiform, subulate 9 acuminate, attenuate 10 lanceolate

tapestry 5 arras, kilim 6 dossal 7 curtain, Gobelin, hanging *pattern:* 7 cartoon

Taphath's father 7 Solomon

tapioca 4 yuca 5 yucca 6 manioc 7 cassava, farinha, pudding

taproom 3 bar, pub 4 café 6 bodega, saloon, tavern 7 cantina 8 dramshop 9 roadhouse

tapster 6 barman 7 barkeep, barmaid, skinker 9 barkeeper, bartender 10 mixologist

tar 3 gob 4 jack, salt, soil, swab 5 pitch, smear, stain, sully, taint 6 defile, hearty, sailor, seaman 7 asphalt, besmear, mariner, shipman 8 besmirch, creosote, deckhand, flatfoot 9 shellback

taradiddle 3 fib, lie 5 hooey, story, trash 6 bunkum, canard 7 baloney, falsity 8 claptrap, nonsense 9 falsehood 10 balderdash 13 prevarication

tarantella 5 dance

tarantula 6 spider 10 wolf spider

Taras Bulba author 5 Gogol (Nikolai)

tarboosh 3 fez, hat

tardy 4 dull, late, lazy, slow 7 belated, delayed, laggard, overdue 8 dilatory, sluggish 10 behindhand, delinquent, unpunctual

tare 4 seed 5 vetch, weigh 6 weight 11 undesirable 13 counterweight

target 3 aim 4 butt, goal, mark, prey 5 aim at 6 object, quarry, victim 9 objective 11 sitting duck *center:* 8 bull's-eye *shooter's:* 10 clay pigeon

Tar Heel State 13 North Carolina

tariff 3 tax 4 cost, duty, levy, rate 5 price 6 charge, impost 7 tribute 10 assessment

Tarkington character 6 Penrod

tarn 4 lake, pool

tarnish 3 dim, mar 4 dull, foul, harm, hurt, soil 5 dirty, muddy, smear, spoil, stain, sully, taint 6 damage, darken, defile, injure, smirch, smudge, smutch 7 begrime, besmear, blemish, vitiate 8 besmirch, discolor

taro 5 aroid 6 yautia 7 dasheen, malanga *product:* 3 poi

tarpaulin 3 gob 4 jack, salt, swab 5 cover, sheet 6 hearty, sailor, seaman 7 mariner, shipman 9 shellback

tarpon 8 ladyfish 10 silverfish

tarry 3 lag 4 bide, drag, stay, wait 5 abide, dally, delay, visit 6 dawdle, linger, loiter, pitchy, remain 7 sojourn

tarsus 5 ankle

tart 3 pie 4 acid, bawd, moll, slut, sour 5 acerb, quean, sharp, tramp, trull, whore 6 biting, harlot, pastry 7 acerbic, cutting, piquant, pungent, tootsie 8 chess pie, strumpet 10 prostitute

tartar 5 argol 6 plaque 8 calculus

Tartar 6 Mongol, Turkic 7 Turkish
9 Mongolian

Tartuffe author 7 Molière

Tarzan *chimpanzee:* 7 Cheetah *creator:*
9 Burroughs (Edgar Rice) *mate:* 4 Jane

task 3 job 4 duty, lade, load, post, slog,
toil, work 5 chare, chore, labor, stint
6 assign, burden, charge, detail, devoir
7 mission, project 8 business, encumber, function 9 challenge, dress down,
reprimand 10 assignment, commission
11 undertaking 12 dressing-down

Tasmanian 4 wolf 5 devil *capital:*
6 Hobart *pine:* 4 Huon

tassel 3 tag 4 tuft 5 adorn 6 fringe 7 pendant, tzitzit 8 ornament 13 inflorescence

Tasso, Torquato *patron:* 4 Este (Alfonso
II d') *work:* 6 Aminta 7 Rinaldo
18 Jerusalem Delivered

taste 3 eat, sip, try 4 tang, zest 5 savor,
smack 6 flavor, liking, palate, relish
7 stomach 8 appetite, elegance, fondness, sapidity, soft spot, weakness
10 experience, partiality, refinement
11 inclination *kind:* 4 salt, sour 5 sweet
6 bitter *organ:* 3 bud

tasteful 4 fine 7 elegant, genteel, refined,
stylish 8 artistic, becoming 9 aesthetic

tasteless 4 dull, flat 5 bland, crass,
gaudy, showy, stale, tacky, vapid 6 vulgar 7 insipid 8 off-color, unsavory
9 inelegant, savorless, unrefined 10 flavorless

tasty 5 sapid, yummy 6 dainty, delish,
savory 8 luscious 9 delicious, flavorful,
palatable, succulent, toothsome
10 appetizing, delectable, flavorsome

tattered 4 torn 5 dingy, seedy 6 frayed,
ragged, ripped, shabby 7 raggedy, run-
down, worn-out 10 bedraggled, threadbare 11 dilapidated

tattle 3 wag, yak 4 blab, buzz, dish, talk
5 clack, prate, rumor 6 gossip, inform,
report, snitch, squeal 7 chatter,
hearsay, prattle 8 chitchat 9 grapevine
11 scuttlebutt

tattletale see TALEBEARER

tatty 5 cheap, dingy, dowdy, dumpy,
seedy, tacky 6 beat-up, cheesy, paltry,
scuzzy, shabby, shoddy, sleazy, trashy
7 run-down, scrubby 8 rubbishy
10 threadbare 11 dilapidated

taunt 3 jab 4 gibe, jeer, mock, quip, razz,
skit, twit 5 scout, tease 6 deride, insult
7 affront, provoke 8 reproach, ridicule
9 challenge

taurine 6 bovine 8 bull-like

Taurus 4 bull *star:* 9 Aldebaran

taut 4 firm, snug, trim 5 rigid, tense,
tight 6 corded 10 high-strung

tautology 8 iterance, pleonasm 9 iteration 10 redundancy, repetition

tavern 3 bar, inn, pub 4 café, dive
6 bistro, bodega, saloon 7 barroom,
cantina, gin mill, taproom 8 alehouse,
pothouse, wineshop 9 roadhouse
11 public house, rathskeller 12 watering hole 13 watering place

taverner 7 barkeep 8 boniface, publican
9 barkeeper, bartender, innkeeper
12 saloonkeeper

taw 3 tan 6 marble 7 partner

tawdry 4 loud 5 cheap, gaudy, tacky
6 brazen, flashy, garish, tinsel 7 chintzy,
glaring, ignoble 9 brummagem, dime-
store 12 meretricious

tawny 3 tan 4 buff 5 beige, brown, sandy
6 copper, tanned

tax 4 duty, lade, levy, load, onus, scot,
toll 5 drain, tithe 6 assess, burden,
cumber, impost, saddle, strain, tariff,
weight 7 tribute 8 encumber 10 imposition *agency:* 3 IRS *feudal:* 7 scutage, tallage *kind:* 4 geld 5 sales, tithe 6 excise,
income 8 property 9 surcharge *on salt:*
7 gabelle *rate:* 10 assessment

taxi 3 cab, car 4 hack 5 cyclo

taxing 5 tough 6 trying 7 exigent, onerous, wearing 8 exacting, grievous, grueling 9 demanding, difficult 10 burdensome, oppressive

Taygeta *father:* 5 Atlas *mother:* 7 Pleione
sisters: 8 Pleiades

tazza 3 cup 4 vase

Tchaikovsky, Pyotr Ilyich *ballet:* 8 Swan
Lake 10 Nutcracker (The) 14 Sleeping
Beauty *opera:* 12 Eugene Onegin
13 Queen of Spades (The)

tea 5 party 6 repast 8 beverage 9 reception *black:* 5 bohea, pekoe 8 souchong
cake: 6 cookie *genus:* 4 Thea *kind:*
4 herb, Java 5 Assam, black, bohea,
green, hyson, pekoe 6 Ceylon, congou,
oolong 7 cambric 8 Earl Grey, souchong 9 sassafras 10 Darjeeling

teach 5 coach, edify, guide, train, tutor
6 impart, school 7 educate, instill, profess 8 instruct 9 enlighten, inculcate
12 indoctrinate

teacher 4 guru, prof 5 coach, guide,
tutor 6 docent, master, mentor, pedant
7 maestro, trainer 8 educator 9 pedagogue, preceptor, professor 10 instructor 12 schoolmaster *Hindu:* 5 swami
Jewish: 5 rabbi, rebbe *Muslim:* 6 mullah
organization: 3 NEA *religious:* 9 catechist 10 mystagogue

Tea for Two composer 7 Youmans (Vincent)

team 4 band, club, crew, gang, join, pair,
side, yoke 5 group, squad, troop,

wagon 6 stable, troupe 8 carriage *baseball:* 4 nine *basketball:* 4 five 7 quintet *football:* 6 eleven *kind:* 6 jayvee 7 varsity

teamster 6 driver 7 trucker

tear 3 cry, cut, fly, rip, run 4 bolt, claw, dash, drop, flaw, gash, hole, lash, pull, race, rend, rift, rive, rush, slit, snag, weep 5 chase, hurry, shoot, shred, slash, speed, split, spree 6 career, charge, course, sunder, tatter, wrench 7 droplet, fissure, rupture 8 lacerate 10 laceration

tear down 4 raze, ruin, slur 5 knock, smash, smear, wreck 6 defame, malign, vilify 7 asperse, traduce, destroy, shatter, slander 8 demolish 9 denigrate, disparage, take apart 10 annihilate, calumniate 11 disassemble

tearful 3 sad 5 misty, moist, weepy 6 crying, watery, woeful 7 bawling, sobbing, weeping 8 mournful, pathetic 9 lamenting, sniveling, sorrowful 10 blubbering, lachrymose

tear-jerking 5 mushy 6 drippy, sticky 7 maudlin, mawkish 8 touching 9 schmaltzy 11 sentimental

teary-eyed 5 blear, moist

tease 3 bug, kid, rag, rip 4 bait, coax, comb, gibe, jive, josh, ride, tear, twit 5 annoy, chaff, chivy, harry, shred, taunt, worry 6 cajole, harass, needle, pester, pick on, plague 7 bedevil, torment 8 ridicule 9 tantalize

teaser 5 promo 7 preview

teched 3 mad 4 daft 5 batty, crazy 6 insane 7 cracked, lunatic 8 demented

technicality 6 detail 8 loophole

technique 4 mode 5 modus 6 method, system 8 approach 9 procedure 13 modus operandi

ted 5 strew 6 spread 7 scatter

tedious 3 dry 4 dull 5 ho-hum, stale 6 boring, dreary 7 irksome, operose 8 drudging, tiresome 9 dryasdust, wearisome 10 monotonous 11 mindnumbing 13 uninteresting

tedium 4 yawn 5 ennui 7 boredom 8 doldrums, dullness, monotony, sameness

teem 4 flow, pour 5 crawl, empty, swarm 6 abound, bustle 7 produce 9 pullulate

teeming 4 lush, rife 5 alive 6 aswarm 7 replete 8 abundant, swarming, thronged 9 abounding 11 overflowing

teen 5 youth 10 adolescent

tee off 4 open 5 begin, drive, enter, start 8 commence, initiate

teeter 4 rock, sway 5 waver 6 falter, seesaw, wobble 9 vacillate

telamon 5 atlas *counterpart:* 8 caryatid

Telamon *brother:* 6 Peleus *father:* 6 Aea-

cus *half-brother:* 6 Phocus *son:* 4 Ajax 6 Teucer

Telegonus *father:* 7 Ulysses 8 Odysseus *mother:* 5 Circe

telegraph 4 wire 5 cable 6 signal *code:* 5 Morse

Telemachus *father:* 7 Ulysses 8 Odysseus *mother:* 8 Penelope

telephone 4 buzz, call, dial, ring 5 phone 6 ring up *inventor:* 4 Bell (Alexander Graham)

Telephus *father:* 8 Heracles, Hercules *mother:* 4 Auge

telescope 5 glass 6 finder 7 compact 8 compress, condense, contract, spyglass 9 reflector, refractor

television 4 tube 5 video 8 boob tube, idiot box *antenna:* 10 rabbit ears *award:* 4 Emmy *British:* 5 telly *children's:* 6 kidvid *frequency:* 3 UHF, VHF *interference:* 4 snow *network:* 3 ABC, BBC, CBS, Fox, NBC, NET, PBS *pioneer:* 5 Baird (John Logie) 8 De Forest (Lee), Zworykin (Vladimir) *program:* 4 news 5 rerun 6 series, sitcom 7 western 8 game show, talk show 9 broadcast, docudrama, soap opera 11 infomercial 12 infotainment *tube:* 9 kinescope

tell 3 say 4 blab, clue, warn 5 break, count, crack, mound, order, spill, state, utter 6 advise, betray, fill in, inform, notify, relate, report, retail, reveal 7 confess, declare, divulge, narrate, recount, reel off 8 describe, disclose, give away 9 come clean

teller 5 clerk 6 banker 7 cashier, counter 8 informer, narrator 12 communicator

telling 5 solid, sound, valid 6 cogent 7 weighty 8 powerful 9 effective 10 convincing, expressive

tell off 4 flay, rate, ream 5 chide, scold 6 berate, rebuke 7 bawl out, chew out, reprove, upbraid 8 admonish, call down 9 dress down, excoriate, reprimand 10 take to task, tongue-lash, vituperate

tell on 6 inform, snitch, tattle

telltale 3 cue 4 clue, fink, lead, sign 5 proof 6 canary, gossip, signal, snitch, tip-off 7 rat fink, tattler 8 evidence, gossiper, informer, quidnunc, signpost, squealer 9 indicator 10 indication, newsmonger 12 blabbermouth, gossipmonger 13 scandalmonger

telluric 6 earthy 7 earthly, mundane, terrene, worldly 9 sublunary 11 terrestrial

temblor 5 quake, shake, shock 6 tremor 8 upheaval 10 aftershock, earthquake

temerarious 4 rash 6 daring 8 heedless, reckless 9 audacious, daredevil, foolhardy, venturous **11** adventurous, venturesome **13** adventuresome

temerity 4 gall **5** cheek, nerve **6** daring **8** audacity, chutzpah, rashness **9** assurance, brashness, hardihood, hardiness **10** effrontery **12** recklessness **13** foolhardiness

temper 4 heat, mean, mind, mood, tone, vein **5** admix, alloy, anger, blood, grain, humor, trend **6** anneal, attune, dander, dilute, govern, hackle, makeup, medium, season, soften, spirit, strain **7** courage, mollify, passion, quality, toughen **8** hardness, moderate, modulate, restrain **9** character, composure, condition **10** resilience, resiliency **11** disposition, personality

temperament 4 mood **5** humor **6** manner, makeup, mettle, nature **9** character **10** complexion **11** disposition, personality

temperamental 5 moody **6** ornery, touchy **7** erratic **8** contrary, ticklish, unstable, variable, volatile **9** mercurial **10** capricious, changeable, high-strung, inconstant **13** unpredictable

temperance 8 sobriety **9** austerity, restraint **10** abstinence, continence, moderation, self-denial **11** self-control *advocate of:* **6** Nation (Carry) **7** Willard (Frances)

temperate 4 calm, even, mild, soft **5** balmy, sober **6** modest, steady **7** clement **8** discreet, moderate **9** abstinent, continent **10** abstemious, controlled, reasonable, restrained **11** abstentious

temperature 4 heat, mood **5** fever **6** degree, warmth **7** hotness **8** coldness **9** intensity

tempered 7 diluted, treated **8** adjusted, hardened, softened **9** mitigated, moderated, qualified **12** strengthened

tempest 3 din **4** blow, gale, rage, wind **5** furor, hurly, storm **6** hubbub, squall, tumult, uproar **8** brouhaha, foofaraw **9** commotion, hurricane **10** hullabaloo, hurly-burly

Tempest, The *character:* **5** Ariel **6** Alonso **7** Caliban, Miranda **8** Prospero **9** Ferdinand

tempestuous 4 wild **5** roily, rough **6** raging, stormy **7** furious, moiling, violent **8** blustery **9** turbulent **10** tumultuous

temple 4 fane **6** church **9** synagogue **10** tabernacle *ancient:* **8** pantheon *Aztec:* **8** teocalli *Buddhist:* **3** wat *Eastern:* **6** pagoda *Greek:* **9** Parthenon *sanctuary:* **5** cella **6** adytum **10** penetralia

tempo 4 pace, rate, time **5** speed **6** rhythm *fast:* **6** presto, vivace **7** allegro

moderate: **7** andante *slow:* **5** grave, lento **6** adagio

temporal 3 lay **5** civil **6** carnal **7** earthly, mundane, profane, secular, worldly **13** chronological, synchronistic

temporary 6 acting **7** Band-Aid, interim **8** fleeting **9** ad interim, makeshift, transient **10** short-lived, substitute, transitory **11** provisional

temporize 5 delay, stall, yield **6** palter **7** draw out **8** gain time **10** equivocate **11** prevaricate

tempt 3 woo **4** bait, lure, risk, sway **5** court, decoy **6** allure, entice, entrap, invite, lead on, seduce **7** provoke **8** inveigle **9** tantalize

temptation 4 bait, lure, trap **5** decoy, siren, snare **6** allure, come-on **9** seduction **10** attraction, enticement

tempting 8 alluring **9** appealing, delicious, seductive **10** attractive, come-hither

temptress 4 vamp **5** siren **7** Lorelei **10** seductress **11** femme fatale

ten *cents:* **4** dime *combining form:* **3** dec, dek **4** deca, deka **5** decem *dollars:* **7** sawbuck *mills:* **4** cent *thousand:* **6** myriad *years:* **6** decade

tenable 5 sound **8** rational **10** defendable, defensible, reasonable **12** maintainable

tenacious 3 set **4** fast, firm, true **5** fixed, stout **6** dogged, secure, sturdy **8** adhesive, clinging, resolute, stalwart, stubborn **9** obstinate, steadfast **10** persistent **11** persevering

tenacity 4 grit, guts **5** moxie, pluck, spunk **6** mettle, spirit **7** courage **8** firmness **10** resolution **11** persistence **13** determination

tenant 6 holder, lessee, lodger, renter **7** boarder, dweller **8** occupant *feudal:* **6** vassal

tenantable 7 livable **9** habitable **11** inhabitable

Ten Commandments 9 Decalogue

tend 4 lean, mind, till, work **5** guard, labor, nurse, serve, watch **6** foster **7** babysit, care for, conduce, incline, nurture, oversee **8** minister **9** cultivate, look after, watch over

tendency 4 bent, bias **5** drift, tenor, trend **7** current, leaning **8** penchant **10** partiality, proclivity, propensity **11** disposition, inclination **12** predilection

tendentious 6 biased **7** colored, partial **8** one-sided, partisan **10** prejudiced

tender 3 bid **4** fond, mild, soft, sore, warm **5** green, money, mushy, offer, young **6** callow, extend, gentle, humane, loving, submit, touchy **7** fragile, hold out, lenient, painful, present, proffer, propose **8** delicate, immature, proposal **9** sensitive, succulent **10** benevolent, solicitous **11** considerate, warmhearted **12** affectionate **13** compassionate

tenderfoot 4 colt, punk, tyro **6** novice, rookie **7** amateur **8** beginner, freshman, neophyte, newcomer **9** cheechako, fledgling, greenhorn, novitiate **10** apprentice

tenderhearted 6 kindly **11** sympathetic **13** compassionate

Tender Is the Night author 10 Fitzgerald (F. Scott)

tendon 4 band, cord **5** nerve, sinew **6** leader **9** hamstring

tendril 4 curl, vine **6** cirrus, spiral **7** ringlet

tenebrific 4 dark, glum, gray, grim **5** black, bleak, sable **6** dismal, dreary, gloomy, somber, sombre **8** desolate, funereal **10** depressing, oppressive **11** dispiriting

tenebrous 3 dim **4** dark, deep, dusk, hazy **5** dusky, foggy, muddy, murky, vague **6** cloudy, gloomy **7** cryptic, obscure, shadowy, unclear **9** ambiguous, lightless **10** caliginous

tenement 4 flat **6** rental, walk-up, warren **7** lodging, rookery **8** building **9** apartment, residence

tenet 3 ism **5** canon, creed, dogma **6** belief **7** paradox **8** doctrine **9** principle **10** empiricism

tenfold 7 decuple

Tennessee *capital:* **9** Nashville *city:* **7** Memphis **9** Knoxville **11** Chattanooga *college, university:* **10** Vanderbilt *mountain, range:* **7** Lookout **10** Great Smoky **13** Clingmans Dome *nickname:* **9** Volunteer (State) *public works:* **3** TVA **9** Norris Dam *river:* **9** Tennessee **11** Mississippi *state bird:* **11** mockingbird *state flower:* **4** iris *state tree:* **11** tulip poplar

tennis *award:* **8** Davis Cup *item:* **3** net **4** ball **6** racket **7** racquet *kind:* **5** table **7** doubles, singles **8** platform *score:* **4** love **5** deuce *serve:* **3** ace *shoe:* **7** sneaker *stroke:* **3** cut, lob **4** chop, drop **5** serve, slice **6** volley **8** backhand, forehand *term:* **3** let, set **5** court, fault **7** service **9** advantage, backcourt

tennis champ 4 Ashe (Arthur), Borg (Bjorn), Cash (Pat), Graf (Steffi), King (Billie Jean), Noah (Yannick), Wade (Virginia) **5** Budge (Don), Chang (Michael), Court (Margaret Smith), Evert (Chris), Gómez (Andres), Laver (Rod), Lendl (Ivan), Perry (Fred), Seles

(Monica), Stich (Michael), Vilas (Guillermo), Wills (Helen) **6** Agassi (André), Austin (Tracy), Becker (Boris), Casals (Rosie), Edberg (Stephan), Fraser (Neale), Gibson (Althea), Hewitt (Lleyton), Hingis (Martina), Kramer (Jack), Muster (Thomas), Pierce (Mary), Stolle (Fred), Tilden (Bill) **7** Connors (Jimmy), Courier (Jim), Emerson (Roy), Federer (Roger), Lacoste (Rene), McEnroe (John), Nastase (Ilie), Novótna (Jana), Sampras (Pete) **8** Connolly (Maureen), González (Pancho), Martínez (Conchita), Newcombe (John), Rosewall (Ken), Sabatini (Gabriela), Wilander (Mats), Williams (Serena, Venus) **9** Davenport (Lindsay) **10** Mandlikova (Hana) **11** Navratilova (Martina) **14** Sánchez Vicario (Arantxa)

Tennyson poem 4 Maud **7** Ulysses **8** Princess (The), Tiresias **10** Enoch Arden, In Memoriam **12** Locksley Hall **23** Charge of the Light Brigade (The)

tenor 4 mood, tone **5** drift, voice **6** singer **7** meaning, purport **8** tendency **9** substance *American:* **5** Lanza (Mario) **6** Hadley (Jerry), Peerce (Jan), Tucker (Richard) **8** Melchior (Lauritz) **9** McCormack (John), McCracken (James) *Canadian:* **7** Vickers (Jon) *Czech:* **6** Slezak (Leo) *German:* **10** Wünderlich (Fritz) *Italian:* **5** Gigli (Beniamino) **6** Alagna (Roberto), Caruso (Enrico) **7** Bocelli (Andrea), Corelli (Franco) **8** Bergonzi (Carlo) **9** del Monaco (Mario), di Stefano (Giuseppe), Pavarotti (Luciano) *Spanish:* **5** Kraus (Alfredo) **7** Domingo (Plácido) **8** Carreras (José) *Swedish:* **5** Gedda (Nicolai) **8** Björling (Jussi) **9** Bjoerling (Jussi)

tenpins 7 bowling

tense 4 edgy, taut **5** nervy, rigid, tight, wired **6** uneasy **7** anxious, jittery, nervous, restive, uptight **8** strained, stressed **10** high-strung *grammatical:* **4** past **6** future **7** perfect, present **8** preterit **9** preterite **10** pluperfect **11** progressive

tension 5 state, steam **6** nerves, strain, stress, unease **7** anxiety, balance **8** edginess, pressure, tautness **9** agitation, hostility, stiffness **10** discomfort, opposition, uneasiness **11** nervousness, uptightness

tent 4 camp **6** canopy, encamp, laager **7** bivouac, shelter *kind:* **3** pup **4** yurt **5** Baker, tepee **6** wigwam **7** marquee **8** pavilion, umbrella *maker:* **4** Omar *material:* **6** canvas *part:* **3** fly, guy, peg **4** pole

tentacle 3 arm 6 barbel, feeler

tentative 4 test 5 chary, loath, probe, trial 6 averse 7 halting 8 hesitant, insecure 9 diffident, makeshift, reluctant, uncertain, undecided, unsettled 10 irresolute 11 conditional, disinclined, problematic, provisional

tenth 5 tithe *combining form:* 4 deci

tenuous 4 slim, thin, weak 5 reedy, shaky 6 feeble, flimsy, slight, stalky 7 fragile, sketchy, slender 8 gossamer 10 precarious 11 implausible 13 insubstantial, unsubstantial

tenure 4 term 6 estate 10 incumbency *feudal:* 7 burgage

tepid 4 mild, warm 7 warmish 8 lukewarm 9 apathetic 11 halfhearted, indifferent

tequila source 5 agave

Terentia's husband 6 Cicero

Tereus *son:* 4 Itys *wife:* 6 Procne

tergiversate 3 haw, hem, rat 5 dodge, evade, hedge 6 defect, desert, waffle, weasel 7 abandon, shuffle 8 renounce, sidestep 9 pussyfoot, repudiate 10 apostatize, equivocate

term 3 dub, end 4 call, name, span, tour, word 5 label, spell, stint, title 6 detail, period, tenure 7 quarter, session 8 duration, semester 9 designate 10 conclusion, denominate, expression, limitation, particular 11 appellation, designation

termagant 5 harpy, scold, shrew, vixen 6 ogress, virago 8 fishwife, harridan 9 Xanthippe

terminable 6 finite

terminal 3 end, lag 4 last 5 depot, fatal, final 6 finial, latest, latter, lethal 7 closing, extreme, station 8 eventual, hindmost, junction, ultimate 9 extremity 10 concluding *negative:* 7 cathode *positive:* 5 anode

terminate 3 end 4 boot, drop, fire, halt, kill, quit, sack, stop 5 abort, cease, close, issue, leave 6 cut off, finish, wind up 7 abolish, dead-end, dismiss 8 complete, conclude, dissolve 9 determine, discharge 10 extinguish 11 assassinate, discontinue

terminology 4 cant 5 argot, idiom, lingo 6 jargon, patois 7 lexicon 8 language, shoptalk 10 vernacular, vocabulary 12 nomenclature

termite 5 alate 8 white ant

ternary 5 third 6 triple 9 threefold

Terpsichore see MUSE

terrace 4 bank, deck, mesa, park, roof, step 5 bench, porch, shelf 6 street 7 balcony, sundeck 8 platform 9 promenade

terra-cotta 4 clay 7 pottery

terra firma 4 dirt, land, soil 5 earth 6 ground

terrain 4 area, land, turf 5 field 6 domain, ground, milieu, sphere 8 province 9 bailiwick, territory 10 topography 11 environment

terrapin 6 turtle

terrestrial 4 land 6 earthy, ground 7 earthly, mundane, worldly 8 everyday, ordinary, telluric, workaday 9 earthlike, planetary, sublunary 10 earthbound

terrible 4 dire 5 awful, dread 6 fierce, grisly, horrid, severe 7 dreaded, fearful, furious, ghastly, hideous, intense, macabre, vicious, violent 8 dreadful, gruesome, horrible, horrific, shocking, vehement 9 abhorrent, appalling, atrocious, desperate, frightful, harrowing, laborious, loathsome, monstrous, strenuous 10 disastrous, formidable, horrendous, horrifying

terrier 3 dog *kind:* 3 fox 4 blue, bull, Skye 5 cairn, Irish, Welsh 6 Boston 8 Airedale, Lakeland 9 Yorkshire

terrific 5 super, swell 6 superb 7 amazing, awesome 8 dreadful, dynamite, glorious 9 appalling, frightful, marvelous, upsetting, wonderful 10 formidable 11 magnificent, sensational 13 extraordinary

terrify 5 alarm, scare 7 scarify, startle 8 affright, frighten 10 intimidate

terrifying 4 grim 5 scary 6 grisly, horrid 7 ghastly, hideous, macabre 8 alarming, dreadful, fearsome, gruesome, horrible, terrible 9 frightful 10 formidable, horrifying

territory 4 area, belt, land, turf, zone 5 field, route, state, tract 6 domain, region, sphere 7 country, demesne, terrain 8 conquest, district, dominion, province 9 bailiwick 10 borderland 12 jurisdiction

terror 4 brat, fear 5 alarm, dread, panic, worry 6 dismay, fright, horror 7 scourge 9 nightmare 11 fearfulness, trepidation

terrorize 3 cow 5 alarm, bully, scare 6 coerce, fright, menace 7 scarify 8 browbeat, bulldoze, frighten, threaten 9 strong-arm 10 intimidate

terry 4 loop 5 cloth 6 fabric 12 Turkish towel

terse 4 curt 5 brief, crisp, pithy, short 6 abrupt 7 brusque, compact, concise, elegant, laconic, summary 8 polished, succinct 11 compendious, sententious, telegraphic 12 monosyllabic

tertiary 5 third

terza ___ 4 rima

tessera 3 die **4** tile **6** tablet, ticket

test 3 try **4** exam, quiz **5** assay, check, essay, final, proof, prove, shell, taste, touch, trial, try on **6** sample, tryout, verify **7** confirm, examine, midterm **8** evaluate, gut check, sounding, trial run **9** benchmark, criterion **10** evaluation, experiment, touchstone **11** demonstrate, examination **12** experimental

testa 6 cupule **7** coating **8** envelope, seed coat, tegument **10** integument

testament 4 will **5** credo, creed, proof **7** tribute, witness **8** evidence **9** scripture **11** attestation **12** confirmation

tester 4 coin **6** canopy, prover **7** analyst, assayer **8** examiner **12** investigator

testifier 7 witness **8** deponent

testify 5 prove, swear **6** affirm, attest, depone, depose, evince **7** certify, witness **11** certificate

testimonial 5 proof **6** salute **7** tribute, witness **8** evidence, affidavit, authority **10** deposition, profession **11** affirmation, attestation, declaration **12** confirmation **13** corroboration, documentation

testimony 5 proof **6** avowal **7** witness **8** evidence **9** affidavit, authority **10** deposition, profession **11** affirmation, attestation, declaration **12** confirmation **13** corroboration, documentation

testy 4 edgy **5** cross, fussy, hasty **6** cranky, ornery, tetchy, touchy **7** fretful, grouchy, peevish **8** choleric **9** crotchety, irascible, irritable **10** ill-humored, out of sorts **12** cantankerous **13** quick-tempered

tetanus 7 lockjaw, trismus

tetchy see TESTY

tête-à-tête 4 chat, talk **5** à deux **7** private, vis-à-vis **8** causerie **10** face-to-face **12** conversation

tether 3 tie **4** bind, rope **5** cable, chain, stake **6** fasten, fetter, lariat, picket **8** restrain **9** restraint

Tethys *daughters:* **9** Oceanides *father:* **6** Uranus *husband:* **7** Oceanus *mother:* **4** Gaea **5** Terra

tetrad 4 four **7** quartet **8** foursome **10** quaternion

Teutonic 6 German **8** Germanic *language:* **5** Dutch **6** Danish, German, Gothic **7** English, Flemish, Frisian, Swedish **9** Afrikaans, Norwegian

Texas *capital:* **6** Austin *city:* **4** Waco **6** Dallas, El Paso **7** Houston **8** Amarillo **9** Arlington, Fort Worth **10** San Antonio *college, university:* **3** SMU **4** Rice **5** Lamar **6** Baylor **9** Texas Tech **15** Sam Houston State *island:* **5** Padre *mountain:*

9 Guadalupe (Peak) *nickname:* **8** Lone Star (State) *park:* **7** Big Bend *river:* **3** Red **5** Pecos **6** Brazos **8** Colorado **9** Rio Grande *state bird:* **11** mockingbird *state flower:* **10** bluebonnet *state tree:* **5** pecan

text 6 script

textbook 6 primer

textile 5 cloth **6** fabric *dealer:* **6** mercer *machine:* **8** calender *shop:* **7** mercery *treat:* **9** mercerize

texture 3 web **4** feel, hand, wale, woof **5** weave **6** fabric

Thackeray novel 9 Pendennis **10** Vanity Fair **11** Barry Lyndon, Henry Esmond

Thailand *capital:* **7** Bangkok *city:* **9** Chiang Mai *former name:* **4** Siam *island:* **6** Phuket *monetary unit:* **4** baht *neighbor:* **4** Laos **5** Burma **7** Myanmar **8** Cambodia, Malaysia *river:* **10** Chao Phraya *sea:* **7** Andaman

Thaïs 7 hetaera, hetaira **9** courtesan *author:* **6** France (Anatole) *composer:* **8** Massenet (Jules) *husband:* **7** Ptolemy *lover:* **9** Alexander (the Great)

thalassic 6 marine **7** oceanic **8** maritime

Thalia see GRACES; MUSE

Thanatopsis author 6 Bryant (William Cullen)

Thanatos 5 death *brother:* **6** Hypnos *mother:* **3** Nyx

thankful 4 glad **8** grateful **12** appreciative

thanks 5 grace **8** blessing **9** gratitude **11** benediction **12** appreciation, gratefulness

Thanksgiving 5 feast **7** holiday *first celebrant:* **6** Indian **7** Pilgrim *food:* **6** turkey

thatch 3 mop **4** hair, roof **5** cover

that is *Latin:* **5** id est

Thaumas *daughter:* **4** Iris **5** Aello, Harpy **7** Celaeno, Ocypete *daughters:* **7** Harpies *father:* **6** Pontus *mother:* **4** Gaea *wife:* **7** Electra

thaumaturgic 5 magic **6** Magian, mystic, witchy **7** magical **8** wizardly **9** marvelous **10** miraculous **11** necromantic **12** supernatural

thaumaturgy 5 magic **7** sorcery **8** cabbalah, kabbalah, witchery, wizardry **10** necromancy

thaw 4 melt **5** deice, relax **6** unbend **7** defrost, liquefy **8** dissolve, unfreeze **10** condescend, deliquesce

the 7 article *French:* **3** les *German:* **3** das, der, die *Spanish:* **3** las, los

Thea *daughter:* **6** Selene *father:* **6** Uranus *husband:* **8** Hyperion *mother:* **4** Gaea

theater 4 nabe **5** drama, stage **6** boards **9** playhouse **10** footlights *award:* **4** Tony *district:* **6** rialto *entrance:* **5** foyer, lobby *Greek:* **5** odeum *movie:* **6** cinema **8** cineplex, megaplex 9 multiplex *outdoor:* 7 drive-in *part:* 3 box, pit 4 loge 5 apron, stage, wings 7 balcony, parquet 8 parterre 9 greenroom, mezzanine, orchestra 10 proscenium

theatrical 5 stagy 6 staged 8 dramatic, thespian 10 artificial, flamboyant, histrionic 11 dramaturgic 12 melodramatic *agent:* 6 Morris (William) *device:* 4 prop *group:* 6 troupe

Theban Eagle 6 Pindar

Thebes *founder:* 6 Cadmus *king:* 5 Laius 7 Oedipus *queen:* 7 Jocasta

theft 5 heist, pinch 6 holdup, piracy 7 break-in, larceny, robbery 8 burglary, stealing, thievery 9 pilferage *combining form:* 5 klept 6 klepto

theme 4 stem, text, tune 5 essay, lemma, motif, paper, point, topic, topos 6 burden, matter, melody, mythos, thesis 7 article, conceit, message, subject 8 argument 11 composition 12 dissertation

Themis *father:* 6 Uranus *goddess of:* 3 law 7 justice *husband:* 4 Zeus 7 Jupiter *mother:* 4 Gaea

then 4 also, anon, ergo, next, thus, when 5 again, hence, later 7 besides, further 8 moreover 9 therefore, thereupon 10 in addition 11 accordingly, furthermore 12 additionally, consequently

thence 4 away 7 thereof 9 from there, therefrom

Theogony poet 6 Hesiod

theologian *American:* 6 Merton (Thomas) 7 Edwards (Jonathan), Niebuhr (Reinhold), Tillich (Paul), Walther (Carl) *Dutch:* 6 Jansen (Cornelis) *English:* 4 Bede (Venerable) 5 Pusey (Edward), Watts (Isaac) 6 Alcuin, Wesley (John) 7 Langton (Stephen) 8 Pelagius, Wycliffe (John) *French:* 6 Calvin (John) 7 Abelard (Peter), William (of Auvergne, of Auxerre) 8 Maritain (Jacques), Sabatier (Auguste), Teilhard (de Chardin, Pierre) *German:* 6 Rahner (Karl) 7 Eckhart (Meister) 8 Albertus (Magnus) 9 Niemöller (Martin) 10 Bonhoeffer (Dietrich) *Greek:* 9 Zygomalas (Theodore) *Italian:* 6 Thomas (Aquinas) 7 Aquinas (Thomas), Socinus (Fausto, Laelius) *Scottish:* 10 Duns Scotus (John) *Spanish:* 6 Suárez (Francisco) 7 Vitoria (Francisco de) 8 Servetus (Michael) *Swedish:* 9 Soderblom (Nathan) *Swiss:* 4 Küng (Hans) 5 Barth (Karl), Vinet (Alexandre-Rodolphe)

theological *school:* 8 seminary *virtue:* 4 hope 5 faith 7 charity ___ **Theologica** 5 Summa

theorbo 4 lute

theorem 3 law 4 rule 5 axiom 7 formula, inverse, stencil 8 converse 9 principle 10 principium 11 fundamental, proposition

theoretical 4 pure 5 ideal 8 abstract, academic, notional, unproved 11 conjectural, speculative 12 hypothetical 13 problematical, suppositional

theorize 5 guess 6 submit 7 suggest 9 formulate, postulate, speculate 10 conjecture 11 hypothesize

theory 7 perhaps, premise, surmise 8 supposal 10 conjecture, hypothesis 11 speculation, supposition *astronomical:* 7 big bang *suffix:* 3 ism

therapeutic 5 tonic 7 healing, helpful 8 curative, remedial, salutary, sanative 9 healthful, medicinal, vulnerary, wholesome 10 beneficial, corrective 11 restorative 12 health-giving

therapy 9 treatment

therefore 4 ergo, then, thus 5 hence 6 thence 11 accordingly 12 consequently

therefrom 4 away 6 thence

thereupon 4 ergo, then, thus 6 at once, at that, thence 8 directly 9 right away, therefore, wherefore 11 accordingly, straightway 12 consequently

thermal unit 3 Btu 6 degree 7 calorie

thermometer 5 gauge 9 indicator *kind:* 7 Celsius, Réaumur 10 centigrade, Fahrenheit

thermos 5 dewar 10 Dewar flask

Theroux work 9 Saint Jack 13 Mosquito Coast (The) 14 Half Moon Street 18 Great Railway Bazaar (The)

Thersites' slayer 8 Achilles

thesaurus editor 5 Roget (Peter Mark)

Theseus *beloved:* 7 Ariadne *father:* 6 Aegeus *mother:* 6 Aethra *slayer:* 9 Lycomedes *son:* 10 Hippolytus *victim:* 6 Sciron 8 Minotaur 10 Procrustes *wife:* 7 Phaedra

thesis 5 essay, point, theme 6 belief 7 premise 8 downbeat, position, tractate, treatise 9 discourse, monograph, postulate, synthesis 10 contention, exposition 11 postulation, proposition, supposition 12 disquisition, dissertation

thespian 5 actor 6 mummer, player 7 actress, trouper 8 dramatic 9 performer 10 histrionic, theatrical 11 dramaturgic 12 impersonator, melodramatic

Thespis' forte 5 drama 7 tragedy

Thessalian hero 5 Jason 8 Achilles ___ **the Terrible** 4 Ivan

Thetis 5 Nereid *father:* 6 Nereus *husband:* 6 Peleus *mother:* 5 Doris *son:* 8 Achilles

theurgist 5 witch 7 warlock 8 magician, sorcerer 12 wonder-worker

thew 4 beef 5 brawn, might, power, sinew, vigor 6 muscle 8 strength, vitality

thick 3 fat 4 wide 5 broad, bulky, burly, close, dense, dumpy, husky, squat, stout 6 chummy, chunky, packed, stocky 7 compact, crammed, crowded, viscous 8 familiar, heavyset, intimate 11 inspissated

thicken 3 set 4 blur, clot, jell 6 curdle 7 broaden, compact, congeal 8 condense 9 coagulate 10 inspissate 11 concentrate, consolidate

thicket 4 bosk, bush, shaw, wood 5 clump, copse, grove, hedge 6 bosket, covert, mallee, tangle 7 boscage, bosquet, coppice, spinney 8 hedgerow, quickset 9 brushwood, canebrake, chaparral

thickness 3 ply 4 loft 5 depth, gauge, layer, sheet 7 density 8 dullness 9 stupidity, viscosity

thickset 5 bulky, burly, husky, pudgy, stout 6 chunky, portly, stocky, sturdy 7 compact 9 corpulent

thief 3 dip 4 prig 5 ganef 6 bandit, lifter, looter, pirate, rascal, robber 7 booster, burglar, filcher, stealer 8 hijacker, larcener, pilferer, water rat 9 larcenist, purloiner 10 cat burglar, highwayman, pickpocket, shoplifter 12 housebreaker

thieve 3 rob 4 hook, lift, pick, roll 5 filch, pinch, pluck, steal, swipe 6 hijack, hold up, pilfer, rip off, snitch 7 purloin 8 knock off 9 knock over

thievery see THEFT

thievish 9 larcenous 13 light-fingered

thigh 3 ham 5 flank 6 gammon *bone:* 5 femur *relating to:* 6 crural 7 femoral

thimble 3 cup 5 cover

thin 4 fine, lank, lean, slim 5 gaunt, lanky, reedy, scant, sharp, spare 6 dilute, flimsy, meager, meagre, rarefy, scanty, skimpy, skinny, slight, sparse, stalky, treble, twiggy, watery 7 diluted, scraggy, scrawny, slender, spindly, squinny, subtile, tenuous 8 rarefied, skeletal 9 attenuate, extenuate 10 attenuated 11 watered-down 13 unsubstantial

thing 4 item 5 being, event 6 entity, matter, object 7 article, concern, element 8 business, incident, material, occasion 9 existence, happening 10 occurrence, phenomenon *in law:* 3 res

thingamajig 5 gizmo 6 dingus, doodad, gadget, jigger, widget 7 whatsit 9 doohickey

things 4 gear 5 goods, stock, stuff 7 baggage, clothes, effects, luggage 8 chattels, clothing, matériel, movables, property, supplies 10 belongings, provisions 11 impedimenta, merchandise 13 accoutrements, paraphernalia

think 4 mull, muse 5 brood, study, weigh 6 ideate, ponder, reason 7 believe, imagine, reflect, suppose, surmise 8 cogitate, consider, meditate, ruminate 9 cerebrate, speculate 10 conjecture, deliberate, excogitate 11 contemplate

Thinker sculptor 5 Rodin (Auguste)

third 8 tertiary *combining form:* 3 tri *power:* 4 cube

third degree 7 torture 8 grilling 11 inquisition, questioning 13 interrogation

third estate 5 plebs 6 people, plebes 8 populace 9 commonage, commoners, plebeians 10 commonalty 11 rank and file

Third Man author 6 Greene (Graham)

Third of May painter 4 Goya (Francisco)

thirst 3 yen 4 itch, long, lust, pine 5 crave, yearn 6 desire, hanker, hunger 7 craving, dryness, longing 8 appetite

thirsty 3 dry 4 arid, avid 5 eager 6 ardent 7 anxious, bone-dry, parched 8 droughty 9 absorbent, waterless

this and that 8 oddments, sundries 9 etceteras 11 miscellanea, odds and ends

Thisbe's lover 7 Pyramus

This Side of Paradise author 10 Fitzgerald (F. Scott)

thistle 4 weed 7 caltrop *Russian:* 10 tumbleweed

thistlebird 9 goldfinch

thither 3 yon 5 there 6 yonder

thole 3 peg, pin 6 endure

Thomas à ___ 6 Becket, Kempis

Thomas's Greek name 7 Didymus

Thomas opera 6 Mignon

Thompson 4 Emma 5 Sadie 6 Hunter 7 Dorothy, Francis, J. Walter 8 Benjamin

thong 4 band, lace, lash, rein, zori 5 lasso, strap, strip, whang 6 sandal 7 latchet 8 flip-flop

Thor 5 Donar *father:* 4 Odin 5 Wotan *god of:* 7 thunder *hammer:* 8 Mjollnir *mother:* 5 Jordh, Jorth

thorax 5 chest, trunk 6 pereon

Thoreau, Henry David *friend:* 7 Emerson (Ralph Waldo) *town:* 7 Concord *work:* 6 Walden

thorn 4 barb 5 briar, spike, spine 7 prickle, spinule 9 annoyance 10 irritation

thorny 5 sharp, spiny 6 briary, touchy, tricky 7 awkward, prickly, spinous 8 ticklish 9 difficult, vexatious 10 nettlesome 11 troublesome

thorough 4 full 6 minute 7 careful, in-depth 8 complete, detailed, diligent, whole-hog 9 downright 10 blow-by-blow, exhaustive, meticulous 11 painstaking 13 conscientious

thoroughbred 8 pedigree, purebred 9 pedigreed, pureblood 10 bloodstock 11 full-blooded

thoroughfare 3 way 4 road 5 track 6 artery, avenue, street 7 highway, parkway 8 corridor 9 boulevard

thoroughgoing 5 utter 6 all-out 7 extreme 8 absolute, complete, outright, whole-hog 9 out-and-out 10 consummate, exhaustive 11 straight-out, unmitigated 13 dyed-in-the-wool

thou 3 you 5 grand *French:* 5 mille

though 3 yet 5 still, while 6 albeit 7 however, whereas 8 after all 11 nonetheless 12 nevertheless

thought 4 idea 6 notion, reason 7 concept, opinion 8 ideation 9 brainwork 10 cogitation, conception, meditation, reflection, rumination 11 cerebration, speculation 12 deliberation, intellection 13 contemplation

thoughtful 6 polite 7 careful, gallant, heedful, mindful, pensive, serious, studied 8 gracious, studious, thinking 9 attentive, courteous, pondering, regardful 10 cogitative, meditative, reflective, ruminative, solicitous 11 considerate 12 deliberative, intellectual 13 contemplative

thoughtless 4 rash, rude 5 brash, hasty 6 madcap 7 selfish 8 careless, feckless, heedless, impolite, reckless, uncaring 9 insensate 10 incautious, ungracious 12 discourteous 13 inconsiderate

thousand *combining form:* 4 kilo *dollars:* 5 grand *years:* 10 millennium

thousandth 10 millesimal *combining form:* 5 milli

thrall 4 peon, serf, yoke 5 helot, slave 7 bondage, bondman, helotry, peonage, serfdom, slavery, villein 9 servitude, villenage 10 absorption 11 enslavement

thrash 3 tan 4 beat, belt, drub, flog, hide, lash, lick, maul, pelt, trim, whip 5 baste, flail, pound, smear, swing, thump, whale, whang 6 batter, buffet, larrup, pummel, stripe, wallop 7 scourge, shellac, trounce 8 flounder, lambaste, work over 10 flagellate

thrash out 4 moot 5 argue 6 debate 7 discuss 10 deliberate, kick around

thread 4 line, vein, yard 5 fiber, trail, weave 6 strand, stream, string 8 filament *ball of:* 4 clew *dental:* 5 floss *holder:* 6 bobbin *kind:* 4 silk, yarn 5 floss, lisle 6 cotton 8 surgical *loose:* 8 raveling 9 ravelling *surgical:* 6 catgut, suture

threadbare 4 hack, worn 5 dingy, faded, seedy, stale, tacky, tatty, tired, trite 6 beat-up, cheesy, cliché, frayed, ragged, shabby, shoddy 7 clichéd, run-down, tedious, worn-out 8 shopworn, slipshod, tattered, timeworn, well-worn 9 destitute, hackneyed 10 down-at-heel 11 commonplace, dilapidated, down-at-heels, stereotyped 13 down-at-the-heel

threadlike 11 filamentous

threads 4 duds 7 clothes 8 clothing, garments

threat 6 danger, duress, menace 7 assault, warning 8 big stick, coercion 11 thunderbolt

threaten 3 cow 4 warn 5 augur 6 coerce, menace 7 caution, portend, presage 8 endanger, forebode, forewarn, overhang 10 intimidate

three 4 trey 5 crowd *combining form:* 3 ter, tri

threefold 5 trine 6 thrice, treble, trinal, triple 7 triplex

Three Musicians artist 7 Picasso (Pablo)

Three Musketeers 5 Athos 6 Aramis 7 Porthos *author:* 5 Dumas (Alexandre) *friend:* 9 D'Artagnan

Threepenny Opera, The *author:* 6 Brecht (Bertolt) *music:* 5 Weill (Kurt)

threescore 5 sixty

Three Sisters, The 4 Olga 5 Irina, Masha *author:* 7 Chekhov (Anton)

threesome 4 trio 5 triad, trine 6 triple, triune, troika 7 trinity 8 triangle 11 triumvirate

three-wheeler 5 cycle, trike 7 pedicab 8 tricycle 10 velocipede

threnody 5 dirge, elegy 6 lament

thresh 3 lam, tan 4 beat, belt, drub, flog, hide, lash, lick, pelt, trim, wave, whip 5 baste, forge, flail, pound, slate, smear, swing, thump, whale, whang 6 batter, buffet, larrup, pummel, strike, stripe, wallop, winnow 7 scourge, shellac, trounce 8 lambaste, work over 10 flagellate

threshold 3 eve 4 door, edge, gate, sill 5 brink, limen, verge 6 outset 8 boundary

thrift 6 saving 7 economy, sea pink 8 prudence 9 frugality, parsimony

thrifty 5 canny 6 frugal, saving 7 sparing 9 provident 10 economical 12 parsimonious

thrill 3 wow 4 bang, boot, kick, rush, send 5 blast, throb 6 charge, excite, shiver, tingle, wallop 7 frisson, tremble, vibrate 9 electrify 10 excitement 11 titillation

thriller 6 gothic **7** chiller, mystery, shocker **8** whodunit **9** dime novel **10** hairraiser **13** penny dreadful

thrive 4 boom, grow **7** advance, burgeon, develop, prosper, succeed **8** flourish, get ahead

throat 3 maw **4** tube **5** gorge **6** groove, gullet **7** channel, weasand *inflammation:* **5** croup **6** angina, quinsy **10** laryngitis *relating to:* **8** guttural *warmer:* **5** scarf

throaty 5 gruff, husky, thick **6** hoarse **8** gravelly, guttural

throb 4 ache, beat, drum **5** pound, pulse **6** thrill **7** pulsate, vibrate **9** palpitate

throe 3 fit **4** pain, pang **5** agony, spasm **6** attack **7** seizure **9** suffering **10** convulsion **11** contraction

thrombus 4 clot **8** blockage, coagulum

throne 4 seat **5** chair, crown, power, reign **8** cathedra, dominion **11** sovereignty

throng 3 jam, mob **4** host, pack, push, rout **5** bunch, crowd, crush, drove, flock, group, horde, press, scrum, shoal, swarm **6** resort **9** multitude **10** assemblage

throttle 3 gun **5** choke **6** throat **7** garrote, trachea **8** strangle, suppress **11** accelerator, strangulate

through 3 per, via **4** done, past **5** due to, ended **6** direct **7** by way of, done for, nonstop, owing to **8** by dint of, complete, finished, washed-up **9** because of, by means of, completed, concluded **10** by virtue of, terminated, throughout *prefix:* **3** dia, per

throughout 3 mid **4** amid **5** midst **6** during **7** all over, overall **10** everywhere, far and near, far and wide, high and low

Through the Looking Glass *author:* **7** Carroll (Lewis) *character:* **5** Alice

throve 9 burgeoned, prospered **10** flourished

throw 3 lob, peg, put **4** cast, fire, hurl, toss **5** chuck, fling, heave, pitch, sling **6** launch, propel **7** buck off, project *in the towel:* **4** quit **6** give up

throw away 4 blow, cast, junk, shed **5** scrap, waste **7** discard, fritter **8** jettison, squander

throwback 7 atavism **9** reversion

throw down the gauntlet 4 defy **8** confront **9** challenge

throw off 4 lose, shed **5** addle, shake **7** confuse, fluster **8** befuddle, bewilder, distract *the track:* **6** derail **7** confuse, mislead

throw out 4 emit, junk, shed **5** chuck, eject, evict, scrap **6** reject **7** discard **8** jettison

throw up 4 barf, cast, hurl, lose, puke, quit, spew, toss **5** heave, retch, vomit **7** upchuck **8** disgorge **11** regurgitate

thrush 5 mavis, ouzel, robin, veery **6** mistle **8** bluebird **9** blackbird, fieldfare, mistletoe **11** nightingale

thrust 3 dig, jab, ram **4** barb, butt, core, cram, dash, dive, duck, gist, hurl, kick, pith, poke, prod, push, stab, tilt **5** barge, crowd, cut in, drive, force, lunge, press, punch, sense, shoot, shove, spear, stick, stuff **6** burden, extend, insert, pierce, plunge, propel, upshot **7** assault, obtrude, project, purport, riposte **8** pressure **9** substance

thud 3 jar **4** bump, jolt, plop **5** clunk, throb, thump **6** impact **10** concussion

thug 3 mug **4** goon, hood, punk **5** bully, rough, rowdy, tough **6** Apache, Capone, gunman, hit man **7** hoodlum, mobster, ruffian **8** enforcer, gangster, hooligan, plug-ugly **9** cutthroat, roughneck

thumb 4 leaf, turn **5** digit, hitch, ovolo **6** pollex, riffle **8** pollices (plural) **9** hitchhike

thumbs-up 3 AOK, nod **4** okay **7** goahead **10** green light

thumb through 4 scan **6** browse, riffle **7** dip into

thump 3 bop, hit **4** bash, beat, belt, blow, drub, jolt, pelt, whip **5** knock, paste, pound, punch, shock, smack, sound, whack **6** batter, buffet, impact, pummel, strike, thrash, thwack, wallop **7** clobber, endorse, promote, shellac, trounce **8** advocate

thunder 4 bang, boom, clap, peal, roar **6** rumble **7** resound **8** rumbling **9** fulminate

thunderbolt 9 lightning

thunder lizard 11 apatosaurus **12** brontosaurus

thunderstruck 5 agape **6** amazed **7** shocked, stunned **8** dismayed **9** astounded, staggered **10** astonished, bewildered, confounded **11** dumbfounded **13** flabbergasted

Thurber character 5 Mitty (Walter)

thus 3 sic **4** ergo, then **5** hence **9** therefore **11** accordingly **12** consequently *French:* **5** ainsi

Thus Spake Zarathustra *author* **9** Nietzsche (Friedrich)

thwack 3 bop **4** belt, biff, blow, pelt, sock, whop **5** crack, pound, smack, thump, whack

thwart 4 balk, beat, dash, foil **5** bench **6** baffle, hinder, oppose, scotch, stymie **9** checkmate, frustrate **10** circumvent, contravene, disappoint

Thyestes *brother:* 6 Atreus *daughter:* 7 Pelopia *father:* 6 Pelops *mother:* 10 Hippodamia *son:* 9 Aegisthus

Tiamat *husband:* 4 Apsu *slayer:* 6 Marduk

tiara 5 crown 6 diadem 8 headband

Tibetan *animal:* 3 yak 5 takin *capital:* 5 Lhasa *coin:* 5 tanga *monk:* 4 lama *people:* 6 Bhotia, Sherpa

tibia 8 shinbone

tic 5 quirk, spasm 6 twitch 9 twitching

tick 5 check 8 arachnid, parasite 9 checkmark 11 bloodsucker

ticker 4 bomb 5 clock, heart, watch

ticket 3 key, tag 4 comp, pass, vote 5 slate 6 ballot 7 receipt 8 passport, password 10 open sesame *seller:* 7 scalper

tickle 4 stir 5 amuse, tease, touch 6 arouse, excite, please, tingle 7 delight, gratify, provoke 9 stimulate, titillate

tickled 5 happy 6 amused 7 pleased 9 delighted

ticklish 6 tender, thorny, touchy, tricky 8 delicate, unstable 9 sensitive 10 precarious 13 oversensitive

tick off 3 ire, irk 5 anger 6 rankle 7 incense, provoke 9 aggravate

tidal flood 4 bore

tidbit 4 bite 5 goody, treat 6 dainty, morsel, nugget

tide 4 flow, flux, rush 5 drift, flood, spate, surge 6 stream 7 current, holiday *type:* 3 ebb, low 4 high, neap 5 flood 6 spring

tidings 4 news, word 6 advice 7 message 11 information 12 intelligence

tidy 4 fair, neat, smug, snug, trim 5 kempt 6 pick up 7 clean up, orderly, precise 9 shipshape 10 acceptable, methodical 11 respectable, spic-and-span, substantial, uncluttered, well-groomed 12 satisfactory, spick-and-span

tie 3 rod 4 band, bind, bond, cord, draw, gird, join, knit, knot, lash, link, moor, rope, yoke 5 equal, leash, match, truss 6 attach, cravat, fasten, fetter, hamper, oxford, ribbon, secure 7 connect, harness, shackle 8 dead heat, deadlock, fastener, ligament, ligature, restrain, shoelace, standoff, vinculum 9 constrain, stalemate 10 attachment, four-in-hand

tied 5 bound 6 joined, united 8 attached, fastened 9 connected

tier 3 row 4 bank, deck, file, line, rank 5 class, grade, group, story 6 league 7 echelon 8 category, grouping

tie-up 3 jam 4 snag 5 crimp, delay, hitch 6 glitch 7 problem 8 gridlock, slow-down, stoppage 10 connection, traffic jam 11 association

tiff 3 row 4 fuss, spat 5 run-in, scrap 6 bicker 7 brabble, dispute, quarrel, wrangle 8 argument, squabble 10 falling-out 11 altercation 12 disagreement

tiffany 5 gauze 11 cheesecloth

tiger 3 cat 6 feline 9 carnivore *young:* 3 cub

tight 4 fast, firm, snug, taut, trim 5 cheap, close, drunk, fixed, tipsy 6 firmly, secure, stingy 7 compact, crowded, drunken, miserly 8 intimate 9 tenacious 10 inebriated 11 closefisted, intoxicated 12 cheeseparing, parsimonious 13 penny-pinching

tighten 4 bind 5 choke, close, cramp, pinch, screw 6 clench, fasten, narrow, secure, shrink 8 compress, restrict 9 clamp down, constrict

tightfisted see STINGY

tight-lipped 6 silent 8 reserved, reticent, taciturn 12 closemouthed

tightwad 5 miser, piker 7 niggard, scrooge 9 skinflint 10 cheapskate 12 penny-pincher

tile 5 plate, slate 6 domino 7 tessera 8 linoleum

till 3 hoe, sow 4 disk, plow, tend, turn, up to, work 6 before, harrow 7 prior to 9 cultivate 11 in advance of 12 cash register

tillable 6 arable 10 cultivable 12 cultivatable

tillage 4 farm, land 5 tilth 7 culture 11 cultivation

tiller 4 helm 5 stalk 6 farmer, sprout 7 planter, steerer 9 sodbuster 10 cultivator

tilt 3 tip 4 bank, bent, bias, cant, cock, heel, lean, list, toss 5 grade, joust, level, lurch, pitch, slant, slope, speed 6 attack, charge, thrust 7 dispute, incline, leaning, recline 8 gradient 11 inclination

timbal 4 drum 10 kettledrum

timber 3 log 4 balk, beam, stud, tree, wood 5 board, joist, plank, trees, woods 6 forest, girder, lumber, rafter 8 woodland *uncut:* 8 stumpage *wolf:* 4 lobo

timbre 4 tone 6 temper 7 quality 9 resonance, tone color

timbrel 4 drum 10 tambourine

time 3 age, era 4 bout, date, hour, pace, span, term 5 clock, epoch, shift, space, spell, stint, tempo, while 6 moment, period, season 7 instant, stretch 8 duration, occasion 11 opportunity *combining form:* 5 chron 6 chrono *gone by:*

4 past **9** yesterday *long:* **3** age, eon, era
4 aeon *of day:* **4** dawn, dusk, noon
5 night **6** sunset **7** evening, morning,
sunrise **8** daybreak, twilight **9** afternoon
olden: **4** yore **10** yesteryear *period:*
3 age, day, eon, era **4** aeon, hour, week,
year **5** epoch, month **6** decade, minute,
moment, second **7** century, instant
9 fortnight **10** millennium *present:*
3 now *relating to:* **8** temporal *short:*
5 jiffy **6** moment, second **7** instant *to
come:* **6** future **8** tomorrow *waste:* **4** loaf
5 dally **6** loiter
time and again 3 oft **5** often **6** hourly
8 commonly, ofttimes **10** constantly, frequently, oftentimes, repeatedly **11** continually, over and over **12** periodically
Time founder 4 Luce (Henry R.) **6** Had-
den (Briton)
timeless 7 ageless, eternal, unaging
8 unageing **9** atemporal, perpetual
11 everlasting
timely 5 early **6** prompt, proper **8** punctual, suitable **9** opportune **10** seasonable **11** appropriate
Time Machine author 5 Wells (H. G.)
Time of Your Life author 7 Saroyan
(William)
time-out 4 rest **5** break, pause **6** hiatus,
recess **7** respite **8** breather **9** interlude
12 interruption
timepiece 5 clock, watch **7** sundial
8 horologe **9** clepsydra, stopwatch
10 water clock **11** chronograph,
chronometer
timetable 6 agenda, docket **7** program
8 calendar, schedule
timeworn 3 old **4** aged, hack **5** hoary,
stale, trite **6** age-old **7** ancient **8** dog-
eared, Noachian **9** hackneyed
10 threadbare
time zone 7 Central, Eastern, Pacific
8 Mountain
timid 3 shy **4** wary **5** chary, mousy
6 afraid, yellow **7** bashful, chicken,
fearful, halting, nervous, panicky
8 cowardly, retiring, timorous **9** diffident, tentative, trepidant, uncertain
11 unassertive **12** apprehensive, fainthearted
timidity 4 fear **7** modesty, shyness
8 meekness **9** hesitancy, reticence
10 diffidence, hesitation
Timon's servant 7 Flavius
timorous 4 wary **5** timid **6** afraid **7** fearful **8** retiring **9** shrinking, tremulous
12 apprehensive
Timothy's associate 4 Paul
tin 3 box, can **5** metal **7** element **9** container *mining region:* **8** stannary *relating
to:* **7** stannic **8** stannous *sheet:* **6** latten

tincture 3 dye **4** cast, hint, tint **5** color,
shade, smack, stain, tinge, touch, trace
6 iodine, streak **8** colorant, dyestuff,
laudanum **9** paregoric **10** intimation,
suggestion
tinder 4 punk **5** spunk **8** kindling
tine 5 point, prong, spike **6** branch
tinge 3 dye, hue **4** cast, hint, tint, tone
5 color, imbue, shade, stain, tinct,
touch **8** tincture **10** intimation
tingle 5 sting **6** thrill **7** prickle **9** sensation
tinker 3 fix **4** mend, mess, muck, play
5 gypsy **6** adjust, diddle, fiddle, mender,
potter, putter, repair **7** bungler, twiddle
9 repairman
tinkle 4 ring, ting **5** chink, clink, plink
6 jingle
tinny 4 thin **5** cheap, harsh **8** metallic
Tin Pan Alley acronym 3 BMI **5** ASCAP
tinsel 5 gaudy **6** flashy, garish, tawdry
7 chintzy, glaring, trinket **8** ornament,
specious **9** clinquant **11** superficial
12 meretricious
tint 3 dye, hue **4** cast, tone, wash **5** color,
shade, tinge, touch **8** tincture **10** coloration **12** pigmentation
tiny 3 wee **5** bitsy, bitty, elfin, pygmy,
teeny, weeny **6** minute, peewee, pocket,
teensy, weensy **8** pint-size **9** itsy-bitsy,
itty-bitty, miniature, minuscule
10 diminutive, pocket-size, teeny-
weeny **11** lilliputian, microscopic
12 teensy-weensy **13** infinitesimal
tip 3 cap, cue, top **4** apex, cant, clue,
cusp, heel, hint, lean, list, peak, perk,
tilt **5** point, slant, slope, steer, upset
6 advice, topple **7** cumshaw, incline
8 gratuity, overturn, turn over **9** baksheesh, lagniappe, pourboire **11** information
tip-off 4 clue, hint, sign **6** advice **7** pointer, warning **8** giveaway, jump ball
10 indication
Tippecanoe and ___ too 5 Tyler
tippet 4 cape **5** scarf **8** liripipe
tipple 3 bib, sip **4** swig, tope **5** booze,
drink **6** guzzle, imbibe **7** swizzle
8 liquor up
tippler 3 sot **4** lush, soak **5** drunk, toper
6 bibber, boozer **7** tosspot **8** drunkard
9 inebriate
tipstaff 7 bailiff
tipster 4 fink **6** canary, snitch **7** adviser,
rat fink, stoolie, tattler **8** informer,
squealer **11** stool pigeon
tipsy 3 lit **4** high **5** askew, drunk, lit up,
oiled, tight **7** drunken, fuddled
8 unsteady **10** inebriated **11** intoxicated
tiptoe 5 creep, steal **9** pussyfoot
tirade 4 rant **6** screed **8** diatribe,
harangue, jeremiad **9** philippic

12 denunciation, vituperation
13 tongue-lashing
tire 3 sap 4 bore, fail, flag, jade, pall, poop, wear 5 drain, droop, ennui, weary, wheel 6 tucker, weaken 7 exhaust, fatigue, wear out 8 enervate, wear down *airless:* 4 flat 7 blowout *kind:* 4 bias, snow 6 radial 7 retread 9 whitewall
tired 4 worn 5 spent, weary 6 done in 7 drained, run-down, worn out 8 fatigued, flagging 9 enervated, exhausted
tiredness 7 fatigue 8 collapse 9 lassitude 10 exhaustion 11 prostration
tireless 10 unflagging 13 indefatigable, inexhaustible
Tiresias 4 seer 10 soothsayer
tiresome 4 dull 5 stale 6 boring 7 irksome, lumpish, operose, tedious
Tirol *capital:* 9 Innsbruck *country:* 7 Austria *mountains:* 4 Alps
Tisiphone see ERINYES
tissue 3 web 4 film, mesh 5 fiber, gauze, paper 6 fabric *anatomical:* 4 tela 5 fiber 6 diploe 8 ganglion 10 epithelium *connective:* 6 stroma, tendon 9 cartilage *kind:* 3 fat 5 nerve 6 muscle 7 nervous 8 muscular 10 connective *layer:* 6 dermis 7 stratum *plant:* 4 bast, wood 5 xylem 6 phloem
titan 5 giant 8 colossus
Titan *father:* 6 Uranus *female:* 4 Rhea 6 Tethys, Themis *male:* 6 Cronus 7 Iapetus, Oceanus *mother:* 4 Gaea
Titan author 7 Dreiser (Theodore)
Titania's husband 6 Oberon
titanic 4 huge, vast 5 great 6 mighty 7 immense, mammoth, massive 8 colossal, enormous, gigantic 9 cyclopean, Herculean, monstrous 10 gargantuan, tremendous
tithe 3 tax 4 levy 5 tenth 12 contribution
Tithonus *beloved by:* 3 Eos *father:* 8 Laomedon
Titian painting 5 Danaë 8 Ecce Homo 10 Assumption (The), Holy Family (The) 12 Rape of Europa (The) 13 Maltese Knight, Medea and Venus, Venus and Cupid 14 Worship of Venus (The) 17 Bacchus and Ariadne
titillate 6 arouse, excite, stir up, thrill, tickle 9 stimulate
title 3 dub, due 4 call, deed, dibs, name, term 5 claim, merit, nomen 7 baptize, caption, heading 8 christen, cognomen, pretense 9 designate 10 denominate, pretension 11 appellation, appellative, designation 12 championship, compellation, denomination *Dutch:* 7 mynheer *ecclesiastic:* 8 reverend *feminine:* 3 Mrs.

4 dame, lady, ma'am, miss 5 madam 6 madame, milady, missus 8 mistress *French:* 6 madame 8 monsieur 12 mademoiselle *German:* 4 Frau, Herr 8 Fräulein *holder:* 5 noble 8 champion *Indian:* 3 sri 5 sahib *Islamic:* 5 hajji 6 sayyid 9 ayatollah *Italian:* 5 donna 6 signor 7 signora 9 signorina *monk's:* 3 fra 7 brother *of nobility:* 3 sir 4 duke, earl, king, lady, lord, sire 5 baron, count, queen 6 prince 7 baronet, duchess, marquis 8 Archduke, baroness, countess, marchesa, marchese, marquise, princess, viscount 11 marchioness, viscountess *Oriental:* 4 khan *Persian:* 5 mirza *Portuguese:* 3 dom 4 dona 6 senhor 7 senhora 9 senhorita *Spanish:* 3 don 4 doña *Turkish:* 3 bey
titmouse 4 bird 6 tomtit 7 bushtit 9 chickadee
Tito 4 Broz (Josip)
titter 5 laugh 6 giggle 7 chortle, chuckle, snicker, snigger
tittle 3 bit, jot 4 atom, iota, mite 5 minim, speck 7 smidgen 8 particle 9 diacritic
titular 5 legal 6 titled 7 nominal 8 so-called 11 designative
Tityus *father:* 4 Zeus *slayer:* 6 Apollo
Tiu see TYR
tizzy 4 flap, fume, snit, stew 5 sweat 6 dither, swivet, uproar
T-man 5 agent 8 revenuer
to *be sure:* 6 indeed 7 granted 9 certainly *Scottish:* 3 tae *wit:* 3 viz 6 namely, that is 8 scilicet
toad 6 anuran, peeper 8 truckler 9 amphibian, brownnose, sycophant 10 batrachian, bootlicker 11 lickspittle *genus:* 4 Bufo
toady 4 fawn 5 cower, leech 6 cringe, flunky, grovel, kowtow, lackey, sponge 7 truckle 8 bootlick, parasite, truckler 9 brownnose, sycophant 10 bootlicker 11 apple-polish, lickspittle
toast 5 bread, drink, skoal 6 cheers, health, l'chaim, pledge, prosit, salute 7 wassail 8 mazel tov *kind:* 5 melba 6 French 8 zwieback
toastmaster 5 emcee
To a Waterfowl author 6 Bryant (William Cullen)
tobacco 4 leaf, weed *cask:* 8 hogshead *chewing:* 4 chaw, quid *ingredient:* 3 tar 8 nicotine *juice:* 6 ambeer *kind:* 4 shag 5 snuff 6 burley 7 caporal, perique, Turkish 9 broadleaf, mundungus *pipe:* 4 heel 6 dottle *rolled:* 5 cigar 9 cigarette *Turkish:* 7 latakia
Tobacco Road author 8 Caldwell (Erskine)

to be *Latin:* 4 esse

Tobias *father:* 5 Tobit *son:* 8 Hyrcanus

toby 3 jug, mug 7 pitcher

tocsin 3 SOS 5 alarm, alert 6 signal

today 3 now 9 currently, presently

toddler 3 tot 4 tyke

to-do 4 fuss, rout, stir 5 hoo-ha, rouse, stink, whirl 6 bother, bustle, clamor, furore, hubbub, hurrah, pother, ruckus, rumpus, uproar 7 turmoil 8 foofaraw 9 agitation, commotion 10 hurly-burly 11 disturbance

toe 5 digit *big:* 6 hallux *combining form:* 6 dactyl

toehold 7 footing

toff 3 fop 4 beau 5 blade, dandy, swell 7 coxcomb, peacock 8 macaroni, popinjay 9 exquisite 12 clotheshorse

toga 4 gown, robe, wrap

together 6 at once, joined, united 7 jointly 8 mutually 10 conjointly 11 concertedly 12 coincidently, collectively, concurrently *prefix:* 3 col, com, con, cor, sym, syn

togetherness 5 union 7 cahoots 8 alliance 10 connection, solidarity 11 affiliation, association, combination, conjunction, partnership

toggle 3 pin 6 fasten, switch 9 alternate 10 crosspiece

Togo *capital:* 4 Lomé *language:* 3 Ewe 6 French *monetary unit:* 5 franc *neighbor:* 5 Benin, Ghana 11 Burkina Faso

togs 3 rig 4 duds, suit 5 dress 6 attire, outfit 7 apparel, clothes, raiment, rigging 8 clothing, ensemble, garments

To His Coy Mistress *author:* 7 Marvell (Andrew)

toil 3 fag, net, tug 4 grub, plod, plug, slog, trap, work 5 grind, labor, slave, snare, sweat 6 drudge 7 slavery, travail 8 drudgery

toiler 4 peon 5 slave 6 drudge, slavey 9 workhorse

toilet 3 loo 4 head, john 5 bidet, potty, privy 6 johnny 7 latrine 8 bathroom, lavatory 11 water closet

toilsome 4 hard 5 heavy 6 uphill 7 arduous, labored 9 difficult, effortful, laborious, strenuous

Tokay 4 wine

token 4 buck, chip, gift, mark, note, sign 5 badge, check, favor, index, piece, plume, prize, relic, scrip 6 copper, emblem, pledge, symbol, ticket, trophy 7 earnest, gesture, memento, symptom, warrant 8 evidence, keepsake, memorial, reminder, security, souvenir 9 indicator 10 expression, indication 11 perfunctory, remembrance

To Kill a Mockingbird *author:* 3 Lee (Harper)

Tokyo *formerly:* 3 Edo *island:* 6 Honshu

tolerable 4 fair 6 common, decent 7 livable 8 adequate, all right, bearable, passable 9 endurable 10 acceptable, sufferable 11 respectable 12 satisfactory

tolerably 4 so-so 5 quite 6 fairly, pretty, rather 8 passably 9 averagely 10 moderately

tolerance 6 leeway 8 patience 9 allowance, endurance, deviation, fortitude, variation 10 indulgence, resistance, sufferance 11 forbearance, habituation

tolerant 4 easy 5 broad 7 lenient, liberal 8 placable 9 easygoing, eurytopic, forgiving, indulgent, tractable 10 openminded, permissive 11 broad-minded, progressive, sympathetic 13 understanding

tolerate 4 bear, bide, hack 5 abide, allow, brook, stand 6 accept, endure, pardon, permit, suffer 7 condone, stomach, swallow 8 bear with, live with 9 put up with 11 countenance

Tolkien *creature:* 3 Ent, Orc 5 Ainur 6 Balrog, Hobbit, Nazgul, Shelob 9 Oliphaunt

toll 3 fee, tax 4 bell, bong, cost, levy, peal, ring 5 chime, knell, price, sound 6 charge, summon, tariff 7 expense 8 casualty 10 assessment

tollbooth 11 customhouse

Tolstoy *novel:* 8 Cossacks (The) 11 War and Peace 12 Anna Karenina 16 Death of Ivan Ilich (The)

tomato 9 love apple

tomb 5 crypt, grave 6 burial 9 mausoleum, sepulcher, sepulchre, sepulture *ancient Egyptian:* 7 mastaba *empty:* 8 cenotaph

tomboy 6 gamine, hoyden

tombstone 4 slab 8 memorial, monument 11 grave marker *inscription:* 3 RIP 8 hic jacet

tome 4 book 6 volume

___ Tomé and Príncipe 3 Sao

tomfool 3 ass 4 dolt, fool, jerk 5 crazy, idiot, loony, ninny, silly, wacky 6 absurd, donkey, stupid 7 doltish, foolish, jackass 8 clodpoll, dummkopf, imbecile 9 blockhead, fantastic, horse's ass, thickhead 10 dunderhead, nincompoop 11 chowderhead, chucklehead, harebrained 12 preposterous

tomfoolery 4 dido, lark 5 antic, caper, prank, shine, trick 6 frolic 8 escapade, fandango 9 high jinks 10 shenanigan 11 monkeyshine

Tom Jones *author:* 8 Fielding (Henry)

tommyrot 4 bull 5 hooey, trash
7 baloney, hogwash, rubbish 8 claptrap,
nonsense 10 balderdash 13 horsefeathers

Tom o'Bedlam 3 nut 4 loon 5 loony
6 madman, maniac 7 lunatic 9 bedlamite

tomorrow 6 future, mañana

Tom Sawyer *author:* 5 Twain (Mark)
7 Clemens (Samuel) *character:* 5 Becky
(Thatcher) 8 Huck Finn, Injun Joe
9 Aunt Polly 10 Muff Potter

Tom Thumb 4 runt 5 dwarf, pygmy
6 midget, peanut, peewee 7 manikin
8 half-pint 10 homunculus 11 lilliputian

ton 3 lot 4 chic 5 bunch, style, trend,
vogue 6 bundle 7 fashion

tone 3 hue 4 cast, mode, mood, note,
tint, vein 5 color, pitch, shade, style,
tinge 6 accent, manner, spirit, strain,
temper, timbre 7 fashion 10 inflection

toned down 4 mute, soft 5 sober 6 low-
key, mellow 7 subdued 8 laid-back,
low-keyed, softened

Tonga *capital:* 9 Nuku'alofa *ethnic group:*
10 Polynesian *explorer:* 4 Cook (Capt.
James) 6 Tasman (Abel) *island group:*
5 Vava'u 6 Haapai 9 Tongatapu *language:* 6 Tongan 7 English *monetary
unit:* 6 pa'anga

tongue 4 lick, pole, tang 6 glossa, lingua,
speech 7 clapper, dialect, languet 8 language 10 vernacular *combining form:*
4 glot 5 gloss, lingu 6 glossa, glosso, lingua, lingui, linguo 7 glossia

tongue-lash 4 lash, rail 5 chide, scold
6 berate, rebuke, revile 7 bawl out,
chew out, tell off, reprove, upbraid
8 admonish, call down, reproach 9 castigate, reprimand 10 vituperate

tongue-lashing 6 rebuke, tirade 7 censure, reproof 8 scolding 9 reprimand,
talking-to 11 castigation
12 dressing-down

tongue-tied 3 mum, shy 4 mute 6 silent
7 bashful 9 diffident 10 speechless
12 inarticulate

tonic 3 pop 4 cola, soda 5 brisk 7 bracing, soda pop 8 curative, salutary
10 refreshing 11 restorative, stimulating
12 exhilarating, invigorating *extract:*
4 cola 9 berberine

tons 4 gobs, lots 5 heaps, loads, piles,
scads

tony 4 chic, posh 5 smart, swank, swish
6 classy, modish, uptown 7 à la mode,
elegant, stylish 9 exclusive 11 fashionable

too 4 also, ever, over, very 5 along 6 as
well, overly, unduly, withal 7 awfully,
besides, further, greatly 8 likewise,
moreover, overmuch 9 extremely,
immensely 10 in addition, remarkably,
strikingly 11 exceedingly, excessively,
furthermore 12 additionally, exorbi-
tantly, immoderately, inordinately
13 exceptionally

tool 4 pawn 5 means 6 puppet, rimmer,
stooge 7 cat's-paw, hayfork, machine,
rounder, utensil 8 picklock 9 appliance,
implement, mechanism 10 instrument
axlike: 4 adze *boring:* 5 auger, drill *carv-
ing:* 6 veiner *cleaving:* 4 froe *cobbler's:*
3 awl *cutting:* 3 axe, saw 4 adze 5 knife
6 shears 8 billhook *digging:* 4 pick
5 spade 6 shovel 7 mattock *engraving:*
5 burin *farm:* 6 seeder *filing:* 4 rasp 7 rif-
fler *garden:* 3 hoe 4 rake 5 spade 6 trowel, weeder *grasping:* 6 pincer 7 tweezer
8 tweezers *mining:* 6 trepan *prehistoric:*
6 eolith *pruning:* 6 shears 8 secateur *rubbing:* 9 burnisher *scooping:* 6 router
toothed: 3 saw 7 rippler *woodworking:*
3 saw 5 bevel, plane 6 chisel, hammer

toot 3 bat, jag 4 bout, bust, tear 5 binge,
blast, drunk, snort, sound, souse, spree
6 bender 7 carouse

tooth 5 molar 7 incisor 8 bicuspid, pre-
molar *combining form:* 4 dent 5 denti,
dento *cuspid:* 6 canine 8 dogtooth, eyetooth 10 carnassial *decay:*
6 caries *doctor:* 7 dentist *pointed:* 4 fang
6 canine, cuspid *small:* 8 denticle

toothless 7 useless 8 edentate 10 edentu-
lous 11 ineffective, ineffectual

toothsome 5 sapid, tasty 6 delish, savory
8 luscious, pleasant, pleasing, tasteful
9 agreeable, delicious, palatable, succulent 10 appetizing, attractive

too-too 6 la-di-da 7 extreme 8 affected,
overdone, overmuch, precious 9 excessive 10 hoity-toity, inordinate 11 exaggerated, overrefined, pretentious

tootsie 3 pet 4 dear 5 honey 7 beloved,
darling, sweetie 10 sweetheart

top 3 cap, tip 4 acme, apex, best, cusp,
head, peak, pick, roof 5 cream, crest,
crown, elite, point, prime, prize 6 apical, choice, climax, height, summit,
utmost, vertex 7 capital, highest, maximal, maximum, surface 8 five-star, loftiest, pinnacle, superior 9 first-rate,
uppermost 10 first-class 11 culmination

tope 3 nip 4 soak 5 booze, drink, shark,
stupa 6 guzzle, imbibe, tipple 7 swizzle
8 liquor up

toper 3 sot 4 lush, soak, wino 5 drunk,
rummy, souse 6 bibber, boozer 7 tippler, tosspot 8 drunkard 9 inebriate

Tophet 4 hell 5 hades, Sheol 6 blazes
7 Gehenna, inferno 9 perdition
10 underworld

topic 4 talk, text 5 issue, motif, point, score, theme 6 burden, matter, motive, thread 7 content, subject 8 argument 11 proposition

topical 5 local 7 current, nominal 8 regional 9 temporary 11 superficial

topmost 7 highest, leading, supreme 8 crowning, ultimate 9 paramount, principal 10 consummate, preeminent 11 culminating

top-notch 5 prime 6 choice 7 capital 8 five-star, superior 9 excellent, first-rate 10 first-class 11 first-string

top off 3 cap 5 crown 6 climax, finish, refill 8 complete, conclude, resupply 9 culminate

topography 7 surface, terrain 8 features

topple 3 tip 4 drop, fall 5 crash, lurch, pitch, slump, upset 6 defeat, falter, plunge, totter, tumble 8 collapse, keel over, overturn 9 overthrow

tops 4 best 5 primo 6 at most 7 highest 8 peerless, superior 9 at the most, first-rate, matchless 11 outstanding

topsy-turvy 7 chaotic, jumbled, mixed-up 8 cockeyed, confused, inverted 10 disjointed, disordered, upside down

toque 3 cap, hat

tor 4 crag, hill, peak 5 butte, cliff, mound, talus

Torah 10 Pentateuch

torch 4 fire 5 flame, light 6 ignite 7 fire-bug 8 arsonist, flambeau, guidance 10 flashlight, incendiary

toreador 6 torero 7 matador 11 bull-fighter

torero 7 matador 11 bullfighter

torment 3 rag, try, vex 4 bait, bane, hell, hurt, pain, pang, rack 5 abuse, agony, curse, grill, harry, tease, worry, wring 6 harass, harrow, heckle, misery, molest, needle, plague 7 afflict, agonize, anguish, crucify, distort, hagride, torture, travail, trouble 8 distress 9 perse-cute, tantalize 10 affliction, excruciate

torn 4 rent 5 split 6 ragged, ripped, unsure 7 mangled 8 tattered, wrenched 9 lacerated, uncertain, undecided

tornado 6 funnel 7 cyclone, twister 9 windstorm, whirlwind

toro 4 bull

torpedo 3 gun, ray 4 mine, thug 5 blast, bravo, smash, wreck 6 gunman, gunsel, hit man, killer, weapon 7 destroy, nulli-fy, scuttle 8 assassin, firework 9 explo-sive, shoot down 10 hatchet man, pro-jectile, triggerman 11 electric ray

torpid 4 dull, lazy, numb 5 dopey, inert 6 sodden, stupid 7 dormant 8 comatose, inactive, sluggish 9 apathetic, lethargic 12 hebetudinous

torpor 4 coma, daze 5 swoon 6 apathy, stupor 7 languor 8 dopiness, dullness, hebetude, lethargy 9 lassitude, passiv-ity, stolidity 10 stagnation 12 listlessness

torque 5 twist

torrent 4 rush 5 flood, spate 6 deluge, stream 7 cascade, Niagara 8 cataract, flooding 9 cataclysm 10 inundation, outpouring

torrid 3 hot 5 fiery 6 ardent, fervid, heat-ed, red-hot, sultry 7 boiling, burning, flaming, parched 8 broiling, white-hot 9 scorching 10 hot-blooded, passionate, sweltering 11 impassioned

tort 5 crime, wrong 7 offense 10 wrong-doing

tortilla dish 4 taco 6 flauta 7 burrito, chalupa, tostada 9 enchilada 10 que-sadilla 11 chimichanga

Tortilla Flat author 9 Steinbeck (John)

tortoise 6 turtle 8 terrapin 9 chelonian *beak:* 3 neb *shell:* 8 carapace

tortuous 5 snaky 6 cranky, tricky 7 crooked, devious, sinuous, winding 8 flexuous, indirect, involute, involved 9 meandrous 10 circuitous, convoluted, meandering, serpentine 11 anfractuous, vermiculate 12 labyrinthine

torture 4 pain, rack, warp 5 agony, wring 6 harrow, martyr 7 afflict, agonize, anguish, crucify, torment 9 martyrdom 10 excruciate 11 third degree

tortured 4 bent 6 racked, warped 7 twist-ed 8 deformed 9 distorted

tory 5 right 7 old-line 8 loyalist, old guard, orthodox, rightist, royalist 12 conservative

Tosca *character:* 5 Mario (Cavaradossi) 7 Scarpia (Baron) *composer:* 7 Puccini (Giacomo)

___ **Toscanini** 6 Arturo

tosh 3 rot 4 bosh, bunk 5 bilge, hooey 6 bunkum, drivel, humbug 7 baloney, eyewash, hogwash, twaddle 8 malarkey, nonsense, tommyrot, trumpery

toss 4 cast, flap, flip, hurl, rock, roll 5 chuck, drink, fling, heave, match, pitch, quaff, sling, surge, throw, vomit 6 imbibe, tumble, welter, writhe 7 dis-card 9 knock back, throw away

tosspot see TIPPLER

tot 3 add, kid, nip, sum 4 dram, shot, slug, tyke 5 child, snort 6 figure, infant, nipper, shaver, squirt 7 snifter, toddler

total 3 add, all, sum 4 foot, full 5 add up, equal, gross, run to, smash, sum to, utter, whole, wreck, yield 6 all-out, amount, budget, entire, figure, number 7 crack up, destroy, full-out, overall, perfect, plenary, quantum 8 absolute, complete, demolish, entirety, outright, positive, quantity **9** aggregate, full-blown, full-scale, inclusive, out-and-out, unlimited **10** consummate, unreserved **11** unmitigated **13** comprehensive, thoroughgoing

totalitarian 8 absolute, despotic **10** autocratic **11** dictatorial **13** authoritarian

totality 3 all, sum **4** lump **5** whole **7** oneness **8** entirety **9** aggregate, wholeness **12** completeness

totalize 3 add, sum **5** sum up **6** figure **7** summate

tote 3 lug **4** cart, haul, load, pack **5** carry, ferry, sum up **6** burden, convey, figure **7** summate **9** transport **10** pari-mutuel

totem 6 emblem, symbol

To the Lighthouse author 5 Woolf (Virginia)

totter 4 reel, sway **5** lurch, shake, waver **6** falter, toddle, topple, wobble **7** stagger

touch 4 abut, feel, meet, move, stir **5** brush, graze **6** adjoin, border, caress, finger, stroke **7** contact, palpate **9** palpation, tactility

touchable 7 tactile **8** palpable, tangible

touch down 4 land **5** light, perch, roost **6** alight, settle

touched 3 odd, off **5** batty, crazy, moved **7** stirred **8** affected **9** emotional

touching 4 as to, in re **5** about, anent, as for **6** moving, tender **7** against, apropos, emotive, meeting, piteous, pitiful, tangent **8** abutting, adjacent, pathetic, pitiable, poignant, stirring **9** adjoining, affecting, apropos of, as regards, bordering, immediate, impinging, regarding **10** as respects, back-to-back, concerning, contiguous, respecting, tangential **11** coterminous **12** conterminous

touch off 5 erupt, spark, start **6** ignite, incite, kindle **7** explode, inflame, provoke, trigger **8** initiate **9** instigate **11** precipitate

touchstone 4 test **5** check, gauge, proof, trial **7** measure **8** standard **9** barometer, benchmark, criterion, yardstick

touch up 3 fix **5** patch **6** rework **7** improve, perfect

touchy 5 dicey, huffy, risky, testy **6** tender, tricky **7** peppery **8** delicate, ticklish **9** explosive, hazardous, irascible, irritable, sensitive **10** precarious **11** inflammable, quarrelsome, thin-skinned **13** oversensitive, temperamental, unpredictable

tough 3 bad, mug **4** goon, hard, hood, lout, punk, stud, thug **5** bully, hardy, harsh **6** rugged, severe, sturdy, unruly **7** arduous, hoodlum, onerous, ruffian **8** bullyboy, exacting, hooligan, obdurate **9** arbitrary, demanding, difficult, effortful, hard-nosed, hidebound, immutable, laborious, resistant, roughneck, strenuous **10** hard-bitten, hard-boiled, hardheaded, inflexible, refractory, unyielding **11** intractable, unbreakable **12** pertinacious

toughen 5 inure **6** anneal, harden, season, temper **9** acclimate, habituate **10** strengthen **11** acclimatize

toughie 4 goon, hood, lout, punk, thug **5** poser, rowdy **7** hoodlum, ruffian, stumper **8** bullyboy, hooligan, plug-ugly **9** roughneck

toupee 3 rug, wig **6** peruke, wiglet **7** periwig **8** postiche **9** hairpiece

tour 4 bout, trip, turn **5** jaunt, round, shift, spell, stint **6** junket, period, travel, troupe **7** circuit, journey **8** progress **9** barnstorm, excursion **10** expedition, rubberneck

tour de force 4 deed, feat **7** classic, display, exploit **10** magnum opus, masterwork **11** achievement, chef d'oeuvre, masterpiece

tour guide 8 cicerone

tourist 7 tripper, visitor **8** traveler **9** sightseer, traveller **10** day-tripper, rubberneck, vacationer **12** excursionist, globe-trotter

tournament 4 open, tilt **5** pro-am **6** jousts, series **7** contest, tourney **8** carousel **10** round-robin **11** competition **12** championship

tourney 4 meet **5** event, games, match **7** compete, contest **8** concours **11** competition

tousle 4 mess, muss **6** rumple **8** dishevel, disorder

tout 3 spy, tip **4** brag, laud, plug **5** watch **6** blow up, peddle, praise, talk up **7** acclaim, crack up, promote, solicit **8** ballyhoo, persuade, proclaim **9** publicize

tovarich 7 comrade

tow 3 lug, tug **4** drag, draw, haul, pull, rope, yarn **5** chain, trail **6** hawser *truck:* **7** wrecker

towel word 3 his **4** hers

tower 4 loom **5** spire **6** turret **8** overlook *on a mosque:* **7** minaret

towering 4 high, tall **5** grand, great, lofty **6** aerial, mighty **7** extreme, soaring, stately **8** imposing, majestic **9** excessive, grandiose **10** exorbitant, immoderate, inordinate, monumental, prodigious **11** extravagant, magnificent, skyscraping **12** altitudinous, overwhelming

towhee 5 finch **7** chewink

to wit 3 viz 6 namely 8 scilicet 9 c'est-à-dire, videlicet

town 4 burg 6 hamlet, podunk 7 borough, village *medieval:* 5 bourg

town and ___ 4 gown 7 country

townsman 7 burgher, citizen

town square 5 plaza *Italian:* 6 piazza

toxic 6 poison 7 harmful 8 venomous, virulent 9 poisonous 10 infectious

toxin 5 venom 6 poison

toy 4 fool, play 5 antic, curio, dally, flirt, knack, mouse, tease 6 bauble, caress, coquet, diddle, fiddle, gewgaw, trifle 7 bibelot, novelty, pastime, trinket, whatnot 8 gimcrack 9 plaything 10 diminutive, knickknack

trace 3 jot, ray, run, tug 4 blip, echo, hint, iota, mark, path, scan, wisp 5 relic, shade, tinge, trail, tread 6 derive, detect, nuance, shadow, strain, streak 7 outline, remains, remnant, run down, soupçon, symptom, vestige 8 discover, tincture, traverse 9 delineate, footprint, remainder, scintilla, suspicion 10 intimation, suggestion

trachea 6 larynx, throat, vessel 7 weasand 8 throttle, windpipe

track 3 way 4 drag, path, road, sign, step, tail 5 chase, cover, print, spoor, trace, trail, tread 6 artery, follow, pursue, shadow, travel 7 footway, imprint, monitor, pathway, vestige 8 footpath, footstep 9 footprint

track-and-field event 4 dash 5 relay 6 discus 7 javelin, hurdles, shot put 8 footrace, high jump, long jump 9 broad jump, decathlon, pole vault 10 heptathlon, triple jump 11 discus throw 12 steeplechase

tract 3 lot 4 area, belt, farm, land, plat, plot, zone 5 block, claim 6 parcel, region 7 leaflet, portion, terrain 8 pamphlet, preserve 9 territory

tractable 4 tame 6 docile, gentle, pliant 7 ductile, plastic, pliable 8 amenable, biddable, flexible, obedient, workable 9 adaptable, breakable, malleable 10 manageable

tractate 5 summa 6 memoir, thesis 7 pandect 8 hornbook, monument, treatise 9 discourse, monograph 10 commentary 12 disquisition, dissertation, introduction

traction 4 drag, pull 5 force 7 drawing, tension 8 friction

tractor maker 5 Deere (John)

trade 4 deal, sell, swap 5 craft, truck 6 barter, change, custom, market, métier, peddle, switch 7 bargain, calling, pursuit, traffic 8 business, commerce, exchange, industry, vocation 10 employment, occupation, profession, substitute 11 merchandise, transaction *illicit:* 11 black market

trademark 3 tag 4 logo 5 brand, label, stamp 6 patent, symbol 8 colophon, logotype 9 brand name

trader 4 ship 6 broker, dealer, vendor 8 merchant

trade route 7 sea-lane

tradition 4 lore, myth 5 habit 6 belief, custom, legacy, legend, mythos, rubric 7 folkway 8 folklore, heredity, heritage, practice 9 mythology 10 convention 12 old wives' tale

traditional 4 oral 5 usual 6 common, spoken, verbal 7 classic, old-line, popular 8 habitual, orthodox 9 classical, customary, old-school, unwritten 10 button-down 11 established 12 acknowledged, buttoned-down, conservative, conventional

traditionalist 6 purist 12 conservative

traditionalistic 4 tory 7 die-hard, old-line 8 orthodox, standpat 12 conservative

traduce 4 slur 5 libel, smear, wrong 6 betray, breach, defame, malign, vilify 7 asperse, slander, violate 8 disgrace, tear down 9 denigrate 10 calumniate

Trafalgar commander 6 Nelson (Horatio)

traffic 4 deal 5 cargo, fence, trade, truck 6 barter, custom 7 bootleg, freight 8 commerce, dealings, exchange, movement 9 patronage, transport 11 black-market *circle:* 6 rotary 10 roundabout *cone:* 5 pylon *jam:* 5 tie-up 6 holdup 8 gridlock 10 bottleneck

trafficker 6 dealer, trader

tragedy 4 woe 6 mishap, plague 8 calamity, disaster 9 cataclysm, mischance 10 misfortune 11 catastrophe 12 misadventure

trail 3 dog, lag, tag 4 drag, flag, path, plod, poke 5 dally, delay, tarry, trace, track 6 dawdle, follow, linger, pursue, shadow 7 draggle, gumshoe, pathway, traipse 8 footpath, footwalk 10 bridle path *emigrant:* 6 Oregon *Florida:* 7 Tamiami *Georgia-Maine:* 11 Appalachian *Indian:* 5 Great

trailer 5 truck 7 preview 9 motor home, transport 10 mobile home

trailer truck 4 semi

train 3 row 4 file, tame 5 coach, drill, teach, track 6 column, convoy, course, school, sequel, series, thread 7 caravan, cortege, educate, prepare, retinue 8 exercise, instruct, sequence 9 cultivate, entourage, following, habituate 10 succession 11 progression

trainee 6 novice 7 learner, new hire 8 beginner 10 apprentice

training 7 tuition 8 teaching, tutelage 9 education, schooling 11 instruction *horses:* 6 manège

traipse 3 gad 4 hoof, pace, roam, rove, step, walk 5 amble, range, trail, tramp, tread 6 ramble, stroll, wander 7 maunder, meander 8 ambulate 9 gallivant

trait 4 mark 5 point, quirk, trace 6 oddity 7 feature, quality 8 hallmark, property, specific 9 attribute

traitor 5 Judas 8 apostate, betrayer, defector, deserter, quisling, renegade, turncoat 9 turnabout

traitorous 5 Punic 8 apostate, disloyal, mutinous, recreant, renegade 9 faithless 10 perfidious, rebellious, unfaithful 11 treacherous

traject 4 beam, pass, pipe, send 5 carry 6 convey, render 7 conduct, forward, impress 8 hand down, transfer, transmit 9 broadcast, transfuse

tram 3 car 7 trolley 9 streetcar

trammel 3 tie 4 bind, curb 5 check, gauge, leash 6 fetter, hamper, hobble 7 compass, confine, ensnare, manacle, pothook, shackle 8 entangle, handcuff 9 restraint

tramontane 8 outsider 9 foreigner, outlander 11 transalpine

tramp 3 bum 4 hike, hobo, jade, plod, slog, thud 5 bimbo, caird, clump, gypsy, march, stamp, stiff, stomp, tread 6 ramble, stroll, travel, trudge, wander 7 chippie, clochard, drifter, floater, saunter, stroller, traipse, vagrant 8 derelict, footslog, homeless, vagabond 10 prostitute

trample 4 mash 5 crush, pound, stamp, stomp, tread, tromp

trance 4 daze, muse 5 swoon 7 ecstasy, rapture, reverie 8 hypnosis 9 catalepsy, enrapture 10 absorption, brown study 11 abstraction

tranquil 4 calm, easy 5 quiet, still 6 dreamy, placid, poised, serene 7 restful 8 composed, peaceful 10 untroubled 13 self-possessed

tranquilize 4 calm, hush, lull 5 quiet, relax, still 6 becalm, pacify, sedate, settle, soothe, subdue 7 compose, mollify

tranquilizer 6 downer 8 diazepam, pacifier, sedative 10 depressant 11 barbiturate

tranquillity 4 calm 5 peace, quiet 8 calmness, serenity 9 composure, placidity

transaction 4 deal 5 trade 7 bargain, dealing 8 contract, covenant 9 agreement

transcend 3 top 4 beat, best 5 excel, outdo 6 better, exceed 7 surpass 8 outshine, outstrip, overcome, surmount

transcendent 5 ideal 7 perfect, sublime, supreme 8 abstract, immanent 10 consummate, surpassing

Transcendentalist 6 Alcott (Bronson), Fuller (Margaret) 7 Emerson (Ralph Waldo), Thoreau (Henry David)

transcribe 4 copy 5 write 6 record 8 transfer 9 translate, write down 13 transliterate

transfer 4 cede, deed, hand, pass, ship 5 carry, grant, shift 6 assign, convey, remove, supply 7 consign, convert, deliver, devolve, dispose 8 alienate, hand over, make over, relocate, turn over 9 carry over 10 assignment, conveyance 11 disposition

transfix 4 spit 5 lance, spear, spike, stick 6 impale, skewer 7 spindle 8 entrance 9 fascinate, hypnotize, mesmerize

transform 5 alter, morph 6 change, mutate 7 commute, convert 12 metamorphose

transformation 8 reaction 10 changeover, conversion 13 metamorphosis

transfuse 5 endue, imbue 7 pervade, suffuse, traject 8 permeate, saturate 9 penetrate, percolate 10 impregnate

transgress 3 err, sin 6 breach, exceed, offend 7 violate 8 infringe, overpass, overstep, trespass 10 contravene

transgression 3 sin 5 crime, error, wrong 6 breach 7 misdeed, offense 9 violation 12 infringement

transient 4 hobo 5 brief, tramp 7 drifter, migrant, passing 8 fleeting, flitting, fugitive, volatile 9 ephemeral, fugacious, momentary, temporary 10 evanescent, fly-by-night, short-lived 11 impermanent

transit 7 passage 8 traverse 10 conveyance

transition 4 leap 5 segue, shift 6 change 7 passage 10 conversion 13 metamorphosis

transitory see TRANSIENT

translate 6 render 7 convert 9 interpret, reproduce 10 paraphrase

translation 9 rendition 10 conversion, paraphrase

transmarine 7 oversea 8 overseas

transmission 7 gearbox 8 handover 9 broadcast, infection

transmit 3 air 4 beam, hand, pass, pipe, send 6 convey, hand on, impart, pass on, render, signal 7 channel, conduct, consign, diffuse, forward, traject 8 bequeath, dispatch, hand down 9 broadcast

transmogrify see TRANSFORM

transmute see TRANSFORM

transoceanic message 4 wire 5 cable 9 cablegram

transparent 5 clear, filmy, gauzy, sheer 6 limpid 7 crystal 8 clear-cut, gossamer, pellucid 10 diaphanous, see-through 11 crystalline

transpire 3 hap 4 leak 5 exude, occur, sweat 6 chance, emerge, happen 7 develop 9 come about, take place 11 come to light

transplant 8 relocate, resettle

transport 3 bus, fly, lag, lug, wow, zap, zip 4 haul, hump, lift, pack, pass, send, ship, taxi, tote 5 carry, ferry, motor, truck 6 convey, excite, ravish, remove, thrill 7 delight, ecstasy, freight, rapture, sealift, trundle, vehicle 8 carriage, displace, railroad, rhapsody 9 carry away, chauffeur, troopship 10 conveyance, helicopter

transportation 6 moving 7 freight, hauling, removal, vehicle 8 carriage, carrying 10 conveyance 12 displacement

transpose 6 invert 7 convert, permute, reorder, reverse 9 rearrange 11 interchange

transude 4 ooze, reek, seep, weep 5 bleed, sweat 7 diffuse, give off 8 permeate 9 transfuse

transverse 5 cross 6 across, thwart 8 crossbar, crossing 9 crossbeam, crosswise 10 crosspiece

trap 3 bag, net 4 bait, snag 5 catch, decoy, set up, snare 6 ambush, enmesh, tangle 7 ensnare, pitfall 8 birdlime, deadfall, entangle, quagmire 9 ambuscade

trappings 4 gear 5 dress 6 finery 8 equipage, ornament 9 adornment, caparison, equipment 10 decoration 11 habiliments 13 accouterments, accoutrements, embellishment, paraphernalia

Trappist 4 monk *writer:* 6 Merton (Thomas)

trash 3 rag, rot 4 bosh, junk, ruin, scum, slop 5 bilge, blast, dreck, dregs, hokum, offal, spoil, tripe, waste, wreck 6 bunkum, debris, insult, litter, refuse, rubble 7 clutter, destroy, garbage, hogwash, put down, rubbish 8 claptrap, malarkey, nonsense 9 disparage, throw away, vandalize 10 balderdash 11 guttersnipe, proletariat

trash can 7 dustbin

trashy 5 bawdy, cheap, tatty 6 cruddy, shoddy, sleazy, smutty, vulgar 8 rubbishy 9 third-rate

trauma 4 blow, pain 5 shock, upset, wound 6 crisis, injury, stress 8 collapse 9 suffering

travail 4 grub, moil, task, toil, work 5 grind, labor, pains 6 drudge, effort 7 slavery, torment 8 drudgery, struggle

travel 4 fare, pass, roam, tour, trek, trip, wend 5 jaunt, tramp 6 junket, push on, voyage 7 explore, journey, passage, proceed, traffic, transit 8 movement, traverse 9 gallivant 10 hit the road

traveler 5 gypsy 7 drummer, tourist 8 salesman, vagabond 9 itinerant, sightseer 10 journeyman 11 peripatetic

traveling library 10 bookmobile

traverse 4 ride, walk 5 cover, cross, march, route, trace, track 6 course, thwart, travel, voyage 7 transit 8 crossing, navigate, pass over 10 crisscross 11 perambulate, peregrinate

travesty 3 ape 4 mock, sham 5 farce, mimic, spoof 6 parody 7 imitate, lampoon, mimicry, mockery, take off 8 ridicule 9 burlesque 10 caricature, distortion *satanic:* 9 Black Mass

Traviata, La *character:* 7 Alfredo (Germont), Germont 8 Violetta (Valéry) *composer:* 5 Verdi (Giuseppe)

trawl 3 net 4 fish 7 setline

tray 6 salver, server 7 platter 8 teaboard *revolving:* 9 lazy Susan

treacherous 5 false, Punic, risky 6 chancy, tricky 7 unsound 8 disloyal, perilous, recreant 9 dangerous, deceptive, faithless, hazardous, insidious 10 perfidious, traitorous, unfaithful, unreliable

treachery 7 perfidy, treason 8 bad faith, betrayal 10 disloyalty, infidelity 11 double-cross 13 dastardliness, double-dealing, faithlessness

treacle 4 mush 5 slush, syrup 8 molasses, schmaltz 11 golden syrup

tread 4 hoof, pace, plod, step, walk 5 dance, march, stamp, stomp, trace, track, tramp, tromp, troop 6 follow, stride 7 footing, traipse, trample 8 footstep

treadle 5 lever, pedal

treadmill 3 rut 4 rote 5 chore, grind 6 groove 7 routine 8 drudgery, turnspit

treason 7 perfidy 8 betrayal, sedition 9 treachery 10 disloyalty, misprision

treasure 4 haul, save 5 adore, cache, hoard, pearl, prize, trove, value 6 esteem, revere, riches, wealth 7 apprize, cherish, idolize, worship 8 conserve, preserve, venerate 9 reverence 10 appreciate

Treasure Island *author:* 9 Stevenson (Robert Louis) *character:* 7 Ben Gunn

8 Long John (Silver) *narrator:* 10 Jim Hawkins

treasurer 6 bursar, purser 7 curator 8 receiver 11 chamberlain

Treasure State 7 Montana

treasure trove 4 find, mine 7 bonanza, pay dirt 8 El Dorado, Golconda, gold mine

treasury 4 fisc, mine 5 cache, chest, hoard 6 argosy, coffer, museum 7 bonanza, gallery, omnibus 8 archives, El Dorado, Golconda, gold mine, war chest 9 anthology, exchequer 10 depositary, depository, repository, storehouse

treat 5 goody, nurse 6 bonbon, dainty, doctor, goodie, handle, manage, morsel, tidbit 7 care for 8 deal with, delicacy, medicate 10 minister to *animals:* 3 vet *leather:* 3 tan, taw 7 tanning

treatise 6 thesis 8 tractate 9 discourse, monograph 10 exposition 12 disquisition, dissertation

treatment 4 care 7 therapy

treaty 4 pact 6 accord 7 charter, compact, concord 8 alliance, contract, covenant 9 agreement, concordat 10 convention

treble 4 high 6 shrill, triple 7 descant, soprano 9 threefold 11 high-pitched

tree *African:* 4 akee, cola, shea 5 limba, sassy 6 baobab 7 avodire, bubinga 8 sasswood 9 berberine *Asian:* 4 dhak, upas 6 banyan, kamala *Australian:* 7 blue gum 8 lacewood, quandong 9 casuarina *branch:* 5 bough *Brazilian:* 3 apa, ule 7 arariba, seringa, wallaba *Chinese:* 4 tung 5 yulan 6 ginkgo, lychee 7 kumquat *citrus:* 4 lime 5 lemon 6 orange 8 bergamot *combining form:* 3 dry 4 dryo 5 arbor, dendr 6 arbori, dendra (plural), dendro *coniferous:* 3 fir, yew 4 pine 5 alder, cedar, larch 6 spruce 7 cypress, hemlock, juniper, redwood, sequoia *dwarf:* 8 arbuscle 10 chinquapin *East Indian:* 4 neem, poon, teak, toon 6 banyan, deodar 7 deodara *elm:* 4 wych *Eurasian:* 5 abele, rowan 6 medlar *European:* 5 osier 8 bourtree *European oak:* 7 murmast *evergreen:* 3 fir, yew 4 atle, pine, titi 5 athel, carob, cedar, piñon, taxus 6 arbute, loquat, mallee, sapota 7 arbutus, camphor, conifer, inkwood, juniper, lentisk, madrona, madrone, redwood, sequoia 8 loblolly, longleaf, tamarisk 9 balsam fir 12 balm of Gilead *evergreen oak:* 6 encina *fig:* 5 pipal *flowering:* 5 sumac 6 acacia 7 dogwood 8 sourwood *hardwood:* 3 oak 5 beech, birch, ebony, maple 6 cherry, cornel, walnut 7 hickory 8 chestnut, mahogany *Japanese:* 4 kaki 7 zelkova *linden:* 8 basswood *mulberry:* 8 sycamine *North African:* 5 babul *nut-bearing:* 4 cola, kola 5 hazel, pecan, piñon 6 almond, cashew 7 buckeye, filbert, hickory 9 pistachio *oak:* 5 roble 8 bluejack *ornamental:* 3 box 5 holly 6 ginkgo, mimosa, myrtle, redbud 8 laburnum, magnolia 9 poinciana 12 rhododendron *palm:* 4 coco, nipa 5 ratan 6 pinang, raffia, rattan 7 coquito 8 carnauba *Peruvian:* 8 cinchona *Philippine:* 4 dita, pili 6 bataan 10 calamondin *resinous:* 10 candlewood *rubber:* 3 ule *shade:* 3 elm, oak 5 maple 6 linden 8 sycamore 10 chinaberry *softwood:* 5 alamo 6 tupelo 8 black gum, corkwood (see also CONIFEROUS) *South American:* 3 apa 4 ombu 7 wallaba 9 Brazil nut *swamp:* 11 bald cypress *tropical:* 4 akee, ohia, palm, sago, teak 5 areca, assai, balsa, cacao, ceiba, lehua, mamey 6 acajou, balata, baobab, citrus 7 genipap, logwood, majagua, palmyra, quassia, soursop 8 allspice, barbasco, mahogany, mangrove, milkwood, palmetto, rosewood, soapbark, sweetsop, tamarind 9 candlenut, jacaranda 10 breadfruit, manchineel 11 candleberry, coconut palm *trunk:* 4 bole *willow:* 5 osier, sauch, saugh 6 poplar *young:* 7 sapling

trefoil 4 leaf 6 clover *part:* 3 arc

trek 4 hike, trip 6 travel, trudge 7 journey 9 migration 10 expedition

trellis 5 arbor 6 screen 7 lattice, pergola 8 espalier 11 latticework

tremble 5 quake, shake 6 dither, quaver, quiver, shiver 7 shudder, twitter, vibrate

tremblor see TEMBLOR

tremendous 4 huge, vast 6 mighty, raging 7 awesome, immense, massive, titanic 8 colossal, enormous, fearsome, gigantic, terrific, towering 9 fantastic, monstrous 10 formidable, gargantuan, incredible, monumental, prodigious, stupendous 13 extraordinary

tremolo 7 vibrato

tremor 5 quake, shock 6 quaver, quiver, shiver 7 shudder, temblor 10 earthquake *muscular:* 8 dystaxia

tremulous 5 shaky, timid 6 afraid 7 aquiver, fearful, quaking, shivery 8 timorous 9 quivering, shivering

trench 4 sink 5 ditch, fosse, gully, verge 6 border, furrow, trough *Caribbean:* 6 Cayman

trenchant 4 keen 5 crisp, sharp 6 biting 7 caustic, cutting, mordant, probing, satiric 8 clear-cut, distinct, incisive, sardonic, scathing 9 sarcastic 11 penetrating

trencher 4 tray 7 platter

trencherman 7 glutton

trend 3 fad, run 4 flow, mode 5 curve, drift, shift, style, swing, tenor, vogue 6 course, temper 7 current, fashion, incline 8 approach, movement, tendency 9 direction

trendy 3 hep, hip, hot 4 cool, tony 5 faddy 6 groovy, modish, with-it 7 à la mode, faddish, stylish 8 downtown, nouvelle, up-to-date 11 fashionable, ultramodern

trepang 10 bêche-de-mer

trepidation 4 fear 5 alarm, dread 6 dismay 7 anxiety 12 apprehension 13 consternation

trespass 3 err, sin 4 debt 5 lapse, poach 6 breach, invade, offend 7 impinge, intrude 8 encroach, entrench, infringe 9 interlope, violation 10 infraction, transgress 12 encroachment, infringement 13 transgression

tress 4 curl, lock 5 braid, plait

trestle 4 buck 6 bridge 7 sawbuck 8 sawhorse

trey 5 three

triad 4 trio 5 chord 6 triple, troika 7 harmony, trinity 9 threesome 11 triumvirate

trial 3 woe 4 care, test 5 agony, cross, essay, grief, rigor, worry 6 dry run, hassle, misery, ordeal, sorrow, tryout 7 anguish, attempt, contest, trouble 8 crucible, distress, endeavor, gauntlet, hardship, struggle, vexation 9 adversity, rehearsal, suffering 10 affliction, coup d'essai, difficulty, experiment, misfortune, proceeding, temptation 11 preliminary, tribulation 12 experimental

trial balloon 6 feeler, tryout

trial run 4 test 5 essay 7 break-in 10 experiment

triangle type 5 acute, right 6 obtuse 7 scalene 9 isosceles 11 equilateral

tribal unit 6 moiety 7 phratry

tribe 4 clan, folk, race 5 house, stock 6 family 7 kindred, lineage

tribulation 3 woe 5 cross, trial 6 burden, ordeal 9 adversity 10 affliction, oppression, visitation 11 persecution

tribunal 3 bar 4 dais 5 bench, court 8 platform 10 consistory 12 court of honor

tributary 5 bayou, creek 6 branch, feeder, stream 7 subject 8 affluent, influent 9 backwater, confluent, dependent, satellite 12 contributory

tribute 5 paean 6 eulogy 8 citation, encomium 9 panegyric 10 salutation 11 recognition, testimonial 12 appreciation

trice 4 lash, wink 5 blink, flash, jiffy, shake 6 moment, second, secure 7 instant 8 eyeblink 9 twinkling 11 split second

trick 3 jig 4 dido, dupe, fool, gull, hoax, lark, play, ploy, ruse, sham 5 antic, caper, dodge, feint, fraud, prank, stunt 6 gambit, outwit, scheme 7 chicane, finagle, gimmick, sleight 8 escapade, flimflam, hoodwink 9 bamboozle, deception, stratagem, victimize 10 red herring, shenanigan, tomfoolery 11 hornswoggle, monkeyshine 13 practical joke

trickery 4 scam, wile 5 cheat, fraud 6 deceit 7 chicane, dodgery 8 jugglery 9 chicanery, deception 10 subterfuge 11 double cross 13 double-dealing, jiggery-pokery, sharp practice

trickle 4 drip, seep 5 creep, trill 7 dribble

trickster 5 cheat, shark 7 cheater, diddler, grifter, sharper 8 conjurer, deceiver, magician, swindler 9 defrauder 11 flimflammer, illusionist 12 doubledealer

tricksy 5 rough 6 trying 7 arduous 8 prankish

tricky 3 sly 4 foxy, wily 5 dodgy 6 catchy, clever, crafty, shifty, sticky, thorny, touchy, trying 7 cunning, knavish 8 delusive, guileful, slippery, ticklish, tortuous, unstable 9 deceptive, difficult, dishonest, ingenious, intricate 10 misleading, nettlesome, precarious, unreliable 11 complicated, treacherous, troublesome 12 undependable

trident 5 spear

tried 6 proved, proven, secure, tested, trusty 7 staunch 8 approved, faithful, reliable, true-blue 9 certified, steadfast 10 dependable 11 trustworthy

tried and true 6 proven, secure, tested, trusty 8 reliable 10 dependable 11 trustworthy

trifle 3 bob, fig, pin, toy 4 doit, fool, mess, play 5 curio, dally, flirt, sport, waste 6 bauble, coquet, diddle, doodle, fiddle, fidget, footle, frivol, gewgaw, monkey, niggle 7 bibelot, conceit, fribble, fritter, novelty, trinket, twiddle, whatnot 8 folderol, gimcrack, kickshaw, nonsense, squander 9 bagatelle, cream puff, dalliance 10 knickknack, triviality 11 small change

trifling 4 tiny 5 petty 6 measly, paltry 7 trivial 8 niggling, picayune, piddling 9 frivolous, worthless 10 negligible 11 unimportant 13 insignificant

trifolium 6 clover 8 shamrock

trig 4 chic, neat, prim, snug, tidy, trim **5** sharp, smart, swank, trick **6** classy, modish, snappy **7** chipper, dashing, orderly, precise, stylish **9** shipshape

trigger 4 fire **5** cause, spark, start **6** ignite, kindle, set off **7** actuate, release **8** activate, initiate, touch off

triggerman 3 gun **5** bravo **6** gunsel, killer **7** torpedo **8** assassin **9** cutthroat, pistolero

trigonometric function see at FUNCTION

trill 4 burr, drop, roll **5** chirr, shake, twirl **6** quaver, warble **7** dribble, revolve, trickle, twitter, vibrato

trillion *combining form:* **4** tera, treg **5** trega

trillionth *combining form:* **4** pico

trim 3 cut, fit **4** clip, crop, deck, neat, pare, snug, tidy, trig **5** adorn, order, prune, shape, shave, shear, skive **6** barber, dapper, fettle, kilter, repair, spruce **7** chipper, dress up, garnish, orderly, shapely **8** clean-cut, decorate, manicure **9** shipshape **11** spic-and-span, streamlined, well-groomed **12** spick-and-span *a tree:* **5** prune **7** pollard

Trinidad and Tobago *capital:* **11** Port of Spain *language:* **7** English *monetary unit:* **6** dollar *sea:* **9** Caribbean

trinity see TRIAD

trinket 3 toy **5** curio, jewel **6** bauble, doodad, gewgaw, trifle **7** bibelot, novelty, whatnot **8** gimcrack, kickshaw **9** bagatelle, plaything, tchotchke **10** knickknack

trinkets 10 bijouterie

trio of goddesses 5 Fates **6** Furies, Graces

trip 3 hop, run **4** fall, ride, skip, slip, step, tour, trek **5** boner, caper, dance, error, lapse **6** bungle, junket, outing, sashay, travel, tumble, voyage **7** blooper, blunder, journey, mistake, misstep, stumble **9** excursion **10** expedition

tripe 4 guts **5** bilge, trash **6** waffle, viscus **7** innards, viscera (plural) **8** entrails, stuffing **9** internals

triple 4 trio **5** triad, trine **6** treble, triune, troika **7** triform, trilogy, trinity **8** trifecta **9** threefold, threesome **11** three-bagger, triumvirate

Triple Crown winner *1919:* **9** Sir Barton *1930:* **10** Gallant Fox *1935:* **5** Omaha *1937:* **10** War Admiral *1941:* **9** Whirlaway *1943:* **10** Count Fleet *1946:* **7** Assault *1948:* **8** Citation *1973:* **11** Secretariat *1977:* **11** Seattle Slew *1978:* **8** Affirmed

tripped out 4 high **5** doped **6** stoned, zonked **7** drugged **8** hopped-up, turned on, wiped out **9** spaced-out **10** freaked-out

Tristan's beloved 6 Iseult, Isolde

Tristan und Isolde composer 6 Wagner (Richard)

triste 3 sad **5** sorry **7** doleful, pensive, wistful **8** mournful **9** depressed, sorrowful **10** melancholy **11** melancholic

Tristram Shandy author 6 Sterne (Laurence)

trite 3 pat, set **4** dull, flat, hack **5** banal, corny, musty, slick, stale, stock, tired, vapid **6** cliché, common, jejune, old-hat **7** prosaic, worn-out **8** bathetic, bromidic, flyblown, ordinary, shopworn, timeworn, well-worn **9** hackneyed **10** threadbare **11** commonplace, stereotyped **13** platitudinous, stereotypical

triton 5 conch **7** mollusc, mollusk **9** shellfish

Triton 6 merman *attribute:* **5** conch *father:* **7** Neptune **8** Poseidon *mother:* **10** Amphitrite

triturate 4 bray **5** crush, grind **6** powder **9** comminute, pulverize

triumph 3 joy, win **4** crow, palm **5** exult, glory, vaunt **6** master **7** conquer, prevail, succeed, success, victory **8** conquest, overcome, surmount **10** exultation, jubilation

triumphant 8 exultant, exulting, jubilant **10** conquering, victorious

triumvirate see TRIAD

Triumvirate, First *member:* **6** Caesar (Julius), Pompey (the Great) **7** Crassus (Marcus Licinius)

Triumvirate, Second *member:* **6** Antony (Marc) **7** Lepidus (Marcus Aemilius) **8** Octavius (Gaius)

trivet 4 rack **5** stand **6** tripod

trivia 8 factoids, minutiae **9** small beer **11** small change **13** small potatoes

trivial 5 light, minor, petty, small **6** casual, measly, paltry, piddly, slight **8** picayune, piddling, piffling, trifling **9** small-beer **10** negligible **11** Mickey Mouse, unimportant **13** insignificant

troche 6 tablet **7** lozenge **8** pastille **9** cough drop

troglodyte 6 hermit **7** caveman, recluse **11** cave dweller

Troilus *beloved:* **8** Cressida, Criseyde *father:* **5** Priam *mother:* **6** Hecuba *slayer:* **8** Achilles

Trojan *horse builder:* **5** Epeus *king:* **5** Priam *priest:* **7** Laocoon *soothsayer:* **7** Helenus **9** Cassandra *warrior:* **5** Paris **6** Aeneas, Agenor, Hector **9** Euphorbus

Trojan Horse builder 5 Epeus **6** Epeius

troll 4 fish, lure, sing, spin **5** angle, dwarf, prowl **6** goblin, search

trolley 3 car **4** cart, tram **8** carriage **9** streetcar

Trollope novel 10 Claverings (The)

11 Ayala's Angel, Phineas Finn
12 Phineas Redux 12 Way We Live Now
(The) 15 Eustace Diamonds (The)
16 Barchester Towers
trombone 7 sackbut
tromp 4 beat, drub, hike, pelt, slog, walk
5 pound, stamp, stomp, stump, tramp,
tread 6 batter, buffet, pummel, thrash,
trudge 7 belabor, trample 8 lambaste
troop 4 army, band, crew, host, pace,
step, walk 5 corps, crowd, flock, tread
6 legion, outfit 7 brigade, company, soldier, traipse 8 assembly 9 associate, battalion, gathering, multitude 10 collection
trooper 3 cop 5 actor, horse 7 soldier
9 policeman 10 cavalryman
trope 6 cliché, simile 8 metaphor,
metonymy 10 synecdoche
Trophonius *brother:* 8 Agamedes *temple
site:* 6 Delphi
trophy 3 cup 5 award, prize, relic, scalp,
token 6 spoils 7 memento 8 hardware,
keepsake, memorial, reminder, souvenir 9 loving cup 11 remembrance
tropical 3 hot 4 lush, warm 5 balmy,
humid 6 jungly, steamy, sultry, torrid
10 equatorial
tropical storm see TYPHOON
Tropic of Cancer author 6 Miller (Henry)
Tros' son 4 Ilus 8 Ganymede
trot 3 jog 4 gait, lope, pony, rack
5 amble, hurry 7 setline 11 translation
troth 6 commit, engage, pledge 7 loyalty
8 affiance, contract, espousal, fidelity
10 engagement 12 faithfulness
trot out 4 show 6 expose, parade 7 display, disport, exhibit, show off
Trotsky, Leon *associate:* 5 Lenin
(Vladimir) *rival:* 6 Stalin (Joseph)
troubadour 4 bard, poet 6 singer 8 jongleur, minstrel, musician 9 balladist
10 folksinger
trouble 3 ado, ail, ill, irk, try, vex, woe
4 care, fret, fuss, pain 5 annoy, beset,
Dutch, grief, harry, haunt, pains, trial,
upset, worry 6 bother, doo-doo, effort,
harass, impose, kiaugh, misery, pester,
plague, put out, ruffle, strain, stress,
unrest 7 afflict, agitate, ailment, bedevil, concern, disturb, oppress, perturb,
torment 8 aggrieve, disquiet, distress,
exertion, hardship, hot water, irritate,
vexation 9 beleaguer, importune, suffering 10 difficulty, disconcert 11 disturbance, predicament
troubled 6 uneasy 7 anxious, worried
9 concerned, disturbed 10 distressed
troublemaker 7 hellion 8 agitator 9 firebrand 10 instigator 11 provocateur
12 rabble-rouser

troublesome 5 pesky 6 thorny, tricky,
trying, vexing 7 carking, onerous,
prickly 8 annoying 9 difficult, upsetting, vexatious 10 bothersome, burdensome, cumbersome, disturbing 11 dis-
quieting, importunate, pestiferous
troublous 5 pesky 6 rugged, stormy
7 onerous 9 turbulent, vexatious
10 tumultuous 11 tempestuous
trough 3 hod 4 bowl, tank 5 basin, drain
6 vessel 7 channel
trounce 4 beat, drub, lick, rout, whip,
whup 5 whomp 6 defeat, larrup, punish, thrash, thresh, wallop 7 clobber,
shellac 9 overwhelm
troupe 4 band 5 corps, party 6 outfit
7 company
trouper 4 mime 5 actor, mimic 6 mummer, player 7 actress, artiste 8 thespian
9 performer 11 entertainer
trousers 5 pants 6 slacks 7 drawers
8 breeches, britches *tartan:* 5 trews
trout *kind:* 3 sea 4 char, lake 5 brook,
brown, river 7 rainbow 8 speckled
9 steelhead
Trovatore, Il *character:* 7 Azucena,
Leonora, Manrico 11 Count di Luna
composer: 5 Verdi (Giuseppe)
trove 4 find, haul 5 hoard, store 8 treasure 10 collection 11 aggregation
12 accumulation
Troy 5 Ilium *epic of:* 5 Iliad *excavator:*
10 Schliemann (Heinrich) *founder:*
4 Ilus *modern site:* 9 Hissarlik (see also
TROJAN)
truant 4 idle 5 shirk 7 shirker, slacker
8 shirking 10 delinquent
truce 4 lull 5 letup, pause, peace
6 accord 7 respite 9 armistice,
cease-fire
truck 3 van 4 semi, swap 5 lorry, trade
6 barter, handle, peddle, retail 7 bargain, traffic 8 commerce, dealings,
exchange *military:* 6 camion
Truckee River city 4 Reno
truckle 4 fawn 5 cower, defer, toady
6 cringe, grovel, kowtow 8 bootlick
11 apple-polish
truckler 5 leech, toady 6 lackey, sponge
7 spaniel 8 parasite 9 sycophant
10 bootlicker 11 lickspittle 13 apple-
polisher
truculent 4 fell, grim 5 cruel, harsh,
rough, sharp 6 brutal, deadly, fierce,
savage, severe 7 abusive, warlike 9 barbarous, bellicose, combative, ferocious
10 pernicious, pugnacious 11 belligerent, contentious, destructive, opprobrious, quarrelsome
trudge 4 plod, slog, trek 5 march, tramp,
tromp 8 footslog

true 4 real, very 5 valid 6 actual, honest, trusty 7 factual, genuine, staunch, upright 8 accurate, bona fide, constant, faithful, resolute, rightful 9 authentic, honorable, steadfast, undoubted, veracious, veritable 10 dependable, legitimate, undeniable 11 indubitable, trustworthy 12 indisputable 13 authoritative

true-blue 5 loyal 6 proven, steady 7 genuine 8 bona fide, constant, faithful 9 steadfast 10 unswerving

truism 3 saw 4 rule 5 adage, axiom, gnome, maxim, moral 6 cliché, dictum, gospel, saying, verity 8 aphorism, apothegm 9 platitude 10 shibboleth 11 commonplace

Truk Island 3 Tol 4 Moen, Udot, Uman 5 Fefan 6 Dublon

truly 4 well 6 easily, indeed, really, surely, verily 7 de facto 8 actually 9 doubtless, genuinely, sincerely, veritably 10 absolutely, definitely, positively, truthfully, undeniably 11 confidently, doubtlessly, undoubtedly

Truman, Harry S *birthplace:* 5 Lamar (Missouri) *predecessor:* 3 FDR *successor:* 3 DDE

trump 3 cap, top 4 beat, best, pass, ruff 5 excel, outdo 6 better 7 manille, surpass 8 clincher, jew's harp, outstrip, override, spadille *up:* 6 invent 7 concoct 9 fabricate 11 manufacture

trumpery 4 bosh, junk, muck, slop, tosh 5 bilge, cheap, dreck, hokum, trash 6 bunkum, cheesy, common, humbug, paltry, piffle, shoddy, trashy 7 baloney, twaddle 8 claptrap, flimflam, malarkey, nonsense, rubbishy, tommyrot 10 double-talk

trumpet 4 horn, tout 6 herald 8 ballyhoo *call:* 6 sennet *ram's horn:* 6 shofar

trumpeter 4 Hirt (Al), swan 5 André (Maurice), Baker (Chet), Brown (Clifford), Davis (Miles), James (Harry) 6 Alpert (Herb), Bolden (Buddy), Farmer (Art), Voisin (Roger) 7 Schwarz (Gerard) 8 advocate, Eldridge (Roy), eulogist, Marsalis (Wynton), Masekela (Hugh) 9 Armstrong (Louis), encomiast, Gillespie (Dizzy), spokesman 10 mouthpiece, panegyrist, Severinsen (Doc)

truncate 3 lop, top 4 crop, trim 5 prune, shear 6 cut off 7 abridge, shorten 10 abbreviate

truncheon 3 bat 4 club 5 baton, billy 6 cudgel, warder 8 bludgeon 9 billy club 10 nightstick, shillelagh

trundle 3 bed, tub 4 cart, haul, roll, spin 5 churn, wheel 6 rotate 7 revolve 9 transport

trunk 3 box 4 body, case, stem 5 chest, torso 7 channel, circuit, luggage *elephant:* 9 proboscis *tree:* 4 bole 5 stump

truss 3 tie 4 band, bind 5 brace 7 bandage, bracket, support 9 framework, supporter 10 strengthen

trust 4 hope, pool, rely 5 faith, stock 6 assume, bank on, belief, cartel, charge, commit, credit, rely on 7 build on, combine, confide, consign, count on, custody, keeping, presume 8 bank upon, credence, depend on, reckon on, reliance, rely upon 9 assurance, certainty, certitude, syndicate 10 confidence, conviction, dependence, depend upon 11 safekeeping 12 conglomerate

trustee 8 guardian 9 custodian, protector 10 supervisor

trustworthy 4 sure, true 5 tried, valid 6 honest, proven, secure 8 accurate, credible, faithful, reliable 9 authentic, realistic, veracious 10 dependable 11 responsible 12 tried and true 13 authoritative

trusty 4 true 5 tried 6 proven, secure, stable, steady 7 certain, convict 8 faithful, reliable 9 truepenny 10 dependable 11 responsible 12 tried and true

truth 5 axiom, maxim, sooth 6 candor, gospel, verity 7 lowdown, reality, veritas 8 veracity 9 rightness 11 genuineness 12 authenticity *goddess:* 4 Maat *serum:* 11 scopolamine

truthful 5 frank 6 candid, honest 7 factual, sincere 8 accurate 9 realistic, veracious, veridical

truthfulness 6 candor, verity 7 honesty 8 veracity

try 3 aim, tax, vex 4 seek, shot, stab, test 5 annoy, assay, essay, judge, offer, prove, study, whack, whirl, worry 6 aspire, harass, harrow, strain, stress, strive 7 afflict, adjudge, attempt, trouble 8 endeavor, struggle 9 undertake 10 adjudicate, experiment

trying 6 taxing, thorny, tricky, vexing 7 arduous, onerous 8 annoying, exacting, grueling 9 demanding, difficult, strenuous, vexatious 10 irritating 11 aggravating, troublesome

try out 8 audition

tryst 4 date 7 meeting 10 engagement, rendezvous 11 appointment, assignation

tsunami 9 tidal wave

tub 3 vat 4 boat 9 container *hot:* 3 spa 7 Jacuzzi

tuba 7 helicon 9 bombardon, euphonium 10 sousaphone

Tubalcain *father:* 6 Lamech *mother:* 6 Zillah

tubby 3 fat 5 plump, podgy, porky, pudgy 6 chubby, chunky, rotund 8 roly-poly

tube 4 duct, hose, pipe 5 buret 6 siphon, subway, tunnel, vessel 7 burette, conduit, cuvette, pipette, syringe 8 pipeline *anatomical:* 3 vas 4 duct, vasa (plural) 7 salpinx 9 salpinges (plural)

tuber 3 set 4 bulb, corm, root, stem 6 potato 7 rhizome 10 prominence

tuberculosis 8 phthisis, scrofula 11 consumption 12 Pott's disease

tucker out 4 do in, poop, tire 5 drain, weary 7 exhaust

tuft 5 clump, mound 7 cluster *of feathers:* 7 panache *ornamental:* 6 pom-pom *vascular:* 6 glomus

tufted 7 crested

tug 3 tow 4 drag, draw, haul, moil, pull, toil 5 labor 6 strain, strive

tug-of-war 5 match 6 strife 7 contest, grapple, rivalry 8 conflict, struggle 10 contention 11 competition

tuition 3 fee 6 charge 8 teaching, training, tutelage 9 education, schooling 11 instruction

tumble 4 drop, fall, trip 5 upset 6 plunge, topple 8 collapse, keel over 9 bring down, overthrow 10 somersault

tumbledown 8 decrepit 10 ramshackle 11 dilapidated

tumbler 5 glass 6 roller 7 acrobat, gymnast 11 cartwheeler

tumbrel 4 cart 5 wagon 7 tipcart

tumescent 6 turgid 7 aureate, bloated, bulging, flowery, swollen 8 inflated, swelling 9 bombastic, dropsical, overblown 10 euphuistic, rhetorical 12 magniloquent 13 grandiloquent

tummy 3 gut 5 belly 6 paunch 7 abdomen, stomach 8 potbelly 9 bay window 11 breadbasket

tumult 3 din 4 flap, riot, to-do 5 babel, broil, hoo-ha, hurly, noise, whirl 6 clamor, dither, hubbub, lather, outcry, pother, racket, strife, uproar 7 ferment, tempest, turmoil 8 disorder, foofaraw, outburst, paroxysm, upheaval 9 agitation, commotion, confusion, kerfuffle, maelstrom 10 convulsion, hullabaloo, hurly-burly, turbulence 11 disturbance, pandemonium

tumultuous 5 rowdy 6 stormy, unruly 7 raucous, riotous 9 clamorous, turbulent 10 boisterous, disorderly 11 rumbustious, tempestuous 12 rambunctious

tumulus 5 grave, knoll, mound 6 barrow 7 hillock

tun 3 keg, vat 4 butt, cask, pipe 6 barrel 8 hogshead, puncheon

tuna 3 ahi 4 pear 6 bigeye, bonito 7 bluefin 8 albacore, skipjack 9 scombroid, yellowfin

tune 3 air 4 dial, lilt, song 5 theme 6 accord, adjust, amount, attune, extent, jingle, melody, strain, temper 7 descant 8 modulate, regulate 9 harmonize 10 coordinate, intonation *out:* 6 ignore

tuneful 5 sweet 6 dulcet 7 melodic 9 melodious 10 euphonious

tungsten 7 wolfram 9 scheelite 10 wolframite

tunic 5 jupon 6 kirtle *Greek:* 6 chiton

tunicate 4 salp 8 ascidian, chordate 9 sea squirt 11 urochordate

Tunisia *capital:* 5 Tunis *city:* 4 Sfax 6 Ariana *island:* 5 Jerba *language:* 6 Arabic *monetary unit:* 5 dinar *neighbor:* 5 Libya 7 Algeria *ruins:* 8 Carthage *sea:* 13 Mediterranean

tunnel 4 tube 6 burrow 7 conduit 8 crawlway *Alps:* 7 Simplon *France:* 4 Rove *Hudson river:* 7 Holland, Lincoln *Nevada:* 5 Sutro *railroad:* 6 Hoosac 7 Cascade

Turandot *character:* 3 Liu 5 Calaf *author:* 5 Gozzi (Carlo) *composer:* 6 Busoni (Ferruccio) 7 Puccini (Giacomo)

turban 7 bandana, pugaree 8 bandanna 9 headdress

turbid 4 dark 5 dense, mucky, muddy, murky, riley, roily, smoky, thick 6 cloudy, opaque, roiled 7 clouded, obscure

turbot 8 flatfish

turbulence 3 din 4 flap, stew 5 babel, fight, hoo-ha 6 dither, fracas, lather, pother, tumult, uproar 7 turmoil 8 foofaraw 9 agitation, commotion, confusion 11 pandemonium

turbulent 4 wild 5 bumpy, roily, rough, rowdy 6 raging, stormy, unruly 7 furious, moiling, raucous, riotous, roaring 8 agitated, blustery, brawling, mutinous, rowdyish, swirling 9 clamorous 10 boisterous, disorderly, tumultuous 11 rumbustious, tempestuous 12 rambunctious

tureen 3 pot 4 bowl 5 crock 6 vessel 9 casserole

turf 3 sod 4 area, peat 5 grass, sward, track 6 domain, region 7 terrain 9 racetrack, territory 11 horse racing 12 neighborhood

turgid see TUMESCENT

Turkey *capital:* 6 Ankara *city:* 5 Adana, Bursa, Izmir, Konya 8 Istanbul 9 Gaziantep *enclave:* 8 Naxçivan *lake:* 3 Van *leader:* 7 Atatürk (Kemal) *monetary unit:* 4 lira *mountain, range:* 6 Ararat,

Taurus *neighbor:* 4 Iran, Iraq 5 Syria 6 Greece 7 Armenia, Georgia 8 Bulgaria *part of:* 7 Balkans *peninsula:* 6 Balkan 9 Asia Minor *river:* 6 Tigris 8 Menderes 9 Euphrates 10 Kizil Irmak *sea:* 6 Aegean 7 Marmara 13 Mediterranean

turkey *buzzard:* 7 vulture *disease:* 9 blackhead *female:* 3 hen *head growth:* 5 snood 7 dewbill *male:* 3 tom 7 gobbler *throat pouch:* 6 wattle *young:* 5 poult

Turkey in the ___ 5 Straw

Turkish *cavalryman:* 5 spahi *empire:* 7 Ottoman *governor:* 4 vali *inn:* 4 kahn 6 imaret *measure:* 3 ohe *music:* 9 janissary *soldier:* 5 nizam 9 janissary *sultan:* 5 Ahmed, Selim 7 Bajazet, Bayezid, Ilderim *sword:* 8 yataghan *title:* 3 aga, bey 4 agha 5 pasha 6 vizier 7 effendi

Turkmenistan *capital:* 8 Ashgabat 9 Ashkhabad *city:* 9 Chardzhou, Dashhowuz *desert:* 7 Kara-Kum *monetary unit:* 5 manat *neighbor:* 4 Iran 10 Kazakhstan, Uzbekistan 11 Afghanistan *river:* 6 Murgab 7 Murghab 8 Amu Dar'ya *sea:* 7 Caspian

Turks and Caicos Islands *capital:* 9 Grand Turk *location:* 10 West Indies *passage:* 6 Caicos 8 Mouchoir *territory of:* 7 Britain

turmeric 3 dye 4 herb 5 spice 6 ginger 8 dyestuff

turmoil 4 coil, flap, moil, riot, stew, stir, to-do 5 chaos, whirl 6 clamor, dither, hassle, hubbub, lather, pother, strife, tumult, unease, unrest, uproar, welter 7 anxiety, ferment 8 disorder, disquiet, distress, upheaval 9 agitation, commotion, confusion 10 disruption, hurlyburly, inquietude, storminess, turbulence, uneasiness 11 anxiousness, disquietude, hurry-scurry, pandemonium, restiveness 12 restlessness 13 helter-skelter, Sturm und Drang

turn 3 yaw, zag, zig 4 bend, bias, bout, cast, grow, gyre, reel, spin, tack, tour, veer, whip, wind 5 angle, curve, pivot, refer, shunt, spell, stint, swirl, train, twirl, whirl 6 detour, divert, gyrate, mutate, revert, rotate, switch, swivel 7 circuit, convert, deflect, deviate, digress, diverge, reverse, revolve 8 gyration, rotation 9 about-face, deviation, pirouette, volte-face 10 deflection, revolution, tergiverse 11 changeabout 12 tergiversate *to stone:* 8 lapidify

turnabout 3 rat 6 coward 7 reverse 8 apostate, defector, recreant, renegade, reversal 9 about-face, reversion, volte-face 11 retaliation 12 merry-go-round 13 tergiversator

turn aside 4 shun, sway, veer 5 avert, repel, shunt, stave 6 divert, refuse, reject, swerve 7 deflect, deviate, digress, dismiss, diverge, fend off, reflect, ward off 8 alienate, estrange, separate 9 sidetrack

turncoat 3 rat, spy 5 Judas 7 traitor 8 apostate, betrayer, defector, deserter, quisling, recreant, renegade 9 traitress, turnabout 13 tergiversator

turn down 4 jilt, veto 5 spurn 6 rebuff, refuse, reject 7 decline, dismiss 9 repudiate 10 disapprove

turned on 4 high 5 doped 6 stoned, zonked 7 aroused, drugged, excited 8 hopped-up, tripping 9 activated, spaced-out, zonked-out 10 passionate 12 enthusiastic

turn in 5 crash, rat on 6 betray, inform, rat out, retire 7 deliver, produce, sack out 8 hand over 10 hit the sack, relinquish

turning point 4 cusp 5 pivot 6 climax, crisis 8 landmark 11 climacteric

turnip 5 swede 8 rutabaga *Scottish:* 4 neep

turnip-shaped 8 napiform

turnkey 6 jailer

turn left 3 haw

Turn of the Screw, The *author:* 5 James (Henry) *character:* 5 Flora, Miles 10 Peter Quint *composer:* 7 Britten (Benjamin)

turn on 5 start 6 excite, ignite 7 start up 8 activate, motivate 9 stimulate, titillate

turn over 4 plow, roll 5 upend, upset 6 assign, commit, give up, rotate 7 capsize, consign, deliver, entrust, furnish, provide, revolve 8 delegate, transfer 9 overthrow, surrender 10 relinquish

turnpike 7 highway

turn right 3 gee

turn up 4 find 6 appear, arrive, reveal 7 uncover, unearth 8 discover 9 encounter 11 materialize

Turnus *beloved:* 7 Lavinia *slayer:* 6 Aeneas

Turow *work* 4 One L 13 Burden of Proof 14 Pleading Guilty 16 Personal Injuries, Presumed Innocent

turpentine 7 galipot, solvent, thinner *ingredient:* 6 pinene *tree:* 4 pine 9 terebinth

turret 5 tower 6 cupola, louver, louvre 7 mirador 8 bartizan 9 belvedere

turtle 8 terrapin, tortoise 9 chelonian *edible part:* 7 calipee 8 calipash *sea:* 6 ridley 8 hawkbill *shell:* 8 carapace *shell part:* 8 plastron

Tuscany *city:* 4 Pisa 8 Florence *river:* 4 Arno *tower:* 4 Pisa *wine:* 7 chianti

tusk 4 fang 5 ivory, tooth

tusker 6 dugong, walrus 7 mammoth,

muntjac, narwhal, warthog **8** elephant, musk deer **11** barking deer

tussle 4 spar **5** scrap, scrum **6** hassle, scrape **7** scuffle, wrangle, wrestle **8** argument, skirmish, struggle **9** scrimmage **11** controversy

tussock 4 tuft **5** clump, mound **7** cluster

tutelage see TUITION

tutor 3 don **5** coach, teach **6** docent, mentor **7** teacher **9** pedagogue, preceptor **10** instructor

Tut's tomb discoverer 6 Carter (Howard)

tutti 3 all

Tuvalu *capital:* **9** Fongafale *ethnic group:* **10** Polynesian *former name:* **6** Ellice (Islands) *monetary unit:* **6** dollar

twaddle 3 jaw, yak **4** bosh, bull, bunk, chat, guff, muck, talk, tosh **5** clack, drool, hooey, prate, run on **6** babble, bunkum, burble, drivel, gabble, hot air, humbug, jabber, tattle **7** baloney, blabber, blarney, blather, chatter, hogwash, prattle, rubbish **8** claptrap, malarkey, nonsense, tommyrot, trumpery **9** poppycock **10** applesauce, balderdash **12** blatherskite **13** horsefeathers

tweak 4 jerk, mock, pull, zing **5** annoy, pinch, pluck **6** adjust, bother, twitch **8** fine-tune **9** poke fun at

tweet 4 call, note **5** cheep, chirp **7** chirrup, twitter

Twelfth Night character 5 Viola **6** Olivia, Orsino (Duke) **7** Antonio, Cesario **8** Malvolio **9** Sebastian, Toby Belch

twelve *combining form:* **5** dodec **6** dodeca

twenty *combining form:* **4** icos **5** icosa, icosi

twerp 4 brat, drip, fool, jerk, nerd, twit **6** squirt

twice 3 bis **7** twofold *combining form:* **3** bis *prefix:* **3** dis

twice a day 3 b.i.d. **8** bis in die **11** semidiurnal

twice a year 8 biannual **10** semiannual, semiyearly

Twice-Told Tales author 9 Hawthorne (Nathaniel)

twig 5 shoot, sprig **6** branch *bundle of:* **5** fagot **6** faggot

twiggy 4 slim, thin **5** reedy **6** slight, stalky **7** slender **9** sticklike

twilight 3 eve **4** dusk **5** gloam, gloom **6** sunset **7** decline **8** gloaming **9** nightfall **10** crepuscule

Twilight of the Gods 8 Ragnarok *composer:* **6** Wagner (Richard)

twill 5 chino, cloth, serge, toile, tweed, weave **6** fabric **7** cheviot **8** dungaree **9** bombazine, gabardine **11** herringbone

twin 4 dual, like, mate **5** clone, match **6** bifold, binary, double, fellow, paired **7** matched, similar, twofold **8** matching **9** companion, duplicate, identical **10** coordinate, reciprocal

Twin Cities 6 St. Paul **11** Minneapolis

twine 4 coil, cord, curl, wind, wrap **5** twist, weave **6** spiral, string **7** embrace, meander, wreathe **8** entangle **9** interlace **10** interweave

twinge 4 ache, pain, pang **5** pluck, shoot, throe, tweak **6** stitch

twinkle 3 bat **4** flit, wink **5** blink, flash, flirt, gleam, glint, light, shake, shine, trice **6** moment, second, winkle **7** flicker, flutter, glimmer, glisten, glitter, instant, shimmer, sparkle **9** coruscate, nictitate **11** coruscation, scintillate, split second

twin stars 6 Castor, Pollux

twirl 4 coil, gyre, spin **5** pitch, trill, whirl, whorl **6** gyrate **7** revolve **9** pirouette

twist 3 wry **4** coil, curl, turn, warp, wind **5** belie, gnarl, pivot, twine, twirl, wring **6** garble, spiral, sprain, squirm, torque, wrench, writhe **7** contort, distort, entwine, falsify, pervert, wriggle **8** misstate **9** corkscrew **12** misrepresent

twisted 3 wry **4** awry, sick **5** askew, kinky **6** swirly, warped **9** perverted

twister 6 funnel **7** tornado **9** dust devil, whirlwind **10** waterspout

twit 4 dolt, fool, gibe, jeer, jive, josh, mock, quiz, razz **5** chide, rally, scout, taunt, tease, twerp **6** deride **8** bonehead, numskull, ridicule **9** blockhead, numbskull **10** nincompoop

twitch 3 tic **4** jerk, pang, pull, yank **5** pluck, spasm, throe, tweak **6** quiver **10** quack grass **11** contraction

twitter 4 chat, peep **5** cheep, chirp, quake, tweet **6** cackle, giggle, jargon, quiver, shiver, titter, tremor, warble **7** chatter, chirrup, chitter, flicker, flitter, flutter, tremble **9** vibration

twittery 6 giggly **8** chattery **9** flustered, tremulous

two 3 duo **4** duet, pair **5** twain **6** couple *combining form:* **3** bis, duo, dyo *divide into:* **4** fork **6** bisect **9** bifurcate *prefix:* **3** twi

two-faced 9 deceitful, dishonest, insincere **11** duplicitous **12** hypocritical **13** double-dealing *god:* **5** Janus

twofold 4 dual, twin **5** binal, duple **6** binary, double, duplex, dyadic, paired **9** dualistic

Two Gentlemen of Verona *author:* **11** Shakespeare (William) *character:* **5** Julia **6** Silvia, Thurio **7** Proteus **9** Valentine

twosome 3 duo **4** dyad, pair **5** brace **6** couple **7** doublet

two-time 4 dupe **6** betray, delude, humbug, take in **7** beguile, cheat on, deceive, mislead **9** bamboozle **11** double-cross

two-wheeler 4 bike **5** cycle **7** bicycle, scooter **10** motorcycle

Two Years Before the Mast author **4** Dana (Richard Henry)

Tybalt cousin: **6** Juliet family: **7** Capulet slayer: **5** Romeo victim: **8** Mercutio

Tyche goddess of: **7** fortune

tycoon 5 mogul, nabob **7** magnate

tyke 3 dog, kid **5** child, hound, puppy **6** canine, moppet, nipper, shaver **7** mongrel

Tyler novel **16** Breathing Lessons **17** Accidental Tourist (The) **29** Dinner at the Homesick Restaurant

tympanum 7 eardrum **9** middle ear

Tyndareus kingdom: **6** Sparta wife: **4** Leda

type 3 cut, ilk, lot, way **4** cast, form, kind, mold, sort **5** breed, class, genre, order, print, serif, stamp **6** kidney, nature, stripe **7** feather, species, variety **8** category **9** character **10** persuasion **11** description bar: **4** slug measure: **4** pica **5** point set: **7** compose setter: **10** compositor size: **4** pica **5** agate, pearl stroke: **5** serif style: **4** bold **5** roman **6** Gothic, italic **7** Fraktur **8** boldface **9** lightface, sans serif tray: **6** galley

Typee author: **8** Melville (Herman) character: **4** Toby

typewriter part: **3** key **6** platen, spacer type size: **4** pica **5** elite

Typhon 3 Set **7** monster **8** Typhoeus offspring: **6** Sphinx **7** Chimera **8** Cerberus, Chimaera wife: **7** Echidna

typhoon 7 cyclone **9** hurricane **13** tropical storm

typical 5 ideal, model, usual **6** common, normal **7** classic, general, natural, regular **8** symbolic

typify 6 embody, mirror **9** epitomize, exemplify, personify, represent, symbolize **10** illustrate **11** emblematize **12** characterize

typo 5 error **7** erratum **8** misprint **11** corrigendum

typographer 7 printer **10** compositor

Tyr 3 Tiu brother: **4** Thor father: **4** Odin god of: **3** war mother: **5** Jordh, Jorth

tyrannical 8 absolute, despotic **9** arbitrary **10** absolutist, autocratic, oppressive **11** dictatorial **12** totalitarian

tyrannize 7 oppress **8** dominate, domineer, overbear **9** terrorize

tyrannous 5 harsh **6** brutal, severe **8** absolute, despotic **9** arbitrary, fascistic **10** autocratic **11** dictatorial **12** totalitarian

tyranny 7 cruelty, fascism **9** autocracy, despotism, monocracy **10** absolutism, domination, oppression **12** dictatorship

tyrant 4 czar, duce, tsar, tzar **5** ruler **6** despot, führer **7** fuehrer, pharaoh, usurper **8** autocrat, dictator **9** oppressor, strongman **10** absolutist **12** totalitarian

Tyrian ___ **6** purple

tyro 4 punk **6** novice, rookie **7** amateur, dabbler, student **8** beginner, freshman, neophyte, newcomer **9** novitiate **10** apprentice, dilettante, tenderfoot **11** abecedarian

Tyrol see TIROL

tzar see CZAR

tzigane 3 Rom **5** gypsy **6** Romany

U

übermensch 8 superman

ubiquitous 7 allover **9** pervasive, universal **10** everywhere, wall-to-wall, widespread **11** omnipresent

U-boat 3 sub **7** pigboat **9** submarine

Uganda capital: **7** Kampala falls: **5** Ripon lake: **5** Kyoga **6** Albert, Edward, George **8** Victoria language: **7** English, Swahili leader: **4** Amin (Idi) monetary unit: **8** shilling mountain: **5** Elgon mountain range: **9** Ruwenzori neighbor: **5** Congo, Kenya, Sudan **6** Rwanda **8** Tanzania river: **4** Nile

ugly 4 vile **7** hideous **8** deformed **9** loathsome, misshapen, offensive, repugnant, repulsive, unsightly **10** disfigured **12** unattractive

Ugly Duckling author 8 Andersen (Hans Christian)

ukase 4 fiat **5** edict, order **6** decree, dictum, ruling **7** command, dictate, mandate **9** directive **10** injunction **12** proclamation **13** pronouncement

Ukraine *capital:* **4** Kiev *city:* **4** Lviv, Lvov **5** Yalta **6** Odessa **7** Kharkiv **9** Chernobyl *ethnic group:* **7** Cossack *monetary unit:* **6** hryvny *mountain range:* **10** Carpathian *neighbor:* **6** Poland, Russia **7** Belarus, Hungary, Moldova **8** Slovakia *peninsula:* **5** Kerch **6** Crimea **7** Crimean *river:* **3** Bug **5** Tisza **6** Donets **7** Dnieper **8** Dniester *sea:* **4** Azov **5** Black

Ulalume author 3 Poe (Edgar Allan)

ulcer 4 sore **6** fester **7** corrupt *kind:* **6** peptic **8** duodenal *mouth:* **10** canker sore

ulna 7 forearm

Ulster hero 6 Fergus **7** Deirdre **9** Conchobar, Cuchulain, Cuchullin **10** Cú Chulainn

ulterior 5 privy **6** covert, future, hidden, latent **7** further, obscure, remoter **9** ambiguous, concealed **10** subsequent, succeeding **11** undisclosed

ultimate 3 end **4** acme, last, peak **5** basic, final **6** summit, utmost, zenith **7** closing, epitome, extreme, maximum, primary, supreme, topmost **8** absolute, deciding, decisive, eventual, farthest, furthest, greatest, original, terminal **9** elemental, paramount **10** apotheosis, concluding, conclusive, consummate, preeminent **11** categorical, fundamental, furthermost, indivisible **12** incomparable, quintessence

ultimatum 5 order **6** demand, threat **7** mandate **9** challenge **12** notification

ultra 5 kinky, outré, rabid **6** beyond, farout, too-too **7** extreme, fanatic, radical **9** excessive, extremist, fanatical **10** outlandish **11** extravagant

ultraconservative 11 reactionary

ultraist 5 rabid **6** zealot **7** extreme, fanatic, radical **9** extremist

ultramarine 7 oversea, sea-blue **8** overseas **11** lapis lazuli

ululate 3 bay **4** howl, wail, yowl

Ulysses *author:* **5** Joyce (James) *character:* **5** Bloom (Leopold), Molly (Bloom) **6** Blazes (Boylan) **7** Dedalus (Stephen) (see also ODYSSEUS)

umber 5 brown, sepia, shade **6** darken, shadow

umbilicus 3 hub **4** core **5** heart, hilum, navel **6** center

umbra 5 shade **6** shadow

umbrage 4 hint, huff **5** anger, pique, shade **6** shadow **7** chagrin, dudgeon, foliage, leafage, offense **9** annoyance, suspicion **10** irritation, resentment **11** displeasure, indignation **12** exasperation

umbrageous 5 shady **6** shaded, touchy **7** shadowy **8** shadowed **9** defensive, sensitive

umbrella 5 cover, guard, shade **6** brolly, pileus, screen **7** parasol, protect, shelter **8** sunshade **10** protection **11** bumbershoot

umph see OOMPH

umpire 3 ref **5** judge **6** decide, settle **7** arbiter, referee **9** arbitrate **10** arbitrator *call:* **3** out **4** balk, ball, safe **6** strike

unabashed 5 blunt, brash, frank, naked, overt **6** arrant, brassy, brazen, candid **7** blatant, forward **8** outright **9** audacious, barefaced, shameless, undaunted **10** unblushing **11** undisguised, unmitigated **12** unapologetic

unabbreviated see UNABRIDGED

unable 5 inept, unfit **8** helpless, impotent **9** incapable, maladroit, powerless, unskilled **10** unequipped **11** incompetent, unqualified **13** incapacitated

unabridged 5 uncut, whole **6** entire, intact **8** complete **10** full-length **11** uncondensed **13** unabbreviated

unacceptable 8 unwanted **9** unwelcome **10** unsuitable **11** intolerable, undesirable **12** inadmissible **13** exceptionable, inappropriate, insupportable, objectionable

unaccompanied 4 lone, sole, solo, stag **5** alone, apart **6** single **8** detached, solitary **9** a cappella **10** unattended, unescorted

unaccountable 6 arcane, mystic **7** strange **8** baffling, puzzling **9** enigmatic **10** mysterious, mystifying, unknowable, unreliable **12** impenetrable, inexplicable, undependable, unfathomable **13** irresponsible, unexplainable

unaccustomed 3 new **5** alien, novel **6** unused **7** strange, unusual **8** singular, uncommon, unwonted **10** unexpected, unfamiliar

unadorned 4 bald, bare **5** naked, plain, spare, stark **6** rustic, severe, simple **7** artless, austere, natural, spartan **11** undecorated **13** unembellished, unembroidered, unpretentious

unadulterated 4 neat, pure **5** sheer, utter **7** genuine, unmixed **8** absolute, straight **9** unalloyed, undiluted **11** unmitigated, unqualified

unaffected 5 naive **6** candid, simple

7 artless, callous, genuine, natural, sincere, unmoved **9** guileless, impassive, ingenuous, unaltered, unchanged, unstudied, untouched **10** hard-boiled, impervious **13** unpretentious

unalloyed 4 pure **5** sheer, total **7** genuine, unmixed **8** absolute, straight **9** authentic, out-and-out, undiluted **11** unmitigated, unqualified **13** thoroughgoing, unadulterated

unalterable 5 fixed **7** binding, bounden, certain, decided **8** constant, required **9** immutable, mandatory, necessary **10** compulsory, invariable **12** unchangeable **13** predetermined

unambiguous 5 clear, lucid, plain **6** patent **7** evident, express, obvious, precise **8** apparent, clean-cut, clear-cut, decisive, definite, distinct, explicit, manifest, specific, univocal **10** definitive, forthright **11** categorical, translucent, transparent, unequivocal **12** transpicuous

unanimous 6 united **8** communal, univocal **9** unopposed **10** collective **11** uncontested **13** consentaneous

unanimously 5 as one **6** wholly **7** en masse **10** altogether

unanticipated 9 unplanned **10** surprising, unexpected, unforeseen **12** out of the blue

unappeasable 4 grim **7** adamant **8** obdurate, resolute **9** insatiate, unbending **10** implacable, insatiable, relentless, unyielding **11** unrelenting **12** unquenchable

unappetizing 4 icky **5** gross, yucky **7** insipid **8** unsavory **9** repugnant **11** unappealing, unpalatable **12** unattractive

unapproachable 5 aloof **6** remote, offish **7** distant **8** reserved **10** unfriendly, unsociable **11** standoffish, unreachable **12** inaccessible, unattainable

unasked 7 willing **8** unbidden, unsought, unwanted **9** uninvited, unwelcome, voluntary **10** gratuitous, unprompted **11** spontaneous, uncalled-for, unrequested, voluntarily

unassailable 6 secure **8** airtight **10** invincible, inviolable, undeniable **11** impregnable, irrefutable **12** indisputable, invulnerable **13** incontestable, unconquerable

unassertive 3 shy **4** meek **5** mousy, timid **6** modest, mousey **7** bashful **8** backward, reticent, retiring, sheepish, timorous **9** diffident, shrinking **10** submissive **12** self-effacing

unassuming 3 shy **6** humble, modest, simple **8** ordinary, retiring **9** diffident

11 unassertive **12** self-effacing **13** unpretentious

unattached 4 free **5** loose **6** single **8** separate **9** unmarried **10** unassigned **11** uncommitted, unconnected **12** disconnected, freestanding, unassociated

unattainable 7 elusive **10** impossible **12** inaccessible

unattractive 4 drab, dull, ugly **5** dowdy, plain **6** homely **8** frumpish **10** unalluring, unsuitable **11** unappealing, undesirable **12** unflattering

unauthentic 4 fake, mock, sham **5** bogus, dummy, faked, false, phony **6** ersatz, forged, pseudo **7** feigned **8** affected, spurious **9** contrived, imitation, pretended, simulated **10** apocryphal, artificial **11** counterfeit, make-believe **12** illegitimate

unavailable 4 busy **6** absent, tied up **7** missing **8** occupied

unavailing 4 idle, vain **5** empty **6** barren, futile **7** useless **8** abortive, bootless **9** fruitless, pointless **11** ineffective, ineffectual **12** unproductive

unavoidable 5 fated **7** certain **8** destined **9** impending, necessary **10** compulsory, inevitable, obligatory **11** ineluctable, inescapable

unavoidably 8 perforce **10** helplessly, inevitably, willy-nilly **11** inescapably, necessarily, whether or no

unaware, unawares 5 aback **7** unready **8** abruptly, heedless, ignorant, off guard, suddenly **9** oblivious, unknowing, unmindful, unwitting **10** by surprise, unfamiliar, uninformed, unprepared **12** unacquainted, unexpectedly

unbalance 11 destabilize

unbalanced 3 mad **4** daft **5** batty, nutty **6** crazed, insane, uneven, wobbly **7** unequal, unsound **8** demented, deranged, lopsided, unhinged, unstable **9** psychotic **10** disordered, moonstruck

unbearable 11 intolerable, unendurable **12** excruciating, insufferable

unbeautiful 4 ugly **5** plain **6** homely **8** uncomely, unlovely **9** unsightly **10** ill-favored, unbecoming, uninviting **12** unattractive

unbecoming 8 improper, unlovely, unseemly, untimely, untoward, unworthy **9** inelegant, tasteless, unfitting **10** indecorous, indelicate, malapropos, unsuitable **11** disgraceful **12** unattractive **13** inappropriate

unbelievable 7 amazing, awesome **8** fabulous **9** fantastic **10** astounding, improbable, incredible, phenomenal, staggering, stupendous **11** astonishing, implausible, spectacular **12** unconvincing, unimaginable **13** extraordinary, inconceivable

unbeliever 5 pagan **6** giaour **7** atheist, doubter, gentile, heathen, heretic, infidel, scoffer, skeptic **8** agnostic **10** Pyrrhonist **11** freethinker

unbelieving 5 leery **6** show-me **8** agnostic, apostate, doubting **9** quizzical, skeptical **10** dissenting, suspicious **11** incredulous, mistrustful, questioning

unbending 5 rigid, stern, stiff **8** hardline, obdurate, resolute **9** inelastic **10** brassbound, inexorable, inflexible, unyielding

unbiased 4 fair, just **5** equal **7** neutral **8** detached, tolerant **9** equitable, impartial, objective, unbigoted **10** even-handed, open-minded **11** broad-minded, uncommitted **12** unprejudiced **13** disinterested, dispassionate

unbidden 7 unasked, willing **8** unsought, unwanted **9** impromptu, uninvited, unwelcome, voluntary **10** gratuitous, unprompted **11** spontaneous, unrequested

unbind 4 free, undo **5** loose, untie **6** detach, loosen **7** manumit, release, unchain, unloose **8** dissolve, liberate, unfasten, unloosen **9** discharge, disengage, unshackle **10** emancipate

unblemished 4 pure **7** perfect **8** flawless, spotless, unmarred, virtuous **9** exemplary, faultless, stainless, undefiled, unspotted, unsullied **10** immaculate **11** untarnished

unbosom 4 bare, open, tell **6** betray, expose, reveal, unveil **7** divulge, express, uncover **8** disclose

unbound 4 free **5** loose, loosed **6** loosed **10** unattached, unconfined, unfastened

unbounded 4 open **6** untold **7** endless **8** infinite, unending **9** excessive, limitless, unchecked, unlimited **10** immoderate, indefinite, inordinate **11** extravagant, measureless **12** immeasurable, incalculable, uncontrolled, unrestrained

unbreakable 7 durable, lasting **10** unyielding **11** everlasting

unbridled 4 free **5** loose **6** madcap **8** reckless, uncurbed **9** dissolute, unchecked **10** immoderate, licentious, unconfined, unfettered, ungoverned **11** spontaneous, uninhibited, unrepressed **12** uncontrolled, unrestrained, unrestricted **13** unconstrained

unbroken 5 solid, sound, whole **6** entire, intact, single **8** complete, constant, enduring **9** ceaseless, steadfast, unceasing, undamaged, undivided, unsub-

dued, unvarying **10** continuous, unimpaired **13** uninterrupted

unburden 3 rid **4** dump, ease, lose **5** shake **6** reveal, unload **7** cast off, confess, confide, off-load, relieve **8** shake off, throw off **9** discharge **10** relinquish **11** disencumber

uncalled-for 8 baseless, needless **9** officious, unfounded **10** gratuitous, groundless **11** unessential, unjustified, unnecessary, unwarranted **13** unjustifiable

uncanny 5 eerie, weird **6** creepy, spooky **7** ghostly, strange **9** unearthly, unnatural **10** mysterious, mystifying, superhuman **11** supernormal, supranormal **12** supernatural

uncared-for 5 dingy **6** beat-up, shabby **7** rickety, run-down, worn-out **8** decrepit, derelict, deserted, desolate, forsaken, tattered, untended **9** neglected **10** broken-down, down-at-heel, ramshackle, tumble-down **11** dilapidated

uncaring 4 cold **7** callous **9** heartless, negligent, oblivious, unfeeling, unheeding **11** coldhearted, hard-hearted, indifferent, insensitive, thoughtless, unconcerned **13** inconsiderate, unsympathetic

unceasing 7 abiding, endless, eternal, nonstop, undying **8** constant, enduring, unbroken, unending **9** continual, perennial, perpetual **10** continuous **11** amaranthine, everlasting, unremitting **12** imperishable, interminable **13** uninterrupted

unceremonious 4 curt, rude **5** bluff, blunt, frank, hasty, sharp, short, terse **6** abrupt, breezy, casual, sudden **7** brusque, hurried, offhand **8** familiar, informal **10** ungracious **11** precipitate, precipitous

uncertain 4 hazy, iffy, moot **5** vague **6** chancy, fitful, unsure, wobbly **7** dubious, erratic, halting, unclear **8** arguable, doubtful, insecure, slippery, unstable, unsteady, variable **9** ambiguous, debatable, undecided, unsettled **10** ambivalent, disputable, inconstant, indefinite, precarious **11** problematic, speculative **12** questionable, undependable **13** indeterminate, problematical, unforeseeable, unpredictable, untrustworthy

uncertainty 5 doubt **7** dubiety **8** distrust, mistrust **9** ambiguity, suspicion **10** indecision, perplexity, puzzlement, skepticism, uneasiness **11** ambivalence **12** doubtfulness, irresolution

unchain 4 free **5** loose **6** loosen, unbind **7** manumit, release **8** liberate, unfasten,

unfetter 9 discharge, unshackle
10 emancipate 11 disenthrall

unchangeable 3 set 4 firm 5 fixed 7 settled 8 constant 9 immutable, permanent
10 continuing, inflexible, invariable
11 established, inalterable

unchanging 5 fixed 6 stable, static, steady 7 abiding, equable, eternal, settled, stabile, uniform 8 constant, enduring 9 immutable, steadfast, unvarying
10 consistent, continuing, invariable

unchaste 4 easy, lewd 5 bawdy, loose
6 impure, vulgar, wanton 7 immoral, lustful, obscene, scarlet, unclean
8 depraved, prurient 9 debauched, dissolute, lecherous, salacious 10 adulterous, lascivious, libidinous, licentious, profligate 11 promiscuous

unchecked 5 loose 7 rampant 9 spreading, unbounded, unbridled 10 widespread 11 uninhibited 12 unrestrained, unrestricted

uncivil 4 rude 5 crass, crude 6 coarse, savage, vulgar 7 boorish, ill-bred, uncouth 8 barbaric, impolite 9 barbarous 10 indecorous, uncultured, ungracious 11 ill-mannered, uncourteous 12 discourteous 13 disrespectful

uncivilized 4 rude, wild 5 crude 6 brutal, coarse, Gothic, savage 7 boorish, Hunnish, ill-bred, loutish, lowbred, uncouth 8 barbaric, churlish 9 barbarian, barbarous, primitive, unrefined
10 mannerless, uncultured, unmannerly, unpolished 12 uncultivated 13 unenlightened

unclad see UNCLOTHED

uncle *cry:* 6 give up 9 surrender *Scottish:* 3 eme *Spanish:* 3 tío *U.S. symbol:* 3 Sam

unclean 4 foul 5 dingy, dirty, grimy
6 filthy, grubby, grungy, impure, soiled, sordid 7 corrupt, defiled, immoral, obscene, squalid, stained, sullied, tainted 8 befouled, indecent, polluted, unchaste 9 tarnished 10 besmirched, desecrated 12 contaminated

unclear 3 dim 4 hazy 5 murky, vague
6 bleary, blurry, cloudy, opaque, unsure 7 clouded, cryptic, dubious, obscure, shadowy 8 doubtful, nebulous, overcast, puzzling 9 ambiguous, enigmatic, tenebrous, unsettled 10 illdefined, indistinct, indefinite, inexplicit
13 indeterminate

Uncle Remus creator 6 Harris (Joel Chandler)

Uncle Tom's Cabin *author:* 5 Stowe (Harriet Beecher) *character:* 5 Eliza, Topsy
6 Legree (Simon) 9 Little Eva

Uncle Vanya author 7 Chekhov (Anton)

unclothe 5 strip 6 denude, divest, expose, unveil 7 display, disrobe, uncloak, uncover, undress

unclothed 4 bare, nude 5 naked
6 peeled, unclad 7 denuded, exposed
8 in the raw, stripped 9 au naturel, buck-naked, undressed 10 stark naked

unclouded 4 fair 5 clear, lucid, sunny
6 bright 7 halcyon 8 rainless, sunshiny

uncluttered 4 neat, tidy, trig, trim
7 orderly 9 organized, shipshape
11 spic-and-span, well-ordered 12 spick-and-span

uncombed 5 messy, mussy 6 matted, mussed 7 ruffled, snarled, tangled, tousled, unkempt 10 disheveled

uncommon 3 odd 4 rare 5 novel
6 choice, scarce, unique 7 special, unusual 8 esoteric, especial, singular, sporadic, unwonted 10 infrequent, noteworthy, remarkable 11 distinctive, exceptional 12 unaccustomed
13 extraordinary

uncommunicative 3 mum 4 dumb
5 aloof 6 offish, silent 7 distant, guarded, private 8 reserved, reticent, taciturn
9 reclusive, secretive, withdrawn
10 antisocial, poker-faced, speechless, tongue-tied, unsociable 11 inscrutable, standoffish, tight-lipped 12 closemouthed, tight-mouthed, unresponsive
13 unforthcoming

uncompassionate 4 cold, hard 5 stony
7 callous 8 obdurate, pitiless, uncaring
9 heartless, unfeeling 10 hard-boiled
11 coldhearted, hardhearted, insensitive 12 stonyhearted 13 unsympathetic

uncomplicated 4 easy 5 basic, clear, plain 6 simple 8 clear-cut 10 effortless, elementary, manageable, uninvolved

uncomplimentary 7 adverse 8 critical
9 degrading 10 belittling, derogatory, pejorative 11 deprecatory, disparaging, unfavorable 12 depreciative, depreciatory, unflattering

uncompromising 4 firm 5 rigid 8 hardline, obdurate, resolute, stubborn
9 hard-nosed, immovable, insistent, unbending 10 brassbound, determined, inexorable, inflexible, unshakable, unyielding 12 intransigent, singleminded

unconcealed 4 bald, bare, open 5 frank, naked, overt, plain 6 candid 7 blatant, evident, exposed, express, obvious, visible 8 apparent, explicit, manifest, palpable 10 forthright 11 openhearted, transparent, undisguised, unvarnished

unconcern 6 apathy 7 neglect 9 aloofness, disregard 10 alienation, detachment, dispassion 11 disinterest, inattention, insouciance, nonchalance **12** care-lessness, heedlessness, indifference **13** preoccupation

unconcerned 4 cool **6** remote **7** unmoved **8** careless, detached, heedless **9** alienated, apathetic, oblivious, unmindful, unruffled **10** insouciant, neglectful, untroubled **11** inattentive, indifferent, unperturbed **12** uninterested **13** disinterested, dispassionate

unconditional 5 sheer, total, utter **8** absolute, definite, explicit, outright **9** downright, out-and-out **10** unreserved **11** unequivocal, unqualified **12** unrestricted **13** thoroughgoing

unconfined 4 free, vast **5** loose **7** at large **9** at liberty, boundless, limitless, unlimited **12** unrestrained, unrestricted

uncongenial 6 at odds **8** unfitted **9** repellent, repugnant, unlikable **10** discordant, unsociable, unsuitable **11** conflicting, displeasing **12** antipathetic, disagreeable, incompatible, unattractive **13** unsympathetic

unconnected 5 alone, apart **8** discrete, detached, disjoint, disjunct, distinct, inchoate, rambling, separate **9** unrelated **10** unattached **11** independent **12** unassociated **13** discontinuous, noncontinuous

unconquerable 10 invincible, inviolable, unbeatable **11** bulletproof, impregnable, indomitable, insuperable **12** invulnerable, unassailable

unconscionable 5 undue **6** unfair, unholy, unjust, wanton, wicked **7** immoral, ungodly **8** barbaric, criminal **9** barbarous, unethical **10** exorbitant, inordinate, outrageous **11** inexcusable, uncivilized **12** unprincipled, unscrupulous

unconscious 3 out **6** asleep, chance **7** out cold, stunned, unaware **8** comatose **9** insensate, passed out, unplanned, unwitting **10** blacked out, insensible, knocked out **11** inadvertent, instinctual, involuntary **12** uncalculated **13** unintentional

unconsciousness 4 coma **5** faint **6** stupor, torpor, trance **7** syncope **13** obliviousness

unconsidered 4 rash **5** brash, hasty **6** casual **7** offhand **8** careless, reckless, slapdash **9** desultory, haphazard, hit-or-miss, hotheaded, impetuous, unplanned **10** ill-advised, incautious, unthinking **11** thoughtless

unconstrained 4 free, open **6** blithe, dégagé, wanton **7** buoyant, gushing, relaxed **8** animated, carefree, effusive, informal, outgoing **9** easygoing, expan-

sive, liberated **10** expressive, nonchalant, unreserved

uncontrollable 4 wild **6** unruly **7** wayward, willful **9** fractious **10** headstrong, refractory, self-willed **11** intractable **12** overwhelming, recalcitrant, ungovernable, unmanageable **13** irrepressible, undisciplined

uncontrolled 4 free, wild **5** loose **6** wanton **9** automatic, excessive, unbounded, unlimited, unmanaged **10** autonomous, immoderate, licentious, ungoverned **11** independent, instinctual, involuntary, unconscious, uninhibited, unregulated **12** disorganized, unrestrained **13** self-governing

unconventional 3 odd **4** beat **5** kinky, kooky, outré **6** casual, far-out, freaky, quirky, unique, way-out, weirdo **7** bizarre, deviant, oddball, offbeat, unusual, wayward **8** aberrant, abnormal, atypical, bohemian, freakish, original, peculiar **9** anomalous, eccentric, irregular **10** avant-garde, unexpected, unorthodox **11** uncustomary **13** idiosyncratic

unconvinced 5 leery **6** unsure **7** dubious **8** doubtful **9** skeptical, undecided **10** suspicious

unconvincing 4 lame **6** feeble, flimsy, forced **7** dubious, suspect **8** doubtful, strained **10** farfetched, improbable, incredible **11** implausible, unrealistic **12** unbelievable **13** unsubstantial

uncooked 3 raw

uncouple 4 part **6** detach, divide **7** disjoin, divorce, unhitch **8** separate, unfasten **9** disengage **10** disconnect, dissociate **12** disaffiliate

uncouth 3 odd, raw **4** rude **5** crass, crude, gross, rough **6** clumsy, coarse, rugged, vulgar **7** awkward, bizarre, boorish, ill-bred, loutish, strange, uncivil **8** barbaric, clownish, impolite, ungainly **9** eccentric, graceless, inelegant, unrefined **10** outlandish, uncultured, unpolished **11** ill-mannered, uncivilized **12** discourteous, uncultivated *person:* **3** oaf **4** boor, dolt, lout **5** clown **7** bumpkin **9** barbarian

uncover 4 bare **5** strip **6** betray, detect, divest, expose, remove, reveal, unmask, unveil **7** display, divulge, unearth **8** disclose

uncritical 5 naive **9** credulous **11** perfunctory

unction 3 oil **4** balm **5** cream, salve **6** balsam, cerate, chrism **7** suavity, unguent **8** liniment, ointment **9** emollient **11** embrocation

unctuous 4 oily **5** fatty, slick, soapy,

suave **6** greasy, smarmy **7** cloying, fawning, fulsome **8** slippery **9** wheedling **10** flattering, oleaginous, saccharine **11** sycophantic

uncultivated 4 wild **5** crass, crude, gross **6** coarse, desert, fallow, savage, vulgar **7** boorish, lowbrow, uncouth **8** barbaric, unplowed, untilled **9** barbarian, barbarous, inelegant, unrefined **10** unpolished **11** uncivilized

uncultured 3 raw **4** rude **5** crass, crude, gross, rough **6** coarse, vulgar **7** artless, boorish, ill-bred, loutish, lowbrow, natural, uncouth **8** barbaric, churlish, cloddish **9** barbarian, barbarous, benighted, inelegant, unrefined **10** unpolished **11** uncivilized **13** unenlightened

uncustomary 4 rare **7** special, strange, unusual **8** aberrant, abnormal, atypical, singular, uncommon **9** anomalous **10** surprising, unfamiliar, unorthodox **11** exceptional **13** extraordinary

uncut 6 whole, entire, intact **8** complete **9** undiluted **10** full-length, unabridged **11** uncondensed **13** unabbreviated

undamaged 5 sound, whole **6** intact, unhurt **8** unbroken, unmarred **9** uninjured, unscathed **10** unimpaired **11** unblemished

undaunted 4 bold **5** brave **6** daring, heroic **7** doughty, Spartan, valiant **8** fearless, intrepid, resolute, unafraid, valorous **9** audacious **10** courageous **11** lionhearted, unconquered, unflinching **12** stouthearted

___ **und Drang 5** Sturm

undeceive 8 disabuse **11** disillusion

undecided 4 iffy, moot, open **6** unsure **7** dubious, pending **8** doubtful, wavering **9** equivocal, tentative, uncertain, unsettled **10** ambivalent, indefinite, unresolved **12** undetermined

undeclared 5 tacit **6** unsaid **7** assumed, implied **8** accepted, implicit, inferred, presumed, unspoken, unstated **10** understood

undecorated 4 bare **5** plain, stark **6** homely, severe, simple **8** no-frills **9** unadorned **12** unornamented **13** unembellished, unembroidered

undefiled 4 pure **6** chaste, intact, vestal, virgin **8** innocent, spotless, virginal, virtuous **9** stainless, unstained, unsullied, untainted **10** immaculate **11** unblemished, untarnished

undefined 3 dim **4** hazy **5** faint, vague **6** bleary **7** obscure, shadowy, unclear **8** inchoate, nebulous, unformed **9** amorphous, shapeless **10** indistinct **12** undetermined

undemonstrative 4 calm, cold, cool **5** aloof, chill **7** aseptic, distant, laconic **8** reserved, retiring **9** contained, inhibited, shrinking, withdrawn **10** restrained, unsociable **11** emotionless, passionless, standoffish, unemotional **12** matter-of-fact, unresponsive **13** self-contained

undeniable 6 patent **7** certain, evident, genuine, obvious **8** manifest **9** veridical **10** inarguable **11** indubitable, irrefutable, unequivocal **12** indisputable **13** incontestable

undependable 6 fickle, tricky, unsafe **7** erratic **10** capricious, fly-by-night, inconstant, unreliable **12** inconsistent, questionable **13** irresponsible, unpredictable, untrustworthy

under 3 low, sub **4** down, less **5** below, lower, short **6** lesser **7** beneath, covered, subject **8** downward, inferior **9** dependent, receiving, secondary, subjacent **11** subordinate *prefix:* **3** hyp, sub **4** hypo

undercarriage 5 frame **9** framework **11** landing gear

undercover 6 covert, hidden, secret **7** furtive, stealth, sub-rosa **8** hush-hush, stealthy **11** clandestine **12** confidential **13** surreptitious *person:* **3** spy **4** mole **5** agent, spook **6** sleuth **9** detective, operative **10** counterspy **11** double agent, secret agent **12** counteragent

undercroft 5 crypt, vault **7** chamber **8** catacomb

undercut 7 subvert **8** sabotage

underdeveloped 4 poor **7** dwarfed, stunted **8** backward, immature **9** unevolved **10** third-world

underdog 5 loser **6** victim **7** also-ran, fall guy **9** dark horse

underdone 3 raw, red **4** rare

underestimate 6 slight **7** dismiss **8** belittle, discount, disprize, minimize **9** deprecate, disparage, sell short **10** depreciate

undergarment 3 bra **4** BVDs, slip **5** teddy **6** bikini, bodice, briefs, corset, girdle, shorts, undies **7** chemise, drawers, panties, stammel, step-ins **8** lingerie, pretties, Skivvies, woollies **9** brassiere, jockstrap, long johns, petticoat, underwear **10** foundation

undergo 4 bear, face **5** abide, brave, brook **6** endure, suffer **7** sustain, weather **8** submit to, tolerate **9** withstand **10** experience

undergraduate 4 coed **5** frosh **6** junior, senior **8** freshman **9** collegian, sophomore

underground 4 tube **5** metro, train

6 buried, hidden, nether, secret, subway **7** illegal, off-beat, railway **8** hypogeal, hypogean **10** undercover **11** alternative, clandestine **12** subterranean **13** surreptitious

underhanded 3 sly **4** wily **5** shady **6** covert, crafty, secret, shifty, sneaky, tricky **7** cunning, devious, elusive, evasive, furtive, sub-rosa **8** guileful, sneaking, stealthy **9** deceitful, deceptive **10** circuitous **11** clandestine, duplicitous **13** surreptitious

underlie 4 bear **6** prop up **7** subtend, support **8** buttress

underline 4 mark **6** play up, stress **9** emphasize, italicize **10** accentuate, underscore

underling 4 aide, peon, serf **5** gofer, scrub, slave **6** flunky, gopher, lackey, menial, minion **7** fall guy **8** inferior **9** assistant, attendant, subaltern **11** subordinate

underlying 4 root **5** basal, basic **7** primary **8** implicit **9** elemental, essential **11** fundamental

Under Milk Wood author 6 Thomas (Dylan)

undermine 3 sap **4** foil **5** blunt, erode **6** impair, thwart, weaken **7** cripple, disable, subvert **8** sabotage **9** attenuate, frustrate **10** debilitate, demoralize

undermost 6 bottom, lowest **9** lowermost **10** bottommost, nethermost, rock-bottom

underneath 4 sole **5** below, lower **6** bottom **7** covered

underpin 4 back, base, prop, root **5** brace **6** uphold **7** bolster, justify, shore up, support **8** buttress, validate **10** strengthen **11** corroborate

underpinning 4 base, prop, root, stay **5** basis, brace **7** bedrock, footing, seating, support **8** buttress **10** foundation, groundwork **12** substructure

underprivileged 4 poor **5** needy **7** hapless, unlucky **8** deprived **11** handicapped, unfortunate **13** disadvantaged

underrate 7 devalue **8** discount, mark down, minimize, write off **9** devaluate, write down **10** depreciate

underscore 6 accent, play up, stress **9** emphasize, italicize **10** accentuate

underside 4 sole **6** bottom **7** reverse

undersized 3 toy **4** baby, mini, puny **5** dinky, dwarf, pygmy, runty, short, small **6** bantam, little, pocket, slight **7** scrubby, stunted **9** miniature **10** diminutive **11** Lilliputian

understand 3 con, ken, see **4** know **5** grasp, guess, infer, savvy, sense, think **6** accept, assume, deduce, expect, fath-

om, figure, follow, gather, reason, reckon, take in, take it **7** believe, discern, imagine, presume, realize, suppose, surmise, suspect **8** conceive, conclude, consider, perceive **9** apprehend, interpret **10** appreciate, comprehend, conjecture

understandable 5 clear, lucid, plain **8** clear-cut, coherent, knowable **9** excusable, graspable, plausible **10** articulate, believable, defensible, fathomable, reasonable **11** justifiable, perceivable, unambiguous **12** intelligible **13** apprehensible

understanding 3 ken, wit **4** deal, pact **5** grasp, sense **6** accord, humane, kindly **7** compact, empathy, entente, insight, mastery **8** sympathy **9** agreement, awareness, knowledge, tolerance **10** acceptance, impression, perception **11** considerate, discernment, explanation, sympathetic **12** apprehension, relationship **13** comprehension

understatement 7 litotes

understood 5 tacit **7** assumed, implied **8** accepted, implicit, inferred, unspoken

understudy 6 double, backup, fill-in **7** standby, stand-in **9** surrogate **10** substitute **11** replacement

undertake 3 try **4** dare **5** assay, begin, essay, start **6** accept, assume, pledge, strive, tackle, take on, take up **7** attempt, certify, execute, perform, promise, warrant **8** commence, contract, covenant, endeavor, set about, set forth, shoulder **9** guarantee

undertaker 8 embalmer **9** mortician

undertaking 3 job **4** task **6** affair, charge, effort **7** calling, emprise, exploit, mission, project, pursuit, venture **8** endeavor **9** adventure, guarantee, operation **10** enterprise **11** proposition, transaction

under-the-table 6 covert, hidden, secret, sneaky **7** furtive, sub-rosa **8** hush-hush, stealthy **9** concealed, underhand **10** undercover **11** clandestine **13** surreptitious

undertone 3 hue, hum **4** cast, hint, tint **5** shade **6** mumble, murmur, mutter **7** inkling **10** suggestion **11** association, connotation, implication

undertow 4 eddy **7** current, riptide, sea puss

undervalue see UNDERRATE

underwater 9 submarine **10** subaquatic, subaqueous *breathing apparatus:* **5** scuba *captain:* **4** Nemo *chamber:* **7** caisson *device:* **8** paravane *missile:* **7** torpedo *sound detector:* **5** sonar

underwear see UNDERGARMENT

underwood 5 brush, copse, hedge, scrub 7 boscage, coppice, thicket 9 shrubbery

underworld 4 hell 5 hades, Sheol 6 Erebus, Tophet 7 Gehenna, inferno 8 gangland 9 antipodes 11 Pandemonium *boatman:* 6 Charon *deity:* 3 Dis 4 Bran 5 Pluto 6 Osiris *goddess:* 6 Hecate 10 Persephone *organization:* 5 Mafia *relating to:* 8 chthonic *watchdog:* 8 Cerberus

underwrite 4 back, fund, sign 5 endow, stake 6 assure, insure, pay for, secure 7 agree to, endorse, finance, sponsor, support 8 bankroll 9 grubstake, guarantee 11 subscribe to

undesigning 5 frank 6 candid, honest 7 artless, earnest, genuine, sincere 9 guileless, ingenuous, unfeigned 10 aboveboard, forthright

undesirable 8 annoying, unwanted 9 offensive, unwelcome 10 ill-favored, unpleasant, unsuitable 11 displeasing, inadvisable, troublesome 12 disagreeable, unacceptable, unattractive 13 inappropriate, objectionable

undesired 8 needless, unsought, unwanted 9 uninvited, unwelcome 10 gratuitous 11 uncalled-for, unnecessary 12 nonessential

undetermined 5 vague 7 dubious, obscure, pending, unclear 8 doubtful 9 ambiguous, equivocal, uncertain, undecided, undefined, unsettled 10 ill-defined, indefinite, indistinct 12 inconclusive

undeveloped 5 crude, green, rough 6 latent 8 backward, immature, inchoate 9 embryonic, incipient, primitive, unevolved 10 unfinished

undiluted 4 neat, pure 5 sheer, utter 7 genuine, unmixed 8 absolute, straight 9 authentic, unalloyed 11 unmitigated, unqualified 13 unadulterated

undiplomatic 4 rash, rude 5 brash, cocky 6 brazen, cheeky 8 impudent, tactless 9 audacious, hotheaded, impolitic, impulsive, maladroit, untactful 10 ill-advised, indiscreet 11 impertinent, injudicious, insensitive, thoughtless 12 presumptuous

undisciplined 4 wild 6 unruly, wanton 7 froward, restive, wayward, willful 8 contrary, untoward 9 fractious 10 disorderly, rebellious, refractory 11 intractable 12 contumacious, noncompliant, obstreperous, recalcitrant, ungovernable, unmanageable

undisclosed 6 hidden, sealed, secret 7 unknown, unnamed 8 ulterior, withheld 9 anonymous 10 unreported, unrevealed 11 clandestine, unmentioned, unspecified 12 confidential, undesignated, unidentified

undisguised 4 bald, open, pure 5 frank, naked, overt, sheer, stark 6 candid, patent 7 obvious 8 apparent, explicit, manifest, palpable 9 barefaced 11 openhearted, unconcealed, unvarnished

undistinguished 5 cheap, stock 6 common 7 humdrum, obscure, routine 8 déclassé, everyday, inferior, low-grade, mediocre, middling, ordinary, workaday 10 second-rate 11 commonplace, nondescript, second-class 12 run-of-the-mill 13 insignificant

undivided 3 one 4 full 5 fixed, total, whole 6 entire, intact, united 8 complete, unbroken 9 unanimous 10 continuous, unswerving 11 indivisible 12 concentrated, undistracted

undo 4 free, open, ruin 5 annul, loose, untie, upset, wrack, wreck 6 cancel, defeat, loosen, negate, stymie, unbind, unsnap 7 abolish, destroy, nullify, release, reverse, vitiate, wipe out 8 abrogate, unfasten, unloosen 9 disengage 10 invalidate 11 disentangle, outmaneuver

undoing 4 bane, doom, ruin, slip 5 shame 7 misstep 8 downfall, reversal 9 destroyer, overthrow, ruination 10 misfortune 11 destruction, humiliation

undoubted 4 real, sure, true 7 certain, genuine 8 definite, positive 9 authentic 10 undisputed

undoubtedly 5 truly 6 indeed, really, surely 7 clearly 8 of course 9 assuredly, certainly 10 definitely, positively, presumably, undeniably 11 indubitably

undress see UNCLOTHE

undressed 4 nude, rude 5 naked 6 unclad 7 exposed 8 in the raw, stripped 9 au naturel, unclothed

undue 5 inapt 7 extreme 8 ill-timed, improper, needless, untimely 9 excessive, unfitting 10 immoderate, indecorous, inordinate, unsuitable 11 extravagant, uncalled-for, unnecessary, unwarranted 12 unreasonable 13 inappropriate, unjustifiable

undulant fever 11 brucellosis

undulate 4 roll, swag, sway, wave 5 heave, snake, swell, swing 6 billow, ripple 7 slither 9 fluctuate, oscillate

unduly 3 too 6 overly 9 extremely, immensely 11 excessively 12 immoderately, inordinately, unreasonably 13 unnecessarily

undying 7 abiding, ageless, endless, eternal 8 enduring, immortal, unending

9 continual, deathless, perennial, perpetual, unceasing 10 continuing 11 amaranthine, everlasting 12 imperishable, unquenchable

unearth 4 find, show 5 dig up, learn 6 exhume, expose, reveal 7 exhibit, find out, root out, uncover 8 come upon, disclose, discover, dredge up, excavate 9 ascertain, determine 10 come across

unearthly 5 eerie, weird 6 absurd, insane, spooky 7 awesome, ghostly, uncanny, ungodly 8 abnormal, ethereal, heavenly, numinous, spectral 9 appalling, fantastic 10 miraculous, mysterious, outlandish, superhuman, suprahuman 12 preposterous, supermundane, supernatural 13 preternatural

unease 4 care, fear 5 angst, worry 6 strain, stress, unrest 7 anxiety, concern, tension 8 disquiet, distress 9 abashment, confusion, misgiving 10 discomfort, discontent, solicitude 11 disquietude, fretfulness, nervousness, uncertainty, uptightness 12 apprehension, discomfiture, discomposure 13 embarrassment

uneasy 4 edgy 5 jumpy, tense 6 afraid 7 anxious, awkward, fearful, fidgety, fretful, nervous, restive, unquiet, uptight, worried 8 agitated, doubtful, insecure, restless, unstable 9 ambiguous, concerned, difficult, disturbed, perturbed, uncertain, unsettled 10 disquieted, precarious, solicitous 11 embarrassed 12 apprehensive 13 uncomfortable

uneducated 5 crude, rough 8 ignorant, untaught 9 benighted, untutored 10 illiterate, unlettered, unschooled 12 uncultivated, uninstructed

unembellished 4 bald, bare 5 blunt, plain, spare, stark 6 severe 7 austere 9 essential, unadorned 11 undecorated, unelaborate, ungarnished, unvarnished 12 unornamented 13 unembroidered, unpretentious

unemotional 4 cold, cool 5 chill, stoic, stony 6 frigid, sedate, serene 7 deadpan, equable, glacial, stoical 8 composed, obdurate, reserved, reticent 9 apathetic, impassive 10 hard-boiled, phlegmatic 11 insensitive, passionless, unexcitable 12 intellectual, thick-skinned, unresponsive 13 dispassionate

unemployed 4 idle 5 fired 6 otiose, unused 7 jobless, laid off, loafing 8 inactive, leisured, workless 10 unoccupied

unending 7 eternal, undying 8 constant, immortal, infinite, timeless 9 boundless, ceaseless, continual, incessant, limitless, perennial, perpetual, unceasing 10 continuous 11 amaranthine, everlasting, unremitting 12 interminable 13 uninterrupted

unenlightened 5 naive 6 unread 7 heathen, unaware 8 backward, ignorant, nescient 9 benighted, unknowing 10 uneducated, uninformed 11 uninitiated 12 uncultivated

unenthusiastic 4 cool 5 tepid 8 grudging, listless, lukewarm 9 apathetic, unexcited 10 lackluster, lacklustre, spiritless 11 halfhearted, indifferent, perfunctory 12 uninterested

unequal 3 odd 6 uneven, unfair 7 diverse 8 inferior, lopsided, one-sided 9 different, disparate, divergent, irregular 10 asymmetric, dissimilar, inadequate, mismatched, off-balance 12 insufficient

unequaled 6 unique 7 supreme 8 foremost, nonesuch, peerless 9 matchless, paramount, unmatched, unrivaled 10 preeminent, surpassing 12 incomparable, transcendent, unparalleled 13 unprecedented

unequivocal 5 clear 6 direct, patent 7 certain, evident 8 apparent, definite, distinct, explicit, manifest, palpable 10 undeniable 11 categorical, indubitable, unambiguous 12 indisputable, undisputable

unerring 5 exact 6 dead-on 7 certain, correct, perfect, precise 8 accurate, reliable 9 faultless, unfailing 10 dependable, infallible 11 trustworthy

unessential 8 marginal, needless, unneeded 9 redundant 10 expendable, gratuitous, irrelevant, peripheral, unrequired 11 dispensable, superfluous, uncalled-for, unimportant, unnecessary 13 insignificant, insubstantial

unethical 5 venal, wrong 7 corrupt, crooked, immoral 9 dishonest, reprobate 12 disreputable, unprincipled, unscrupulous

uneven 3 odd 4 wavy 5 bumpy, erose, harsh, jaggy, rough 6 craggy, jagged, patchy, ragged, random, rugged, spotty 7 scraggy, unequal, varying 8 lopsided, scabrous, scraggly, variable 9 haphazard, hit-or-miss, irregular 10 asymmetric, imbalanced, unbalanced

unevenness 4 bump, wave 7 anomaly 8 asperity, imparity 9 disparity, imbalance, roughness, variation 10 inequality 12 irregularity, lopsidedness 13 disproportion

uneventful 5 usual 6 placid 7 humdrum, prosaic, routine 8 ordinary 10 unexciting 11 commonplace 12 unremarkable

unexampled 4 lone, only, sole, solo
5 alone 6 unique 8 singular, solitary
9 matchless, unequaled, unmatched,
unrivaled 10 consummate, inimitable,
sui generis, unequalled, unrivalled
12 incomparable, unparalleled
13 unprecedented

unexcited 4 calm 5 blasé, stoic 6 placid,
sedate, serene 7 relaxed, stoical 8 composed, tranquil 9 apathetic, collected,
unruffled 10 nonchalant 11 indifferent
12 uninterested 13 dispassionate

unexciting 4 arid, dull, tame 5 banal,
bland, ho-hum 6 boring, stodgy 7 humdrum, insipid, prosaic, tedious 8 lifeless, tiresome 10 monotonous 11 commonplace 13 uninteresting

unexpected 10 surprising, unforeseen
11 unpredicted 13 unanticipated

unexpectedly 5 aback, short 6 sudden
7 unaware 8 abruptly, suddenly,
unawares 9 forthwith 11 unwittingly
12 accidentally 13 inadvertently

unexpended 5 saved 7 reserve, surplus
8 left over, reserved 9 remaining

unexpired 5 valid 9 operative

unexpressed 5 tacit 6 silent, unsaid
7 assumed, implied 8 implicit, presumed, unspoken, wordless 9 unuttered 10 undeclared, understood

unfailing 4 fast, sure 7 certain, devoted
8 constant, faithful, reliable, resolute,
surefire, unerring 9 steadfast, unvarying 10 consistent, dependable, infallible, invariable, persistent, unchanging,
unflagging, unwavering 11 everlasting,
persevering, unrelenting 12 tried-and-
true 13 inexhaustible

unfair 4 foul 5 wrong 6 biased, shabby,
uneven, unjust 7 unequal 8 wrongful
9 arbitrary, dishonest, unethical
10 prejudiced 11 inequitable, underhanded, unrighteous

unfaithful 5 false 6 untrue 8 cheating,
disloyal, recreant, turncoat 9 faithless,
two-timing 10 adulterous, inaccurate,
perfidious, traitorous 11 treacherous
13 untrustworthy

unfaltering 3 set 4 firm 6 steady 7 abiding 8 constant, enduring, resolute, tireless 9 steadfast, unfailing 10 continuous, unflagging, unwavering
11 persevering 12 never-failing, wholehearted

unfamiliar 3 new 5 alien, novel 6 exotic
7 foreign, strange, unaware, unknown
8 peculiar 11 incognizant, out-of-the-
way 12 unaccustomed, unacquainted

unfashionable 5 dated, dowdy, passé,
stale 6 bygone, démodé, old-hat, shabby 7 outworn 8 outdated, outmoded
9 out-of-date, unstylish 10 antiquated,
oldfangled

unfasten 4 free, open, undo 5 loose,
unbar, unfix, unpin, untie 6 detach,
loosen, unbind, unbolt, unlace, unlock,
unsnap 7 release, unclasp, unhitch,
unlatch, unleash, unloose, unstrap
8 unbuckle, unfetter, unloosen, unteth-
er 9 disengage

unfathomable 7 abysmal, obscure 8 profound 9 boundless, enigmatic,
unplumbed 10 bottomless, fathomless,
unknowable 11 inscrutable 12 immeasurable, impenetrable

unfavorable 3 bad, ill 4 poor 6 averse,
unfair, unkind 7 adverse, hostile,
opposed 8 contrary, damaging, inimical, negative 9 disliking, troubling
11 detrimental, displeasing 12 antagonistic, disapproving, inauspicious *prefix:* 3 dys

unfavorably 4 awry 5 amiss, badly
6 astray, poorly 7 wrongly 10 nega-
tively, unsuitably 13 unfortunately

unfeasible 8 quixotic 9 visionary
10 chimerical, impossible, unworkable
11 impractical, speculative, theoretical,
unrealistic 12 unattainable, unrealizable 13 impracticable

unfeeling 4 cold, hard, numb 5 cruel,
harsh, stern, stony 6 brutal, leaden,
marble, numbed, severe, stolid, unkind
7 callous 8 benumbed, deadened, hardened, obdurate, pitiless, ruthless,
uncaring 9 apathetic, heartless,
indurated, insensate, senseless 10 hard-
boiled, insensible, insentient 11 cold-
blooded, coldhearted, hardhearted,
insensitive, unemotional 12 anesthetized 13 unsympathetic

unfeigned 4 real, true 6 actual, hearty,
honest 7 artless, earnest, genuine, natural, sincere 8 innocent 9 guileless,
heartfelt, ingenuous 11 undesigning
12 wholehearted

unfinished 3 raw 5 crude, rough
7 sketchy 9 imperfect, roughhewn,
undressed 10 incomplete, unpolished

Unfinished Symphony composer
8 Schubert (Franz)

unfit 4 sick, weak 5 inapt, inept 6 faulty
7 deprive, disable, unsound, useless
8 disabled, improper, unsuited 9 ill-suited, incapable, maladroit 10 disqualify,
ill-adapted, inadequate, ineligible,
unsuitable 11 incompetent, unqualified
12 disqualified, incompatible 13 inappropriate, incapacitated

unfitting 5 inapt 8 improper, unseemly
9 imprudent 10 ill-advised, inapposite,

malapropos, unbecoming, unsuitable 11 inadvisable 13 inappropriate

unfix 4 part, undo 5 loose, sever 6 cut off, detach, loosen, sunder, unbind 7 unloose 8 uncouple, unfasten, unloosen 9 disengage 10 disconnect, dissociate

unflagging 6 steady 7 staunch 8 constant, tireless, untiring 9 unceasing, unfailing, unwearied 11 persevering, unfaltering, unrelenting, unremitting 13 indefatigable, inexhaustible

unflappable 4 calm 6 poised, serene 7 assured, equable 8 composed, laid-back 9 collected, unruffled 10 deliberate, nonchalant 11 self-assured 13 imperturbable, self-possessed

unfledged 5 green, young 6 callow, jejune, unripe 7 puerile 8 immature, juvenile 10 unseasoned 11 undeveloped, unfeathered 13 inexperienced

unflinching 4 firm, grim 6 dogged 7 doughty, staunch, valiant 8 intrepid, resolute 9 dauntless, steadfast 10 relentless, unwavering, unyielding 11 unfaltering, unrelenting 12 stouthearted

unfold 4 open 6 deduce, evolve, expand, expose, extend, flower, mature, reveal, unwrap 7 blossom, burgeon, clear up, develop, display, dope out, exhibit, explain, resolve 8 decipher, disclose, evidence, manifest 9 elaborate, explicate, figure out, puzzle out, transpire 10 effloresce, outstretch 11 come to light

unforced 4 easy 7 natural, willing, witting 8 elective, optional 9 available, easygoing, voluntary 10 deliberate, volitional 11 intentional 12 unprescribed 13 discretionary, noncompulsory

unforeseeable 9 uncertain, unplanned 10 accidental

unforeseen 6 chance 8 surprise 10 accidental, surprising, unexpected 11 unlooked-for, unpredicted 13 unanticipated

unforgivable 9 untenable 10 censurable, inexpiable, outrageous 11 blameworthy, inexcusable, intolerable 12 indefensible, unacceptable, unpardonable 13 insupportable, reprehensible, unjustifiable

unformed 4 rude 5 crude, rough, vague 6 callow 8 immature, inchoate, nebulous, unshaped 9 amorphous, roughhewn, shapeless 10 indefinite, unfinished, unpolished 11 undeveloped, unfashioned 12 unstructured 13 indeterminate

unfortunate 3 bad, sad 4 dire, poor

6 woeful, wretch 7 adverse, awkward, hapless, unhappy, unlucky 8 grievous, ill-fated, luckless, untoward, wretched 9 desperate, graceless, ill-chosen, miserable 10 afflictive, calamitous, deplorable, disastrous, ill-starred, lamentable, unsuitable 11 distressing, regrettable, star-crossed, unfavorable 12 disagreeable, inauspicious, infelicitous, unsuccessful 13 heartbreaking

unfounded 4 idle, vain 5 false 8 baseless, spurious, unproven 9 deceptive, dishonest, untenable 10 fabricated, fallacious, gratuitous, groundless, mendacious, misleading, untruthful 11 uncalled-for, unsupported, unwarranted

unfriendly 4 cold, cool 5 alien, aloof, chill, gruff, surly 6 chilly, frosty, remote 7 distant, grouchy, hostile, opposed, warlike 8 inimical, unsocial 10 antisocial, censorious, inimicable, unsociable 11 ill-disposed, uncongenial 12 antagonistic, disagreeable, inhospitable, misanthropic, unneighborly 13 unsympathetic

unfruitful 4 arid, idle 5 empty, waste 6 barren, desert, effete, fallow, futile, wasted 7 parched, sterile, useless 8 abortive, bootless, depleted, impotent 9 infertile, pointless 10 unavailing 11 ineffective, ineffectual 12 impoverished, unproductive, unprofitable

unfurl 4 open 6 expose, reveal, spread, unfold, unroll, unwind 7 develop, display, exhibit, uncover 8 disclose 9 elaborate, spread out

unfurnished 4 bare 5 empty 6 vacant

unfussy 5 loose 6 breezy, casual, common, dégagé, folksy, mellow 7 cursory, relaxed 8 familiar, informal, laid-back 9 easygoing 10 unreserved 11 low-pressure, pococurante, unconcerned 12 unparticular 13 unceremonious, uncomplicated

ungainly 5 gawky, lanky, splay 6 clumsy, klutzy, oafish 7 awkward, boorish, hulking, loutish, lumpish, uncouth 8 bungling, clownish, lubberly, unwieldy 9 lumbering, maladroit 10 blundering

ungarnished 5 plain 6 modest, simple 9 unadorned 11 undecorated, unelaborate 12 unornamented 13 unembellished, unembroidered

ungenerous 4 mean 5 petty, tight 6 paltry, shabby, skimpy, stingy 7 chintzy, miserly 8 grudging, picayune, ungiving 9 illiberal, niggardly, penurious 11 closefisted, tightfisted 12 parsimonious 13 penny-pinching

ungodly see UNHOLY

ungovernable 4 wild **6** unruly **7** froward, lawless, willful **8** mutinous, untoward **9** fractious, turbulent, unbridled **10** disorderly, headstrong, rebellious, refractory, tumultuous **11** intractable **12** recalcitrant, uncontrolled, unmanageable **11** irrepressible, undisciplined

ungraceful 5 crude, gawky, inept, stiff **6** clumsy, gauche, klutzy, oafish, wooden **7** artless, awkward, halting, labored, stilted **8** bumbling, bungling, ungainly, untoward **9** all thumbs, inelegant, lumbering, maladroit **10** blundering

ungracious 4 rude **5** gruff **6** crusty **7** brusque, uncivil **8** churlish, impolite **9** offensive **10** unmannerly **11** disobliging, ill-mannered, impertinent, thoughtless, uncalled-for **12** disagreeable, discourteous **13** disrespectful, inconsiderate, unceremonious

ungraspable 6 opaque **7** obscure **8** baffling **9** enigmatic **10** unknowable **12** impenetrable, inexplicable, unfathomable

ungrateful 9 thankless

unguarded 5 frank, hasty **6** candid, direct, unwary **7** offhand **8** careless, heedless, reckless **9** impolitic, imprudent, impulsive **10** incautious, indiscreet, unthinking **11** defenseless, thoughtless, unprotected

unguent 4 balm **5** cream, salve **6** balsam, cerate, chrism, lotion **8** ointment **9** emollient, lubricant **11** embrocation

ungulate 3 hog, pig **4** deer **5** horse, tapir **6** hoofed **8** elephant **10** rhinoceros

unhallowed 4 evil **6** impure, unholy, wicked **7** immoral, impious, profane, ungodly **8** infernal **9** nefarious **10** desecrated, iniquitous, irreverent **13** unconsecrated

unhampered 4 free, open **5** frank, loose **6** direct **8** uncurbed **9** unbridled, unchecked, unimpeded, unlimited **10** unhindered **11** uninhibited, untrammeled **12** unrestrained, unrestricted, unobstructed **13** unconstrained

unhand 5 let go **7** release

unhandy 5 bulky, inept **6** clumsy, gauche, klutzy **7** awkward, halting, hulking **8** bumbling, bungling, cumbrous, unwieldy **9** all thumbs, hamhanded, maladroit, ponderous **10** cumbersome, unskillful **12** inconvenient

unhappiness 3 woe **5** blues, dolor, dumps, gloom, grief, worry **6** misery, mishap, sorrow **7** anxiety, sadness **8** distress **9** dejection **10** depression, desolation, discontent, heartbreak, melancholy **11** despondency, dolefulness **12** mournfulness, wretchedness **13** cheerlessness

unhappy 3 sad **4** down, grim **5** sorry **6** dismal, dreary, gloomy **7** joyless **8** dejected, downcast, mournful, saddened, troubled, wretched **9** cheerless, depressed, sorrowful, woebegone **10** despondent, dispirited, melancholy **11** melancholic, unfortunate **12** disconsolate, heavyhearted

unharmed 4 safe **5** sound **6** intact, secure, unhurt **8** unbroken, unmarred **9** protected, undamaged, undefiled, uninjured, unscathed **10** unimpaired **11** unblemished

unhealthiness 7 ailment, disease, illness, malaise **8** debility, sickness **9** infirmity **10** affliction, sickliness **11** decrepitude **13** indisposition

unhealthy 3 ill **4** sick **6** ailing, infirm, sickly, unwell **7** baneful, noisome, noxious, unsound **8** diseased **9** injurious **11** deleterious, unwholesome **12** insalubrious

unheard-of 3 new **6** unique **7** obscure, unknown, unnoted **8** nameless **10** phenomenal, unrenowned **12** uncelebrated **13** extraordinary, unprecedented

unhesitating 7 assured, earnest **8** decisive, positive, resolute **9** confident, immediate, unchecked **10** determined, forthright, purposeful **11** unflinching **12** wholehearted

unhinge 5 addle, craze **6** madden, ruffle **7** derange **9** unbalance

unhinged 3 mad **4** daft, loco, nuts **5** balmy, crazy, loony, wacky **6** insane **7** lunatic, unglued **8** demented, deranged **9** disturbed **10** unbalanced

unholy 4 base, evil, vile **6** impure, sinful, wicked **7** heinous, immoral, impious, profane, ungodly **8** dreadful, fiendish, god-awful, shocking **9** atheistic, barbarous **10** iniquitous, irreverent, outrageous, scandalous, unhallowed **11** irreligious, unbelieving **12** sacrilegious, unsanctified **13** reprehensible

unhorse 5 pitch, throw **6** topple, tumble, unseat **7** buck off **8** dislodge, dismount, overturn, unsaddle **9** overthrow

unhurried 4 easy, slow **7** laggard, relaxed **8** dilatory, laid-back **9** easygoing, leisurely **10** deliberate **11** low-pressure

unhurt 4 safe **5** sound, whole **6** entire, intact **7** perfect **8** unbroken, unharmed, unmarred **9** undamaged, uninjured, unscathed, untouched **10** unimpaired **11** unblemished

unification 5 union **6** fusion, hookup, merger **7** amalgam, joining, linkage, melding, merging **8** alliance, coupling

9 coalition 10 connection, federation
11 affiliation, coalescence, combination
12 amalgamation 13 confederation,
consolidation

uniform 4 even, like, suit 5 alike, dress,
equal, level 6 attire, outfit, stable,
steady 7 ordered, orderly, regular, similar, stabile 8 constant, unvaried 9 consonant, unvarying 10 comparable, consistent, invariable, unchanging
11 homogeneous 13 unfluctuating *combining form:* 3 iso *type:* 5 blues, habit,
khaki 6 livery, whites

uniformity 6 parity 7 oneness 8 equality,
evenness, identity, monotony, sameness
9 agreement, congruity, constancy
11 consistency 13 invariability

uniformly 6 always, evenly 7 equally
8 smoothly 10 comparably 11 analogously, identically 12 equivalently

unify 3 tie, wed 4 bind, bond, fuse, knit,
link, mesh 5 blend, marry, merge, unite
6 cement, couple 7 combine, conjoin
8 coalesce, compound, federate 9 integrate 10 amalgamate, centralize, synthesize 11 concatenate, consolidate

unimaginable 10 incredible, unknowable
11 unthinkable 12 mind-boggling,
unbelievable 13 extraordinary, inconceivable, indescribable

unimaginative 4 dull, flat 5 banal, bland,
trite, vapid 6 common 7 literal, prosaic,
routine, vanilla 8 bromidic 10 derivative, pedestrian, uncreative, uninspired
11 commonplace

unimpaired 4 safe 5 sound 6 intact,
unhurt 7 perfect 8 unbroken,
unharmed, unmarred 9 undamaged,
uninjured, unscathed 11 unblemished

unimpassioned 4 calm, cool 5 sober,
stoic 6 placid, remote, stolid 7 deadpan
8 detached, lukewarm, reserved, tranquil 9 impassive, temperate 10 phlegmatic, spiritless 11 cold-blooded, emotionless 12 matter-of-fact

unimpeachable 5 valid 7 correct 8 flawless, reliable, virtuous 9 blameless,
exemplary, faultless, unspotted, unsullied 10 conclusive, impeccable, undisputed 11 unblemished, untarnished
13 authoritative

unimportant 5 minor, petty 6 casual,
minute, paltry 7 trivial 8 piddling
9 small-beer, worthless 10 expendable,
immaterial, irrelevant, negligible
11 dispensable, meaningless, superfluous 13 insignificant

uninformed 7 unaware 8 ignorant, nescient 9 oblivious, unknowing, unwitting
10 unfamiliar 11 incognizant, superficial 12 unacquainted, undiscerning

uninhabited 5 empty, waste 6 barren,
vacant 7 vacated 8 deserted, desolate,
forsaken 9 abandoned, evacuated
10 unoccupied

uninhibited 3 lax 4 free 5 loose
8 uncurbed 9 expansive, fancy-free, liberated, unbridled 10 boisterous,
ungoverned, unhampered, unreserved
11 spontaneous, unrepressed, untrammeled 12 unrestrained, unsuppressed
13 unconstrained

uninjured 4 safe 5 sound, whole 6 intact,
unhurt 8 unharmed, unmarred
9 undamaged, undefiled, unscathed,
untouched 10 unimpaired 11 unblemished

uninspired 4 blah, drab, dull 5 banal,
stock, trite, vapid 6 boring, leaden, old-
hat, stodgy 7 humdrum, insipid, plastic,
sterile, vanilla 8 bromidic, lifeless, ordinary 9 colorless 10 lackluster, lacklustre, pedestrian, uncreative, unoriginal
11 commonplace 13 unimaginative

unintelligent 4 dumb 5 dense 6 obtuse,
stupid 7 asinine, brutish, doltish, fatuous, foolish, moronic, vacuous, witless
8 mindless 9 brainless, ludicrous
10 half-witted, ill-advised, irrational,
ridiculous, weak-minded 11 harebrained, lamebrained 12 feebleminded

unintentional 6 chance, random 9 haphazard, unplanned, unwitting 10 accidental, fortuitous, incidental, unexpected, unforeseen, unthinking
11 inadvertent, unconscious, unlooked-
for 12 adventitious, coincidental
13 unanticipated

uninterested 5 aloof, blasé, bored, jaded
9 apathetic, incurious, unexcited
10 uninvolved 11 indifferent, unconcerned

uninteresting 3 dry 4 arid, blah, drab,
dull, flat 5 banal, dusty, ho-hum, stale
6 boring, jejune 7 humdrum, insipid,
prosaic, tedious 8 bromidic, plodding,
tiresome 9 colorless, dryasdust, wearisome 10 monotonous, pedestrian,
uneventful, unexciting 11 uninspiring

uninterrupted 6 direct 7 endless, nonstop
8 constant, unbroken, unending
9 ceaseless, continual, incessant, perpetual, sustained, unceasing 10 continuous 11 undisturbed, unremitting
12 interminable

uninvited 7 unasked 8 unbidden,
unsought 9 intruding 10 gratuitous
11 uncalled-for, unrequested, unsolicited 12 presumptuous

union 4 bloc, bond, club 5 alloy, group,
guild, joint 6 fusion, league, merger

7 amalgam, joining, melding, merging, society **8** alliance, congress, coupling, junction, juncture, marriage, sodality **9** coalition **10** connection, federation, fellowship **11** association, brotherhood, coalescence, combination, confederacy, cooperative, unification **13** confederation, consolidation *labor:* **3** AFL, CIO, UAW, UMW **5** ILGWU

unique 3 odd, one **4** lone, only, sole, solo **5** alone, novel **6** single **8** peculiar, peerless, singular, solitary, uncommon, unwonted **9** anomalous, exclusive, matchless, unequaled, unmatched, unrivaled **10** inimitable, particular, sui generis, unequalled, unexampled, unrivalled **11** distinctive, exceptional **12** incomparable, unparalleled, unrepeatable **13** extraordinary, idiosyncratic, unprecedented

uniqueness 8 identity **10** singleness **11** peculiarity, singularity **13** individuality

___-Unis **5** Etats

unit 3 arm, one **4** area, item, part, wing **5** digit, group, monad, piece, whole **6** entity **7** element, measure **8** molecule **9** component **10** individual **11** constituent *administrative:* **6** agency, bureau, sector **8** district *boy scout:* **5** troop *educational:* **6** course *military:* (see at MILITARY) *of acceleration:* **3** gal *of action:* **7** episode *of advertising space:* **4** line **6** column *of an element:* **4** atom **8** molecule *of angular measure:* **6** radian *of area:* **3** are **4** acre **6** morgen **7** hectare **9** square rod **10** square mile, square yard *of astronomical distance:* **6** parsec **9** light-year *of brightness:* **7** lambert *of capacity:* **3** cup, tun **4** cord, dram, gill, peck, pint **5** liter, litre, minim, ounce, quart **6** barrel, bushel, firkin, gallon *of computer information:* **3** bit, gig, meg **4** byte **8** gigabyte, megabyte *of conductance:* **3** mho **7** siemens *of distance:* **4** mile, yard **5** meter **6** league **7** furlong *of electricity:* **3** amp **4** volt, watt **6** ampere **7** coulomb *of energy:* **3** erg **5** joule **7** quantum **8** watt-hour *of explosive force:* **7** megaton *of fineness:* **5** carat, karat *of force:* **4** dyne **6** newton **7** poundal *of frequency:* **5** hertz **7** fresnel *of grain:* **5** sheaf *of heat:* **3** BTU **5** therm **7** calorie *of illumination:* **3** lux **5** lumen *of inductance:* **5** henry *of length:* **3** mil, rod **4** foot, hand, inch, mile, rood, yard **5** chain, fermi, meter **6** fathom, micron **7** furlong **9** kilometer *historic:* **5** cubit *of loudness:* **4** sone **7** decibel *of lumber:* **9** board foot *of magnetic flux:* **5** gamma, gauss, tesla, weber **7** maxwell *of magnetic intensity:* **7** oersted *of magnetomotive force:* **7** gilbert *of pressure:* **3** bar **4** torr **6** pascal **10** atmosphere *of radiation:* **3** rad **8** roentgen *of radioactivity:* **5** curie *of resistance:* **3** ohm *of solar radiation:* **7** langley *of sound absorption:* **5** sabin *of speech:* **4** word **6** toneme **7** phoneme **8** morpheme, syllable *of speed:* **3** CPS, MPH, RPM **4** knot *of temperature:* **6** degree, kelvin *of time:* **3** day **4** beat, bell, hour, week, year **5** month **6** minute, season, second **8** svedberg *of viscosity:* **5** poise *of volume:* **9** cubic foot, cubic yard **10** cubic meter *of weight:* **3** cwt, ton **4** dram, gram, tael **5** carat, grain, ounce, pound, tonne **6** drachm **7** gigaton, kiloton, quintal, scruple **8** kilogram, millieme **9** metric ton, microgram, milligram *historic:* **3** tod **5** gerah, libra *Indian:* **4** tola *Russian:* **4** pood *of work:* **3** erg **5** ergon, joule *social:* **4** clan **5** tribe **6** family **7** chapter

unite 3 mix, tie, wed **4** ally, band, bind, bond, fuse, join, knit, link, meld, pool, weld **5** blend, graft, marry, merge, unify **6** cement, couple, gather, league, mingle, splice **7** combine, conjoin, connect **8** assemble, coadjute, coalesce, compound, federate **9** affiliate, aggregate, commingle **10** amalgamate, federalize **11** confederate, incorporate

united 3 one, wed **5** joint **6** allied, linked, merged, wedded **7** made one **8** agreeing, combined, in accord **10** harmonious

United Arab Emirates *capital:* **8** Abu Dhabi *city:* **5** Dubai **6** Dubayy *coast:* **6** Pirate **7** Trucial *emirate:* **5** Dubai **6** Dubayy **8** Abu Dhabi *former name:* **13** Trucial States *gulf:* **4** Oman **7** Persian *monetary unit:* **6** dirham *neighbor:* **4** Oman **11** Saudi Arabia *peninsula:* **7** Arabian *strait:* **6** Hormuz

United Kingdom *capital:* **6** London *city:* **3** Ely **4** Bath **5** Derby, Dover, Leeds **6** Exeter, Oxford **7** Bristol, Cardiff, Glasgow, Paisley **8** Bradford, Brighton, Coventry, Plymouth **9** Cambridge, Edinburgh, Leicester, Liverpool, Newcastle, Sheffield **10** Birmingham, Manchester, Nottingham **11** Bournemouth *colony:* **8** Falkland (Islands) *component:* **5** Wales **7** England **8** Scotland **12** Great Britain *conqueror:* **6** Caesar (Julius) **7** William (the Conqueror) *island:* **3** Man **4** Jura, Skye **5** Islay, Lewis, Wight **6** Jersey **8** Anguilla, Guernsey, Mainland *island group:* **6** Orkney **7** Channel **8** Hebrides, Shetland *language:* **5** Welsh **6** Gaelic **7** English *leader:* 8 Cromwell (Oliver) 9 Churchill (Winston) *monarch:* 4 Anne, Mary 5 Henry, James 6 Alfred (the Great), Edward, George 7 Charles, Richard, William 8 Victoria 9 Elizabeth *monetary unit:* 5 pence, penny, pound *monetary unit, former:* 3 bob 5 crown, groat 6 florin, guinea 7 ha'penny 8 farthing, shilling, sixpence 9 halfpenny 10 threepence *mountain, range:* 7 Scafell (Peak), Snowdon 8 Ben Nevis, Cumbrian, Grampian 12 Cheviot Hills *peninsula:* 7 Kintyre *prehistoric site:* 7 Avebury 9 Skara Brae 10 Stonehenge *river:* 3 Dee, Exe, Wye 4 Aire, Avon, Ouse 5 Clyde 6 Mersey, Severn, Thames *sea:* 5 Irish, North 6 Celtic *territory:* 8 Anguilla

United Nations *secretary-general:* 3 Lie (Trygve) 5 Annan (Kofi), Thant (U) 8 Waldheim (Kurt) 12 Boutros-Ghali (Boutros), Hammarskjöld (Dag) 14 Pérez de Cuéllar (Javier)

United States *desert:* 6 Mojave 7 Sonoran 8 Colorado *highest point:* 6 Denali (Mt.) 8 McKinley (Mt.) *island:* 6 Hawaii, Kodiak, Unimak 7 Nunivak 9 Admiralty, Chichagof 10 St. Lawrence 13 Prince of Wales *island group:* 3 Fox 6 Hawaii 8 Aleutian, Pribilof, Thousand *lowest point:* 11 Death Valley *mountain range:* 5 Coast, Green, Ozark, Rocky, White 7 Cascade, Olympic 9 Blue Ridge, Catskills 10 Adirondack, Great Smoky 11 Appalachian 12 Sierra Nevada *national park:* 4 Zion 6 Denali 7 Glacier, Olympic, Redwood, Sequoia 8 Badlands, Carlsbad, Wind Cave, Yosemite 9 Mesa Verde, Mt. Rainier 10 Everglades, Grand Teton, Hot Springs, Isle Royale, Shenandoah 11 Dry Tortugas, Grand Canyon, Kenai Fjords, Mammoth Cave, Yellowstone *possession:* 10 Puerto Rico *state:* 4 Iowa, Ohio, Utah 5 Idaho, Maine, Texas 6 Alaska, Hawaii, Kansas, Nevada, Oregon 7 Alabama, Arizona, Florida, Georgia, Indiana, Montana, New York, Vermont, Wyoming 8 Arkansas, Colorado, Delaware, Illinois, Kentucky, Maryland, Michigan, Missouri, Nebraska, Oklahoma, Virginia 9 Louisiana, Minnesota, New Jersey, New Mexico, Tennessee, Wisconsin 10 California, Washington 11 Connecticut, Mississippi, North Dakota, Rhode Island, South Dakota 12 New Hampshire, Pennsylvania, West Virginia 13 Massachusetts, North Carolina, South Carolina *territory:* 4 Guam 13 American Samoa, Virgin Islands

unity 5 union 6 accord 7 concord, harmony, oneness 8 identity, soleness 9 agreement, consensus 10 continuity, singleness, solidarity

universal 3 all 5 broad, total, whole 6 common, cosmic, entire, global 7 general, generic 8 catholic 9 extensive, planetary, unlimited, worldwide 10 ecumenical, ubiquitous 11 omnipresent 12 all-embracing, all-inclusive, cosmopolitan 13 comprehensive *combining form:* 4 omni

universe 3 all 5 whole, world 6 cosmos, system 8 creation 9 macrocosm

unjust 5 wrong 6 biased, shabby, unfair 7 partial, unequal 8 one-sided, improper, wrongful 9 inequable 10 prejudiced, undeserved 11 inequitable, unrighteous

unjustifiable 5 undue 7 invalid 8 baseless 9 unfounded, untenable 10 groundless 11 inexcusable, unsupported, unwarranted 12 indefensible

unkempt 5 messy 6 frowsy, frowzy, shaggy, sloppy, untidy 7 ruffled, rumpled, scruffy, tousled 8 scraggly, slipshod, slovenly, uncombed 10 bedraggled, disarrayed, disheveled, disordered, unpolished 11 disarranged

unkind 4 mean, vile 5 cruel, harsh, rough, stern 6 severe 7 callous 8 uncaring 9 inclement, malicious 10 ungenerous, ungracious 11 insensitive, thoughtless, unfavorable 12 uncharitable 13 unsympathetic

unknowable 6 arcane, hidden, mystic, occult, secret 7 cryptic 8 mystical, numinous 9 enigmatic, recondite 10 mysterious 11 inscrutable, ungraspable 12 impenetrable, unfathomable

unknowing 6 unwary 7 unaware 8 heedless, ignorant 9 oblivious, unmindful, unwitting 10 insensible, unfamiliar, uninformed 11 incognizant 12 unsuspecting

unknown 6 hidden, nobody, secret 7 obscure, strange 8 nameless 9 anonymous, incognito

unlawful 6 banned 7 bootleg, corrupt, crooked, illegal, illicit, immoral 8 criminal, outlawed, wrongful 9 forbidden, felonious, nefarious 10 contraband, flagitious, indictable, iniquitous, prohibited, proscribed, unlicensed 11 black-market 12 illegitimate, unauthorized

unlearned 5 naive 6 unread 7 unaware 8 ignorant, nescient, untaught 10 illiterate, uneducated, unlettered, unschooled 11 instinctive 13 unenlightened

unleash 4 free, vent 5 let go, loose,

untie, visit, wreak 6 unbind 7 inflict, release 8 carry out, liberate 10 bring about

unless 3 but 4 save 6 except, saving 7 barring, but that, without 9 excepting, excluding

unlettered see UNEDUCATED

unlikable 9 obnoxious, offensive, repellent 10 unpleasant 11 displeasing, distasteful 12 disagreeable

unlike 5 mixed 7 diverse, unequal, various 8 assorted 9 different, disparate, divergent 10 dissimilar 11 distinctive, diversified 13 heterogeneous

unlikely 5 faint, unfit 6 remote, slight 7 distant, dubious 8 doubtful 10 farfetched, improbable, unsuitable 11 implausible, unpromising 12 questionable

unlimited 4 full, vast 5 total 6 untold 7 endless, immense 8 absolute, infinite, wide-open 9 boundless, countless, unbounded, universal 10 unconfined, unfettered 11 unqualified, untrammeled 12 immeasurable, interminable, unrestrained, unrestricted 13 comprehensive, unconditional, unconstrained

unlit 4 dark, inky 6 gloomy 9 lightless

unload 4 drop, dump, junk 5 chuck, ditch, empty 6 debark, remove 7 confess, confide, deep-six, deliver, discard, divulge, lighten, relieve 8 disclose, disgorge, jettison 9 disburden, discharge, disembark, eighty-six, stevedore 11 disencumber

unloose 4 free, undo 5 let go, relax, untie 6 detach, unbind 7 break up, manumit, release, set free, slacken 8 liberate, uncouple, unfasten 9 disengage, extricate, untighten 10 disconnect

unlucky 6 jinxed 7 hapless, ominous 8 ill-fated, untoward 9 ill-boding 10 illstarred 11 detrimental, inopportune, regrettable, star-crossed, unfavorable, unfortunate 12 inauspicious, unpropitious

unmanageable 4 wild 5 balky, bulky 6 unruly 7 awkward 8 contrary, cumbrous, perverse, stubborn, unwieldy 9 fractious, obstinate 10 cumbersome, disorderly, headstrong, inflexible, rebellious, refractory 11 intractable 12 obstreperous, recalcitrant, ungovernable 13 uncooperative, undisciplined

unmannered 4 rude 5 crude, rough 6 coarse, gauche 7 boorish, ill-bred, loutish 8 impolite 10 indecorous, ungracious 12 discourteous 13 disrespectful

unmarred 5 sound, whole 6 intact,

unhurt 7 perfect 8 pristine, unflawed, unharmed 9 undamaged, undefiled, unscathed, unstained 10 unimpaired 11 unblemished, untarnished

unmask 6 debunk, detect, expose, reveal, show up, unveil 7 deflate, uncover 8 disclose, discover, disprove 9 demystify

unmatched 3 odd 4 only 5 alone 6 unique 8 peerless, singular 9 unequaled, unrivaled 10 inimitable, unequalled, unrivalled 11 exceptional 12 incomparable, unparalleled

unmerciful 5 cruel, harsh 6 brutal 7 callous, extreme 8 inhumane, pitiless, ruthless, uncaring, vengeful 9 heartless, unfeeling, unsparing 10 relentless

unmindful 7 unaware 8 careless, heedless 9 forgetful, negligent, oblivious, unheeding, unwitting 10 abstracted, distracted, neglectful 11 inattentive

unmistakable 5 clear, frank, plain 6 patent 7 certain, decided, evident, express, obvious 8 apparent, definite, distinct, explicit, manifest, palpable 11 unambiguous, unequivocal

unmitigated 4 pure, rank 5 gross, sheer, utter 6 arrant 7 perfect, unmixed 8 absolute, clearcut, complete, outright 9 downright, out-and-out, unalloyed, undiluted 10 consummate, unmodified, unrelieved 11 straight-out, unqualified 12 unalleviated 13 thoroughgoing, unadulterated

unmixed 4 mere, neat, pure 5 plain, sheer, utter 6 simple 7 perfect, sincere 8 absolute, straight 9 unalloyed, unblended, undiluted, undivided 11 unmitigated, unqualified 13 unadulterated

unmoved 4 calm, cool, firm 5 aloof, stony 6 stolid 7 adamant, callous, stoical 8 obdurate 9 impassive, untouched 10 insensible, untroubled 11 unconcerned, unemotional, unimpressed 12 unresponsive

unnamed 5 incog 6 secret 7 obscure, unknown 9 anonymous, incognito 11 unspecified 12 unidentified

unnatural 7 uncanny 8 aberrant, abnormal 9 anomalous, contrived, irregular, synthetic 10 artificial, fabricated, factitious

unnecessary 6 excess 7 surplus 8 needless, optional, prodigal 9 redundant 10 expendable, extraneous, gratuitous, unrequired 11 dispensable, inessential, superfluous, uncalled-for, unessential 12 nonessential

unnerve 5 daunt, shake, throw, upset 6 dismay, rattle 7 agitate, fluster, per-

turb, unhinge **8** bewilder, confound
9 undermine **10** demoralize, disconcert,
discourage, dishearten, intimidate
unobstructed 4 open **5** clear **8** passable
9 unblocked, unimpeded **10** unhampered, unhindered **12** unrestricted
unobtrusive 5 quiet **6** modest **7** subdued
8 reserved, retiring, tasteful
10 restrained **13** inconspicuous
unoccupied 4 free, idle **5** empty **6** vacant
7 jobless, vacated **8** deserted **9** abandoned, available **10** employable, unemployed **11** uninhabited
unofficial 7 pirated, private, wildcat
8 informal **9** irregular **10** unapproved,
unorthodox **12** unauthorized, unsanctioned
unorganized 7 aimless, chaotic, muddled **8** confused, inchoate, nebulous,
rambling, unformed **9** amorphous,
arbitrary, haphazard, shapeless,
unplanned **10** disjointed, disordered,
incoherent, incohesive **11** spontaneous
unoriginal 5 banal, stock **6** copied, old-
hat **7** clichéd, humdrum, prosaic, sterile **8** borrowed, ordinary **9** hackneyed,
imitative **10** derivative, uninspired
11 commonplace, plagiarized, uninventive **12** conventional **13** unimaginative
unornamented 4 bare **5** plain, spare,
stark **6** chaste, modest, severe, simple
7 austere **9** unadorned **11** unelaborate,
ungarnished **13** unembellished, unembroidered
unorthodox 3 odd **5** kinky, novel, weird
6 far-out **7** strange, unusual **8** abnormal
9 different, dissident, eccentric, heretical, irregular, sectarian **10** schismatic,
unexpected **13** nonconformist
unorthodoxy 6 heresy, schism **7** dissent
8 variance **9** disbelief, ingenuity, recusancy **10** contention, dissidence, innovation **13** nonconformism, nonconformity
unpaid 3 due **5** owing **6** mature **7** donated, overdue, payable, pro-bono
8 freewill, honorary, wageless **9** unsettled, voluntary, volunteer **10** delinquent, gratuitous, receivable, unsalaried **11** contributed, outstanding
13 uncompensated, unremunerated
unpalatable 8 unsavory **10** flavorless
11 distasteful **12** unappetizing
unparalleled 6 unique **8** peerless, singular **9** matchless, unequaled, unmatched,
unrivaled **10** inimitable, unequalled,
unrivalled **11** exceptional **12** incomparable
unplanned 5 fluky **6** chance, random
7 aimless **9** desultory, haphazard, hit-or-miss **10** accidental, unexpected,

unforeseen, unintended **11** inadvertent
12 adventitious, coincidental, unconsidered **13** unintentional
unpleasant 4 sour **5** seamy **7** painful
8 annoying **9** offensive, troubling **10** disturbing, irritating **11** displeasing, distasteful, distressing **12** disagreeable
13 objectionable
unpolished 4 rude **5** crude, gruff, rough
6 crusty, unhewn, vulgar **7** brusque,
uncivil, uncouth **8** homespun,
unworked **9** inelegant, roughhewn,
unrefined **10** amateurish, uncultured,
unfinished, ungracious **11** ill-mannered,
uncivilized **12** discourteous
unpredictable 4 iffy **5** dicey, fluky
6 chancy, fickle, random, touchy
7 erratic, mutable **8** unstable, variable,
volatile **9** arbitrary, mercurial, uncertain, whimsical **10** capricious, changeable **13** unforeseeable
unprejudiced 4 fair, just **5** equal **8** balanced, unbiased **9** equitable, impartial,
objective, unbigoted, uncolored
10 even-handed, fair-minded, open-
minded **11** nonpartisan **12** uninfluenced
13 disinterested, dispassionate
unpressed 7 rumpled, wrinkly **8** crinkled, puckered, wrinkled
unpretentious 5 frank, plain **6** candid,
honest, modest, simple **7** genuine
8 ordinary **9** unadorned **10** forthright,
unaffected, unassuming **11** plainspoken
unprincipled 5 venal **7** corrupt, crooked,
immoral **9** deceitful, dishonest, dissolute, mercenary, reprobate, unethical
10 inconstant, iniquitous, profligate,
unfaithful **11** underhanded
12 unscrupulous
unproductive 4 vain **6** barren, futile
7 sterile, useless **8** bootless, depleted,
feckless, impotent **9** fruitless, infertile
10 unavailing **11** ineffectual **12** hardscrabble
unprofitable 4 idle, vain **6** barren, futile
7 useless **8** bootless **9** fruitless
10 unavailing **11** ineffective **12** unproductive, unsuccessful
unprogressive 8 orthodox **9** illiberal
11 traditional **12** conservative
unpropitious 4 grim **5** bleak **7** ominous,
unlucky **9** ill-boding, ill-omened
10 foreboding **11** inopportune, threatening, unfavorable **12** discouraging
13 disheartening
unprosperous 4 poor **5** needy **8** strapped
9 penurious **11** impecunious
unprotected 6 unsafe **7** exposed **8** helpless, insecure **9** unguarded **10** endangered, undefended, unshielded, vulner-

able **11** defenseless, susceptible, unsheltered

unproved 7 untried **8** untested **10** postulated **11** conjectural, preliminary, provisional, speculative, theoretical **12** experimental, hypothetical

unpunctual 4 late **5** tardy **6** remiss **7** belated, delayed, overdue **10** behindhand, delinquent

unqualified 4 firm, rank **5** sheer, total, unfit, utter **7** express **8** absolute, explicit, unfitted **9** incapable, out-and-out, steadfast, unalloyed, undiluted, unskilled **10** ineligible, unequipped, unreserved, unsuitable **11** ill-equipped, incompetent, unmitigated **12** wholehearted **13** unadulterated, unconditional

unquenchable 6 crying **7** buoyant, exigent **8** pressing, yearning **9** demanding, insatiate, insistent **10** insatiable **12** effervescent, unrestrained **13** irrepressible, unconstrained

unquestionable 4 real, sure, true **7** certain, genuine **8** absolute, bona fide **9** authentic, undoubted **10** sureenough, undeniable **11** established, indubitable, self-evident, well-founded **12** indisputable, well-grounded **13** authoritative, incontestable, unimpeachable

unquestioning 4 firm, sure **5** fixed **6** steady **7** abiding **8** enduring, gullible, resolute, trusting, unshaken **9** accepting, believing, credulous, steadfast **10** uncritical, undoubting, unshakable, unwavering **11** unfaltering, unqualified **12** never-failing, unhesitating, unsuspecting, unsuspicious, wholehearted

unravel 5 break, solve **6** answer, decode, unknit, unwind **7** clear up, dope out, explain, resolve, unsnarl **8** decipher, dissolve, untangle **9** elucidate, extricate, figure out, interpret, puzzle out, translate **11** disentangle

unreadable 7 deadpan **9** illegible **10** poker-faced **11** inscrutable **12** hieroglyphic **13** cacographical

unreal 4 fake **5** false **6** fabled **7** fictive **8** chimeric, fanciful, illusory, mythical **9** fantastic, fictional, imaginary, imitation **10** artificial, chimerical, fictitious, improbable, incredible **11** nonexistent **12** unbelievable *combining form:* **5** pseud **6** pseudo

unrealistic 7 blue-sky, idyllic, utopian **8** fanciful, quixotic, romantic **9** distorted, idealized, overblown **10** farfetched, ivory-tower, overstated, starryeyed, unworkable **11** exaggerated, extravagant, impractical, sensational

unreasonable 5 undue **6** absurd **7** invalid **9** arbitrary, excessive, illogical, senseless, sophistic **10** exorbitant, fallacious, headstrong, immoderate, inordinate, irrational, peremptory, ridiculous **11** extravagant, incongruous, nonsensical, uncalled-for, unwarranted **12** preposterous **13** unjustifiable

unreasoned 7 invalid, unsound **9** deceptive, illogical, sophistic, unfounded **10** fallacious, ill-founded, irrational, misleading, ungrounded **11** nonrational

unrefined 3 raw **4** rude **5** crass, crude, rough, tacky **6** coarse, earthy, impure, vulgar **7** natural, uncouth **9** graceless, inelegant, maladroit, roughhewn **10** uncultured, unpolished **11** illmannered, uncivilized, unprocessed **12** uncultivated

unreflective 6 casual **7** offhand **8** careless, feckless, heedless, mindless **9** imprudent, impulsive, oblivious, unheeding **10** indiscreet, nonchalant, unthinking **11** inadvertent, perfunctory, thoughtless **13** ill-considered

unrehearsed 7 offhand **8** informal **9** extempore, impromptu, unstudied **10** improvised, off-the-cuff, unprepared **11** extemporary, spontaneous **12** extemporized

unrelated 8 discrete, separate **9** different, disparate **10** dissimilar, extraneous, irrelevant **11** independent

unrelenting 3 set **4** grim **5** stern **7** adamant, endless **8** constant, resolute, ruthless, tireless **9** ceaseless, continual, hard-nosed, incessant, tenacious, unbending, unsparing **10** continuous, determined, implacable, inexorable, inflexible, persistent, unflagging, unshakable, unwavering, unyielding **12** unappeasable

unreliable 6 fickle, shifty, tricky, unsafe **7** dubious **8** fallible, slippery, two-faced **9** deceitful, deceptive, faithless, trustless, unassured, uncertain **10** capricious, fly-by-night, inaccurate, inconstant, perfidious, unfaithful **11** vacillating **12** falsehearted, questionable, unconvincing, undependable **13** irresponsible, unpredictable, untrustworthy

unremarkable 4 so-so **5** plain, usual **6** common, decent, normal **7** average, mundane, prosaic, routine, vanilla **8** adequate, everyday, familiar, habitual, mediocre, ordinary, workaday **9** customary, quotidian, tolerable **11** commonplace, nondescript **12** run-of-the-mill **13** unexceptional

unremitting 7 abiding, chronic, endless,

lasting, nonstop 8 constant, enduring, unending 9 ceaseless, continual, incessant, perennial, perpetual, sustained, unceasing 10 continuous, persistent, persisting, relentless 12 interminable 13 uninterrupted

unrepentant 10 impenitent 11 remorseless 12 unregenerate

unrepresentative 7 deviant, unusual 8 aberrant, abnormal, atypical 9 anomalous, divergent, eccentric, irregular, untypical 11 exceptional, heteroclite 13 nonconforming

unreserved 4 open 5 frank, plain 6 candid 7 sincere 8 effusive, explicit, informal, outgoing, outright 9 expansive, talkative 10 definitive 11 forthcoming, openhearted, unconcealed, undisguised, unqualified, unvarnished 13 demonstrative, unconstrained

unresolved 4 moot 7 pending 8 hesitant, wavering 9 faltering, tentative, uncertain, undecided, unsettled 10 ambivalent, hesitating, indecisive, irresolute, unanswered 11 vacillating

unrespectable 3 low 5 shady 6 shabby, shoddy 8 shameful, unworthy 10 inglorious 11 disgraceful, ignominious 12 dishonorable, disreputable 13 discreditable

unresponsive 4 cold 5 aloof, stoic 6 frigid, remote, stolid 7 distant, passive 8 detached, reserved 9 inhibited, withdrawn 10 forbidding, insentient 11 insensitive, passionless, unemotional 12 uninterested 13 insusceptible, unsusceptible

unrest 6 strife, tumult 7 anarchy, anxiety, ferment, tension, turmoil 8 disorder, disquiet, distress, edginess, upheaval 9 agitation, commotion, confusion 10 inquietude, turbulence, uneasiness 11 disquietude, disturbance, instability 12 perturbation 13 Sturm und Drang

unrestrained 5 bluff, blunt, frank 6 candid, wanton 7 rampant 8 outgoing, uncurbed 9 audacious, excessive, expansive, indulgent, unbridled 10 forthright, immoderate, implacable, inordinate, ungoverned, unhampered 11 extravagant, impassioned, intemperate, overwrought, plainspoken, spontaneous, uninhibited, untrammeled 12 uncontrolled 13 demonstrative, irrepressible, overindulgent

unrestricted 4 free, full, open 9 boundless, extensive, unlimited 10 accessible, unconfined, unfettered, unhampered 11 far-reaching, unqualified, wide-ranging 12 unobstructed 13 unconditional

unripe 3 raw 5 green, young 6 callow, jejune 7 untried 8 emergent, immature, juvenile, unformed, youthful 9 unfledged, untrained 10 unprepared, unseasoned 11 undeveloped 13 inexperienced

unrivaled 4 only, sole 5 alone 6 unique 7 leading, stellar, supreme 8 champion, foremost, greatest, peerless 9 matchless, paramount, principal, unequaled, unmatched 10 inimitable, preeminent, unequalled 11 outstanding, predominant, unsurpassed 12 incomparable, transcendent, unparalleled

unroll 6 expose, extend, reveal, unfurl, unwind 7 exhibit, open out 8 disclose 9 spread out

unromantic 5 sober 8 sensible 9 practical, pragmatic, realistic 10 hard-boiled, hardheaded 11 down-to-earth, levelheaded, utilitarian 12 businesslike, matter-of-fact 13 unsentimental

unruffled 4 calm, cool 6 poised, placid, serene, smooth 7 equable, unmoved 8 composed, tranquil 9 collected, unexcited 10 nonchalant, untroubled 11 unconcerned, undisturbed, unflappable 13 imperturbable, self-possessed

unruly 4 wild 5 rowdy 7 froward, naughty, raucous, wayward, willful 8 contrary, perverse, untoward 9 fractious, obstinate, turbulent 10 boisterous, disorderly, headstrong, ill-behaved, rebellious, refractory, tumultuous 11 disobedient, indomitable, intractable 12 contumacious, incorrigible, obstreperous, rambunctious, recalcitrant, ungovernable, unmanageable 13 undisciplined

unsafe 5 risky, shaky 6 chancy 7 erratic, harmful, parlous, rickety, tottery, unsound 8 insecure, perilous, slippery, unstable 9 dangerous, hazardous, uncertain 10 precarious, ramshackle, unreliable, vulnerable 11 threatening, treacherous 12 undependable

unsaid 5 known, tacit 6 silent 7 assumed, implied 8 accepted, implicit, indirect, inferred, presumed, unspoken, unstated, wordless 9 customary, unuttered 10 insinuated, undeclared, understood 11 traditional, unexpressed

unsatisfactory 3 bum 4 lame 5 amiss 8 mediocre 9 defective, deficient 10 inadequate 11 displeasing, substandard 12 unacceptable 13 disappointing,

unsavory 4 rank 5 gross, shady 6 rancid 7 insipid 9 repugnant, repulsive, sickening, tasteless 10 disgusting, flavorless 11 distasteful, ill-flavored, unpalatable 12 disagreeable, unappetizing

unsay 4 lift, void 6 abjure, cancel, disown, recall, recant, revoke 7 nullify, rescind, retract, reverse, suspend 8 abnegate, abrogate, disclaim, forswear, renounce, take back, withdraw 11 countermand

unscathed 4 safe 5 sound, whole 6 intact, unhurt 8 unharmed 9 uninjured, unscarred, untouched 11 unscratched

unscented 8 odor-free, odorless

unschooled 5 naive 7 artless, natural, vacuous 8 ignorant, untaught 9 ingenuous, unstudied, untrained, untutored 10 illiterate, unaffected, uneducated, unlettered 11 empty-headed 12 unartificial, uninstructed

unscramble 5 solve, untie 6 unwind 7 clarify, resolve, restore, sort out, unravel, untwine 8 untangle 9 extricate 11 disentangle 12 disembarrass

unscrupulous 5 shady, venal 7 corrupt, crooked, knavish 8 scheming, wrongful 9 deceitful, dishonest, mercenary, shameless, underhand, unethical 11 underhanded 12 dishonorable, exploitative, unprincipled

unseasonable 8 ill-timed, untimely 12 inconvenient

unseasoned 3 raw 4 flat 5 bland, fresh, green, young 6 callow 7 untried 8 immature 9 credulous, tasteless, unfledged, untrained 10 flavorless 11 unpracticed 13 inexperienced

unseat 3 axe, can 4 boot, buck, fire, oust, sack 5 eject, pitch, purge, throw 6 depose, recall, remove 7 buck off, dismiss, unhorse 8 dethrone, dislodge, displace 9 ostracize

unseemliness 5 gaffe 7 blunder, faux pas 8 solecism 9 barbarism, gaucherie, immodesty, impudence, indecency, vulgarity 10 coarseness, imprudence, incivility, indelicacy 11 impropriety 12 indiscretion

unseemly 8 improper, untoward 9 inelegant, unrefined 10 indecorous, indelicate, malapropos, unbecoming, unsuitable 11 unbefitting 13 inappropriate

unseen 6 hidden 9 concealed, invisible, unnoticed 10 overlooked, unobserved 11 unsuspected

unsentimental see UNROMANTIC

unserviceable 7 useless 10 inoperable, unfeasible, unworkable 11 impractical, unrealistic 13 impracticable, nonfunctional

unsettle 3 vex 4 faze 5 spook, upset 6 bother, flurry, jumble, rattle, ruffle 7 agitate, disturb, fluster, perturb, trouble, unhinge, unnerve 8 bewilder, con-

found, disarray, disorder, disquiet 9 discomfit 10 disarrange, discompose, disconcert 11 disorganize

unsettled 3 due 4 open 5 fluid, owing, shaky 6 mobile, queasy, shaken, uneasy, unpaid 7 anxious, dubious, mutable, overdue, payable, pending, restive 8 agitated, bothered, doubtful, frontier, restless, troubled, unstable, unsteady, variable 9 disturbed, uncertain, undecided 10 changeable, indecisive, unbalanced, unresolved 11 outstanding, problematic 12 undetermined

unsex 3 fix 4 geld, spay 5 alter 6 change, neuter 8 castrate 9 sterilize 10 emasculate

unshackle 4 free 5 loose 6 loosen, unbind 7 manumit, release, unchain 8 liberate, unfetter 10 emancipate

unshakable 4 firm, sure 5 fixed 6 stable, steady 7 abiding, adamant, settled, staunch 8 resolute 9 steadfast, tenacious, unbending 10 determined, persistent, unwavering, unyielding 11 unfaltering, unrelenting 12 neverfailing 13 unquestioning

unshaped 5 vague 7 nascent 8 formless, inchoate, unformed 9 amorphous, embryonic 11 preliminary, undeveloped 13 indeterminate

unshared 4 sole 6 single, unique 7 private 8 singular 9 exclusive, undivided 10 individual 11 distinctive

unshod 8 barefoot, shoeless 9 discalced 10 barefooted

unsightly 4 ugly 5 gross 6 grisly 7 hideous 9 repulsive 10 ill-favored 12 unattractive

unskillful 5 inept 6 clumsy, gauche 7 awkward, unhandy 8 bumbling, bungling, inexpert 9 ham-handed, incapable, maladroit, stumbling, untrained 11 unpracticed 13 unworkmanlike

unsnarl see UNTANGLE

unsociable 3 shy 4 cold, cool 5 aloof, timid 6 offish, remote, shut-in 7 distant 8 reserved, secluded, solitary 9 diffident, reclusive, unbending, withdrawn 10 unfriendly 11 introverted, standoffish 12 inaccessible, unneighborly

unsoiled 5 clean 8 spotless 9 unspotted, unstained, unsullied, untainted 10 immaculate 11 unblemished, untarnished

unsophisticated 5 corny, green, naive 6 callow, folksy, rustic, simple 7 artless, natural, sincere, uncouth 8 gullible, innocent 9 childlike, ingenuous, unrefined, unworldly

unsorted 5 mixed 6 divers, motley, sundry, varied 7 diverse, jumbled, mingled **8** ungraded **9** disparate, scrambled, unmatched, unrefined **10** variegated **11** diversified **12** multifarious **13** heterogeneous, miscellaneous

unsought 7 unasked, willing **8** unbidden, unwanted **9** undesired, uninvited, unwelcome, voluntary **10** gratuitous, unprompted **11** spontaneous, unrequested, unsolicited

unsound 3 mad **4** weak **5** false, frail, shaky, wrong **6** faulty, flawed, flimsy, infirm, insane, sickly, untrue, weakly **7** cracked, damaged, fragile, invalid **8** decrepit, demented, deranged, specious **9** defective, erroneous, imperfect, incorrect, unhealthy **13** insubstantial

unsparing 5 ample, harsh, stern, tough **6** lavish, severe, strict **7** copious, liberal, onerous, profuse **8** abundant, exacting, generous, prolific, rigorous, ruthless **9** bounteous, bountiful, demanding, plenteous **10** freehanded, munificent, openhanded, unmerciful **11** magnanimous

unspeakable 4 dire, evil **5** awful **6** grisly **7** beastly, ghastly, hateful, heinous, hideous **8** dreadful, ghoulish, gruesome, horrific, shocking **9** appalling, atrocious, execrable, frightful, loathsome, monstrous, obnoxious, repugnant, repulsive, revolting **10** abominable, detestable, disgusting, horrendous, outrageous, scandalous **11** unutterable **13** inexpressible

unspoiled 5 ideal **6** intact, virgin **7** halcyon, idyllic, perfect, untamed **8** arcadian, pastoral, pristine, virginal **9** idealized, undamaged, undefiled, untouched **10** unimpaired **11** unblemished, uncorrupted

unspoken 4 mute **5** tacit **6** hinted, silent, unsaid **7** assumed, implied **8** implicit, inferred, presumed, unstated, wordless **9** intimated, suggested, unuttered **10** undeclared, understood **11** unexpressed

unstable 5 fluid, shaky **6** fickle, shifty, tricky, wobbly **7** dubious, protean, rickety, suspect **8** insecure, rootless, slippery, ticklish, unsteady, variable, volatile, wavering **9** ambiguous, changeful, fluctuant, irregular, mercurial, teetering, uncertain, unsettled **10** capricious, inconstant, precarious **11** vacillating **13** temperamental, unpredictable

unstated 5 tacit **6** latent, unsaid **7** assumed, implied **8** implicit **10** understood

unsteady 5 rocky, shaky, tippy **6** uneven, wobbly **7** erratic, mutable, rickety,

varying **8** shifting, unstable, variable **9** changeful, irregular, tottering **10** changeable, inconstant *British:* **5** wonky

unstudied 5 naive **6** casual, improv, simple **7** artless, natural, offhand **8** careless, informal, unforced, unversed **9** extempore, guileless, impromptu, ingenuous, makeshift, unlabored, unlearned, unplanned, untutored **10** improvised, nonchalant, unaffected, unpolished, unschooled **11** extemporary, spontaneous, uncontrived, unrehearsed **13** improvisatory

unstylish 4 drab, dull **5** dated, dowdy, fusty, passé, ratty, tacky **6** démodé, frumpy, old-hat, shabby, stodgy **7** vintage **8** outdated, outmoded **9** inelegant, moth-eaten, out-of-date **10** antiquated, oldfangled **12** old-fashioned **13** unfashionable

unsubstantial 4 thin **5** frail, shaky **6** feeble, flimsy, infirm **7** fragile, shadowy, tenuous, unsound **8** ethereal, illusory **9** dreamlike, imaginary, spiritual, unearthly **10** immaterial, impalpable, intangible **11** implausible, incorporeal, nonmaterial, nonphysical **12** metaphysical

unsuitable 5 inapt, undue, unfit **7** awkward, jarring **8** ill-timed, improper, unfitted, unseemly, untimely **9** ill-suited **10** ill-adapted, inadequate, inapposite, malapropos, mismatched, unbecoming **11** inadvisable, inopportune, unbefitting, unqualified **12** incompatible, infelicitous, unacceptable, unseasonable **13** inappropriate

unsullied 4 pure **5** clean **6** chaste **8** flawless, spotless, unsoiled **9** blameless, exemplary, guiltless, stainless, taintless, undefiled **10** immaculate **11** unblemished, untarnished

unsure 5 dicey, shaky **6** wobbly **7** dubious, unclear **8** doubtful, insecure, unstable, wavering **9** fluctuant, skeptical, uncertain, undecided **10** ambivalent, indecisive, irresolute, unreliable **11** unconvinced, vacillating **12** questionable, undependable **13** indeterminate, untrustworthy

unsurpassable 7 supreme **8** ultimate **9** matchless **10** consummate, preeminent **12** transcendent

unsusceptible 6 immune, inured **8** hardened **9** impassive, resistant **10** impervious **11** insensitive **12** invulnerable, unresponsive

unsuspecting 5 naive **6** unwary **8** gullible, trustful, trusting **9** confiding, credulous, imprudent **10** incautious

unswerving see UNFALTERING

unsympathetic 4 cold, cool **5** chill, stony **6** averse **7** callous, haughty, unmoved **8** detached, lukewarm **9** apathetic, unfeeling, unpitying **10** disdainful, hard-boiled **11** coldhearted, hardhearted, indifferent, insensitive, unconcerned, uncongenial **12** contemptuous, stonyhearted, unresponsive **13** disinterested

untactful 4 flip, rash, rude **5** brash, nervy **6** brazen **8** flippant, insolent **9** audacious, impolitic, imprudent, maladroit **10** indiscreet **11** impertinent, thoughtless **12** presumptuous, undiplomatic

untamed 4 wild **5** brute, feral **6** carnal, fierce, savage **7** bestial, brutish **8** barbaric **9** primitive **11** uncivilized

untangle 5 solve **7** clear up, explain, resolve, unravel, unsnarl, untwine, untwist **9** elucidate, extricate, interpret **10** disembroil, disentwine, straighten, unscramble **11** disencumber **12** disembarrass

untaught 5 naive **7** natural **8** ignorant, nescient **9** intuitive, untrained, untutored **10** uneducated, unlettered, unschooled **11** empty-headed, instinctive, instinctual, spontaneous **12** uncultivated, uninstructed

untempered 6 wanton **7** extreme **9** excessive **10** gratuitous, immoderate, inordinate **11** extravagant **12** unrestrained

untenable 5 wrong **6** faulty, flimsy **10** inadequate **12** indefensible

untended 5 seedy **7** rickety, run-down **8** decrepit, derelict, deserted, forsaken, tattered **9** neglected **10** ramshackle, tumbledown, uncared-for **11** dilapidated

Unter den ___ 6 Linden

untested 6 intact, unused **7** untried **8** unproved, unproven **11** unpracticed

unthinkable 10 impossible, incredible, outlandish **12** preposterous, unimaginable **13** extraordinary, inconceivable, unprecedented

unthinking 8 careless, feckless, habitual, heedless, knee-jerk, uncaring **9** automatic, reflexive, unheeding, unmindful **10** distracted, unintended **11** inattentive, inadvertent, instinctive, instinctual, involuntary, perfunctory, spontaneous **12** unreflective

unthrifty 6 lavish, wanton **7** ruinous **8** prodigal, wasteful **9** imprudent **10** profligate **11** extravagant, improvident **12** uneconomical

untidy 5 messy **6** sloppy **7** chaotic, jumbled, unkempt **8** confused, littered, slapdash, slipshod, slovenly **9** cluttered **10** disheveled, disordered, disorderly, topsy-turvy **11** disarranged, dishevelled **12** disorganized, unsystematic

untie 5 let go **6** loosen, unbind, unknot, unlace, unlash **7** release, resolve, set free **8** unstring **9** extricate **11** disencumber, disentangle **12** disembarrass

until 4 up to **6** before **7** prior to **11** in advance of

untimely 5 early, undue **9** premature **10** malapropos **11** ill-seasoned, inopportune **12** unseasonable **13** inappropriate

untiring 7 devoted, patient **8** diligent, enduring **9** assiduous, ceaseless, dedicated, energetic, unceasing **10** determined, persistent, unflagging, unwavering, unwearying **11** persevering, unfaltering **13** indefatigable, inexhaustible

untold 4 huge, vast **7** immense **8** enormous, gigantic **9** countless **10** prodigious **11** innumerable, uncountable **12** incalculable **13** indescribable

untouchable 5 leper **6** pariah **7** outcast **8** outcaste

untouched 4 pure **5** sound, whole **6** intact, virgin **7** unmoved **8** flawless, pristine, unharmed, unmarred, untapped, virginal **9** undamaged, unspoiled **10** unaffected **11** unblemished, unconcerned, unimpressed

untoward 6 unruly **7** adverse, awkward, froward, ungodly, unhappy, unlucky **8** ill-fated, improper, indecent, luckless, unseemly **9** fractious, unfitting, vexatious **10** ill-starred, indecorous, indelicate, refractory, unbecoming **11** detrimental, intractable, star-crossed, troublesome, unfortunate **12** inconvenient, recalcitrant, ungovernable, unmanageable, unpropitious

untrained see UNSKILLED

untrammeled 8 uncurbed **9** unimpeded **10** unconfined, unfettered, ungoverned, unhampered **11** uninhibited **12** unobstructed, unrestrained, unrestricted

untried 3 raw **5** fresh, green **6** callow, rookie **8** unproved, untested **10** innovative, pioneering, unseasoned **11** unpracticed **13** inexperienced, unprecedented

untroubled 4 calm **5** still **6** blithe, placid, serene **7** halcyon **8** carefree, composed, peaceful, tranquil **9** easygoing, unruffled **10** insouciant, nonchalant **11** unconcerned, unperturbed **12** lighthearted

untrue 4 fake **5** false, wrong **7** inexact **8** disloyal, specious **9** erroneous, faithless, imprecise, incorrect **10** fictitious, inaccurate, unfaithful *combining form:* 5 pseud 6 pseudo

untrustworthy 5 shady 6 shifty, unsafe, unsure 7 devious, dubious 8 disloyal, slippery, two-faced 9 deceptive, negligent, two-timing 10 fly-by-night, unreliable 11 duplicitous 12 questionable, undependable 13 double-dealing, irresponsible

untruth 3 fib, lie 4 sham 5 error 6 canard, deceit 7 blarney, fallacy, falsity, fiction, hogwash 9 deception, duplicity, falsehood, falseness, hypocrisy, mendacity 11 fabrication, insincerity 12 misstatement 13 prevarication

untruthful 4 sham 5 bogus, false, lying, phony 7 knavish 8 specious 9 deceitful, dishonest, erroneous, incorrect 10 fictitious, inaccurate, mendacious

untutored see UNSCHOOLED

unusable 7 outworn, useless 8 obsolete 9 worthless 10 inoperable, unavailing, unworkable 11 impractical, unrealistic 12 inapplicable 13 nonfunctional

unused 3 new 4 idle 5 fresh 6 excess 7 dormant, surplus 8 leftover, residual 9 untouched

unusual 3 odd 4 rare 6 quaint, unique 7 bizarre, curious, special, strange 8 aberrant, abnormal, peculiar, singular, uncommon, atypical, unwonted 9 anomalous, different, eccentric, irregular 11 exceptional 13 extraordinary

unusually 4 very 5 extra 6 rarely, seldom 8 markedly 9 curiously, extremely, strangely 10 abnormally, especially, peculiarly, remarkably, strikingly, uncommonly 11 exceedingly 12 infrequently, particularly

unutterable 5 taboo 7 awesome 9 ineffable 11 unspeakable 13 indescribable, inexpressible

unvaried 4 like, same 5 alike 7 uniform 9 identical 10 consistent, unchanging 11 undeviating

unvarnished see UNDISGUISED

unvarying see UNCHANGING

unveil see UNCOVER

unversed 3 raw 5 fresh, green 6 callow 7 untried 8 inexpert 9 unfledged 10 unfamiliar, unseasoned 11 uninitiated, unpracticed 12 unaccustomed 13 inexperienced

unwanted see UNWELCOME

unwarranted 5 undue 8 baseless 9 misguided, unfounded 10 gratuitous, groundless, immoderate, unprovoked 11 extravagant, inexcusable, injudicious, uncalled-for, unjustified 12 indefensible, unreasonable 13 insupportable, unjustifiable, unsupportable

unwary 5 brash, hasty 8 careless, gullible, heedless, reckless 9 credulous, impetuous, imprudent, unguarded 10 ill-advised, incautious, indiscreet 11 thoughtless 12 unsuspecting

unwavering see UNFALTERING

unwelcome 7 unasked 8 unsought, unwanted 9 undesired, uninvited 11 undesirable 12 unacceptable 13 objectionable

unwell 3 ill 4 sick 5 frail, shaky 6 ailing, feeble, infirm, offish, peaked, queasy, sickly, wobbly 8 diseased, stricken 9 afflicted, enfeebled, unhealthy 10 indisposed 11 debilitated

unwholesome 4 foul 5 toxic 6 sickly 7 adverse, baneful, corrupt, harmful, immoral, noisome, noxious, obscene, ruinous, unsound 8 diseased 9 injurious, loathsome, offensive, unhealthy 10 disgusting, pernicious, subversive 11 deleterious, detrimental, unhealthful 12 insalubrious

unwieldy 5 bulky 7 awkward, massive 8 cumbrous 9 ponderous 10 burdensome, cumbersome 12 unmanageable

unwilling 5 loath 6 averse 8 grudging, hesitant 9 obstinate, reluctant 10 indisposed 11 disinclined

unwind 4 rest, undo 5 let go, relax 6 loosen, unbend, uncoil, unfold, unreel, unroll 7 ease off, slacken, unravel 8 calm down, kick back, loosen up

unwise 4 rash 5 silly 6 stupid 7 asinine, fatuous, foolish, idiotic, witless 8 reckless 9 brainless, foolhardy, ill-judged, imbecilic, impolitic, imprudent, ludicrous, misguided, senseless 10 illadvised, indiscreet, ridiculous 11 impractical, injudicious, thoughtless, undesirable, unfortunate 13 unintelligent

unwitting 6 chance 7 unaware 8 ignorant, innocent 9 haphazard, oblivious, unknowing, unmindful, unplanned 10 unfamiliar, uninformed, unintended 11 inadvertent 12 unacquainted

unwonted 4 rare 6 signal, unique 7 notable, unusual 8 singular, uncommon 10 remarkable, unexpected 11 exceptional 12 unaccustomed 13 extraordinary

unworkable 7 useless 8 quixotic 9 halfbaked 10 impossible, infeasible, inoperable, unfeasible 11 impractical, unrealistic 12 inapplicable 13 impracticable, nonfunctional

unworldly 5 naive 6 astral, dreamy, simple 7 artless, natural 8 ethereal, innocent, trusting 9 celestial, ingenuous,

spiritual, unearthly, visionary
11 impractical 13 inexperienced

unworthy 6 no-good 7 ignoble 8 shameful, unseemly 9 no-account, unmerited, worthless 10 unbecoming 11 disgraceful, inexcusable, undeserving

unwrap see UNCOVER

unwritten 4 oral 5 blank, tacit 6 latent, spoken, verbal 7 assumed 8 accepted, implicit 10 understood 11 traditional, word-of-mouth 12 conventional

unyielding 4 firm, grim, hard 5 fixed, rigid, stern, stiff, tough 6 dogged, mulish 7 adamant 8 hard-core, obdurate, stubborn 9 hard-nosed, insistent, obstinate, pigheaded, steadfast, unbending 10 determined, headstrong, implacable, inexorable, inflexible, persistent, relentless 11 intractable, unrelenting 12 pertinacious, single-minded, unappeasable

up 4 hike, jump, lift, rise 5 above, ahead, arise, boost, built, mount, raise, risen 6 ascend, arisen, lifted, versed 7 abreast, promote 8 familiar, increase, informed, positive 9 au courant, northward 10 acquainted, conversant *prefix:* 3 ana, sur

up-and-coming 7 go-ahead, hot-shot 8 aspiring 9 promising 11 presumptive, prospective 12 enterprising

upbeat 4 rosy 6 cheery 7 buoyant, hopeful 8 cheerful, positive, sanguine 9 confidant, expectant, promising 10 heartening, optimistic 12 Pollyannaish

upbraid 4 lash, rate 5 chide, scold 6 berate, rail at, rebuke, revile, scorch 7 bawl out, censure, chasten, chew out, reprove, scourge, tell off 8 admonish, chastise, reproach 9 castigate, criticize, dress down, reprimand 10 tongue-lash, vituperate

upbringing 7 nurture, rearing 8 training 9 schooling

upchuck 4 barf, hurl, puke, spew 5 heave, retch, vomit 6 spit up 7 bring up, throw up 8 disgorge 11 regurgitate

upcoming 7 looming, nearing, pending 8 expected, foreseen, imminent 9 advancing, impending, onrushing 11 anticipated, approaching, forthcoming, prospective

up-country 4 bush 6 inland, sticks, upland 7 outback 8 backland, frontier, interior, outlying, woodland 9 backwater, backwoods, boondocks 10 hinterland, timberland

update 5 amend, brief, renew 6 inform, revamp, revise, revive 7 apprise, enhance, improve, refresh, restore,

rundown, upgrade 8 renovate 9 modernize, refurbish 10 rejuvenate

upend 4 beat, best, drub, flip, lick, skin, trim, whip 5 cream, crush, upset 6 invert, subdue, thrash, topple, unseat, wallop 7 capsize, clobber, conquer, overrun, shellac, trounce 8 dethrone, lambaste, overcome, overturn, vanquish 9 overpower, overwhelm, subjugate

upgrade 4 hike, rise 5 boost, raise 6 prefer 7 advance, elevate, enhance, improve, promote 8 increase 9 promotion 10 betterment 11 advancement, improvement 12 breakthrough

upheaval 6 clamor, outcry, tumult, upturn 7 ferment, turmoil 8 churning, disaster, disorder 9 cataclysm, commotion 10 alteration, convulsion, disruption 11 catastrophe

uphill 4 hard 6 rising, rugged, taxing 7 arduous, labored, operose, tedious 8 climbing, grueling, toilsome 9 ascending, difficult, effortful, gruelling, laborious, punishing, strenuous, wearisome

uphold 3 aid 4 back, help, lift, prop 5 brace, carry, hoist, raise 6 assist, back up, bear up, buoy up, defend, second 7 bolster, elevate, justify, shore up, support, sustain 8 advocate, backstop, buttress, champion, maintain, side with 9 vindicate

upkeep 4 cost 7 expense 8 overhead 11 expenditure, maintenance

upland 4 mesa 5 table 7 plateau

uplift 4 buoy 5 cheer, hoist, raise 6 take up 7 animate, elevate, enliven, gladden, hearten 8 brighten, embolden, inspirit 9 encourage 10 exhilarate, strengthen

upon 4 atop *prefix:* 3 epi

upper class 4 rank 5 elite 6 gentry 7 peerage, quality, society, who's who 8 affluent, nobility, noblesse, well-to-do 9 blue blood, gentility, haut monde 10 patricians, patriciate 11 aristocracy 13 carriage trade, Establishment

upper hand 4 edge, sway 5 leg up 7 control, mastery 8 leverage 9 advantage, dominance 10 ascendancy 11 superiority 12 predominance

uppermost 3 top 6 apical 7 highest 8 loftiest

uppity 4 smug 5 aloof, brash 6 lordly, sniffy, snippy, snooty, snotty 7 forward, haughty, pompous 8 arrogant, cavalier 9 conceited, egotistic, imperious, know-it-all, presuming 10 disdainful, high-handed 11 overweening, pretentious 12 contemptuous, presumptuous, supercilious 13 self-asserting, self-assertive, self-important

upright 4 fair, good, just, pure, true
5 erect, moral, noble, piano **6** honest,
raised **7** correct, ethical **8** elevated,
goalpost, standing, vertical, virtuous
9 equitable, exemplary, honorable,
impartial **10** principled, scrupulous
13 conscientious, perpendicular
uprightness 5 honor **6** repute, virtue
7 honesty, probity **8** morality, nobility
9 character, integrity, rectitude **13** righteousness
uprising 4 riot **6** mutiny, revolt
8 upheaval **9** rebellion **10** insurgence,
revolution **12** insurrection
uproar 3 din, row **4** coil, fuss, to-do, riot
5 babel, brawl, broil, chaos, furor, hoo-
ha, melee, whirl **6** bedlam, clamor, fracas, furore, hassle, hubbub, mayhem,
pother, racket, ruckus, rumpus, shindy,
tumult **7** shindig, turmoil **8** brouhaha,
disorder, foofaraw **9** commotion, confusion **10** hullabaloo, hurly-burly, turbulence **11** pandemonium
uproarious 5 noisy, rowdy **7** comical,
rackety, raucous, riotous **8** brawling,
clattery, mirthful, strident **9** clamorous,
hilarious **10** clangorous, hysterical,
resounding, rollicking, tumultuous
12 obstreperous **13** sidesplitting
uproot 4 grub, move, weed **8** displace,
overturn, supplant **9** eradicate, extirpate, overthrow, supersede **10** annihilate, transplant **11** exterminate
upset 3 ail, ill **5** worry **6** bother, defeat,
dismay, invert, jumble, muddle, topple,
tumble **7** afflict, agitate, capsize, disturb, fluster, invalid, jittery, jumbled,
muddled, perturb, rattled, reverse, tip
over, toppled, trouble, unnerve, worried **8** agitated, bewilder, bothered,
confound, confused, disarray, dismayed, disorder, distress, overturn,
troubled, turn over, unnerved **9** afflicted, confusion, disturbed, flustered,
knock over, overthrow, perturbed
10 bewildered, confounded, disconcert,
disordered, distracted, distressed, indisposed, invalidate, overthrown, over-
turned, tipped over **11** overwrought
12 apprehensive, disconcerted
upshot 5 issue **6** burden, climax, effect,
ending, finish, result **7** outcome, purport **9** substance **10** conclusion,
denouement **11** consequence, culmination, termination **12** significance
upside-down 7 chaotic, haywire, jumbled **8** backward, confused, inverted,
pell-mell, reversed **10** disordered, over-
turned, topsy-turvy **13** helter-skelter
upstanding see UPRIGHT
upstart 5 comer **7** parvenu **8** outsider

9 arriviste, pretender **12** nouveau riche
13 social climber
upsurge 4 gain, jump, rise, wave
5 boost, spurt **6** growth **7** advance
8 increase
uptight 4 edgy **5** riled, tense **6** uneasy
7 anxious, nervous, restive, worried
up to 4 till **5** until **6** before **11** in
advance of
up-to-date 6 modern, modish, timely,
trendy **7** abreast, à la mode, current,
stylish **8** advanced, brand-new, contempo **9** au courant **10** avant-garde **11** cutting-edge, fashionable **12** contemporary
13 state-of-the-art
upturn 4 jump, rise **6** growth **8** increase
11 improvement
Urania see MUSE
Uranus 6 planet *mother, wife:* **4** Gaea *offspring:* **6** Titans **8** Cyclopes *overthrower,
son:* **6** Cronus
urban 9 municipal **12** metropolitan
urbane 5 suave **6** poised, smooth **7** elegant, genteel, politic, refined **8** cultured, debonair, gracious, polished
9 civilized, distingué **10** cultivated,
diplomatic **12** cosmopolitan **13** sophisticated
urbanize 6 citify
urchin 3 imp **4** brat **5** child, gamin,
scamp **10** ragamuffin
Urdur see NORN
urge 3 egg, sic, yen **4** coax, goad, itch,
lust, prod, push, spur, wish **5** drive, egg
on, impel, press, prick, set on, tar on
6 adjure, cajole, compel, demand,
desire, exhort, incite, induce, needle,
prompt, propel **7** beseech, conjure,
craving, entreat, implore, impulse,
inspire, longing, passion, promote, propose, provoke, solicit, wheedle **8** advocate, appetite, blandish, pressure,
yearning **9** encourage, instigate, stimulate **12** high-pressure
urgency 6 duress, stress **8** exigence, exigency, pressure **9** necessity **10** compulsion, insistence
urgent 5 vital **6** crying **7** burning, clamant, crucial, driving, exigent, instant,
present **8** critical, pressing **9** clamorous,
demanding, immediate, impelling,
insistent, momentous **10** compelling,
imperative **11** importunate
Uriel 9 archangel
Uris novel 3 Haj (The) **5** QB VII **6** Exodus **7** Trinity **9** Battle Cry, Mitla Pass
10 Angry Hills (The), Redemption
urn 4 vase **6** vessel **7** samovar *Greek:*
7 amphora
Ursa Major 9 Great Bear **11** Great Dipper
Ursa Minor 10 Little Bear **12** Little Dip-

per *star:* 7 Polaris 8 polestar
9 North Star
Uruguay *capital:* 10 Montevideo *language:* 7 Spanish *monetary unit:* 4 peso
neighbor: 6 Brazil 9 Argentina *river:*
7 La Plata 8 Río Negro
usable 6 liquid 7 running, working
9 adaptable, available, operative
10 accessible, applicable, employable,
expendable, functional, marketable,
negotiable 11 exploitable, operational,
serviceable
usage 3 way 4 form, mode, wont
5 habit, sense 6 action, amount, custom, manner, method, praxis 7 process
8 habitude, practice 9 formality, procedure 10 convention
use 3 ply 4 wont, work 5 apply, avail,
habit, serve, treat, value, wield, worth
6 custom, demand, employ, handle, liking, manage, manner 7 benefit, exploit,
operate, purpose, service, utility, utilize
8 deal with, exercise, exertion, function, impose on, occasion, practice,
regulate 9 advantage, habituate, objective, relevance 10 employment, manipulate 11 application
used 8 pre-owned, shopworn 10 secondhand
used up 5 all in, spent 6 bleary, effete,
sapped, wasted 7 drained, emptied, fargone, worn-out 8 consumed, depleted
9 exhausted, washed-out
useful 3 fit 4 meet 5 handy, utile 7 helpful 8 fruitful, suitable, valuable 9 favorable, practical 10 beneficial, convenient, functional, productive, profitable,
propitious, worthwhile 11 appropriate,
practicable, serviceable, utilitarian
12 advantageous
usefulness 5 value, worth 7 fitness, service, utility 8 function 9 advantage, relevance, substance 10 expedience, expediency 12 practicality 13 applicability
useless 4 idle, vain 5 inept 6 futile
7 inutile 8 bootless, hopeless, unusable
9 fruitless, pointless, worthless
10 unavailing, unworkable 11 impractical, ineffective, ineffectual, inoperative
12 unproductive, unprofitable
13 impracticable, nonfunctional
user 5 buyer 6 addict 8 consumer, customer, utilizer
use up 5 drain, spend 6 devour, expend
7 consume, deplete, exhaust 8 draw
down 10 run through
usher 5 lead, seat 5 guide 6 escort 7 conduct, precede 9 conductor 10 doorkeeper
usher in 5 begin, greet, start 6 launch
7 kick off, trumpet, welcome

8 announce, commence, initiate, proclaim 9 institute, introduce, originate
10 inaugurate
usual 5 stock, typic 6 common, kosher,
normal, wonted 7 average, regular,
routine, typical, vanilla 8 accepted,
everyday, expected, familiar, habitual,
ordinary, orthodox, standard, workaday 9 customary, prevalent, quotidian
10 accustomed, prevailing 11 commonplace, established 12 conventional,
unremarkable
usually 6 mainly, mostly 7 as a rule
8 commonly, normally 9 generally, routinely 10 habitually, ordinarily 11 customarily
usurer 7 Shylock 9 loan shark 11 moneylender
usurp 5 wrest 6 assume 7 preempt
8 arrogate, displace, supplant 10 commandeer 11 appropriate
Utah *capital:* 12 Salt Lake City *city:*
4 Orem 5 Ogden, Provo *college, university:* 12 Brigham Young *lake:* 6 Powell
9 Great Salt *motto:* 8 Industry *mountain:*
5 Kings (Peak) *nickname:* 7 Beehive
(State) *park:* 4 Zion 5 Bryce 6 Arches
11 Canyonlands *river:* 5 Green 6 Sevier
state bird: 14 California gull *state flower:*
8 sego lily *state tree:* 10 blue spruce
utensil 3 pan, pot 4 fork, tool 5 knife,
spoon 6 device, vessel 8 saucepan, teaspoon 9 implement 10 instrument
uterus 4 womb
Uther Pendragon *son:* 6 Arthur *wife:*
6 Ygerne 7 Igraine
utile 5 handy 6 useful 7 working 9 available, operative, practical 10 accessible,
convenient, dependable, functional
11 practicable, serviceable
utilitarian 6 useful 9 practical, pragmatic
10 functional *philosopher:* 4 Mill (John
Stuart) 7 Bentham (Jeremy)
utility 3 use 7 benefit, fitness, service
8 function 9 advantage, relevance
10 efficiency, usefulness 12 practicality
13 applicability
utilize 3 use 5 apply, spend 6 bestow,
deploy, employ, handle, occupy
7 exploit 8 exercise 11 appropriate
utmost 3 top 4 acme, apex, best, peak
6 height, zenith 7 extreme, highest,
maximal, maximum, supreme 8 farthest, furthest, greatest, pinnacle,
remotest, ultimate 9 damnedest,
extremity
utopia 4 Eden, Zion 5 bliss 6 heaven
7 Elysium 8 paradise 9 Cockaigne,
dreamland, Shangri-la 10 dreamworld
12 promised land 13 Elysian fields
Utopia author 4 More (Thomas)

utopian 5 ideal, lofty **6** edenic **7** dreamer **8** arcadian, fanciful, idealist, quixotic **9** grandiose, ideologue, visionary **10** chimerical, idealistic, impossible, millennial, unfeasible **11** impractical **12** otherworldly **13** castle-builder, impracticable

utter 3 say **4** damn, dang, darn, rank, talk, tell **5** sheer, speak, stark, state, total, voice **6** arrant, dashed, deuced, reveal **7** blasted, blessed, declare, deliver, divulge, flat-out **8** absolute, bring out, complete, crashing, disclose, infernal, outright, positive, throw out **9** downright, out-and-out, pronounce, verbalize **10** confounded, consummate **11** come out with, straight-out, unmitigated, unqualified **13** thoroughgoing

utterance 4 rant, vent, word **5** voice **6** speech **7** oration **8** delivery, speaking **9** assertion, discourse, statement **10** expression, revelation **11** declaration **12** announcement, articulation **13** pronouncement, verbalization

utterly 4 just **5** plumb, quite **6** in toto **7** totally **8** entirely **9** perfectly **10** absolutely, altogether, completely, thoroughly

uttermost 4 last **5** final **7** extreme, outmost **8** farthest, furthest, remotest

Utu see SHAMASH

Uzbekistan *capital:* **8** Tashkent *city:* **7** Bokhara, Bukhara **9** Samarkand, Samarqand *desert:* **8** Kyzyl Kum *enclave:* **10** Karakalpak *monetary unit:* **3** sum *neighbor:* **9** Kazakstan **10** Kazakhstan, Kyrgyzstan, Tajikistan **11** Afghanistan **12** Turkmenistan *river:* **8** Amu Dar'ya, Syr Dar'ya **9** Zeravshan *sea:* **4** Aral

V

vacancy 4 void **6** vacuum **7** opening **8** idleness **9** blankness, emptiness

vacant 4 bare, free, idle, open, void **5** blank, clear, empty, inane, stark **6** unused **7** deadpan, vacuous **8** deserted, unfilled **9** abandoned, impassive **10** tenantless, unoccupied **11** emptyheaded **12** inexpressive

vacate 4 quit, void **5** annul, clear, empty, leave **6** bow out, give up, repeal, revoke **7** abandon, rescind, retract, reverse **8** abrogate, check out, dissolve, evacuate **9** discharge **10** relinquish

vacation 4 rest, trip **5** break, leave **6** recess **7** holiday, leisure, respite, time off **8** furlough, interval **10** sabbatical **12** intermission

vacationer 7 tourist, tripper **9** weekender **10** rubberneck **12** holidaymaker

vaccination 4 shot **7** booster **9** injection **11** inoculation

vaccine 4 shot **5** serum **9** antiserum **11** preparation *inventor:* **6** Jenner (Edward)

vacillate 4 sway, yo-yo **5** waver **6** dither, falter, teeter, waggle **7** swither, whiffle **8** hesitate **9** alternate, fluctuate, oscillate **10** equivocate **12** shilly-shally

vacillating 4 weak **6** fickle, unsure, wobbly **8** hesitant, shifting, unstable, unsteady **9** fluctuant, tentative, uncertain, undecided, unsettled **10** changeable, inconstant, indecisive, irresolute **12** shilly-shally

vacillation 5 doubt **8** to-and-fro, wavering **9** hesitancy **10** fickleness, indecision **12** irresolution, shilly-shally

vacuity 4 hole, void **6** cavity, hollow, vacuum **7** inanity **9** black hole, blankness, ditsiness, ditziness, emptiness, stupidity **10** hollowness **11** nothingness

vacuous 4 idle, void **5** blank, empty, inane, silly **6** stupid, vacant **7** foolish, shallow **11** birdbrained, empty-headed, superficial

vacuum 4 void **5** space **7** suction **9** emptiness **11** nothingness *bottle:* **5** dewar **7** thermos

vacuum tube 5 diode **6** triode **7** tetrode *casing:* **4** bulb

vade mecum 5 guide **6** manual **8** Baedeker, handbook **9** guidebook **11** enchiridion

___**Vadis** 3 Quo

vagabond 3 bum 4 hobo 5 gypsy, idler, rogue, rover, tramp 6 picaro, roamer 7 drifter, migrant, nomadic, vagrant, wastrel 8 bohemian, clochard, picaroon, runabout, runagate, traveler, wanderer 9 itinerant, transient, wandering 11 peripatetic

vagarious 6 fickle 7 erratic, flighty, mutable, wayward 8 unstable, volatile 9 impulsive, mercurial, whimsical 10 capricious, inconstant 13 unpredictable

vagary 3 bee 4 whim 5 crank, fancy, freak, humor, quirk 6 megrim, whimsy 7 caprice, fantasy 8 crotchet

vagrancy 6 roving 7 roaming 8 drifting, nomadism, rambling 9 wandering 10 itinerancy

vagrant see VAGABOND

vague 3 dim 4 hazy 5 blear, faint, foggy, fuzzy, gauzy, misty, muddy, woozy 6 bleary, blurry, cloudy, dreamy, slight, vacant 7 inexact, obscure, shadowy, unclear 8 confused, nebulous, vaporous 9 ambiguous, dreamlike, enigmatic, imprecise, uncertain 10 diaphanous, indefinite, indistinct 13 indeterminate, unsubstantial

vain 4 idle 5 empty, proud 6 futile, hollow, otiose 7 foppish, haughty, stuck-up, trivial, useless 8 abortive, arrogant, boastful, bootless, nugatory 9 conceited, fruitless, valueless, worthless 10 egocentric, profitless, sophomoric, unavailing 11 egotistical, ineffective, ineffectual 12 narcissistic, unproductive, unprofitable, unsuccessful 13 self-important

vainglorious 8 arrogant, boastful, bragging, puffed-up, vaunting 9 conceited, egotistic 10 swaggering 11 egotistical 12 supercilious

vainglory 4 pomp 5 pride 6 egoism, vanity 7 conceit, egotism 9 arrogance 10 pretension 11 haughtiness 12 boastfulness

valance 5 drape 6 pelmet 7 curtain, drapery 10 lambrequin

vale 4 dale, dell, glen 5 combe 6 dingle, hollow, valley

valediction 5 adieu 7 good-bye 8 farewell 11 leave-taking

valedictory see VALEDICTION

valentine 4 card, dear, love 7 beloved, darling, tribute 10 sweetheart

valet 7 servant 9 attendant 10 manservant

valiant 4 bold 5 brave 6 heroic, plucky 7 doughty, gallant, valiant 8 fearless, intrepid 10 chivalrous, courageous 11 lionhearted 12 greathearted, stouthearted

valid 4 just, true 5 legal, solid, sound 6 cogent, lawful, potent, proven 7 binding, in force, logical, telling 8 attested, bona fide, credible, forceful 9 effective, effectual, operative 10 acceptable, compelling, convincing, legitimate, persuasive 11 justifiable, trustworthy 12 well-grounded

validate 5 prove 6 affirm, ratify, verify 7 approve, bear out, certify, confirm, endorse, justify, probate 8 legalize, sanction 10 legitimate, legitimize 11 corroborate, rubber-stamp 12 authenticate, substantiate

validity 5 force, proof 7 cogency, potency 8 efficacy 9 soundness 10 lawfulness 13 effectiveness

valise 3 bag 4 grip 6 kit bag, suiter 7 handbag, Pullman 8 gripsack, suitcase 9 gladstone, two-suiter 10 weekend bag 11 portmanteau 12 overnight bag, traveling bag 13 traveling case

Valjean's pursuer 6 Javert

Valkyrie 6 maiden 8 Brynhild

valley 4 dale, dell, glen, vale, wadi 5 basin, combe, gulch, gully, swale 6 canyon, dingle, hollow, ravine 10 depression *Africa-Asia:* 4 Rift 9 Great Rift *Alps:* 11 Grindelwald *ancient Greece:* 5 Nemea *Asia:* 7 Fergana *California:* 4 Napa 5 Death, Squaw 7 Central 8 Imperial, Yosemite 11 San Fernando *Dead Sea area:* 6 Arabah *Dominican Republic:* 5 Cibao *Egypt:* 6 Kharga *England:* 5 Doone *Germany:* 4 Ruhr *Greece:* 5 Tembi, Tempe *India:* 4 Kulu 7 Kashmir (Vale of) *Ireland:* 5 Avoca, Ovoca *Israel:* 4 Elah *Lebanon:* 4 Biqa 5 Bekaa *moon:* 4 rill 5 rille *New York:* 12 Sleepy Hollow *Pennsylvania:* 7 Nittany *Scotland:* 7 Glen Roy *Switzerland:* 5 Hasli 8 Engadine 11 Grindelwald *Virginia:* 10 Shenandoah *Washington:* 11 Grand Coulee

Valmiki's epic 8 Ramayana

valor 4 guts 6 mettle, spirit, virtue 7 bravery, courage, heroism, prowess, stomach 8 chivalry, valiance, valiancy 9 fortitude, gallantry 10 resolution

valorous see VALIANT

valse 5 waltz

valuable 4 dear 6 costly, prized, useful, worthy 8 precious 9 expensive, important, rewarding, treasured 10 satisfying, worthwhile

valuate 4 rate 5 assay, price 6 assess, survey 7 adjudge 8 appraise, estimate

valuation 4 cost, rate 5 price, worth 6 rating 7 opinion 8 estimate, judgment

9 appraisal **10** assessment, estimation **12** appreciation

value 4 cost, rate **5** assay, gauge, judge, price, prize, scale, worth **6** assess, assign, charge, esteem, figure, reckon, regard, return, survey **7** account, apprize, care for, cherish, compute, quality, respect, utility **8** appraise, estimate, evaluate, quantity, treasure **9** appraisal, principle **10** appreciate, assessment, equivalent, importance **11** market price **12** denomination

valve 3 tap **4** cock, flap, gate **6** device, faucet, poppet, spigot **7** hydrant, petcock, shutoff **8** stopcock **9** regulator *cardiac:* **6** mitral **8** bicuspid

vamoose 3 git **4** scat **5** leave, scram, split **6** beat it, begone, cut out, decamp, depart, get out **7** run away, skiddoo, take off **8** clear out **9** skedaddle

vamp 3 fix **4** fake, lure, mend, wile **5** ad-lib, flirt, intro, patch, siren, tempt **6** cook up, entice, groove, lead-in, make up, repair, seduce **7** beguile, charmer, rebuild **8** inveigle **9** fabricate, formulate, improvise, refurbish, temptress **10** gold digger, seductress **11** enchantress, extemporize, femme fatale

vampire 3 bat **5** lamia **6** undead **7** Dracula **9** Nosferatu **11** bloodsucker

van 3 car **4** head, lead, wing **5** front, truck, wagon **7** minibus **11** cutting edge, leading edge

vandal 3 Hun **5** yahoo **6** looter **8** pillager **9** despoiler, destroyer, plunderer, spoliator

vandalize 5 smash, trash, wreck **6** damage, deface, ravage, tear up **7** destroy **8** demolish, sabotage

Vandal king 8 Gaiseric, Genseric

Vandyke 5 beard **6** border, collar, edging, goatee

vane 3 web **7** feather, wind tee **8** vexillum **10** bellwether **11** weathercock

vanguard 4 lead **5** front **9** forefront **11** cutting edge, leading edge

vanilla 4 tame **5** beige, cream, plain **7** extract **8** ordinary **9** innocuous **10** white-bread **12** conventional **13** garden-variety

vanish 3 die, fly **4** fade, flee, melt **5** clear **8** dissolve, evanesce **9** disappear, dissipate, evaporate **13** dematerialize

vanity 3 ego **5** pride **6** egoism **7** conceit, egotism **8** self-love, smugness **9** vainglory **10** narcissism, pretension **13** dressing table

Vanity Fair author 9 Thackeray (William Makepeace)

vanquish 4 beat, best, drub, lick, rout

5 cream, crush, quell **6** defeat, humble, subdue, thrash **7** clobber, conquer, destroy, smother, trounce **8** surmount **9** overpower, overthrow, subjugate **10** annihilate

vantage 4 edge, odds **8** handicap **9** head start, upper hand *point:* **3** POV **5** perch **7** lookout, outlook **8** position **10** watchtower

Vanuatu *capital:* **8** Port-Vila *ethnic group:* **10** Melanesian *explorer:* **4** Cook (Capt. James) *former name:* **11** New Hebrides *island:* **3** Epi **5** Efate, Maéwo, Tanna **6** Ambrim **8** Aneityum, Malekula **9** Erromango, Pentecost **13** Espíritu Santo *language:* **6** French *monetary unit:* **4** vatu

vapid 4 dull, flat, weak **5** banal, bland, ditsy, ditzy, inane, silly **6** jejune **7** fatuous, insipid, sapless, vacuous **9** brainless, colorless, innocuous **10** namby-pamby, wishy-washy **13** uninteresting

vapor 3 fog, gas **4** brag, haze, mist, smog **5** brume, cloud, smoke, steam **6** breath, miasma, nimbus **7** bluster **8** phantasm *condensed:* **3** dew *frozen:* **4** hoar, rime **5** frost **9** hoarfrost

vaporize 5 steam **6** ablate **8** disperse, dissolve, evanesce **9** dissipate, evaporate

vaporous 4 airy, hazy **5** foggy, misty, vague, wispy **6** cloudy, unreal **7** gaseous **8** ethereal, illusory, volatile **10** evanescent **13** unsubstantial

vaquero 5 waddy **6** cowboy, gaucho, herder, waddie **7** cowpoke **8** buckaroo, herdsman, wrangler **10** cowpuncher

varia 6 medley **7** mélange, mixture, omnibus **8** treasury **9** anthology **10** compendium, miscellany **11** compilation

variable 5 fluid **6** fickle, fitful, mobile, symbol **7** mutable, protean **8** unstable, unsteady, volatile **9** irregular, mercurial, uncertain, unsettled, versatile **10** capricious, changeable, inconstant **13** temperamental

variance 3 war **4** odds **6** change, strife **7** discord, dispute, dissent **8** conflict, disunity, division **9** variation **10** contention, difference, dissension, dissidence **11** fluctuation **12** disagreement

variation 4 riff **5** shade, shift **6** change, nuance **7** partita **8** mutation **9** disparity **10** alteration, difference, divergence **11** fluctuation, declination, discrepancy, oscillation **12** modification **13** dissimilarity

varicolored see VARIEGATED

varicose 7 bulging, dilated, swollen

varied 5 mixed **6** motley, sundry **7** diverse, various **8** assorted **9** different,

disparate, divergent 10 dissimilar
12 multifarious 13 heterogeneous,
kaleidoscopic, miscellaneous

variegated 4 pied 5 mixed, pinto 6 calico, motley 7 checked, dappled, diverse,
mottled, piebald, spotted 8 skewbald,
stippled, streaked 9 checkered, multihued 10 multicolor, parti-color, poly-
chrome 12 multicolored, parti-colored
13 kaleidoscopic, polychromatic

variety 3 ilk 4 kind, mode, sort, type
5 array, breed 6 flavor, medley, nature,
stripe 8 mixed bag 9 diversity, variation
10 assortment, collection, miscellany,
subspecies 12 multiformity, multiplicity

various 4 some 5 mixed 6 divers, sundry,
unlike 7 diverse, several, unalike
8 assorted, separate 9 different, disparate, divergent, unsimilar 10 dissimilar 12 multifarious 13 heterogeneous,
miscellaneous

varlet 3 cur 4 page 5 knave, rogue,
skunk 6 menial, rascal, wretch
8 coistrel 9 attendant, miscreant,
scoundrel 10 blackguard

varmint 4 pest 5 knave, rogue, scamp,
skunk, sneak 6 rascal 7 critter
9 scoundrel

varnish 4 coat 5 adorn, cover, glaze,
gloss, japan 6 veneer 7 coating, conceal, cover up, shellac 8 covering
9 embellish, gloss over, sugarcoat,
whitewash *component:* 5 resin

vary 5 alter, range 6 change, depart, differ, modify, mutate 7 deviate, digress,
diverge 8 modulate 9 diversify

vase 3 urn 5 tazza 6 crater, krater, vessel
7 amphora

Vashni's father 6 Samuel

Vashti's husband 6 Xerxes 9 Ahasuerus

vassal 4 leud, serf 5 helot, liege, slave
6 tenant 7 bondman, homager, peasant,
servant, subject 8 bondsman, liege man
9 dependent, underling 11 subordinate
12 feudal tenant *high-ranking:* 7 vavasor
8 vavasour

vast 4 huge, mega 5 giant, great, jumbo
6 untold 7 immense, mammoth, oceanic, titanic 8 colossal, enormous, gigantic, spacious, whopping 9 boundless,
expansive, humongous 10 gargantuan,
tremendous, widespread 12 astronomical

vastness 5 sweep 8 enormity, hugeness
9 immensity, magnitude 13 expan-
siveness

vat 3 tub, tun 4 beck, butt, cask, kier,
tank 5 keeve, kieve 6 barrel, liquor,
vessel 7 cistern 8 cauldron *cheese:*
7 chessel

vatic 6 mantic 7 fatidic 8 oracular

9 fatidical, prophetic, sibylline 10 predictive 11 apocalyptic

Vatican City 10 papal state *army:* 11 Swiss
Guards *chapel:* 7 Sistine *church:*
11 Saint Peter's *ruler:* 4 Pope *site:*
4 Rome

vaticinal see VATIC

vaticinate 5 augur 6 divine 7 portend,
predict, presage 8 forebode, forecast,
foretell, prophesy, soothsay 9 adumbrate 13 prognosticate

vaudeville 5 revue 9 burlesque, music
hall 11 variety show 12 song and dance

vaudevillian 11 entertainer

vault 3 pit, sky 4 arch, cave, dome,
jump, leap, room, safe, tomb 5 bound,
crypt 6 cavern, cellar, cupola, hurdle,
spring, welkin 7 archway, dungeon
8 catacomb, overleap 9 firmament
10 undercroft

vaulting 4 arch, dome 7 emulous 8 aspiring 9 ambitious 12 enthusiastic
13 opportunistic

vaunt 4 blow, brag, crow, puff, rant
5 boast, strut 6 flaunt, parade 7 bluster,
display, exhibit, show off 8 brandish
9 gasconade 11 rodomontade

veal 4 calf *cutlet:* 9 schnitzel *roasted:*
10 fricandeau *shank:* 8 osso buco

vector 5 agent 7 carrier 9 direction
10 pollinator

Vedic religion *country:* 5 India *god:*
4 Agni, deva, Soma 5 Indra 6 Varuna
language: 8 Sanskrit *priest:* 7 Brahman
treatise: 9 Upanishad *writing:* 7 Rig
Veda, Samhita

veer 3 yaw 4 cast, chop, slew, sway, turn
5 fetch, sheer, shift, trend 6 depart,
swerve 7 deflect, deviate, digress,
diverge

vegetable 3 pea, soy, yam 4 bean, beet,
corn, kale, leek, okra, soya, taro, wort
5 chard, chive, cress, green, onion,
plant 6 carrot, celery, cowpea, endive,
garlic, legume, lentil, peanut, pepper,
potato, radish, sorrel, squash, tomato,
turnip 7 cabbage, chayote, dullard, lettuce, mustard, parsley, parsnip, pumpkin, rhubarb, salsify, shallot, soybean,
spinach 8 broccoli, collards, cucumber,
eggplant, kohlrabi, lima bean, rutabaga, scallion, snap bean 9 artichoke,
asparagus, muskmelon 10 watermelon
11 cauliflower, horseradish, sweet potato *bog:* 6 muskeg *dish:* 5 salad *mold:*
5 humus *seller:* 6 grocer 7 grocery
12 costermonger *sponge:* 5 luffa
6 loofah *spread:* 4 oleo 9 margarine

vegetarian 9 herbivore 11 herbivorous

vegetate 4 idle, laze, loaf, loll 5 chill,
slack 6 loiter, lounge 7 goof off, hang

out 8 languish, lollygag, slack off, stagnate 9 goldbrick, hibernate

vegetation 5 flora 6 growth, plants 7 verdure 8 greenery 9 plant life *floating:* 4 sudd 8 pleuston

vehement 3 hot 4 wild 5 fiery, rabid 6 ardent, bitter, fervid, fierce, heated 7 excited, fervent, vicious, violent, zealous 8 forceful, powerful 9 perfervid 10 passionate 11 impassioned 12 antagonistic

vehicle 3 ATV, bus, cab, car, SUV, van 4 auto, bike, taxi, tool 5 agent, buggy, means, organ, plane, sedan, train, truck, wagon 6 agency, binder, medium, vector 7 bicycle, carrier, channel, machine, solvent, travois 8 airplane, ministry 9 ambulance, implement, motor home, transport 10 automobile, conveyance, instrument, motorcycle *baby's:* 4 pram 8 carriage, stroller 9 baby buggy *child's:* 5 trike 7 scooter 8 tricycle *farm:* 4 wain 7 tractor *horse-drawn:* 4 cart, dray 5 buggy, lorry, sulky, wagon 6 hansom, landau, troika 7 calèche, phaeton 8 carriage 9 buckboard *military:* 4 jeep, tank 6 Humvee *one-wheeled:* 8 unicycle *passenger:* 3 bus, cab, car 4 auto, taxi 7 ricksha 8 cable car, rickshaw *public:* 3 bus 4 tram 5 train 6 subway 7 omnibus, trolley *Roman:* 7 chariot *winter:* 4 sled 6 sleigh 8 snowplow 10 snowmobile

veil 4 caul, hide, mask, wrap 5 cloak, cloth, cloud, cover, velum 6 mantle, screen, shield, shroud 7 conceal, cover up, curtain, obscure, secrete 8 covering, disguise, enshroud 10 camouflage, false front *Muslim:* 7 yashmak *netting:* 6 maline 7 malines

vein 3 bed, way 4 line, lode, mind, mode, mood, seam, tone, tube 5 style, tenor 6 manner, nature, spirit, strain, streak, vessel 7 channel, fashion, pattern, quality, stratum 8 aptitude 11 blood vessel *combining form:* 3 ven 4 veni, veno *deposit:* 3 ore *fluid:* 5 blood *heart:* 8 vena cava *leaf:* 3 rib *leg:* 7 saphena 9 saphenous *neck:* 7 jugular *small:* 6 venule *varicose:* 5 varix

velar 8 guttural

veld 7 prairie 9 grassland

velleity 4 bent, wish 5 fancy 6 desire, liking 7 leaning 10 propensity 11 inclination

velocipede 4 bike 5 cycle, trike 6 tandem 7 bicycle, pedicab 8 tricycle

velocity 4 pace 5 haste, speed, tempo 7 headway 8 celerity, rapidity 9 quickness, swiftness 12 acceleration

velum 4 caul, veil 8 membrane 10 soft palate

velvet 4 gain, mild, rich, soft 5 cloth 6 fabric, profit, smooth 8 winnings 10 antler skin

velvety 4 mild, soft 5 plush 6 smooth

venal 4 paid 6 sordid 7 corrupt 8 bribable 9 mercenary, unethical 11 corruptible, purchasable 12 unprincipled, unscrupulous

vend 4 hawk, sell, toot 6 market, monger, peddle, retail 8 huckster 9 advertise, broadcast

vendee 5 buyer 6 client 8 customer 9 purchaser

vendetta 4 feud 7 rivalry 9 blood feud

vendible 7 salable 8 sellable 10 marketable 12 merchantable

vendor 6 dealer, duffer, hawker, seller 7 packman, peddler 8 huckster, merchant, retailer, salesman

vendue 4 sale 7 auction 10 public sale

veneer 3 ply 4 burl, coat, face, mask, show, veil 5 cover, front, gloss, layer, plate 6 facade, facing 7 conceal, overlay 8 disguise

venerable 3 old 4 aged 5 hoary 6 sacred 7 ancient, antique, elderly, honored, revered, stately 8 esteemed 9 admirable, dignified, estimable, honorable, respected

venerate 5 adore, honor, prize 6 admire, esteem, revere 7 cherish, idolize, respect, worship 8 treasure 9 reverence

veneration 3 awe 5 honor 6 esteem, homage 7 respect, worship 9 adoration, reverence 10 admiration 11 hero worship

venery 3 sex 4 game, prey 5 chase 7 hunting

venesection 10 phlebotomy

Venetian *boat:* 7 gondola *boatman:* 9 gondolier *product:* 5 glass 9 glassware *ruler:* 4 doge *school:* 6 Titian 7 Bellini, Tiepolo 8 Veronese 9 Giorgione 10 Tintoretto *street:* 5 canal *suburb:* 6 Murano

Venezuela *capital:* 7 Caracas *city:* 8 Valencia 9 Maracaibo 12 Barquisimeto *island:* 9 Margarita *lake:* 8 Valencia 9 Maracaibo *language:* 7 Spanish *monetary unit:* 7 bolívar *mountain, range:* 5 Andes 6 Parima (Serra, Sierra) 7 Bolívar (Pico) 9 Pacaraima 11 Pico Bolívar, Serra Parima 12 Sierra Parima *neighbor:* 6 Brazil, Guyana 8 Colombia *peninsula:* 9 Paraguaná *river:* 7 Orinoco *sea:* 9 Caribbean *waterfall:* 10 Angel Falls

Venezuelan *herdsman:* 7 llanero *liberator:* 7 Bolívar (Simón) *people:* 5 Carib 6 Timote

vengeance 6 payoff **7** payback, redress, revenge **8** reprisal, revanche **9** repayment **10** punishment **11** retaliation, retribution

vengeful 8 punitive **10** vindictive **11** retaliatory

venial 5 minor **7** trivial **8** harmless, trifling **9** allowable, excusable, tolerable **10** condonable, forgivable, pardonable, remissible, remittable **13** insignificant

Venice of the East 7 Bangkok, Udaipur

Venice of the North 6 Bruges, Brugge **9** Amsterdam, Stockholm **12** St. Petersburg

Veni, Creator ___ 8 Spiritus

venison 4 deer

veni, vidi, ___ 4 vici

venom 4 bane, hate **5** spite **6** malice, poison, rancor **7** ill will, vitriol **8** embitter **9** contagion, malignity, virulence **11** malevolence

venomous 5 toxic **6** deadly, malign, poison **7** baneful, malefic, noxious **8** spiteful, viperish, viperous, virulent **9** malicious, malignant, poisonous **10** malevolent, pernicious **12** vituperative

vent 3 air **4** emit, flue, hole, pipe, pour, slit **5** burst, expel, issue, loose, utter, voice **6** broach, nozzle, outlet **7** chimney, exhaust, express, give off, opening, orifice, release, take out, unleash, volcano **8** breather, fumarole, spiracle **9** discharge **11** black smoker

venter 3 gut **5** belly **6** paunch **7** abdomen, stomach

ventilate 3 air **5** state, utter **6** aerate, expose **7** discuss, express **9** advertise, broadcast, circulate, verbalize **11** investigate

ventral area 7 abdomen, stomach

ventricle 6 cavity **7** chamber

ventriloquist 9 performer **11** entertainer *companion:* **5** dummy *famous:* **6** Bergen (Edgar)

venture 3 bet, try **4** dare, face, feat, gest, risk **5** brave, peril, stake, wager **6** chance, expose, gamble, hazard **7** attempt, daresay, emprise, exploit **8** endanger, jeopardy, long shot, make bold **9** challenge, crapshoot, speculate **10** enterprise **11** speculation, undertaking

venturesome 4 bold, rash **5** brave **6** daring **8** reckless **9** audacious, daredevil, foolhardy **11** adventurous, temerarious

venue 4 site **5** arena, forum, place, scene **6** locale, outlet **7** setting **8** locality

Venus 6 planet, Vesper **7** daystar, Lucifer **8** Hesperus (see also APHRODITE)

Venus de ___ 4 Milo

___ vera 4 aloe

veracious 4 just, true **5** exact, frank, right, valid **6** candid, honest **7** correct, factual, sincere **8** accurate, truthful

veracity 4 fact **5** truth **6** candor **7** honesty **8** accuracy, trueness **9** actuality, exactness **11** correctness **12** truthfulness

veranda 5 lanai, porch, stoop **6** piazza **7** gallery, portico

verb *auxiliary:* **3** are, can, did, had, has, may, was **4** have, must, were, will, word **5** could, might, shall, would **6** should *form:* **6** active, gerund **7** passive **10** infinitive, participle *kind:* **10** transitive **12** intransitive *linking:* **6** copula *mood:* **8** optative **10** imperative, indicative **11** subjunctive *tense:* **4** past **6** aorist, future **7** perfect, present **9** predicate **10** pluperfect

verbal 4 oral **5** wordy **6** gerund, spoken **7** literal **9** unwritten **10** infinitive, participle, rhetorical **11** word-for-word

verbalism 4 term **6** phrase **7** wording **8** phrasing **9** prolixity, windiness, wordiness **11** phraseology

verbalization 4 talk **6** speech **8** speaking **9** discourse, utterance **12** articulation, vocalization

verbalize 3 air, say **4** talk **5** speak, state, utter, voice, write **6** broach **7** express **8** bloviate, vocalize **9** ventilate

verbatim 5 exact **6** direct **7** exactly, literal, precise **8** directly **9** literally, literatim, precisely **10** accurately **11** word-for-word

verbiage 4 talk **6** phrase **7** diction, wording **8** parlance, phrasing, pleonasm **9** wordiness **10** redundancy **11** phraseology

verbose 5 gassy, windy, wordy **6** prolix **7** diffuse **9** garrulous, redundant, talkative **10** loquacious, pleonastic **11** tautologous

verbosity 9 prolixity, windiness, wordiness **10** redundancy

verboten 5 taboo **6** banned **7** illegal **8** outlawed **9** forbidden **10** prohibited

verdant 4 lush **5** green, leafy, naive **6** grassy, unripe

verdict 6 assize, ruling **7** finding, opinion **8** decision, judgment **9** judgement

Verdi opera 4 Aïda **6** Ernani, Oberto, Otello **7** Nabucco **8** Don Carlo, Falstaff, Lombardi (I), Traviata (La) **9** Don Carlos, Rigoletto, Trovatore (Il) **15** Simon Boccanegra

verdure 7 foliage **8** greenery **9** greenness **10** vegetation

verge 3 hem, lip, rim **4** abut, cusp, edge, sink **5** bound, brink, skirt, staff, touch

6 adjoin, border, fringe, margin 7 selvage 8 approach, shoulder 9 threshold 10 borderline

veridical see VERACIOUS

verifiable 4 true 6 proven 7 certain 8 provable 9 undoubted

verification 5 proof 10 validation 11 attestation 12 confirmation 13 corroboration

verify 4 aver, test 5 check, prove, vouch 6 attest, settle 7 bear out, confirm 8 document, validate 9 establish, factcheck 11 corroborate, demonstrate 12 authenticate, substantiate

verily 5 truly 6 indeed 7 in truth 9 assuredly, certainly 11 confidently, undoubtedly

veritable 4 real, true 6 actual 7 factual, genuine 8 bona fide 9 authentic, undoubted 10 sure-enough 11 indubitable

verity 5 truth 6 gospel, truism 7 honesty, reality 9 actuality 12 truthfulness

vermiform 8 wormlike

vermilion 3 red

vermin 4 lice, mice, pest, rats, scum 5 fleas, pests, trash 7 bedbugs, varmint

Vermont *capital:* 10 Montpelier *city:* 7 Rutland 10 Burlington *college, university:* 7 Norwich 8 Marlboro 10 Bennington, Middlebury *mountain, range:* 5 Green 9 Mansfield *nickname:* 13 Green Mountain (State) *river:* 11 Connecticut *state bird:* 12 hermit thrush *state flower:* 9 red clover *state tree:* 10 sugar maple

vernacular 4 cant 5 argot, idiom, lingo, slang 6 common, jargon, patois, patter, speech, tongue, vulgar 7 dialect, vulgate 8 language 9 dialectal 10 colloquial 12 mother tongue

vernal 5 fresh, green 6 spring 8 youthful 10 springlike

Verne, Jules *character:* 4 Fogg (Phileas), Nemo 12 Passepartout *submarine:* 8 Nautilus *work:* 16 Mysterious Island (The) 21 From the Earth to the Moon 26 Around the World in Eighty Days

versant see CONVERSANT

versatile 5 handy 6 adroit, facile 7 protean 8 variable 9 all-around, competent, many-sided 10 changeable 11 well-rounded 12 ambidextrous

verse 3 lay, ode 4 epic, poem, rune 5 lyric, poesy, rhyme 6 ballad, jingle, poetry, sonnet, stanza 7 passage 8 acquaint 11 composition, familiarize *analysis:* 8 scansion *four-line:* 8 quatrain *free:* 5 blank 8 unrhymed *six-line:* 6 sestet *three-line:* 6 tercet *two-line:* 7 couplet *writer:* 4 poet

versed 5 adept 6 au fait 7 abreast, skilled, veteran 8 familiar, informed, seasoned 9 au courant, competent, practiced 10 acquainted 11 experienced 13 knowledgeable

versifier 4 bard, poet 6 rhymer 9 poetaster, rhymester, sonneteer

version 4 copy 5 draft, model 6 flavor, remake 7 account, edition, reading, variant 8 revision 9 iteration, narrative, redaction, rendition, rewording 10 adaptation, paraphrase 11 arrangement, description, incarnation, restatement, translation

versus 4 anti 6 contra 7 against, vis-à-vis 11 over against

vertebra 7 segment *kind:* 6 dorsal, lumbar, sacral 8 cervical, thoracic 9 coccygeal

vertebrae 4 back 5 spine 6 coccyx, rachis, sacrum 8 backbone, tailbone 12 spinal column

vertebrate 9 animal *characteristic:* 5 spine 7 cranium 12 spinal column *kind:* 4 bird, fish, frog 6 mammal 7 reptile 9 amphibian

vertex 3 cap, top 4 acme, apex, peak 5 crest, crown 6 apogee, summit, tiptop, zenith

vertical 5 erect, plumb, sheer, steep 7 upright 8 straight 10 lengthwise, straight-up 13 perpendicular

vertiginous 5 dizzy, giddy, woozy 6 fickle, rotary 11 light-headed

vertigo 6 megrim 9 dizziness, giddiness

verve 3 pep, vim, zip 4 brio, dash, élan, fire, life, zest, zing 5 flair, gusto, moxie, oomph, style, vigor 6 bounce, energy, spirit, spring 7 panache 8 vitality, vivacity 10 enthusiasm, liveliness 13 sprightliness

very 3 too 4 bare, mere, most, much, pure, real, same, true 5 exact, ideal, model, plain, quite, sheer, super, truly, utter 6 actual, ever so, highly, hugely, mighty, really, simple 7 awfully, genuine, greatly, notably, perfect, precise, special 8 absolute, actually, bona fide, selfsame, terribly 9 authentic, extremely, genuinely, identical, undoubted 10 absolutely, particular 11 exceedingly *French:* 4 très *German:* 4 sehr *Italian:* 5 molto *Scottish:* 3 gey *Spanish:* 3 muy

vesicle 3 sac 4 cell, cyst 5 bulla 6 cavity 7 blister, vacuole

vespers 8 evensong

___ **Vespucci** 7 Amerigo

vessel 3 can, cup, jar, pan, pot, tub, urn 4 boat, bowl, cask, drum, duct, ewer, pail, ship, tank, tube, vase, vein 5 canal, craft, cruse 6 artery, barrel, bottle, bucket, firkin, flagon, kettle, krater, pottle 7 cresset, pitcher 8 crucible 9 container 10 receptacle, watercraft *combining form:* 3 vas 4 angi, vaso 5 angio *drinking:* 3 cup, mug 4 toby 5 flask, glass, gourd, stein, stoup 6 goblet, seidel 7 tankard, tumbler *Indian:* 4 lota 5 lotah *Scottish:* 6 quaich, quaigh

vest 6 weskit 9 waistcoat

Vesta see HESTIA

vestal 4 pure 6 chaste, virgin 8 celibate, virginal, virtuous

vestibule 5 entry, foyer, lobby 6 cavity 7 hallway, narthex, passage 8 anteroom, entrance, entryway 10 antechapel 11 antechamber

vestige 4 echo 5 dregs (plural), relic, scrap, stump, trace, track 6 shadow 7 memento, remains, remnant 8 leftover 9 remainder 10 hide or hair 11 hide nor hair

vestment 3 alb 4 cope, garb, gown, robe 5 amice, cotta, dress, habit, stole, tunic 6 attire, rochet 7 apparel, cassock, garment, maniple, pallium, tunicle 8 chasuble, cincture, clothing, covering, dalmatic, parament, surplice *ancient Hebrew:* 5 ephod 11 breastplate

vestry 6 closet 8 sacristy 9 sacrarium

vesture 4 robe 6 clothe 7 apparel, garment 8 clothing 10 habiliment

Vesuvius 7 volcano

vet 5 check 6 go over, review 7 analyze, examine, inspect 8 appraise, check out, evaluate, look over 10 old soldier

vetch 4 herb, tare 6 legume *type:* 4 milk (vetch) 5 crown (vetch), hairy (vetch)

veteran 4 ex-GI 5 adept 6 expert, master 7 old hand, skilled 8 old-timer, warhorse 9 practiced, shellback 10 past master 11 experienced

veto 3 nix 4 kill 6 defeat, forbid, refuse, reject 7 decline 8 disallow, negative, prohibit 9 blackball 10 disapprove 11 prohibition 12 interdiction

vex 3 bug, irk 4 fret, gall, itch, roil 5 annoy, chafe, gripe, harry, rowel, tease, worry 6 badger, baffle, bother, harass, harrow, nettle, pester, plague, puzzle, rankle, ruffle 7 chagrin, torment, trouble 8 bullyrag, distress, irritate

vexation 4 fret, sore 5 chafe, trial 6 bother 7 problem, torment 8 distress, headache 9 annoyance, troubling 10 affliction, harassment, irritation 11 aggravation, bedevilment, provocation

vexatious 5 pesky 7 prickly 8 annoying, tiresome 9 troublous 10 bothersome, irritating 11 distressing, troublesome 12 exasperating

vexed 6 sticky, touchy 7 debated, weighty 8 ticklish 9 difficult, discussed, troubling

vexing 5 tough 7 irksome 8 annoying 9 difficult, harassing, upsetting 10 bothersome, irritating 11 distressing, troublesome

via 3 per 4 over, with 5 along 7 by way of, through 9 by means of

viable 6 doable 7 capable 8 feasible, possible, workable 11 practicable, sustainable

vial 6 ampule 7 ampoule

viands 4 eats, fare, feed, food, grub 7 aliment, edibles, vittles 8 victuals 9 provender 10 provisions 11 comestibles

vibrant 5 alive, vital, vivid 6 bright, lively, punchy 7 ringing 8 resonant 9 consonant, pulsating 10 resounding 11 oscillating 12 effervescent

vibrate 3 jar 4 ring 5 quake, shake, swing, throb, waver 6 quiver, shimmy, thrill, tremor 7 flutter, pulsate 8 undulate 9 fluctuate, oscillate, vacillate

vibration 4 aura 5 quake, shake, trill 6 motion, quaver, quiver, shimmy, spirit, tremor 7 flutter, shaking 8 fremitus, wavering 9 emanation, trembling 11 fluctuation, oscillation, vacillation

vicar 6 pastor, priest 8 minister, reverend 9 clergyman

Vicar of Wakefield, The *author:* 9 Goldsmith (Oliver) *character:* 8 Primrose

vice 3 sin 4 evil, flaw 5 crime, fault 6 defect 7 devilry, failing, frailty, offense, scandal 8 iniquity 9 deformity, depravity, indecency 10 corruption, debauchery, immorality, perversion, wickedness 11 shortcoming

vice-president 4 veep 6 deputy 7 officer 9 executive *American:* 4 Burr (Aaron), Bush (George), Ford (Gerald), Gore (Albert), King (William) 5 Adams (John), Agnew (Spiro), Dawes (Charles), Gerry (Elbridge), Nixon (Richard), Tyler (John) 6 Arthur (Chester), Cheney (Richard), Colfax (Schuyler), Curtis (Charles), Dallas (George), Garner (John Nance), Hamlin (Hannibal), Hobart (Garret), Morton (Levi), Quayle (Dan), Truman (Harry), Wilson (Woodrow) 7 Barkley (Alben), Calhoun (John Caldwell), Clinton (George), Johnson (Andrew, Lyndon Baines, Richard Mentor), Mondale (Walter), Sherman (James Schoolcraft), Wallace (Henry), Wheeler (William) 8 Coolidge (Calvin), Fillmore (Millard), Humphrey (Hubert Horatio), Marshall (Thomas), Tompkins (Daniel),

Van Buren (Martin) 9 Fairbanks (Charles), Hendricks (Thomas), Jefferson (Thomas), Roosevelt (Theodore), Stevenson (Adlai) 11 Rockefeller (Nelson) 12 Breckinridge (John)

viceroy 5 nabob 6 exarch, satrap 7 khedive 8 alderman, governor 9 butterfly 11 stadtholder

vice versa 10 conversely 12 contrariwise

vicinity 4 area 5 range 6 extent, locale, region, shadow 7 suburbs 8 ballpark, district, environs, locality, nearness, precinct 9 closeness, magnitude, proximity 12 neighborhood

vicious 4 evil, mean, vile 5 cruel 6 fierce, malign, savage, sinful, wicked 7 brutish, corrupt, hateful, immoral, noxious, violent 8 depraved, horrible, perverse, spiteful 9 barbarous, ferocious, malicious, malignant, monstrous, nefarious, reprobate 10 degenerate, flagitious, iniquitous, malevolent, villainous, vindictive

vicissitude 5 rigor, trial 6 chance, change 7 weather 8 hardship, mutation, reversal 9 adversity, mischance 10 affliction, difficulty, misfortune, mutability 11 permutation, progression, tribulation

victim 4 butt, dupe, gull, mark, prey 5 chump, patsy 6 pigeon, martyr, quarry, sucker 7 fall guy 8 casualty, fatality, offering, underdog 9 sacrifice

victimize 4 dupe, fool, gull, hoax 5 cheat, cozen, trick 7 deceive, swindle 8 flimflam, hoodwink 9 bamboozle, sacrifice 11 hornswoggle

victor 5 champ 6 top dog, winner 7 subduer 8 champion 9 conqueror 10 vanquisher

Victorian 4 prim 6 prissy, stuffy 7 prudish 8 priggish 11 puritanical, straitlaced 12 old-fashioned

Victoria, Queen *family:* 7 Hanover *father:* 6 Edward *husband:* 6 Albert *prime minister:* 8 Disraeli (Benjamin) 9 Gladstone (William), Melbourne (Lord) *son:* 6 Edward

victory 3 win 5 sweep 6 defeat 7 mastery, success, triumph 8 conquest, walkaway, walkover 10 overcoming 11 superiority *costly:* 7 Pyrrhic *easy:* 8 cakewalk, walkaway *monument:* 4 arch 13 Arc de Triomphe *reward:* 6 spoils *sign:* 3 vee *symbol:* 4 flag 6 laurel, wreath

Victory author 6 Conrad (Joseph)

victuals 4 chow, eats, feed, food, grub, prog 6 viands 7 edibles, vittles 9 provender 10 provisions 11 comestibles

___ **Vidal** 4 Gore

videlicet 3 viz 5 to wit 6 namely, that is 8 scilicet 11 that is to say

vie 3 pit 5 match 6 oppose, strive 7 compete, contend, contest, counter 8 struggle

Viennese *city hall:* 7 Rathaus *family:* 8 Habsburg, Hapsburg *palace:* 7 Hofburg *park:* 6 Prater *river:* 6 Danube

Vietnam *capital:* 5 Hanoi *city:* 3 Hue 6 Da Nang, Saigon 8 Haiphong 13 Ho Chi Minh City *delta:* 6 Mekong *gulf:* 6 Tonkin 8 Thailand *monetary unit:* 4 dong *mountain:* 8 Fan-si-pan *neighbor:* 4 Laos 5 China 8 Cambodia 9 Kampuchea *river:* 3 Red 6 Mekong *sea:* 10 South China

Vietnamese New Year 3 Tet

view 3 eye, see 4 espy, look, plan, scan 5 scene, sight, vista, watch 6 behold, belief, look at, notice, notion, regard, review, survey 7 close-up, examine, inspect, lookout, observe, opinion, outlook, picture, scenery, vantage 8 judgment, panorama, perceive, prospect, scrutiny, snapshot 10 conviction, inspection, scrutinize 11 contemplate, examination

viewer 7 witness 8 looker-on, onlooker 9 bystander, spectator 10 eyewitness

viewing instrument 5 glass, scope 6 binocs 7 glasses 9 telescope 10 binoculars, microscope 12 field glasses *combining form:* 5 scope

viewpoint 3 eye 5 angle, slant, stand 6 stance 7 outlook 8 attitude, position 9 direction 11 perspective

vigil 4 wake 5 watch 7 lookout, prayers 9 devotions 10 deathwatch 11 wakefulness 12 surveillance, watch and ward

vigilance 5 watch 9 alertness 12 surveillance, watchfulness

vigilant 4 keen, wary 5 alert, awake, aware, chary, sharp 7 careful, jealous, on guard 8 cautious, open-eyed, watchful 9 attentive, sharp-eyed, wide-awake

vignette 5 scene 6 sketch 7 glimpse, picture 8 ornament

vigor 3 pep, vim, zip 4 brio, push, snap, tuck 5 ardor, drive, force, gusto, moxie, oomph 6 energy, mettle, muscle, spirit, starch 7 potency 8 dynamism, strength, tonicity, virility, vitality 9 hardihood, lustiness, puissance 10 get-up-and-go, robustness, sturdiness

vigorous 5 brisk, hardy, lusty, stout, tough, vital 6 active, hearty, lively, potent, robust, strong, sturdy, virile 7 dashing, driving, dynamic, healthy 8 athletic, forceful, muscular, powerful, spirited, youthful 9 energetic, strenuous 10 mettlesome, red-blooded

Viking see NORSE

vile 4 base, evil, foul, mean, ugly 5 gross, nasty, slimy 6 filthy, horrid, sordid, vulgar, wicked 7 low-down, noisome, obscene, squalid 8 depraved, wretched 9 abhorrent, loathsome, obnoxious, offensive, perverted, repugnant, repulsive, revolting 10 despicable, disgusting 12 contemptible

vilify 5 abuse, libel, smear 6 assail, attack, berate, defame, malign 7 asperse, run down, slander, spatter, traduce 8 denounce, tear down 9 denigrate, disparage 10 calumniate

villa 5 dacha, manor 6 estate, quinta 7 château, mansion 9 residence

village 4 burg, town 5 bourg, thorp 6 hamlet 7 townlet *African:* 4 dorp 5 kraal *Indian:* 6 pueblo *Japanese:* 4 mura *Jewish:* 6 shtetl *Malay:* 7 kampong *Russian:* 3 mir

Village Blacksmith author 10 Longfellow (Henry Wadsworth)

villain 4 boor, heel 5 demon, devil, heavy, knave, rogue 6 rascal, sinner 7 lowlife 8 antihero, criminal, evildoer, offender, scalawag 9 character, miscreant, reprobate, scoundrel 10 blackguard, malefactor *classic:* 4 Iago 5 Judas (Iscariot) 6 Brutus (Marcus Junius) 8 Quisling (Vidkun)

villainous 4 evil 6 rotten, wicked 7 corrupt, debased, heinous, vicious 8 depraved, wretched 9 atrocious, felonious, miscreant, nefarious 10 detestable, diabolical, flagitious, iniquitous, perfidious, traitorous 11 treacherous

villainy 4 vice 5 crime 8 evilness 9 depravity, treachery, turpitude 10 corruption, wickedness

villein 7 peasant 8 villager

villenage 4 yoke 6 tenure, thrall 7 bondage, serfdom 9 servitude, thralldom

vim 3 zip 4 brio, dash, élan, gimp, zing 5 gusto, oomph, verve, vigor 6 bounce, energy, esprit, spirit 7 vinegar 9 animation 10 enthusiasm, razzmatazz

___ **vincit omnia** 4 Amor

vinculum 3 tie 4 bond, knot, link, yoke 5 nexus 8 ligament, ligature

vindicable 7 tenable 9 excusable 10 condonable, defendable, defensible, pardonable 11 justifiable, warrantable

vindicate 4 free 5 clear, guard, prove, right 6 acquit, avenge, defend, excuse, refute, shield, uphold, verify 7 absolve, bear out, confirm, deliver, justify,

redress, revenge, support, warrant 8 maintain 9 exculpate, exonerate, safeguard 11 corroborate 12 substantiate

vindictive 5 catty, nasty 6 malign 7 hateful, hurtful, vicious 8 punitive, spiteful, vengeful, venomous 9 malicious, malignant, poisonous

vine 3 hop, ivy, pea 5 grape, kudzu, liana, liane, maile, plant 6 maypop 7 chayote, climber, creeper 8 catbrier, clematis 11 bittersweet *Asian:* 6 pikake

vinegar 3 vim 6 liquid 8 ill humor, sourness 9 condiment 12 preservative *relating to:* 10 acetic acid *steep in:* 6 pickle

vinegarish 4 sour 6 bitter, cranky, ornery 7 bearish, waspish 8 snappish 9 crotchety, irascible 12 cantankerous, cross-grained, disagreeable

Vinegar Joe 8 Stilwell (Joseph)

vineyard *French:* 3 cru 7 château, domaine

Vinland discoverer 4 Leif (Ericsson, Eriksson) 12 Leif Ericsson, Leif Eriksson

vintage 3 age, old 4 crop, wine 5 yield 7 antique, classic, harvest 8 outdated 9 classical 10 antiquated 12 old-fashioned

Viola *brother:* 9 Sebastian *husband:* 6 Orsino *play:* 12 Twelfth Night

viola da ___ 5 gamba

violate 4 rape 5 break, wrong 6 breach, defile, offend, ravish 7 disturb, outrage, profane, traduce 8 fracture, infringe, trespass 9 desecrate, disregard 10 contravene, transgress

violation 4 foul, rape 5 break, crime, wrong 6 breach, injury 7 offense, outrage, perjury, scandal 8 trespass 9 blasphemy, injustice, sacrilege 10 illegality, infraction, ravishment 11 desecration, disturbance, misdemeanor, profanation 12 encroachment, infringement, interruption 13 contravention, transgression

violence 4 fury, riot 5 clash 6 frenzy, mayhem 7 assault, outrage, rampage 8 foul play, savagery 9 onslaught 10 distortion, roughhouse

violent 5 cruel, harsh, rabid 6 fierce, raging, savage, stormy 7 berserk, furious, intense, vicious 8 slam-bang, vehement 9 explosive, ferocious 10 hellacious 11 acrimonious, destructive

violet 5 mauve 6 purple 8 amethyst, lavender 10 heliotrope

violin 6 fiddle 10 instrument *kind:* 5 Amati, Strad 8 Guarneri 10 Guarnerius, Stradivari 12 Stradivarius *part:* 3 bow, nut, peg 4 neck 6 bridge, scroll, string 8 chin rest 9 tailpiece 10 sound-

board 11 fingerboard *precursor:* 5 rebec
6 rebeck
violinist *American:* 4 Hahn (Hilary)
5 Elman (Mischa), Fodor (Eugene),
Ricci (Ruggiero), Stern (Isaac)
6 Midori, Powell (Maud) 7 Heifetz
(Jascha), Menuhin (Yehudi), Szigeti
(Joseph) 8 Kreisler (Fritz), Milstein
(Nathan) 9 Zimbalist (Efrem) *Belgian:*
5 Ysaÿe (Eugene) 8 Grumiaux (Arthur)
Czech: 3 Suk (Josef) *English:* 7 Menuhin
(Yehudi) *French:* 12 Francescatti (Zino)
German: 6 Mutter (Anne-Sophie) *Hun-
garian:* 7 Joachim (Joseph) *Israeli:*
7 Perlman (Itzhak) 8 Zukerman (Pin-
chas) *Italian:* 6 Viotti (Giovanne Bat-
tista) 7 Corelli (Arcangelo), Vivaldi
(Antonio) 8 Paganini (Niccolo) 9 Gemi-
niani (Francesco) *Romanian:* 6 Enescu
(George) *Russian:* 8 Oistrakh (David)
violin maker 4 Salò (Gasparo da)
5 Amati (Andrea, Antonio, Girolamo,
Nicolo) 7 Maggini (Giovanni Paolo),
Stainer (Jacob) 8 Guarneri (Andrea, del
Gesù, Giuseppe, Pietro) 10 Guarnerius
(Andrea, Giuseppe, Pietro), Stradivari
(Antonio, Francesco, Omobono)
12 Stradivarius (Antonio, Francesco,
Omobono)
VIP 4 BMOC, lion 5 mogul, nabob 6 big
gun, biggie, bigwig, fat cat, honcho
7 big shot, notable, someone 8 big
wheel, luminary, mandarin, somebody
9 big cheese, dignitary 10 panjandrum
13 high-muck-a-muck
viper 3 asp 5 adder, snake 7 serpent
10 bushmaster, copperhead, fer-de-
lance 11 rattlesnake 13 water moccasin
virago 5 harpy, scold, shrew, vixen
6 amazon, dragon, gorgon, ogress
8 battle-ax, fishwife, harridan, Xantippe 9 battle-axe, termagant, Xanthippe
Virgil 4 poet 5 guide 6 orator 8 cicerone
epic: 6 Aeneid *poems:* 8 Eclogues,
Georgics
virgin 3 new 4 pure 5 first, fresh, unwed
6 chaste, intact, maiden, modest,
unused, vestal 7 initial 8 celibate, innocent, primeval, pristine, spotless
9 abstinent, undefiled, unmarried,
unspoiled, unsullied, untouched
10 immaculate
virginal 4 pure 5 fresh 6 chaste, intact,
maiden, spinet 8 pristine, virtuous
9 undefiled, unspoiled, unsullied,
untouched
Virgin Goddess 5 Diana 6 Hestia
7 Artemis
Virginia *capital:* 8 Richmond *city:* 7 Norfolk, Roanoke 10 Alexandria 11 New-

port News 13 Virginia Beach *college,
university:* 3 VMI 7 Hampton 10 Sweet
Briar 11 George Mason, Old Dominion
12 James Madison 13 Randolph-Macon
14 William and Mary *historical site:*
10 Monticello 11 Mount Vernon
12 Williamsburg *mountain, range:*
6 Rogers 9 Blue Ridge *nickname:* 11 Old
Dominion *river:* 5 James 7 Potomac
10 Shenandoah *state bird:* 8 cardinal
state flower: 7 dogwood (American)
state tree: 7 dogwood (American)
Virginian, The *author:* 6 Wister (Owen)
character: 7 Trampas
Virgin Island 5 Peter 6 Norman, St. John
7 Anegada, St. Croix, Tortola 8 St.
Thomas
Virgin Islands (U.S.) *capital:* 15 Charlotte
Amalie *island:* 6 St. John 7 St. Croix
8 St. Thomas *location:* 10 West Indies
territory of: 12 United States
Virgin Islands, British *capital:* 8 Road
Town *island:* 5 Peter 6 Norman 7 Anegada, Tortola 11 Jost Van Dyke, Virgin
Gorda *location:* 10 West Indies
virginity 6 purity 8 celibacy, chastity
10 chasteness, maidenhead, maidenhood
Virgin Queen 9 Elizabeth
Virgo star 5 Spica
virgule 5 comma, slant, slash 7 solidus
8 diagonal
viridity 5 green 7 naïveté 9 freshness,
greenness, innocence
virile 4 male 5 macho, manly 6 manful,
potent, robust 7 manlike 8 forceful,
vigorous 9 energetic, masculine
virtual 5 moral, tacit 7 de facto 8 implicit
9 essential, practical 10 electronic
11 fundamental
virtuality 4 core, pith, soul 5 being, juice,
stuff 6 effect, marrow, nature 7 essence,
makings 8 quiddity 9 substance
10 capability 12 essentiality, quintessence, potentiality
virtually 4 nigh 6 all but, almost, fairly,
nearly, next to 7 morally 8 as good as,
in effect, well-nigh 9 basically, in
essence, literally 10 implicitly 11 effec-
tively, essentially, practically
13 approximately, fundamentally, substantially
virtue 5 merit, power, right, trait, valor,
value, vigor, worth 7 courage, feature,
potency, probity, quality 8 chastity,
goodness, morality, strength 9 attribute, character, puissance, rectitude,
rightness 10 excellence, excellency, perfection 11 uprightness *cardinal:* 4 hope,
love 5 faith 7 charity, justice 8 prudence 9 fortitude 10 temperance

virtuosic 5 showy 6 expert, flashy 7 hotshot, skilled 9 brilliant, masterful 10 consummate, prodigious 12 razzle-dazzle

virtuoso 4 whiz 6 expert, master, savant, wizard, wonder 7 artiste, hotshot, maestro, prodigy 10 past master, wunderkind

virtuous 4 good, pure 5 moral, noble, pious, right 6 chaste, decent, modest, proper 7 ethical, sinless 8 innocent, spotless 9 blameless, faultless, guiltless, righteous, unsullied, untainted 10 inculpable, moralistic 11 respectable, right-minded, untarnished

virulent 5 harsh, toxic 6 biting, bitter, malign, poison 7 cutting, hateful, hostile 8 scathing, spiteful, venomous 9 malicious, malignant, pestilent, poisonous, rancorous, vitriolic 10 pathogenic

virus 3 bug 8 pathogen 9 contagion, infection

vis 5 force, might, power

visage 3 mug, pan 4 cast, face, look, mien, phiz, puss 6 aspect, kisser 8 features 9 semblance 10 expression 11 countenance

vis-à-vis 4 date 6 escort, facing, toward 7 against 8 fronting, opposite, together 9 tête-à-tête 10 face-to-face 11 counterpart

visceral 3 gut 4 deep 5 inner 8 internal, intimate 9 intuitive 10 intestinal 11 instinctive, instinctual

viscid see VISCOUS

viscount 4 lord, peer 8 nobleman

viscous 4 limy, ropy 5 gluey, gooey, gummy, limey, slimy, thick 9 glutinous, semifluid 10 gelatinous 12 mucilaginous

vise 5 clamp, screw 7 squeeze

Vishnu 4 Hari *avatar:* 4 Rama 5 Kurma 6 Buddha, Matsya, Vamena, Varaha 7 Krishna 9 Narasinha *consort:* 3 Sri 4 Shri 7 Lakshmi *home:* 4 Meru

visible 6 patent 7 obvious 8 apparent, viewable 9 available, well-known 10 detectable 11 conspicuous, discernible, perceivable, perceptible 12 recognizable

Visigoth *conquest:* 4 Rome *king:* 6 Alaric

vision 3 eye 5 dream, fancy, image, sense, sight 6 beauty, seeing 7 concept, fantasy, feature, picture, specter 8 daydream, eyesight, phantasm, presence, prophecy 9 foresight, nightmare 10 apparition, perception, phenomenon, revelation 13 manifestation *combining form:* 4 opto 5 opsis *deceptive:* 6 mirage *relating to:* 5 optic 6 visual 7 optical

visionary 4 seer 5 ideal, lofty, noble 6 unreal 7 blue-sky, dreamer, utopian 8 fanciful, idealist, illusory, quixotic, romantic 9 ambitious, ideologue, imaginary 10 abstracted, daydreamer, idealistic, starry-eyed 11 impractical

visionless 5 blind

Vision of Sir Launfal *author:* 6 Lowell (James Russell)

visit 3 gam, see 4 call, chat, stay, talk, tour 5 pop in, run in 6 call on, come by, drop by, drop in, look in, look up, stay at, stop by, stop in 7 force on, sojourn 8 come over, converse, stay with, stopover 10 social call

visitation 3 woe 4 wake 5 cross, trial 6 misery, ordeal, plague 8 calamity 9 martyrdom 10 affliction 11 tribulation

visitor 5 alien, guest 6 caller, drop-in 7 company, invitee 8 stranger, visitant 9 transient 10 houseguest

visor 4 bill, mask 6 domino 8 eyeshade, disguise, face mask, sunshade

vista 4 view 5 scene, sight 7 lookout, outlook 8 panorama, prospect 9 landscape 11 perspective

visual 5 optic 6 ocular 7 graphic, optical, seeable 8 viewable 9 pictorial 11 discernible, perceivable, perceptible

visualize 3 see 4 view 5 fancy, image 6 call up 7 feature, imagine, picture 8 conceive, envisage, envision 9 conjure up

vital 4 dire 5 alive 6 lively, living, mortal, urgent 7 animate, crucial, pivotal 8 animated, cardinal, critical, decisive, integral, pressing, required, vigorous 9 essential, important, necessary, requisite 10 imperative, red-blooded 11 fundamental, life-or-death 12 invigorating 13 indispensable

vitality see VIGOR

vitalize 5 liven 6 arouse, excite, infuse, perk up, spirit, vivify 7 animate, enliven, quicken 8 energize 9 encourage, galvanize, stimulate 10 invigorate

vitals see VISCERA

vitamin 6 biotin, niacin 7 choline, folacin, retinal, retinol 8 thiamine 9 carnitine, cobalamin, folic acid 10 calciferol, pyridoxine, riboflavin, tocopherol 12 ascorbic acid

Vita Nuova *author:* 5 Dante (Alighieri)

vitelline 5 yolky 6 yellow

vitiate 3 mar 4 harm, soil, undo 5 annul, spoil, sully, taint 6 damage, debase, defile, impair, negate 7 blemish, corrupt, debauch, deprave, nullify, pervert, tarnish 8 abrogate 9 undermine 10 bastardize, demoralize, invalidate

vitreous 6 glassy

vitriol 4 bile 5 spite, venom 6 malice, rancor 7 sulfate 8 acrimony 9 virulence 12 sulfuric acid

vitriolic 4 acid 5 acrid 7 acerbic, caustic, cutting, mordant 8 scathing, stinging, virulent 9 rancorous, truculent

vituperate 3 rag 4 lash, rail, rant, rate 5 abuse, baste, curse, scold, score 6 berate, malign, revile, scorch 7 asperse, bawl out, chew out, condemn, cuss out, upbraid 8 lambaste 9 castigate 10 tongue-lash

vituperation 5 abuse 6 rebuke 7 censure, obloquy, reproof 8 scolding 9 contumely, invective 10 scurrility 11 fulmination, mudslinging 12 billingsgate 13 tongue-lashing

vituperative 7 abusive, railing, scurril 8 scathing, scolding, scurrile, venomous, viperish 9 invective 10 censorious, scurrilous 11 opprobrious 12 contumelious

vivace 5 brisk 6 lively 8 animated, spirited

vivacious 3 gay 4 airy, pert 5 perky, spicy, sunny, zesty 6 bouncy, breezy, bubbly, jaunty, lively, sparky 7 buoyant, chipper 8 animated, pixieish, spirited 9 ebullient, sprightly 12 effervescent, high-spirited

vivacity see VERVE

Vivaldi epithet 9 red priest (the)

___ **vivant** 3 bon

vivarium 9 terrarium

viva voce 4 oral 6 orally, spoken 11 word-of-mouth

vivid 5 alive, sharp 6 bright, garish, lively, punchy, visual 7 graphic, intense, vibrant 8 animated, colorful, eloquent, lifelike 9 chromatic, pictorial 10 expressive 11 picturesque

vivify 5 liven, renew 6 excite, infuse, kindle, revive 7 animate, enliven, quicken, refresh, restore 9 stimulate

vixen 3 fox, nag 5 harpy, scold, shrew 6 ogress, virago 8 fishwife, harridan, Xantippe 9 termagant, Xanthippe

viz 5 to wit 6 namely, that is 8 scilicet 9 videlicet 12 in other words

vizard 4 face, mask 5 guise, visor 6 domino 8 disguise

vocabulary 4 cant 5 argot, lingo, slang, words 6 jargon, patois 7 lexicon 8 glossary 9 word-hoard 10 vernacular 11 terminology

vocal 4 oral 5 blunt, frank 6 phonic, spoken, voiced 7 uttered 8 eloquent 9 outspoken 10 articulate, expressive, free-spoken

vocalic 5 vowel

vocalist 4 diva 6 belter, canary, singer 7 crooner, warbler, yodeler 8 minstrel, songbird 9 balladeer, chanteuse, chorister 10 cantatrice, prima donna

vocalization 4 song 5 voice 6 speech 7 diction 8 speaking 9 utterance 11 enunciation 12 articulation 13 pronunciation

vocalize 3 air, hem 4 sing, talk 5 chant, croon, speak, state, utter, voice 6 warble 7 express 9 enunciate, pronounce

vocal organ 6 larynx 8 voice box *bird:* 6 syrinx

vocation 3 art, job 4 call, work 5 craft, trade 6 career, métier 7 calling, mission, pursuit 8 business, lifework 10 employment, handicraft, occupation, profession

vociferate 3 bay, cry 4 bark, bray, call, roar, yawp, yell 5 shout 6 bellow, clamor, holler 7 thunder

vociferous 4 loud 5 noisy 6 shrill 7 blatant, clamant, raucous 8 strident 9 clamorous 11 openmouthed 12 obstreperous

vogue 3 cry, fad, ton 4 chic, mode, pose, rage 5 craze, favor, furor, style, trend 6 furore 7 fashion 10 dernier cri, popularity 11 stylishness

voice 3 put, say 4 part, talk, tell, vent 5 say-so, sound, speak, state, utter 6 assert, choice, medium, singer, speech 7 declare, express, opinion, present 8 vocalize 9 condition, enunciate, formulate, pronounce, statement, utterance, verbalize 10 articulate, expression, instrument *female:* 4 alto 5 mezzo 7 soprano 9 contralto *high:* 5 tenor 7 soprano 8 falsetto *in grammar:* 6 active 7 passive *Latin:* 3 vox *male:* 4 bass 5 tenor 8 baritone *quality:* 5 pitch 6 timbre *quiet:* 7 whisper *relating to:* 5 vocal 8 phonetic *without:* 4 dumb, mute

voice box 6 larynx

voiced 4 oral 5 vocal 6 sonant, spoken 7 uttered 8 phonated 9 expressed

voiceless 3 mum 4 dumb, mute, surd 6 silent 8 breathed 12 inarticulate

void 3 gap, nix 4 emit, hole, idle, lack, null, undo 5 abyss, annul, blank, clear, empty, inane, quash 6 bereft, cancel, cavity, hollow, negate, remove, vacant, vacate, vacuum 7 absence, give off, negated, nullify, rescind, reverse, vacuity, vacuous 8 abrogate, deserted, evacuate 9 black hole, discharge, eliminate, emptiness 10 extinguish 11 nothingness

volant 4 fast, spry, yare 5 agile, fleet, quick, zippy 6 flying, lively, nimble 9 dexterous, sprightly

volar 6 palmar

volatile 5 flaky 6 fickle, flying, lively 7 erratic, essence, flighty 8 fleeting, fugitive, skittery, skittish, unstable, variable, volcanic 9 ephemeral, explosive, fugacious, mercurial, momentary, transient 10 capricious, changeable, evanescent, inconstant, short-lived, transitory 11 impermanent 13 temperamental

volatility 10 fickleness 11 flightiness, inconstancy, instability 13 changeability

volcanic 7 violent 8 volatile 9 explosive *explosion:* 8 eruption *glass:* 8 obsidian *matter:* 3 ash 4 lava, tufa, tuff 5 magma 6 scoria *mound:* 4 cone *passage:* 6 throat 7 conduit *vent:* 8 fumarole 9 solfatara

volcano 4 hill, vent 8 mountain *Alaska:* 6 Katmai (Mount) 8 Wrangell (Mount) 9 Aniakchak (Crater) *Andes:* 5 Omate 12 Huaina Putina *Antarctica:* 6 Erebus (Mount) *Azores:* 4 Alto (Pico) *California:* 6 Lassen (Peak) *Canaries:* 5 Teide (Pico de), Teyde (Pico de) 8 Tenerife (Pico de) *Colombia:* 5 Huila (Nevado del), Pasto 6 Purace 7 Galeras *Costa Rica:* 4 Poás 5 Barba, Irazú *Ecuador:* 6 Sangay 8 Antisana, Cotopaxi *extinct:* 4 Popa (Mount) 5 Iriga, Kenya (Mount) 8 Mauna Kea 9 Haleakala (Crater) *Guatemala:* 4 Agua 5 Fuego 7 Atitlán *Hawaii:* 7 Kilauea 8 Mauna Loa *Honshu:* 4 Nasu 5 Asama, Azuma 6 Bandai 8 Nasudake 9 Asamayama *Iceland:* 5 Askja, Hecla, Hekla *Indonesia:* 3 Awu (Gunung) 5 Agung (Gunung) 7 Tambora (Gunung) *island:* 5 Thera, Thira 8 Krakatau, Krakatoa, Santorin 9 Santorini *Italy:* 8 Vesuvius 9 Stromboli *Iwo Jima:* 9 Suribachi (Mount) *Japan:* 3 Aso 5 Unzen 6 Asosan *Java:* 4 Gede (Gunung) 5 Bromo, Gedeh (Gunung), Kelud (Gunung), Salak (Gunung) *Madeira:* 5 Ruivo (Pico) *Martinique:* 5 Pelée (Mount) *Mexico:* 6 Colima 7 Orizaba 9 Paricutín 12 Popocatepetl *New Zealand:* 7 Ruapehu (Mount) 9 Ngauruhoe, Tongariro *Peru:* 5 Misti (El) *Philippines:* 3 Apo (Mount) 4 Taal 5 Mayon (Mount) 8 Pinatubo (Mount) *Sicily:* 4 Etna *Solomons:* 5 Balbi *South America:* 5 Lanín, Maipo, Maipu *Sumatra:* 5 Dempo (Gunung) 7 Kerinci 8 Kerintji *type:* 6 shield 10 cinder cone *Washington:* 11 Saint Helens (Mount) *West Indies:* 9 Soufrière

___ **volente** 3 Deo

volition 4 will 6 choice, desire, intent, option 8 decision, election 9 selection 10 preference

volley 4 hail, shot 5 burst, round, salvo, storm 6 return, shower 7 barrage 8 drumfire 9 broadside, cannonade, discharge, fusillade

volplane 5 glide

Volpone 3 Fox (The) *author:* 6 Jonson (Ben) *servant:* 5 Mosca

Volsung *grandson:* 6 Sigurd 9 Siegfried *great-grandfather:* 4 Odin *son:* 7 Sigmund

voltage 5 power 6 energy 9 intensity

Voltaire *drama:* 5 Zaïre 6 Alzire, Brutus, Mèrope, Oedipe 7 Mahomet 8 Tancrède *novel:* 5 Zadig 7 Candide *real name:* 6 Arouet (François Marie)

volte-face 5 U-turn 8 flip-flop, reversal, turnover 9 about-face, inversion, turnabout 10 switcheroo 13 change of heart

voluble 4 glib 5 gabby, talky, windy 6 chatty, fluent, mouthy, prolix 7 verbose 8 effusive, vocative 9 garrulous, talkative 10 long-winded, loquacious

volume 4 body, book, bulk, mass, size, tome 5 album, flood, folio, space 6 amount, scroll 7 content 8 capacity, loudness, quantity 9 aggregate 12 displacement

voluminous 4 full 5 bulky 6 legion, prolix 7 copious 8 numerous, prolific 9 capacious 10 convoluted 13 multitudinous

Volumnia's son 10 Coriolanus

voluntary 4 free 7 willful, willing, witting 8 elective, freewill, optional 10 autonomous, deliberate, volitional 11 independent, intentional, spontaneous 13 discretionary

volunteer 5 offer 6 enlist, join up, sign up 7 present, propose, suggest *hospital:* 12 candy striper

Volunteer State 9 Tennessee

voluptuous 4 sexy 5 ample, buxom 6 wanton 7 languid, sensual 8 luscious, sensuous 9 bodacious, luxurious 10 curvaceous

volute 5 helix, shell 6 scroll, spiral 7 mollusc, mollusk 8 curlicue

vomit 3 gag 4 barf, cast, gush, hurl, lose, puke, spew, toss 5 expel, retch 6 spit up 7 bring up, throw up, upchuck 8 disgorge 11 regurgitate

vomiting 6 emesis

Vonnegut work 9 Galapagos, Timequake 10 Cat's Cradle, Hocus Pocus 11 Player Piano 17 Sirens of Titan (The) 18 Slaughterhouse Five 20 Breakfast of Champions 22 Happy Birthday Wanda June

voodoo 3 hex 4 jinx, juju, mojo 5 charm, magic, spell 6 amulet, whammy 7 bewitch, enchant, sorcery 8 ensorcel, wizardry 9 ensorcell 10 hocus-pocus, mumbo jumbo, necromancy, witch-craft **11** abracadabra, implausible, unrealistic

voracious 4 avid **5** eager **6** ardent, greedy, hungry **7** piggish, starved **8** edacious, famished, ravenous, starving **9** rapacious **10** gluttonous, insatiable, omnivorous, quenchless

vortex 4 eddy, gyre **5** swirl **7** tornado **9** hurricane, maelstrom, whirlpool, whirlwind **11** tourbillion

votary 3 bug, fan, nut **4** buff **5** lover **6** addict, zealot **7** admirer, apostle, devotee, groupie, habitué **8** adherent, advocate, believer, disciple, follower **9** worshiper **10** aficionado, enthusiast, worshipper

vote 3 opt **4** poll **5** elect, judge, offer **6** ballot, choice, choose, decide, ratify, select, ticket **7** adjudge, declare, endorse, express, opinion, propose, suggest, verdict **8** election, suffrage **9** franchise **10** expression *affirmative:* **3** aye, nod, yea, yes **6** placet *kind:* **5** proxy, straw, voice **6** secret **7** write-in **8** absentee **10** plebiscite, referendum *negative:* **3** nay *right to:* **8** suffrage **9** franchise

votive 8 grateful **10** devotional

vouch 5 prove **6** affirm, assert, assure, attest, uphold, verify **7** certify, confirm, support, witness **8** accredit **9** guarantee **11** corroborate **12** substantiate

voucher 3 IOU **4** chit **5** proof **6** coupon, surety **7** receipt **9** affidavit, indenture **10** credential **11** certificate **13** authorization

vouchsafe 4 give **5** award, favor, grant **6** accord, bestow, confer, oblige **7** concede, furnish

vow 4 aver, oath, word **5** swear, troth **6** assert, attest, pledge, plight **7** confirm, declare, promise, warrant **8** covenant **9** assertion, guarantee **10** obligation **11** declaration

vowel 6 letter, symbol **11** speech sound *kind:* **4** high, long **5** glide, schwa, short **9** diphthong **11** monophthong *omission:* **7** aphesis **11** contraction *variation:* **6** ablaut, umlaut

voyage 4 sail, trek, trip **5** jaunt **6** cruise, junket, outing, travel **7** journey, odyssey, set sail **8** traverse **9** excursion **10** expedition, pilgrimage

voyeur 6 peeper **10** peeping Tom

Vronski's lover 12 Anna Karenina

Vulcan see HEPHAESTUS

vulgar 3 low, raw **4** base, lewd, rude, vile **5** crass, crude, gaudy, gross, rough, tacky **6** coarse, earthy, flashy, garish, ribald, sordid, tawdry **7** kitschy, low-bred, lowbrow, obscene, profane, uncouth **8** churlish, improper, indecent, off-color, unseemly **9** barbarous, graceless, low-minded, offensive, tasteless, unrefined **10** indecorous, indelicate, scurrilous, unpolished, vernacular **11** pretentious

vulgate 10 vernacular

Vulgate translator 6 Jerome

vulnerability 8 exposure, soft spot, weakness **10** underbelly **12** Achilles' heel

vulnerable 4 open, weak **6** liable **7** exposed **10** assailable **11** susceptible

vulnerary 4 balm **5** salve, tonic **7** healing, unguent **8** curative, ointment, remedial, salutary, sanative **9** medicinal, wholesome **10** salubrious **11** restorative, therapeutic **12** healthgiving

vulpine 3 sly **4** foxy, wily **5** slick **6** artful, astute, crafty, shrewd, tricky **7** cunning, foxlike **8** guileful

vulture 4 bird **6** condor **11** lammergeier, lammergeyer *food:* **7** carrion *relative:* **4** hawk **5** eagle **6** falcon **7** buzzard

vulturine 8 ravenous **9** predatory, rapacious, raptorial **10** predaceous, predacious, scavenging

W

wacky 3 fey, mad **4** daft, nuts **5** batty, daffy, crazy, flaky, kooky, loony, loopy, silly **6** absurd, fruity, insane, screwy **7** bonkers, cracked, foolish, idiotic, lunatic, offbeat **8** crackers, demented **9** eccentric **10** irrational **11** harebrained **12** preposterous

wad 3 gob **4** lump, mint, pile, plug, quid, roll, swab **5** chunk, stuff **6** boodle, bundle, packet, pellet **7** fortune **8** bankroll

waddle 6 toddle

waddy 4 club, cosh **6** cowboy, cudgel **7** rustler **8** bludgeon

wade 4 ford, plod **5** labor **6** drudge, trudge *into:* **5** set to **6** attack, plunge, tackle **9** undertake

wadi 3 bed **4** wash **5** gully **6** arroyo, coulee, course, ravine **9** streambed **10** depression **11** watercourse

wafer 4 chip, disk, host **5** matzo, slice **6** matzoh **7** cracker

waffle 4 yo-yo **5** tripe, waver **6** dither, drivel, seesaw **7** blather **8** flip-flop **9** fluctuate, vacillate **10** equivocate

waft 4 flag, gust, puff, wave **5** drift, float, hover **7** pennant

wag 3 bob, nod, wit **4** card, lash, wave **5** clown, cutup, joker, shake, swing, whisk **6** kidder, switch, twitch, waddle **8** brandish, comedian, funnyman, jokester

wage 3 fee, pay **6** income, reward, salary **7** carry on, payment, stipend **8** earnings, pittance, receipts **9** emolument **10** recompense **12** compensation, remuneration

wager 3 bet, lay, pot **4** ante, game, risk **5** stake **6** chance, gamble, hazard **7** venture

waggery 3 gag **4** jest, joke **5** prank, sport **7** devilry, kidding, roguery **8** deviltry, drollery, mischief **10** impishness, pleasantry **11** roguishness **12** sportiveness **13** practical joke

waggish 4 arch, pert **5** antic, comic, droll, saucy, witty **6** impish, jocose **7** comical, jocular, playful, puckish, roguish **8** humorous, prankish, sportive **9** facetious **10** frolicsome **11** mischievous

waggle 3 bob **4** reel, sway

Wagner, Richard *birthplace:* **7** Leipzig *father-in-law:* **5** Liszt (Franz) *festival site:* **8** Bayreuth *opera:* **4** Ring **6** Rienzi **8** Parsifal **9** Lohengrin, Rheingold (Das), Siegfried **10** Die Walküre, Tannhäuser **12** Das Rheingold **13** Meistersinger (Die) **14** Flying Dutchman (The) **15** Götterdämmerung **16** Tristan und Isolde **17** Ring of the Nibelung (The) *recurring theme:* **9** leitmotif, leitmotiv *wife:* **5** Minna **6** Cosima

wagon 3 van **4** cart, dray, tram, trek, wain **7** caravan, coaster, hayrack

wahoo 3 ono **8** mackerel **9** winged elm **11** burning bush

waif 5 gamin, stray **6** gamine, orphan, urchin **8** wanderer **9** foundling **10** ragamuffin **11** guttersnipe

wail 3 bay, cry **4** bawl, blub, fuss, howl, keen, weep, yowl **5** mourn, whine **6** bemoan, lament, plaint, repine **7** blubber, ululate **8** complain **9** complaint **11** lamentation

wain 5 wagon **9** Big Dipper

waistband 3 obi **4** belt, sash **6** girdle **8** ceinture, cincture **10** cummerbund

waistcoat 4 vest **6** jerkin, weskit

wait 4 bide, idle, stay **5** abide, dally, delay, serve, tarry, watch **6** expect, hold on, linger, remain **8** hang fire, mark time, sit tight **10** anticipate **11** stick around

waiter 4 tray **6** garçon, salver, server **7** servant **9** attendant

Waiting for ___ 5 Godot, Lefty

wait on 4 tend **5** serve **6** attend, tend to **7** cater for, cater to **9** look after

waive 4 cede, stay **5** allow, defer, delay, forgo, table, yield **6** give up, hold up, put off, shelve **7** abandon, concede, dismiss, hold off, suspend **8** hand over, hold over, postpone **9** surrender **10** relinquish

wake 4 path, stir, wash **5** alert, arise, get up, rally, rouse, track, vigil, watch **6** arouse, bestir, excite, kindle, stir up **7** roll out **8** backwash **9** aftermath, stimulate

wakeful 5 alert **8** restless, vigilant **9** insomniac, sleepless

waken see WAKE

Walden author 7 Thoreau (Henry David)

wale 3 rib **4** bend, welt **5** brace, ridge **6** strake

walk 3 pad **4** gait, hike, hoof, pace, path, plod, roam, slog, step, trip **5** alley, amble, clump, mince, paseo, stave, strut, stump, trail, tramp, tread, troop **6** prance, ramble, sashay, stride, stroll, toddle, trudge, waddle, wander **7** saunter, shamble, shuffle, stumble, swagger, traipse **8** ambulate, traverse **9** promenade **11** base on balls, perambulate, peregrinate

walkaway 4 romp, rout

walking shorts 8 Bermudas

walking stick 4 cane **5** staff **6** crutch, insect **7** phasmid, whangee

walk out 5 leave **6** strike

walk out on 5 leave **6** desert **7** abandon, forsake

Walküre composer 6 Wagner (Richard)

walkway 4 path **7** passage **9** promenade

wall 3 bar, hem **4** side, stop **5** block, close, fence, hedge **6** immure **7** barrier, close in, enclose **8** blockade, surround **9** barricade, enclosure, roadblock, structure *bearing:* **7** support *hanging:* **8** tapestry *painting:* **5** mural *protective:* **7** parapet, rampart *top of:* **6** coping

wallaby 8 kangaroo

wallet 5 funds **6** folder **8** billfold **9** accessory, resources **10** pocketbook

Wallis and Futuna Islands *capital:* **7** Mata-Utu *island:* **4** Uvéa *territory of:* **6** France

wallop 3 bop, hit **4** bang, bash, beat, belt, blow, boil, bust, clip, drub, lick, pelt, slam, slug, sock, whip, whop, whup **5** baste, paste, pound, punch, smack, whack **6** buffet, pummel, thrash, thwack **7** shellac, trounce **8** lambaste

walloping 4 huge **5** giant **7** immense, mammoth, monster **8** colossal, enormous, gigantic, smashing **10** gargantuan, impressive, incredible, prodigious

wallow 4 bask, roll **5** enjoy, revel **6** billow, welter **7** delight, indulge **9** luxuriate

___ **Walpole 4** Hugh **6** Horace

___ **Walton 3** Sam **5** Izaak

waltz 5 dance, valse

Waltz King 7 Strauss (Johann)

Wampanoag chief 9 Massasoit, Metacomet **10** King Philip

wampum 5 beads, money **6** shells

wan 3 dim **4** ashy, gray, pale, waxy, weak, worn **5** ashen, faint, livid, lurid, pasty, waxen **6** anemic, doughy, feeble, infirm, pallid, peaked, sallow, sickly **7** ghastly, languid **8** blanched **9** bloodless, colorless, washed-out **10** cadaverous, white-faced

wand 3 rod **4** pole, tube **5** baton, staff

wander 3 bat, bum, gad **4** mill, roam, rove, swan **5** amble, dally, drift, float, gypsy, mooch, prowl, range, stray, tramp **6** ramble, stroll **7** deviate, digress, diverge, maunder, meander, saunter, traipse **8** divagate, straggle, vagabond **9** expatiate, gallivant **10** kick around

wanderer 4 waif **5** gypsy, nomad, rover, stray **7** pilgrim, vagrant **8** runabout, vagabond

wandering 7 erratic, migrant, nomadic, vagrant **8** vagabond **9** itinerant, migratory, walkabout, wayfaring **10** roundabout **11** peripatetic

wane 3 dim, ebb **4** fail, fall **5** abate, let up **6** lessen, recede, reduce, relent, shrink, weaken **7** decline, dwindle, slacken, subside **8** decrease, diminish, moderate, slack off, taper off

wangle 6 scheme **7** finagle, wheedle **8** inveigle, scrounge **10** manipulate

wannabe 5 clone **7** also-ran, copycat, hopeful, wishful **8** apparent, aspiring, desiring, desirous **9** ambitious, lookalike, potential

want 4 lack, like, need, void, wish **5** covet, crave, fault **6** dearth, desire, penury **7** absence, poverty, require **8** exigency **9** indigence, necessity, neediness, privation **10** deficiency, desiderate, inadequacy, scantiness **11** destitution, requirement **13** insufficiency

wanting 4 away, less, sans **5** minus, scant, short **6** absent, scanty, scarce **7** lacking, missing, without **9** deficient **10** inadequate, incomplete **12** insufficient

wanton 4 doxy, jade, lewd, minx, rank, slut **5** bawdy, cruel, hussy, loose, tramp, trull, wench **6** coquet, floozy, harlot, lavish, trifle, unruly **7** baggage, cyprian, immoral, jezebel, lustful, obscene, Paphian, sensual, trollop, wayward **8** inhumane, pitiless, ruthless, slattern, spiteful, sportive, strumpet **9** dissolute, luxuriant, malicious, merciless **10** gratuitous, lascivious, malevolent, outrageous, prostitute **11** extravagant, mischievous, uncalled-for

wapiti 3 elk **7** red deer

war 4 feud, odds **5** fight **6** battle, combat, strife **7** contest **8** conflict, struggle, variance **9** hostility **10** antagonism **11** competition *German:* **5** Krieg **10** blitzkrieg *god:* **3** Tiu, Tyr **4** Ares, Mars, Odin **5** Woden, Wotan *goddess:* **4** Enyo **5** Anath **6** Inanna, Ishtar **7** Bel-

Iona *Latin:* 6 bellum *Muslim:* 5 jehad, jihad *relating to:* 7 martial

War and Peace *author:* 7 Tolstoy (Leo) *composer:* 9 Prokofiev (Sergey)

warble 4 sing 5 carol, chirp, trill, tweet 6 gadfly, maggot, quaver 7 descant, melisma, twitter

warbler 4 bird 6 singer 7 kinglet 8 songster 9 blackpoll 11 gnatcatcher *European:* 10 chiffchaff

war cry 5 motto 6 slogan *Greek:* 5 alala *Japanese:* 6 banzai

ward 4 care 5 aegis, stave 6 barrio, charge 7 custody, defense, keeping 8 district, division, precinct, security 9 bishopric 10 protection 11 safekeeping 12 guardianship

warden 6 jailer, keeper, regent 7 provost 8 governor, guardian, official 9 castellan, constable, custodian, protector 10 commandant, supervisor

ward off 5 avert, parry, rebut, repel 6 divert 7 deflect 8 turn away 9 forestall

wardrobe 5 trunk 6 closet 7 apparel, armoire, clothes 8 clothing 9 garderobe 12 clothespress

warehouse 4 stow 5 depot, lodge, stock, store 7 confine, deposit, shelter, storage, stowage 8 building 9 stockroom, storeroom 10 depository, repository 11 accommodate *oriental:* 6 godown

wares 4 line 5 goods, stock 9 vendibles 11 commodities, marketables, merchandise

warfare 6 battle, combat, strife 8 conflict, struggle 10 operations 11 hostilities *type:* 4 germ 6 trench 10 biological

warhorse 4 hack 7 charger, courser, veteran 8 chestnut, standard

warlike 7 hawkish, martial 8 militant, military 9 bellicose, combative, truculent 10 aggressive, pugnacious 11 belligerent

warlock 3 wiz 4 mage 5 magus 6 wizard 8 conjurer, conjuror, magician, satanist, sorcerer 9 diabolist, enchanter 11 necromancer

warm 4 bask, heat, kind 5 angry, fresh 6 ardent, genial, heated, heat up, loving, reheat, secure, tender 7 affable, cordial, excited, fervent, sincere 8 friendly, gracious, spirited 9 heartfelt 10 passionate, responsive 11 kindhearted, sympathetic 12 affectionate, enthusiastic, wholehearted 13 compassionate *air:* 7 thermal

warmed-over 5 banal, stale, tired, trite 6 old-hat 7 clichéd 8 shopworn, timeworn 9 hackneyed

warmhearted 4 kind 6 benign, kindly, loving, tender 7 cordial 8 generous

9 benignant, unselfish 10 benevolent 11 magnanimous, sympathetic 12 affectionate 13 compassionate

warmth 4 glow, heat 7 comfort 8 fondness 9 affection 10 cordiality

warn 3 tip 4 clew, clue 5 alert 6 advise, inform, notify, tip off 7 apprise, caution, counsel 8 admonish

warning 3 tip 4 hint 5 alarm, alert 6 caveat, notice, signal, tip-off 7 caution, counsel, summons 8 monition, monitory 10 admonition, cautionary 12 admonishment *legal:* 6 caveat

War of the Worlds author 5 Wells (H. G.)

warp 4 base, bend, cast, kink, rope, wind 5 color, curve, twist 6 buckle, debase, deform, wrench 7 confuse, contort, corrupt, deflect, distort, pervert, torture, vitiate 10 bastardize 12 misrepresent

warrant 4 pawn, writ 5 proof, prove, token 6 affirm, assert, assure, attest, avouch, ensure, ground, insure, pledge, secure 7 certify, contend, declare, justify, precept 8 guaranty, maintain, mittimus, sanction, security 9 assurance, authority, authorize, guarantee 10 foundation 11 certificate 12 confirmation 13 justification

warranty 4 bail, bond 6 surety 8 covenant, security 9 guarantee

warren 4 maze 7 network, rabbits 8 tenement

warrior 4 hero 7 battler, fighter, soldier 8 champion 9 combatant 10 serviceman *female:* 6 Amazon *Japanese:* 7 samurai

Warsaw *castle:* 5 Zamek *river:* 7 Vistula

wart 4 flaw 6 defect, growth 7 blemish, verruca 11 excrescence

wary 5 alert, cagey, canny, chary, leery 7 careful, dubious, guarded, mindful 8 cautious, skittish, vigilant, watchful 10 suspicious 11 circumspect, distrustful

wash 3 lap, pan, tub 4 hose, lave, suds, wadi 5 bathe, clean, creek, douse, drift, float, flush, marsh, scrub, slosh, swill 6 drench, shower, sluice, splash 7 cleanse, coating, launder, laundry, shampoo, suffuse 8 backwash

washed-out 4 beat 5 all in, faded, spent, tired, weary 6 bushed, effete, sapped, used-up, wasted 7 drained 8 depleted 9 exhausted

washed-up 4 beat, done 5 kaput, spent 6 done in 7 also-ran, defunct, done for, through 8 finished

washing 4 bath 6 lavage 7 laundry 8 ablution, lavation *ceremonial:* 6 lavabo

Washington *capital:* 7 Olympia *city:*

6 Tacoma 7 Seattle, Spokane 9 Vancouver 10 Walla Walla *college, university:* 7 Gonzaga, Whitman 9 Evergreen *dam:* 11 Grand Coulee *mountain, range:* 7 Cascade, Olympic, Rainier 8 St. Helens *nickname:* 9 Evergreen (State) *river:* 6 Yakima 8 Columbia *state bird:* 9 goldfinch *state flower:* 12 rhododendron *state tree:* 7 hemlock

Washington, D.C., designer 7 L'Enfant (Pierre-Charles)

Washington, George *home:* 11 Mount Vernon *wife:* 6 Martha

Washington Square author 5 James (Henry)

wasp 5 mason 6 digger, hornet, vespid 9 ichneumon, mud dauber 12 yellow jacket

waspish 5 testy 6 snappy, snarky, snippy, touchy 7 peevish, vespine 8 petulant, snappish, vinegary 9 crotchety, fractious, irritable, querulous 10 vinegarish 12 cantankerous, cross-grained

wassail 5 binge, carol, drink, revel, spree, toast 6 bender 7 carouse, revelry, roister 8 carousal, drinking

Wasserstein play 15 Heidi Chronicles (The) 17 Sisters Rosensweig (The)

waste 4 arid, fail, kill, loss, ruin, sack, wild 5 empty, offal, scrap, trash 6 barren, damage, debris, desert, devour, litter, ravage, refuse, sewage, shrink; weaken 7 badland, consume, despoil, destroy, fritter, garbage, pillage, plunder, rubbish 8 decrease, desolate, emaciate, enfeeble, misspend, prodigal, spoilage, squander, wear away, wildland 9 devastate, dissipate, excrement, sweepings, throw away 10 desolation, wilderness 11 prodigality 12 extravagance, extravagancy *maker:* 5 haste *time:* 5 dally 6 dawdle, footle, piddle, trifle

waste away 4 fade, fail 6 molder, shrink 7 atrophy, decline, dwindle, shrivel 10 degenerate

wasted 3 lit 4 high 5 drunk, gaunt 6 peaked, sickly, stoned 7 elapsed, ravaged 8 skeletal 9 emaciated 10 cadaverous, skeletonic 11 intoxicated

wasteful 6 lavish 8 prodigal 9 throwaway 10 profligate, thriftless, uneconomic 11 extravagant, improvident, inefficient, spendthrift

wastefulness 6 excess 10 lavishness 11 prodigality 12 extravagance, immoderation

wasteland 4 wild 5 heath 6 barren 10 desolation, wilderness

Waste Land author 5 Eliot (T. S.)

wastrel 3 rip 4 rake, roué 7 rounder,

spender 8 prodigal 9 fritterer, libertine 10 dissipater, high roller, ne'er-do-well, profligate, squanderer 11 scattergood, spendthrift

watch 3 eye, see, spy 4 bide, look, tend, tout, wait, wake, ward 5 guard, shift, vigil 6 attend, follow, look at, notice, sentry 7 care for, lookout, monitor, observe, surveil 8 bulletin, eagle eye, scrutiny, sentinel, watchman 9 attention, timepiece, vigilance 10 duty period, observance 11 chronometer, observation 12 surveillance *chain:* 3 fob *maker:* 10 horologist

watchdog 5 guard 6 keeper 8 Cerberus, guardian 9 custodian, protector

watcher 6 viewer 7 guarder, lookout 8 beholder, follower, guardian, observer, onlooker 9 spectator

watchful 4 wary 5 alert, chary 7 on guard, wakeful 8 cautious, vigilant 9 attentive, observant, sleepless, wideawake 10 unsleeping *Scottish:* 5 tenty 6 tentie

watchman 5 guard, scout 6 patrol, picket, sentry, warder 7 lookout 8 sentinel

watch out 6 beware 8 take care

watchtower 6 turret 7 lookout 8 barbican, bartizan 10 lighthouse

watchword 3 cry 5 motto 6 mantra, parole, signal, slogan 8 password 9 principle 10 shibboleth 11 catchphrase, countersign

water 4 soak, thin, tide 5 drink, fluid, spray 6 dilute, liquid, supply 7 moisten 8 irrigate, moisture, snowmelt, sprinkle 10 excellence 13 amniotic fluid *body:* 3 bay, sea 4 gulf, lake, pool 5 ocean 6 lagoon, strait 9 reservoir *combining form:* 4 aqui, aquo, hydr 5 hydro *French:* 3 eau *goddess:* 4 Nina 7 Anahita, Anaitis *Latin:* 4 aqua *Spanish:* 4 agua

water buffalo 4 arna 5 bovid 7 carabao *female:* 5 arnee

water clock 9 clepsydra

water closet 3 loo 4 head, john 5 privy 6 toilet 7 latrine 8 bathroom, lavatory

watercourse 4 dike, duct 5 bayou, canal, ditch 6 arroyo 7 channel, conduit 8 aqueduct, headrace, tailrace 9 streambed

water cow 6 dugong 7 manatee

watered-down 5 washy 6 dilute 7 diluted

waterfall 5 chute, sault, shoot 7 cascade 8 cataract *Brazil:* 6 Iguaçú (Falls), Iguazú (Falls) *California:* 8 Yosemite (Falls) *Canada:* 5 Grand (Falls) 8 Takkakaw 9 Churchill (Falls) *Canada-U.S.:* 7 Niagara (Falls) *Congo:* 6 Boyoma (Falls) 7 Stanley (Falls) *former Nile:* 4 Owen (Falls) 5 Ripon (Falls) *Ken-*

tucky: 10 Cumberland (Falls) *New Zealand:* 10 Sutherland (Falls) *Niagara:* 8 American, Canadian 9 Horseshoe *Norway:* 6 Rjukan (Falls) *Oregon:* 9 Multnomah (Falls) *South Africa:* 6 Tugela (Falls) *Snake River:* 4 Twin (Falls) 8 Shoshone (Falls) *Venezuela:* 5 Angel (Falls) *Washington:* 10 Snoqualmie (Falls) *world's highest:* 5 Angel (Falls) *Wyoming:* 11 Yellowstone (Falls) *Zambezi River:* 8 Victoria

water finder 6 dowser 11 divining rod

waterfront 8 seacoast 9 lakeshore, riverside

water hole 5 oasis

watering hole 3 bar, pub 4 café 5 oasis 6 lounge, nitery, resort, saloon, tavern 7 barroom, cabaret 9 nightclub, nightspot, roadhouse 10 supper club

waterless 3 dry 4 arid, sere 7 bone-dry 8 droughty 9 anhydrous 10 dehydrated

waterlog 8 saturate

waterloo 4 ruin 6 defeat 7 failure 8 disaster, downfall

water nymph 4 lily 5 naiad 6 mayfly, Nereid 7 Oceanid 9 dragonfly *female:* 3 nix 5 nixie

water oscillation 6 seiche

water pipe 4 bong 5 spout 6 hookah 8 narghile, nargileh 12 hubble-bubble

water plant 7 aquatic, seaweed 8 duckweed, wild rice 9 arrowhead, tape grass 10 hydrophyte, manna grass 11 bladderwort

water rat 6 nutria

watershed 6 crisis, divide 12 turning point

water spirit 3 nix 5 nixie, nymph 6 sprite, undine

water tank 7 cistern

watery 4 pale, thin, weak 5 banal, bland, vapid, washy 6 dilute, serous 7 diluted, insipid

wattle 4 gill, grid, jowl 5 frame 8 caruncle 9 framework, interlace 10 interweave

wattle and___ 4 daub

wave 3 wag 4 flag, flap 5 heave, ridge, surge, sweep, swell 6 comber, influx, marcel, motion, period, ripple, signal, waggle 7 breaker, dismiss, flutter, gesture, upsurge 8 activity, brandish, flourish, undulate 9 disregard *large:* 7 tsunami

waver 4 reel, sway 5 swing, weave 6 dither, falter, quaver, quiver, teeter, totter, wobble 7 flicker, stagger, whiffle 8 hesitate, undulate 9 oscillate, vacillate 12 shilly-shally

wavering 4 weak 5 shake, shaky 6 unsure, wobbly 7 halting 8 doubtful, insecure, to-and-fro, unstable 9 equivocal, faltering, fluctuant, hesitancy, undecided, vibration, whiffling 10 hesitating, hesitation, indecision, irresolute 11 fluctuating, vacillating, vacillation 12 irresolution, shilly-shally

Waverly author 5 Scott (Walter)

wavy 7 rolling 8 rippling, swelling 9 fluctuant 10 undulating 11 fluctuating

wavy pattern 5 moiré 8 squiggle 10 undulation 11 crenulation

wax 4 come, grow, rise 5 boost, build, mount 6 become, expand, record 7 augment, enlarge 8 heighten, increase, multiply, paraffin, simonize 9 secretion, substance

waxen 3 wan 4 ashy, pale 5 ashen, livid 6 pallid, smooth 7 pliable 8 blanched, moldable 9 colorless

way 3 ilk 4 door, kind, mode, much, path, road, sort, type, very 5 entry, habit, means, order, route, state, style, usage 6 access, artery, action, avenue, course, custom, degree, manner, method, street 7 ability, fashion, feature, ingress, opening, outcome, respect 8 distance, entrance, practice 9 boulevard, condition, direction, procedure, technique 11 opportunity, possibility 12 thoroughfare

wayfarer 5 gypsy, hiker, nomad, tramp 8 traveler 9 itinerant, journeyer

wayfaring 6 roving 7 nomadic, vagrant 8 vagabond 9 itinerant, traveling, wandering 10 travelling 11 peripatetic 13 perambulatory

waylay 5 brace 6 ambush, attack 8 surprise 9 bushwhack, still-hunt

Way of All Flesh author 6 Butler (Samuel)

Way of the World author 8 Congreve (William)

wayward 5 balky 6 fickle, unruly 7 froward, restive, vagrant 8 contrary, perverse, untoward 9 whimsical 10 capricious, headstrong 11 intractable, wrongheaded 12 ungovernable 13 unpredictable

we *French:* 4 nous *German:* 3 wir *Italian:* 3 noi *Spanish:* 8 nosotros

weak 3 dim, wan 4 puny, soft, thin 5 faint, frail, shaky, timid 6 dilute, feeble, flimsy, infirm, sickly, unsure, watery, wobbly 7 brittle, diluted, fragile, rickety, spindly, tenuous, unsound 8 decrepit, delicate, helpless, impotent, inferior, insecure, timorous, unstable, wavering 9 deficient, enfeebled, inaudible, powerless, spineless, uncertain 10 improbable, inadequate, unreliable, unstressed 11 debilitated, implausible, ineffective, ineffectual, vacillating, watered-down **12** unconvincing, undependable **13** insubstantial, unsubstantial

weaken 3 lag, sap **4** fail, flag, thin, wane **5** abate **6** damage, dilute, impair, lessen, reduce, soften **7** corrode, decline, disable, dwindle, subvert, unbrace **8** enervate, enfeeble, moderate **9** attenuate, grind down, honeycomb, undermine **10** debilitate, demoralize, invalidate

weak-kneed 5 timid **6** wobbly **7** gutless **8** cowardly, wavering **9** faltering, uncertain, whiffling **10** irresolute **11** lily-livered, vacillating **12** fainthearted, shilly-shally **13** pusillanimous

weakling 4 wimp, wuss **5** mouse, sissy **7** doormat, milksop, sad sack **8** pushover **9** jellyfish **10** namby-pamby **11** milquetoast, mollycoddle **12** invertebrate

weakness 4 flaw, hole, vice **5** crack, fault, taste **6** defect, desire, liking, relish **7** failing, frailty **8** appetite, debility, fondness, soft spot **9** infirmity **10** feebleness **11** decrepitude, shortcoming **12** Achilles' heel

weal 4 welt **5** ridge **7** welfare **9** well-being

weald 5 woods **6** forest **8** woodland **10** timberland, wilderness

wealth 5 goods, worth **6** assets, estate, plenty, riches **7** capital, fortune **8** holdings, opulence, property **9** abundance, affluence, profusion, resources **11** possessions

Wealth of Nations author 5 Smith (Adam)

wealthy 4 rich **5** flush **6** loaded **7** moneyed, opulent, well-off **8** affluent, well-to-do **9** well-fixed **10** prosperous, well-heeled **12** silk-stocking

wean 4 free, part **5** alien **6** detach **8** accustom, estrange, separate

weapon 3 bow, gun **4** bill, bolo, bomb, club, dart, dirk, mace, nuke, pike **5** A-bomb, arrow, H-bomb, knife, lance, prick, rifle, saber, sabre, sling, spear, steel, sword **6** dagger, Magnum, musket, pistol, poleax, rapier, rocket **7** bazooka, broadax, car bomb, carbine, firearm, gisarme, halberd, javelin, machete, missile, shotgun, sidearm, stun gun, torpedo, war club **8** battle-ax, bludgeon, broadaxe, catapult, crossbow, death ray, nerve gas, nunchaku, partisan, partizan, petronel, revolver, spontoon, tomahawk **9** battle-axe, blackjack, boomerang, derringer, slingshot **10** atomic bomb, machine gun, projectile **11** blunderbuss, depth

charge, nuclear bomb **12** quarterstaff **13** brass knuckles

weapons 4 arms **7** arsenal, battery **8** ordnance **9** armaments, artillery, munitions **13** armamentarium

wear 3 rub **4** fray, tire **5** chafe, dress, erode, grind **6** abrade, attire, endure, impair **7** corrode, exhibit, fatigue, fashion **8** abrasion, clothing *and tear:* **12** depreciation *thin:* **4** fray **5** chafe **6** tatter **7** hackney

wear down 5 drain, erode, grind **6** abrade, weaken **7** corrode, degrade, exhaust, fatigue

weariness 5 ennui **7** boredom, fatigue, languor **8** lethargy **9** lassitude **10** enervation, exhaustion **12** taedium vitae

wearing 6 taxing, tiring, trying **9** difficult, fatiguing

wearisome see TIRESOME

wear out 3 fag **4** bust, do in, fray, poop, tire **5** drain **6** efface, tucker **7** consume, deplete, exhaust, frazzle **8** overstay

weary 4 beat, jade, limp, tire, worn **5** drain, jaded, spent, tired **6** bushed, done in, pooped, tucker, wasted **7** drained, fatigue, worn-out **8** dog-tired, fatigued, tiresome **9** apathetic

weasand 6 gullet, throat **7** trachea **8** windpipe **9** esophagus

weasel 5 dodge, evade, hedge, slink, sneak, stoat **6** ermine, escape, ferret, mammal **7** sneaker **8** sidestep **9** pussyfoot **10** equivocate *Scottish:* **8** whittret

weather 4 rain **5** storm **6** bear up, endure, expose **7** climate, ride out, undergo **9** withstand *forecasting:* **11** meteorology

weathercock 4 vane

weathered 8 hardened, seasoned, tempered

weave 4 cane, lawn, leno, spin, sway **5** braid, cloth, lurch, twine, waver **6** careen, fabric, pleach, raddle, wobble, zigzag **7** pattern, stagger, textile, texture **8** contrive **9** interlace **10** crisscross, intertwine

web 3 net **4** mesh, vane **5** snare, snarl **6** enmesh, fabric, tangle **7** ensnare, netting, network **8** entangle **10** enmeshment **12** entanglement

Weber opera 6 Oberon **9** Euryanthe **10** Freischütz (Der)

____ **Webster 4** Noah **6** Daniel

wed 4 join, link, mate, yoke **5** hitch, marry, merge, unite **6** splice **7** combine, conjoin, connect, espouse **10** tie the knot

wedded 7 marital, nuptial **8** conjugal, hymeneal **9** connubial **11** matrimonial

wedding 6 bridal 7 spousal 8 espousal, marriage, nuptials

wedding anniversary *fifteenth:* 7 crystal *fifth:* 6 wooden *fiftieth:* 6 golden *first:* 5 paper *seventy-fifth:* 7 diamond *tenth:* 3 tin *twentieth:* 5 china *twenty-fifth:* 6 silver

wedge 4 shim 5 chock, stuff 8 golf club, golf shot, keystone 10 force apart

wedge-shaped 7 cuneate 8 cottered, sphenoid 9 cuneiform

wedlock 4 knot, yoke 8 espousal, marriage 9 matrimony 11 conjugality 12 connubiality

wee 4 tiny 5 bitsy, bitty, early, small, teeny 6 little, minute, teensy 9 itty-bitty, miniature 10 diminutive, teeny-weeny 11 Lilliputian, little bitty 12 teensy-weensy

weed 4 dock, tare 5 chess, clear, plant 6 cockle, darnel, dodder, nettle, remove 7 burdock, burseed, ragweed, ruderal 8 amaranth, charlock, purslane 9 chickweed, cocklebur, dandelion, knotgrass, marijuana, poison ivy, poison oak, stickseed 10 cheatgrass, lady's thumb, sow thistle *European:* 6 spurry 7 spurrey *killer:* 8 paraquat 9 herbicide *Western:* 4 loco

weedy 4 lean, thin 5 lanky 6 skinny 7 scrawny, stringy, willowy 8 untended 9 overgrown

week 6 period 8 hebdomad *two weeks:* 9 fortnight

weep 3 cry, sob 4 drip, moan, ooze, tear, wail 5 bleed, exude, sweat 6 lament 7 blubber, dribble, trickle 8 transude

weepy 5 misty, moist, teary 7 tearful 10 lachrymose

weevil 7 billbug 8 curculio

weft 3 web 4 pick, woof, yarn 6 fabric, thread

weigh 3 way 4 heft, rate, tare 5 count, judge, scale, study 6 burden, ponder 7 balance, measure, oppress, perpend 8 appraise, bear down, consider, evaluate, militate 11 contemplate

weigh down 4 load 5 press 6 burden, sadden 7 depress, oppress 8 encumber 10 discourage, overburden

weight 3 tax 4 heft, lade, load, mass, onus, task 5 class, force, power 6 amount, assign, burden, charge, credit, import, moment, saddle 7 oppress, potency, quality 8 encumber, poundage, pressure, prestige, quantity 9 authority, influence, magnitude 10 corpulence, importance 11 consequence 12 significance *allowance:* 4 tare *apothecary:* 4 dram 5 grain, pound 7 scruple *Asian:* 6 cattie *gem:* 5 carat

measure of: 3 ton 4 dram, gram 5 grain, ounce, pound 7 long ton, scruple 8 kilogram, short ton 9 metric ton *system:* 3 net 4 troy 6 metric 10 apothecary 11 avoirdupois

weightiness 4 pith 6 import, moment 7 dignity, gravity 9 heaviness, magnitude, solemnity 10 importance 11 consequence, massiveness 12 significance 13 momentousness

weight lift 4 pull 5 clean, press, shrug 6 snatch 12 clean and jerk

weighty 3 fat 5 grave, gross, heavy, hefty, obese, sober, staid 6 fleshy, portly, sedate, severe, solemn, somber 7 massive, serious, telling 8 cumbrous, grievous, powerful 9 corpulent, effective, important, momentous, ponderous 10 burdensome, convincing, cumbersome 11 significant, substantial 12 considerable 13 consequential

weir 3 dam 5 stank

weird 3 odd 5 eerie, queer 6 creepy, freaky, spooky 7 bizarre, curious, oddball, strange, uncanny 8 freakish, peculiar, singular, sinister 9 eccentric, fantastic, unearthly 10 mysterious 11 inscrutable 12 supernatural 13 preternatural

weirdo 4 geek, kook 5 freak 7 nutcase, oddball 8 crackpot 9 eccentric, screwball

welcome 4 hail 5 cheer, greet, hello, howdy 6 accept, invite, salute 7 embrace, invited, receive 8 greeting, pleasant, pleasing 9 agreeable, favorable, reception 10 gratifying, hospitable 11 hospitality, pleasurable

weld 4 bond, fuse, join 5 braze, joint, merge, unite 6 solder

welfare 3 aid 4 dole, help, weal 5 pogey 6 health, relief, succor 7 benefit, fortune, success, support 8 interest 9 advantage, happiness, well-being 10 assistance, commonweal, prosperity

welkin 3 sky 5 ether, vault 6 heaven 7 heavens 8 empyrean 9 firmament

well 3 far, fit, pit 4 easy, emit, hale, hole, pool, rise, sane 5 amply, clear, cured, fully, quite, shaft, sound, truly 6 easily, freely, healed, indeed, justly, kindly, likely, nicely, origin, rather, really, source, spring, wholly 7 clearly, healthy, perhaps, readily, rightly 8 entirely, expertly, pleasing, possibly, probably, properly, sensibly, smoothly, suitably 9 advisable, correctly, desirable, elegantly, favorably, fittingly, fortunate, perfectly, wholesome 10 acceptably, adequately, affluently, becomingly, completely, pleasantly, pleasingly, prosperous, reasonably, thoroughly **11** attentively, comfortable, compartment, fortunately, substantial **12** considerably, prosperously, satisfactory, successfully **13** appropriately, significantly

well-being 4 weal **6** health **7** welfare **8** thriving **9** happiness **10** prosperity

well-bred 6 urbane **7** genteel, refined **8** cultured, highborn, polished **9** civilized, patrician **10** cultivated **11** blueblooded, gentlemanly

well-built 4 buff **5** hunky, solid **8** muscular **9** strapping

well-developed 5 curvy **7** fulsome, rounded, shapely **8** advanced **9** Junoesque **10** curvaceous

well-disposed 7 amiable **8** friendly **9** favorable, receptive **11** sympathetic **13** understanding

Welles movie 5 Trial (The) **7** Macbeth, Othello **8** Jane Eyre, Stranger (The), Third Man (The) **11** Citizen Kane, Touch of Evil **15** Journey into Fear **16** Chimes at Midnight, Lady from Shanghai (The) **20** Magnificent Ambersons (The)

well-favored 4 fair **6** comely, lovely, pretty **8** gorgeous, handsome **9** beauteous, beautiful **10** attractive **11** good-looking

well-fixed see WELL-TO-DO

well-founded 5 sound, valid **6** cogent **8** rational **9** justified **10** convincing

well-groomed 4 neat, snug, tidy, trig, trim **5** natty, smart **6** dapper, snappy, spiffy, spruce, sprucy **7** orderly **8** cleancut **9** shipshape

well-heeled see WELL-TO-DO

Wellington 4 duke **7** general **8** Iron Duke *horse:* **10** Copenhagen *original name:* **9** Wellesley (Arthur) *victory:* **7** Vitoria **8** Talavera, Waterloo **9** Salamanca

well-known 5 noted **6** famous **7** bigname, eminent, popular **8** renowned **9** notorious, prominent **10** celebrated **11** illustrious

well-liked 7 beloved, favored, popular **8** favorite **9** cherished, preferred

well-mannered 5 civil, suave **6** poised, polite, proper, urbane **7** genteel, tactful **9** courteous **10** diplomatic

well-nigh 6 all but, almost, fairly, nearly, next to **8** as good as **9** just about, virtually **11** essentially, practically

well-off see WELL-TO-DO

well-paying 7 gainful **9** lucrative, rewarding **10** profitable, worthwhile **11** moneymaking **12** advantageous, remunerative

wellspring 4 font, root **5** fount **6** origin,

source **7** genesis **8** fountain **10** provenance **11** provenience **12** fountainhead

well-thought-of 6 valued, worthy **7** admired, reputed **9** estimable, reputable **10** creditable **11** respectable

well-timed 6 timely **7** apropos, fitting, timeous **9** favorable, opportune **10** auspicious, felicitous, fortuitous, propitious, seasonable

well-to-do 4 rich **5** flush **6** loaded **7** moneyed, upscale, wealthy **8** affluent **10** prosperous **11** comfortable

well-turned 4 trim **5** plump **7** rounded, shapely **10** curvaceous, felicitous, Rubenesque, statuesque **11** cleanlimbed

well-worn 5 banal, musty, stale, stock, tired, trite **6** frayed, old-hat, shabby **7** clichéd **8** bromidic, cobwebby, dogeared, overused **9** hackneyed **10** threadbare **11** commonplace, stereotyped

Welsh see CYMRIC

welsh 5 dodge **6** renege, resile **7** back out, default

welt 4 blow, edge, seam, wale, weal **5** ridge, wheal, whelk **6** insert

welter 4 coil, moil, toss **5** chaos, churn, steep, surge **6** flurry, hassle, hubbub, jumble, lather, ruckus, seethe, thrash, wallow, writhe **7** ferment, turmoil **8** disorder **9** confusion

___ **Welty 6** Eudora

wen 4 bleb, cyst **5** blain **6** growth **7** vesicle **11** excrescence

wench 3 gal **4** girl, jade, lass, maid, minx, miss, puss, slut, tart **5** hussy, nymph, tramp, trull, whore, woman **6** damsel, gamine, harlot, hoyden, lassie, maiden, wanton **7** jezebel, servant, trollop **8** slattern, strumpet

wend 3 hie **4** fare, pass **6** direct, push on, repair, travel **7** journey, proceed

werewolf 9 loup-garou **11** lycanthrope

Werther's beloved 5 Lotte **9** Charlotte

Wesleyan 9 Methodist

West 8 Occident

western 5 oater **9** Hesperian **10** horse opera, occidental *hemisphere:* **8** Americas, New World

Western novelist 4 Grey (Zane), Ross (Dana Fuller) **5** Brand (Max), Faust (Frederick), Short (Luke) **6** Judson (E. Z. C.), L'Amour (Louis), Patten (Lewis), Wister (Owen) **7** Guthrie (A. B.), Leonard (Elmore) **8** Buntline (Ned), McMurtry (Larry)

West Indies *country:* **4** Cuba **5** Haiti **7** Bahamas, Grenada, Jamaica **8** Barbados, Dominica **10** Guadeloupe, Martinique, Puerto Rico, Saint Lucia **17** Dominican Republic *island group:*

6 Virgin (Islands) 7 Bahamas, Leeward (Islands) 8 Antilles (Greater, Lesser), Windward (Islands)

West Point *father of:* 6 Thayer (Sylvanus) *freshman:* 5 plebe *student:* 5 cadet

West Side Story *composer:* 9 Bernstein (Leonard) *heroine:* 5 Maria *lyricist:* 8 Sondheim (Stephen)

West Virginia *capital:* 10 Charleston *city:* 8 Wheeling 10 Huntington *mountain:* 10 Spruce Knob *nickname:* 8 Mountain (State) *river:* 4 Ohio *state bird:* 8 cardinal *state flower:* 12 rhododendron *state tree:* 10 sugar maple

west wind see at WIND

wet 3 sop 4 damp, dank, rain, soak, wash, weak 5 douse, drown, drunk, humid, moist, rainy, soggy, soppy, souse, water 6 dampen, drench, soaked, sodden, soused, sweaty, watery 7 moisten, raining, soaking, sopping 8 drenched, dripping, humidify, irrigate, moisture, saturate, slippery 9 saturated, spineless *combining form:* 4 hygr 5 hygro

wet blanket 6 grinch 7 killjoy 8 sourpuss 9 pessimist 10 spoilsport 11 party pooper

wether 4 goat 5 sheep

wetland 3 bog, fen 4 mire, quag 5 marsh, swamp 6 morass, muskeg, slough

whack 3 bat, hit, pop, try 4 bash, belt, biff, blow, chop, cuff, kill, pelt, shot, sock, stab, wham, whap, whop 5 crack, punch, smack, smash 6 attack, defeat, murder, strike, wallop 7 bump off 8 knock off, lambaste *up:* 4 part 5 divvy, split 6 divide 7 portion 9 apportion

whale 3 hit 4 beat, flog, hide, lash, whip 5 giant 6 defeat, strike, stripe, thrash 7 mammoth 8 cetacean, behemoth 9 leviathan 10 flagellate *arctic:* 7 bowhead *group:* 3 pod *killer:* 4 orca *kind:* 3 sei 4 blue 5 right, sperm 6 baleen, beluga, killer 7 narwhal, rorqual 8 cachalot *tale:* 8 Moby Dick *toothed:* 5 pilot (whale) 9 blackfish *young:* 4 calf

whalebone 9 scrimshaw

wham 3 hit 4 bang, beat, blow, boom, clap, slam 5 blast, burst, crack, crash, smash, whack 6 impact, propel, strike 7 explode

whammy 3 hex, zap 4 jinx, juju 5 curse, spell 6 hoodoo, voodoo 7 evil eye

wharf 4 dock, pier, quay 5 jetty, levee

Wharton novel 10 Buccaneers (The), Ethan Frome 12 House of Mirth (The) 14 Age of Innocence (The) 18 Custom of the Country (The)

whatnot 7 étagère

wheal 4 lump, welt 5 ridge, whelk

wheat 4 crop 5 emmer, flour, grain, grass, spelt 6 cereal 7 einkorn *beard:* 3 awn *beat:* 6 thresh *chaff:* 4 bran *crushed:* 6 bulgur *disease:* 4 rust, smut *type:* 4 club 5 durum

wheedle 3 con 4 coax 5 cozen 6 cajole, entice, seduce 7 blarney, flatter 8 blandish, inveigle, scrounge, soft-soap 9 sweet-talk

wheel 3 VIP 4 auto, gyre, move, reel, spin, turn 5 cycle, drive, motor, pilot, pivot, round, whirl 6 bigwig, circle, gyrate, league, rotate, totter, travel 7 big shot, circuit, revolve 8 rotation 9 about-face, volte-face *part:* 3 hub, rim 4 tire 5 felly, spoke *spoke:* 6 radius *toothed:* 3 cog 4 gear

wheeze 3 saw, yuk 4 gasp, hiss, joke, puff, rasp 5 adage, cough 6 saying 7 proverb, whistle 8 chestnut, rhonchus

whelk 4 wale, weal, welt 5 wheal

whelm 4 bury, sink 5 cover, drown, flood, swamp 6 deluge, engulf 8 bear down, inundate, overbear, overcome, submerge 9 devastate

whelp 3 cub, kid, pup 4 bear 5 child, puppy 9 youngster

whereas 5 since, while 6 seeing, though 7 howbeit 8 although 11 considering

wherefore 3 why 4 thus 5 proof 6 ground, reason, whence 8 argument 11 explanation

wherewithal 5 funds, means, money 9 resources

wherry 4 boat 5 barge, scull 7 lighter, rowboat

whet 4 edge, goad, hone 5 drink, rally, rouse, waken 6 arouse, awaken, excite, kindle 7 sharpen, starter 8 aperitif 9 appetizer, challenge, stimulate 10 incitement 11 hors d'oeuvre

whiff 3 fan 4 blow, gust, hint, puff, waft 5 expel, smoke, tinge, trace 6 breath, exhale, inhale 7 soupçon, whisper 9 strikeout 10 indication, inhalation

whiffet 6 nobody, squirt 9 nonentity

whiffle 4 blow, gust, puff 5 waver 6 dither, falter 9 fluctuate, vacillate 12 shilly-shally

while 4 pass, time, when 5 spell 6 albeit, moment, though 7 howbeit, stretch, whereas 8 although, as long as, so long as

whilom 6 bygone, former 7 onetime, quondam 8 formerly, previous, sometime 9 erstwhile

whim 3 bee 4 idea, kink 5 dream, fancy, freak, humor 6 maggot, megrim, notion, vagary 7 caprice, capstan, conceit, thought 8 crotchet

whimper 3 cry **4** fret, mewl, pule, wail **5** bleat, whine **6** snivel

whimsical 4 iffy, zany **5** droll, fancy, flaky **6** chancy, fickle, fitful, quirky, random **7** erratic, flighty, mutable, puckish, wayward **8** fanciful, freakish, volatile **9** eccentric, impulsive, pixilated, screwball, uncertain, vagarious **10** capricious **13** unpredictable

whimsy 3 bee **4** play **5** dream, fancy, freak, humor **6** levity, maggot, megrim, notion, vagary **7** caprice, conceit, fantasy **9** capriccio, frivolity

whim-wham 4 dido **5** curio, fancy, frill **6** bauble, gewgaw, ruffle, trifle **7** bibelot, flounce, trinket **8** furbelow, gimcrack, kickshaw **9** objet d'art **10** knickknack

whine 3 cry **4** cant, fret, fuss, kick, moan, pule, wail **5** bleat, gripe **6** grouse, repine, snivel, whinge, yammer **7** grumble, snuffle, whimper **8** complain **9** bellyache

whinny 5 neigh **6** nicker **7** whicker

whiny 5 fussy **7** fretful, grouchy, peevish **8** petulant **9** irritable, querulous

whip 3 cut, hem, set **4** beat, cane, crop, dash, flog, hide, jerk, lash, lick, pull, rout, wind, wrap **5** abuse, mop up, quirt, spank, sting, whale, whisk **6** defeat, lather, snatch, strike, stroke, subdue, switch, thrash, urge on **7** agitate, dessert, provoke, rawhide, shellac, trounce, utensil **8** coachman, lambaste, overcome, vanquish **9** instigate, overwhelm **10** flagellate **13** cat-o'-nine-tails *braided:* **10** blacksnake

whippersnapper see WHIFFET

whipping boy 4 goat **5** patsy **7** fall guy **9** scapegoat

whippy 6 supple **7** elastic, springy **8** flexible **9** resilient

whir 3 fly, hum **4** burr, buzz, whiz **5** chirr, churr, drone, whizz **7** revolve, vibrate **9** bombinate

whirl 3 ado, gig, pop, try **4** eddy, flit, fuss, gyre, moil, reel, shot, spin, stab, stir, swim, turn, veer **5** hurry, pivot, swirl, whack, wheel **6** bustle, circle, gyrate, hassle, hubbub, pother, rotate **7** circuit, dervish, turmoil **8** ballyhoo, gyration, rotation **9** commotion, pirouette **10** revolution

whirligig 4 gyre, spin **6** beetle, gyrate **8** carousel **9** pirouette **12** merry-go-round

whirlpool 3 ado **4** eddy, fuss **6** bustle, flurry, furore, tumult, vortex **7** turmoil **8** vortices (plural) **9** commotion, maelstrom

whirlwind 4 rush, stir, to-do **5** hasty, spout, swift **6** bustle **7** cyclone, tornado, twister, typhoon **8** headlong **9** commotion, dust devil, dust storm, hurricane **10** waterspout **11** tourbillion

whish 4 fizz, hiss **6** fizzle **8** sibilate

whisk 3 mix, nip, wag, zip **4** beat, flit, whip **5** broom, brush, fluff, hurry, speed **6** switch

whisker 4 hair **7** bristle **8** filament, vibrissa **9** outrigger **11** hairbreadth

whiskered 5 hairy **6** pilose **7** bearded, bristly, hirsute **8** stubbled, unshaven

whiskers 5 beard **6** goatee **7** stubble, weepers **8** bristles **9** burnsides, peach fuzz, sideburns **11** muttonchops

whiskey 3 rye **6** liquor, Scotch **7** alcohol, bourbon *with beer chaser:* **11** boilermaker

whisper 4 buzz, hint, hiss, whiz **5** rumor, shade, tinge, touch, trace, whiff **6** breath, gossip, murmur, mutter **8** sibilate, susurrus **9** suspicion, undertone **11** susurration

whist 4 game, hush **5** quiet, still **6** silent **9** noiseless, soundless

whistle 4 pipe, toot **5** flute, whiff **6** signal, tootle, wheeze

whistle-stop 5 stump **8** campaign, politick **9** barnstorm **11** electioneer

whit 3 bit, fig, jot, rap **4** atom, damn, hoot, iota, mite **5** crumb, scrap, shred, speck, whoop **7** dribble, modicum, smidgen **8** molecule, particle

white 4 pure **5** livid, milky, snowy **6** albino, blanch, bleach, pallid **7** silvery **9** colorless *combining form:* **4** leuc, leuk **5** leuco, leuko *egg's:* **5** glair, glaire **7** albumen

White novel 12 Stuart Little **13** Charlotte's Web

white cliffs of____ 5 Dover

White Fang author 6 London (Jack)

White House *designer:* **5** Hoban (James) *first occupant:* **5** Adams (Abigail, John)

white lightning 5 hooch **7** bootleg, whiskey **9** moonshine **10** bathtub gin **11** mountain dew

whiten 4 fade, pale **5** frost **6** blanch, bleach, blench **8** etiolate **10** decolorize

white plague 8 phthisis **11** consumption **12** tuberculosis

whitewash 6 parget **7** cover up **9** gloss over, gloze over, sugarcoat

whither 5 where **7** whereto **9** whereunto

whiting 3 cod **4** hake **10** silver hake

Whitsunday 9 Pentecost

Whittier poem 9 Snow-Bound **10** Maud Muller **11** Barefoot Boy **16** Barbara Frietchie

whittle 4 chip, form, fret, pare, trim

5 carve, shape, shave, skive 6 reduce, sculpt 8 diminish

whiz 3 fly, hum, zip 4 buzz, flit, hiss, zoom 5 hurry, speed, swish, whirl 6 expert, fizzle, genius, phenom, rotate, whoosh 8 virtuoso 10 wunderkind

whoa 3 hey 4 slow, stop 6 hold up

whole 3 all, fit, sum 4 full, hale, sane 5 sound, total, uncut, unity 6 entire, entity, healed, intact, system, unhurt 7 healthy, perfect, plenary 8 complete, entirely, entirety, flawless, restored, totality, unbroken, unmarred 9 recovered, undamaged, undivided, uninjured, untouched 10 unimpaired, unmodified 11 unblemished 12 concentrated, undistracted *combining form:* 3 hol, pan 4 holo

wholehearted 6 ardent 7 devoted, earnest, fervent, sincere 8 bona fide 9 committed, heartfelt, steadfast, unfeigned 10 passionate, unwavering 11 impassioned 12 enthusiastic 13 unquestioning

whole-hog 6 all-out, gung-ho 8 complete, thorough 9 full-scale 11 straight-out 13 thoroughgoing

wholeness 7 oneness 8 entirety, totality 9 integrity, soundness 10 intactness, perfection

whole note 9 semibreve

whole number 5 digit 6 cipher 7 integer, numeral

wholesome 3 fit 4 good, hale, safe, sane, well 5 right, sound 6 benign 7 healthy 8 hygienic, salutary 9 favorable, healthful 10 beneficial, salubrious

wholly 3 all 4 only 6 in toto, singly, solely, purely 7 totally 8 entirely 10 altogether, completely 11 exclusively

whomp 3 hit 4 beat, drub, slap, whip, whup 5 crash, thump 6 crunch, strike, thrash, wallop 7 clobber, shellac, trounce 8 lambaste

whomp up 4 stir 5 rouse, spark 6 arouse, excite, foment

whoopee 3 fun 5 revel, yahoo 6 gaiety, hoopla, yippee 7 jollity, revelry, wassail, whoopla 8 hilarity 9 festivity, high jinks, merriment 10 hurly-burly 11 merrymaking

whoopla see HOOPLA

whop 3 bat, bop 4 bash, beat, biff, blow, drub, lick, sock 5 baste, pound, smack, thump, whack 6 batter, buffet, defeat, hammer, pummel, strike, thrash, thwack, wallop 7 trounce 8 lambaste

whopping 4 huge, vast 6 mighty 7 amazing, immense, massive 8 colossal, enormous, gigantic, whacking 9 bodacious,

humongous, monstrous 10 gargantuan, incredible, prodigious 13 extraordinary

whorl 4 coil, eddy, turn 5 swirl 6 spiral

why 5 cause 6 enigma, motive, puzzle, reason, riddle 7 mystery, problem, what for 9 conundrum, rationale, therefore, wherefore 10 puzzlement 11 explanation

wicked 4 evil, mean, very, vile 5 awful, black, wrong 6 fierce, malign, sinful, unholy 7 corrupt, hateful, heinous, immoral, naughty, ungodly, vicious 8 depraved, devilish, fiendish 9 atrocious, barbarous, dangerous, extremely, hazardous, injurious, malicious, malignant, nefarious 10 iniquitous, malevolent, outrageous 11 treacherous

wickedness 3 sin 4 evil, vice 7 devilry 8 enormity, iniquity, satanism 9 depravity 10 corruption, immorality 12 devilishness, fiendishness

wicker 4 twig 5 osier, withe 6 branch

wicket 4 arch, door, gate, hoop 6 window *sticky:* 3 fix, jam 4 knot 7 toughie 9 conundrum, tight spot

wide 4 vast 5 broad, fully 8 extended, spacious, straying, sweeping 9 deviating, expansive, extensive, inclusive 10 completely 13 comprehensive

widen 4 ream 6 dilate, expand, extend, open up, spread 7 broaden, distend, enlarge

widespread 4 rife, vast 6 common 7 current, general, popular, rampant, regnant 8 far-flung 9 extensive, pervasive, prevalent 10 far-ranging, ubiquitous

widget 5 gizmo 6 device, dingus, doodad, gadget, hickey, jigger 7 gimmick, whatsit 9 doohickey, thingummy 11 contraption, thingamabob, thingamajig, thingumajig

width 4 gape, kerf, span 5 depth, range 6 spread 7 breadth 9 extension

wield 3 use 5 exert 6 handle 7 control 8 exercise 10 manipulate *the gavel:* 7 preside

wiener 3 dog 5 frank 6 hot dog 7 sausage 11 frankfurter 13 Vienna sausage

wife 3 Mrs. 4 mate 5 bride, woman 6 female, matron, missis, missus, spouse 7 consort, partner 8 helpmate, helpmeet *Latin:* 4 uxor *of a rajah:* 4 rani 5 ranee

wifely 7 uxorial

wig 3 jaw, rap, rug 4 flip, rail, rate 5 chide, freak, scold 6 berate, peruke, rebuke, revile, toupee 7 bawl out, chew out, reproof, upbraid 8 postiche, reproach 9 hairpiece, reprimand 10 tongue-lash

wiggle 4 jerk **5** shake, twist **6** fidget, squirm, writhe *Scottish:* **5** hotch

wight 3 man **5** human **6** animal, mortal, person **7** critter **8** creature **10** human being, individual

wild 3 mad **4** fast **5** crazy **6** barren, raging, savage, stormy, unruly **7** erratic, frantic, furious, natural, untamed, vicious **8** barbaric, blustery, desolate, frenetic, frenzied, reckless **9** barbarian, barbarous, delirious, fantastic, turbulent, wasteland **10** incautious, outlandish **11** extravagant, intractable, sensational, tempestuous, uncivilized, uninhabited **12** preposterous, uncontrolled, uncultivated, ungovernable, unmanageable **13** irresponsible, undisciplined

wild ass 5 kiang **6** onager

Wild Duck author 5 Ibsen (Henrik)

wildebeest 3 gnu

wilderness 4 bush **5** heath, waste **6** barren, desert **9** backlands, wasteland **10** hinterland **11** backcountry

Wilder play 7 Our Town **10** Matchmaker (The) **14** Skin of Our Teeth (The)

wild-eyed 6 raving **7** blue-sky, radical **9** visionary

wile 4 ploy, ruse, vamp **5** charm, feint, guile, trick **6** allure, deceit, entice, gambit **7** attract, beguile, bewitch, chicane, cunning, enchant, gimmick **8** artifice, inveigle, maneuver, trickery **9** captivate, chicanery, fascinate, magnetize, stratagem **10** subterfuge

wiliness 5 guile **7** cunning

will 4 like, wish **5** cause, elect, leave, order **6** choice, choose, decree, desire, direct, intend, intent, liking, option, ordain, please **7** bequest, consent, control, passion, purpose **8** appetite, bequeath, pleasure, volition **9** intention, testament **10** discipline **11** disposition, inclination, self-control **13** determination, self-restraint *addition:* **7** codicil *maker:* **8** testator **9** testatrix *without:* **9** intestate

willful 5 heady **6** dogged, mulish, unruly **8** perverse, stubborn **9** obstinate, pigheaded, voluntary **10** deliberate, hardheaded, headstrong, purposeful, self-willed **11** intentional, intractable, wrongheaded **12** contumacious, pertinacious, ungovernable

Williams play 10 Camino Real, Rose Tattoo (The) **14** Glass Menagerie (The), Summer and Smoke **16** Cat on a Hot Tin Roof, Night of the Iguana (The), Sweet Bird of Youth **18** Suddenly Last Summer **20** Streetcar Named Desire (A)

William Tell composer 7 Rossini (Gioacchino)

willies 6 creeps, shakes **7** jimjams, jitters, shivers **9** whim-whams **10** goose bumps **13** heebie-jeebies

willing 3 apt **4** fain, game, glad, open **5** prone, ready **6** minded **7** forward, witting **8** amenable, disposed, inclined, obliging, unforced **9** agreeable, compliant, favorable, receptive, voluntary **10** deliberate, volitional **11** intentional, predisposed

williwaw 4 gust, wind **5** blast **8** outburst, paroxysm **9** commotion

will-o'-the-wisp 7 fantasy, figment, phantom **8** daydream, delusion **11** ignis fatuus

willow 5 osier, salix **6** sallow **10** cricket bat *flower cluster:* **6** catkin *kind:* **5** crack, pussy, white **6** basket **7** weeping

willowy 4 tall **5** lithe **6** pliant, supple, svelte **7** lissome, pliable, slender **8** graceful

Wilson play 6 Fences **11** Piano Lesson (The) **12** Talley's Folly **13** Hot l Baltimore (The) **20** Ma Rainey's Black Bottom

wilt 3 sag **4** swag **5** droop, dry up, wizen **6** wither **7** shrivel **8** languish

wily 3 sly **4** foxy **5** cagey, canny, slick **6** artful, astute, clever, crafty, shrewd, tricky **7** cunning, devious, vulpine **8** guileful, scheming **10** serpentine

wimble 4 bore **5** auger, borer, brace, drill **6** gimlet

Wimbledon's game 6 tennis

wimp 4 nerd, wuss **5** sissy **7** doormat, nebbish **9** jellyfish **11** milquetoast

wimple 4 bend, veil, wrap **5** cover, curve **6** ripple *wearer:* **3** nun

wimp out 6 beg off, cave in, give in **8** back down

wimpy 4 lame, puny, weak **5** dinky, inept, timid **6** craven, feeble **7** gutless **8** cowardly, feckless, impotent, pathetic **9** spineless **10** namby-pamby, wishy-washy **11** ineffective, ineffectual

win 3 get **4** beat, earn, gain **5** reach, score **6** attain, defeat, obtain, secure **7** achieve, acquire, conquer, procure, produce, realize, succeed, success, triumph, victory **8** conquest, persuade **9** influence **10** accomplish *over:* **6** disarm, induce **8** convince, persuade, talk into **9** prevail on

wince 4 cower, quail, start **6** blanch, blench, cringe, flinch, recoil, shrink **7** squinch

wind 3 air, dry, fan, gas **4** bend, blow, clue, coil, curl, gale, gird, gust, haul, hint, reel, rest, talk, turn, warp, wrap

5 cover, crank, curve, force, hoist, raise, sound, spool, twine, twist 6 breath, breeze, circle, enlace, girdle, notion, zephyr 7 enclose, entwine, envelop, inkling, involve, monsoon, nothing, tighten 8 easterly, encircle, entangle, surround, tendency, westerly 9 direction, idle words, influence, insinuate 10 indication, intimation, suggestion *cold:* 4 bora 7 mistral, pampero 8 williwaw *combining form:* 4 anem 5 anemo, venti, vento *gentle:* 6 breeze, zephyr *god:* 6 Boreas 8 Zephyrus *hot:* 6 simoom 7 sirocco *instrument:* 3 sax 4 horn, oboe, tuba, vane 5 flute 7 bassoon, trumpet 8 trombone 9 saxophone 10 anemometer 11 weather vane *into:* 8 aweather *measure of speed:* 4 knot *Mediterranean:* 7 sirocco 8 levanter, libeccio *scale:* 8 Beaufort *stormy:* 4 gale 7 cyclone, tornado, twister 9 hurricane 11 northeaster *warm:* 4 föhn 5 foehn 7 chinook

windbag 6 gabber 7 blabber 8 bigmouth, blowhard, braggart

windfall 4 boon, gain 5 break 7 jackpot 8 fortuity

winding 4 curl, kink 5 snaky 6 spiral 7 coiling, curving, devious, sinuous 8 flexuous, indirect, tortuous, twisting 9 meandrous 10 circuitous, convoluted, meandering, roundabout, serpentine 11 anfractuous 12 labyrinthine

windmill 4 spin 5 wheel 7 machine *fighter:* 10 Don Quixote

window 3 bay, eye 4 pane 5 oriel 6 dormer 7 opening 8 aperture, casement, jalousie *cover:* 5 blind 7 curtain, shutter *French:* 7 fenêtre *over a door:* 7 transom 8 fanlight *part:* 4 pane, sash, sill 5 frame *projecting:* 3 bay 5 oriel *roof's:* 6 dormer 7 lucarne 8 skylight *Scottish:* 7 winnock *ship's:* 4 port 8 porthole

windpipe 7 trachea *combining form:* 6 trache 7 tracheo

windrow 4 bank, heap, hill, mass, pile 5 mound, ridge, stack

wind up 3 end 4 halt 5 close 6 finish, settle 8 complete, conclude 9 terminate

windup 3 end 5 close 6 ending, finale, finish 8 backswing 10 completion, conclusion 11 termination

windy 4 airy 5 blowy, gassy, gusty, inane, tumid, wordy 6 breezy, prolix, stormy, turgid 7 diffuse, orotund, pompous, verbose 8 blustery, inflated 9 bombastic, overblown 11 tempestuous 13 grandiloquent

wine 4 vino 5 drink, juice 8 beverage *aromatized:* 8 vermouth 9 hippocras *beverage:* 5 negus, punch 6 bishop, cooler 7 sangria 8 sangaree, spritzer 9 hippocras *bottle:* 6 fiasco, magnum 8 decanter, jeroboam 10 methuselah *cabinet:* 8 cellaret *cask:* 3 tun, vat 4 butt, pipe *cellar:* 6 bodega *combining form:* 3 eno, oen 4 oeno *discoverer:* 4 Noah *distillate:* 6 brandy, cognac *dry:* 3 sec 4 brut *flavor:* 4 mull *fortified:* 4 port 6 Malaga, sherry 7 Madeira, marsala, oloroso 8 muscatel *fragrance:* 4 nose 7 bouquet *lover:* 9 oenophile 11 oenophilist *maker:* 7 vintner 8 vigneron 10 winegrower 13 viticulturist *merchant:* 7 vintner *red:* 4 port 5 Gamay, Macon, Medoc, Rioja 6 Barolo, Beaune, claret, Shiraz 7 Chianti 8 Bordeaux, Burgundy, cabernet 9 Lambrusco, Pinot Noir, St. Emilion, zinfandel 10 Beaujolais, Sangiovese 11 Petite Sirah 12 Valpolicella *relating to:* 6 vinous *residue:* 4 marc *rice:* 4 sake *richness:* 4 body *sediment:* 4 lees 5 dregs *shop:* 6 bistro, bodega, tavern *sparkling:* 8 cold duck, sparkler, Spumante 9 champagne, Lambrusco *specialist:* 9 enologist 10 oenologist *spiced:* 6 mulled (wine) 9 hippocras *steward:* 9 sommelier *study of:* 7 enology 8 oenology *sweet:* 4 port 5 Tokay 6 canary, Malaga, muscat 7 Catawba, Madeira, malmsey, marsala, oloroso, Vouvray 8 Malvasia, muscatel, sauterne 9 Sauternes 11 scuppernong *sweeten:* 4 mull *vessel:* 7 chalice *white:* 4 hock 5 Rhine, Soave 7 Catawba, Chablis, Moselle, Orvieto, Vouvray 8 Bordeaux, Riesling, Semillon, vermouth 9 champagne, Hermitage, Meursault 10 chardonnay, Montrachet 11 Chenin Blanc, scuppernong 13 liebfraumilch 14 sauvignon blanc *year:* 7 vintage

wing 3 ala, arm, ell, fly 4 sail, unit, vane 5 annex, flank, fleet, pinna, wound 6 flight 7 airfoil, faction, flanker, section 9 appendage, expansion, extension, improvise *combining form:* 3 ali 4 pter 5 ptero *relating to:* 4 alar 5 alary

wingding 4 bash, fete, gala 5 binge, party 7 blowout, shindig 9 festivity

winged 5 alate, fleet, rapid, swift 7 soaring 8 elevated *deity:* 4 Amor, Eros, Nike 5 Cupid 6 Hermes 7 Mercury *horse:* 7 Pegasus *monster:* 5 harpy

wingless 8 apterous

winglike 4 alar 5 alary *part:* 3 ala 4 alae (plural)

wink 3 bat, nap 5 flash, jiffy, shake, trice 6 moment, second, signal 7 connive, flicker, instant, twinkle 9 nictitate, twinkling 11 split second

winner 3 ace 4 lulu 5 doozy 6 doozie, top dog, victor 7 success 8 champion 9 conqueror 11 titleholder

Winnie-the-Pooh *author:* 5 Milne (A. A.) *character:* 3 Roo 5 Kanga 6 Piglet, Tigger

winning 8 charming, engaging, pleasing 9 agreeable 10 delightful, successful, triumphant, victorious 11 captivating 13 prepossessing

winnow 3 fan 4 blow, cull, pare, sift, sort 6 delete, filter, narrow, reduce, remove, screen, select 8 separate

winsome 5 sweet 6 dulcet, lovely 8 charming, cheerful, engaging, pleasing 9 easygoing 12 lighthearted

winter 6 season 9 hibernate *French:* 5 hiver *Spanish:* 8 invierno

Winter's Tale, A *author:* 11 Shakespeare (William) *character:* 7 Camillo, Leontes, Paulina, Perdita 8 Florizel, Hermione 9 Antigonus, Autolycus, Polixenes

wintry 3 icy 4 cold 5 bleak, hoary, nippy, snowy 6 frigid, frosty 8 chilling, freezing, hibernal 12 bone-chilling

wipe 3 dry, rub 4 swab 5 towel, whisk 6 napkin, smudge, sponge 8 squeegee

wipe out 4 rout 5 crash, erase, smear, sweep 7 blot out, destroy, expunge 8 decimate 9 eradicate, extirpate 10 annihilate, obliterate

wipeout 4 fall, rout 5 crash 8 drubbing 11 destruction 12 annihilation

wire 3 rod 4 cord, line, send 5 cable, metal 6 thread 7 message 8 meshwork, telegram 9 cablegram, telegraph 10 finish line *measure:* 3 mil 5 gauge

wiry 4 lean, ropy 6 sinewy, supple 7 fibrous, stringy

Wisconsin *capital:* 7 Madison *city:* 6 Racine 7 Kenosha 8 Green Bay 9 Milwaukee *college, university:* 5 Ripon 6 Beloit 9 Marquette *lake:* 7 Mendota *motto:* 7 Forward *nickname:* 6 Badger (State) *peninsula:* 4 Door *river:* 7 St. Croix 9 Menominee, Wisconsin 11 Mississippi *state bird:* 5 robin *state flower:* 6 violet *state tree:* 10 sugar maple

wisdom 5 sense 7 insight, science 8 judgment, learning, sagacity, sageness, sapience 9 good sense, knowledge 10 horse sense 11 common sense, information

wise 3 hep, hip 4 bold, keen, sage, sane, tell, warn, wily 5 alert, aware, brash, cagey, canny, cocky, fresh, learn, nervy, quick, sassy, sharp, smart 6 artful, astute, bright, cheeky, clever, crafty, fill in, inform, notify, shrewd, sophic, tricky 7 cunning, gnostic, knowing, politic, prudent, sapient 8 discreet, flippant, impudent, insolent, sensible, tactical 9 advisable, bold-faced, expedient, judicious, sagacious, scholarly 10 discerning, insightful, perceptive, reflective, thoughtful 11 foresighted, impertinent, intelligent, quick-witted, sharp-witted, smart-alecky 13 contemplative, knowledgeable, perspicacious *old man:* 6 Nestor *person:* 4 sage 6 savant 7 scholar

wiseacre see WISE GUY

wisecrack 3 dig, gag 4 gibe, jape, jest, joke, quip 5 sally 9 witticism

wise guy 6 smarty 7 mobster 8 gangster, smart-ass 9 know-it-all, swellhead 10 smart aleck 11 smarty-pants, wisenheimer

wise man 4 guru, sage 5 magus 6 savant

Wise Men see MAGI

wish 3 bid 4 care, goal, like, long, lust, want 5 covet, crave, fancy, foist, order, yearn 6 desire, impose 7 request 10 desiderate

wishbone 7 furcula

wishful 5 eager 7 anxious, hopeful, longing 8 desirous

wishy-washy 4 lame, weak 5 banal, bland, vapid, wimpy 6 jejune, watery 7 insipid, languid 10 namby-pamby 11 ineffective, ineffectual 13 characterless

wisp 3 bit 5 shred, strip, trace 6 sliver, snatch, streak 7 smidgen, snippet 8 fragment 9 scintilla

wispy 4 slim 5 frail 6 flimsy, slight 7 slender, tenuous 8 fleeting, nebulous 10 evanescent

Wister novel 9 Virginian (The)

wistful 3 sad 6 dreamy, triste 7 longing, pensive 8 yearning 9 nostalgic 10 melancholy

wit 3 wag 5 brain, comic, droll, humor, irony, joker 6 banter, esprit, jester, reason, satire, wisdom 7 farceur, punster 8 banterer, comedian, funnyman, judgment, humorist, jokester, quipster, repartee 9 alertness, ingenuity, intellect 10 cleverness, persiflage

witch 3 hag, hex 5 dowse, spell 6 voodoo, Wiccan 7 charmer 8 magician, sorcerer 9 sorceress 11 enchantress *companion:* 3 cat *group:* 5 coven *male:* 6 wizard 7 warlock *meeting:* 6 sabbat *town:* 5 Endor *vehicle:* 5 broom

witchcraft 5 magic, wicca 6 hoodoo, voodoo 7 devilry, hexerei, sorcery 8 wizardry 9 diablerie, sortilege, voodooism 10 black magic, hocus-pocus, mumbo jumbo, necromancy 11 abracadabra, thaumaturgy

witch hazel 5 shrub 6 lotion

witchy 6 Wiccan **7** magical **8** wizardly
9 sorcerous **11** necromantic **12** thaumaturgic

with 3 for, per, pro, via **4** over, upon
5 about **6** having **7** against, by way of,
through **8** as well as **9** by means of, in
favor of **10** by virtue of *French:* **4** avec
German: **3** mit *Italian, Spanish:* **3** con
Latin: **3** cum

withal 3 too, yet **4** also **5** still **6** as well,
though **7** besides, howbeit, however
8 after all, moreover **11** furthermore,
nonetheless **12** additionally, nevertheless

withdraw 4 exit, quit **5** demit, leave,
unsay **6** depart, bow out, call in, cash
in, desert, detach, recall, recant,
recede, recoil, retire, secede, shrink
7 back out, drop out, pull out, retract,
retreat, scratch, take off, take out
8 back down, evacuate, fall back, pull
away, push back, separate, take back,
turn away **9** disengage, stand down
10 disconnect, give ground

withdrawal 4 exit **6** exodus **7** exiting,
pullout, removal, retreat **9** departure
10 alienation, detachment, retirement,
retraction, revocation

withdrawn 4 cool **5** aloof **6** casual,
remote **7** distant, removed **8** detached,
isolated, reserved, retiring, solitary
9 incurious, unaffable, uncurious
10 unsociable **11** indifferent, introverted, standoffish, unconcerned, unexpansive **12** uninterested, unresponsive

wither 3 age, dry **4** fade, sear, wilt **5** dry
up, parch, quail, wizen **6** scorch
7 mummify, shrivel

withered 4 sere **7** sapless **8** shrunken,
wrinkled **9** shriveled

withhold 4 deny **5** check **6** deduct,
detain, refuse, retain **7** abstain, deprive,
forbear, inhibit, refrain, reserve
8 restrain, subtract **9** constrain

within 4 into **5** among **6** inside **7** indoors,
inwards **8** enclosed, interior, inwardly
10 inner place *prefix:* **5** infra, intra, intro

with-it 6 modern, modish, trendy **7** à la
mode, current, faddish, stylish **8** up-to-
date **11** fashionable **12** contemporary

without 4 open, past, sans **5** minus
6 absent **7** lacking, open air, outside,
wanting **8** outdoors **10** externally, out-
of-doors *Latin:* **4** sine

with respect to 4 as to, in re **5** as for
7 apropos **8** touching **9** as regards,
regarding **10** concerning

withstand 4 bear, buck, defy **5** fight,
repel **6** endure, oppose, resist, suffer
7 hold off, survive, sustain **8** tolerate,
traverse

withy 4 twig **5** osier **6** branch, willow
8 flexible **9** resilient

witless 3 mad **4** daft, nuts **5** crazy, daffy,
dotty, nutty, silly **6** insane, simple, stupid **7** asinine, cracked, foolish, idiotic
8 demented, deranged, mindless **9** bedlamite, brainless, senseless **10** weak-
minded, unbalanced

witlessness 5 folly **6** idiocy, lunacy
7 inanity **8** insanity **9** absurdity, stupidity

witness 3 see **4** note, sign, view **5** proof,
vouch **6** attest, depone, depose, notice,
viewer **7** bear out, confirm, betoken,
certify, testify, watcher **8** attester,
beholder, deponent, evidence, looker-
on, observer, onlooker **9** bystander,
spectator, testament, testifier, testimony **11** affirmation, attestation, corroborate, testimonial **12** confirmation

witticism 3 dig, gag, mot **4** gibe, jape,
jest, jibe, joke, quip **5** crack, sally **6** bon
mot **8** one-liner, repartee **9** throwaway,
wisecrack

witting 5 aware **7** knowing, willful **8** sensible, sentient **9** cognizant, conscious,
voluntary **10** deliberate **11** intentional

witty 5 funny **6** clever, jocose **7** amusing,
jocular **8** humorous **9** facetious **13** scintillating

wiz 3 ace **5** adept, fiend **6** artist, expert,
phenom **7** artiste **8** virtuoso

wizard 3 ace **4** mage **5** adept, druid,
fiend, magus **6** expert, phenom **7** warlock **8** conjurer, magician, sorcerer, virtuoso **9** enchanter **10** past master
11 necromancer, thaumaturge **13** thaumaturgist

wizardly 5 magic **6** mystic, witchy **7** magical **9** sorcerous **10** mysterious **11** necromantic **12** thaumaturgic

Wizard of Menlo Park 6 Edison (Thomas
Alva)

Wizard of Oz *author:* **4** Baum (L. Frank)
character: **7** Dorothy **9** Scarecrow
10 Tin Woodman **12** Cowardly Lion
dog: **4** Toto

wizardry 5 magic **6** voodoo **7** sorcery
8 witchery **9** diablerie, sortilege
10 black magic, necromancy, witchcraft **11** bewitchment, conjuration,
enchantment

wizen 3 dry **4** sere, wilt **5** dry up **6** shrink,
wither **7** dried-up, shrivel, wrinkle

wizened 4 aged, sere **5** dried **6** shrunk
7 pinched **8** shrunken, withered, wrinkled

wobble 4 reel, rock, sway **5** quake,
shake, waver, weave **6** dither, falter,
quaver, teeter, totter **7** stagger, stumble,
tremble **8** nutation **9** vacillate

wobbly 4 weak **5** rocky, shaky **6** unsure **7** rackety, rickety **8** insecure, rachitic, unstable, unsteady, wavering **9** faltering, teetering, tottering **10** nutational **11** vacillating

Wodehouse, P. G. *castle:* **9** Blandings *character:* **6** Bertie (Wooster), Gussie (Fink-Nottle), Jeeves, Psmith **7** Wooster (Bertie) **8** Emsworth (Lord), Mulliner (Mr.) **10** Threepwood (Clarence, Freddie) **12** Lord Emsworth *club:* **6** Drones

Woden see ODIN

woe 3 rue **4** bale, bane, care **5** grief **6** misery, regret, sorrow **7** anguish, sadness, trouble **8** calamity **9** heartache **10** affliction, heartbreak **11** lamentation, unhappiness **12** wretchedness

woebegone 3 low, sad **4** blue, down, worn **6** shabby **7** doleful, forlorn, ruthful **8** dejected, dolorous, downcast, wretched **9** depressed, miserable, sorrowful **10** despondent, melancholy **11** crestfallen, downhearted, low-spirited **12** disconsolate

woeful 3 sad **5** heavy, sorry **6** dismal, rueful, tragic, triste **7** ruthful **8** dejected, dolorous, downcast, grievous, mournful, stricken, tortured, wretched **9** afflicted, aggrieved, depressed, heartsick, miserable, plaintive, sorrowful **10** deplorable, lamentable, lugubrious, melancholy **11** distressing, downhearted, low-spirited **12** disconsolate **13** heartbreaking

wolf 4 bolt, lobo, rake, roué **5** canid **6** canine, coyote, devour, gobble, masher **7** Don Juan, poverty **8** Casanova, lothario **10** starvation *genus:* **5** Canis *group:* **4** pack *young:* **5** whelp

Wolfe *novel* **17** Look Homeward Angel, Of Time and the River **18** You Can't Go Home Again **20** Bonfire of the Vanities (The)

wolfish 4 wild **5** cruel, feral **6** fierce, lupine, savage **7** bestial, brutish, vicious **9** ferocious

wolverine *European:* **7** glutton *genus:* **4** Gulo

Wolverine State 8 Michigan

woman 4 dame, lady **5** madam **6** female, matron **8** mistress **10** girlfriend *attractive:* **5** belle **6** beauty, eyeful, looker **7** stunner **8** knockout *combining form:* **4** gyny **5** gynec **6** gynaec, gyneco, gynous **7** gynaeco *courageous:* **7** heroine *dignified:* **6** matron **7** dowager **10** grande dame *dowdy:* **5** frump *English:* **6** milady *first, biblical:* **3** Eve *first, mythological:* **7** Pandora *French:* **5** femme *German:* **4** Frau **8** Fräulein *Hawaiian:* **6** wahine *Indian:* **5** squaw *Ital-*

ian: **5** donna **7** signora *old:* **3** hag **4** dame **6** beldam, carlin, gammer, granny *pregnant:* **7** gravida *resembling:* **8** gynecoid *royal:* **5** queen **8** princess *sailor:* **4** Wave *servant:* **4** maid *soldier:* **3** Wac *Spanish:* **4** doña **6** señora *strong:* **6** amazon, virago *unmarried:* **4** miss **6** maiden **8** spinster *young:* **4** girl, lass **6** lassie, maiden

womanize 4 wolf **9** gallivant, philander **10** fool around, mess around

womanizer 4 stud, wolf **6** masher **7** Don Juan, gallant, playboy **8** Casanova, lothario **9** ladies' man **10** lady-killer **11** philanderer

womb 6 uterus *combining form:* **6** hyster **7** hystero

women *hatred of:* **8** misogyny *organization of:* **3** DAR, NOW **8** sorority

Women in Love *author* **8** Lawrence (D. H.)

wonder 3 awe **4** muse **5** doubt **6** marvel **7** dubiety, miracle, portent, prodigy **8** mistrust, question **9** amazement, speculate, suspicion **10** admiration, skepticism **11** incertitude, uncertainty **12** astonishment

wonderful 4 keen **5** grand, great, nifty, super, swell **6** divine, groovy, peachy, spiffy **7** amazing, strange, too much, topping **8** dynamite, fabulous, glorious, spiffing, terrific **9** admirable, excellent, marvelous, wunderbar **10** astounding, delightful, miraculous, out-of-sight, stupendous **11** astonishing, outstanding

wondrous 6 mystic **7** amazing, awesome, strange **9** marvelous **10** astounding, formidable, miraculous, portentous, prodigious, remarkable, stupendous, surprising **11** astonishing, spectacular **13** extraordinary

wonky 4 awry **5** geeky, nerdy, shaky **7** bookish **8** unsteady

wont 3 apt **4** used **5** habit, usage **6** custom, manner **8** accustom, habitude, inclined, practice **10** accustomed, consuetude

wonted 5 usual **7** routine **8** habitual, ordinary **9** customary **10** accustomed

woo 4 sue **5** court **6** pursue **7** address, entreat, solicit

wood 5 weald **6** forest, lumber, timber **8** golf club **10** timberland *combining form:* **3** xyl **4** lign, xylo **5** ligni, ligno *decayed:* **4** punk *eater:* **7** termite *for burning:* **5** fagot **6** tinder **8** kindling *golf:* **6** driver *hard:* **3** elm, oak **4** ebon, rata, teak **5** beech, birch, ebony, maple **6** cherry, walnut **8** chestnut, mahogany, sycamore *imperfection:* **4** knot **5** gnarl *light:* **5** balsa *made of:* **5** treen *pattern in:*

5 grain 6 figure *product:* 3 tar 5 paper
10 turpentine *soft:* 4 pine

wood alcohol 6 methyl 8 carbinol,
methanol

woodchuck 6 marmot 9 groundhog

wood coal 7 lignite

wooded 5 bosky, treed 6 sylvan 8 forested, timbered

wooden 5 rigid, stiff 6 clumsy 7 awkward, stilted 8 ligneous 10 inflexible

woodland 5 copse, taiga, weald 6 forest,
pinery 7 coppice 10 rain forest

wood nymph 5 dryad

woodpecker 4 bird 7 flicker, wryneck
9 sapsucker *genus:* 5 Picus *kind:*
5 downy, green, hairy 8 imperial, pileated 9 redheaded 11 ivory-billed

woodsman 6 logger 8 forester
10 bushranger 11 bushwhacker

wood sorrel 3 oca 6 oxalis 8 shamrock
9 carambola

woodsy 6 rustic, sylvan

woodwind 4 oboe, reed 5 flute, shawm
7 bassoon, piccolo 8 clarinet 9 saxophone 10 instrument 11 English horn
13 contrabassoon

woodworker 9 carpenter 12 cabinetmaker

woody 8 ligneous 12 station wagon

wooer 4 beau 5 lover, spark, swain
6 suitor 7 admirer, gallant, sparker

woof 4 bark, crow, weft, yarn 5 boast,
weave 6 fabric, thread 7 texture

wool 3 fur 4 coat, hair 6 fabric, fleece
cut: 5 shear *fabric:* 4 felt 5 baize, crepe,
serge, tweed 6 covert, kersey, mohair,
poplin, shoddy, velour 7 flannel,
worsted 8 cashmere, chenille 9 gabardine 10 broadcloth *fat:* 7 lanolin *kind:*
4 hogg 6 angora, hogget, virgin *lowquality:* 5 mungo 6 shoddy *musk-ox:*
6 qiviut *process:* 7 carding *source:*
4 goat, lamb 5 camel, llama, sheep
6 alpaca

woolly 5 fuzzy, hairy, nappy 6 fleecy,
shaggy 7 blurred, hirsute 9 roughness
10 indistinct

woozy 4 hazy, sick, weak 5 dazed, dizzy,
faint, fuzzy, muzzy, vague 6 addled,
blurry, groggy, punchy 8 confused,
nauseous 9 nauseated, slaphappy
11 light-headed

word 3 vow 4 buzz, news, oath, term
5 logos, order, rumor 6 advice, gospel,
gossip, phrase, pledge, plight, remark,
report, saying, signal 7 command, message, promise 8 locution 9 assurance,
directive, discourse, guarantee, statement, utterance 10 commitment,
expression 11 declaration, information
12 announcement, conversation, intelligence *connective:* 11 conjunction *group:*
6 clause, phrase 8 sentence *misused:*
8 malaprop 11 malapropism *naming:*
4 noun *new:* 7 coinage 9 neologism *of
action:* 4 verb *of honor:* 4 oath 7 promise
origin: 9 etymology *part:* 8 syllable *root:*
6 etymon *scrambled:* 7 anagram *shortened:* 11 contraction 12 abbreviation
square: 10 palindrome *with opposite
meaning:* 7 antonym *with same meaning:*
7 synonym *with same pronunciation:*
7 homonym 9 homophone *with same
spelling:* 7 homonym 9 homograph

wordbook 5 vocab 7 lexicon 8 glossary
9 thesaurus 10 dictionary, vocabulary

word-for-word 7 literal 8 ad verbum, verbally, verbatim

wordiness 8 verbiage 9 logorrhea, prolixity, verbosity 10 bloviation

word-of-mouth 4 oral 6 spoken, verbal
8 viva voce 9 unwritten

wordy 5 windy 6 prolix, verbal 7 diffuse,
verbose 9 dictional, garrulous, iterative,
redundant, vocabular 10 long-winded,
logorrheic, loquacious, rhetorical

work 3 act, fix, job, run, tug, use 4 duty,
line, make, opus, take, task, tend, till,
toil 5 chore, craft, drive, forge, grind,
guide, labor, shape, solve, sweat, trade
6 create, effect, effort, energy, excite,
métier, result, strain, strive 7 arrange,
calling, control, exploit, fashion, operate, perform, product, provoke, pursuit, resolve, succeed, travail 8 activity,
business, contrive, drudgery, exertion,
function, operate, slogging, striving,
vocation 9 cultivate, embroider, execution 10 assignment, employment, handicraft, occupation, profession *together:*
9 cooperate 11 collaborate *unit:* 3 erg
5 joule

workaday 5 plain, usual 7 mundane, prosaic, routine 8 ordinary 9 quotidian
11 commonplace 12 run-of-the-mill

worker 4 doer, hand, serf 5 prole 6 toiler,
wallah 7 artisan, laborer 8 employee,
mechanic, operator 9 craftsman, operative 10 roustabout, wage earner 11 proletarian *fellow:* 7 comrade, partner
9 colleague *group:* 4 crew, gang 5 shift,
staff, union *hard:* 5 slave 6 beaver,
drudge *insect:* 3 ant, bee 4 wasp 7 termite *itinerant:* 6 boomer 7 migrant *slow:*
7 plodder *unskilled:* 4 peon 7 jackleg,
laborer

working 4 busy, live 6 active, useful,
viable 7 dynamic, engaged, running
8 employed, occupied 9 operative
11 functioning *not:* 5 kaput 6 broken

workman see WORKER

work out 3 fix 5 solve, train 6 devise, settle **7** arrange, develop, resolve **8** exercise

workout 4 test **5** drill **8** exercise, practice **10** daily dozen

work over 4 beat, redo **5** scrag, study **6** beat up, mess up, redraw, rehash, revamp, revise **7** examine, redraft, restyle, rewrite, rough up **9** manhandle

workroom 3 lab **4** shop **6** studio **7** atelier **10** laboratory

works 4 mill **5** plant **7** factory **8** workshop **11** manufactory

Works and Days author 6 Hesiod

world 5 class, earth, globe, realm **6** career, cosmos, nature, planet, public, sphere, system **7** kingdom, society **8** creation, division, everyone, renowned, universe **9** human race, macrocosm, microcosm **13** distinguished *combining form:* **4** cosm **5** cosmo

worldly 5 blasé **6** carnal, earthy, urbane **7** earthly, fleshly, mundane, profane, secular, sensual, terrene **8** material, telluric, temporal **9** sublunary **11** terrestrial **12** cosmopolitan **13** sophisticated

worldly-wise 12 cosmopolitan **13** sophisticated

World War I *battle:* **5** Aisne, Marne, Somme, Ypres **6** Isonzo, Verdun **7** Jutland **9** Caporetto **10** Tannenberg **11** Dardanelles *battle line:* **9** Siegfried *general:* **4** Foch (Ferdinand), Haig (Douglas) **7** Allenby (Edmund) **8** Pershing (John) **10** Hindenburg (Paul von), Ludendorff (Erich) *hero:* **4** York (Alvin) **8** Red Baron (The) **10** Richthofen (Manfred von) **12** Rickenbacker (Eddie) *treaty:* **10** Versailles

World War II *admiral:* **6** Halsey (William "Bull"), Nimitz (Chester) *alliance:* **4** Axis **6** Allies *battle:* **4** St.-Lô **5** Anzio, Bulge **6** Bataan, Midway, Tarawa, Warsaw **7** Britain, Iwo Jima, Okinawa, Saint-Lô **8** Coral Sea, Normandy **9** El Alamein, Leyte Gulf **10** Stalingrad **11** Guadalcanal *general:* **6** Patton (George), Rommel (Erwin), Zhukov (Georgy) **7** Bradley (Omar) **9** MacArthur (Douglas) **10** Eisenhower (Dwight David), Montgomery (Bernard) *hero:* **6** Murphy (Audie) *journalist:* **4** Pyle (Ernie) *vehicle:* **4** jeep *weapon:* **5** A-bomb **6** rocket **8** buzz bomb

worldwide 6 cosmic, global **8** catholic **9** planetary, universal **10** ecumenical **12** cosmopolitan

worm 3 cad, cur **4** grub, lout **5** borer, creep, fluke, leech, louse, screw, treat **6** edge in, maggot, no-good, squirm,

thread, wiggle, wretch, writhe **7** extract, lowlife, serpent, triclad, wriggle **8** helminth, nematode, squiggle **9** insinuate, planarium, trematode **10** infiltrate *marine:* **6** nereid **7** annelid, tubifex *parasitic:* **5** fluke, leech **7** ascarid, ascaris, cestode, filaria **8** helminth, trichina **9** strongyle

worn 3 old, wan **4** aged, beat **5** drawn, jaded, tatty, tired, weary **6** eroded, frayed, ragged, shabby **7** haggard **8** fatigued **9** woebegone **10** threadbare

worn-out 4 beat **5** all in, spent, tired, weary **6** bleary, bushed, ragged, used-up **7** drained, run-down **8** decrepit, depleted, fatigued, overused **9** exhausted, worm-eaten **10** broken-down, threadbare, tumbledown **11** debilitated, dilapidated

worried 6 afraid, on edge **7** anxious, nervous **8** bothered, distrait, troubled **9** concerned, tormented **10** distracted, distraught, distressed **12** apprehensive

worry 3 nag, try, vex **4** care, fret, fuss, gnaw, goad, pain, stew, test **5** annoy, beset, shake, tease, trial, upset **6** assail, attack, bother, harass, needle, pester, plague, pull at, unease **7** afflict, anguish, anxiety, concern, disturb, oppress, torment, trouble **8** aggrieve, distress, irritate **9** agitation, annoyance, misgiving **10** irritation, uneasiness

worrywart 7 fusspot **9** Cassandra, doomsayer, pessimist **10** fussbudget

worse 8 inferior

worsen 4 sink **7** decline **10** degenerate **11** deteriorate

worship 4 love **5** adore, honor **6** admire, dote on, homage, revere **7** idolize, lionize, liturgy, respect **8** devotion, idolatry, venerate **9** adoration, affection, reverence **10** admiration, veneration **11** idolization *object of:* **3** god **4** icon, idol *place of:* **5** altar **6** church, mosque, shrine, temple **9** cathedral, synagogue

worshipper 3 fan **6** votary **7** admirer, devotee **8** adherent, believer, disciple **10** enthusiast

worsted 4 yarn **5** stuff **6** caddis, fabric **7** cheviot, etamine, flannel, lasting **8** shalloon **9** bombazine, sharkskin **10** broadcloth

worth 4 rate **5** merit, price, value **6** regard, riches, wealth **7** caliber, calibre, fortune, quality, stature **9** resources, substance, valuation **10** excellence

worthless 4 vain **6** futile, no-good **7** inutile **8** nugatory **9** no-account

worthwhile 6 paying **7** gainful **9** estimable, honorable, lucrative

10 profitable, well-paying 11 meritorious, moneymaking 12 advantageous, remunerative

worthy 4 good 5 noble 8 laudable, standout 9 admirable, deserving, desirable, estimable, honorable 10 acceptable, creditable 11 commendable, meritorious

Wotan see ODIN

Wouk novel 4 Hope (The) 5 Glory (The) 10 Winds of War (The) 11 Caine Mutiny (The) 19 Marjorie Morningstar

would-be 7 hopeful, wishful 8 apparent, aspiring, desiring, desirous 9 ambitious, potential

wound 3 cut 4 blow, harm, hurt, pain, rift 6 damage, injure, injury, insult, lesion, trauma 8 lacerate 10 laceration *discharge:* 3 pus *sign:* 4 scab, scar 5 blood 7 blister

wow 3 hit 4 boff, grab 5 amaze, boffo, smash 6 dazzle 7 astound, impress, success 8 bedazzle

Wozzeck composer 4 Berg (Alban)

wrack 4 kelp, raze, ruin 5 smash, total 7 destroy, flotsam, remnant, seaweed 8 decimate, demolish, shambles, wreckage 11 destruction

wraith 5 ghost, shade, spook 6 double, shadow, spirit 7 phantom, specter, spectre 8 phantasm 10 apparition

wrangle 3 row 4 spar, spat, tiff 5 argue, brawl, fight, scrap 6 bicker, fracas, haggle, hassle 7 brabble, dispute, fall out, finagle, quarrel, quibble 8 squabble 11 altercation

wrangler 6 cowboy 8 buckaroo 9 ranch hand

wrap 3 fur 4 bind, cape, coat, roll 5 cloak, drape, shawl, stole 6 bundle, clothe, enfold, invest, jacket, mantle, muffle, parcel, shroud, swathe 7 bandage, blanket, conceal, dress up, embrace, enclose, engross, envelop, involve, package, swaddle 8 bundle up, enshroud, surround

wrapped up 4 deep 6 intent 7 engaged 8 absorbed, consumed, immersed 9 engrossed 10 preoccupied

wrapper 5 cover 6 jacket 10 dust jacket 12 dressing gown

wrap up 6 muffle 8 close out, complete, conclude 9 summarize

wrap-up 4 coda 5 close 6 capper, closer, finale, report 7 closing 8 epilogue 9 summation 10 denouement

wrath 3 ire 4 fury, rage 5 anger 6 choler 8 ferocity 9 vengeance 10 punishment 11 retribution 12 chastisement

wrathful 3 mad 5 angry, irate 6 heated,

raging 7 enraged, furious 8 choleric, incensed, inflamed 10 infuriated

wreak 5 cause, exact, visit 6 effect, impose 7 inflict 10 bring about

wreath 3 bay, lei 5 crown 6 anadem, laurel 7 chaplet, circlet, coronal, coronet, garland, laurels

wreathe 4 coil, curl, wind 5 twine, twist 6 spiral 7 entwine 9 corkscrew 10 interweave

wreck 4 do in, heap, hulk, raze, ruin 5 beach, crack, crash, cream, smash, total 6 beater, damage, jalopy, junker, pileup, ravage, strand 7 clunker, crackup, destroy, scuttle, smashup, torpedo 8 decimate, demolish 9 vandalize 11 destruction

wreckage 5 wrack 6 debris 7 flotsam 8 detritus, shambles 11 destruction

wrecker 8 salvager, tow truck

wrench 4 jerk, pull, rack, tool, turn, warp, yank 5 force, twist, wrest, wring 6 change, injure, injury, snatch, socket, sprain, strain 7 disable, distort, pervert, squeeze 8 distress, twisting *kind:* 6 monkey 7 ratchet

wrest 4 rend, rive 5 exact, twist, wring 6 elicit, extort, snatch, wrench 7 extract, squeeze

wrestle 6 combat, strain, strive, tussle 7 contend, grapple, scuffle 8 struggle

wrestling *hold:* 4 lock 6 nelson 8 headlock, scissors *kind:* 4 sumo *term:* 3 pin 4 fall 5 throw 8 takedown

wretch 3 cur, dog 4 scum, toad, worm 5 devil, knave, louse, rogue, skunk, snake 6 rascal, rotter 7 caitiff, hangdog, lowlife, outcast, rat fink, stinker, villain 8 scalawag, stinkard 9 scoundrel 10 blackguard, sleazeball 11 rapscallion

wretched 3 low, sad 4 base, foul, mean, vile 6 abject, dismal, horrid, scurvy, sordid, woeful 7 abysmal, doleful, forlorn, ignoble, ruthful, servile, squalid, unhappy 8 dejected, dolorous, hopeless, inferior 9 afflicted, execrable, miserable, sorrowful 10 despairing, despicable, deplorable, despondent, melancholy, villainous

wretchedness 3 woe 6 misery 7 anguish 8 distress

wriggle 4 worm 5 slink 6 squirm, writhe

wring 3 wry 5 choke, exact, screw, twist, wrest 6 extort, squirm, wrench, writhe 7 afflict, draw out, extract, squeeze, torment *the neck:* 5 scrag

wringing-wet 4 soppy 6 soaked, sodden, soused 7 soaking, sopping 8 drenched, dripping 9 saturated

wrinkle 4 fold, ruck, ruga, seam 5 crimp, crisp, plica, ridge, wizen 6 cockle, crease, fillip, furrow, pucker, rumple **7** crumple, novelty, scrunch, shrivel **8** contract **9** corrugate, crow's-foot, worry line **10** innovation **11** corrugation **12** imperfection, irregularity

wrinkled 5 lined **6** rugose, rumply **7** creased **8** puckered, rugulose

Wrinkle in Time author: **6** L'Engle (Madeleine)

wrist 5 joint **6** carpus **bone: 6** carpal, hamate **8** pisiform

writ 5 brief, order **6** assize, capias, decree, elegit, extent **7** mandate, process, summons, warrant **8** detainer, document, mandamus, mittimus, praecipe, replevin, subpoena **9** execution **10** attachment, certiorari, court order, injunction **11** fieri facias, scire facias, supersedeas **12** habeas corpus, venire facias **13** sequestration

write 3 ink, jot, pen **4** note **5** chalk, draft, print, score, spell **6** answer, author, byline, draw up, indite, ordain, pencil, record, scrawl, scribe **7** compose, dissert, engross, fire off, put down, scratch, set down **8** inscribe, scribble, spell out **9** autograph, transpose **10** correspond, underwrite

write down 4 note **6** record, reduce **10** transcribe

write off 6 cancel **7** dismiss, expense **8** amortize, discount **9** eliminate **10** depreciate

write-off 4 debt, loss **7** expense **8** donation **9** allowance, deduction, reduction

writer 4 poet **6** author, penman, scribe **8** composer, novelist **9** scribbler, wordsmith **bad: 4** hack

write-up 5 blurb, story **7** account, article

writhe 4 curl, worm **5** twist **6** squirm, suffer, wallow, welter, wiggle, wrench **7** agonize, contort, distort, wriggle **8** convolve, squiggle **10** intertwine

writing 4 book, hand, note **5** essay, paper, print, prose, style, words **6** letter, notice, record, script **7** epistle **8** document, longhand **9** signature **10** authorship, literature, manuscript, penmanship **11** calligraphy, composition, inscription, publication **character: 6** letter **9** cuneiform **10** hieroglyph **combining form: 4** gram **6** grapho, graphy **for the blind: 7** braille **instrument: 3** pen **5** chalk, quill **6** pencil, stylus **kind: 5** prose, verse **6** poetry **sacred: 5** Bible,

Koran **6** Talmud, Tantra **9** scripture **secret: 4** code **surface: 5** board, paper, slate **6** scroll **9** parchment

wrong 3 bad, ill, off, sin **4** awry, evil, harm, hurt, tort **5** abuse, amiss, badly, crime, false, inapt, unfit **6** afield, astray, injure, injury, malign, offend, sinful, unfair, unjust, untrue **7** defraud, immoral, oppress, outrage, violate **8** aggrieve, ill-treat, improper, inequity, iniquity, maltreat, mistaken, mistreat, opposite **9** discredit, erroneous, grievance, incorrect, injustice, misguided, persecute, unethical, unfitting, violation **10** inaccurate, iniquitous, mistakenly, unfairness, unjustness, unsuitable, wickedness **11** erroneously, incorrectly, unfavorably **12** inaccurately, infelicitous **13** inappropriate

wrongdoer 5 felon **6** sinner **8** criminal, offender **9** miscreant, reprobate **10** accomplice, delinquent, malefactor **12** transgressor

wrongdoing 3 sin **4** evil **5** crime **7** misdeed, offense **8** iniquity **10** misconduct **11** malefaction, malfeasance, misbehavior

wrongful 6 unjust, unfair **7** illegal, illicit, lawless **8** criminal, improper, unlawful **12** illegitimate

wrongheaded 6 mulish **7** froward **8** contrary, perverse **9** obstinate

wrought 4 made **6** formed, shaped, worked **7** created **8** finished, hammered **9** decorated, fashioned, processed **10** ornamented **11** embellished **12** manufactured **up: 7** excited, stirred

wry 4 bent **5** askew, twist, wrest **6** ironic, wrench **7** crooked, twisted **8** humorous, sardonic **11** wrongheaded

wryneck 10 woodpecker **11** torticollis

wurst 7 sausage

Wuthering Heights author: **6** Brontë (Emily) **character: 5** Cathy **9** Catherine **10** Heathcliff **family: 6** Linton **8** Earnshaw

Wycliffite 7 Lollard

Wyoming capital: **8** Cheyenne **city: 6** Casper **7** Laramie **mountain, range: 5** Rocky **7** Gannett (Peak) **9** Wind River **10** Grand Teton **nickname: 8** Equality (State) **river: 5** Green, Snake **6** Powder **7** Bighorn **11** Yellowstone **state bird: 10** meadowlark **state flower: 16** Indian paintbrush **state tree: 10** cottonwood

X

x 3 chi, ten 4 kiss 5 annul, cross, erase, error, times, wrong 6 cancel, delete, efface 7 mistake, unknown 8 abscissa 9 signature

Xanthippe 3 nag 5 scold, shrew 6 nagger 9 termagant *husband:* 8 Socrates

Xenophon work 8 Anabasis 9 Cyropedia, Hellenica

xerophyte 6 cactus

Xerxes *crossing site:* 10 Hellespont *defeat:* 7 Plataea, Salamis *father:* 6 Darius *kingdom:* 6 Persia *mother:* 6 Atossa *victory:* 11 Thermopylae

Xmas 4 Noel, yule 8 Nativity, yuletide

X-ray *discoverer:* 8 Roentgen (Wilhelm) *science:* 9 radiology

xylophone relative 7 marimba

Y

yacht 4 race, sail 6 cruise 7 cruiser 8 sailboat 12 cabin cruiser

yahoo 3 hun, yay 4 boor, clod, dolt, hood, lout, punk, thug 5 brute, chuff, churl, clown, rough, rowdy, tough 6 hoorah, hooray, hurrah, savage, terror, vandal, yippie 7 buffoon, bumpkin, hoodlum, ruffian, toughie 8 bullyboy, hooligan 9 roughneck 10 clodhopper

Yahweh 3 God 6 Adonai, Elohim 7 Jehovah

yak 3 gab, jaw 4 blab, chat 5 clack, prate 6 babble, gabble, jabber, natter, yammer 7 blabber, blather, chatter, palaver, prattle 11 confabulate

Yalta participant 6 Stalin (Joseph) 9 Churchill (Winston), Roosevelt (Franklin Delano)

yam 7 boniato 11 sweet potato

yammer 3 cry 4 bawl, crab, fuss, moan, wail, yawp, yell 5 bleat, gripe, whine 6 babble, bellow, clamor, gabble, grouch, grouse, jabber, natter, snivel, squawk 7 blather, prattle, whimper 8 complain 9 bellyache, caterwaul

yank 3 tug 4 grab, jerk, pull, tear 5 hoick 6 snatch, wrench 7 extract

yap 3 gab 4 bark, hick 5 mouth, prate 6 babble, bowwow, gabble, jabber, natter, rustic, yammer 7 blather, bumpkin, chatter, hayseed, prattle 9 hillbilly 10 clodhopper

yard 3 pen 4 herd, quad, spar, unit 5 court, garth, glass 6 length 7 grounds, measure 9 curtilage, enclosure 10 playground, quadrangle *five and one-half:* 3 rod *part of:* 4 foot *two hundred and twenty:* 7 furlong

yardstick 4 norm, test 5 basis, gauge, model 7 measure, pattern 8 paradigm, standard 9 barometer, benchmark, criterion, guideline 10 touchstone

yare 4 deft, spry 5 agile, brisk, handy, lithe, quick, ready, zippy 6 lively, nimble, volant 7 lissome 9 sprightly

yarn 4 tale, talk 5 fiber, story 6 caddis, cotton, crewel, strand, thread 7 account, caddice 8 anecdote, tall tale 9 adventure, narration, narrative *ball of:* 4 clew *coil:* 5 skein 6 skeane *cotton:* 10 candlewick *for fastening a sail:* 6 roband *woolen:* 6 crewel 7 worsted 8 shetland

yaw 4 rock, swag, veer 5 lurch 6 swerve 7 deviate 9 alternate, deviation 10 deflection

yawn 3 gap 4 bore, gape 5 ennui 6 cavity,

tedium 7 boredom, bromide 10 dullsville
yawning 4 deep 5 agape 6 gaping
7 abyssal 9 cavernous
yawp 3 bay, cry, nag 4 bark, bawl, beef,
crab, fuss, gape, wail 5 bleat, gripe
6 clamor, outcry, squall, squawk, yammer 8 complain 9 bellyache
yaws 9 frambesia
yclept 5 named 6 called
yea 3 aye, too 4 also, amen, even, more,
okay 5 truly 6 agreed, assent, as well,
indeed, really, verily 7 besides, granted
8 likewise, moreover, positive 9 certainly 10 definitely 11 affirmation, affirmative 12 additionally
yeanling 3 kid 4 lamb
year 4 time 5 cycle 6 period *academic
division:* 4 term 7 quarter, session
8 semester 9 trimester *French:* 5 année
kind: 4 leap 5 solar 6 fiscal 8 academic,
calendar, sidereal *Latin:* 5 annus *Scottish:* 7 towmond *Spanish:* 3 año
yearbook 5 annal 6 annual 7 almanac
yearling 4 colt, foal 5 filly
Yearling, The *author:* 8 Rawlings (Marjorie Kinnan) *character:* 4 Jody *fawn:*
4 Flag
yearly 6 annual 8 annually
yearn 4 ache, burn, itch, long, lust, pant,
pine, sigh, wish 5 dream, spoil 6 hanker, hunger, thirst
yearning 4 wish 5 ardor, drive, eager
6 desire, thirst 7 craving, wistful
8 appetite 10 aspiration
years 3 age, era *five:* 7 lustrum 12 quin-
quennial, quinquennium *four:* 11 quad-
rennial, quadrennium *one hundred:*
7 century 9 centenary 10 centennial
one thousand: 10 millennium *ten:*
6 decade 9 decennial, decennium *three:*
9 triennial, triennium *two:* 8 biennial,
biennium
yeast 4 barm, foam, suds 5 froth, spume
6 lather, leaven 7 ferment
yeasty 5 dizzy, giddy, light 6 frothy
7 flighty 8 immature, restless, seething
9 exuberant, frivolous, unsettled
11 light-headed
Yeats, William Butler *beloved:* 9 Maud
Gonne *birthplace:* 6 Dublin *play:*
7 Deirdre 9 Herne's Egg (The)
16 Countess Cathleen (The) *poetry:*
5 Tower (The) 10 Easter 1916 12 Second
Coming (The) 16 Wild Swans at Coole
(The) 18 Sailing to Byzantium *theater:*
5 Abbey
yegg 5 thief 6 robber 7 burglar 8 picklock 11 safecracker
yell 3 cry 4 call, howl, roar, wail 5 cheer,
hallo, hollo, shout, whoop 6 bellow,

clamor, holler, outcry, scream, shriek,
squall 10 vociferate
yellow 3 age 4 buff, mean, weak, yolk
5 amber, blond, color, lemon, straw,
tawny, topaz 6 coward, craven, flaxen,
golden, sallow 7 gutless, ignoble, mustard, saffron 8 cowardly, discolor 9 dastardly, jaundiced, spunkless 11 sensational 12 dishonorable 13 pusillanimous
brownish: 3 dun 5 amber, ocher *dye:*
7 annatto *greenish:* 5 olive 6 acacia
10 chartreuse
yellowhammer 5 finch 7 bunting, flicker
yelp 3 cry, yap 4 bark 6 outcry, squeal
Yemen *capital:* 4 Sana 5 Sanaa *city:*
4 Aden 5 Ta'izz *desert:* 10 Rub' al-Khali
gulf: 4 Aden *island:* 7 Socotra *island
group:* 7 Kamaran *language:* 6 Arabic
monetary unit: 4 rial *neighbor:* 4 Oman
11 Saudi Arabia *peninsula:* 7 Arabian
sea: 3 Red 7 Arabian
yen 4 ache, itch, long, lust, pine, sigh,
urge 5 taste, yearn 6 desire, hanker,
hunger, thirst 7 craving, longing, passion 8 appetite, yearning 9 hankering
yeoman 5 clerk 6 farmer 7 freeman
8 retainer 9 attendant, beefeater,
landowner 10 freeholder 11 home-
steader
yeomanly 5 loyal 6 sturdy 8 faithful
yes 3 aye, yea, yeh, yep, yup 4 okay,
yeah 5 agree 6 agreed, assent, gladly
7 consent, exactly 8 all right 9 assuredly, certainly, willingly 11 affirmation,
affirmative, undoubtedly *French:* 3 oui
yeshiva 6 school 8 seminary
yes-man 5 toady 6 minion, stooge
7 spaniel 8 groveler, truckler 9 flatterer,
sycophant 10 bootlicker 13 apple-
polisher
yesterday 4 past, yore 8 recently
10 recent time *French:* 4 hier *Spanish:*
4 ayer
yesteryear 4 past, yore 7 history 8 foretime, lang syne
yet 3 but, too 4 also, even, more, only,
save 5 so far, still 6 as well, though,
withal 7 besides, earlier, finally, howbeit, however, someday, thus far 8 after
all, hitherto, moreover, sometime
10 eventually, ultimately 11 furthermore, nonetheless, still and all 12 additionally, nevertheless
Yevtushenko poem 7 Babi Yar, Baby Yar
Ygerne see IGRAINE
yield 3 bow, net, pay 4 bear, bend, cave,
cede, crop, fold 5 defer, grant, waive
6 accede, bounty, buckle, comply,
impart, output, profit, relent, render,
resign, return, reward, submit, supply,
tender 7 abandon, bring in, concede,

consent, deliver, furnish, harvest, produce, product, proffer, provide, revenue, succumb **8** abdicate, collapse, generate, hand over **9** acquiesce, surrender **10** bring forth, capitulate, production, relinquish

yielding 4 soft **6** pliant, supple **7** bearing, passive, pliable **8** flexible **9** adaptable, tractable **10** manageable, productive, submissive **11** acquiescent, unresistant

yin and ___ 4 yang

yip 3 cry **4** bark, yelp

yippee 6 hoorah, hooray, hurrah, hurray

yoga posture 5 asana

yoke 3 bar, tie, wed **4** bond, join, link, pair, span, team **5** clamp, frame, hitch, marry, unite **6** attach, couple, inspan **7** bondage, connect, control, harness, peonage, serfdom, slavery **8** marriage **9** servitude **7** crosspiece, oppression *combining form:* **3** zyg **4** zygo *part:* **5** oxbow

yokel 3 oaf **4** boor, clod, hick, rube **5** churl, swain **6** rustic **7** bucolic, bumpkin, hayseed **9** chawbacon, hillbilly **10** clodhopper, countryman

yolk 4 food **6** yellow **10** ovum center

yon see YONDER

yonder 5 there **7** farther, further, thither **8** outlying

yore 3 old **7** history **8** foretime, lang syne **9** antiquity, yesterday **10** yesteryear

you 3 one **4** thee, thou *French:* **4** vous *German:* **3** Sie *Spanish:* **5** usted **7** ustedes

young 3 fry, new **4** baby, tyro **5** brood, fresh, green **6** babies, callow, infant, junior, litter, tender, unripe **7** untried **8** childish, immature, juvenile, unformed, youthful **9** unfledged **10** unfinished, unseasoned **11** unpracticed **13** inexperienced *animal:* **3** cub, fry, kid, kit, pup **4** calf, colt, fawn, foal, joey **5** puppy **6** kitten, heifer, piglet *bird:* **5** chick **7** gosling *hare:* **7** leveret *sheep, goat:* **4** lamb **8** yeanling

younger 6 junior

youngster 3 boy, cub, kid, lad, tad, tot **4** girl, lass, tike **5** chick, child **6** moppet, shaver **8** juvenile **9** fledgling

youth 5 prime **6** period, spring **8** juvenile, preadult, teenager **9** stripling **10** adolescent, springtide, springtime **12** inexperience *ancient Greek:* **6** ephebe **7** ephebus *goddess of:* **4** Hebe *mythological:* **6** Adonis, Apollo, Icarus **8** Ganymede *time of:* **9** salad days

youthful 5 fresh, green, young **6** boyish, callow, maiden, unripe **7** puerile **8** immature, juvenile, virginal **9** beardless, unfledged

yowl 3 bay, cry **4** bawl, howl, wail **6** scream, squall, squeal **7** ululate **9** caterwaul

yucca 7 cassava **9** bear grass

Yukon *bay:* **9** Mackenzie *capital:* **10** Whitehorse *city:* **6** Dawson *mountain:* **5** Logan *river:* **5** Yukon **8** Klondike

yule 4 Noel, Xmas **8** Nativity **9** Christmas **13** Christmastide

Z

Zambia *capital:* **6** Lusaka *city:* **5** Kitwe, Ndola **11** Livingstone *lake:* **5** Mweru **9** Bangweulu **10** Tanganyika *language:* **7** English *monetary unit:* **6** kwacha *mountain range:* **8** Muchinga *neighbor:* **5** Congo **6** Angola, Malawi **7** Namibia **8** Tanzania, Zimbabwe **10** Mozambique *river:* **5** Kafue **7** Luangwa, Zambezi *waterfall:* **13** Victoria Falls

zany 3 nut, wag **4** card, fool, kook **5** antic, campy, clown, comic, crazy, cutup, dotty, goofy, idiot, joker, kooky, loony, nutty, wacky **6** jester, madcap **7** buffoon, farceur, half-wit **8** clowning, clownish, comedian, funnyman, jokester **9** harlequin, prankster, screwball, simpleton, trickster **11** merry-andrew

zap 3 hit **4** blow, kill, nuke **5** blast, snuff **6** attack **7** destroy, wipe out **8** dissolve **9** eliminate, irradiate, liquidate **10** annihilate

Zauberflöte composer 6 Mozart (Wolfgang Amadeus)

zeal 4 brio, fire, zest **5** ardor, drive,

mania 6 desire, energy, esprit, fervor, spirit **7** avidity, passion, urgency **8** devotion, dynamism, keenness **9** eagerness, intensity, vehemence **10** enthusiasm, fanaticism, fierceness

zealot 3 bug, fan, nut **4** buff **5** fiend, freak **6** maniac, votary **7** devotee, fanatic, sectary **8** partisan **10** aficionado, enthusiast **12** true believer

zealous 4 avid, keen **5** afire, eager, fiery, fired, nutty, rabid **6** ardent, fervid, gung-ho **7** devoted, fanatic, fervent **8** frenetic, obsessed, wild-eyed **9** dedicated, fanatical, possessed **10** passionate **11** impassioned **12** enthusiastic

zebra 6 equine **7** referee **9** crosswalk *extinct:* **6** quagga *type:* **6** Grevy's **8** mountain **9** Burchell's

zebu 4 oxen

Zebulun 9 lost tribe *brother:* **4** Levi **5** Judah **6** Simeon *father:* **5** Jacob *mother:* **4** Leah

zecchino 6 sequin

Zechariah 7 prophet

Zedekiah 9 Mattaniah *father:* **6** Josiah

zenana 5 harem, serai **8** seraglio

zenith 3 top **4** acme, apex, peak **6** apogee, height, summit, vertex **8** capstone, pinnacle **12** culmination **12** highest point *opposite:* **5** nadir

Zenobia *husband:* **9** Odenathus *kingdom:* **7** Palmyra

Zeno follower 5 Stoic

Zephaniah 7 prophet **9** Sophonias

zephyr 6 breeze **8** west wind

Zephyrus *father:* **8** Astraeus *mother:* **3** Eos **6** Aurora

zeppelin 5 blimp **7** airship **9** dirigible

zero 3 aim, nil, zip **4** love, nada, none, null, void **5** aught, nadir, zilch **6** cipher, naught, nobody **7** nothing, nullity **8** goose egg **9** nonentity

zest 4 élan, peel, tang, zeal **5** ardor, gusto, taste **6** fervor, flavor, relish **7** delight, ecstasy, elation, passion, sparkle **8** appetite, dynamism, piquancy, pleasure **9** eagerness, enjoyment **10** enthusiasm **11** delectation **12** exhilaration, satisfaction

zesty 4 racy, tart **5** sharp, spicy, tangy **6** biting, lively, savory, snappy **7** peppery, piquant, pungent **8** exciting, poignant, seasoned, spirited **9** flavorful

Zetes *brother:* **6** Calais *father:* **6** Boreas *mother:* **8** Orithyia *slayer:* **8** Heracles, Hercules

Zethus *brother:* **7** Amphion *father:* **4** Zeus **7** Jupiter *mother:* **7** Antiope

Zeus 7 Jupiter *brother:* **5** Hades **8** Poseidon *daughter:* **3** Ate **4** Hebe **5** Helen **6** Athena **7** Artemis **9** Aphrodite

10 Persephone, Proserpina *father:* **6** Cronus *home:* **7** Olympus (Mt.) *lover:* **4** Leda, Leto, Maia **5** Danae, Dione, Metis **6** Aegina, Europa, Latona, Semele, Themis **7** Alcmene, Antiope, Demeter **8** Callisto, Eurynome *mother:* **4** Rhea *nurse:* **9** Almathaea *oracle:* **6** Dodona *shield:* **5** aegis *sister:* **4** Hera, Juno *son:* **4** Ares **5** Arcas, Argus, Minos **6** Aeacus, Apollo, Hermes, Zethus **7** Amphion, Perseus **8** Dionysus, Heracles, Hercules, Sarpedon, Tantalus *tree:* **3** oak *wife:* **4** Hera, Juno *weapon:* **11** thunderbolt

zigzag 4 tack, turn **5** angle, crank, weave **6** jagged **7** chevron **8** flexuous, indirect, serrated

zilch 3 nil, zip **4** zero **5** aught, squat **6** cipher, naught, nobody **7** nothing, nullity **8** goose egg **9** nonentity **11** diddly-squat

Zimbabwe *capital:* **6** Harare *city:* **5** Gweru **6** Kwekwe, Mutare **8** Bulawayo, Maxvingo **11** Chitungwiza *ethnic group:* **5** Shona **7** Ndebele *former name:* **8** Rhodesia *lake:* **6** Kariba *language:* **5** Bantu **7** English *monetary unit:* **6** dollar *neighbor:* **6** Zambia **8** Botswana **10** Mozambique **11** South Africa *river:* **4** Sabi **7** Limpopo, Zambezi *waterfall:* **13** Victoria Falls

zinc 7 element *ingot:* **7** spelter *ore:* **6** blende **10** sphalerite

zing 3 pan, pep, rap, vim, zap, zip **4** brio, dash, élan, slam, snap, zeal **5** ardor, flair, oomph, verve, vigor **6** energy, esprit, fervor, spirit **7** panache, passion, sparkle **8** dynamism, vitality **9** animation, eagerness **10** ebullience, enthusiasm

Zion 5 bliss **6** heaven, Israel **7** Elysium **8** eternity, paradise **12** New Jerusalem, promised land

Zionist *American:* **5** Szold (Henrietta) *English:* **7** Sokolow (Nahum) **8** Zangwill (Israel) *German:* **6** Nordau (Max Simon) *Hungarian:* **5** Herzl (Theodor) *Israeli:* **5** Buber (Martin) **8** Weizmann (Chaim)

zip 3 fly, nil, nix, pep, run, vim **4** brio, dash, hiss, rush, nada, snap, tear, whiz, zero, zest, zing, zoom **5** drive, gusto, hurry, oomph, speed, squat, whisk, zilch **6** bustle, energy, hasten, hustle **7** nothing **8** vitality **10** excitement, liveliness **11** diddly-squat

zippy 4 keen, spry, yare **5** agile, alert, brisk, peppy, quick, ready **6** lively, nimble, snappy, speedy **7** dynamic **8** spirited **9** sprightly

zircon 6 jargon **7** jargoon, mineral *variety:* **7** jacinth **8** hyacinth

zit 6 pimple

zither 10 instrument *Chinese:* 3 kin 4 ch'in *Japanese:* 4 koto *relative:* 8 autoharp, dulcimer

zodiac sign 3 Leo (the Lion) 5 Aries (the Ram), Libra (the Balance), Virgo (the Virgin) 6 Cancer (the Crab), Gemini (the Twins), Pisces (the Fishes), Taurus (the Bull) 7 Scorpio (the Scorpion) 8 Aquarius (the Water Bearer) 9 Capricorn (the Goat) 11 Sagittarius (the Archer)

Zola, Emile *work:* 4 Nana 7 J'accuse 8 Drunkard (The), Germinal 9 La Débâcle 10 L'Assommoir 13 Thérèse Raquin

zombie 5 robot 8 cocktail 9 automaton

zone 4 area, band, belt 5 layer, tract 6 region, sector 7 portion, quarter, section, segment, stretch 8 district, division, encircle, surround 9 partition, territory

zonked 4 high 5 dazed, doped, drunk, tight 6 ripped, stoned 7 drugged, drunken, smashed 8 hopped-up, tripping, turned on, wiped out 9 spaced-out, strung out, stupefied 10 inebriated, tripped out 11 intoxicated

zoologist *American:* 5 Clark (Eugenie), Hyatt (Alpheus) 6 Carson (Rachel), Fossey (Dian), Osborn (Henry Fairfield), Yerkes (Robert) 7 Agassiz (Alexander), Ditmars (Raymond), Merriam (Clinton) 8 Hornaday (William) *Austrian:* 6 Frisch (Karl von) *British:* 6 Darwin (Charles), Huxley (Julian, Thomas) 7 Goodall (Jane), Medawar (Peter) 9 Lankester (Edwin) *Dutch:* 10 Swammerdam (Jan) *French:* 6 Buffon (G.-L. Leclerc), Cuvier (Georges) *German:* 7 Haeckel (Ernst) *Norwegian:* 6 Nansen (Fridtjof) *South African:* 5 Broom (Robert) *Swedish:* 8 Linnaeus (Carolus)

zoom 3 hum, zip 4 buzz, dash, whiz, zero 5 focus, speed, whizz 6 streak 7 shoot up 9 skyrocket

zoophyte 5 coral 6 sponge 8 bryozoan 9 gorgonian 10 sea anemone

Zoroastrian *demon:* 4 deva *god:* 10 Ahura Mazda *sacred writings:* 6 Avesta

zounds 3 gad 4 egad 8 gadzooks 11 odd's bodkins

zucchetto 7 calotte 8 skullcap

zwieback 5 toast 7 biscuit

zygomatic bone 5 malar 9 cheekbone

zygote 4 cell 6 oocyst